THE MERCERS' SERIES

Oil Paintings in Public Ownership in Leicestershire, Lincolnshire & Rutland

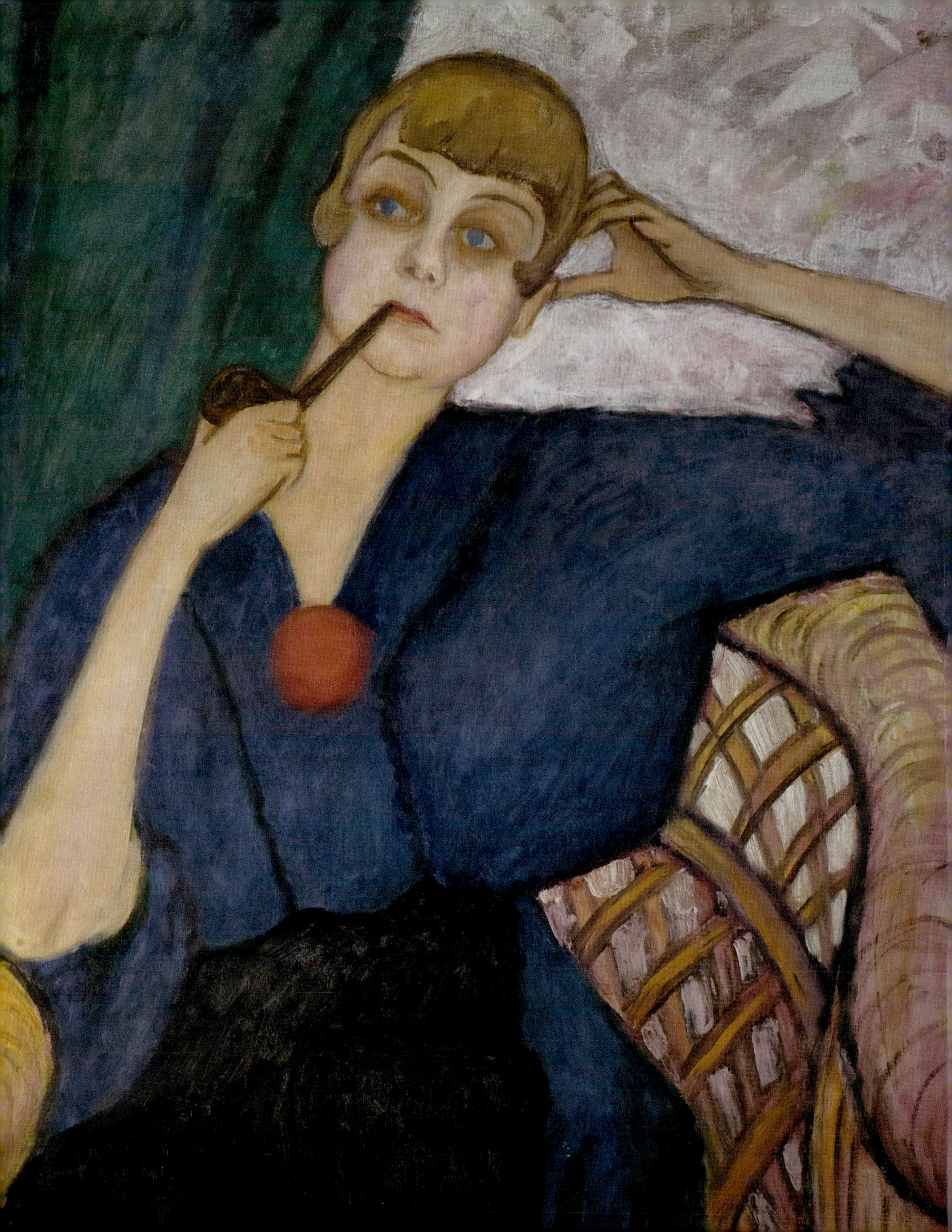

The *Oil Paintings in Public Ownership* series of catalogues is an extraordinary work in progress. Published by The Public Catalogue Foundation, it is the result of the determined efforts of a small team of administrative staff, researchers and photographers spread across the United Kingdom.

Our national collection of oil paintings in public ownership is probably one of the finest anywhere in the world. It is held not just by our museums and galleries but is also to be found in hospitals, universities and other civic buildings throughout the United Kingdom. A large proportion of these paintings are not on display and many have never before been reproduced.

This series of books for the first time allows the public to see an entire photographic record of these works – a collection likely to number some 200,000 in total. In doing so, these volumes provide a unique insight into our nation's artistic and cultural history.

As Patron of The Public Catalogue Foundation, my visits to collections across the country have highlighted to me not only the desire of curators to publicise their paintings, but also the limited resources at their disposal. The Foundation's work goes a long way towards helping to create access to these collections, while at the same time giving the British public the opportunity to see and enjoy *all* the paintings that they own.

I wish The Public Catalogue Foundation every success in its continuing endeavours.

Camilla

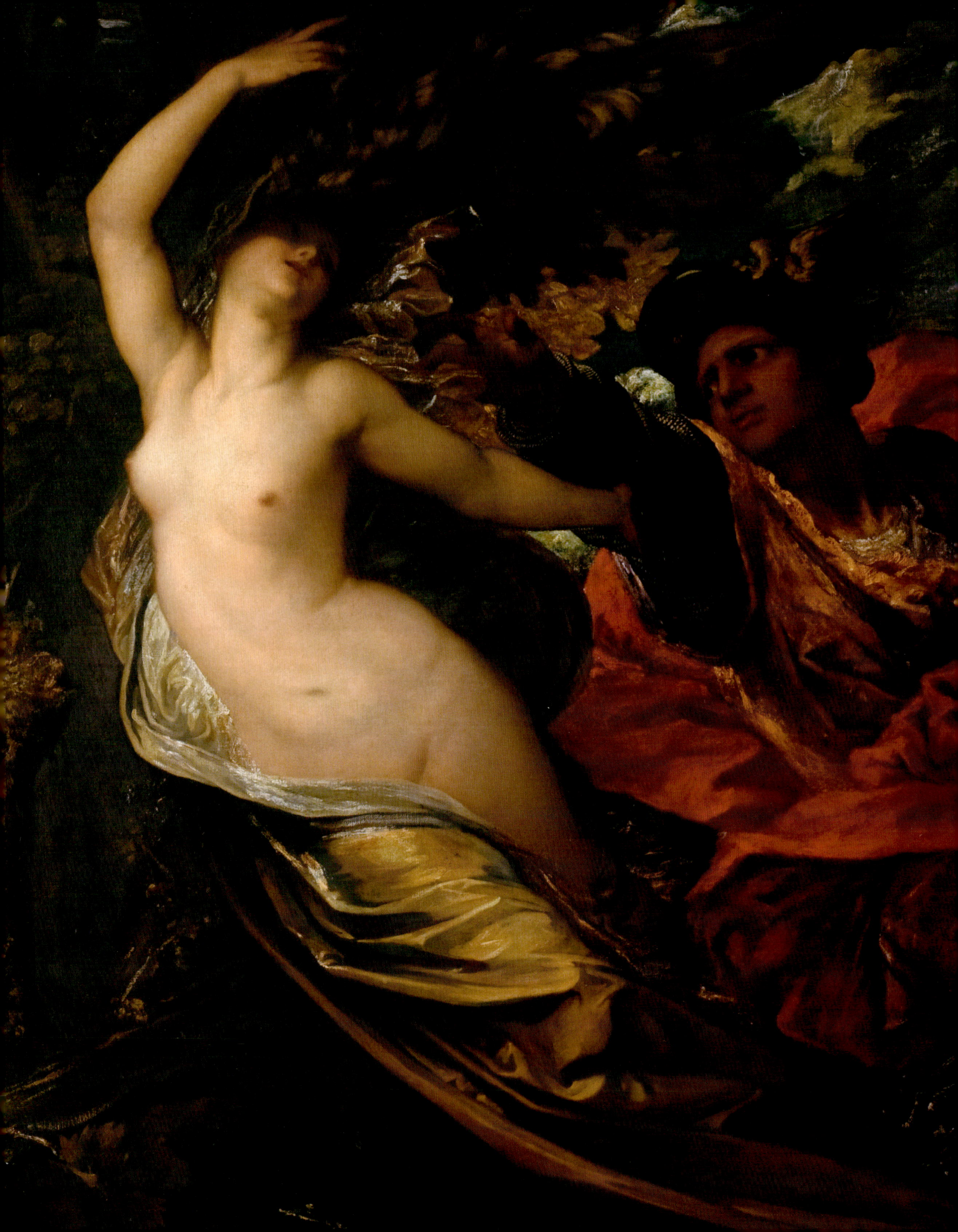

Oil Paintings in Public Ownership in Leicestershire, Lincolnshire & Rutland

Funding Patron
The Mercers' Company

Coordinators: Yasmin Canvin & Hazel Buchan-Cameron
Photographer: John MacLean

The Public Catalogue Foundation
Patron
HRH The Duchess of Cornwall

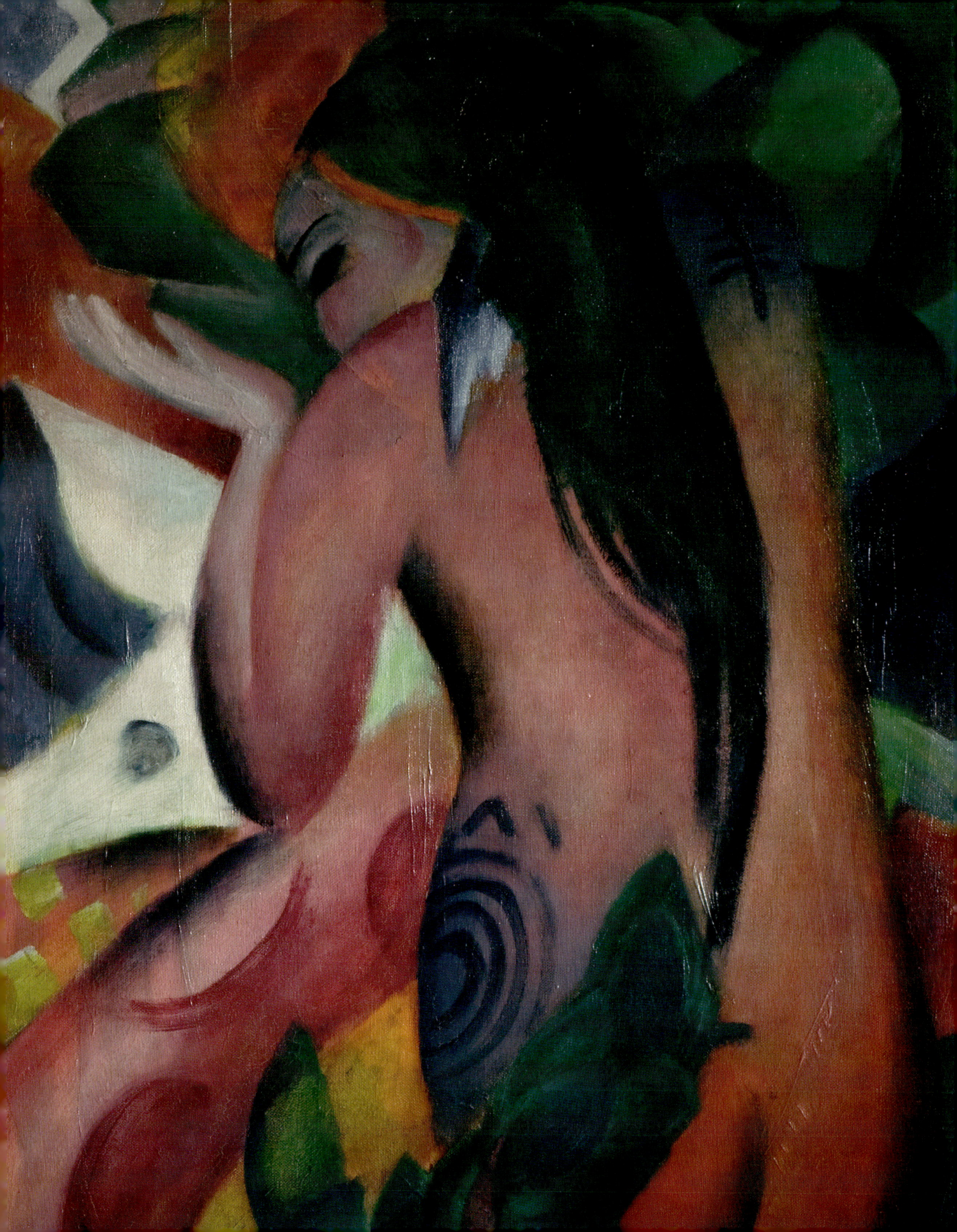

Contents

Facing page: Marc, Franz, 1880–1916, *Rote Frau* (detail), 1912, Leicester Arts and Museums Service, (p. 62)

Image opposite HRH The Duchess of Cornwall's statement: Munter, Gabriele, 1877–1962, *Anna Roslund (1891–1941)* (detail), Leicester Arts and Museums Service (p. 68)
Image opposite title page: Watts, George Frederick, 1817–1904, *Orlando Pursuing the Fata Morgana* (detail), 1846–1848, Leicester Arts and Museums Service, (p. 94)

i Leicester Arts and Museums Service, Leicester City Council (Adult Skills and Learning) and Leicester Town Hall are all managed by Leicester City Council.
ii Leicestershire County Council Artworks Collection, Leicestershire County Council Beaumanor Collection, Leicestershire County Council Civic Collection, Leicestershire County Council Museums Service and Leicestershire Libraries are all managed by Leicestershire County Council.
iii Gainsborough Old Hall, Grantham Museum, Museum of Lincolnshire Life, The Collection: Art & Archaeology in Lincolnshire (Usher Gallery), The Royal Lincolnshire Regimental Museum Trust and Stamford Museum are all managed by Lincolnshire County Council.
iv Grimsby Town Hall and North East Lincolnshire Museum Service are managed by North East Lincolnshire Council.
v The Guildhall, Lincoln and The Lawn are owned by the City of Lincoln Council.

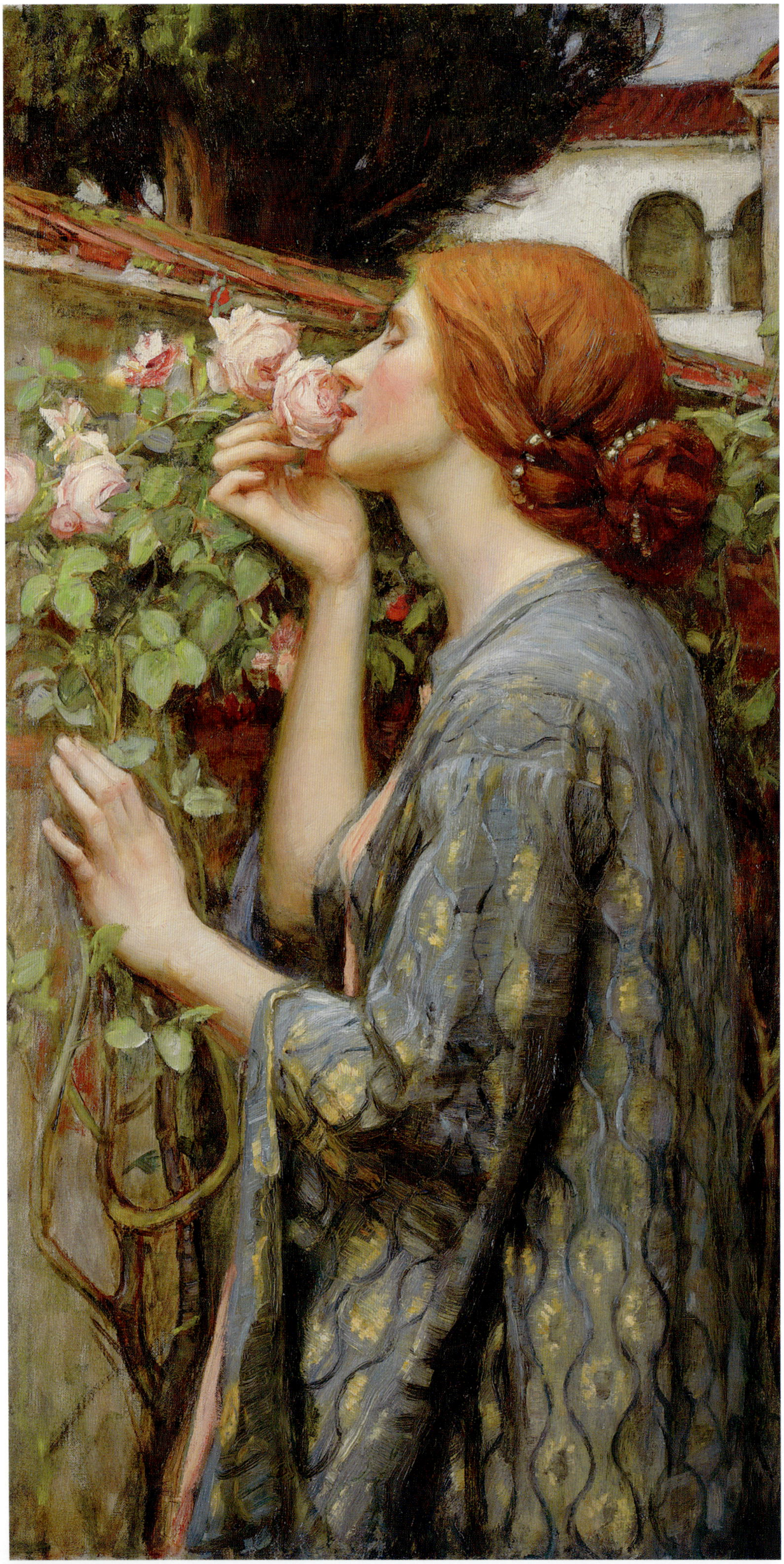

The Public Catalogue Foundation: People Involved

Trustees & Advisors

Staff

Financial Supporters and Others

The Public Catalogue Foundation would like to express its profound appreciation to the following organisations and individuals who, alongside the Mercers' Company, have made the publication of this catalogue possible:

Mr Tim Haywood

Yasmin Canvin and Hazel Buchan-Cameron, Coordinators
John MacLean, Photographer
Daniel Whibley
The Team at Maiden Lane
Sophie Kullmann
Ruth Chadwick

Catalogue Scope and Organisation

Medium and Support

The principal focus of this series is oil paintings. However, tempera and acrylic are also included as well as mixed media, where oil is the predominant constituent. Paintings on all forms of support (e.g. canvas, panel, etc.) are included as long as the support is portable. The principal exclusions are miniatures, hatchments or other purely heraldic paintings and wall paintings *in situ*.

Public Ownership

Public ownership has been taken to mean any paintings that are directly owned by the public purse, made accessible to the public by means of public subsidy or generally perceived to be in public ownership. The term 'public' refers to both central government and local government. Paintings held by national museums, local authority museums, English Heritage and independent museums, where there is at least some form of public subsidy, are included. Paintings held in civic buildings such as local government offices, town halls, guildhalls, public libraries, universities, hospitals, crematoria, fire stations and police stations are also included.

Geographical Boundaries of Catalogues

The geographical boundary of each county is the 'ceremonial county' boundary. This county definition includes all unitary authorities. Counties that have a particularly large number of paintings are divided between two or more catalogues on a geographical basis.

Criteria for Inclusion

As long as paintings meet the requirements above, all paintings are included irrespective of their condition and perceived quality. However, painting reproductions can only be included with the agreement of the participating collections and, where appropriate, the relevant copyright owner. It is rare that a collection forbids the inclusion of its paintings. Where this is the case and it is possible to obtain a list of paintings, this list is given in the Paintings Without Reproductions section. Where copyright consent is refused, the paintings are also listed in the Paintings Without Reproductions section. All paintings in collections' stacks and stores are included, as well as those on display. Paintings which have been lent to other institutions, whether for short-term exhibition or long-term loan, are listed under the owner collection. In addition, paintings on long-term loan are also included under the borrowing institution when they are likely to remain there for at least another five years from the date of publication of this catalogue. Information relating to owners and borrowers is listed in the Further Information section.

Layout

Collections are grouped together under their home town. These locations are listed in alphabetical order. In some cases collections that are spread over a number of locations are included under a single owner collection. A number of collections, principally the larger ones, are preceded by curatorial forewords. Within each collection paintings are listed in order of artist surname. Where there is more than one painting by the same artist, the paintings are listed chronologically, according to their execution date.

The few paintings that are not accompanied by photographs are listed in the Paintings Without Reproductions section.

There is additional reference material in the Further Information section at the back of the catalogue. This gives the full names of artists, titles and media if it has not been possible to include these in full in the main section. It also provides acquisition credit lines and information about loans in and out, as well as copyright and photographic credits for each painting. Finally, there is an index of artists' surnames.

Key to Painting Information

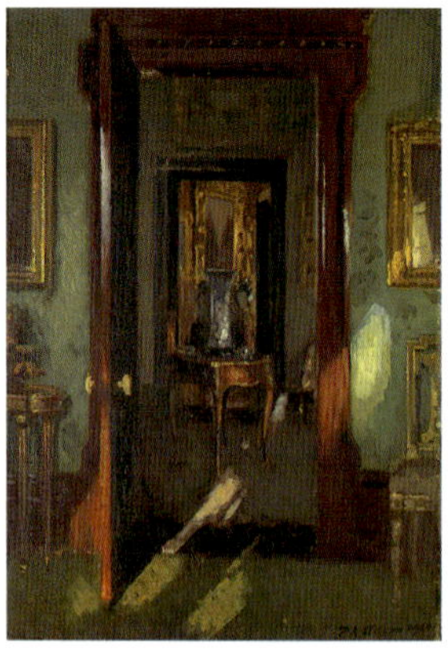

Almost all paintings are reproduced in the catalogue. Where this is not the case they are listed in the Paintings Without Reproductions section. Where paintings are missing or have been stolen, the best possible photograph on record has been reproduced. In some cases this may be black and white. Paintings that have been stolen are highlighted with a red border. Some paintings are shown with conservation tissue attached to parts of the painting surface.

Adam, Patrick William 1854–1929
Interior, Rutland Lodge: Vista through Open Doors 1920
oil on canvas 67.3 × 45.7
LEEAG.PA.1925.0671.LACF

Artist name This is shown with the surname first. Where the artist is listed on the Getty Union List of Artist Names (ULAN), ULAN's preferred presentation of the name is given. In a number of cases the name may not be a firm attribution and this is made clear. Where the artist name is not known, a school may be given instead. Where the school is not known, the painter name is listed as *unknown artist*. If the artist name is too long for the space, as much of the name is given as possible followed by (...). This indicates the full name is given at the rear of the catalogue in the Further Information section.

Painting title A painting title followed by *(?)* indicates that the title is in doubt. Where the alternative title to the painting is considered to be better known than the original, the alternative title is given in parentheses. Where the collection has not given a painting a title, the publisher does so instead and marks this with an asterisk. If the title is too long for the space, as much of the title is given as possible followed by *(...)* and the full title is given in the Further Information section.

Execution date In some cases the precise year of execution may not be known for certain. Instead an approximate date will be given or no date at all.

Artist dates Where known, the years of birth and death of the artist are given. In some cases one or both dates may not be known with certainty, and this is marked. No date indicates that even an approximate date is not known. Where only the period in which the artist was active is known, these dates are given and preceded with the word *active*.

Medium and support Where the precise material used in the support is known, this is given.

Dimensions All measurements refer to the unframed painting and are given in cm with up to one decimal point. In all cases the height is shown before the width. An (E) indicates where a painting has not been measured and its size has been calculated by sight only. If the painting is circular, the single dimension is the diameter. If the painting is oval, the dimensions are height and width.

Collection inventory number In the case of paintings owned by museums, this number will always be the accession number. In all other cases it will be a unique inventory number of the owner institution. (P) indicates that a painting is a private loan. Details can be found in the Further Information section. Accession numbers preceded by 'PCF' indicate that the collection did not have an accession number at the time of catalogue production and therefore the number given has been temporarily allocated by The Public Catalogue Foundation. The symbol indicates that the reproduction is based on a Bridgeman Art Library transparency (go to www.bridgemanart.com) or that Bridgeman administers the copyright for that artist.

Facing page: Monaco Lorenzo, c.1370–1425, *St John the Baptist Entering the Wilderness* (detail), Leicester Arts and Museums Service (p. 60)

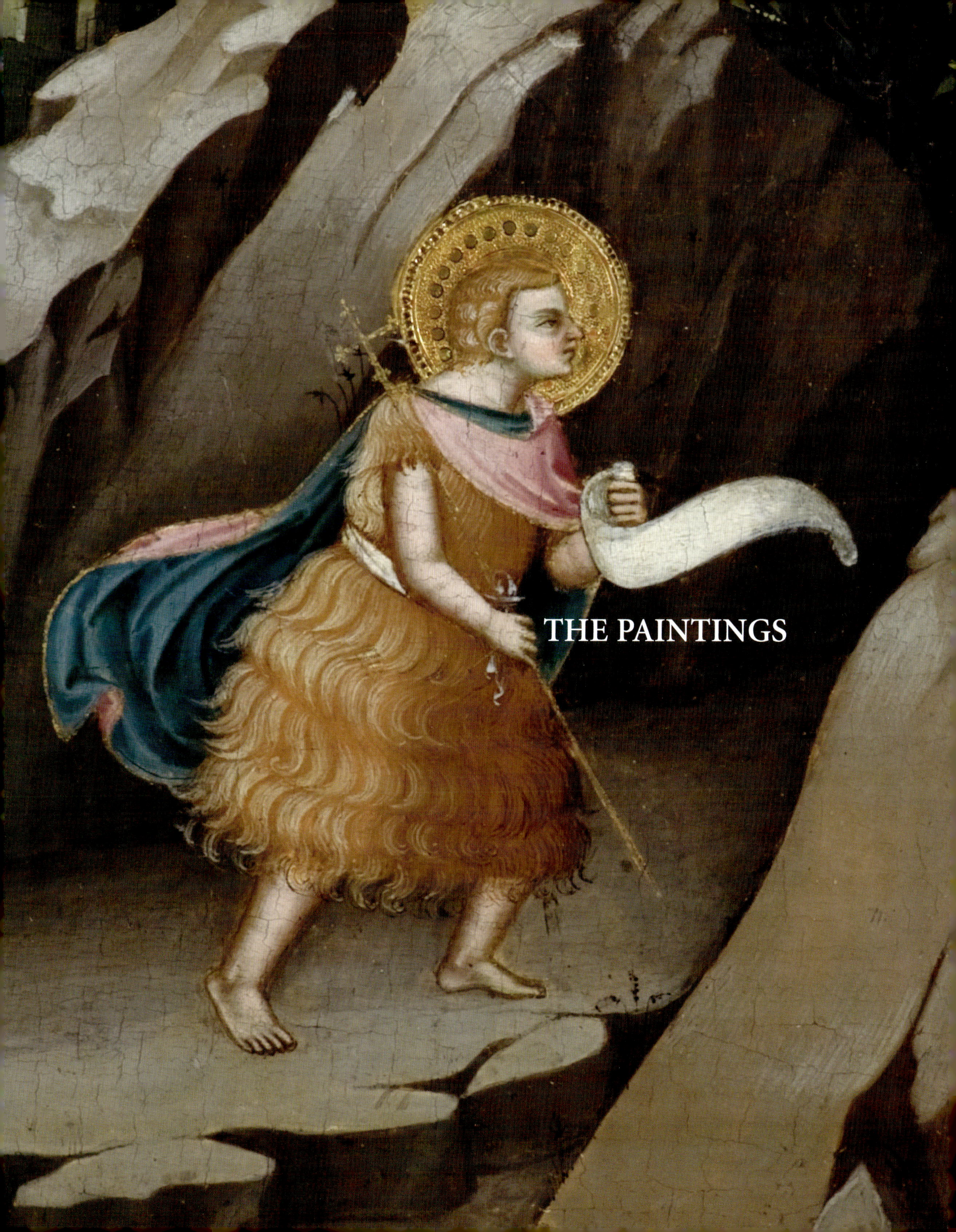

THE PAINTINGS

Ashby-de-la-Zouch Museum

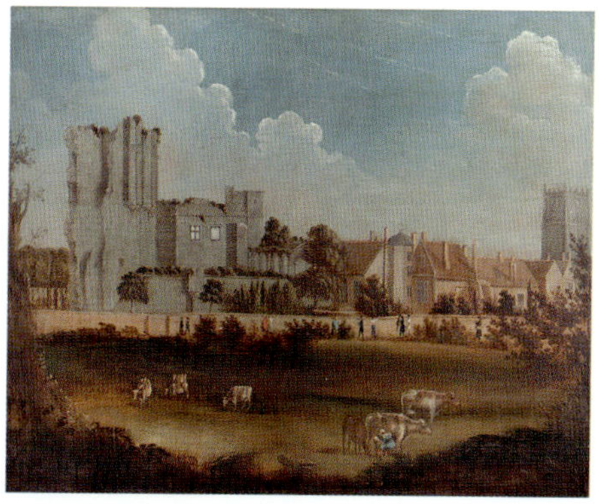

British (English) School
View of Ashby-de-la-Zouch Castle, Leicestershire, with Passers-By 1828–1830
oil on canvas 87.6 x 114.9
AYZMU/2008/415

Castle Donington Museum

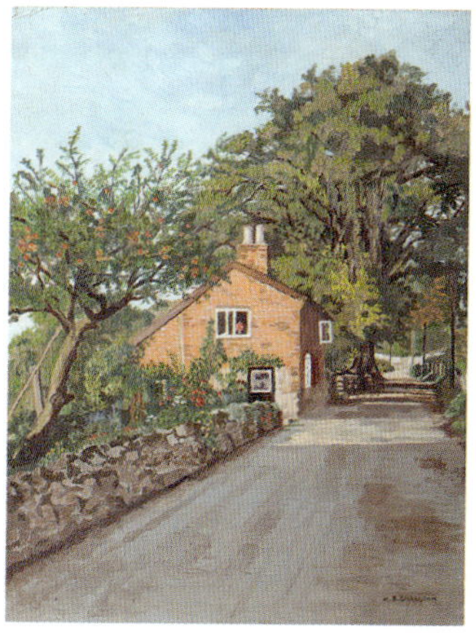

Charlton, Margaret c.1905–c.1980
Little Lane in Derbyshire
oil on board 40.5 x 30.5
CADMT.2000.19.37

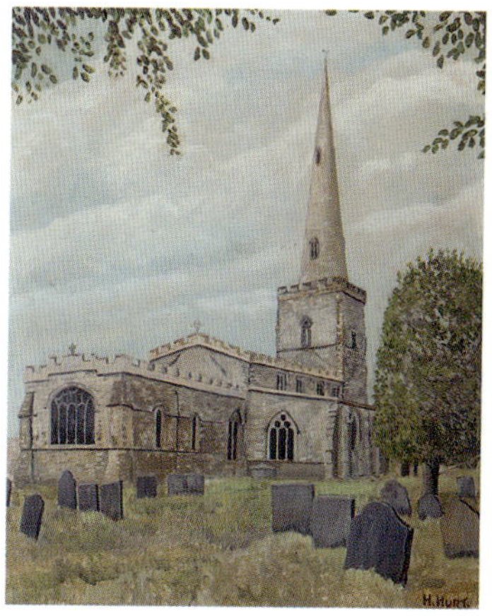

Hurt, Henry d.c.1980
St Edward's Church, Castle Donington, Leicestershire
oil on board 38 x 29.5
CADMT.2006.99

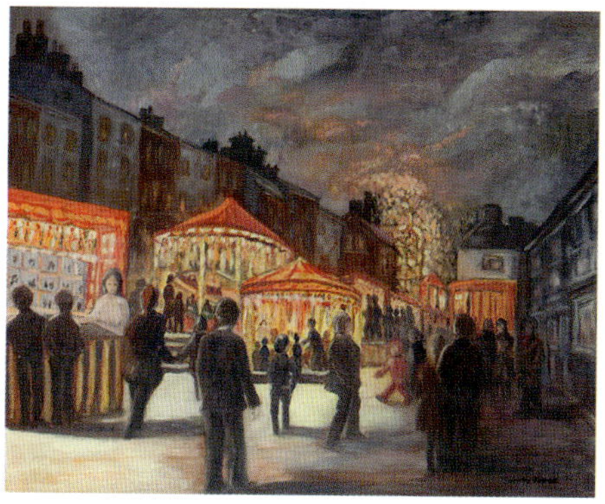

Jones, Dorothy d.c.1990
Castle Donington Wakes, Leicestershire 1970s
oil on board 50.8 x 61
CADMT.2000.19.36

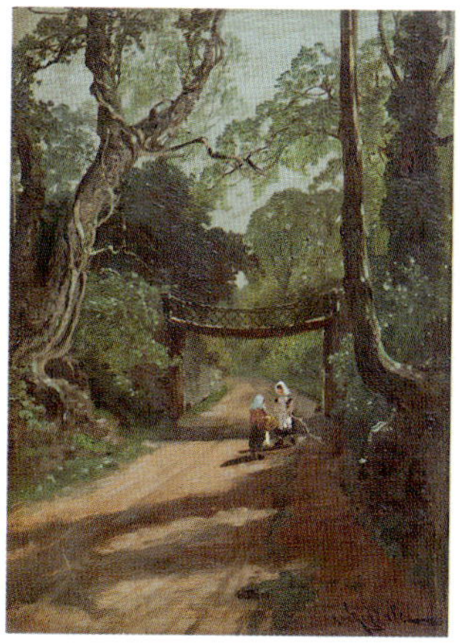

Redgate, Arthur Walker 1860–1906
Chain Bridge, King's Mills, Leicestershire c.1891
oil on wood 25.5 x 18
CADMT.2000.19.33

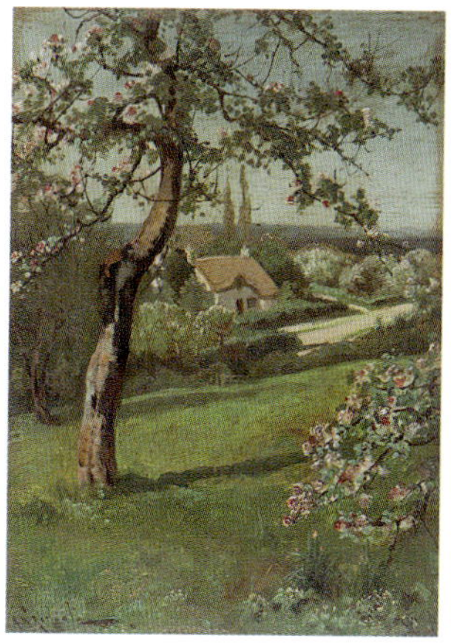

Redgate, Arthur Walker 1860–1906
Cottage in Fields c.1891
oil on wood 25.5 x 18
CADMT.2000.19.34

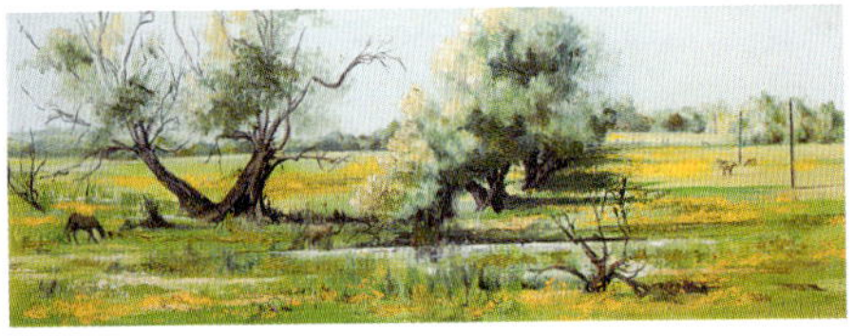

Trotter, Diana b.1923
Shardlow Water Meadows, Derbyshire 1975
oil on canvas 36 x 92
CADMT.2009.52

Hinckley and District Museum

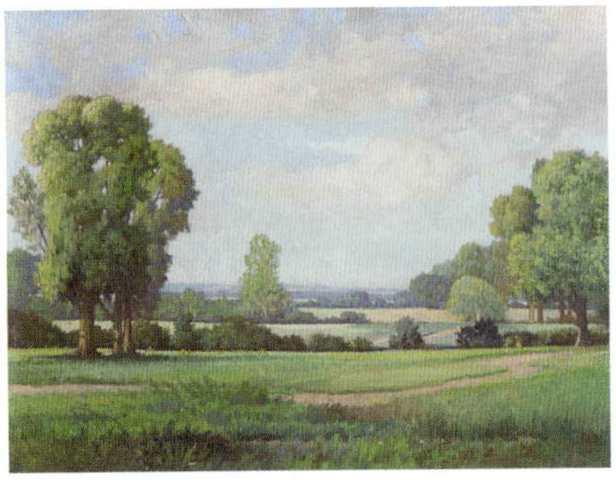

Billinghame, Wilfred Ernest c.1882–1965
Open Country 1940s
oil on canvas 43 x 53.5
HNKDM/1998/25

John Cleveland College

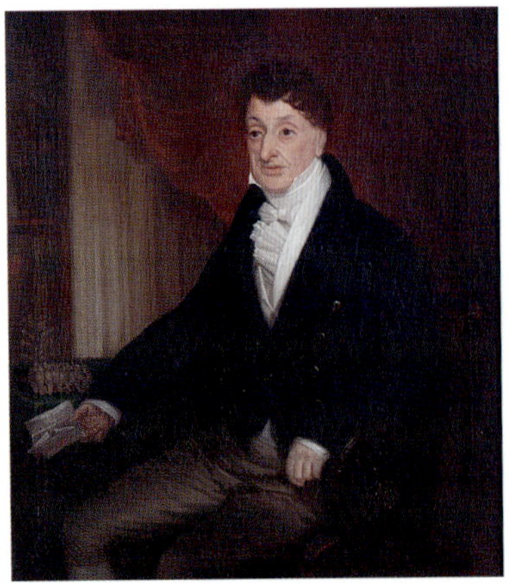

Bass, Stanley
Dr Cheshire, First British Orthopaedic Surgeon c.1820
oil on canvas 50 x 43.5
2

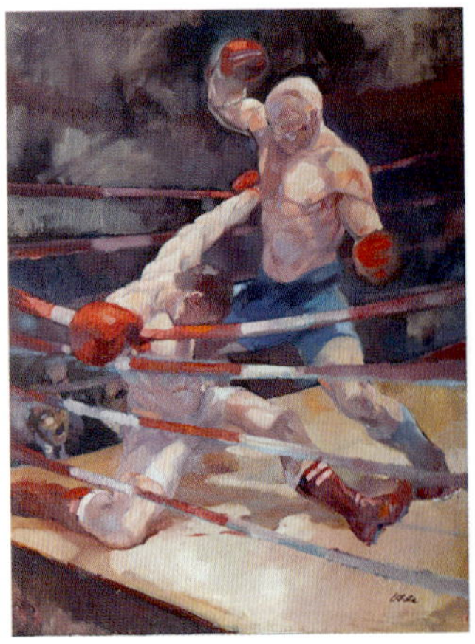

Bate, William
Boxers 1987
oil on canvas 122 x 91
6

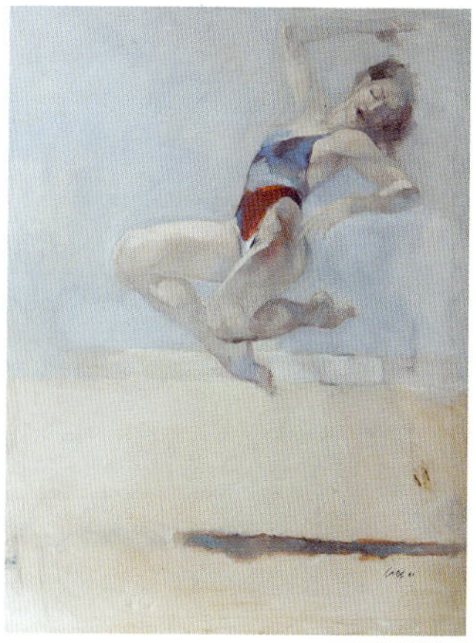

Bate, William
Gymnast 1988
oil on canvas 122 x 91
7

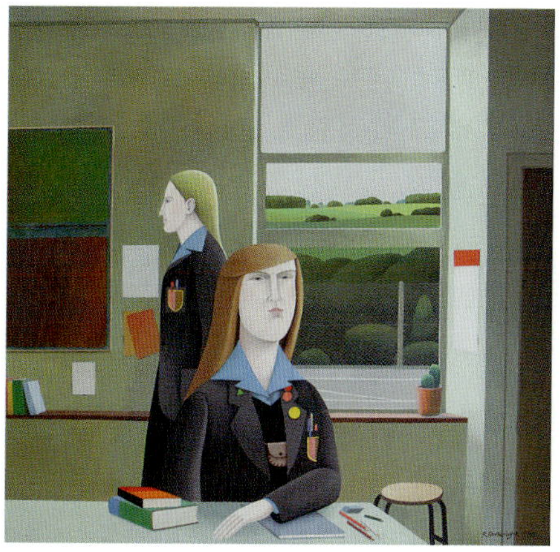

Cartwright, Reg b.1938
The Schoolgirl 1980
oil on canvas 91 x 91
4

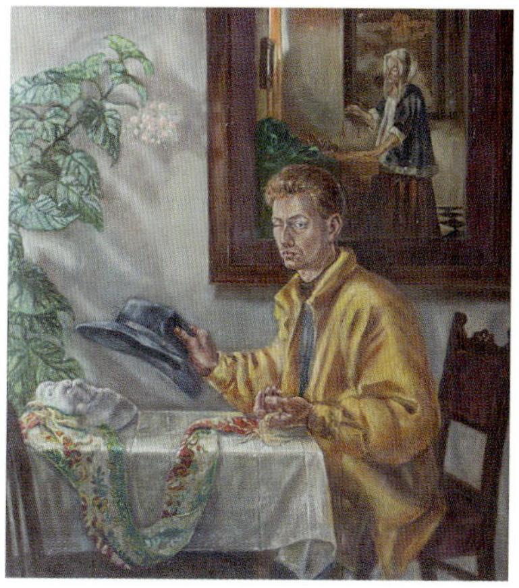

Jarvis, Timothy
Age of Aspirations 1986
oil on canvas 123 x 107
9

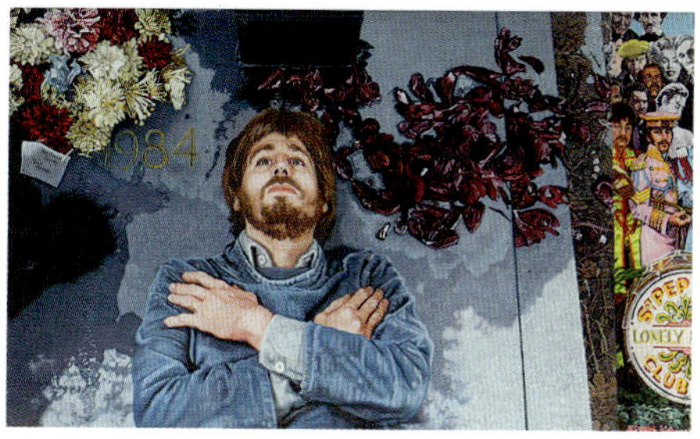

Littlehales, Thomas Paul b.1945
Endangered Species 1980
oil on canvas 92 x 153
8

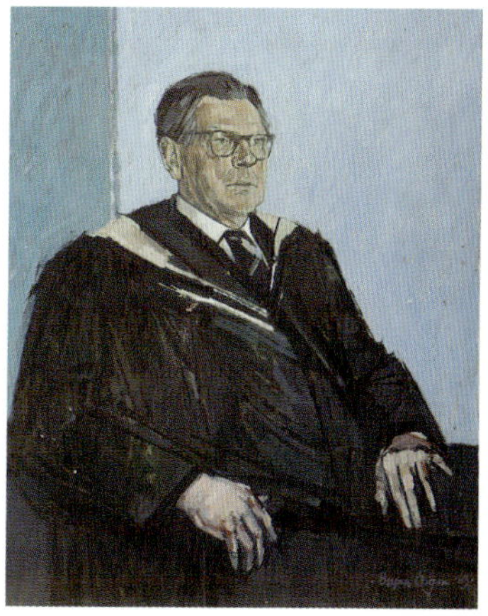

Organ, Bryan b.1935
Frank Oldham, Former Headmaster of John Cleveland College 1963
oil on canvas 91 x 71
1

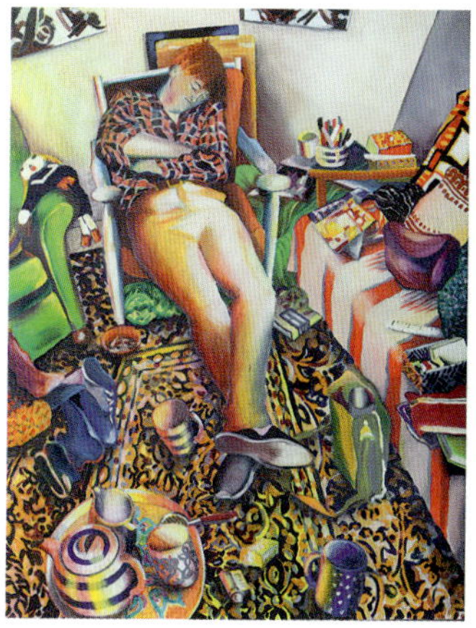

Whitrow, Kirsty b.1960
The Beast Is Asleep 1983
oil on canvas 154 x 123
5

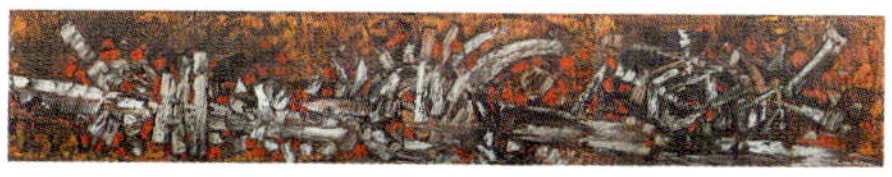

Wilson, Frank Avray 1914–2009
Paris (3 panels) 1959
oil on canvas 76 x 152; 76 x 152; 76 x 152
3

Kegworth Museum

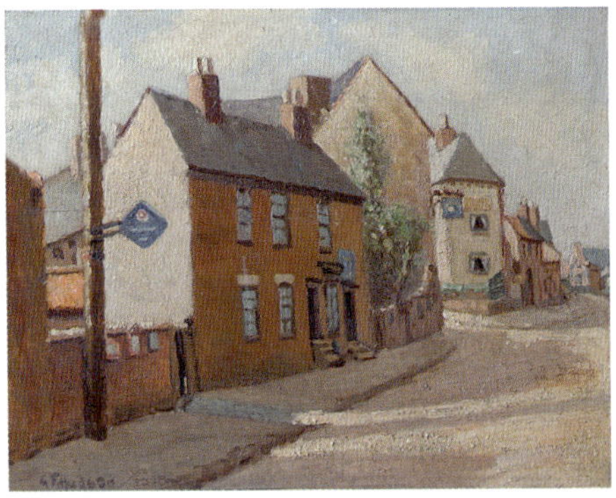

Hudson, George Frederick 1895–1966
Sir John Kirk's Birthplace
oil on board 24 x 30
2 (P)

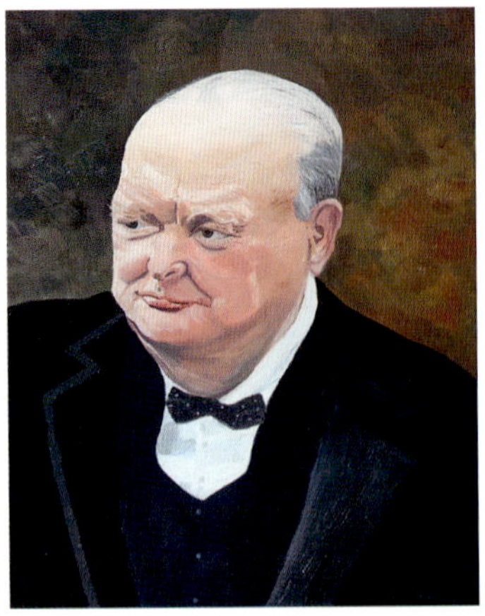

Stanway, S.
Sir Winston Churchill (1874–1965)
oil on board 50 x 40
3

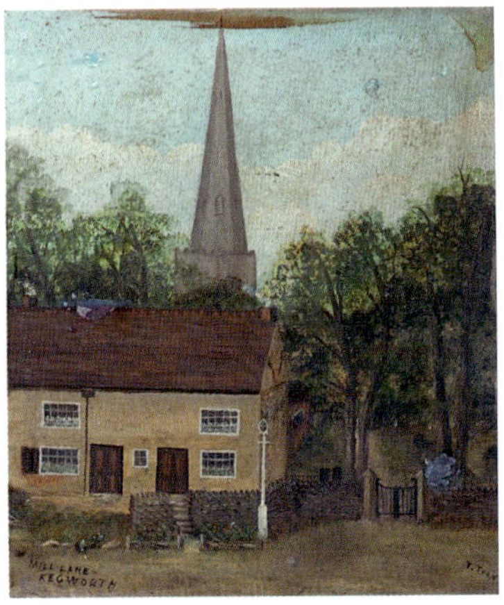

Toon, Tommy d.1962
Mill Lane, Kegworth, Leicestershire
oil on board 30 x 25
1

Kibworth C. of E. Primary School

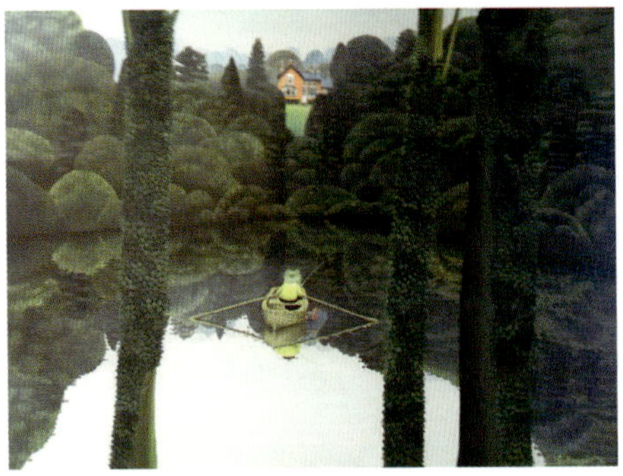

Cartwright, Reg b.1938
View of Gumley Lake, Leicestershire
oil on canvas 60 x 90 (E)
1

Leicester Arts and Museums Service

To say that Leicester seized the invitation to join The PCF's series of catalogues with both hands is an understatement. We are delighted that this catalogue presents the Leicester Arts and Museums Service's art collections in a stunning new light, and marks the first major survey publication of the collections since 1978.

The New Walk Museum and Art Gallery opened its first dedicated art gallery in 1885, and by 1893 some 87 paintings had been purchased by the Art Gallery Committee. In the past 125 years the Collection has grown to include over 750 oil, tempera and acrylic paintings and approximately 3,000 works on paper. Paintings date from the fifteenth to the twenty-first centuries, the earliest an exquisite panel from c.1400 of *Saint John the Baptist Entering the Wilderness* by Lorenzo Monaco, with further pieces of international importance by Edgar Degas, Georges de la Tour, Camille Pissarro, Alfred Sisley, Michael Sweerts and Aert van der Neer.

The British works demonstrate breadth and variety, forming one of the leading collections of British art to be found in a local authority museums service. Examples include eighteenth-century portraiture by Arthur Devis, Allan Ramsay and Joseph Wright of Derby and nineteenth-century landscape, mythological and classical scenes by Frank Dicksee, William Powell Frith, John Fulleylove, Frederic Leighton and Joseph Mallord William Turner. L. S. Lowry's great vision of smoking factories, *Industrial Landscape, River Scene,* connects to the similarly bleak interior of *Lying Figure No.1* by the twentieth-century master of human angst, Francis Bacon.

In contrast, Sarup Singh's *Martin Luther King Junior (1929–1968)* and Aubrey Williams' *Maya Confrontation* join contemporary portraits by Alan Parker in exploring and celebrating aspects of cross-cultural identity, echoing our city's dynamic, diverse character.

Leicester also possesses an internationally acclaimed collection of early twentieth-century German Expressionist art, which is the best of its kind in the UK, crowned by Franz Marc's 1912 masterpiece *Rote Frau* (The Red Woman).

The first acquisitions were made from the 1944 'Mid-European Art' exhibition held at Leicester Museum and Art Gallery which featured works brought out of Germany by émigré and refugee artists and collectors. Treasures here include paintings by Lovis Corinth, Lyonel Feininger, Gabriele Munter, Ernst Neuschul and Hermann Max Pechstein.

Our grateful thanks go to The PCF team; also to Mary Hider, Documentation Manager, and Claire Cooper, Documentation Officer (Leicester Arts and Museums), for their unstinting attention to detail regarding catalogue entries.

We acknowledge the generous support of The Art Fund and Victoria and Albert Museum Purchase Grant Fund; also the City of Leicester Museums Trust, the Friends of Leicester and Leicestershire Museums and the many individual supporters whose contributions have helped to build this wonderful Collection.

Simon Lake, Senior Curator of Art, New Walk Museum and Art Gallery

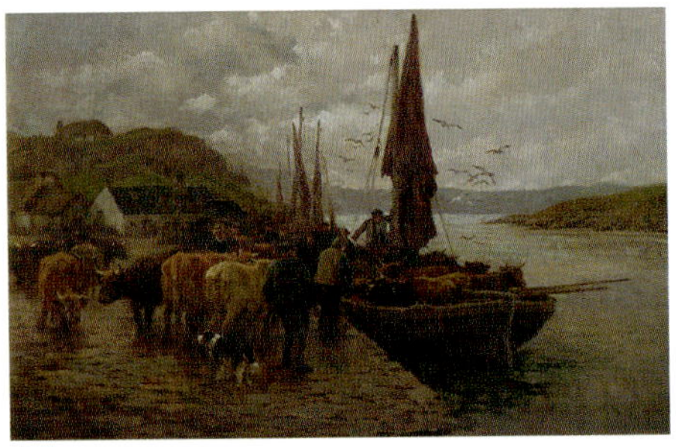

Adams, Charles James 1859–1931
The Ferry
oil on canvas 31 x 45.8
L.F310.1973.0.0

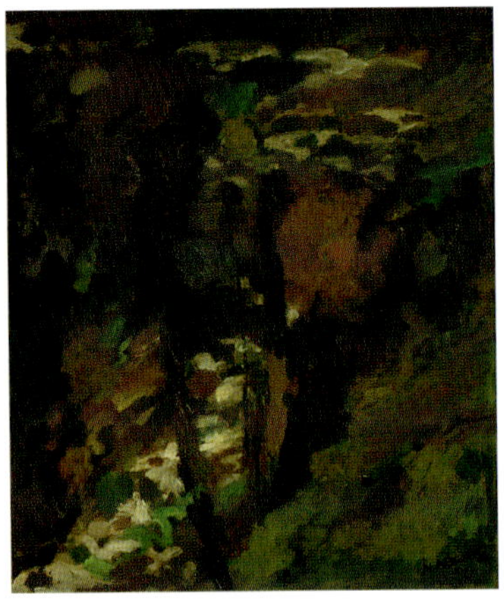

Adams, Norman 1927–2005
Brants Ghyll, North Yorkshire, through Foliage 1957
oil on canvas 96.5 x 78.7
L.F9.1958.0.0

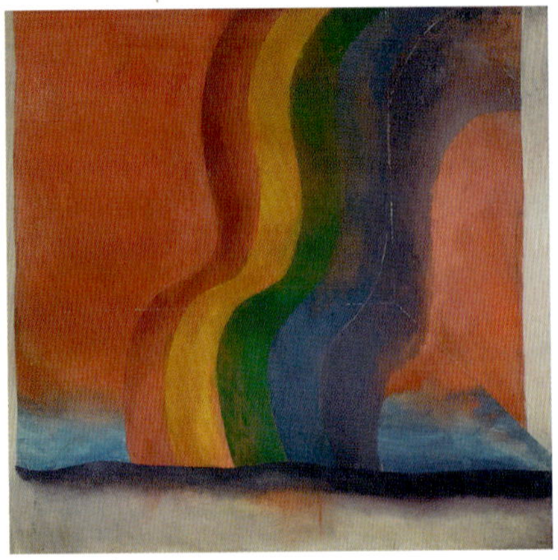

Adams, Norman 1927–2005
Rainbow Painting 4, Easter Series 1966
oil on canvas 127 x 127
L.F79.1973.0.0

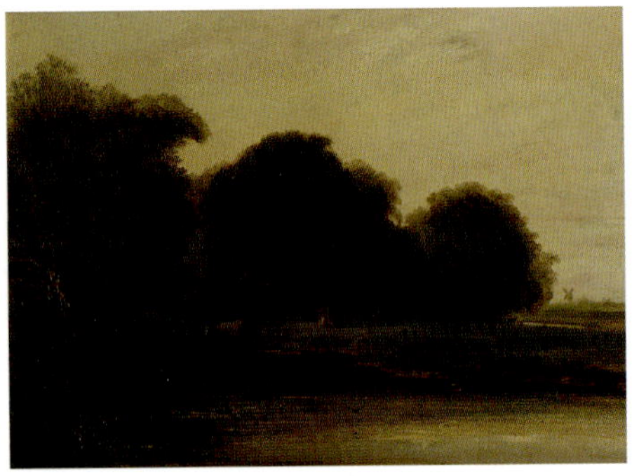

Adcock, John Wilton 1863–1930
Cattle at a Stream
oil on canvas 45.5 x 61
Y.F7.2009.0.0

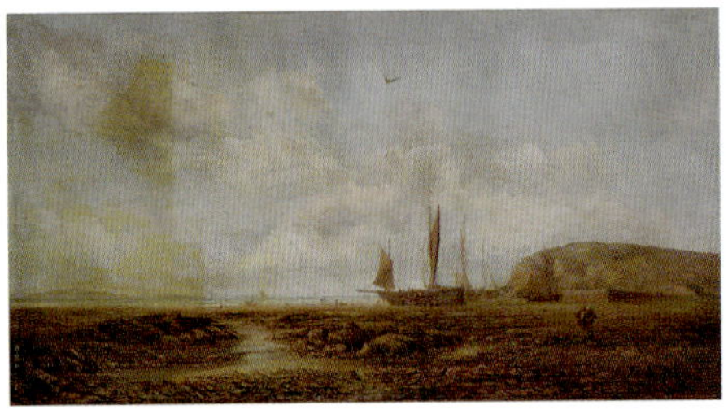

Adcock, John Wilton 1863–1930
On the Cornish Coast
oil on canvas 45.7 x 81.3
Y.F18.2009.0.0

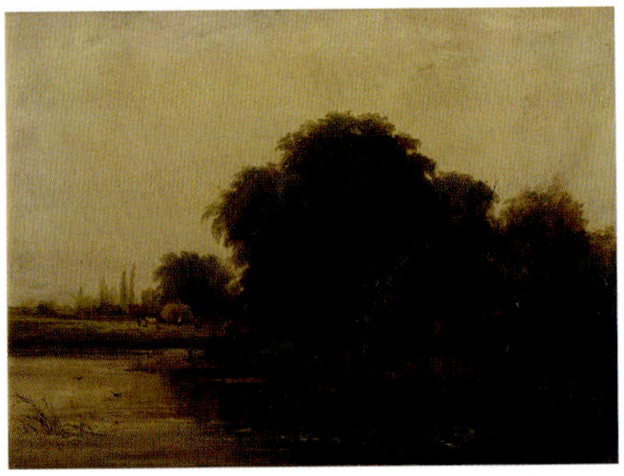

Adcock, John Wilton 1863–1930
Stream with Harvesters
oil on canvas 43.7 x 57.4
Y.F10.2009.0.0

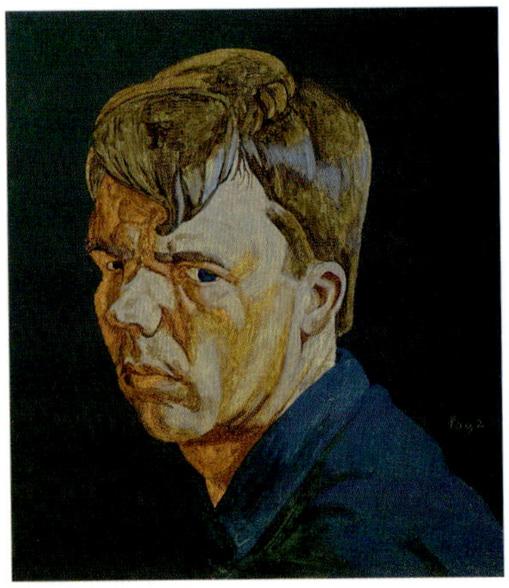

Akkerman, Philip b.1957
Self Portrait No.92 1992
oil on board 40 x 34
Y.F14.2000.0.0

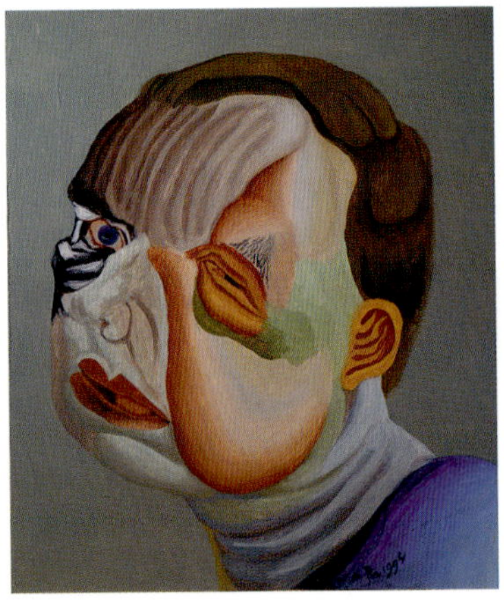

Akkerman, Philip b.1957
Self Portrait No.42 1994
oil on board 40 x 34
Y.F13.2000.0.0

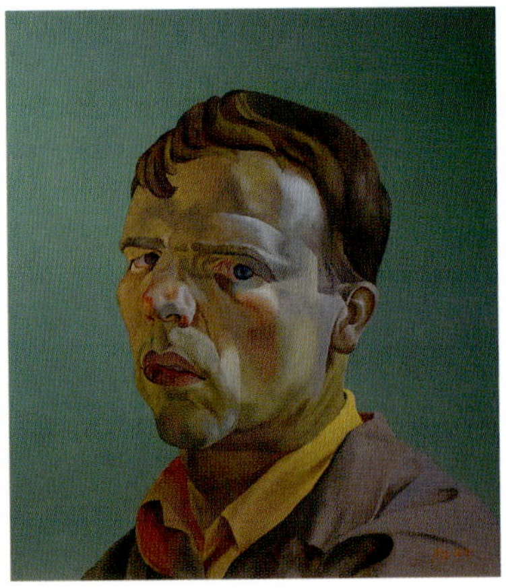

Akkerman, Philip b.1957
Self Portrait No.31 1995
oil on board 50 x 43
Y.F16.2000.0.0

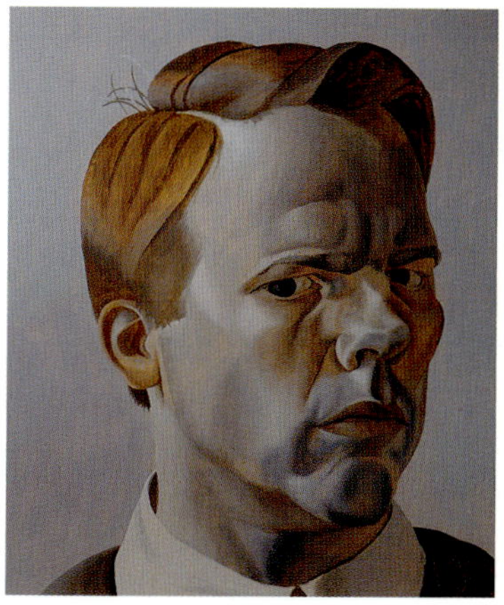

Akkerman, Philip b.1957
Self Portrait No.38 1996
oil on board 40 x 34
Y.F15.2000.0.0

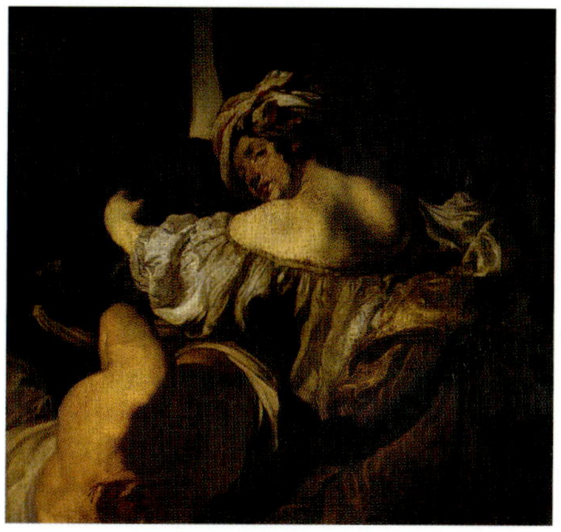

Alberti, Cherubino (follower of) 1553–1615
Judith with the Head of Holofernes
oil on canvas 102 x 108
L.F113.1981.0.0

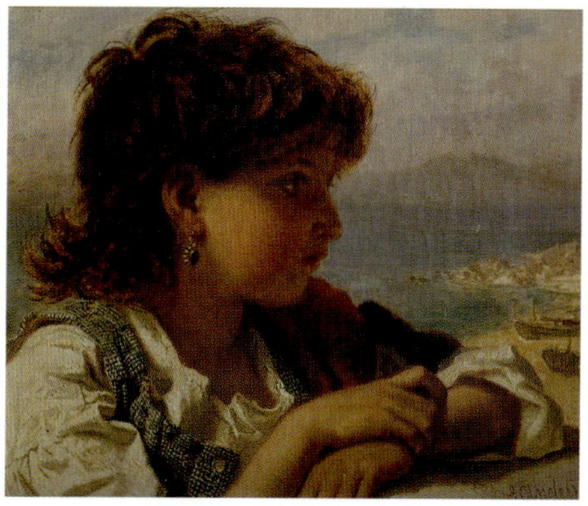

Anderson, Sophie 1823–1912
A Neapolitan Boy
oil on canvas 31.8 x 37.7
L.F4.1908.0.0

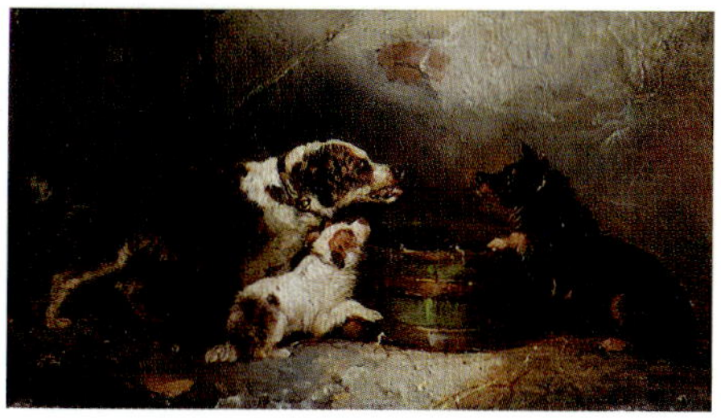

Armfield, George 1810–1893
The Breakfast Party
oil on panel 12.5 x 22
L.F7.1900.0.0

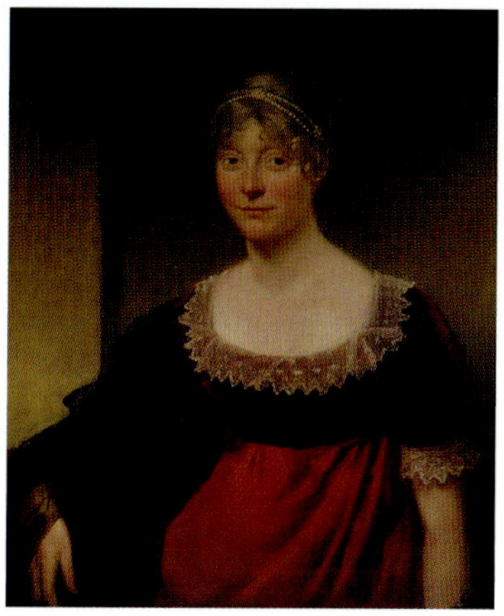

Artaud, William 1763–1823
Portrait of a Lady 1809
oil on canvas 75.6 x 62.2
L.F8.1900.0.0

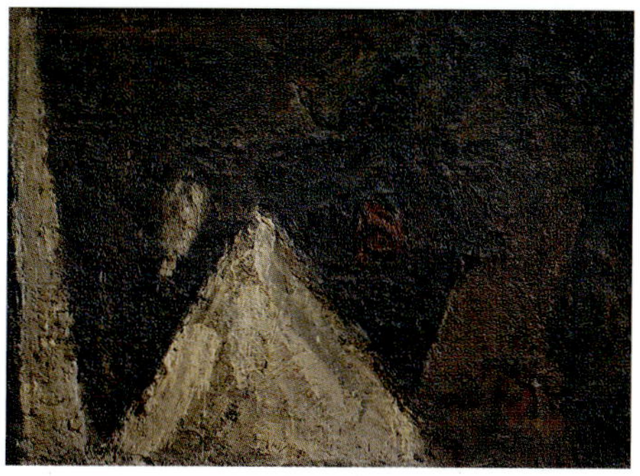

Auerbach, Frank Helmuth b.1931
Bruton Street Building Site, London 1953
oil on millboard 76 x 100.2
L.F395.1976.0.0

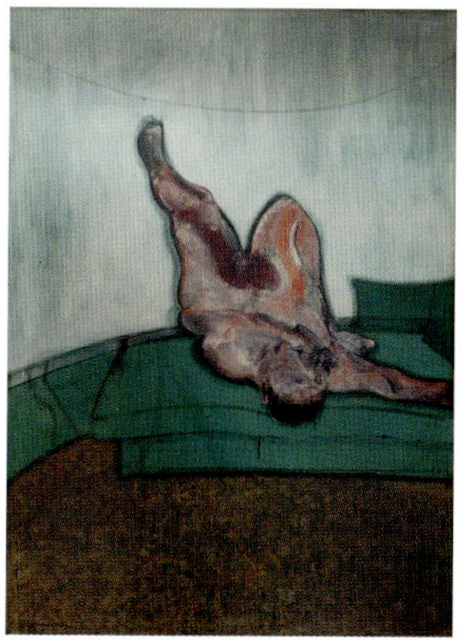

Bacon, Francis 1909–1992
Lying Figure No.1 1959
oil on canvas 196 x 141.5
L.F7.1960.0.0

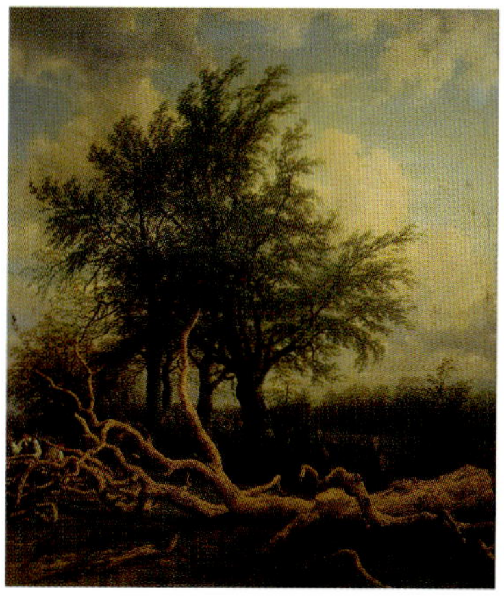

Baker, Thomas 1809–1869
Felling Timber 1850
oil on canvas 85 x 72
L.F4.1881.0.0

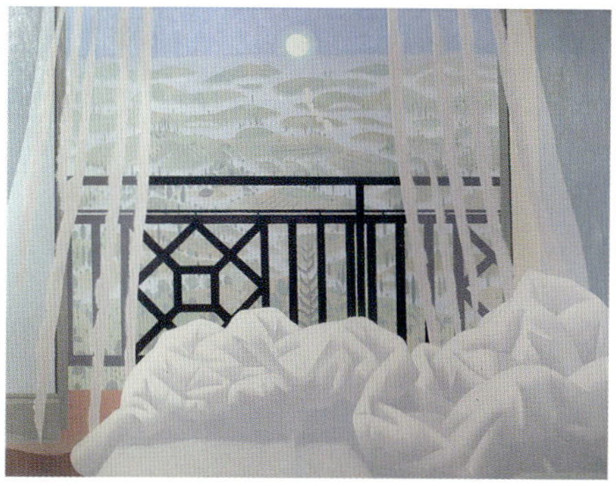

Balmer, Barbara b.1929
Domenica 1993
oil on panel 107 x 137.5
L.F2.1997.0.0

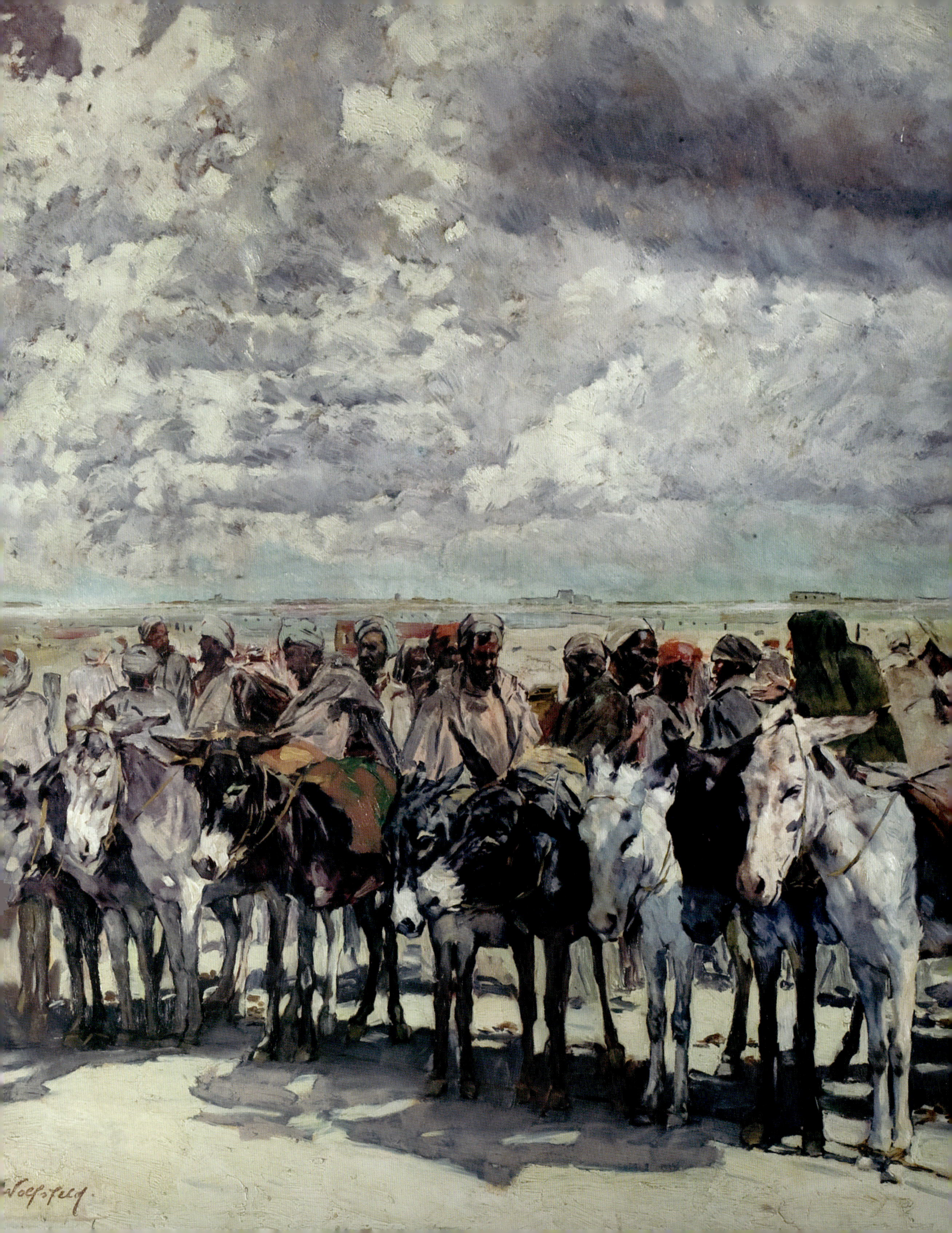

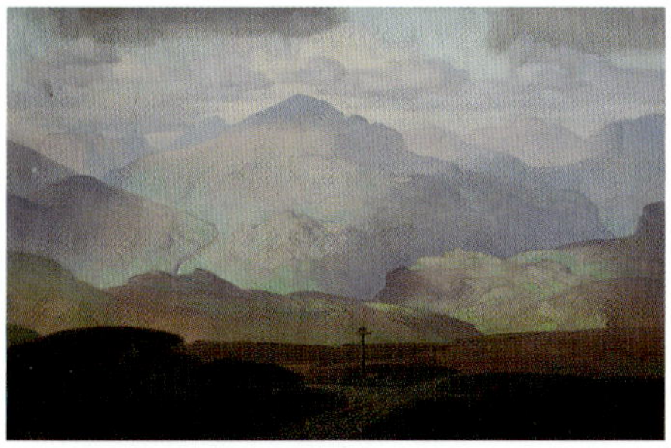

Banner, Delmar Harmond 1896–1983
Scafell from Birker Moor, Eskdale, Cumberland
1943–1944
oil on canvas 61 x 91.5
L.F36.1948.0.0

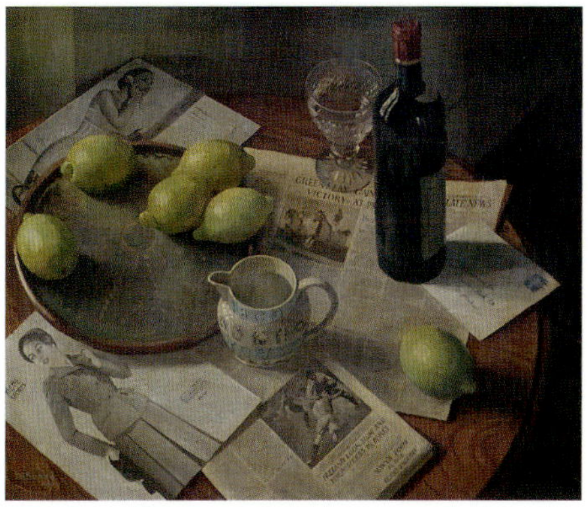

Barnard, Thomas Henslow 1898–1992
Still Life
oil on canvas 51 x 60.8
L.F3.1996.40.0

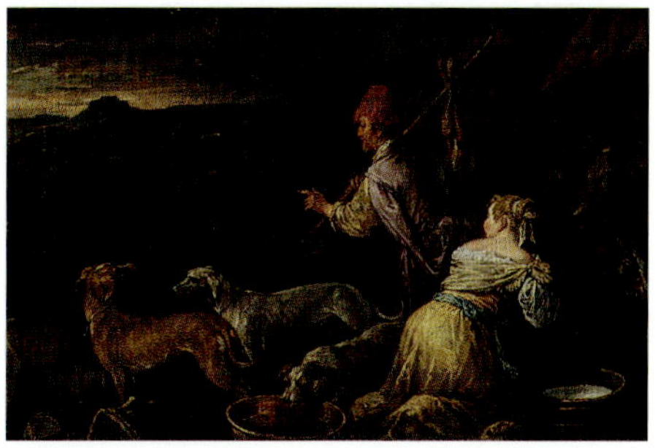

Bassano, Jacopo the elder (follower of)
c.1510–1592
Two Peasants with Animals
oil on canvas 38.1 x 57.1
L.F34.1939.0.0

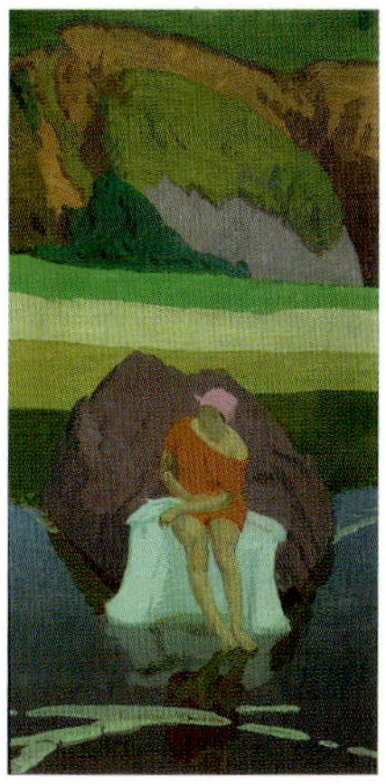

Bayes, Walter 1869–1956
The Bather 1917
oil on canvas 115.5 x 56
L.F3.1929.0.0

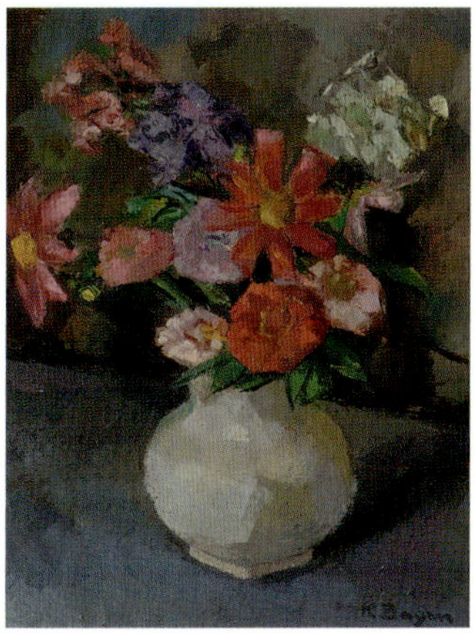

Baynes, Keith 1887–1977
Still Life, Flowers
oil on canvas 45.7 x 35.5
L.F3.1944.0.0

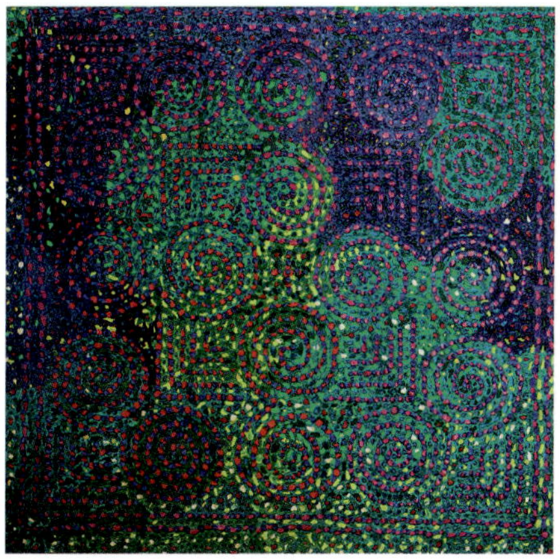

Beaton, Angus b.1948
Sid Barrett's Garden 2005
oil on canvas 122 x 122
Y.F7.2006.0.0

Beaumont, George Howland 1753–1827
Derwentwater, Cumberland c.1798
oil on canvas & millboard 38.5 x 54
L.F8.1953.1.0

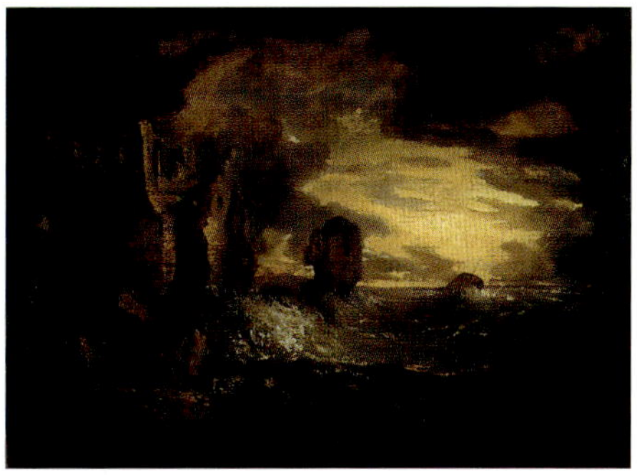

Beaumont, George Howland 1753–1827
Peel Castle in a Storm, Isle of Man c.1800
oil on canvas 73.6 x 99
L.F49.1986.0.0

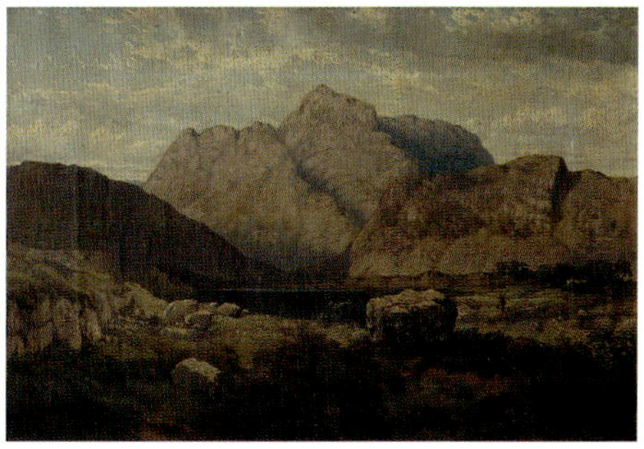

Beaumont, George Howland 1753–1827
View near Keswick, Cumberland 1803
oil on canvas 32 x 45
L.F5.1971.0.0

Facing page: Wolfsfeld, Erich, 1884–1956, *Caravan Resting* (detail), The Collection: Art & Archaeology in Lincolnshire (Usher Gallery) (p. 342)

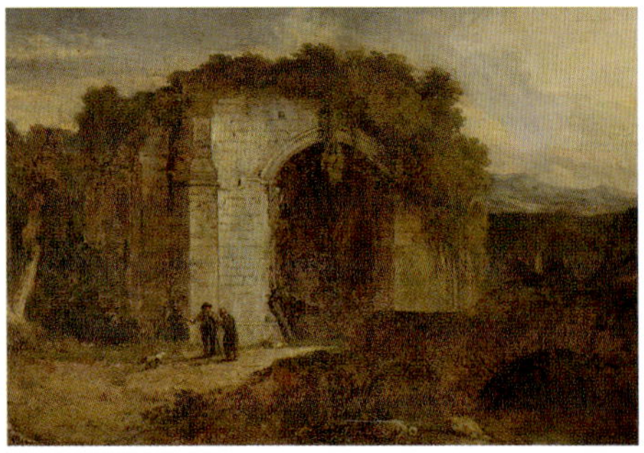

Beaumont, George Howland 1753–1827
A Ruined Abbey before 1807
oil on millboard 29.7 x 42.2
L.F8.1953.7.0

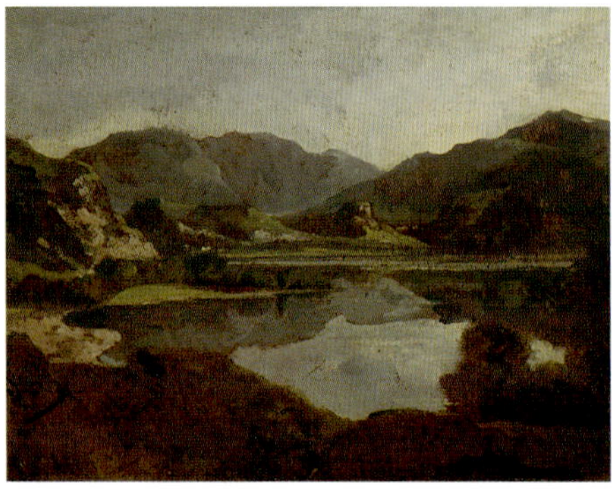

Beaumont, George Howland 1753–1827
Keswick Lake, Cumberland 1807
oil on millboard 24.6 x 30.5
L.F8.1953.14.0

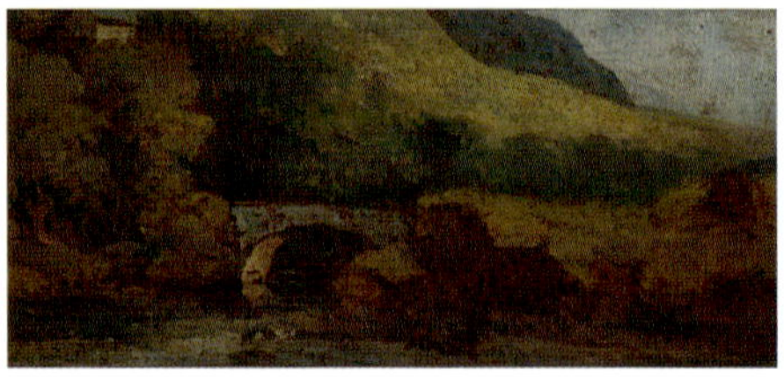

Beaumont, George Howland 1753–1827
Landscape with a Bridge 1807
oil on millboard 11.5 x 24
L.F8.1953.5.0

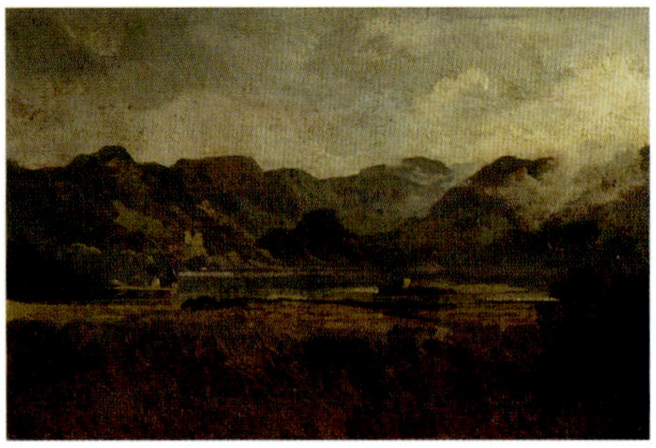

Beaumont, George Howland 1753–1827
Derwentwater, Cumberland c.1807
oil on millboard 22 x 31.5
L.F8.1953.3.0

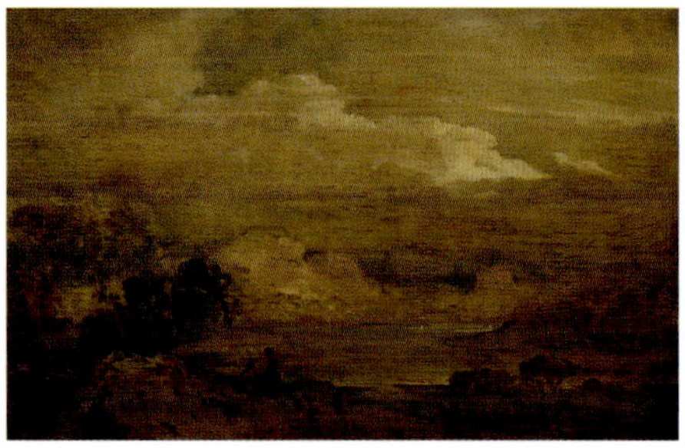

Beaumont, George Howland 1753–1827
Derwentwater, Cumberland c.1807–c.1818
oil on millboard 31.4 x 47
L.F51.1986.0.0 (P)

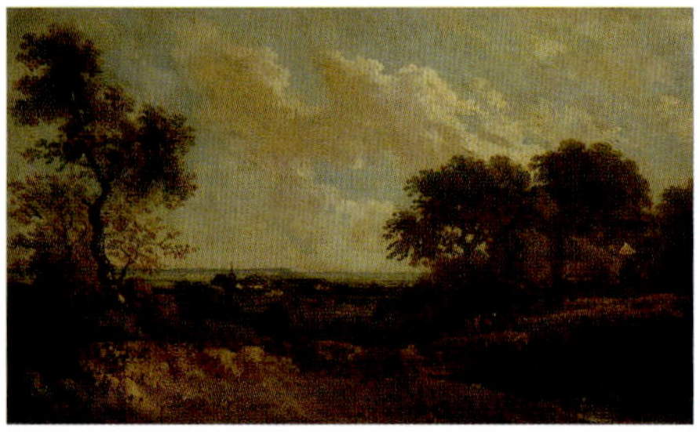

Beaumont, George Howland 1753–1827
Coleorton, Leicestershire 1810
oil on millboard 27.7 x 44.5
L.F3.1916.0.0

Beaumont, George Howland 1753–1827
Wooded Landscape c.1810
oil on canvas 37 x 31.5
L.F22.1946.0.0

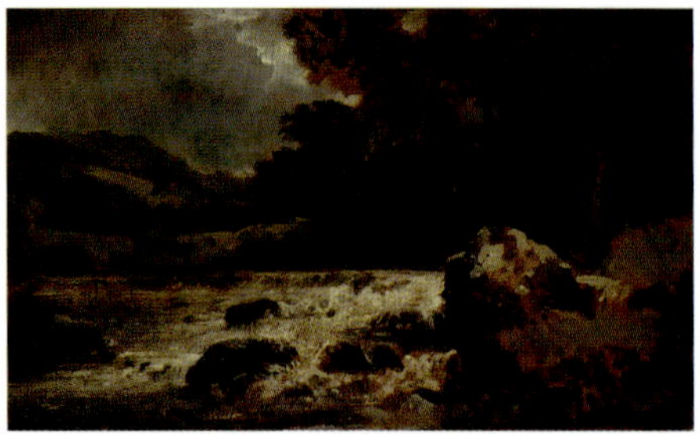

Beaumont, George Howland 1753–1827
Banks of the Greta, Keswick, Cumberland
1815–1821
oil on panel 27.7 x 44.5
L.F8.1953.6.0

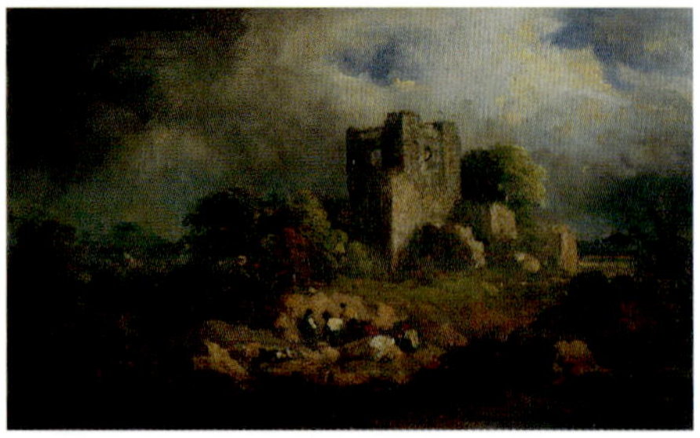

Beaumont, George Howland 1753–1827
Broughton Castle, Lancashire c.1815
oil on board 27.5 x 44
L.F8.1953.12.0

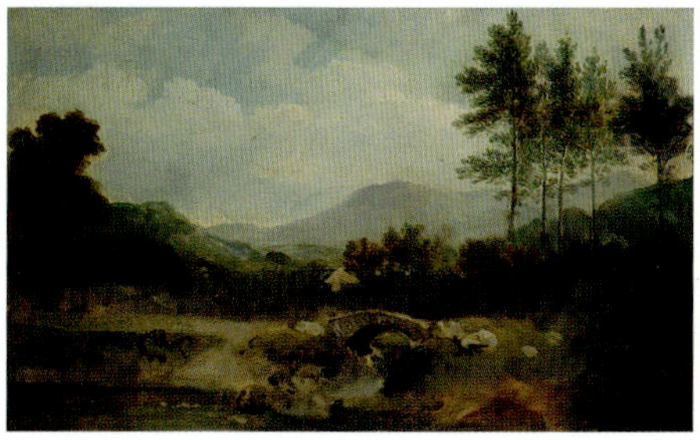

Beaumont, George Howland 1753–1827
Grange Bridge in Borrowdale, Cumberland c.1815
oil on millboard 27.7 x 44.4
L.F8.1953.11.0

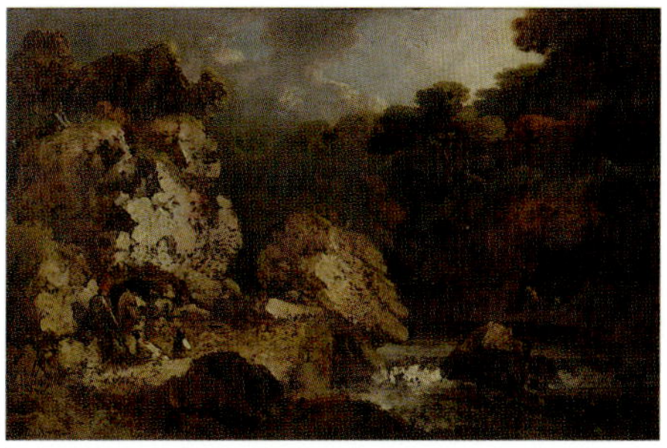

Beaumont, George Howland 1753–1827
River Scene with Figures c.1815
oil on millboard 31.6 x 47
L.F8.1953.10.0

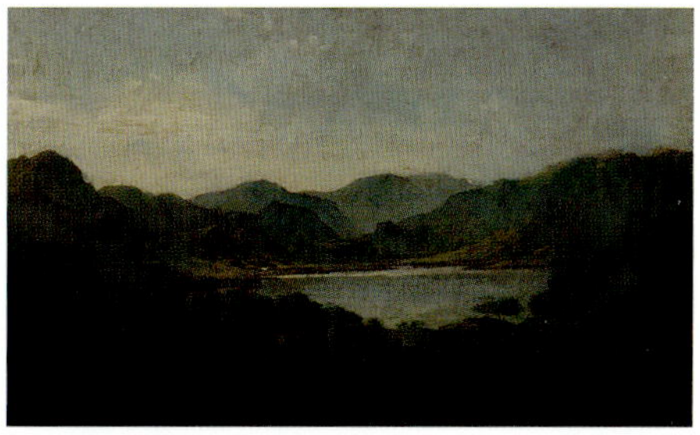

Beaumont, George Howland 1753–1827
Keswick Lake, Cumberland (recto) c.1818
oil on millboard 27.5 x 44.5
L.F57.1986.0.0 (P)

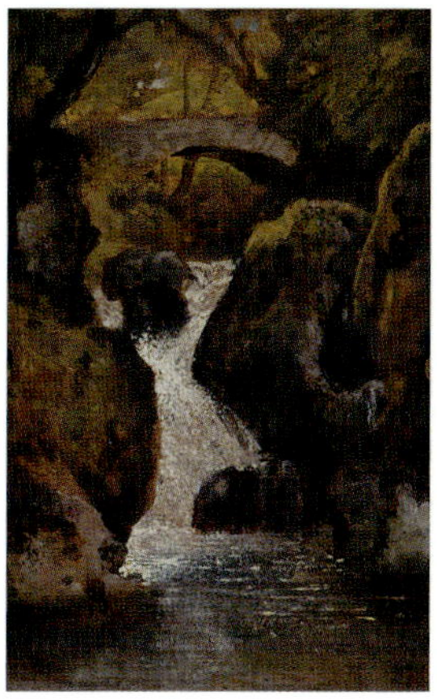

Beaumont, George Howland 1753–1827
Landscape with a Waterfall (verso) c.1818
oil on millboard 44.5 x 27.5
L.F57.1986.0.0B (P)

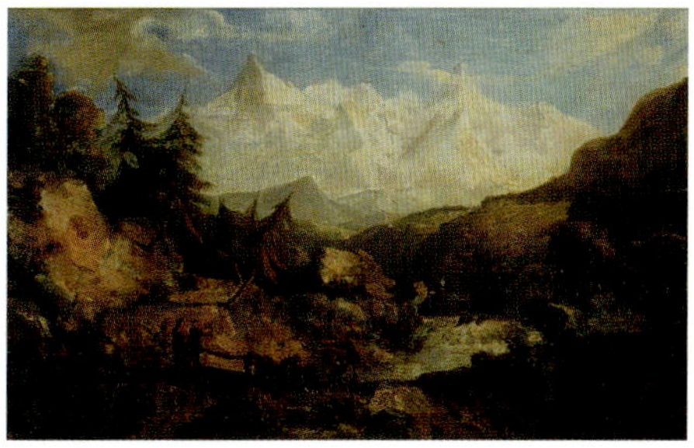

Beaumont, George Howland 1753–1827
Swiss Landscape 1819
oil on panel 28.7 x 45
L.F8.1953.8.0

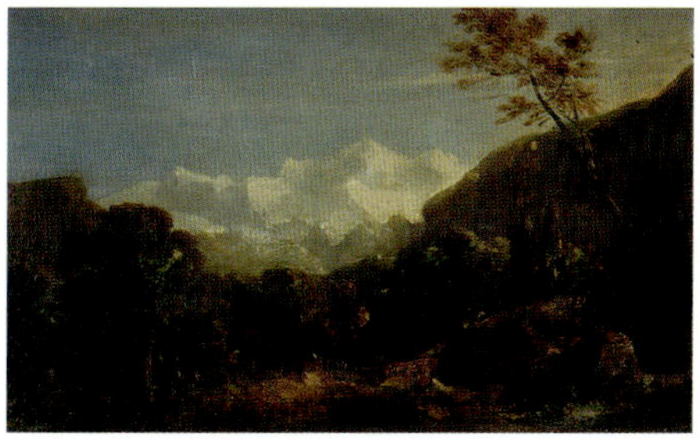

Beaumont, George Howland 1753–1827
Swiss Landscape 1819
oil on millboard 27.8 x 44.3
L.F8.1953.9.0

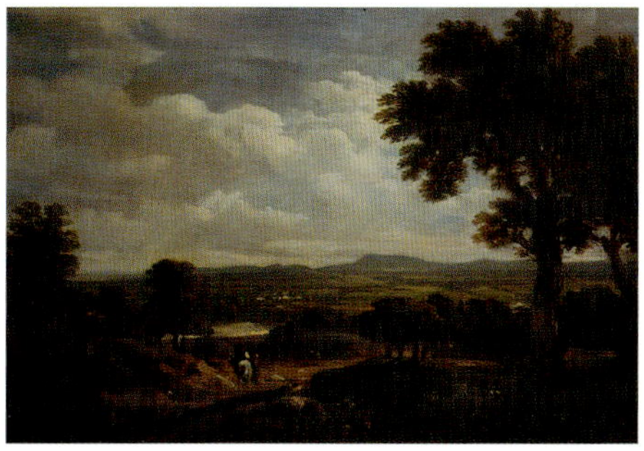

Beaumont, George Howland 1753–1827
View near Coleorton, Leicestershire 1819–1827
oil on canvas 36 x 51
L.F8.1953.2.0

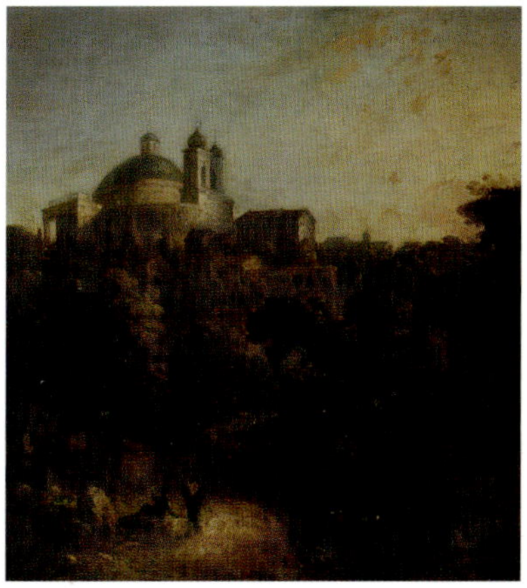

Beaumont, George Howland 1753–1827
St Lorice, Ariccia, Albano, Italy 1822
oil on canvas 47.3 x 42
L.F8.1953.13.0

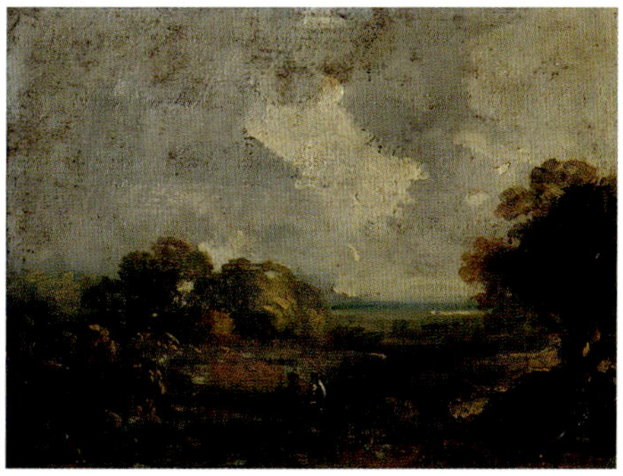

Beaumont, George Howland 1753–1827
Landscape with Figures 1823–1827
oil on millboard 25.8 x 32.8
L.F8.1953.4.0

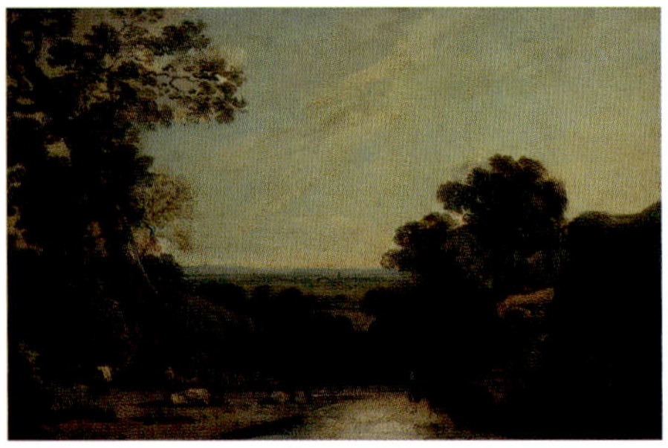

Beaumont, George Howland 1753–1827
Near Coleorton, Leicestershire after 1823
oil on millboard 31 x 47
L.F52.1986.0.0 (P)

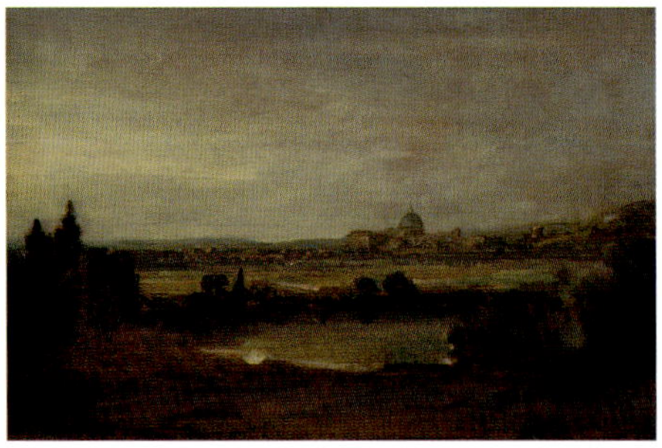

Beaumont, George Howland 1753–1827
A View in Italy
oil on millboard 31 x 47.5
L.F59.1986.0.0 (P)

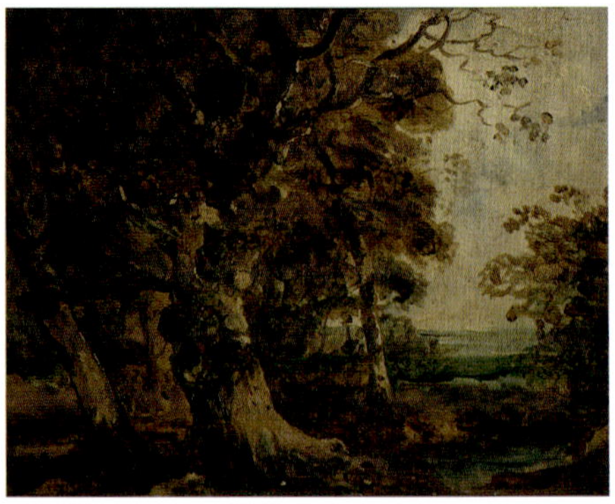

Beaumont, George Howland 1753–1827
An Autumn Wood
oil on panel 25.6 x 31.7
L.F50.1986.0.0 (P)

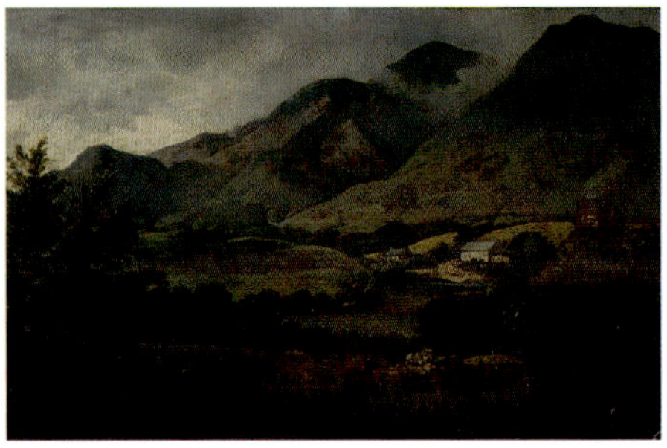

Beaumont, George Howland 1753–1827
Applethwaite, Cumberland
oil on millboard 31 x 47.2
L.F56.1986.0.0 (P)

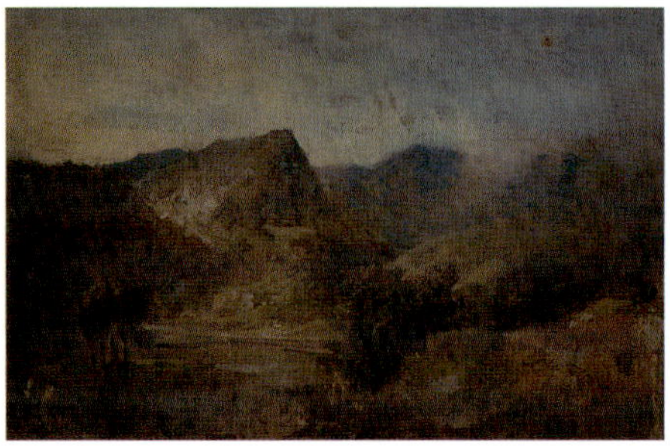

Beaumont, George Howland 1753–1827
Hills with Trees in the Foreground (recto)
oil on millboard 19.7 x 32.7
L.F60.1986.0.0 (P)

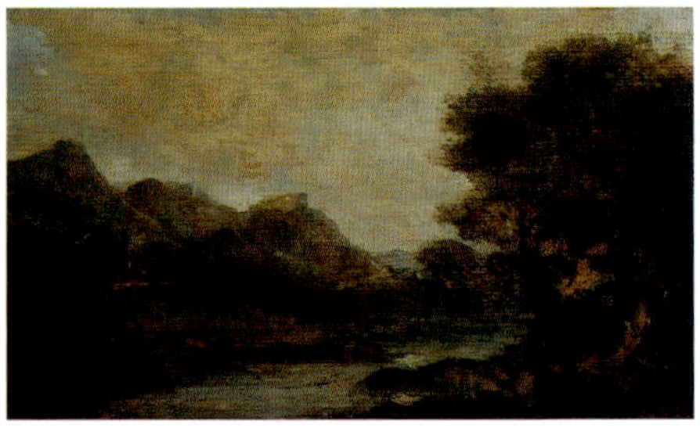

Beaumont, George Howland 1753–1827
Landscape (verso)
oil on millboard 19.7 x 32.7 (E)
L.F60.1986.0.0B (P)

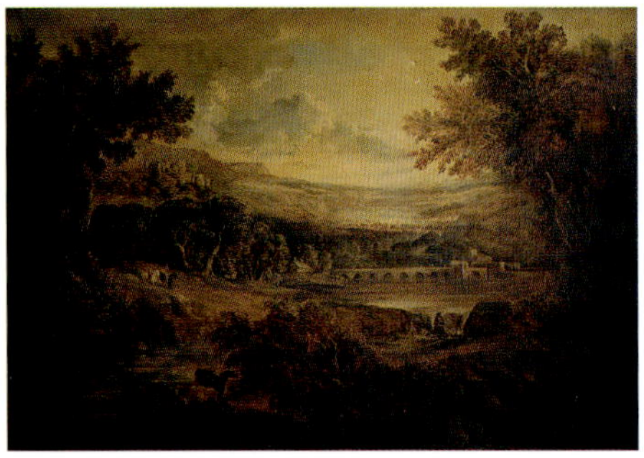

Beaumont, George Howland 1753–1827
Landscape
oil on canvas 76 x 106
IL7.1964.14.0 (P)

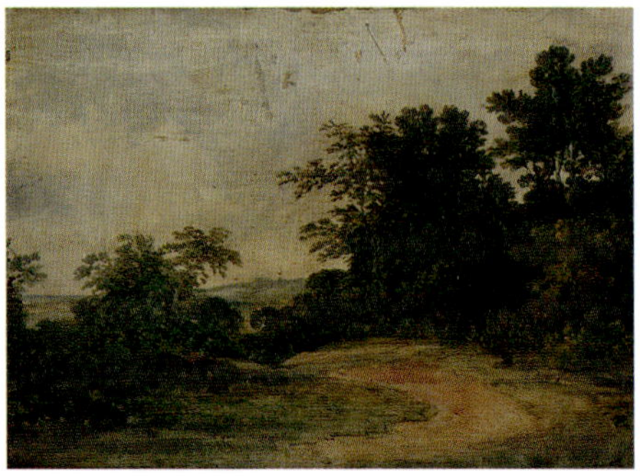

Beaumont, George Howland 1753–1827
Landscape
oil on panel 31 x 41.5
L.F4.1962.0.0

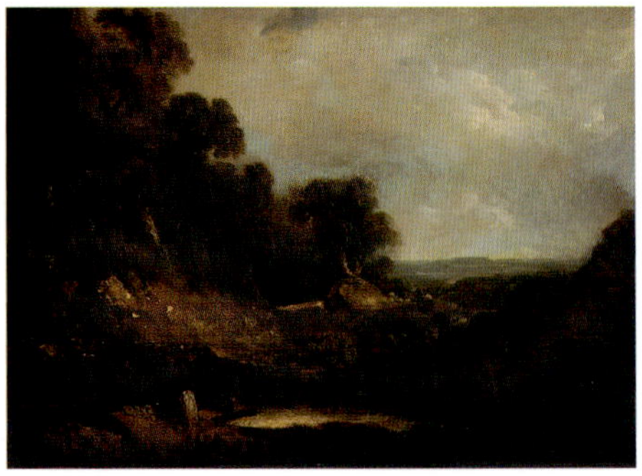

Beaumont, George Howland 1753–1827
Landscape
oil on canvas 57.5 x 79
L.F56.1953.0.0

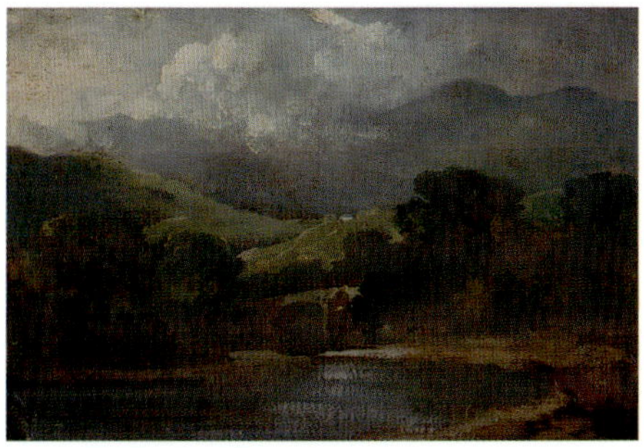

Beaumont, George Howland 1753–1827
Landscape with a Bridge
oil on millboard 21.7 x 31.6
L.F54.1986.0.0 (P)

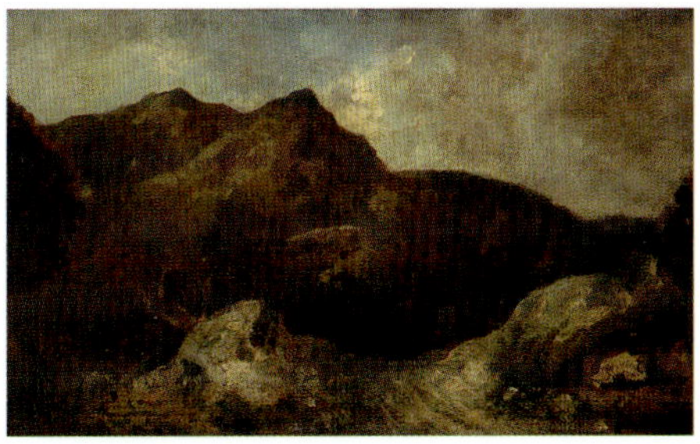

Beaumont, George Howland 1753–1827
Mountain Road
oil on millboard 27 x 44.5
L.F61.1986.0.0 (P)

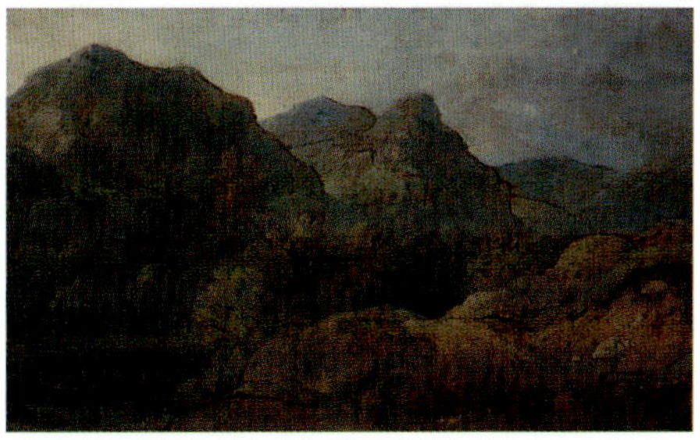

Beaumont, George Howland 1753–1827
Mountain Scenery
oil on millboard 27.8 x 44
L.F58.1986.0.0 (P)

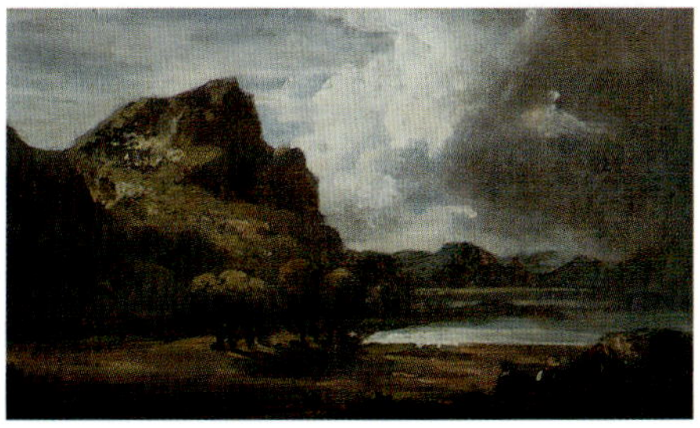

Beaumont, George Howland 1753–1827
Mountain, Trees and a Lake
oil on millboard 19.7 x 32.7
L.F53.1986.0.0 (P)

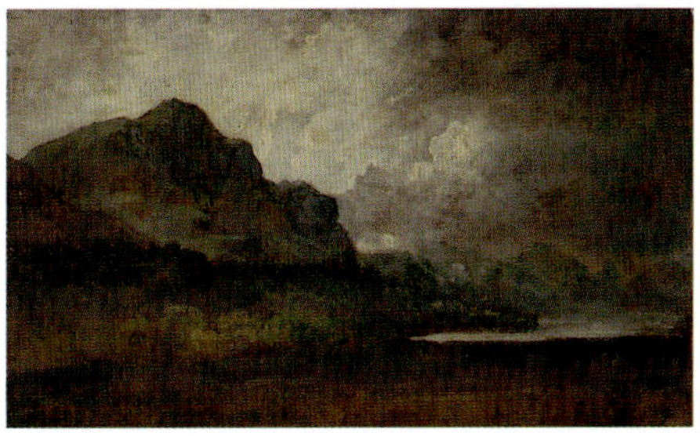

Beaumont, George Howland 1753–1827
Mountainous Landscape with a Lake
oil on millboard 28 x 44.3
L.F64.1986.0.0 (P)

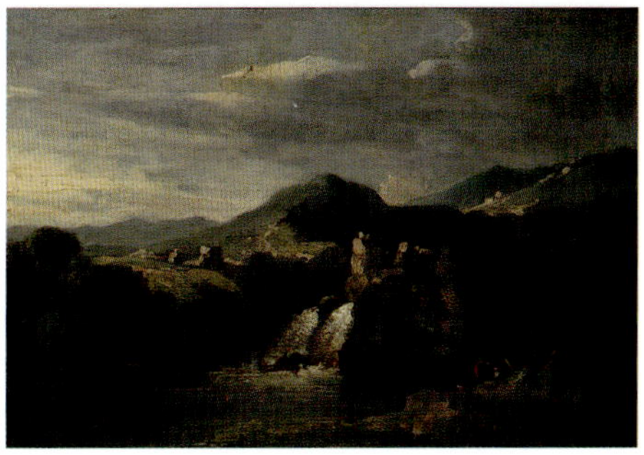

Beaumont, George Howland 1753–1827
Mountainous Landscape with a Waterfall and Figures
oil on tin 25 x 35
L.F62.1986.0.0 (P)

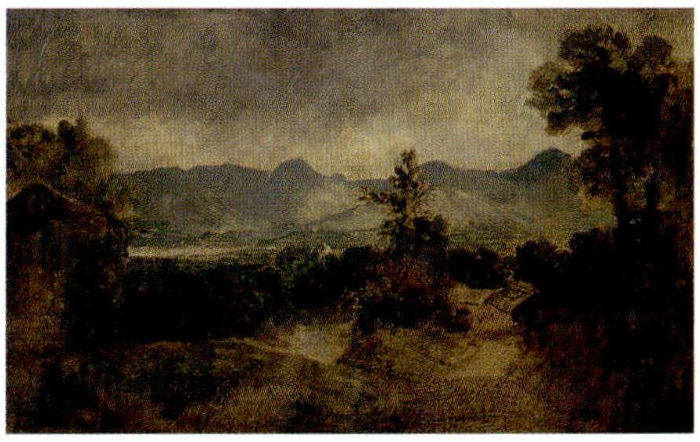

Beaumont, George Howland 1753–1827
View near Applethwaite, Cumberland
oil on millboard 28 x 44.5
L.F63.1986.0.0 (P)

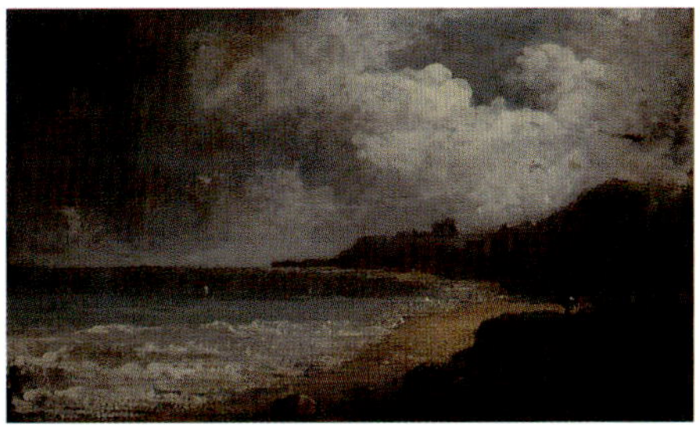

Beaumont, George Howland 1753–1827
Weymouth Bay, Dorset
oil on millboard 28 x 44.2
L.F65.1986.0.0

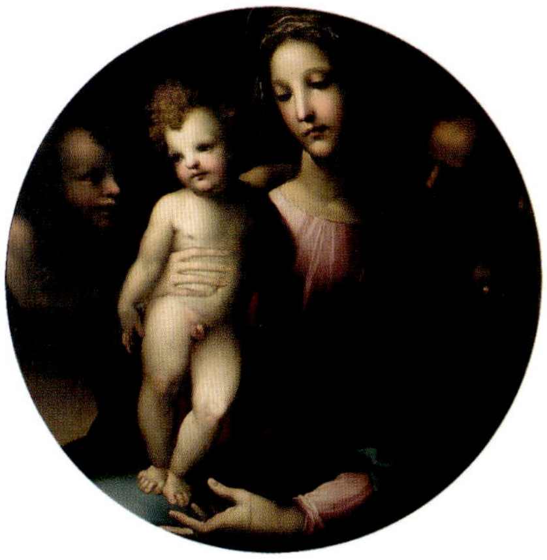

Beccafumi, Domenico 1484–1551
The Holy Family with Saint John the Baptist
c.1530
oil on panel 87
L.F42.1965.0.0

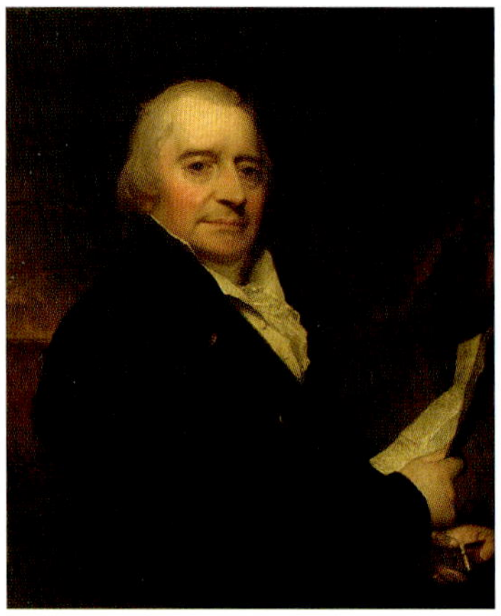

Beechey, William 1753–1839
William Salte (c.1746–1817)
oil on canvas 76.2 x 63.5
L.F52.1924.0.0

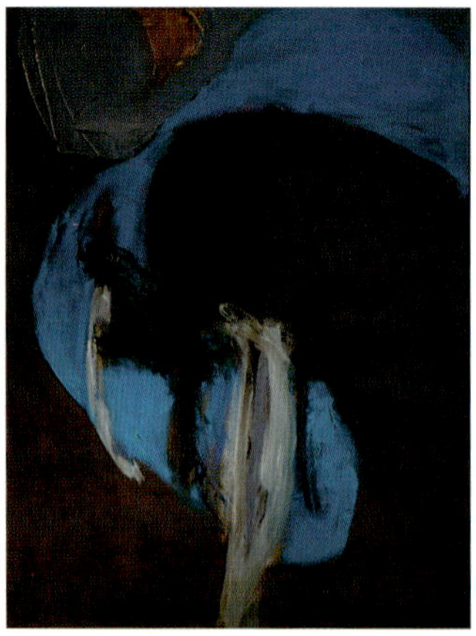

Bell, Trevor b.1930
Strange Blue
oil on canvas 121.5 x 91
L.F11.1960.0.0

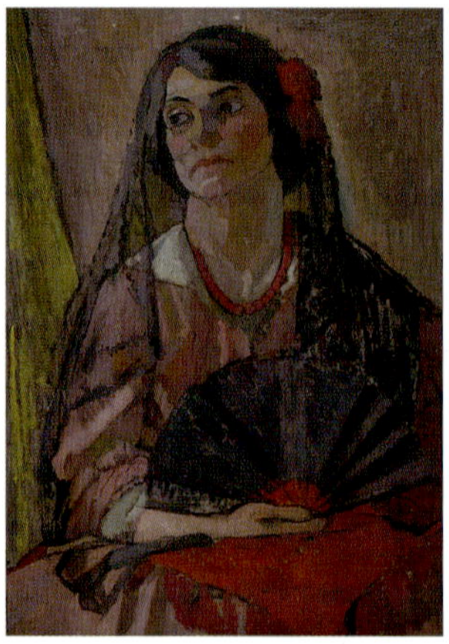

Bell, Vanessa 1879–1961
The Spanish Lady 1912
oil on millboard 75.6 x 53
L.F2.1924.0.0

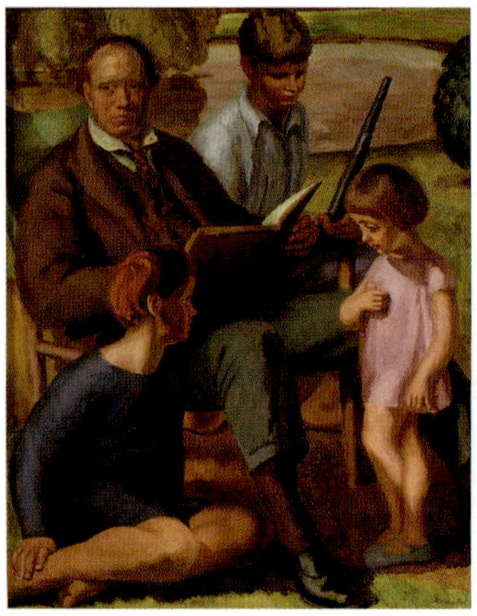

Bell, Vanessa 1879–1961
Clive Bell (1881–1964), and Family 1924
oil on canvas 127 x 101.5
L.F23.1927.0.0

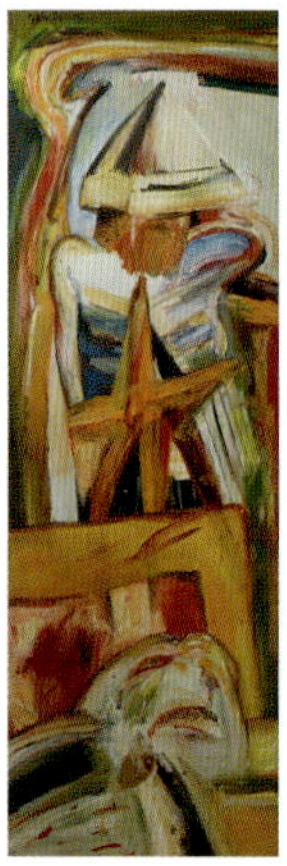

Bellany, John b.1942
Lune de miel (Towards the Lighthouse) (triptych, left wing) 1980
oil on canvas 183 x 61
L.F54.1982.0.0

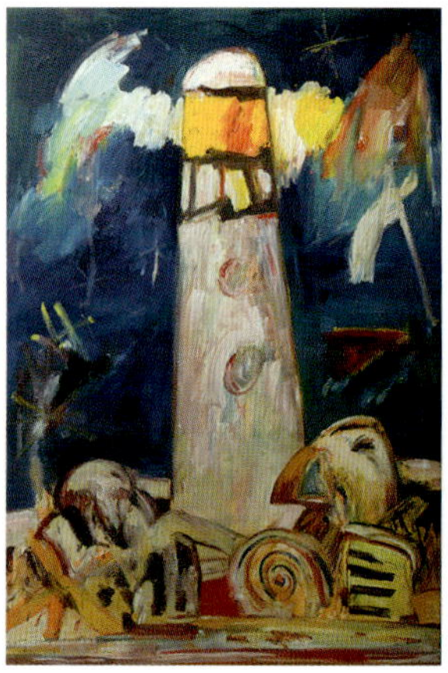

Bellany, John b.1942
Lune de miel (Towards the Lighthouse) (triptych, centre panel) 1980
oil on canvas 183 x 122.5
L.F54.1982.0.0

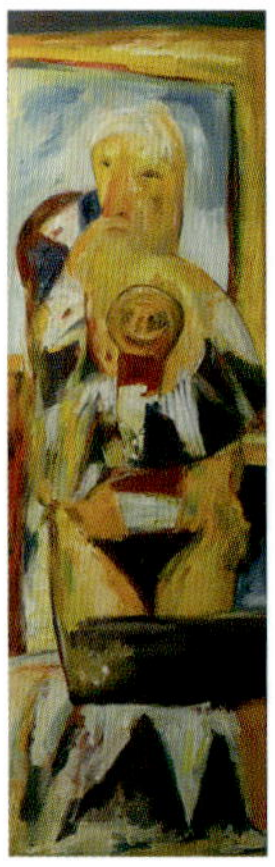

Bellany, John b.1942
Lune de miel (Towards the Lighthouse) (triptych, right wing) 1980
oil on canvas 183 x 61
L.F54.1982.0.0

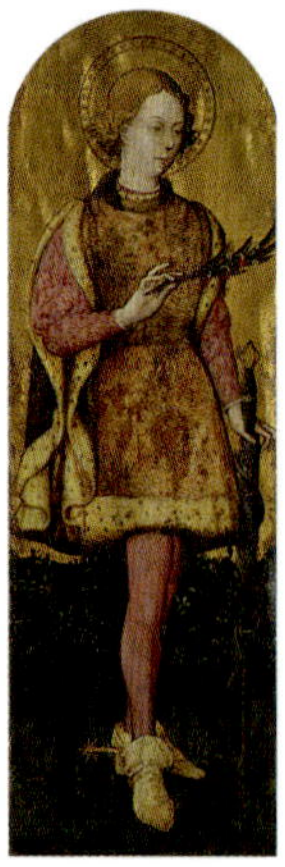

Bembo, Bonifazio (attributed to) c.1420–1482
A Martyr 1440–1470
oil on canvas 72.4 x 23.5
L.F26.1950.0.0

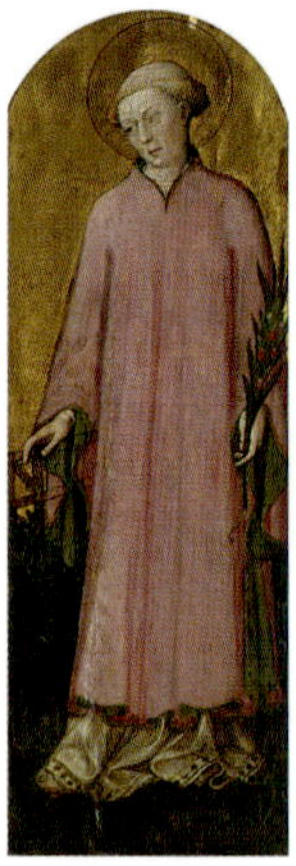

Bembo, Bonifazio (attributed to) c.1420–1482
Saint Lawrence 1440–1470
oil on panel 72.4 x 23.5
L.F25.1950.0.0

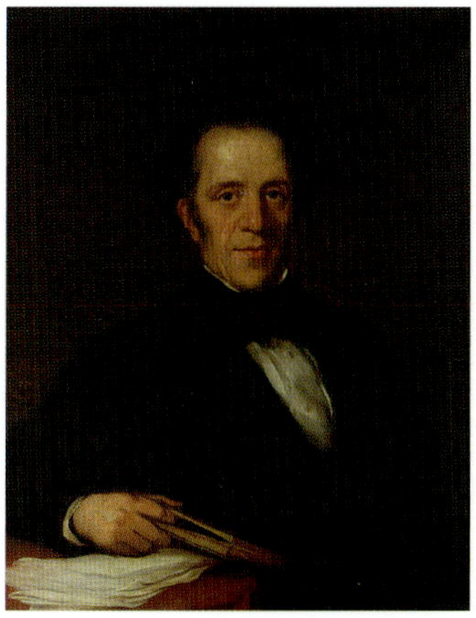

Benson, Edward 1808–1863
George Bristow (1803–1896) 1852
oil on canvas 76.2 x 63.5
L.F1.1943.0.0

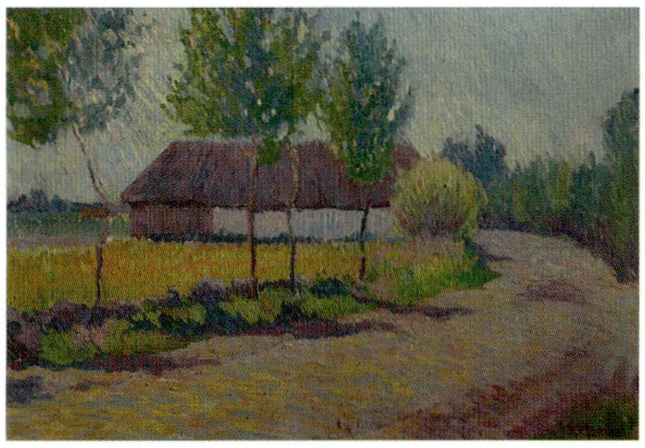

Bevan, Robert Polhill 1865–1925
Polish Landscape 1901
oil on canvas 38.7 x 54.6
L.F33.1937.0.0

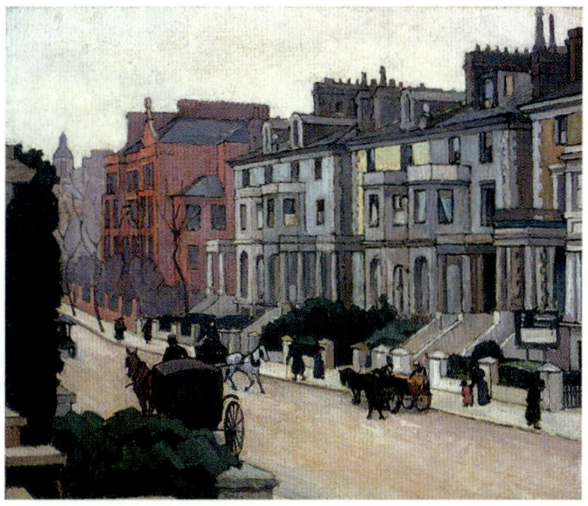

Bevan, Robert Polhill 1865–1925
From the Artist's Window 1915–1916
oil on canvas 62.2 x 75
L.F25.1944.0.0

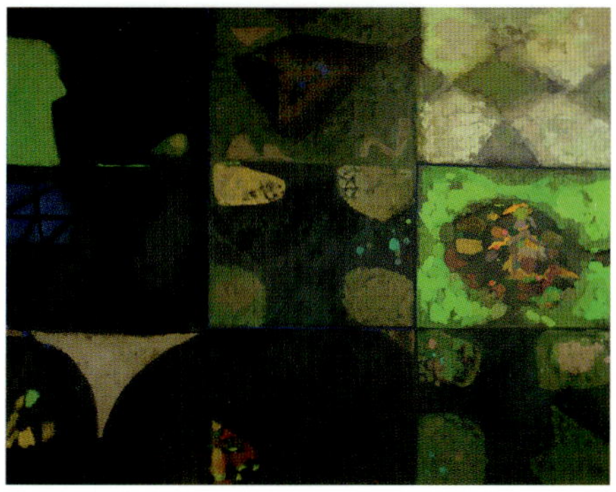

Bizley, Roy 1930–1999
Terrace 1982–1983
oil on canvas 122 x 153
Y.F4.2008.0.0

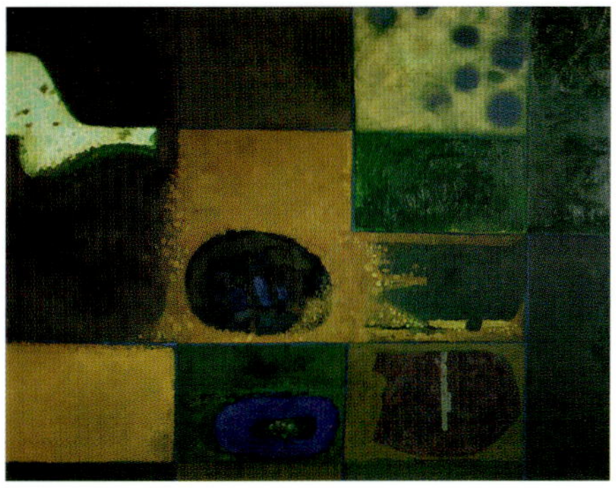

Bizley, Roy 1930–1999
Terrace 1982–1983
oil on canvas 122 x 151
Y.F5.2008.0.0

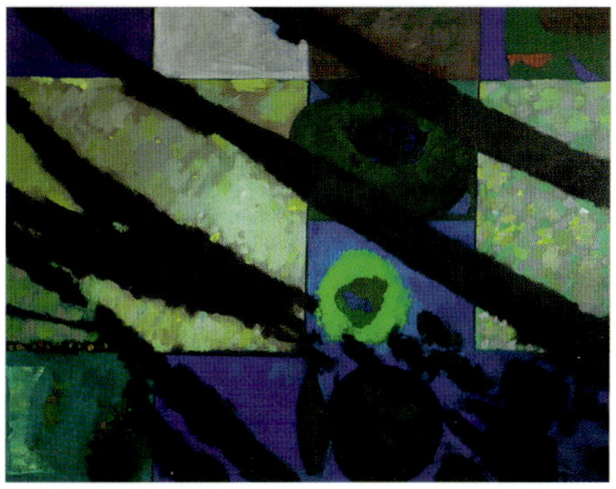

Bizley, Roy 1930–1999
Terrace 1982–1983
oil on canvas 120 x 151
Y.F6.2008.0.0

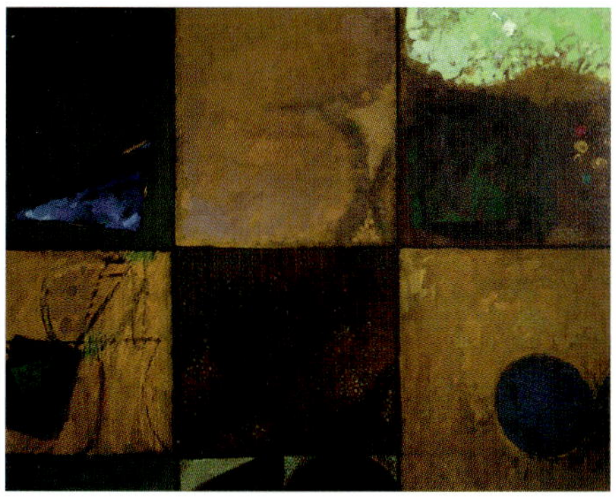

Bizley, Roy 1930–1999
Terrace 1982–1983
oil on canvas 120.5 x 151
Y.F7.2008.0.0

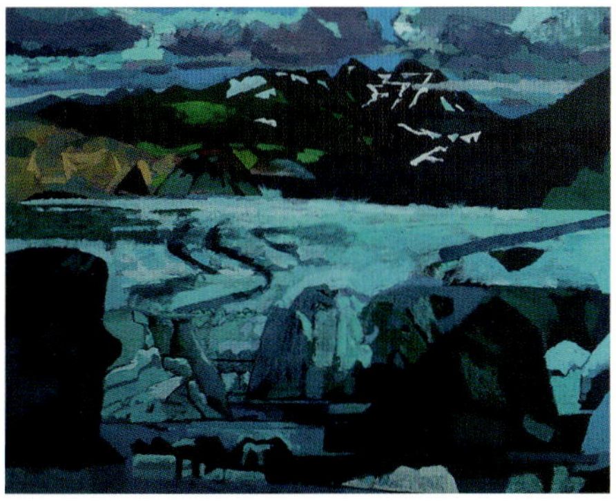

Bizley, Roy 1930–1999
Iceland I c.1994
acrylic on hardboard 101.8 x 126.7
Y.F8.2002.0.0

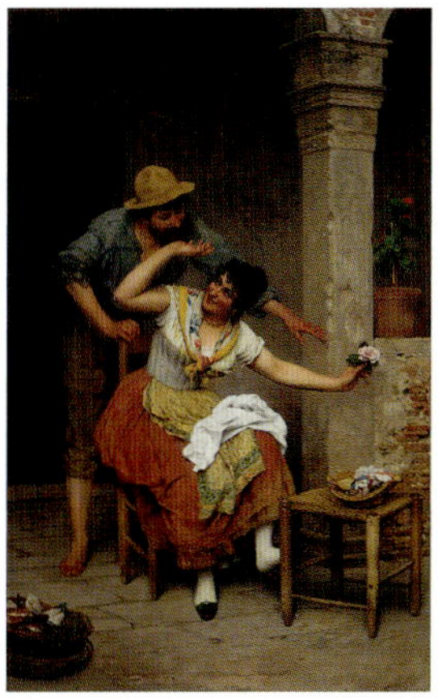

Blaas, Eugen von 1843–1931
A Venetian Courtship 1891
oil on canvas 107 x 66.3
L.F2.1907.0.0

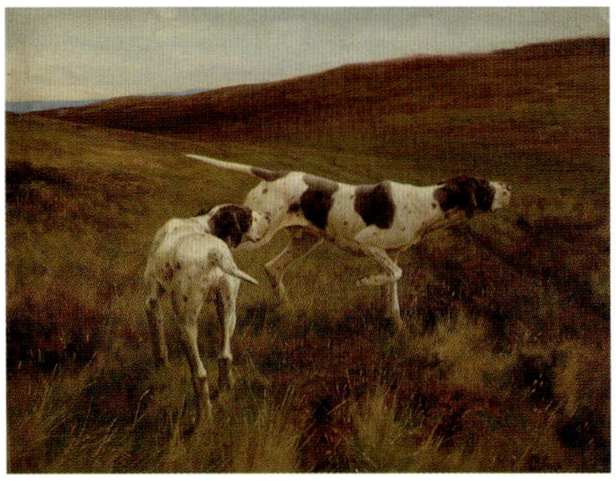

Blinks, Thomas 1860–1912
Pointers in a Landscape
oil on canvas 36 x 46
L.F77.1955.0.0

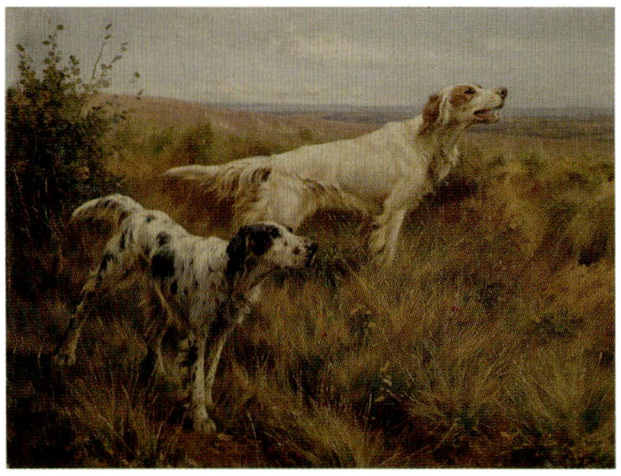

Blinks, Thomas 1860–1912
Two Setters in a Landscape
oil on canvas 35.5 x 45.7
L.F76.1955.0.0

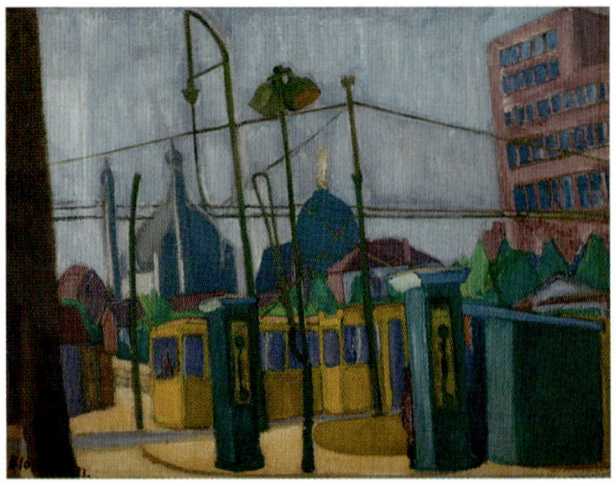

Bloch, Martin 1883–1954
Fehrbelliner Platz, Berlin 1933
oil on canvas 76 x 96
L.F7.1981.0.0

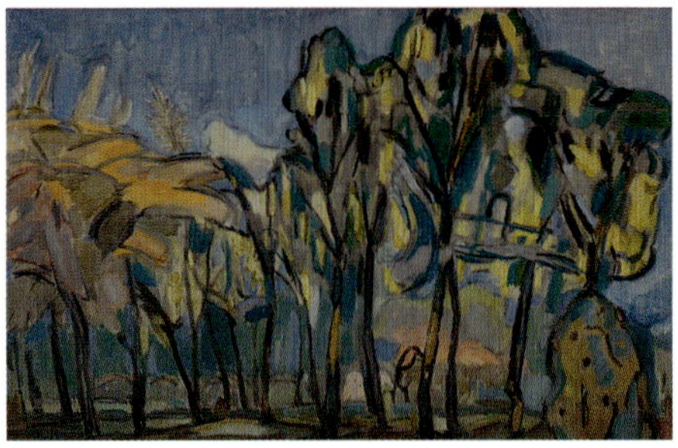

Bloch, Martin 1883–1954
Laburnum and May Trees 1941
oil on canvas 53 x 80.5
L.F16.1955.0.0

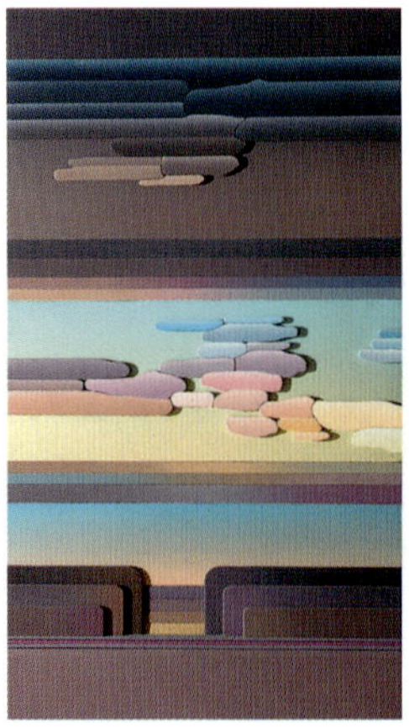

Bloomfield, Rib b.1948
Landscape 19 c.1976
acrylic on canvas 149.5 x 83.8
L.F177.1976.0.0

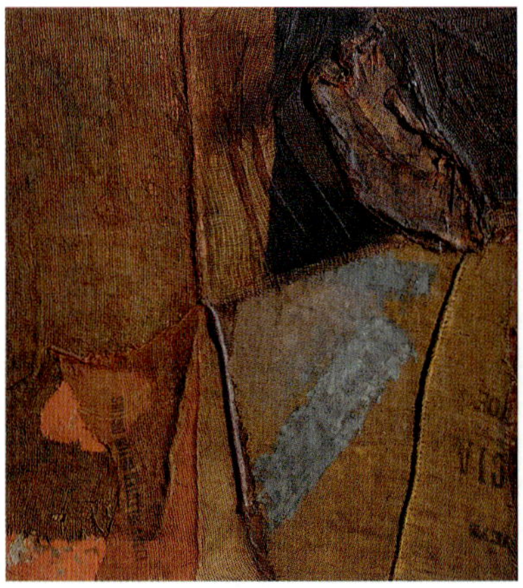

Blow, Sandra 1925–2006
Composition
oil & hessian on hardboard 122 x 108
L.F106.1963.0.0

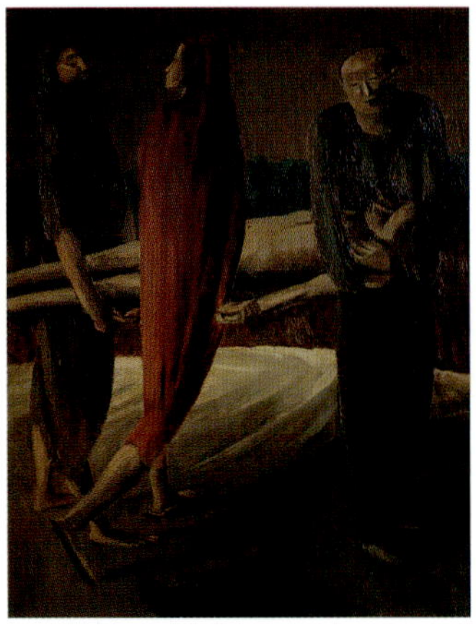

Bomberg, David 1890–1957
Grief 1922
oil on canvas 91.5 x 71
L.F5.1982.0.0

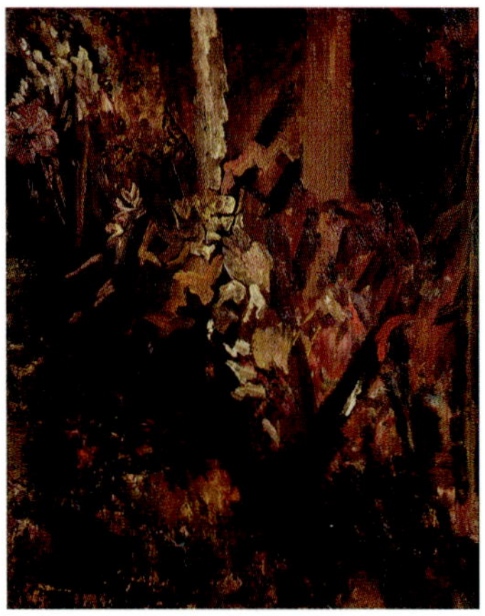

Bomberg, David 1890–1957
Flowers in Sunlight 1943
oil on canvas 85.7 x 67.3
L.F44.1987.0.0

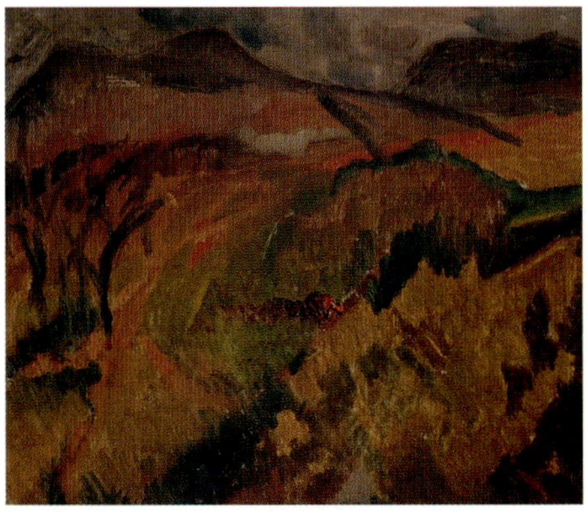

Bomberg, David 1890–1957
Landscape 1947
oil on canvas 66.3 x 76.3
L.F7.1961.0.0

Facing page: Reynolds, Joshua, 1723–1792, *Isabella Thorold of Syston (d.1803)* (detail), 1754, The Collection: Art & Archaeology in Lincolnshire (Usher Gallery) (p. 321)

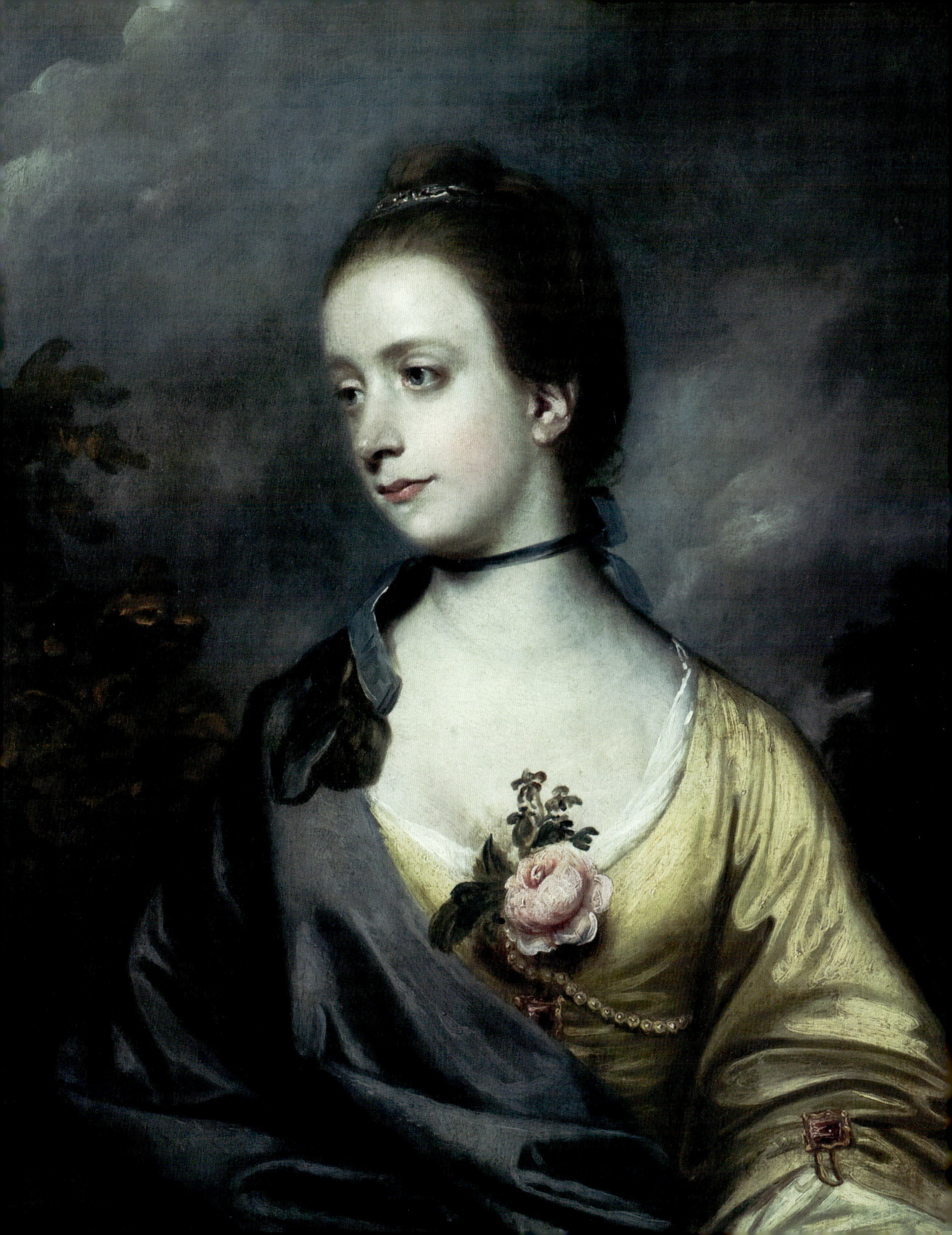

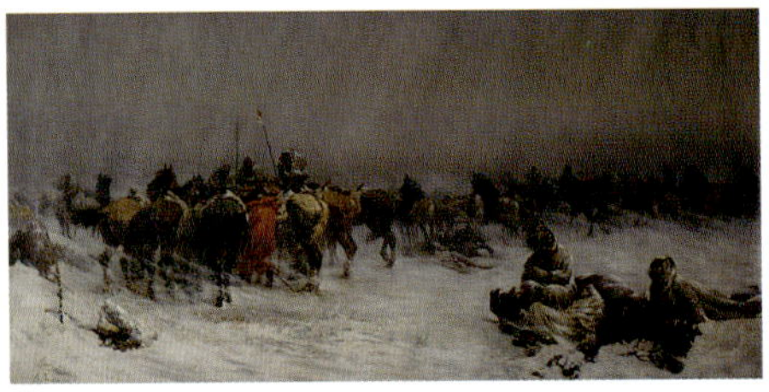

Bombled, Louis Charles 1862–1927
A Squall from the North-East
oil on canvas 60.3 x 120.4
L.F3.1881.0.0

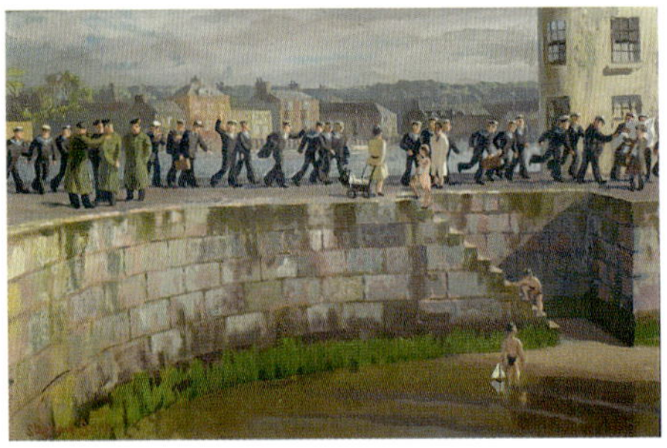

Bone, Stephen 1904–1958
Liberty Men, Weymouth, Dorset
oil on canvas 50 x 75.5
L.F3.1996.39.0

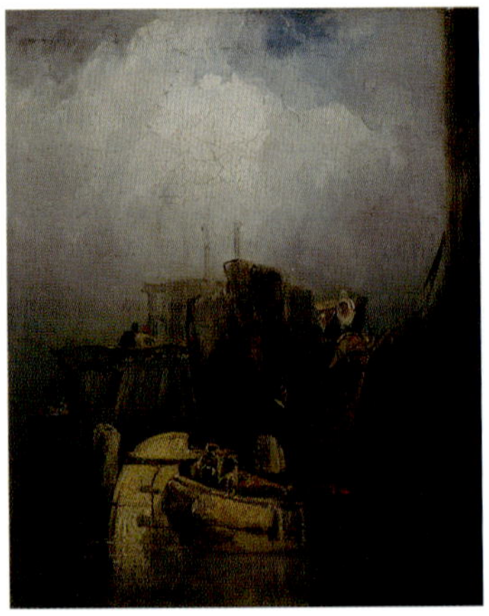

Bonington, Richard Parkes 1802–1828
The Old Jetty, Boulogne, France
oil on millboard 30.7 x 25
L.F21.1936.0.0

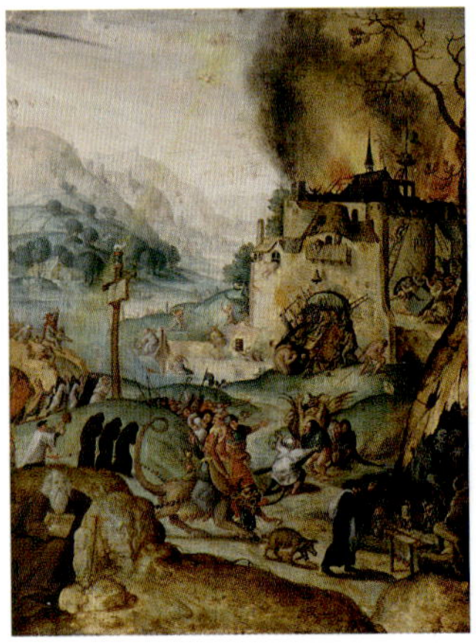

Bosch, Hieronymus (follower of) c.1450–1516
The Temptation of Saint Anthony 16th C
oil on panel 43.5 x 32.1
L.F90.1936.0.0

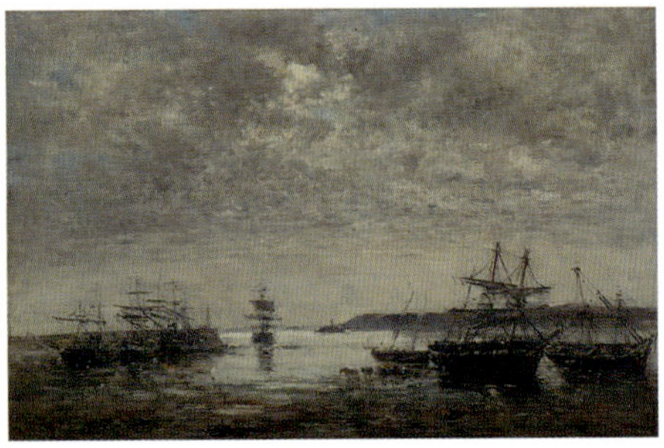

Boudin, Eugène Louis 1824–1898
Le Havre, France, l'avant-port
oil on canvas 49.3 x 74.5
L.F121.1981.0.0

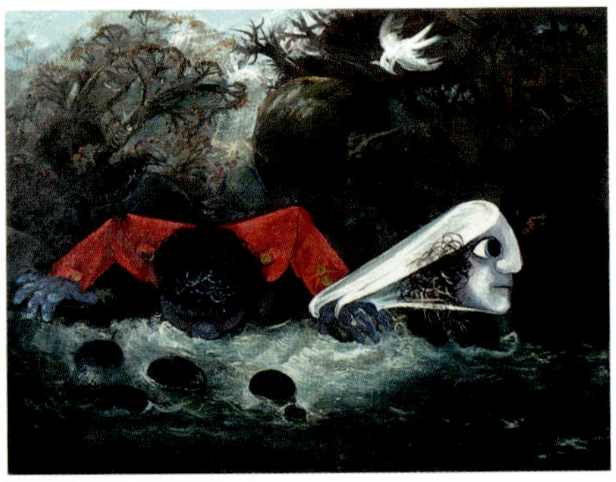

Boyd, Arthur 1920–1999
Bridegroom Drinking from a Creek 1957–1959
oil & tempera on board 106.8 x 137.2
L.F85.1963.0.0

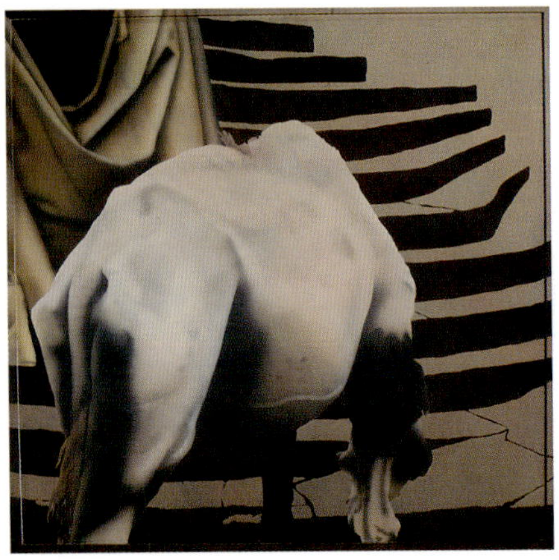

Boyd, Fionnuala b.1944 & **Evans, Leslie** b.1945
Old Picture 1970
acrylic on board 93.3 x 93.3
L.F338.1977.0.0

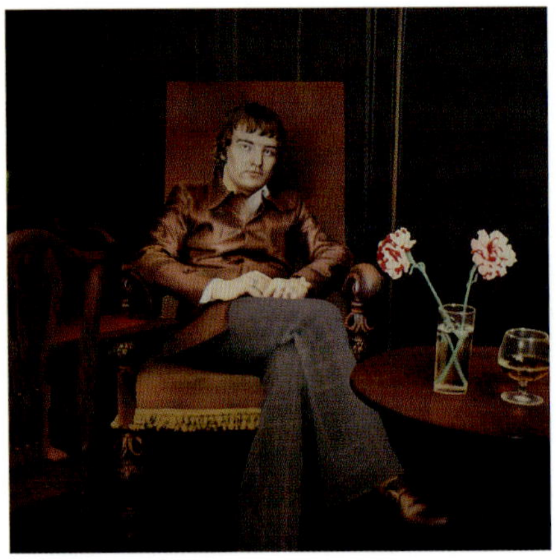

Boyd, Fionnuala b.1944 & **Evans, Leslie** b.1945
Christopher Wright (b.1945) 1971
acrylic on board 90 x 90
L.F66.1988.0.0

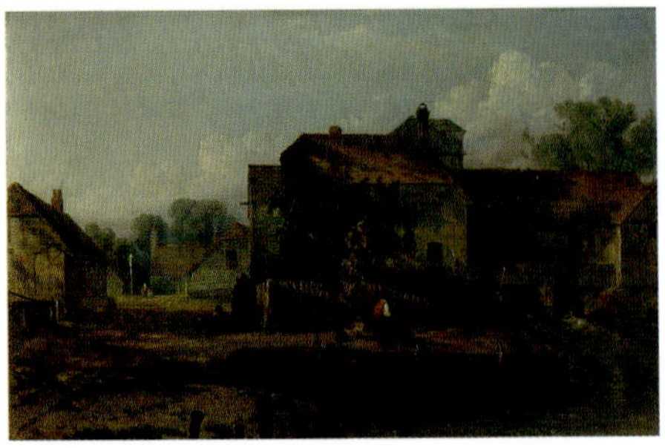

Brandard, Robert 1805–1862
Landscape
oil on canvas 30.5 x 45.6
L.F6.1882.0.0

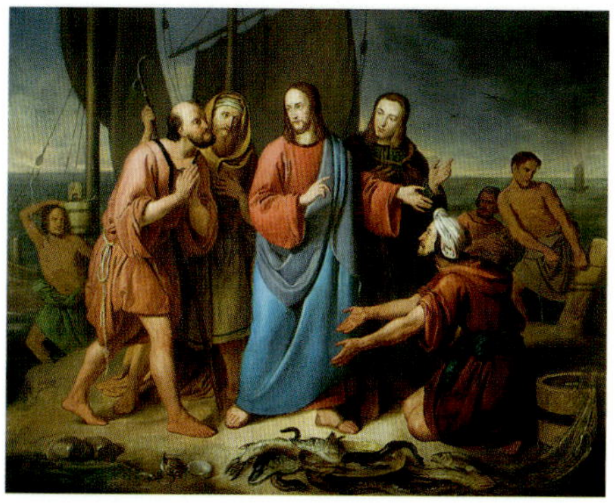

Brenner, Adam 1800–1891
Christ Calling His First Disciples 1839
oil on canvas 62.4 x 78.8
L.F146.1964.0.0

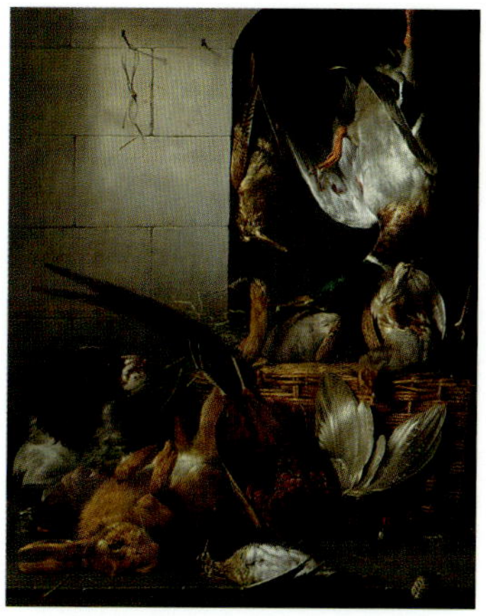

Bristow, Edmund 1787–1876
Still Life, Spaniel and Dead Game 1827
oil on canvas 97 x 70.5
L.F2.1889.0.0

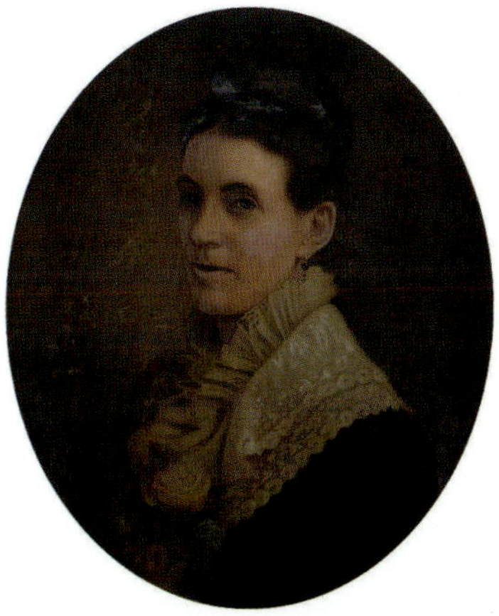

British (English) School late 19th C
Catherine Elizabeth Biggs, née Holland
oil on canvas 61 x 50.5
Y.F7.2005.3.0

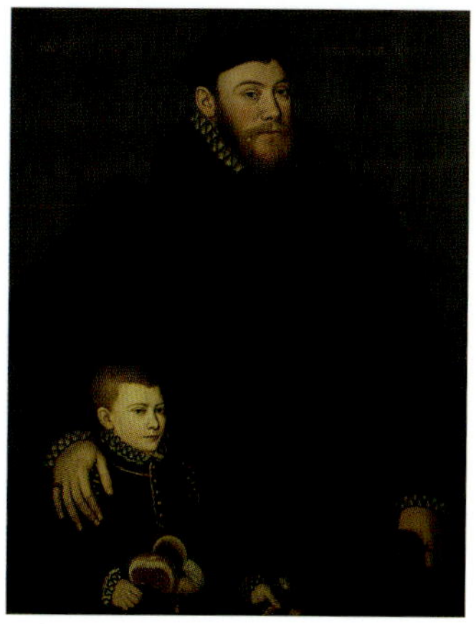

British School
Sir George Hastings (1540–1604), Later 4th Earl of Huntingdon, and His Son Francis 1565
oil on panel 102.8 x 79.5
L.F91.1938.0.0

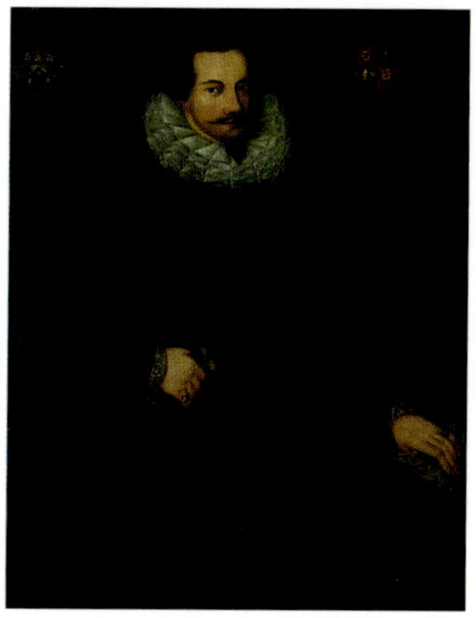

British School
Sir William Herrick (1557–1653) 1594
oil on panel 110.5 x 86.4
L.F48.1926.0.0

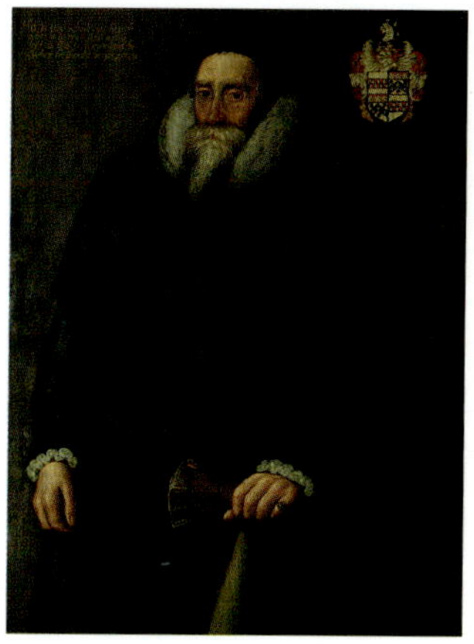

British School
Sir Robert Herrick (1540–1618) 1600–1650
oil on panel 113.7 x 83.6
L.F50.1926.0.0

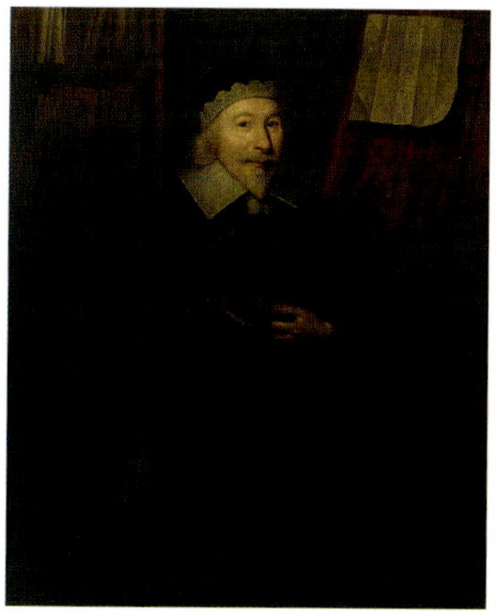

British School
Reverend Thomas Hayne (1582–1645), MA
c.1656
oil on canvas 110 x 91
L.F52.1926.0.0

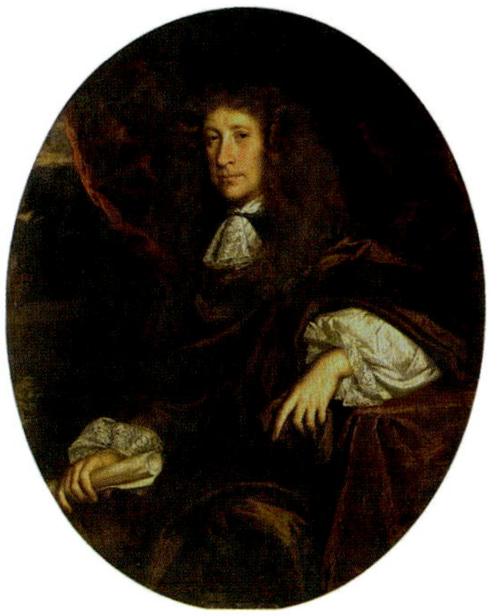

British School 17th C
Thomas Staveley (1626–1684)
oil on canvas 112.4 x 90.2
L.F60.1946.1.0

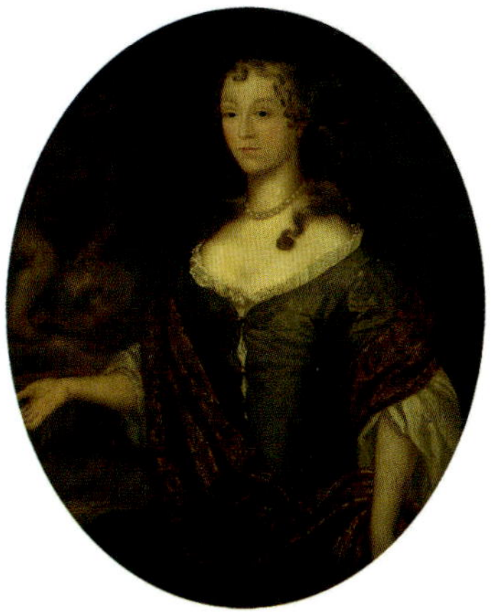

British School 17th C
Mary Staveley (d.1699)
oil on canvas 113 x 91.4
L.F60.1946.2.0

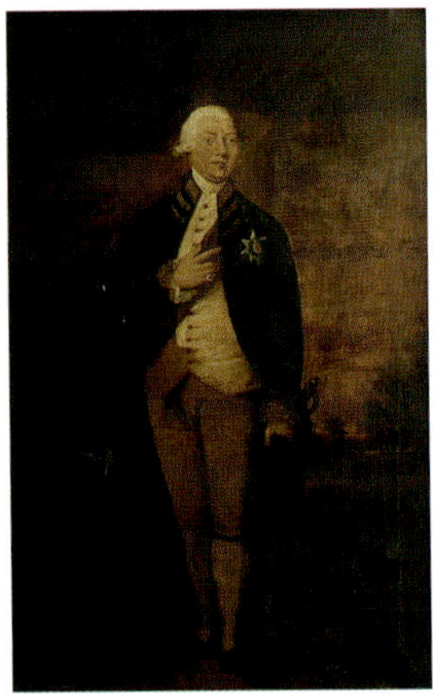

British School
George III (1738–1820) c.1760
oil on canvas 109.9 x 63.5
Y.F14.2008.0.0

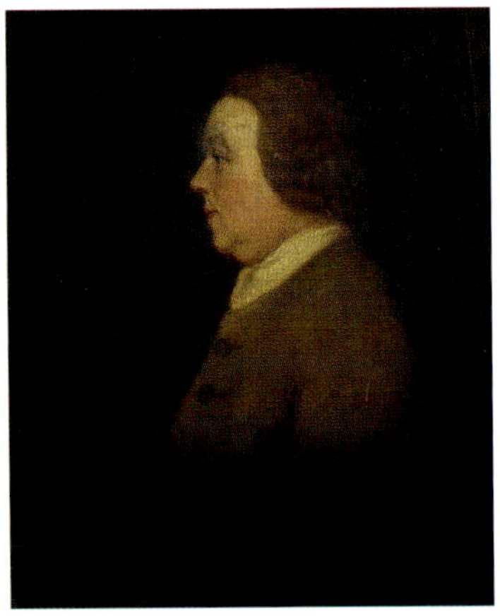

British School 18th C
John Darker (1722–1784)
oil on canvas 76 x 63
L.F53.1926.0.0

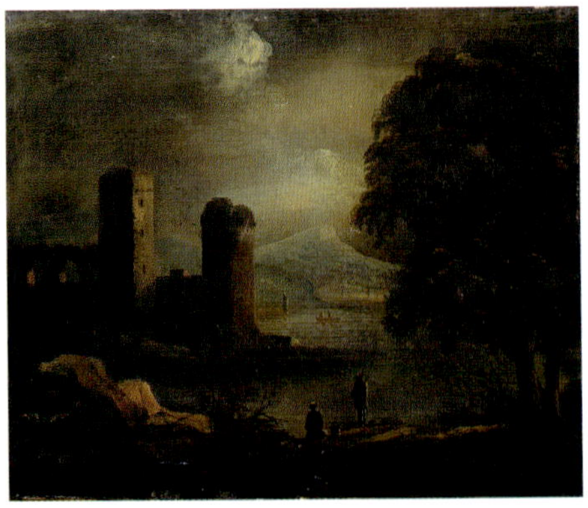

British School 18th C
Landscape, a Castle and a Man Fishing
oil on canvas 25 x 30
L.F20.1935.13.2

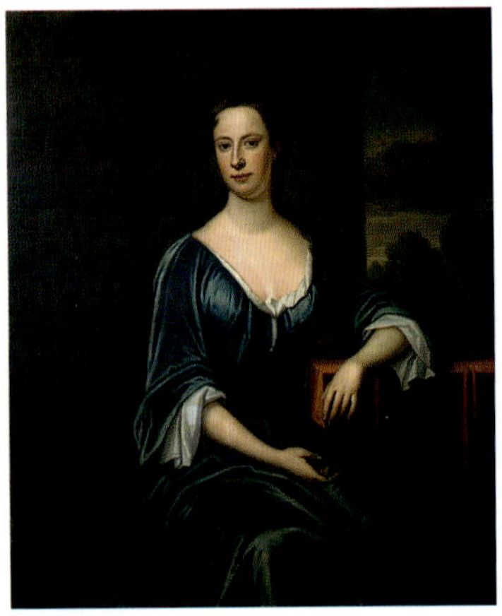

British School 18th C
Portrait of a Lady
oil on canvas 127 x 101.6
L.F1.1947.0.0

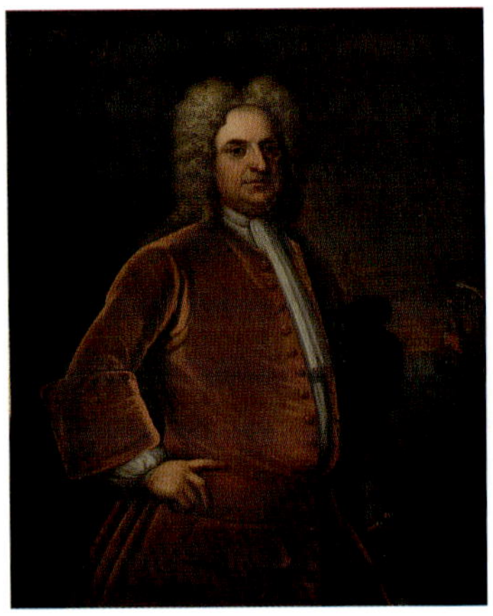

British School 18th C
Rear Admiral Sir Cloudesley Shovell (1650–1707)
oil on canvas 126.5 x 101.5
L.F9.1943.1.0

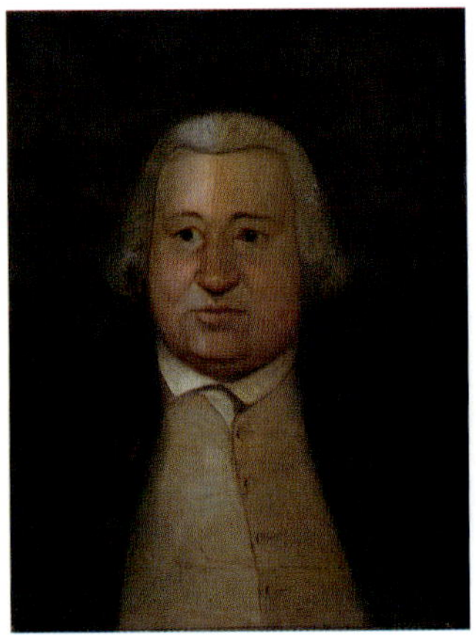

British School late 18th C
John Valentine (1730–1792)
oil on canvas 58.4 x 43.1
Y.F3.2000.0.0

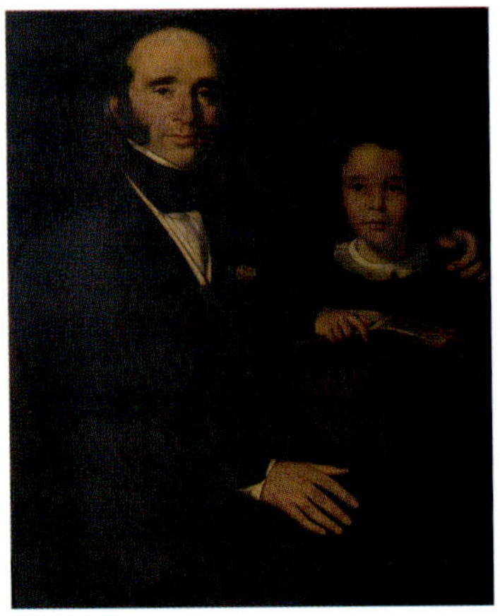

British School
John Biggs (1801–1871), MP, and His Nephew Arthur Biggs c.1840
oil on canvas 101.5 x 80
Y.F7.2005.1.0

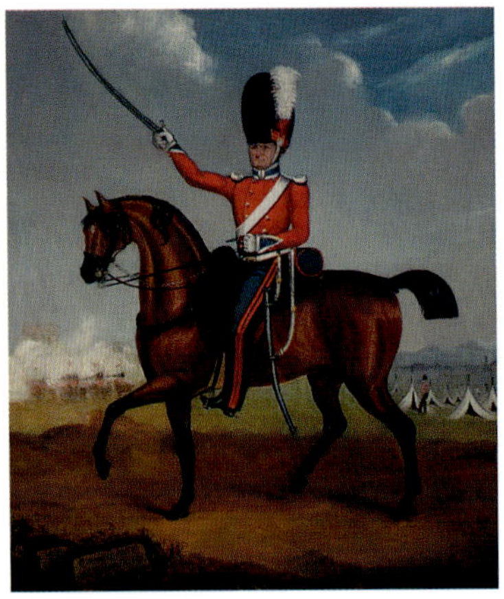

British School
Quartermaster J. Kirk, Leicestershire Yeomanry 1841
oil on canvas 63.8 x 54.5
L.F41.1987.0.0

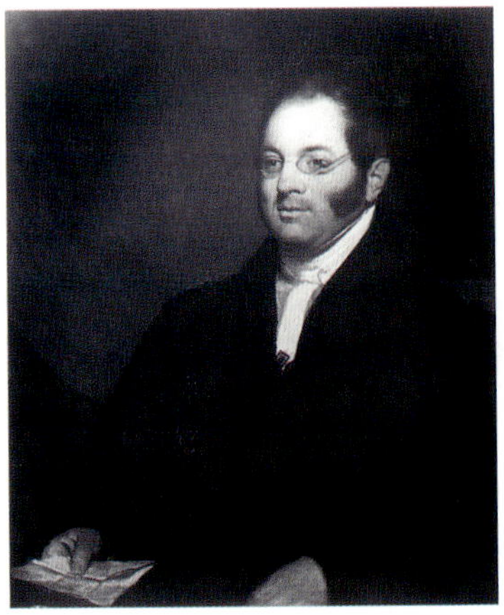

British School
Thomas Burbidge (1784–1855) 1855
oil on canvas 76.2 x 63.5
L.F4.1957.0.0

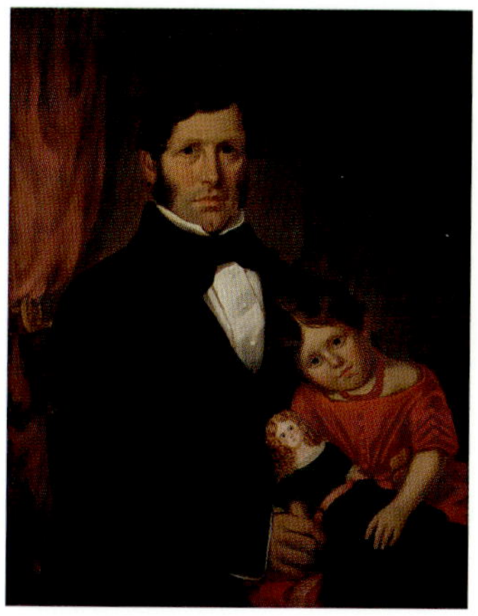

British School
Mr Creswell and His Daughter Charlotte (1854–1918) 1858
oil on canvas 91.4 x 73
L.F49.1967.0.0

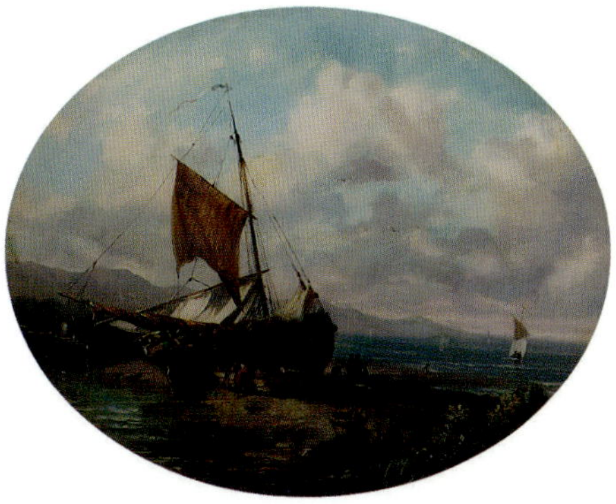

British School
Seascape c.1860
oil on glass 36.5 x 44.5
L.F958.1977.1.0

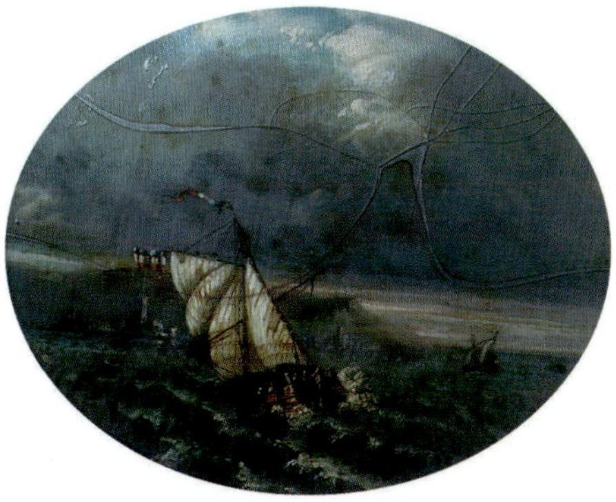

British School
Seascape c.1860
oil on canvas 38 x 45.5
L.F958.1977.2.0

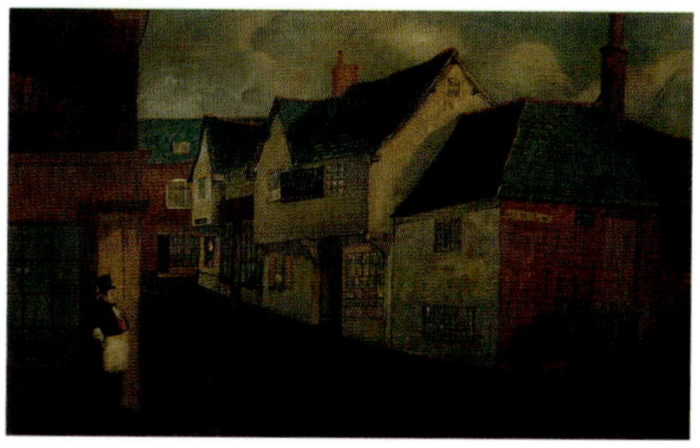

British School
The East Side of West Bridge, Leicester c.1865
oil on canvas 50.8 x 85.1
L.F1.1951.0.0

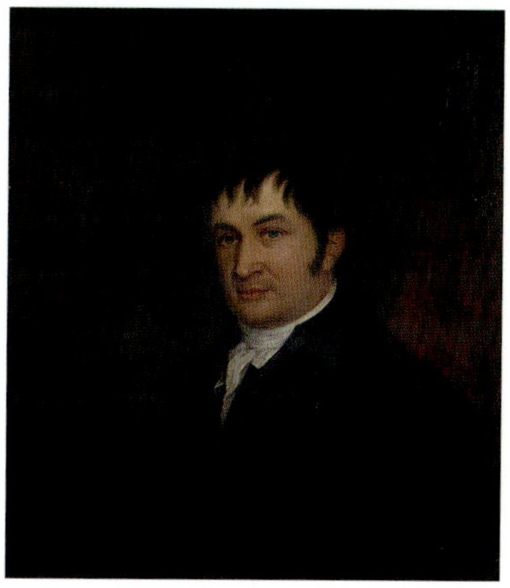

British School 19th C
Alderman James Richards (1765–1845)
oil on canvas 76.2 x 63.5
L.F24.1949.0.0

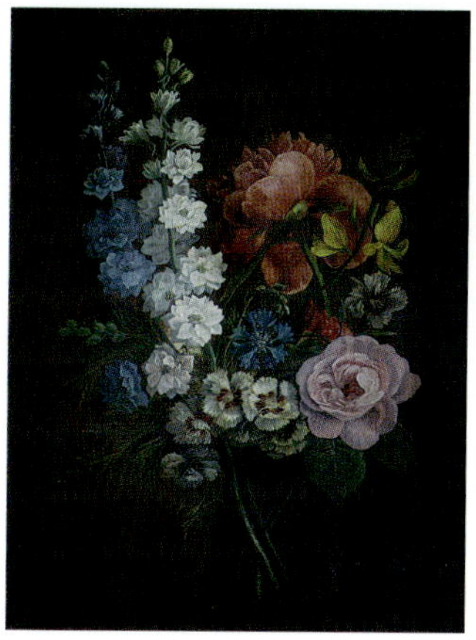

British School 19th C
Flower Piece
oil & paper on canvas 38.7 x 28.9
L.F9.1943.11.0

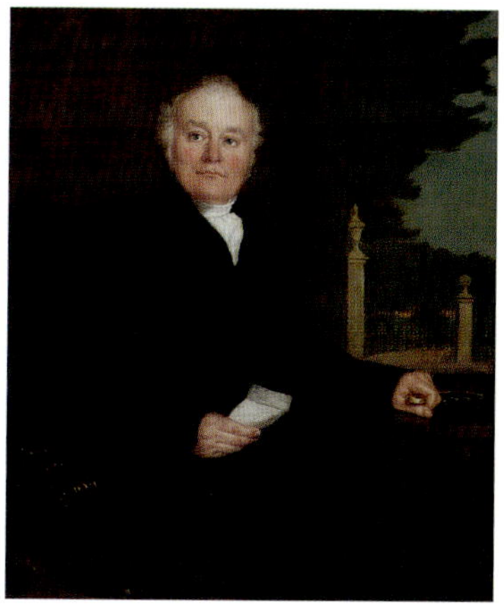

British School 19th C
John Ellis (1789–1862)
oil on canvas 63.5 x 50.8
L.F34.1951.0.0

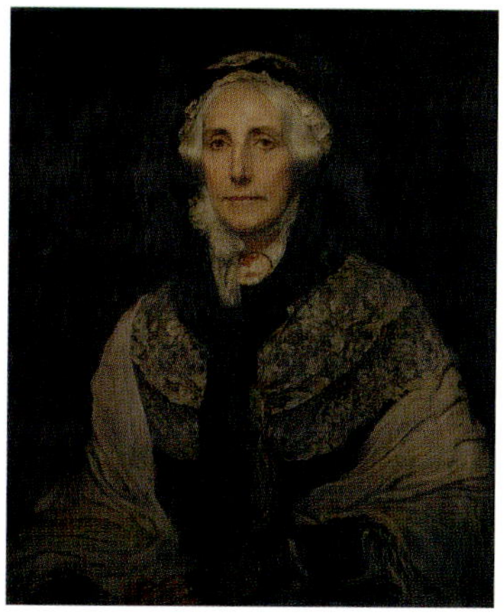

British School late 19th C
Mrs Holland
oil on canvas 75 x 62.3
Y.F7.2005.2.0

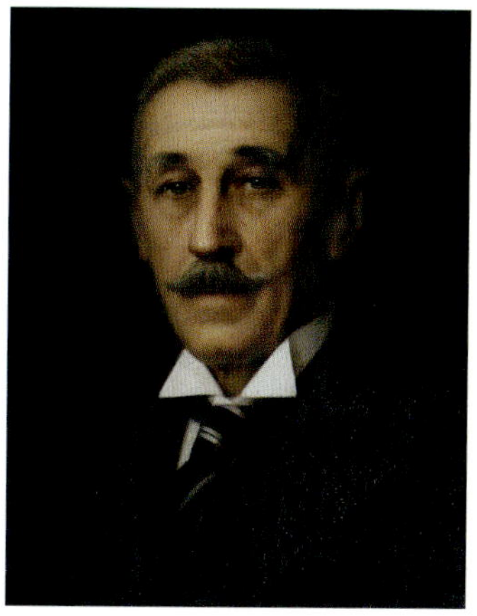

British School 20th C
Alderman John Parsons
oil on canvas 45.7 x 36.2
L.F45.1957.0.0

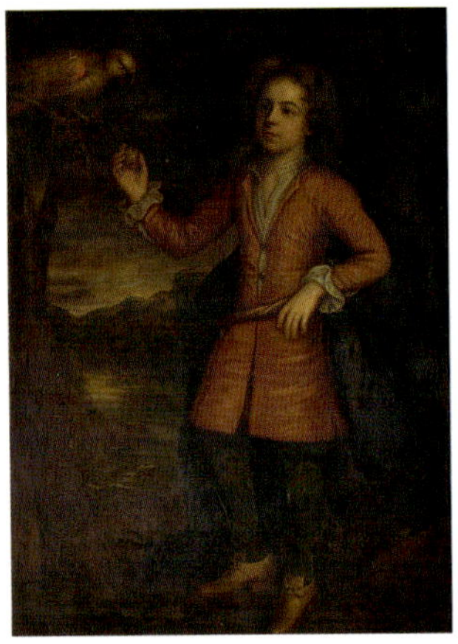

British School
A Boy with a Parrot
oil on canvas 145.7 x 98.4
L.F9.1943.3.0

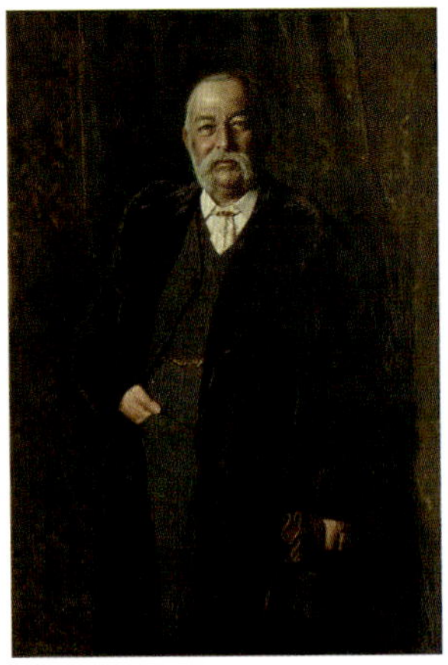

British School
Alderman Edward Wood (1839–1917)
oil on canvas 66 x 43
Y.F16.2009.0.0

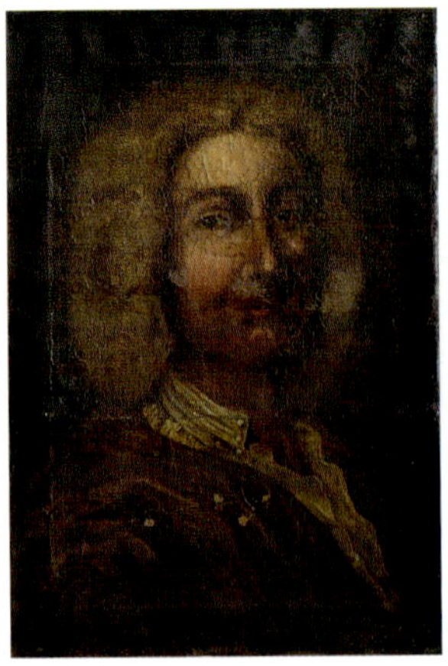

British School
Bishop Dodridge
oil on canvas 52 x 35.2
L.F61.1920.0.0

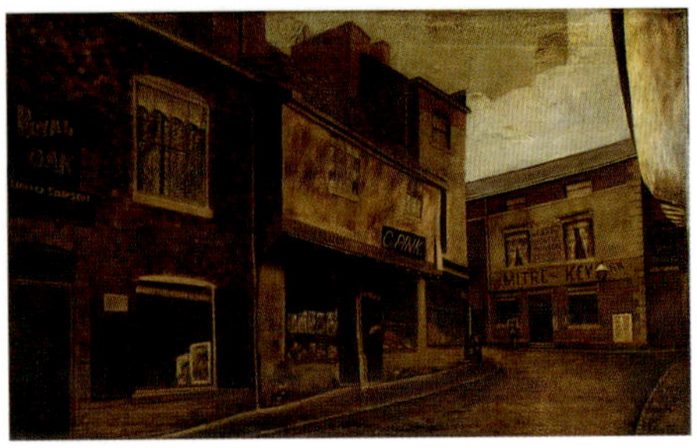

British School
Bridge Street, View of 'The Mitre and Keys Inn', Leicester
oil on canvas 89.1 x 138
L.F353.1957.0.0

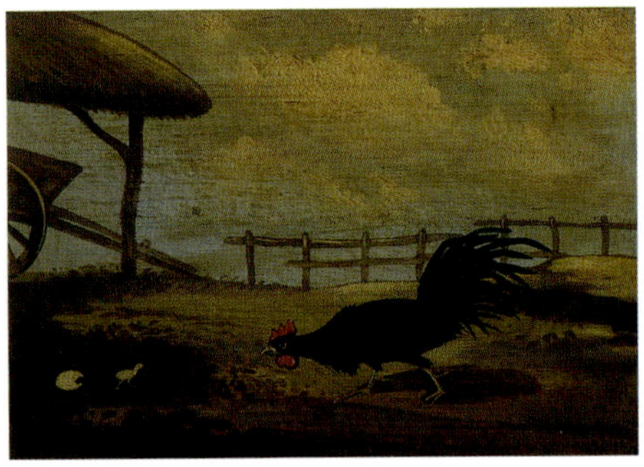

British School
Cock with a Hatched Chick
oil on card 12 x 15.8
L.F132.1961.2.0

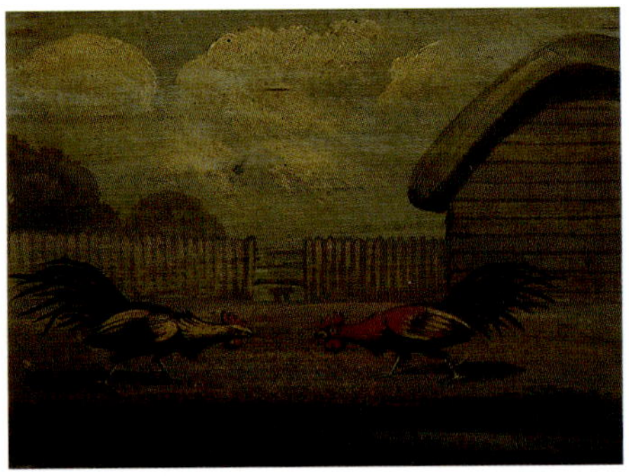

British School
Two Cocks Fighting
oil on card 12 x 15.8
L.F132.1961.1.0

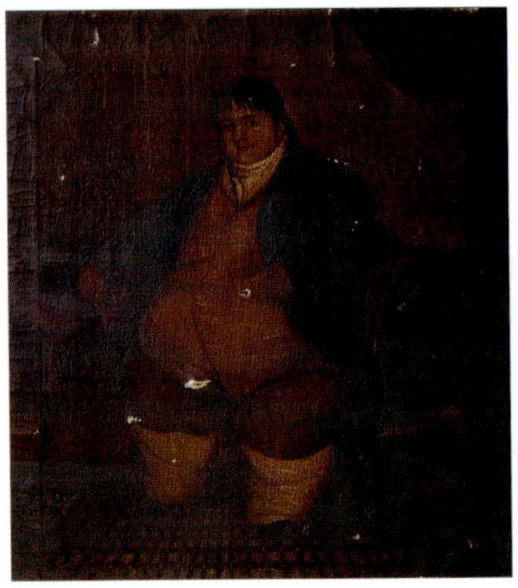

British School
Daniel Lambert (1770–1809)
oil on canvas 63.5 x 58.5
L.F11.1957.0.0

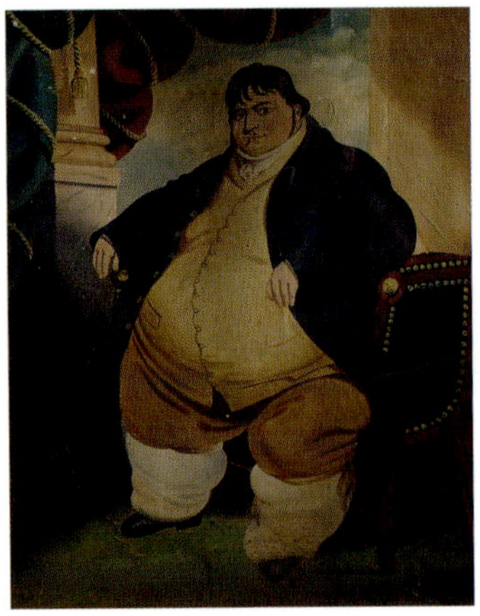

British School
Daniel Lambert (1770–1809)
oil on card 58 x 45
L.F389.1956.0.0

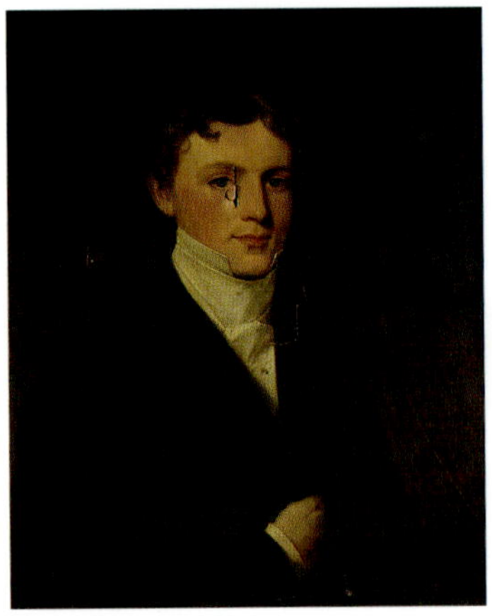

British School
Dr George Shaw (1801–1888), MD
oil on canvas 76.5 x 64
L.F56.1966.0.0

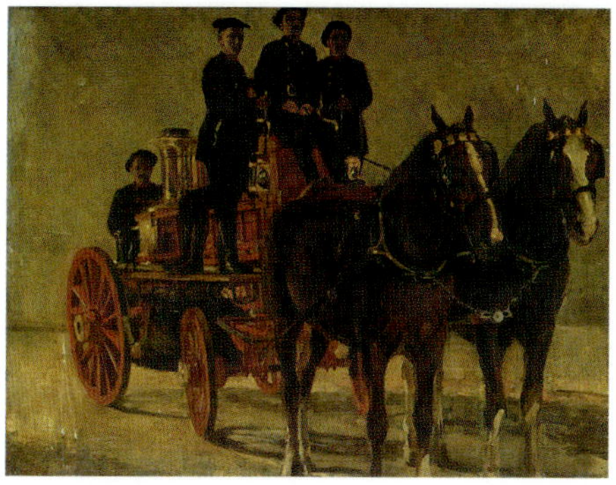

British School
Horse-Drawn Fire Engine
oil on canvas 86.4 x 112.4
L.F135.1967.0.0

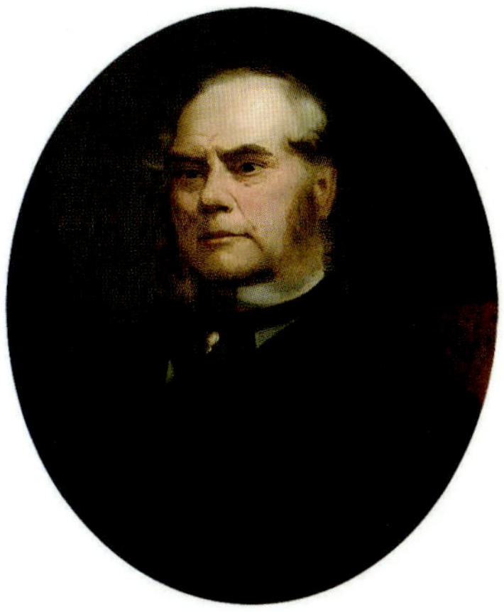

British School
Joseph Goddard (1813–1877)
oil on canvas 60.5 x 50.8
L.F106.1969.0.0

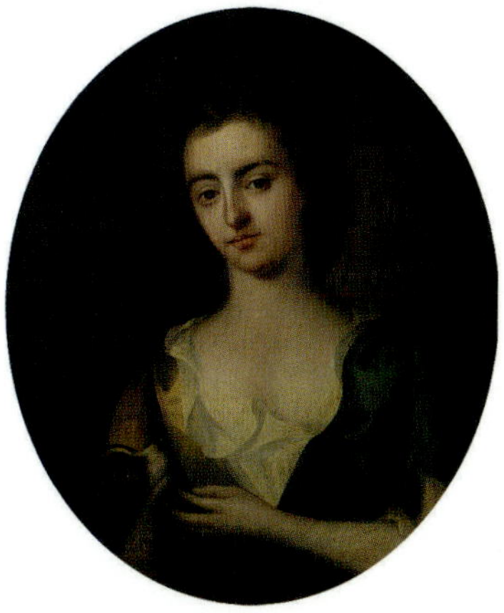

British School
Lady Rachel Russell
oil on canvas 76 x 65
L.F7.1894.0.0

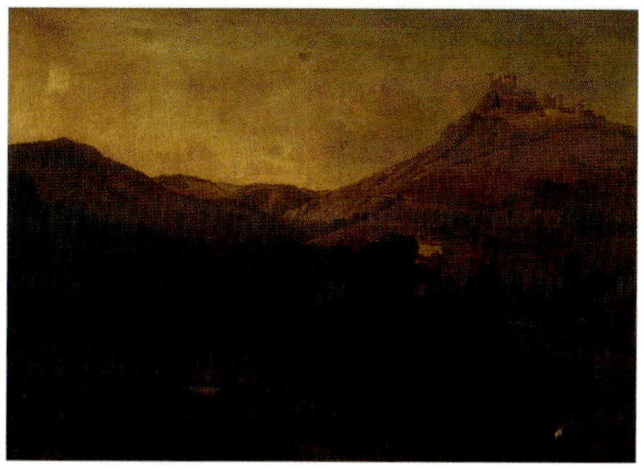

British School
Landscape with Cattle
oil on canvas 94 x 128
Y.F13.2009.0.0

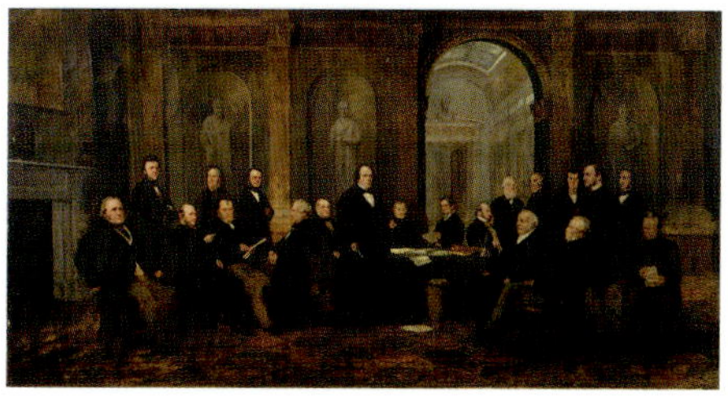

British School
The Midland Counties Railway Board
oil on canvas 87 x 160.5
L.F648.1973.0.0

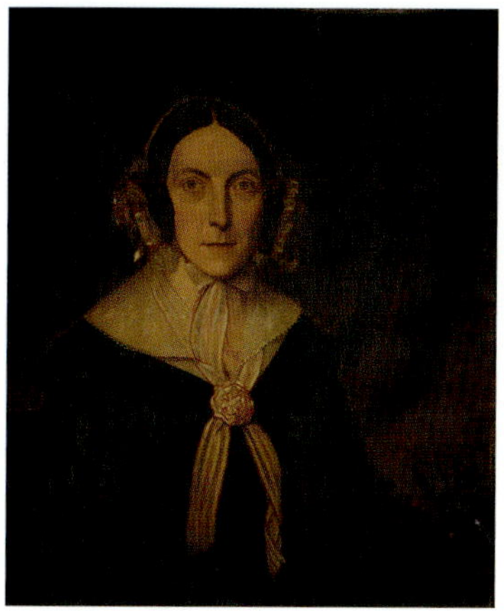

British School
Miss Harriman
oil on canvas 76 x 63.5
L.F2.1981.0.0

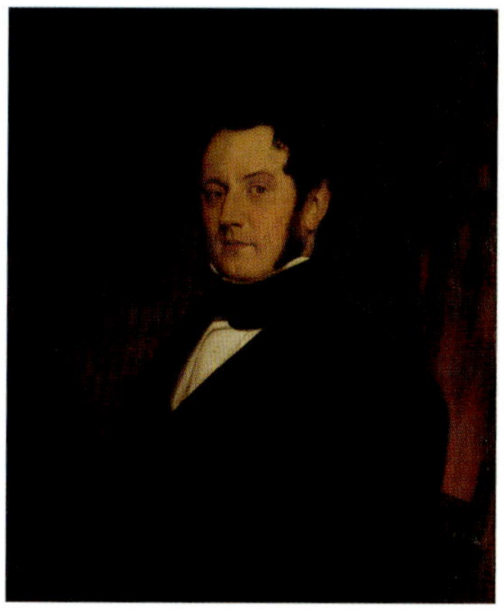

British School
Mr Harriman
oil on canvas 76 x 63.5
L.F1.1981.0.0

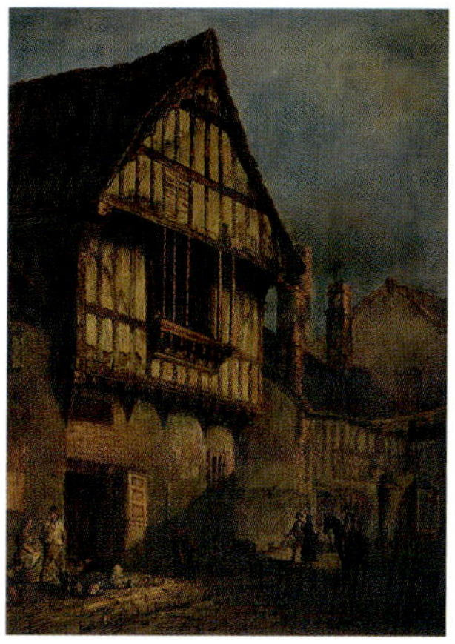

British School
'Old Blue Boar' Inn, Leicester
oil on canvas 42.5 x 31
L.F32.1920.0.0

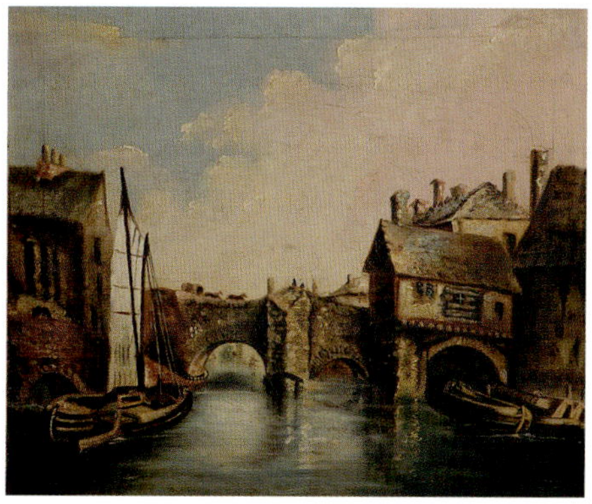

British School
Old West Bridge, Leicester
oil on canvas 33.6 x 38.7
L.F346.1957.0.0

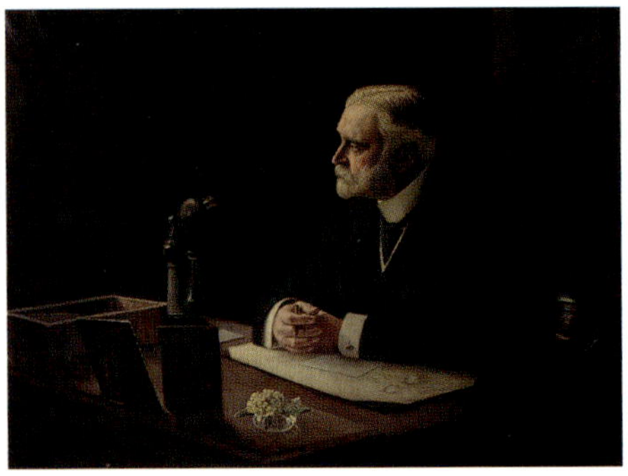

British School
Portrait of a Gentleman at a Desk
oil on canvas 89 x 120
L.F25.1987.0.0

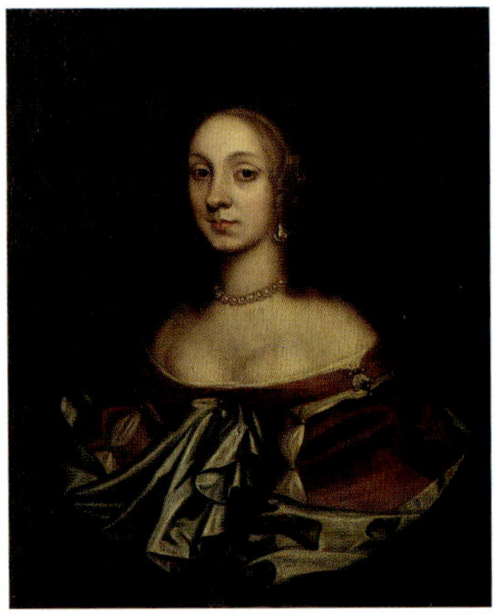

British School
Portrait of a Lady (possibly Queen Caroline or Queen Elizabeth)
oil on canvas 75.9 x 63.5
L.F9.1943.6.0

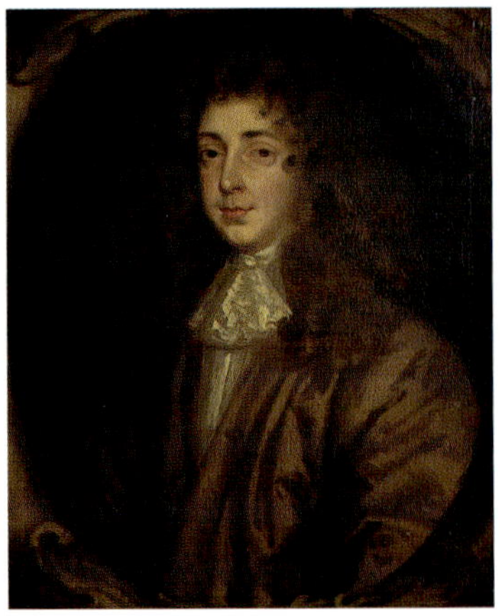

British School
Portrait of an Unknown Gentleman
oil on canvas 74 x 61
L.F9.1900.0.0

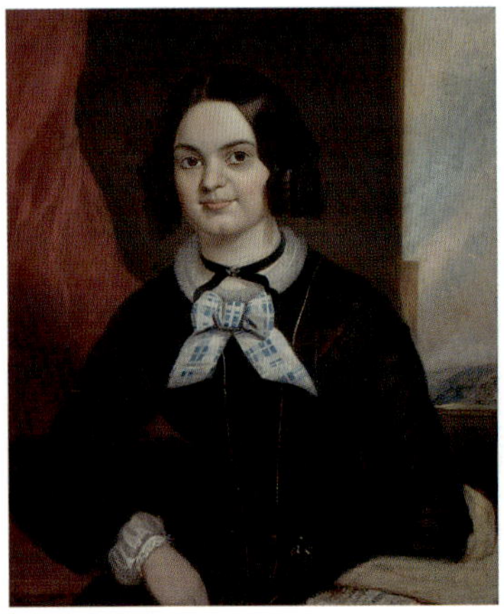

British School
Portrait of an Unknown Lady
oil on canvas 76.5 x 64
Y.F14.2009.0.0

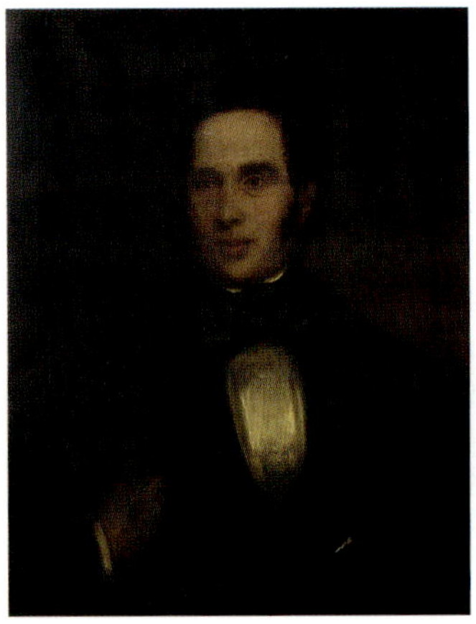

British School
Portrait of an Unknown Man
oil on canvas 70.5 x 53.5
Y.F2.2009.0.0

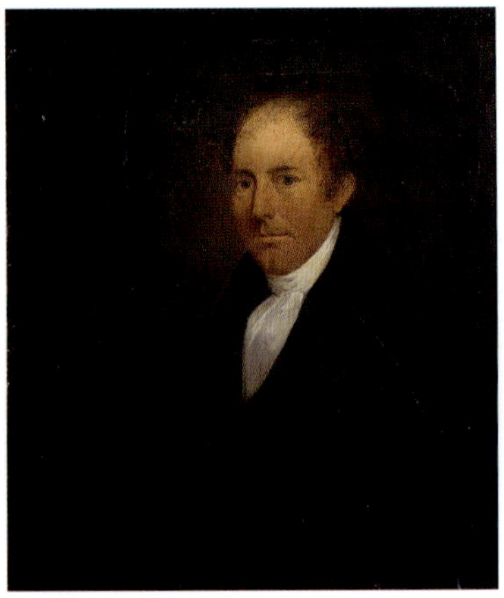

British School
Portrait of an Unknown Man
oil on canvas 76.5 x 63.4
Y.F6.2009.0.0

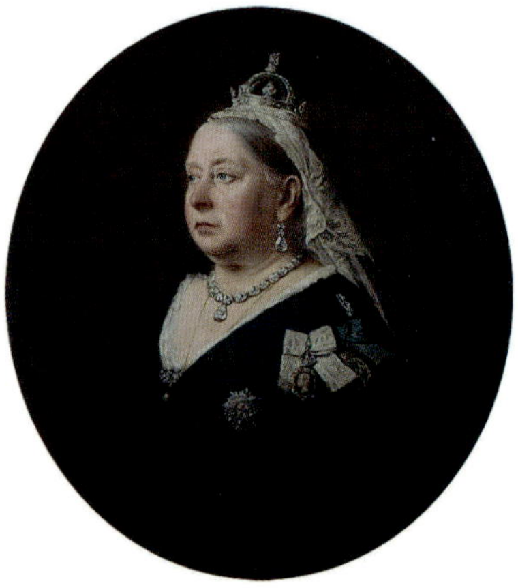

British School
Queen Victoria (1819–1901)
oil on canvas 81.2 x 71
L.F1.1990.0.0

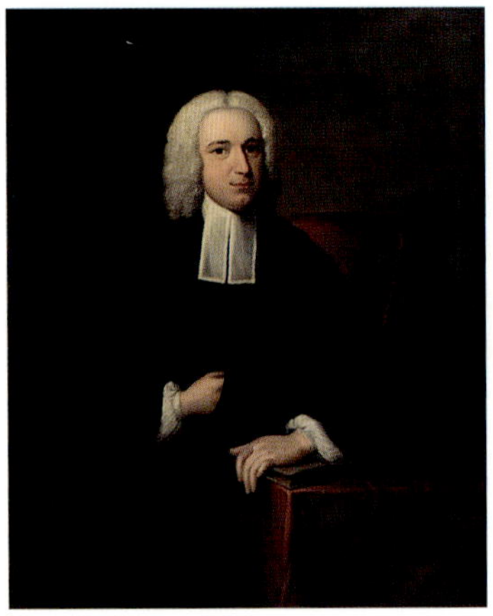

British School
Reverend John Taylor (1711–1772)
oil on canvas 124.5 x 99
L.F148.1964.0.0

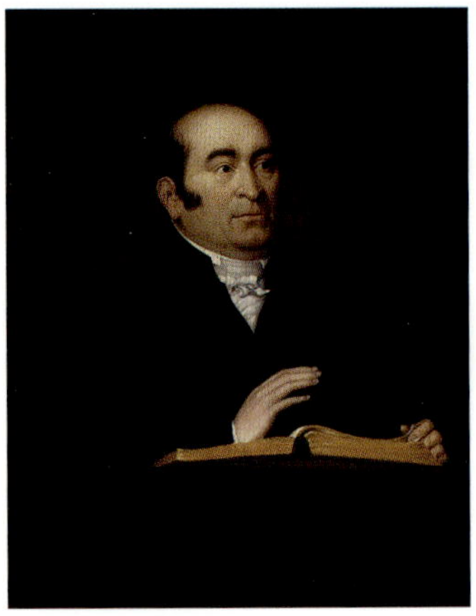

British School
Reverend Robert Hall (1764–1831)
oil on canvas 51 x 40
L.F106.1958.0.0

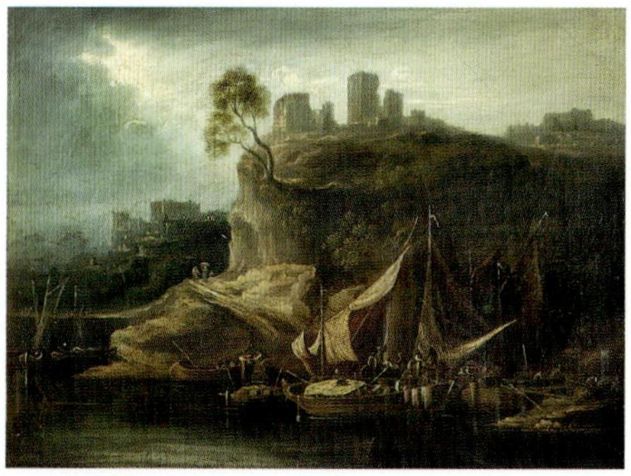

British School
Romantic Landscape
oil on canvas 51.3 x 67
L.F73.1993.0.0

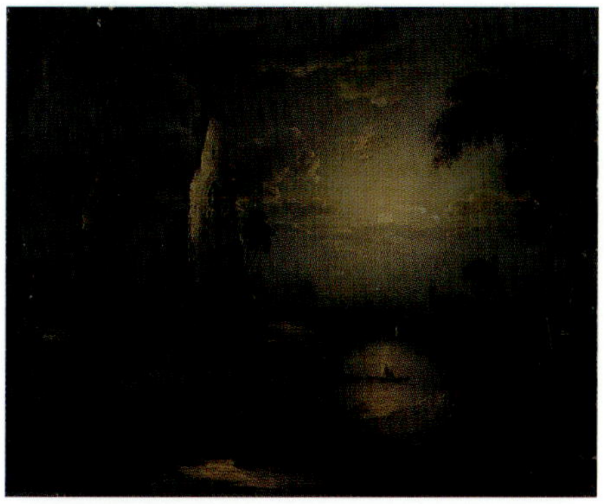

British School
Romantic Landscape, Ruins in the Moonlight
oil on canvas 50 x 60.8
L.F30.1947.0.0

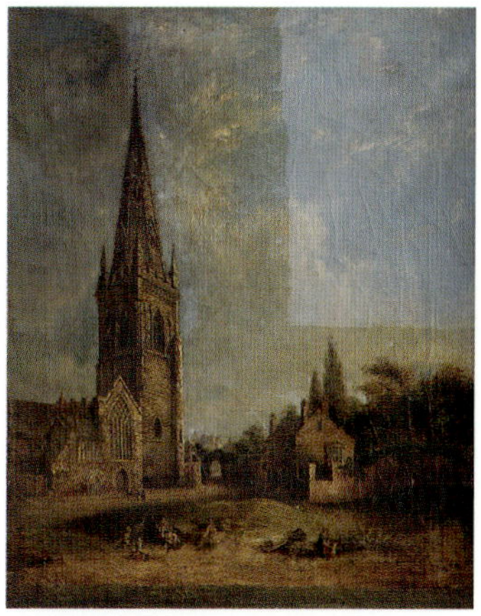

British School
St Mary de Castro, Leicester
oil on canvas 50.7 x 40.3
L.F97.1914.0.0

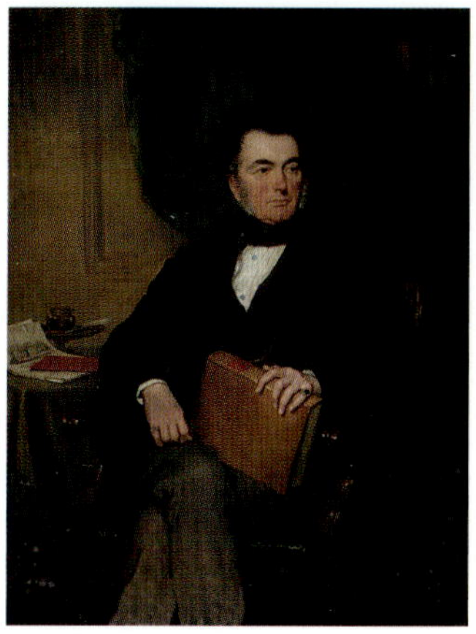

British School
Sir Charles William Packe (1792–1867), MP
oil on canvas 139 x 109
L.F26.1987.0.0

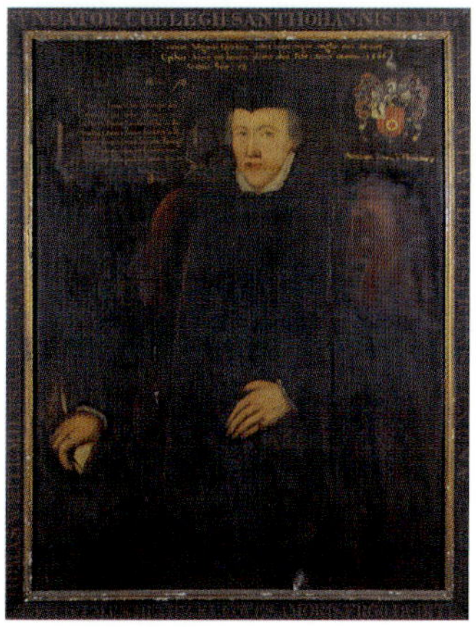

British School
Sir Thomas White (1492–1566)
oil on panel 113.7 x 85.7
L.F51.1926.0.0

British School
Sir William Herrick (1557–1653)
oil on canvas 72.4 x 59.6
L.F25.1937.3.0

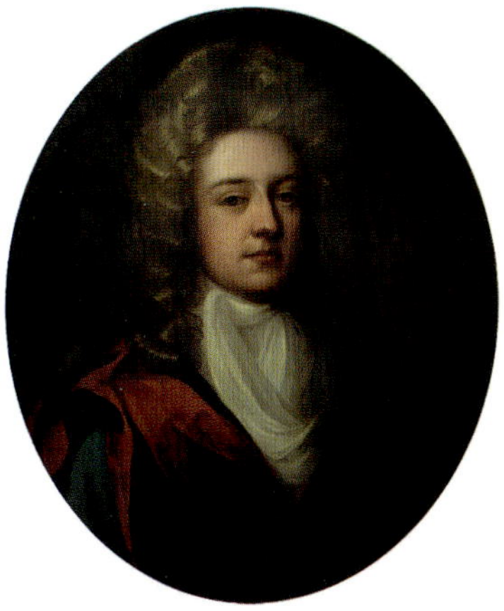

British School
Sir William Russell
oil on canvas 77.2 x 64.5
L.F8.1894.0.0

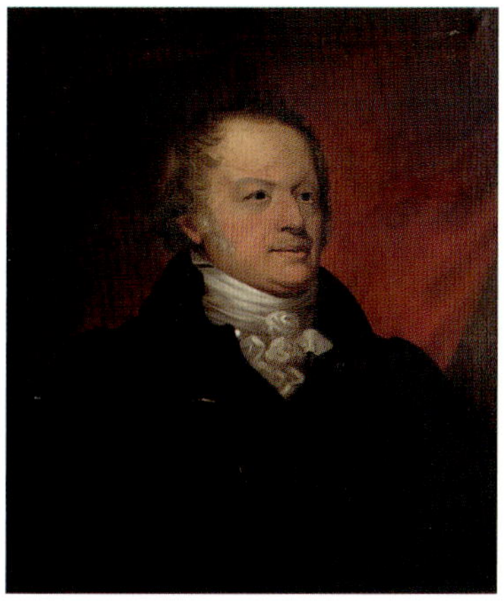

British School
Sir William Walker
oil on canvas 76.2 x 63.4
L.F29.1949.0.0

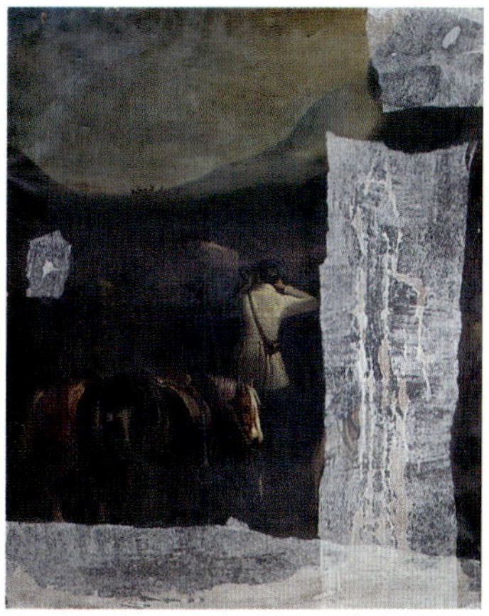

British School
Stag Shooting in Mountainous Country
oil on canvas 112 x 87.5
L.F20.1935.18.0

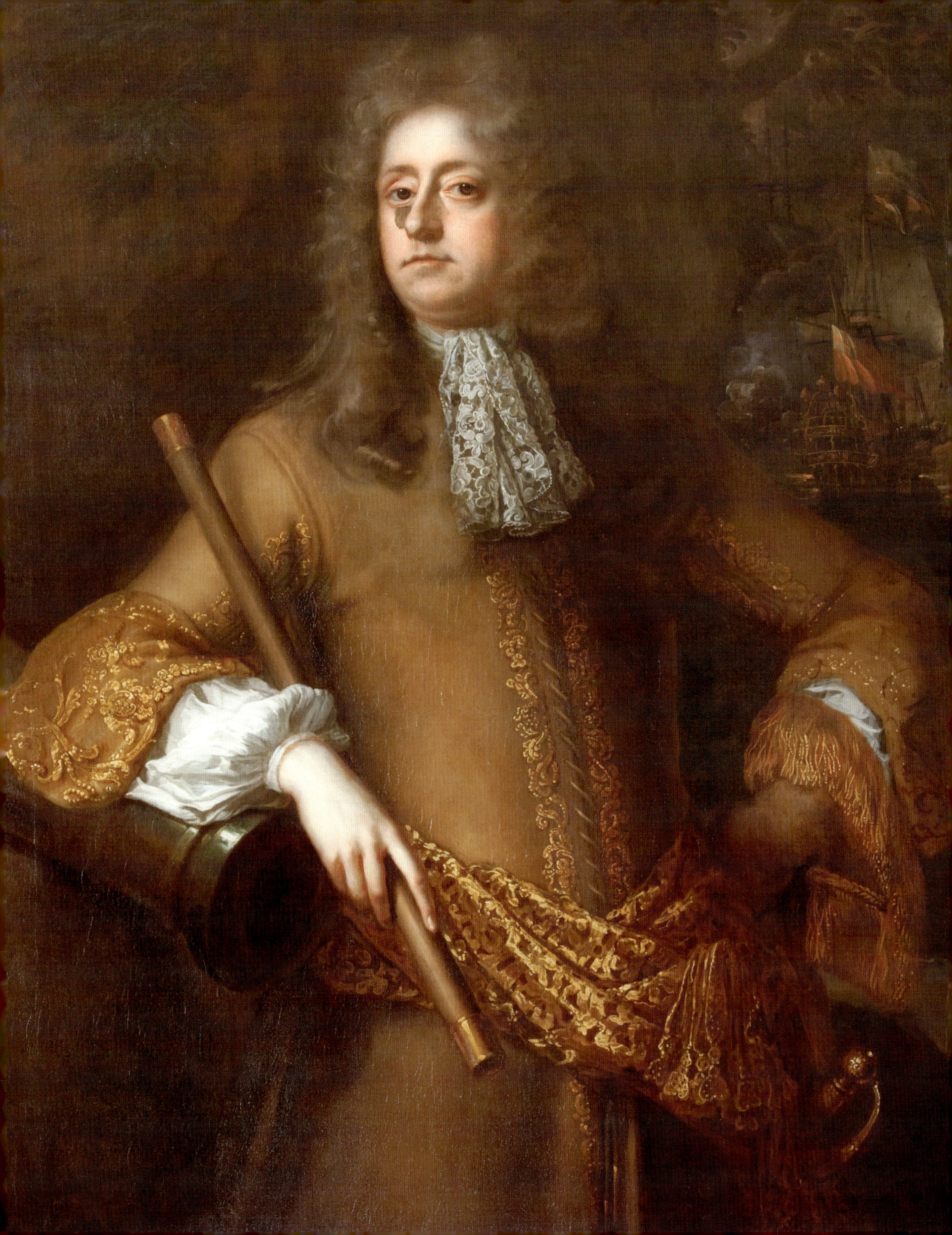

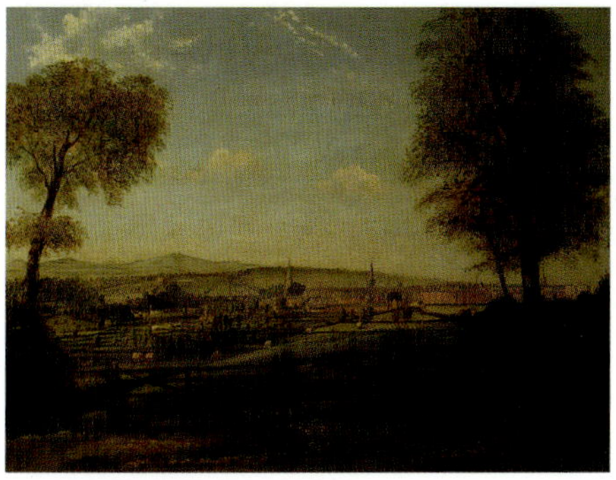

British School
View of Leicester
oil on canvas 71.5 x 91.5
Y.F9.2009.0.0

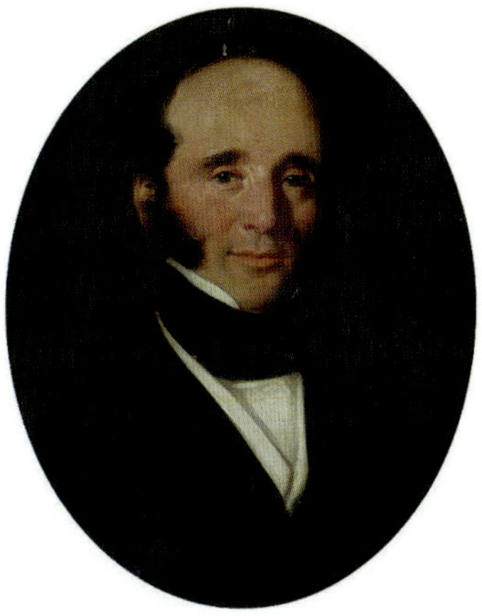

British School
William Biggs (1804–1881), 19th Lord Mayor of Leicester
oil on canvas 57.5 x 45
L.F2.1996.0.0

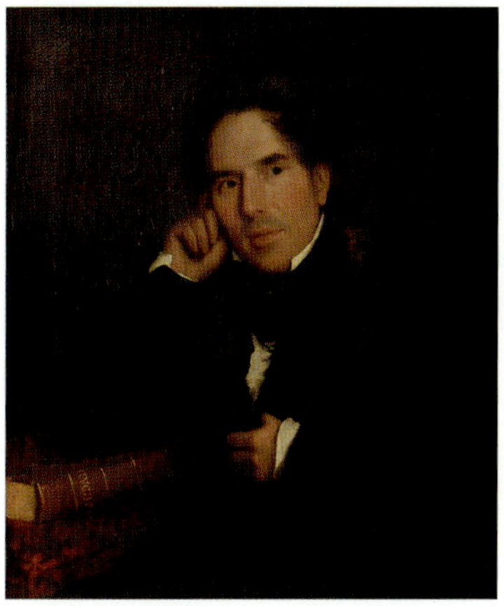

British School
William Gardiner (1770–1853)
oil on canvas 76.2 x 63.5
Y.F13.2008.0.0

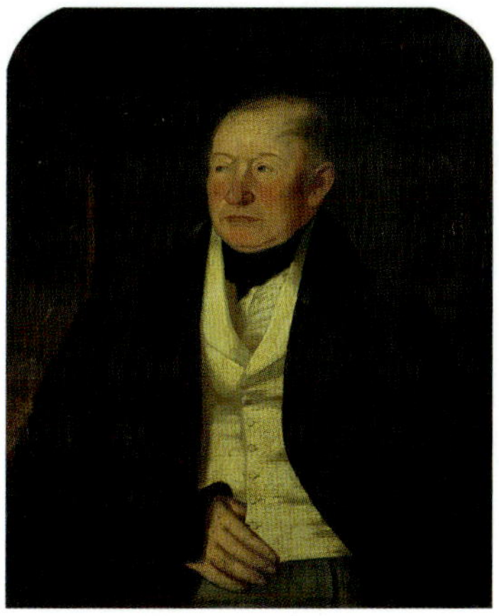

British School
William Stenson of Whitwick (1771–1861)
oil on canvas 91.2 x 71
L.F2.1960.0.0

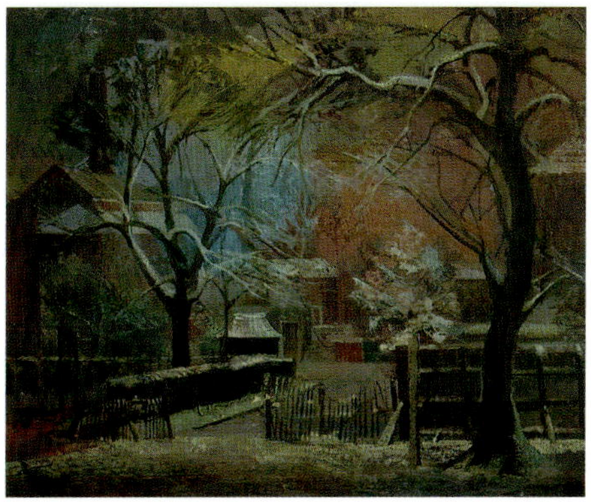

British School
Winter Scene
oil on canvas 50 x 60
L.F3.1996.42.0

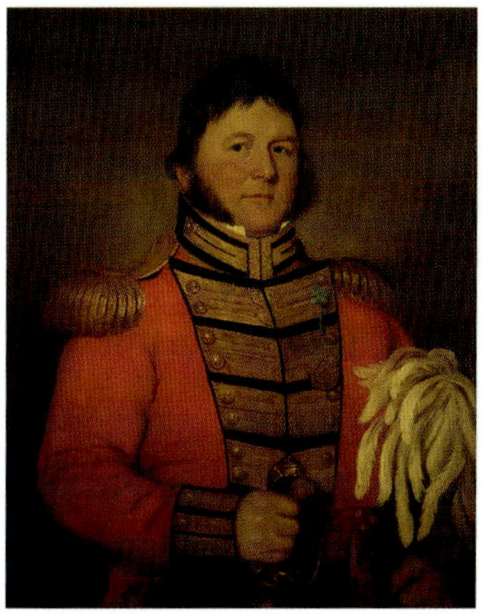

Brown, W.
Captain James Jones (1777–1866), RM 1830
oil on canvas 85.8 x 64.7
L.F6.1945.1.0

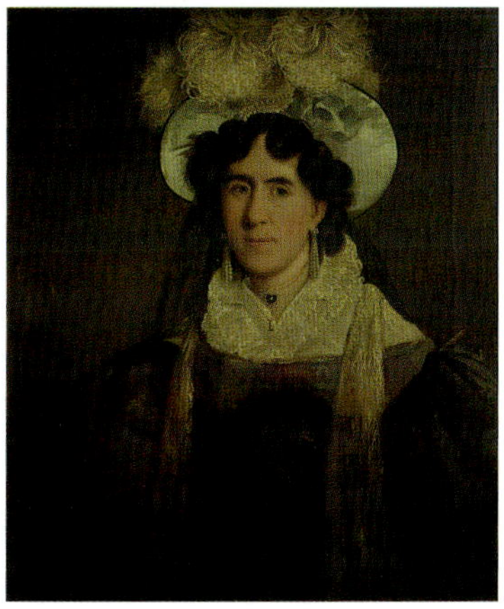

Brown, W.
The Wife of Captain James Jones 1830
oil on canvas 76.2 x 63.5
L.F6.1945.2.0

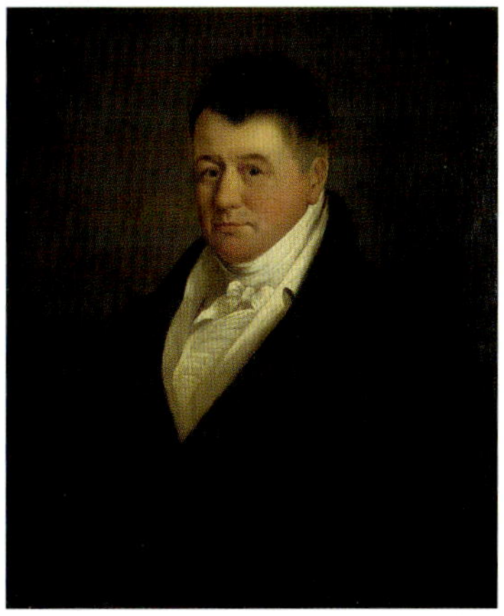

Brown, W.
John Mansfield (1739–1798)
oil on canvas 77 x 64
L.F35.1918.0.0

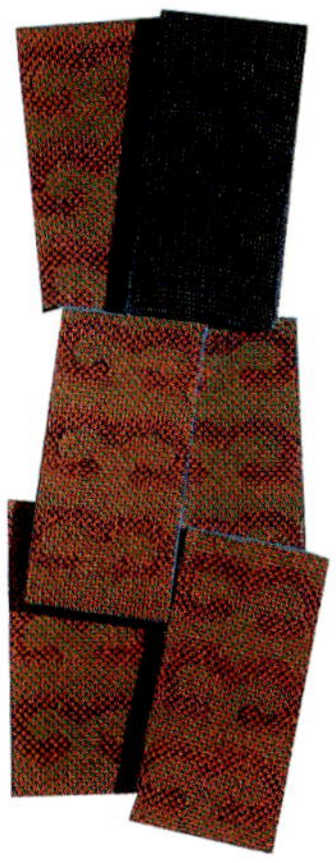

Buckley, Stephen b.1944
Two Step 1990–1999
oil & enamel on canvas 98 x 39
Y.F5.2007.1.0

Facing page: Closterman, John, 1660–1711, *Arthur Herbert (c.1648–1716), 1st Earl of Torrington* (detail), c.1700, North Lincolnshire Museums Service (p. 358)

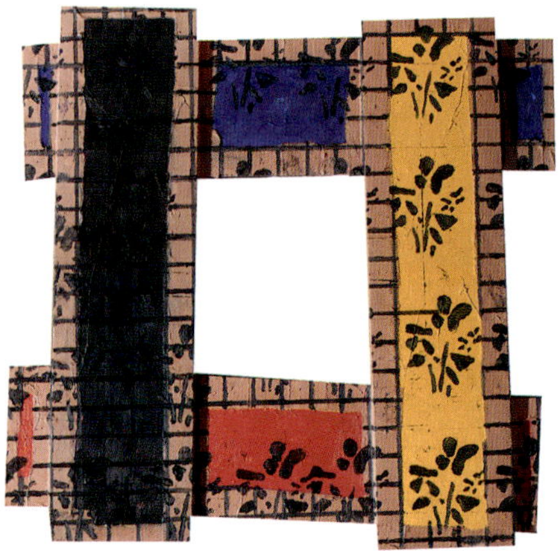

Buckley, Stephen b.1944
Dosover 1998
oil on canvas 110 x 110
Y.F5.2007.2.0

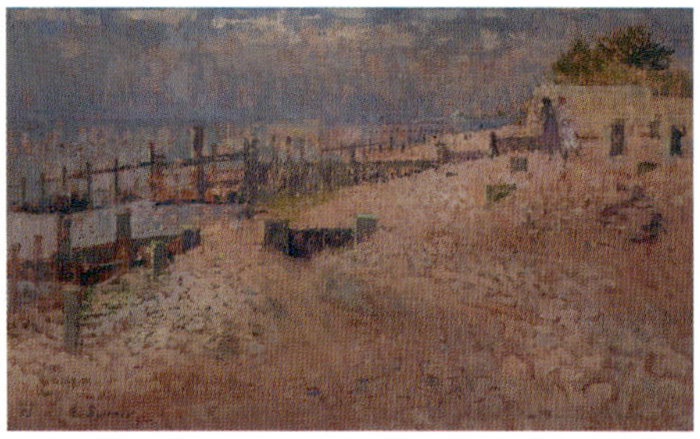

Bulmer, Lionel 1919–1992
The Shelving Beach 1955
oil & muslin on hardboard 16.5 x 37.5
L.F28.1956.0.0

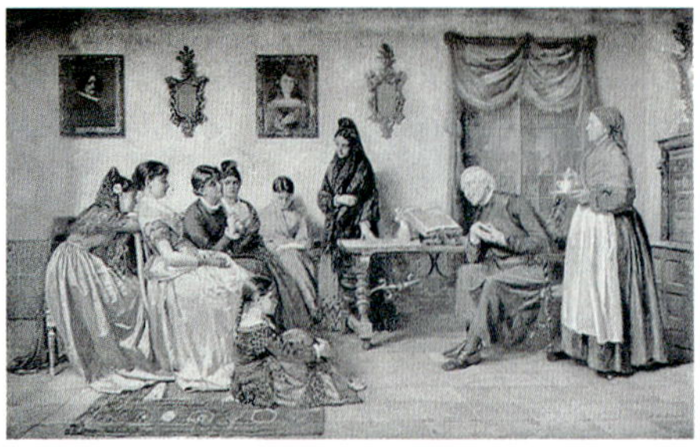

Burgess, John Bagnold 1830–1897
Catechising 1878
oil on panel 84.3 x 132.5
L.F9.1890.0.0

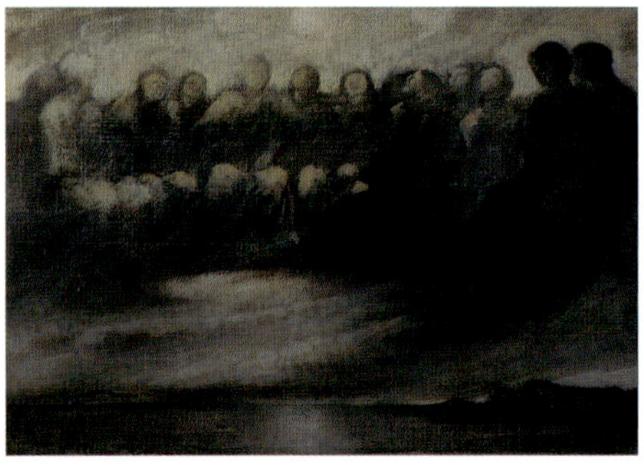

Burne-Jones, Edward 1833–1898
Christ and the Twelve Apostles
oil on canvas 25.1 x 35.3
L.F2.1947.0.0

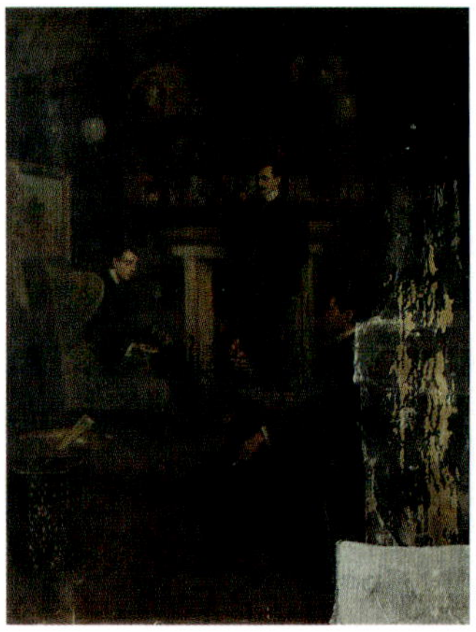

Burroughs, Albert Leicester 1865–after 1915
Interior with Three Men round a Fire
oil on canvas 126.5 x 91.5
L.F37.1990.0.0

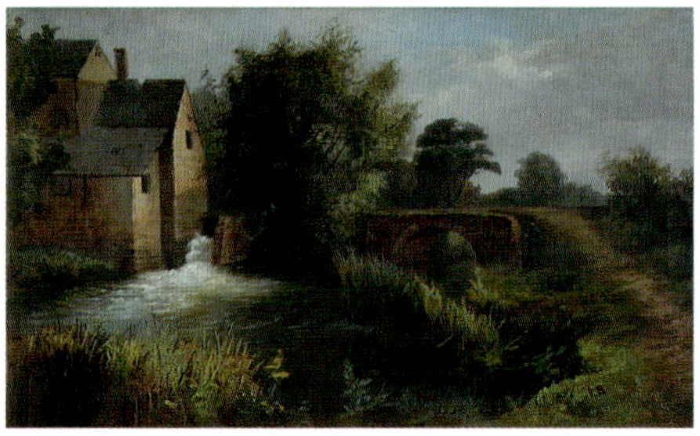

Burton, Ida
Aylestone Mill, Leicestershire
oil on canvas 41 x 66.5
L.F122.1955.0.0

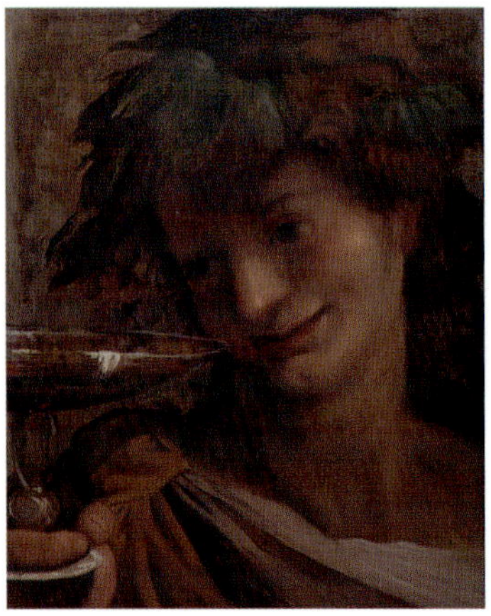

Carracci, Annibale 1560–1609
Youthful Bacchus
oil on canvas 46.4 x 36.1
L.F17.1967.0.0

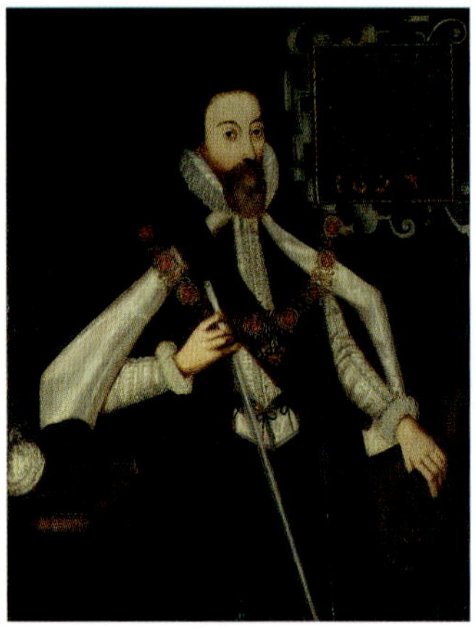

Carter, Chirstopher
Henry Hastings (c.1535–1595), 3rd Earl of Huntingdon 1623
oil on panel 116.8 x 90.2
L.F49.1926.0.0

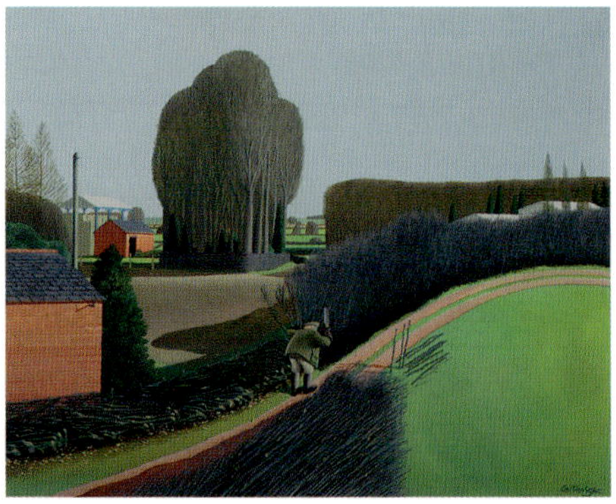

Cartwright, Reg b.1938
The Hedge Layer 1974
oil on canvas 61 x 76
L.F22.1981.0.0

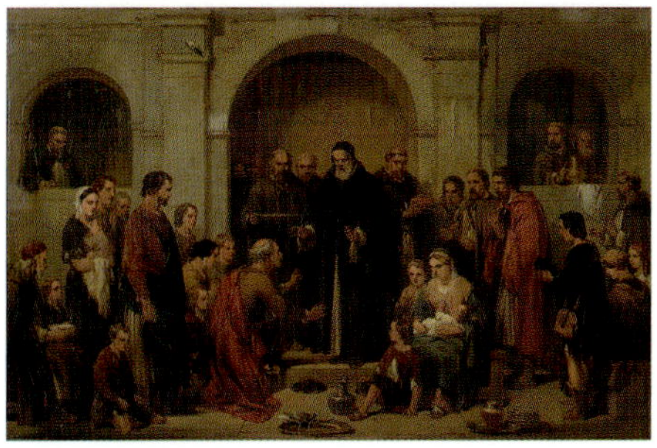

Cattermole, George 1800–1868
The Monastery Door 1862
oil on canvas 50.2 x 75
L.F5.1882.0.0

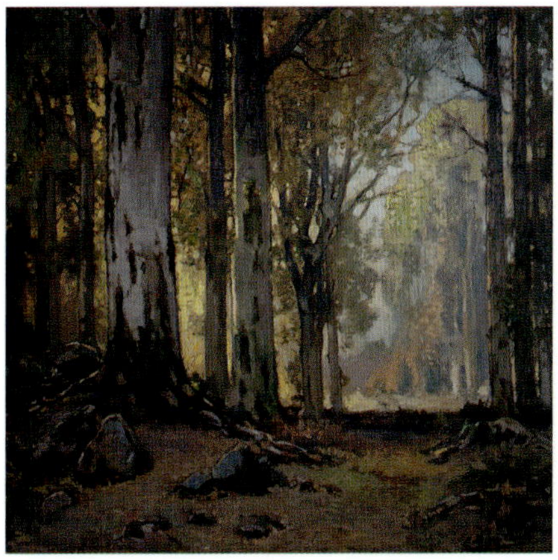

Clarke, Harry Harvey 1869–1948
The Silver Beeches of Pentre Du, Conwy
oil on canvas 96.5 x 101.6
L.F13.1925.0.0

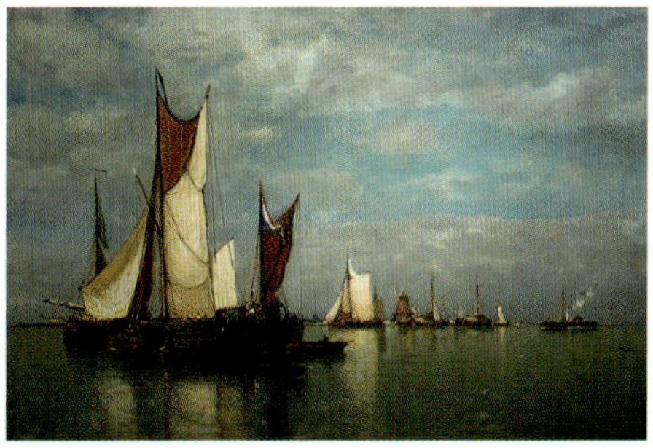

Clays, Paul Jean 1819–1900
A Calm on the Kel near Dordrecht, The Netherlands 1870
oil on canvas 76 x 110.5
L.F3.1891.0.0

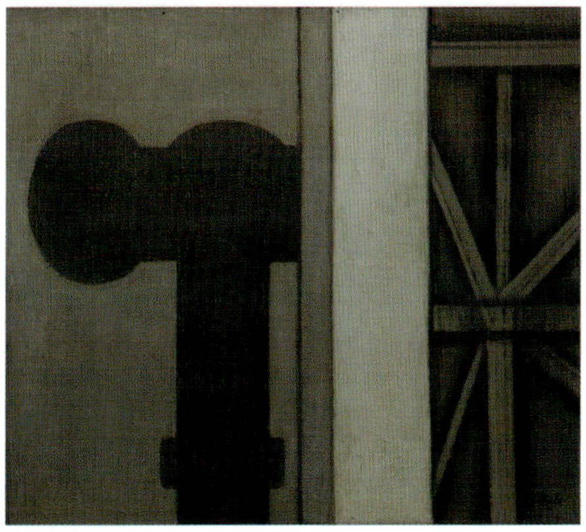

Clough, Prunella 1919–1999
Industrial Interior 1 1956
oil on canvas 54.7 x 61
L.F358.1975.0.0

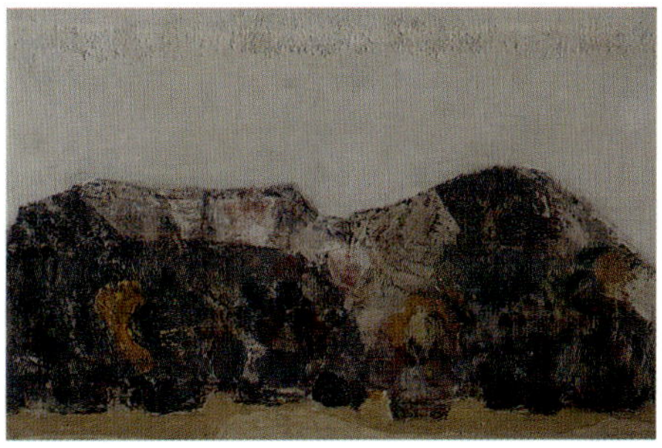

Clough, Prunella 1919–1999
Slag Heap 1959
oil on canvas 30.5 x 46
L.F52.1982.0.0

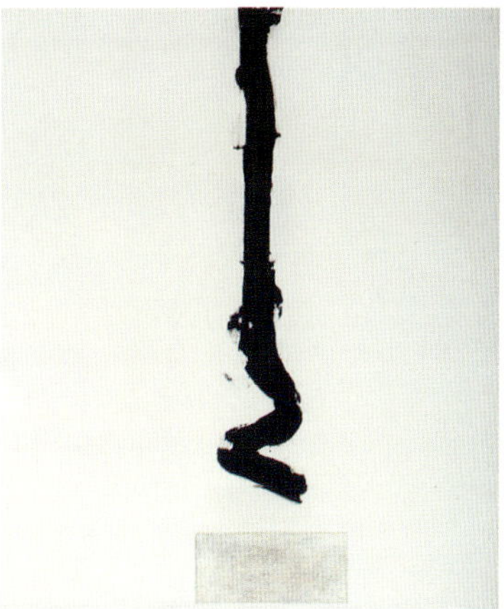

Clough, Prunella 1919–1999
Commemorate 1976
oil on canvas 184 x 152.5
L.F779.1977.0.0

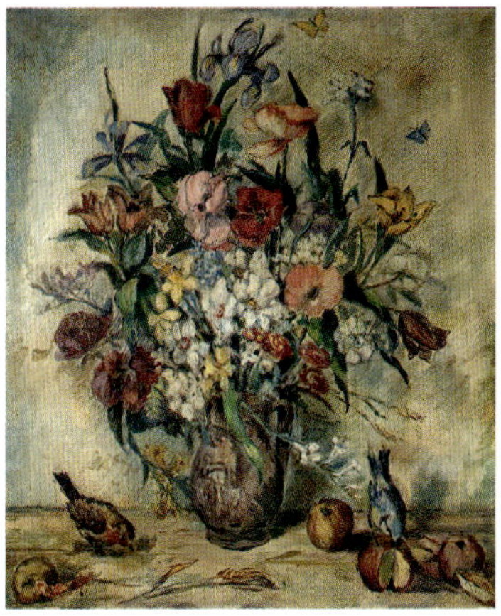

Clutton-Brock, Evelyn Alice b.1876
Flower Study
oil on canvas 76 x 64
L.F3.1996.32.0

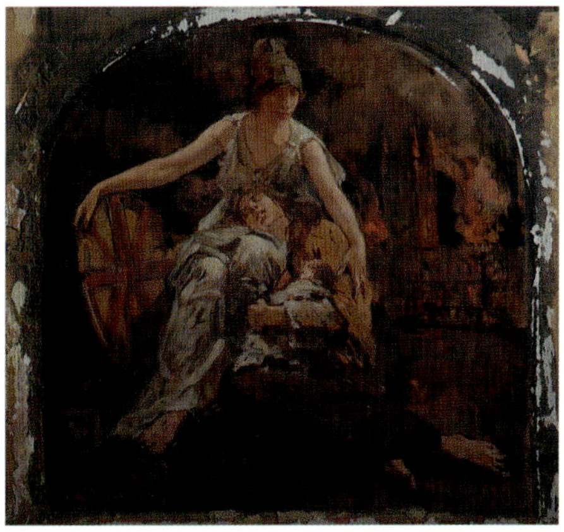

Cluysenaar, André 1872–1939
Britannia with Belgian Refugees
oil on board 40.6 x 45.5
L.F81.1987.0.0

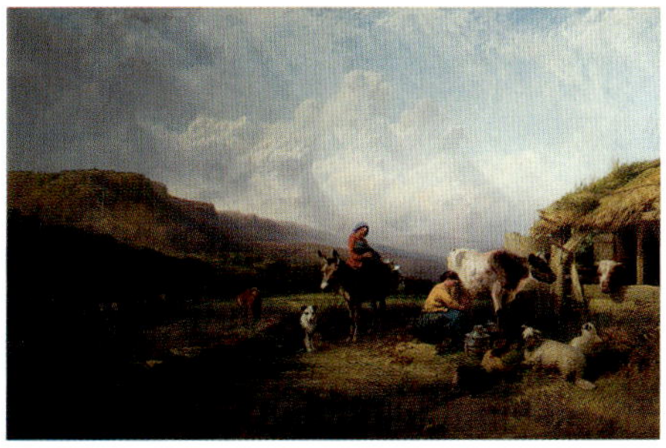

Cole, George 1810–1883
Milking Time on the Swale, Yorkshire 1863/1868
oil on canvas 107 x 153.2
L.F5.1902.0.0

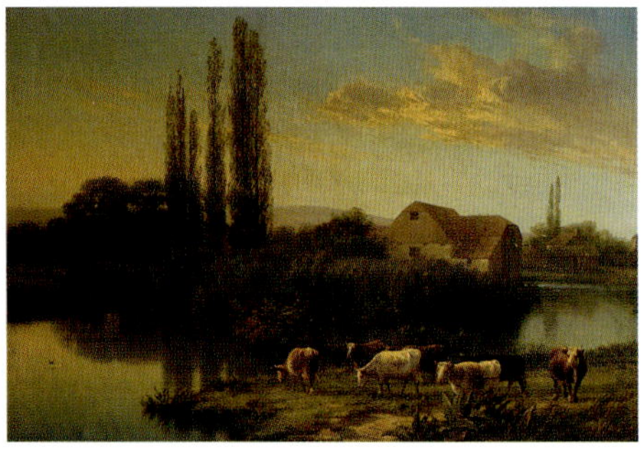

Cole, George 1810–1883
Fittleworth Old Mill, River Rother, Sussex 1881
oil on canvas 104 x 150
L.F3.1908.0.0

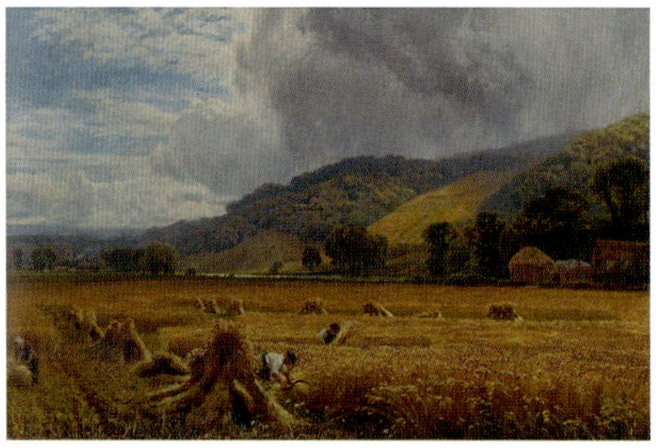

Cole, George Vicat 1833–1893
Harvesting in the Thames Valley 1888
oil on canvas 51 x 76.5
L.F14.1939.0.0

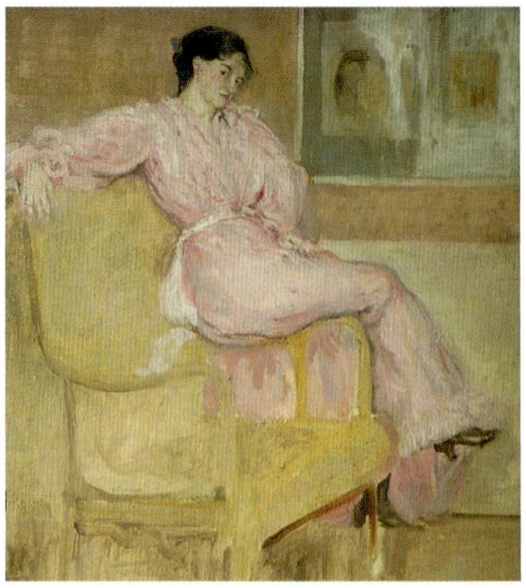

Conder, Charles 1868–1909
Mrs Conder in Pink
oil on canvas 48 x 44.3
L.F43.1956.0.0

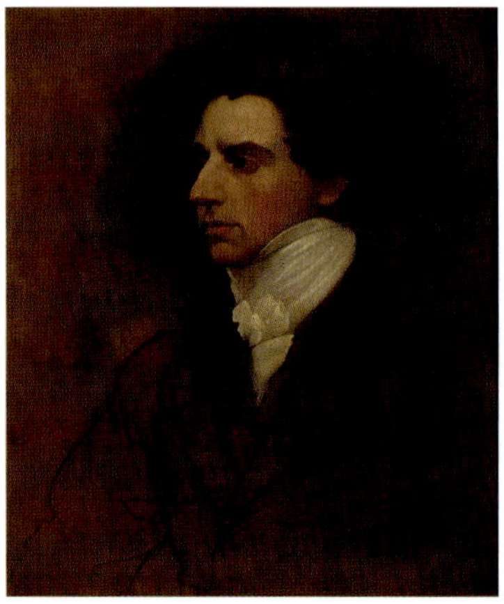

Constable, John 1776–1837
Portrait of a Gentleman (unfinished) 1803–1804
oil on canvas 71.2 x 59.1
L.F11.1936.0.0

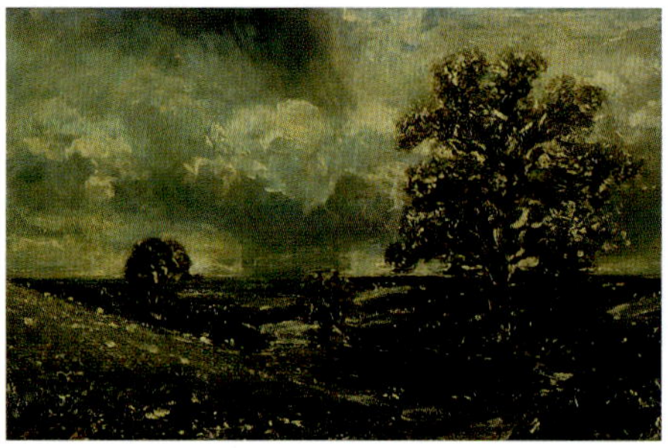

Constable, John (after) 1776–1837
Noon, West End Fields, Hampstead, London (sketch)
oil on canvas 38 x 55.5
L.F38.1948.1.0

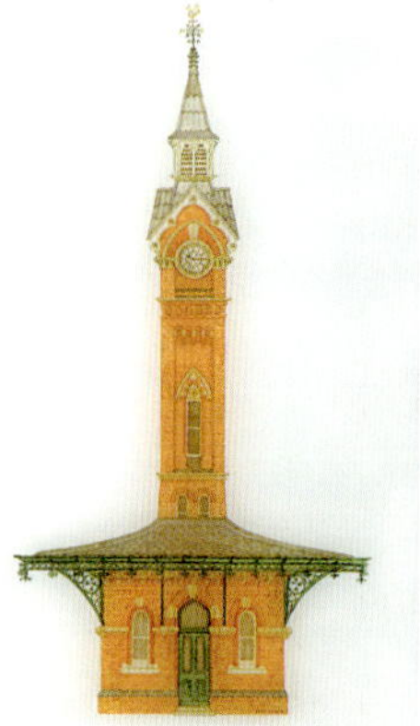

Cook, Jenny b.1942
Cattle Market Clock Tower, Leicester
oil on acrylic sheet 32.1 x 19
L.F59.1982.0.0

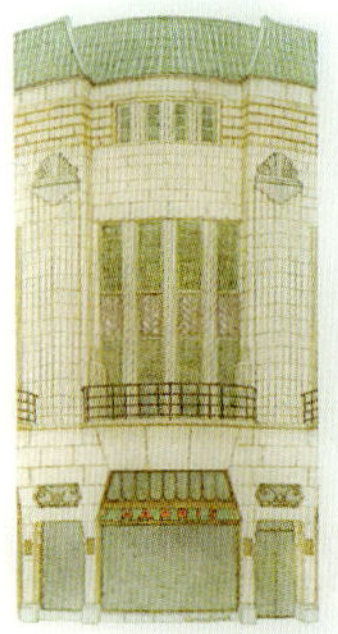

Cook, Jenny b.1942
'Harris', Granby Corner, Leicester
oil on acrylic sheet 32.1 x 19.5
L.F58.1982.0.0

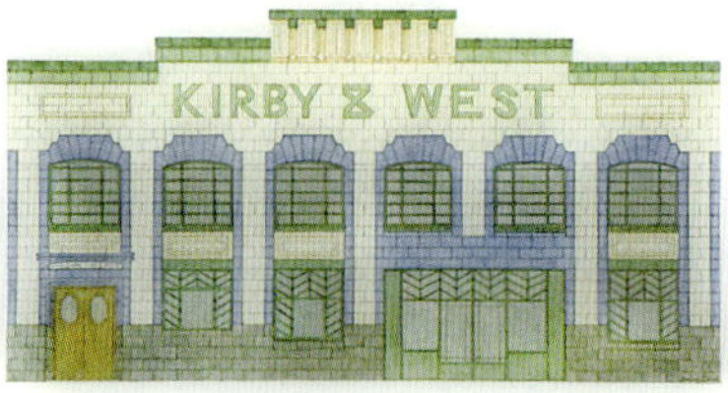

Cook, Jenny b.1942
'Kirby & West' Building, Western Boulevard, Leicester
oil on acrylic sheet 20.6 x 37.2
L.F60.1982.0.0

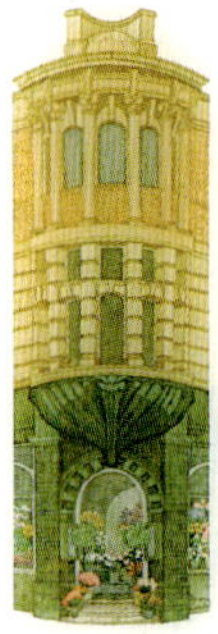

Cook, Jenny b.1942
'Roy Vickers' Flower Shop, YMCA Corner, Granby Street, Leicester
oil on acrylic sheet 32.1 x 19.5
L.F57.1982.0.0

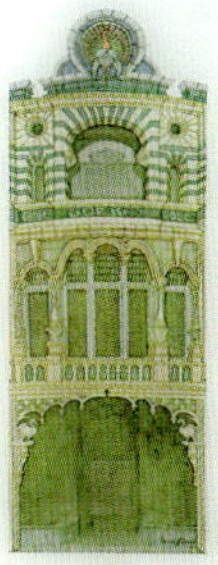

Cook, Jenny b.1942
Turkey Café, Granby Street, Leicester
oil on acrylic sheet 32.1 x 19.6
L.F56.1982.0.0

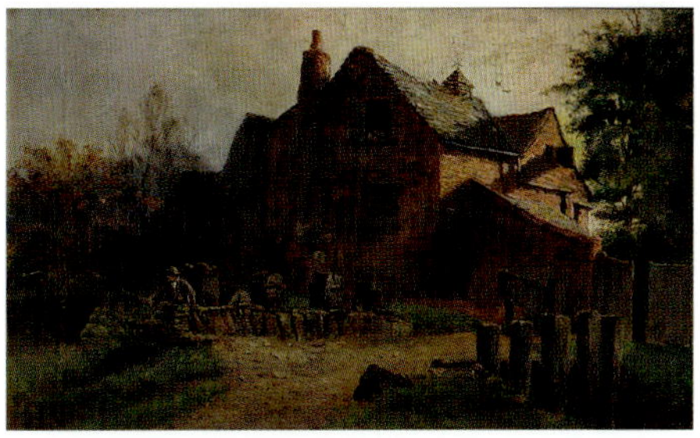

Cooke, Edward William 1811–1880, **Francis, Charles & unknown artist**
The Old Mill, Kirby Bellars, Leicestershire 1876
oil on canvas 24.1 x 39.4
L.F216.1954.7.0

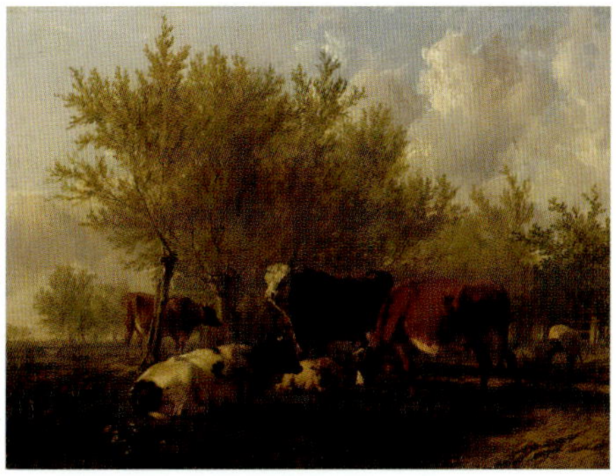

Cooper, Thomas Sidney 1803–1902
Cattle in a Landscape 1832
oil on canvas 34.2 x 40.1
L.F5.1887.0.0

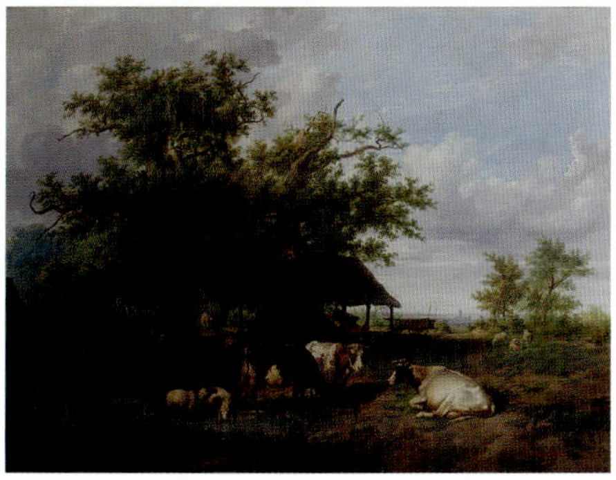

Cooper, Thomas Sidney 1803–1902
Landscape with Cattle 1832
oil on canvas 104.7 x 134
L.F14.1990.0.0

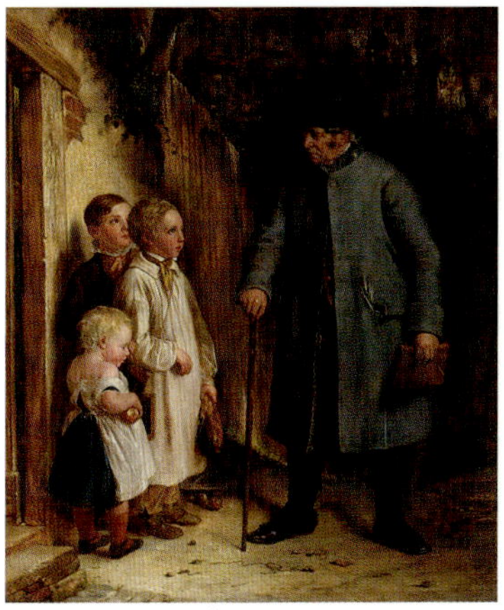

Cope, Charles West 1811–1890
The Village Schoolmaster 1842
oil on canvas 75.5 x 63
L.F5.1888.0.0

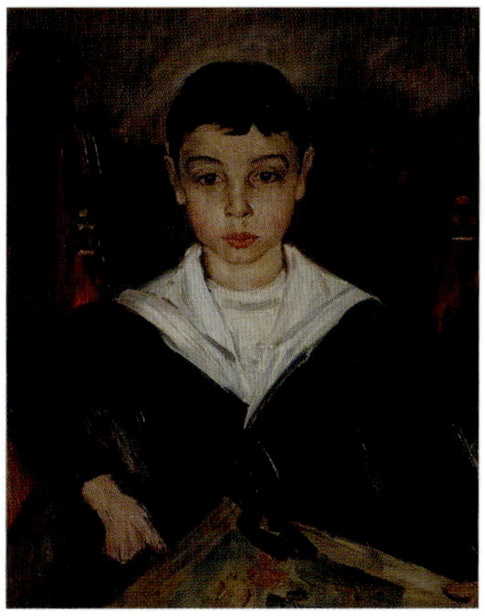

Corinth, Lovis 1858–1925
Carl Ludwig Elias, Aged 7 1/4 1899
oil on canvas 68.5 x 54.5
L.F48.1968.0.0

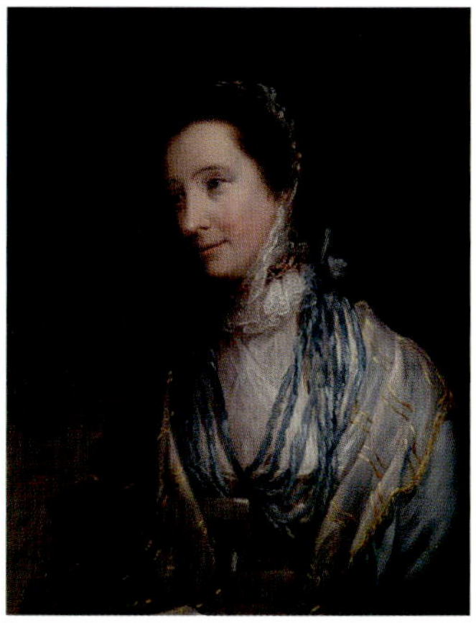

Cotes, Francis 1726–1770
Miss Elizabeth Adney (d.1783) 1760
oil on canvas 67 x 51.5
L.F1.1908.0.0

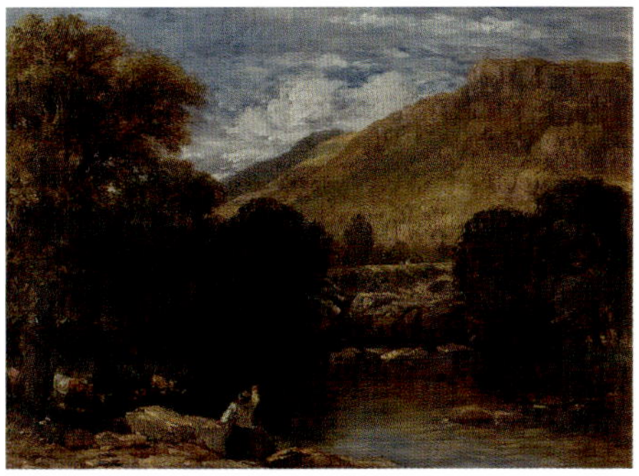

Cox, David the elder 1783–1859
Pont-y-Pair, Conwy 1851
oil on canvas 46.3 x 61.5
L.F4.1892.0.0

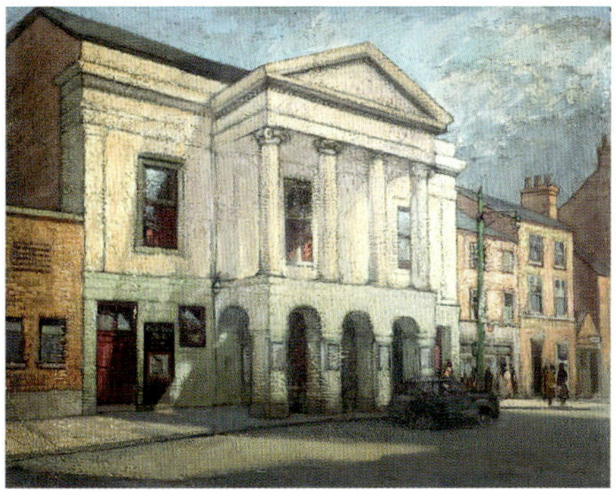

Cramphorn, Frank Leslie 1908–2000
The Theatre Royal, Leicester c.1957
oil on hardboard 61 x 75.9
Y.F1.2002.0.0

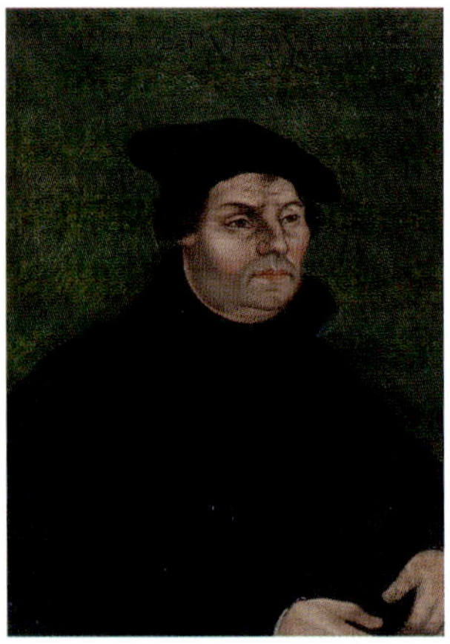

Cranach, Lucas the elder (follower of) 1472–1553
Martin Luther (1483–1546)
oil on panel 20.4 x 14.5
L.F14.1941.3.0

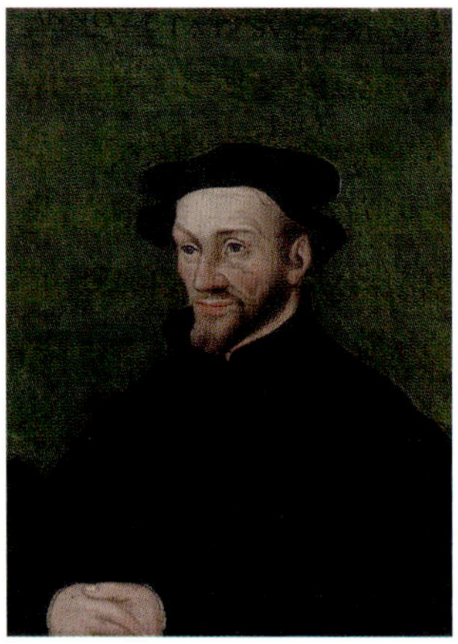

Cranach, Lucas the elder (follower of) 1472–1553
Philip Melanchthon (1497–1560)
oil on panel 36 x 33.5
L.F14.1941.2.0

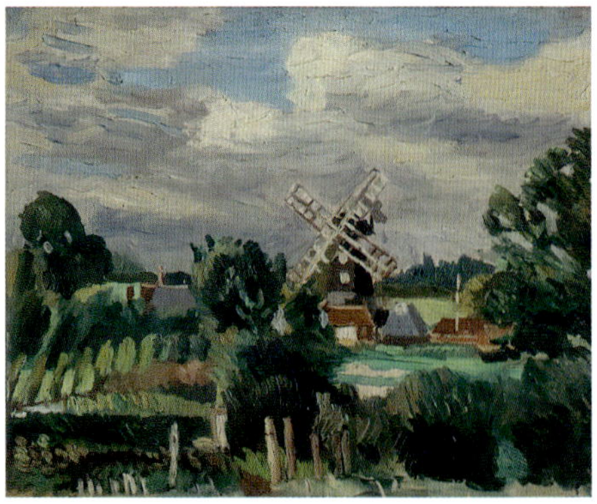

Daintrey, Adrian Maurice 1902–1988
The Windmill
oil on canvas 50.7 x 61
L.F23.1931.0.0

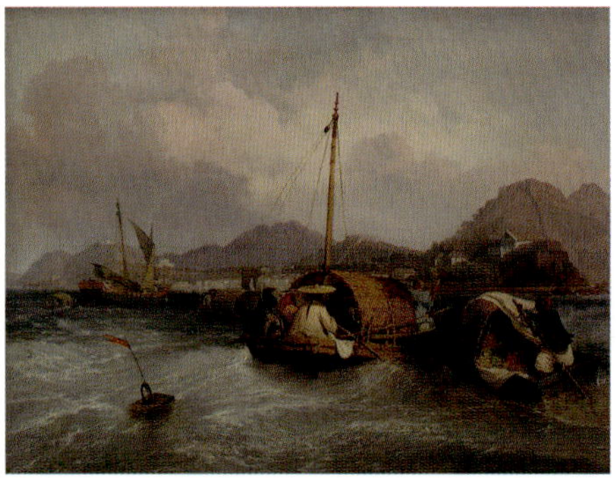

Daniell, William (attributed to) 1769–1837
Egg Boats off Macao, China
oil on canvas 71 x 91.5
L.F56.1955.0.0

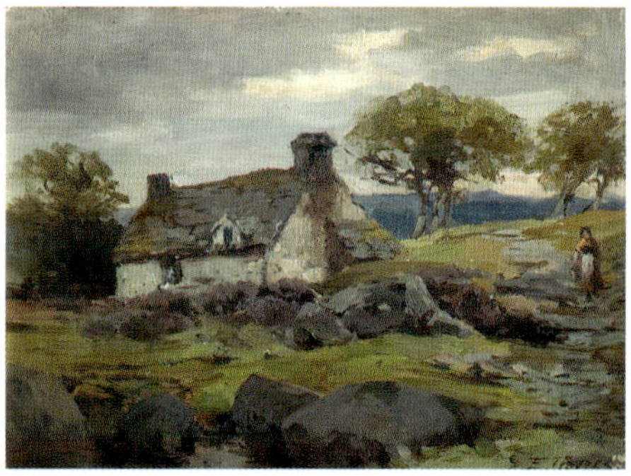

Davies, Edward 1841–1920
A Welsh Cottage
oil on board 23 x 31
L.F18.1910.0.0

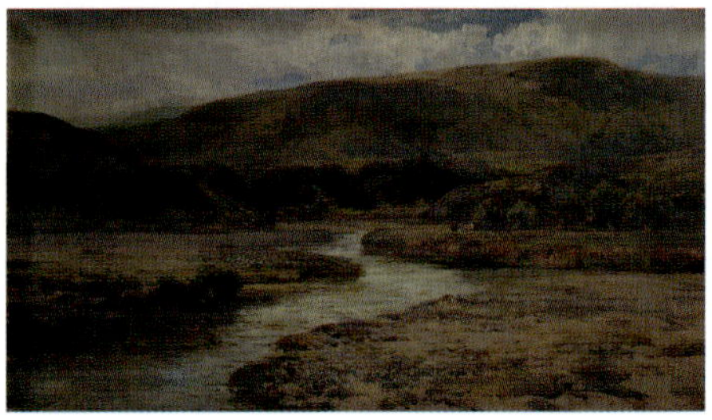

Davies, Edward 1841–1920
Landscape, near Peel, Isle of Man
oil on canvas 88.9 x 152.4
L.F3.1919.0.0

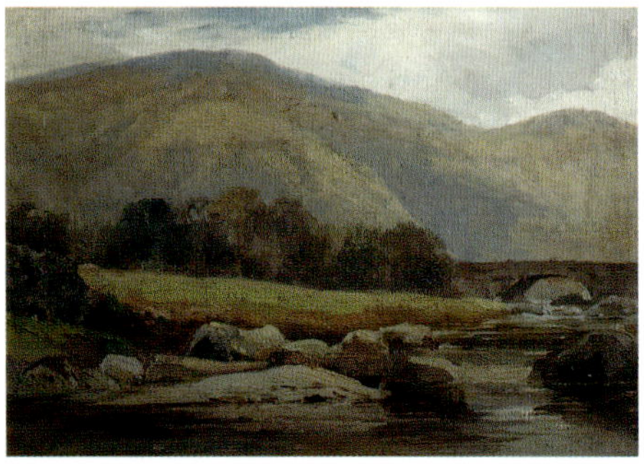

Davies, Edward 1841–1920
Llugwy, Betws-y-Coed, Conwy
oil on board 25 x 35
L.F19.1910.0.0

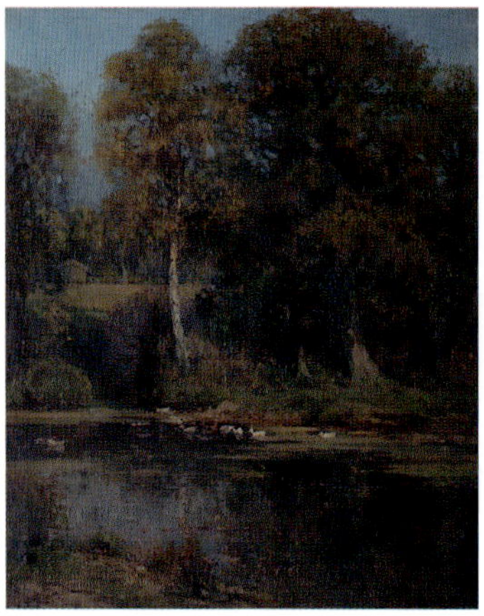

Davies, Edward 1841–1920
The Duck Pond
oil on canvas 51 x 40.5
L.F20.1910.0.0

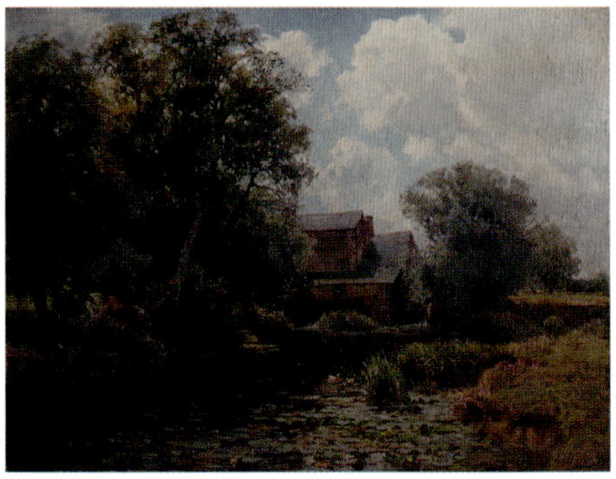

Davies, Edward 1841–1920
The Old Mill, Aylestone, Leicestershire
oil on canvas 71.2 x 91.5
L.F12.1900.0.0

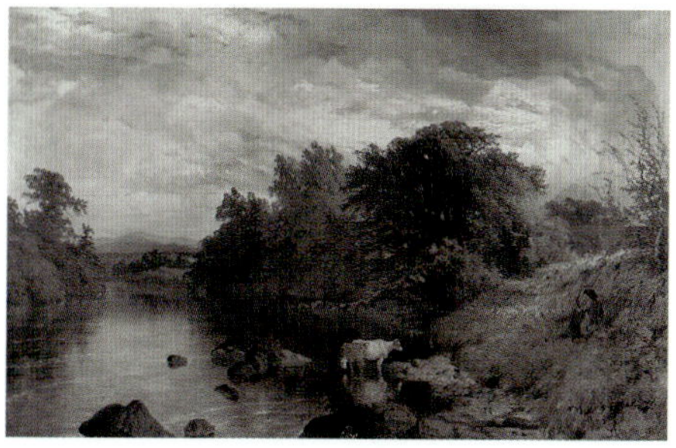

Dawson, Henry 1811–1878
On the Ribble 1847
oil on canvas 87.5 x 135.5
L.F2.1881.0.0

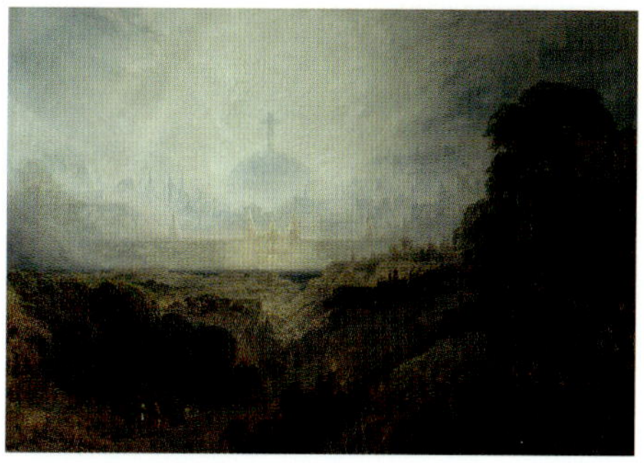

Dawson, Henry 1811–1878
Pilgrims in Sight of the Celestial City 1854
oil on canvas 76.2 x 106.7
L.F4.1911.0.0

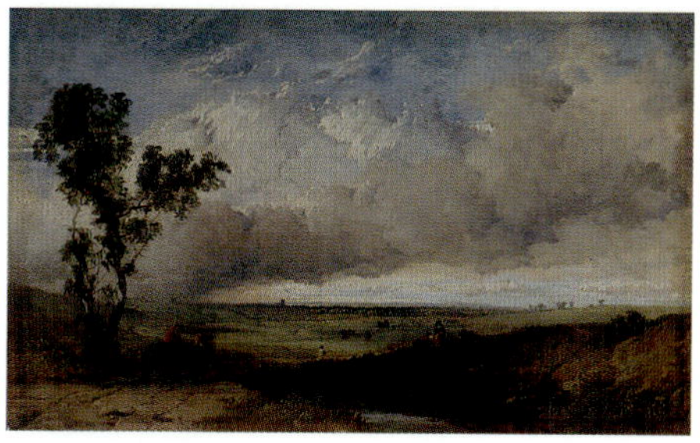

Dawson, Henry 1811–1878
Landscape Sketch
oil on canvas 42.5 x 68
L.F1.1881.0.0

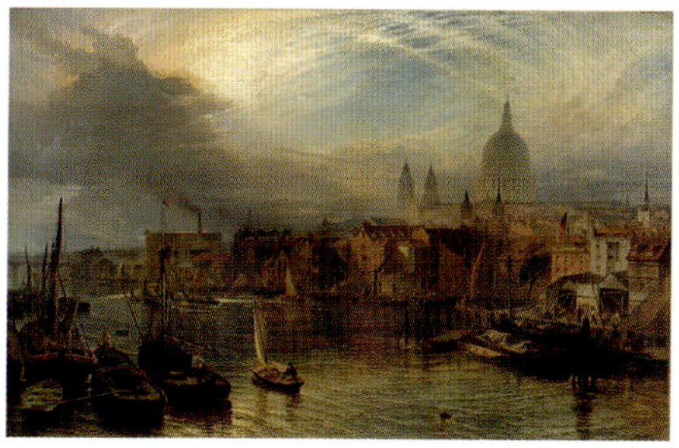

Dawson, Henry 1811–1878
St Paul's, London
oil on canvas 135.5 x 212
L.F1.1893.0.0

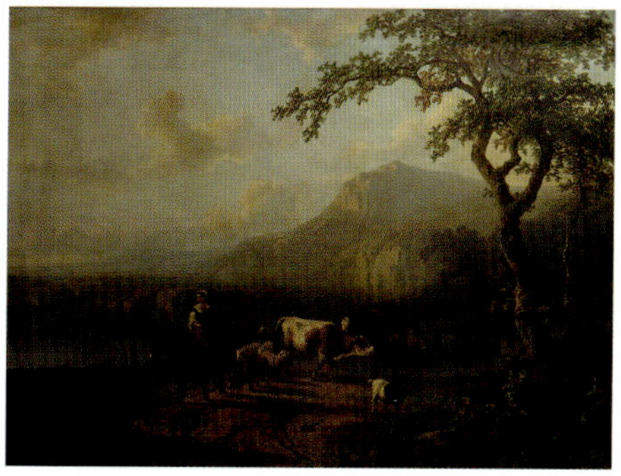

de Bylant, Alfred active 1853–1879
Italian Landscape 1856
oil on canvas 129 x 169
L.F39.1990.0.0

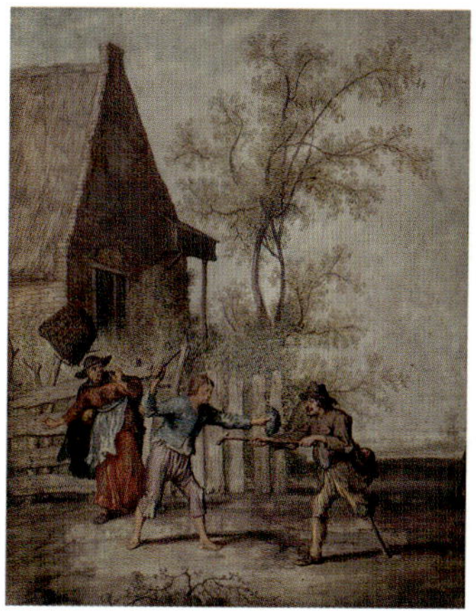

De Heer, Margarethe c.1603–c.1665
Two Frisian Beggars Fighting
oil on panel 36.2 x 28.6
L.F44.1937.0.0

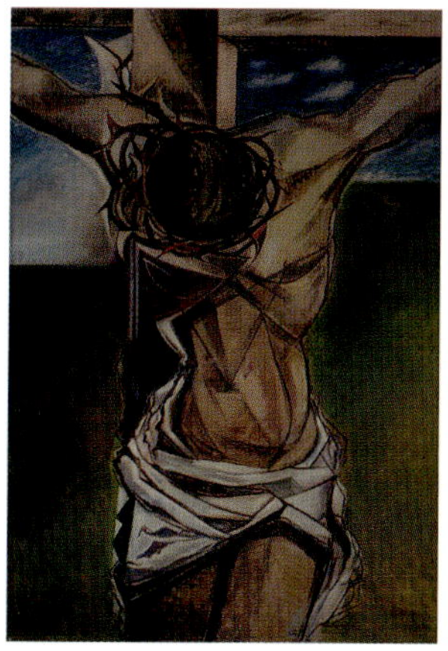

de Maistre, Leroy Leveson Laurent Joseph 1894–1968
The Crucifixion 1942–1944
oil on canvas 130 x 91.5
L.F22.1952.0.0

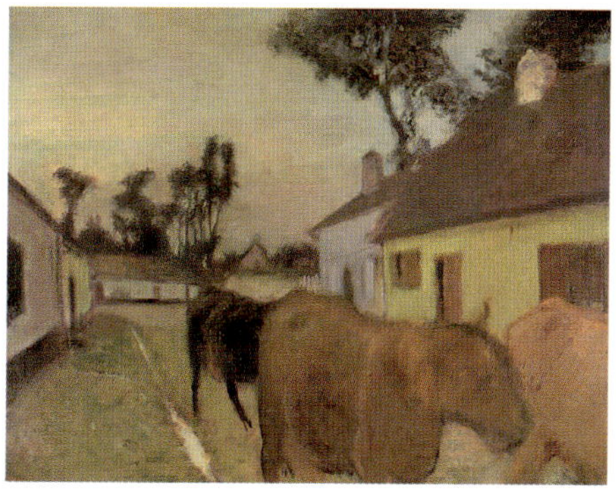

Degas, Edgar 1834–1917
La rentrée du troupeau 1898
oil on canvas 71 x 92
L.F11.1969.0.0

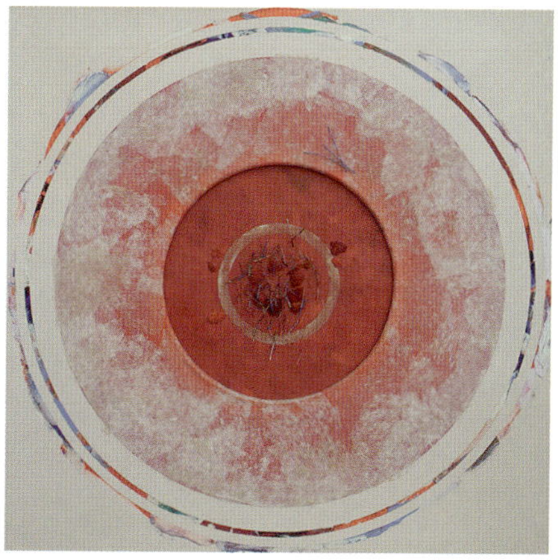

Delaney, Barbara b.1941
Mikado's Gambit 1995–1996
acrylic & mixed media on canvas
137.3 x 137.3
Y.F20.2003.0.0

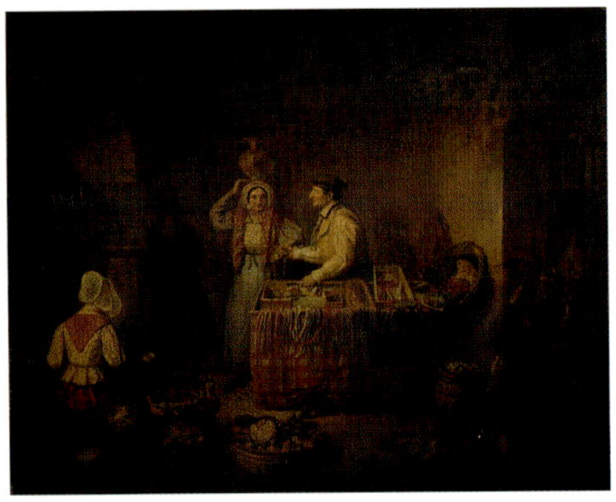

Deloos, H. active 19th C
The Pedlar
oil on canvas 64 x 80
L.F32.1987.0.0

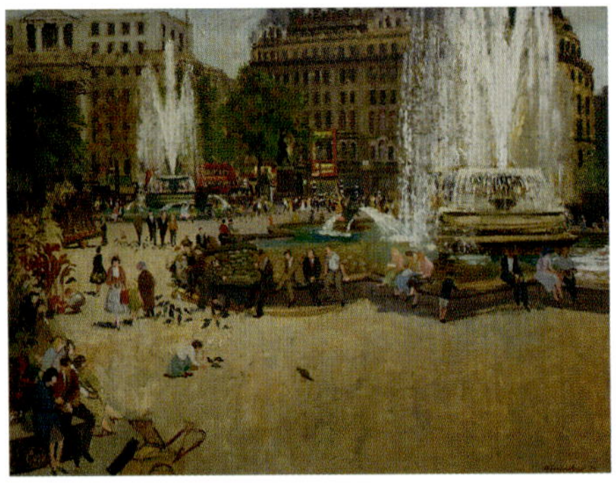

Dent, Ann Langford b.1924
Trafalgar Square, London
oil on board 70.8 x 91.5
L.F3.1996.5.0

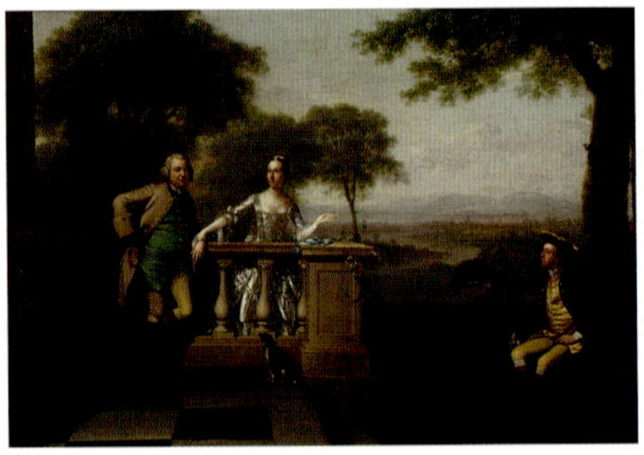

Devis, Arthur 1712–1787
Edward Gordon, His Sister Mrs Miles, and Her Husband in Their Garden at Bromley 1756
oil on canvas 67 x 102.2
L.F98.1955.0.0

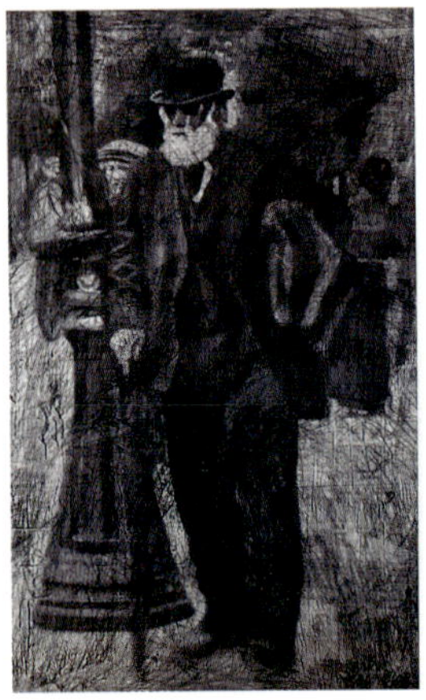

Di Stefano, Arturo b.1955
Edgar Degas (1834–1917) 1990
oil on linen 168 x 97
L.F7.1992.0.0

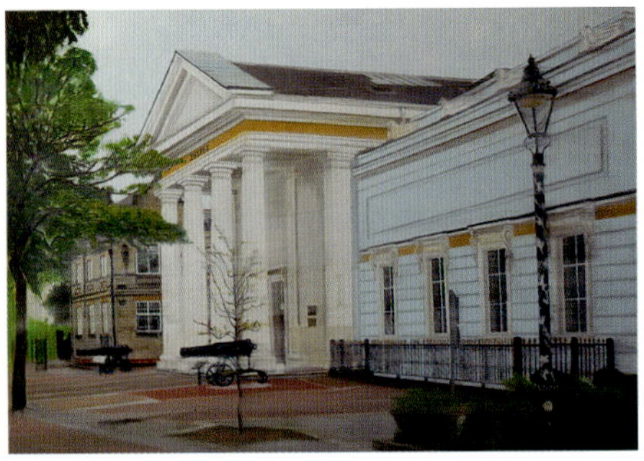

Di Stefano, Arturo b.1955
The New Walk Museum and Art Gallery, Leicester 1999
oil on canvas 151.5 x 212.3
Y.F5.2000.0.0

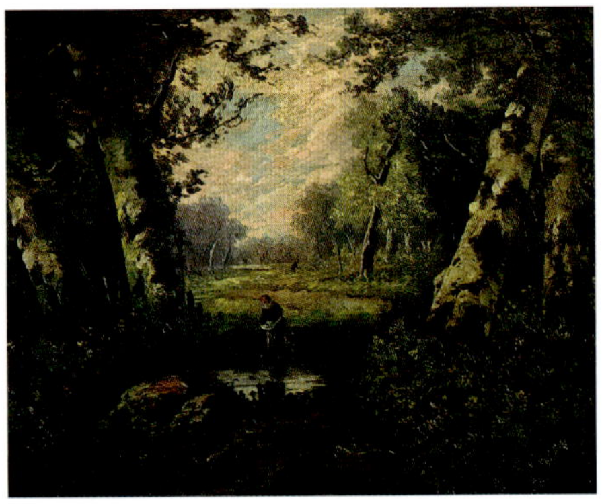

Diaz de la Peña, Narcisse Virgile (after) 1808–1876
A Wooded Landscape
oil on canvas 53.3 x 66
L.F7.1938.0.0

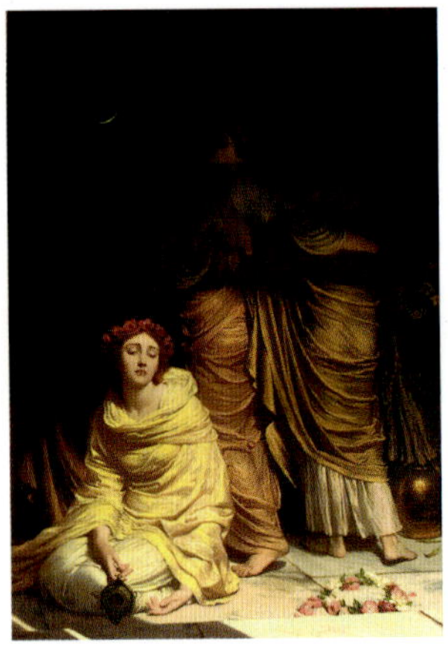

Dicksee, Frank 1853–1928
The Foolish Virgins, 'Too late, ye cannot enter now' 1883
oil on canvas 233.7 x 160.5
L.F7.1902.0.0

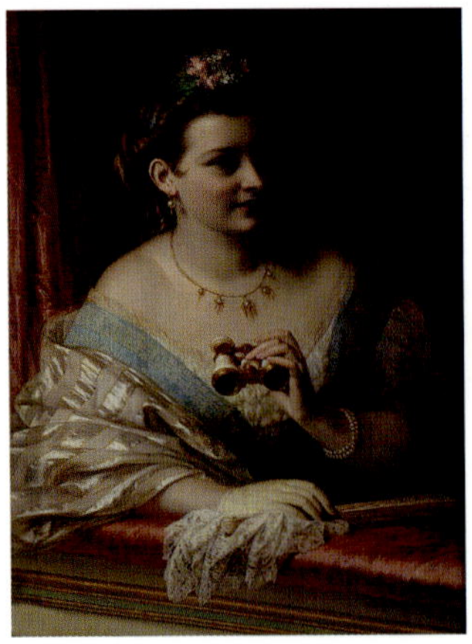

Dicksee, Thomas Francis 1819–1895
At the Opera
oil on canvas 45.7 x 35.6
L.F15.1941.3.0

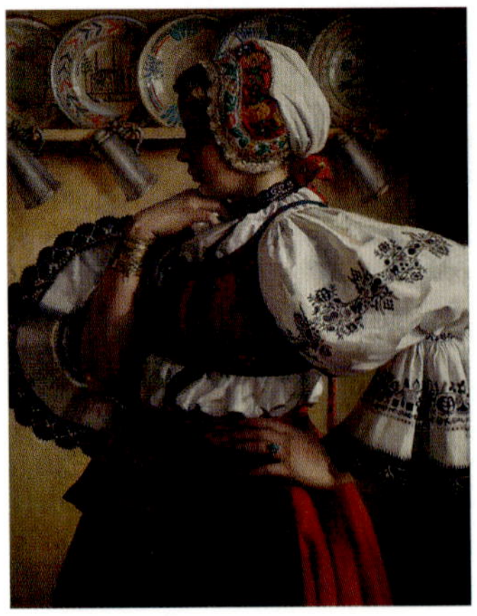

Dodd, Phyllis 1899–1995
Girl in National Costume, in an Interior
oil on canvas 91.5 x 71
L.F14.1981.0.0

Facing page: Morley, Harry, 1881–1943, *A Wayside Madonna* (detail), 1927, Leicester Arts and Museums Service (p. 67)

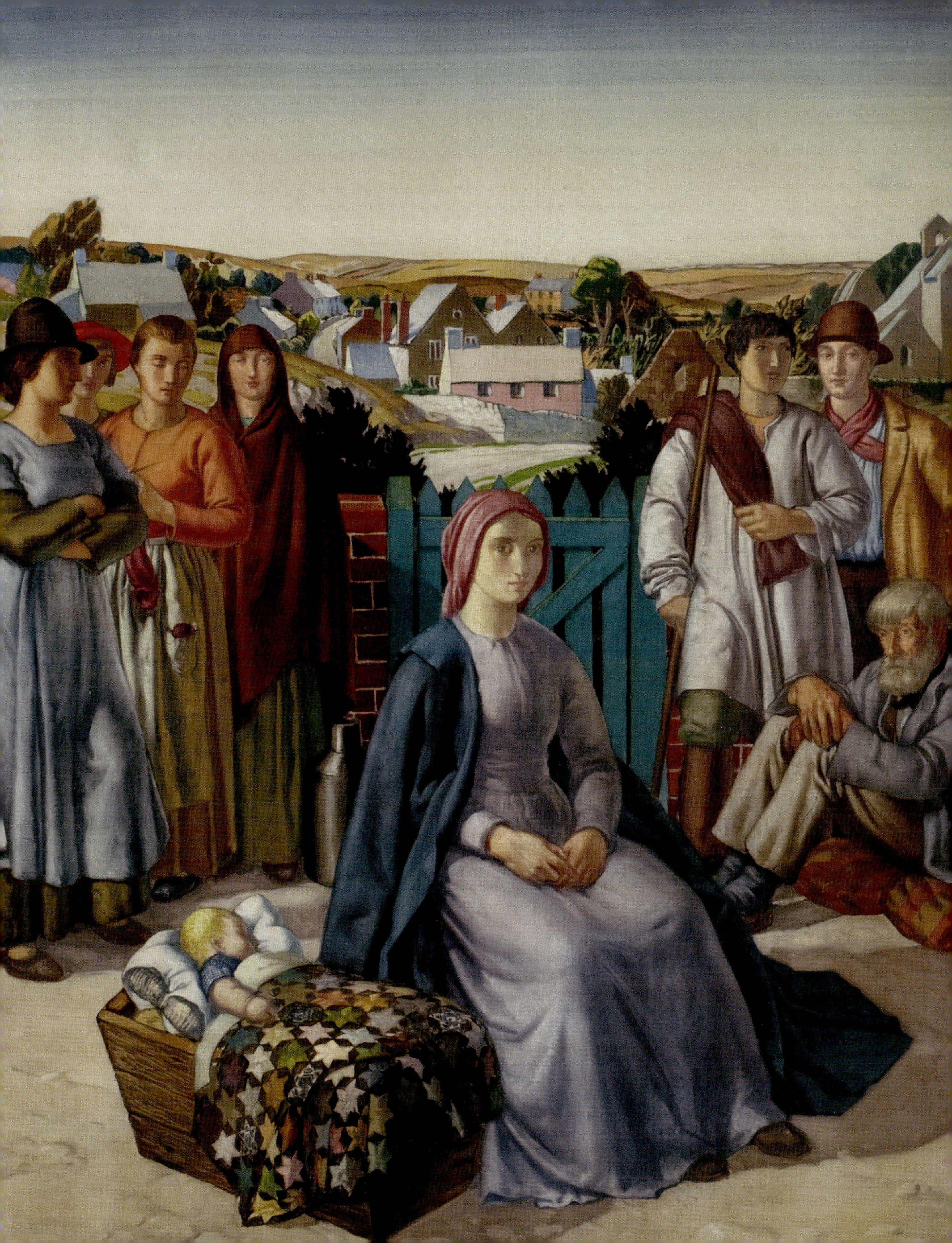

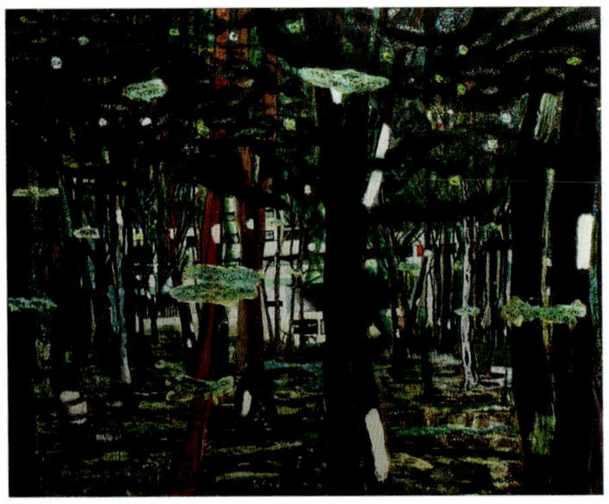

Doig, Peter b.1959
Concrete Cabin 1991–1992
oil on canvas 200.5 x 241
L.F9.1996.0.0

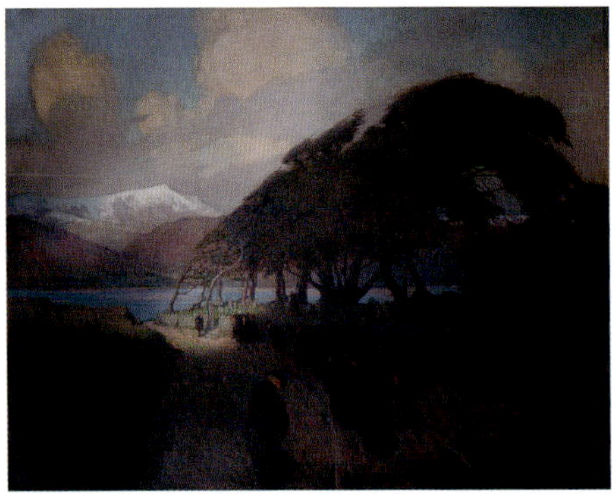

Donne, Walter J. 1867–1930
God's Acre 1911
oil on canvas 162.5 x 207.5
L.F1.1929.0.0

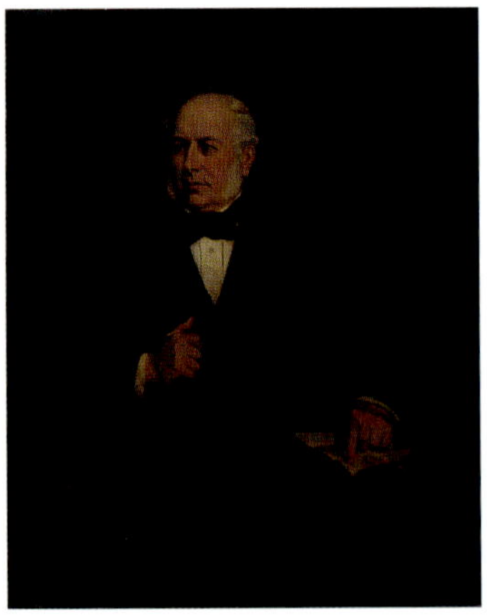

Dowling, Robert Hawke 1827–1886
Edward Shipley Ellis (1817–1879) 1878
oil on canvas 127.3 x 111.7
L.F38.1949.0.0

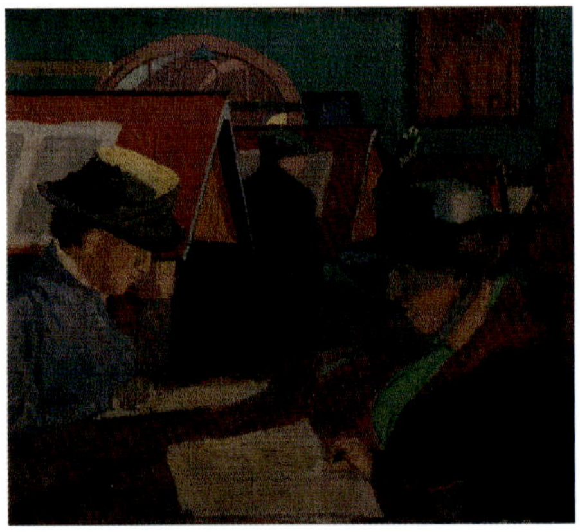

Drummond, Malcolm 1880–1945
Chelsea Public Library 1920
oil on canvas 39 x 43.2
L.F4.1981.0.0

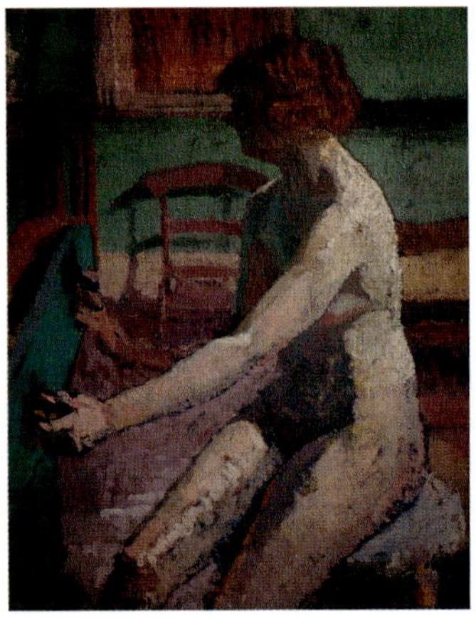

Drummond, Malcolm 1880–1945
Seated Nude 1923–1925
oil on canvas 65.5 x 50.5
L.F117.1981.0.0

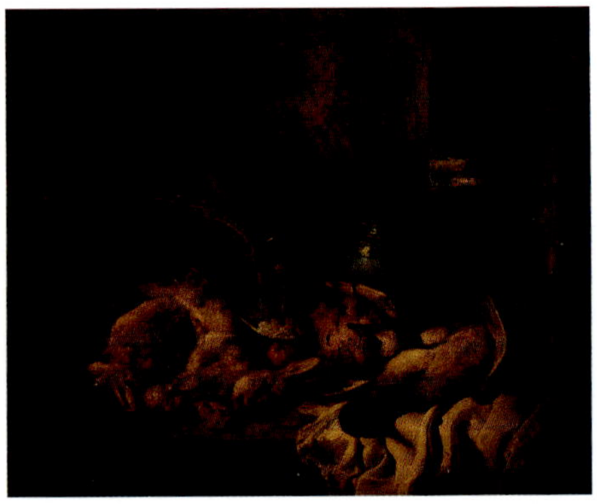

Duffield, William 1816–1863
Still Life with Dead Rabbits
oil on canvas 50.8 x 61
L.F12.1882.0.0

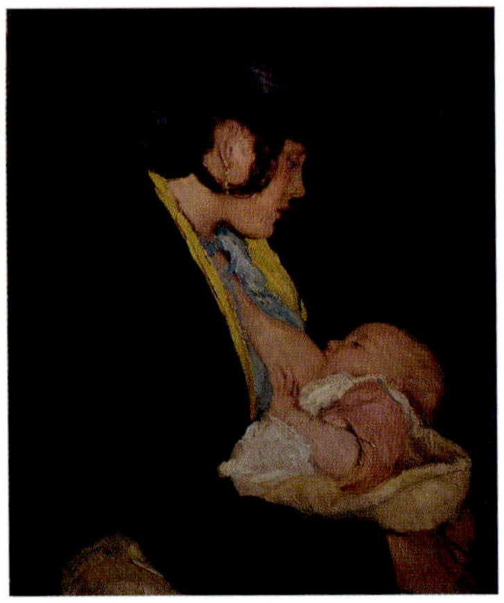

Dugdale, Thomas Cantrell 1880–1952
Motherhood
oil on canvas 75.5 x 62.2
L.F28.1923.0.0

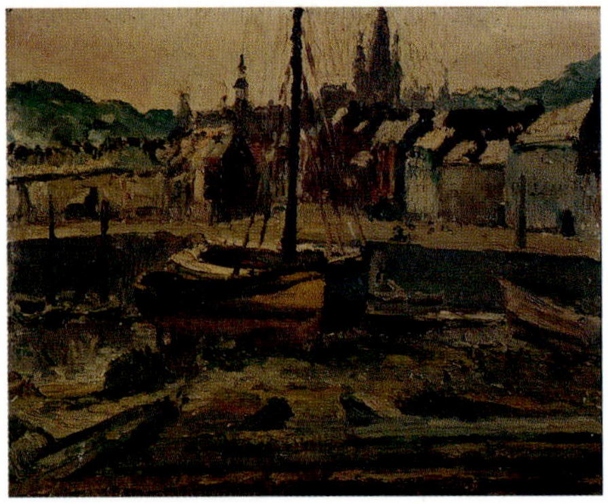

Dunlop, Ronald Ossory 1894–1973
Les deux bateaux
oil on canvas 50.5 x 61
L.F3.1996.41.0

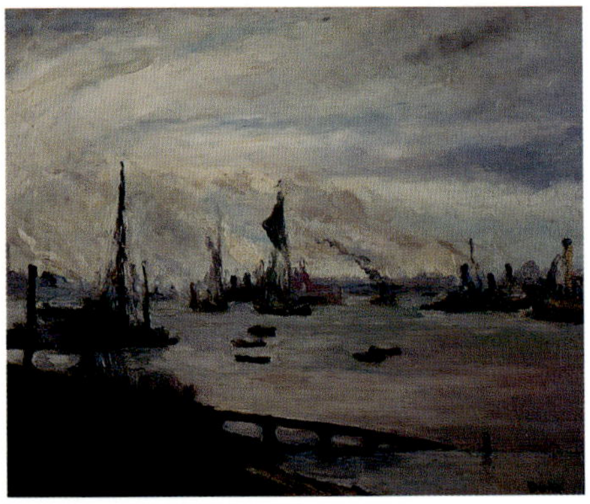

Dunlop, Ronald Ossory 1894–1973
The Thames near Rotherhithe, London
oil on canvas 62 x 74.5
L.F32.1936.0.0

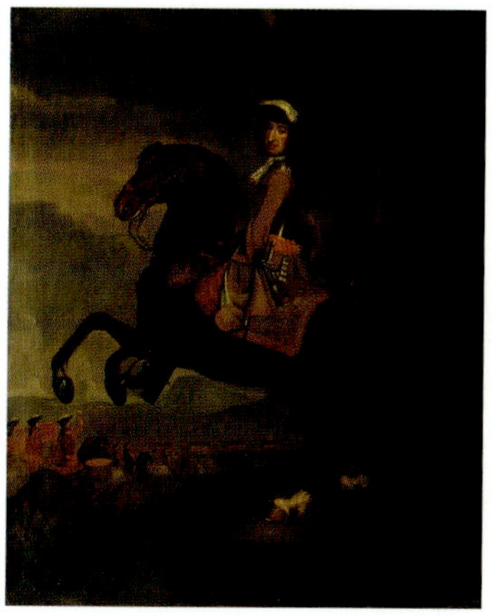

Dutch School 17th C
William III (1650–1702), on Horseback
oil on canvas 127 x 102.2
L.F20.1935.8.0

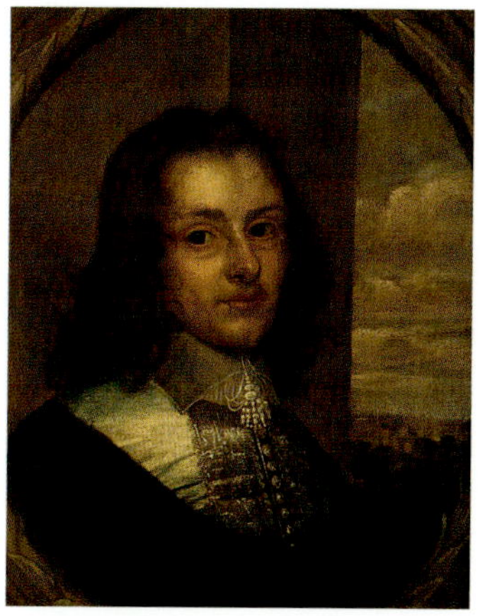

Dutch School
Portrait of a Boy in the Reign of Charles II
oil on canvas 52.5 x 41.5
L.F9.1943.9.0

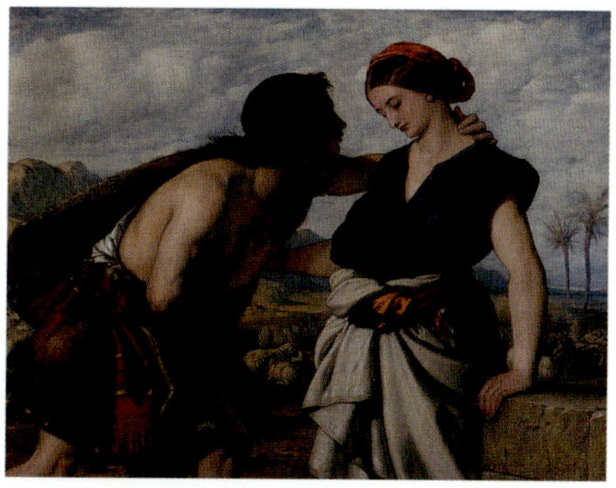

Dyce, William 1806–1864
The Meeting of Jacob and Rachel 1850
oil on canvas 70.5 x 91
L.F32.1937.0.0

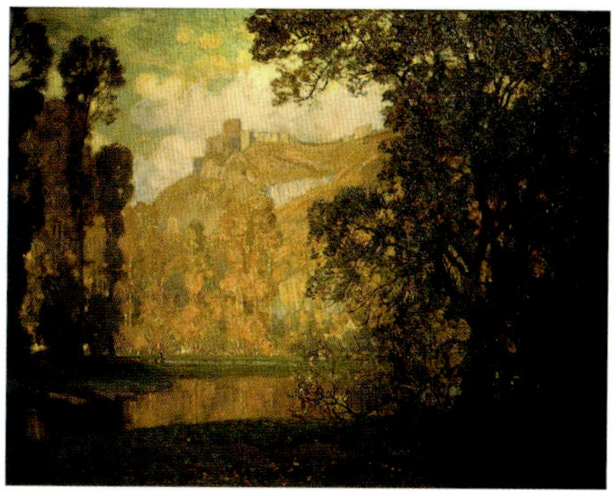

East, Alfred 1844–1913
Autumn in the Valley of the Seine
oil on canvas 122 x 151
L.F42.1910.0.0

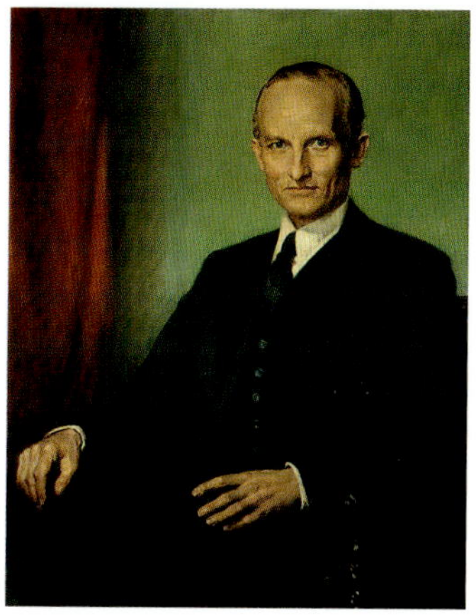

Eastham, Frank
Harold Trevor Hawsley Peck 1954
oil on canvas 91.5 x 71
L.F23.1991.0.0

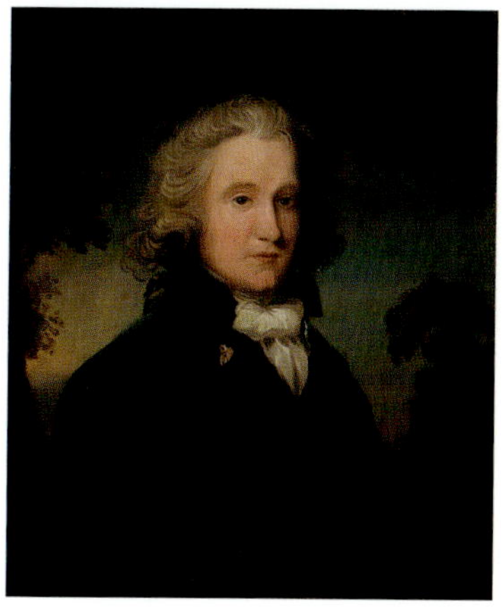

Eddis, Eden Upton 1812–1901
Sir George Beaumont (1828–1882), 9th Bt
oil on canvas 76.2 x 64.1
L.F573.1973.0.0

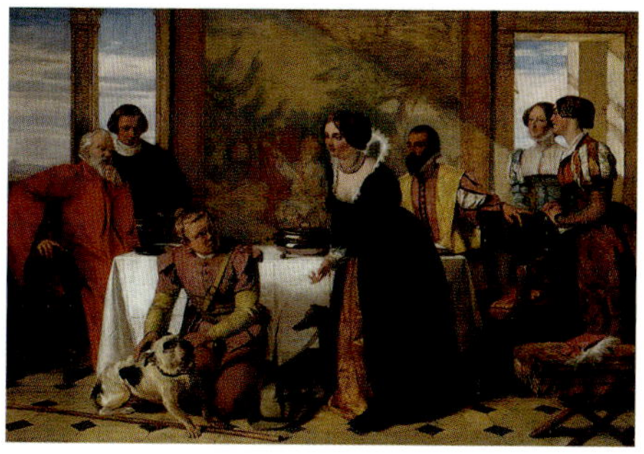

Egg, Augustus Leopold 1816–1863
Launce's Substitute for Proteus' Dog (from 'The Two Gentlemen of Verona' by William Shakespeare) 1849
oil on canvas 56 x 80.5
L.F9.1891.0.0

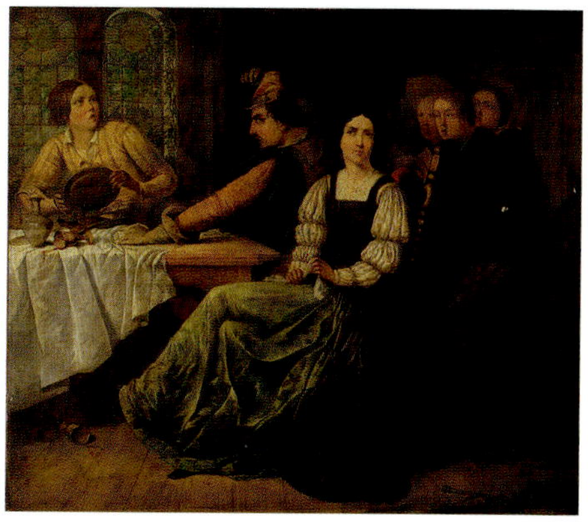

Egg, Augustus Leopold 1816–1863
'The Taming of the Shrew' (from the play by William Shakespeare)
oil on canvas 61.5 x 101.5
L.F19.1947.0.0

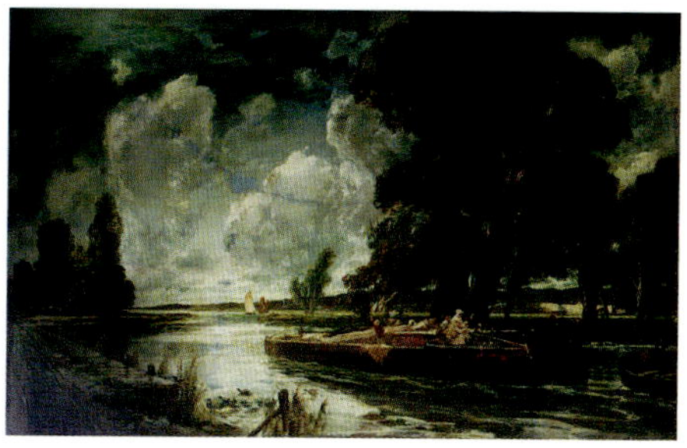

Ellis, Edwin 1841–1895
The Captain's Birthday
oil on canvas 136.7 x 213.7
L.F4.1905.0.0

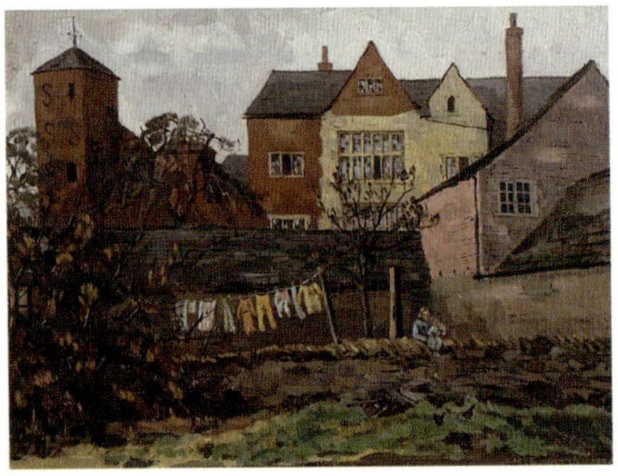

Ellis, Norman 1913–1971
Old Hall Farm, Groby, Leicestershire 1950
oil on board 30.5 x 39.4
L.F457.1971.0.0

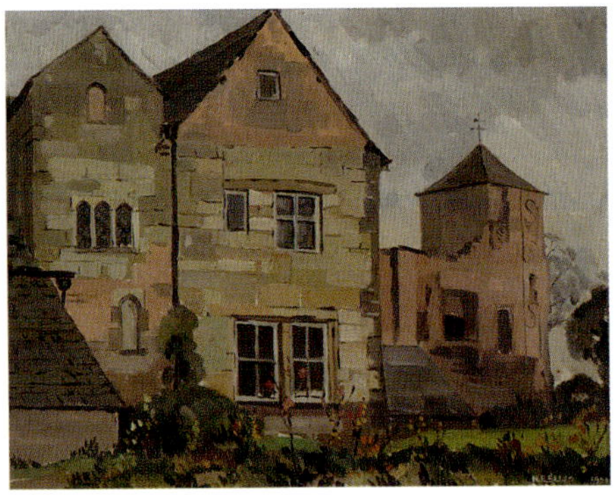

Ellis, Norman 1913–1971
Old Manor Farm, Groby, Leicestershire 1951
oil on board 31.8 x 40.8
L.F458.1971.0.0

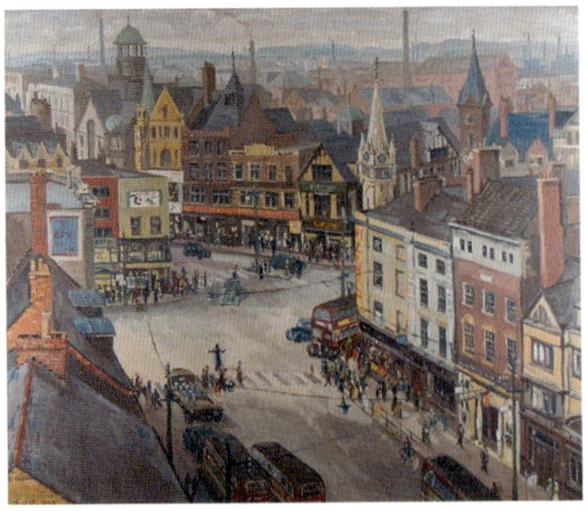

Ellis, Norman 1913–1971
Leicester City Centre 1952
oil on canvas 68.5 x 82.5
L.F460.1971.0.0

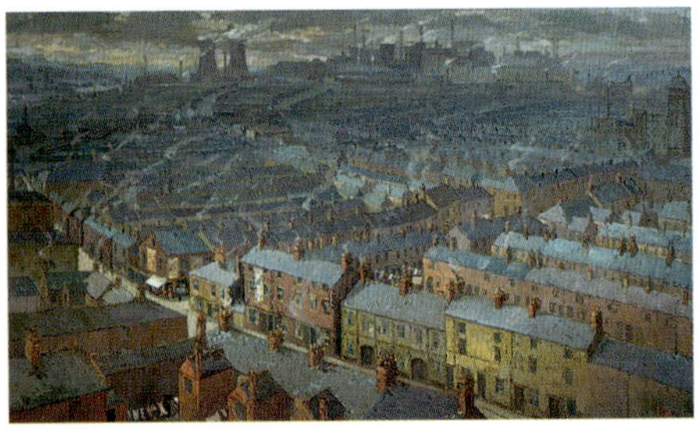

Ellis, Norman 1913–1971
A Leicester Vista 1955
oil on hardboard 71.1 x 116.8
L.F15.1956.0.0

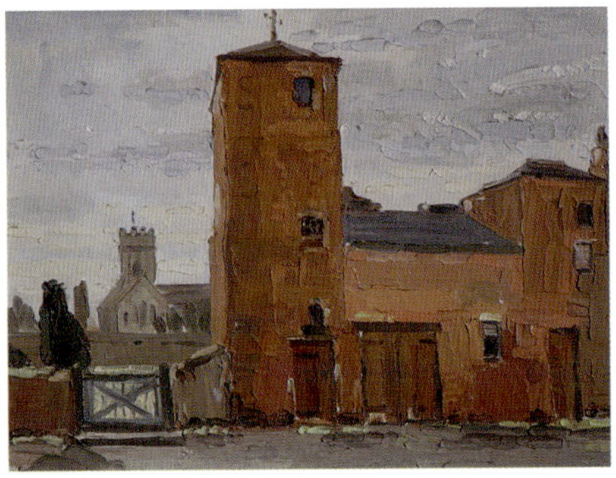

Ellis, Norman 1913–1971
Old Hall Farm, Groby, Leicestershire 1970
oil on canvas 30.5 x 40.5
L.F455.1971.0.0

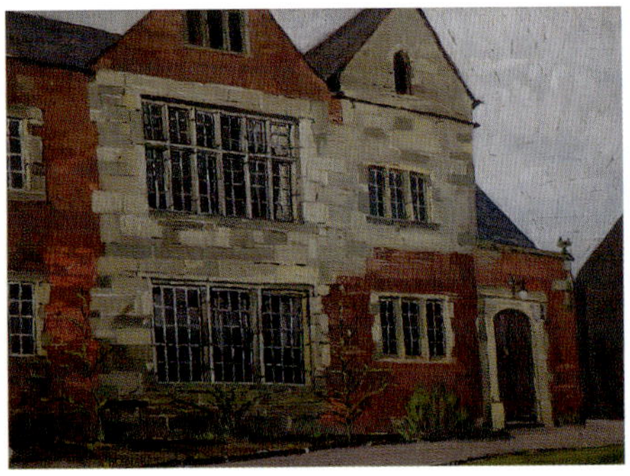

Ellis, Norman 1913–1971
Old Hall Farm, Groby, Leicestershire 1970
oil on board 32.5 x 47
L.F456.1971.0.0

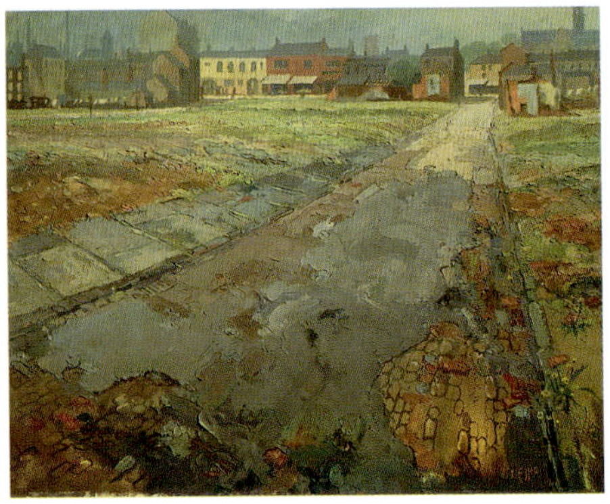

Ellis, Norman 1913–1971
Wharf Street Vista, Leicester 1970
oil on board 61 x 76
L.F459.1971.0.0

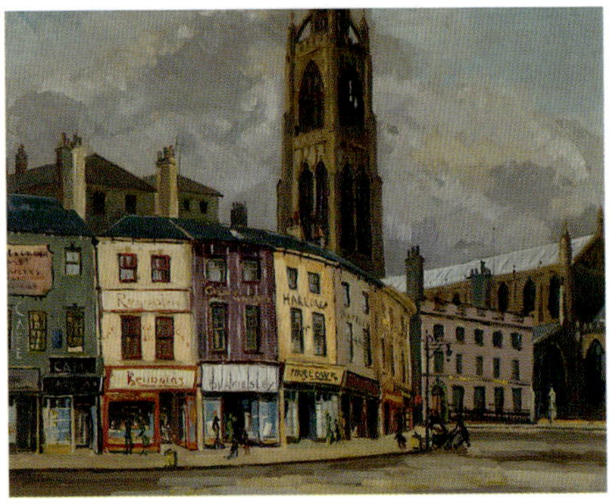

Ellis, Norman 1913–1971
Boston Stump, Leicestershire
oil on board 42.5 x 53
L.F164.1971.7.0

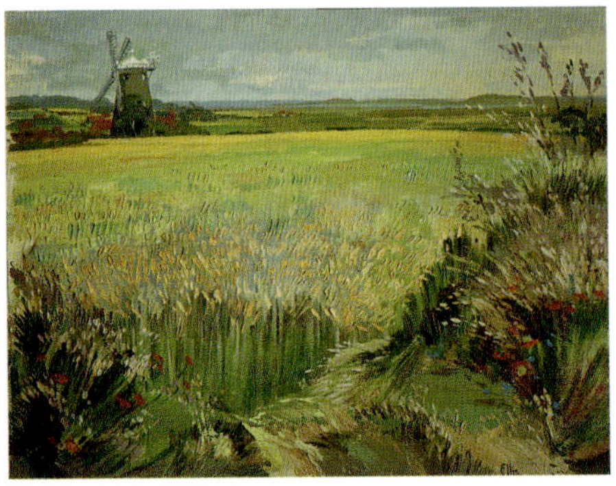

Ellis, Norman 1913–1971
Burnham Overy Mill across the Cornfield, Norfolk
oil on board 38 x 48.5
L.F164.1971.6.0

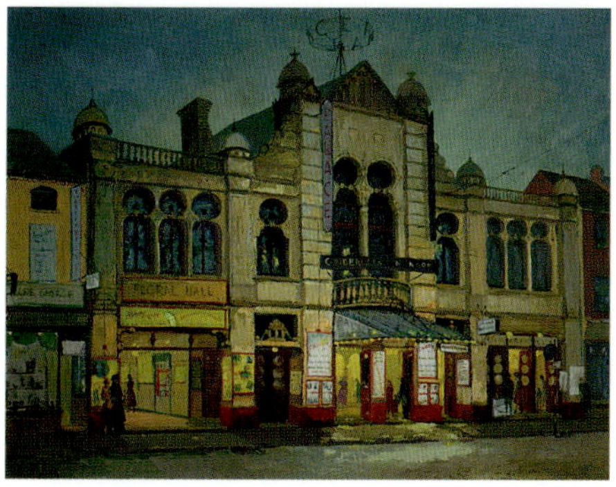

Ellis, Norman 1913–1971
The Last Days of Leicester Palace
oil on hardboard 76 x 98.7
L.F461.1971.0.0

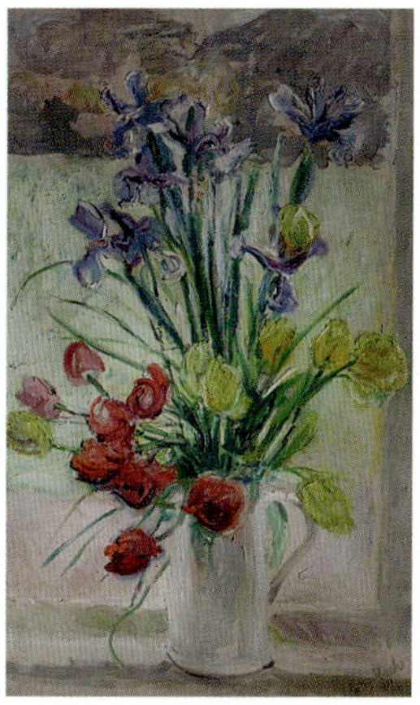

Engelbach, Florence 1872–1951
Tulips and Irises 1931
oil on canvas 92.2 x 55.6
L.F12.1933.0.0

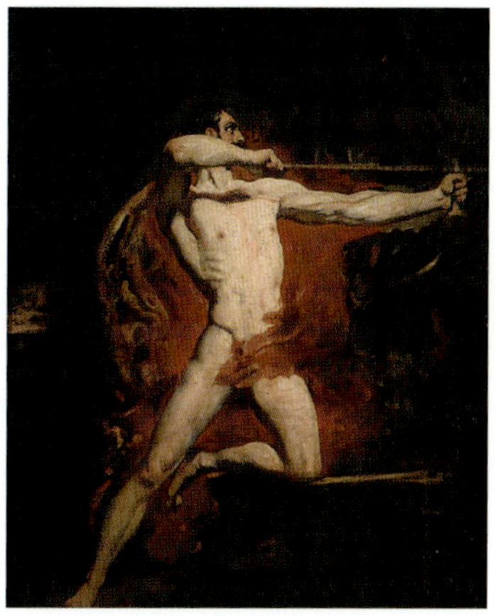

Etty, William 1787–1849
The Bowman 1825–1830
oil on millboard on panel 89 x 70
L.F47.1947.0.0

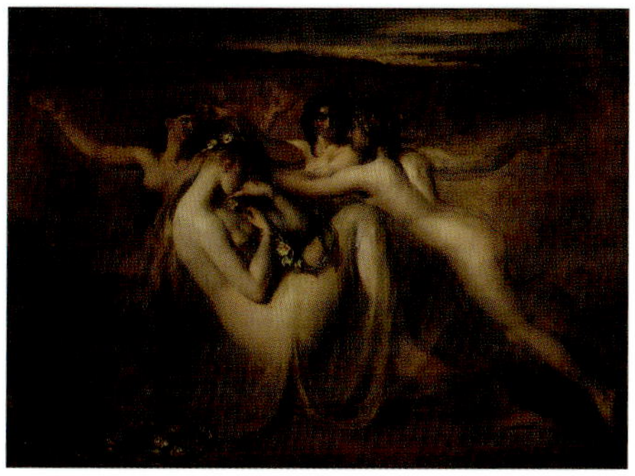

Etty, William 1787–1849
Sabrina and Her Nymphs 1841
oil on canvas 59.5 x 80
L.F22.1936.0.0

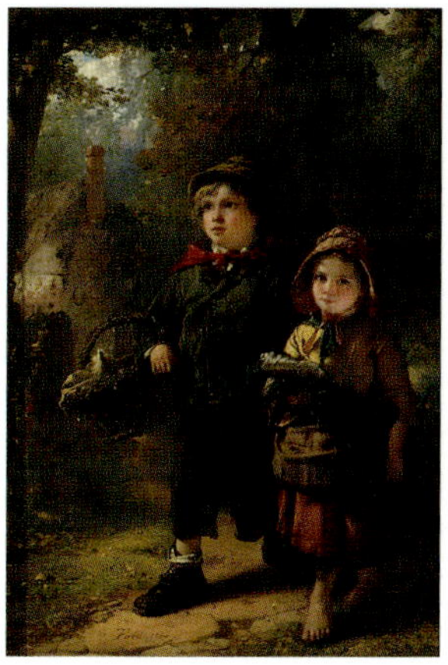

Faed, Thomas 1826–1900
The Orphans 1854
oil on canvas 36.5 x 26
L.F7.1944.0.0

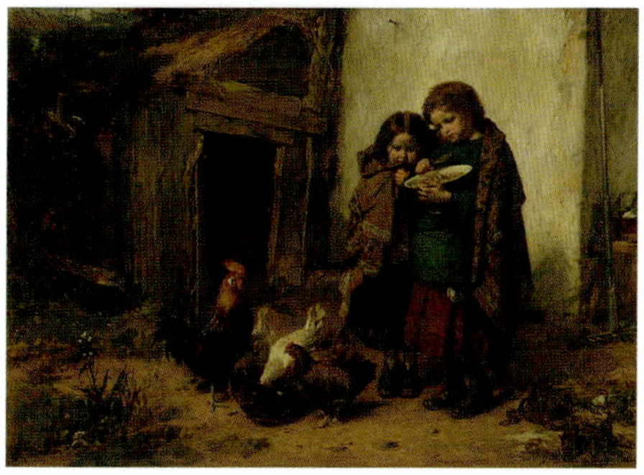

Faed, Thomas 1826–1900
Pot Luck 1866
oil on canvas 90.4 x 122
L.F11.1890.0.0

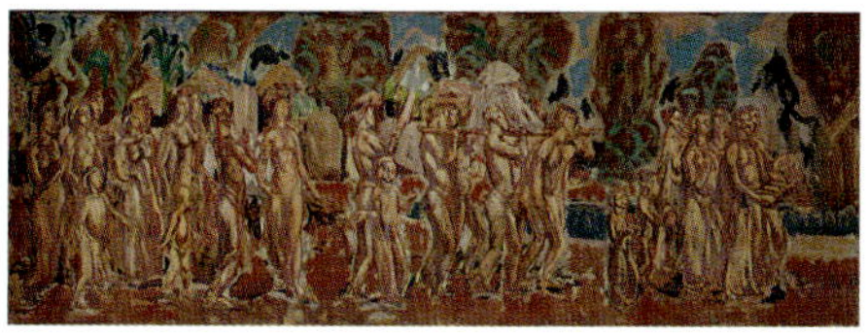

Fairweather, Ian 1891–1974
Procession in Bali 1933
oil & paper on canvas 52 x 143
L.F33.1936.0.0

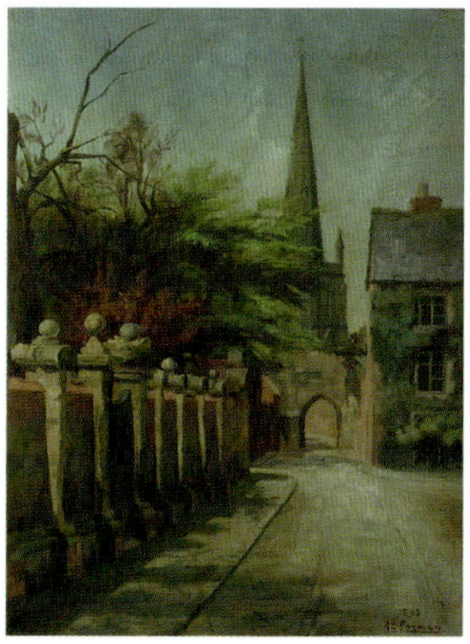

Farman, Agnes Ethel 1863–1947
Castle View, Gateway, Chantry House and St Mary de Castro Church, Leicester 1895
oil on canvas 40.5 x 30.5
L.F28.1951.0.0

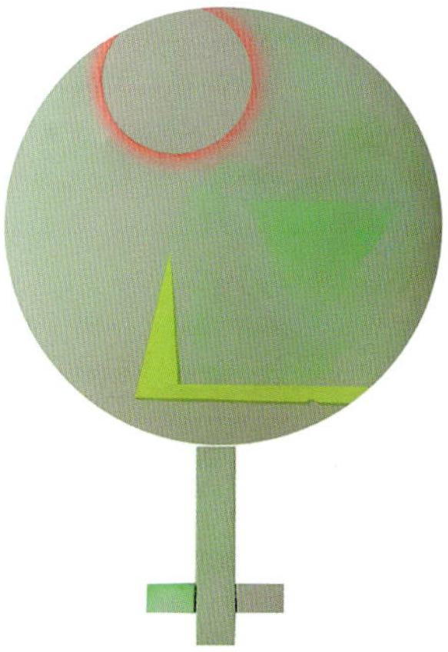

Farquhar, Keith b.1969
'Woman I can hardly express' 2000
acrylic on canvas 125 x 91.5
Y.F1.2006.2.0

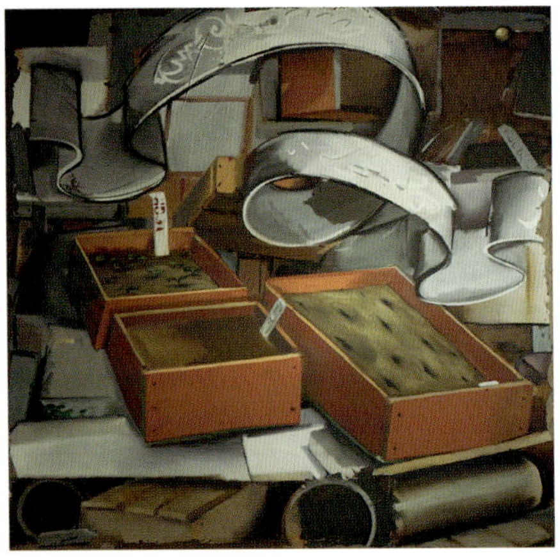

Farthing, Stephen b.1950
Monument to a Propagator
acrylic on canvas 153 x 152.5
L.F2.1985.0.0

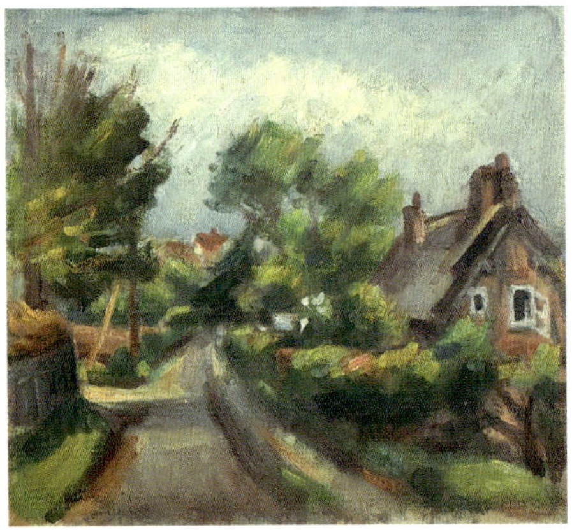

Feigl, Bedrich 1884–1965
Knighton, Church Lane, Leicester
oil on canvas 61 x 66
L.F517.1977.0.0

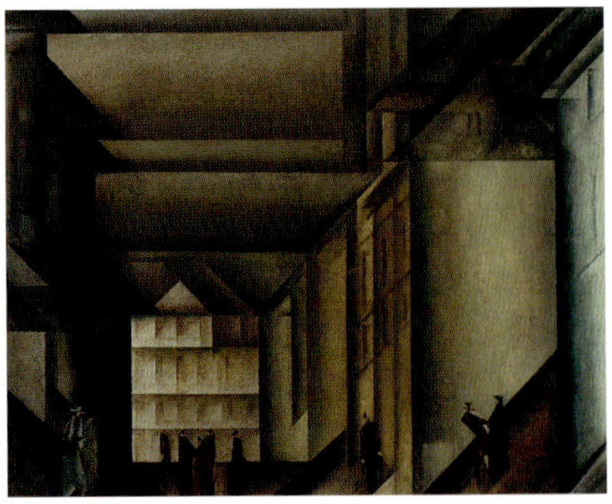

Feininger, Lyonel 1871–1956
Hinter der Stadtkirche 1916
oil on canvas 73.5 x 90
L.F9.1944.0.0

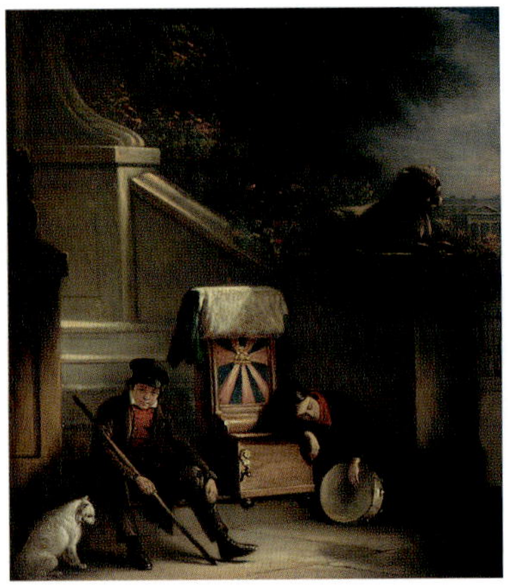

Ferneley, John E. 1782–1860
Two Children with a Hurdy-Gurdy 1847
oil on canvas 76.5 x 65.5
L.F77.1973.0.0

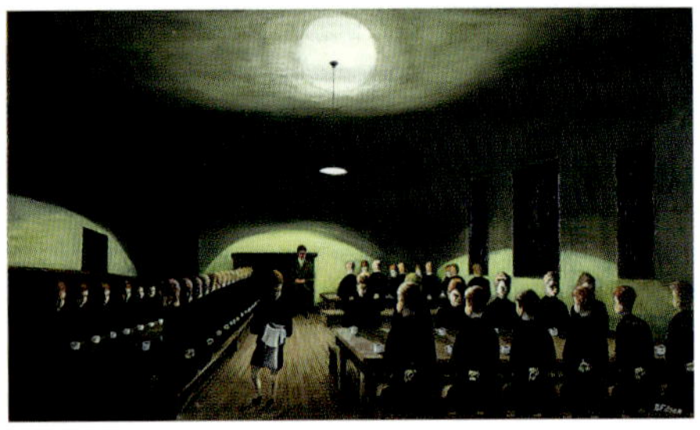

Filmer, D. active c.1972
'For what we are about to receive'
oil on canvas 61 x 101.6
L.F47.1972.0.0

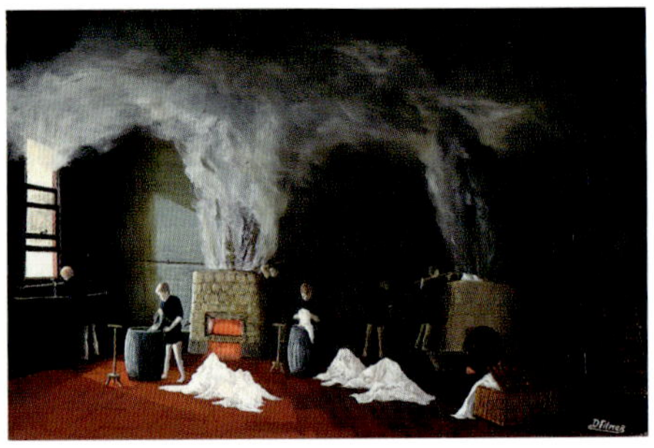

Filmer, D. active c.1972
The Dolly Boys Tuning Up
oil on canvas 50.8 x 76.2
L.F46.1972.0.0

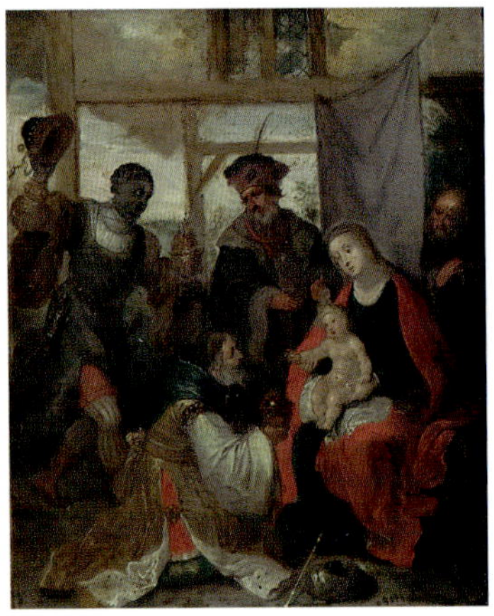

Flemish School
Adoration of the Magi 1500–1700
oil on wood 13.5 x 10.5
Y.F20.2009.0.0

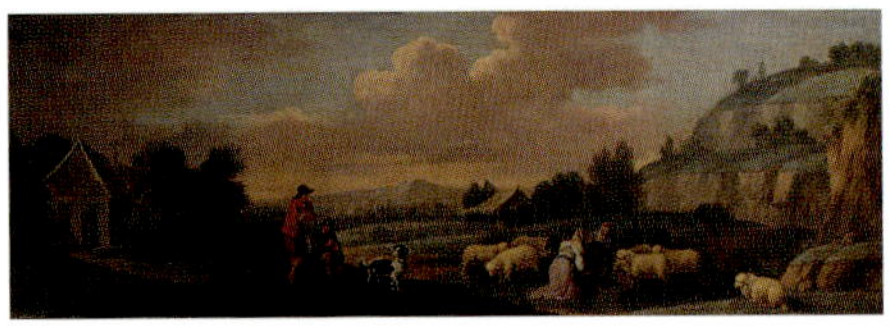

Flemish School
A Pastoral Scene
oil on canvas 53.3 x 145.4
L.F21.1935.0.0

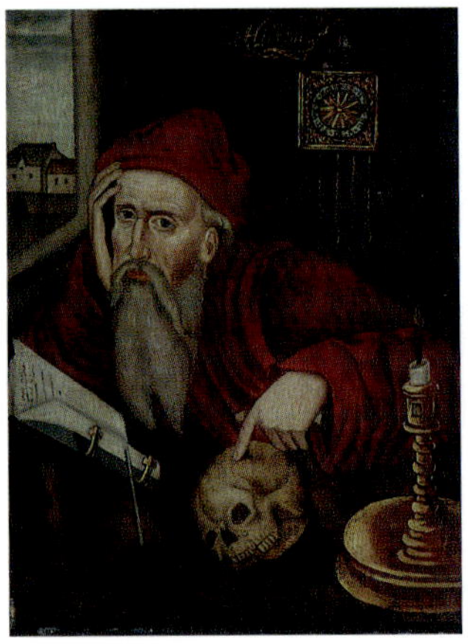

Flemish School
Saint Jerome
oil on oak panel 38.5 x 28
L.F55.1926.0.0

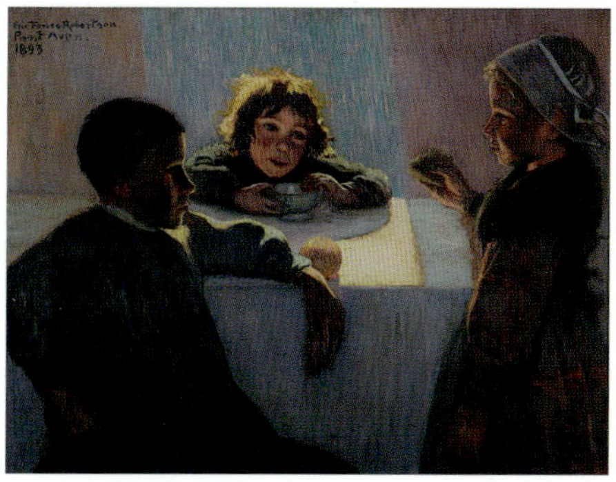

Forbes-Robertson, Eric 1865–1935
Breton Children, Pont Aven, France 1893
oil on canvas 70.5 x 91
L.F41.1968.0.0

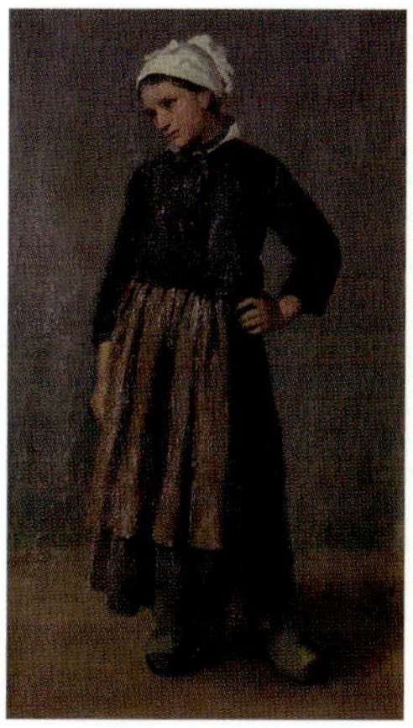

Foster, Herbert Wilson 1846–1929
Breton Girl
oil on canvas 40 x 24
L.F67.1968.0.0

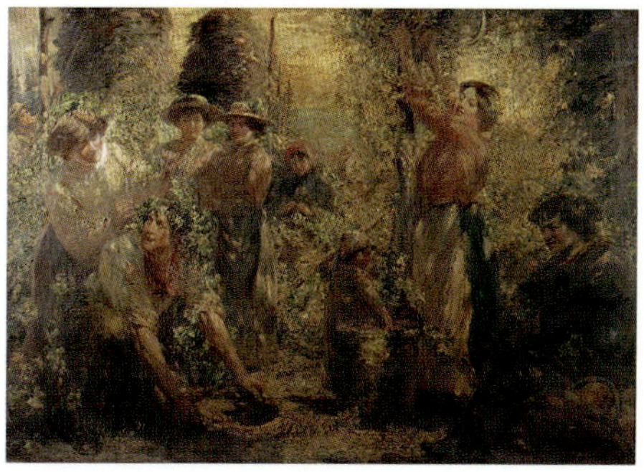

Fowler, Robert 1853–1926
Light and Laughter in the Kent Hopfields
oil on canvas 169.5 x 231
L.F7.1932.0.0

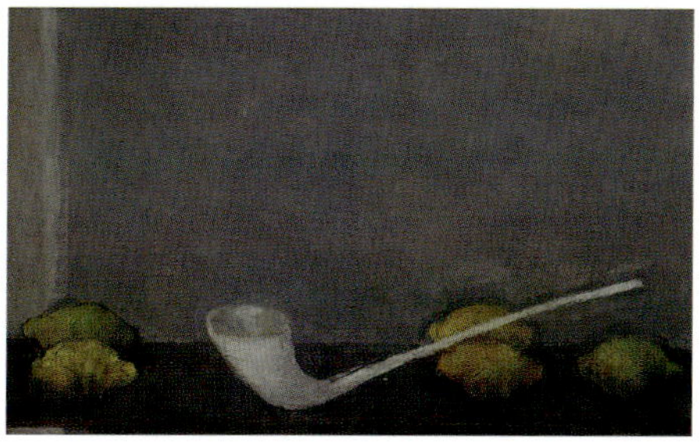

Frankl, Gerhardt 1901–1965
Still Life: Lemons and a Clay Pipe 1965
oil on canvas 40.3 x 60.7
Y.F2.2006.1.0

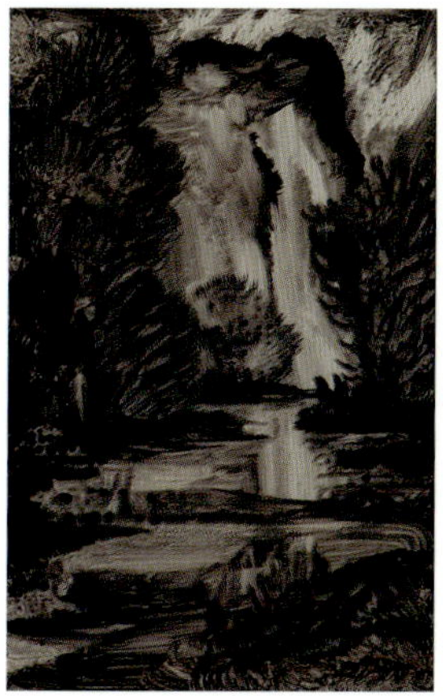

Freer, Allen b.1926
Ilam Tor, Derbyshire
oil on glass 25.5 x 16.4
Y.F1.2005.8.0

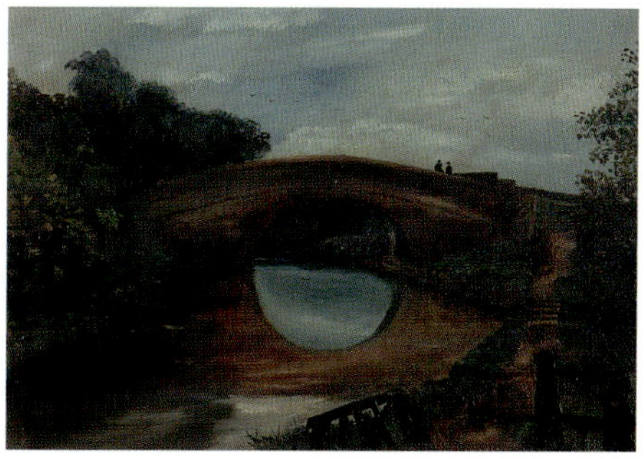

Freestone, William Henry 1876–1953
Canal Bridge at Aylestone, Leicestershire
oil on canvas 25.5 x 35.8
L.F203.1958.0.0

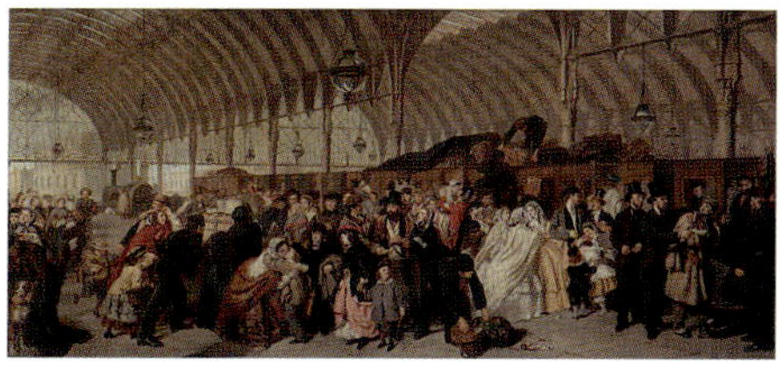

Frith, William Powell 1819–1909
The Railway Station 1863
oil on canvas 41.7 x 90.7
L.F1.1892.0.0

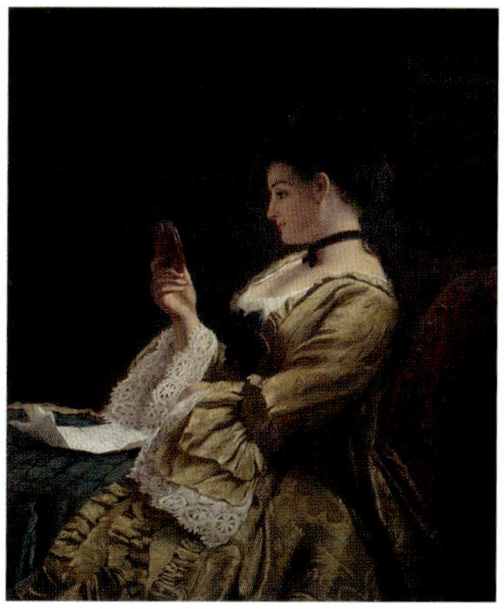

Frith, William Powell 1819–1909
The Miniature 1883
oil on canvas 46.3 x 38
L.F9.1953.0.0

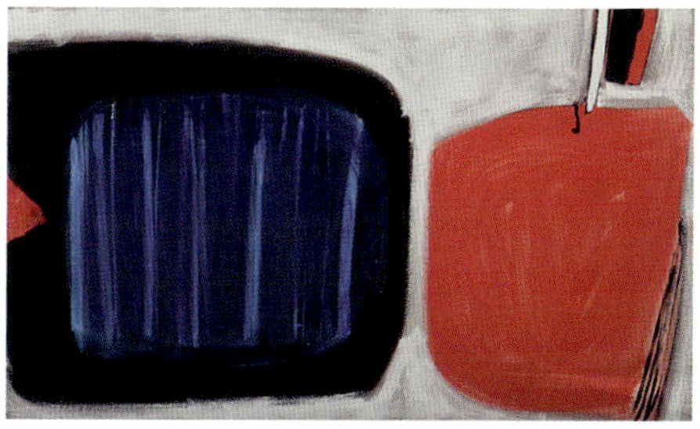

Frost, Terry 1915–2003
Red and Blue 1959
oil on canvas 76 x 127
L.F778.1977.0.0

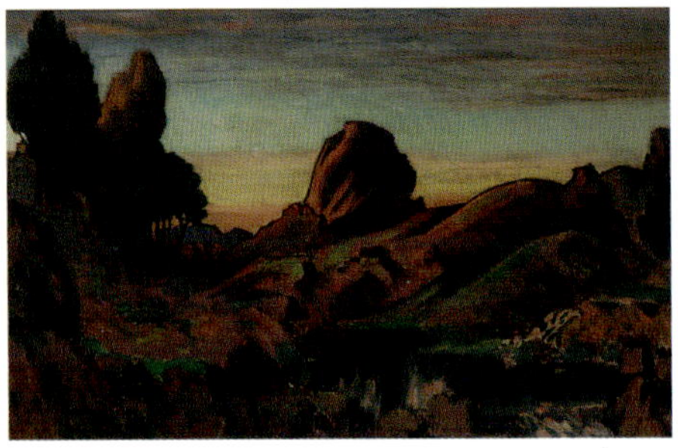

Fry, Roger Eliot 1866–1934
Samothrace, Greece 1912
oil on panel & canvas 20.4 x 30.5
L.F26.1934.0.0

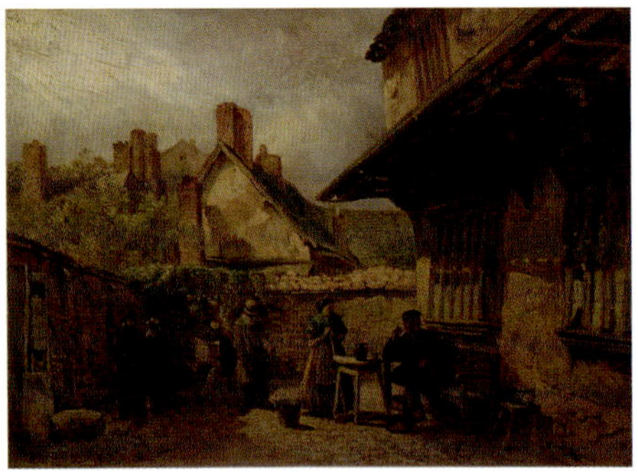

Fulleylove, John 1845–1908
The Old Wyggeston Hospital, Leicester 1872
oil on board 25.4 x 34
L.F76.1926.0.0

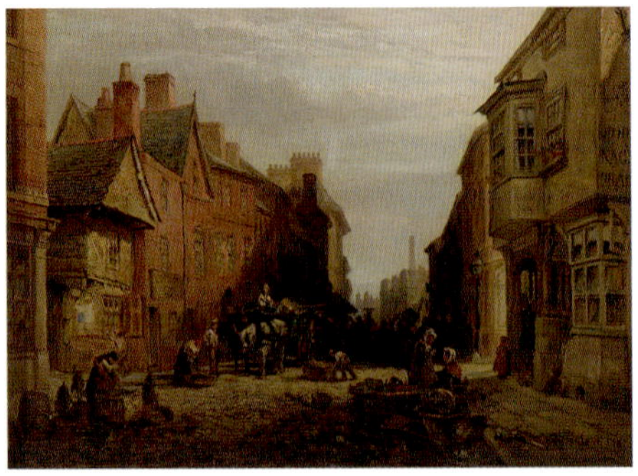

Fulleylove, John 1845–1908
High Cross Street and 'The Nag's Head', Leicester 1874
oil on canvas 28 x 38
L.F103.1993.0.0

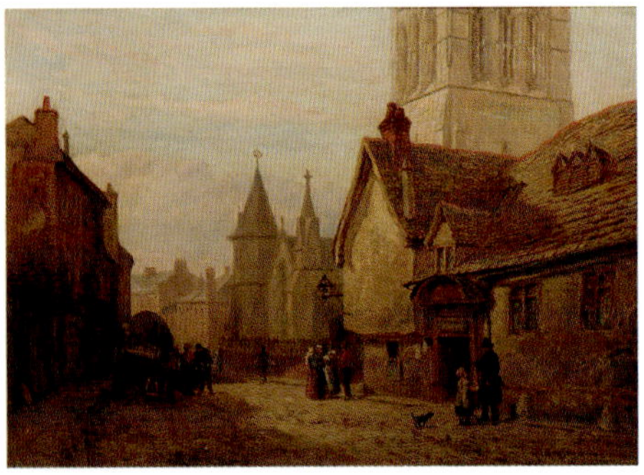

Fulleylove, John 1845–1908
The Old Town Hall, Leicester 1874
oil on canvas 33 x 43
Y.F19.2008.0.0

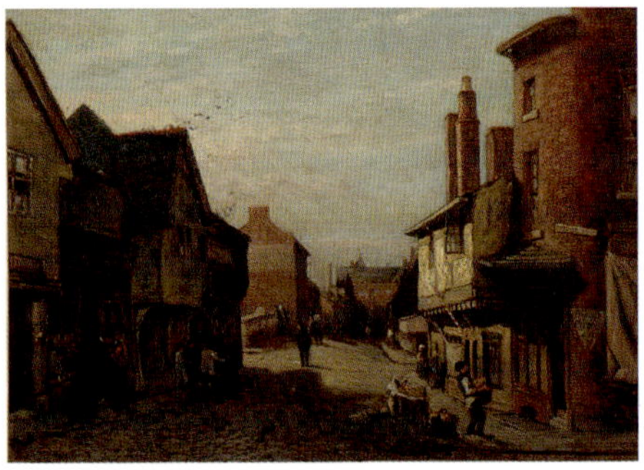

Fulleylove, John 1845–1908
Old West Bridge Street, Leicester 1875
oil on canvas 28 x 38
L.F118.1937.0.0

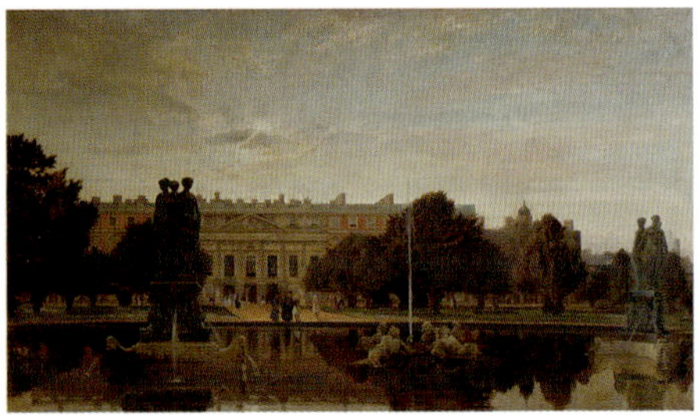

Fulleylove, John 1845–1908
Hampton Court 1889
oil on canvas 91.3 x 152.7
L.F6.1891.0.0

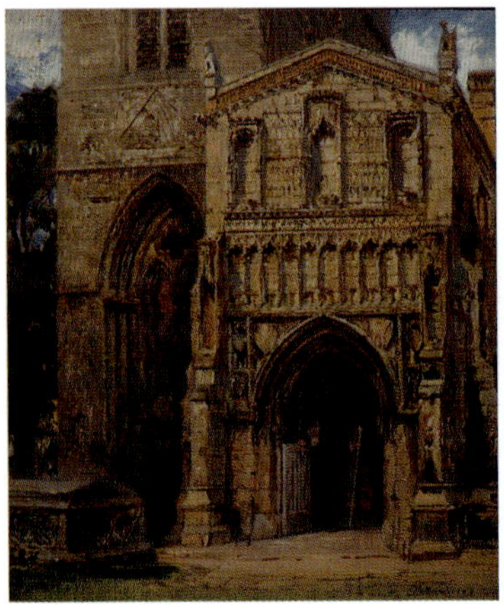

Fulleylove, John 1845–1908
South Porch, St Nicholas, King's Lynn, Norfolk
oil on canvas 30 x 25.5
L.F4.1914.0.0

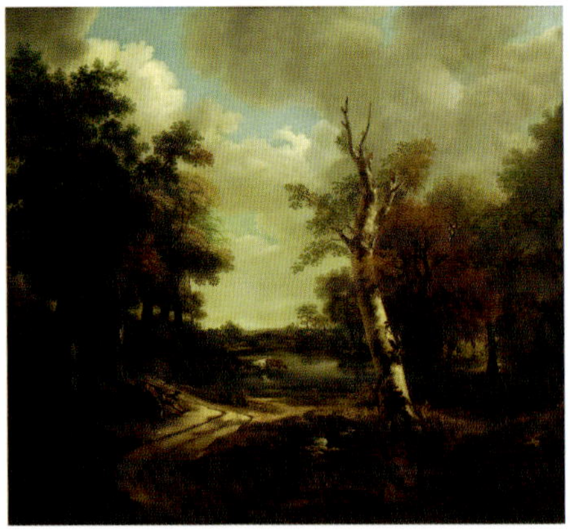

Gainsborough, Thomas (after) 1727–1788
View of Drinkstone Park, Stowmarket, Suffolk
oil on canvas 146 x 159
L.F72.1955.0.0

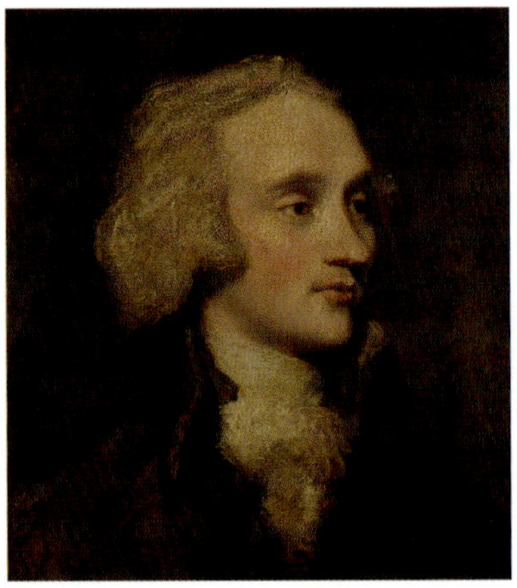

Gardner, Daniel 1750–1805
Wilson Gale-Braddyll (1756–1818), MP
oil on canvas 49.7 x 44.7
L.F2.1905.0.0

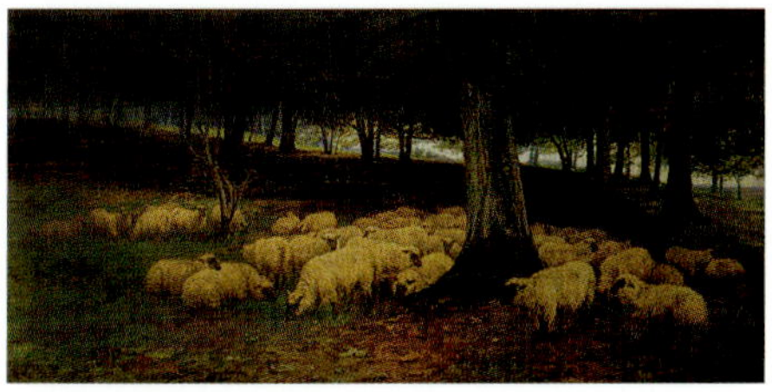

Garland, Henry 1834–1913
A Cool Retreat 1881
oil on canvas 76.1 x 160
L.F10.1882.0.0

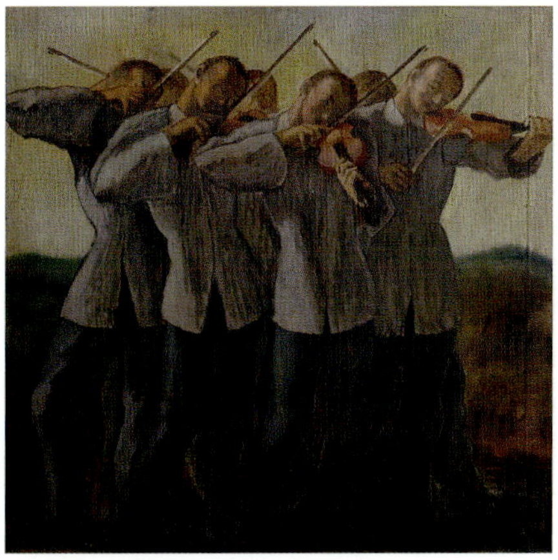

Gerstl, Arnold 1888–1956
The Violinists
oil on hessian 110 x 110
L.F29.1989.0.0

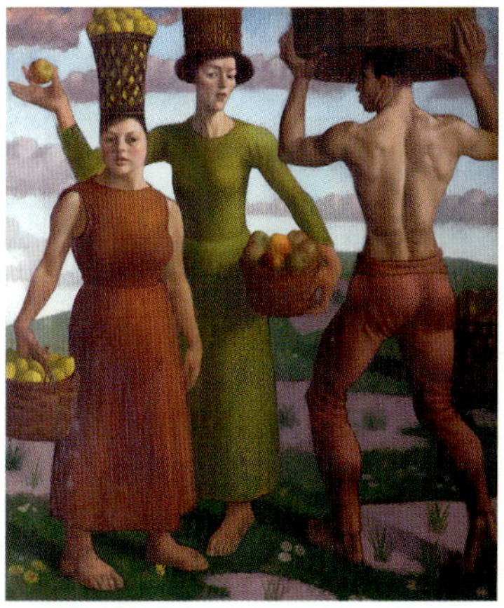

Gertler, Mark 1891–1939
The Fruit Sorters 1914
oil on canvas 76.2 x 63.5
L.F3.1924.0.0

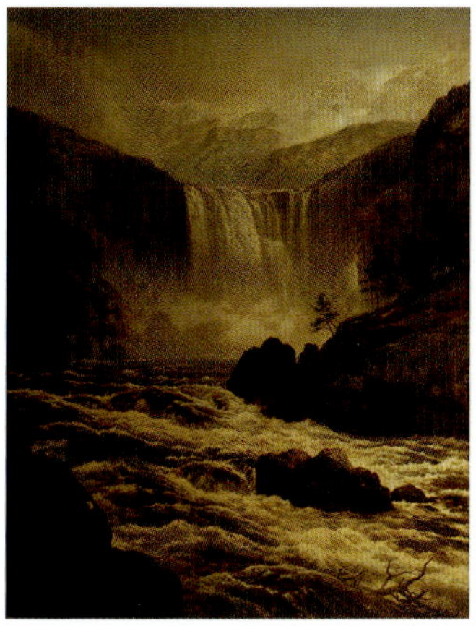

Gill, Edmund Marriner 1820–1894
The Yellowstone Falls, Wyoming, USA 1885
oil on canvas 152.6 x 116.5
L.F2.1917.0.0

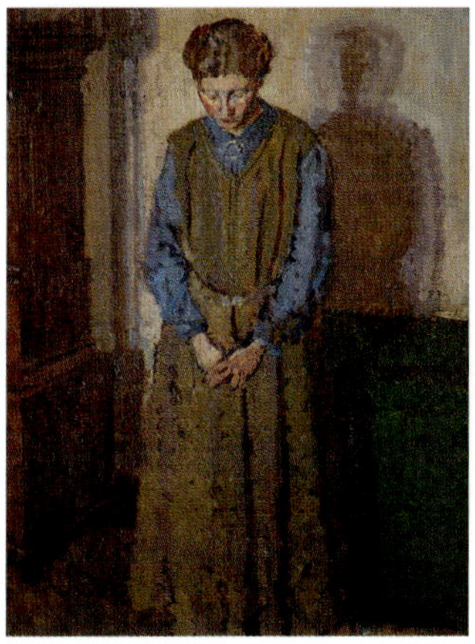

Gilman, Harold 1876–1919
Meditation 1910–1911
oil on canvas 59 x 44
L.F3.1981.0.0

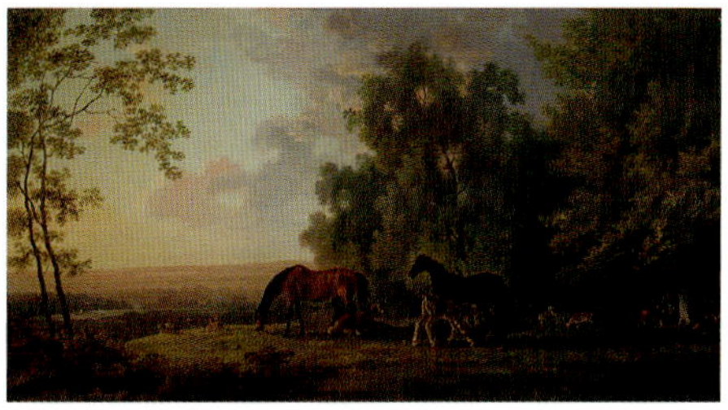

Gilpin, Sawrey (attributed to) 1733–1807 & **Barret, George the elder (attributed to)** 1728/1732–1784
Landscape with Mares, Foals and Deer
oil on canvas 96.5 x 132.7
L.F8.1970.0.0

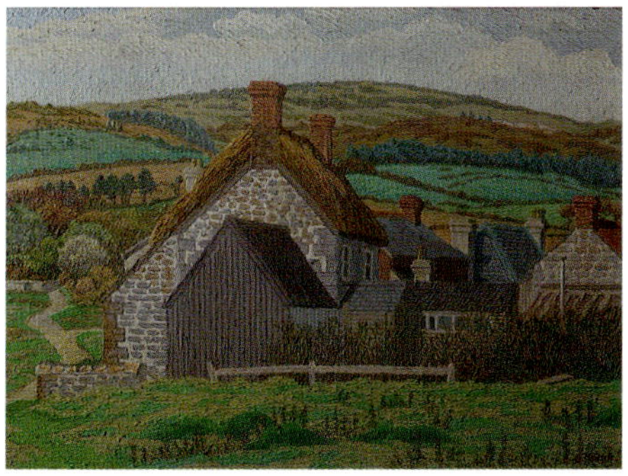

Ginner, Charles 1878–1952
Cottages, Brook Green, Isle of Wight 1929
oil on canvas 53 x 71
L.F9.1956.0.0

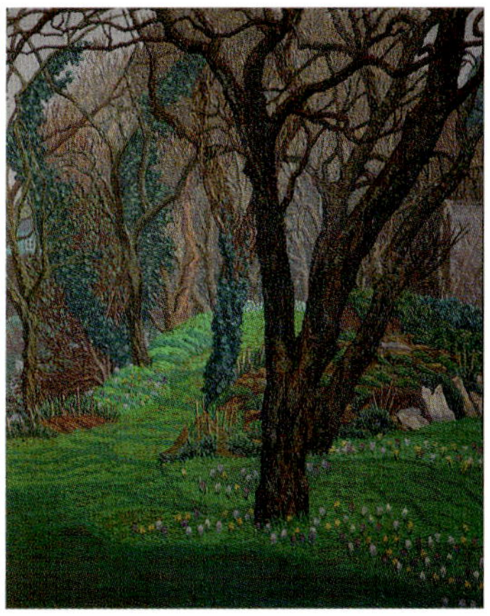

Ginner, Charles 1878–1952
Garden in Spring 1940
oil on canvas 50.8 x 40.7
L.F4.1944.0.0

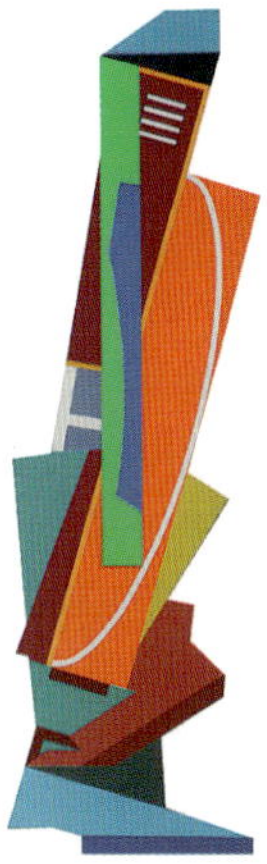

Ginsborg, Michael b.1943
The Harp 1979
acrylic on canvas 186 x 56.3
L.F123.1981.0.0

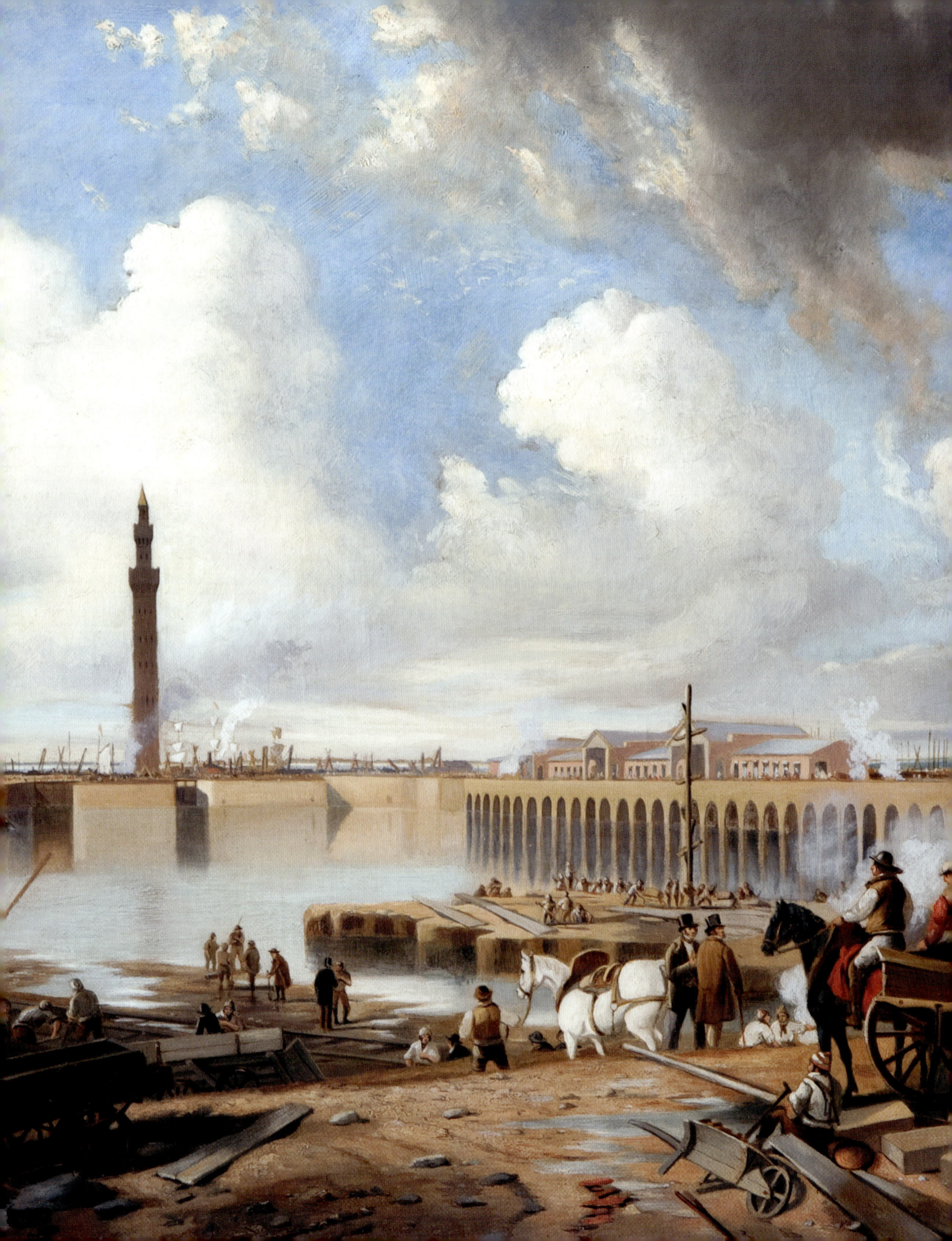

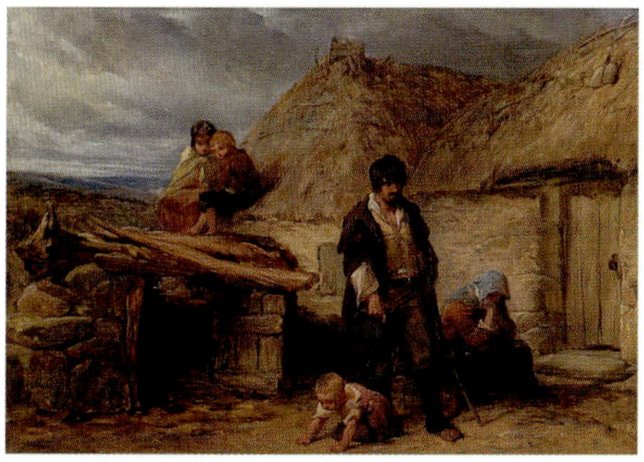

Goodall, Frederick 1822–1904
An Irish Eviction 1850
oil on panel 22.7 x 30.3
L.F4.1890.0.0

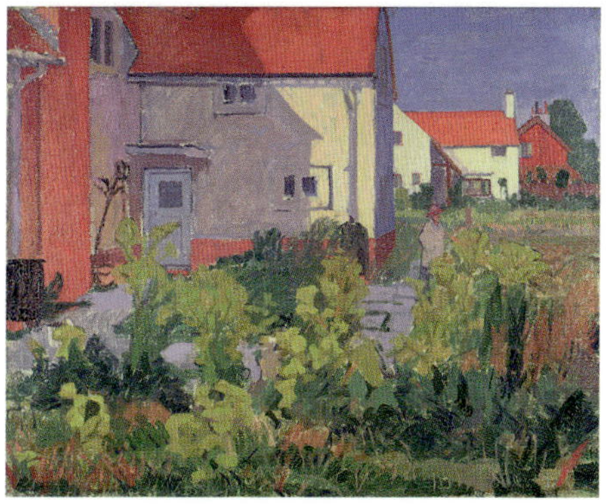

Gore, Spencer 1878–1914
Harold Gilman's House at Letchworth, Hertfordshire 1912
oil on canvas 63.5 x 76.2
L.F345.1974.0.0

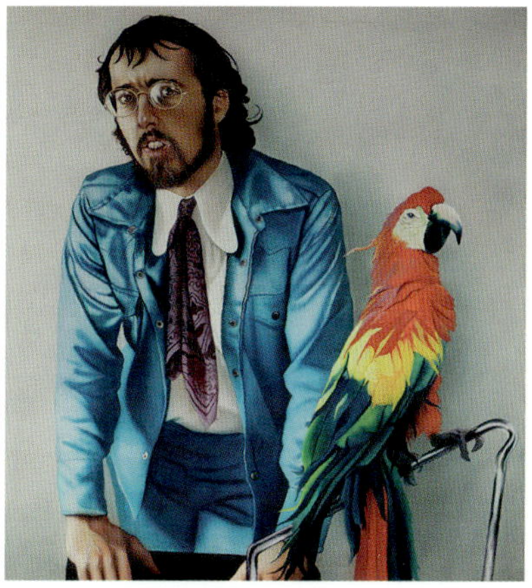

Gorman, Michael b.1938
Mr Treadwell Meets the Critics 1973
acrylic on canvas 137 x 127
L.F806.1975.0.0

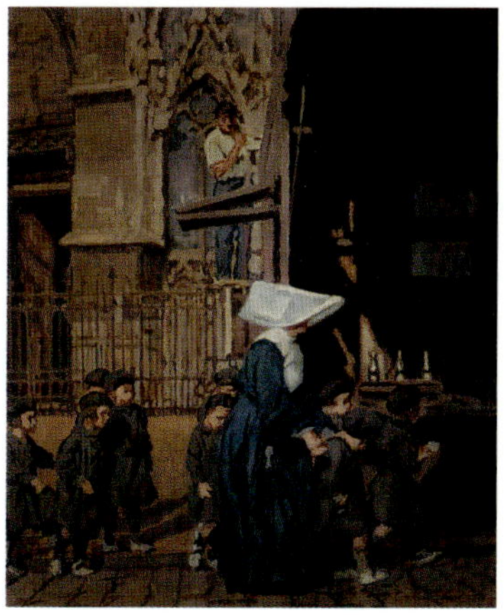

Gosse, Laura Sylvia 1881–1968
A Nun with Children
oil on canvas 70.8 x 61.5
L.F1.1952.0.0

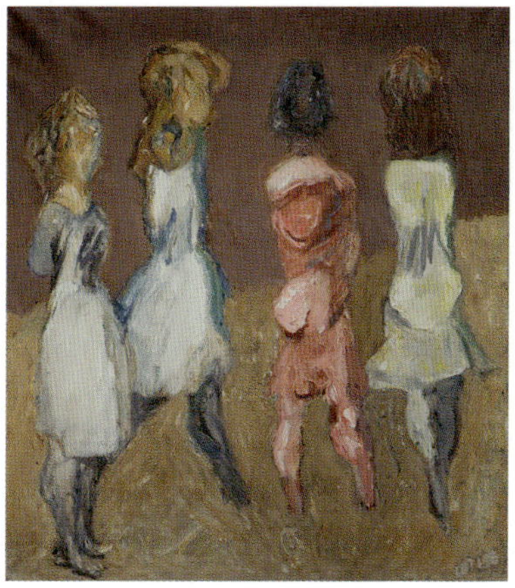

Gotlib, Henryk 1890–1966
Four Girls at Forte dei Marmi, Italy
oil on canvas 70 x 60.5
L.F118.1981.0.0

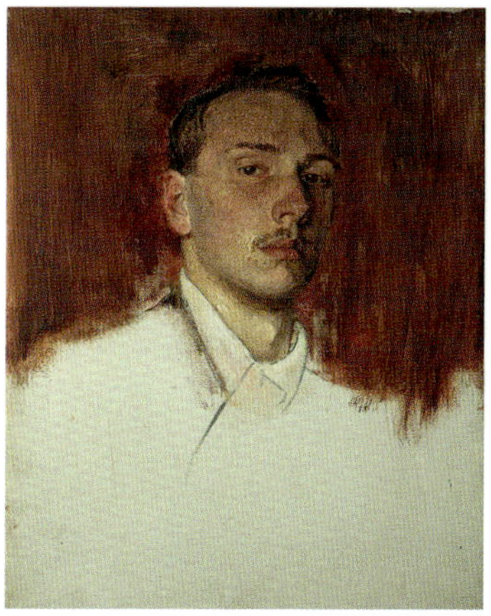

Gould, Julian 1891–1917
Self Portrait 1914
oil on canvas 54 x 43.2
L.F22.1967.0.0

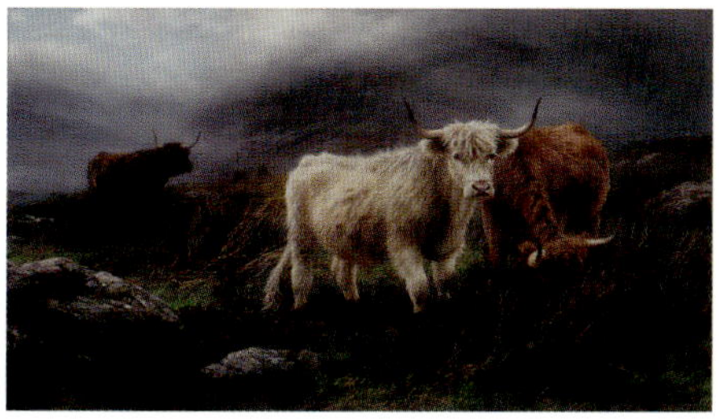

Graham, Peter 1836–1921
The Highland Pastures 1897
oil on canvas 108.2 x 184
L.F1.1897.0.0

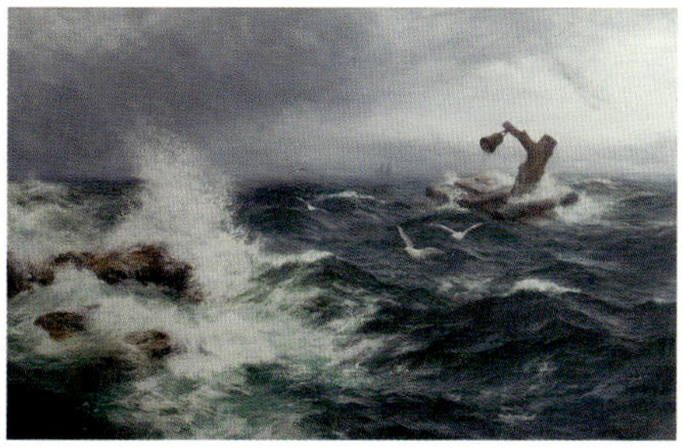

Graham, Peter 1836–1921
The Inchcape Rock 1908
oil on canvas 122 x 186
L.F4.1909.0.0

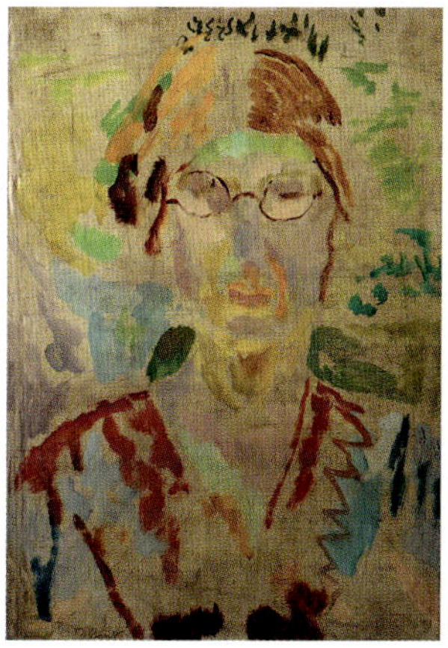

Grant, Duncan 1885–1978
Vanessa Bell (1879–1961) 1914–1915
oil on canvas & panel 51 x 35
L.F15.1955.0.0

Facing page: Carmichael, John Wilson, 1799–1868, *The Construction of the Royal Dock, Grimsby, Lincolnshire* (detail), 1852, North East Lincolnshire Museum Service (p. 237)

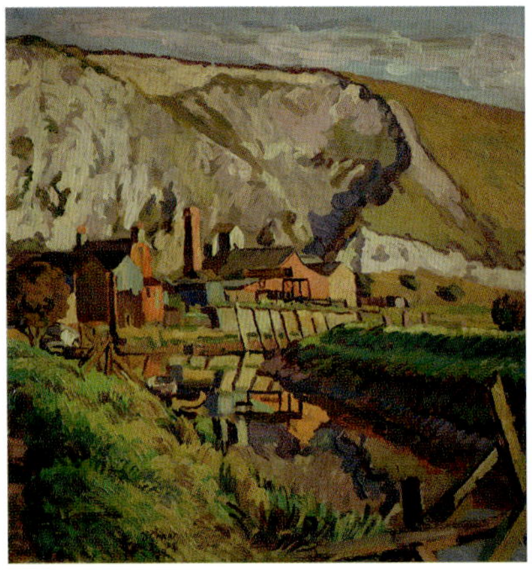

Grant, Duncan 1885–1978
Lewes Landscape, East Sussex 1933–1934
oil on paper on board 60.2 x 57.2
L.F8.1945.0.0

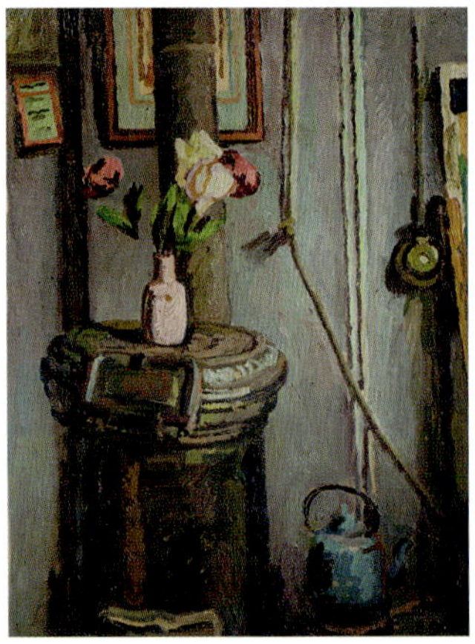

Grant, Duncan 1885–1978
The Pink Vase 1934
oil on paper on panel 76.8 x 56.5
L.F54.1937.0.0

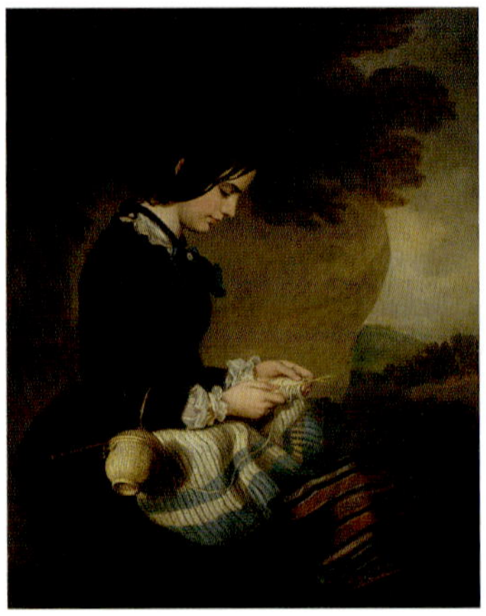

Grant, Francis 1803–1878
Mary Isabella Grant (d.1854)
oil on canvas 127 x 101.6
L.F25.1954.0.0

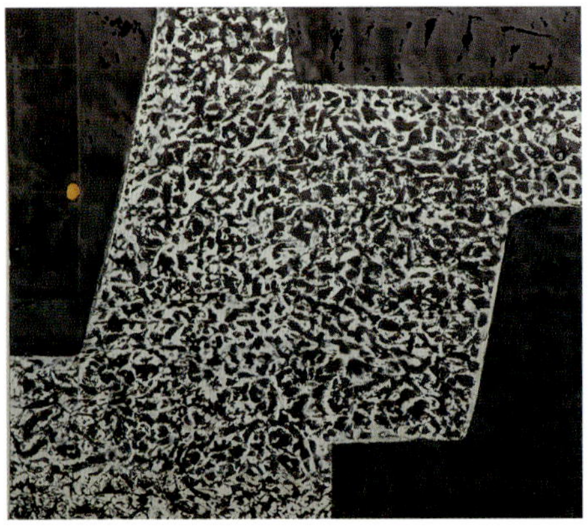

Gray, Eileen 1878–1976
Collage 1940–1949
oil & collage on paper 33.5 x 37.2
L.F9.1976.0.0

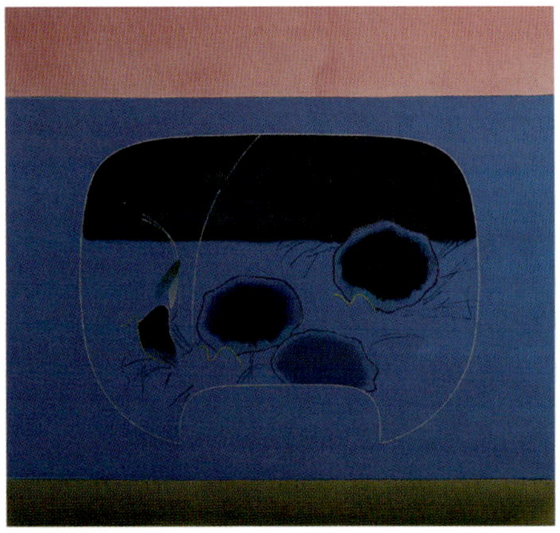

Greaves, Derrick b.1927
Studies for Hiroshige II 1974
acrylic on canvas 127 x 132
L.F356.1975.0.0

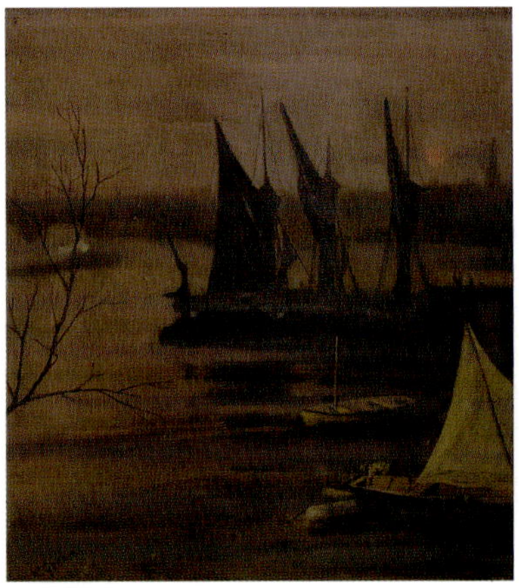

Greaves, Walter 1846–1930
The River in Winter, Sunset 1865
oil on canvas 51.3 x 45.7
L.F33.1947.0.0

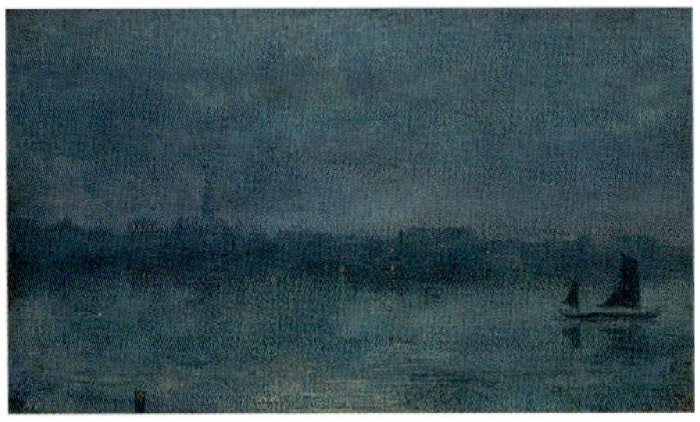

Greaves, Walter 1846–1930
Nocturne in Blue and Gold
oil on canvas 28.3 x 46.5
L.F37.1944.0.0

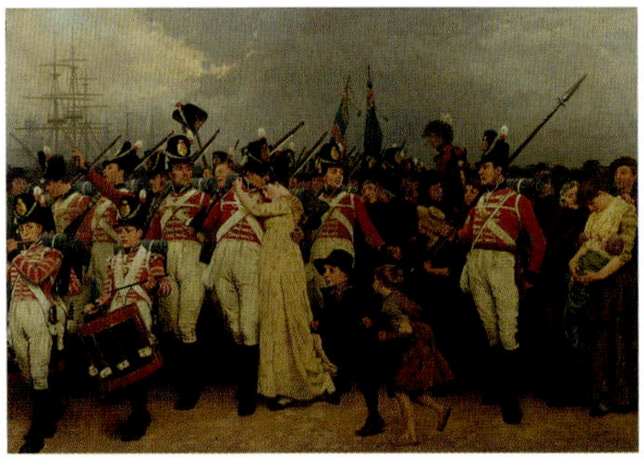

Green, Charles 1840–1898
The Girl I Left behind Me 1880
oil on canvas 129.5 x 183
L.F2.1882.0.0

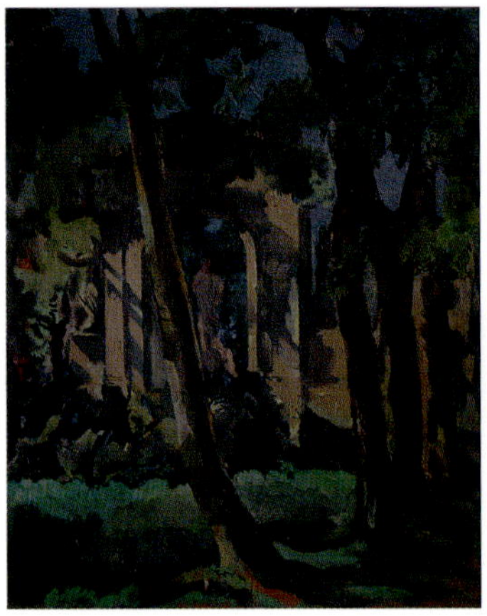

Green, Kenneth 1905–1986
Borghese Gardens, Rome 1945
oil on canvas 76.5 x 61
L.F7.1945.0.0

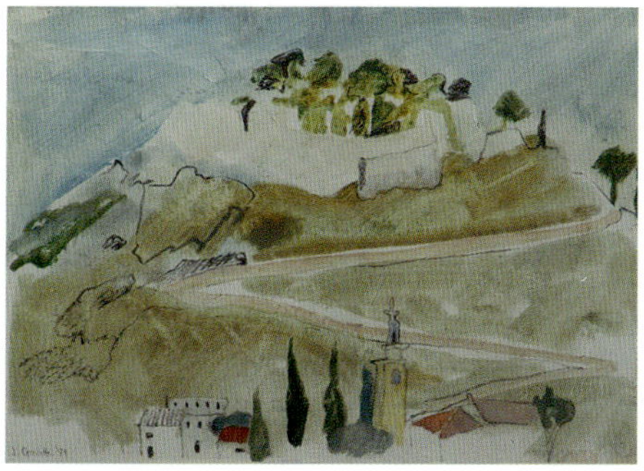

Grevatte, Jenny b.1951
Castle in Cephalonia, Greece 1989
gesso on paper 18.5 x 25.5
L.F3.1992.0.0

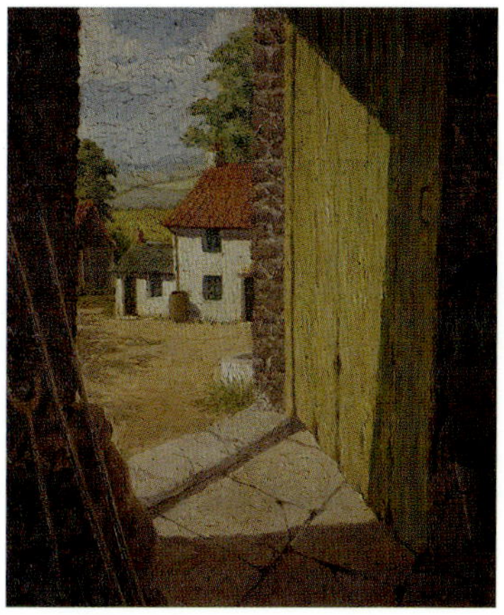

Grigg, Ronald Edwin 1917–1957
A Barn Door 1942
oil on canvas 55.8 x 45.7
L.F2.1943.0.0

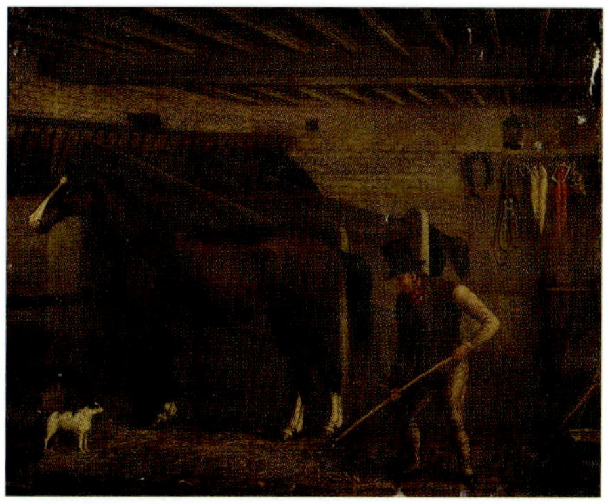

Groves, T.
*Hunter and Groom**
oil on canvas 63.5 x 74
Y.F24.2009

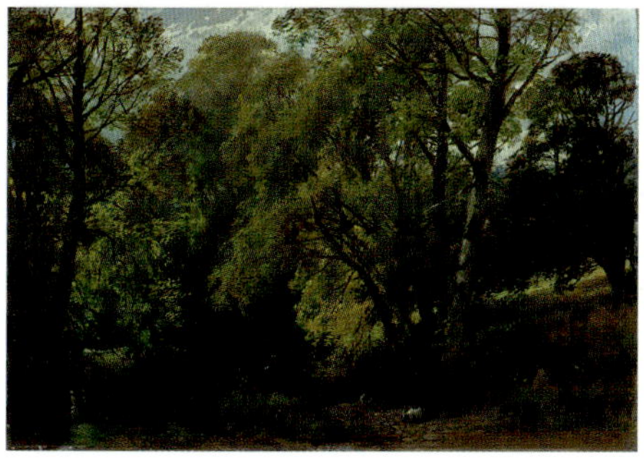

Harding, James Duffield 1798–1863
A Shady Nook 1858
oil on board 30.5 x 43
L.F1.1890.0.0

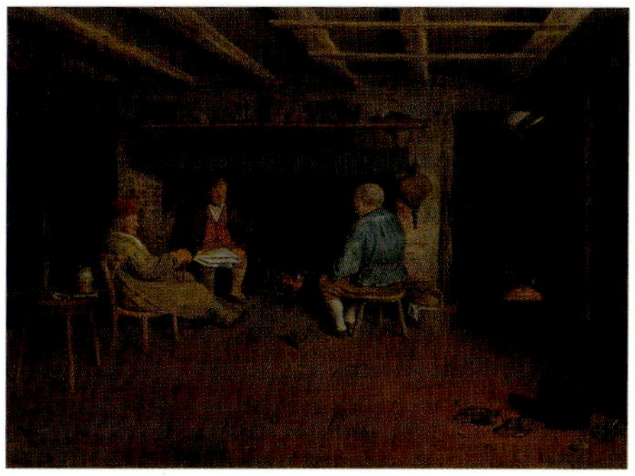

Hardy, Frederick Daniel 1827–1911
Interior of a Sussex Farmhouse
oil on panel 15 x 20.3
L.F3.1890.0.0

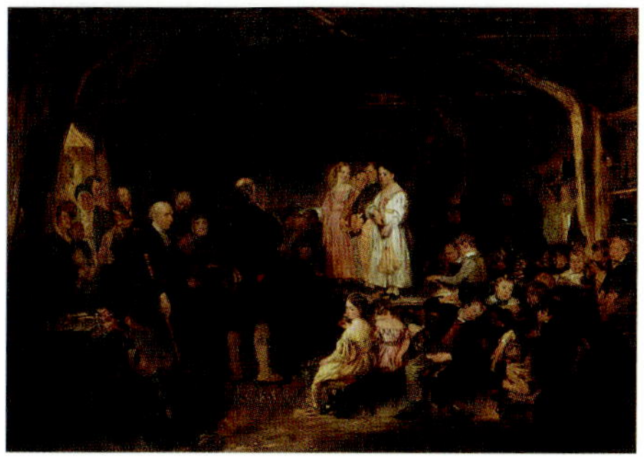

Harvey, George 1806–1876
Catechising in a Scottish School 1832
oil on panel 96.5 x 127
L.F8.1886.0.0

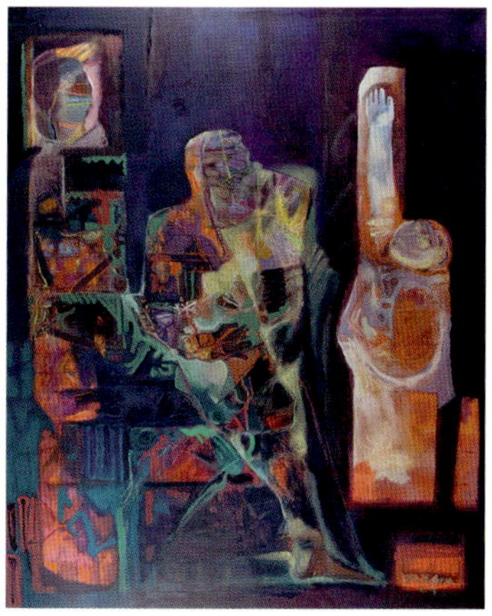

Hashem, Satta b.1959
Freedom No.1 2007
acrylic on canvas 180 x 140
Y.F2.2010.0.0

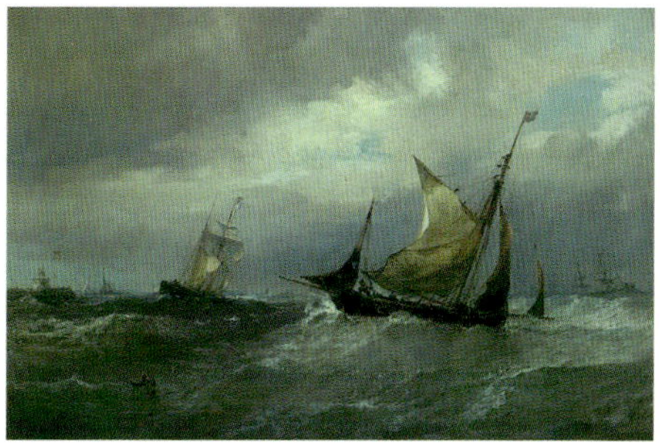

Hayes, Edwin 1819–1904
Trawling off Gorleston Harbour, Norfolk
oil on canvas 55.7 x 86.5
L.F7.1881.0.0

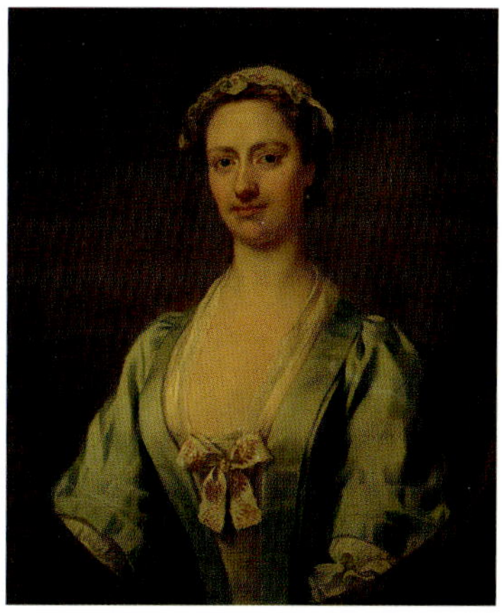

Hayman, Francis (attributed to) 1708–1776
Portrait of a Lady (possibly the actress Margaret 'Peg' Woffington, 1720?–1760) c.1730
oil on canvas 76.2 x 63.5
L.F21.1937.0.0

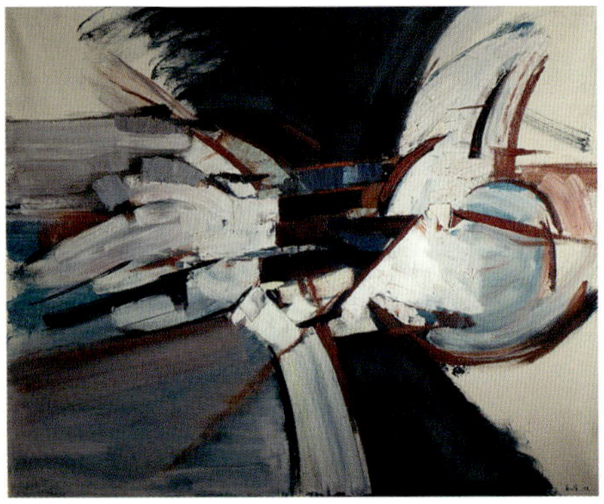

Heath, Adrian 1920–1992
Painting Blue and White 1959
oil on canvas 101.5 x 142
L.F2.1961.0.0

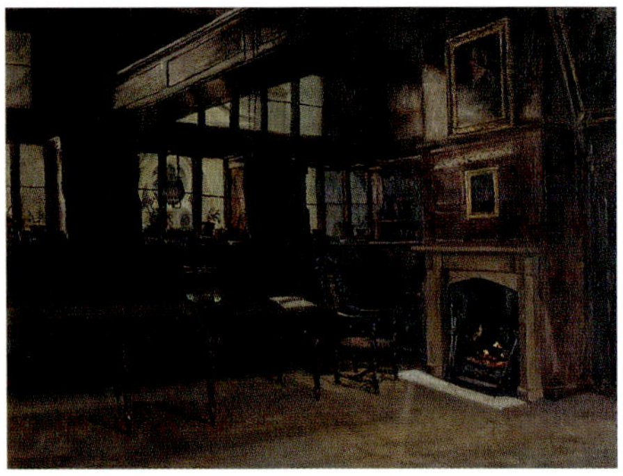

Henton, George W. Moore 1861–1924
Old Town Hall Library, Guildhall, Leicester 1881
oil on canvas 29 x 39.8
L.F19.1934.78.0

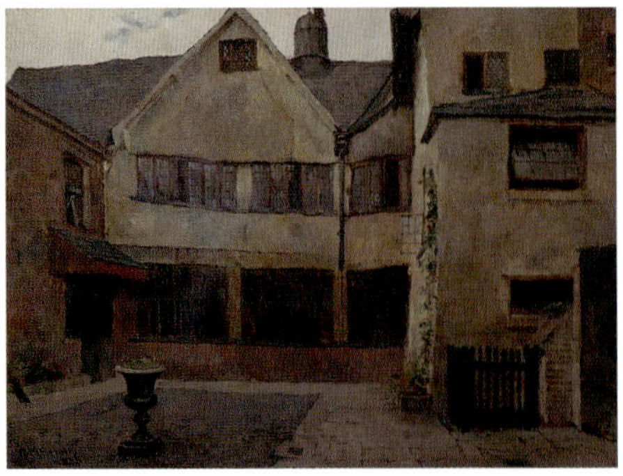

Henton, George W. Moore 1861–1924
Courtyard, Guildhall, Leicester 1882
oil on canvas 30.5 x 40.5
L.F6.1989.0.0

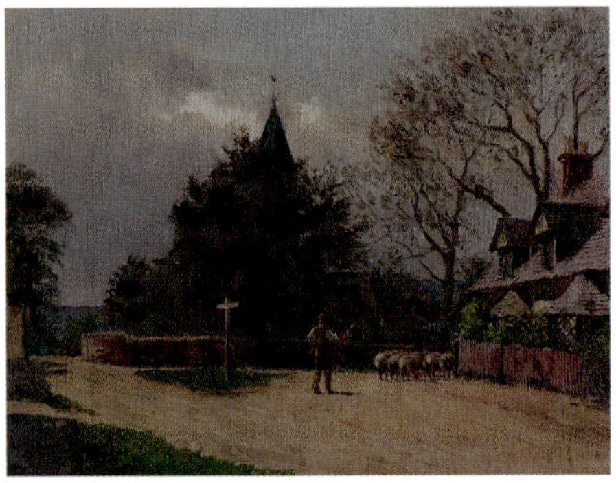

Henton, George W. Moore 1861–1924
St Mary-in-the-Elms, Woodhouse, Leicestershire 1904
oil on board 21.6 x 28
L.F19.1934.68.0

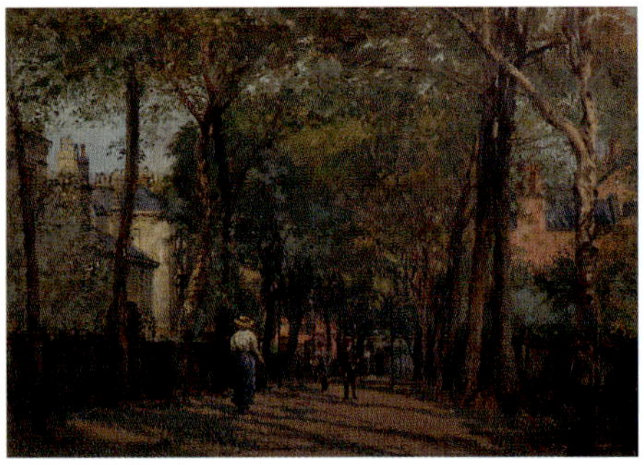

Henton, George W. Moore 1861–1924
The New Walk, Leicester 1914
oil on canvas 30.5 x 40.6
L.F190.1960.0.0

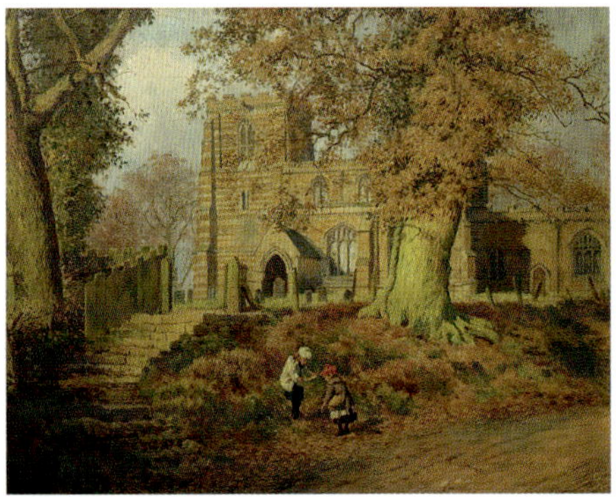

Henton, George W. Moore 1861–1924
November Sunshine, Lowesby Church, Leicestershire 1915
oil on canvas 63.5 x 76.9
L.F19.1934.77.0

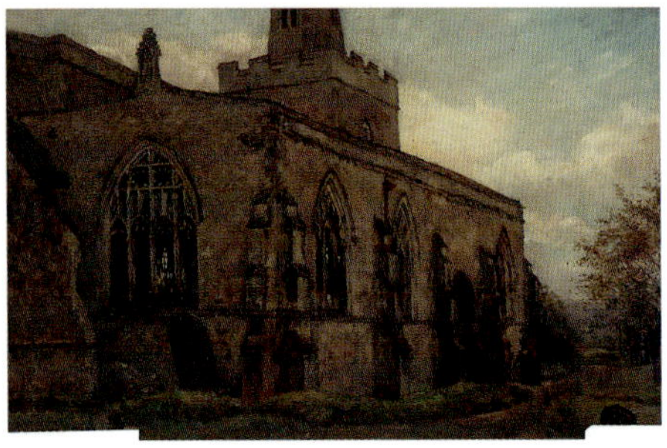

Henton, George W. Moore 1861–1924
St Denys' Church, Evington, Leicestershire
oil on canvas 29.5 x 44.5
L.F19.1934.55.0

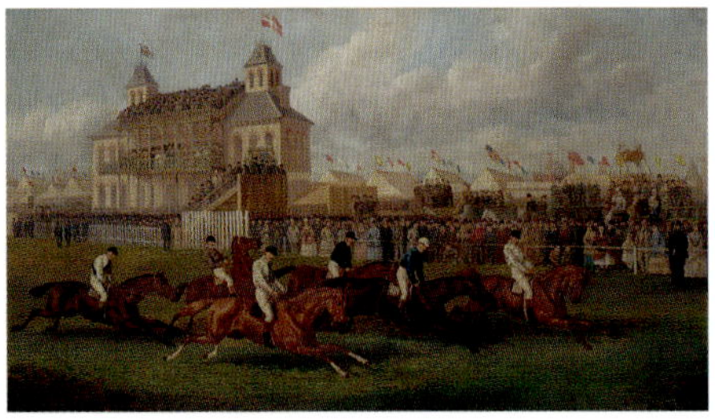

Herberte, Edward Benjamin active 1857–1893
A Horse Race in Victoria Park, Leicester 1874
oil on canvas 71 x 122
L.F34.1953.0.0

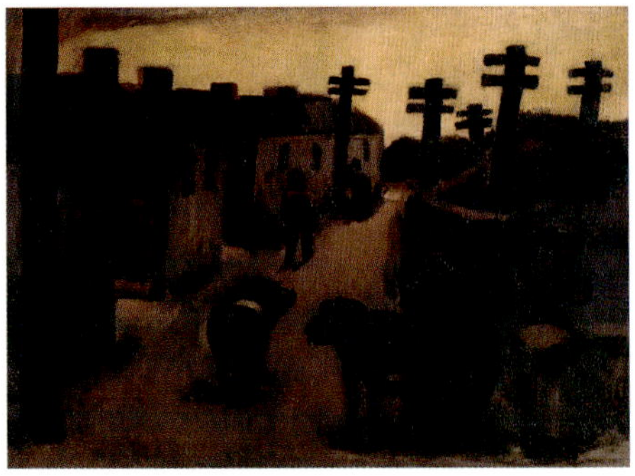

Herman, Josef 1911–2000
Evenfall, Ystradgynlais, Powys 1948
oil on canvas 76.5 x 101.5
L.F11.1950.0.0

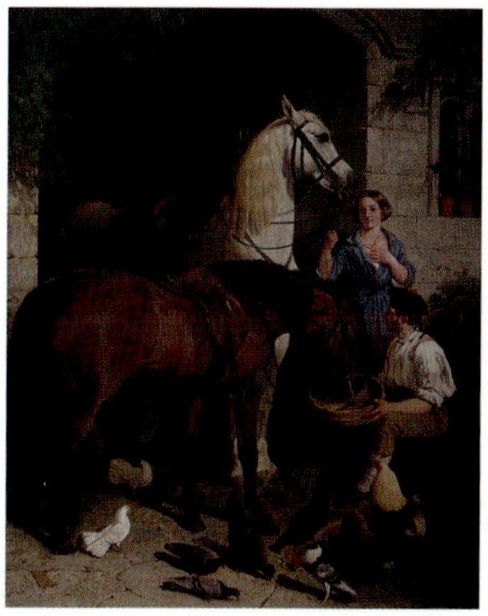

Herring, John Frederick I 1795–1865
The Halt 1854
oil on canvas 126 x 101.5
L.F3.1902.0.0

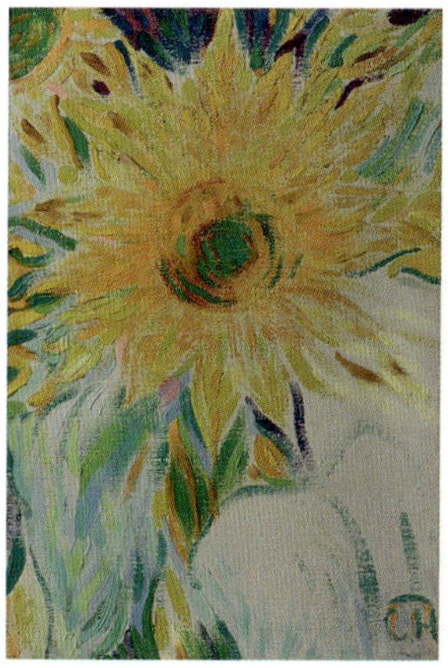

Herrmann, Curt 1854–1929
Sunflowers
oil on canvas 47 x 32
L.F12.1986.0.0

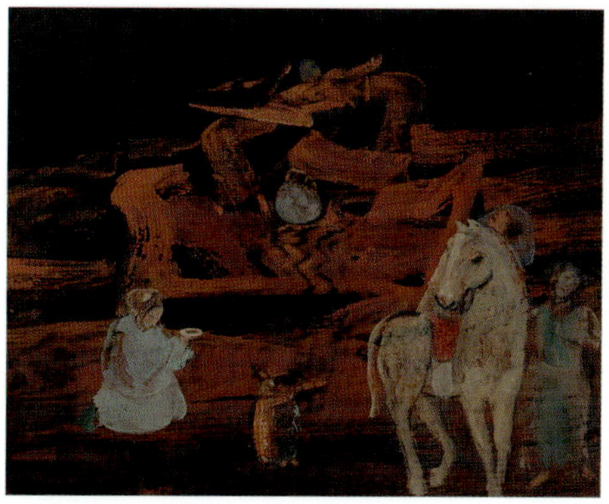

Higgins, Charles S. 1893–1980
La lutte angelique 1948
oil on panel 37.5 x 45.7
L.F21.1952.0.0

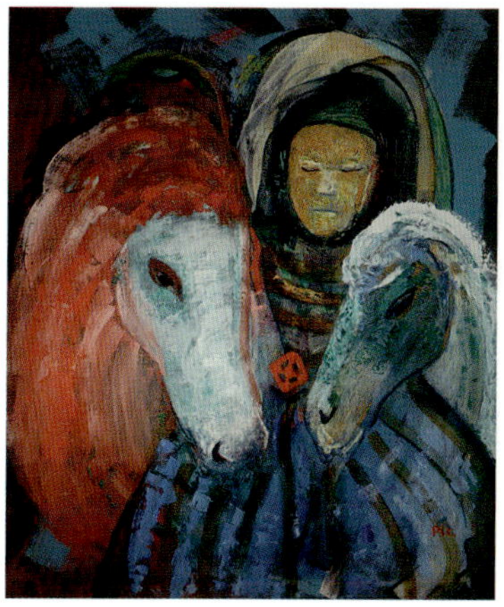

Higgins, Charles S. 1893–1980
Bedouin and Horses
oil on board 112.7 x 95
L.F4.1983.0.0

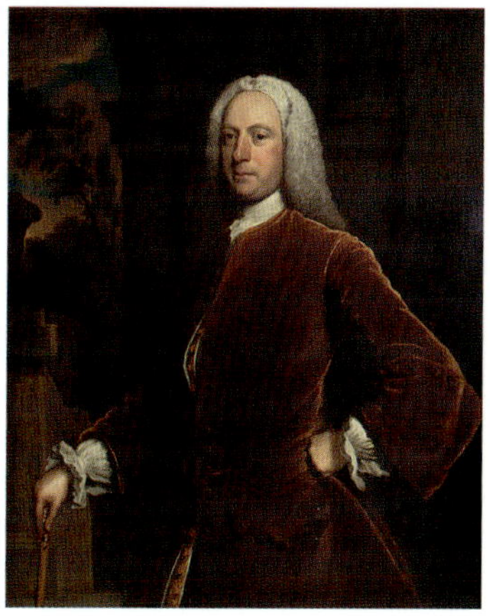

Highmore, Joseph 1692–1780
James Wigley of Scraptoft Hall (c.1700–1765) 1741
oil on canvas 127 x 105.6
L.F54.1926.0.0

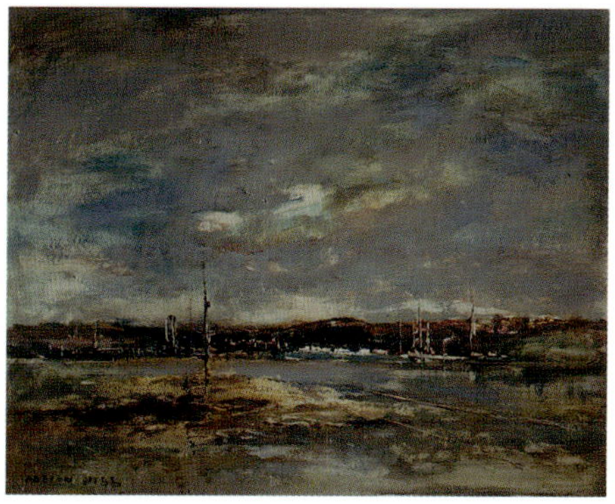

Hill, Adrian Keith Graham 1895–1977
The Estuary
oil on board 50.7 x 60.5
L.F3.1996.7.0

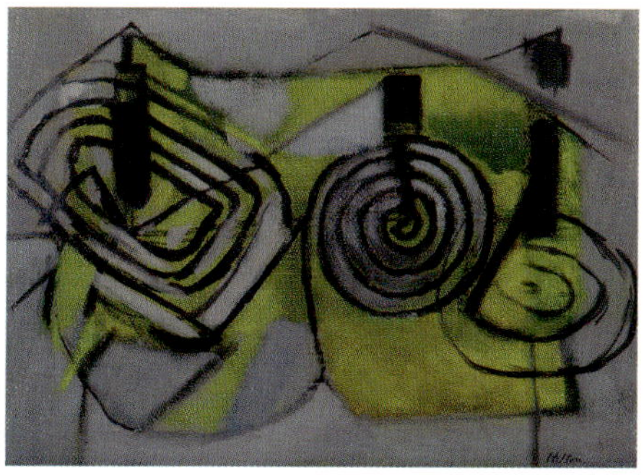

Hilton, Roger 1911–1975
Spiral 1953
oil on canvas 25.3 x 35.3
L.F18.1962.0.0

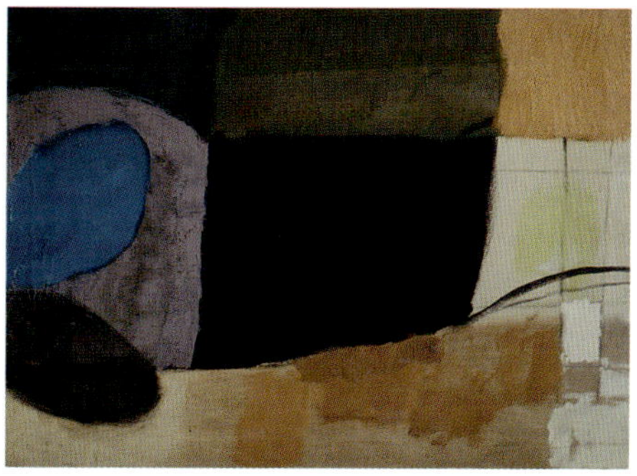

Hilton, Roger 1911–1975
Untitled 1956
oil on canvas 55.5 x 76
L.F354.1975.0.0

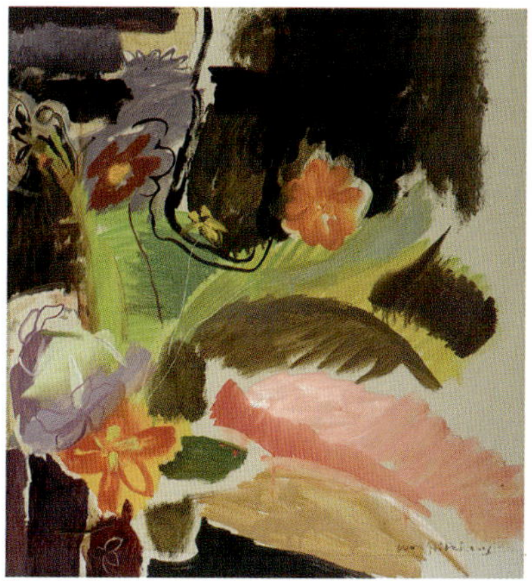

Hitchens, Ivon 1893–1979
Flower Piece
oil on canvas 61 x 55.7
L.F4.1942.0.0

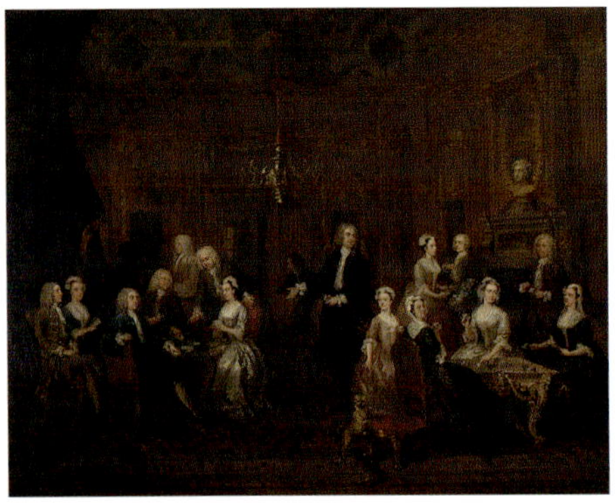

Hogarth, William 1697–1764
The Wollaston Family 1730
oil on canvas 102.5 x 126.4
L.F40.1982.0.0 (P)

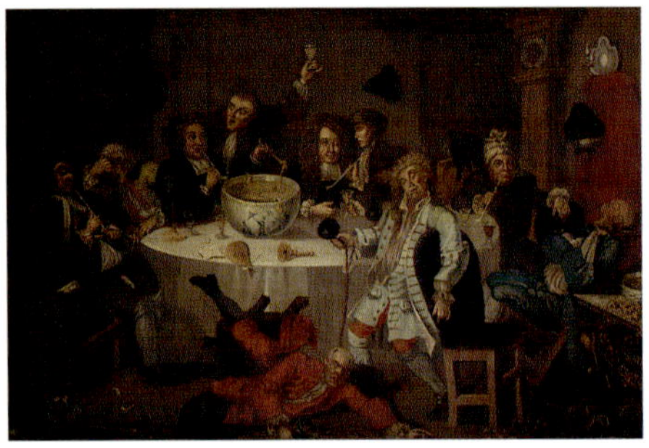

Hogarth, William (after) 1697–1764
A Modern Midnight Conversation 18th C
oil on canvas 80.5 x 116.5
L.F5.1905.0.0

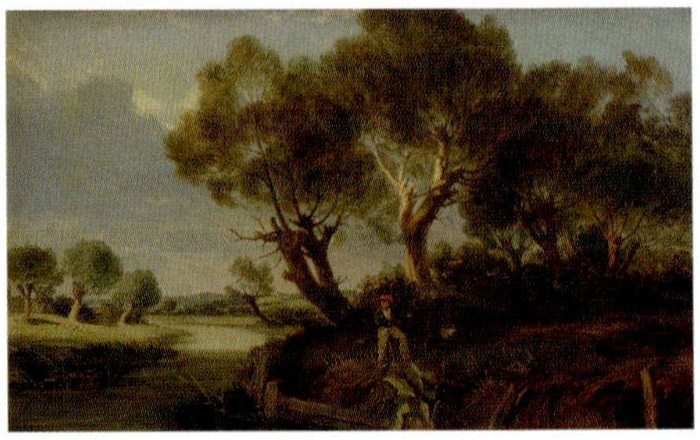

Holland, James 1799–1870
English Landscape 1841
oil on canvas 49.5 x 78.7
L.F4.1887.0.0

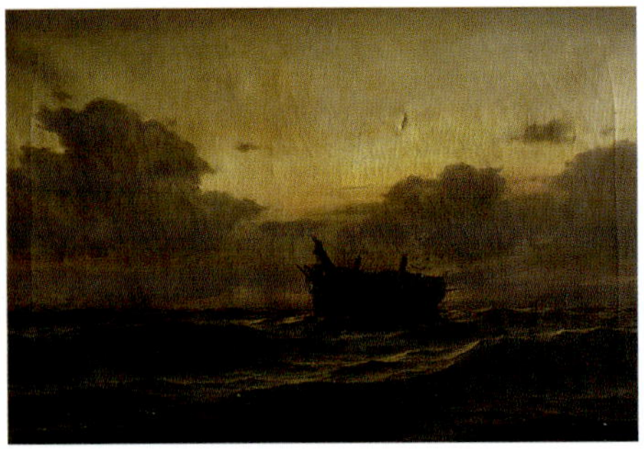

Holst, Laurits Bernhard 1848–1934
The Derelict, Morning after a Storm 1878
oil on canvas 62.5 x 90.3
Y.F11.2009.0.0

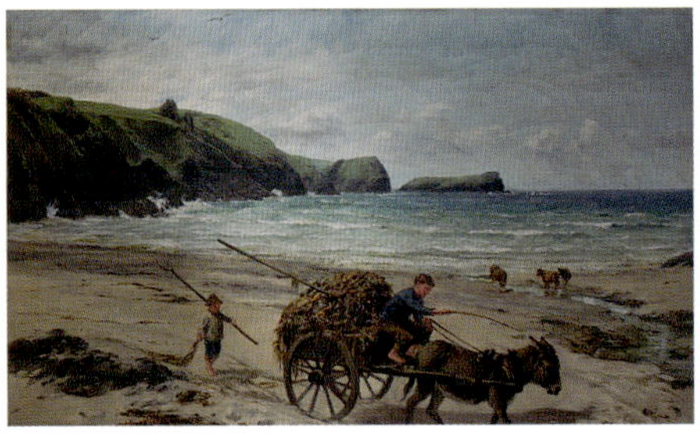

Hook, James Clarke 1819–1907
Carting for Farmer, Pengelly, Cornwall 1872
oil on canvas 87 x 142
L.F11.1900.0.0

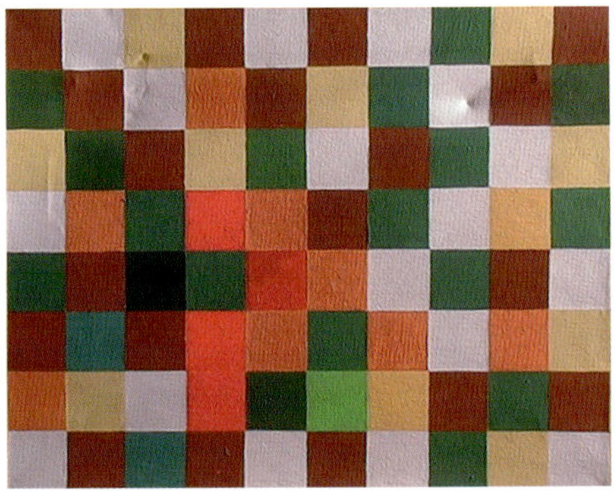

Hooper, John b.1939
Untitled (To Bernstein's 'Big Bluff') 1994
acrylic on canvas 41 x 51.5
Y.F1.2006.3.0

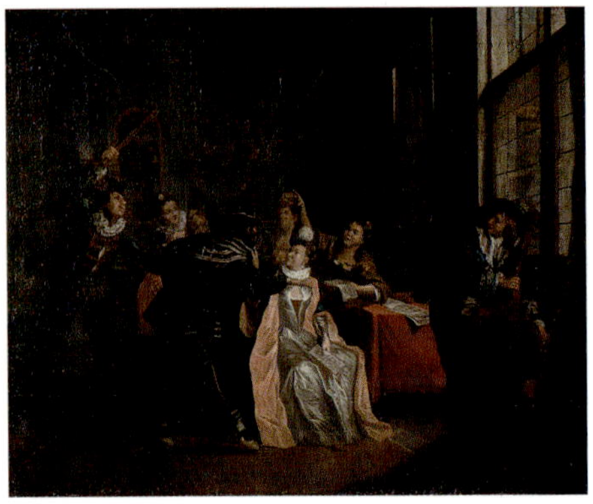

Horemans, Jan Josef the elder 1682–1752 &
Horemans, Jan Josef the younger 1714–1790
A Music Party 18th C
oil on canvas 48 x 56.5
L.F20.1935.11.0

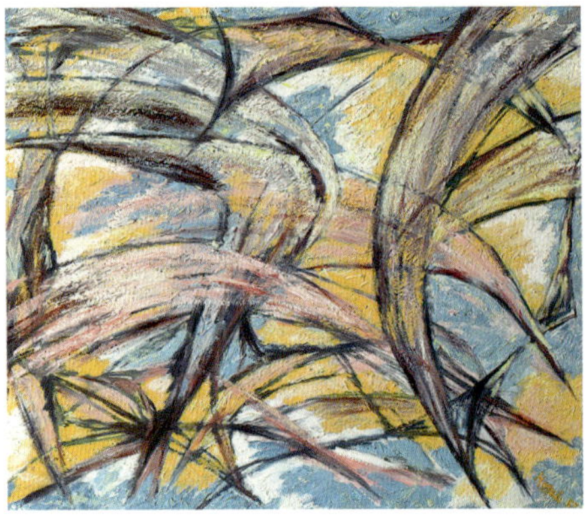

Hosali, Nina 1898–1987
Movement 3, Dance at Sunrise 1957
oil on canvas 54 x 76
L.F67.1988.0.0

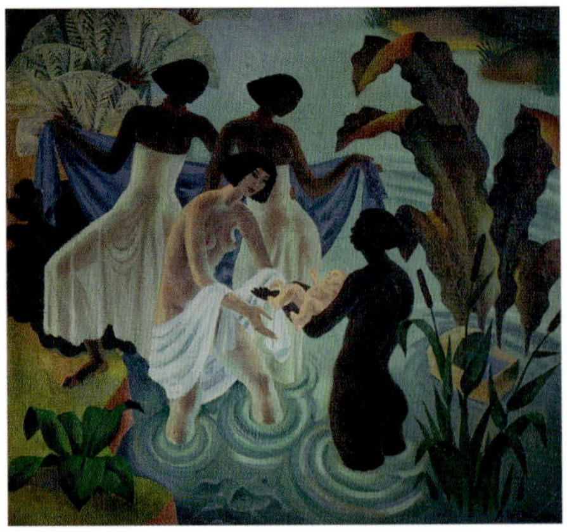

Hosking, Hugh Richard 1904–1991
The Finding of Moses
oil on canvas 76.5 x 81.3
L.F7.1933.0.0

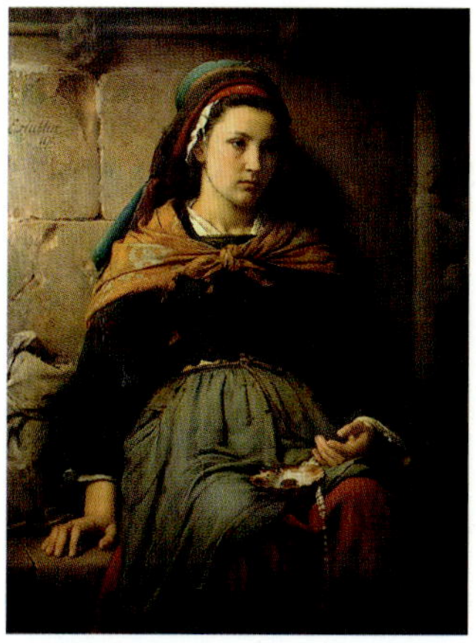

Hublin, Émile Auguste 1830–1891
The Orphan 1876
oil on canvas 109.2 x 81.3
L.F1.1891.0.0

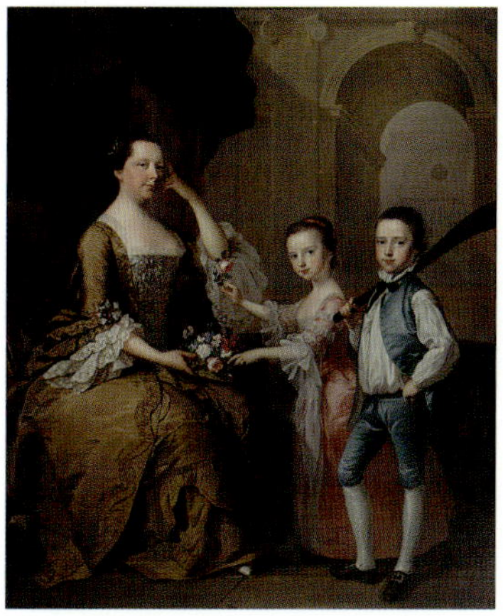

Hudson, Thomas 1701–1779
Mrs Matthew Michell and Her Children, Matthew and Anne 1757–1758
oil on canvas 191.8 x 161.6
L.F9.1938.0.0

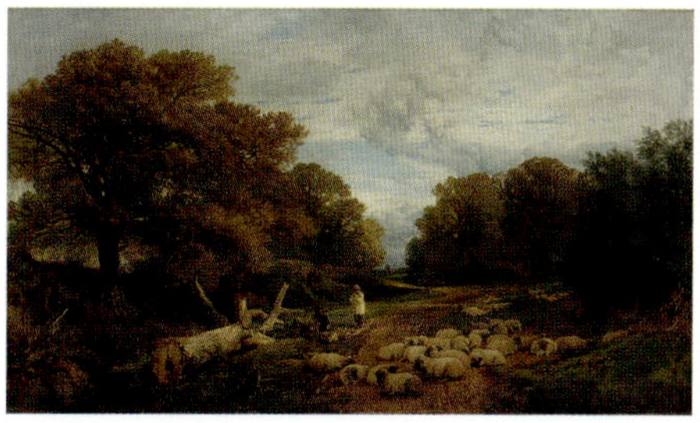

Hulme, Frederick William 1816–1884
Scene in Sussex 1867
oil on canvas 76.5 x 128.3
L.F4.1902.0.0

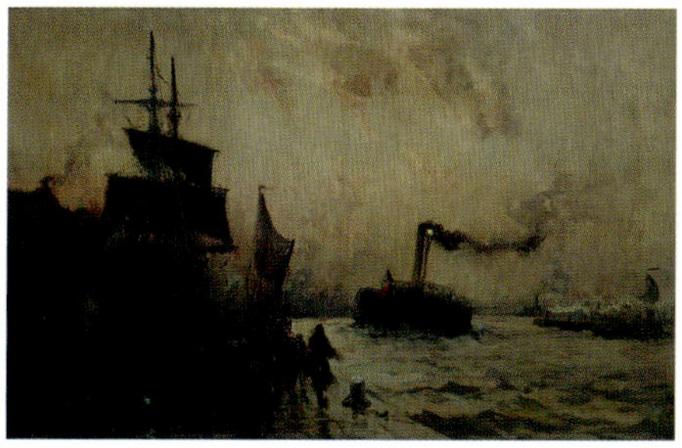

Hunt, Edward Aubrey 1855–1922
Greenwich Reach, London, Evening
oil on canvas 54.5 x 85.2
L.F2.1914.0.0

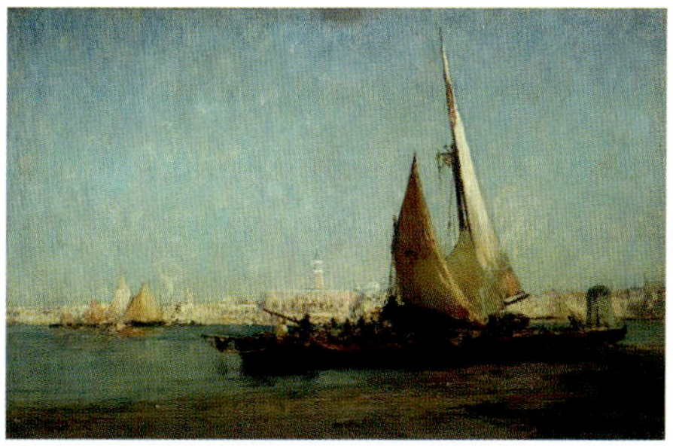

Hunt, Edward Aubrey 1855–1922
Venice
oil on canvas 50.7 x 76.3
L.F3.1905.0.0

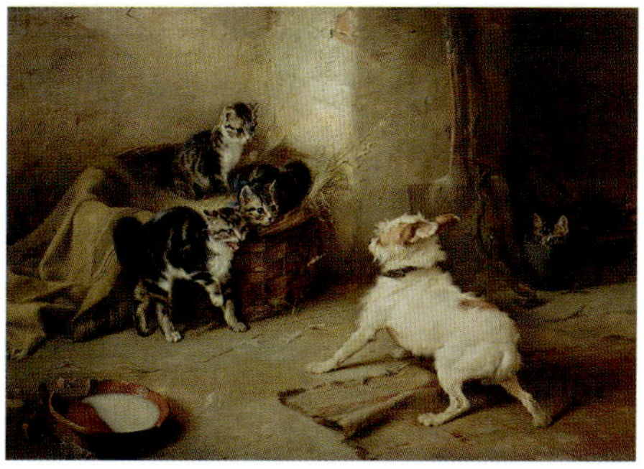

Hunt, Walter 1861–1941
Kittens and a Dog 1881
oil on canvas 86 x 118.7
IL.2104.1996 (P)

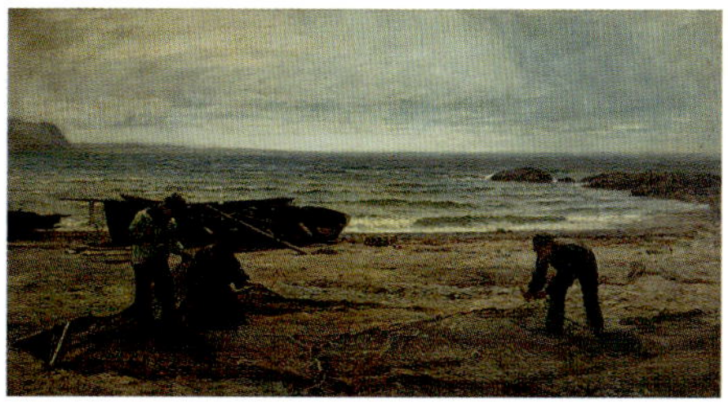

Hunter, Colin 1841–1904
Three Fishers 1873
oil on canvas 66.4 x 123
L.F4.1891.0.0

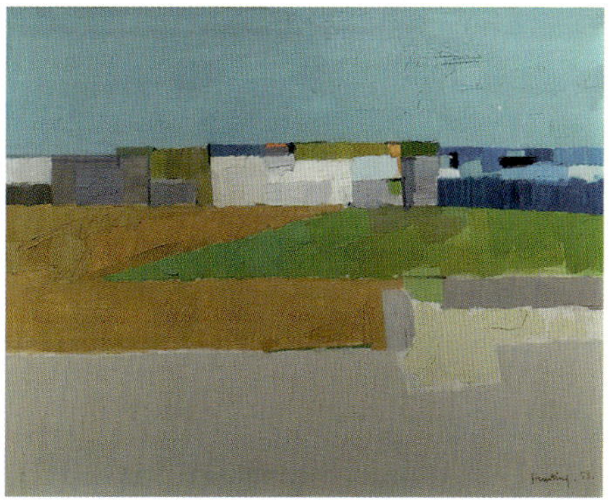

Hunting, Leonard b.1926
Landscape, Martigues, France 1958
oil on canvas 54 x 64.7
L.F13.1958.0.0

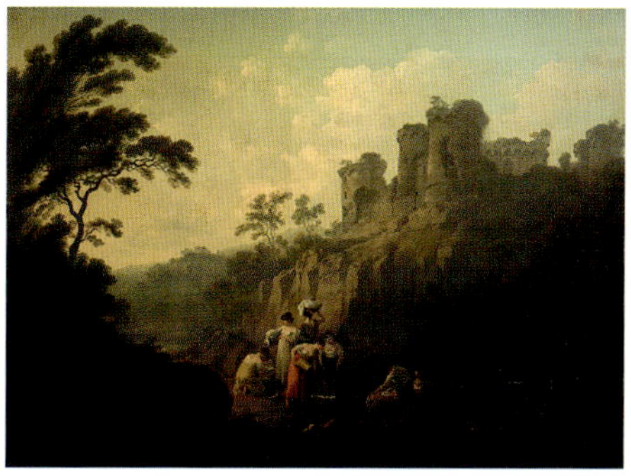

Ibbetson, Julius Caesar 1759–1817
Masham Castle, North Yorkshire 1811
oil on canvas 47 x 63
L.F7.1882.0.0

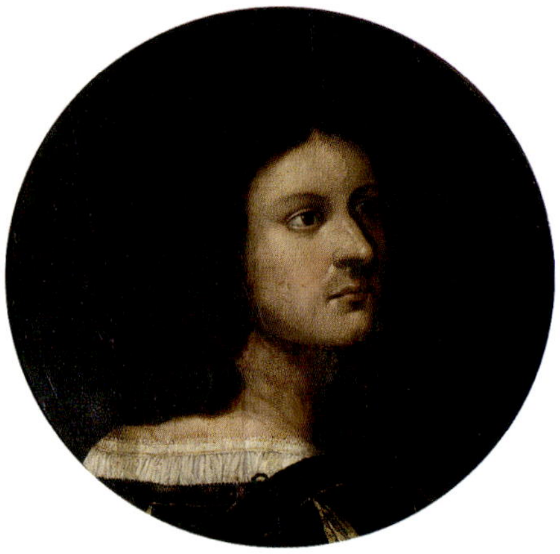

Italian School 19th C
Andrea del Sarto (1486–1530)
oil on panel 48
L.F14.1935.0.0

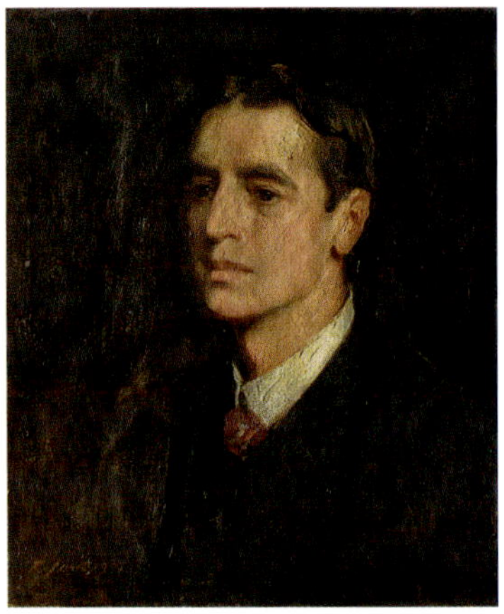

Jack, Richard 1866–1952
Colin McAlpin (1870–1942) 1907
oil on canvas 58.4 x 48.3
L.F65.1968.0.0

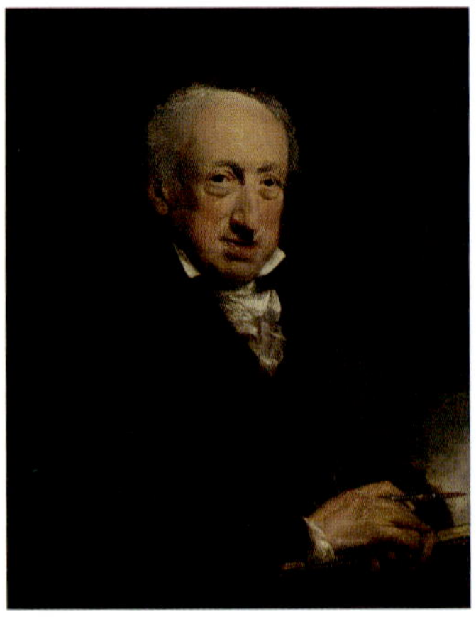

Jackson, John 1778–1831
George Dance (1741–1825)
oil on canvas 76.2 x 63.5
L.F35.1948.0.0

Jacquemon, Pierre 1936–2002
Triptych 1962
oil on panel 71 x 30.5; 71 x 84; 71 x 30.5
L.F11.1963.0.0

Jessel, Jeremy George b.1939
Winter of '47 1972
oil on canvas 178.5 x 305
L.F499.1975.0.0

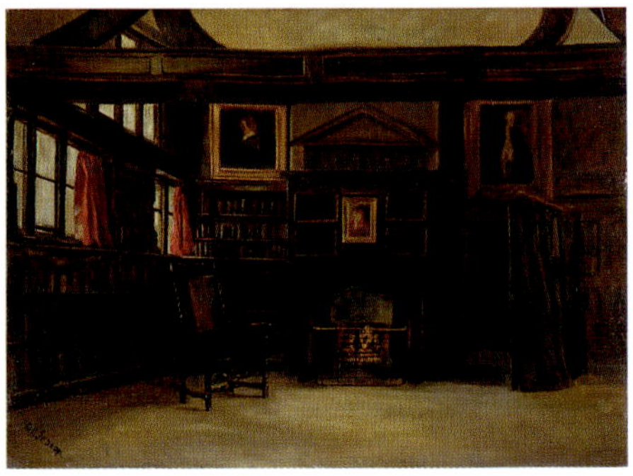

Jessop, D. E.
South End of the Library in the Guildhall, Leicester
oil on canvas 29.2 x 39.4
L.F626.1951.0.0

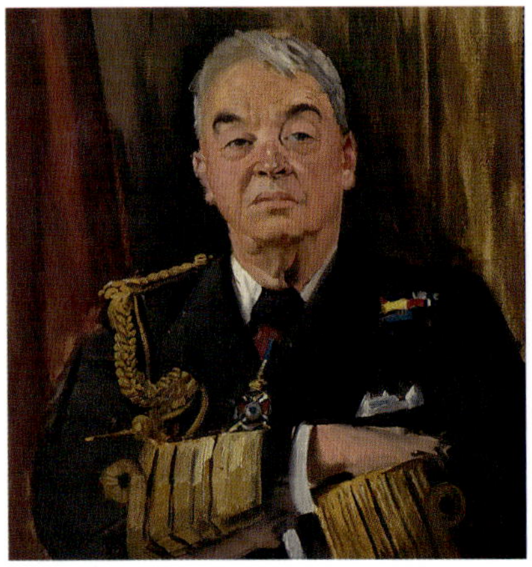

John, Augustus Edwin 1878–1961
Admiral Lord Fisher of Kilverstone (1841–1920), GCB, OM, GCVO, First Sea Lord (1905–1910) 1916
oil on canvas 76.3 x 71.1
L.F1.1920.0.0

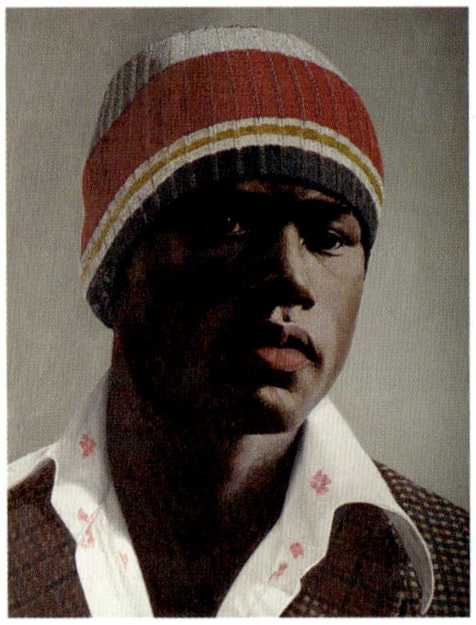

Johnson, Frank 1917–1998
Paul Oxford
oil on board 91.5 x 71
Y.F6.2007.0.0

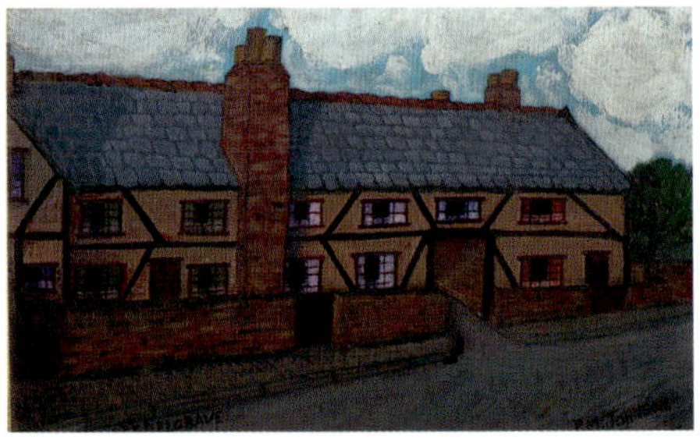

Johnson, P. M. b.1916
Old Belgrave, Leicester 1970
oil on board 23 x 37
Y. F25.2009.0.0

Facing page: Spencer, Stanley, 1891–1959, *Adoration of Old Men* (detail), 1937, Leicester Arts and Museums Service (p. 85)

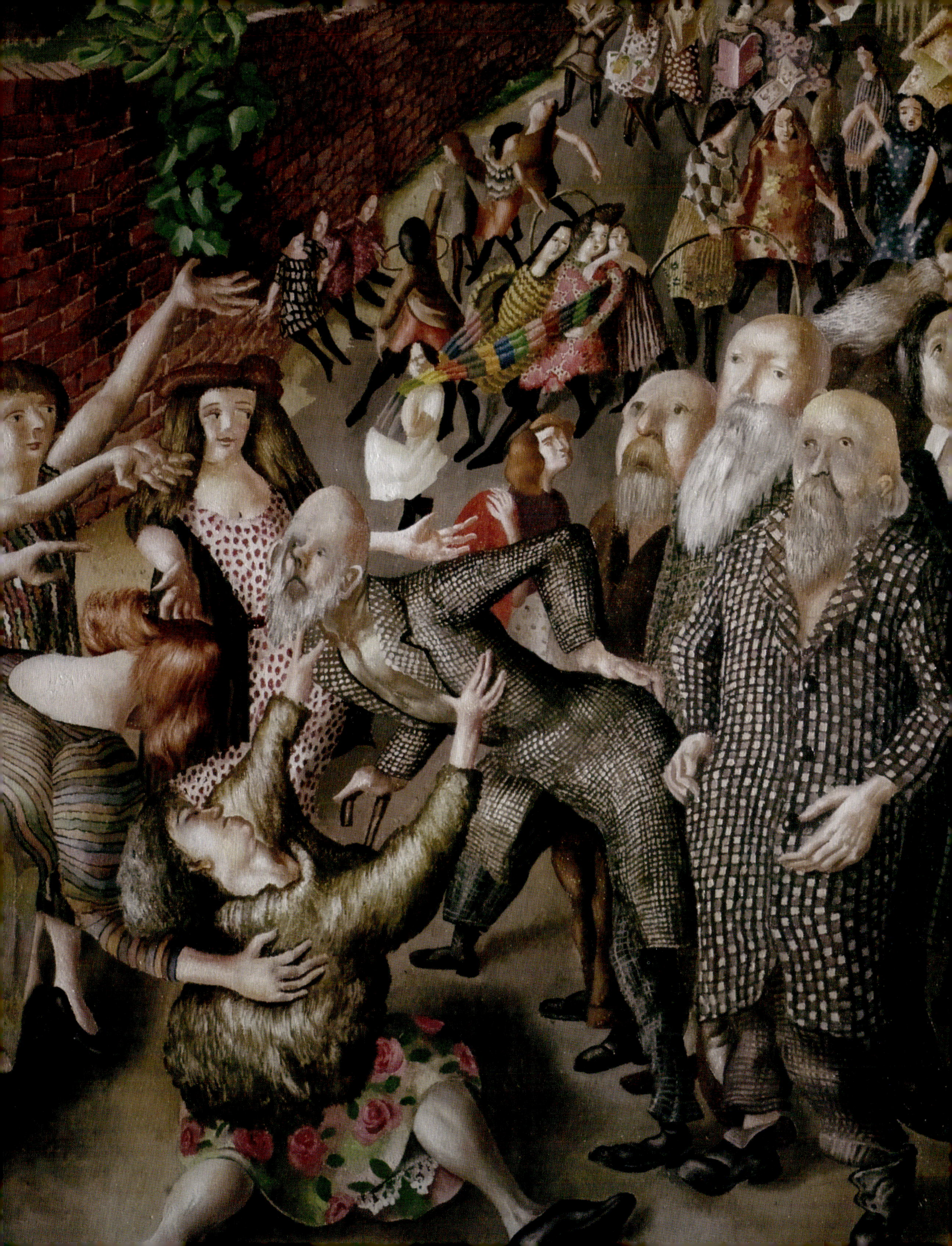

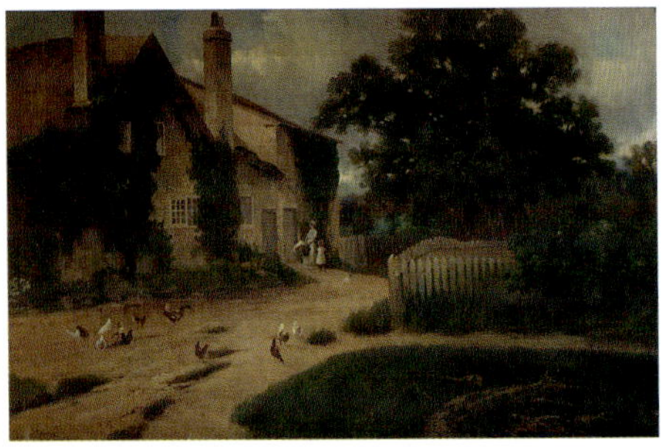

Keene, Ezra Elmer 1853–1929
Old Evington Village, Leicester, c.1900
oil on canvas 61 x 91.4
Y.F5.2009.0.0

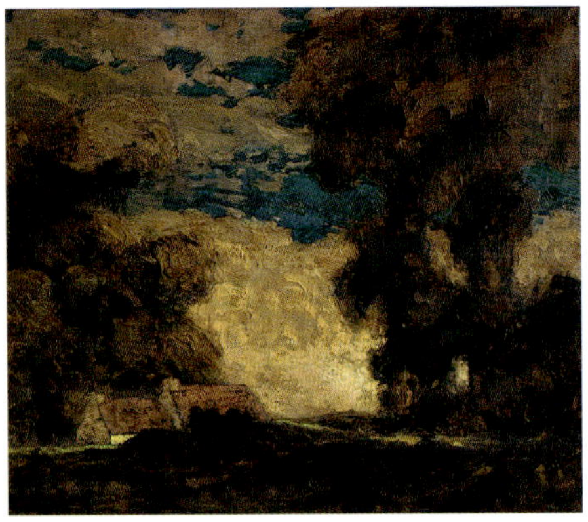

Kiddier, William 1859–1934
The Cottage
oil on canvas 109.5 x 122
L.F15.1933.0.0

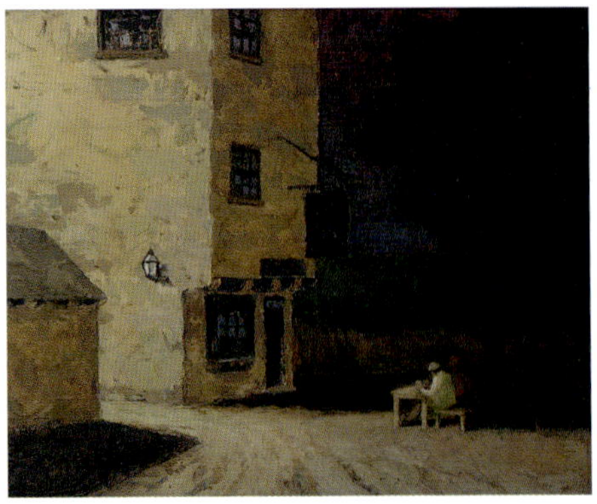

Kiddier, William 1859–1934
The Inn
oil on canvas 61 x 73.5
L.F1.1934.0.0

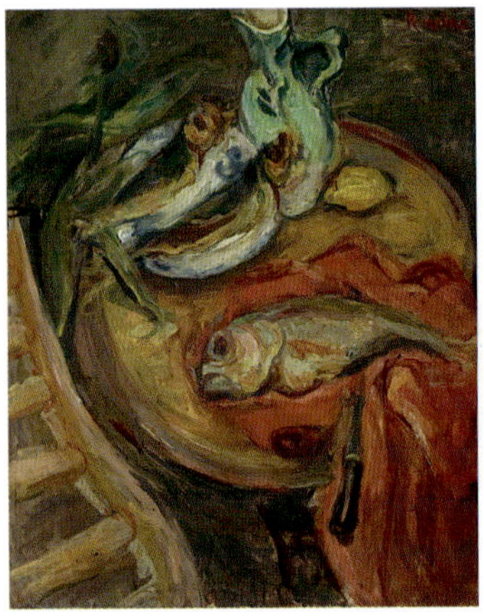

Kikoine, Michel 1892–1968
Still Life with Fish before 1925
oil on canvas 73 x 60
L.F86.1963.0.0

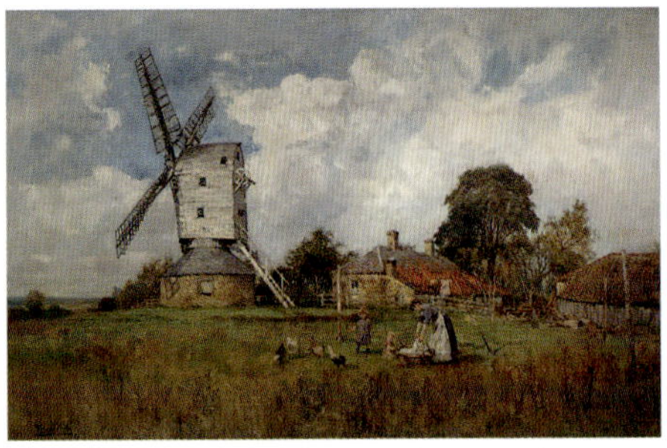

King, Henry John Yeend 1855–1924
Landscape with a Windmill
oil on canvas 120 x 180
L.F24.1987.0.0

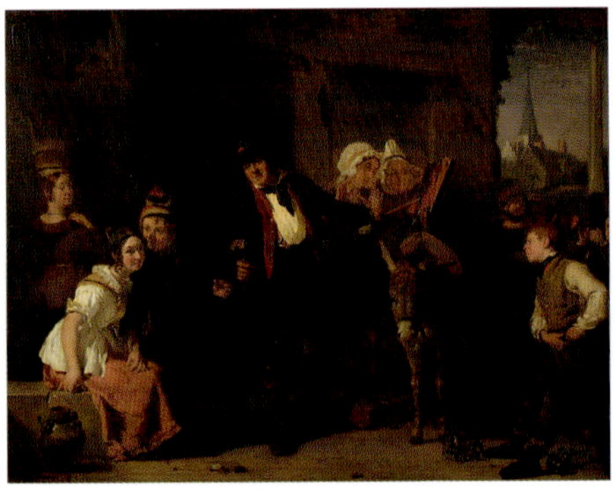

Knight, John Prescott 1803–1881
The Merry Pedlar
oil on panel 70.5 x 91.5
L.F2.1891.0.0

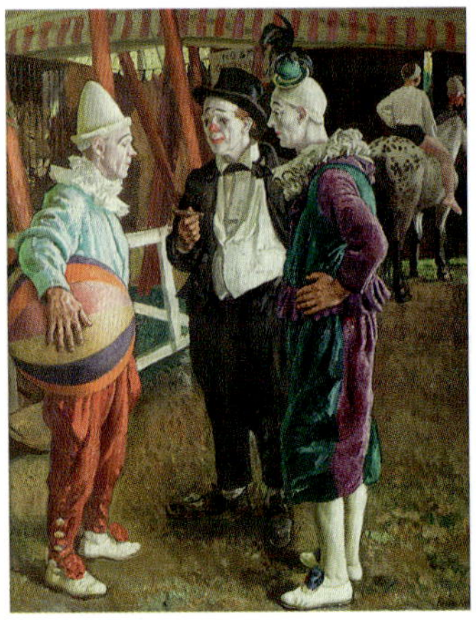

Knight, Laura 1877–1970
The Three Clowns
oil on canvas 77 x 63.5
L.F7.1934.0.0

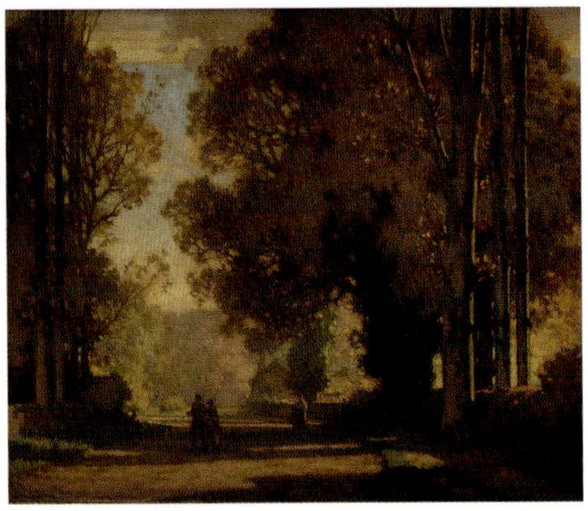

Knight, William 1872–1958
Autumn Afternoon
oil on canvas 85.5 x 100.5
Y.F22.2009.0.0

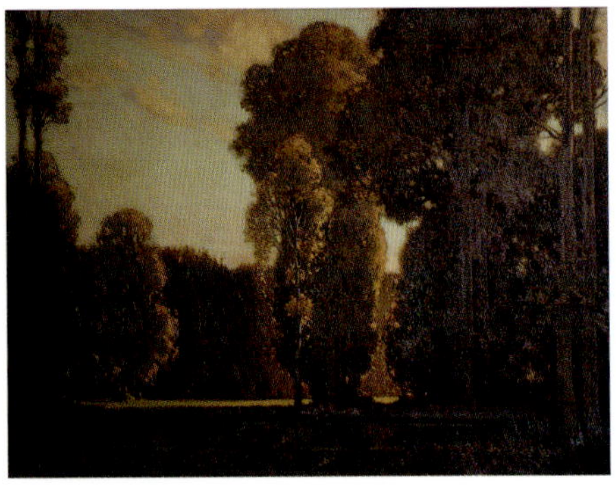

Knight, William 1872–1958
Autumn Evening
oil on canvas 71 x 90.2
L.F17.1925.0.0

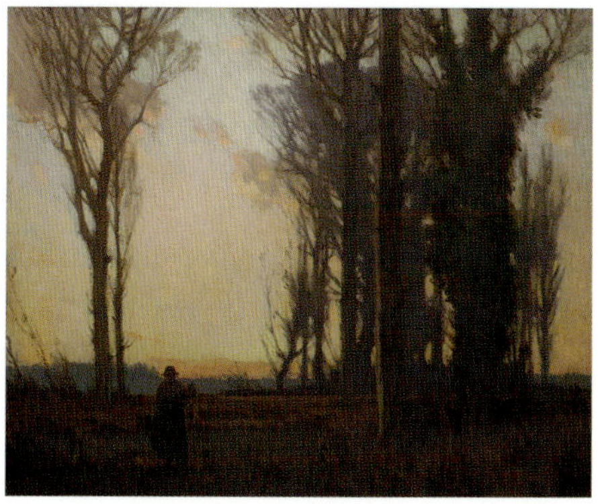

Knight, William 1872–1958
Russet and Gold
oil on canvas 49.5 x 60.2
L.F18.1925.0.0

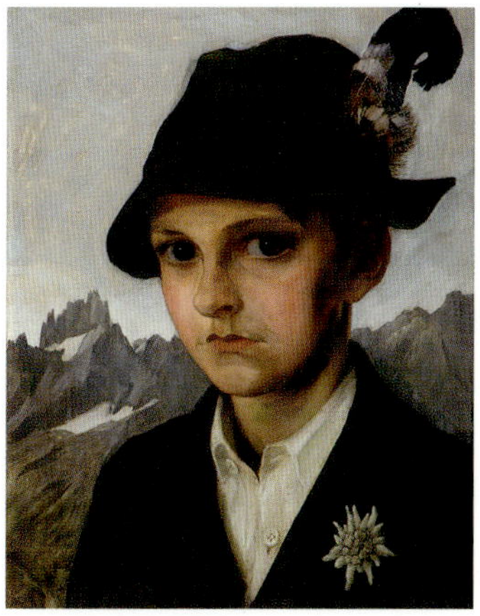

Koelz, Johannes Mattheus 1895–1971
Portrait of the Artist's Son, Siegfried, Aged 12
1935
oil on panel 38.3 x 30
Y.F19.1998.0.0

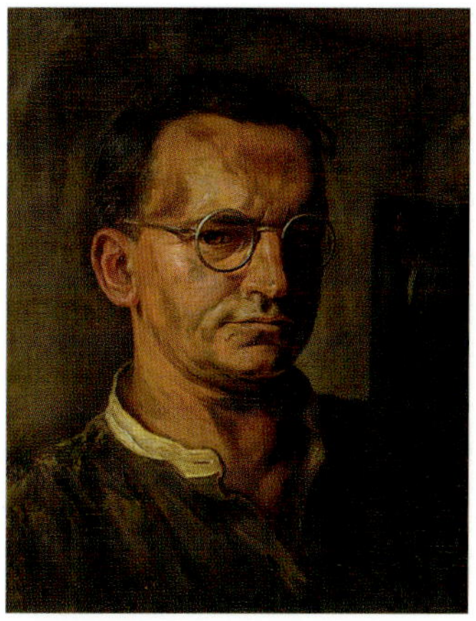

Koelz, Johannes Mattheus 1895–1971
Self Portrait 1943
oil on panel 52.7 x 41.3
Y.F18.1998.0.0

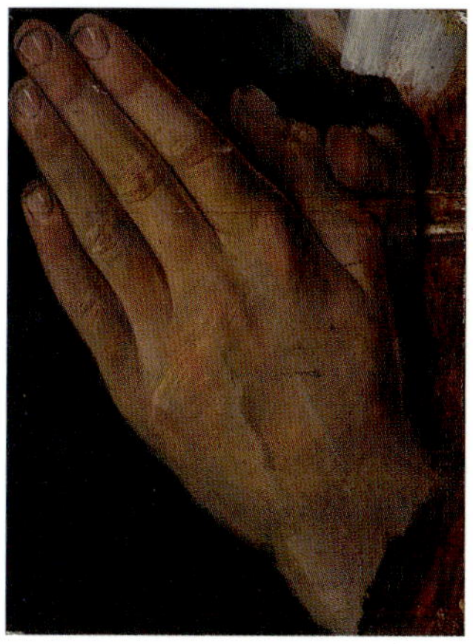

Koelz, Johannes Mattheus 1895–1971
Boy's Praying Hands
oil on panel 16.5 x 12.2
Y.F17.1998.0.0

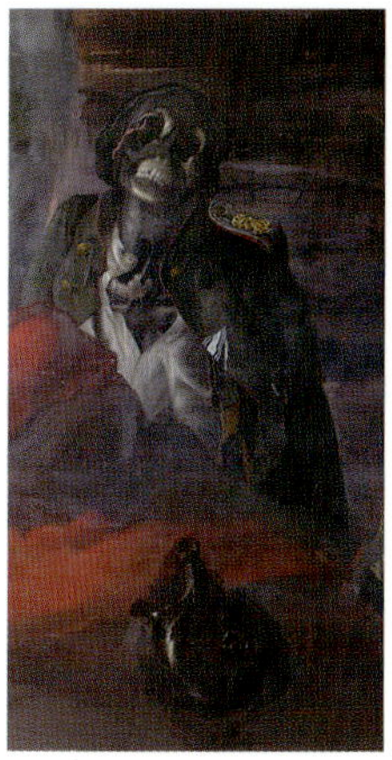

Koelz, Johannes Mattheus 1895–1971
Dead Soldier
oil on panel 133.8 x 68.5
Y.F15.1998.0.0

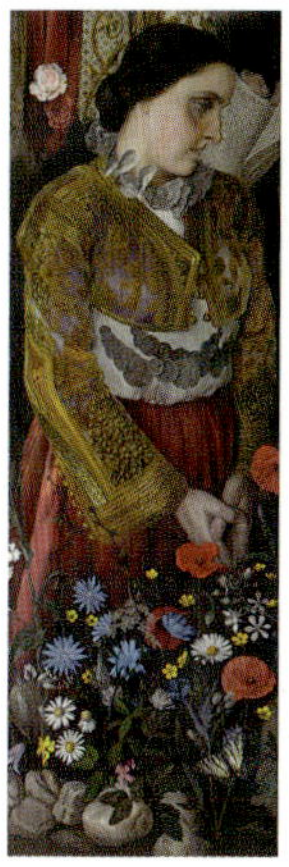

Koelz, Johannes Mattheus 1895–1971
Girl in National Costume
oil on panel 144.3 x 46.7
Y.F16.1998.0.0

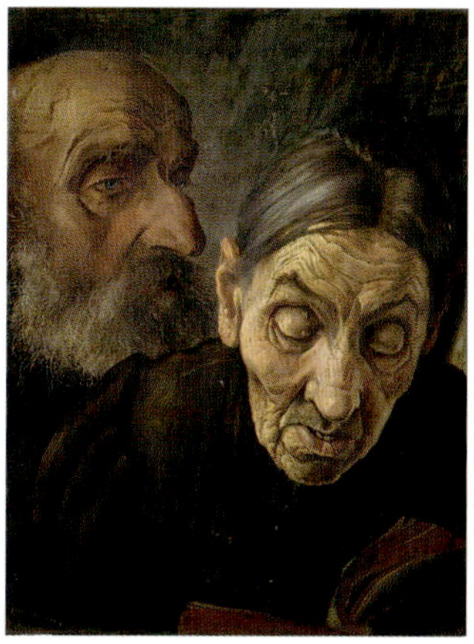

Koelz, Johannes Mattheus 1895–1971
Heads of Two Old People
oil on panel 48.3 x 35.8
Y.F14.1998.0.0

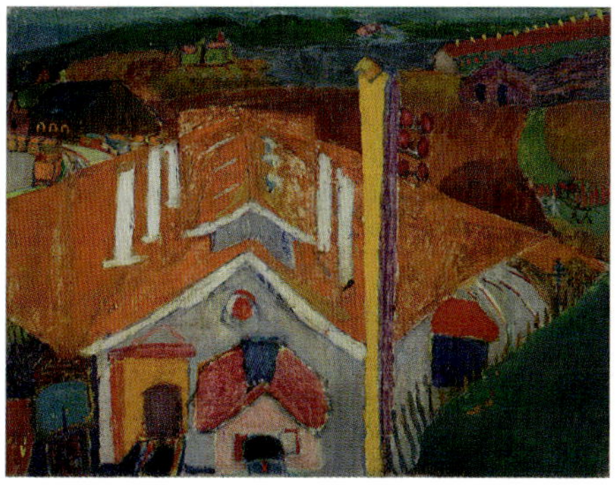

Koppel, Heinz 1919–1980
The Engine Shed, Dowlais (recto) 1951
oil on paper 58.5 x 76.5
L.F2.1989.0.0

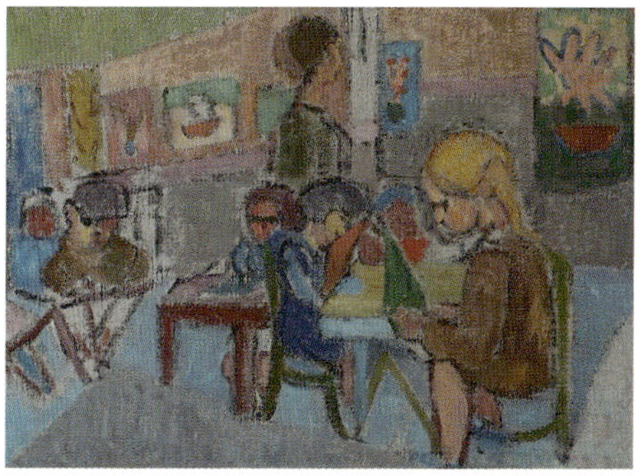

Koppel, Heinz 1919–1980
Classroom (verso) 1951
oil on paper 58.5 x 76.5 (E)
L.F2.1989.0.0B

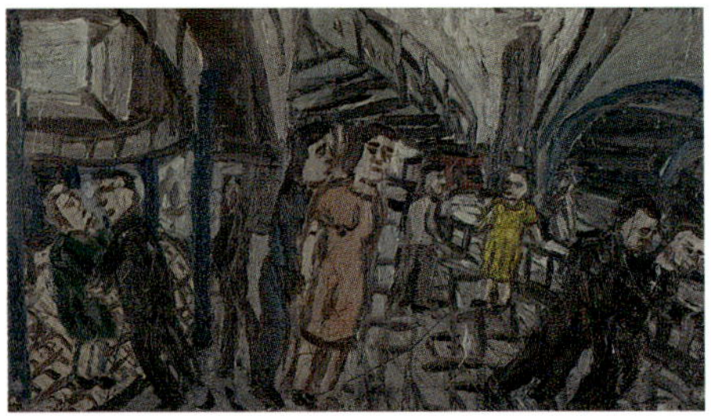

Kossoff, Leon b.1926
Outside Kilburn Underground, Summer 1976
1976
oil on board 107.5 x 184
L.F6.1981.0.0

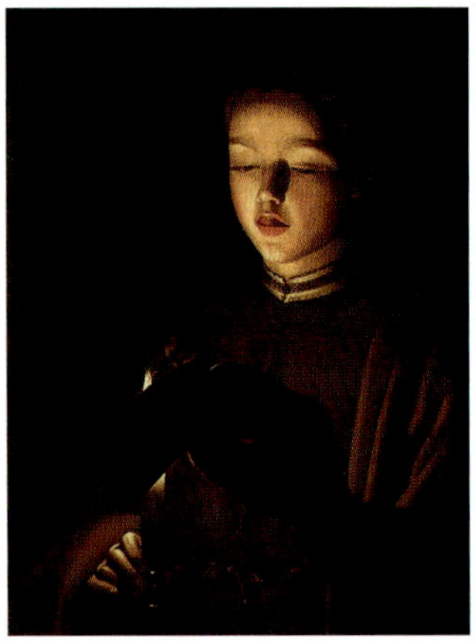

La Tour, Georges de 1593–1652
The Choirboy c.1645
oil on canvas 66.7 x 50.2
L.F19.1983.0.0

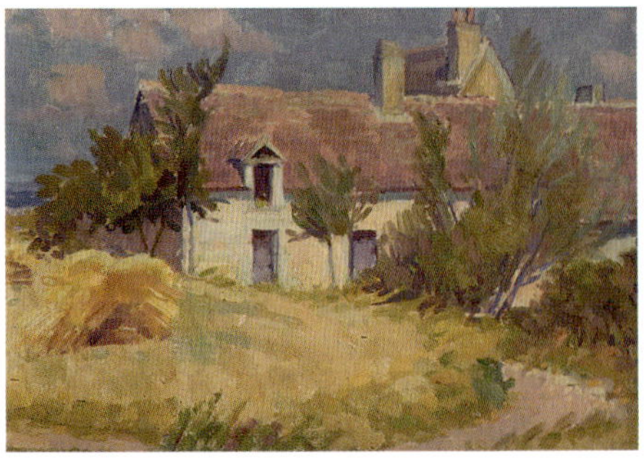

Lamb, Henry 1883–1960
A French Farm
oil on board 26.5 x 35.5
L.F445.1980.0.0 (P)

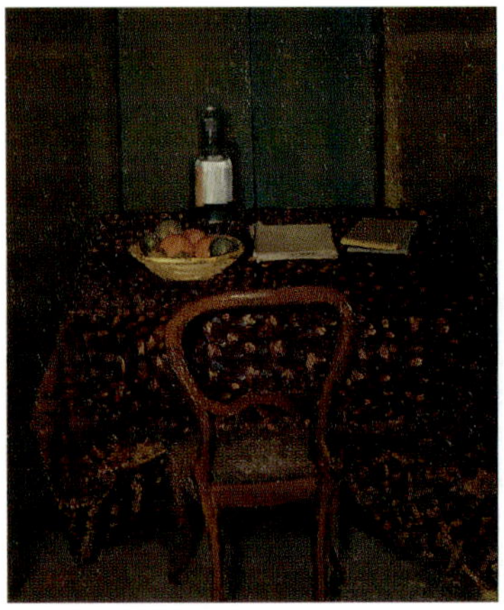

Lamb, Lynton Harold 1907–1977
The Victorian Chair
oil on canvas 60.8 x 50.6
L.F181.1981.0.0

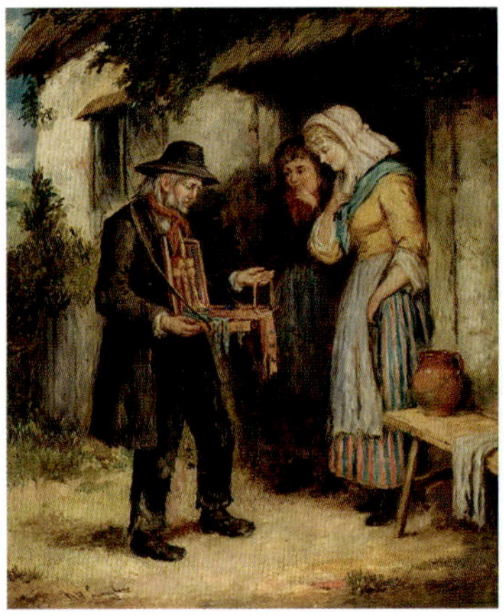

Langlois, Mark William 1848–1924
The Tinker
oil on canvas 53 x 43
L.F44.1990.0.0

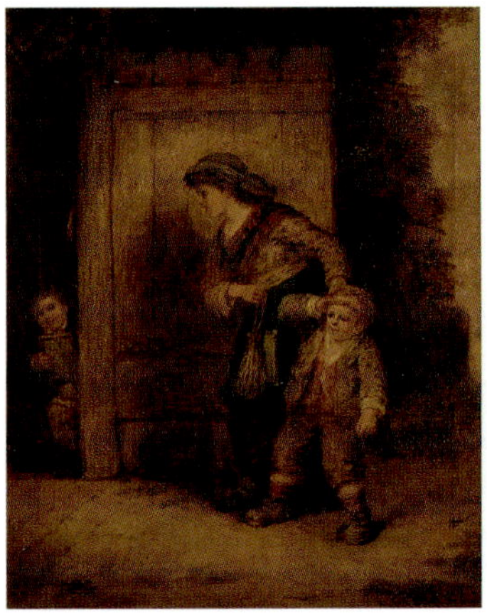

Langlois, Mark William 1848–1924
Unwilling to School
oil on canvas 53 x 43
L.F45.1990.0.0

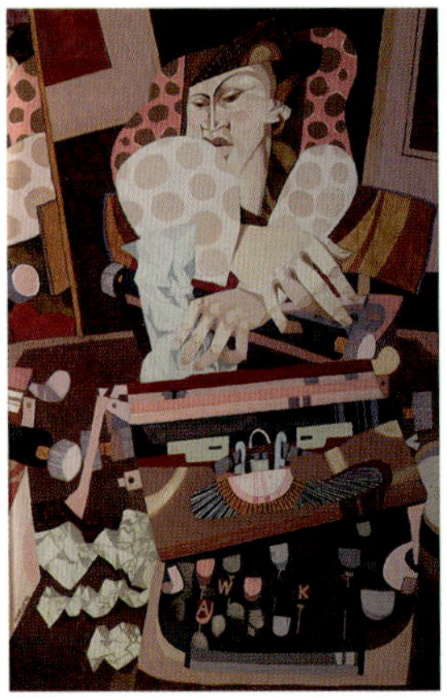

Large, George b.1936
Typist 1993
oil on canvas 91.2 x 61
Y.F6.2005.0.0

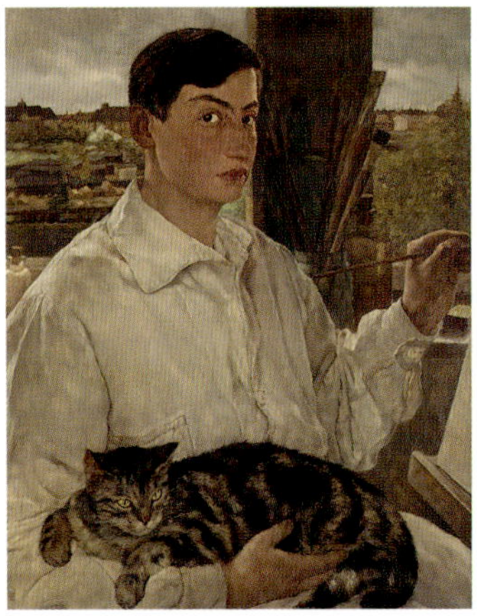

Laserstein, Lotte 1898–1993
Self Portrait with a Cat 1928
oil on panel 61 x 51
L.F3.1988.0.0

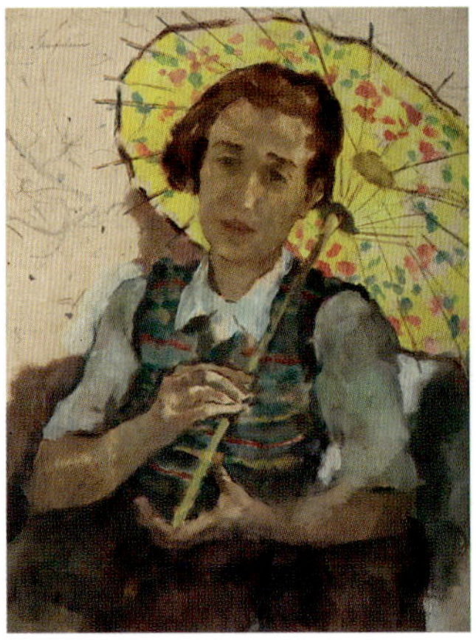

Laserstein, Lotte 1898–1993
The Yellow Parasol 1935
oil on paper 58 x 44
L.F4.1988.0.0

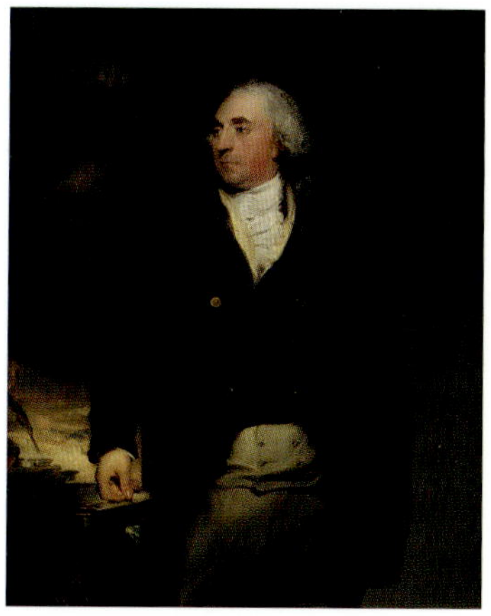

Lawrence, Thomas 1769–1830
William Brabazon (1744–1806), 1st Baron Ponsonby 1805
oil on canvas 122.5 x 100
L.F296.1973.0.0

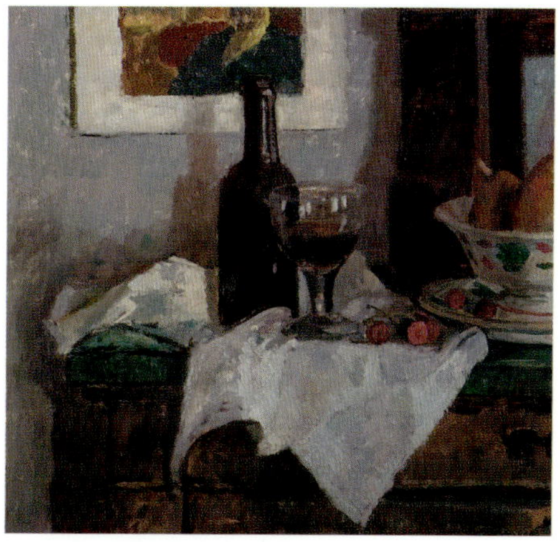

Le Bas, Edward 1904–1966
Still Life with a Wine Bottle and a Glass
oil on canvas 46.6 x 55.5
L.F2.1944.0.0

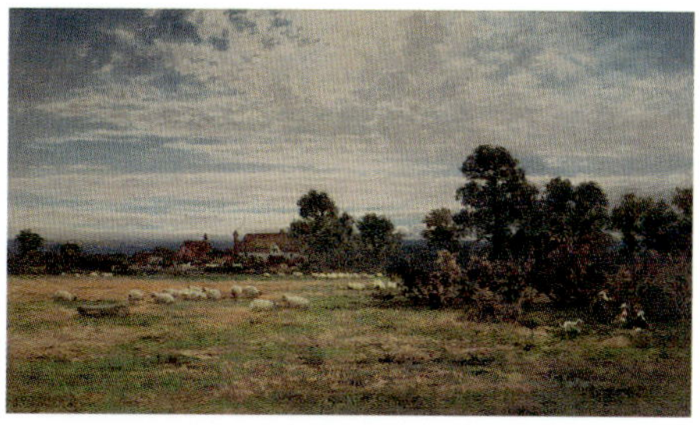

Leader, Benjamin Williams 1831–1923
A Surrey Meadow 1902
oil on canvas 45.8 x 76.5
L.F17.1936.0.0

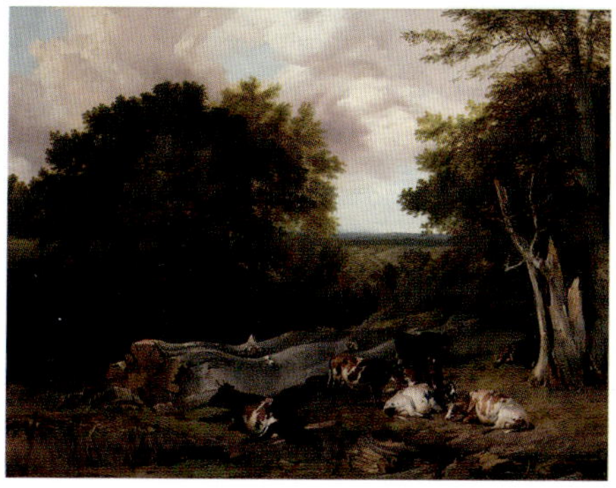

Lee, Frederick Richard 1798–1879 & **Cooper, Thomas Sidney** 1803–1902
Cattle in a Landscape
oil on canvas 101.5 x 127.5
L.F10.1943.0.0

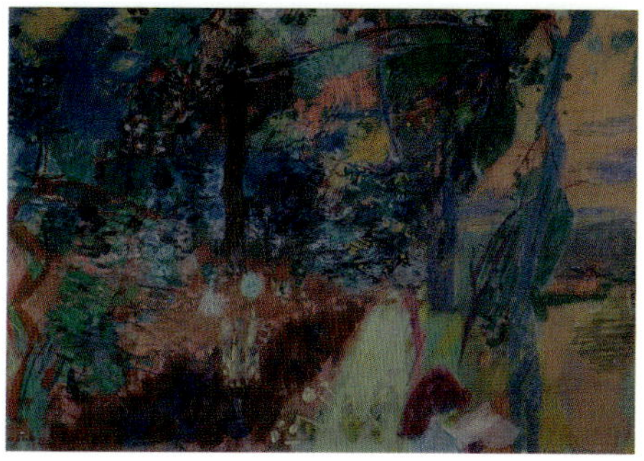

Legueult, Raymond Jean 1898–1971
Le bocage 1948
oil on canvas 66 x 91.5
L.F27.1956.0.0

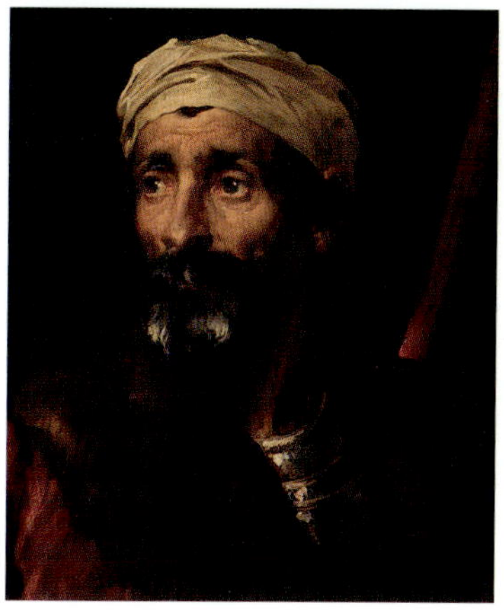

Leighton, Frederic 1830–1896
Head of an Arab 1857
oil on canvas 46.1 x 38.2
L.F15.1941.1.0

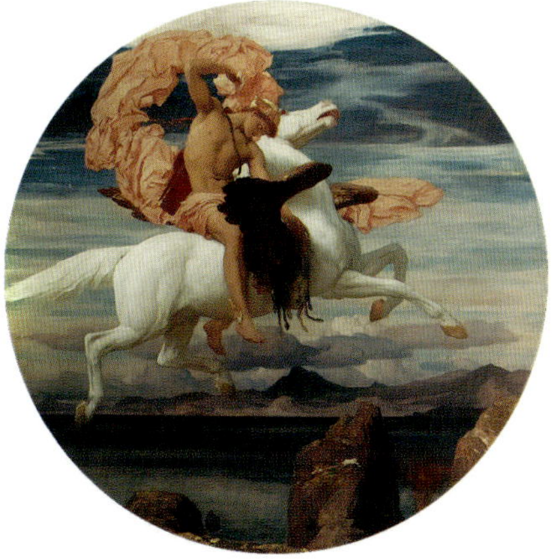

Leighton, Frederic 1830–1896
Perseus, on Pegasus, Hastening to the Rescue of Andromeda c.1896
oil on canvas 18.4
L.F6.1902.0.0

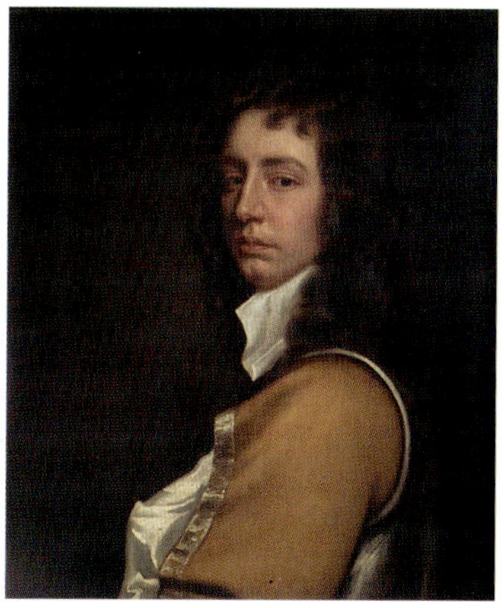

Lely, Peter 1618–1680
Sir Thomas Lee (1635–1691), 1st Bt 1655
oil on canvas 73.1 x 60.3
L.F92.1938.0.0

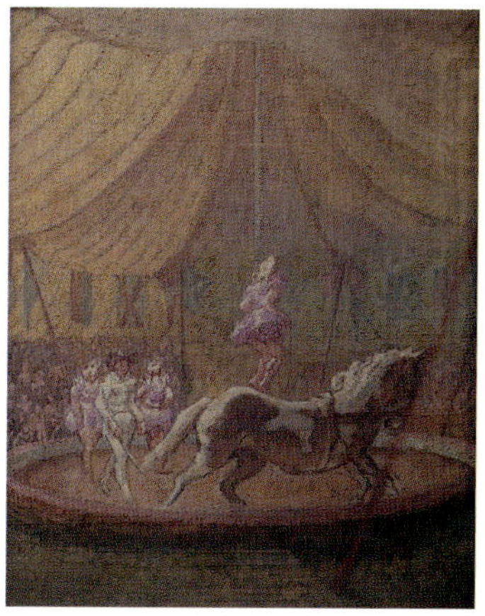

Lessore, Thérèse 1884–1945
Circus at Bath
oil on canvas 88 x 68
L.F21.1947.0.0

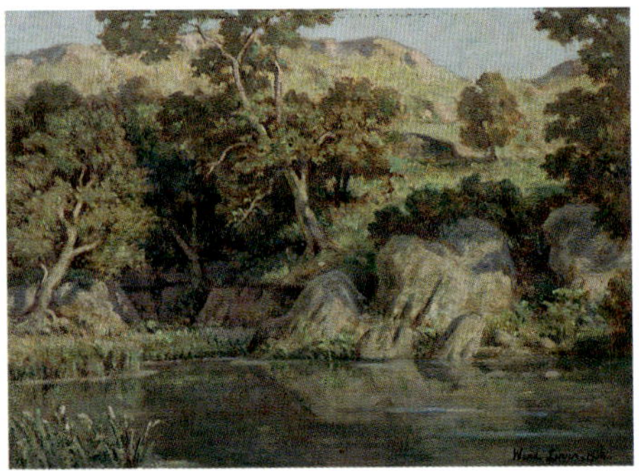

Lever, Ward active 1920–1959
Tarn 1954
oil on board 29.5 x 39.5
L.F3.1996.9.0

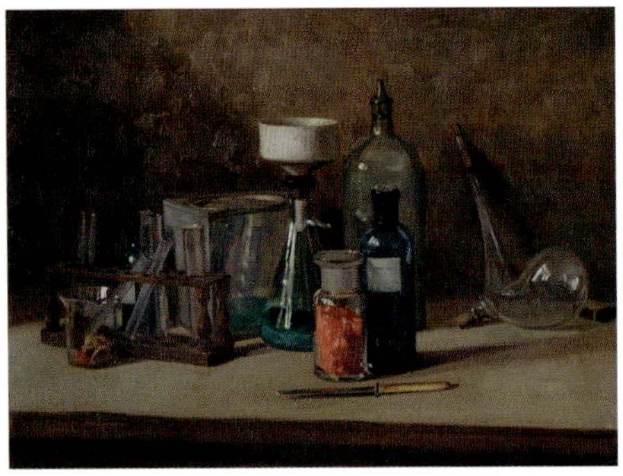

Lewis, Kathleen Edith 1907–2003
Bottles
oil on canvas 45.8 x 61.3
Y.F3.2007.3.0

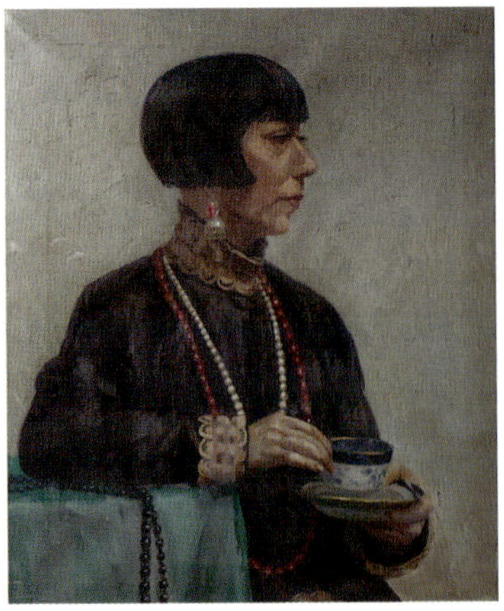

Lewis, Kathleen Edith 1907–2003
Chinese Lady
oil on canvas 61 x 51
Y.F3.2007.2.0

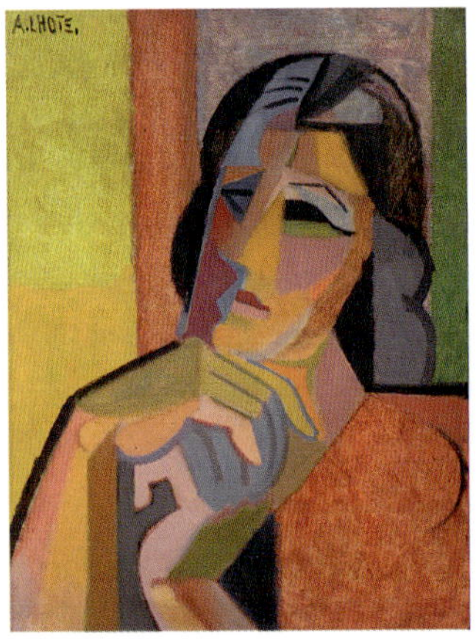

Lhote, André 1885–1962
Bust of a Young Woman 1910
oil on canvas 65.2 x 48
L.F23.1971.0.0

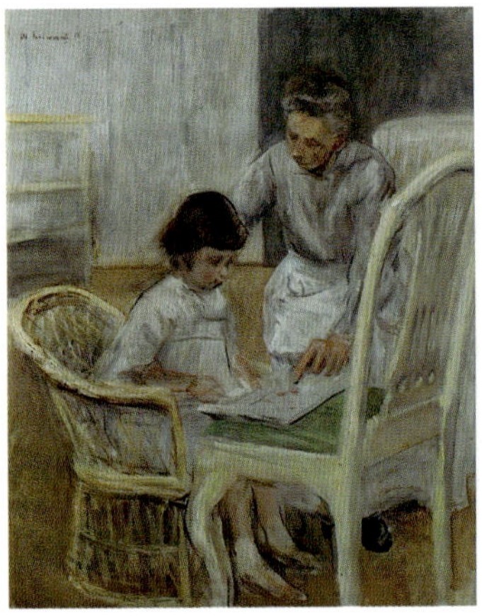

Liebermann, Max 1847–1935
Die Enkelin des Künstlers mit ihrem Kindermädchen 1919
oil on canvas 52 x 41
L.F958.1974.0.0

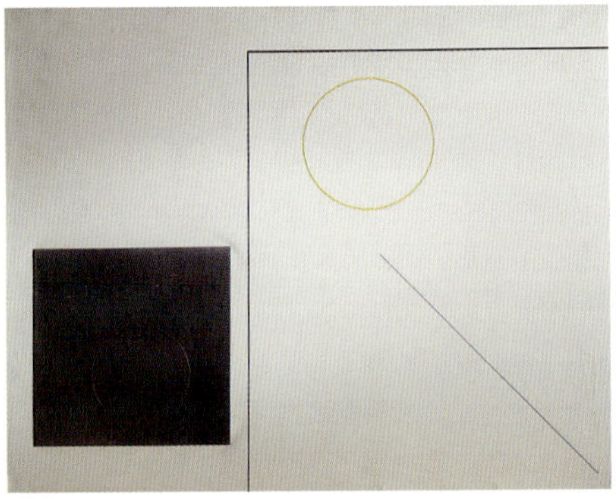

Lin, Richard b.1933
Painting, Relief with Aluminium Square 1960
oil on canvas 101.5 x 127
L.F1.1961.0.0

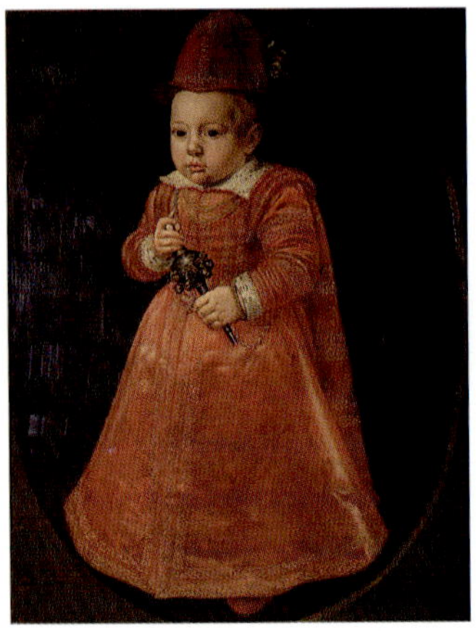

Linde, Adriaen van der (attributed to)
c.1560–1609
Portrait of a Child with a Rattle
oil on canvas 68.5 x 52.5
L.F41.1944.0.0

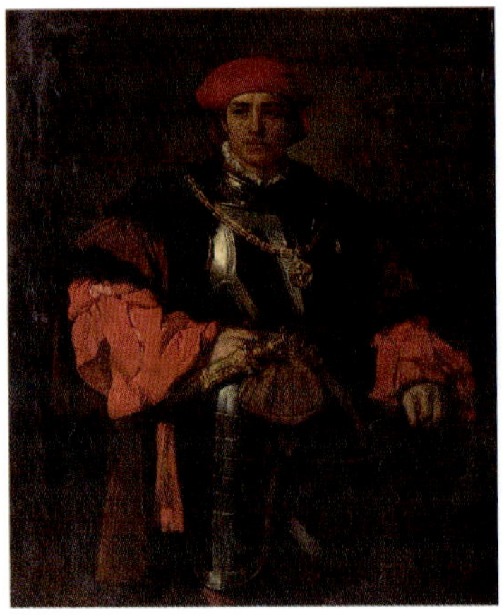

Linton, James Dromgole 1840–1916
Valentine
oil on canvas 61 x 51
L.F3.1882.0.0

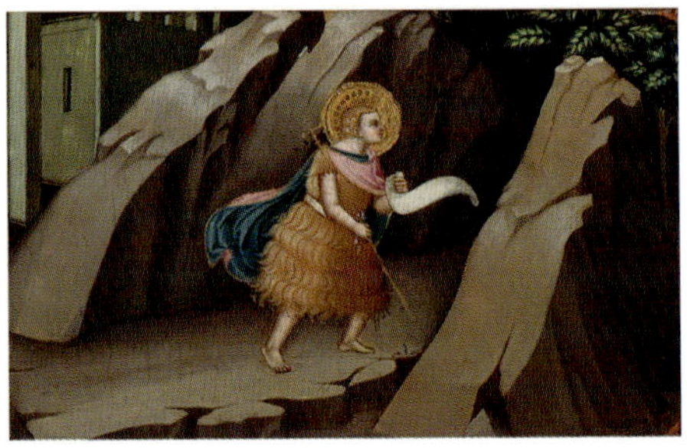

Monaco, Lorenzo c.1370–1425
Saint John the Baptist Entering the Wilderness
c.1400
tempera on wood 23 x 34
L.F33.1959.0.0

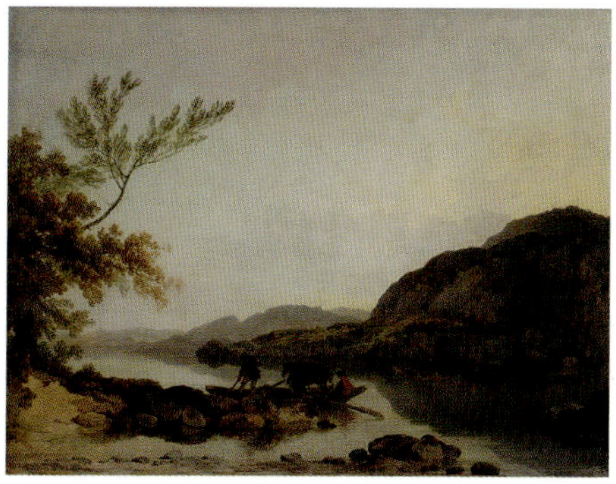

Loutherbourg, Philip James de 1740–1812
A River Scene with a Ferry 1785–1786
oil on canvas 58.5 x 76.2
L.F4.1882.0.0

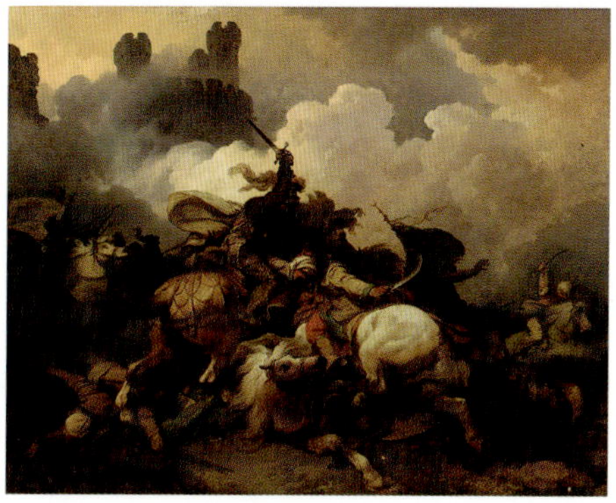

Loutherbourg, Philip James de 1740–1812
The Battle between Richard Coeur de Lion and Saladin in Palestine c.1807
oil on canvas 152 x 184
L.F755.1977.0.0

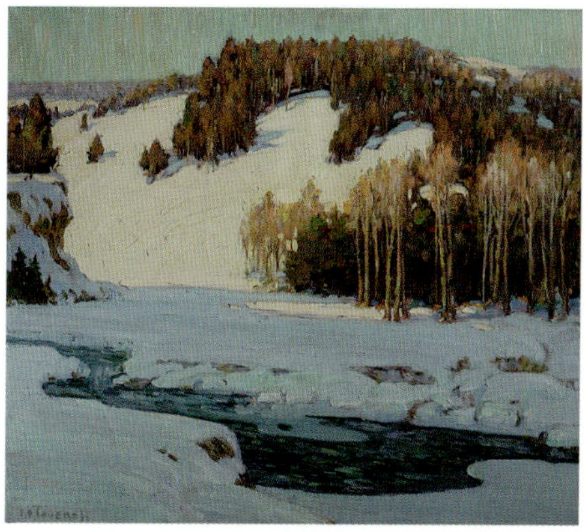

Loveroff, Frederick Nicholas 1894–1960
Snow on the Hillside 1924
oil on canvas 86.4 x 95.3
L.F1.1925.0.0

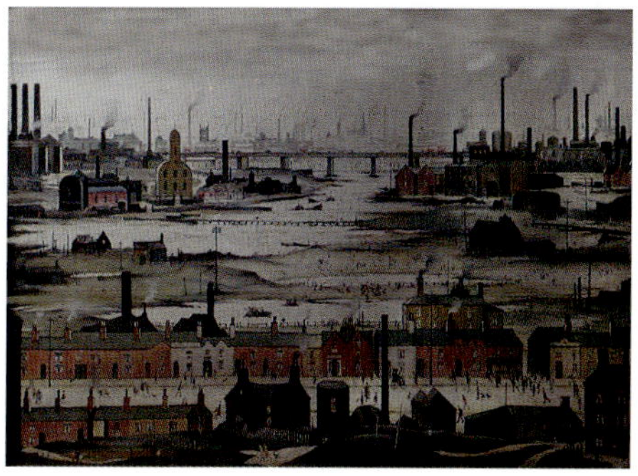

Lowry, Laurence Stephen 1887–1976
Industrial Landscape, River Scene 1950
oil on canvas 110.2 x 148.3
L.F20.1952.0.0

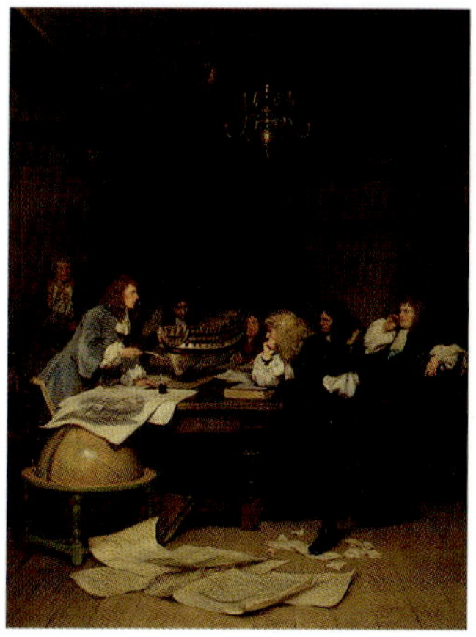

Lucas, Seymour 1849–1923
A Whip for Van Tromp, the Admiralty 1883
oil on canvas 163.8 x 121.3
L.F5.1892.0.0

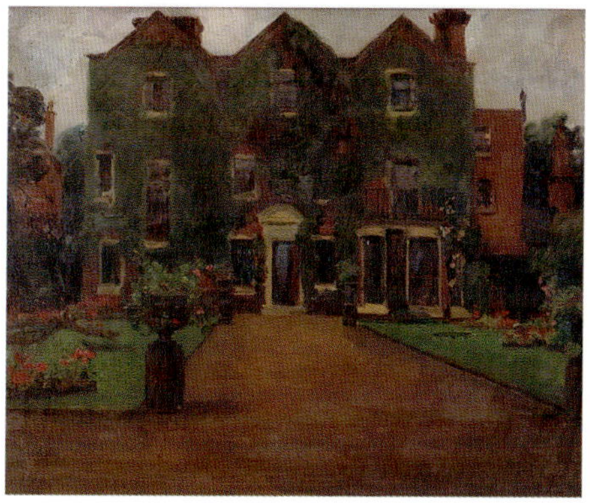

Ludlow, Mary Sophia 1869–1951
Belgrave Hall, Leicestershire
oil on canvas 50 x 60
L.F152.1937.0.0

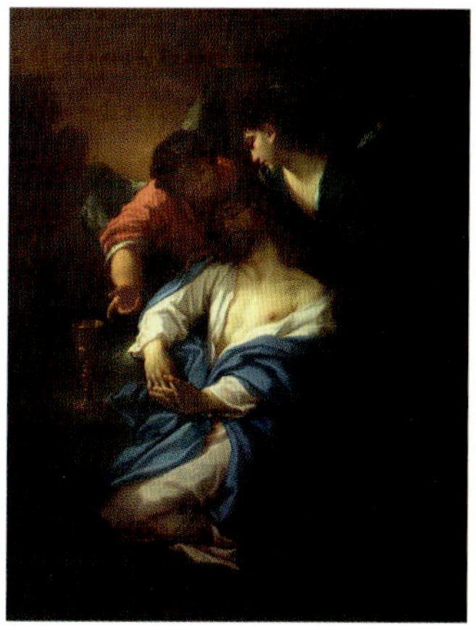

Luti, Benedetto 1666–1724
The Agony in the Garden
oil on canvas 102.5 x 78.5
L.F6.1961.0.0

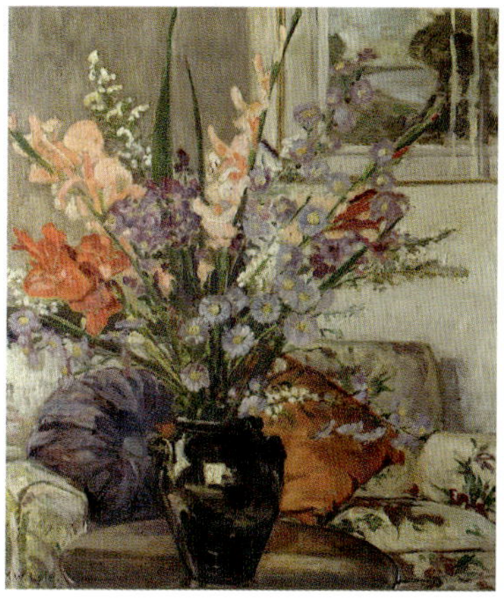

Lyle, M. W.
Flowers and Cushions
oil on canvas 63.5 x 55
L.F3.1996.33.0

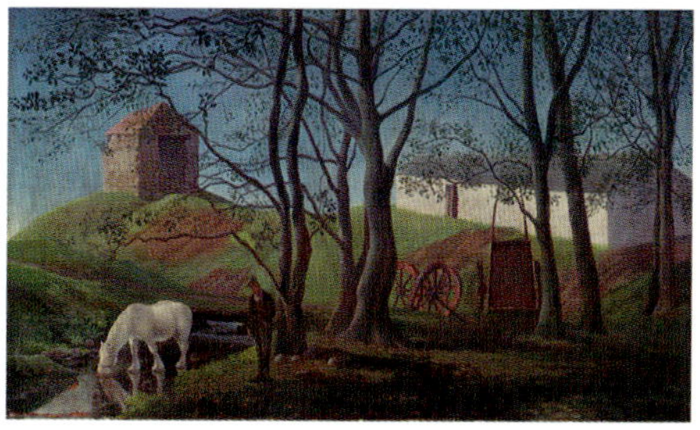

MacKinnon, Sine 1901–1996
A White Horse Drinking from a Stream
oil on canvas 40.5 x 68.3
L.F36.1990.0.0

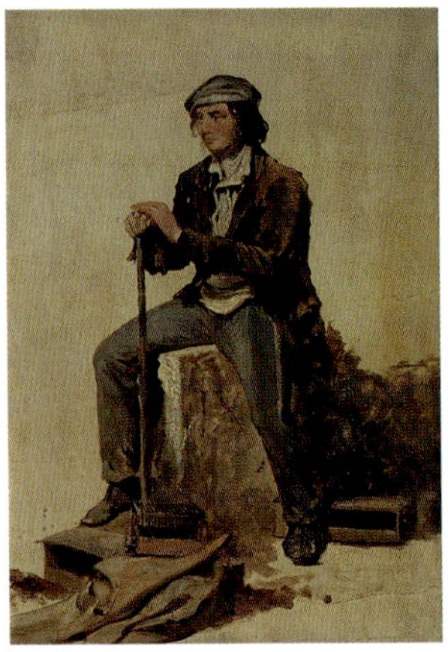

Maclise, Daniel 1806–1870
The Rat Catcher
oil & paper on panel 48.1 x 31.5
L.F15.1939.0.0

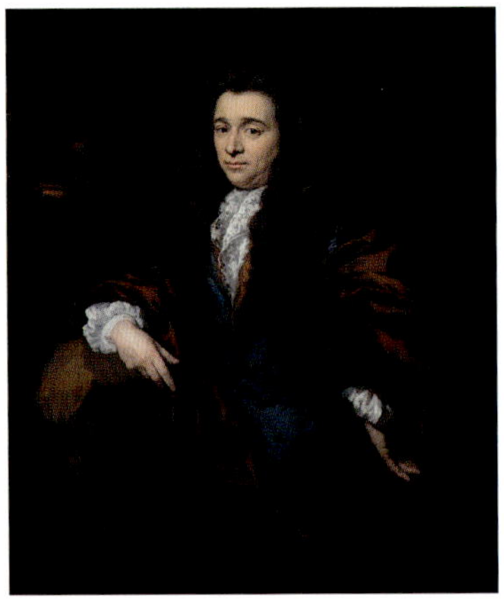

Maes, Nicolaes 1634–1693
Portrait of an Unknown Gentleman 1689
oil on canvas 69.2 x 57.2
L.F14.1941.1.0

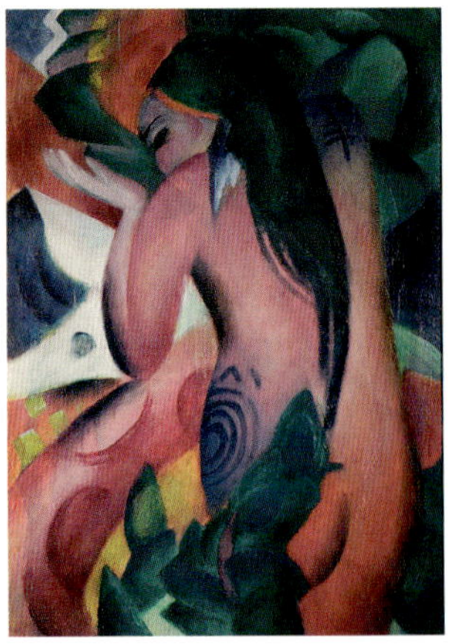

Marc, Franz 1880–1916
Rote Frau 1912
oil on canvas 100.5 x 70
L.F10.1944.0.0

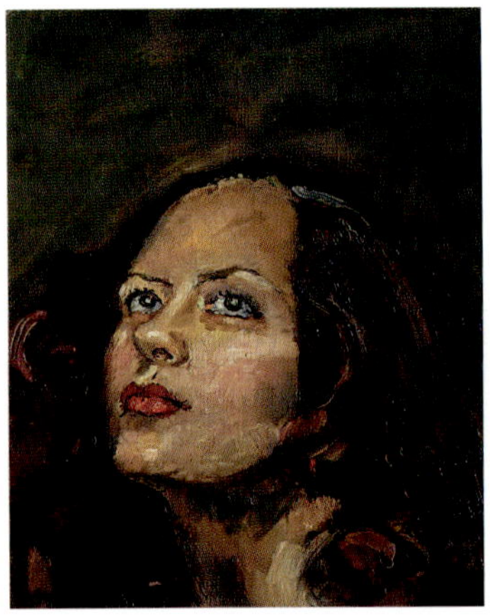

Marinot, Maurice 1882–1960
Femme à la tête levée 1946
oil on canvas 41 x 33
L.F250.1974.3.0

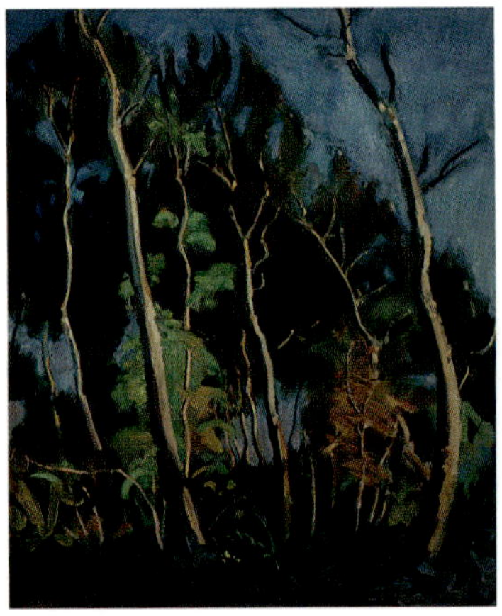

Marinot, Maurice 1882–1960
Paysage aux grands arbres 1947
oil on canvas 73 x 60
L.F250.1974.1.0

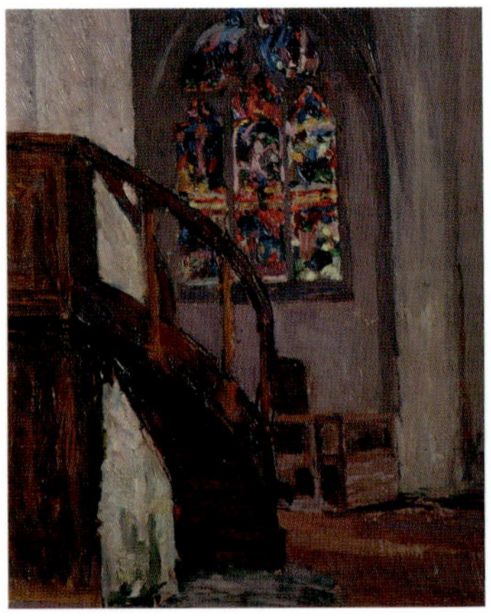

Marinot, Maurice 1882–1960
Intérieur d'église
oil on canvas 40 x 31
L.F250.1974.4.0

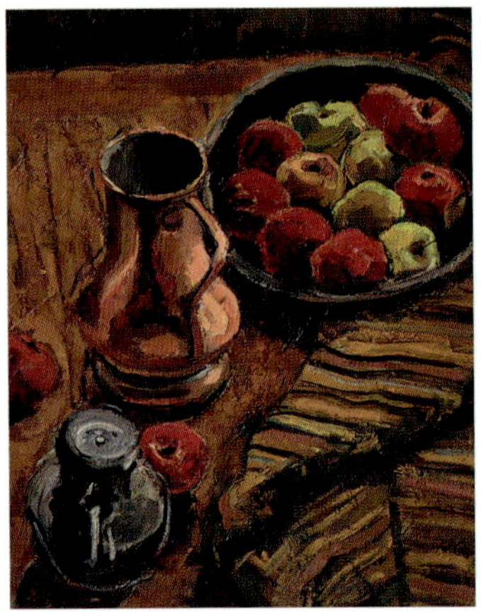

Marinot, Maurice 1882–1960
Nature mort aux pommes
oil on canvas 65 x 50
L.F250.1974.2.0

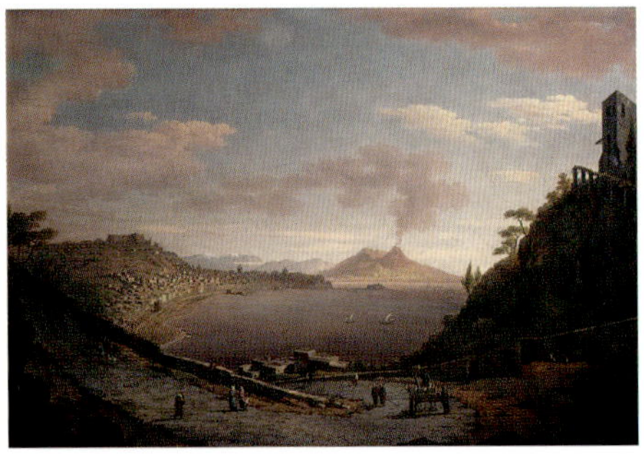

Marlow, William 1740–1813
View of the Bay of Naples with Vesuvius in the Distance c.1776
oil on canvas 63.5 x 91.3
L.F220.1981.0.0

Marlow, William (attributed to) 1740–1813
Classical Landscape
oil on canvas 59.6 x 45.1
L.F15.1941.2.0

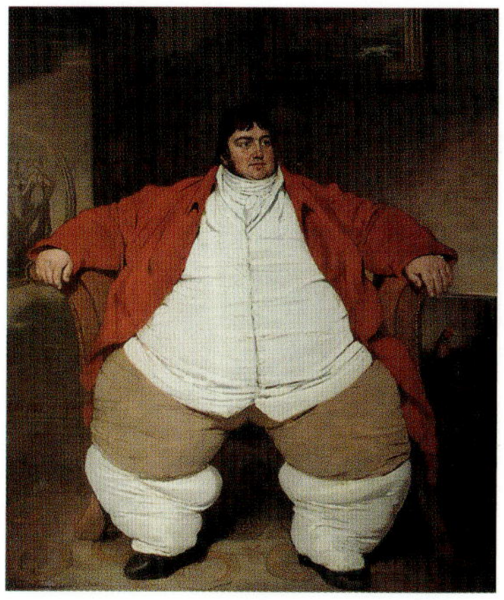

Marshall, Benjamin 1767–1835
Daniel Lambert (1770–1809) 1806
oil on canvas 76.2 x 62.9
L.F12.1919.0.0

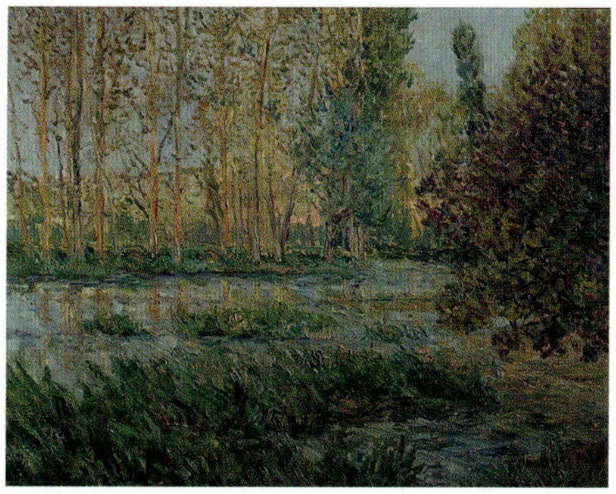

Maufra, Maxime 1861–1918
Bords du Loire 1907
oil on canvas 65.3 x 81.3
L.F10.1946.0.0

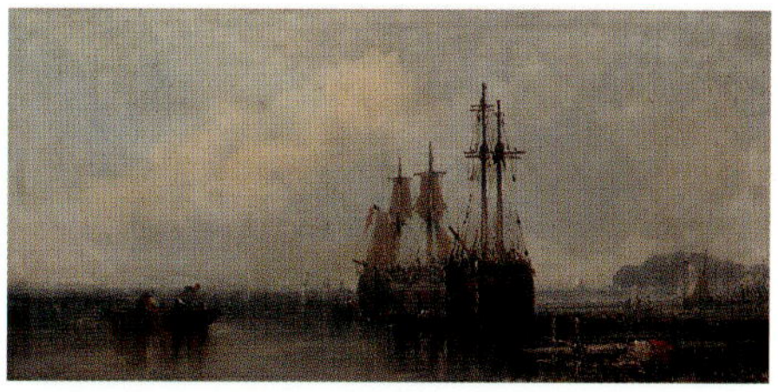

McAlpine William (attributed to) active 1840–1880
Off Sheerness, Kent
oil on canvas 20 x 40.6
L.F5.1900.0.0

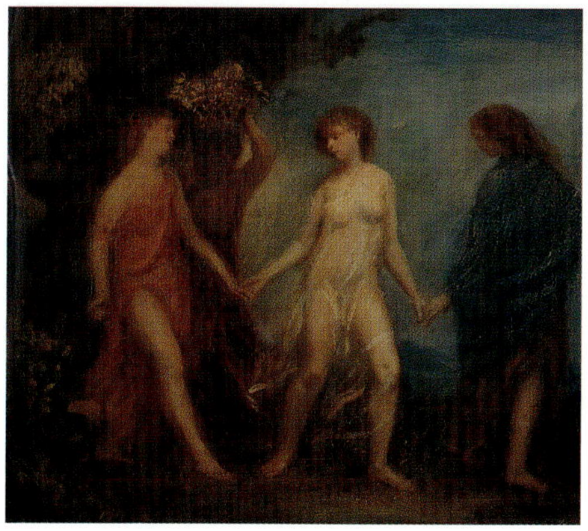

McEvoy, Ambrose 1878–1927
The Seasons c.1904
oil on canvas 43.8 x 50
L.F7.1946.0.0

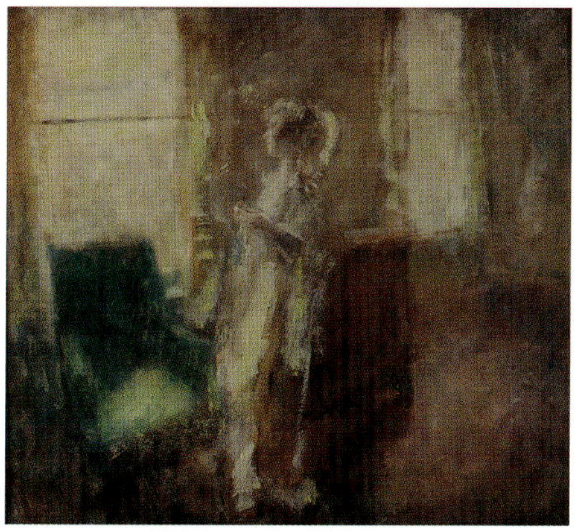

McEvoy, Ambrose 1878–1927
The Artist's Wife in an Interior 1912
oil on canvas 94 x 101.5
L.F9.1970.0.0

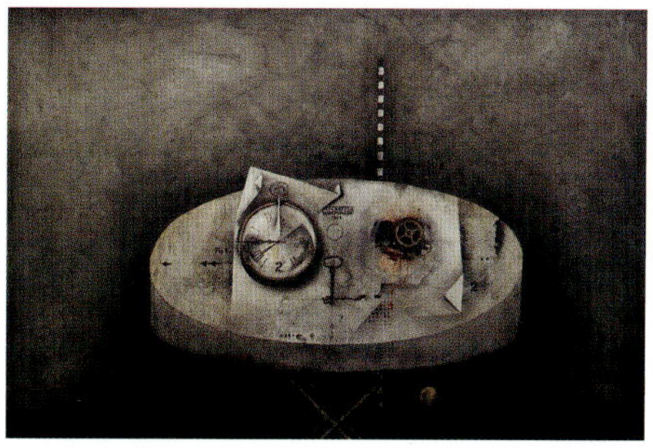

Meckseper, Friedrich b.1936
Magia horographica 1962
oil on board 58.4 x 83.8
L.F49.1963.0.0

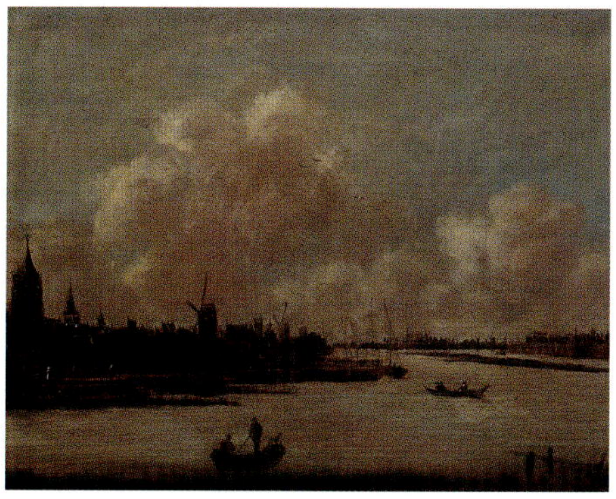

Meerhout, Jan (attributed to) 1633–1677
View of Gorinchem (or Gorkum?), *The Netherlands*
oil on panel 33.5 x 40
L.F24.1937.0.0

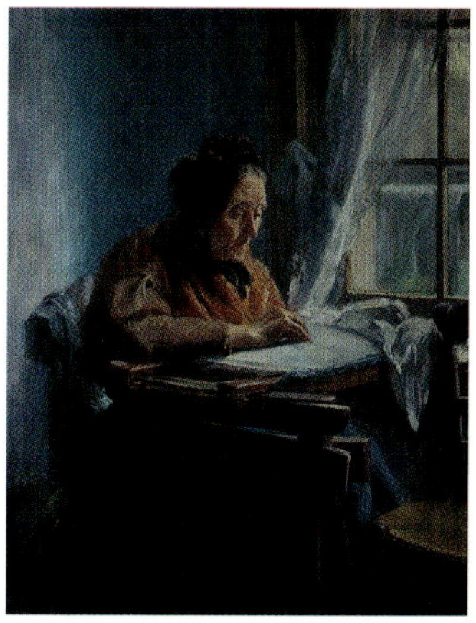

Mees, Jérôme active 1915
A Flemish Lace Embroiderer
oil on canvas 68 x 52.5
L.F1.1915.0.0

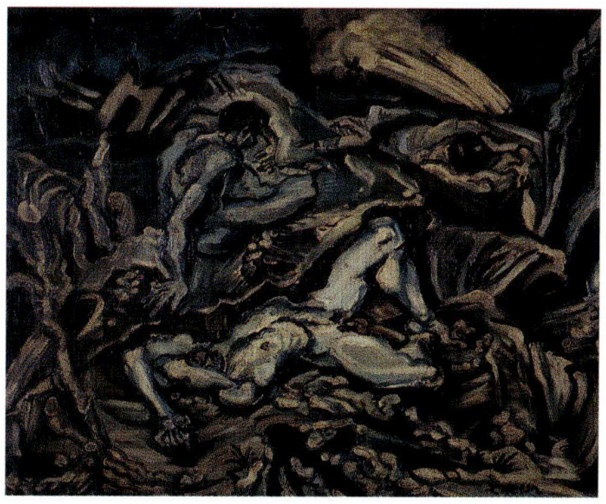

Meidner, Ludwig 1884–1966
Apocalyptic Vision 1912
oil on canvas 72.8 x 88.4
L.F49.1968.0.0

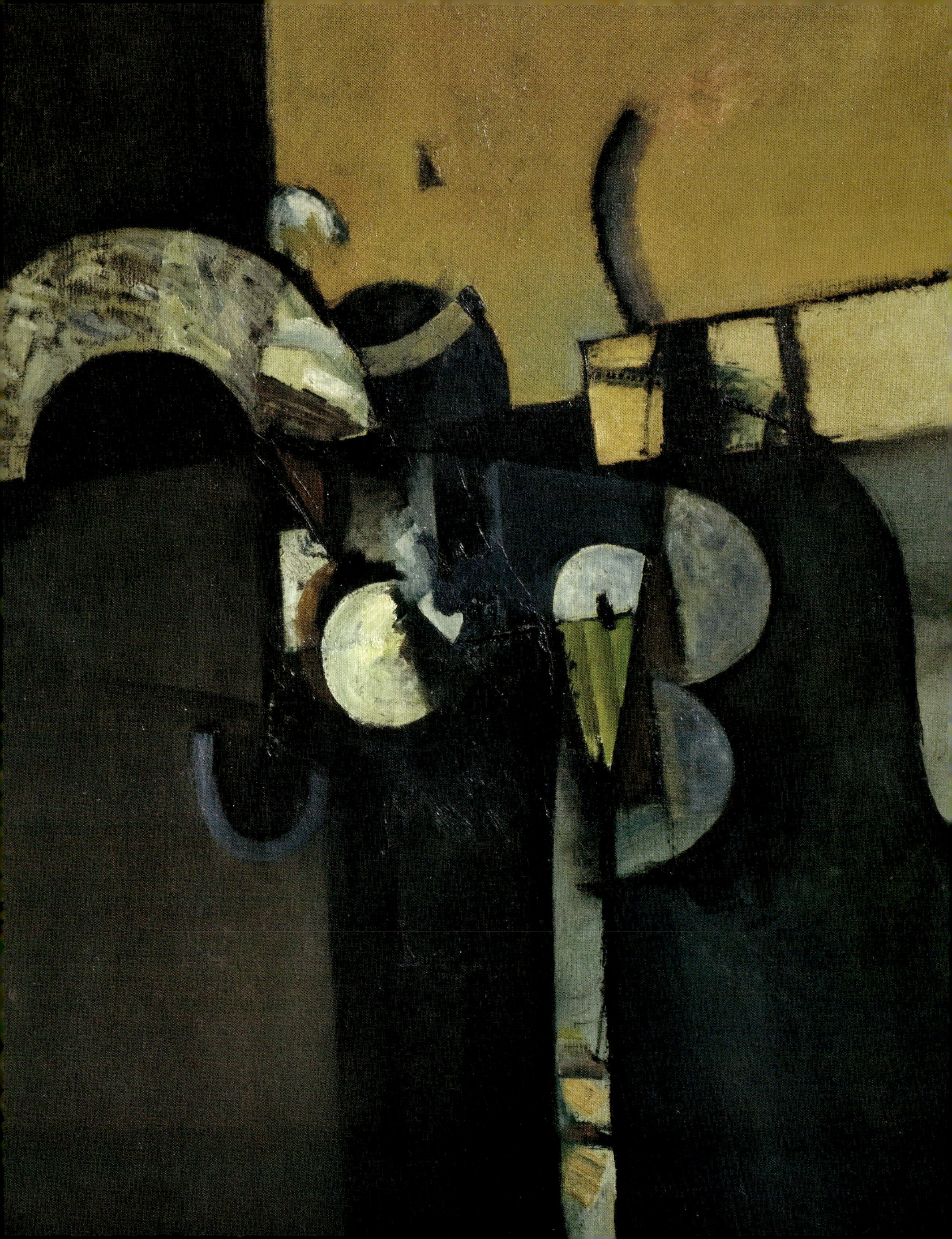

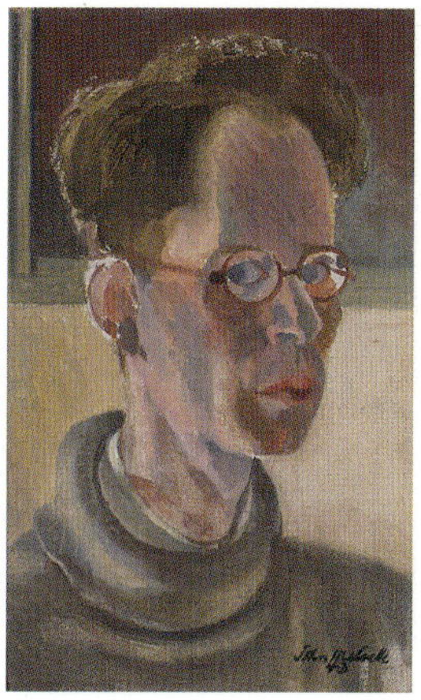

Melville, John 1902–1986
Self Portrait 1943
oil on canvas 29 x 17.5
L.F16.1946.0.0

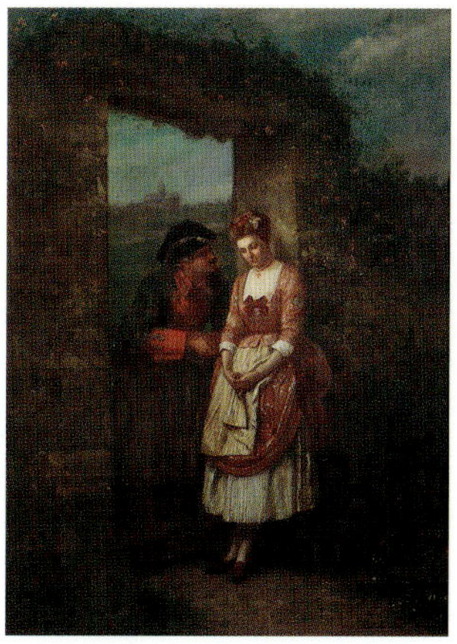

Metzmacher, Emile Pierre 1815–1890
Courtship
oil on canvas 52 x 37.3
Y.F12.2008.0.0

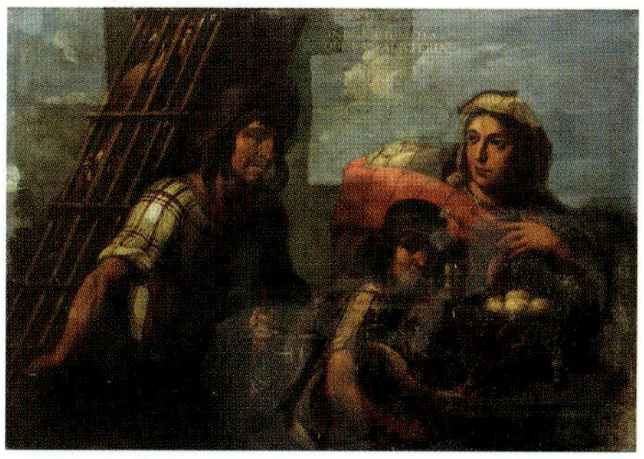

Mexican School
Indios otomíes que ban a la feria
oil on canvas 103 x 146
L.F224.1852.1.0

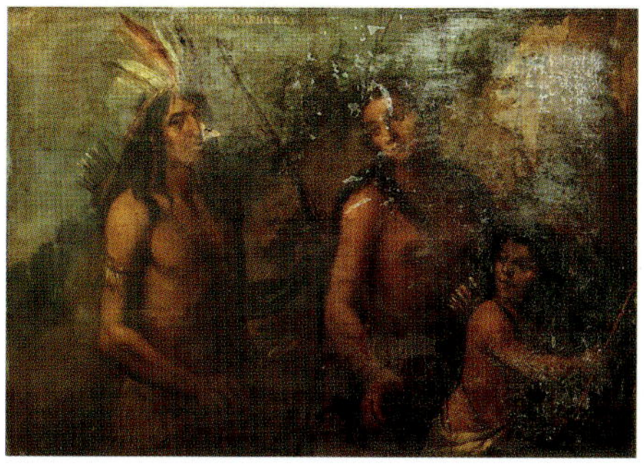

Mexican School
Indios bárbaros
oil on canvas 104 x 146
L.F224.1852.2.0

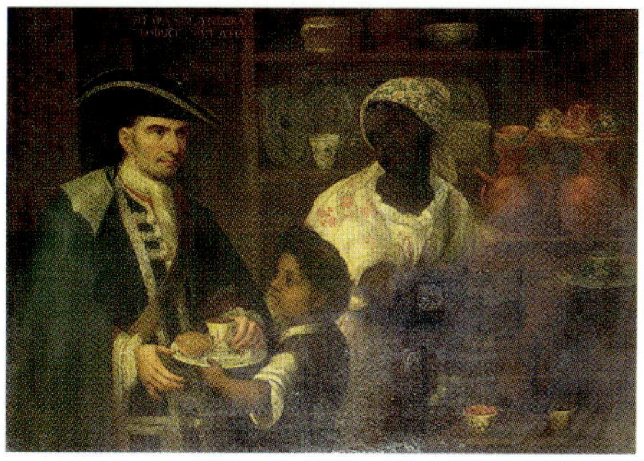

Mexican School
De español y negra se produce un mulato
oil on canvas 104 x 145
L.F224.1852.3.0

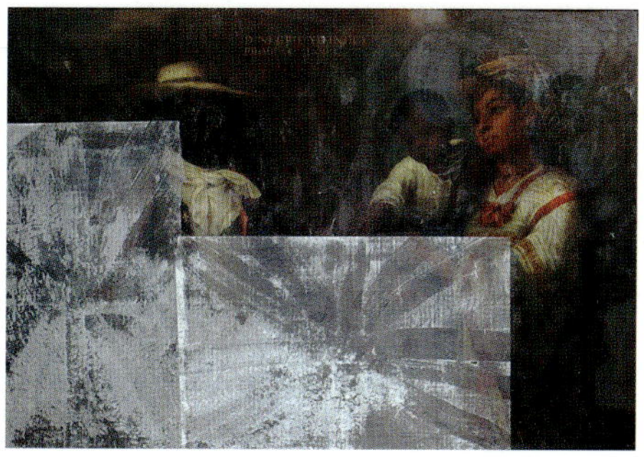

Mexican School
De negro y india se produce un lobo
oil on canvas 103 x 147
L.F224.1852.4.0

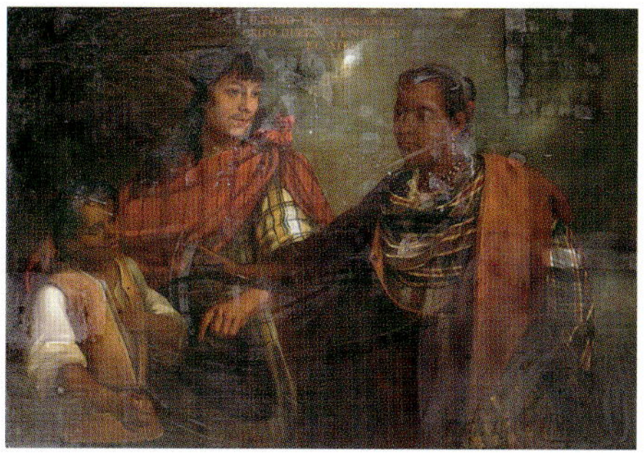

Mexican School
De indio y lobo se produce un grifio que es tente en el aire
oil on canvas 104 x 145
L.F224.1852.5.0

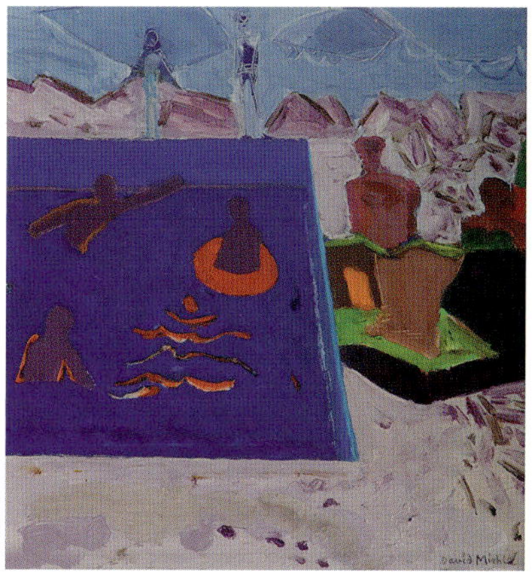

Michie, David Alan Redpath b.1928
The Swimming Pool
oil on panel 30.5 x 28.3
Y.F16.2003.0.0

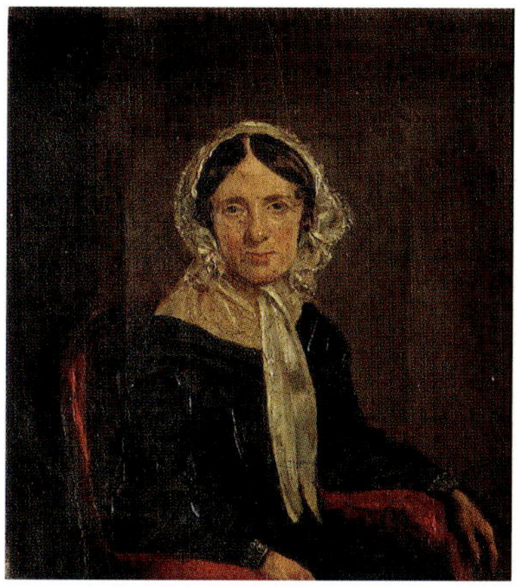

Miller, William P. active 1843
Elizabeth Thompson
oil on canvas 13.2 x 11.5
L.F68.1955.0.0

Facing page: Vaughan, John Keith, 1912–1977, *Vertical Tree Forms* (detail), 1956, Leicester Arts and Museums Service (p. 90)

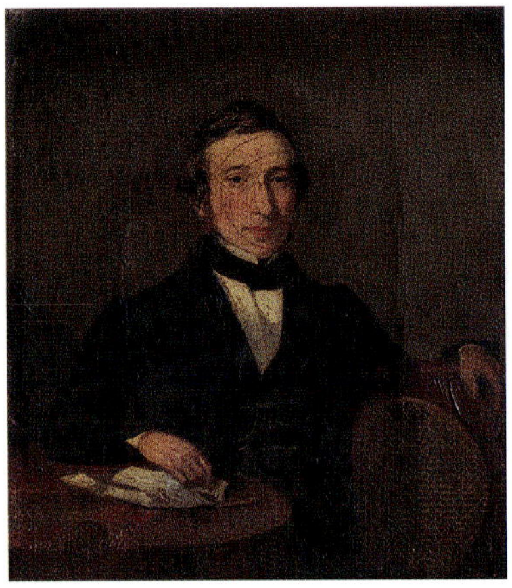

Miller, William P. active 1843
James Thompson (1817–1877)
oil on canvas 16 x 13 (E)
L.F67.1955.0.0

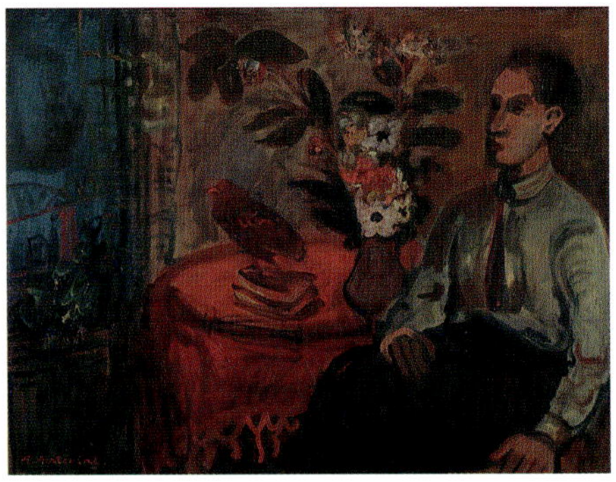

Mintchine, Abraham 1898–1931
Personnage assis et bouquet de fleurs c.1928
oil on canvas 50.2 x 65.5
L.F13.1963.0.0

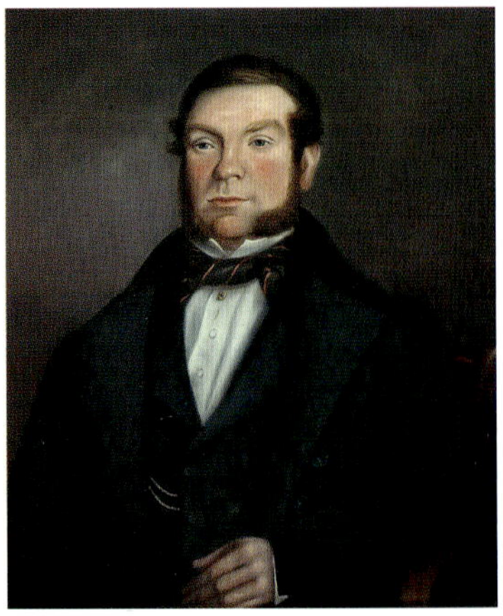

Mobbs, William (attributed to)
John Kelley, Leicester Chimney Sweep 1870–1880
oil on board 74.3 x 61.6
L.F258.1965.0.0

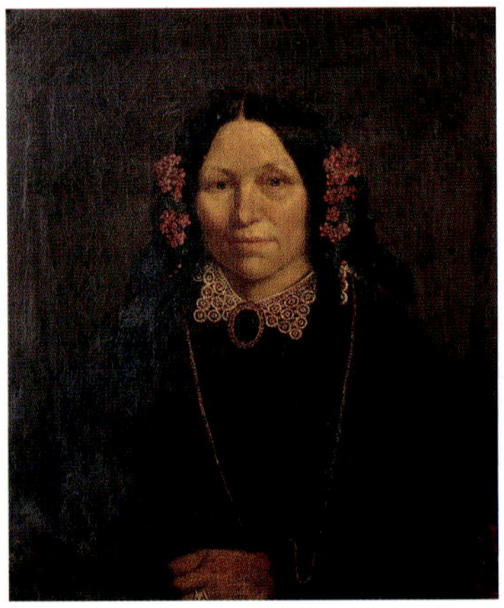

Mobbs, William (attributed to)
Sarah Kelley 1870–1880
oil on canvas 74.3 x 61.6
L.F259.1965.0.0

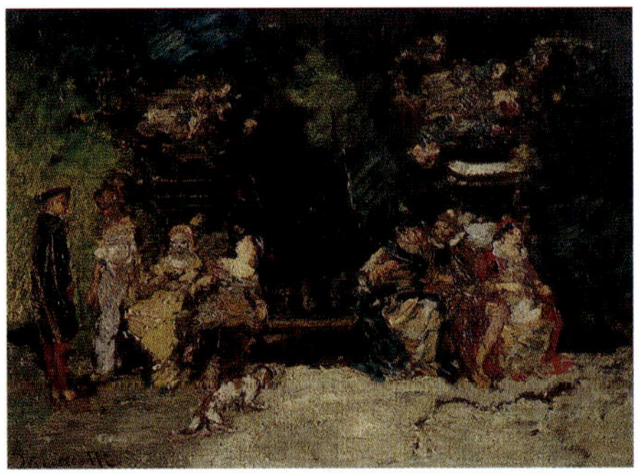

Monticelli, Adolphe Joseph Thomas 1824–1886
Réunion dans un parc
oil on canvas 38.7 x 51.4
L.F105.1963.0.0

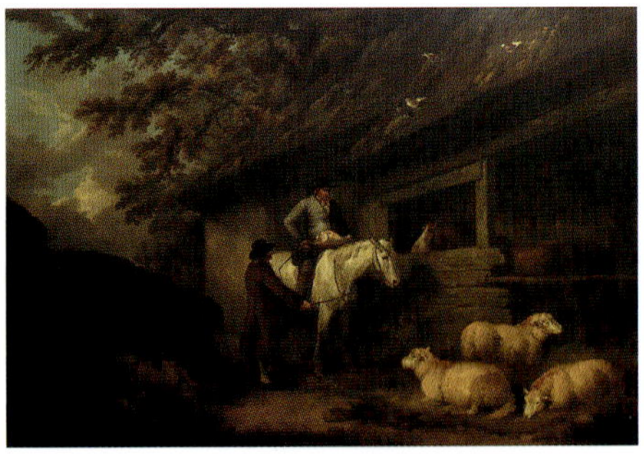

Morland, George 1763–1804
Bargaining for Sheep 1794
oil on canvas 139.7 x 198.1
L.F75.1955.0.0

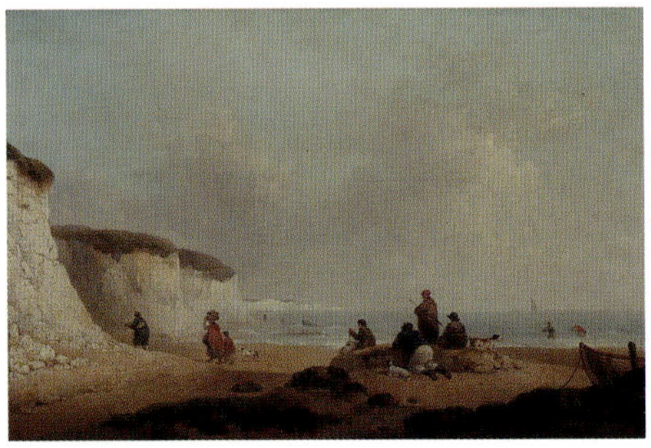

Morland, George 1763–1804
Calm off the Coast of the Isle of Wight 1799–1804
oil on panel 27.6 x 40.7
L.F7.1890.0.0

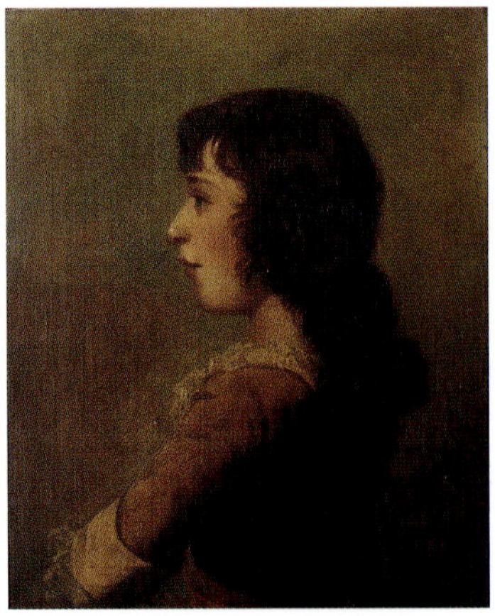

Morland, George 1763–1804
Portrait of a Girl
oil on canvas 53.3 x 43.2
L.F35.1944.0.0

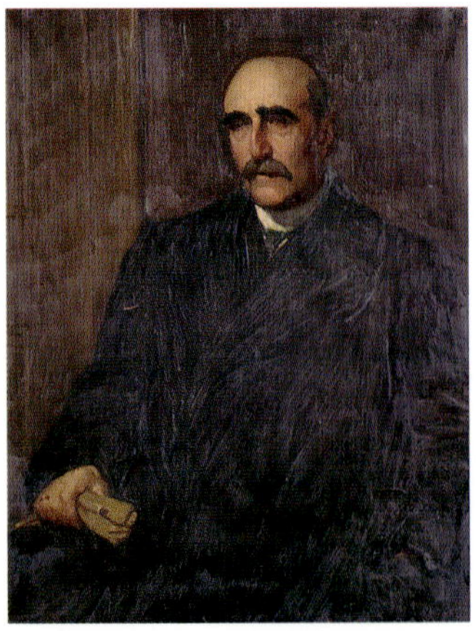

Morley, Harry 1881–1943
Doctor Alfred Wilson Emms (1850–1920) 1905
oil on canvas 101.5 x 76.2
L.F42.1957.0.0

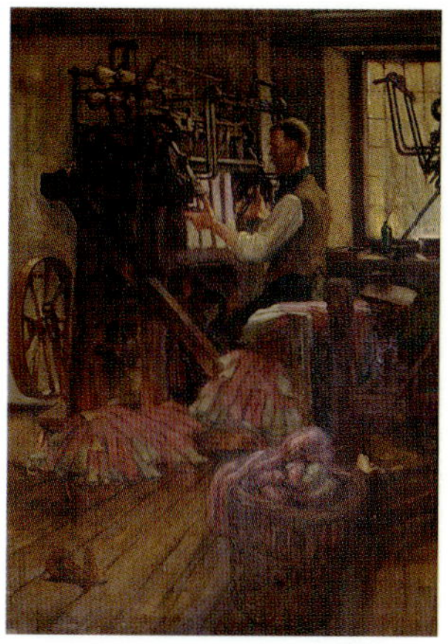

Morley, Harry 1881–1943
A Framework Knitter 1908
oil on canvas 101.5 x 70.9
L.F29.1952.0.0

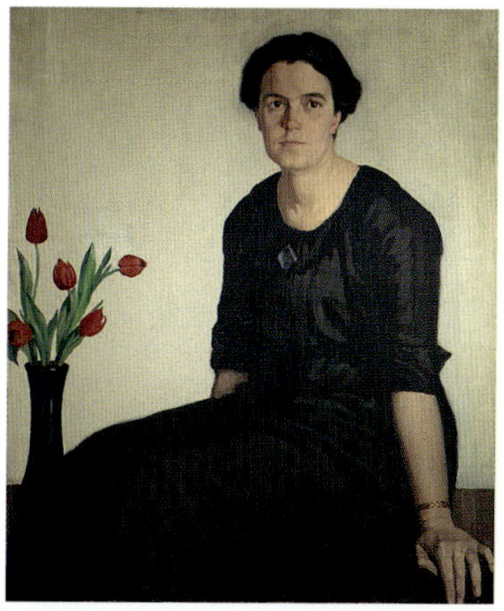

Morley, Harry 1881–1943
Jessie Elizabeth Morley, the Artist's Sister
c.1914
oil on canvas 76.2 x 63.5
L.F9.1959.0.0

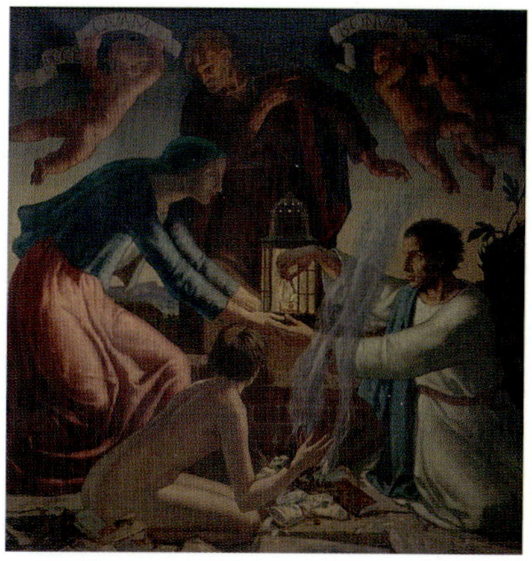

Morley, Harry 1881–1943
Lighting the Lamp of Peace 1922
oil on canvas 107 x 102
L.F106.1938.0.0

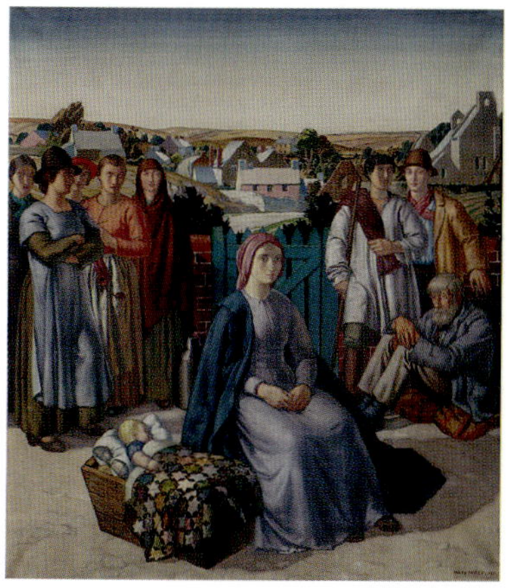

Morley, Harry 1881–1943
A Wayside Madonna 1927
oil on canvas 108.3 x 96.5
L.F2.1929.0.0

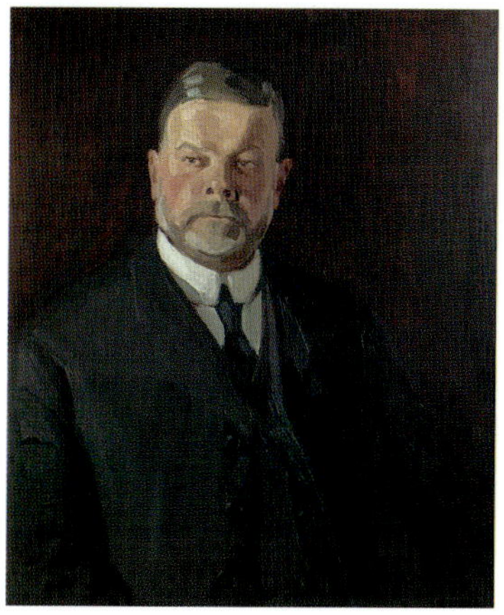

Morley, Harry 1881–1943
Arthur Richard Johnson (1854–1918), Co-Founder of Hawley and Johnson
oil on canvas 76.5 x 63.5
L.F120.1981.0.0

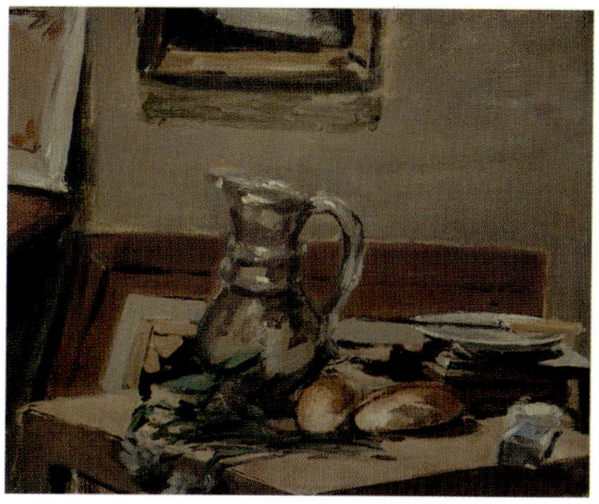

Moynihan, Rodrigo 1910–1990
Still Life with a Jug 1937
oil on canvas 51 x 62
L.F1.1941.6.0

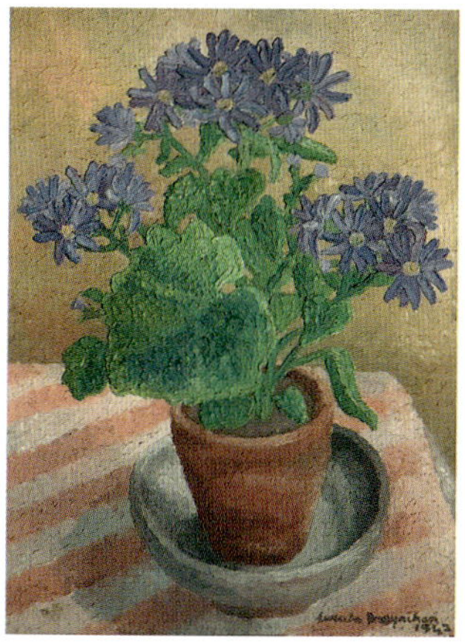

Moynihan, Ursula 1912–1995
Blue Cineraria 1942
oil on canvas 38.6 x 28.5
L.F3.1943.0.0

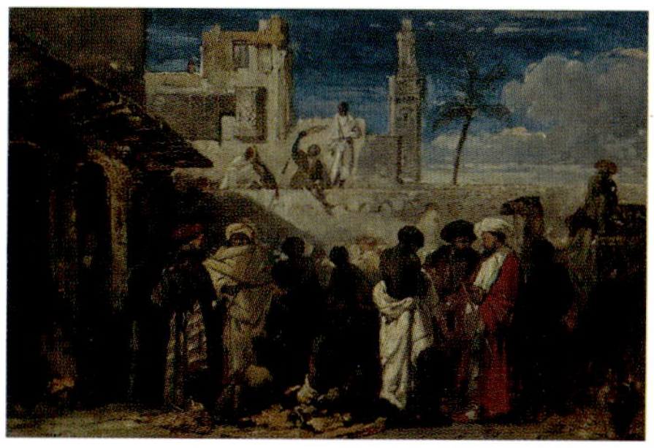

Muller, William James 1812–1845
The Slave Market, Cairo 1840
oil on panel 27.3 x 40.6
L.F3.1907.0.0

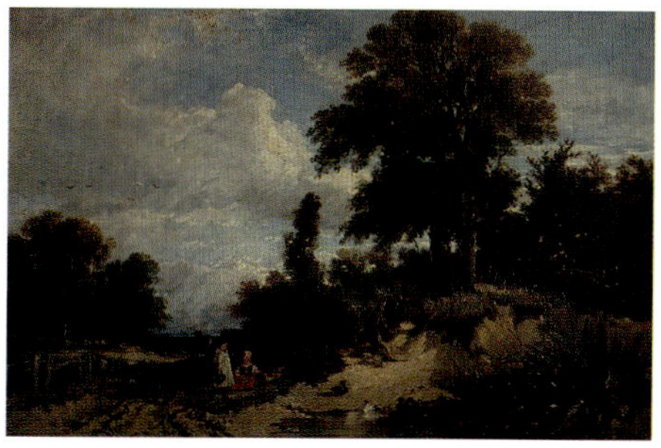

Muller, William James 1812–1845
A Wooded Landscape 1844
oil on canvas 62.5 x 90.5
L.F12.1890.0.0

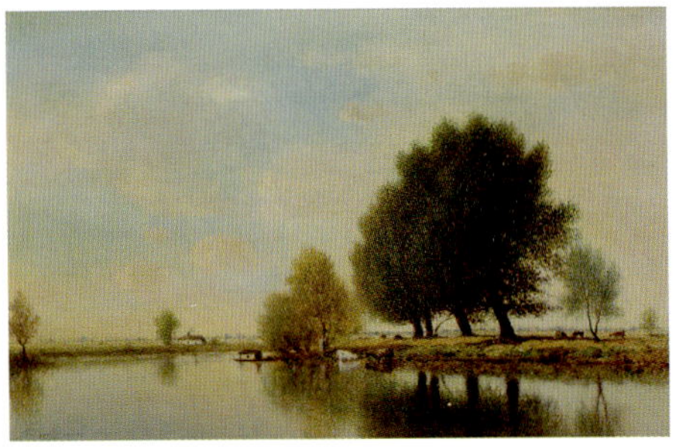

Munger, Gilbert Davis 1837–1903
On the Seine
oil on panel 31 x 46
L.F24.1948.0.0

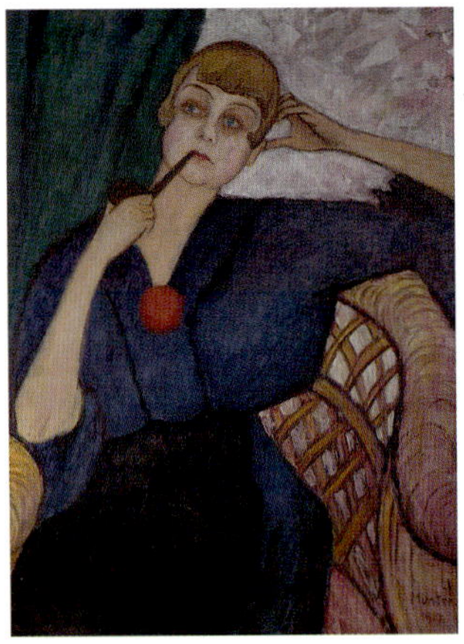

Munter, Gabriele 1877–1962
Anna Roslund (1891–1941) 1917
oil on canvas 94 x 68
L.F10.1991.0.0

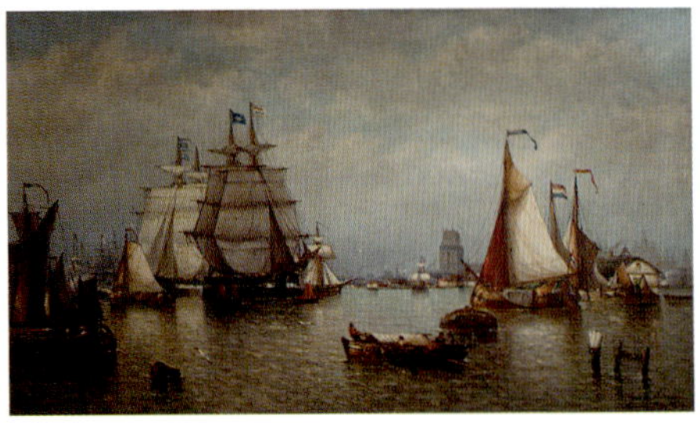

Musin, Auguste Henri 1852–1920
Rotterdam Harbour, The Netherlands 1876
oil on canvas 76.6 x 127.2
L.F18.1946.0.0

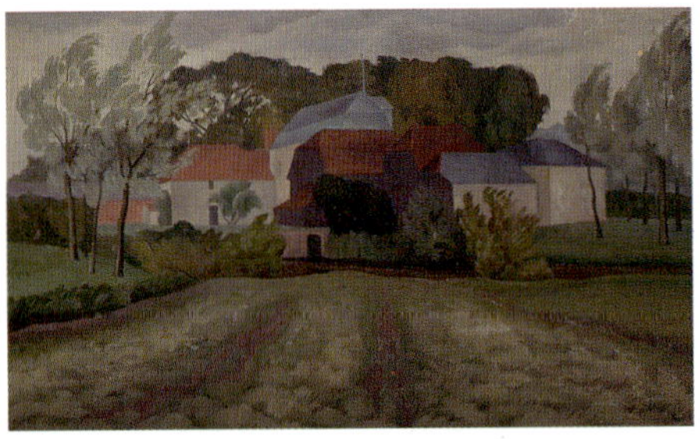

Nash, John Northcote 1893–1977
Wakes Colne Mill, Colchester, Essex 1931
oil on canvas 50.8 x 81.5
L.F9.1941.0.0

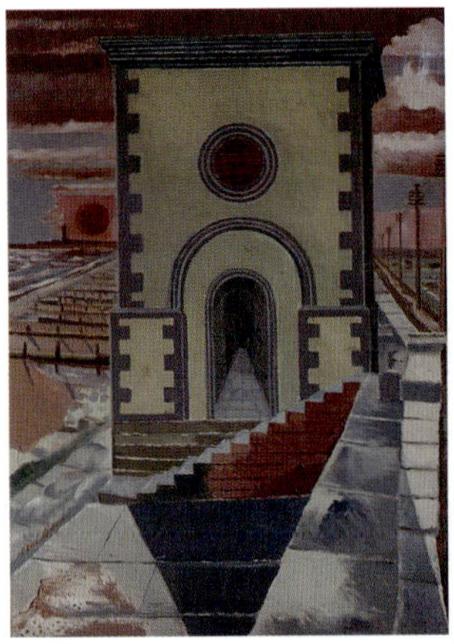

Nash, Paul 1889–1946
Nostalgic Landscape 1923–1938
oil on canvas 71.2 x 50.8
L.F49.1947.0.0

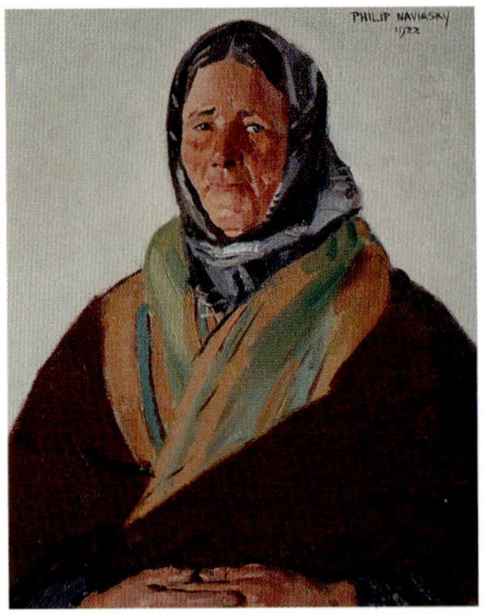

Naviasky, Philip 1894–1982
Head of a Woman 1922
oil on canvas 51 x 40.8
L.F22.1931.0.0

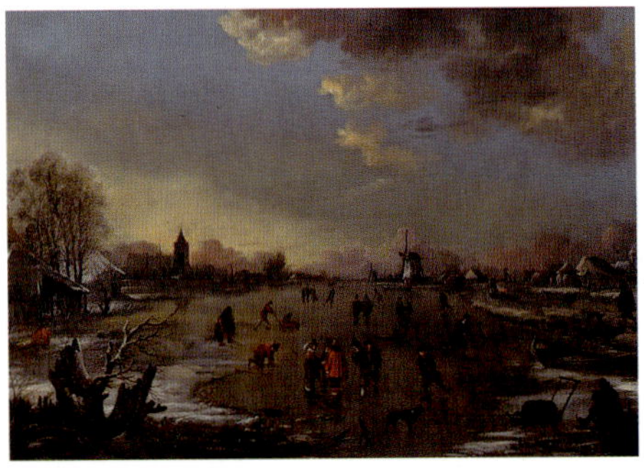

Neer, Aert van der 1603–1677
Winter Landscape at Sunset 1650–1655
oil on canvas 104.5 x 145
L.F15.1981.0.0

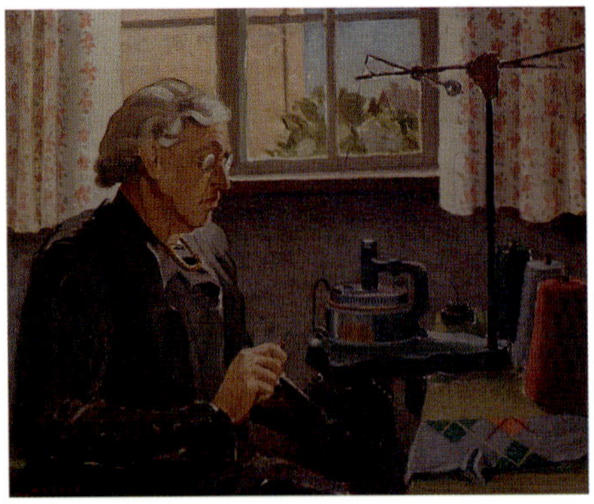

Nesbit, Ian
Griswold Knitting Machine 1949
oil on canvas 51 x 61
L.T920.1978.0.0

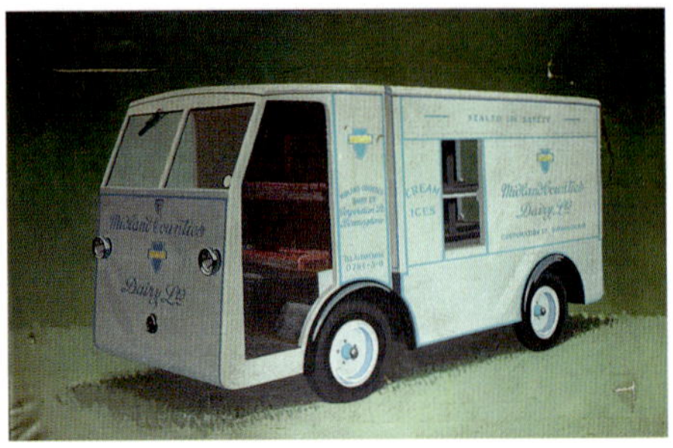

Nesbit, Ian
Partridge Wilson Milk Float
oil on canvas 100 x 151
L.T37.1986.11

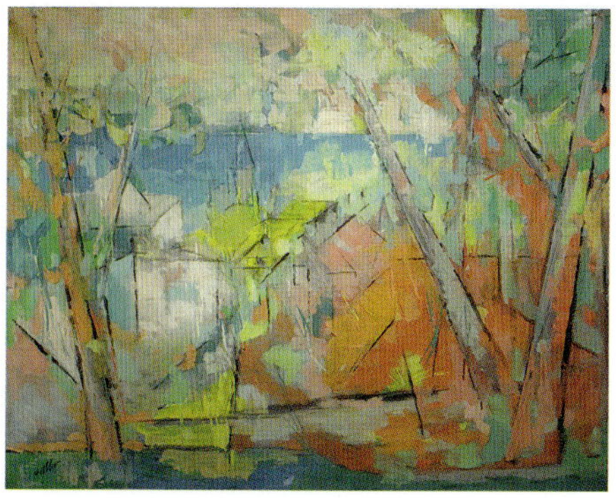

Nessler, Walter H. 1912–2001
Southern Landscape 1955
oil on canvas 61 x 76.2
L.F19.1956.0.0

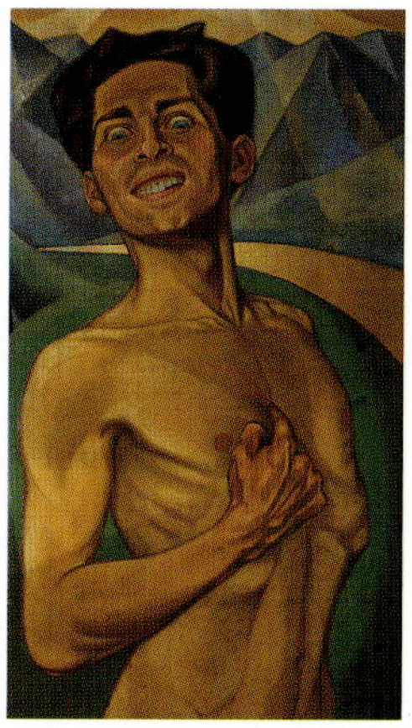

Neuschul, Ernst 1895–1968
Messias 1919
oil on card 95.5 x 55.5
Y.F2.2007.0.0

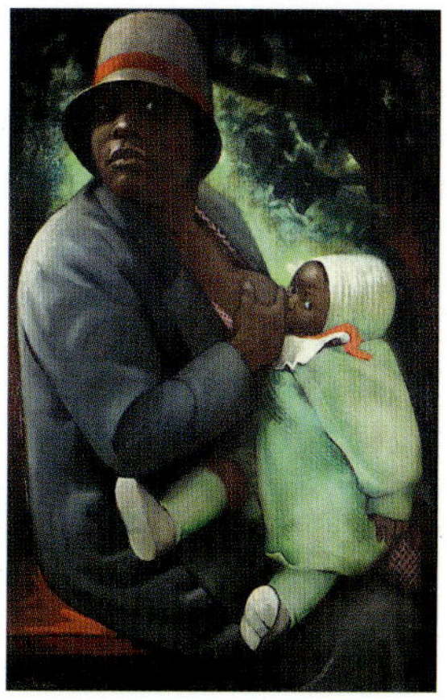

Neuschul, Ernst 1895–1968
Negermutter c.1927–1931
oil on canvas 100.5 x 65.5
L.F453.1978.0.0

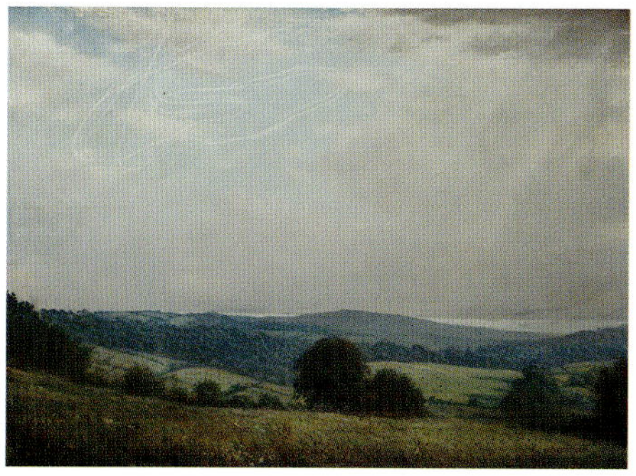

Nevinson, Christopher 1889–1946
One Summer's Day
oil on canvas 76.2 x 101.6
L.F27.1947.0.0

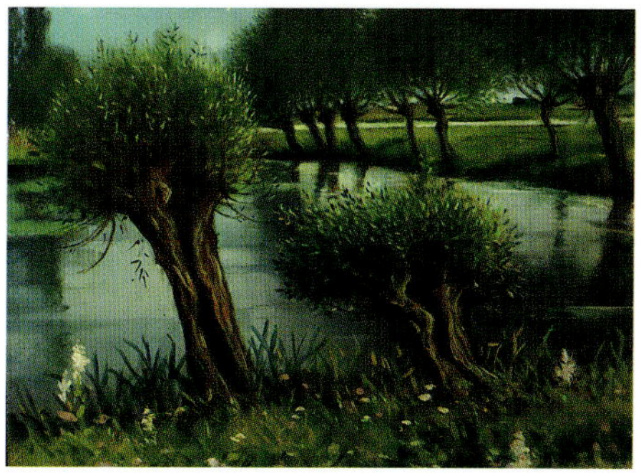

Nevinson, Christopher 1889–1946
Oxford, on the Cherwell
oil on canvas 51 x 68.5
L.F4.1924.0.0

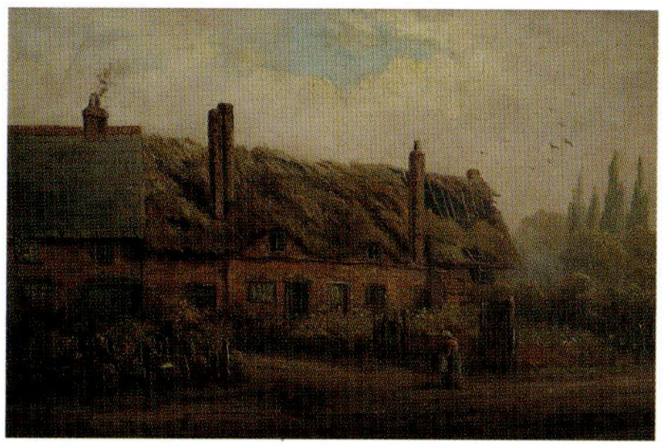

Newton, George
The Old Workhouse (Poor House), the Green, Belgrave, Leicestershire
oil on canvas 29.2 x 43.8
L.F292.1968.0.0

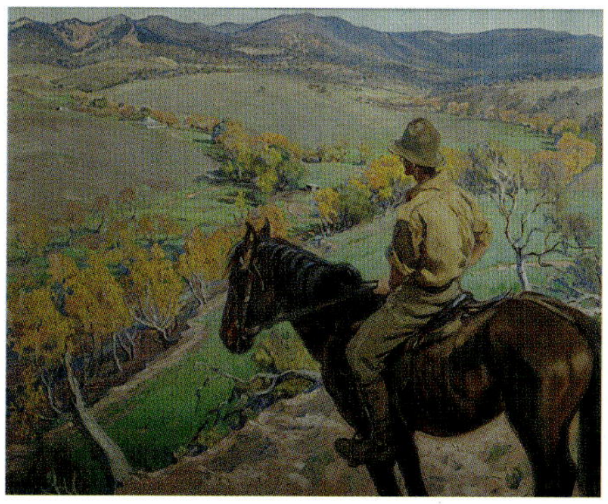

Nicholas, Hilda Rix 1884–1961
His Land
oil on canvas 80.5 x 98
L.F2.1928.0.0

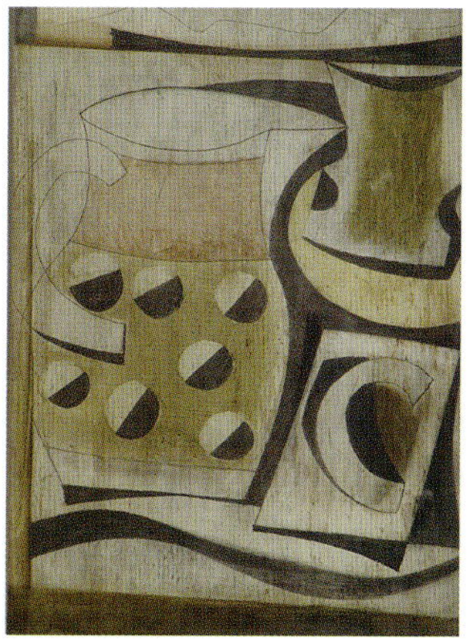

Nicholson, Ben 1894–1982
1948 (still life)
oil & graphite on board 35 x 24.8
L.F7.1962.0.0

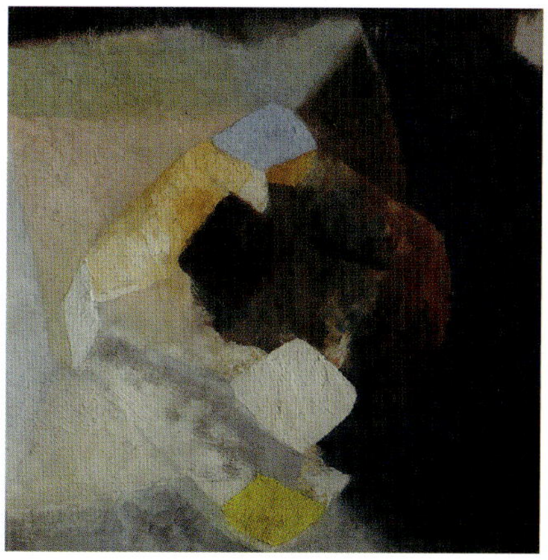

Nicholson, Winifred 1893–1981
Crystals 1930
oil on canvas 51 x 51
L.F780.1977.0.0

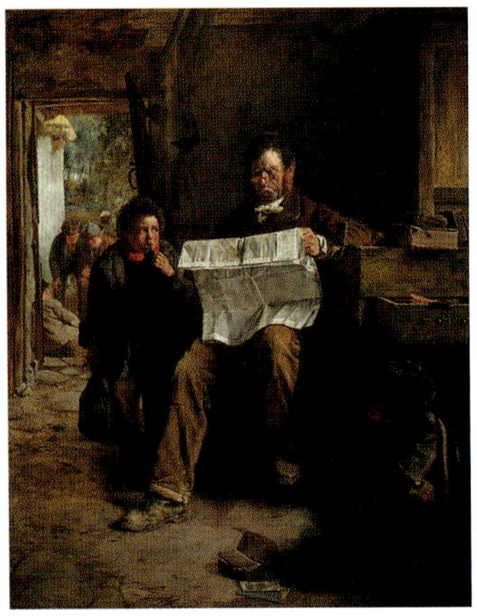

Nicol, Erskine 1825–1904
Kept In 1866
oil on canvas 108 x 83
L.F215.1924.0.0

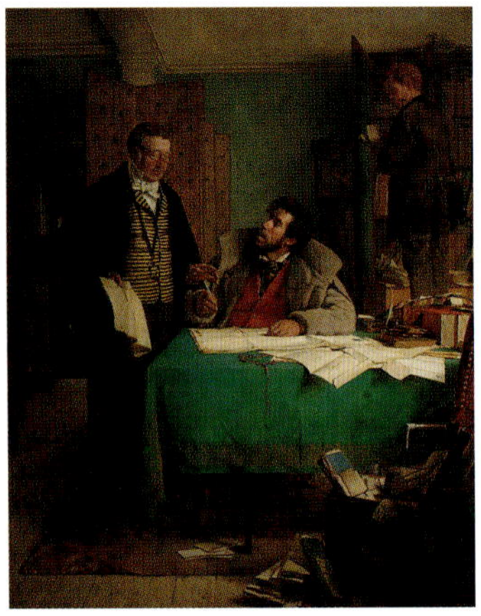

Nicol, Erskine 1825–1904
Signing the New Lease 1868
oil on canvas 122 x 93.4
L.F15.1900.0.0

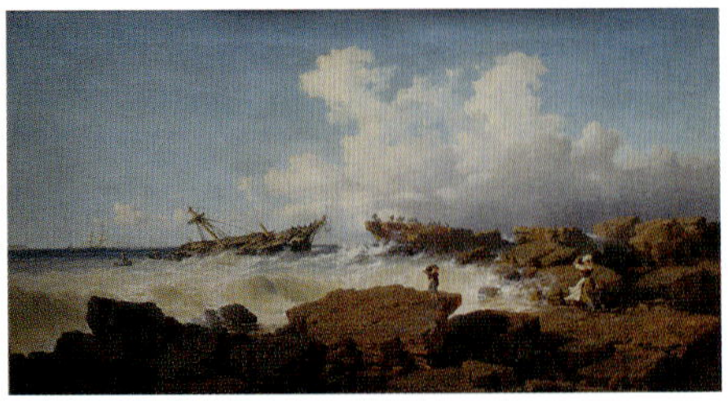

Niemann, Edmund John 1813–1876
Filey Brigg, North Yorkshire 1868
oil on canvas 63.5 x 114.3
L.F2.1918.0.0

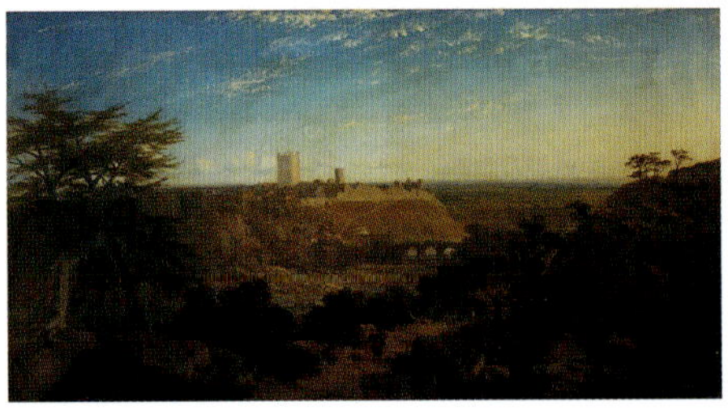

Niemann, Edmund John 1813–1876
Richmond, North Yorkshire, from the Swale
1870
oil on canvas 61 x 112.5
L.F1.1918.0.0

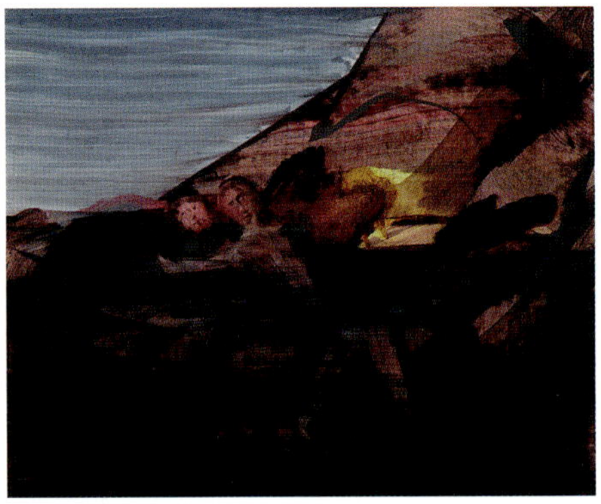

Nolan, Sidney 1917–1992
Mrs Fraser with Convict 1958
oil on paper 25.5 x 30.5
L.F115.1981.0.0

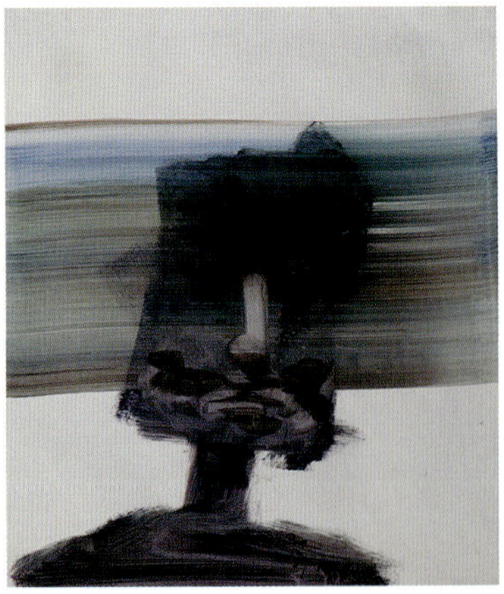

Nolan, Sidney 1917–1992
Kelly 1959
oil on paper 30.5 x 25.5
L.F114.1981.0.0

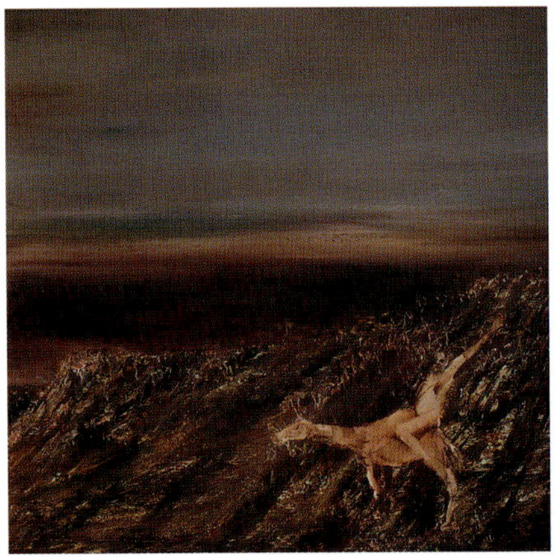

Nolan, Sidney 1917–1992
The Explorer Burke on a Camel 1966
oil on board 122 x 122
L.F4.1967.0.0

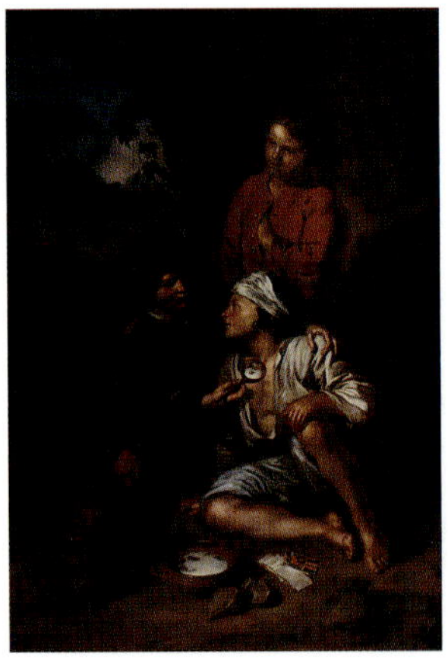

Núñez de Villavicencio, Pedro 1644–1700
Two Boys Feeding a Beggar
oil on canvas 170.5 x 117.3
L.F25.1949.0.0

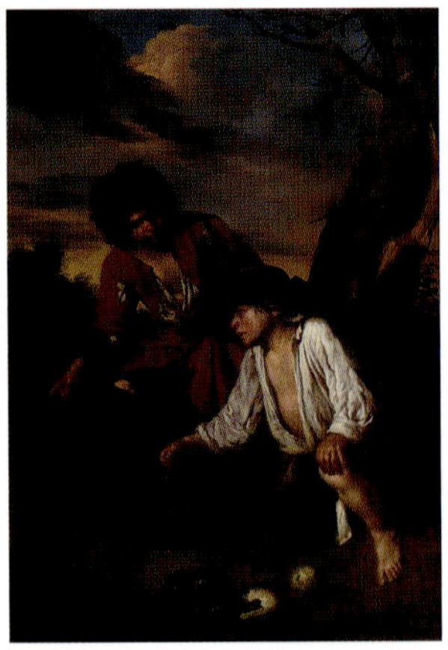

Núñez de Villavicencio, Pedro 1644–1700
Two Boys Playing Pitch-and-Toss
oil on canvas 174 x 120.2
L.F8.1950.0.0

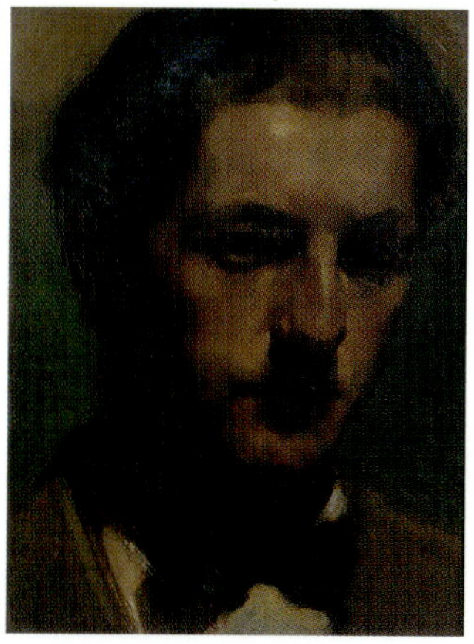

Nunney, Reginald 1895–1922
Self Portrait
oil on canvas & millboard 30.5 x 23
L.F3.1939.0.0

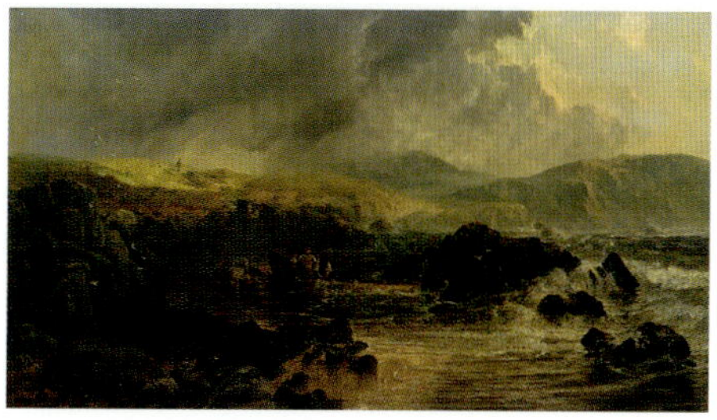

Oakes, John Wright 1820–1887
Picking up Wreckage on a Rocky Shore 1864
oil on canvas 51.5 x 87
L.F8.1888.0.0

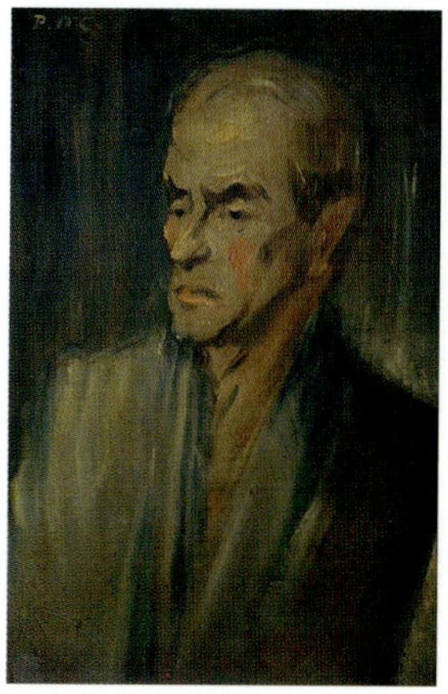

O'Connor, Patrick 1909–1997
Jack Butler Yeats (1871–1957) 1940
oil on canvas 38 x 25.5
L.F30.1987.0.0 (P)

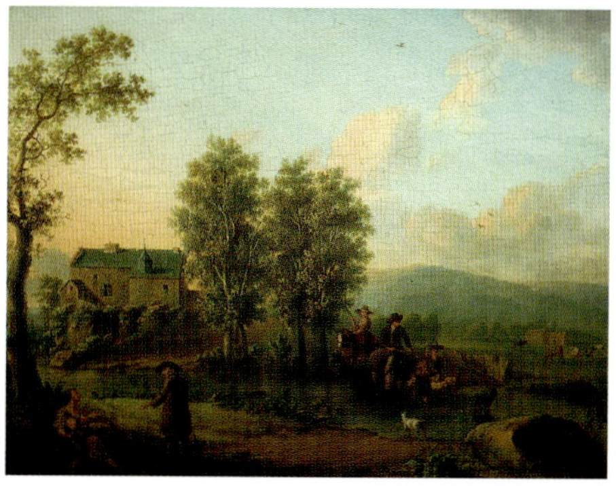

Ommeganck, Balthazar Paul 1755–1826
Landscape with Figures
oil on panel 42.5 x 54
L.F20.1935.5.0

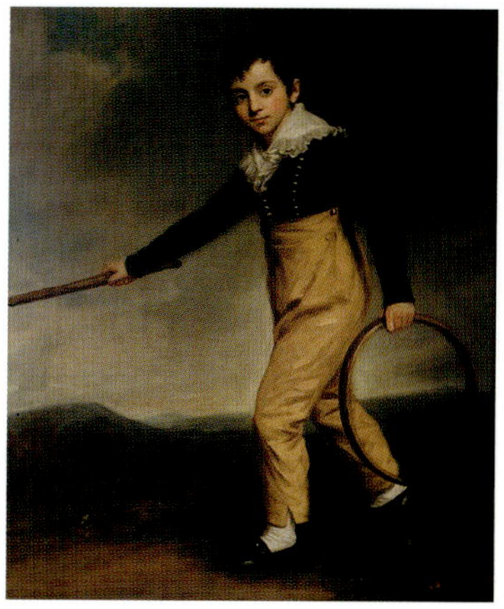

Opie, John 1761–1807
Boy with a Hoop
oil on canvas 145 x 118
L.F54.1953.0.0

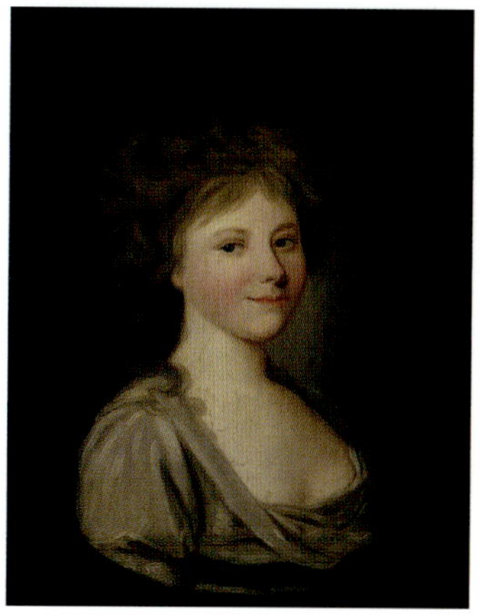

Opie, John 1761–1807
Head of a Girl
oil on canvas 55 x 41.5
L.F9.1943.5.0

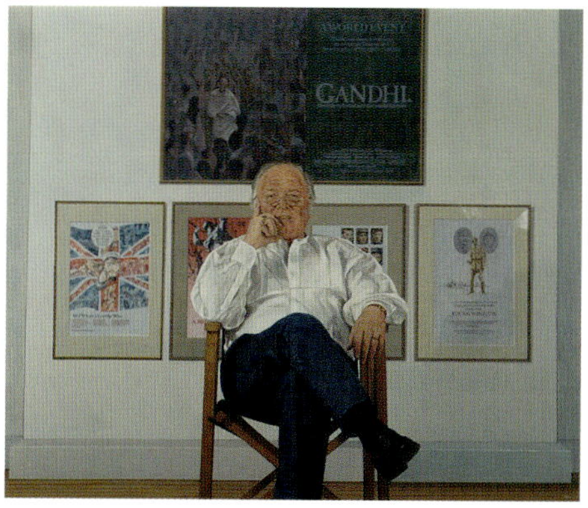

Organ, Bryan b.1935
Sir Richard Attenborough (b.1923) 1985–1986
acrylic on canvas 127 x 152.5
L.F4.1986.0.0

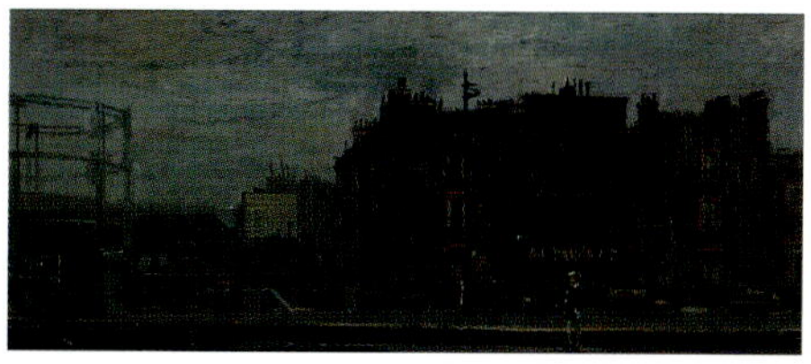

Organ, Bryan b.1935
St Pancras Station, London
oil on hardboard 44 x 122
L.F2.1969.0.0

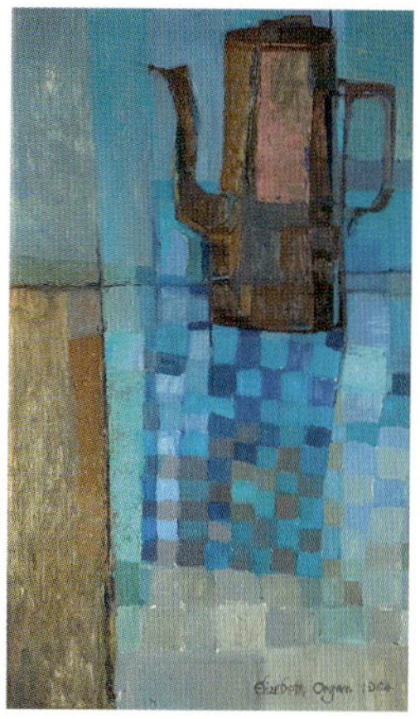

Organ, Elizabeth 1934–2009
Coffee Pot 1964
oil on canvas 68 x 39
L.F454.1977.0.0

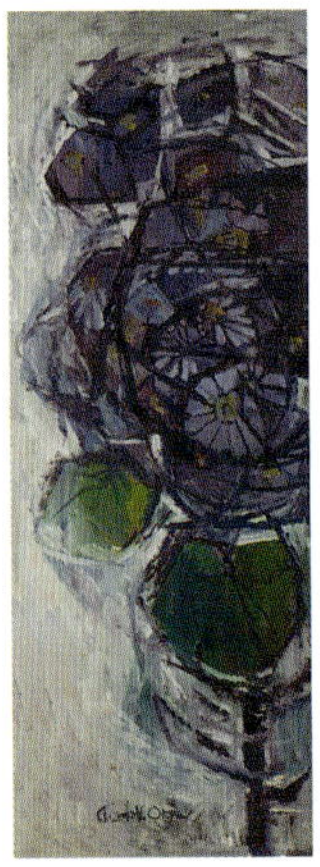

Organ, Elizabeth 1934–2009
Blue Flowers
oil on canvas 94 x 33
L.F452.1977.0.0

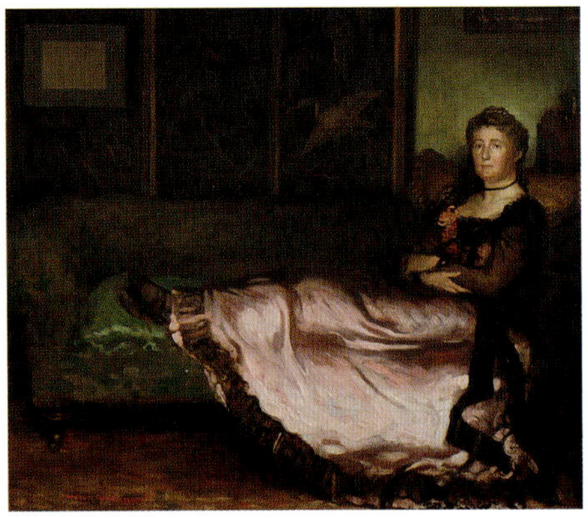

Orpen, William 1878–1931
Lady on a Couch 1900
oil on canvas 80 x 89
L.F15.1945.0.0

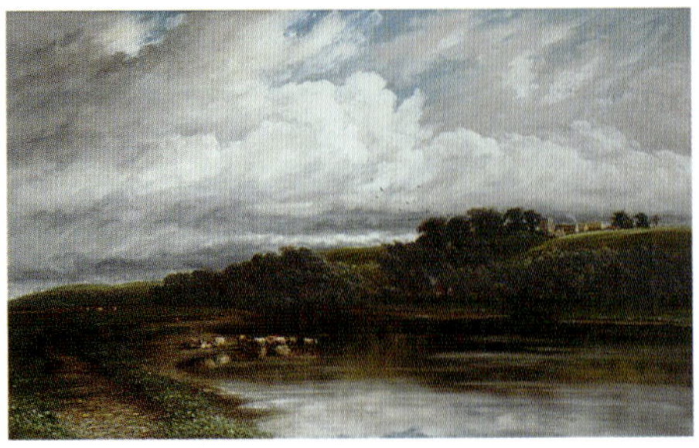

Orrock, James 1829–1913
Kneeton Ford, Nottingham, on the Trent 1884
oil on canvas 86.5 x 127.3
L.F2.1884.0.0

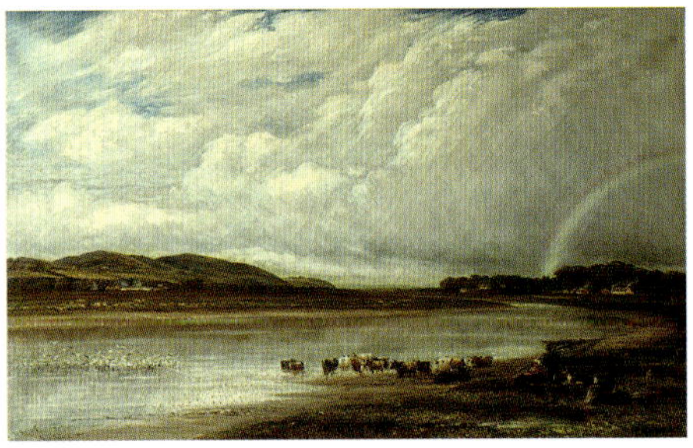

Orrock, James 1829–1913
On the Nith, Scotland 1899
oil on canvas 81.3 x 127.3
L.F13.1945.0.0

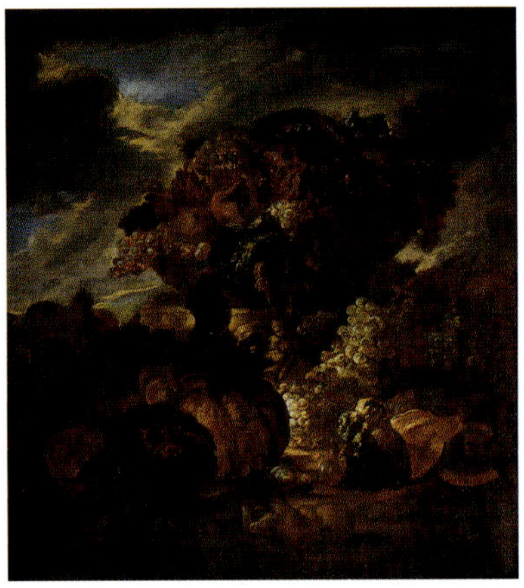

Pace del Campidoglio, Michele (attributed to) 1610–probably 1670
Still Life with Fruit
oil on canvas 117 x 103.5
L.F123.1964.0.0

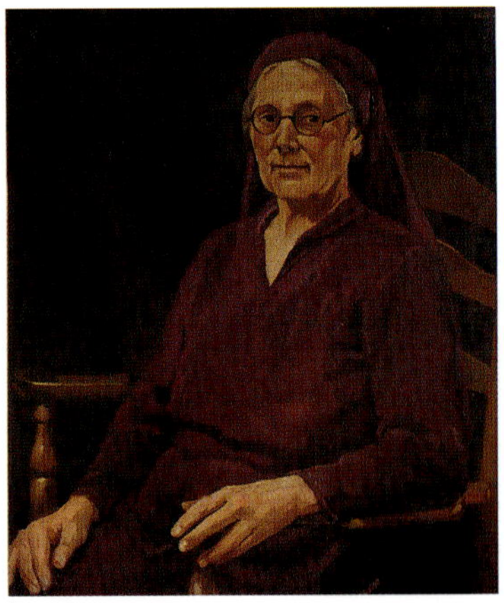

Parker
Emily Comber Fortey (1866–1946), Councillor
oil on canvas 61 x 51
L.F28.1987.0.0

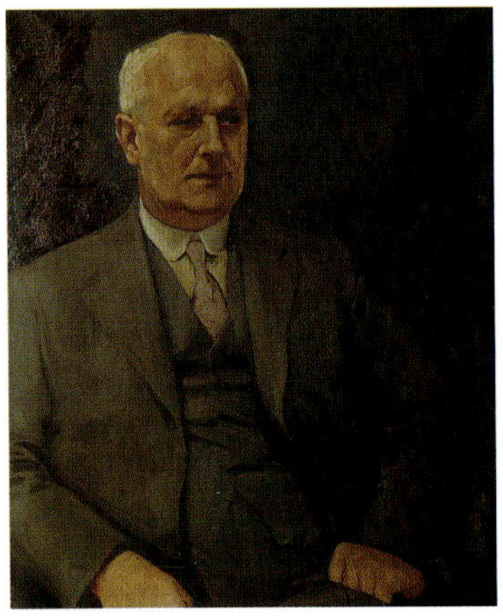

Parker
Francis Paul Armitage, Esq., Director of Education, Leicester County Borough (1910–1940)
oil on canvas 61 x 51
L.F27.1987.0.0

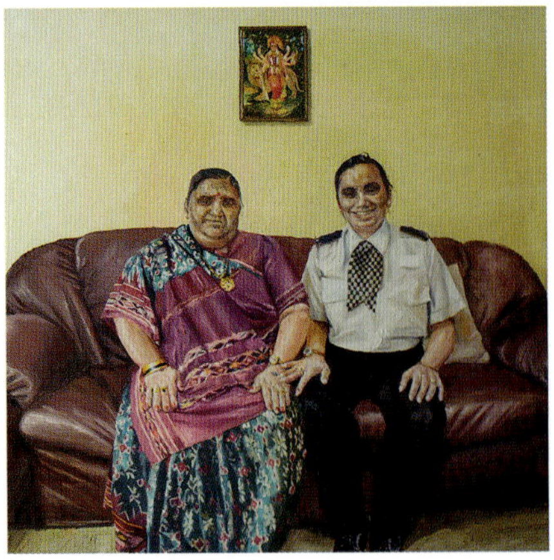

Parker, Alan b.1965
Muktaben Bhogaita and Daughter Alka 2001
oil on canvas 122.5 x 121.5
Y.F4.2005.0.0

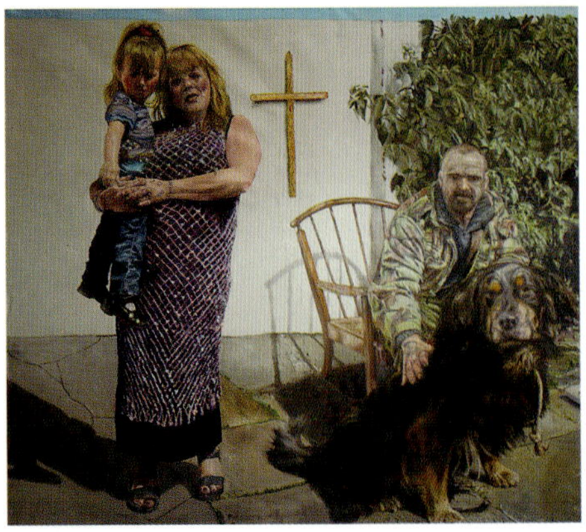

Parker, Alan b.1965
Debbie Loves Jesus 2002
oil on canvas 126.5 x 137
Y.F3.2005.0.0

Facing page: Bayes, Walter, 1869–1956, *The Bather* (detail), 1917, Leicester Arts and Museums Service (p. 11)

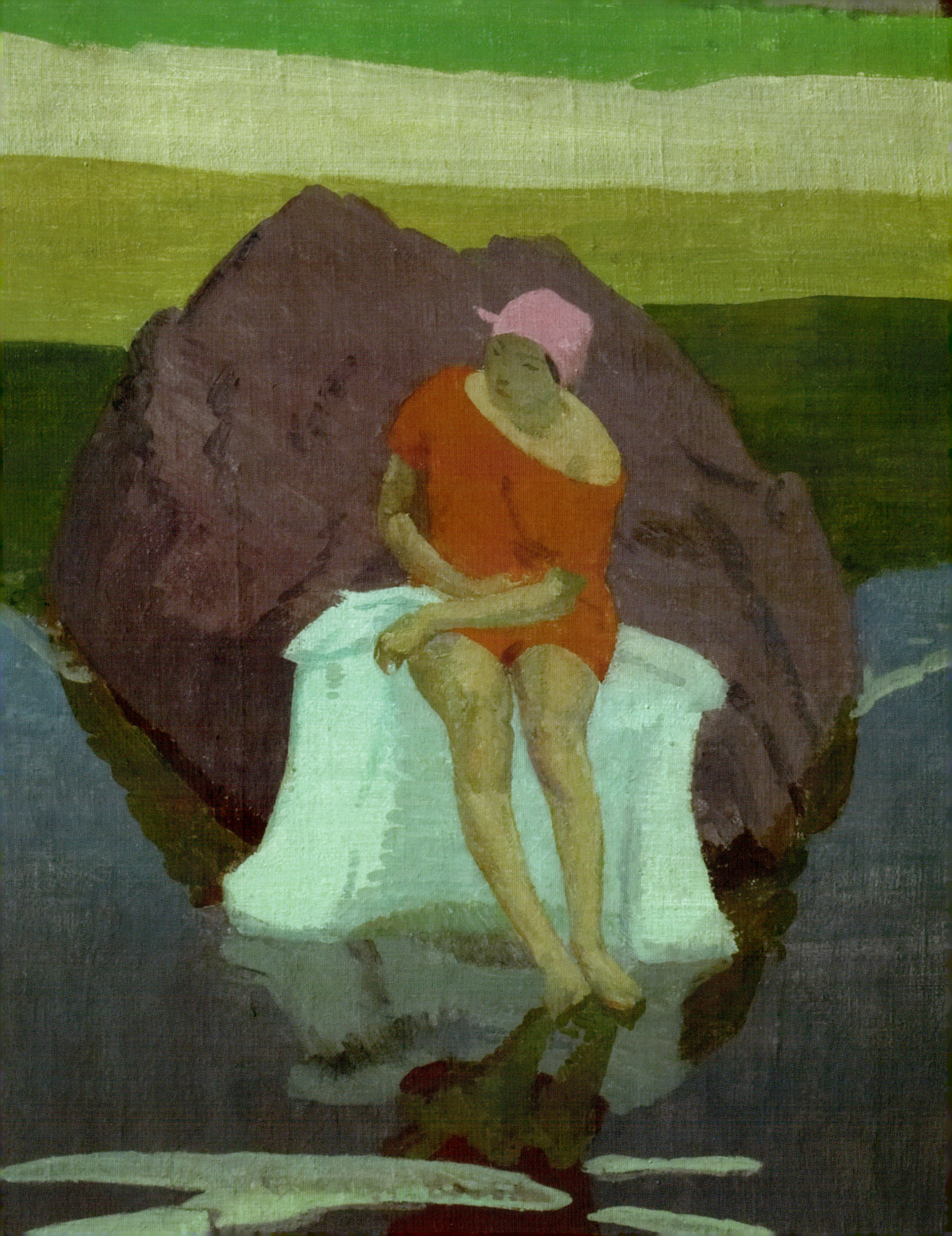

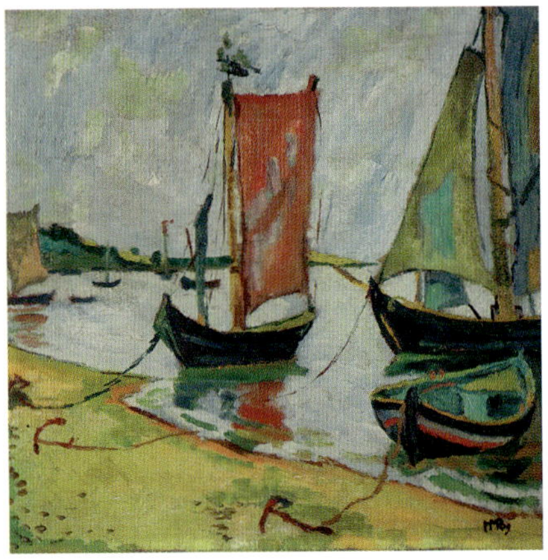

Pechstein, Hermann Max 1881–1955
Nidden Coastline with Fishing Boats 1909
oil on canvas 50 x 50
L.F43.1952.0.0

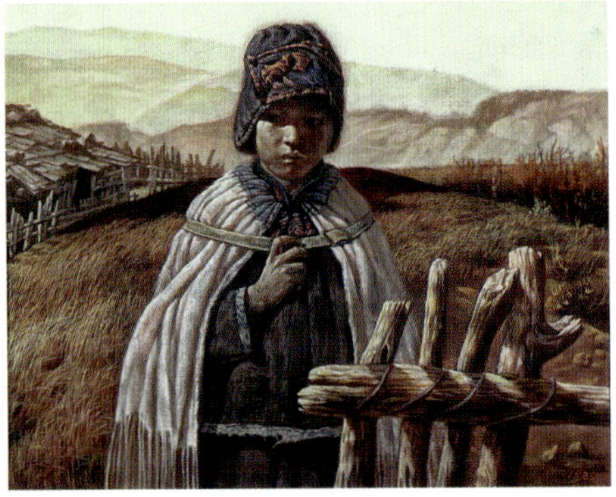

Peng, Shi b.1954
A Mountain Boy 1989
acrylic on cloth 8 x 14.5
L.F7.1990.0.0

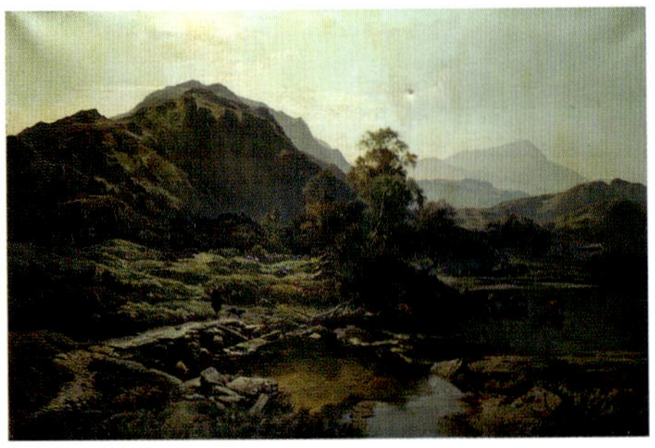

Percy, Sidney Richard 1821–1886
Highland Landscape 1853
oil on canvas 125.7 x 182.9
Y.F11.2008.0.0

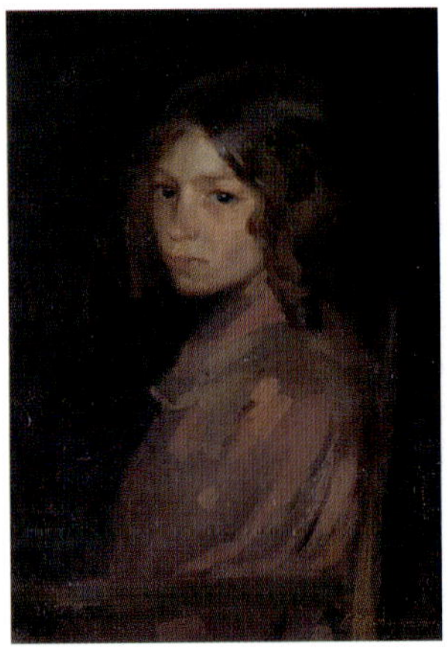

Pettinger, John Frederick 1877–1939
Wee Annie 1910
oil on canvas & panel 54 x 37.5
L.F5.1943.0.0

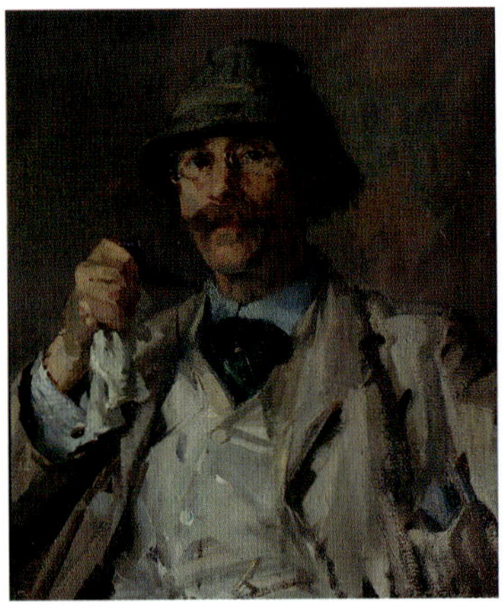

Pettinger, John Frederick 1877–1939
Percival James Atkins (1871–1955) 1930
oil on canvas 61 x 50.7
Y.F13.1998.0.0

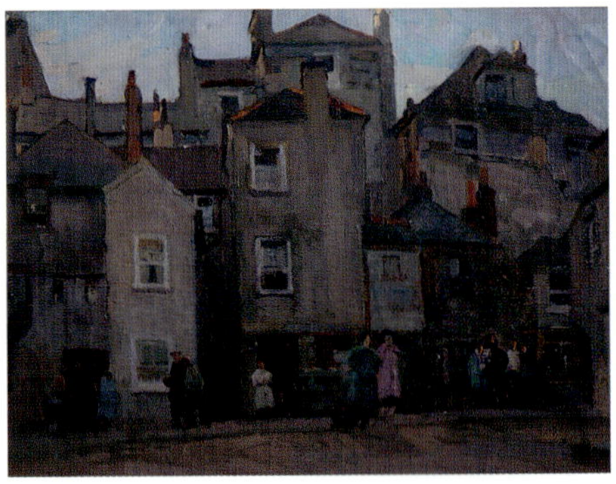

Pettinger, John Frederick 1877–1939
From the Artist's Window, Leicester Art School
oil on canvas 26.7 x 30.5
L.F40.1944.2.0

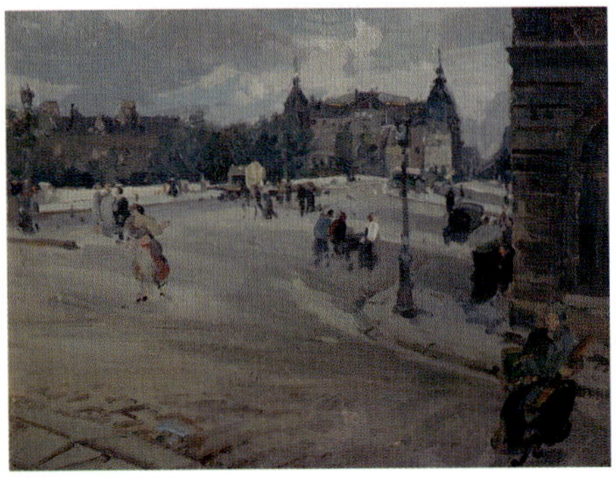

Pettinger, John Frederick 1877–1939
Pont Neuf, Paris
oil on canvas 35.6 x 45.7
L.F10.1925.0.0

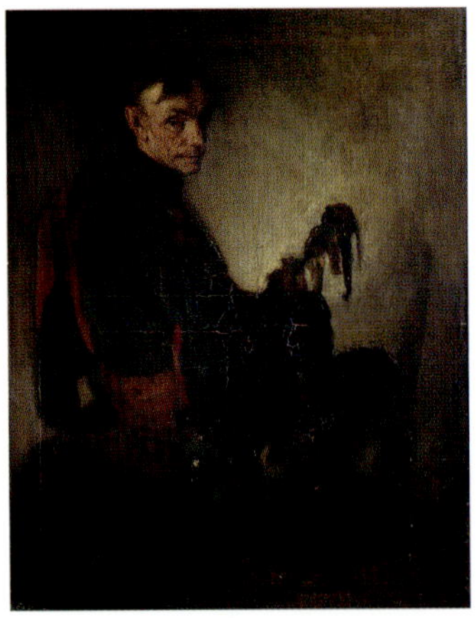

Pettinger, John Frederick 1877–1939
The Jester
oil on canvas 112 x 86.3
L.F2.1946.0.0

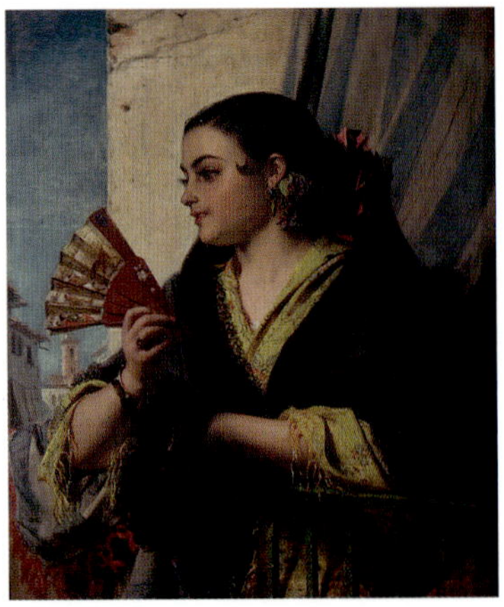

Phillip, John 1817–1867
The Balcony 1857
oil on canvas 61 x 48.3
L.F10.1891.0.0

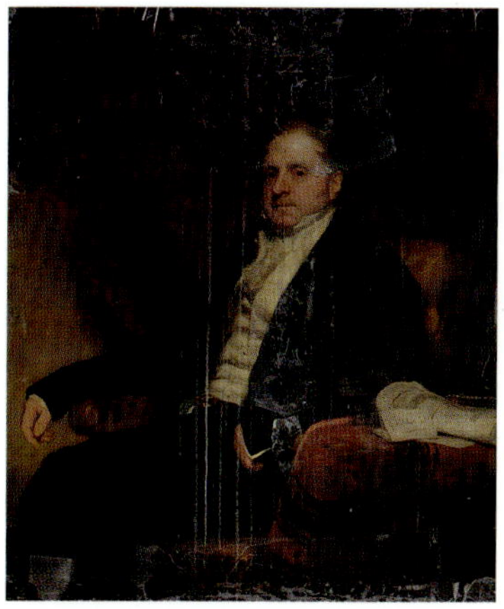

Phillips, Thomas 1770–1845
George Anthony Legh-Keck (1774–1860) 1830
oil on canvas 127 x 101.6
L.F43.1957.0.0

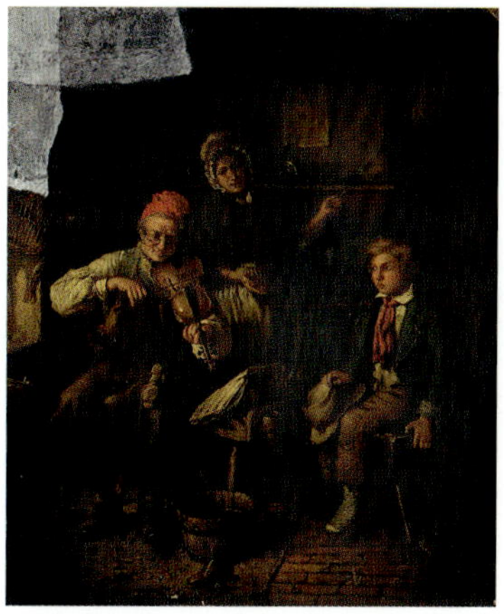

Pidding, Henry James 1797–1864
The Enthusiast
oil on canvas 68.5 x 55.7
L.F1.1889.0.0

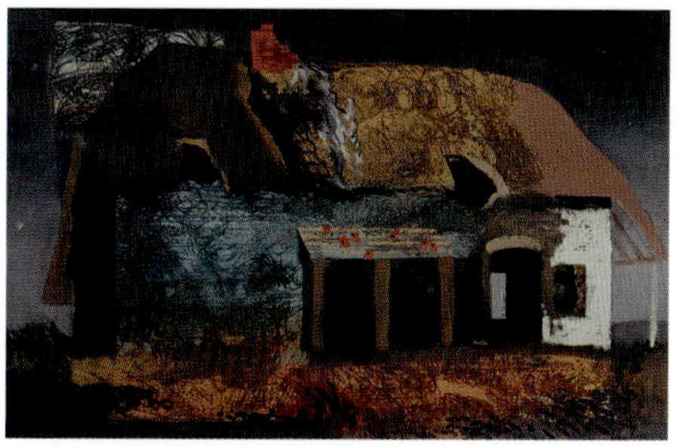

Piper, John 1903–1992
Derelict Cottage, Deane, Hampshire 1940
oil on canvas & panel 51 x 76
L.F3.1942.0.0

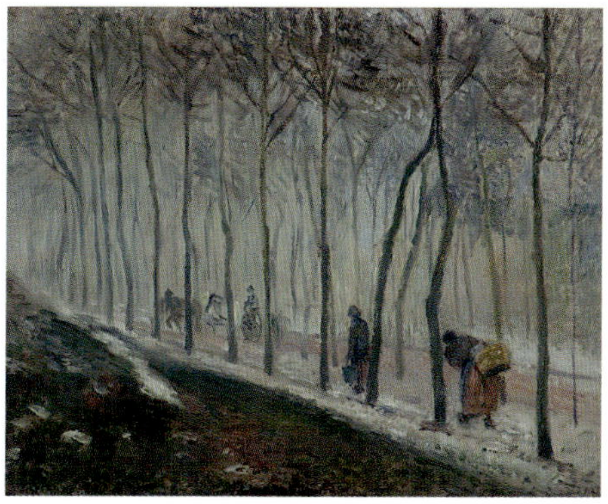

Pissarro, Camille 1831–1903
La route, effet de neige 1879
oil on canvas 45.5 x 55.1
L.F122.1981.0.0

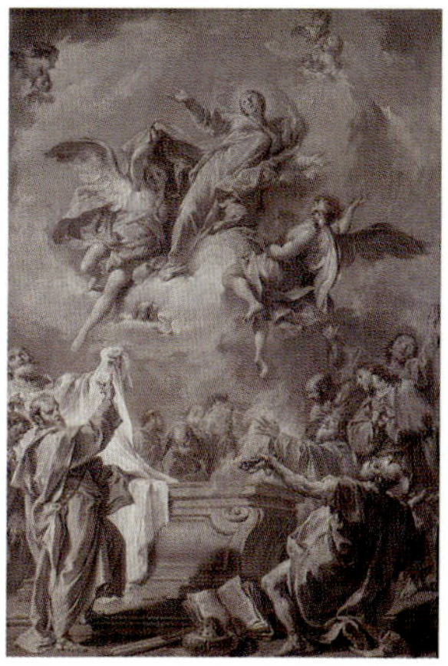

Pittoni, Giovanni Battista the younger 1687–1767
The Assumption of the Virgin
oil on canvas 71.5 x 48.2
L.F83.1964.0.0

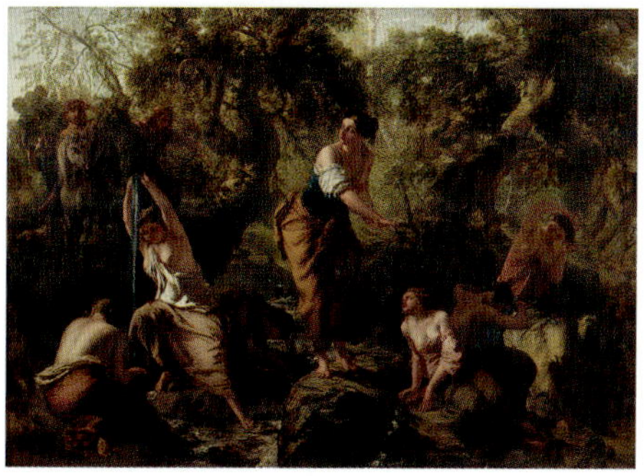

Poole, Paul Falconer 1807–1879
Arlète, a Peasant Girl of Falaise in Normandy, First Discovered by Duke Robert le Diable 1848
oil on canvas 115.5 x 153
L.F11.1891.0.0

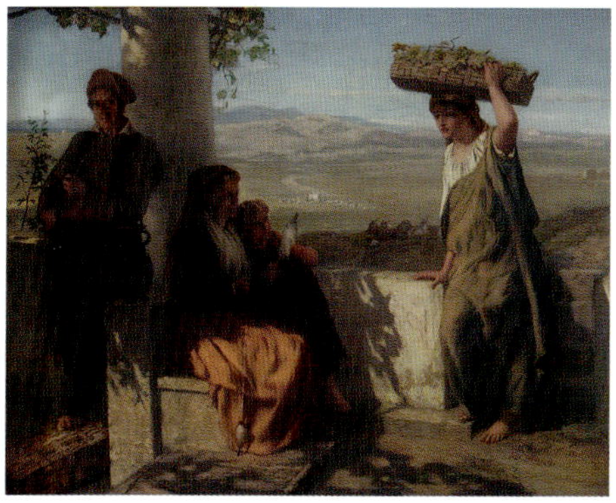

Poole, Paul Falconer 1807–1879
An Italian Family 1856
oil on canvas 53 x 66
L.F12.1891.0.0

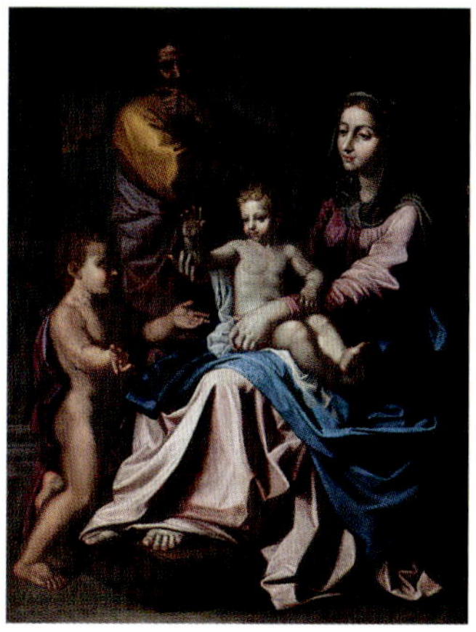

Poussin, Nicolas (attributed to) 1594–1665
The Holy Family with the Infant Saint John 1660
oil on canvas 97.5 x 73
L.F9.1943.4.0

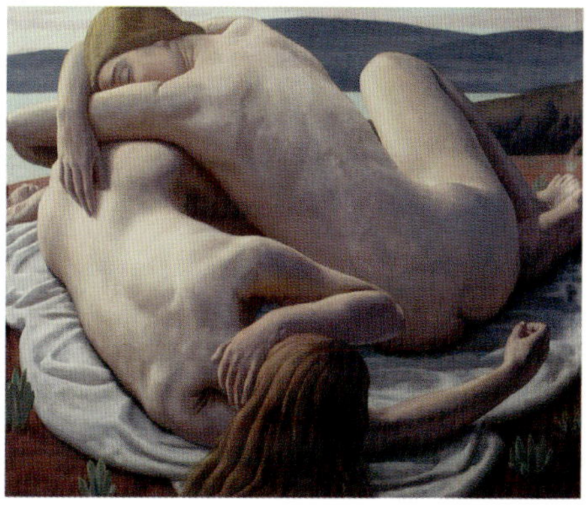

Procter, Ernest 1886–1935
The Day's End 1927
oil on canvas 91.5 x 106.5
L.F3.1928.0.0

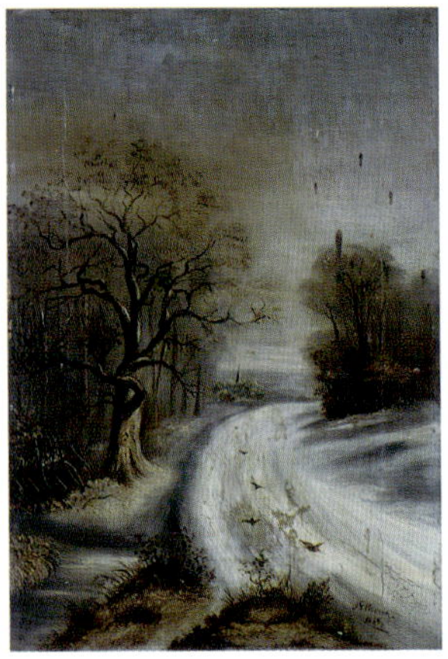

Proctor, J. F.
Winter in South Wales 1886
oil on canvas 46 x 30.6
Y.F19.2009.0.0

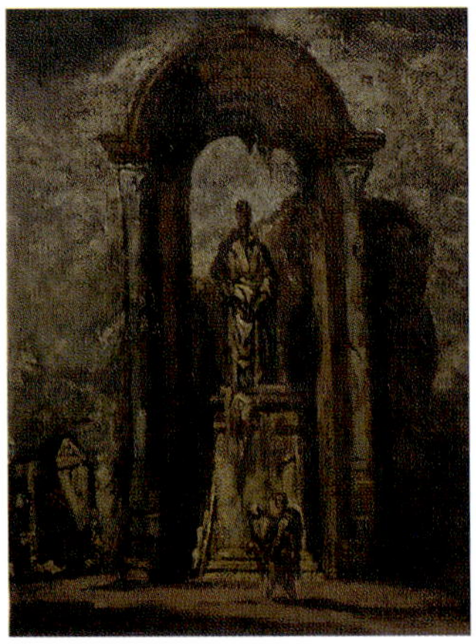

Pryde, James 1866–1941
The Monument
oil on canvas 41 x 30.6
L.F21.1941.0.0

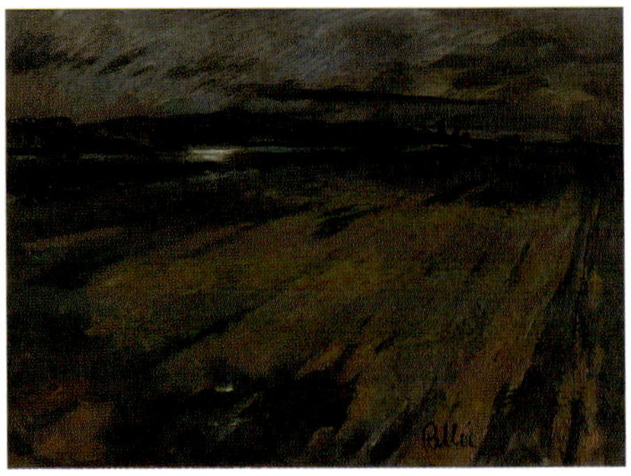

Pullée, Edward 1907–2002
Receding Floodwater
oil on hardboard 30.2 x 40.2
L.F4.1961.0.0

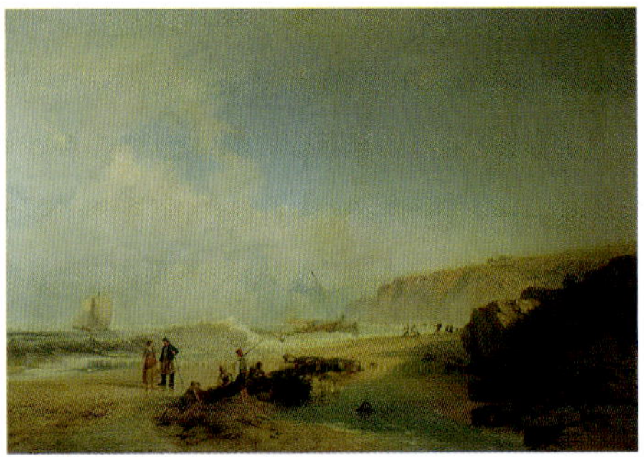

Pyne, James Baker 1800–1870
Whitby, North Yorkshire
oil on canvas 79 x 111.7
L.F2.1892.0.0

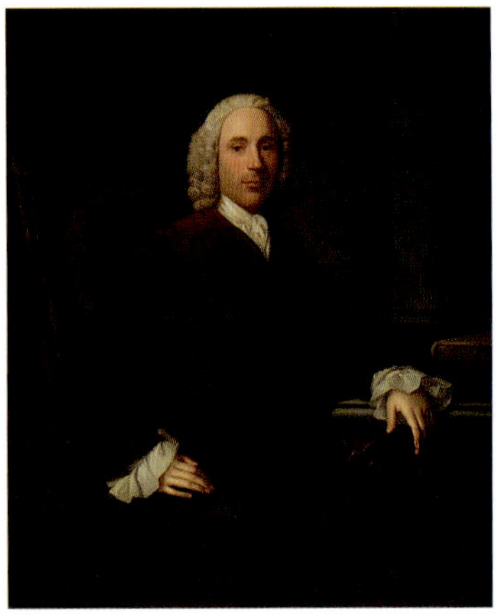

Ramsay, Allan 1713–1784
The Honourable William Finch 1744
oil on canvas 127.3 x 101.5
L.F39.1982.0.0

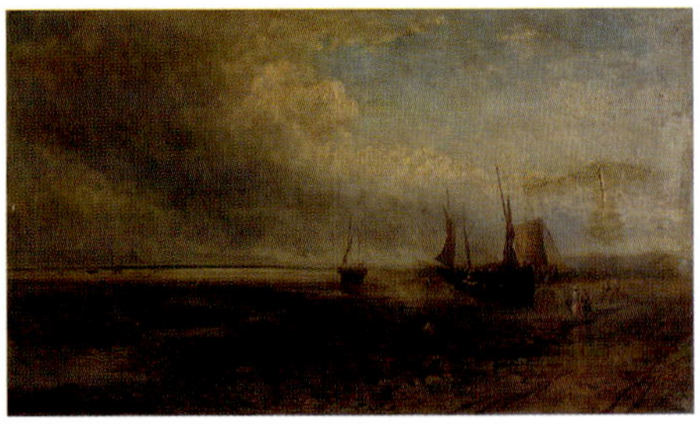

Read, Ada
Carting Fish at Mount's Bay, Cornwall (copy after Edmund Morison Wimperis) 1885
oil on canvas 79 x 130
Y.F12.2009.0.0

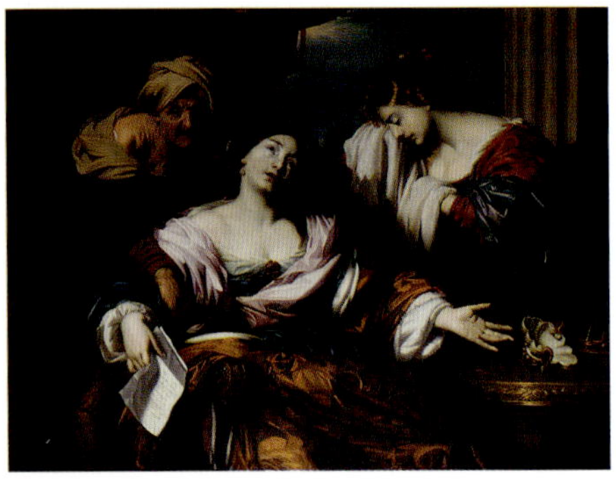

Régnier, Nicolas (attributed to) c.1590–1667
The Death of Sophonisba 1665–1667
oil on canvas 131.5 x 167
L.F22.1949.0.0

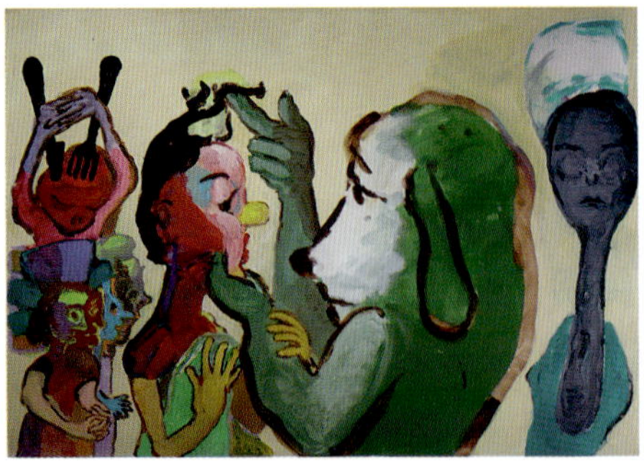

Rego, Paula Figueiroa b.1935
Three Guchi Faces, Guchi Face with Cutlery 1983
acrylic on paper 76.5 x 101.5
L.F18.1984.0.0

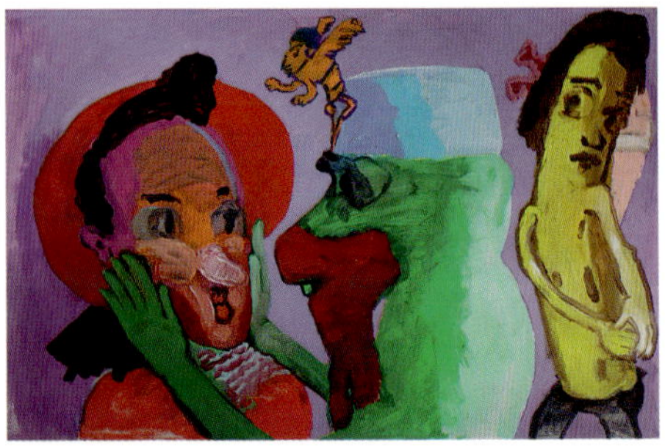

Rego, Paula Figueiroa b.1935
Three Guchi Faces, Guchi Face with Banana 1983
acrylic on paper 68.5 x 101.5
L.F19.1984.0.0

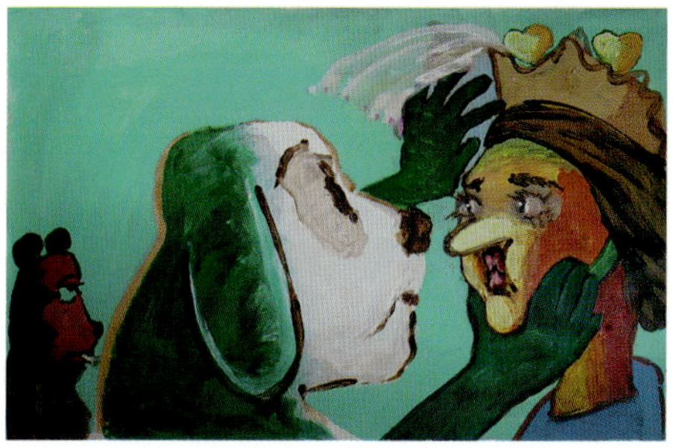

Rego, Paula Figueiroa b.1935
Three Guchi Faces, Guchi Face with Bride
1983
acrylic on paper 68.8 x 101.5
L.F20.1984.0.0

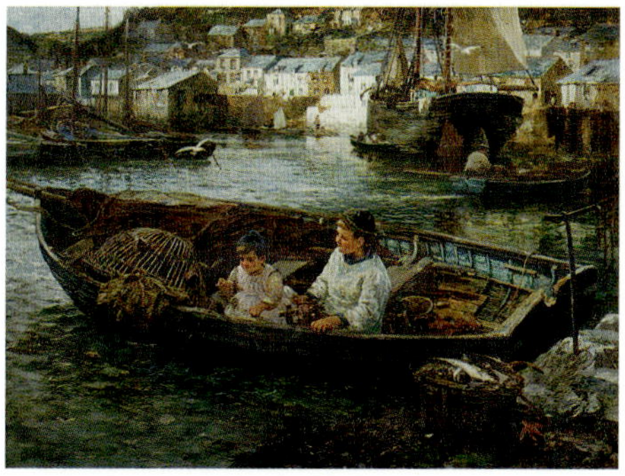

Reid, John Robertson 1851–1926
Little Cornish Fishermen, Polperro
oil on canvas 99.5 x 130.8
L.F1.1906.0.0

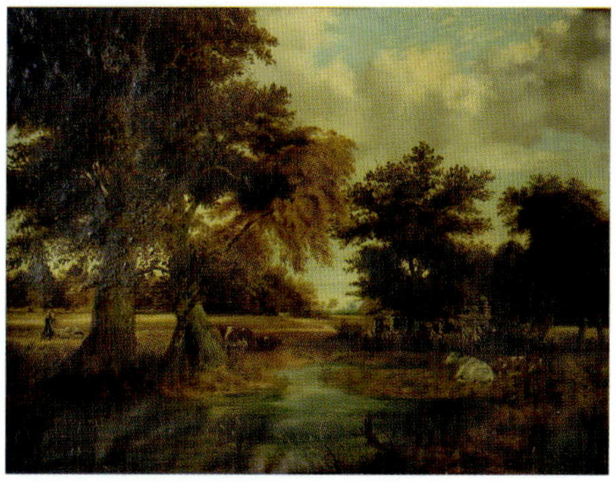

Renals, Richard Beswick 1833–1900
Landscape with Cattle and Sheep by a Stream
oil on canvas 72 x 91.5
L.F80.1988.0.0

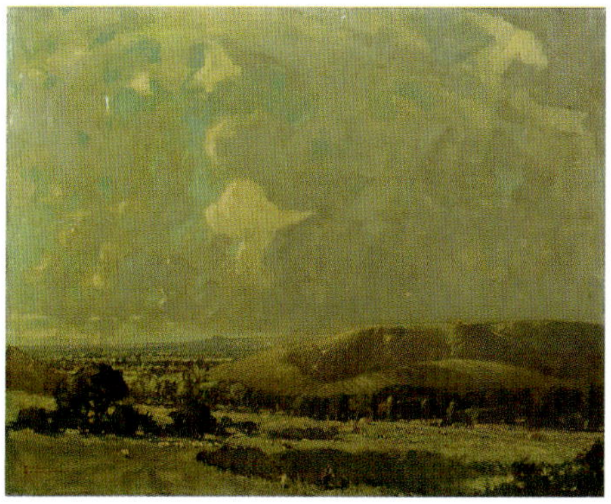

Renison, G.
Summer Landscape with Hills
oil on canvas 50.7 x 60.6
L.F3.1996.8.0

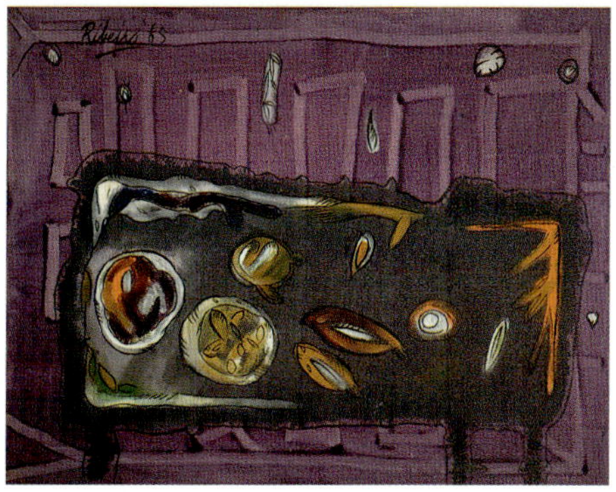

Ribeiro, Lancelot 1933–2010
Purple Still Life 1965
oil on canvas 50 x 62
L.F53.1990.0.0

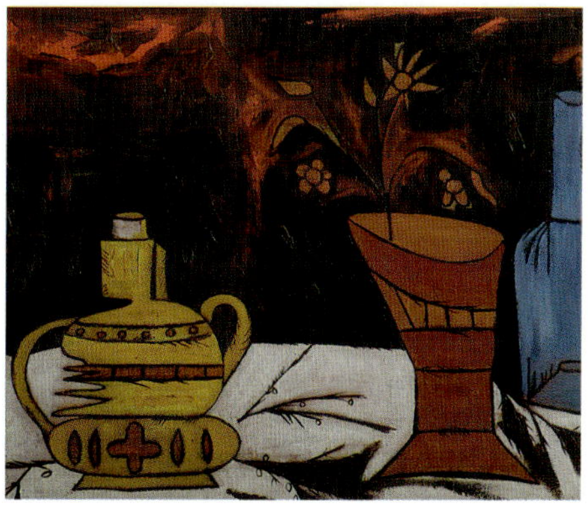

Ribeiro, Lancelot 1933–2010
Still Life with a Pitcher 1965
PVA & oil on canvas 42.7 x 48.5
L.F4.1990.0.0

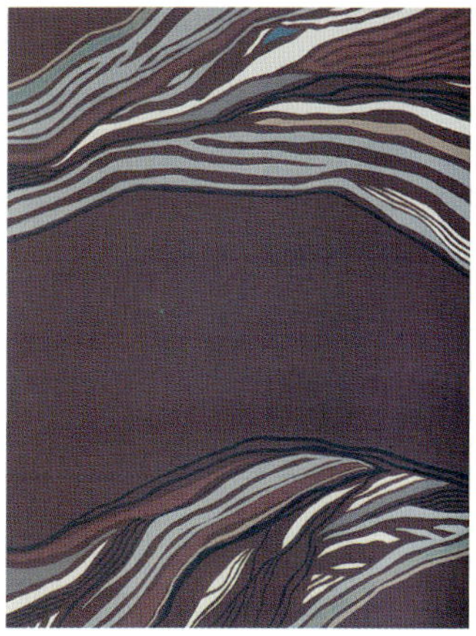

Ribeiro, Lancelot 1933–2010
Accented Landscape, Series 1 1979
PVA on canvas 77.5 x 57
L.F3.1990.0.0

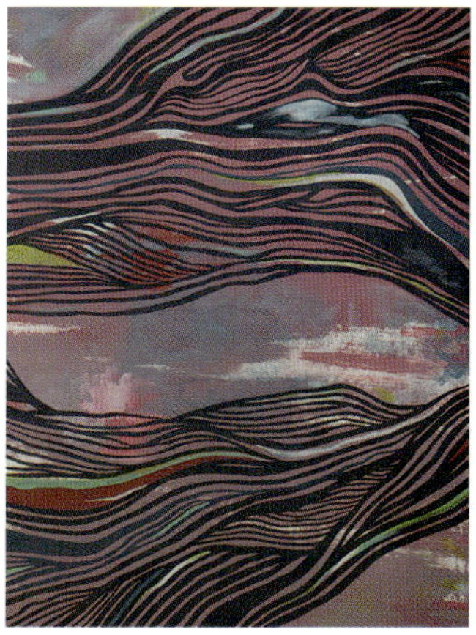

Ribeiro, Lancelot 1933–2010
Accented Landscape, Series 2 1980
PVA on canvas 92.5 x 68.5
L.F54.1990.0.0

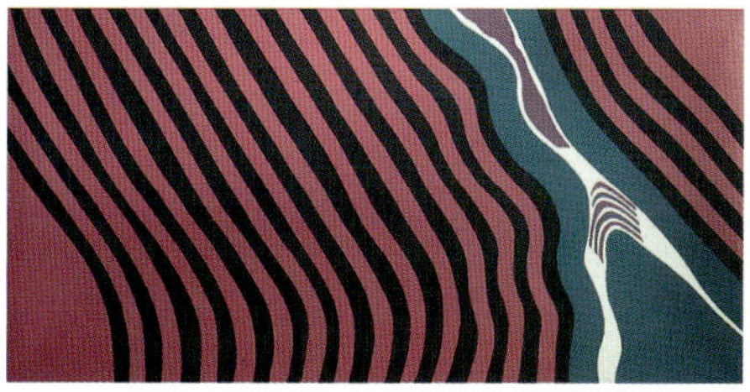

Ribeiro, Lancelot 1933–2010
Curvilinear Directions II 1980
PVA on canvas 61.5 x 121.8
L.F2.1990.0.0

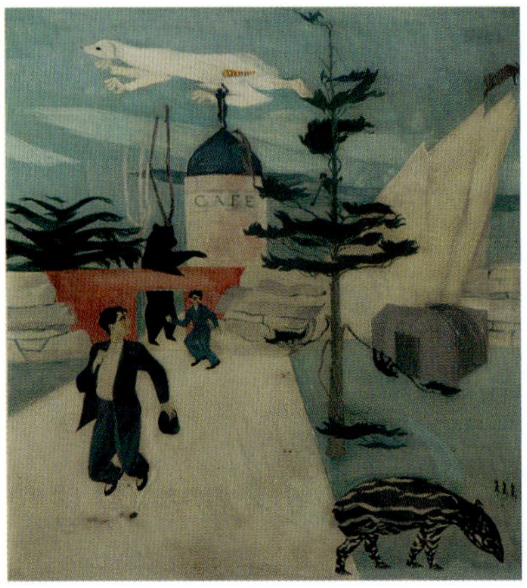

Richards, Albert 1919–1945
Escape from the Circus 1938
oil on canvas 45.5 x 41.5
L.F16.1981.0.0

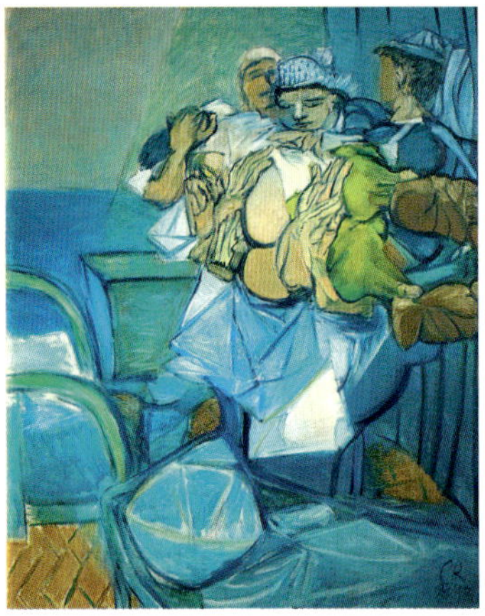

Richards, Ceri Geraldus 1903–1971
Return of the Patient (version 1) 1953
oil on canvas 126.5 x 102
L.F5.1981.0.0

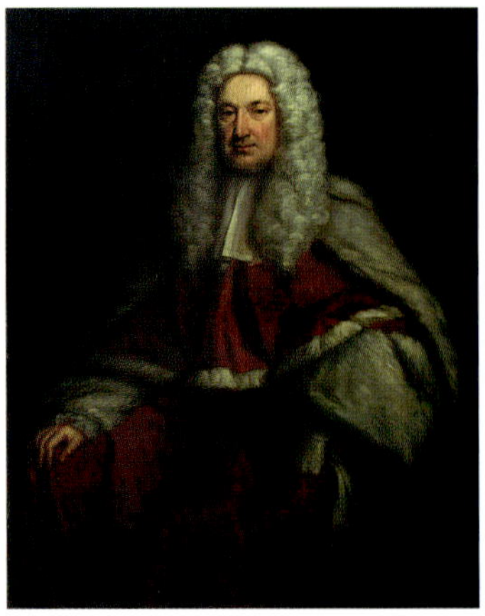

Richardson, Jonathan the elder (after) 1664/1665–1745
Baron Carter, Lord Chief Justice Carter
oil on canvas 126.4 x 102.2
L.F120.1900.0.0

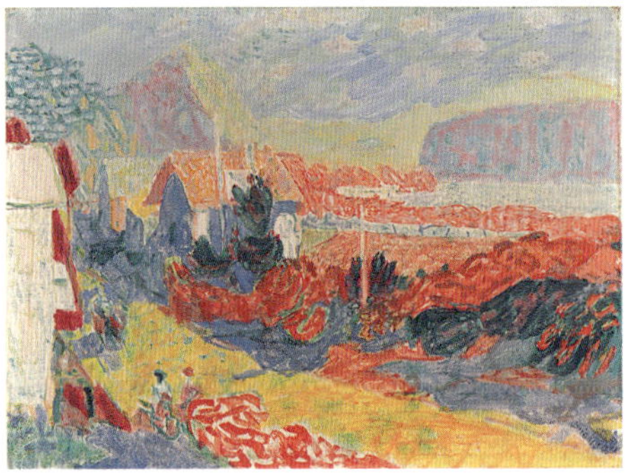

Robb, Brian 1913–1979
Weesen, Switzerland 1954
oil on canvas 50.8 x 60.3
L.F7.1955.0.0

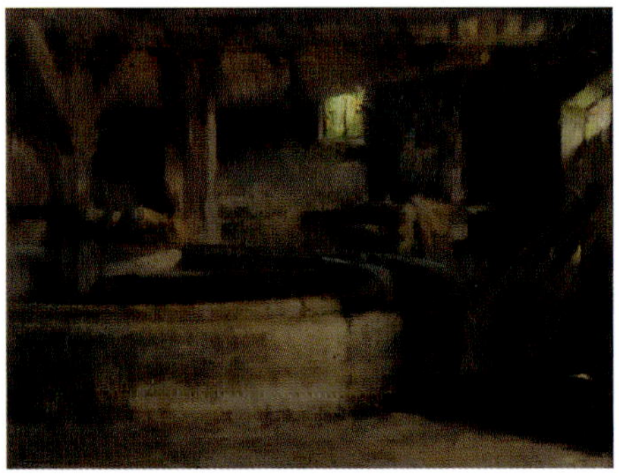

Roberts, Albert Thomas 1868–1923
Cider Press, Normandy, France
oil on millboard 26.5 x 34.5
L.F18.1923.0.0

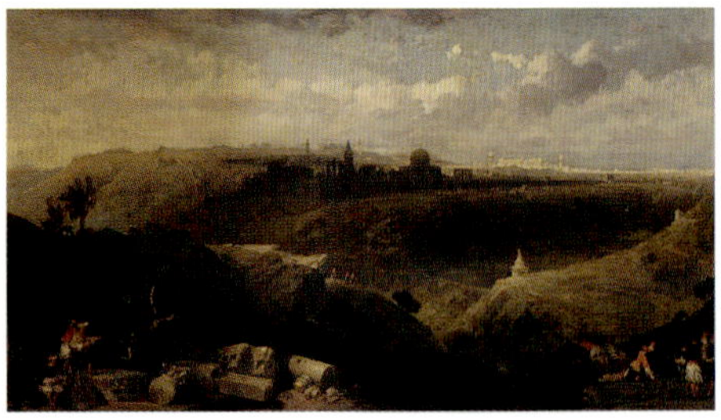

Roberts, David 1796–1864
Jerusalem from the Mount of Olives 1860
oil on canvas 52.2 x 89.5
L.F5.1890.0.0

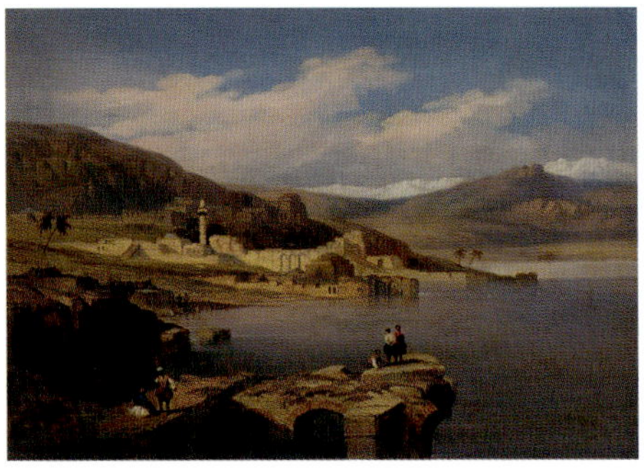

Roberts, David 1796–1864
View of Tiberias on the Sea of Galilee
oil on canvas 39.3 x 54.5
L.F54.1966.0.0

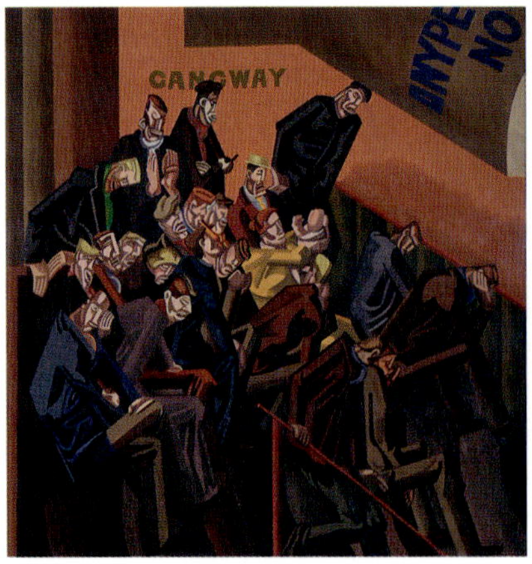

Roberts, William Patrick 1895–1980
At the Hippodrome 1921
oil on canvas 95 x 90.6
L.F23.1935.0.0

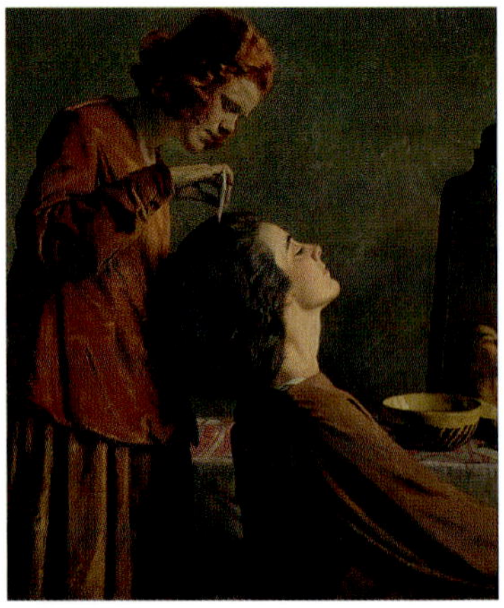

Rothenstein, William 1872–1945
The Toilet 1924
oil on canvas 91.5 x 76.4
L.F16.1931.0.0

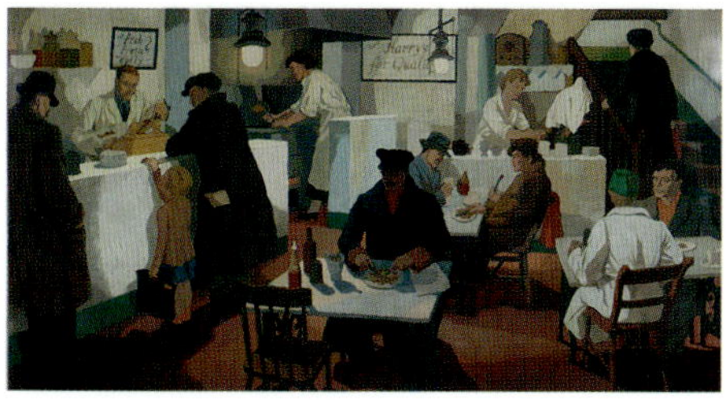

Rowe, Cliff 1904–1989
The Fried Fish Shop 1936
oil on panel 59.5 x 112.8
L.F41.1936.0.0

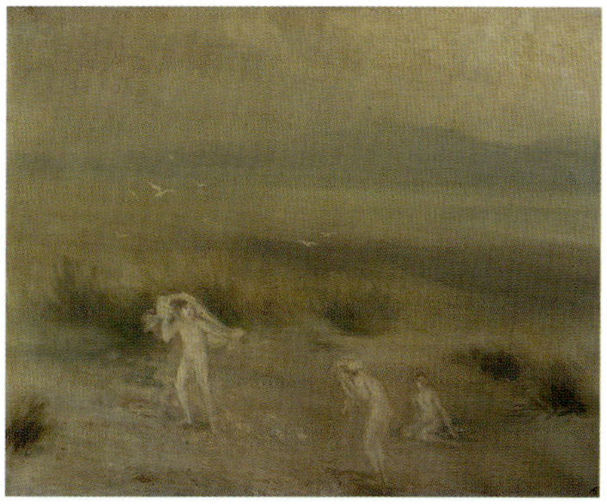

Russell, George William (attributed to)
1867–1935
Three Figures in a Landscape with Birds
oil on canvas 53.5 x 64
L.F38.1990.0.0

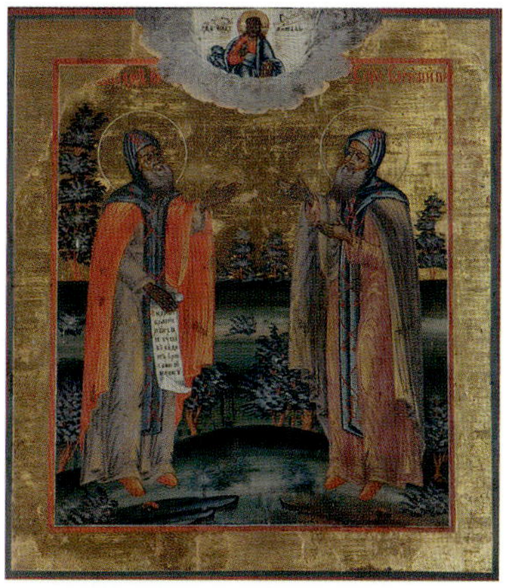

Russian School 17th C
Ikon with Saint Theodore and Saint Aloysius
oil on panel 35.5 x 31
L.F143.1856.0.0

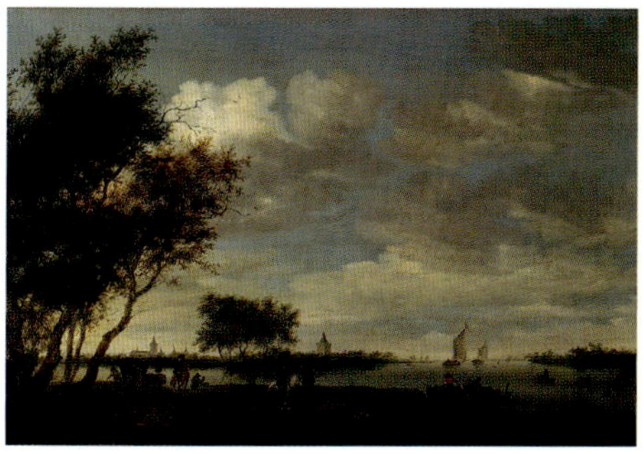

Ruysdael, Salomon van c.1602–1670
River Scene with a Distant View of Vianen, The Netherlands 1645
oil on canvas 77.5 x 114.3
L.F74.1955.0.0

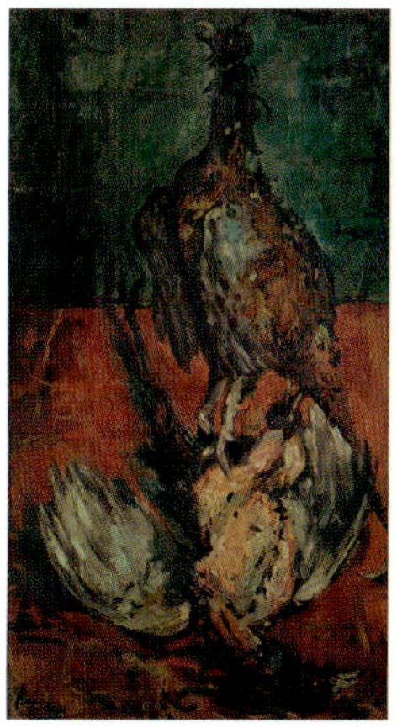

Ryan, Adrian 1920–1998
Pheasants before 1953
oil on canvas 96.5 x 50.8
L.F43.1953.0.0

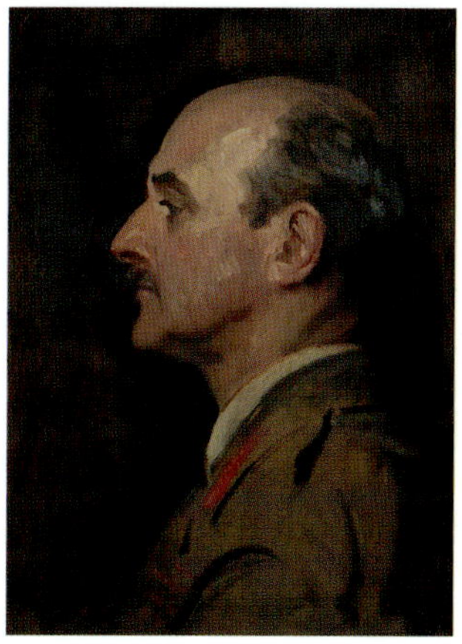

Sargent, John Singer 1856–1925
Field Marshal Viscount Allenby (1861–1936), GCB, GCMG (sketch) 1922
oil on canvas 56.3 x 41.2
L.F15.1925.0.0

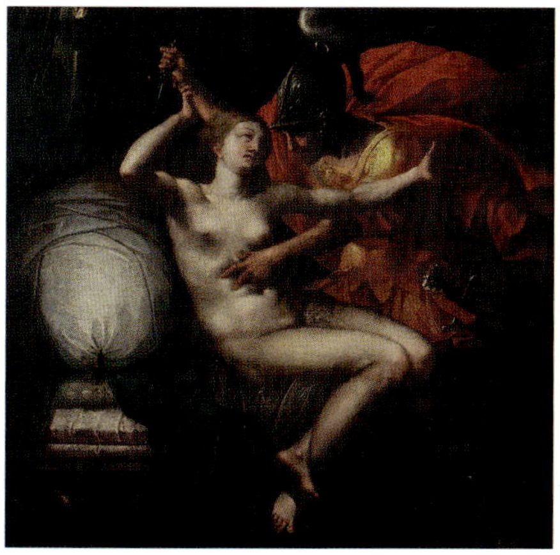

School of Fontainebleau
The Rape of Lucrece (from the poem by William Shakespeare) 18th C
oil on canvas 58.4 x 61
L.F20.1935.27.0

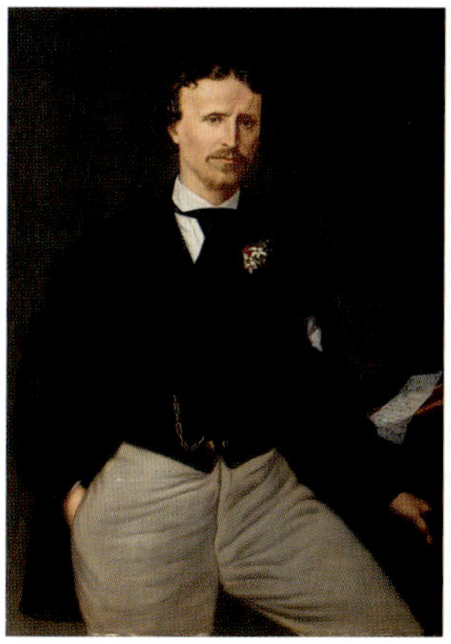

Scott, A.
Thomas Crick (d.1879) 1867
oil on canvas 124 x 86
L.F58.1993.0.0 (P)

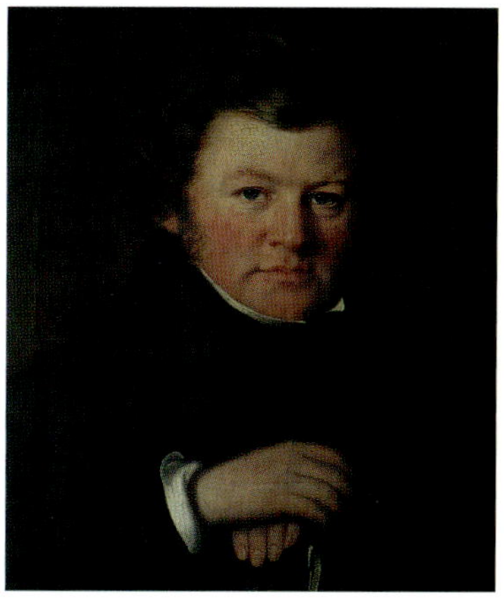

Scott, William 1797–1862
John Flower (1793–1861) 1841
oil on canvas 56 x 45.8
Y.F3.2008.0.0

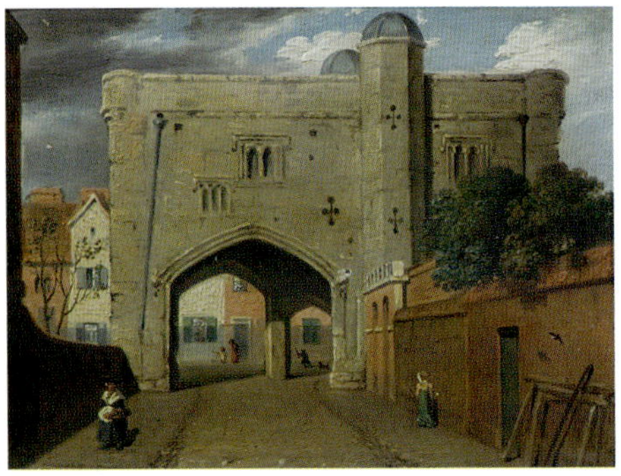

Seguier, John 1785–1856
Newarke Gateway, Leicester
oil on wood 10.5 x 13.4
Y.F19.2009.0.0

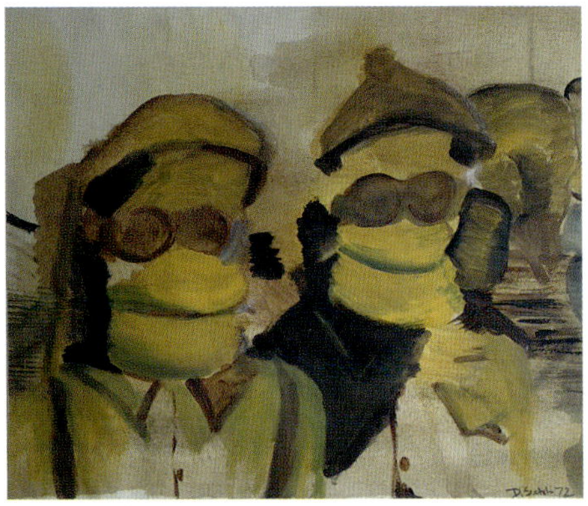

Setch, Dianne b.1945
Soldiers 2 c.1982
acrylic on paper 54 x 62.3
Y.F4.2006.1.0

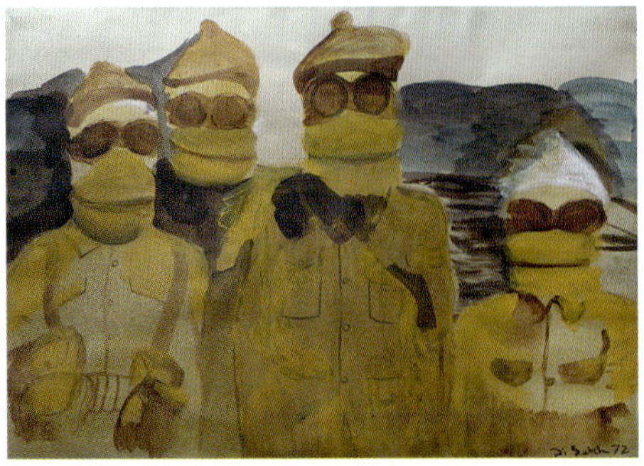

Setch, Dianne b.1945
Soldiers 4 c.1982
acrylic on paper 49 x 67
Y.F4.2006.2.0

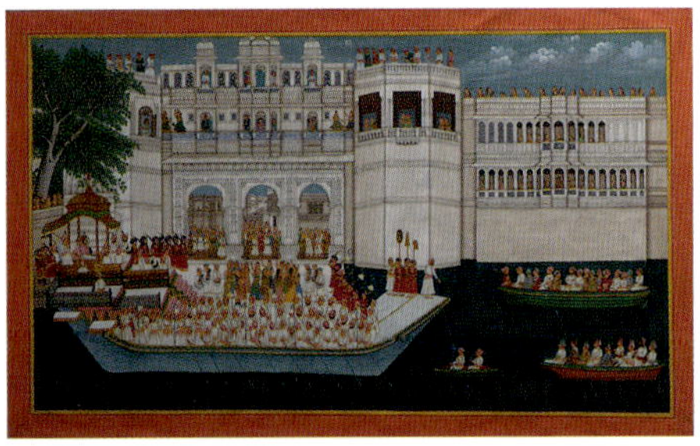

Sharma, Ram Krishan
Bagor House, Gangor Festival, India
tempera on silk 53.6 x 85.8
Y.F7.2001.0.0

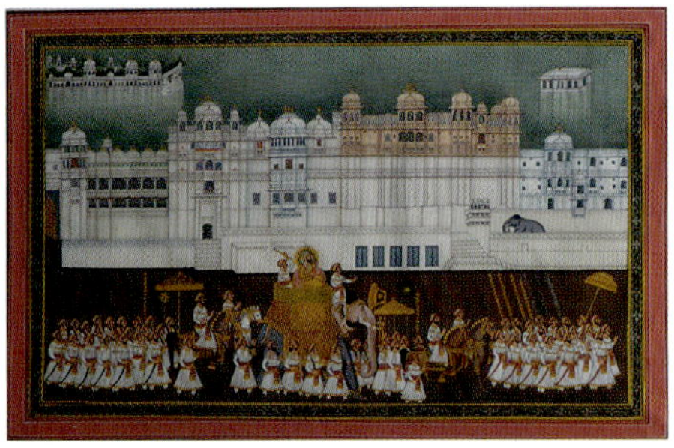

Sharma, Ram Krishan
City Palace, Sawar, India
tempera on silk 35.5 x 54.3
Y.F10.2001.0.0

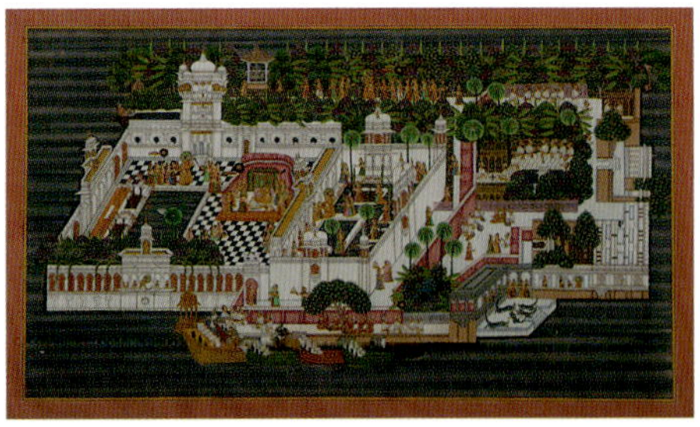

Sharma, Ram Krishan
Jag Mandir, India
tempera on silk 50 x 81.5
Y.F8.2001.0.0

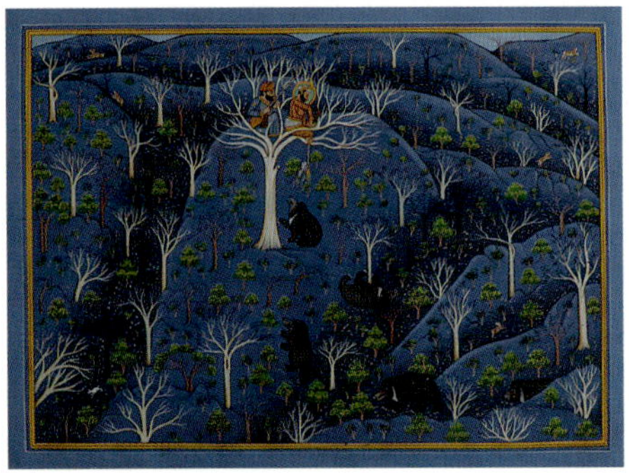

Sharma, Ram Krishan
Small Hunting Scene
tempera on silk 24 x 31
Y.F9.2001.0.0

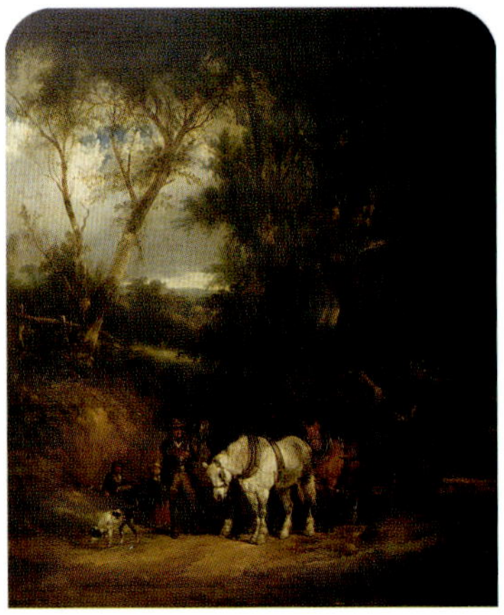

Shayer, William 1788–1879
The Timber Wagon
oil on canvas 101.5 x 84
L.F2.1883.0.0

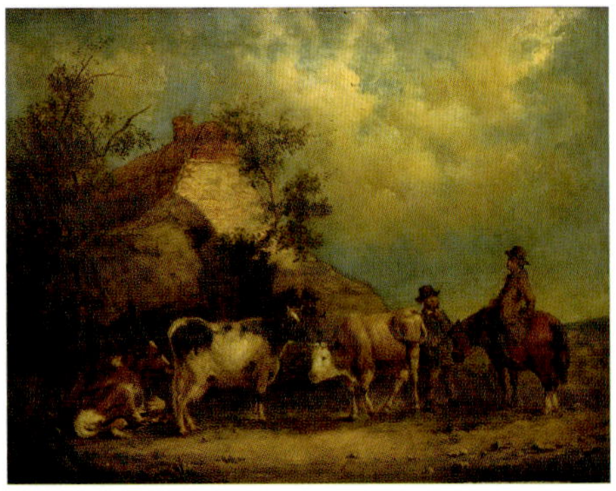

Shayer, William (style of) 1788–1879
At the Farm 1840
oil on canvas 38.5 x 48.5
L.F4.1946.0.0

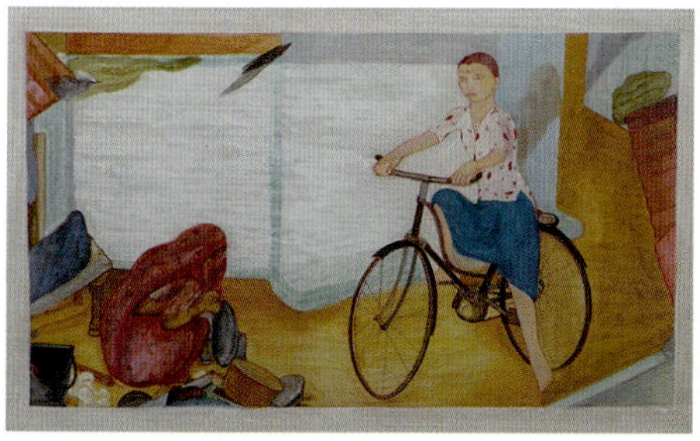

Sheikh, Nilima b.1945
Champa, before Her Marriage, and with Her Mother 1984–1985
tempera on sanghaneri paper 22 x 35 (E)
L.F35.1990.1.0

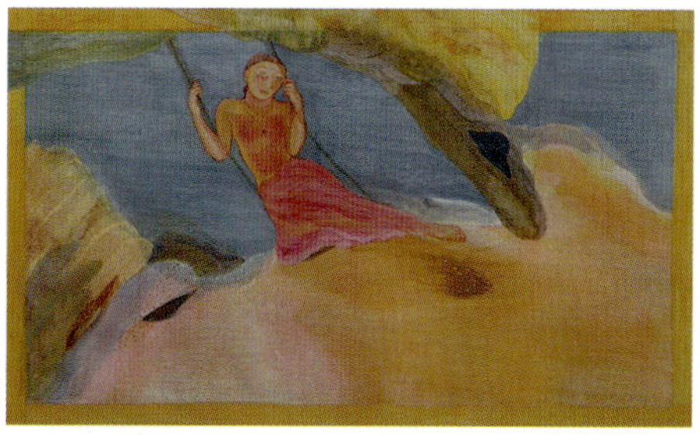

Sheikh, Nilima b.1945
Champa, on the Swing, a Traditional Motif of Love and Girlhood, on the Eve of Her Marriage 1984–1985
tempera on sanghaneri paper 22 x 35 (E)
L.F35.1990.2.0

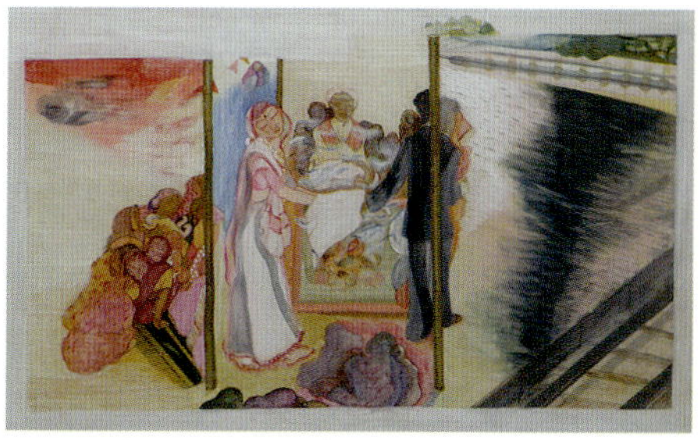

Sheikh, Nilima b.1945
Marriage and Departure to the In-Laws' Village 1984–1985
tempera on sanghaneri paper 22 x 35 (E)
L.F35.1990.3.0

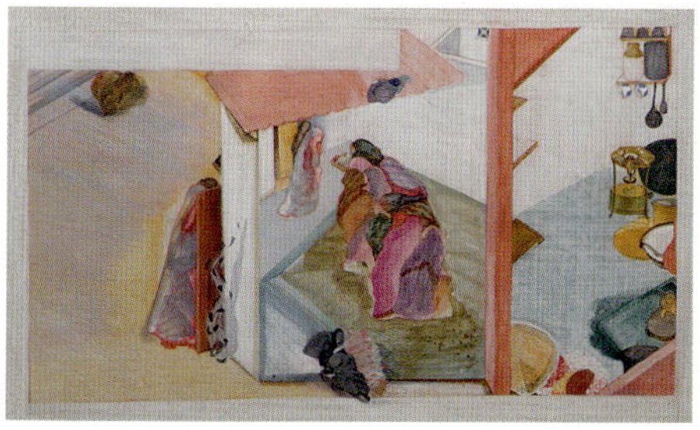

Sheikh, Nilima b.1945
Arrival and Welcome 'aati' at the In-Laws and the Kitchen, the Bride's Place 1984–1985
tempera on sanghaneri paper 22 x 35 (E)
L.F35.1990.4.0

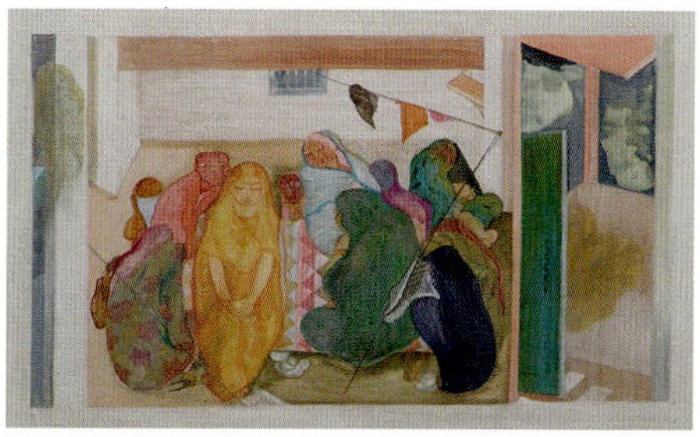

Sheikh, Nilima b.1945
The Womenfolk of the House Inspect Champa, the New Bride 1984–1985
tempera on sanghaneri paper 22 x 35 (E)
L.F35.1990.5.0

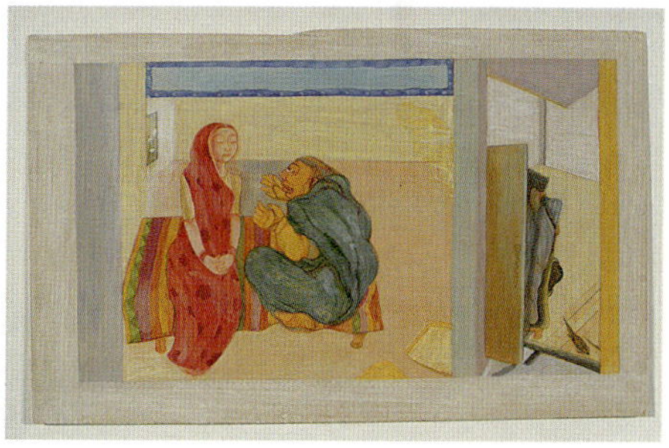

Sheikh, Nilima b.1945
Conflict between the Daughter-in-Law and Mother-in-Law, while the Husband Enjoys a Rest 1984–1985
tempera on sanghaneri paper 22 x 35 (E)
L.F35.1990.6.0

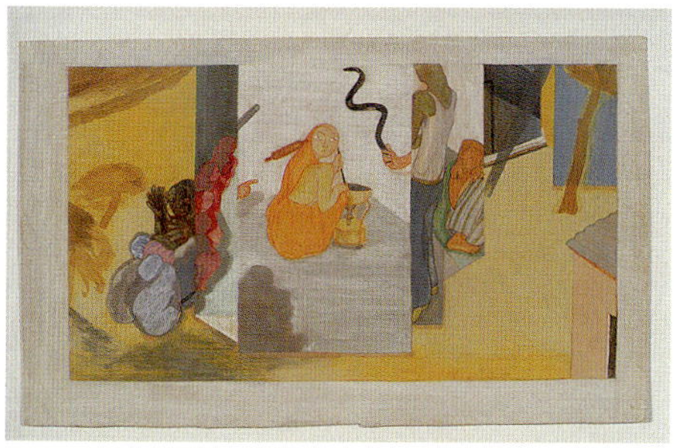

Sheikh, Nilima b.1945
Tensions in the Household and Persecution of the New Bride 1984–1985
tempera on sanghaneri paper 22 x 35 (E)
L.F35.1990.7.0

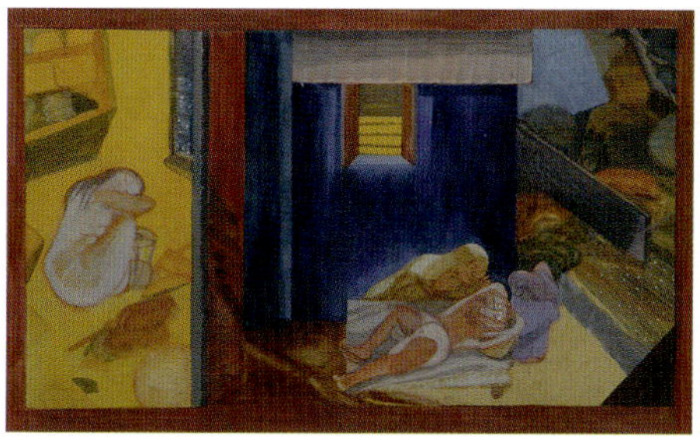

Sheikh, Nilima b.1945
The Husband, Sister-in-Law and Mother-in-Law Plot to Kill Champa, while She Dozes Battered and Exhausted from (...) 1984–1985
tempera on sanghaneri paper 22 x 35 (E)
L.F35.1990.8.0

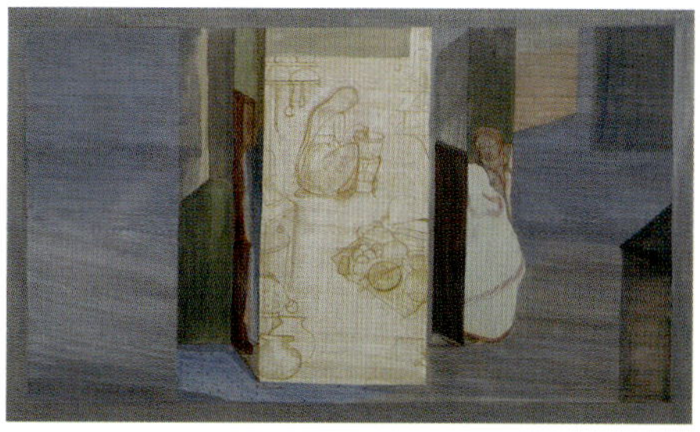

Sheikh, Nilima b.1945
Conspiracy to Murder while Champa Works in the Kitchen 1984–1985
tempera on sanghaneri paper 22 x 35 (E)
L.F35.1990.9.0

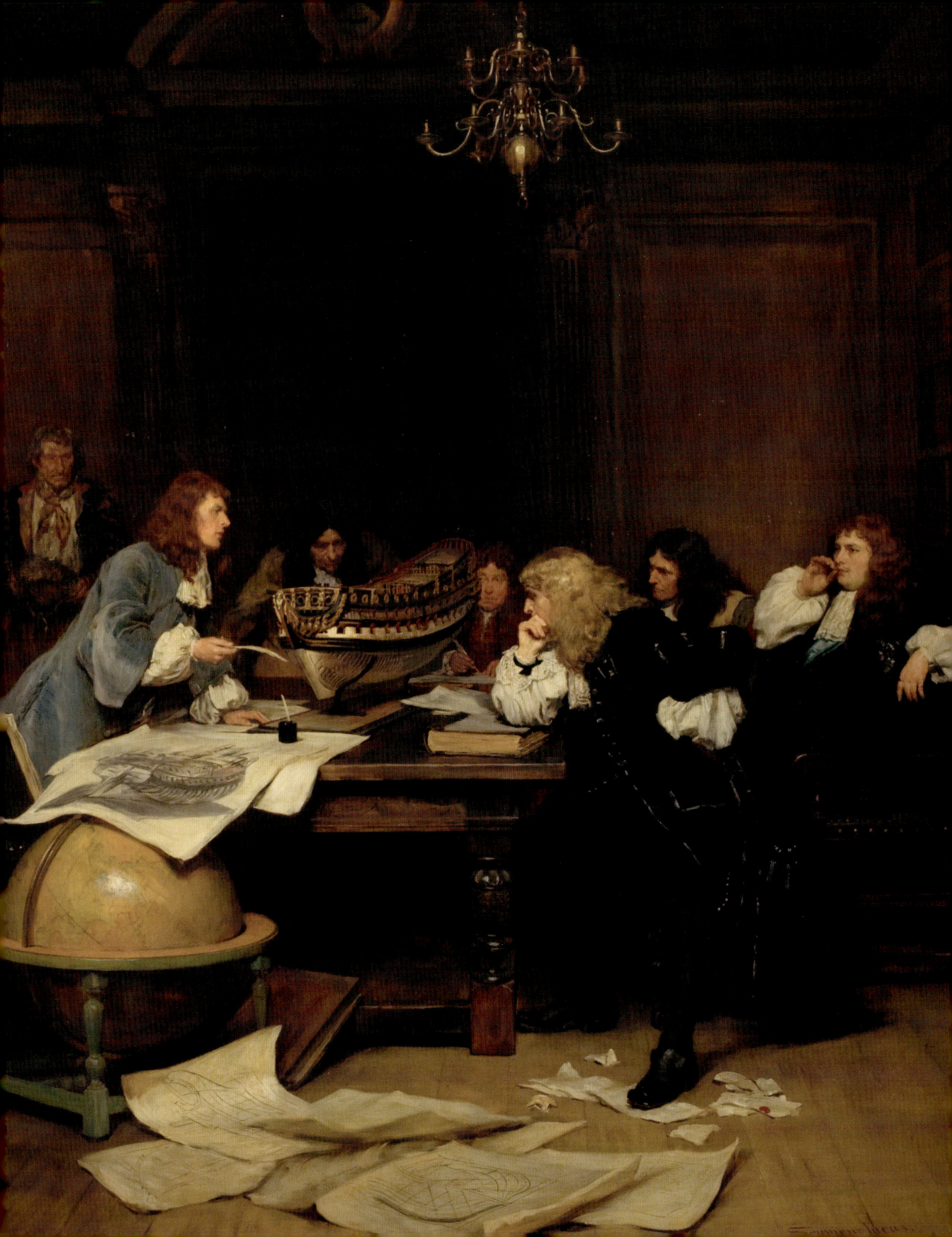

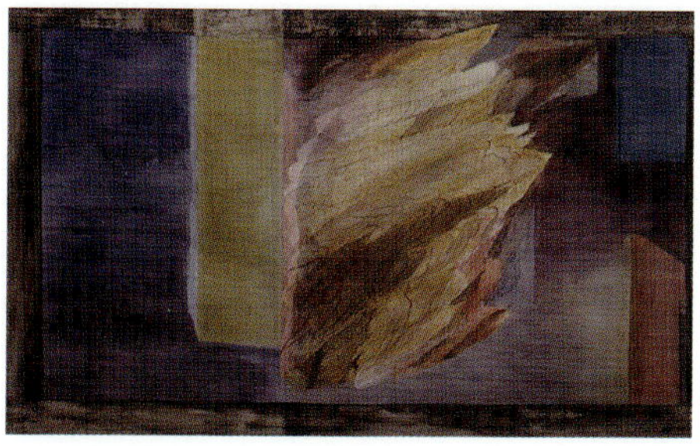

Sheikh, Nilima b.1945
Fire and Smoke from the Kitchen 1984–1985
tempera on sanghaneri paper 22 x 35 (E)
L.F35.1990.10.0

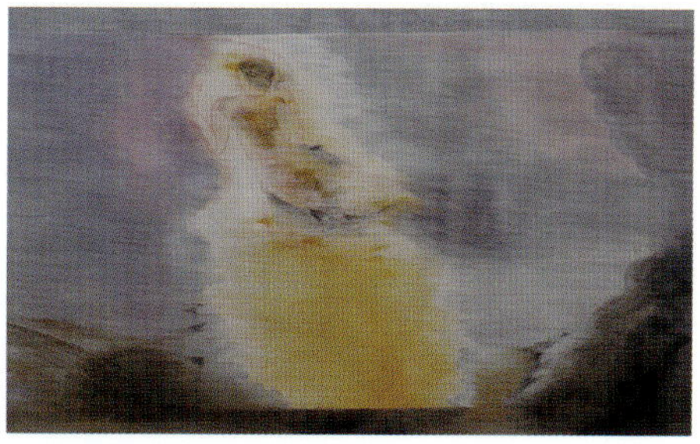

Sheikh, Nilima b.1945
Champa's Funeral Pyre 1984–1985
tempera on sanghaneri paper 22 x 35 (E)
L.F35.1990.11.0

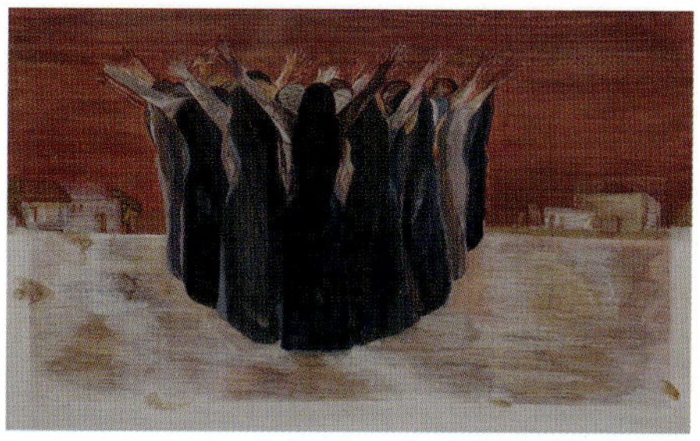

Sheikh, Nilima b.1945
Ritualised Mourning, Marshia 1984–1985
tempera on sanghaneri paper 22 x 35 (E)
L.F35.1990.12.0

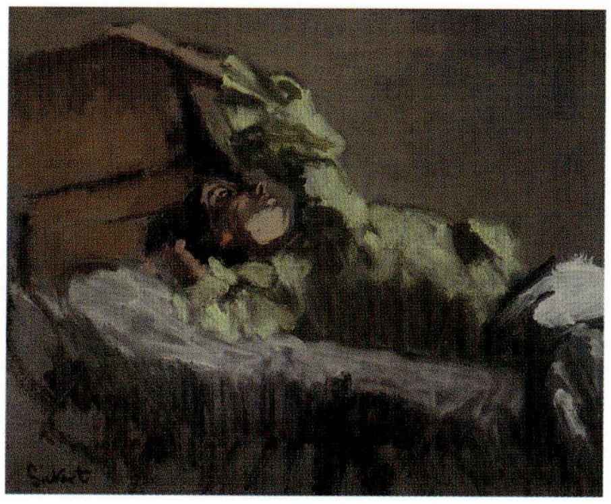

Sickert, Walter Richard 1860–1942
The Yellow Sleeve 1903–1904
oil on canvas 38.5 x 46.1
L.F840.1974.0.0

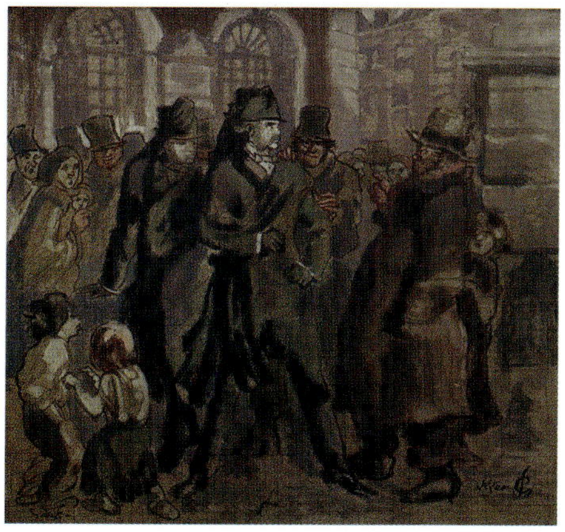

Sickert, Walter Richard 1860–1942
The Bart and the Bums (after John Gilbert)
1930
oil on canvas 59.5 x 63.5
L.F17.1931.0.0

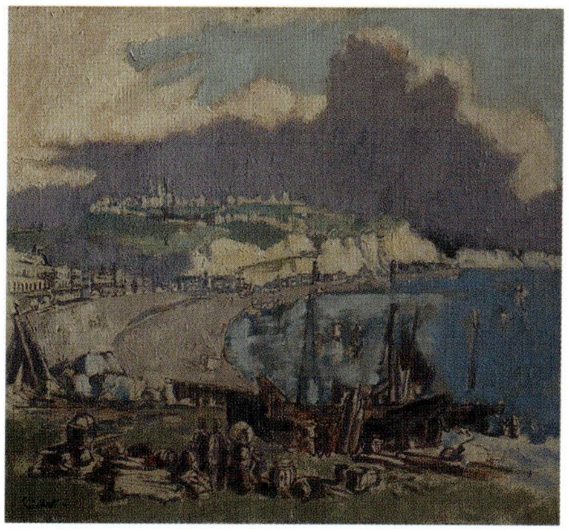

Sickert, Walter Richard 1860–1942
Dover, Kent
oil on canvas 53 x 57.3
L.F4.1945.0.0

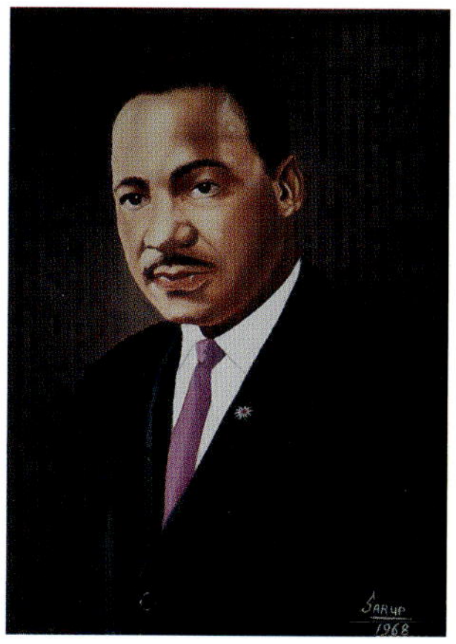

Singh, Sarup active 1968–2001
Martin Luther King Junior (1929–1968) 1968
oil on canvas 71 x 50.5
Y.F19.2003.0.0

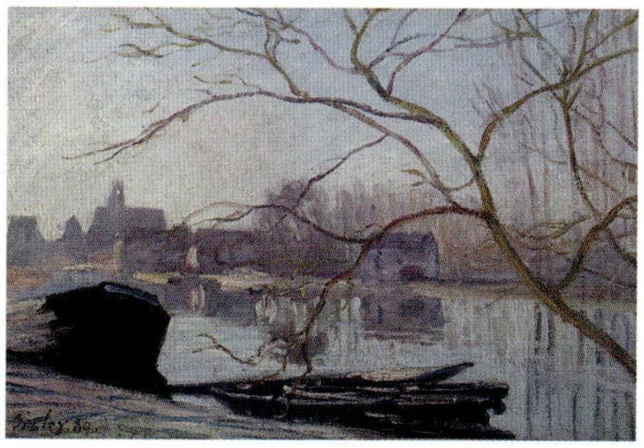

Sisley, Alfred 1839–1899
Le Loing, gelée blanche 1889
oil on canvas 37 x 54
L.F15.1935.0.0

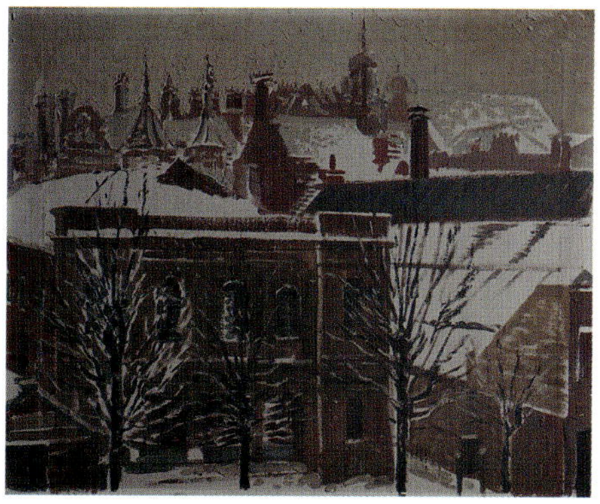

Slater, Joseph Edward 1902–1994
Charles Street, Leicester 1947
oil on canvas 48.9 x 59.1
L.F453.1977.0.0

Facing page: Lucas, Seymour, 1849–1923, *A Whip for Van Tromp, the Admiralty* (detail), 1883, Leicester Arts and Museums Service (p. 61)

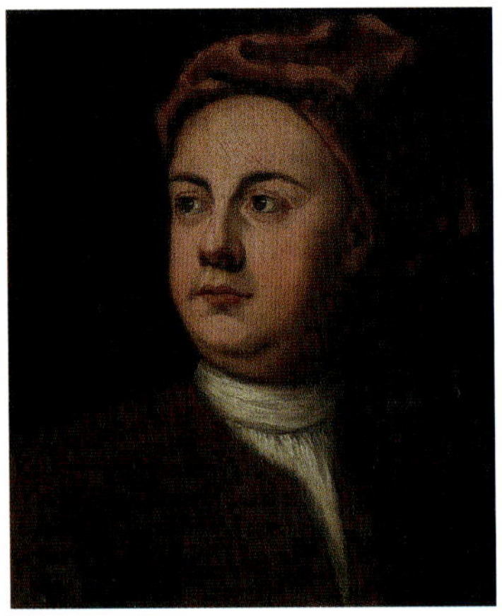

Slaughter, Stephen 1697–1765
James Thomson (1700–1748), Poet
oil on canvas 45 x 37
L.F28.1937.0.0

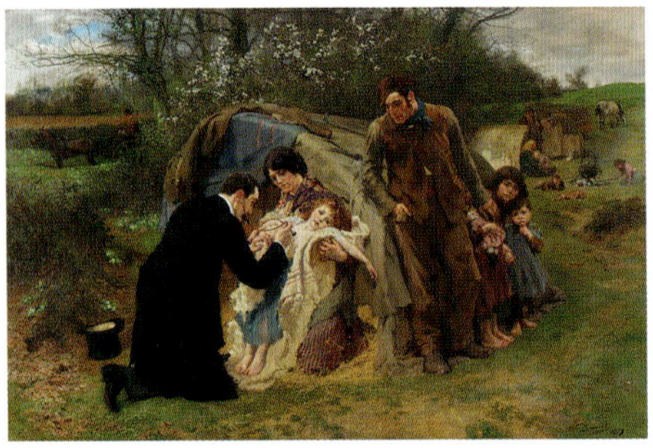

Small, William 1843–1931
The Good Samaritan 1899
oil on canvas 155.5 x 230
L.F16.1900.0.0

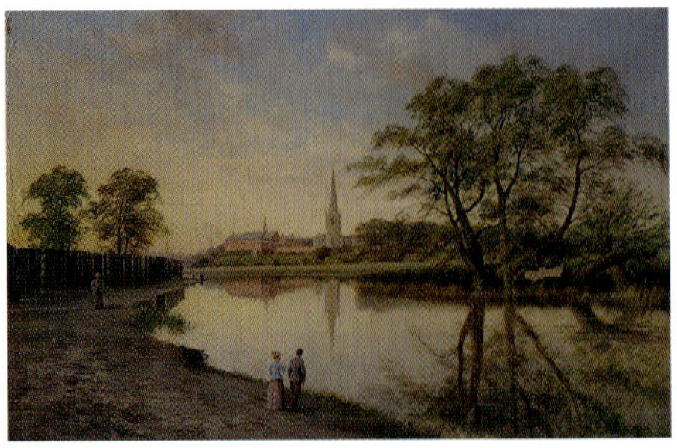

Smith, J. H.
Leicester from the River c.1900
oil on canvas 51 x 76
Y.F8.2009.0.0

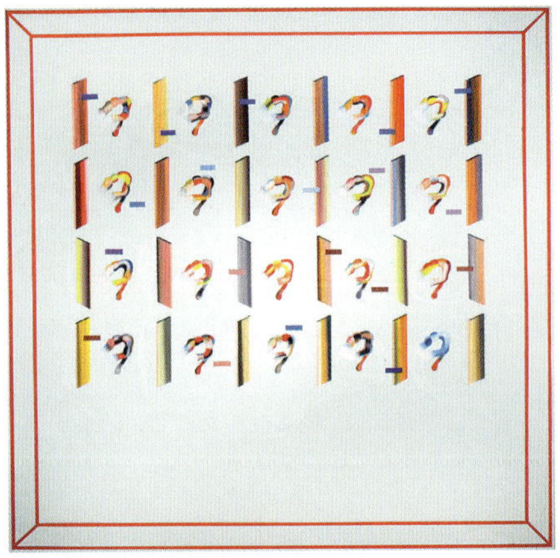

Smith, Jack 1928–2011
64 Activities in Blue 1943
oil on canvas 107 x 106.5
L.F355.1975.0.0

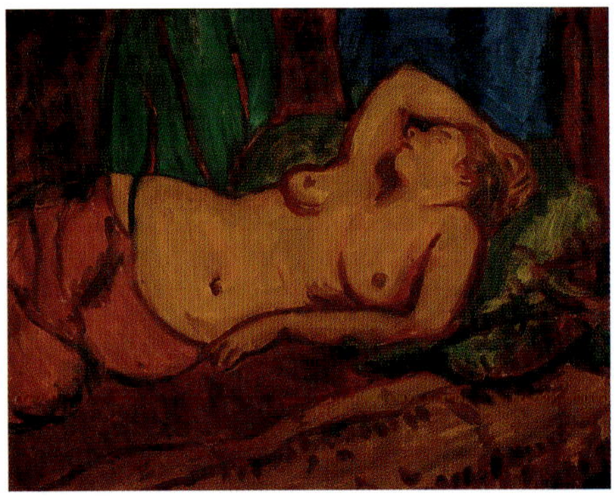

Smith, Matthew Arnold Bracy 1879–1959
Reclining Nude 1924
oil on canvas 66 x 82
L.F29.1948.0.0

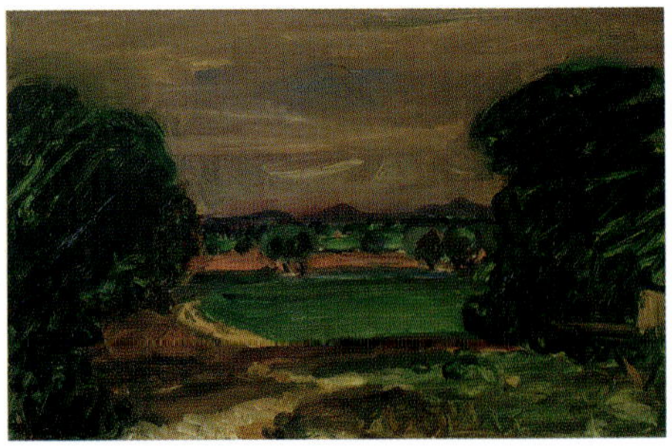

Smith, Matthew Arnold Bracy 1879–1959
Landscape, South of France 1930–1940
oil on canvas 35.7 x 53.6
L.F107.1955.0.0

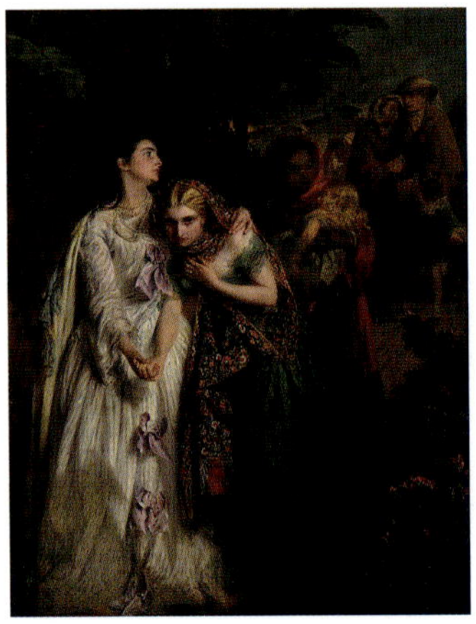

Solomon, Abraham 1824–1862
The Flight from Lucknow 1858
oil on canvas 61 x 45.7
L.F13.1891.0.0

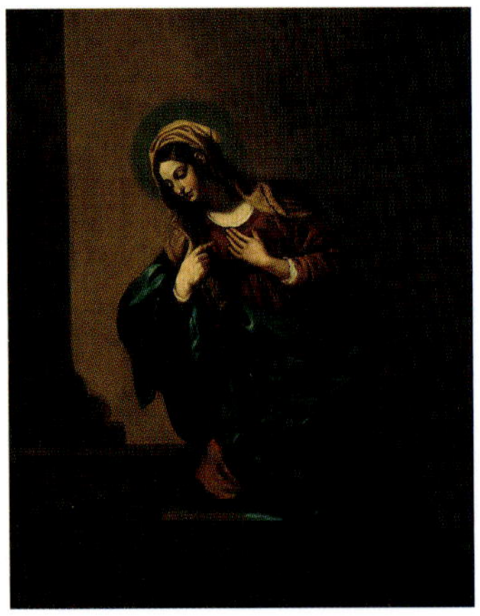

Spanish School early 18th C
The Virgin
oil on canvas 91 x 70.7
L.F11.1954.0.0

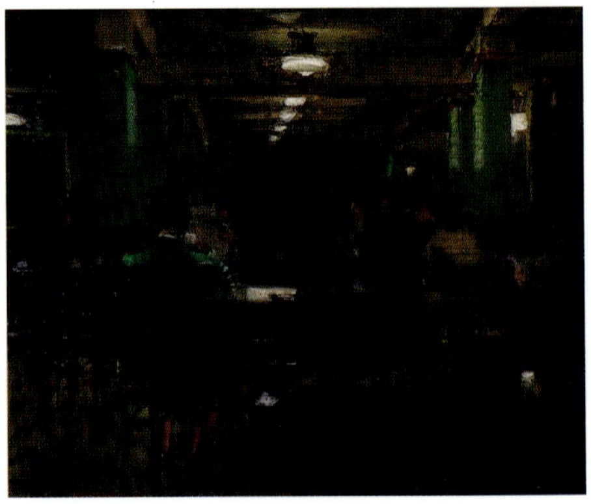

Spear, Ruskin 1911–1990
The Tea Shop
oil on panel 42.3 x 49.5
L.F7.1947.0.0

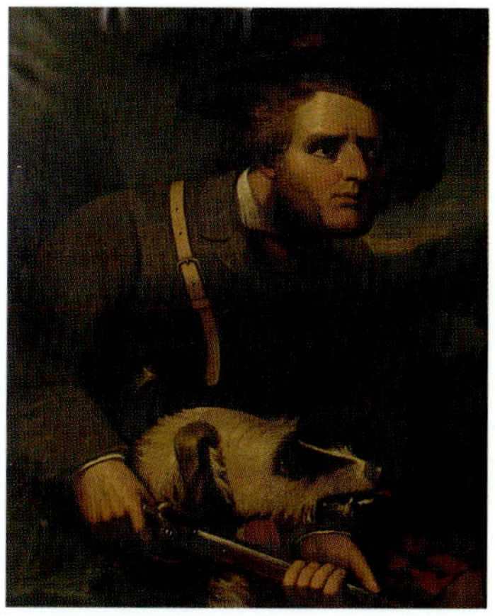

Spencer, J. L.
Portrait of a Scottish Huntsman 1863
oil on canvas 92.4 x 72.4
Y.F15.2009.0.0

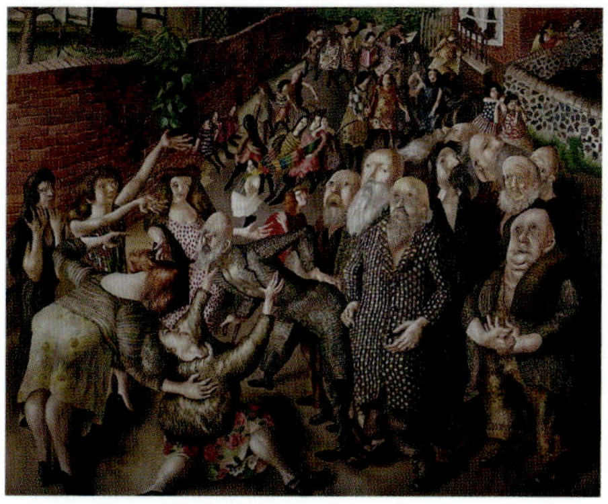

Spencer, Stanley 1891–1959
Adoration of Old Men 1937
oil on canvas 90.6 x 110.5
L.F82.1964.0.0

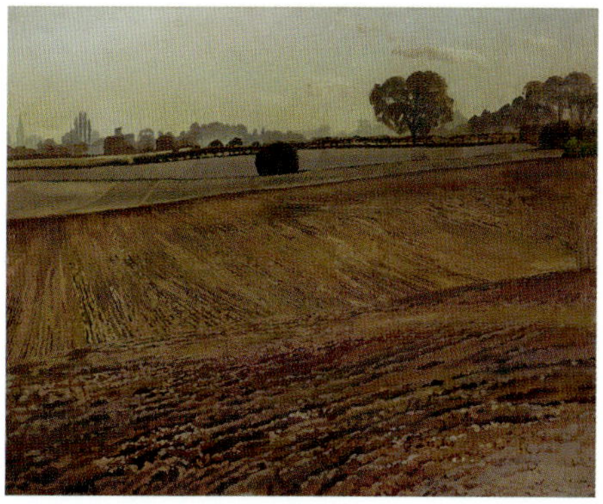

Spencer, Stanley 1891–1959
Distant View of Maidenhead, Berkshire 1939
oil on canvas 45.6 x 56
Y.F7.2000.0.0

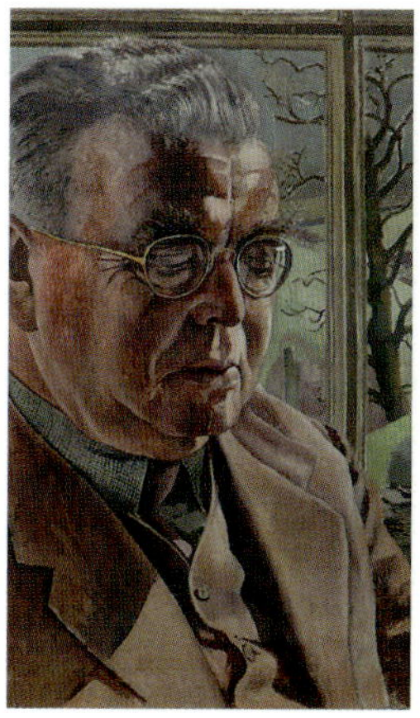

Spencer, Stanley 1891–1959
J. L. Behrend 1956
oil on canvas 51 x 30.5
Y.F6.2000.0.0

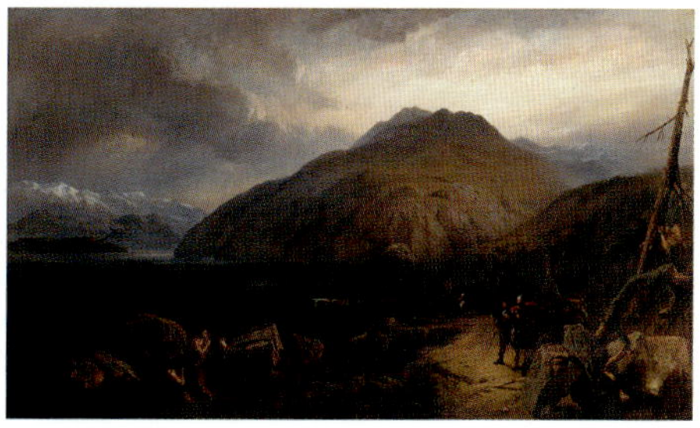

Stanfield, Clarkson 1793–1867
Macbeth and the Witches 1850
oil on canvas 80.6 x 132.1
L.F10.1890.0.0

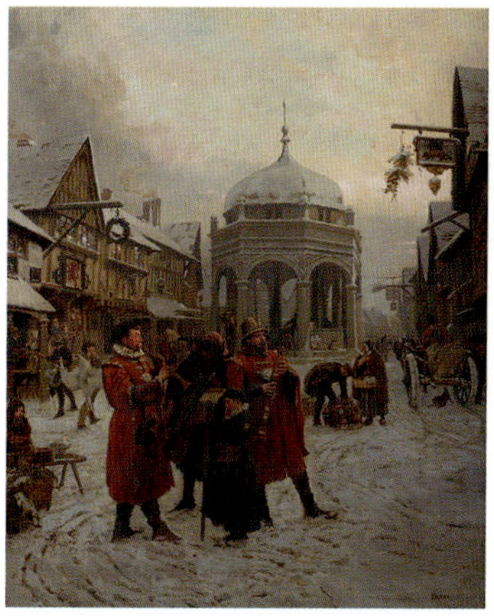

Steer, Henry Reynolds 1858–1928
Christmas Eve, Highcross Market, Leicester, Sixteenth Century c.1900
oil on canvas 147.5 x 101.5
Y.F6.1997.0.0

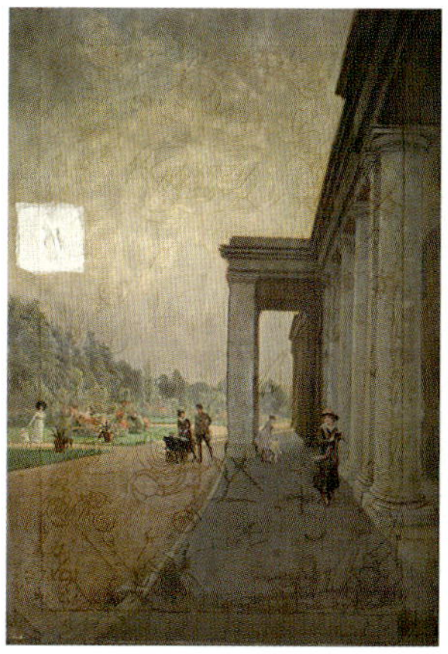

Steer, Henry Reynolds 1858–1928
De Montfort Hall Gardens, Leicester 1917
oil on canvas 91 x 61.5
L.F503.1975.0.0

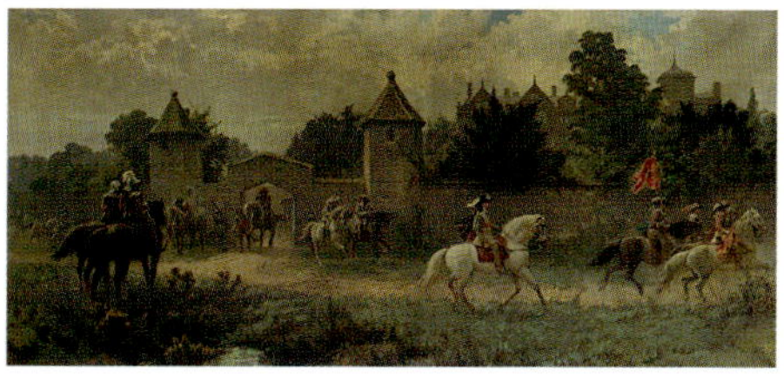

Steer, Henry Reynolds 1858–1928
Charles I Leaving the Cavendish Mansion, Leicester, on His Way to Relieve Oxford, May 1645
oil on canvas 91.5 x 177.8 (E)
Y.F10.2008.0.0

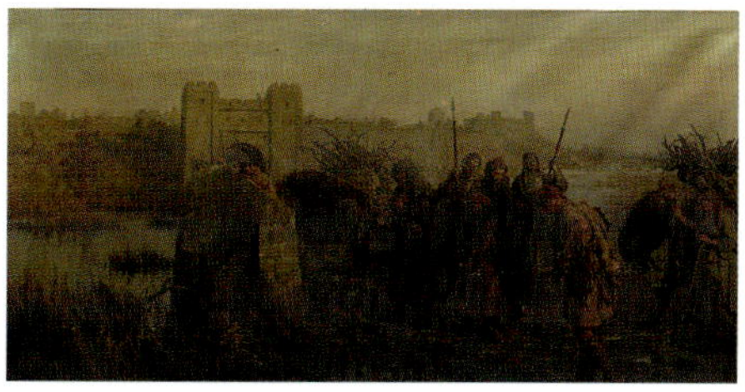

Steer, Henry Reynolds 1858–1928
The Old Woodgate, Leicester
oil on canvas 93.5 x 177.8 (E)
Y.F9.2008.0.0

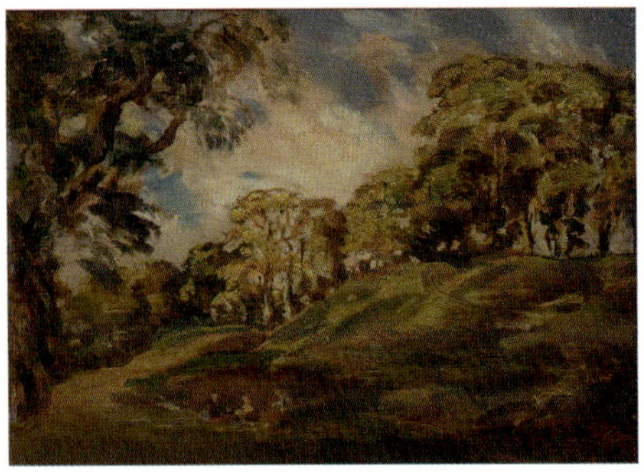

Steer, Philip Wilson 1860–1942
Evening, near Bridgnorth, Shropshire 1941
oil on board 26 x 35
L.F31.1987.0.0 (P)

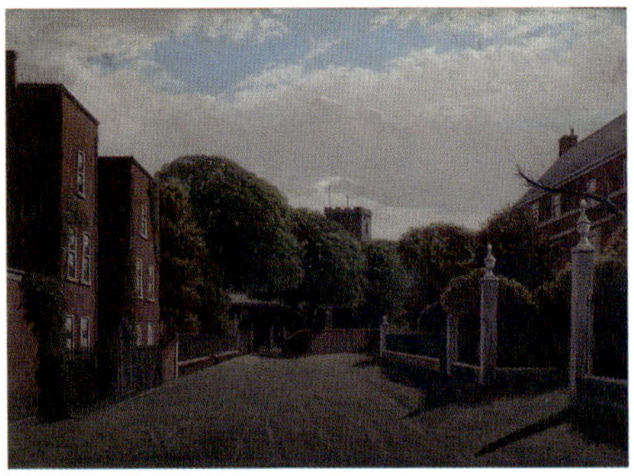

Stevenson, William Grant 1849–1919
Church Road, Belgrave, Leicestershire 1892
oil on canvas 27.9 x 38
L.F14.1982.0.0

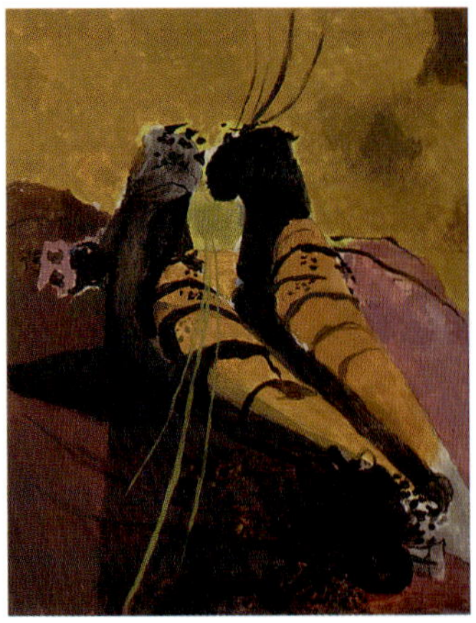

Sutherland, Graham Vivian 1903–1980
Narrow Road between Hedges 1938–1939
oil on canvas 68.6 x 50.8
L.F6.1946.0.0

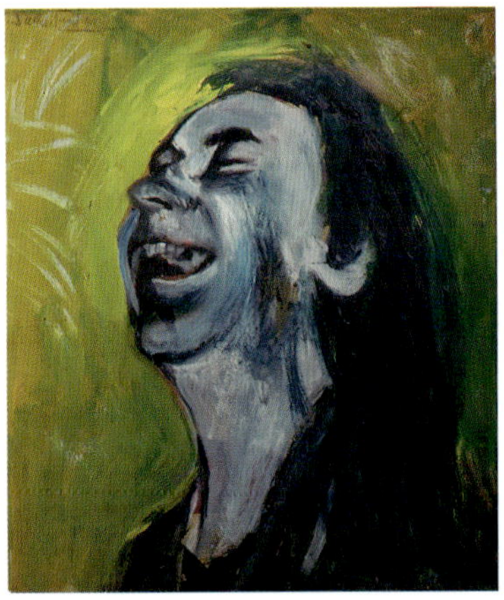

Sutherland, Graham Vivian 1903–1980
The Laughing Woman (study) 1946
oil on canvas 45.5 x 37
L.F3.1983.0.0

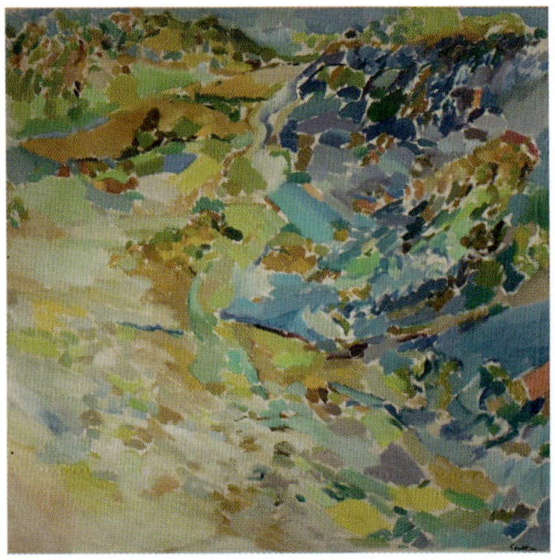

Sutton, Philip b.1928
Landscape
oil on canvas 87.3 x 87.3
L.F42.1956.0.0

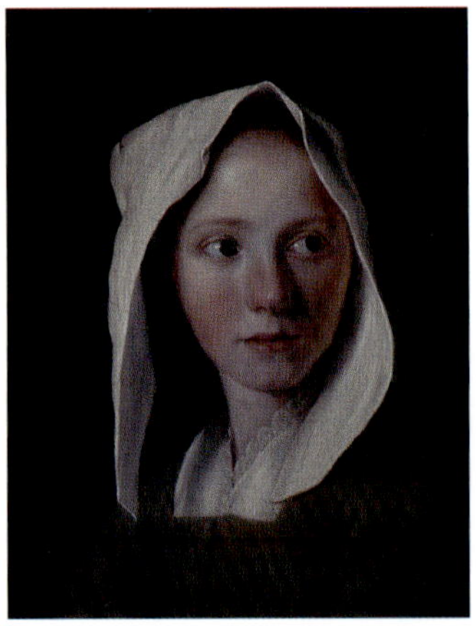

Sweerts, Michael 1618–1664
Portrait of a Girl
oil on canvas 43.5 x 36.5
L.F201.1975.0.0

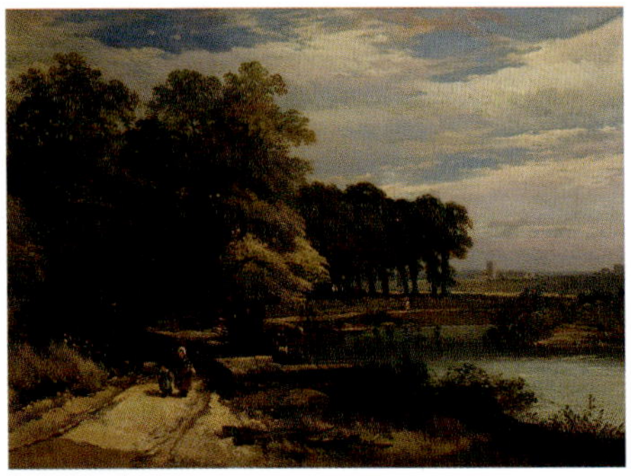

Syer, John 1815–1885
Landscape
oil on canvas 45.5 x 60.5
L.F2.1893.0.0

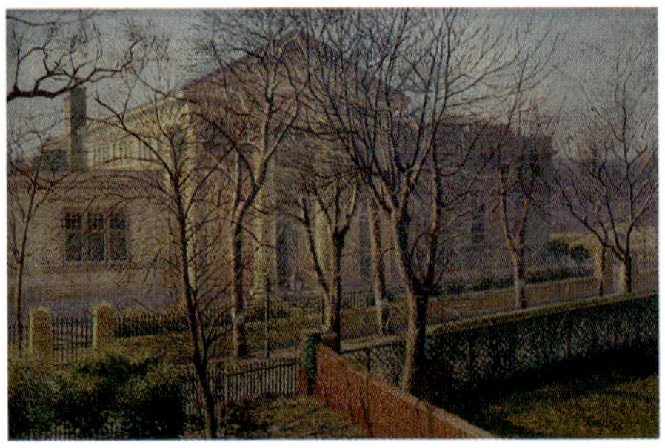

Tempest, Herbert Victor 1913–2003
View of Leicester Museum
oil on canvas 50.8 x 76.2
L.F11.1941.0.0

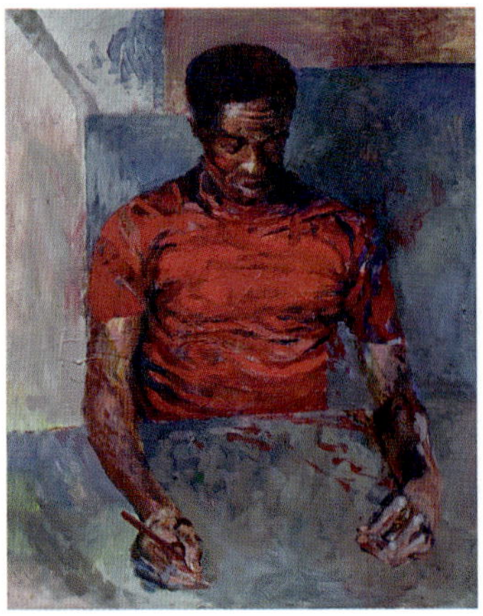

Thomas, Susan
Chris Ofili (b.1968) 1989
acrylic on canvas 76 x 58
Y.F16.2008.0.0

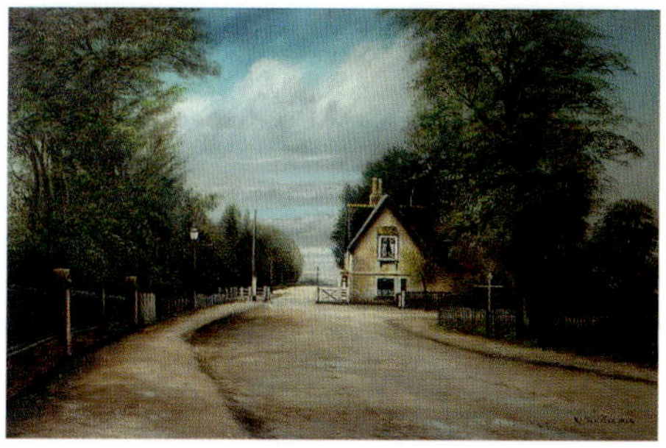

Thornton, Albert James 1873–1947
View of the New Granby Toll House, London Road, Leicester 1924
oil on canvas 76.2 x 101.6
L.F542.1969.0.0

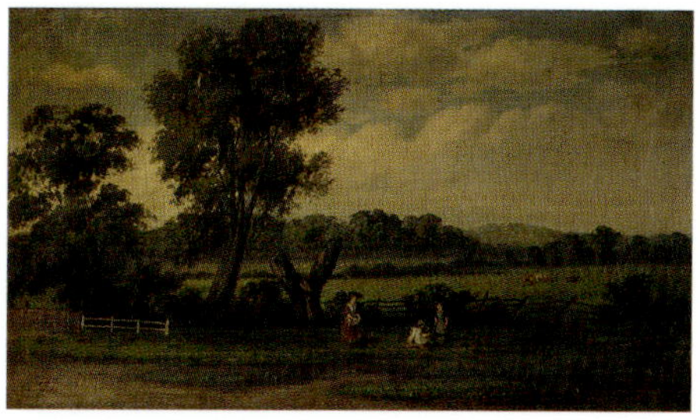

Thorpe, George O.
View from Narborough, Leicestershire, Looking towards Lubbesthorpe 1848
oil on canvas 53.3 x 91.4
L.F36.1952.0.0

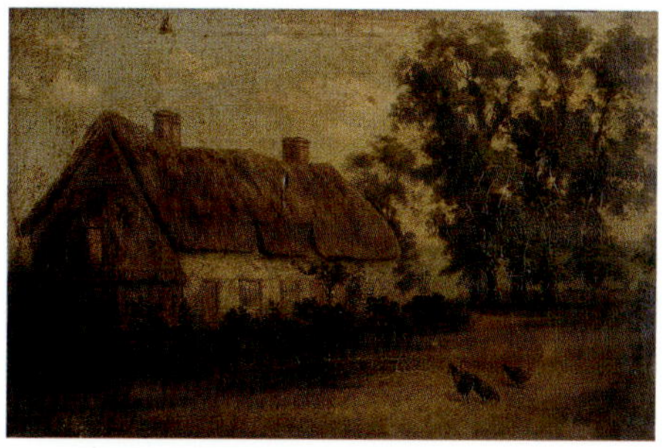

Thorpe, George O.
Old Cottage, Knighton, Leicester
oil on canvas 55.9 x 85.1
L.F34.1952.0.0

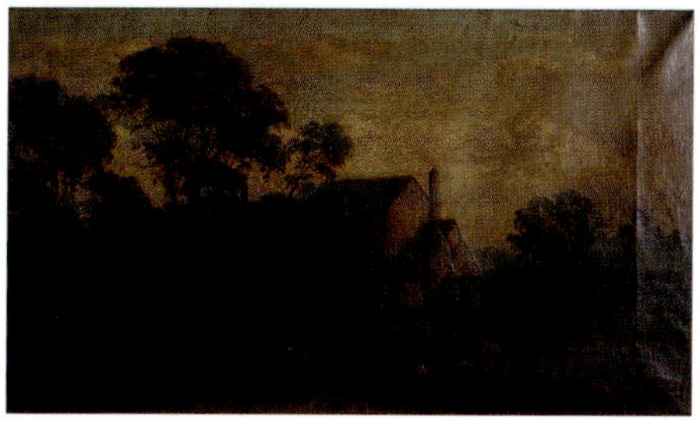

Thorpe, George O.
The Old Mill, Aylestone, Leicestershire
oil on canvas 68.6 x 91.4
L.F37.1952.0.0

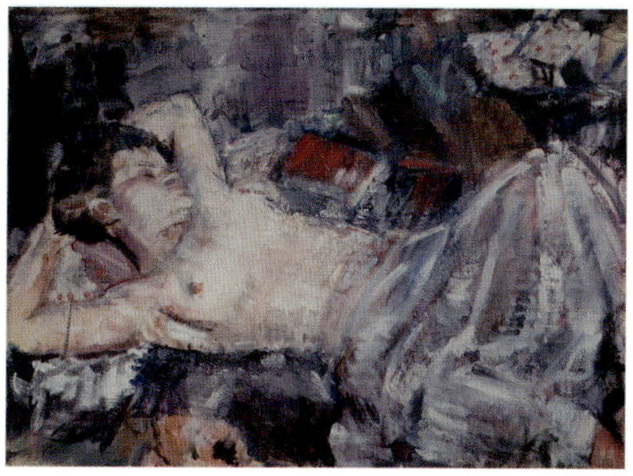

Tibble, Geoffrey Arthur 1909–1952
Reclining Woman 1938
oil on canvas 91.5 x 121.8
L.F13.1938.0.0

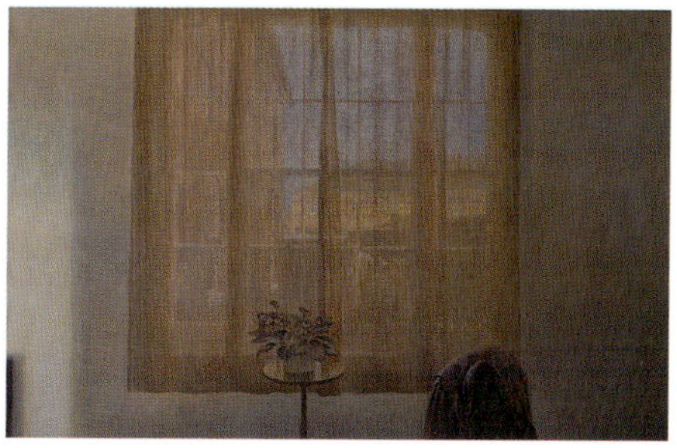

Tindle, David b.1932
Back Room 1987
tempera on canvas 81.2 x 121.9
L.F110.1988.0.0

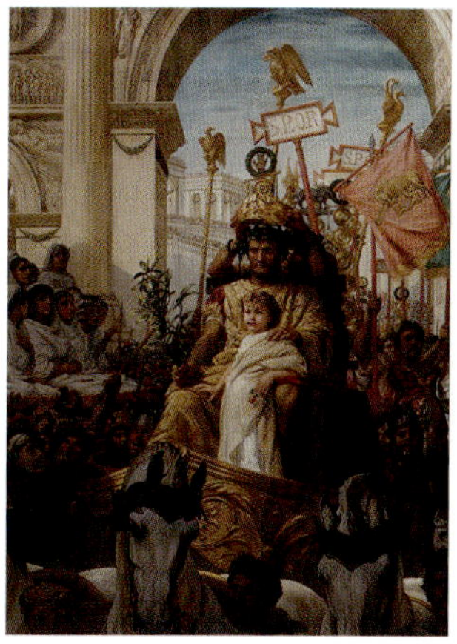

Topham, Frank William Warwick 1838–1924
A Roman Triumph 1883
oil on canvas 193.4 x 138
L.F2.1888.0.0

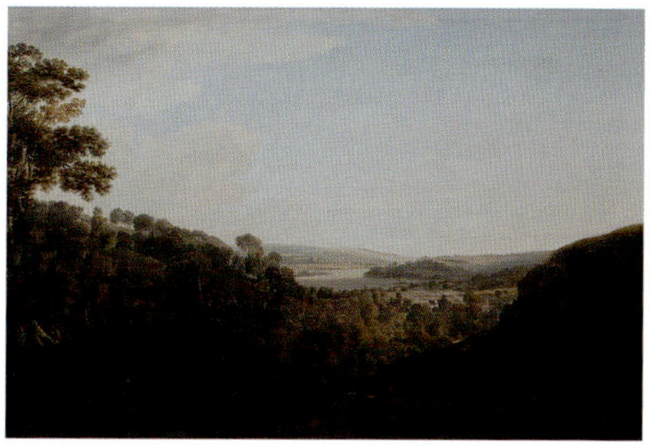

Towne, Francis 1739/1740–1816
The Valley of the Teign, Devonshire 1780
oil on canvas 81.7 x 114.3
L.F55.1953.0.0

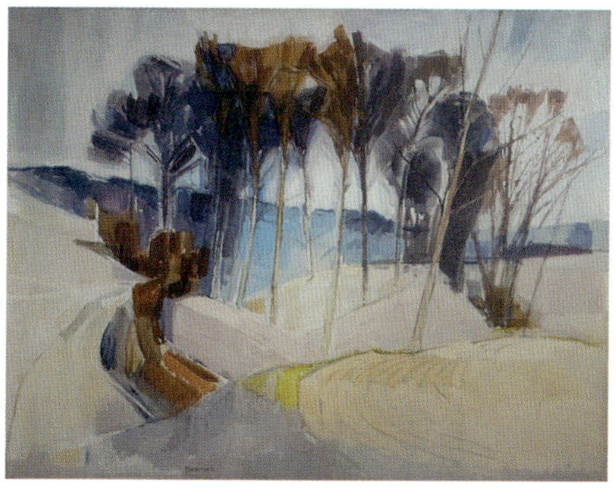

Townsend, William 1909–1973
Trees at Rolvenden, Kent 1956
oil on canvas 71.3 x 91.4
L.F12.1957.0.0

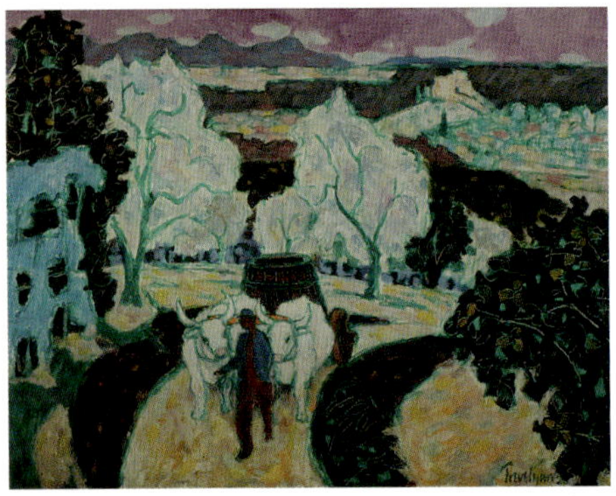

Trevelyan, Julian 1910–1988
Tuscan Landscape 1954
oil on canvas 60.4 x 76
L.F8.1955.0.0

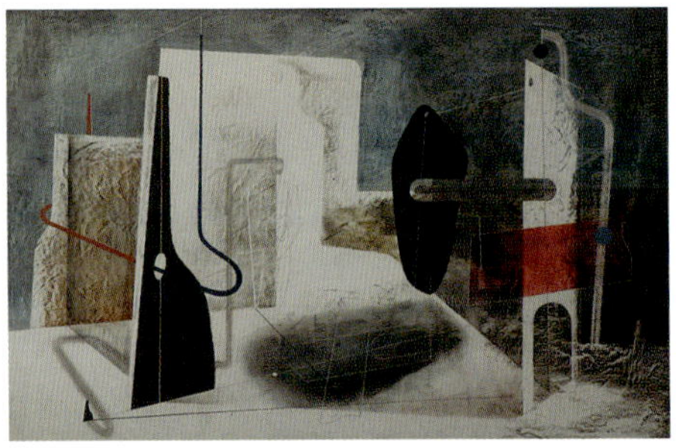

Tunnard, John 1900–1971
Metamorphosis 1942
oil on hardboard 31.5 x 61
L.F22.1941.0.0

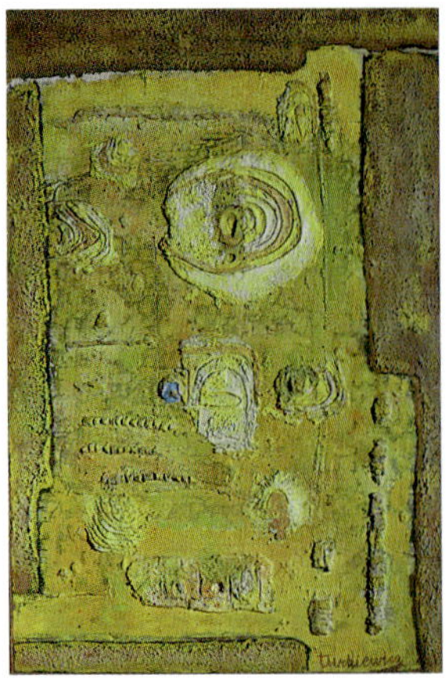

Turkiewicz, Zygmunt 1913–1973
The Sun c.1960
oil & mixed media on hardboard 94 x 61
L.F1.1969.0.0

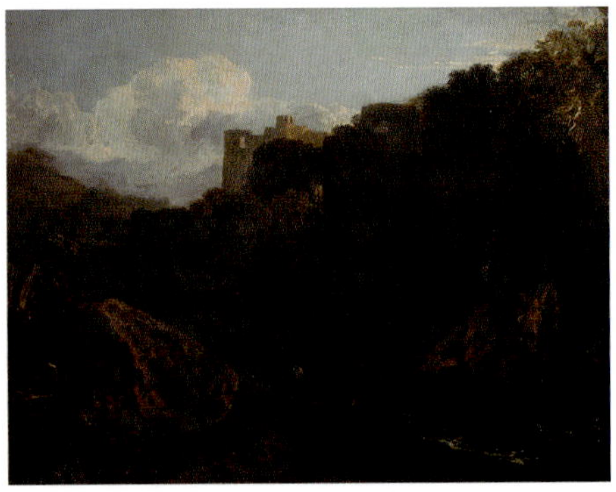

Turner, Joseph Mallord William 1775–1851
Cilgerran Castle
oil on canvas 75.5 x 93.5
L.F71.1955.0.0

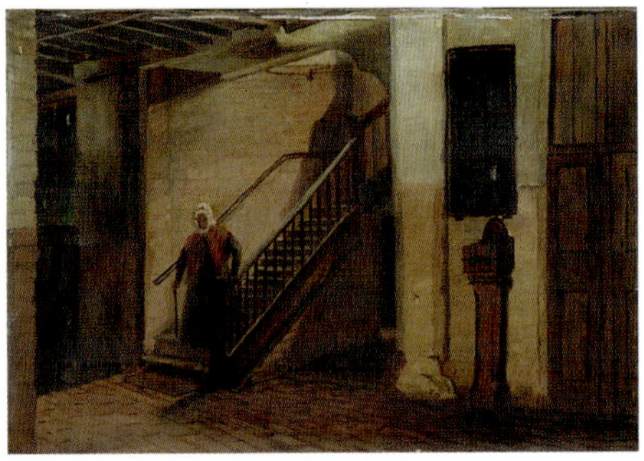

Uff, Emmeline Sarah 1872–1942
Trinity Hospital, Leicester c.1890
oil on canvas 25.4 x 35.5
L.F161.1963.0.0

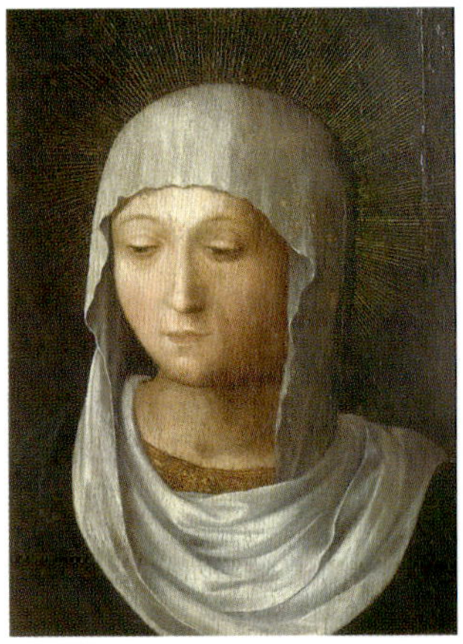

unknown artist late 15th C
Head of the Virgin
oil on panel 41.9 x 30.8
L.F78.1955.0.0

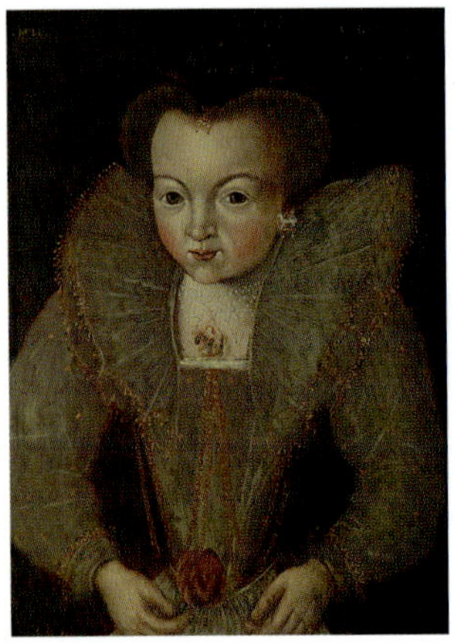

unknown artist
Mary Herrick 1592
oil on panel 47 x 34.8
L.F25.1937.2.0

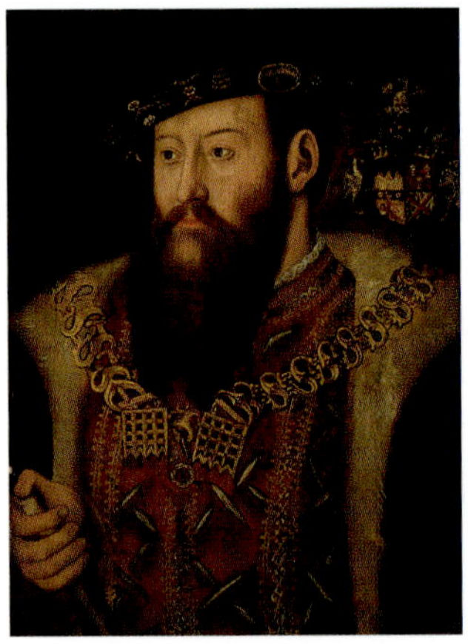

unknown artist 16th C
Portrait of a Man (said to be James Butler, 2nd Earl of Ormonde)
oil on panel 20.4 x 14.5
L.F14.1941.4.0

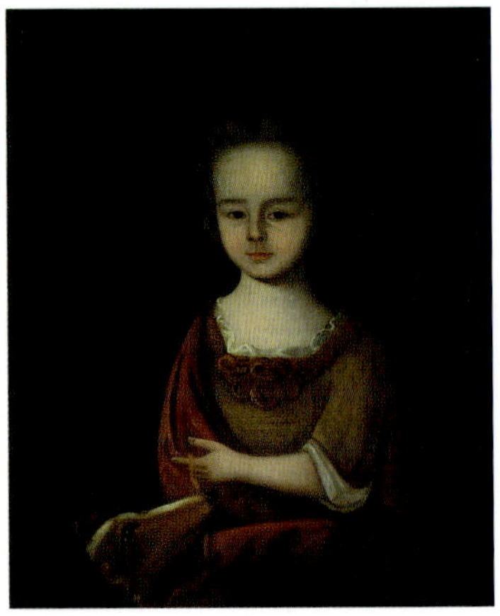

unknown artist
Portrait of a Herrick Boy 1698
oil on canvas 76.2 x 63.5
L.F25.1937.6.0

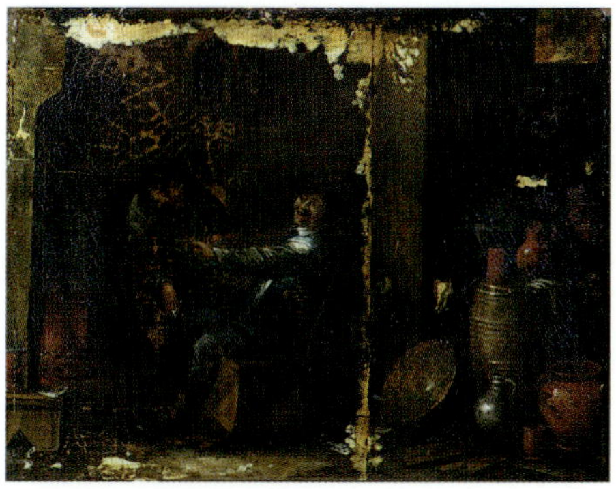

unknown artist 17th C
Interior, Tavern Scene
oil on wood & canvas 28.4 x 35.2
L.F20.1935.28.0

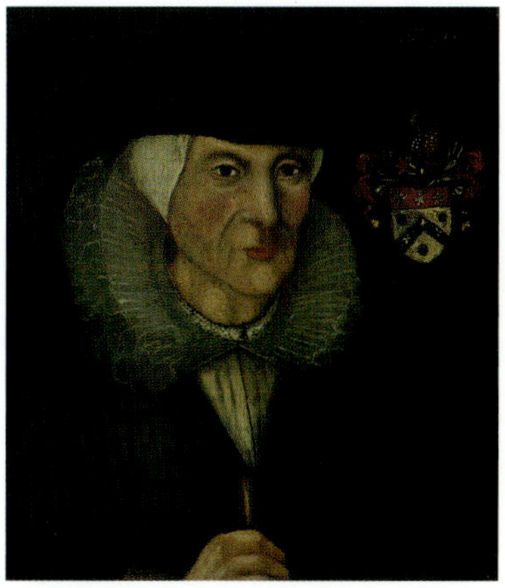

unknown artist 17th C
Mary Bond (1514–1611)
oil on panel 49.5 x 41.3
L.F25.1937.1.0

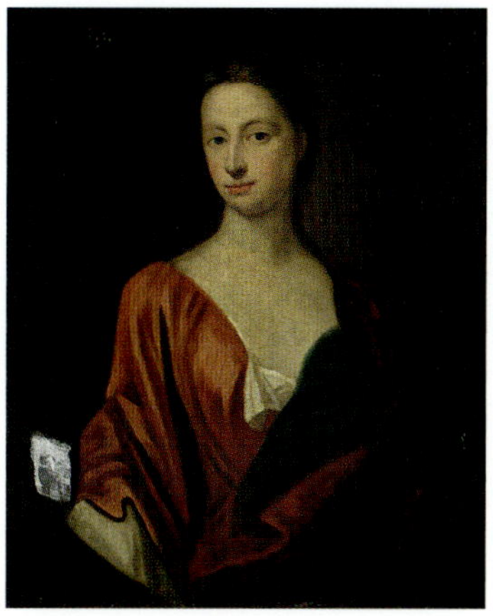

unknown artist early 18th C
Portrait of a Lady
oil on canvas 76.2 x 61
L.F96.1955.0.0

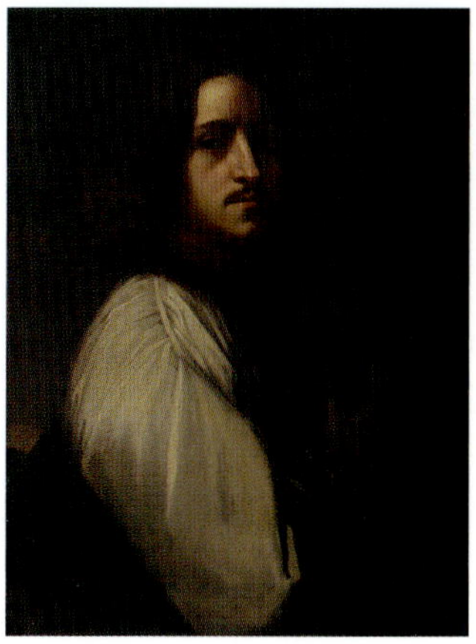

unknown artist 18th C
Portrait of the Artist
oil on canvas 79 x 58.5
L.F18.1935.0.0

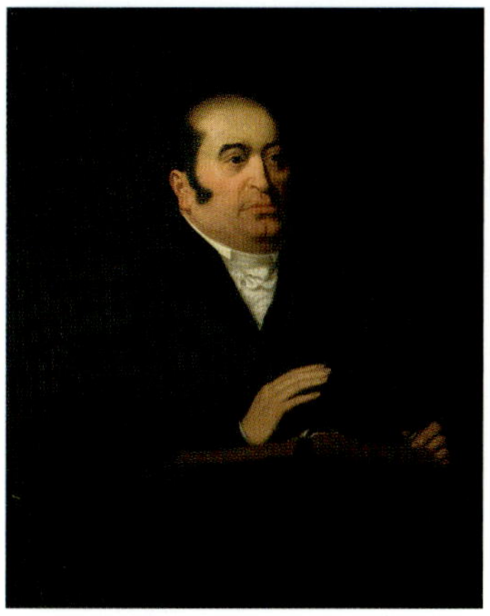

unknown artist 19th C
Reverend Robert Hall (1764–1831)
oil on canvas 51 x 40
L.F39.1987.0.0 (P)

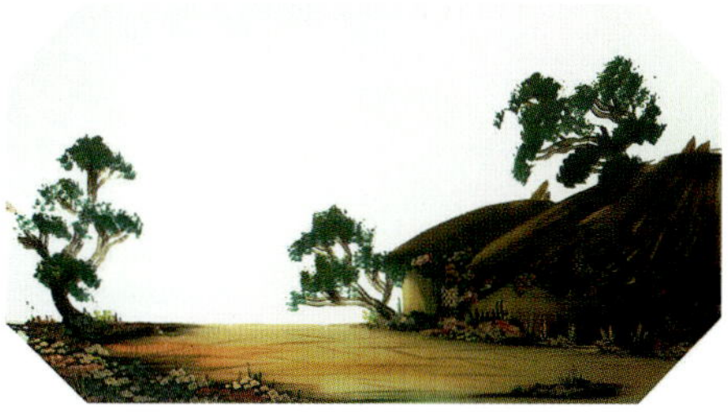

unknown artist
Landscape 1920s
oil on mirror glass 32.5 x 56
L.H88.1993.0.0

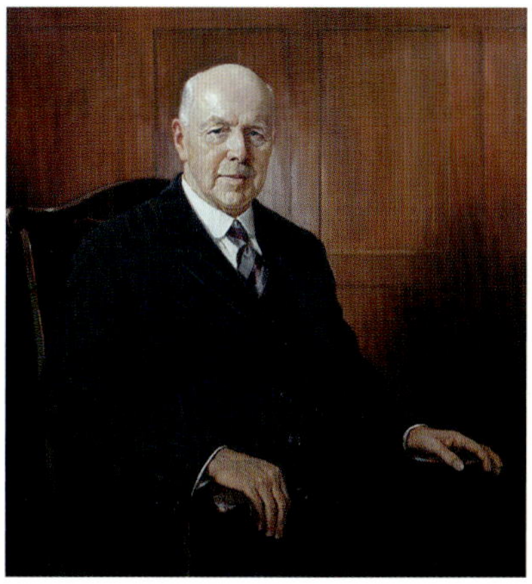

unknown artist
Portrait of an Unknown Man 1930s/1940s
oil on canvas 101.5 x 91.3
Y.F17.2009.0.0

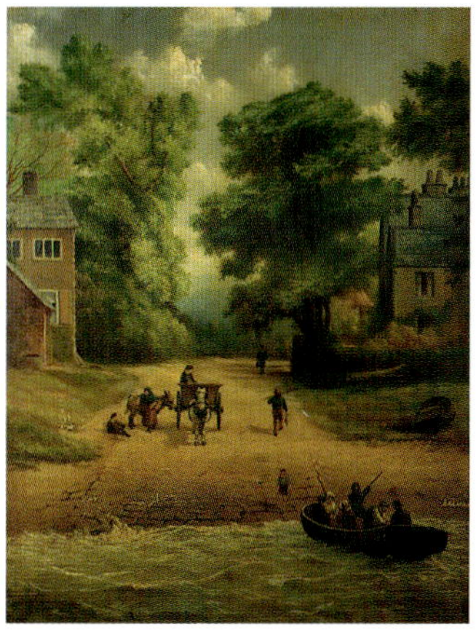

unknown artist
Country Ford
oil on canvas 123 x 91.5
L.F3.1996.30.0

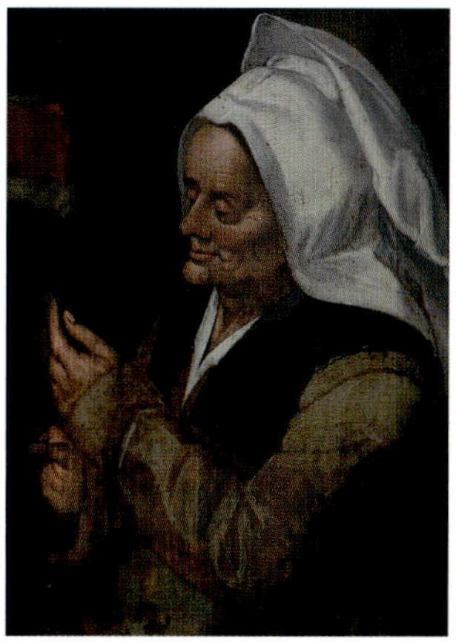

unknown artist
Head of an Old Woman
oil on oak panel 28.2 x 20
L.F16.1935.0.0

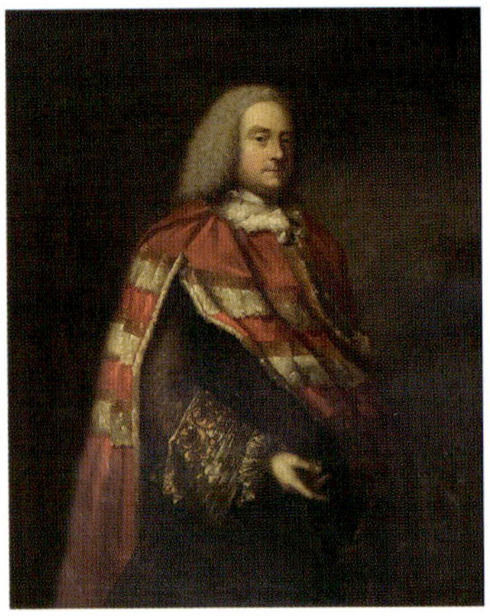

unknown artist
Portrait of a Gentleman in Robes (possibly Sir John Vaughan, 1769–1839)
oil on canvas 126 x 99
L.F9.1943.2.0

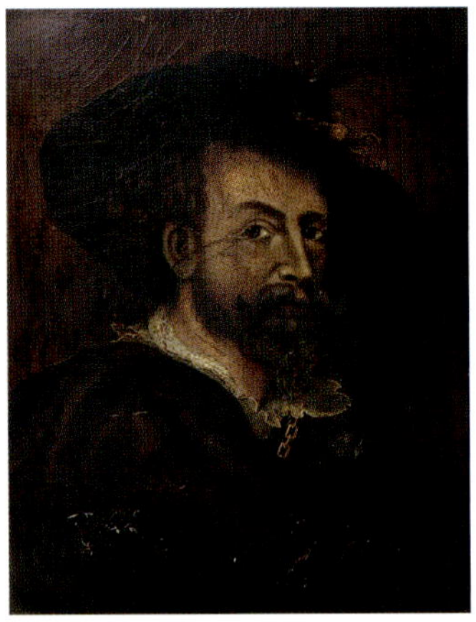

unknown artist
Portrait of a Man (copy of an earlier painting)
oil on board 36.5 x 28
L.F62.1993.0.0

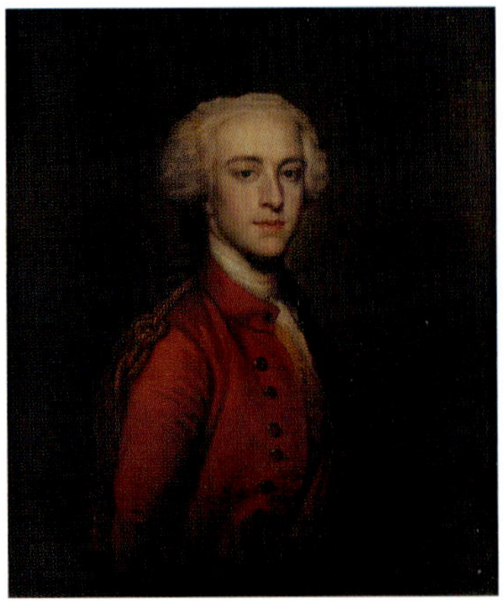

unknown artist
Portrait of a Young Man in Military Costume
oil on canvas laid on panel 76.8 x 61
L.F9.1943.10.0

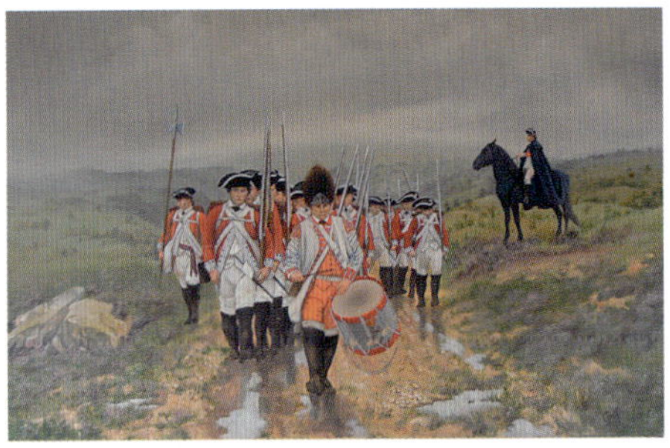

unknown artist
The Return of the Princeton Heroes
oil on canvas 50.5 x 76
L.H72.1988.0.0

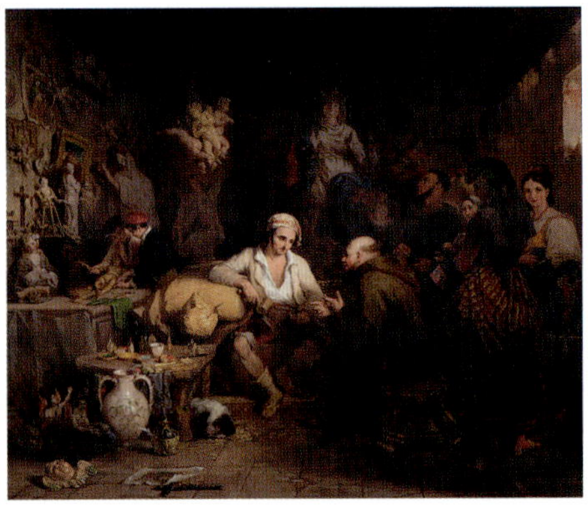

Uwins, Thomas 1782–1857
A Neapolitan Saint Manufactory 1832
oil on canvas 75 x 86.4
L.F7.1892.0.0

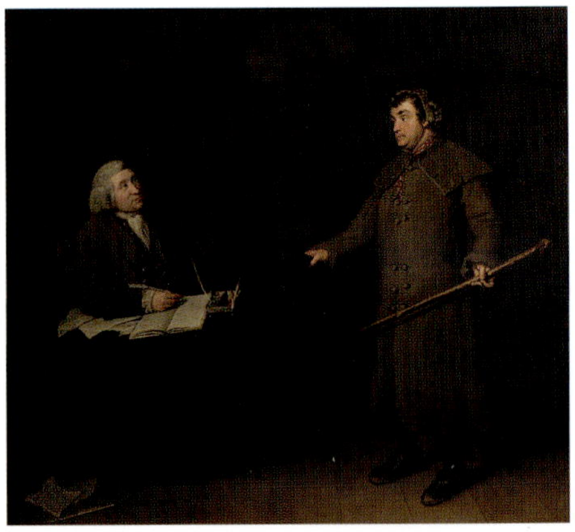

Vandergucht, Benjamin 1753–1794
Scene from 'The Register Office' by Joseph Reed
oil on canvas 105.7 x 113
L.F26.1954.0.0

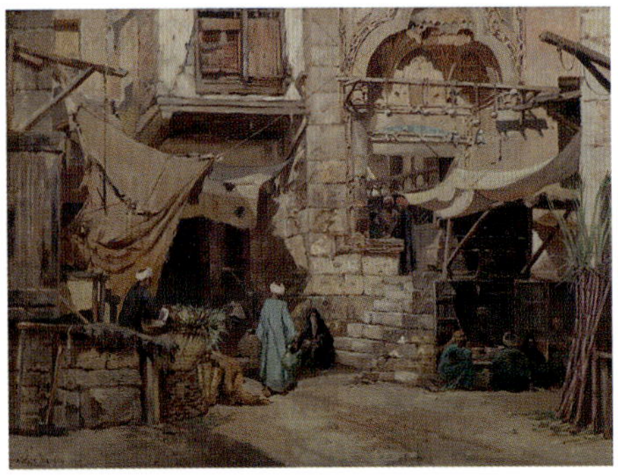

Varley, John II 1850–1933
Mosque of Mohammed Bey, Cairo 1882
oil on canvas 45.7 x 61
L.F15.1882.0.0

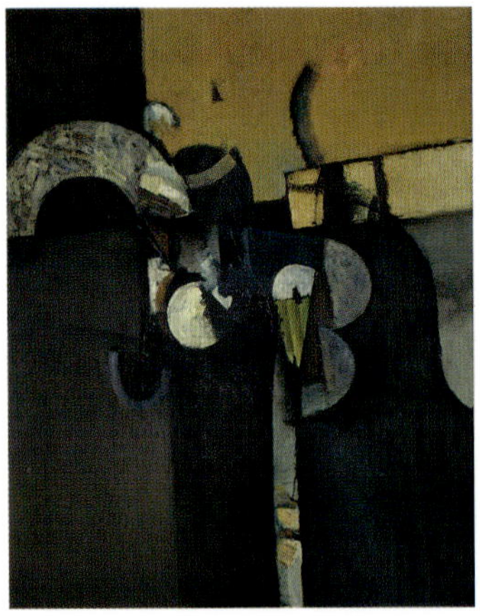

Vaughan, John Keith 1912–1977
Vertical Tree Forms 1956
oil on canvas 91.5 x 71
L.F10.1960.0.0

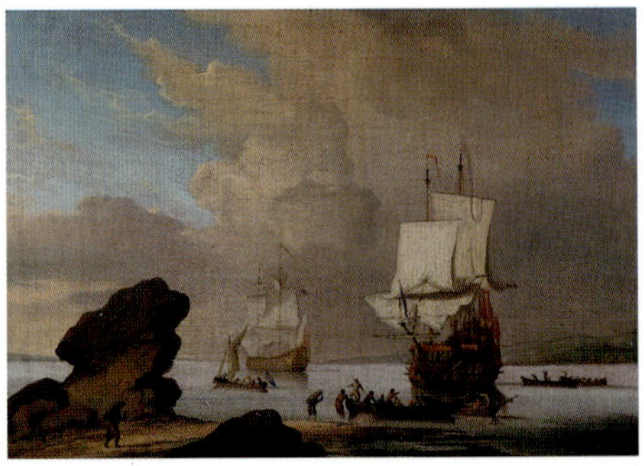

Velde, Willem van de II 1633–1707
Seascape, Ships and Boats in a Calm off a Rocky Shore
oil on canvas 35.2 x 48.2
L.F17.1935.0.0

Facing page: Carline, Sydney William, 1888–1929, *Village by Lake Orta, Italy* (detail), The Collection: Art & Archaeology in Lincolnshire (Usher Gallery) (p.290)

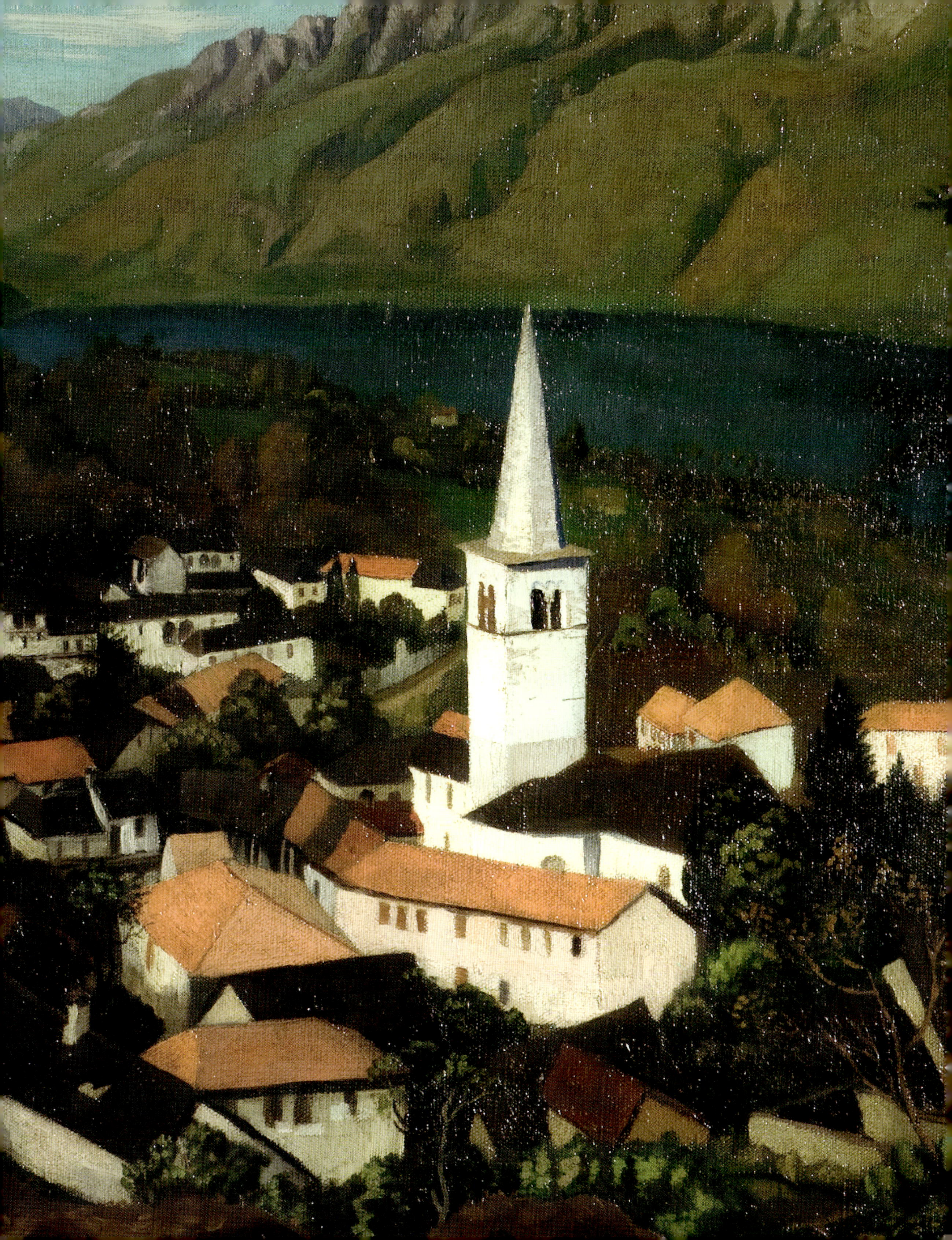

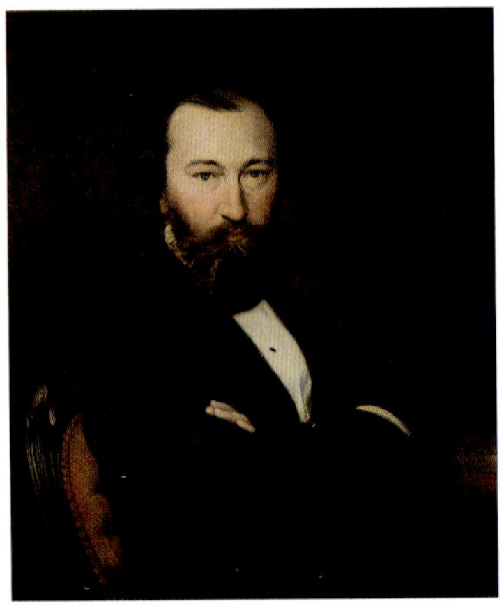

Venables, Adolphus Robert (attributed to) c.1805–1892
Peter Alfred Taylor (1819–1891), MP for Leicester (1868)
oil on canvas 76.2 x 50.8
L.F219.1924.0.0

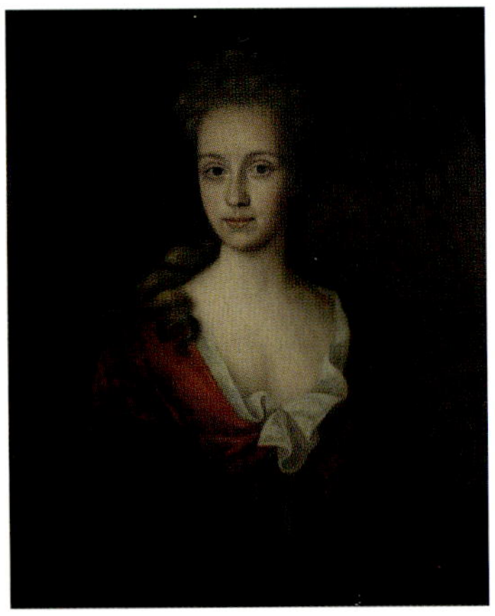

Verelst, Johannes d.1734
Portrait of a Lady 1699
oil on canvas 76 x 63.5
L.F97.1955.0.0

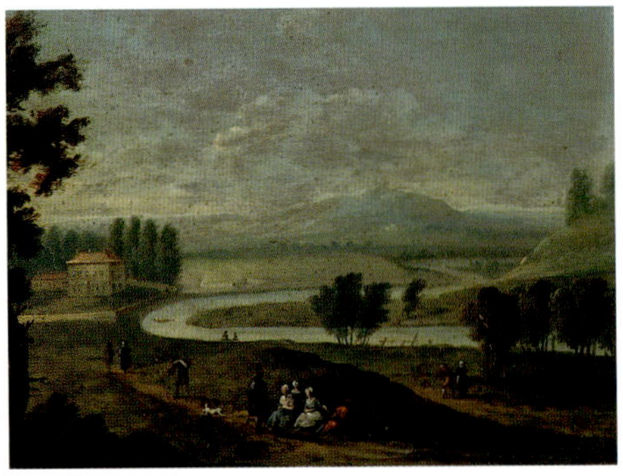

Vernet, Antoine-François 1730–1779
A River Landscape 1771
oil on copper 18 x 22.6
L.F20.1935.1.1

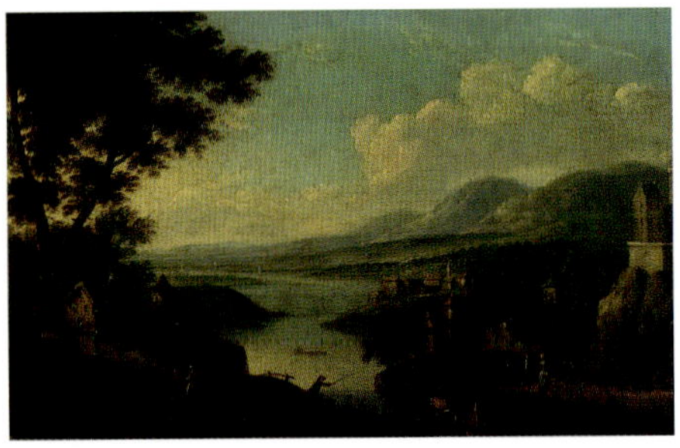

Vernet, Antoine-François 1730–1779
A River Landscape 1771
oil on canvas 35.5 x 55.8
L.F20.1935.14.0

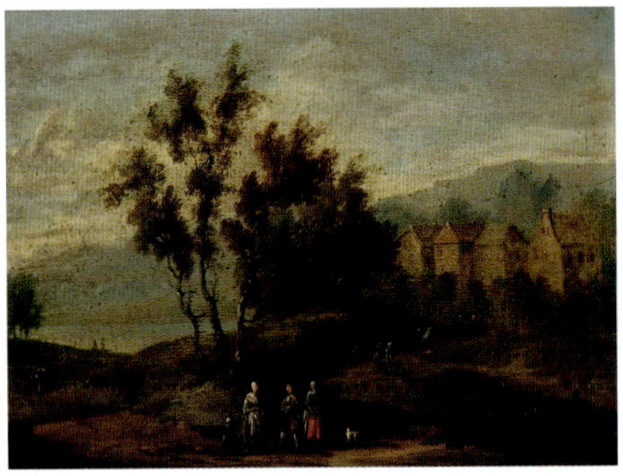

Vernet, Antoine-François 1730–1779
A River Landscape
oil on copper 18 x 22.6
L.F20.1935.1.2

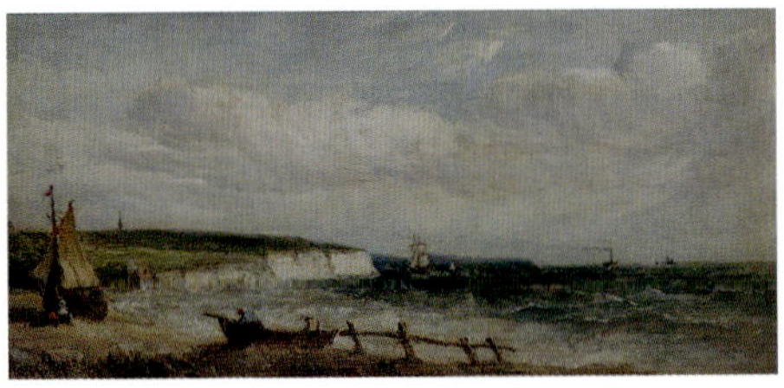

Vickers, Alfred 1786–1868
The Undercliff, Isle of Wight 1866
oil on paper & panel 17.5 x 35.3
L.F4.1900.0.0

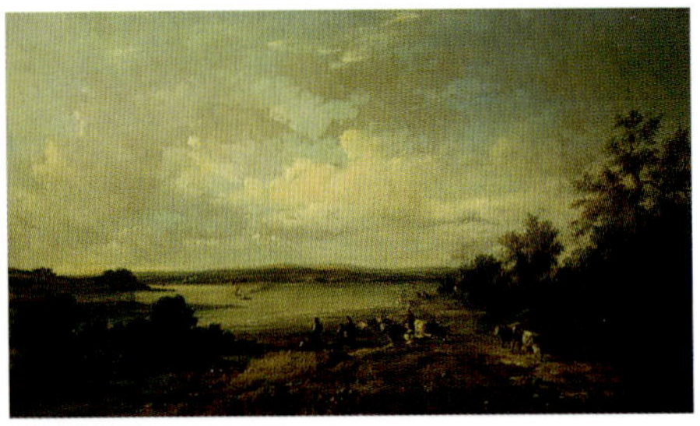

Vickers, Alfred 1786–1868
Morning, Pen Pole Point, Bristol Channel
oil on canvas 61 x 101.6
L.F3.1888.0.0

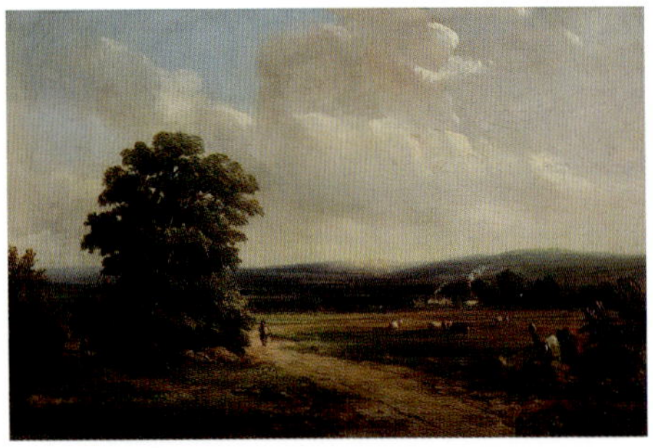

Vickers, Alfred 1786–1868
Okehampton, Devon
oil on canvas 20.5 x 30.2
L.F2.1900.0.0

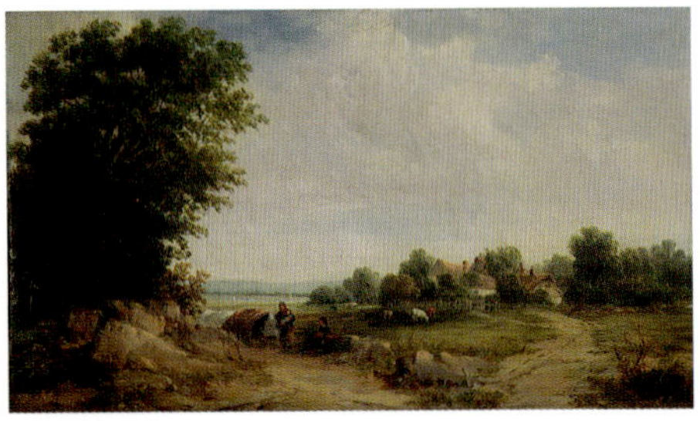

Vickers, Alfred 1786–1868
Plumstead Common, London
oil on canvas 22.8 x 38.2
L.F3.1900.0.0

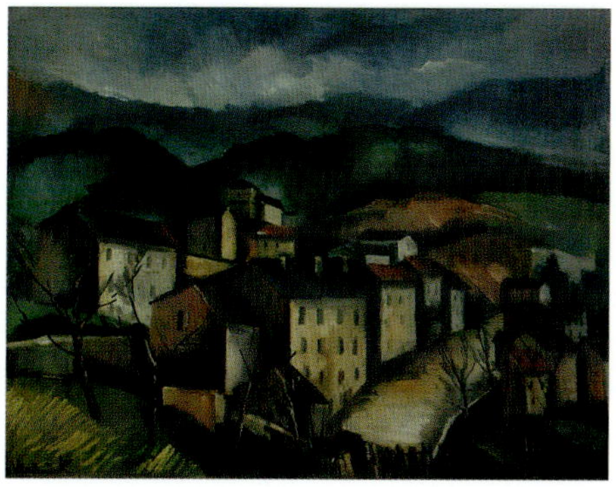

Vlaminck, Maurice de 1876–1958
La route Napoléon 1912–1914
oil on canvas 73 x 92
L.F6.1943.0.0

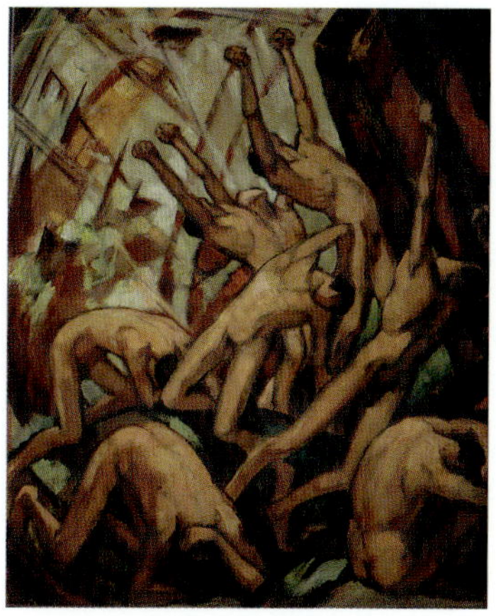

Von Hofmann, Ludwig 1861–1945
Zusammenbruch c.1918
oil on canvas 88.9 x 69.8
L.F24.1971.0.0

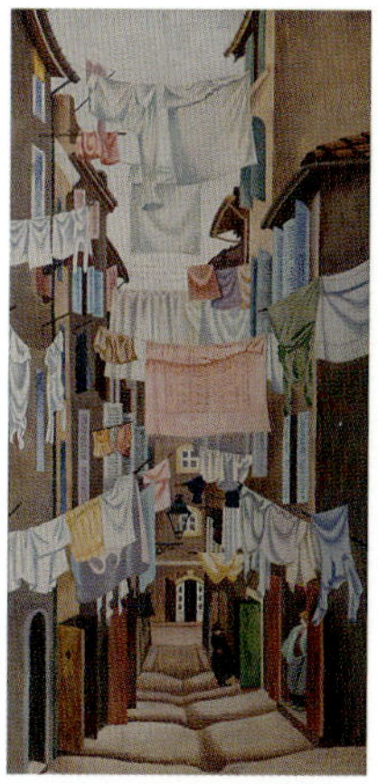

Wadsworth, Edward Alexander 1889–1949
Rue Fontaine de Caylus, Marseilles, France
1924
tempera on panel 94 x 45.3
L.F13.1937.0.0

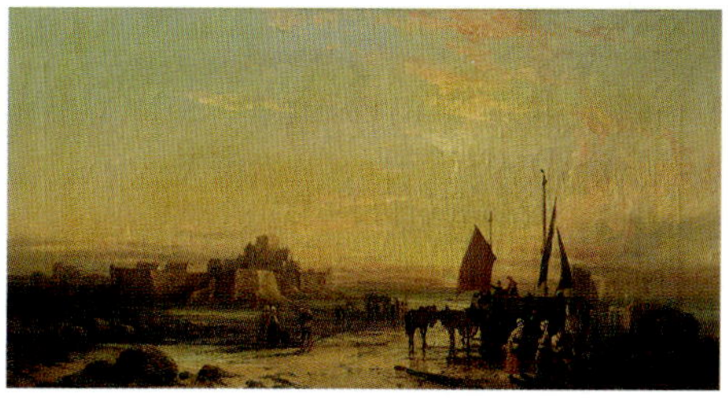

Wake, John Cheltenham c.1837–1882
Landing the Catch
oil on canvas 51 x 92
Y.F1.2009.0.0

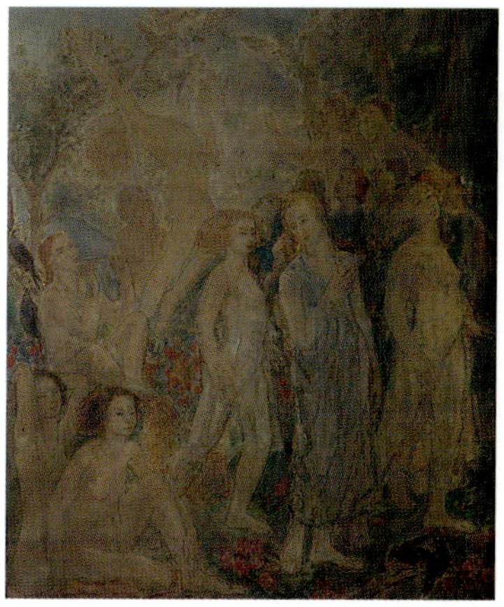

Walker, Ethel 1861–1951
In the Land of Ecstasy 1933–1935
oil on canvas 169 x 138.5
L.F13.1955.0.0

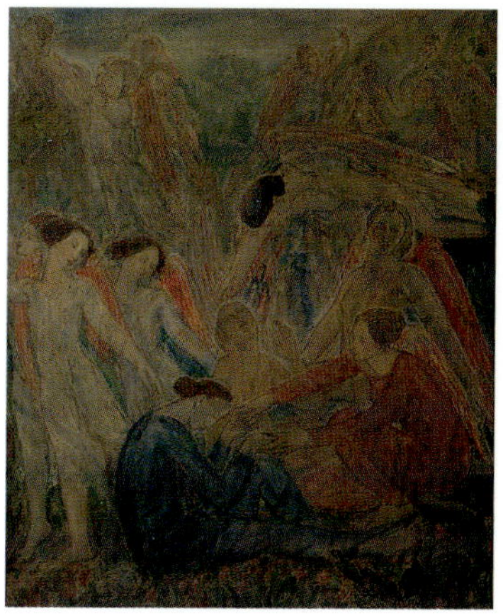

Walker, Ethel 1861–1951
The Arrival 1933–1935
oil on canvas 169 x 138.5
L.F14.1955.0.0

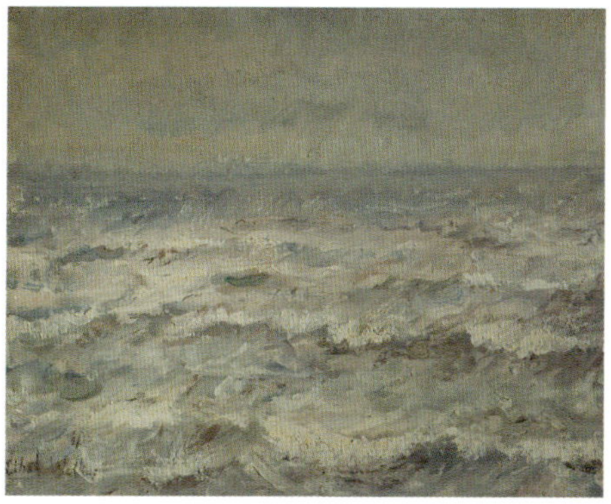

Walker, Ethel 1861–1951
September Morning
oil on canvas 50.8 x 61
L.F24.1944.0.0

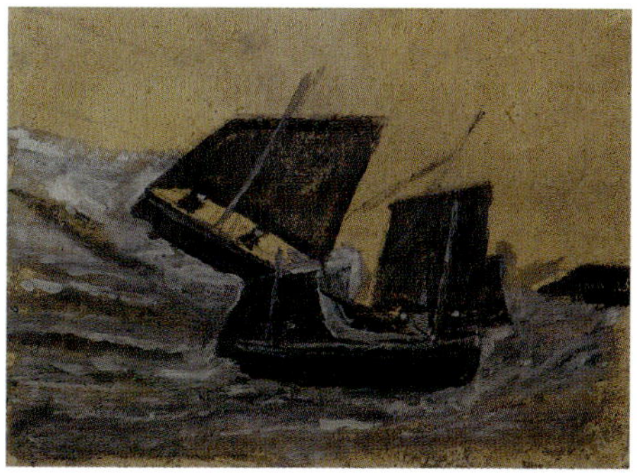

Wallis, Alfred 1855–1942
Two Black Boats Sailing up Dark Grey Waves
oil on card 17.8 x 23.8
L.F396.1976.0.0

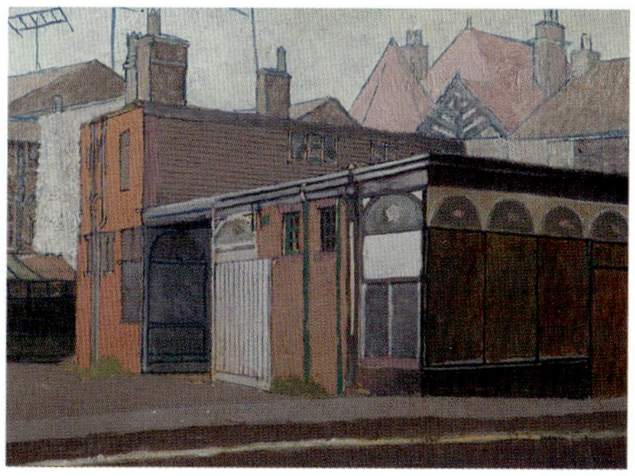

Ward, Bryan 1921–1987
Small Building in Buxton, Derbyshire 1979
oil on board 23 x 30
L.F47.1988.0.0

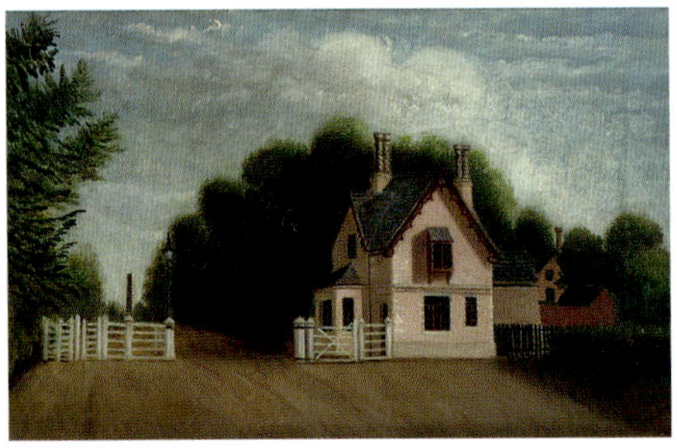

Ward, George
New Granby Toll House, London Road, Leicester
oil on panel 26 x 39.3
L.F632.1951.0.0

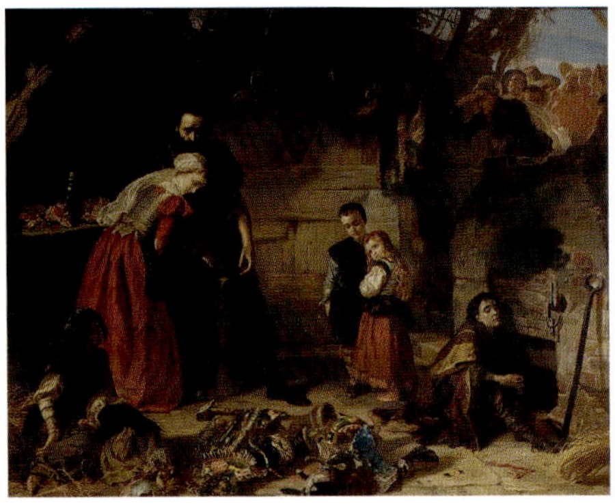

Ward, Henrietta Mary Ada 1832–1924
Palissy the Potter 1866
oil on canvas 108 x 133.4
L.F2.1887.0.0

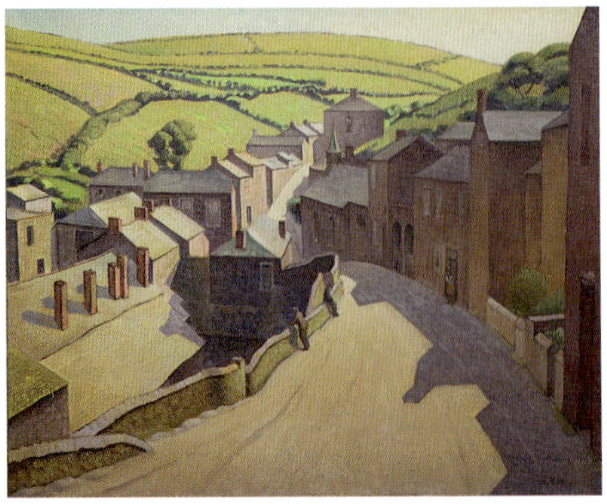

Watson, Sydney Robert 1892–1971
Portloe, Cornwall 1932
oil on canvas 49.5 x 60.5
L.F6.1933.0.0

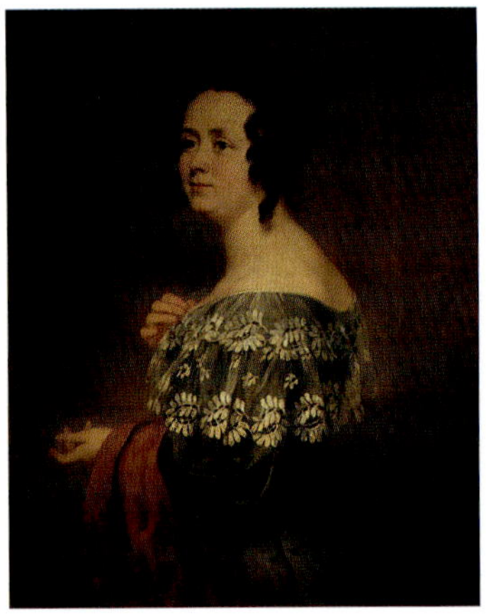

Watts, George Frederick 1817–1904
Mrs Anne Gertrude Toller 1843
oil on canvas 91.5 x 71
L.F8.1931.0.0

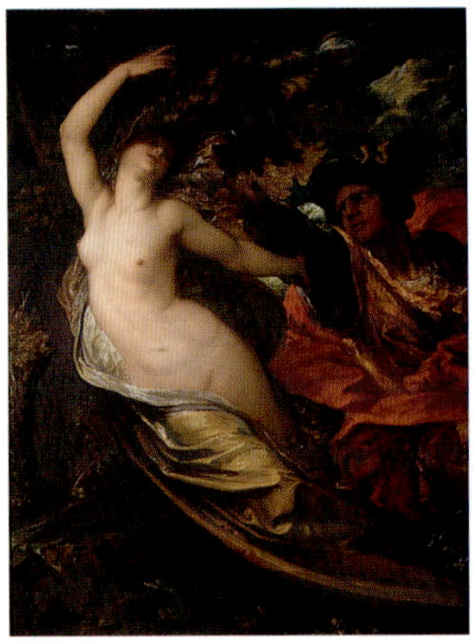

Watts, George Frederick 1817–1904
Orlando Pursuing the Fata Morgana 1846–1848
oil on canvas 165 x 120
L.F5.1889.0.0

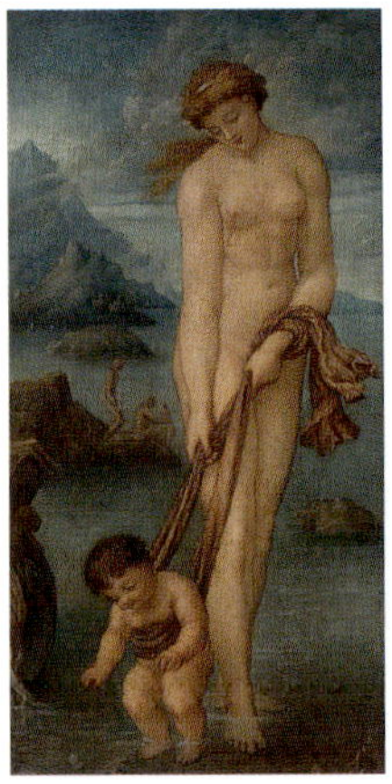

Watts, George Frederick 1817–1904
Woman and Child
oil on canvas 63.5 x 32
L.F8.1961.0.0

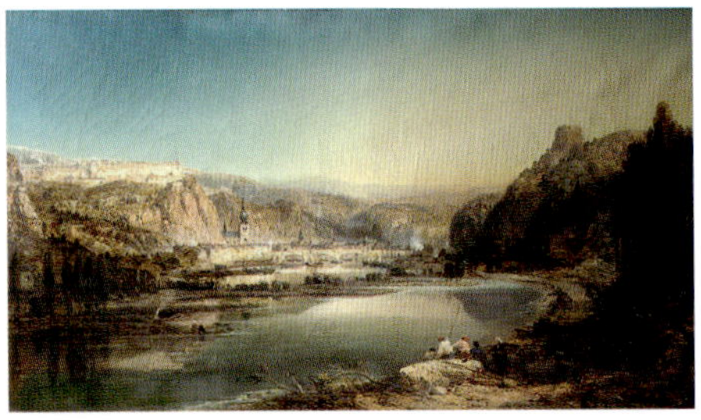

Webb, James 1825–1895
Dinant, Belgium 1876
oil on canvas 76 x 127
Y.F4.2009.0.0

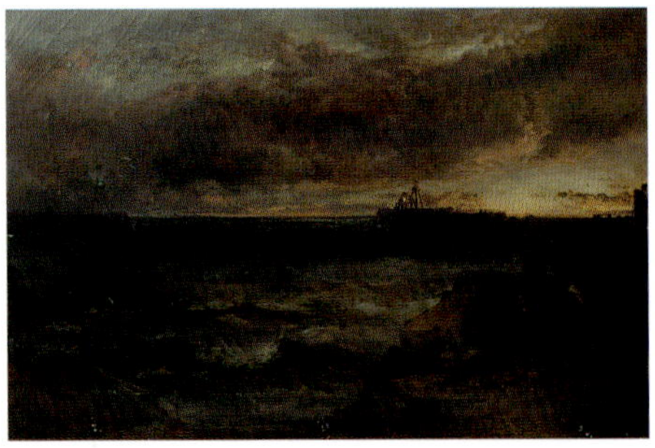

Webb, James 1825–1895
Men Must Work and Women Must Weep 1877–1878
oil on canvas 86.5 x 127
L.F1.1884.0.0

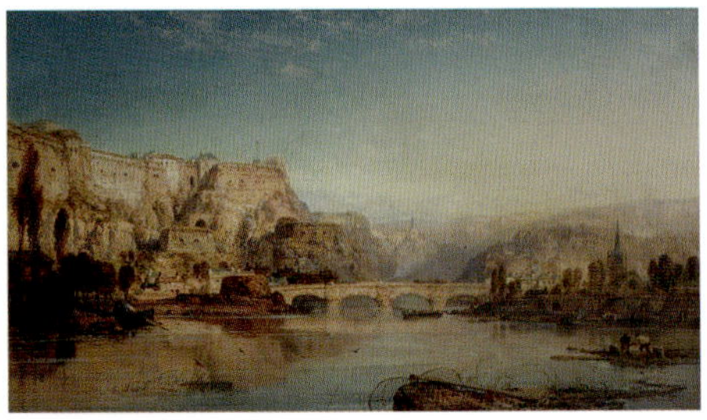

Webb, James 1825–1895
Namur, Belgium 1878
oil on canvas 76.5 x 128
L.F1.1907.0.0

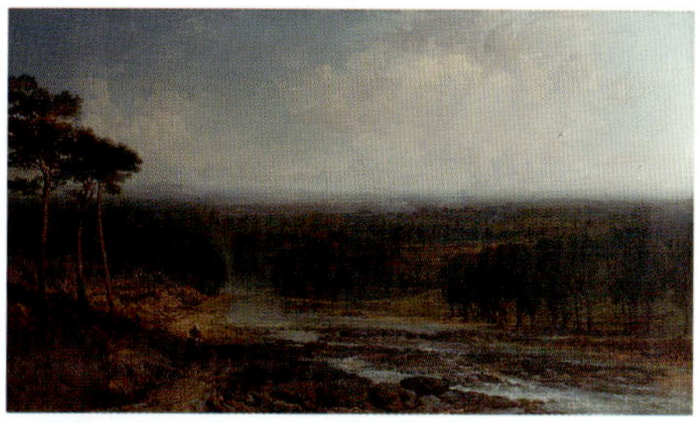

Webb, James 1825–1895
The Vale of Ross
oil on canvas 90.2 x 152.4
L.F11.1882.0.0

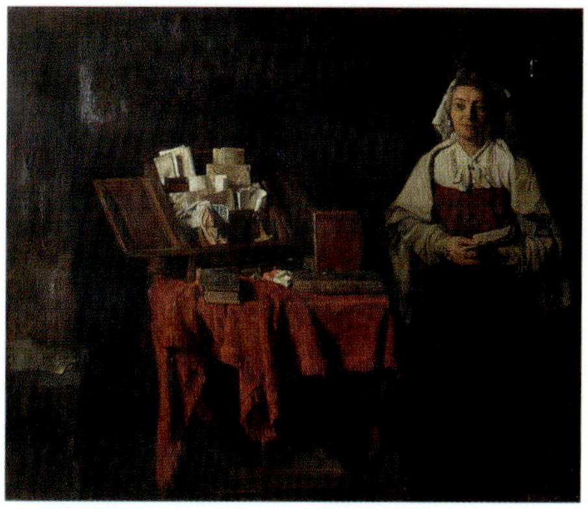

Weissbon, G.
Portrait of a Woman with Books 1958
oil on canvas 63.8 x 73.8
L.F3.1996.1.0

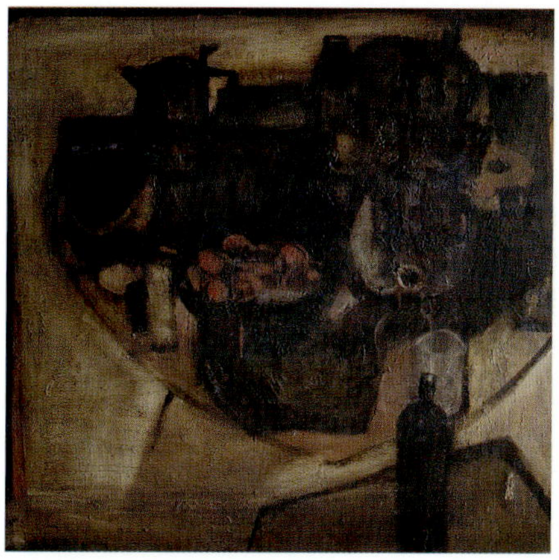

Whishaw, Anthony b.1930
Still Life on a Round Table
oil on board 124.5 x 122
L.F11.1959.0.0

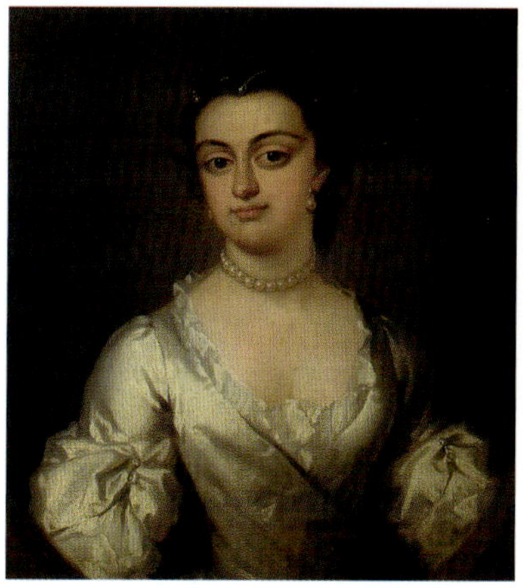

Whood, Isaac 1688/1689–1752
Portrait of a Lady in White Satin
oil on canvas 69.8 x 58.4
L.F9.1943.8.0

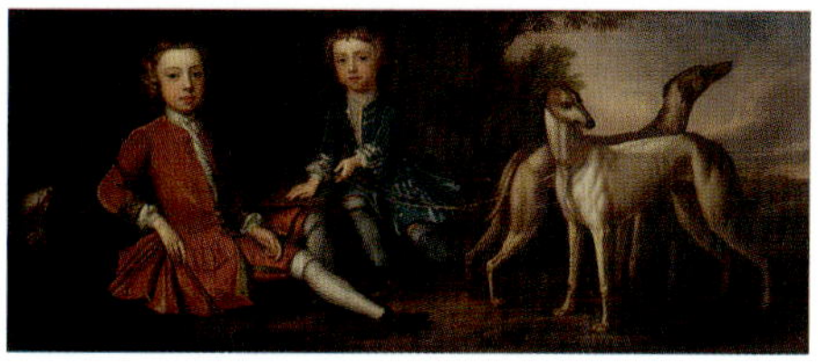

Whood, Isaac 1688/1689–1752
Two Boys with Greyhounds
oil on canvas 44.5 x 102.5
L.F9.1943.7.0

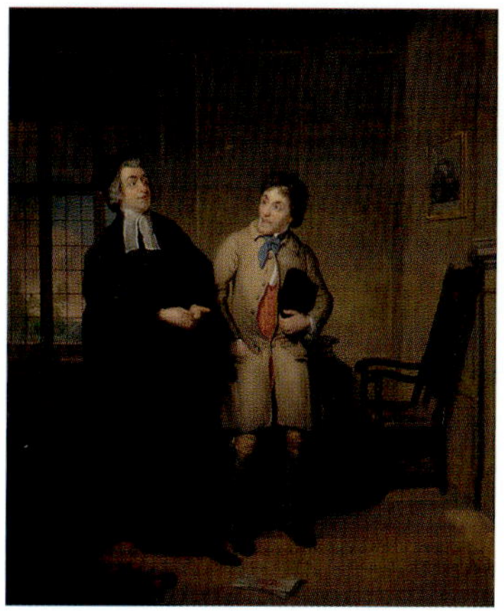

Wilde, Samuel de 1748–1832
Mr Bannister Junior and Mr Parsons as Scout and Sheepface in 'The Village Lawyer' c.1796
oil on canvas 61.6 x 51.2
L.F3.1941.0.0

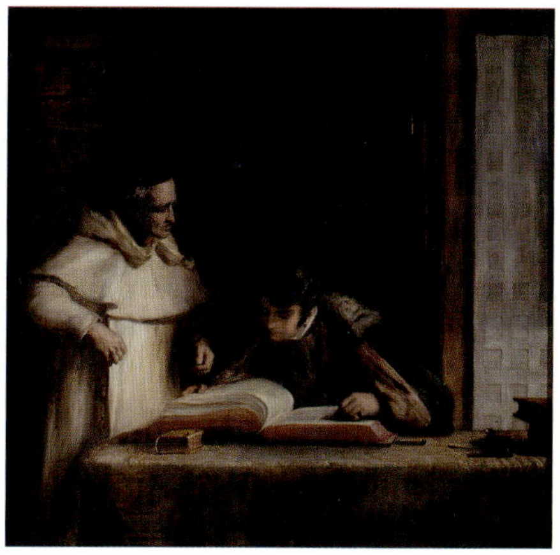

Wilkie, David 1785–1841
Washington Irving in the Archives of Seville
1828–1829
oil on canvas 122.6 x 122.6
L.F2.1890.0.0

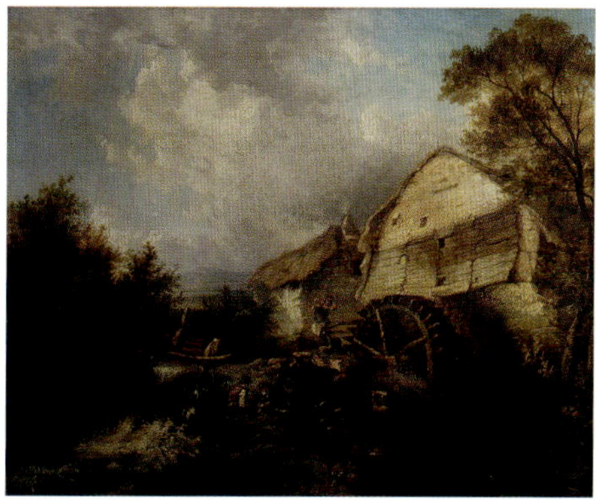

Willcock, George Burrell 1811–1852
Holy Street Mill, Chagford, Devon
oil on canvas 63 x 75.6
L.F25.1948.0.0

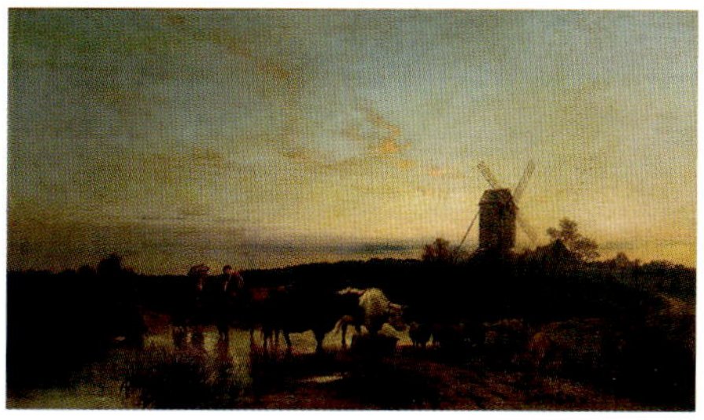

Williams, Alfred Walter 1823–1905
Reigate Heath, Surrey 1857
oil on canvas 107 x 183
L.F5.1881.0.0

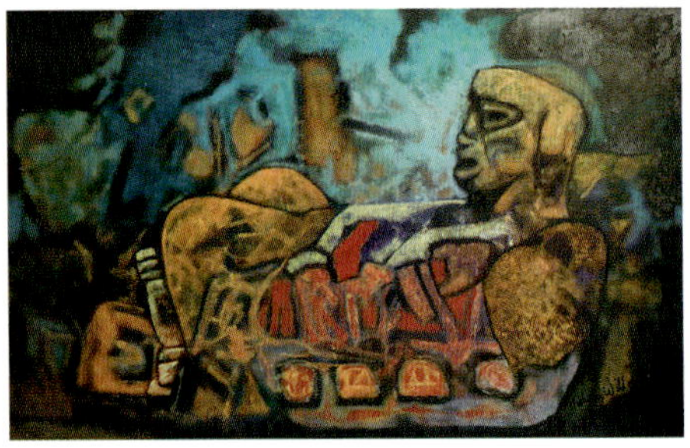

Williams, Aubrey 1926–1990
Chac-Mool 1983
oil on canvas 120 x 178.5
L.F17.1985.0.0

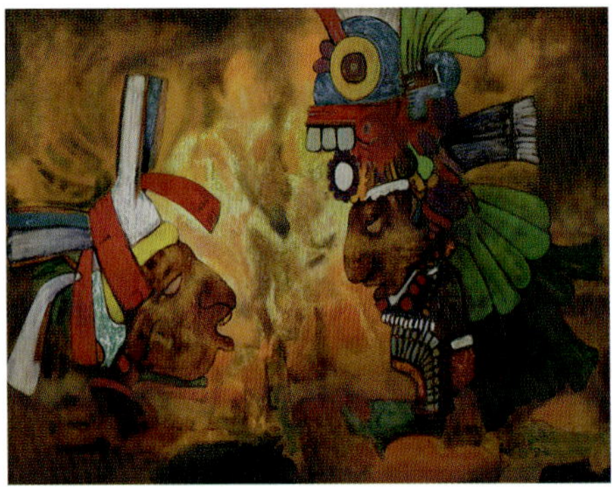

Williams, Aubrey 1926–1990
Maya Confrontation 1983
oil on canvas 117 x 176.5
L.F18.1985.0.0

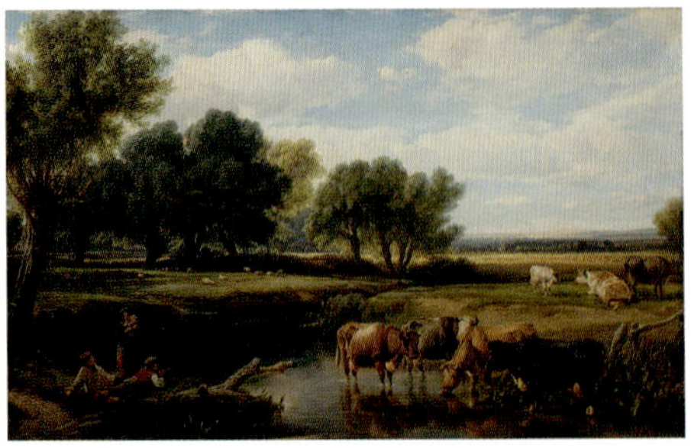

Willis, Henry Brittan 1810–1884
Cattle Watering at a Stream 1853
oil on canvas 91.5 x 143.5
L.F7.1891.0.0

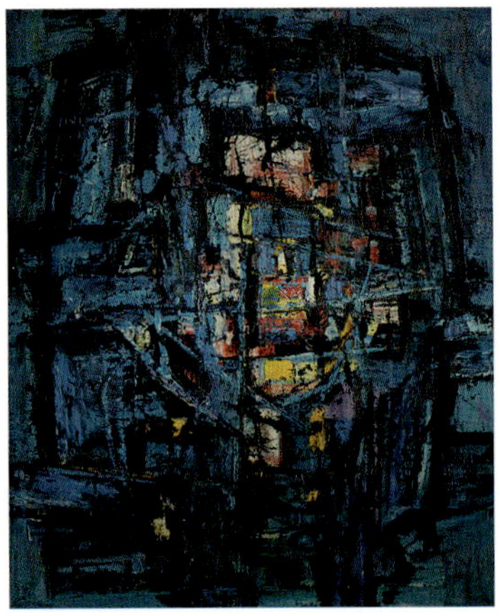

Wilson, Frank Avray 1914–2009
Configuration, Black and Blue
oil on canvas 152.5 x 122
L.F14.1958.0.0

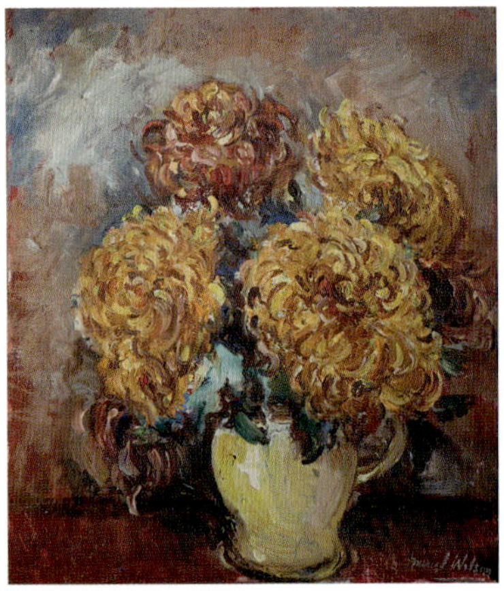

Wilson, Muriel Gertrude 1893–1977
Chrysanthemums
oil on canvas 61.2 x 50.7
L.F21.1931.0.0

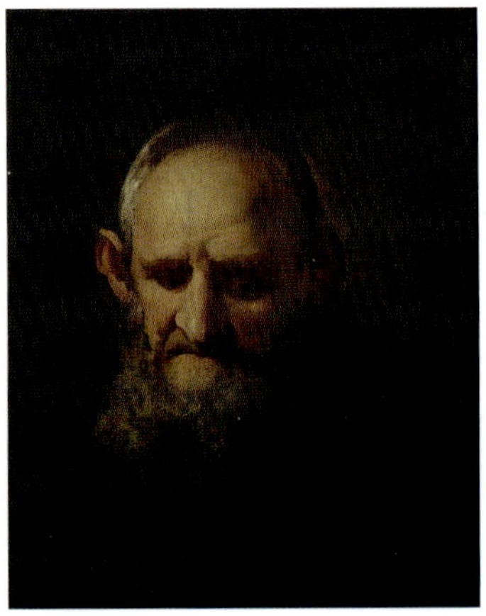

Wilson, Richard 1712/1713–1782
Head of a Capuchin 1752
oil on canvas 48.2 x 38.2
L.F48.1955.0.0

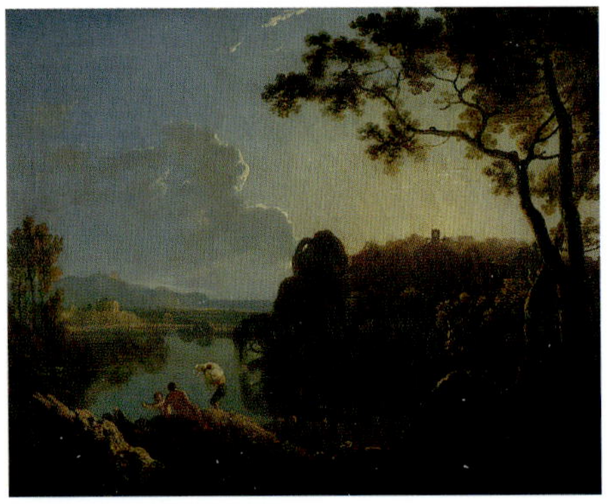

Wilson, Richard 1712/1713–1782
Landscape with Bathers 1770–1775
oil on canvas 61 x 76.2
L.F55.1937.0.0

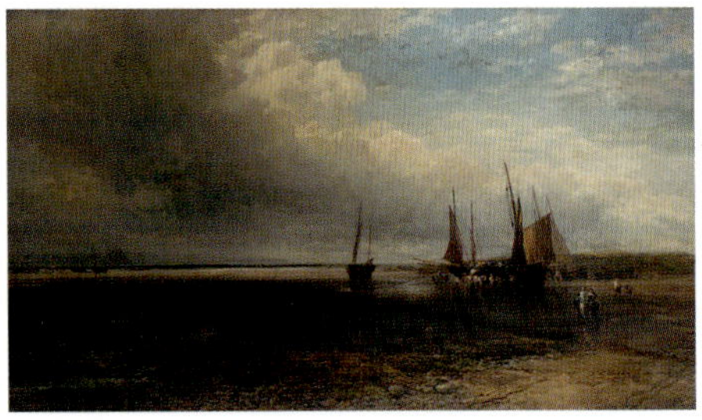

Wimperis, Edmund Morison 1835–1900
Carting Fish, Mount's Bay, Cornwall 1882
oil on canvas 76 x 127.5
L.F9.1882.0.0

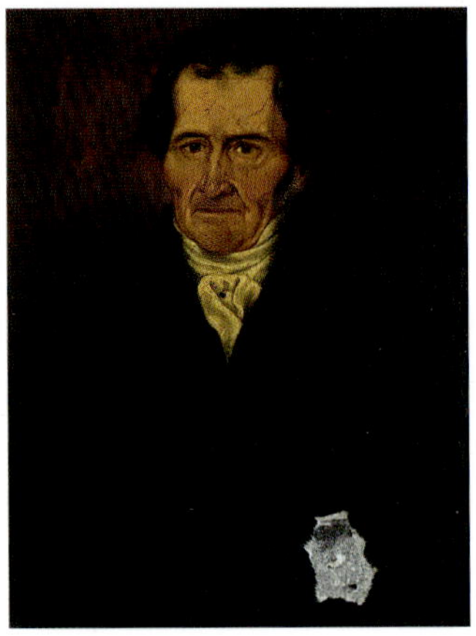

Winks, Frederick c.1805–1880
Joseph Winks (1767–1835), the Artist's Father
1830
oil on canvas 53.3 x 43.2
L.F30.1959.0.0

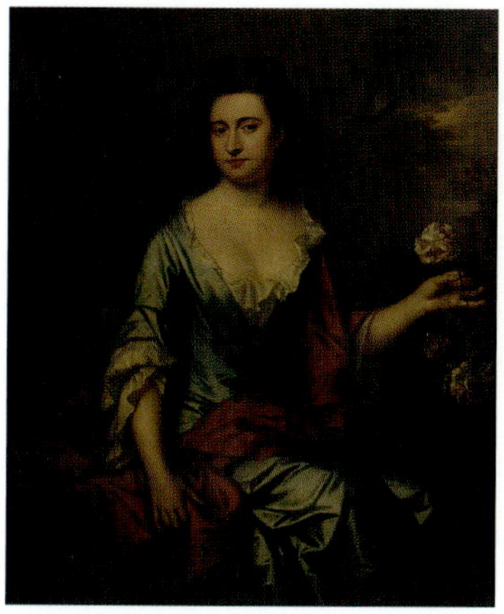

Wissing, Willem (school of) 1656–1687
Portrait of a Lady
oil on canvas 124.5 x 101.6
L.F45.1947.1.0

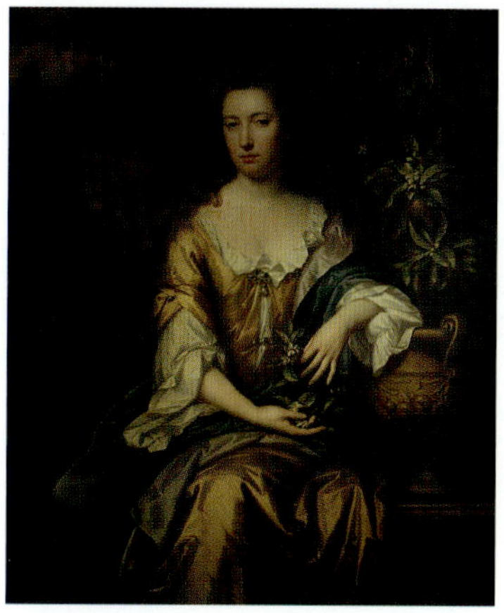

Wissing, Willem (school of) 1656–1687
Portrait of a Lady
oil on canvas 126 x 102
L.F45.1947.2.0

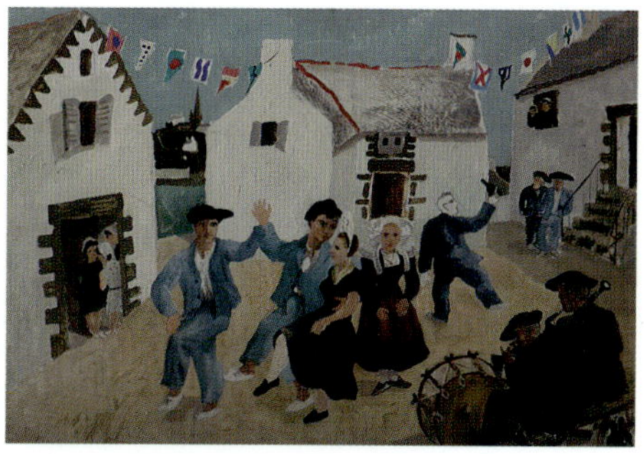

Wood, Christopher 1901–1930
Dancing Sailors, Brittany, France 1930
oil & household paint on board 57.5 x 82
L.F21.1981.0.0

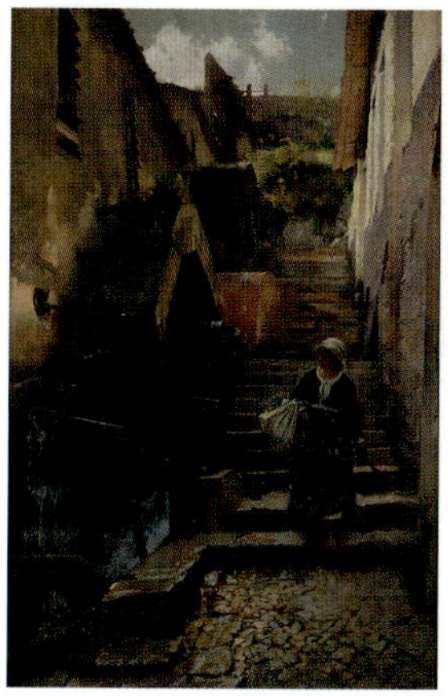

Woods, Henry 1846–1921
The Water Wheels at Savassa, Italy 1886
oil on canvas 119 x 75
L.F13.1900.0.0

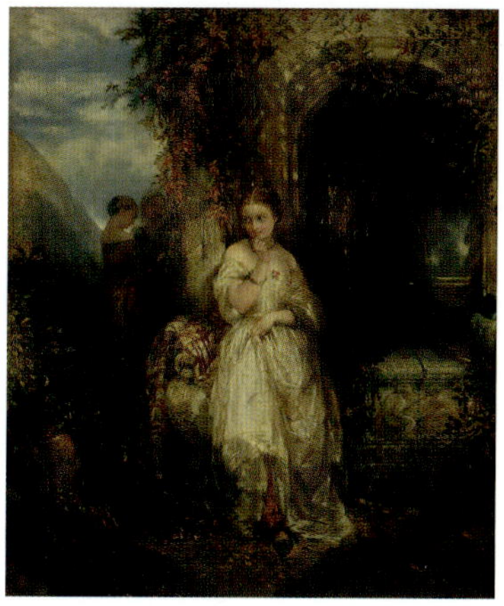

Woolmer, Alfred Joseph 1805–1892
Lalla Rookh (from the poem by Thomas Moore) 1861
oil on canvas 72.4 x 60.4
L.F11.1943.0.0

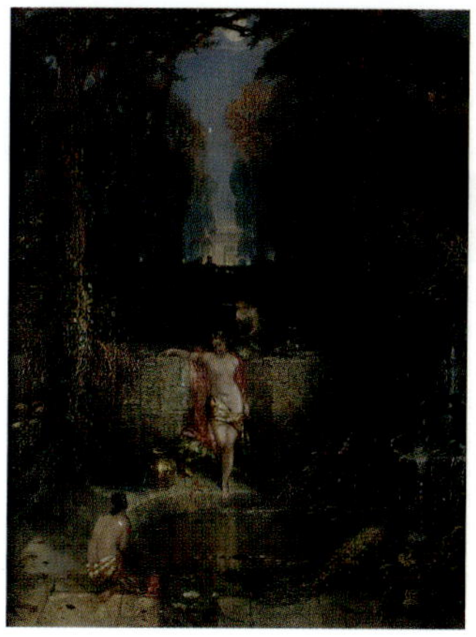

Woolmer, Alfred Joseph 1805–1892
The Bathers
oil on canvas 112 x 86.5
L.F1.1903.0.0

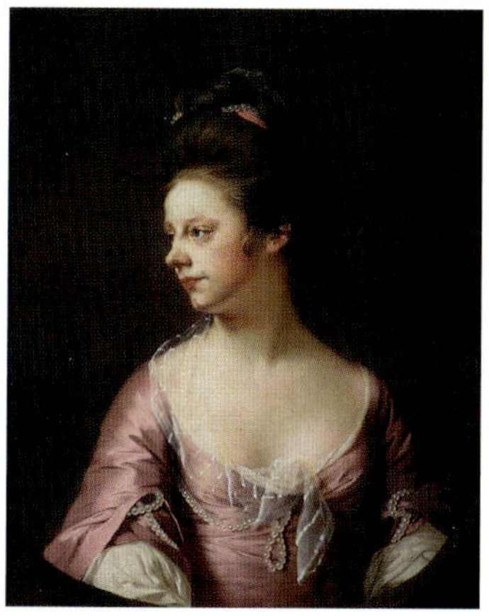

Wright, Joseph of Derby 1734–1797
Mrs Catherine Swindell 1769–1772
oil on canvas 71.5 x 55.6
L.F8.1938.0.0

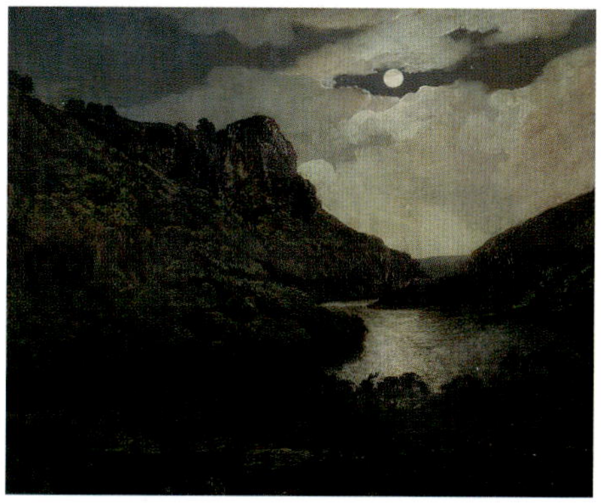

Wright, Joseph of Derby 1734–1797
High Tor, Matlock, Derbyshire
oil on canvas 61 x 73.7
L.F12.1946.0.0

Leicester City Council (Adult Skills and Learning)

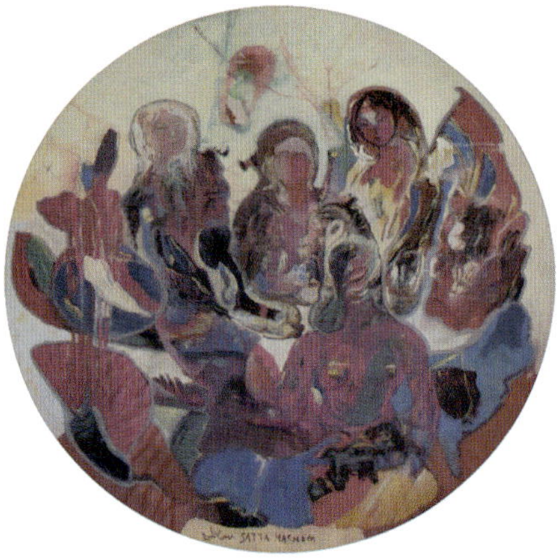

Hashem, Satta b.1959
Sight and Insight 1 2002
acrylic on paper on wood 300
PCF1

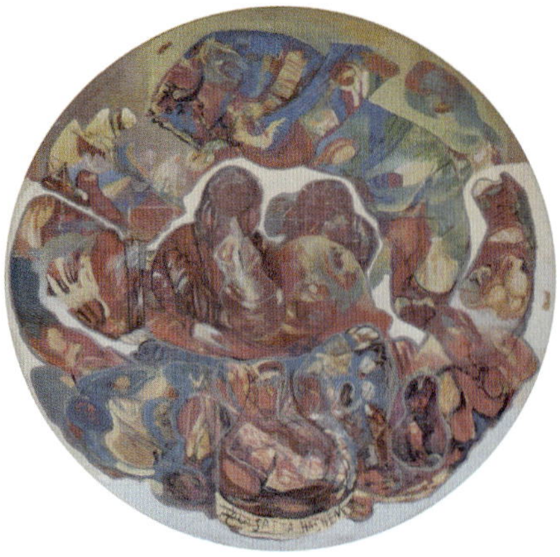

Hashem, Satta b.1959
Sight and Insight 2 2002
acrylic on paper on wood 300
PCF2

Leicester Town Hall

Built in the Queen Anne style, Leicester Town Hall was opened in August 1876. It was not long before more accommodation was required and the building was substantially altered and extended in the 1920s to form a complete quadrangle. The original Victorian Court Room remains, however the original Council Chamber was significantly altered during this refurbishment. Leicester City Council services provided from the building include civic, democratic, registry service and coronial functions.

Most of the paintings are on display and may be most easily viewed on the first Wednesday of each month during the free public tour conducted by a Blue Badge guide affiliated to Leicester Tourist Information Office.

Joseph Martin, Civic Attendant

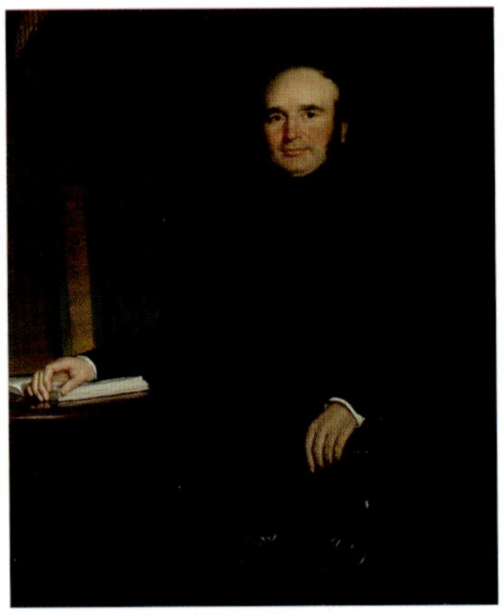

British School 19th C
Alderman John Biggs (1801–1871), Mayor of Leicester (1840, 1847 & 1855)
oil on canvas 124.5 x 99
L.F37.1949.0.0

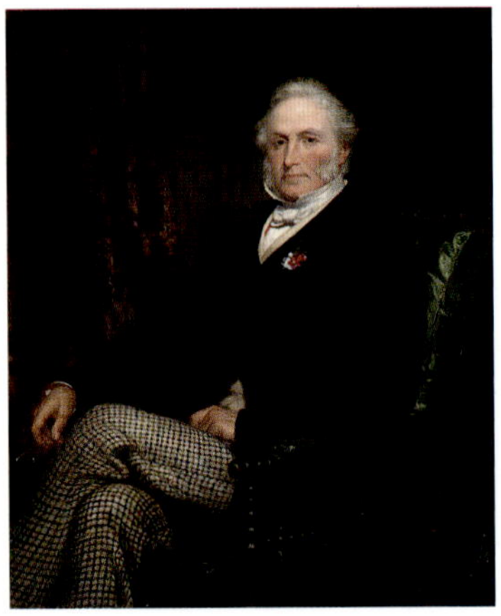

British School 19th C
Thomas Paget (1778–1862), Mayor of Leicester (1836–1837)
oil on canvas 125.7 x 99
L.F42.1949.0.0

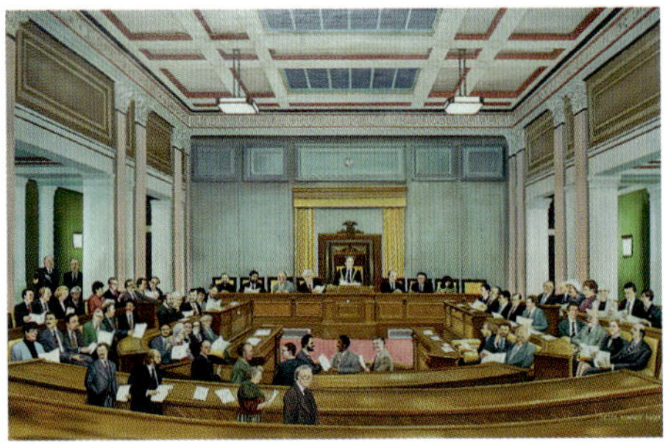

Bunney, Peter b.1932
Council Chambers 1993
oil on board 85.2 x 125
L.F12

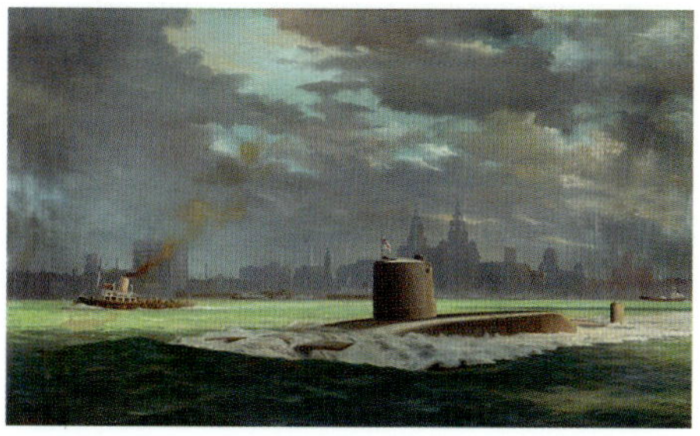

Cobb, J.
HMS 'Renown' Polaris Submarine's Maiden Voyage 1999
oil on canvas board 49.5 x 80
L.F1

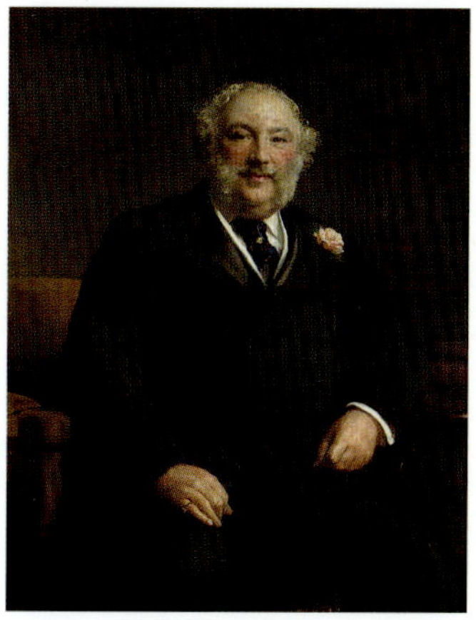

Cope, Arthur Stockdale 1857–1940
Sir Israel Hart (1935–1911), Mayor of Leicester (1884–1888 & 1893–1894) 1896
oil on canvas 119.4 x 93
L.F41.1949.0.0

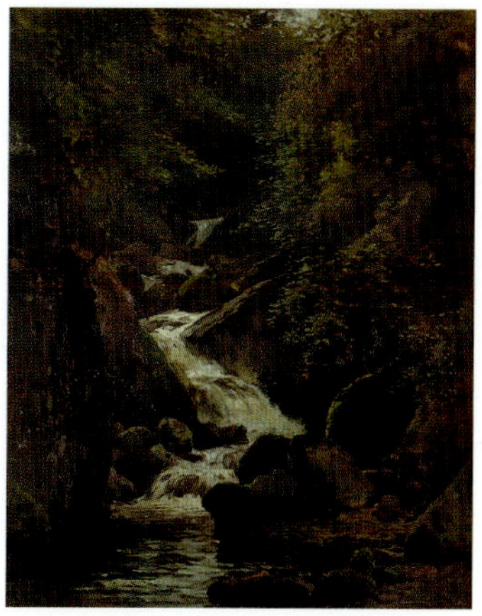

Davies, Edward 1841–1920
A Stream from the Hills, Brecon, Powys
oil on canvas 91.5 x 71.2
L.F18.1936.0.0

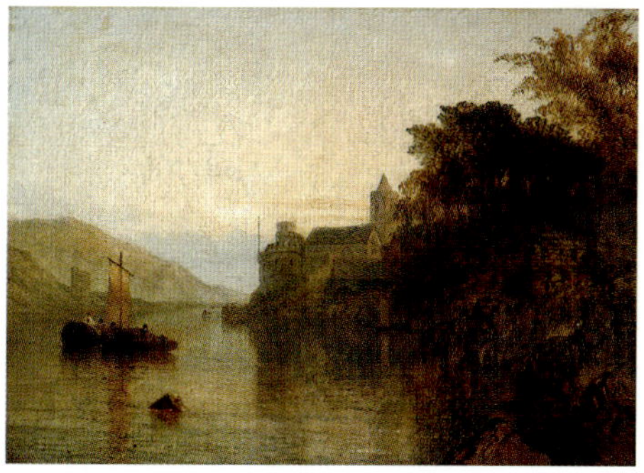

Dawson, Henry 1811–1878
The Mouth of the Dart, Devon 1854
oil on canvas 30.8 x 40.5
L.F6.1888.0.0

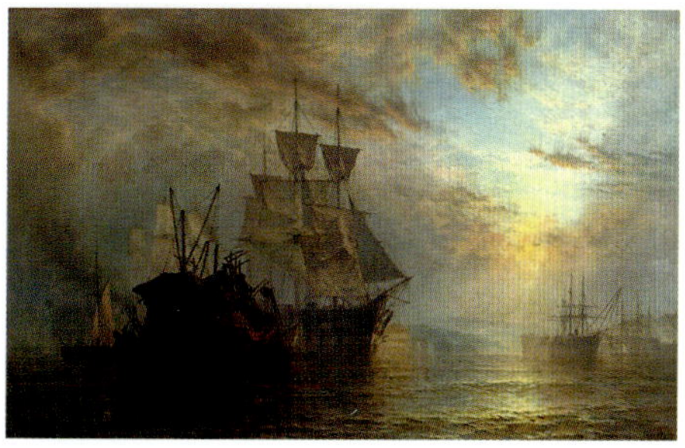

Dawson, Henry Thomas 1841/1842–after 1896
The River Tamar 1873
oil on canvas 81.3 x 122
L.F2.1908.0.0

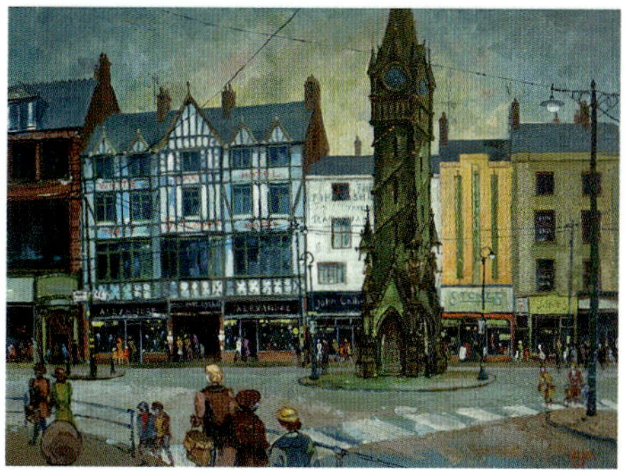

Ellis, Norman 1913–1971
Haymarket, Leicester 1970
oil on canvas 50 x 65.5
L.F462.1971.0.0

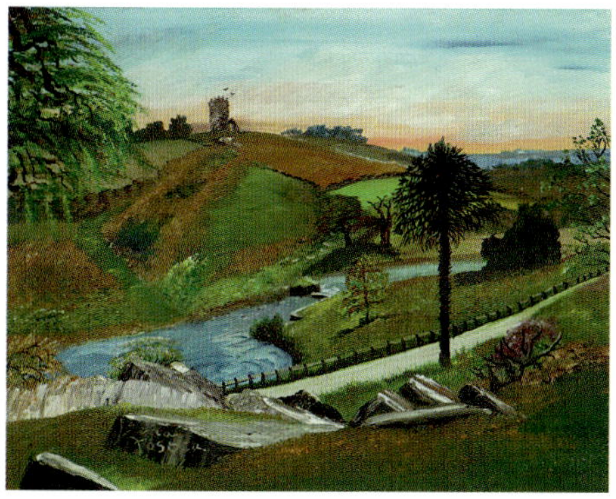

Foster, Zena b.1931
View of Old John, Bradgate Park, Leicestershire c.2000
oil on canvas 41 x 51
L.F10

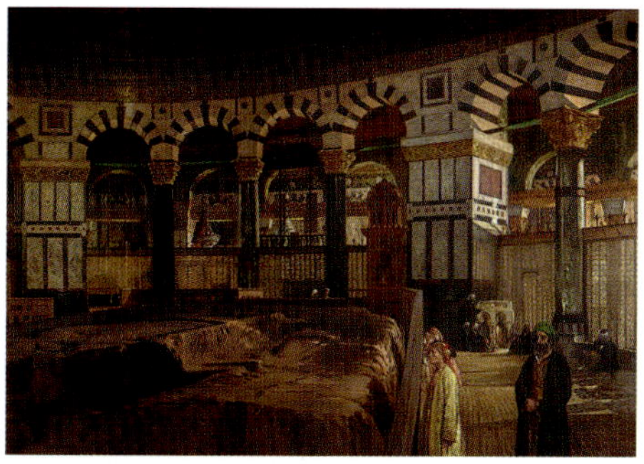

Fulleylove, John 1845–1908
Interior of the Mosque of Omar, Jerusalem
oil on canvas 135.3 x 191.8
L.F1.1923.0.0

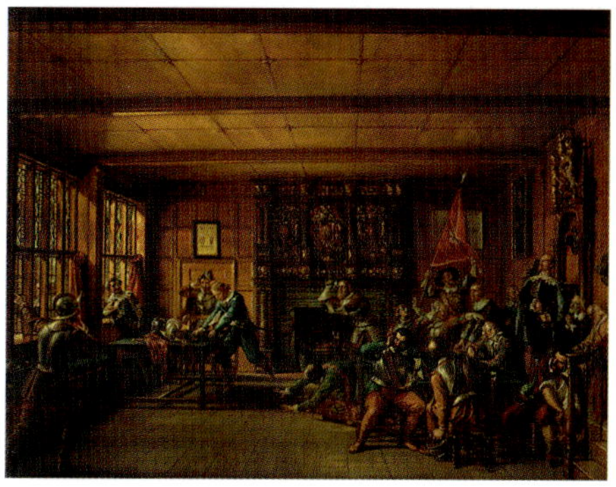

Gotzenburg
The Mayor and Town Council of Leicester in the Mayor's Rooms 1854
oil on canvas 63.5 x 81.3
L.F65.1952.0.0

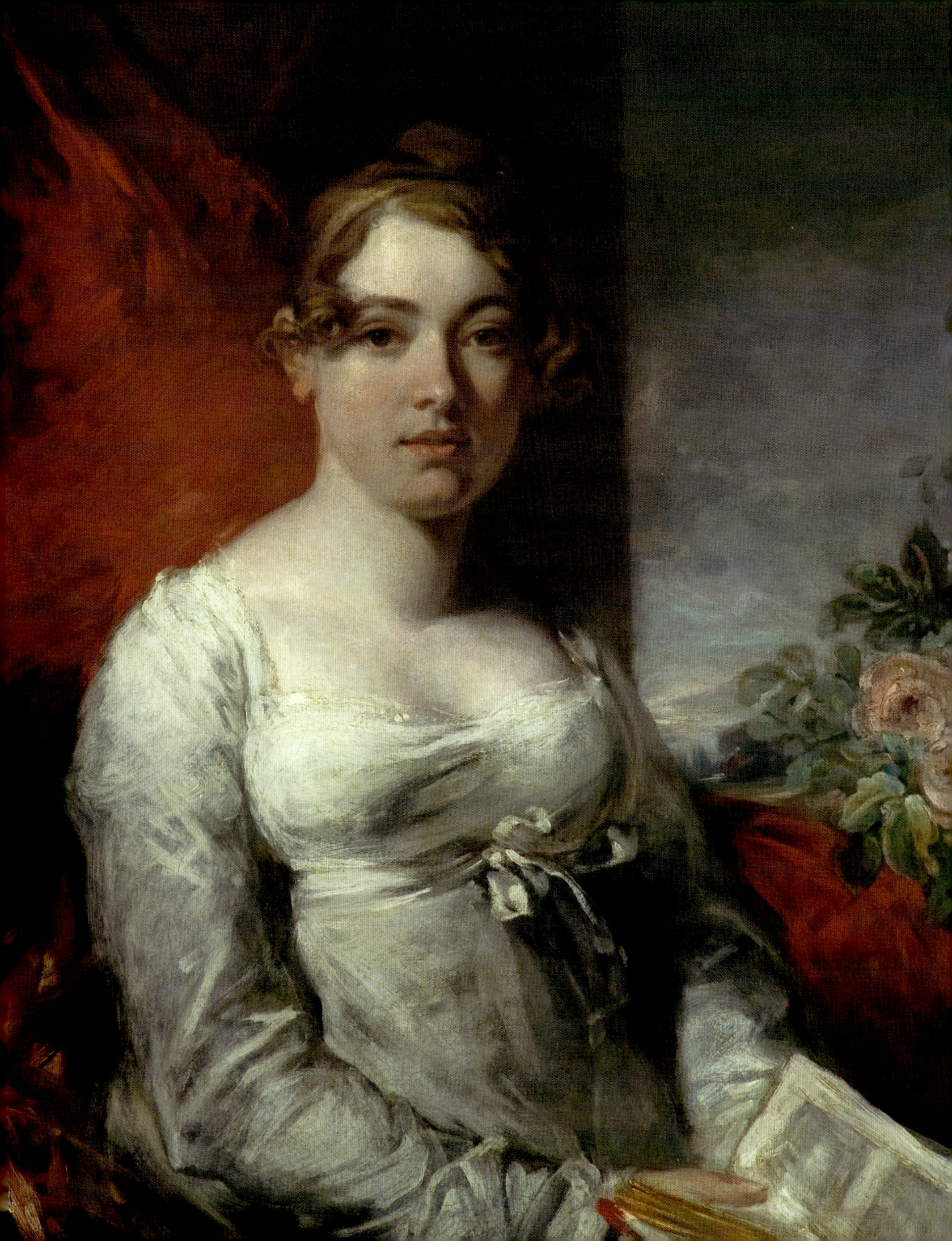

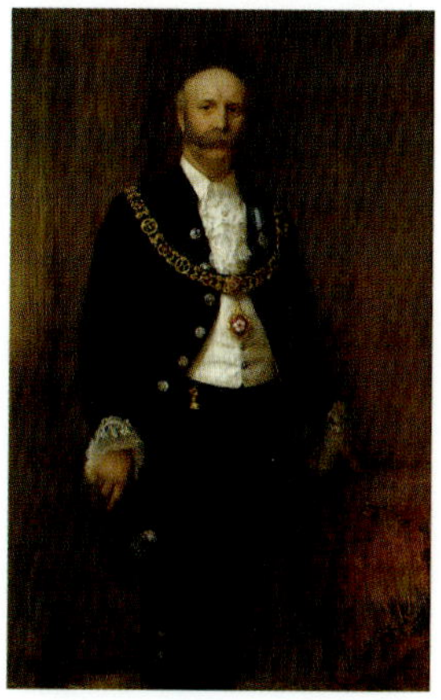

Hacker, Arthur 1858–1919
Sir Herbert Marshall (1851–1918), Mayor of Leicester (1896–1897) 1898
oil on canvas 170.2 x 106.7
L.F32.1949.0.0

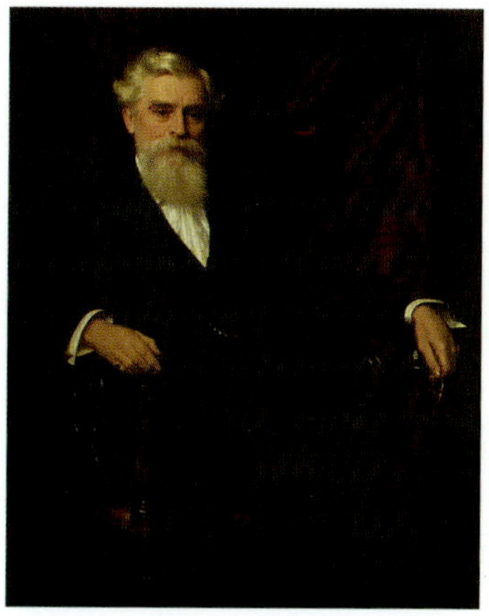

Hare, St George 1857–1933
Alderman Thomas Windley (1835–1932), Mayor of Leicester (1899) 1901
oil on canvas 124.5 x 100.3
L.F36.1949.0.0

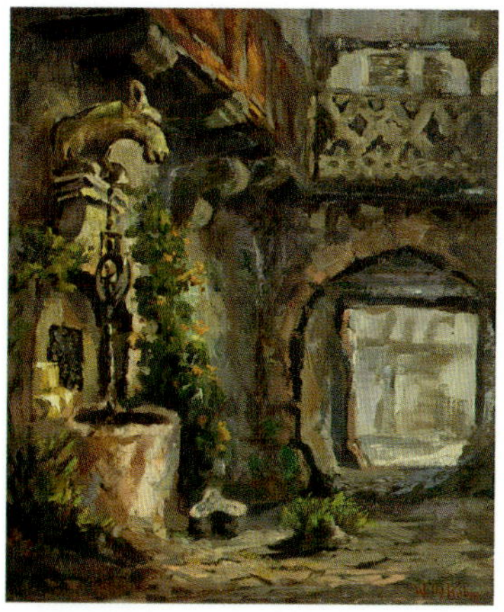

Kuhn, Willy
Cour du Corbeau, Strasbourg, France
oil on canvas 55.7 x 46.5
L.F11

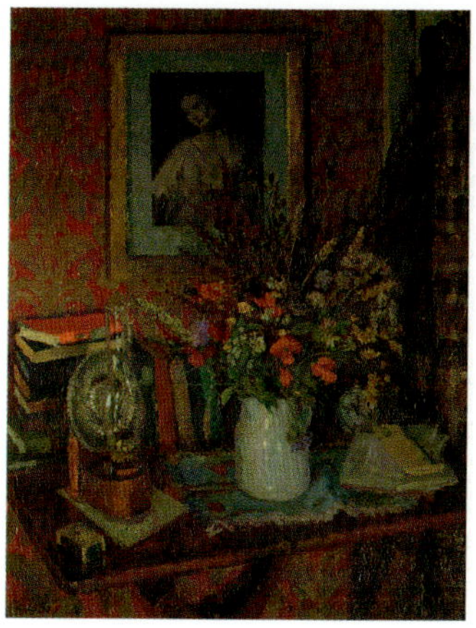

Le Bas, Edward 1904–1966
Still Life with Flowers 1936
oil on millboard 73.6 x 56.2
L.F25.1947.0.0

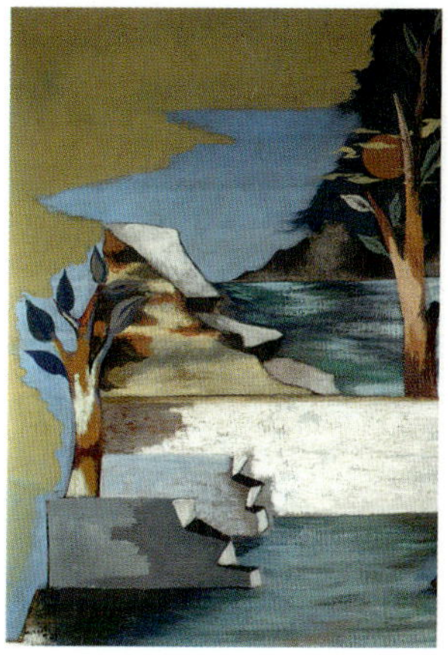

Lurçat, Jean 1892–1966
The Olive Tree 1938
oil on canvas 75.5 x 50
L.F5.1983.0.0

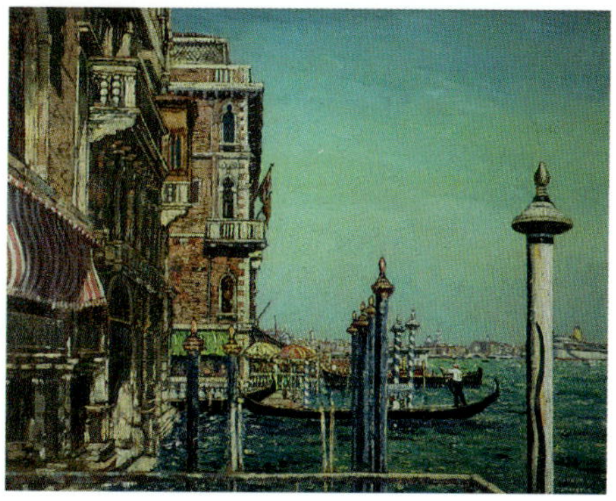

Muncaster, Claude 1903–1974
Landing Stage, Venice
oil on board 39.4 x 49.5
L.F3.1996.6.0

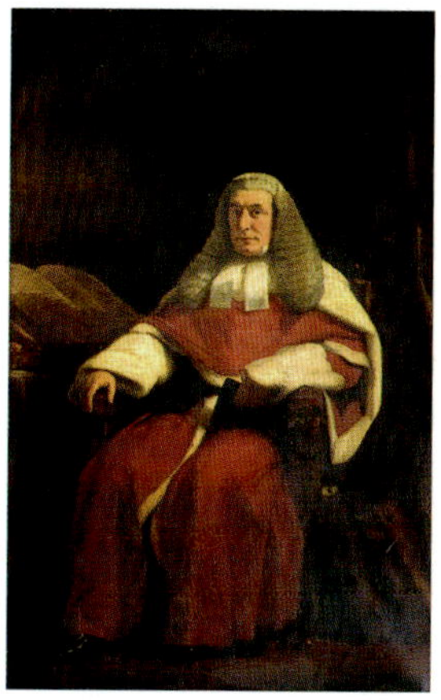

Napier, John James 1831–1877
The Right Honourable Sir John Mellor (1808–1887), Bt, Judge c.1876
oil on canvas 274 x 167
L.F43.1949.0.0

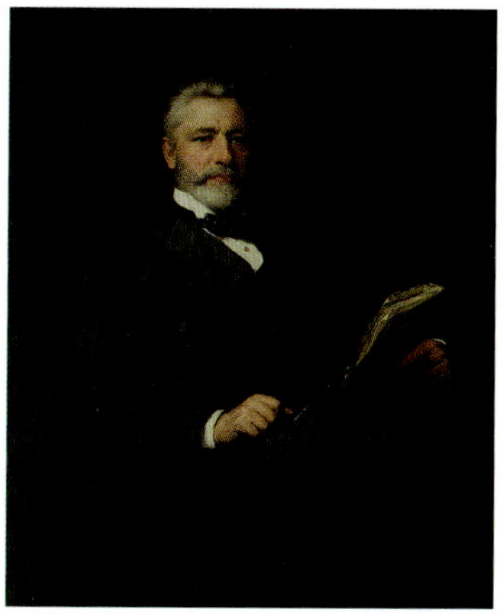

Ouless, Walter William 1848–1933
Alderman Edward Wood (1839–1917), JP, Mayor of Leicester (1888, 1895, 1901 & 1906) 1898
oil on canvas 124.5 x 99
L.F40.1949.0.0

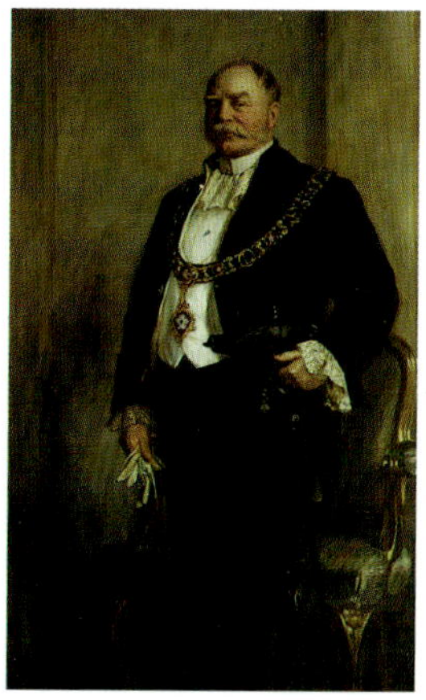

Pettie, John 1839–1893
Sir Thomas Wright (1838–1905)
oil on canvas 238.8 x 101.6
L.F33.1949.0.0

Facing page: De Wint, Peter, 1784–1849, *Mrs Peter De Wint (1791–1866)* (detail), The Collection: Art & Archaeology in Lincolnshire (Usher Gallery) (p. 294)

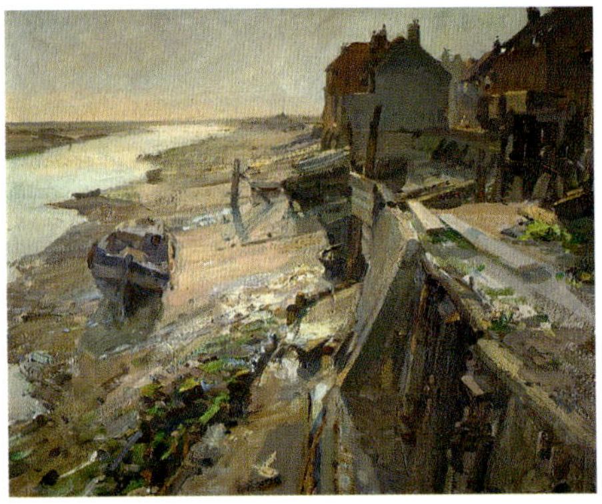

Pettinger, John Frederick 1877–1939
Low Tide
oil on canvas 129 x 154.9
L.F13.1930.0.0

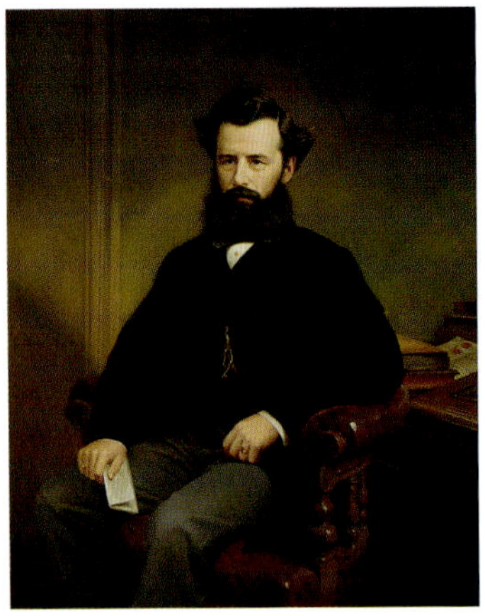

Pratt, Jonathan 1835–1911
Alderman William Grimsley (1832–1878), Mayor of Leicester (1878) after 1878
oil on canvas 124.5 x 99
L.F35.1949.0.0

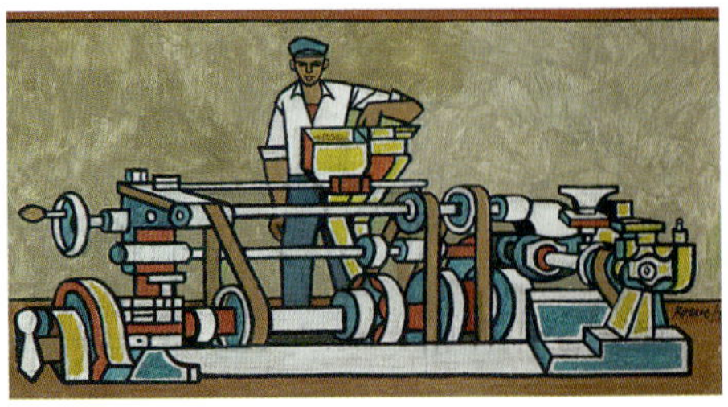

Rowe, Cliff 1904–1989
Machine Minder 1976
oil on hardboard 23.7 x 42
L.F2.1986.0.0

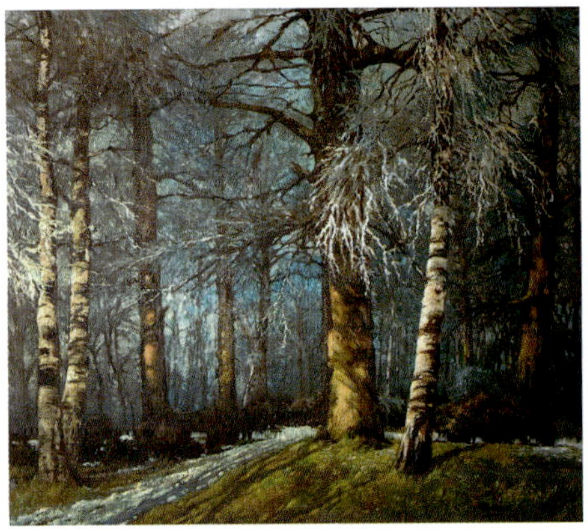

Sarson, George 1880–1969
Changing Moods, near Stoneleigh Abbey, Kenilworth, Warwickshire 1964
oil on cloth on hardboard 72.5 x 78.6
Y.F2.2000.0.0

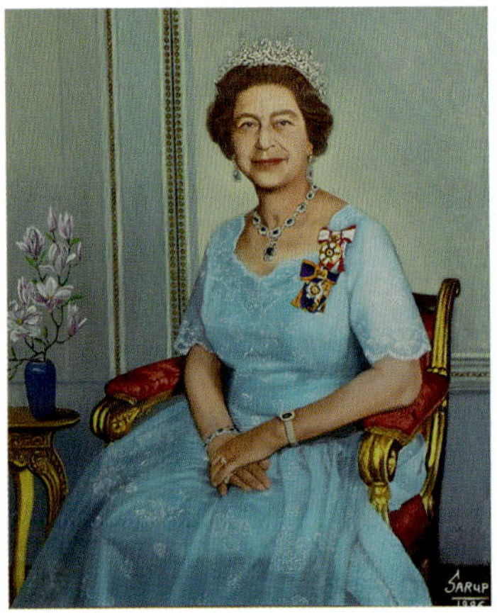

Singh, Sarup active 1968–2001
Elizabeth II (b.1926) 1986
acrylic on canvas 76.5 x 61
L.F7

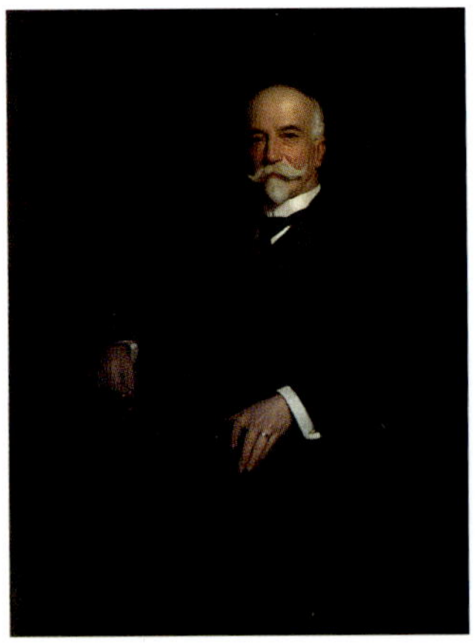

unknown artist 19th C
Sir William Wilkins Vincent (1843–1916), Mayor of Leicester (1902 & 1910)
oil on canvas 133.3 x 99
L.F44.1949.0.0

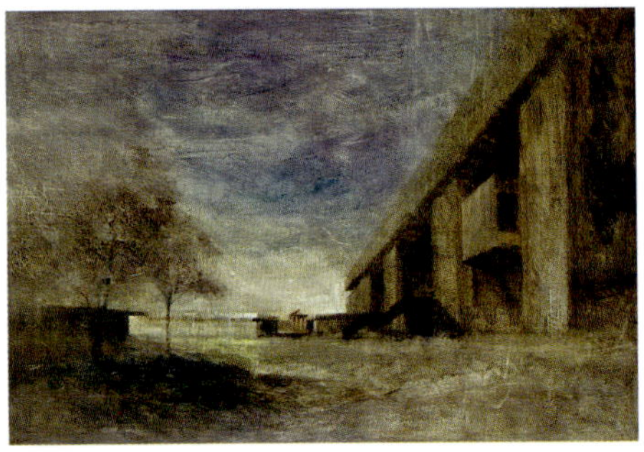

unknown artist
Plans for Civic Centre 1 (Albion Hill Project)
oil on board 86.5 x 122
L.F8

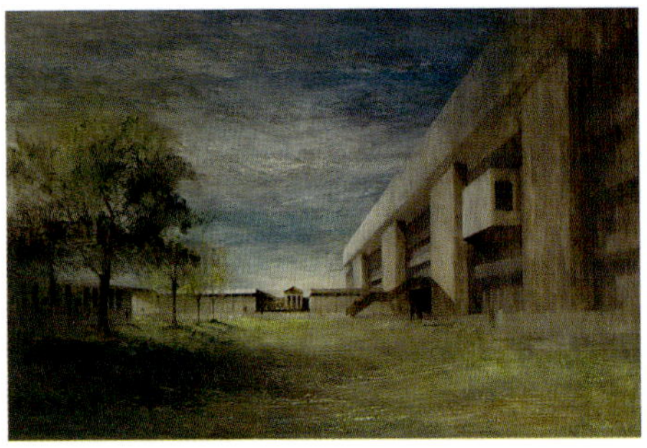

unknown artist
Plans for Civic Centre 2 (Albion Hill Project)
oil on board 86 x 122
L.F9

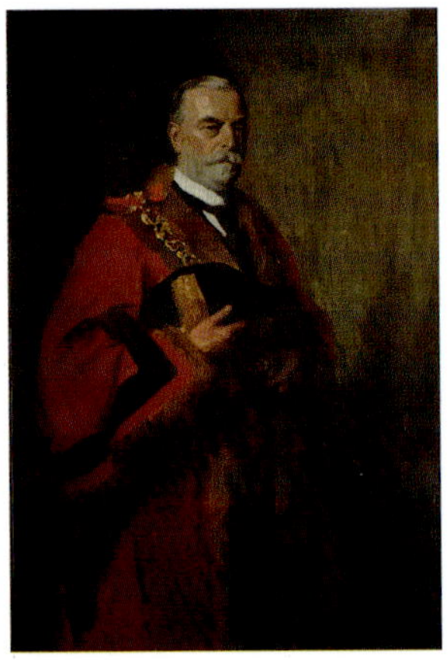

Watt, George Fiddes 1873–1960
Alderman Sir Jonathan North (1855–1939), JP 1923
oil on canvas 144.8 x 94
L.F34.1949.0.0

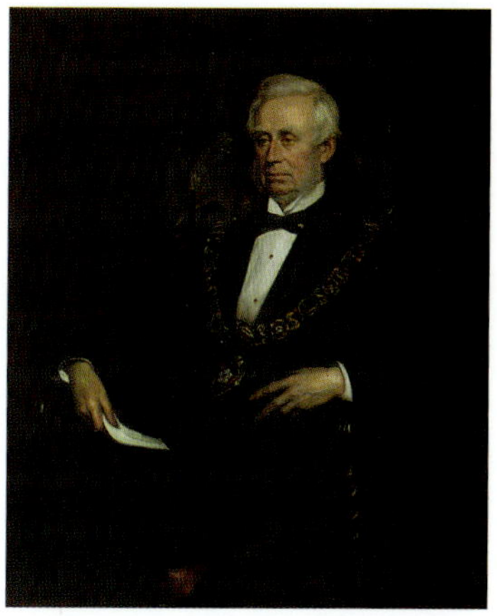

Wirgman, Theodore Blake 1848–1925
Alderman William Kempson (1805–1893), JP, Mayor of Leicester (1873 & 1890)
oil on canvas 124.5 x 99
L.F39.1949.0.0

Leicestershire County Council Artworks Collection

'Art is both a form of communication and a means of expression of feelings which ought to permeate the whole curriculum and the whole life of the school…'
The Plowden Report, 1967

Leicestershire County Council Artworks Collection was established in 1947 under the vision of Stewart Mason, the then Director of Leicestershire Education. The royalties received from the publication of books by county officials allowed Mason to realise a lifetime ambition: to provide schools and colleges with original contemporary works of art. Mason felt that it was important to have art in places where people congregate daily as much as in museums and galleries. He particularly wanted children to experience art from an early age.

Over 60 years later, the Artworks Loan Scheme is now administered by the Open Museum Team of Leicestershire County Council Environment and Heritage Services and continues to bring art into schools and communities where it can be enjoyed, appreciated and more significantly used in the classroom to support and encourage creative and critical thinking.

The Artworks Collection comprises over 1,000 original paintings, drawings, prints, photographs, sculpture and textiles from the twentieth and twenty-first centuries. The Collection includes works by Christopher Wood, William George Scott, Patrick Heron, and John Piper. More recent additions to the Collection have included paintings by Patrick Hughes and P. J. Crook, and prints by David Hockney, Peter Howson, Paula Rego and Bridget Riley (not included in this catalogue due to their medium). Leicestershire County Council Environment and Heritage Services continues to maintain the vibrancy of the Collection with an active collecting policy and new works being purchased each year. They are selected on grounds of artistic merit and in conjunction with an ongoing understanding of what types of work will be most effective and useful within different school environments and community groups – some of our artworks and sculptures are selected with the intention of providing tactile stimulus for people with physical or learning disabilities. The Artworks scheme also provides supporting information to accompany the selected works, providing a catalyst for further inspiration and projects.

Artworks may be used in different ways according to the requirements of the borrowing organisation. The art may be used in formal education activities and linked into the national curriculum, to inform and inspire discussion, or to stimulate project work or to allow a general appreciation of original art. The scheme encourages and explores ways which art can be applied across the curriculum, and inspires innovative projects involving artists working with students and local communities, which give teachers the confidence to use art in schools in a pro-active way. The scheme arranges for the works to be delivered to a venue then collected at the end of a termly or yearly loan period. The scheme also provides continuous support and information on how users can make the most of the art they have on loan.

Lisa Webb, Artworks Officer

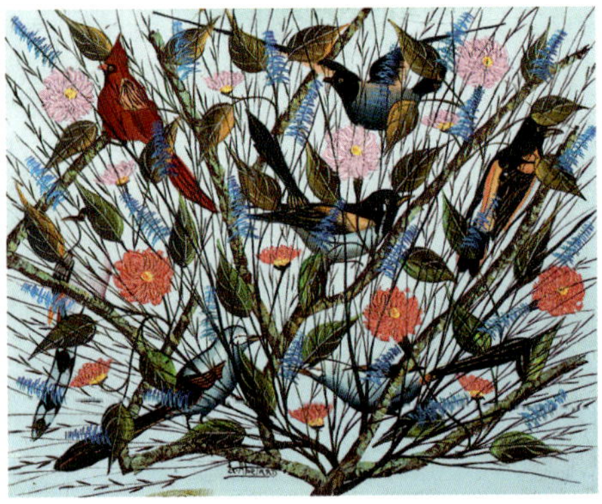

Aberlard, Gesner b.1922
Birds and Flowers 1969
acrylic on board 53.3 x 64
0669

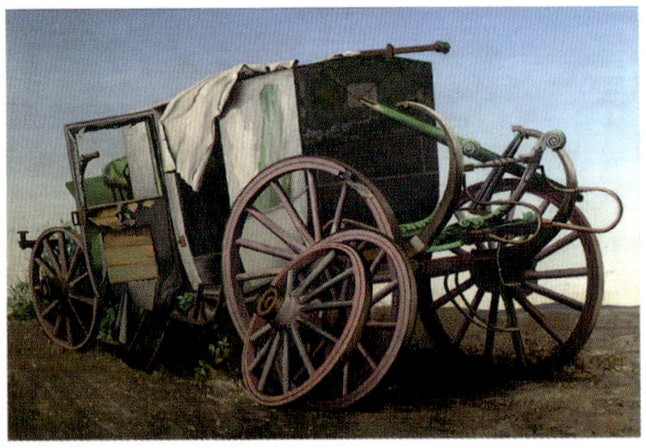

Adnams, Marion Elizabeth 1898–1995
Coloured Ending 1962
acrylic on board 68 x 93
0646

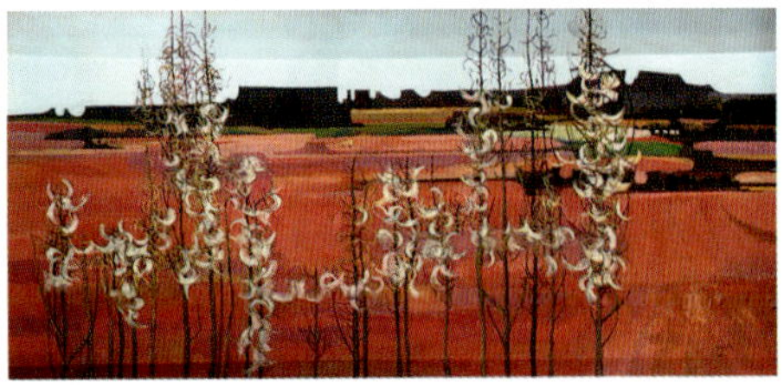

Akers, John Michael 1936–2009
Willowherb 1970
oil on board 64.5 x 125
0676

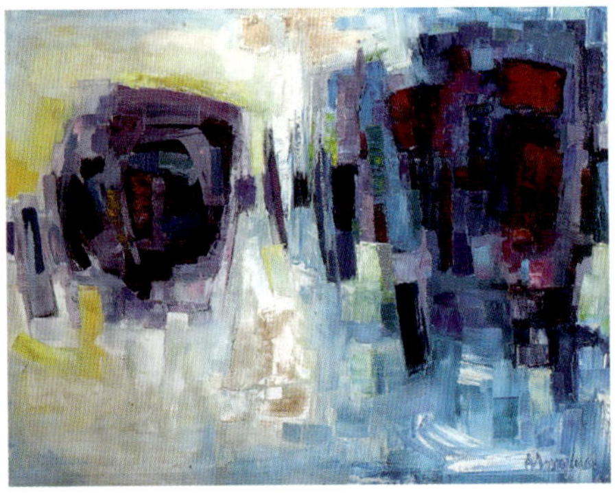

Almquist, John
Exiles 1960
oil on canvas 100 x 123
0668

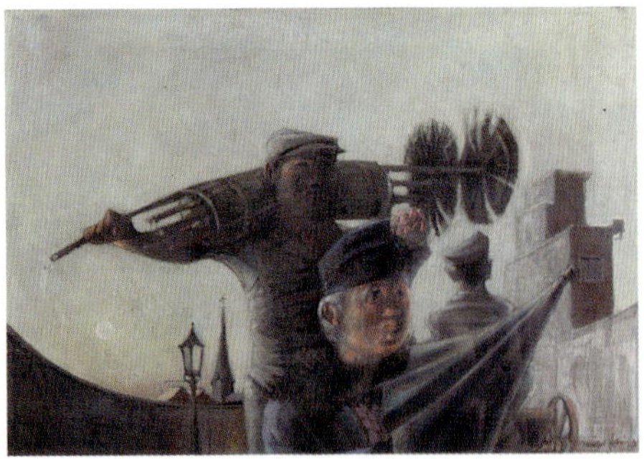

Ayrton, Michael 1921–1975
The Sweep and Others 1951
oil on canvas 75 x 100
0666

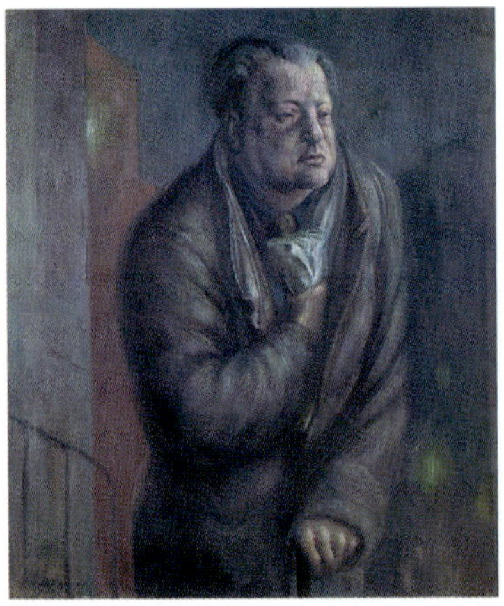

Ayrton, Michael 1921–1975
Constant Lambert (1905–1951) 1954
oil on canvas 91 x 78.5
0667

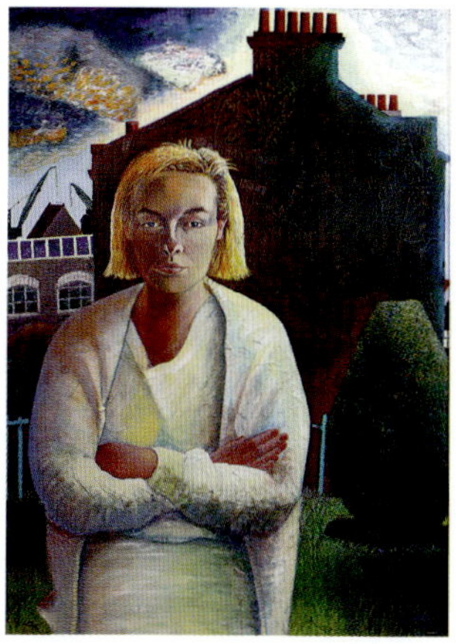

Banks, Lesley b.1962
From Bearsden to Partick 1990
acrylic on board 125.5 x 93
0632

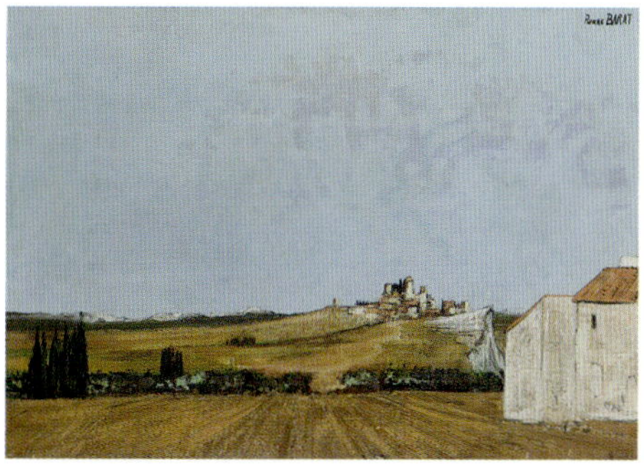

Barat, Pierre b.1935
Village in the Camargue, France 1971
oil on canvas 65.5 x 84
0672

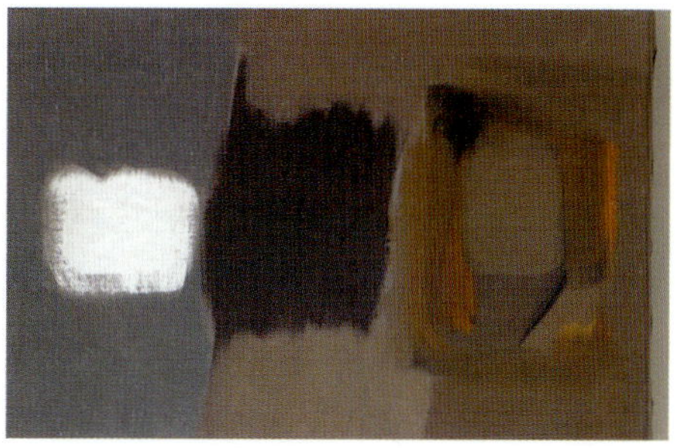

Barker, Kit 1916–1988
Tranquil Forms 1962
oil on canvas 41.5 x 57
0665

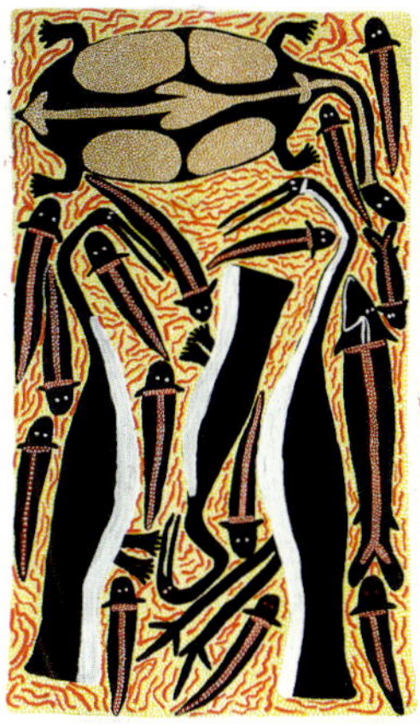

Barra Barra, Sambo b.c.1946
Waterbirds Feeding in Yellow 2001
acrylic on canvas 125 x 64
0962

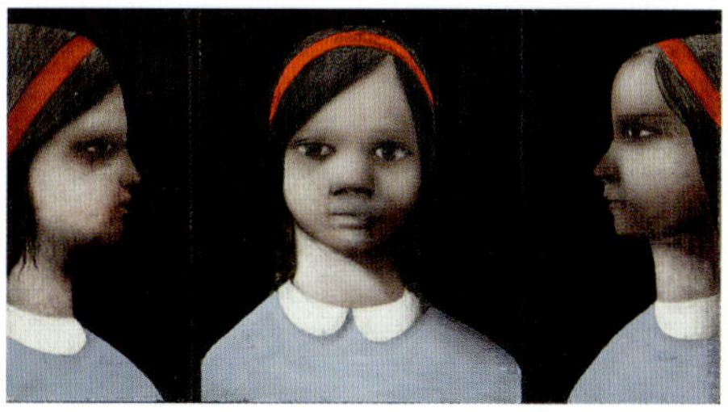

Bassingthwaighte, Lewin 1928–1983
Girl with a Headband 1970
oil on board 38 x 62
0674

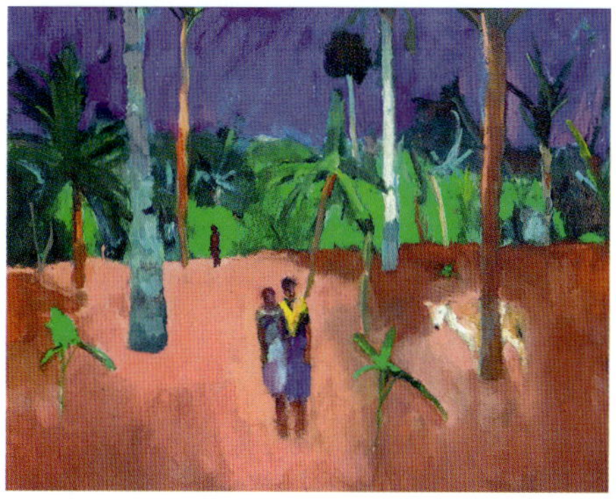

Bassingthwaighte, Paul b.1963
Red Earth, Forest
oil on canvas 43.5 x 54
0821

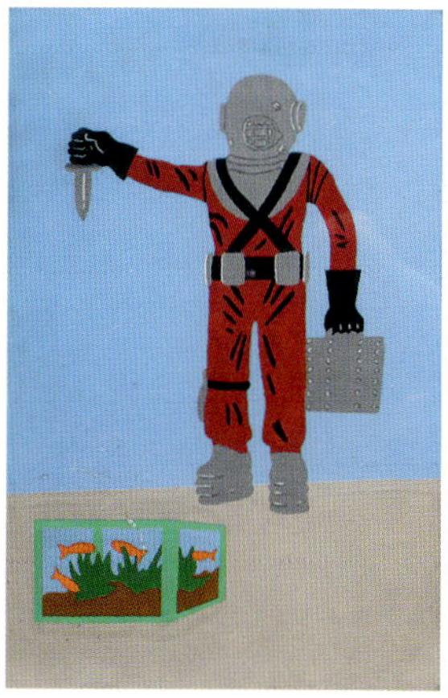

Baxter, G.
Diver 1972
acrylic on board 73 x 39
0670

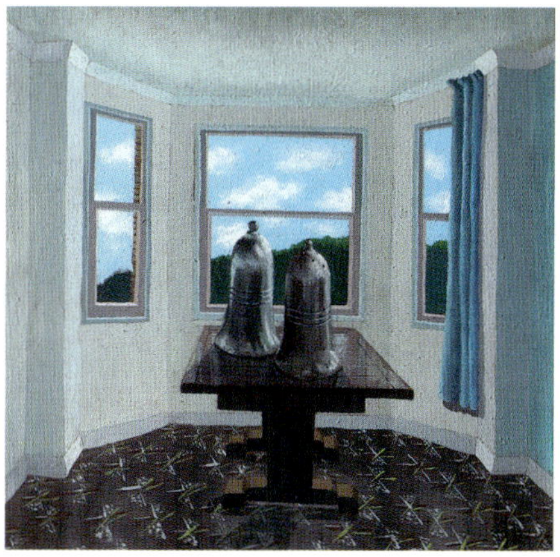

Beers, Robin b.1943
Pepper and Salt 1978
oil on canvas 61.5 x 62
0675

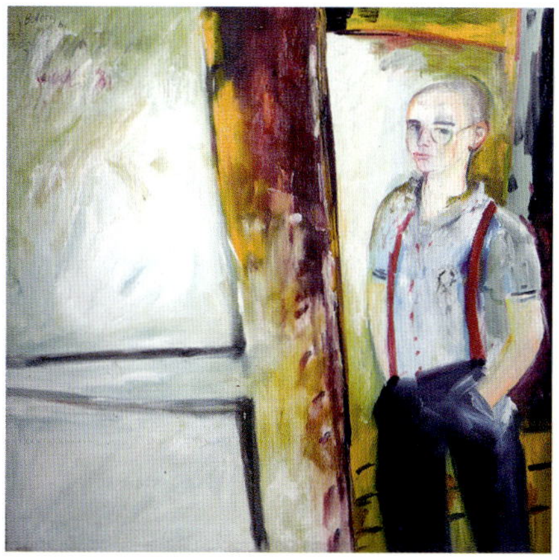

Bellany, John b.1942
My Son, Tristan
oil on canvas 172 x 172
0769

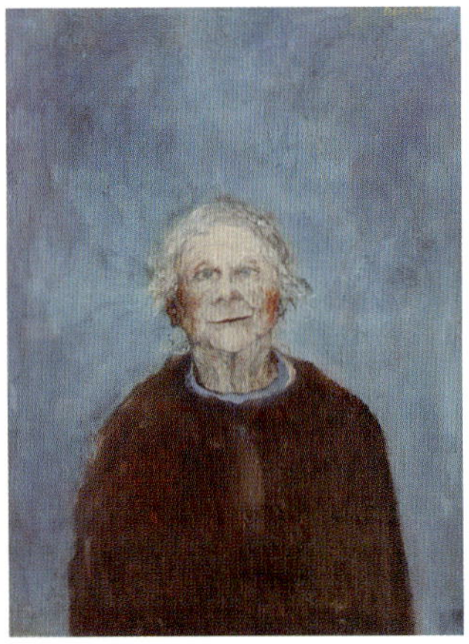

Bellany, John b.1942
Portrait of My Grandmother
oil on board 84 x 64
0644

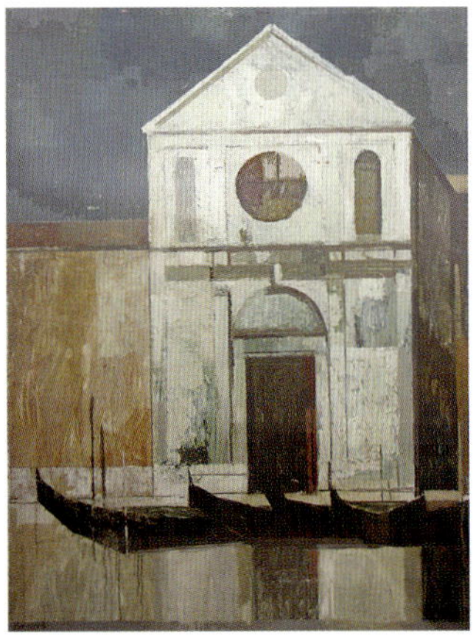

Berrisford, Peter 1932–2003
Church and Gondolas 1965
oil on board 104.5 x 78
0677

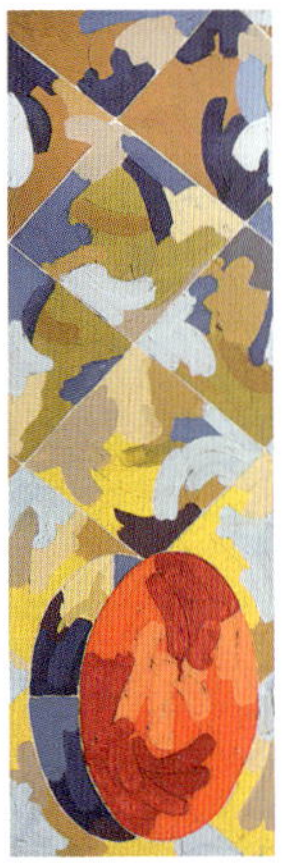

Billington, Bob b.1948
Pentimento 1977
oil on canvas 150 x 48
0771

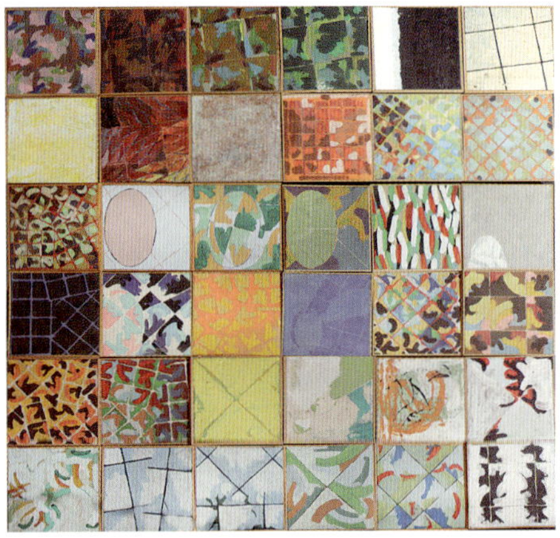

Billington, Bob b.1948
Seriatim (36 elements) 1977
oil & acrylic on canvas 193.5 x 193.5
0770

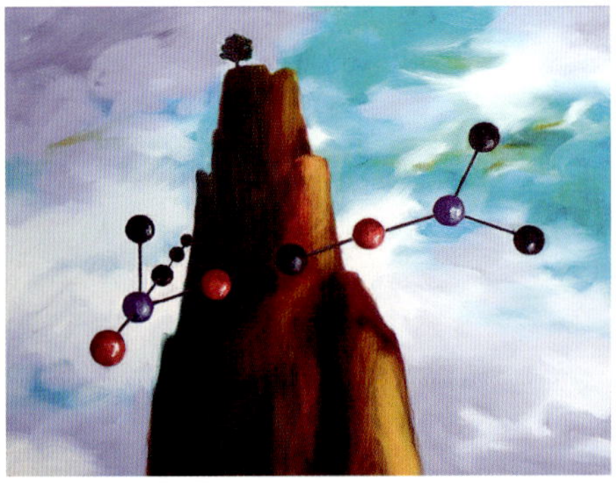

Blackett, Vivien b.1955
Mountains and Molecules II 1989
oil on canvas 71 x 91.5
0647

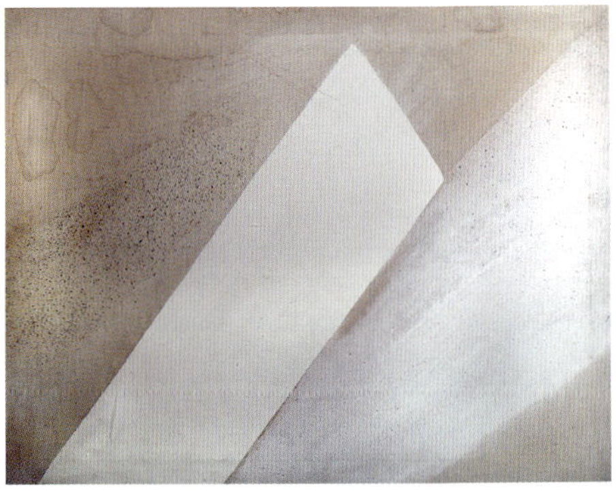

Blow, Sandra 1925–2006
Small Painting 1969
acrylic on canvas 62 x 77
0663

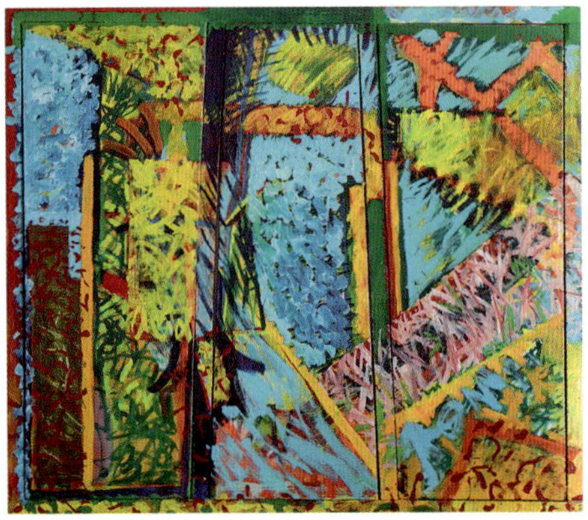

Bodimeade, Nick b.1957
Triptych 1982
oil on canvas 131 x 146.5
0634

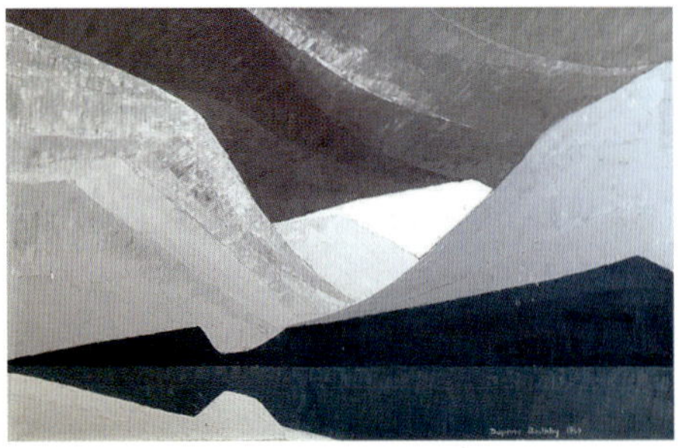

Boothby, Daphne b.1931
Sea Inlet 1969
oil on canvas 63.5 x 94
0671

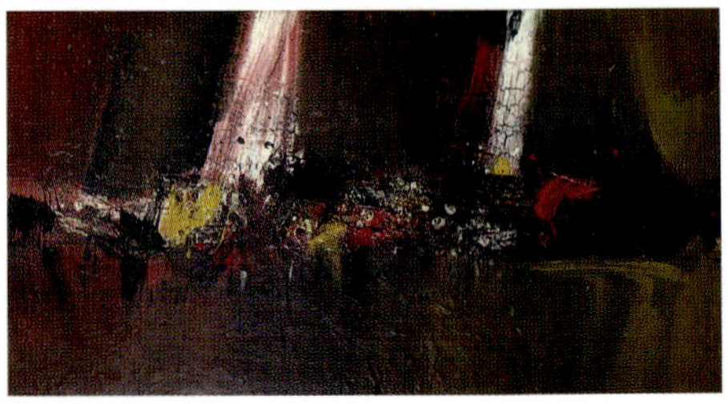

Bowen, Denis A. 1921–2006
Atomic Image 1952
oil on board 76 x 137
0662

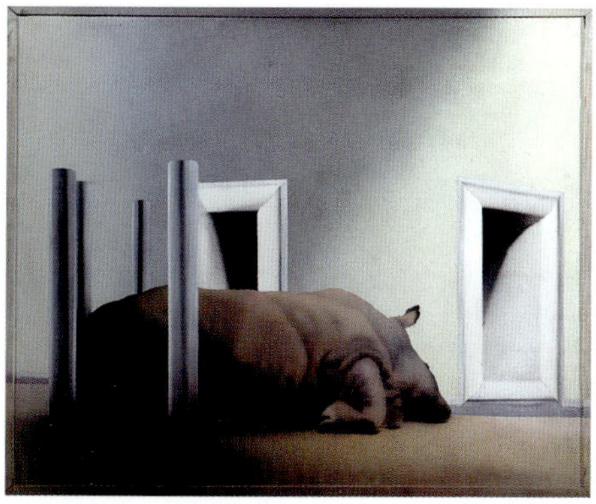

Boyd, Fionnuala b.1944 & **Evans, Leslie** b.1945
Rhinoceros 1968
acrylic on board 98 x 116.5
0002

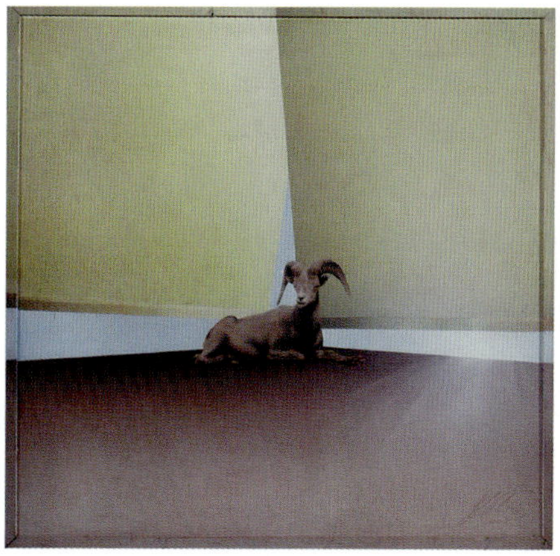

Boyd, Fionnuala b.1944 & **Evans, Leslie** b.1945
Vacuum Raft 1968
acrylic on board 93 x 93
0003

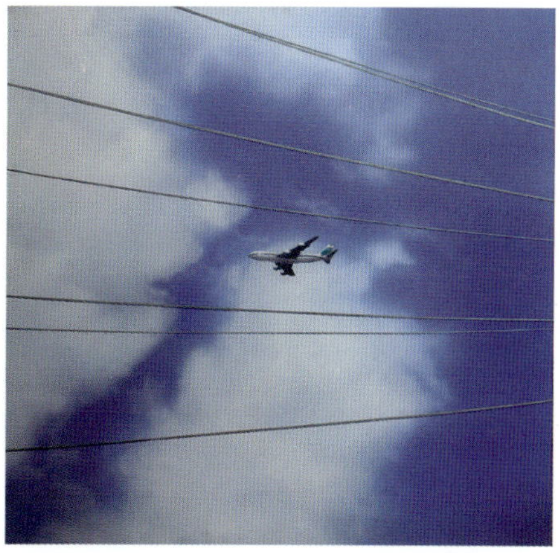

Boyd, Fionnuala b.1944 & **Evans, Leslie** b.1945
Air Corridor 1972
acrylic on board 94 x 94
0001

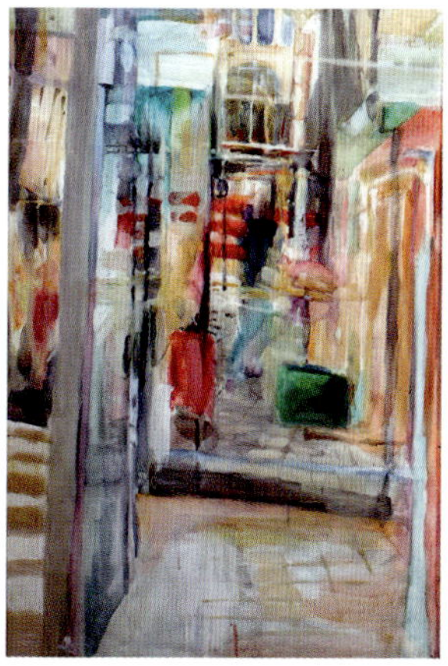

Bradford, Jill active 1990–1991
Doorway 1990
oil on canvas 144 x 97
0004

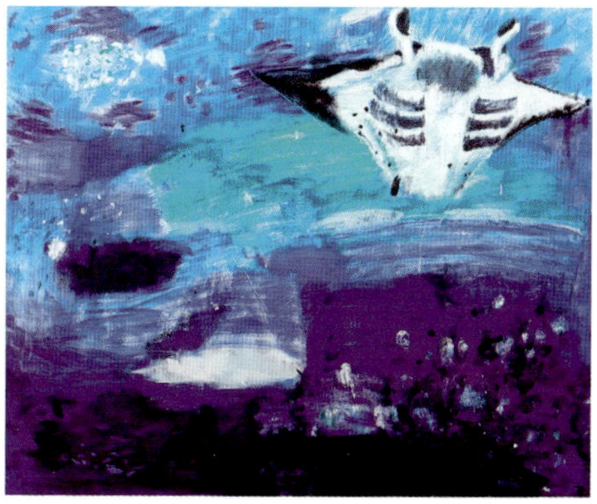

Bramble, Richard b.1968
Manta Rays 1990
oil on canvas 149.5 x 179
0005

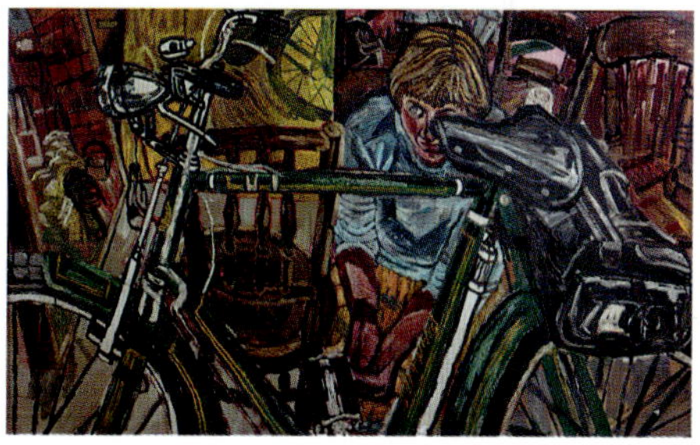

Bratby, John Randall 1928–1992
Jean with a Bicycle 1955
oil on board 133 x 200
0006

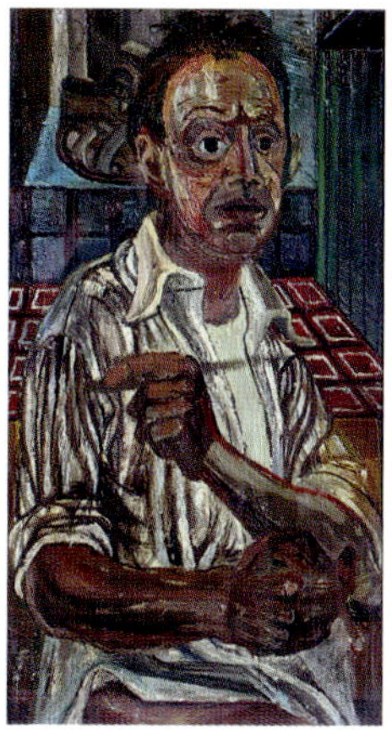

Bratby, John Randall 1928–1992
Self Portrait with Sandals 1958
oil on board 119 x 70.9
0007

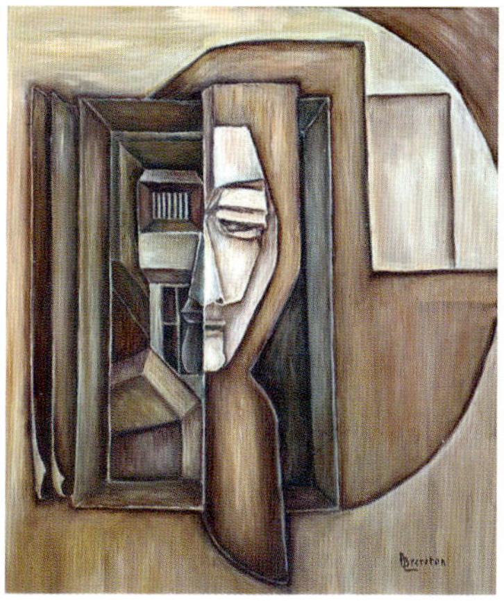

Brereton, Ann
Introversion 1974
oil on board 79 x 69
0008

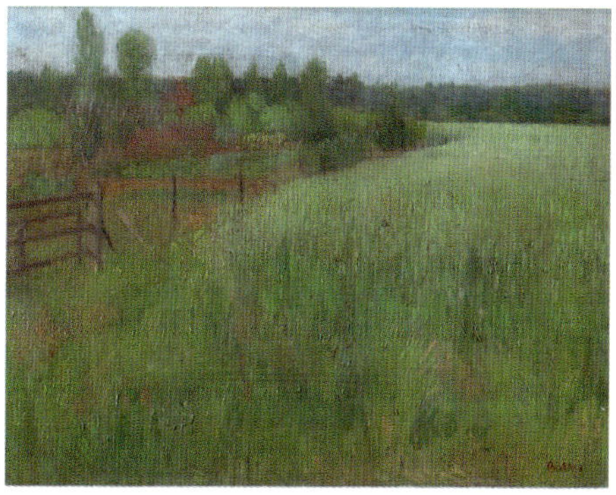

Buhler, Robert A. 1916–1989
Cornfield, Rogate, Hampshire 1945
oil on board 49.7 x 59.8
0009

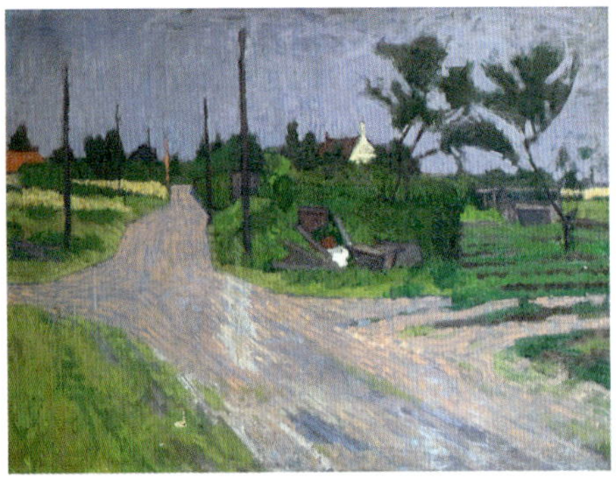

Buhler, Robert A. 1916–1989
Suffolk Lane
oil on canvas 75.5 x 95
0010

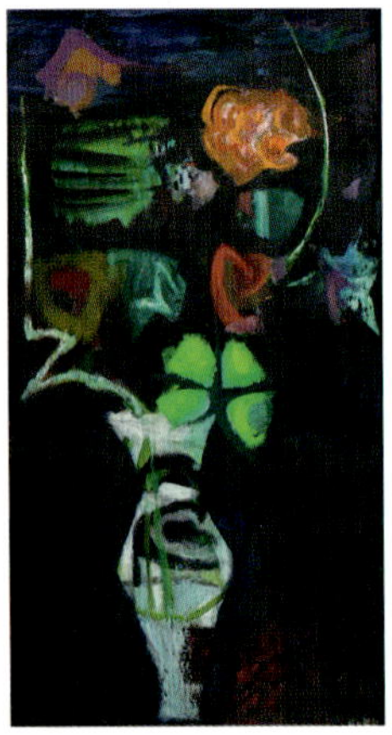

Burr, James b.1926
Night Flowers 1966
oil on board 120 x 63.5
0011

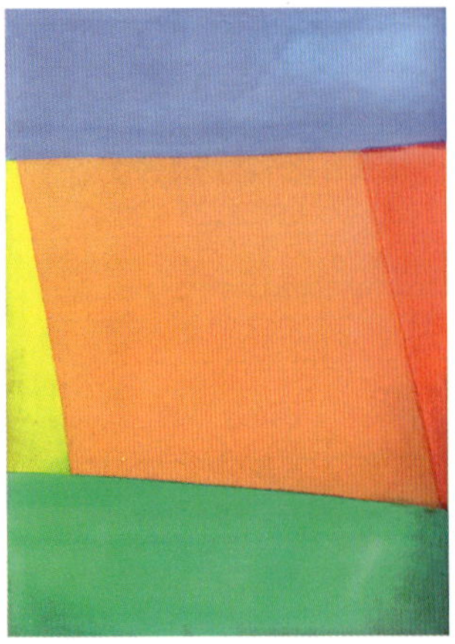

Bush, Jack 1909–1977
Tan Band 1969
oil on canvas 179 x 124
0012

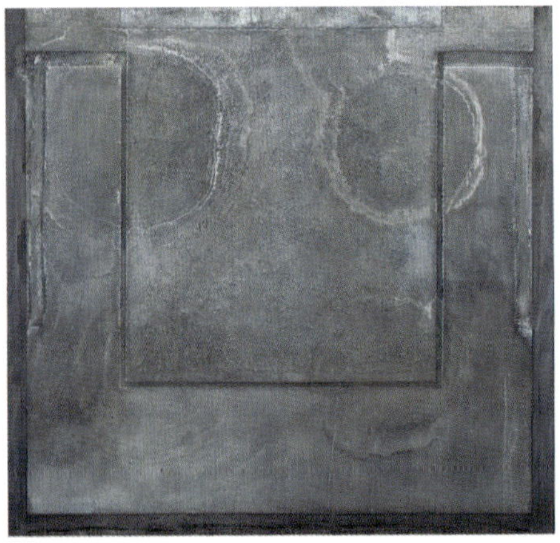

Butler, Elizabeth
6/77 1977
acrylic on canvas 177 x 182.5
0772

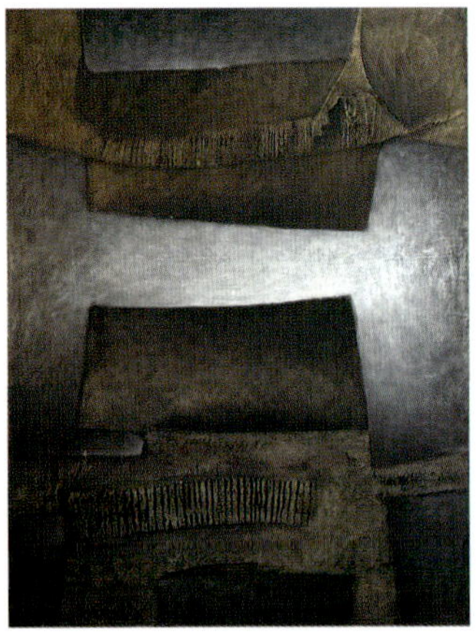

Caloutsis, Valerios b.1927
Stress
oil on canvas 134 x 101
0013

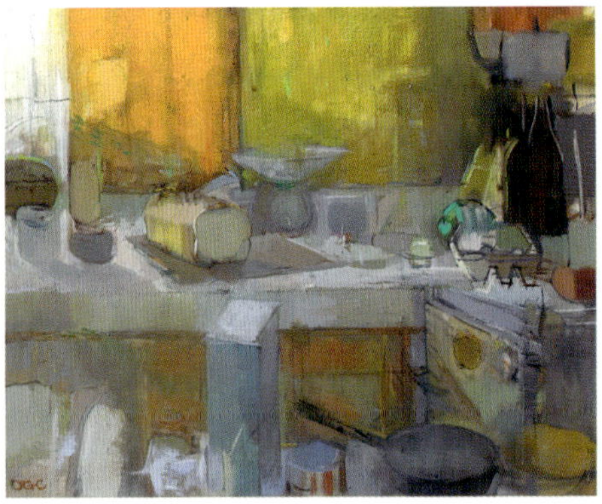

Campion, Oliver 1928–2000
The Kitchen 1968
oil on canvas 64 x 74.5
0014

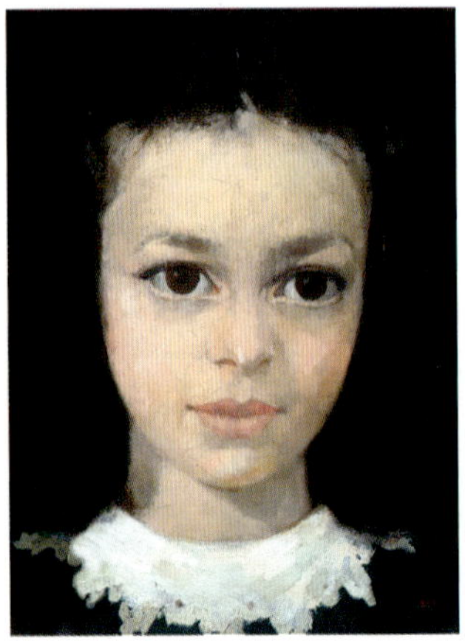

Carr, Thomas James 1909–1999
Girl with a Lace Collar 1954
oil on canvas 52.5 x 42
0015

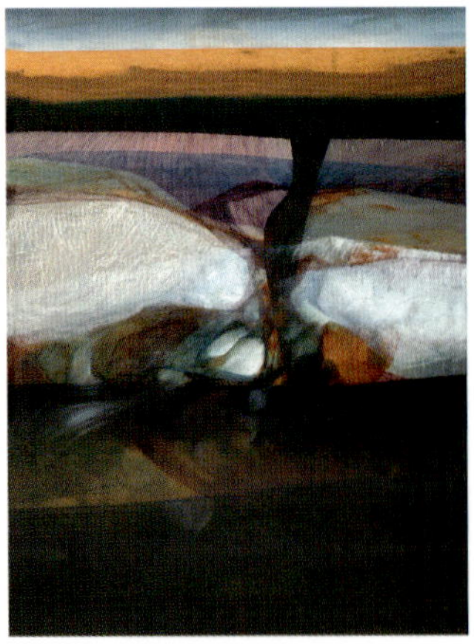

Carradice, Michael
Irontide 1971
oil on board 77.5 x 57.5
0016

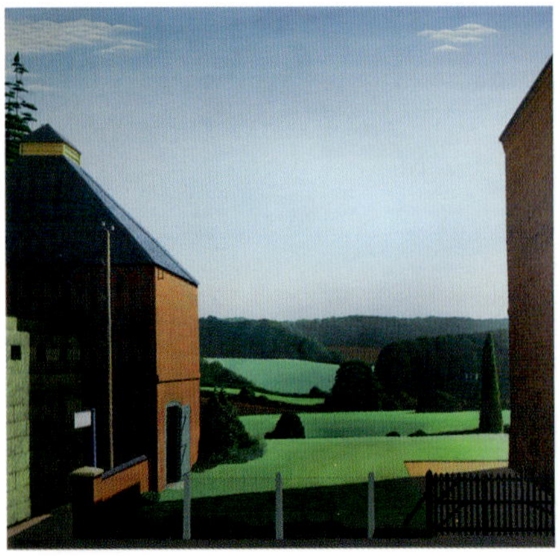

Cartwright, Reg b.1938
Landscape between Two Buildings 1978
oil on canvas 93.6 x 93.6
0019

Facing page: Large, George, b.1936, *Typist* (detail), 1993, Leicester Arts and Museums Service (p. 58)

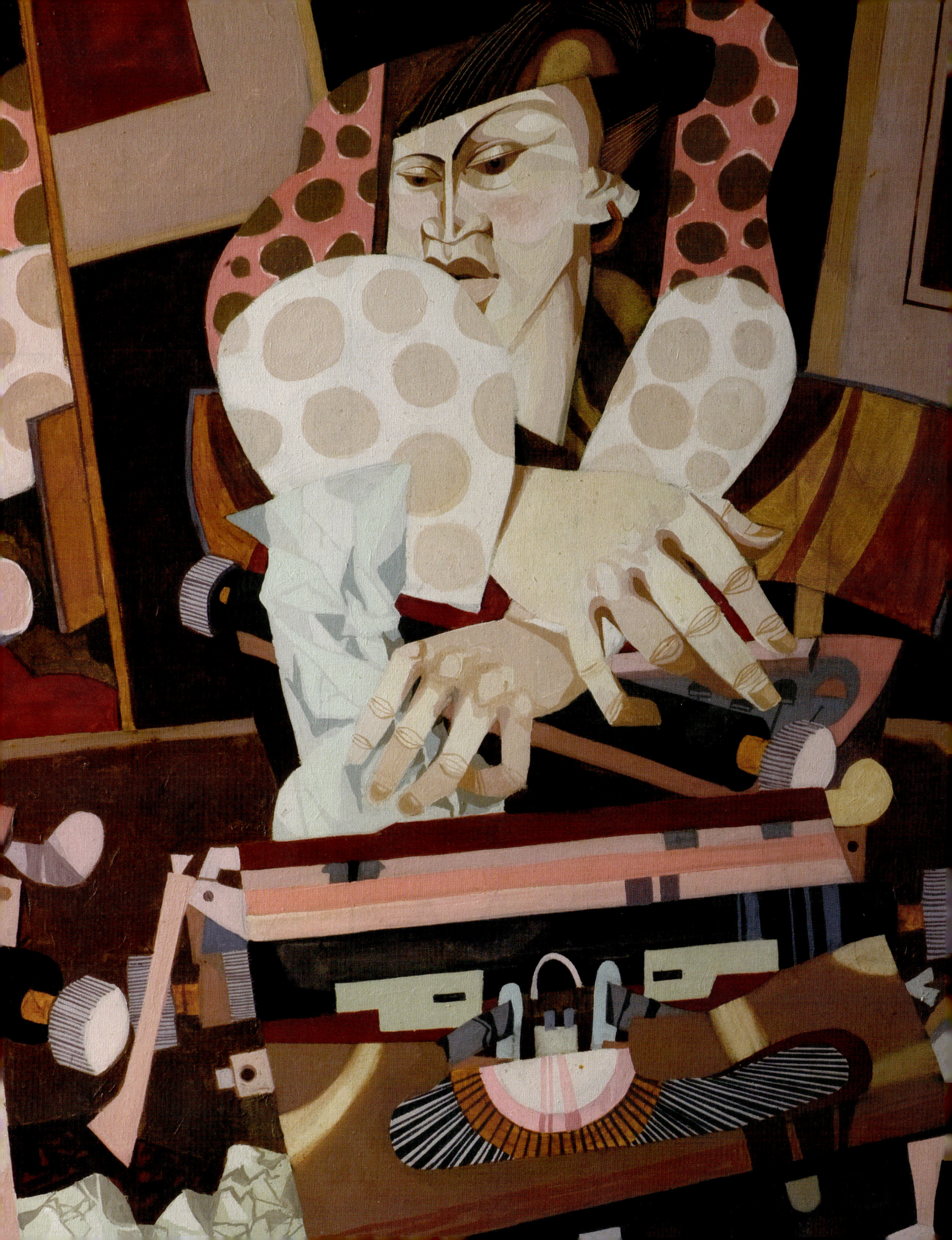

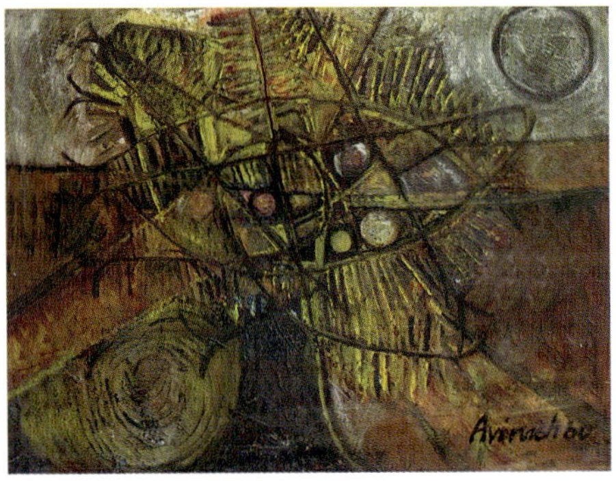

Chandra, Avinash 1931–1991
Crab Tree 1960
oil on canvas 75 x 93
0022

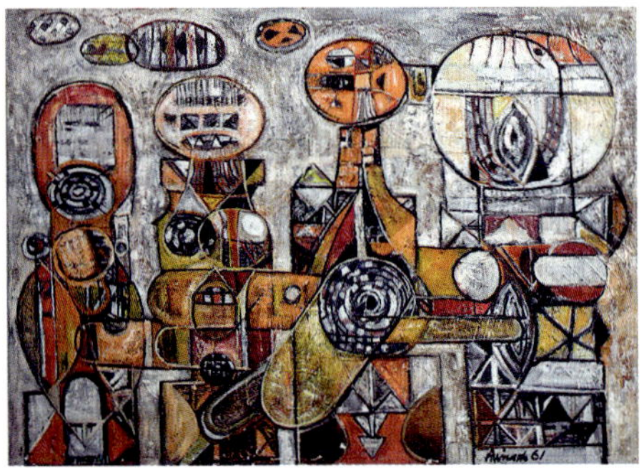

Chandra, Avinash 1931–1991
Early Figures 1961
oil on board 94 x 124.5
0020

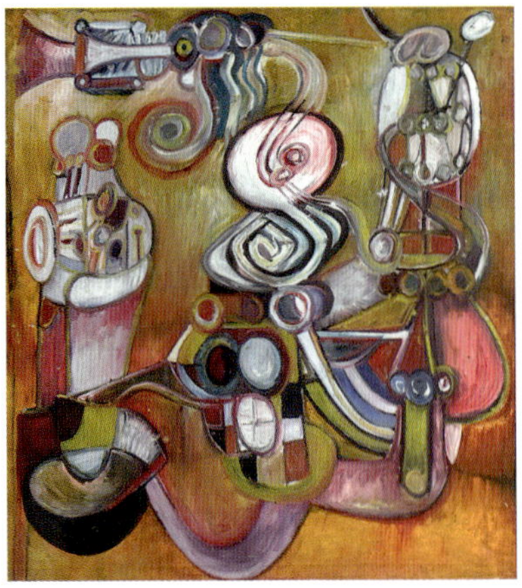

Chandra, Avinash 1931–1991
Figures in the Sand 1967
oil on canvas 131 x 115.5
0021

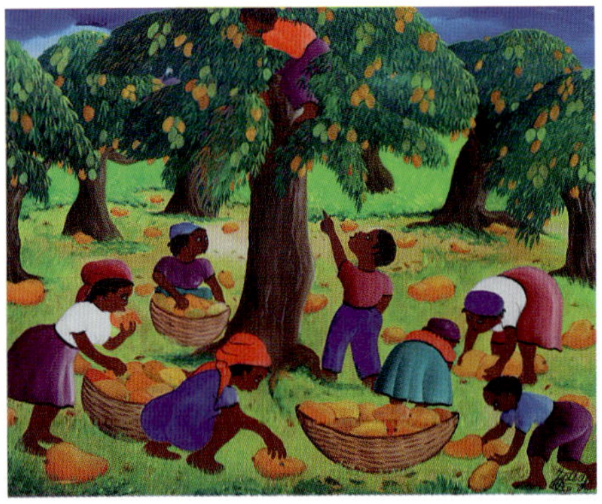

Chery, Jacques-Richard b.1928
Picking Fruit 1969
oil on board 66.5 x 76.5
0023

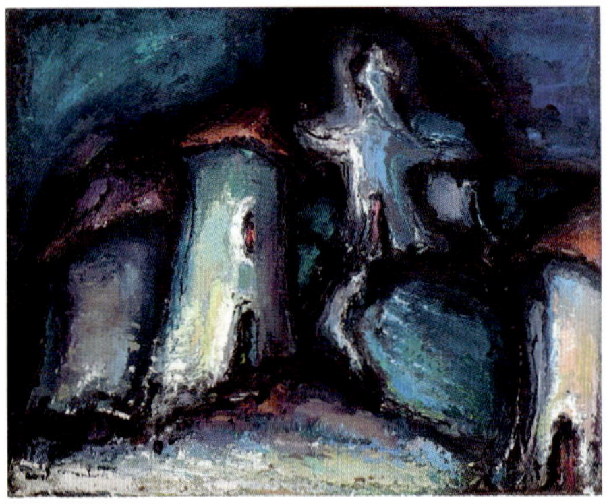

Christoforou, John b.1921
Landscape with a Church 1949
oil on board 63.5 x 74.5
0024

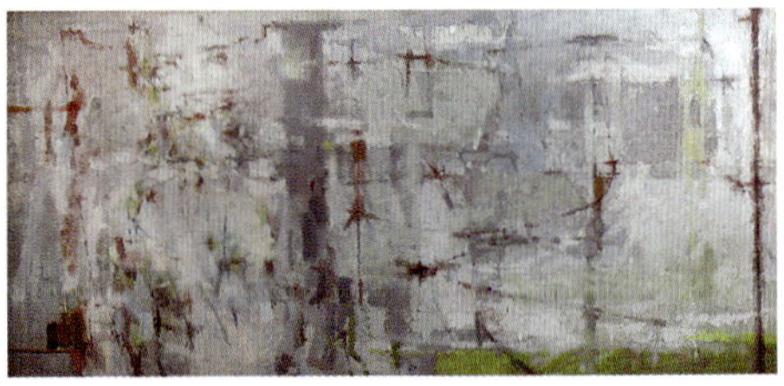

Cohen, Harold b.1928
Woman in the Window 1954
oil on board 70 x 131
0029

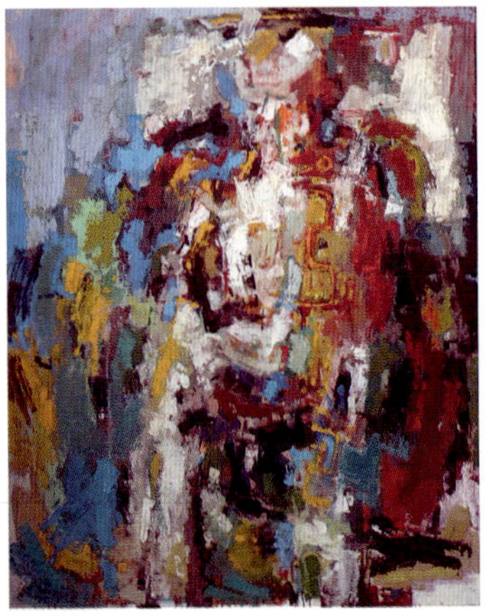

Cohen, Harold b.1928
Gentleman in Academic Dress 1957
oil on board 171.5 x 141.5
0025

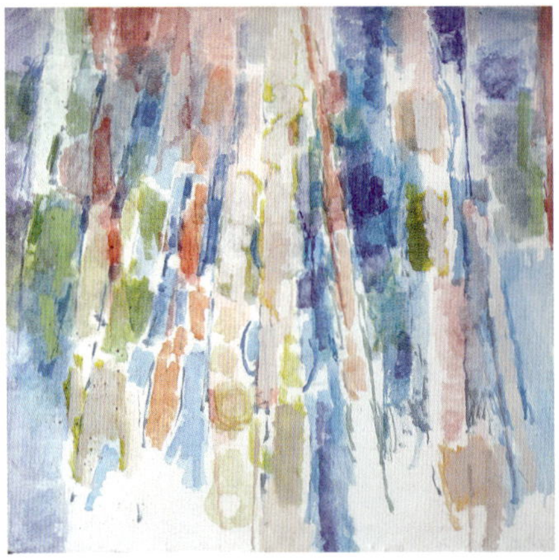

Cohen, Harold b.1928
Water Garden 1957
oil on canvas 93.5 x 93.5
0028

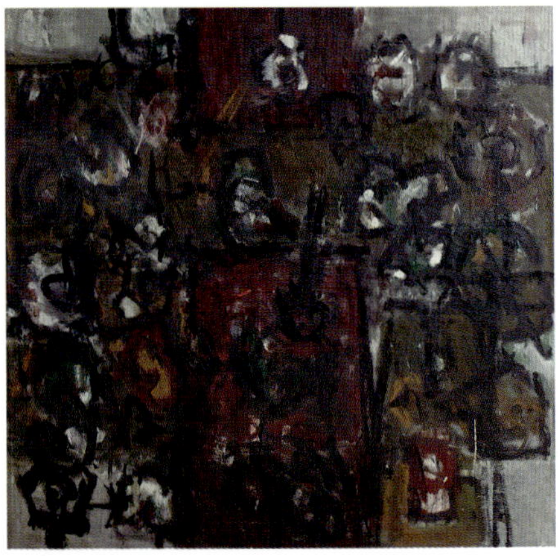

Cohen, Harold b.1928
Fiesta 1958
oil on canvas 132.3 x 132.1
0026

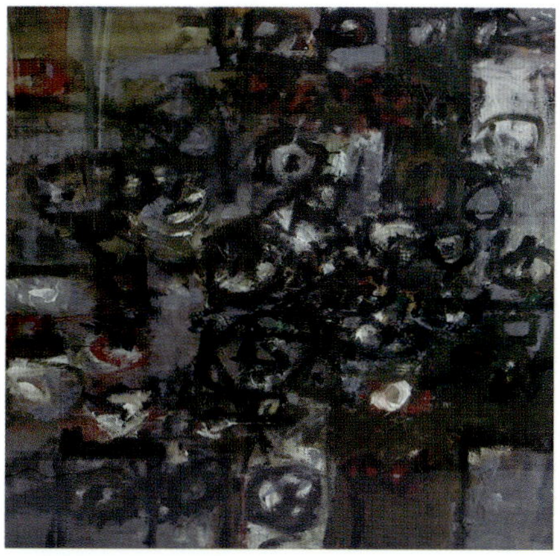

Cohen, Harold b.1928
Plan for a City 1958
oil on canvas 130.5 x 130.5
0027

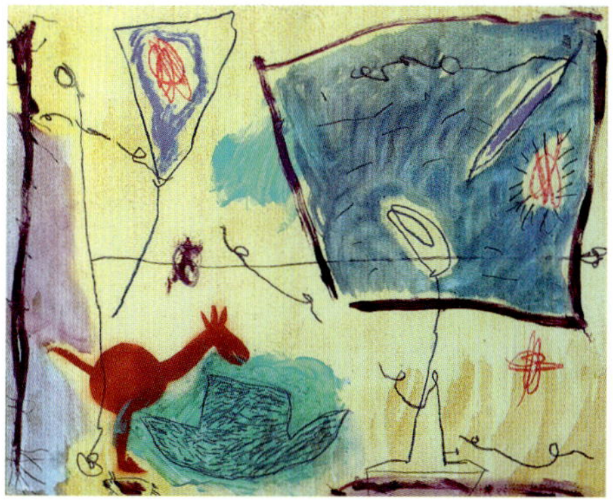

Collins, Niamh b.1956
Red Kangaroo 1985
oil on paper 65 x 73
0030

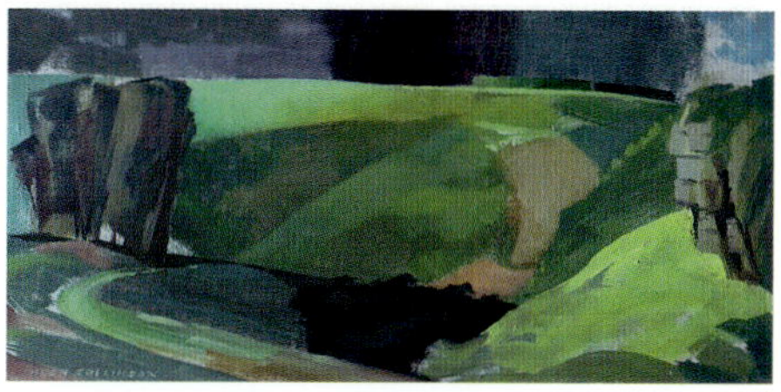

Collinson, Hugh 1909–2009
The Green Bowl, Derbyshire Limestone 1969
oil on board 52.5 x 93.5
0031

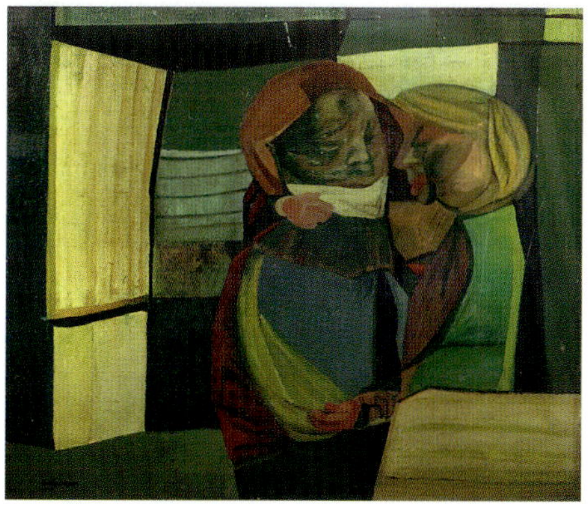

Colquhoun, Robert 1914–1962
The Peasant Woman 1944
oil on canvas 55.5 x 63
0033

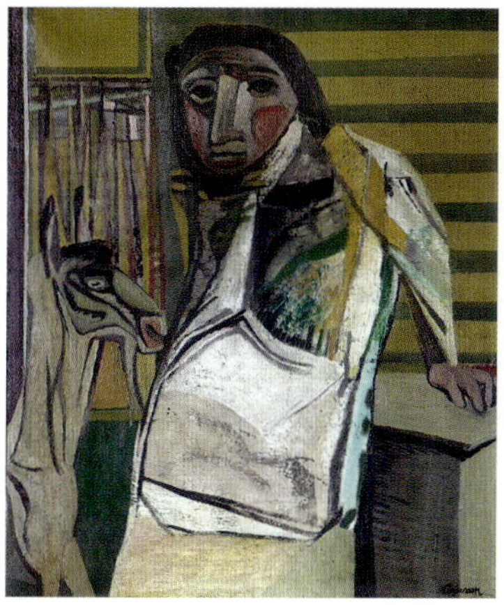

Colquhoun, Robert 1914–1962
The Goatherd 1948
oil on canvas 67 x 56.5
0032

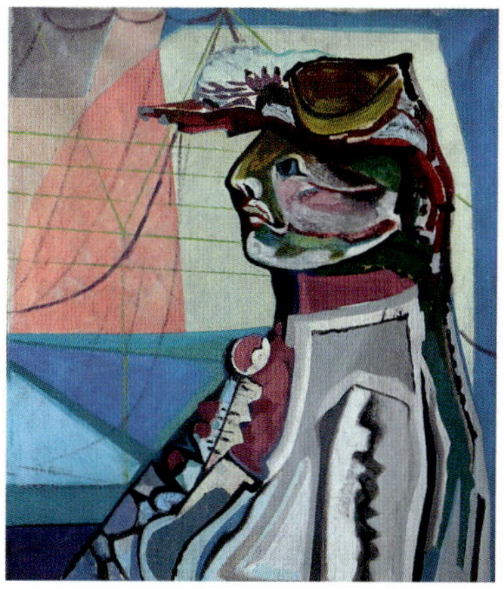

Colquhoun, Robert 1914–1962
Seated Figure 1949
oil on canvas 102 x 90
0034

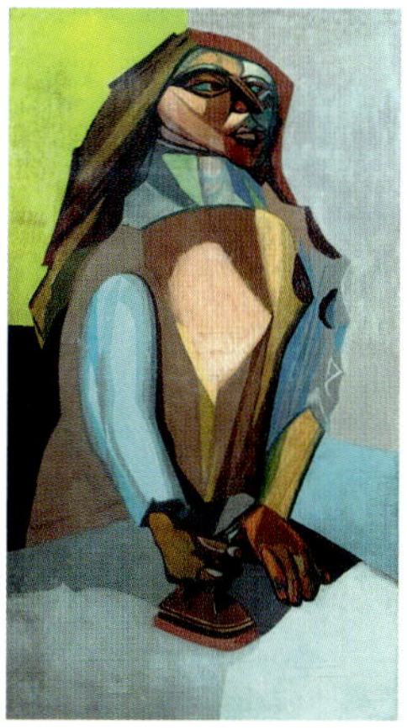

Colquhoun, Robert 1914–1962
Woman Ironing 1958
oil on canvas 156.9 x 90.4
0429

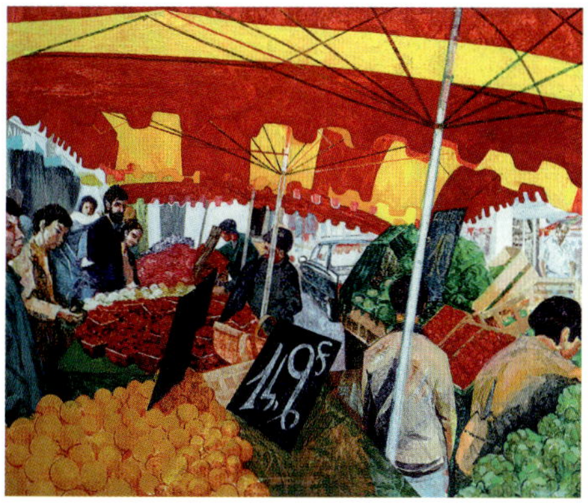

Cook, Frank b.1940
Fécamp Market, France
acrylic on canvas 90 x 105
0690

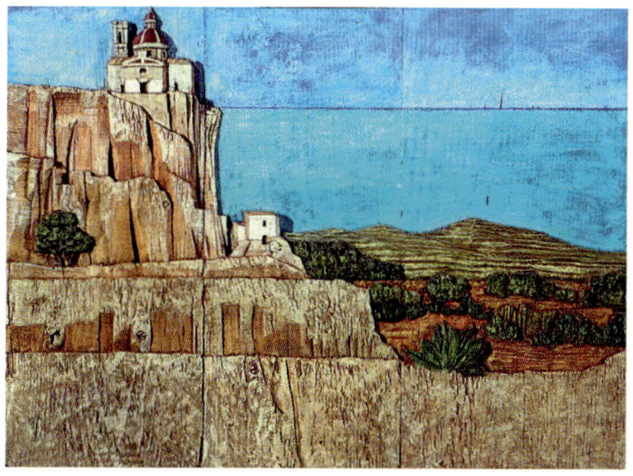

Cook, Jenny b.1942
Mtahleb, Malta II 2003
acrylic on wood 30 x 43
0958

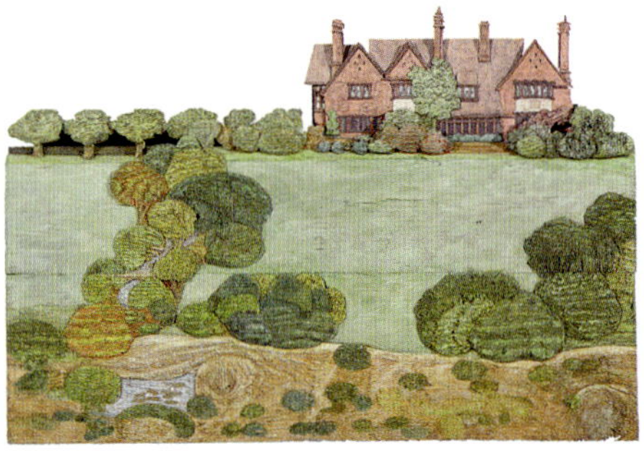

Cook, Jenny b.1942
Return to Beaumont 2003
acrylic on wood 25 x 43
0960

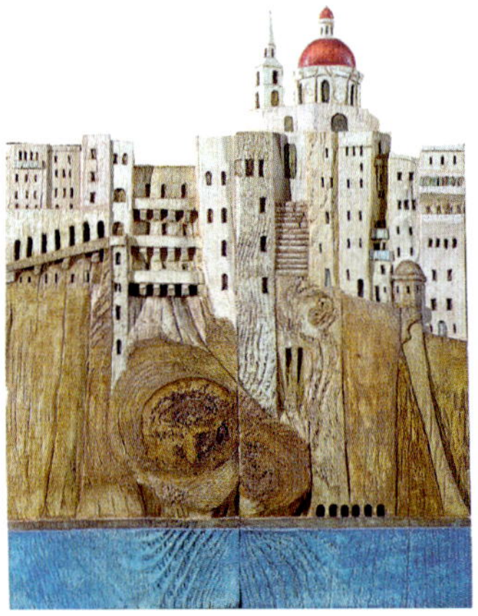

Cook, Jenny b.1942
Spirit of Malta 2003
acrylic on wood 39 x 30
0959

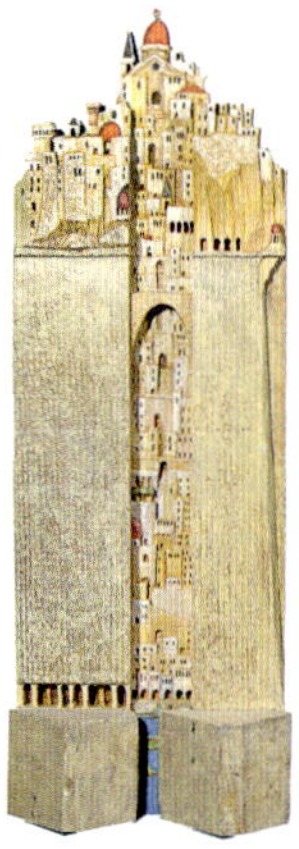

Cook, Jenny b.1942
Citadel Valetta, Malta 2004
acrylic on wood 57 x 25
0973

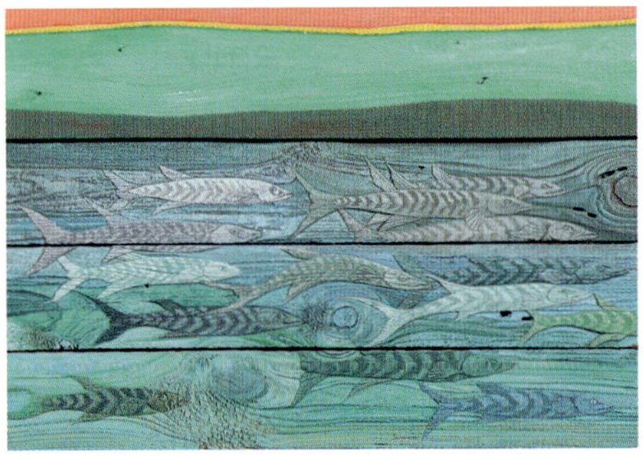

Cook, Jenny b.1942
Chevron Fish
acrylic on wood 30 x 45
0826

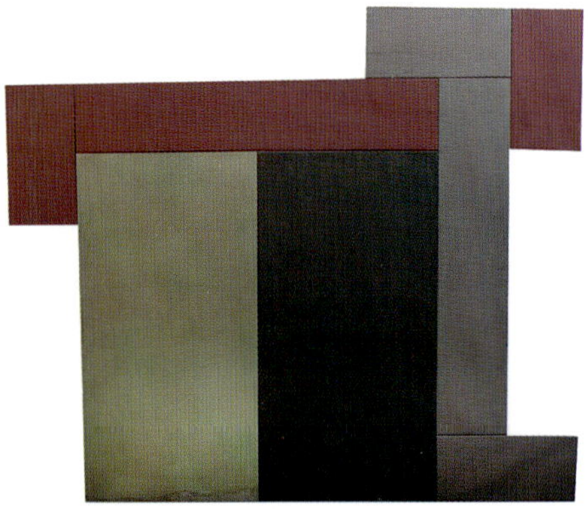

Cook, Roger b.1940
Slightly Imperfect 1966
oil on canvas 213 x 243.5
0777

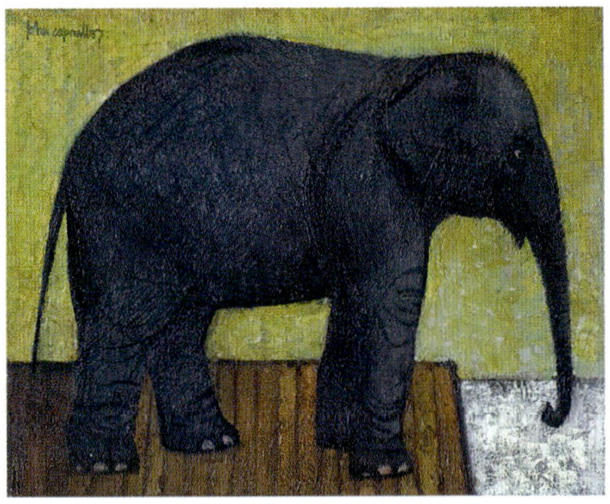

Copnall, John 1928–2007
Elephant 1957
oil on board 53.3 x 62.9
0036

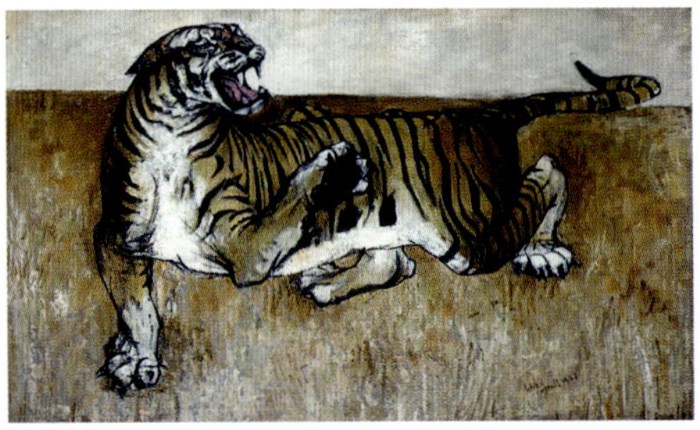

Copnall, John 1928–2007
Tiger 1957
oil on canvas 121.5 x 197.5
0687

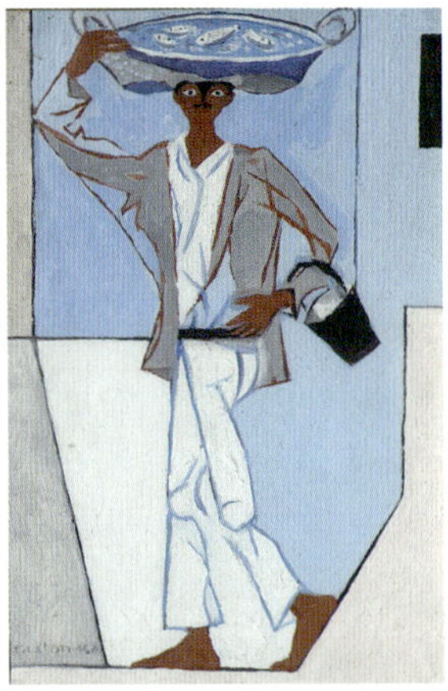

Craxton, John 1922–2009
Fish Hawker, Athens 1950
oil on canvas 50.5 x 39
0039

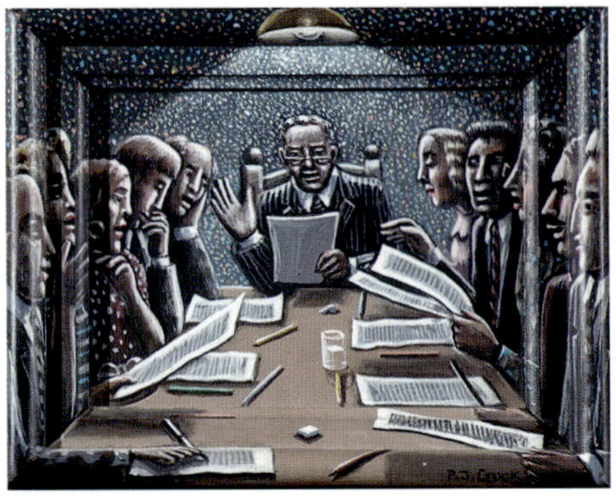

Crook, P. J. b.1945
Staff Meeting 1990
acrylic on board 22 x 27
0700

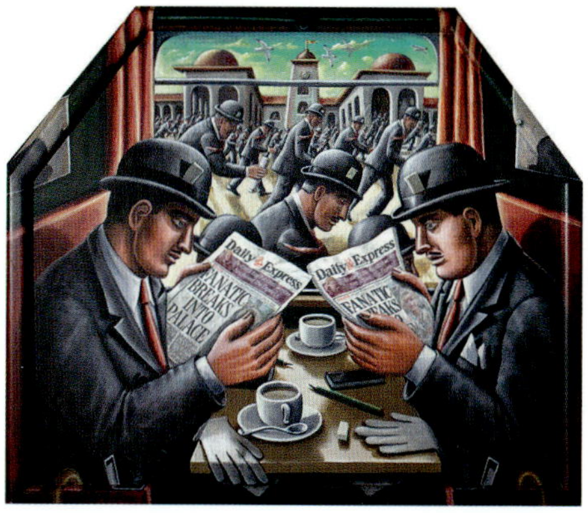

Crook, P. J. b.1945
Expresso 1997
acrylic on canvas 103 x 122.5
0894

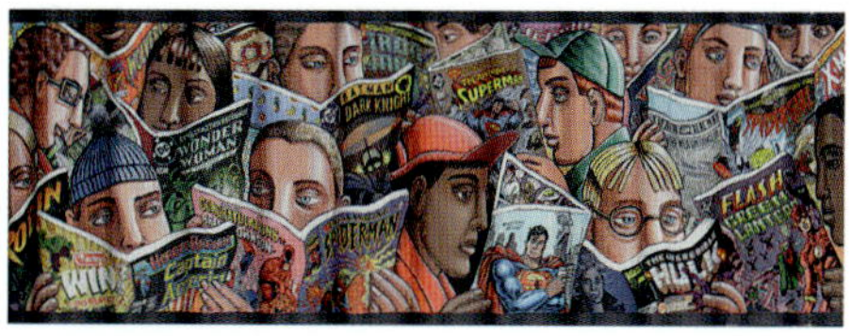

Crook, P. J. b.1945
Comic Strip 2001
acrylic on board 48 x 127
0928

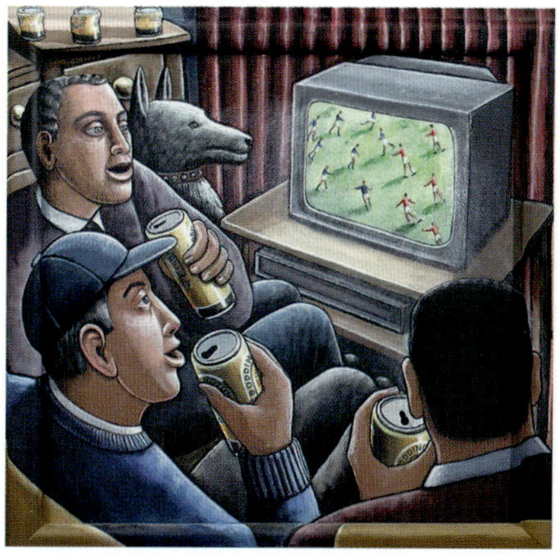

Crook, P. J. b.1945
Armchair Supporters 2004
acrylic on board 71 x 71
0974

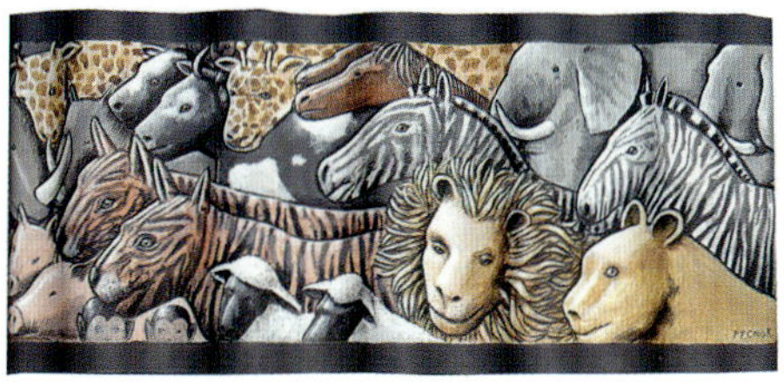

Crook, P. J. b.1945
The Ark 2004
acrylic on board 30 x 50
0972

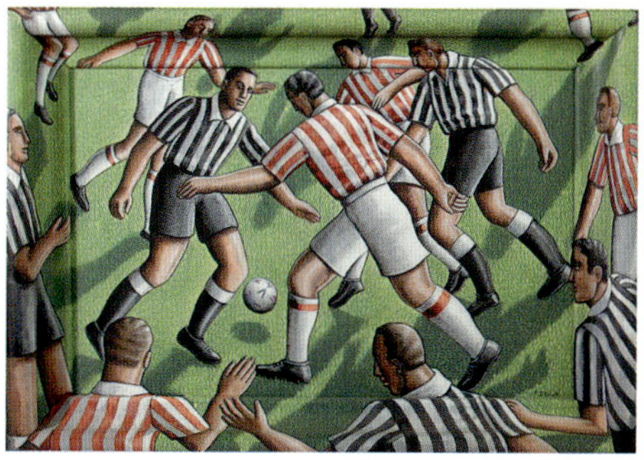

Crook, P. J. b.1945
The Beautiful Game 2004
acrylic on canvas 55 x 70
0971

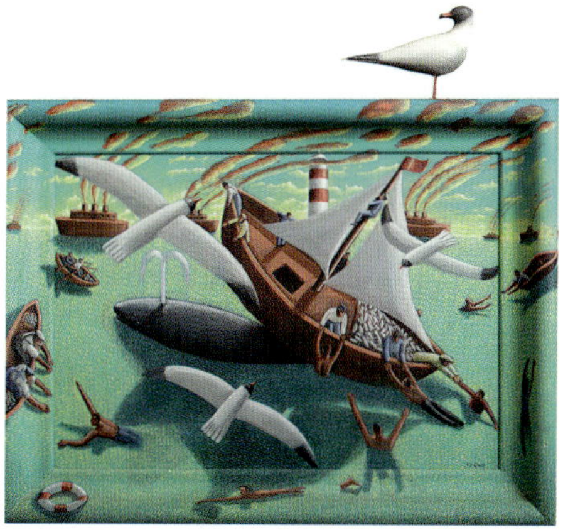

Crook, P. J. b.1945
The Whale
acrylic on board 87 x 92
0895

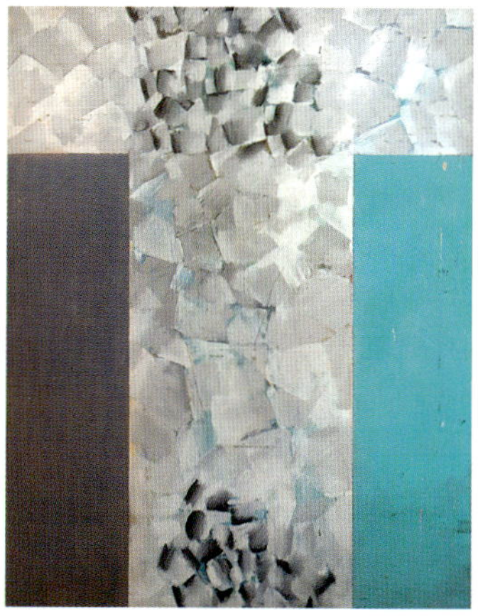

Culbert, Bill b.1935
Descent from Château Lacoste II 1962
oil on board 125.5 x 97.9
0042

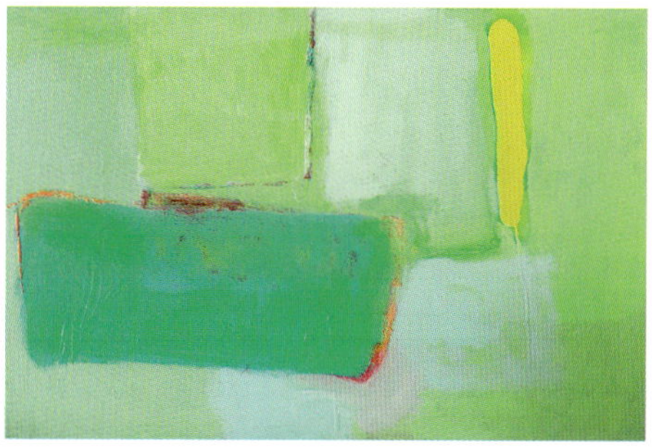

Cyster, Poppy b.1983
Tormaukin I 2005
oil on canvas 70 x 110
0986

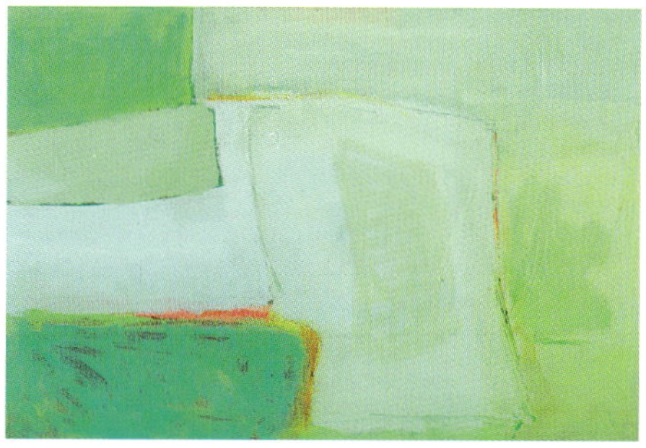

Cyster, Poppy b.1983
Tormaukin II 2005
oil on canvas 70 x 110
0987

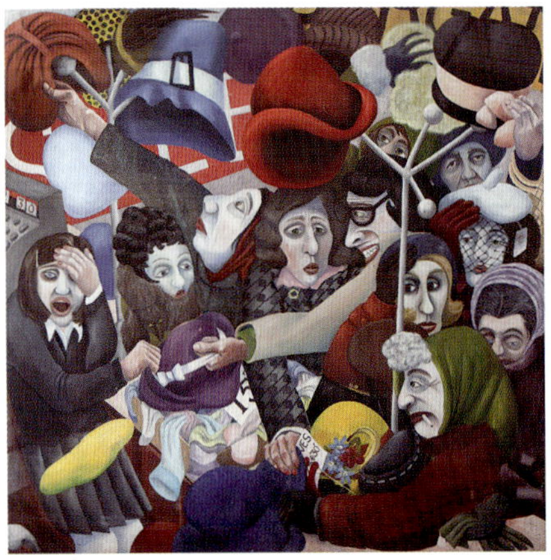

Daborn, Erica b.1951
Hat Bargains 1972
oil on canvas 123.5 x 123.5
0043

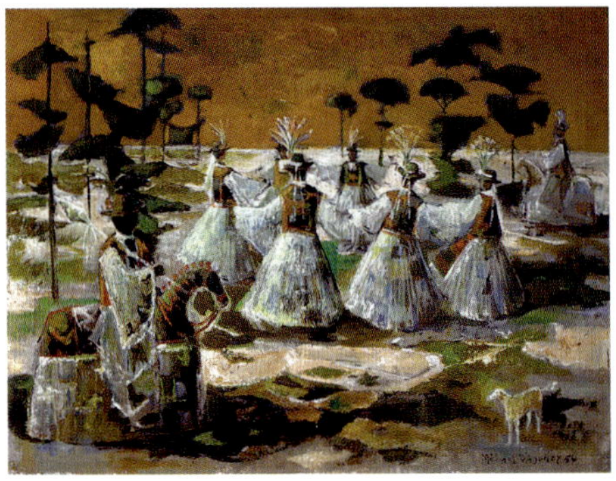

D'Aguilar, Michael b.1924
Folk Dancers, Spain 1956
oil on canvas 71 x 91.5
0045

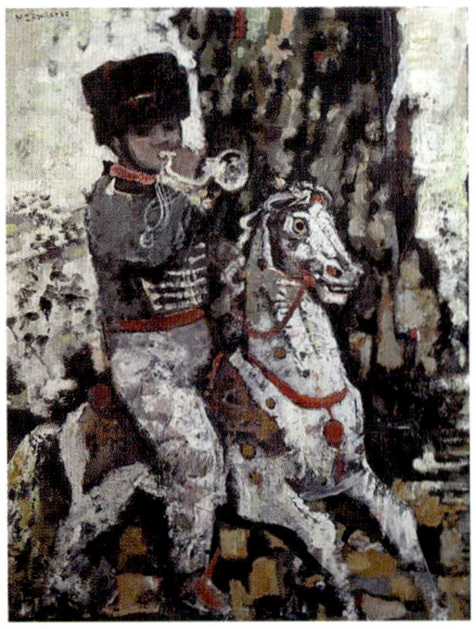

D'Aguilar, Michael b.1924
Boy Trumpeter 1960
oil on board 134 x 104.5
0044

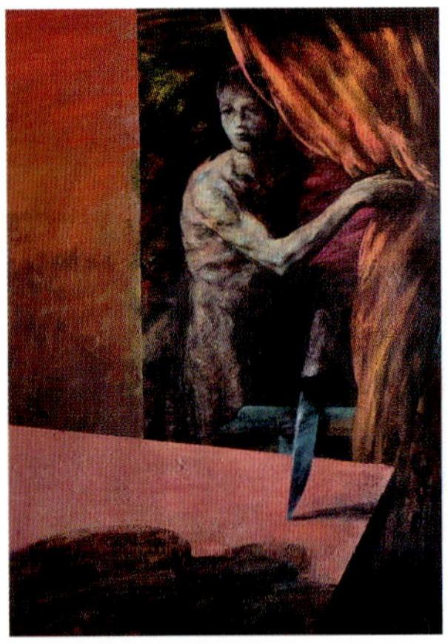

Davies, Hugh b.1946
Youth 1985
acrylic on paper 92 x 70
0047

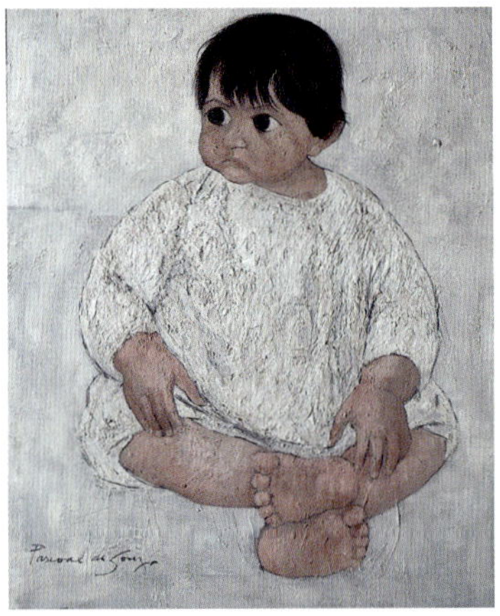

De Souza, Pascoal b.1928
Child Study 1961
oil on board 89 x 76
0050

Deacon, Peter b.1945
Aberration I 1976
acrylic on canvas 120 x 120
0048

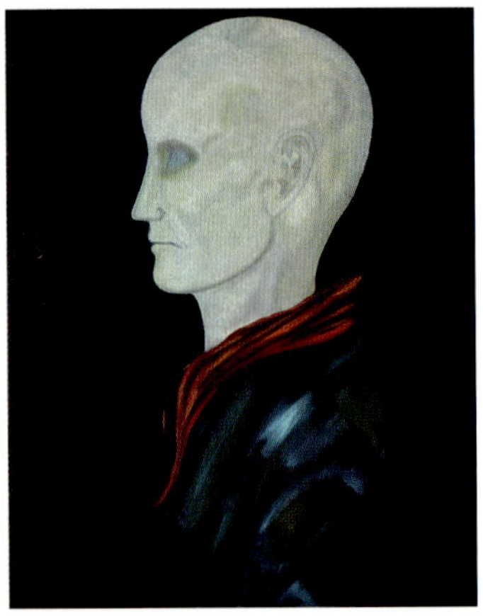

Denison, David b.1939
Bald Blindman 1977
oil on board 73.5 x 57.5
0049

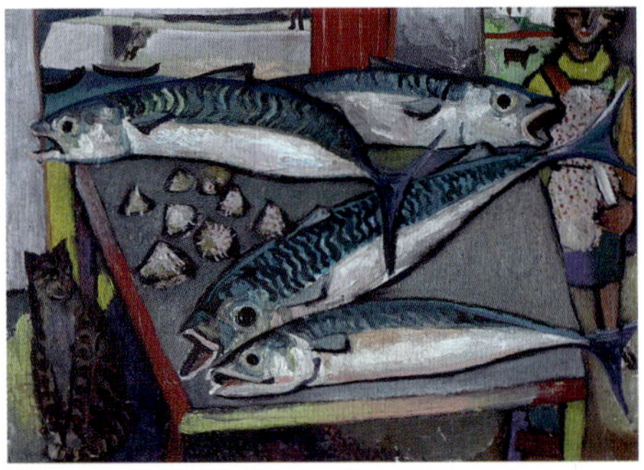

Dillon, Gerard 1916–1971
Still Life with Mackerel 1954
oil on board 44 x 60
0918

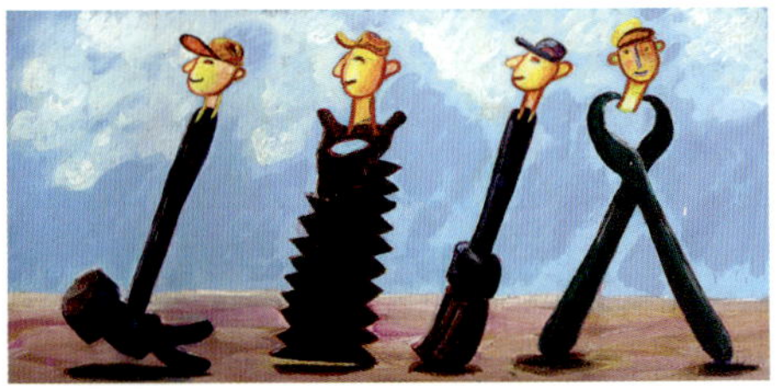

Dixon, Bob
Walk This Way
oil on canvas 122.5 x 243
PCF7

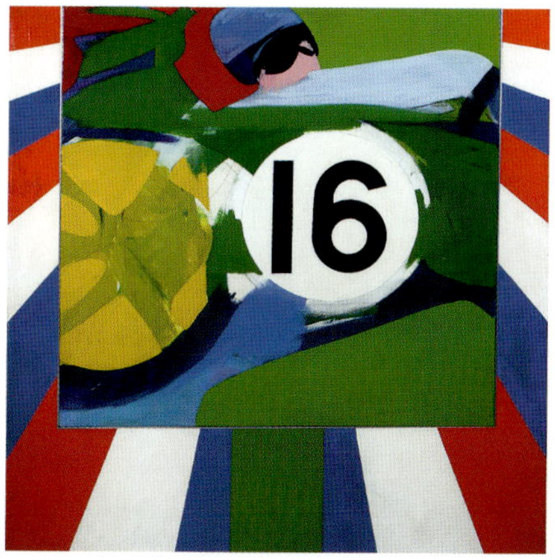

Donaldson, Antony b.1939
Medal for Jim Clark 1963
oil on board 162 x 155.5
0052

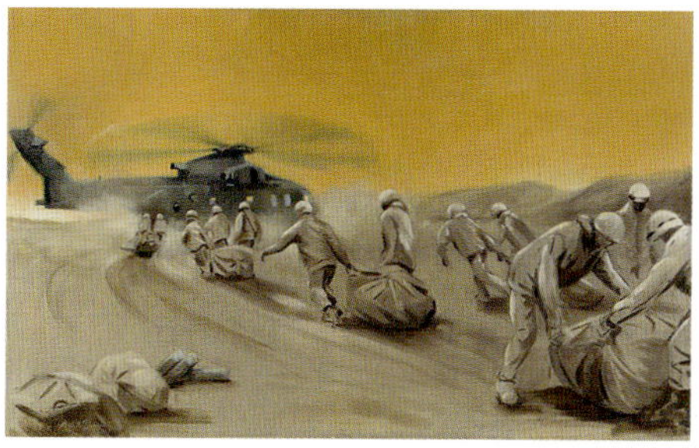

Dorman, Arabella b.1975
A Quick Turnaround, the Queen's Royal Lancers, Maysaan 2009
oil on canvas 81 x 127.5
PCF11

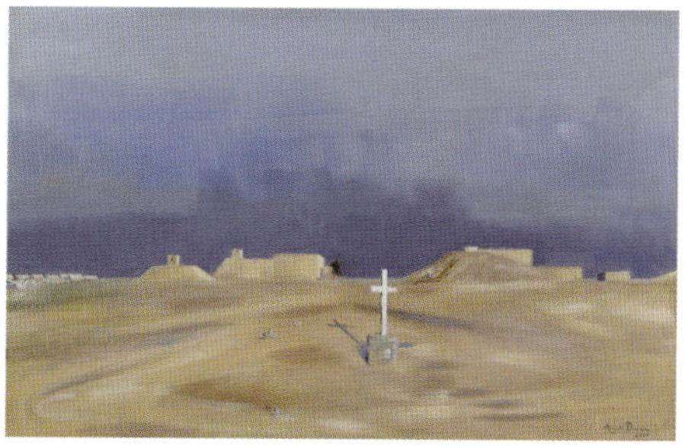

Dorman, Arabella b.1975
Another Beautiful Day in Shaibah 2009
oil on canvas 76 x 116
PCF10

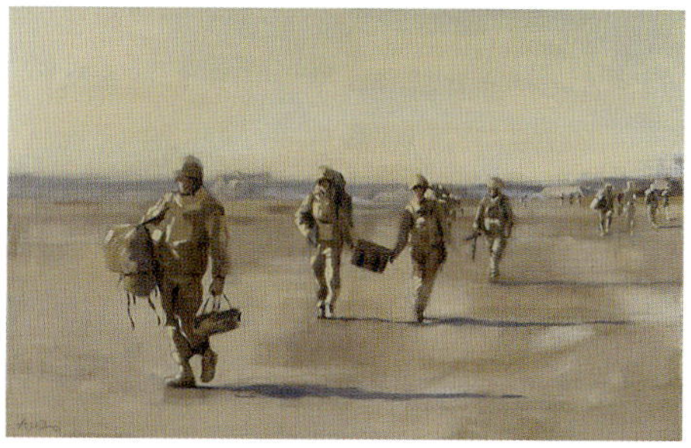

Dorman, Arabella b.1975
Leaving Camp 2009
oil on canvas 76 x 116
PCF9

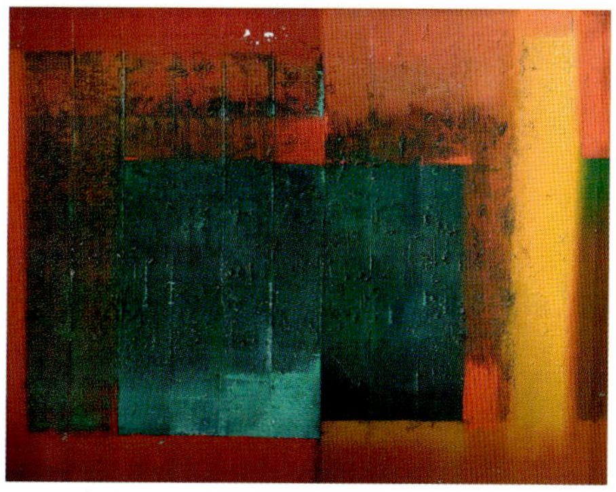

Drawbridge, John 1930–2005
Crustacea 1962
oil on canvas 109.5 x 135
0054

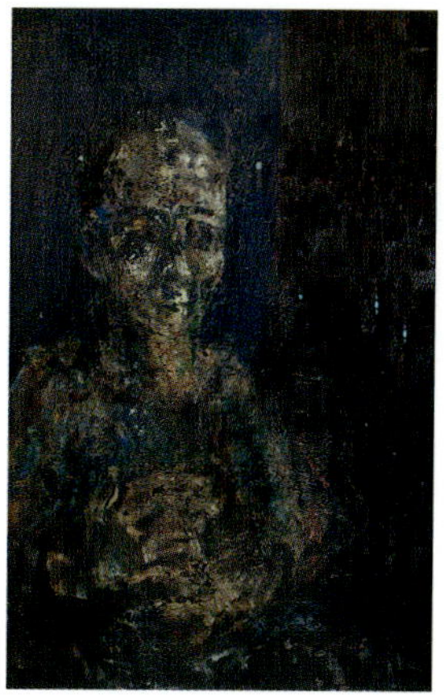

Drawbridge, John 1930–2005
Portrait of a Man 1962
oil on canvas 132 x 89
0055

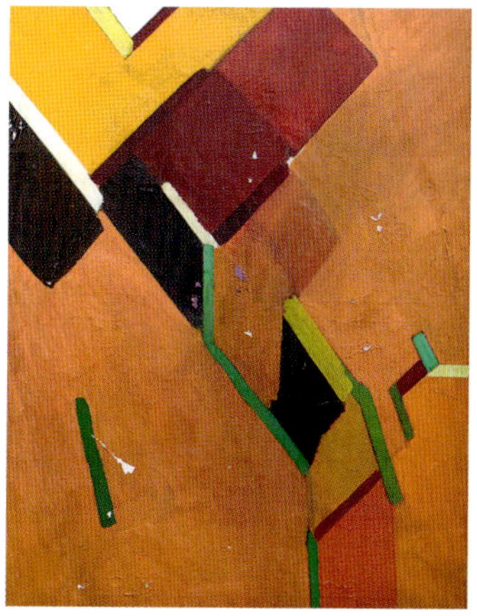

Dubsky, Mario 1939–1985
Flying High
oil on canvas 170.5 x 130.5
0056

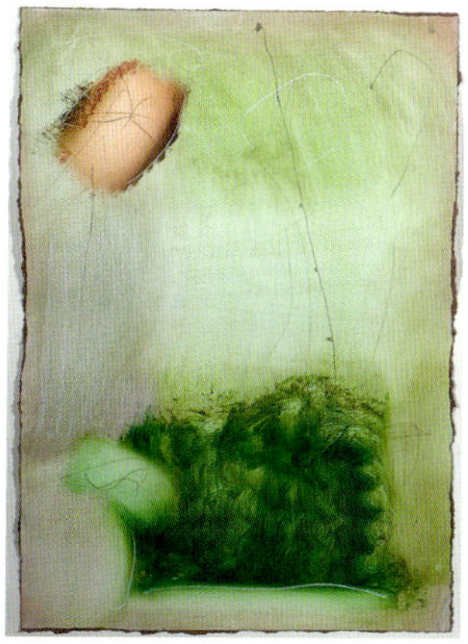

Duffy, Terry b.1948
Out of the Green 1990
oil on paper 147 x 108
0057

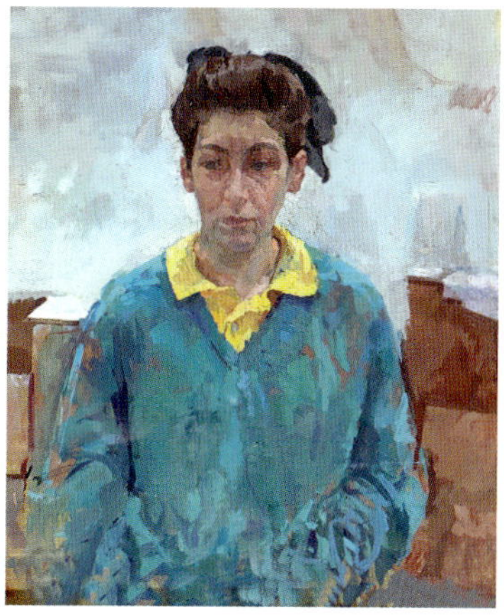

Dukes, Robert b.1965
Portrait of a Girl 1987
oil on board 61.5 x 51.5
0759

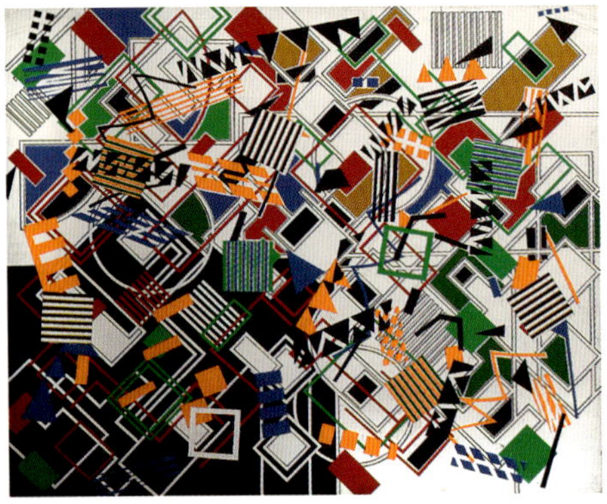

Dunn, Stephen
Black Corner 1978
acrylic on canvas 102 x 121.5
0689

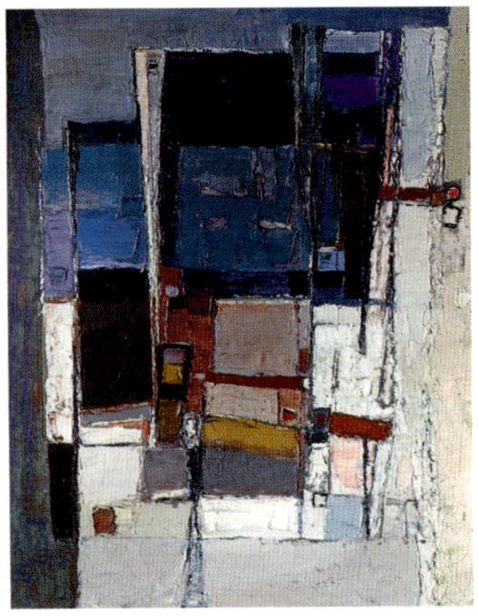

Feiler, Paul b.1918
Italian Village Square with a Lake 1954
oil on canvas 110.2 x 88.9
0059

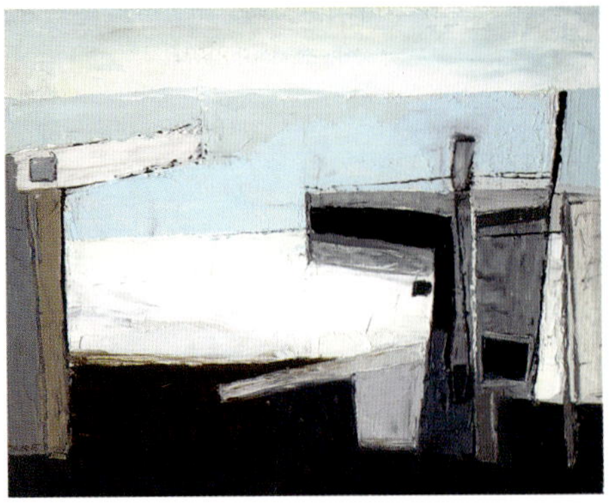

Feiler, Paul b.1918
Lamorna Grey and Black 1955
oil on board 51.5 x 61.5
0060

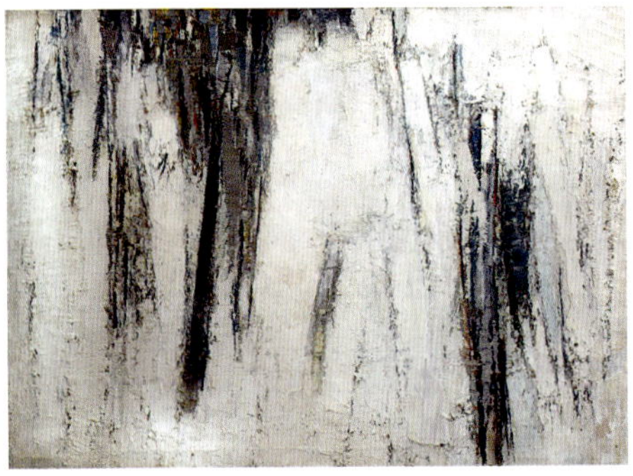

Feiler, Paul b.1918
Porth Ledden Grey 1958
oil on canvas 101 x 132
0061

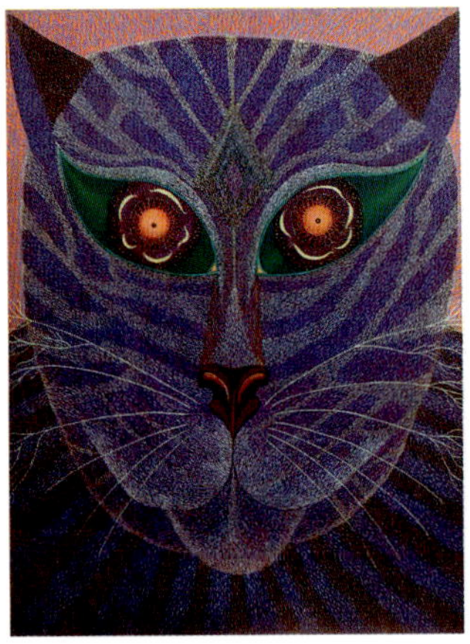

Fletcher, David 1948–2008
Temple Cat 1973
oil on canvas 124 x 94
0062

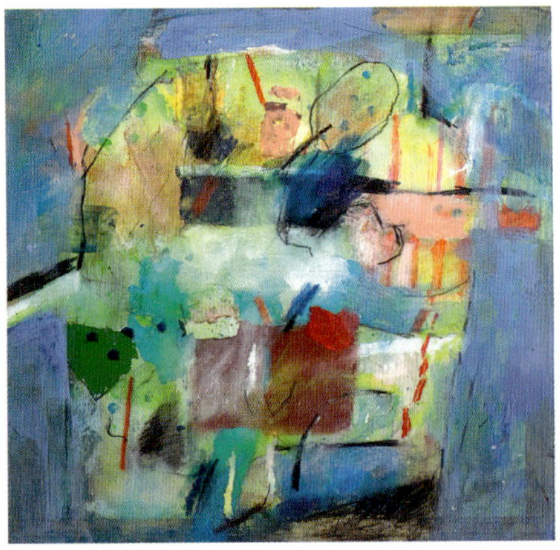

Foord, Susan b.1945
Untitled 1984
oil & oil pastel on board 56.5 x 56.5
0063

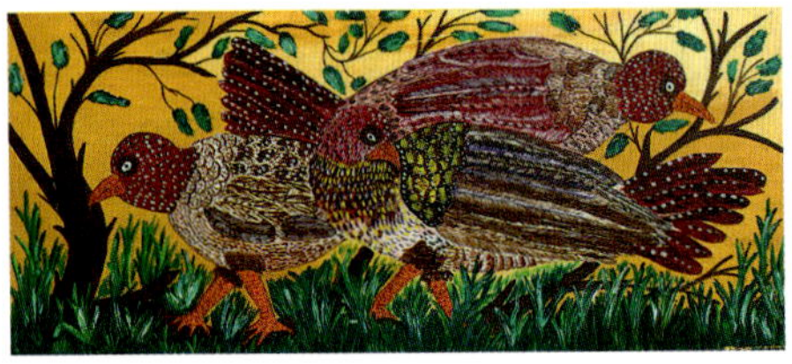

Francois, Roger b.c.1928
Birds 1969
oil on board 48.5 x 104.5
0065

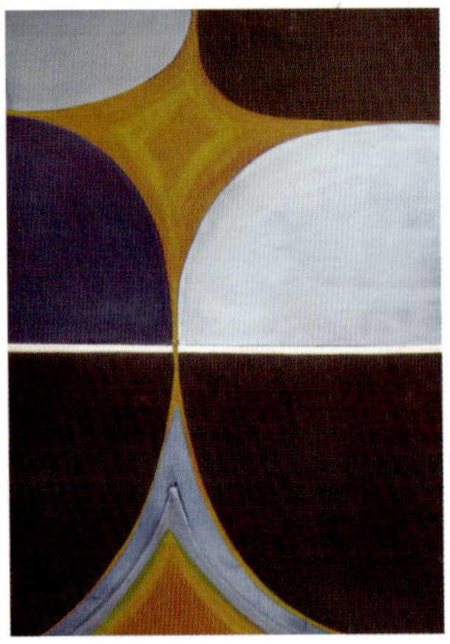

Frost, Terry 1915–2003
Blues 1966
acrylic on canvas 205 x 143.5
0067

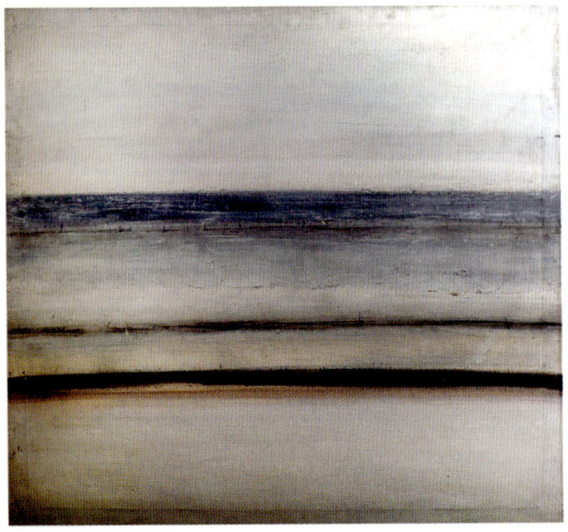

Fussell, Michael 1927–1974
Low Tide, Aldeburgh, Suffolk 1959
oil on canvas 103 x 108
0068

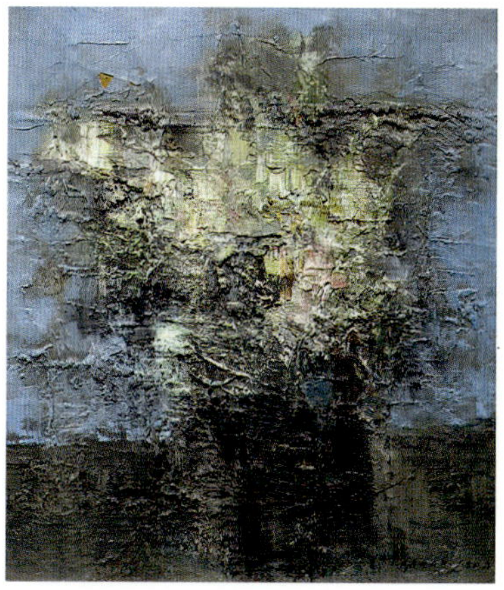

Garanjoud, Claude 1926–2005
Flowers II 1957
oil on canvas 59 x 50.5
0070

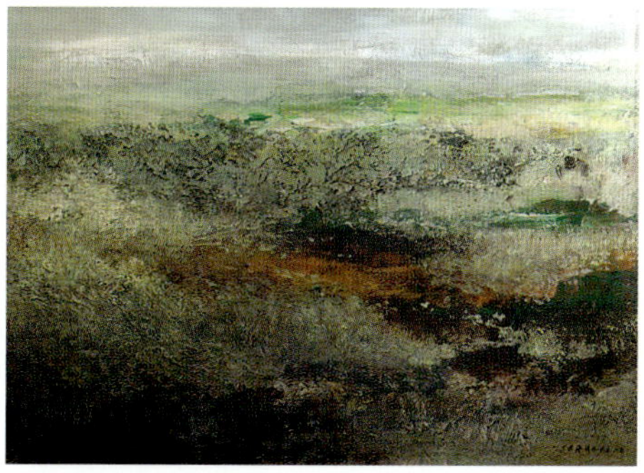

Garanjoud, Claude 1926–2005
Valansole, Provence, France 1957
oil on canvas 73 x 94
0071

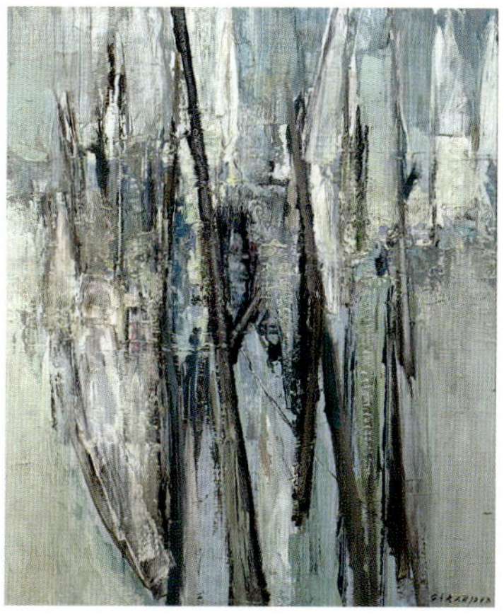

Garanjoud, Claude 1926–2005
Composition with Sails 1959
oil on canvas 87.5 x 74.5
0069

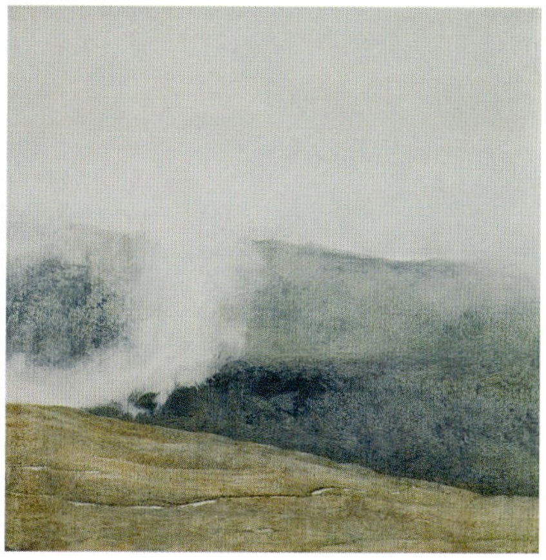

George, Andrew Scott b.1952
Cairngorms, Highlands 2002
tempera on board 54.5 x 53.5 (E)
0975

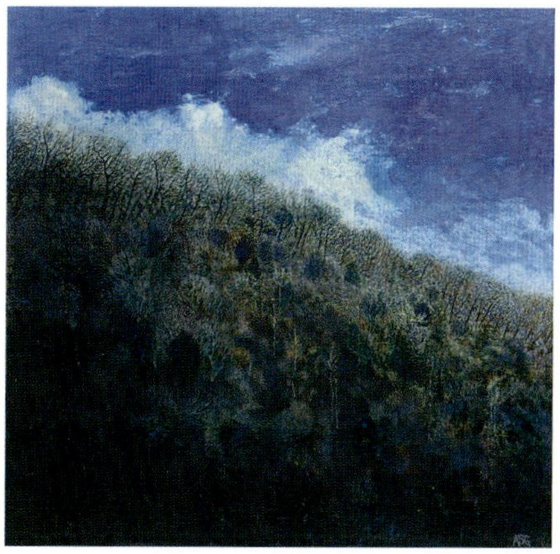

George, Andrew Scott b.1952
Dream Topping 2002
tempera on board 54 x 54 (E)
0977

George, Andrew Scott b.1952
Rothiemurchus, Inverness 2002
tempera on board 54.5 x 53.5 (E)
0976

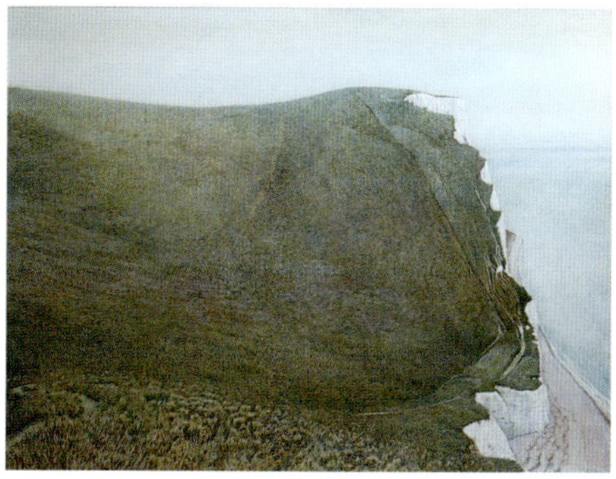

George, Andrew Scott b.1952
Above the Swyre, Dorset 2005
tempera on board 90 x 120
0979

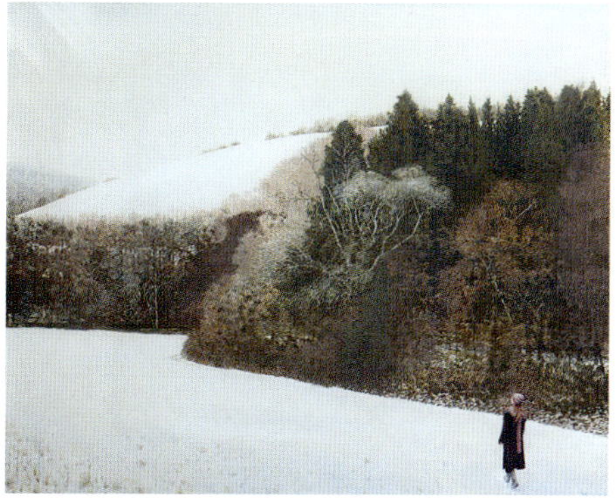

George, Andrew Scott b.1952
Bullock's Hill 2005
tempera on board 79 x 95
0978

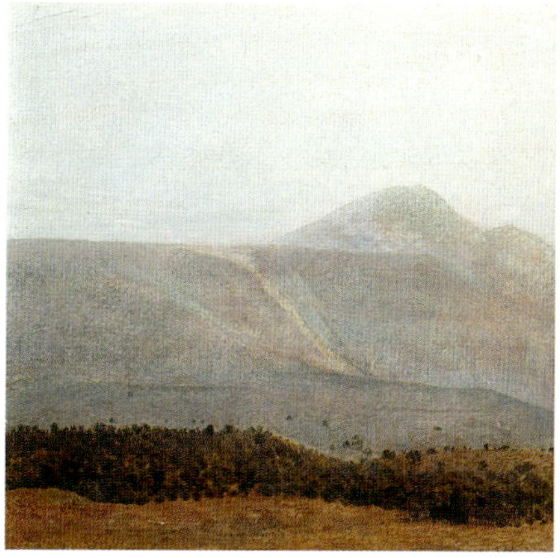

George, Andrew Scott b.1952
Abernethy, Perthshire
tempera on board 36 x 34
0982

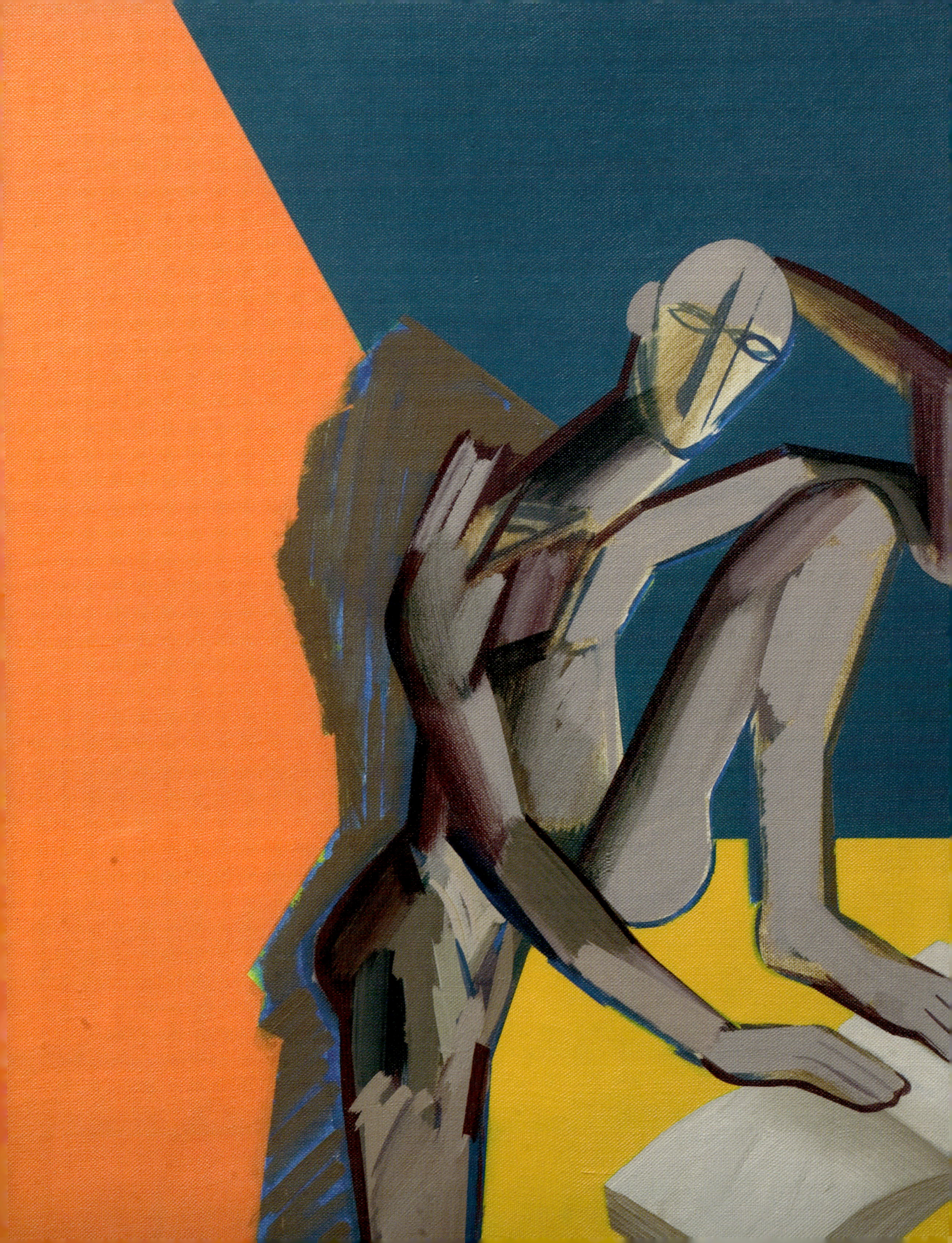

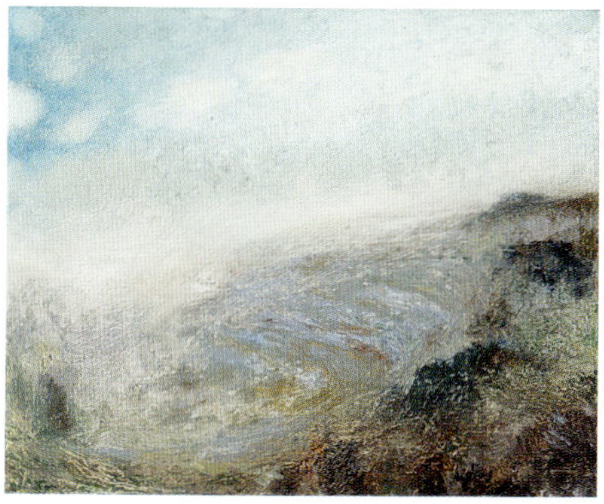

George, Andrew Scott b.1952
Downland
oil on board 26 x 30
0980

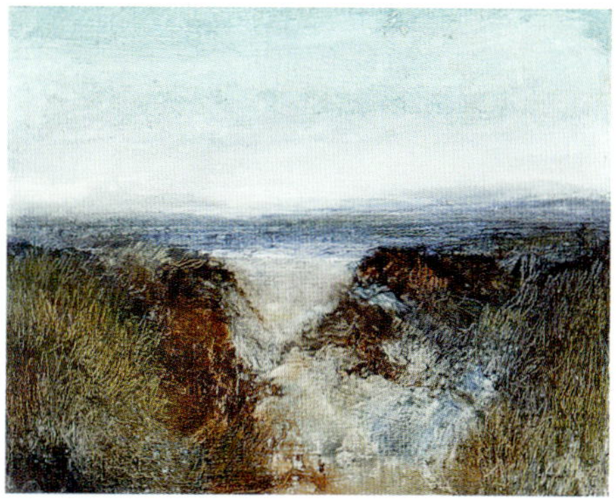

George, Andrew Scott b.1952
Dunes
oil on board 24 x 30
0981

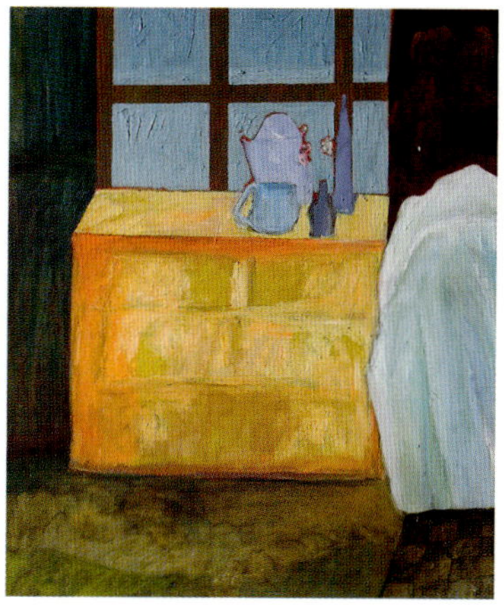

Ghosh, Amal b.1933
Secrets
oil on canvas 78.5 x 65.5
0072

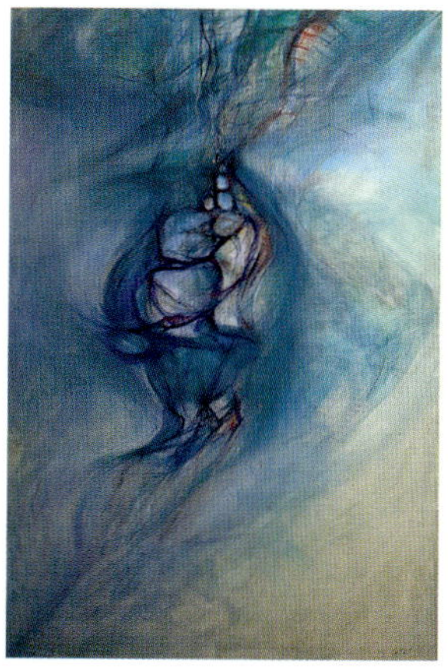

Gibbs, Evelyn 1905–1991
Erosion 1970
oil on canvas 153.3 x 103.3
0073

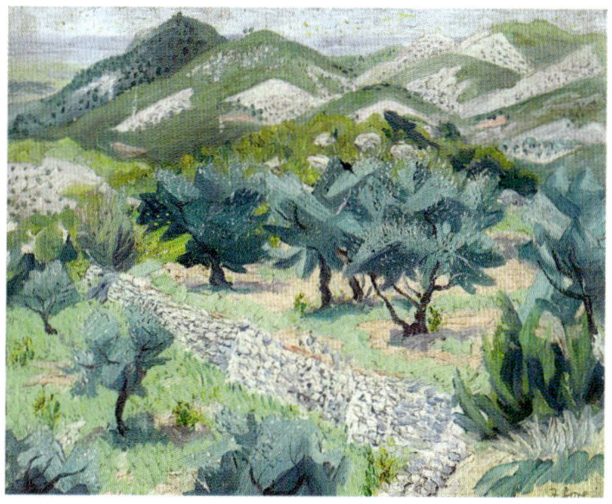

Gore, Frederick John Pym 1913–2009
Provence in Silver 1953
oil on canvas 56 x 67
0083

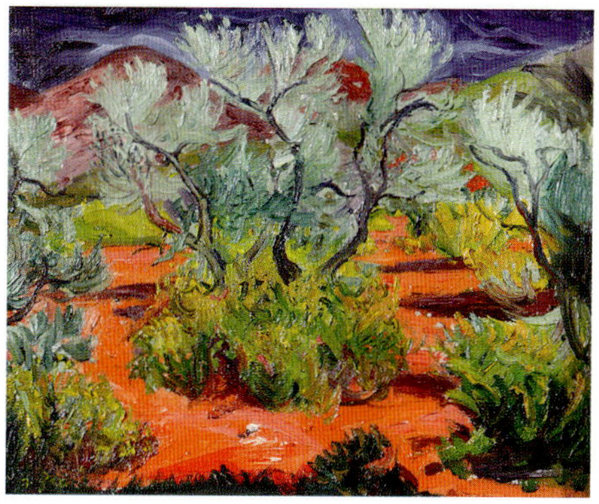

Gore, Frederick John Pym 1913–2009
Swirly Olive Trees, Les Baux, France 1954
oil on canvas 57 x 67.5
0084

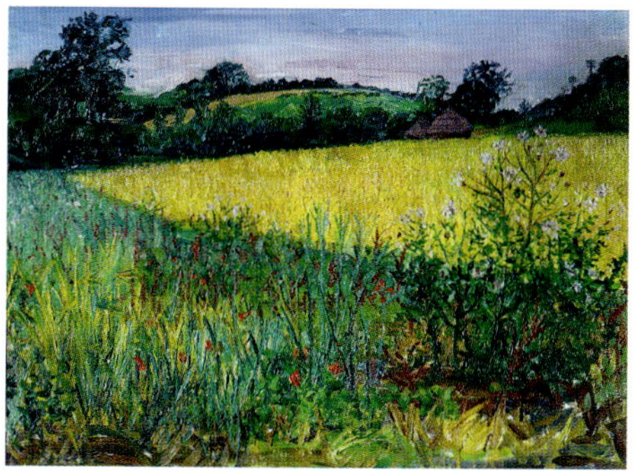

Gore, Frederick John Pym 1913–2009
Cornfield, Meopham, Kent 1956
oil on board 70.7 x 91
0081

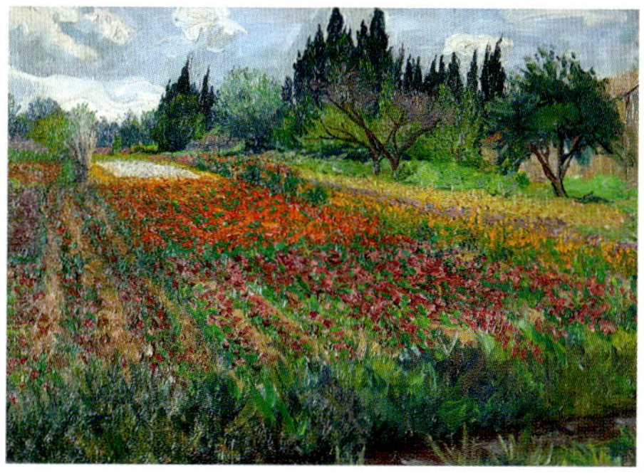

Gore, Frederick John Pym 1913–2009
Flower Farm, near Arles, France 1959
oil on canvas 67 x 88
0082

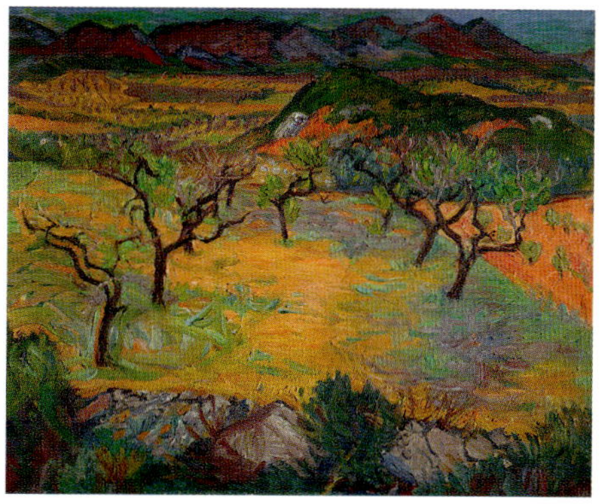

Gore, Frederick John Pym 1913–2009
Near Les Baux, Provence, France
oil on canvas 66.5 x 79
0080

Facing page: Norwich, Anne, b.1929, *Reading* (detail), 1973, The Collection: Art & Archaeology in Lincolnshire (Usher Gallery) (p. 317)

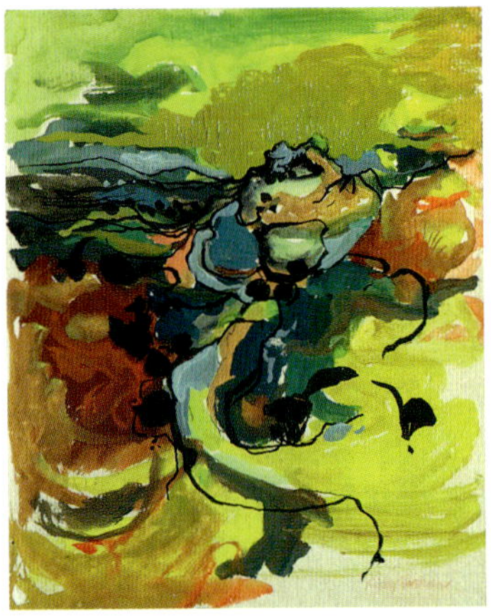

Graham, Rigby b.1931
Turbulent Landscape, Dorset 1966
oil on board 43 x 38
0087

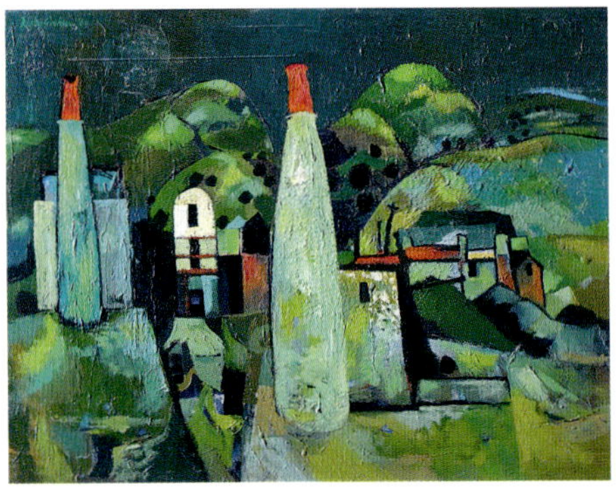

Graham, Rigby b.1931
Cornish Landscape with Lime Workings 1969
oil on board 59 x 69
0085

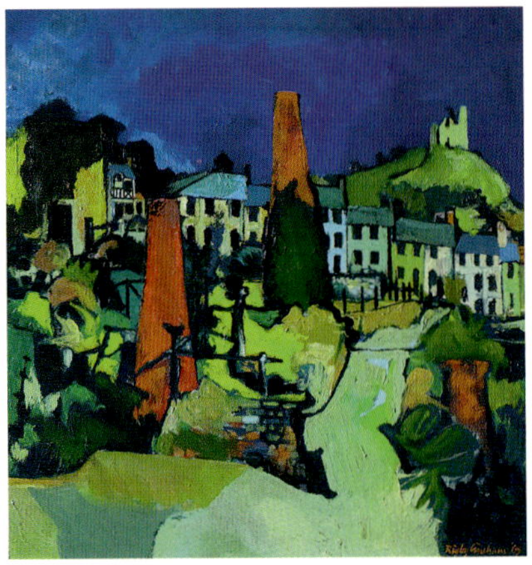

Graham, Rigby b.1931
Mine Workings, East Cornwall 1969
oil on board 67 x 63
0086

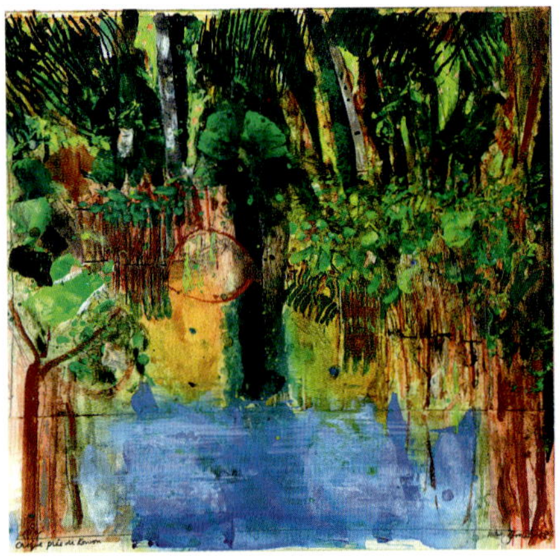

Grant, Keith b.1930
Swamp on the Road to Sinnamary, French Guiana 1983
acrylic on paper 58.5 x 57
0088

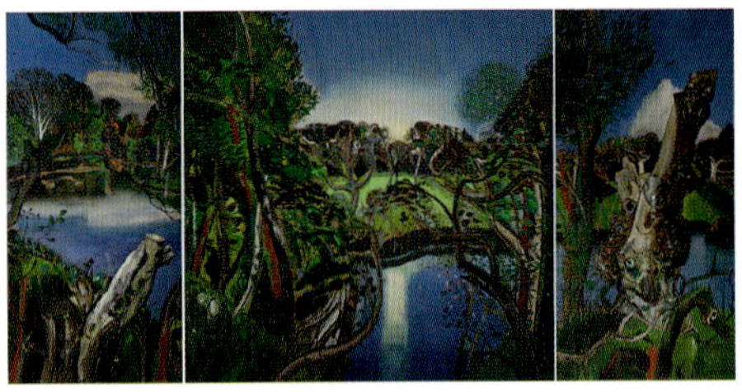

Grant, Keith b.1930
Spring, the North Tyne, Chollerford, Northumberland
oil on canvas 140 x 80; 140 x 170; 140 x 80
0781

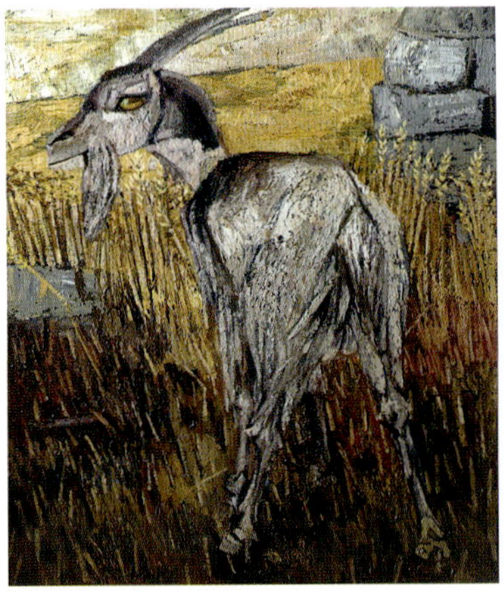

Greaves, Derrick b.1927
Goat 1956
oil on canvas 91 x 79
0090

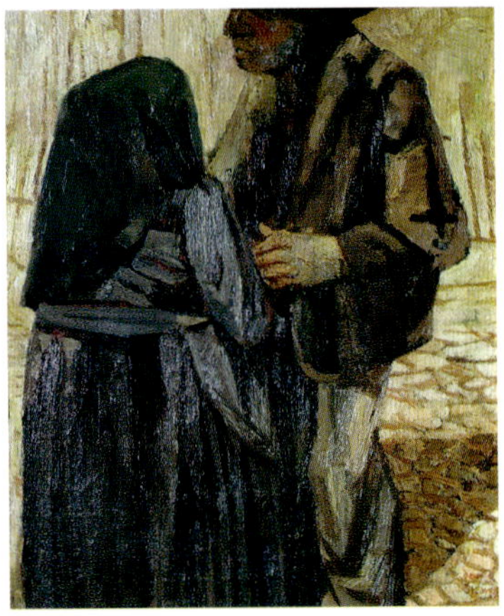

Greaves, Derrick b.1927
Italian Peasants 1959
oil on canvas 71.5 x 60.5
0092

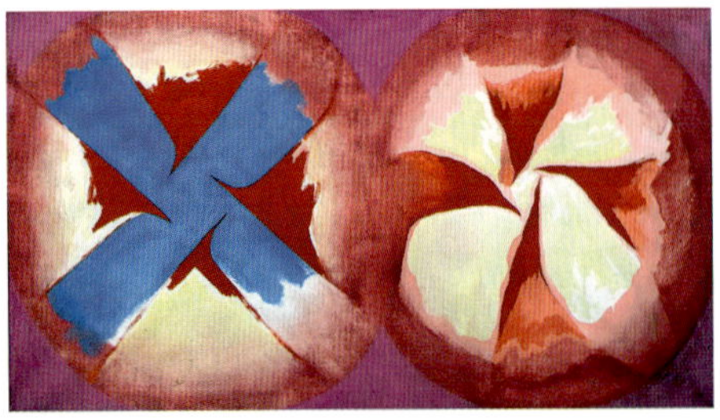

Greaves, Derrick b.1927
Bloomfield 1962
oil on canvas 79 x 135
0089

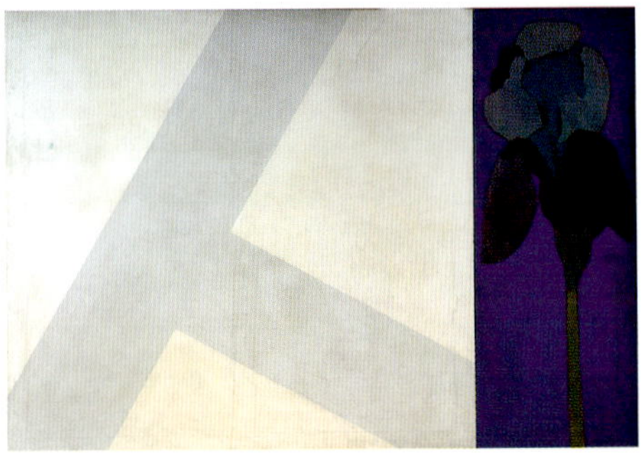

Greaves, Derrick b.1927
Iris 1964
oil on canvas 146.4 x 204.8
0091

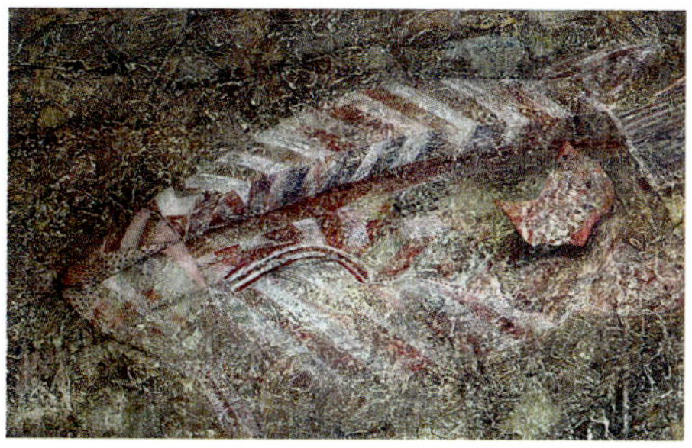

Grebby, Anne b.1944
Duladna Moonshine 1981
acrylic on paper 52.5 x 70
0093

Green, Alan 1932–2003
Key 1974
oil on canvas 177 x 176.5
0094

Green, Alan 1932–2003
Painting with Grey, Yellow and Ochre
acrylic on canvas 122 x 167.5
0095

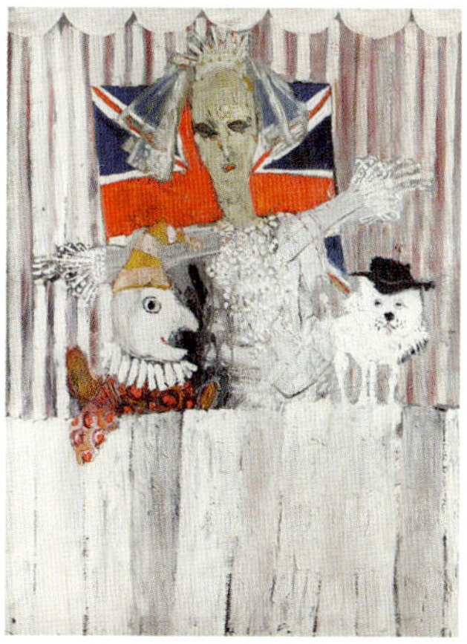

Green, Anthony b.1939
Punch and Judy 1961
oil on board 128 x 93.1
0096

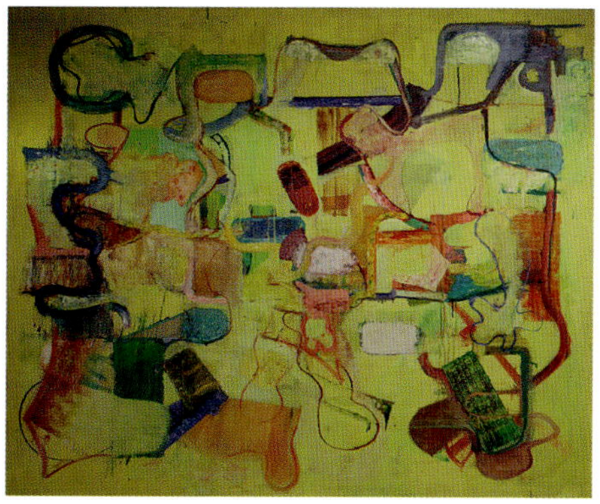

Greep, Jenny
Gleaming Things 1991
oil on canvas 214 x 244
0097

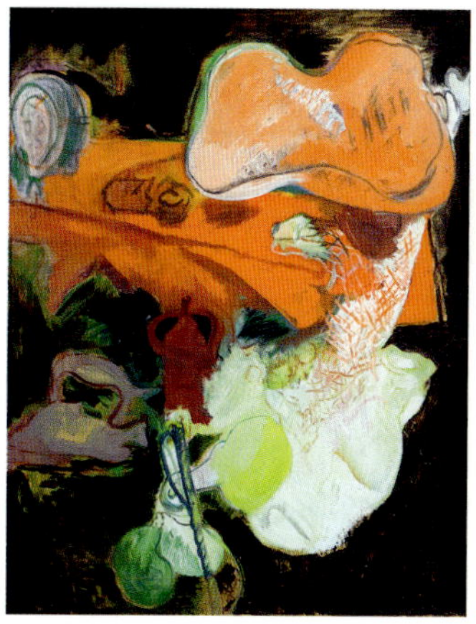

Gurney, Julia b.1955
Hot Water Bottle Still Life No.2 1982
oil on canvas 105.5 x 79
0099

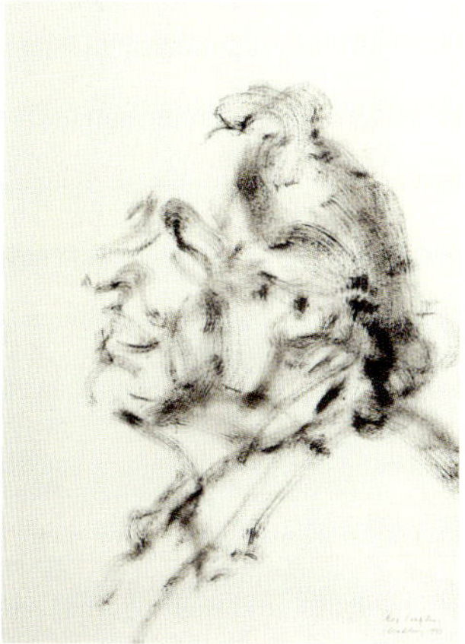

Hambling, Maggi b.1945
Mac Laughing 1981
oil on paper 63.3 x 50.7
0100

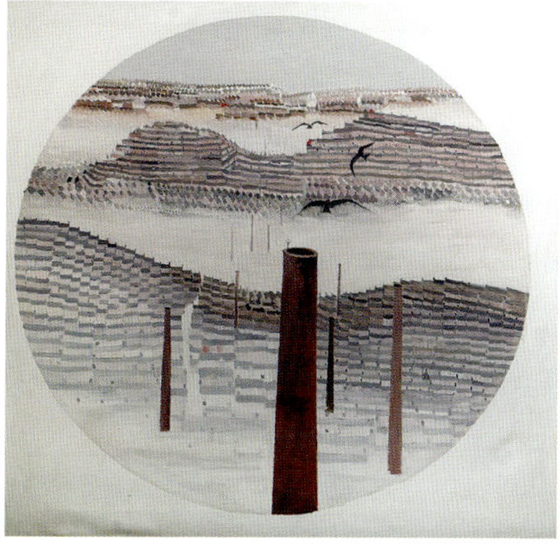

Hanley, Liam b.1933
The Chimney
oil on canvas 97 x 97
0102

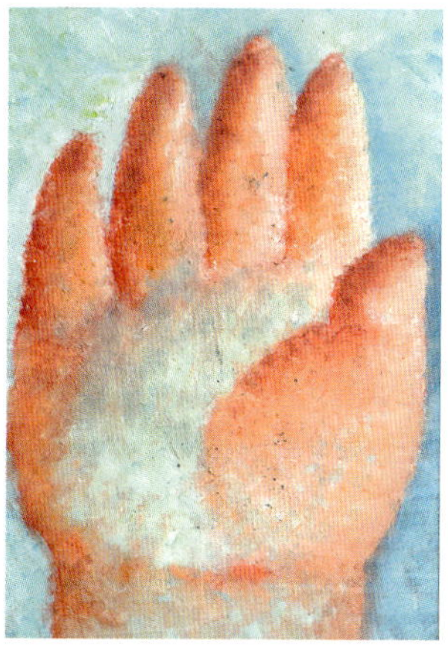

Hardie, Gwen b.1962
Hand Two 1986
oil on paper 105 x 74.5
0103

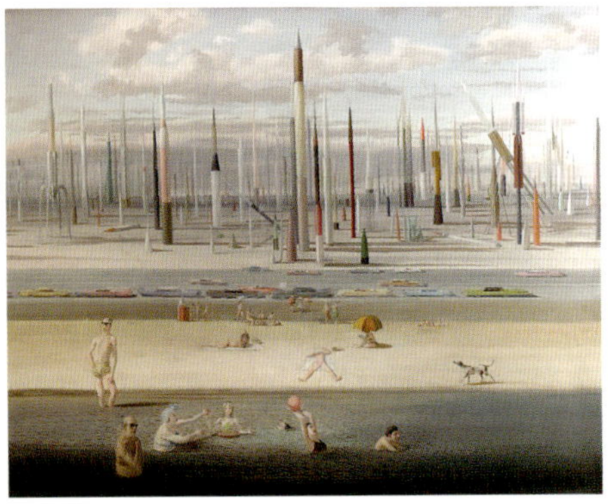

Harrison, Claude 1922–2009
Fête Canaveral 1967
oil on board 103.5 x 123
0104

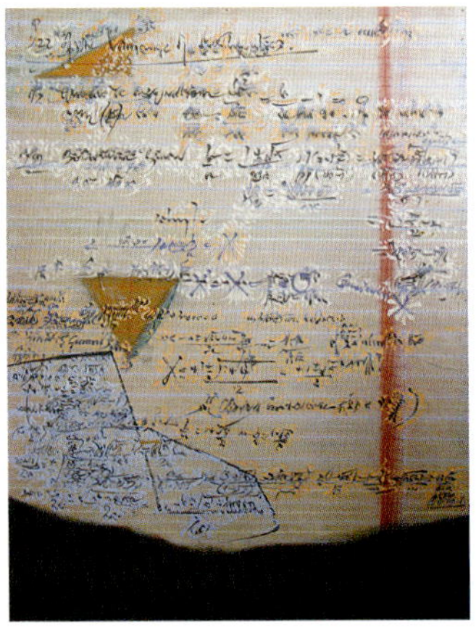

Hart, John 1921–1996
Imps of Fancy on the Moors 1973
oil on board 74 x 62
0105

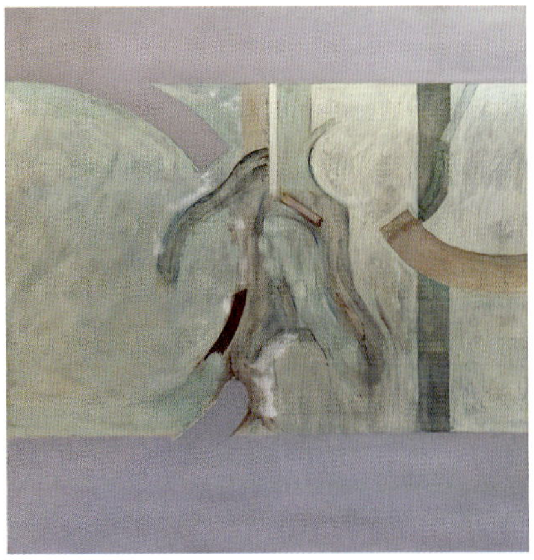

Heath, Adrian 1920–1992
Taza 1965
oil on canvas 184 x 173.5
0106

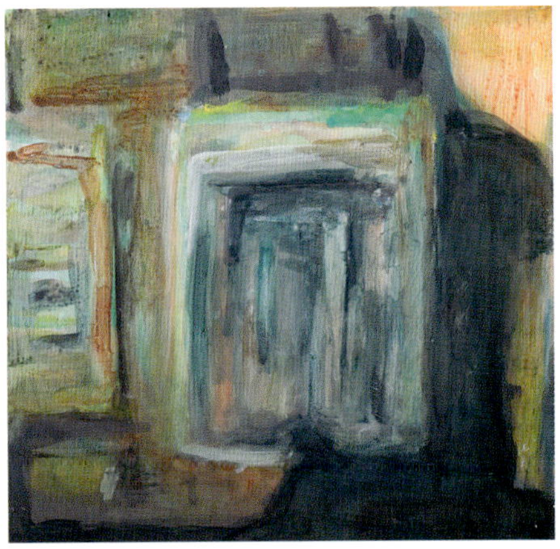

Henderson, Sonia
Untitled (Green Window) 2004
oil on board 50 x 50
0983

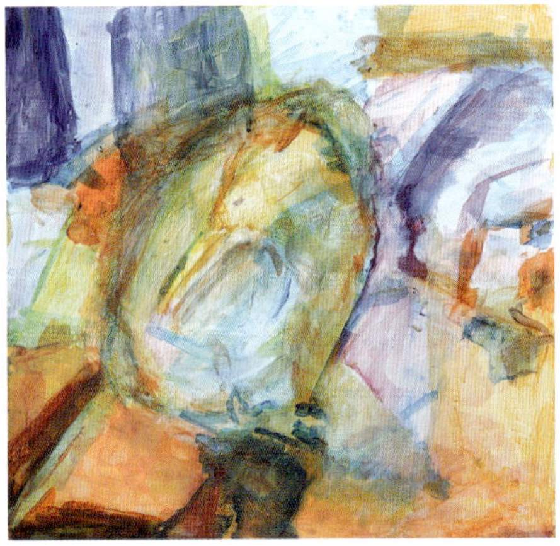

Henderson, Sonia
Untitled (Kiwi) 2004
oil on board 50 x 50
0985

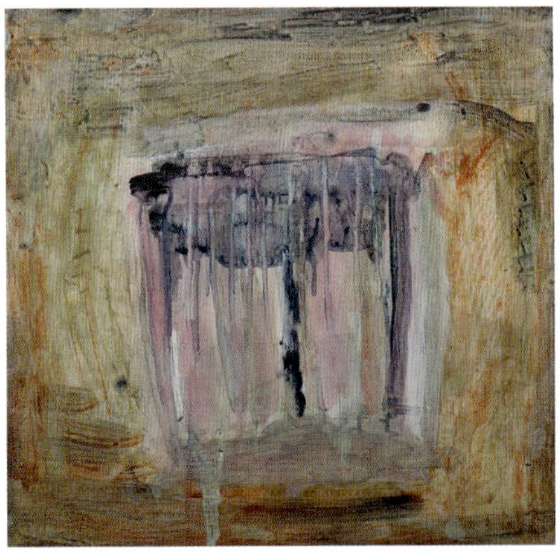

Henderson, Sonia
Untitled (Pink Window) 2004
oil on board 50 x 50
0984

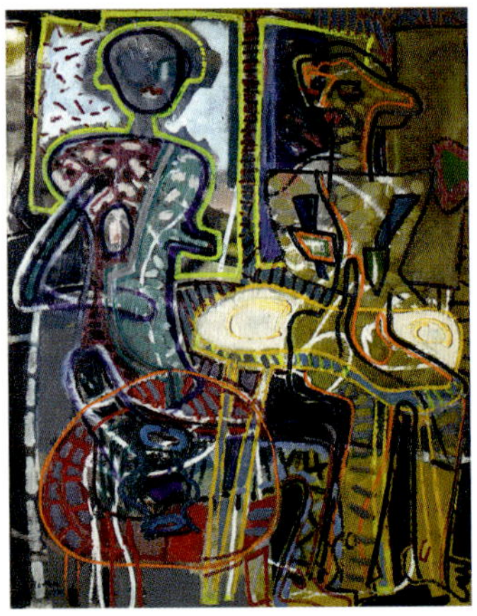

Heron, Patrick 1920–1999
Two Women in a Café 1950
oil on canvas 114 x 95
0109

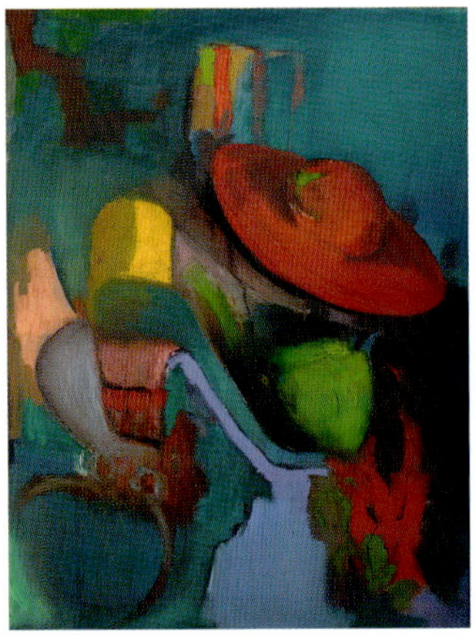

Hill, Elizabeth
Sombrero 1989
oil on canvas 247 x 186
0111

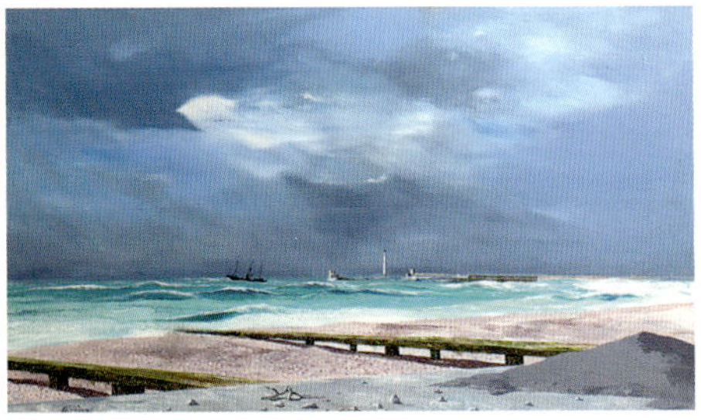

Hillier, Tristram Paul 1905–1983
The Breakwater at Dieppe, France 1948
oil on board 46 x 63
0112

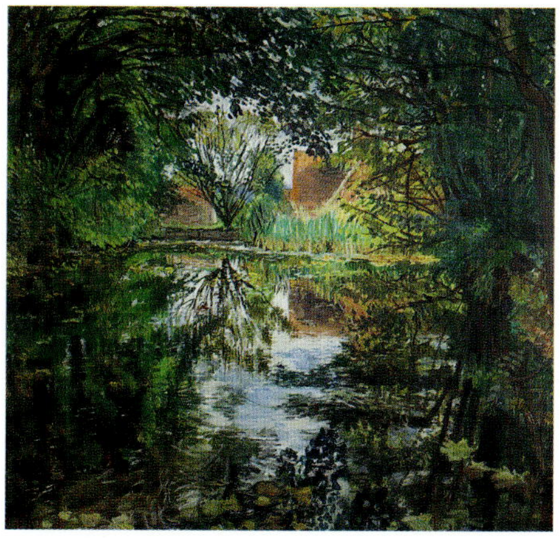

Hippisley, Julian 1938–1972
Old Mill Pond, Leeds, Kent 1969
oil on canvas 75.5 x 81
0113

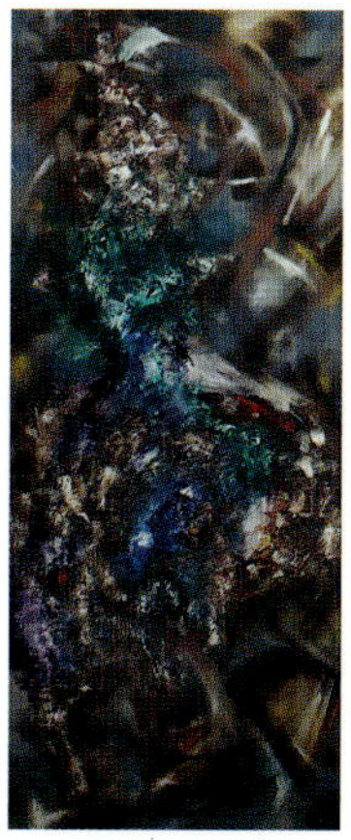

Hitchcock, Raymond 1922–1992
Falling Soldier 1963
oil on canvas 155 x 63
0114

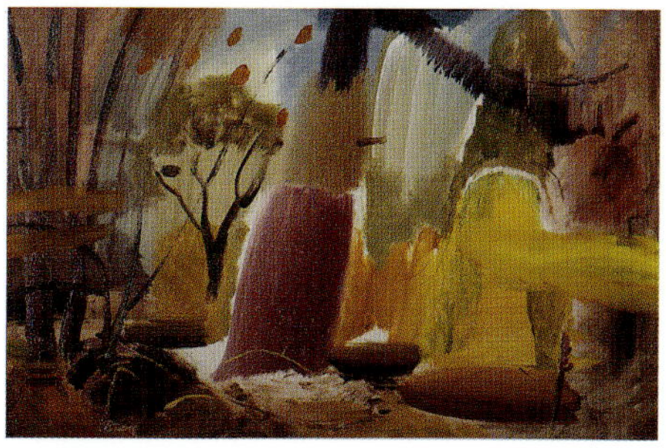

Hitchens, Ivon 1893–1979
Woodpecker Tree
oil on canvas 69.5 x 95
0115

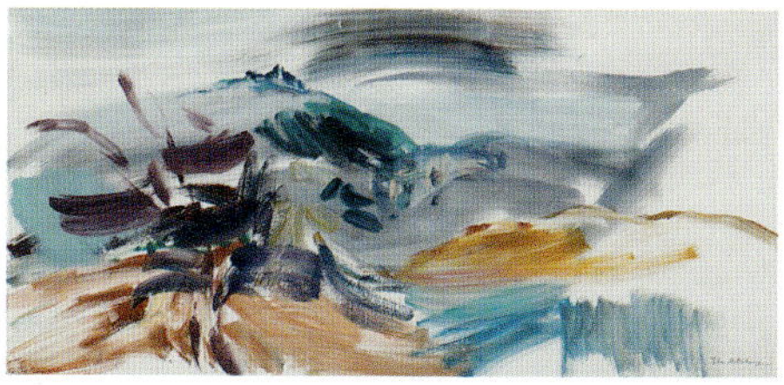

Hitchens, John b.1940
Torn Hill Landscape 1963
oil on canvas 61 x 114.5
0117

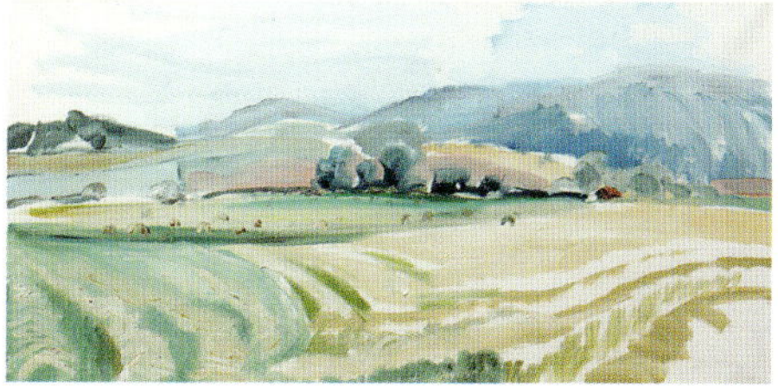

Hitchens, John b.1940
June Hay 1965
oil on canvas 60 x 110.5
0116

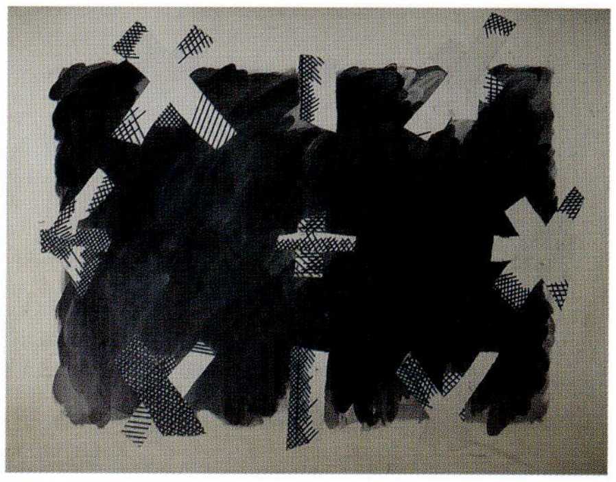

Hosking, Knighton Stephen b.1944
Earth, Sky and Water 1973
acrylic on canvas 214 x 276
0785

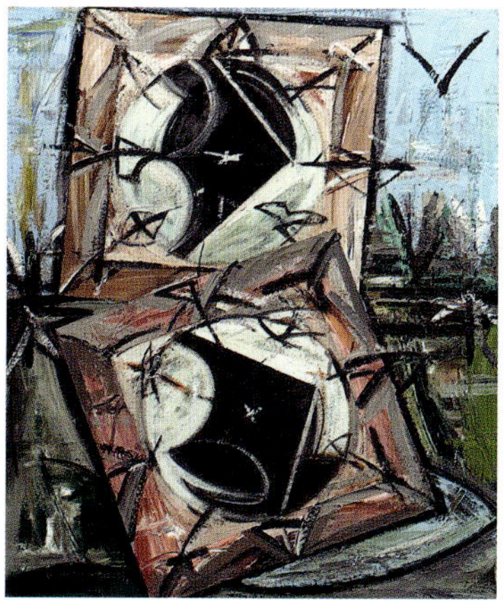

Hosking, Knighton Stephen b.1944
Sun Maker 1980
oil on canvas 93.2 x 77.5
0915

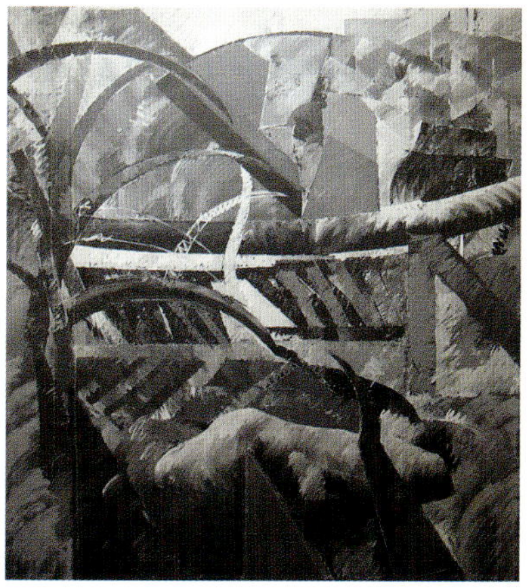

Hosking, Knighton Stephen b.1944
Pool of Water (study)
oil on canvas 213.4 x 182.9
786

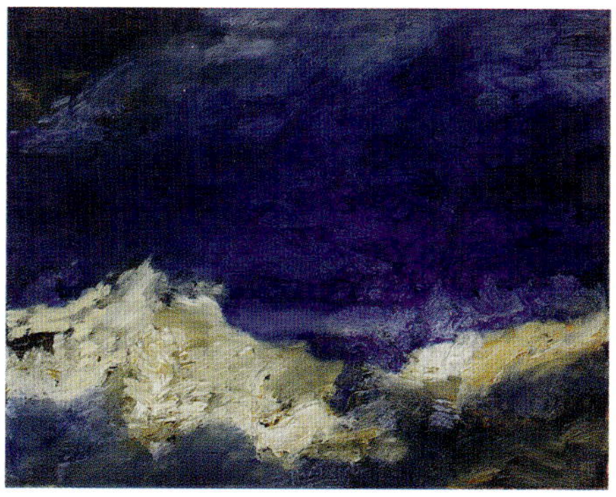

Houthuesen, Albert Anthony 1903–1979
Barrier 1968
acrylic on canvas 43.5 x 54.5
0119

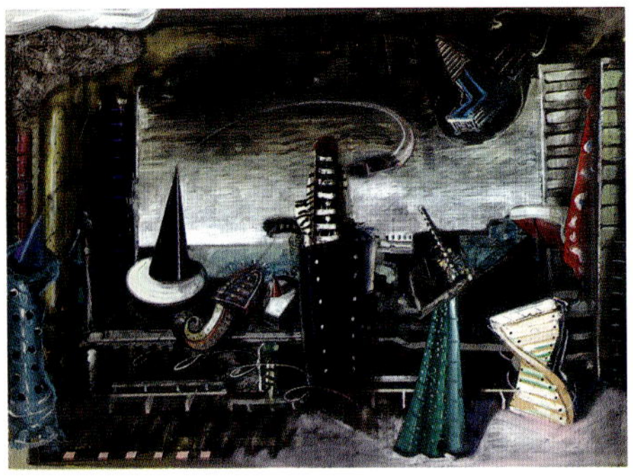

Howard, Ian b.1952
Staged 1988
acrylic gel & chalk on paper 104.5 x 140.5
0120

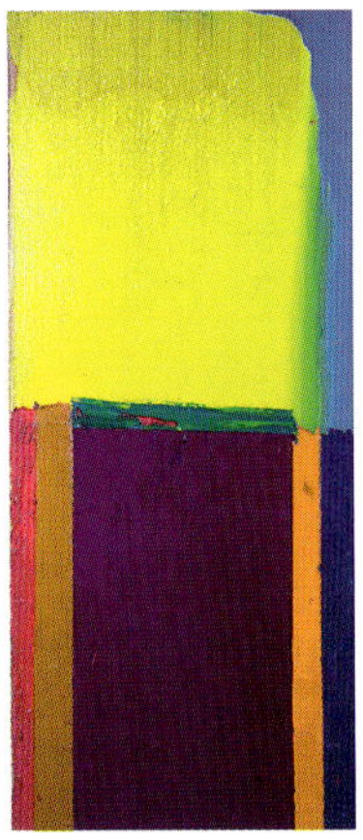

Hoyland, John 1934–2011
31.3.69 1969
acrylic on canvas 216 x 92
0121

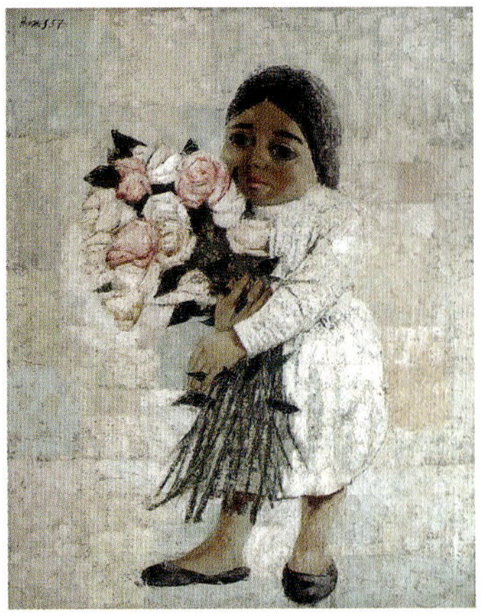

Hughes, Jack
Nina with Flowers 1957
oil on canvas 104 x 84
0123

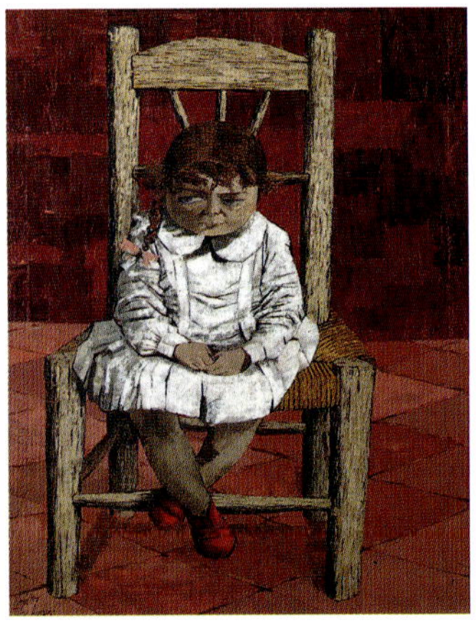

Hughes, Jack
Small Girl in a Chair 1957
oil on canvas 96.7 x 76.7
0125

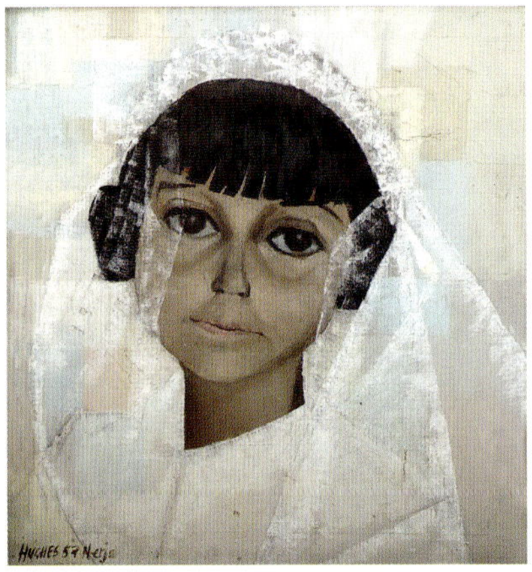

Hughes, Jack
The Bridesmaid 1957
oil on canvas 59 x 55
0122

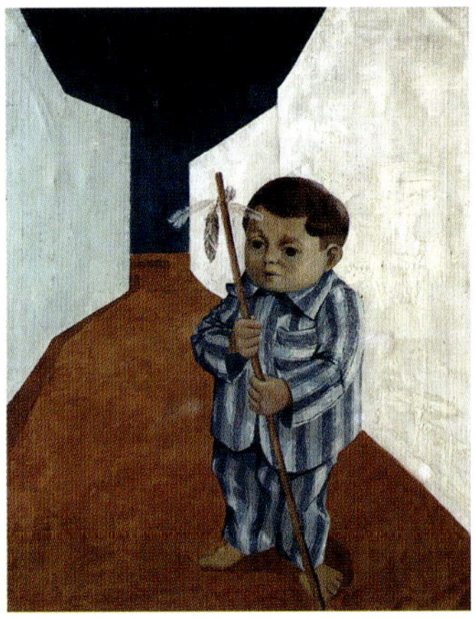

Hughes, Jack
Small Boy with a Feather 1958
oil on canvas 104.5 x 84
0124

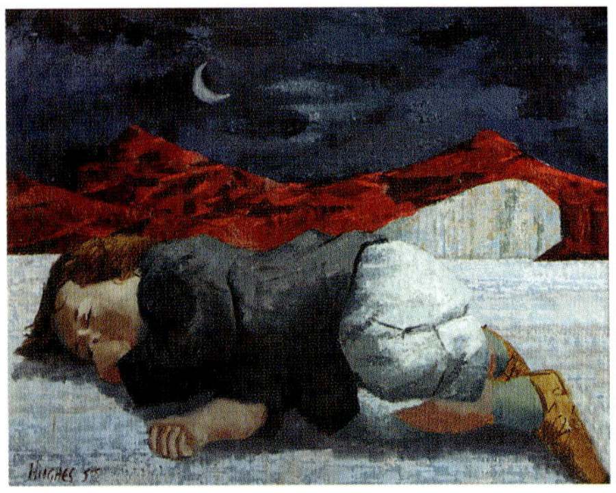

Hughes, Jack
Boy Sleeping under the Moon
oil on canvas 79 x 94
0730

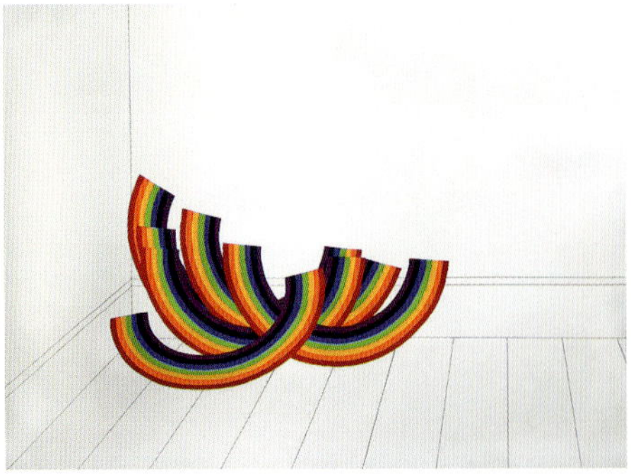

Hughes, Patrick b.1939
Pile of Discarded Rainbows 1972
gloss paint on board 122.5 x 162.5
0126

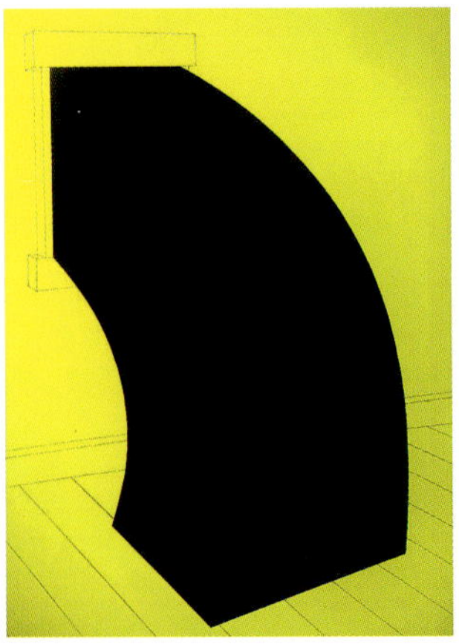

Hughes, Patrick b.1939
Darkness Falls 1977
gloss paint on board 168 x 122
0787

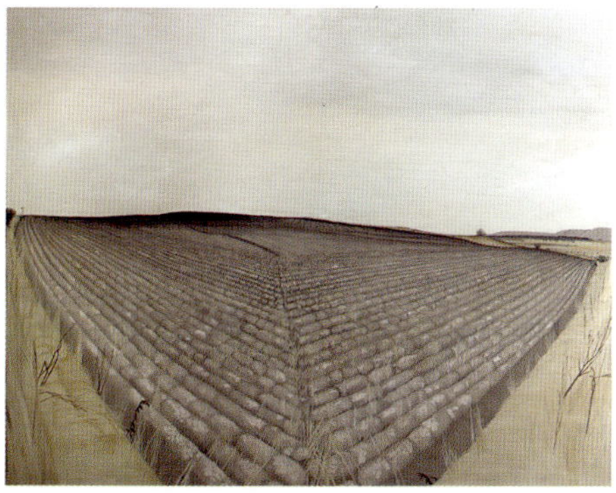

Huson, Eric b.1930
A Ploughed Field 1965
oil on board 71 x 86
0129

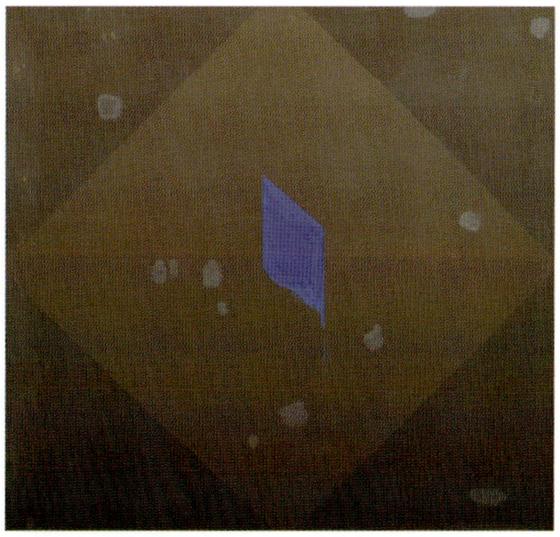

Huxley, Paul b.1938
Ceriff 1962
acrylic on canvas 127.5 x 127.5
0696

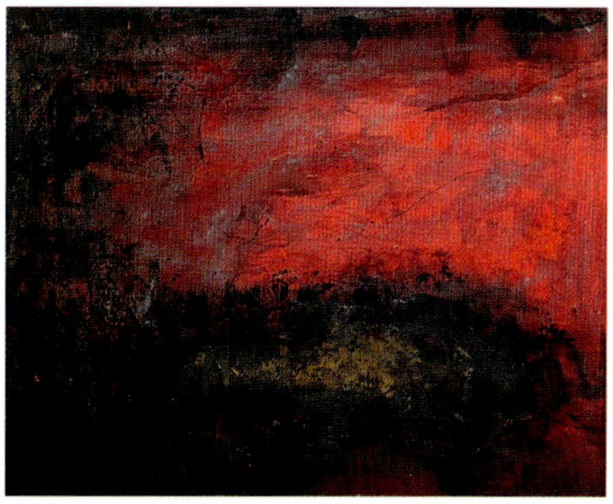

Jacquemon, Pierre 1936–2002
Composition in Crimson 1961
oil on canvas 59.5 x 69
0130

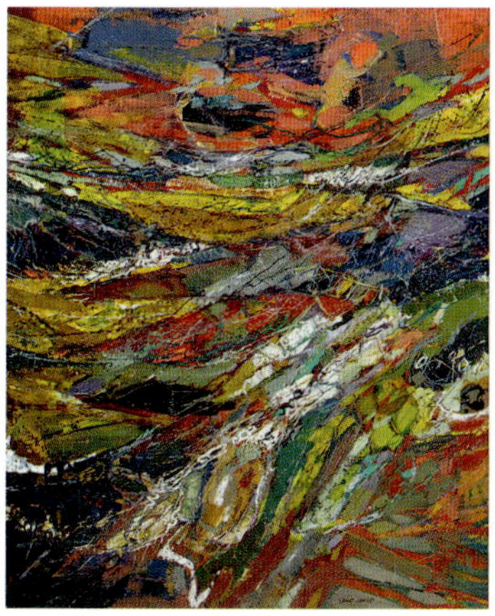

James, Louis 1920–1996
Evening Panorama, Spain 1957
oil on canvas 138.2 x 112.5
0132

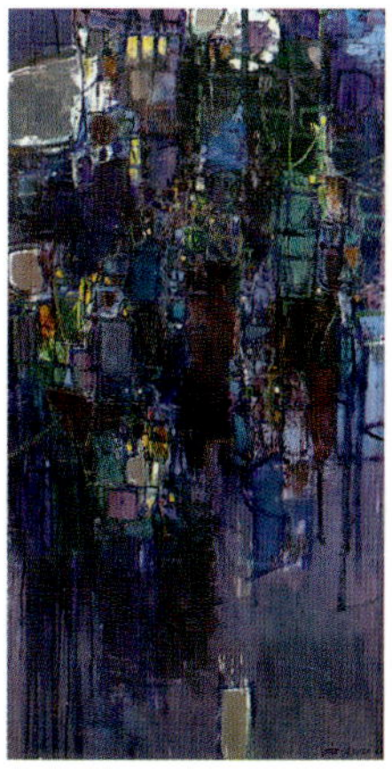

James, Louis 1920–1996
The Port I 1960
oil on canvas 138 x 75
0133

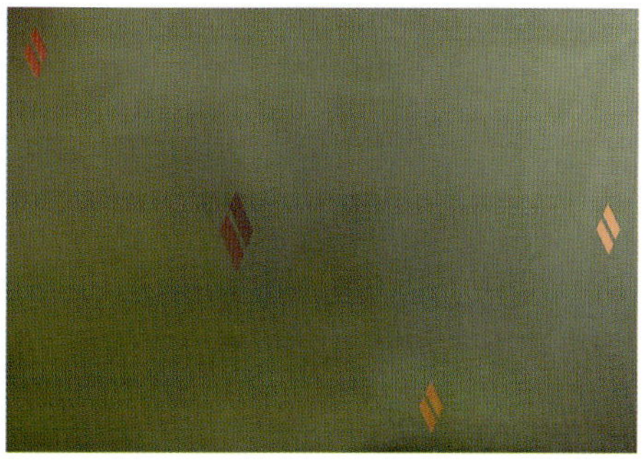

Jaray, Tess b.1937
Dark Green with Four 1971
acrylic on canvas 91 x 129.5
0136

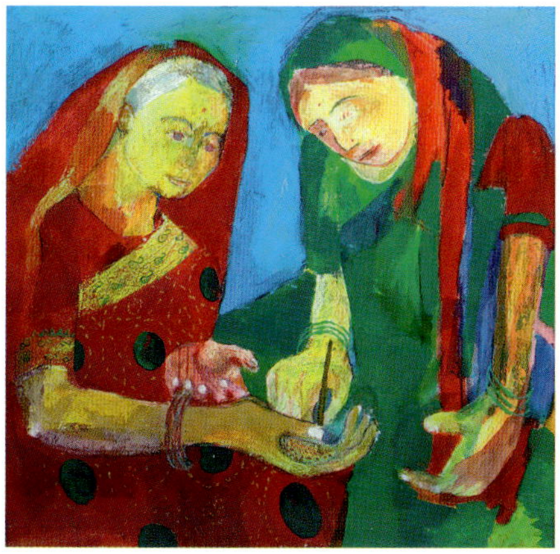

Jariwala, Caroline b.1965
Mendi Hands 1990
oil on paper 90.5 x 91
0137

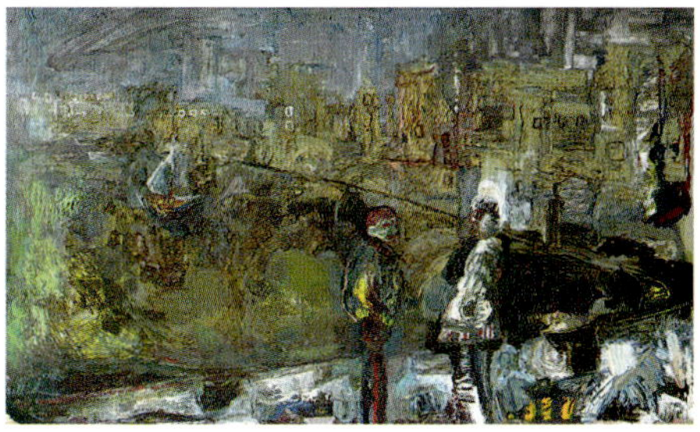

Jefferson, Anna b.1965
Harbour
oil on canvas 129.5 x 206
0138

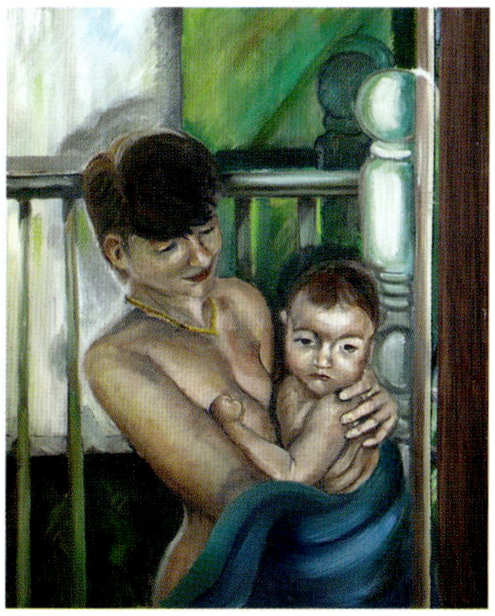

Jennings, Ceri active 1989–1991
Mother and Baby 1989
oil on canvas 130.5 x 106
0139

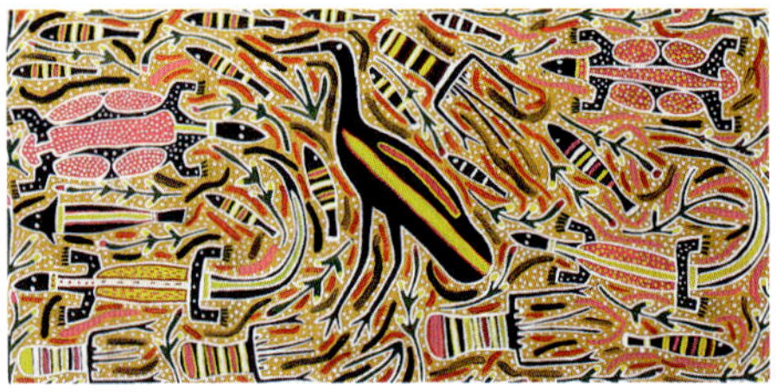

Jirwulurr, Amy Johnson b.1953
River Life in Pink
acrylic on canvas 64 x 125
0961

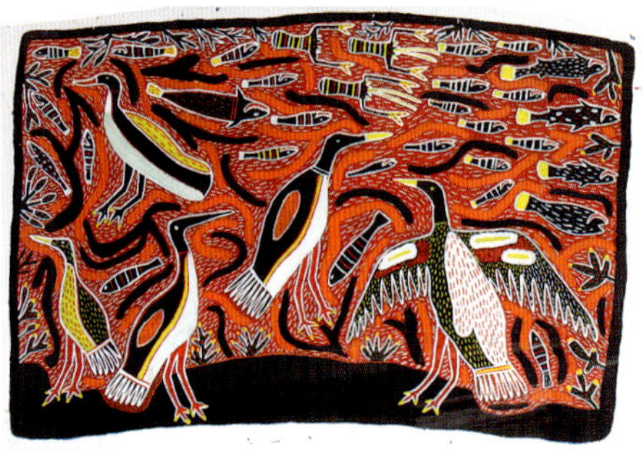

Jirwulurr, Amy Johnson b.1953
River Life in Red
acrylic on canvas 75 x 125
0963

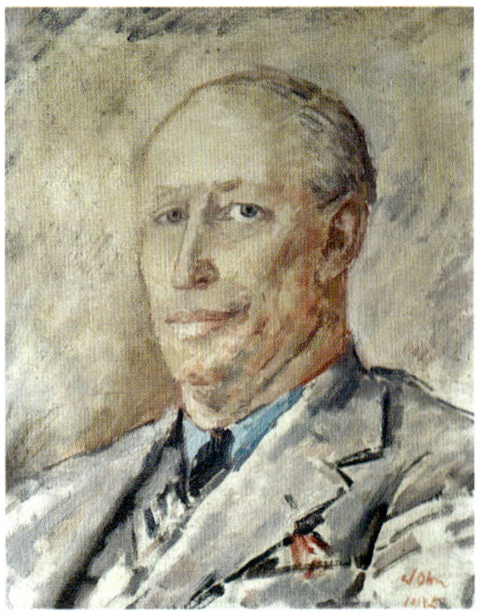

John, Augustus Edwin 1878–1961
B. O. Schonegevel 1938
oil on canvas 56 x 45.5
0140

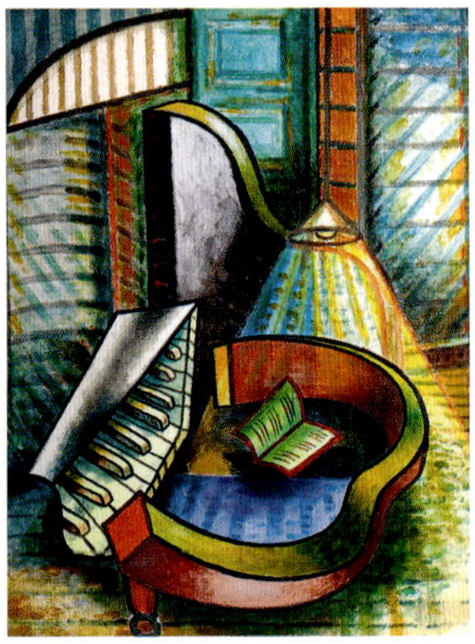

Jones, Tim b.1950
Piano with Light 1980
oil on canvas 91 x 70
0141

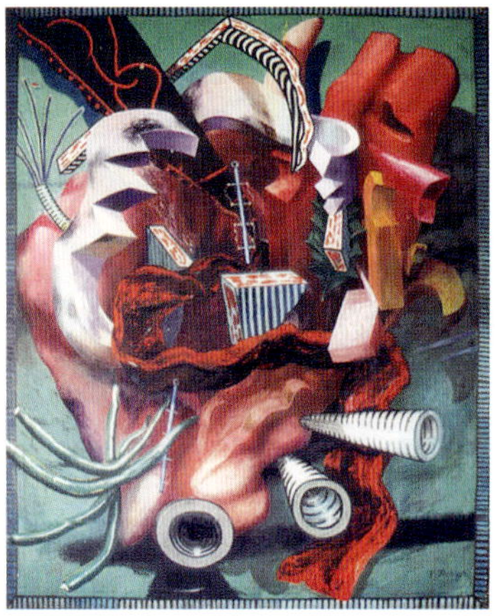

Jones, Tim b.1950
Construct II
oil on canvas 243.8 x 211.4
0788

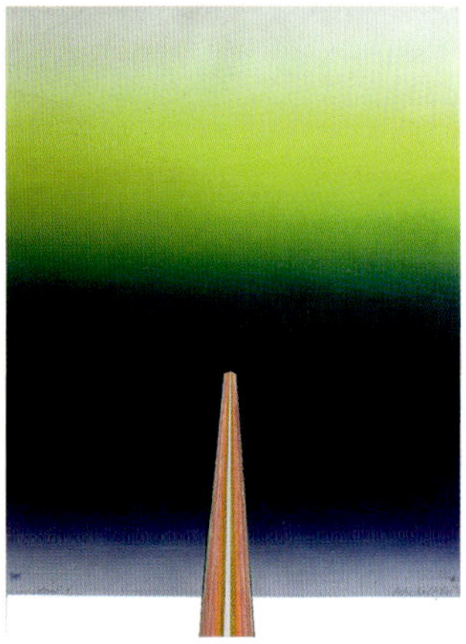

Kalkhof, Peter b.1933
Space and Colour I 1971
acrylic on paper 77 x 63
0142

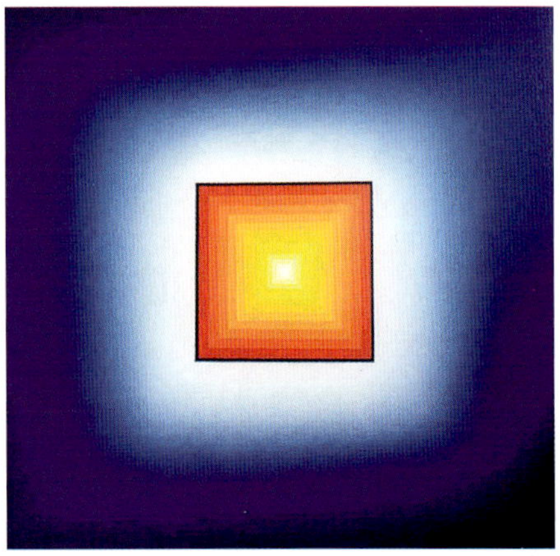

Kalkhof, Peter b.1933
Hot Centre
oil on canvas 125 x 125
789

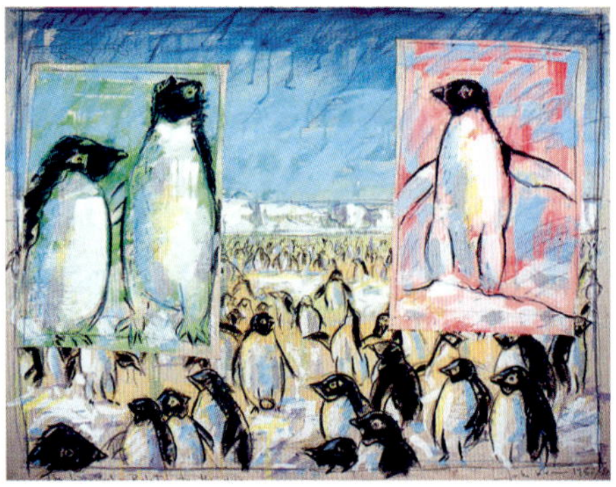

Keane, John b.1954
Individual in Relation to the Masses
1962/1963
acrylic on canvas 121.9 x 170.7
790

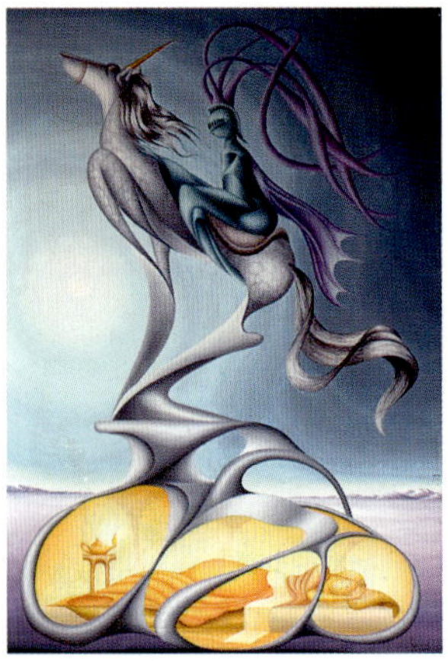

Keirle, Gordon
Guardian of Sleep 1969
oil on canvas 84 x 59.5
0143

Facing page: Souza, Francis Newton, 1924–2002, *The Emperor* (detail), 1958, Leicestershire County Council Artworks Collection (p. 143)

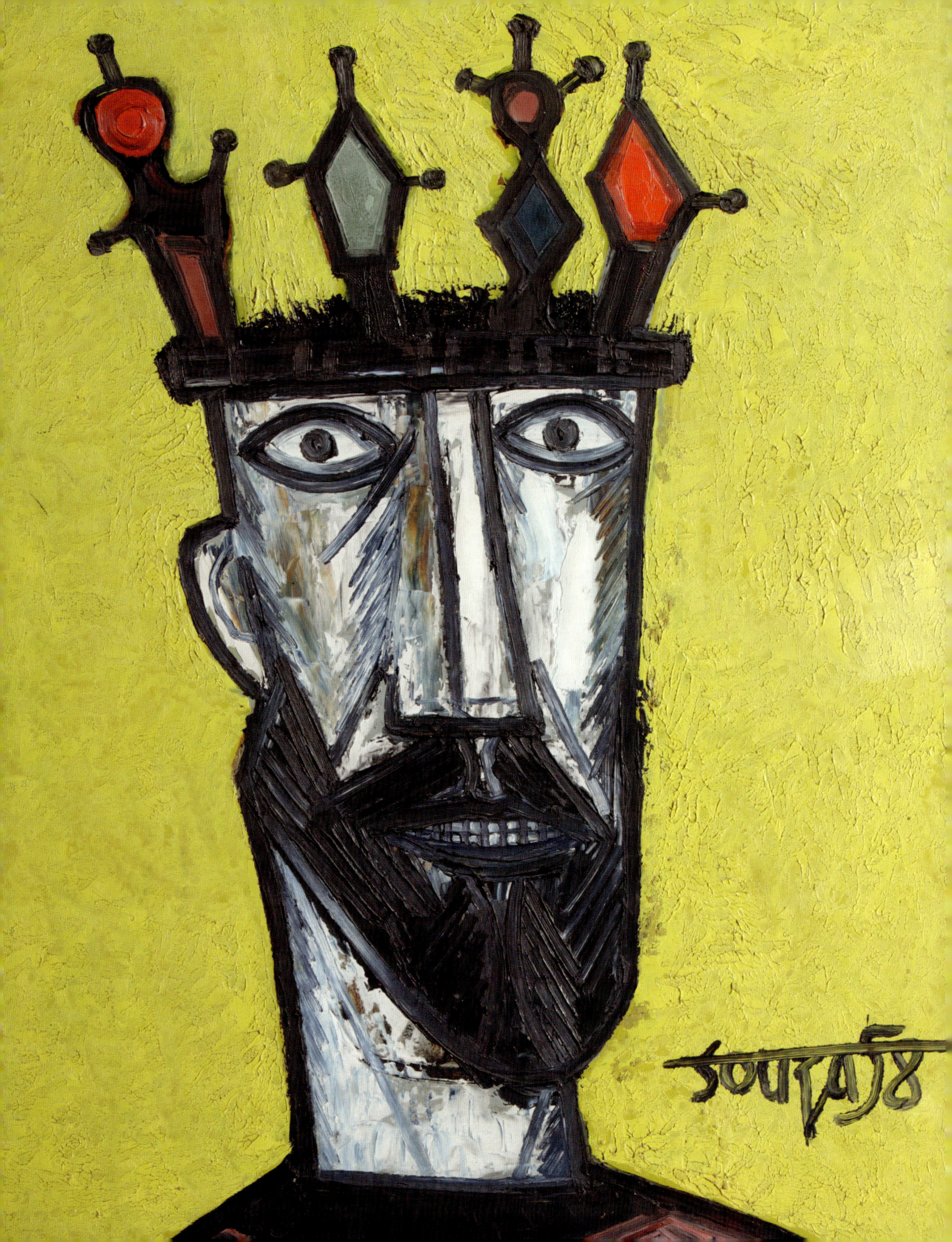
Souza 58

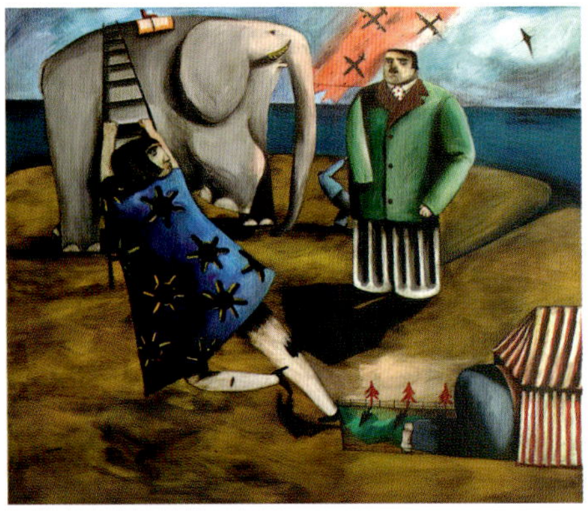

Kennelly, Peter b.1965
On the Beach 1989
oil on canvas 160 x 183
0144

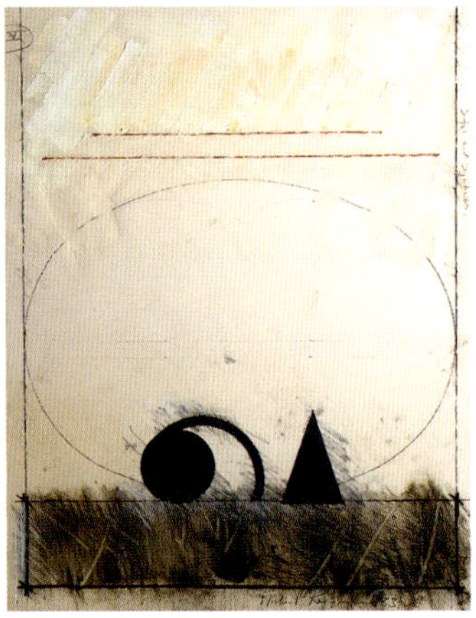

Kenny, Michael 1941–1999
Signs and Symbols IV 1983
oil, charcoal, graphite & pastel on paper
73 x 55
0145

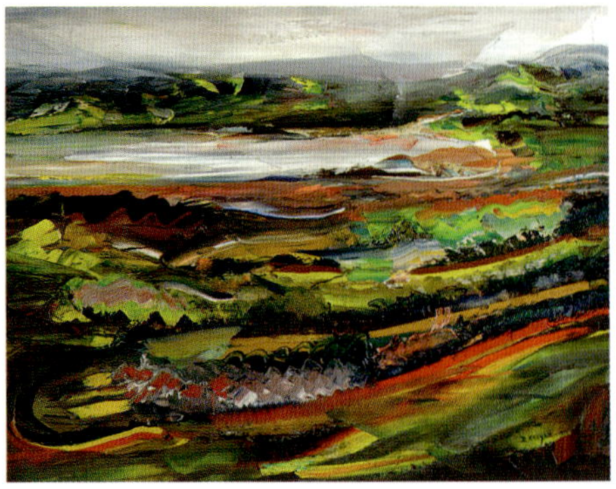

Khayatt, Dora c.1912–1986
Downhill to the Severn 1950
oil on canvas 42 x 52.5
0146

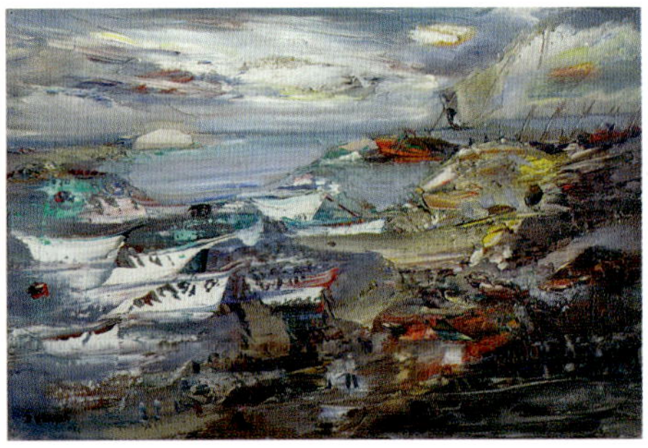

Khayatt, Dora c.1912–1986
The Little Port 1950
oil on canvas 39 x 56
0147

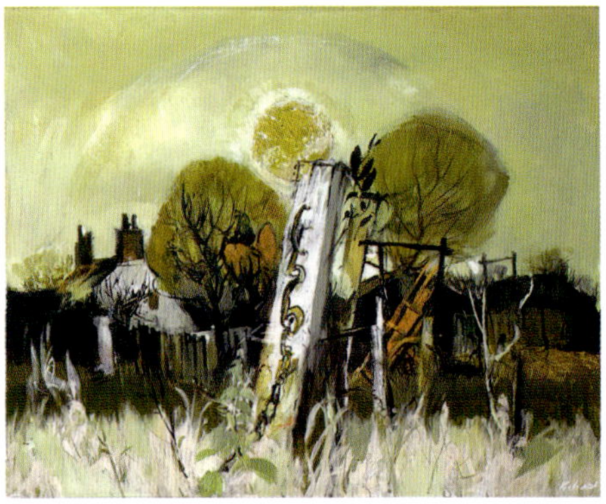

Kibart, James b.1912
Leicestershire Landscape 1970
acrylic on canvas 69.7 x 83.9
0148

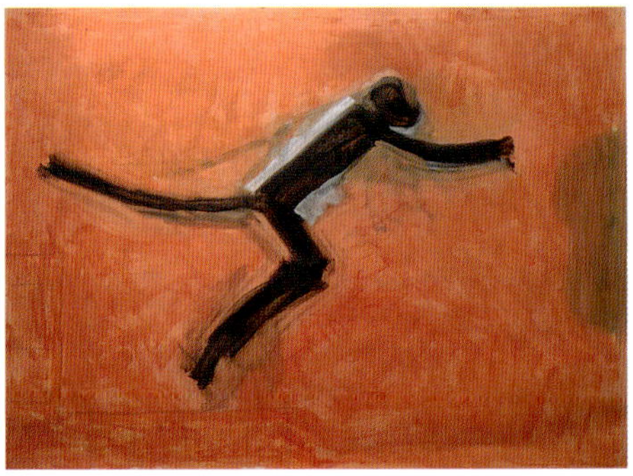

Kinley, Peter 1926–1988
Monkey (study) 1984
oil on paper 79 x 102
0149

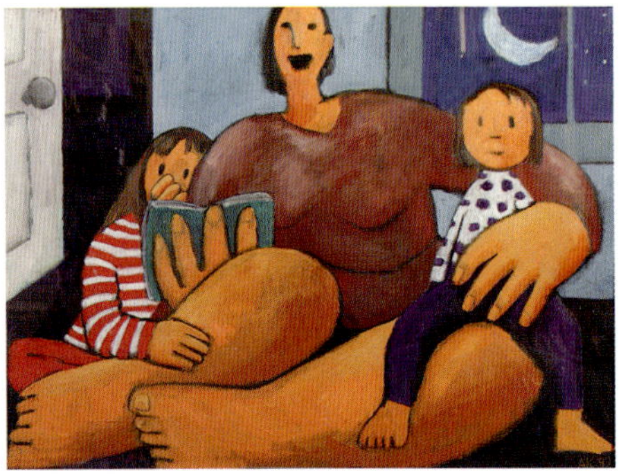

Klein, Anita b.1960
Bedtime Story 1992
oil on board 92 x 122
0642

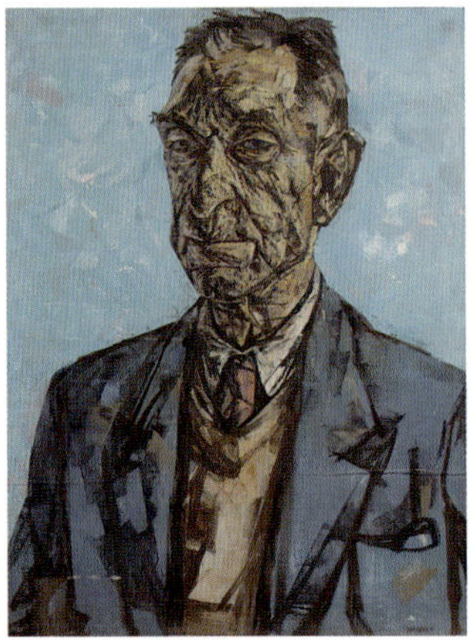

Kneale, Bryan b.1930
Head of a Man 1956
oil on canvas 107 x 82
0151

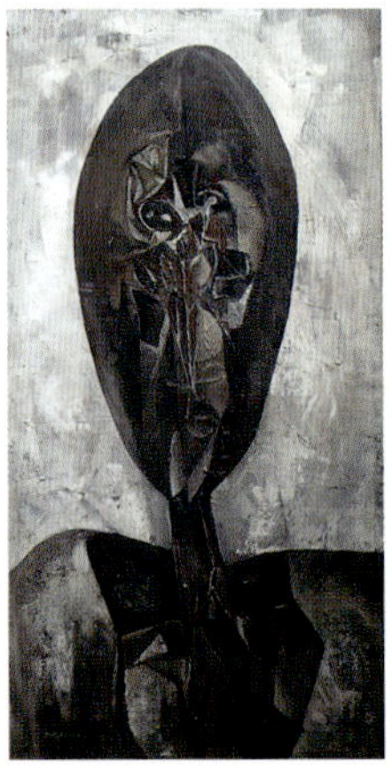

Kneale, Bryan b.1930
Watching Head 1960
oil on board 124.5 x 63.5
0153

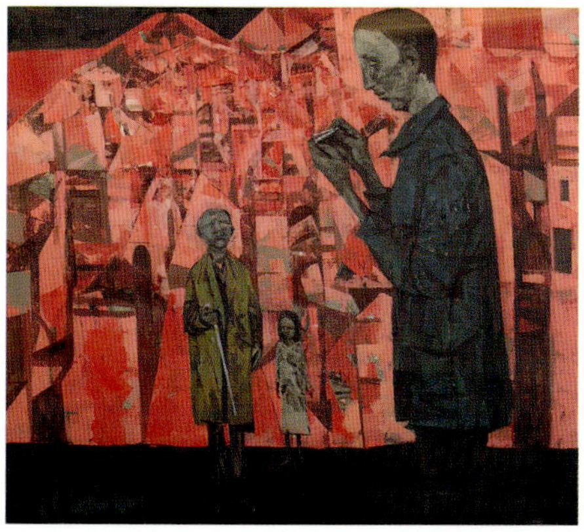

Kneale, Bryan b.1930
Blind Man
oil on canvas 99 x 109.5
0150

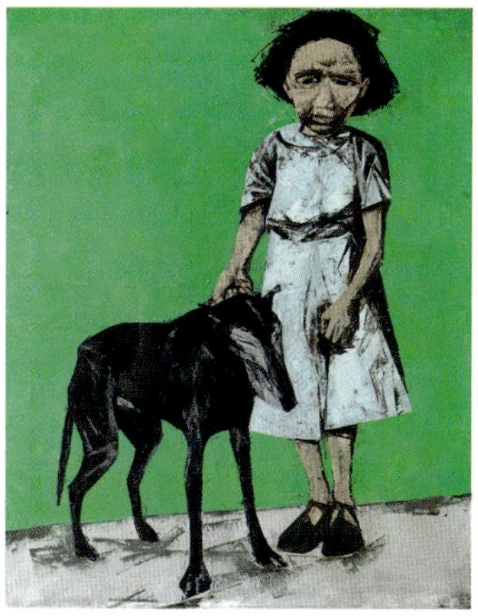

Kneale, Bryan b.1930
Peel Child
oil on canvas 102 x 85
0152

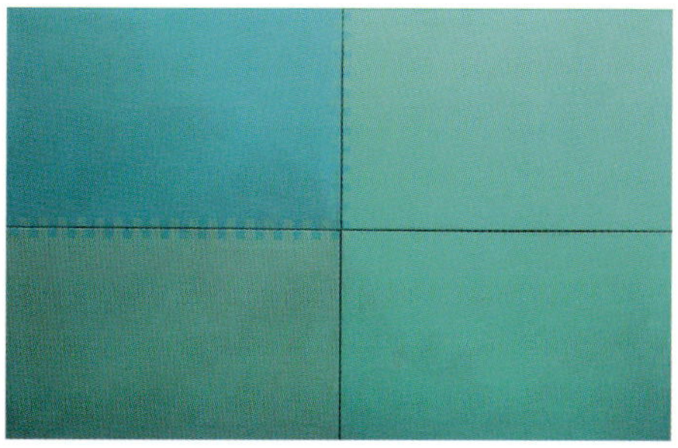

Lancaster, Mark b.1938
Bloomingdale 1965
oil on canvas 124 x 186
0154

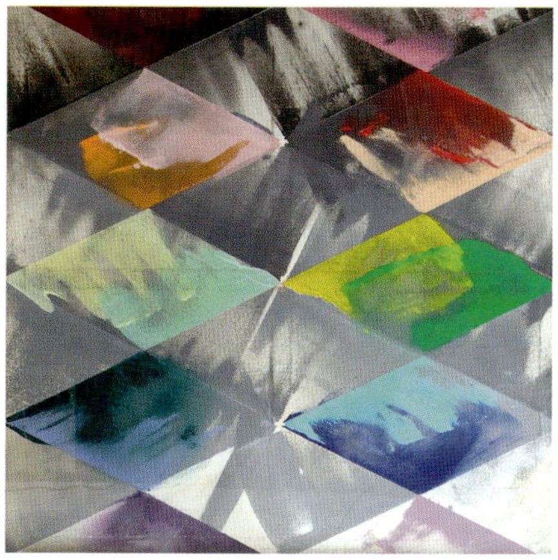

Lancaster, Mark b.1938
King Study II 1970
acrylic on canvas 112.5 x 112.5
0155

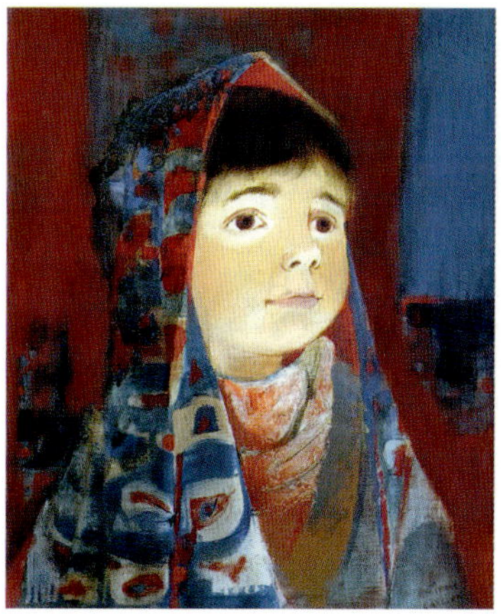

Lavarenne, Pierre b.1928
Head of a Girl 1959
oil on canvas 57.5 x 49.5
0157

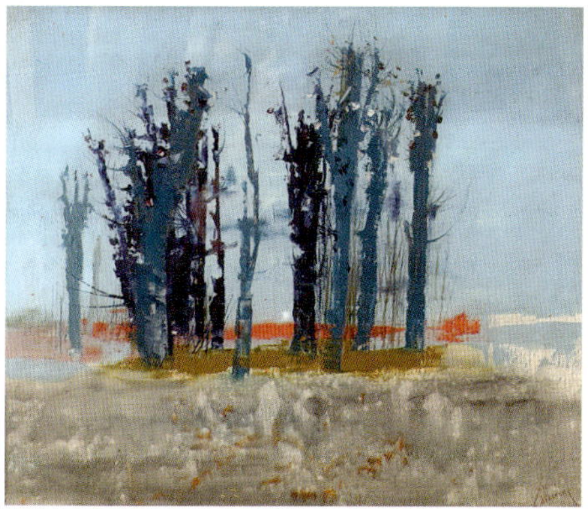

Lavarenne, Pierre b.1928
Arbres bleus 1960
oil on canvas 48.5 x 57.7
0156

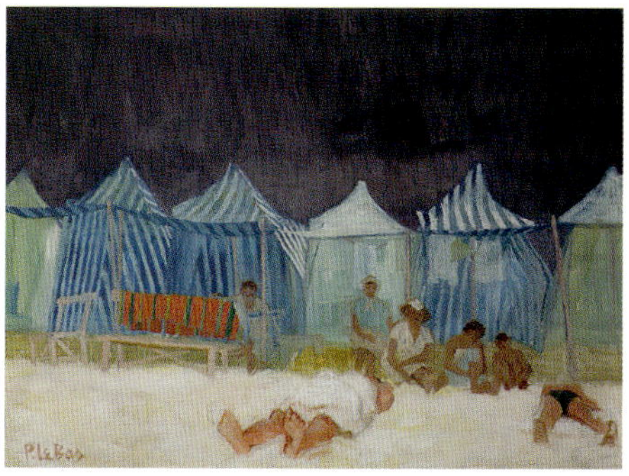

Le Bas, Philip Hubert b.1925
Beach Scene
oil on canvas 79 x 99.5
0688

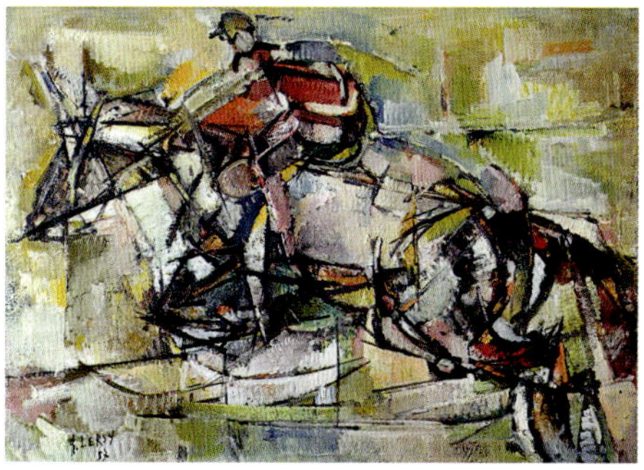

Lersy, Roger b.1920
Concours hippique 1957
oil on canvas 77.5 x 104.5
0158

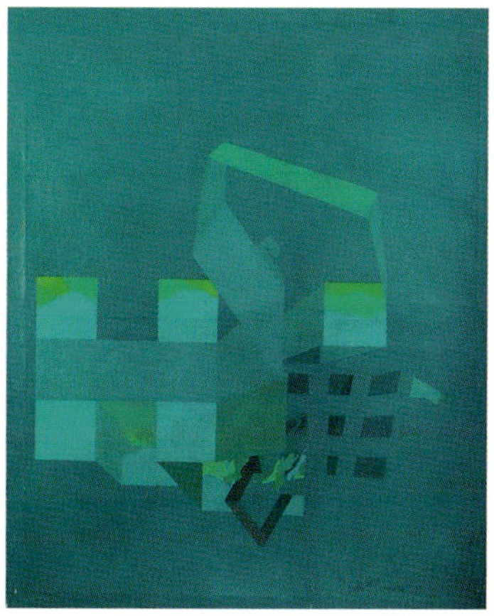

Leverett, David b.1938
Greenfields 1965
acrylic on canvas 152 x 122
0159

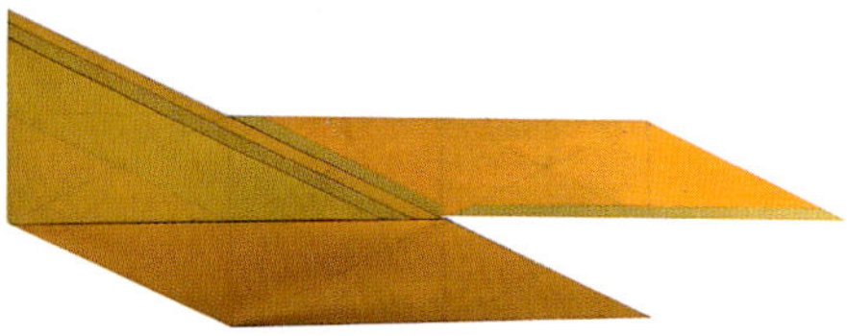

Leverett, David b.1938
Split Shift 1969
acrylic on canvas 43 x 126
0160

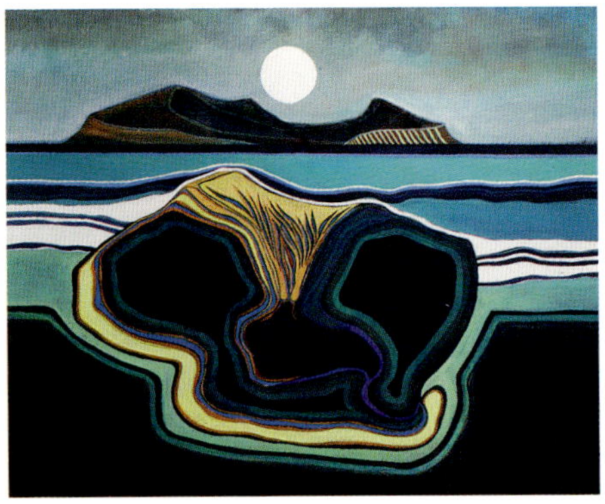

Liddell, Peter b.1954
Galloway 1972
oil on canvas 78 x 93
0162

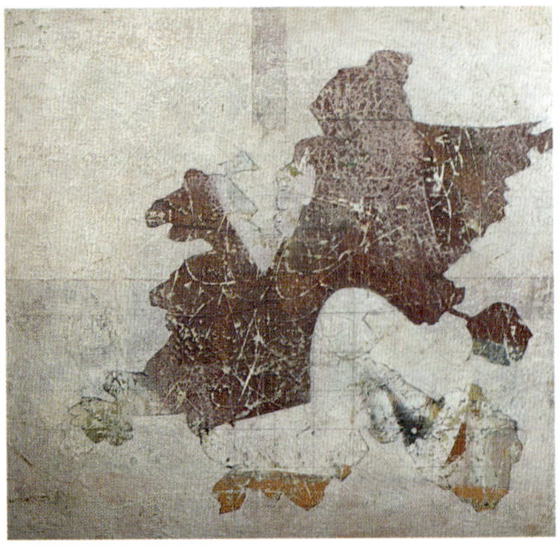

Lurlinski, David
Hanoko
acrylic, primer paint & pencil on board
70.5 x 76
0163

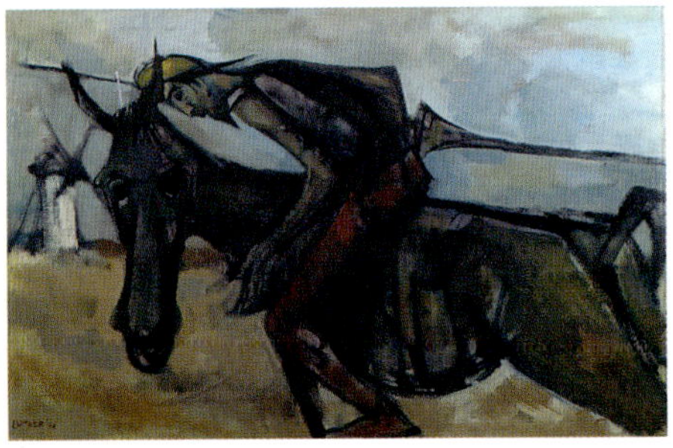

Luther, Peter b.1926
Don Quixote Number 2 1964
oil on canvas 49 x 69
0165

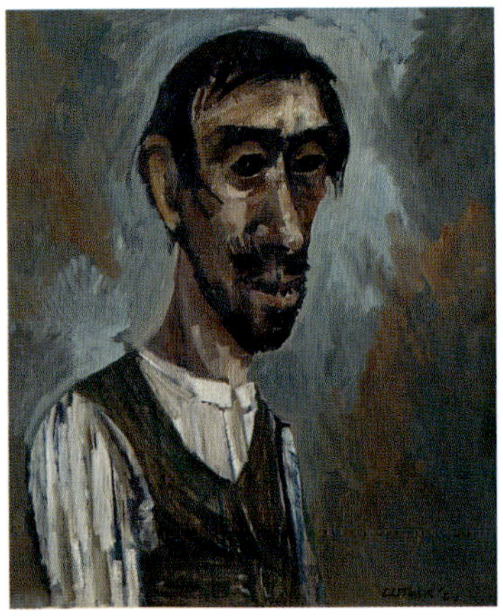

Luther, Peter b.1926
French Farm Hand 1964
oil on board 74.5 x 64.5
0166

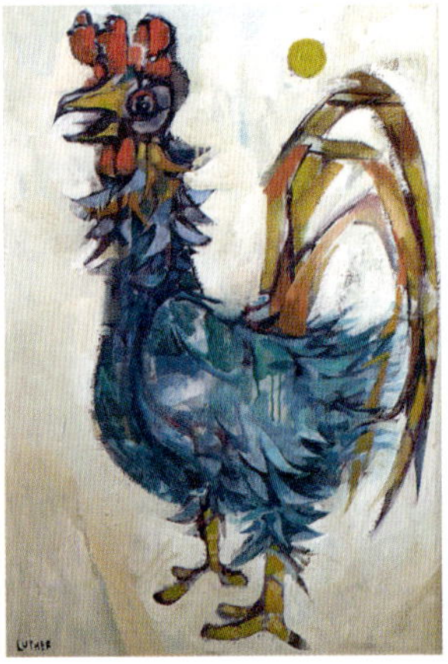

Luther, Peter b.1926
The Cockerel 1970
oil on board 100.5 x 70
0164

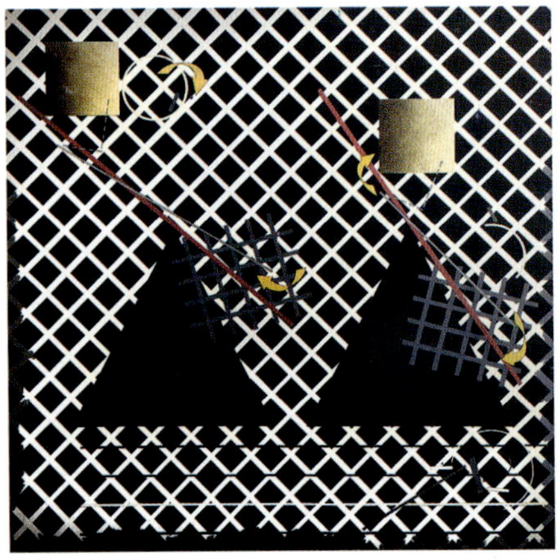

Lyons, Peter active 1970–1972
Spacemaker II 1972
acrylic on canvas 122 x 122
0167

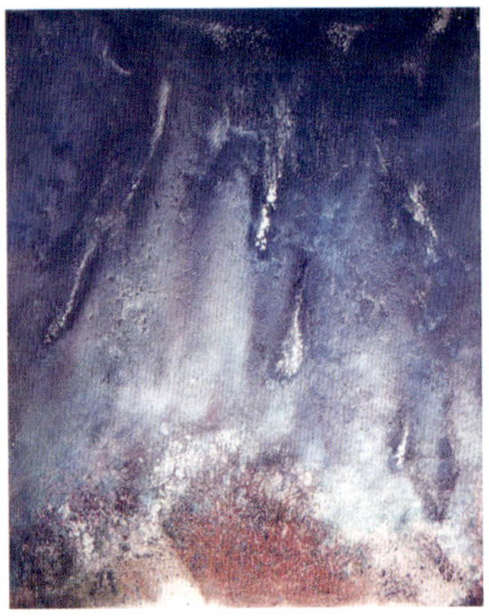

MacBeth, Lorna Barbara b.1948
Apocalypse
oil on canvas 215 x 170
793

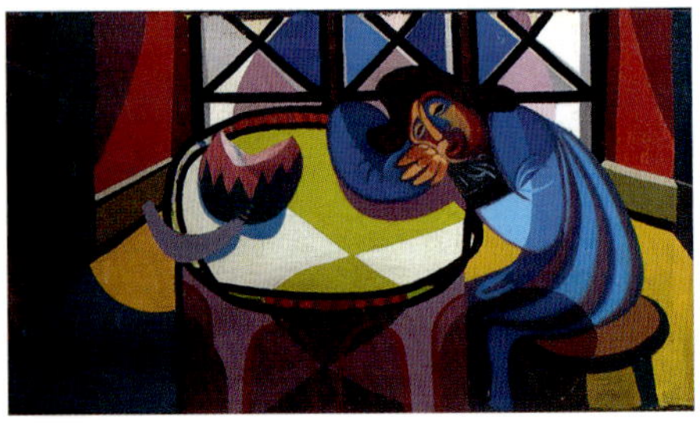

MacBryde, Robert 1913–1966
Man with a Melon 1952
acrylic on canvas 102 x 155
0168

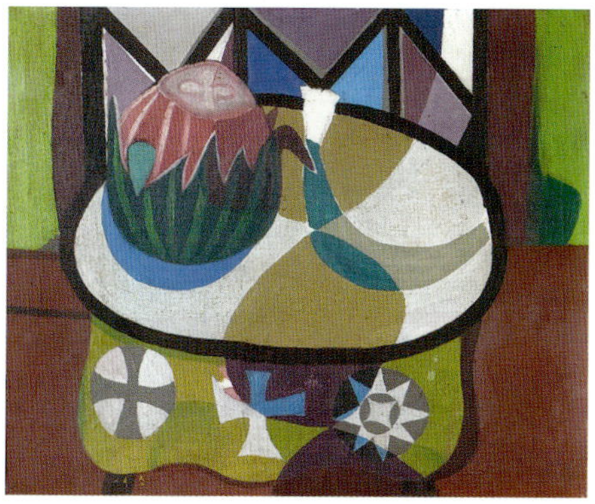

MacBryde, Robert 1913–1966
Melon on a Table 1953
acrylic on canvas 54.5 x 64.5
0169

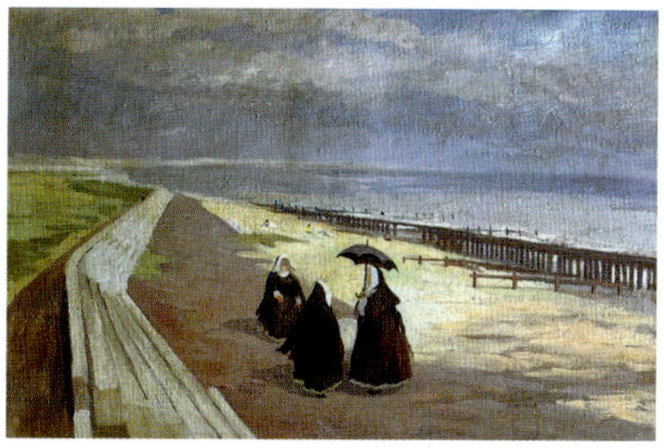

Manchester, George 1922–1996
Nuns on the Beach (recto) 1954
oil on canvas 56 x 76
0728A

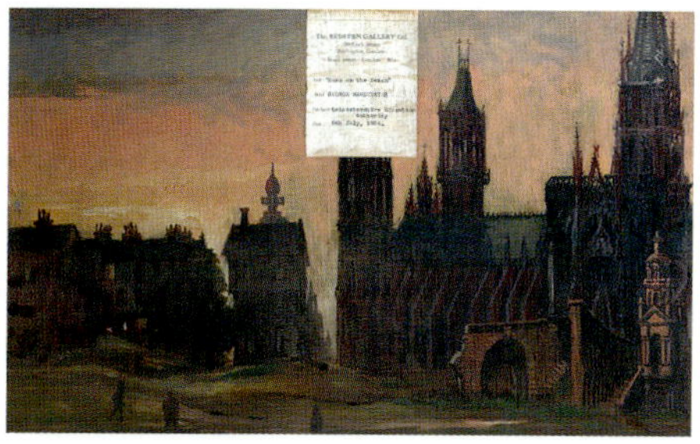

Manchester, George 1922–1996
*City View** (verso)
oil on canvas 56 x 76 (E)
0728B

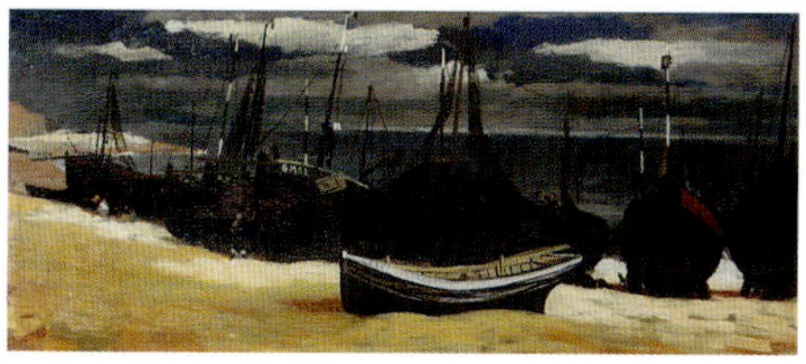

Manchester, George 1922–1996
Black Boats
oil on board 32 x 72
0917

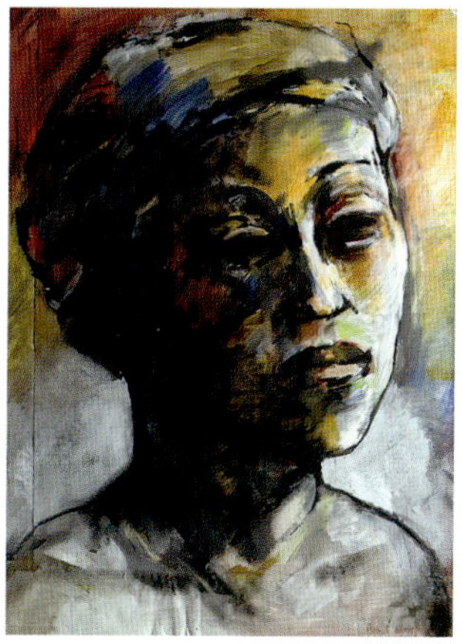

Martin, Patrick b.1958
Woman's Head 1991
oil & distemper on paper 105 x 75
0172

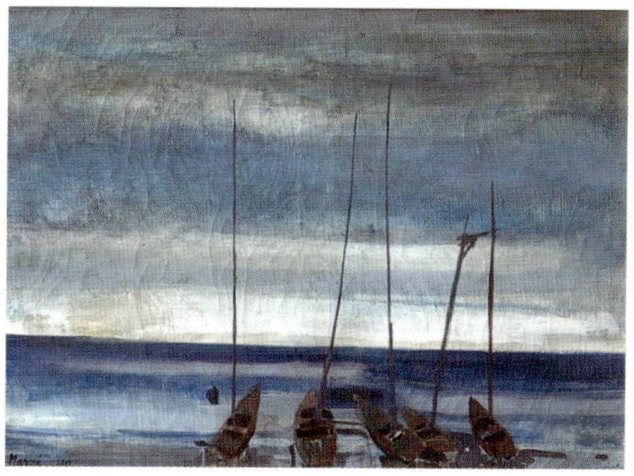

Marzé, Émile b.1930
Boats by the Mediterranean 1959
oil on canvas 67 x 86
0173

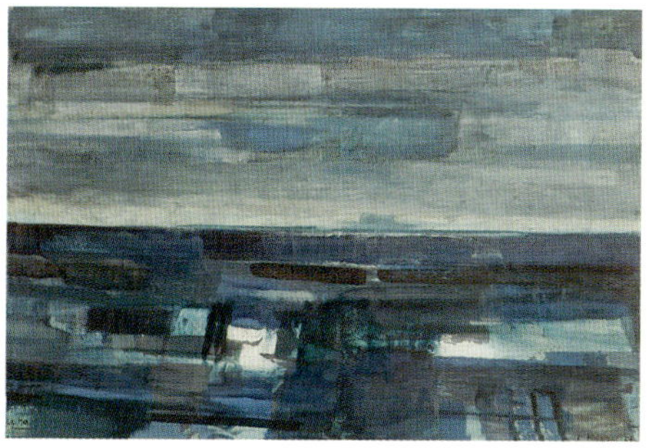

Marzé, Émile b.1930
La mer 1959
oil on canvas 51.5 x 74
0174

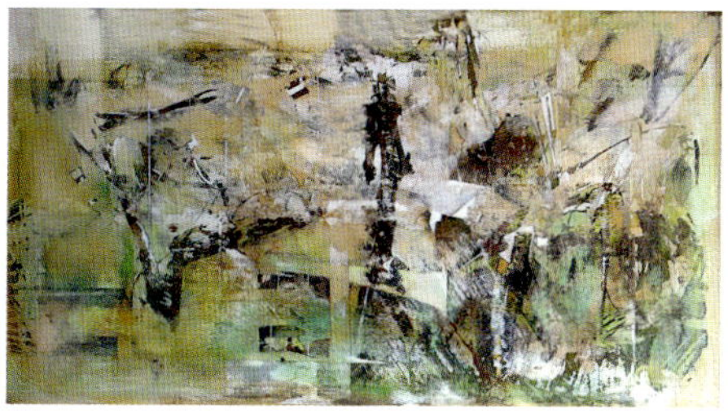

Mason, Robert b.1946
From Oumach 1977
acrylic & rhoplex on paper 82.5 x 140.5
0175

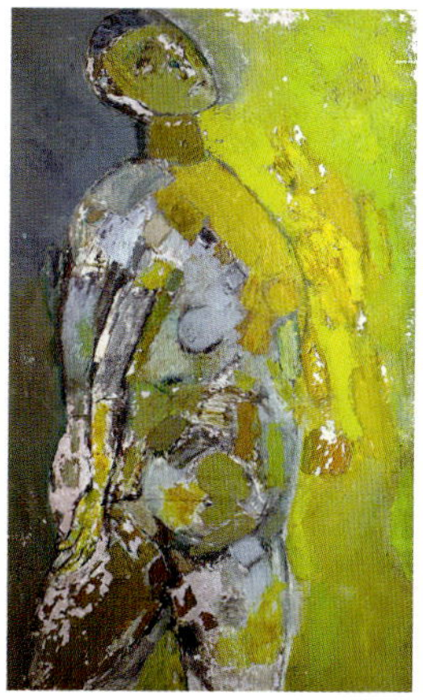

Mehta, Tyeb 1925–2009
The Fall 1962
oil on board 152 x 91
0796

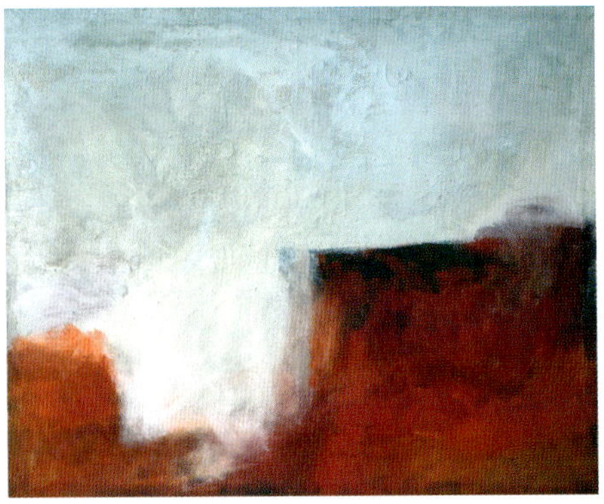

Messenger, Tony 1936–2001
Composition 1963
oil on canvas 154 x 182.5
0177

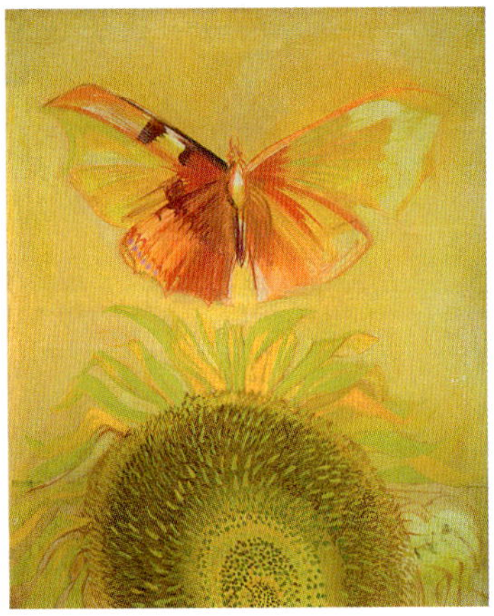

Middleditch, Edward 1923–1987
Butterfly and Sunflower 1958
oil on canvas 130 x 105
0178

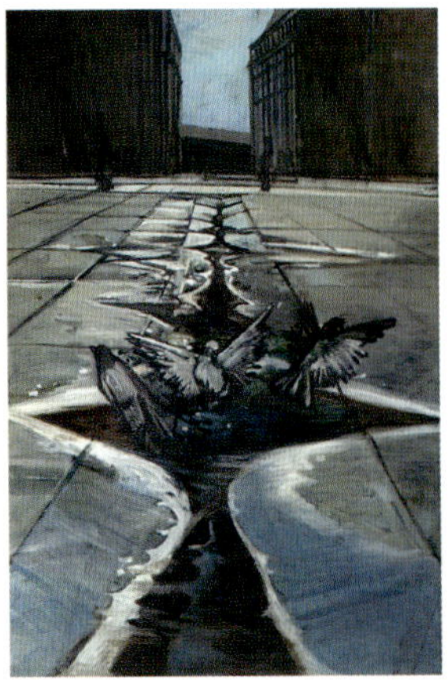

Middleditch, Edward 1923–1987
Pigeons in Trafalgar Square 1958
oil on canvas 200 x 140
0797

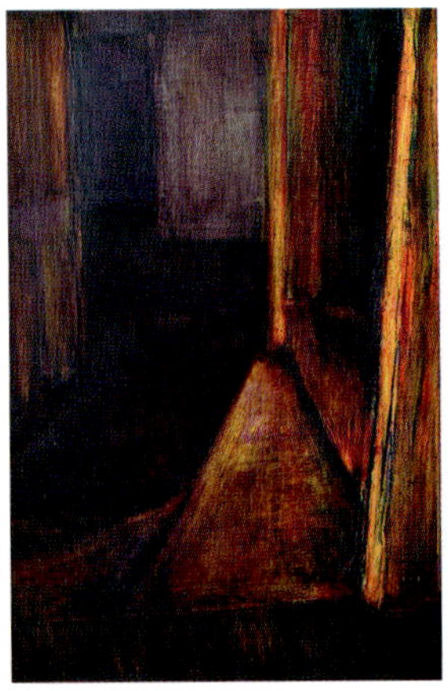

Miller, Elaine
Staircase 2008
gloss paint on board 61 x 43
0998

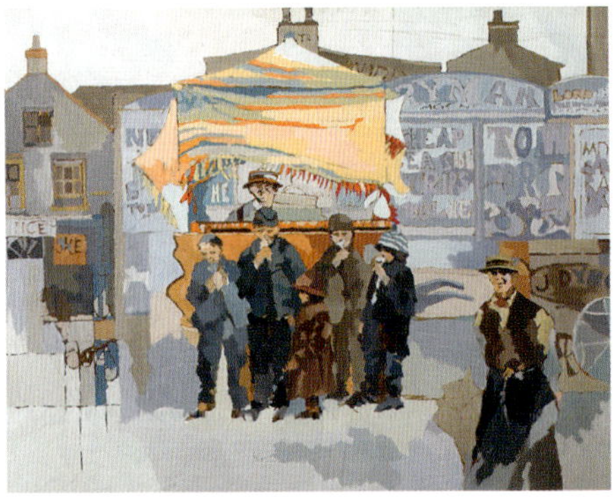

Miller, Peter active 1970–1989
Hokey Pokey Man 1971
oil on canvas 53.5 x 64
0180

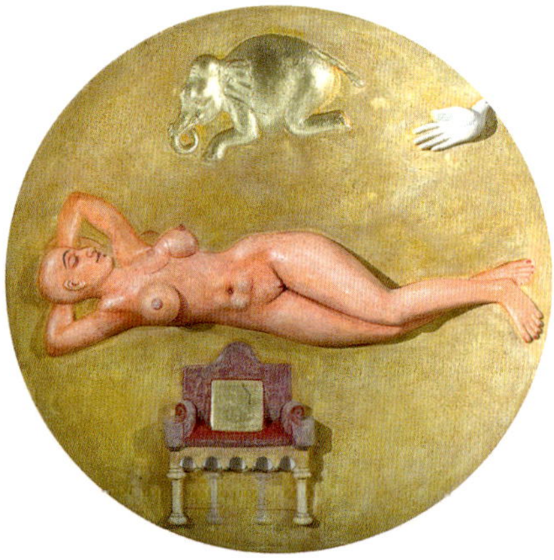

Mistry, Dhruva b.1957
Maya Medallion 1987
acrylic on plaster 116
0799

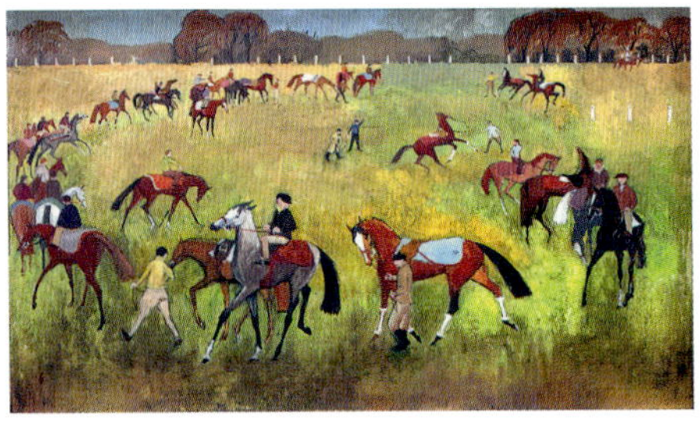

Moddy, Coleen
Morning Exercises
oil on board 52 x 90
0710

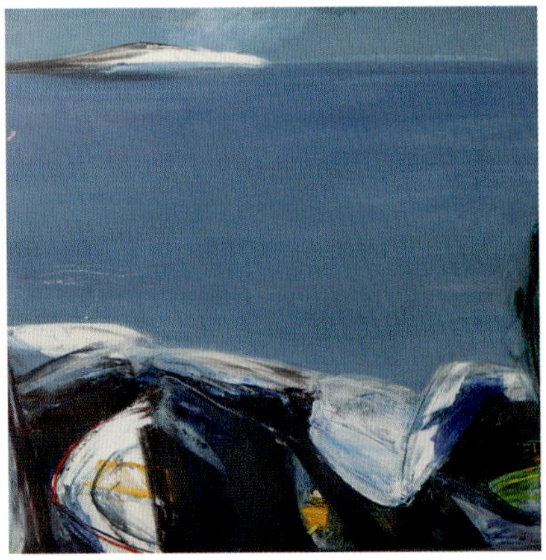

Murison, Neil b.1930
South Coast Blue 1986
oil on canvas 97 x 96.5
0184

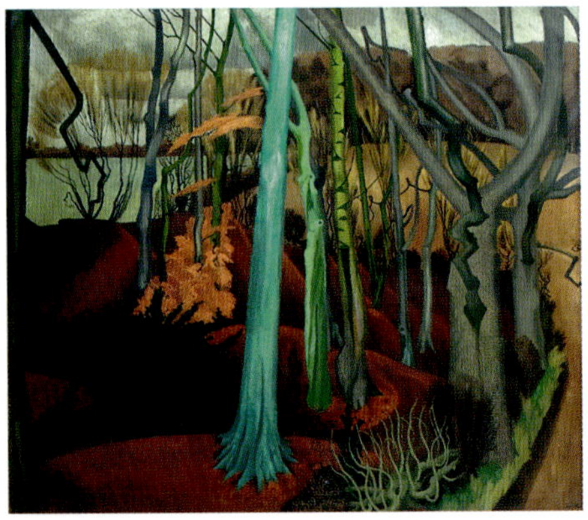

Nash, John Northcote 1893–1977
The Dingle Winter 1949
oil on board 107.5 x 120.5
0187

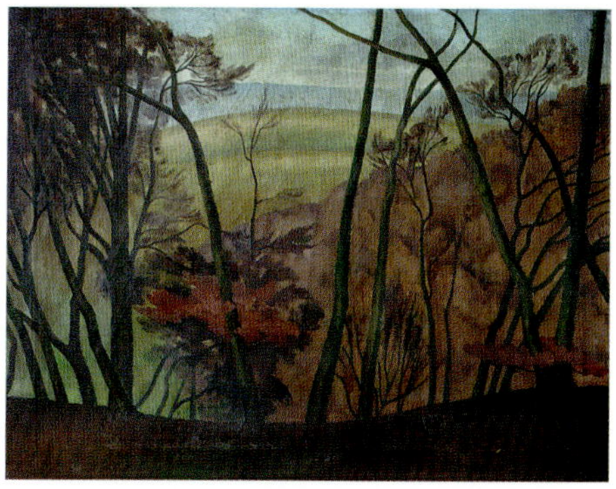

Nash, John Northcote 1893–1977
Autumn Berkshire 1951
oil on canvas 68.5 x 84
0186

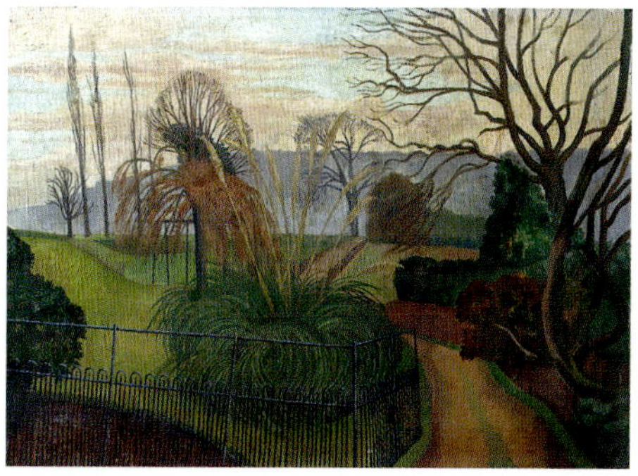

Nash, John Northcote 1893–1977
The Garden 1951
oil on canvas 58.7 x 79
0185

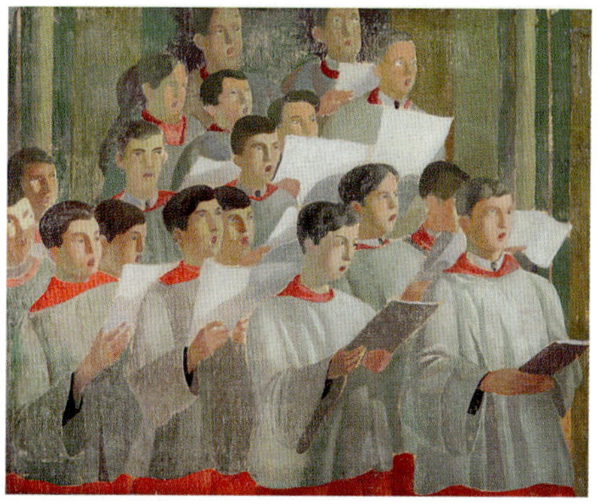

Nash, Thomas Saunders 1891–1968
Choristers 1951
oil on board 55 x 63
0920

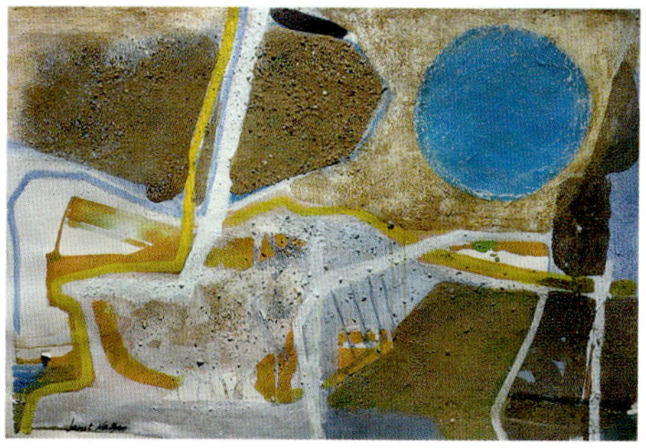

Nathan, Janet b.1938
Ionian Sound 1986
acrylic on paper 82 x 115
0189

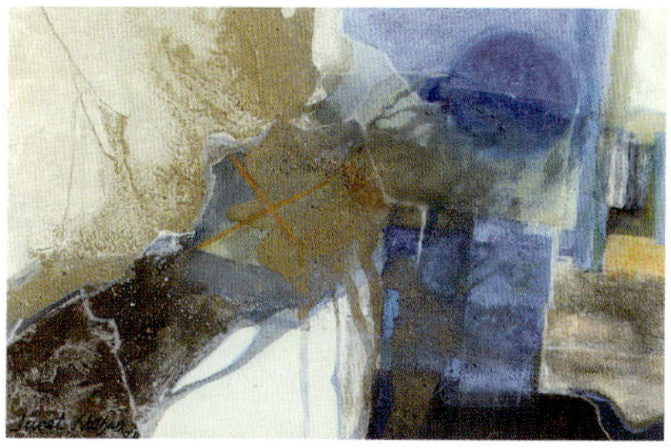

Nathan, Janet b.1938
Off-Shore Sound 1987
acrylic, gouache & sand on paper 72 x 104
0188

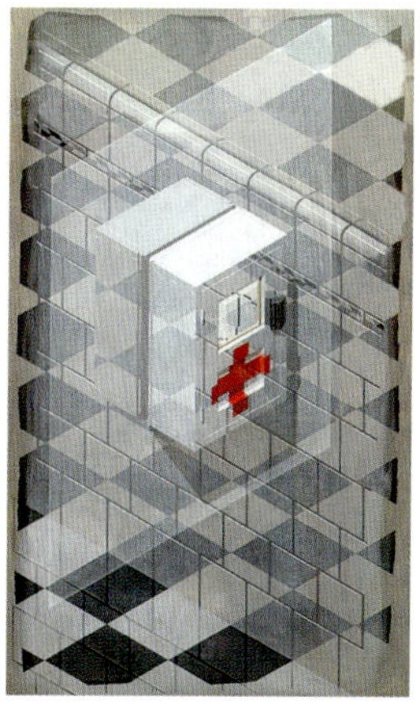

Newsome, Victor b.1935
Medicine Chest 1975
acrylic on wood 111.5 x 71.5
0191

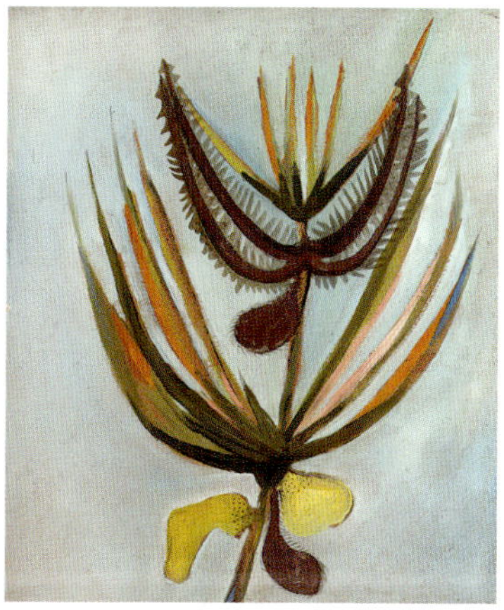

Nolan, Sidney 1917–1992
Blackboy Flower 1948
oil on board 77.5 x 65
0195

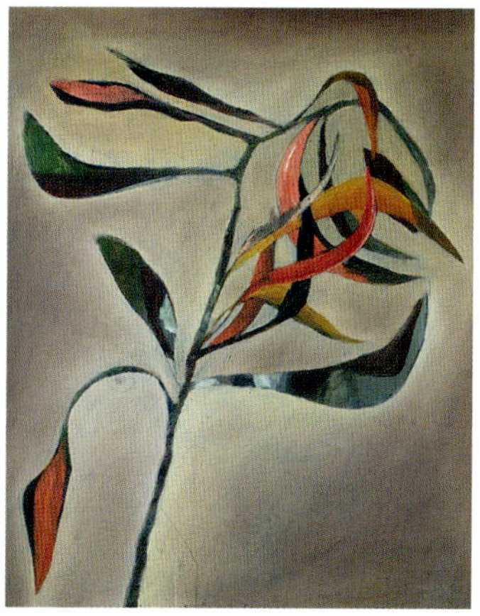

Nolan, Sidney 1917–1992
Australian Foliage 1954
oil on board 77.5 x 62.5
0192

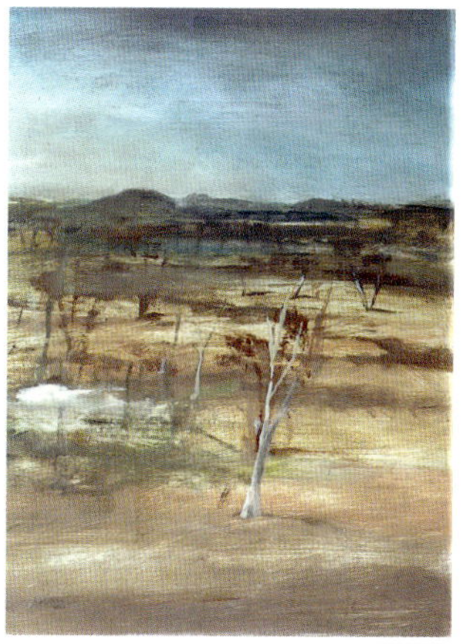

Nolan, Sidney 1917–1992
Australian Landscape 1954
oil on board 61.8 x 44.5
0194

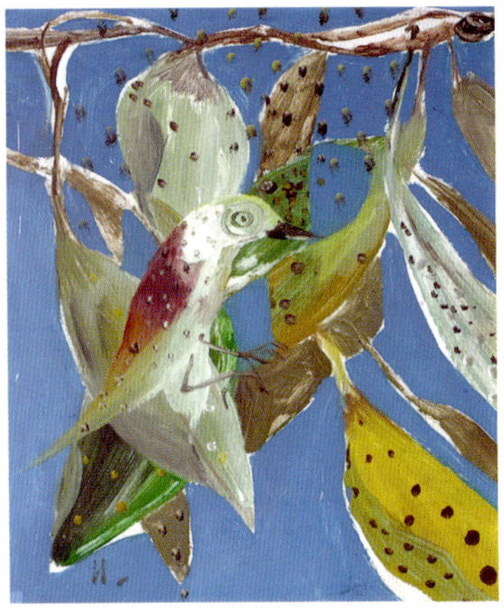

Nolan, Sidney 1917–1992
Australian Honeyeater
oil on board 74 x 64.5
0193

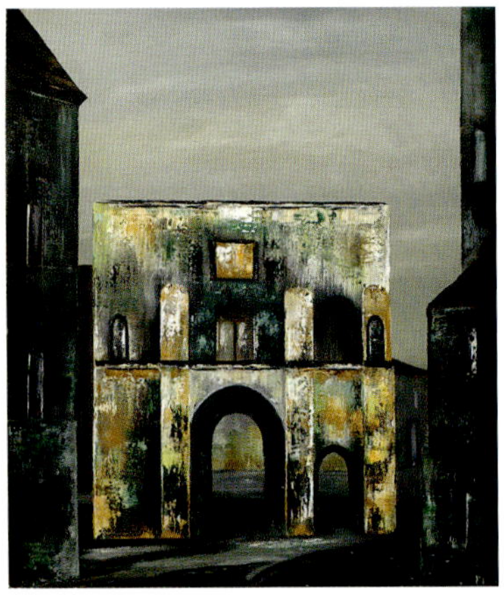

Norton, Margaret
West Gate, Winchester, Hampshire 1968
oil on canvas 60.2 x 50.5
0196

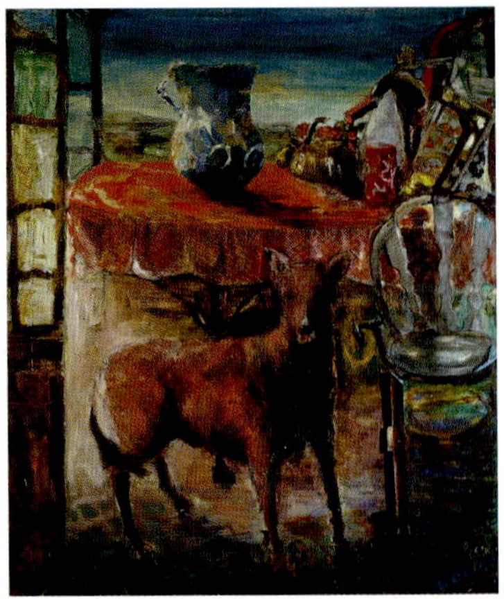

O'Brien, Kevin b.1956
Circus Animals' Desertion 1983
oil on canvas 197.5 x 162
0197

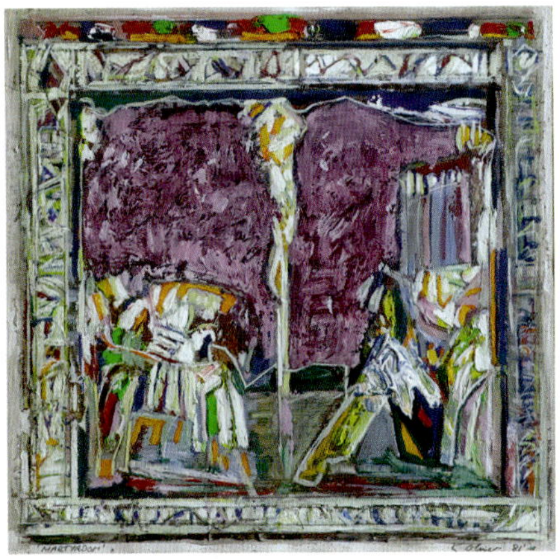

Oliver, Ken b.1948
Martyrdom 1981
acrylic on paper 43.5 x 43.5
0198

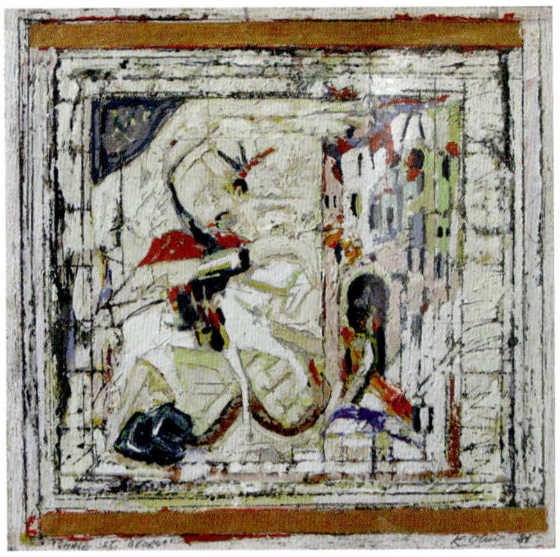

Oliver, Ken b.1948
Small Saint George
acrylic & mixed media on paper 43.5 x 44
0199

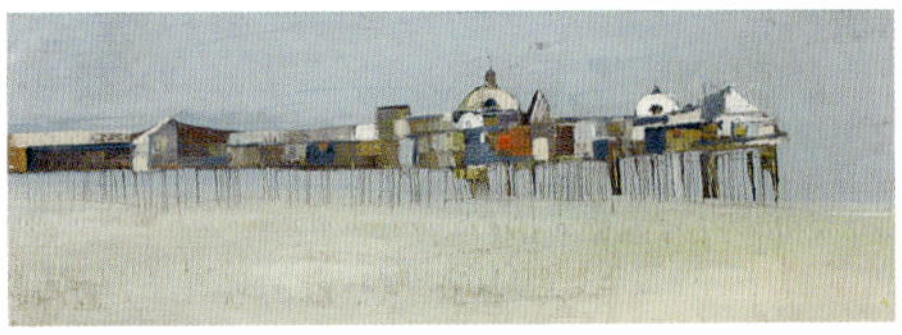

Oliver, Peter 1927–2006
Winter Pier
oil on board 58.5 x 134.5
0200

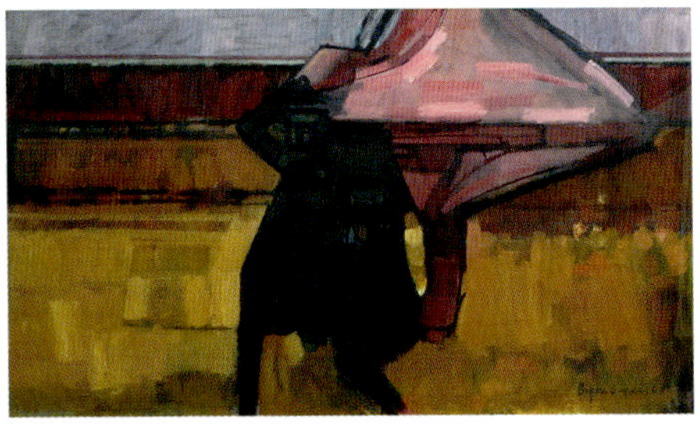

Organ, Bryan b.1935
Number 3 Composition 1962
oil on canvas 98 x 147
0201

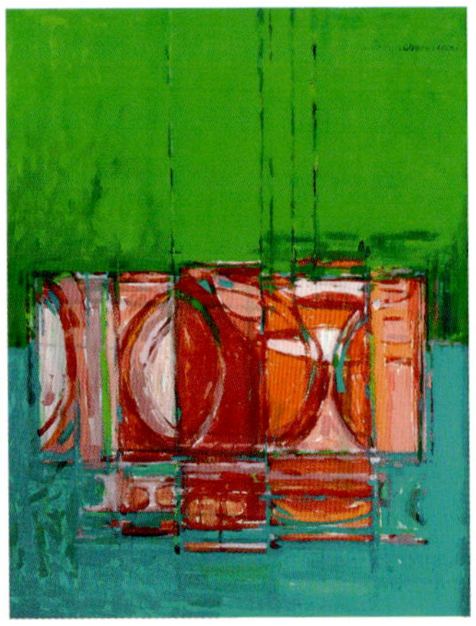

Organ, Bryan b.1935
Pendulum Number 3 1965
oil on board 94.5 x 75.5
0202

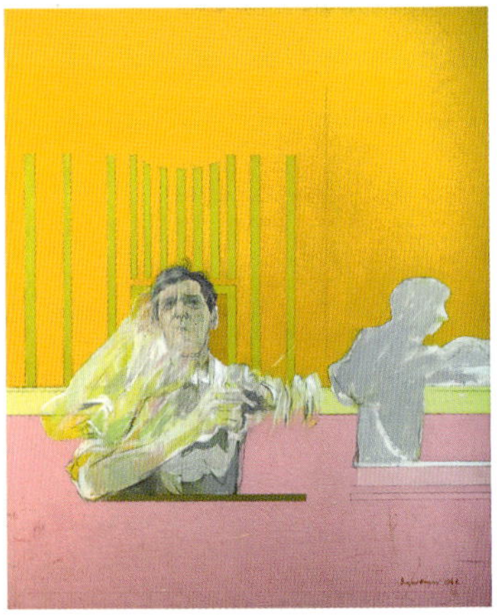

Organ, Bryan b.1935
Tippett at De Montfort Hall 1966
oil on canvas 152 x 121
0805

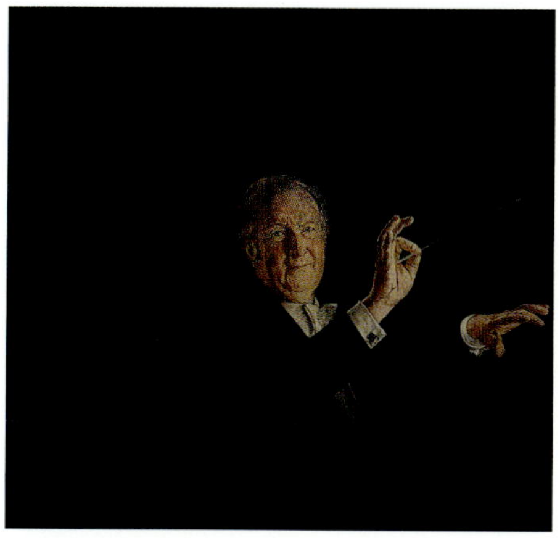

Organ, Bryan b.1935
Eric Pinkett (1911–1979) 1978
oil on canvas 147.3 x 147.3
0804

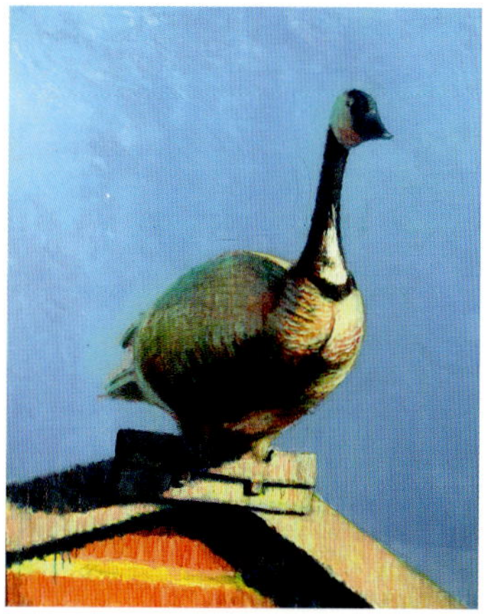

Ormond, Tom b.1974
Garden Folly (Goose) 1995
oil on canvas 150 x 120
0829

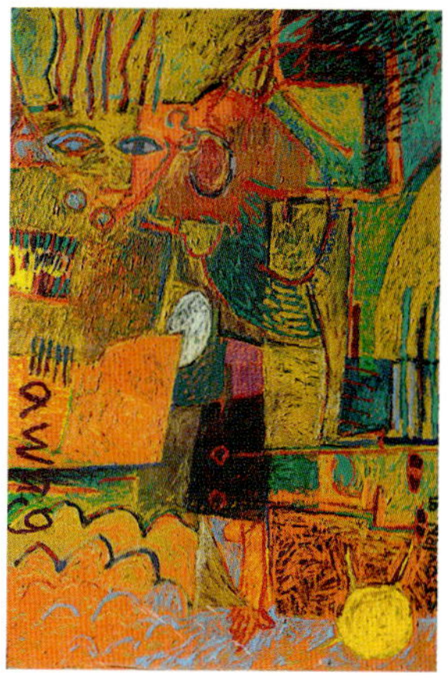

Owen, Sally
Figure in a Frame No.1 1990
oil on board 93 x 62
0203

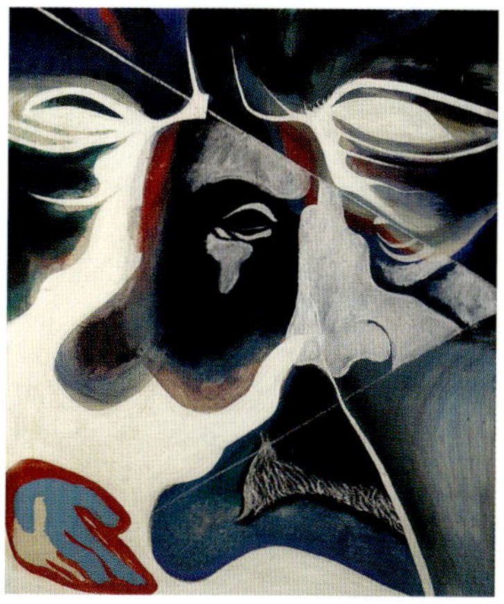

Oxtoby, David Jowett Greaves b.1938
Ecclusiastics 1964
oil on canvas 84.5 x 72
0204

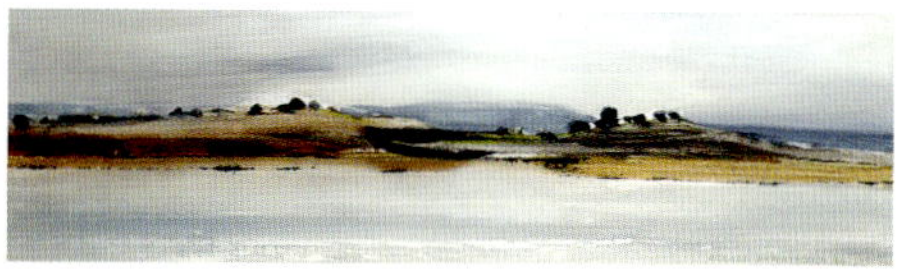

Parkinson, Gerald b.1926
Brittany Landscape III 1969
oil on board 38.5 x 89.5
0206

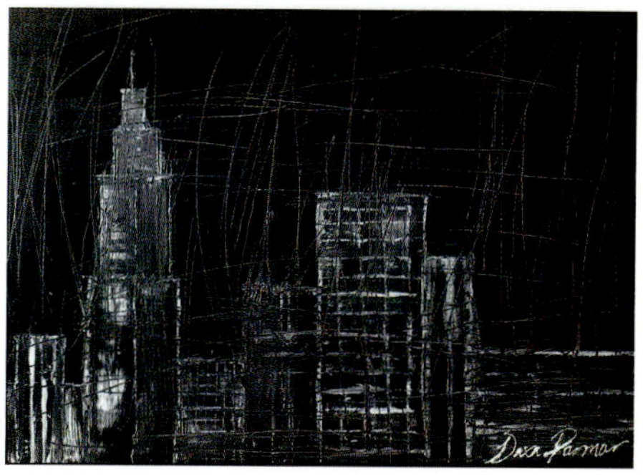

Parmar, Daxa b.1972
Cityscape
oil on canvas 56 x 76
0999

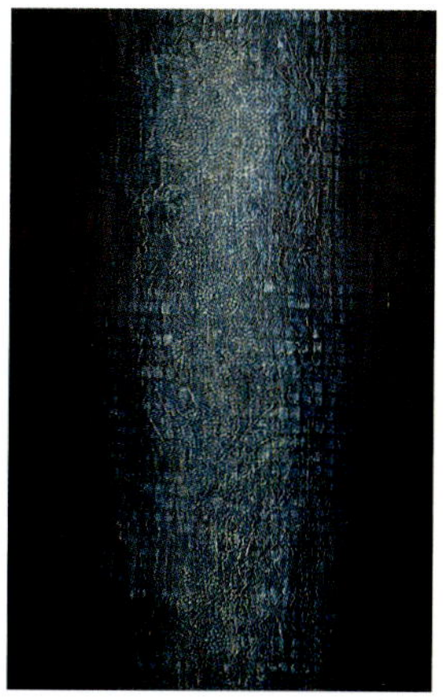

Partridge, David 1919–2006
Mesozoic No.1 1967
oil on board 169 x 109
0207

Partridge, Susan
Disappear
oil on board 40.5 x 40.5
0899

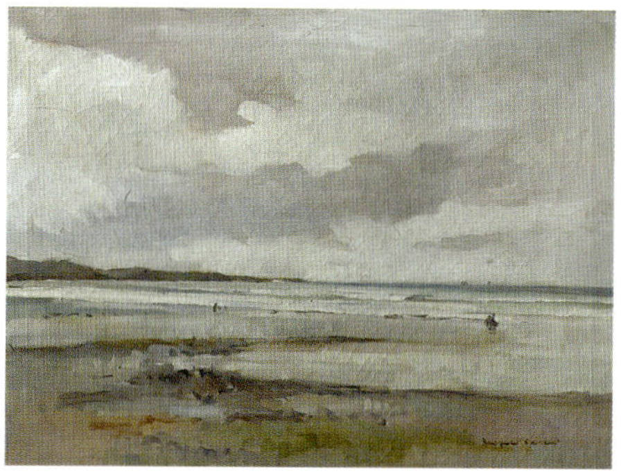

Pascal, Léopold 1900–1957
Brittany Beach Scene, France 1956
oil on canvas 61.7 x 77.3
0208

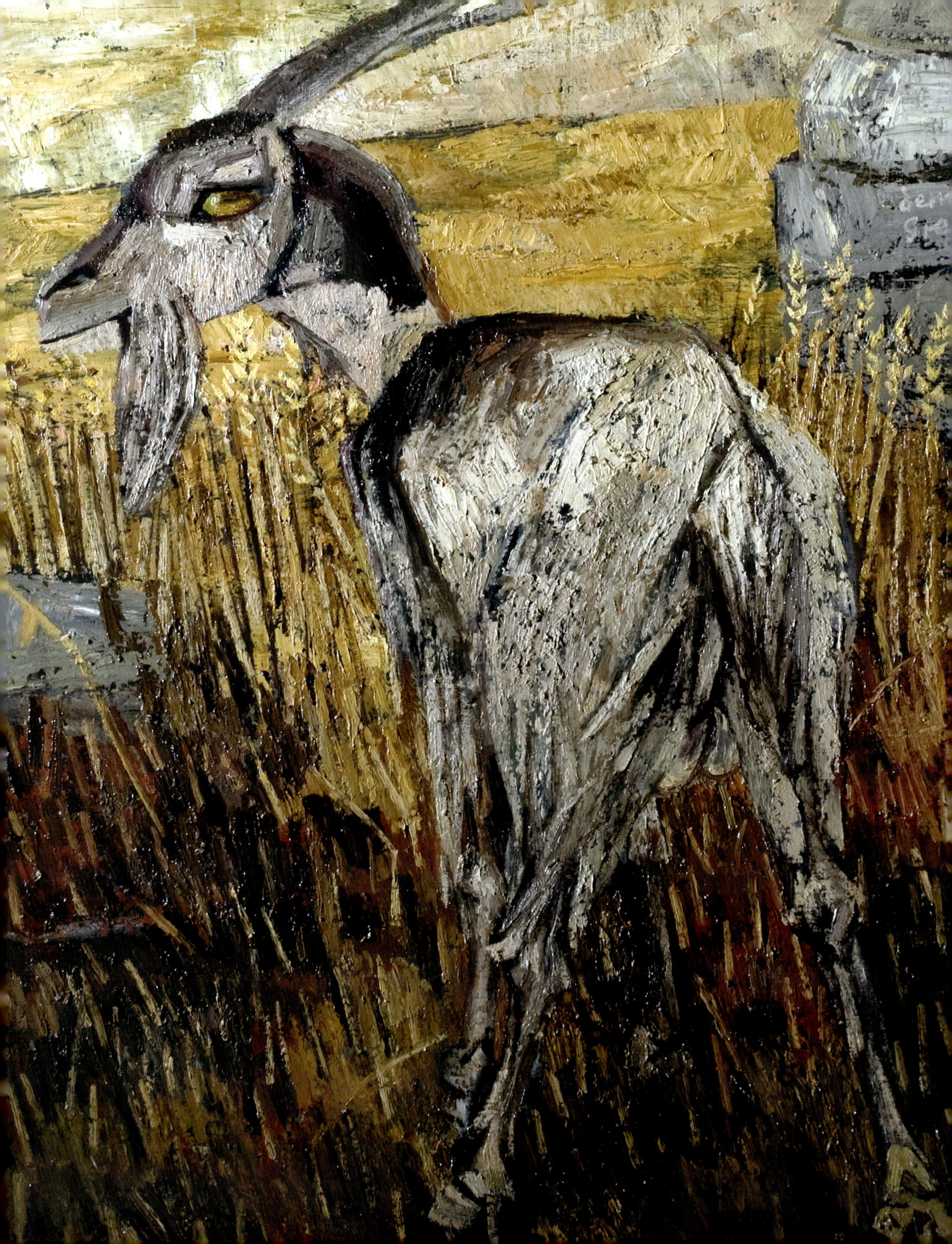

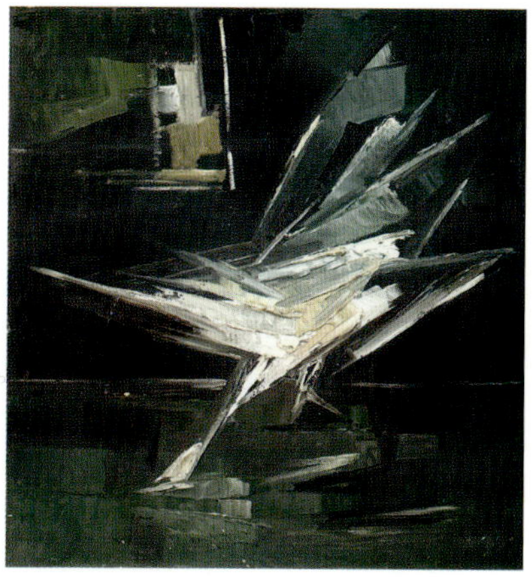

Pass, David
Swan Alighting
oil on canvas 62 x 57
0209

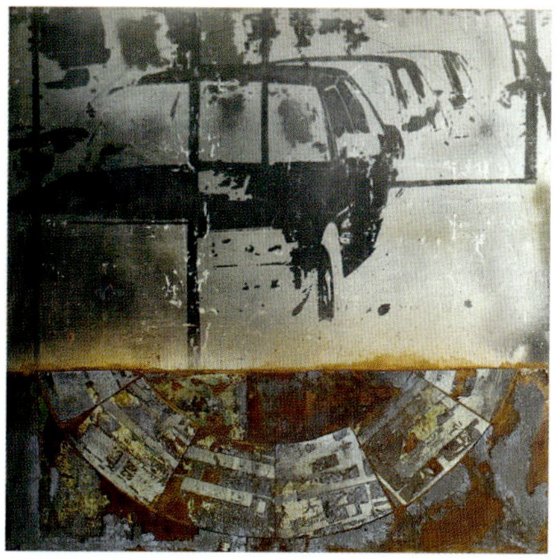

Paterson, Guy
Breakers 1990
oil & concrete on canvas 144 x 144
0211

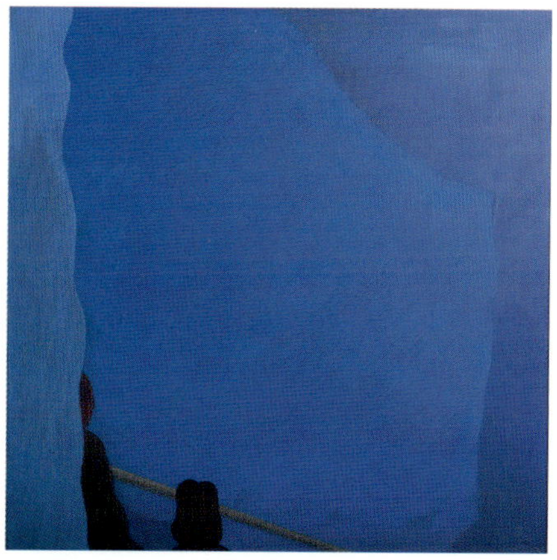

Peacock, Brian 1935–2004
Hotel Balcony 1967
oil on canvas 76 x 76
0212

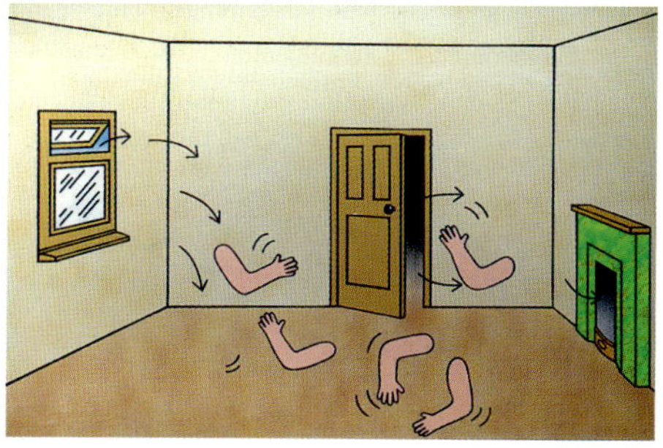

Pearson, John
Untitled 1973
oil on canvas 109 x 154
0213

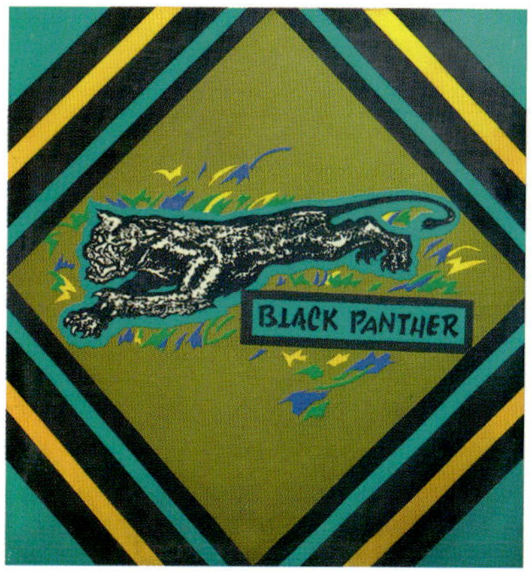

Phillips, Peter b.1939
Black Panther 1963
oil on canvas 111 x 103.5
0214

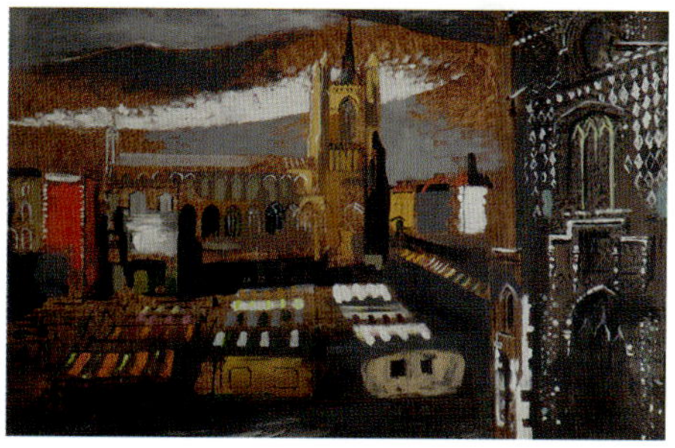

Piper, John 1903–1992
Norwich Market, Norfolk 1952
oil on canvas 70 x 96
0216

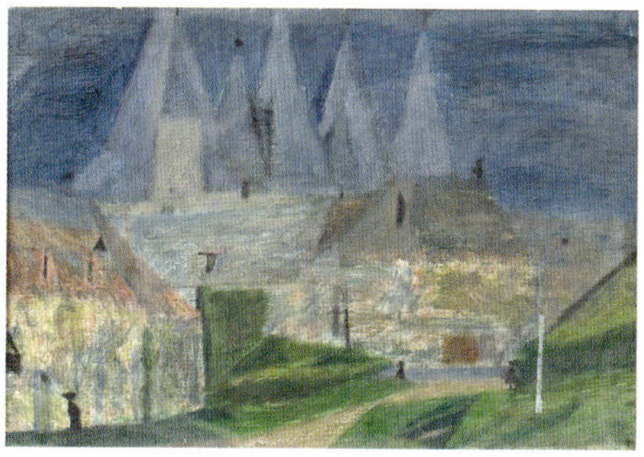

Potworowski, Peter 1898–1962
Château de Jumilhac-le-Grand, France
oil on board 51.5 x 66
0221

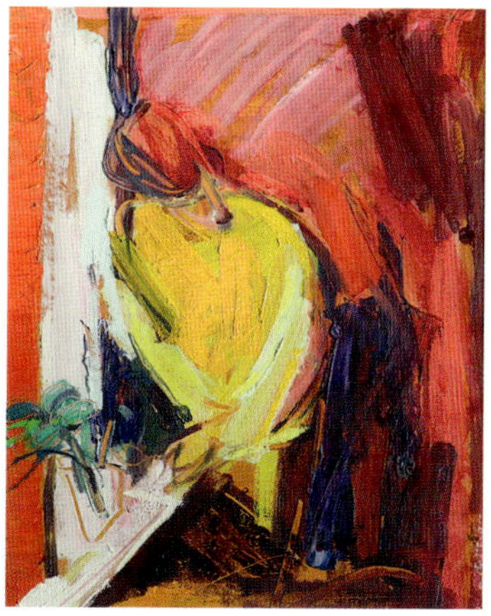

Price, Rebecca b.1966
Sunshine 1989
oil on paper 54 x 43.7
0222

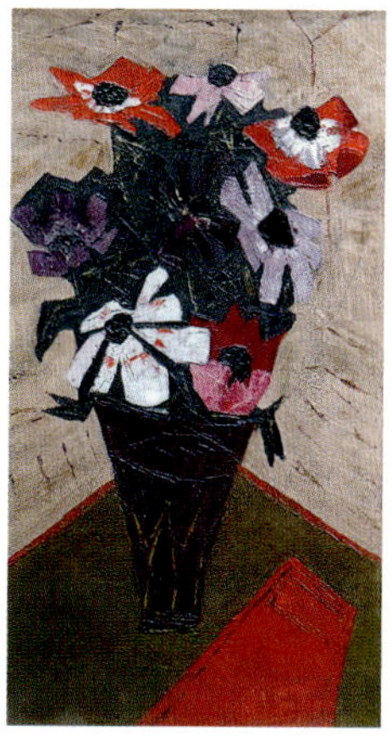

Procktor, Patrick 1936–2003
Anemones: The Last Day 1959
oil on board 80 x 49.5
0223

Facing page: Greaves, Derrick, b.1927, *Goat* (detail), 1956, Leicestershire County Council Artworks Collection (p. 120)

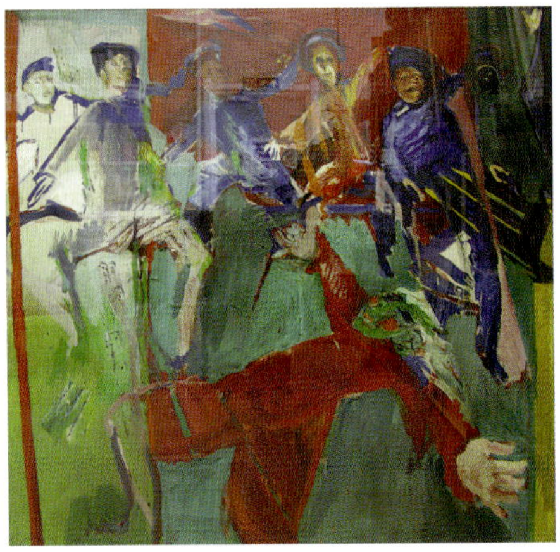

Procktor, Patrick 1936–2003
Red Army Ensemble 1963
oil on canvas 122.5 x 122.5
0224

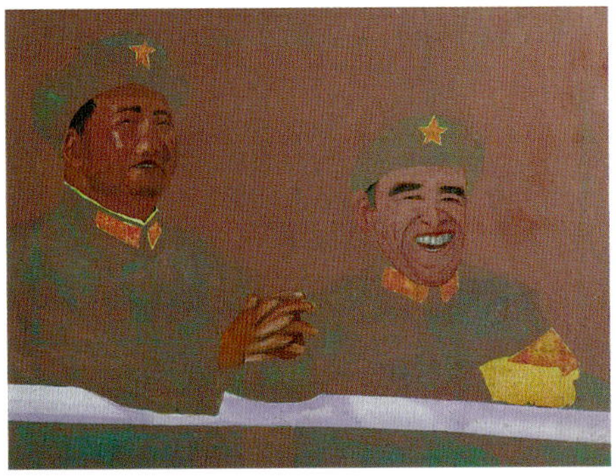

Procktor, Patrick 1936–2003
Two Chinese Generals 1968
oil on canvas 36.3 x 46.3
0225

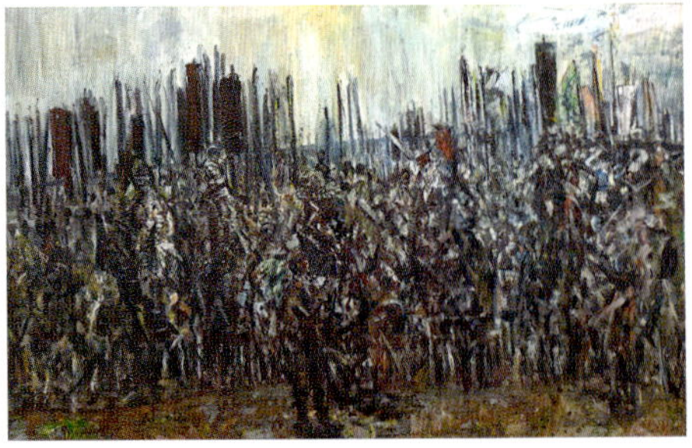

Reason, Cyril b.1931
Cavalry 1959
oil on board 127 x 188
0226

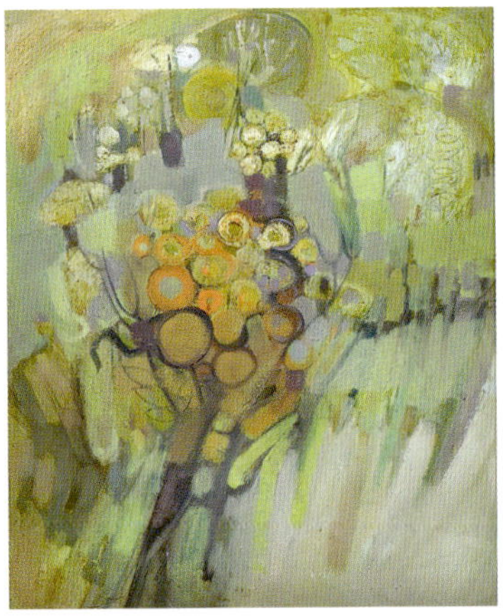

Reiman, Maarja
Summertime 1960
oil on board 77.5 x 62
0227

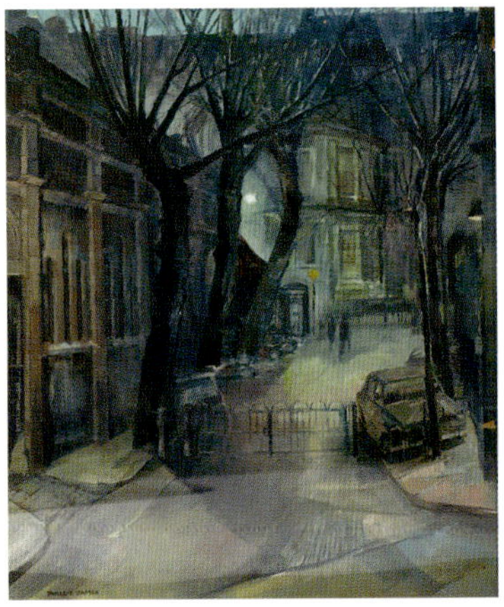

Reynette James, Phyllis May 1911–1973
New Walk at Night, Leicester
oil on canvas 87 x 72.5
0135

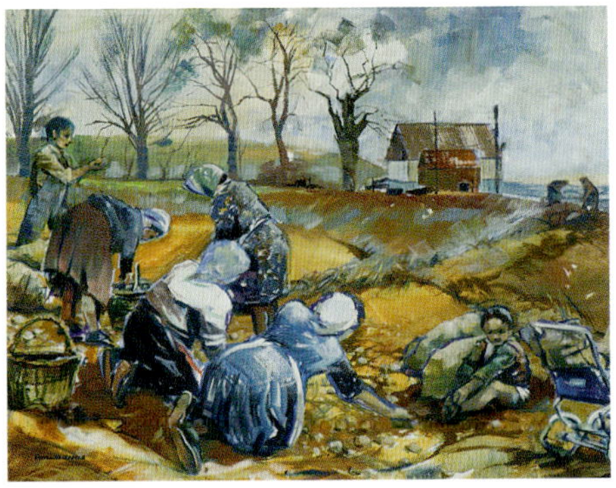

Reynette James, Phyllis May 1911–1973
Potato Pickers near Melton, Leicestershire
oil on canvas 63.5 x 78
0134

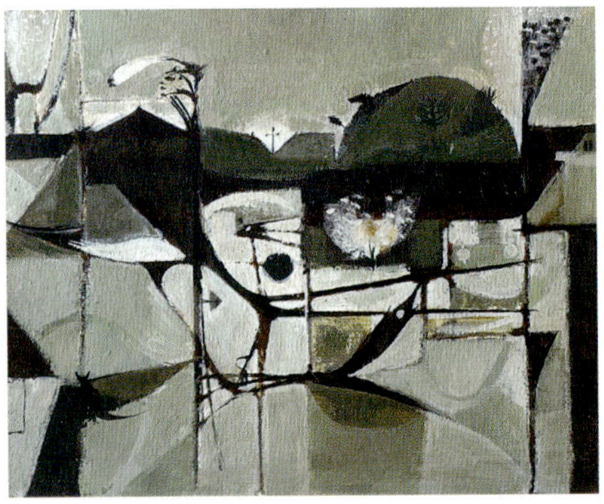

Reynolds, Alan b.1926
Moth Barn Interior 1952
oil on board 42 x 51
0231

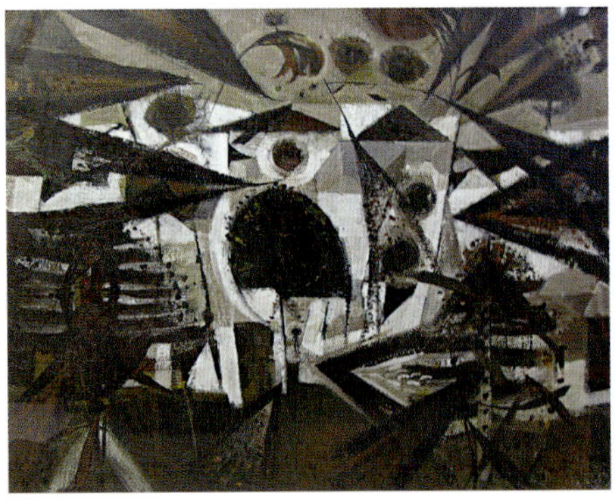

Reynolds, Alan b.1926
Autumn Movement 1953
oil on board 62 x 76.5
0228

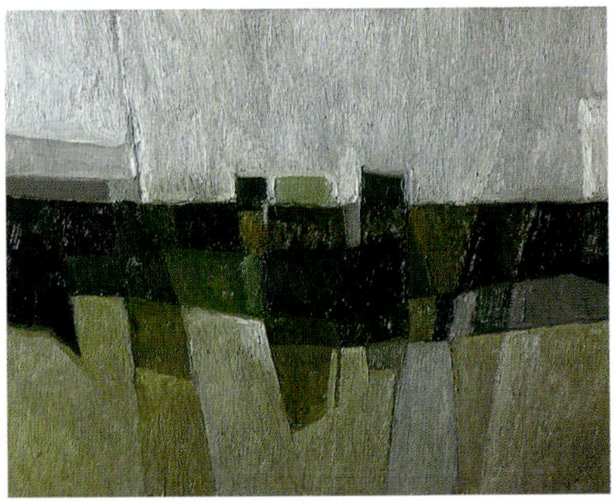

Reynolds, Alan b.1926
Forms Grey and Green 1959
oil on board 62.5 x 74.5
0230

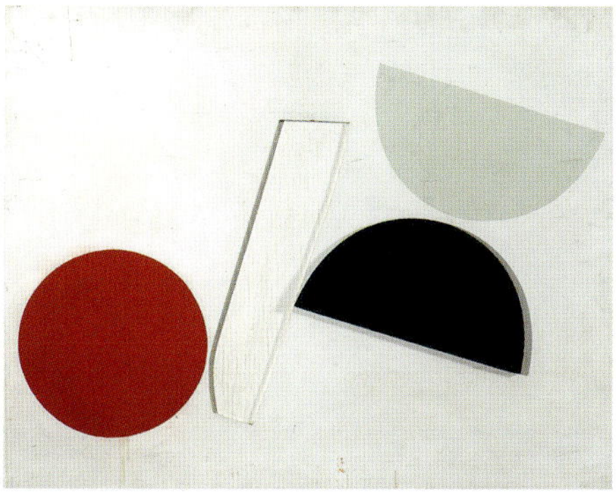

Reynolds, Alan b.1926
Dialogue 1972
emulsion paint on board 78.5 x 96
0229

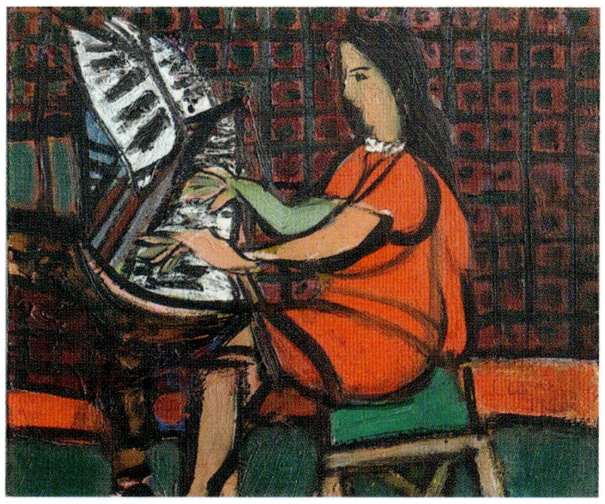

Richards, Ceri Geraldus 1903–1971
Girl at a Piano 1948
oil on canvas 41 x 45.8
0234

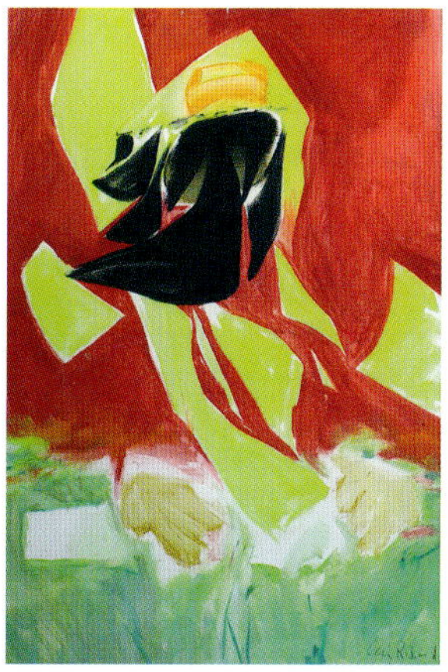

Richards, Ceri Geraldus 1903–1971
The Beekeeper 1956
oil on canvas 123.5 x 86
0233

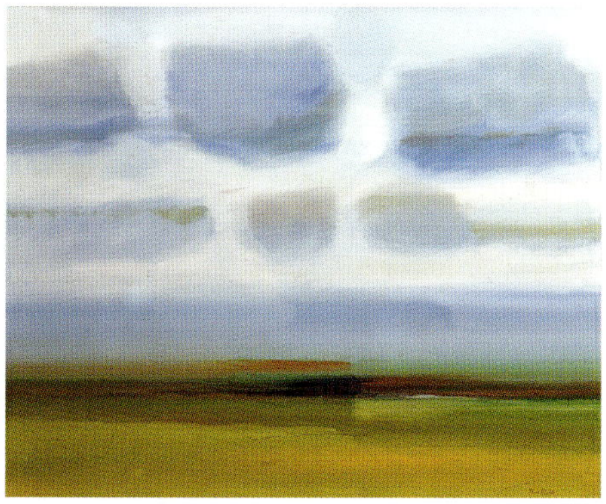

Robb, Tom b.1933
Summer Clouds 1972
oil on board 57.5 x 68
0236

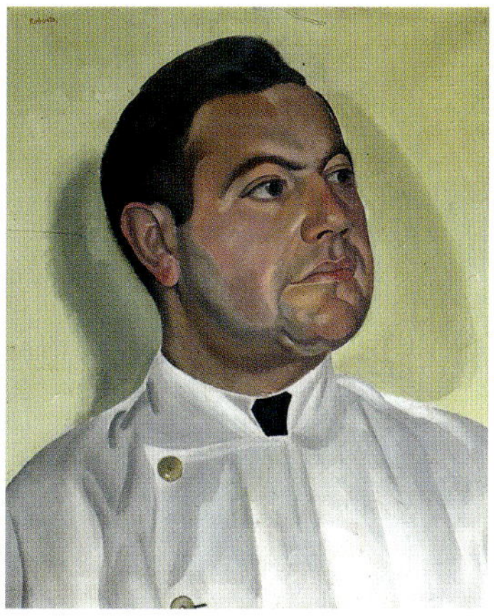

Roberts, William Patrick 1895–1980
The Dentist 1925
oil on canvas 69.5 x 59.5
0237

Romyn, Dick 1915–2007
No.1 (Figures on a Beach) 1971
oil on board 129 x 59
0239

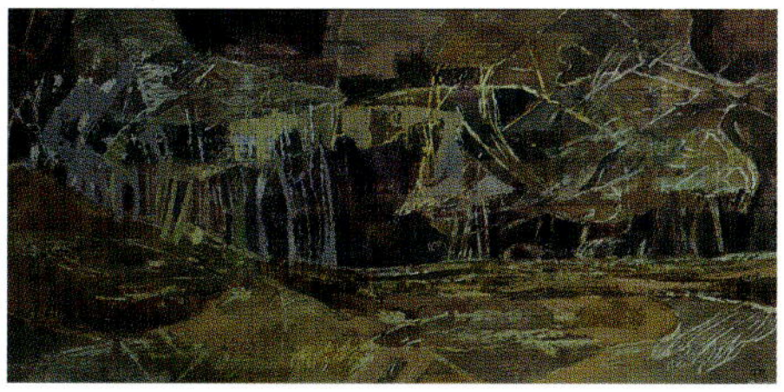

Roobottom, Joan b.1919
Woodland Landscape 1971
oil on board 59 x 110
0241

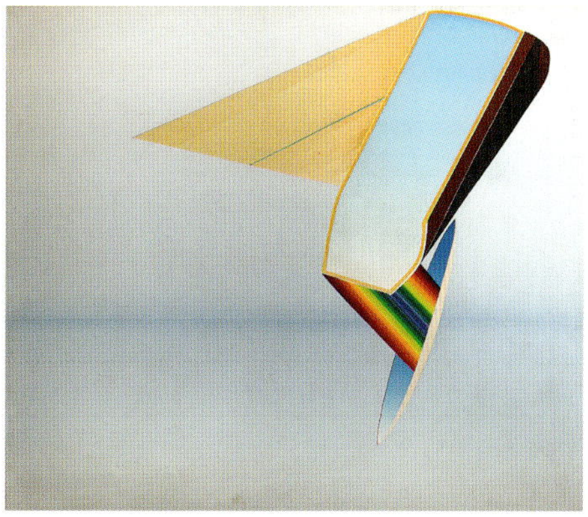

Roth, Frank b.1936
Spirit for Annie 1966
oil on canvas 117 x 132
0240

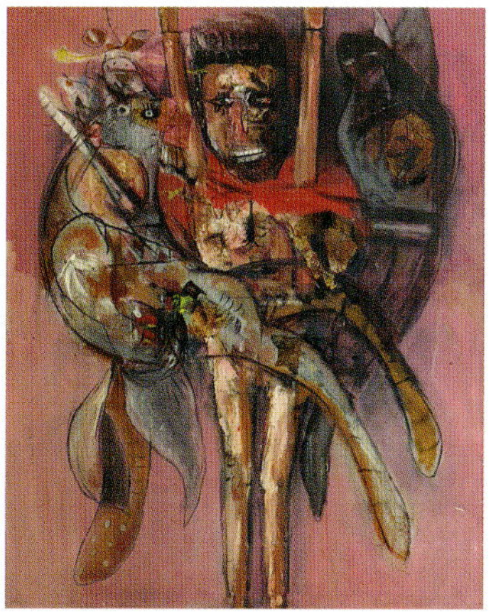

Rowell, Kenneth Leslie 1920–1999
Man and Spectres 1963
oil on canvas 154.5 x 124
0242

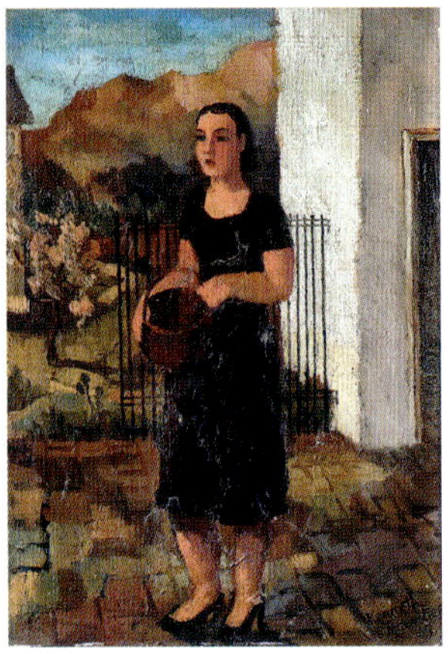

Rowntree, Kenneth 1915–1997
Spanish Girl 1935
oil on canvas 43.7 x 33.2
0243

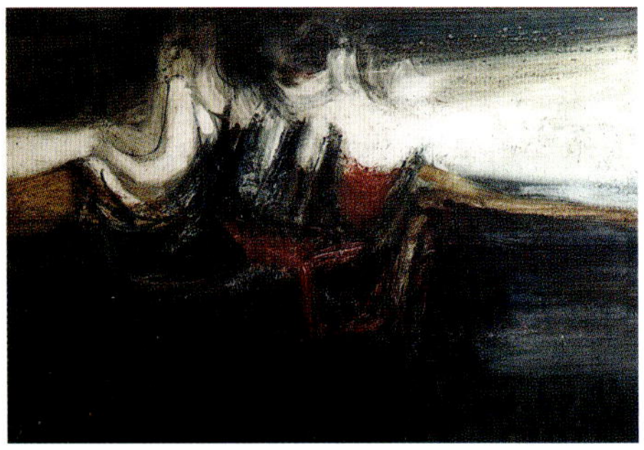

Saxton, Colin b.1927
Dark Horizon
oil on board 77 x 106.5
0245

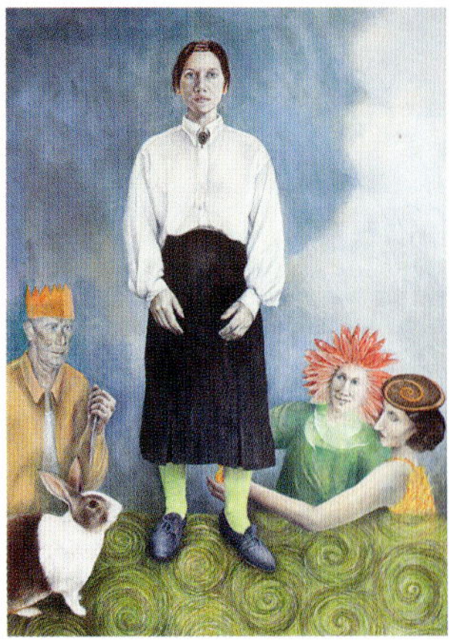

Schwab, Linda b.1960
Painting Myself
acrylic on canvas 128 x 92
0913

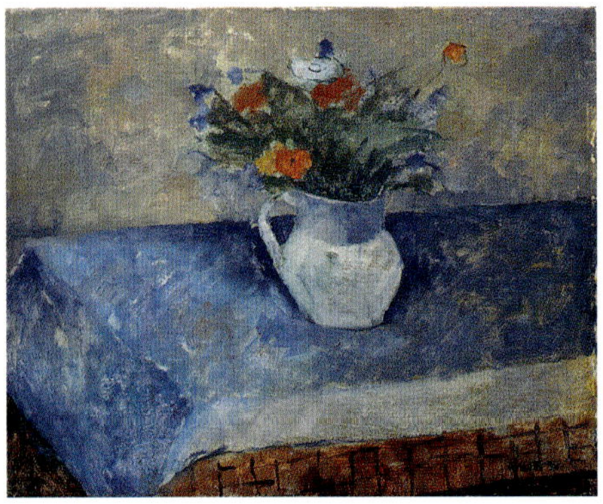

Scott, William George 1913–1989
Flowers on a Blue Cloth 1938
oil on canvas 53.3 x 62.2
0246

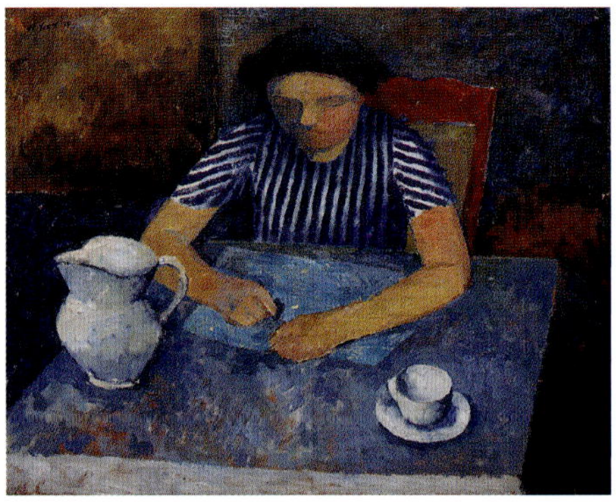

Scott, William George 1913–1989
Girl at a Blue Table 1938
oil on canvas 65.9 x 81
0247

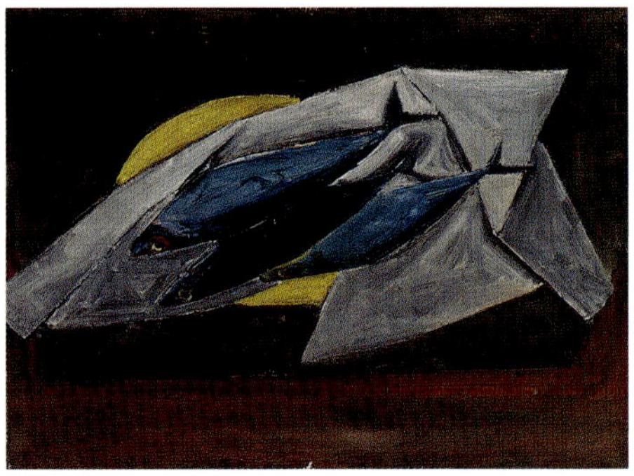

Scott, William George 1913–1989
Still Life, Fish 1946
oil on canvas 45.9 x 61
0249

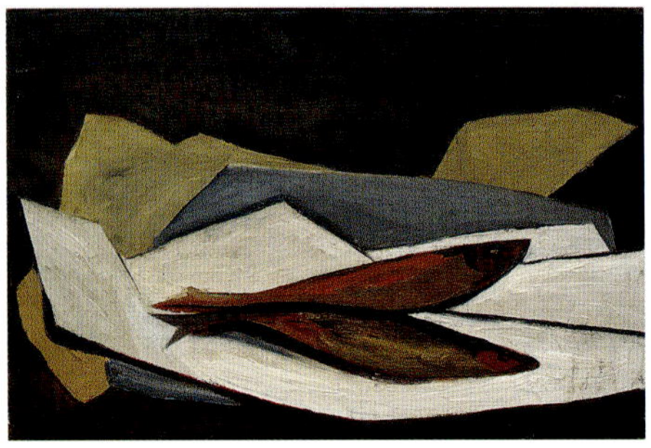

Scott, William George 1913–1989
Red Herrings 1946/1947
oil on canvas 36.9 x 54
0248

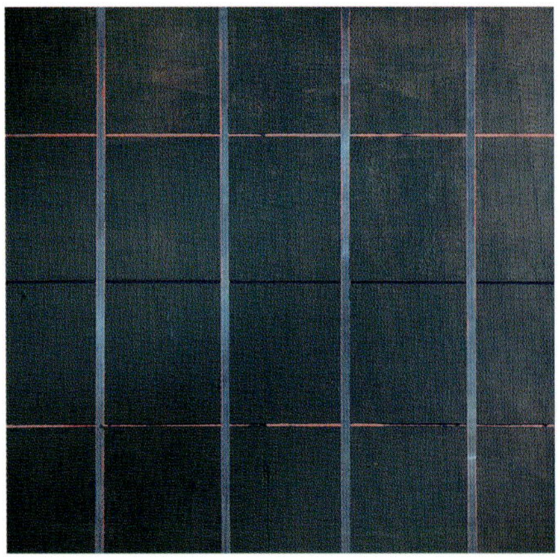

Scully, Sean b.1945
20.7.74, No.2 1974
acrylic on cotton duck 124 x 124
0251

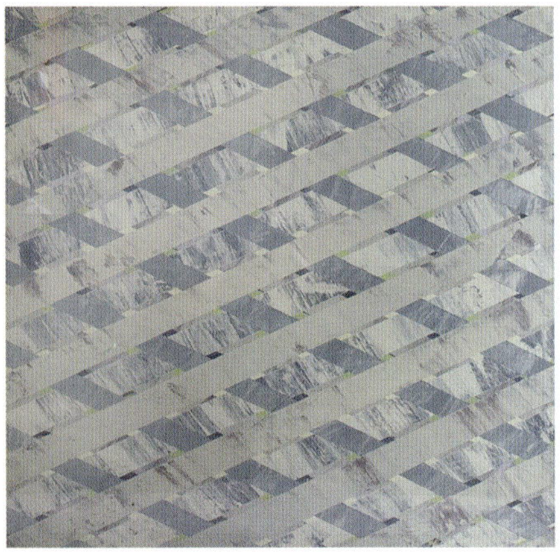

Scully, Sean b.1945
Jan 4/74 1974
acrylic on cotton duck 124 x 124
0250

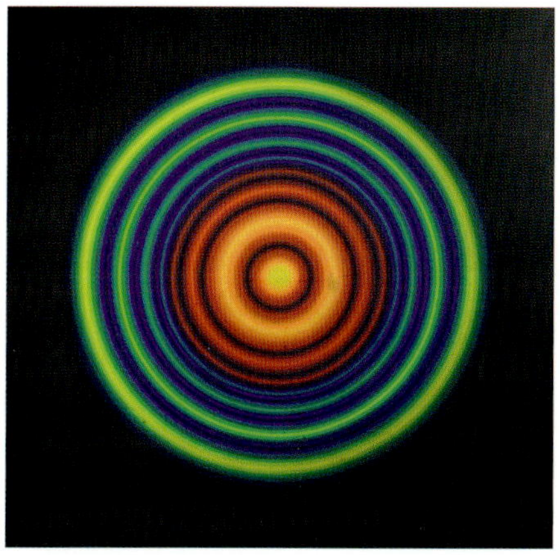

Sedgley, Peter b.1930
Target Dive 1966
acrylic on canvas 183.5 x 183.5
0252

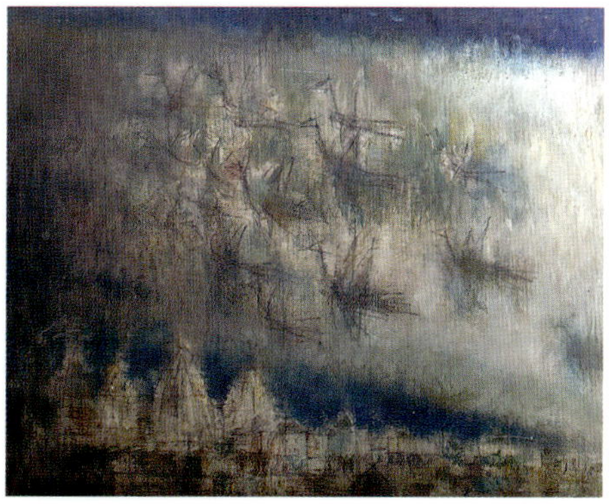

Sen, Paritosh b.1918
Rain over Benares, India 1962
oil on canvas 79 x 93.5
0253

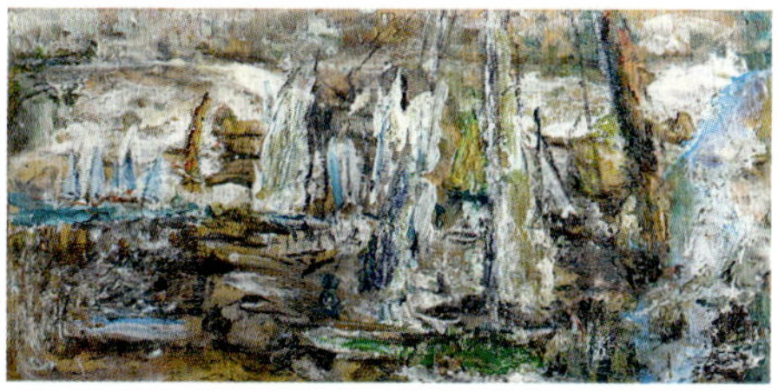

Setch, Terry b.1936
Racing in the Bay 1989
oil on board 49.5 x 80
0254

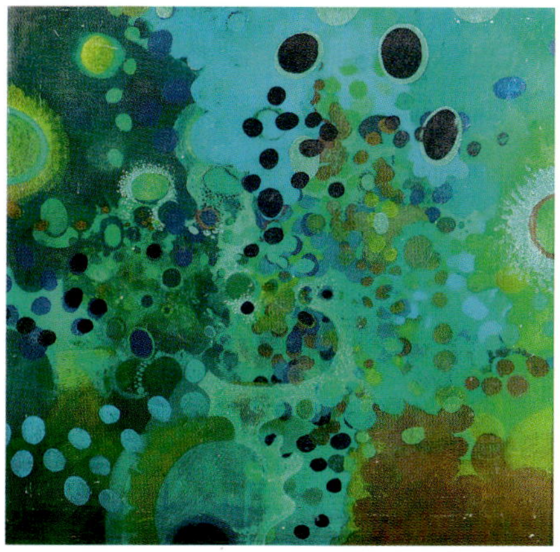

Shaw, Jack
Feeling through a Bach Brandenburg Concerto
1966
oil on canvas 79.5 x 79.8
0255

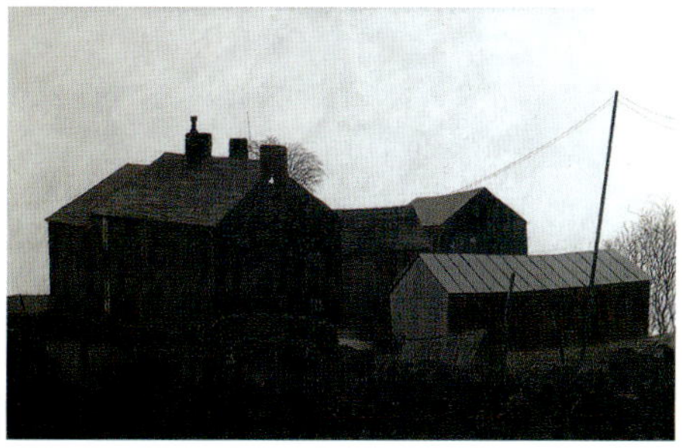

Simcock, Jack b.1929
The Farm, Mow Cop, Staffordshire 1961
oil on board 70.5 x 101
0257

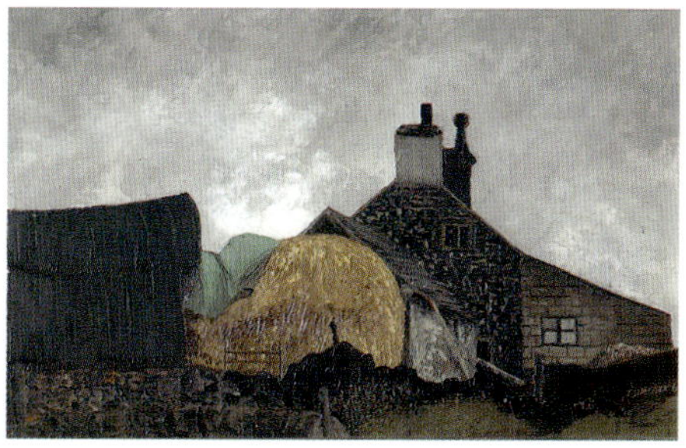

Simcock, Jack b.1929
The Haystack 1961
oil on board 41.7 x 59.2
0256

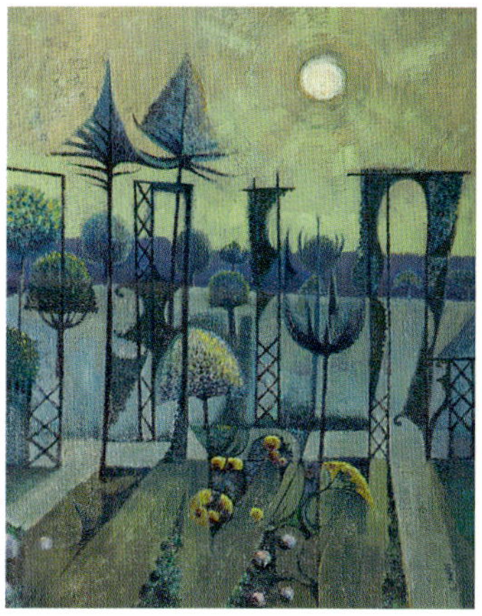

Slater, Richard b.1927
Garden Trellis, Evening 1971
oil on board 76 x 61
0259

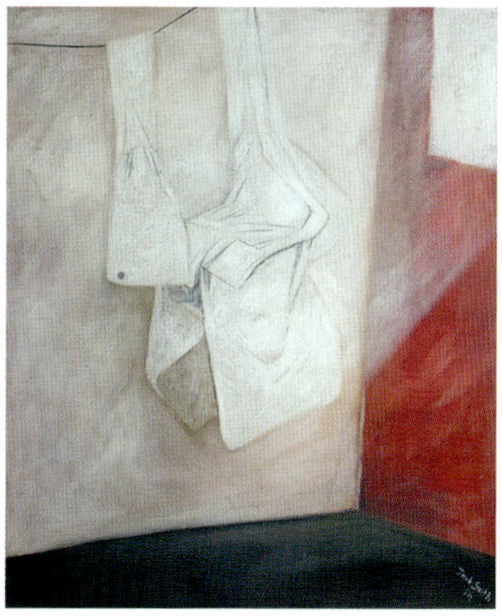

Smith, Jack 1928–2011
Shirt in Sunlight 1956
oil on canvas 170.5 x 140
0260

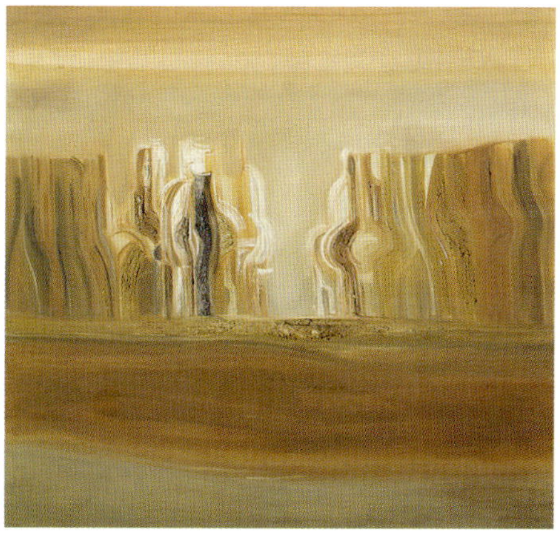

Smith, Jack 1928–2011
Bottles III 1959
oil on canvas 99.5 x 103
0261

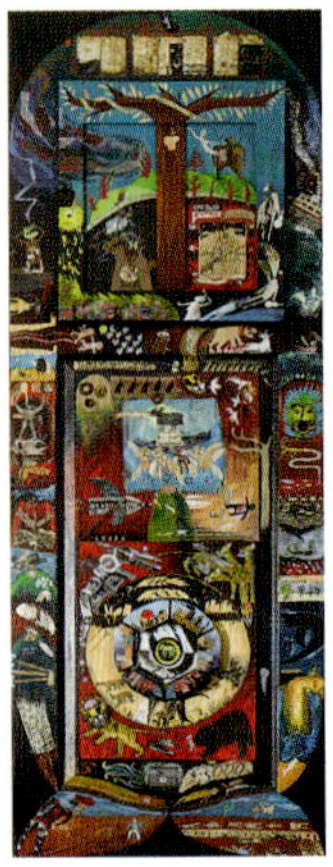

Smith, Paul
The Old Testament 2005
oil on wood 203.2 x 72.4
0989

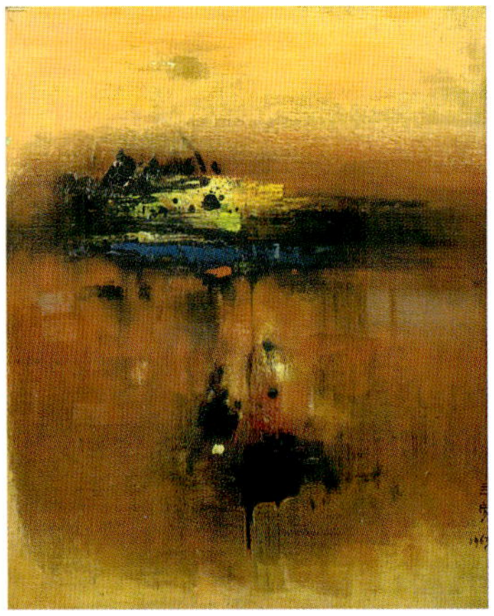

Soo Pieng, Cheong 1917–1983
Paysage chinois 1963
oil on canvas 76 x 61
0215

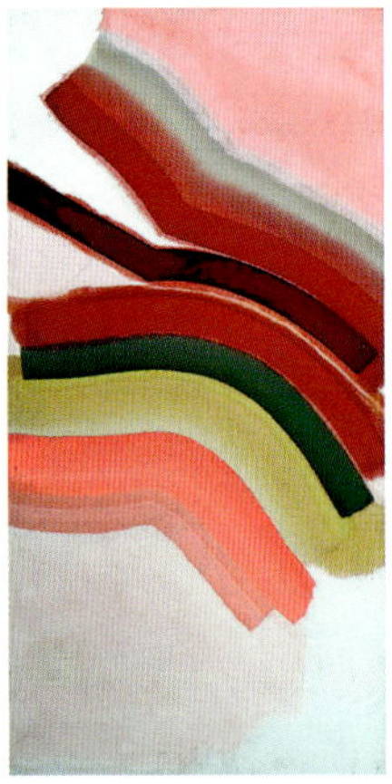

Southall, Derek b.1930
Small Painting 1965
acrylic on canvas 123 x 61.5
0265

Southall, Derek b.1930
Pale Fire No.2 1968
oil on canvas 183 x 122
0810

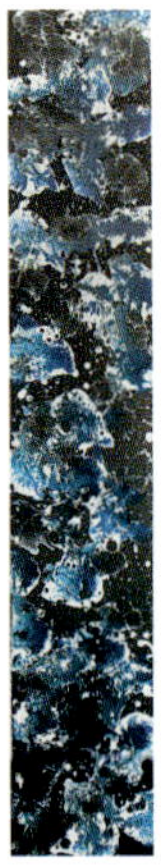

Southall, Derek b.1930
Blue Orchid 1970
oil on canvas 183 x 30.5
0263

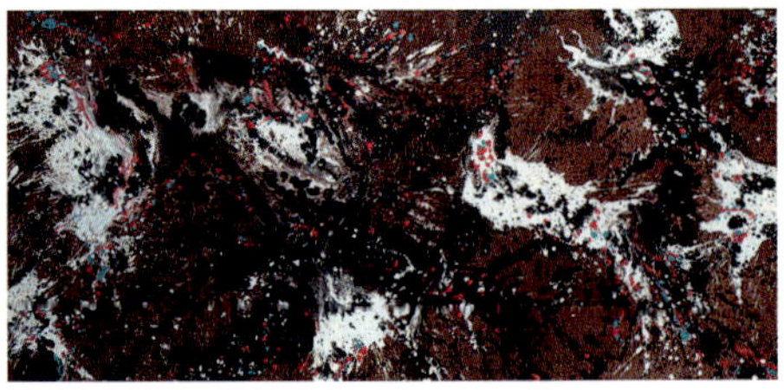

Southall, Derek b.1930
Implode 1970
acrylic on canvas 122 x 244
0264

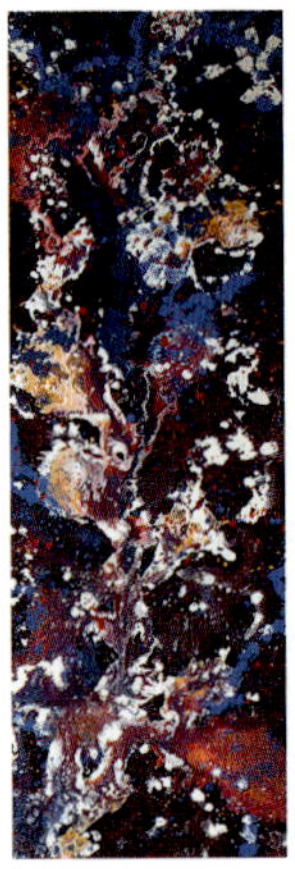

Southall, Derek b.1930
Song I 1970
oil on canvas 183 x 61
0266

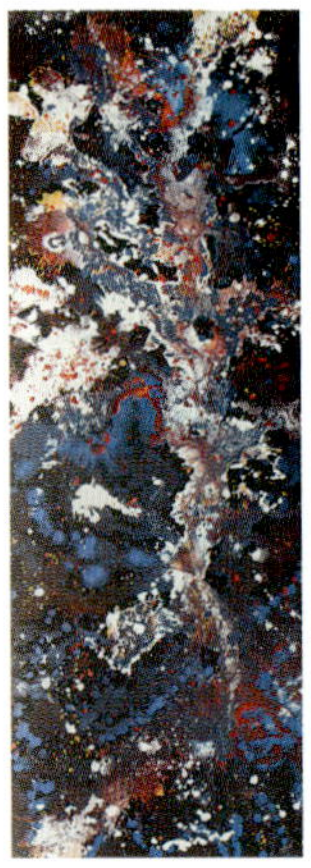

Southall, Derek b.1930
Song II 1970
oil on canvas 183 x 60.5
0267

Southall, Derek b.1930
Song III 1970
oil on canvas 153.5 x 60.5
0268

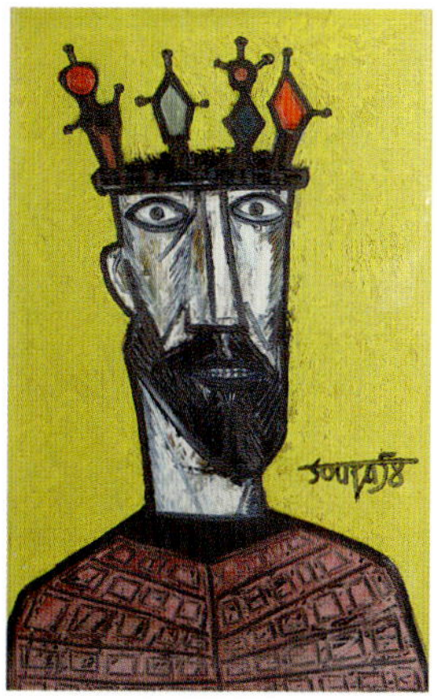

Souza, Francis Newton 1924–2002
The Emperor 1958
oil on board 110.2 x 70
0269

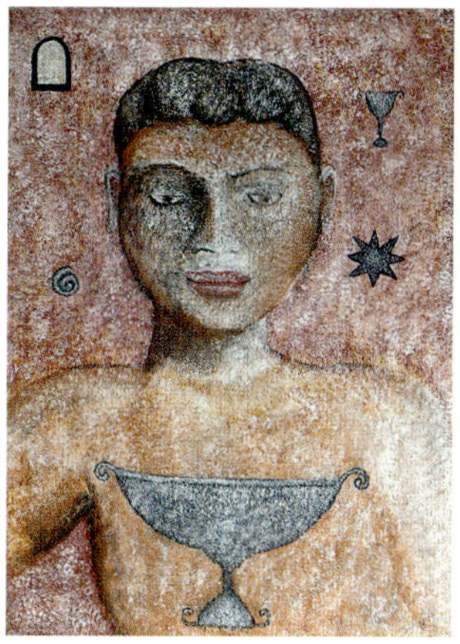

Stahl, Andrew b.1954
Head and Window 1984
acrylic on paper 70 x 53
0270

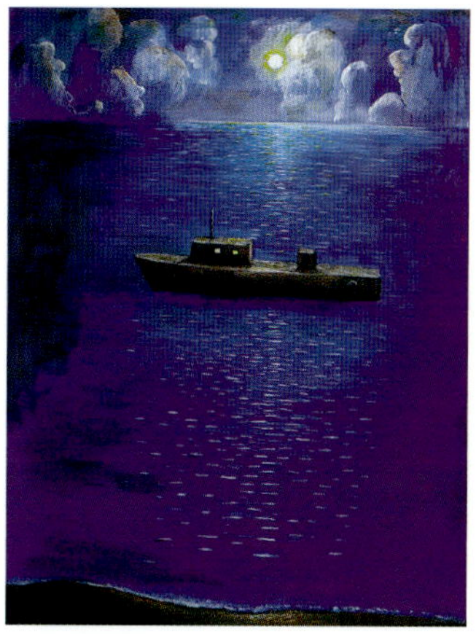

Stahl, Andrew b.1954
Boat 1990
acrylic on paper 90.6 x 70
0271

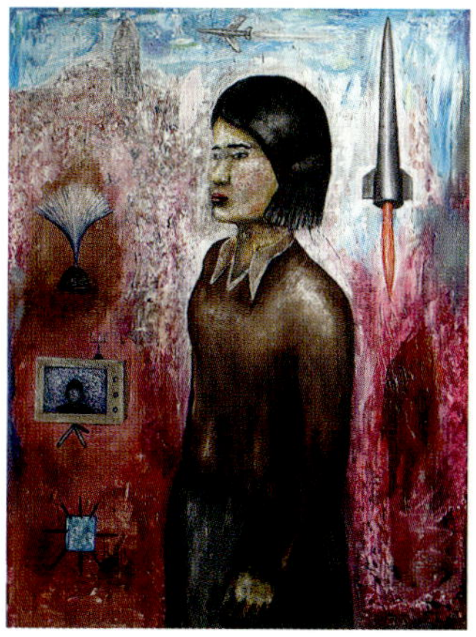

Stahl, Andrew b.1954
Figure and Rocket 1990
acrylic on paper 90.5 x 69
0272

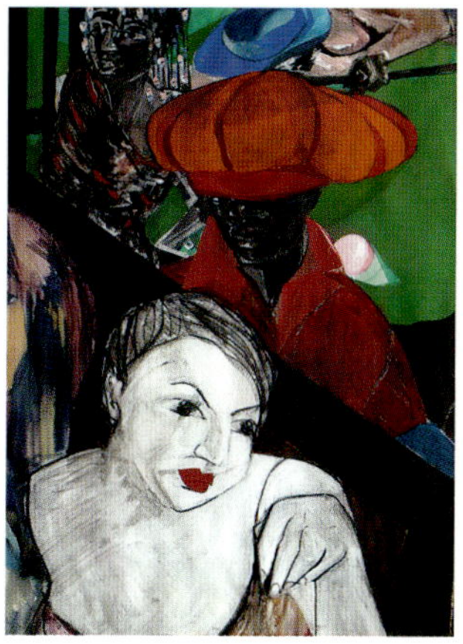

Steele, Elaine active 1983–1984
Miss Victoria 1983
oil & watercolour on paper 83.5 x 63
0273

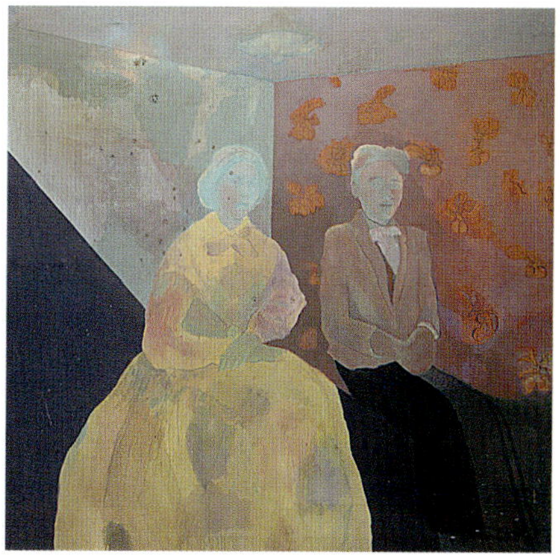

Sujo, Glenn b.1952
Gentle Portrait of the Artist and His Sister
oil on canvas 152.5 x 152.5
812

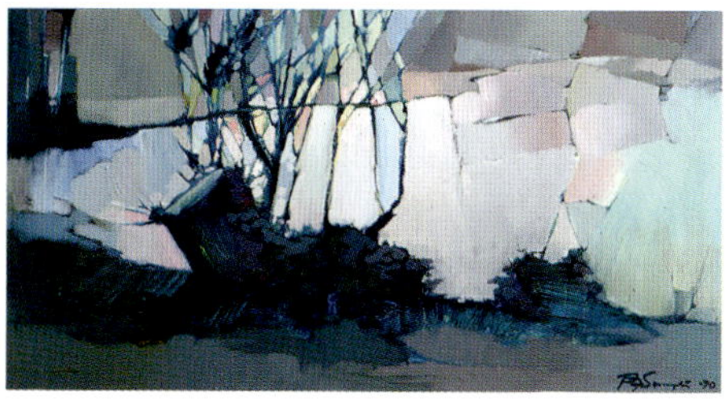

Sumpter, Peter b.1933
Tree Form, Rolleston, Leicestershire c.1970
oil on board 40.7 x 66
0276

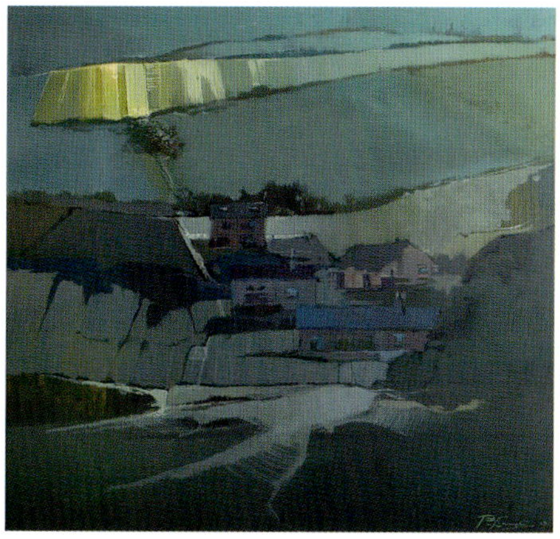

Sumpter, Peter b.1933
Yellow Field on Greys, Praa Sands, Cornwall c.1970
oil on board 102.5 x 104.5
0277

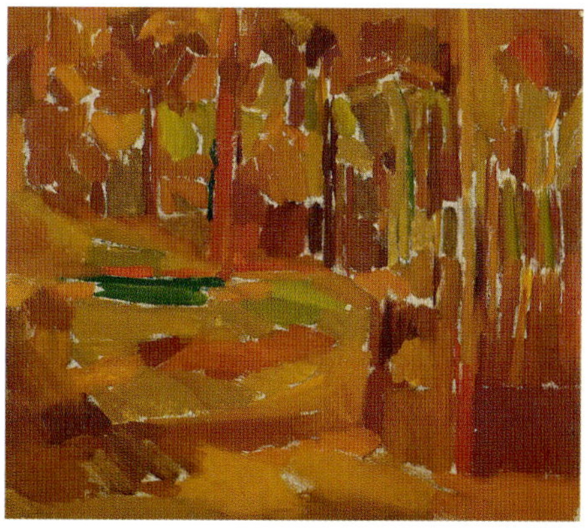

Sutton, Philip b.1928
Iken Wood, Suffolk
oil on canvas 47 x 52
0278

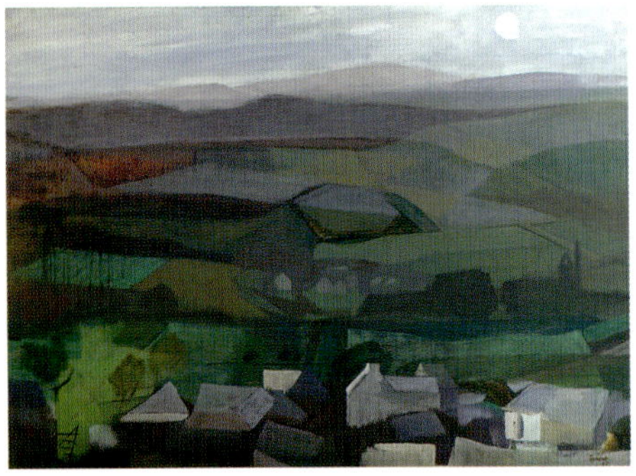

Symonds, Ken b.1927
Godolphin Landscape
oil on canvas 108 x 137.5
0279

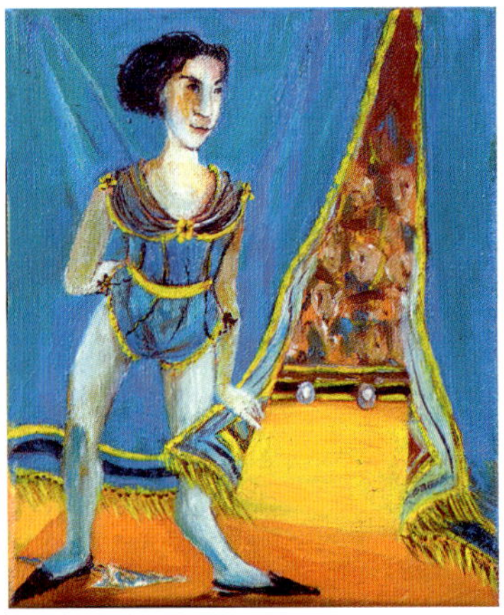

Taylor, Anita b.1961
Revealed, Concealed
oil on canvas 23 x 18
0280

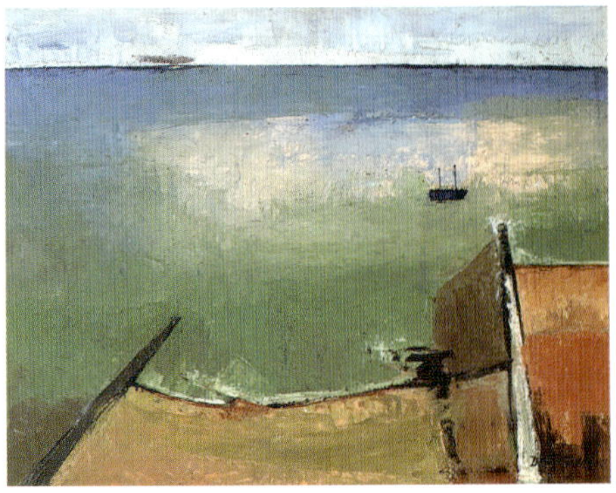

Tindle, David b.1932
Hastings Harbour, East Sussex 1956
oil on canvas 63 x 79
0283

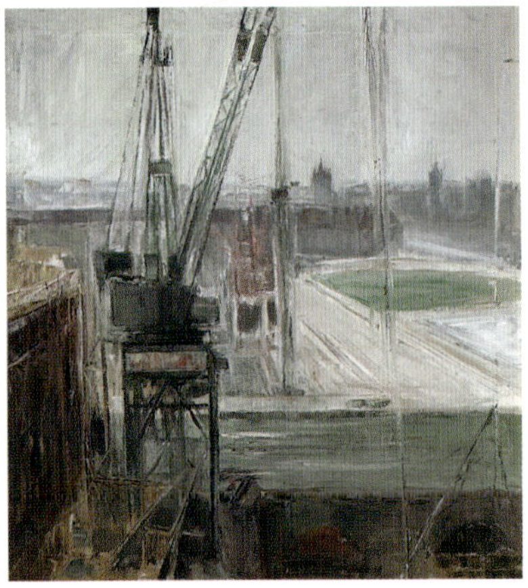

Tindle, David b.1932
Shell Site, South Bank, London
oil on canvas 86.5 x 79
0282

Tippett, Bruce b.1933
Untitled
acrylic on wood 173 x 173
0284

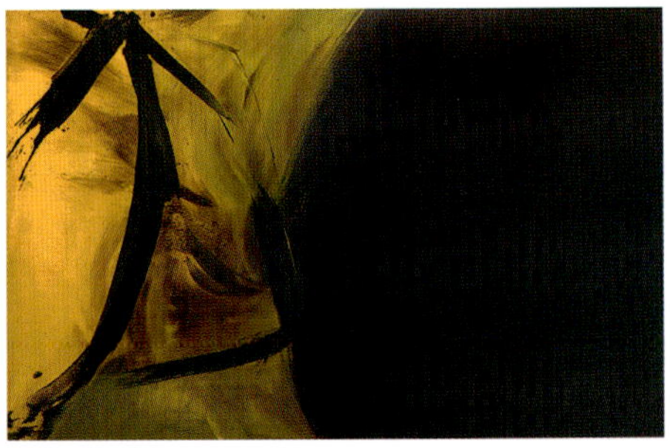

Tirr, Willy 1915–1991
Yellow and Black 1963
oil on canvas 123 x 182
0285

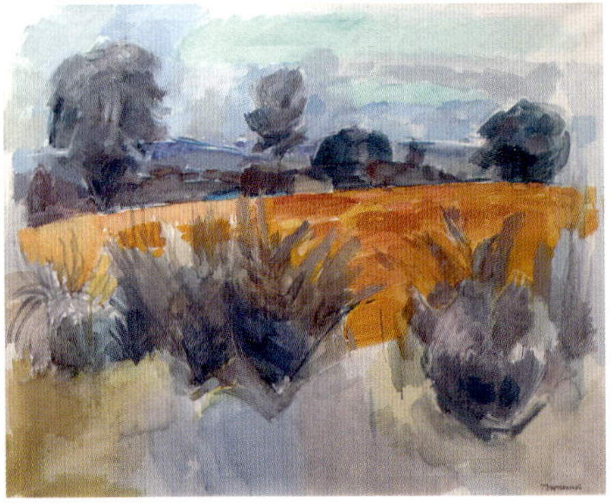

Townsend, William 1909–1973
Cornfield, August
oil on canvas 67 x 78
0286

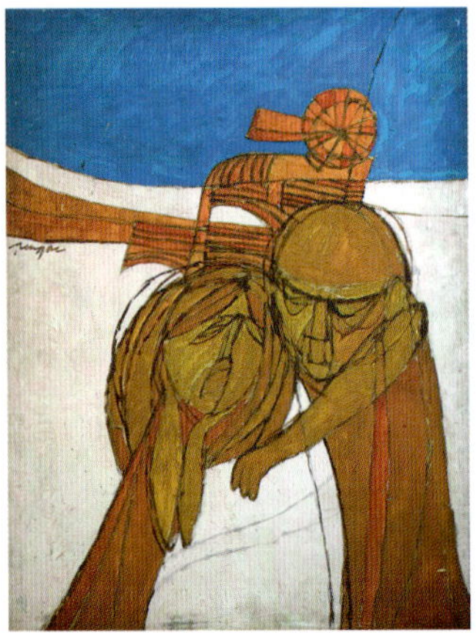

Trengrove, Barry
Himmelfarb and Miss Hare
oil on board 121.5 x 91.5
0287

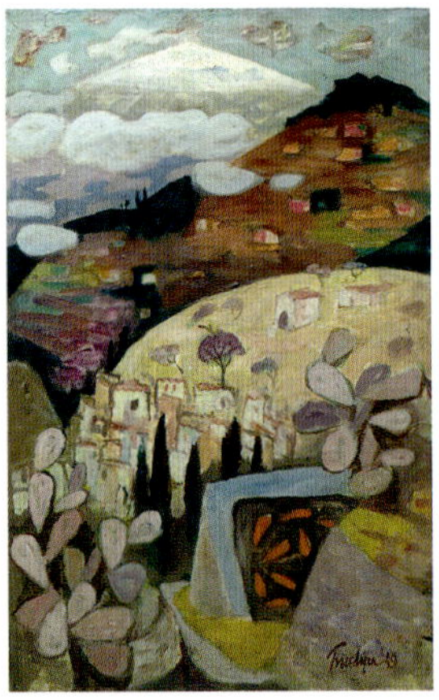

Trevelyan, Julian 1910–1988
Taormina, Sicily 1949
oil on canvas 69.1 x 46.5
0288

Facing page: Rowe, Cliff, 1904–1989, *The Fried Fish Shop* (detail), 1936, Leicester Arts and Museums Service (p. 79)

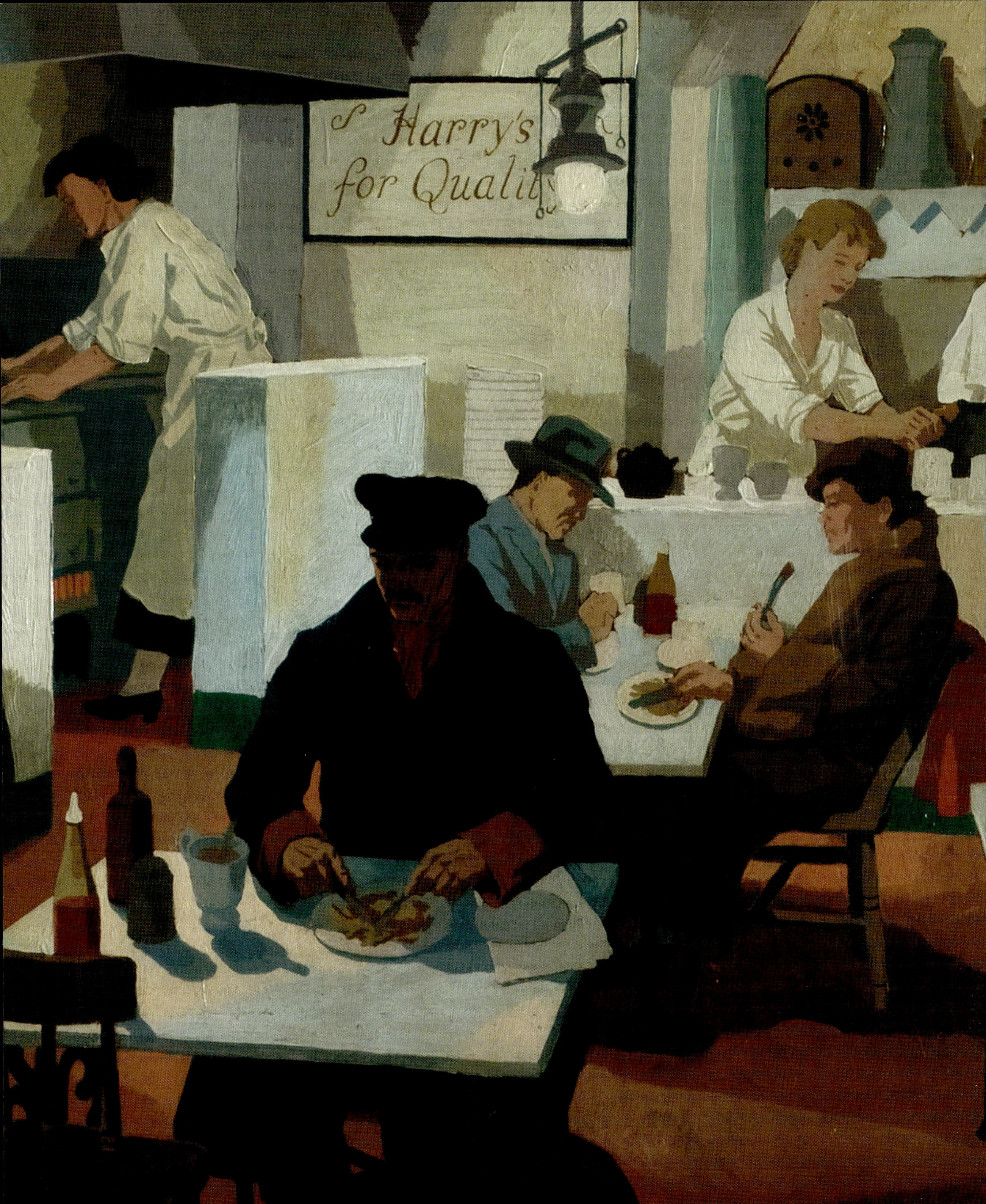
Harry's
for Quali

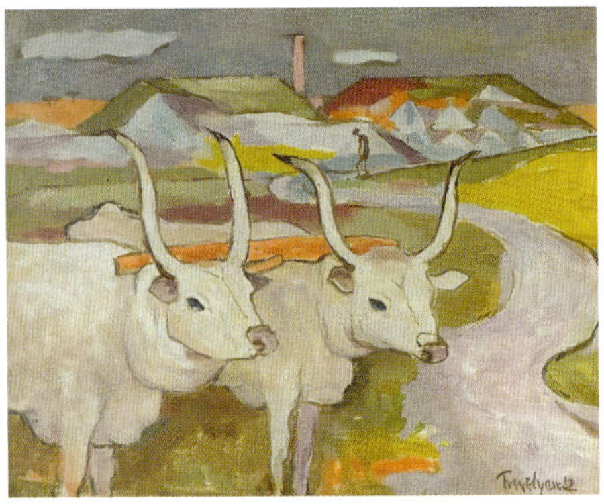

Trevelyan, Julian 1910–1988
White Oxen
oil on canvas 54 x 60
0919

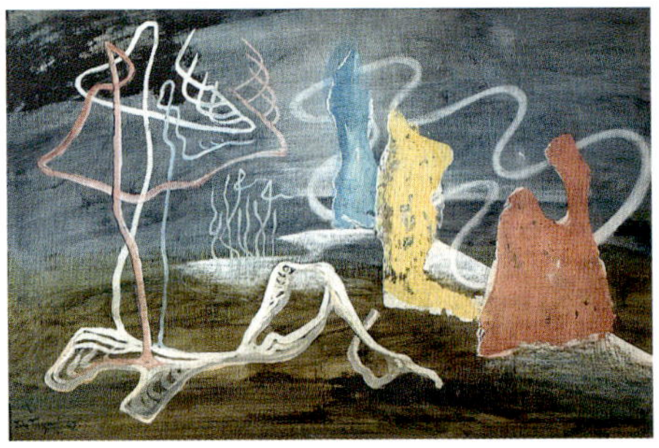

Tunnard, John 1900–1971
Trio 1947
oil on board 52 x 76
0289

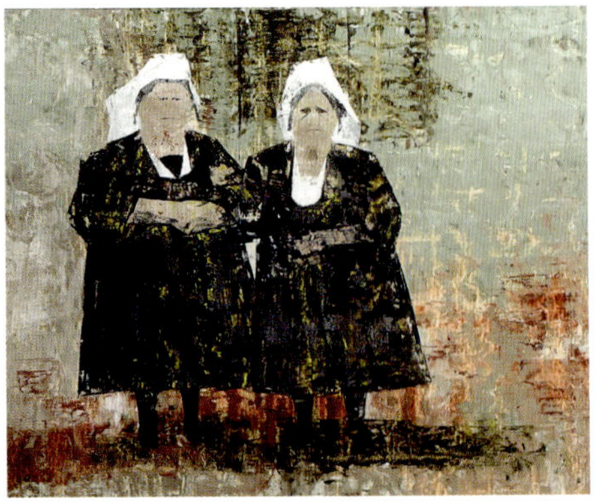

Twist, Anthony
Breton Peasant Women 1972
oil on board 88.5 x 103.5
0291

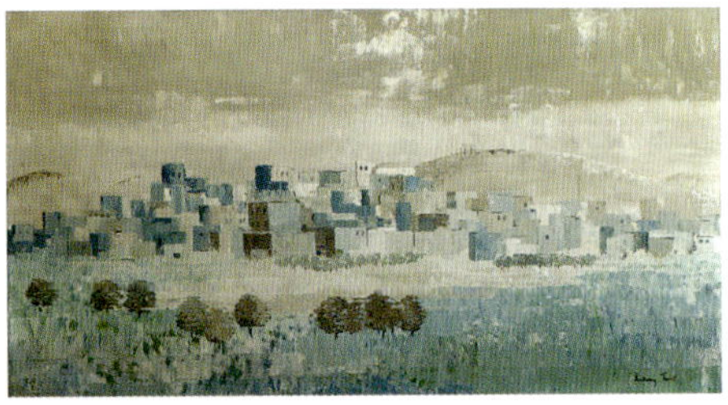

Twist, Anthony
Cyprus Village
oil on board 52 x 92.5
0290

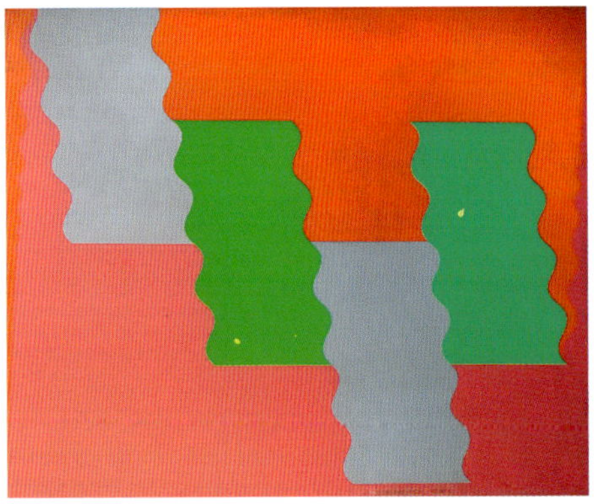

Tyzack, Michael 1933–2007
Saratoga 1967
oil on canvas 183 x 213
0292

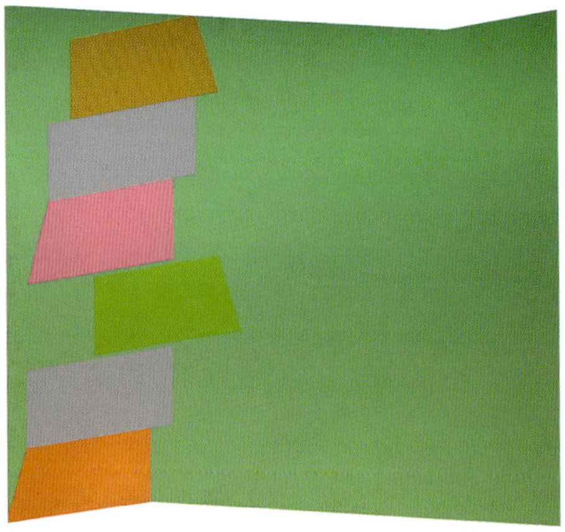

Tyzack, Michael 1933–2007
Pavan
acrylic on canvas 152 x 167
0293

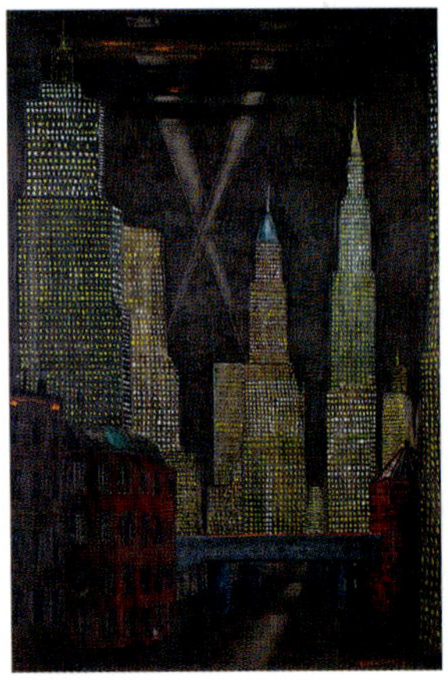

Uhlman, Fred 1901–1985
New York 1955
oil on canvas 108.5 x 78.5
0295

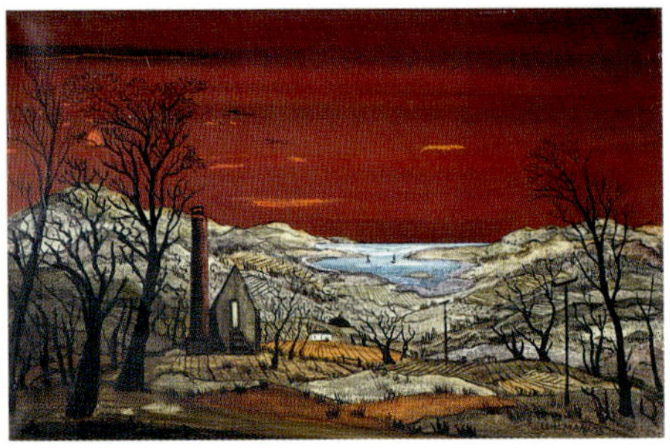

Uhlman, Fred 1901–1985
Lead Mine 1958
oil on canvas 80 x 111
0294

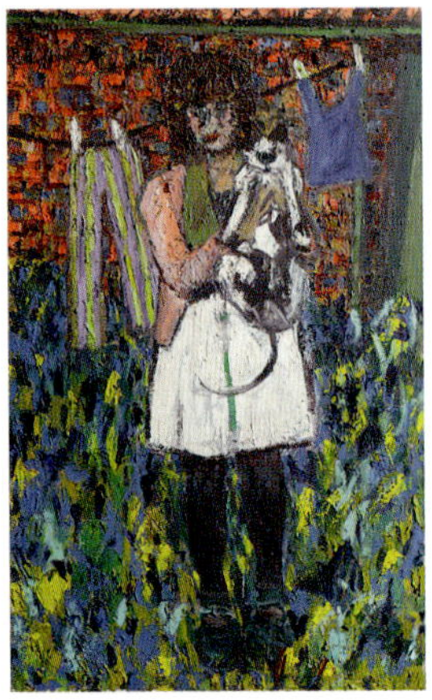

unknown artist
Girl Holding a Cat
oil on canvas 152 x 91
0845

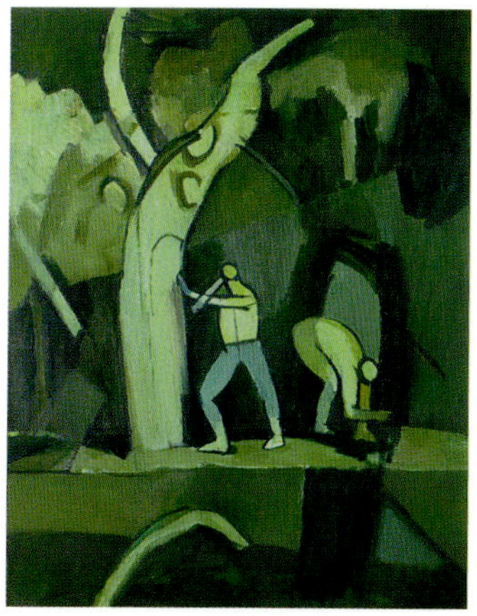

Vaughan, John Keith 1912–1977
Woodmen in a Clearing 1953
oil on canvas 105.5 x 85
0297

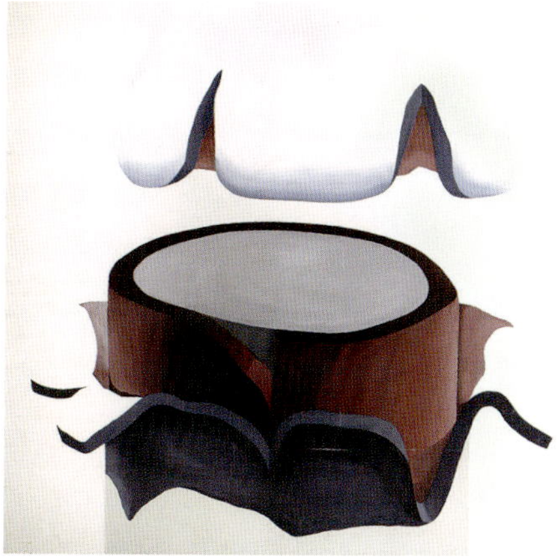

Vaughan, Michael b.1938
Food Objects
oil on board 120 x 121
0298

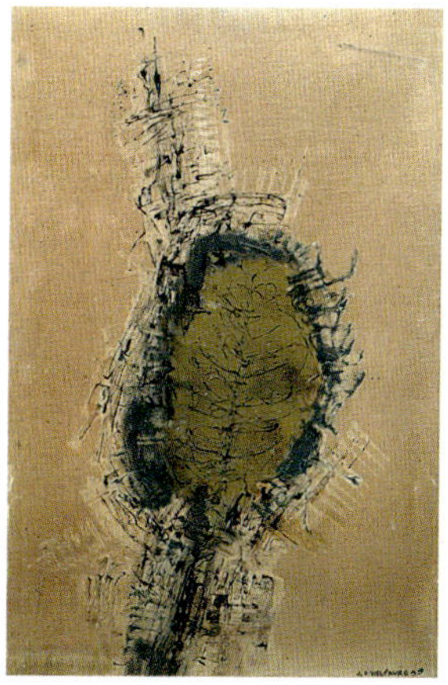

Vielfaure, Jean-Pierre b.1930
Vision d'apocalypse 1959
oil on canvas 105 x 64.5
0299

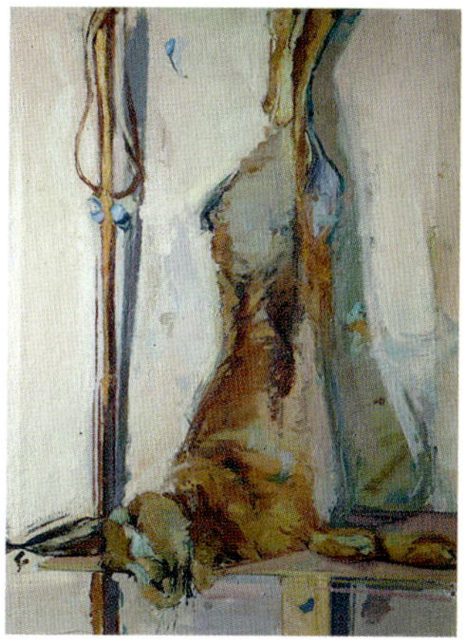

Volley, Nicholas 1950–2006
Hare
oil on canvas 84.5 x 64
0301

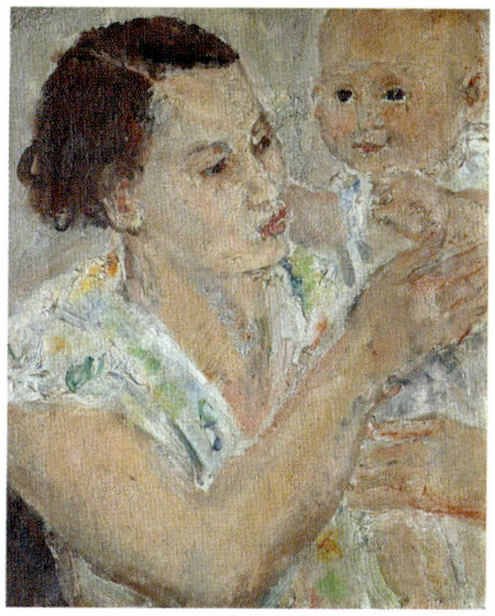

Walker, Ethel 1861–1951
Mother and Baby
oil on board 61 x 50.5
0302

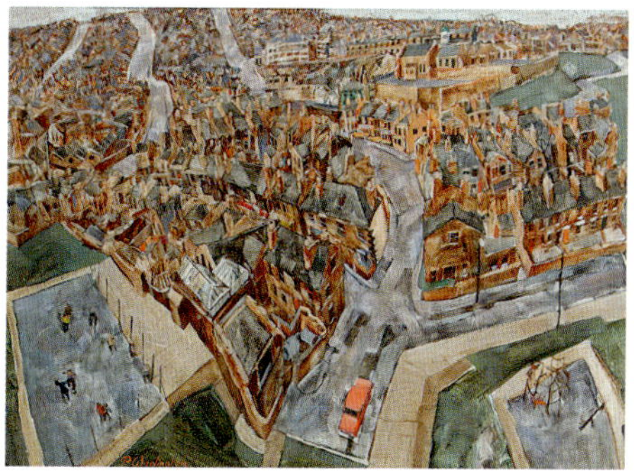

Waplington, Paul Anthony b.1938
Kelvin Flats, Sheffield
acrylic on canvas 91 x 121
0815

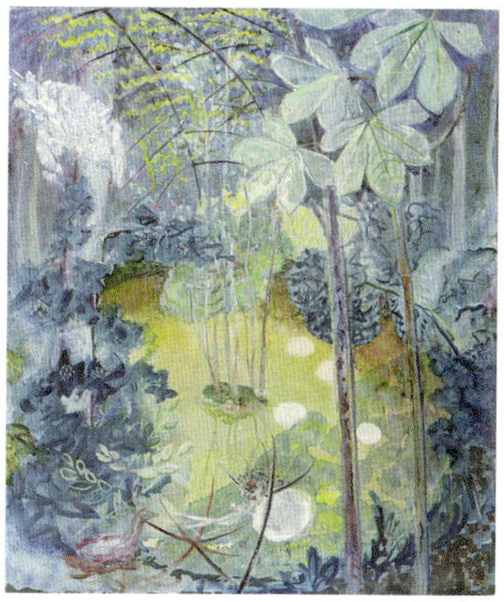

Ward, Irene
The Eel Pond
oil on board 72.9 x 60.8
0303

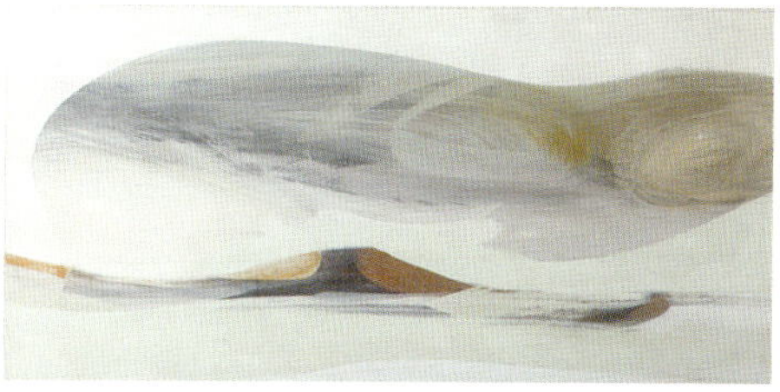

Watkiss, Reg b.1933
North Coast
oil on board 68 x 129
0304

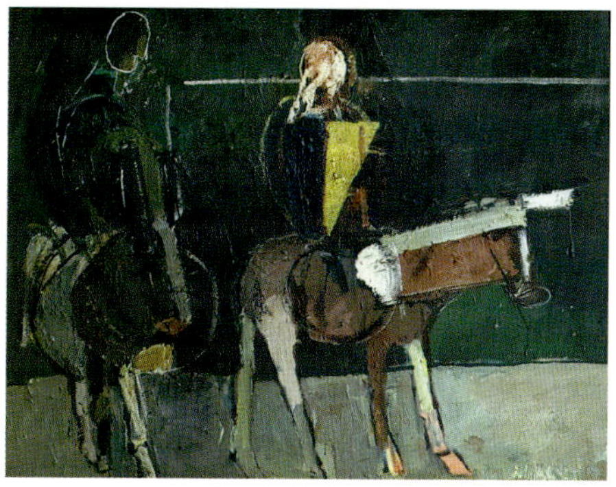

Watson, John 1923–1992
The Cockle Woman of Llansaint
oil on canvas 76 x 94
0305

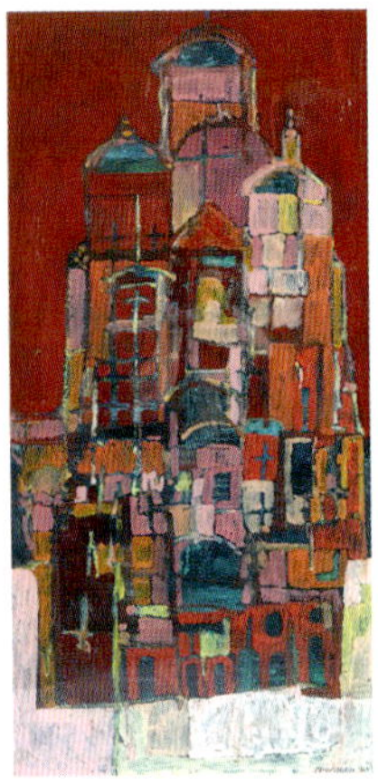

Watts, Percy active c.1962–1969
Untitled Red Abstract with Crucifixes 1963
acrylic on board 118 x 56
0712

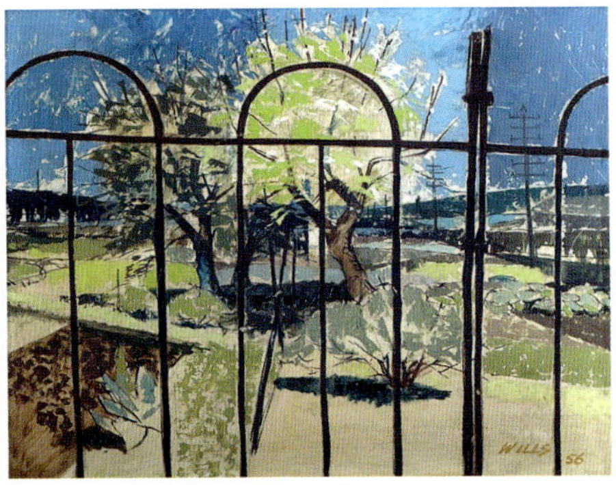

Wills, Dennis Frederick b.1928
City Allotments
oil on board 69 x 84
0308

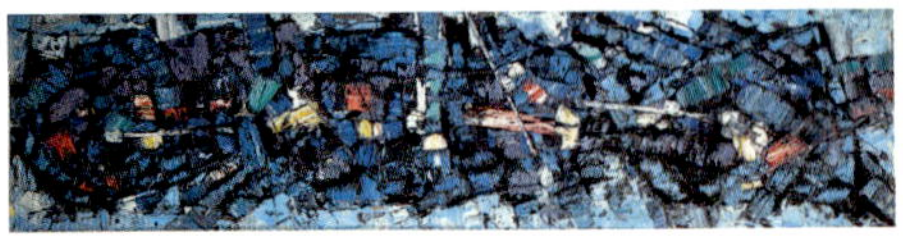

Wilson, Frank Avray 1914–2009
Alleluia 1958
oil on canvas 60 x 244
0816

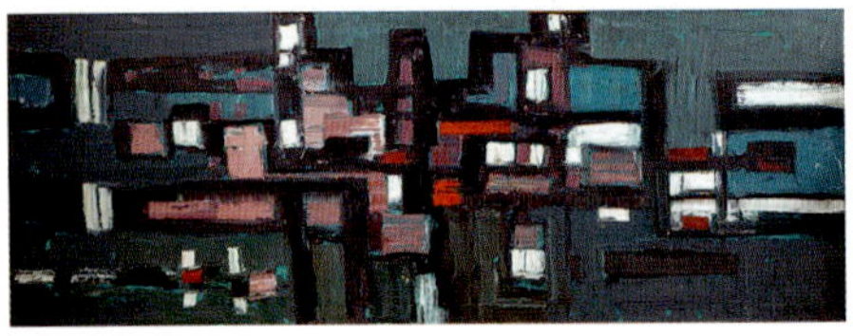

Wilson, Frank Avray 1914–2009
Abstract Composition
oil on canvas 81 x 209
0309

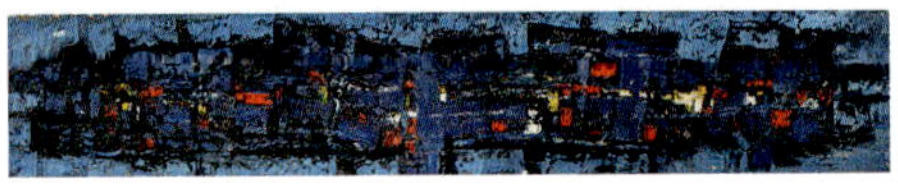

Wilson, Frank Avray 1914–2009
Blue Effigy
oil on canvas 46.5 x 259
0310

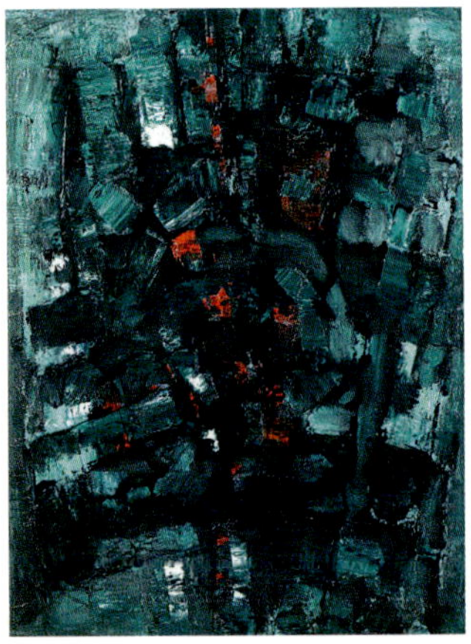

Wilson, Frank Avray 1914–2009
Participate
oil on canvas 91 x 66
0753

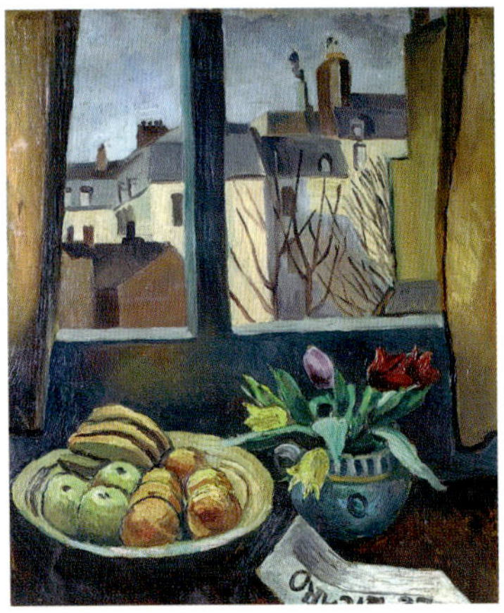

Wood, Christopher 1901–1930
Studio Window, Rue des Saints-Pères, Paris 1923
oil on canvas 69 x 58
0314

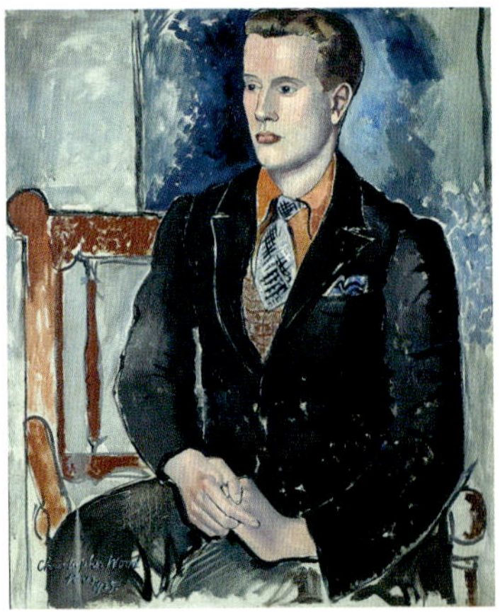

Wood, Christopher 1901–1930
Constant Lambert (1905–1951), as a Young Man 1925
oil on canvas 93 x 80
0311

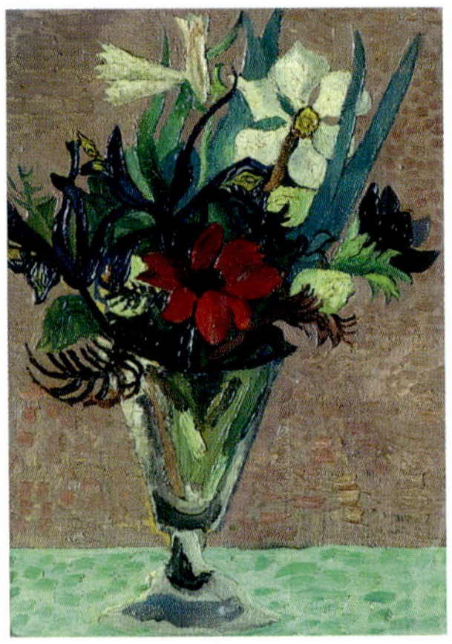

Wood, Christopher 1901–1930
Flowers in a Glass
oil on canvas 50.5 x 40.5
0312

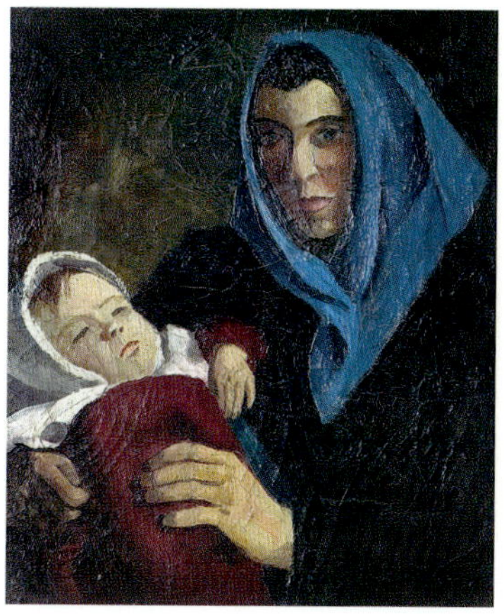

Wood, Christopher 1901–1930
Mother and Sleeping Child
oil on canvas 64 x 55
0313

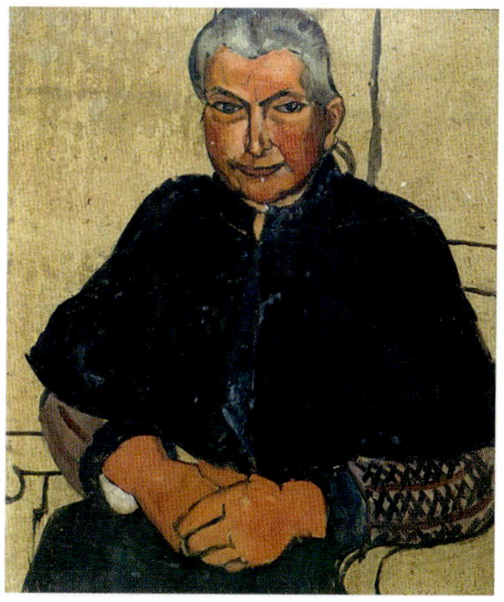

Wood, Christopher 1901–1930
Woman in Black
oil on board 74.5 x 64
0315

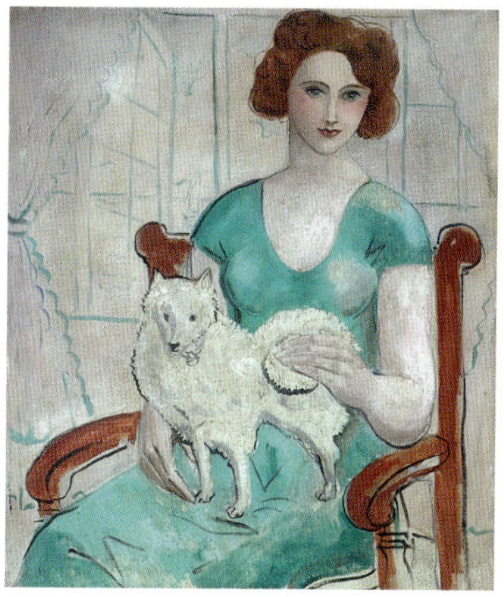

Wood, Christopher 1901–1930
Woman with a Dog
oil on canvas 80 x 70
0316

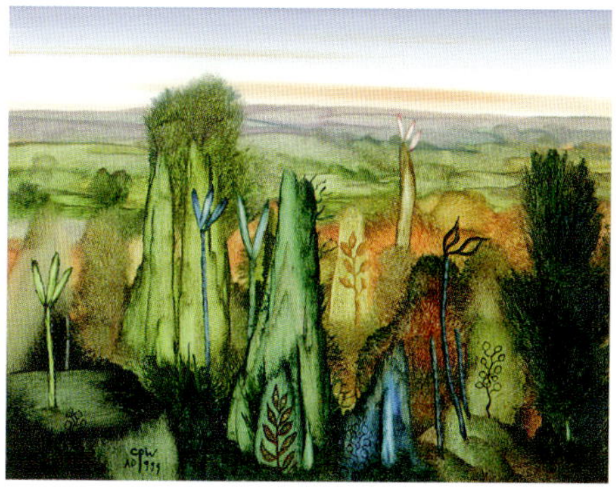

Wood, Christopher P. b.1961
Undersea World No.5 1999
oil on canvas 58.5 x 68.5
0970

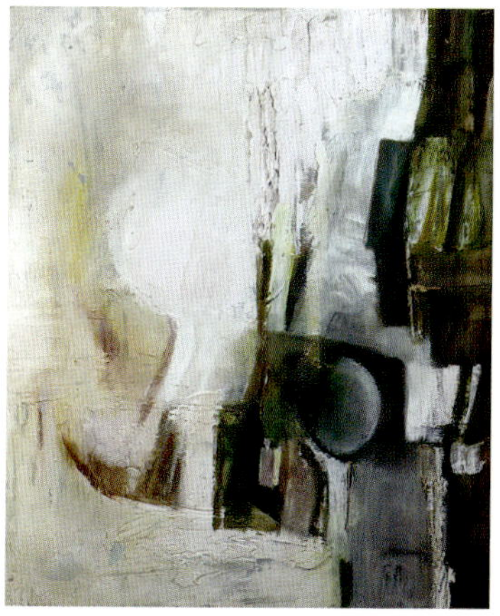

Worthington, Maurice
Cliff Wall
oil on canvas 82 x 67
0317

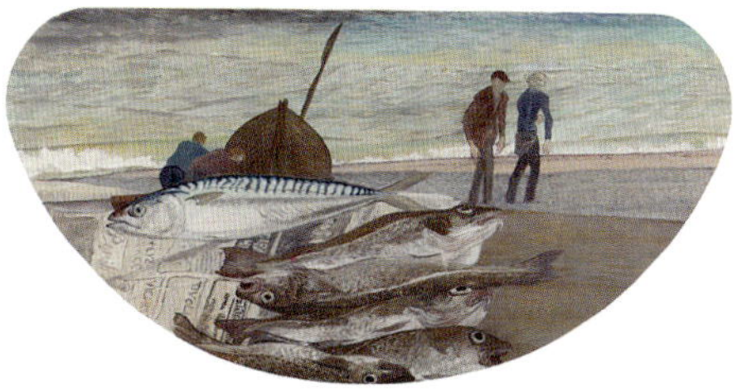

Yhap, Laetitia b.1941
Mackerel and Cod and Oxo and Leon Coming up the Beach 1977
oil on board 48 x 92
0318

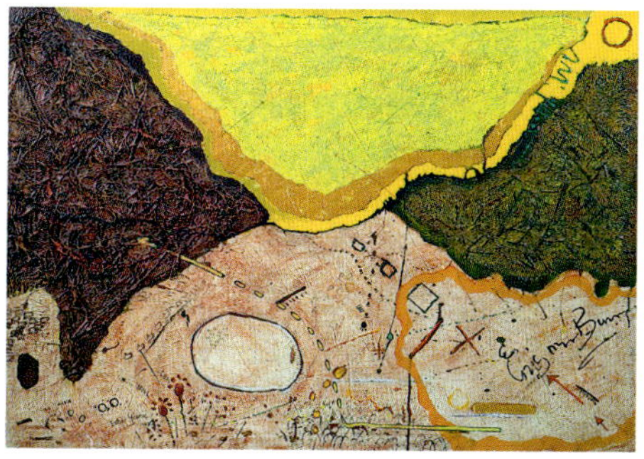

Younie, Esther
Ten Paces Left 1982
acrylic on board 105 x 138
0319

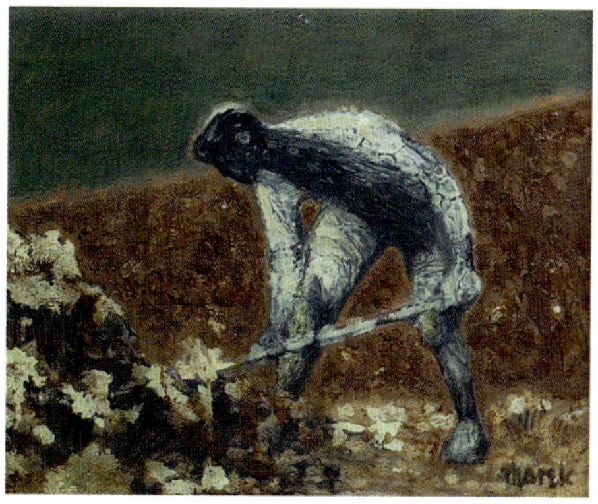

Żulawski, Marek 1908–1985
The Gardener 1959
oil on canvas 78.5 x 91
0320

Leicestershire County Council Beaumanor Collection

The Beaumanor Collection comprises works that were purchased by Leicestershire County Council Education Department between the 1950s and 1980s. This was a scheme to give young people direct access to original works of art for their educational benefit and enjoyment. Some of the works purchased during this time formed the 'County Collection', which was available for schools to borrow on a yearly basis. Now known as 'Artworks', this Collection has a separate section within this catalogue.

Beaumanor Hall was built in the 1840s in the Elizabethan style by the architect William Railton for the Herrick family. The family lived on the Beaumanor Estate, near Woodhouse, Leicestershire for around 350 years until 1946 when it was sold by Lieutenant Colonel Assheton Penn Curzon Howe Herrick. During the Second World War, the War Office requisitioned Beaumanor Estate for war work and it became a strategic intercept station, known as a 'Y station'. Enemy radio transmissions were intercepted and the information was sent everyday by motorbike to Bletchley Park, 'Station X', for decryption and analysis. When the estate was sold the War Office bought the Hall and some of the land.

Beaumanor Hall is now owned by Leicestershire County Council and is a busy venue for conferences, weddings and social events, therefore the works in the Collection are seen by a wide cross-section of Leicestershire residents and visitors to the county. Also on site is the Beaumanor Outdoor Learning Centre, a thriving children's residential and activity centre which accommodates a large number of Leicestershire school children throughout the year.

Alan Jacobs, Outdoor & Residential Learning Service Manager

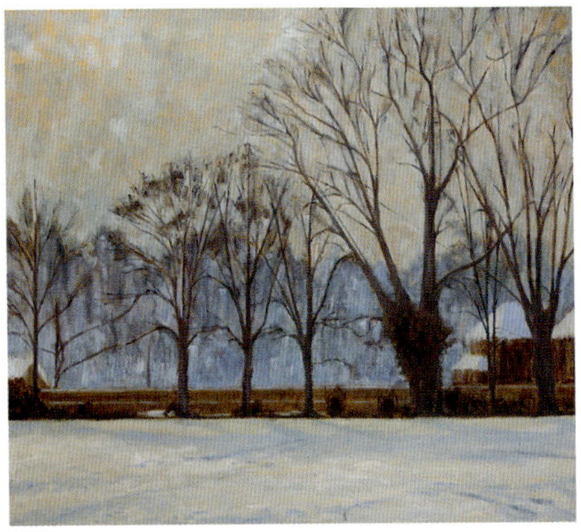

Bartram, David
Trees and Snow 1985
oil on canvas 79 x 89.5
30

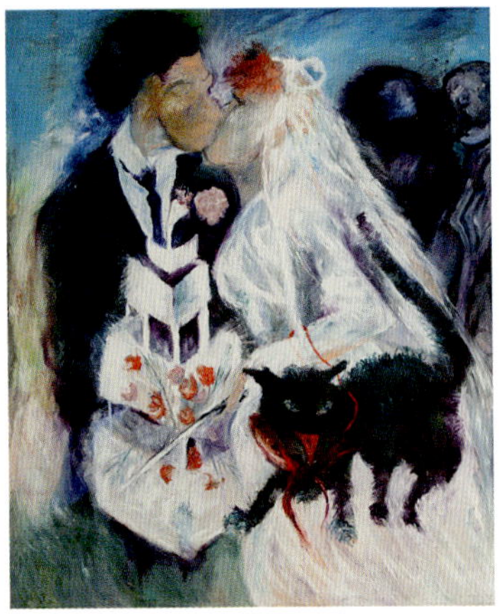

Bramall, Janella
Untitled 2
acrylic on canvas 213 x 183
14

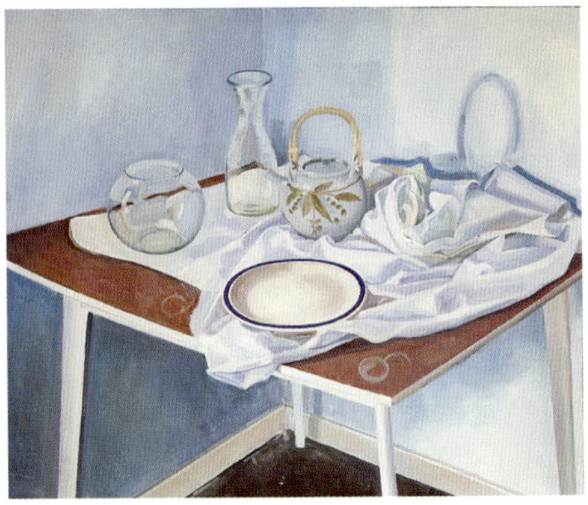

Breen, Bernadette
Still Life on a Table 1983
acrylic & oil on canvas 76 x 91.5
27

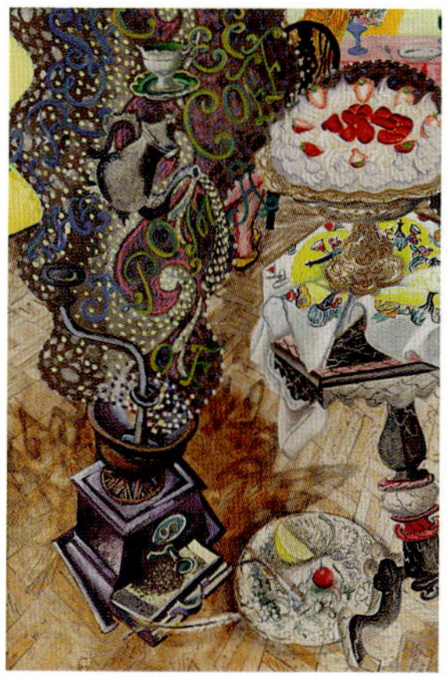

Brill, Vicky
The Aroma of Coffee
oil on wood 91 x 59
7

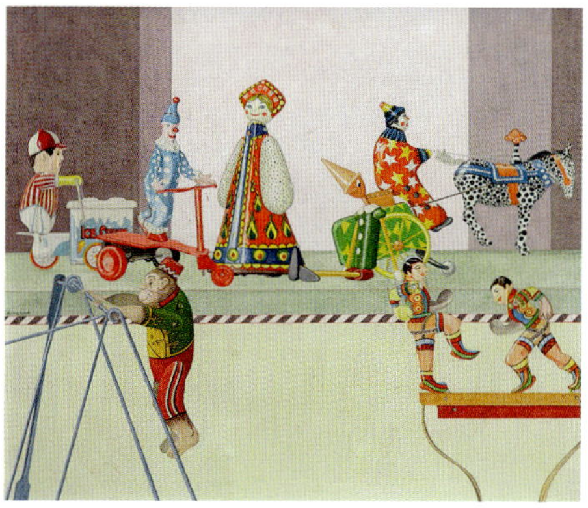

Cook, Jenny b.1942
Chinese Creatures 1985
oil on board 42 x 49.5
1

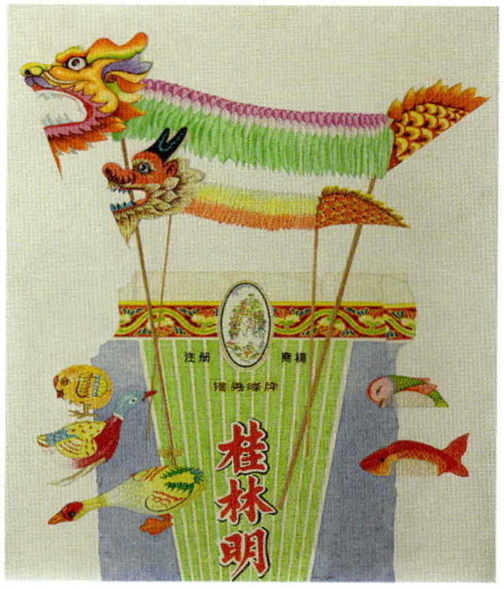

Cook, Jenny b.1942
Circus Toys 1985
oil on board 45.5 x 35
2

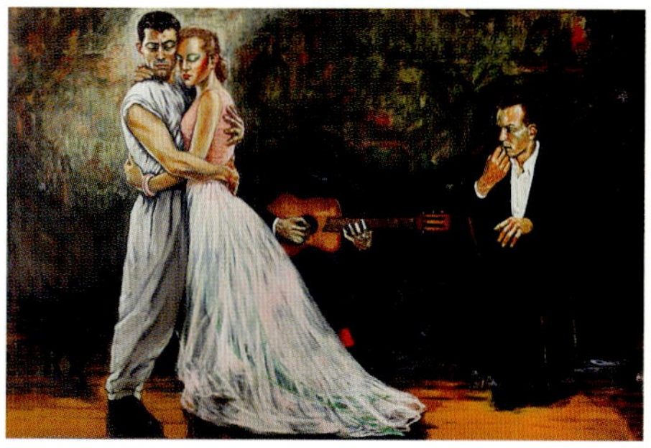

Cottam, Haydn b.1959
Between the Devil and the Deep Blue Sea
oil on canvas 183 x 274.5
22

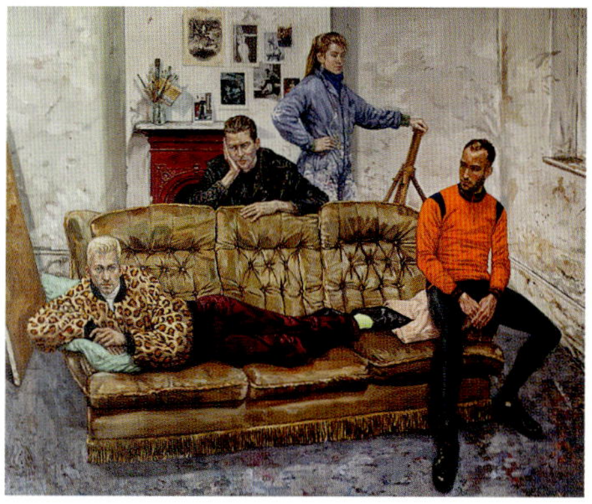

Cottam, Haydn b.1959
The Venus de Mile End
oil on canvas 240 x 305
8

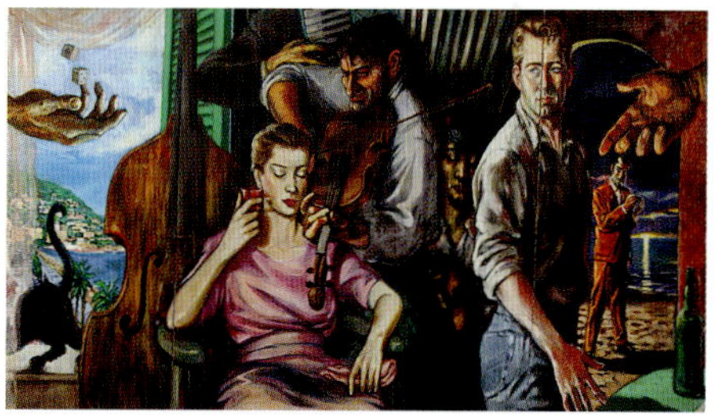

Cottam, Haydn b.1959
View through the Eye of the Great Northern Shore
oil on canvas 122 x 244
20

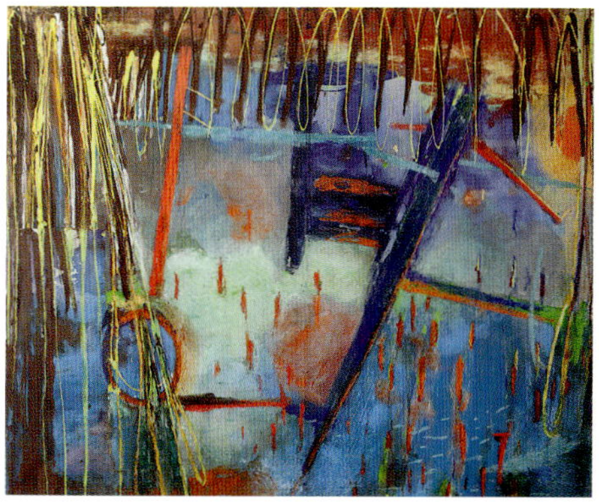

Croft, Tamsen
Reflections on Derwentwater
oil & mixed media on paper (?) 104.5 x 149.5
4

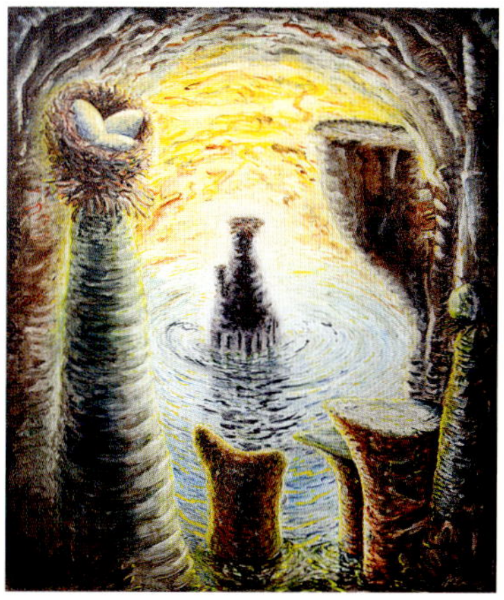

Crowley, Graham b.1950
Sanctuary 1982
oil on canvas 122 x 91
25

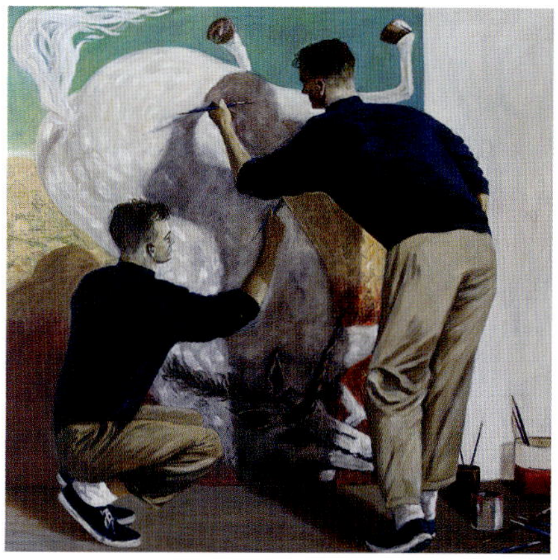

Doubleday, Peter
Is It Only Virgins That Can Catch a Unicorn?
oil on canvas 122 x 122
3

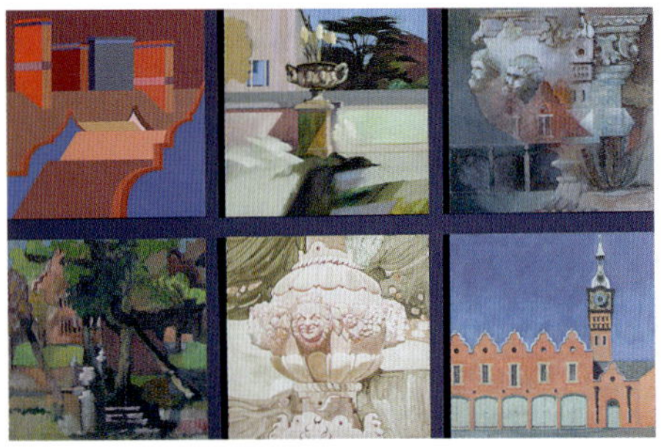

Four Unknown Artists
Six Scenes of Beaumanor, Leicestershire 1977
oil on board 95 x 146
34

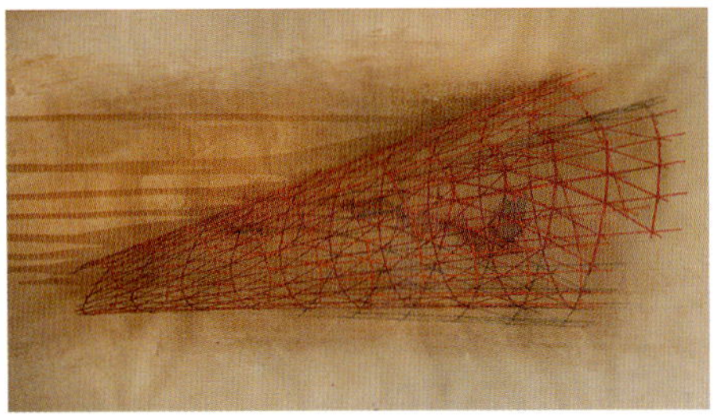

Haselden, Ron b.1944
Water Trap 1980
acrylic on paper 90 x 152
9

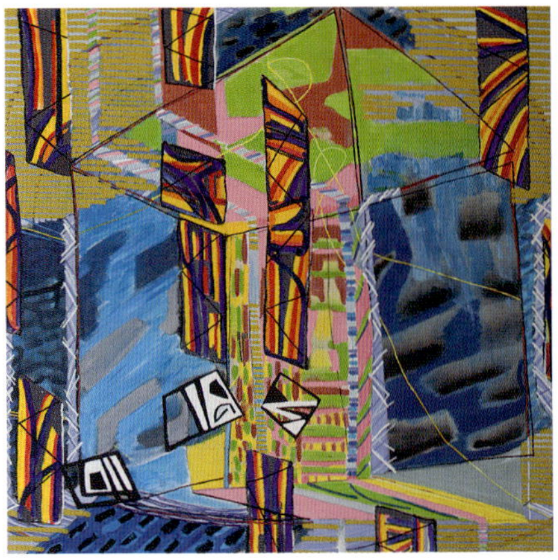

Hatton, Rosamunde
Record
acrylic on canvas 188 x 184.5
11

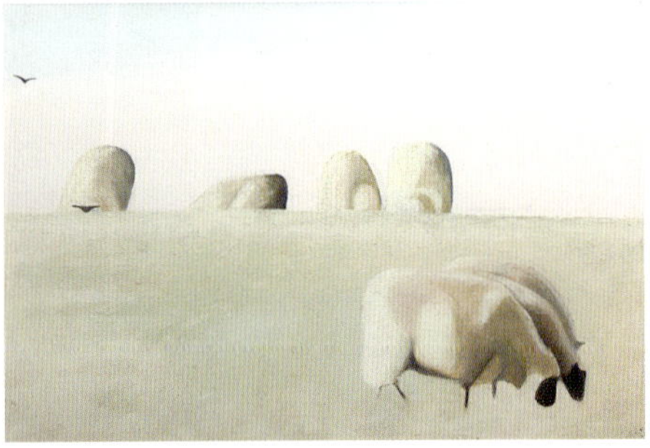

Haywood, Rosie
Where Sheep May Safely Graze II 1988
acrylic on board 50 x 77
24

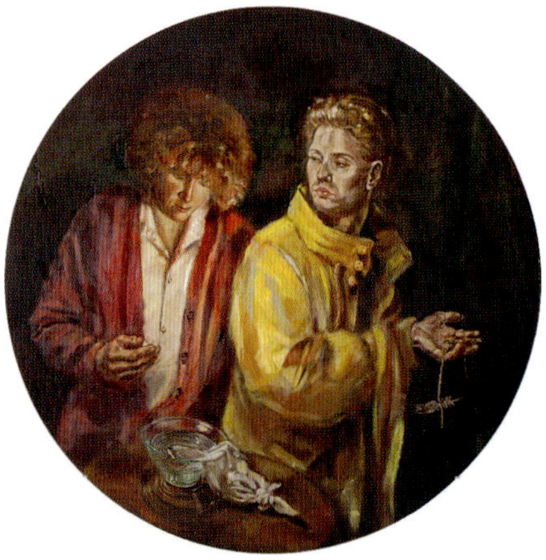

Jarvis, Timothy
The Wavering Balance of My Feeling
oil on canvas 119
21

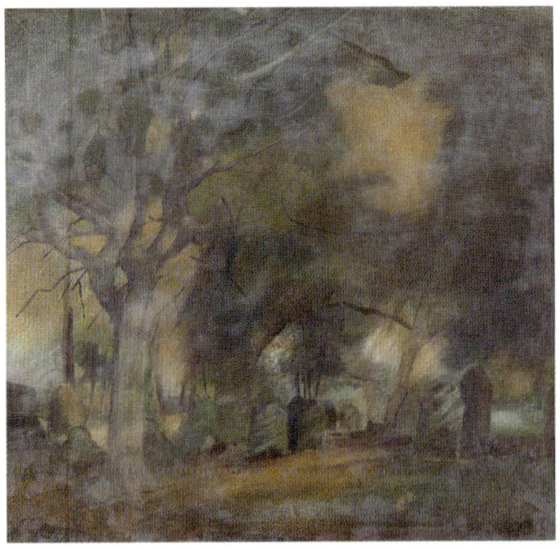

Lawley, Madonna
Graves in Sun and Wind 1987
tempera on canvas 61.5 x 61.5
29

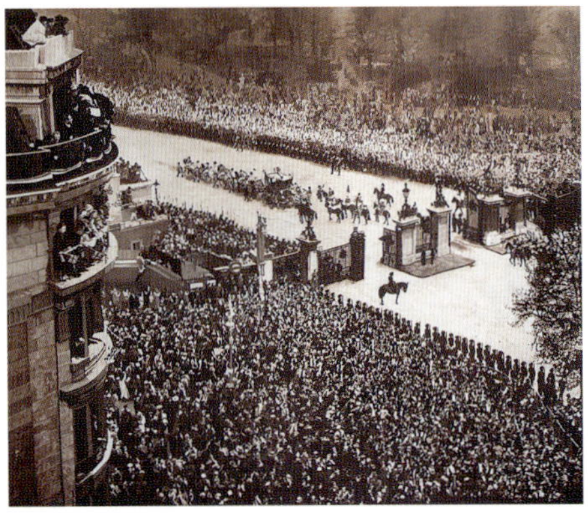

Littlehales, Thomas Paul b.1945
Untitled
oil on sail cloth 181.5 x 211
12

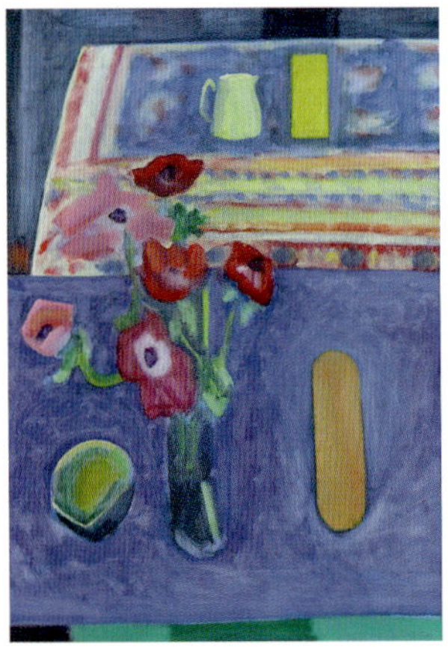

Martin, Ross active 1985–1990
Still Life: 3/11/86
acrylic on paper 87 x 61
18

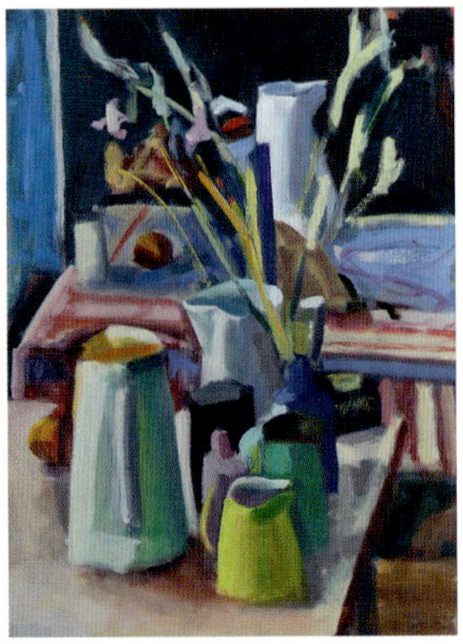

Martin, Ross active 1985–1990
Still Life: 26/11/85
acrylic on paper 87 x 61
17

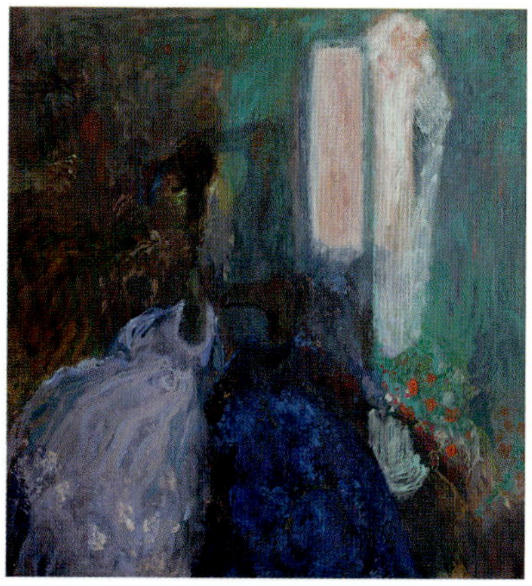

Murdoch, Sadie b.1965
Amoureuse (Marie Bashkirtseff)
oil on canvas 199 x 194.5
13

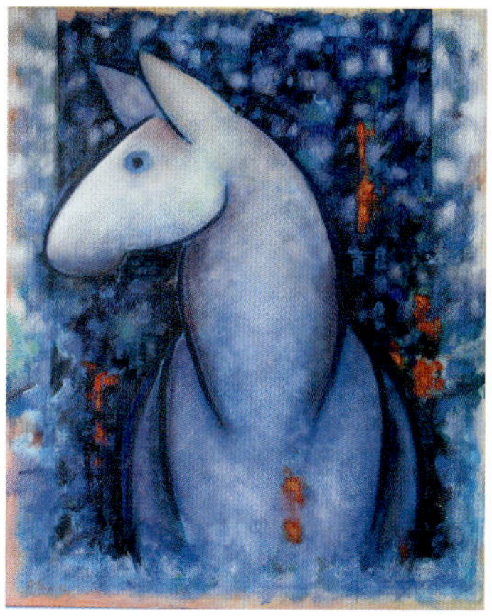

Norton, Paul b.1946
Horse 1982
oil on canvas 92 x 73
26

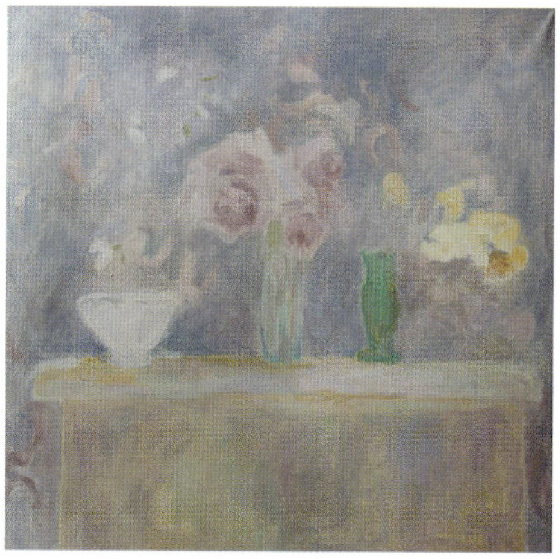

Potter, Clare
Untitled 1
oil on canvas 92 x 92 (E)
28

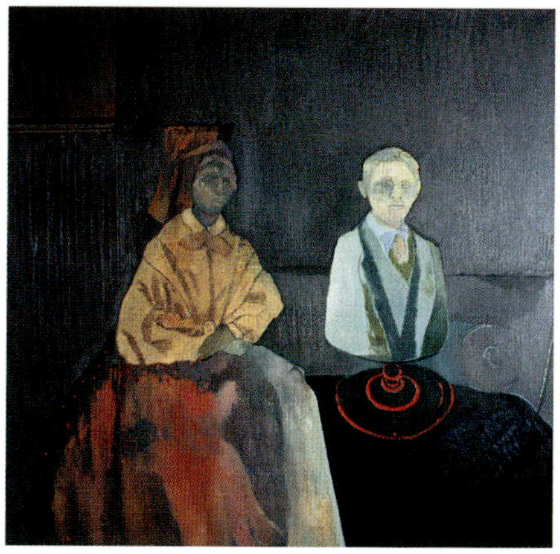

Sujo, Glenn b.1952
Gentle Portrait of the Artist and His Sister: Anxious Moments 1980–1981
oil on canvas 152.5 x 152.5
PCF3

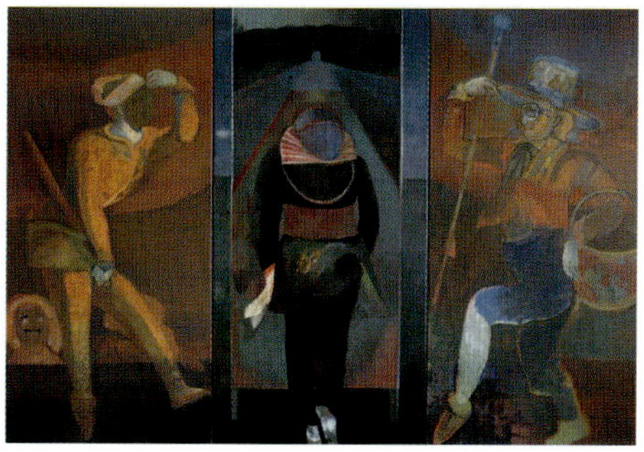

Sujo, Glenn b.1952
Triptych I: Harlequin, une parade (left panel); *Crispin, Diary of an Insurgent* (centre panel); *Ce qui joue le rôle d'un fou (...)* 1980–1981
oil on canvas 172.7 x 243.8
PCF1

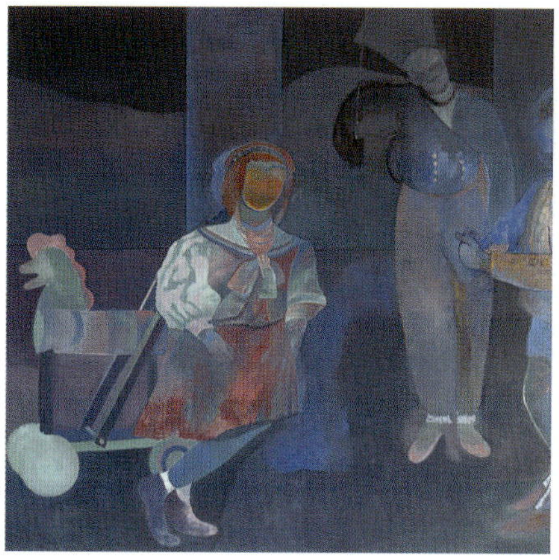

Sujo, Glenn b.1952
Where Play Ends (Come Out and Play)
c.1981
oil on canvas 152.5 x 152.5
PCF2

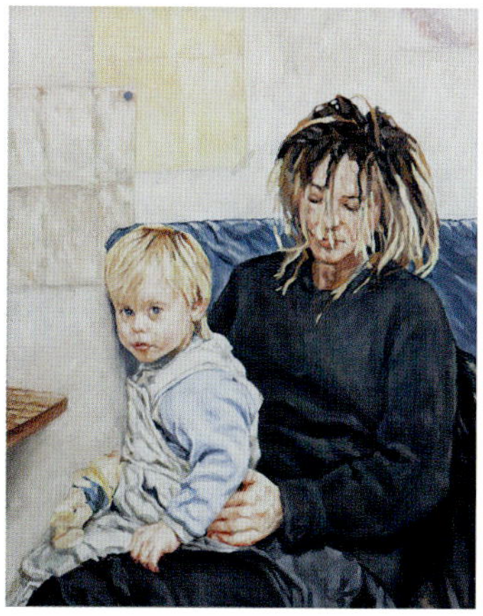

Tiffany, Francis
Mother and Child
oil on canvas 74.5 x 59.5
10

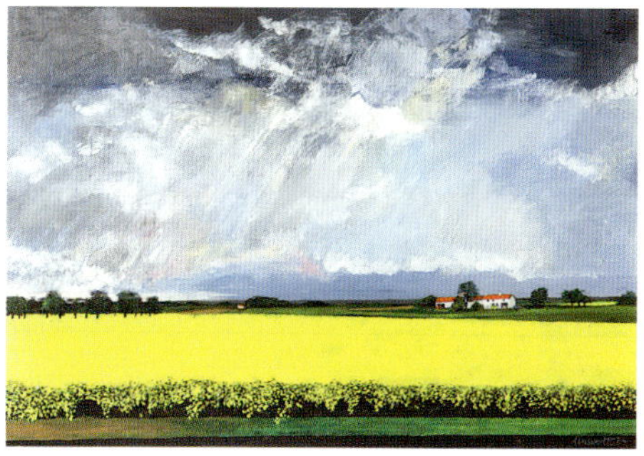

Unsworth, Peter
*Landscape, Rape Field** 1984
oil on canvas 60 x 91
19

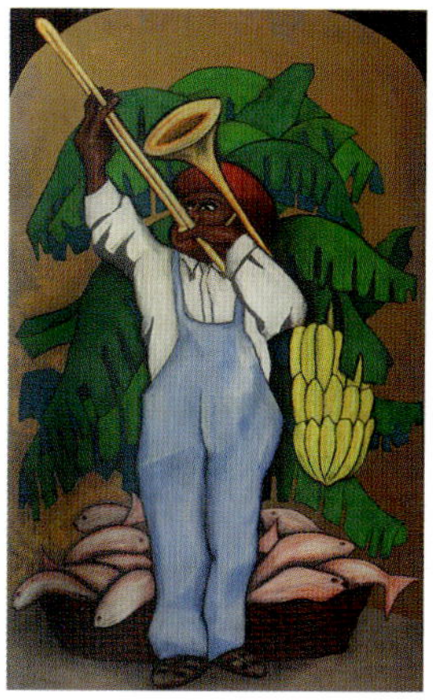

Vaughan, Alan b.1959
Trombone Player with Bananas and Fish
tempera & pastel on wood 142 x 91.5
6

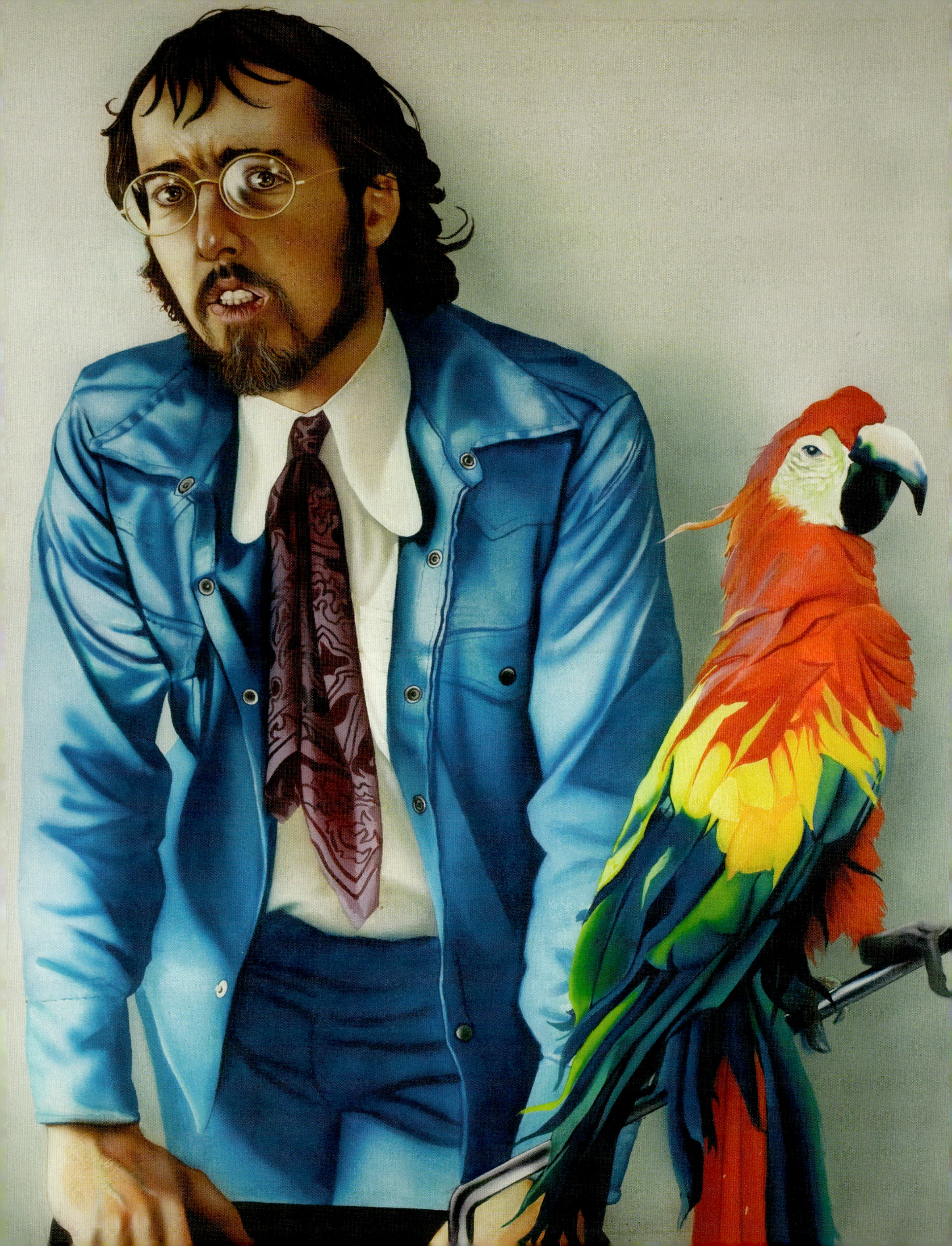

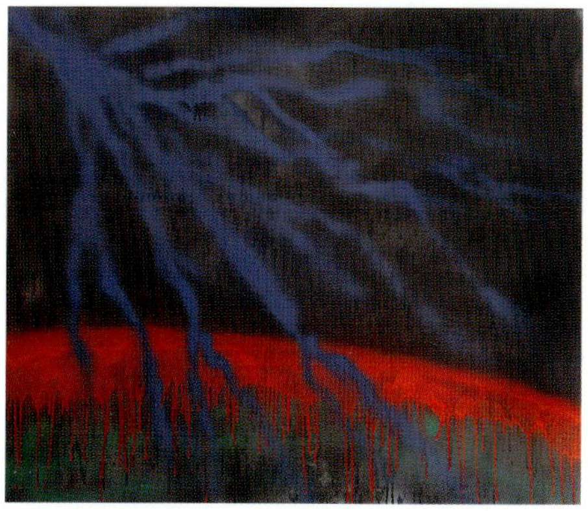

Vaughan, Kraig
Untitled Abstract
acrylic on canvas 101.5 x 126.5
32

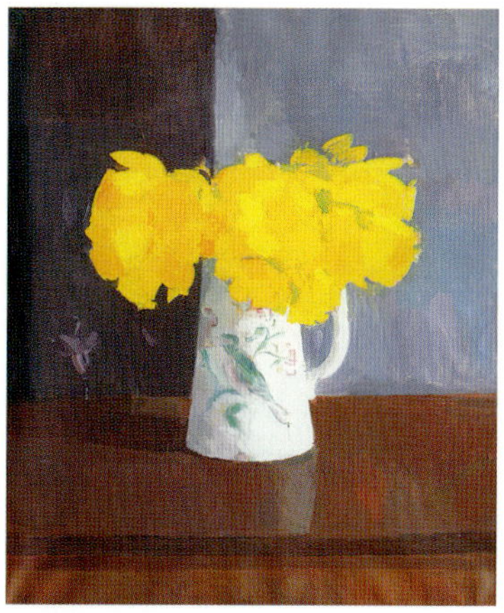

Volley, Jo b.1953
Daffodils
oil on canvas 47 x 39
16

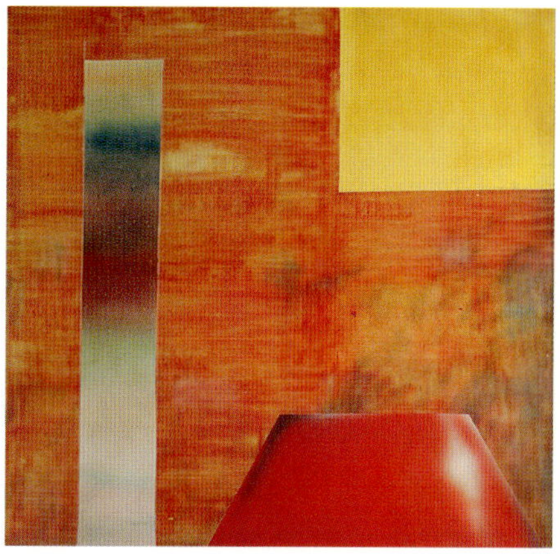

Walker, John b.1939
Tense Study 1 1966/1967
acrylic on canvas 210 x 212
15

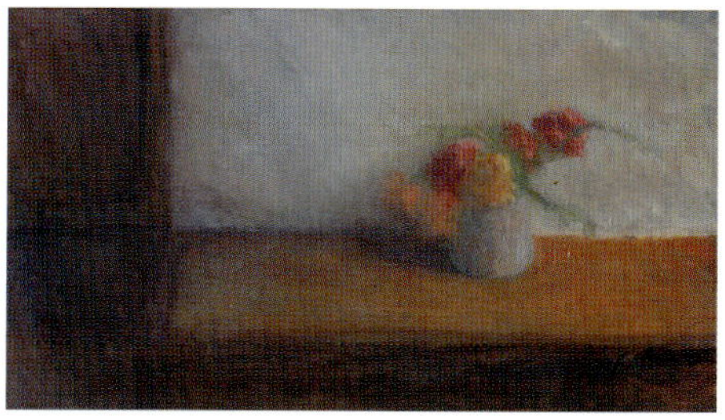

Whitehouse, Mark
Vase of Flowers
oil on canvas 40 x 76
33

Leicestershire County Council Civic Collection

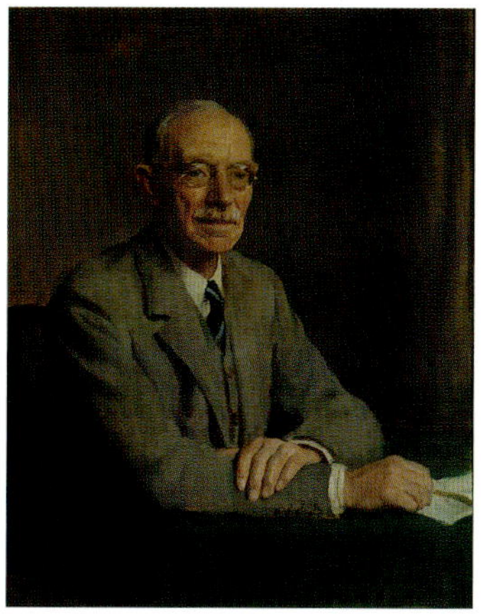

Birley, Oswald Hornby Joseph 1880–1952
Lieutenant Colonel Sir Robert Martin, CMG, TD, JP, DL, Chairman of Leicestershire County Council (1924–1960) 1949
oil on canvas 89 x 69
4

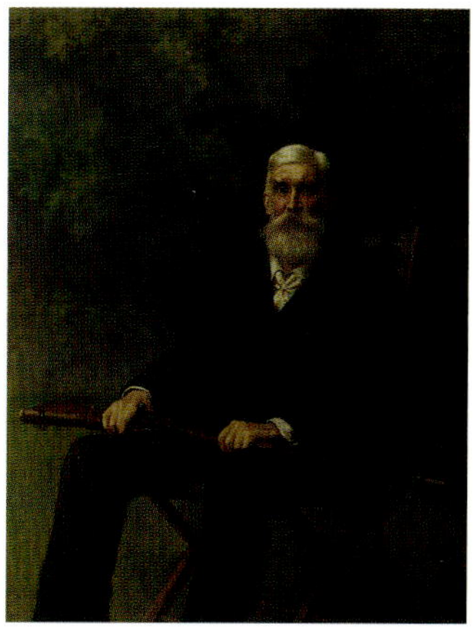

Collier, John 1850–1934
Colonel Sir Henry St John Halford (1828–1897), Bt, CB, VD, Chairman of Leicestershire County Council (1889–1893) 1896
oil on canvas 140 x 110.5
1

Facing page: Gorman, Michael, b.1938, *Mr Treadwell Meets the Critics* (detail), 1973, Leicester Arts and Museums Service (p. 47)

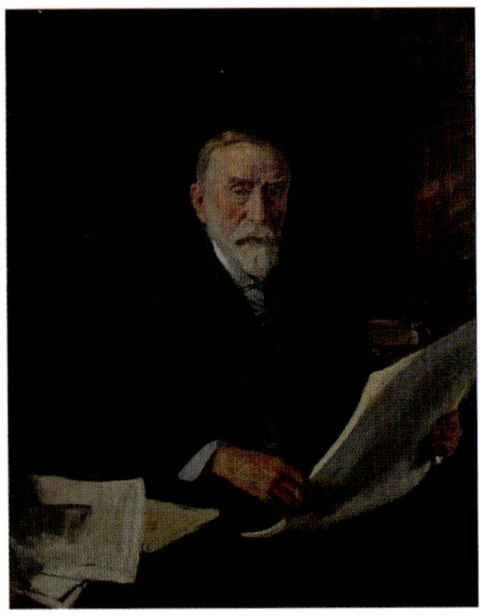

Eves, Reginald Grenville 1876–1941
Sir Thomas Cope (1840–1924), Bt, DL, Chairman of Leicestershire County Council (1908–1922)
oil on canvas 109.5 x 86
6

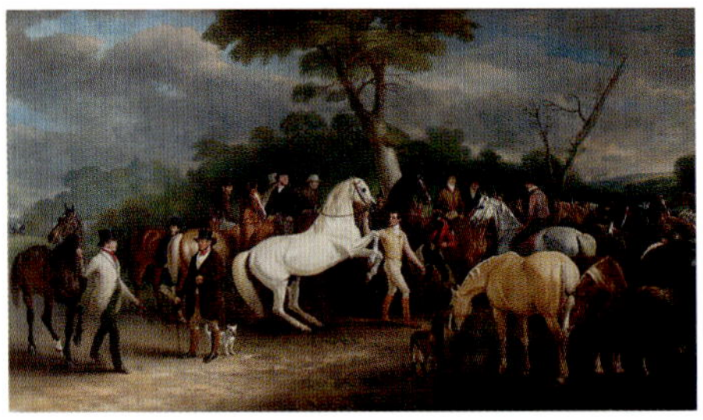

Ferneley, John E. 1782–1860
Melton Mowbray Horse Fair
oil on canvas 152 x 256
8

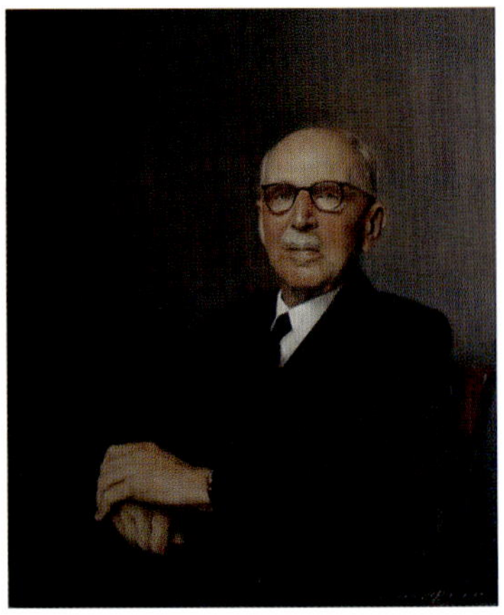

Hepple, Norman 1908–1994
Victor Robert Pochin, CBE, JP, DL, Chairman of Leicestershire County Council (1960–1961)
1968
oil on canvas 75 x 62
2

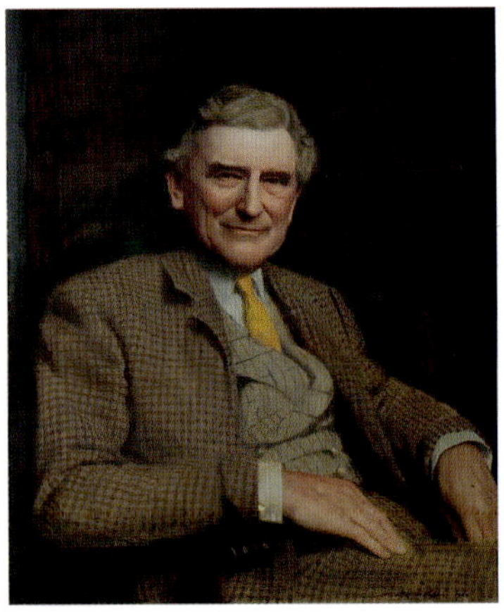

Hepple, Norman 1908–1994
Colonel Philip Henry Lloyd, CBE, TD, JP, DL, Chairman of Leicestershire County Council (1961–1974) 1969
oil on canvas 74.5 x 62
5

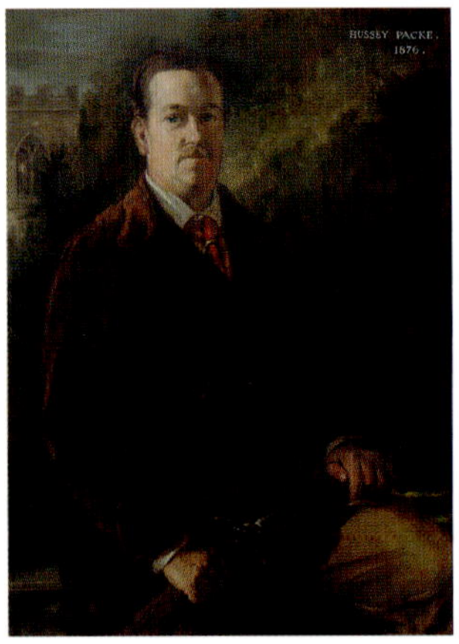

unknown artist
Mr Hussey Packe, DL, Chairman of Leicestershire County Council (1893–1908)
1876
oil on canvas 100 x 75
7

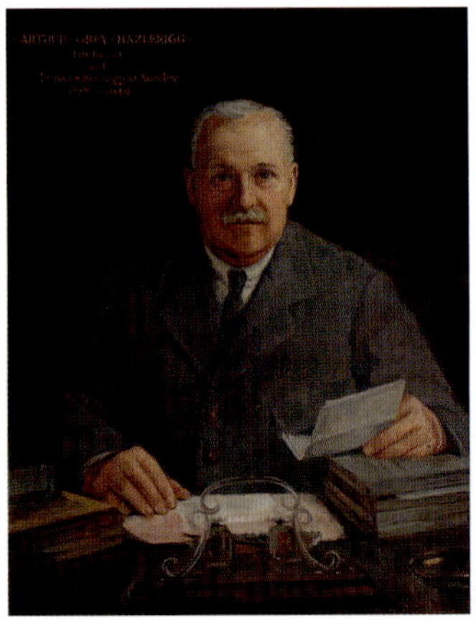

unknown artist
The Right Honourable Arthur Grey Hazlerigg (1878–1949), 1st Baron Hazlerigg of Noseley, Lord Lieutenant of Leicestershire (...) 1968
oil on canvas 99.5 x 74.5
3

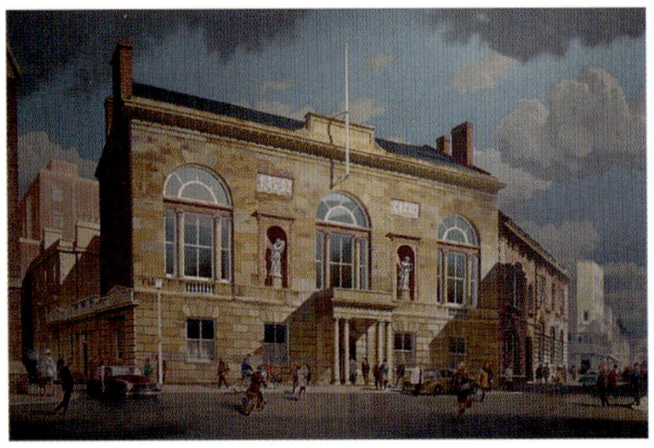

Wright, Lawrence 1906–c.1985
The County Rooms Leicester, Exterior View
1968
oil on board 82 x 120
9

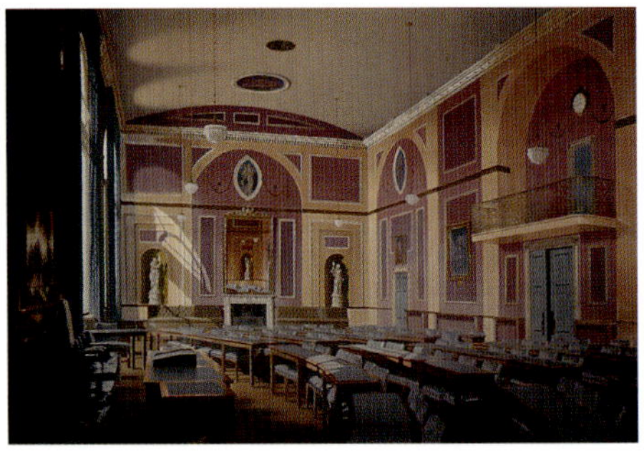

Wright, Lawrence 1906–c.1985
The County Rooms Leicester, Interior of the Council Chamber 1968
oil on board 82 x 120
10

Leicestershire County Council Museums Service

Leicestershire Museums' art collection began with the formation of a core collection of paintings at the Leicester Town Museum in the 1850s. Today, the focus of the Collection is on the landscape and built environment of the county, and local sporting pursuits. The lives of local people are recorded in a series of portraits and in scenes of working life in some of the county's principal industries. The Collection is strong in representing the work of local artists who painted their surroundings and interests.

The Collection has benefited from support from the Friends of Leicester and Leicestershire Museums and grants from the Museums, Libraries and Archives Council/Victoria and Albert Museum Purchase Grant Fund. The focus on recent collecting has been on smaller topographical works on paper which are outside the remit of this catalogue.

The portrait collection includes politicians, social reformers, dignitaries, innovators, landowners and private individuals. Notable sitters include Robert Bakewell, the agriculturalist who introduced stockbreeding methods that transformed the quality of Britain's cattle, horses and sheep, painted on a Bay Cob horse by John Boultbee. Science is represented by Thomas Beach's painting of *Dr Richard Pulteney (1730–1801), FRS, FLS*, the eminent naturalist and pioneer of Leicestershire botany, and a portrait of *Dr John Bowles (1765–1834)*, the early equestrian veterinary surgeon, by Benjamin Marshall.

The realm of politics and ceremonial life is reflected in portraits of *George Villiers (1592–1628), 1st Duke of Buckingham*, by Cornelius Janssens van Ceulen, *John Manners (1676–1721), 2nd Duke of Rutland*, by Charles Jervas, portraits of Viscount and Lady Wentworth by Thomas Hudson, and also *Ambassador John Burnaby (1701–1774), Minister to the Swiss at Turin (1743–1749)* attributed to Emmanuel Jakob Handmann, after Pompeo Batoni.

There are also important portraits by an unknown artist of two social and political reformers; John Skevington, the Loughborough Chartist, and Levi Lovett, one of the founders of the Leicestershire Miners' Association.

Local landowners and gentry include Sir John Palmer painted, by John E. Ferneley, with his shepherd John Green and their prize Leicester Longwool sheep, and a fine collection of portraits of the Herrick family of Beaumanor Hall.

Leicestershire has been a centre for country sports, especially fox hunting, for centuries and it is unsurprising that a number of paintings depicting the sport form a major group within the Collection.

Most notable amongst the sporting art collection are the works painted by John E. Ferneley of Melton Mowbray, including a triple portrait of the Grant brothers in the field (including Francis Grant, President of the Royal Academy from 1866 to 1878). The sporting art collection was brought up-to-date with *The Melton Mowbray Hunt Meet* by Tim Fisher, painted in 2000.

One of the earliest paintings of industrial change in the Collection is the *The Opening of the Leicester and Swannington Railway (The Arrival of the First Train at Bagworth, 17 July 1832)* by John E. Ferneley. The railway made economic the movement of coal from the North West of Leicestershire to local markets and onward transport links across the country. It heralded a new age in Leicestershire's industrial development which has since been depicted by artists including Bryan Organ and Paul Anthony Waplington, with images of railways, coal mining, quarrying, metalworking and aeronautics.

Alexandra Davy, Collections Access Officer (Exhibitions & Fine Art)

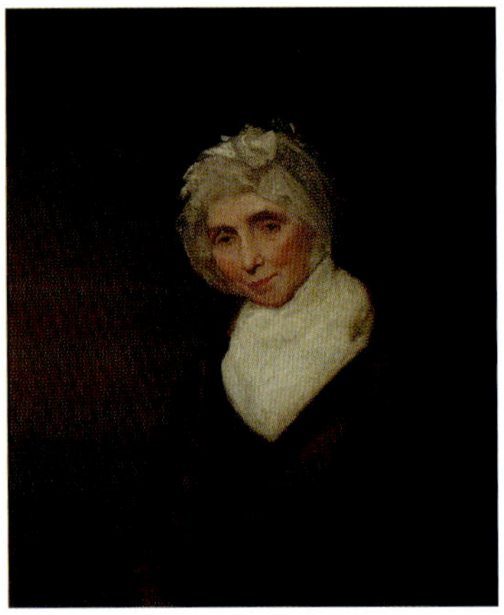

Artaud, William 1763–1823
Portrait of a Lady of the Herrick Family 1813
oil on canvas 75 x 62.5
L.F25.1937.11.0

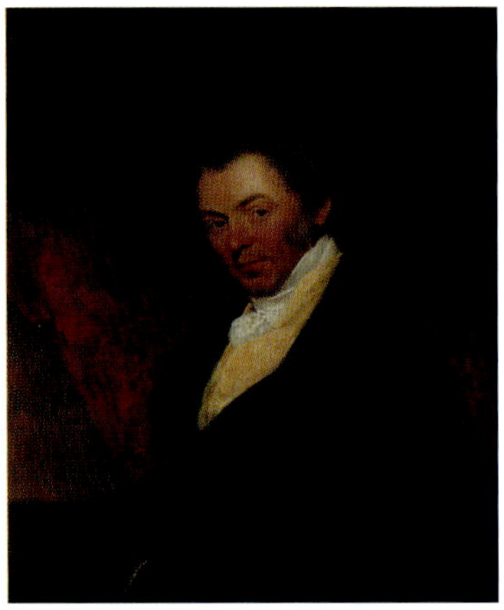

Artaud, William 1763–1823
Portrait of a Gentleman of the Herrick Family
oil on canvas 75 x 62.5
L.F25.1937.10.0

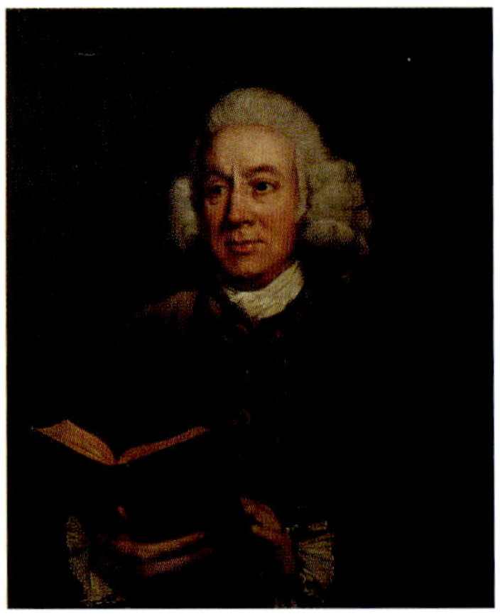

Beach, Thomas 1738–1806
Dr Richard Pulteney (1730–1801), FRS, FLS 1788
oil on canvas 76.2 x 63.2
L.F3.1911.0.0

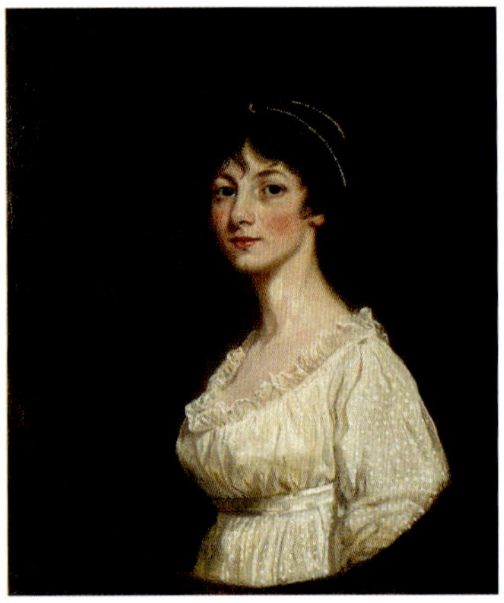

Beach, Thomas 1738–1806
Portrait of a Girl of the Burnaby Family 1801
oil on canvas 71.5 x 61.5
X.F1.2010.0.0

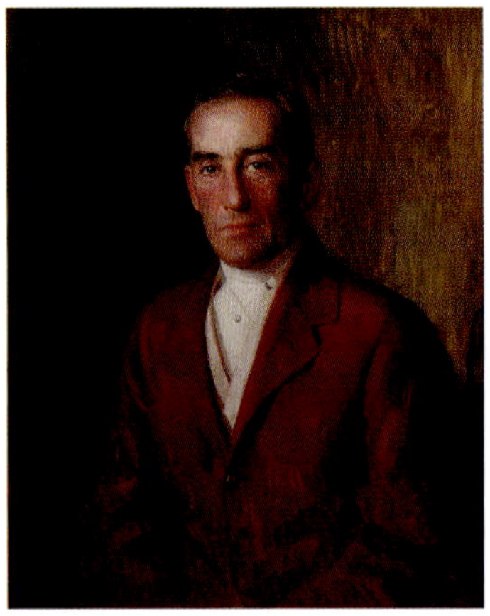

Becker, Nicolas active 1922–1932
Algernon Burnaby (1868–1938) 1928
oil on canvas 81.3 x 66
L.F8.1957.0.0

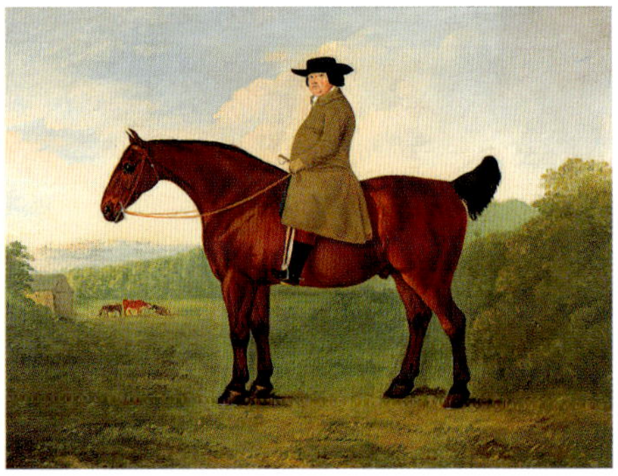

Boultbee, John 1753–1812
Robert Bakewell Mounted on a Bay Cob
oil on canvas 68.8 x 88.4
L.F7.1967.0.0

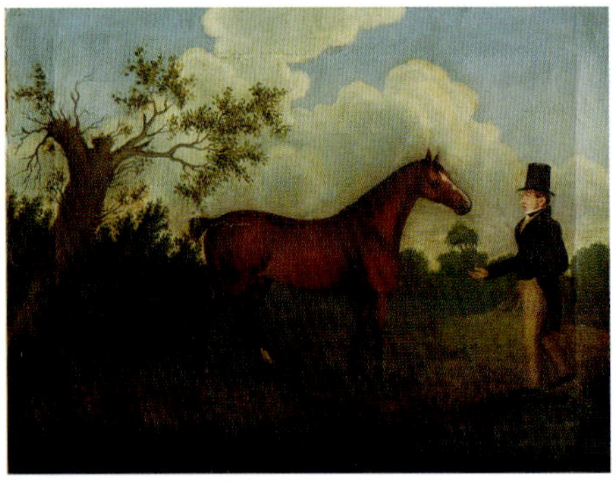

Bown, Sydney
A Hunter 1833
oil on canvas 50.8 x 61
L.F151.1957.0.0

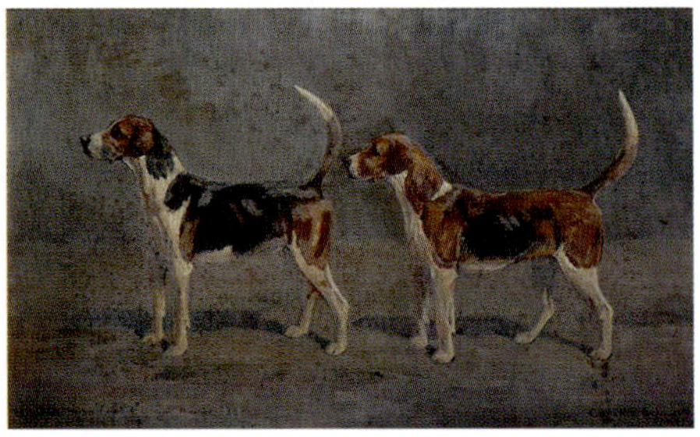

Bradley, Cuthbert 1861–1943
'Fallible' and 'Ranter' 1926
oil on canvas 31 x 48.5
L.H80.1994.5.0

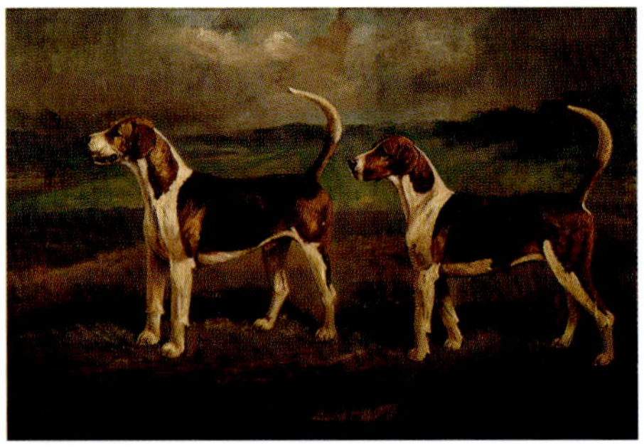

Bradley, Cuthbert 1861–1943
Quorn Hounds, 'Cruiser' and 'Woeful' 1926
oil on canvas 50 x 75.5
L.F278.1957.2.0

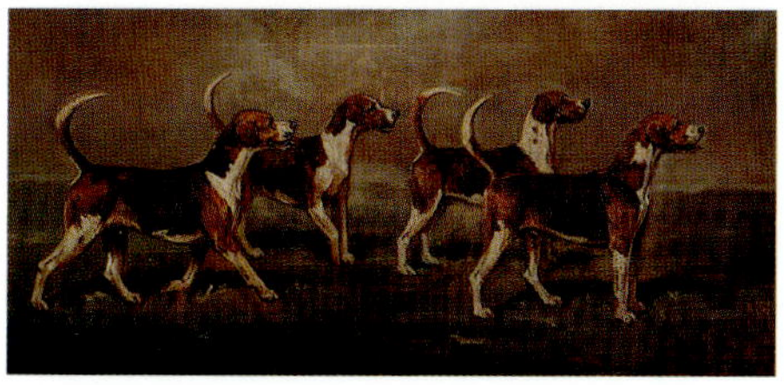

Bradley, Cuthbert 1861–1943
Quorn Hounds, 'Batsman', 'Baffler', 'Weaver' and 'Batchelor' 1927
oil on canvas 30.7 x 61
L.F278.1957.3.0

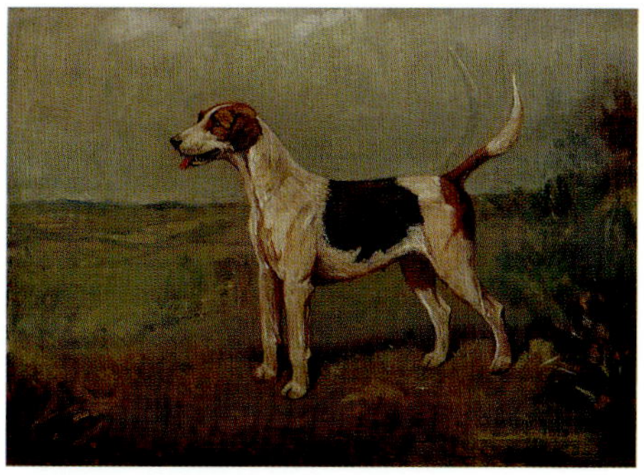

Bradley, Cuthbert 1861–1943
Quorn Hound 'Wonderful' 1929
oil on board 27.9 x 38.1
L.F278.1957.4.0

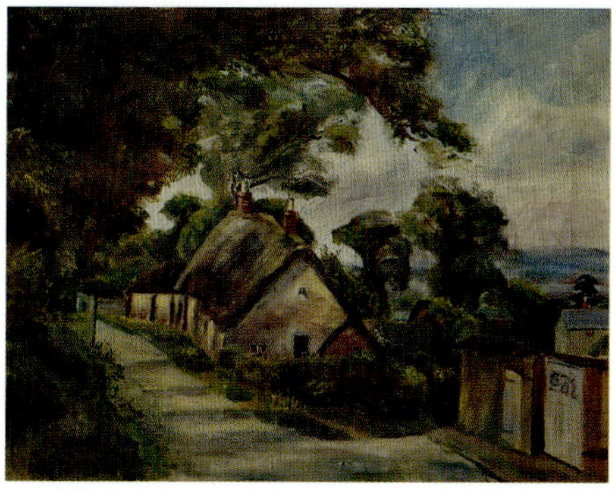

Cave, F.
East Farndon, Leicestershire 1901
oil on canvas 35.3 x 45.5
M.H100.1983.3069.0

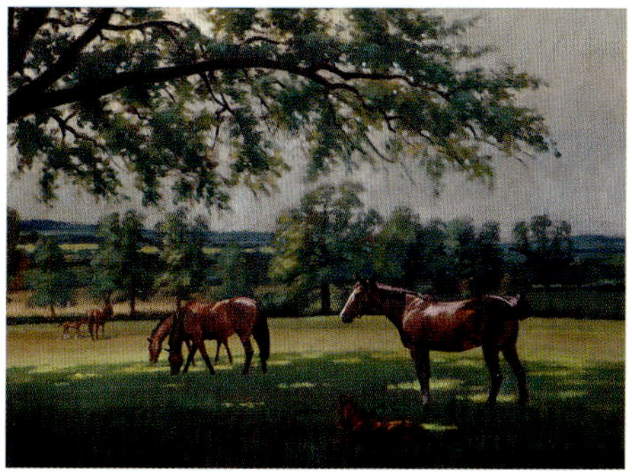

Cawthorne, Neil b.1936
Summer Days
oil on canvas 22 x 38.5
X.F2.2003.0.0

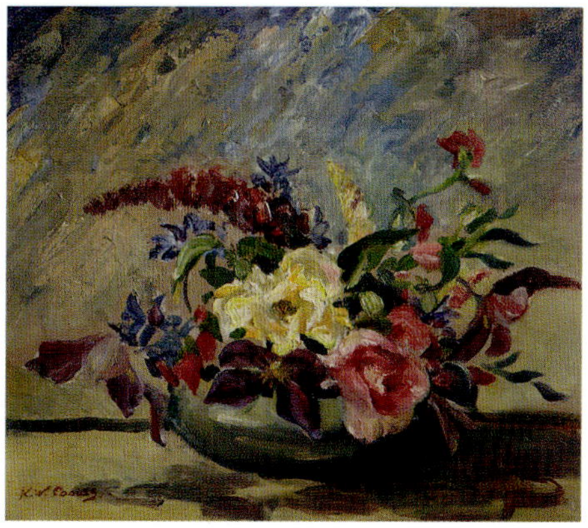

Coales, Kathleen Wallis 1893–1982
Still Life
oil on board 49 x 53
M.H64.1998.0.0

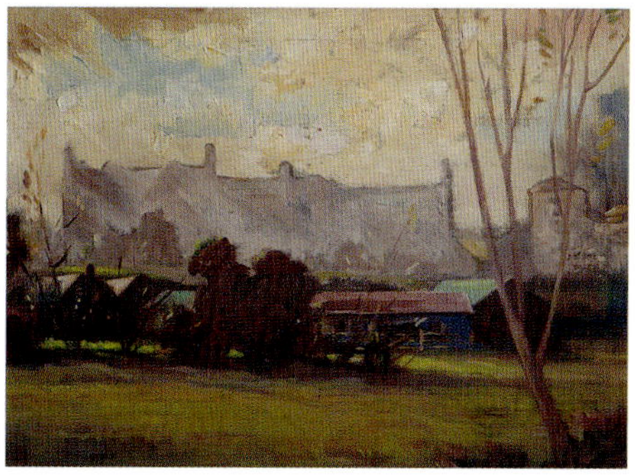

Cooke, Arthur Claude 1867–1951
Ragdale Hall, Leicestershire
oil on card 29.5 x 40
L.F23.1984.3.0

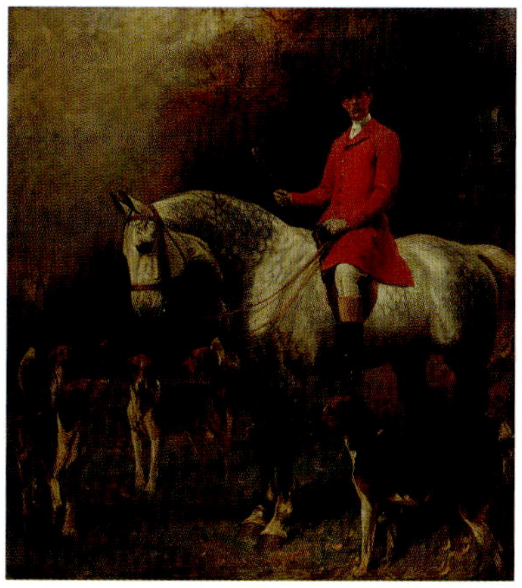

Cope, Arthur Stockdale 1857–1940
Equestrian Portrait of Captain Burns Hartopp with Hounds 1906
oil on canvas 163 x 143
L.F23.1987.0.0

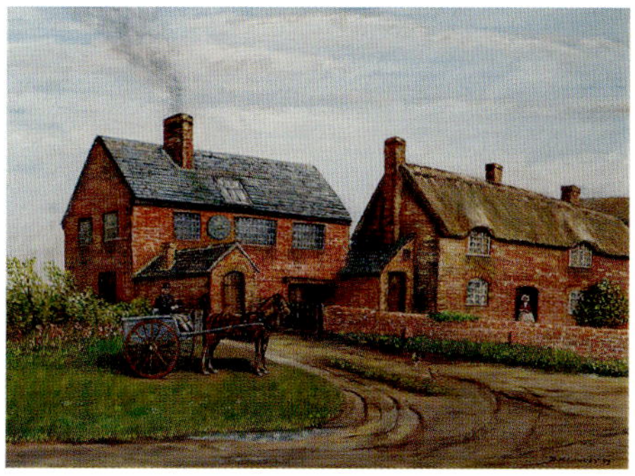

Cowley, David M.
View of the Deacon Workshop, Barton in the Beans, Leicestershire
oil on canvas 45.5 x 61
X.W11.2010.0.0

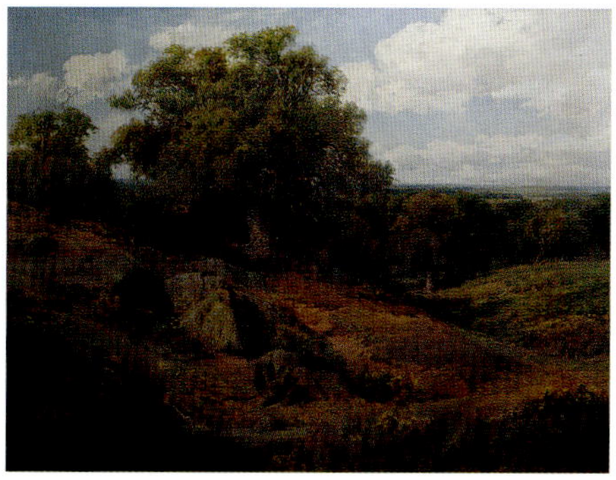

Davies, Edward 1841–1920
Raven Hill, Charnwood Forest, Leicestershire 1901
oil on canvas 137.8 x 183
L.F1.1902.0.0

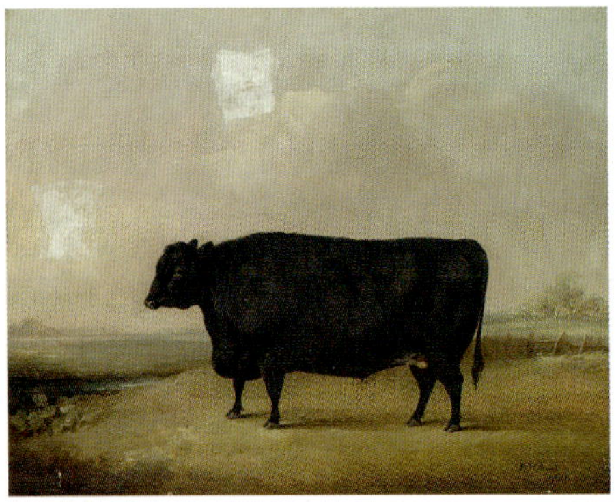

Davis, William Henry 1786–1865
Black Bull 1841
oil on canvas 71.1 x 83.8
L.F346.1956.0.0

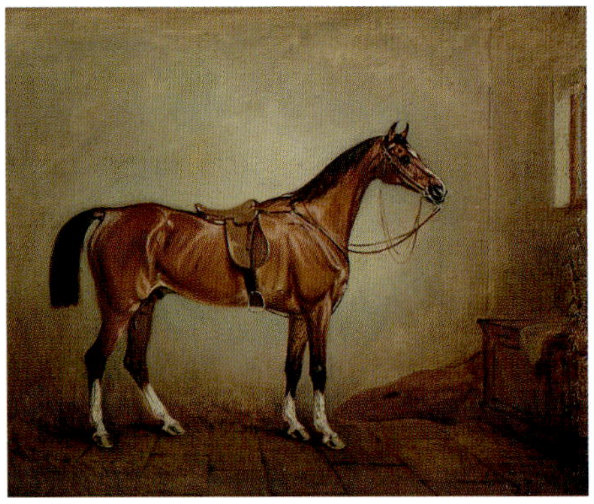

Ferneley, Claude Lorraine 1822–1891
A Hunter 1845
oil on canvas 30.5 x 35.5
L.F20.1935.16.4

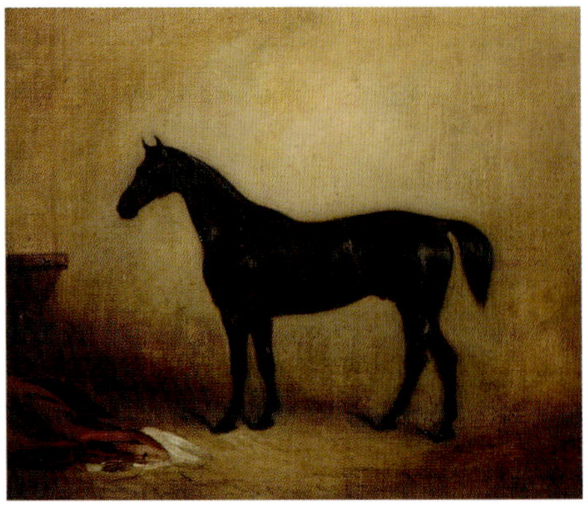

Ferneley, Claude Lorraine 1822–1891
A Hunter 1847
oil on canvas 31 x 36
L.F20.1935.16.3

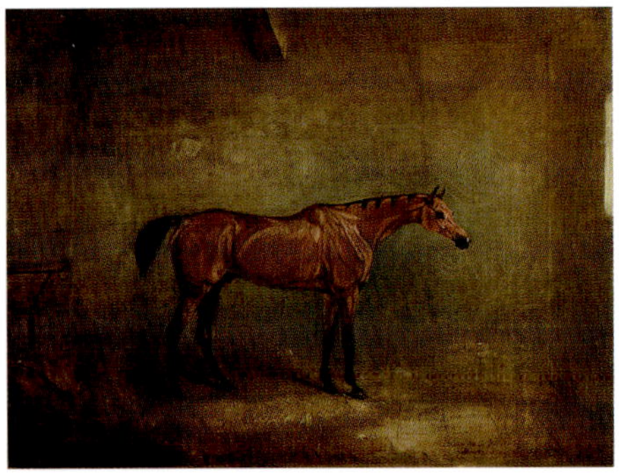

Ferneley, Claude Lorraine 1822–1891
A Hunter
oil on canvas 38 x 51 (E)
L.F20.1933.16.1

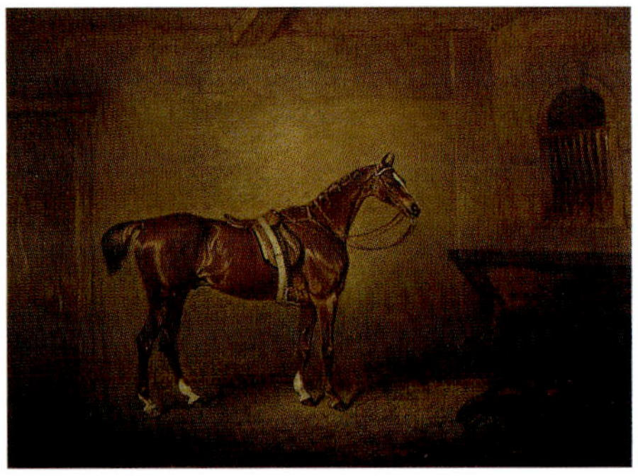

Ferneley, Claude Lorraine 1822–1891
A Hunter
oil on canvas 38 x 51 (E)
L.F20.1935.16.1

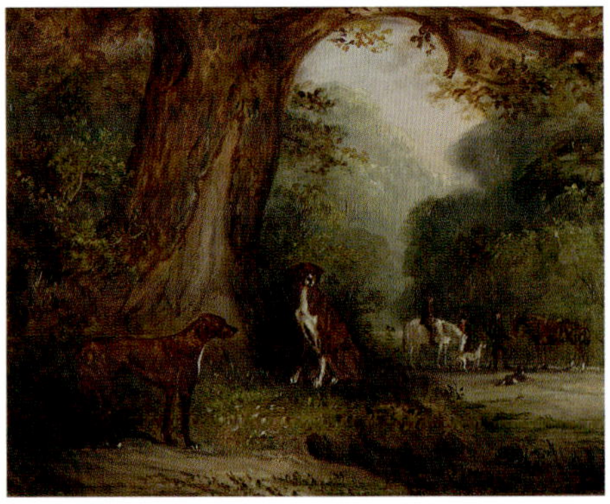

Ferneley, Claude Lorraine 1822–1891
A Shooting Party in a Wood
oil on canvas 26.5 x 31.5
L.F20.1935.16.5

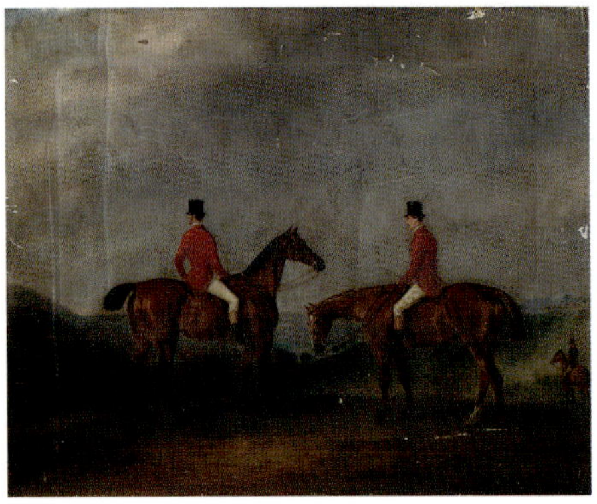

Ferneley, Claude Lorraine 1822–1891
Two Huntsmen in a Landscape
oil on canvas 43.5 x 51.8
L.F20.1935.16.2

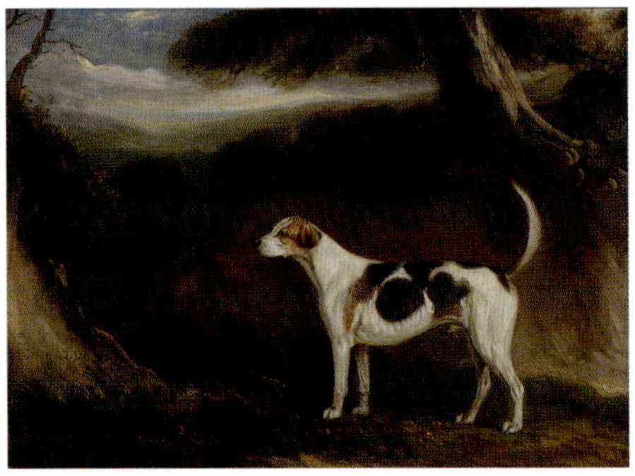

Ferneley, John II 1814–1862
Playmate 1847
oil on canvas 43.8 x 59.7
L.F25.1982.0.0

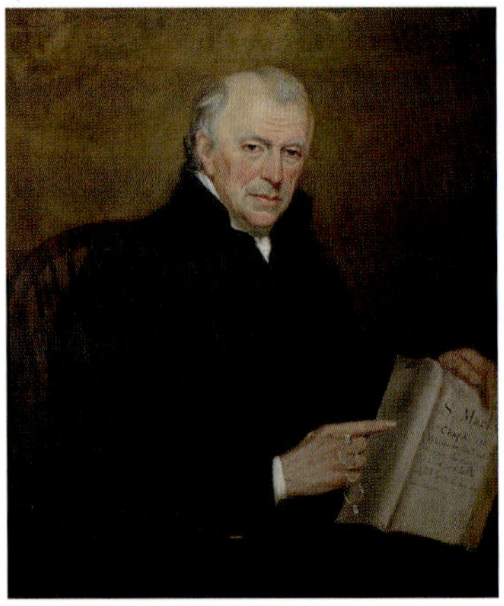

Ferneley, John E. 1782–1860
Dr Thomas Ford (1742–1821) 1820
oil on canvas 73.5 x 61
L.IL1289.1993 (P)

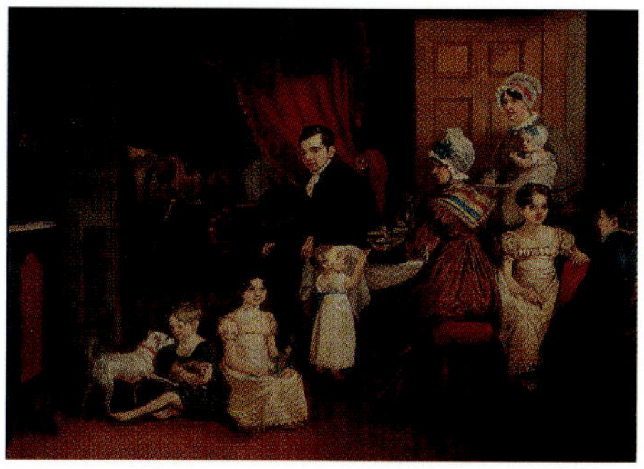

Ferneley, John E. 1782–1860
Portrait of the Artist and His Family in His Studio 1822–1823
oil on canvas 49 x 67
L.F184.1981.0.0

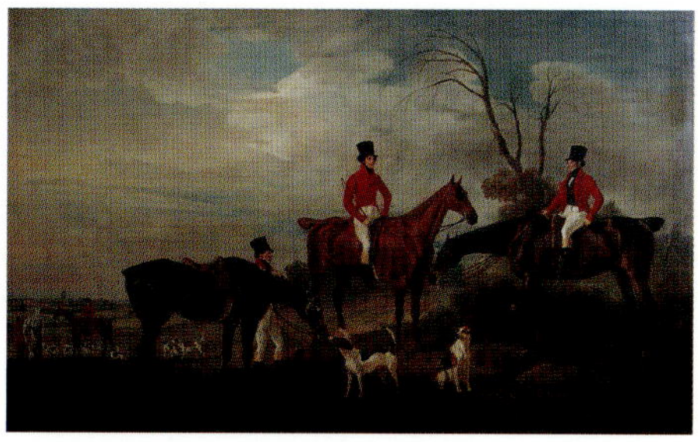

Ferneley, John E. 1782–1860
John, Henry and Francis Grant at Melton 1823
oil on canvas 107.5 x 170.5
L.F8.1967.0.0

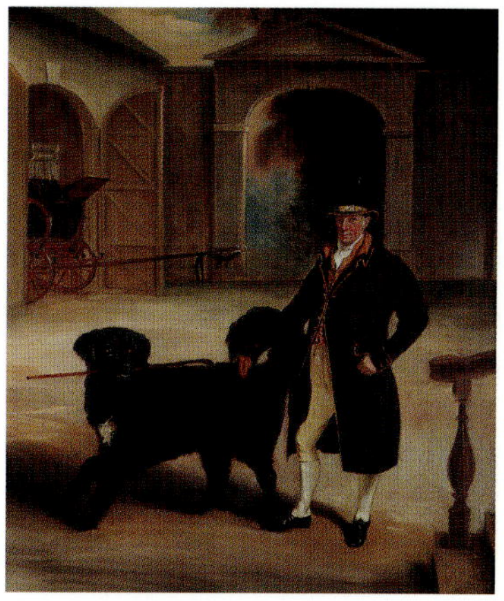

Ferneley, John E. 1782–1860
Mr Pare's Coachman with a Newfoundland Dog 1823
oil on canvas 59.2 x 49.7
L.F24.1982.0.0

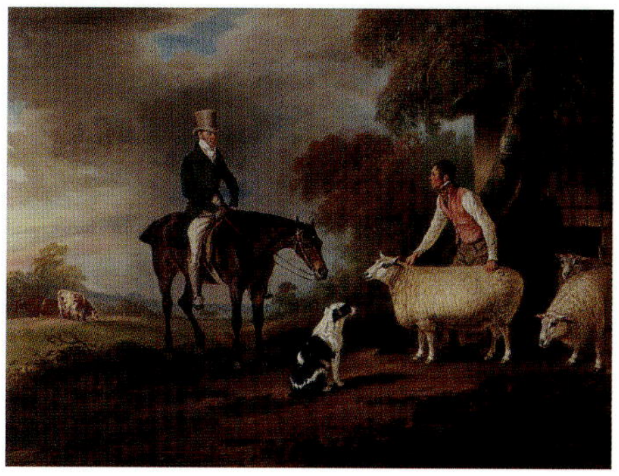

Ferneley, John E. 1782–1860
Sir John Palmer on His Favourite Mare with His Shepherd, John Green, and His Prize Leicester Longwool Sheep 1823
oil on canvas 84.4 x 109.4
L.F23.1982.0.0

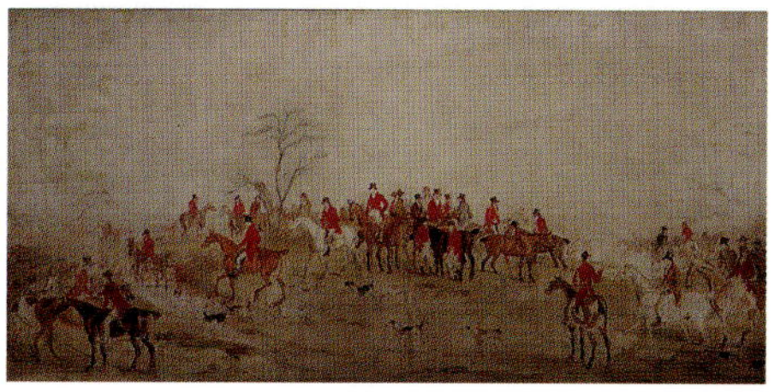

Ferneley, John E. 1782–1860
The Quorn at Quenby (sketch) 1823
oil on canvas 47.7 x 96.5
L.F68.1936.0.0

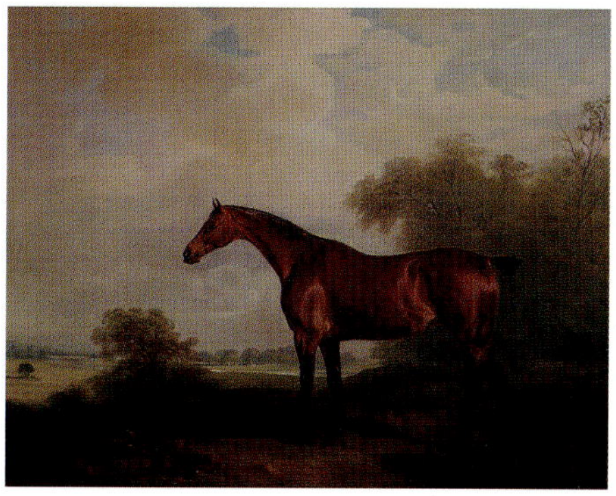

Ferneley, John E. 1782–1860
Mr Green's Bay Mare 1825
oil on canvas 85.5 x 105.5
L.F26.1948.0.0

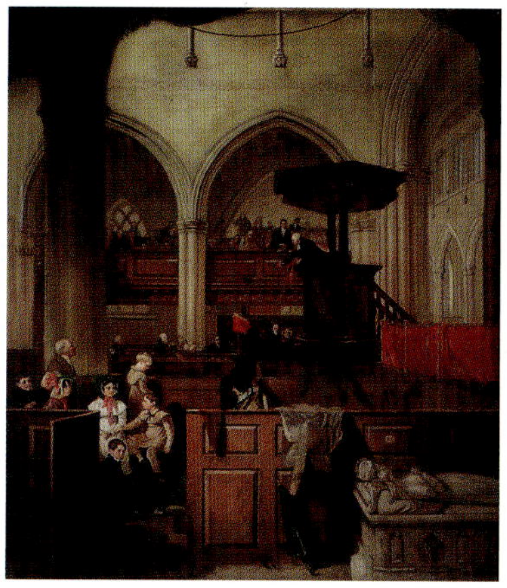

Ferneley, John E. 1782–1860
The Ferneley Family Pew in Melton Mowbray Parish Church, Leicestershire 1828
oil on canvas 129.5 x 111.7
L.F4.1972.0.0

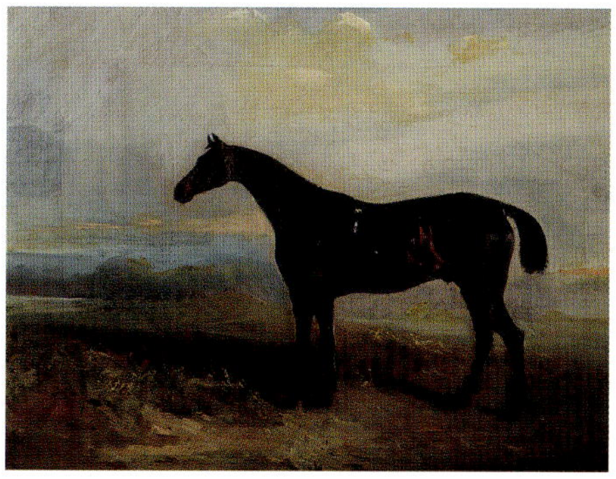

Ferneley, John E. 1782–1860
Hunter in a Landscape 1830–1839
oil on canvas 24 x 30.2
L.F20.1935.3.0

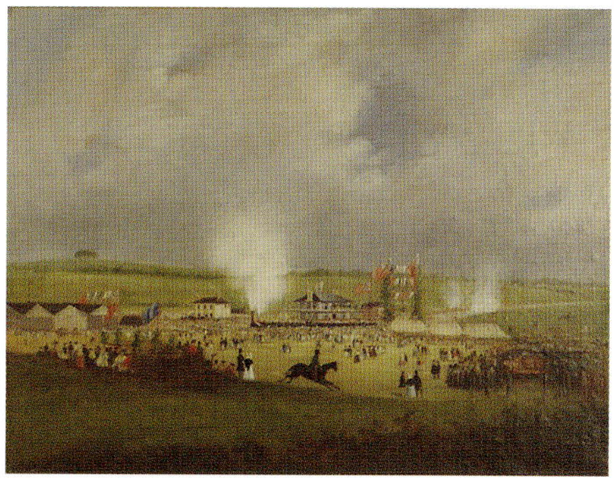

Ferneley, John E. 1782–1860
The Opening of the Leicester and Swannington Railway (The Arrival of the First Train at Bagworth, 17 July 1832) 1832
oil & paper on canvas 35.5 x 45.5
L.F962.1978.0.0

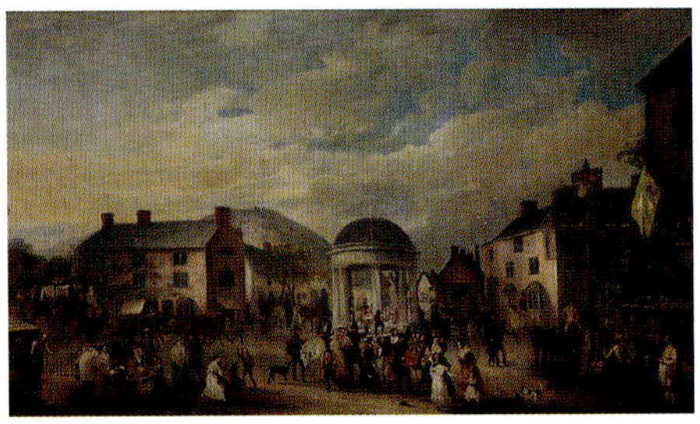

Ferneley, John E. 1782–1860
Mountsorrel, Leicestershire, the Market Place
1842
oil on canvas 90 x 154
L.F18.1949.0.0

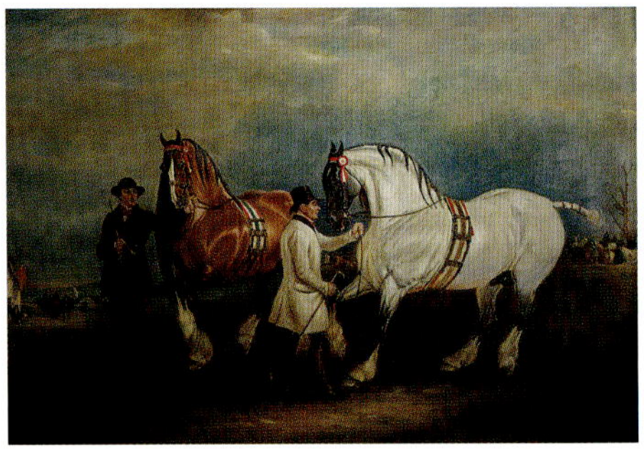

Ferneley, John E. 1782–1860
Carthorses with Grooms at a Fair c.1856
oil on canvas 105 x 149
L.F20.1935.17.0

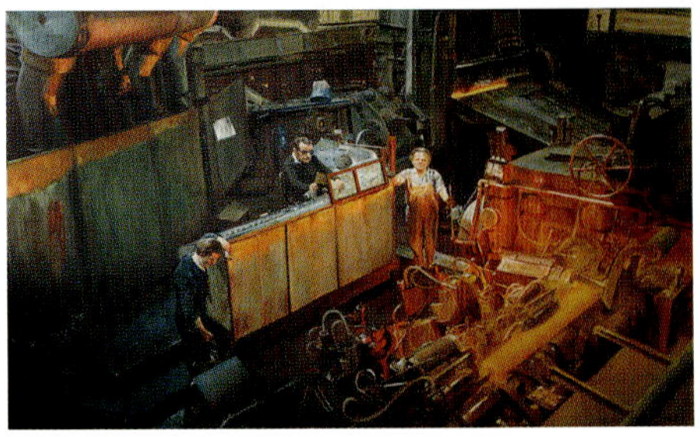

Ferrow, Anton Mark active 1974–1989
Tubes Factory, Desford, Leicestershire 1974
oil on canvas 95 x 150
X.W1.2008.0.0

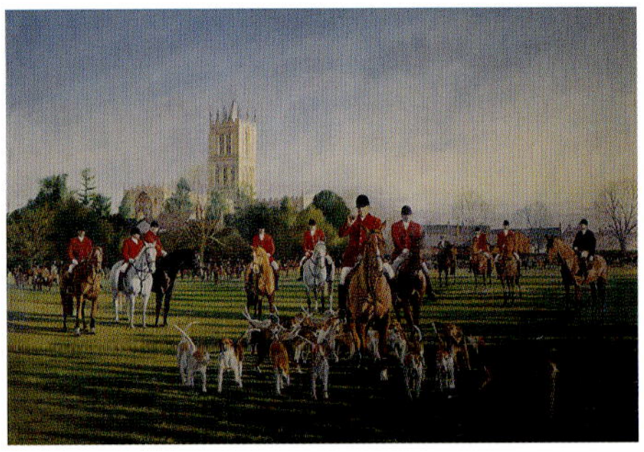

Fisher, Tim b.1958
The Melton Mowbray Hunt Meet 2000
acrylic on canvas 69 x 99
X.F3.2003.0.0

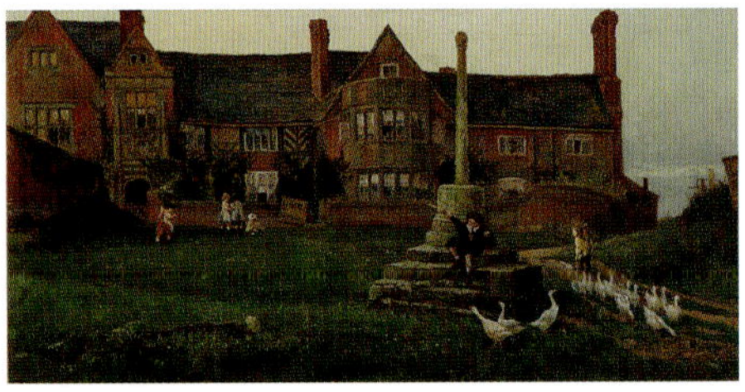

Fulleylove, John 1845–1908
Ragdale Hall, Leicestershire 1876
oil on board 35.5 x 49
X.F1.2008.0.0

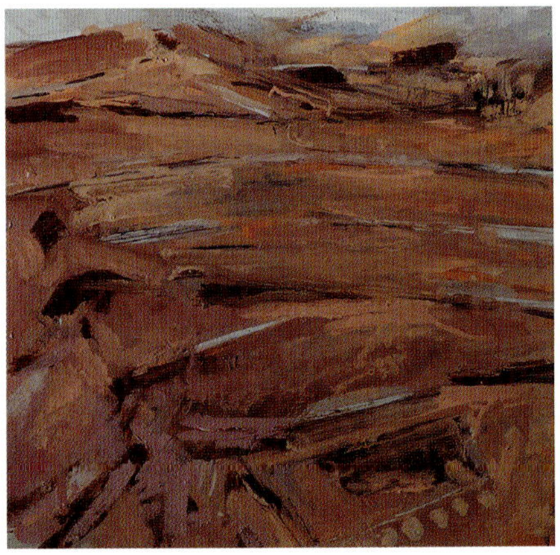

Hancock, Lulu
Dawn, Mountsorrel Quarry, Leicestershire
1999
enamel on board 20 x 20
X.F3.2000.0.0

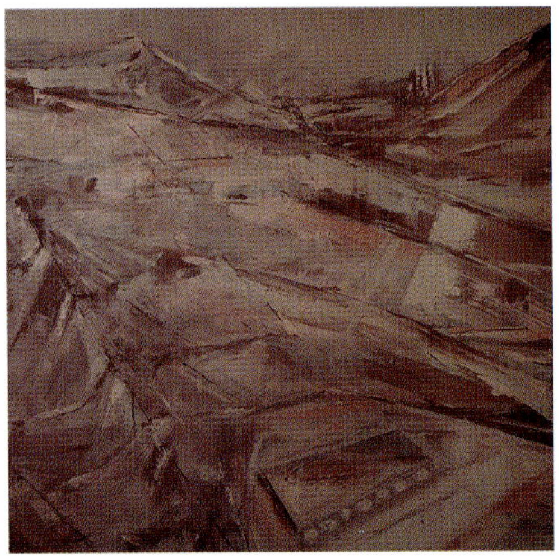

Hancock, Lulu
Dusk, Mountsorrel Quarry, Leicestershire
1999
oil on canvas 122 x 122
X.F1.2000.0.0

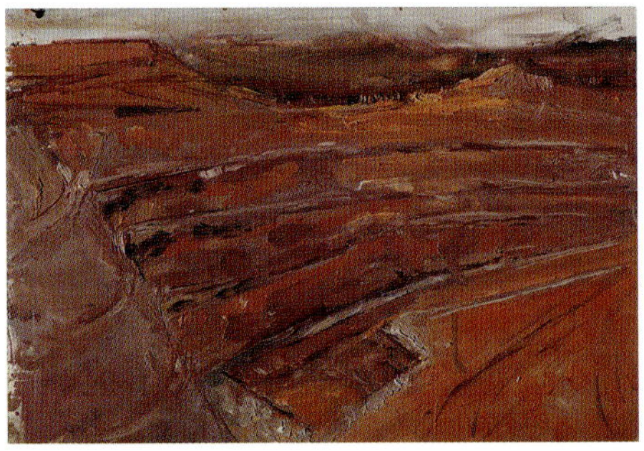

Hancock, Lulu
Dusk, Mountsorrel Quarry, Leicestershire
1999
oil on board 20.7 x 30
X.F2.2000.0.0

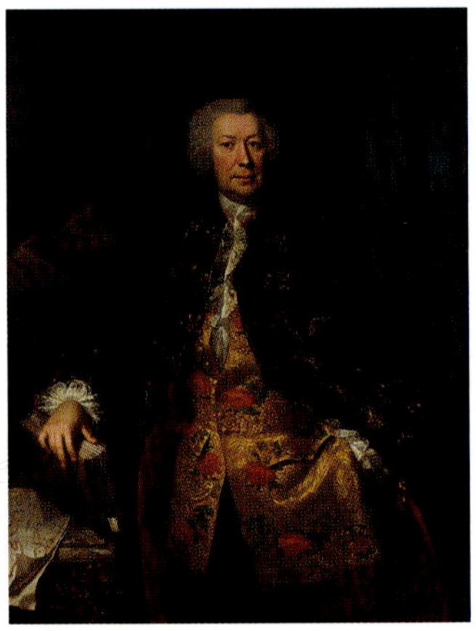

Handmann, Emmanuel Jakob (attributed to) 1718–1781
Ambassador John Burnaby (1701–1774), Minister to the Swiss at Turin (...) 1747
oil on canvas 165 x 127
L.F5.1957.0.0

Facing page: Roberts, William Patrick, 1895–1980, *At the Hippodrome* (detail), 1921, Leicester Arts and Museums Service (p. 78)

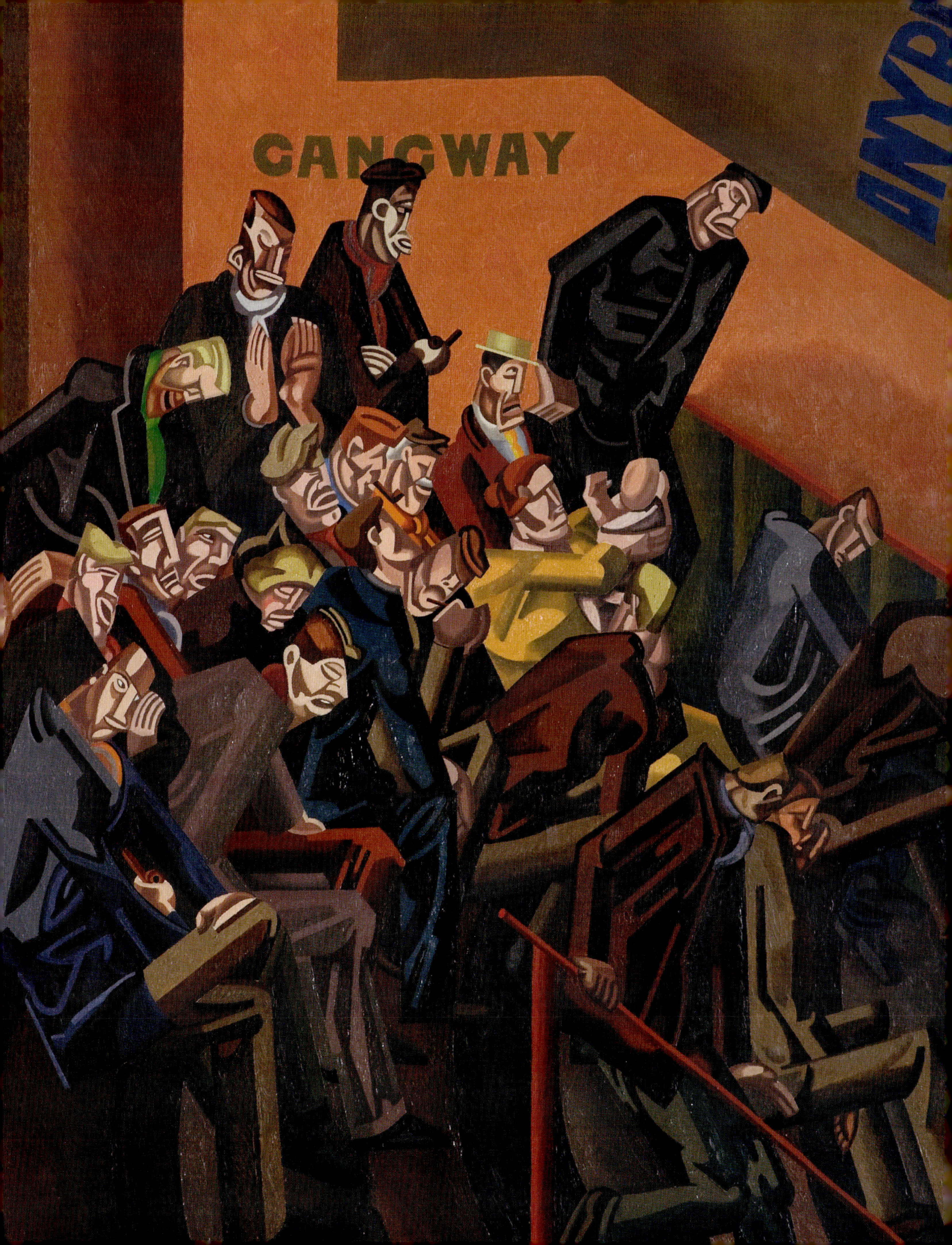
GANGWAY

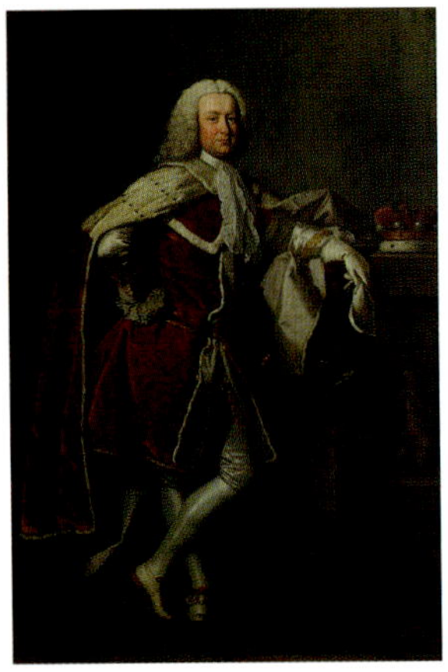

Hudson, Thomas 1701–1779
Lord Edward Noel (1715–1774), 9th Baron, 1st Viscount Wentworth
oil on canvas 210.8 x 138.4
L.F39.1944.1.0

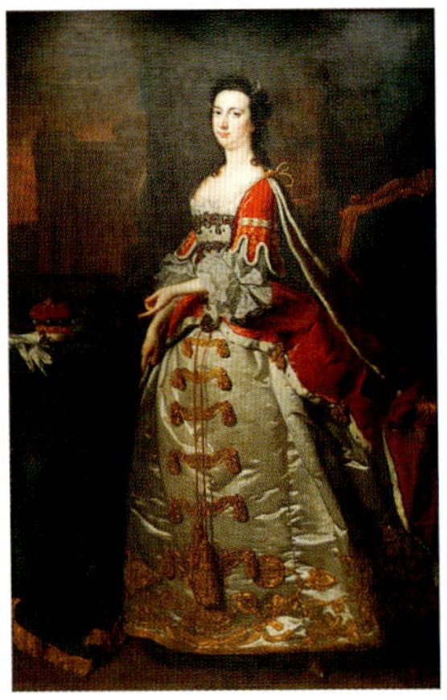

Hudson, Thomas 1701–1779
Judith Lamb (1726–1797), Lady Wentworth
oil on canvas 210.8 x 138.4
L.F39.1944.2.0

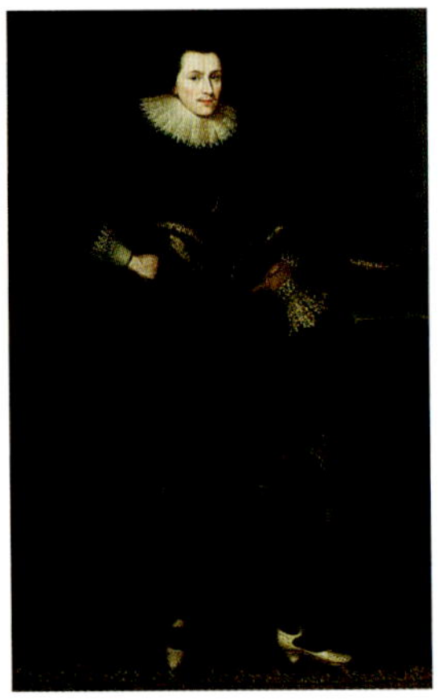

Janssens van Ceulen, Cornelis 1593–1661
George Villiers (1592–1628), 1st Duke of Buckingham 1619
oil on canvas 208.5 x 126
L.F46.1938.0.0

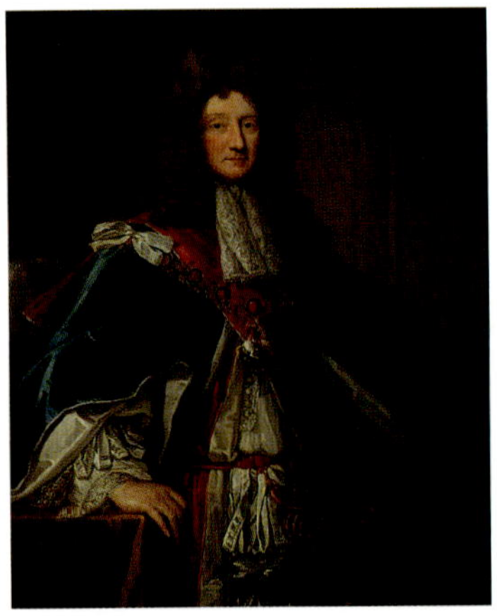

Jervas, Charles c.1675–1739
John Manners (1676–1721), 2nd Duke of Rutland c.1714–1721
oil on canvas 124 x 99.5
L.F6.1935.0.0

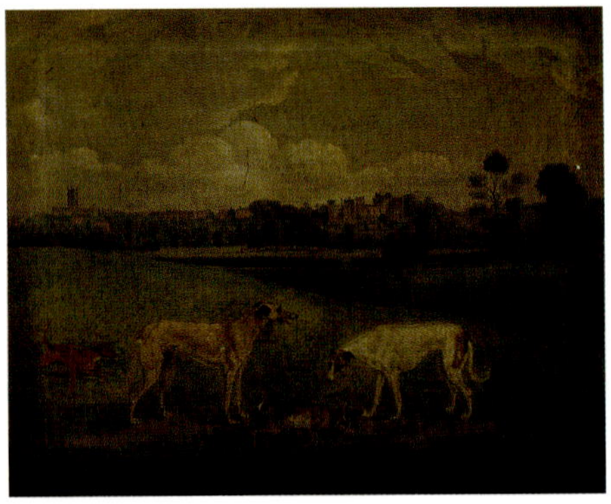

Jill, E. W.
Two Greyhounds and a Hare
oil on canvas 51 x 61.5
M.H100.1983.3070.0

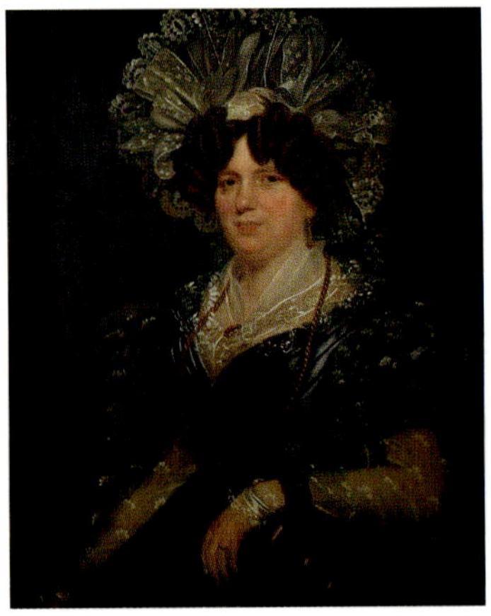

Kirkby, Thomas 1775–c.1848
Charlotte Jane Cope 1831
oil on canvas 89.5 x 70
L.F38.1968.0.0

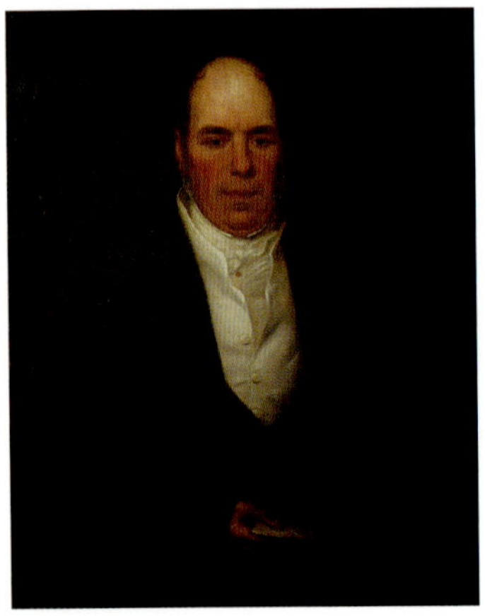

Kirkby, Thomas 1775–c.1848
Thomas Cope 1831
oil on canvas 89 x 70
L.F39.1968.0.0

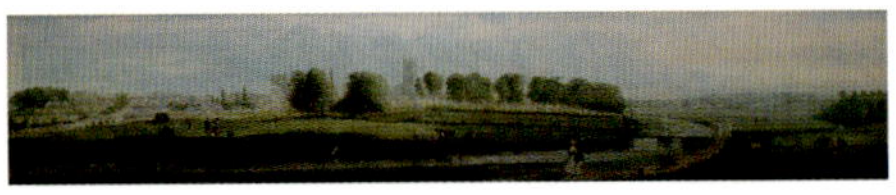

Latham, William
Melton Mowbray, Leicestershire, from the Canal 1835
oil on canvas 22 x 109.5
L.F37.1987.0.0

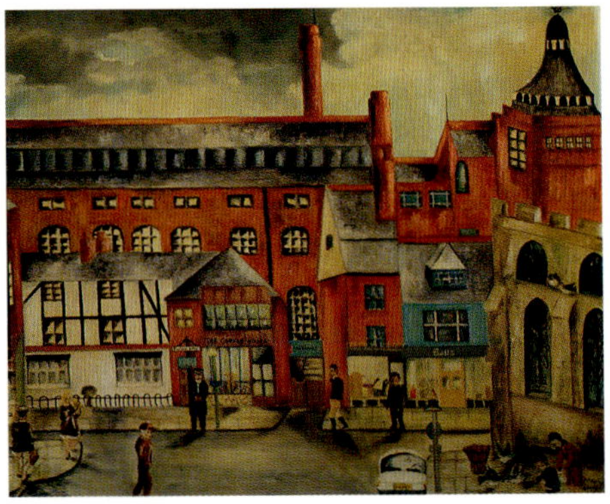

Madin, M.
The Square
oil on board 49 x 59.5
M.H1.2009.0.0

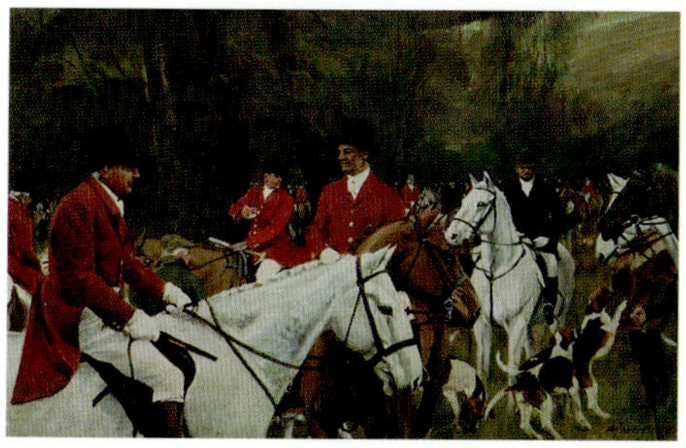

Marriott, Samuel 1932–1997
The Meet of the Fernie Hunt
oil on board 38 x 58.5
X.F5.2008.0.0

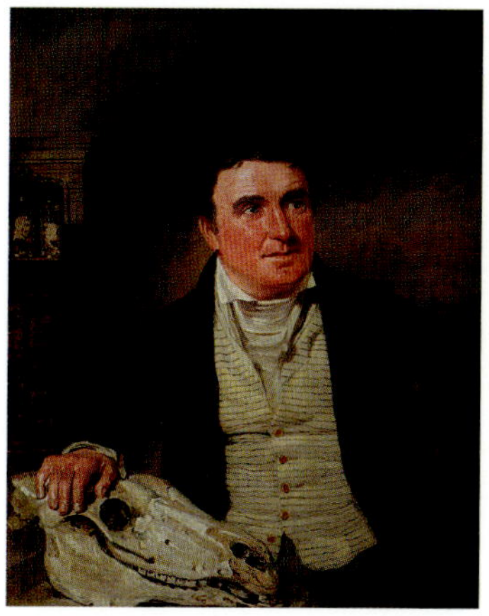

Marshall, Benjamin 1767–1835
Dr John Bowles (1765–1834) 1825
oil on canvas 91 x 69
L.F7.1972.0.0

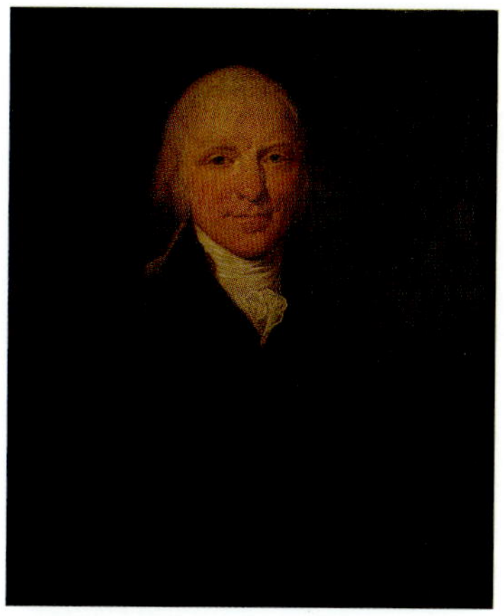

Millar, James 1735–1805
Reverend John Fisher (1755–1837) 1789
oil on canvas 76.5 x 64.3
L.F20.1981.0.0

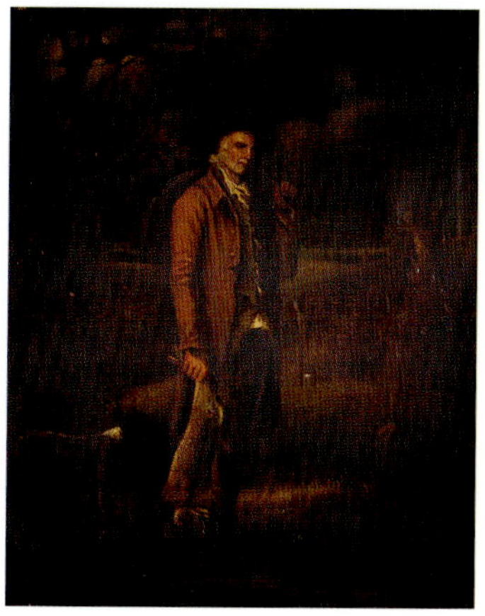

Nedham, William active 1815–1849
The Poacher 1815
oil on canvas 109.2 x 86.5
L.F418.1963.0.0

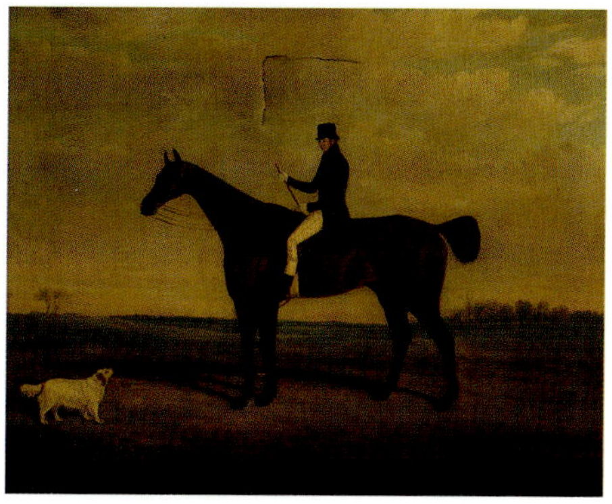

Nedham, William active 1815–1849
Horse and Rider 1836
oil on canvas 77 x 92
L.F12.1950.0.0

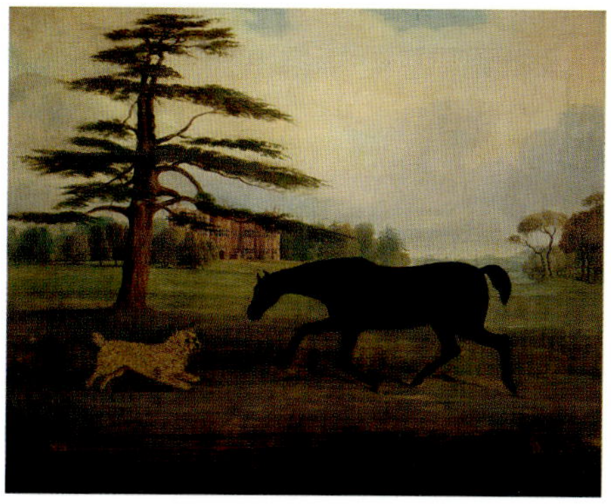

Nedham, William active 1815–1849
A Hunter and Dog in the Grounds of Quenby Hall, Leicestershire 1838
oil on canvas 63.5 x 77.5
L.F8.1958.0.0

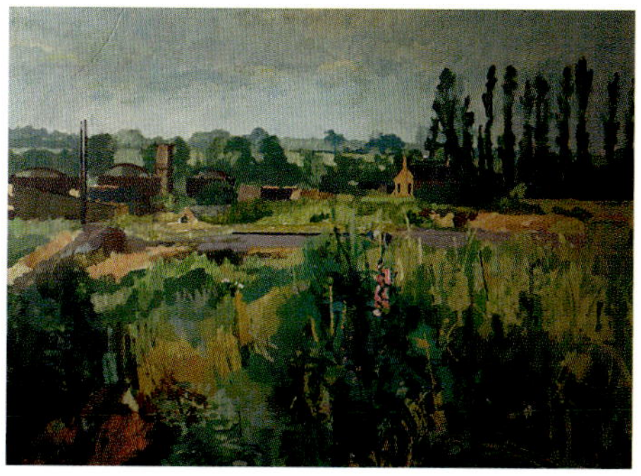

Organ, Bryan b.1935
The Brickyard, Glenfield, Leicestershire
oil on hardboard 77 x 102.5
L.F10.1959.0.0

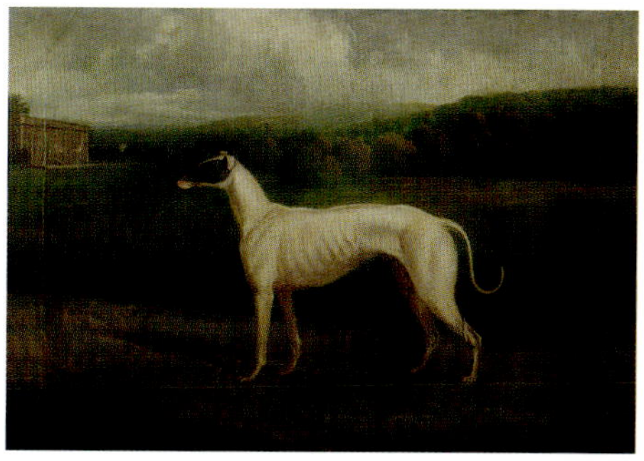

Paul, John Dean 1775–1852
Greyhound in a Landscape
oil on canvas 40.6 x 56
L.F20.1935.15.1

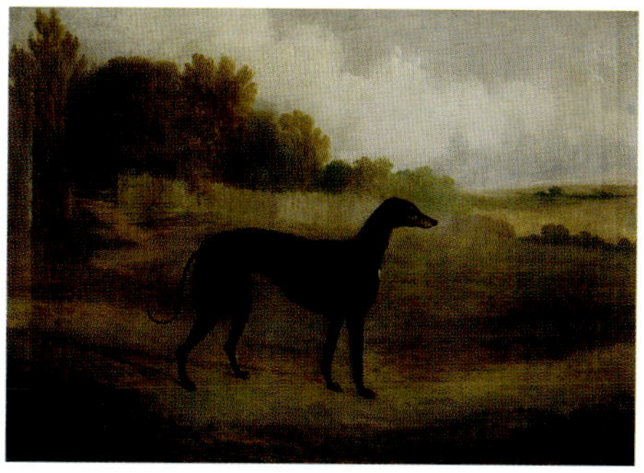

Paul, John Dean 1775–1852
Greyhound in a Landscape
oil on canvas 40.6 x 56
L.F20.1935.15.2

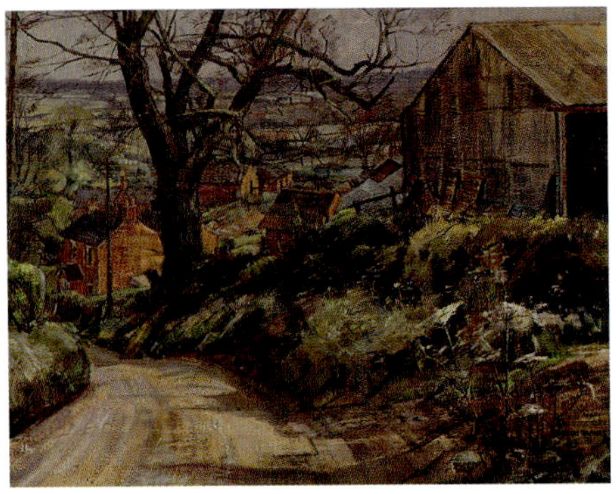

Reynette James, Phyllis May 1911–1973
A Leicestershire Landscape
oil on board 60 x 75
L.F502.1976.0.0

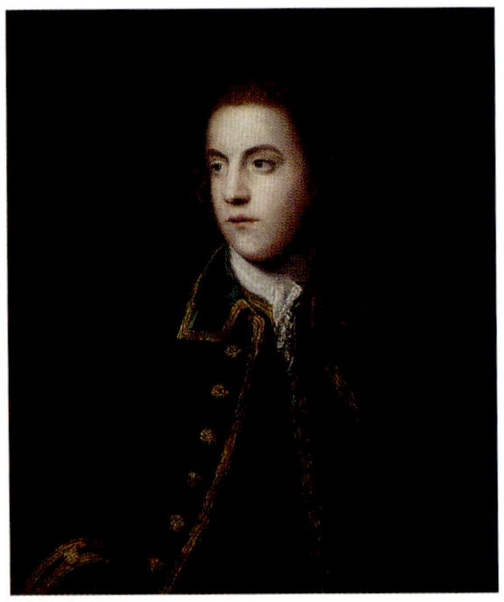

Reynolds, Joshua 1723–1792
Charles Boothby Skrymshire (1740–1800)
1758
oil on canvas 76.2 x 63.5
L.F11.1949.0.0

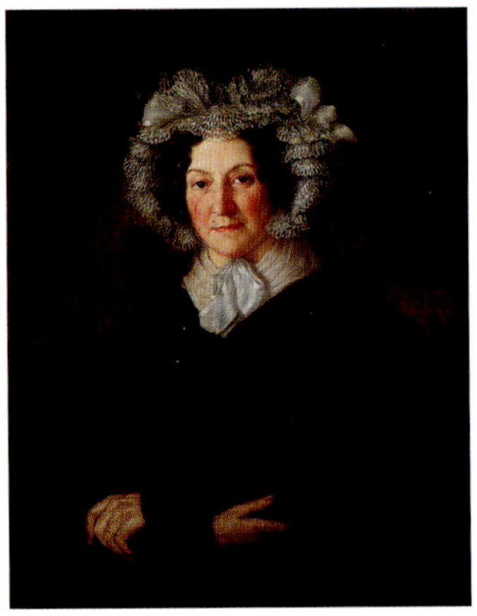

Scott, William Wallace 1820–1905
Mrs William Scott c.1840
oil on canvas 91.5 x 71
L.F79.1988.0.0

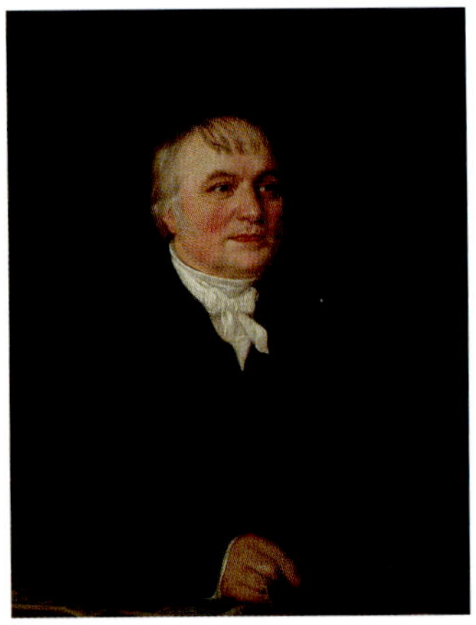

Scott, William Wallace 1820–1905
William Scott of Barsby, Leicestershire (1797–1862)
oil on canvas 90 x 70
L.F78.1988.0.0

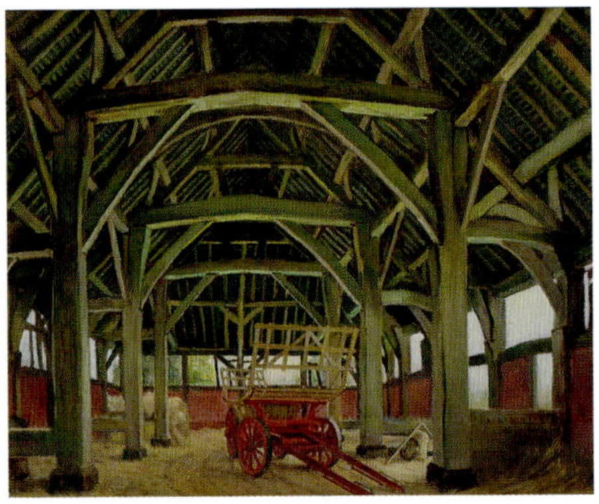

Sharp, Miles Balmford 1897–1973
Barn at Sheepy Magna, Leicestershire 1968
oil on canvas 63.5 x 76.2
L.F536.1968.0.0

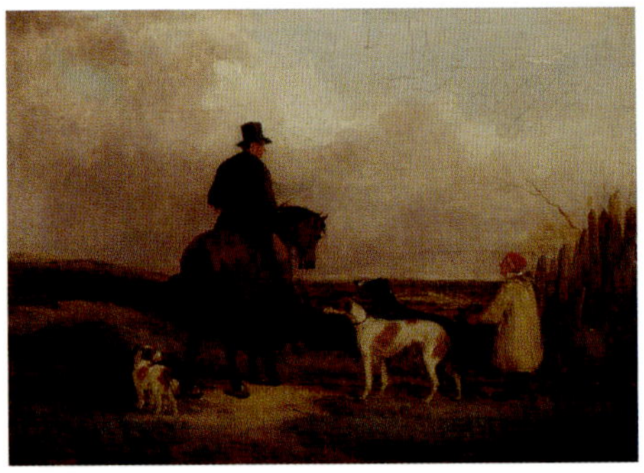

Shayer, William Joseph 1811–1892
Coursing 1842
oil on canvas 30.5 x 40.7
L.F6.1890.0.0

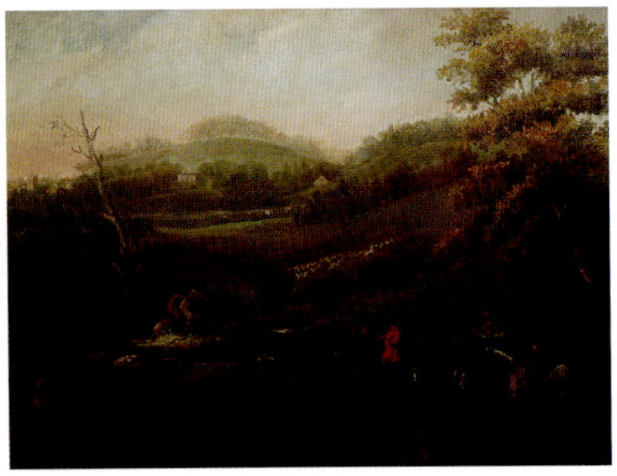

Smith, Charles Lorraine 1751–1835
The Billesdon Coplow Run, Leicestershire
oil on canvas 70 x 91.5
L.F11.1958.0.0

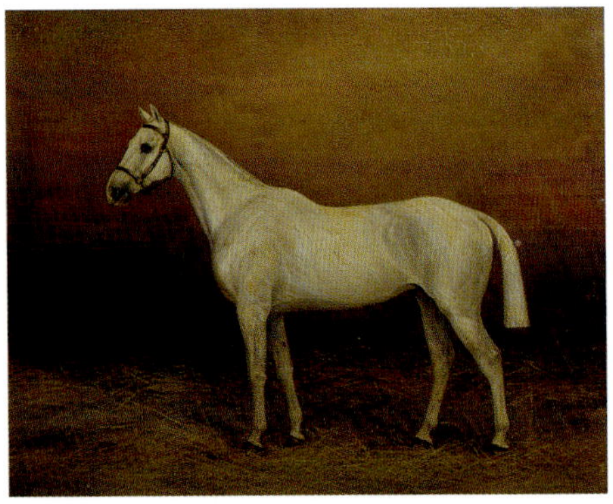

Stirling-Brown, Albert Edward D. G.
active 1896–1929
'Tiger', Grey Mare 1925
oil on canvas 40.5 x 51
L.H80.1994.4.0

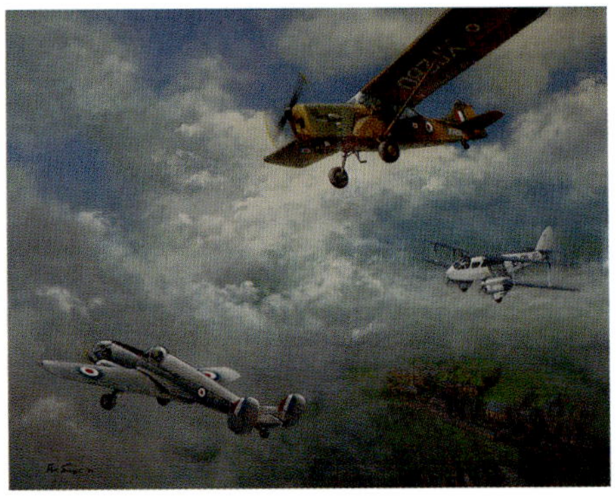

Sumpter, Peter b.1933
Aviation 1993
oil on canvas 61.2 x 76.3
L.F4.1994.0.0

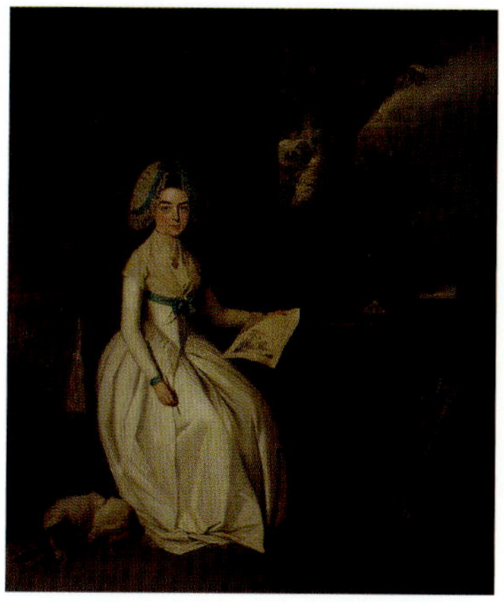

Towne, Francis 1739/1740–1816
Mrs Martha Nichols (1756–1788)
oil on canvas 76.5 x 64
L.F2.1982.0.0

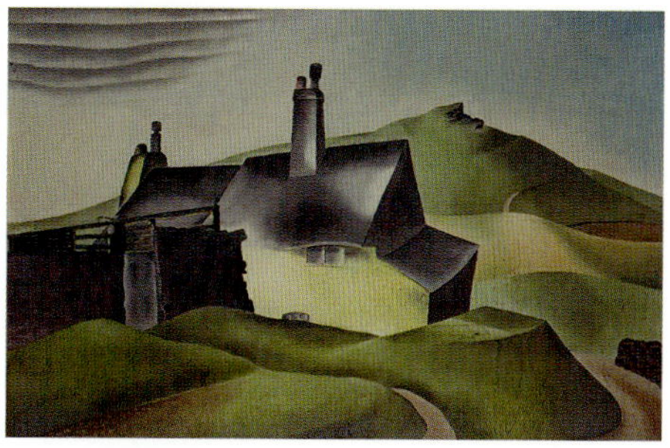

Treen, James
Mountsorrel Cottage, Leicestershire 1943
oil on canvas 41 x 61
L.F14.1943.0.0

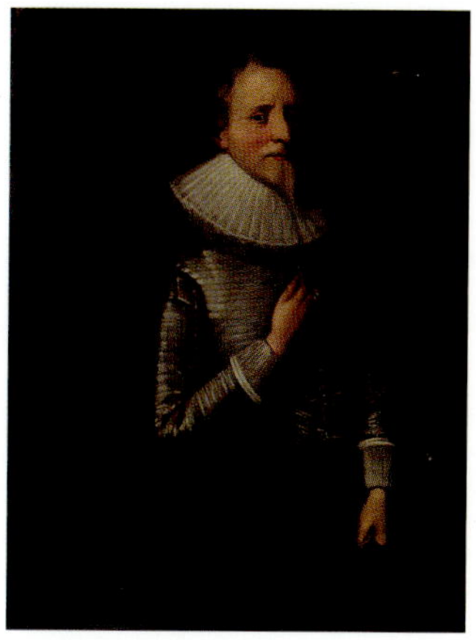

unknown artist
Sir William Herrick (1562–1653) 1628
oil on canvas 109.2 x 80.6
L.F34.1959.0.0

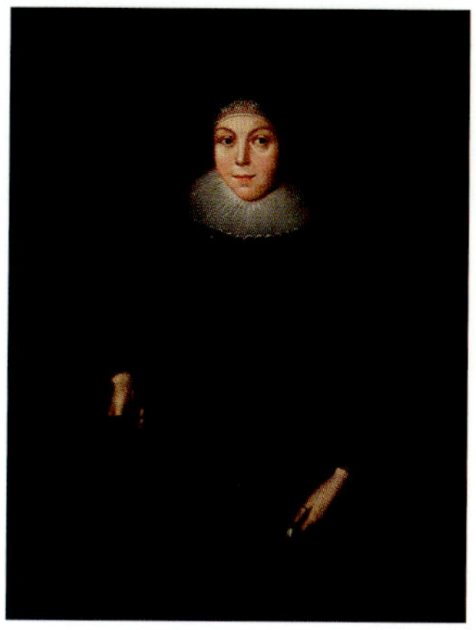

unknown artist
Mary, Lady Herrick 1632
oil on canvas 110 x 81
L.F35.1959.0.0

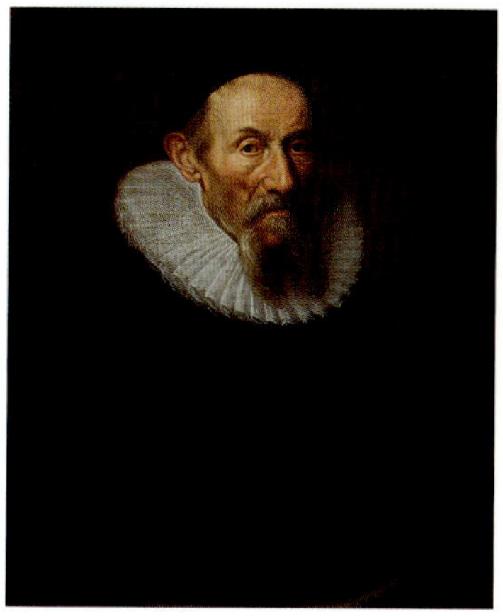

unknown artist
Humphrey de Burnaby 1648
oil on canvas 68 x 59.5
L.F9.1957.0.0

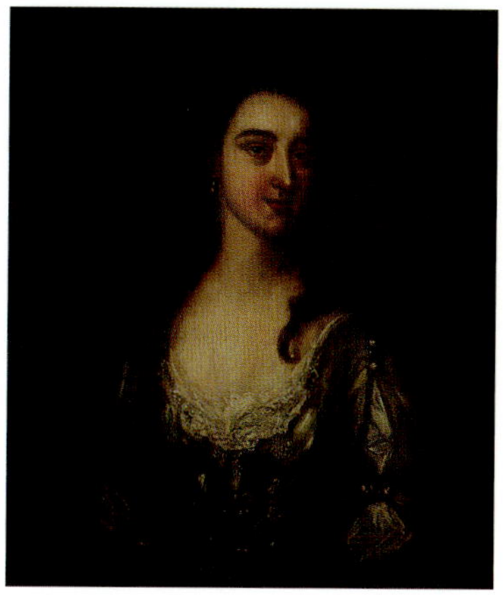

unknown artist
Portrait of a Lady of the Herrick Family
1650–1700
oil on canvas 76.2 x 63.5
L.F25.1937.8.0

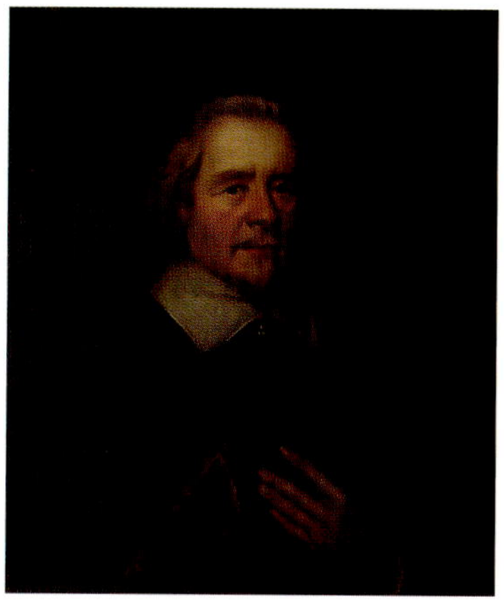

unknown artist
David Papillon (1581–1659) 1654
oil on canvas 76 x 63.5
L.F182.1981.0.0

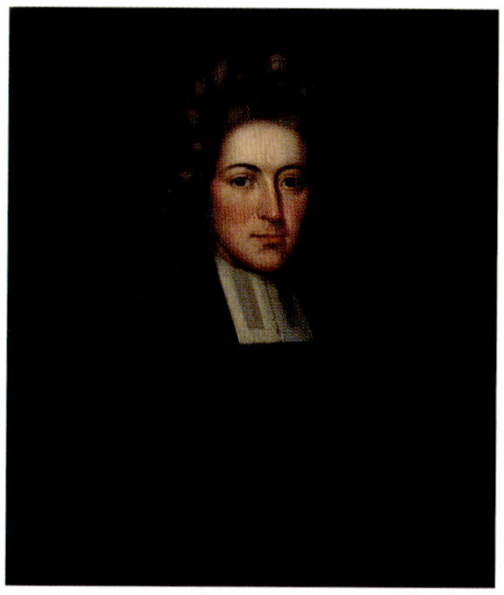

unknown artist
Portrait of a Gentleman of the Herrick Family
1698
oil on canvas 74 x 62
L.F25.1937.4.0

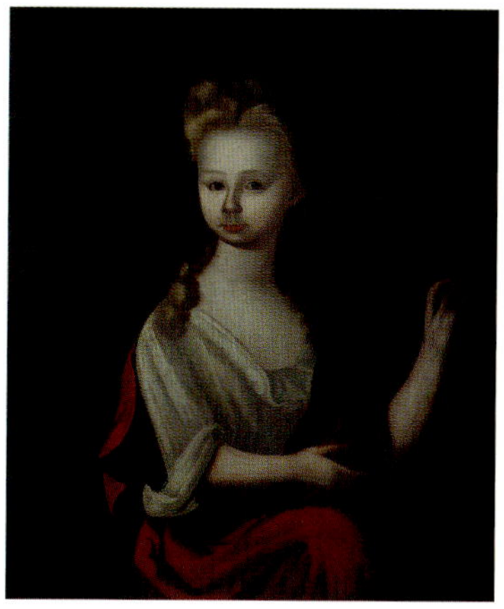

unknown artist
Portrait of a Girl of the Herrick Family 1698
oil on canvas 76.2 x 63.5
L.F25.1937.7.0

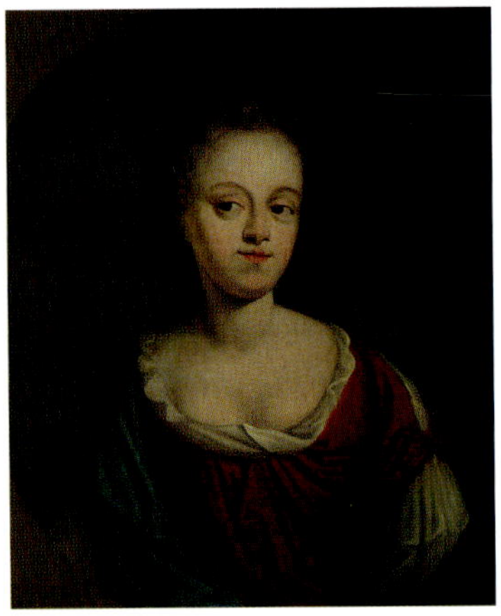

unknown artist
Portrait of a Young Lady of the Herrick Family 1698
oil on canvas 74 x 61.5
L.F25.1937.5.0

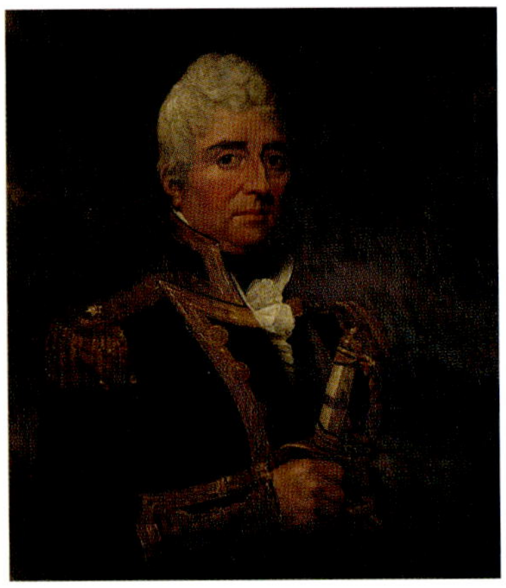

unknown artist
Captain Burnaby 1780
oil on canvas 76.2 x 65.7
L.F6.1957.0.0

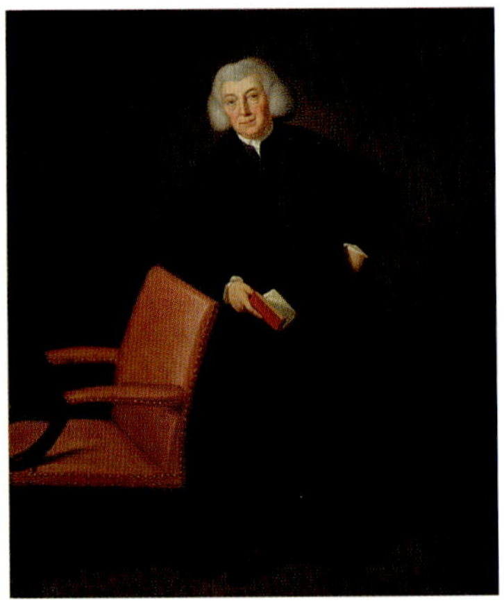

unknown artist
Reverend Andrew Burnaby (1734–1812) 1789
oil on canvas 90.8 x 75.6
L.F7.1957.0.0

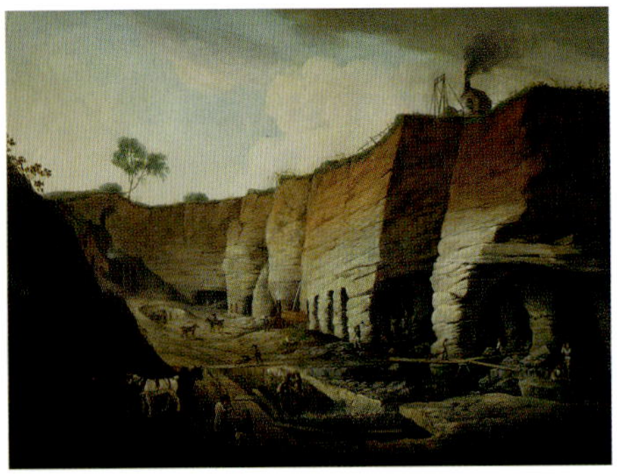

unknown artist
Dimminsdale Quarries on the Ferrers Estate, Staunton Harold, Leicestershire c.1810
oil on canvas 69 x 89
L.F49.1990.0.0

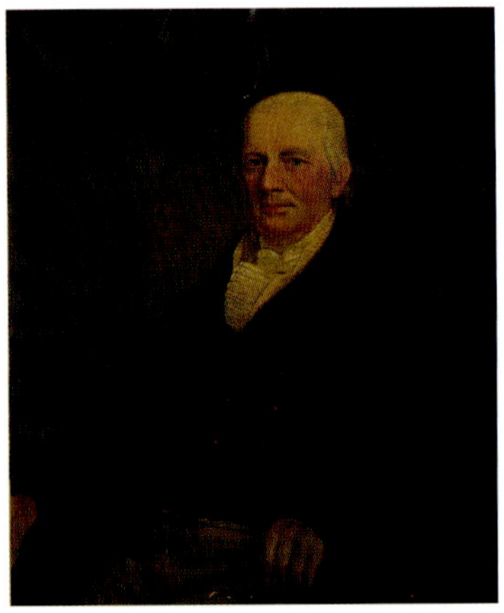

unknown artist
John Heycock of Ouston (1758–1823) 1822
oil on canvas 78.1 x 64.1
L.F774.1972.0.0

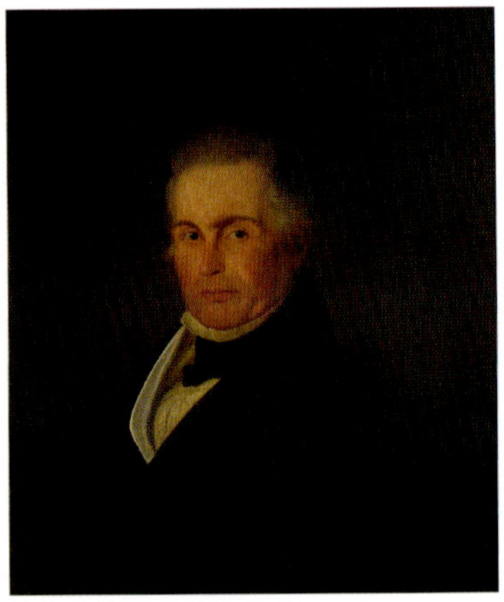

unknown artist
John Hippisley Heycock (b.1793) 1843
oil on canvas 76.2 x 63.5
L.F773.1972.0.0

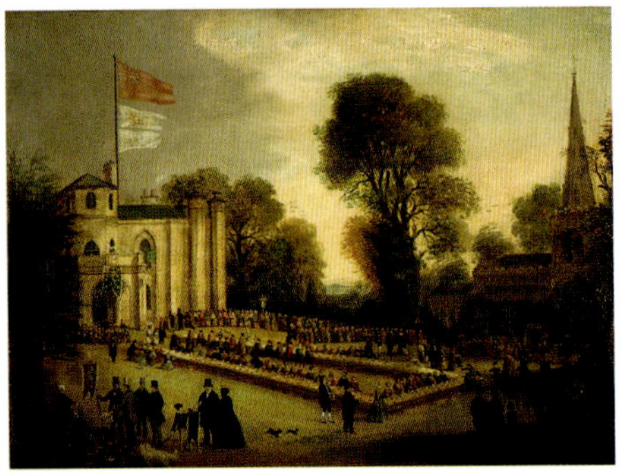

unknown artist
The Village Feast, Coleorton Hall, Leicestershire 1849
oil on canvas 71.8 x 94.2
L.F7.1953.0.0

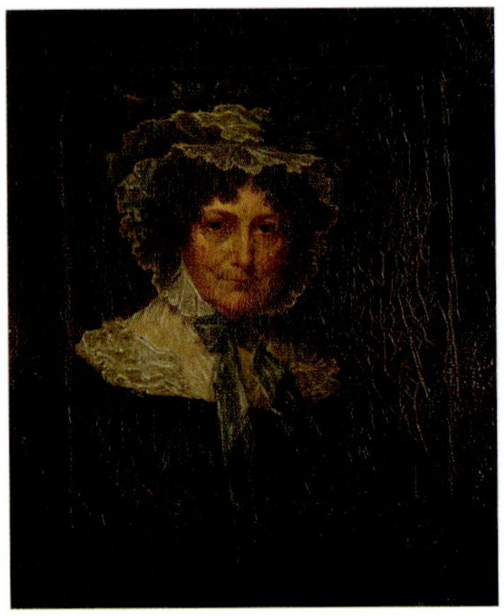

unknown artist
Jane Anne Oakley, née Fisher (b.1828) 1870s
oil on canvas 25.2 x 20.3
L.F17.1981.0.0

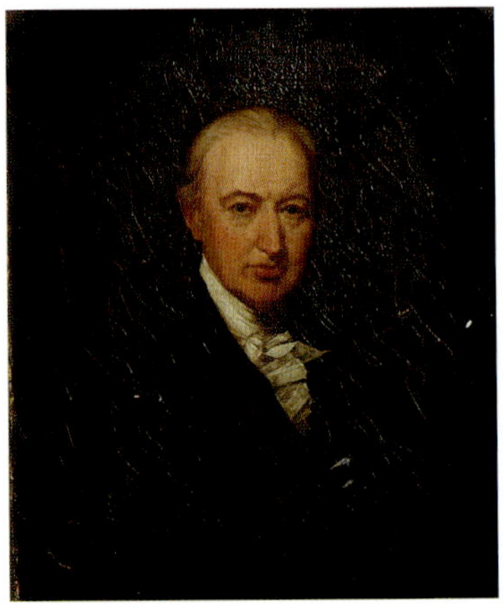

unknown artist
Thomas William Oakley 1870s
oil on canvas 25.5 x 20.4
L.F18.1981.0.0

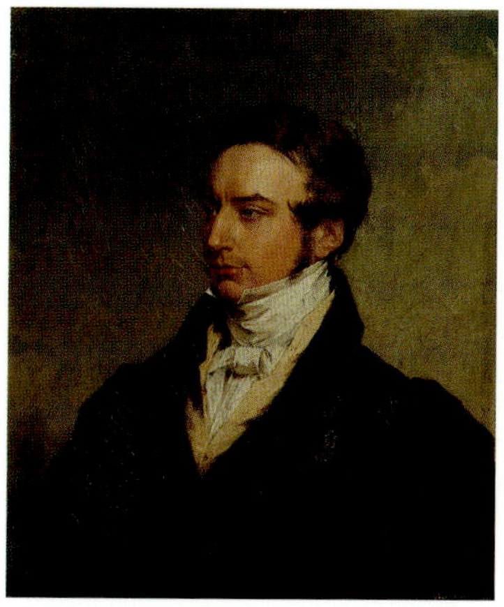

unknown artist
Mr Oakley Junior (b.1852) 1870s
oil on canvas 25.4 x 20.4
L.F19.1981.0.0

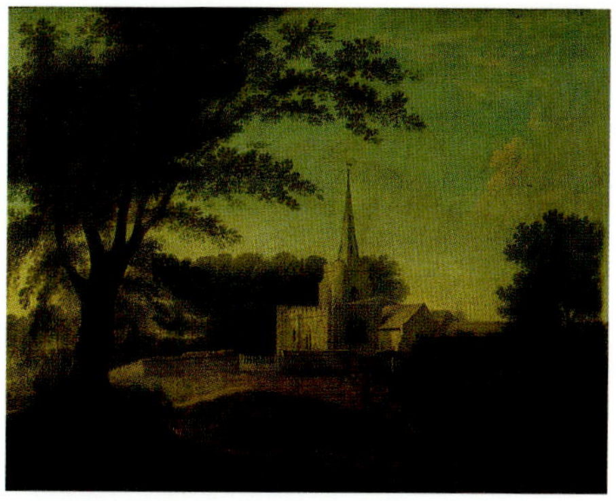

unknown artist 19th C
Coleorton Church, Leicestershire
oil on canvas 54.6 x 66.4
L.F6.1953.0.0

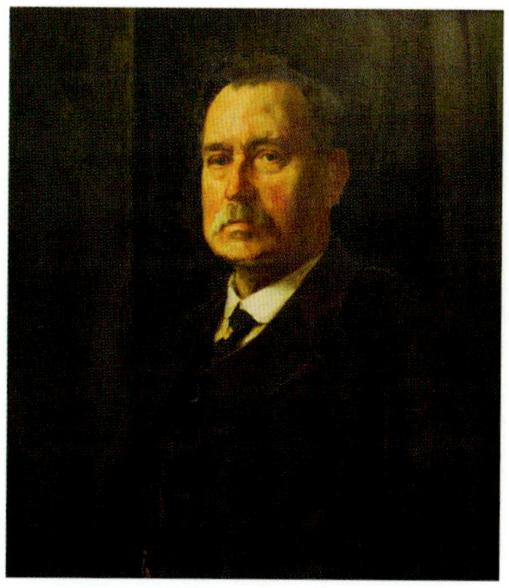

unknown artist
Levi Lovett, Secretary of the Leicestershire Miners' Association (1887–1919) 1924
oil on canvas 73.5 x 63.5
X.F3.2009.0.0

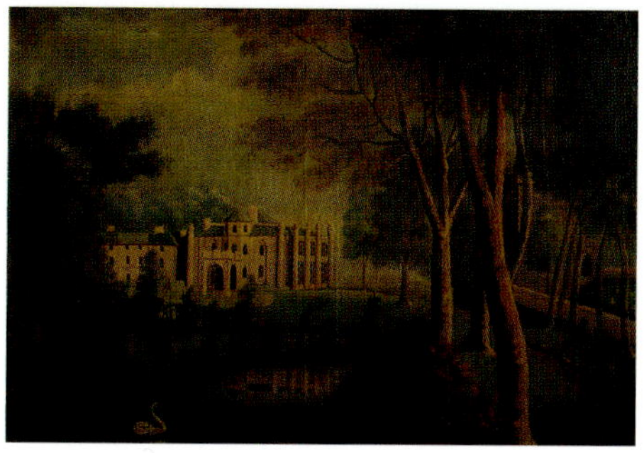

unknown artist
Coleorton Hall, Leicestershire
oil on canvas 64 x 92
M.H46.1997.0.0

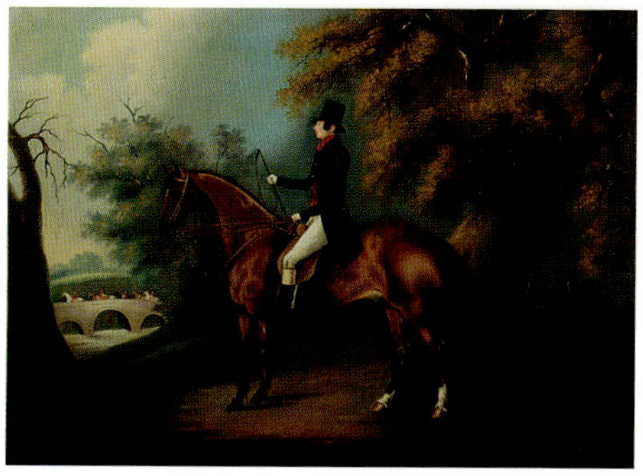

unknown artist
H. W. Penistone, Esq., of Oakham
oil on canvas 57 x 78.8
L.F8.1946.0.0

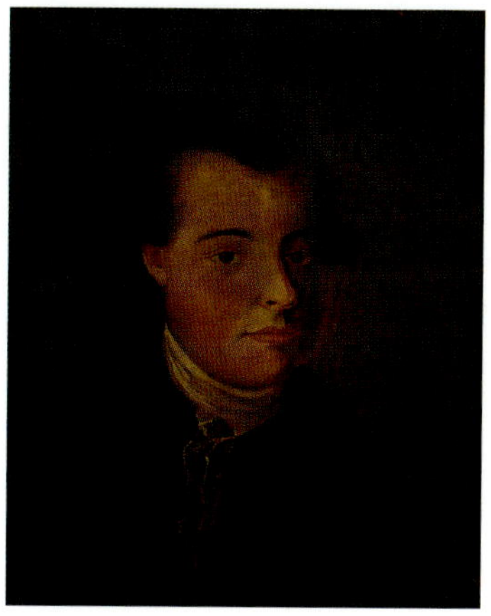

unknown artist
Henry Woodcock (b.1775), LLB
oil on canvas 50.8 x 40.5
L.F44.1957.0.0

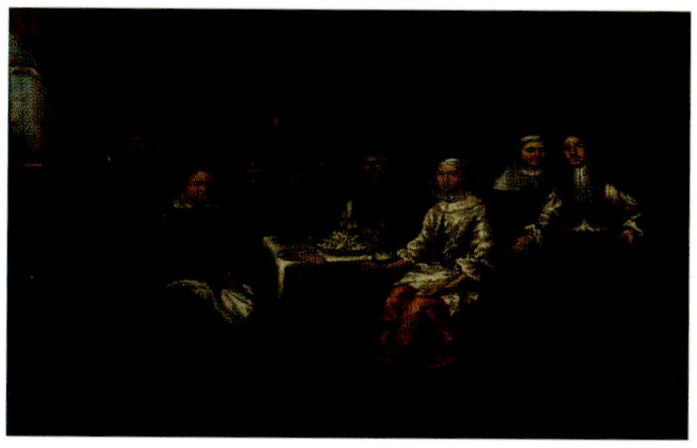

unknown artist
Interior, the Marriage Breakfast
oil on panel 72.5 x 88
L.F19.1935.0.0

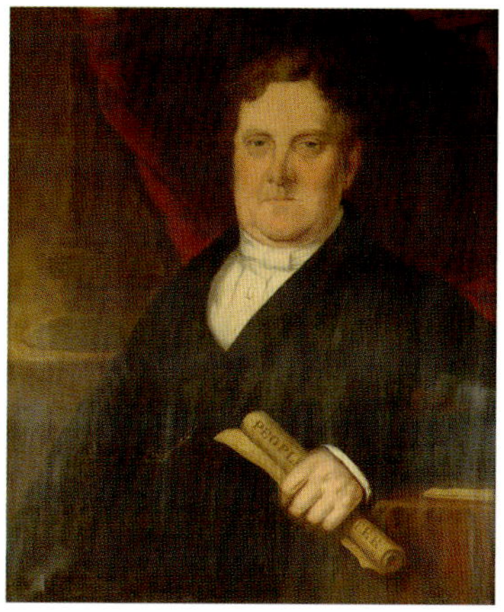

unknown artist
John Skevington (1801–1850)
oil on canvas 75 x 61
L.F70.1955.0.0

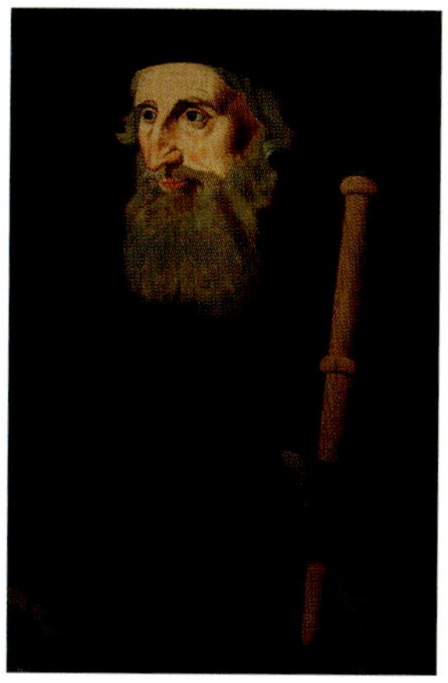

unknown artist
John Wycliffe (1330–1384), Rector of Lutterworth
oil on panel 62.2 x 42
L.F150.1898.0.0

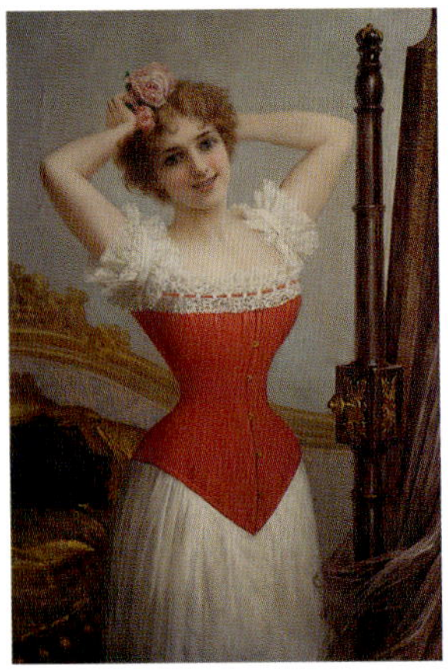

unknown artist
Lady in a Red Corset
oil on canvas 102 x 71
L.H161.1968.0.0

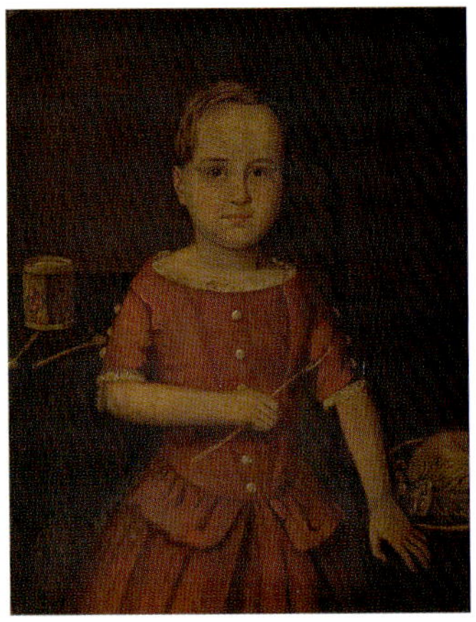

unknown artist
Portrait of a Child
oil on canvas 38.5 x 29
L.F1233.1951.61.0

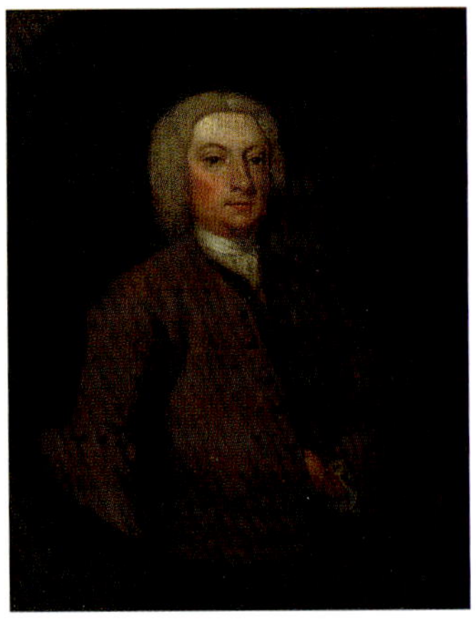

unknown artist
Portrait of a Gentleman of the Herrick Family
oil on panel 27 x 21.5
L.F25.1937.13.0

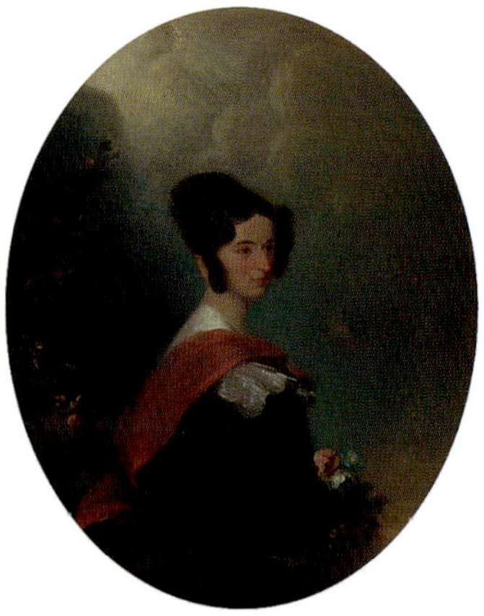

unknown artist
Portrait of a Young Lady of the Herrick Family
oil on panel 25.7 x 21
L.F25.1937.12.0

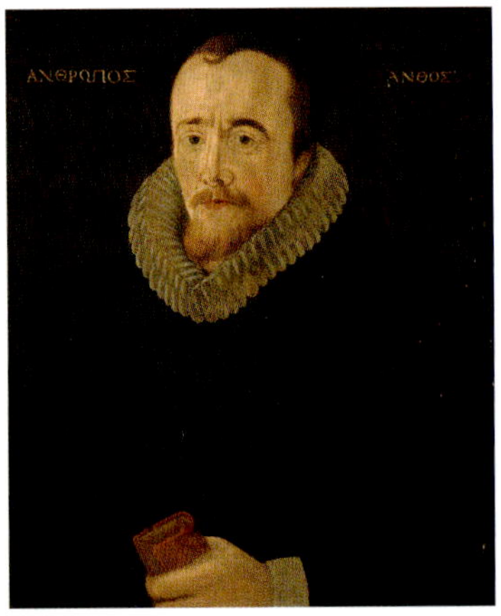

unknown artist
Tobias Herrick, Rector (1605–1627)
oil on panel 48.7 x 39.8
L.F25.1937.14.0.0

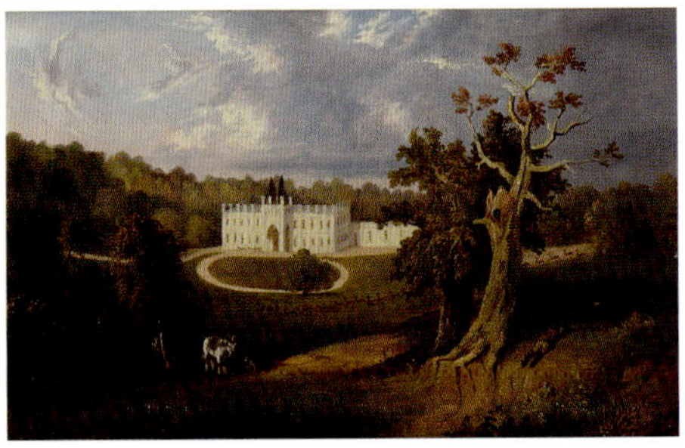

unknown artist
View of Donington Hall and Grounds, Leicestershire
oil on canvas 31.5 x 49.5
L.F112.1981.0.0

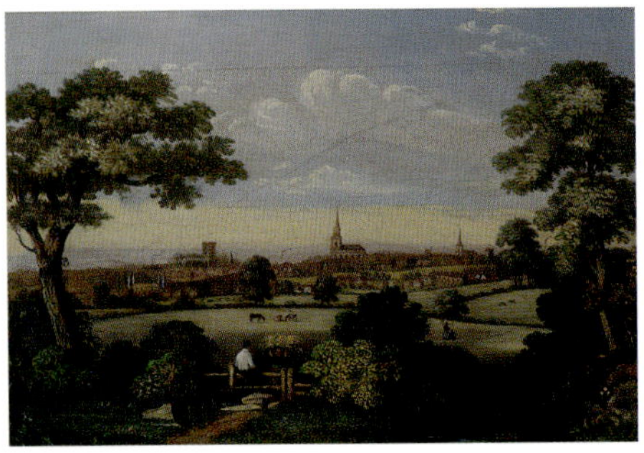

unknown artist
View of Hinckley, Leicestershire
oil on canvas 25.4 x 35.5
L.F215.1981.0.0

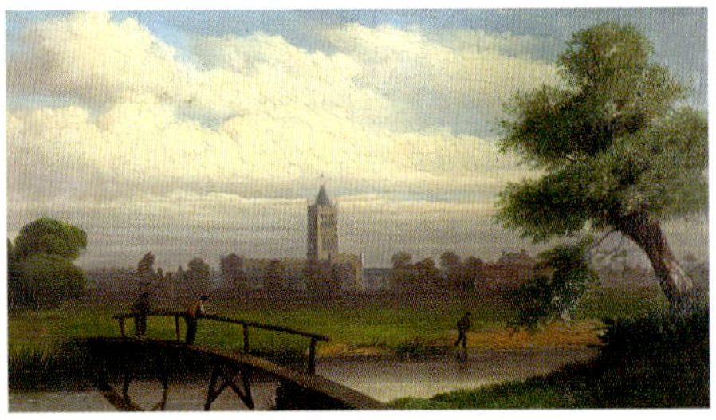

unknown artist
View of Melton Mowbray, Leicestershire
oil on canvas 23.5 x 40.5
L.F209.1981.0.0

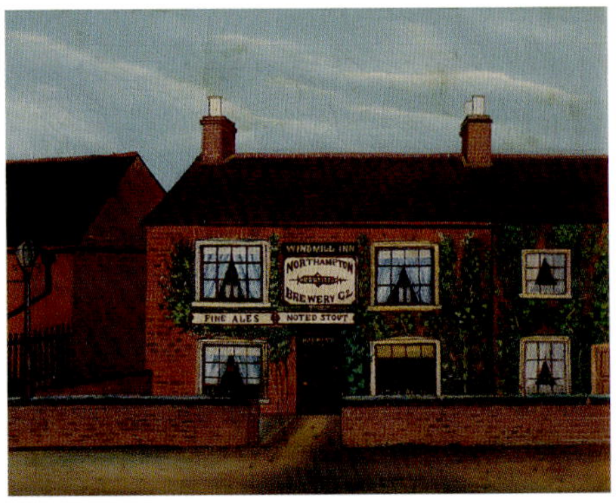

unknown artist
'Windmill Inn'
oil on canvas 41.5 x 51
M.H2.2009.0.0

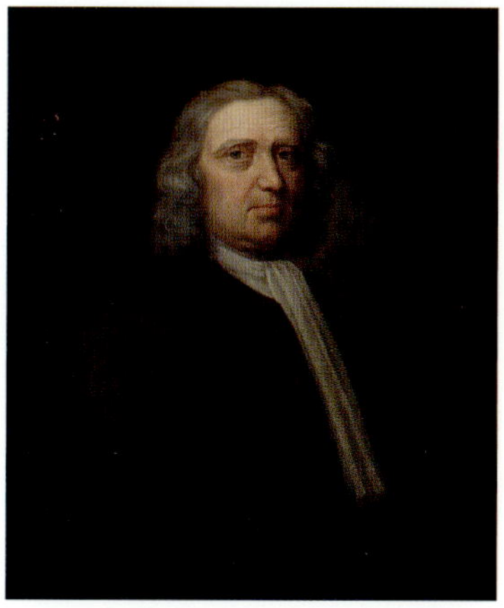

Verelst, Johannes (attributed to) d.1734
Honest George Ashby (1656–1728), the Planter
oil on canvas 76.2 x 63.5
L.F17.1935.10.0

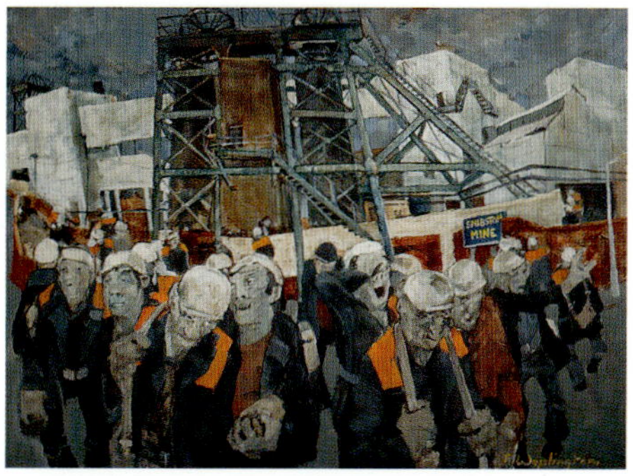

Waplington, Paul Anthony b.1938
Snibston Mine, Leicestershire
oil on canvas 90 x 121
X.F1.2001.0.0

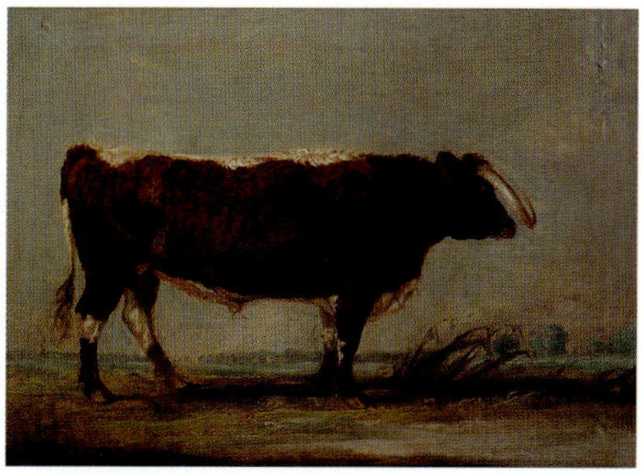

Ward, James 1768–1859
Leicestershire Longhorn Bull
oil & paper on canvas 31.4 x 42.9
L.F116.1981.0.0

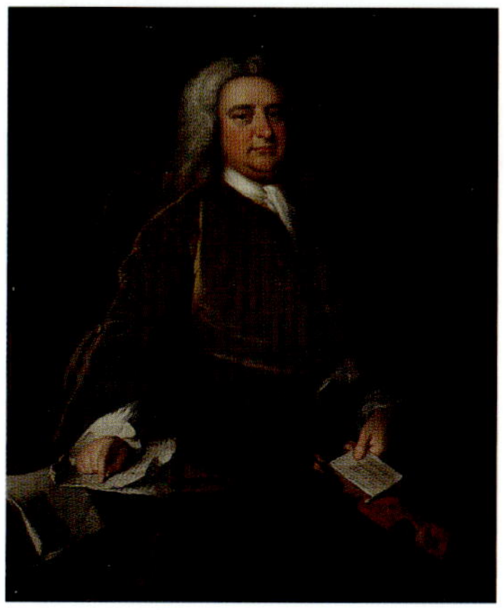

Whood, Isaac 1688/1689–1752
David Papillon (1691–1762), MP 1739
oil on canvas 122.5 x 100
L.F183.1981.0.0

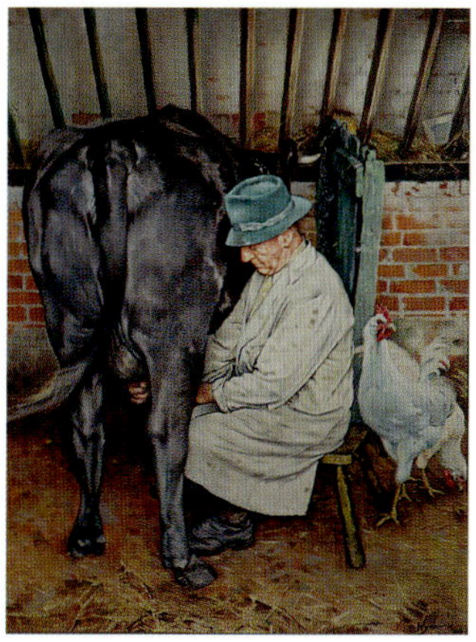

Wynn, Kenneth James 1922–2009
The Glenfield Farmer 1946
oil on panel 47 x 35.5
L.F8.1984.0.0

Leicestershire County Cricket Club

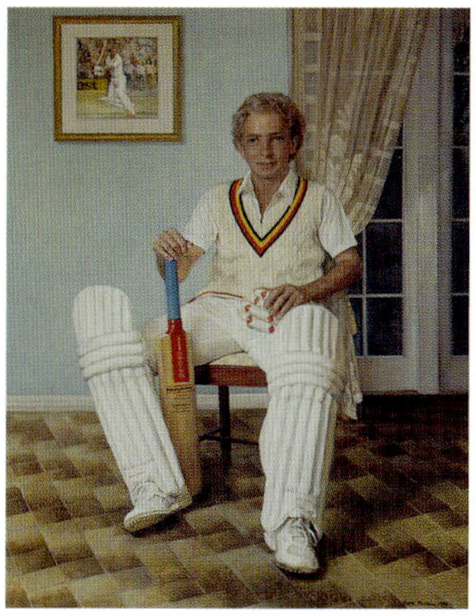

Ferrow, Anton Mark active 1974–1989
David Gower (b.1957) 1988
oil on canvas 256 x 128
1988/1

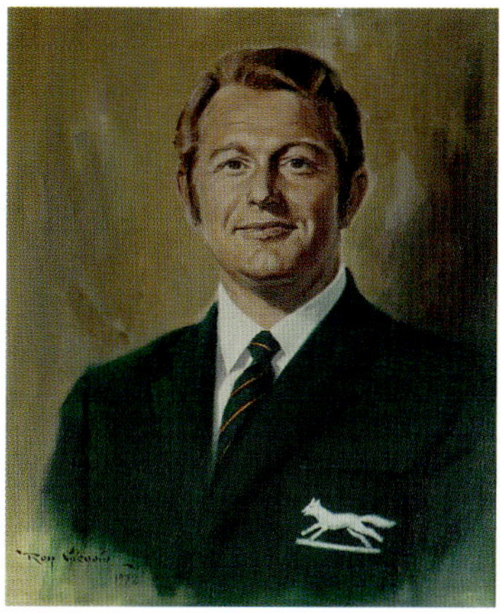

Gregory, Roy
F. M. Turner 1972
oil on canvas 57 x 47.5
1972/2

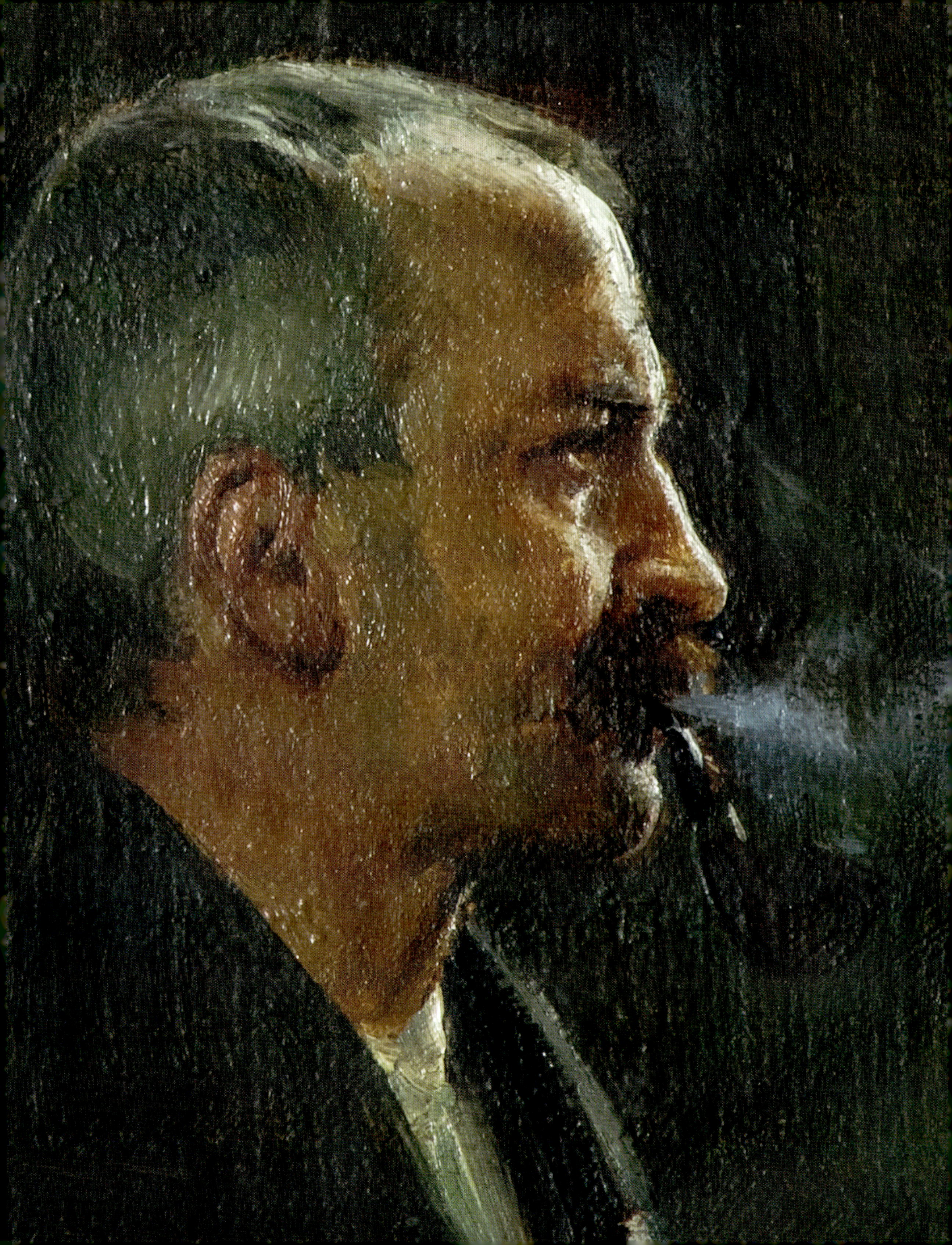

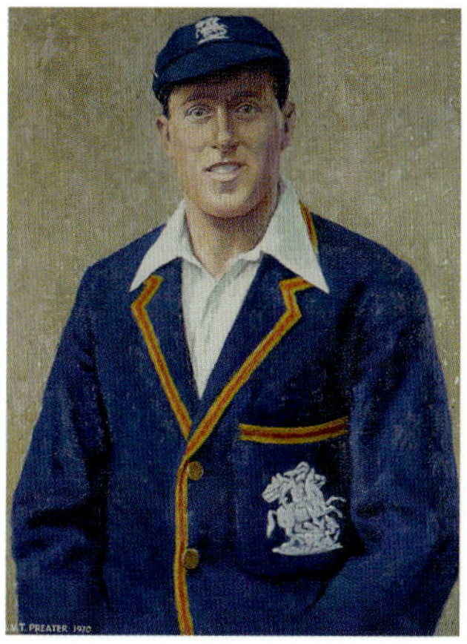

Preater, L. V. T. active 1970–1972
George Geary (1893–1981) 1970
oil on canvas 60 x 45
1970/2

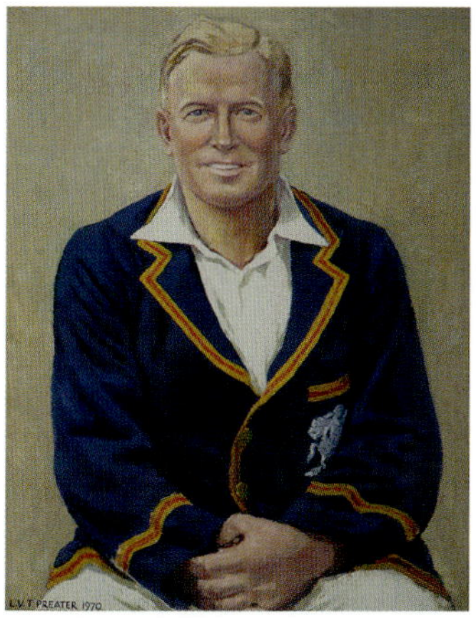

Preater, L. V. T. active 1970–1972
William Ewart Astill (1888–1948) 1970
oil on canvas 59 x 45
1970/1

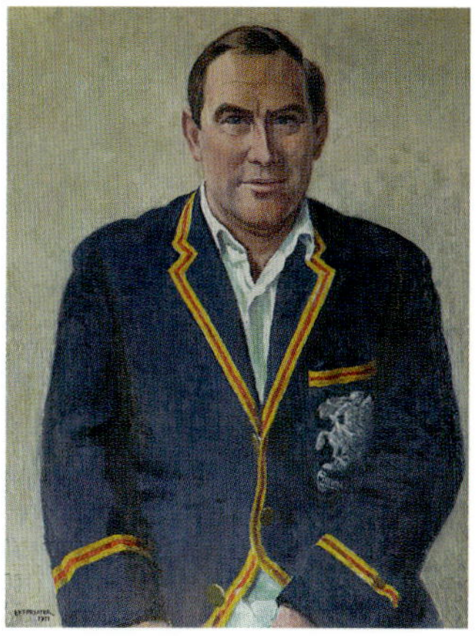

Preater, L. V. T. active 1970–1972
Raymond Illingworth (b.1932) 1971
oil on canvas 60 x 45
1971/1

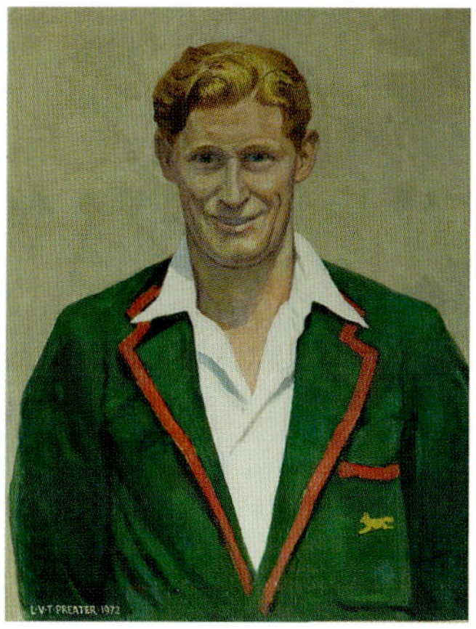

Preater, L. V. T. active 1970–1972
Maurice Tompkin (1919–1956) 1972
oil on canvas 59 x 45
1972/1

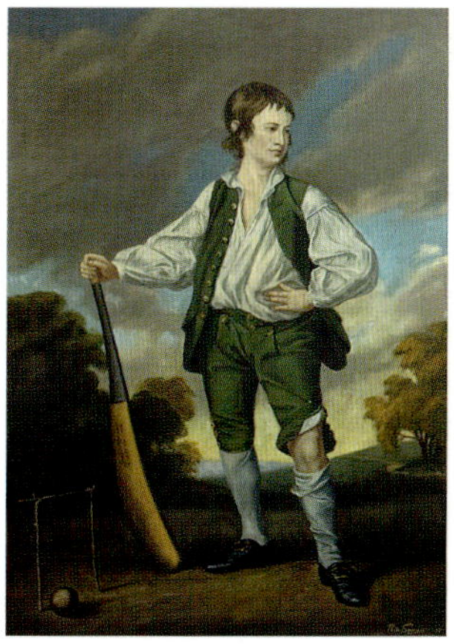

Sumpter, Peter b.1933
Lewis Cage, Aged 13, 1763 (after Francis Cotes) 1976
oil on canvas 120 x 80 (E)
1976/1

Leicestershire Libraries

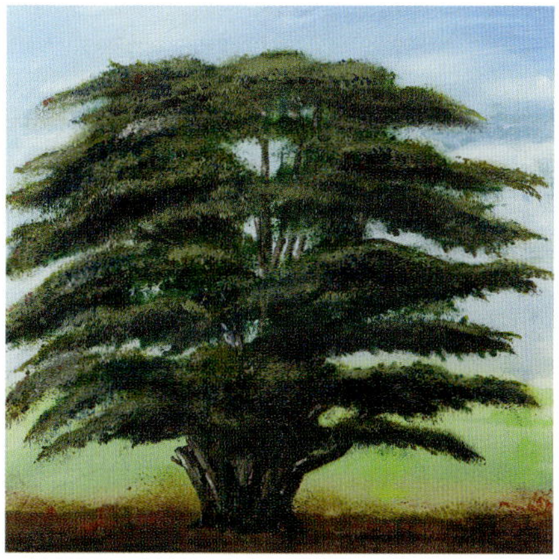

Gowham, Roger
The Birstall Cedar Tree c.2008
oil on board 31.5 x 30
2

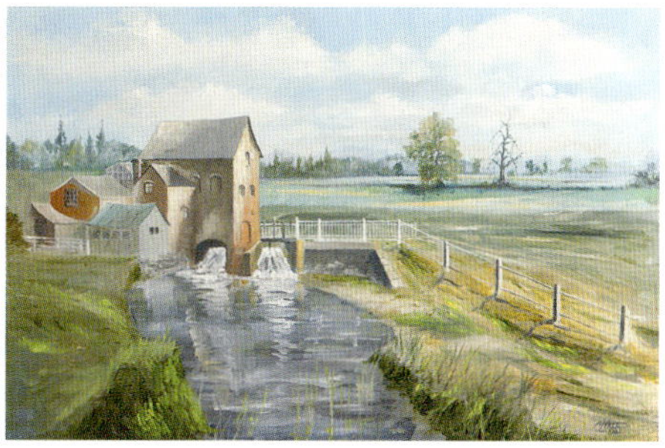

Mason, A.
The Mill, Anstey, Leicestershire 1982
oil on canvas 50 x 75
3

Facing page: Logsdail, William, 1859–1944, *Self Portrait* (detail), The Collection: Art & Archaeology in Lincolnshire (Usher Gallery) (p. 313)

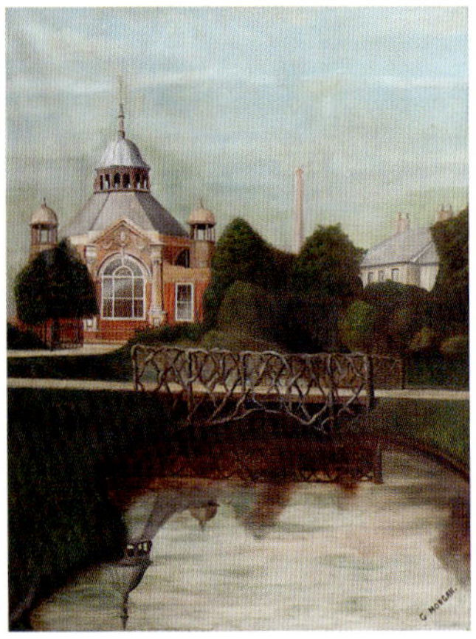

Morgan, G.
Loughborough Library, Leicestershire
oil on canvas 83 x 60.5
1

The Leicestershire Fire and Rescue Service Collection

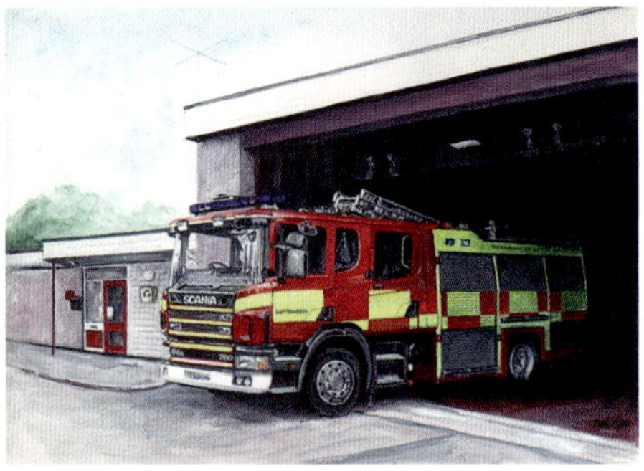

Lowe, Pamela Ann
The Old Lutterworth Fire Station, Leicestershire 2004–2005
acrylic on paper 24 x 33
2

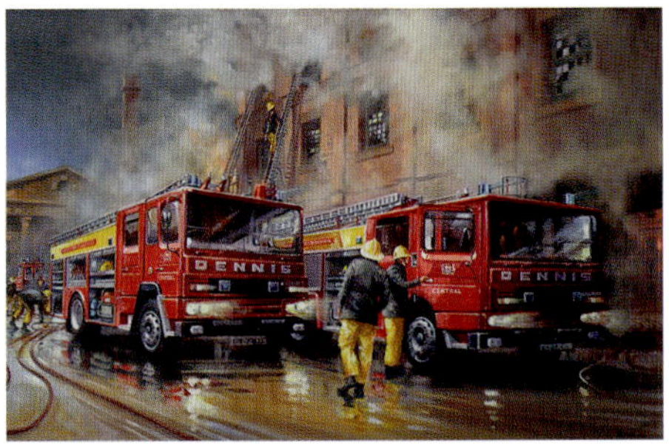

Weston, David b.1935
Men of Fire 1990
oil on canvas 59.5 x 90
1

The Royal Leicestershire Regiment Museum

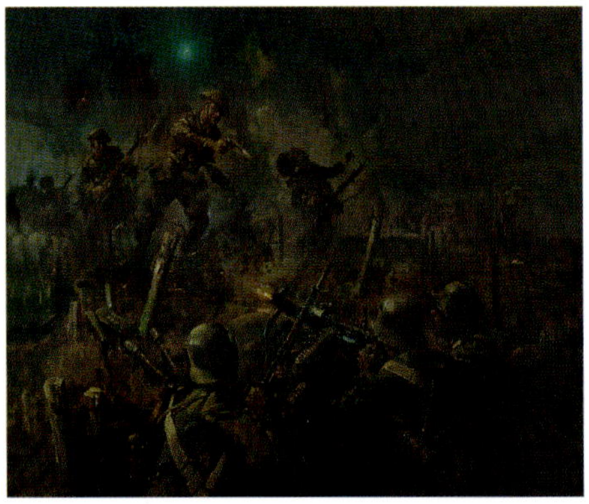

Cuneo, Terence Tenison 1907–1996
Lieutenant John Cridlan Barrett, VC, 1/5th Battalion, Leicestershire Regiment during the Attack on Machine Guns in Forgan's (...) 1958
oil on canvas 135 x 160
L.H38.1988.2.0

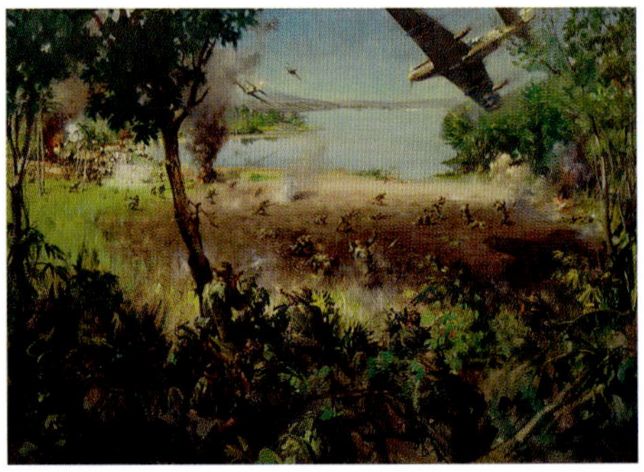

Cuneo, Terence Tenison 1907–1996
2nd Battalion The Leicestershire Regiment, as Chindits, during Operations against the Japanese at Indaw Lake, Burma, 1944 1961
oil on canvas 148 x 196
L.H38.1988.3.0

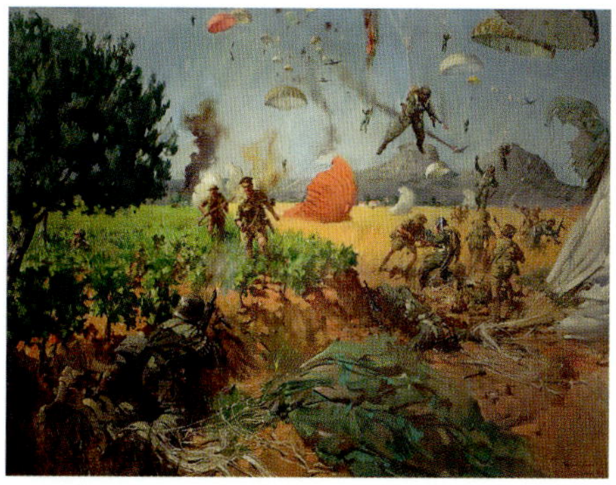

Cuneo, Terence Tenison 1907–1996
German Paratroops Landing on Top of the 2nd Battalion, The Leicestershire Regiment in Crete, 20 May 1941 1961
oil on canvas 150 x 196
L.H38.1988.1.0

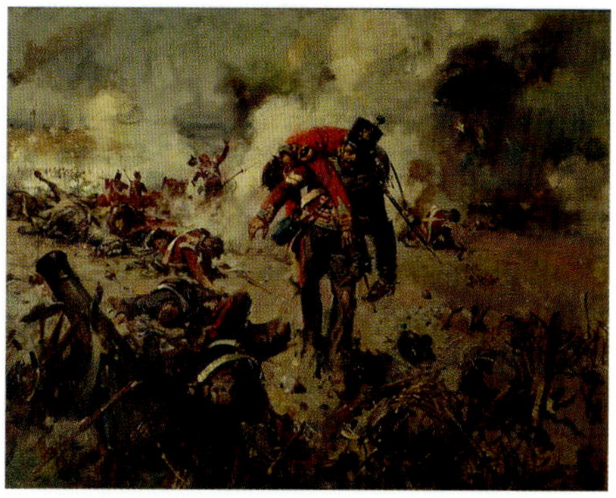

Cuneo, Terence Tenison 1907–1996
Lance Sergeant Philip Smith Winning the Leicestershire Regiment's First Victoria Cross for Bringing In Wounded Comrades at the (...)
oil on canvas 82 x 95.5
L.H38.1988.4.0

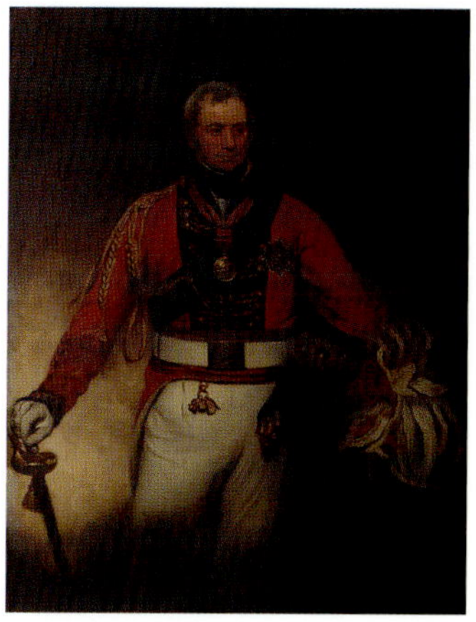

unknown artist
General Sir Frederick Augustus Wetherall (1754–1842), GCH
oil on canvas 151.5 x 115.2
L.H578.1995.275.0

William Carey Museum

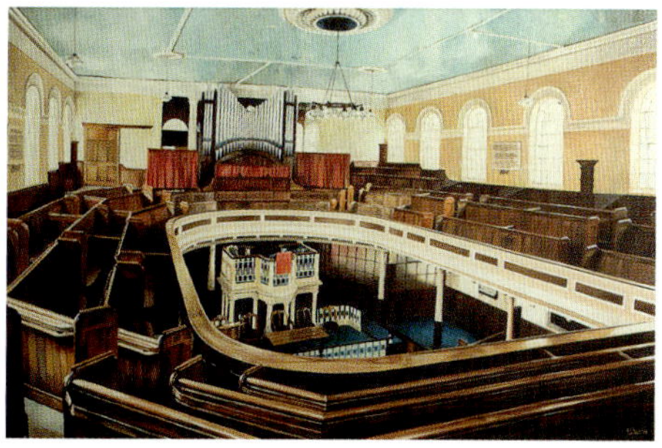

Scott, F. J.
Interior of the Central Baptist Church, Leicester (1920–1983)
oil on canvas 60 x 90
2 (P)

University of Leicester

The University of Leicester was founded in the late 1950s, growing out of University College Leicester, which had opened in 1921. Leicester was established at a time of widespread university growth that saw the development of a number of other civic universities such as Nottingham, Reading and Southampton. Some of these universities were fortunate enough to have wealthy benefactors who were able to invest heavily in land, buildings and subsequently collections of artwork. Leicester's main benefactor was Thomas Fielding Johnson who provided six acres of land for the development of University College, and there were also individual benefactions from local manufacturers in the hosiery industry and in local footwear companies.

For many years the University did not benefit from having a clear policy for building up an art collection, yet it did ensure that portraits of its Chancellors, Vice-Chancellors, Chairmen of Council and Treasurers were commissioned and hung in the University's Council Chamber. Many of the recently commissioned portraits were painted by the esteemed artist Bryan Organ, who lives in Leicestershire. The lack of a systematic policy for collecting art dismayed the current Vice-Chancellor, Professor Sir Robert Burgess, who on his arrival at the University in 1999 initiated an annual Sculpture Show in the University's Botanic Gardens which resulted in a number of long-term loans and donations of sculpture to the University. He also took advantage of the Leicestershire County Council schools and colleges art collection loan scheme to provide artwork in the main administrative building. Subsequently Sir Robert discovered a trust fund that had been established for the purpose of enhancing the University in this way and, along with Assistant Registrar, Jo Wood, began systematically purchasing art for the University as well as engaging in a loan and donation scheme to promote the work of local and regional artists. Whilst the majority of work purchased is watercolours, acrylic, mixed media or prints, there are some oils that feature in the collection, as illustrated in the catalogue.

Robert Burgess, Vice-Chancellor & Jo Wood, Assistant Registrar

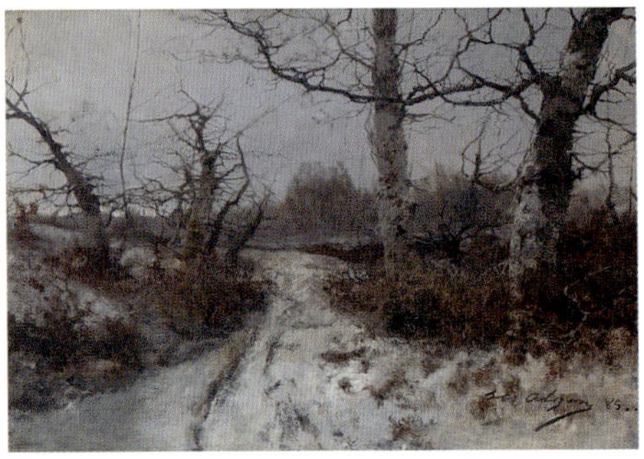

Alizon, Henri active 1885–1886
Winter Scene 1885
oil on canvas 63 x 90
17

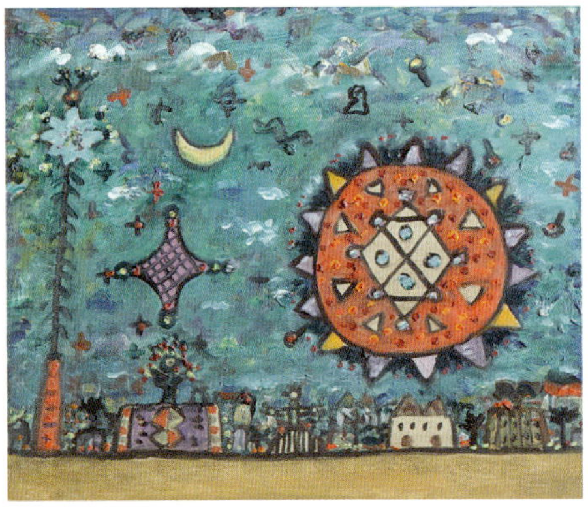

Davie, Alan b.1920
Untitled Abstract
oil on board 35 x 40.5
20

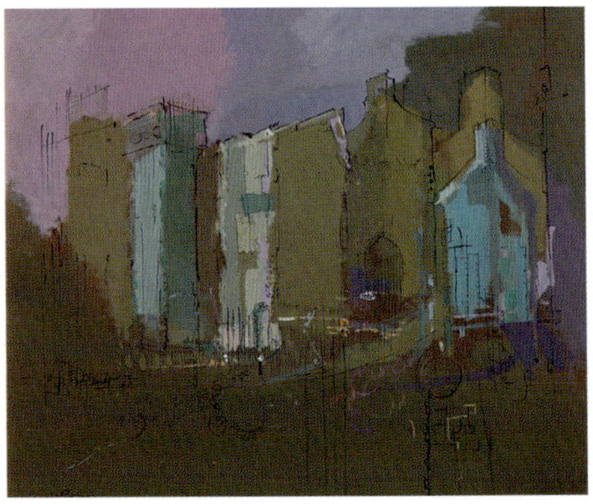

Goodwin, Leslie Albert b.1929
Blaemauon, South Wales
acrylic on board 57 x 72
12

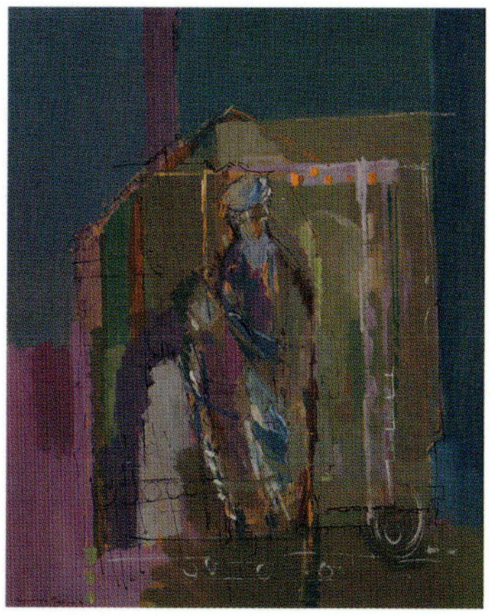

Goodwin, Leslie Albert b.1929
Tapestry Study
acrylic on board 72 x 57
14

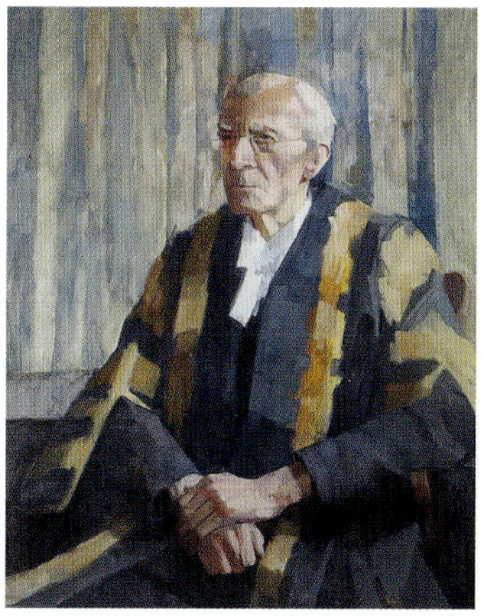

Gowing, Lawrence 1918–1991
Lord Adrian 1962
oil on canvas 100 x 80
10

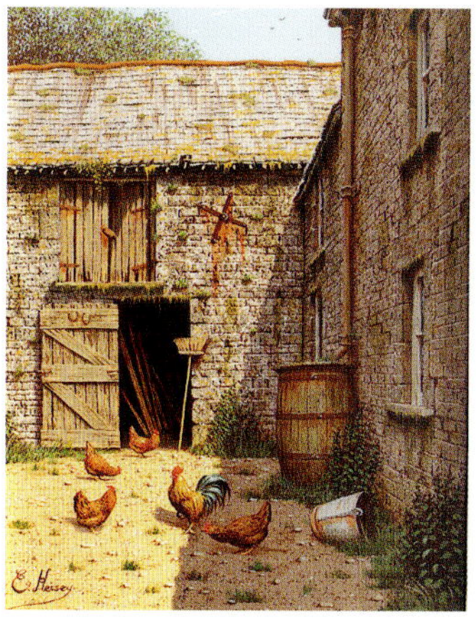

Hersey, Edward b.1948
Wooden Water Butt
oil on canvas 129 x 89
19

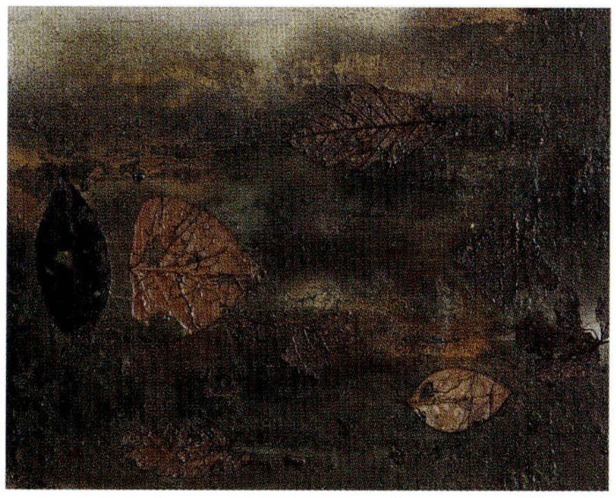

Ismay, D. B.
Study with Leaves
oil on canvas 37 x 49
13

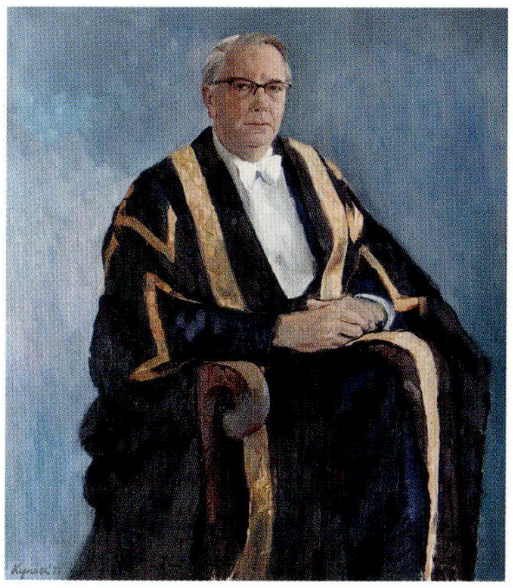

Kynoch, Kathryn b.1942
Sir Fraser Noble (1918–2003), MBE 1977
oil on canvas 124 x 110
1

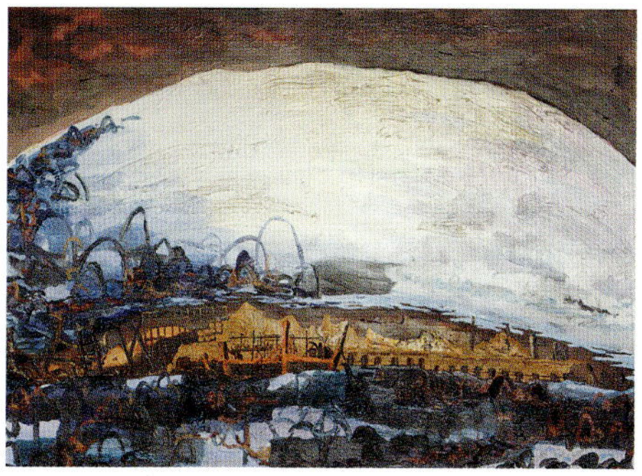

Lancaster, John b.1930
Tundra Excavation I
oil on board 109 x 149
21 (P)

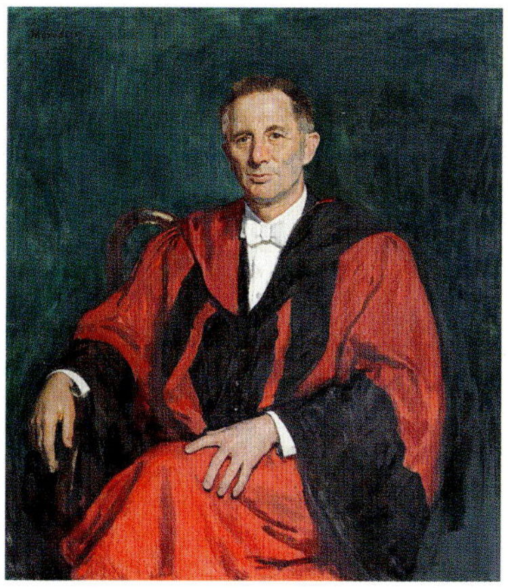

Morrocco, Alberto 1917–1998
Sir Charles Wilson (1909–2002)
oil on canvas 125 x 110
5

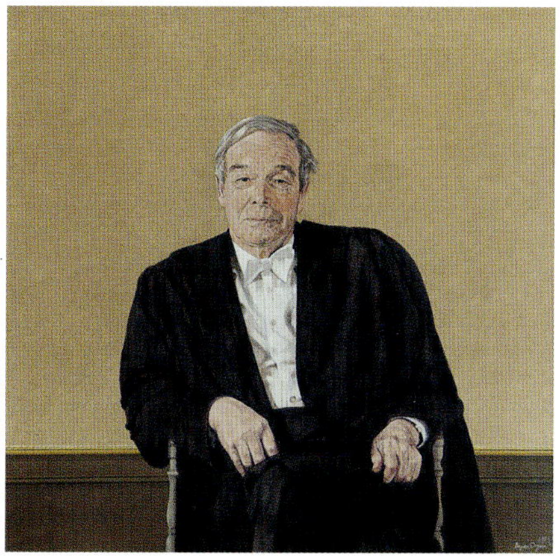

Organ, Bryan b.1935
Sir Alan Hodgkin (1914–1998) 1983
oil on canvas 100 x 100
8

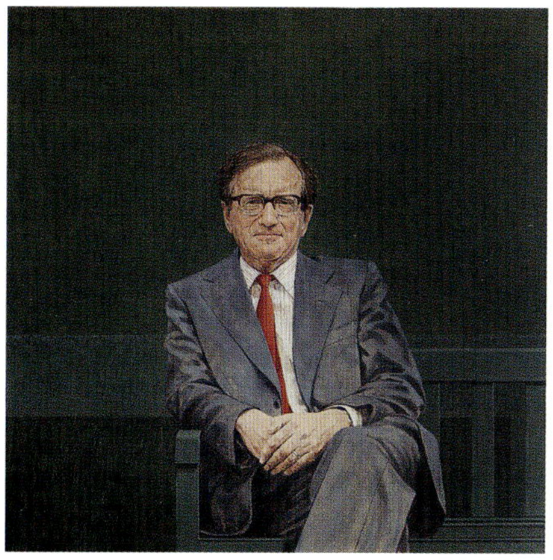

Organ, Bryan b.1935
Sir Maurice Shock 1983
oil on canvas 100.5 x 100.5
9

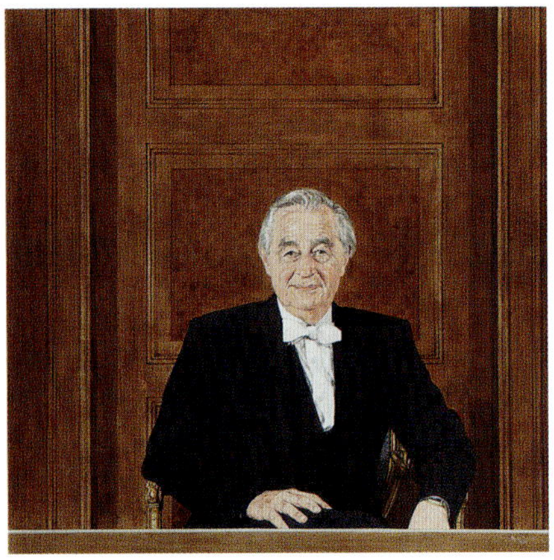

Organ, Bryan b.1935
Lord Potter 1984
oil on canvas 100 x 100
4

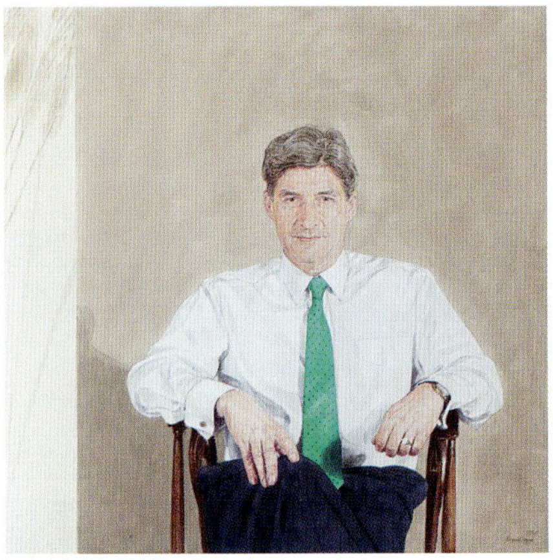

Organ, Bryan b.1935
Dr Ken Edwards 1995
oil on canvas 80.5 x 80.5
6

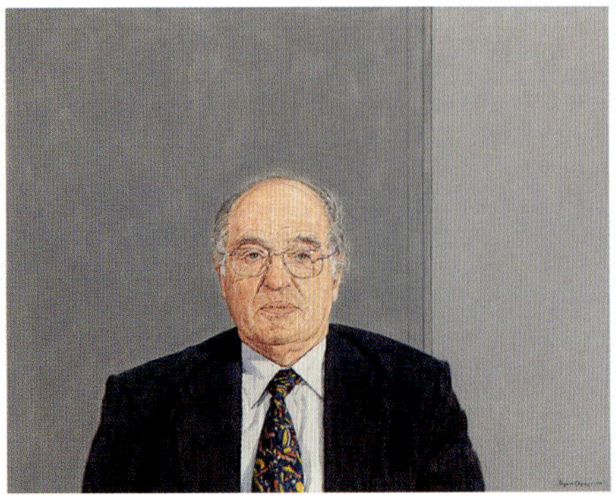

Organ, Bryan b.1935
Michael Atiyah (b.1929) 2000
oil on canvas 60 x 76
7

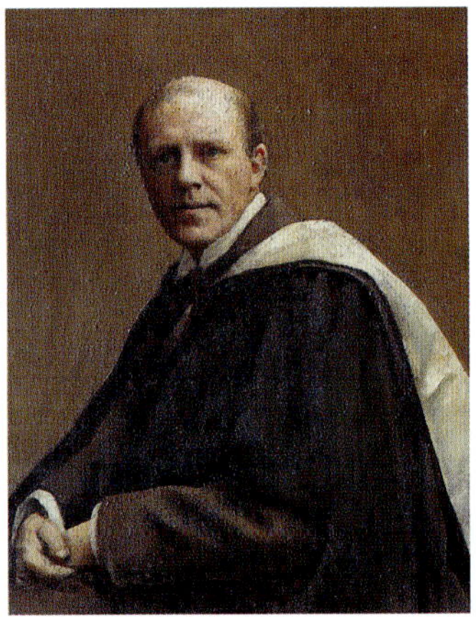

Perry, A. F.
F. L. Attenborough
oil on canvas 87 x 67
11

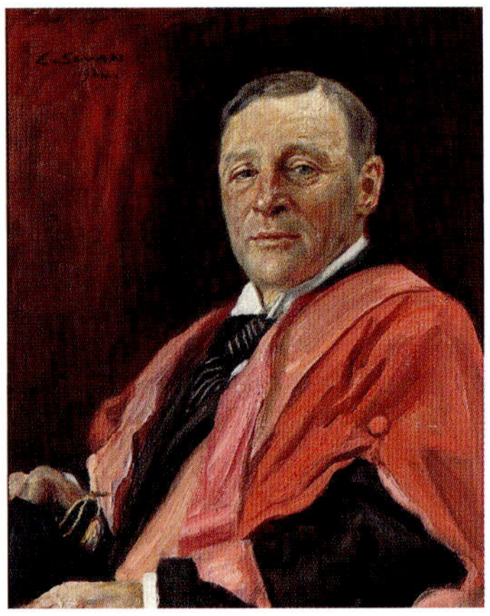

Swann, Edwin b.1873
Dr Astley V. Clarke (1870–1945) 1924
oil on canvas 52 x 42
3

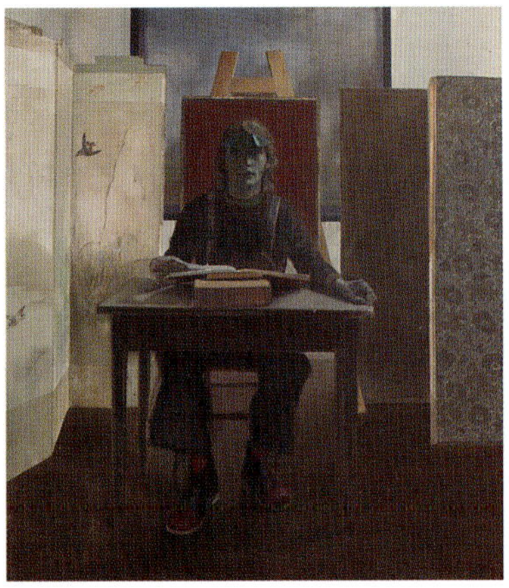

Tindle, David b.1932
The Reader 1972
oil on canvas 144 x 126
15

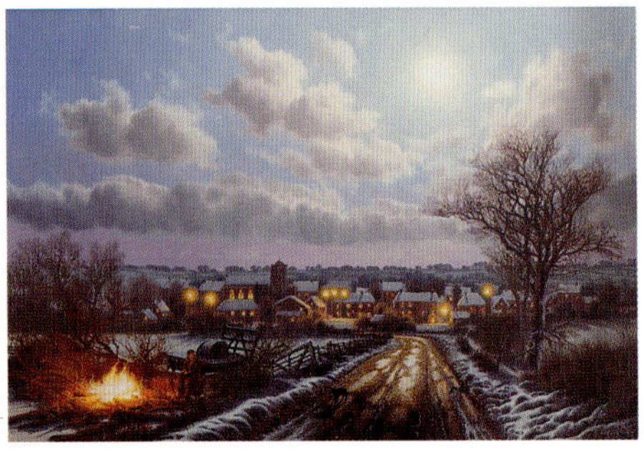

van der Putten, Daniel
Winter Hill at Sulgrave, Northamptonshire
oil on panel 24 x 34
18

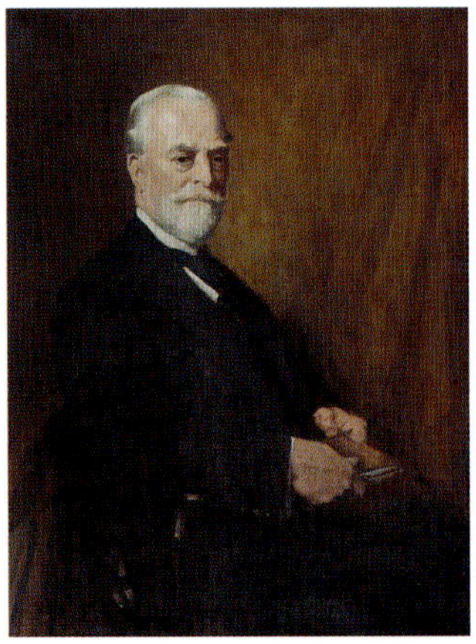

Watt, George Fiddes 1873–1960
Sir Jonathan North (1855–1939)
oil on canvas 97 x 65
2

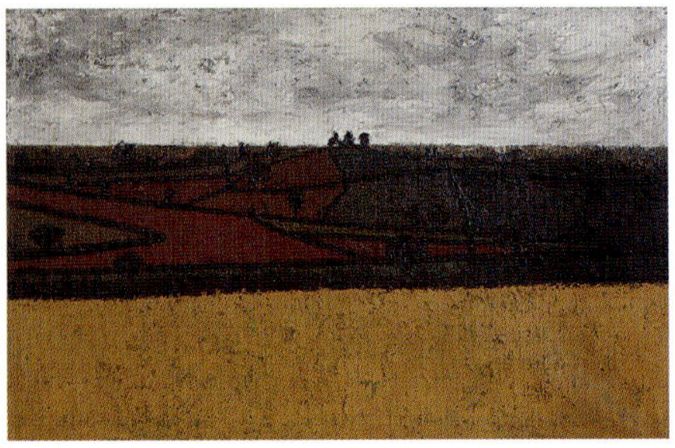

Wright, Peter
Ambio Hill, Leicestershire
oil on canvas 29 x 39
16

Charnwood Borough Art Collection

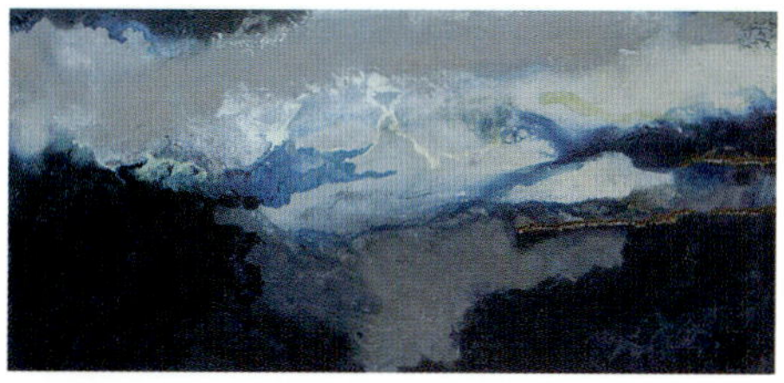

Bird, Lynsey active 1999
Interaction
oil & graphite powder on board 29 x 60
APPW9

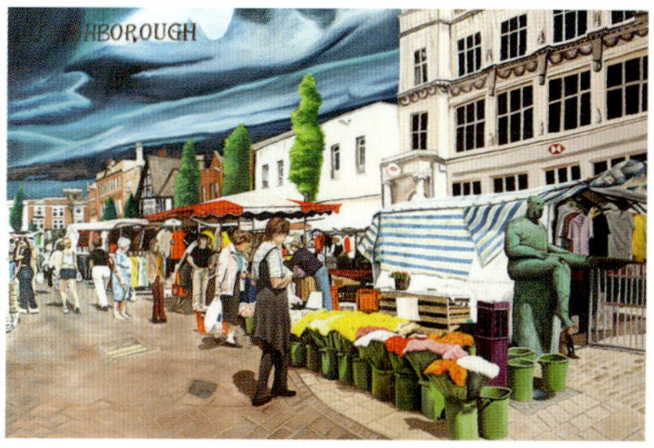

Cumming, Gemma b.1983
Loughborough, Leicestershire 2006
oil on canvas 122 x 185
APPW32

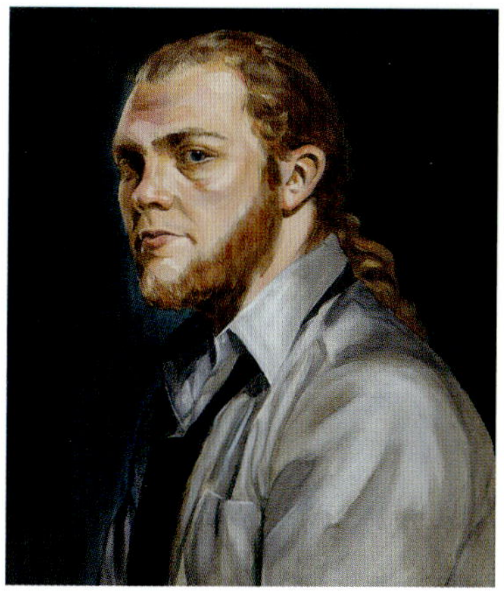

Fraser, Rhiannon b.1986
David 2008
oil on canvas 60 x 50.5
APPW42

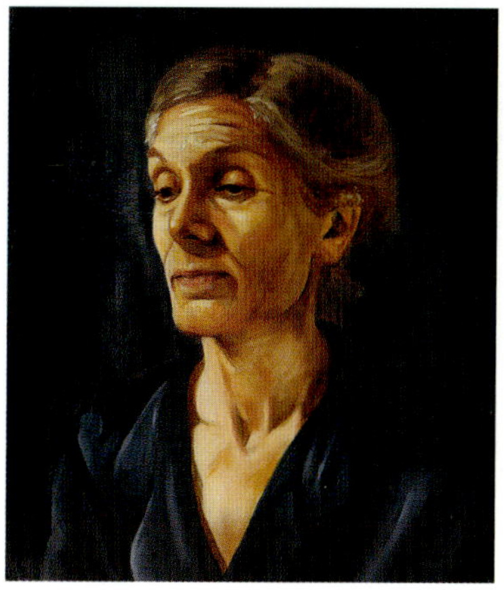

Fraser, Rhiannon b.1986
Ethel 2008
oil on canvas 60 x 50.5
APPW41

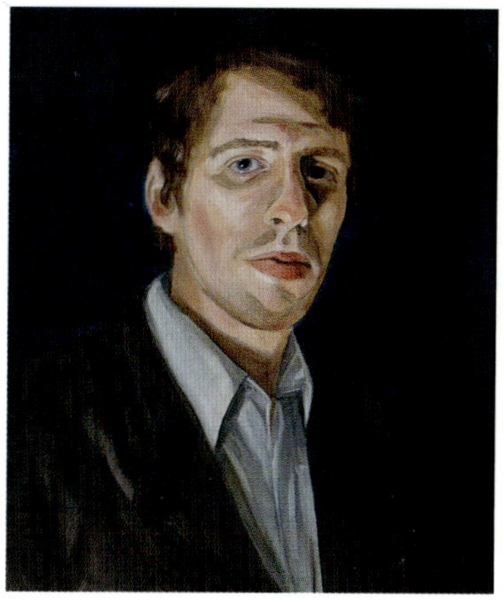

Fraser, Rhiannon b.1986
Graham 2008
oil on canvas 60 x 50.5
APPW38

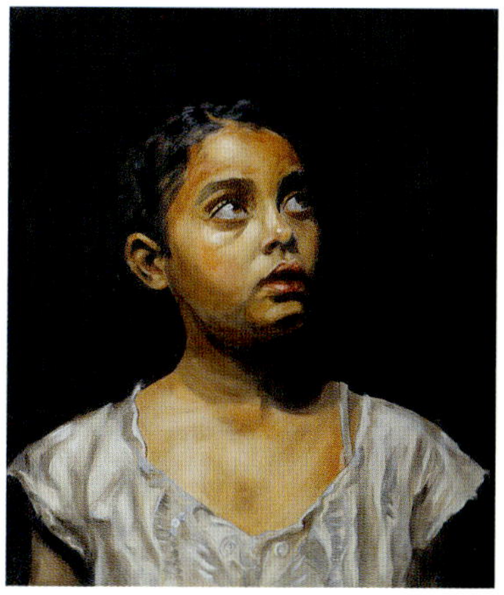

Fraser, Rhiannon b.1986
Jaida 2008
oil on canvas 60 x 50.5
APPW39

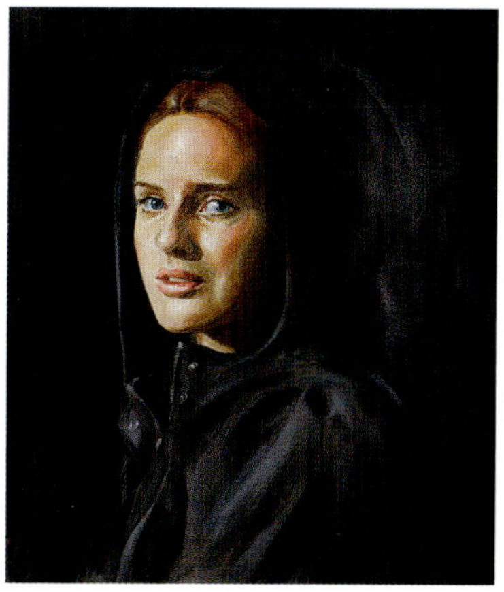

Fraser, Rhiannon b.1986
Rose 2008
oil on canvas 60 x 50.5
APPW40

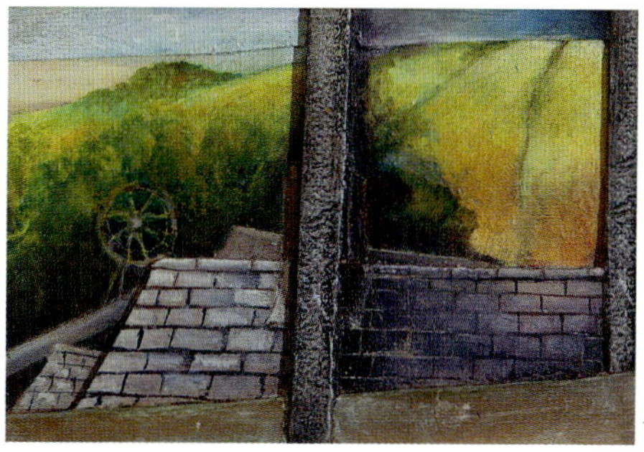

Hantman, Anne
Durham Coastal Town
oil & wood on board 11.5 x 16.5
APPW3

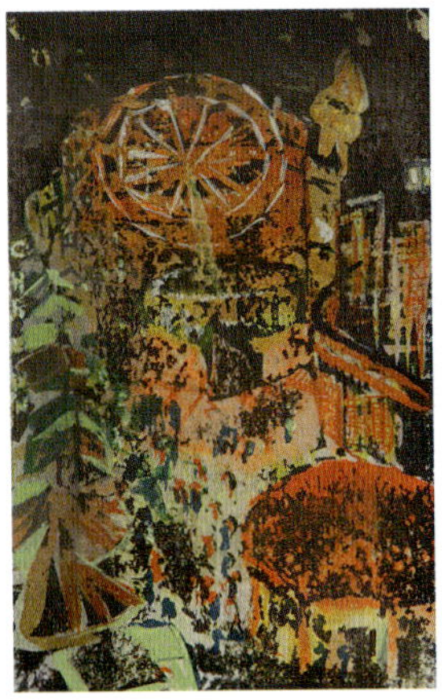

Mitchell, Sue active 1994
Loughborough Fair, Leicestershire
oil on paper 12.5 x 8
APPW5

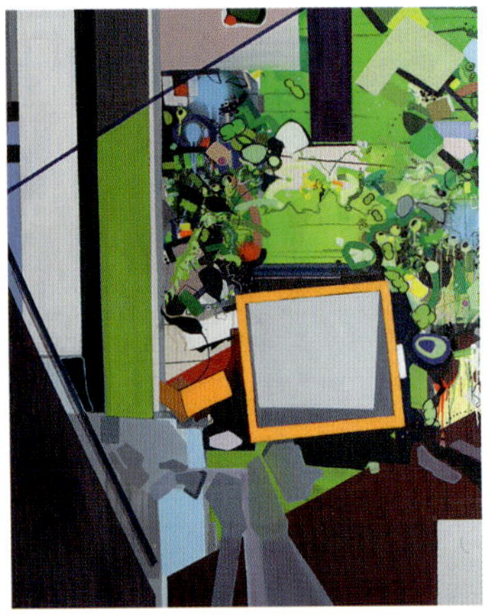

Ratcliff, Charlotte
Blue Circle Study 2009
oil, acrylic & spray paint on canvas 180 x 140
APPW1

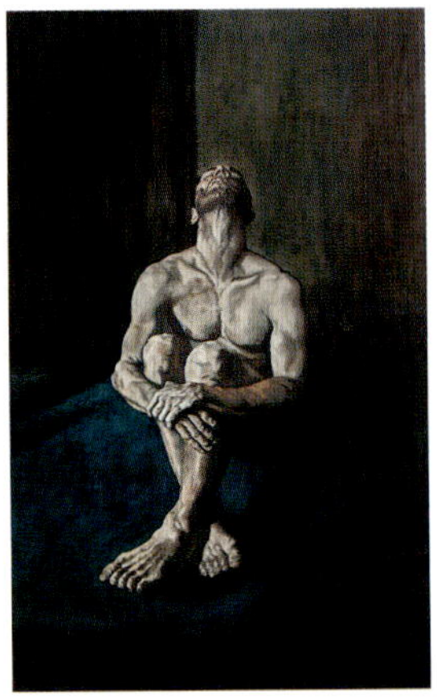

Rutter, Neil
Self 1 2007
oil on board 240 x 122
APPW35

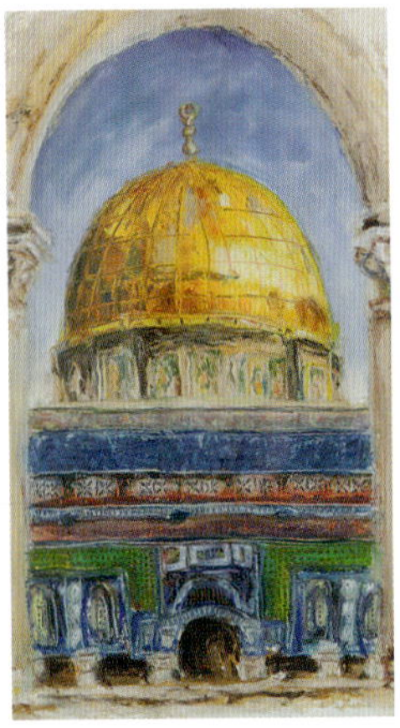

Tomlinson, Rachel
Jewish Temple 1998
oil & pencil on paper 52 x 28
APPW7

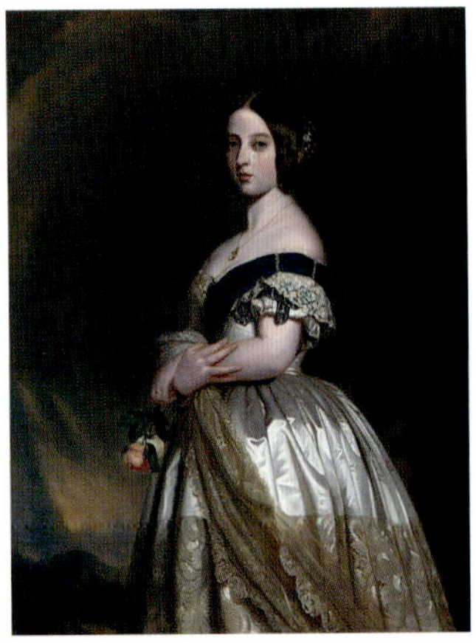

unknown artist
Queen Victoria (1819–1901)
oil on canvas 160 x 110 (E)
APPW0

Facing page: Ysenbrandt, Adriaen, c.1500–before 1551 (attributed to), *Crucifixion* (detail), The Collection: Art & Archaeology in Lincolnshire (Usher Gallery) (p. 344)

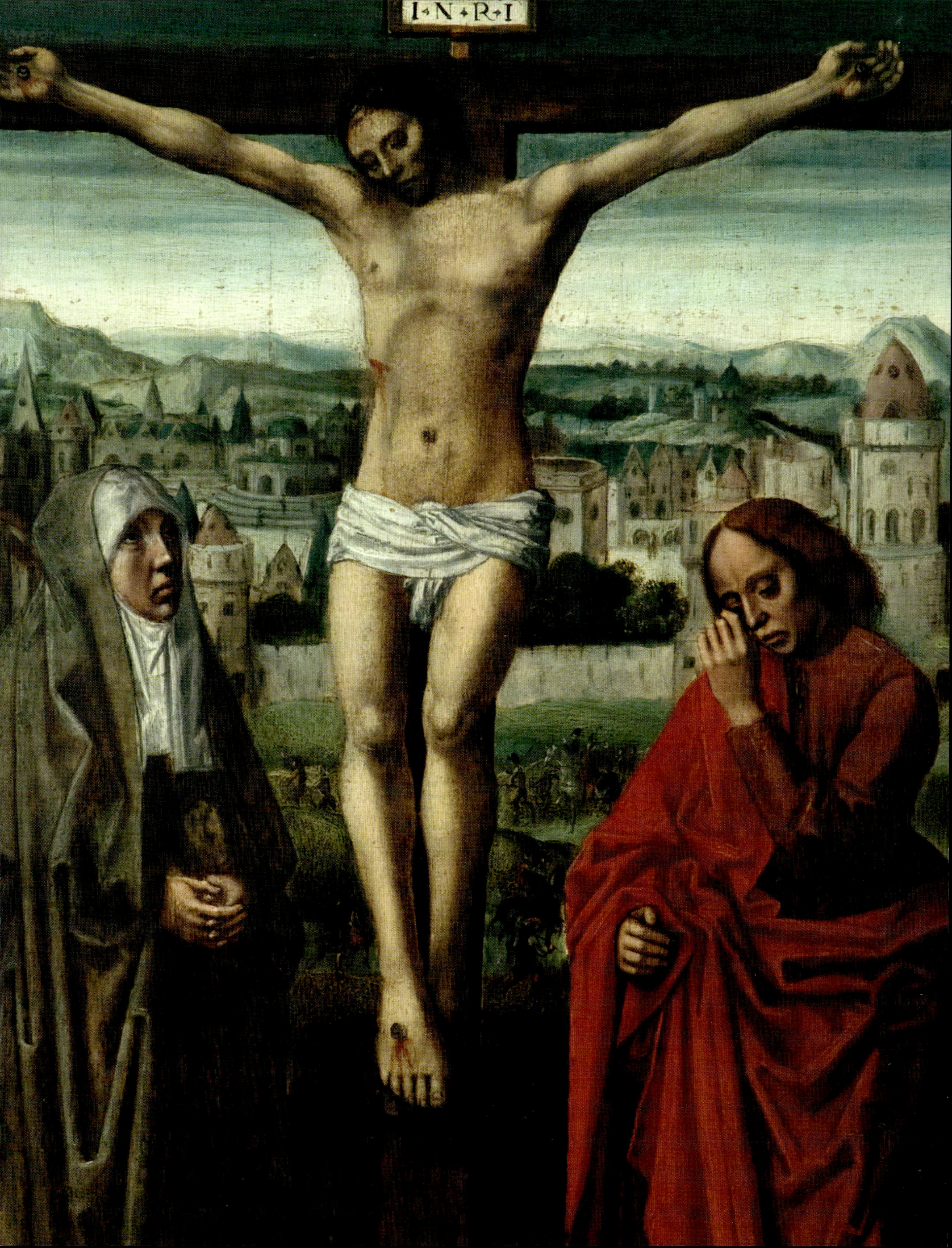
I·N·R·I

Loughborough University

The University, which first opened its doors in 1909, has a rich body of work dating from 1950 to the present day, including pieces by commissioned artists as well as some by former students of the School of Art. The Collection encompasses varying styles of realism and abstraction influenced by the trends of the day, and reflects the high standard for which the University is renowned.

There is a large collection of portraits of people who have made a great contribution to the University. These include Oswald Hornby Joseph Birley's portrait of Herbert Schofield, Principal of Loughborough College from 1915 to 1950, who supported the war effort in the First World War by turning the Institute into a munitions factory, training over 2,000 men and women. The Collection also contains Lionel Brooke's painting of Dr Herbert Leslie Haslegrave, the first Vice-Chancellor of the University, who managed the transition from College to University, and June Mendoza's portrait of Sir David Wallace, Vice-Chancellor of Loughborough University from 1994 to 2006, who was awarded a knighthood in 2004 in recognition of his services to UK science.

The Collection houses work by renowned artists such as British abstract expressionist painter and printmaker Frank Avray Wilson, and works by British painter John Hitchens.

More recent acquisitions include Matt Howell's 2006 *Mission Statement*, commissioned by the Students' Union, portraying the variety of student life experienced at the University, and *Rehersal* by artist Rhiannon Fraser, a graduate of the School of Art and Design.

Looking through the University's Collection, with all the history and diversity it holds, allows one both to recognise its past and welcome future acquisitions.

Lucie Chapman, Programme Assistant

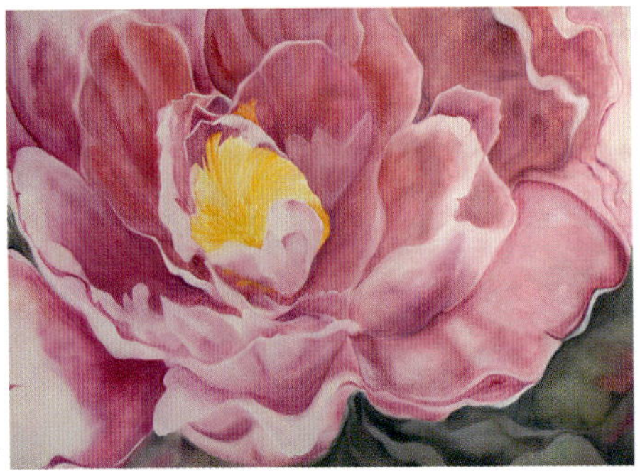

Aldridge, Sue active 1994–1997
Pink Flower 1997
oil on canvas 125 x 199
PCF1

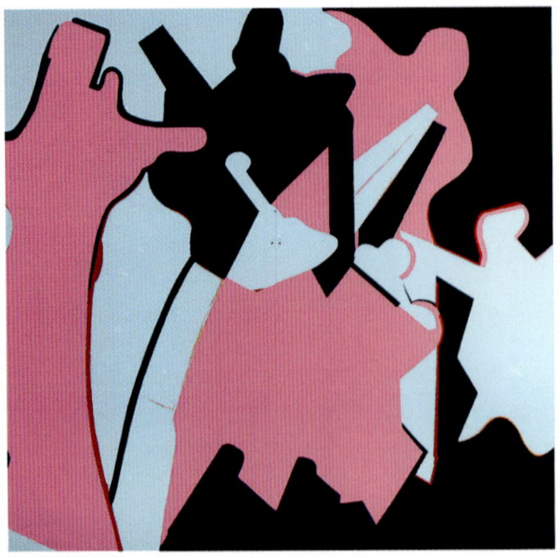

Allen, Lara Z.
Guitarist 2004
oil on hardboard 238 x 244
PCF2

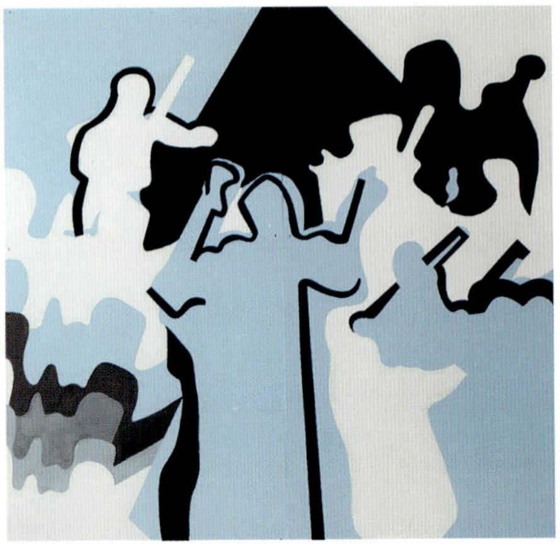

Allen, Lara Z.
Orchestra 2004
oil on hardboard 238 x 244
PCF3

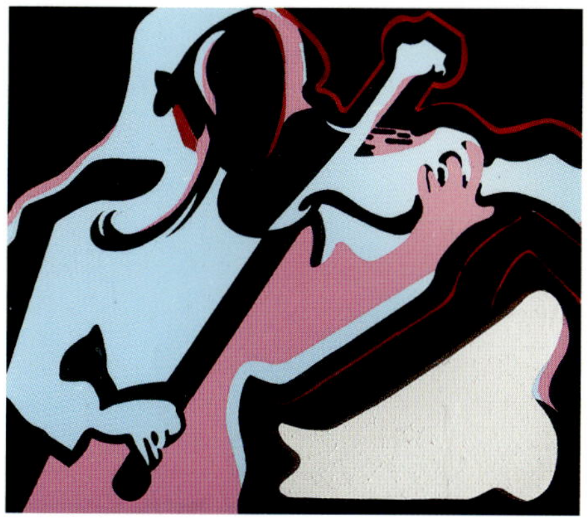

Allen, Lara Z.
Violinist 2004
oil on hardboard 109 x 122
PCF4

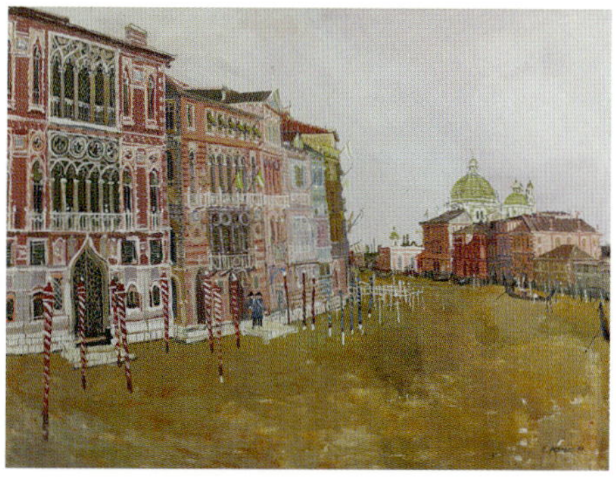

Atkinson, Eric b.1928
Grand Canal, Venice 1954
oil on canvas 68 x 89
PCF5

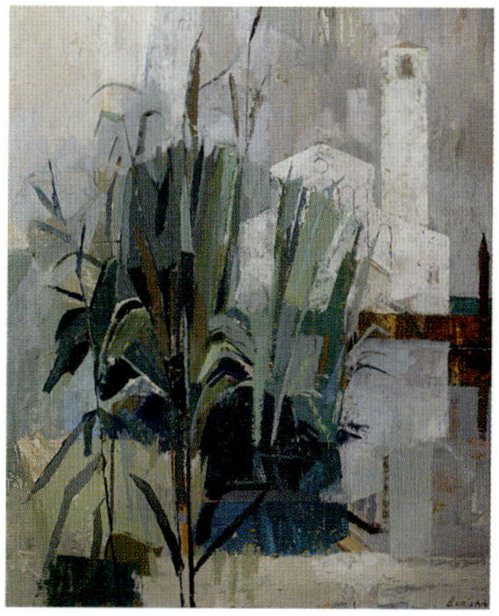

Berrisford, Peter 1932–2003
Torcello, Italy
acrylic on hardboard 94.5 x 74.5
PCF6

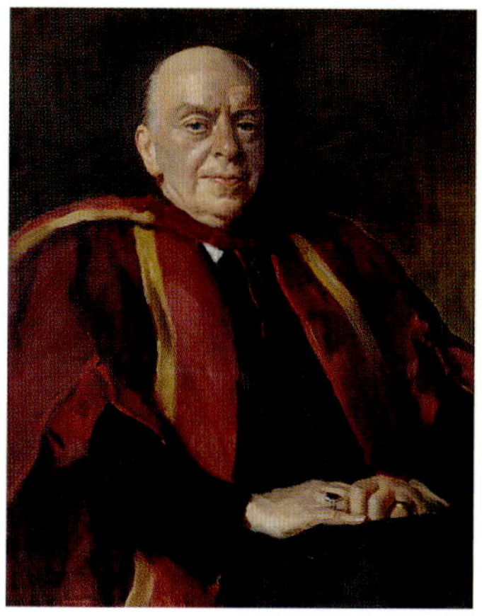

Birley, Oswald Hornby Joseph 1880–1952
Herbert Schofield (1882–1963), Principal of Loughborough College (1915–1950) 1950
oil on canvas 87 x 67.5
PCF7

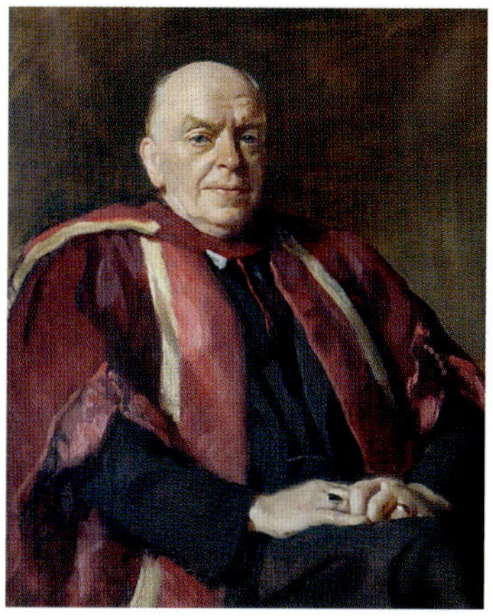

Birley, Oswald Hornby Joseph 1880–1952
Herbert Schofield (1882–1963), Principal of Loughborough College (1915–1950) 1950
oil on canvas 89 x 70
PCF8

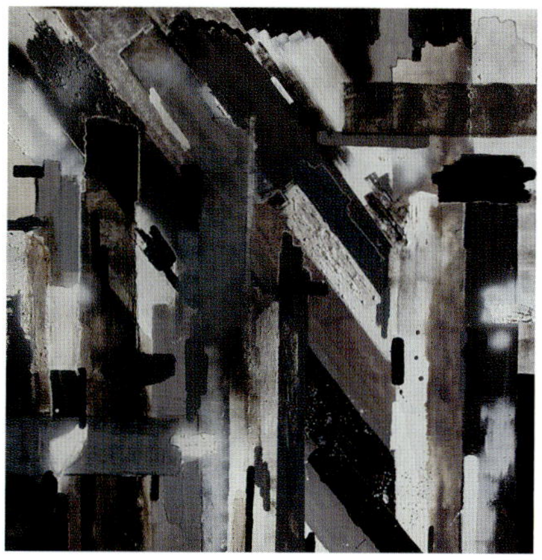

Boswell, Sophie
Untitled 1
oil on canvas 115 x 114.5
87

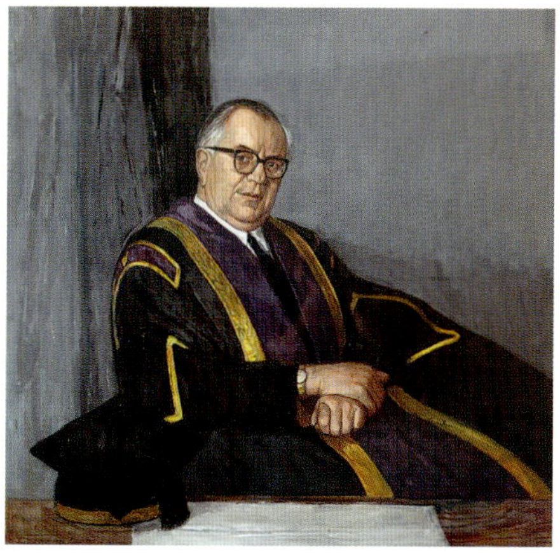

Bowyer, William b.1926
Professor E. J. Richards (1914–1995), Vice-Chancellor of Loughborough University (1967–1975)
oil on canvas 102 x 99
PCF9

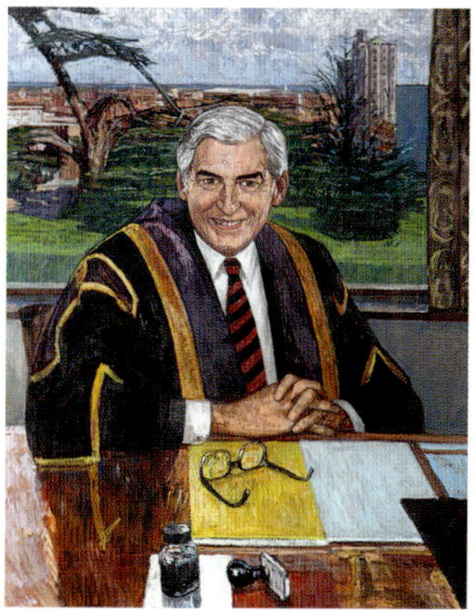

Bowyer, William b.1926
Professor J. G. Phillips (1933–1987), Vice-Chancellor of Loughborough University (1986–1987)
oil on canvas 93 x 72
PCF10

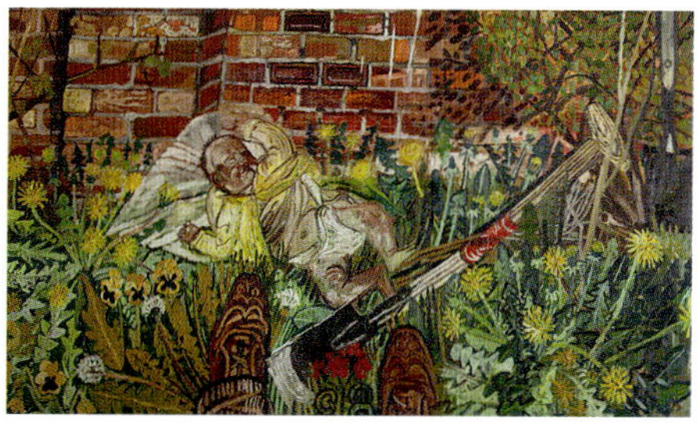

Bratby, John Randall 1928–1992
Baby Asleep in the Garden 1961
oil on canvas 127 x 220
PCF11

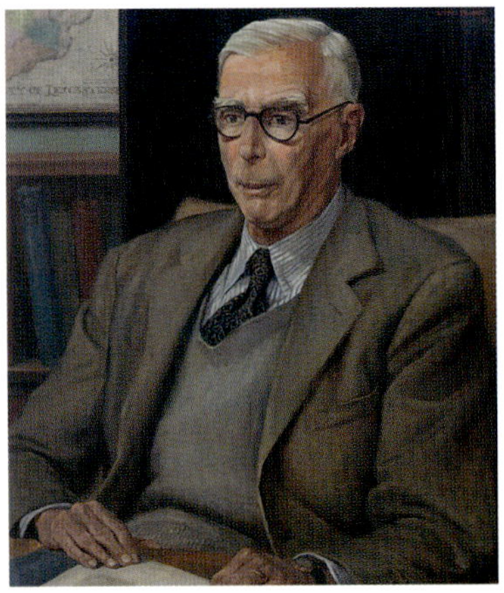

Brookes, Lionel b.1915
Sir William Brockington (1871–1959), Director of Education for Leicestershire (1903–1946) 1952
oil on canvas 77 x 62
PCF12

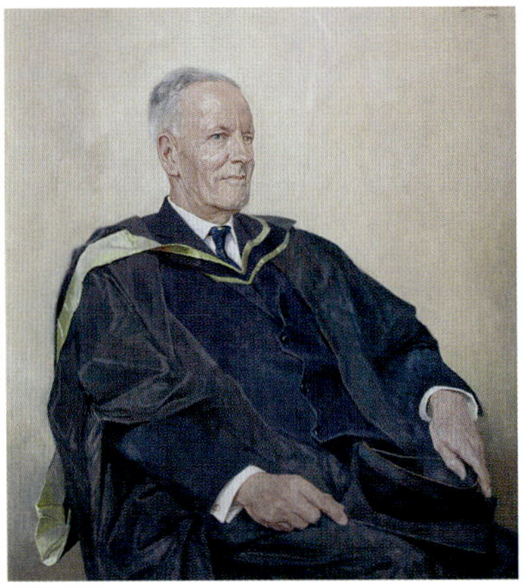

Brookes, Lionel b.1915
Professor J. F. Peck (1897–1971), Emeritus Professor of Engineering at Loughborough College of Technology 1969
oil on canvas 90 x 84
PCF13

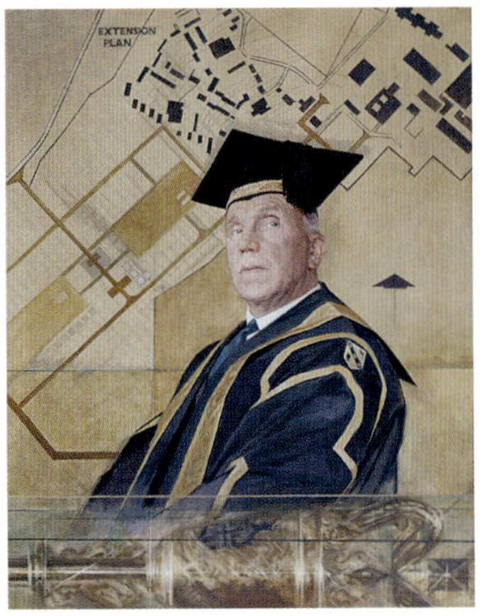

Brookes, Lionel b.1915
Dr Herbert Leslie Haslegrave (1902–1999), Principal at Loughborough College of Technology (1953–1966), First (...)
oil on canvas 125 x 95
PCF14

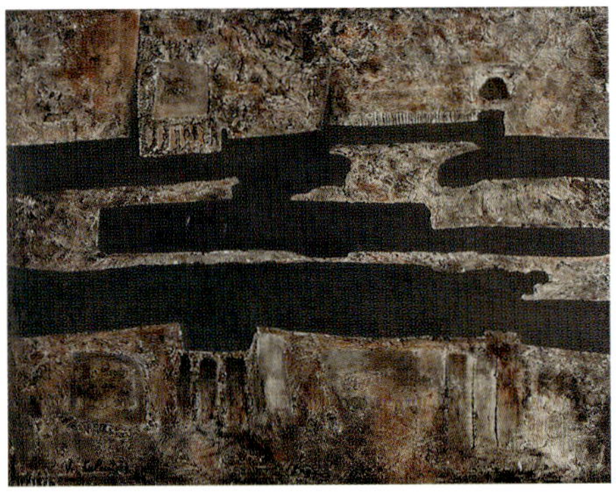

Caloutsis, Valerios b.1927
London 1960
oil on canvas 129 x 163
PCF15

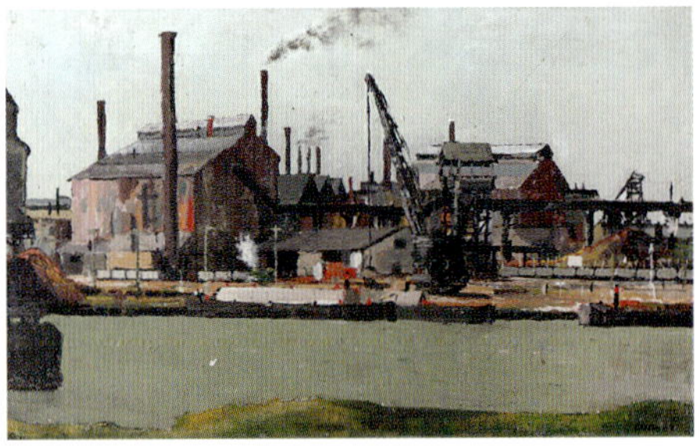

Challinor, T.
Industrial Scene 1957
oil on hardboard 56 x 90
LCE 75

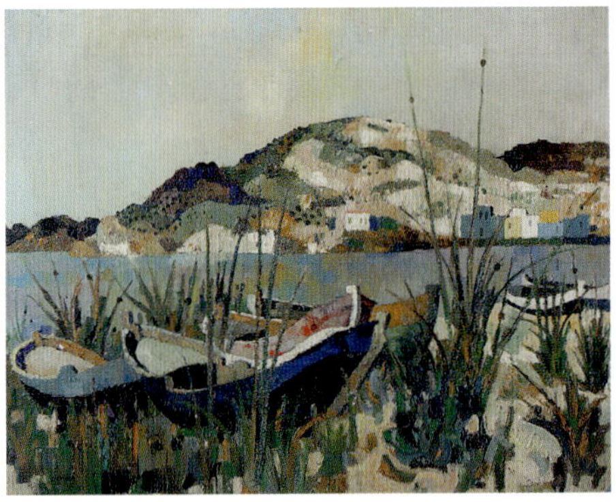

Charon, Guy b.1927
The Canal Saint-Martin
oil on hardboard 73 x 93
LCE 82

Chatburn, Margaret active 1994–1997
Heavy Rain 1997
oil on canvas 92 x 92
PCF16

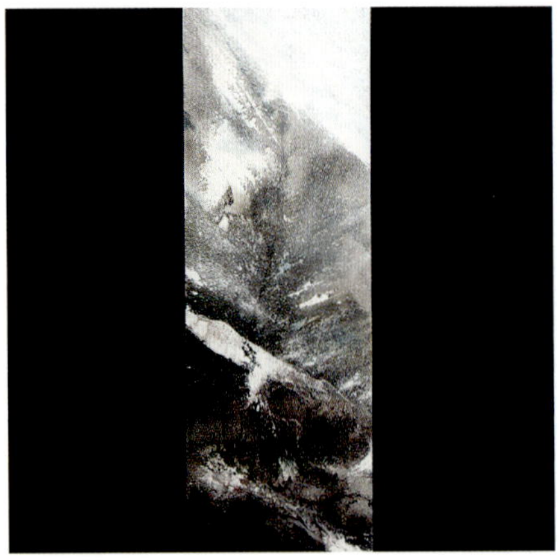

Clarke, Matthew b.1970
Roaches 15
oil & acrylic on canvas 180 x 180
PCF20

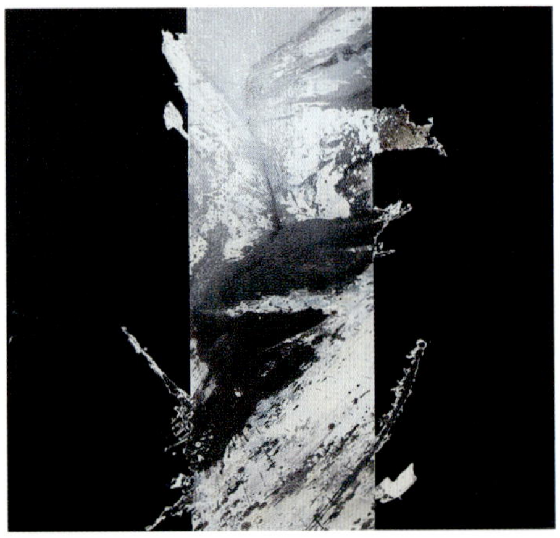

Clarke, Matthew b.1970
Roaches 18
oil & acrylic on canvas 59 x 59
PCF17

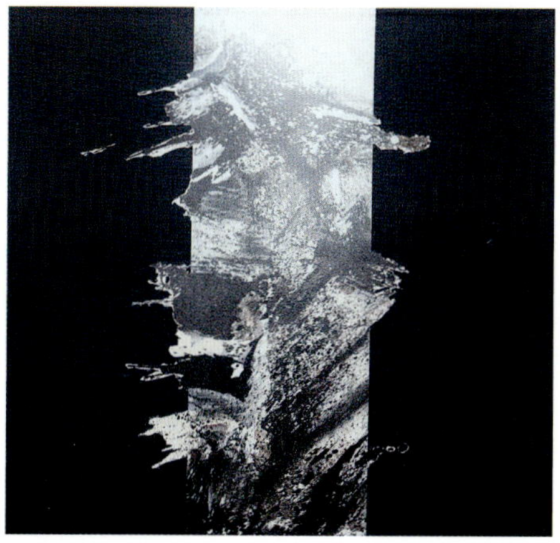

Clarke, Matthew b.1970
Roaches 19
oil & acrylic on canvas 59 x 59
PCF18

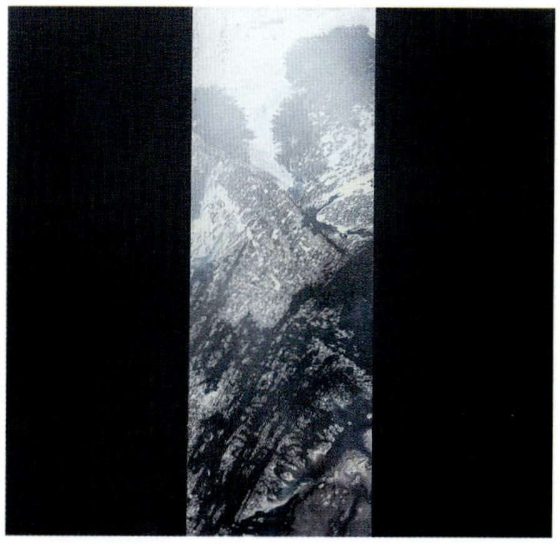

Clarke, Matthew b.1970
Roaches 20
oil & acrylic on canvas 59 x 59
PCF19

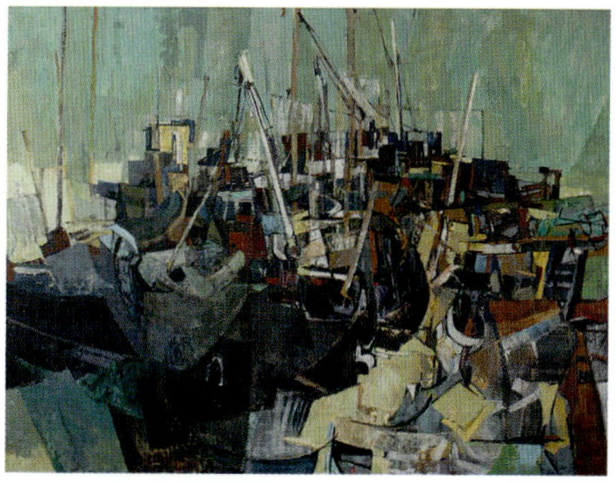

Coantury, R. (attributed to)
Untitled 1965
oil on hardboard 90 x 121
PCF21

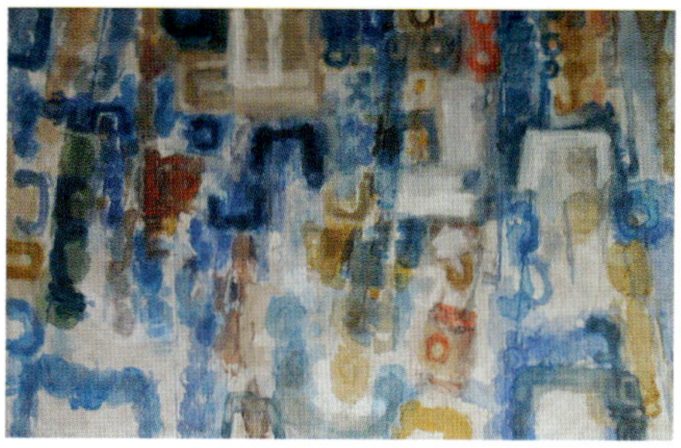

Cohen, Harold b.1928
Happy Day
oil on canvas 280 x 356
PCF22

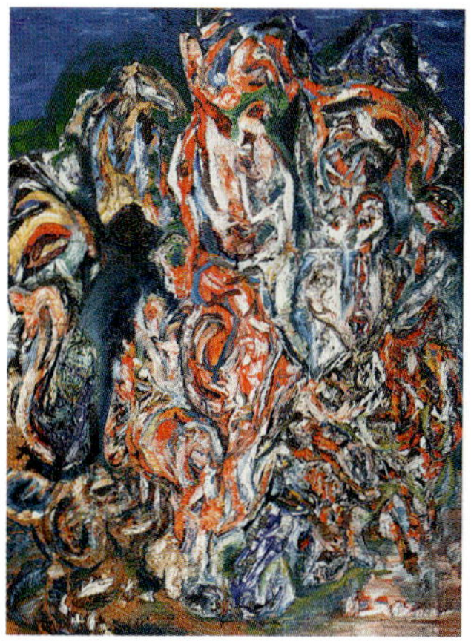

Cole, Dan
Monkey
oil on canvas 213 x 157
PCF23

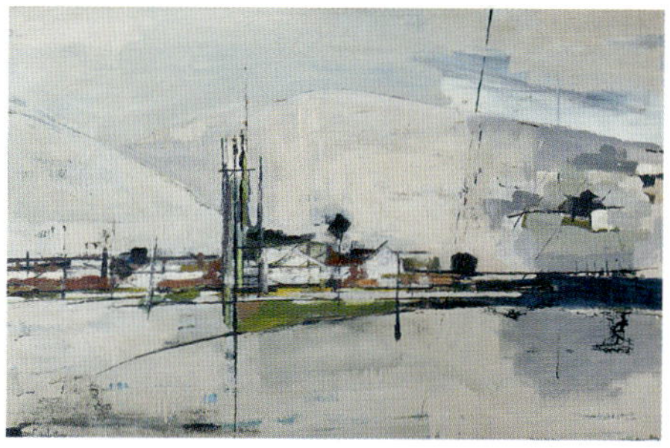

Copplestone, Trewin b.1921
Dartmoor Village, Devon
oil on hardboard 59 x 89
PCF24

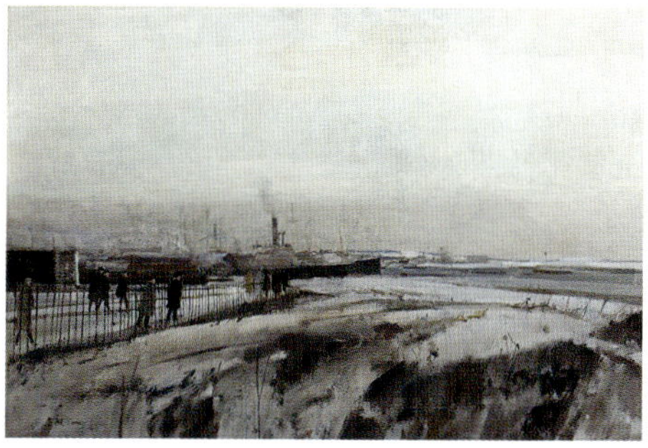

Cuming, Frederick b.1930
Rochester Snowscape, Kent before 1964
oil on canvas 140 x 190
PCF25

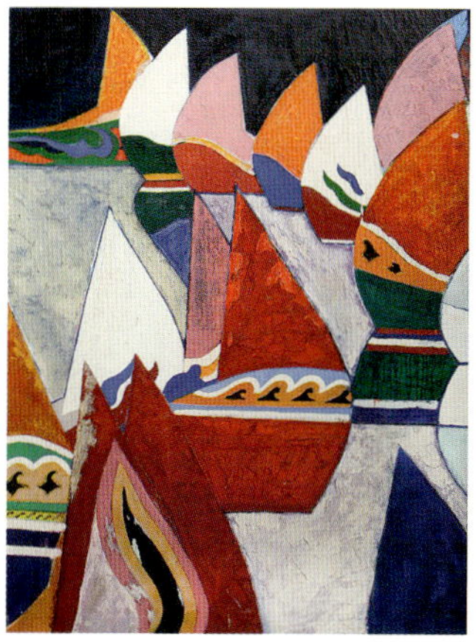

Davies, L.
Ships at Sea
oil on canvas 122 x 92
PCF26

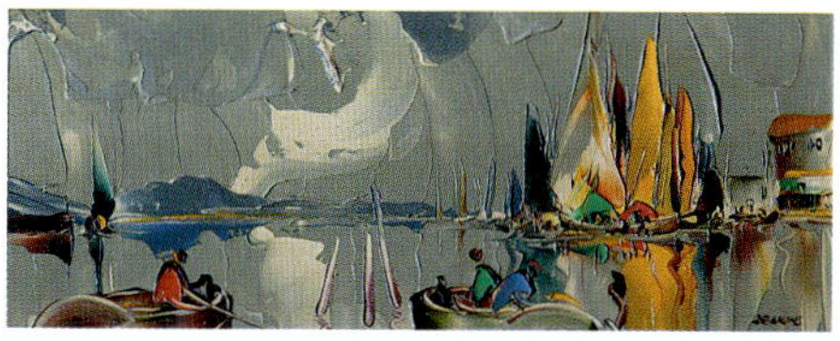

Deakins, George 1911–1981
Sail Cluster
oil on canvas 23 x 59
PCF27

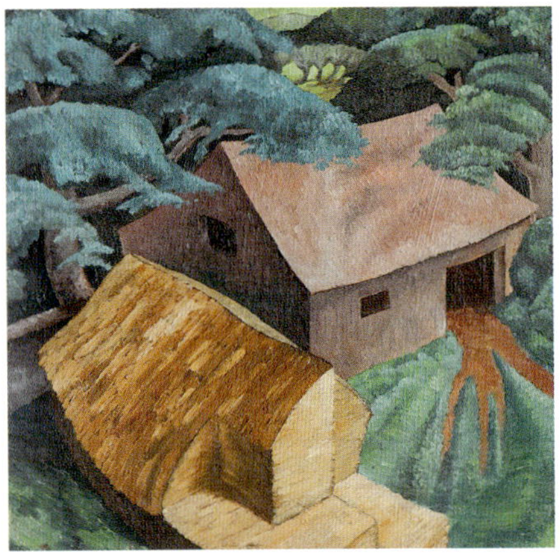

Divine, Jack A. F. 1912–1960
Haystack and Barn
oil on canvas 43 x 45
PCF28

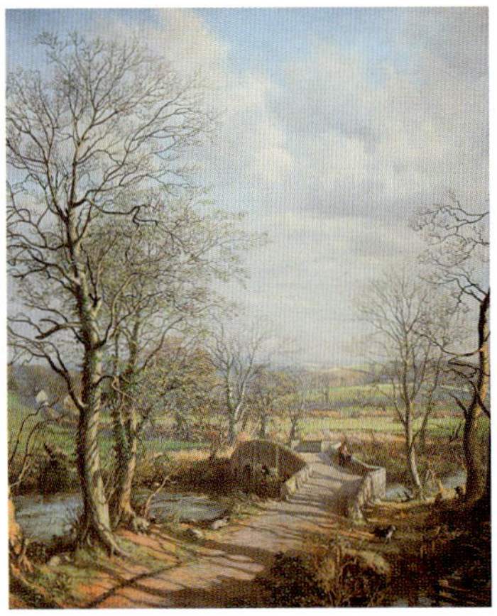

Elford, Victor 1911–2003
April Sunshine c.1971
oil on hardboard 70 x 54
PCF29

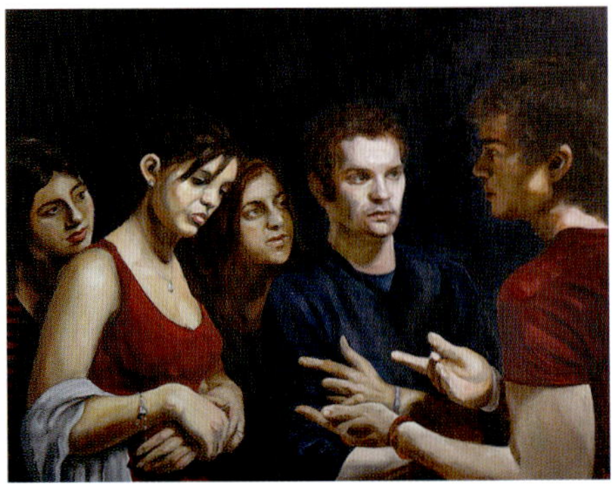

Fraser, Rhiannon b.1986
Rehearsal 2008
oil on canvas 98 x 123
PCF30

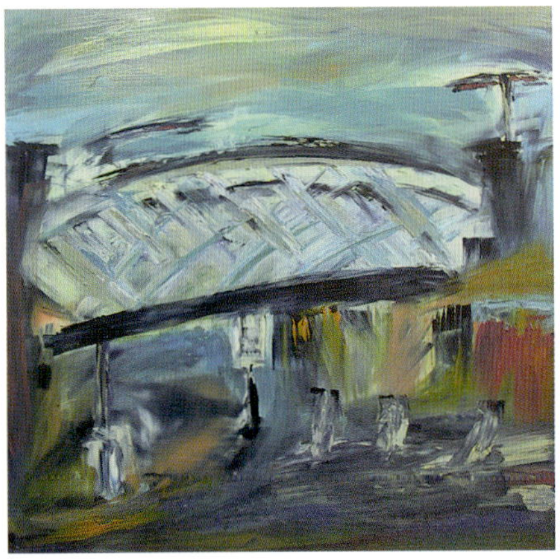

Gaff, David b.1959
Bowstring Bridge, Leicester 2008
oil on canvas 102 x 102
PCF81

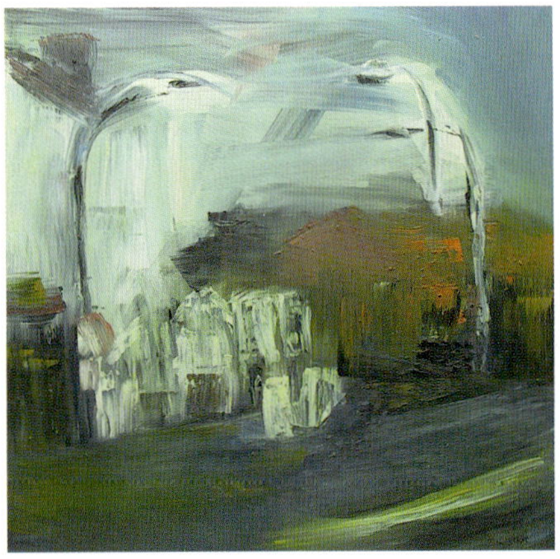

Gaff, David b.1959
Braunstone High Street, Leicester 2008
oil on canvas 102 x 102
PCF82

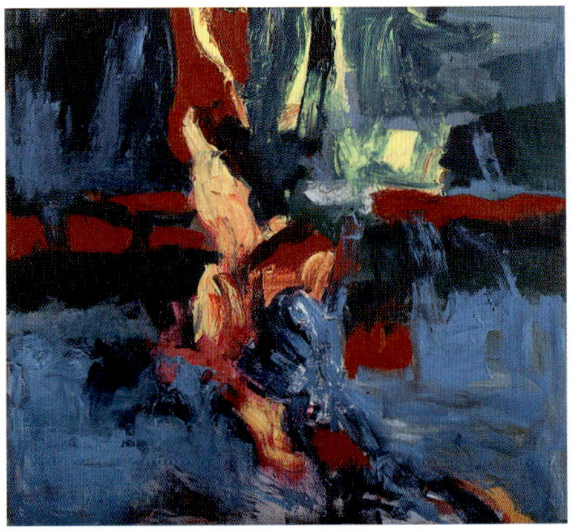

Gallagher, Rachel b.1953
The Applause Grew Louder 1995
oil on canvas 151 x 160
PCF31

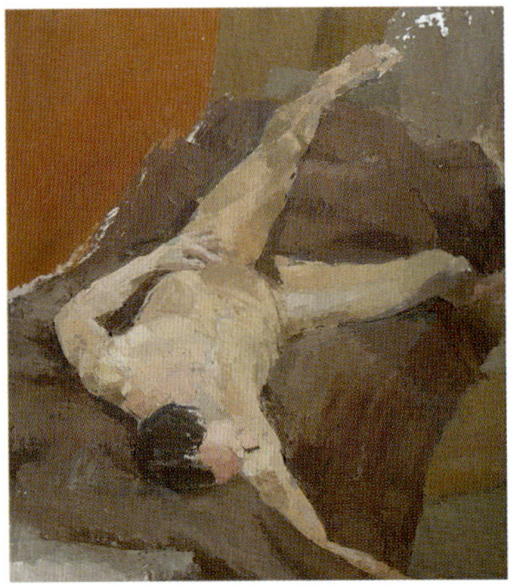

Gray, W.
Life Painting
oil on canvas 108 x 92
PCF32

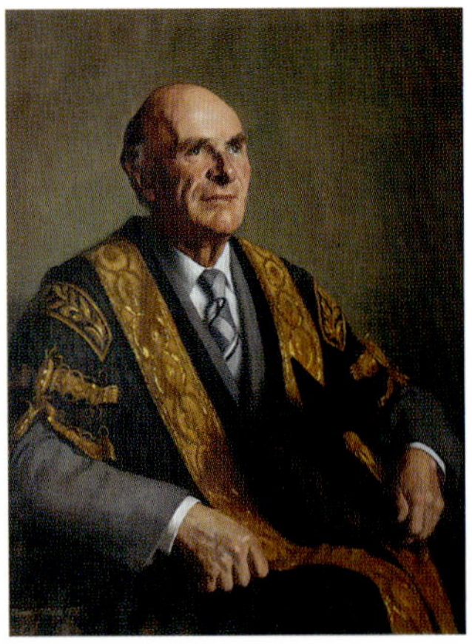

Halliday, Edward Irvine 1902–1984
Sir Harry Pilkington (1905–1983), Chancellor of Loughborough University of Technology (1966–1980) 1979
oil on canvas 100 x 74
PCF33

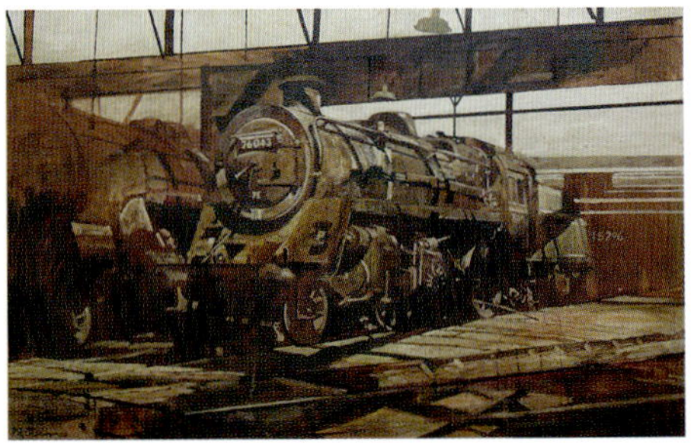

Hammonds, A. L.
Loco Sheds at Saltley, Birmingham
oil on canvas 99 x 150
PCF34

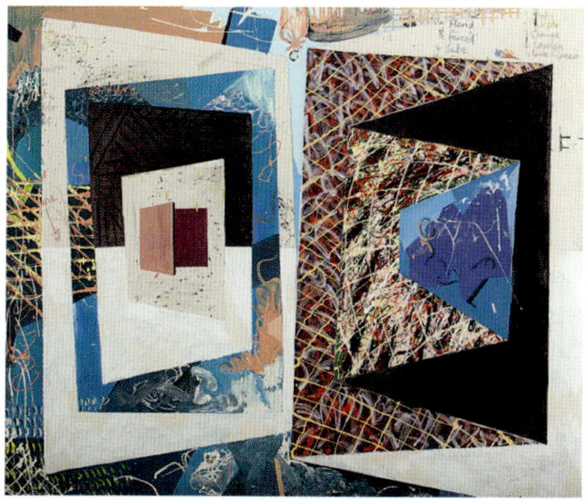

Hartshorne, Ian b.1968
Cardinal Humerment 1995
oil on canvas 132 x 154
PCF36

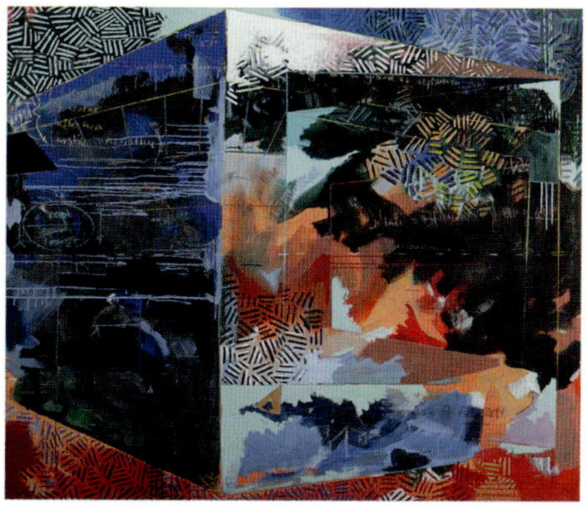

Hartshorne, Ian b.1968
Keeping Mum 1995
oil on canvas 180.5 x 207
PCF35

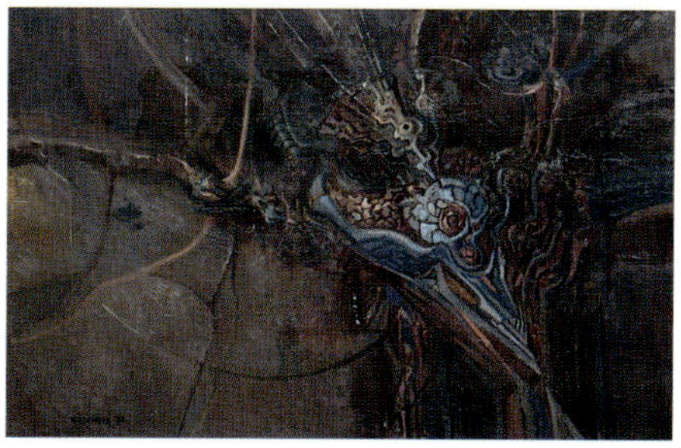

Hellawell, Edward
Tree Form 1972
oil on canvas 69 x 102
PCF37

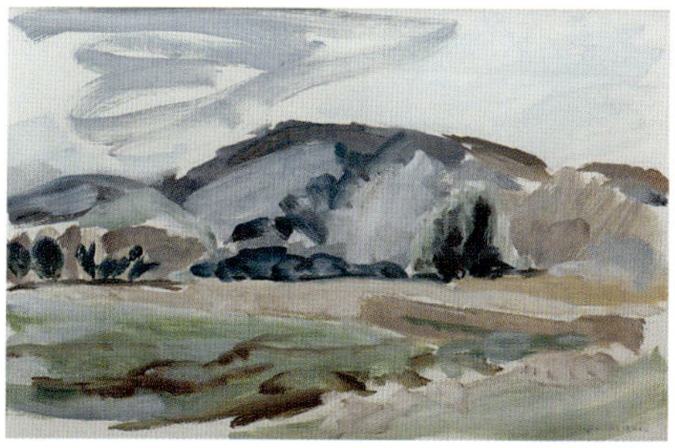

Hitchens, John b.1940
September Hills 1959
oil on board 50 x 76
PCF39

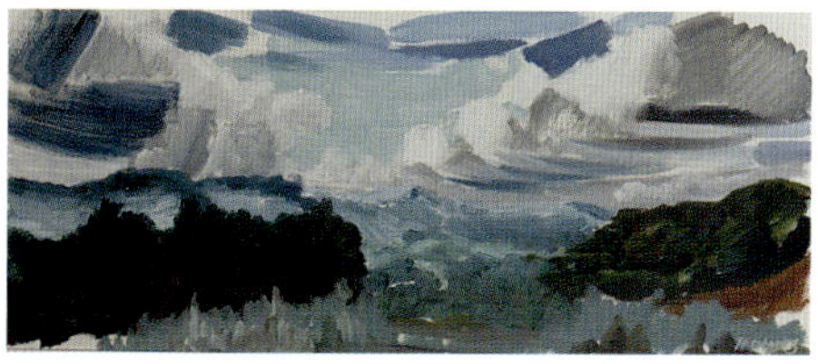

Hitchens, John b.1940
West Wind 1959
oil on board 44 x 104
PCF38

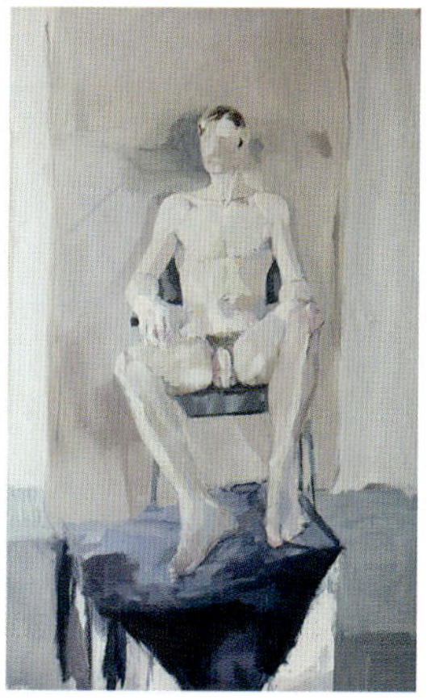

Holt, Stephen
Life Painting 1982
oil on canvas 127.5 x 77
PCF40

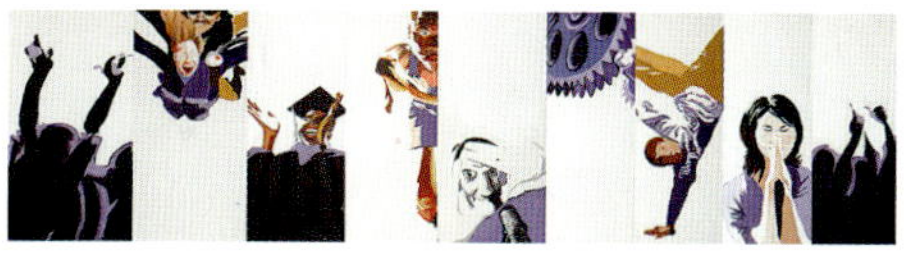

Howell, Matt
Mission Statement 2006
acrylic on canvas 33.5 x 150
86

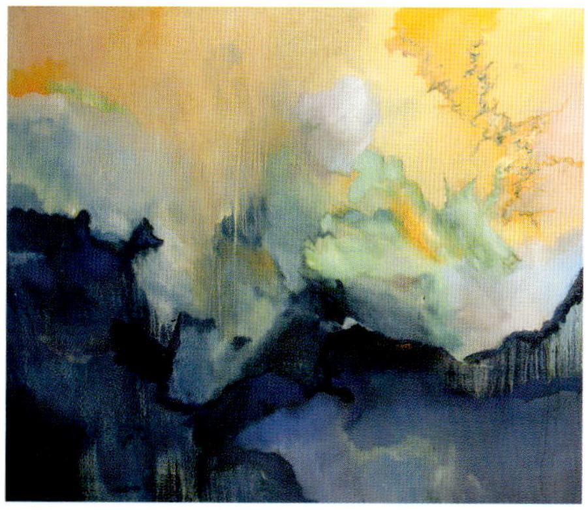

Huggins, Anna Michela active 1994–1997
To See a Sea 1997
oil on canvas 150 x 180
PCF41

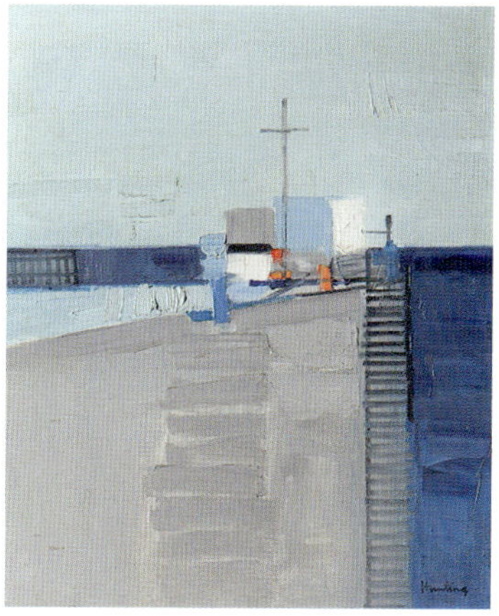

Hunting, Leonard b.1926
The Harbour at Dieppe, France
oil on canvas 39.5 x 26.5
LCE 84

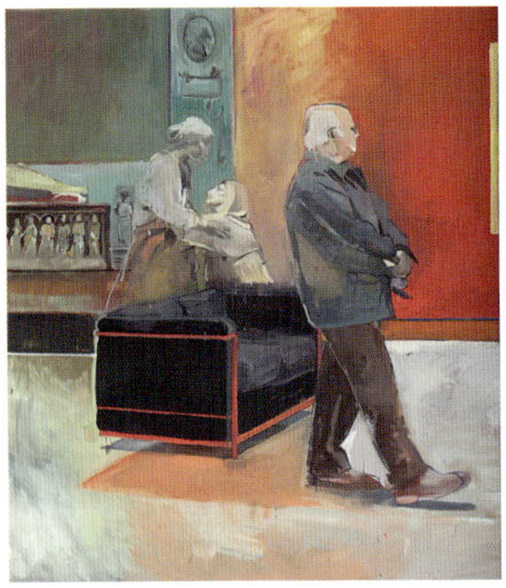

McConkey, Sarah b.1973
Can We Go Home Yet? 1995
oil on canvas 154 x 132
PCF42

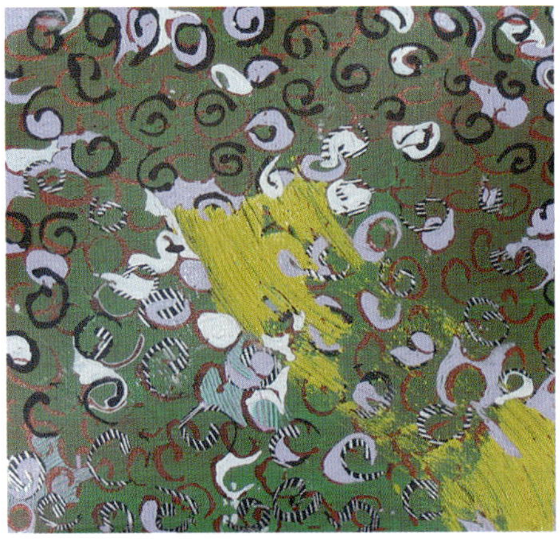

McGraw, Rachel
Untitled 2002
acrylic on canvas 95 x 105 (E)
91

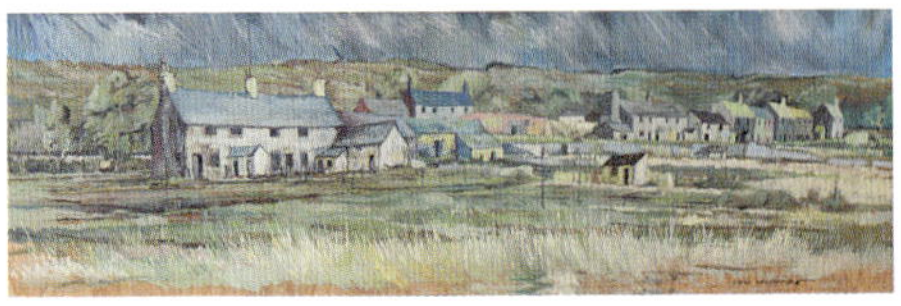

McIntyre, Ian
Blackbrook, Derbyshire
oil on canvas 42 x 103
PCF43

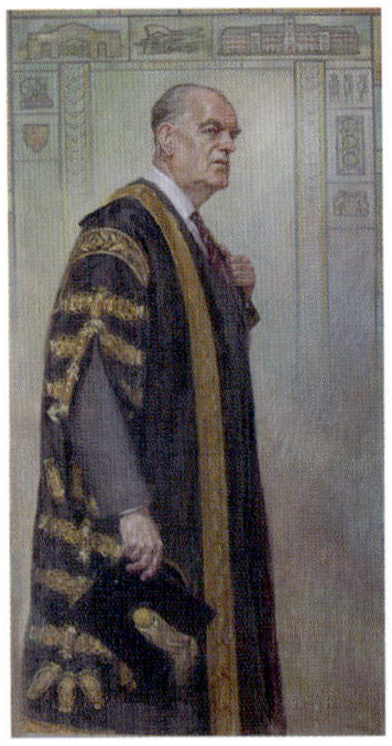

Mendoza, June b.1945
Sir Denis Rooke (1924–2008), Chancellor of Loughborough University (1986–2003) c.1994
oil on canvas 180 x 80 (E)
85

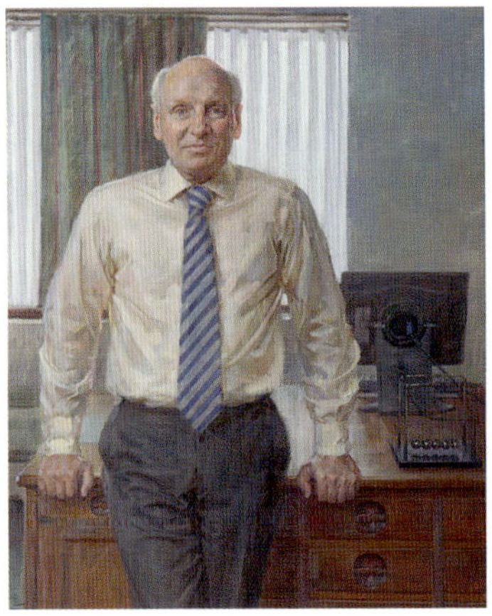

Mendoza, June b.1945
Sir David Wallace (b.1945), Vice-Chancellor of Loughborough University (1994–2006)
oil on canvas 114 x 88
PCF64

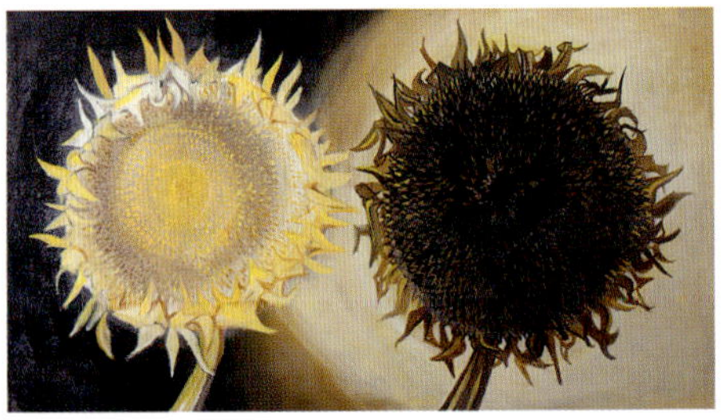

Middleditch, Edward 1923–1987
Sunflowers
oil on canvas 106 x 186
PCF44

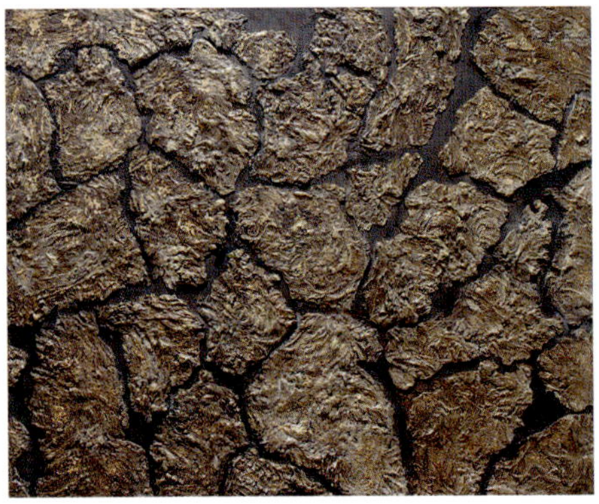

Nuttall, Matthew
Greed
oil, gold leaf & plaster on canvas 151 x 182
90

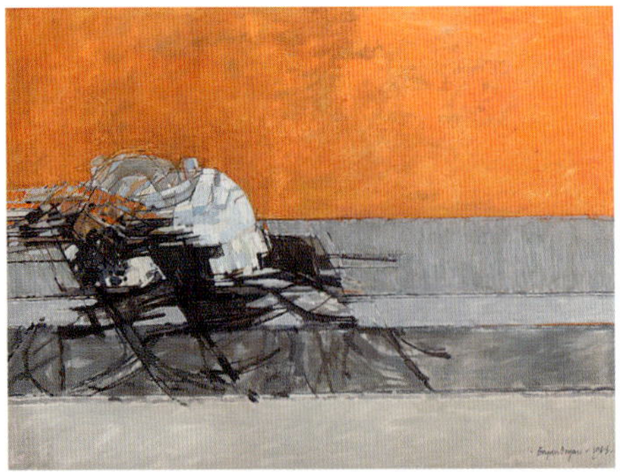

Organ, Bryan b.1935
Race Meeting
oil on canvas 119 x 157
PCF46

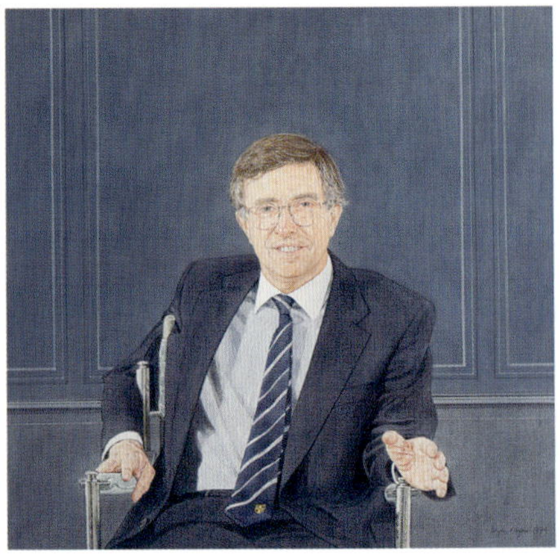

Organ, Bryan b.1935
Sir David E. N. Davies (b.1935), Vice-Chancellor of Loughborough University (1988–1993)
oil on canvas 76 x 76
PCF47

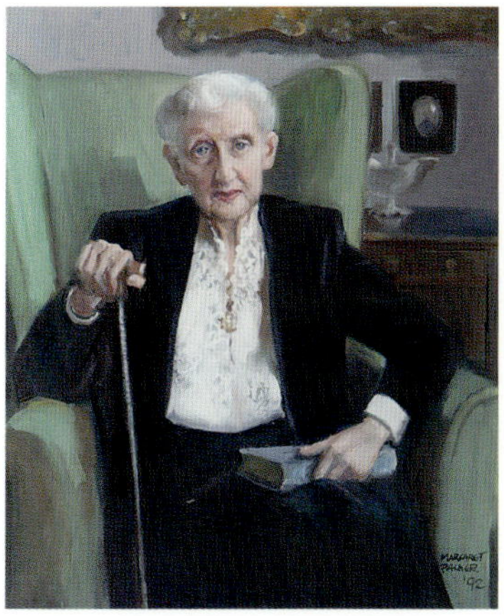

Palmer, Margaret b.1922
Claudia Parsons (1900–1998), First Woman to Circumnavigate the World by Car 1992
oil on canvas 72 x 62
PCF48 (P)

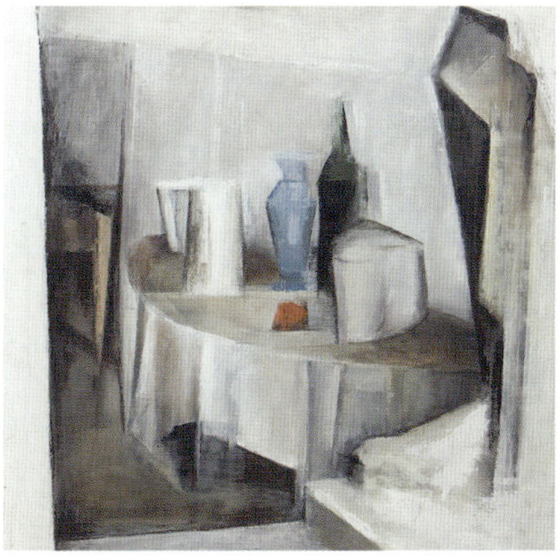

Parker, Elizabeth
Still Life
oil on canvas 69 x 69
PCF49

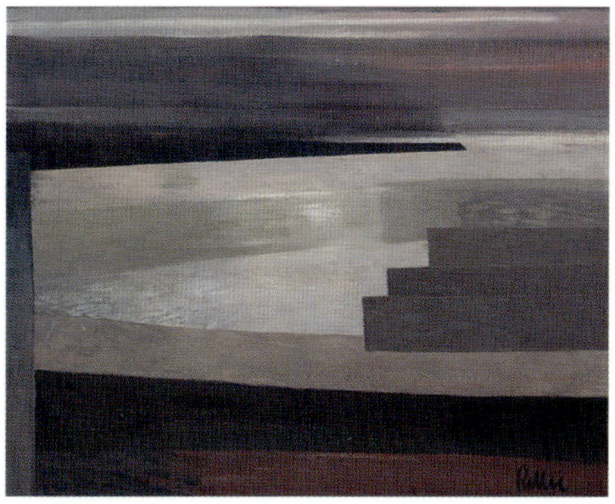

Pullu
Twilight
oil on hardboard 50 x 60
PCF50

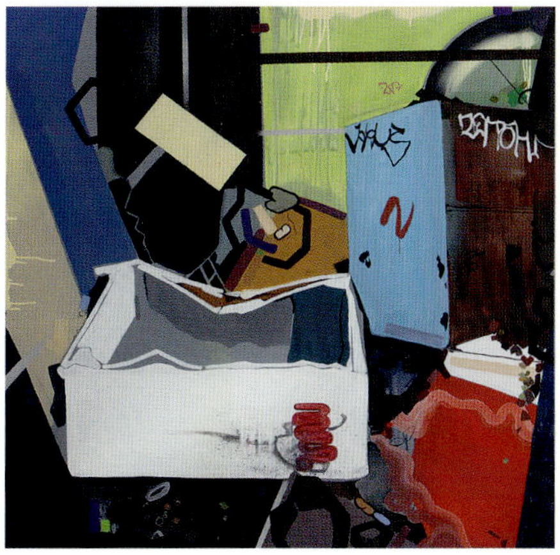

Radcliffe, Charlotte
Scrapyard
oil on canvas 119.5 x 120.5
88

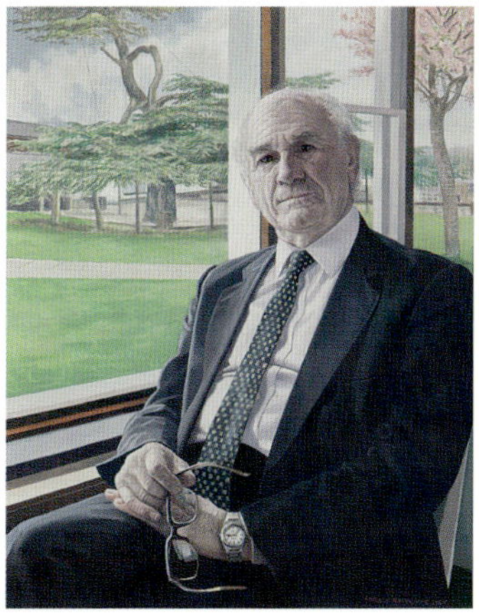

Ratcliffe, Andrew b.1948
Sir Clifford Butler (1922–1999), Vice-Chancellor of Loughborough University (1975–1985) 1987
oil on canvas 90 x 70
PCF51

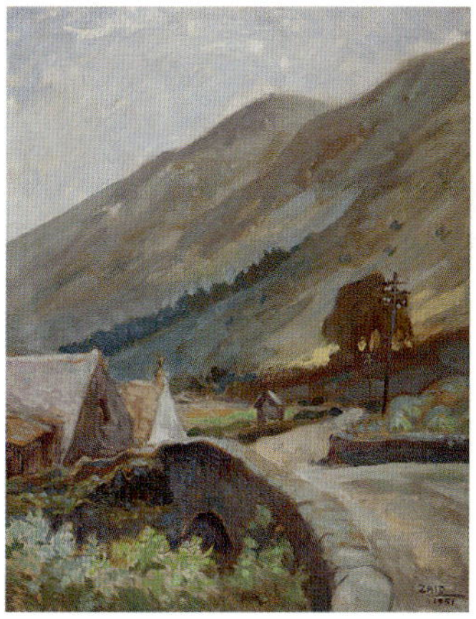

Salih, Zaid
Crianlarich, Stirling 1951
oil on canvas 54 x 36 (E)
PCF52

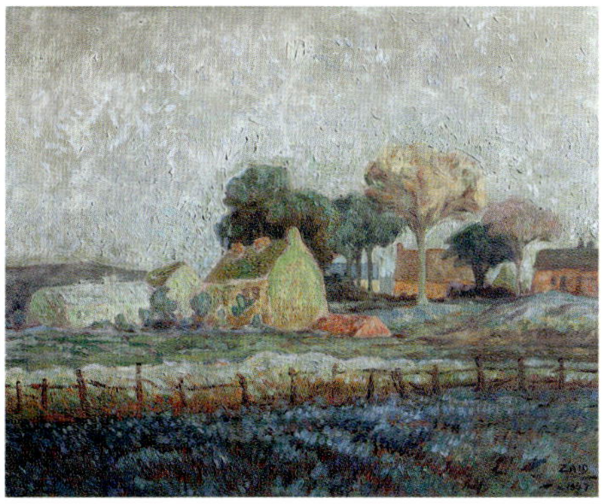

Salih, Zaid
Thorpe Acre, Leicestershire 1951
oil on canvas 61 x 75
PCF53

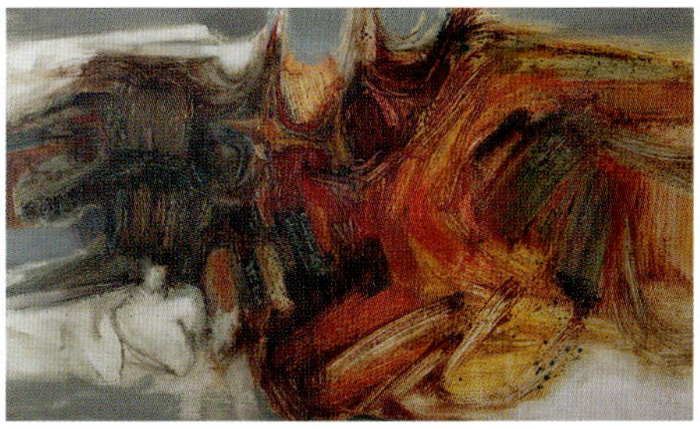

Saxton, Colin b.1927
Fiery Landscape c.1980
oil on canvas 129 x 221
PCF55

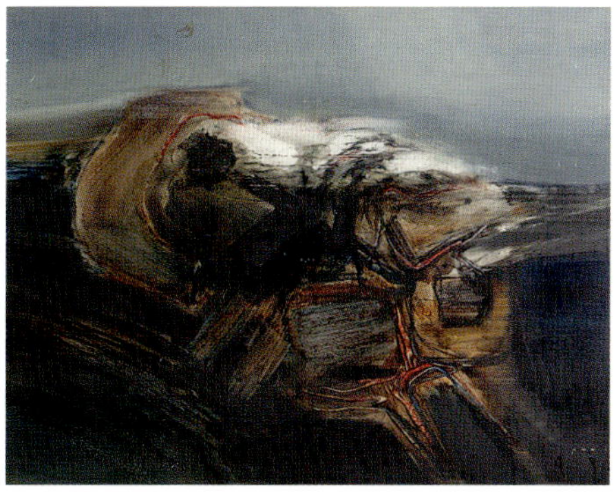

Saxton, Colin b.1927
Fallen Giant 2004
oil on hardboard 100 x 135 (E)
PCF54

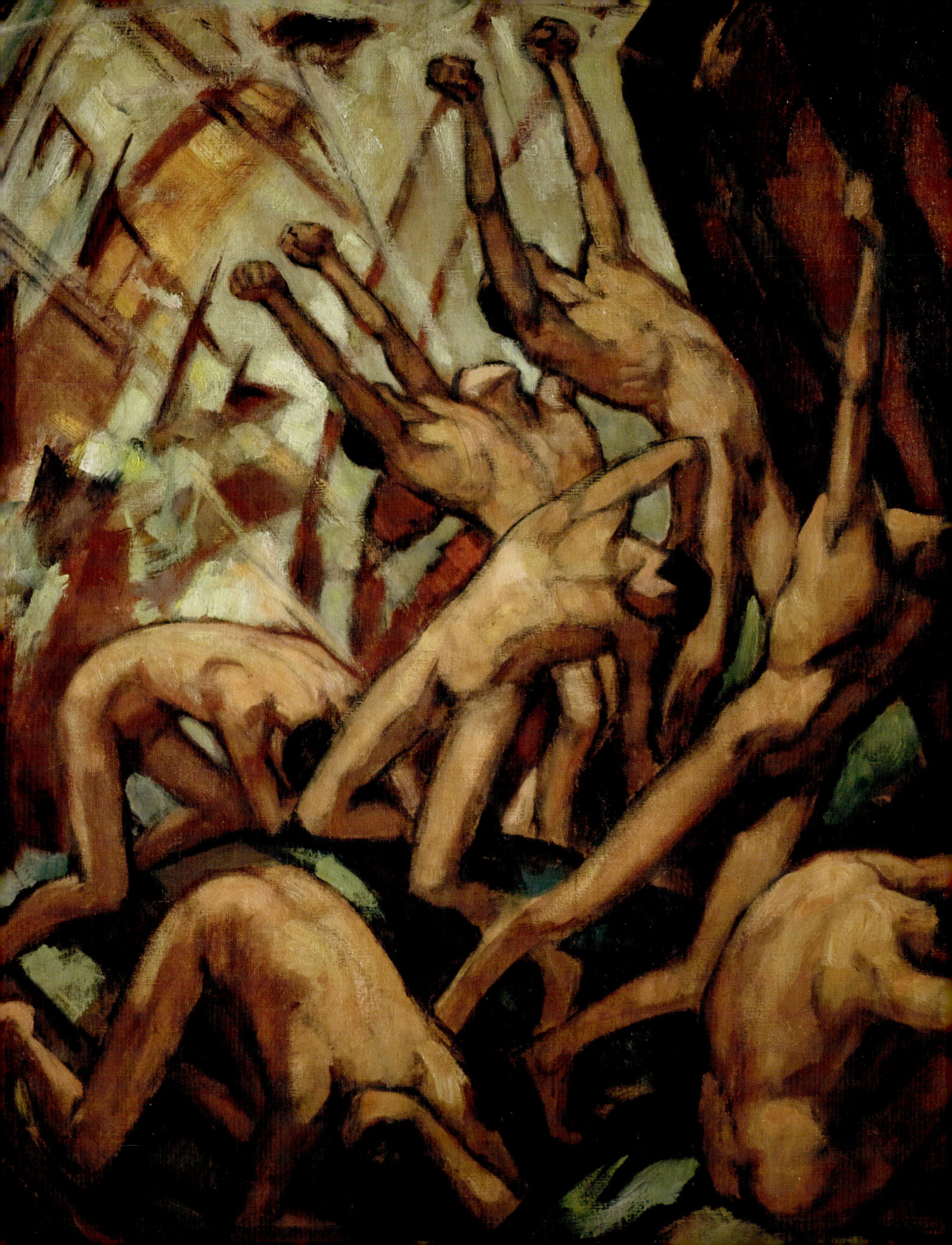

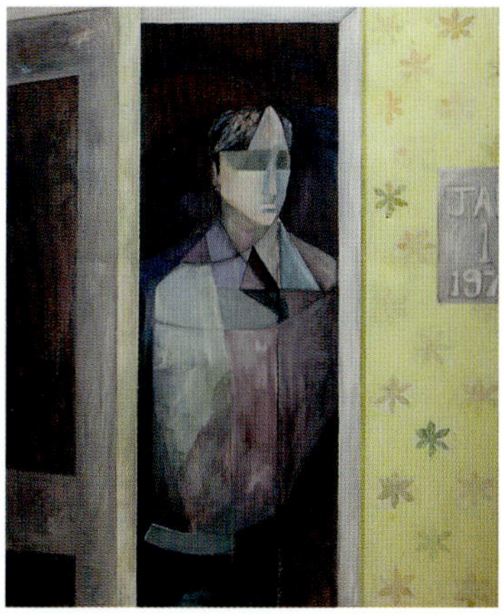

Stevenson, Lesley
Male Figure 1970
oil on canvas 115 x 92
PCF58

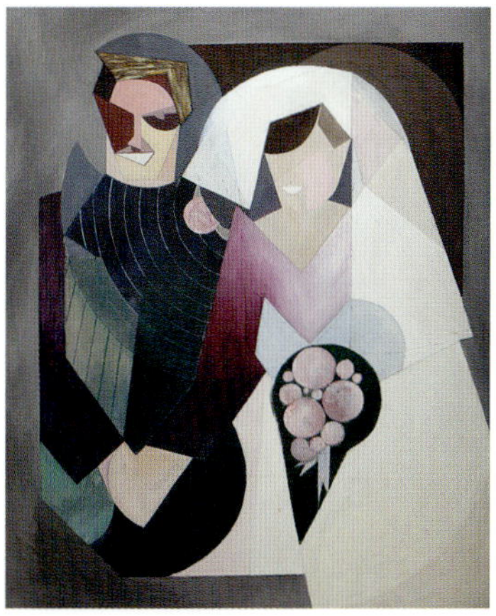

Stevenson, Lesley
Bride and Groom c.1970
oil on canvas 153 x 122
PCF56

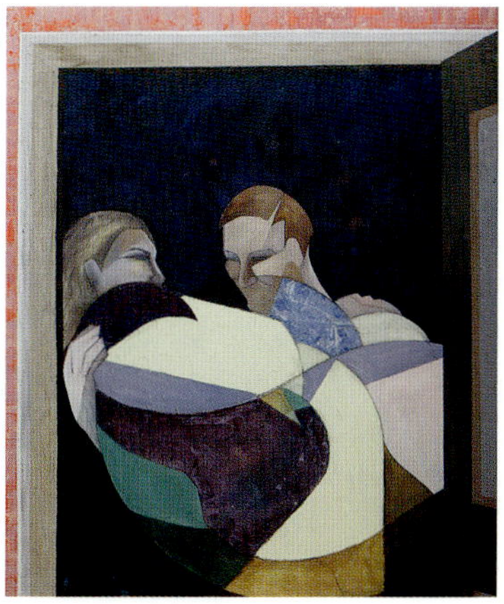

Stevenson, Lesley
Man Carrying a Lady c.1970
oil on canvas 116 x 93
PCF59

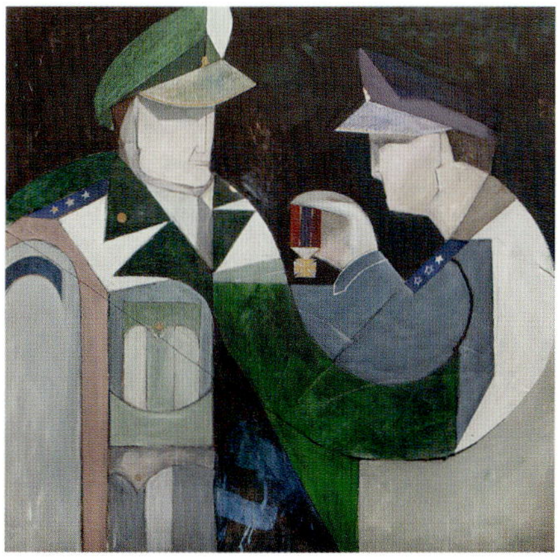

Stevenson, Lesley
Military Award c.1970
oil on canvas 90 x 90
PCF57

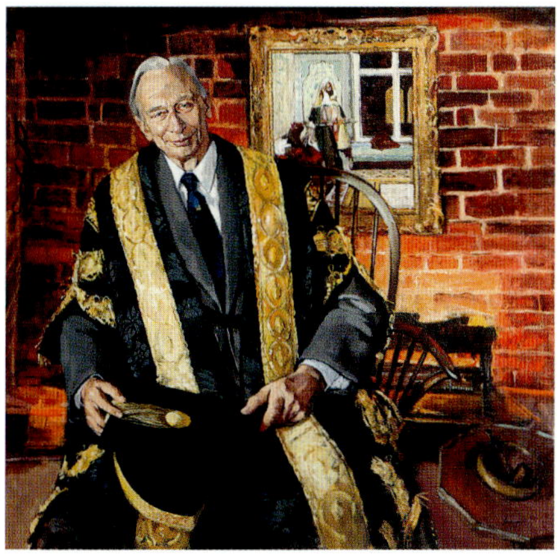

Stubley, Trevor 1932–2010
Sir Arnold Hall (1915–2000), Chancellor of Loughborough University (1980–1989)
oil on canvas 100 x 100
PCF60

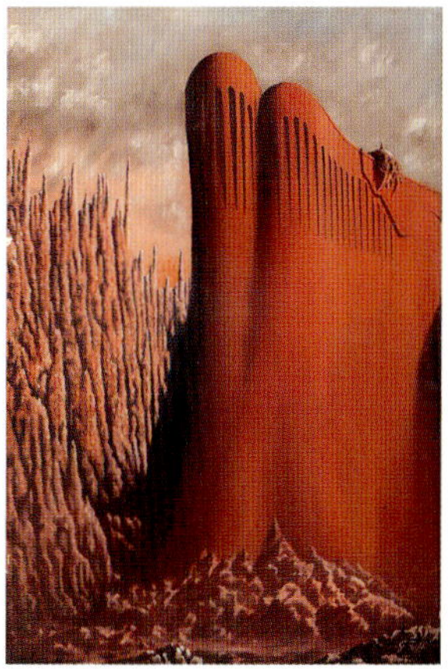

Suff, Gregory b.1949
The Iron Gate
oil on hardboard 76 x 51
PCF61

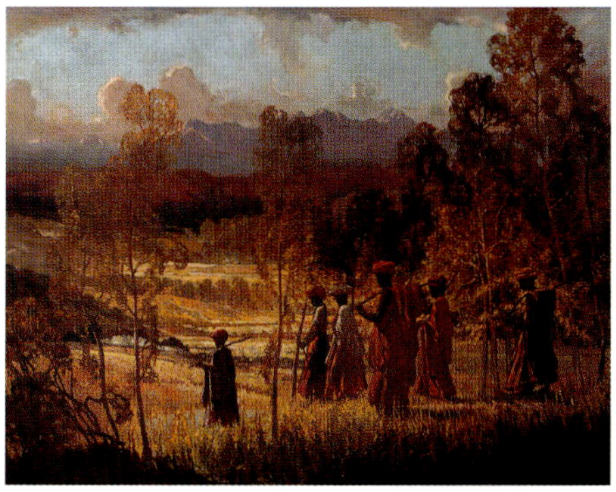

Timlin, William Mitcheson 1893–1943
Bush Landscape with Figures
oil on canvas 101 x 151
PCF62

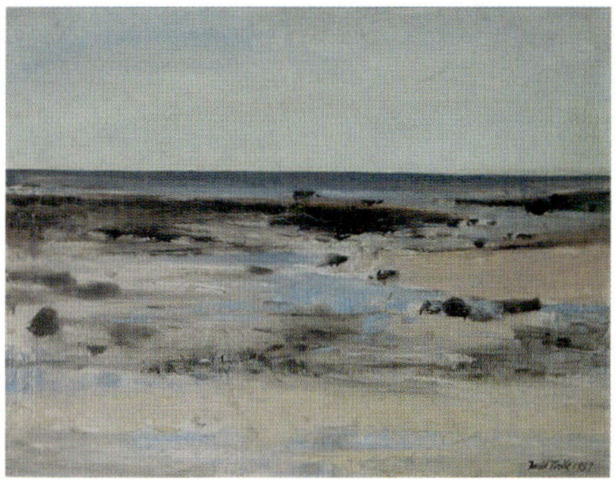

Tindle, David b.1932
Seascape 1957
oil on canvas 71 x 94
PCF63

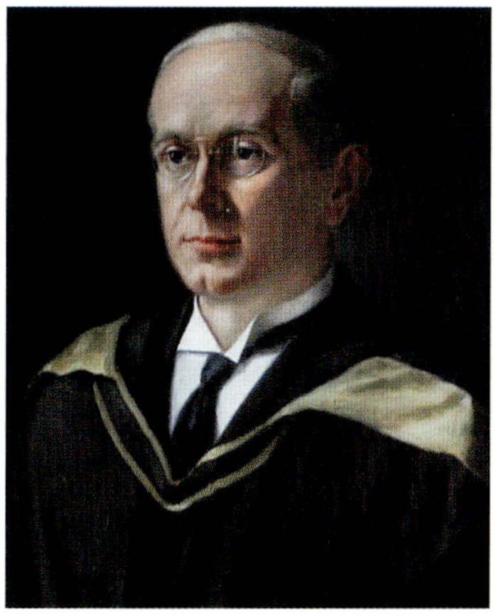

Trautmann, M. B.
James White, Lecturer in Civil Engineering (1924–1955)
oil on canvas 55 x 45
PCF65

Facing page: Von Hofmann, Ludwig, 1861–1945, *Zusammenbruch* (detail), c.1918, Leicester Arts and Museums Service (p. 93)

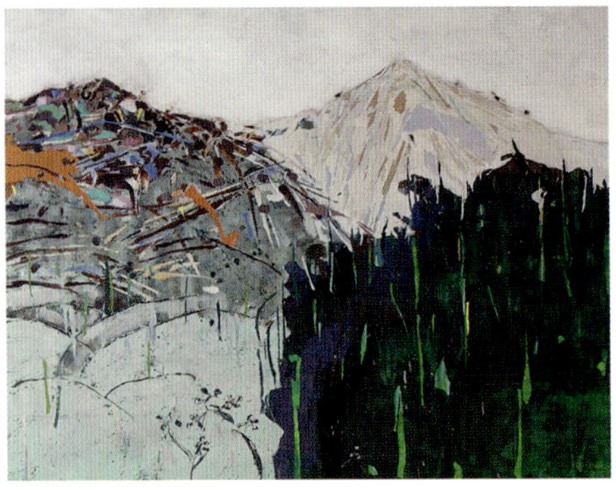

Turnbull, Julie
Where the Grass Is Greener 1996
oil & collage on canvas 157 x 204
PCF66

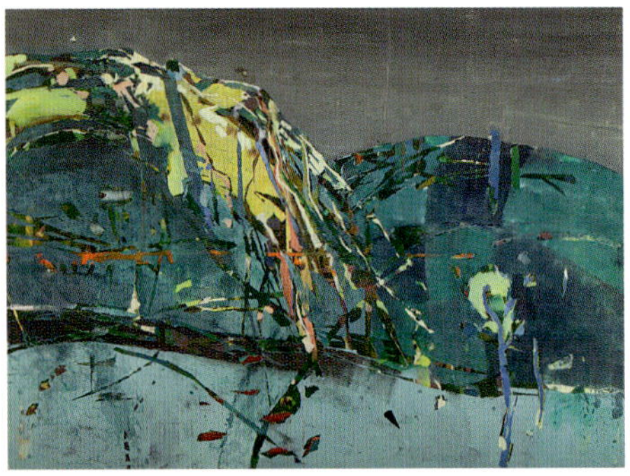

Turnbull, Julie
Still Breathing
oil & collage on canvas 151 x 199
30

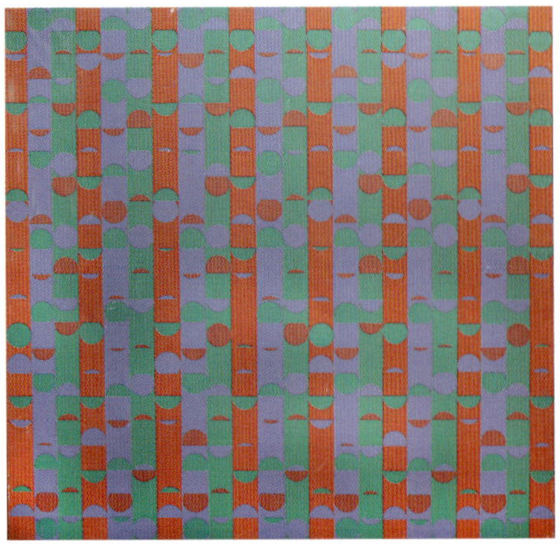

unknown artist
Geometry 1947
oil on canvas 122 x 125
PCF70

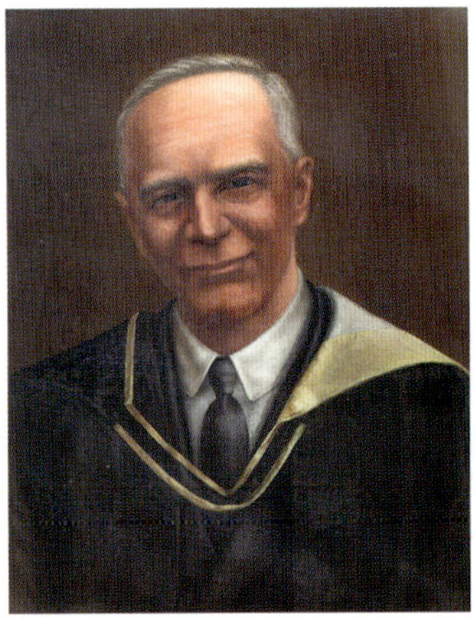

unknown artist
A. T. Eggington (1888–1982), Headmaster of Loughborough College School (1919–1952)
oil on canvas 60 x 45
PCF76

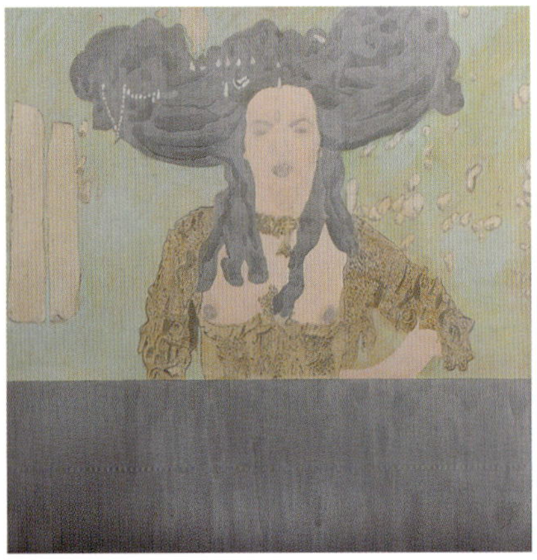

unknown artist
Baroque Lady
oil on canvas 180 x 170
PCF77

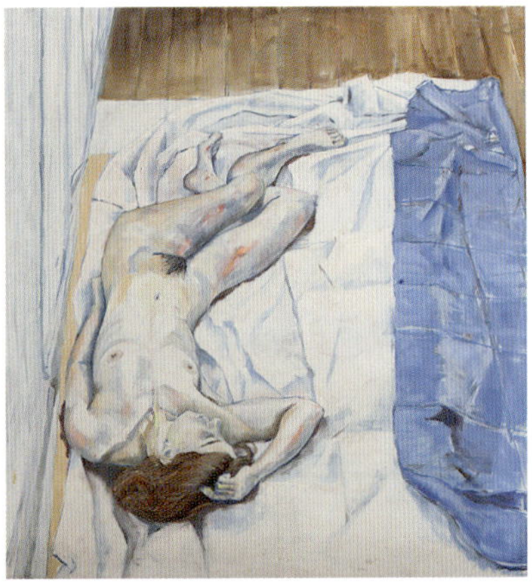

unknown artist
Life Painting
oil on canvas 152 x 137
PCF68

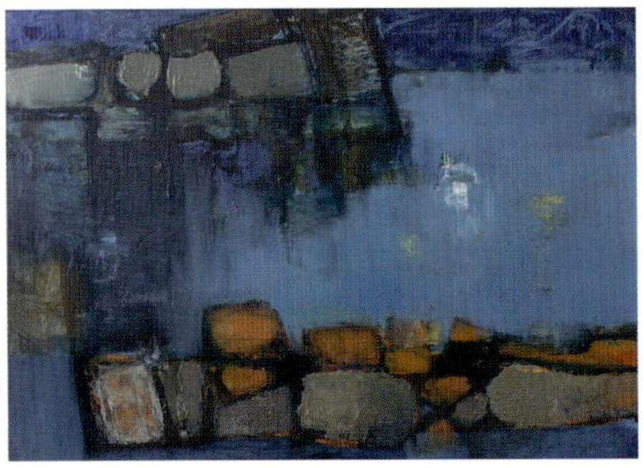

unknown artist
Lights on the Water
oil on canvas 60 x 82
PCF67

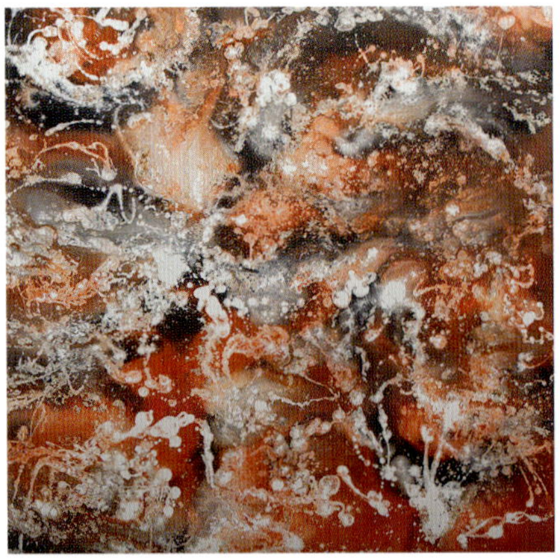

unknown artist
Red Abstract
oil on canvas 137 x 137
PCF71

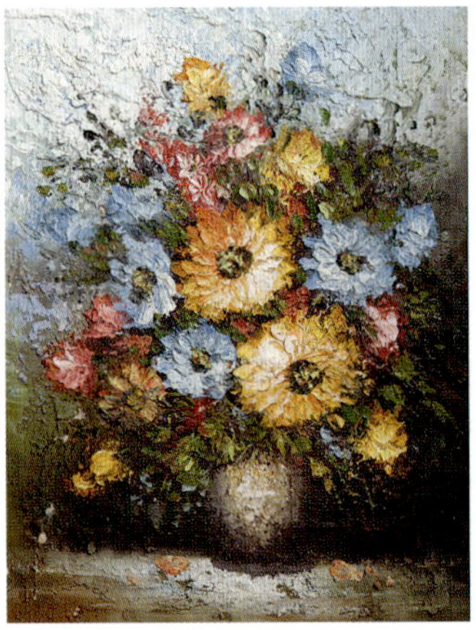

unknown artist
Still Life (Flowers)
oil on hardboard 40 x 30
PCF69

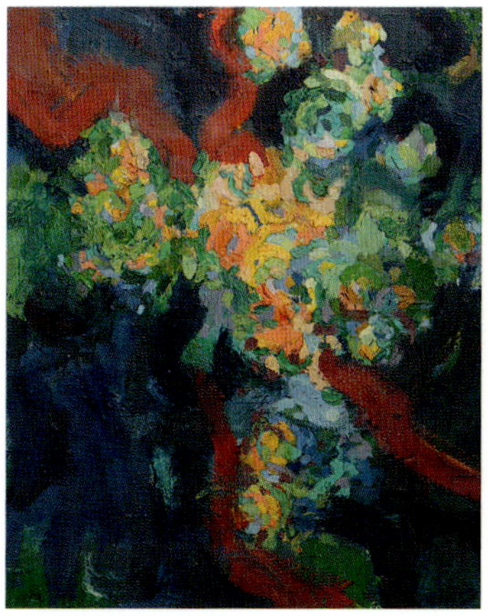

unknown artist
Still Life (Flowers)
oil on hardboard 123 x 93
PCF74

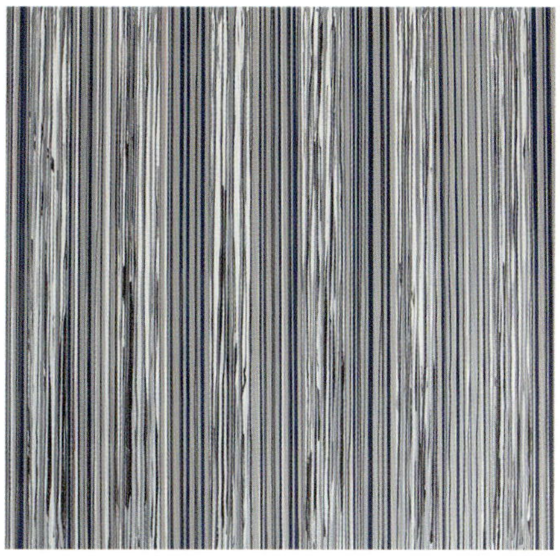

unknown artist
Stripe Painting
oil on canvas 222 x 222
PCF75

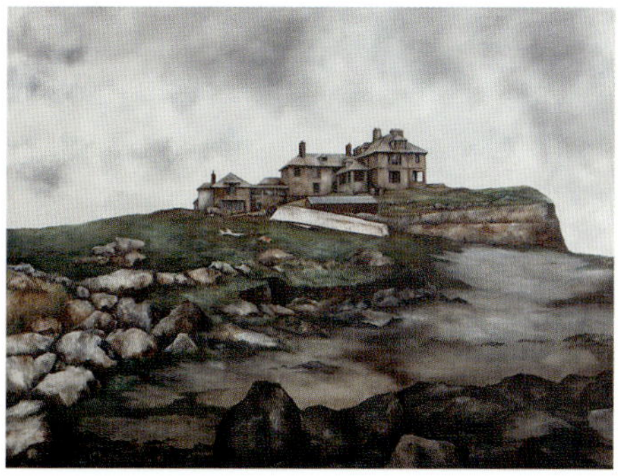

unknown artist
The Haunted House
oil on canvas 183 x 243
PCF73

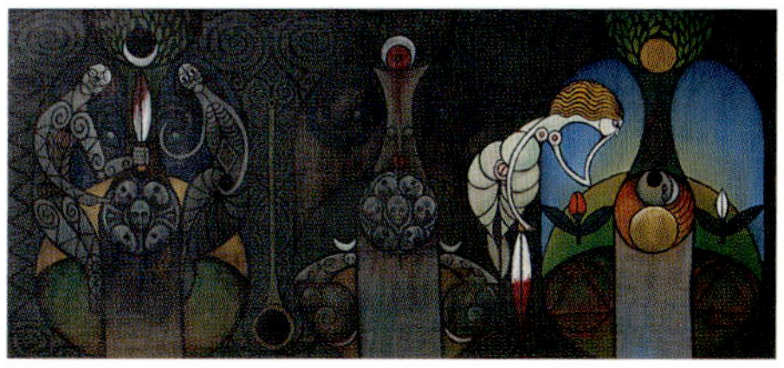

unknown artist
Voodoo
oil on canvas 77 x 169
PCF72

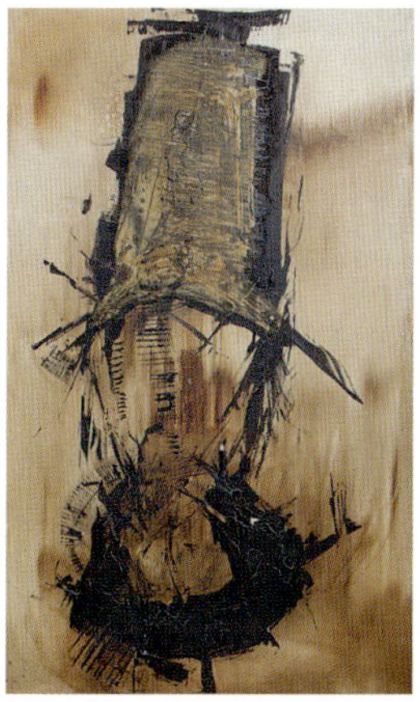

Vielfaure, Jean-Pierre b.1930
Accusé Einstein levez-vous! 1959
oil on canvas 178 x 102
PCF78

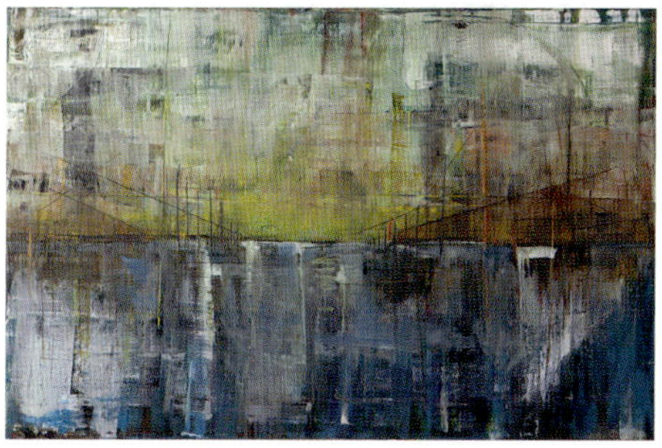

Whittall, Sam
Landscape: Horizontal Line, Blue and Green Tones
oil on canvas 123 x 183
89

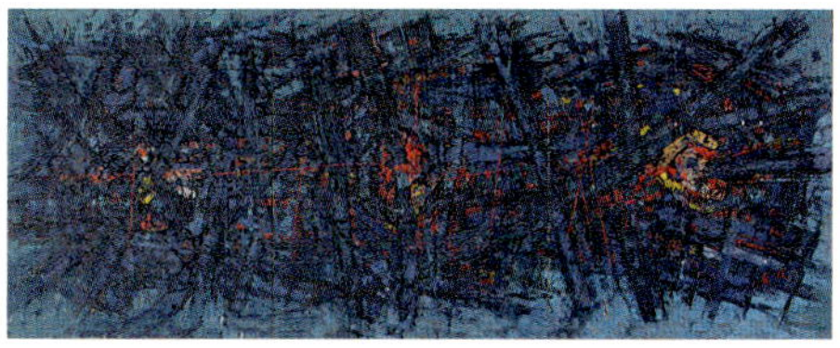

Wilson, Frank Avray 1914–2009
Deep End
oil on canvas 211 x 587
PCF79

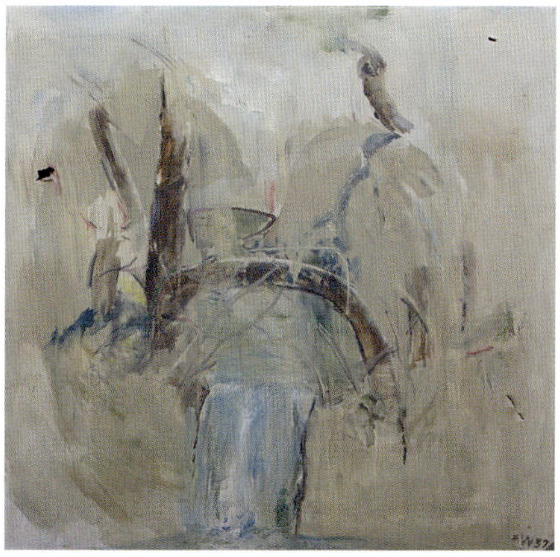

Wishart, John Michael 1928–1996
Waterfall 1957
oil on canvas 76 x 76
PCF80

Loughborough War Memorial Museum

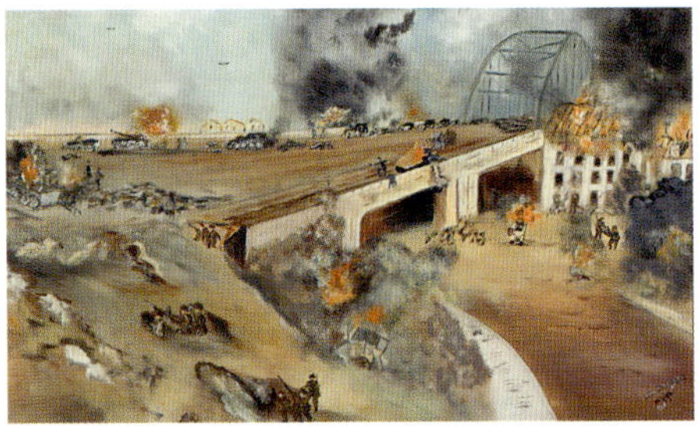

Bradley, Jack
Nijmegen Bridge, The Netherlands 1982
oil on board 50 x 90 (E)
3

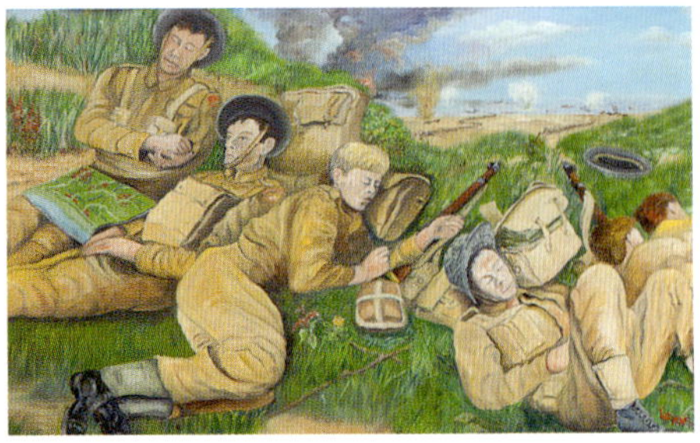

Byrne, E. H.
Soldiers at Rest
oil on canvas 45 x 75 (E)
1

RNIB College Loughborough

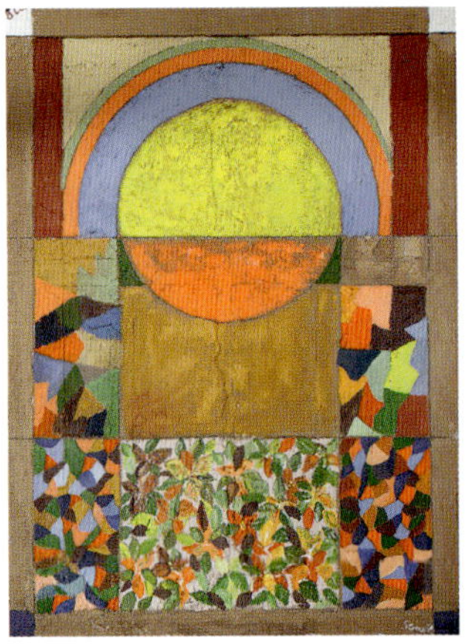

Cook, S.
Sun Garden
oil & sand on canvas 250 x 180
1

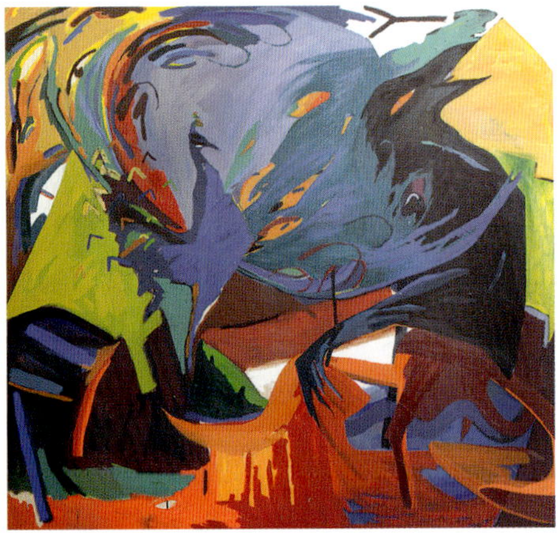

Hadley, Ross
Constellation of Eyes 1989
oil on canvas 244.5 x 260
7

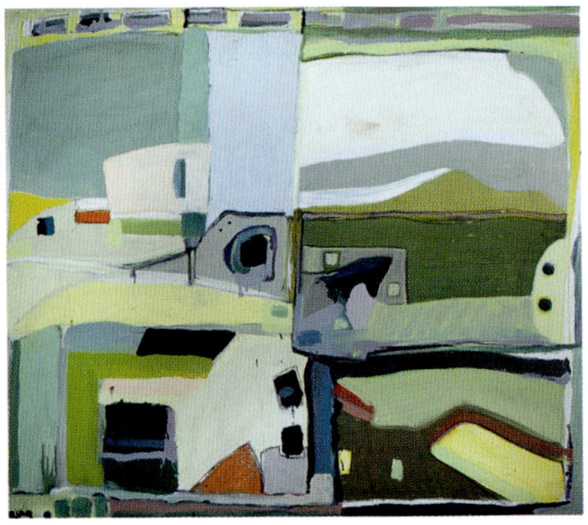

Hall, Louise M.
Ariel 1988
oil on canvas 121 x 152
7

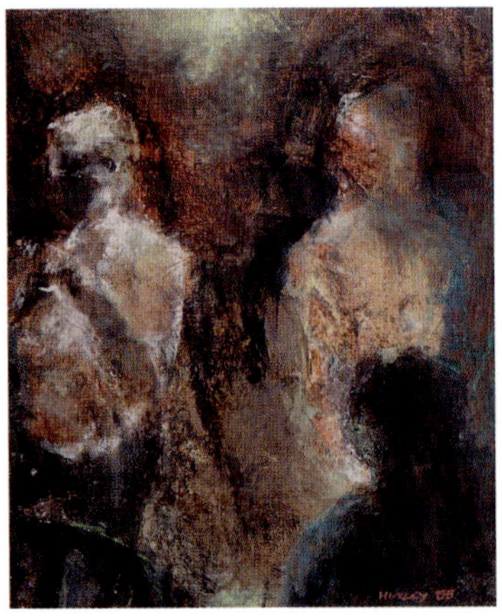

Huxley
Figures (sketch) 1988
oil & mixed media on paper 63 x 51.5
2

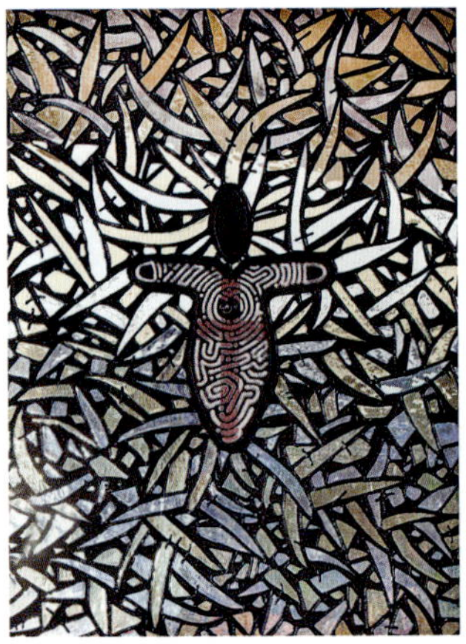

Lakey, Andrew b.1959
Angel of Hope 1992
oil & mirror on canvas 122 x 91
11

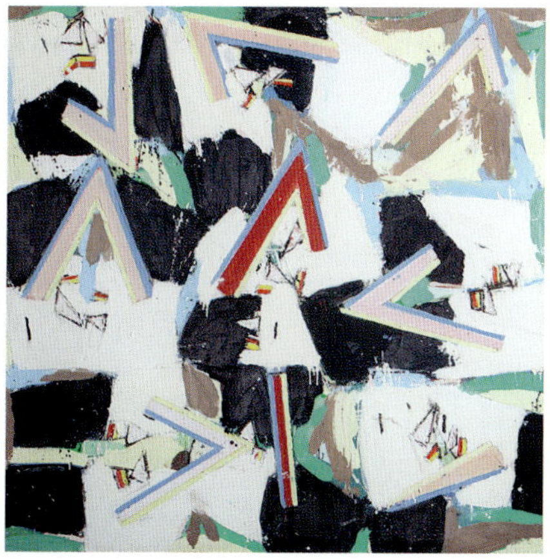

March, Tony
Abstract 1976
oil on canvas 194 x 194
3

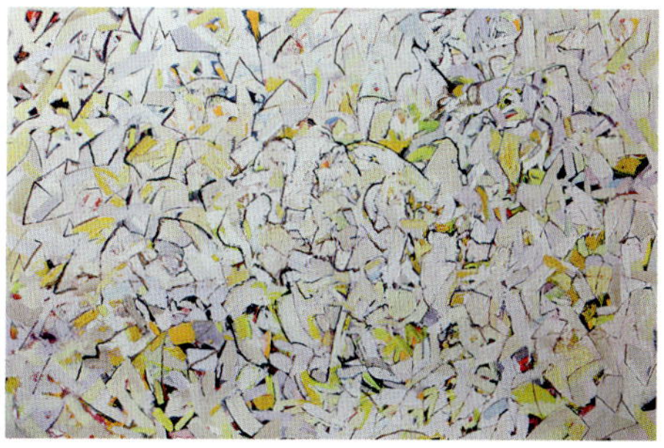

Scott, Margaret
Ettrick
oil & acrylic on canvas 123 x 184.5
8

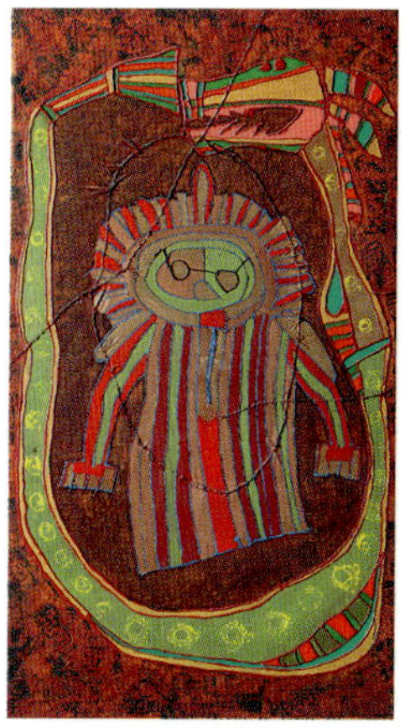

unknown artist
Dragon and Figure 1989
oil on canvas 169 x 93
9

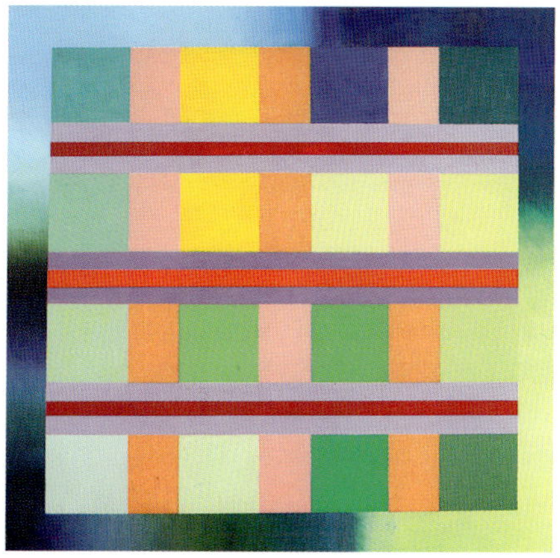

unknown artist
Abstract Geometry
oil on canvas 169 x 169
10

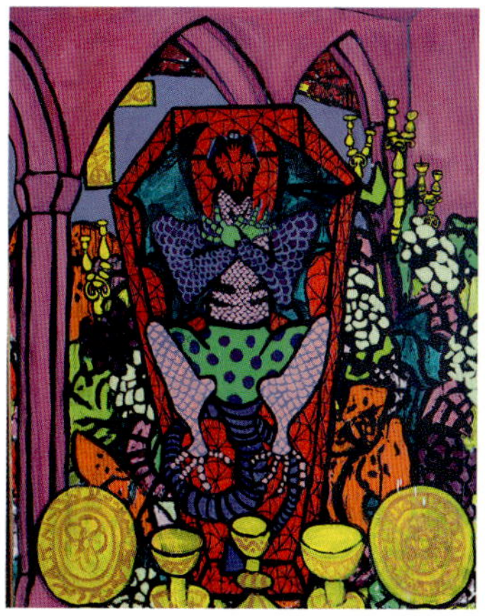

unknown artist
Batman
oil on canvas 209 x 167
6

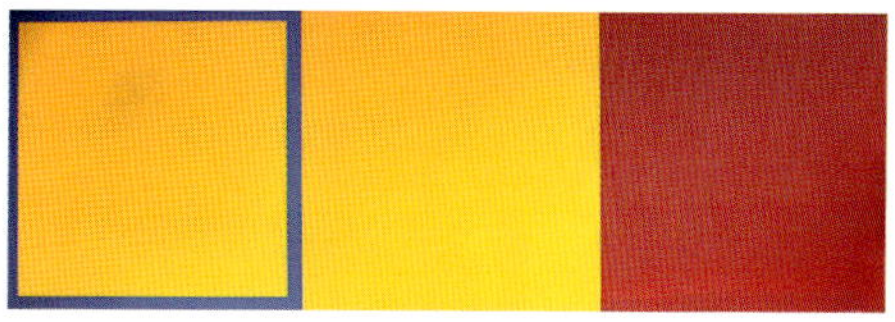

unknown artist
Four Squares
oil on canvas 107 x 321
12

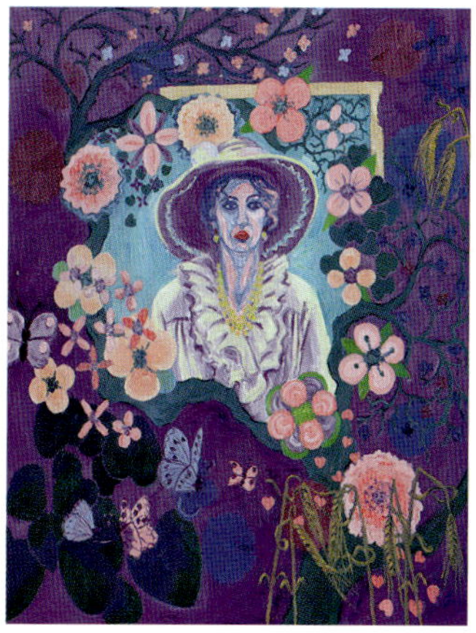

unknown artist
The Purple Lady
oil on canvas 182.5 x 152
5

Allington Parish Council

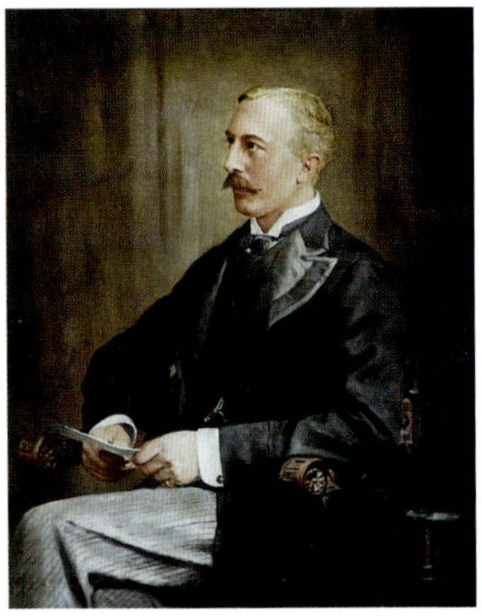

Hayman, Godfrey
Sir George Welby (1851–1936) 1935
oil on canvas 92 x 72
1

Boston Borough Council

Boston St Mary's Guildhall is one of the most significant religious Guildhalls in the country. Until recently it was thought to have been built in the fifteenth century, but during its recent restoration it was discovered that the building was erected in the 1390s. This would have been almost immediately after religious guilds were given permission to own property for the first time. The building has had many uses since Henry VIII dissolved the religious guilds in the 1500s, from Town Hall to Sessions Court and a gaol – where the band of religious Separatists (later to be known as the Pilgrim Fathers) were tried and held in 1607. Latterly, the building became the repository for the Borough's museum Collection.

Boston Borough Council's Collection of art and artefacts became a formalised museum collection with a constitution in 1926. There are paintings, alongside archaeological, photographic, social history (which includes boat-making tools, printing tools, costume, ceramics, kitchen equipment, banners and furniture) and natural history collections.

The Haven Gallery, a glass-fronted contemporary arts and resource centre, is used for temporary exhibitions of arts and crafts. The permanent Collection is stored within The Haven Gallery while displays supporting the story of Boston are on view in the Guildhall.

The painting collection includes a portrait of *Sir Joseph Banks (1743–1820), 1st Bt, GCB, PRS* by the artist Thomas Phillips, which is on permanent display within the Boston Guildhall, *Cupid Guarding Psyche* painted by Samuel George Enderby in 1900, three works by the artist William Etty, a painting of *John Wesley Preaching from His Father's Tomb at Epworth* by the artist George Washington Brownlow, portraits of a some of the past mayors of the Borough and a selection of works of local scenes both within and around Boston by various artists, both historic and contemporary. We would like to thank the Friends group for their support with conservation projects within the Collection.

Boston Guildhall and The Haven Gallery hold full Museums, Libraries and Archives Council-accredited status and are award-winning venues, including winning Lincolnshire Museum of the Year 2008 and both Royal Institute of Chartered Surveyors East Midlands Best Conservation and Best Overall Project of the Year 2008.

Polly Stanley, Collections Officer

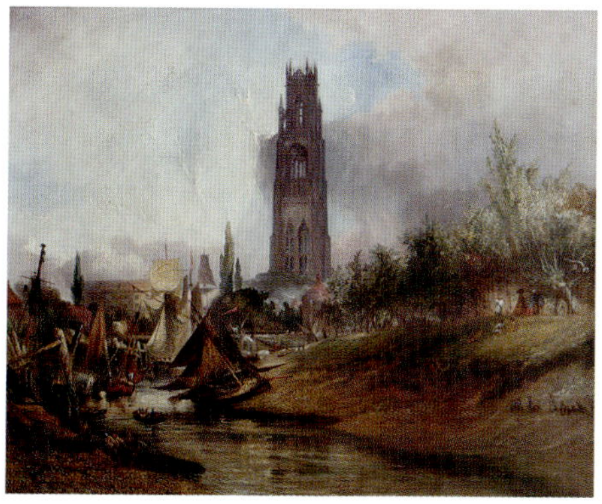

Baines, Henry 1823–1894
St Botolph's from the Witham, Boston, Lincolnshire 1857
oil on canvas 62 x 75
1926.82

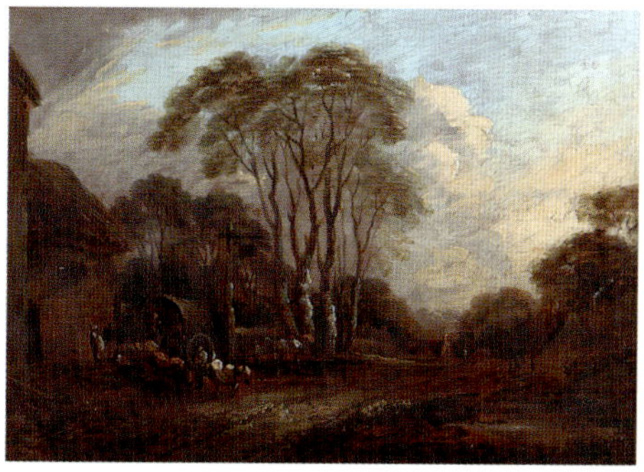

Baker, Thomas 1809–1869
Wooded Landscape with a Village
oil on canvas 27 x 37
1926.93

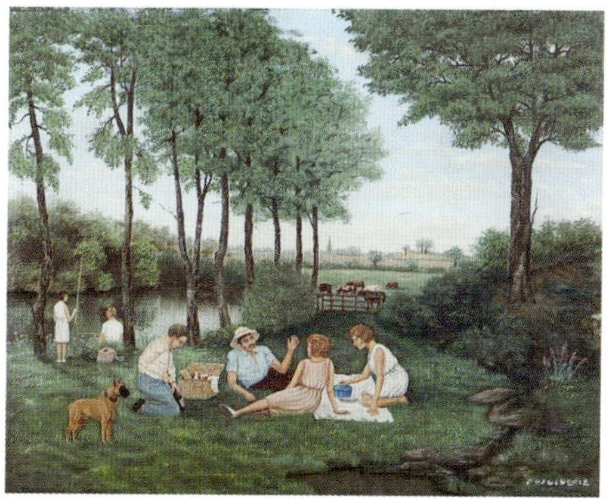

Beucherie, Paul
Scène champêtre Mayennaise, France
oil on canvas 49 x 60
1969.15

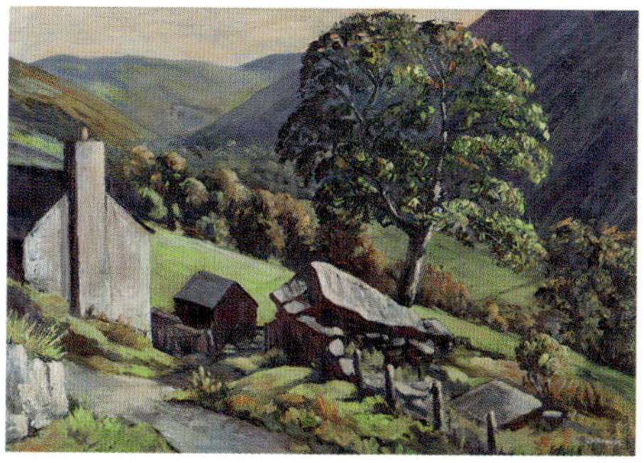

Brough, M.
September Evening
oil on card 61 x 84
1964.3

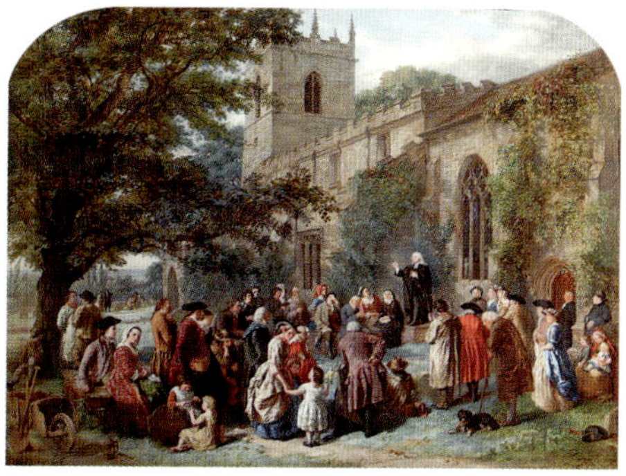

Brownlow, George Washington 1835–1876
John Wesley Preaching from His Father's Tomb at Epworth
oil on canvas 102 x 142
1926.81

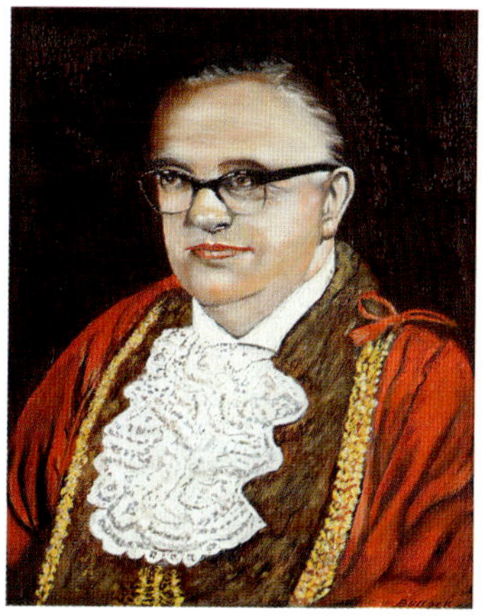

Bullock, George Henry d.1999
Bruce James Veal (1917–1990), Mayor of Boston (1968–1969) 1968
oil on board 44.5 x 35.5
2009.13.1

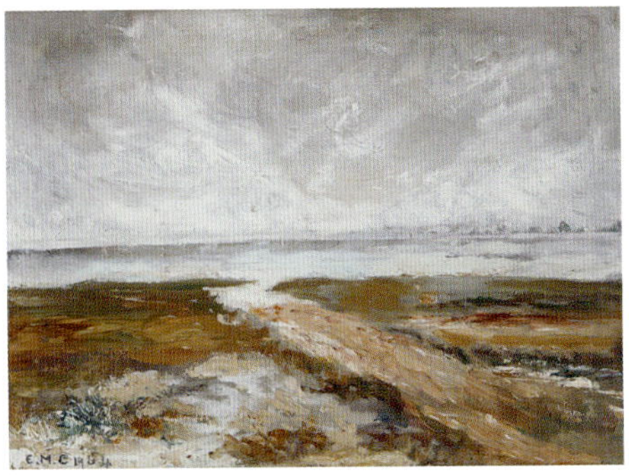

Cheales, Edith May 1872–1964
Freiston Shore, Boston, Lincolnshire 1964
oil on canvas 45 x 52
1966.4

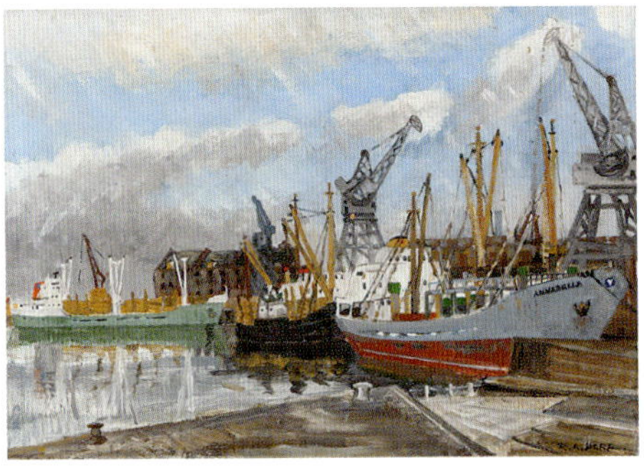

Dorr, Ray
Boston Dock, Lincolnshire c.1970
acrylic on board 53 x 74
1995.16

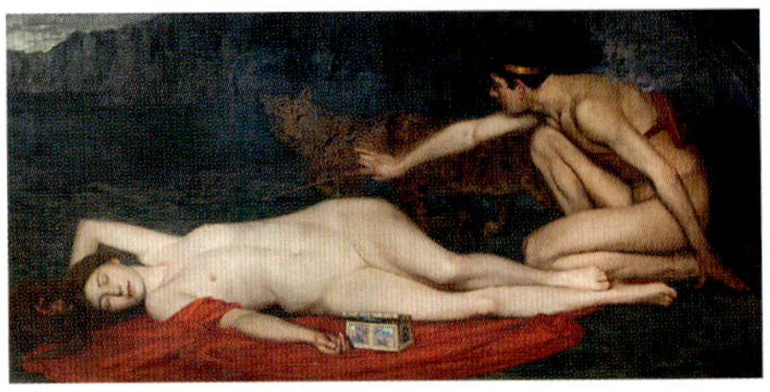

Enderby, Samuel George 1860–1921
Cupid Guarding Psyche 1900
oil on canvas 97.5 x 197
1926.98

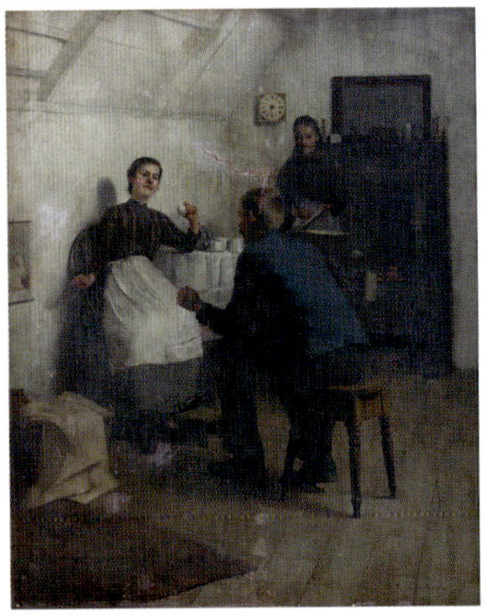

Enderby, Samuel George 1860–1921
Entangled
oil on canvas 115 x 83
1971.27

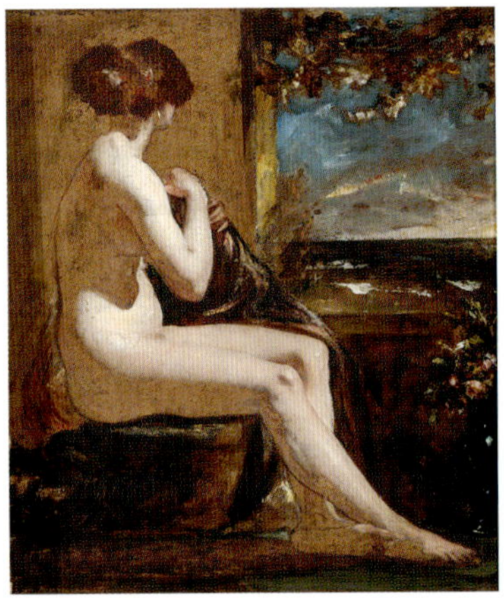

Etty, William 1787–1849
Hero Waiting for Leander
oil on panel 60 x 49
1926.88

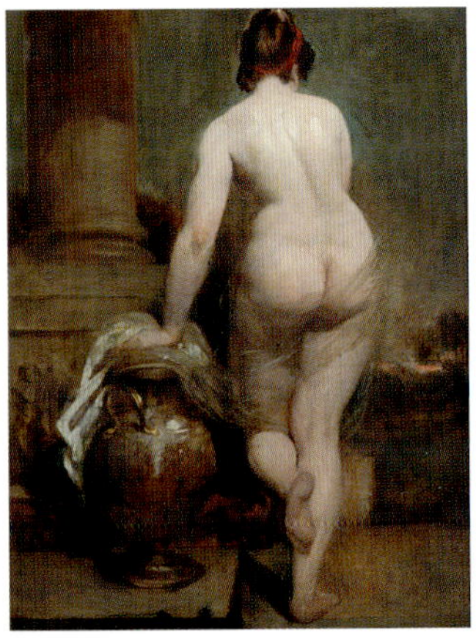

Etty, William 1787–1849
Study of a Female Nude
oil on canvas 52 x 38
1926.87

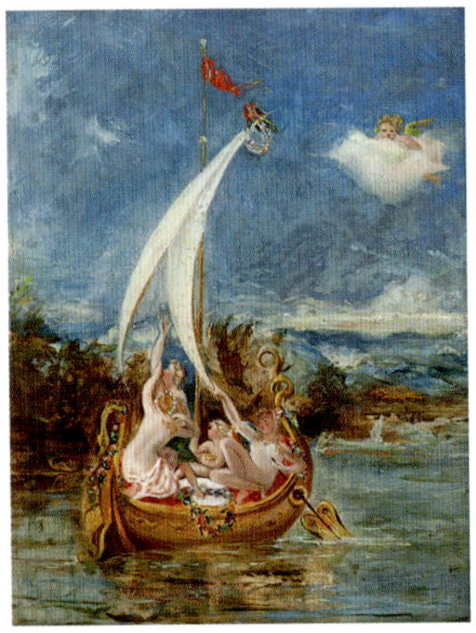

Etty, William 1787–1849
Youth at the Prow and Pleasure at the Helm
oil on panel 42 x 32
1926.90

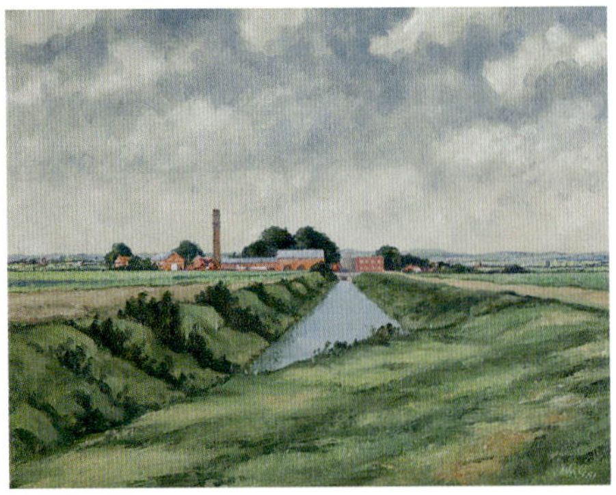

Grimble, John d.1997
Lade Bank Pumping Station, Hobhole Drain, East Fen 1981
oil on canvas 41 x 51
2002.57

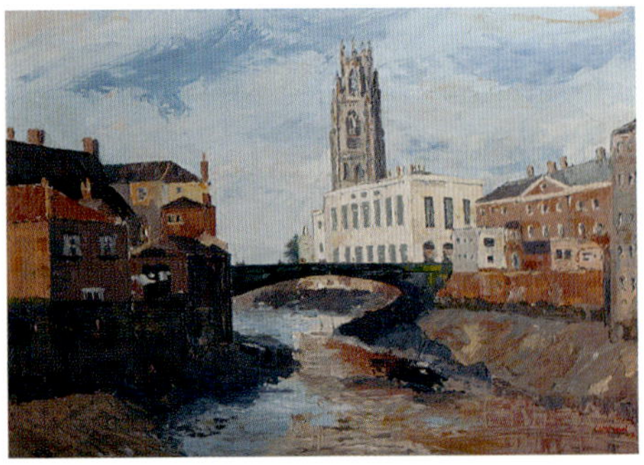

Grimble, John d.1997
River Haven, Boston, Lincolnshire
oil on canvas 49 x 68
1966.2

Facing page: Bacon, Francis, 1909–1992, *Lying Figure No.1* (detail), 1959, Leicester Arts and Museums Service (p. 9)

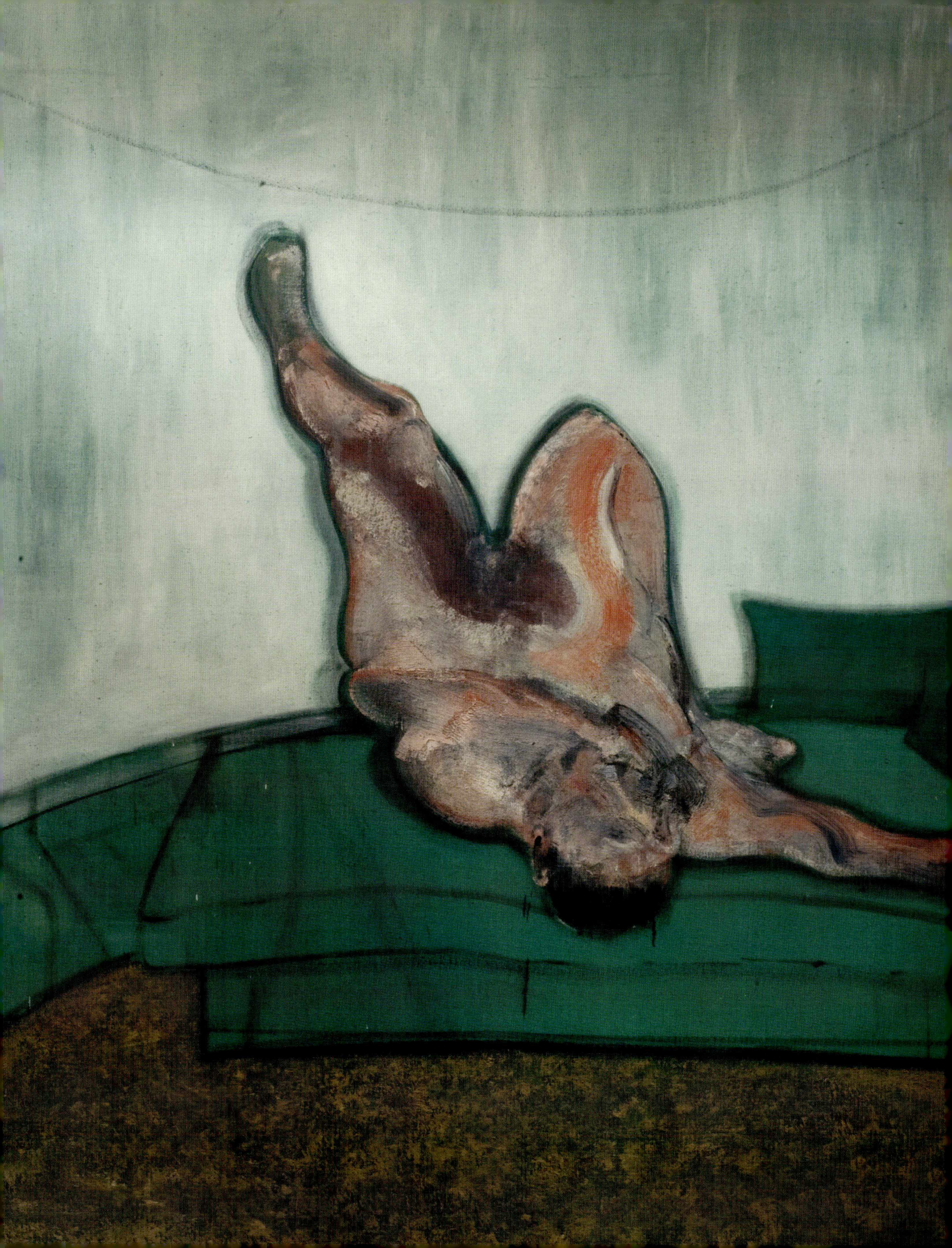

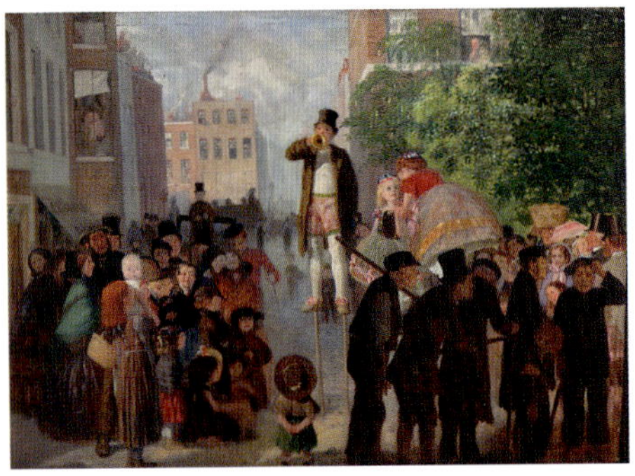

Houghton, Arthur Boyd 1836–1875
Street Gymnasts c.1860
oil on panel 29 x 39
1926.91

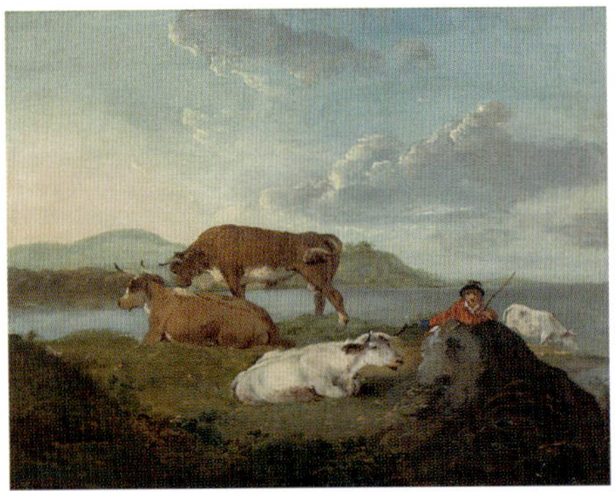

Ibbetson, Julius Caesar 1759–1817
Cows
oil on canvas 34 x 43.5
1926.83

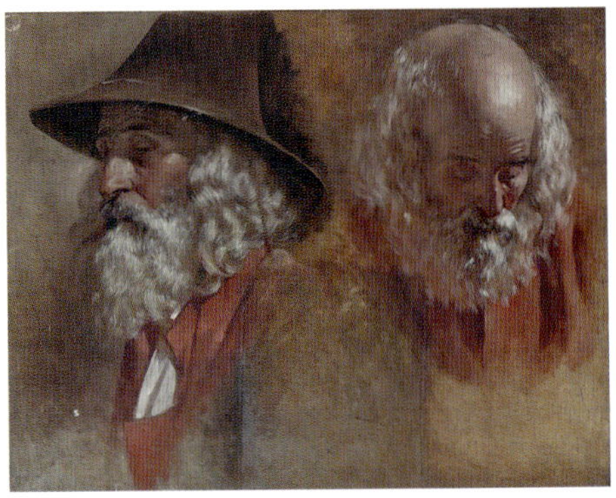

Kennedy
Portrait Study of a Bearded Gentleman from Two Angles
oil on canvas 58 x 72
1926.80

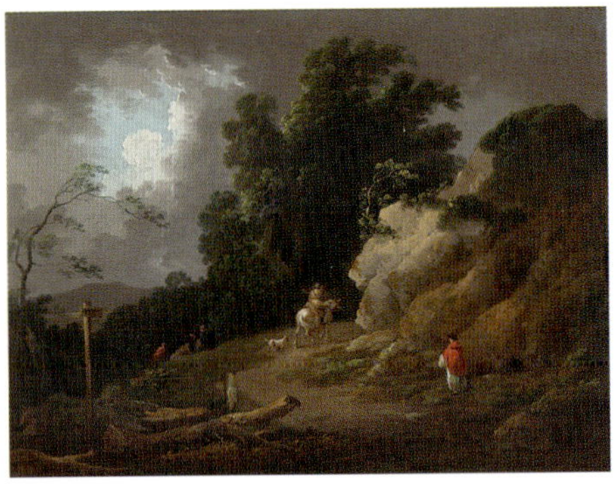

Morland, George 1763–1804
Landscape with an Approaching Storm 1800
oil on canvas 29 x 37
1926.96

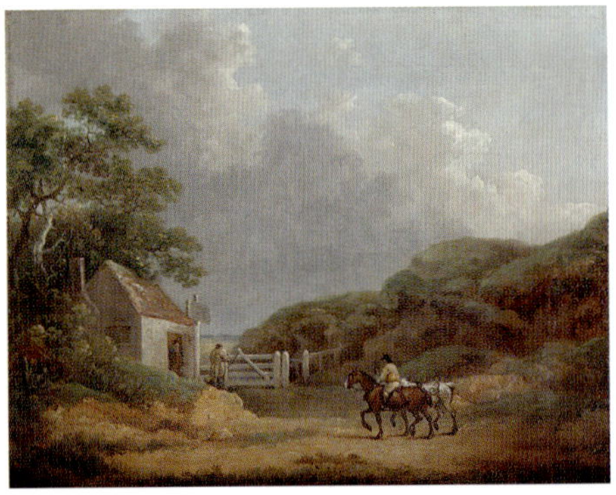

Morland, George 1763–1804
Wooded Landscape with a Toll Gate
oil on canvas 29.5 x 37.3
1926.97

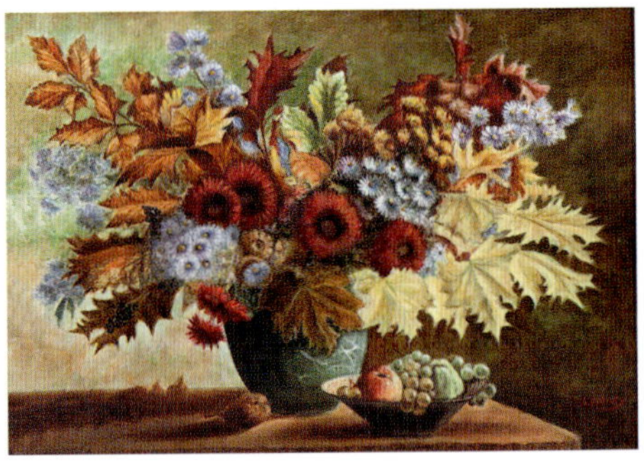

Pawley, A.
Flower Study
oil on paper 41 x 59
1967.21

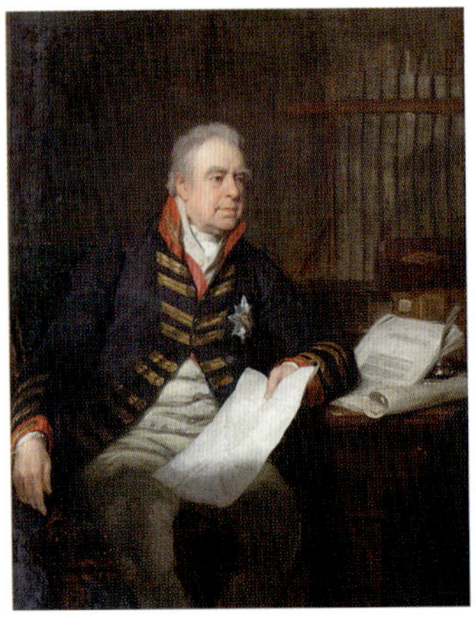

Phillips, Thomas 1770–1845
Sir Joseph Banks (1743–1820), 1st Bt, GCB, PRS 1814
oil on canvas 140 x 109
1964.6

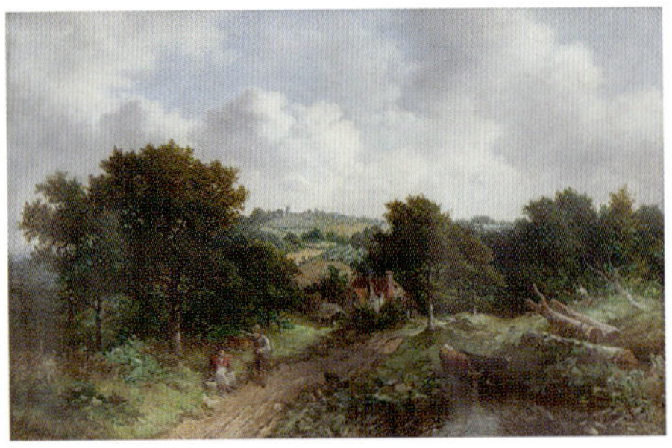

Rose, William S. 1810–1873
Wooded Landscape
oil on millboard 28.5 x 44.5
1926.84

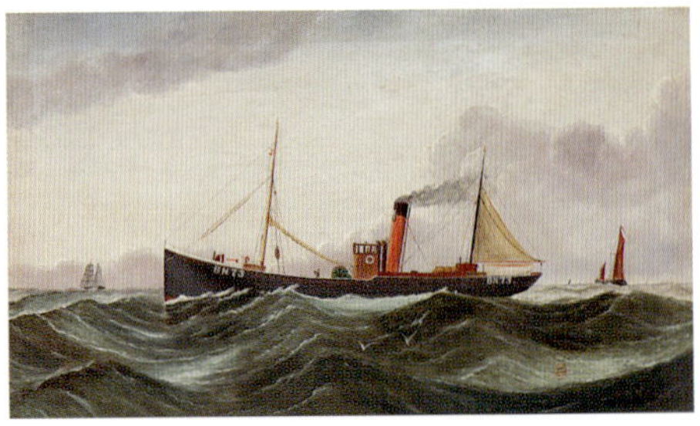

Smith, H.
Fishing Boat 'Alsatian' BN73 1905
oil on canvas 46 x 73
1987.19

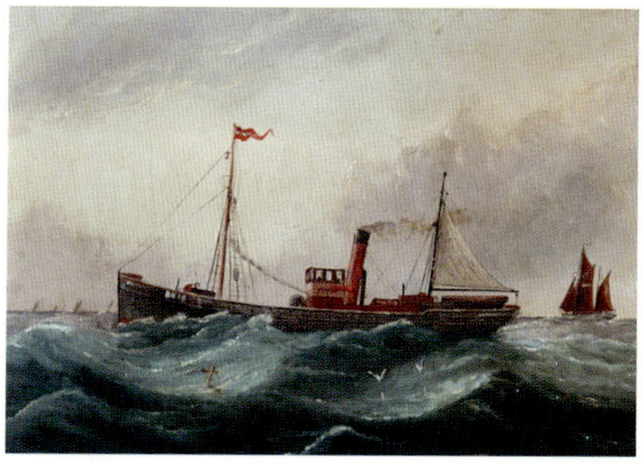

Smith, H.
Steam Trawler 1905
oil on board 20.8 x 29
1957.6

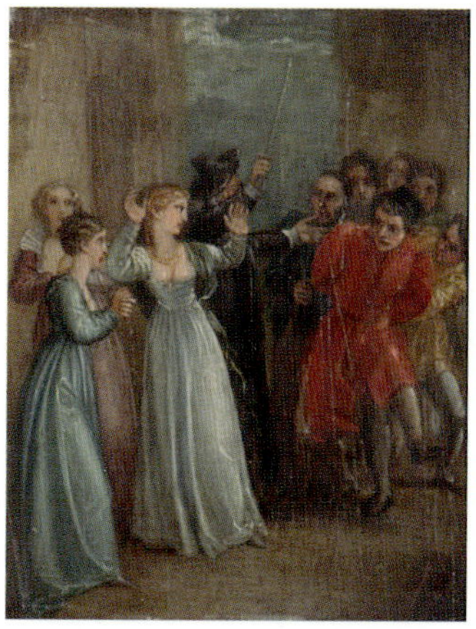

Stothard, Thomas 1755–1834
A Scene from William Shakespeare's 'A Comedy of Errors'
oil on board 21 x 16
1926.86.2

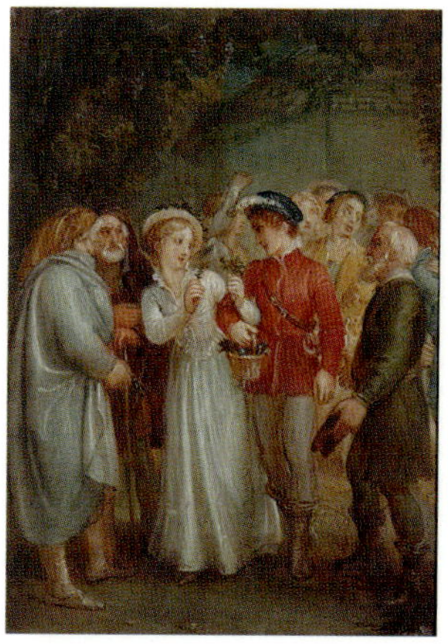

Stothard, Thomas 1755–1834
A Scene from William Shakespeare's 'A Winter's Tale'
oil on board 21 x 16
1926.86.1

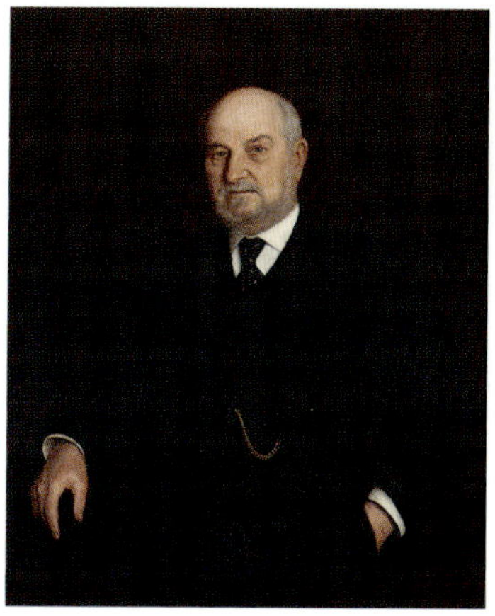

Thistlewaite, Clara Olive
William Bedford 1905
oil on canvas 100 x 76
PCF1

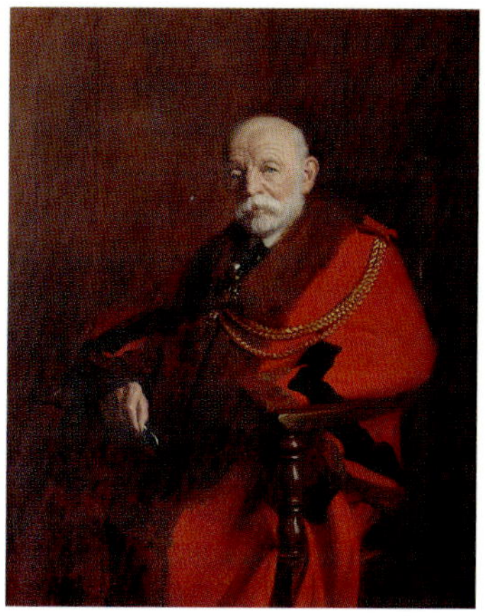

Townsend, Ernest 1885–1944
Mayor John Beaulah (1841–1926), Mayor of Boston (1921–1922)
oil on canvas 107 x 81.5
1989.43

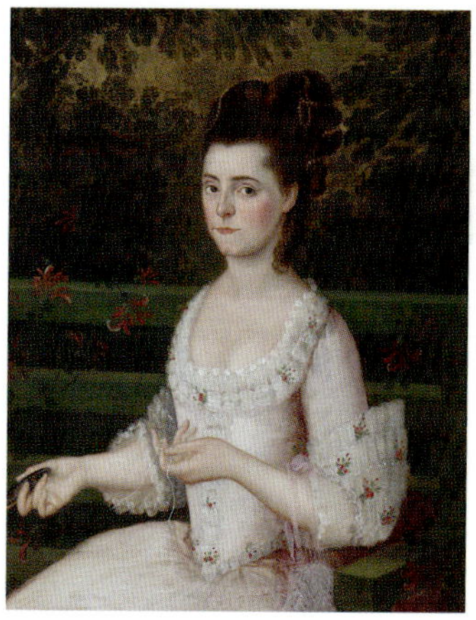

unknown artist
Ann Twell, Wife of Charles Twell c.1700–1750
oil on canvas 107 x 88
1954.11

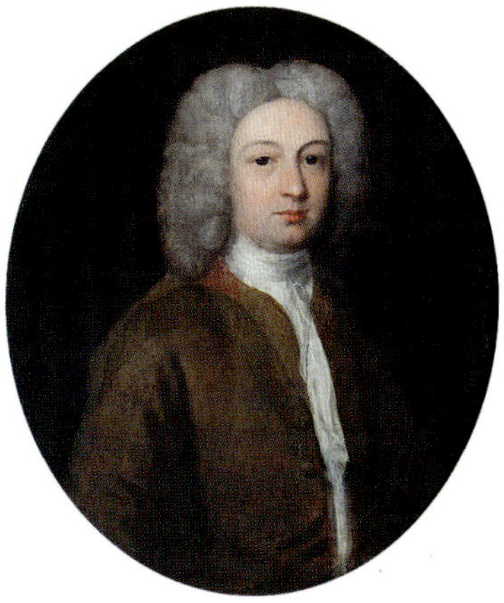

unknown artist
Charles Twell, Mayor of Boston (1729–1730) c.1700–1750
oil on canvas 73 x 61.5
1954.10

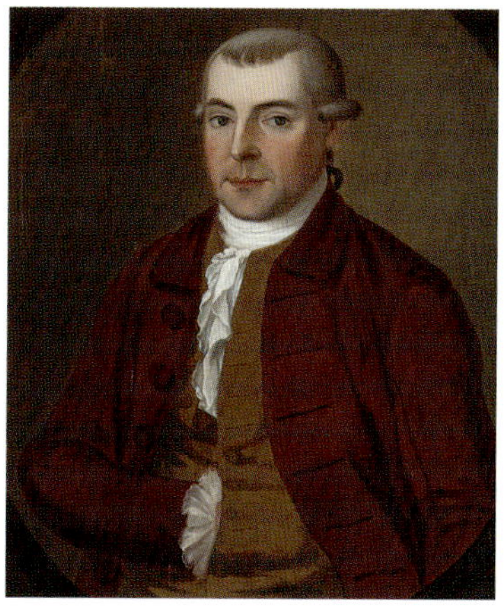

unknown artist
Samuel Thornton c.1740
oil on canvas 66.5 x 55.5
1954.12

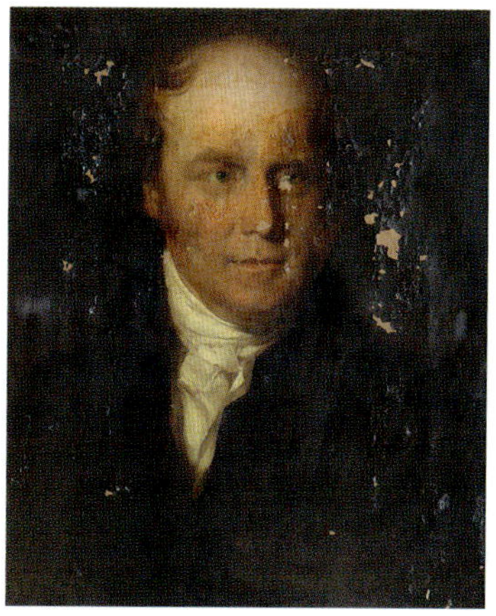

unknown artist
John Caistor, Mayor of Boston (1838–1839) 1837
oil on canvas 53.3 x 42.3
1987.54

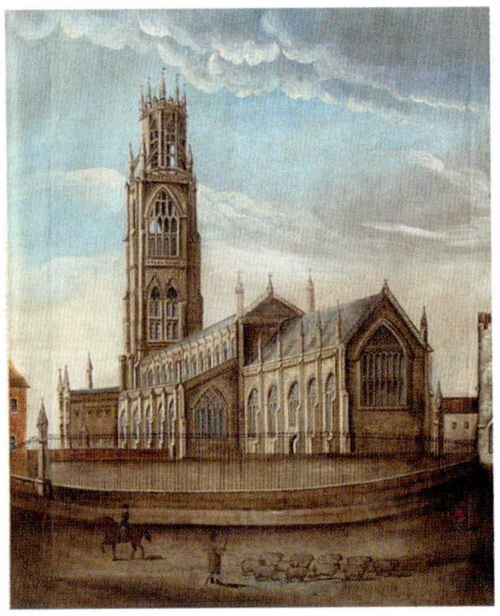

unknown artist
Boston Stump from the Market Place, Licolnshire 1840–1850
oil on canvas 61 x 50
1977.719

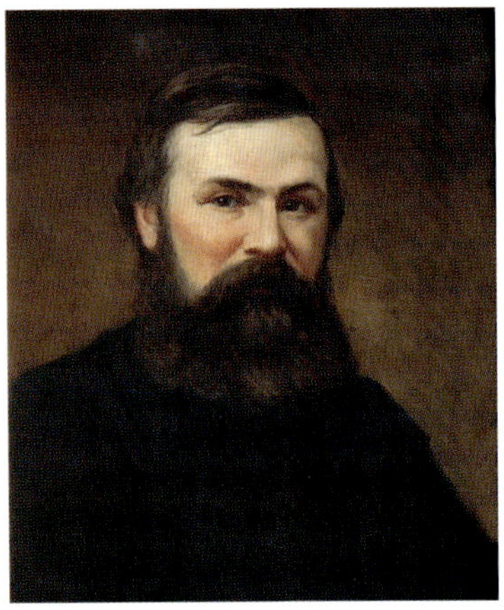

unknown artist
William Caistor, Mayor of Boston (1865–1866) 1865–1866
oil on canvas 52.5 x 42.3
1987.53

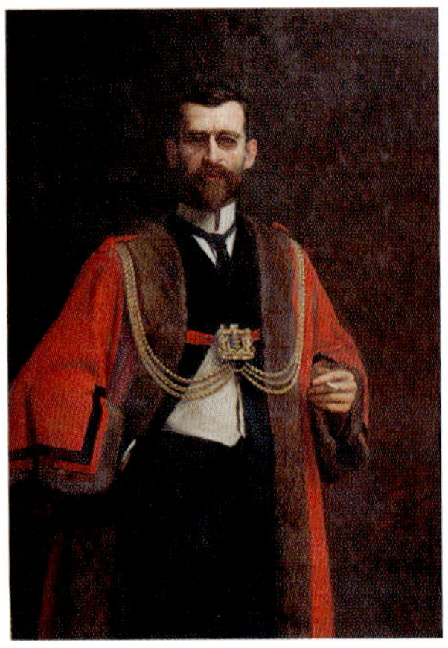

unknown artist
Alderman Joseph Cooke, Mayor of Boston (1902–1904)
oil on canvas 141 x 95
1989.44

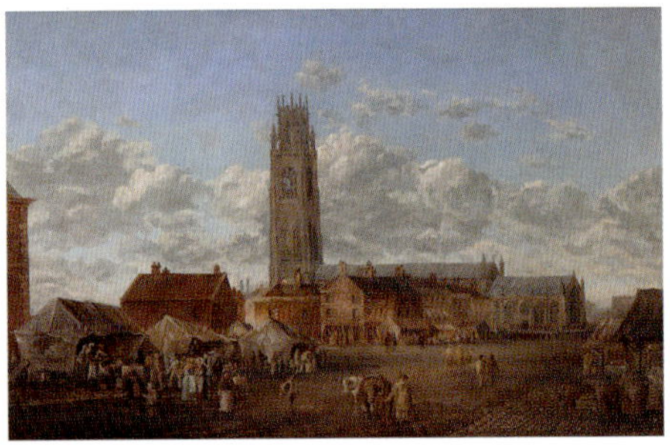

unknown artist
Boston Market Place and St Botolph's, Lincolnshire
oil on panel 29 x 43
2002.55

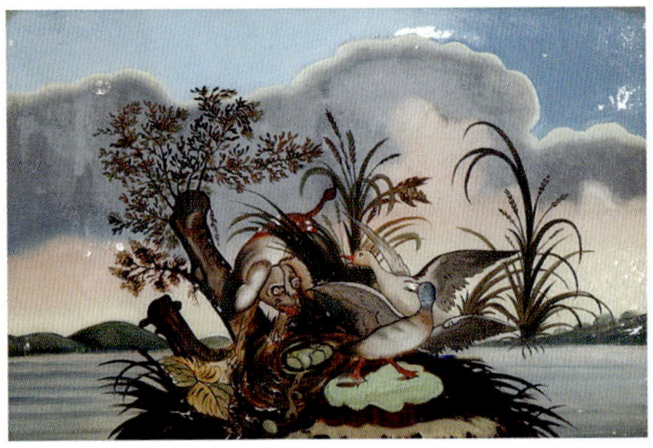

unknown artist
Dog and Ducks
oil on glass 26.5 x 39
1996.40

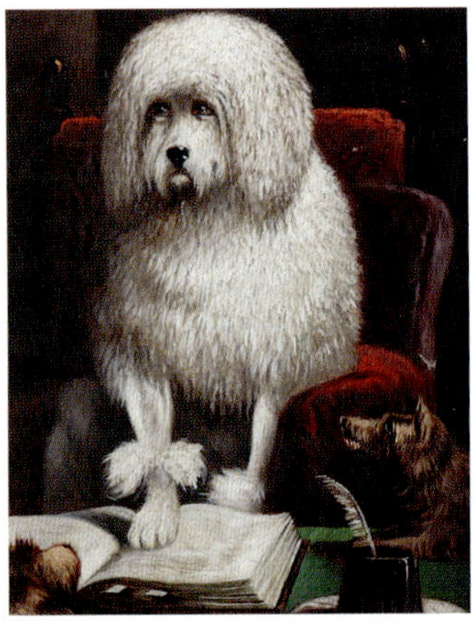

unknown artist
Poodle
oil on canvas 42 x 32
1987.35

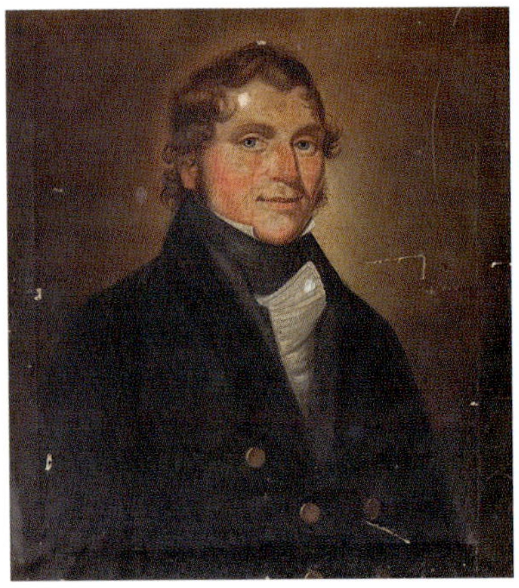

unknown artist
Portrait of an Unknown Man
oil on canvas 65 x 57
1987.55

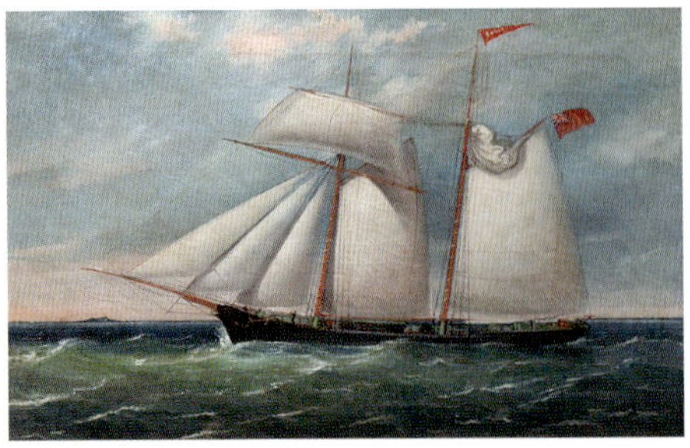

unknown artist
Sailing Ship 'Eagle'
oil on canvas 46.8 x 72
1961.5

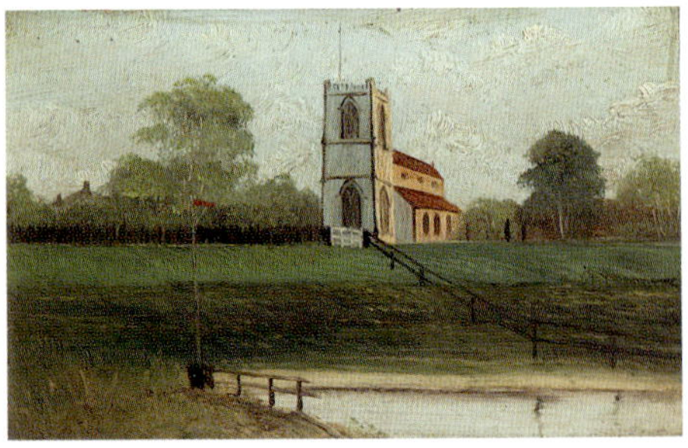

unknown artist
Skirbeck Church, Lincolnshire
oil on board 15.3 x 23
2009.4

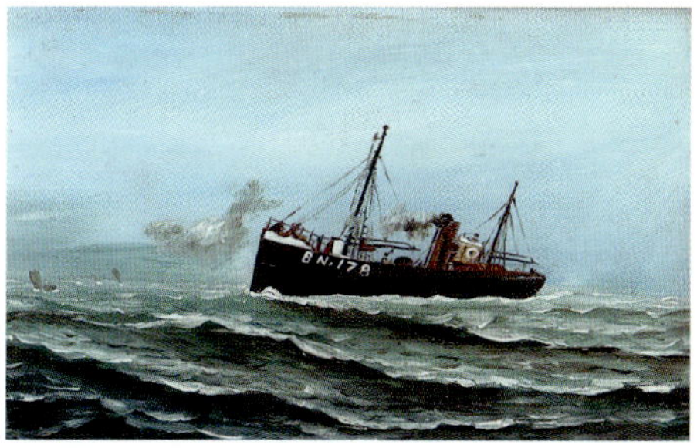

unknown artist
Steam Trawler BN178
oil on canvas 14 x 22.5
2002.176

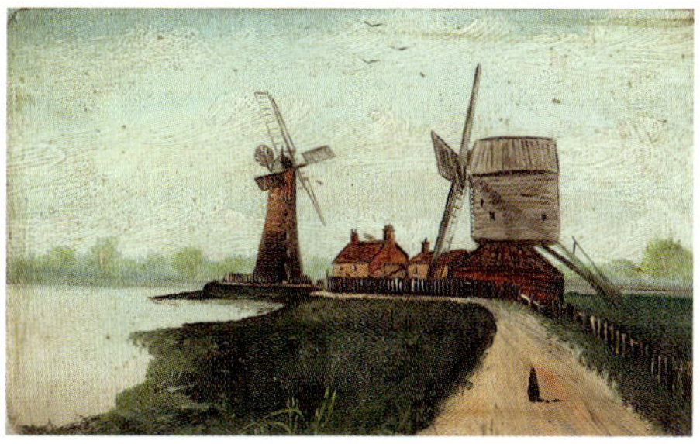

unknown artist
Windmill
oil on board 15.3 x 23.5
2009.3

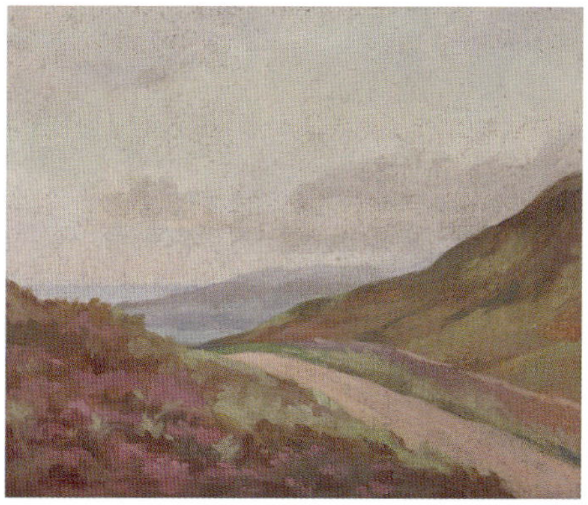

White, Charles Ernest 1890–1971
Landscape Scene
oil on canvas & board 24.5 x 29.5
1971.30

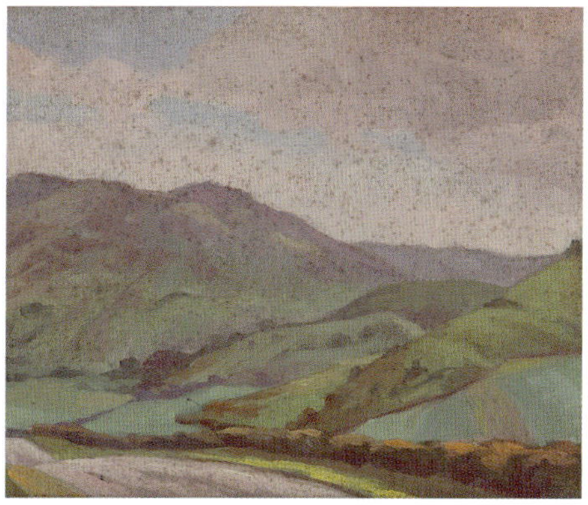

White, Charles Ernest 1890–1971
Landscape Scene
oil on canvas & board 24.5 x 29.5
1971.31

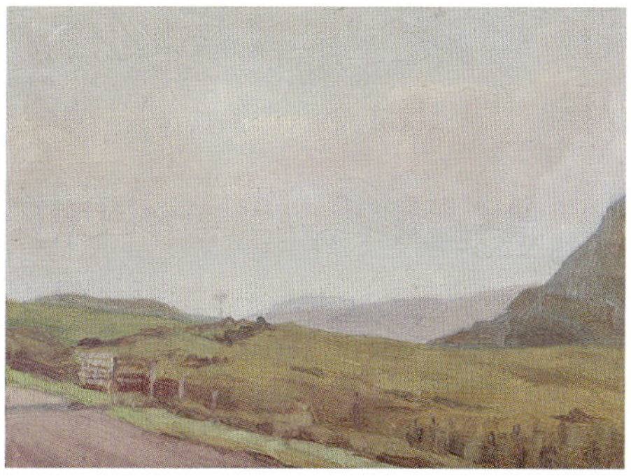

White, Charles Ernest 1890–1971
Landscape Scene
oil on canvas & board 22 x 29
1971.33

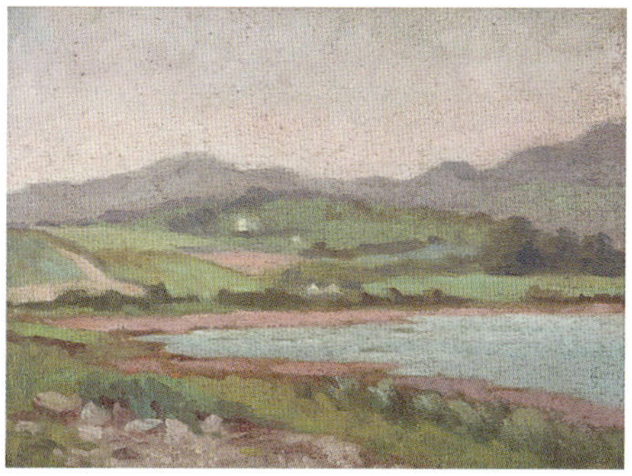

White, Charles Ernest 1890–1971
Landscape Scene
oil on canvas & board 22 x 29.5
1971.34

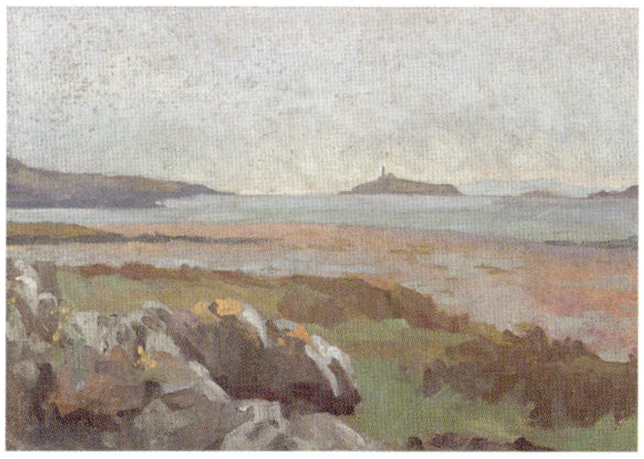

White, Charles Ernest 1890–1971
Landscape Scene
oil on canvas & board 24.5 x 34.5
1971.35

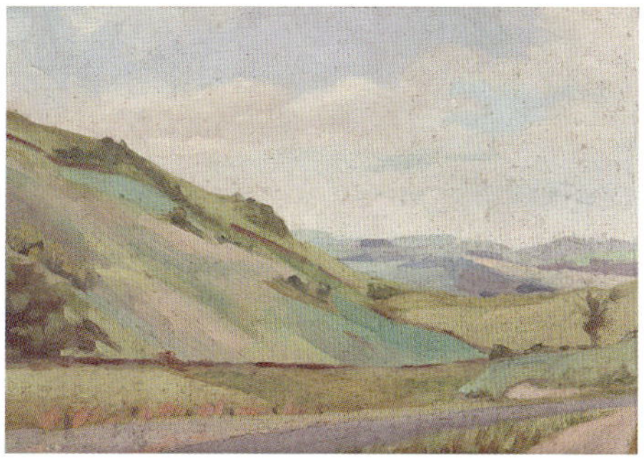

White, Charles Ernest 1890–1971
Landscape Scene
oil on canvas & board 24.5 x 34.5
1971.36

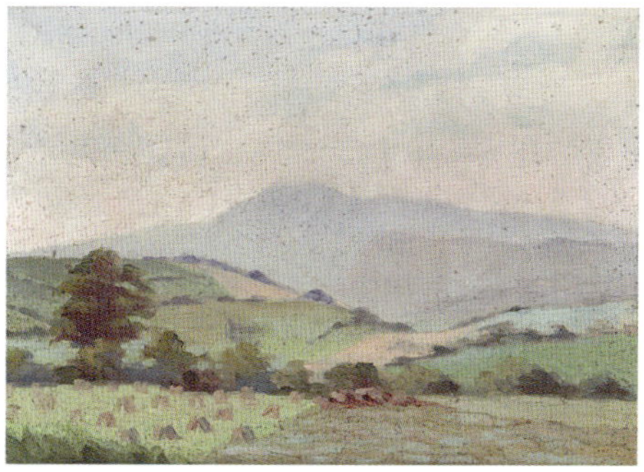

White, Charles Ernest 1890–1971
Landscape Scene
oil on canvas & board 24.5 x 34.5
1971.37

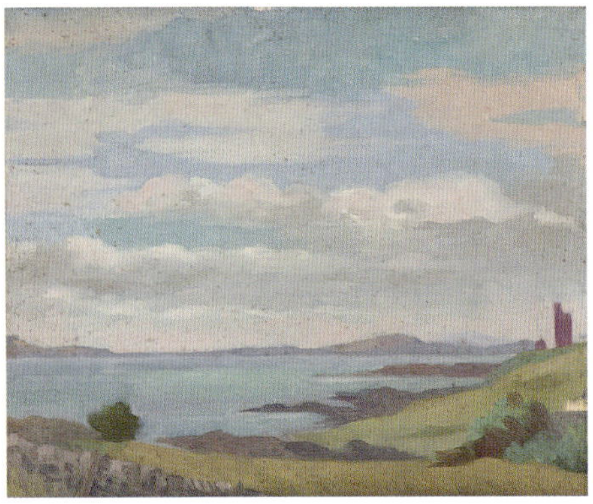

White, Charles Ernest 1890–1971
Landscape Scene
oil on canvas & board 24.5 x 30 (E)
1971.38

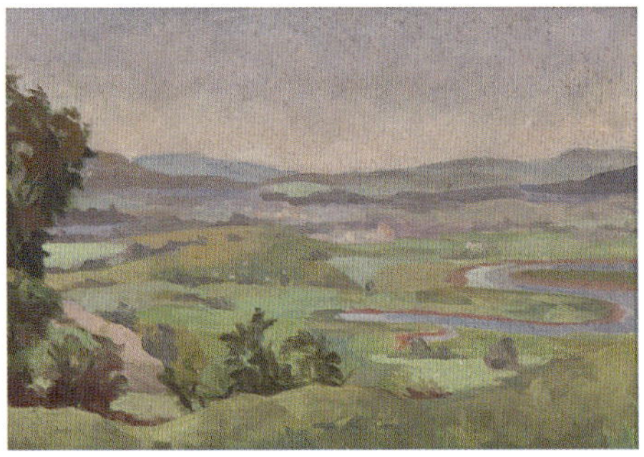

White, Charles Ernest 1890–1971
Landscape Scene
oil on canvas & board 24.5 x 34.5
1971.39

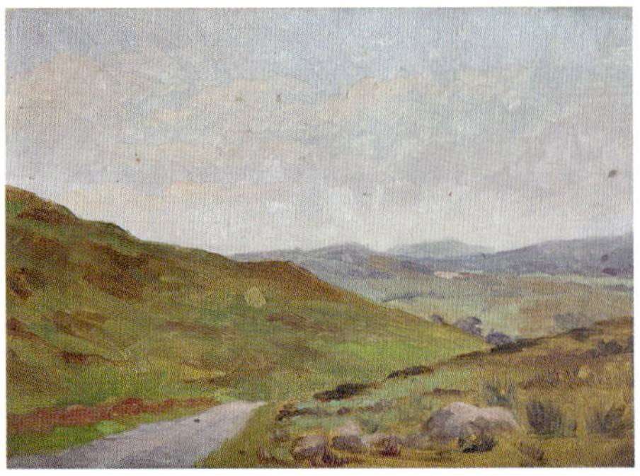

White, Charles Ernest 1890–1971
Landscape Scene
oil on canvas & board 27 x 37
1971.40

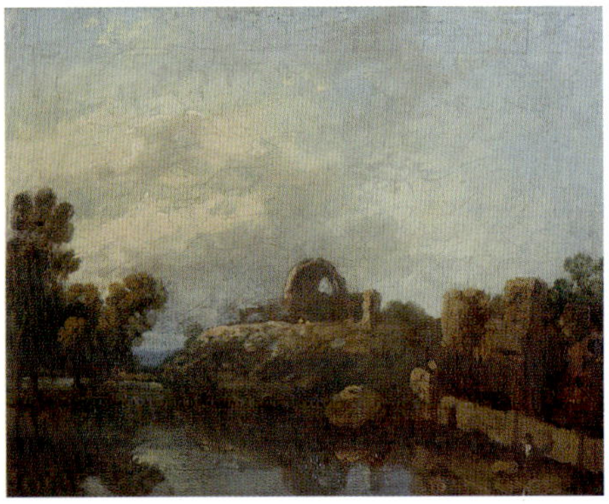

Wilson, Richard 1712/1713–1782
River Landscape
oil on canvas 28 x 35
1926.94

Fydell House

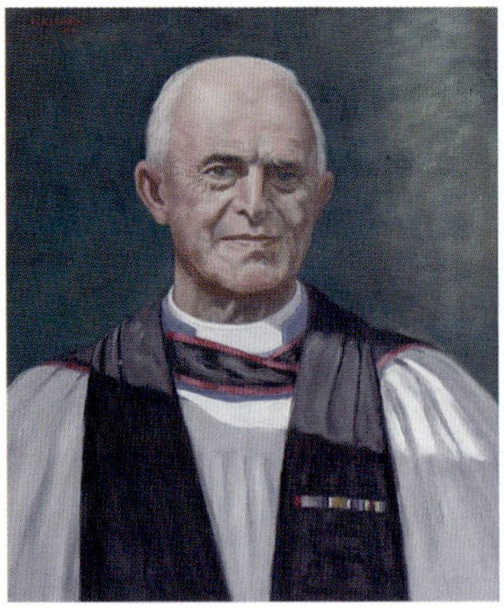

Kiddey
Canon A. M. Cook (d.1964), Vicar of St Botolph's, Boston, Lincolnshire (1932–1946)
1964
oil on canvas 59 x 49
3

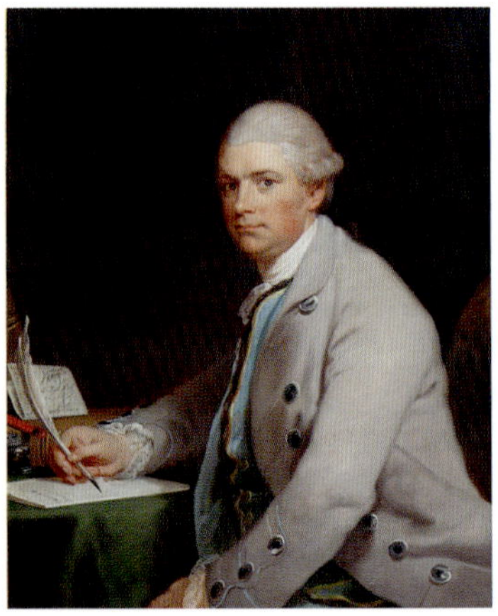

Pine, Robert Edge c.1720/1730–1788
Richard Fydell, Junior (1747–1793) 1777
oil on canvas 89 x 71
1

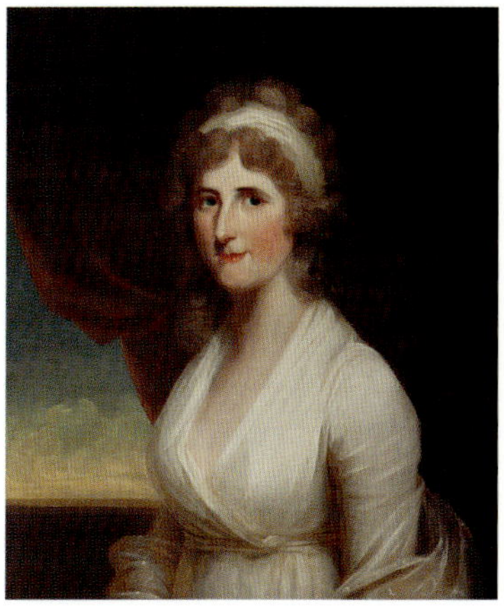

unknown artist
Elizabeth Fydell (1767–1797), Niece of Richard Fydell
oil on canvas 70.5 x 58
2

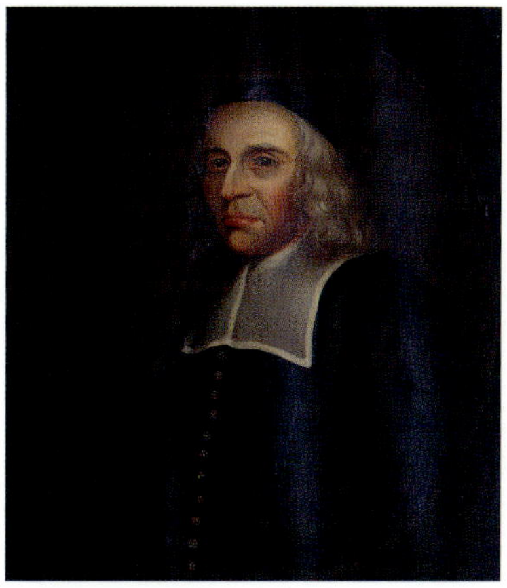

unknown artist
Sir John Leverett (1616–1679), Governor of Massachusetts (1673–1679)
oil on canvas 73 x 61
4

Bourne Heritage Centre

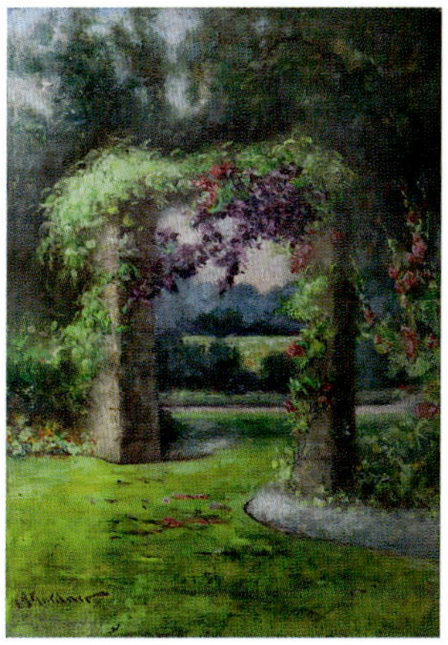

Gardner, Robert Arthur
1850–1926
Rose Garden
oil on canvas 38 x 28
1

Epworth Old Rectory

Epworth Old Rectory is a Queen Anne house, built in 1709 to replace the previous rectory on the site, which burnt down in the famous fire from which the Wesley family only just escaped. Samuel Wesley came to Epworth in 1695 to become the rector of the parish of St Andrews. He and Susanna Wesley had nineteen children, ten of whom survived infancy. The most famous were John and Charles Wesley, but they also had an elder brother Samuel and seven sisters. Samuel (senior) died in 1735 and Susanna then left Epworth to live with various of her children. She spent her last days in London.

The house continued to be a rectory until 1954, when it was purchased by the Methodist Church to become a museum. Many people from all over the world visit the Old Rectory to see the place where the seeds of the eighteenth-century religious revival in England were planted. Many people believe that it was Susanna's disciplined teaching and religious devotion that inspired her children.

The Trustees are currently working on a development plan to restore the house to its condition in around 1716, and to build a new visitors' centre. Epworth Old Rectory is also applying to be an accredited museum. The collection of paintings is diverse, with pieces ranging from the eighteenth century to the modern day. Two modern artists have produced several works illustrating episodes in the lives of the Wesley family. The eighteenth-century highlights of the collection are the 'Lily' portrait of Charles Wesley, the portrait of John Wesley after John Jackson, the portrait of John Wesley after John Michael Williams and the portrait of Susanna Wesley by an unknown artist in the mid-eighteenth century.

Claire Potter, Development Manager

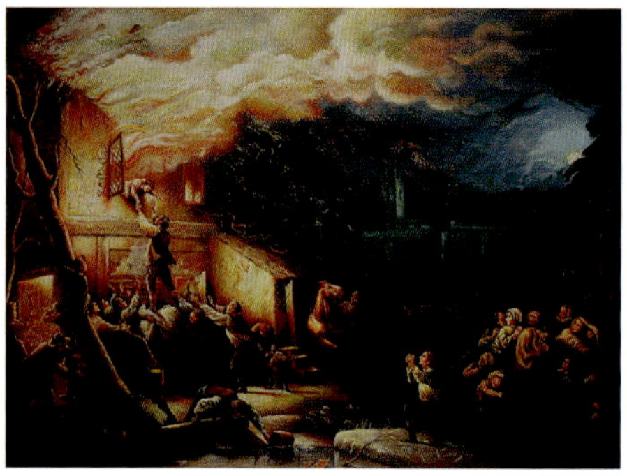

Douglas, Richard Gilmore b.c.1937
Epworth Rectory Fire, 1909 (after Henry Perlee Parker) 1991
oil on board 91.5 x 122
EPWOR 2008 - 134

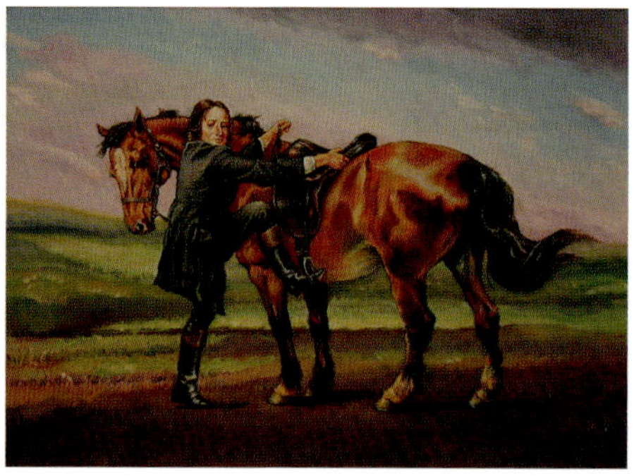

Douglas, Richard Gilmore b.c.1937
John Wesley (1703–1791), Mounting His Horse 1992
oil on canvas board 45.8 x 61
EPWOR 2009 - 284

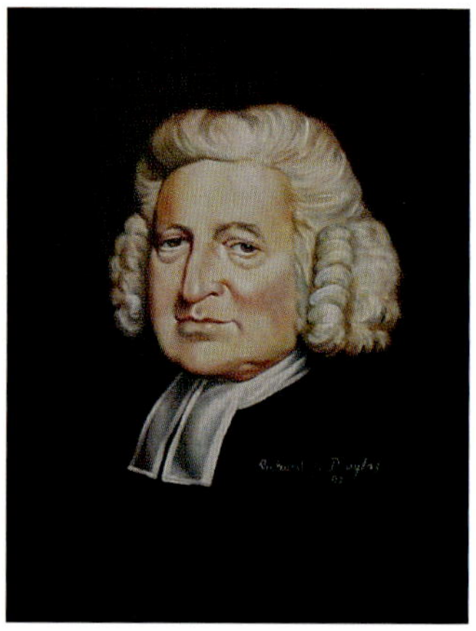

Douglas, Richard Gilmore b.c.1937
Charles Wesley (1707–1788), Epworth (after John Russell) 1997
oil on board 40.8 x 30.5
EPWOR 2009 - 306

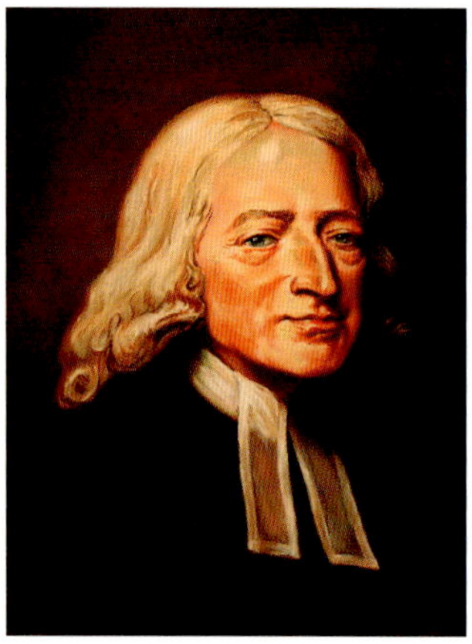

Douglas, Richard Gilmore b.c.1937
John Wesley (1703–1791) (after George Romney) 1997
oil on panel 40.6 x 30.5
EPWOR 2009 - 286

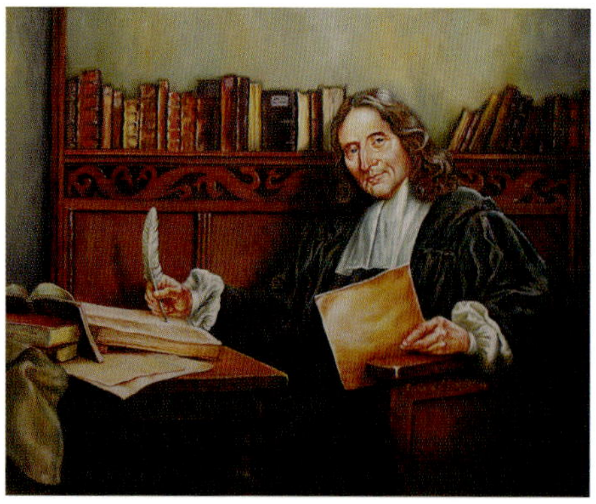

Douglas, Richard Gilmore b.c.1937
Samuel Wesley, Senior (1662–1735) 1998
oil on board 51 x 61.5
EPWOR 2009 - 287

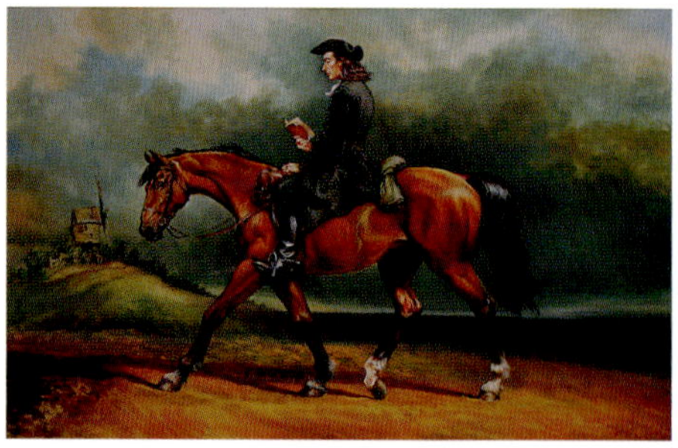

Douglas, Richard Gilmore b.c.1937
John Wesley (1703–1791), Riding a Horse Whilst Reading a Book 1999
oil on canvas 60.2 x 91.5
EPWOR 2009 - 283

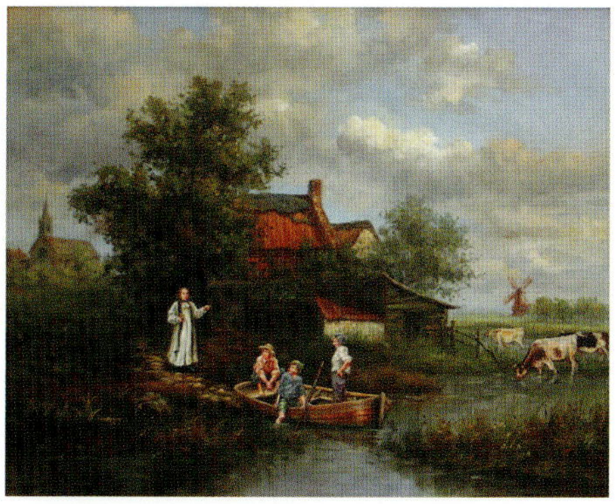

Douglas, Richard Gilmore b.c.1937
John Wesley at Wroot, Lincolnshire c.2000
oil on canvas 50.9 x 61
EPWOR 2009 - 307

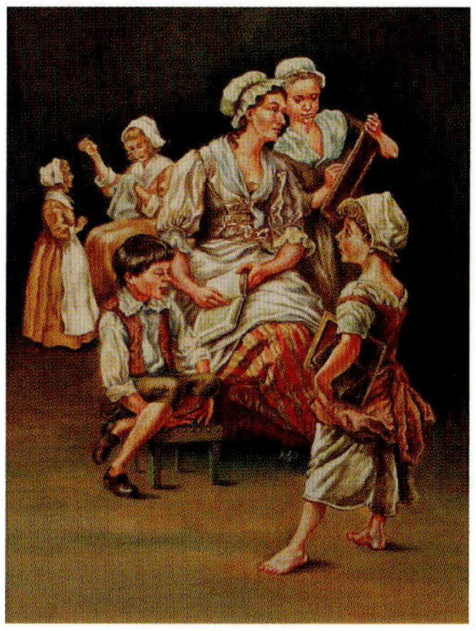

Douglas, Richard Gilmore b.c.1937
Susanna Wesley with Five Children c.2000
oil on board 40.6 x 33
EPWOR 2009 - 290

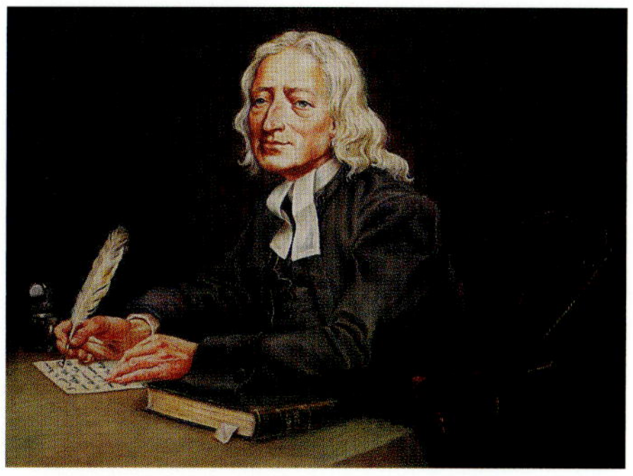

Douglas, Richard Gilmore b.c.1937
John Wesley (1703–1791), Holding a Quill Pen 2002
oil on board 45.6 x 61
EPWOR 2009 - 285

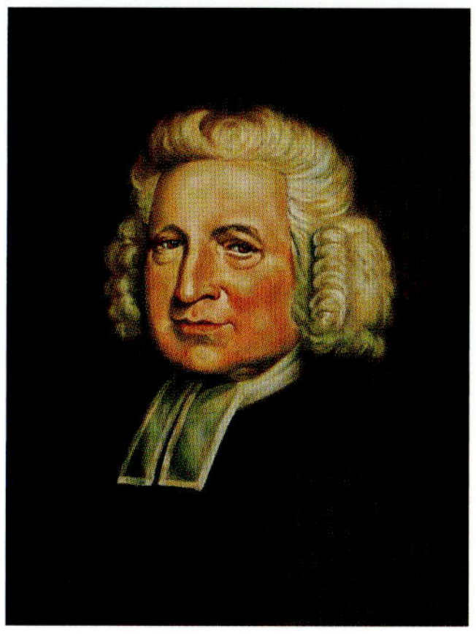

Douglas, Richard Gilmore b.c.1937
Charles Wesley (1707–1788), Epworth (after John Russell) 2003
oil on board 40.8 x 30.5
EPWOR 2009 - 292

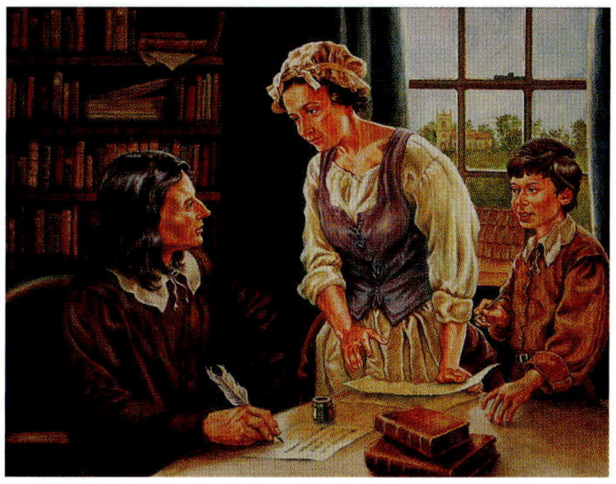

Douglas, Richard Gilmore b.c.1937
Samuel Wesley, Senior (1662–1735), Susanna Wesley and Samuel Wesley, Junior 2003
oil on board 40.7 x 51
EPWOR 2009 - 289

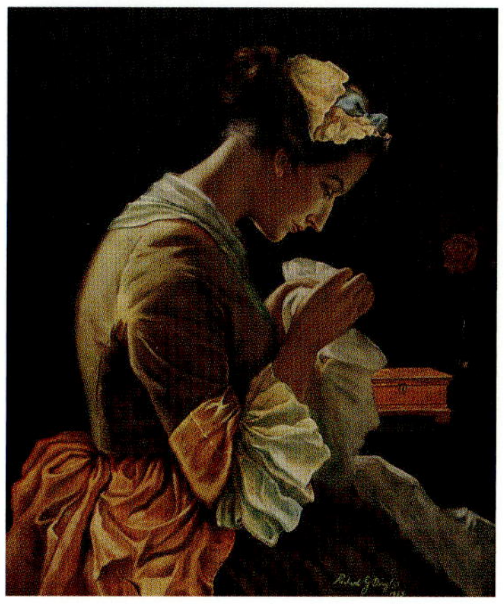

Douglas, Richard Gilmore b.c.1937
Susanna Wesley, Sewing 2003
oil on hardboard 60.9 x 55
EPWOR 2009 - 291

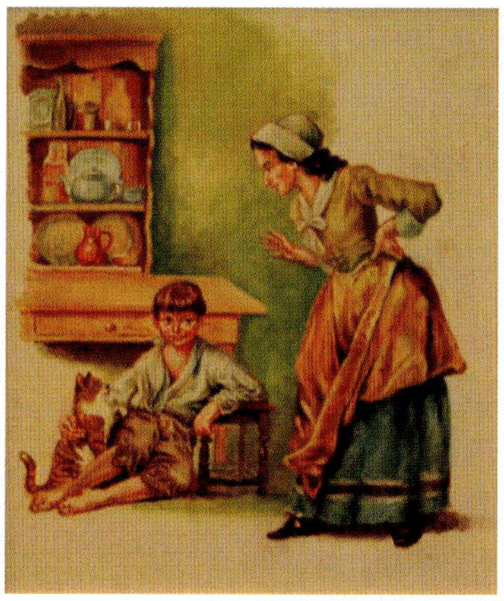

Douglas, Richard Gilmore b.c.1937
Susanna Wesley with Samuel Wesley, Junior and a Cat 2003
oil on hardboard 30.5 x 25.5
EPWOR 2009 - 288

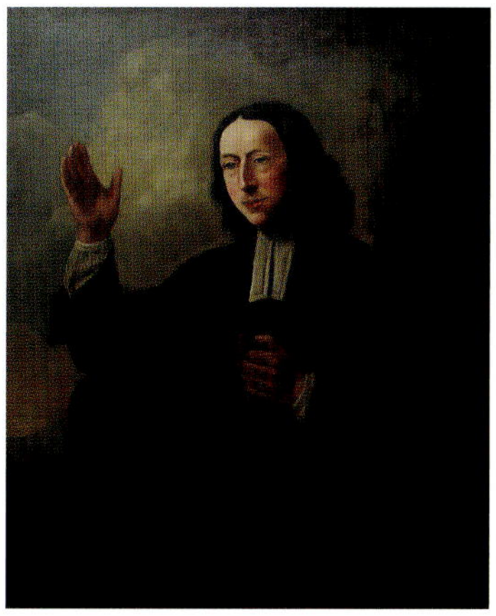

Grose, Margaret active early 20th C
John Wesley (1703–1791) (after Nathaniel Hone) 1920
oil on canvas 76.2 x 63.3
EPWOR 2009 - 410

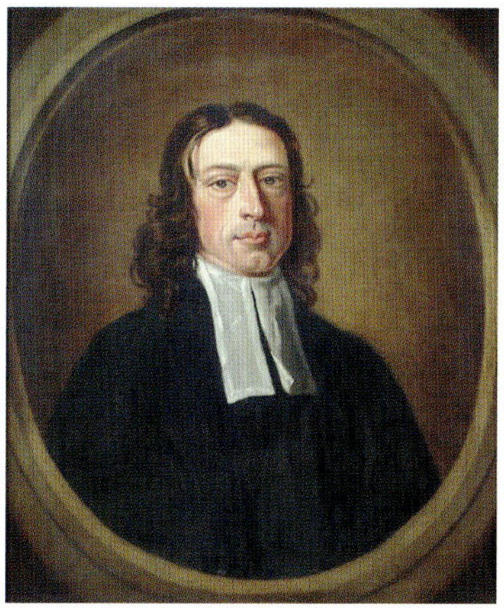

Harley, J.
Reverend John Wesley (1703–1791) (after John Michael Williams) 1745
oil on canvas 75 x 62.3
EPWOR 2009 - 384

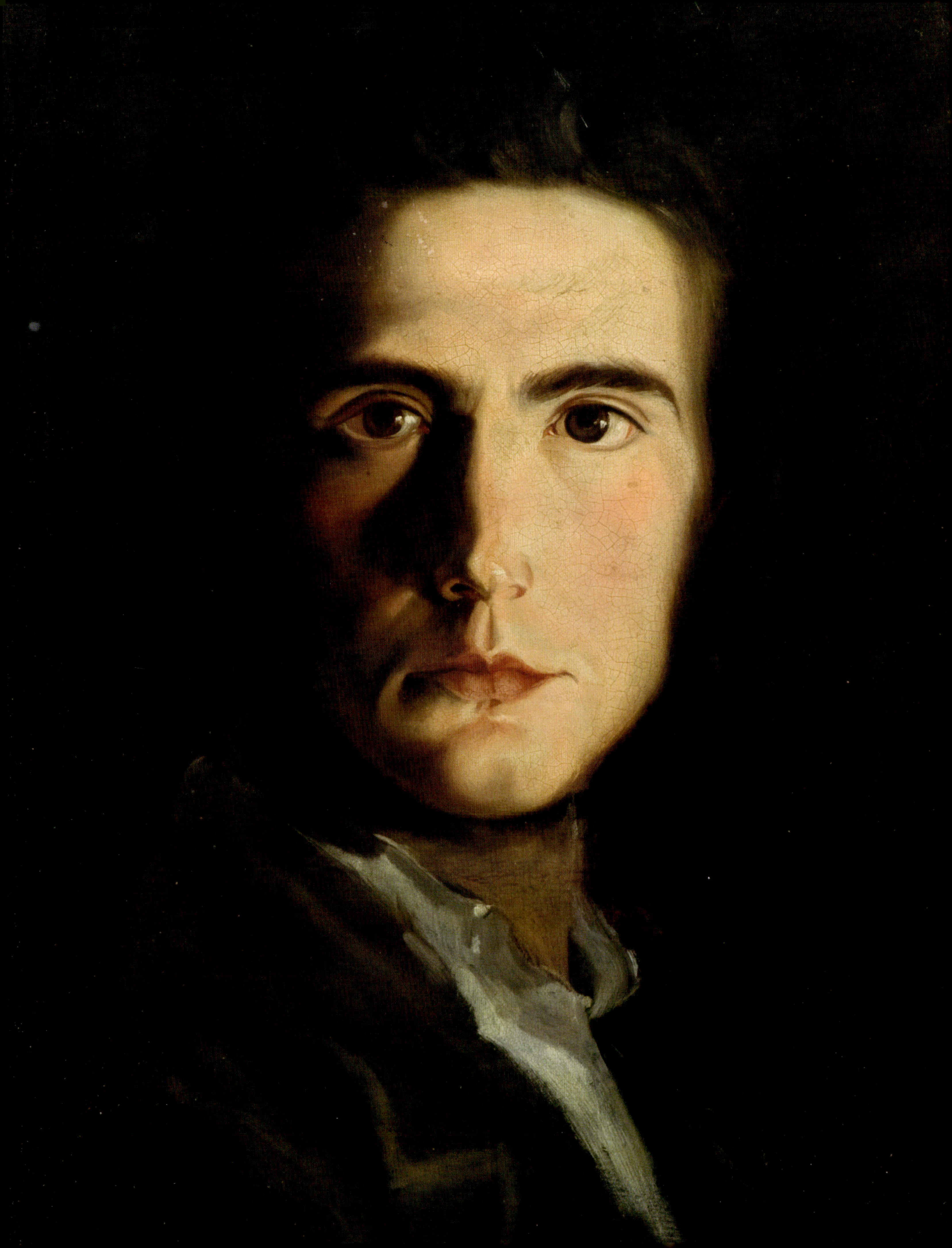

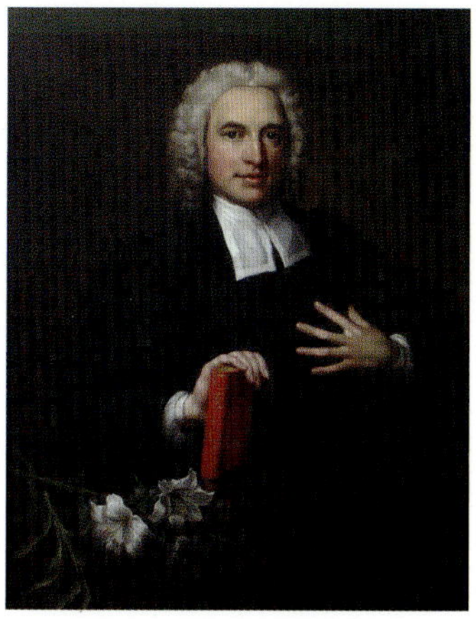

Hudson, Thomas (after) 1701–1779
Reverend Charles Wesley (1707–1788) 1749
oil on canvas 92.7 x 72.4
EPWOR 2009 - 383

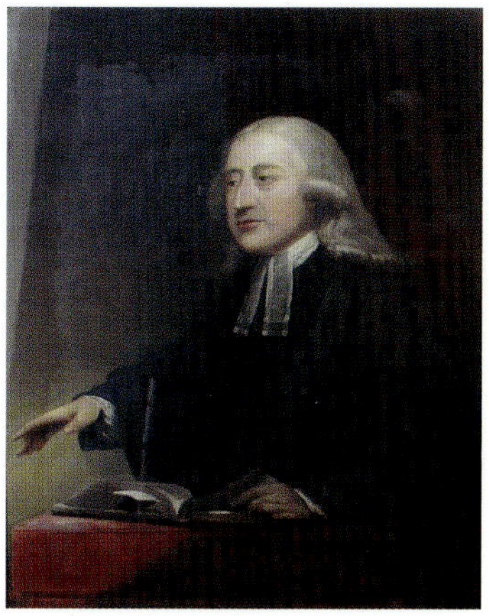

Jackson, John (after) 1778–1831
Reverend John Wesley (1703–1791) 1827
oil on canvas 96 x 75
EPWOR 2009 - 385

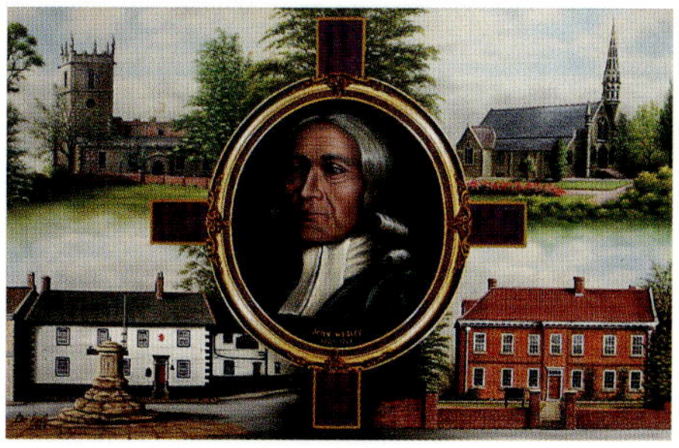

Keal, David Ernest b.1930
John Wesley (1703–1791) (superimposed on a purple cross, surrounded by four views of Epworth, Lincolnshire) 1989
oil on canvas 50.2 x 76.2
EPWOR 2008 - 212

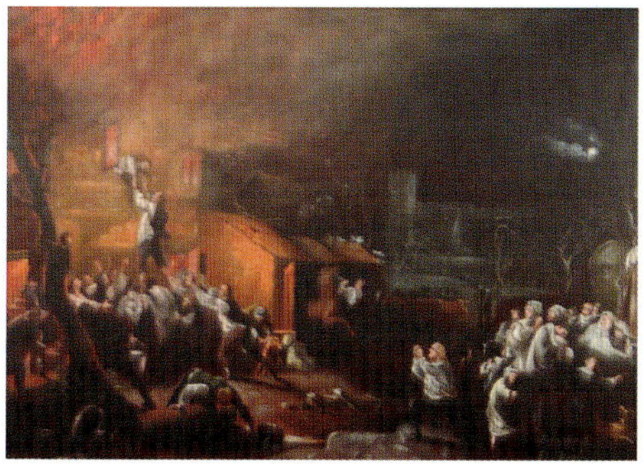

Keal, David Ernest b.1930
The Epworth Rectory on Fire and the Rescue of John Wesley, Aged 6 (after Henry Perlee Parker) c.1990
oil on board 28 x 38.1
EPWOR 2008 - 213

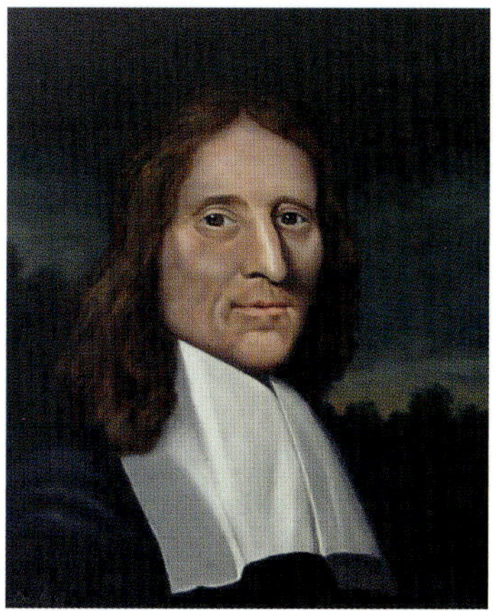

Keal, David Ernest b.1930
Samuel Wesley Senior (1662–1735) 2003
oil on board 45.7 x 38.1
EPWOR 2008 - 136

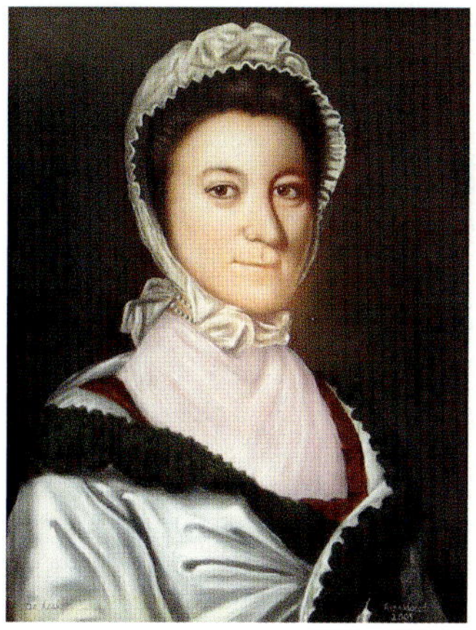

Keal, David Ernest b.1930
Sarah Wesley, née Gwynne (1726–1822) 2005
oil on board 49.6 x 38.1
EPWOR 2008 - 209

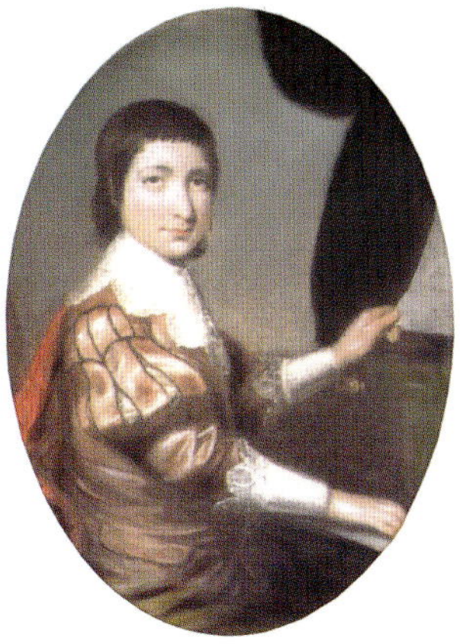

Keal, David Ernest b.1930
Charles Wesley Junior (1757–1834) 2007
oil on board 17.8 x 12.8
EPWOR 2008 - 210A

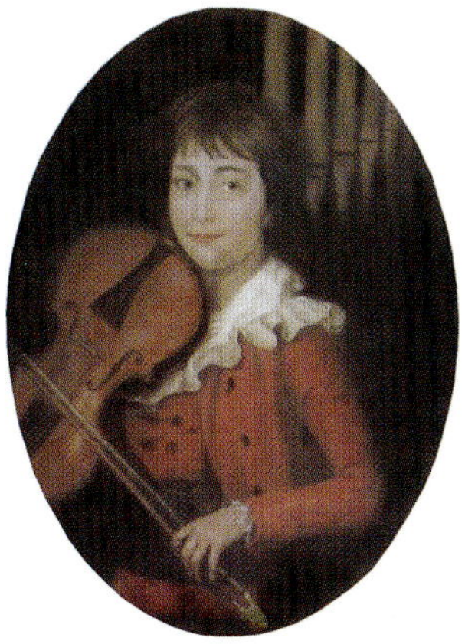

Keal, David Ernest b.1930
Samuel Wesley (1766–1837), Son of Charles 2007
oil on board 17.8 x 12.8
EPWOR 2008 - 210C

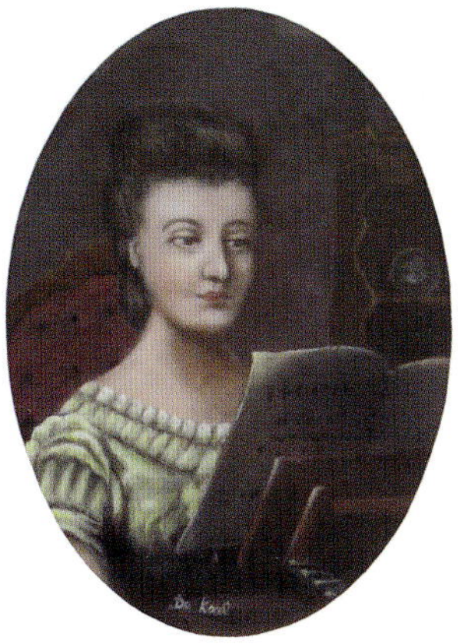

Keal, David Ernest b.1930
Sarah Wesley Junior (1759–1823) 2007
oil on board 17.8 x 12.8
EPWOR 2008 - 210B

Facing page: Dawson, Henry, 1811–1878, *Self Portrait* (detail), Grantham Museum (p. 220)

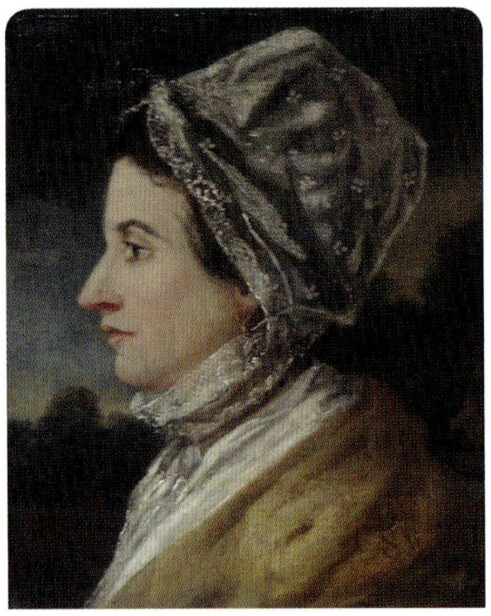

unknown artist mid-18th C
Mrs Susanna Wesley
oil on canvas 45.1 x 36.8
EPWOR 2000 - 020

Gainsborough Old Hall

Gainsborough Old Hall is a part brick and part timber-framed medieval manor house situated in the middle of Gainsborough. It was rescued from dereliction in 1949 by the Friends of the Old Hall, who opened it to the public and built up its social history and art collection. The Old Hall was given to the nation by Sir Edmund Bacon in 1970.

The art collection comprises two parts – works donated by the public and those on loan from a privately-owned collection. The former consists mostly of Victorian paintings depicting local scenes and the Old Hall itself. Several works are by William Edward Millner, who was born in Gainsborough in 1849 and lived all his life there. His father, William, was also a professional painter and art teacher in the town. Local agricultural scenes, including horses and other animals, feature strongly in his work and give an insight to agricultural life at this time. Such examples include *Two Horses Grazing, with a Parish Church Tower in the Distance* (1893) and *Thonock Lodge Gates, Lincolnshire* (1875). Thonock Hall was a property just outside Gainsborough, which has now been demolished. Milner exhibited work at the Royal Academy, although he was never made a member. He died in 1895 and in December of that year a sale of 35 of his paintings was held at the Gainsborough Coffee Tavern.

The greater part of the privately-owned collection includes family portraits dating from the sixteenth century to the Victorian period. There are many interesting sitters, although not all lived at the Old Hall. Most notable are *Francis Bacon (1561–1626), Baron Verulam, Viscount St Albans*, who was Lord High Chancellor at the court of Queen Elizabeth I, as well as a philosopher and writer. Also by unknown artists, portraits of his father, *Sir Nicholas Bacon (1510–1597), Lord Keeper*, are also included in the collection. Sir Nicholas was knighted by Elizabeth I in 1558 and appointed Lord Keeper of the Privy Seal in the same year. The Collection also features two portraits of Henry VIII, who visited the Old Hall in 1541 with his fifth wife, Catherine Howard.

Gainsborough Old Hall is grateful to The Public Catalogue Foundation for increasing access to and raising the profile of its art collection.

Sara Basquill, Collections Officer

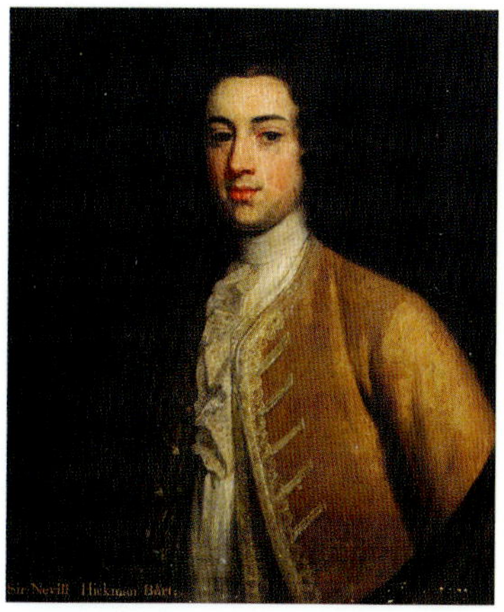

Devis, Arthur (attributed to) 1712–1787
Sir Neville Hickman (1725–1781), Bt
oil on canvas 73 x 60
GANOHL 77 (P)

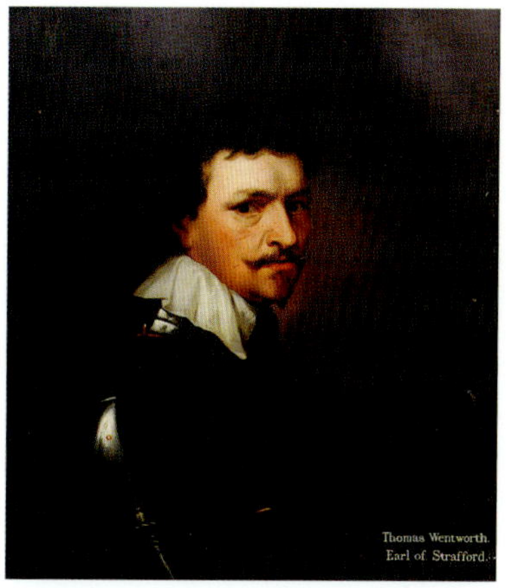

Dyck, Anthony van (after) 1599–1641
Thomas Wentworth (1593–1641), Earl of Strafford c.1636
oil on canvas 74.5 x 62
GANOHL 75 (P)

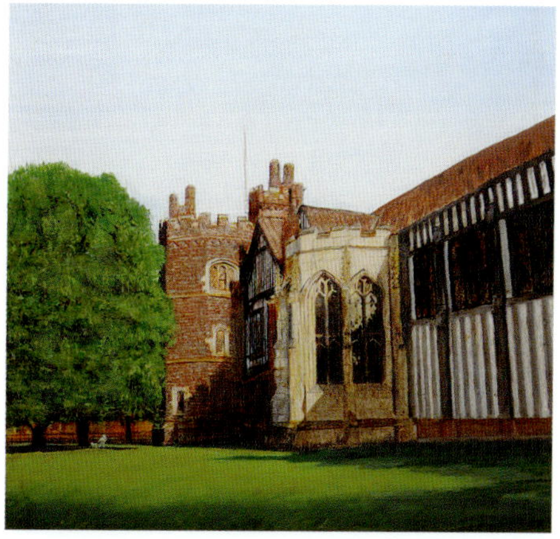

Gordon, R.
Gainsborough Old Hall, Lincolnshire 1996
oil on board 60 x 60
PCF1

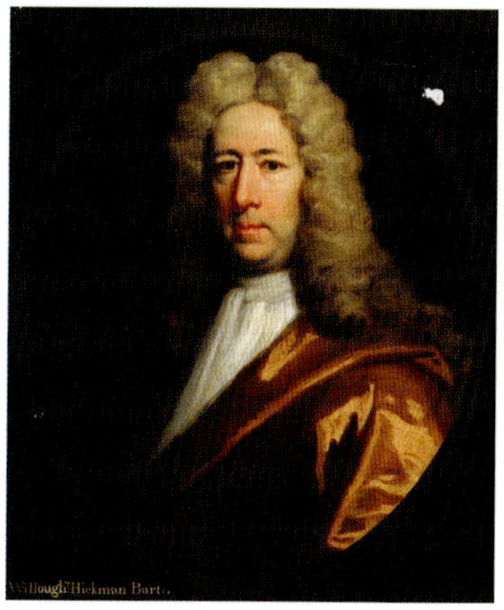

Jackson, Gilbert active 1615–1658
Willoughby Hickman (1659–1720), Bt
oil on canvas 74.8 x 60.8
GANOHL 72 (P)

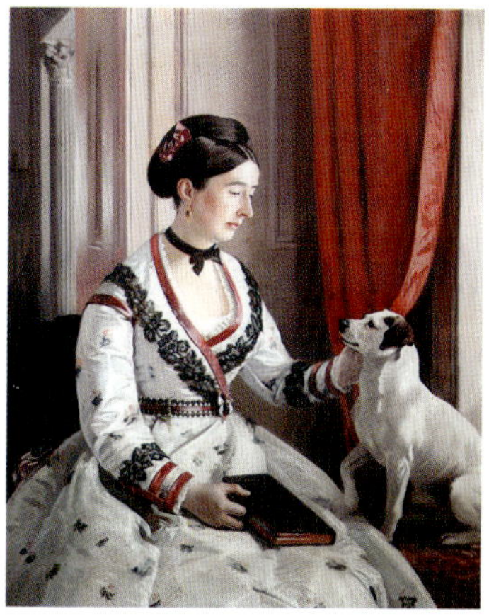

Lutyens, Charles Augustus Henry 1829–1915
Elizabeth (1829–1885), Daughter of Sir Thomas Beckett, Bt, Wife of Sir Henry (...)
oil on canvas 126 x 100
GANOHL 84 (P)

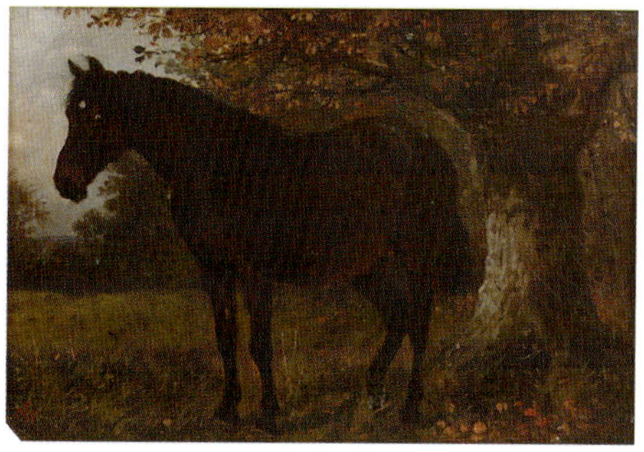

Millner, William Edward 1849–1895
Brown Horse 1873
oil on millboard 24.4 x 36.8
GANOH4199

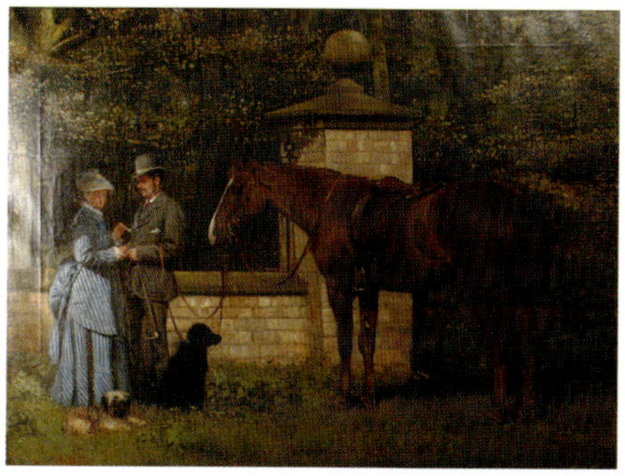

Millner, William Edward 1849–1895
Thonock Lodge Gates, Lincolnshire 1875
oil on canvas 75.5 x 101
GANOH4203

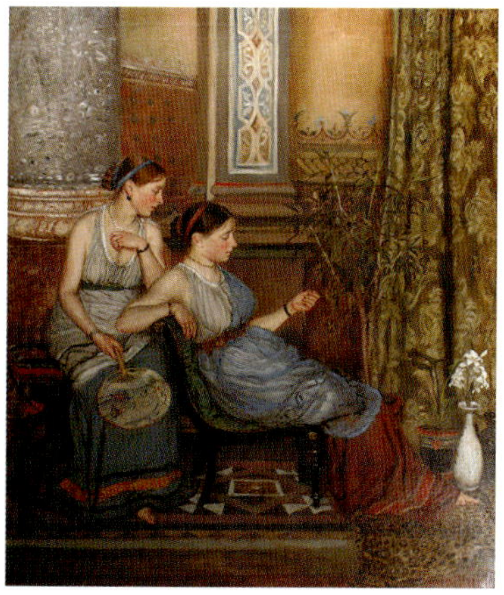

Millner, William Edward 1849–1895
Two Women (Greek Girls) 1877
oil on canvas 74.5 x 62
GANOH1354

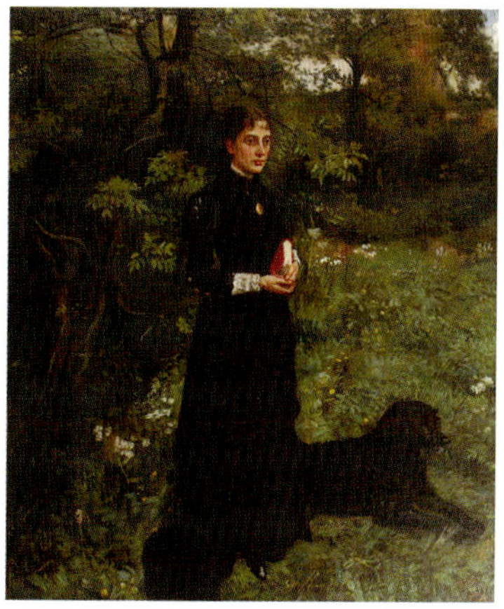

Millner, William Edward 1849–1895
'Will he come?' 1881
oil on canvas 51.5 x 41.5
GANOH4206

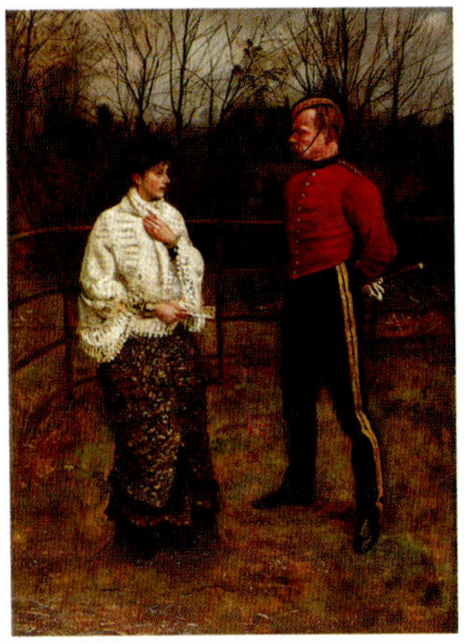

Millner, William Edward 1849–1895
A Woman with a Soldier 1882
oil on canvas 74.5 x 49.5
GANOH4207

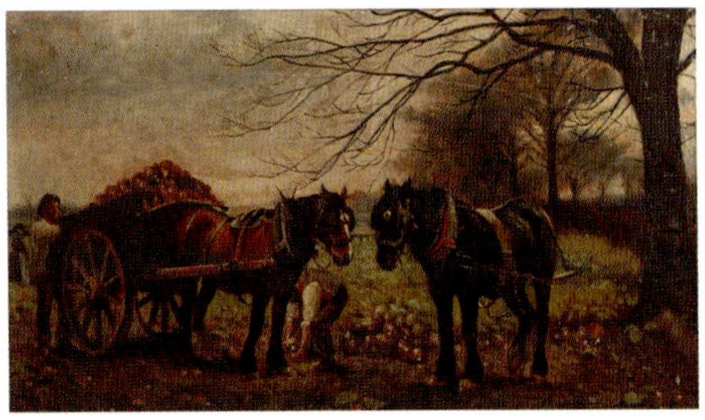

Millner, William Edward 1849–1895
Loading Mangold Wurzels into a Tumbril 1885
oil on card 25.5 x 49.5
GANOH4205

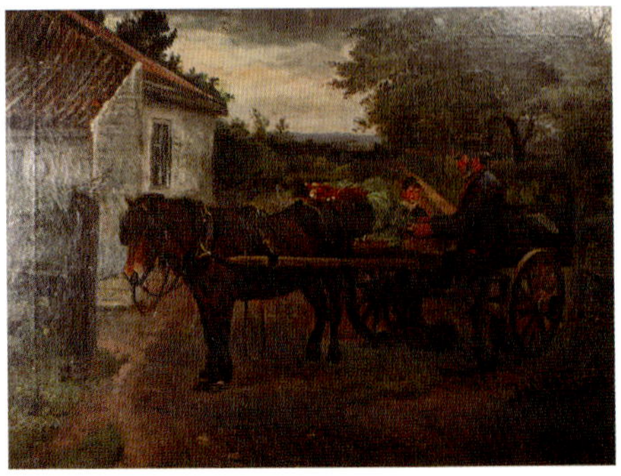

Millner, William Edward 1849–1895
Preparing for Market, a Man and a Boy Loading Rhubarb 1890
oil on canvas 75.2 x 101
GANOH4209

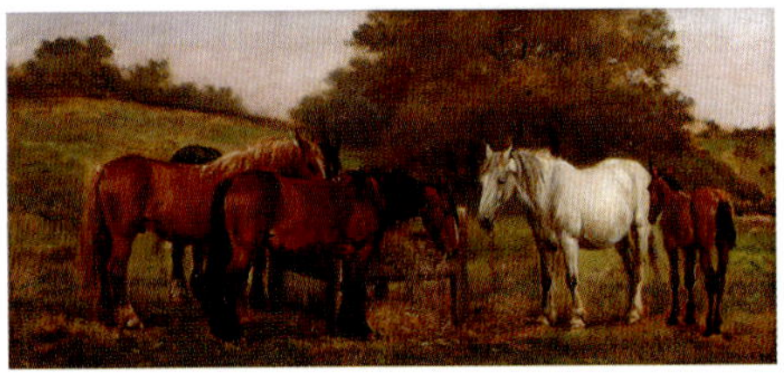

Millner, William Edward 1849–1895
Group of Horses and a Foal 1892
oil on millboard 21 x 49.5
GANOH4198

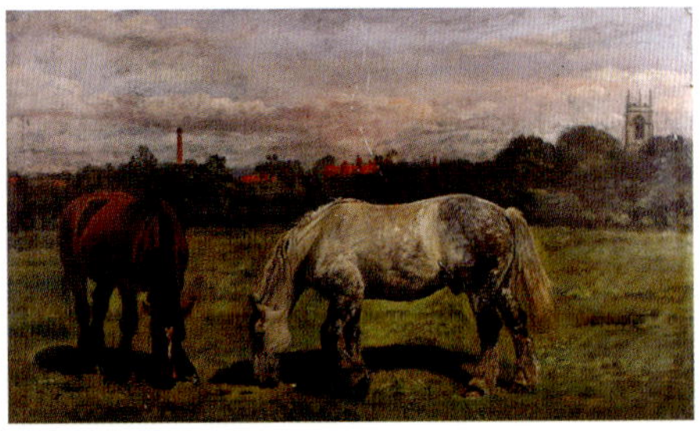

Millner, William Edward 1849–1895
Two Horses Grazing, with a Parish Church Tower in the Distance 1893
oil on hardboard 36.5 x 62
GANOH1375

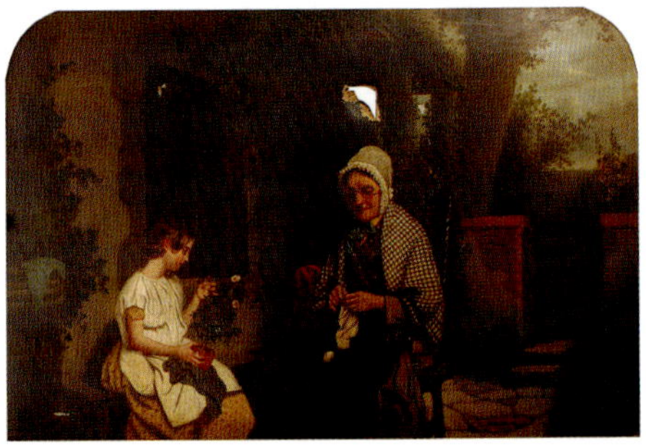

Millner, William Edward 1849–1895
An Old Woman Knitting and a Girl Holding a Pot Plant
oil on canvas 49.3 x 74.7
GANOH1374

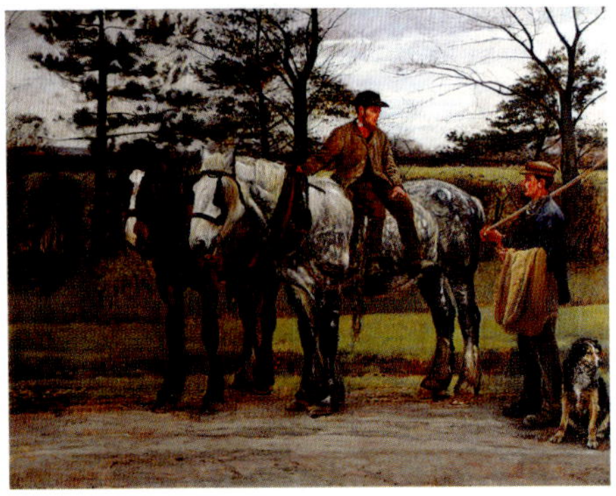

Millner, William Edward 1849–1895
Homeward Bound
oil on canvas 99.5 x 126
GANOH1386

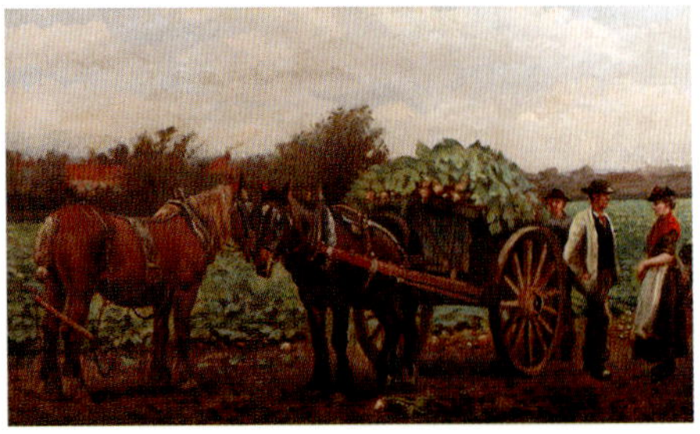

Millner, William Edward 1849–1895
Horses and Figures in a Turnip Field
oil on canvas 31.5 x 59.4
GANOH4217

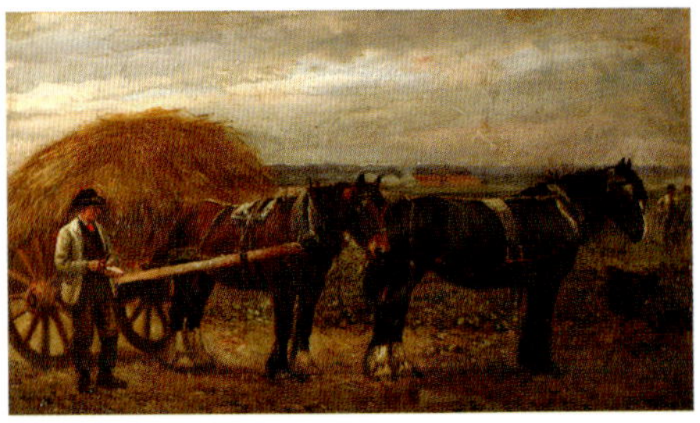

Millner, William Edward 1849–1895
Men, Horses and a Hay Cart
oil on hardboard 28.5 x 50
GANOH4202

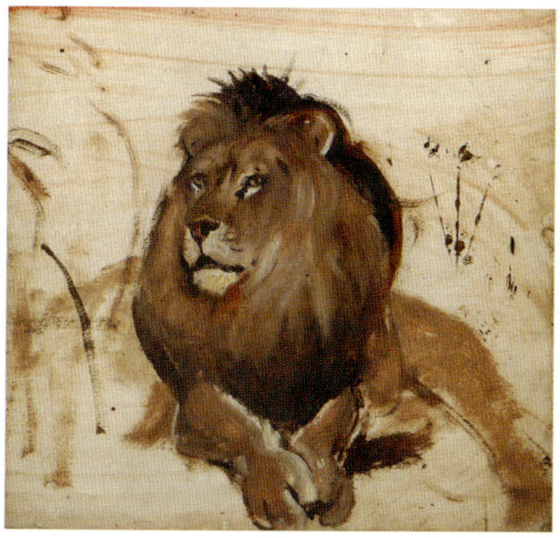

Millner, William Edward 1849–1895
Reclining Lion
oil on paper 24.6 x 24.3
GANOH4201

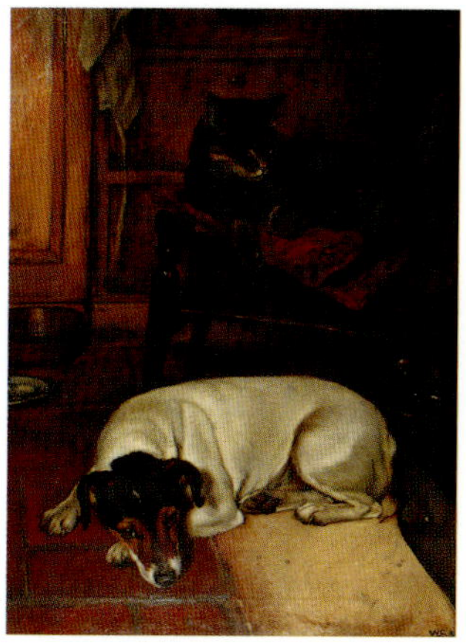

Millner, William Edward 1849–1895
'Spot' and His Friend
oil on canvas 75 x 52
GANOH4204

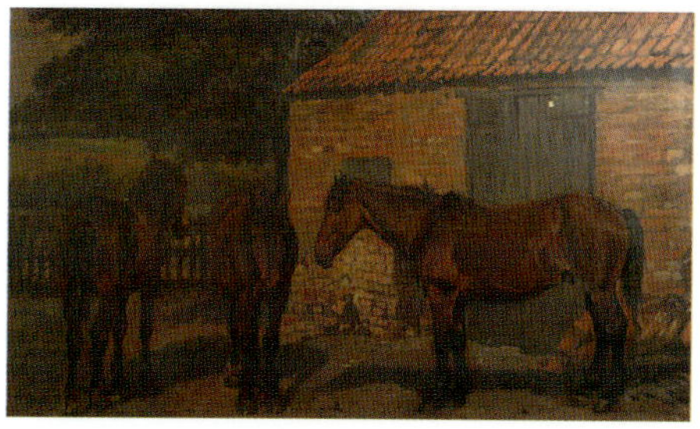

Millner, William Edward 1849–1895
Three Brown Horses Standing Outside a Stable
oil on card & strawboard 35.5 x 61.5
GANOH4211

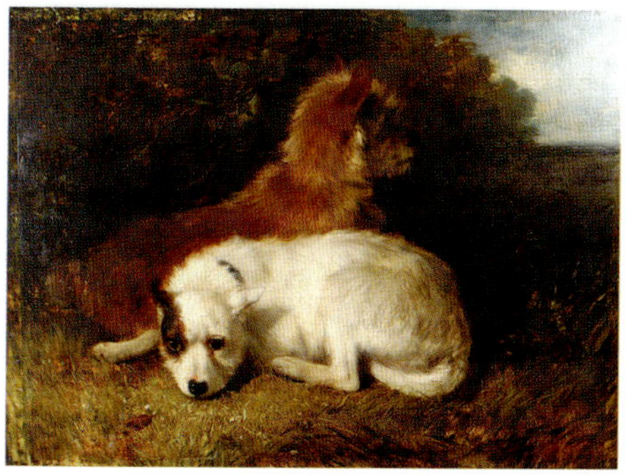

Millner, William Edward 1849–1895
Two Dogs
oil on canvas 62 x 81.5
GANOH4208

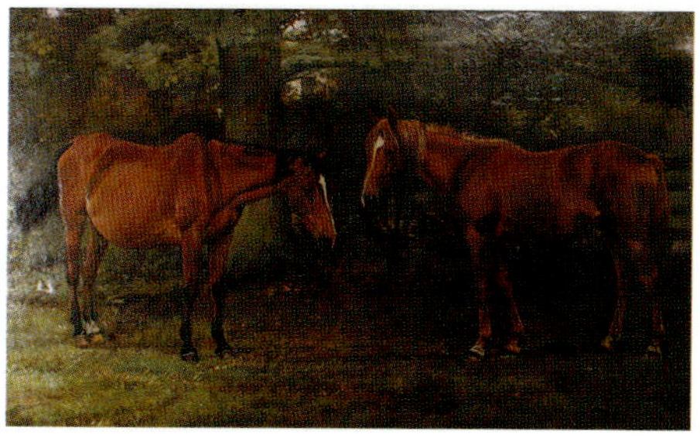

Millner, William Edward 1849–1895
Two Horses by a Wood
oil on canvas 75.5 x 126
GANOH4210

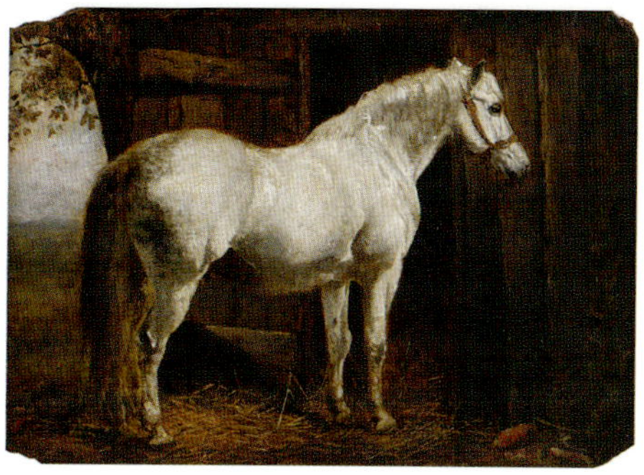

Millner, William Edward 1849–1895
White Horse
oil on millboard 24.1 x 34.2
GANOH4197

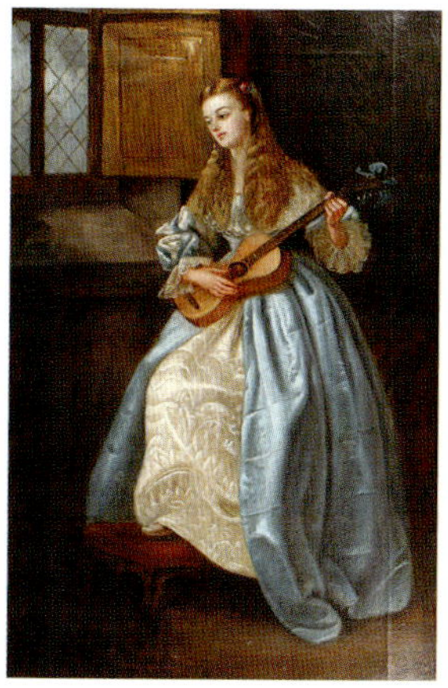

Millner, William Edward (attributed to)
1849–1895
A Lady with a Guitar
oil on canvas 59 x 36.8
GANOH4200

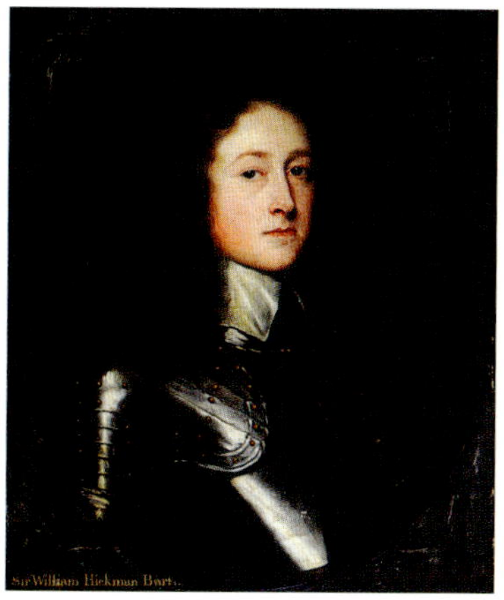

Squint Master active c.1660–c.1685
Sir William Hickman (1629–1682), Bt
oil on canvas 75 x 61
GANOHL 71 (P)

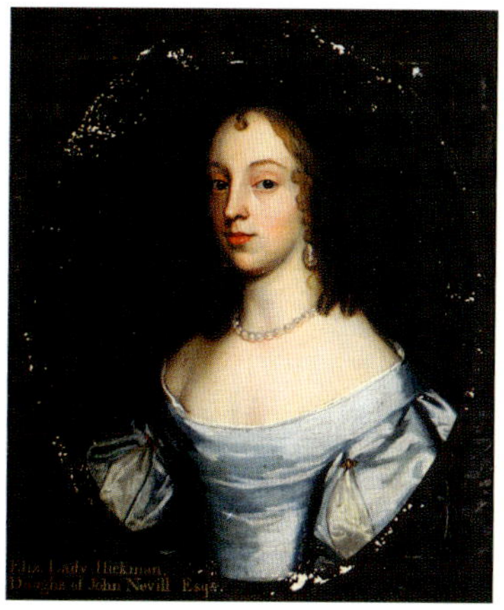

Squint Master active c.1660–c.1685
Elizabeth Hickman (1635–1691), Lady Hickman, Daughter of John Nevill
oil on canvas 75 x 61
GANOHL 65 (P)

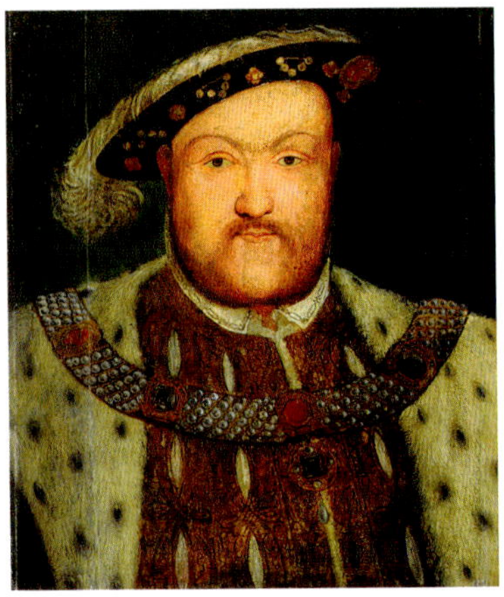

unknown artist
Henry VIII (1491–1547) c.1509–1547
oil on oak panel 62 x 52
GANOHL 62 (P)

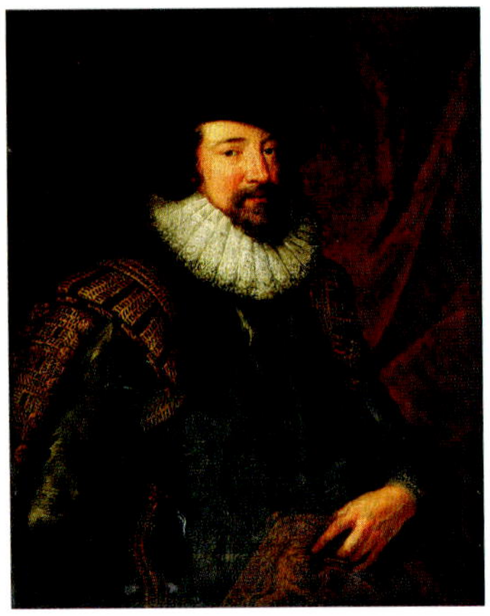

unknown artist
Francis Bacon (1561–1626), Baron Verulam, Viscount St Albans c.1590
oil on canvas 95 x 76
GANOHL 73 (P)

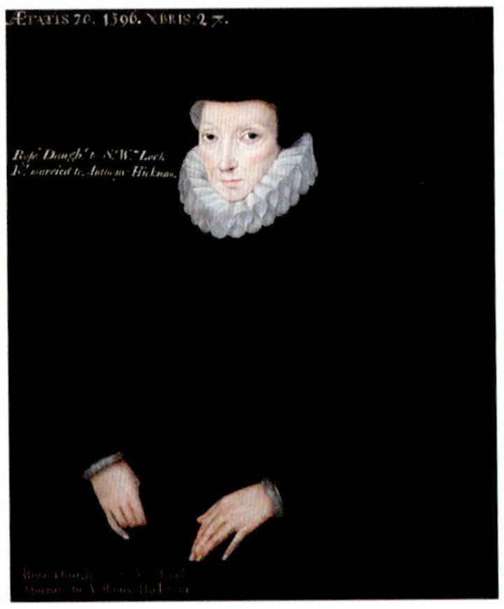

unknown artist
Rose Hickman (1526–1596), Daughter of Sir William Lock, Wife of Anthony Hickman 1596
oil on oak panel 75.5 x 61.5
GANOHL 66 (P)

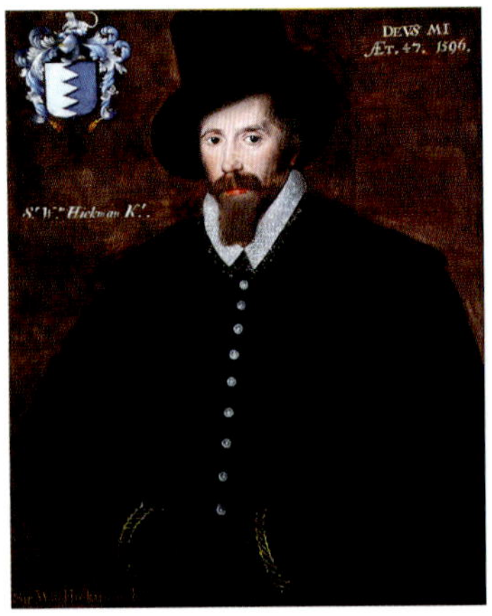

unknown artist
Sir William Hickman (d.1625), Kt 1596
oil on oak panel 76.5 x 61
GANOHL 69 (P)

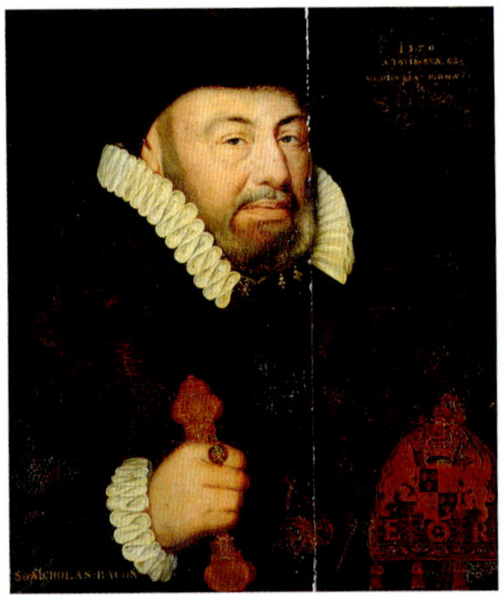

unknown artist 16th C
Sir Nicholas Bacon (1510–1597), Lord Keeper
1579 (?)
oil on oak panel 59 x 48.5
GANOHL 78 (P)

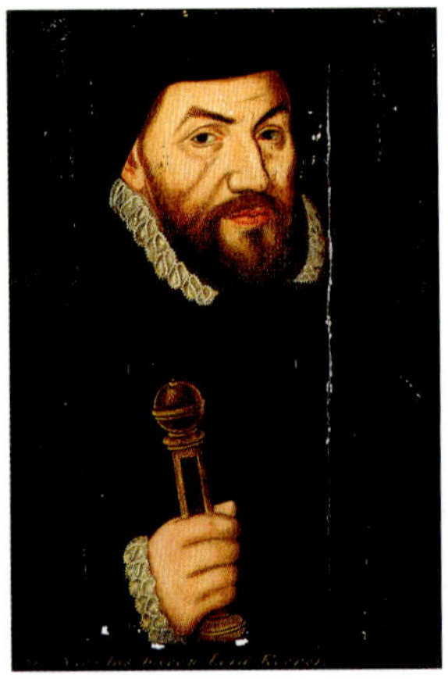

unknown artist 16th C
Sir Nicholas Bacon (1510–1597), Lord Keeper
oil on oak panel 51.5 x 33
GANOHL 60 (P)

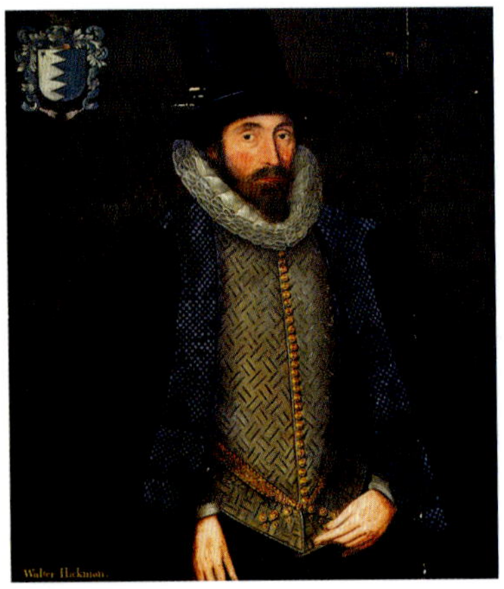

unknown artist
Walter Hickman c.1600
oil on oak panel 88 x 73
GANOHL 67 (P)

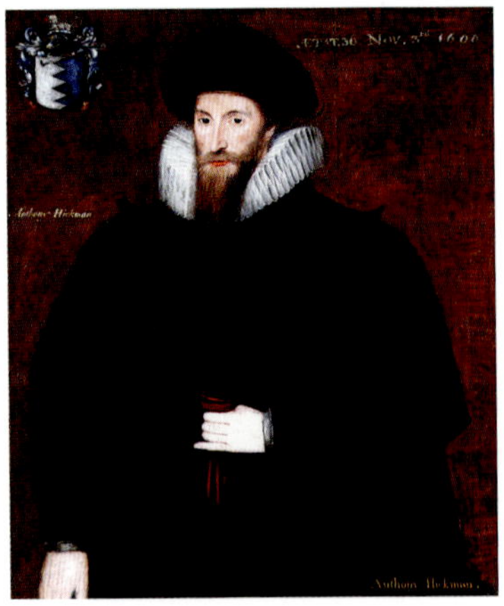

unknown artist
Antony Hickman 1606
oil on panel 90 x 70 (E)
PCF5 (P)

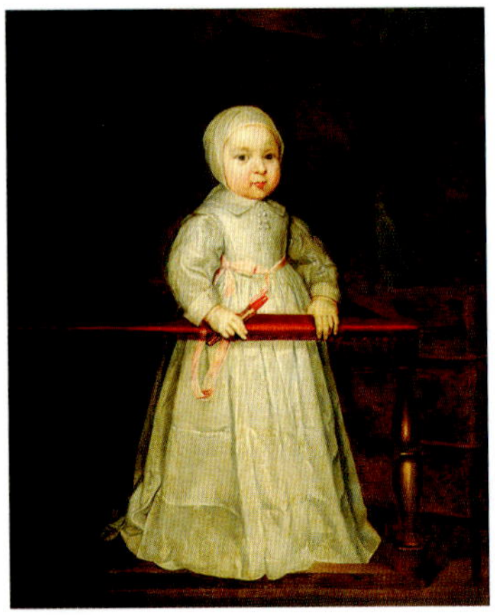

unknown artist
Lady Anne Wentworth c.1620
oil on canvas 104 x 82.5
GANOHL 58 (P)

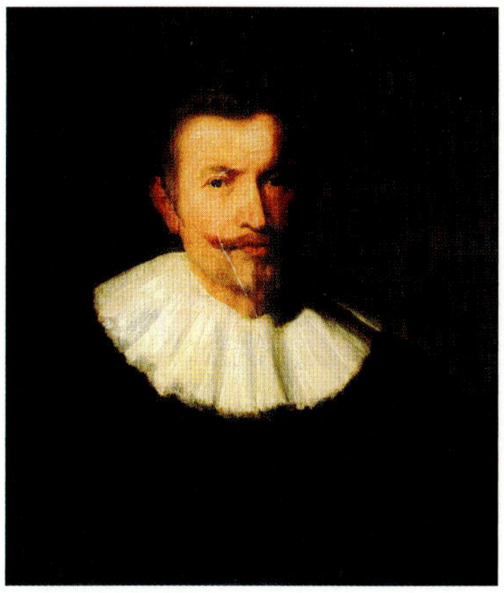

unknown artist
Portrait of a Bearded Gentleman c.1620
oil on canvas 62.5 x 52
GANOHL 59 (P)

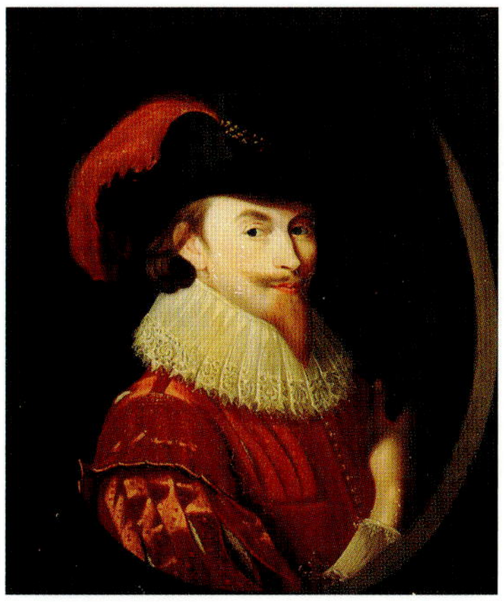

unknown artist
Sir Nathaniel Bacon (1585–1627), KB c.1620
oil on canvas 75 x 62
GANOHL 74 (P)

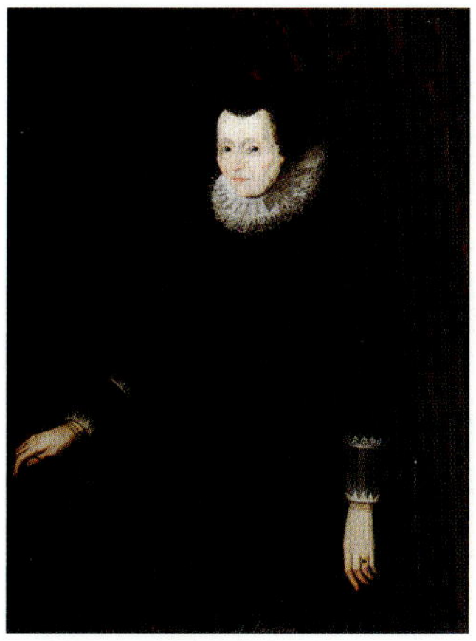

unknown artist
Elizabeth Willoughby, Lady Hickman, Daughter of William, Lord Willoughby of Parham c.1625
oil on oak panel 112 x 83
GANOHL 68 (P)

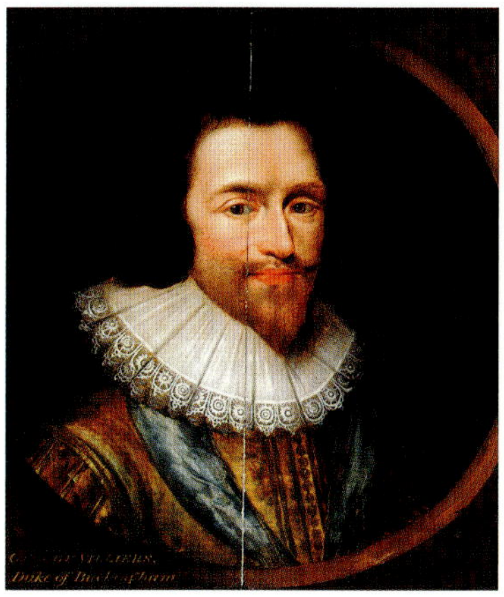

unknown artist
George Villiers (1592–1628), Duke of Buckingham c.1627
oil on oak panel 59 x 48.5
GANOHL 79 (P)

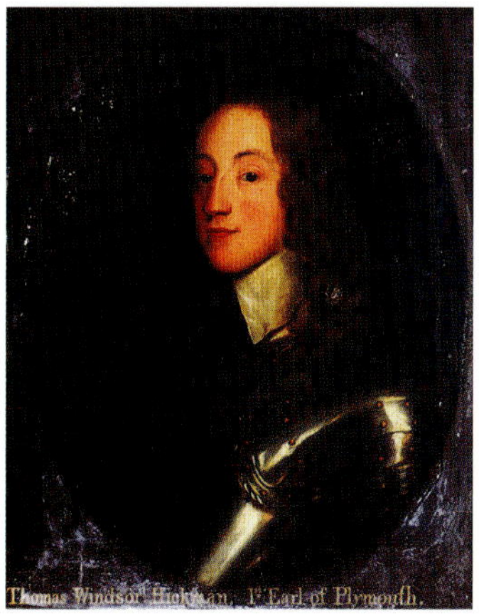

unknown artist
Thomas Windsor Hickman (c.1627–1687), 1st Earl of Plymouth c.1660
oil on canvas 73.5 x 59.5
GANOHL 76 (P)

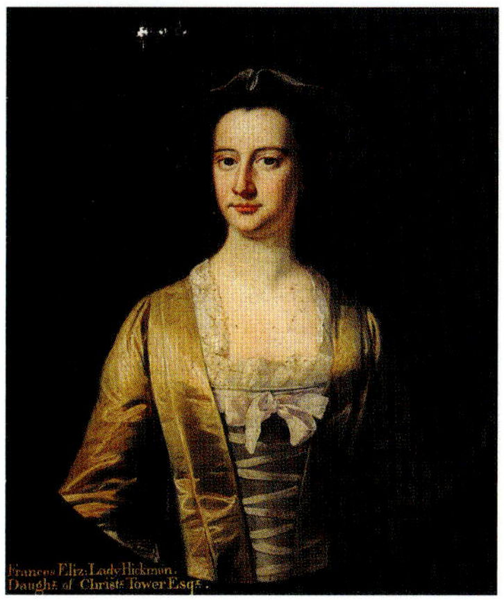

unknown artist
Frances Elizabeth, Lady Hickman, Daughter of Christopher Tower, Esq. c.1700–1750
oil on canvas 73.5 x 60.5
GANOHL 63 (P)

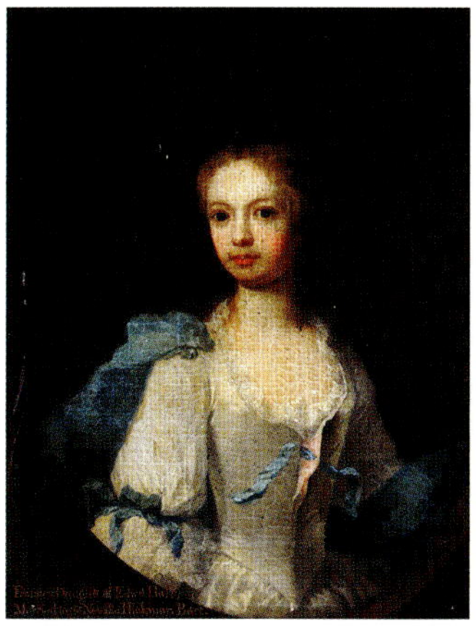

unknown artist
Frances Hickman, Daughter of Edward Hall, Wife of Sir Neville Hickman, Bt c.1720
oil on canvas 74 x 61.5
GANOHL 64 (P)

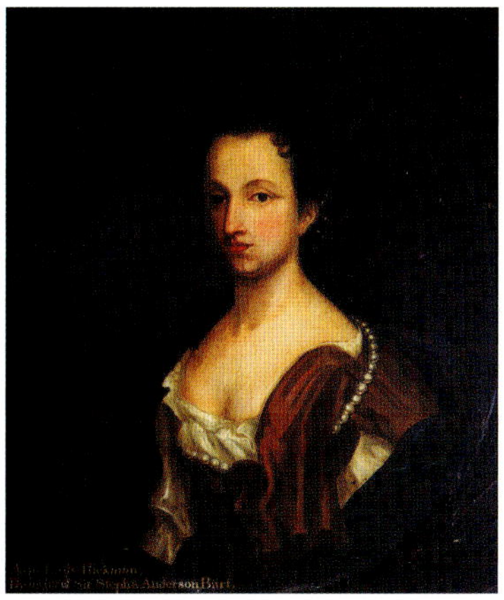

unknown artist 18th C
Ann Hickman, Lady Hickman, Daughter of Sir Stephen Anderson, Bt
oil on canvas 74.8 x 60.8
GANOHL 70 (P)

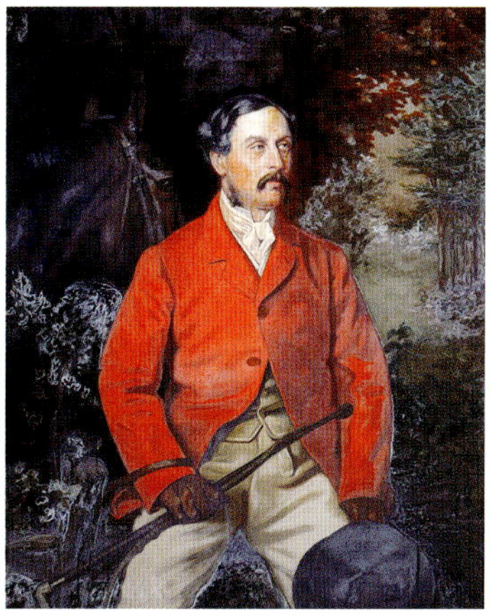

unknown artist
Sir Henry Hickman Bacon (1820–1872), Bt c.1860
oil on canvas 125.5 x 100.5
GANOHL 81 (P)

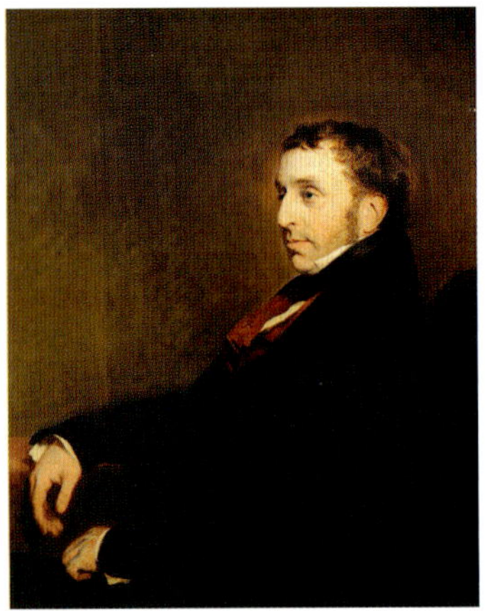

unknown artist
Sir Henry Hickman Bacon (1820–1872), Bt
c.1860
oil on canvas 90 x 70
GANOHL 83 (P)

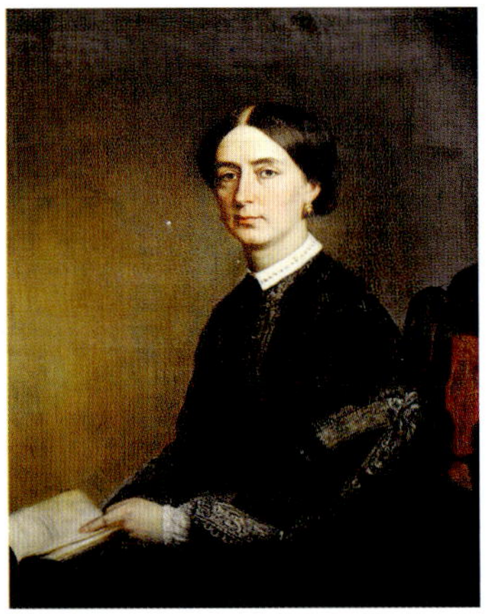

unknown artist
Elizabeth Beckett (1829–1885), Daughter of Sir Thomas Beckett, Wife of Sir Hickman Bacon, Bt c.1880
oil on canvas 90 x 70
GANOHL 82 (P)

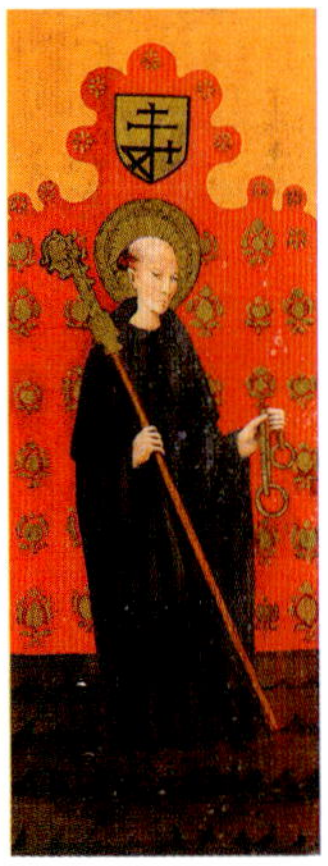

unknown artist
*Cloaked Man with a Staff and Keys**
oil on panel 73.5 x 27
PCF2

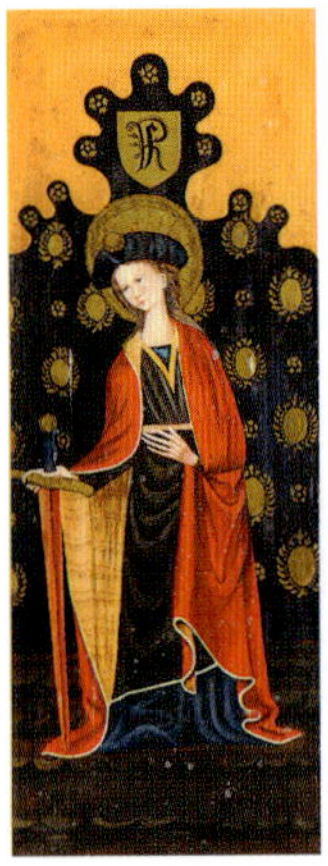

unknown artist
*Lady with a Sword**
oil on panel 73.5 x 27
PCF3

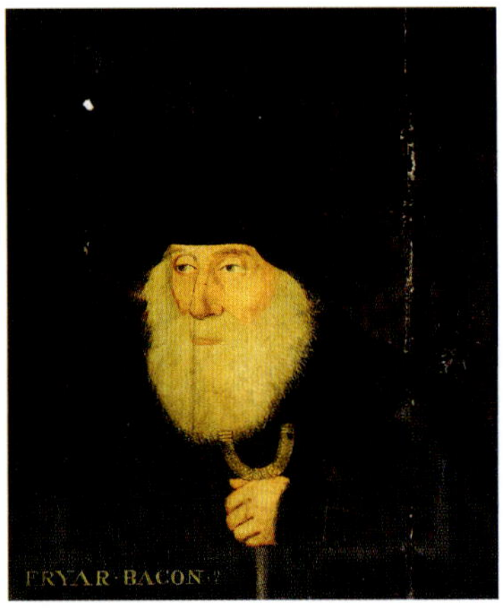

unknown artist
Fryar Bacon
oil on oak panel 59 x 48.5
GANOHL 80 (P)

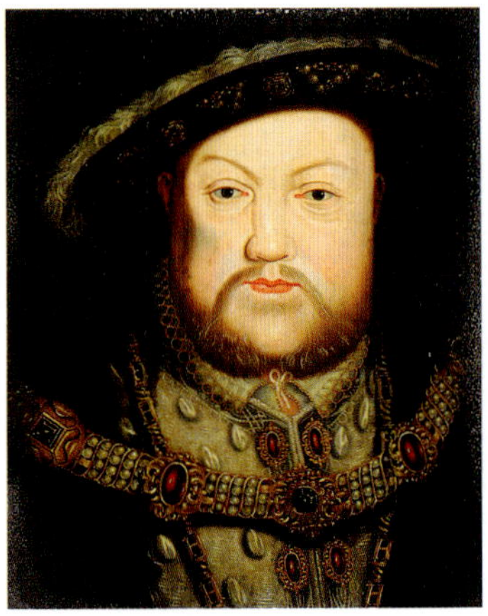

unknown artist
Henry VIII (1491–1547)
oil on oak panel 51.5 x 40.5
GANOHL 61 (P)

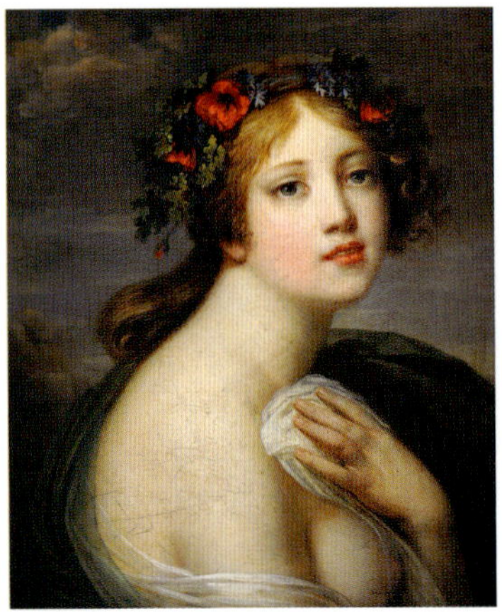

unknown artist
Portrait of a Young Lady
oil on canvas 44.5 x 36.5
GANOH4560

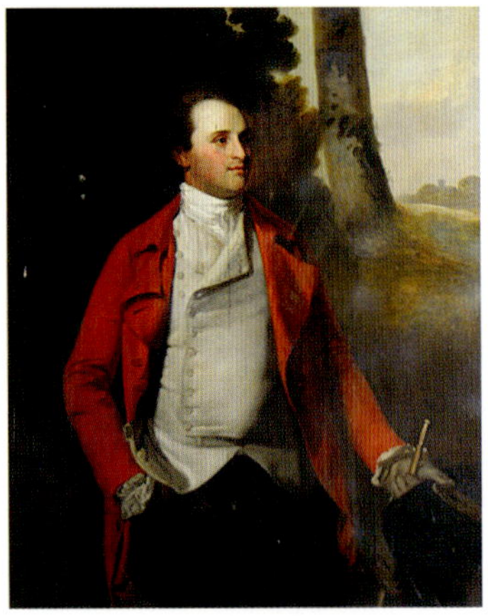

Walton, Henry 1746–1813
Sir Edmund Bacon (1749–1820), 8th Bt
oil on canvas 125 x 99.5
GANOHL 85 (P)

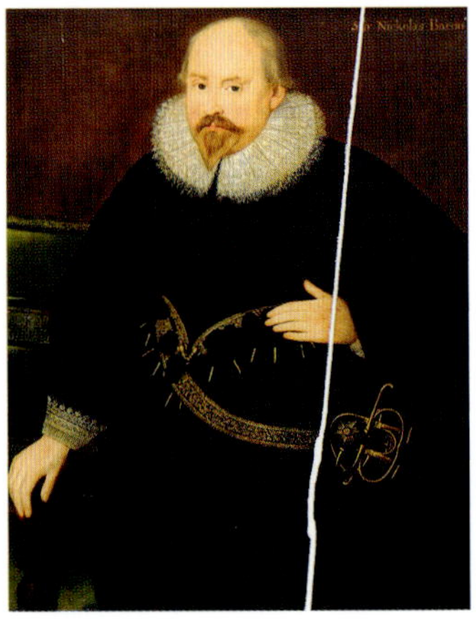

Zuccaro, Federico (attributed to) c.1541–1609
Sir Nicholas Bacon (d.1624)
oil on oak panel 101.5 x 77
GANOHL 57 (P)

Facing page: Bower, Edward, 1597–1667, *Portrait of a Gentleman Cleric* (detail), North Lincolnshire Museums Service (p. 357)

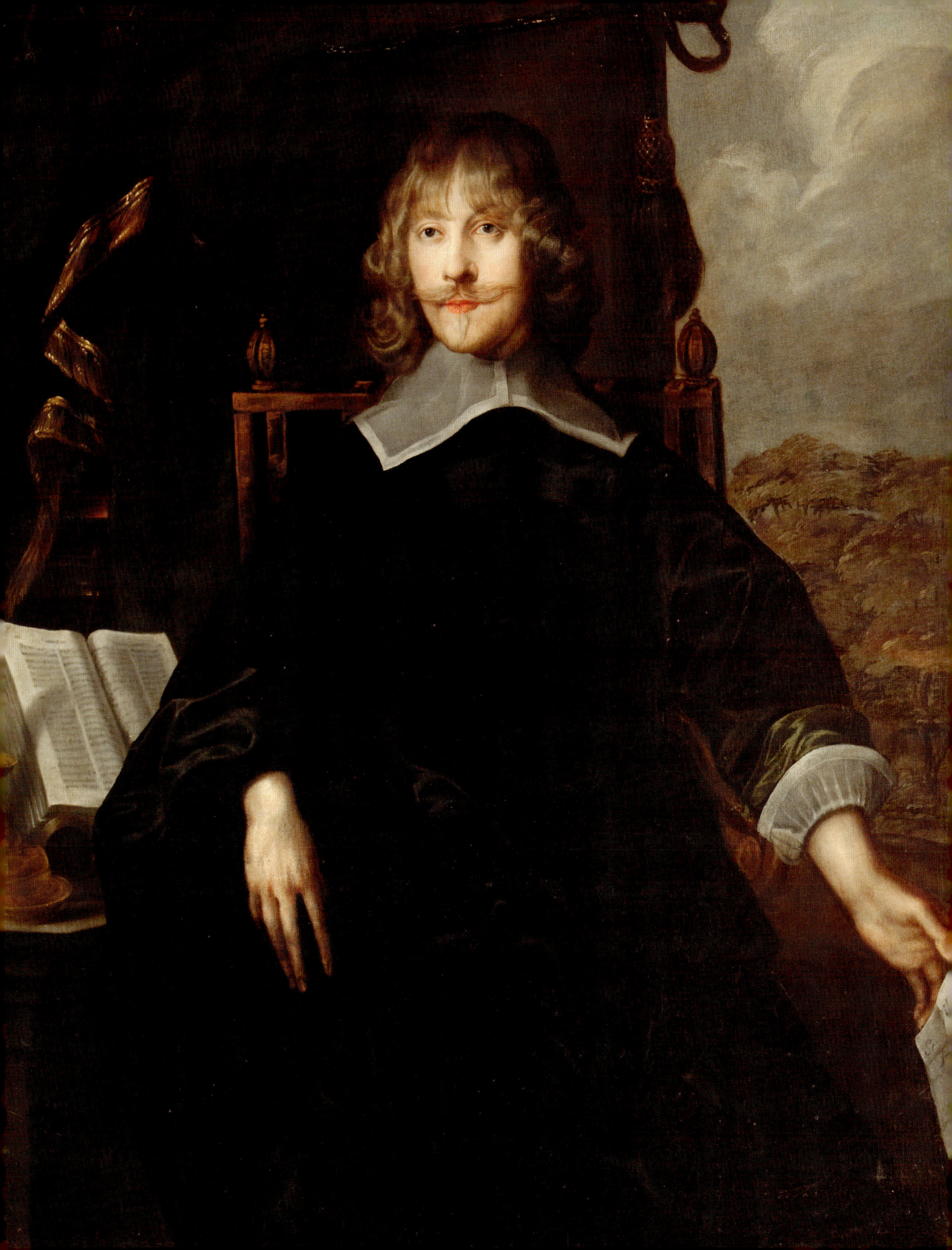

West Lindsey District Council

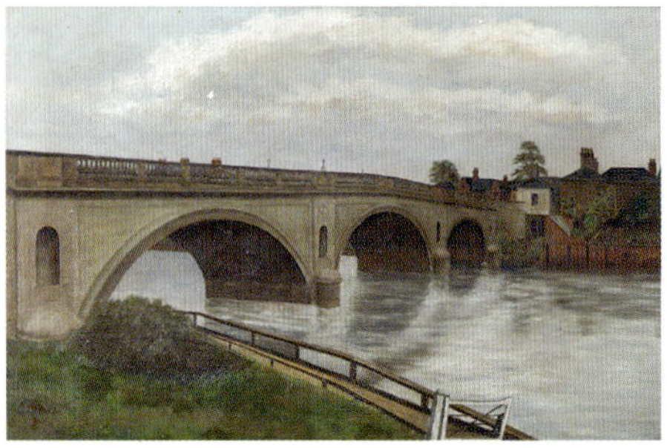

Bell, A.
Trent Bridge 1897
oil on canvas 30 x 45
2

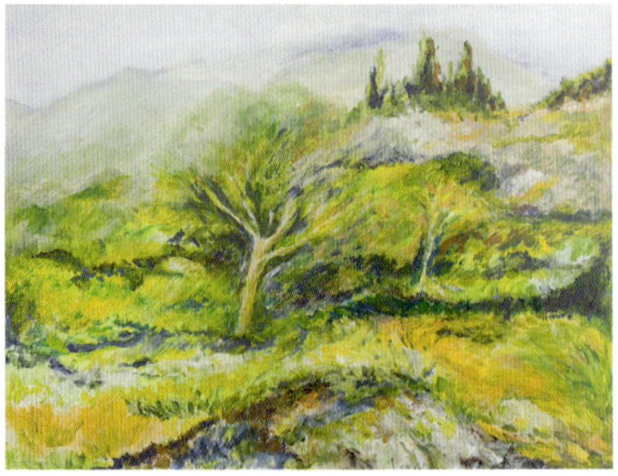

Schublaus, A. M. (attributed to)
Dingle Halbinsel, Süd-Irland 2007
oil on canvas 41 x 55
3

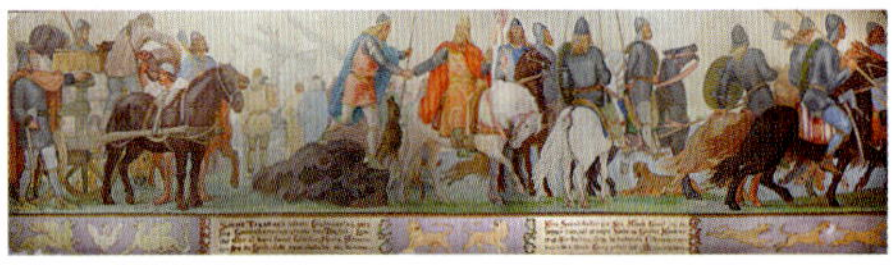

unknown artist
Sweyn's Last Journey to England, 1013
oil on canvas on board 98 x 350
1

Grantham Museum

Grantham Museum is a local history museum, founded in 1926, which forms part of Lincolnshire County Council Heritage Service. The artworks which were added to the Collection in its early days were collected largely on the criteria of their being old. This accounts for the eclectic mix of paintings showing still life or romantic landscapes, with little or no local connection.

In recent years, however, collecting has been confined to paintings which show local scenes or buildings, or those which are by local artists.

Paintings of local topographical scenes include views of St Wulfram's Church, Grantham wharf and the famous 'Beehive Inn', named so for the live beehive within its sign. In 1989 the Museum acquired the painting of the *Mid Lent Fair, Grantham Market Place, Lincolnshire* with assistance from the Victoria and Albert Museum Purchase Grant Fund, adding a rare naïve impression by an unknown artist of the fair dating from the early-nineteenth century to our Collection.

Within the collection at Grantham Museum are some interesting paintings by local artists, such as Joe Cross and Isa Connett. Another local artist, Alice M. Edwards, trained at the Slade School of Art in London. She joined Grantham Art Club in the 1930s, and worked mainly in the field of portraiture. She gave up painting in 1939 because of the War. Her portrait of *Mr Forsgate-Weekly (b.1872), Mayor of Grantham (1920–1937)* commemorates both Edwards as an artist and the sitter's contribution to local government in the early-twentieth century.

A contemporary local Grantham artist represented in the collection is Terry Shelbourne, who draws the weekly cartoon for the *Grantham Journal.* His portrait of *Baroness Margaret Thatcher (b.1925)* illustrates an additional feature to our collecting policy; acquiring portraits of famous local people. Also in this category falls the painting of *Sir Isaac Newton (1642–1727)* by Godfrey Kneller, which was acquired with assistance from the Victoria and Albert Museum Purchase Grant Fund, the Art Fund and local support in 1987. The Museum also collects portraits of less well-known but locally important people, such as *Richard Hornsby Senior (1790–1864)*, the industrial magnate of the late-nineteenth century, who is depicted in a portrait by an unknown artist. Also in this vein is the collection of portraits of members of the Middlemore family, a local family of note in the late-eighteenth and early-nineteenth century. Similarly, a painting of an unknown sitter may actually be of William Knott Dunn, a local man who lived in the early-nineteenth century and was connected with the Gregory family of nearby Harlaxton Manor.

In common with many small museums, it can be seen that Grantham Museum is indebted to the Museums, Libraries and Archives/Victoria and Albert Museum Purchase Grant Fund and the Art Fund for their generous assistance, and many of the most important paintings in our Collection could not have been acquired without their help. We are also indebted to the many people who have kindly donated works of art to us.

Deborah Bircham, Collections Officer, Stamford and Grantham Museums

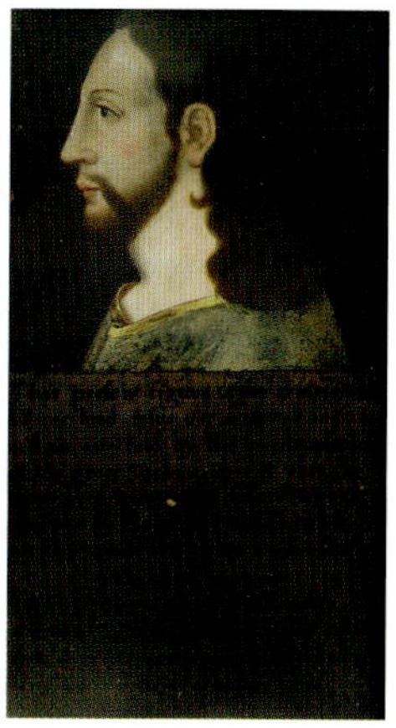

Clef, M.
Christ
oil on wood 27 x 14.5
LCNGR:1991.792

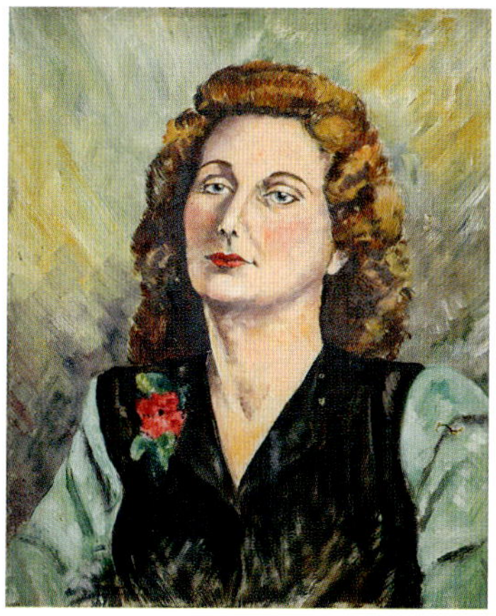

Connett, Isa
Self Portrait
acrylic on canvas 51 x 40.5
LCNGR:876

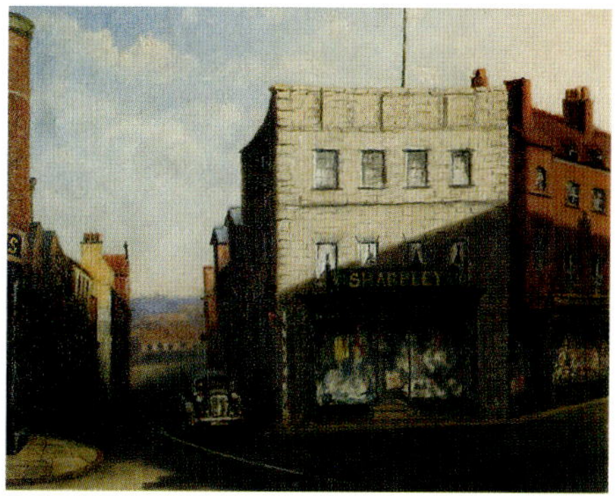

Cross, Joe
View of Watergate with Sharpley's Building, Grantham, Lincolnshire 1939
oil on canvas 29.5 x 37
LCNGR:1995.175

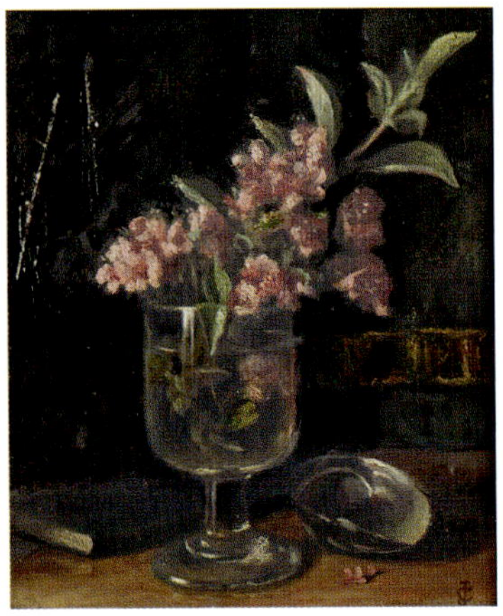

Cross, Joe
Still Life
oil on canvas 28 x 23
LCNGR:1994.58

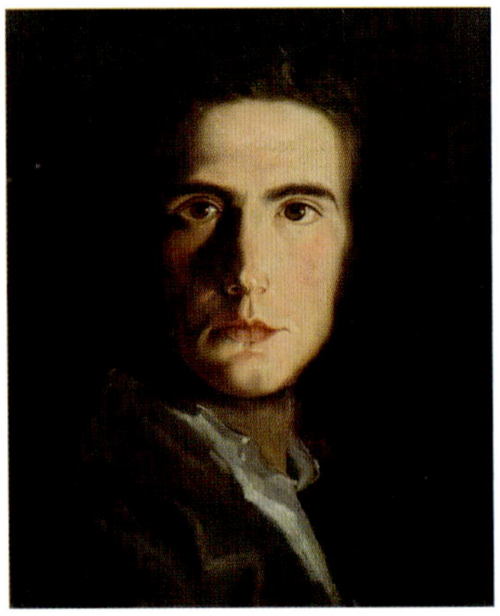

Dawson, Henry 1811–1878
Self Portrait
oil on wood 40 x 32
LCNGR:1995.230

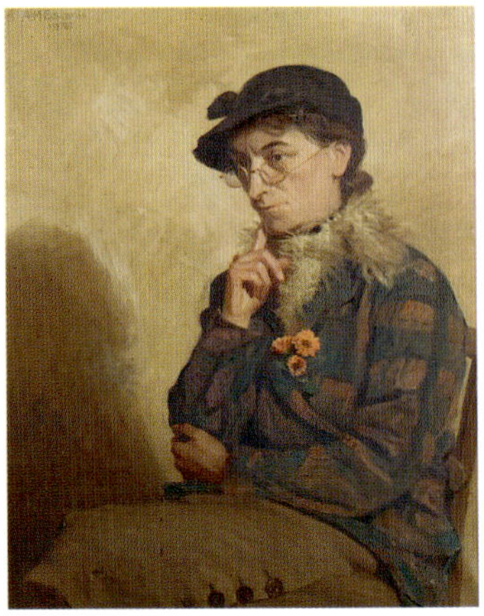

Edwards, Alice M. active c.1930–1938
Miss Norah Hall as Mrs Milsom in 'Call It a Day' by Dodie Smith c.1930
oil on canvas 89 x 70
LCNGR:1994.19

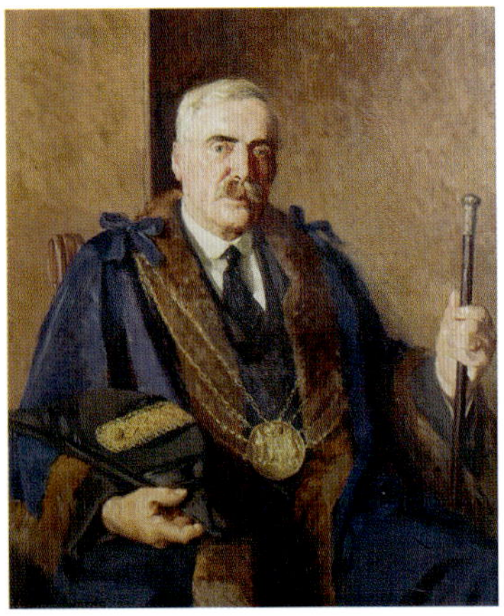

Edwards, Alice M. active c.1930–1938
Mr Forsgate-Weekly (b.1872), Mayor of Grantham (1920–1937) 1937
oil on canvas 107.5 x 87.5
LCNGR:2004.28

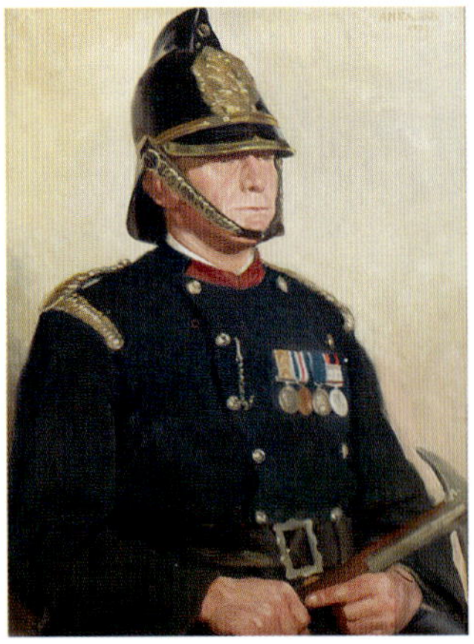

Edwards, Alice M. active c.1930–1938
Captain Spriggs, Ruston and Hornsby Fire Brigade 1938
oil on canvas 90.5 x 64.5
LCNGR:1995.249

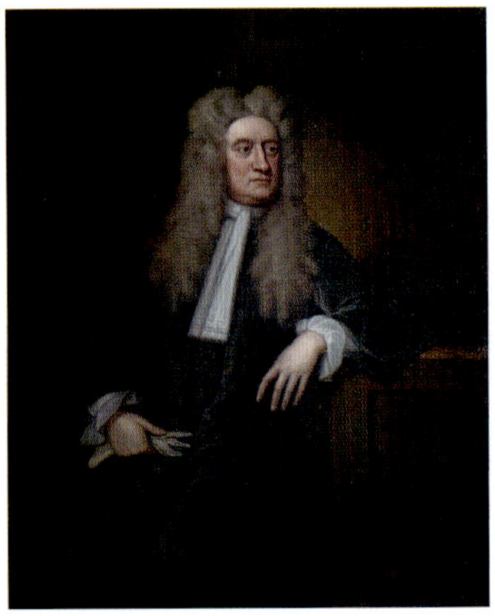

Kneller, Godfrey 1646–1723
Sir Isaac Newton (1642–1727)
oil on canvas 126 x 100 (E)
LCNGR:1995.3806

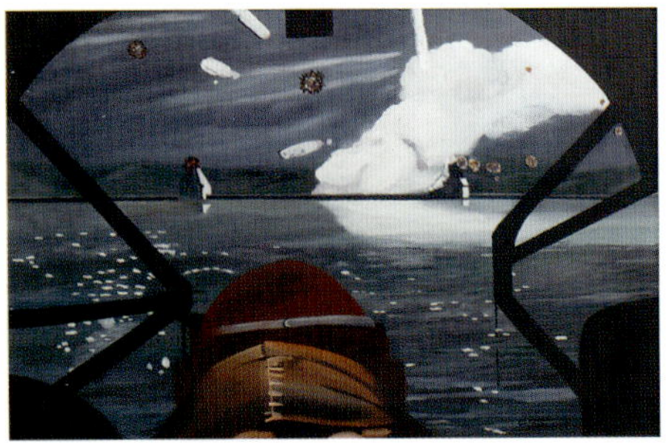

Massey, George Edward 1919–2007
Lancaster Crew's View of a Dam, 1943 (painted from a still of the film 'The Dam Busters') 1992
oil on canvas 49.5 x 75
LCNGR:1997.135

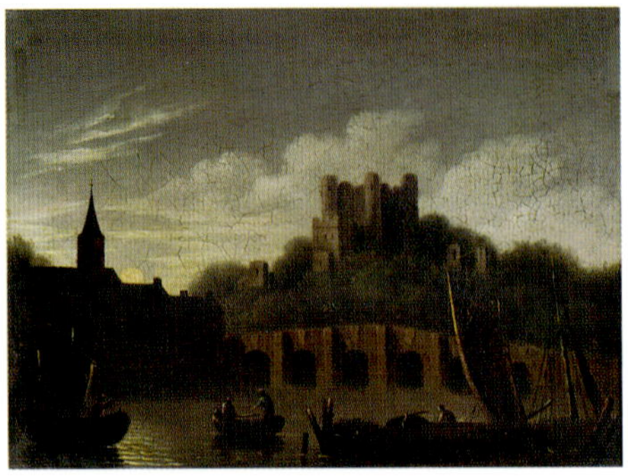

Pether, William 1731–1819
View of a Castle
oil on card 22.5 x 29
LCNGR:1995.197

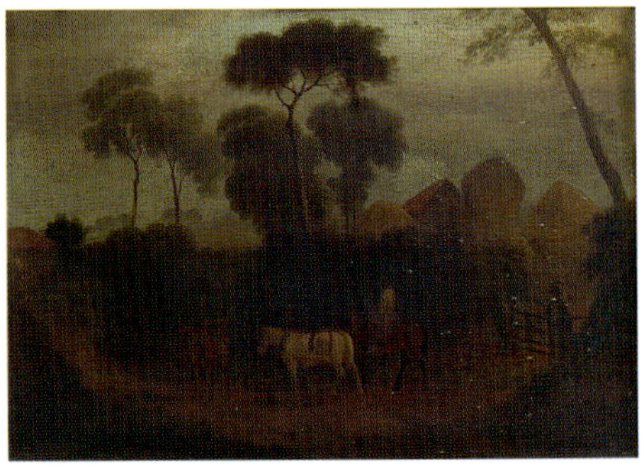

Rhodes
My Father's Old Hovel
oil on wood 29.7 x 41.7
LCNGR:1995.227

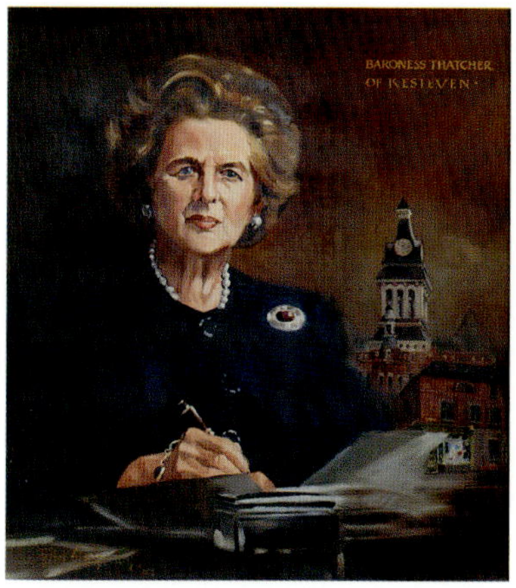

Shelbourne, Terry b.1930
Baroness Margaret Thatcher (b.1925) 1996
oil on canvas 71 x 61
LCNGR:1996.503

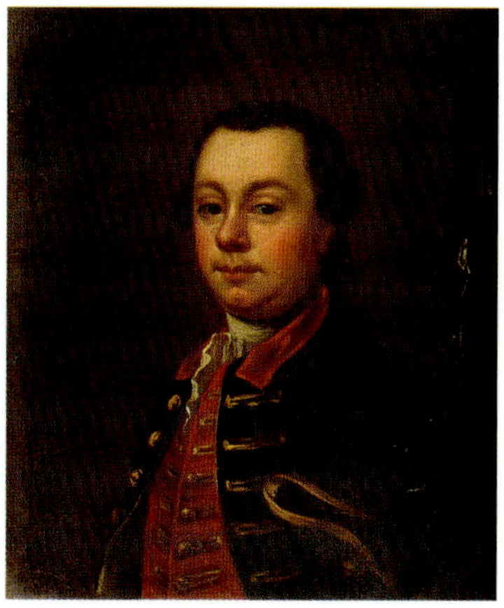

unknown artist
William Richard Middlemore of Grantham and Somerby Hall (1731–1772) c.1750
oil on wood 18.5 x 14.7
LCNGR:1991.771

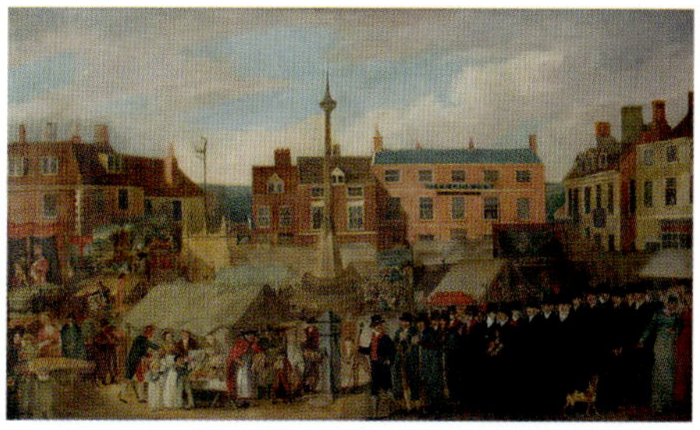

unknown artist
Mid Lent Fair, Grantham Market Place, Lincolnshire c.1800
oil on canvas 63.5 x 104
LCNGR:1991.315

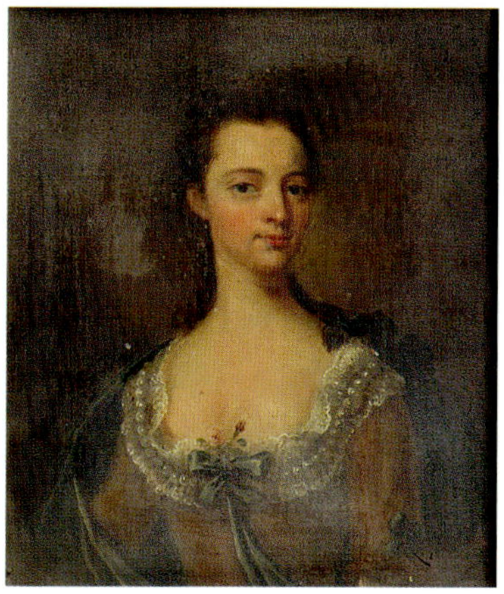

unknown artist
Mrs Mary Middlemore c.1800
oil on wood 18.3 x 15
LCNGR:1991.772

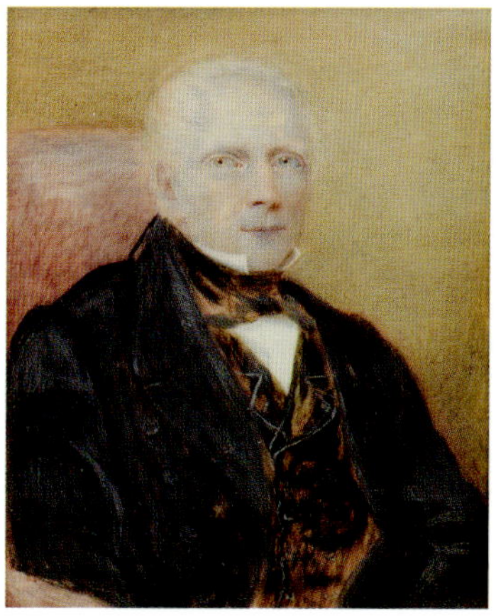

unknown artist
William Richard Middlemore of Nottingham (1767–1815) c.1800
oil on card 10.3 x 8
LCNGR:1991.775

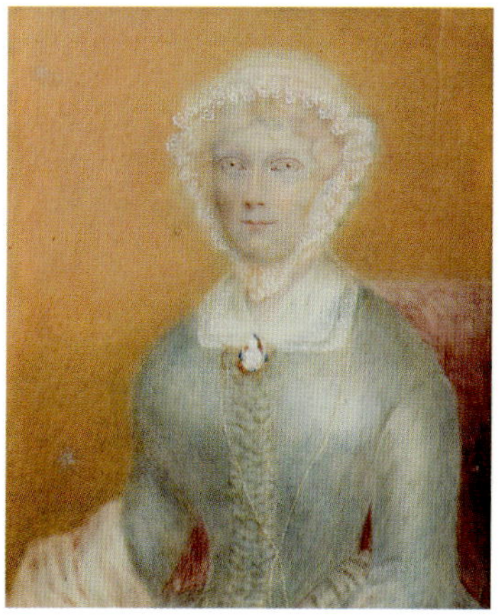

unknown artist
Mrs Susanna Middlemore of Orston Hall (c.1770–1849), Wife of William Richard Middlemore of Nottingham c.1800
oil on card 10.1 x 8
LCNGR:1991.774

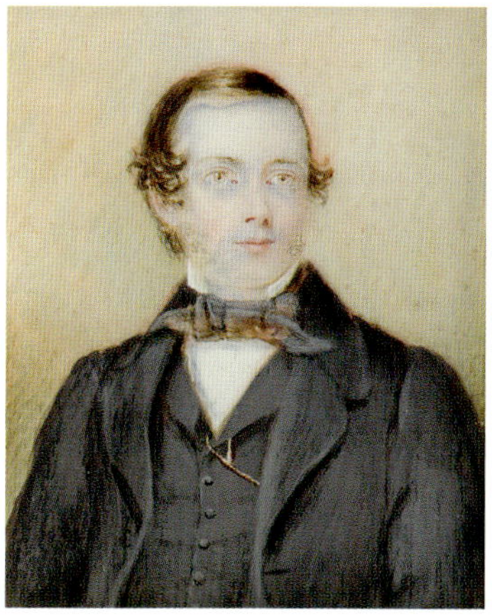

unknown artist
Robert Frederick Middlemore (1816–1890), Colonel of 91st Regiment c.1850
oil on card 9.5 x 7.5
LCNGR:1991.773

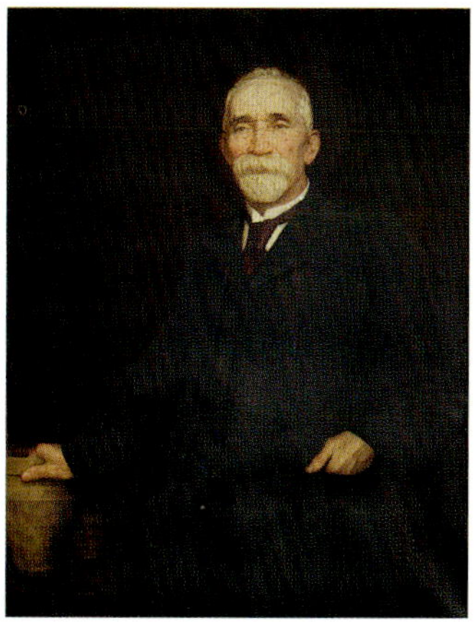

unknown artist
Henry Preston, Founder of Grantham Museum 1926
oil on canvas 110 x 85
LCNGR:1995.3588

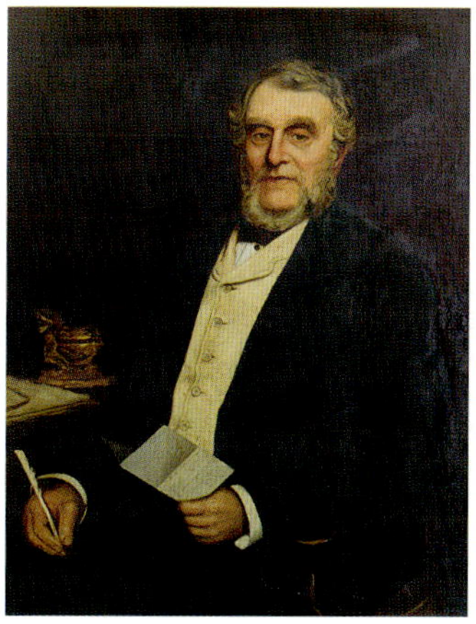

unknown artist
Algernon Gray Tollemache (1805–1892)
oil on canvas 115.5 x 89
LCNGR:1997.131

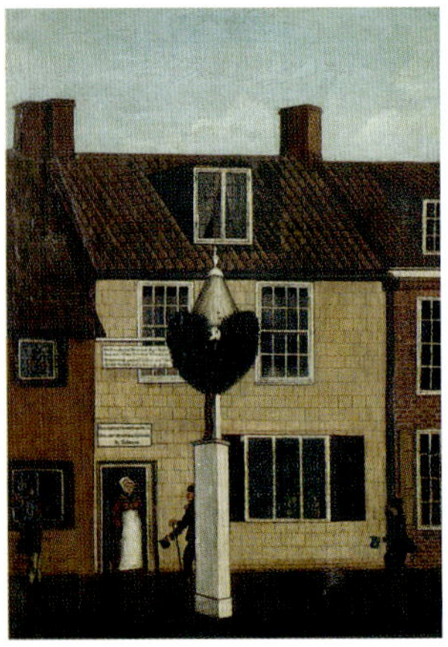

unknown artist
'Beehive' Public House and Landlady Elizabeth Wood
oil on canvas 64.6 x 46.4
LCNGR:1995.235

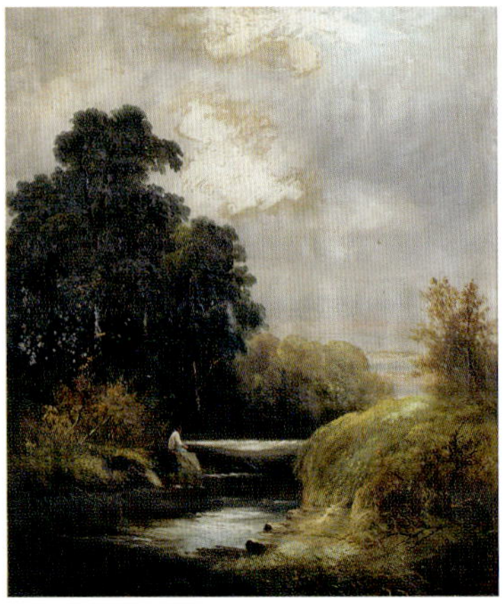

unknown artist
Landscape with a River and Trees
oil on canvas 59.7 x 49.3
LCNGR:1995.250

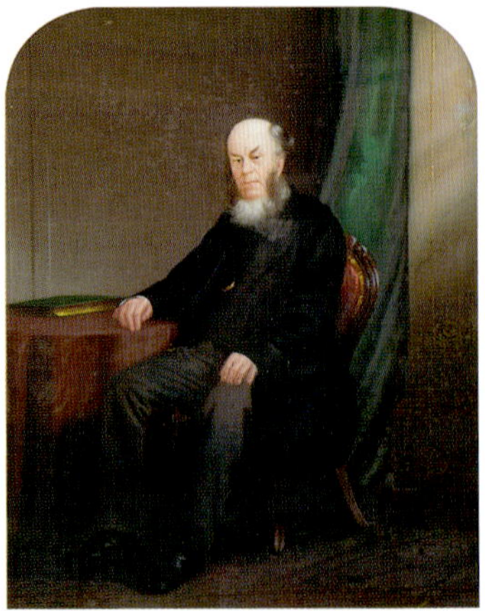

unknown artist
Mr Palmer of Manthorpe Mill
oil on board 38.5 x 29.5
LCNGR:1995.208

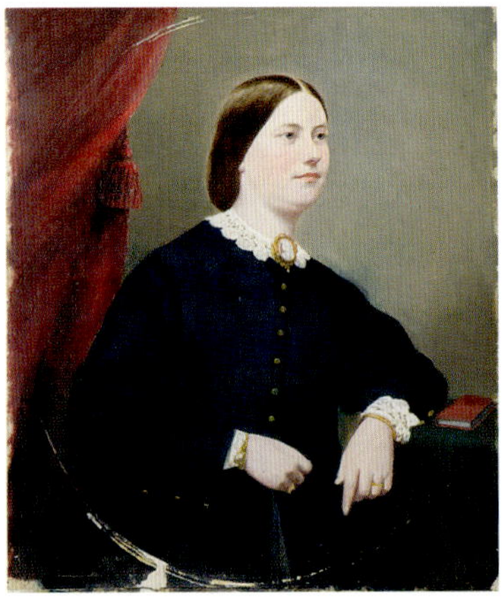

unknown artist
Mrs William Hornsby
oil on card 33 x 27.2
LCNGR:1991.807

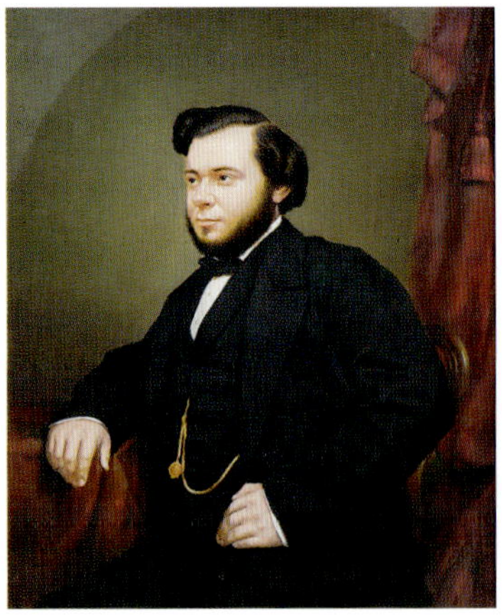

unknown artist
Richard Hornsby Senior (1790–1864)
oil on canvas 38.5 x 32
LCNGR:1995.3809

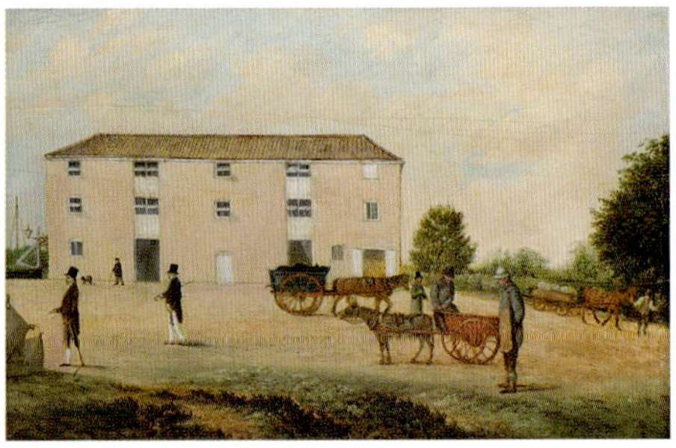

unknown artist
Ponies and Carts on Grantham Wharf, Lincolnshire
oil on wood 25.8 x 38.7
LCNGR:1995.181

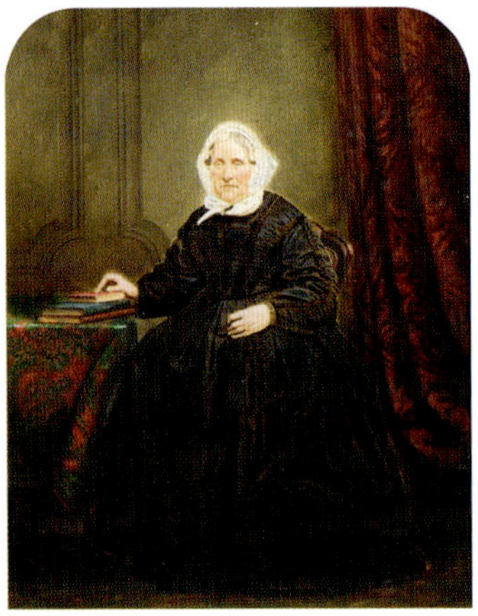

unknown artist
Portrait of an Unknown Lady
oil on card 35.5 x 27.3
LCNGR:1995.209

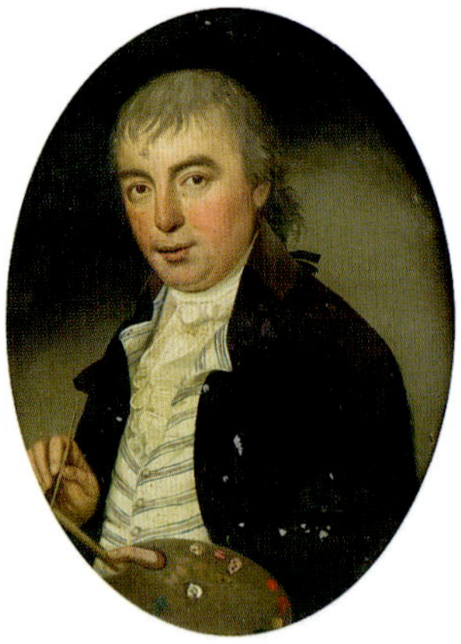

unknown artist
Portrait of an Unknown Man (possibly William Knott Dunn)
oil on tin 28.4 x 21.4
LCNGR:1991.806

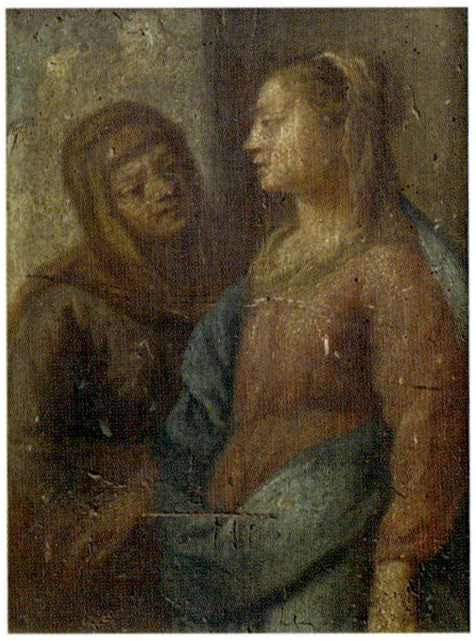

unknown artist
Portrait of Two Unknown Ladies
oil on wood 34.7 x 25.5
LCNGR:1995.228

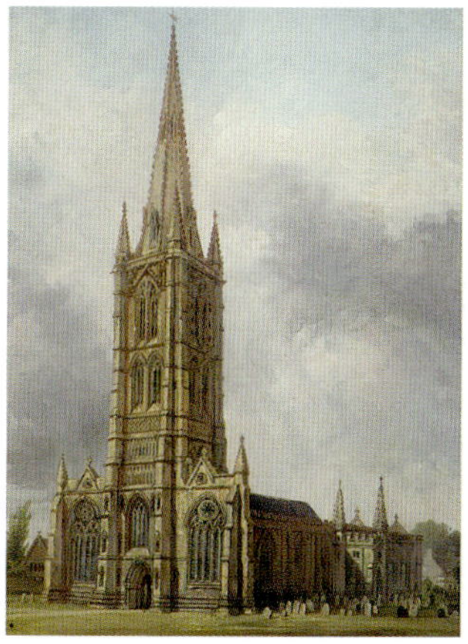

unknown artist
St Wulfram's Church, Grantham, Lincolnshire
oil on wood 28.9 x 22
LCNGR:1991.805

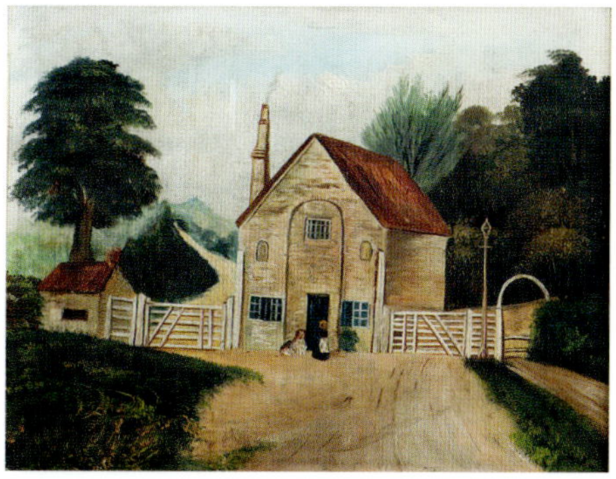

unknown artist
Toll House
oil on card 29.6 x 37.1
LCNGR:1995.182

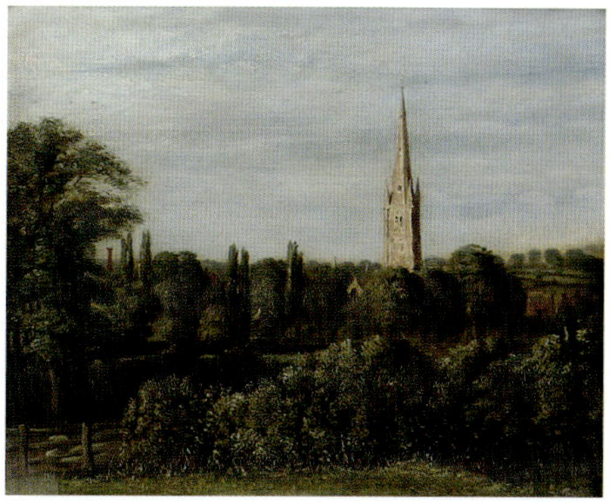

unknown artist
View of Grantham from Sedgwick Meadows, Lincolnshire
oil on card 17.8 x 21.6
LCNGR:1995.225

Grimsby Institute of Further & Higher Education

For over 120 years, the 'Art School', now known as Grimsby Institute of Further & Higher Education's East Coast School of Art & Design, has been providing high quality education in the arts. During that time the Art School has secured its reputation by producing some highly successful and nationally recognised artists and designers.

Included in the Collection are pieces by Nicholas Volley who attended the Art School in the 1960s. Nicholas went on to study at the Slade, where he was taught by William Coldstream and Euan Uglow. Nick enjoys a successful career and his paintings are included in many international collections. We were privileged to include Nick's work in our Retrospective Exhibition celebrating the Art School's 120-year anniversary in 2006.

Amanda Rudolph, Dean of Faculty, Creative Arts

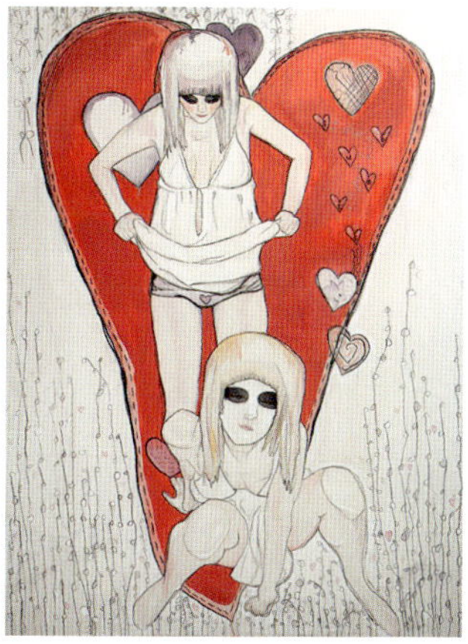

Green, Roberta
Love Birds c.2005
oil on canvas 200 x 150
12

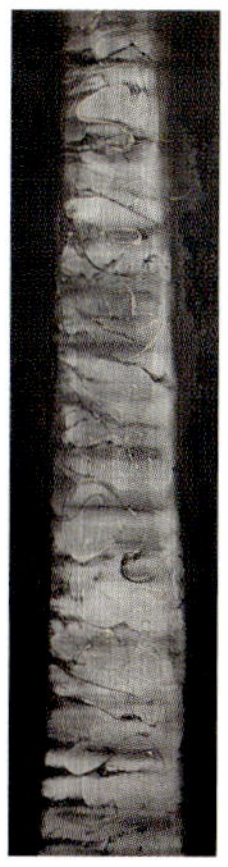

Green, Tracy
Black 2008
oil on canvas 240 x 60
28

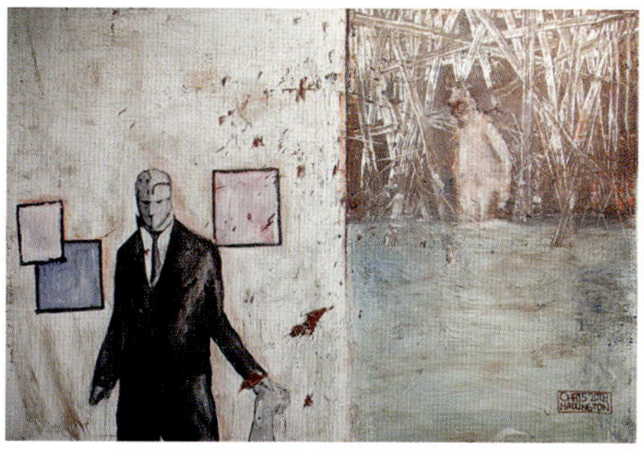

Hadlington, Chris
Man in a Suit 2003
oil on canvas 150 x 180
19

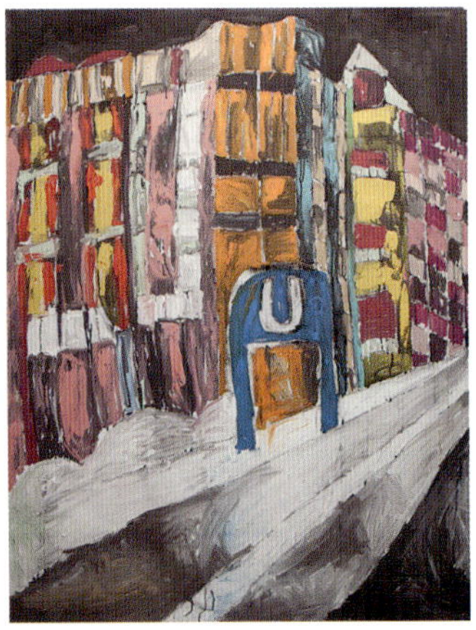

Holnb, Louiza
Berlin in Pink c.2006
oil on canvas 180 x 120
13

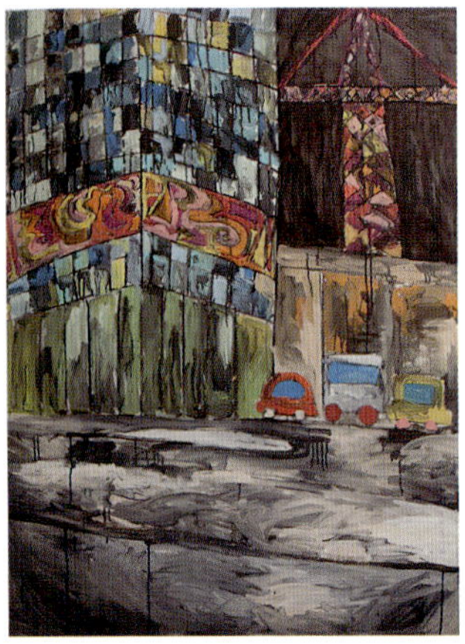

Holnb, Louiza
Berlin with Cars c.2006
oil on canvas 180 x 120
14

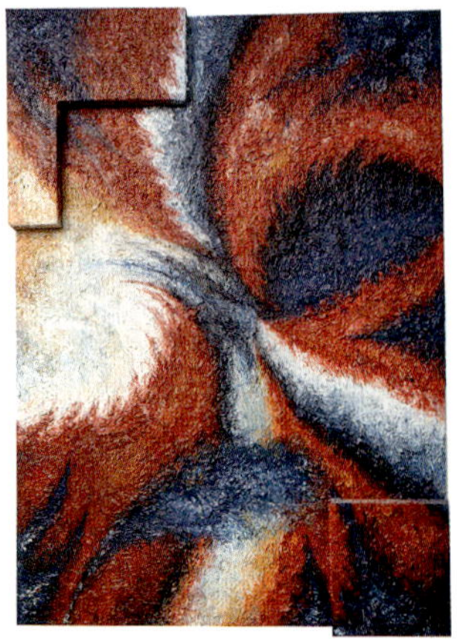

Jerome, Lindsey
Untitled
oil on canvas 130 x 102
29

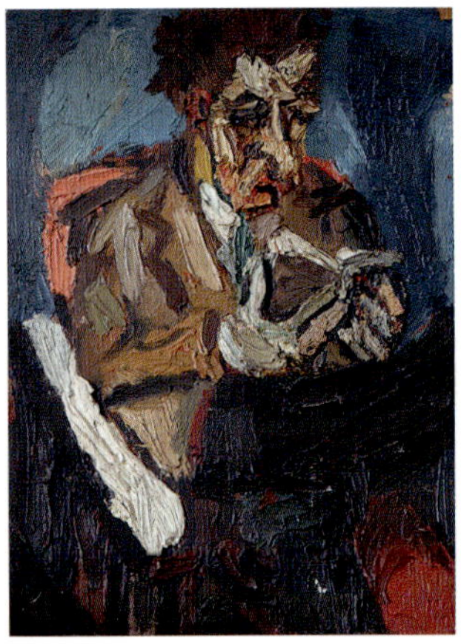

King, John
Man with a Book 1963–1965
oil on board 58 x 42
2

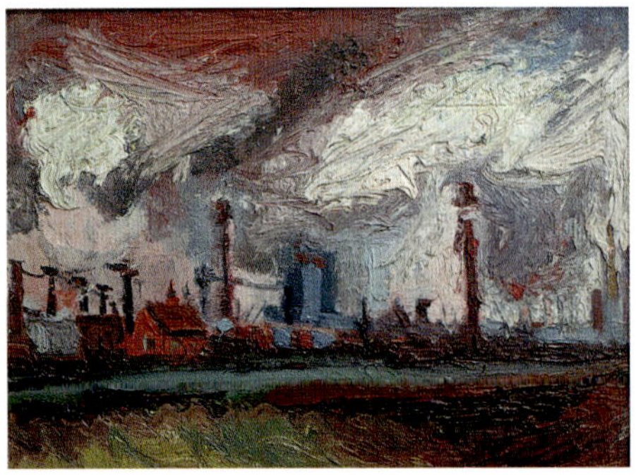

King, John
Humber Factories
oil on canvas 42 x 56
25

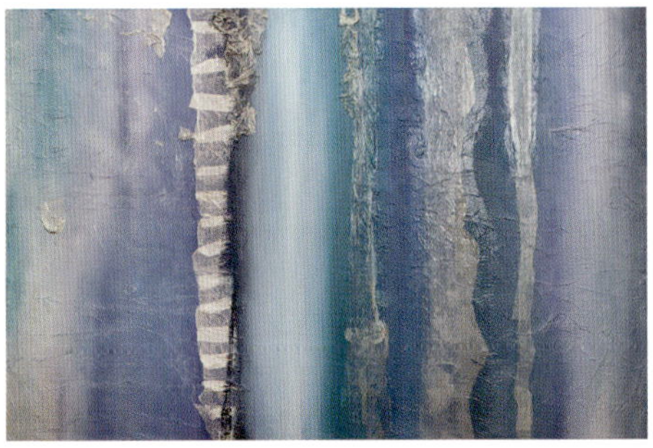

Mather, Louise
Blue
oil on canvas 98 x 150
26

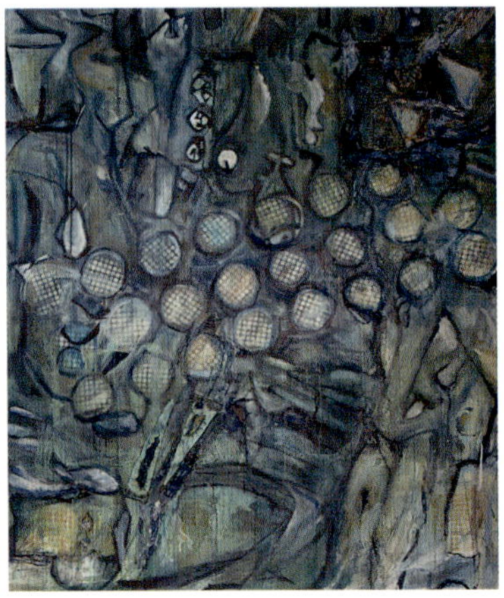

Maughton, Jane
Underwater 2005–2006
oil on canvas 160 x 115
21

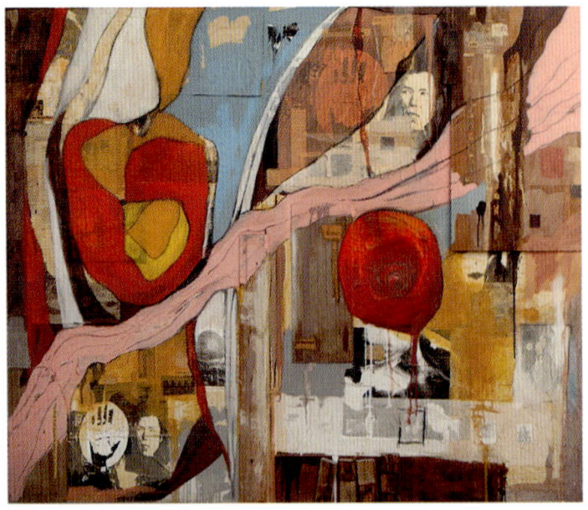

McCoy, Debbie
Mixed Media c.1989
oil, acrylic, collage, wood & cloth on canvas 180 x 250
7

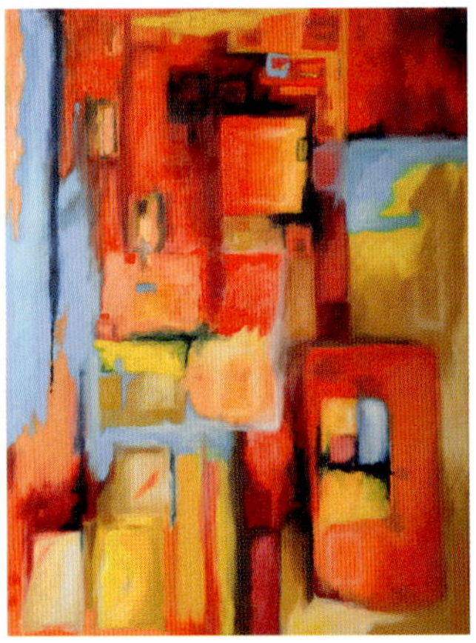

McCoy, Debbie
*Orange Squares**
oil on canvas 180 x 146
10

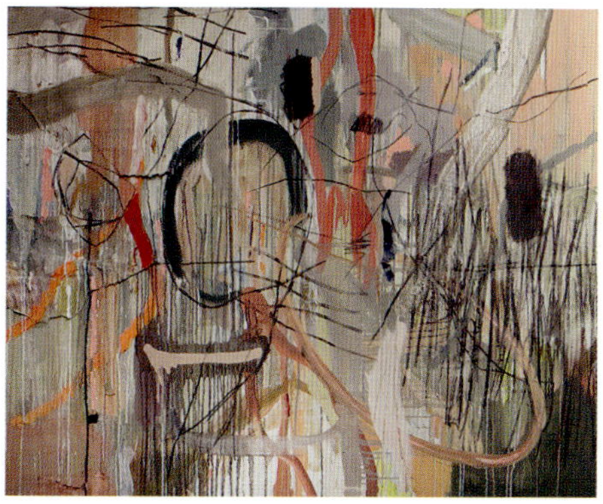

Mumby, John
*Abstract**
oil on canvas 150 x 180
18

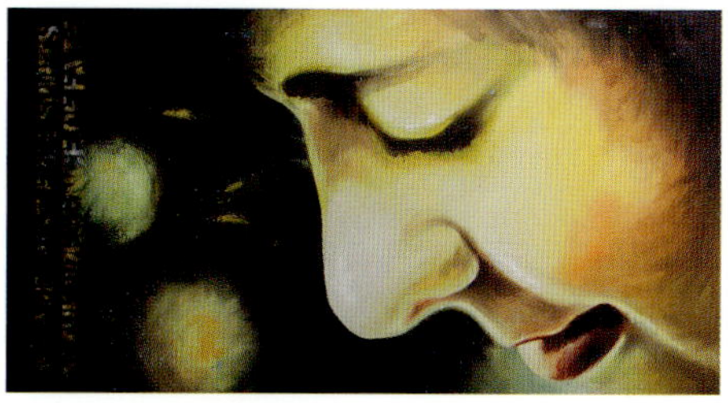

Osborne, Robert
We are Just Free Spirits in the Presence of Fate
2007
oil on canvas 123 x 230
27

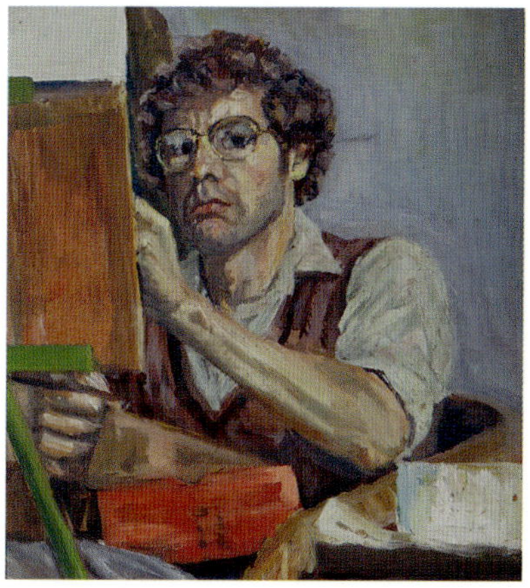

Owen, David active 1981–1982
Self Portrait 1981
oil on canvas 102 x 80
4

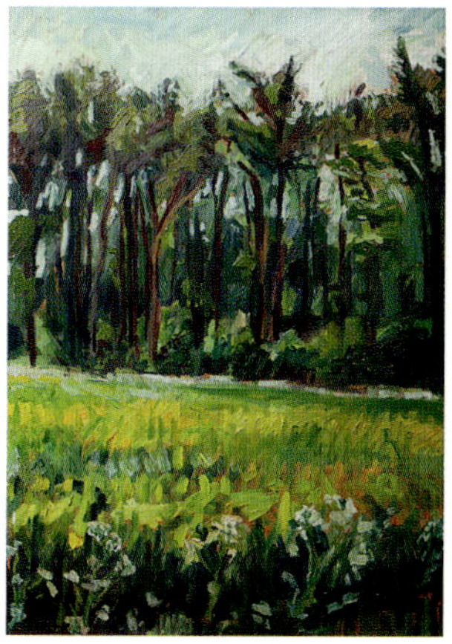

Owen, Mark b.1963
Wooded Scene 1981
oil on board 88 x 61
17

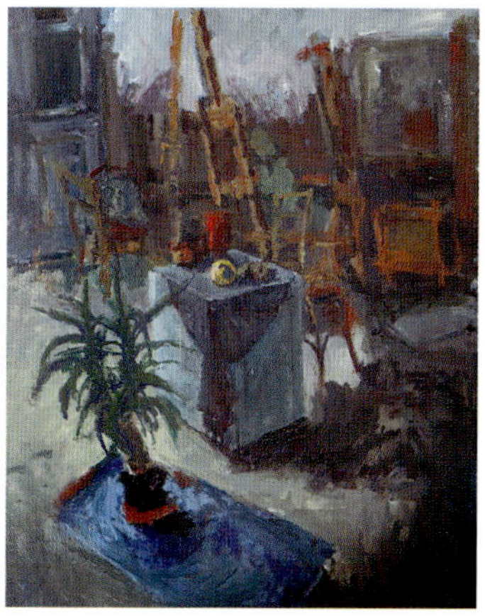

Penketh, Andrew b.1966
Art Studio 1985
oil on board 120 x 90
6

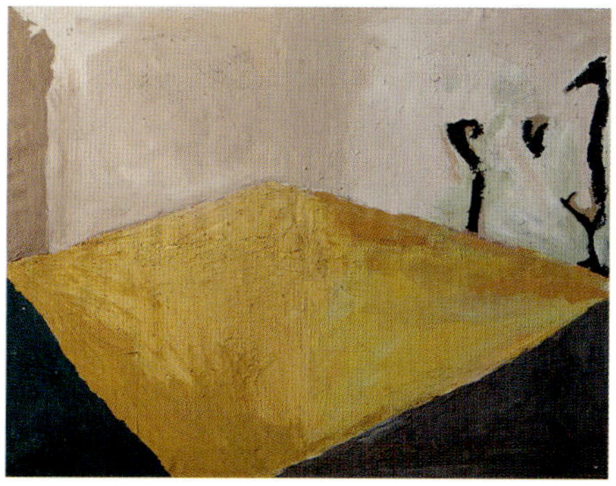

Reeves, Aimie b.1971
Yellow Field 1989
oil on canvas 179 x 200
22

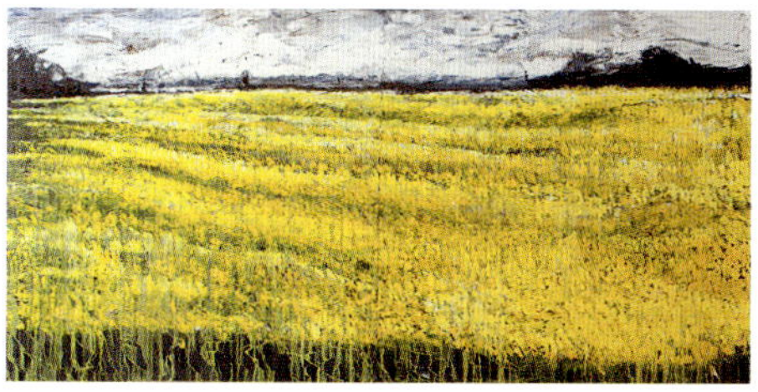

Roberts, Darren
Yellow Rape Field 2008
oil on canvas 121 x 243
1

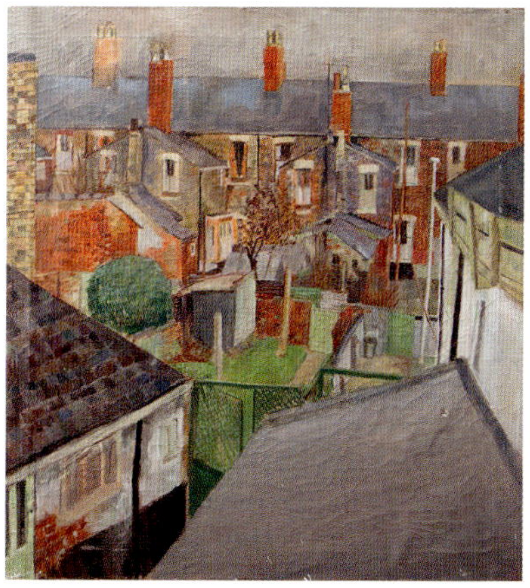

unknown artist
Backyard Scene
oil on canvas 78 x 76
15

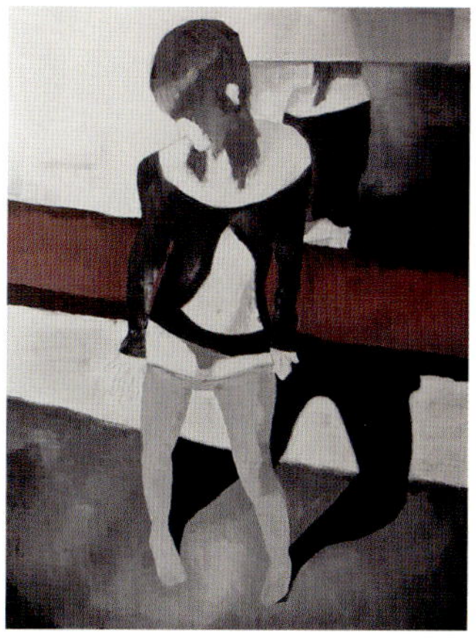

unknown artist
Black Pants
oil on canvas 120 x 95
31

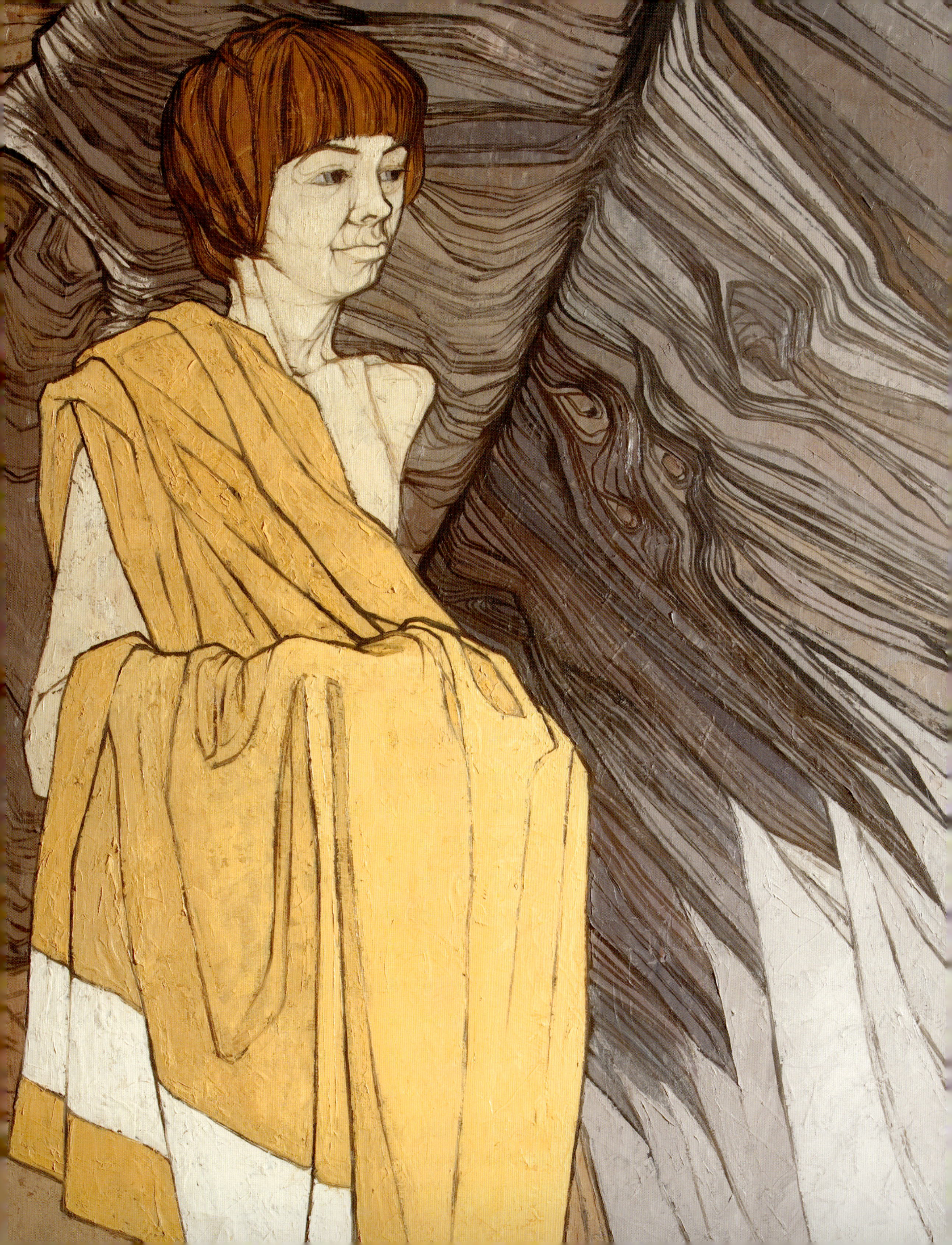

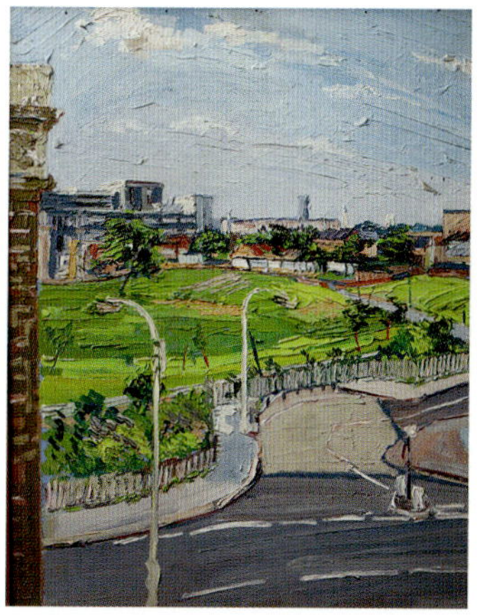

unknown artist
City Parkland
oil on wood 68 x 53
16

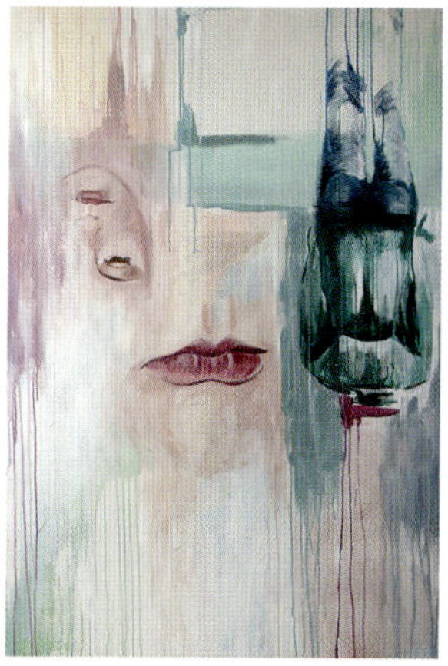

unknown artist
Lips
oil on canvas 140 x 100
30

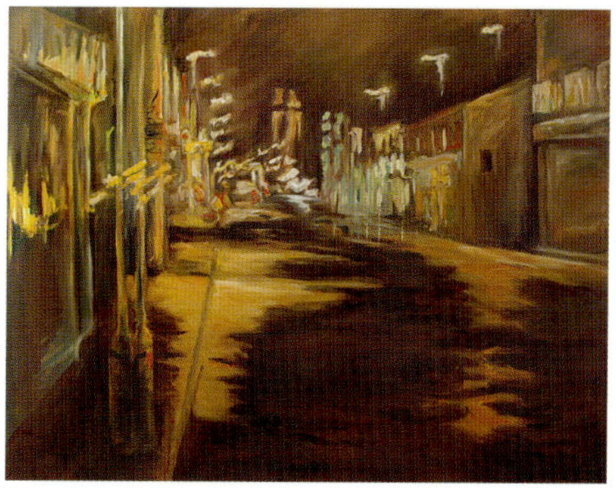

unknown artist
Street Scene at Night
oil on canvas 190 x 270
8

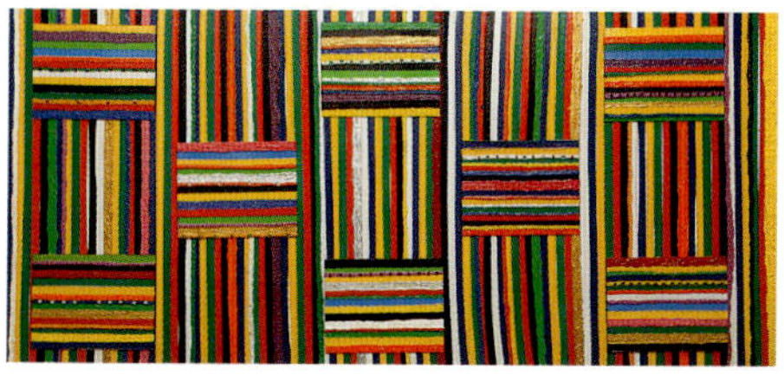

unknown artist
Stripes and Beads
oil on chipboard 76 x 163
23

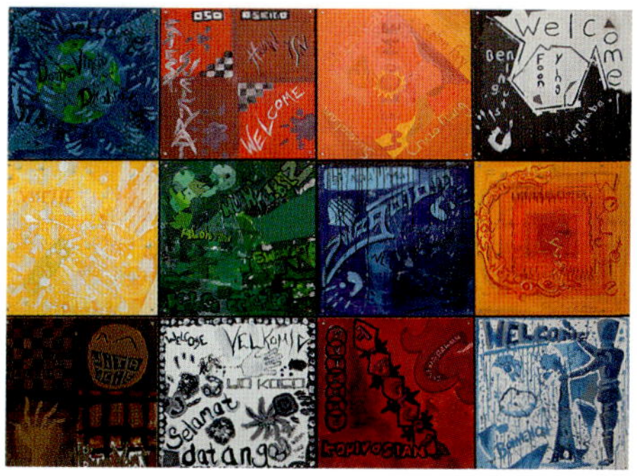

unknown artist
Welcome
oil on board 184 x 247
11

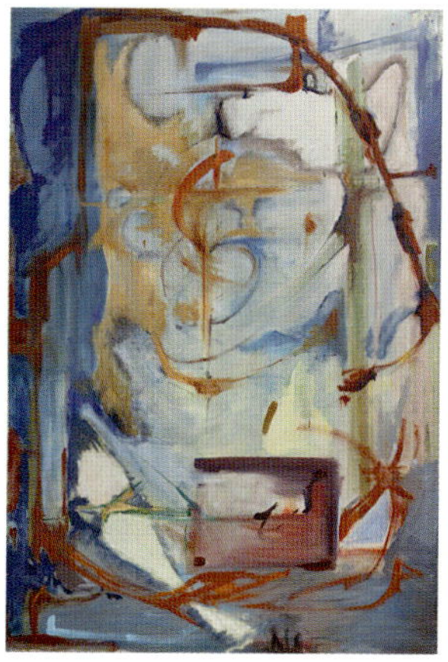

Vernau, Madeleine
Fraser 1991
oil on canvas 180 x 125
24

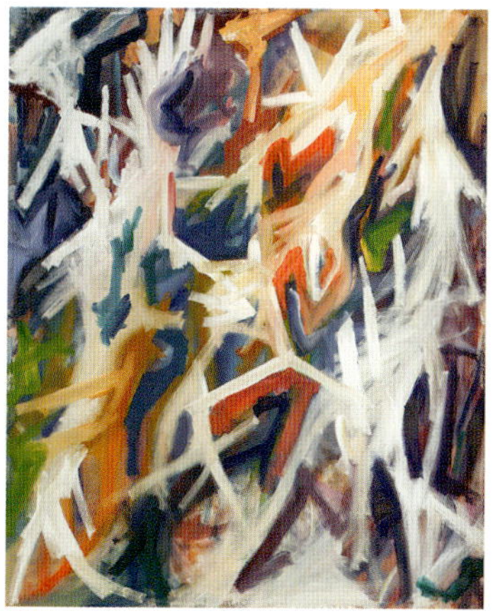

Vernau, Rosie
Abstract 1999
oil on canvas 152 x 126
9

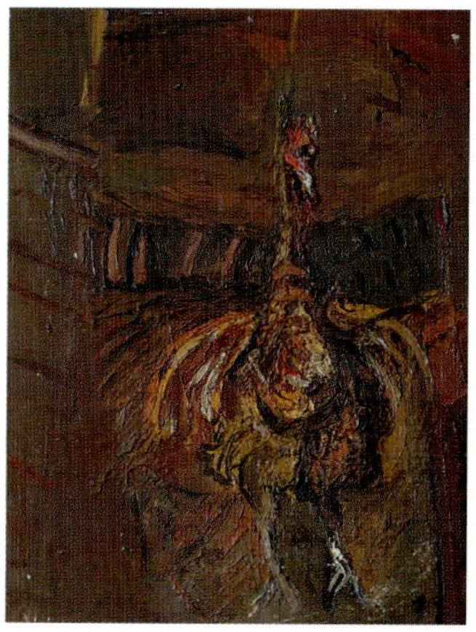

Volley, Nicholas 1950–2006
Brown Cockerel 1968
oil on board 49 x 27
3

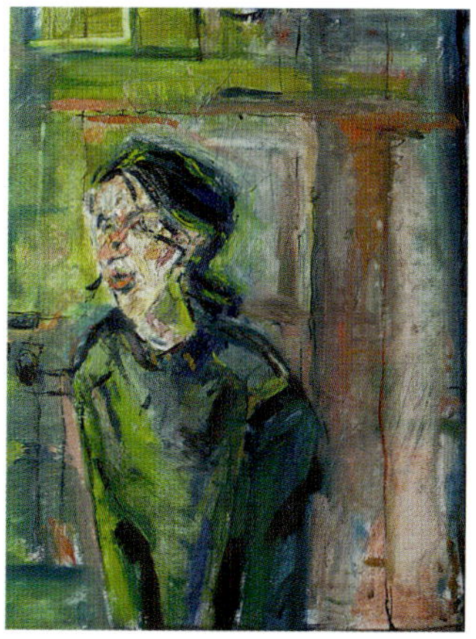

Volley, Nicholas 1950–2006
Green Girl c.1968
oil on board 80 x 59
5

Facing page: Teed, Shirley Brenda, b.1933, *Rockface with a Boy in a Yellow Towel* (detail), 1973, North Lincolnshire Museums Service (p. 367)

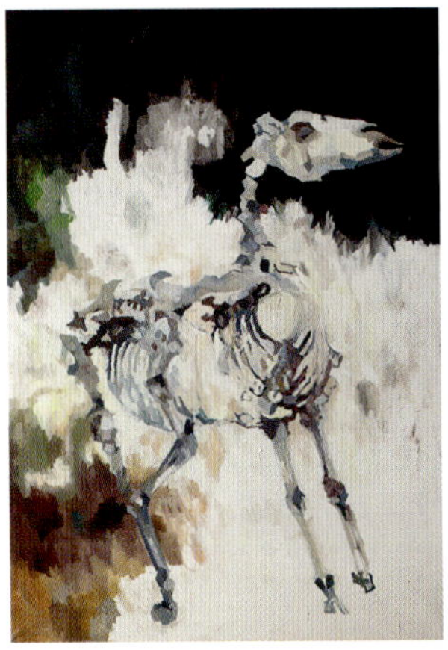

Walters, Claire
Horse Skeleton 2005–2006
oil on canvas 136 x 96 (E)
20

Grimsby Town Hall

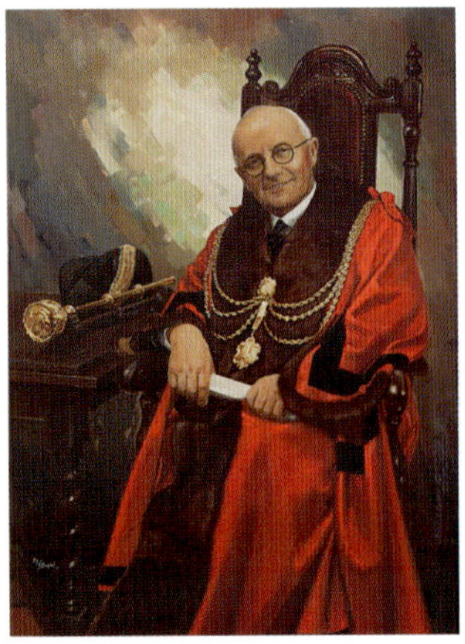

Bugion, S.
Councillor James Keay, Mayor of Grimsby (1941–1942)
oil on board 99.2 x 72.3
GRTH.1

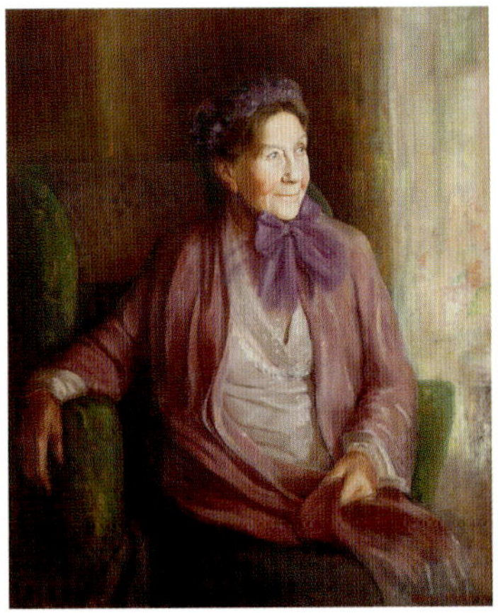

Fildes, Denis 1889–1974
Dame Madge Kendal (1848–1935), CBE
oil on canvas 83 x 69.7
GRTH.2

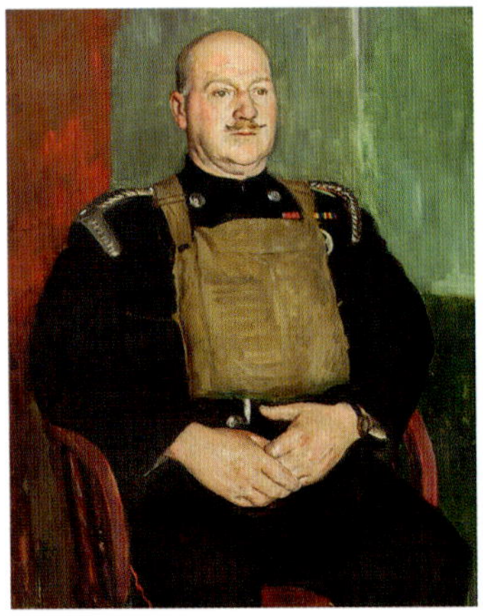

Hailstone, Bernard 1910–1987
Councillor C. H. Wilkinson, MBE, JP
oil on canvas 100.7 x 74.5
GRTH.3

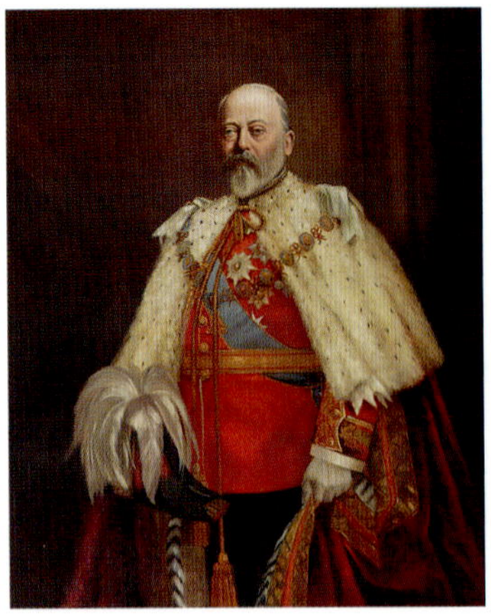

Jennison, George
Edward VII (1841–1910) 1910
oil on canvas 140 x 109
GRTH.13

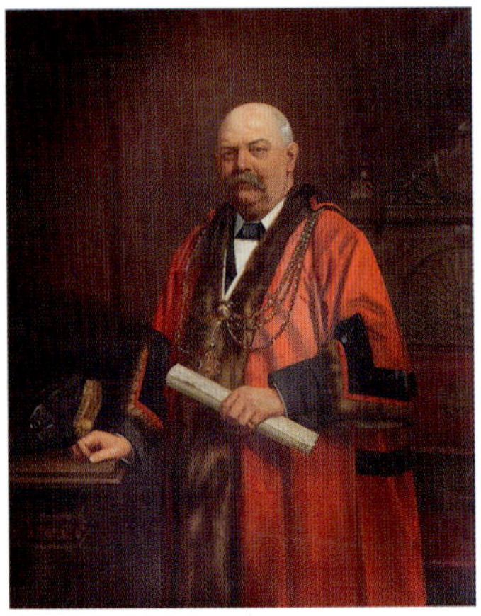

Jennison, George
Robert William Roberts, Mayor of Grimsby (1909) 1910
oil on canvas 139 x 109.5
GRTH.14

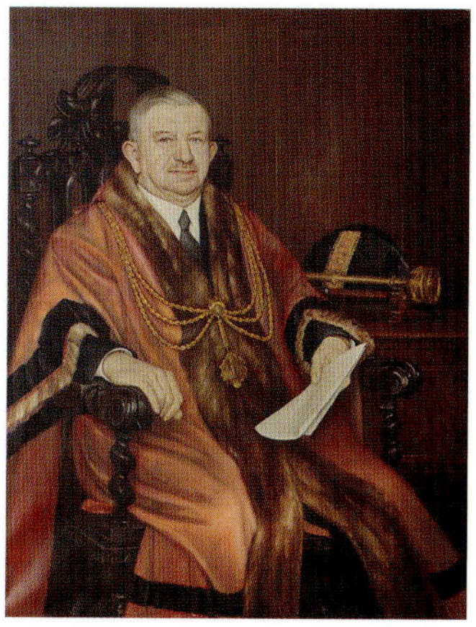

Jennison, George
Alderman C. W. Hewson, JP, Mayor of Grimsby (1944–1945)
oil on canvas 132.5 x 100.2
GRTH.5

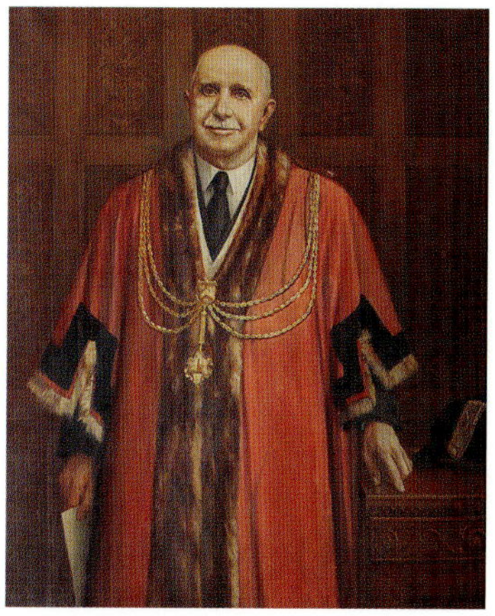

Jennison, George
Alderman J. H. Tate, JP, Mayor of Grimsby (1913–1914)
oil on canvas 126 x 99.7
GRTH.4

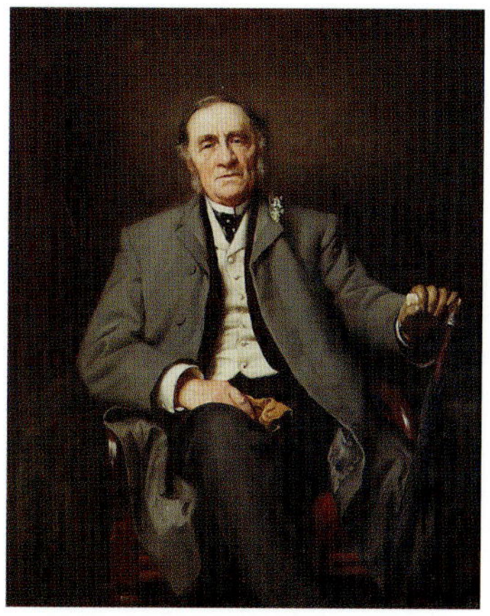

Kennington, Thomas Benjamin 1856–1916
Edward John Bannister, Mayor of Grimsby (1868–1869)
oil on canvas 126 x 103.5
GRTH.8

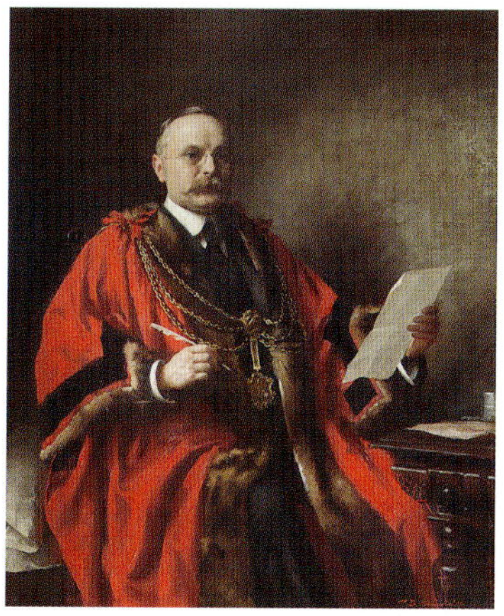

Kennington, Thomas Benjamin 1856–1916
Frank Barrett, Mayor of Grimsby (1908 & 1924)
oil on canvas 126 x 99.5
GRTH.10

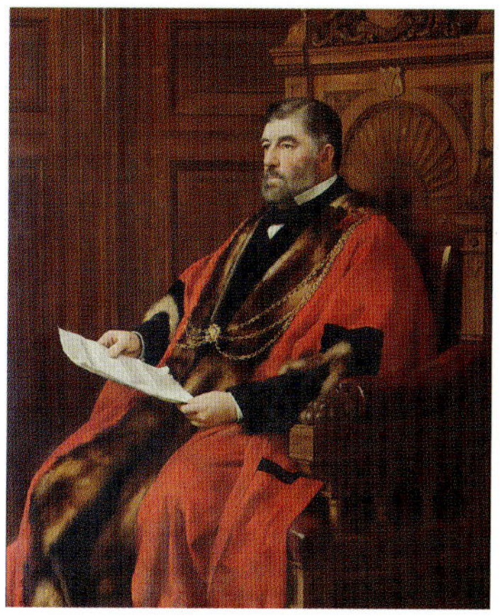

Kennington, Thomas Benjamin 1856–1916
Henry James Veal, Mayor of Grimsby (1877–1878)
oil on canvas 150 x 120
GRTH.9

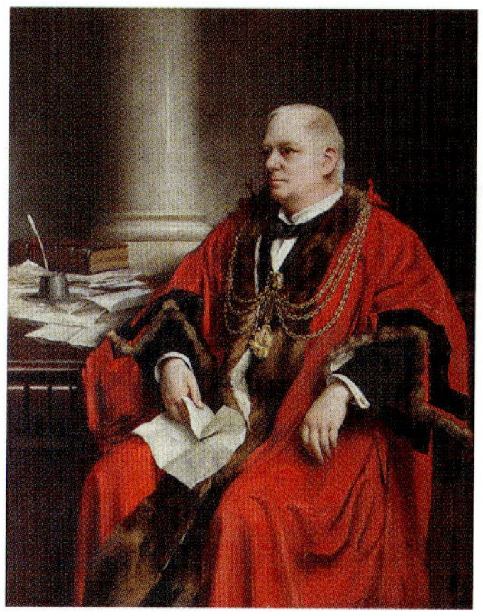

Kennington, Thomas Benjamin 1856–1916
Jack Sutcliffe, Mayor of Grimsby (1896–1897)
oil on canvas 151 x 120
GRTH.6

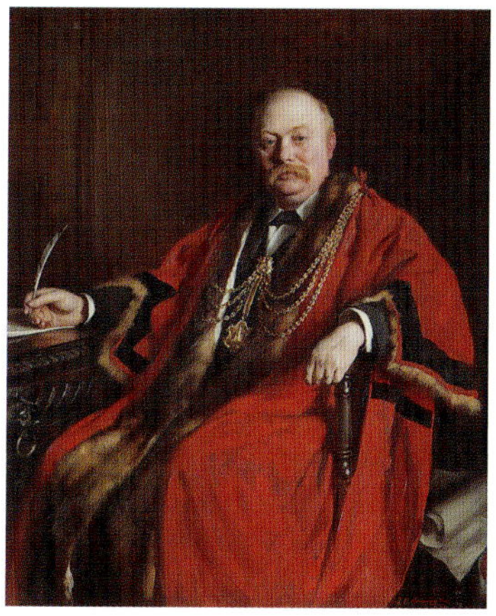

Kennington, Thomas Benjamin 1856–1916
Sir George Doughty, MP (1895), Mayor of Grimsby (1892–1893)
oil on canvas 125.5 x 100.5
GRTH.7

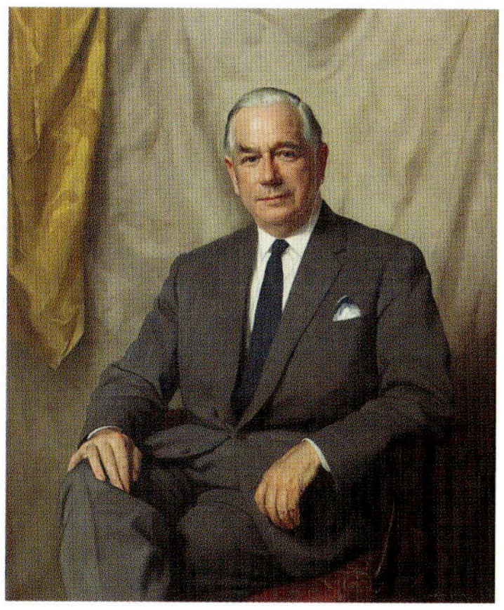

Turner, James (attributed to)
J. Carl Ross, Esq., High Steward of the Borough of Great Grimsby 1964
oil on canvas 111.5 x 88.9
GRTH.16

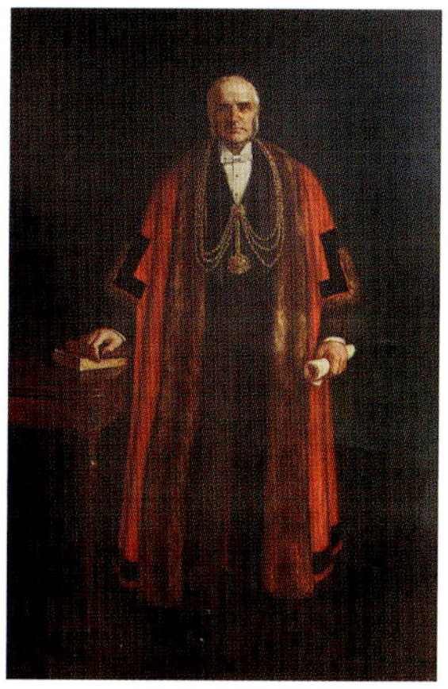

unknown artist
Henry Smethurst Senior, Mayor of Grimsby (1885–1886)
oil on canvas 195.2 x 122.2
GRTH.11

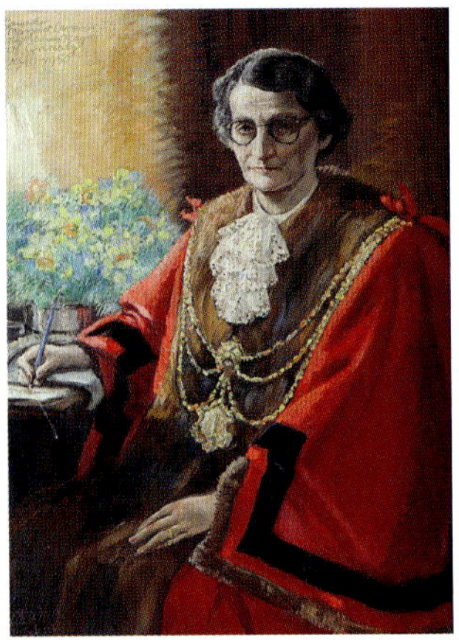

Wade, George A. active 1950–1960
Margaret Larmour, Mayor of Grimsby (1949)
oil on canvas 96 x 67
GRTH.15

North East Lincolnshire Museum Service

North East Lincolnshire Museum Service is part of North East Lincolnshire Council, which covers the towns of Grimsby, Cleethorpes and Immingham and a number of the surrounding villages. The Museum Service is responsible for holding the Council's art collection, which, though small, contains many fine pieces, made by local, national and international artists.

Much of the Collection has come from a single donation: the Doughty Bequest. This bequest was left to the town of Grimsby in the will of Wilfrid Vere Doughty on his death in 1941 and is made up of a large number of paintings (particularly maritime scenes), a wide range of ship models and a great deal of chinaware.

The majority of this collection was put together by Wilfrid's father Sir George Doughty, a long-time local councillor and then Member of Parliament for the town at the end of the nineteenth and beginning of the twentieth centuries. Sir George was a hugely important local businessman, being, amongst other things, a ship owner, ship builder and newspaper magnate, as well as having other national and international business interests. This success made the Doughtys one of the wealthiest and most influential families in the town. A great deal of this wealth was spent on developing the family's collection, which shows an excellent taste, particularly in the choices of maritime scenes. Though the Doughty Bequest forms the core of the Collection, many other donators, often from the surrounding area, have contributed pieces to the Collection.

Amongst the finest works in the Collection are Edward William Cooke's *A Dutch Galliot Entering Aberdeen Harbour in a Storm*, a quite stunning seascape which was the product of a real event that the artist witnessed and sketched; John Wilson Carmichael's fascinating painting of *The Construction of the Royal Dock, Grimsby, Lincolnshire*; as well as a number of portraits by the Grimsby-born but later London-based Victorian-era society artist Sir Thomas Benjamin Kennington. There are also works held which are attributed to the eminent artists Sir Peter Lely and Nicholas Pocock. Local artists such as Albert Edward Wade, David Tarttelin, George Race and John Hopkinson are well-represented too, giving the Collection a richness and diversity, whilst also representing the artistic talent that this region has long had. Recently, the Collection has begun to expand, with new acquisitions coming in from contemporary artists local to the Grimsby region, further strengthening the Collection's connection to this area.

The Collection is frequently displayed in exhibitions across the North East Lincolnshire area.

Mark T. Tindle, Collections and Access Officer

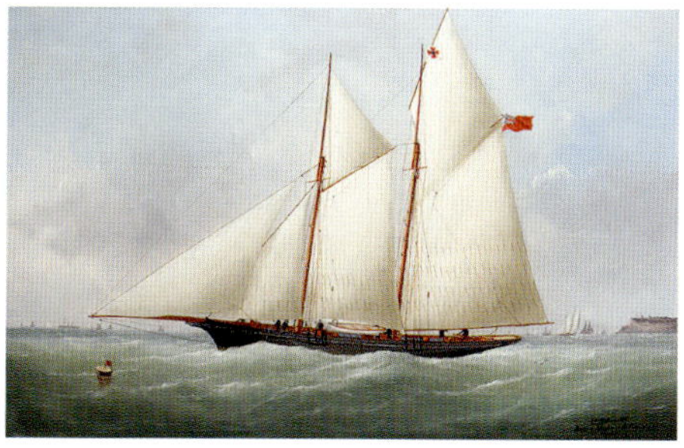

Adam, Edouard Marie 1847–1929
Schooner off the Coast 1887
oil on canvas 59.5 x 91
A.110

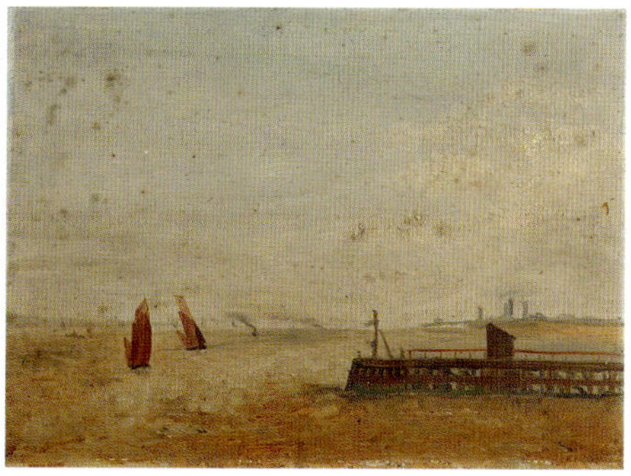

Anderson, W. I. L.
The Mouth of the Humber from Grimsby Docks, Lincolnshire
oil on card 25 x 32.5
A.56

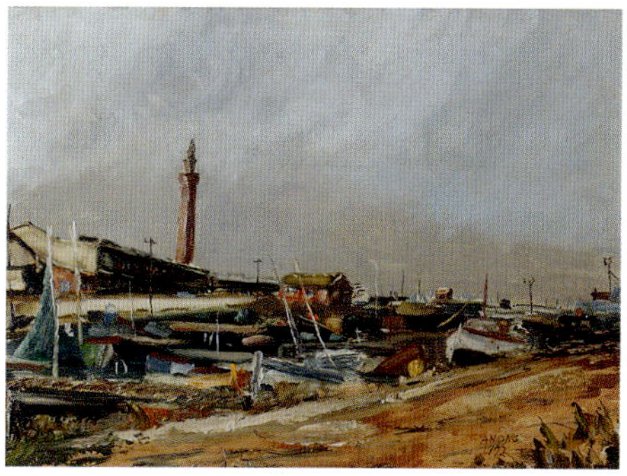

Anong (attributed to)
Dock Tower, Grimsby Dock, Lincolnshire 1972
oil on board 45 x 61
A.441

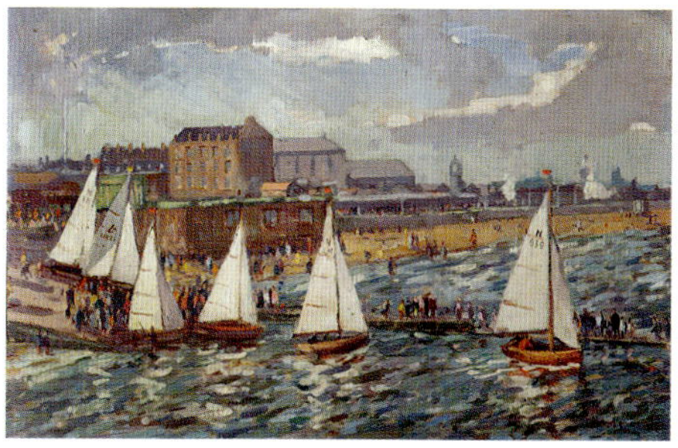

Appleyard, Frederick 1874–1963
Yachts c.1920
oil on canvas 50 x 75.5
Z728

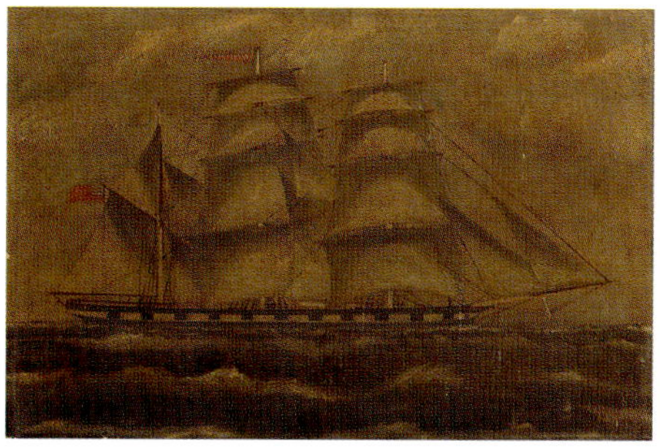

Barclay (Captain)
Three-Masted Sailing Ship 'Gladova' of Sunderland 1822
oil on board 31 x 47.5
GRIMS:2010.3

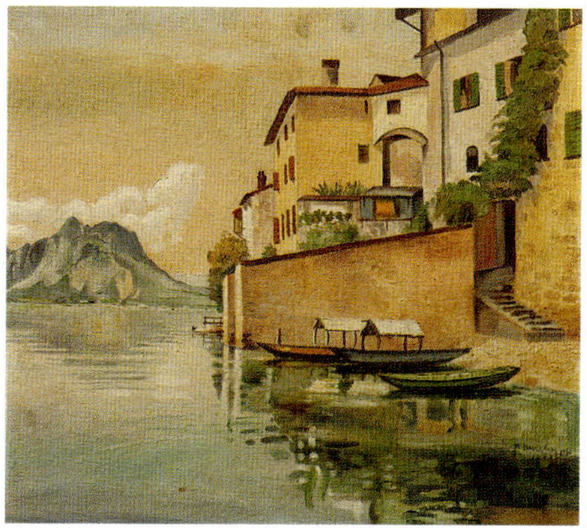

Bauckham, R.
Waterside Scene 1946
oil on board 48 x 56
A.54

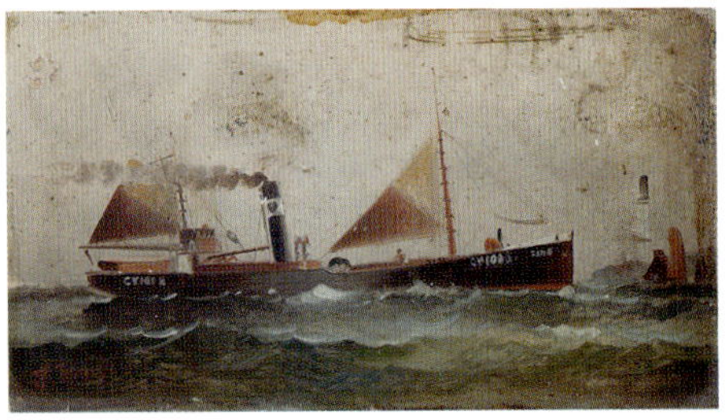

Boulen, J.
The 'Fawn', GY 1008
oil on board 17.1 x 30.2
A.190

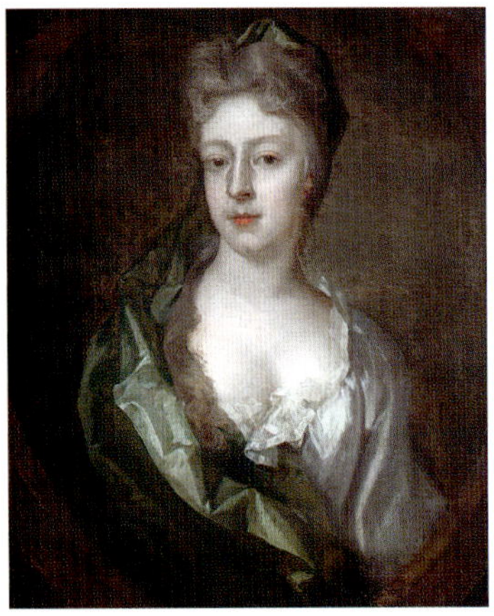

British (English) School
Lady Anne Meres c.1658
oil on canvas 73 x 60.5
A.85

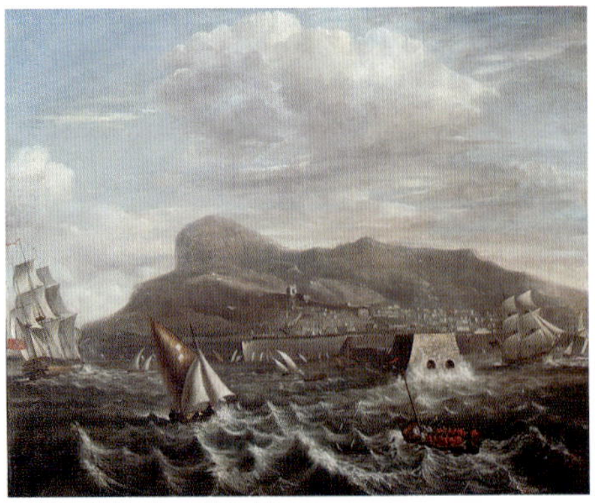

British (English) School
Man-of-War with Shipping off Gibraltar c.1800
oil on canvas 61 x 75
A.3

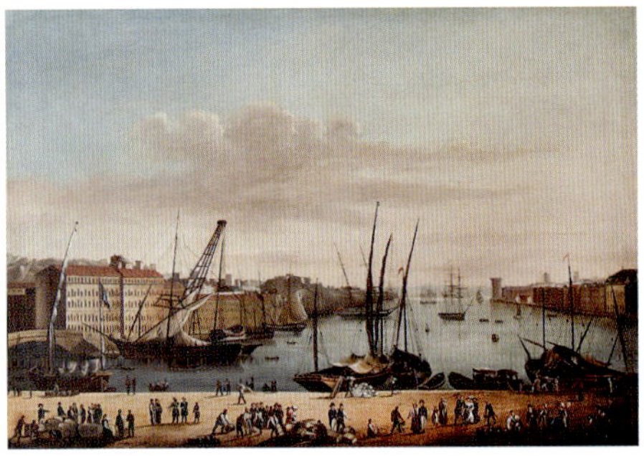

British (English) School
Malta 1813
oil on canvas 72 x 105.5
A.48

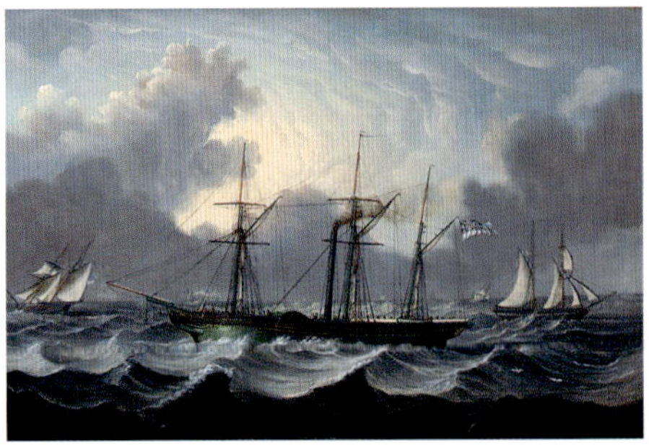

British (English) School
The 'Yorkshireman' at Sea with a Storm Threatening c.1820
oil on canvas 49.5 x 71
A.154

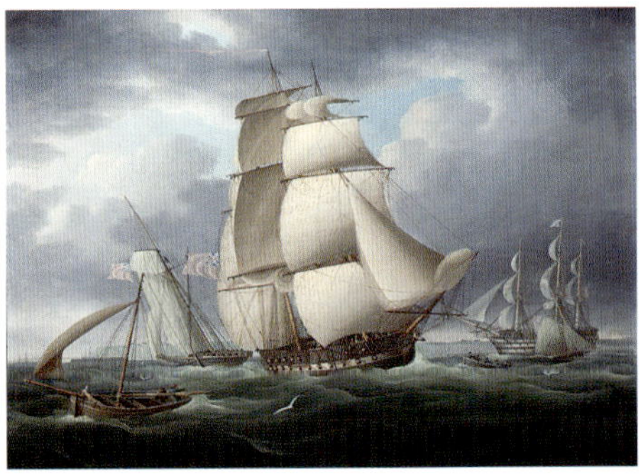

British (English) School
Ships off the Coast c.1830
oil on canvas 44 x 59
A.209

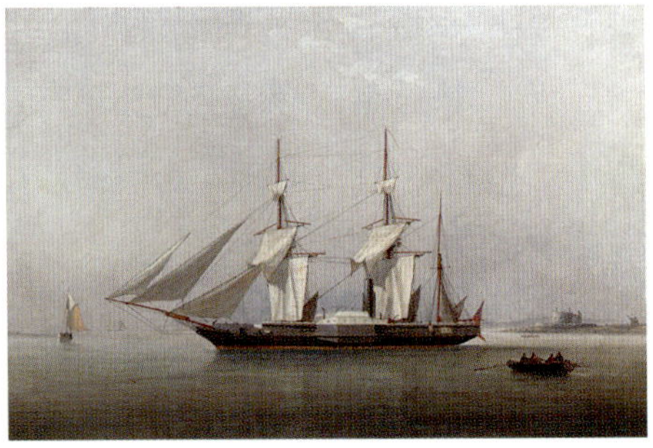

British (English) School
The 'Fury', Moored in the Medway c.1840
oil on canvas 30 x 44
A.101

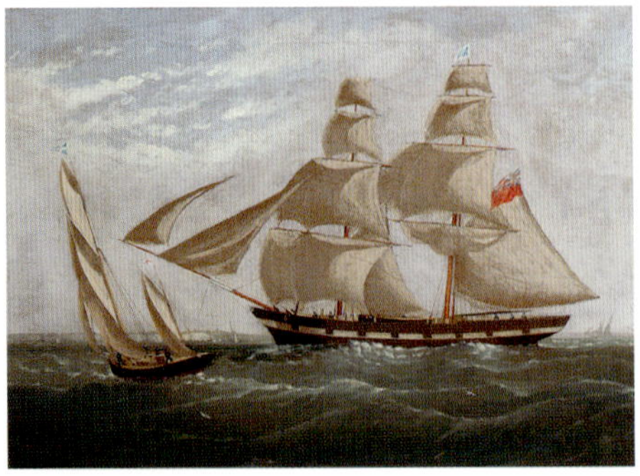

British (English) School
The 'Tigress' c.1840
oil on canvas 44 x 59
A.79

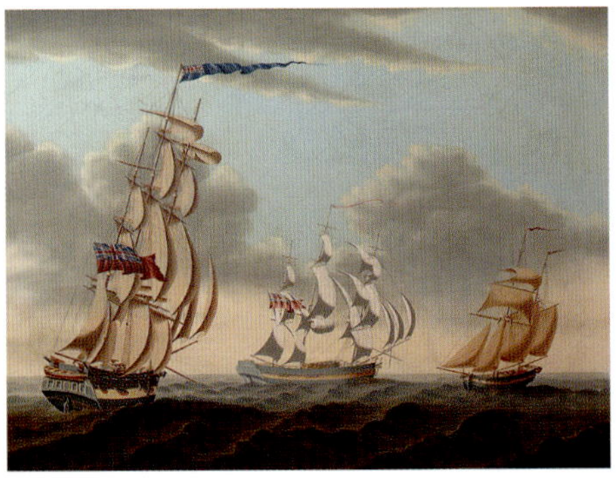

British (English) School
Three English Sailing Ships c.1840
oil on canvas 64 x 82
A.130

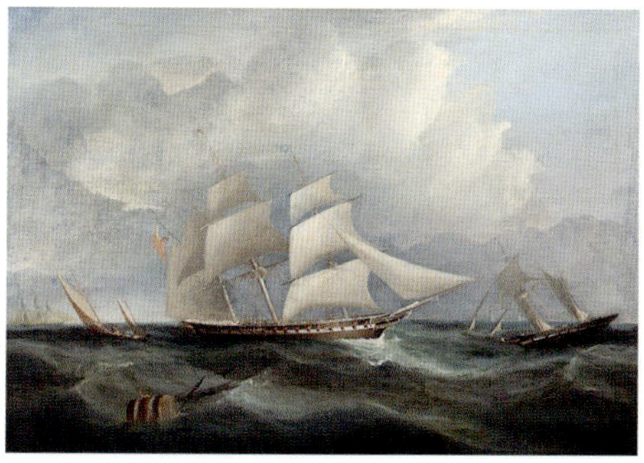

British (English) School
Three-Masted Frigate c.1840
oil on canvas 51 x 72
A.93

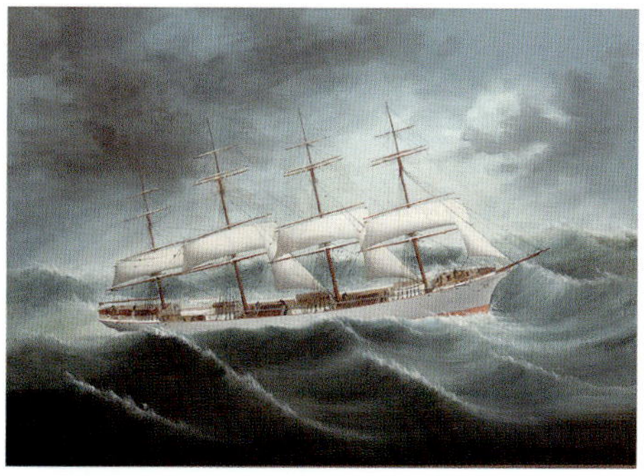

British (English) School
The 'Falls of Dee' c.1850
oil on canvas 64 x 87
A.74

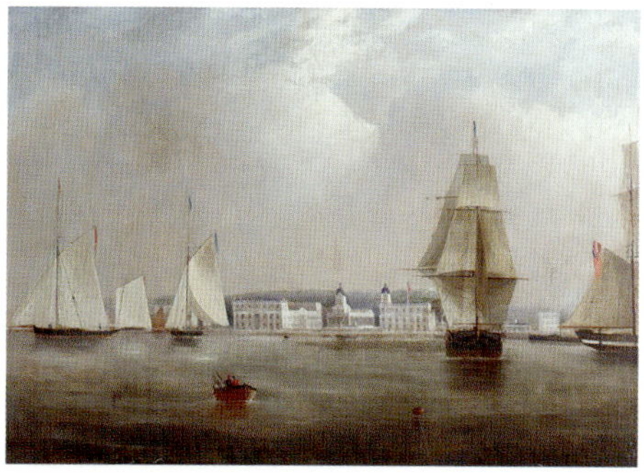

British (English) School
The Thames at Greenwich, London c.1850
oil on canvas 49 x 72.5
A.95

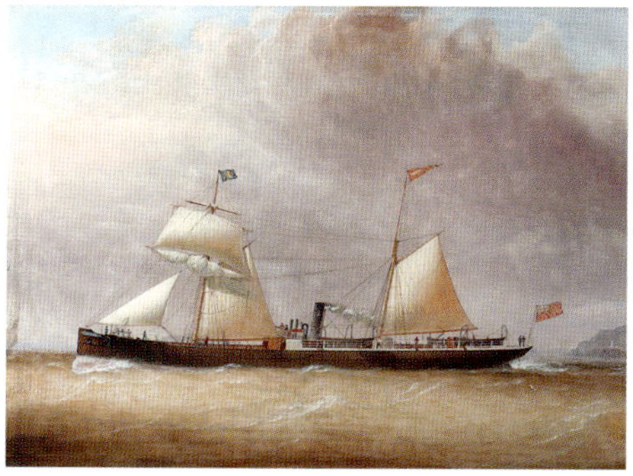

British (English) School
The 'Campanil' c.1870
oil on canvas 61 x 83
A.89

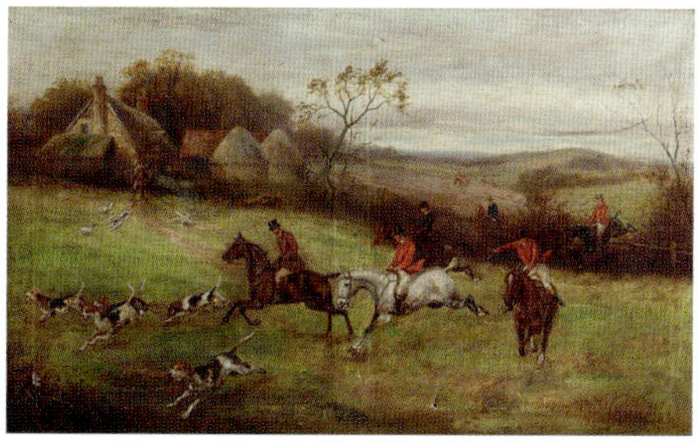

British (English) School
Hunting Scene 1880
oil on canvas 75 x 126
A.21

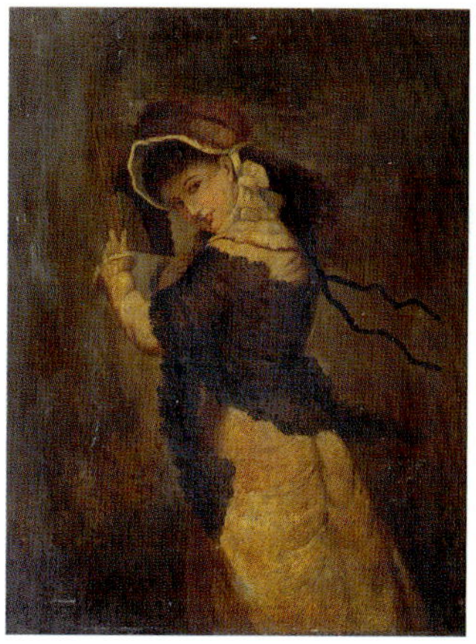

British (English) School 19th C
Lady with a Fan
oil on canvas 61 x 45.5
A.100

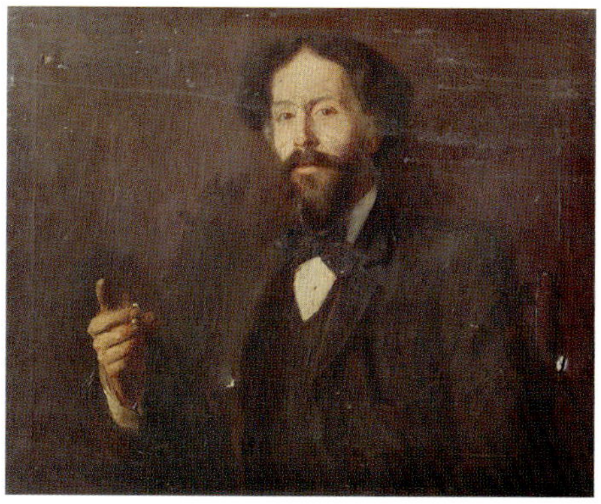

British (English) School late 19th C
Portrait of an Unknown Gentleman
oil on canvas 61 x 76.5
A.2

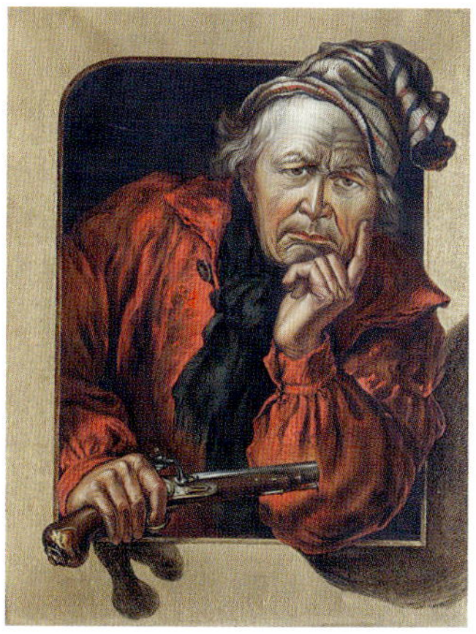

British (English) School
A Man with a Flintlock Pistol
oil on canvas 54.5 x 44
A.427

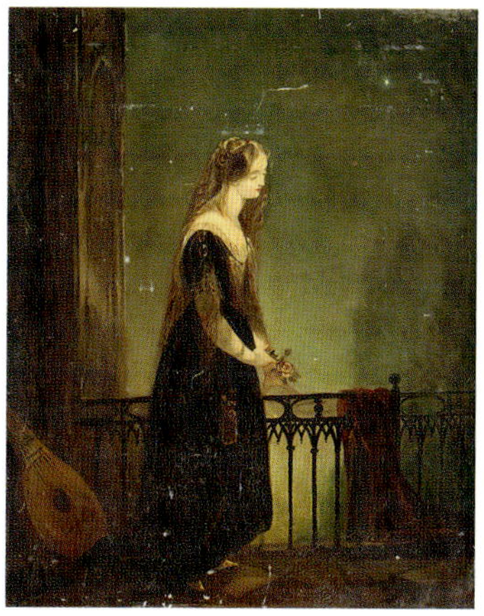

British (English) School
A Woman on a Balcony at Night
oil on canvas 91 x 76
A.77

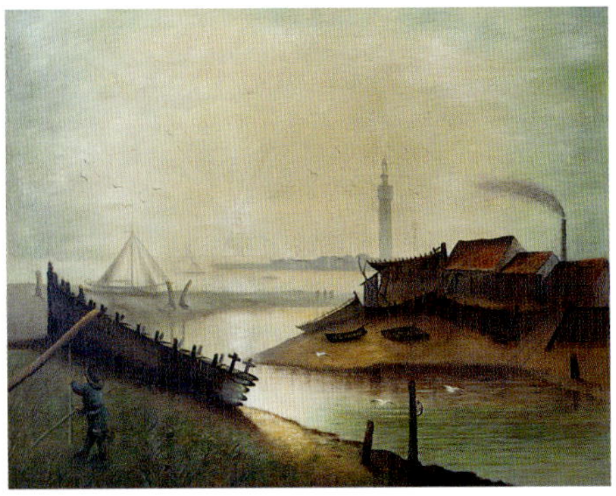

British (English) School
Grimsby Docks and Tower, Lincolnshire
oil on canvas 61 x 76.5
A.1

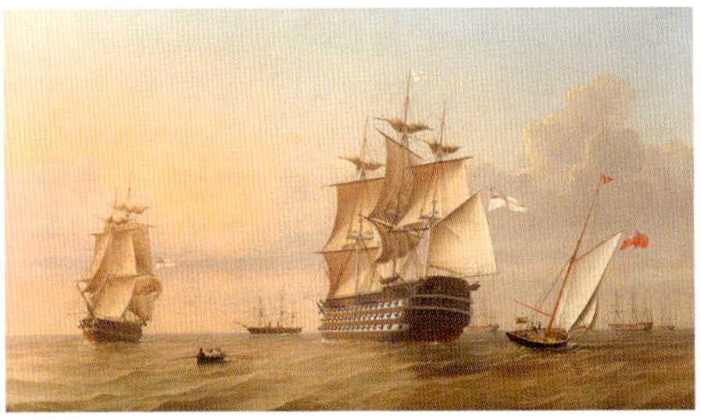

British (English) School
Man-of-War and Other Shipping
oil on canvas 73.8 x 125.4
A.132

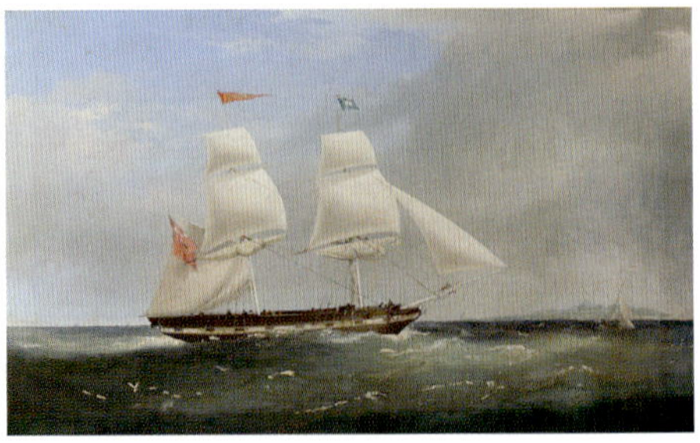

British (English) School
The 'Horwood'
oil on canvas 50.5 x 79.5
A.156

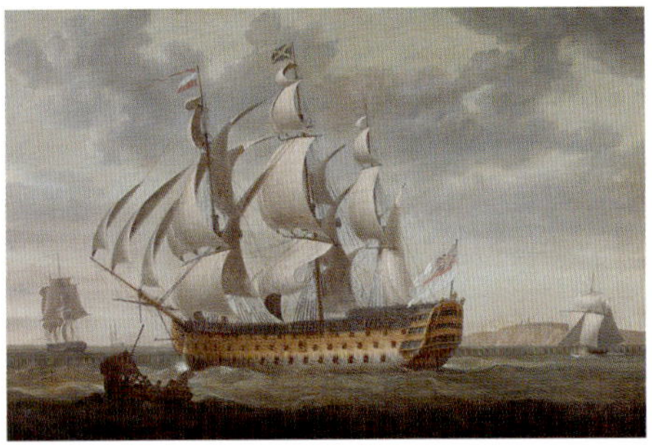

Brooking, Charles (attributed to)
1723–1759
Man-of-war off the Coast
oil on canvas 105 x 150
A.31

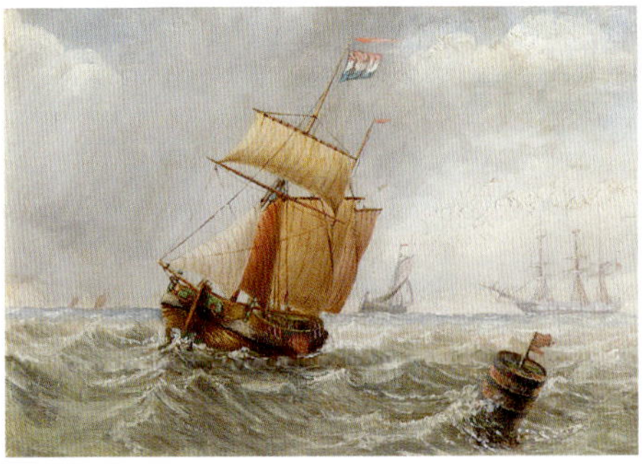

Bunting, William Richard 1866–c.1944
Two-Masted Ship at Sea 1886
oil on canvas 25.7 x 36
A.188

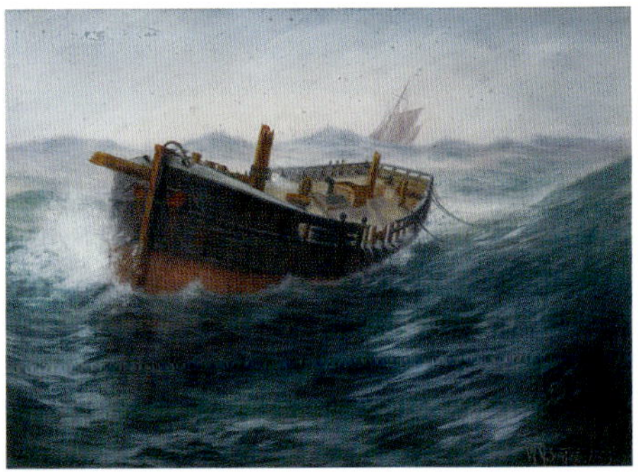

Bunting, William Richard 1866–c.1944
Help at Last 1905
oil on canvas 30.7 x 40.8
A.38

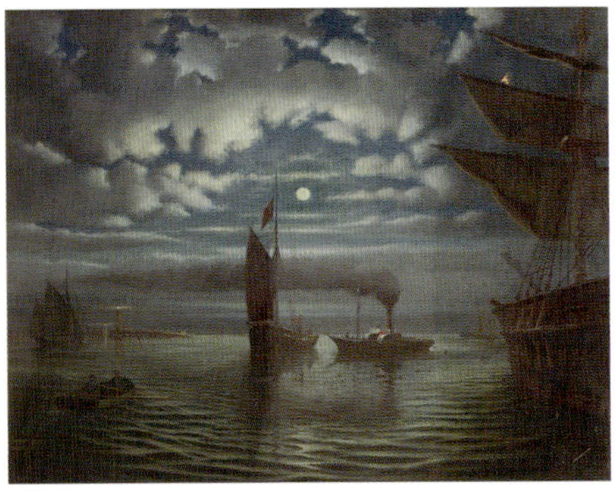

Bunting, William Richard 1866–c.1944
Each Fishing Boat Seemed Scarce Afloat 1908
oil on canvas 64.5 x 80.5
A.105

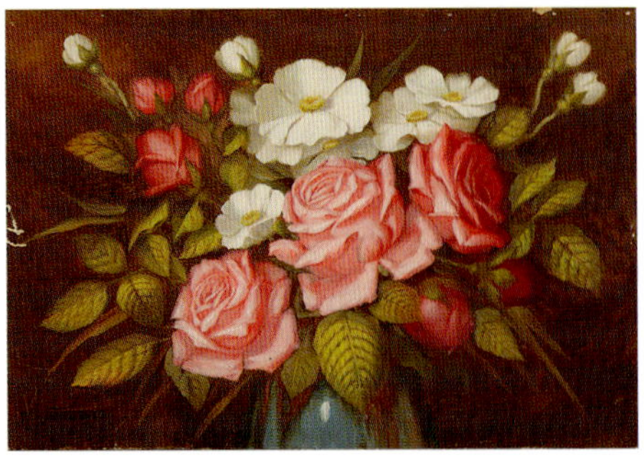

Bunting, William Richard 1866–c.1944
Still Life, Roses 1910
oil on board 28 x 45
GRIMS:2010.6

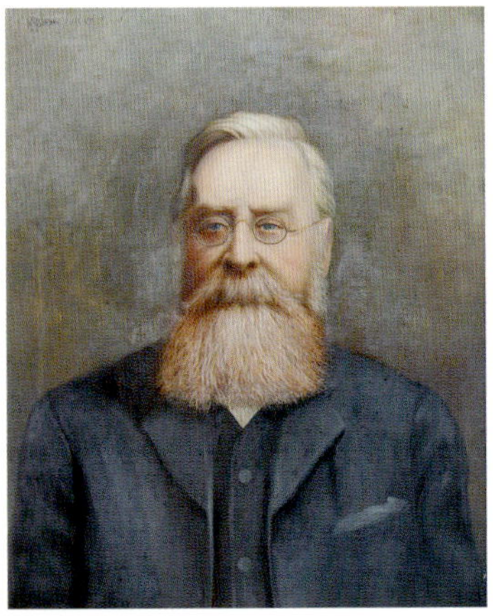

Bunting, William Richard 1866–c.1944
Jack Bell, Shipbuilder 1911
oil on canvas 59 x 49
A.5

Facing page: Carmichael, John Wilson, 1799–1868, *The Brayford Pool and Lincoln Cathedral* (detail), 1858, The Collection: Art & Archaeology in Lincolnshire (Usher Gallery) (p. 290)

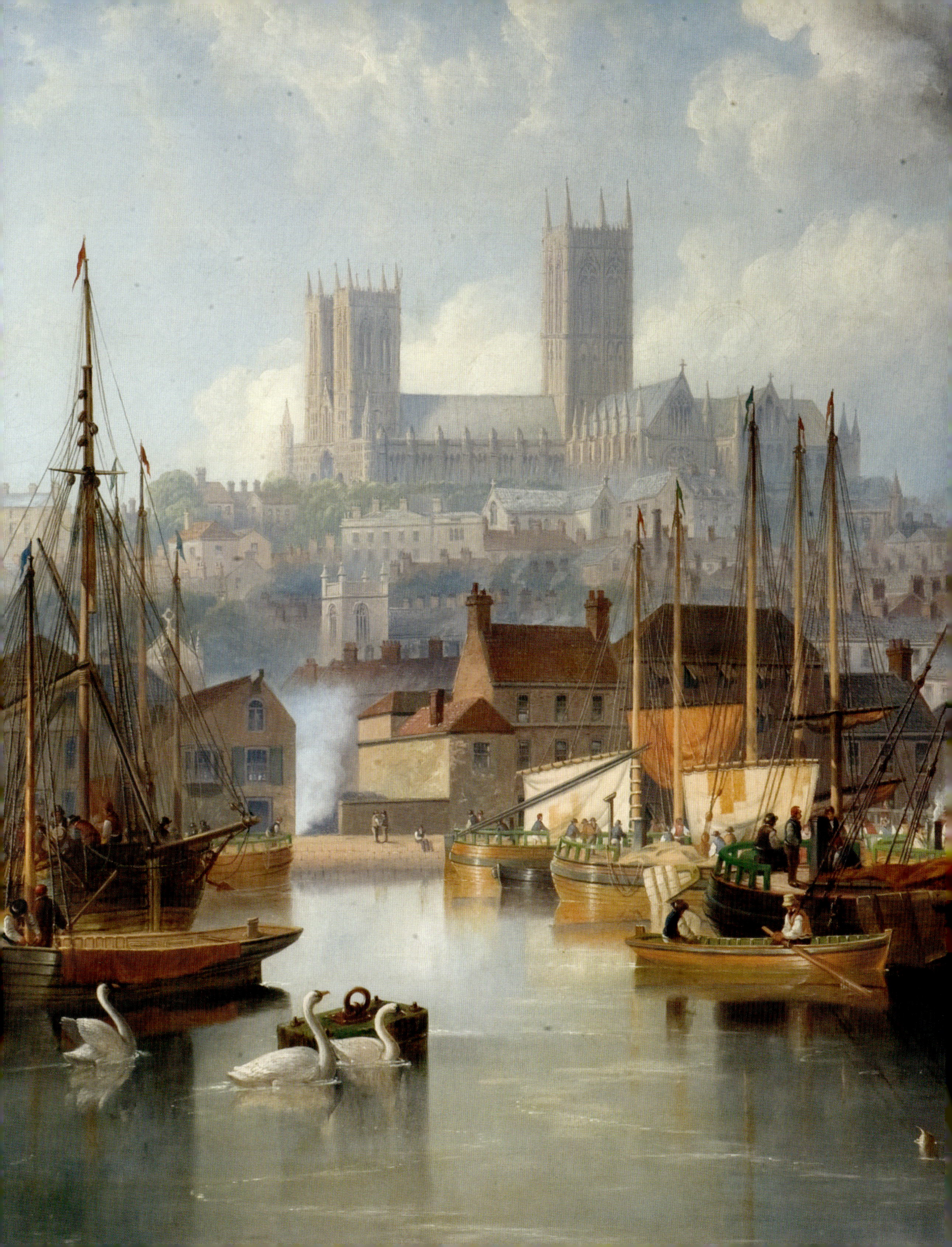

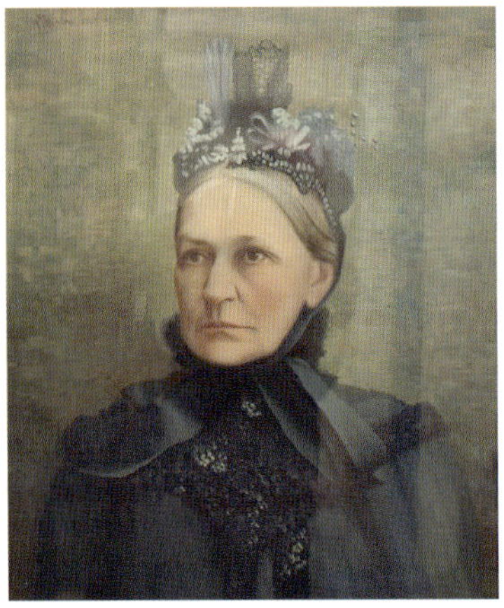

Bunting, William Richard 1866–c.1944
Mrs Jack Bell 1911
oil on canvas 59 x 49
A.4

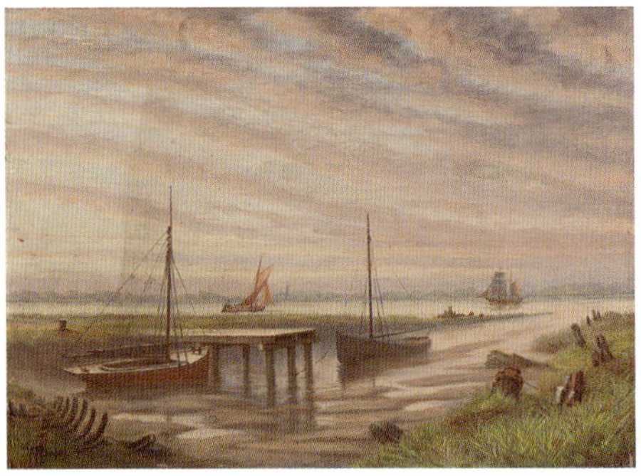

Bunting, William Richard 1866–c.1944
The Last Phase of Grimsby's Old Harbour Entrance, Lincolnshire 1927
oil on board 30.4 x 40.6
GRIMS.2010.5

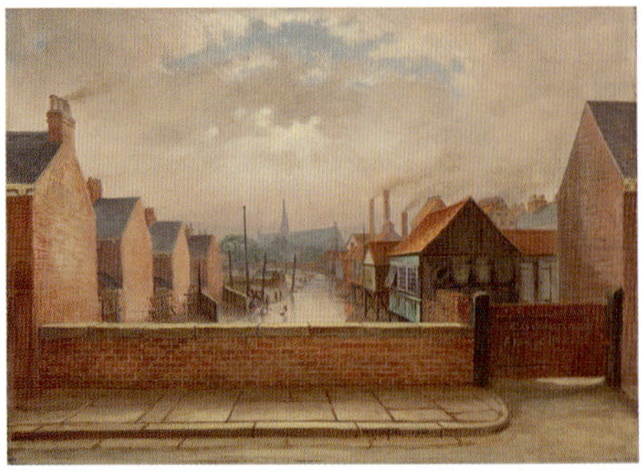

Bunting, William Richard 1866–c.1944
The Old Boundary Mark, Oxford Street and Albert Street, Grimsby, Lincolnshire 1936
oil on canvas 30.4 x 40.8
GRIMS:2010.4

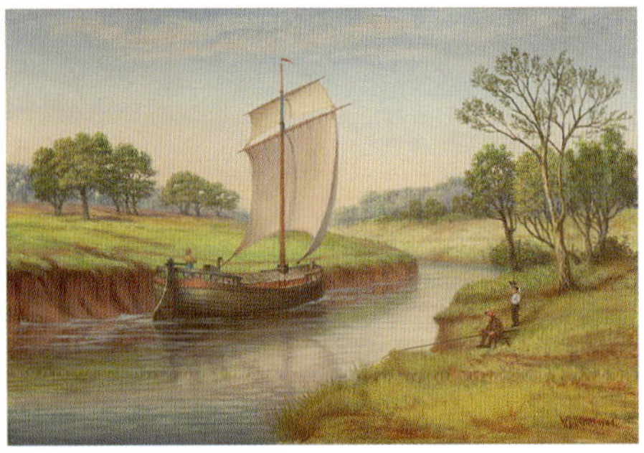

Bunting, William Richard 1866–c.1944
Riverside Pastime and Pleasure 1944
oil on board 28 x 40.6
GRIMS:2010.7

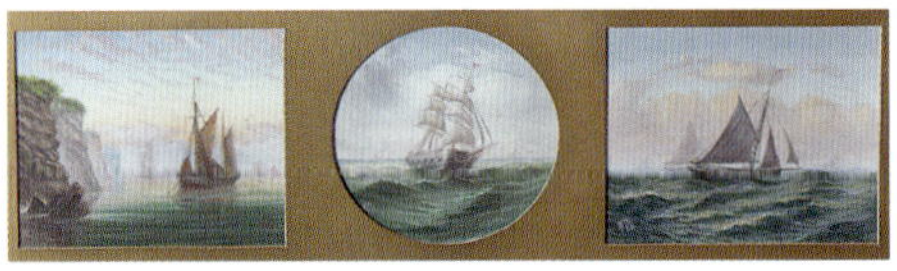

Bunting, William Richard 1866–c.1944
Ships at Sea
oil on card 19 x 72
A.51

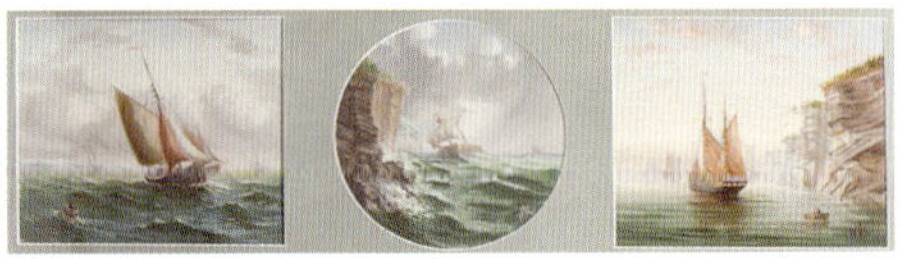

Bunting, William Richard 1866–c.1944
Ships at Sea
oil on card 18.5 x 72.5
A.52

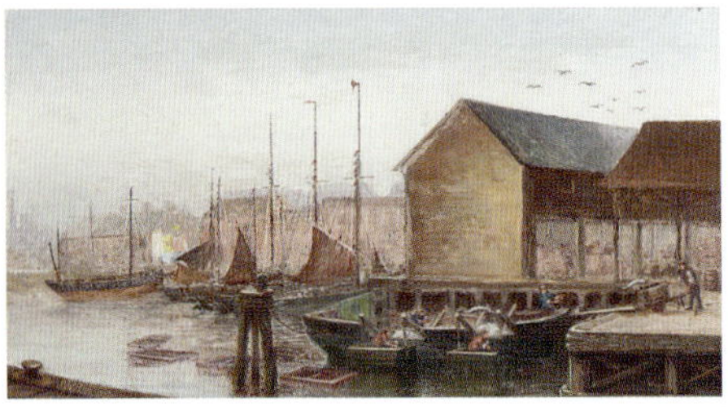

Bunting, William Richard 1866–c.1944
The Stowboat, No.2 Fish Dock, Grimsby, Lincolnshire
oil on panel 24 x 44
A.61

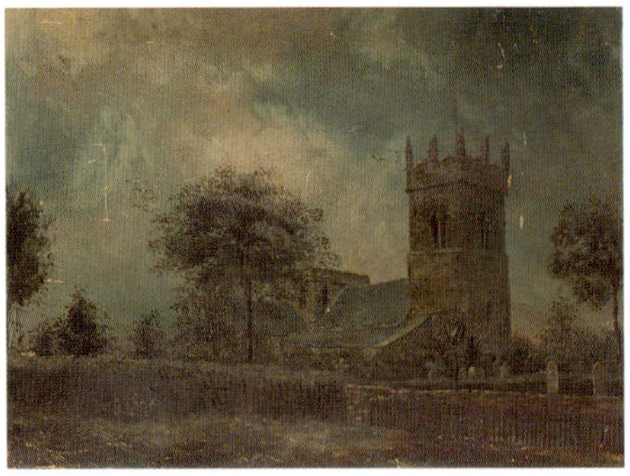

Burton, Thomas
Old Clee Church, Lincolnshire 1878
oil on board 52 x 72
A.42

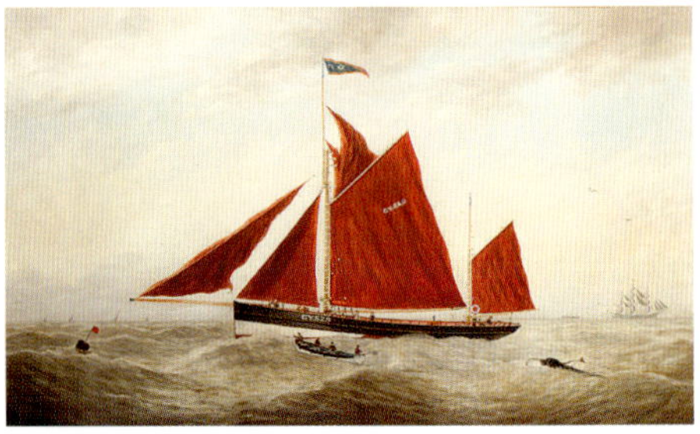

Burwood, George Vemply 1844–1917
The 'Leslie' 1890
oil on canvas 61 x 100
A.87

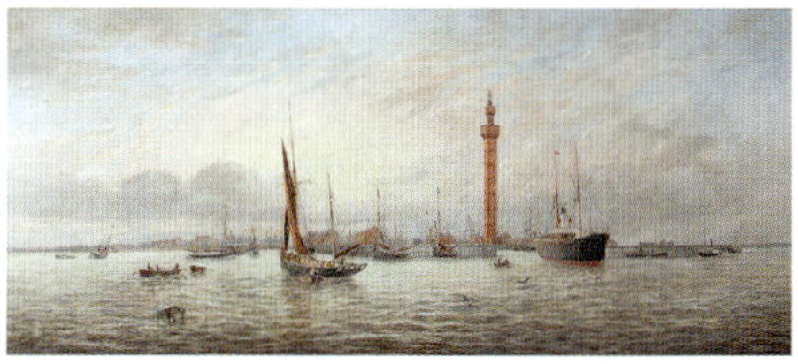

Burwood, George Vemply 1844–1917
Grimsby Docks, Lincolnshire 1896
oil on canvas 67.4 x 152.7
A.32

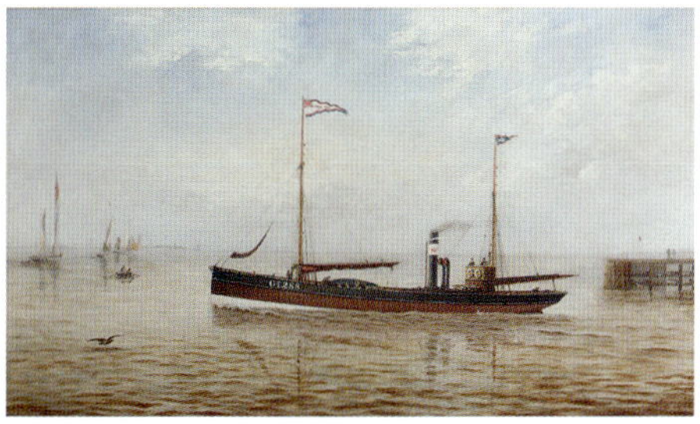

Burwood, George Vemply 1844–1917
The 'Tubal Cain' 1899
oil on canvas 59.5 x 99.5
A.88

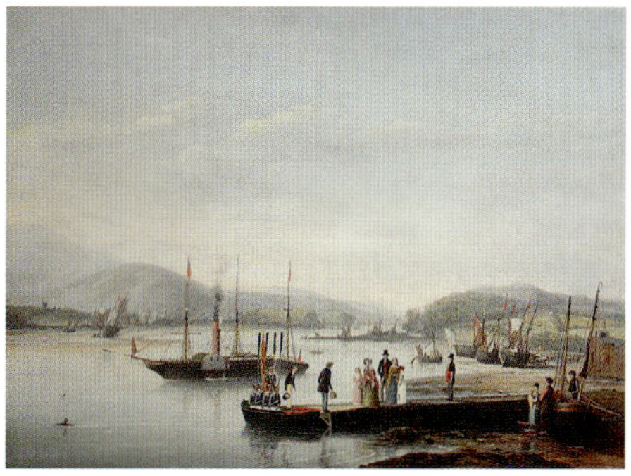

Butler, Joseph
The Departure of Princess Victoria 1832
oil on canvas 64.5 x 86
A.75

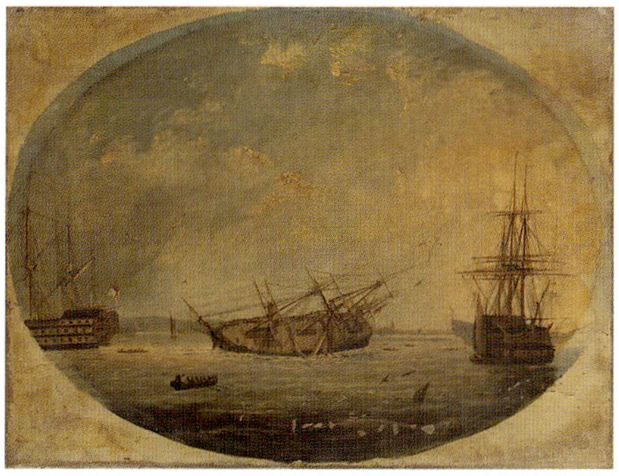

Calvert, Frederick c.1785–c.1845
The Wreck of the 'Royal George'
oil on canvas 35.6 x 45.8
GRIMS:2010.8

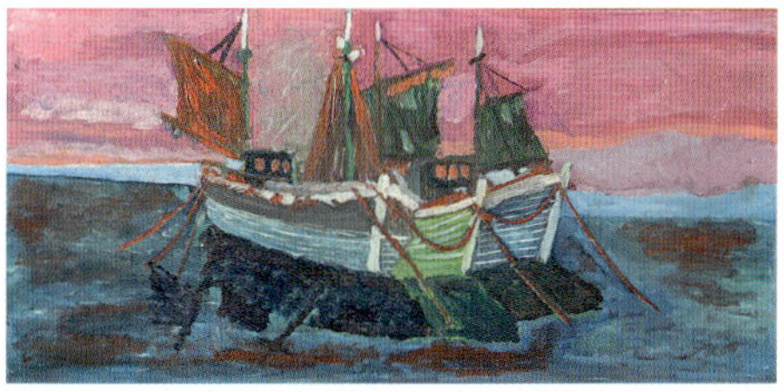

Campling, Herbert John 1879–1939
Three Boats Tied up for the Night
oil on board 24 x 49.5
A.237

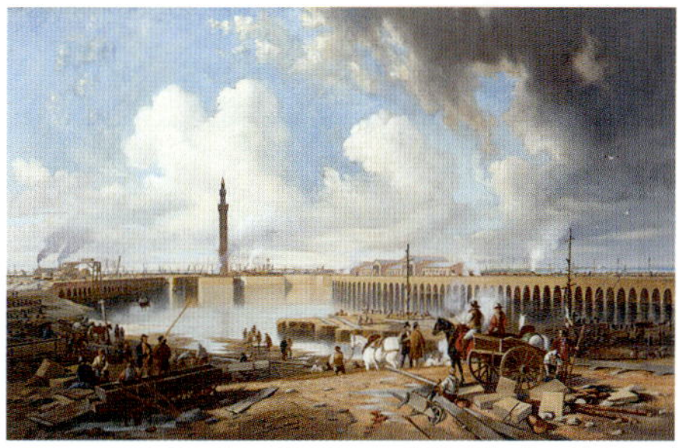

Carmichael, John Wilson 1799–1868
The Construction of the Royal Dock, Grimsby, Lincolnshire 1852
oil on canvas 39.7 x 57
A.204

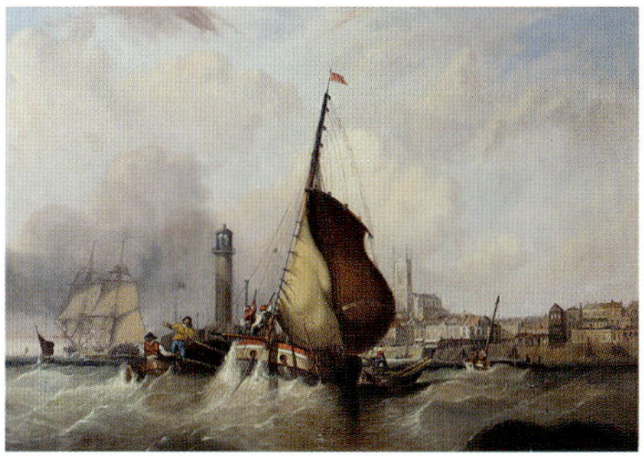

Carmichael, John Wilson 1799–1868
Margate Harbour, Kent
oil on canvas 65 x 90.5
A.205

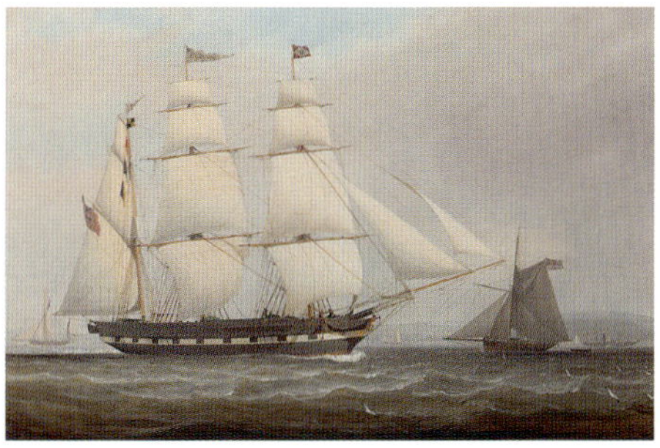

Carmichael, John Wilson 1799–1868
The 'Peruvian'
oil on canvas 36 x 55
A.210

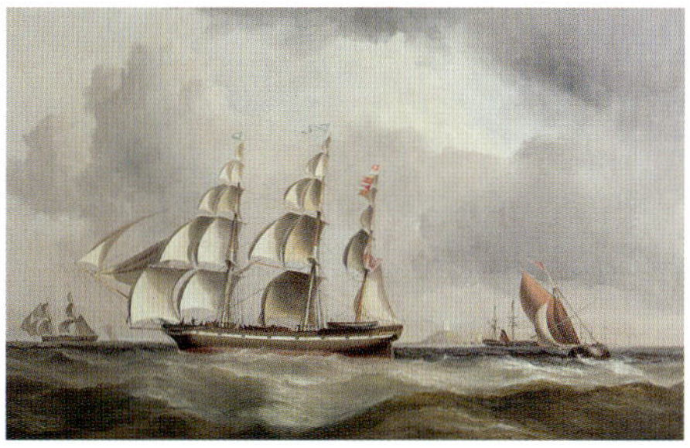

Carmichael, John Wilson 1799–1868
Three-Masted Ship near a Lighthouse
oil on canvas 49 x 81.5
A.152

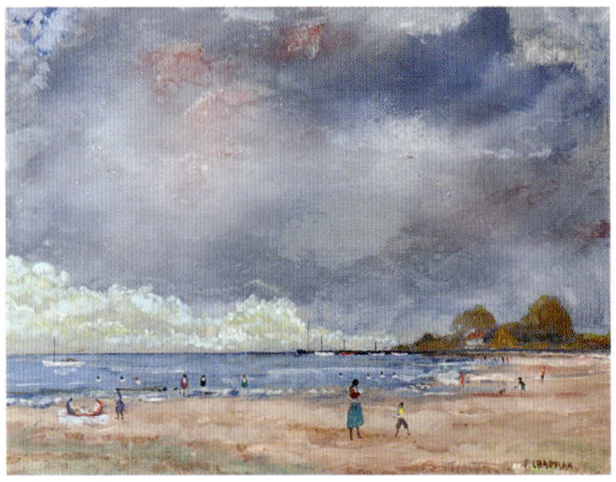

Chapman, E.
Near Sandilands, Lincolnshire
oil on board 36 x 46
A.444

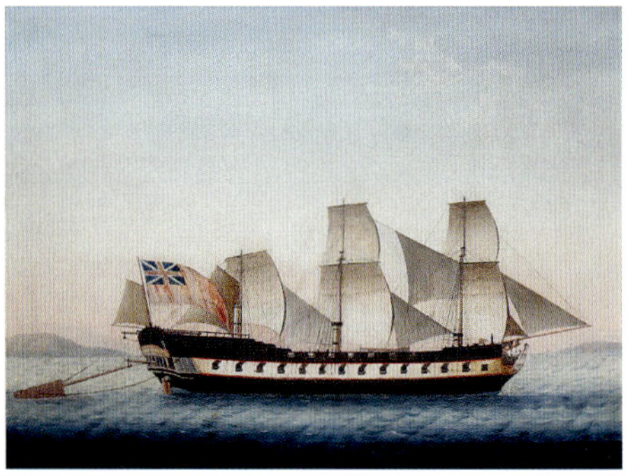

Chinese School
A Three-Masted British Man-of-War
oil on canvas 49 x 59
A.81

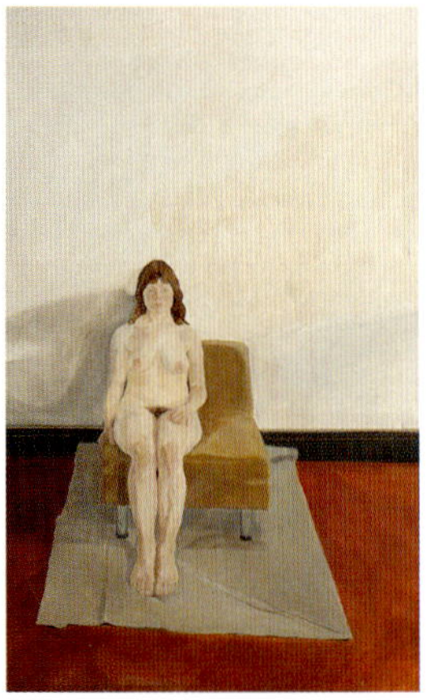

Codd, Tony active 2009
Life Painting, Woman Seated
oil on canvas 141 x 81.5
GRIMS:2009.10.4

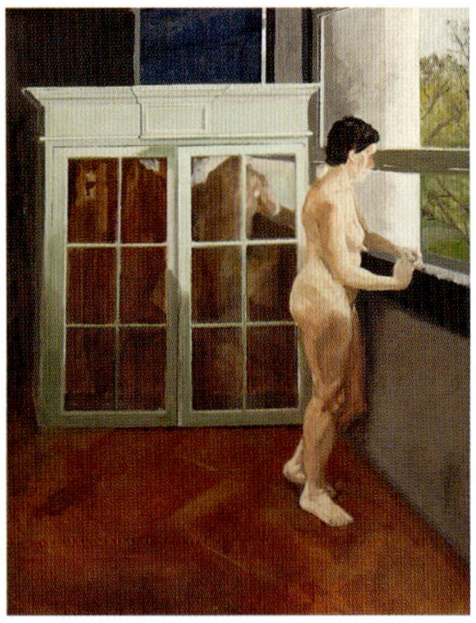

Codd, Tony active 2009
Life Painting, Woman Standing
oil on canvas 104 x 80.5
GRIMS:2009.10.3

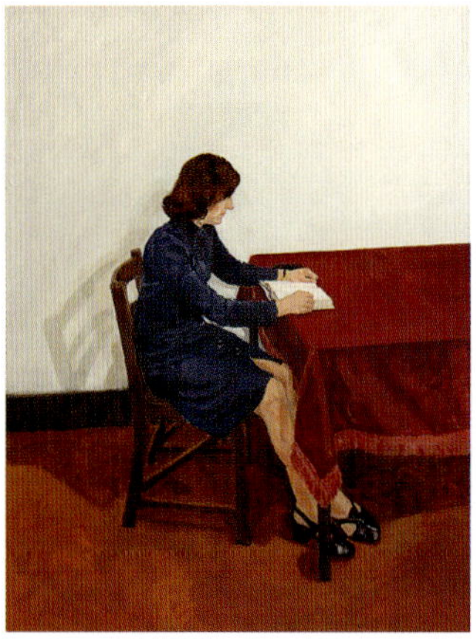

Codd, Tony active 2009
Portrait of a Woman Reading
oil on canvas 121 x 91
GRIMS:2009.10.2

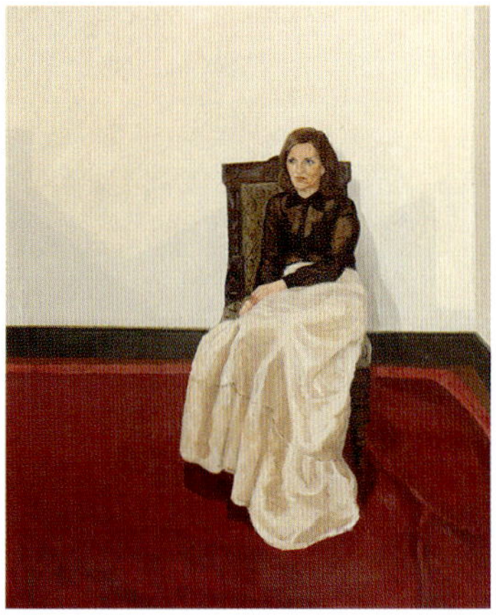

Codd, Tony active 2009
Portrait of a Woman Seated
oil on canvas 98 x 78
GRIMS:2009.10.1

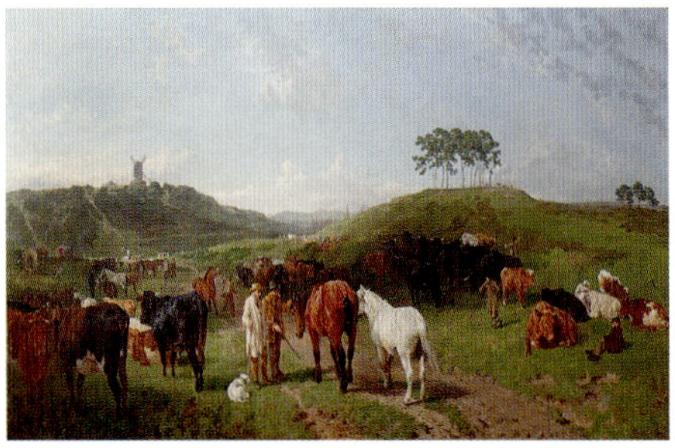

Collins, Charles II 1851–1921
Gypsy Encampment with Horses and Cattle 1877
oil on canvas 110 x 160 (E)
A.27

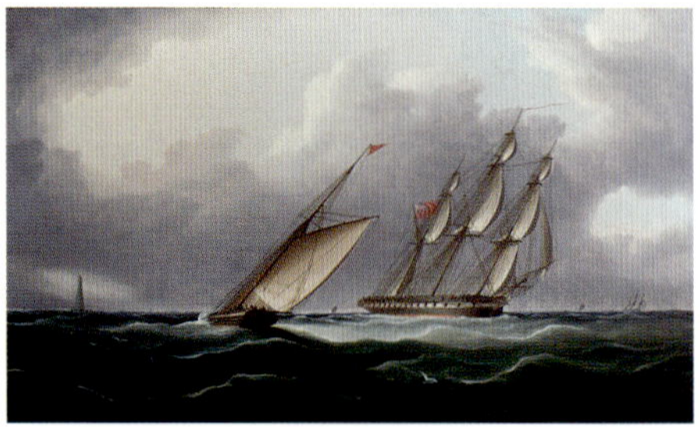

Condy, Nicholas (attributed to) 1793–1857
Two Ships near a Lighthouse
oil on canvas 37.5 x 59.5
A.131

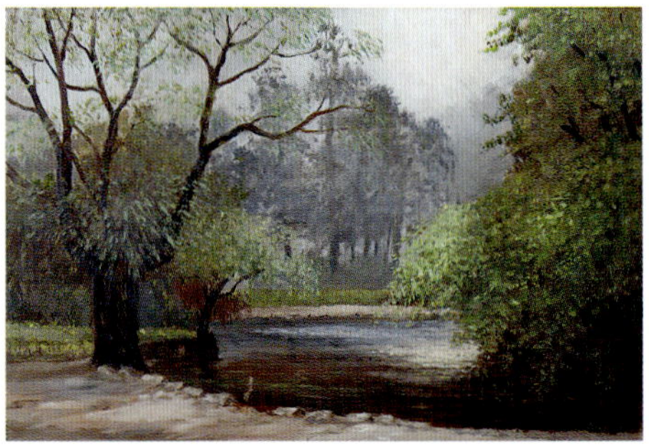

Cook, A. R.
People's Park, Grimsby, Lincolnshire
oil on board 46 x 65
GRIMS:2010.9

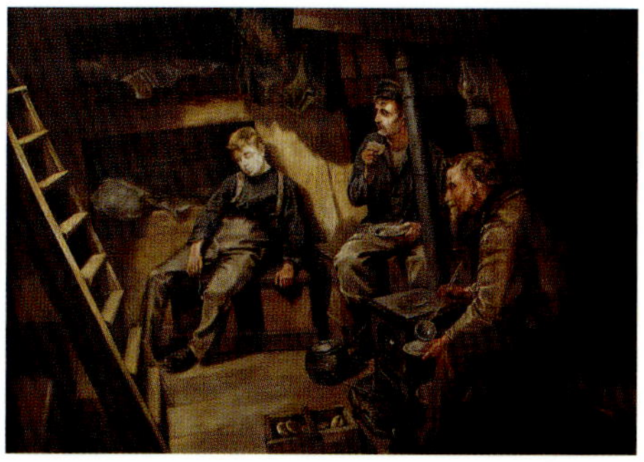

Cooke, A.
The Apprentice's First Voyage
oil on canvas 71.5 x 101.5
A.138

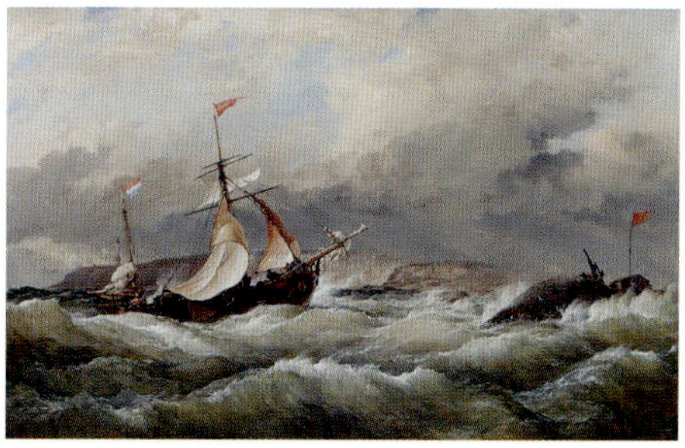

Cooke, Edward William 1811–1880
A Dutch Galliot Entering Aberdeen Harbour in a Storm 1860
oil on canvas 104.5 x 165
A.148

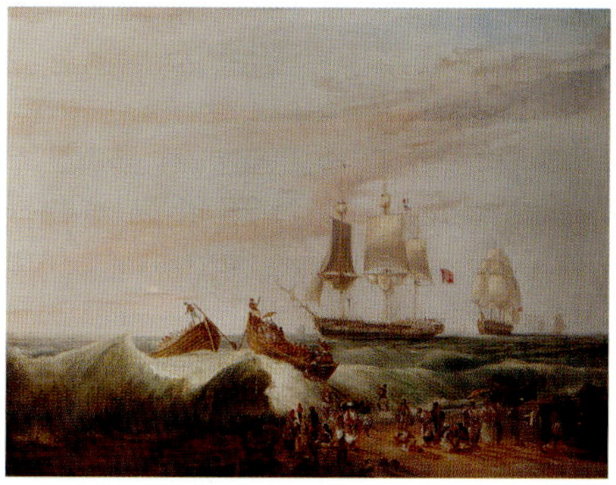

Daniell, William 1769–1837
Landing on the Beach at Madras, India
oil on canvas 70 x 90
A.147

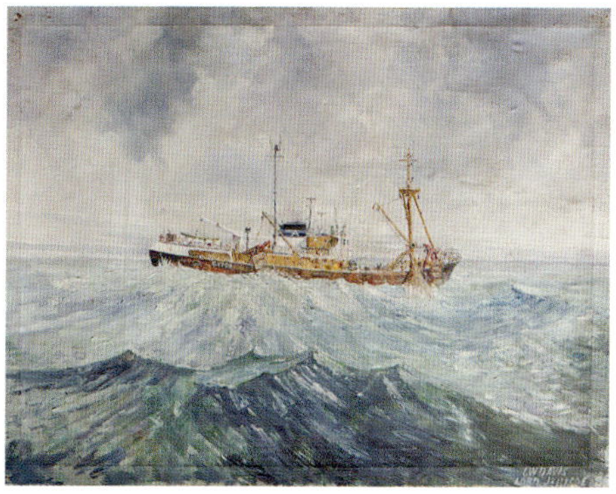

Davis, G. W.
The 'Lord Jellicoe', GY 709
oil on canvas 74.5 x 96
A.180

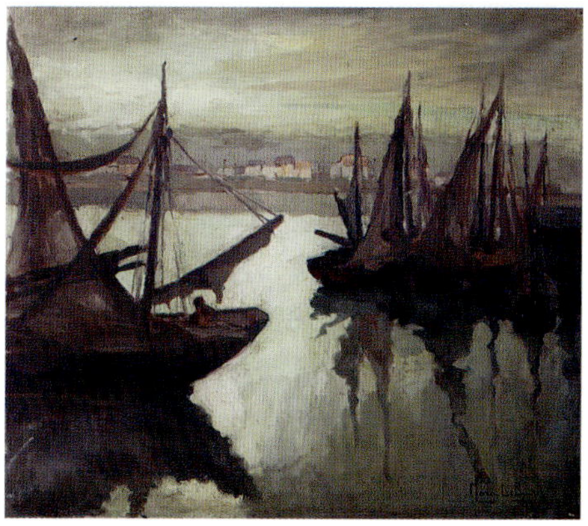

De Baeker, Mary
Zeebruge, Belgium
oil on canvas 69.5 x 80
A.112

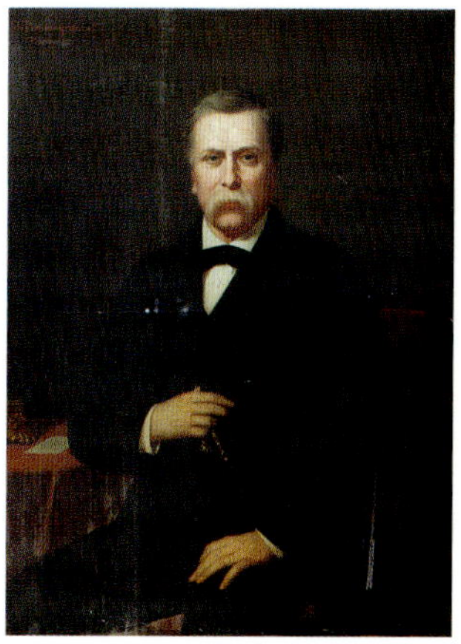

De Pommayrac, Pierre Paul 1807–1880
Henri Josse (1828–1893), MP for Great Grimsby 1873
oil on canvas 115 x 84.5
A.103

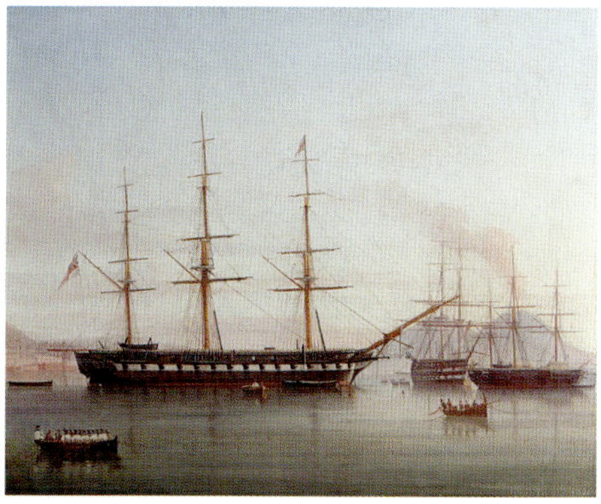

De Simone, Tommaso 1805–1888
British Man-of-War 'Hong Kong' in the Bay of Naples, Italy 1841
oil on canvas 41.5 x 52
A.206

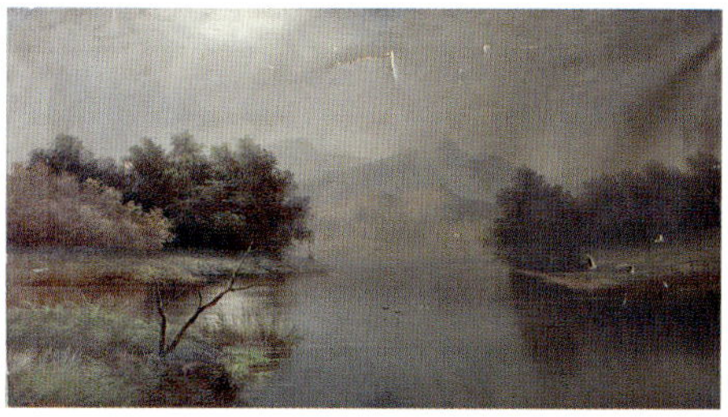

Deleware, V.
River Scene
oil on canvas 61 x 106.5
A.109

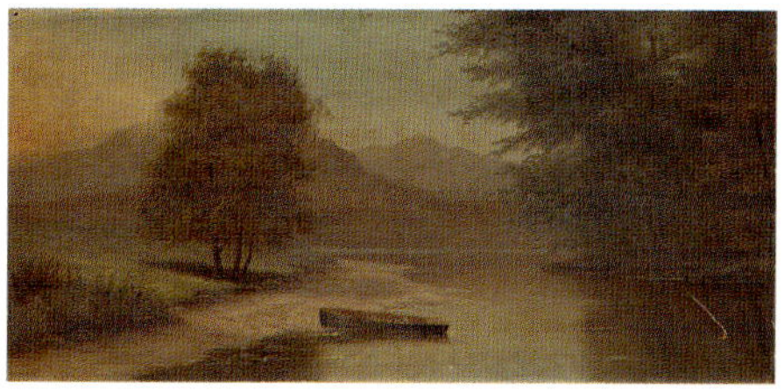

Deleware, V.
River Scene
oil on canvas 30.5 x 61
GRIMS:2010.10

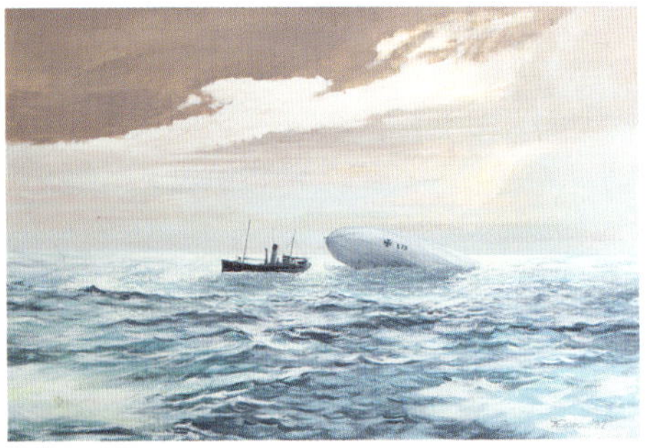

Easton, J.
Trawler GY174 with Zeppelin L19 1982
acrylic on board 60 x 88
Z469

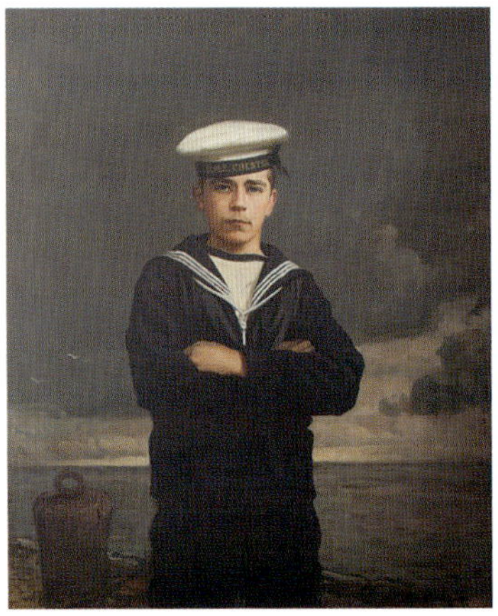

Elwell, Frederick William 1870–1958
John Travers Cornwell (1900–1916), VC 1916
oil on canvas 125.5 x 100.8
Z.13

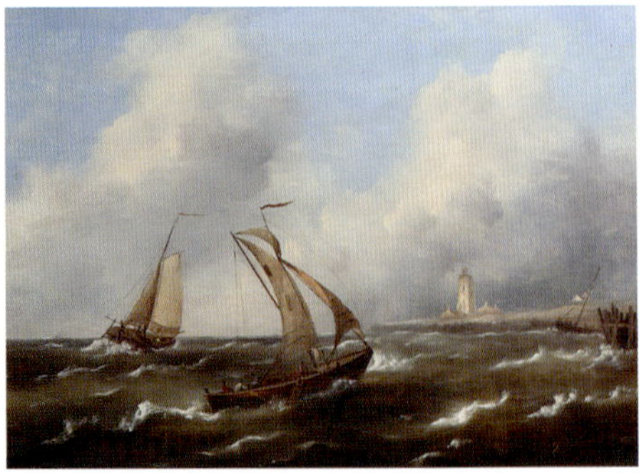

Emmerson, Henry Hetherington 1831–1895
Fishing Vessels off the Coast 1848
oil on canvas 49.5 x 71
A.13

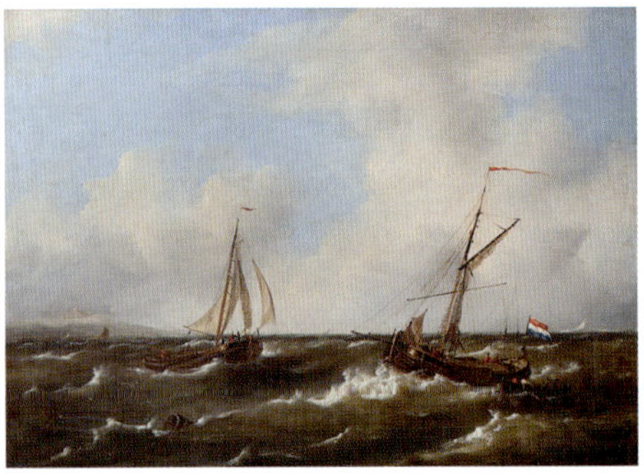

Emmerson, Henry Hetherington (attributed to) 1831–1895
Two Fishing Smacks
oil on canvas 50 x 71.5
A.135

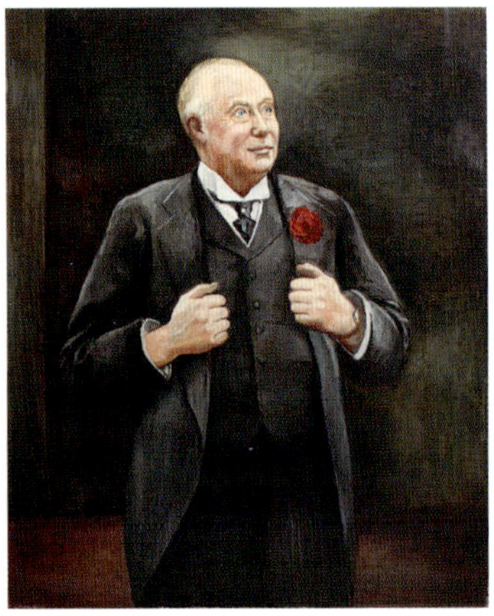

Engers
Sir George Doughty, MP (1895), Mayor of Grimsby (1892–1893)
oil on canvas 127 x 100
A.25

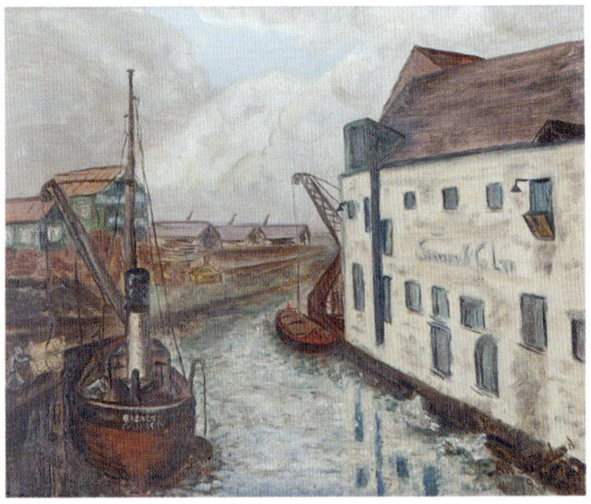

England, Reg
Riverhead, Grimsby, Lincolnshire 1951
oil on canvas 27 x 32
A.431

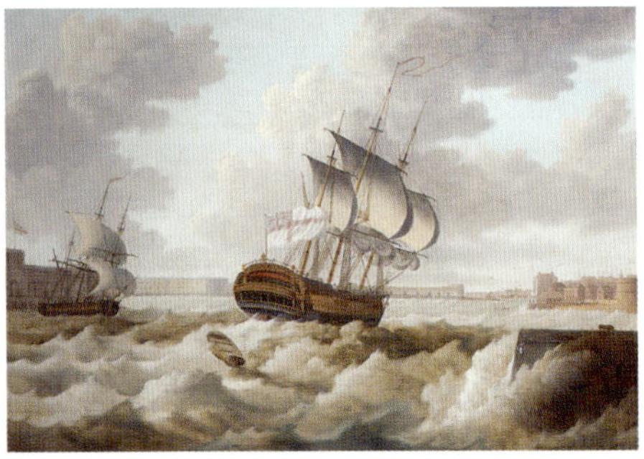

Erdy, John William (attributed to) b.1760
Two Ships in a Harbour
oil on canvas 64 x 90
A.91

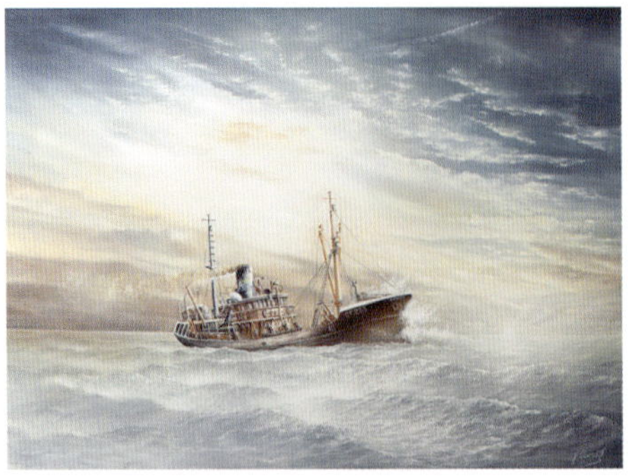

Everett, John 1876–1949
The 'Viveria'
oil on canvas 90 x 119.5
A.402

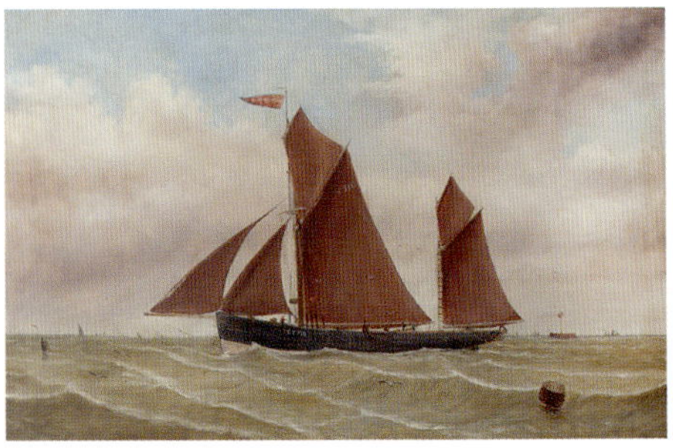

Friston, Frederick Edwin c.1844–1901
The 'Harry Sinclair' 1879
oil on canvas 59 x 89.5
A.435

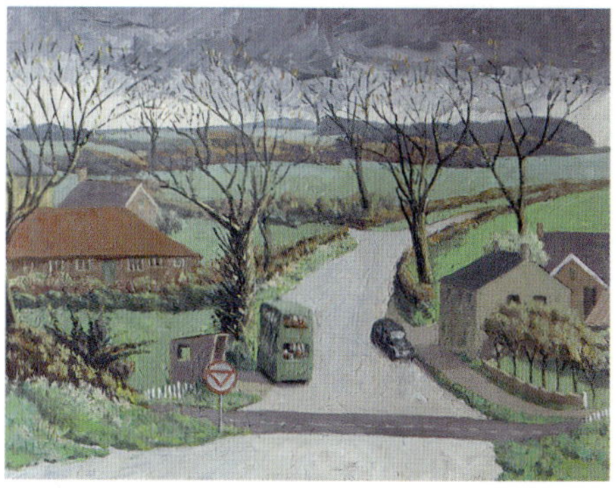

Green, Peter H.
Swallow Crossroads, Grimsby, Lincolnshire
oil on board 41 x 51
A.446

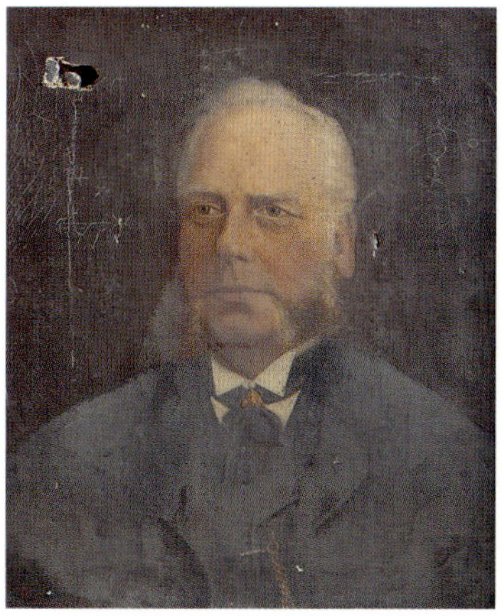

Greensmith, W.
Portrait of an Unknown Gentleman
oil on canvas 61 x 50.5
A.12

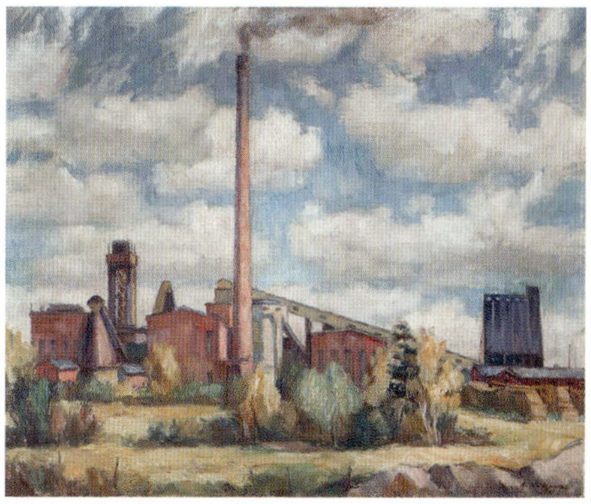

Hakava, Aale 1909–1995
Ogakeghtio Toppila 1951
oil on canvas 72.5 x 92.5
A.114

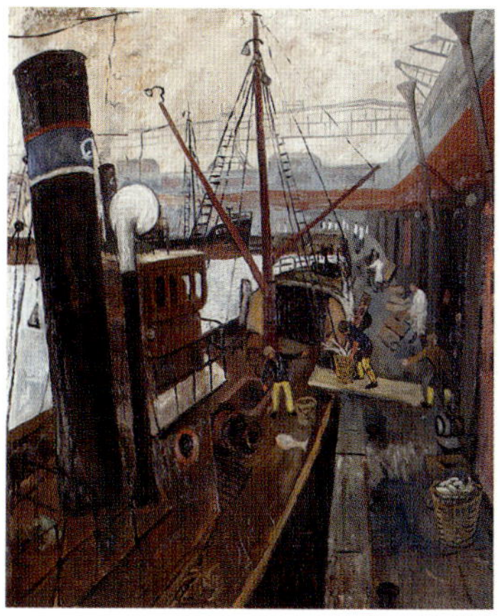

Hancocks, Peter
Grimsby Fish Docks, Lincolnshire 1957
oil on card 85 x 71
A.183

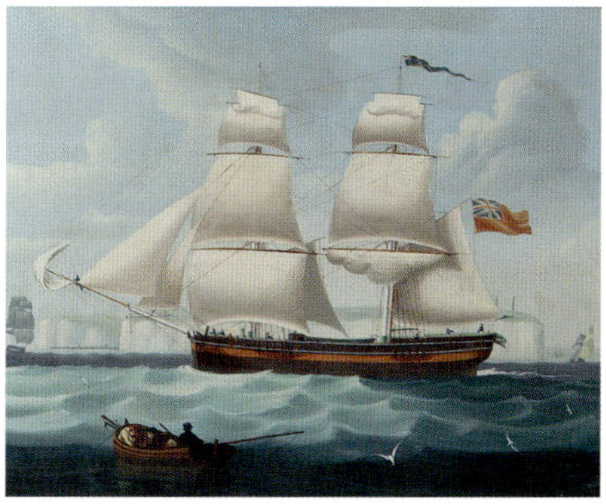

Headgren
The 'Alchemist' off Dover, Kent
oil on canvas 61 x 73.5
A.92

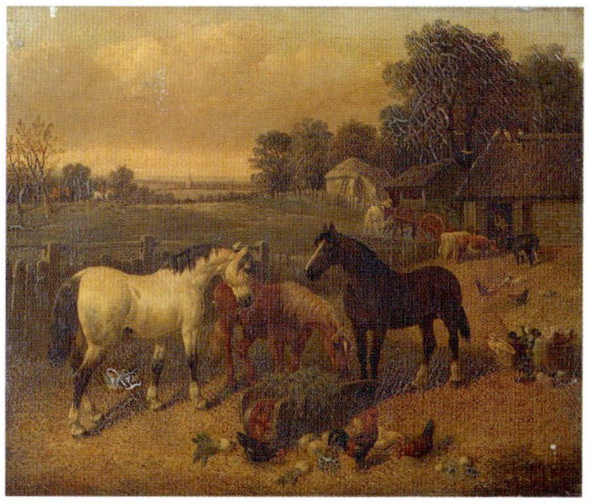

Herring, John Frederick I (school of) 1795–1865
Farmyard Scene
oil on canvas 51 x 61
A.98

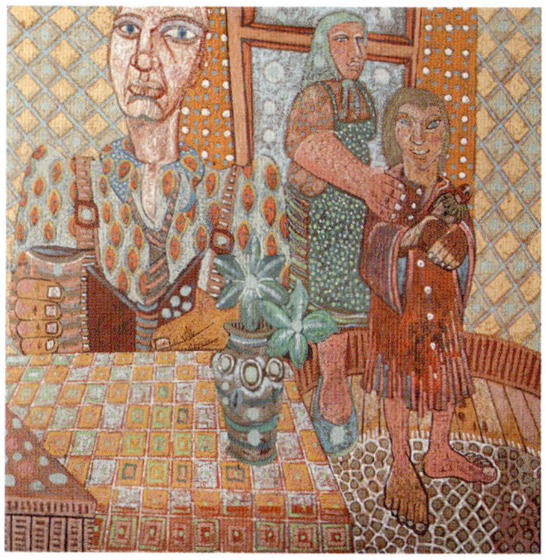

Hopkinson, John b.1941
The Family c.1970
oil on board 89 x 89
A.408a

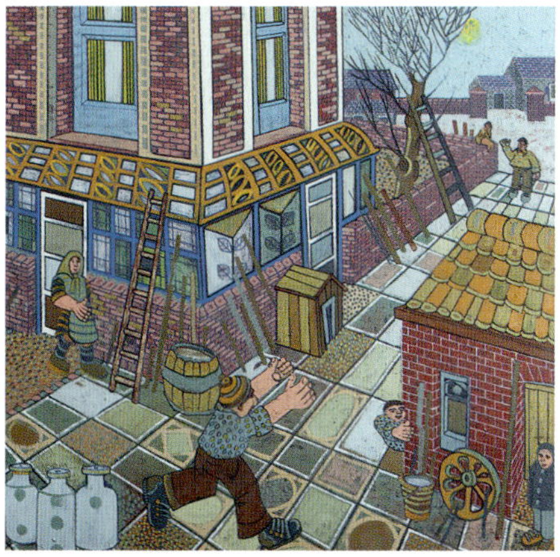

Hopkinson, John b.1941
The Return of the Prodigal Son c.1970
oil on board 89 x 89
A.409

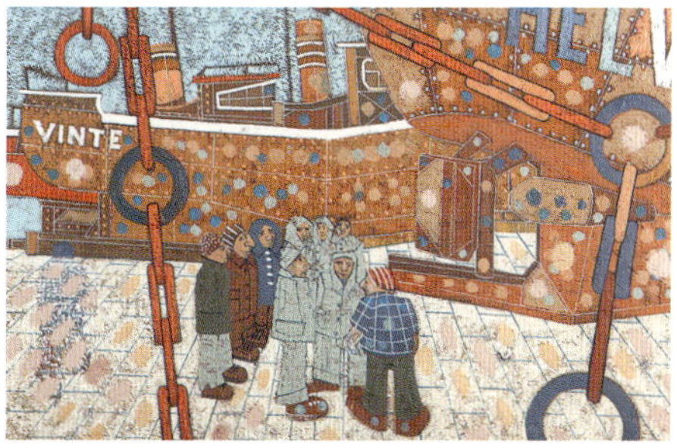

Hopkinson, John b.1941
Shipyard 1979
oil on board 58.5 x 89
A.410

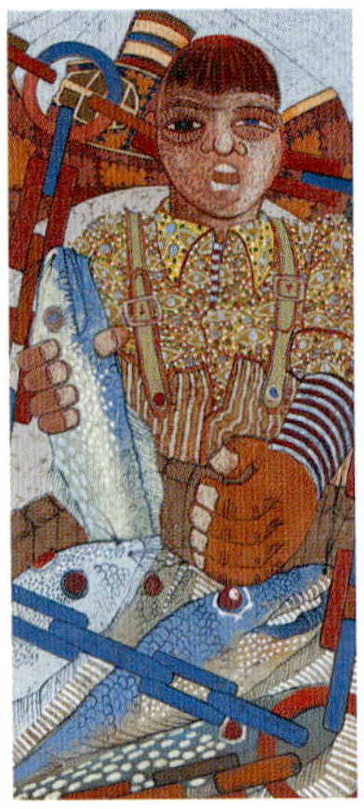

Hopkinson, John b.1941
Resentment 1980
oil on board 150 x 65.5
A.411

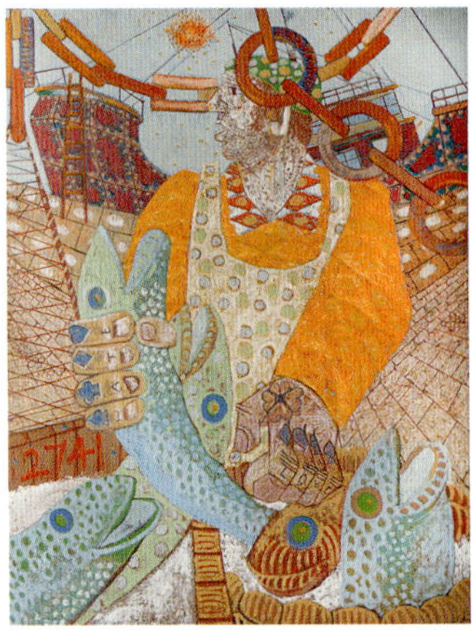

Hopkinson, John b.1941
Souvenirs 1980
oil on board 119 x 89
A.412

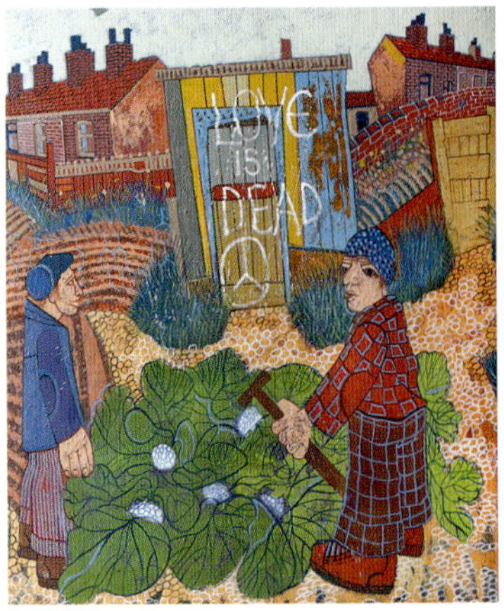

Hopkinson, John b.1941
Conversation 1981
oil on board 89.5 x 81.5
GRIMS:2010.11

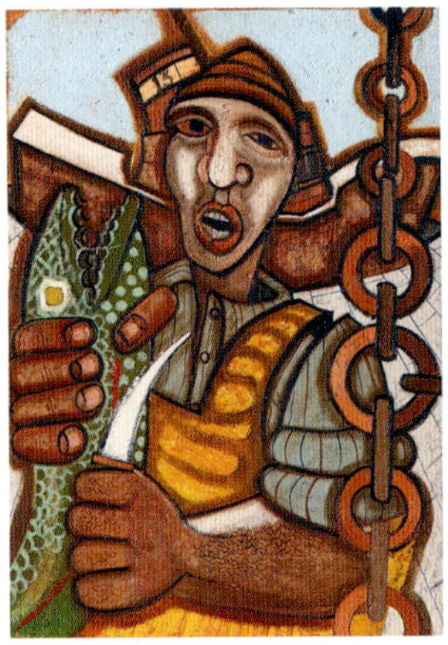

Hopkinson, John b.1941
Do Fish Scream? 1981
oil on board 89 x 62
A.413

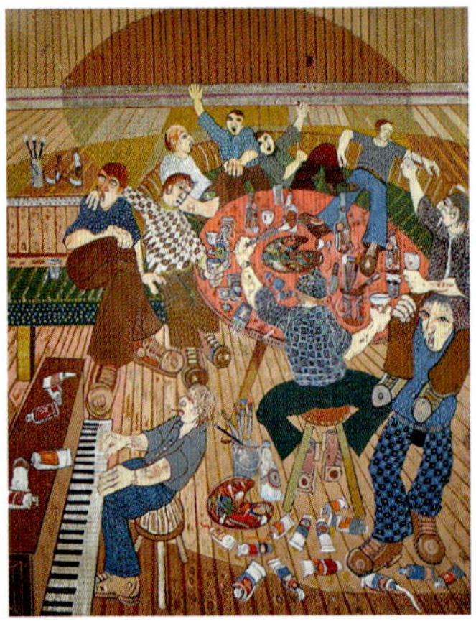

Hopkinson, John b.1941
Artists in the Pub
oil on board 121 x 90
GRIMS:2009.14.1

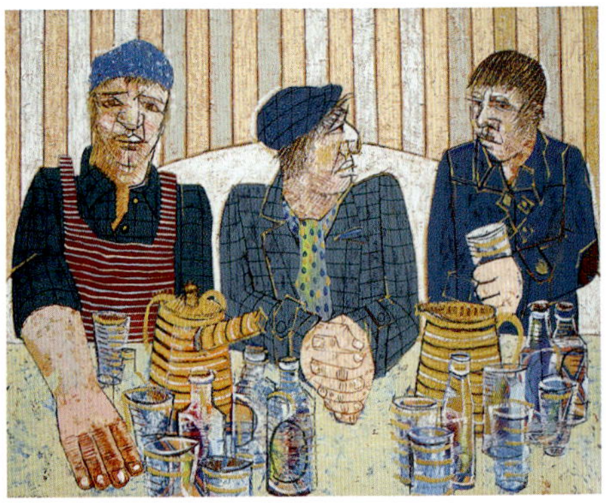

Hopkinson, John b.1941
Fish Workers' Canteen
oil on board 51 x 60
GRIMS:2009.14.3

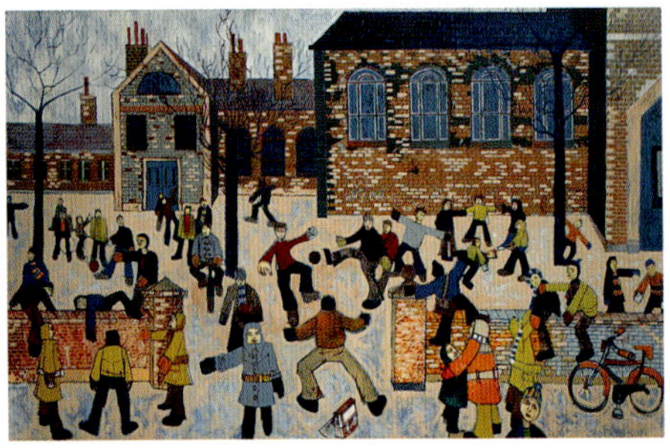

Hopkinson, John b.1941
School Playground
oil on board 74.5 x 120.5
GRIMS:2009.14.2

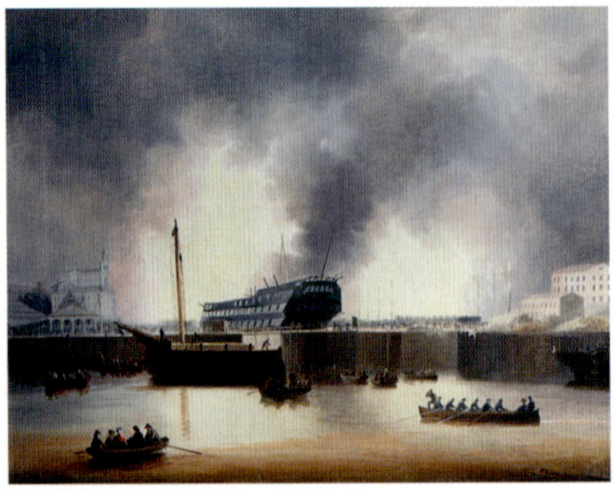

Hornbrook, Thomas Lyde 1780–1850
Dockyard Fire, 1840
oil on canvas 43.5 x 60
A.141

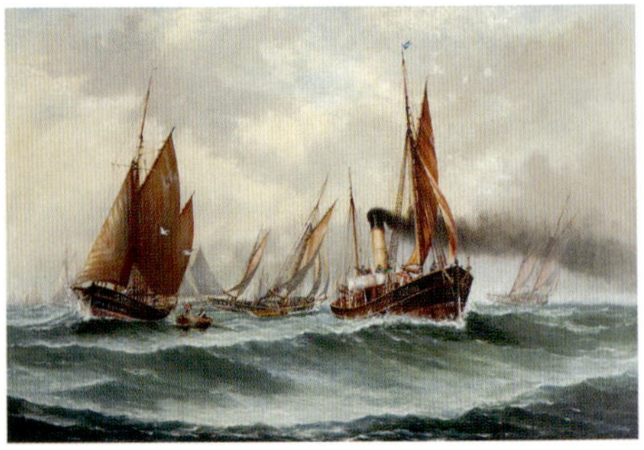

Hote, Kenneth
Fleeting c.1890
oil on canvas 50 x 75.5
A.137

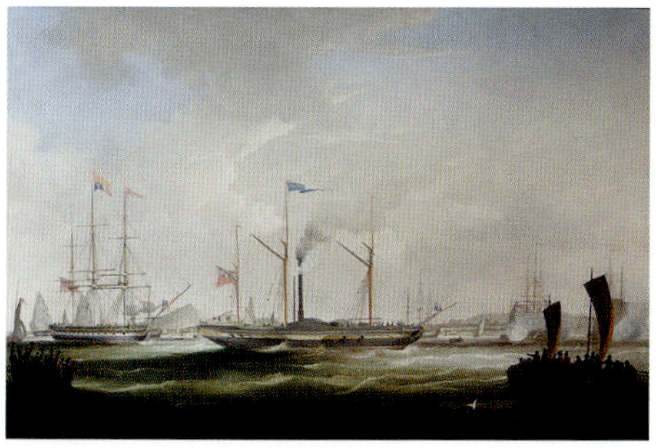

Huggins, William John 1781–1845
SS 'James Wyatt' Towing the Royal Yacht, 'Royal George' on the Visit of George IV to Edinburgh, August 1824
oil on canvas 90 x 151
A.30

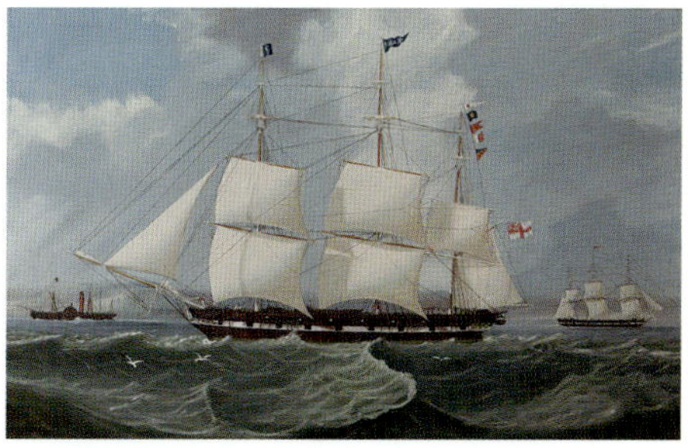

Huggins, William John 1781–1845
The 'Leguan'
oil on canvas 52.5 x 81.5
A.111

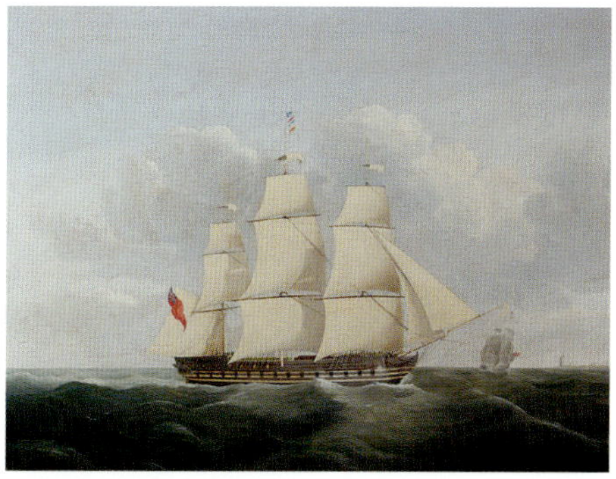

Huggins, William John 1781–1845
Three-Masted Frigate
oil on canvas 71 x 91
A.90

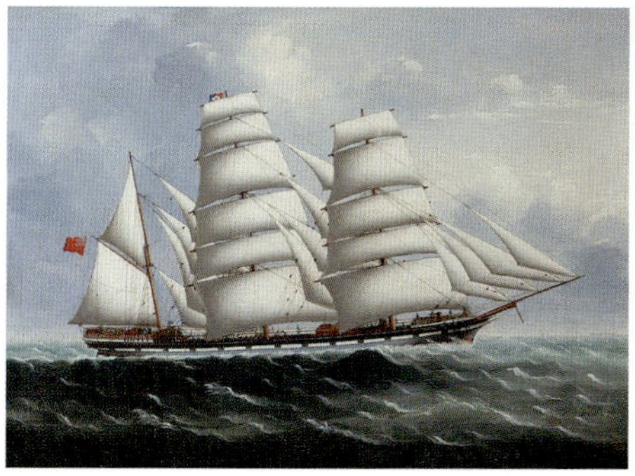

Huggins, William John (attributed to) 1781–1845
The 'Newark' 1840
oil on canvas 45.3 x 59.6
A.80

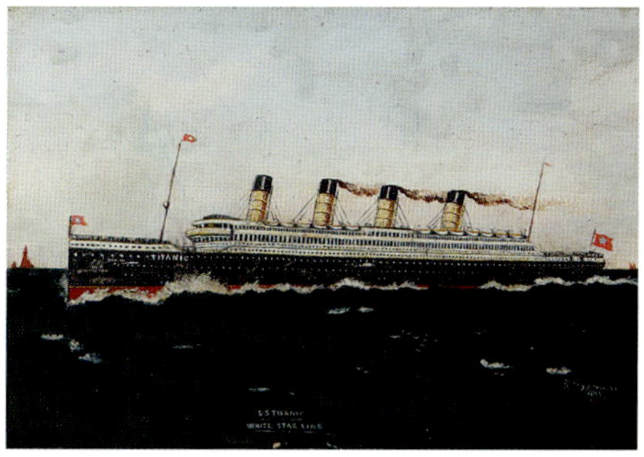

Hyam, B. active 1912–1914
SS 'Titanic' 1912
oil on board 22.5 x 31
GRIMS:2010.12

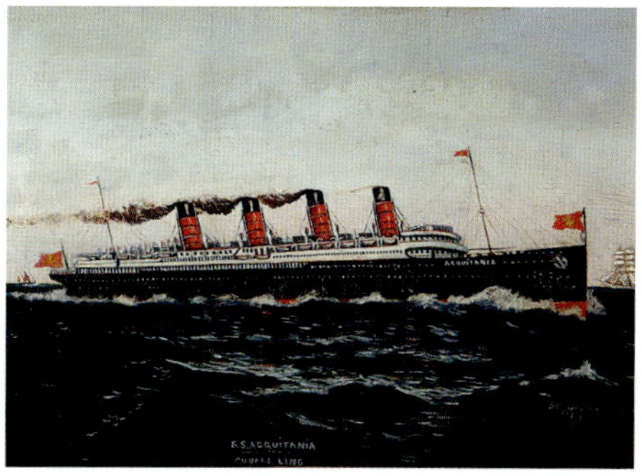

Hyam, B. active 1912–1914
The 'Acquitania' 1914
oil on board 23 x 31
GRIMS:2010.13

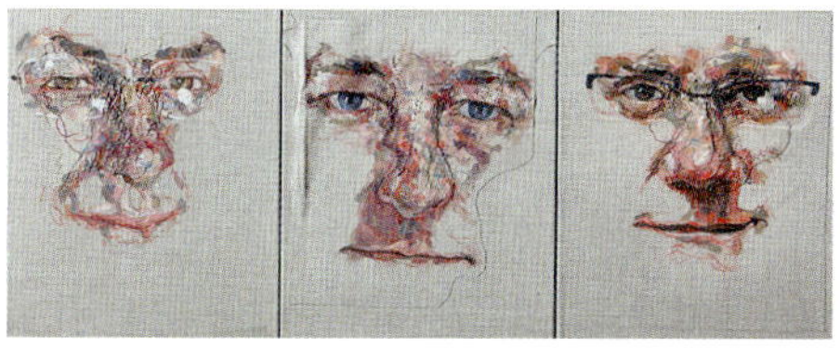

Ingham, Linda b.1964
Three Generations (Thomas Brian Ingham, Richard Coulbeck, Richard Harris)
oil on canvas
25.5 x 20.4; 25.6 x 20.5; 25.7 x 20.3
GRIMS.2009.4

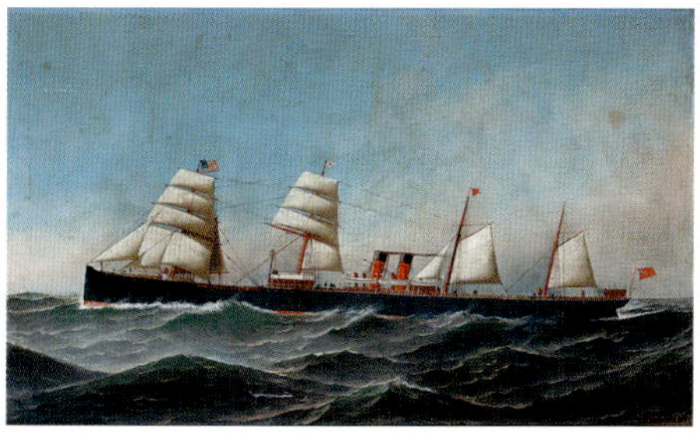

Jacobsen, Antonio 1850–1921
SS 'Buffalo' 1887
oil on canvas 56 x 91.5
A.78

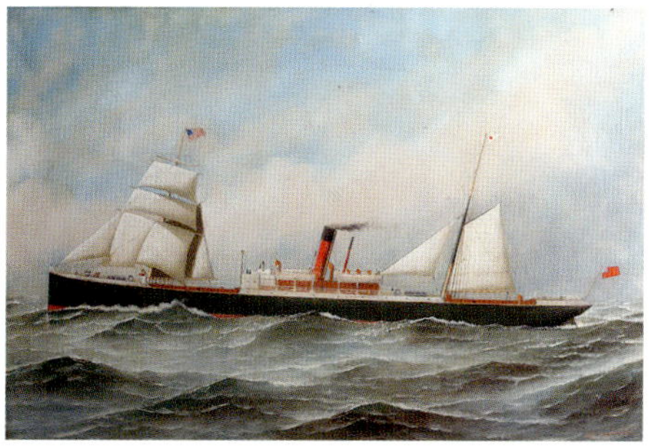

Jacobsen, Antonio 1850–1921
The 'Hindoo' 1893
oil on canvas 54 x 90
A.182

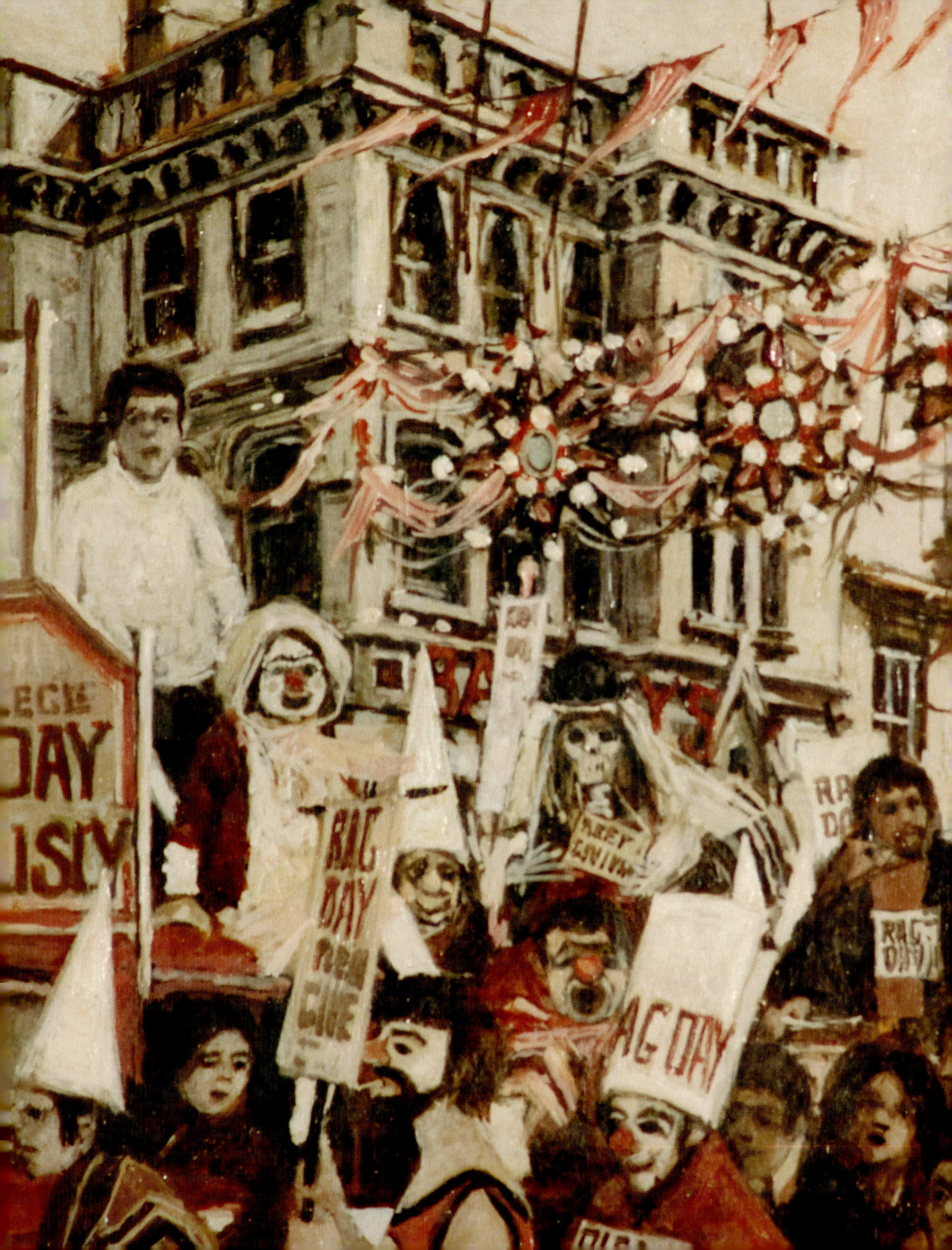
RAG DAY

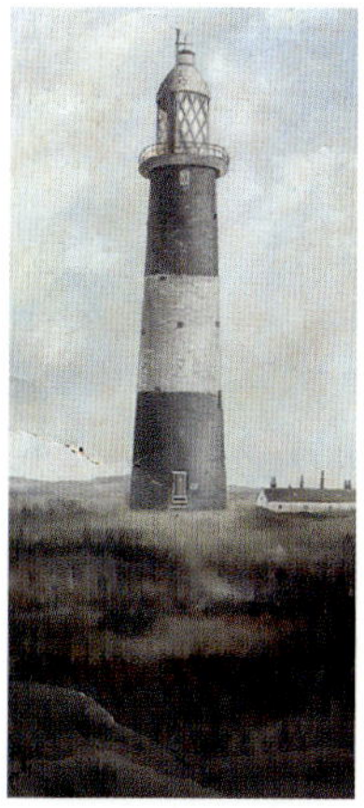

James, Frederick Charles 1873–1926
Lighthouse 1911
oil on card 45 x 19.5
A.170

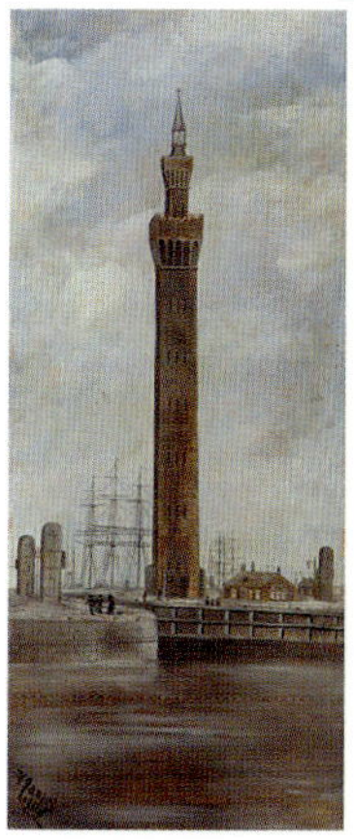

James, Frederick Charles 1873–1926
Royal Dock Tower, Grimsby, Lincolnshire 1911
oil on card 51 x 20.3
A.171

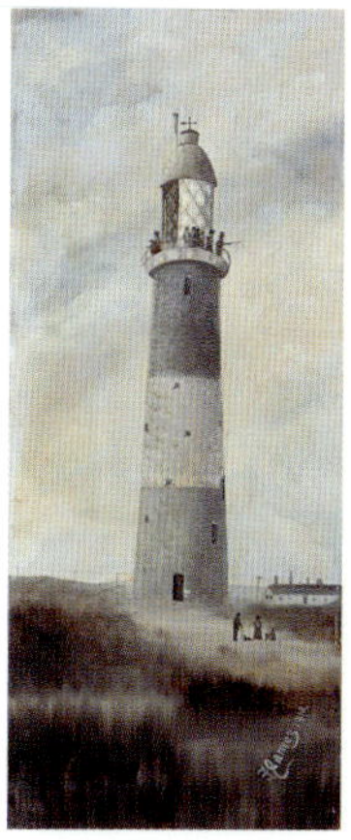

James, Frederick Charles 1873–1926
Lighthouse 1912
oil on card 51.2 x 21.2
A.169

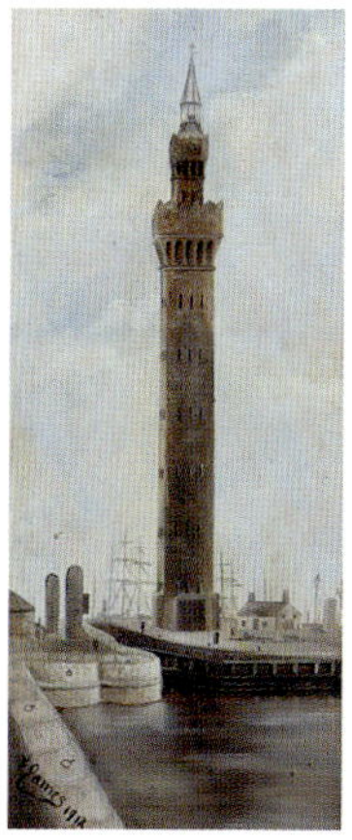

James, Frederick Charles 1873–1926
Royal Dock Tower, Grimsby, Lincolnshire 1912
oil on card 48 x 20
A.99

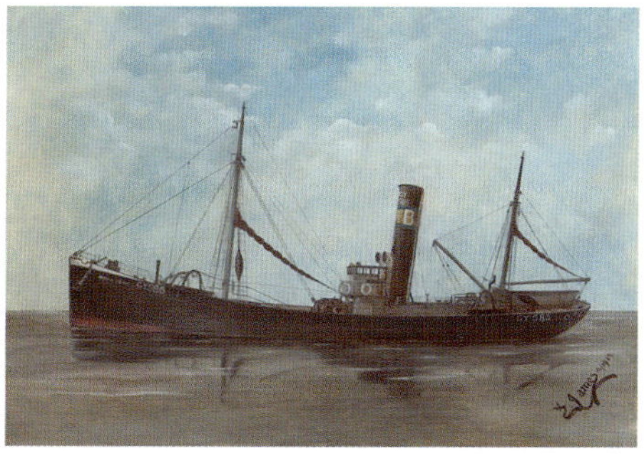

James, Frederick Charles 1873–1926
The 'Manx Hero', GY 585 1914
oil on board 42.4 x 62.7
A.184

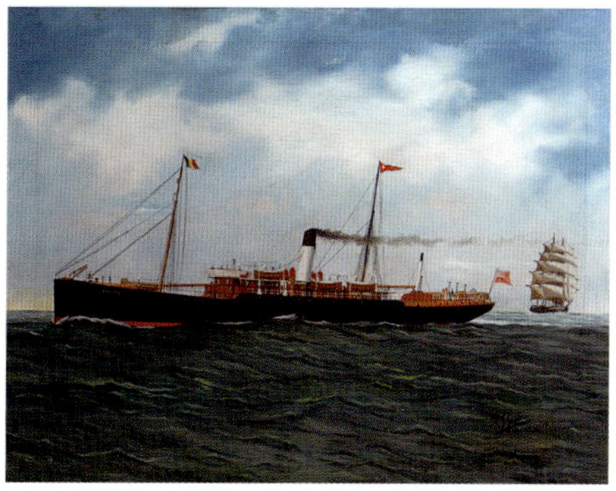

Jansen, A. J. active 1906–1933
The 'Ashton' 1906
oil on canvas 53.5 x 76
A.165

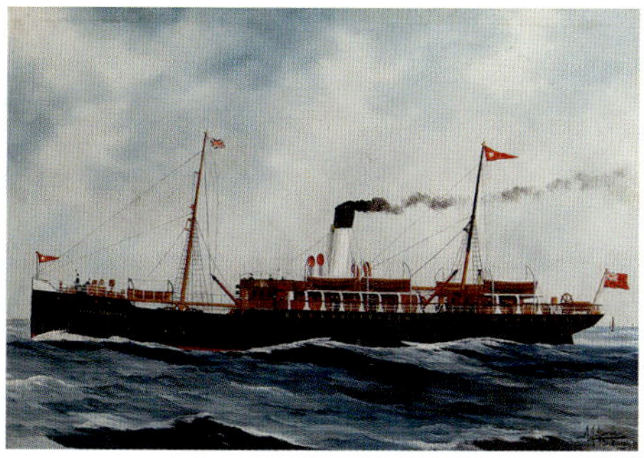

Jansen, A. J. active 1906–1933
The 'City of Bradford' 1916
oil on canvas 40.9 x 62.2
A.82

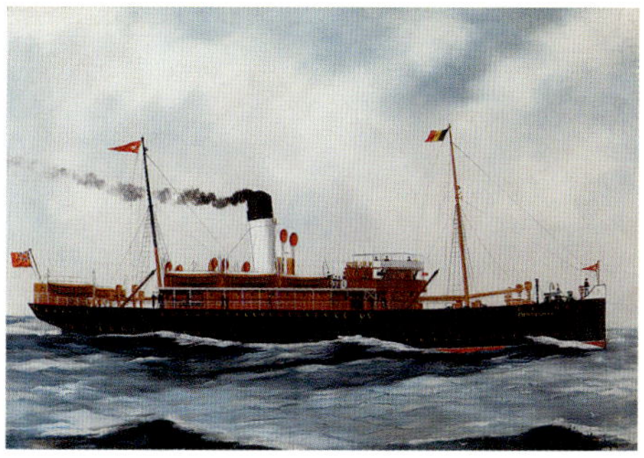

Jansen, A. J. active 1906–19332
The 'Immingham' 1916
oil on canvas 41 x 63
A.177

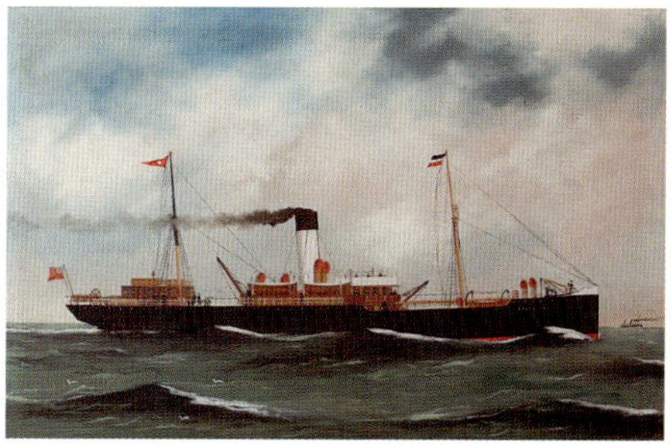

Jansen, A. J. active 1906–1933
The 'Staveley'
oil on canvas 53 x 72.5
A.144

Facing page: Brannan, Peter, 1926–1994, *Rag Day, Lincoln* (detail), 1973, The Collection: Art & Archaeology in Lincolnshire (Usher Gallery) (p. 286)

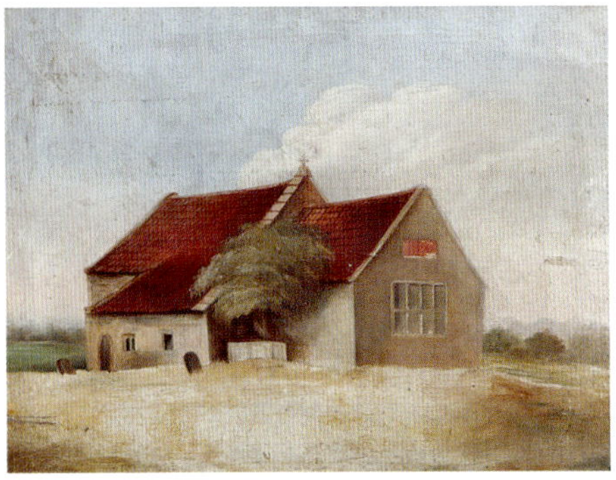

Jillot, James (attributed to) 1800–1880
Landscape with a Church
oil on canvas 27.5 x 35
A.407

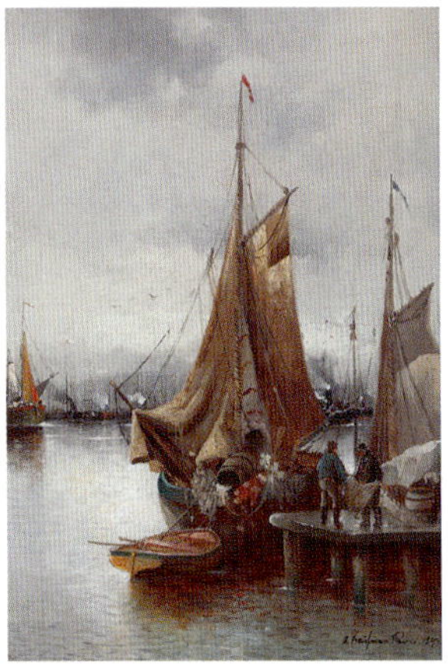

Kaufman, Adolf 1848–1916
Unloading a Boat at a Quayside, Paris c.1890
oil on canvas 46.4 x 30.8
A.65

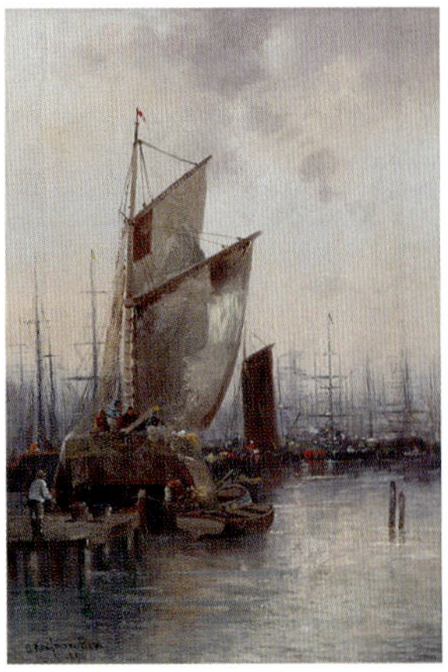

Kaufman, Adolf 1848–1916
Harbour Scene 1894
oil on canvas 45.9 x 30.5
A.129

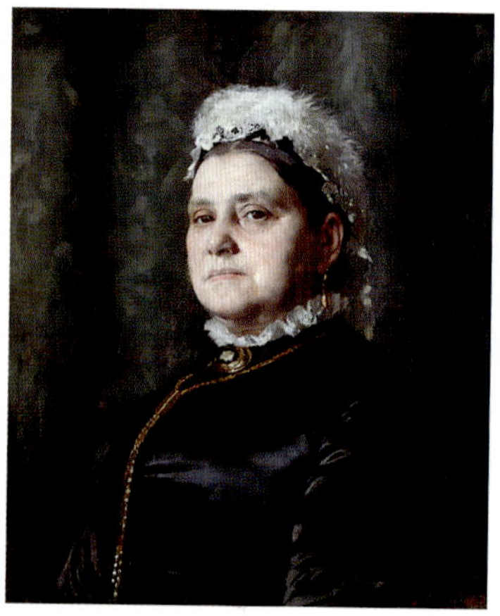

Kennington, Thomas Benjamin 1856–1916
Portrait of a Lady with a White Cap 1893
oil on canvas 60 x 50
A.44

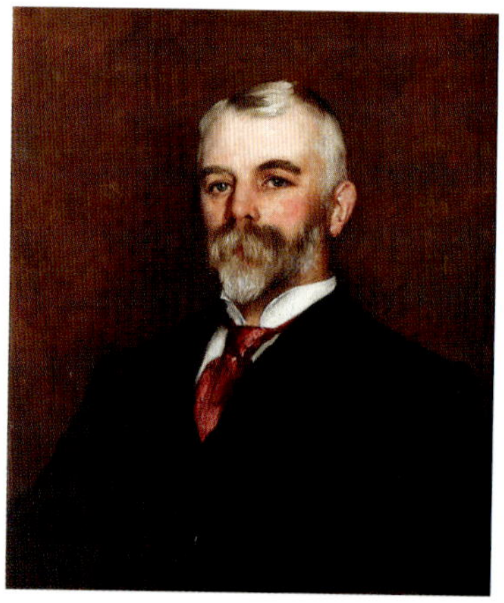

Kennington, Thomas Benjamin 1856–1916
Portrait of an Unknown Man with a Beard
1895
oil on canvas 69 x 58
A.45

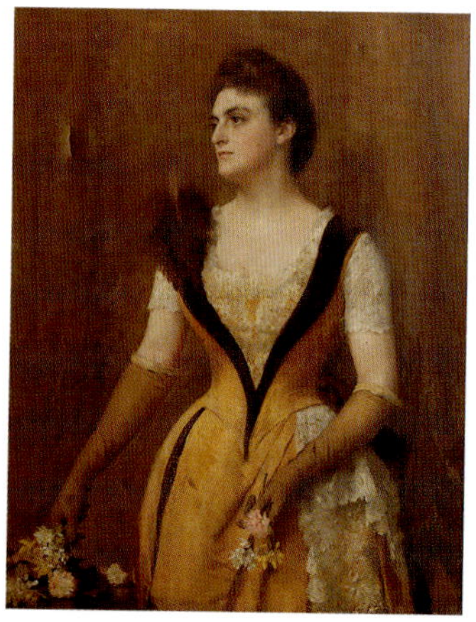

Kennington, Thomas Benjamin 1856–1916
Portrait of an Unknown Lady c.1900
oil on canvas 110.3 x 85
A.10

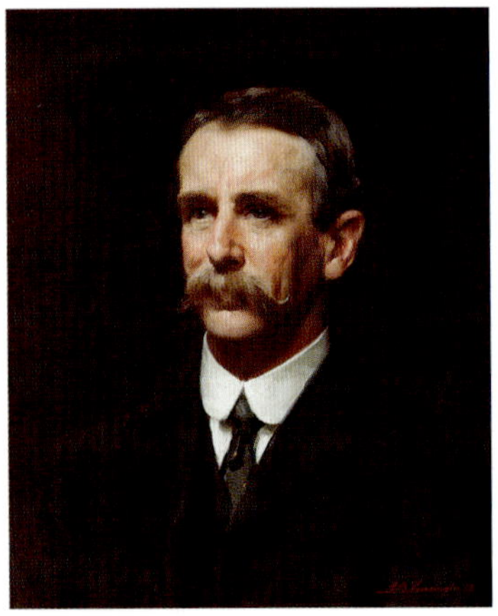

Kennington, Thomas Benjamin 1856–1916
George Skelton (1855–1932) 1913
oil on canvas 54.5 x 44
A.434

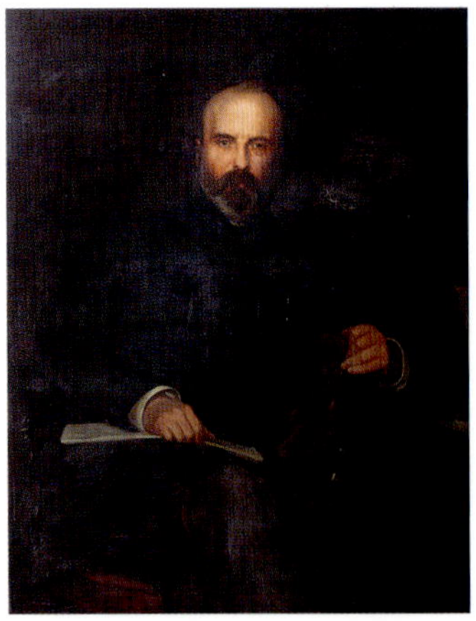

Kennington, Thomas Benjamin 1856–1916
John Wintringham, Mayor of Grimsby (1864–1865)
oil on canvas 127 x 101.5
A.270

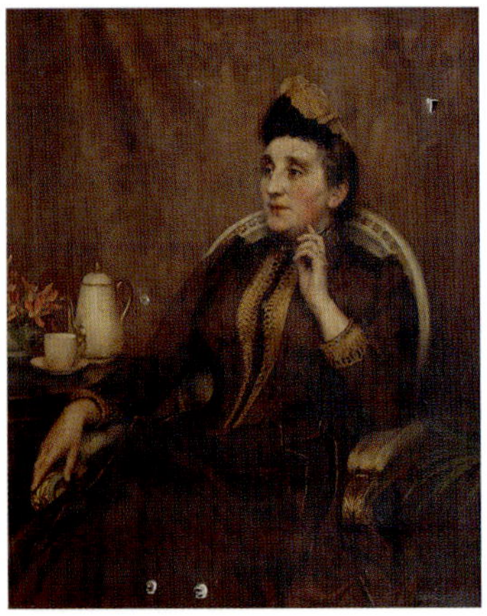

Kennington, Thomas Benjamin 1856–1916
Mrs Wintringham
oil on canvas 126 x 100.5
A.259

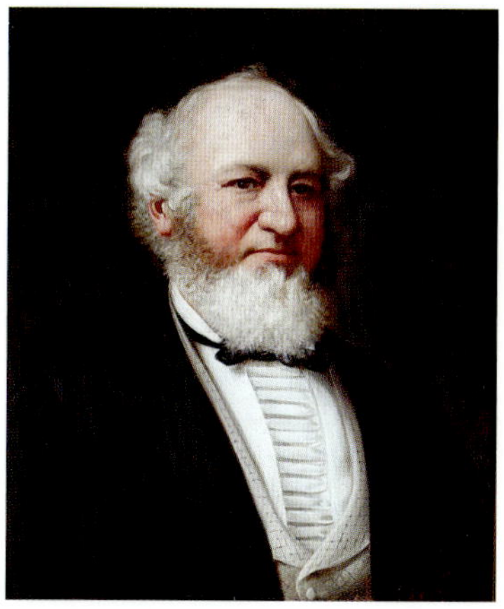

Kennington, Thomas Benjamin 1856–1916
Portrait of an Unknown Man
oil on canvas 60 x 50
A.8

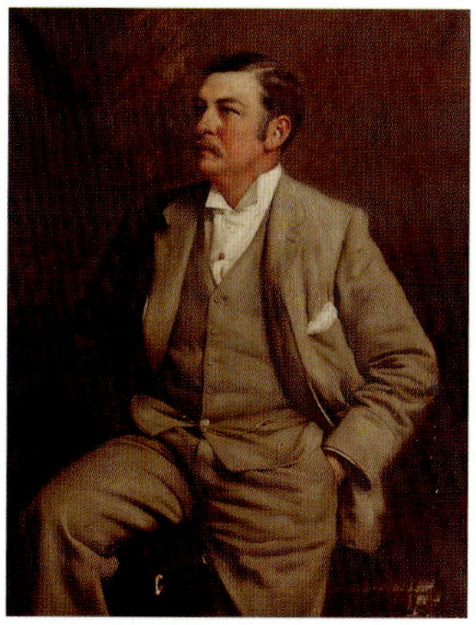

Kennington, Thomas Benjamin 1856–1916
Portrait of an Unknown Man
oil on canvas 111.5 x 85
A.17

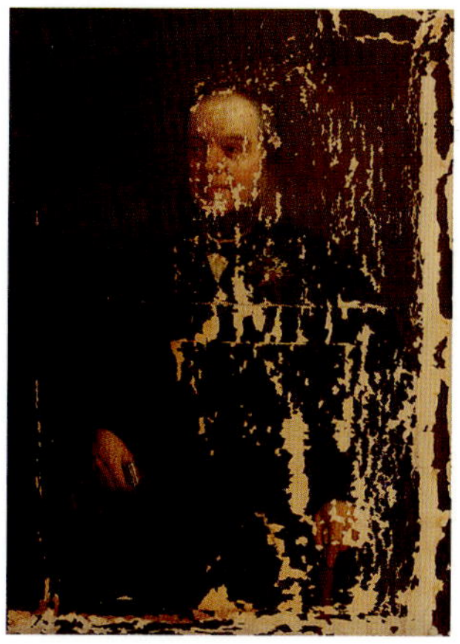

Kennington, Thomas Benjamin (attributed to) 1856–1916
Charles Bartholomew Moody, Mayor of Grimsby (1855–1856)
oil on canvas 120 x 83
A.104

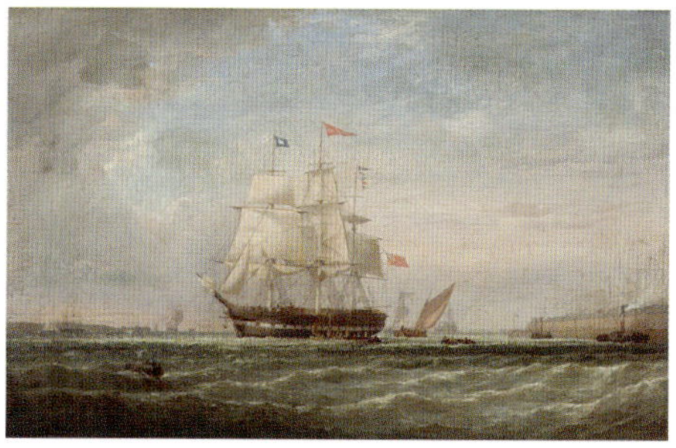

Knell, William Adolphus 1802–1875
A Man-of-War and Other Shipping in Harbour c.1840
oil on canvas 39.3 x 59.6
A.153

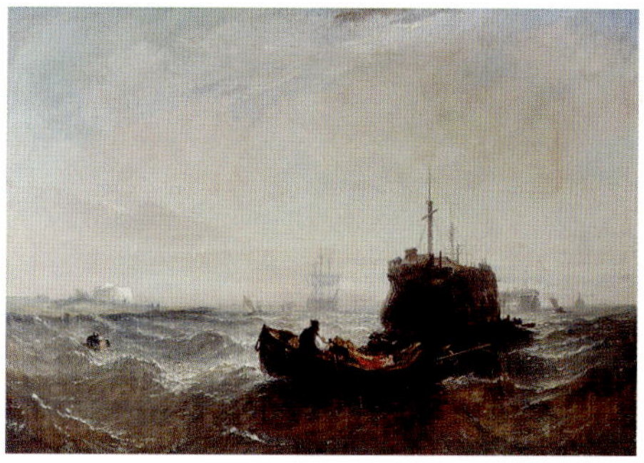

Knell, William Adolphus 1802–1875
The Old Hulk
oil on canvas 62 x 90
A.149

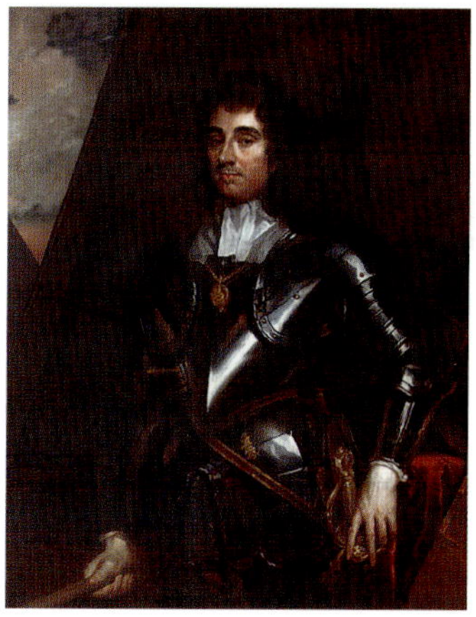

Lely, Peter (attributed to) 1618–1680
George Monck (b.1608), 1st Duke of Abermarle
oil on canvas 123.5 x 97.5
A.34

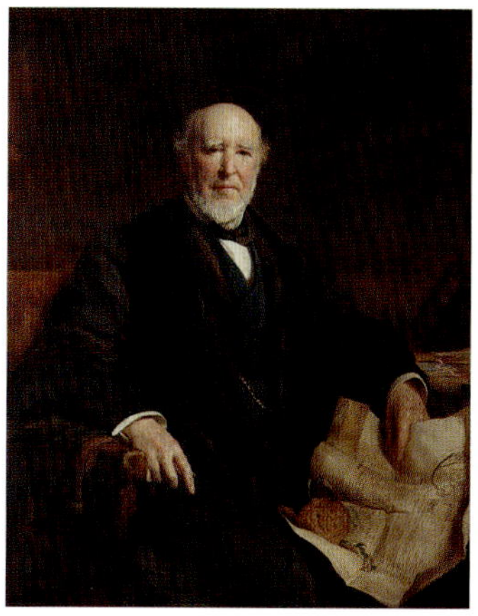

Lolie, M.
William Grange (1861–1913), Town Clerk of Grimsby 1899
oil on canvas 125.7 x 100.5
A.231

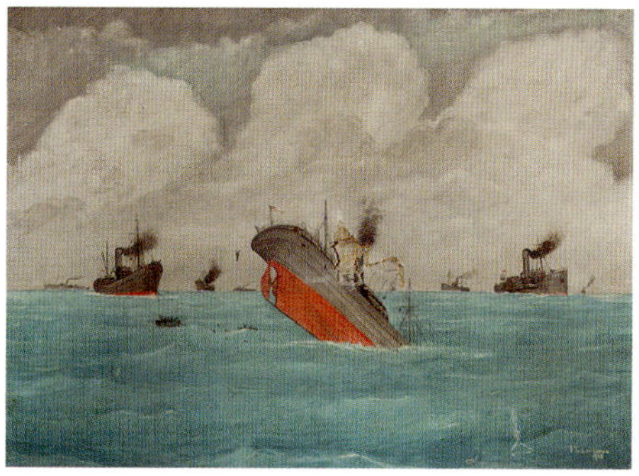

Lonsdale, F. G.
A Ship Sinking 1915
oil on canvas 49 x 67
A.16

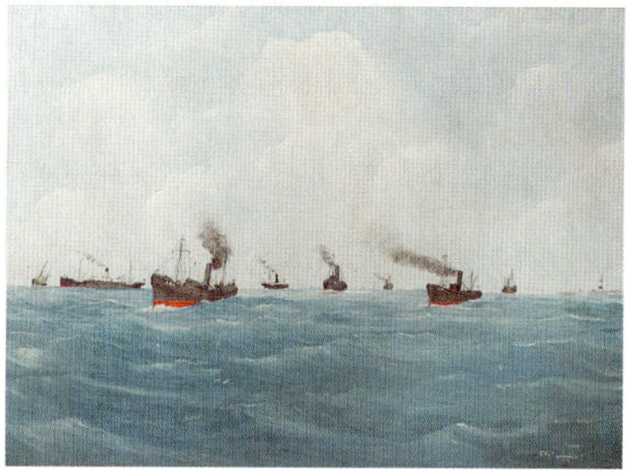

Lonsdale, F. G.
Convoy off a Lighthouse 1915
oil on canvas 49 x 67
A.15

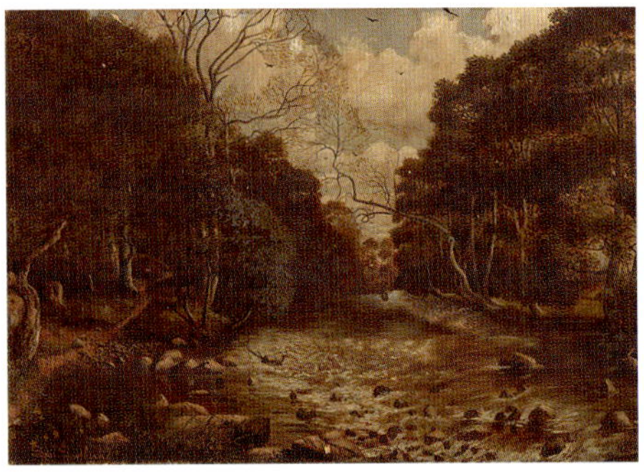

Lothian, Lewis
River Scene with Fishermen
oil on card 40.6 x 55.2
GRIMS:2010.14

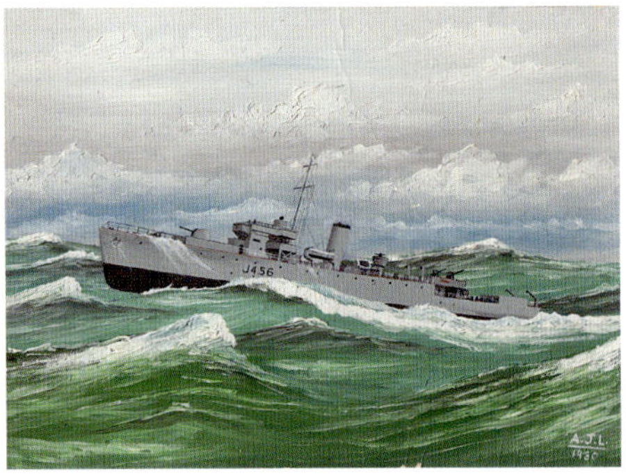

Loveridge, Alan John 1950–2005
HMS 'Nerissa' 1980
oil on board 30.5 x 40.8
A.211

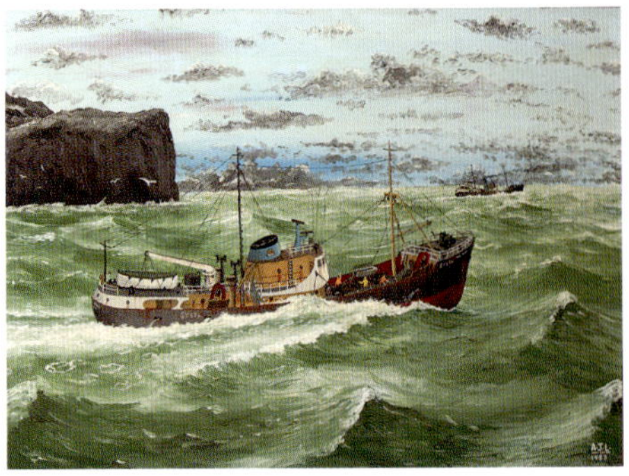

Loveridge, Alan John 1950–2005
The 'Real Madrid', GY 674 1983
oil on canvas 49 x 74
A.250

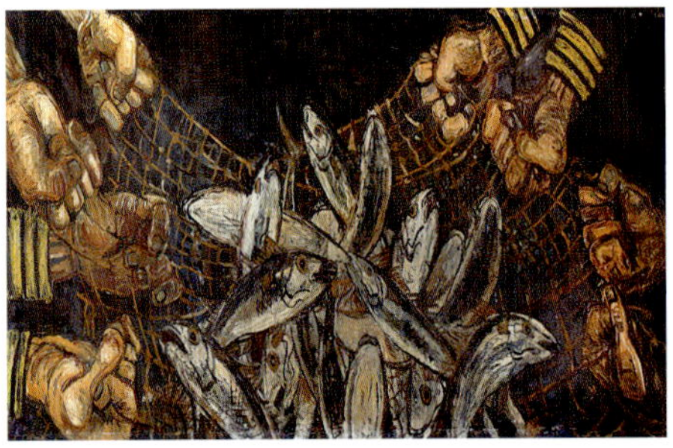

Ludlam, Alf b.1941
Cod War 1960
oil on board 122 x 179 (E)
GRIMS:2009.2

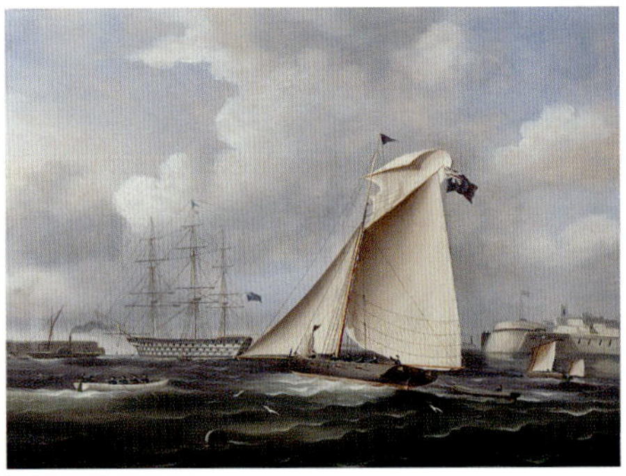

Luny, Thomas 1759–1837
Portsmouth Harbour, Hampshire
oil on canvas 51 x 66
A.96

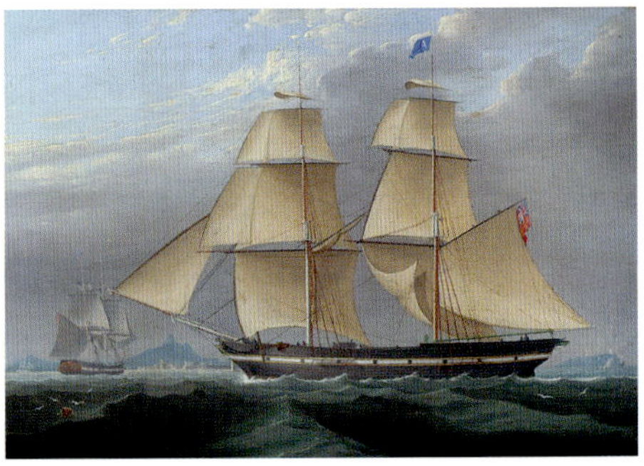

Lynn, John 1826–1869
Shipping off the Coast 1827
oil on canvas 48 x 67
A.208

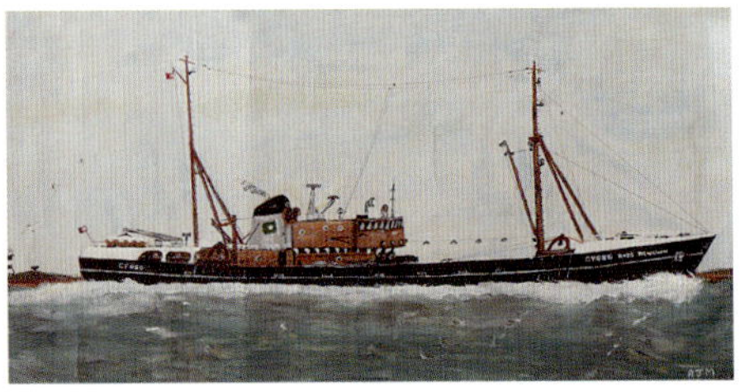

A. J. M.
The 'Ross Renown', GY 666
oil on paper 23 x 45
A.239

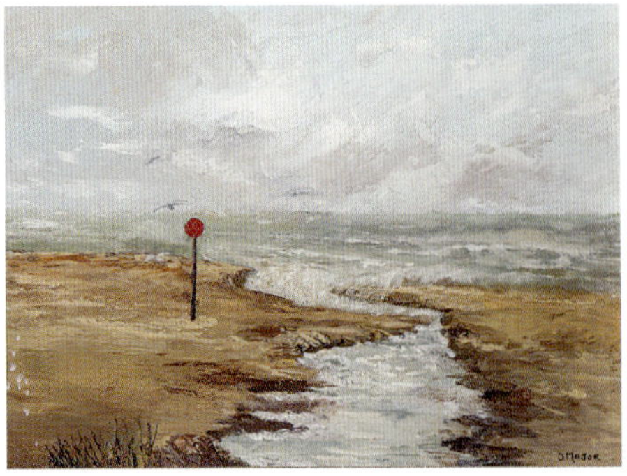

Major, O.
Foreshore
oil on board 31 x 41
GRIMS:2010.15

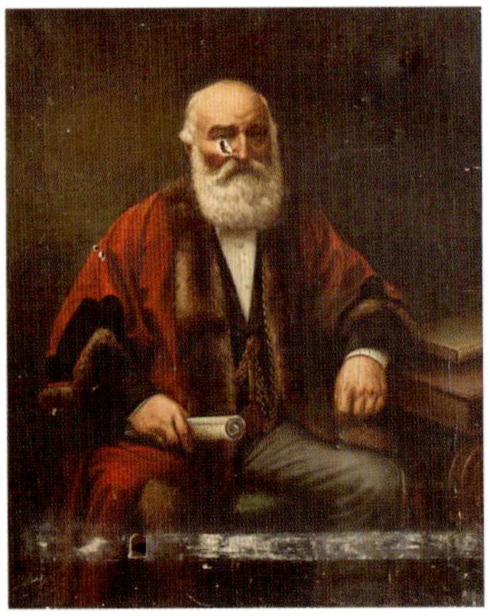

Marsden, Walter Major 1851–after 1900
Dr Thomas Bell Keetley, Mayor of Grimsby (1883–1884) 1885
oil on canvas 112 x 86.3
A.18

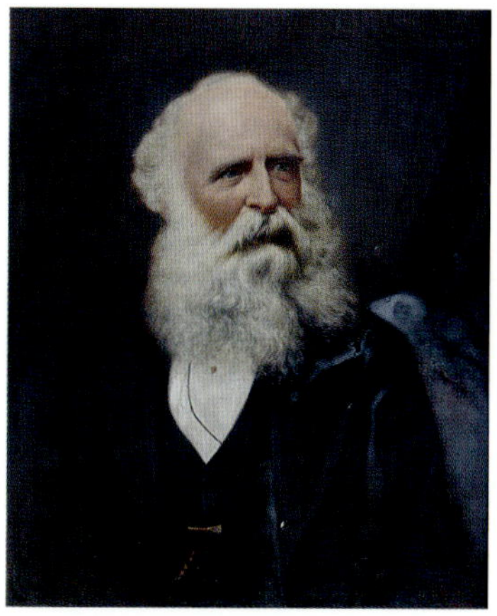

Marsden, Walter Major 1851–after 1900
Portrait of an Unknown Gentleman
oil on board 60 x 50
A.107

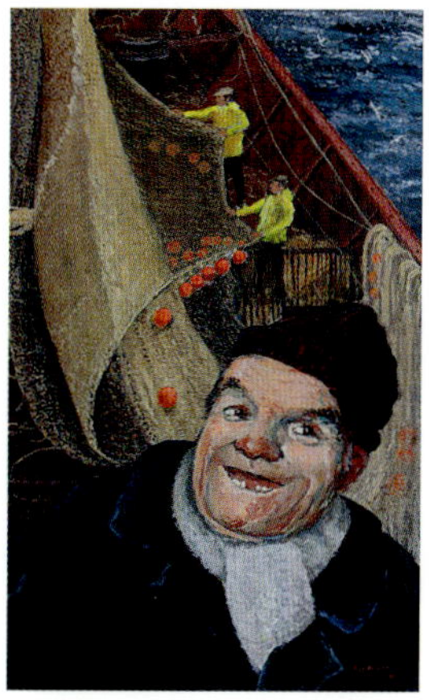

Marston, Frank William b.1931
Checking the Nets 1990
acrylic on board 149.3 x 91.3
A.267

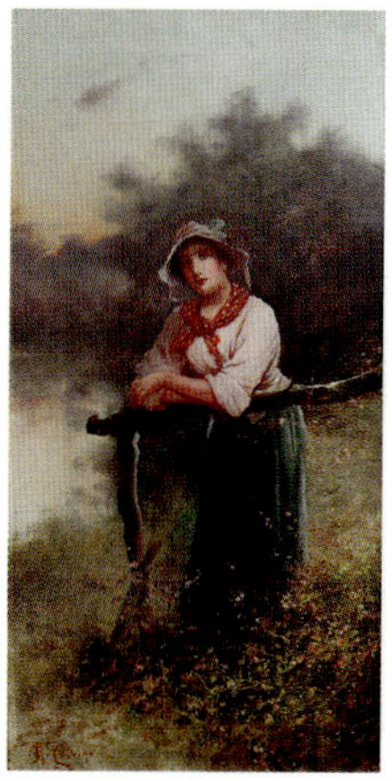

McColvin, John A. 1864–1920
Girl Leaning on a Fence
oil on canvas 60 x 30
A.63

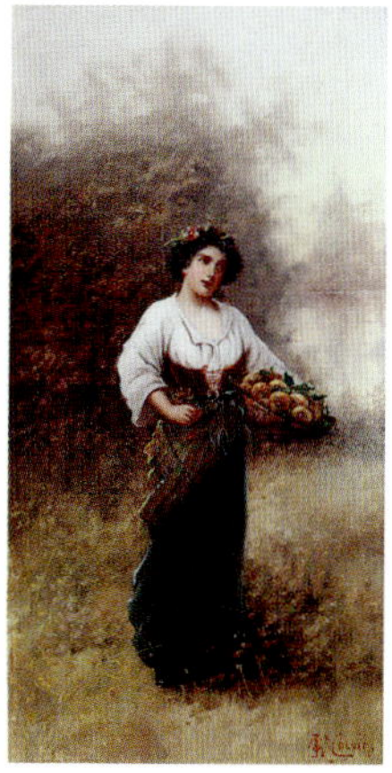

McColvin, John A. 1864–1920
Gypsy Fruit Seller
oil on canvas 60 x 30
A.14

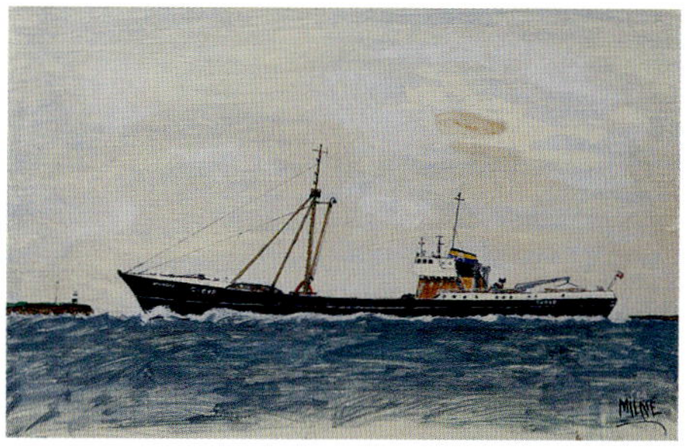

Milnie
The 'Vivaria', GY 648
oil on board 26 x 39.6
A.240

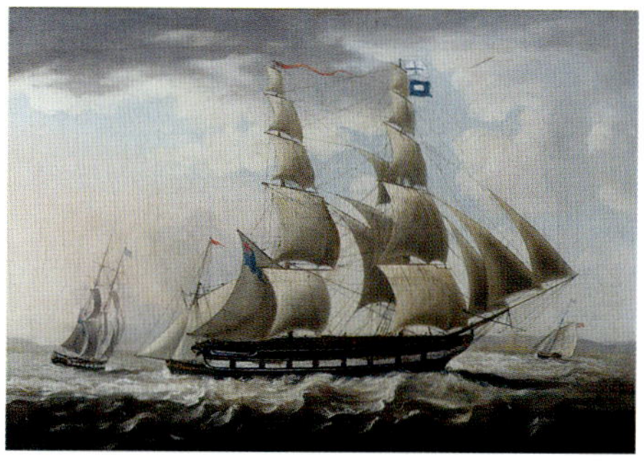

Mitchell, Alfred 1854–1914
Two-Masted Brig
oil on canvas 42 x 59
A.134

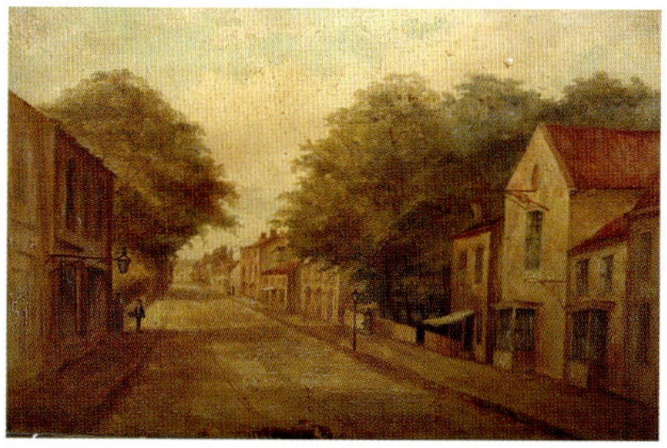

Moore, H. (attributed to)
Street Scene
oil on canvas 34.5 x 52
Z467

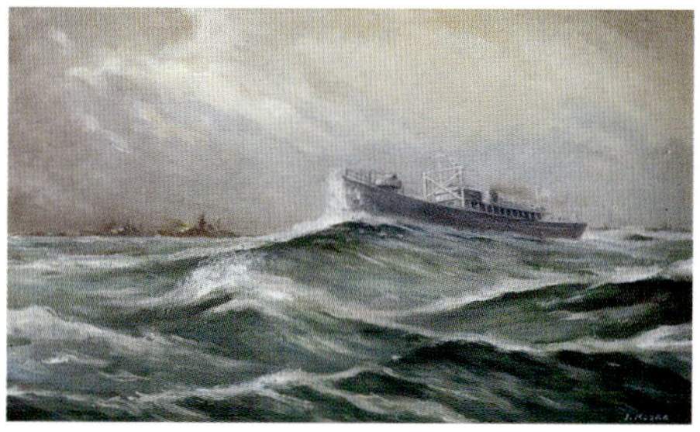

Moore, Jack
HMS 'St Barbe' 1944
oil on board 35 x 58
A.241

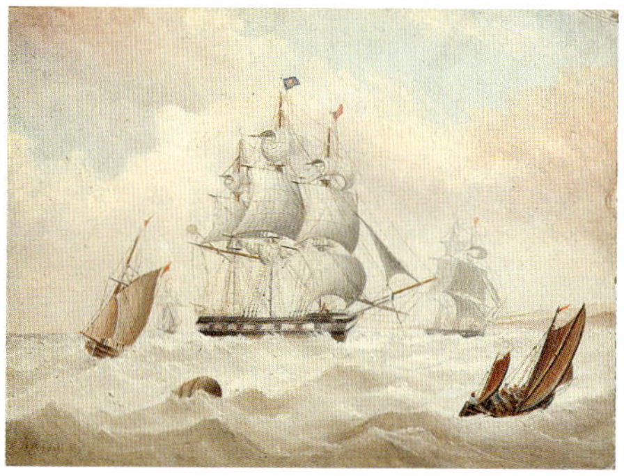

Moorhall, R.
Ship Taking Pilots in the Channel
oil on board 23.6 x 31
GRIMS:2010.16

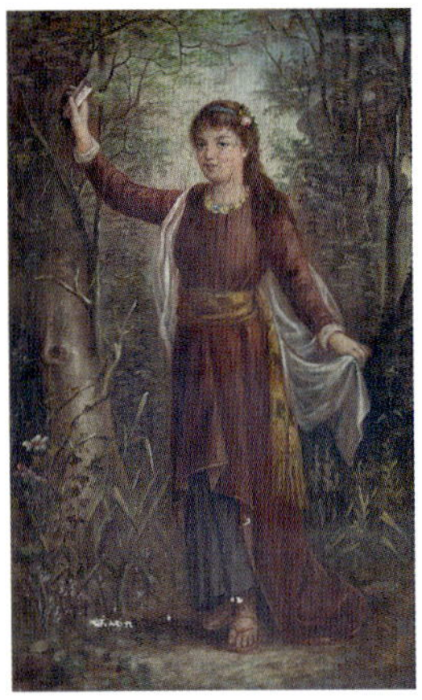

Moras, S. (attributed to)
A Girl in a Wood with a Letter 1891
oil on canvas 80.5 x 49
A.9

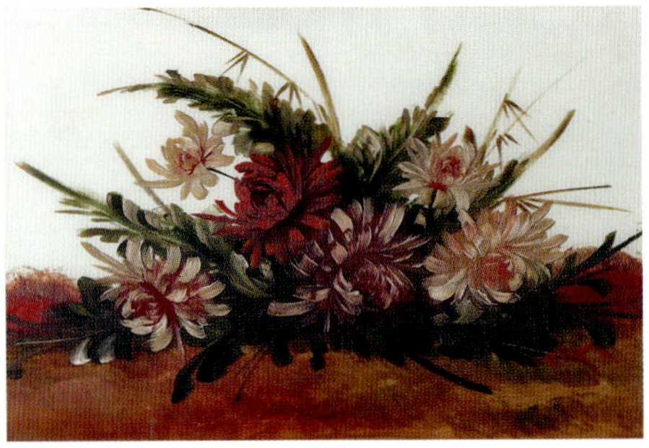

Munga, G.
Still Life, Flowers
oil on glass 37.5 x 54
A.41a

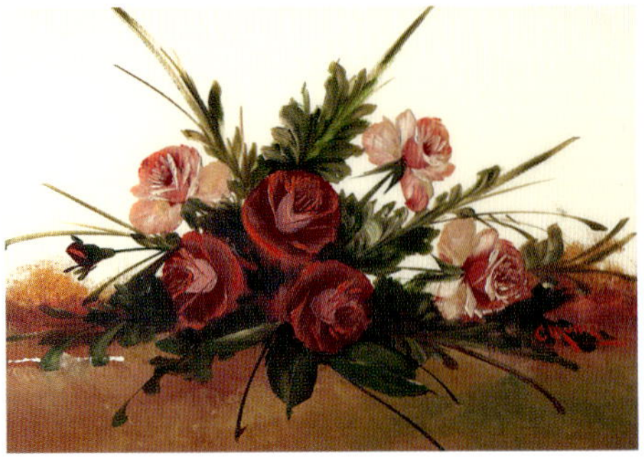

Munga, G.
Still Life, Flowers
oil on glass 35 x 52
A.41b

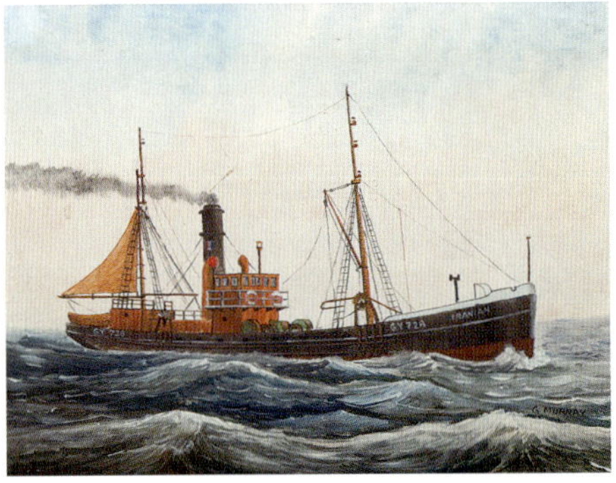

Murray, G.
The 'Iranian'
oil on board 34.6 x 45.7
A.414

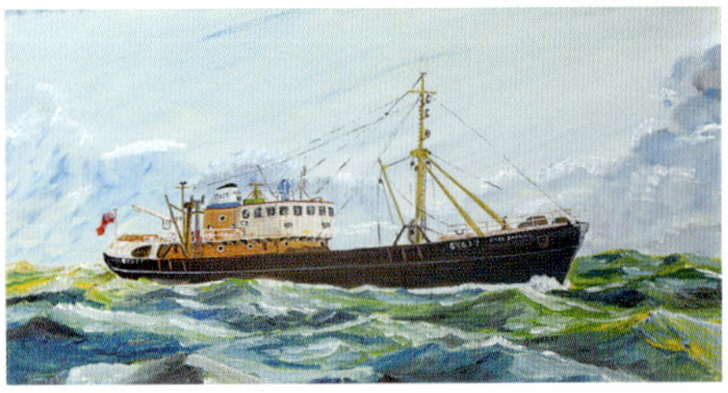

Murray, G.
The 'Ross Jackal', GY 637
oil on board 37 x 71
A.255

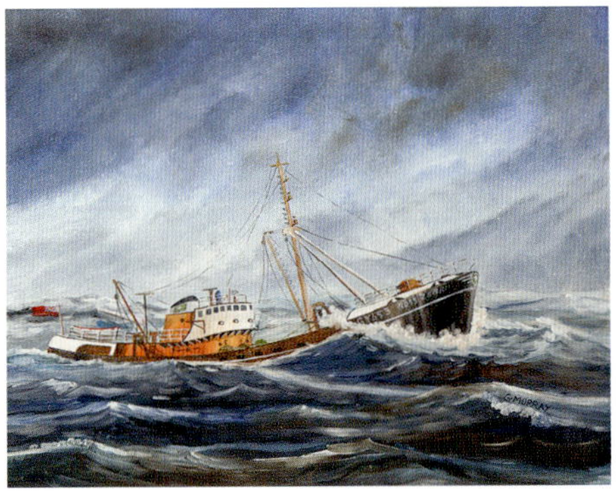

Murray, G.
The 'Ross Zebra', GY 653
oil on board 39.5 x 49.5
A.260

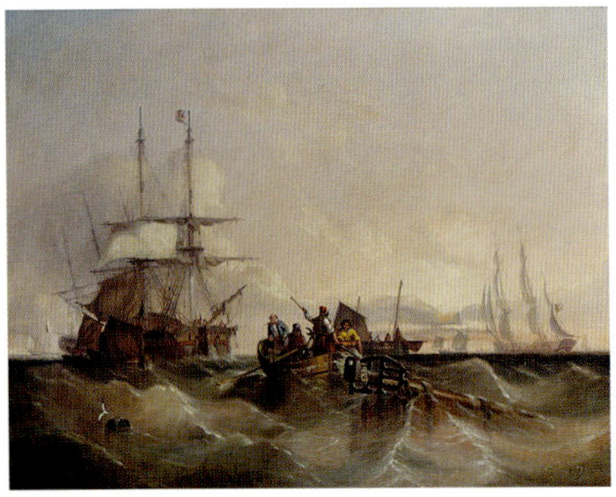

Ovenden, F. W. active 1834–1843
Recovering Wreckage 1839
oil on canvas 70 x 90
A.142

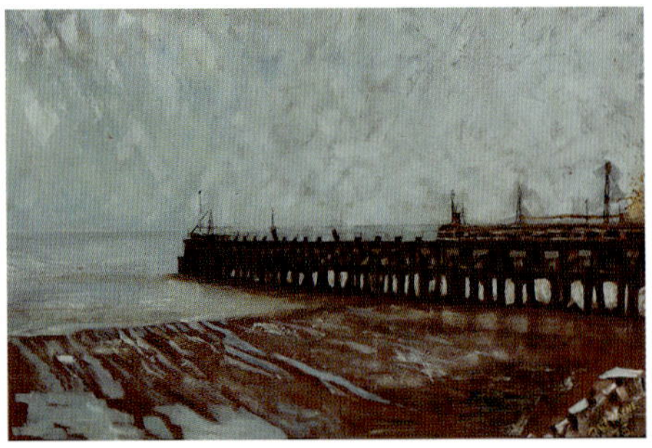

Payne, Roland W.
The Old Pier, Grimsby, Lincolnshire, 1975
oil on board 60 x 91
A.445

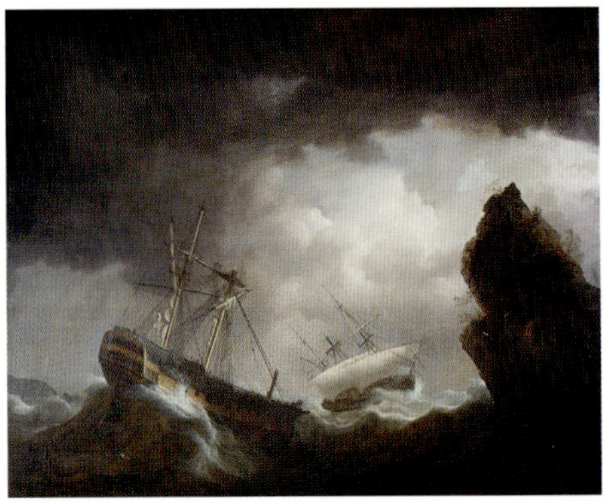

Pocock, Nicholas (attributed to) 1740–1821
HMS 'Endymion' Rescuing a French School Two-Decker off the Coast of Spain, 1805
oil on canvas 105 x 150
A.158

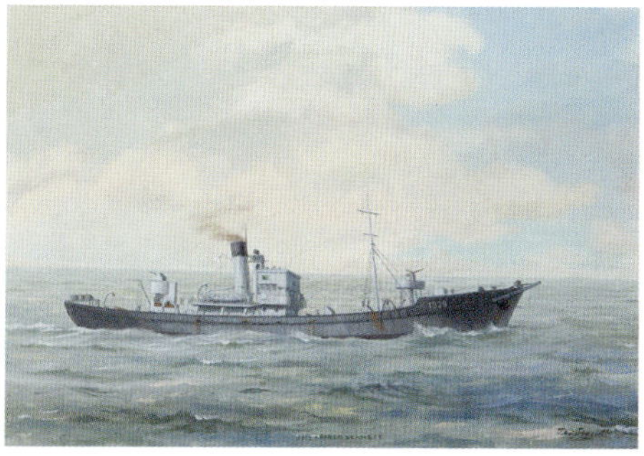

Prescott, David
HMS 'Arnold Bennett'
oil on canvas 34.5 x 49
Z621

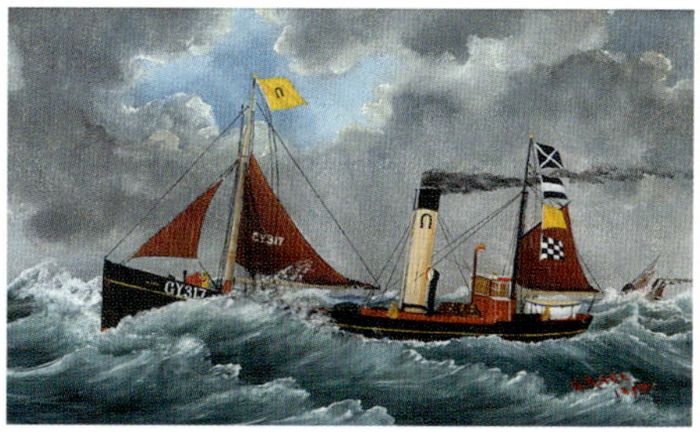

Race, George 1872–1957
The 'Clyde', GY317 1897
oil on board 26 x 42.5
A.59

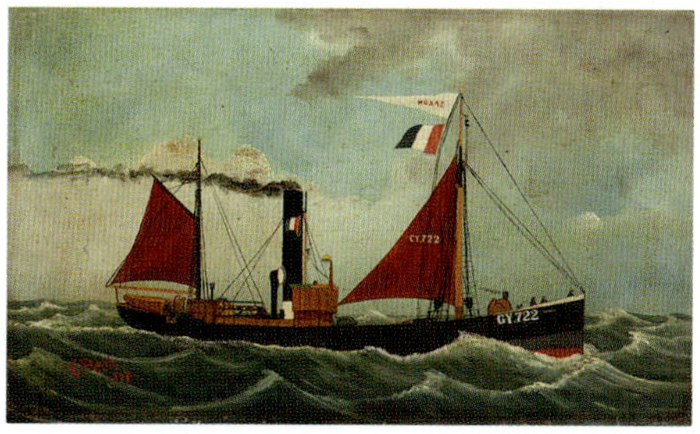

Race, George 1872–1957
The 'Saxon', GY722, Outward Bound 1897
oil on board 27.8 x 44.9
GRIMS:2010.17

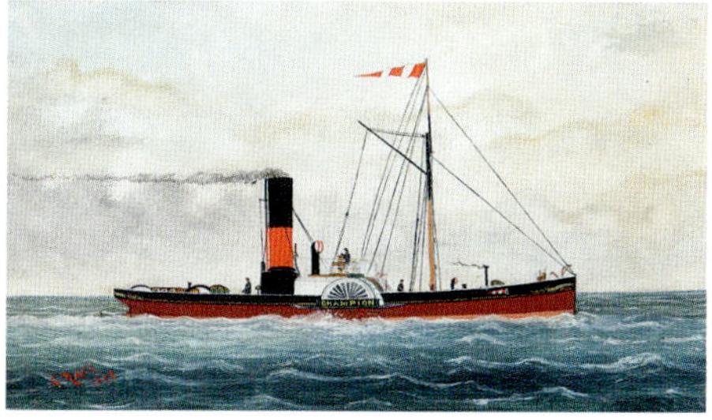

Race, George 1872–1957
The 'Champion' 1898
oil on cardboard 26 x 42.5
A.57

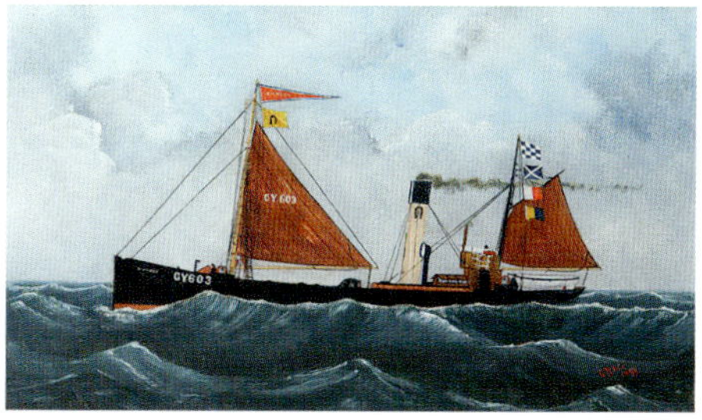

Race, George 1872–1957
The 'Diamond', GY603 1899
oil on cardboard 26 x 43.5
A.60

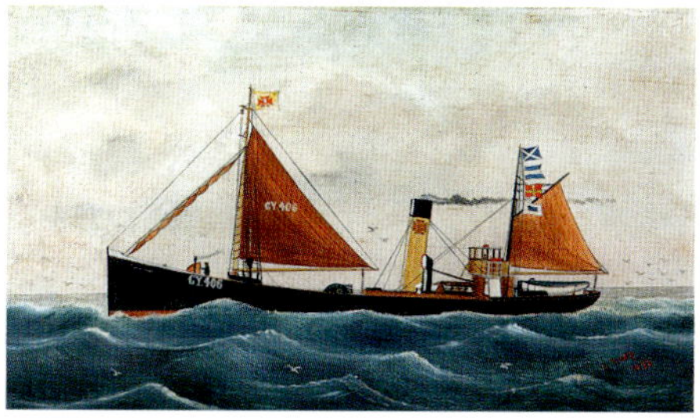

Race, George 1872–1957
The 'Dominican', GY406 1899
oil on cardboard 25.5 x 42
A.72

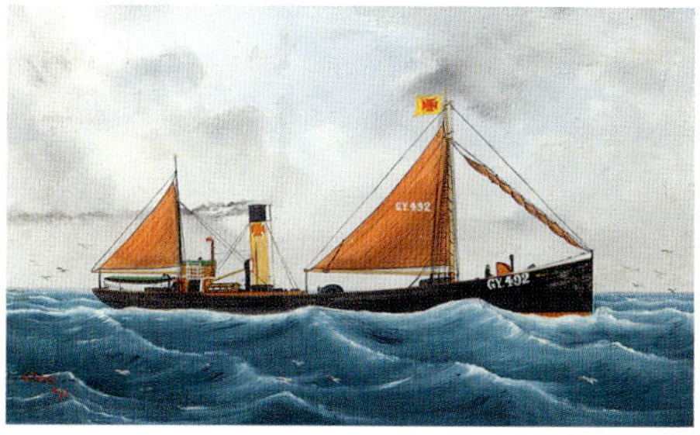

Race, George 1872–1957
The 'Egyptian', GY492 1899
oil on board 25.5 x 42.5
A.73

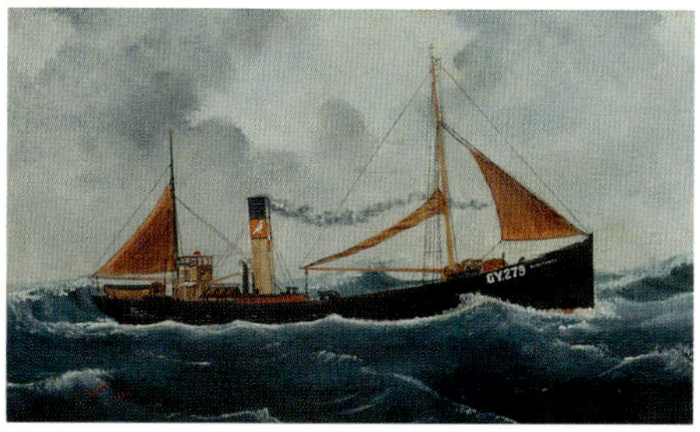

Race, George 1872–1957
The 'Albatross', GY 279, Outward Bound
1900
oil on board 24 x 42 (E)
A.221

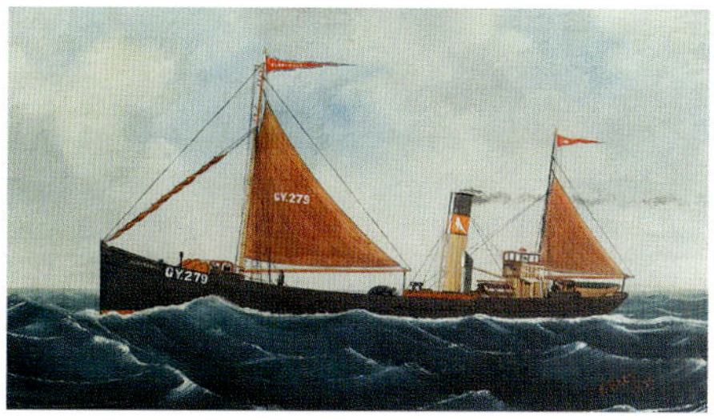

Race, George 1872–1957
The 'Albatross', GY 279, Homeward Bound
1900
oil on cardboard 26 x 41 (E)
A.222

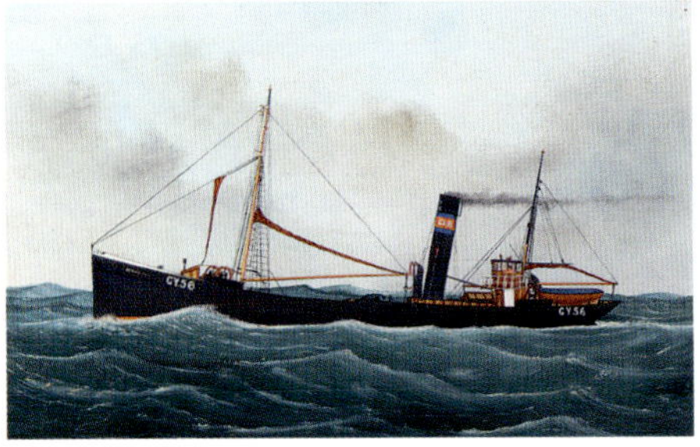

Race, George 1872–1957
The 'Bermuda', GY56 1905
oil on board 26.5 x 41
A.173

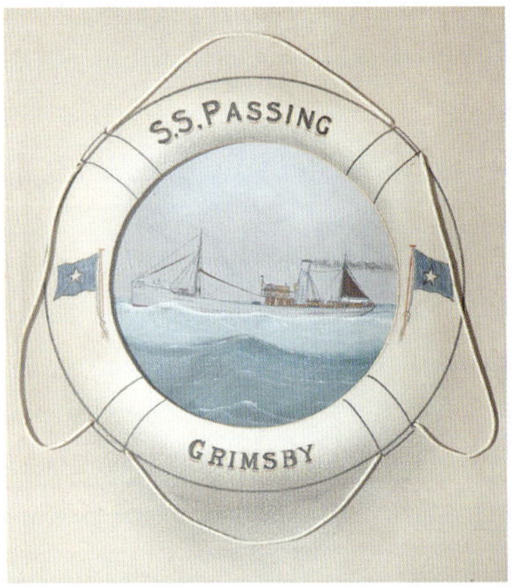

Race, George 1872–1957
SS 'Passing', GY 877 1913
oil on cardboard 38.5 x 34
A.224

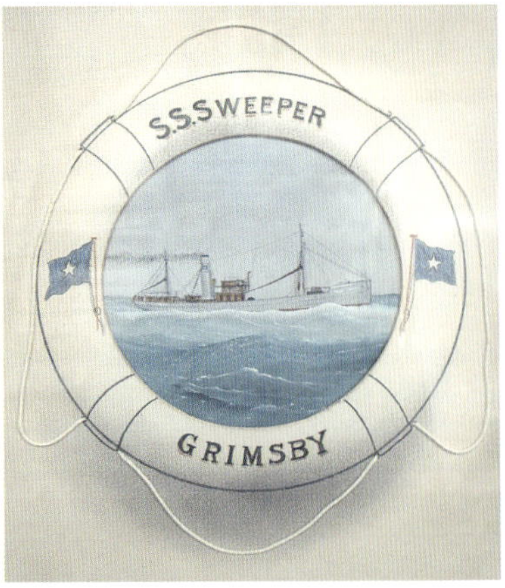

Race, George 1872–1957
SS 'Sweeper', GY 853 1913
oil on cardboard 38.5 x 34
A.225

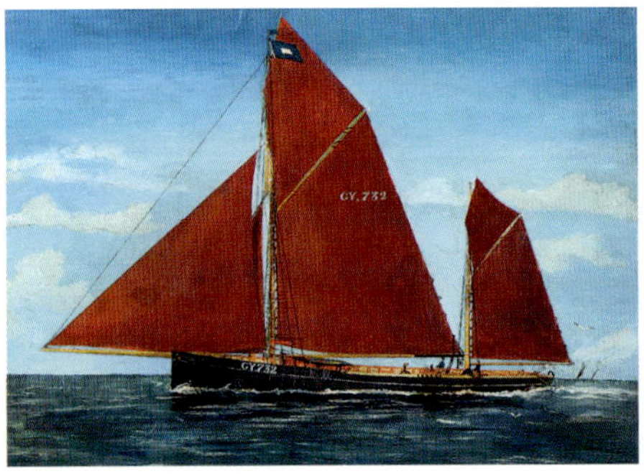

Race, George 1872–1957
Fishing Smack, GY732
oil on cardboard 33 x 46.5
A.102

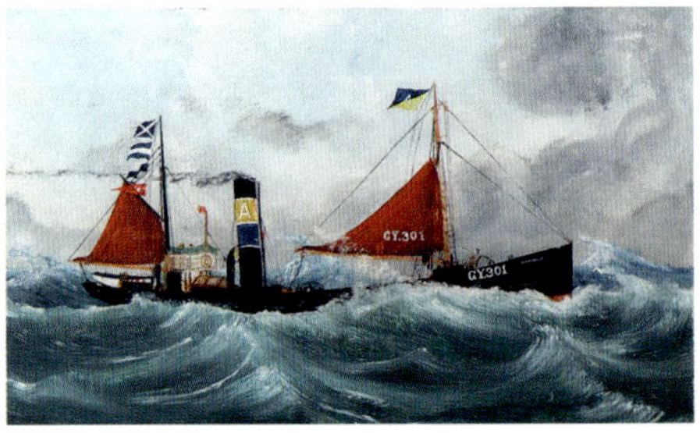

Race, George 1872–1957
The 'Somerville', GY301, Homeward Bound
oil on cardboard 26.5 x 43
A.53

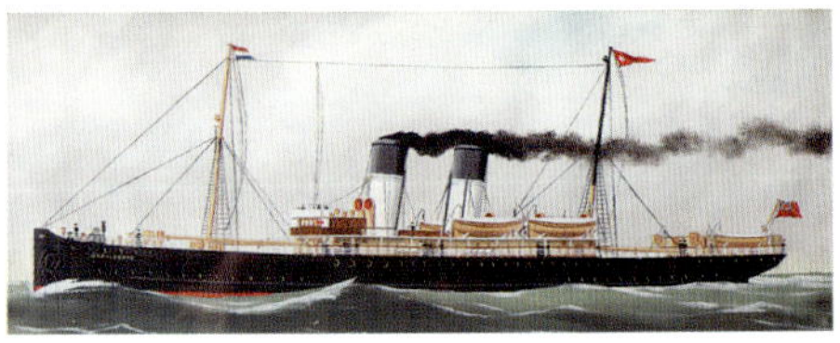

Race, George (attributed to) 1872–1957
The 'Marylebone' c.1905
oil on cardboard 20 x 50
A.226

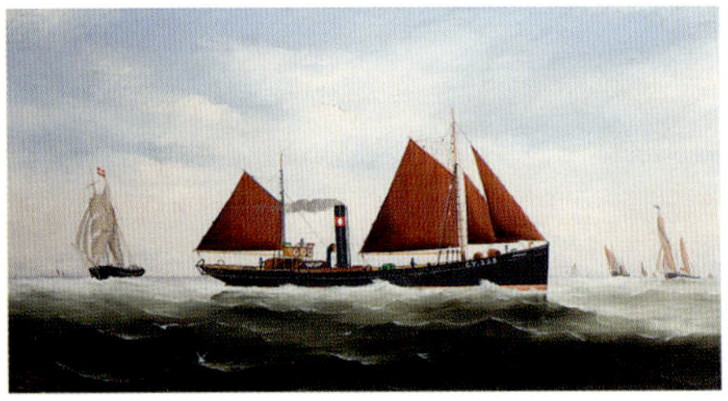

Ramsey, G. active 1856–1889
The 'Dahlia', GY223 1889
oil on canvas 43.5 x 82
A.166

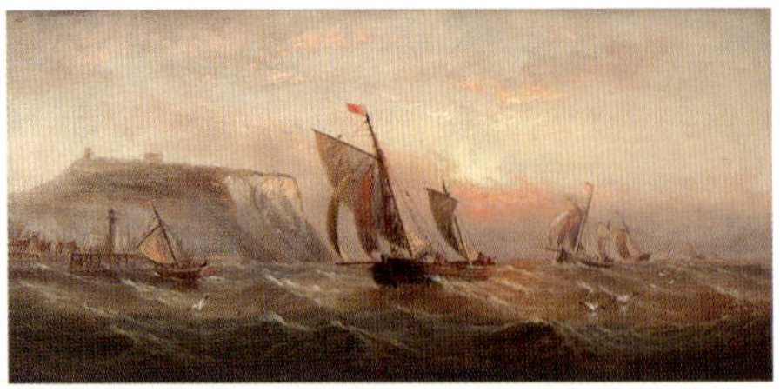

Redmore, Edward King 1860–1941
Fishing Vessels off the Coast
oil on canvas 29 x 59.5
A.86

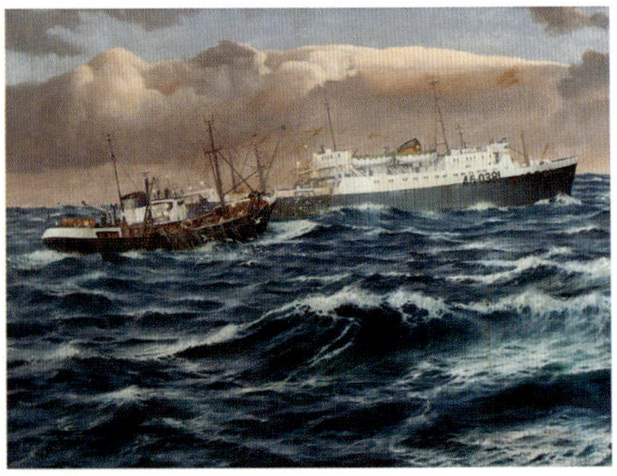

Reynolds, Roy Peter b.1929
Across the Bows c.1970
oil on canvas 74 x 99.5
A.432

Facing page: Gertler, Mark, 1891–1939, *The Fruit Sorters* (detail), 1914, Leicester Arts and Museums Service (p. 45)

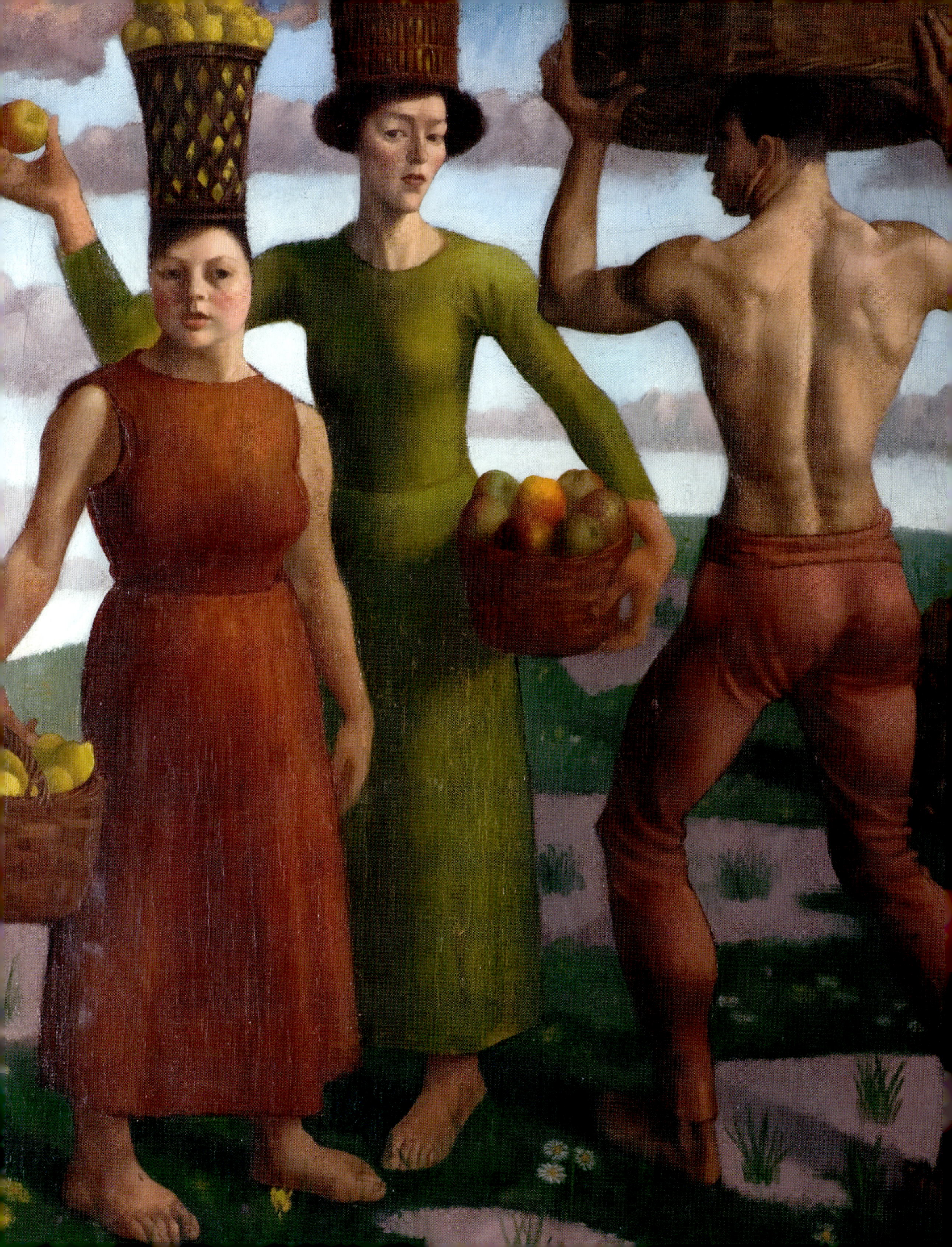

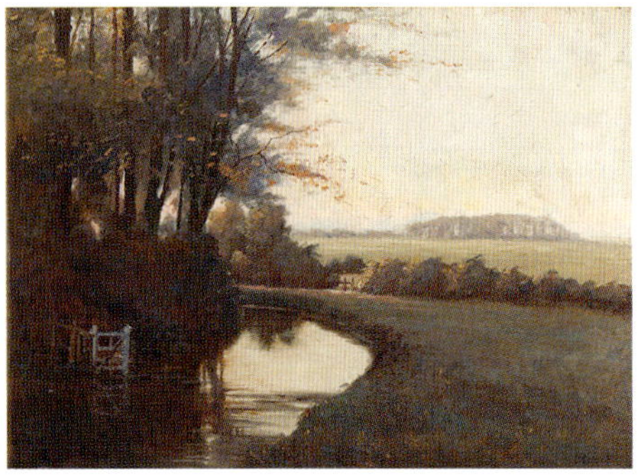

Rollett, Herbert 1872–1932
Lincolnshire Scene c.1920
oil on canvas 34.5 x 50
A.223

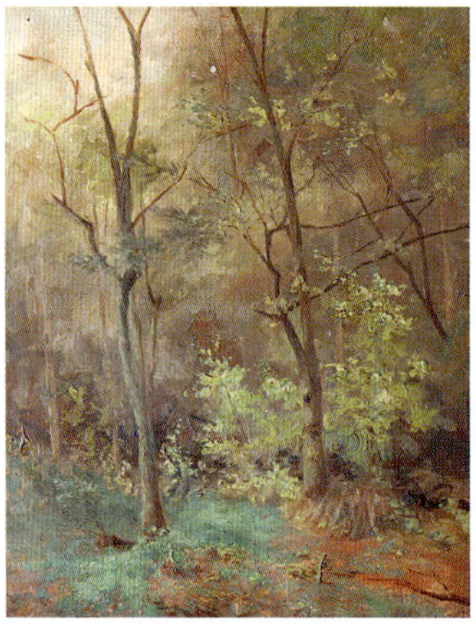

Rollett, Herbert 1872–1932
Arden Wood, Healing, Lincolnshire
oil on canvas 44 x 34.5
A.229

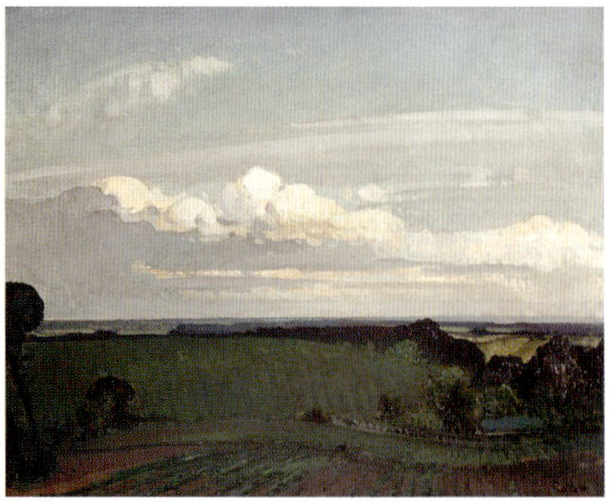

Rollett, Herbert 1872–1932
Landscape with a Large Cloud
oil on canvas 62 x 75
A.252

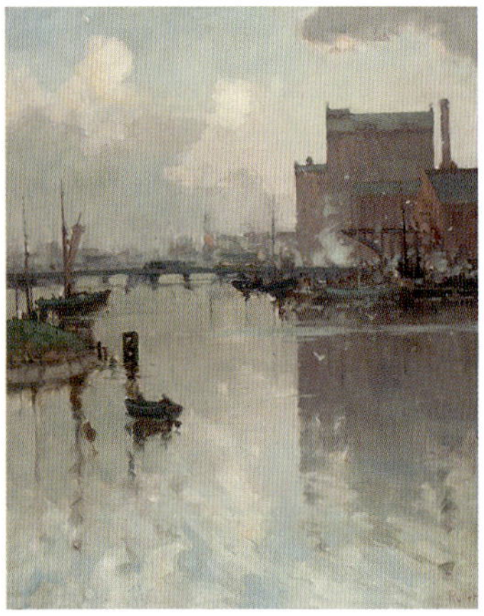

Rollett, Herbert 1872–1932
Victoria Mill and Alexandra Dock, Grimsby, Lincolnshire
oil on canvas 100 x 75
A.268

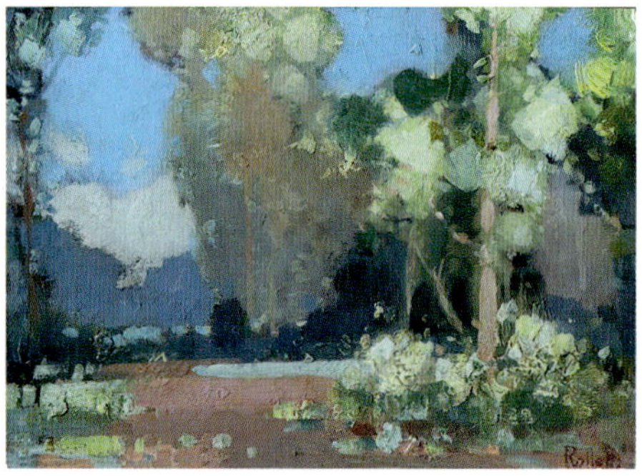

Rollett, Herbert 1872–1932
Woodland Scene
oil on board 25 x 34
A.254

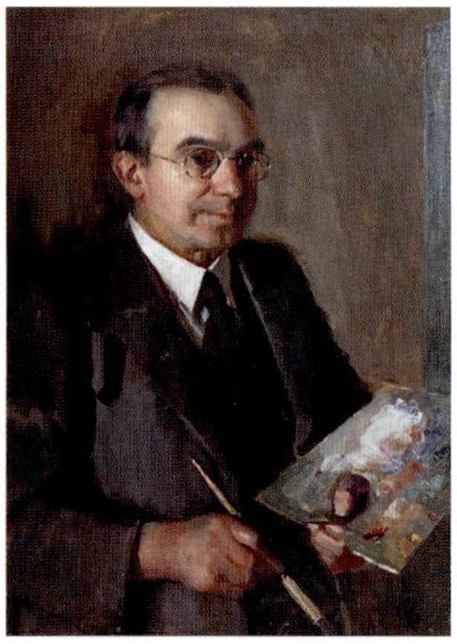

C. V. S.
Herbert Rollett (1872–1932)
oil on canvas 90 x 60
A.106

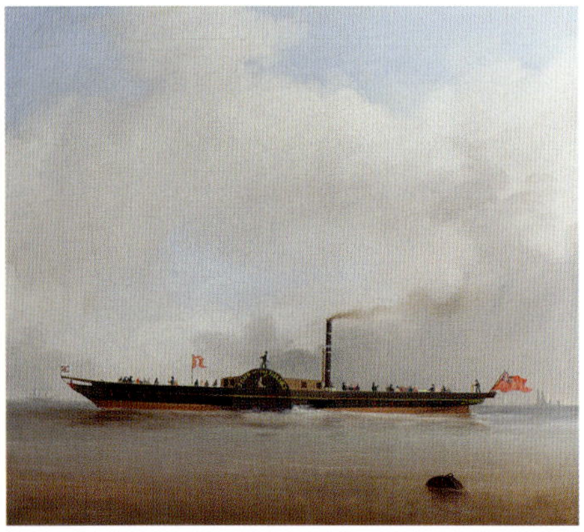

S. S.
The 'Sons of the Thames' 1841
oil on canvas 49 x 58
A.97

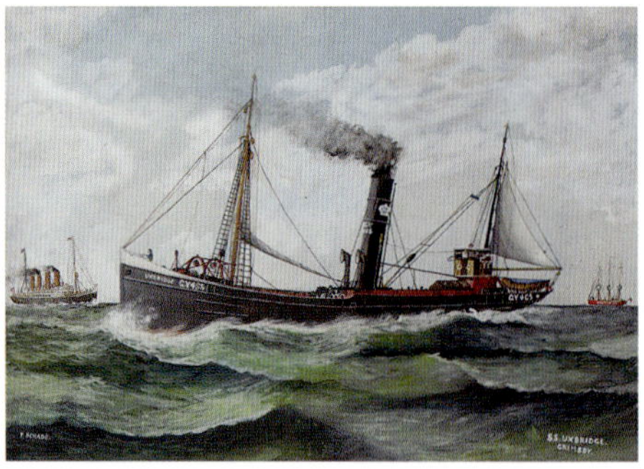

Schade, Frederick
SS 'Uxbridge', Grimsby c.1910
oil & mixed media on paper 55 x 79
A.58

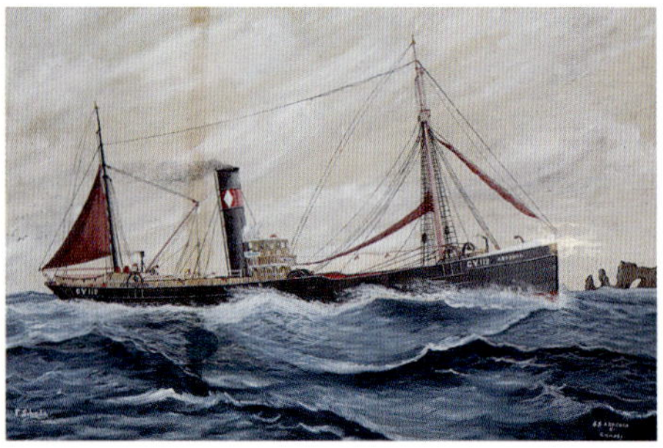

Schade, Frederick
The 'Abronia', Grimsby c.1910
oil & watercolour on paper 46 x 68
A.6

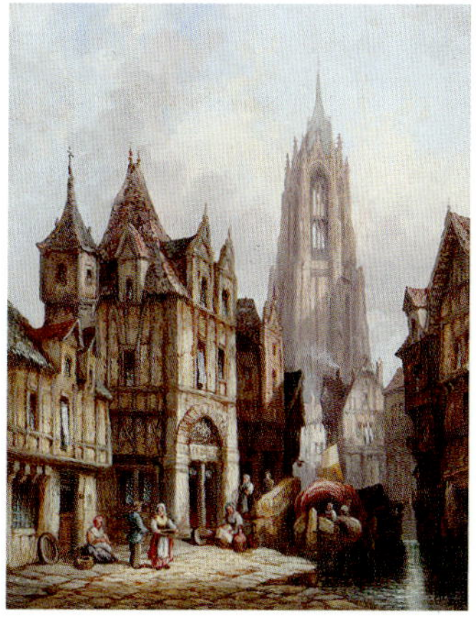

Schäfer, Heinrich c.1815–1905
Utrecht, The Netherlands 1885
oil on canvas 39.5 x 29.5
A.64

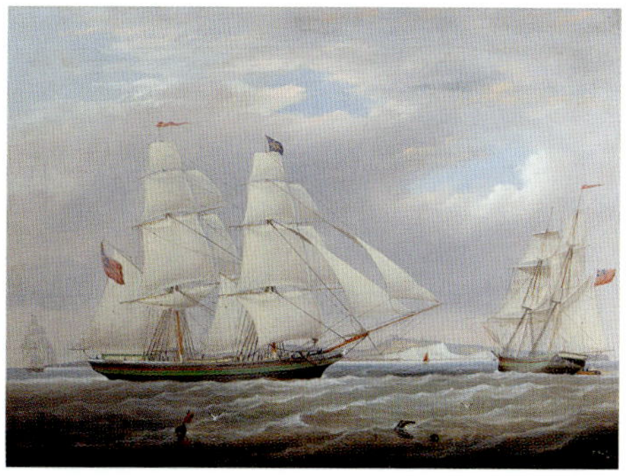

Scott, F.
Two-Masted Ship off the Coast in Three Positions 1856
oil on canvas 65 x 90
A.151

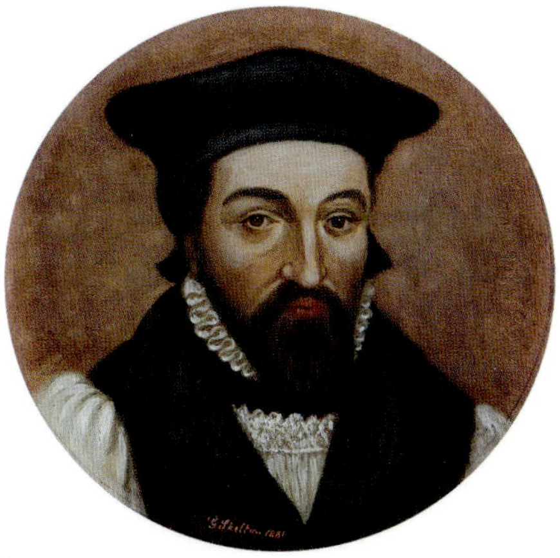

Skelton, George 1855–1932
Tudor Portrait of an Unknown Gentleman 1880
oil on board 25.3 x 23
1998.3.4

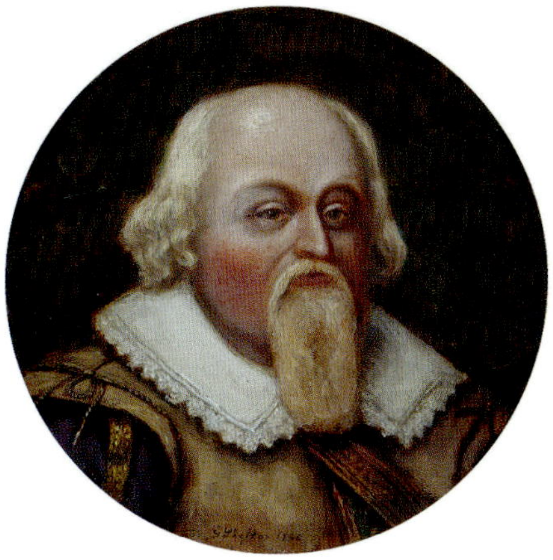

Skelton, George 1855–1932
Elizabethan Portrait of an Unknown Gentleman 1890
oil on board 26.8 x 22.5
1998.3.5

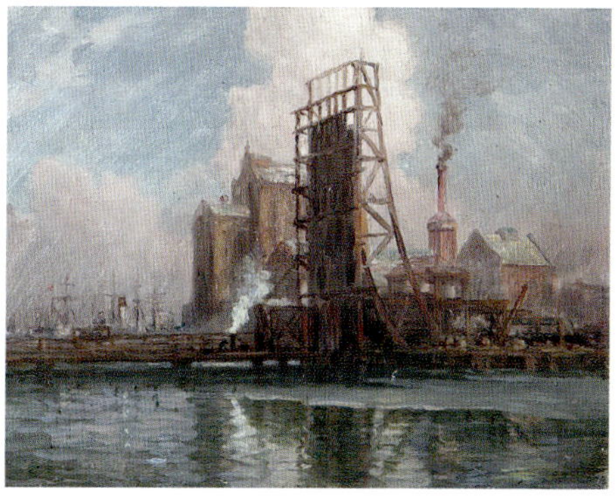

Skelton, George 1855–1932
Building of the Second Corporation Road Bridge, Lincolnshire 1927
oil on board 21.5 x 26
A.220

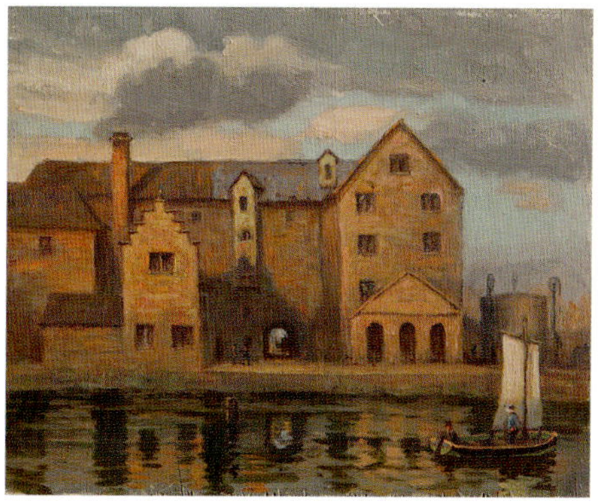

Skelton, George 1855–1932
The Back of Bennett's Mill, Old Bone Mill and Gasworks, Grimsby, Lincolnshire 1928
oil on board 21.6 x 25.8
GRIMS:2010.18

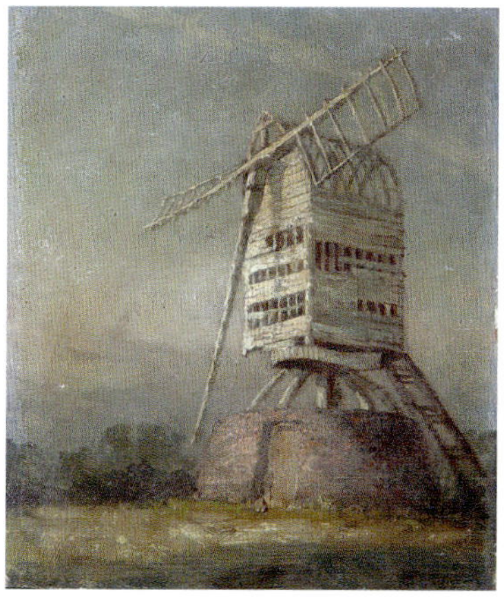

Skelton, George 1855–1932
The Moll All Alone 1928
oil on board 26 x 21.7
A.216

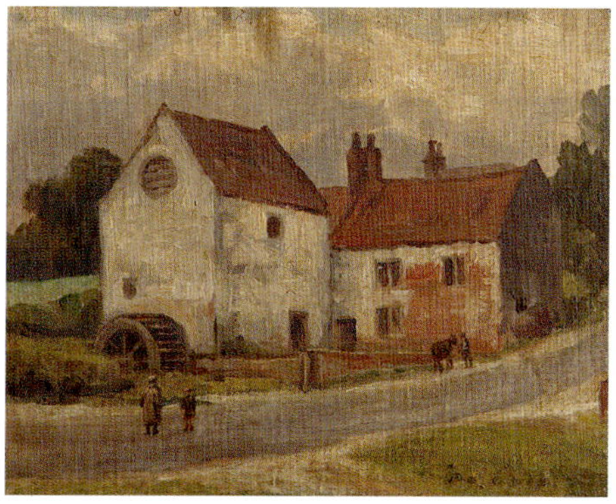

Skelton, George 1855–1932
Beelsby Mill, Grimsby, Lincolnshire 1929
oil on board 21.7 x 26.6
GRIMS:2010.19

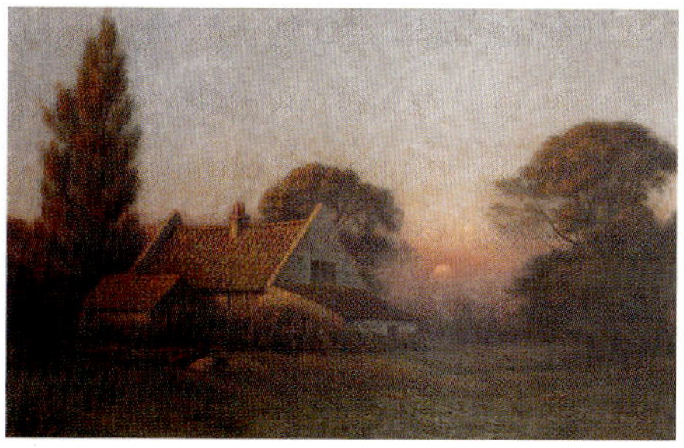

Skelton, George 1855–1932
Nun's Farm, Sunset
oil on canvas 38.5 x 59.5
GRIMS:2010.20

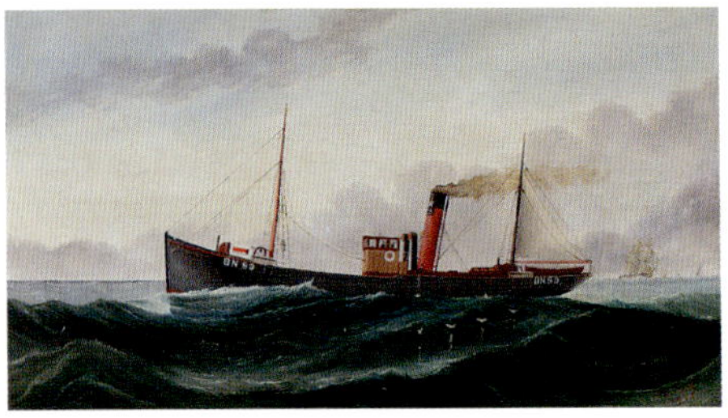

Smith, H.
The 'Hungarian', BN89 1905
oil on canvas 44 x 75
A.84

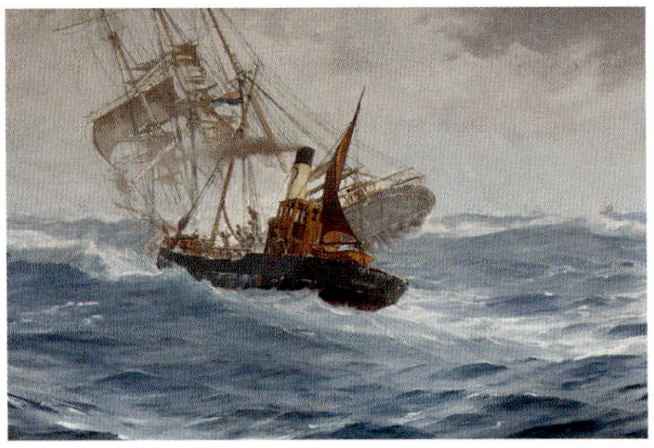

Somerscales, Thomas Jacques 1842–1927
The Rescue of the 'Anna Mathilda' by the Trawler 'Clyde', GY 317 1906
oil on canvas 121 x 180
A.253

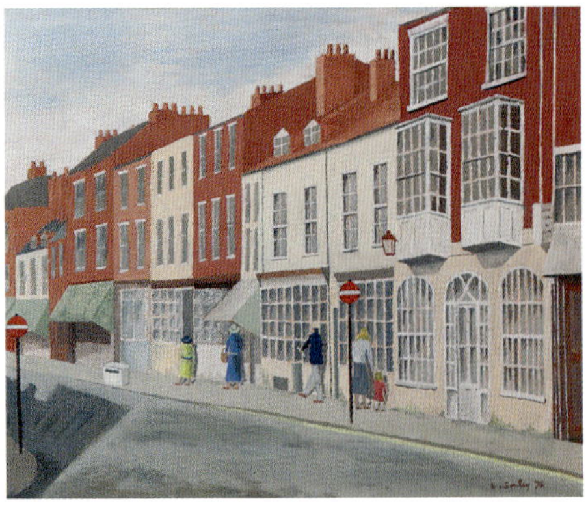

Sonley, L.
High Street, Bridlington, East Riding of Yorkshire 1976
oil on board 41 x 50.5
GRIMS:2010.21

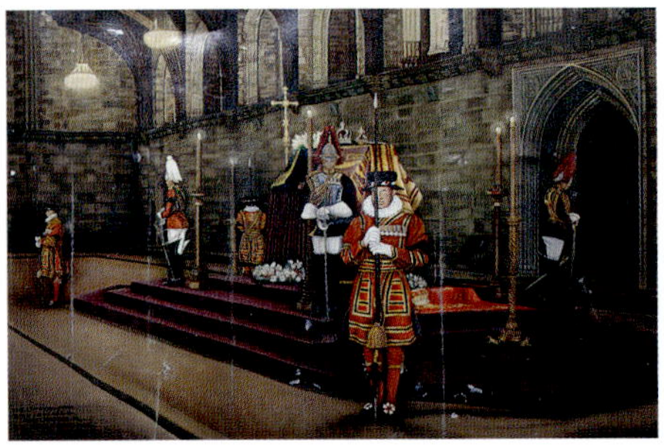

Speechley, J. H.
The Lying in State of George VI 1952
oil on canvas 82.2 x 105
A.238

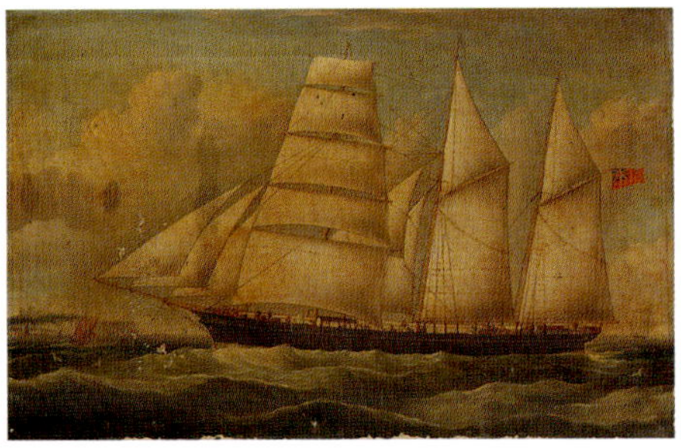

Spencer, William Barnett c.1810–c.1880
Three-Masted Sailing Ship off the Coast
oil on canvas 40.5 x 61
GRIMS:2010.22

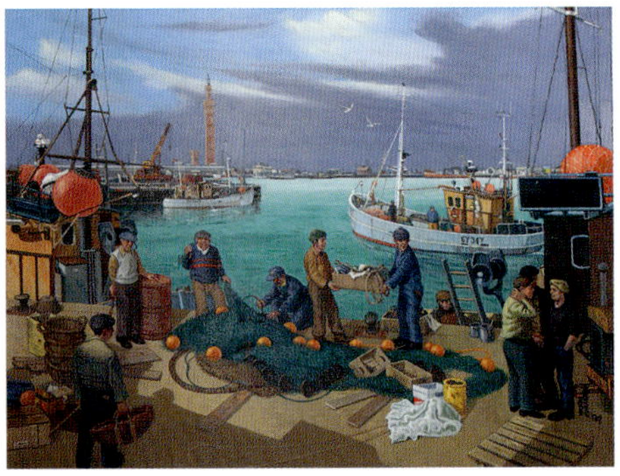

Tarttelin, David
South Quay, No.3 Fish Dock, Grimsby, Lincolnshire 1970
oil on canvas 69 x 89.5
GRIMS:2010.23

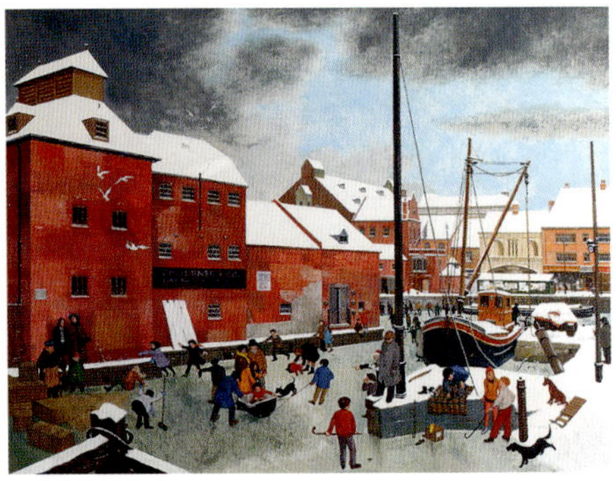

Tarttelin, David
The Riverhead in Winter
oil on canvas 90 x 120.5
A.159

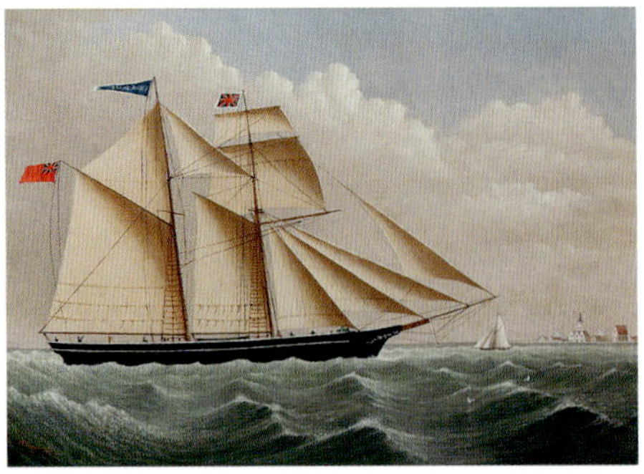

Tindall, J. T.
The 'Emma Sharp' 1922
oil on canvas 49 x 67
A.143

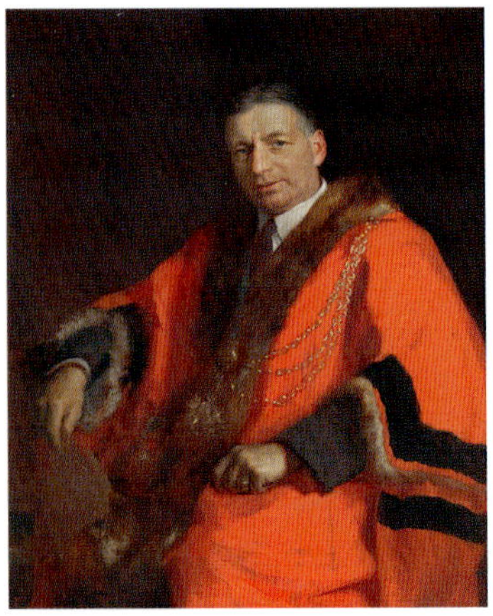

Townsend, Ernest 1885–1944
Councillor W. R. Womersley, Mayor of Grimsby (1922–1923)
oil on canvas 110.7 x 85.2
A.23

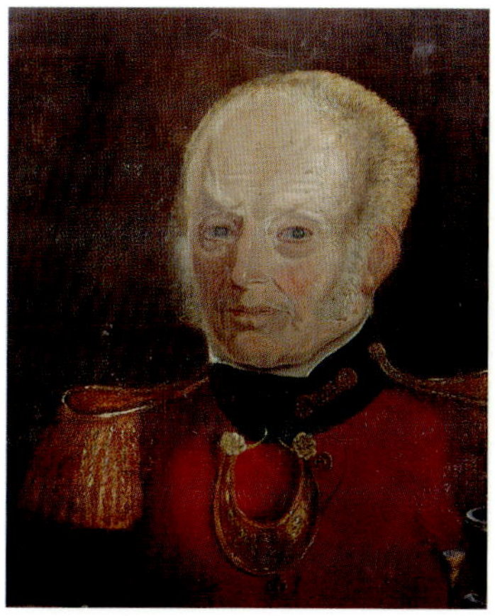

Truman, P. J.
Major Lushby 1852
oil on canvas 91 x 48
A.133

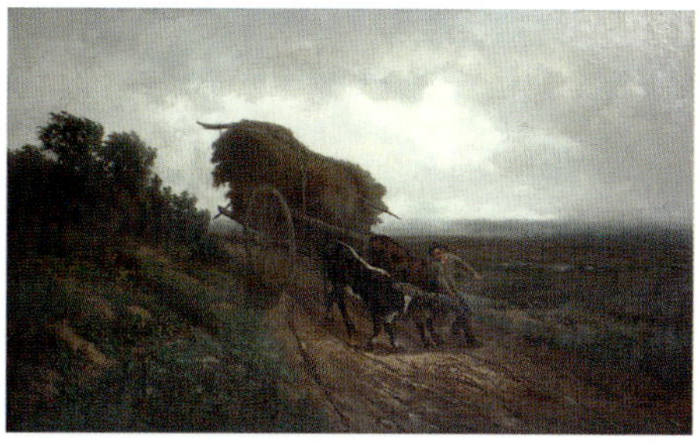

Tscharner, Theodore
Evening Scene with a Hay Cart
oil on canvas 98 x 154
A.28

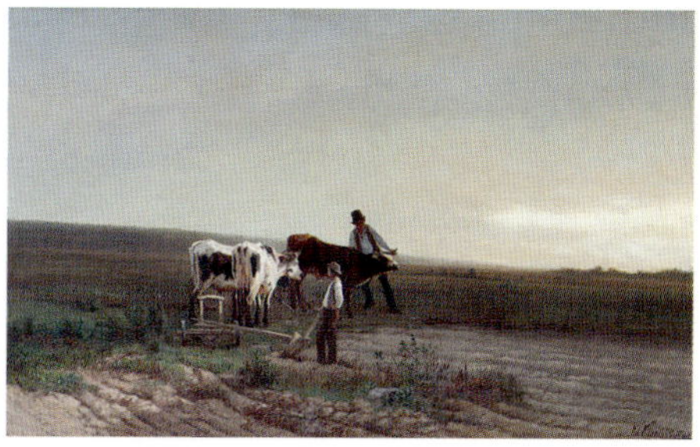

Tscharner, Theodore
Evening Scene with a Plough
oil on canvas 96 x 154
A.29

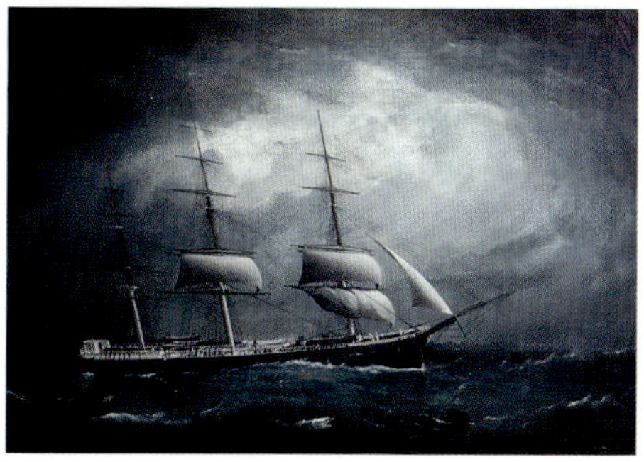

Tudgay, Frederick J. 1841–1921
Three-Masted Ship by Night 1869
oil on canvas 60 x 90
A.47

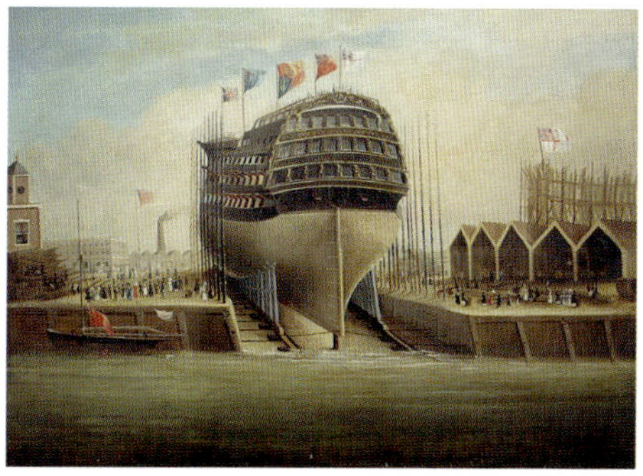

Tudgay, Frederick J. 1841–1921
Launching of the 'Royal George'
oil on canvas 71 x 91.5
A.155

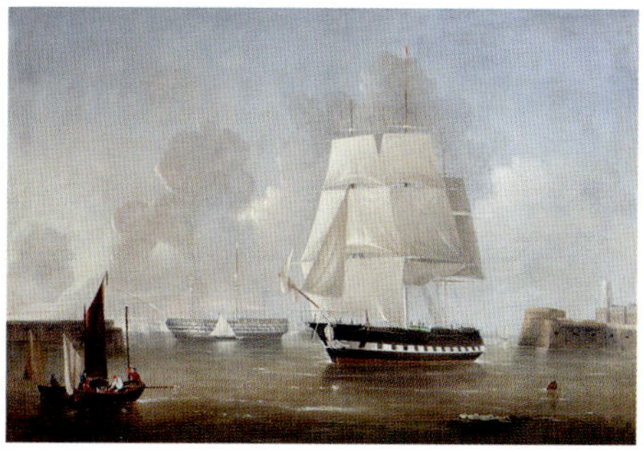

Tudgay, Frederick J. 1841–1921
Shipping at a Harbour Entrance
oil on canvas 64.5 x 95
A.150

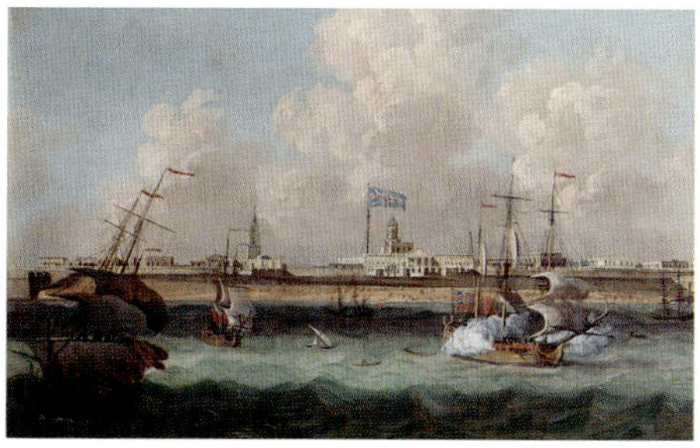

unknown artist
Ships off Madras, India c.1780
oil on canvas 52 x 85.5
A.136

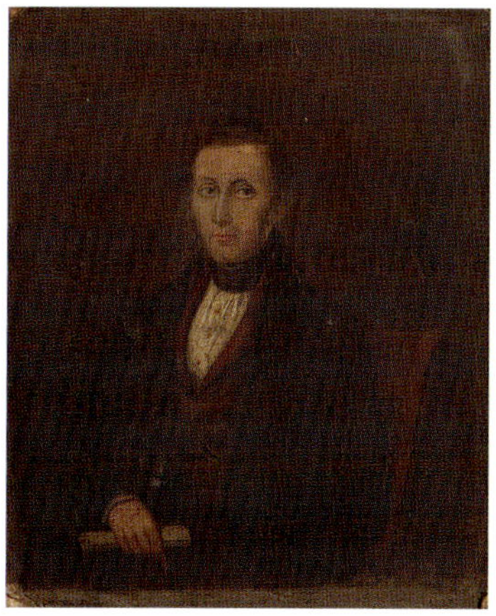

unknown artist
John Skelton, JP 1840
oil on board 21.5 x 17.5
GRIMS:2010.26

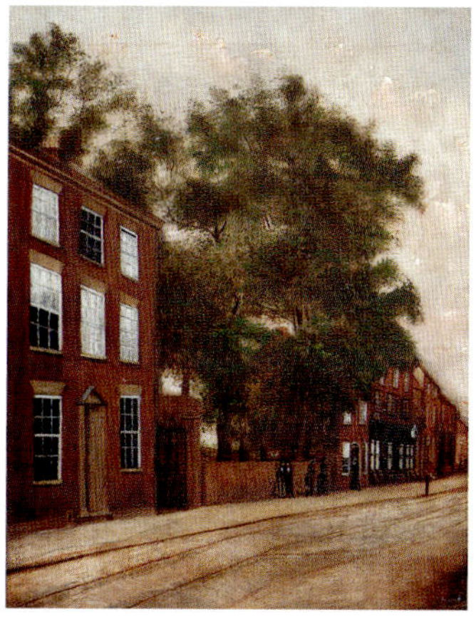

unknown artist
Victoria Street c.1880
oil on canvas 49.5 x 39.5
A.235

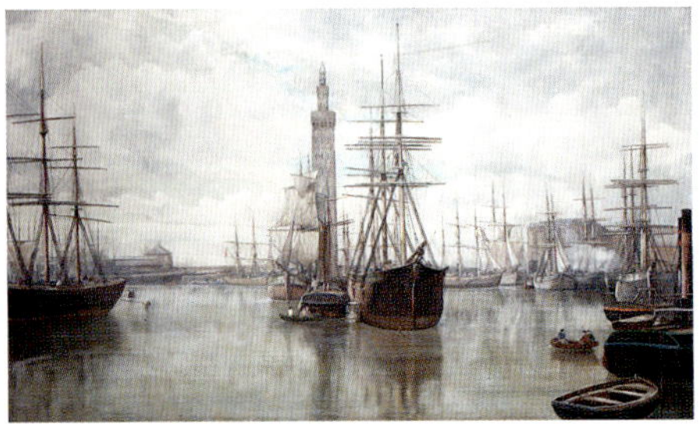

unknown artist
Royal Dock, Grimsby, Lincolnshire 1890
oil on canvas 75.5 x 126
A.22

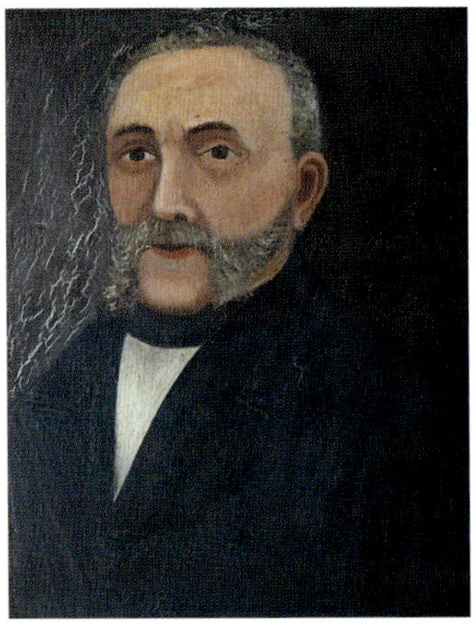

unknown artist
Portrait of a Man with a Moustache c.1900
oil on board 47 x 37
A.108

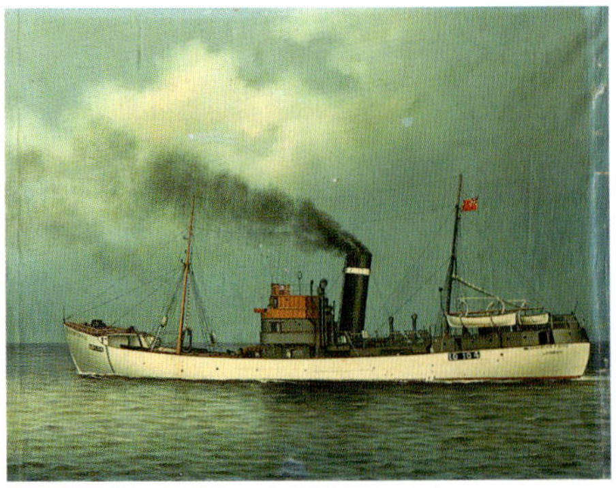

unknown artist
'Northern Pride', Arctic Trawler, Built in Germany for 'Northern Trawlers', Grimsby 1939
oil on silk 39.5 x 50.7
A.403

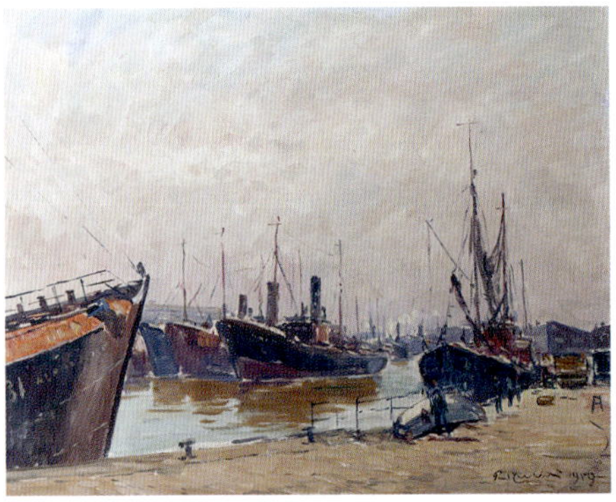

unknown artist
Bremerhaven Docks, Germany 1959
oil on canvas 58.4 x 78.5
A.116

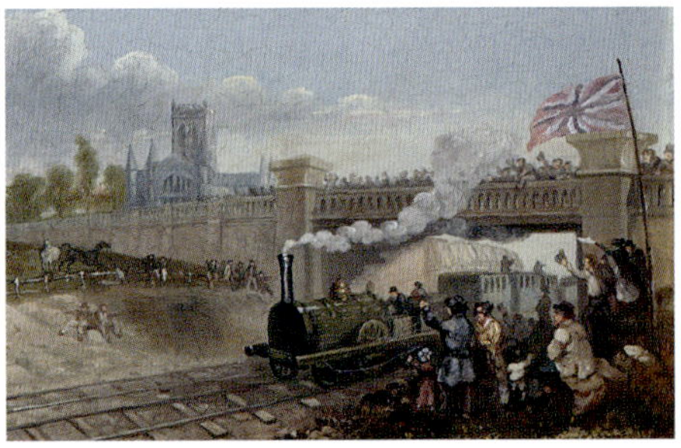

unknown artist
First Train Leaving Grimsby, Lincolnshire, 1848
oil on board 21 x 30.5
A.433

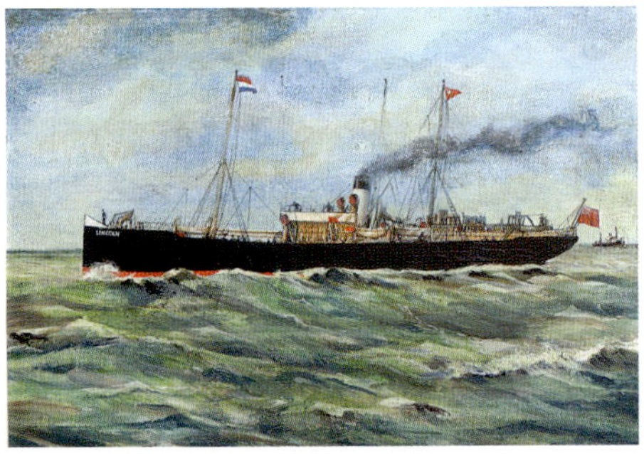

unknown artist
GER Steamship 'Lincoln'
oil on board 45.5 x 66
A.437

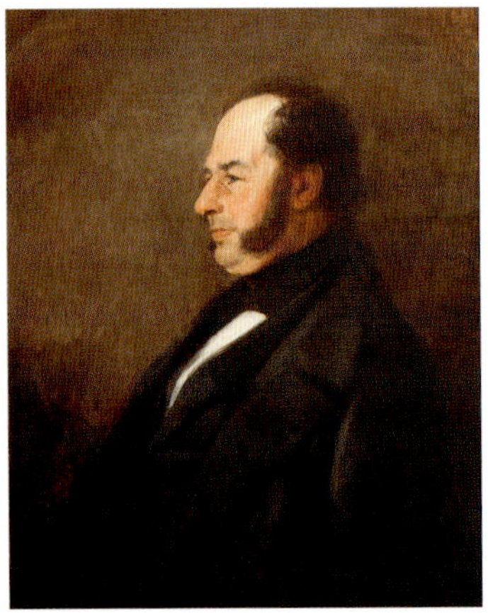

unknown artist
John James Earle (Smack Owner)
oil on canvas 86 x 72.5
A.11

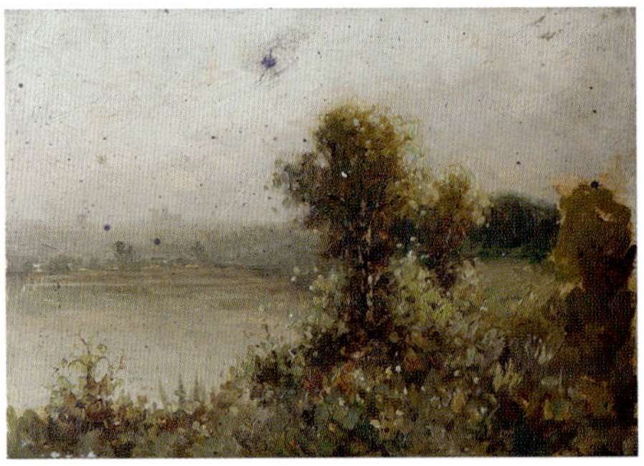

unknown artist
Landscape
oil on board 25.5 x 35.5
A.276

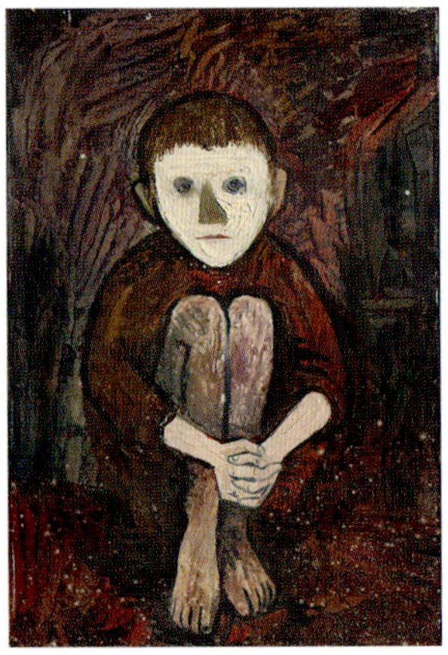

unknown artist
Portrait of a Child with a White Face
oil on board 61 x 41
A.113

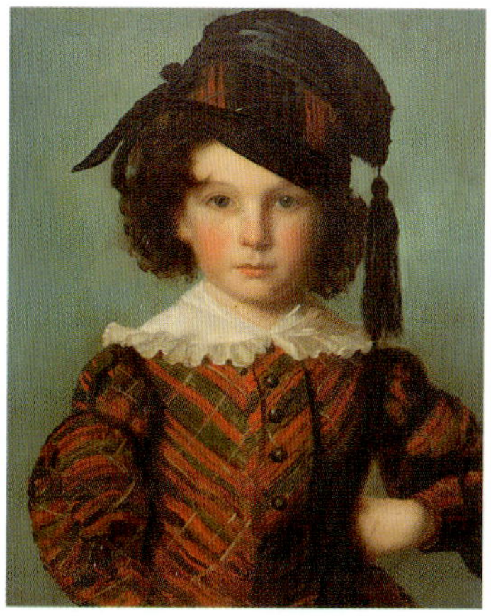

unknown artist
Portrait of a Young Boy Dressed in Tartan
oil on board 53 x 42.5
704/9

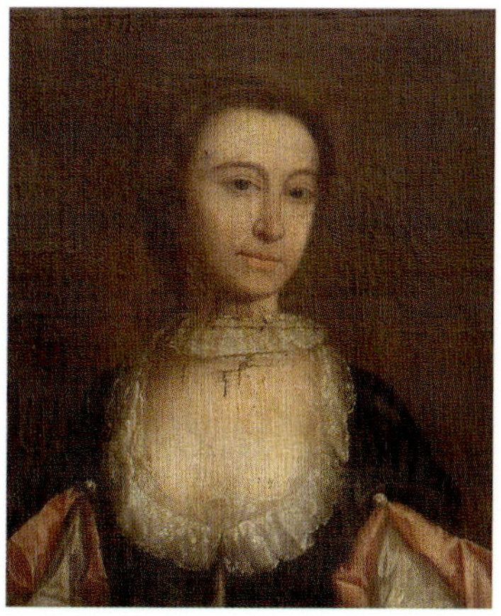

unknown artist
Portrait of an Unknown Lady
oil on canvas 61 x 50.7
GRIMS:2010.27

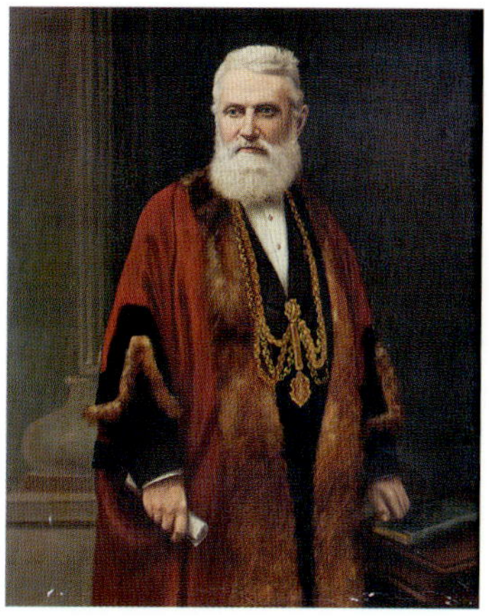

unknown artist
Portrait of an Unknown Mayor
oil on canvas 74.5 x 62
A.7

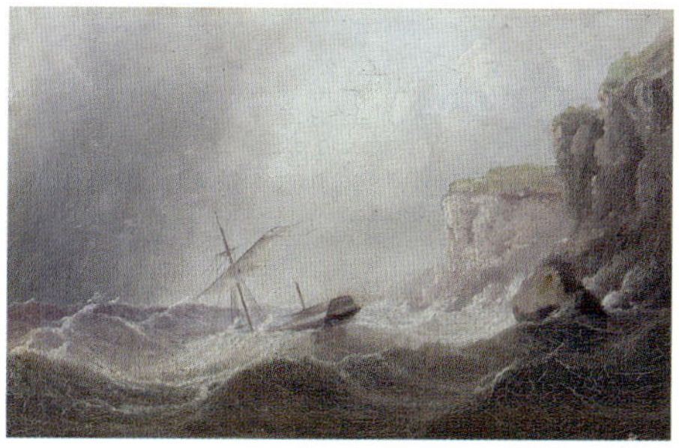

unknown artist
Ship in Distress off the Coast
oil on board 26.5 x 40.5
A.275

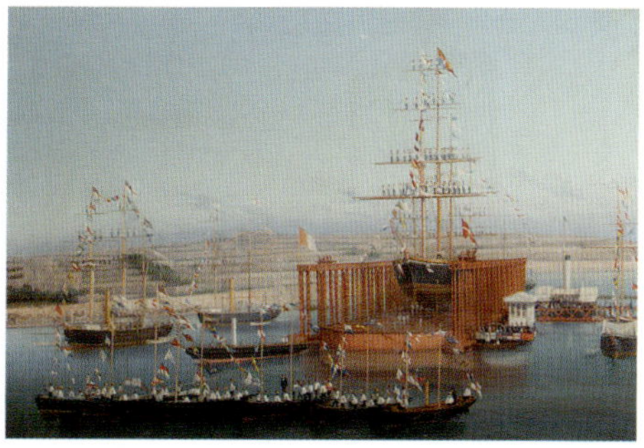

unknown artist
Ship in Dry Dock
oil on canvas 59 x 86
GRIMS:2010.24

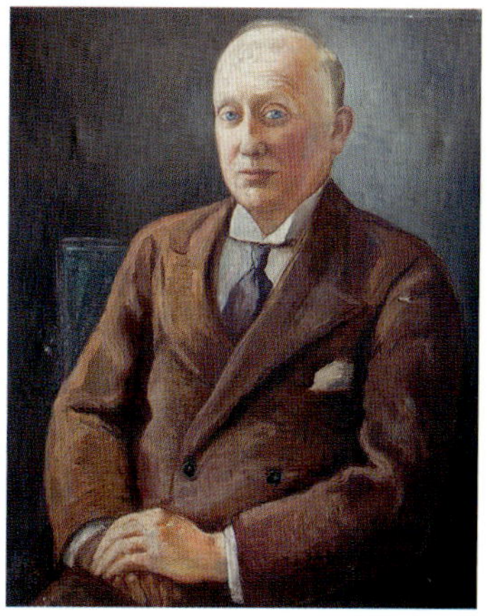

unknown artist
Sir George Doughty, MP (1895), Mayor of Grimsby (1892–1893)
oil on canvas 74.5 x 60
A.94

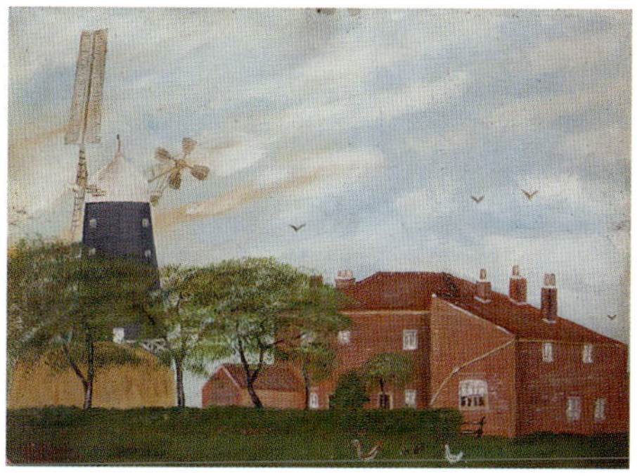

unknown artist
Sluice Mill, South Ferriby, Lincolnshire
oil on board 23.5 x 31
A.280

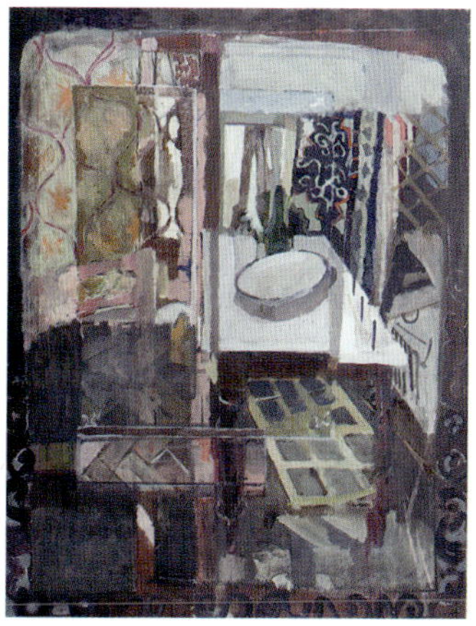

unknown artist
Still Life, Interior
oil on canvas 141 x 119
A.274

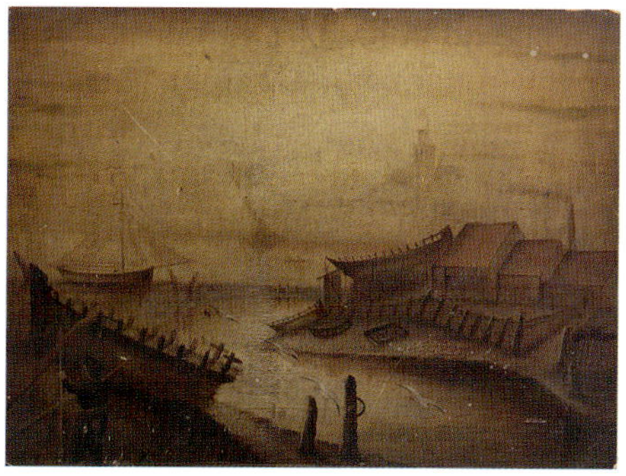

unknown artist
Sunrise, Old Outfall, Grimsby, Lincolnshire
oil on board 46.5 x 62
A.124

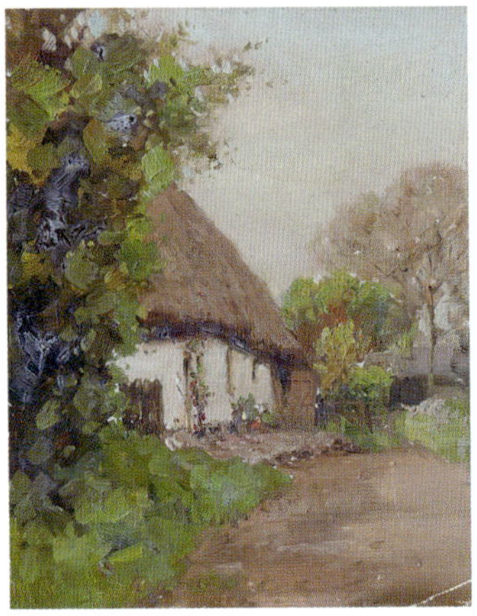

unknown artist
Thatched Cottage
oil on card 33 x 25.3
A.69

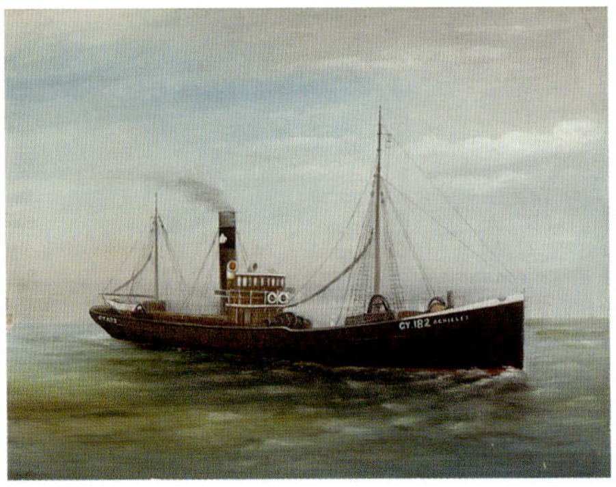

unknown artist
The 'Achilles', GY182
oil on card 39.2 x 50
GRIMS:2010.25

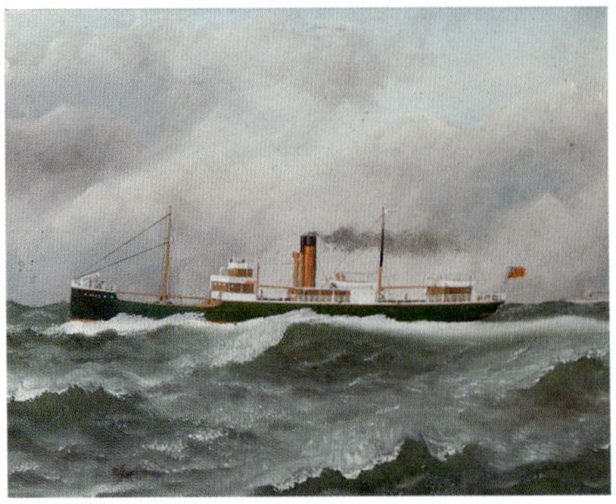

unknown artist
The 'Argo'
oil on board 33.2 x 40
A.174

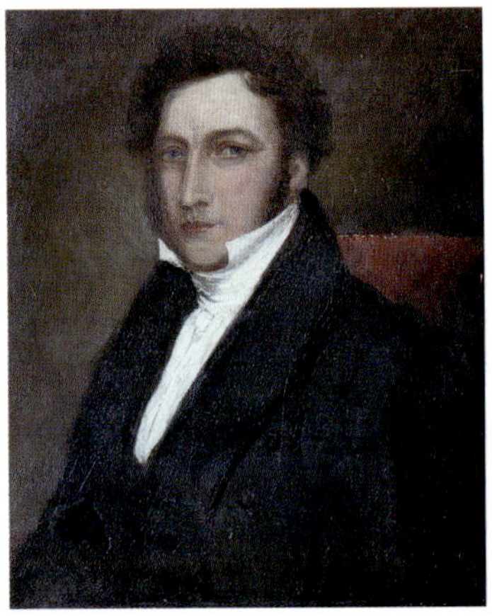

unknown artist
'The Commodore', Charles Anderson-Pelham (1781–1846), 1st Earl of Yarborough
oil on board 24 x 19.5
A.70

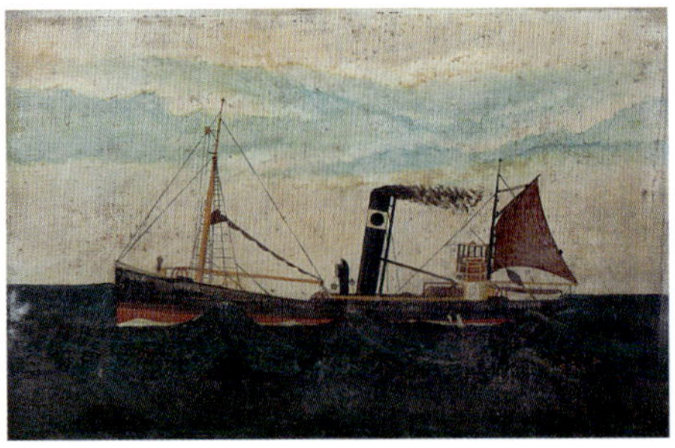

unknown artist
The 'Elk'
oil on metal 23.2 x 35.9
F.98.20.1

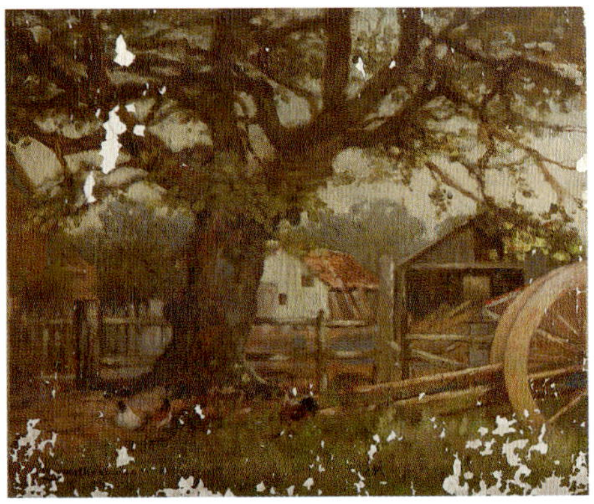

unknown artist
The Wheelright's Shed
oil on board 31 x 36
GRIMS:2010.28

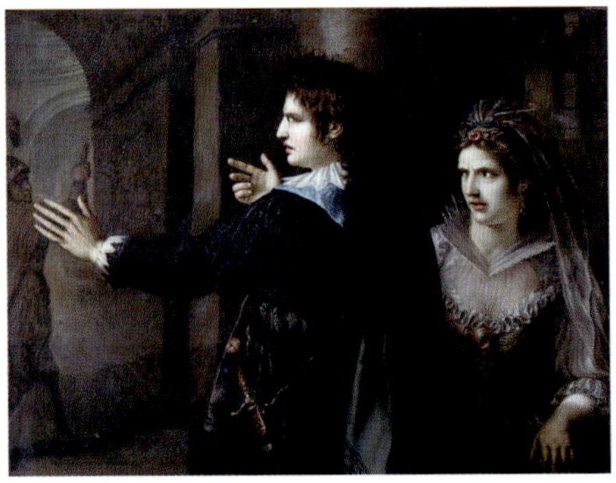

unknown artist
Theatrical Scene
oil on canvas 97 x 122
A.26

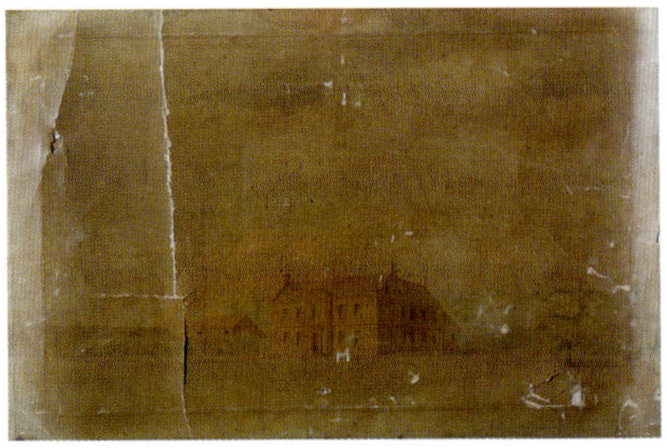

unknown artist
Waltham Hall, Melton Mowbray (?)
oil on canvas 40.5 x 58
A.125

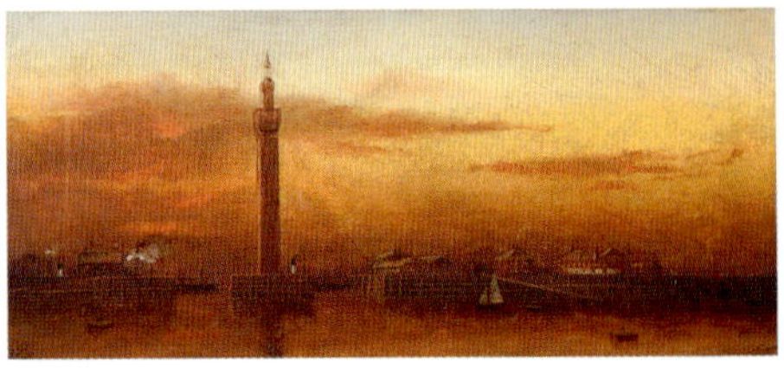

H. W.
Grimsby Docks from the West Pier, Lincolnshire 1894
oil on canvas 18.5 x 40
A.67

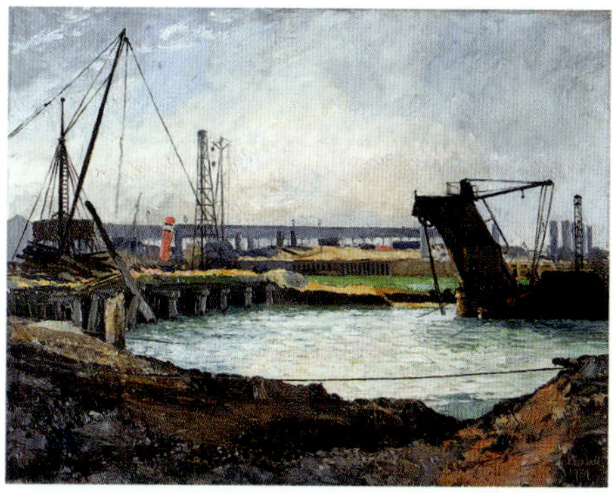

Wade, Albert Edward active 1911–1948
Last of Pie Jetty, Grimsby Fish Dock, Lincolnshire 1934
oil on canvas 60 x 76
A.430

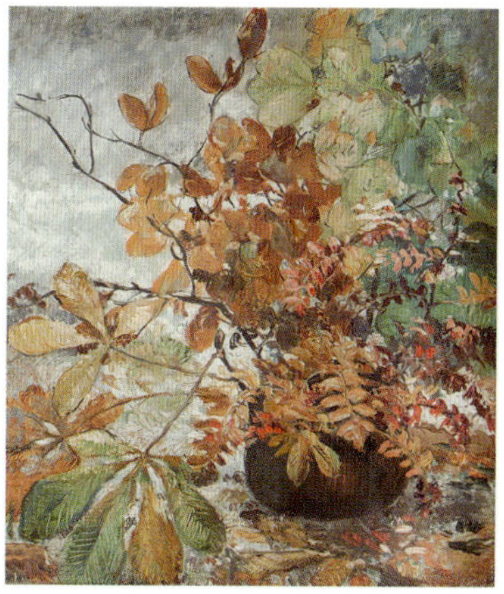

Wade, Albert Edward active 1911–1948
Still Life, Autumn 1935
oil on canvas 59.5 x 50.5
A.439.1

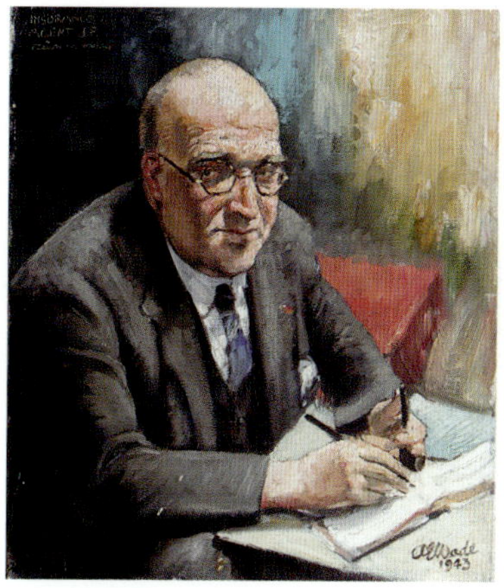

Wade, Albert Edward active 1911–1948
Jesse Flower 1943
oil on canvas 61 x 52
A.36

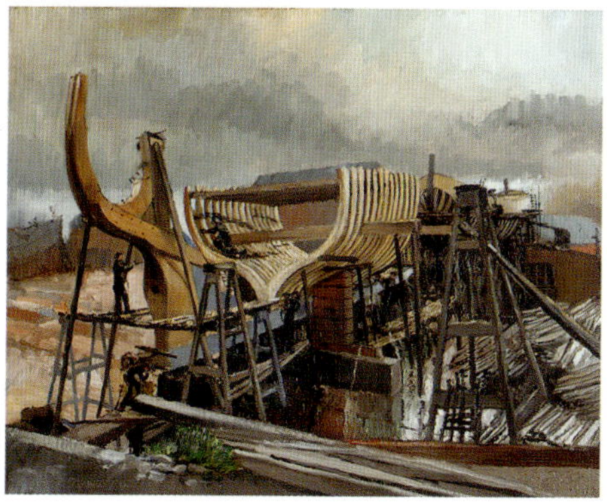

Wade, Albert Edward active 1911–1948
Slipway, Grimsby Docks, Lincolnshire 1943
oil on canvas 50 x 60
A.40

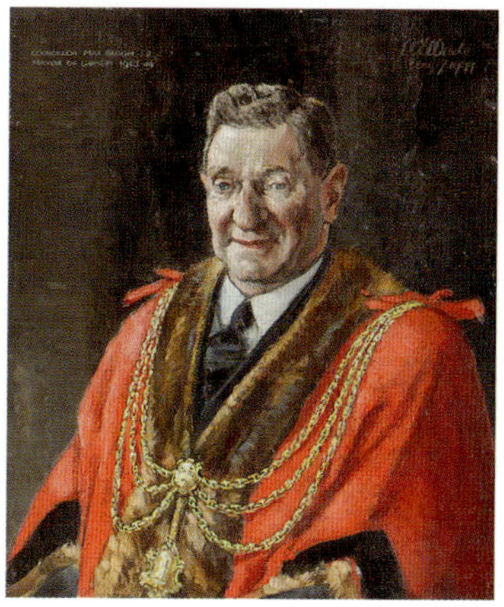

Wade, Albert Edward active 1911–1948
Councillor Max Bloom, JP, Mayor of Grimsby (1943–1944) 1944
oil on canvas 62 x 50.5
A.176

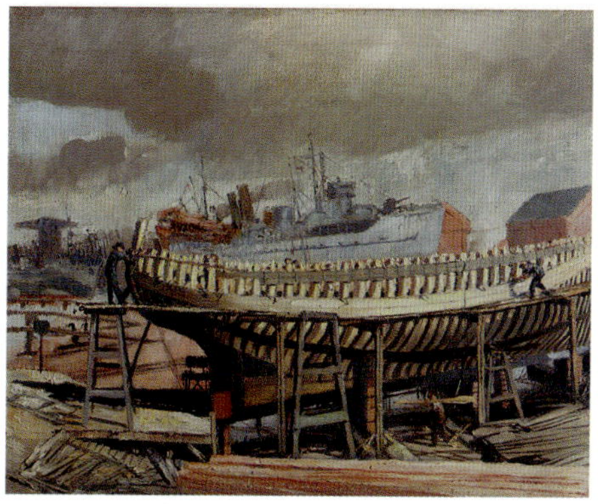

Wade, Albert Edward active 1911–1948
Ship Building, Grimsby Docks, Lincolnshire 1945
oil on canvas 50 x 60
A.43

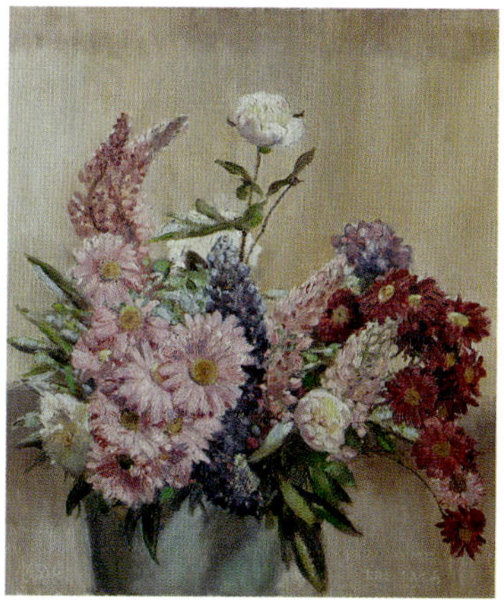

Wade, Albert Edward active 1911–1948
Still Life, Flowers 1946
oil on canvas 61 x 51
A.438.1

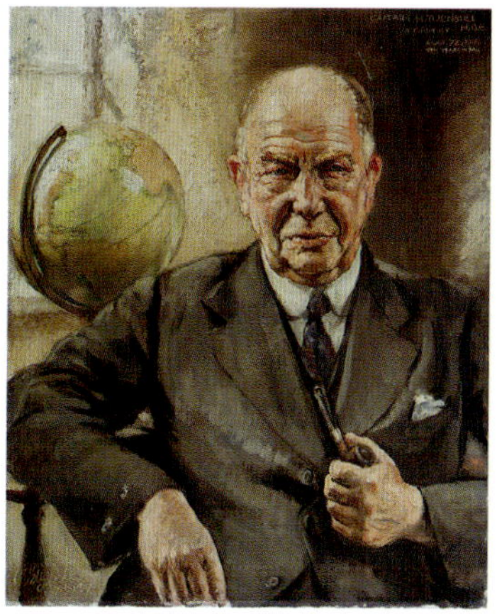

Wade, Albert Edward active 1911–1948
Captain H. Turnbull, MBE, Former Harbour Master of Grimsby 1947
oil on canvas 61.5 x 51
A.37

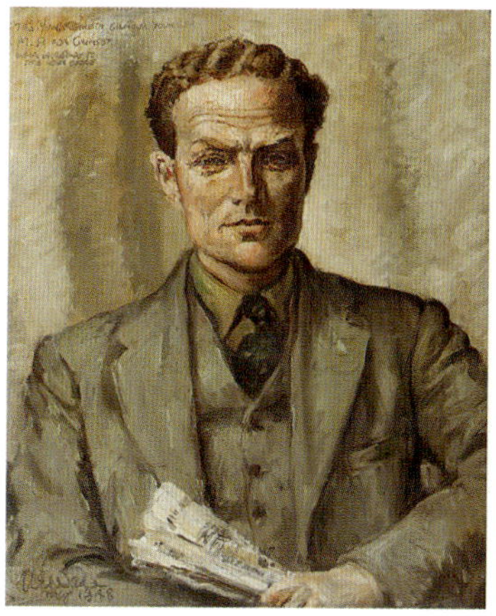

Wade, Albert Edward active 1911–1948
Kenneth Gilmour Younger, MP 1948
oil on canvas 60 x 50
A.35

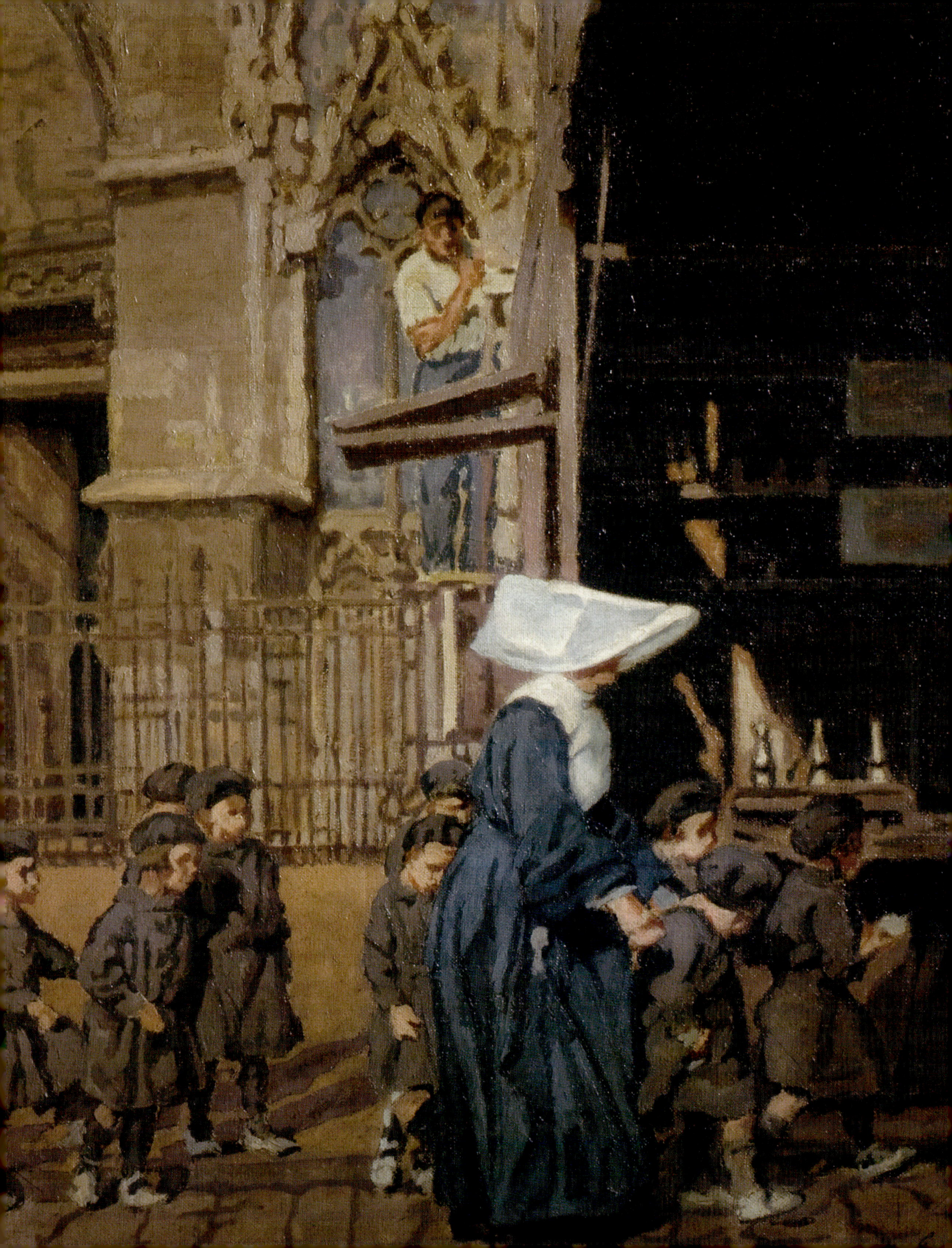

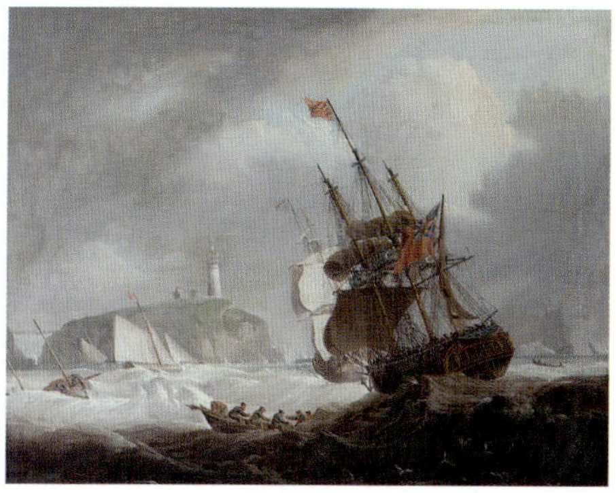

Webster, George 1797–1864
Ships off Holyhead at the Beginning of a Storm
oil on canvas 35 x 43.5
A.139

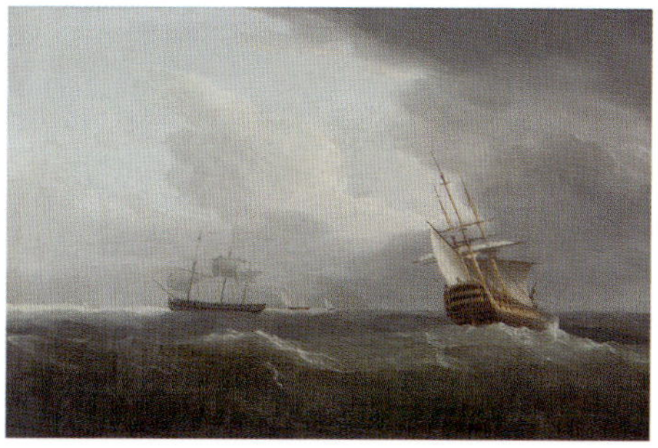

Whitcombe, Thomas c.1752–1824
Ships at Sea
oil on canvas 36 x 53
A.207

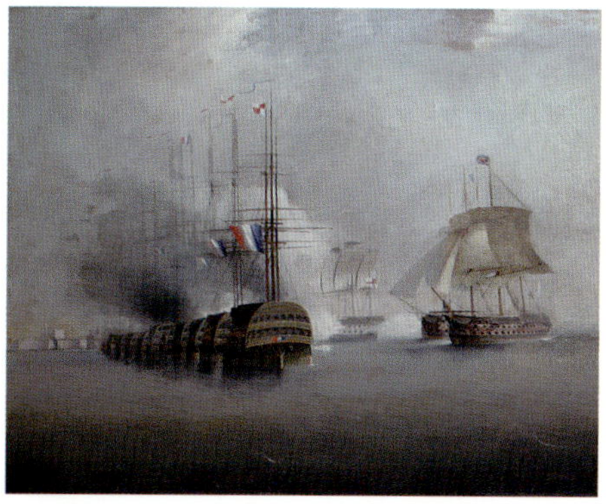

Whitcombe, Thomas (attributed to)
c.1752–1824
The Battle of the Nile, 1–2 August 1798
oil on canvas 62.5 x 75.5
A.46

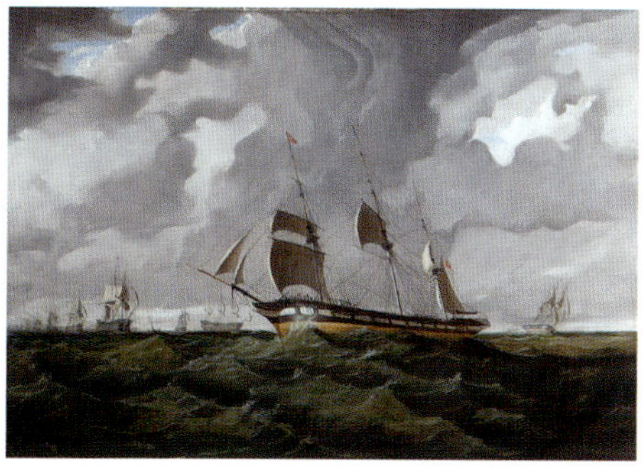

William, A. G.
Men-of-War at the Beginning of a Storm
oil on canvas 65 x 90.2
A.157

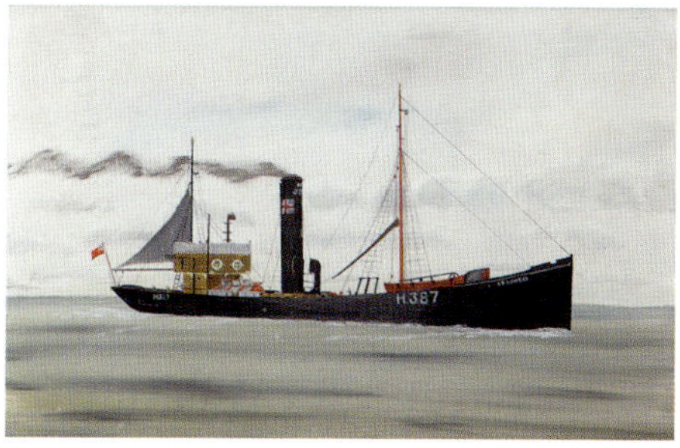

Wilson, G. (attributed to)
The 'Ronsay', H387 1915
oil on board 29 x 45
A.49

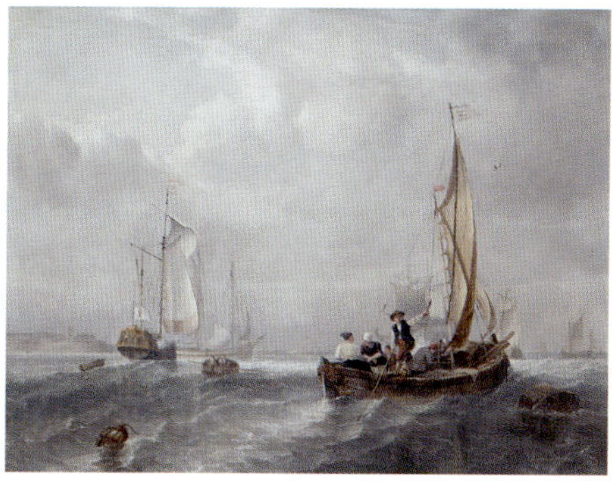

Wilson, John H. 'Jock' 1774–1855
Small Ships and Boats off the Coast
oil on canvas 70 x 90
A.140

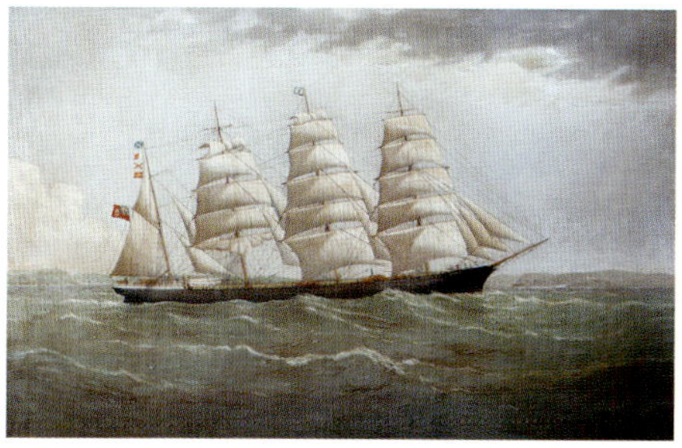

Witham, Isaac Joseph 1832–1901
The 'Oweenee'
oil on canvas 64 x 105.5
A.76

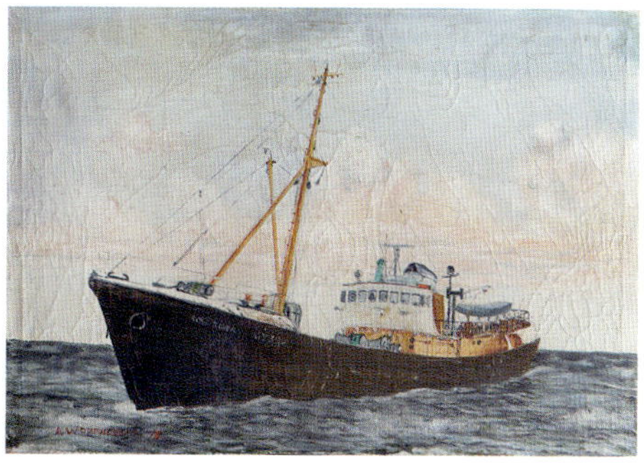

Wozencroft, A.
The 'Ross Tiger', GY 398 1973
oil on canvas 51 x 76
A.245

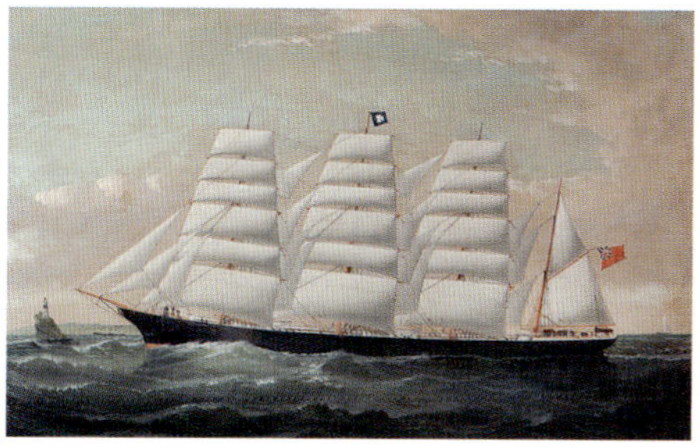

Yorke, William Horde 1847–1921
The 'Lord Templeshore' 1892
oil on canvas 44 x 68
A.83

Facing page: Gosse, Laura Sylvia, 1881–1968, *A Nun with Children* (detail), Leicester Arts and Museums Service (p. 47)

The Franklin Trust

Founded in 1970, the Jack Franklin Memorial Trust commemorates the services to education of Councillor Jack Franklin, OBE. As a lasting tribute to his work, the Franklin Trust instigated a collection of works representing the best artistic achievements of students, teachers and artists in Lincolnshire, using the monies donated by the public. Many of the works of art have also been donated to the trust by artists, and others have been purchased using the fund set up in 1970. The fund also allows for the Collection to be maintained in good order and to be expanded; alongside this, the Trust is able to give bursaries to students wishing to continue with their art education.

Members of the public are invited to view the Collection which is displayed on the walls of the Franklin College in Grimsby. Groups wishing to view the collection should first contact the College to ensure easy access at a mutually convenient time.

Geoffrey Baxter, Secretary of the Trust

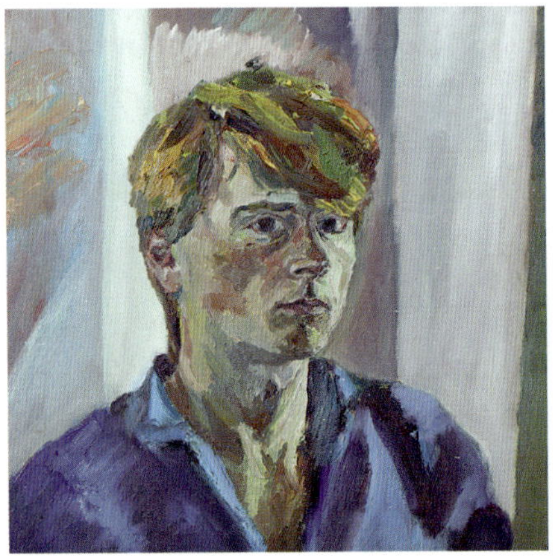

Ashton, Stuart
Self Portrait
oil on canvas 43.2 x 43.2
39

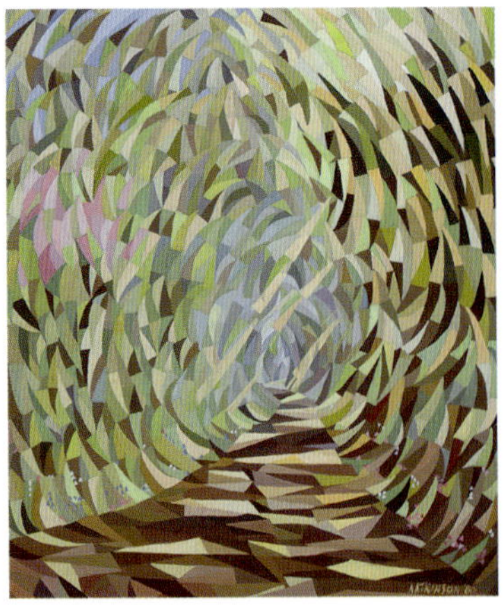

Atkinson, Albert
My Road through the Woods 1980
oil on panel 84 x 70
101

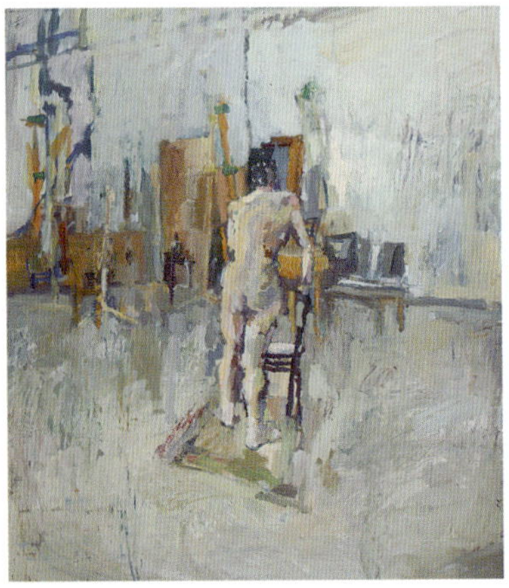

Avison, Michelle b.1965
Nude 1984
oil on board 130 x 93
58

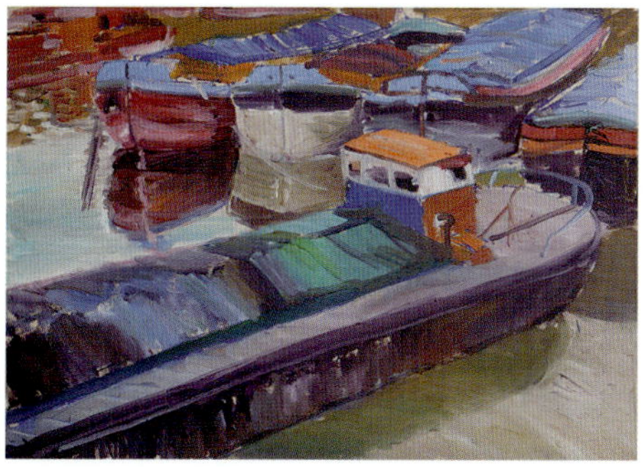

Barker, Geoffrey
Barges
oil on canvas 55 x 75
126

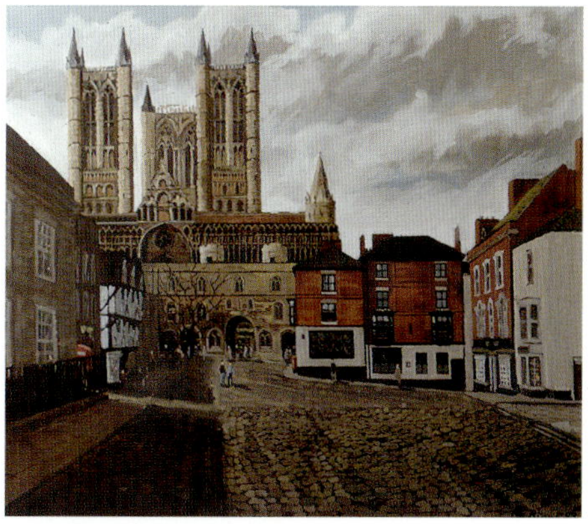

Binns, Andrew b.1964
Lincoln Cathedral
oil on canvas 112 x 127
153

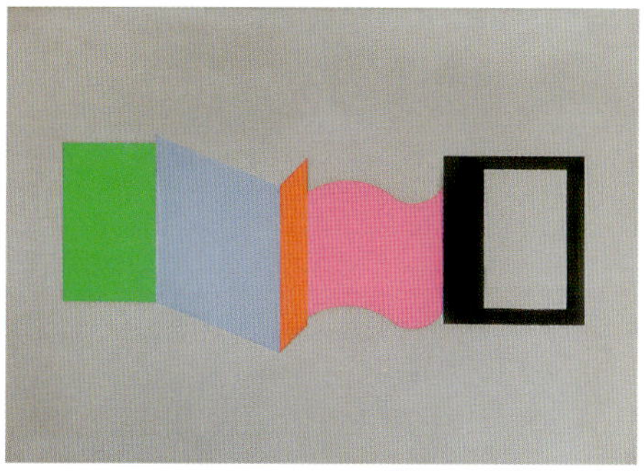

Boucher, John
Drawing
acrylic & collage on paper 55 x 81
115

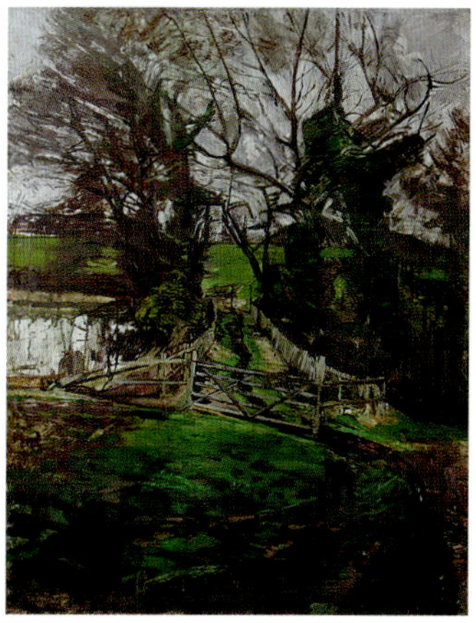

Bowey, Olwyn b.1936
Landscape
oil on canvas 100 x 75
51

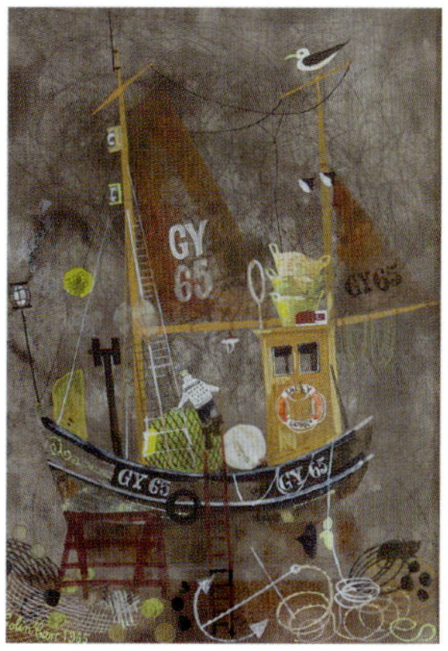

Carr, Colin b.1929
Blue Seiner
oil on paper 28 x 20
116

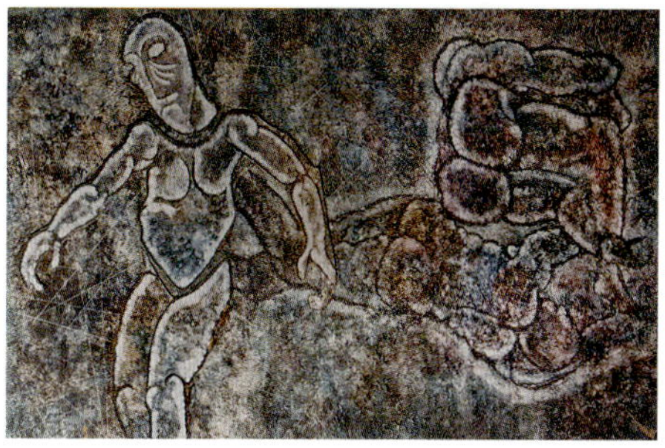

Clatter, Malcolm b.1953
Full Fathom Five
oil on board 122 x 244
35

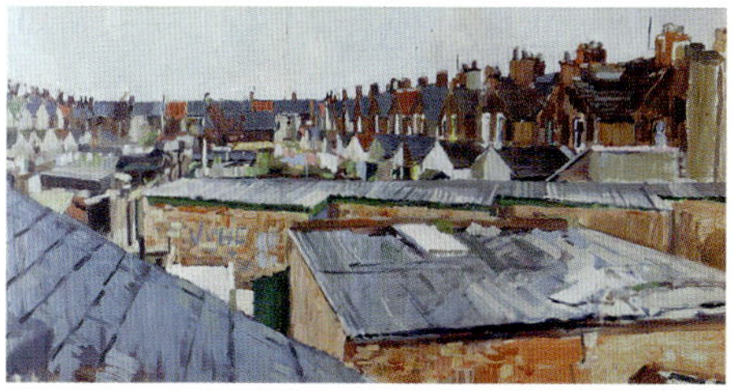

Clilverd, Jason
Rooftops
oil on board 48 x 89
45

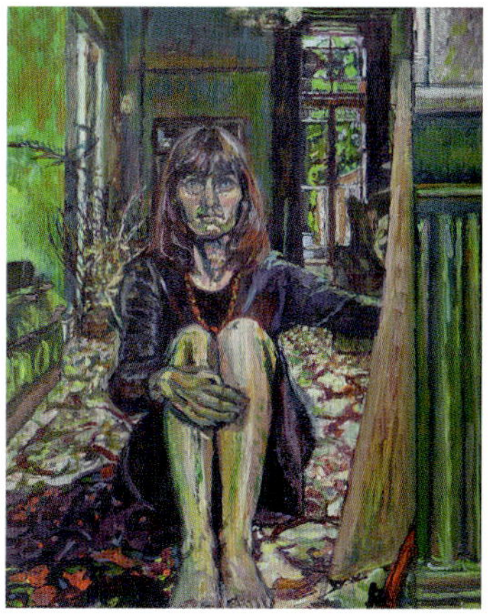

Collins, Lesley
Self Portrait
oil on board 74 x 58
56

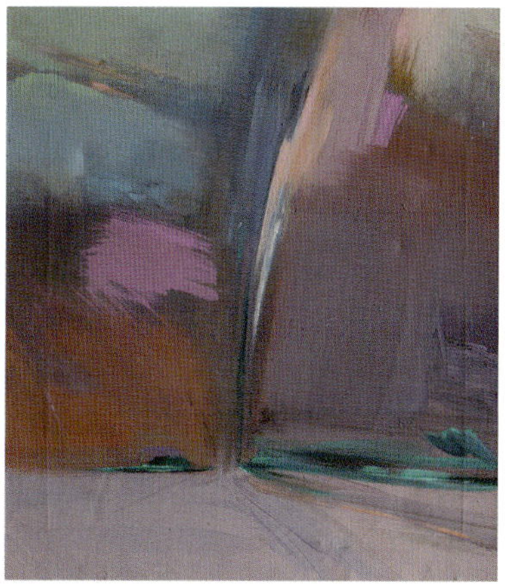

Constance, Diana 1934–2011
Abstract Landscape
oil on canvas 50 x 43
68

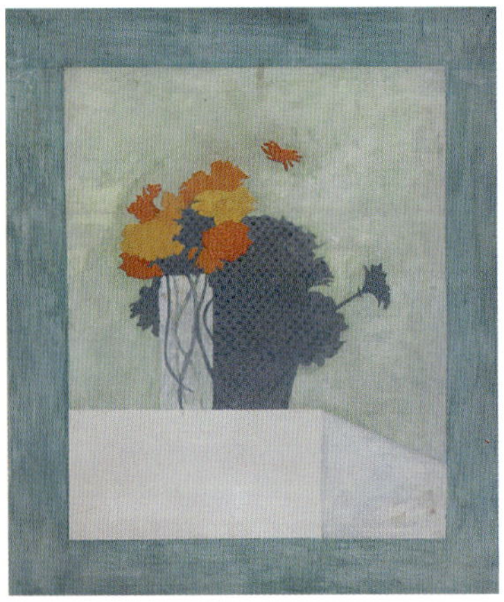

Crowe, Victoria b.1945
Flowers on the Fridge
oil on panel 73 x 60
111

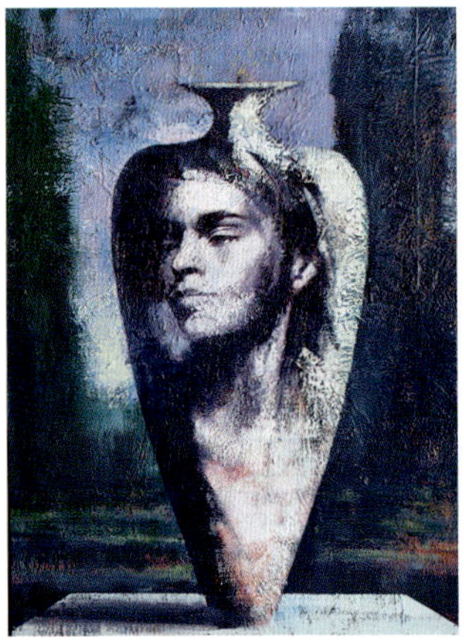

Davies, Hugh b.1946
The Neapolitan Girl
oil on panel 92 x 66
148

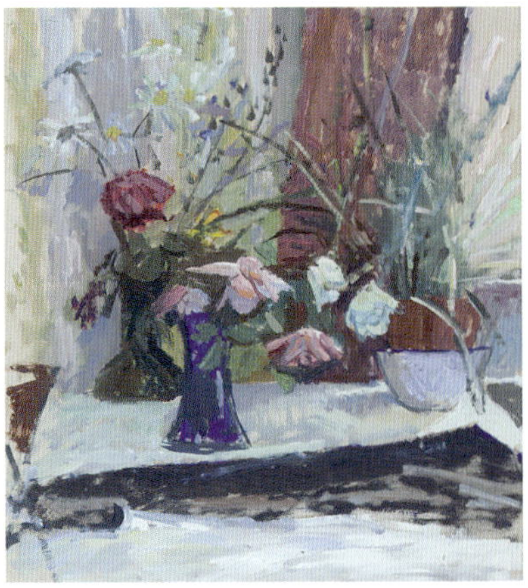

Davis, Katherine
Still Life, Flowers
oil on canvas 66 x 53
4

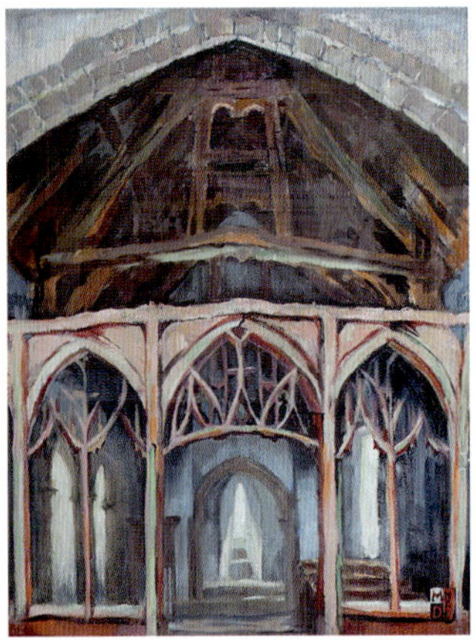

Dean, Margaret b.1939
Church Interior
oil on paper 76 x 55
147

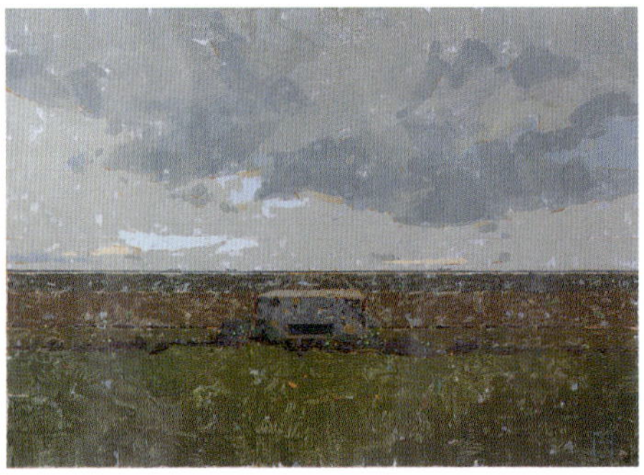

Ellerby, Nick b.1958
Pillbox, Horseshoe Point, Lincolnshire 2009
oil on board 40 x 53
169

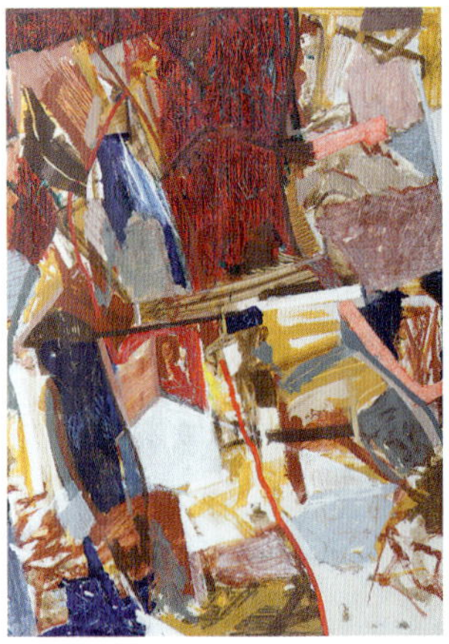

Elliott, Mike
Hello
oil on board 72 x 50
138

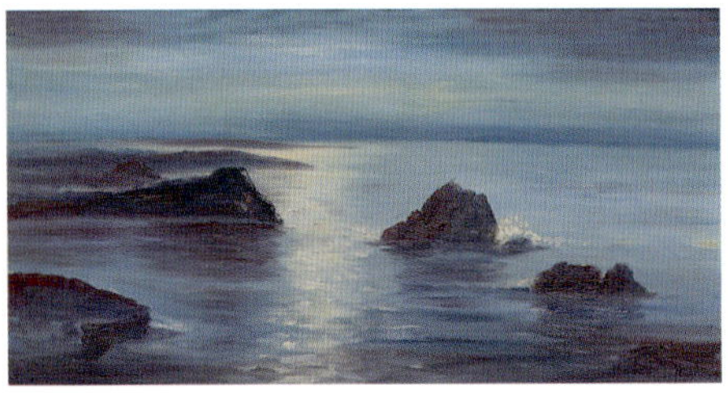

Fegan, David 1955–2006
Seascape
oil on panel 44 x 83
155

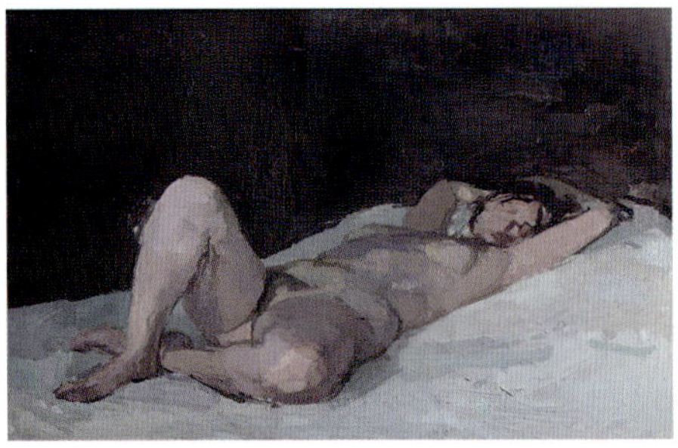

Felcey, Trevor b.1945
Nude
oil on canvas 93 x 130
25

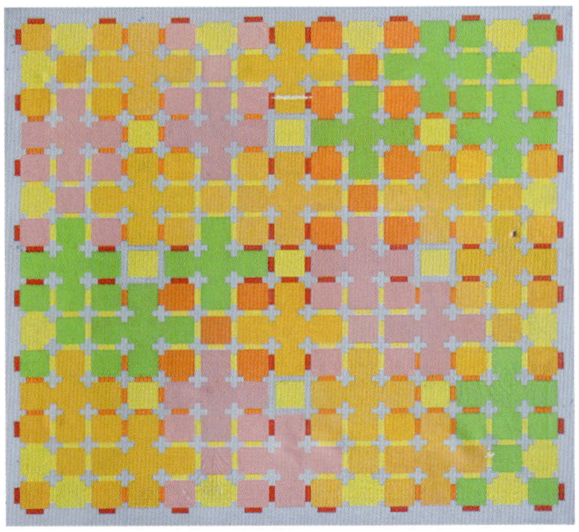

Foster, John
Sierpinski Curve Variation
oil on canvas 91 x 91 (E)
113

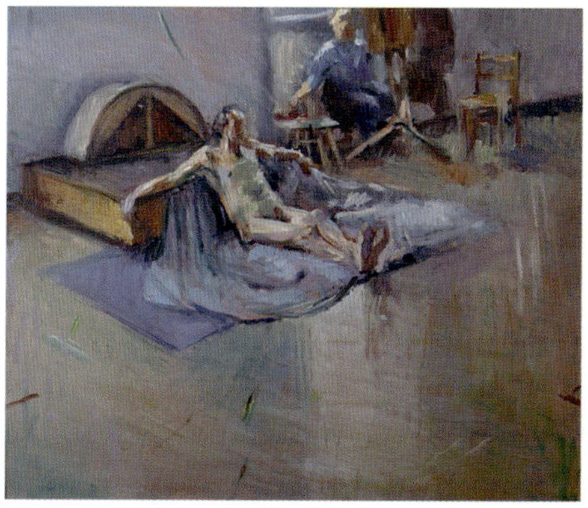

Gables, Gina
Reclining Male
oil on canvas 62 x 72
60

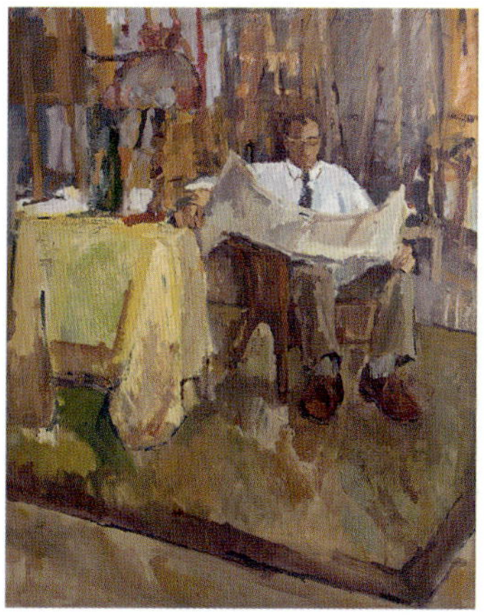

Gillett, Stephen
Man Reading a Newspaper
oil on board 130 x 90
57

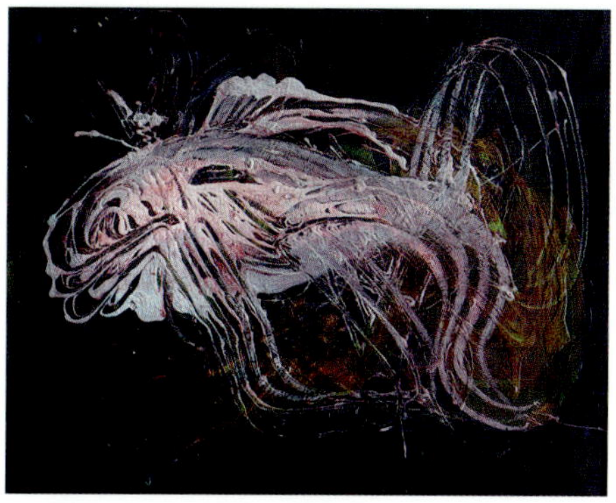

Haddock, Edwin Aldridge 1921–1996
Pink Pride (Pink Perfection)
acrylic & oil on panel 90 x 120
100

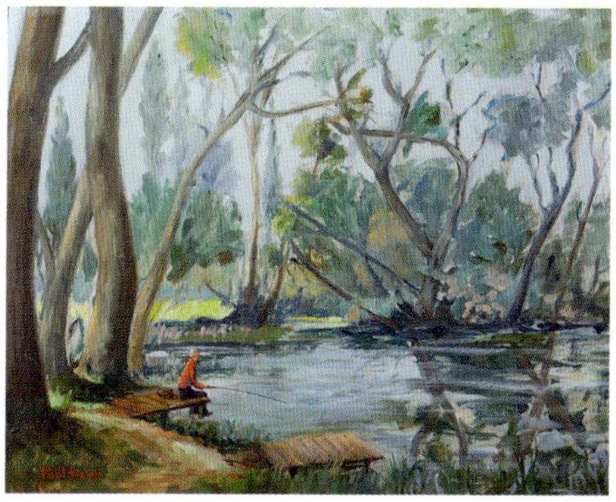

Haigh, Paul active 1983–1990
Boy Fishing
oil on board 34.2 x 42
171

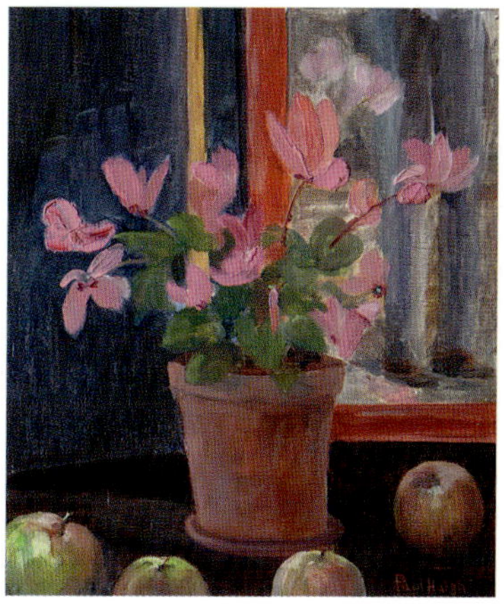

Haigh, Paul active 1983–1990
Cyclamen with Apples
oil on panel 29 x 24
105

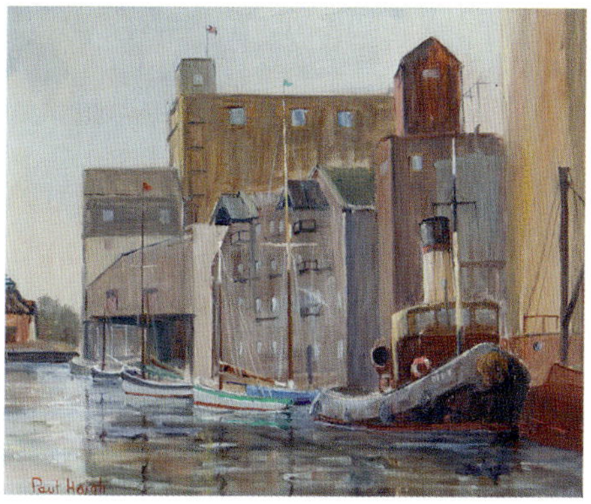

Haigh, Paul active 1983–1990
Ipswich Docks, Suffolk
oil on board 27.5 x 34
84

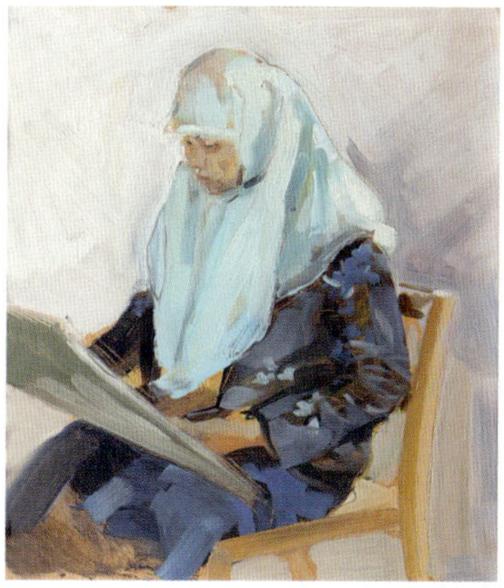

Haswell, Malcolm
Model
oil on panel 34 x 29
28

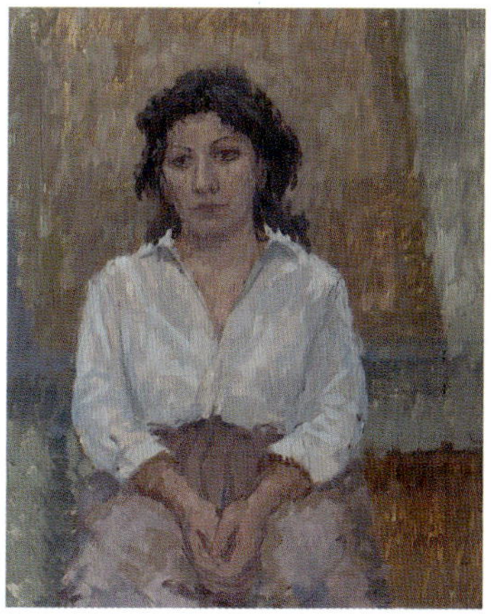

Hennes, Jolyon b.1950
Greek Girl
oil on panel 46 x 39
6

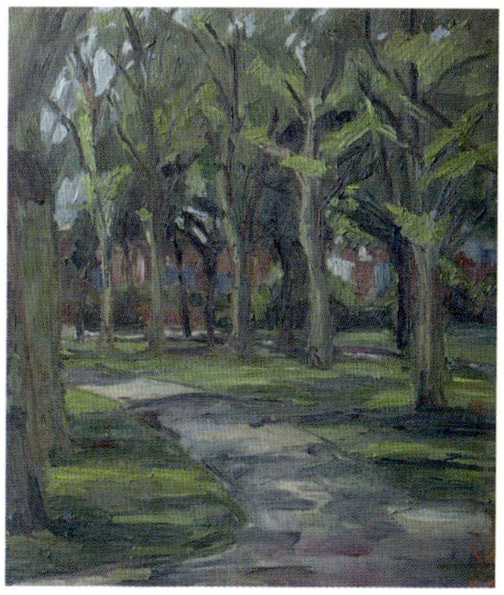

Hill, Carol
Grant Thorold Park, Grimsby, Lincolnshire
oil on board 68 x 58
55

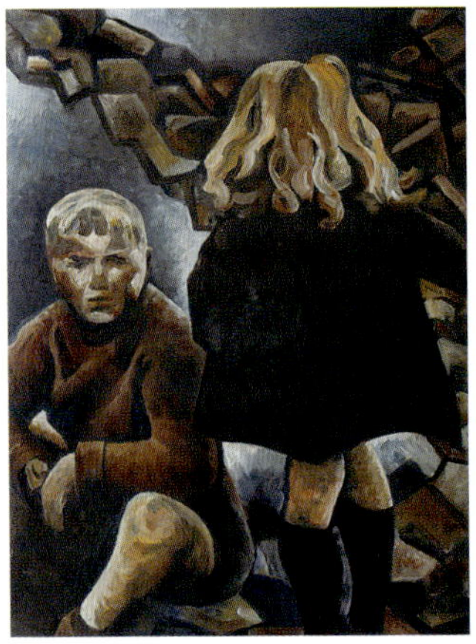

Holmes, Mark
Children
oil on board 84 x 58
97

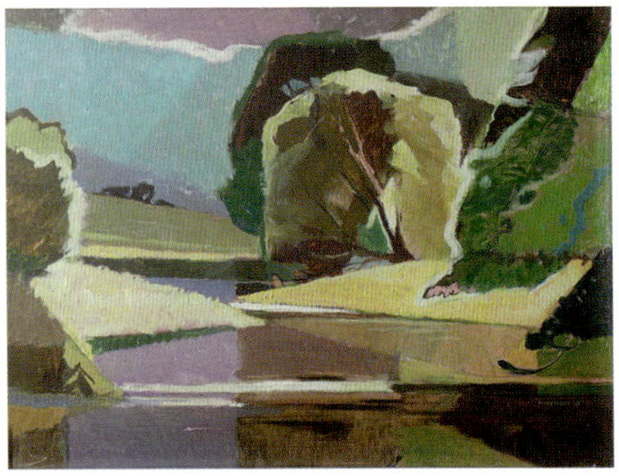

Holzer, Henry 1907–2007
Sun over Willows
oil on canvas 40 x 54
122

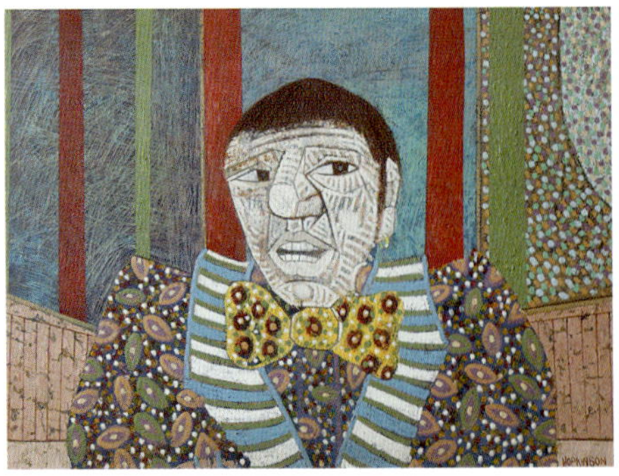

Hopkinson, John b.1941
Mr Beau Williams, Outsider
oil on board 46 x 61
7

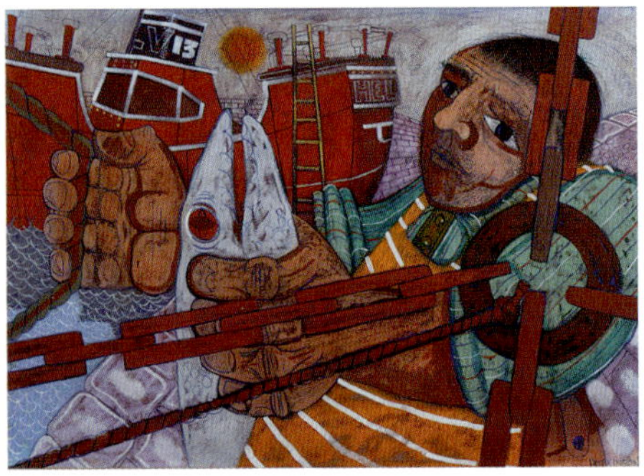

Hopkinson, John b.1941
Trawler (Still Life)
oil on board 51 x 71
89

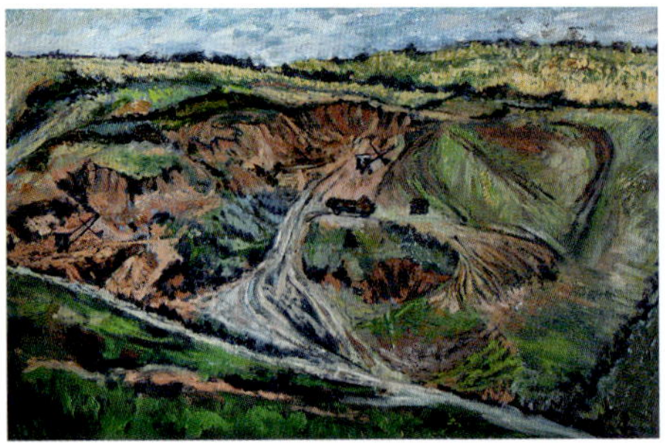

Hoult, Ken 1928–1990
Hurdis Sandpits, Nettleton, Lincolnshire
oil on board 39 x 60
124

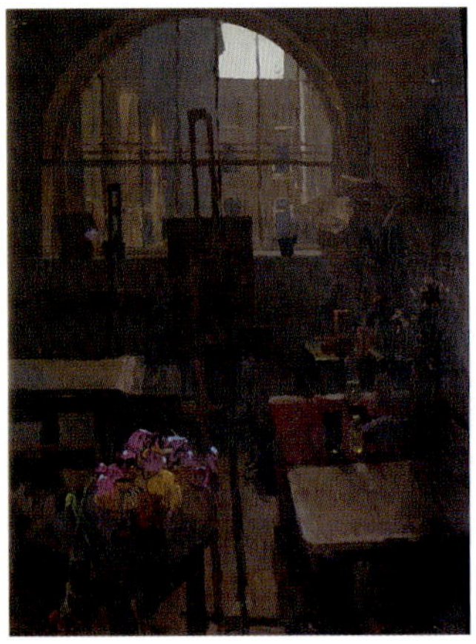

Humphreys, Geoff b.1959
Studio Interior
oil on board 82 x 59
44

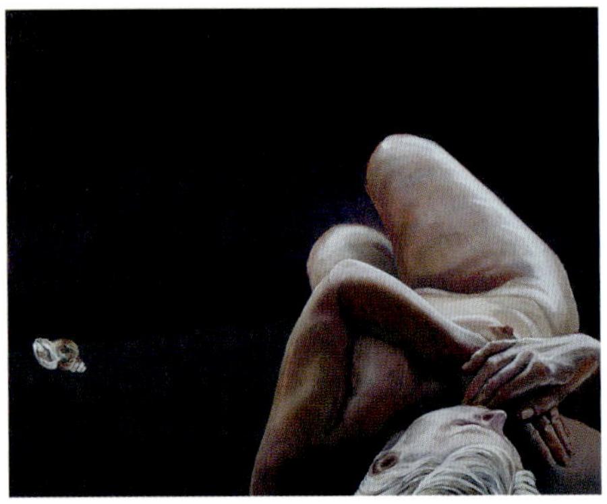

Ingham, Linda b.1964
Shell (study) 2007
oil on canvas 50 x 60
164

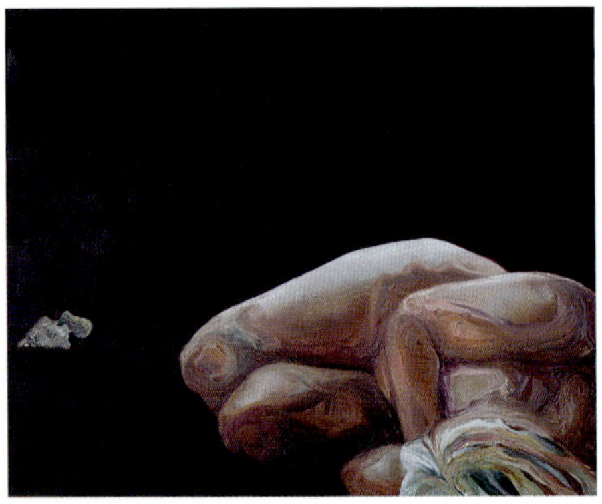

Ingham, Linda b.1964
Shell 2007
oil on canvas 50 x 61
165

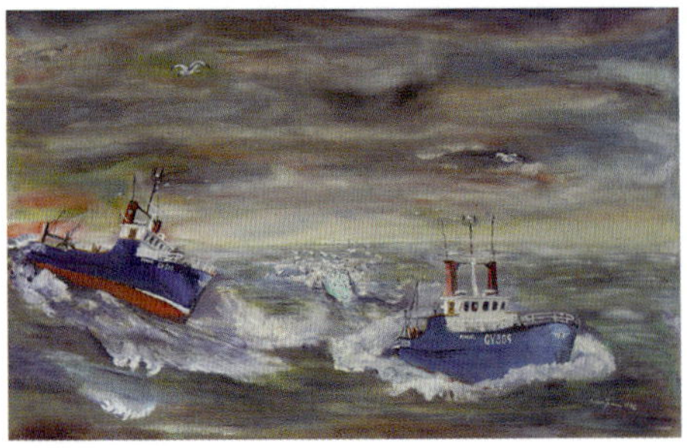

Jensen, Andreas
The Pair Fishers 1976
oil on board 61 x 91
156

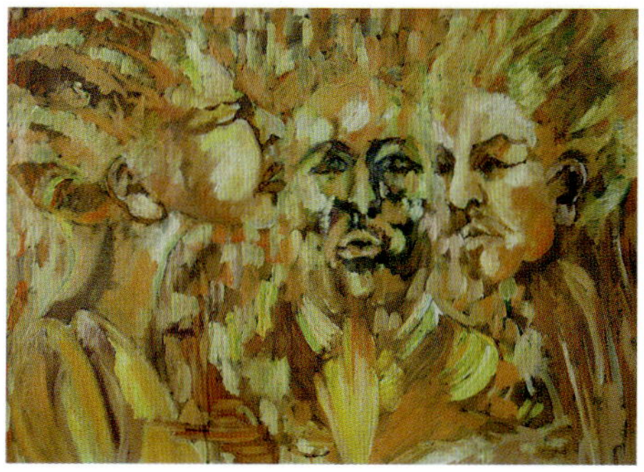

Jessup, Ann
Triple Echo
oil on paper 42 x 60
90

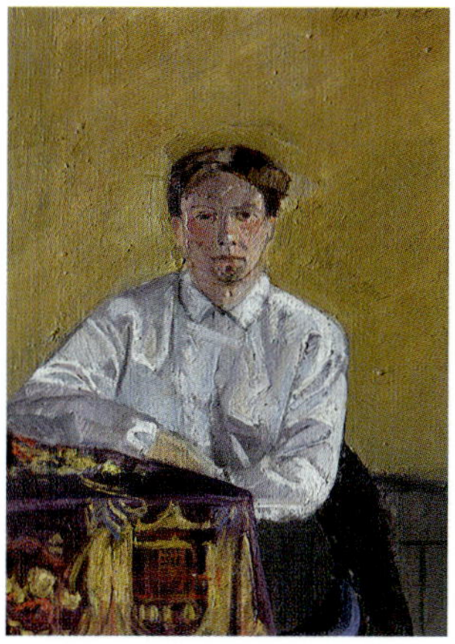

Ludlam, Alf b.1941
Portrait of a Young Lady
oil on panel 28 x 19
102

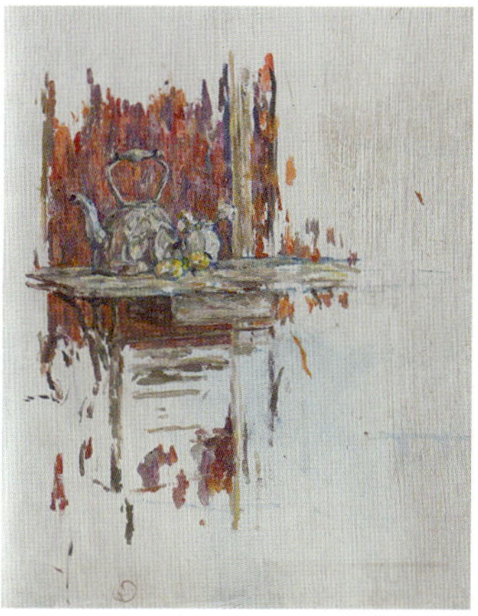

Lundy, Fiona b.1963
Still Life with a Kettle
oil on panel 32 x 25
22

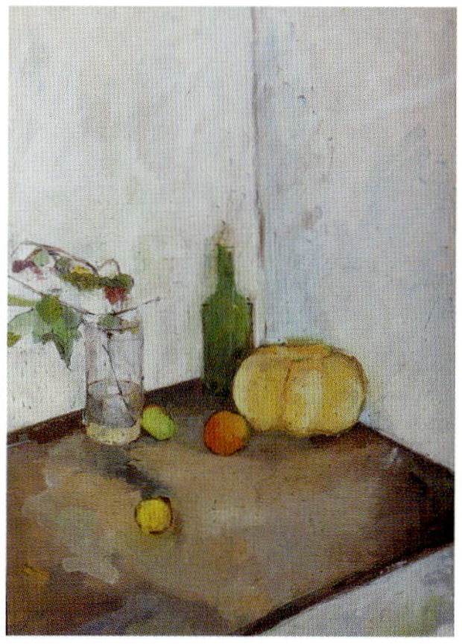

Moffat, Mark J.
Still Life
oil on board 90 x 63
70

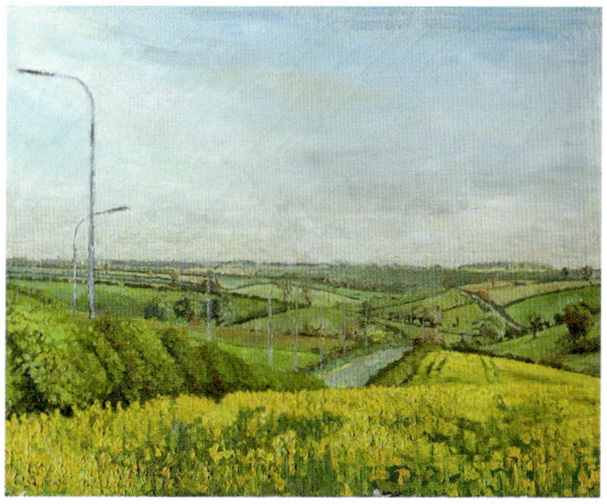

Owen, David active 1981–1982
Rape Field at Caistor, Lincolnshire
oil on canvas 64 x 78
40

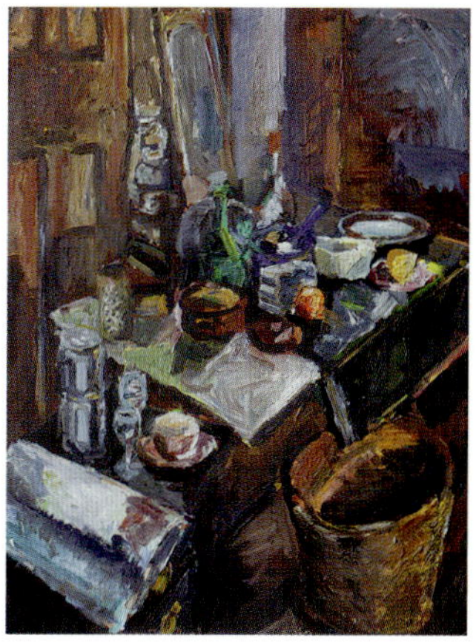

Owen, Mark b.1963
Still Life
oil on panel 140 x 85 (E)
36

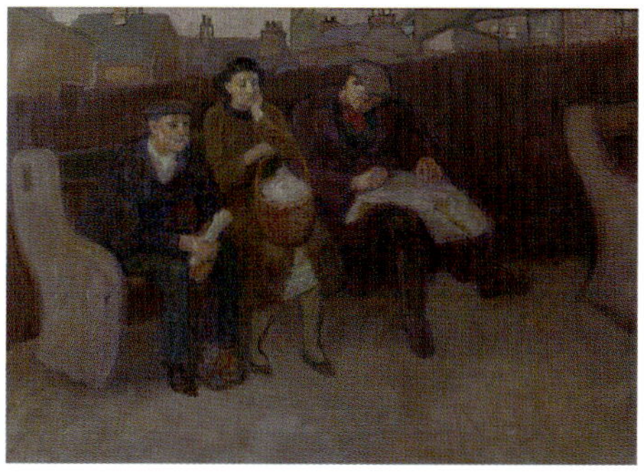

Palmer, Albert Harold 1911–1985
Park Bench
oil on canvas 50 x 70
109

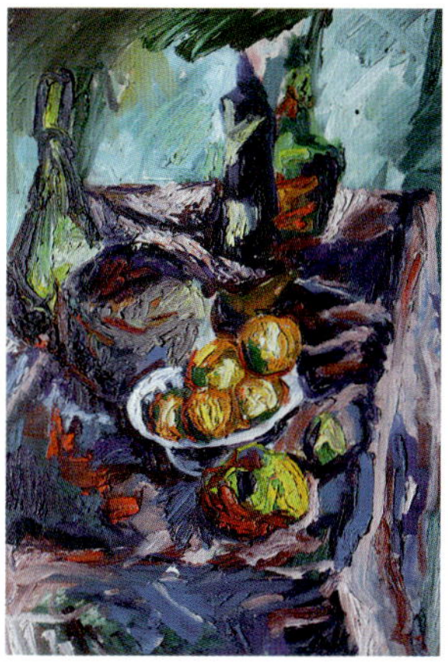

Penketh, Andrew b.1966
Still Life
oil on board 87 x 56
71

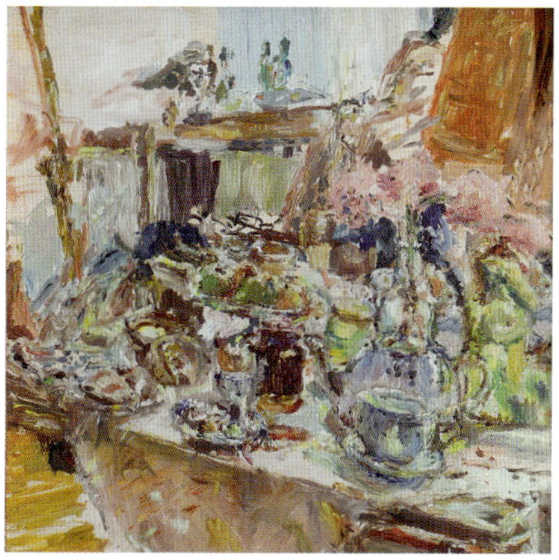

Rae, Annette
Still Life
oil on panel 37.3 x 37.3
59

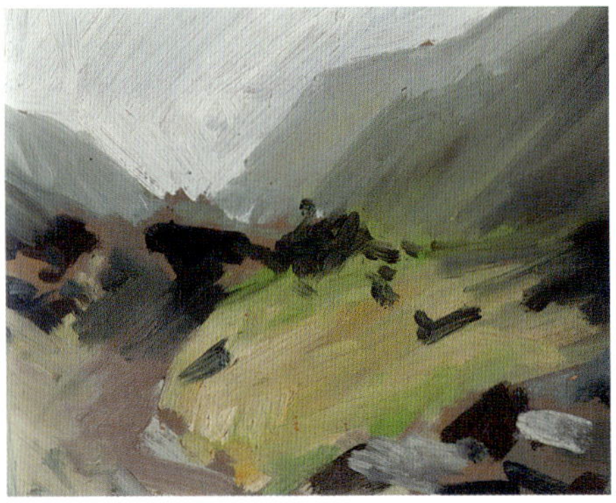

Rawson, Philip 1924–1995
Landscape
oil on panel 17.5 x 23.9
17

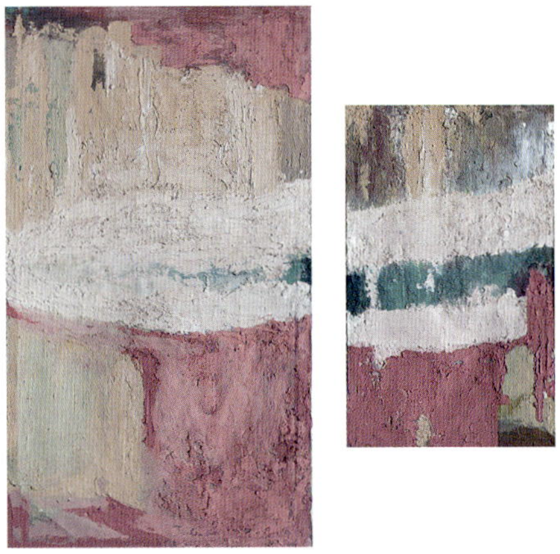

Reeves, Aimie b.1971
Diptych
oil on canvas 127 x 65; 80 x 45
98

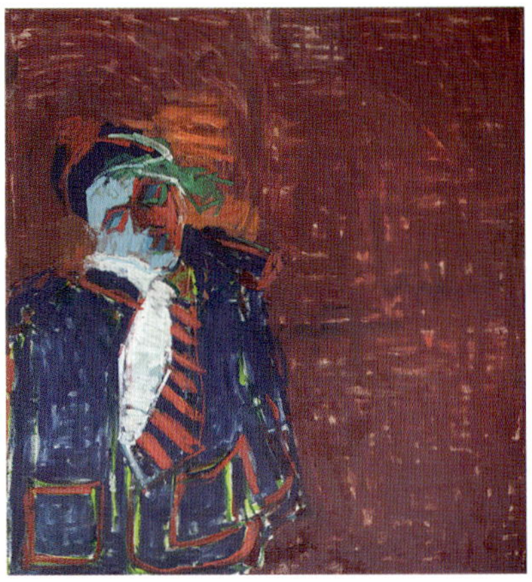

Rider, Gordon
Figure
oil on board 187 x 148
52

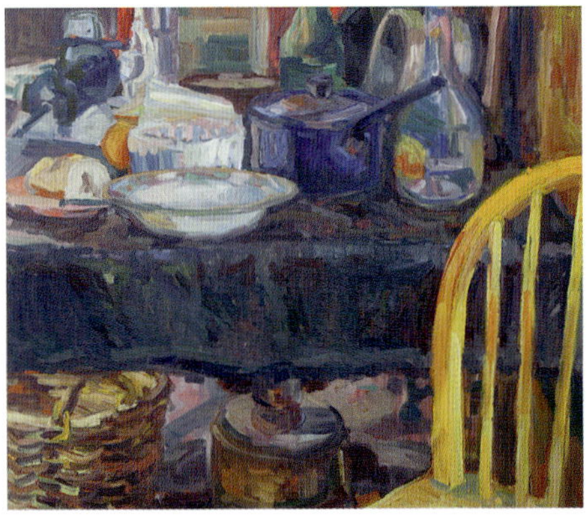

Robinson, Mark active 1982
Still Life
oil on board 53 x 60
41

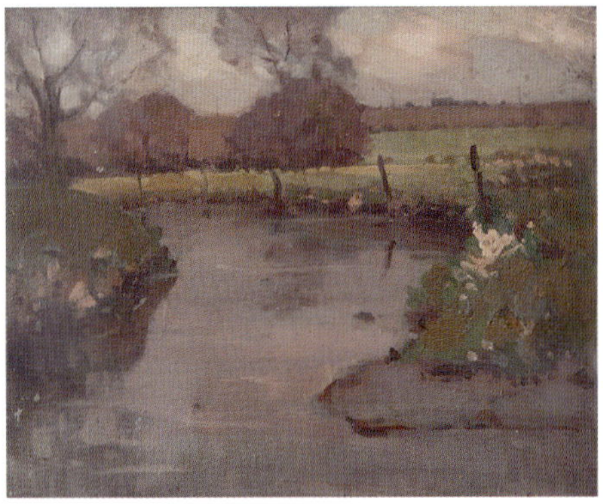

Rollett, Herbert 1872–1932
The Freshney, Lincolnshire
oil on board 26 x 31
152

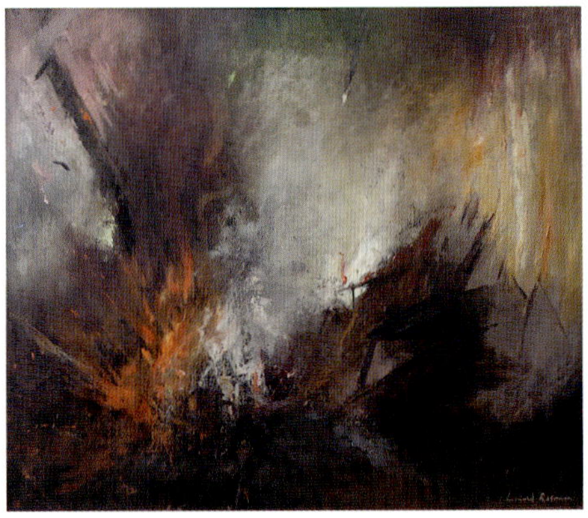

Rosoman, Leonard Henry 1913–2012
'Blitz' (London Docks)
oil on canvas 72 x 88
150

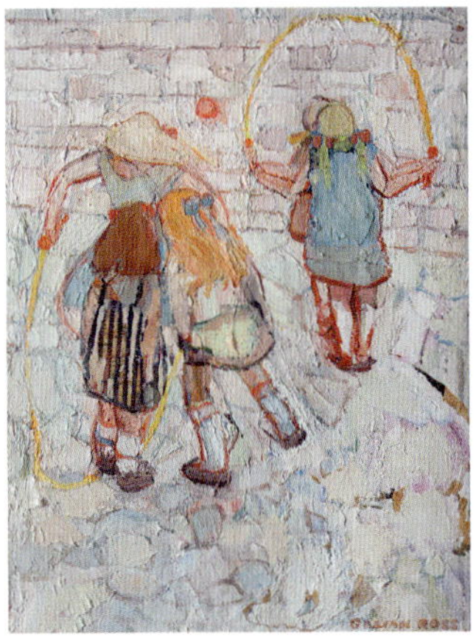

Ross-Kelsey, Gillian
Children at Play
oil on panel 46 x 36
62

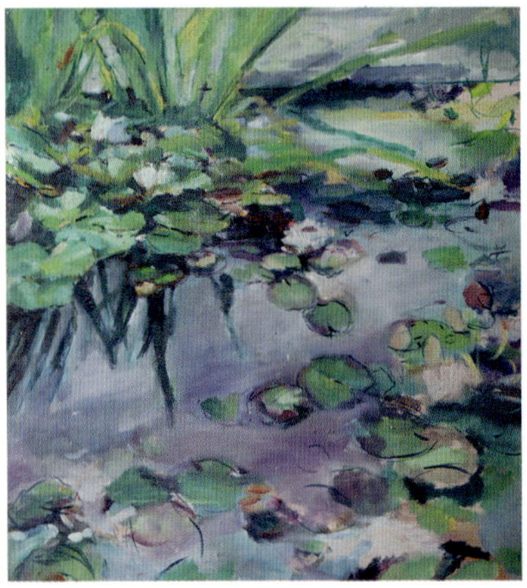

Smith, David
Lily Pool at Healing, Lincolnshire 1967
oil on board 82 x 72
154

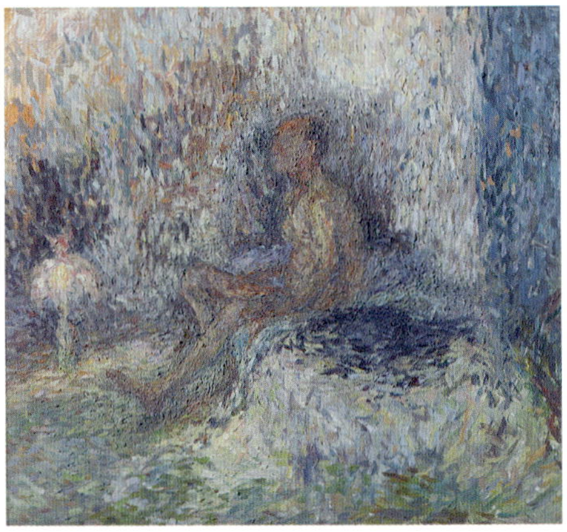

Smith, Margaret
Seated Nude
oil on board 57 x 60
83

Facing page: Knight, Laura, 1877–1970, *The Three Clowns* (detail), Leicester Arts and Museums Service (p. 56)

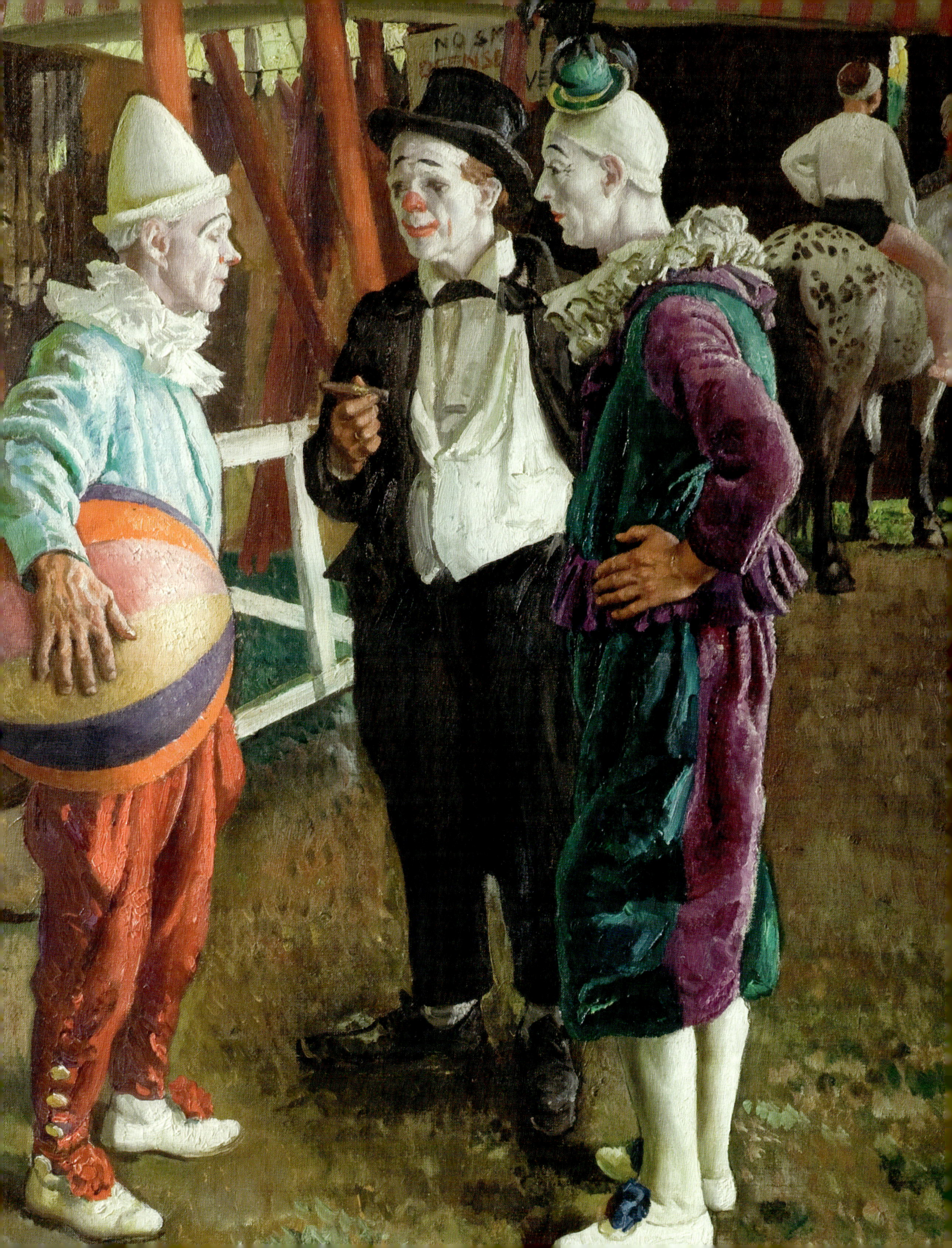

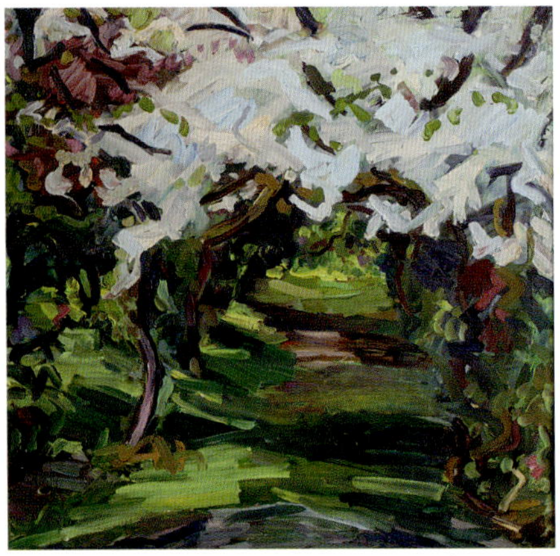

Swift, Nigel
Trees
oil in canvas 86.2 x 85
18

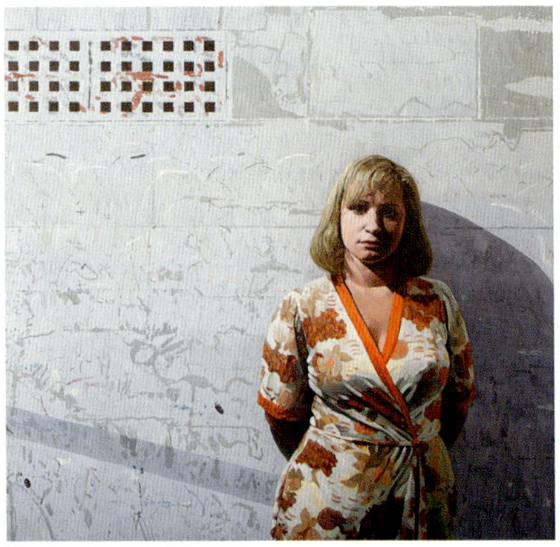

Upton, Steve b.1947
Molly
acrylic on canvas 105 x 105
168

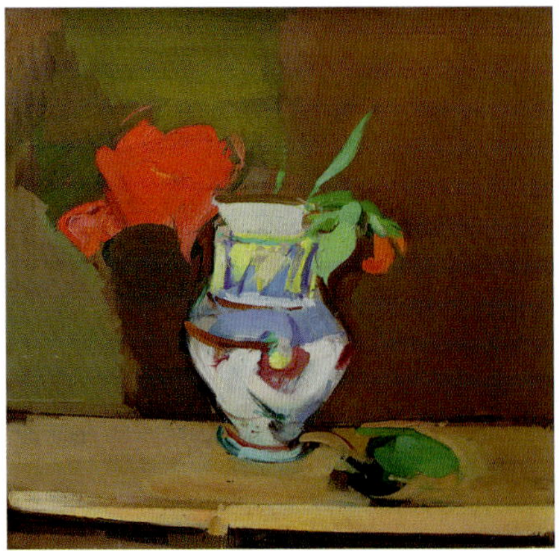

Volley, Nicholas 1950–2006
Flowers
oil on board 53 x 53
21

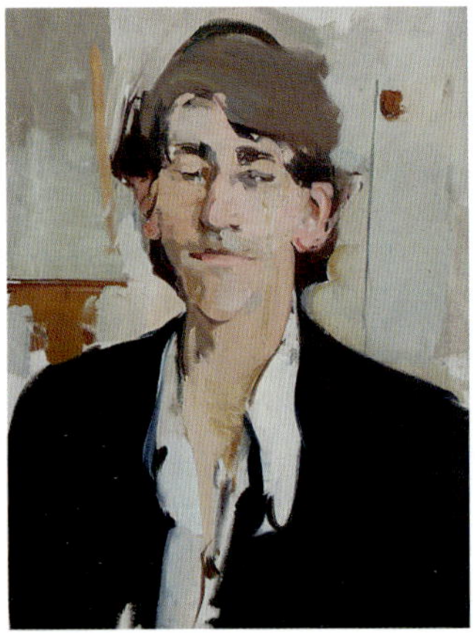

Volley, Nicholas 1950–2006
Self Portrait
oil on canvas 60 x 45
23

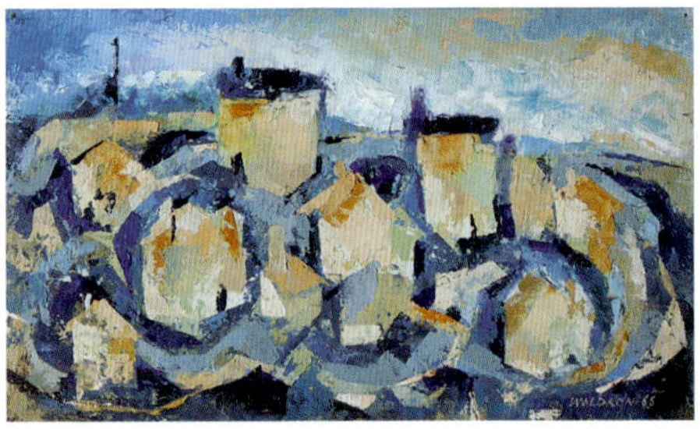

Waldron, E. W.
Hillside Community No.2 1966
oil on panel 30 x 49
120

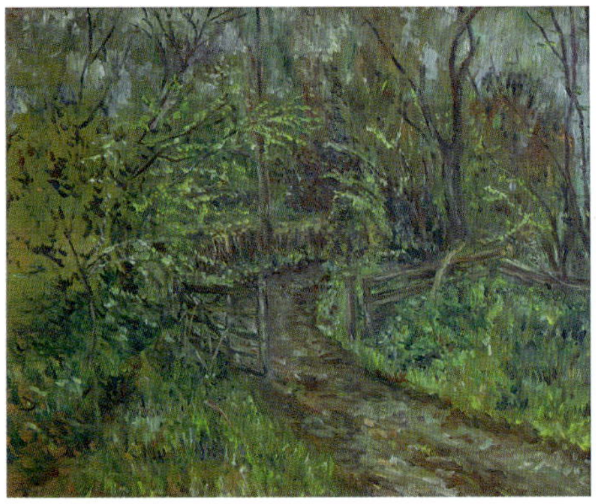

Warmoth, Pip Todd b.1962
Church Lane
oil on panel 39 x 49
42

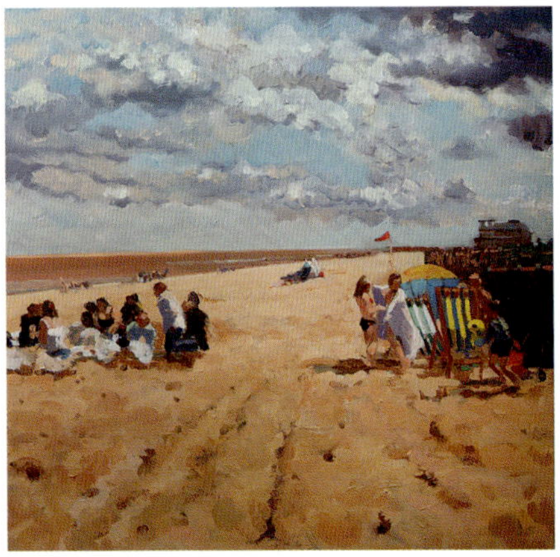

Webb, Sarah b.1964
The Point, Cleethorpes, Lincolnshire 2009
oil on canvas 50 x 50
170

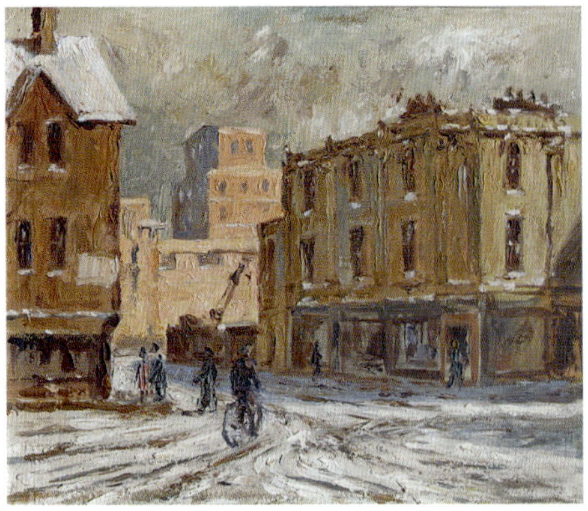

White, Harry
Central Market
oil on board 37 x 44
14

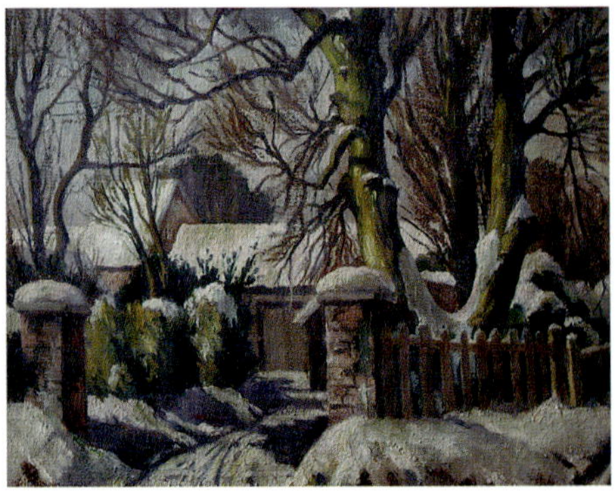

Worrall, Ernest J. 1898–1972
Snow Scene, Healing, Lincolnshire
oil on canvas 60 x 78
50

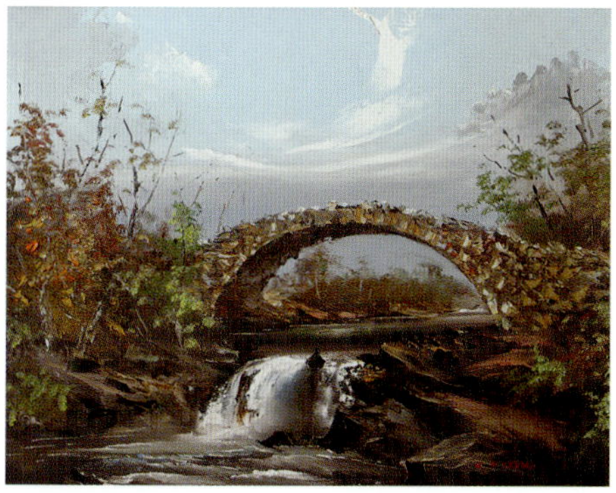

Yeung, Hai Shuet b.1936
Bridge
oil on canvas 60 x 80
103

Immingham Museum

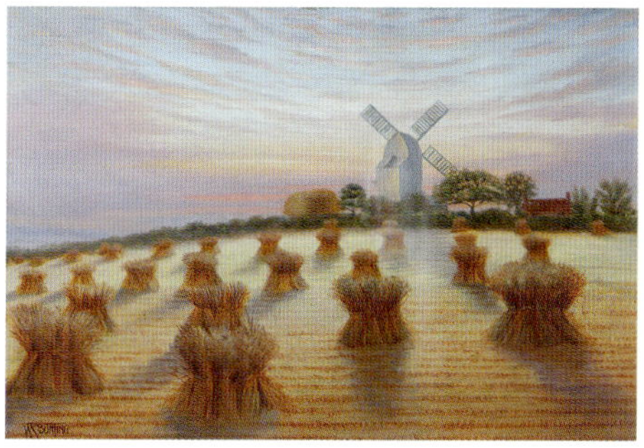

Bunting, William Richard 1866–c.1944
Habrough Mill, Lincolnshire 1903
oil on board 26 x 36.5
PCF1

Bishop Grosseteste University College Lincoln

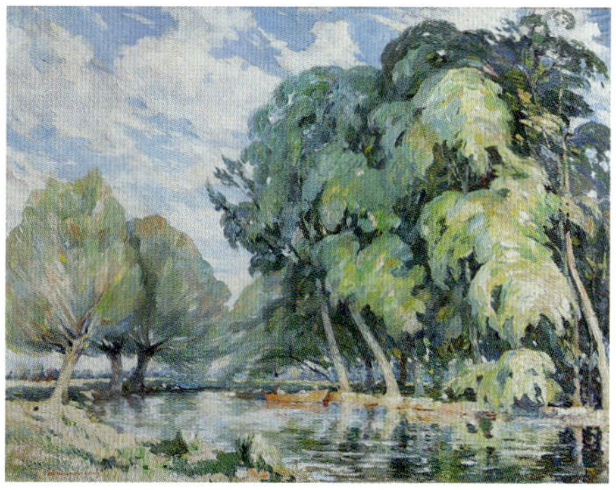

Adams, Bernard 1884–1965
*River Scene**
oil on canvas 100 x 126
1

Doddington Hall

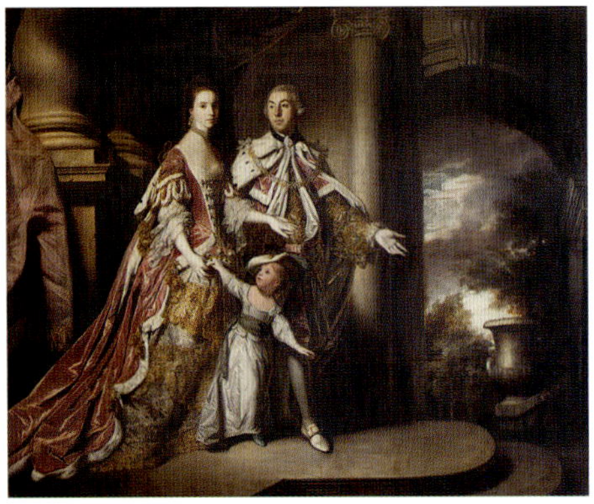

Reynolds, Joshua 1723–1792
The Earl and Countess of Mexborough with Their Son, Lord Pollington (1719–1778)
c.1763
oil on canvas 233.7 x 292.1 (E)
1

Museum of Lincolnshire Life

The art collection at the Museum of Lincolnshire Life has been developed mainly through public donations and reflects the Museum's primary collecting areas. These areas include topography, military, industry and – not surprisingly for a county famous for its agriculture – farming and livestock.

The Museum is housed in the former barracks which was once home to the Lincolnshire Yeomanry. It is fitting therefore that the Collection should hold Arthur James Wetherall Burgess' painting of the *SS 'Mercian'*, shelled by a German Submarine in November 1915 whilst transporting the 1st Lincolnshire Yeomanry across the Mediterranean Sea to Egypt. The ship failed to sink, but 23 lives were lost. Also significant is the caricature by an unknown artist of Gainsborough banker, William Hornsby, which was transferred from the Lincolnshire Local History Society; the society's core collection was used to found the Museum in the 1960s.

A large section of the art collection comprises work by a local amateur artist, Miss E. M. C. Morris, who bequeathed many of her paintings – a varied selection of local scenes and the surreal – to the Museum in the early 1970s. Little is known of the artist's life. Other topographical works of note include Rowland Wright Alston's painting of *Teapot Hall, Lincolnshire,* an unusual eighteenth-century dwelling so named because of its small size and shape – it measured just 19 feet square. Located near the village of Dalderby, on the road to Horncastle, Teapot Hall was demolished in the 1960s.

The museum also holds a significant collection of nineteenth- and early twentieth-century agricultural livestock portraits – farmers were very proud of their prize-winning animals and often commissioned portraits of them. A large portion of the agricultural collection was donated by the Dudding family; mainly photographs of livestock, and medals and trophies. Henry Dudding of Riby Grove was a well-known Lincolnshire sheep breeder, famous for the Panton breed. Portraits of Henry and his mother, Mary Ann, are held in the Collection. In 1906 Sybil Hutchinson painted *Henry Dudding and His Shepherd, Richard Aves*. This was the year Henry auctioned a Lincoln ram, obtaining 1450 guineas – the highest price ever in the United Kingdom. Is it possible the painting was commissioned to celebrate this event? Hutchinson's painting was generously purchased for the Museum by the Friends of Lincoln Museums and Art Gallery in 1984.

Two small oil paintings of a threshing drum and steam engine at work have been a recent and exciting discovery. Undated, and painted by William Cave Day, an accomplished artist who exhibited at both the Royal Academy and the Royal Society of British Artists, these scenes depict what was once a common sight in the fields of Lincolnshire.

The Museum of Lincolnshire Life is grateful to The Public Catalogue Foundation for increasing access to, and raising the profile of, its art collection.

Sara Basquill, Collections Officer

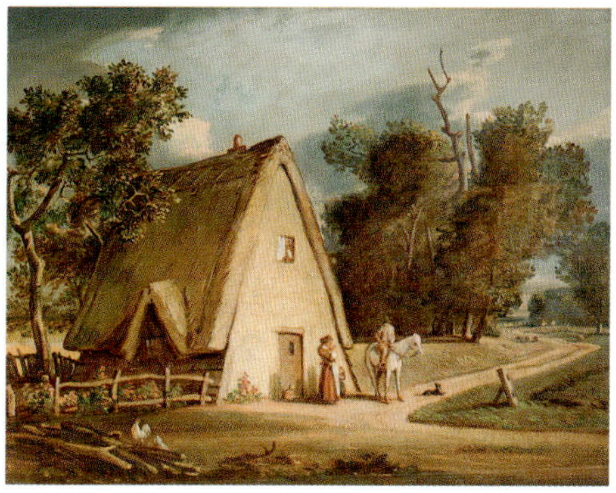

Alston, Rowland Wright 1895–1958
Teapot Hall, Lincolnshire
oil on board 47.5 x 60.5
2006/28/1

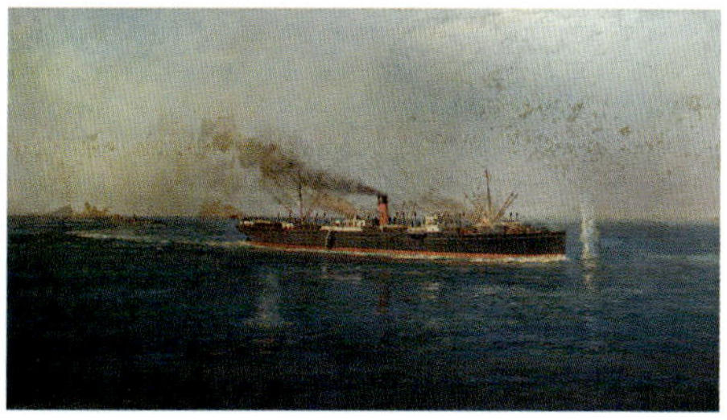

Burgess, Arthur James Wetherall 1879–1957
SS 'Mercian'
oil on canvas 110 x 186.5
1974/973

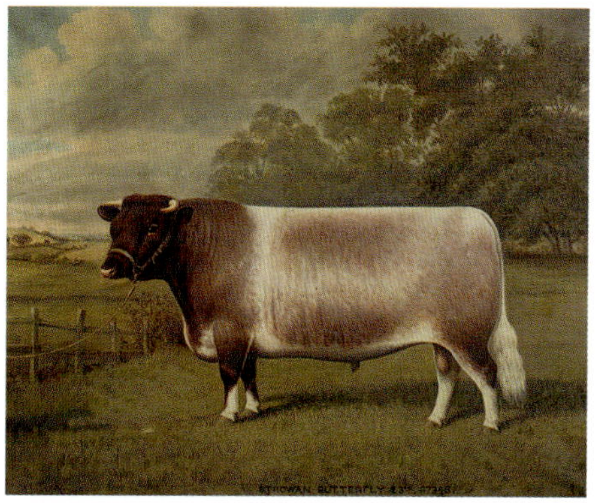

Clark, William Albert 1880–1963
'Strowan Butterfly' 1908
oil on canvas 51.5 x 62
1972/721

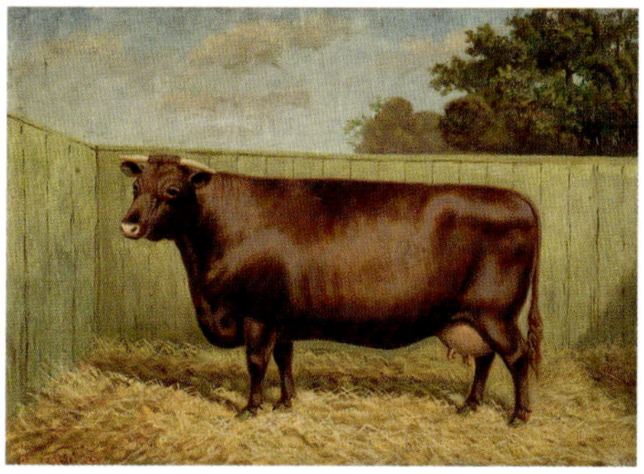

Clark, William Albert 1880–1963
Lincoln Red Cow 1910
oil on canvas 31 x 40.5
1982/575/1

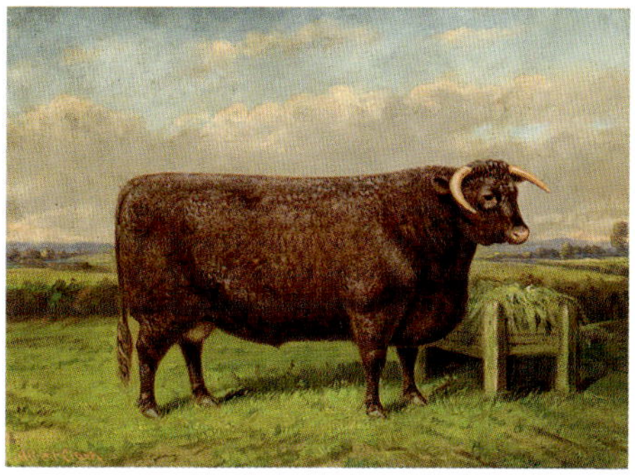

Clark, William Albert 1880–1963
The Heaviest Beast of the Smithfield Show 1910
oil on canvas 30.5 x 40.9
1982/575/2

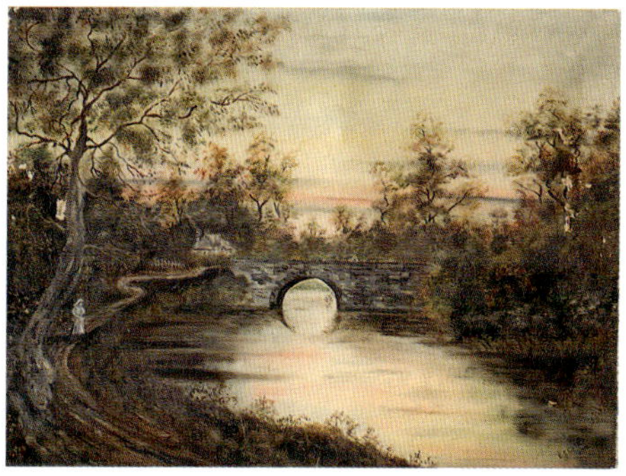

Cook, Evelyn active 1897–1918
Pastoral Scene 1918
oil on canvas 46 x 61
1990/40/1

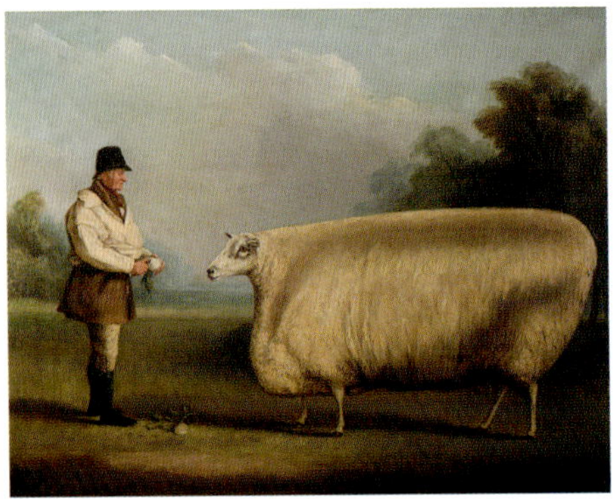

Davis, William Henry 1786–1865
Prize Sheep 1838
oil on canvas 54.5 x 67.5
1971/188

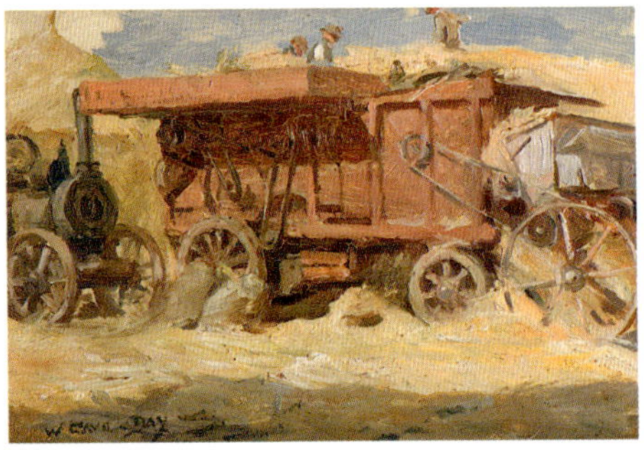

Day, William Cave 1862–1924
Threshing Drum 1
oil on board 15.5 x 22
2009/73

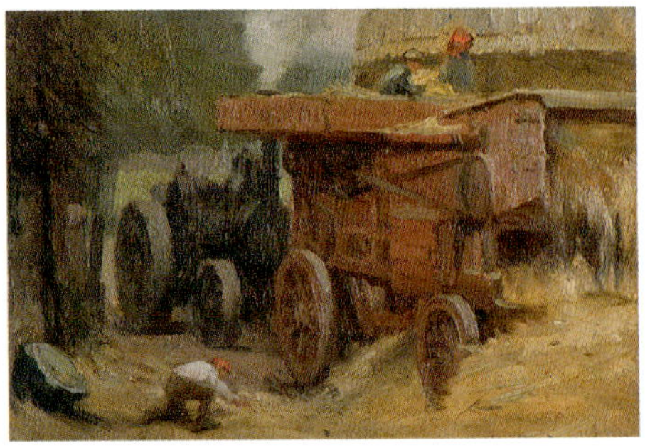

Day, William Cave 1862–1924
Threshing Drum 2
oil on board 15.5 x 22
2009/74

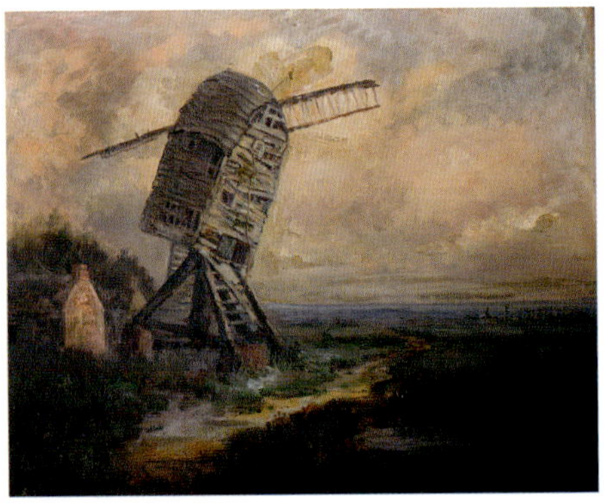

Garnt, F. M.
Derelict 1933
oil on canvas 62 x 75
PCF4

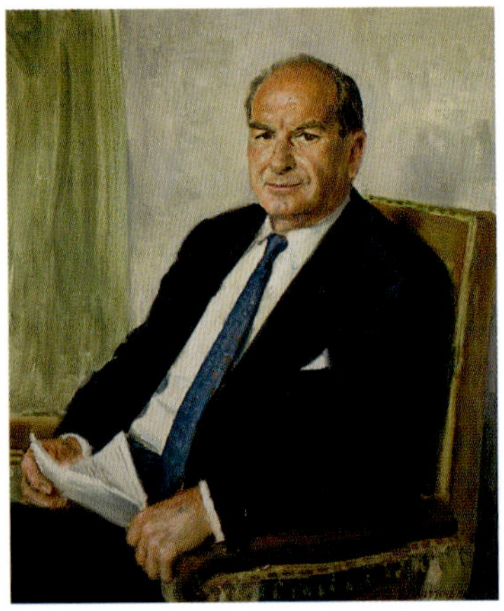

Hailstone, Bernard 1910–1987
Charles W. Heathcote, Chairman of Robey & Co. Ltd of Lincoln (1969–1972)
oil on canvas 75.5 x 62.5
1997/5

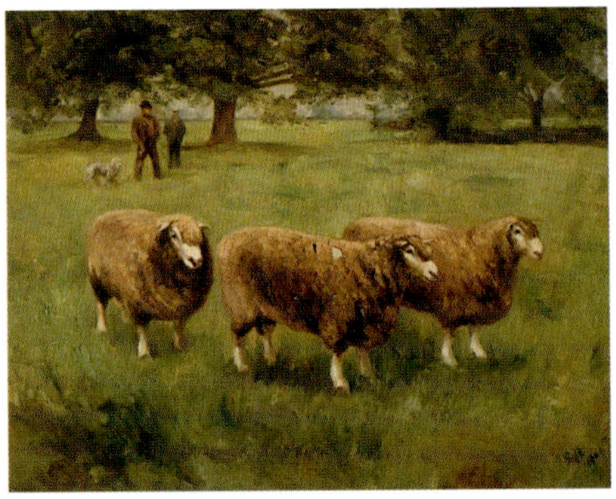

Hutchinson, Sybil
Henry Dudding and His Shepherd, Richard Aves 1906
oil on canvas 50.5 x 61
1985/15

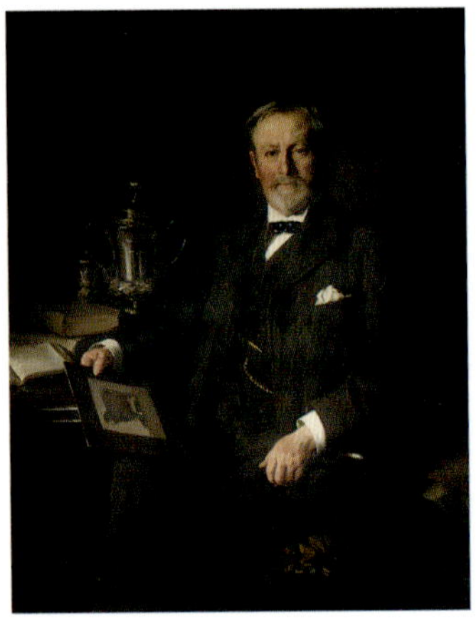

Kennington, Thomas Benjamin 1856–1916
Henry Dudding 1911
oil on canvas 130 x 102
1972/725

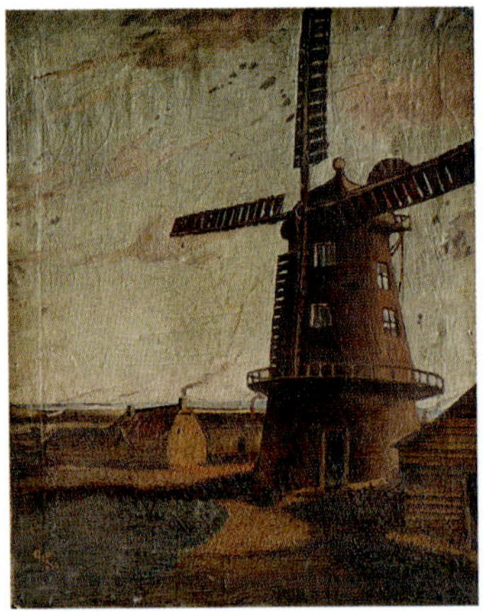

Lee, G.
Windmill by the Sea 1933
oil on canvas 49 x 38
1981/830.2

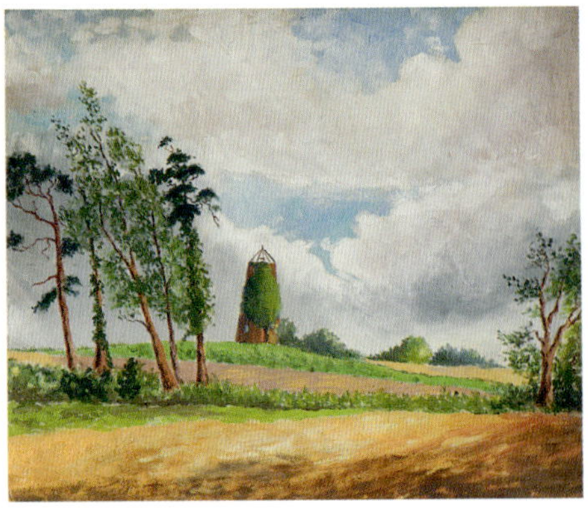

Morris, E. M. C. d.1970
Bicker Windmill, Lincolnshire
oil on canvas 30.5 x 36
1972/28

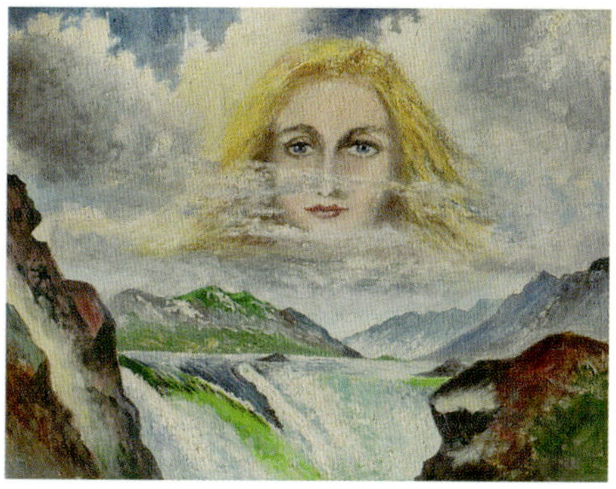

Morris, E. M. C. d.1970
Girl in the Sky over the Sea
oil on canvas 40.5 x 51
1972/38

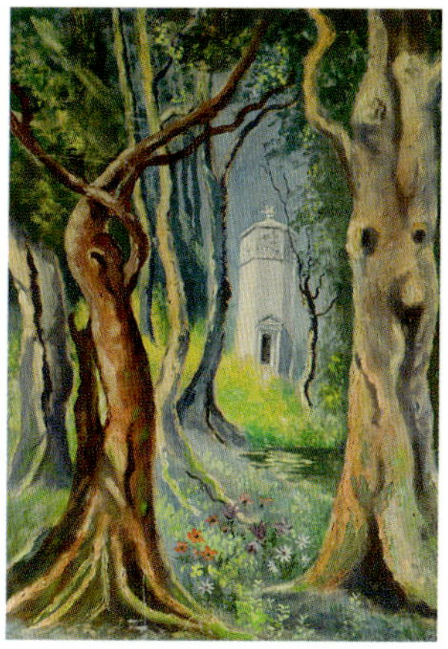

Morris, E. M. C. d.1970
Heathen Shrine
oil on board 50 x 34.5
1972/35

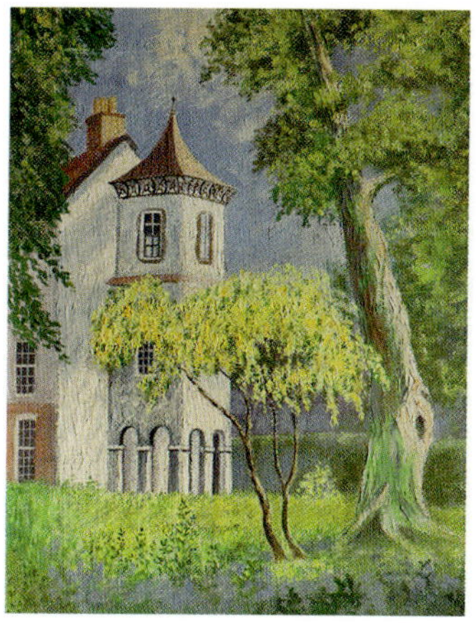

Morris, E. M. C. d.1970
House at Skegness, Lincolnshire
oil on canvas 45.5 x 35.5
1972/26

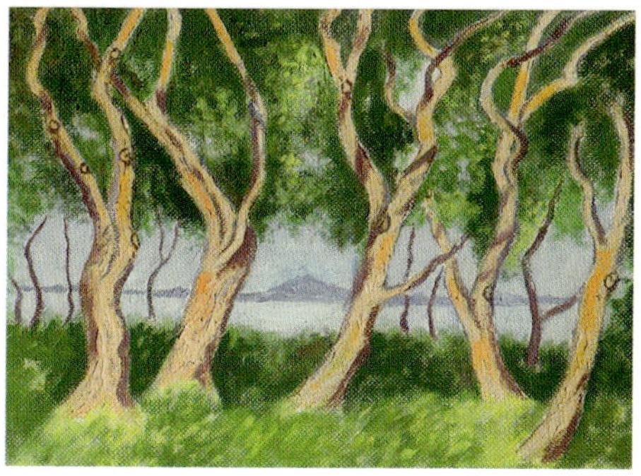

Morris, E. M. C. d.1970
Landscape with Trees
oil on board 31 x 41
1972/34

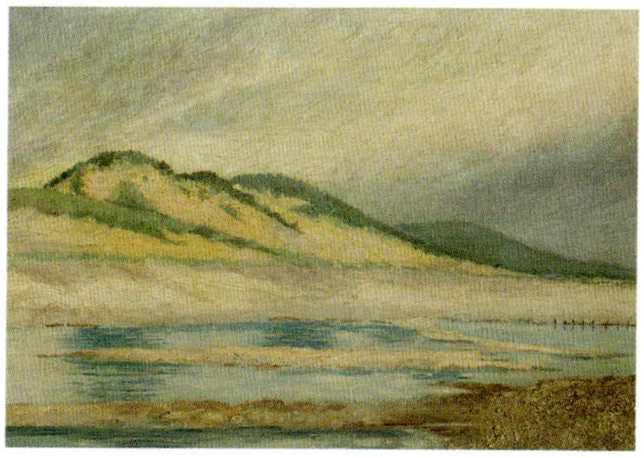

Morris, E. M. C. d.1970
Sand Dunes at Gibraltar Point, Lincolnshire
oil on board 28 x 38
1972/33

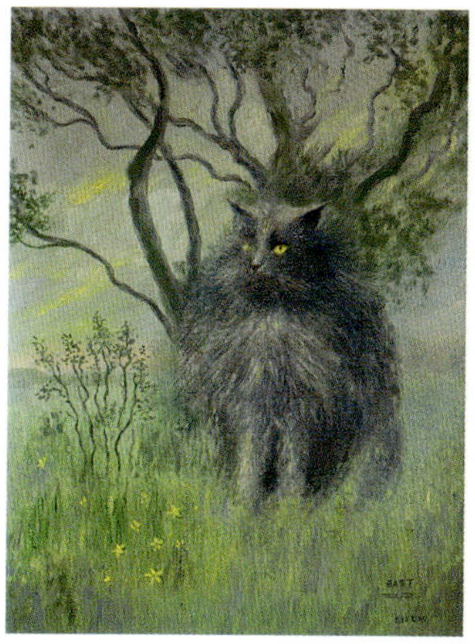

Morris, E. M. C. d.1970
The Mysterious Being (A Donington Cat)
oil on canvas 41 x 31
1972/36

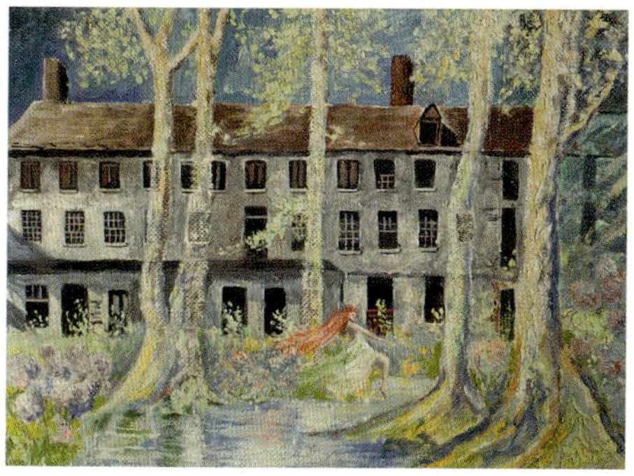

Morris, E. M. C. d.1970
The Parallel Universe
oil on board 38.5 x 52
1972/39

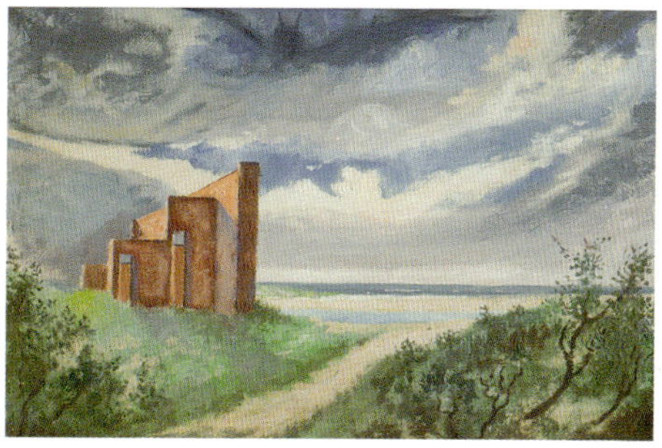

Morris, E. M. C. d.1970
The Rifle Range at Skegness, Lincolnshire
oil on canvas 35 x 51
1972/25

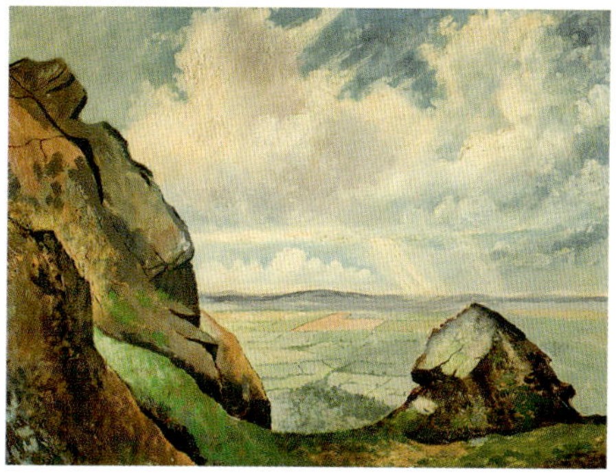

Morris, E. M. C. d.1970
The Wrekin, Shropshire
oil on board 52 x 69.5
1972/22

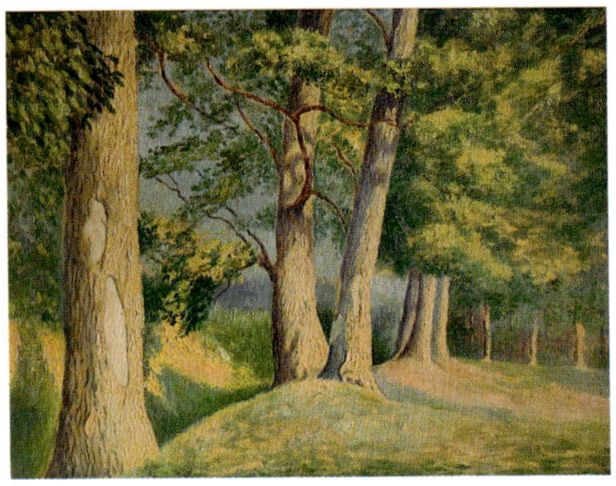

Morris, E. M. C. d.1970
Trees on a River Bank
oil on board 48.5 x 61
1972/32

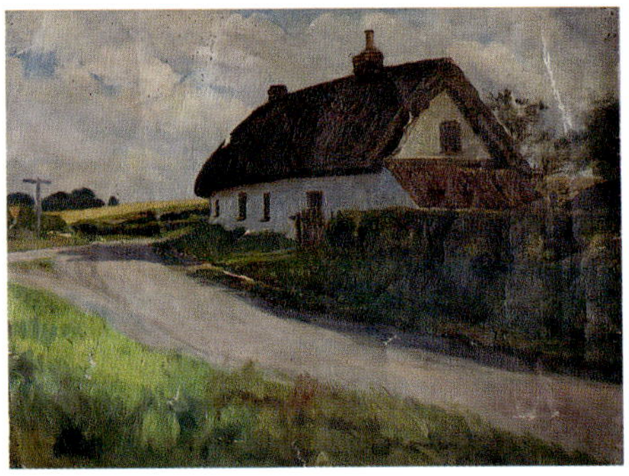

Pears (Mrs)
Thatched Cottage, Driby Top, Lincolnshire
oil on canvas 33 x 43
1976/633

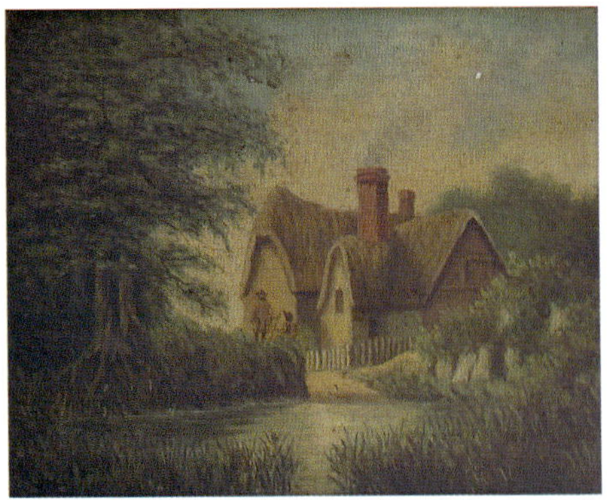

J. R.
Thatched Cottage by a Pool
oil on canvas 26.5 x 30
1973/5155

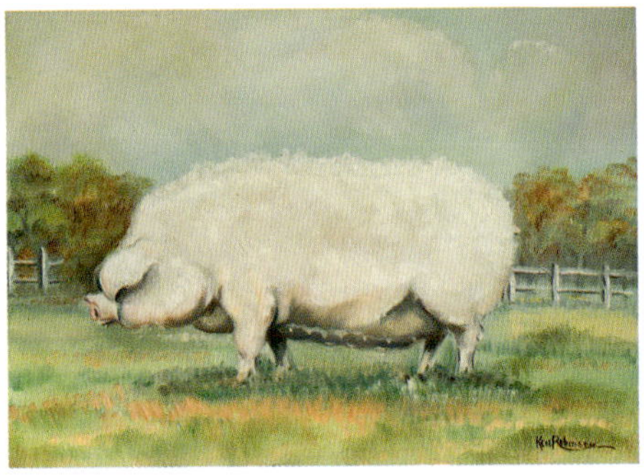

Robinson, Ken
Curly-Coated Pig 1977
oil on board 41 x 55.5
1979/1004/1

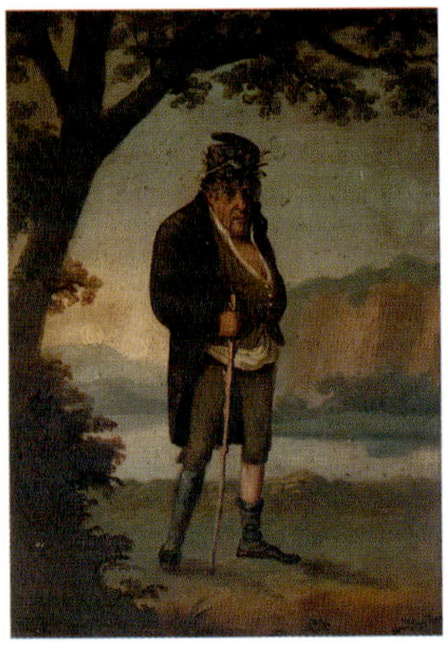

unknown artist
William Hornsby, Manager of Hornsby's Bank, Gainsborough, Lincolnshire 1802
oil on metal 38.5 x 28
1970/257

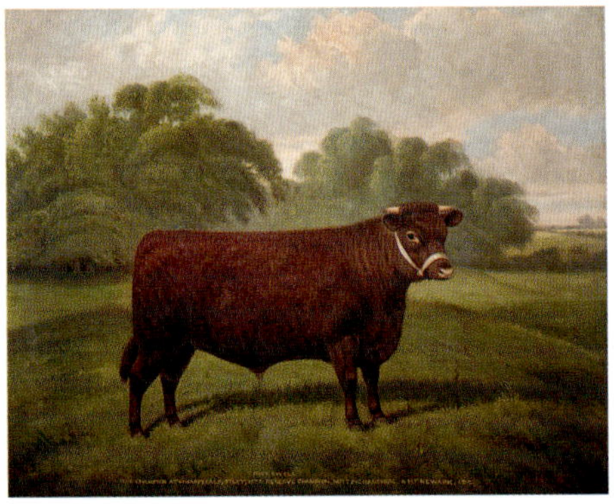

unknown artist
'Riby Swell', First and Champion at Wharfedale and Otley, First and Reserve Champion at Nottinghamshire, First (...) 1910
oil on canvas 50 x 61
PCF5

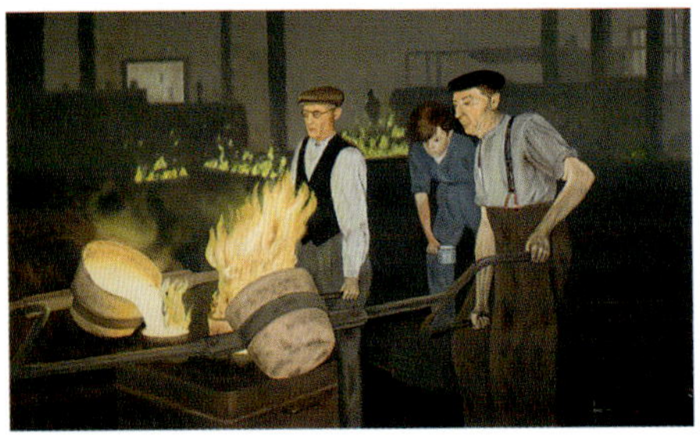

unknown artist
Ley Maleable Works, Lincoln 1920
oil on board 46 x 75
1976/316

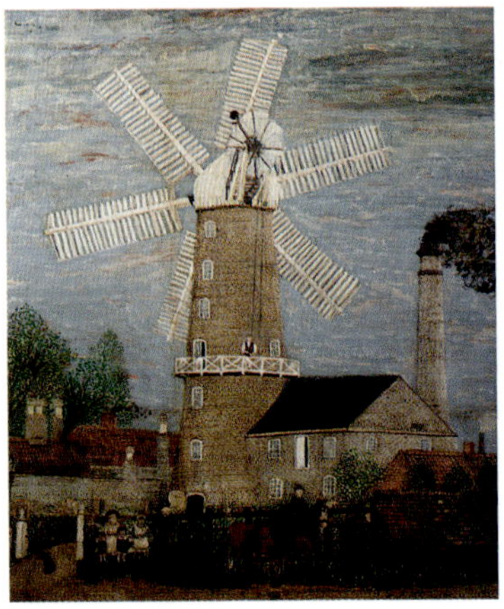

unknown artist
Bardney Mill, Lincolnshire
oil on canvas 69.5 x 57
1984/1056

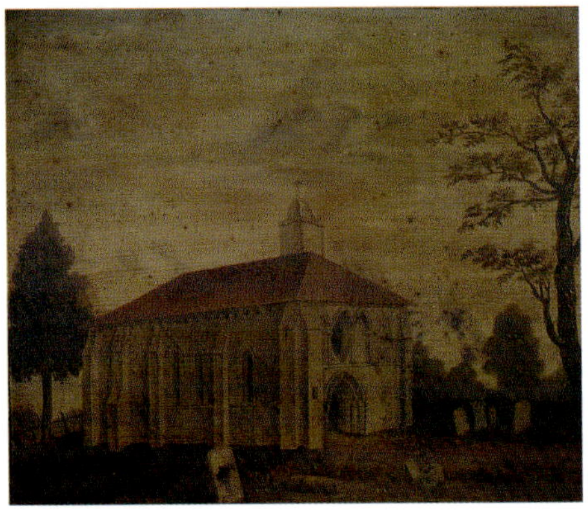

unknown artist
Church
oil on metal 27 x 31.5
1975/526/1

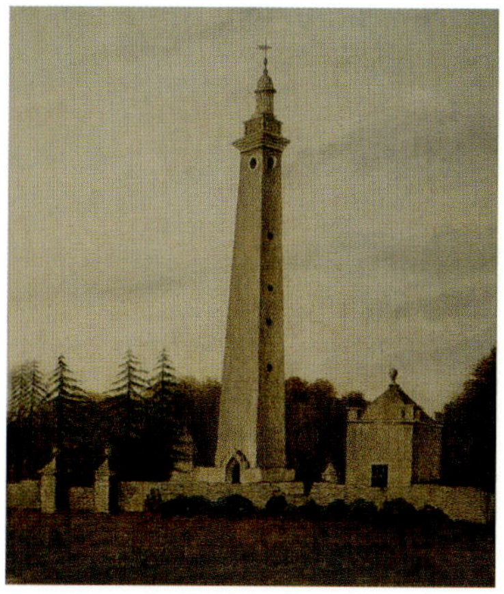

unknown artist
Dunston, Lincolnshire
oil on board 28 x 24
1975/527

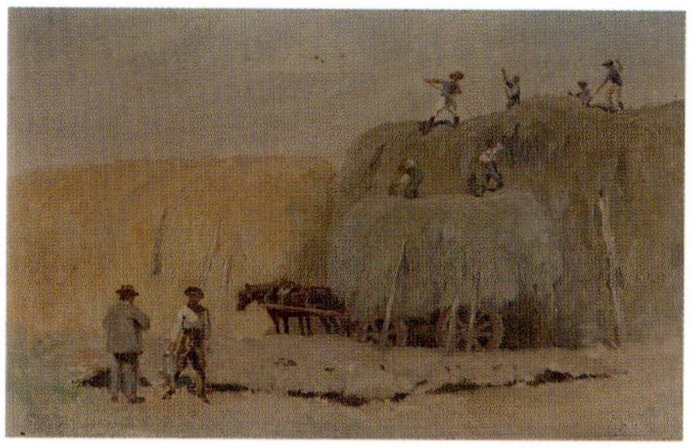

unknown artist
Harvesting
oil on board 26.5 x 37
1972/726

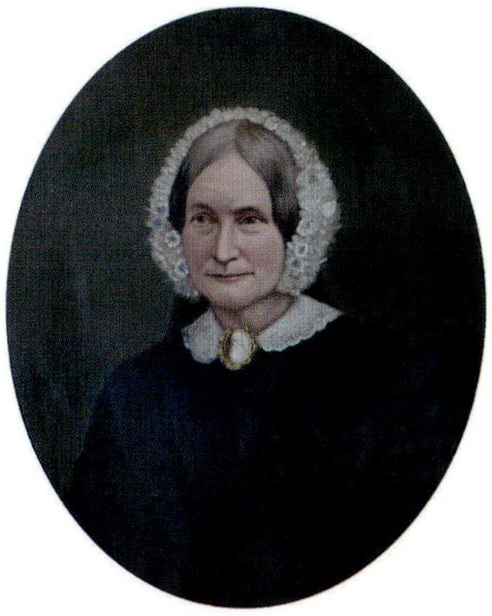

unknown artist
Mary Ann Dudding
oil on canvas 93 x 83
1972/724

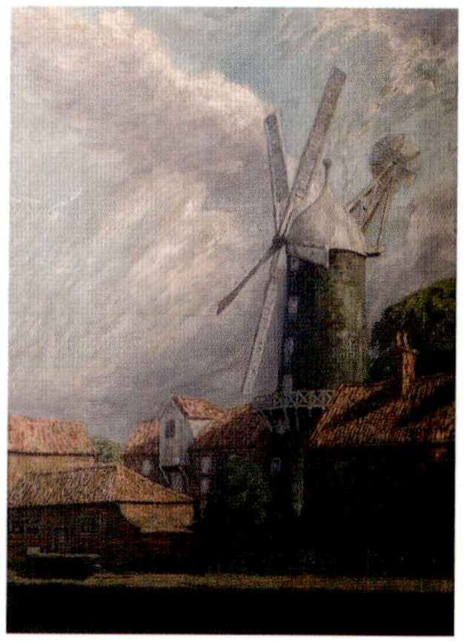

unknown artist
Maud Foster Mill, Boston, Lincolnshire
oil on canvas 144 x 102.5
1974/1088

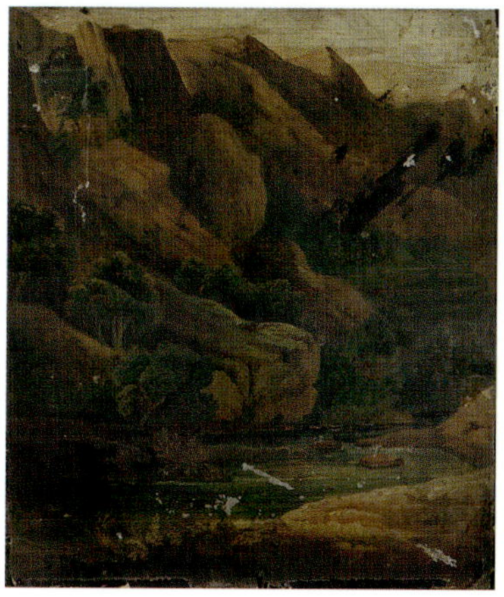

unknown artist
Mountains
oil on metal 31.5 x 27
1975/526/2

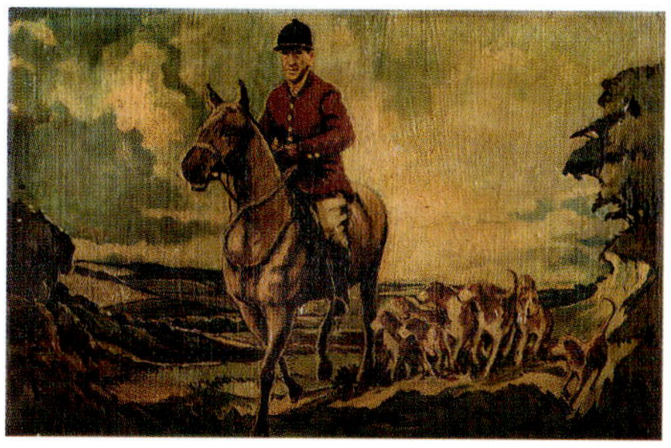

unknown artist
Mr Wardall in Hunting Clothes
oil on board 30.5 x 45.5
1978/900

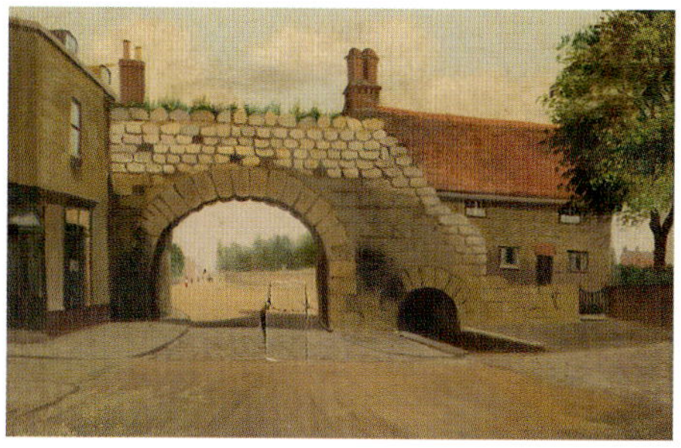

unknown artist
Newport Arch, Lincoln
oil on canvas 25.5 x 36
1968/68

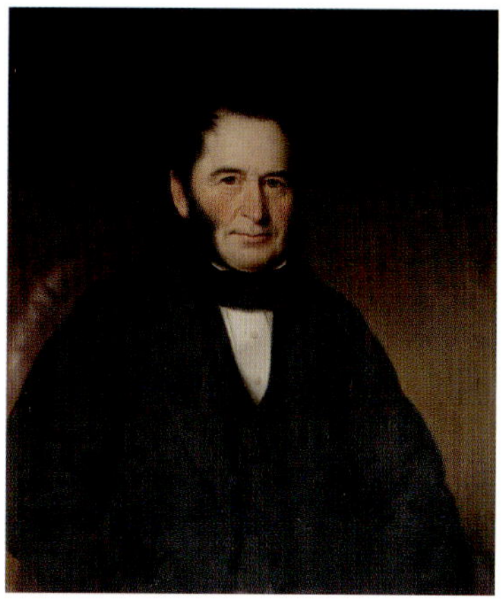

unknown artist
Portrait of an Unknown Man
oil on canvas 77 x 61
PCF3

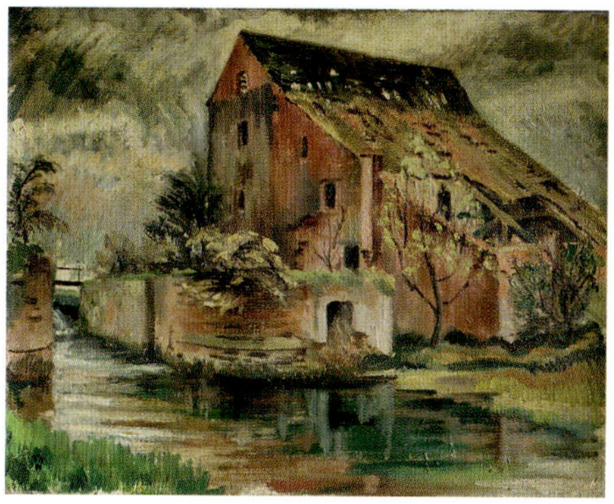

Wells, F. V.
Paper Mill at Washdyke Bridge, Evedon, Lincolnshire 1958
oil on canvas 56 x 69.5
1973/21

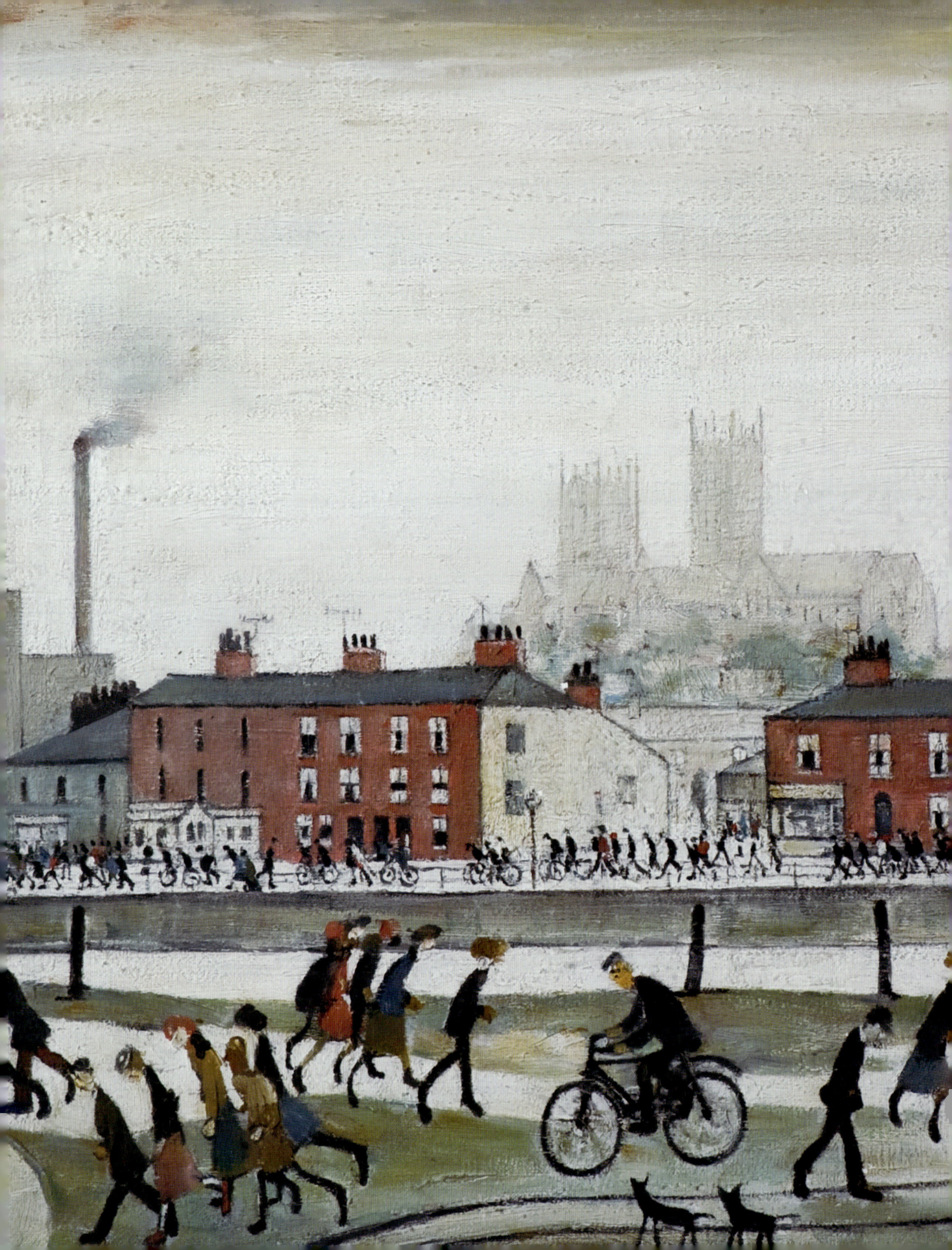

The Collection: Art & Archaeology in Lincolnshire (Usher Gallery)

The Usher Gallery, part of The Collection: Art and Archaeology in Lincolnshire, has a collection of fine and decorative arts and is the only purpose-built public art gallery in the county of Lincolnshire.

The Gallery was founded in 1927 through a bequest to the City Corporation by James Ward Usher, a Lincoln watchmaker and jeweller. The bequest stipulated that a Gallery should be built to house and display the collection he brought together comprising silver, watches, miniatures and porcelain. The fine art collection has since grown alongside the decorative arts.

The Collection has strong local associations including topographical views of the historic county of Lincolnshire, portraits of local personalities, for example the explorer and antiquarian *Sir Joseph Banks,* painted by Benjamin West, and work by Lincolnshire-born artists including William Hilton, William Logsdail, Charles Haslewood Shannon and William Tom Warrener. The Collection also features works by nationally-renowned artists such as Duncan Grant, John Piper, L. S. Lowry and Leon Underwood. The non-British collection includes a small but distinctive group of Italian, Dutch and Flemish sixteenth-, seventeenth- and eighteenth-century oil paintings.

The Collection has developed through gifts, bequests and acquisitions and these have been generously supported by the Art Fund, Victoria and Albert Museum Purchase Grant Fund, Contemporary Art Society, the Heslam Trust, Friends of Lincoln Museums and Art Gallery and the Usher Gallery Trust, plus many individual contributions.

The twentieth century fine art collections were greatly enhanced by a major bequest in 1985 from Mrs Dora Bond. The paintings had been brought together by Dora Bond and her late husband John Stuart Bond for over 30 years and include works by Ivon Hitchens and Ronald Ossory Dunlop.

More recent acquisitions have included a pair of portraits by Sir Joshua Reynolds of *Thomas Middleton Trollope of Casewick (1721–1779)*, near Sleaford, and *Isabella Thorold of Syston (d.1803),* in Grantham, painted just before their marriage in 1759. A portrait of *Maria van Wassenaer Hanecops (c.1542–after 1612)* by Michiel Jansz. van Miereveld, in the possession of the family of a former Mayor of Lincoln, has recently been given to the Gallery enhancing our seventeenth-century collections.

In recent years a small collection of contemporary work has been developed (by purchase and commission) mainly in relationship to an exhibition programme at the Gallery. These include work by Craigie Ronald John Aitchison, Jean Cooke, Susan Wilson, Mary Mabbutt, Lucy Jones, Shani Rhys-James, Barbara Walker and J. Chuhan.

We are pleased that The Public Catalogue Foundation has given us this opportunity to publish the oil and acrylic paintings in our collection and hope it will bring them to a wider audience.

Dawn Heywood, Collections Officer

Facing page: Lowry, Laurence Stephen, 1887–1976, *Lincoln* (detail), The Collection: Art & Archaeology in Lincolnshire (Usher Gallery) (p. 314)

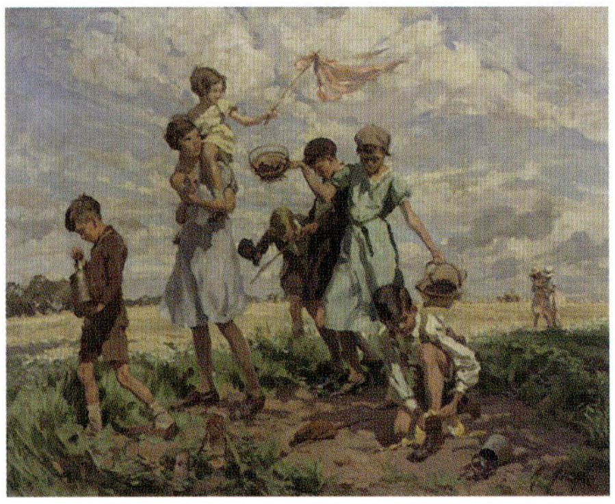

Airy, Anna 1882–1964
Children Blackberrying
oil on canvas 61 x 76.2
LCNUG 1927.956

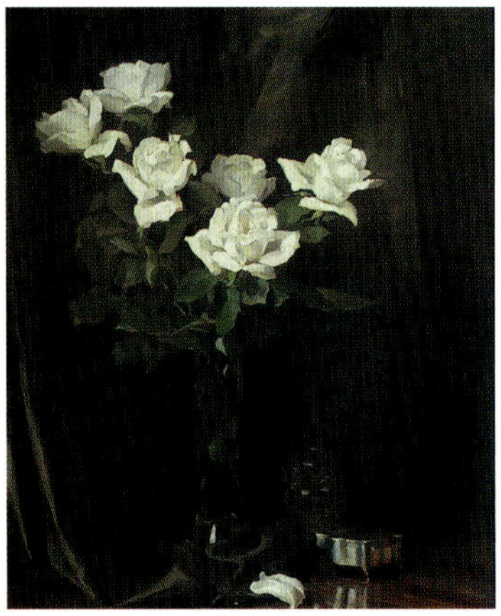

Airy, Anna 1882–1964
Roses Triumphant
oil on canvas 89 x 76.2
LCNUG 1927.168

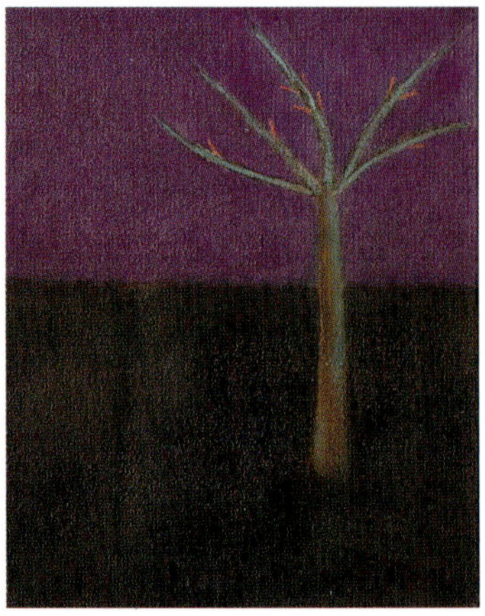

Aitchison, Craigie Ronald John 1926–2009
The Tree 1968
oil on canvas 25.2 x 20.5
LCNUG 2007.38

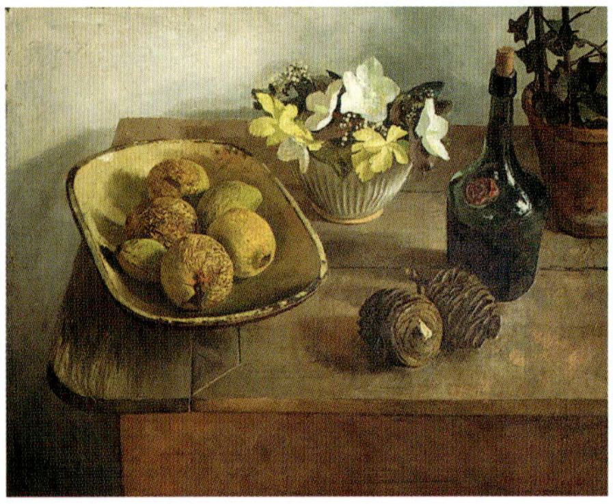

Aldridge, John Arthur Malcolm 1905–1983
Still Life 1958
oil on canvas 45.7 x 63.5
LCNUG 1927.2675

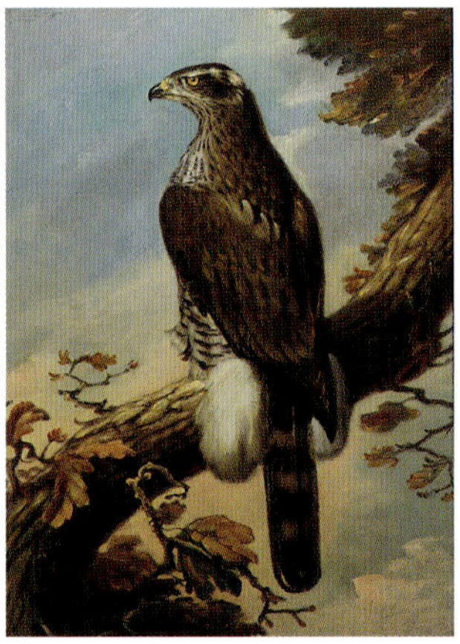

Alston, Rowland Wright 1895–1958
Peregrine Falcon
oil on board 54.5 x 40.5
LCNUG 1927.2383

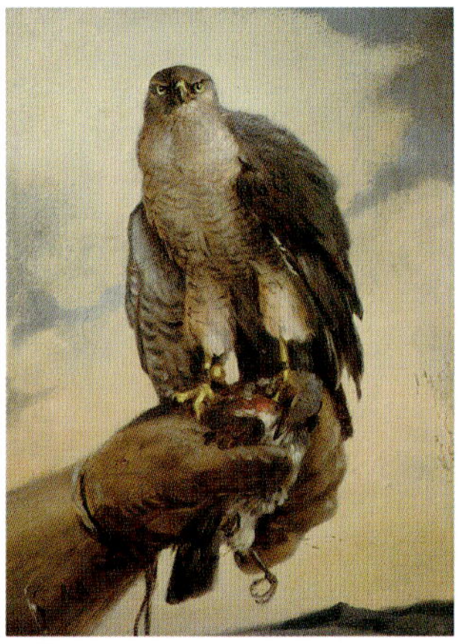

Alston, Rowland Wright 1895–1958
Trained Hawk on the Fist
oil on canvas 37.8 x 28
LCNUG 1927.2382

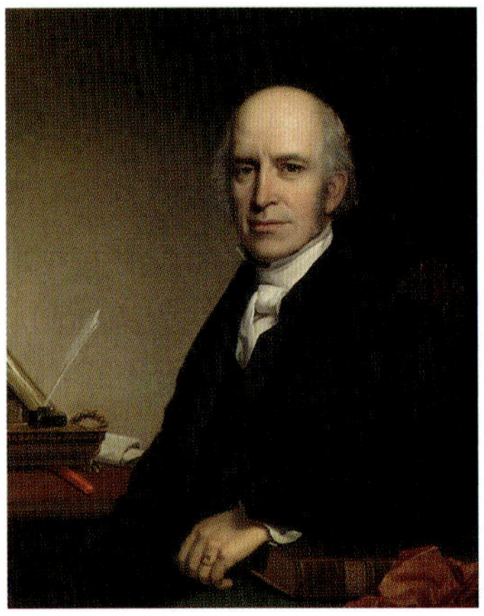

Andrew
Alderman Edward James Willson 1843
oil on canvas 91.8 x 71.3
LCNUG 1927.1843

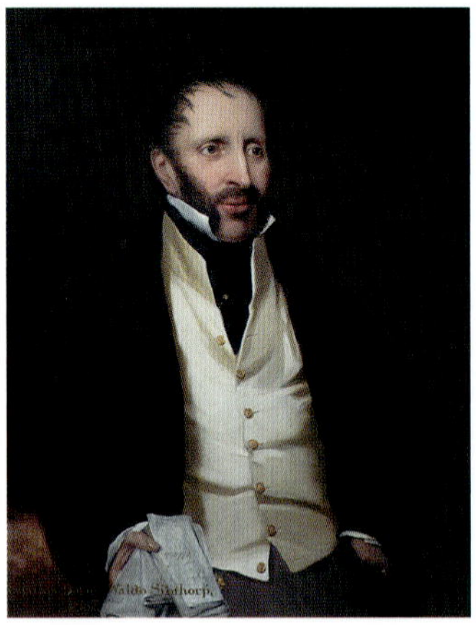

Andrews, John active 1824–1870
Charles Delaet Waldo Sibthorp (1815–1861)
1837
oil on canvas 91.5 x 71
LCNUG 1972.145

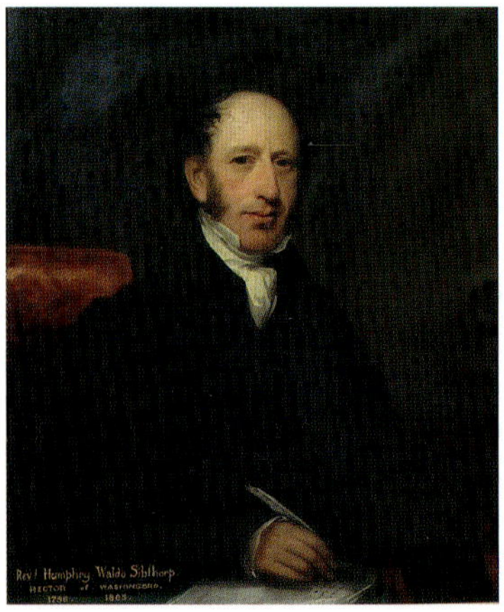

Andrews, John active 1824–1870
Reverend Humphrey Waldo Sibthorp (1786–1865) 1838
oil on canvas 91.5 x 71.5
LCNUG 2001.11

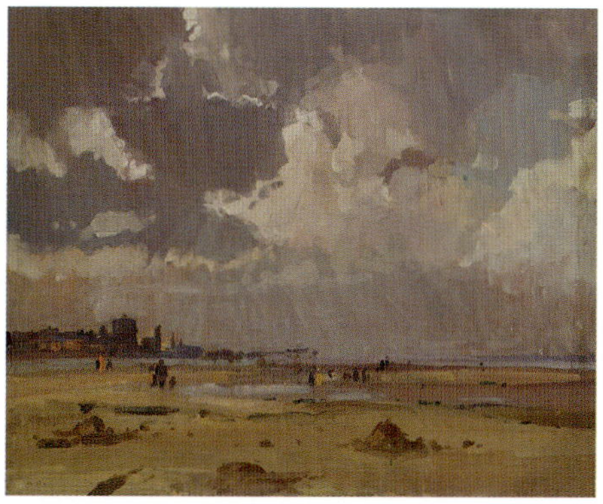

Appleyard, Frederick 1874–1963
Cleethorpes Foreshore, Lincolnshire 1930
oil on panel 51 x 61
LCNUG 1927.174a

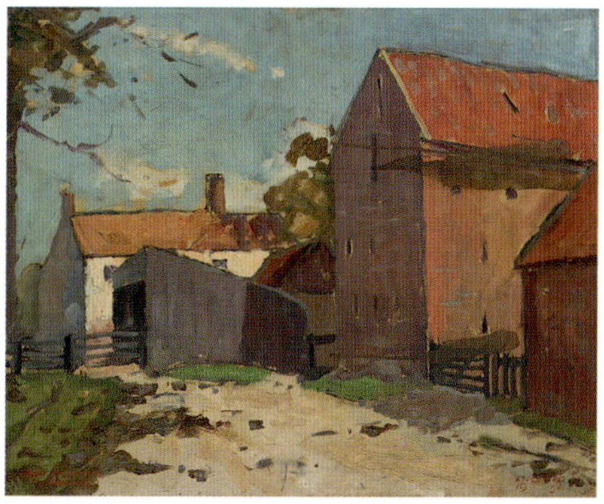

Appleyard, Frederick 1874–1963
Farm Buildings 1930
oil on panel 51 x 61
LCNUG 1927.174b

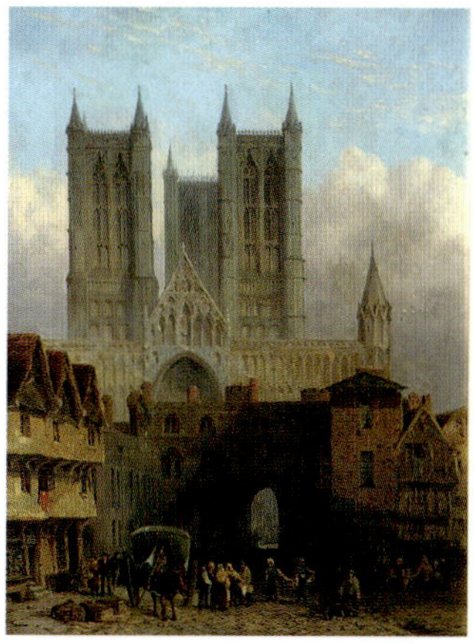

J. D. B.
Lincoln Cathedral and the Exchequer Gate 1869
oil on canvas 51 x 38
LCNUG 1927.2336

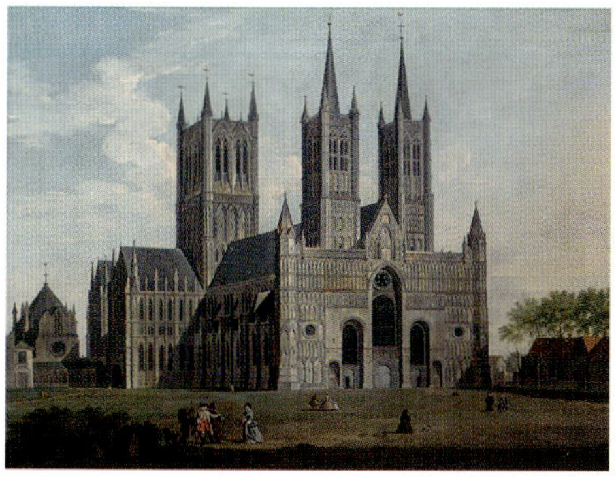

Baker, Joseph d.1770
A View of Lincoln Cathedral from the West 1742
oil on canvas 104.2 x 133.3
LCNUG 1976.14

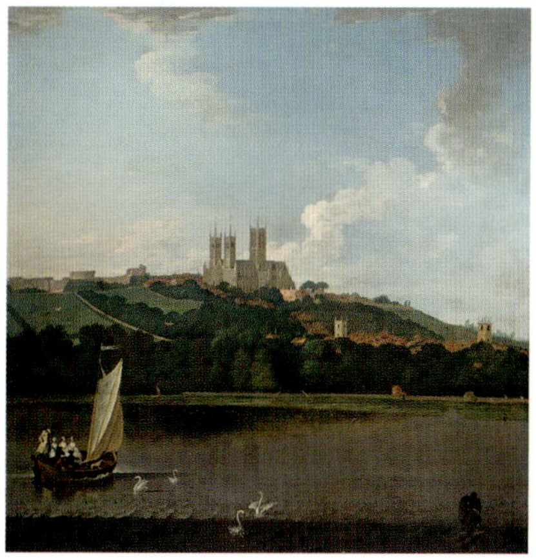

Baker, Joseph (attributed to) d.1770
Lincoln from Brayford 1730
oil on canvas 128.2 x 122
LCNUG 1927.176

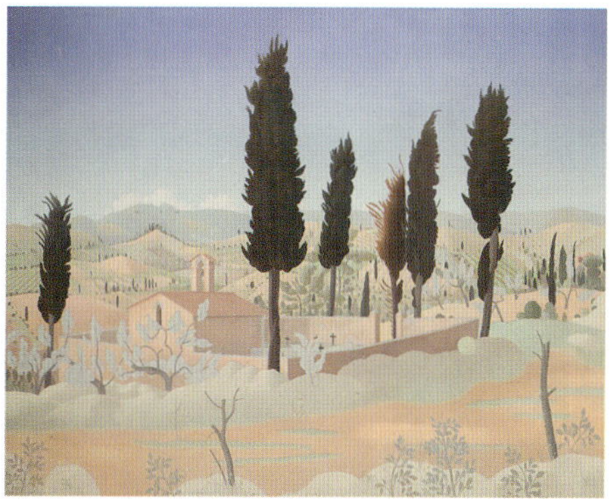

Balmer, Barbara b.1929
Deserted Cemetery 1995
oil on canvas 120 x 151
LCNUG 1995.69

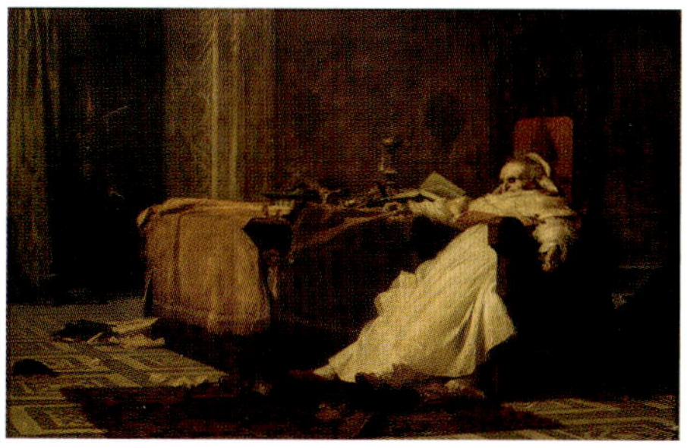

Barabino, Nicolò 1832–1891
The Death of Pope Boniface VIII 1866
oil on canvas 182 x 257.5
LCNUG 1927.163

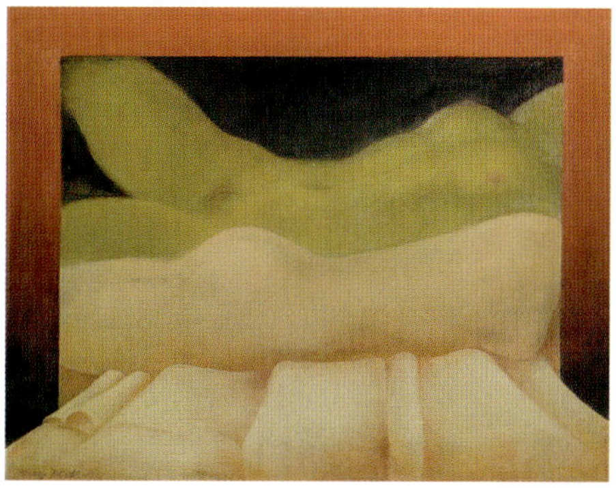

Bartl, Antonin Karel 1912–1998
Reclining Nude 1977
oil on board 39.5 x 50
LCNUG 1997.1

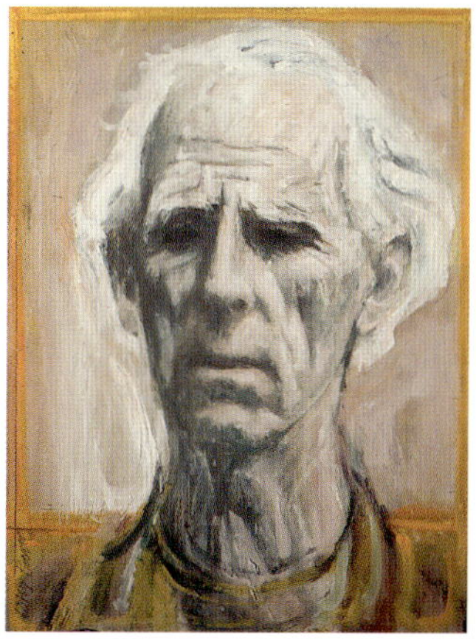

Bartl, Antonin Karel 1912–1998
John Piper (1903–1992)
oil on board 40.5 x 31
LCNUG 1977.19

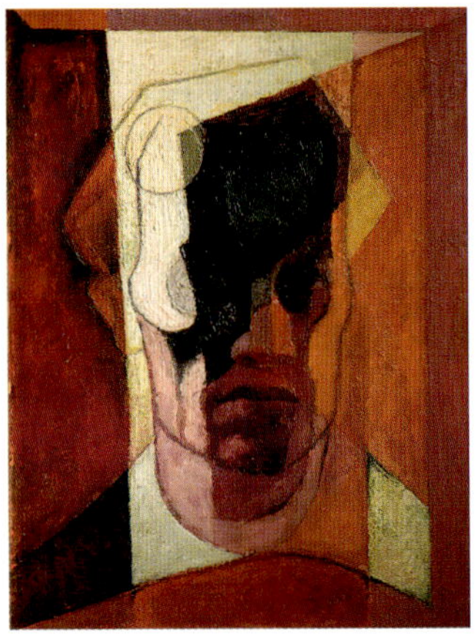

Bartl, Antonin Karel 1912–1998
Portrait of an Architect
oil on board 70 x 53.5
LCNUG 1927.2394

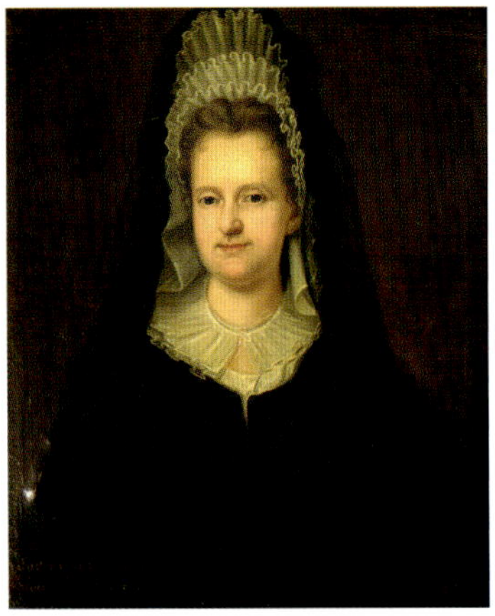

Beale, Mary 1633–1699
Judith Sibthorp 1683
oil on canvas 74 x 61
LCNUG 1972.144

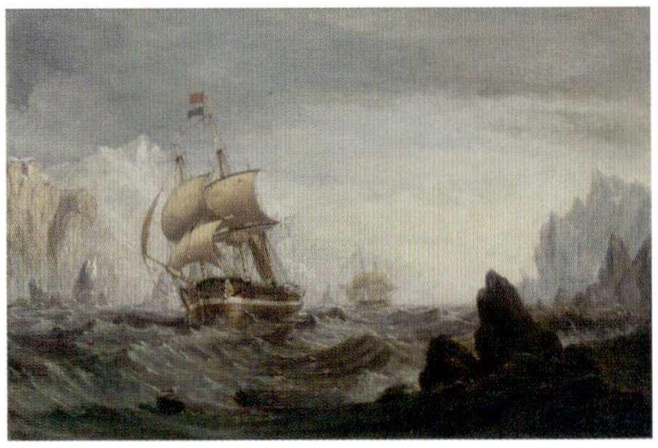

Bell, Stuart Henry 1823–1896
The Expedition Entering Baffin Bay in Search of John Franklin 1850
oil on canvas 45.6 x 66.5
LCNUG 1980.3

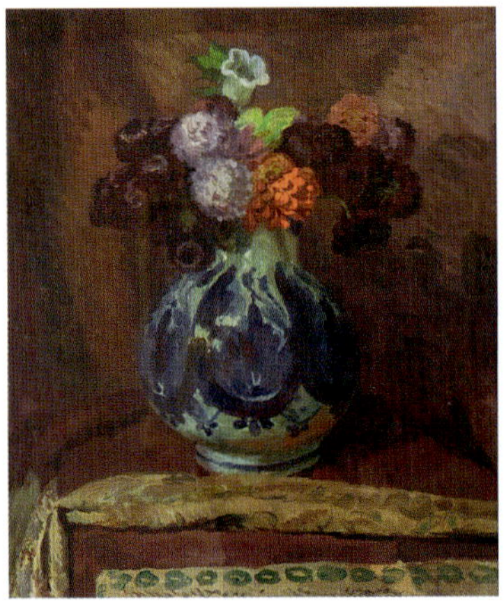

Bell, Vanessa 1879–1961
Zinnias 1943
oil on canvas 61.2 x 50.3
LCNUG 1927.2232

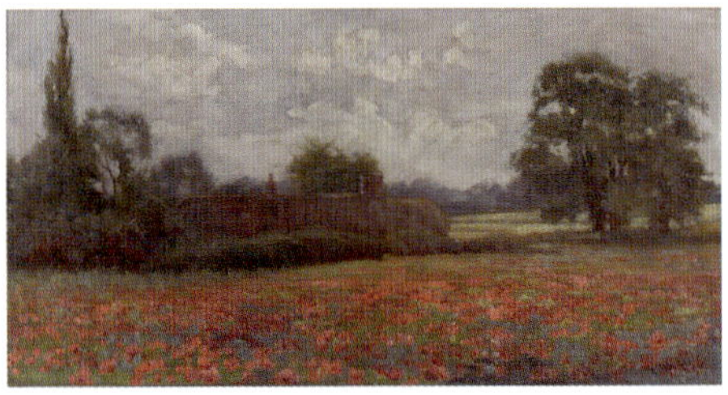

Blakesley, Alicia 1861–1939
Thatched Cottage and a Poppy Field c.1890
oil on canvas 24 x 44.6
LCNUG 1975.135

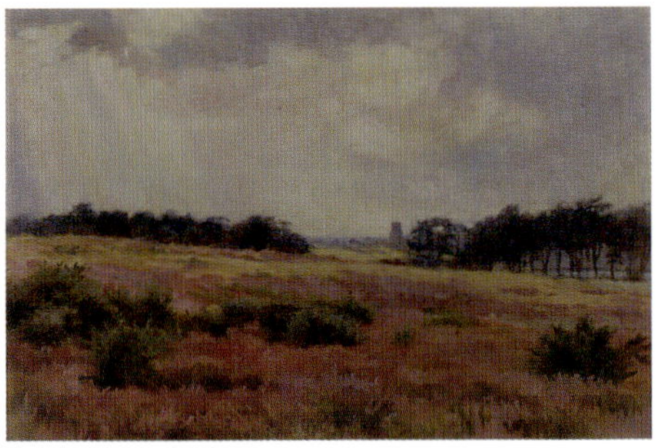

Blakesley, Alicia 1861–1939
Common with Gorse and a Distant Church
oil on panel 30 x 45
LCNUG 1927.1849

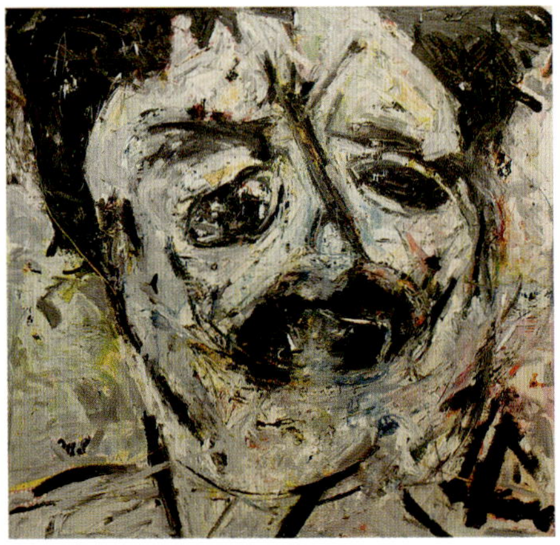

Blane, Frances Aviva b.1954
Self Portrait 1993
oil on canvas 198 x 198
LCNUG 1996.2

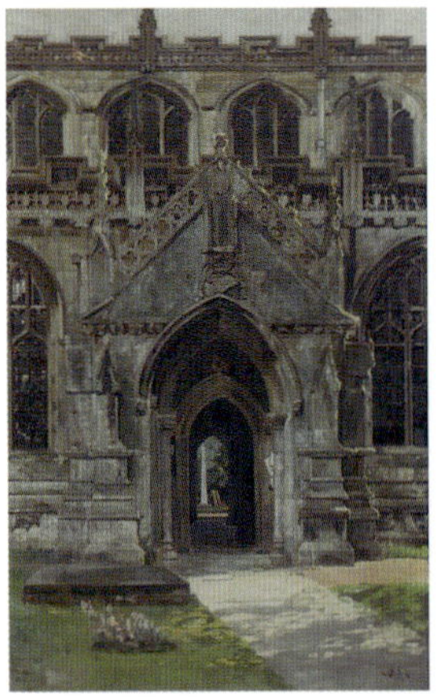

Boden, George Alfred 1888–1956
Church, Brant Broughton, Lincolnshire 1925
oil on panel 64.5 x 43
LCNUG 1927.2333

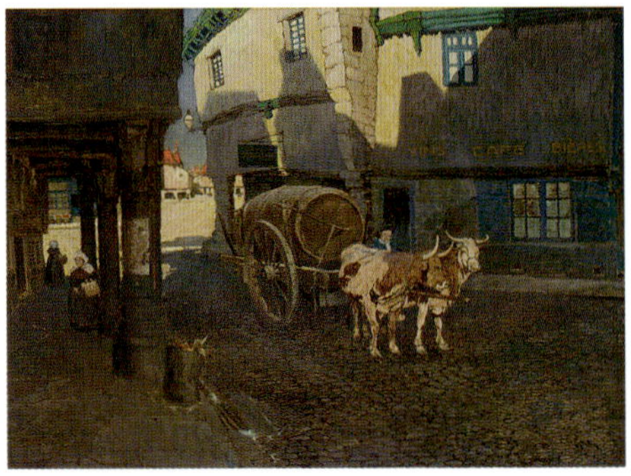

Boden, George Alfred 1888–1956
Breton Oxcart
oil on board 61 x 81
LCNUG 1927.2651

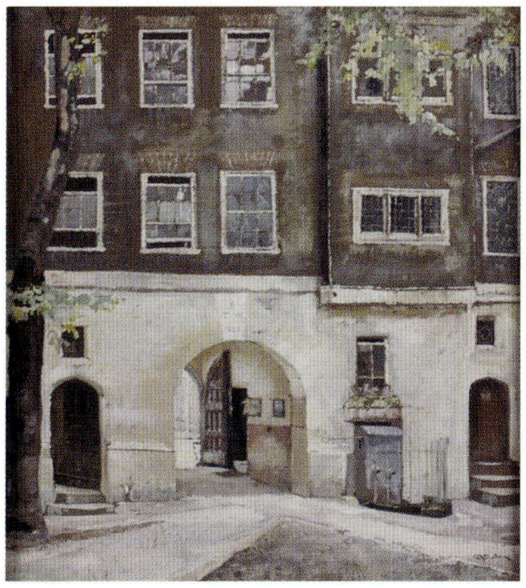

Boden, George Alfred 1888–1956
Staple Inn, Holborn, London
oil on board 41.5 x 37
LCNUG 1927.2425

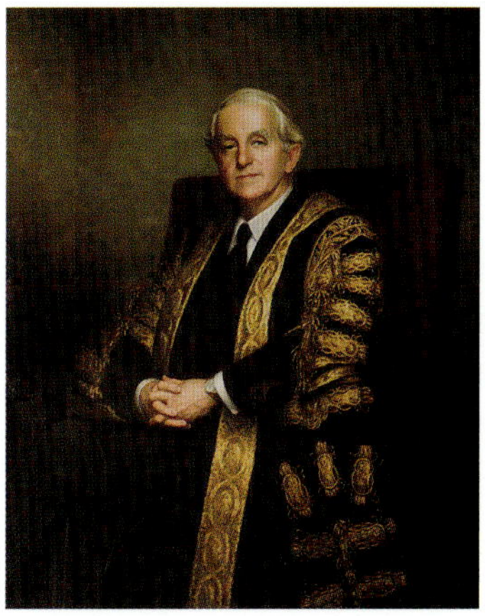

Boden, Leonard 1911–1999
Sir Francis Hill (1899–1980) 1984
oil on canvas 128 x 101
LCNUG 1985.2

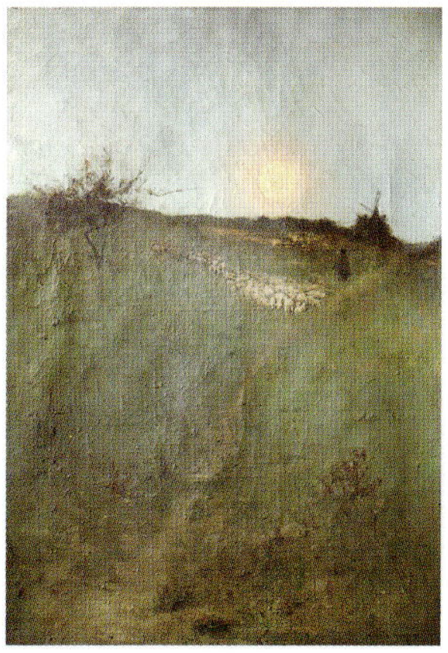

Bonjean, Antonia active 19th C
Sheep on a Hillside
oil on canvas 81.5 x 55
LCNUG 1927.2318

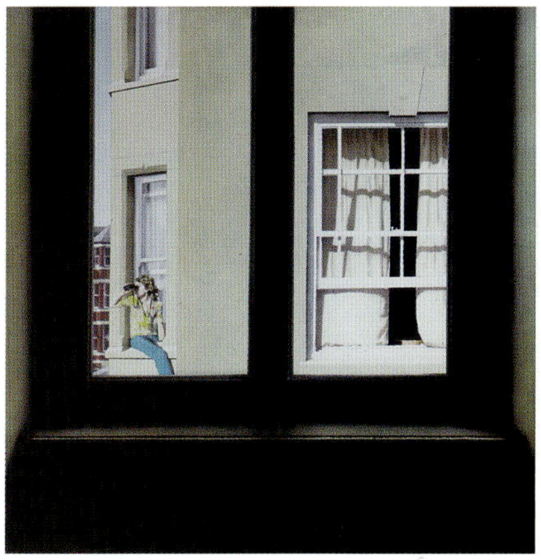

Boyd, Fionnuala b.1944 & **Evans, Leslie** b.1945
Looking Out 1974
oil on canvas 122 x 121.5
LCNUG 1979.121

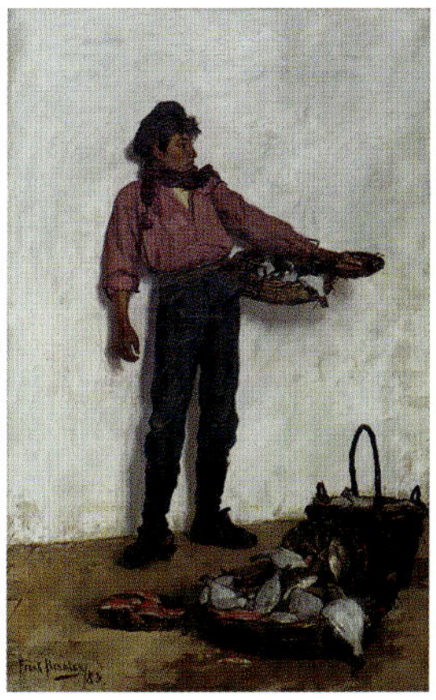

Bramley, Frank 1857–1915
Neapolitan Fisher Boy 1883
oil on canvas 69.2 x 41.3
LCNUG 1927.701

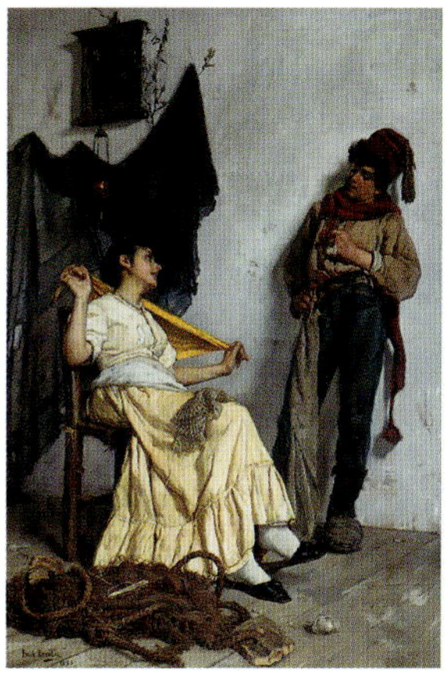

Bramley, Frank 1857–1915
Weaving Nets 1883
oil on canvas 114.5 x 75
LCNUG 1927.41

Bramley, Frank 1857–1915
Self Portrait 1897
oil on canvas 32 x 30.5
LCNUG 1996.25

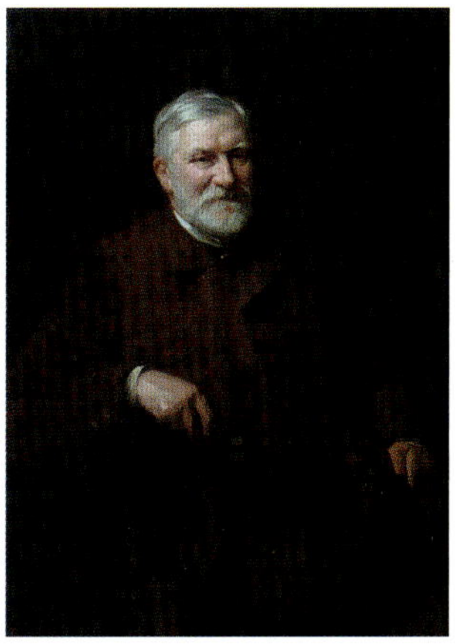

Bramley, Frank 1857–1915
Alexander S. Leslie Melville of Lincoln (d.1881)
oil on canvas 125.5 x 92.2
LCNUG 1927.921

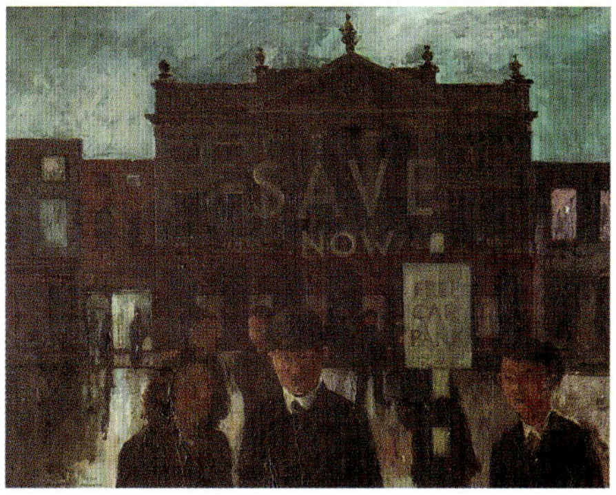

Brannan, Peter 1926–1994
Street Scene before 1953
oil on panel 41 x 50.5
LCNUG 1927.2179

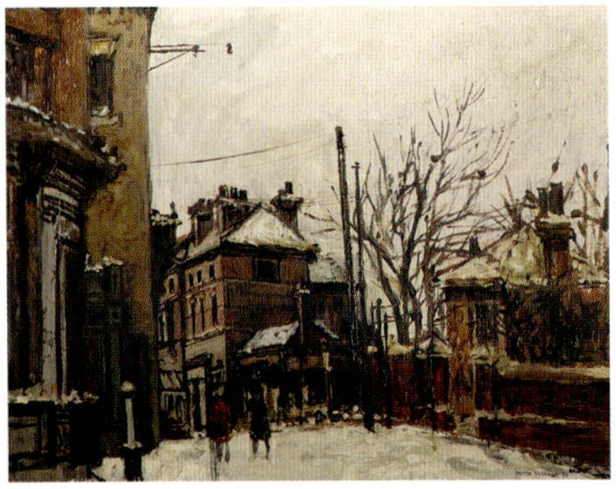

Brannan, Peter 1926–1994
Winter Street Scene 1959
oil on board 31.5 x 40
LCNUG 2001.4

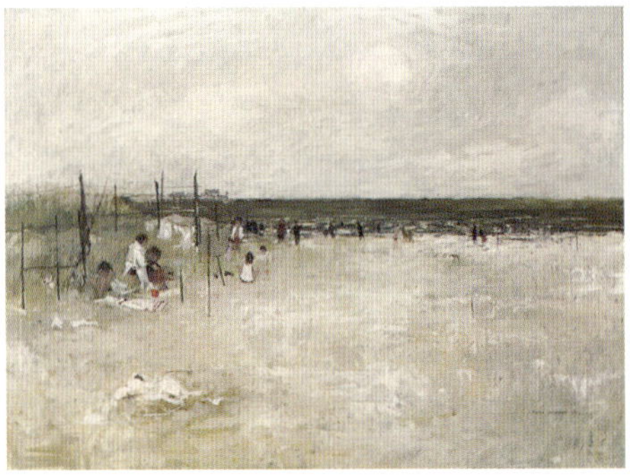

Brannan, Peter 1926–1994
On the Beach 1960
oil on canvas 54.6 x 81.3
LCNUG 1927.2392

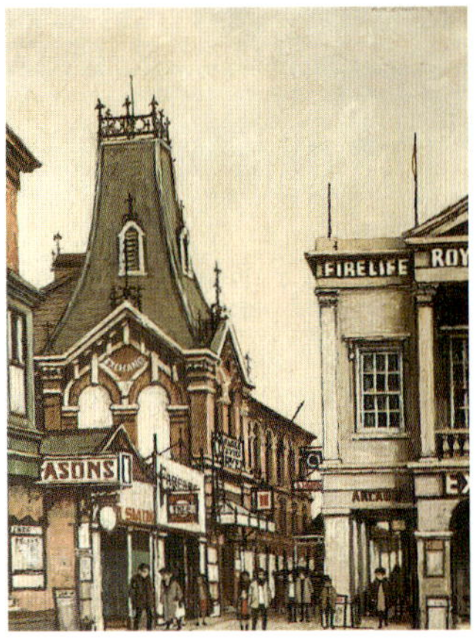

Brannan, Peter 1926–1994
Corn Exchange, Lincoln 1973
oil on hardboard 40 x 30.4
LCNUG 1974.17

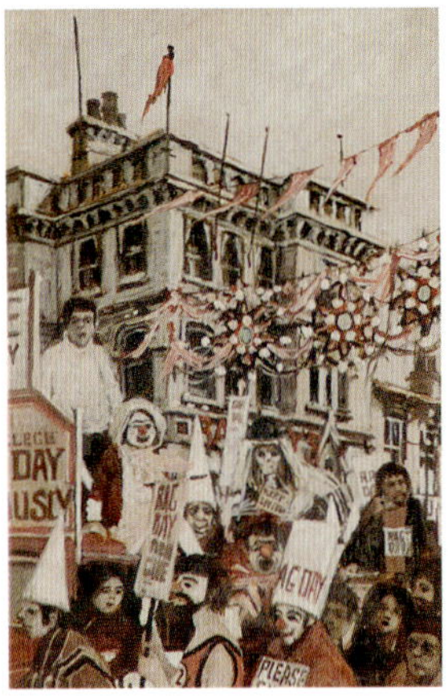

Brannan, Peter 1926–1994
Rag Day, Lincoln 1973
oil on hardboard 32.5 x 22.5
LCNUG 1974.16

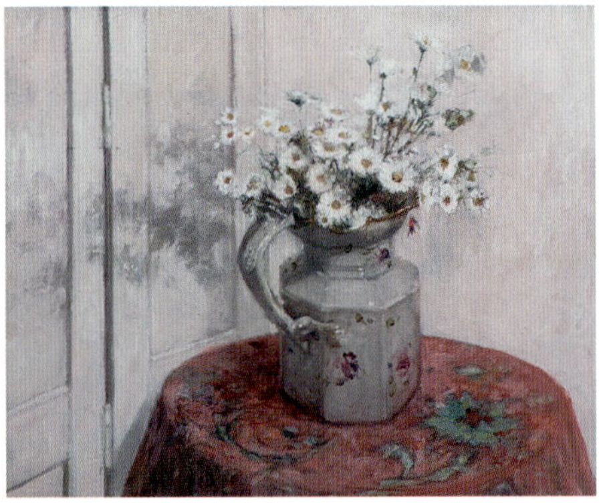

Brannan, Peter 1926–1994
Flowers in a Jug 1980
oil on board 51.5 x 61.5
LCNUG 1995.58

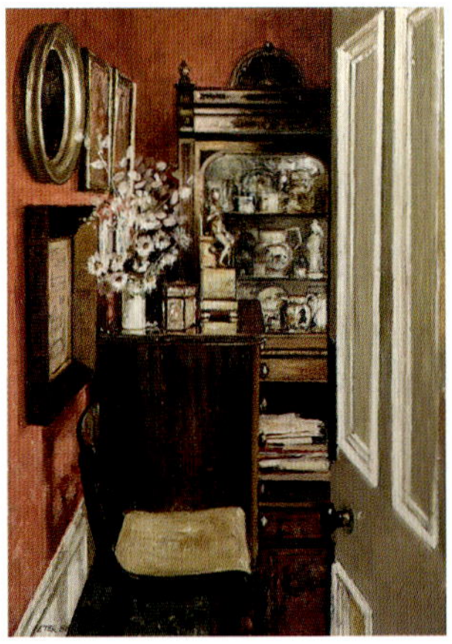

Brannan, Peter 1926–1994
At Frank's, Bradford, West Yorkshire 1985
oil on card 35.8 x 25.4
LCNUG 1995.59

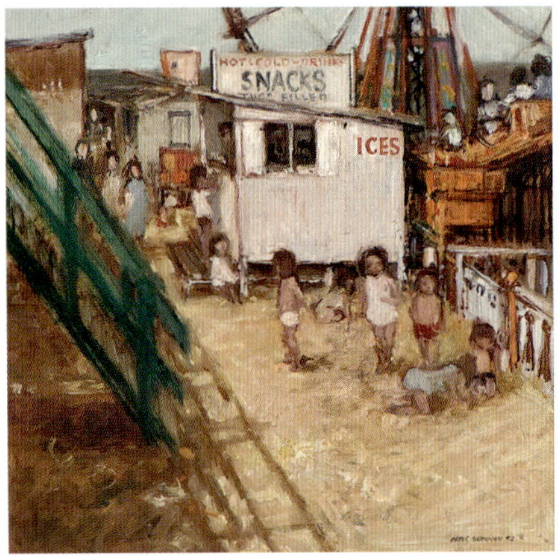

Brannan, Peter 1926–1994
Cleethorpes, Beach Scene, Lincolnshire 1992
oil on board 32.5 x 32.5
LCNUG 1995.60

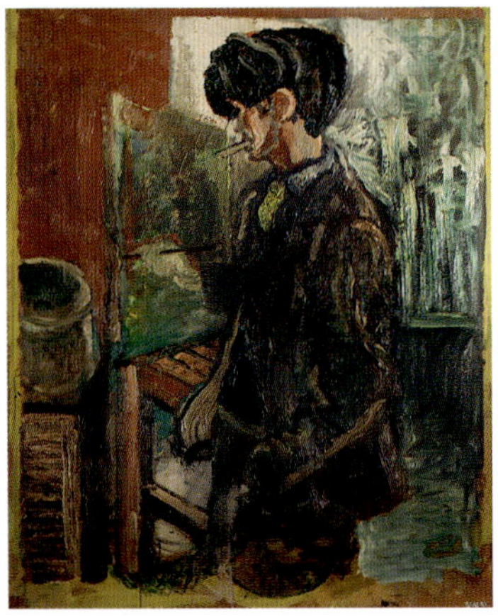

Bratby, John Randall 1928–1992
Taffy Roberts 1952
oil on board 109.2 x 84
LCNUG 1927.2658

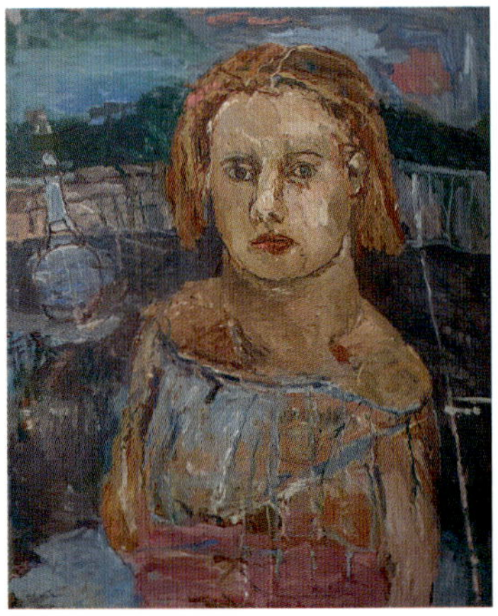

Brigham, Isobel b.1963
Tennis Court Self Portrait 1991
oil on canvas 152.5 x 122
LCNUG 1996.3

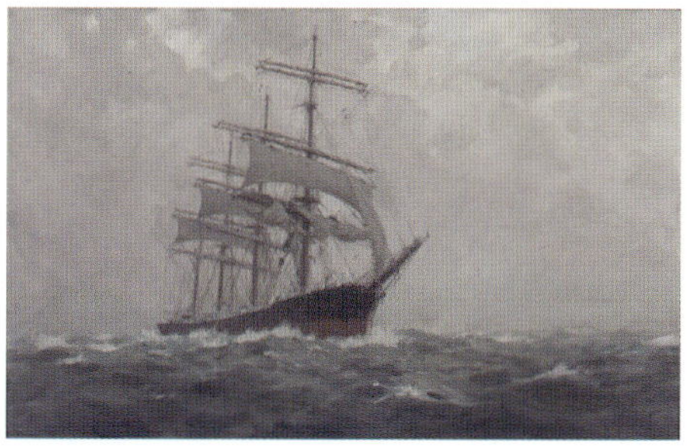

Briscoe, Arthur John Trevor 1873–1943
In Ballast 1934
oil on canvas 65 x 102
LCNUG 1927.671

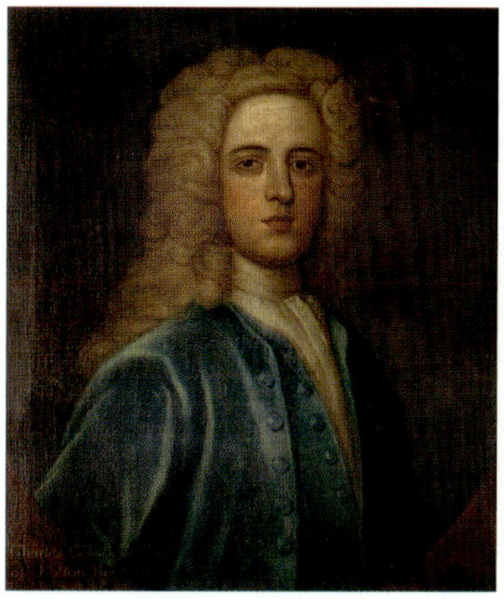

British (English) School
Charles Caldecote, Esq., of Holton Beckering
oil on canvas 76.5 x 63
LCNUG 2001.7

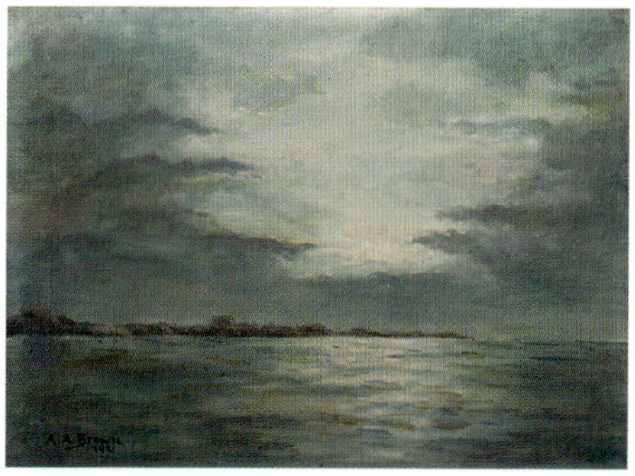

Brown, Agnes Augusta 1847–1932
Moonlight on the Yorkshire Coast
oil on canvas 31 x 41
LCNUG 1927.144

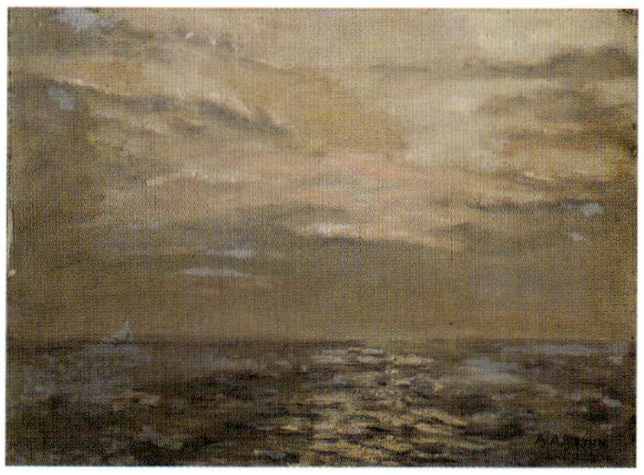

Brown, Agnes Augusta 1847–1932
North Sea Sunrise
oil on canvas 30.5 x 40.5
LCNUG 1927.639

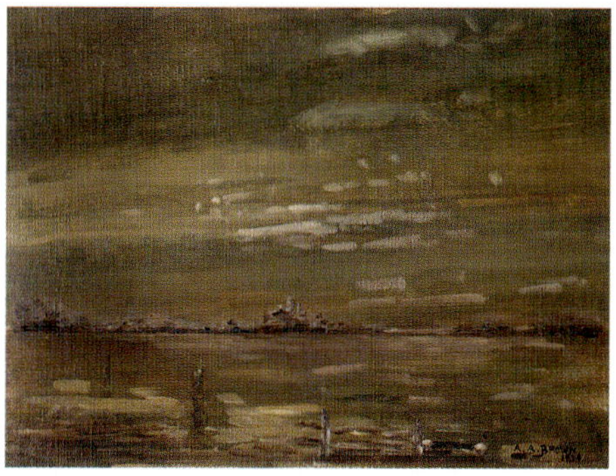

Brown, Agnes Augusta 1847–1932
Shades of Evening
oil on canvas 31 x 40.5
LCNUG 1927.183

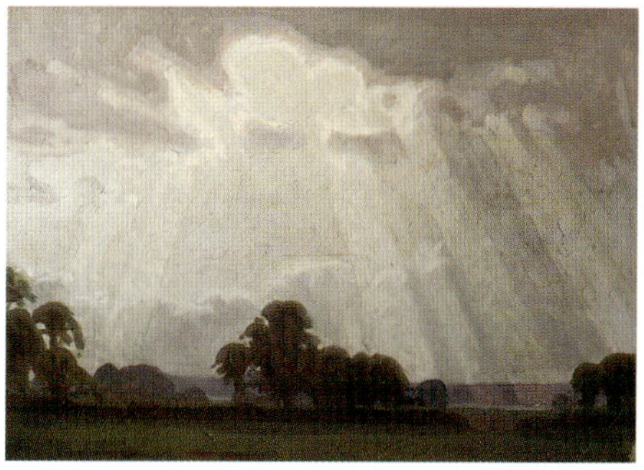

Brown, John 1887–1966
A Break in the Clouds
oil on canvas 29.5 x 40
LCNUG 1927.219

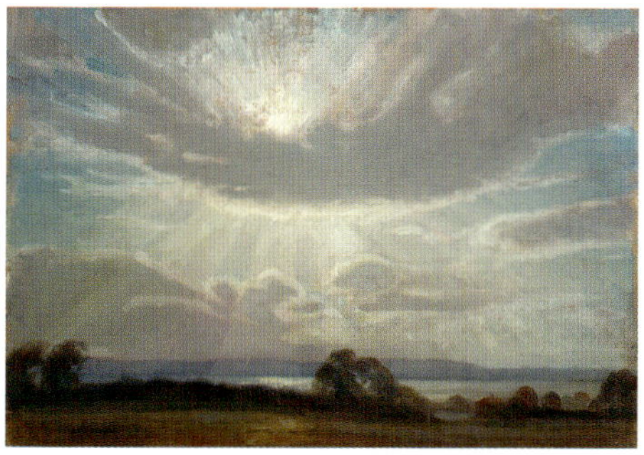

Brown, John 1887–1966
November Sky
oil on panel 25.5 x 35.5
LCNUG 1927.638

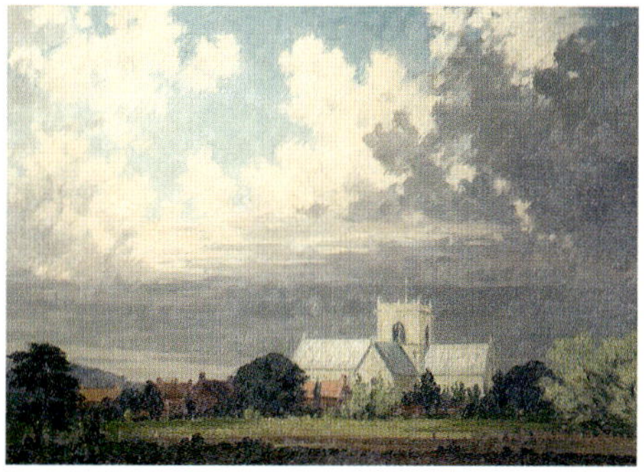

Browne, Clive Richard 1901–1991
St Mary's Church, Stow, Lincolnshire c.1950
oil on canvas 46 x 61
LCNUG 1980.2

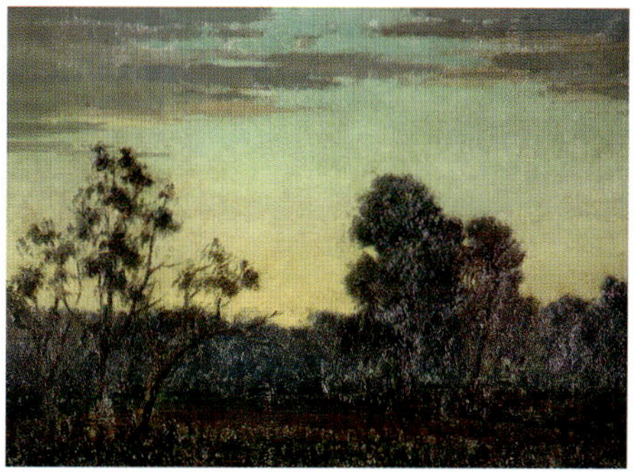

Browne, Clive Richard 1901–1991
Before Sunrise
oil on canvas 31 x 41
LCNUG 1927.729

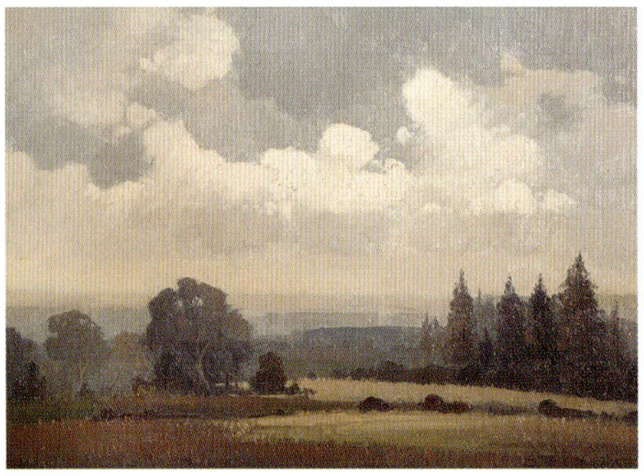

Browne, Clive Richard 1901–1991
Early Morning
oil on canvas 30 x 40
LCNUG 1927.641

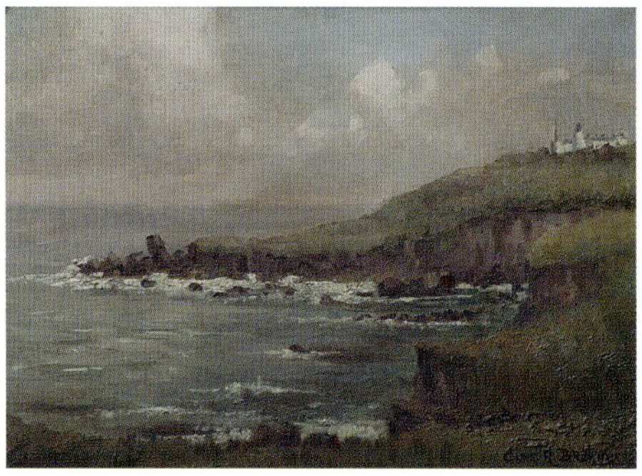

Browne, Clive Richard 1901–1991
Housel Bay, Cornwall
oil on canvas 29 x 40.5
LCNUG 1927.179

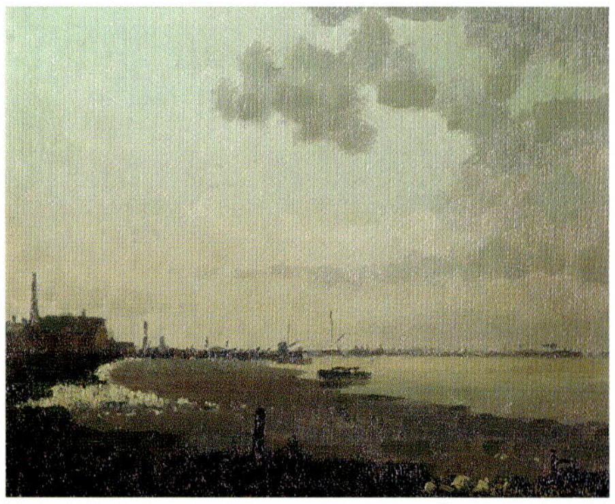

Browne, Clive Richard 1901–1991
Low Tide on the Humber
oil on canvas 25.5 x 31
LCNUG 1927.218

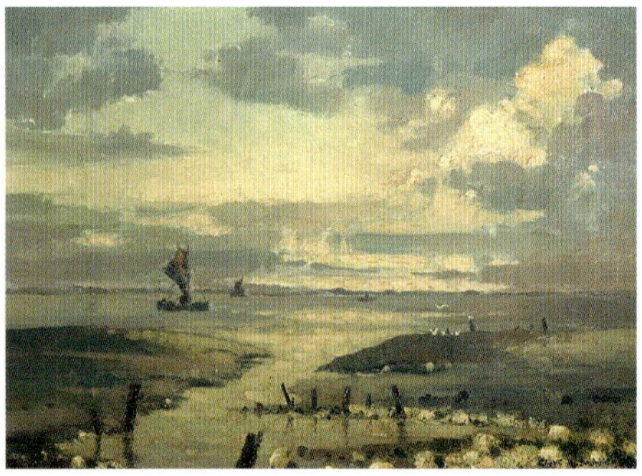

Browne, Clive Richard 1901–1991
The Haunt of the Seagull
oil on canvas 32 x 41
LCNUG 1927.156

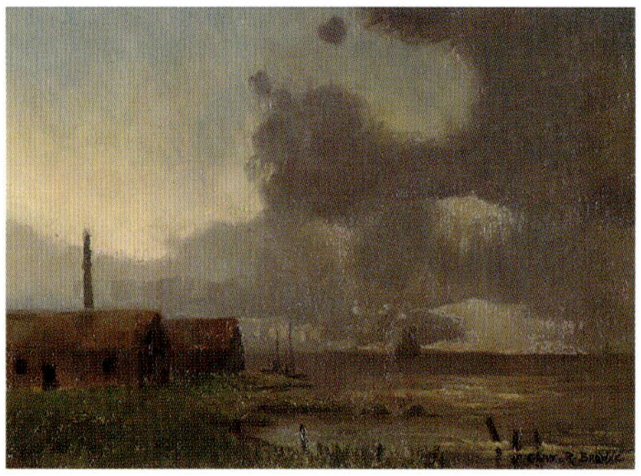

Browne, Clive Richard 1901–1991
The Humber in a Sullen Mood
oil on canvas 29.3 x 39
LCNUG 1927.217

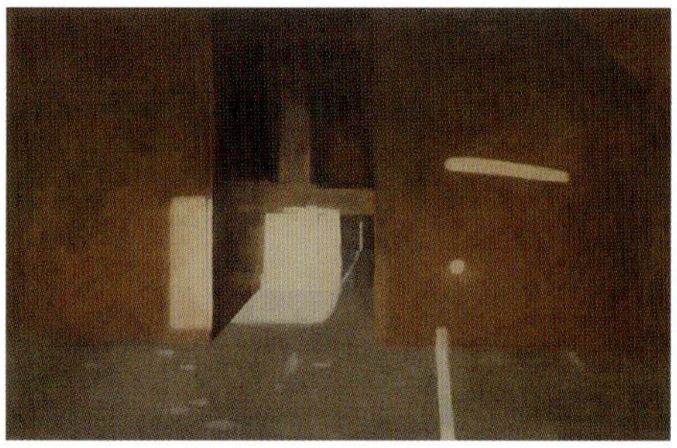

Bruce, Allan b.1943
Interior V
oil on paper 37 x 56
LCNUG 1983.42

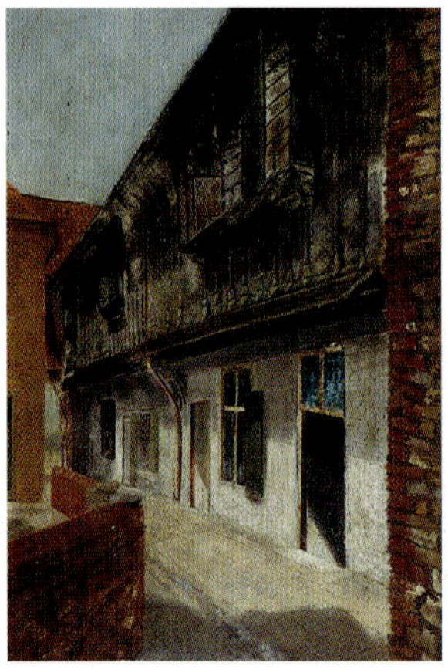

Buffam, H. M.
Whitefriars House, Akrill's Passage, Lincoln
1885
oil on millboard 32.3 x 22
LCNUG 1976.30

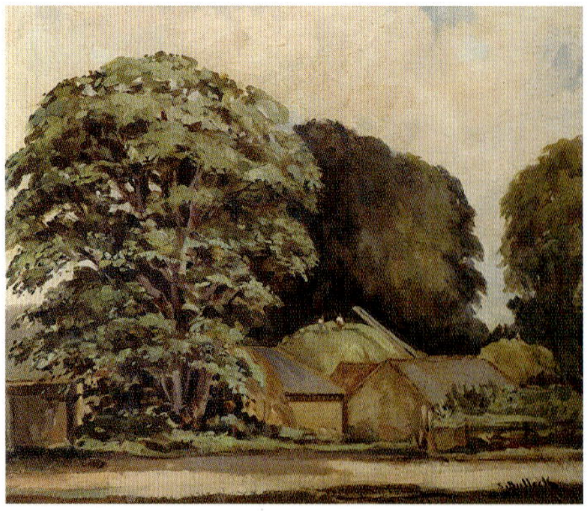

Bullock, Stephen 1889–1971
Farmstead, Donington On Bain, Lincolnshire
oil on board 44 x 51
LCNUG 1927.2581

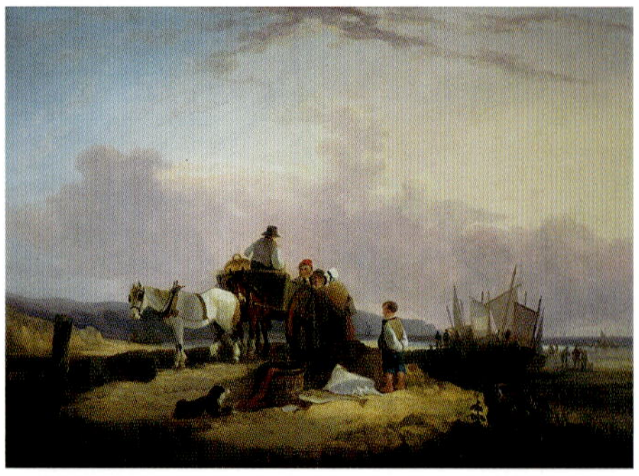

Callcott, Augustus Wall 1779–1844
Sea Pier
oil on canvas 76 x 102
LCNUG 1927.221

Facing page: Clausen, George, 1852–1944, *A. G. Webster (1852–1916)* (detail), 1881, The Collection: Art & Archaeology in Lincolnshire (Usher Gallery) (p. 290)

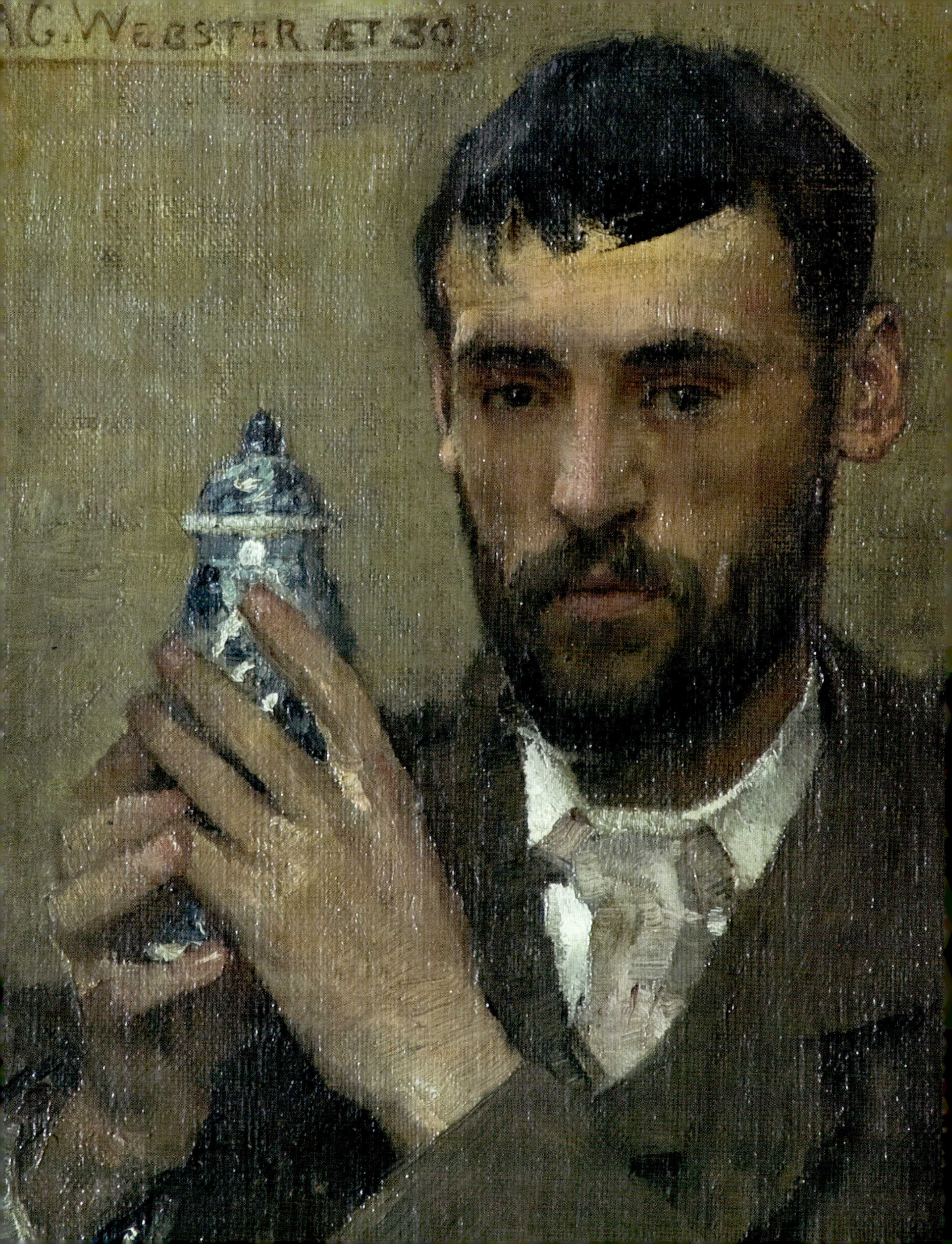
G. WEBSTER ÆT 30

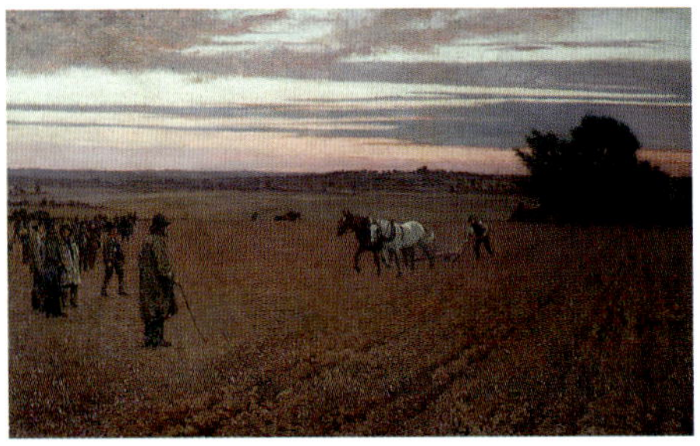

Carline, George F. 1855–1920
The Ploughing Match 1892
oil on canvas 79 x 160
LCNUG 1927.123

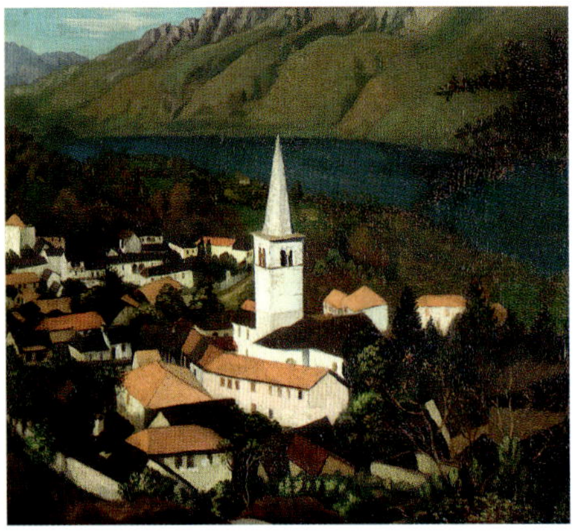

Carline, Sydney William 1888–1929
Village by Lake Orta, Italy
oil on canvas 64 x 71
LCNUG 1927.131

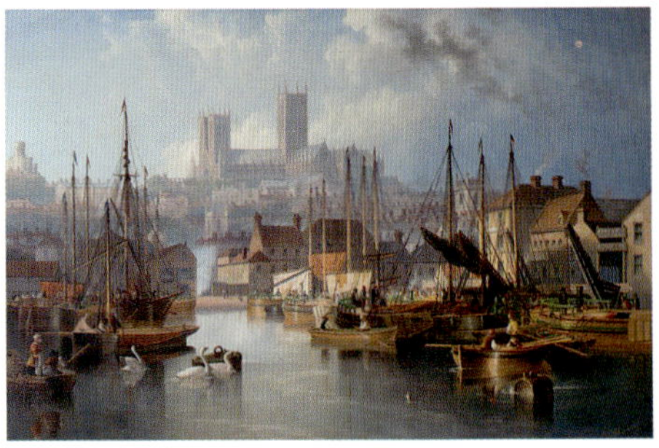

Carmichael, John Wilson 1799–1868
The Brayford Pool and Lincoln Cathedral 1858
oil on canvas 89 x 134.5
LCNUG 1927.2686

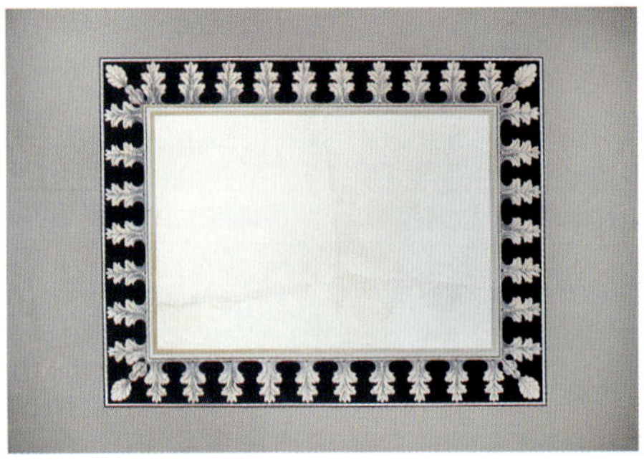

Carter, Tony b.1943
Flag for Pericles 1967
oil on hardboard 122 x 182.8
LCNUG 1980.162

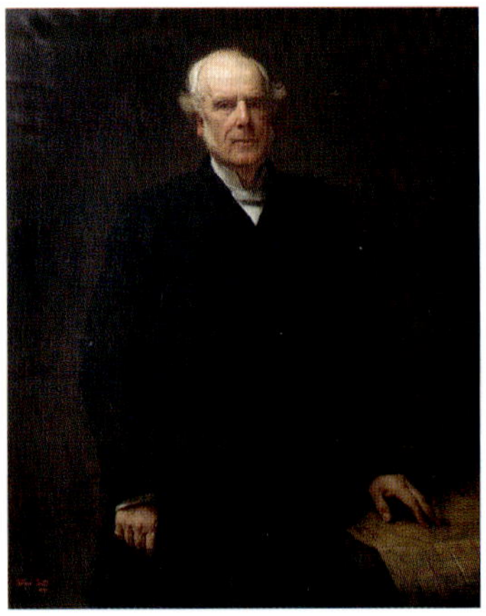

Carter, William 1863–1939
Reverend Canon Frederic Pretyman (1820–1905) 1891
oil on canvas 127.5 x 102.2
LCNUG 1982.59

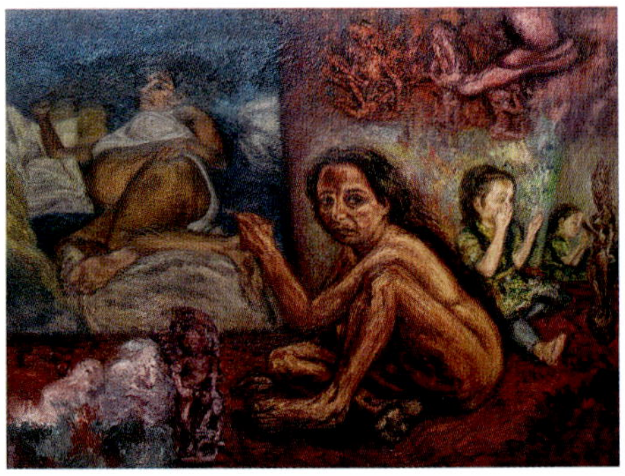

Chuhan, J. b.1955
Self Portrait II 1996
oil on canvas 143 x 175
LCNUG 1996.4

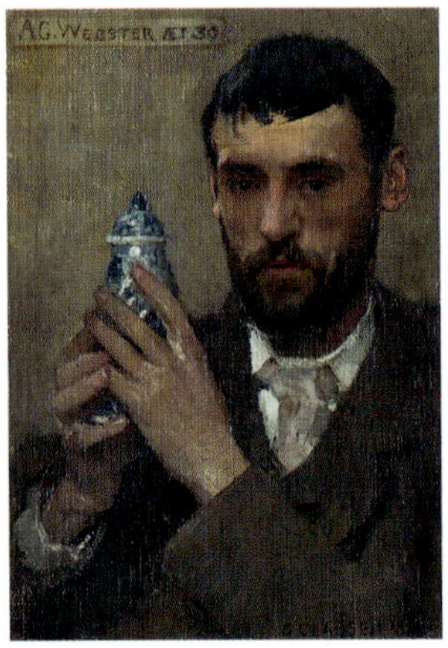

Clausen, George 1852–1944
A. G. Webster (1852–1916) 1881
oil on canvas 20.4 x 14.6
LCNUG 1927.2316

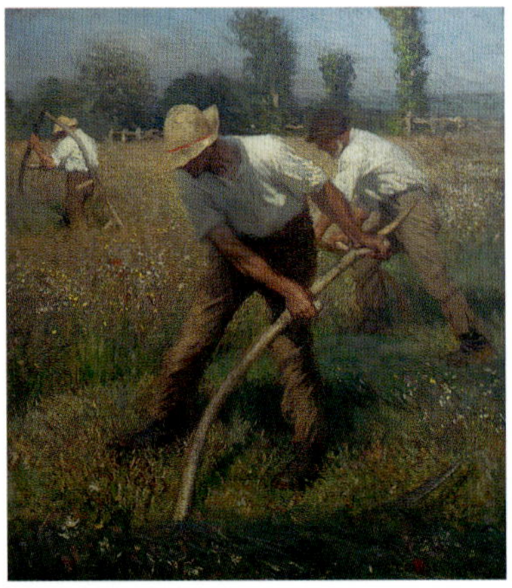

Clausen, George 1852–1944
The Mowers 1891
oil on canvas 97.2 x 76.2
LCNUG 1927.1893

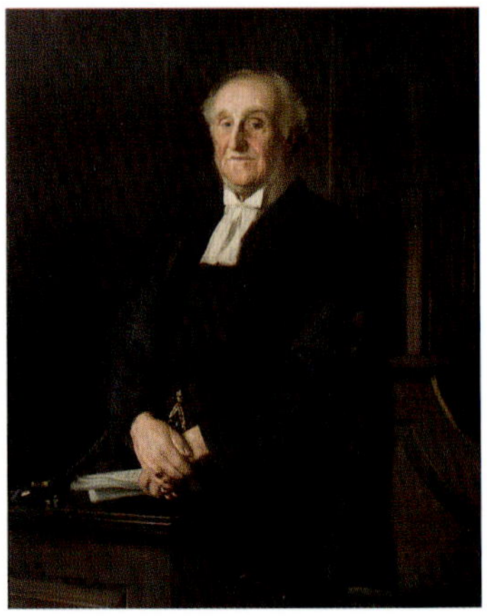

Clausen, George 1852–1944
John Thomas Tweed (1823–1910), Town Clerk of Lincoln (1855–1905) 1906
oil on canvas 127.2 x 101.6
LCNUG 1927.2039

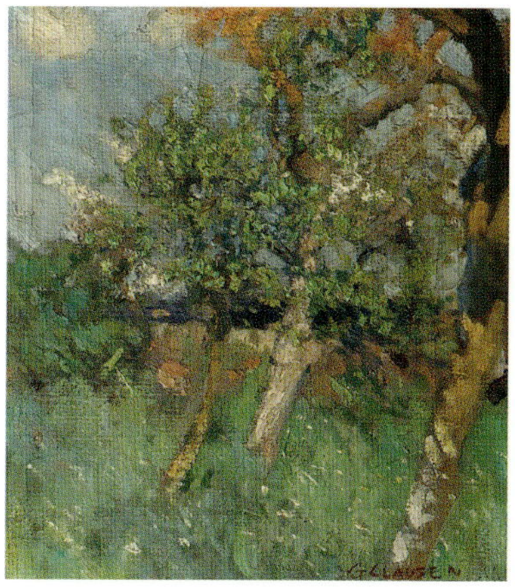

Clausen, George 1852–1944
Orchard Scene
oil on canvas 33 x 29
LCNUG 1927.2317.

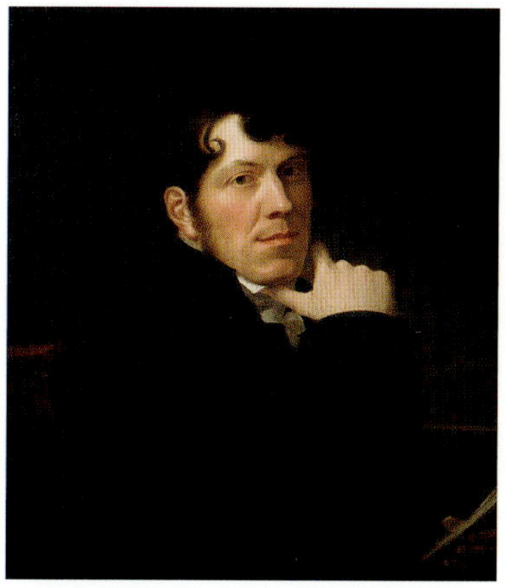

Clayton, G.
George Clayton Tennyson (1778–1831), Father of Alfred Tennyson
oil on canvas 77 x 64
TENN.T2010.01

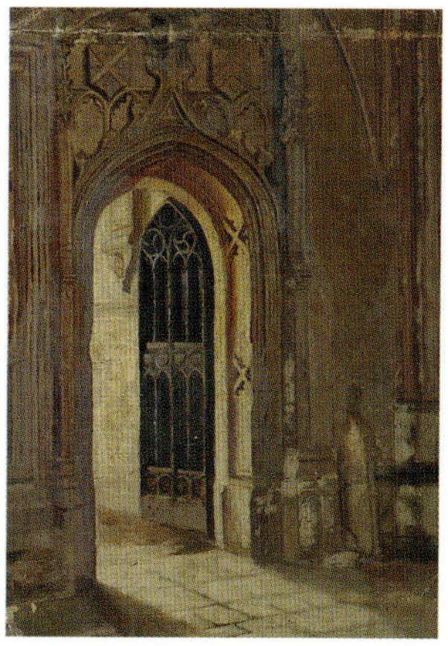

Clements, Helen d.1934
Chapel Doorway, Lincoln Cathedral
oil on canvas 40 x 28
LCNUG 1927.224

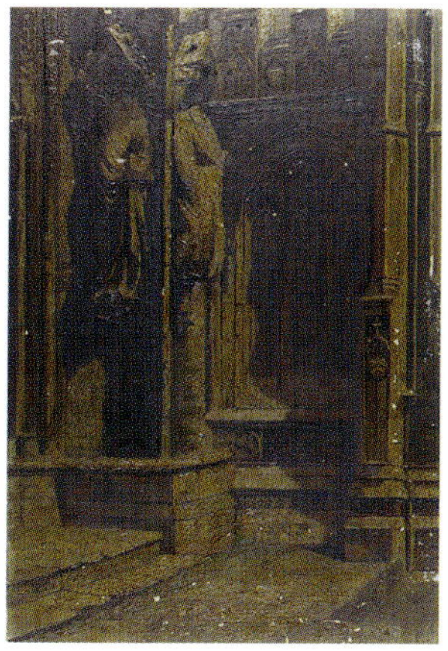

Clements, Helen d.1934
Corner of Judgement Porch, Lincoln Cathedral
oil on canvas 45 x 30
LCNUG 1927.225

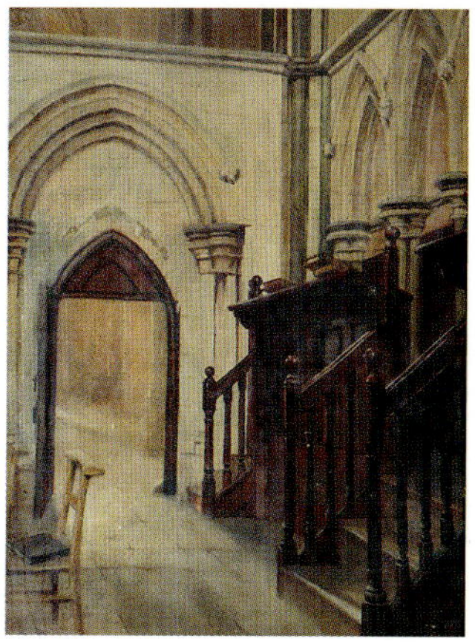

Clements, Helen d.1934
Morning Chapel, Lincoln Cathedral
oil on canvas 37.5 x 27
LCNUG 1927.238

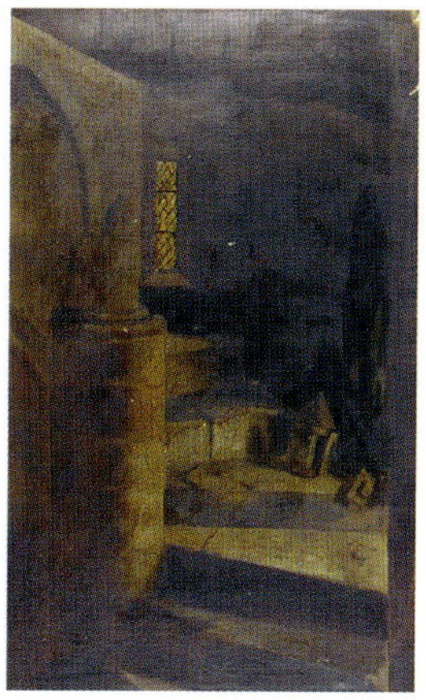

Clements, Helen d.1934
Staircase, Lincoln Cathedral
oil on canvas 51 x 31
LCNUG 1927.229

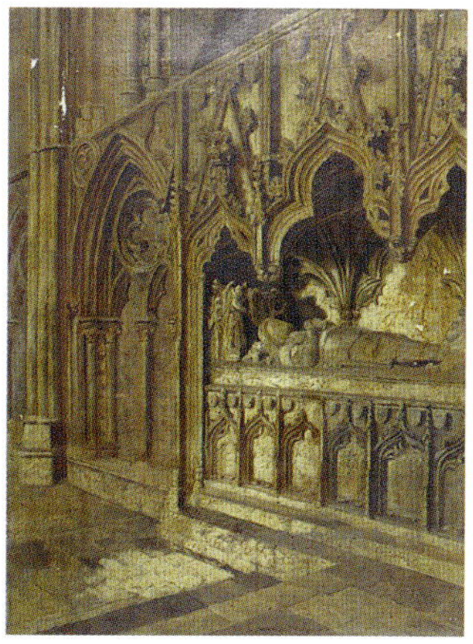

Clements, Helen d.1934
The Tomb of Sir Bartholomew Burghersh, Lincoln Cathedral
oil on canvas 56 x 40.5
LCNUG 1927.230

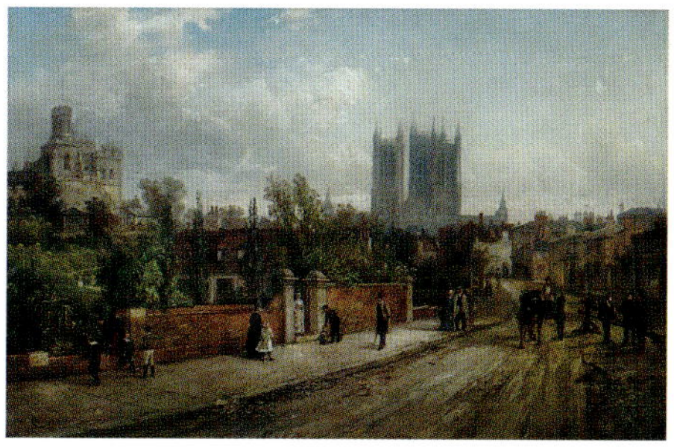

Clouse, M. 1820–1880
A View of Lincoln Cathedral from Drury Lane 1886
oil on canvas 51 x 76.5
LCNUG 1995.6

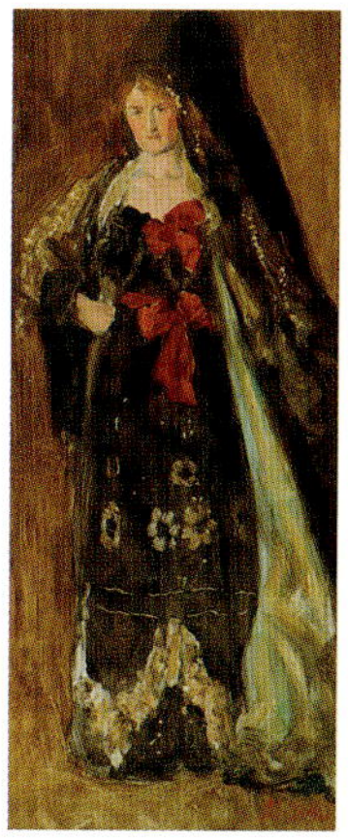

Collier, John 1850–1934
The Prodigal Daughter (sketch) 1903
oil on board 58.5 x 24.5
LCNUG 1987.1

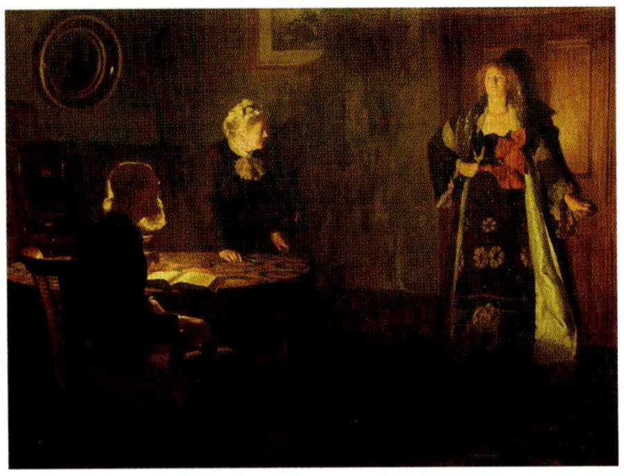

Collier, John 1850–1934
The Prodigal Daughter 1903
oil on canvas 166 x 217
LCNUG 1927.186

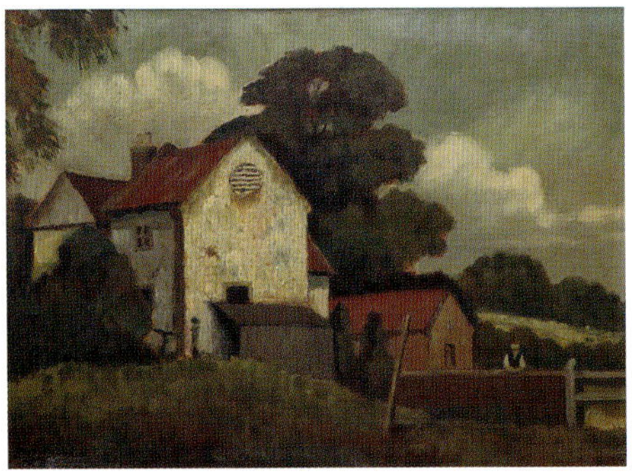

Cook, A. active 20th C
Watermill, Hatcliffe, Lincolnshire
oil on panel 38 x 50.5
LCNUG 1927.284

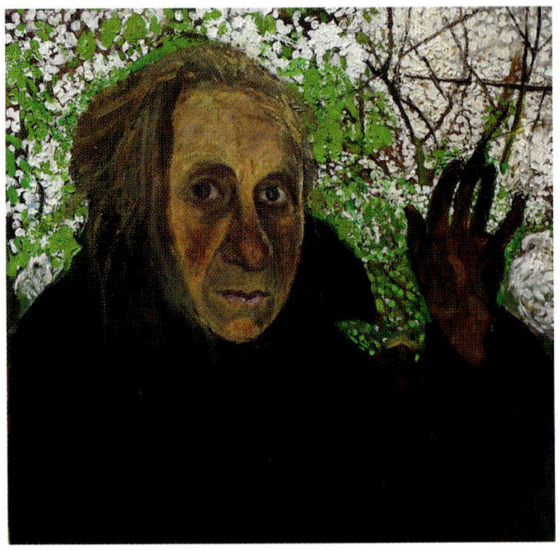

Cooke, Jean 1927–2008
Not Waving, Just Painting 1996
oil on canvas 45 x 45
LCNUG 1996.5

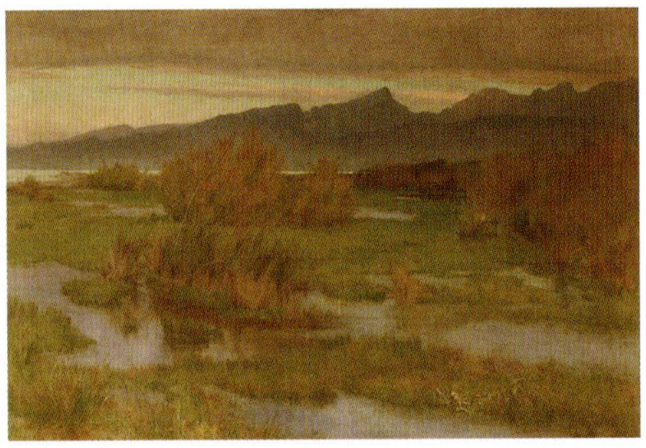

Corbet, Matthew Ridley 1850–1902
Autumn Rains, the Marshes of Florence, Italy
oil on canvas 122 x 190.2
LCNUG 1927.46

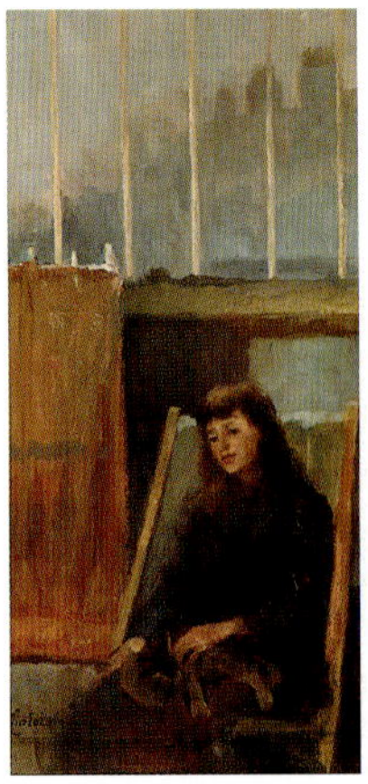

Curtois, Mary Henrietta Dering 1854–1929
Young Girl Sitting in a Deck Chair 1880
oil on canvas 45 x 22
LCNUG 1986.3

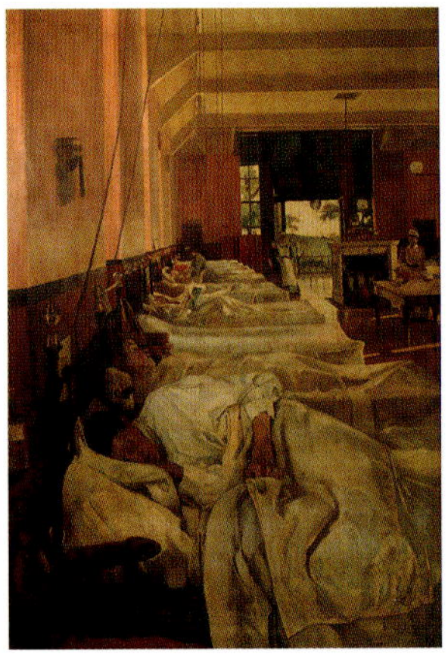

Curtois, Mary Henrietta Dering 1854–1929
Ruston Ward, Lincoln County Hospital 1891
oil on canvas 152.5 x 104
LCNUG 1927.37

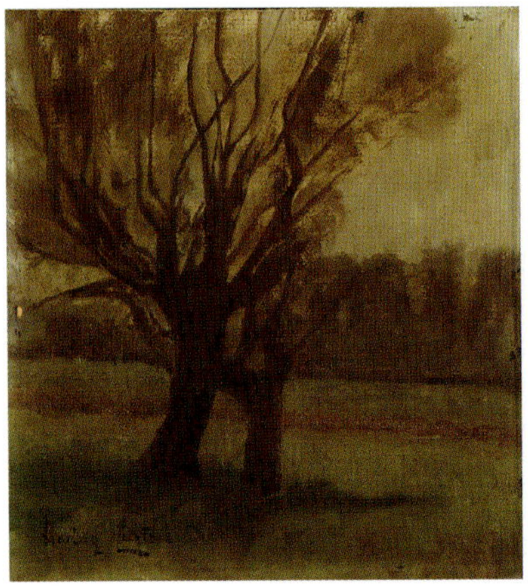

Curtois, Mary Henrietta Dering 1854–1929
Willow Trees, Winter
oil on cardboard 25 x 22.5
LCNUG 1927.2579

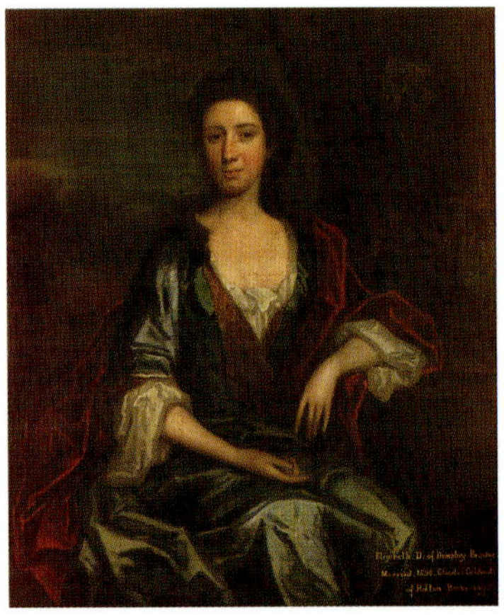

Dahl, Michael I (style of) 1656/1659–1743
Elizabeth Browne, Daughter of Humphry Browne late 17th C–early 18th C
oil on canvas 123 x 100.5
LCNUG 1972.151

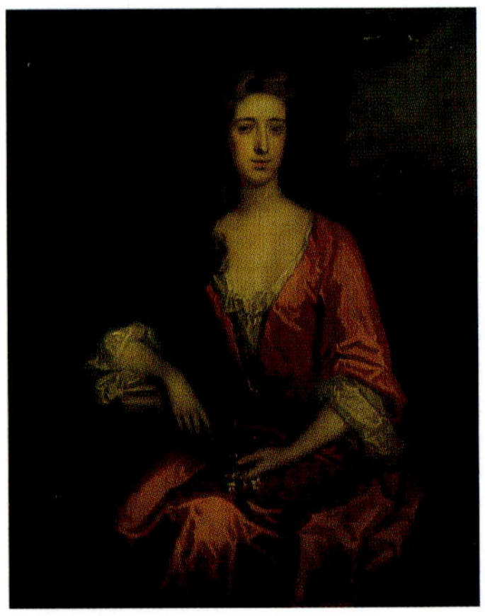

Dahl, Michael I (style of) 1656/1659–1743
Mary Sibthorp, Wife of John Sibthorp 18th C
oil on canvas 125 x 99.5
LCNUG 1972.150

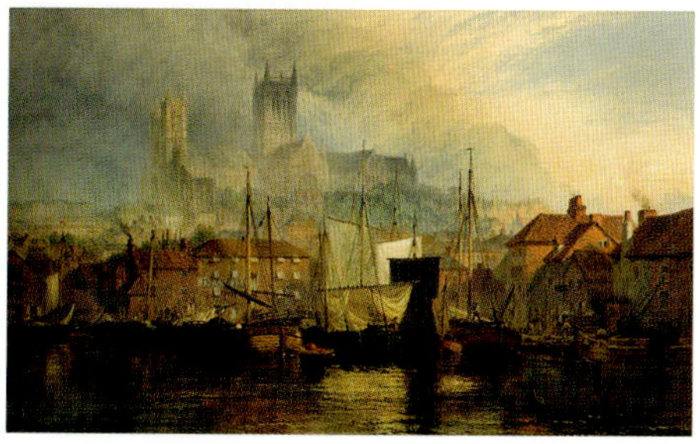

Dawson, Henry 1811–1878
Lincoln Cathedral from Brayford 1867
oil on canvas 81 x 126
LCNUG 1927.938

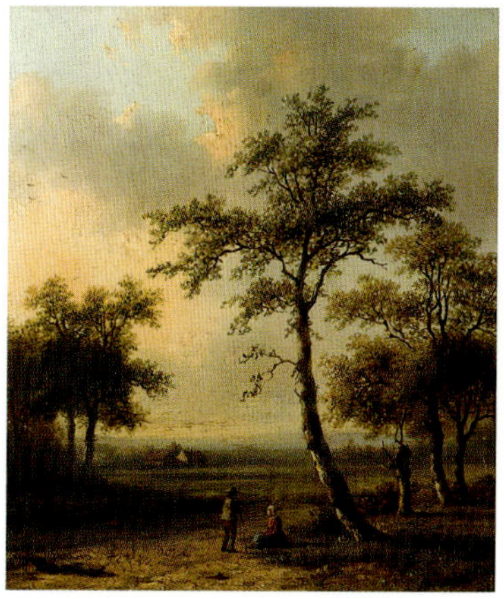

De Coene, Jean Henri 1798–1866
Landscape
oil on panel 33 x 28
LCNUG 1927.912

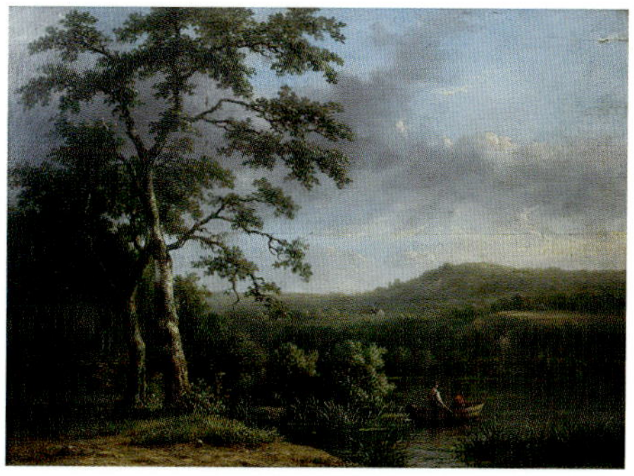

De Coene, Jean Henri 1798–1866
River Scene with Men in a Boat
oil on panel 33.2 x 44.1
LCNUG 1927.909

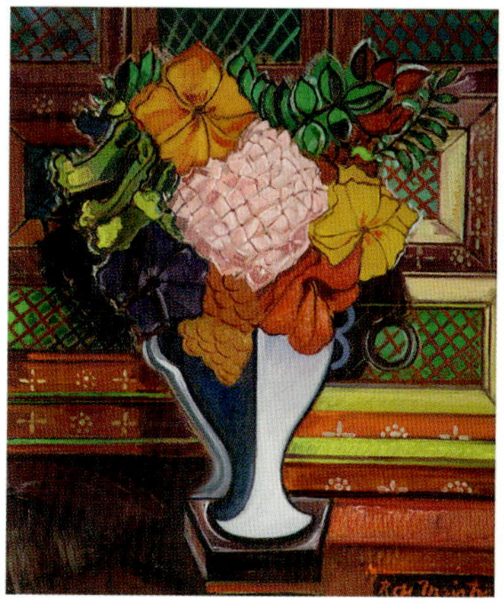

de Maistre, Leroy Leveson Laurent Joseph 1894–1968
Flowers
oil on board 60 x 50
LCNUG 1985.21

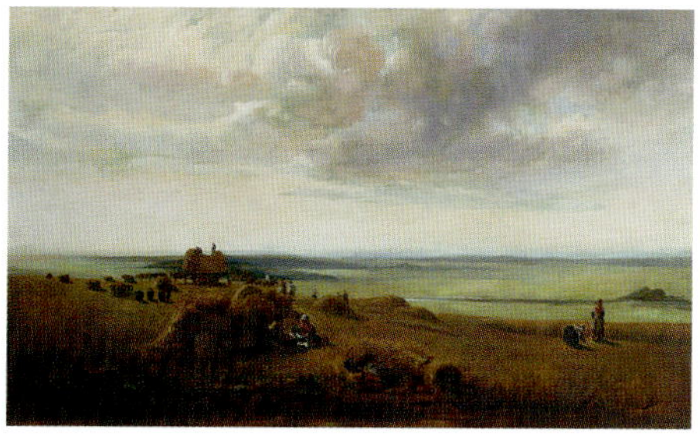

De Wint, Peter 1784–1849
Lincolnshire Cornfield near Horncastle 1815
oil on canvas 107 x 171
LCNUG 1927.1684

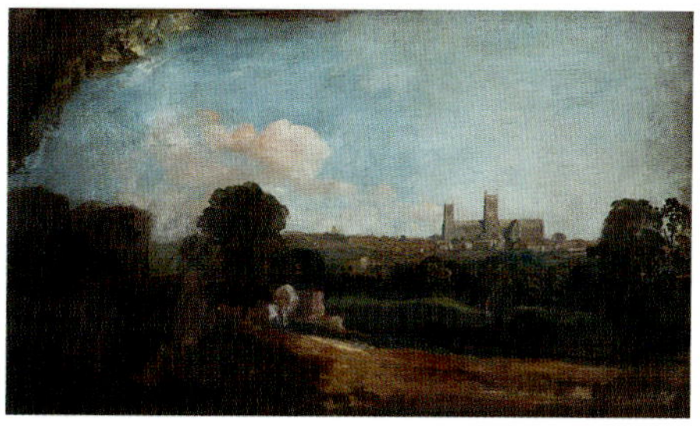

De Wint, Peter 1784–1849
A View of Lincoln from the South at Little Bargate c.1824
oil on millboard 31 x 50.5
LCNUG 1995.4

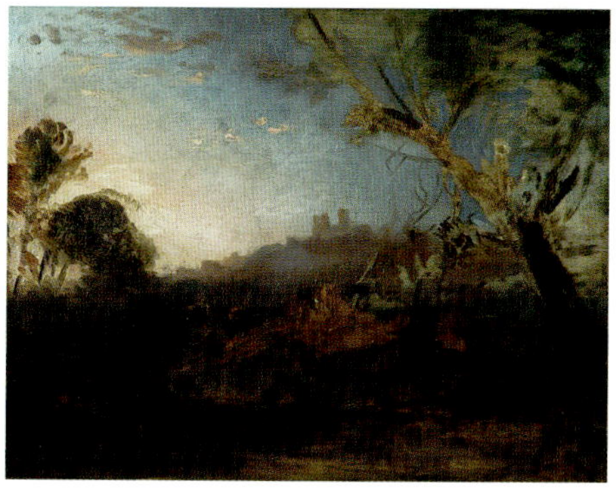

De Wint, Peter 1784–1849
A Drover at the Edge of a Wood, Lincoln in the Distance c.1830
oil on canvas 35.7 x 44.3
LCNUG 1995.5

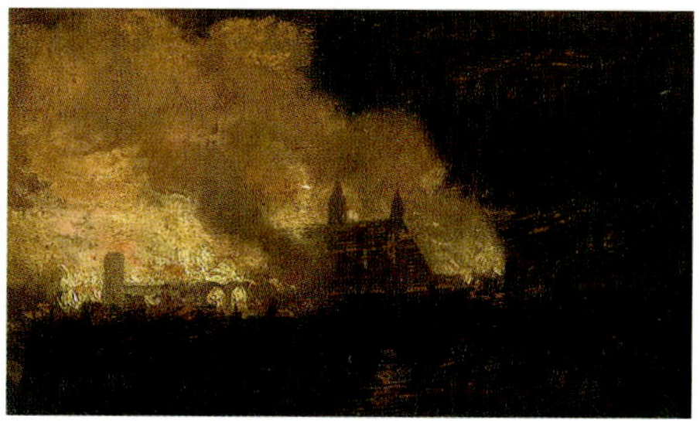

De Wint, Peter 1784–1849
The Burning of the Houses of Parliament 1834
oil on panel 13.5 x 21
LCNUG 1927.1962

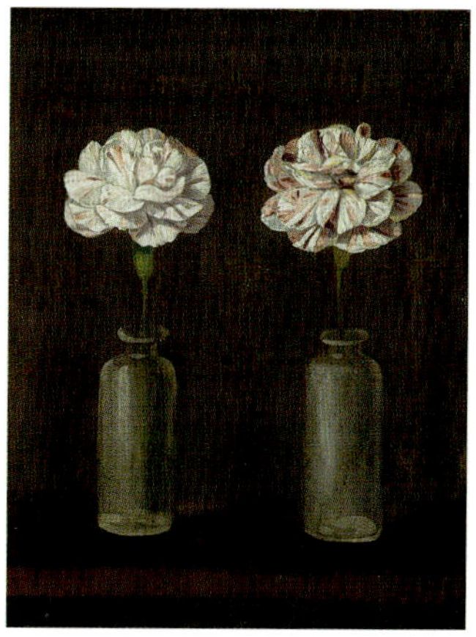

De Wint, Peter 1784–1849
Carnations
oil on canvas 30.5 x 25.4
LCNUG 1927.1961

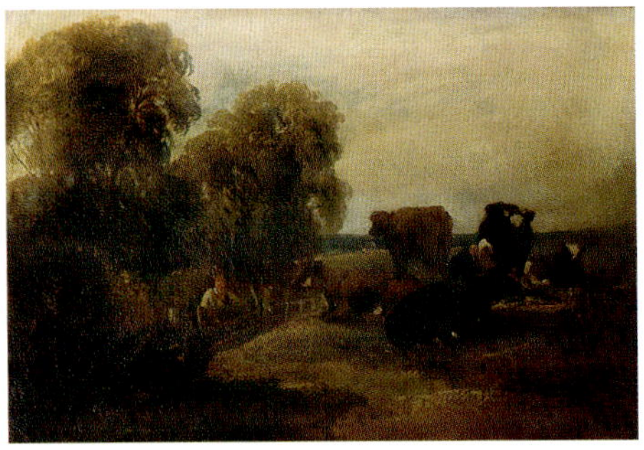

De Wint, Peter 1784–1849
Cattle in a Landscape
oil on canvas 33 x 47.5
LCNUG 1927.943

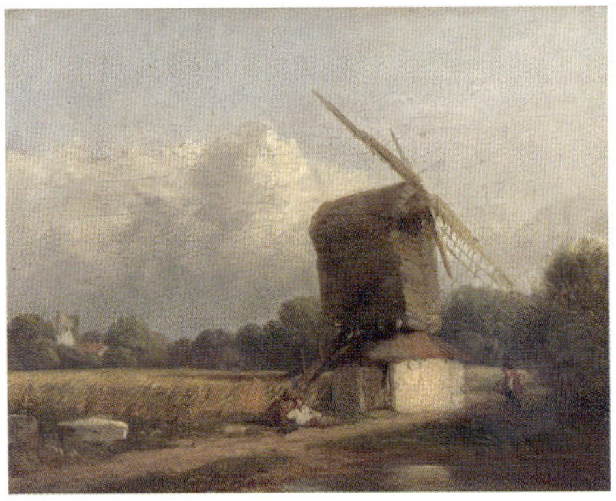

De Wint, Peter 1784–1849
Cornfield with a Windmill
oil on panel 20.5 x 25.5
LCNUG 1927.1499

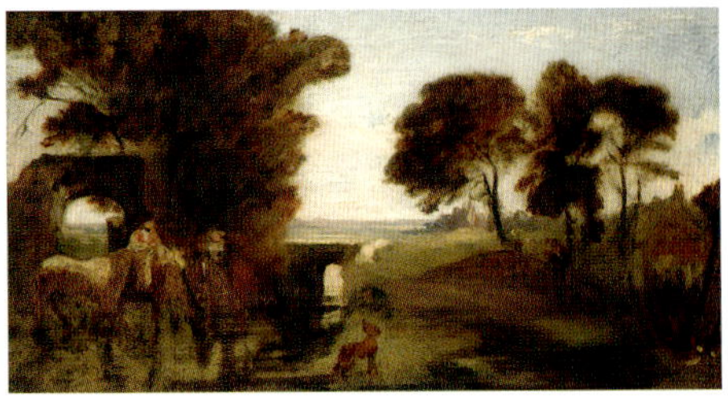

De Wint, Peter 1784–1849
Horses and Figures at a Ford
oil on canvas 31.2 x 55.1
LCNUG 1977.2787

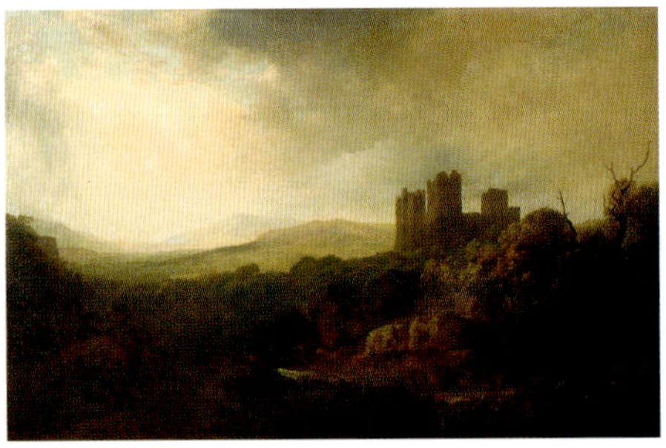

De Wint, Peter 1784–1849
Landscape with a Castle
oil on canvas 108.5 x 166
LCNUG 1927.675

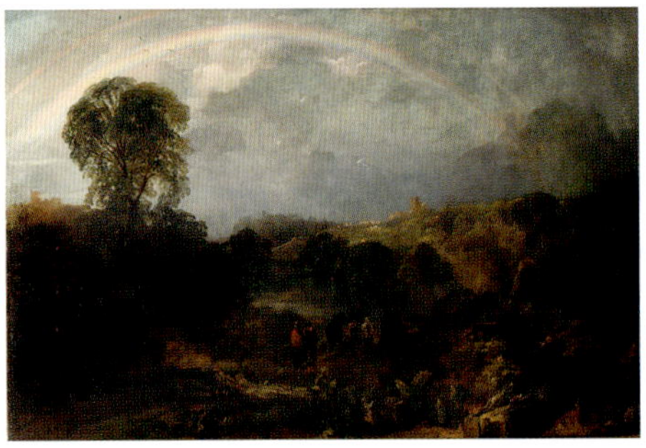

De Wint, Peter 1784–1849
Landscape with a Rainbow
oil on canvas 109 x 165.5
LCNUG 1927.681

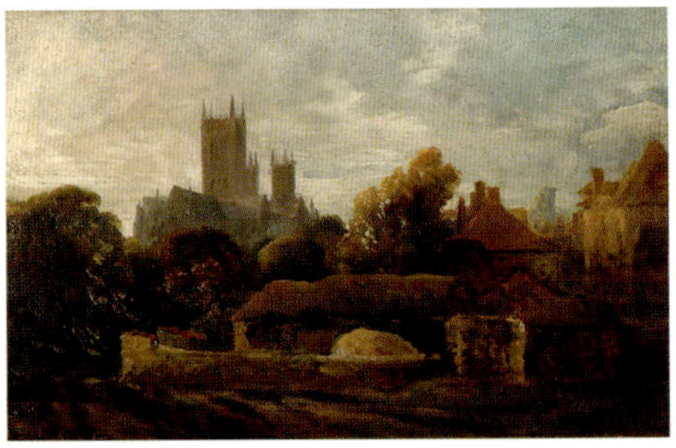

De Wint, Peter 1784–1849
Lincoln Cathedral from the North East
oil on canvas 30 x 45
LCNUG 2009.27

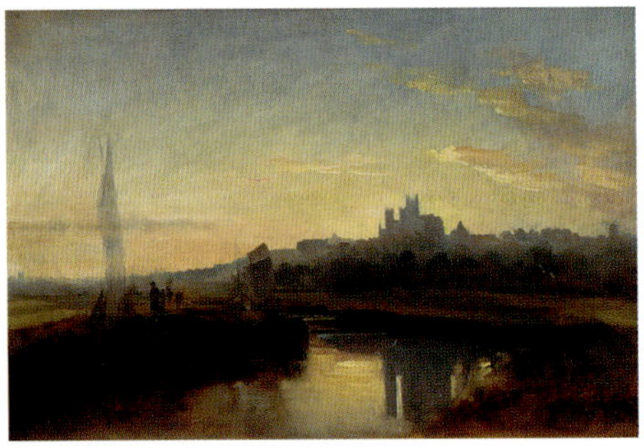

De Wint, Peter 1784–1849
Lincoln from the River at Sunset
oil on paper laid on canvas 39.5 x 56
LCNUG 1985.1

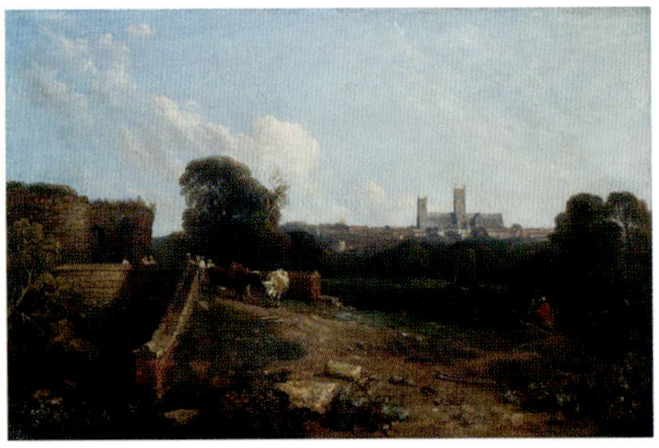

De Wint, Peter 1784–1849
Lincoln from the South
oil on canvas 61 x 92
LCNUG 1927.878

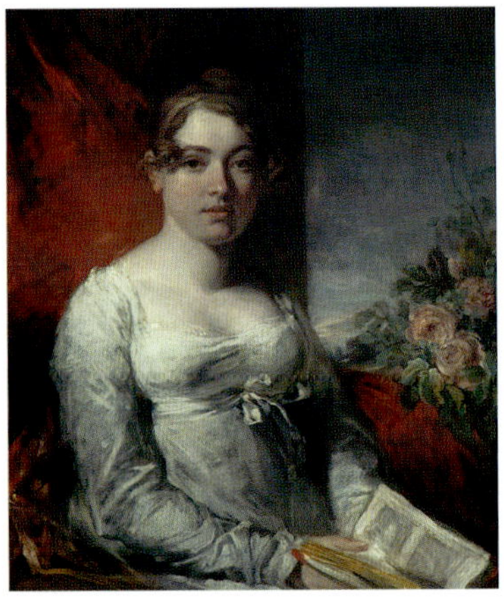

De Wint, Peter 1784–1849
Mrs Peter De Wint (1791–1866)
oil on canvas 78.8 x 64.3 (E)
LCNUG 1927.306

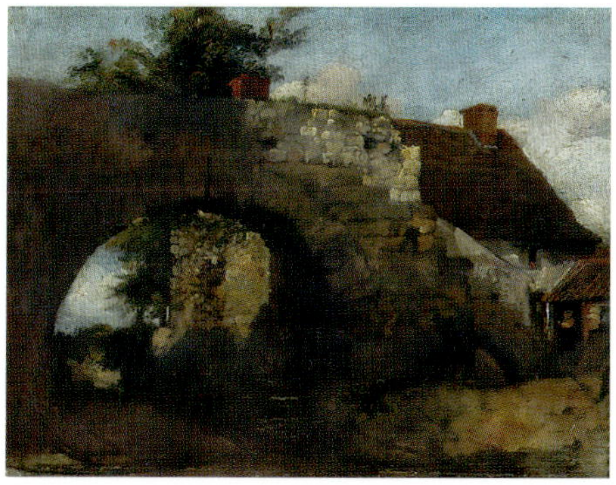

De Wint, Peter 1784–1849
Newport Arch, Lincoln
oil on panel 29 x 37
LCNUG 1927.705

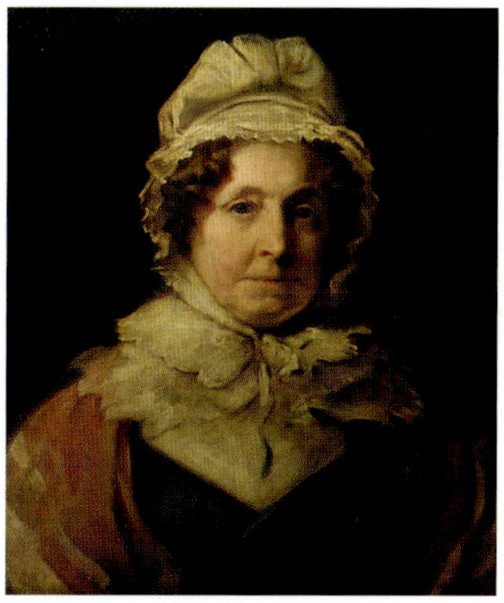

De Wint, Peter 1784–1849
Portrait of the Artist's Mother
oil on canvas 59.5 x 53.2
LCNUG 1927.1813

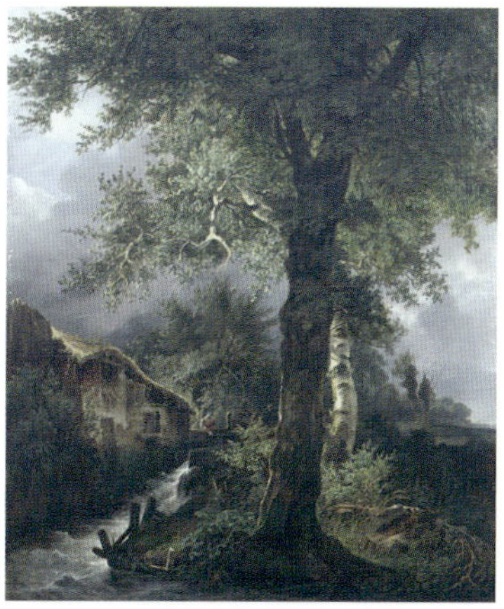

Delvaux, Edouard 1806–1862
Trees by the Side of a Watermill 1843
oil on panel 99.7 x 83
LCNUG 1927.907

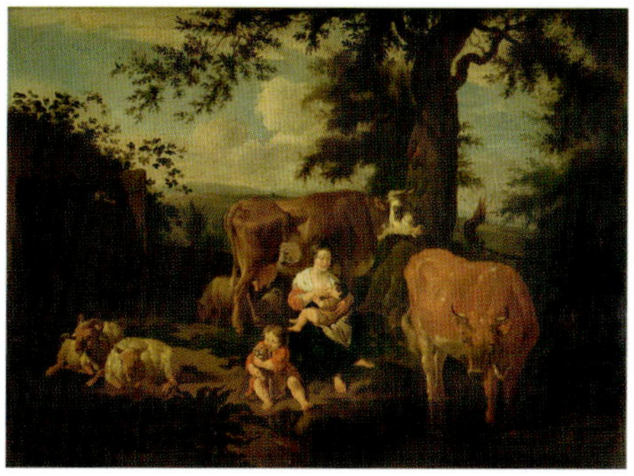

Does, Jacob van der the elder 1623–1673
Mother and Child with Cattle in a Landscape
oil on canvas 49.5 x 65
LCNUG 1927.1528

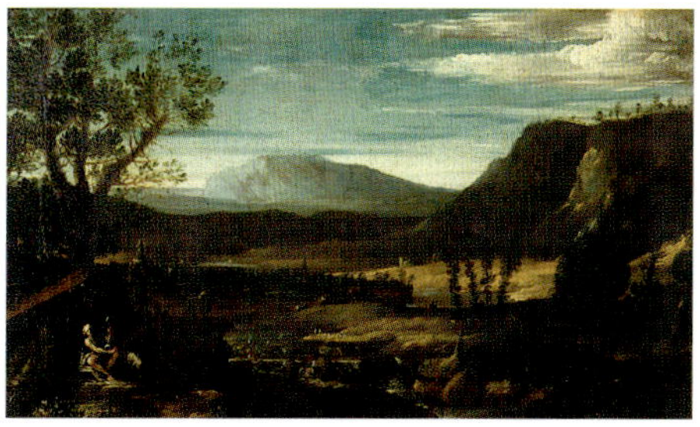

Domenichino (attributed to) 1581–1641
Saint John in a Mountain Landscape
oil on canvas 32 x 50.5
LCNUG 1927.1529

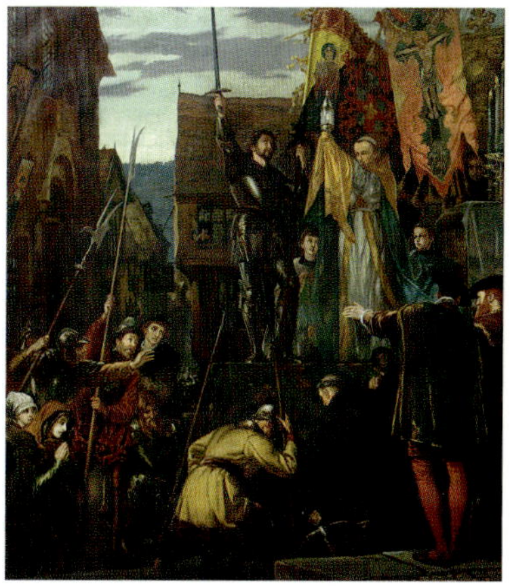

Donaldson, Andrew Benjamin 1840–1919
The Beginning of the Pilgrimage of Grace Lincoln, 1537
oil on canvas 153 x 133.8
LCNUG 1927.234

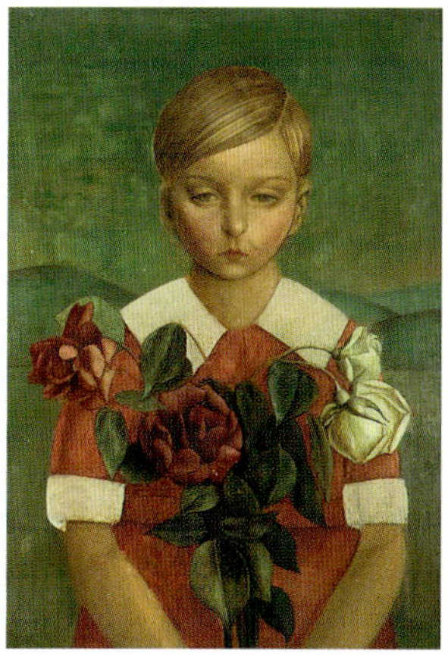

Downton, John 1906–1991
Child with Roses c.1936
tempera on brass 42.8 x 29.1
LCNUG 1997.7

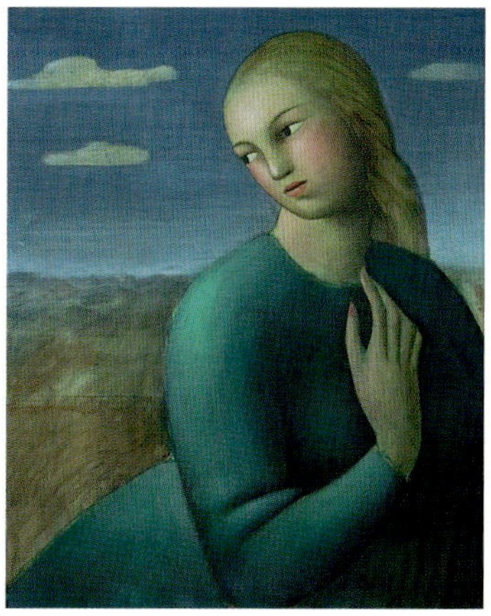

Downton, John 1906–1991
Young Woman in a Landscape 1948
tempera on panel 52.5 x 41
LCNUG 1997.6

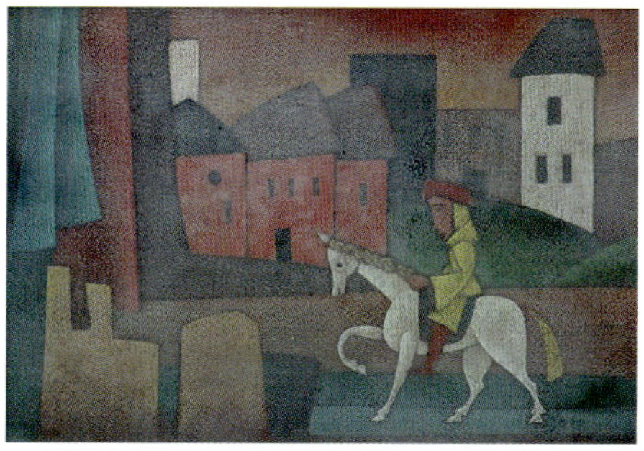

Downton, John 1906–1991
The Arrival
tempera on panel 17.9 x 25.2
LCNUG 1997.4

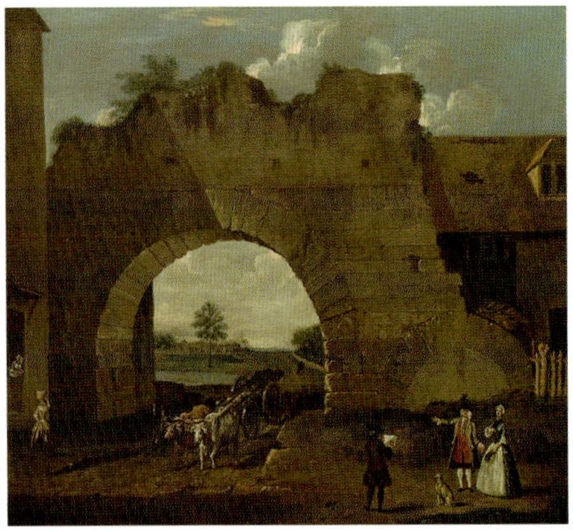

Drake, Nathan c.1728–1778
Newport Arch, Lincoln 1756
oil on canvas 83.5 x 99
LCNUG 1927.47

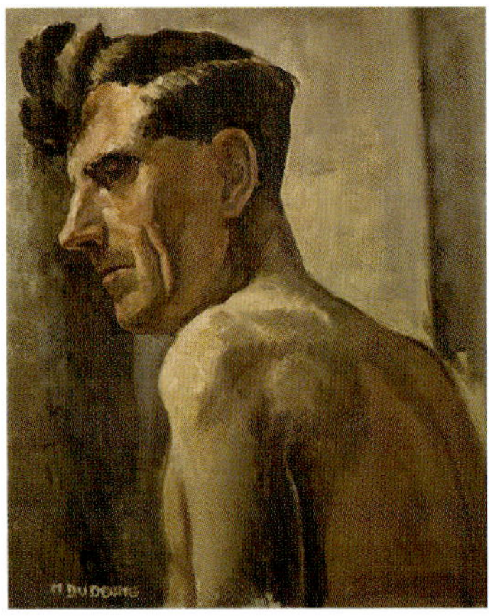

Dudding, Mary 1914–1994
A Lincoln Model
oil on canvas 50.9 x 40.7
LCNUG 1992.4

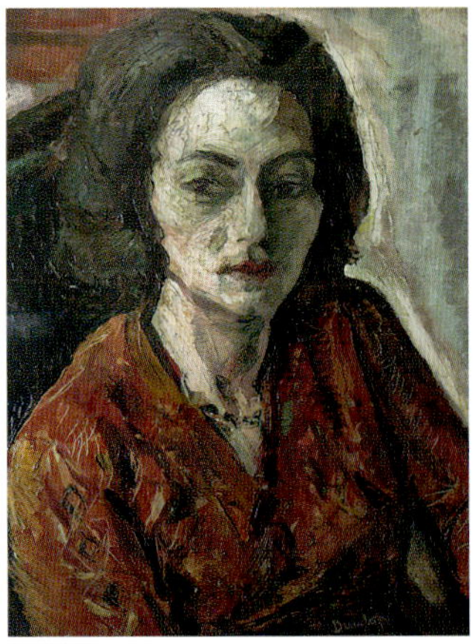

Dunlop, Ronald Ossory 1894–1973
The Girl of Montparnasse 1932
oil on canvas 60.5 x 44
LCNUG 1985.32

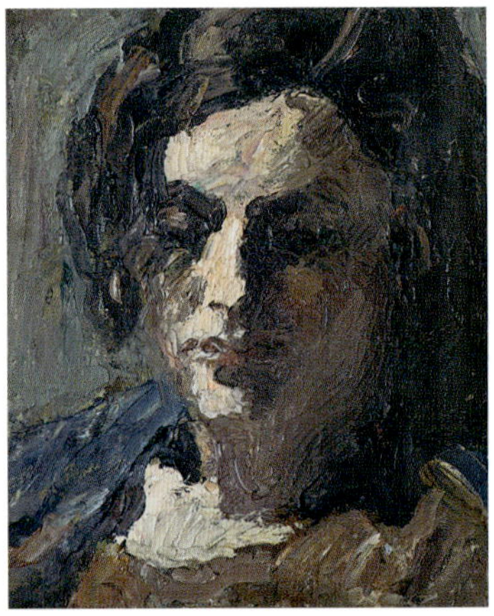

Dunlop, Ronald Ossory 1894–1973
Girl's Head
oil on board 33.4 x 27.3
LCNUG 1985.22

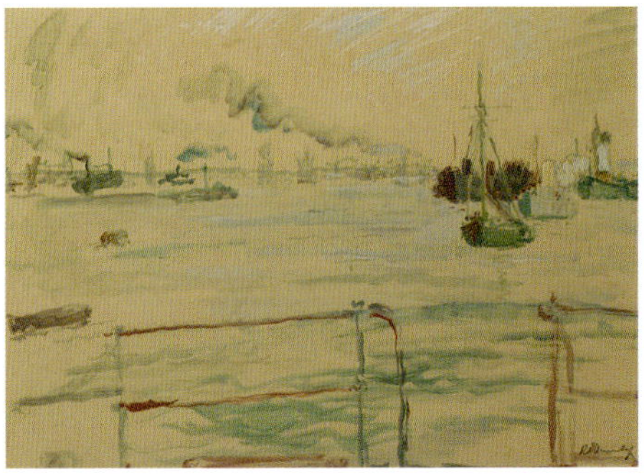

Dunlop, Ronald Ossory 1894–1973
Gravesend, Kent
oil wash on paper 35.5 x 48.5
LCNUG 1985.29

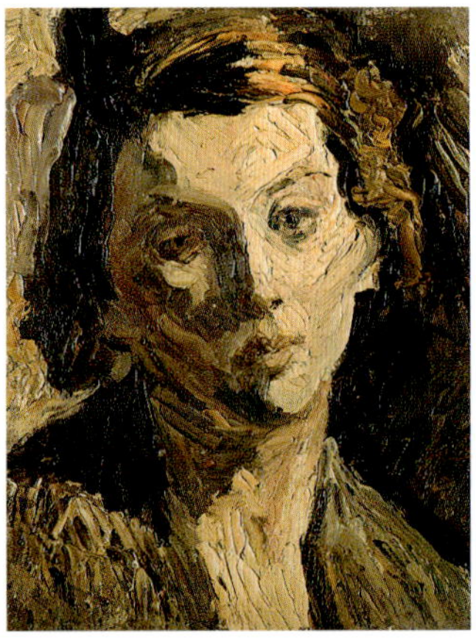

Dunlop, Ronald Ossory 1894–1973
Head of a Girl
oil on canvas 40.5 x 30.5
LCNUG 1985.23

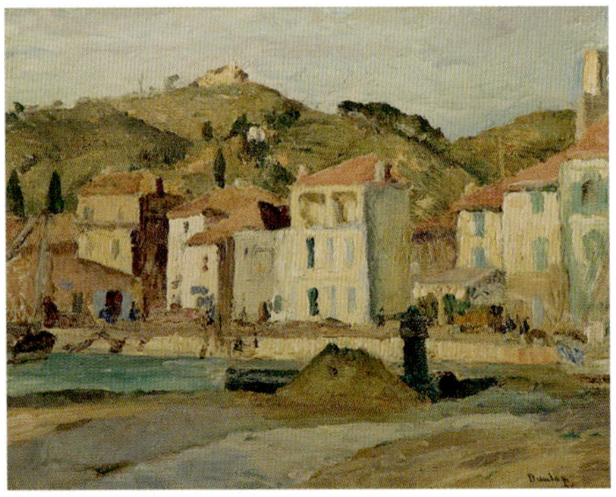

Dunlop, Ronald Ossory 1894–1973
Martigues, France
oil on canvas 40.5 x 50.7
LCNUG 1985.24

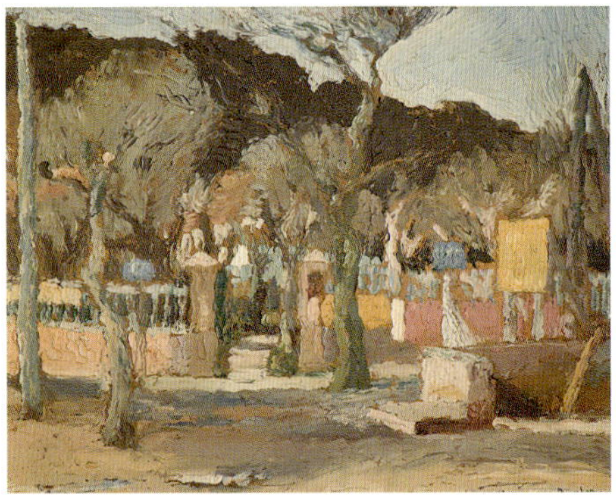

Dunlop, Ronald Ossory 1894–1973
Near Cannes, France
oil on panel 40 x 50
LCNUG 1985.26

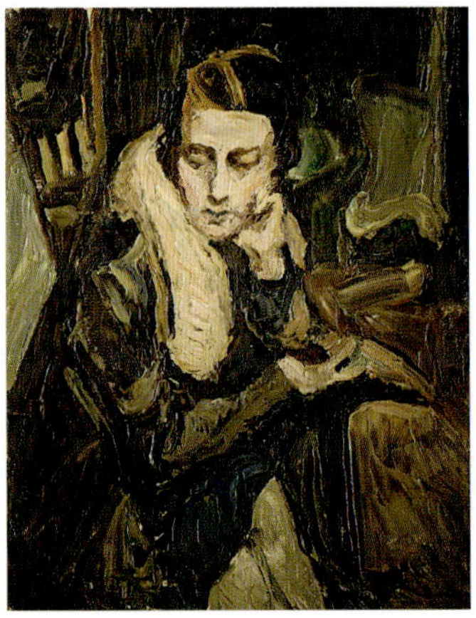

Dunlop, Ronald Ossory 1894–1973
Portrait of an Unknown Woman
oil on canvas 66 x 51
LCNUG 1985.31

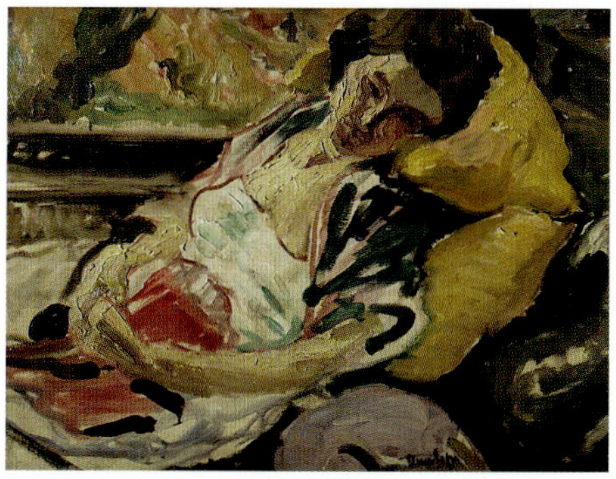

Dunlop, Ronald Ossory 1894–1973
Portrait of an Unknown Woman
oil on canvas 51 x 66
LCNUG 1985.33

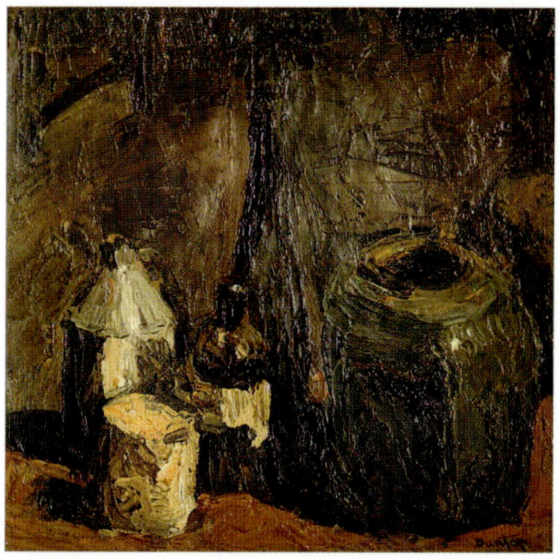

Dunlop, Ronald Ossory 1894–1973
Still Life
oil on canvas 44.7 x 44.7
LCNUG 1985.28

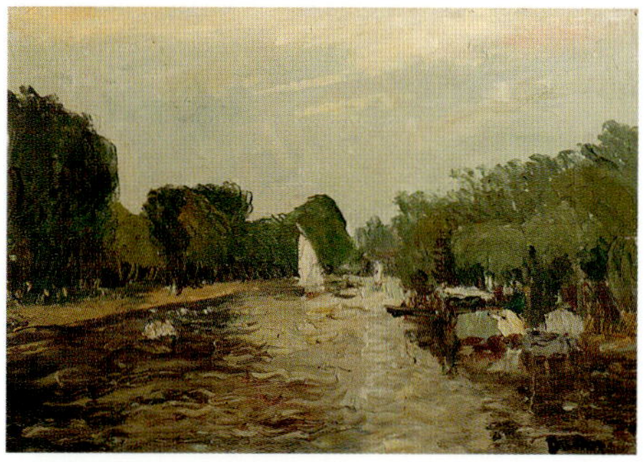

Dunlop, Ronald Ossory 1894–1973
Teddington, Middlesex
oil on canvas 25 x 35.5
LCNUG 1985.25

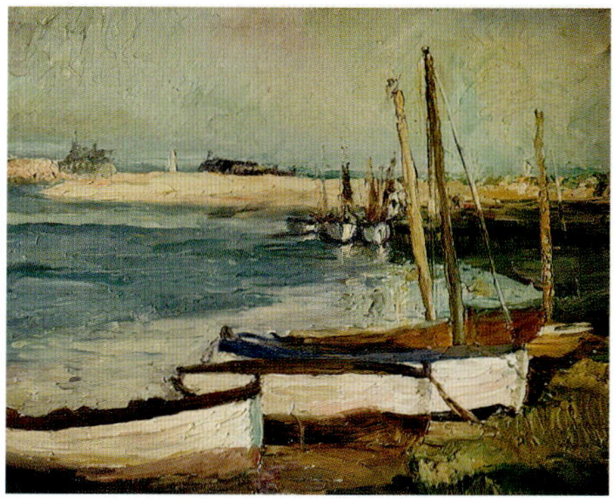

Dunlop, Ronald Ossory 1894–1973
Walberswick, Suffolk
oil on canvas 40.6 x 50.8
LCNUG 1985.27

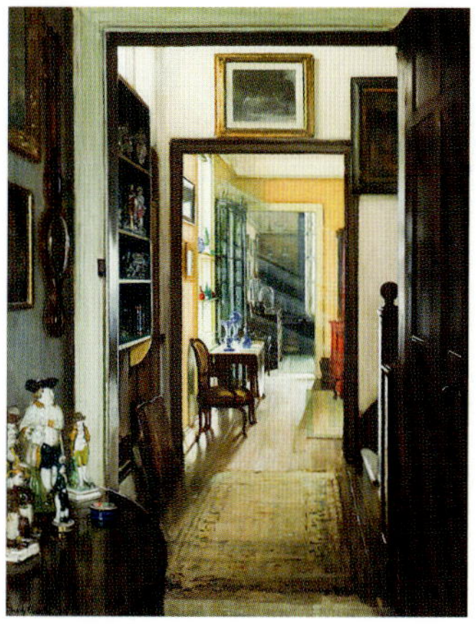

Elwell, Frederick William 1870–1958
Bric-à-brac 1931
oil on canvas 91.4 x 71.1
LCNUG 1927.1586

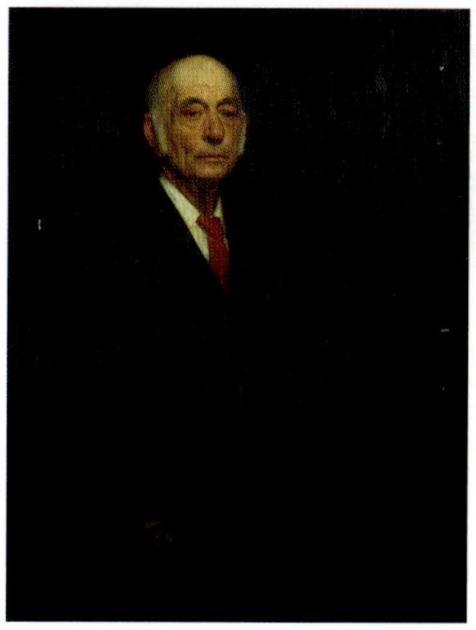

Enderby, Samuel George 1860–1921
Portrait Study 1906
oil on canvas 109 x 81
LCNUG 1927.236

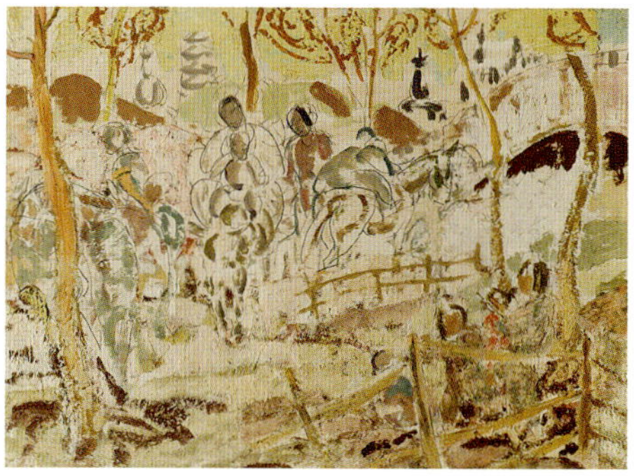

Fairweather, Ian 1891–1974
Outside Hangchow, China 1930–1939
oil & pencil on paper 45 x 61
LCNUG 1985.34

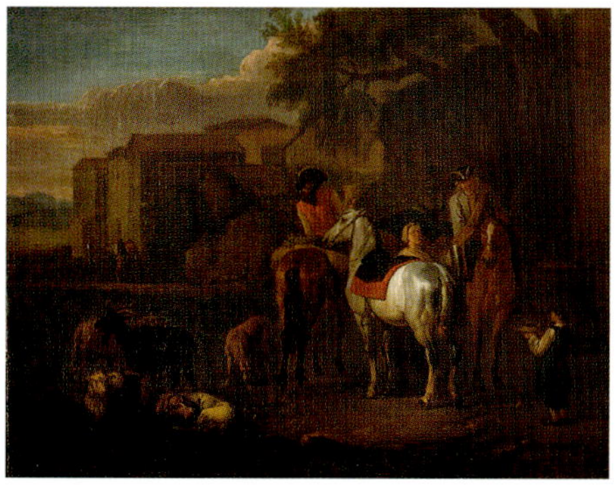

Falens, Carel van 1683–1733
Soldier on Horseback
oil on canvas 48.8 x 60.6
LCNUG 1980.6

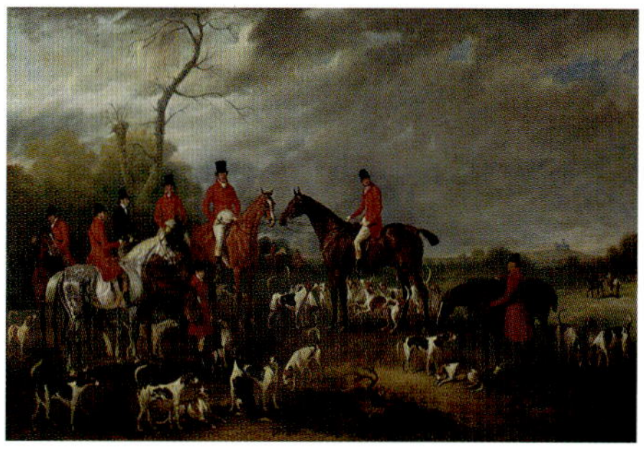

Ferneley, John E. 1782–1860
The Burton Hunt 1830
oil on canvas 152.3 x 246.3
LCNUG 1975.1

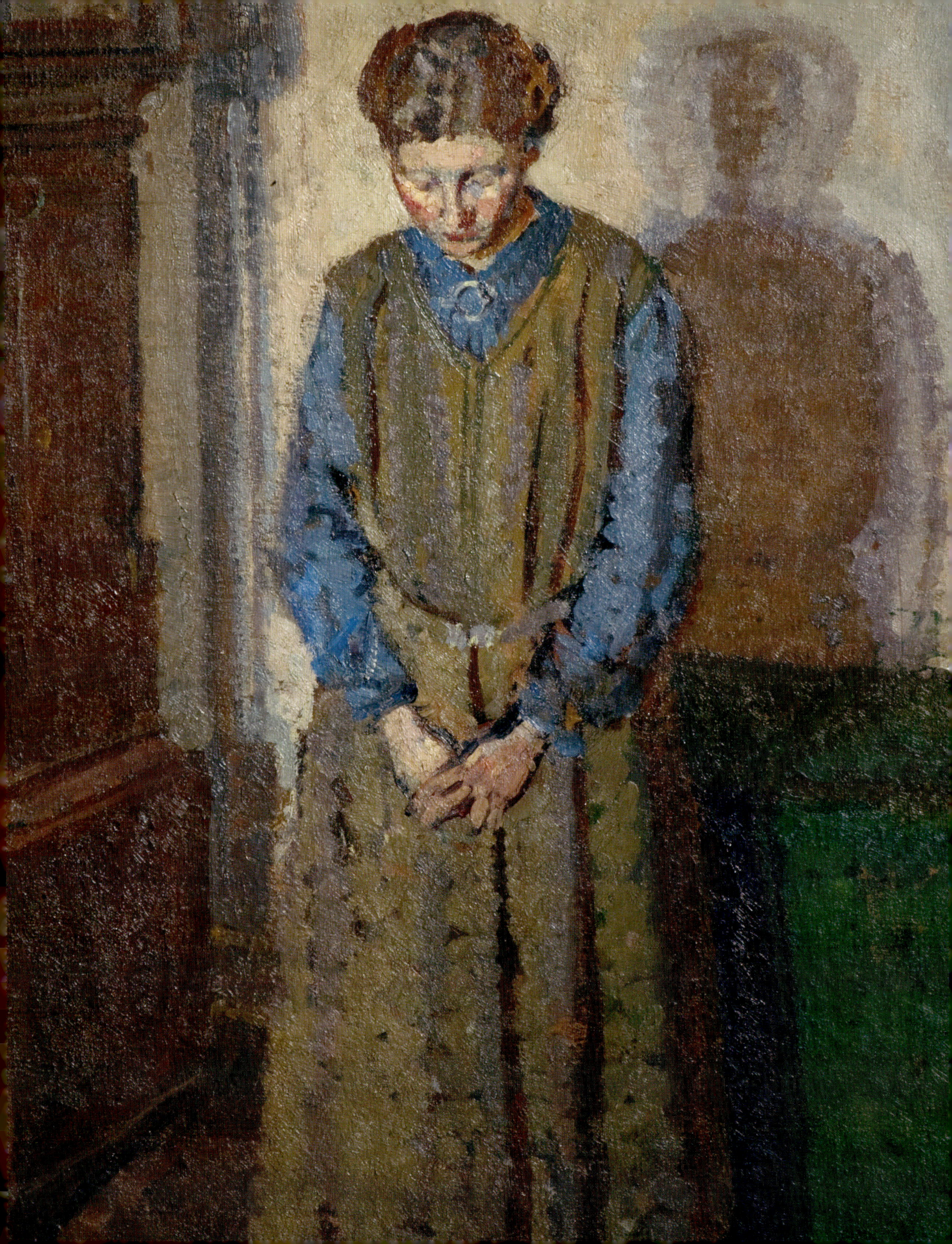

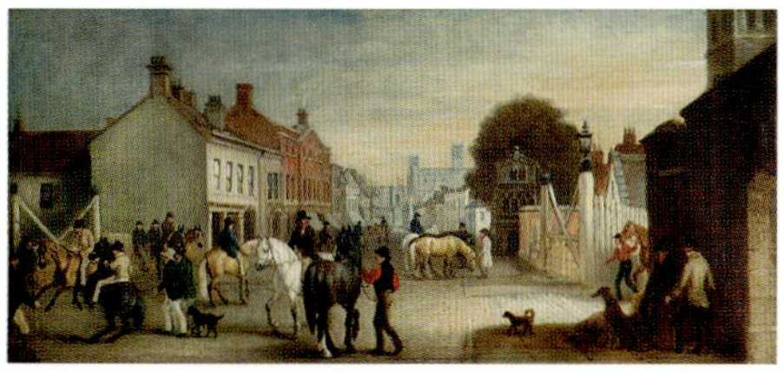

Ferneley, John E. 1782–1860
Lincoln High Street, Two Years after the Coming of the Railways
oil on canvas 33 x 66
LCNUG 1927.2231

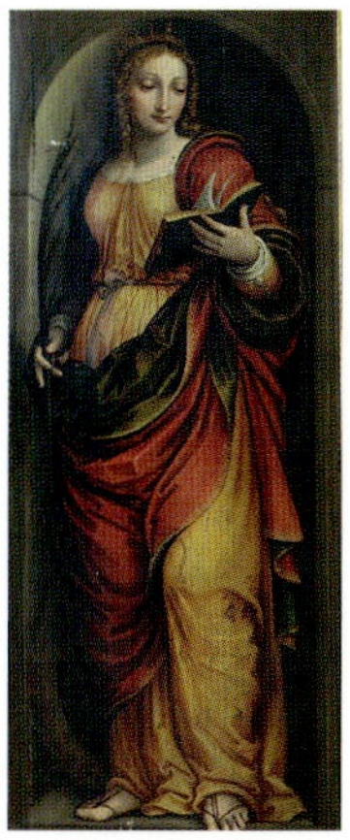

Ferrari, Gaudenzio c.1470–1546
Saint Catherine of Alexandria
oil on panel 190 x 68.5
LCNUG 1927.648

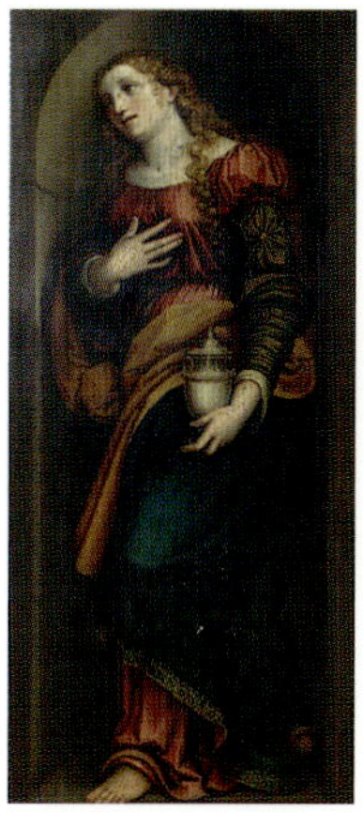

Ferrari, Gaudenzio c.1470–1546
Saint Mary Magdalene
oil on panel 193 x 68.5
LCNUG 1927.647

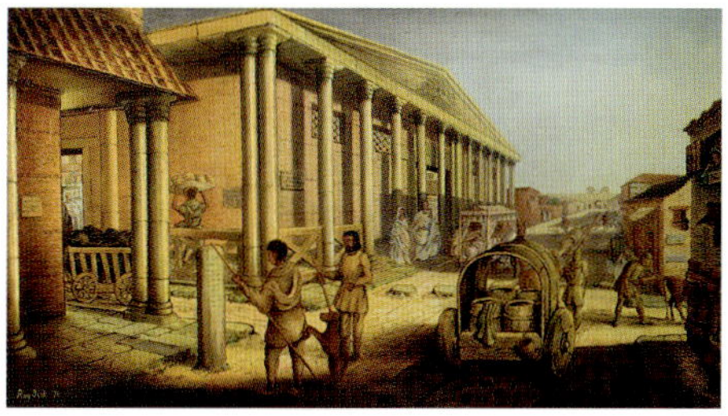

Fisk, Roy 1916–2008
Roman Bailgate, Lincoln 1978
oil on canvas 84 x 150.3
LCNUG 1979.78

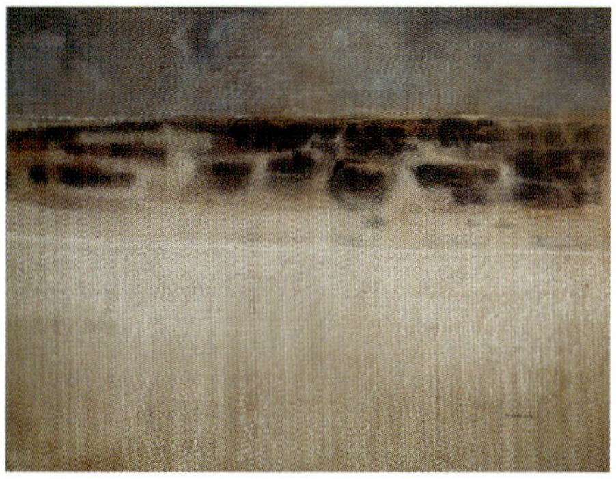

Flanagan, Terence Philip 1929–2011
Sand Dunes
oil on canvas 46 x 61
LCNUG 1972.2

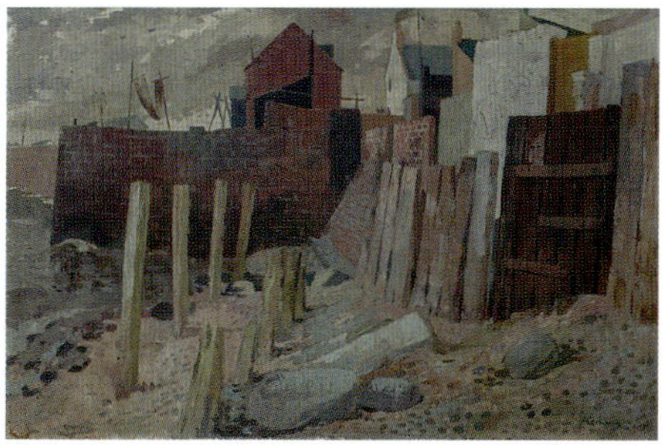

Fleming, Ian 1906–1994
Danger Point, Arbroath, Scotland 1949
oil on canvas 61.5 x 91.5
LCNUG 1988.2

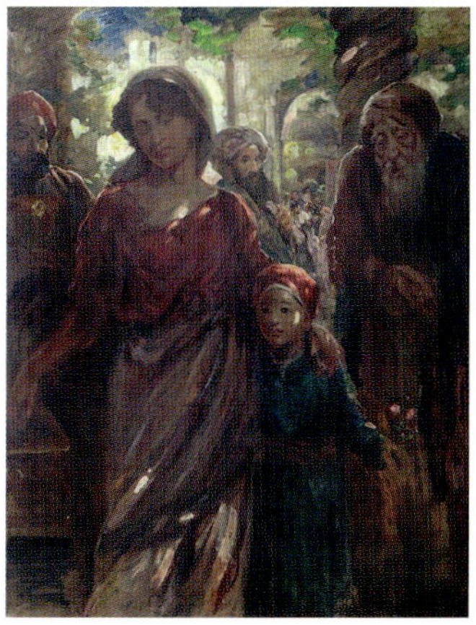

Fowler, Robert 1853–1926
The Widow's Mite
oil on canvas 127.5 x 102
LCNUG 1927.130

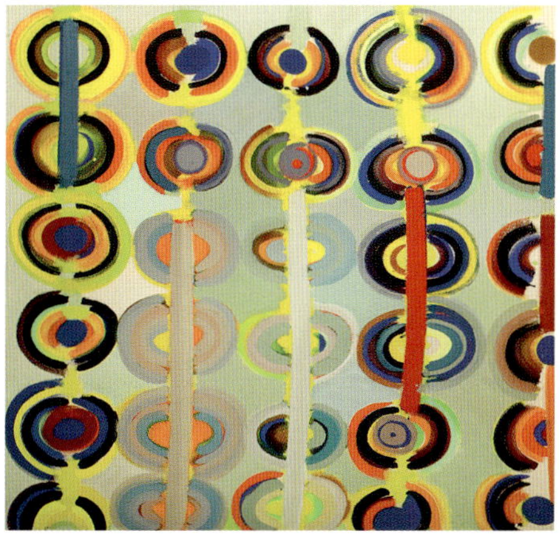

Frost, Terry 1915–2003
Autumn Rings Andeuze, September 1971 1983
acrylic on canvas 164.2 x 164.2
LCNUG 1986.11

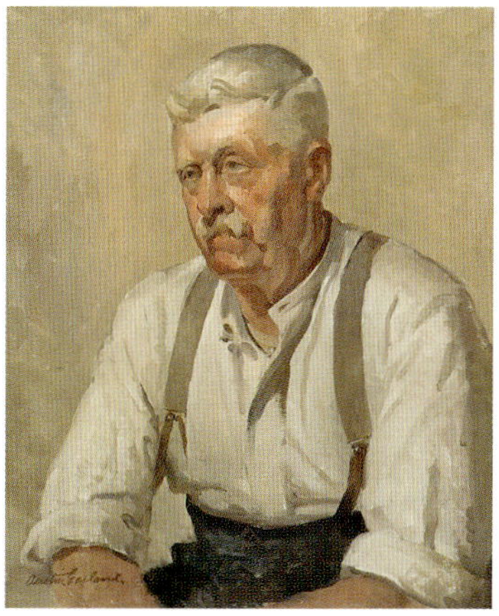

Garland, Austin 1887–1966
Portrait of an Unknown Man
oil on canvas 58 x 48
LCNUG 1927.1734

Facing page: Gilman, Harold, 1876–1919, *Meditation* (detail), 1910–1911, Leicester Arts and Museums Service (p. 45)

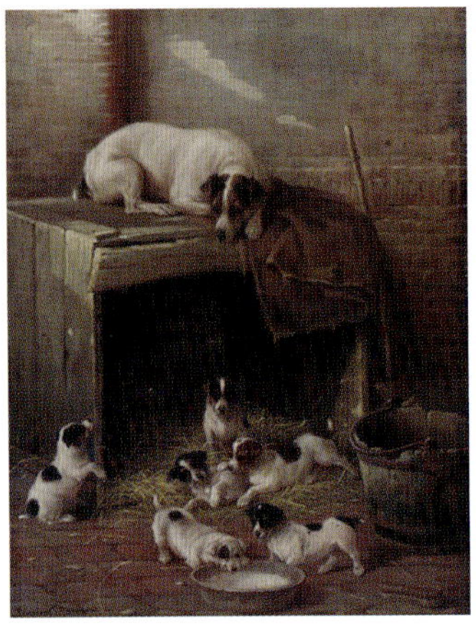

Garland, Valentine Thomas 1840–1914
An Anxious Mother 1891
oil on canvas 33.2 x 25.6
LCNUG 1927.237

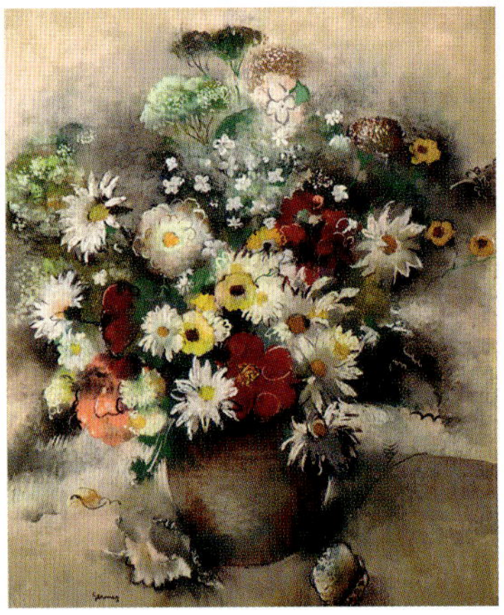

Gernez, Paul-Elie 1888–1948
Dahlias et marguerites
oil on canvas 54 x 45.5
LCNUG 1985.36

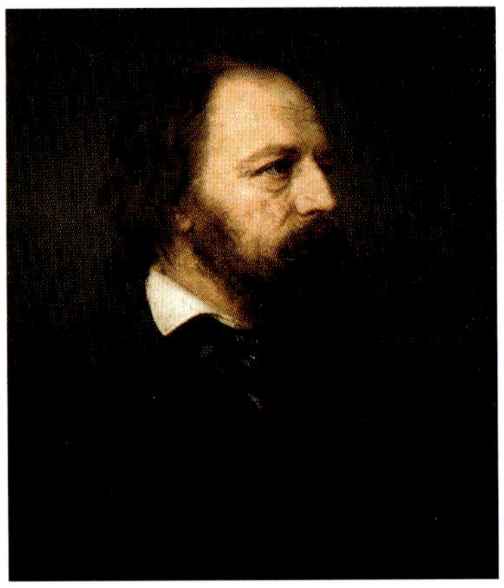

Girardot, Ernest Gustave 1840–1904
Alfred Tennyson (1809–1892)
oil on canvas 57 x 47
TENN.T2010.05

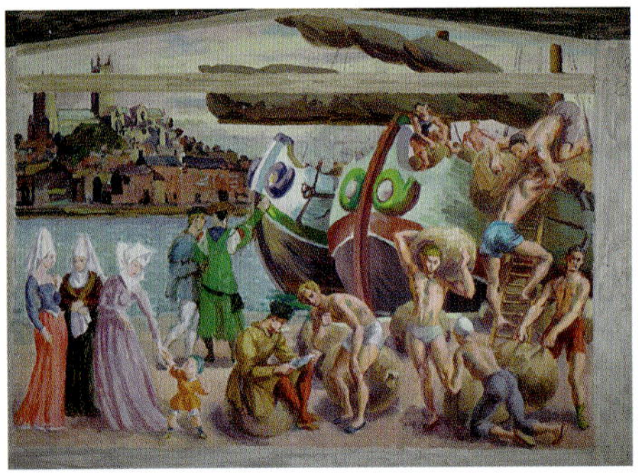

Grant, Duncan 1885–1978
The Wool Staple in Medieval Lincoln c.1957
oil on wood 77 x 105
LCNUG 1999.4

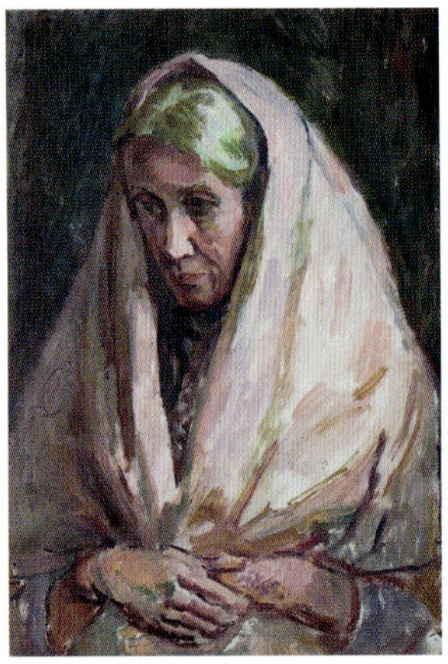

Grant, Duncan 1885–1978
Woman in a Shawl c.1957
oil on paper 55 x 37
LCNUG 1990.10

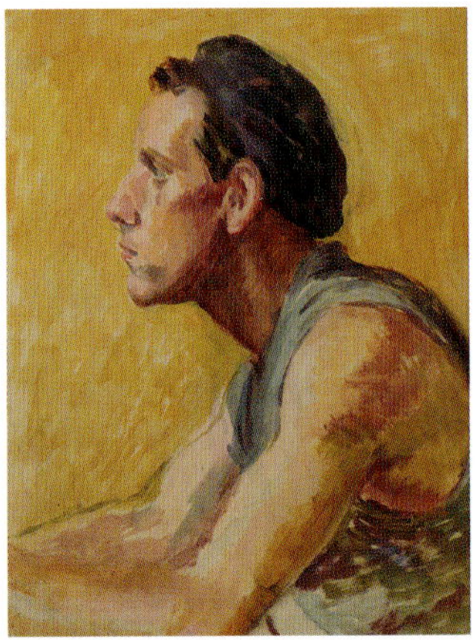

Grant, Duncan 1885–1978
Sheep Shearer (study for 'The Russell Chantry, Lincoln Cathedral')
oil on paper 50.5 x 38
LCNUG 2007.18

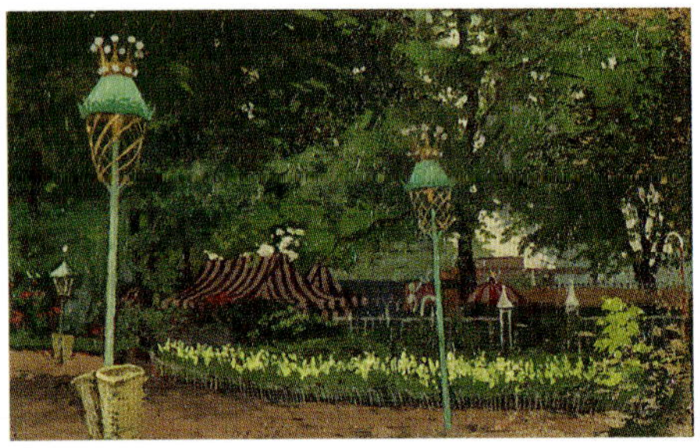

Green, Margaret 1925–2003
Festival Gardens
oil on board 18 x 27.7
LCNUG 1985.37

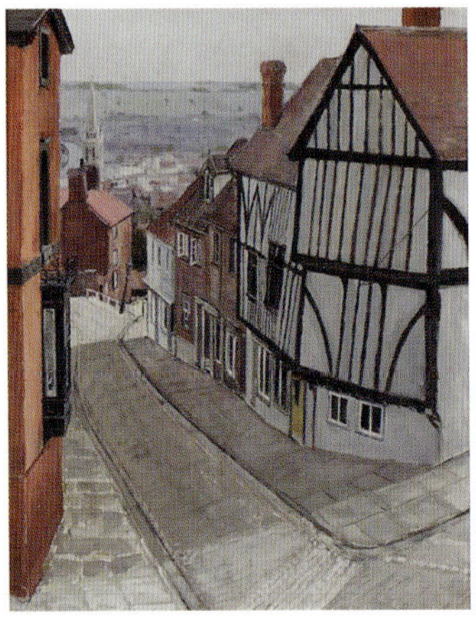

Gribble, Kenneth 1925–1995
Steep Hill, Lincoln
oil on canvas 91.5 x 71
LCNUG 1927.2629

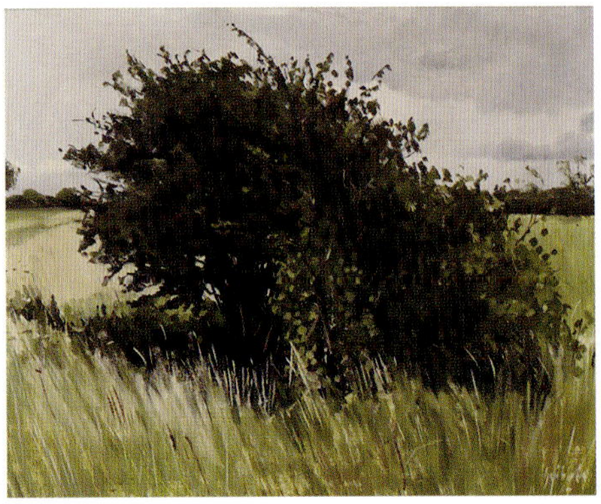

Gribble, Kenneth 1925–1995
The Spinney
oil on board 51 x 61
LCNUG 1927.2571

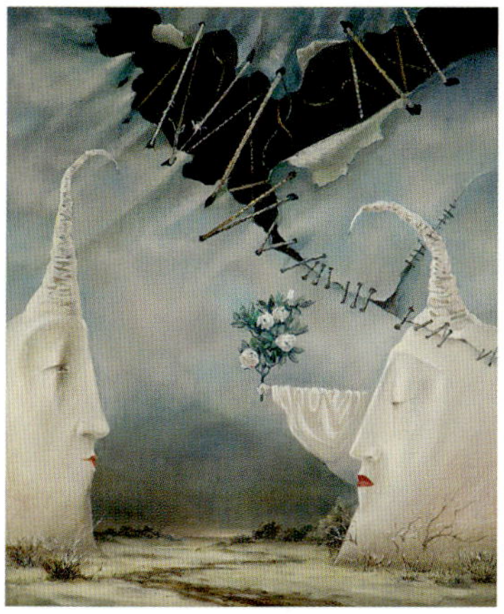

Grigoriev, Alexei b.1949
Bound by Love 1997
oil & gesso on canvas & wood 52 x 43
LCNUG 1997.13

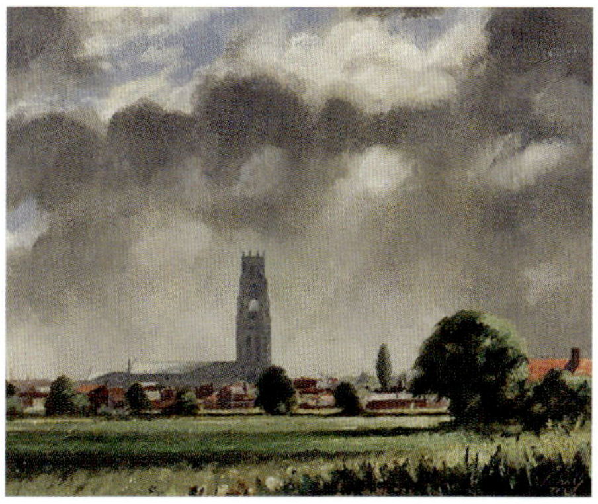

Grimble, John d.1997
Boston Skyline, Lincolnshire
oil on canvas 26 x 31.1
LCNUG 1927.2743

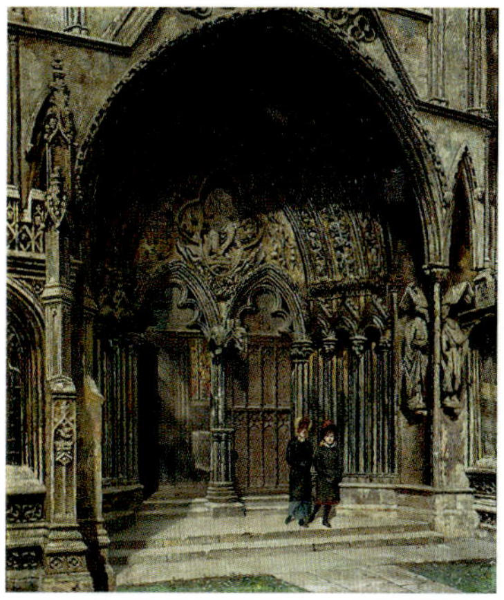

Hall, Frederick 1860–1948
The Judgement Porch, Lincoln Cathedral 1881
oil on canvas 61.2 x 51.2
LCNUG 1985.4

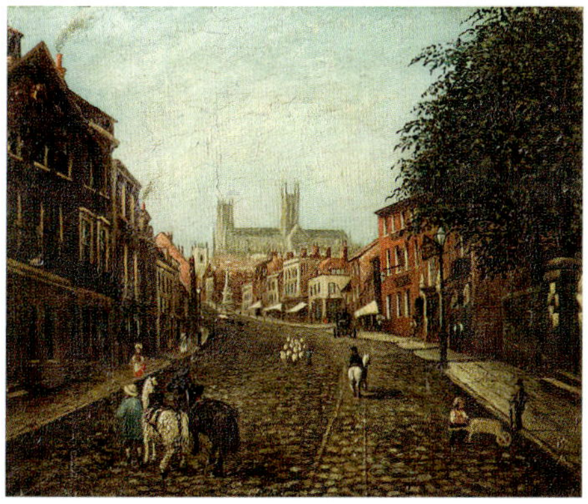

Hall, Henry active late 19th C
Distant View of Lincoln Cathedral from the South
oil on canvas 16.5 x 19
LCNUG 1980.4

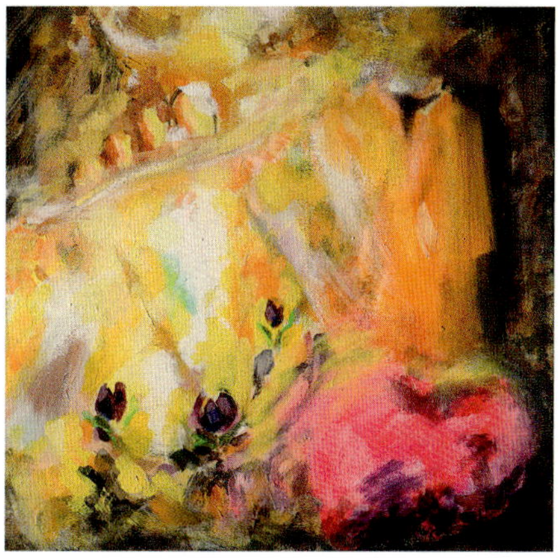

Hammad, Medina b.1963
Father's Robe, Fountain Lamp and Satin Cushion 1991
oil or acrylic on canvas 36 x 35.5
LCNUG 1991.11

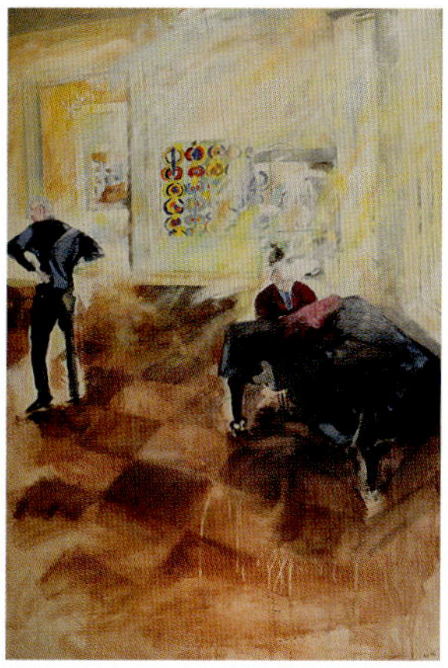

Hammad, Medina b.1963
Fred and Trevor 1995
oil on canvas 149.2 x 99.3
LCNUG 1995.66

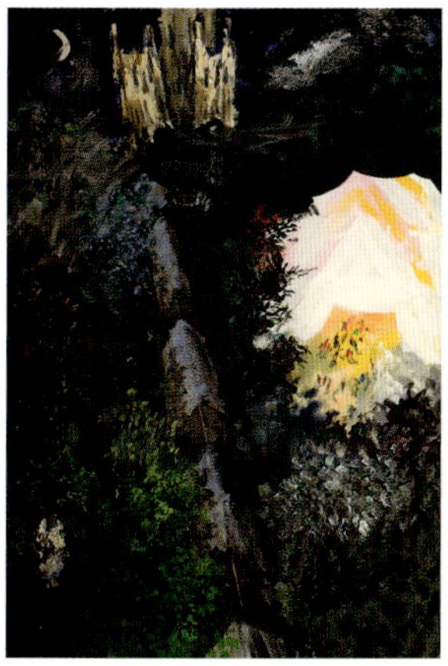

Hammad, Medina b.1963
Midsummer Ball 1995
oil on canvas 149.2 x 99.3
LCNUG 1995.68

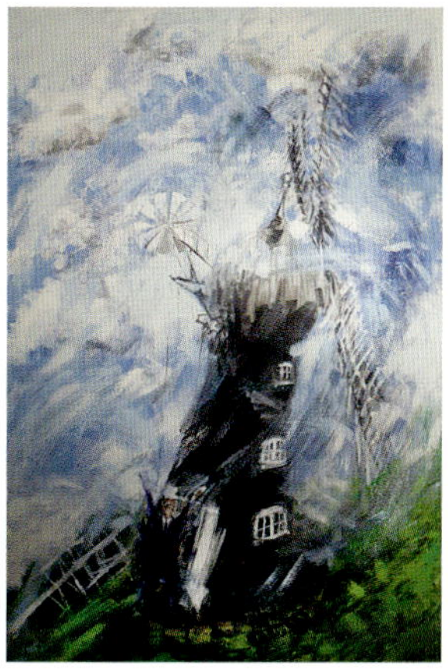

Hammad, Medina b.1963
From Sea to Sky
oil on canvas 149.2 x 99.3
LCNUG 1995.67

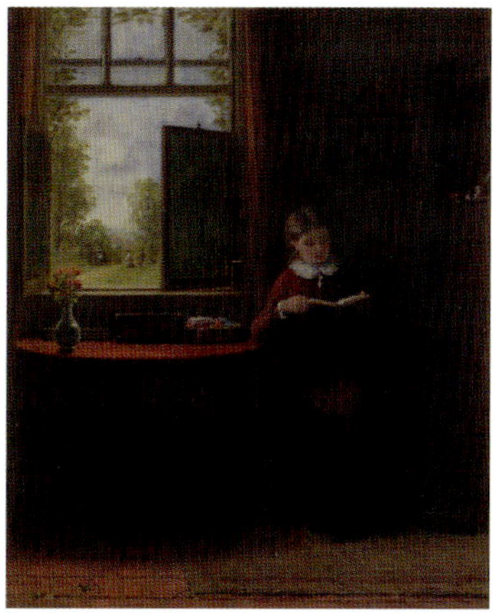

Hardy, Frederick Daniel 1827–1911
An Interesting Story 1884
oil on panel 30.4 x 25.1
LCNUG 1927.241

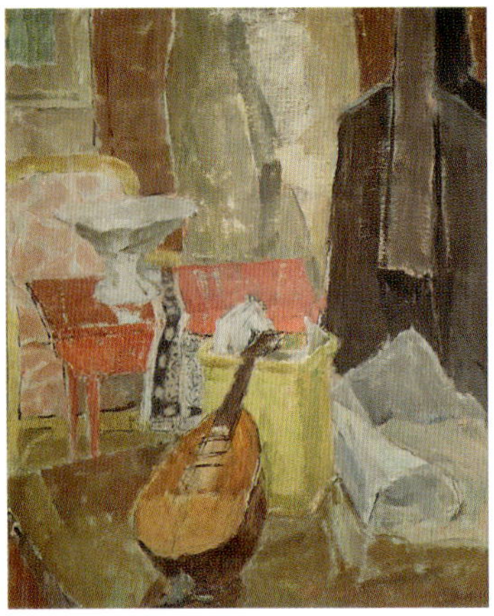

Hartnell, Kathleen 1886–c.1965
Still Life
oil on canvas 74.4 x 61
LCNUG 1985.38

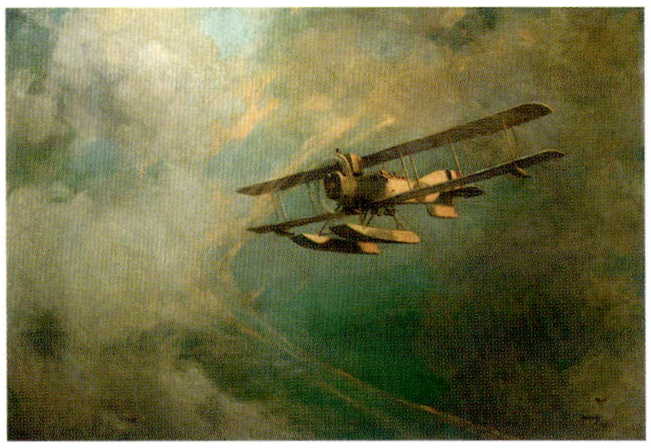

Hassall, John 1868–1948
Short Seaplane 1915
oil on canvas 101 x 150
LCNUG 2001.44

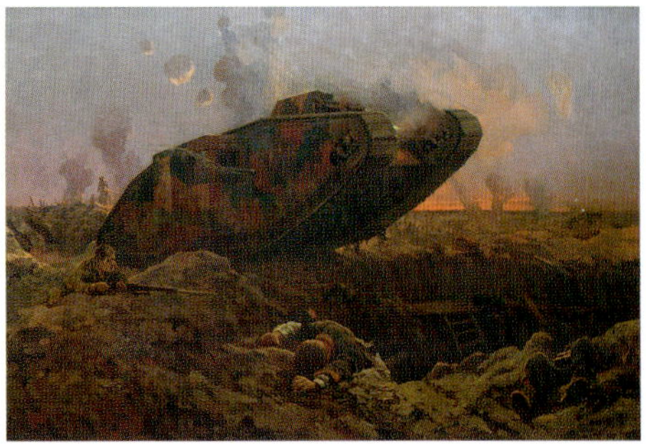

Hassall, John 1868–1948
A Tank in Action
oil on canvas 101.7 x 152
LCNUG 1927.2667

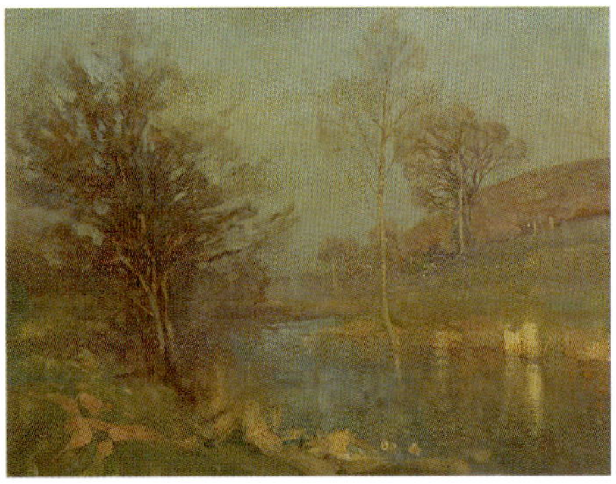

Haughton, Benjamin 1865–1924
Winter Morning on the Otter
oil on panel 32 x 39
LCNUG 1927.674

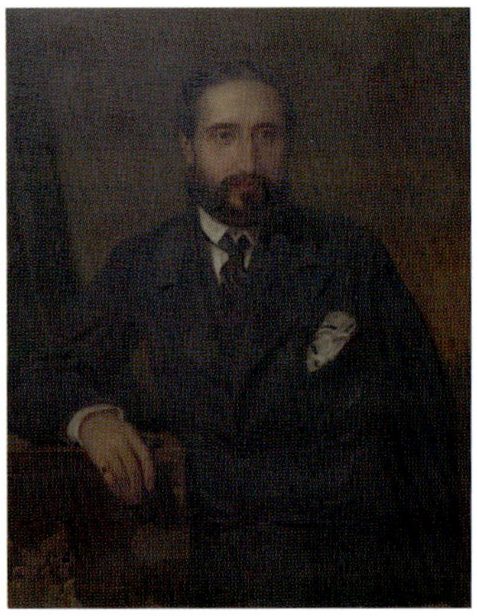

Havell, Edmund the younger 1819–1894
Henry A. M. Waldo Sibthorp 1873
oil on canvas 90.5 x 68
LCNUG 1972.148

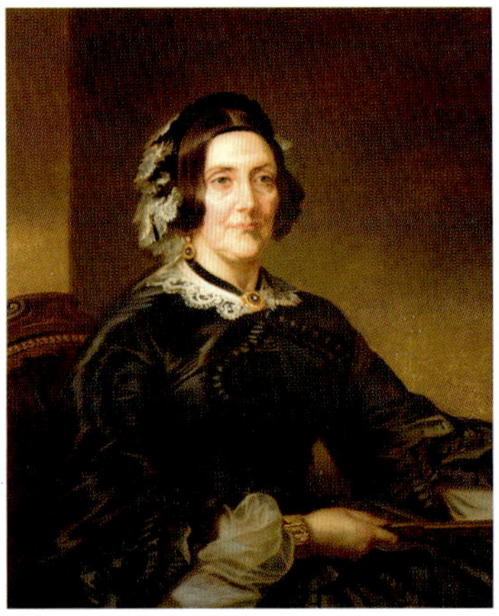

Havell, Edmund the younger 1819–1894
Maria, Widow of Charles Delaet Waldo Sibthorp
oil on canvas 89.5 x 69
LCNUG 1972.146

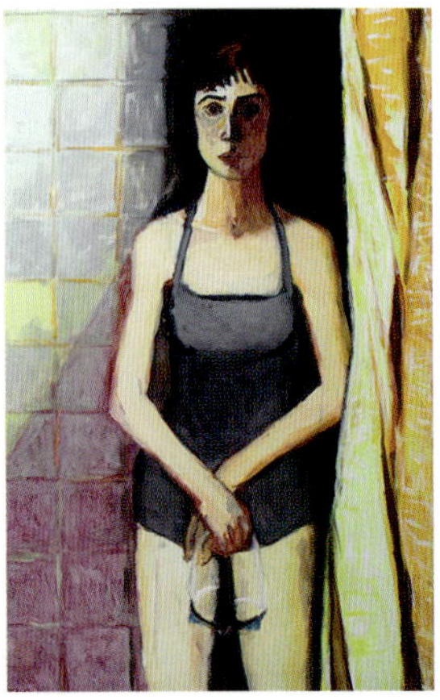

Held, Julie b.1958
The Swimmer (Cosham Painting) 1996
oil on canvas 175 x 143
LCNUG 1996.7

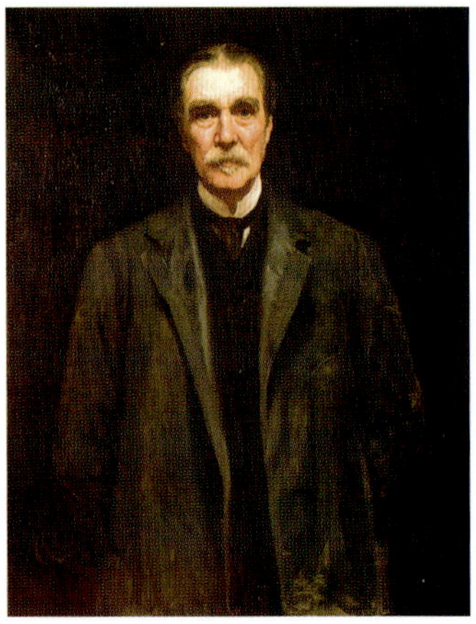

Herkomer, Hubert von 1849–1914
Captain Philip Blundell Bicknell (1818–1905)
oil on canvas 112.2 x 86.3
LCNUG 1985.72

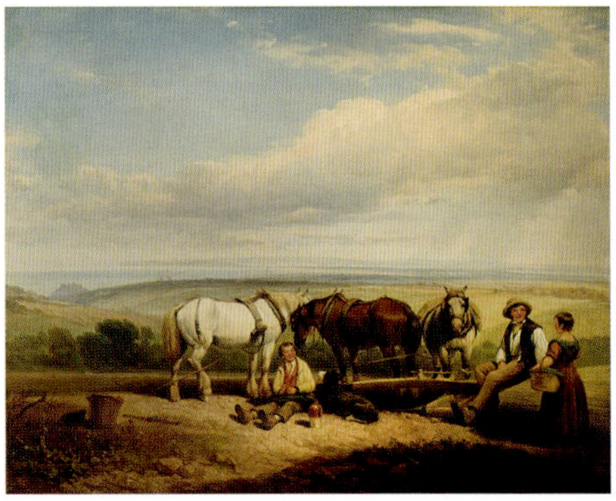

Herring, John Frederick I 1795–1865
Midday Rest
oil on canvas 110.5 x 143.5
LCNUG 1927.78

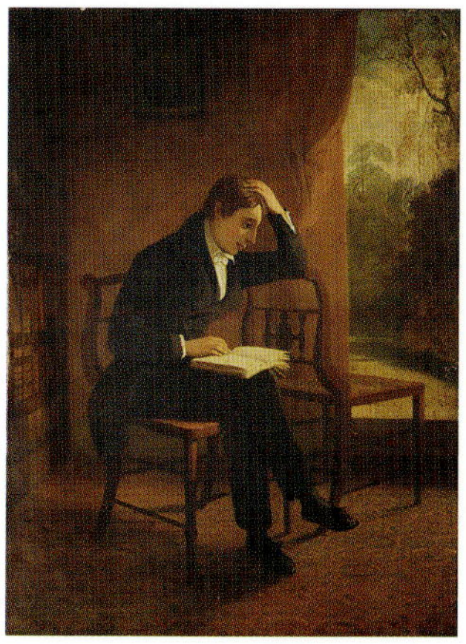

Hilton, Joseph or **Hilton, William II** 1786–1839 or **De Wint, Peter** 1784–1849
John Keats (1795–1821) (copy of Joseph Severn)
oil on canvas 58.5 x 42
LCNUG 1927.1992

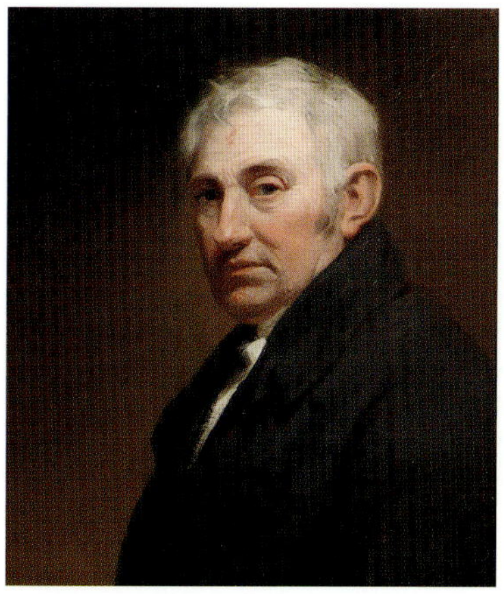

Hilton, William I 1752–1822
Self Portrait
oil on canvas 62.3 x 54
LCNUG 1927.892

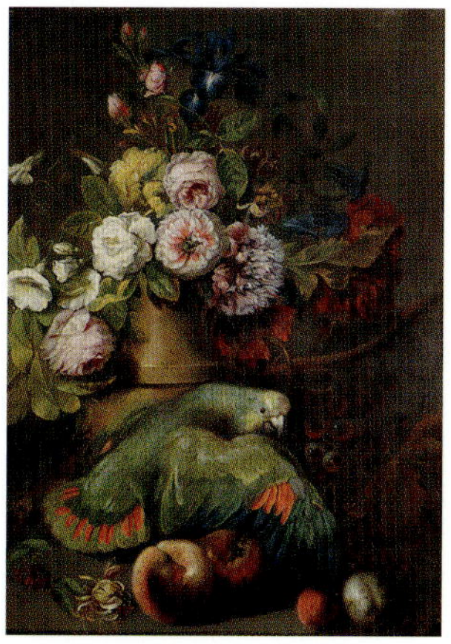

Hilton, William I 1752–1822
Still Life with Parrot
oil on canvas 75 x 52.5
LCNUG 1927.244

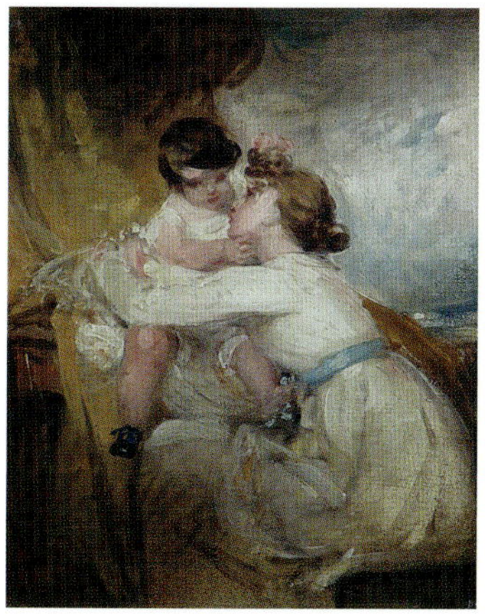

Hilton, William II 1786–1839
Harriet Hilton (1791–1866) and Child (Helen Hilton, 1811–1873) (sketch) c.1812
oil on canvas 28.5 x 23
LCNUG 1994.3

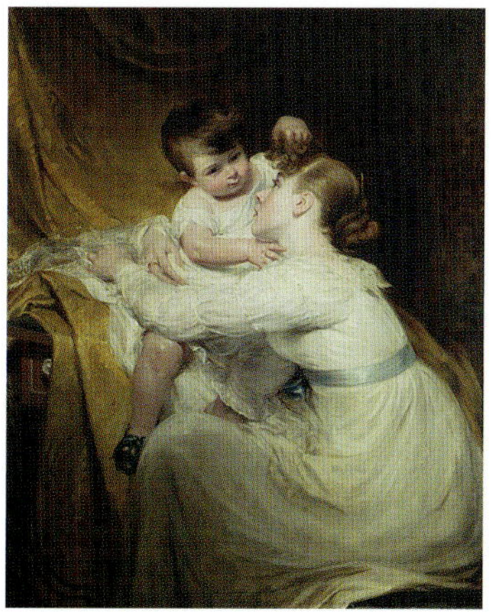

Hilton, William II 1786–1839
Harriet Hilton (1791–1866) and Child (Helen Hilton, 1811–1873)
oil on canvas 127 x 99
LCNUG 1927.881

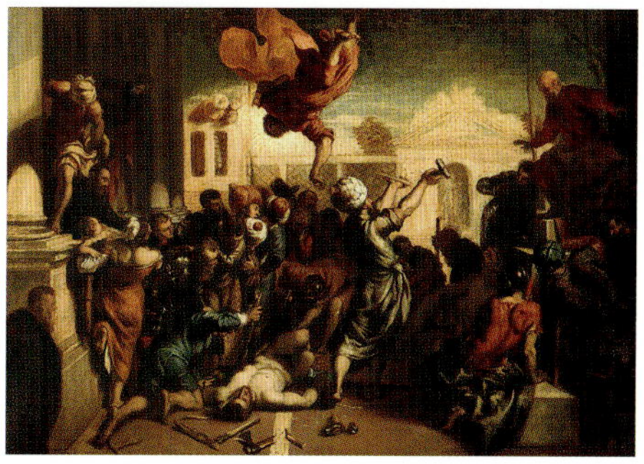

Hilton, William II 1786–1839
The Miracle of Saint Mark (after Jacopo Tintoretto) 1823
oil on canvas 55 x 78
LCNUG 1927.246

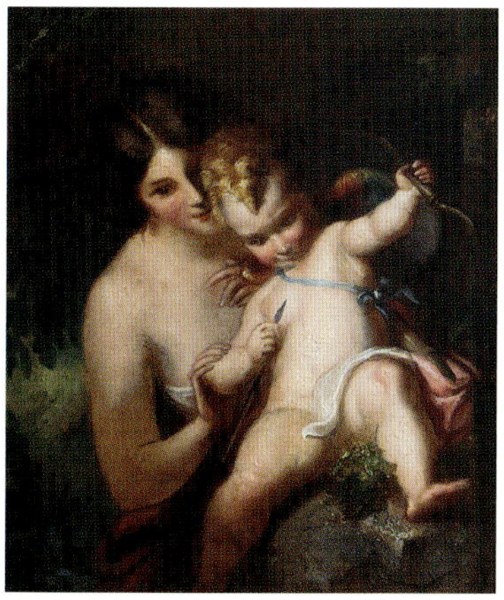

Hilton, William II 1786–1839
Cupid Armed
oil on board 30.5 x 26.5
LCNUG 1927.2085

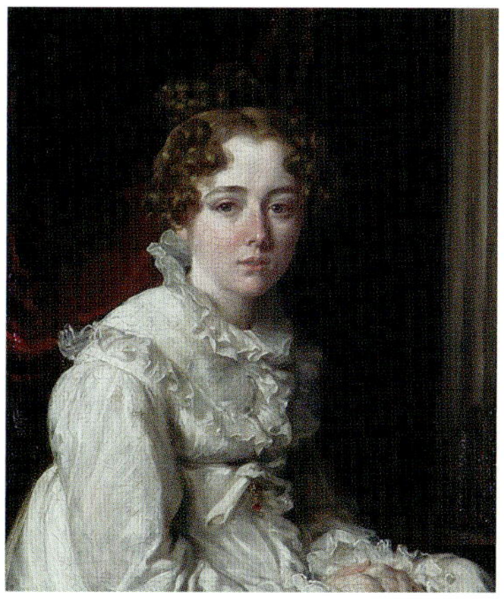

Hilton, William II 1786–1839
Harriet Hilton (1791–1866)
oil on canvas 34.2 x 28.6
LCNUG 1999.3

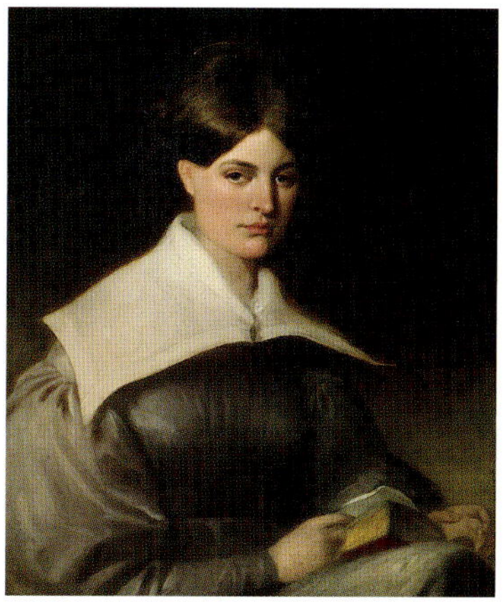

Hilton, William II 1786–1839
Justina Hilton, née Kent
oil on canvas 74 x 61
LCNUG 1927.2574

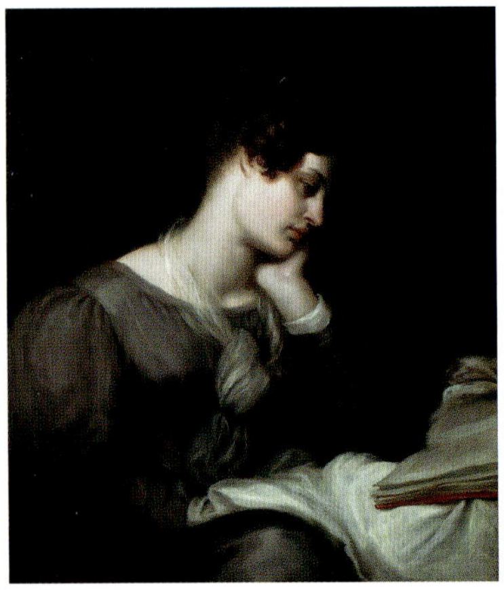

Hilton, William II 1786–1839
Justina Hilton, née Kent
oil on canvas 76 x 63.5
LCNUG 1927.2575

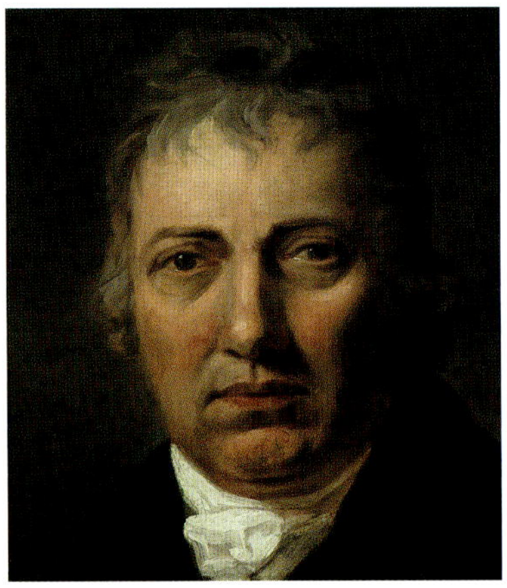

Hilton, William II 1786–1839
Portrait of an Unknown Man
oil on canvas 36 x 30.5
LCNUG 1927.2576

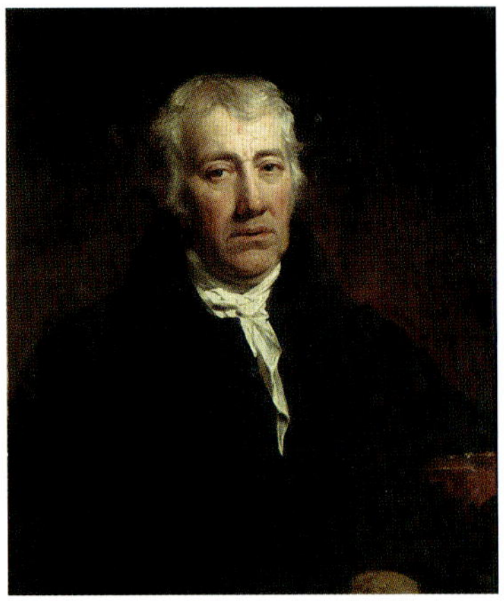

Hilton, William II 1786–1839
Portrait of the Artist's Father
oil on canvas 76 x 62.5
LCNUG 1927.1683

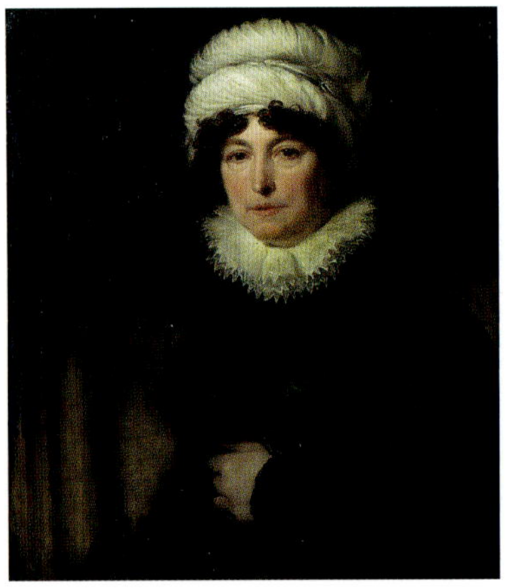

Hilton, William II 1786–1839
Portrait of the Artist's Mother
oil on canvas 76 x 61
LCNUG 1927.1682

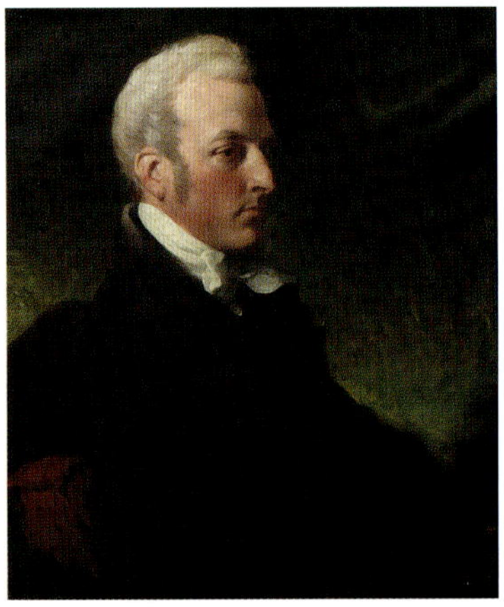

Hilton, William II 1786–1839
Reverend la Tour
oil on canvas 76 x 64
LCNUG 2001.5

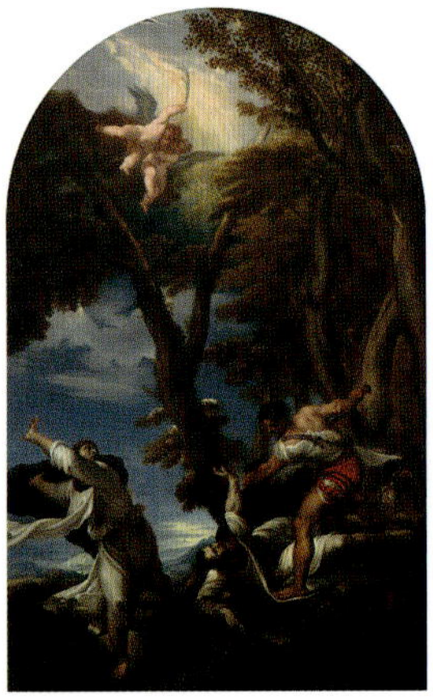

Hilton, William II 1786–1839
Saint Peter, Martyr (after Titian)
oil on canvas 109 x 76
LCNUG 1927.247

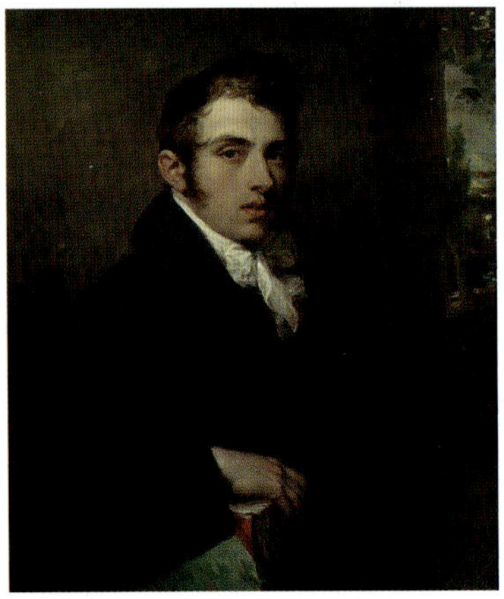

Hilton, William II 1786–1839
Self Portrait
oil on canvas 76 x 61
LCNUG 1927.85

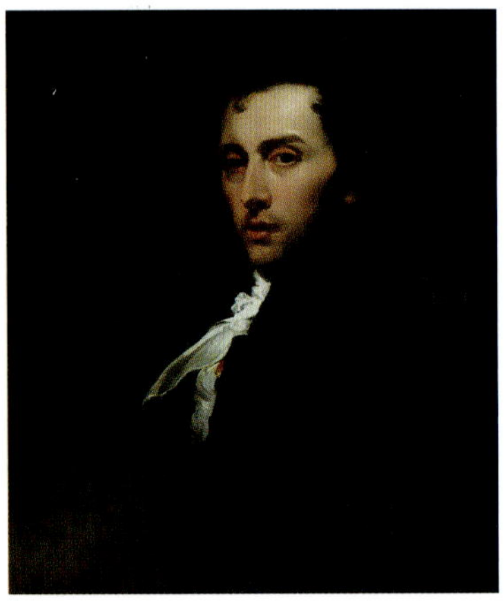

Hilton, William II 1786–1839
Self Portrait
oil on canvas 76.8 x 64.4
LCNUG 1927.2573

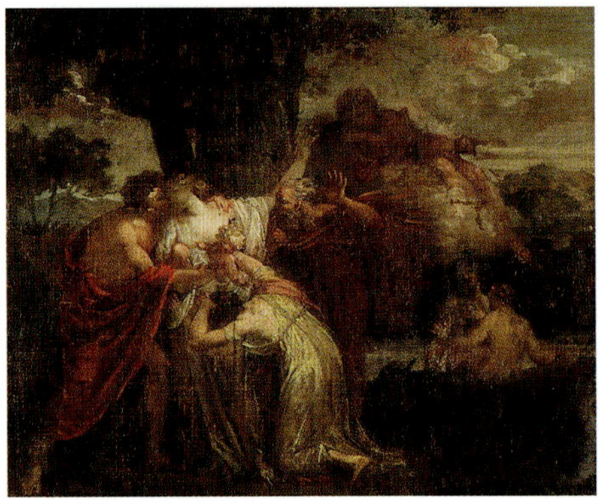

Hilton, William II 1786–1839
Study of a Classical Subject
oil on canvas 33 x 38
LCNUG 1927.814

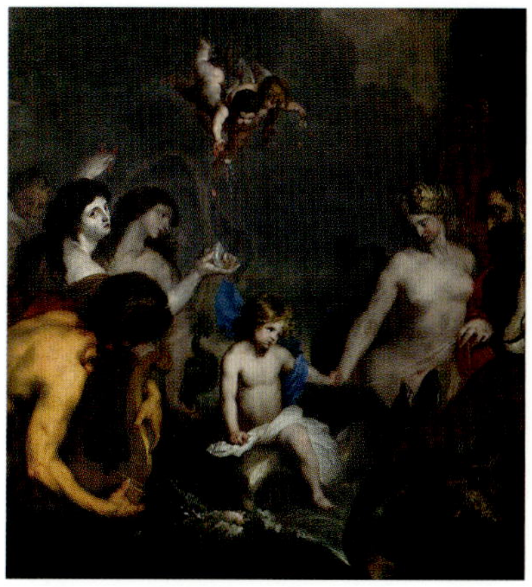

Hilton, William II 1786–1839
The Birth of Triton
oil on canvas 137 x 127.5
LCNUG 1927.2323

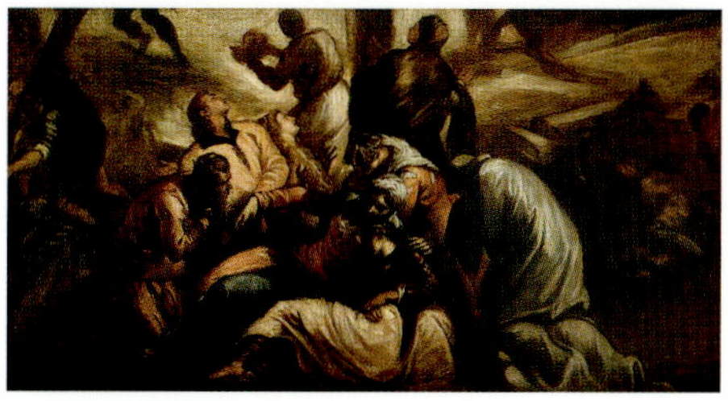

Hilton, William II 1786–1839
The Crucifixion
oil on canvas 44 x 75
LCNUG 1927.243

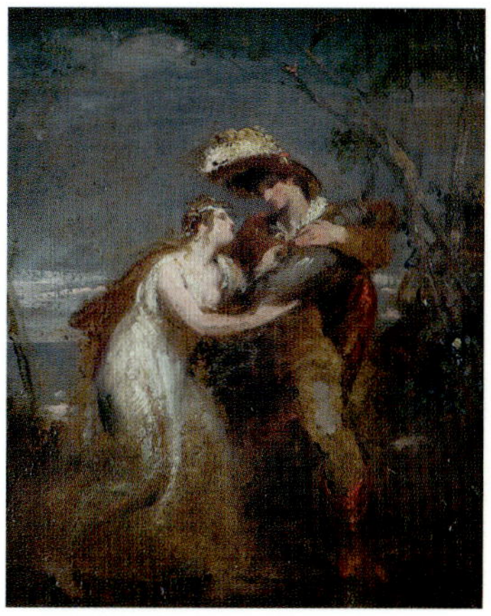

Hilton, William II 1786–1839
The Elopement
oil on panel 43.2 x 31.8
LCNUG 1927.2237

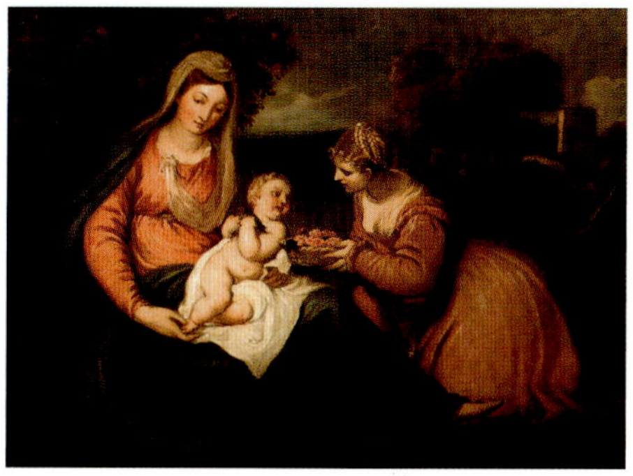

Hilton, William II 1786–1839
The Holy Family (after Jacopo Palma il vecchio)
oil on canvas 56 x 73.5
LCNUG 1927.245

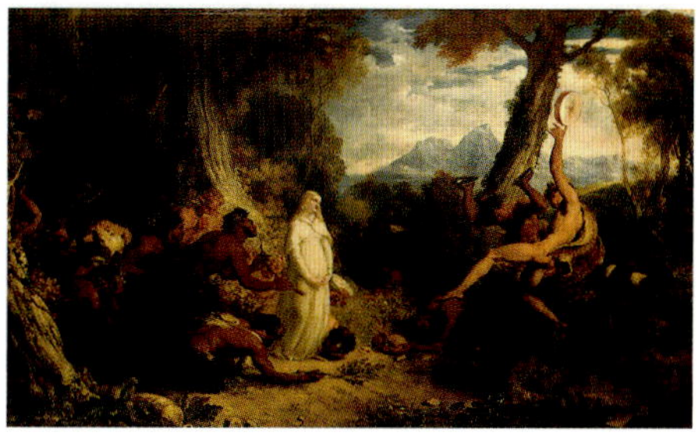

Hilton, William II 1786–1839
Una and the Satyrs
oil on canvas 157.5 x 240
LCNUG 1927.147

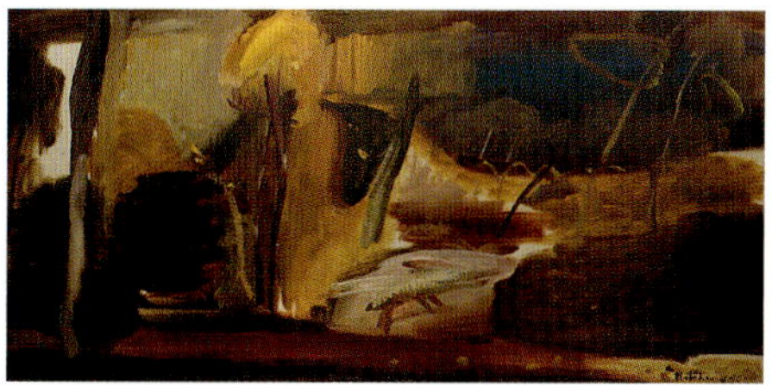

Hitchens, Ivon 1893–1979
Autumn Painting 1945
oil on canvas 52.5 x 104.8
LCNUG 1985.41

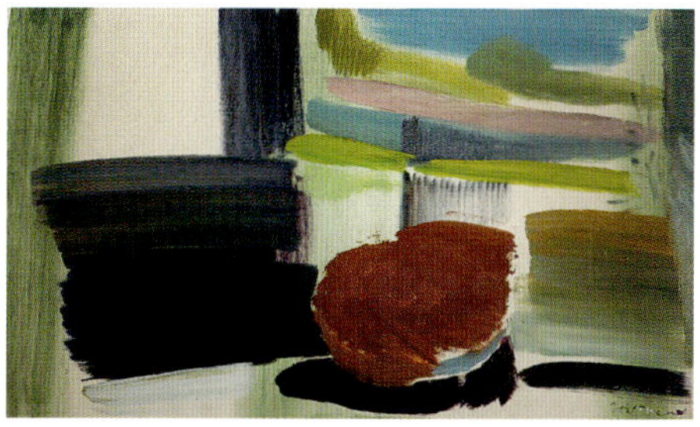

Hitchens, Ivon 1893–1979
Boat on a Lake No.2
oil on canvas 51 x 83.5
LCNUG 1985.42

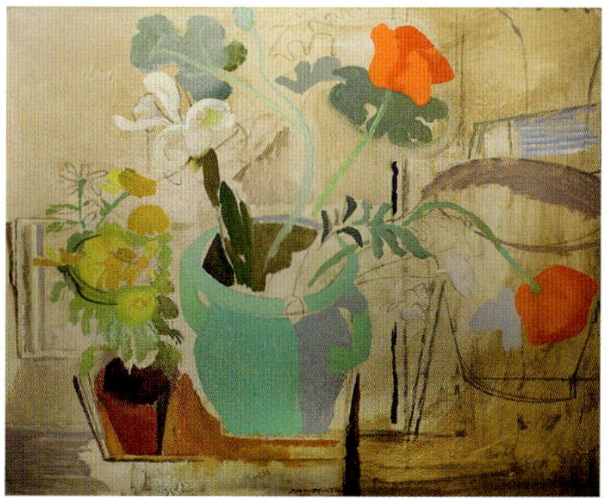

Hitchens, Ivon 1893–1979
Poppies in a Green Bowl
oil on canvas 63.5 x 76.4
LCNUG 1985.39

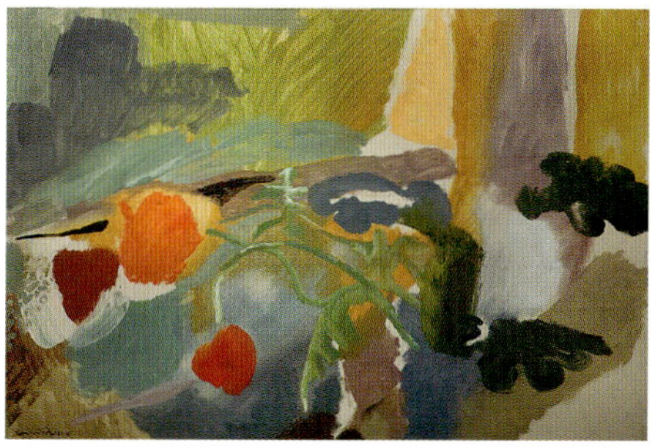

Hitchens, Ivon 1893–1979
Study for a Painting
oil on canvas 55.8 x 83.8
LCNUG 1985.40

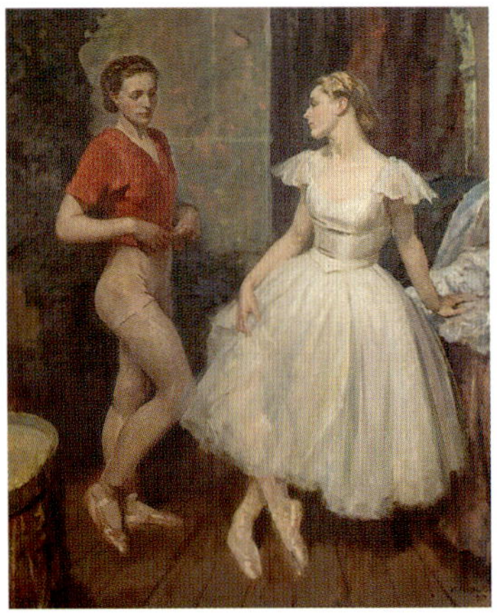

Hodge, Francis Edwin 1883–1949
Preparation for the Ballet
oil on canvas 127 x 102
LCNUG 1927.1927

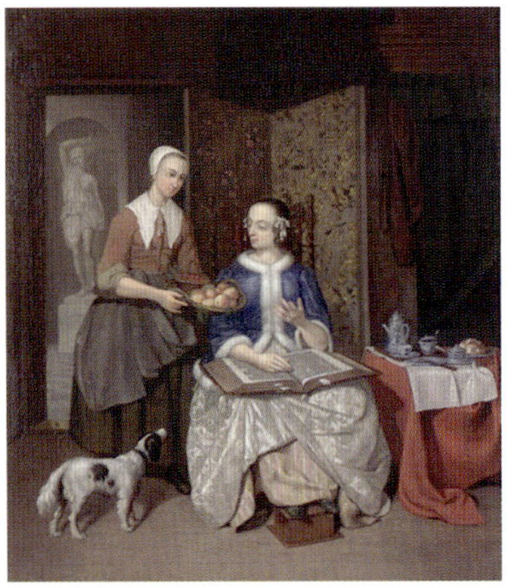

Hoevenaar, Cornelis William 1802–1873
Interior Scene with Two Ladies
oil on panel 47 x 40.5
LCNUG 1927.908

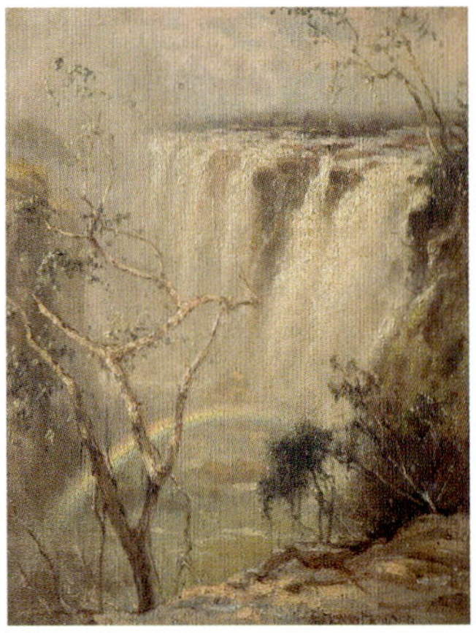

Holder, Edward Henry 1847–1922
Victoria Falls on the Zambezi, Zimbabwe
oil on board 23 x 17.7
LCNUG 1974.54

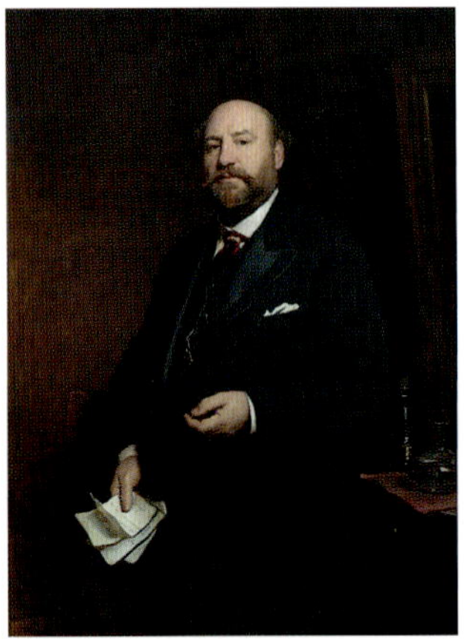

Holl, Frank 1845–1888
Joseph Ruston (1835–1897) 1883
oil on canvas 142.5 x 102
LCNUG 1990.13

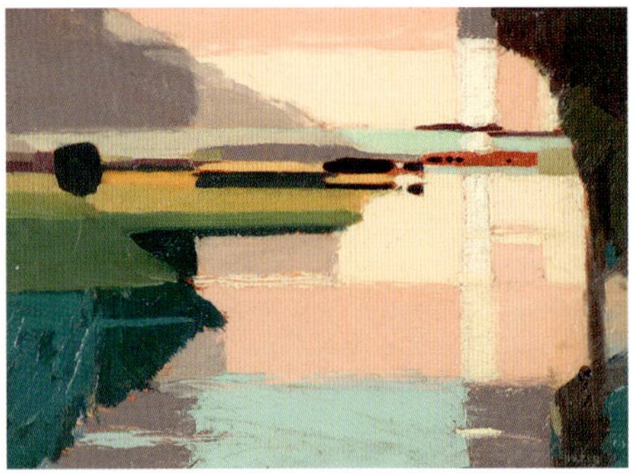

Holzer, Henry 1907–2007
Summer Evening after Rain before 1971
oil on board 15.5 x 20
LCNUG 1971.89

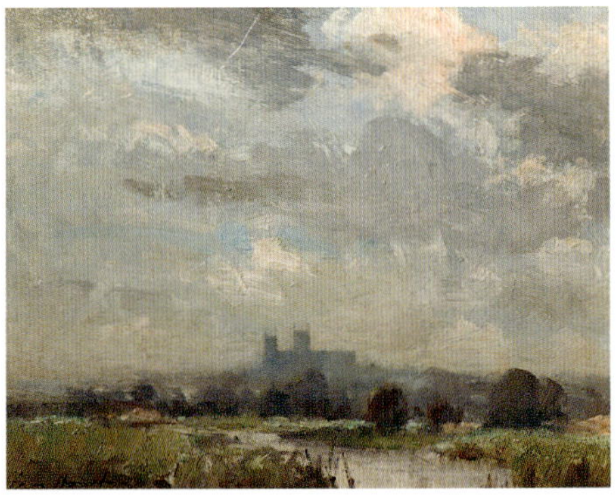

Houston, Ian b.1934
Lincoln Cathedral from the Water Meadows c.1965
oil on board 27.6 x 32.6
LCNUG 1980.5

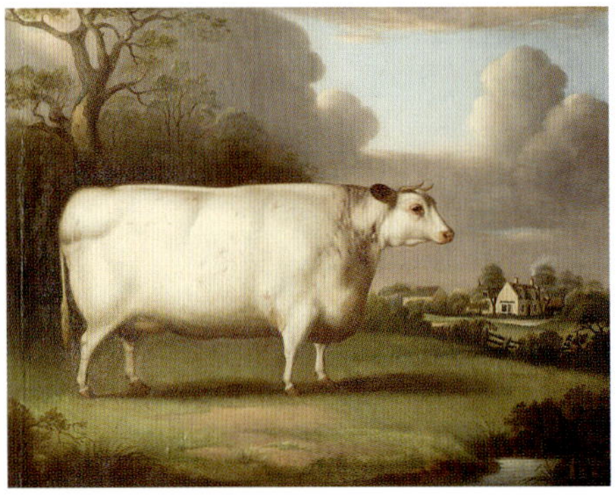

Hubbard, Bennett 1806–1870
The Habertoft Heifer 1841
oil on canvas 63.5 x 76.5
LCNUG 1994.7

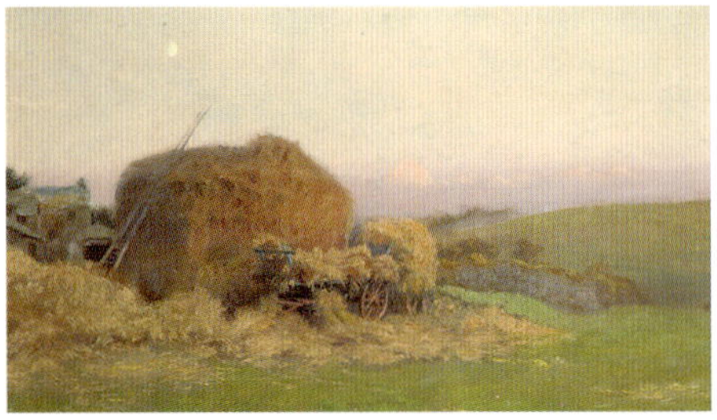

Hughes, Arthur 1832–1915
Rest 1890
oil on panel 22 x 37
LCNUG 1927.250

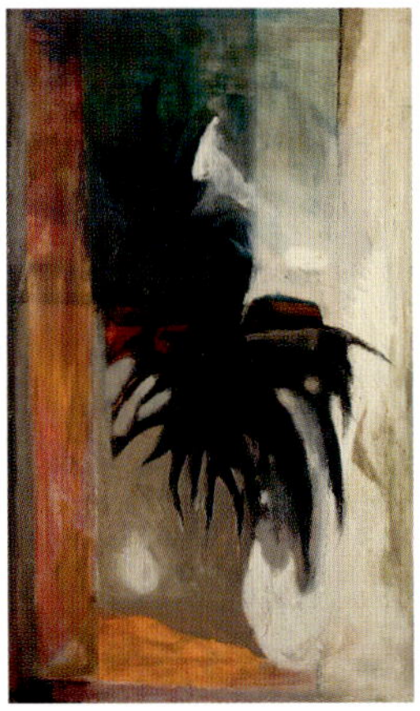

Hulbert, Thelma 1913–1995
Leaves and Gauze Screen 1964
oil on board 140 x 78.4
LCNUG 1927.2668

Facing page: Sweerts, Michael, 1618–1664, *Portrait of a Girl* (detail), Leicester Arts and Museums Service (p. 86)

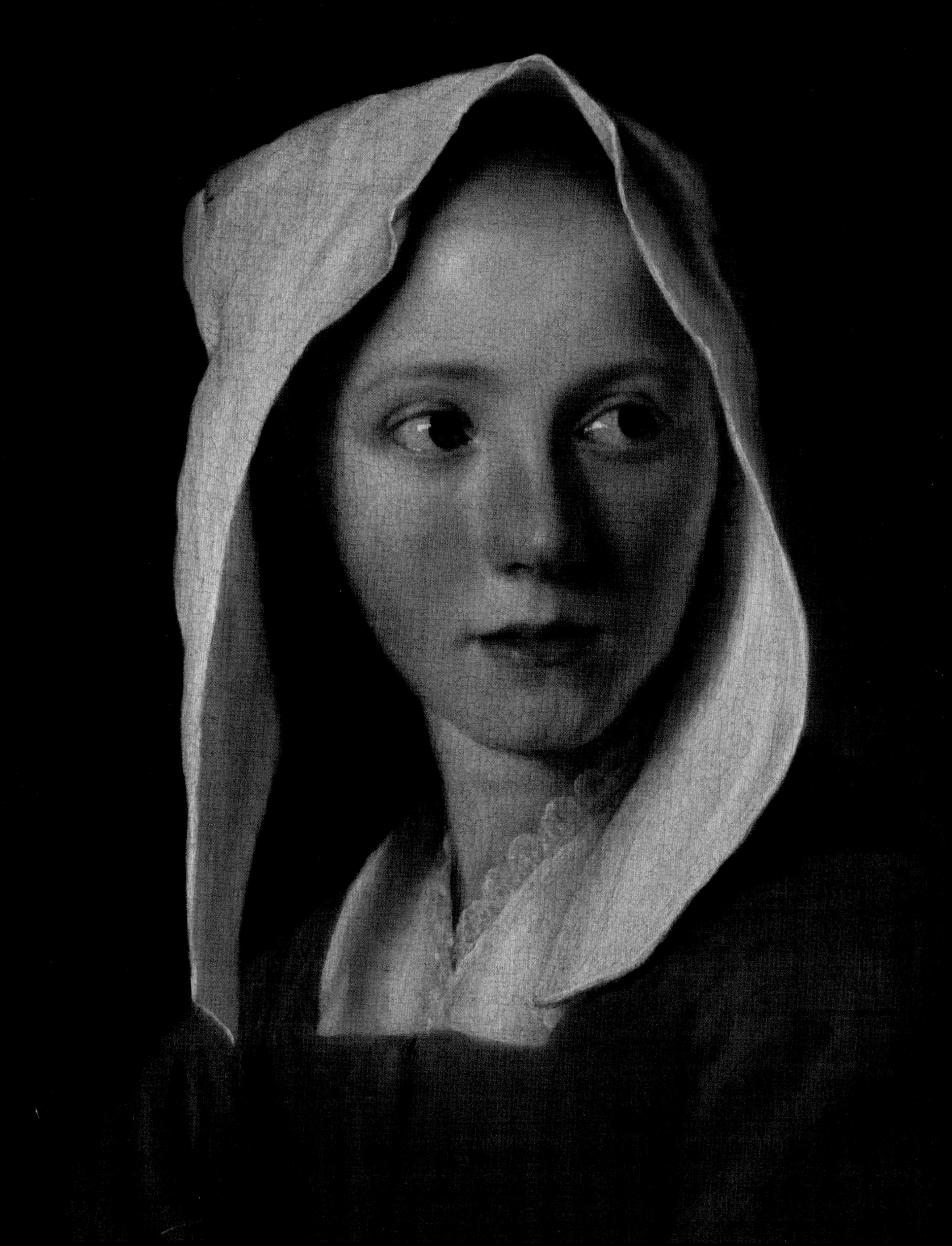

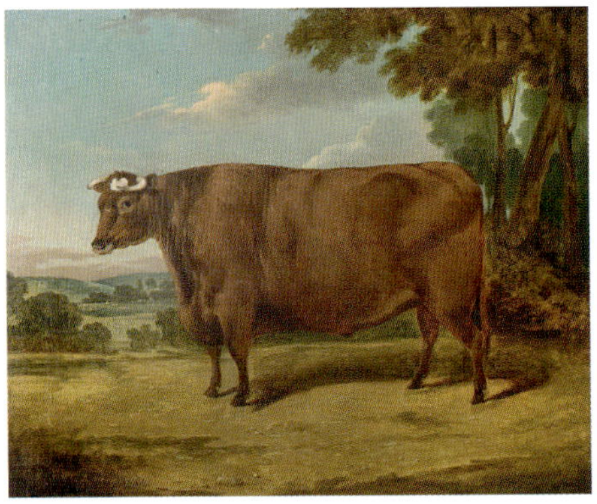

Hutton, R. W.
A Lincoln Red Prize Shorthorn Bullock, Aged 4 Years and 10 Months 1857
oil on board 63.5 x 77
LCNUG 1988.29

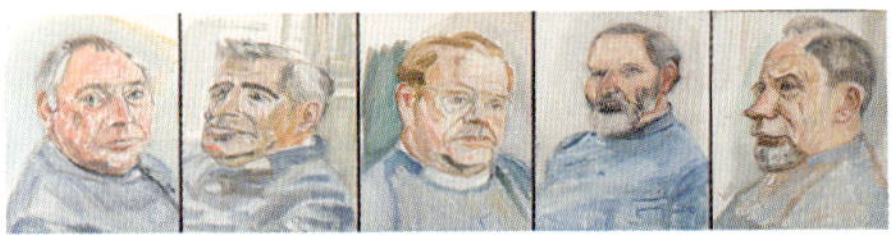

Hyman, Timothy b.1946
The Dean and Chapter Meeting in the Martha and Mary Room
oil on canvas board 30.5 x 152.5
LCNUG 1984.44

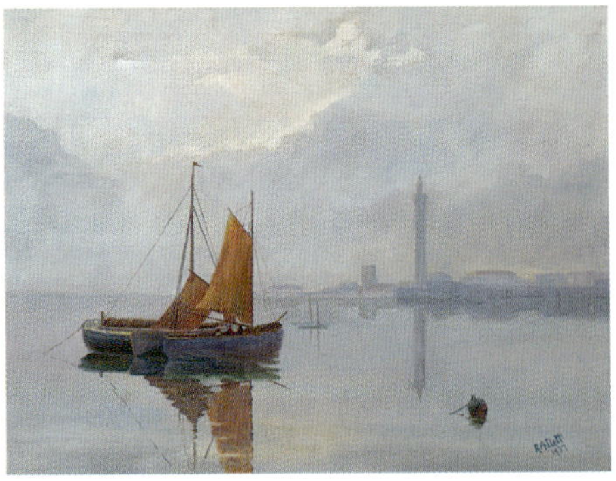

Ilett, R. A.
Morning Tide 1937
oil on canvas 45 x 51
LCNUG 1927.694

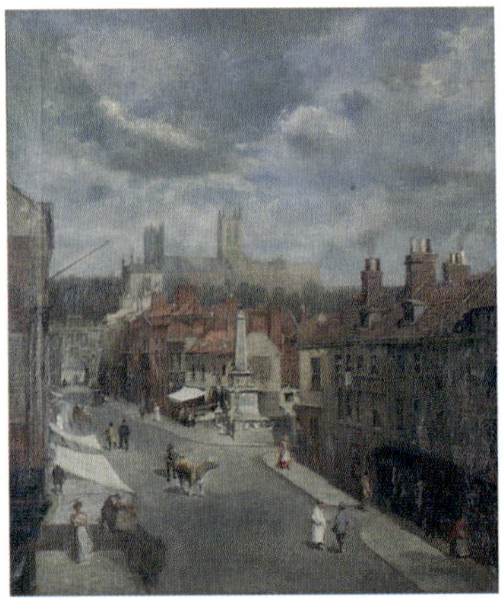

Jackson, F. A. active c.1900
Lincoln High Street
oil on canvas 76.2 x 63.8
LCNUG 1927.2364

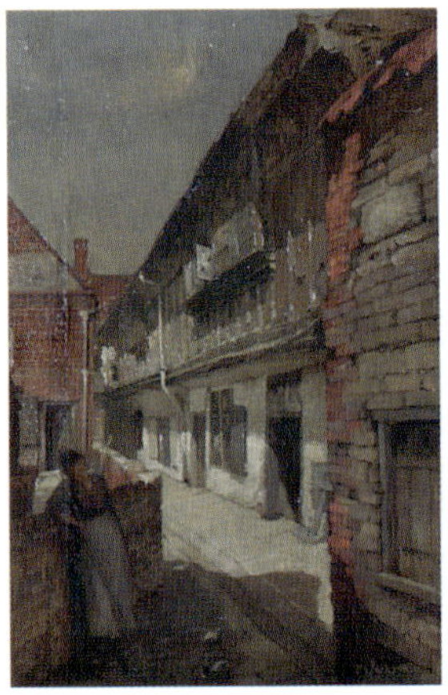

Jackson, F. A. active c.1900
Lincoln High Street
oil on canvas 46 x 30
LCNUG 1927.2378

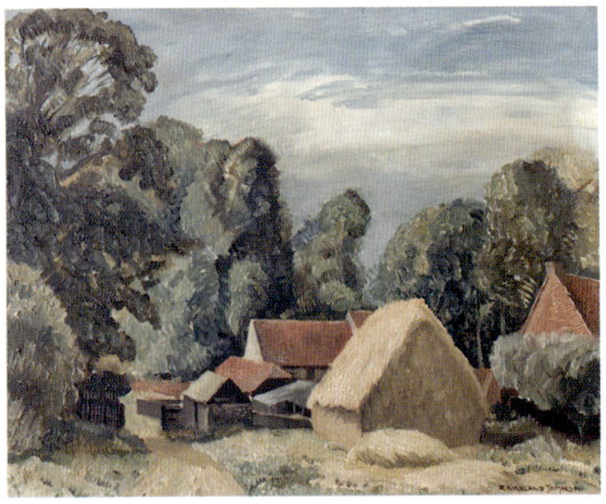

Jamieson, Robert Kirkland 1881–1950
Essex Farm
oil on canvas 64 x 76.8
LCNUG 1927.1886

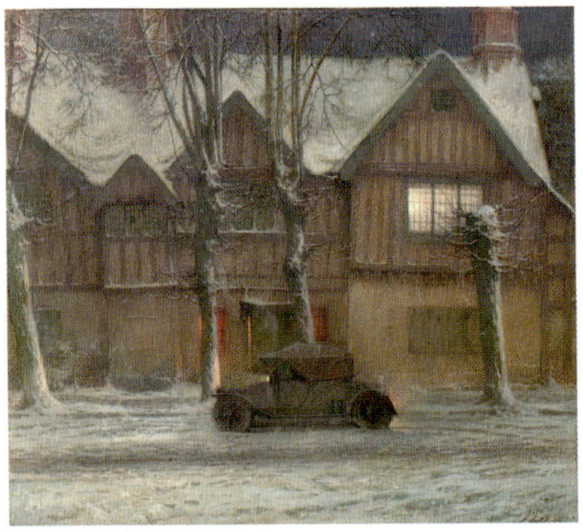

Jelley, James Valentine 1856–1950
The Doctor's Car
oil on board 62 x 68.6
LCNUG 1927.771

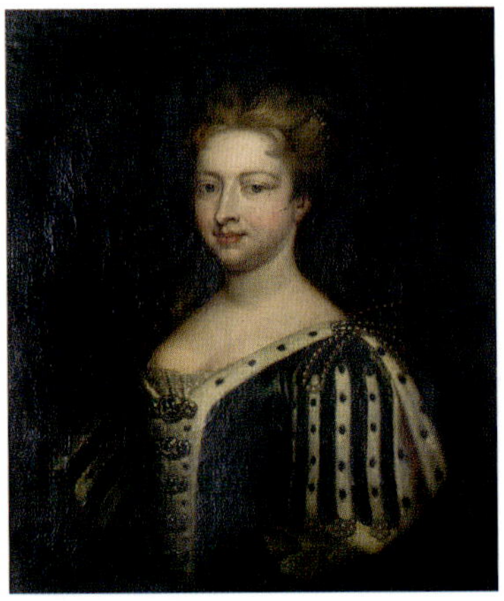

Jervas, Charles c.1675–1739
Queen Caroline (1768–1821)
oil on canvas 161 x 74
LCNUG 1927.2041

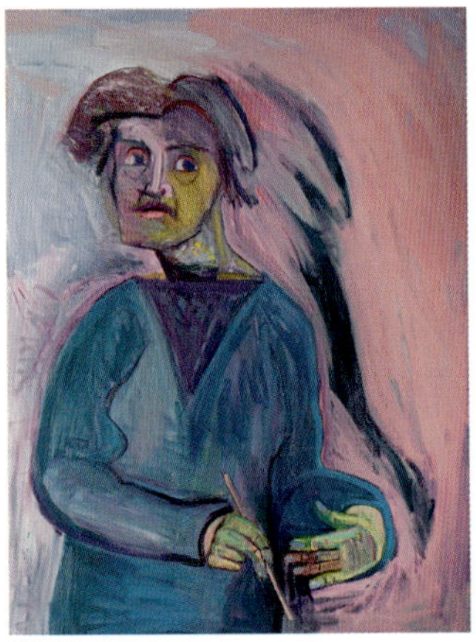

Jones, Lucy b.1955
Self Portrait 1991
oil on canvas 122 x 91
LCNUG 1996.8

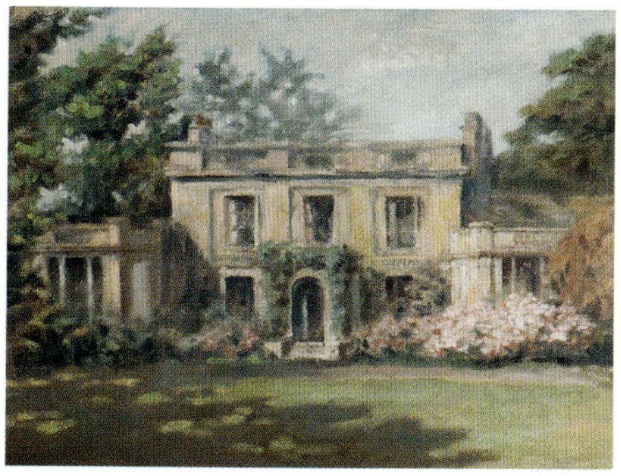

Kelly, J. E. T.
Kingston Manor, Angmering-on-Sea, Sussex
oil on board 35.5 x 45.5
LCNUG 1977.2857

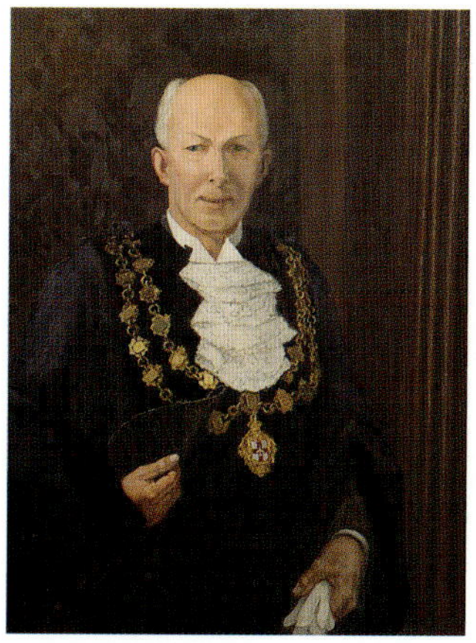

Kennedy, Alex G.
Major John Hermaine Smith, City Sheriff
oil on canvas 103 x 76
LCNUG 2009.31

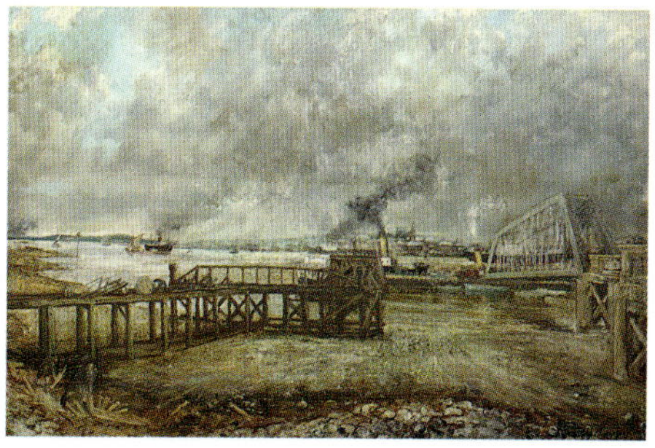

Kerr, Antony b.1924
Ferry at Tilbury, Essex
oil on board 61 x 91.5
LCNUG 1927.2539

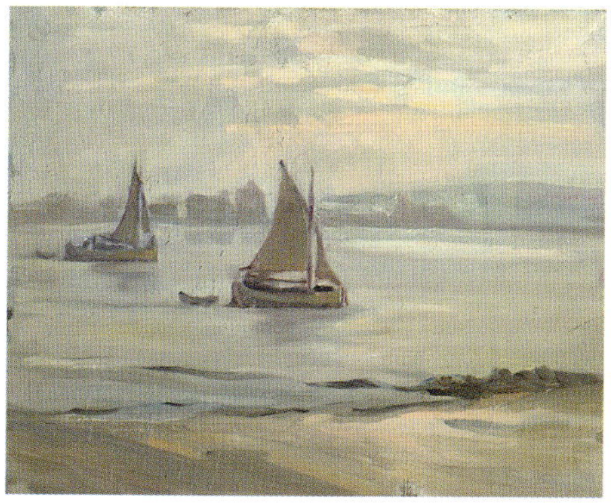

Kidder, Norah b.1888
Humber Foreshore
oil on panel 24 x 29
LCNUG 1927.770

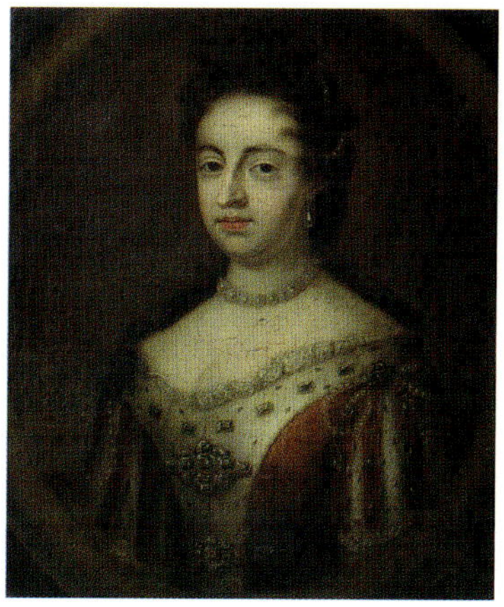

Kneller, Godfrey 1646–1723
Mary II (1662–1694) early 18th C
oil on canvas 74 x 62
LCNUG 1927.2043

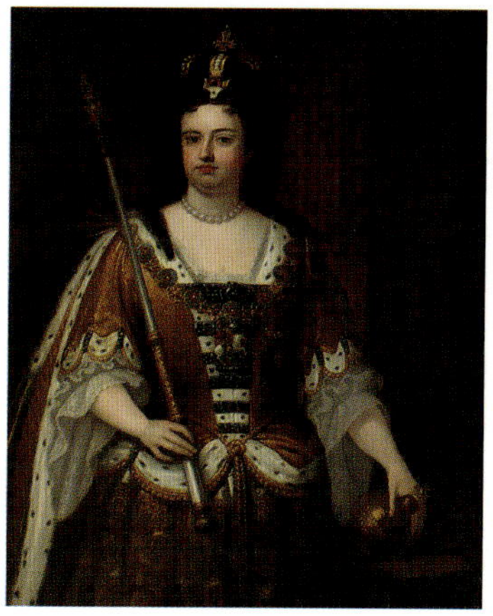

Kneller, Godfrey 1646–1723
Queen Anne (1665–1714)
oil on canvas 125 x 100
LCNUG 1927.2038

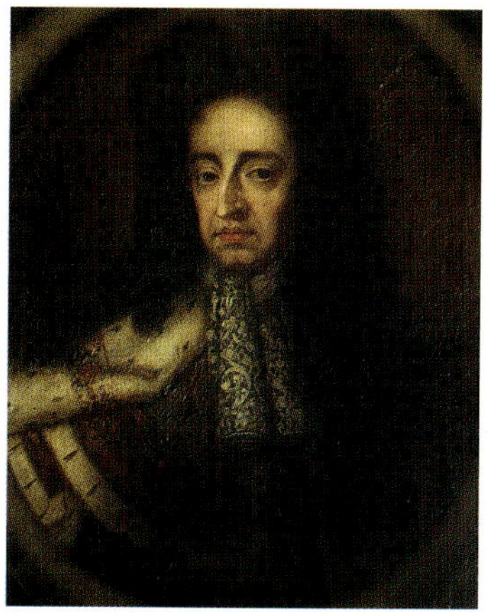

Kneller, Godfrey (after) 1646–1723
William III (1650–1702) early 18th C
oil on canvas 71 x 58
LCNUG 1927.2040

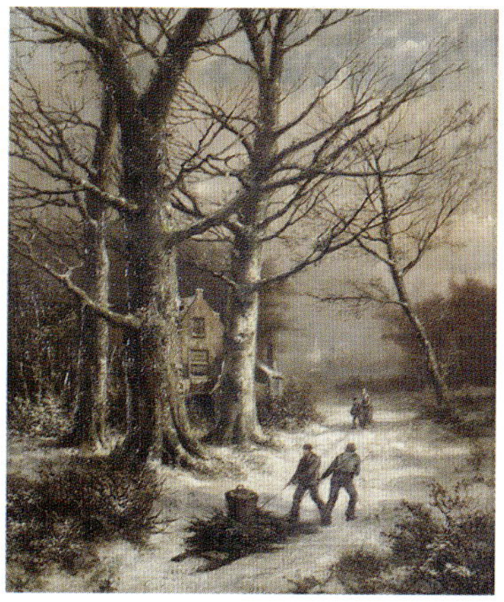

Koekkoek, Johannes Herman Barend
1840–1912
Snow Scene
oil on canvas 76.8 x 63.8
LCNUG 1975.14

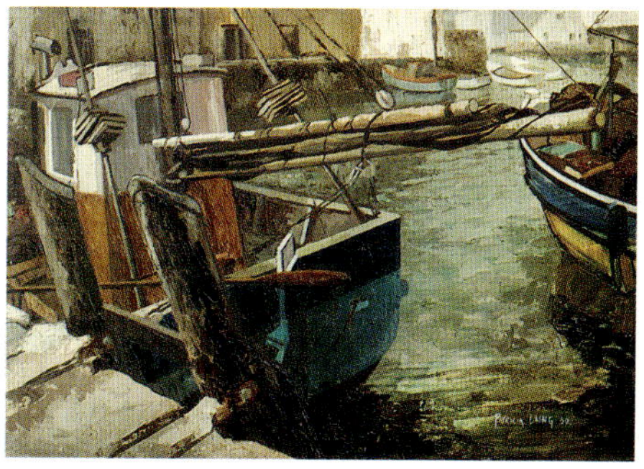

Laing, Patricia b.1928
Cornish Fishing Boat
oil on canvas 53.4 x 73.2
LCNUG 1927.2395

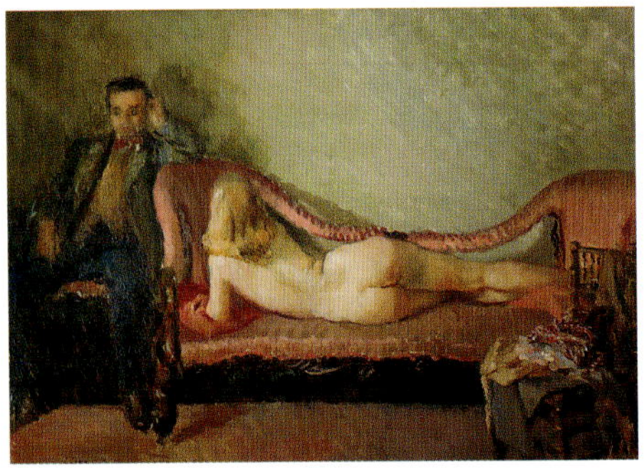

Lamb, Lynton Harold 1907–1977
Nude
oil on canvas 50.7 x 68.5
LCNUG 1927.2233

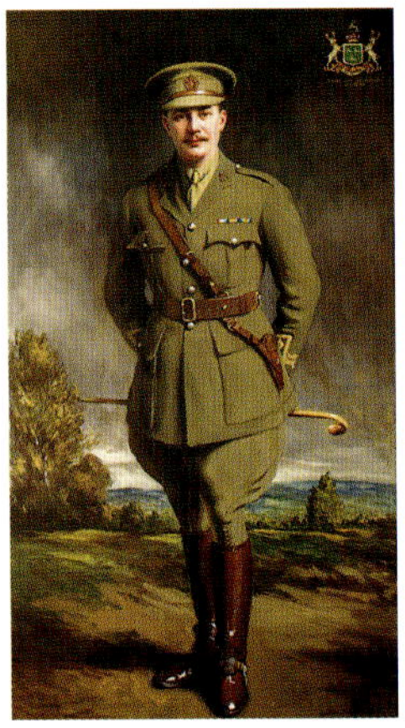

Lander, John Saint-Hélier 1869–1944
Captain T. D. Trollope-Bellew 1921
oil on canvas 212 x 112
LCNUG 1976.47

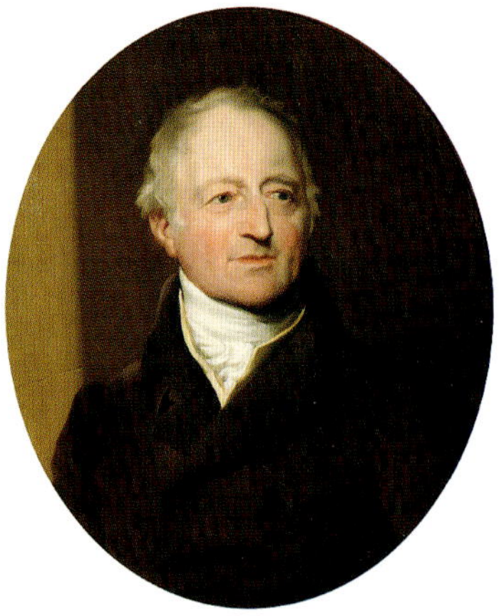

Lane, Samuel 1780–1859
John Willis
oil on canvas 72.6 x 57.2
LCNUG 1927.173

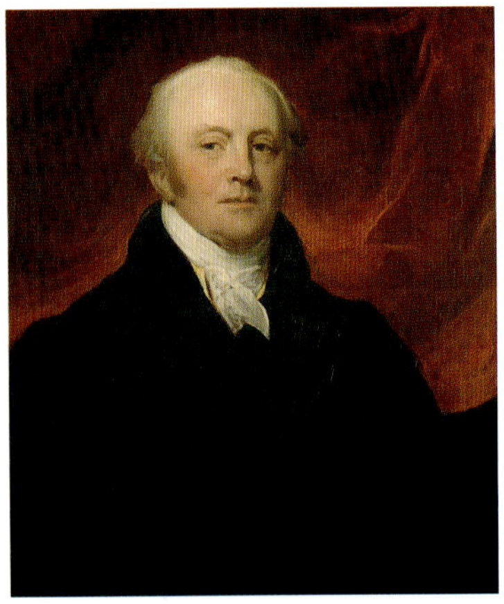

Lawrence, Thomas 1769–1830
George Tennyson (1749/1750–1835), Grandfather of Alfred Tennyson
oil on canvas 75 x 62
TENN.T2010.04

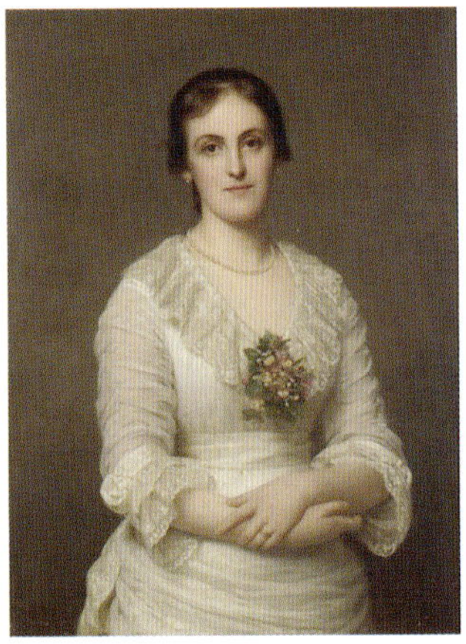

Lehmann, Rudolph 1819–1905
Maria Albina 1883
oil on canvas 91.5 x 67
LCNUG 1972.147

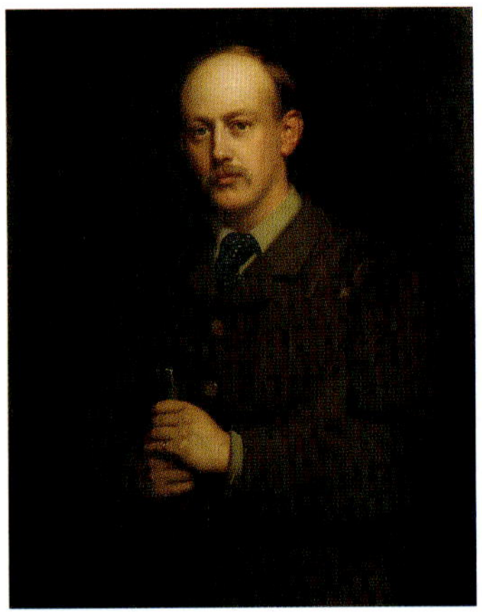

Lehmann, Rudolph 1819–1905
Montagu Richard Waldo Sibthorp 1883
oil on canvas 92 x 71
LCNUG 1972.149

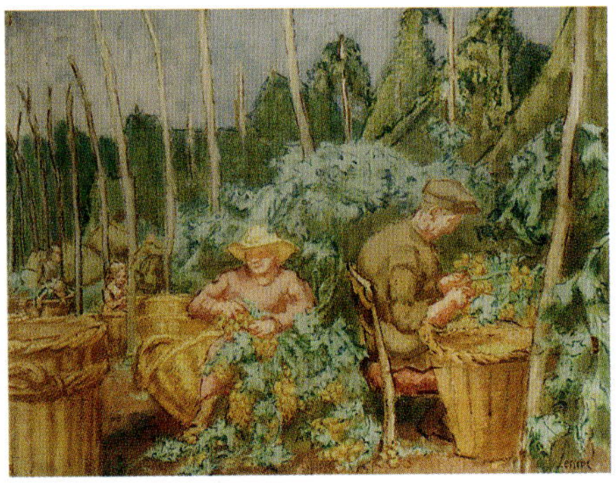

Lessore, Thérèse 1884–1945
Hop-Pickers c.1938
oil on canvas 65.5 x 76
LCNUG 1927.1750

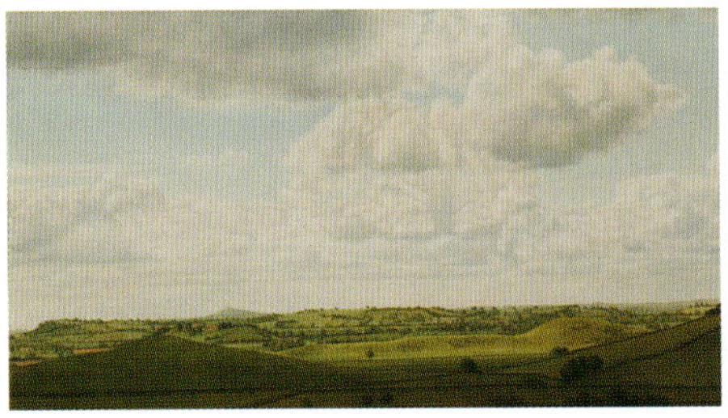

Lewis, Simon b.1965
'Step inside luv' 1993
oil & gesso on board 10.2 x 17.8
LCNUG 1996.18

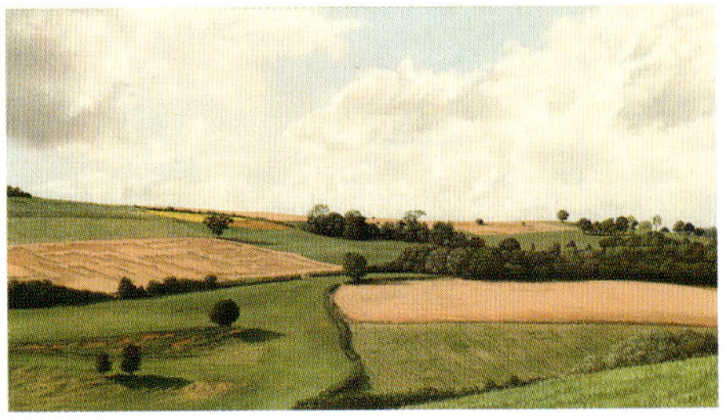

Lewis, Simon b.1965
Where's Walter? 1993
oil & gesso on board 10.7 x 17.8
LCNUG 1996.17

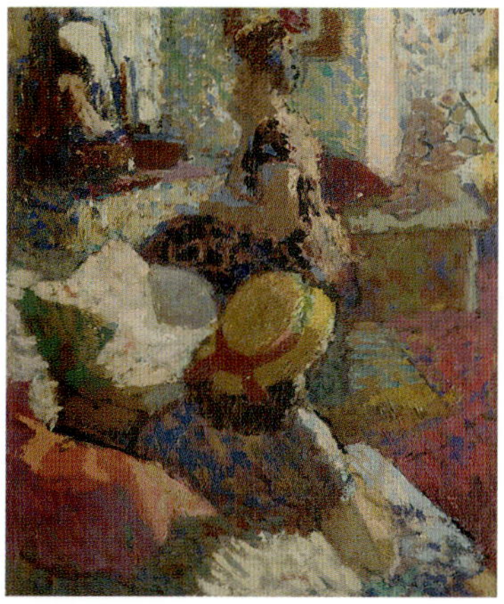

McCall, Charles James 1907–1989
Maquillage
oil on canvas 55.2 x 46.2
LCNUG 1927.2063

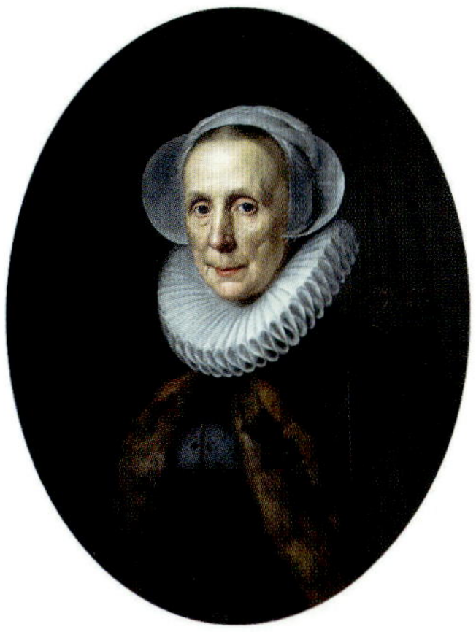

Miereveld, Michiel Jansz. van 1567–1641
Maria van Wassenaer Hanecops (c.1542–after 1612) 1612
oil on board 69 x 52
LCNUG 2008.6

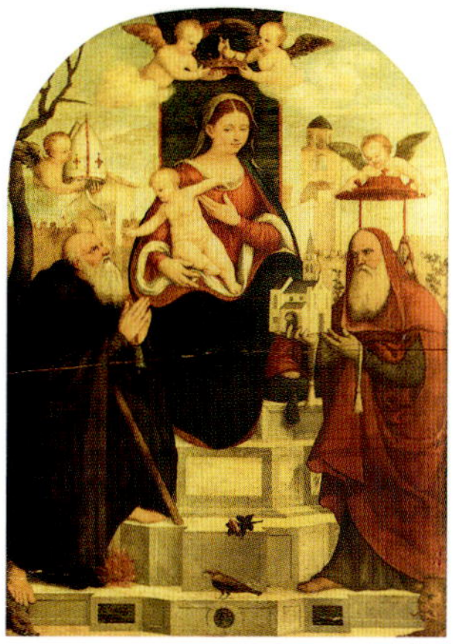

Milano, Francesco Figini active 1502–1548
Madonna and Child Enthroned c.1522–1538
oil on panel 205.7 x 144
LCNUG 1927.146

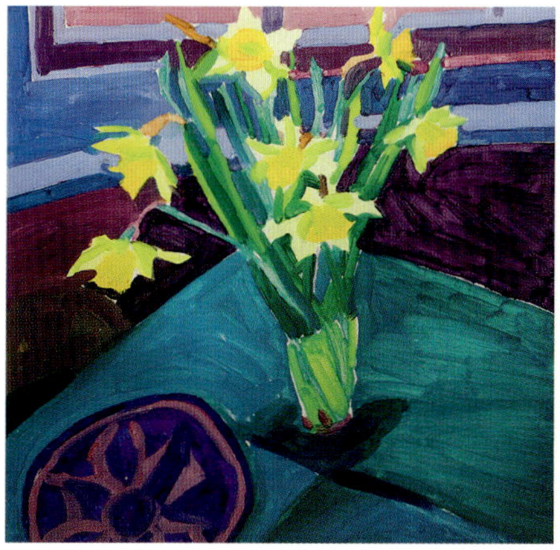

Montford, Rosemary b.1951
Daffodils on a Green Cloth 1987
oil on canvas 127.5 x 122.2
LCNUG 1988.44

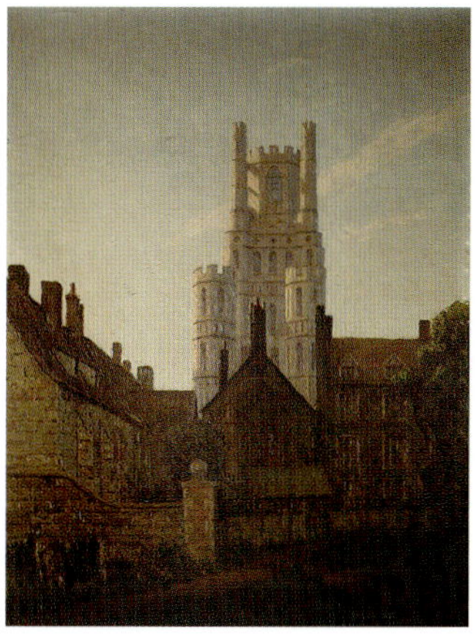

Morton, Charles Reginald active 1917–1936
Ely Cathedral, Cambridgeshire
oil on board 121.5 x 91
LCNUG 1927.700

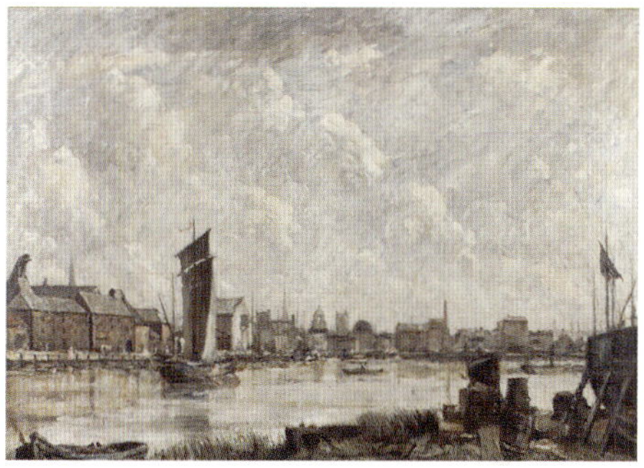

Muirhead, David 1867–1930
Lincoln, 1913
oil on canvas 76.2 x 104.2
LCNUG 1927.2155

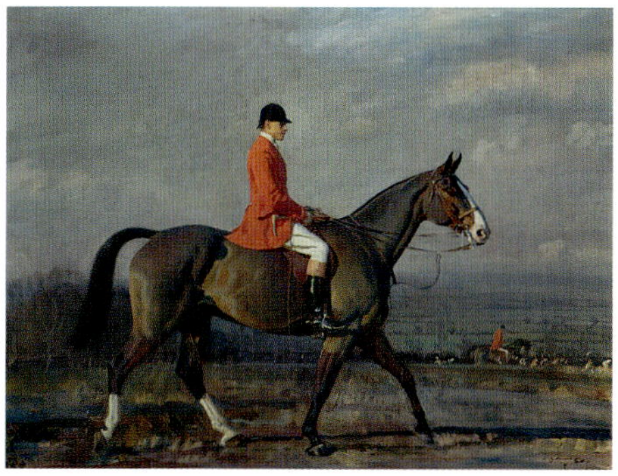

Munnings, Alfred James 1878–1959
Colonel Lord Barnby on 'Crusader' with the Blankney Hounds 1929
oil on canvas 28 x 36
LCNUG 1991.10

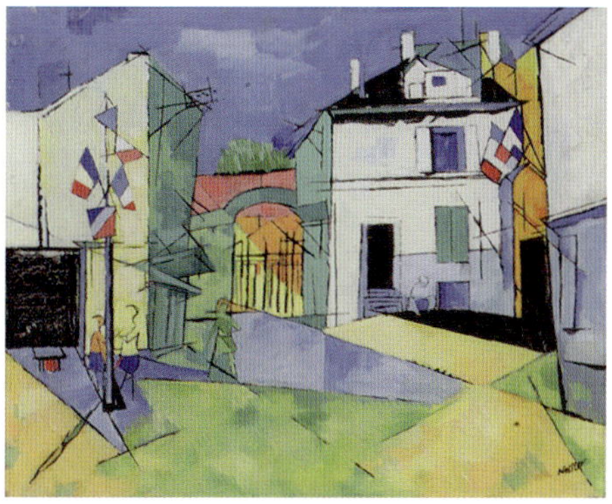

Nessler, Walter 1912–2001
Sèvres, France 1952
oil on canvas 50.5 x 61.2
LCNUG 1927.2314

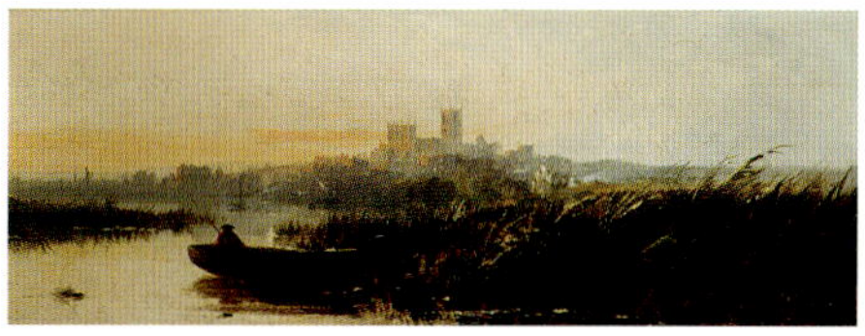

Niemann, Edmund John 1813–1876
Distant View of Lincoln 1857
oil on panel 17.5 x 46.1
LCNUG 1980.1

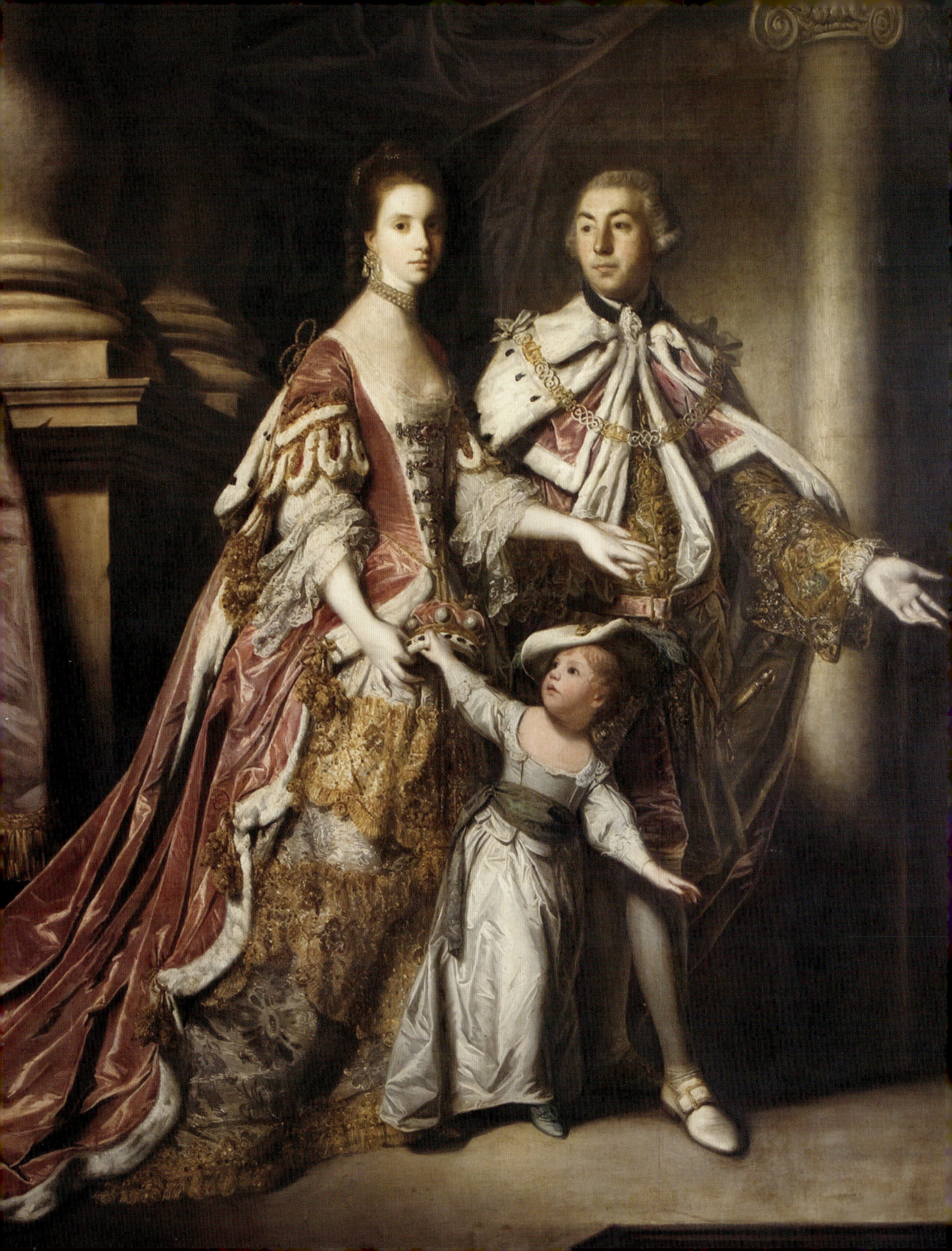

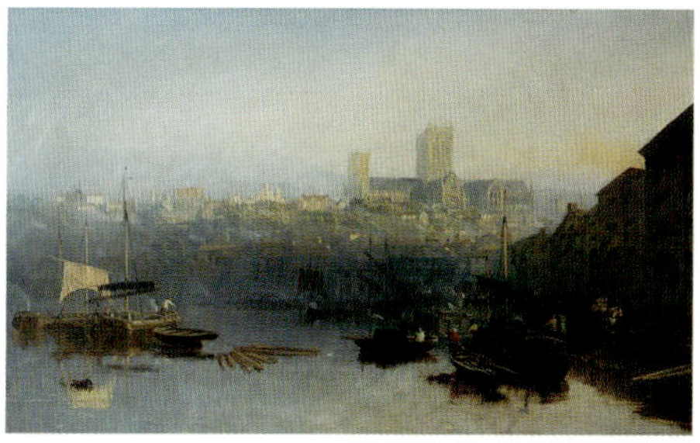

Niemann, Edmund John 1813–1876
Lincoln from Brayford 1858
oil on canvas 81.3 x 127
LCNUG 1927.2591

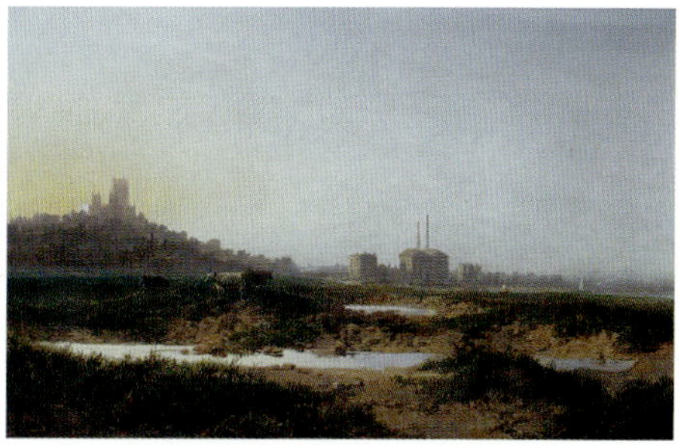

Niemann, Edmund John 1813–1876
Lincoln from the Holmes 1860
oil on canvas 34 x 51
LCNUG 1927.2180

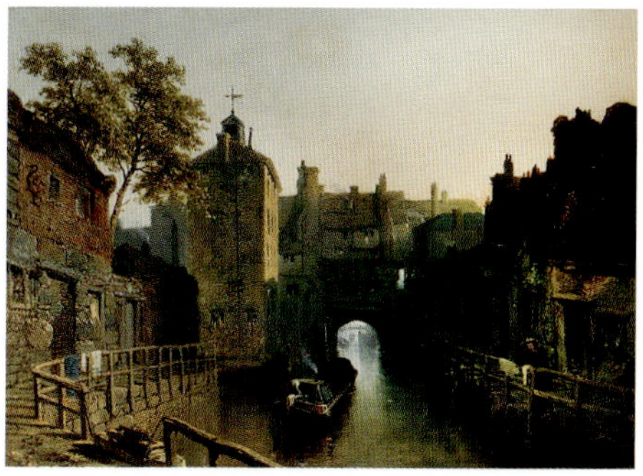

Niemann, Edmund John 1813–1876
The Glory Hole, Lincoln 1860
oil on canvas 29.8 x 40
LCNUG 1927.1845

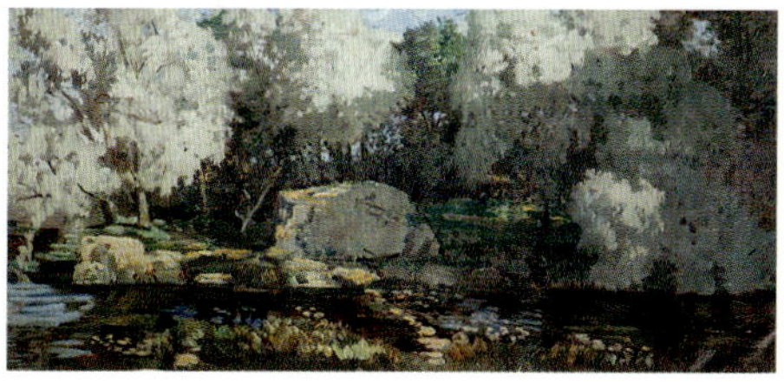

Noble, Robert 1857–1917
On the Dean, East Linton, Scotland
oil on canvas 30.5 x 61.5
LCNUG 1927.74

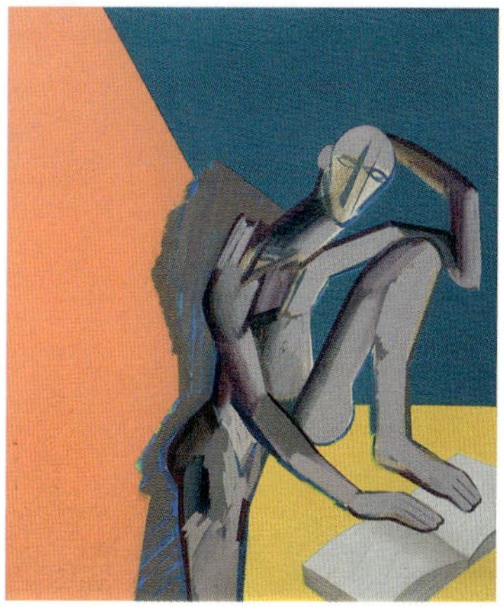

Norwich, Anne b.1929
Reading 1973
acrylic on canvas 61 x 50.5
LCNUG 1980.161

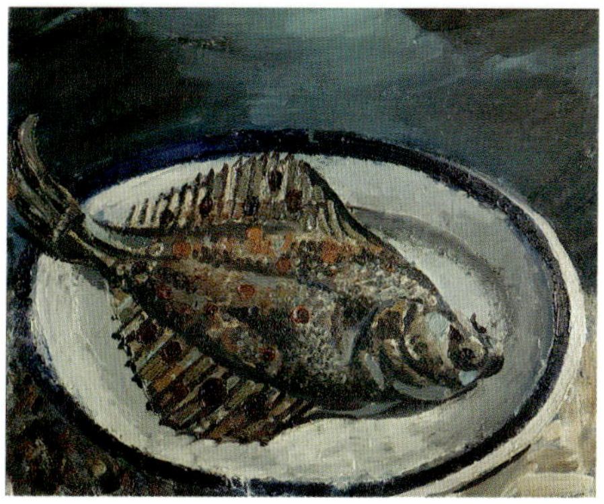

Nyberg, Henning 1903–1964
Plaice
oil on panel 51 x 61
LCNUG 1924.2064

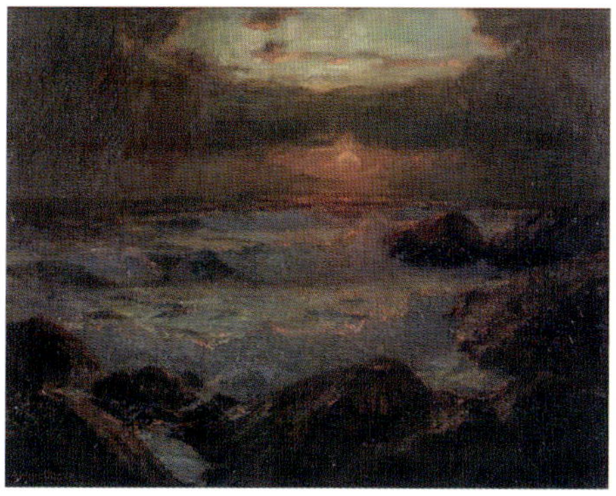

Olsson, Albert Julius 1864–1942
Seascape Evening
oil on canvas 61 x 76
LCNUG 1927.1510

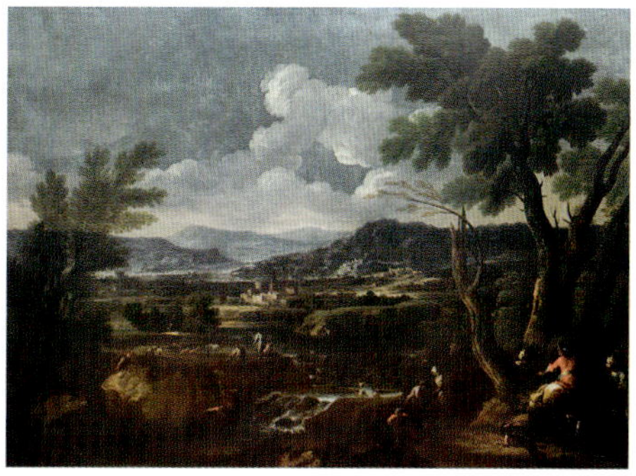

Onofri, Crescenzio (attributed to)
c.1632–c.1712
Classical Landscape
oil on canvas 178 x 235.5
LCNUG 1927.2251

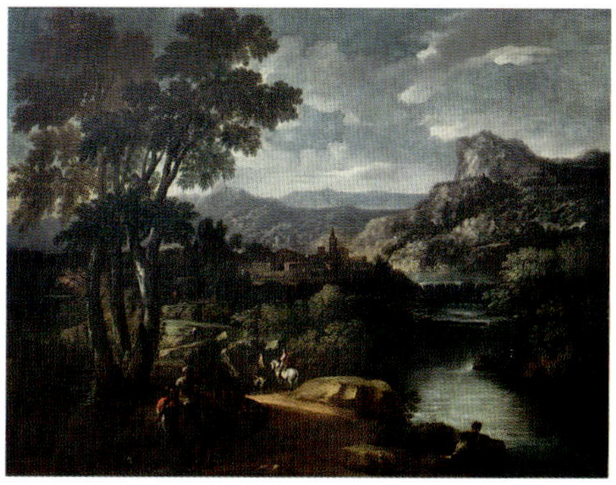

Onofri, Crescenzio (attributed to)
c.1632–c.1712
Classical Landscape
oil on canvas 177 x 236.5
LCNUG 1927.2252

Facing page: Reynolds, Joshua, 1723–1792, *The Earl and Countess of Mexborough with Their Son, Lord Pollington (1719–1778)* (detail), c.1763, Doddington Hall (p. 274)

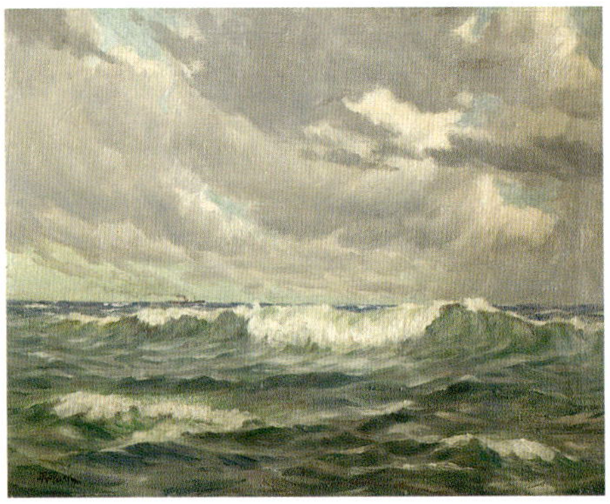

Park, J. R. S. active 20th C
Breezy Sea
oil on canvas 50 x 60
LCNUG 1927.669

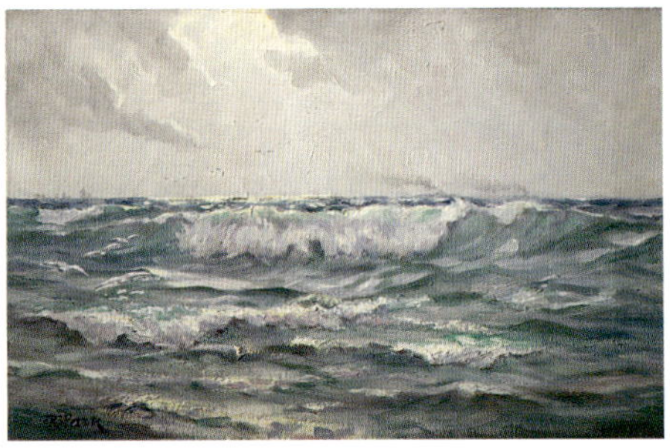

Park, J. R. S. active 20th C
Seascape
oil on canvas 35.5 x 53.5
LCNUG 1927.685

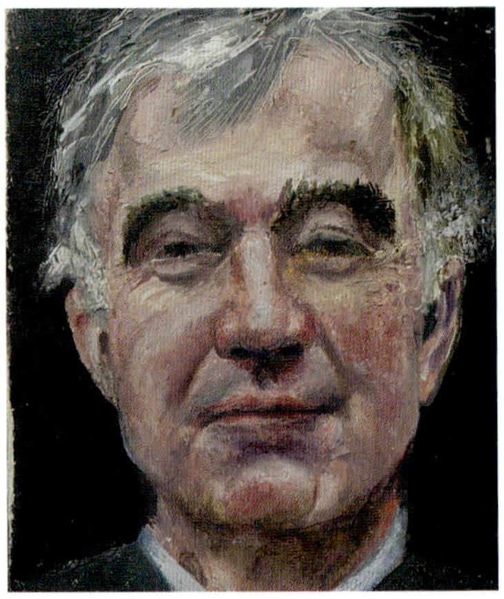

Parker, Alan b.1965
Study for Cathedral Painting I
oil on board 12 x 10
LCNUG 2010.18.1

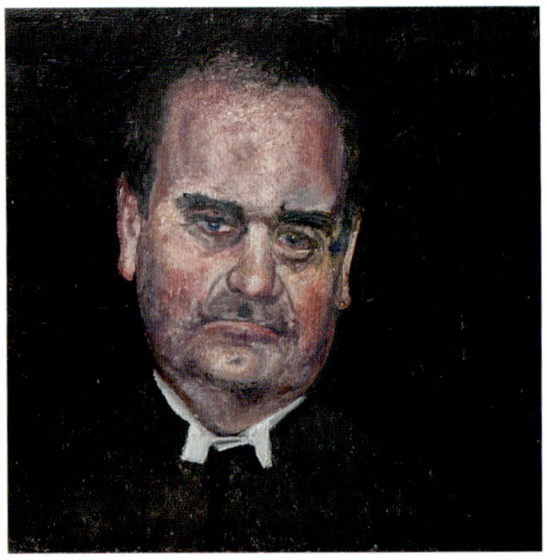

Parker, Alan b.1965
Study for Cathedral Painting II
oil on board 15 x 15
LCNUG 2010.18.2

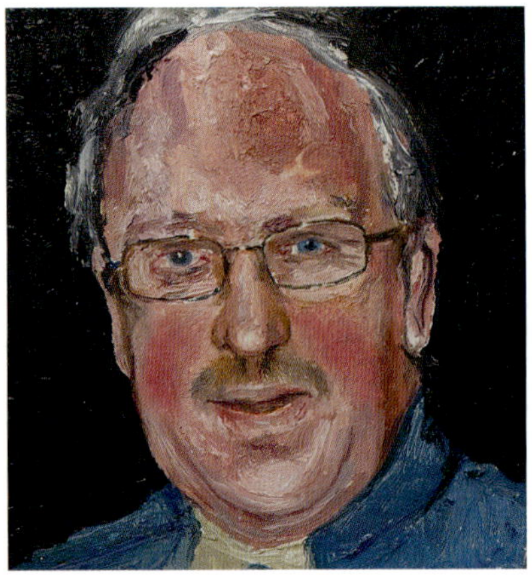

Parker, Alan b.1965
Study for Cathedral Painting III
oil on board 13.5 x 12
LCNUG 2010.18.3

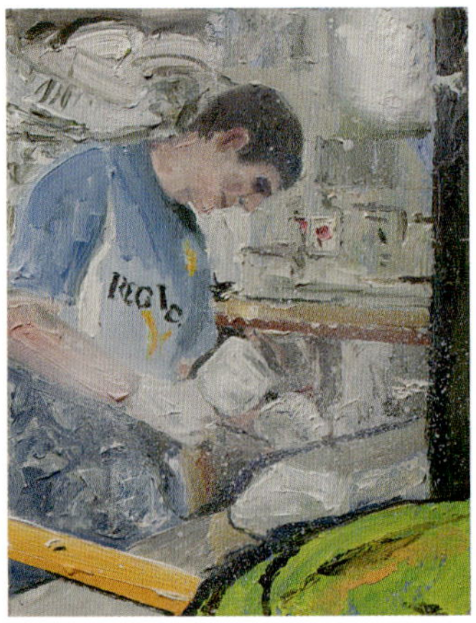

Parker, Alan b.1965
Study for Cathedral Painting IV
oil on board 31 x 23
LCNUG 2010.18.4

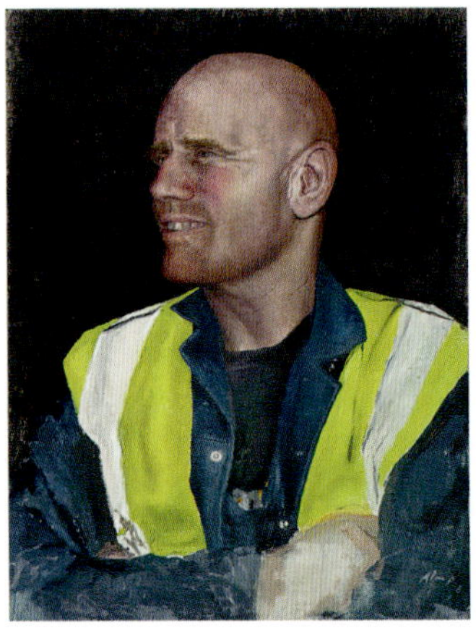

Parker, Alan b.1965
Study for Cathedral Painting V
oil on board 40 x 30
LCNUG 2010.18.5

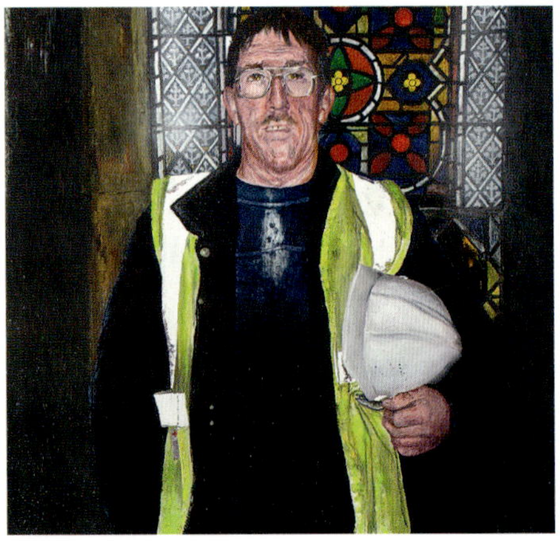

Parker, Alan b.1965
Study for Cathedral Painting VI, Stuart Bonfield, Supervisor
oil on board 60.5 x 60.5
LCNUG 2010.18.6

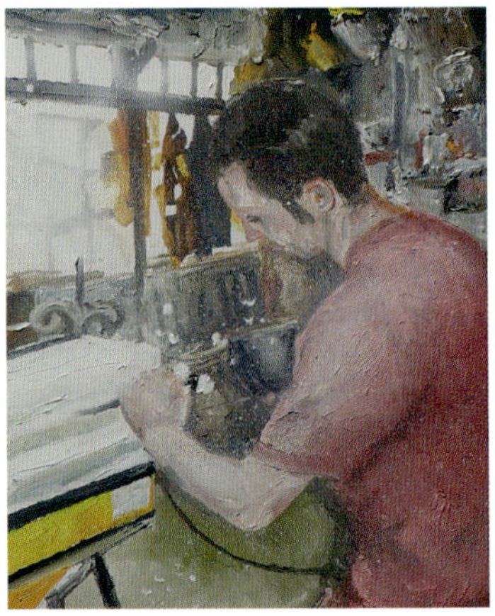

Parker, Alan b.1965
Study for Cathedral Painting VII
oil on canvas 50.5 x 40.5
LCNUG 2010.18.7

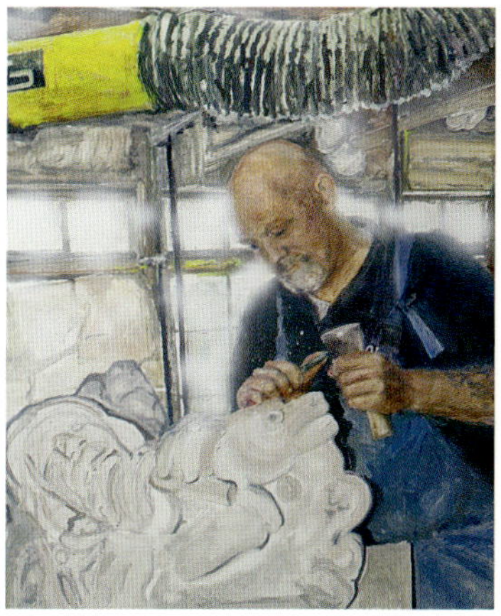

Parker, Alan b.1965
Study for Cathedral Painting VIII, Paul Ellis, Master Carver
oil on canvas 100 x 80
LCNUG 2010.18.8

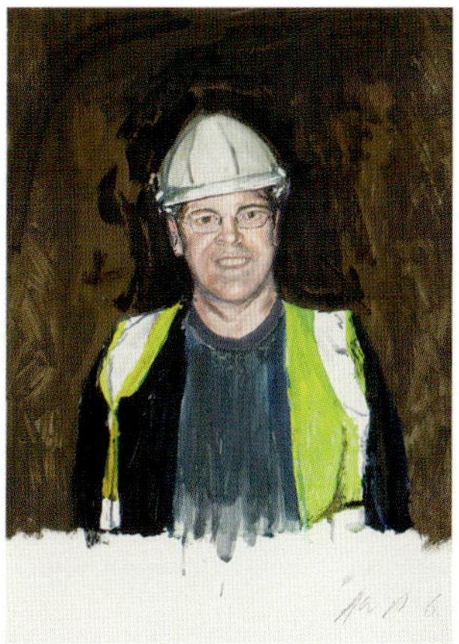

Parker, Alan b.1965
Study for Cathedral Painting IX
oil on card 60 x 51
LCNUG 2010.18.9

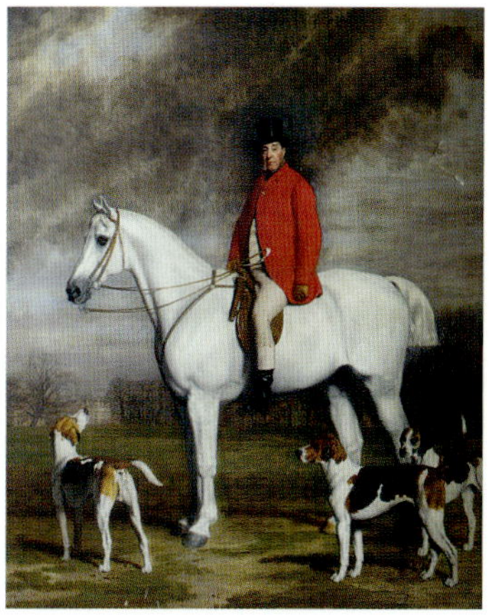

Pearce, Stephen 1819–1904
Lord Kesteven on a Horse, with Hounds 1871
oil on canvas 184 x 152.5
LCNUG 1976.48

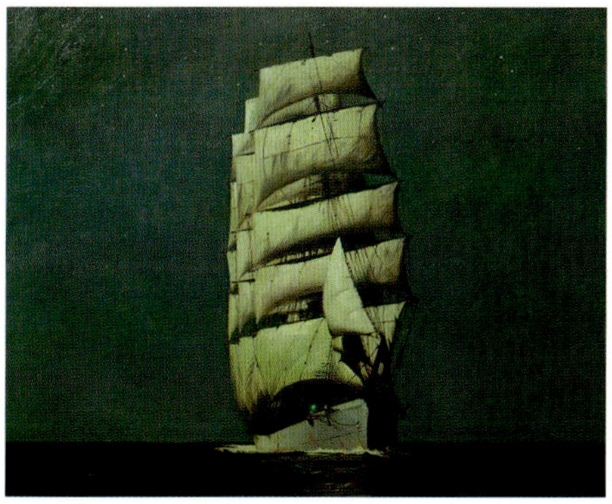

Pears, Charles 1873–1958
Moonlight Barque
oil on canvas 102 x 127
LCNUG 1927.672

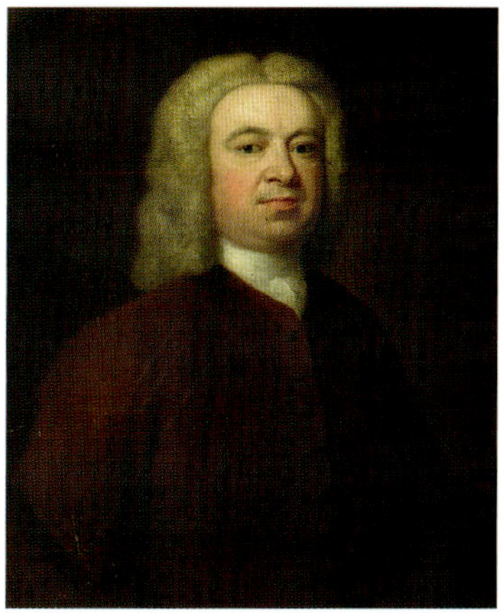

Philips, Charles 1708–1747
Thomas Becke (1690–1757)
oil on canvas 77 x 64
LCNUG 1927.2250

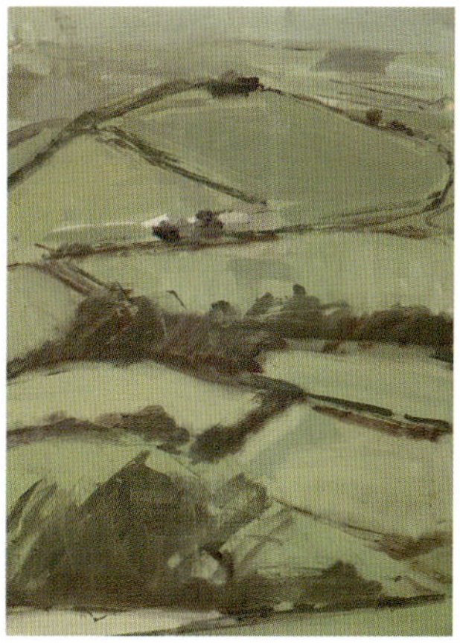

Pickering, Roy b.1954
Landscape, Derbyshire I
oil on canvas 72.2 x 51.5
LCNUG 1984.54

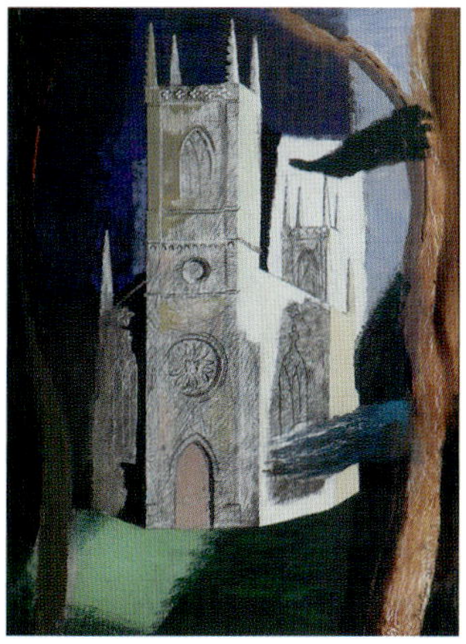

Piper, John 1903–1992
Octagonal Church, Hartwell, Buckinghamshire 1939
oil on canvas 55.8 x 40.7
LCNUG 1927.1599

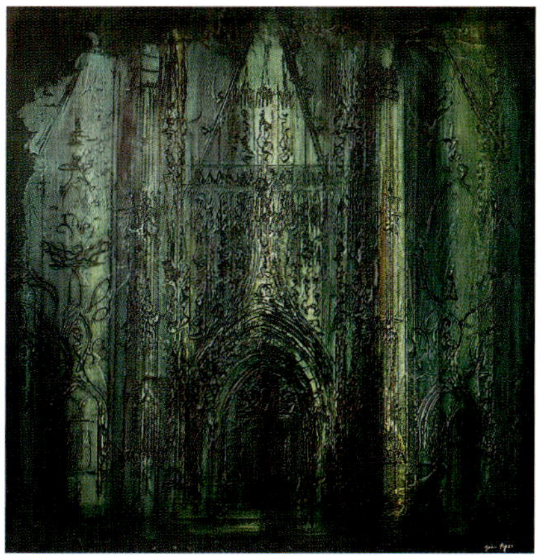

Piper, John 1903–1992
Saint-Riquier, Somme, France 1972
oil on canvas & board 122 x 122
LCNUG 1972.42

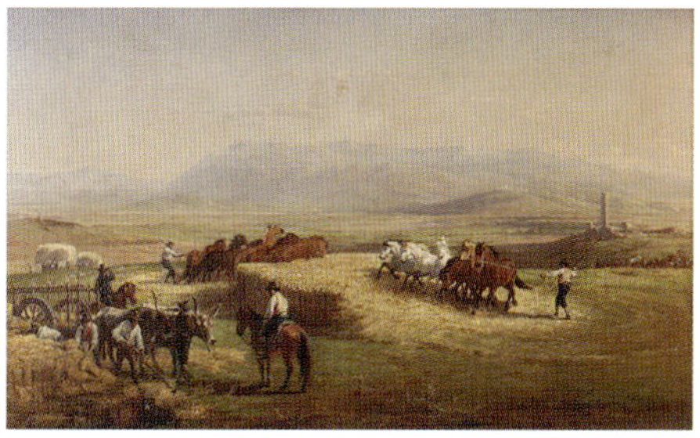

Poingdestre, Charles 1825–1905
Italian Harvest Scene 1850
oil on canvas 38.7 x 63.5
LCNUG 1927.1538

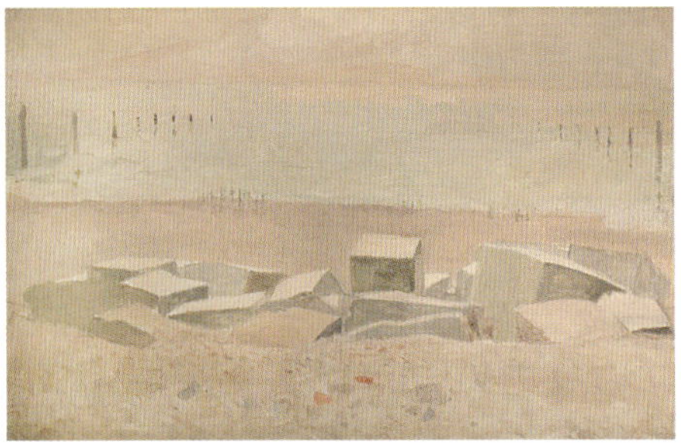

Potter, Mary 1900–1981
Sea Defences
oil on canvas 51.3 x 76.2
LCNUG 1985.51

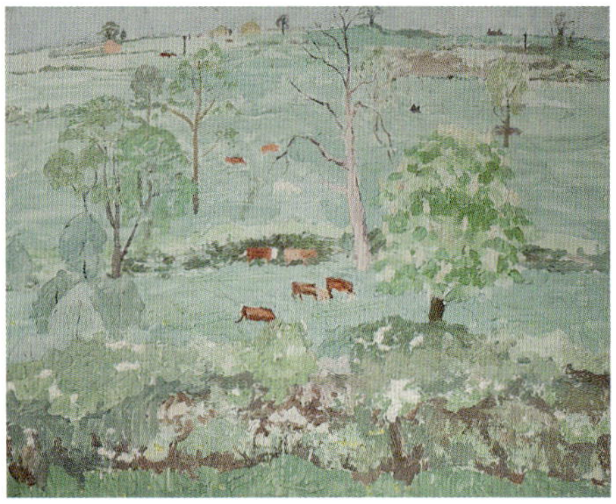

Potter, Mary 1900–1981
Spring Landscape
oil on wood panel 50.6 x 60.8
LCNUG 1985.52

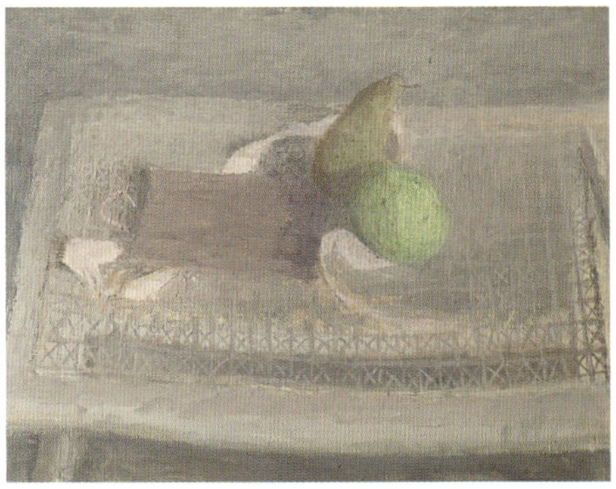

Potter, Mary 1900–1981
Still Life
oil on canvas 40.5 x 57
LCNUG 1985.53

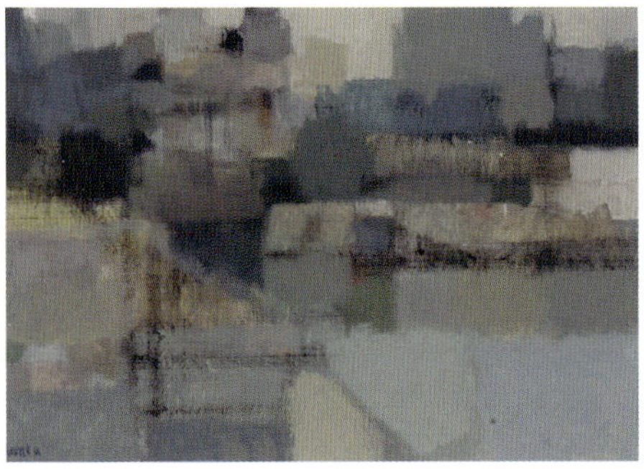

Poulsen, Georg 1911–1997
Seine
oil on canvas 33 x 47
LCNUG 1927.2583

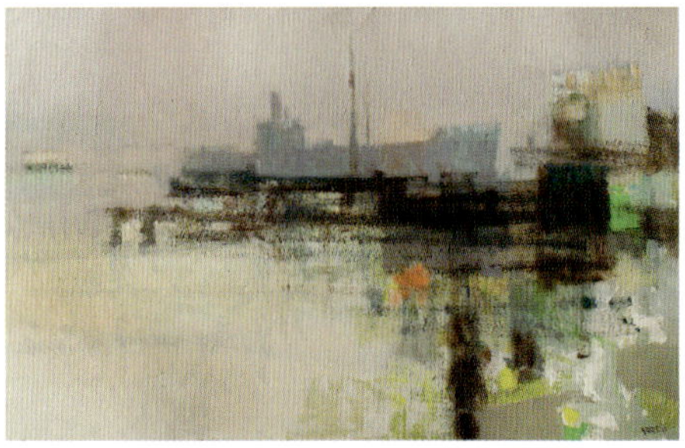

Poulsen, Georg 1911–1997
Shorescape
oil on canvas 48.5 x 76
LCNUG 1927.2584

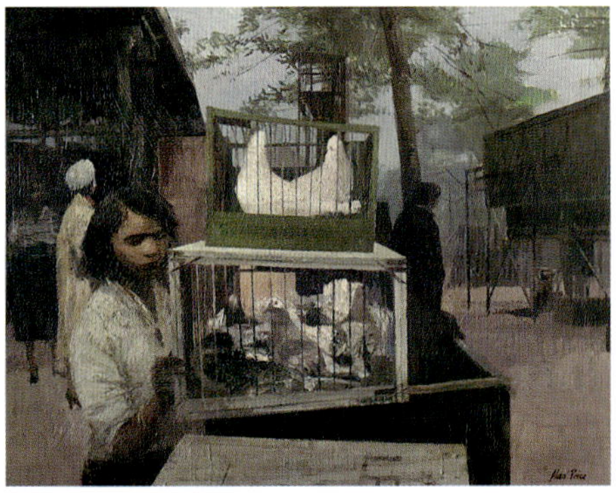

Price, Alan 1926–2002
The Bird Market
oil on board 39.5 x 52
LCNUG 1927.2170

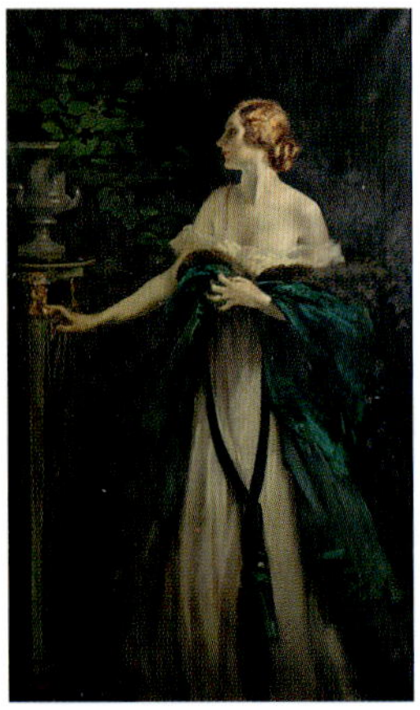

Ranken, William Bruce Ellis 1881–1941
Portrait of a Lady in Green 1928
oil on canvas 212.5 x 121.5
LCNUG 1927.1600

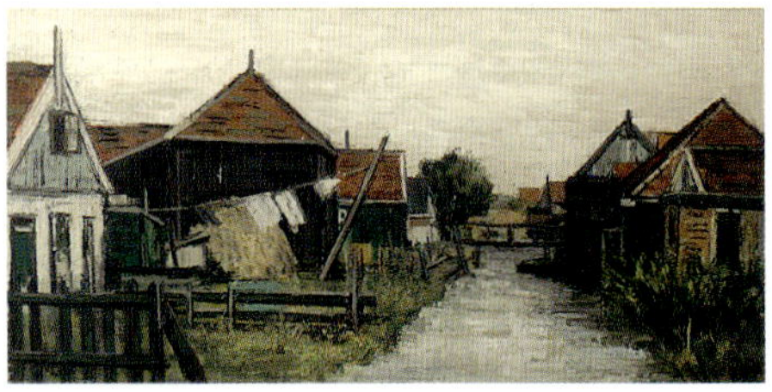

Rapp, Ginette 1928–1998
Canal in Volendam, The Netherlands
oil on canvas 40.2 x 80.2
LCNUG 1985.54

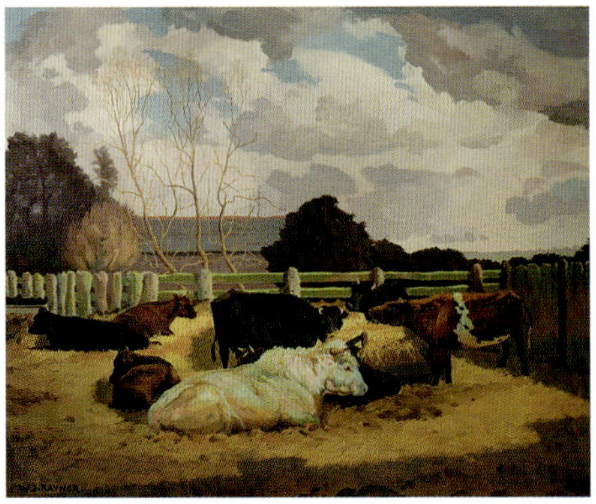

Rayner, W. J. active early 20th C
The White Bull
oil on canvas 56 x 66
LCNUG 1927.1998

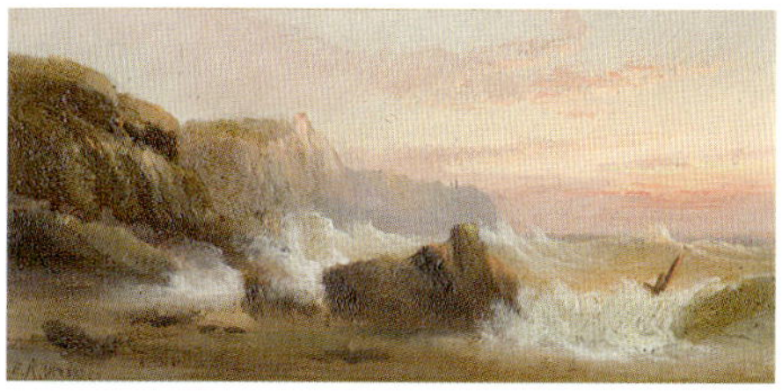

Redmore, Edward King 1860–1941
Seascape
oil on panel 9.5 x 20
LCNUG 1927.957a

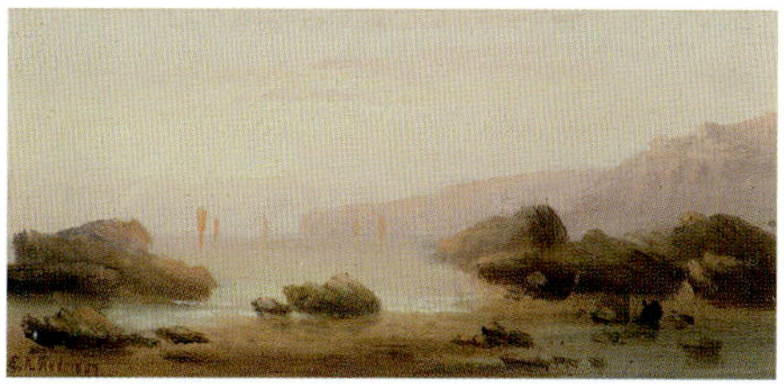

Redmore, Edward King 1860–1941
Seascape
oil on panel 9.5 x 20
LCNUG 1927.957b

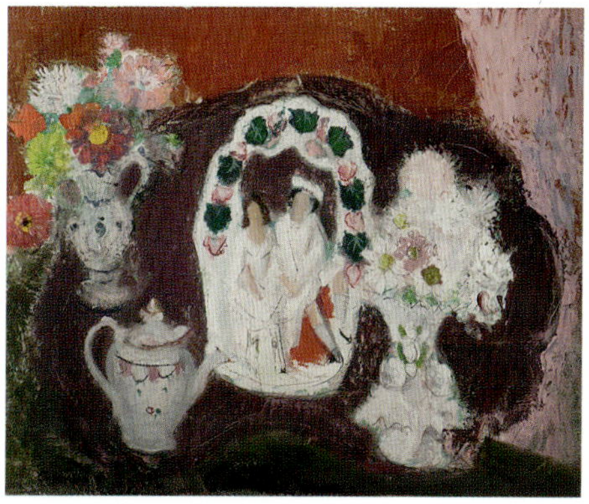

Redpath, Anne 1895–1965
Sweethearts
oil & crayon on board 54.6 x 63.5
LCNUG 1985.56

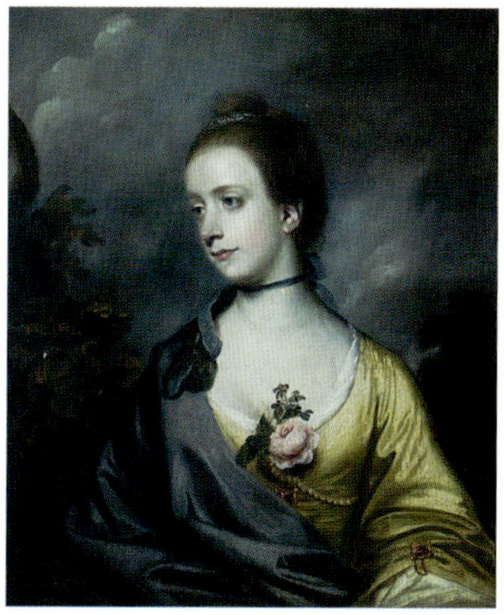

Reynolds, Joshua 1723–1792
Isabella Thorold of Syston (d.1803) 1754
oil on canvas 76 x 62
LCNUG 2008.21

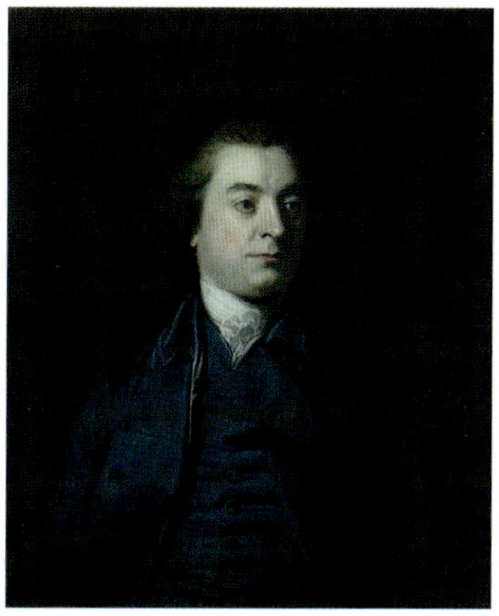

Reynolds, Joshua 1723–1792
Thomas Middleton Trollope of Casewick (1721–1779) 1754
oil on canvas 76 x 62
LCNUG 2008.20

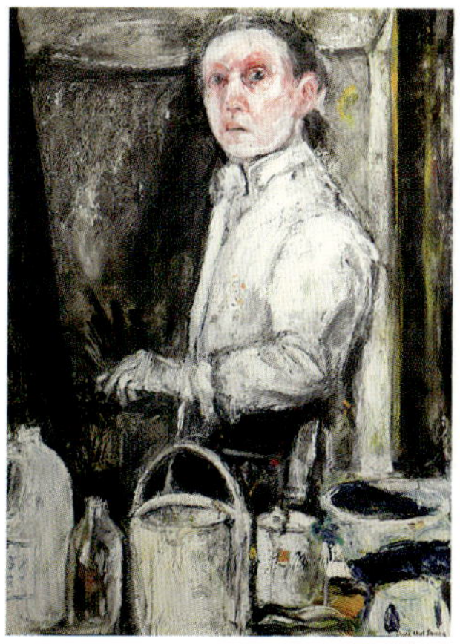

Rhys-James, Shani b.1953
Lead White 1995
oil on canvas 122 x 91.5
LCNUG 1996.10

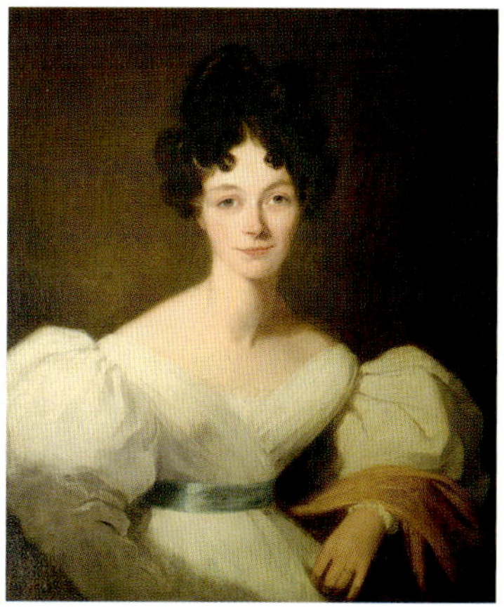

Richard, Frederick active c.1800–1850s
Mrs Richard Mason
oil on canvas 76.5 x 63
LCNUG 2001.6

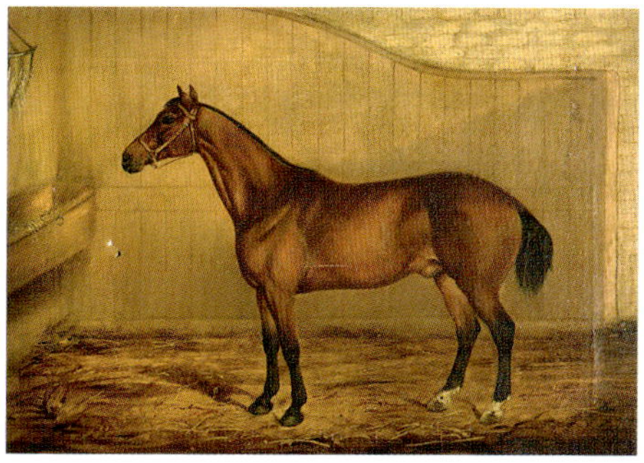

Robinson, William H.
'The Flea' 1833
oil on canvas 33 x 47
LCNUG 2001.37

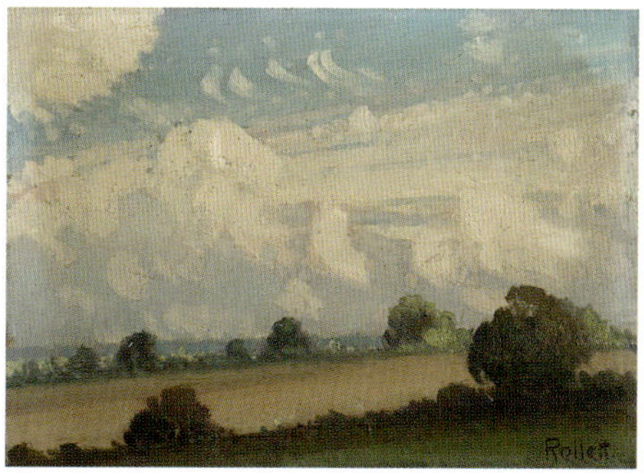

Rollett, Herbert 1872–1932
Summer Fallows 1931
oil on panel 30.5 x 40.5
LCNUG 1984.12

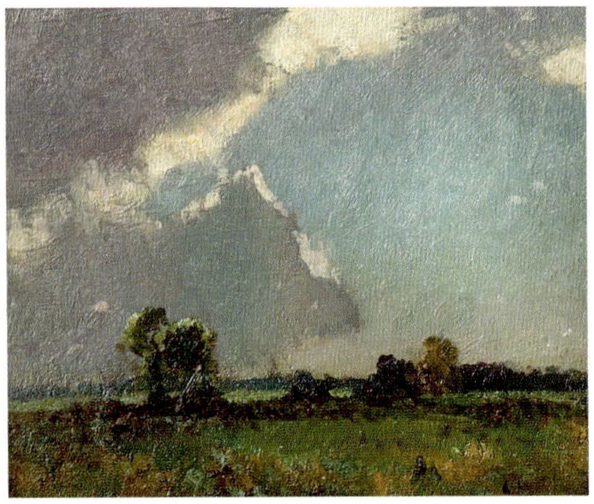

Rollett, Herbert 1872–1932
Blue Sky
oil on panel 22 x 27
LCNUG 1996.22

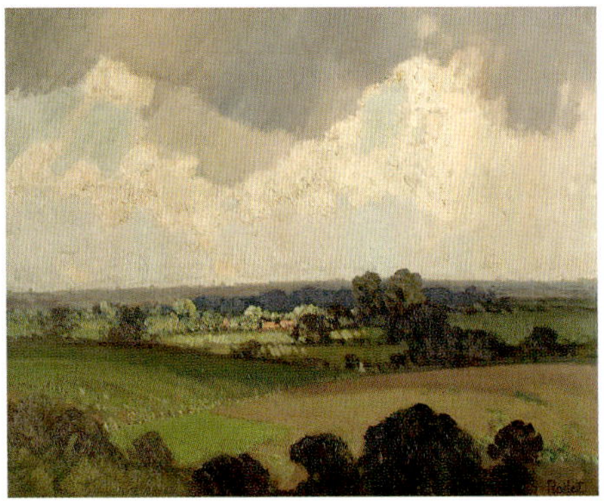

Rollett, Herbert 1872–1932
June Morning
oil on canvas 50.8 x 61
LCNUG 1927.259

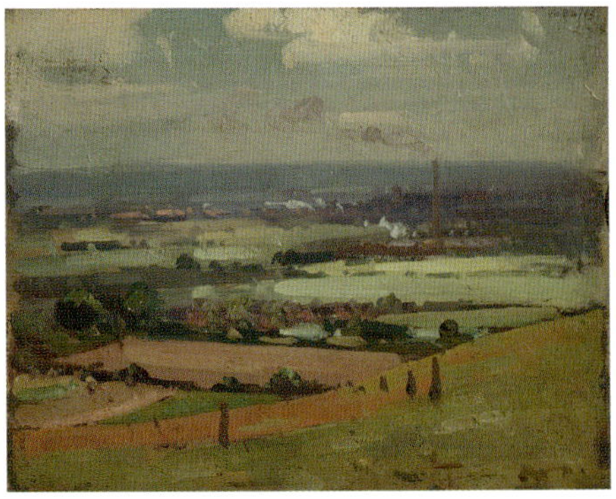

Rollett, Herbert 1872–1932
Landscape (recto)
oil on panel 22 x 27
LCNUG 1984.13a

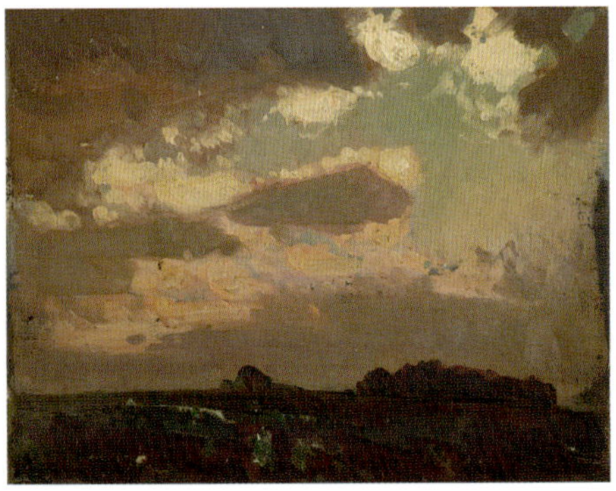

Rollett, Herbert 1872–1932
Landscape (verso)
oil on panel 22 x 27
LCNUG 1984.13b

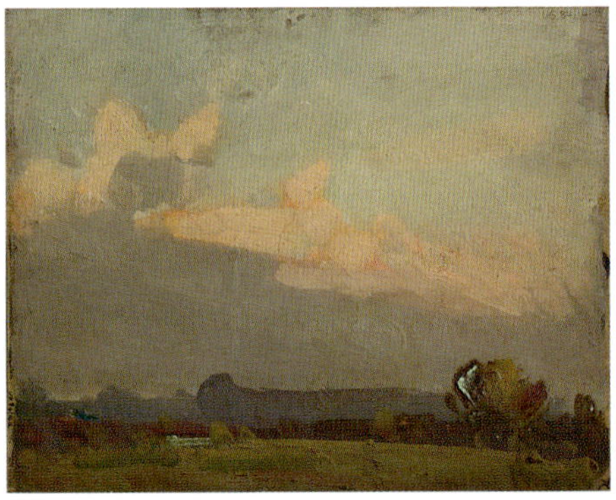

Rollett, Herbert 1872–1932
Landscape (recto)
oil on panel 22 x 27
LCNUG 1984.14a

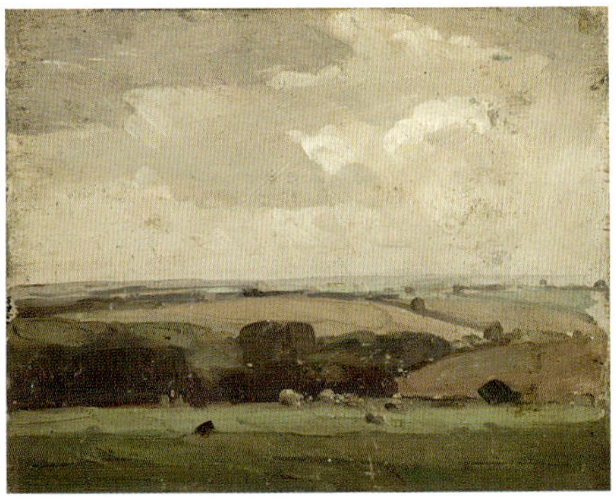

Rollett, Herbert 1872–1932
Landscape (verso)
oil on panel 21.9 x 27
LCNUG 1984.14b

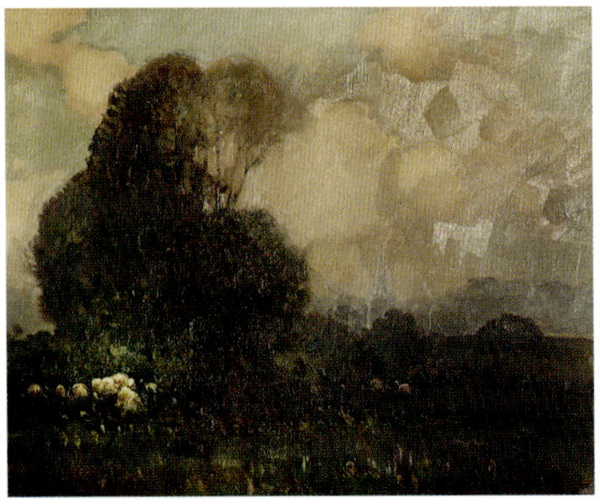

Rollett, Herbert 1872–1932
Louth, Lincolnshire
oil on canvas 51 x 61
LCNUG 1984.11

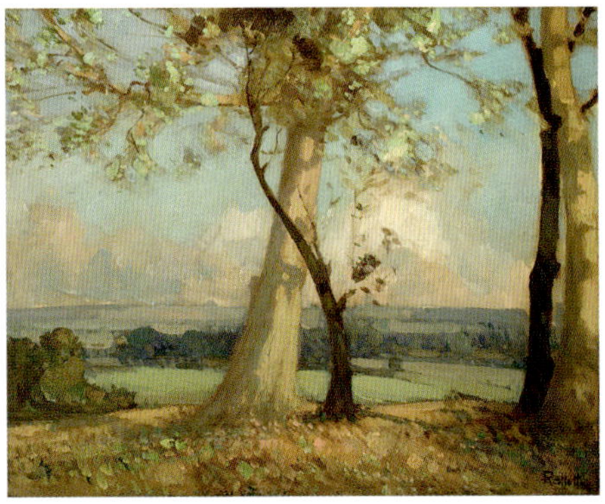

Rollett, Herbert 1872–1932
Louth, Lincolnshire
oil on panel 51.5 x 61
LCNUG 1996.24

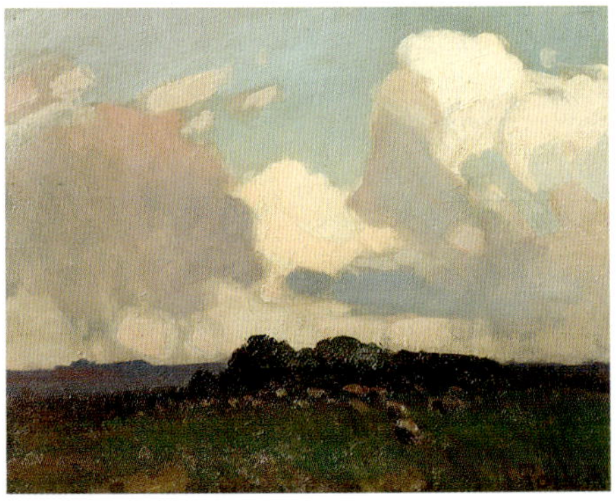

Rollett, Herbert 1872–1932
Sheep
oil on panel 21.5 x 26.5
LCNUG 1996.23

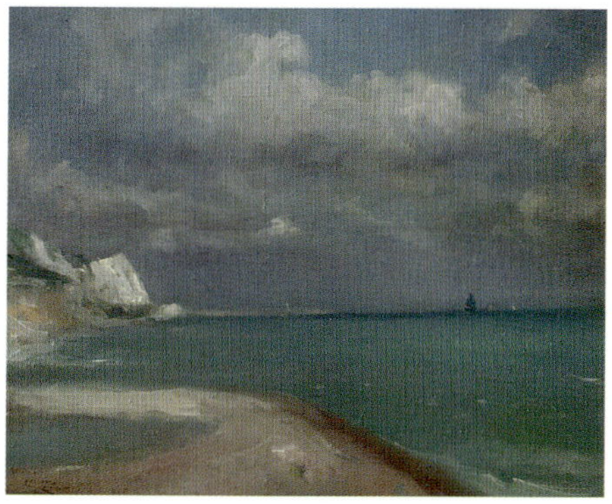

Roussel, Théodore Casimir 1847–1926
Approaching Storm, Dover, Kent
oil on canvas 70 x 80
LCNUG 1927.1699

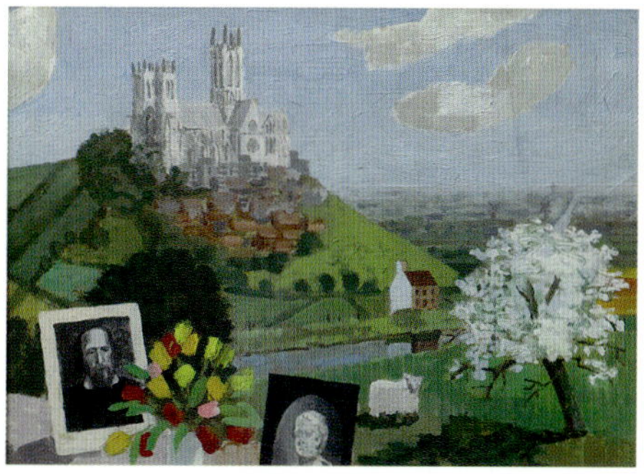

Rowntree, Kenneth 1915–1997
View of Lincoln Cathedral
oil on board 31.5 x 41.5
LCNUG 2009.29

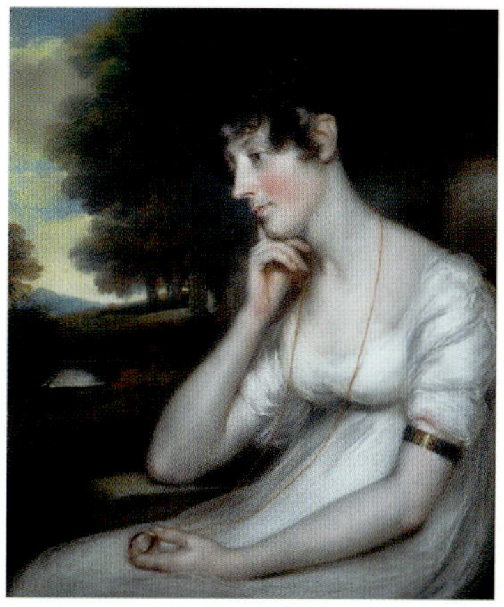

Russell, J. active late 19th C
Elizabeth Russell, née Tennyson
oil on canvas 75 x 62
TENN.T2010.12

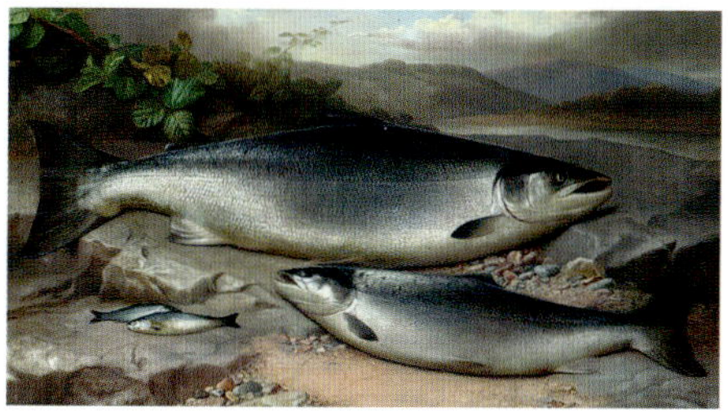

Russell, John Bucknell 1819–1893
Salmon 1887
oil on canvas 60.2 x 107.6
LCNUG 1927.819

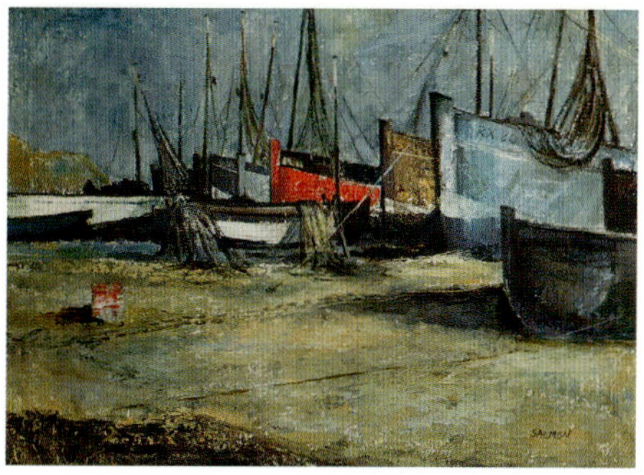

Salmon, James Marchbank 1916–1994
Boats and Nets, South Coast
oil on board 43 x 58.5
LCNUG 1927.2396

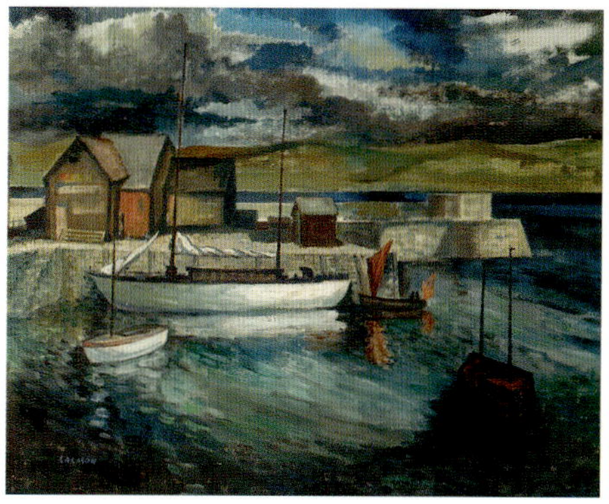

Salmon, James Marchbank 1916–1994
The White Yacht
oil on canvas 51 x 76.5
LCNUG 1927.1993

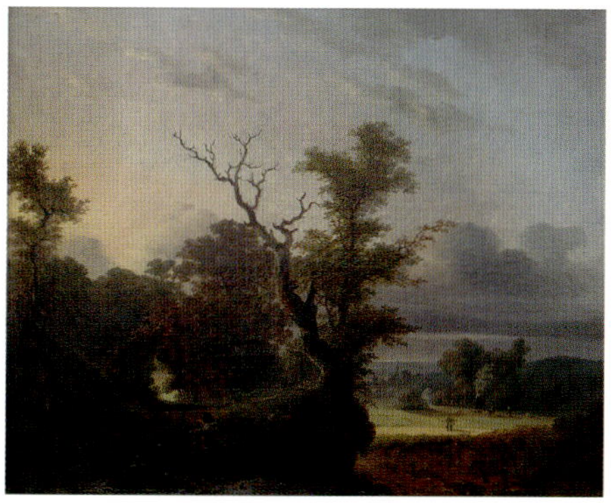

Schoor, Lodewijk van 1666–1726 or **Schoor, Nicholas van** active c.1690
Landscape with a Tree
oil on canvas 33 x 39.3
LCNUG 1927.1531

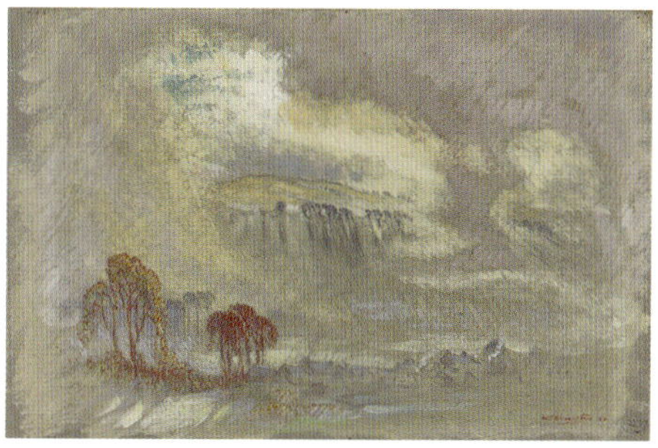

Shackleton, William 1872–1933
Winter Sunrise, Malham, Yorkshire 1924
oil on paper 19 x 28
LCNUG 1927.2337

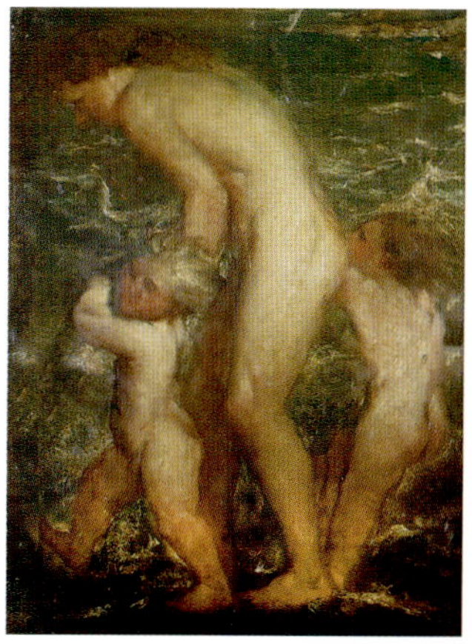

Shannon, Charles Haslewood 1863–1937
Salt Water 1902
oil on canvas 76 x 56.2
LCNUG 1927.2177

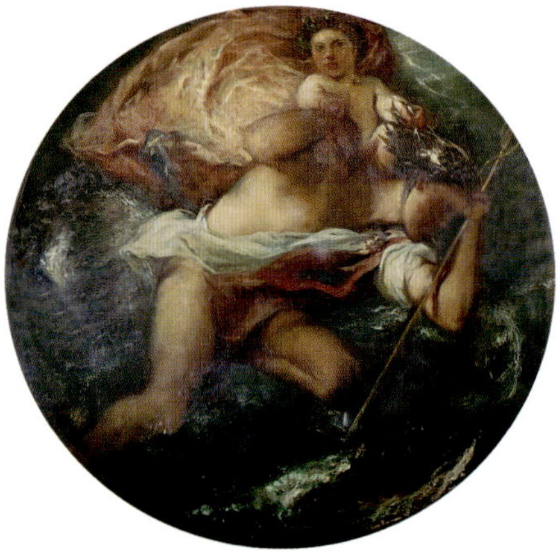

Shannon, Charles Haslewood 1863–1937
The Infant Bacchus 1906
oil on canvas 78.5
LCNUG 1927.2176

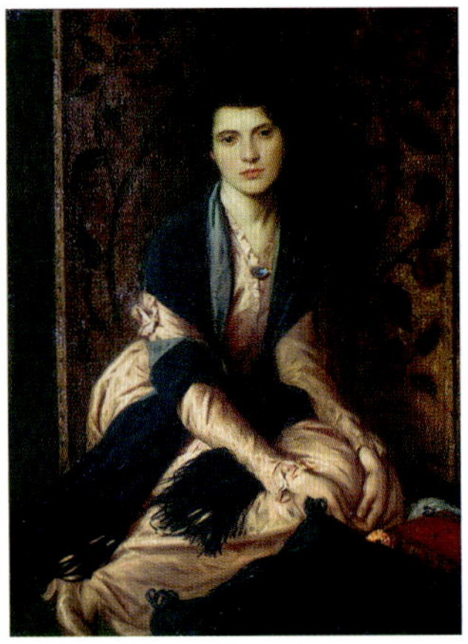

Shannon, Charles Haslewood 1863–1937
Miriam 1918
oil on canvas 110.5 x 85.5
LCNUG 1990.11

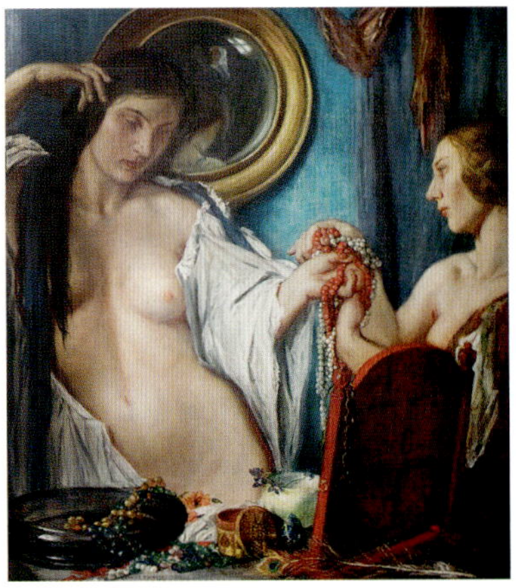

Shannon, Charles Haslewood 1863–1937
The Toilet 1927
oil on canvas 97.2 x 85.8
LCNUG 1927.683

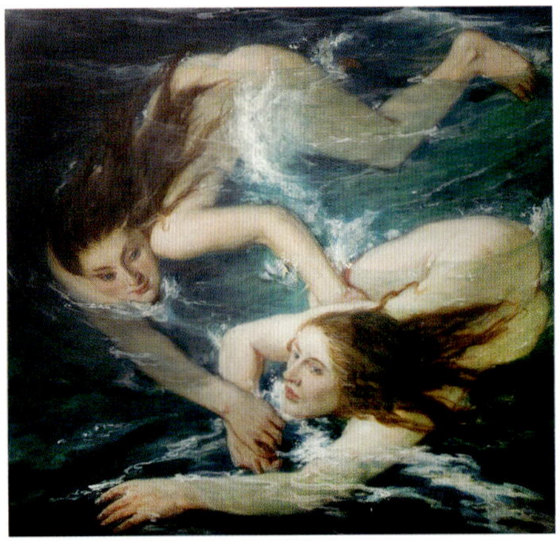

Shannon, Charles Haslewood 1863–1937
The Capture 1928
oil on canvas 92.2 x 96.5
LCNUG 1927.684

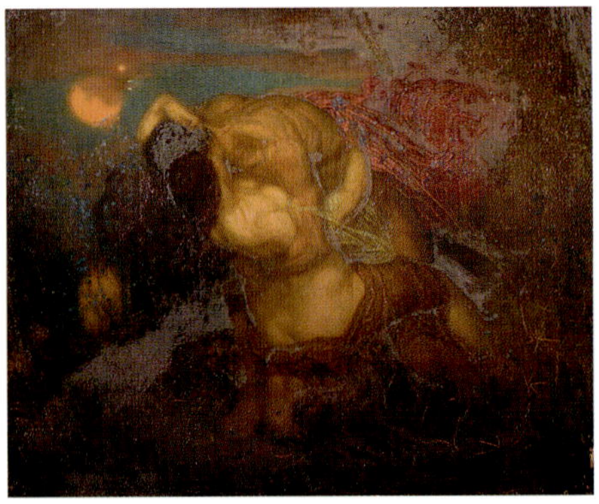

Shannon, Charles Haslewood 1863–1937
Study
oil on canvas 56 x 66.5
LCNUG 2009.30

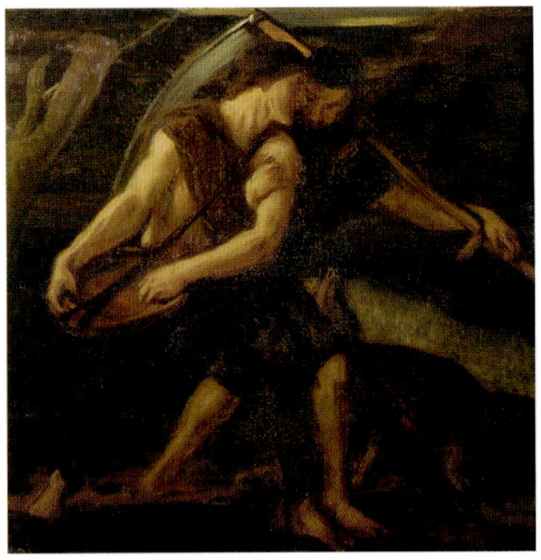

Shannon, Charles Haslewood 1863–1937
The Sower and the Reaper
oil on panel 61 x 62
LCNUG 1927.1930

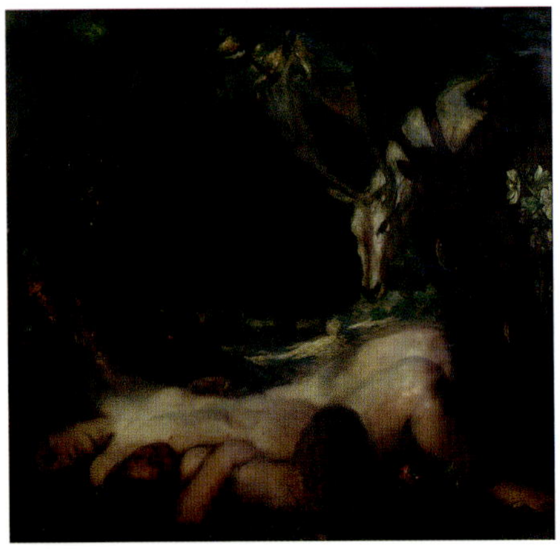

Shannon, Charles Haslewood 1863–1937
The Wood Nymph
oil on canvas 111 x 114
LCNUG 1977.2848

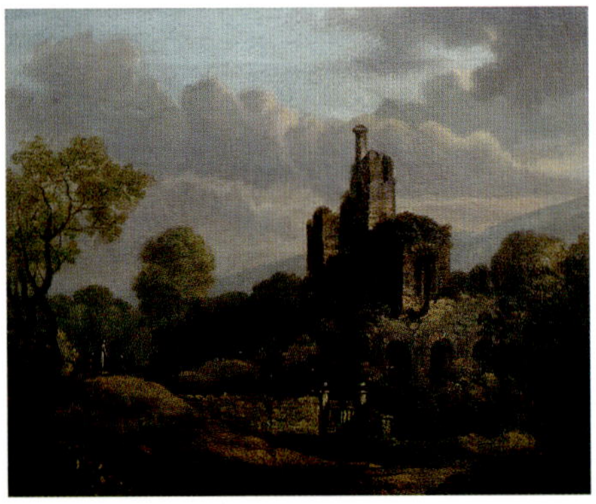

Shayer, William 1788–1879
Landscape with a Ruined Castle
oil on canvas 26 x 31
LCNUG 1927.1537

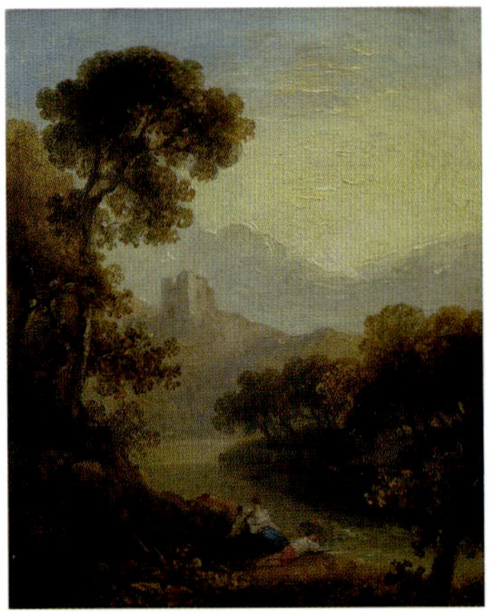

Sherlock, William P. 1780–1825
Landscape with a Castle and a River
oil on canvas 26.5 x 20.5
LCNUG 1927.1533

Facing page: Downton, John, 1906–1991, *Child with Roses* (detail), c.1936, The Collection: Art & Archaeology in Lincolnshire (Usher Gallery) (p. 295)

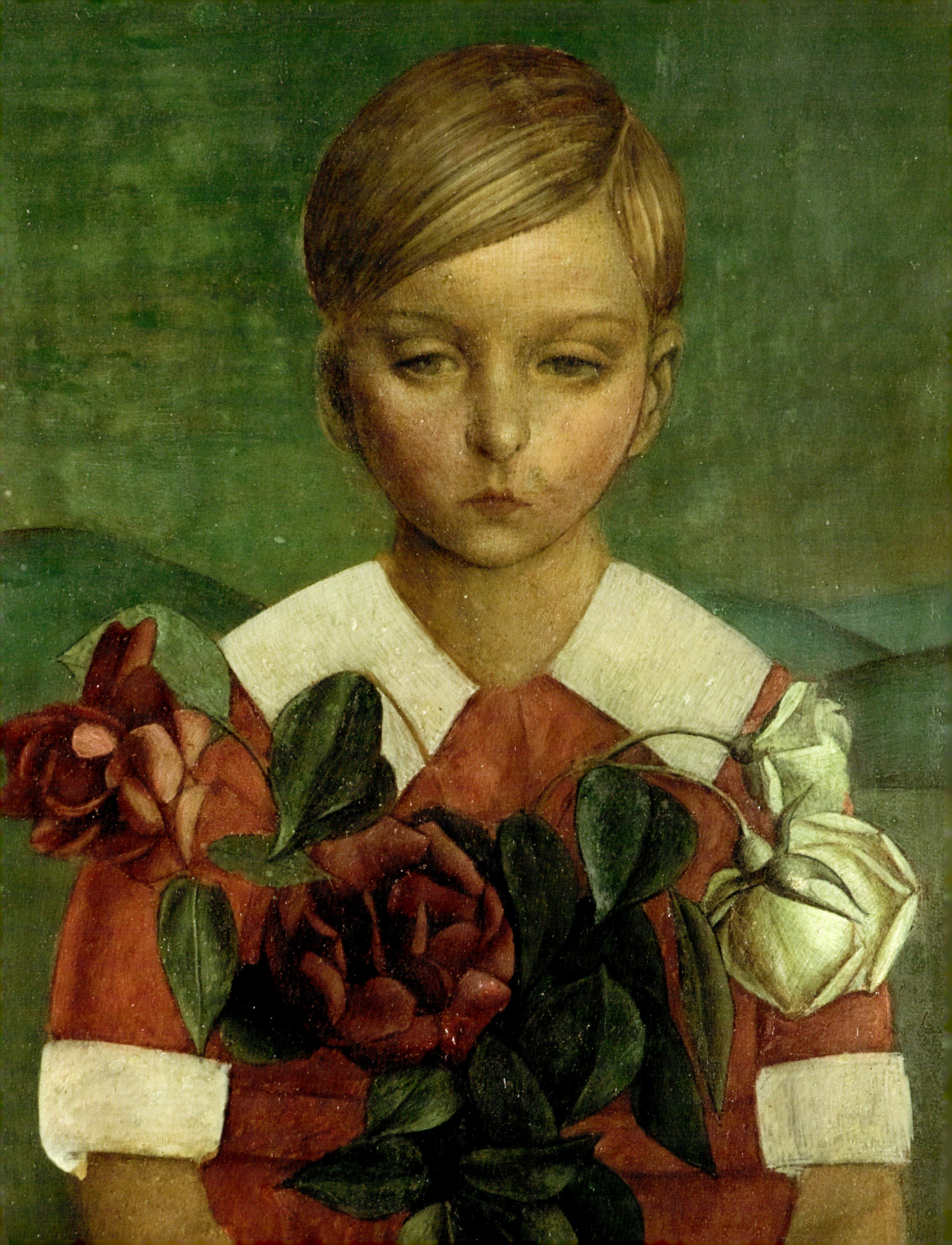

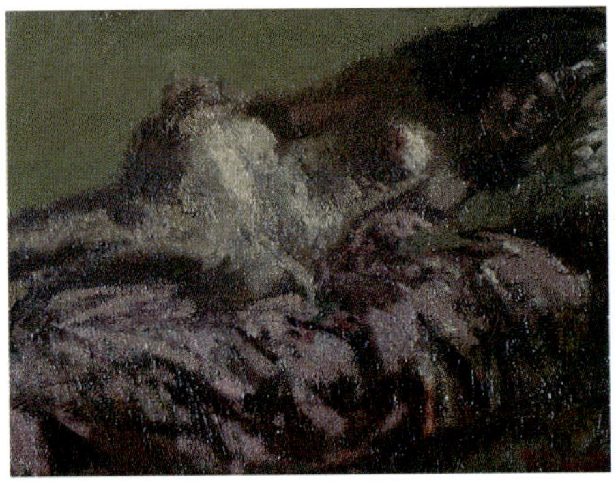

Sickert, Walter Richard 1860–1942
Nude Figure Reclining 1912
oil on canvas 40.9 x 51.2
LCNUG 1927.636

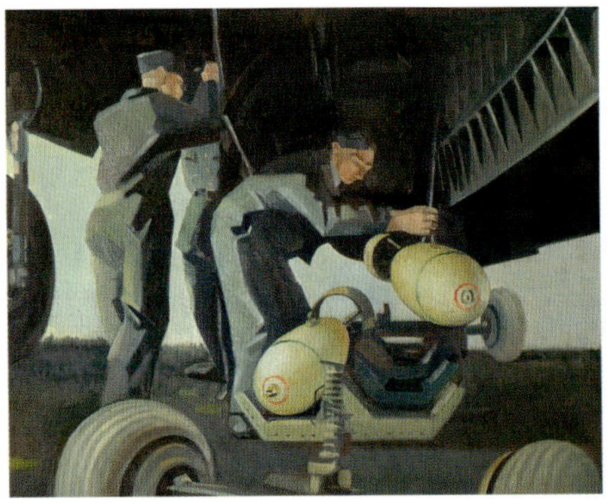

Smith, David T. b.1920
Bombing Up
oil on canvas 41 x 51
LCNUG 1927.1768

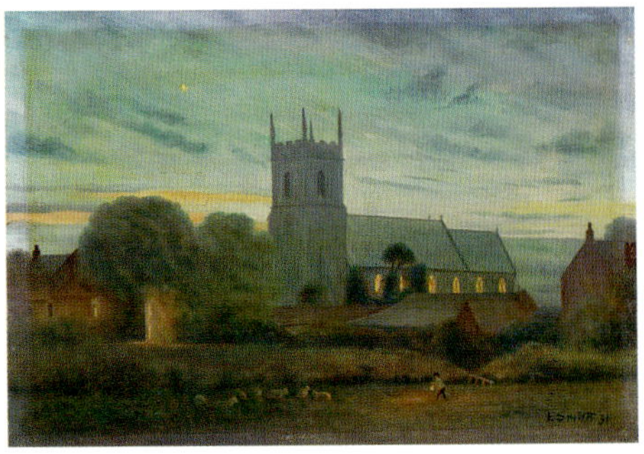

Smith, Edward Blount (attributed to) active 1877–1898
Nettleton Church, Lincolnshire
oil on board 25 x 35.5
LCNUG 1927.693

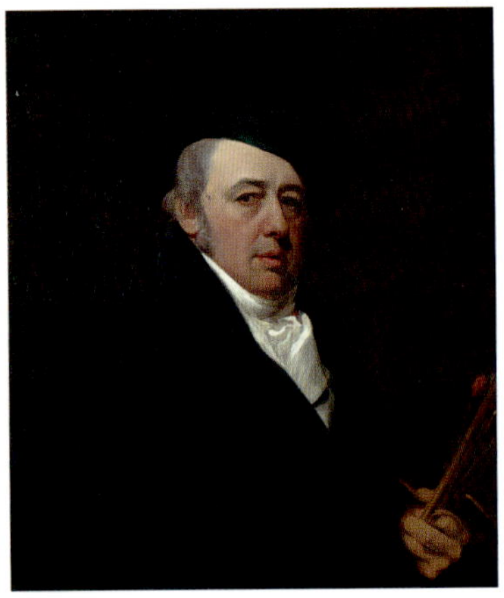

Smith, John Raphael 1752–1812
Self Portrait 1785–1787
oil on canvas 78.8 x 64.3
LCNUG 1978.66

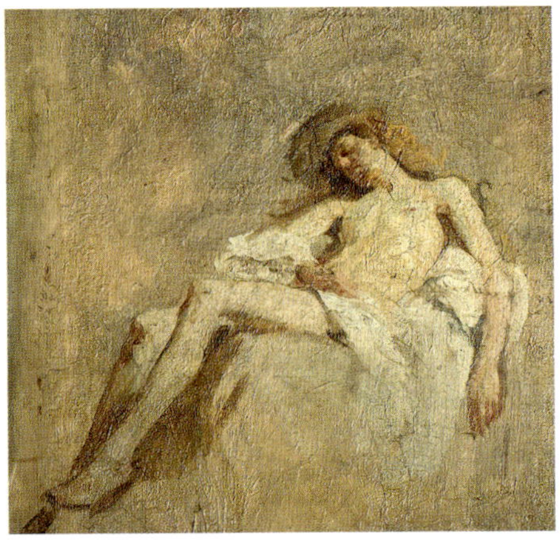

Solomon, Solomon Joseph 1860–1927
An Allegory of the Dead Christ (study)
oil on canvas 45.5 x 51
LCNUG 1927.263

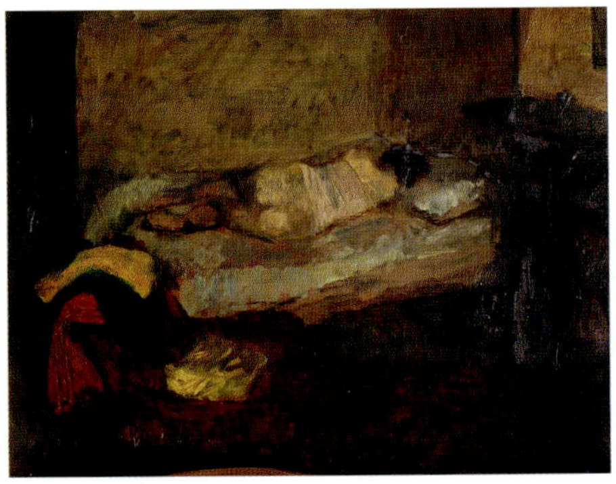

Spear, Ruskin 1911–1990
Interior with Nude
oil on panel 50.5 x 63.3
LCNUG 1927.1921

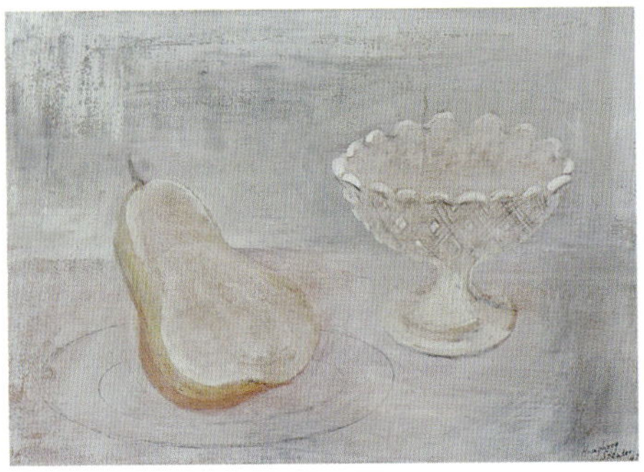

Spender, John Humphrey 1910–2005
Still Life in White 1947
oil on board 27.7 x 37.8
LCNUG 1985.59

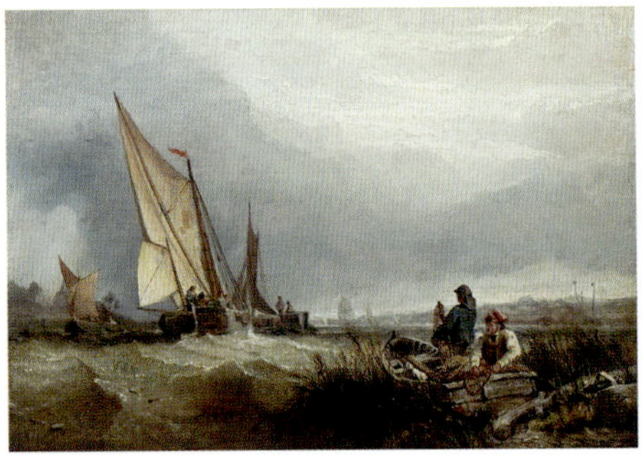

Stanfield, William Clarkson 1793–1867
River Scene with Shipping
oil on canvas 26 x 36.5
LCNUG 1927.1532

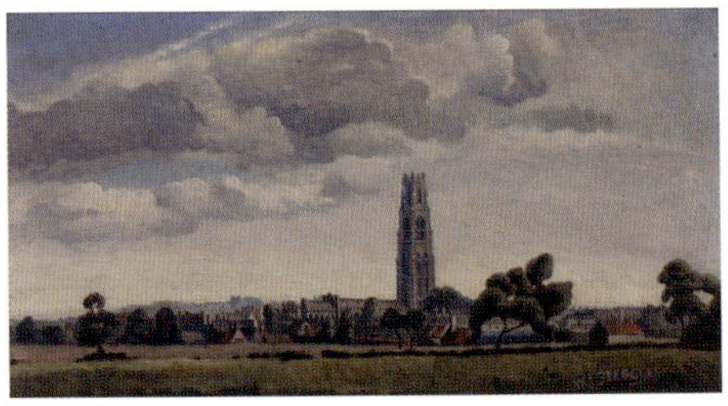

Steggles, Walter James 1908–1997
Boston, Lincolnshire
oil on panel 18.8 x 33.3
LCNUG 1927.150

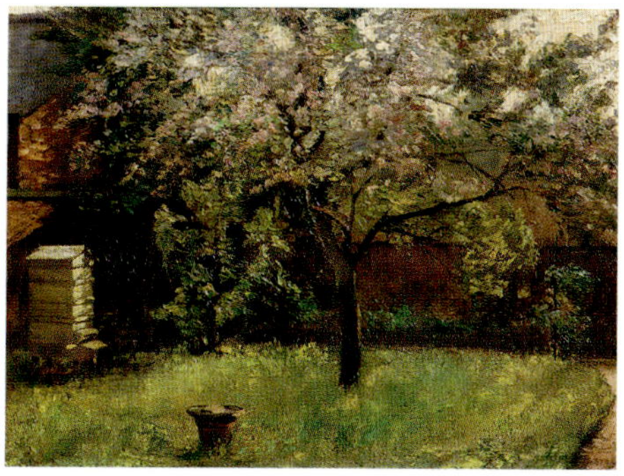

Storey, Thomas George 1865–1935
Blossom
oil on canvas 36 x 46
LCNUG 1995.7

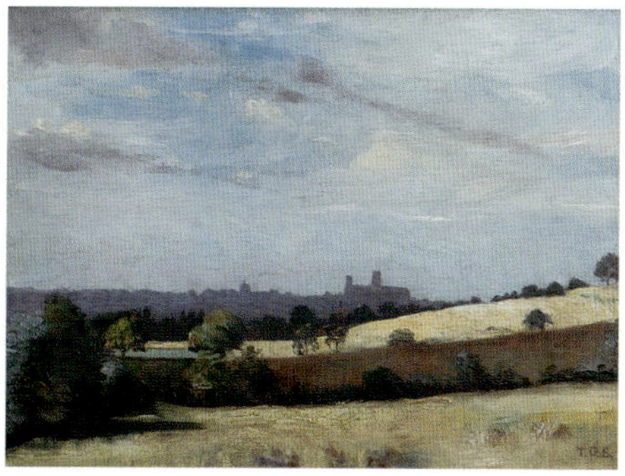

Storey, Thomas George 1865–1935
Lincoln from the South
oil on canvas 36 x 46.2
LCNUG 1995.8

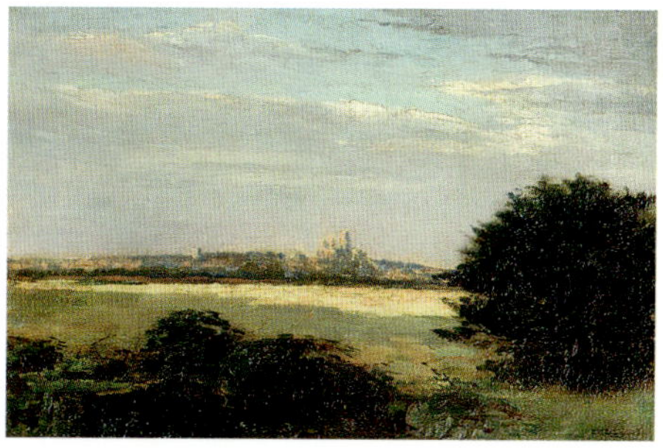

Storey, Thomas George 1865–1935
Lincoln from the South West
oil on canvas 28.2 x 41
LCNUG 1995.9

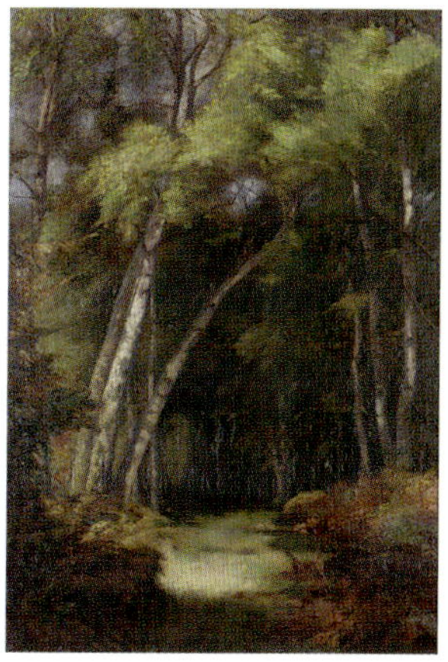

Storey, Thomas George 1865–1935
The Sanctuary
oil on canvas 129.5 x 86.5
LCNUG 1978.64

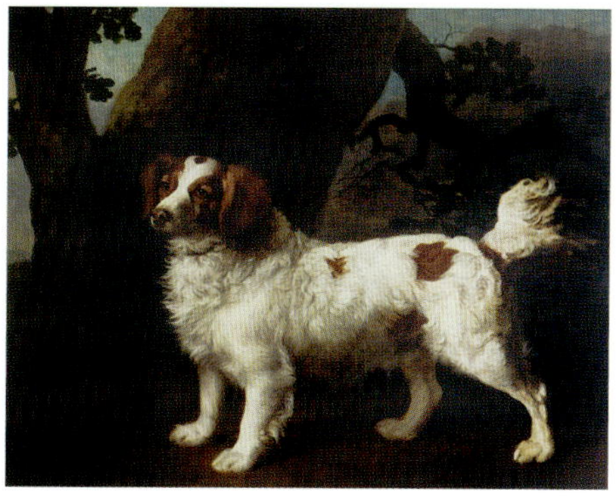

Stubbs, George 1724–1806
A Clumber Spaniel
oil on oak panels 83 x 101.3
LCNUG 1996.14

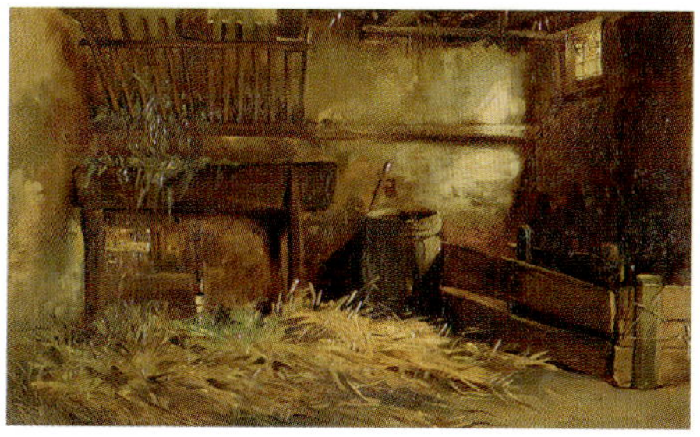

Sully, Thomas 1783–1872
Old Stables of the 'Dolpinn' Inn, Lincoln 1827
oil on panel 22.3 x 35.9
LCNUG 1927.223

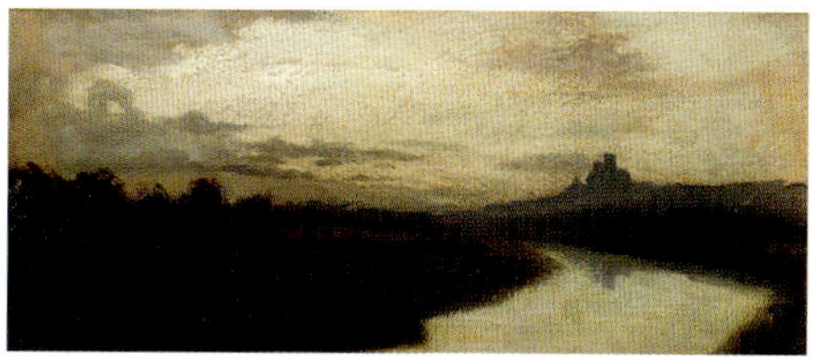

Taylor, Edward Richard 1838–1912
Lincoln Cathedral from the Witham
oil on millboard 19.7 x 39.4
LCNUG 1927.2597

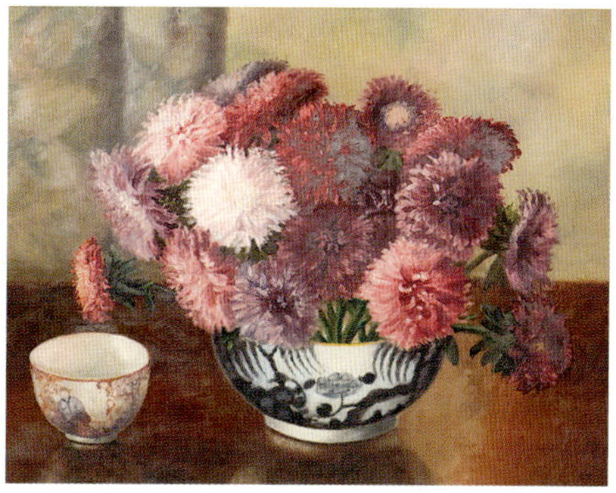

Taylor, George active 1911–1931
Double Asters
oil on board 41 x 51
LCNUG 1971.107

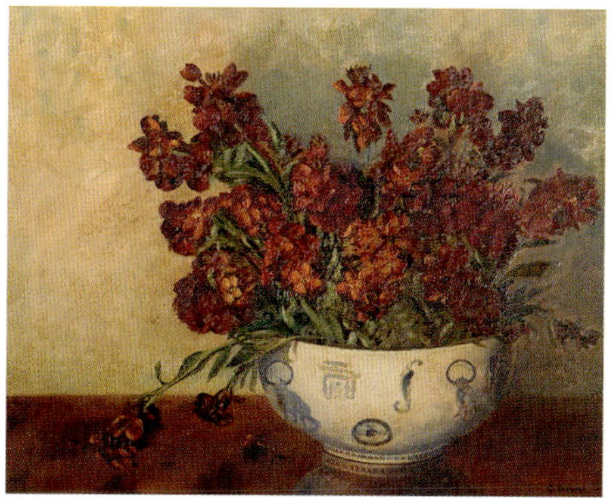

Taylor, George active 1911–1931
Wallflowers
oil on canvas 51 x 61
LCNUG 1971.106

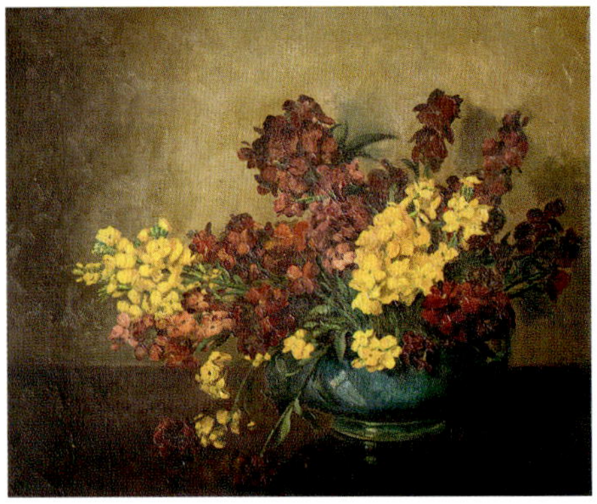

Taylor, George active 1911–1931
Wallflowers
oil on canvas 52 x 61
LCNUG 1971.109

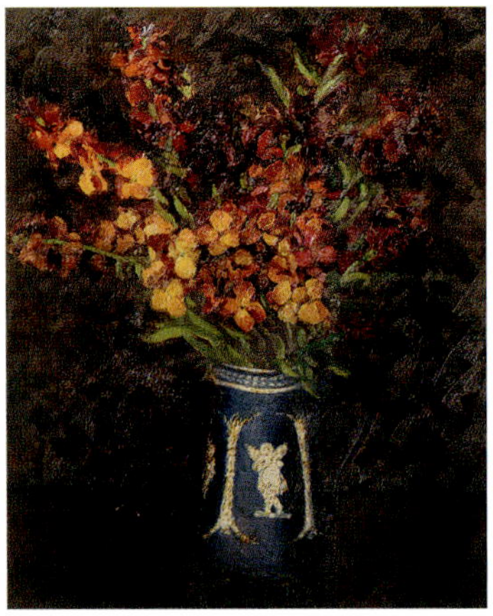

Taylor, George active 1911–1931
Wedgwood and Wallflowers
oil on canvas 51 x 41
LCNUG 1971.108

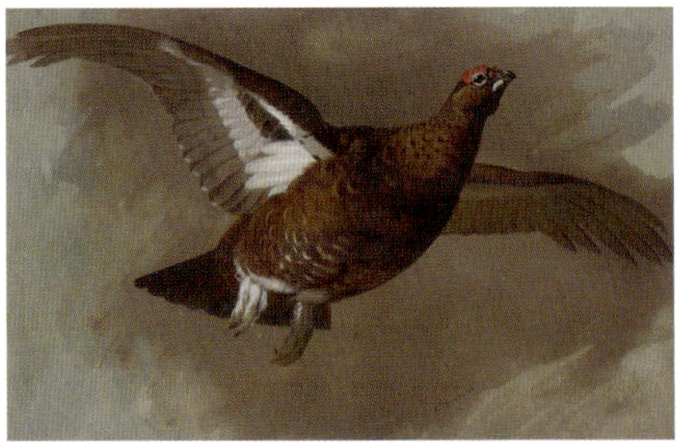

Thorburn, Archibald 1860–1935
Grouse
oil on board 22 x 27.5
LCNUG 2001.38

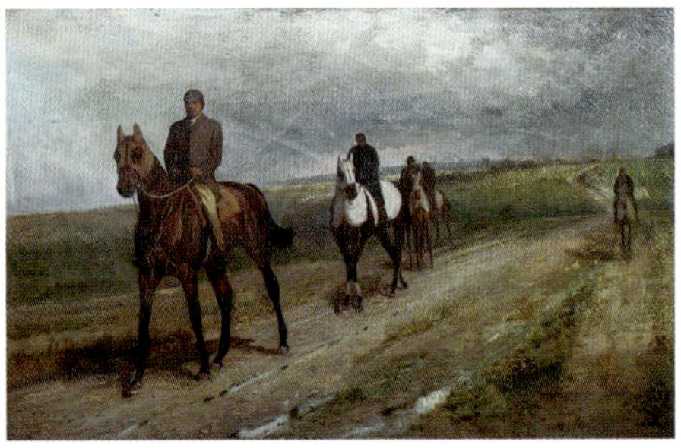

Townsend, Arthur Louis b.1848
Horses Returning from Exercise, Newmarket Heath, Suffolk 1886
oil on canvas 29 x 44.5
LCNUG 1927.2236

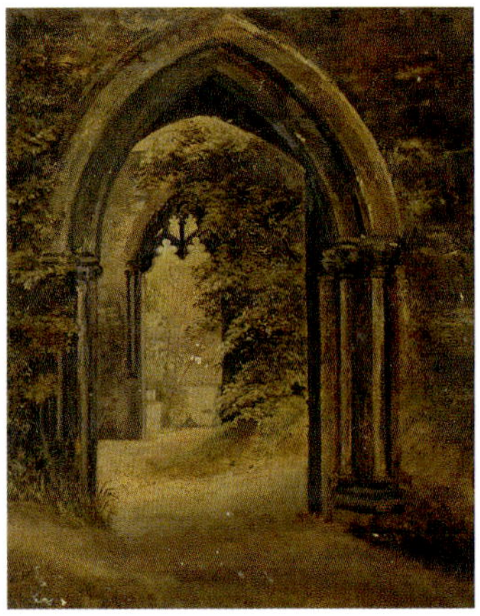

Toynbee, Edith
The Ruins of the Bishop's Palace, Lincoln
oil on canvas 38.5 x 30
LCNUG 1927.271

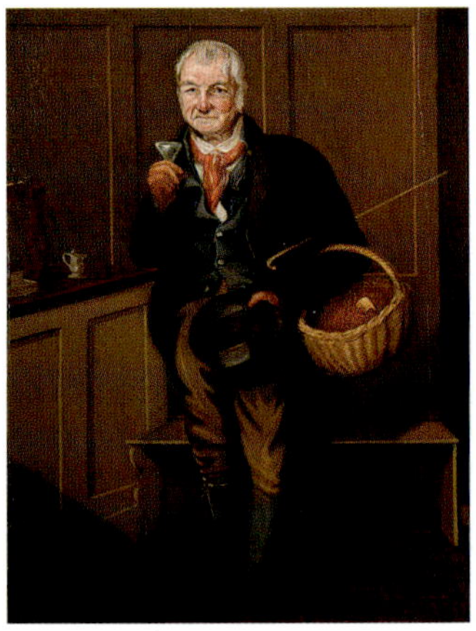

Tuke, Samuel 1797–1857
Mr Kendal 1842
oil on wood panel 41.9 x 33.5
LCNUG 1976.9

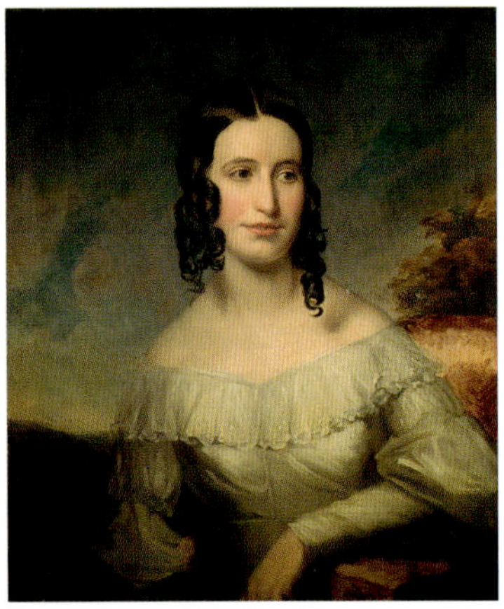

Tuke, Samuel 1797–1857
Miss Emma Tuke
oil on canvas 76.5 x 63
LCNUG 1976.158

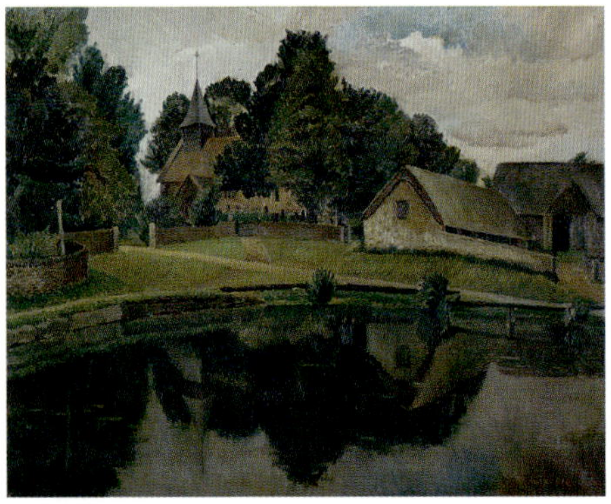

Tyson, Kathleen 1898–c.1982
Westwell, Kent (?)
oil on canvas 64.7 x 76
LCNUG 1927.2627

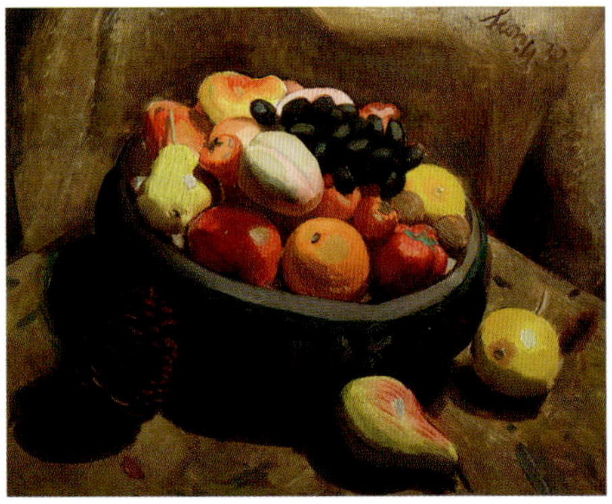

Underwood, Leon 1890–1975
Still Life 1930
oil on canvas 50.8 x 61
LCNUG 1927.149

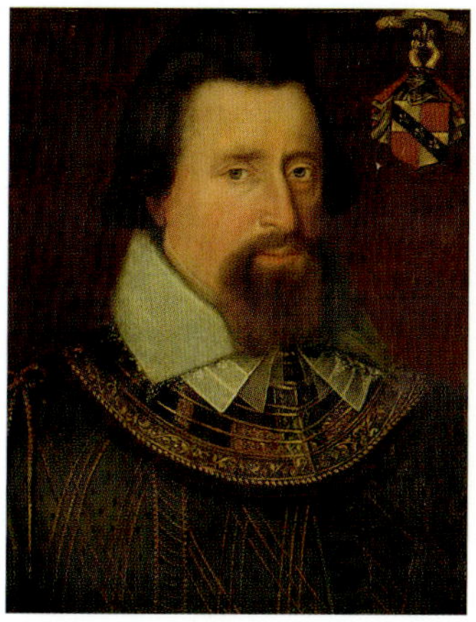

unknown artist
Sir Peter Eure (1549–1612) 1593
oil on panel 50.4 x 38.8
LCNUG 1927.38

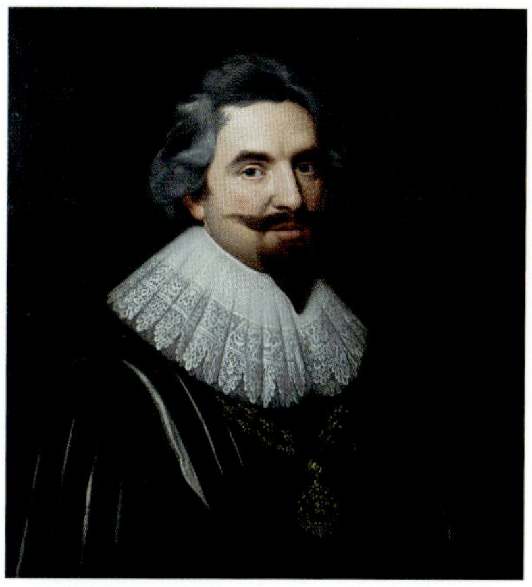

unknown artist
Sir Philibert Vernatti (c.1590–1646) c.1626
oil on panel 69 x 62
LCNUG 1979.77

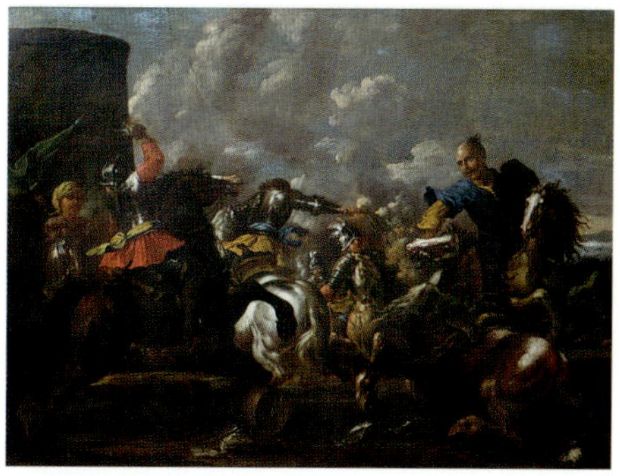

unknown artist 17th C
Turkish Battle Piece
oil on canvas 113.5 x 147.5
LCNUG 1927.1584

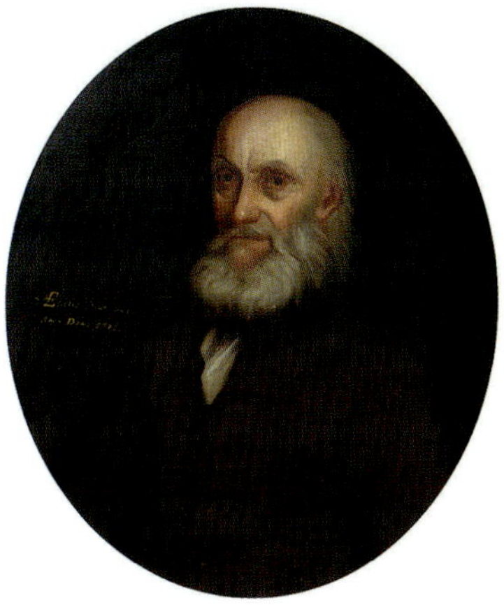

unknown artist
Reverend John Cunnington 1706
oil on canvas 76.5 x 63.5
LCNUG 1927.2537

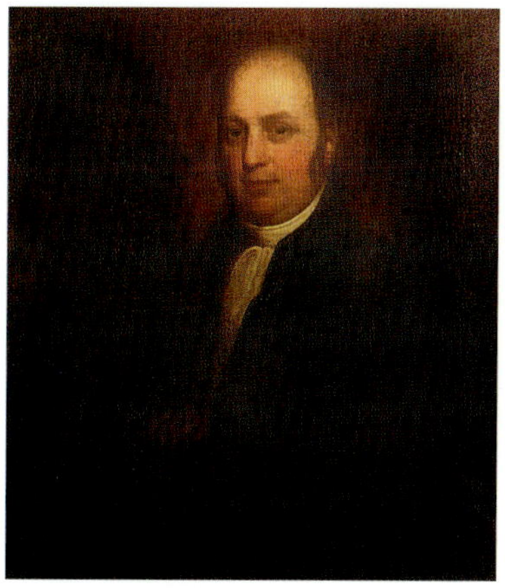

unknown artist
William Mawer c.1773
oil on canvas 76.5 x 64
LCNUG 1984.22

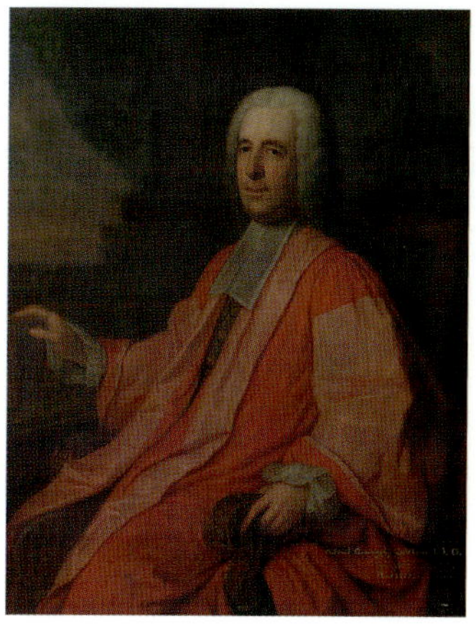

unknown artist 18th C
Colonel Coningsby Sibthorp (1706–1779), LLD
oil on canvas 125 x 100
LCNUG 2001.39

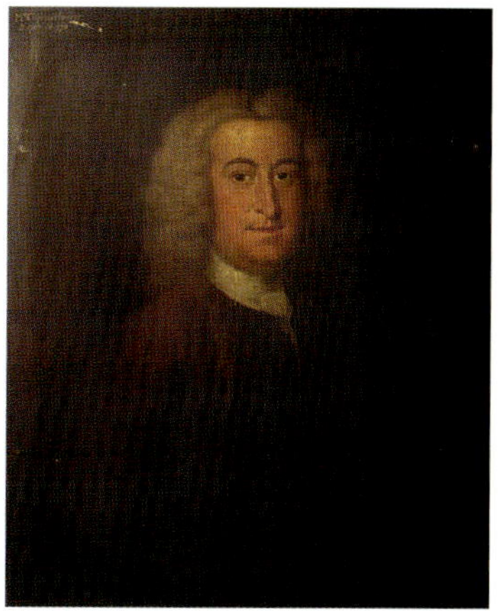

unknown artist 18th C
Mr Gibbon Hawker (1703–1778)
oil on canvas 76 x 63.5
LCNUG 2001.8

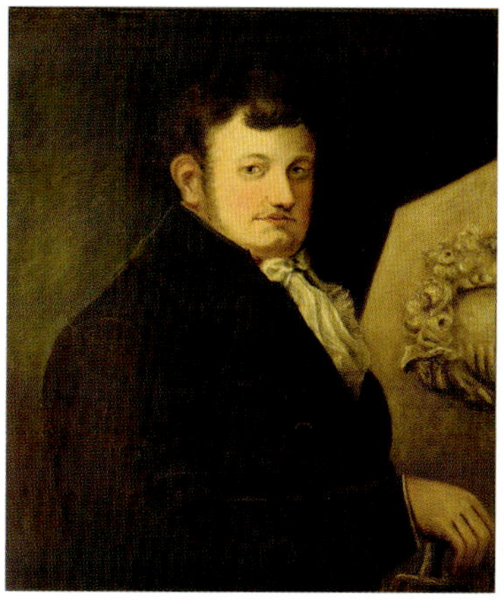

unknown artist
Charles Hayward, Town Clerk 1820
oil on canvas 78 x 63.5
LCNUG 1927.2045

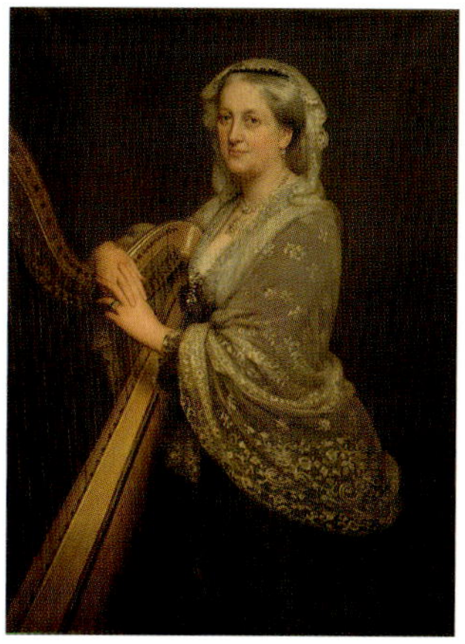

unknown artist
Louisa Amcotts Cracroft (1590–1643), Wife of Gervais Tottenham Waldo Sibthorp 1880
oil on canvas 127 x 93
LCNUG 1972.153

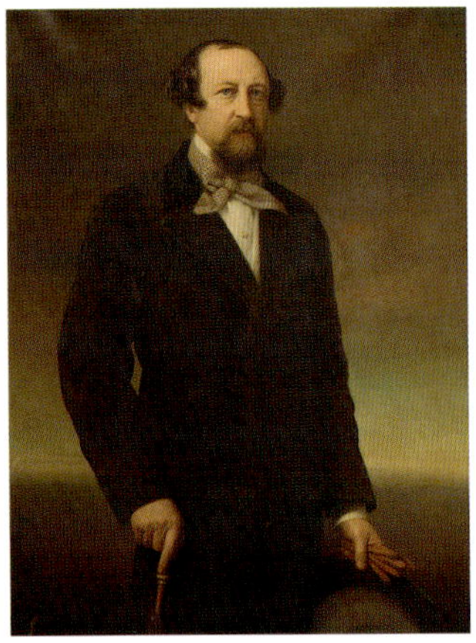

unknown artist
Gervaise Tottenham Waldo Sibthorp (1815–1861) 1882
oil on canvas 125 x 99
LCNUG 1972.152

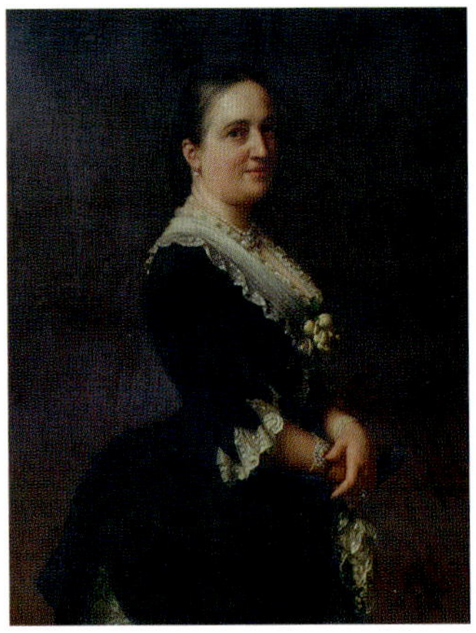

unknown artist
Mary Georgiana, Wife of Coningsby Charles Sibthorp 1883
oil on canvas 91.5 x 71.5
LCNUG 2001.2

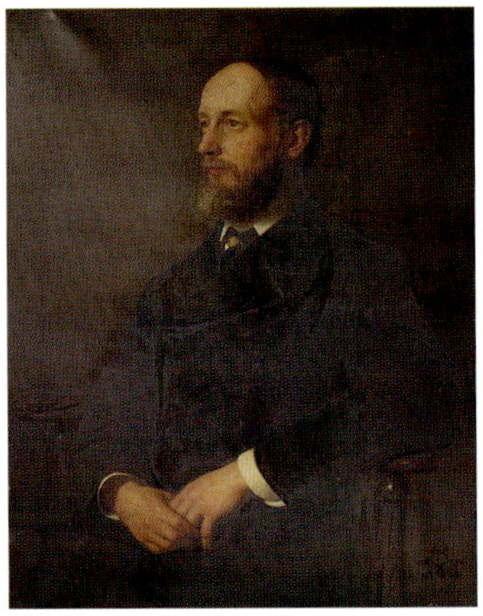

unknown artist
Coningsby Charles Sibthorp 1883
oil on canvas 90.5 x 70.5
LCNUG 2001.1

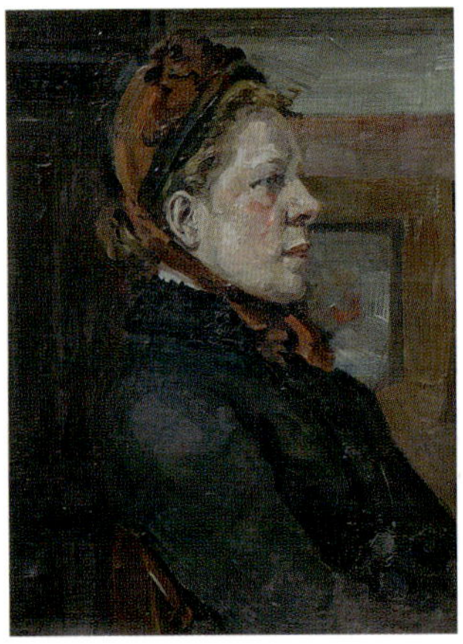

unknown artist
Madame Frieda Rholl c.1885
oil on canvas laid on board 33.4 x 24.5
LCNUG 1995.61

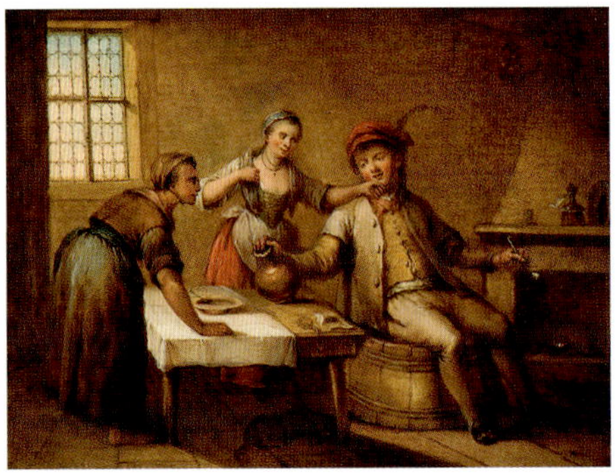

unknown artist early 19th C
Interior Scene with a Man Smoking a Pipe
oil on panel 19.6 x 25.8
LCNUG 1980.151

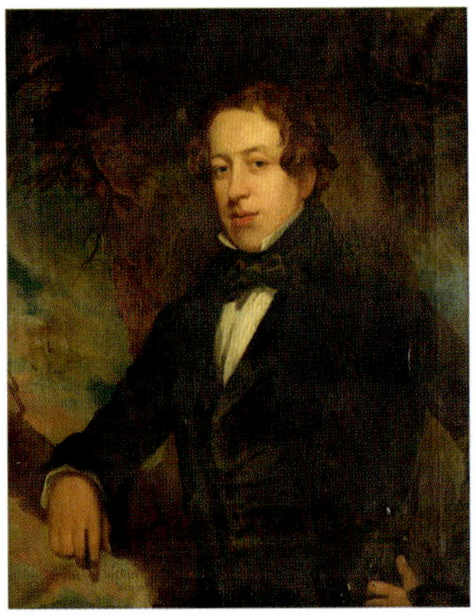

unknown artist mid-19th C
Gervaise Tottenham Waldo Sibthorp (1815–1861)
oil on canvas 92 x 72
LCNUG 2001.40

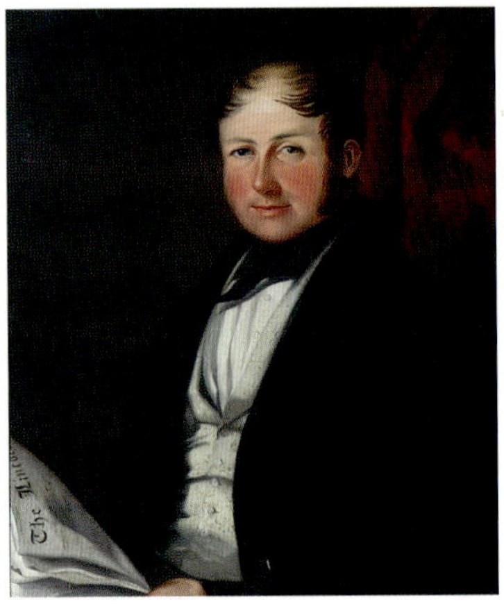

unknown artist 19th C
Portrait of an Unknown Man
oil on canvas 76 x 63.5
LCNUG 2001.15

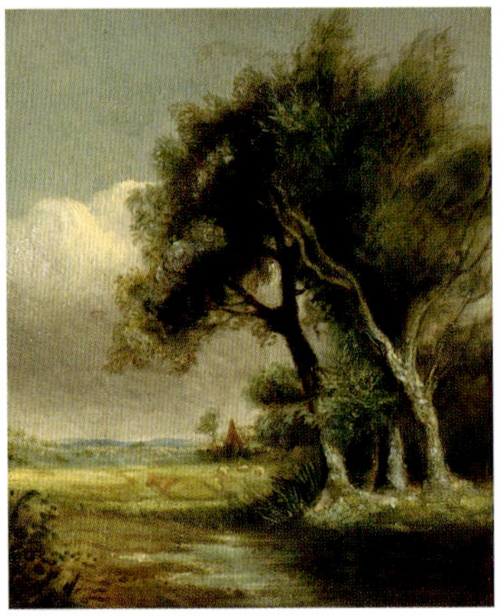

unknown artist 19th C
Tree Study
oil on panel 28.5 x 23.5
LCNUG 1927.1534

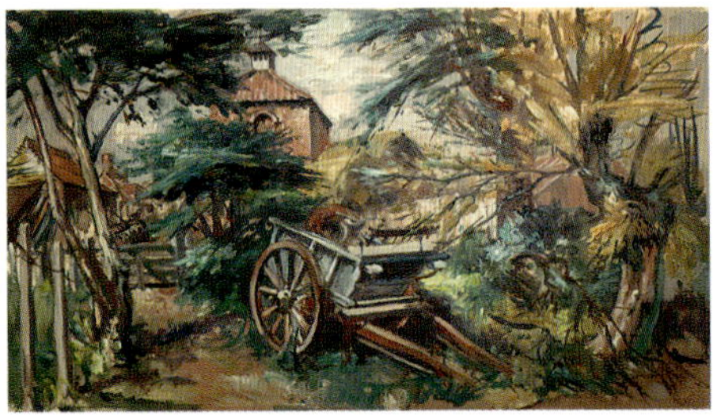

unknown artist mid-20th C
Farm Buildings and a Wagon
oil on board 56 x 96.5
LCNUG 2001.3

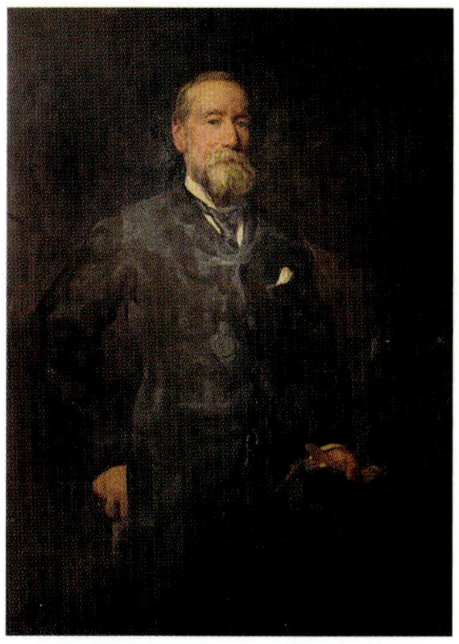

unknown artist
Alfred Shuttleworth (1843–1925), JP for Lincoln
oil on canvas 147 x 100
PCF25

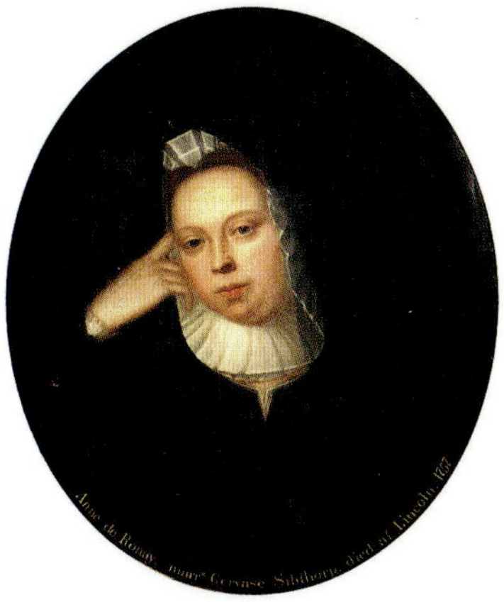

unknown artist
Anne de Ronay (d.1757), Wife of Gervaise Tottenham Waldo Sibthorp
oil on canvas 96 x 83
LCNUG 1972.143

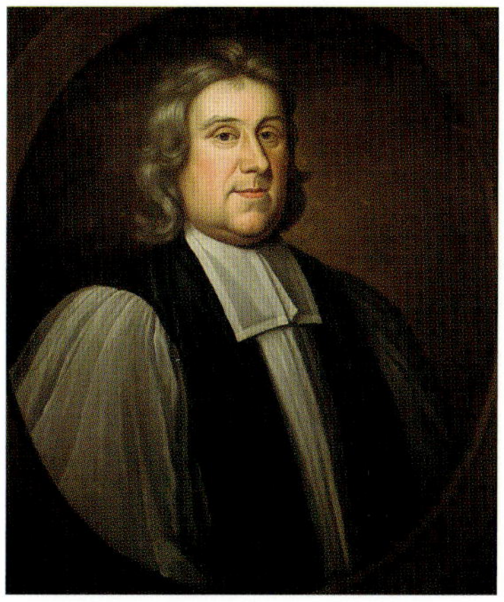

unknown artist
Archbishop Thomas Tenison (1636–1715), Archbishop of Canterbury
oil on canvas 75 x 61
TENN.T2010.06

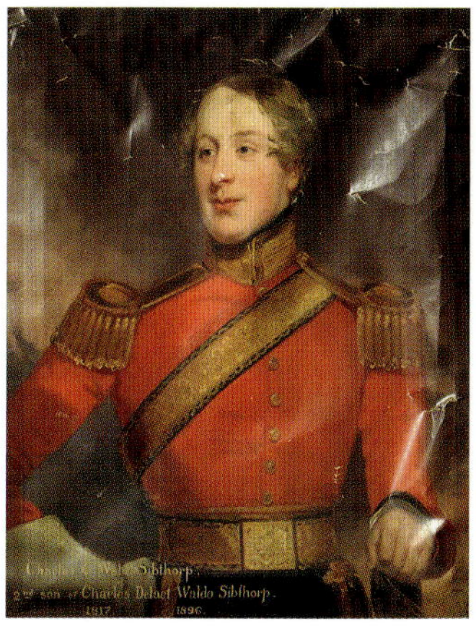

unknown artist
Charles C. Waldo Sibthorp (1817–1896)
oil on canvas 88 x 68
PCF24

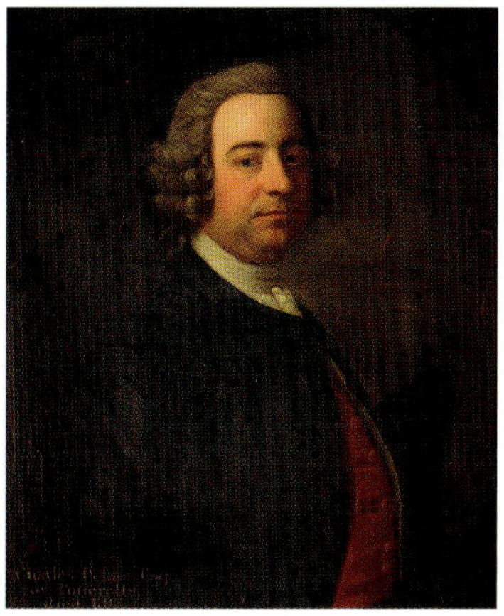

unknown artist
Charles Delaet, Esq. of Potterells (d.1792)
oil on canvas 73 x 61
PCF24B

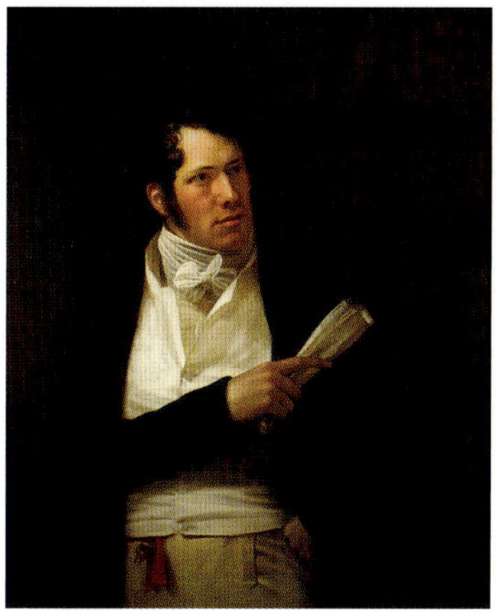

unknown artist
Charles Tennyson Turner (1808–1879)
oil on canvas 95 x 75
TENN.T2010.07

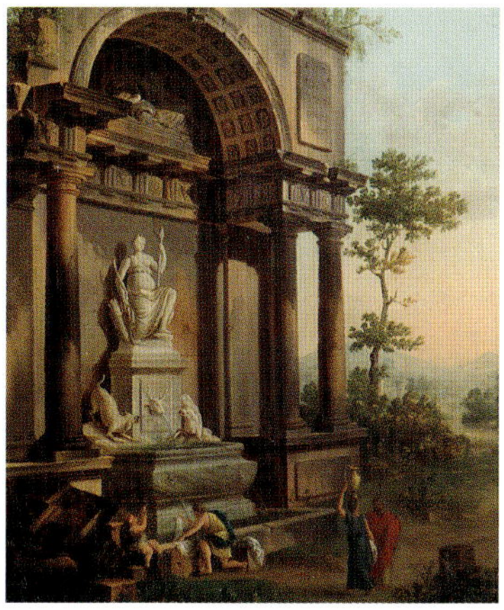

unknown artist
Classical Scene
oil on canvas 54 x 45.5
LCNUG 1927.1546

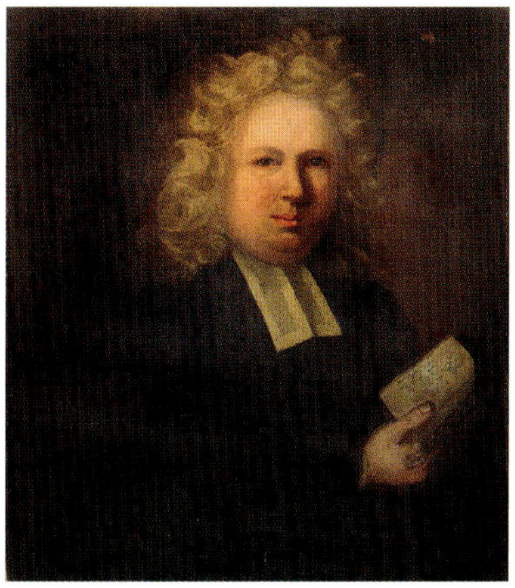

unknown artist
Dr William Dodd (1729–1777)
oil on canvas 72.5 x 62.5
LCNUG 1927.2355

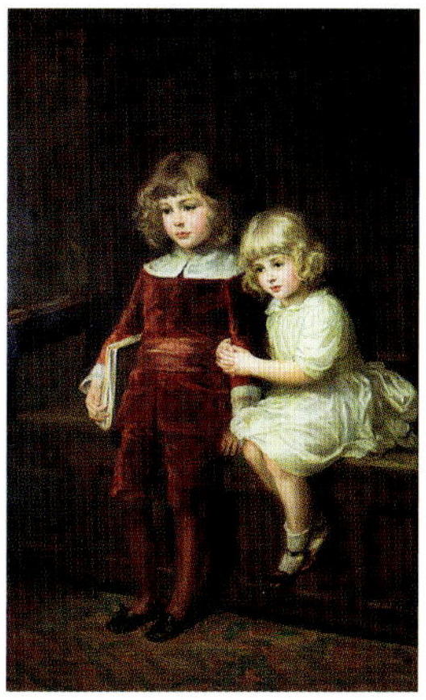

unknown artist
Eleanor and Lionel, Grandchildren of Alfred Tennyson
oil on canvas 146 x 90
TENN.T2010.10

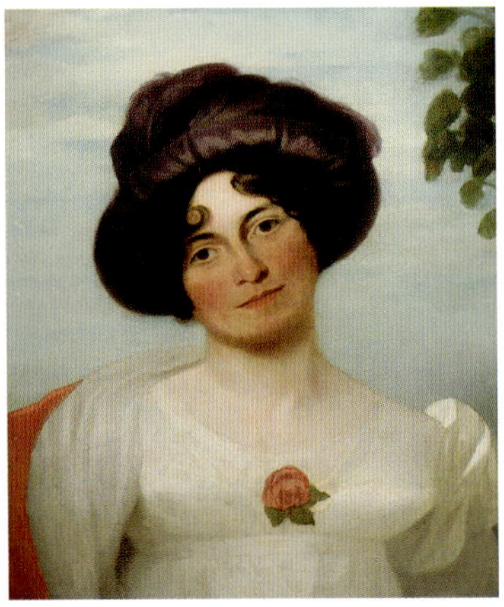

unknown artist
Elizabeth Tennyson, née Fytche (1781–1865), Mother of Alfred Tennyson
oil on canvas 61 x 51
TENN.T2010.13

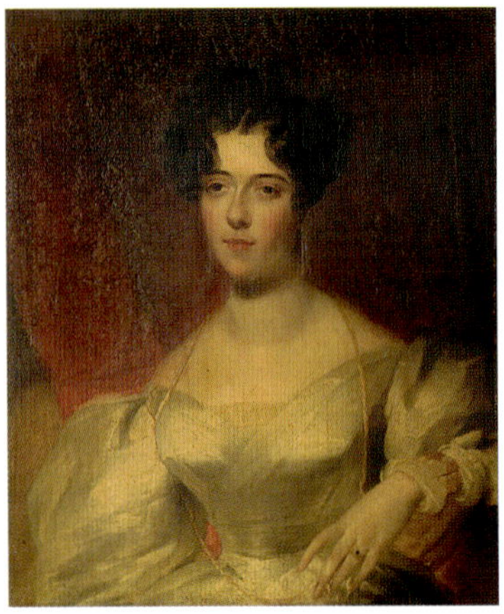

unknown artist
Emma Maria Russell (d.1870), Viscountess Boyne
oil on canvas 76 x 63
TENN.T2010.08

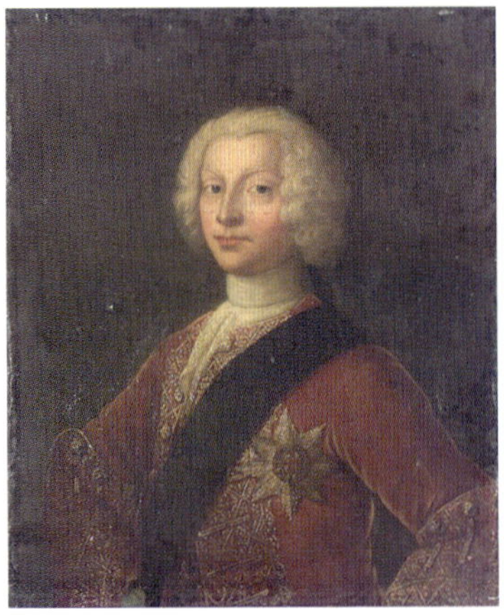

unknown artist
Frederick Louis (1707–1751), Prince of Wales
oil on canvas 76.5 x 63.5
LCNUG 1927.2042

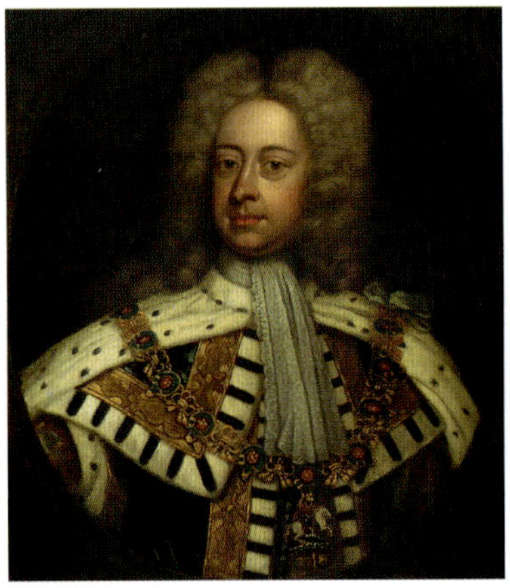

unknown artist
George II (1683–1760)
oil on canvas 76 x 63
LCNUG 1927.2044

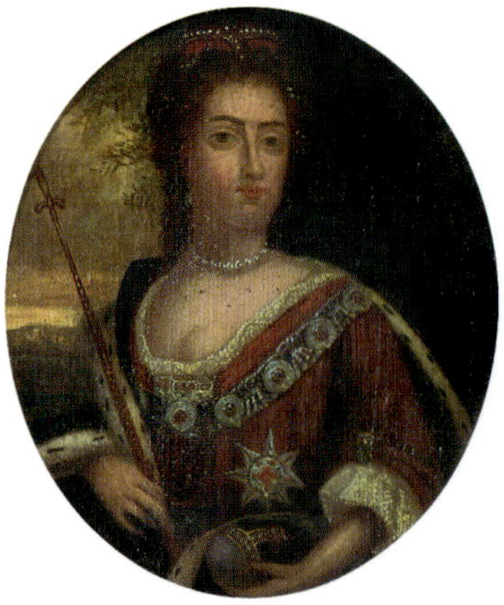

unknown artist
Caroline (1768–1821), Wife of George II
oil on canvas 35.5 x 32
LCNUG 1927.2049

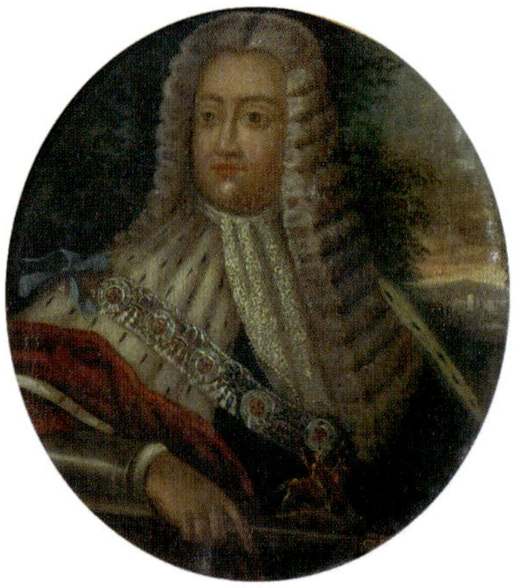

unknown artist
George II (1683–1760)
oil on canvas 35.5 x 32
LCNUG 1927.2048

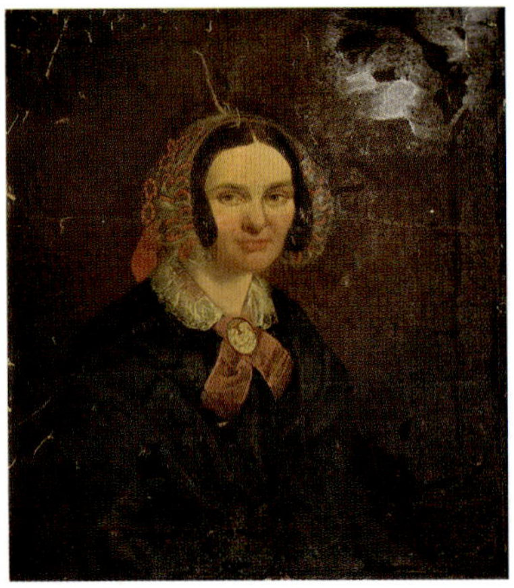

unknown artist
Jane Usher
oil on canvas 75 x 62
LCNUG 1927.213

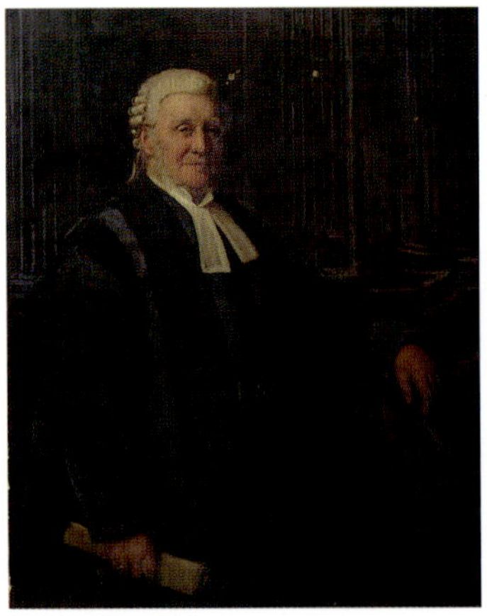

unknown artist
John Thomas Tweed (1823–1910), Town Clerk of Lincoln (1855–1905)
oil on canvas 128 x 97.5
LCNUG 1927.902

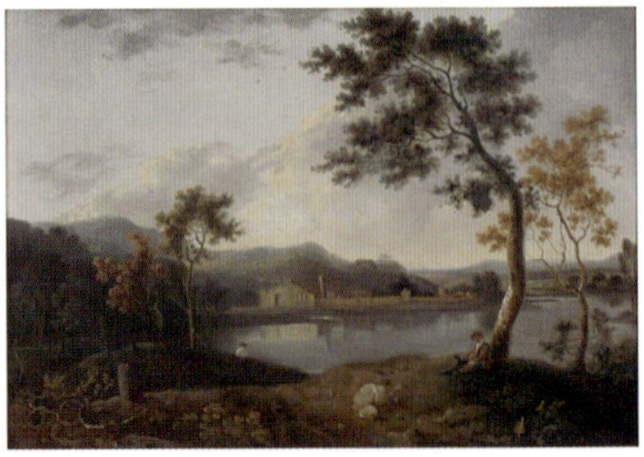

unknown artist
Landscape in Wales
oil on canvas 49.5 x 70
LCNUG 1927.1514

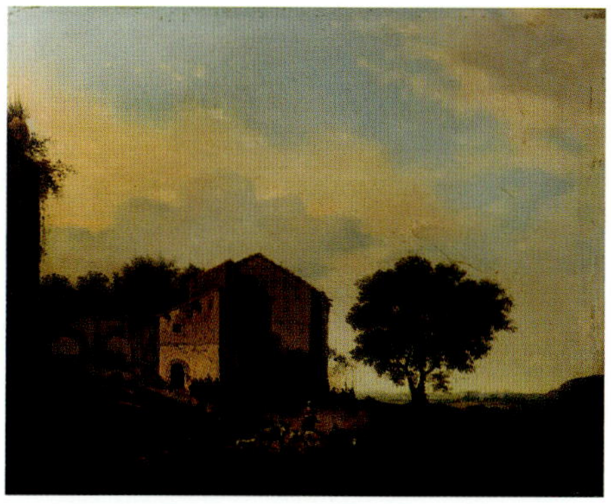

unknown artist
Landscape with a Building, Cows and Sheep
oil on panel 24 x 28.5
LCNUG 1927.913

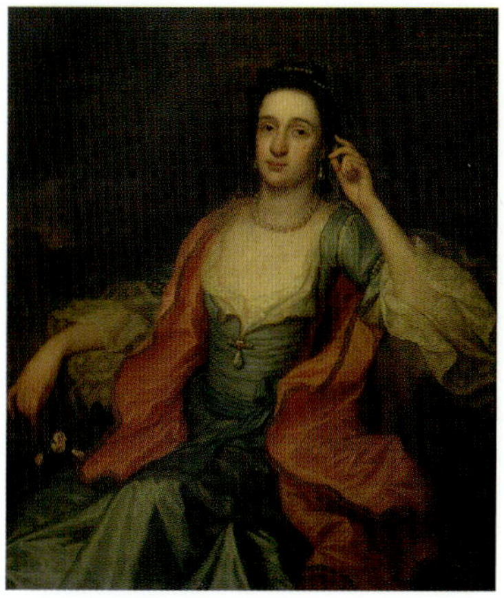

unknown artist
Mary Elizabeth, Daughter of Humphrey Sibthorp
oil on canvas 117.5 x 98
LCNUG 2001.47

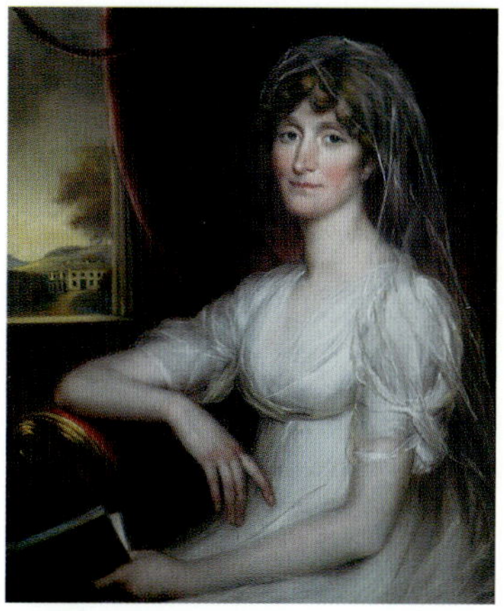

unknown artist
Mary Tennyson, née Turner (d.1825), Grandmother of Alfred Tennyson
oil on canvas 75 x 62
TENN.T2010.11

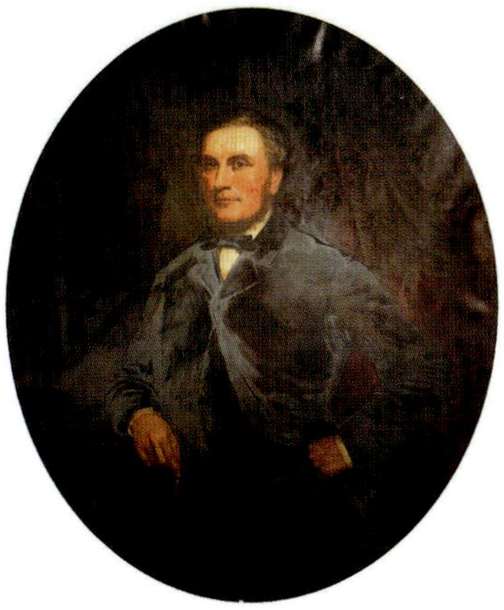

unknown artist
Nathaniel Clayton (1811–1890)
oil on canvas 131 x 108
LCNUG 1927.178

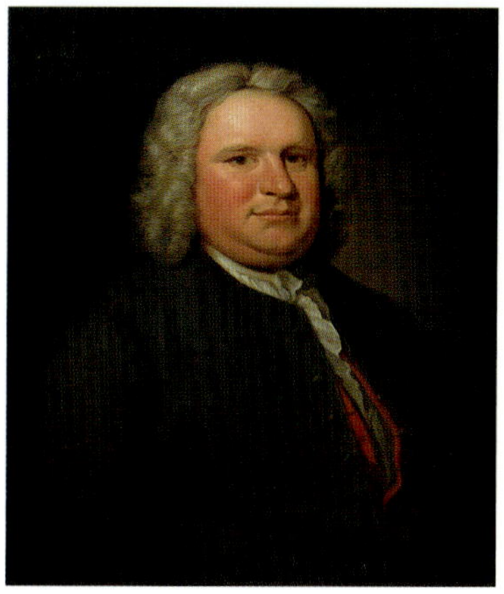

unknown artist
Portrait of a Man
oil on canvas 78 x 65
LCNUG 2009.33

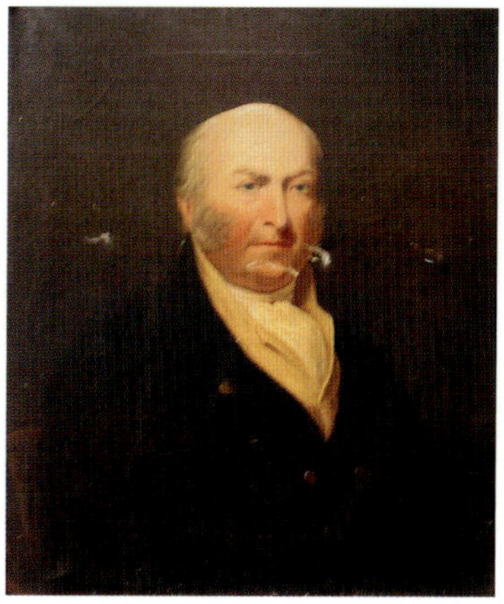

unknown artist
Portrait of a Man
oil on canvas 82 x 70
LCNUG 2009.34

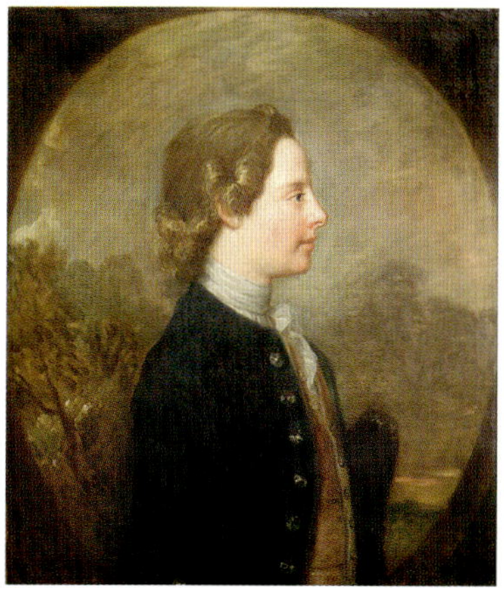

unknown artist
Portrait of an Unknown Boy
oil on canvas 75.5 x 63
LCNUG 2001.19

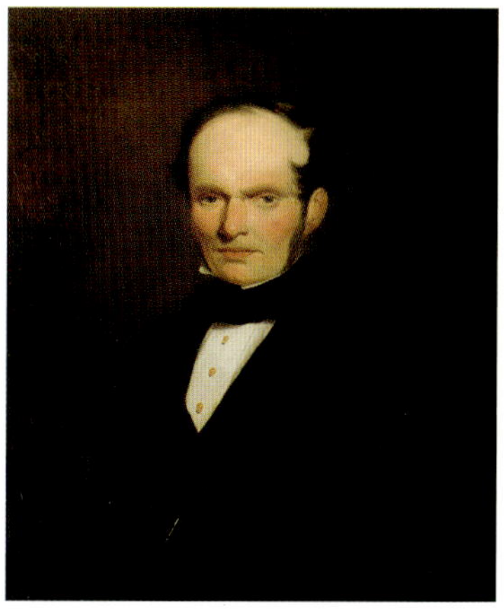

unknown artist
Portrait of an Unknown Man
oil on canvas 76.5 x 64
LCNUG 2001.18

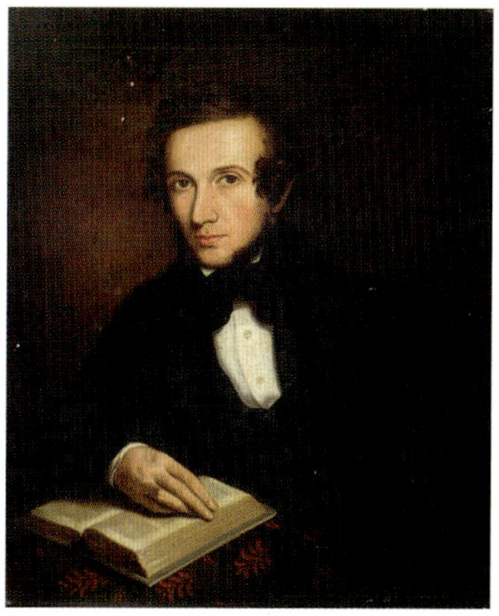

unknown artist
Portrait of an Unknown Man with a Book
oil on canvas 75.5 x 62.5
LCNUG 2001.14

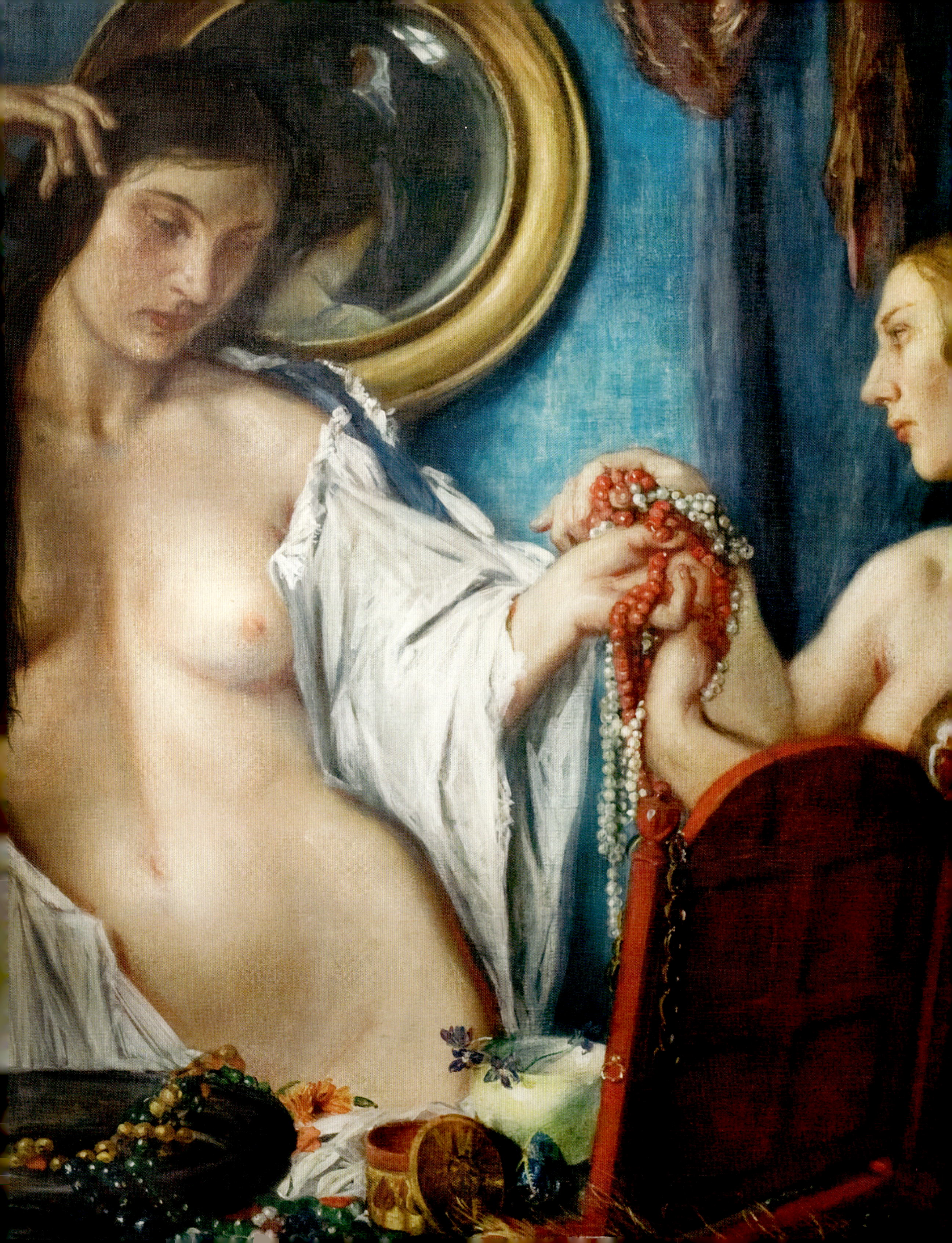

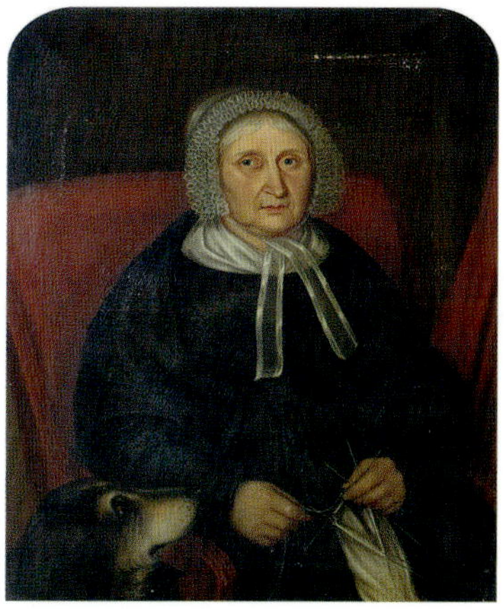

unknown artist
Portrait of an Unknown Woman
oil on canvas 76.5 x 63
LCNUG 2001.16

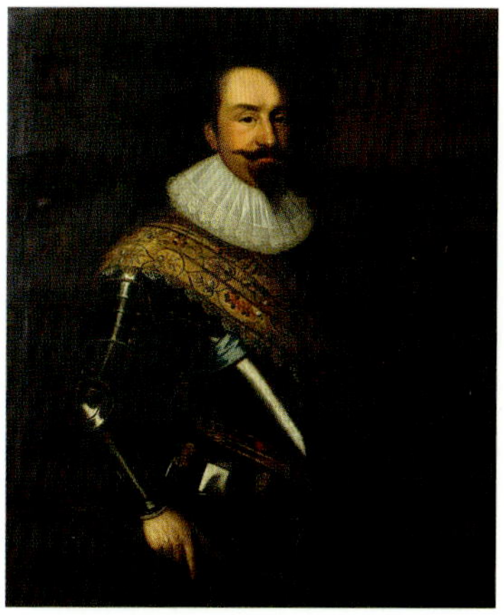

unknown artist
Robert Bertie (1582–1642), Earl of Lindsey
oil on canvas 123 x 105
LCNUG 1927.1922

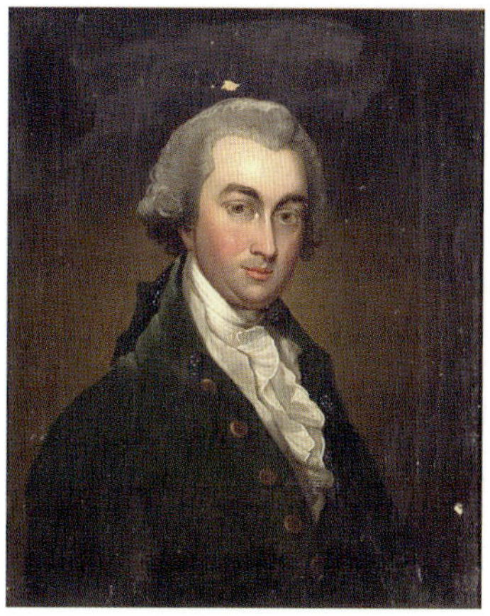

unknown artist
Sir Richard Worsley (1751–1805)
oil on canvas 26.5 x 21.5
LCNUG 2001.24

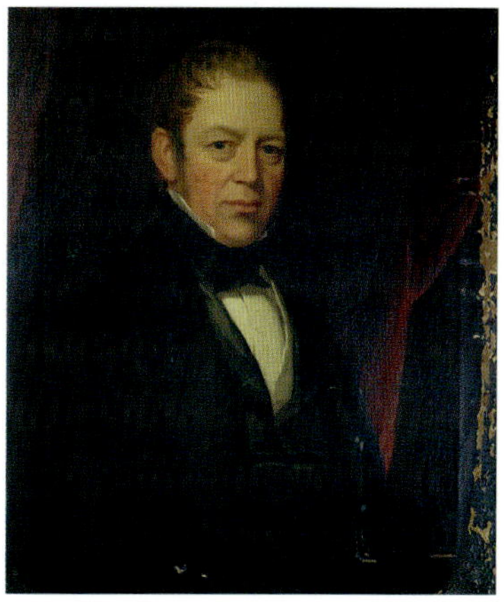

unknown artist
William Rudgard, Mayor of Lincoln (1839)
oil on canvas 76 x 63
LCNUG 1927.2046

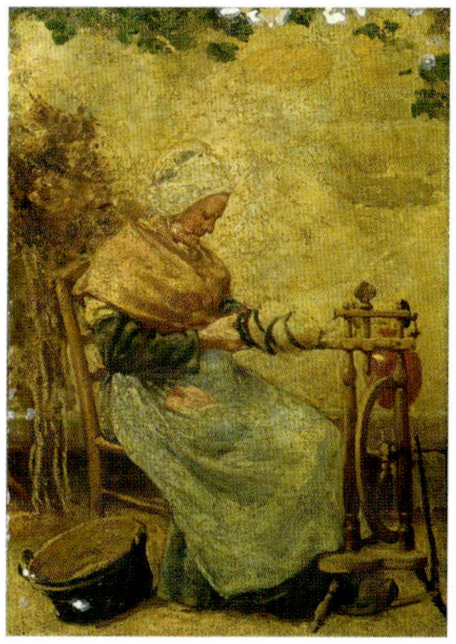

unknown artist
Woman at a Spinning Wheel
oil on canvas 65.5 x 45.5
LCNUG 1927.2319

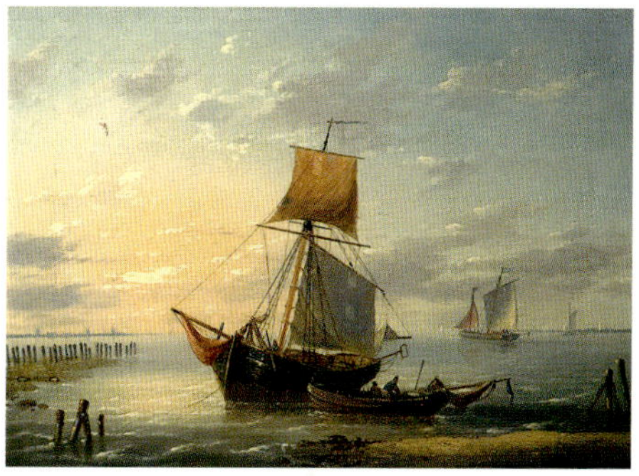

Verboeckhoven, Charles Louis 1802–1889
Seascape
oil on canvas 26 x 35
LCNUG 1927.910

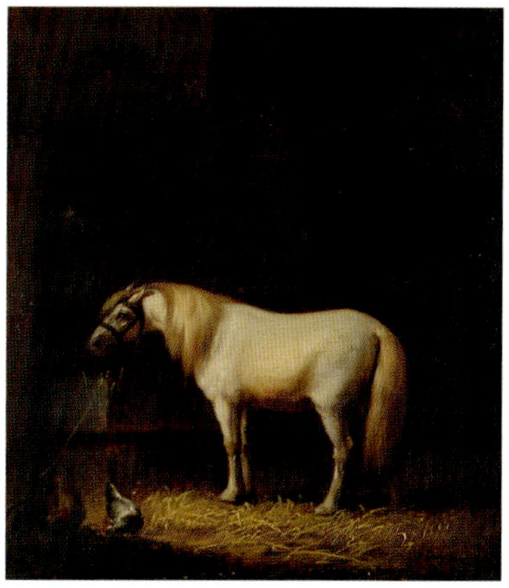

Verboeckhoven, Eugène Joseph 1799–1881
A Horse Feeding in a Stable
oil on panel 24.1 x 20.6
LCNUG 1927.911

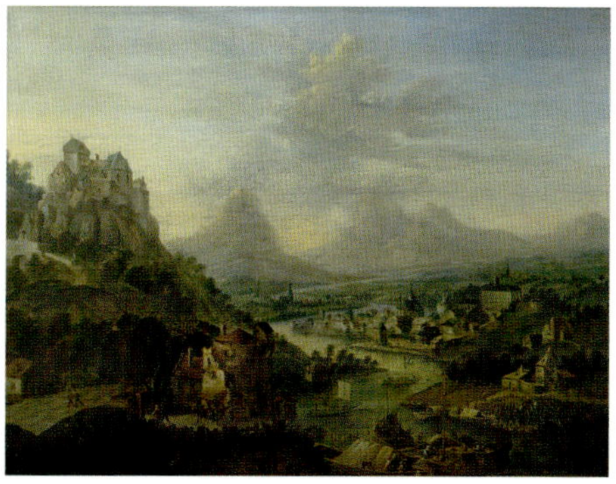

Verdonck, Cornelis active c.1715
Mountainous Landscape with a River and a Castle
oil on panel 30.5 x 38
LCNUG 1927.2167

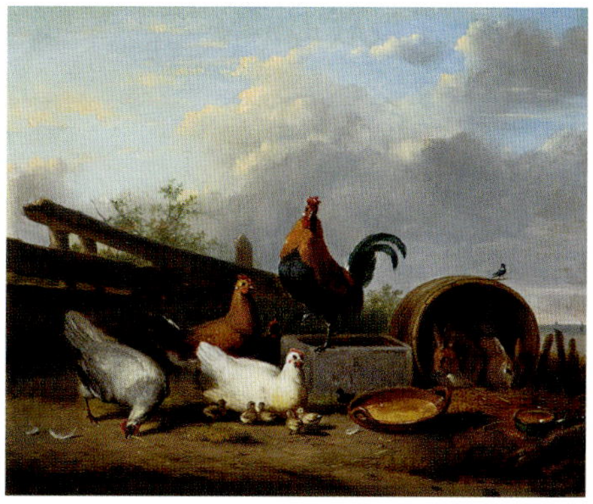

Verhoesen, Albertus 1806–1881
Farmyard Scene
oil on panel 20 x 23.9
LCNUG 1927.231

Facing page: Shannon, Charles Haslewood, 1863–1937, *The Toilet* (detail), 1927, The Collection: Art & Archaeology in Lincolnshire (Usher Gallery) (p. 324)

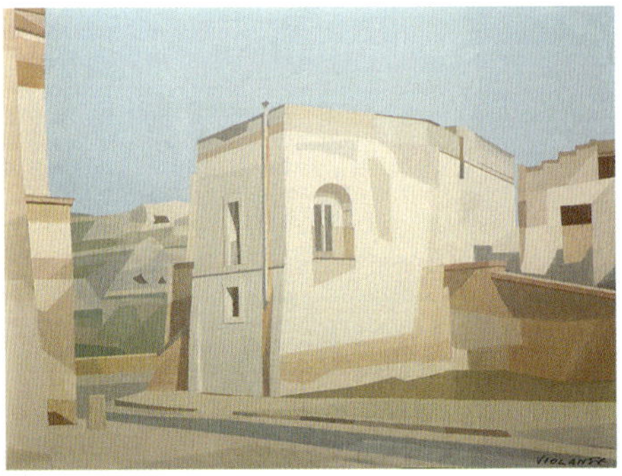

Violante, Italo b.1916
I Sassi, Matera, Italy 1974
oil on board 30 x 40
LCNUG 1979.116

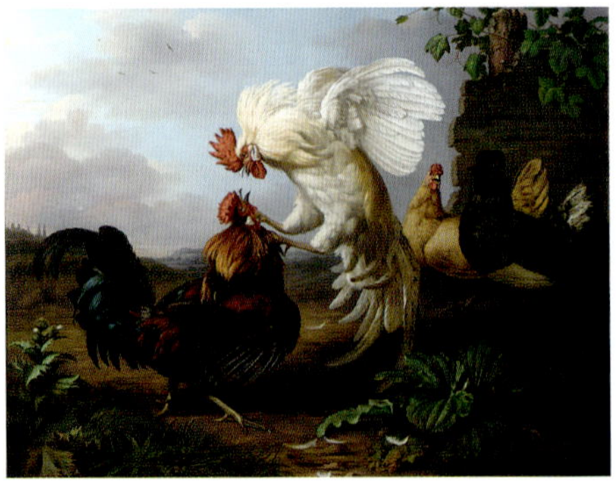

Voordecker, Henri 1779–1861
Cocks Fighting
oil on canvas 108 x 138
LCNUG 1927.270

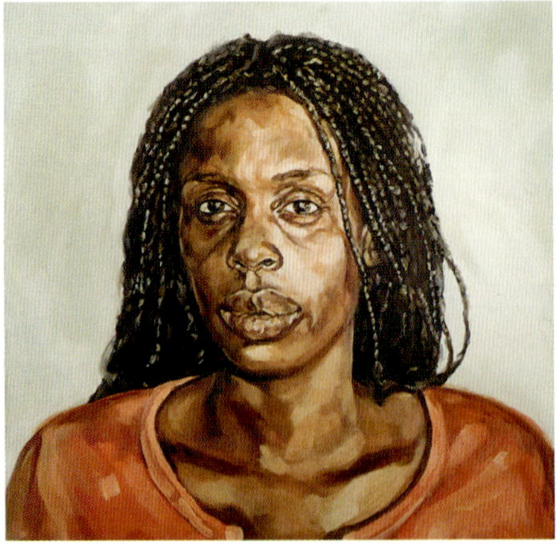

Walker, Barbara b.1964
Self Portrait 2000
oil on canvas 69 x 69
LCNUG 2000.1

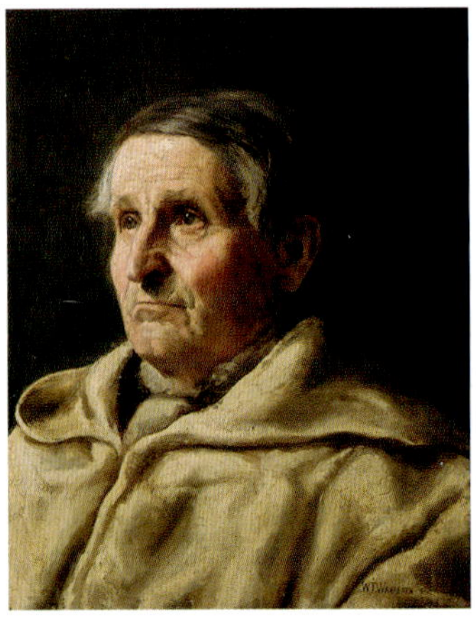

Warrener, William Tom 1861–1934
Portrait of an Unknown Man 1882
oil on canvas 45.9 x 35.9
LCNUG 1973.16

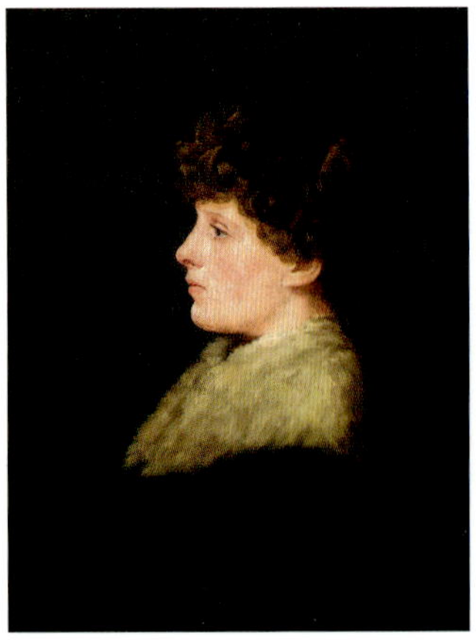

Warrener, William Tom 1861–1934
Oephea c.1884
oil on canvas 61.5 x 45
LCNUG 1981.38

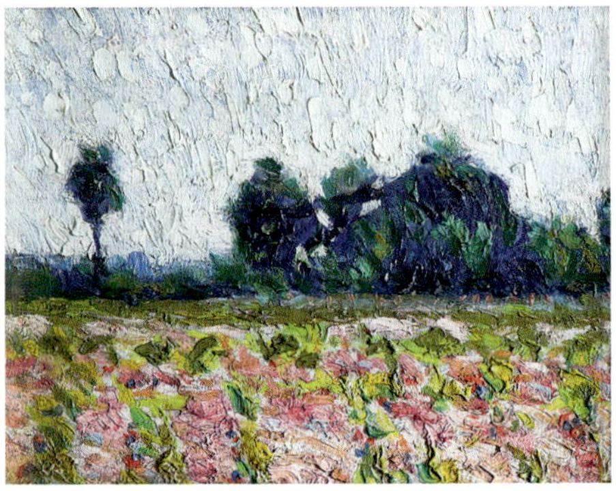

Warrener, William Tom 1861–1934
Landscape with Trees c.1890
oil on canvas 22.5 x 27.5
LCNUG 1993.5

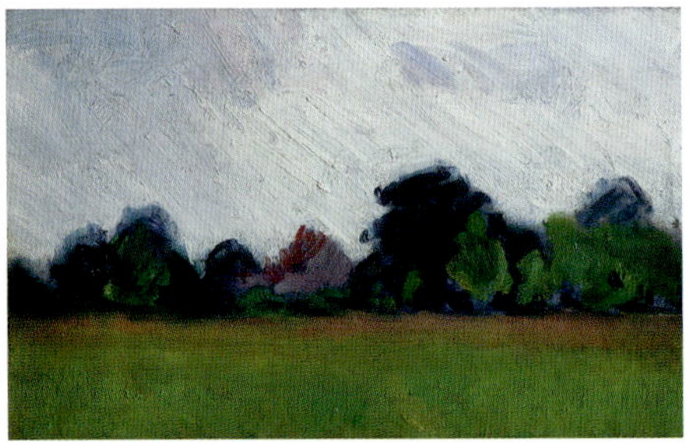

Warrener, William Tom 1861–1934
Landscape with Trees c.1890
oil on canvas 22.5 x 35
LCNUG 1993.6

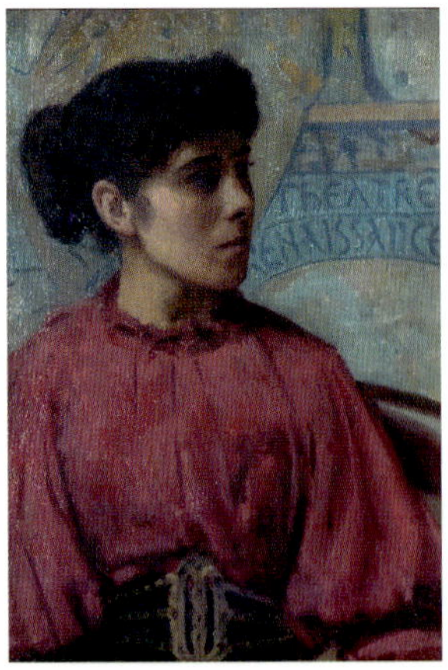

Warrener, William Tom 1861–1934
Leonline c.1890
oil on canvas 35 x 25
LCNUG 1993.1

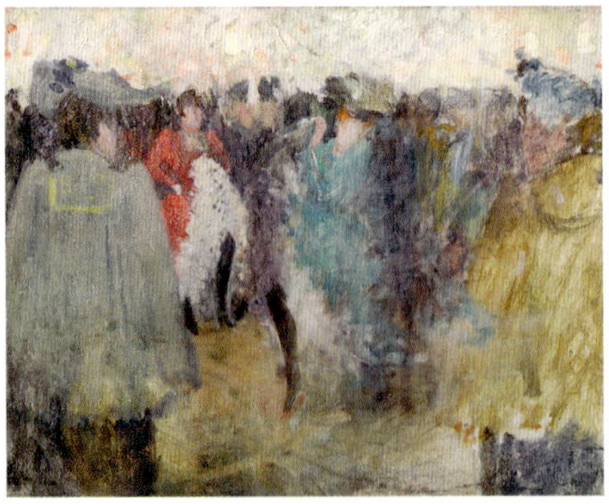

Warrener, William Tom 1861–1934
Quadrille I c.1890
oil on canvas 46 x 55
LCNUG 1993.3

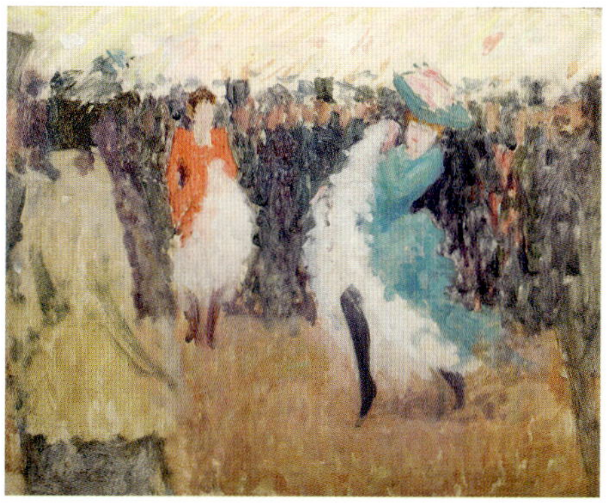

Warrener, William Tom 1861–1934
Quadrille II c.1890
oil on canvas 46.5 x 56
LCNUG 1993.4

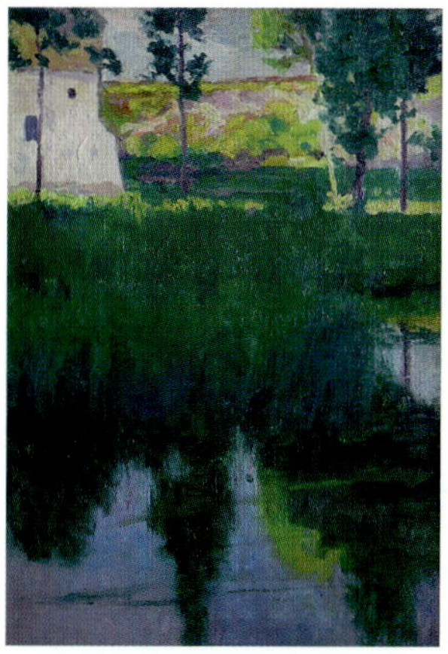

Warrener, William Tom 1861–1934
Reflections c.1890
oil on canvas 54 x 37.5
LCNUG 1993.7

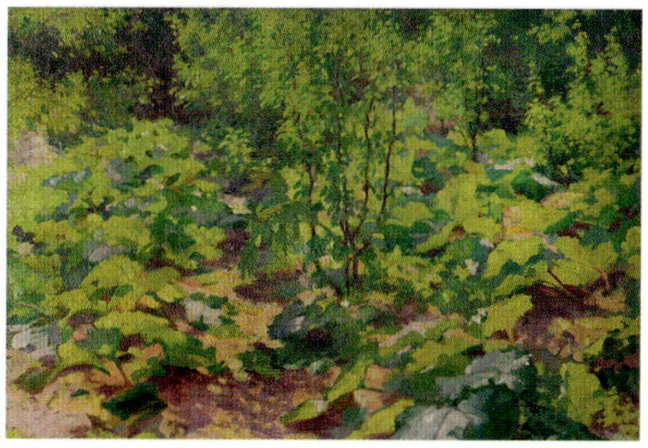

Warrener, William Tom 1861–1934
Undergrowth c.1890
oil on canvas 38.2 x 56
LCNUG 1993.9

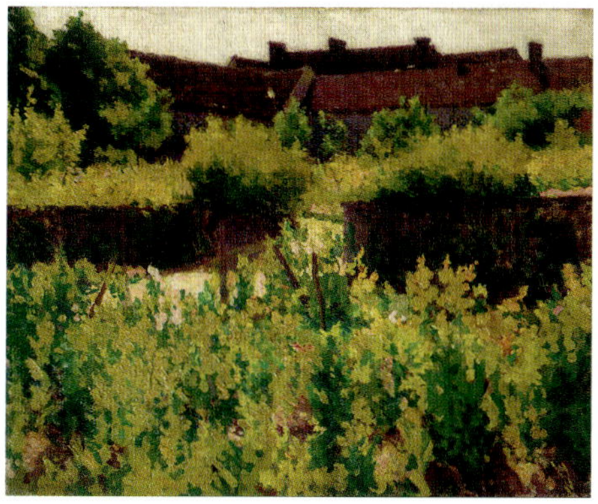

Warrener, William Tom 1861–1934
Vineyard c.1890
oil on canvas 46 x 55
LCNUG 1993.8

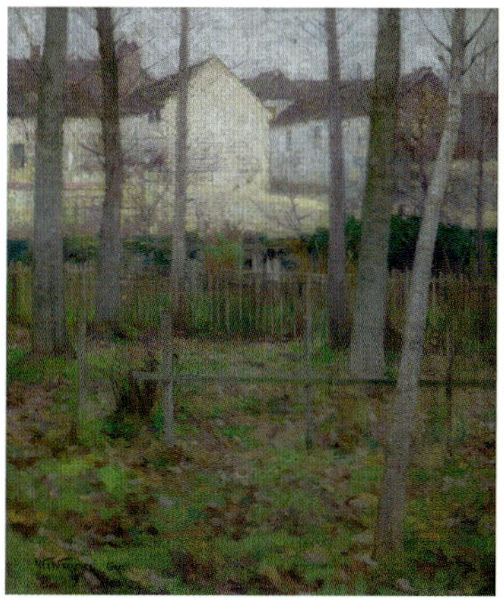

Warrener, William Tom 1861–1934
December Day at Grez-sur-Loing, France
c.1890–1891
oil on canvas 73.4 x 61
LCNUG 1993.2

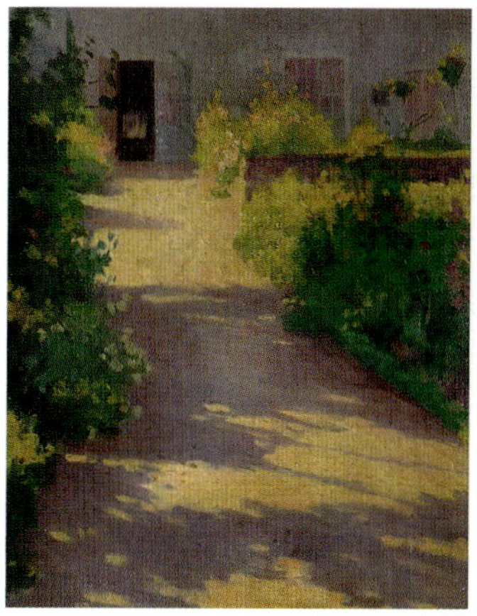

Warrener, William Tom 1861–1934
Garden Pathway
oil on canvas 41 x 32.3
LCNUG 1973.17

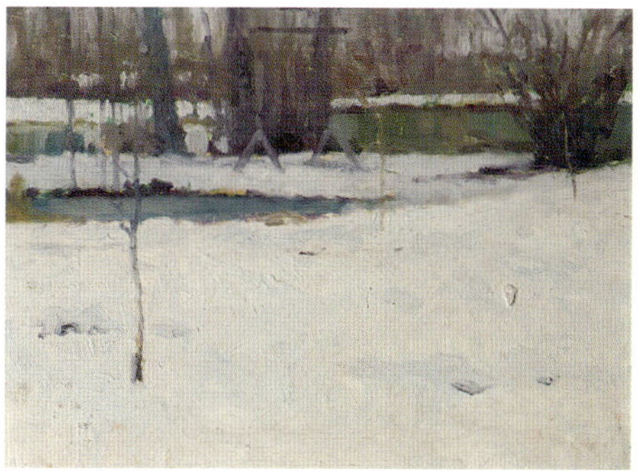

Warrener, William Tom 1861–1934
Grez-sur-Loing, France
oil on wood 24.3 x 32
LCNUG 1972.193

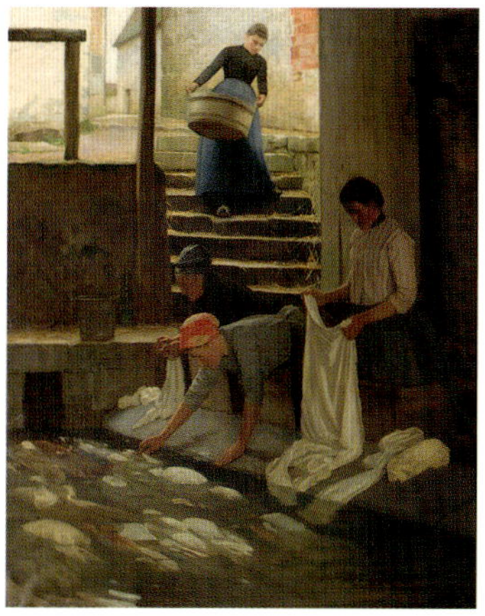

Warrener, William Tom 1861–1934
Le lavoir
oil on canvas 144.7 x 109.3
LCNUG 1927.70

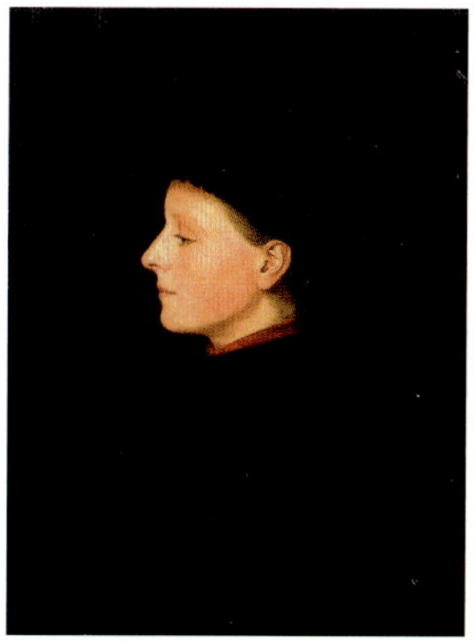

Warrener, William Tom 1861–1934
Mary Ann Carlton
oil on canvas 59.3 x 44
LCNUG 1973.6

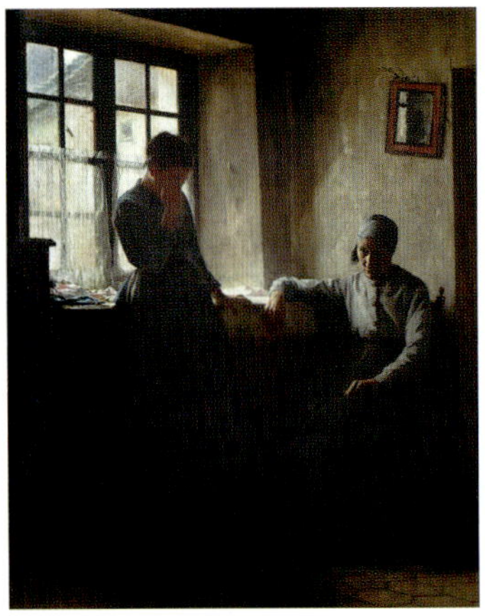

Warrener, William Tom 1861–1934
Un aveu
oil on canvas 92.5 x 73.2
LCNUG 1976.151

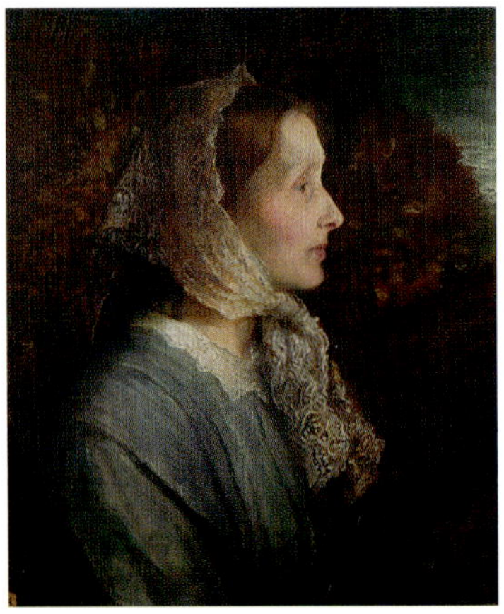

Watts, George Frederick 1817–1904
Emily Tennyson (1813–1896), Wife of Alfred Tennyson 1862
oil on canvas 63.5 x 53.5
TENN.T2010.03

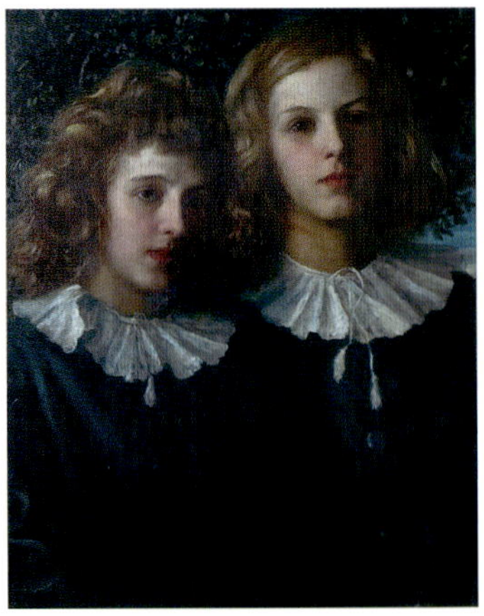

Watts, George Frederick 1817–1904
Hallam and Lionel Tennyson 1865
oil on canvas 66 x 54
TENN.T2010.09

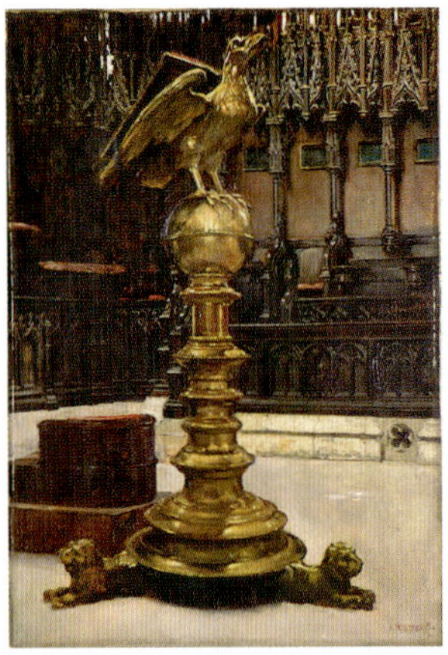

Webster, Alfred George 1852–1916
Lectern, Lincoln Cathedral 1894
oil on canvas 41.1 x 28.2
LCNUG 1927.2147

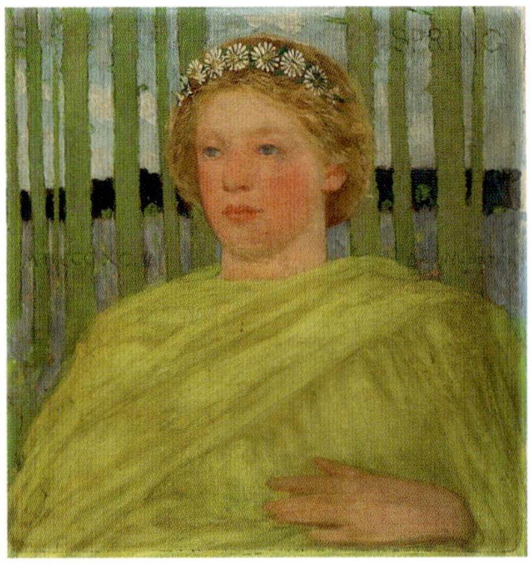

Webster, Alfred George 1852–1916
Spring 1896
oil on board 24.1 x 22.8
LCNUG 1927.2140

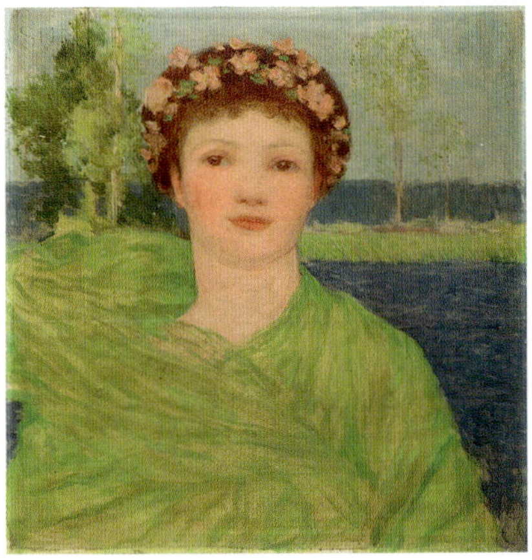

Webster, Alfred George 1852–1916
Summer
oil on board 24.5 x 23.5
LCNUG 1927.2141

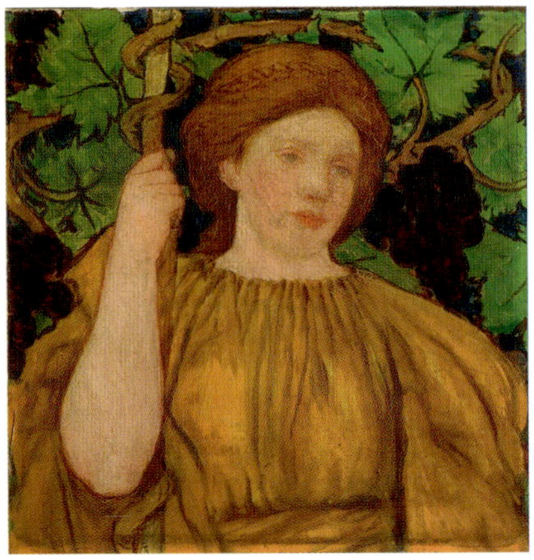

Webster, Alfred George 1852–1916
Autumn
oil on board 24.5 x 23.5
LCNUG 1927.2142

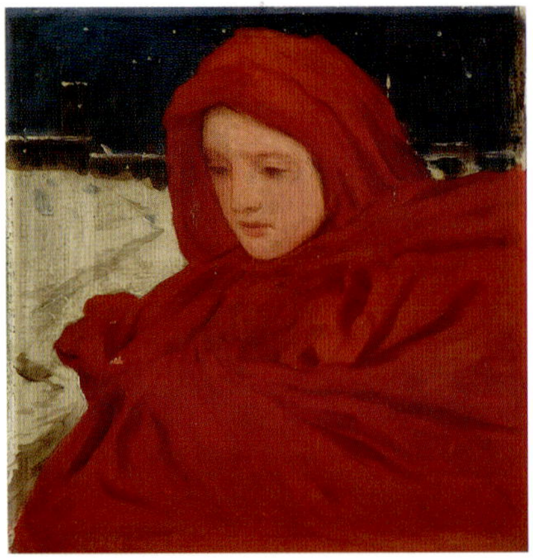

Webster, Alfred George 1852–1916
Winter
oil on board 24.6 x 23.2
LCNUG 1927.2143

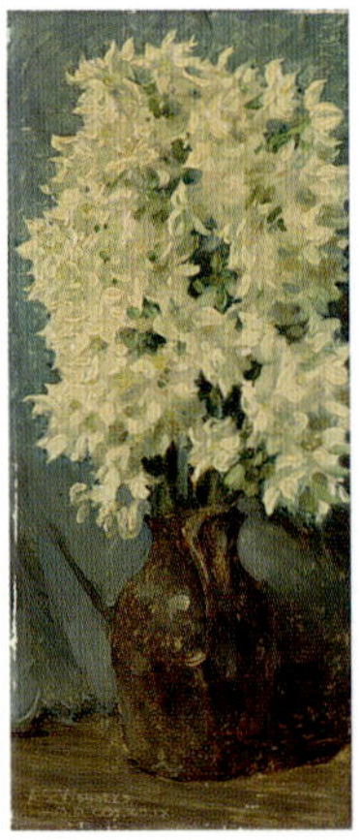

Webster, Alfred George 1852–1916
Narcissus 1899
oil on panel 40.5 x 17
LCNUG 1927.2146

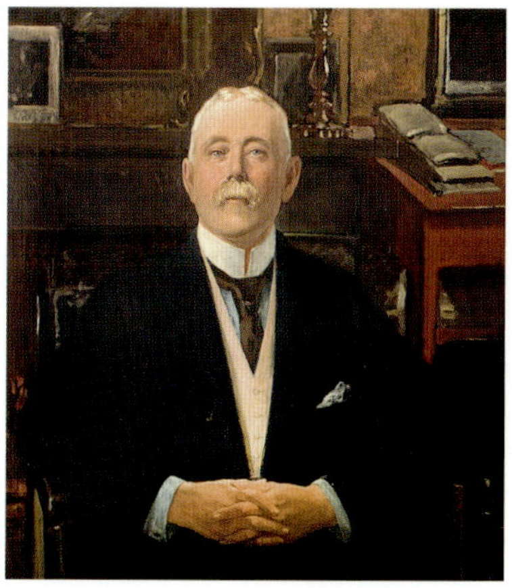

Webster, Alfred George 1852–1916
Frederick Andrew (1840–1916) 1916
oil on canvas 86.5 x 76
LCNUG 1985.63

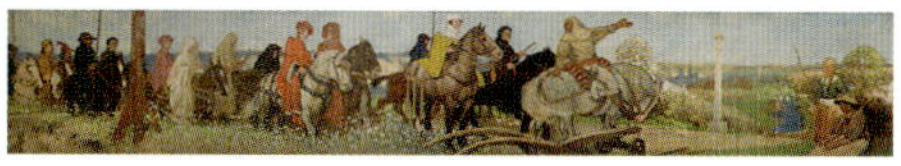

Webster, Alfred George 1852–1916
Canterbury Pilgrims
oil on canvas 23.5 x 135
LCNUG 1927.1502

Webster, Alfred George 1852–1916
Castle Hill, Lincoln
oil on panel 18.8 x 6.8
LCNUG 1927.2145

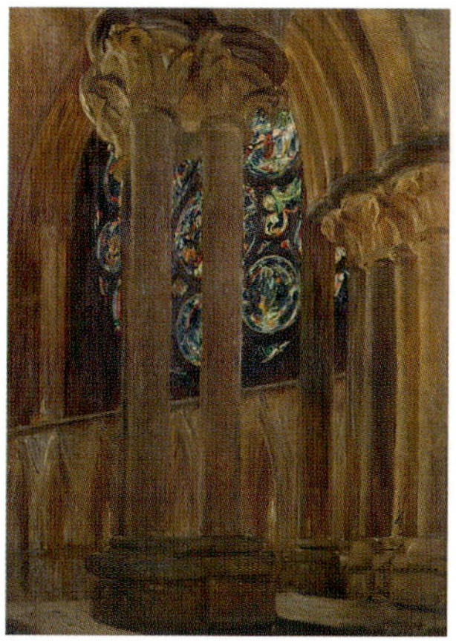

Webster, Alfred George 1852–1916
Dean's Eye, Lincoln Cathedral from the Clerestory
oil on canvas 39.4 x 27.5
LCNUG 1927.2151

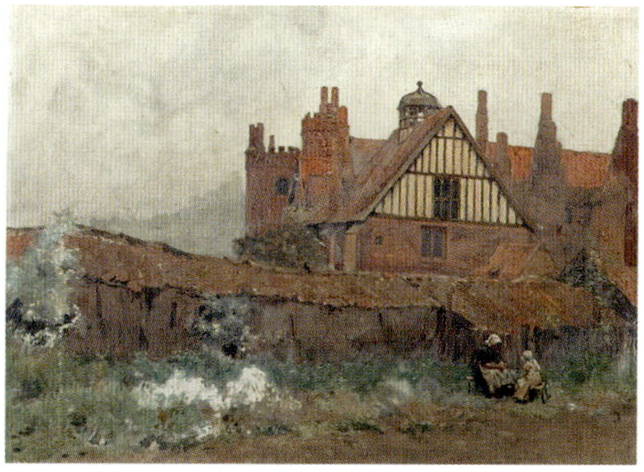

Webster, Alfred George 1852–1916
Gainsborough Old Hall, Lincolnshire
oil on board 33 x 40.5
LCNUG 1927.2149

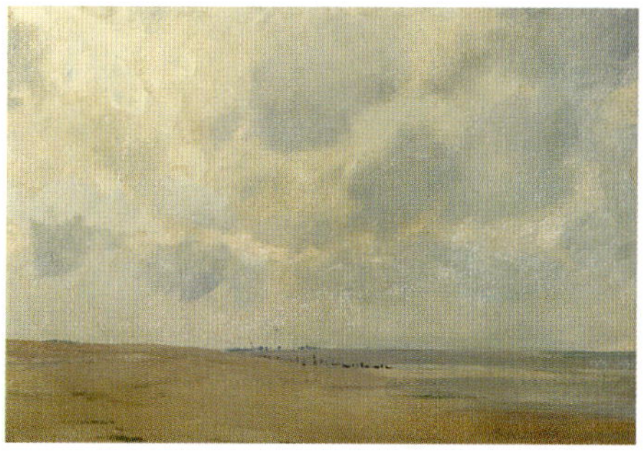

Webster, Alfred George 1852–1916
Mablethorpe Shore, Lincolnshire
oil on canvas 28 x 33
LCNUG 1927.2148

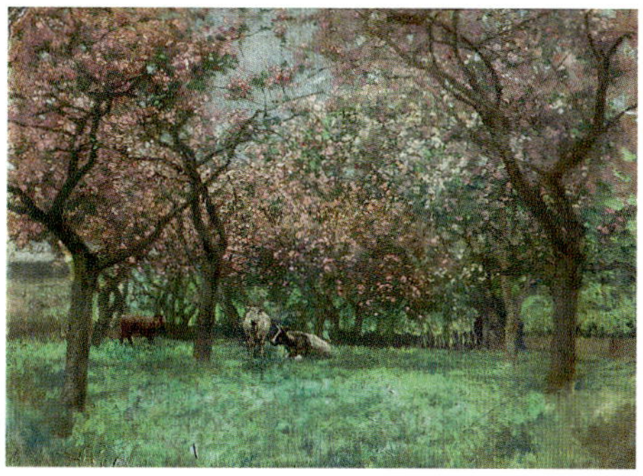

Webster, Alfred George 1852–1916
Mr Bland's Orchard, Heighington, Lincoln
oil on millboard 30 x 40.5
LCNUG 1976.31

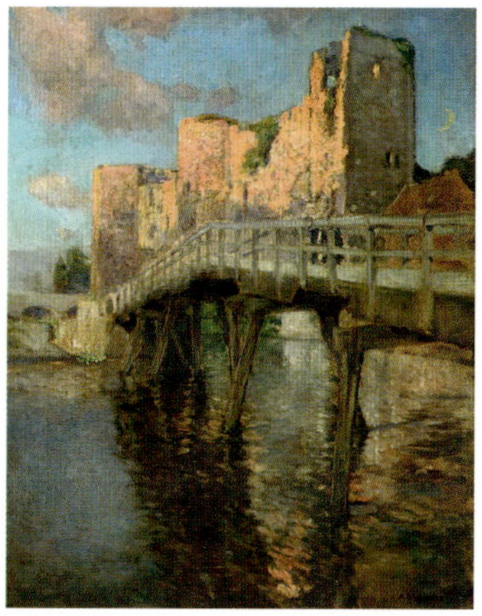

Webster, Alfred George 1852–1916
Newark Castle, Nottinghamshire
oil on canvas 45.8 x 35.6
LCNUG 1927.2152

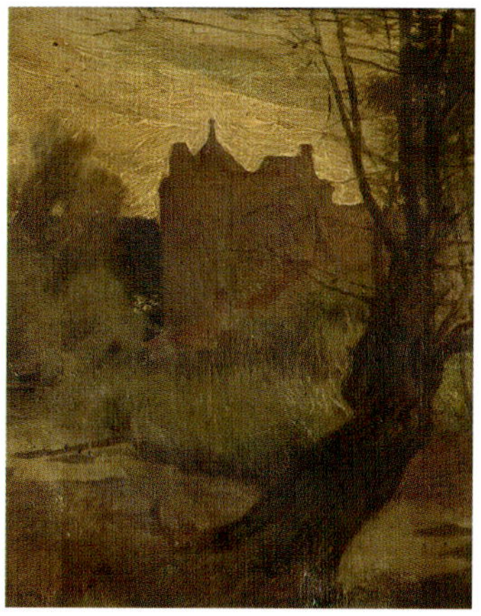

Webster, Alfred George 1852–1916
Somerton Castle, Lincolnshire
oil on canvas 33.6 x 26.2
LCNUG 1927.2150

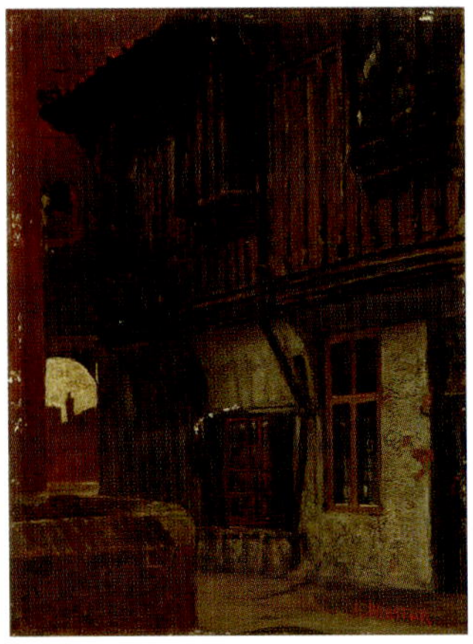

Webster, Alfred George 1852–1916
Whitefriars, Lincoln
oil on board 24 x 17.8
LCNUG 1927.2144

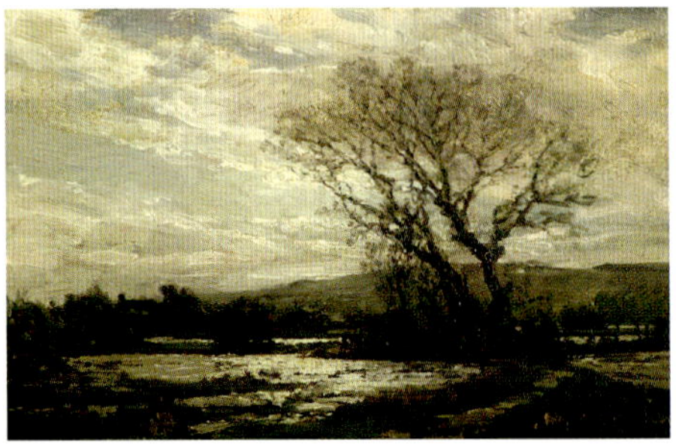

Weiss, José 1859–1919
Landscape
oil on panel 24.5 x 37.5
LCNUG 1927.952

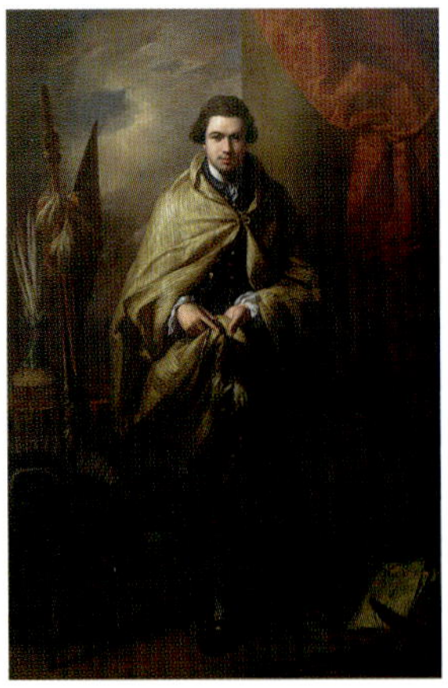

West, Benjamin 1738–1820
Sir Joseph Banks (1743–1820), 1st Bt, GCB, PRS 1771–1772
oil on canvas 234 x 160
LCNUG 1989.9

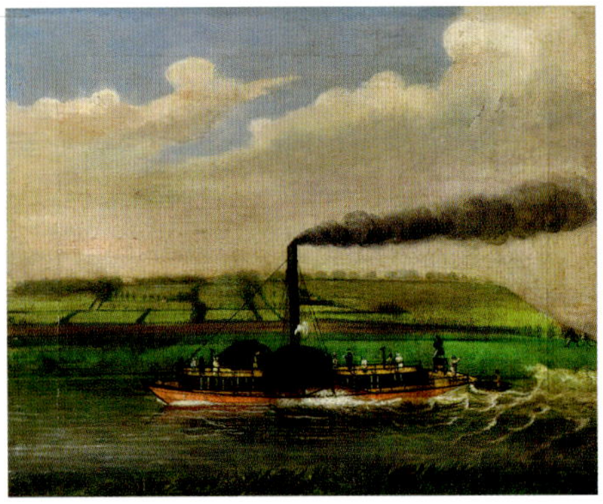

West, John active 1839–1844
'Celerity' 1839
oil on canvas 50.5 x 61
LCNUG 1975.61

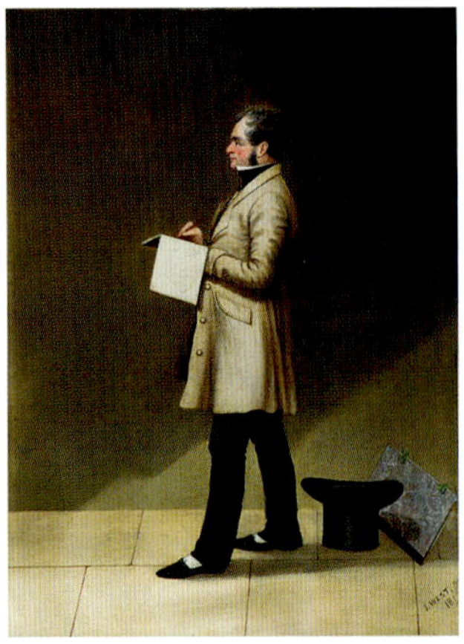

West, John active 1839–1844
Samuel Tuke (1784–1857) 1844
oil on canvas 35.5 x 24.7
LCNUG 1975.62

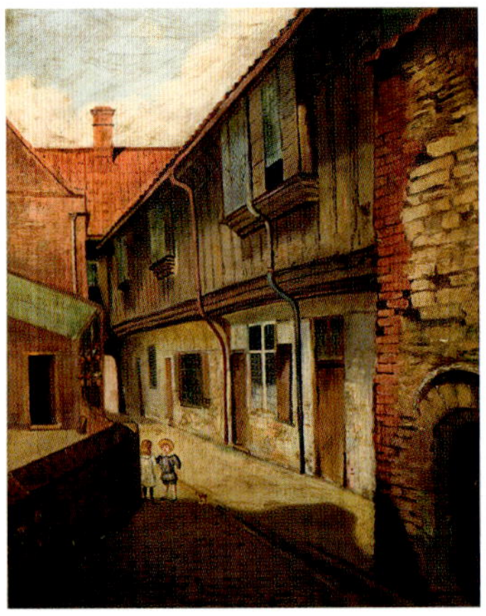

White, Alfred Ernest 1873–1953
Akrill's Passage, Lincoln
oil on canvas 46 x 33
LCNUG 1927.2278

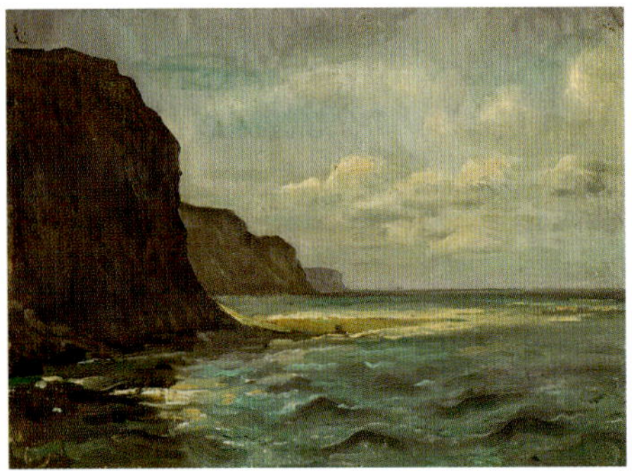

White, Harry active 20th C
Boulby Cliffs, Yorkshire
oil on panel 25.9 x 29
LCNUG 1927.734

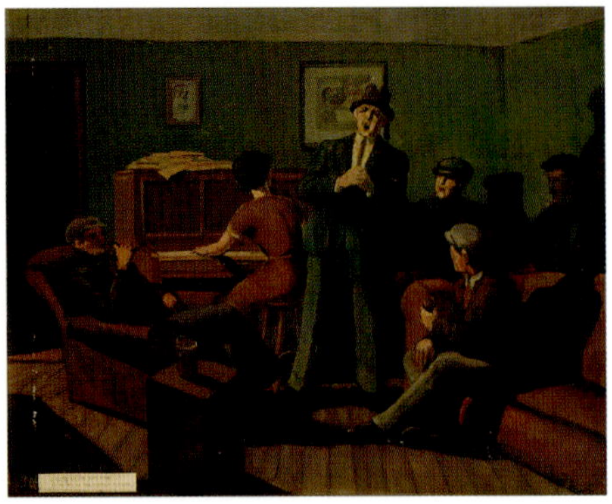

White, Harry active 20th C
Concert in the Club Room
oil on panel 51 x 61
LCNUG 1927.813

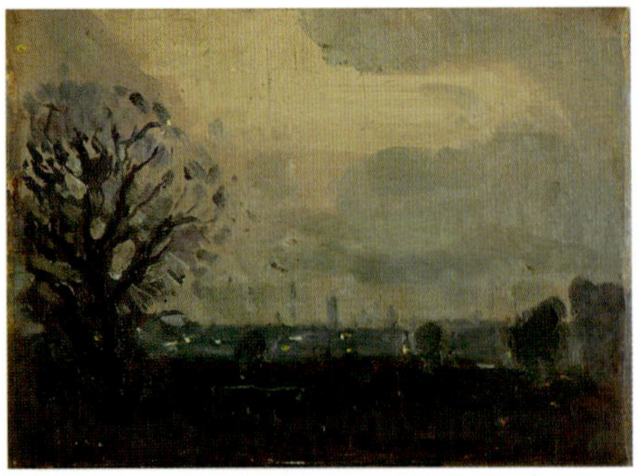

White, Harry active 20th C
Evening Effect over Grimsby, Lincolnshire (sketch) (recto)
oil on panel 19 x 25.5
LCNUG 1927.264

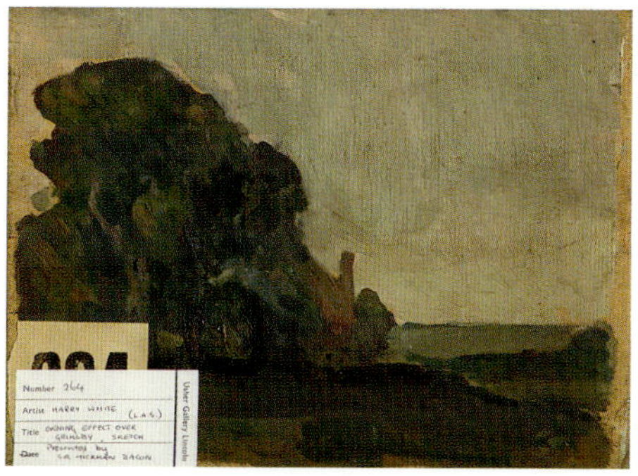

White, Harry active 20th C
Unfinished Sketch (verso)
oil on panel 19 x 25.5
LCNUG 1927.264b

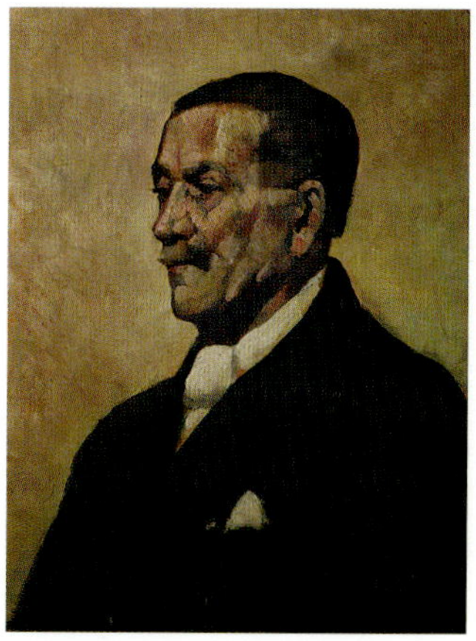

White, Harry active 20th C
Portrait
oil on board 43 x 33
LCNUG 1927.283

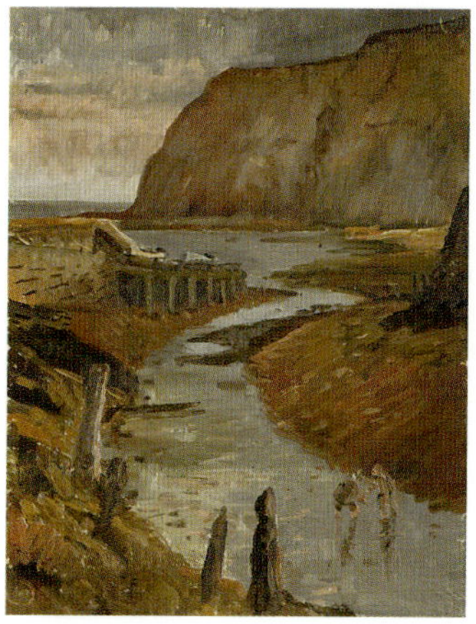

White, Harry active 20th C
Seashore at Whitby, North Yorkshire
oil on board 39.5 x 29
LCNUG 1927.756

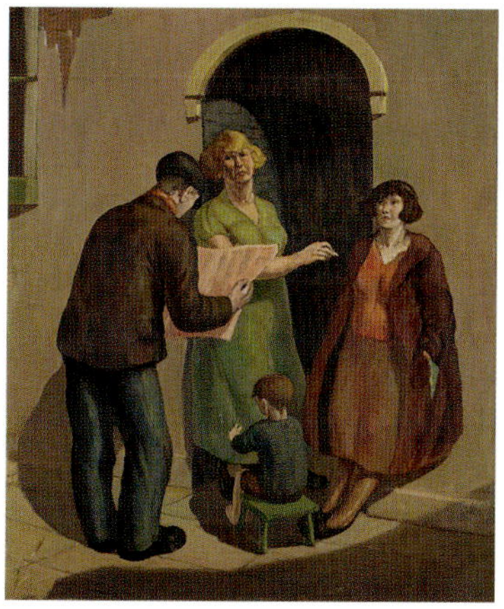

White, Harry active 20th C
Sporting Pink
oil on board 76 x 60
LCNUG 1927.281

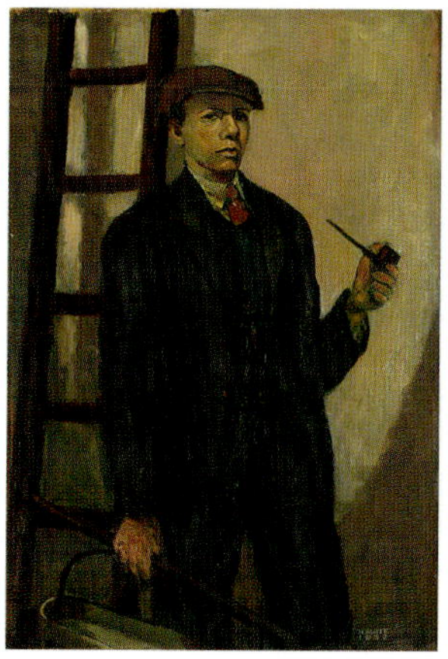

White, Harry active 20th C
The Billposter
oil on board 76.2 x 51
LCNUG 1927.143

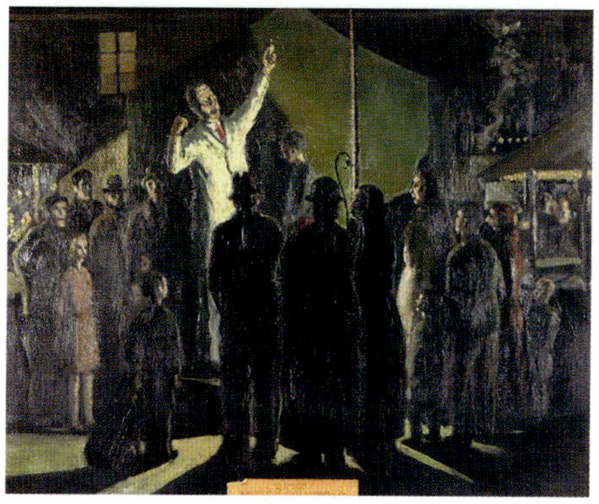

White, Harry active 20th C
The Charlatan
oil on panel 51 x 62
LCNUG 1927.670

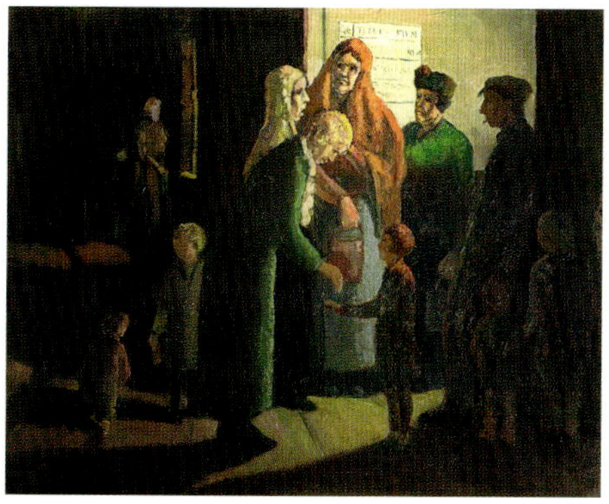

White, Harry active 20th C
The Fourpenny Entrance
oil on canvas 51 x 61
LCNUG 1927.266

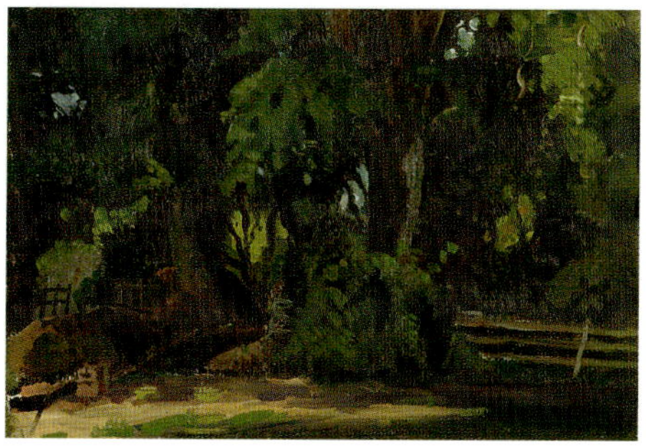

White, Harry active 20th C
Woodland Study
oil on board 17.5 x 25.5
LCNUG 1927.698

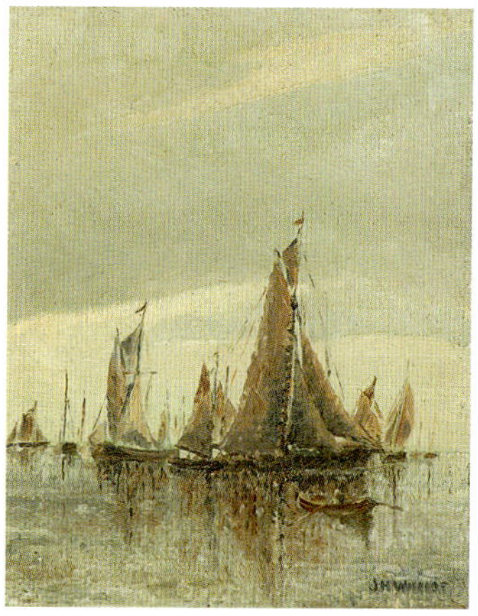

Wilmot, J. H.
Brixham Trawlers
oil on panel 24 x 19
LCNUG 1927.658

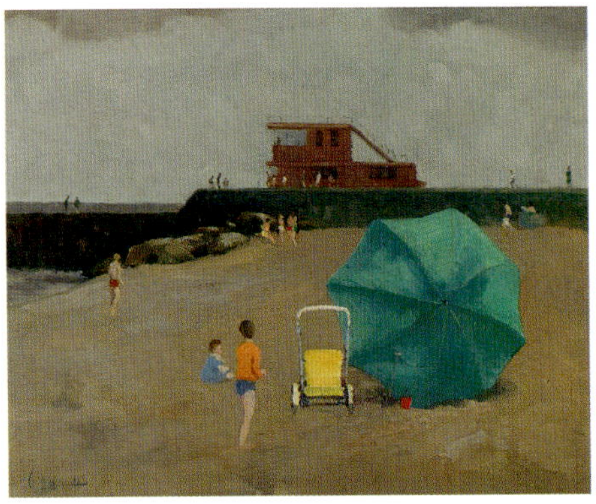

Wilson, Geoffrey b.1920
The Green Umbrella
oil on board 48.5 x 57
LCNUG 1927.2684

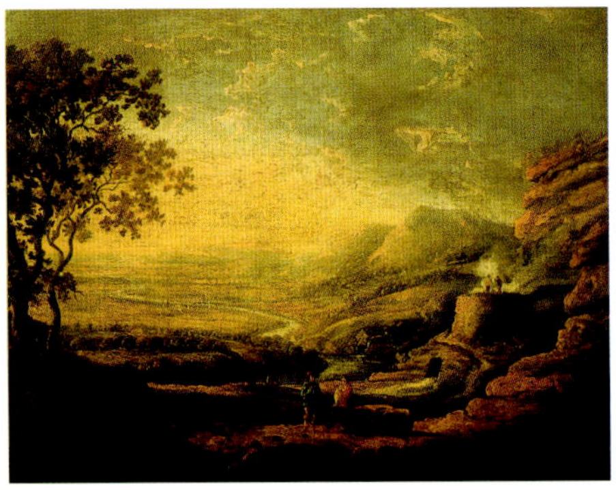

Wilson, Richard 1712/1713–1782
View in the Wye Valley, Wales
oil on canvas 77 x 99
LCNUG 1927.937

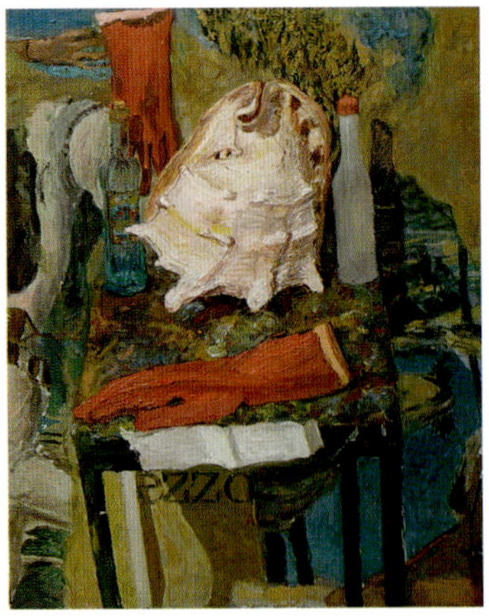

Wilson, Susan b.1951
On the Gothic Line 1990
oil on canvas 91.4 x 71
LCNUG 1992.3

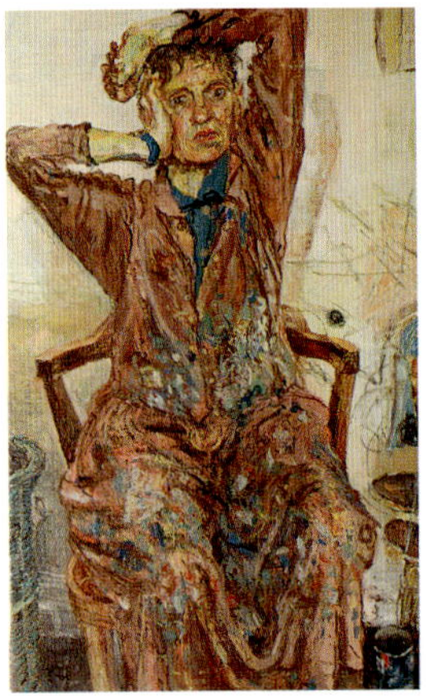

Wilson, Susan b.1951
Self Portrait with Hands 1995–1996
oil on canvas 126.5 x 75.7
LCNUG 1996.11

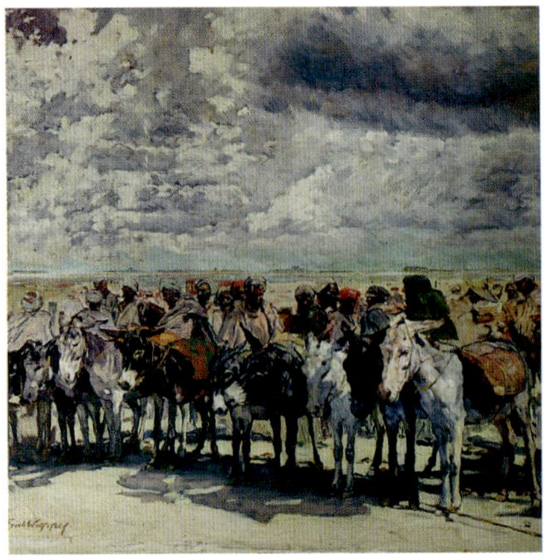

Wolfsfeld, Erich 1884–1956
Caravan Resting
oil on panel 115.5 x 113
LCNUG 1927.2351

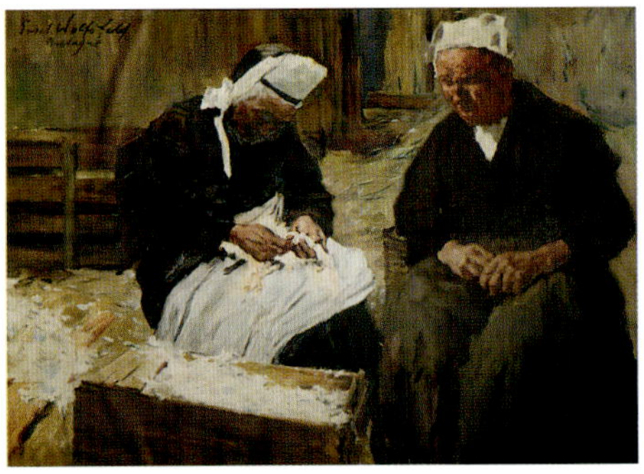

Wolfsfeld, Erich 1884–1956
Plucking Chickens
oil on canvas 51 x 69
LCNUG 1927.2350

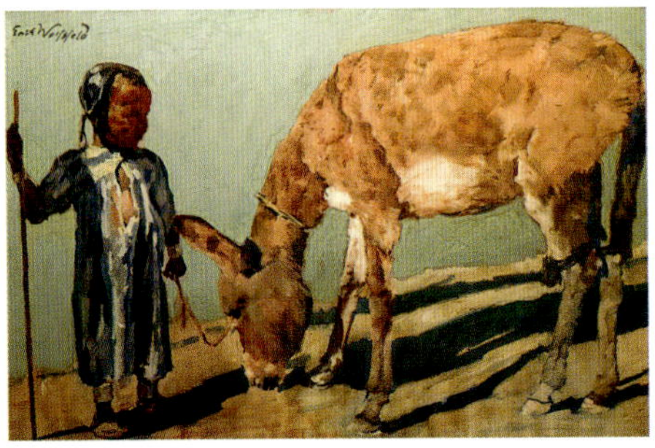

Wolfsfeld, Erich 1884–1956
Young Arab with a Donkey
oil on canvas 63.5 x 96.5
LCNUG 1927.2349

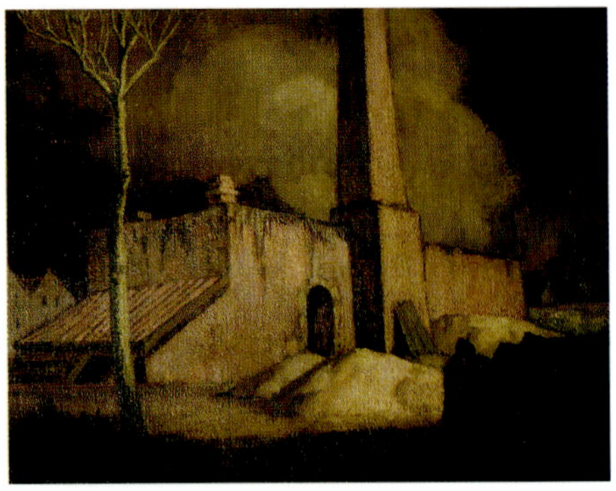

Worrall, Ernest J. 1898–1972
Limekilns 1933
oil on canvas 71.5 x 92
LCNUG 1927.187

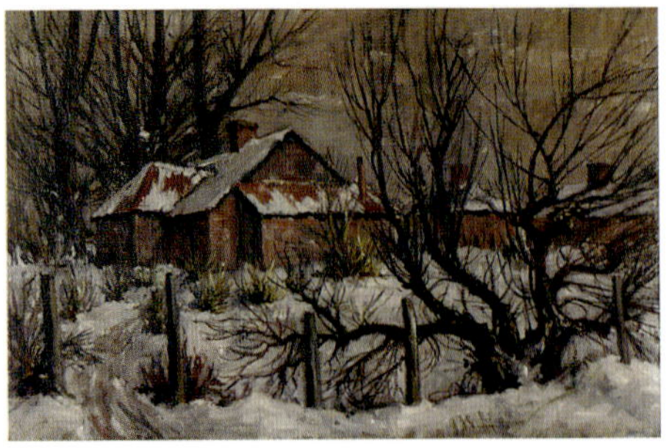

Worrall, Ernest J. 1898–1972
Snow at Healing, Lincolnshire
oil on canvas 56 x 83.5
LCNUG 1927.2238

Facing page: Doubleday, Peter, *Is It Only Virgins That Can Catch a Unicorn?* (detail), Leicestershire County Council Beaumanor Collection (p. 151)

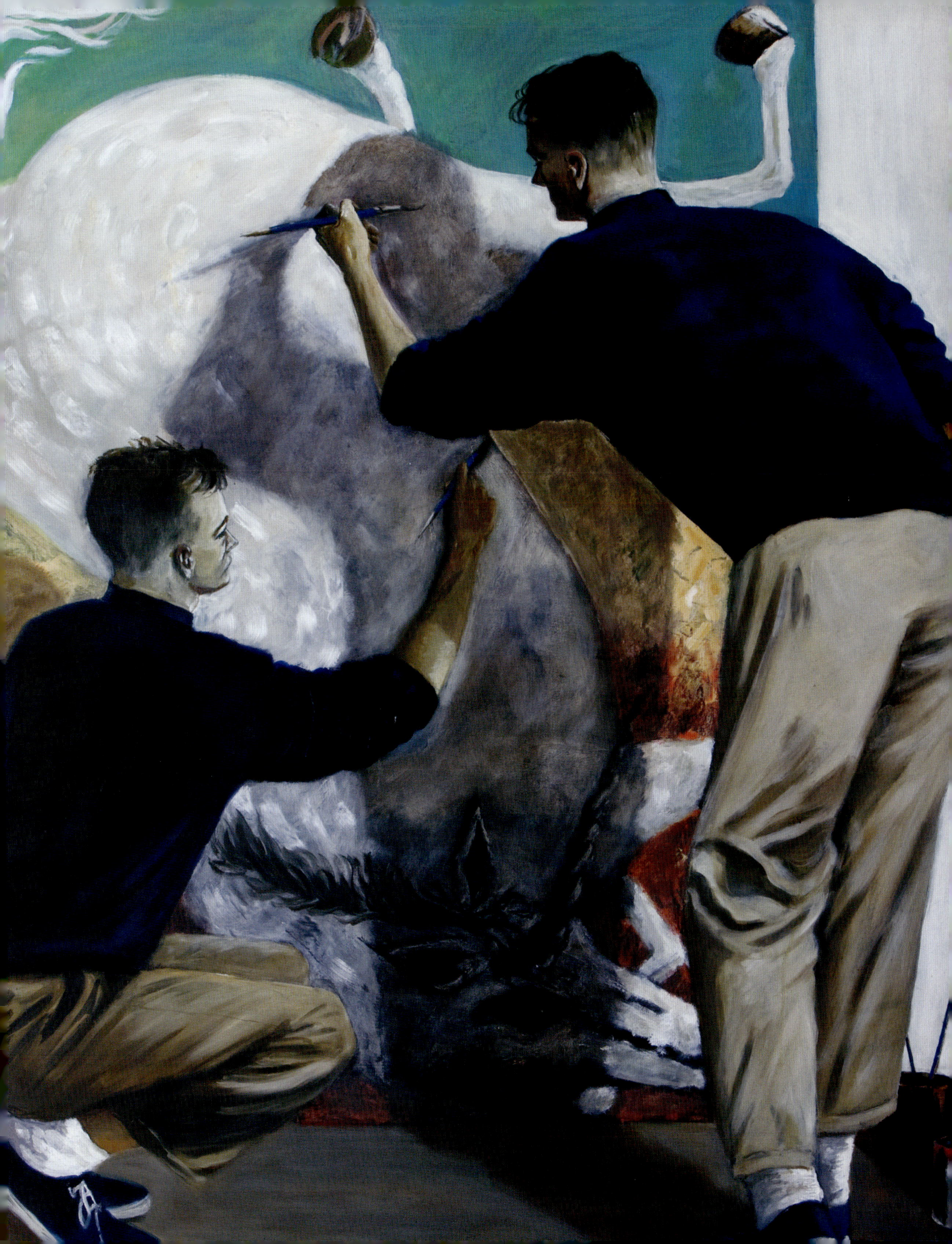

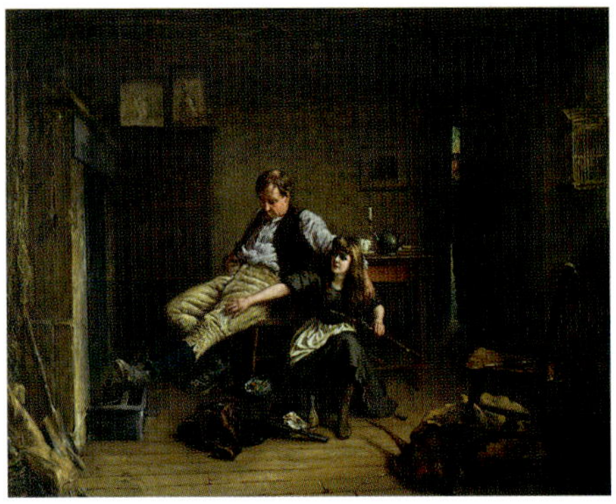

Wortley, Archibald J. Stuart 1849–1905
The Poacher's Daughter 1884
oil on canvas 112.5 x 160.5
LCNUG 1927.1997

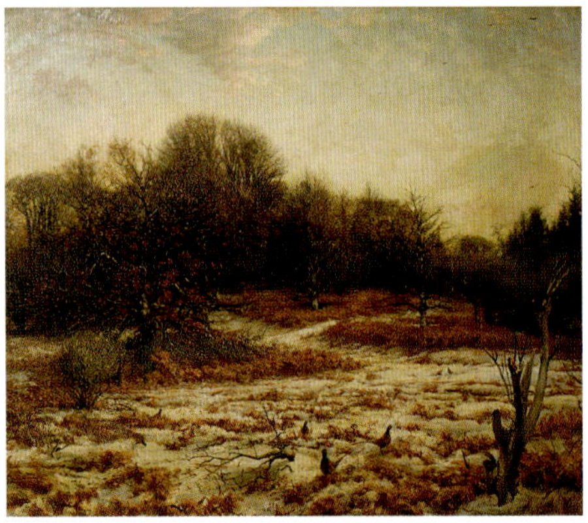

Wortley, Archibald J. Stuart 1849–1905
The Sleep of an Acorn 1884
oil on canvas 139.5 x 160.5
LCNUG 1927.72

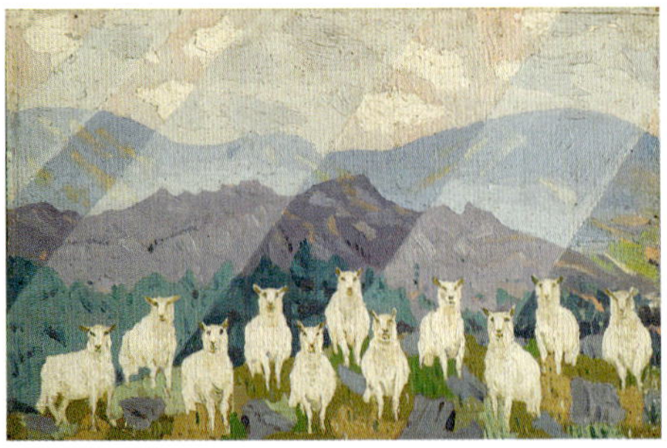

Wright, Nora active 20th C
Sheep
oil on board 19.7 x 29.2
LCNUG 1927.898

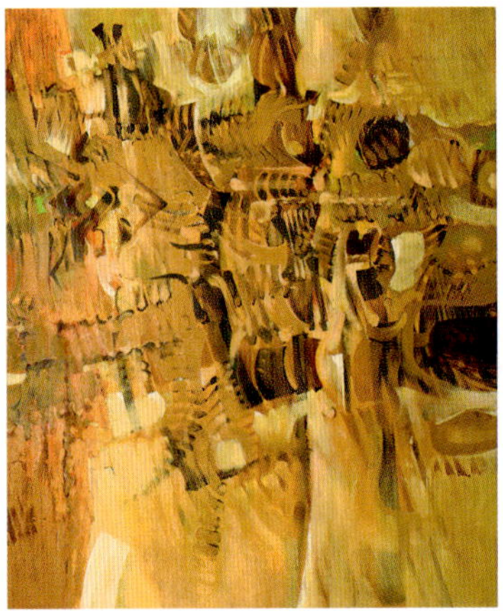

Wynter, Bryan 1915–1975
Sandspoor III c.1961
oil on canvas 152.5 x 122
LCNUG 1927.2567

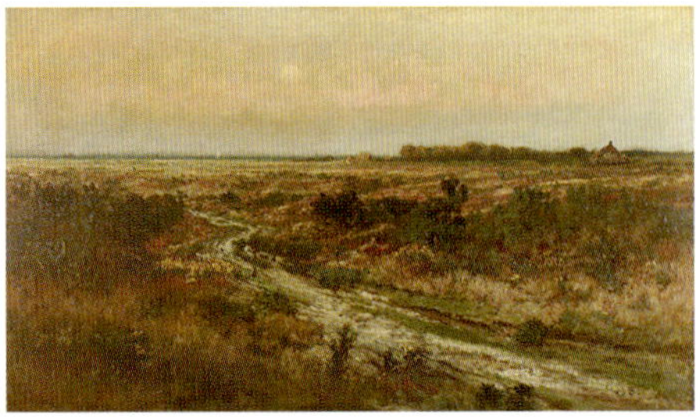

Yglesias, Vincent Philip 1845–1911
The Golden Common 1893
oil on canvas 101.5 x 168.5
LCNUG 1927.39

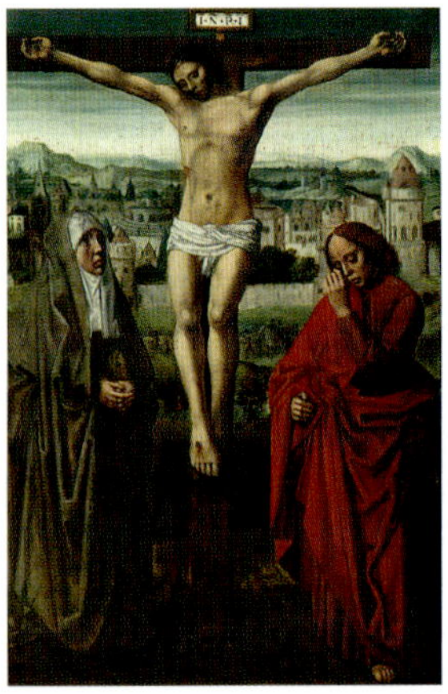

Ysenbrandt, Adriaen (attributed to)
c.1500–before 1551
Crucifixion
oil on panel 42 x 28
LCNUG 1927.2315

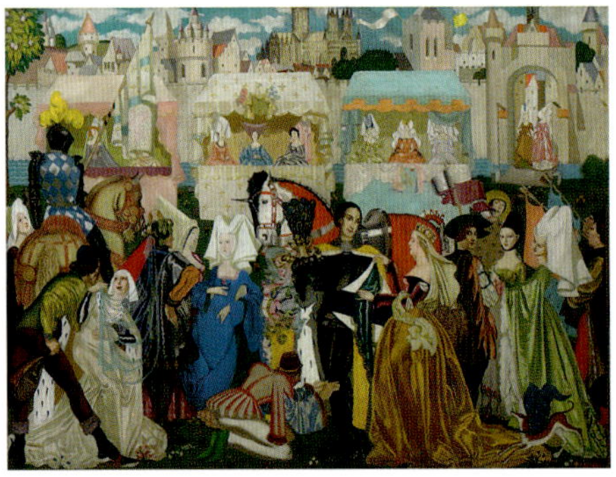

Zinkeisen, Anna Katrina 1901–1976
Mediaeval Lincoln
oil on canvas 77 x 102
LCNUG 1927.682

The Guildhall, Lincoln

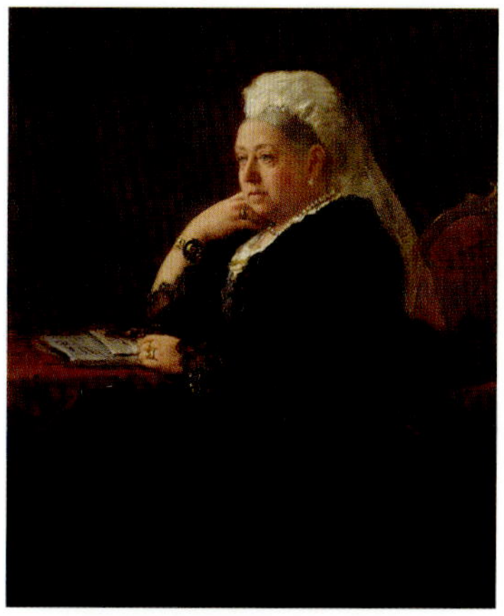

Bentley, Joseph Herbert 1866–1934
Queen Victoria (1819–1901)
oil on canvas 160 x 134.6
4

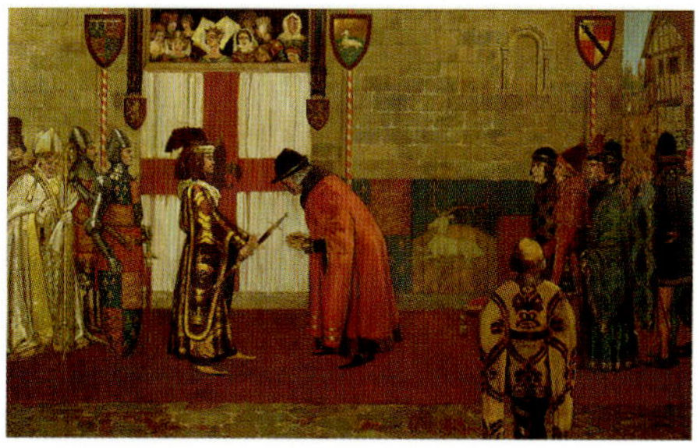

Boden, George Alfred 1888–1956
Richard II Presenting the Sword to the Mayor of Lincoln, 1386
oil on board 78.5 x 127
1

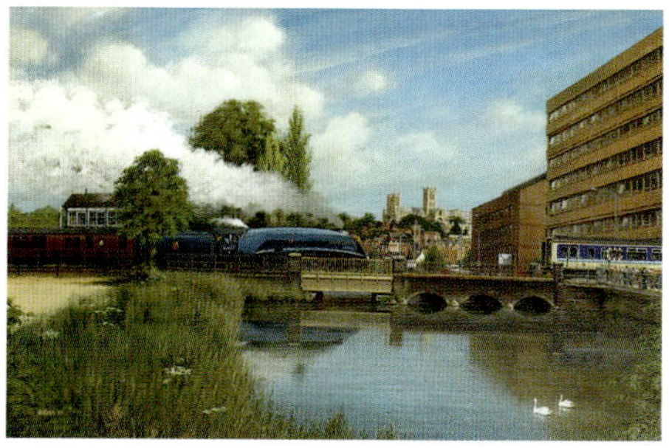

Brian
'Sir Nigel Gresley' Steam Train 1996
oil on canvas 62.5 x 90.5
3

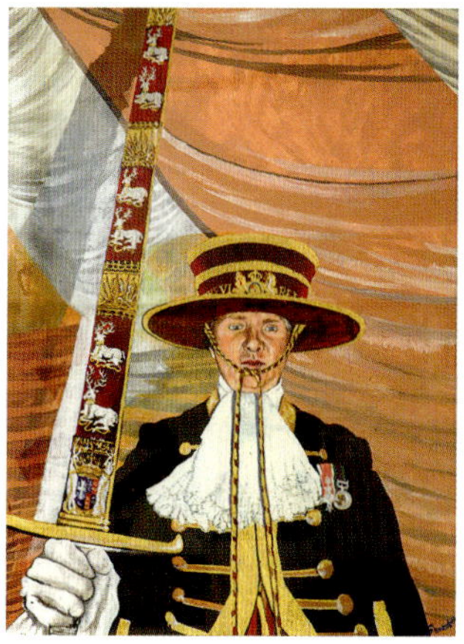

Pearson, Stewart
Sword Bearer 2004
acrylic on canvas (?) 111.8 x 74.9
2 (P)

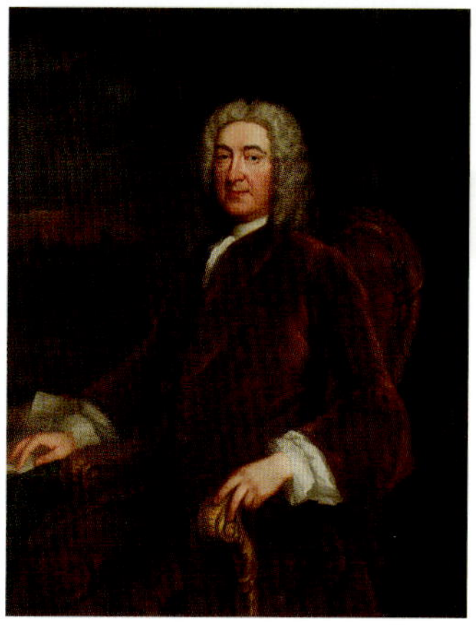

Philips, Charles 1708–1747
William Gylby 1740
oil on canvas 124 x 100
7

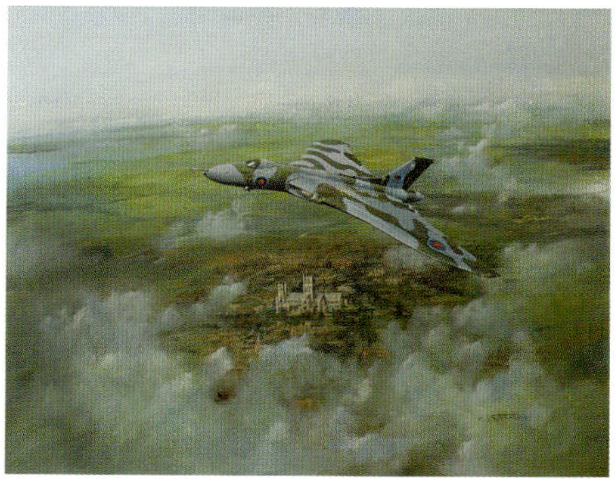

Stotthard, C. J.
Vulcan over Lincoln 1984
oil on canvas 61 x 77
9

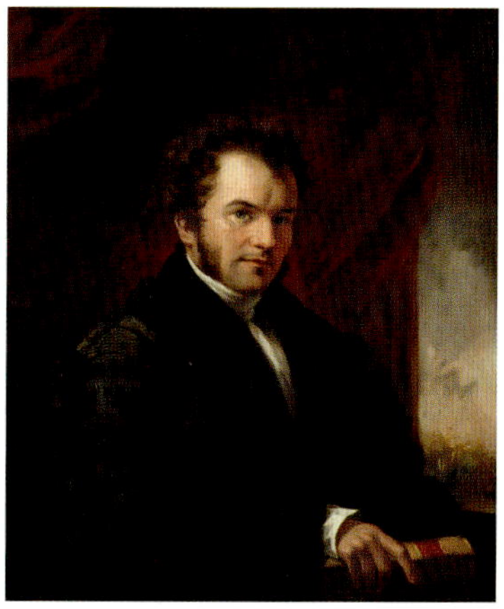

Stratt, J. G.
Richard Mason (1827–1855)
oil on canvas 76 x 61
6

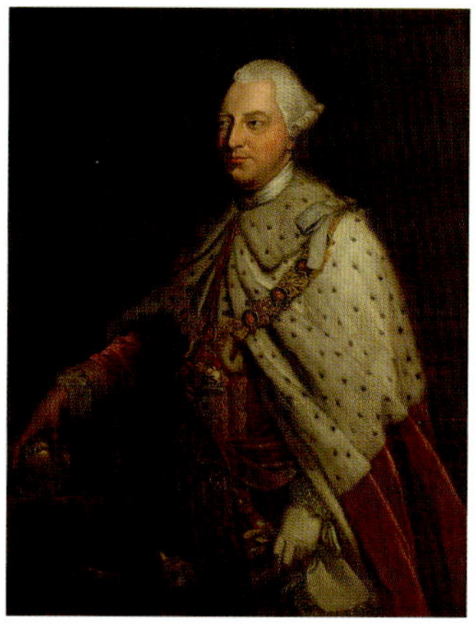

unknown artist
George III (1738–1820)
oil on canvas 160 x 134.6
5

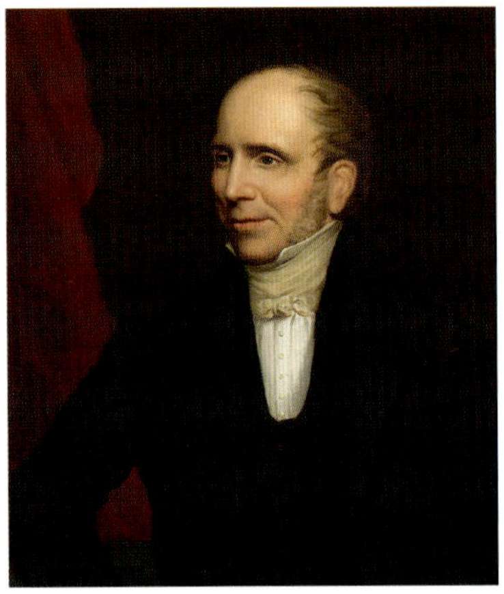

unknown artist
John Rudyard, Mayor of Lincoln (1836)
oil on canvas 74 x 61
8

The Lawn

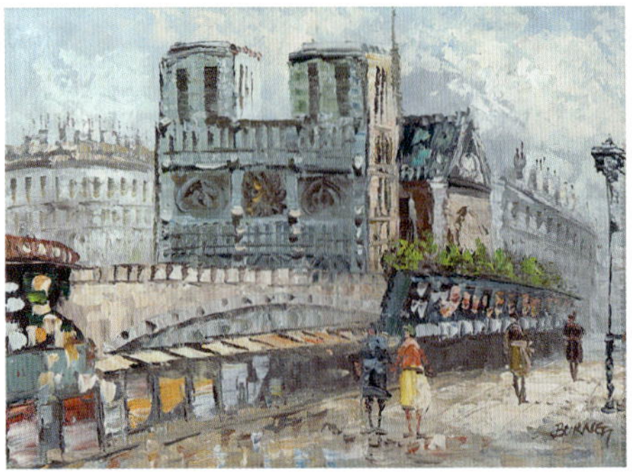

Burnett
Bridge in Neustadt, Germany
oil on canvas 30 x 40
2

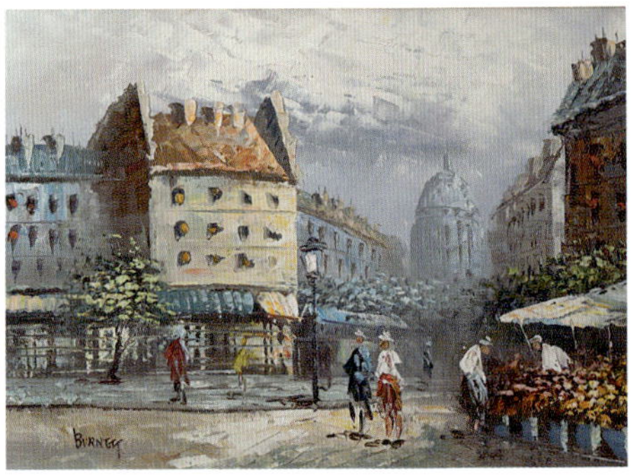

Burnett
Neustadt, Germany, Street Scene 1
oil on canvas 30 x 40
1

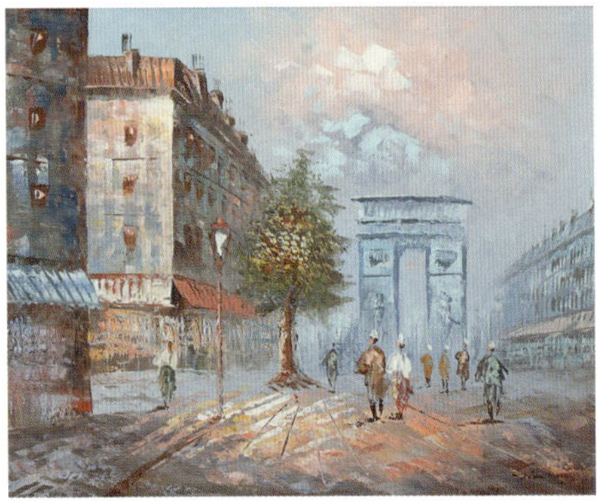

Gina
Neustadt, Germany, Street Scene 3
oil on canvas 50 x 65
4

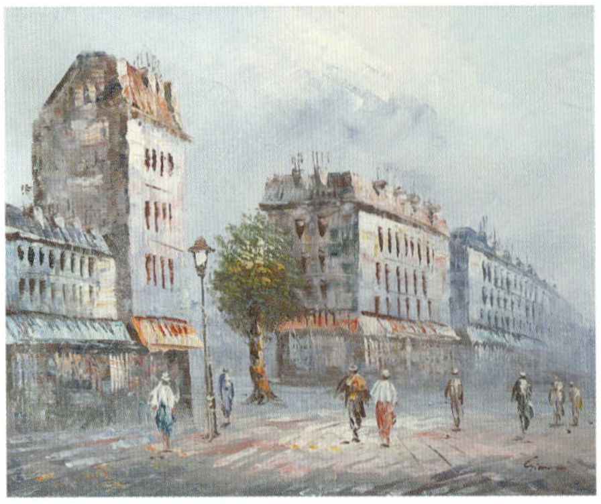

Gina
Neustadt, Germany, Street Scene 4
oil on canvas 50 x 65
5

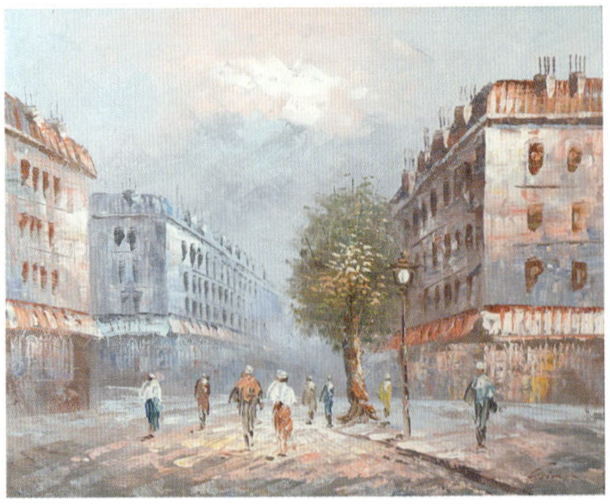

Gina
Neustadt, Germany, Street Scene 5
oil on canvas 50 x 65
6

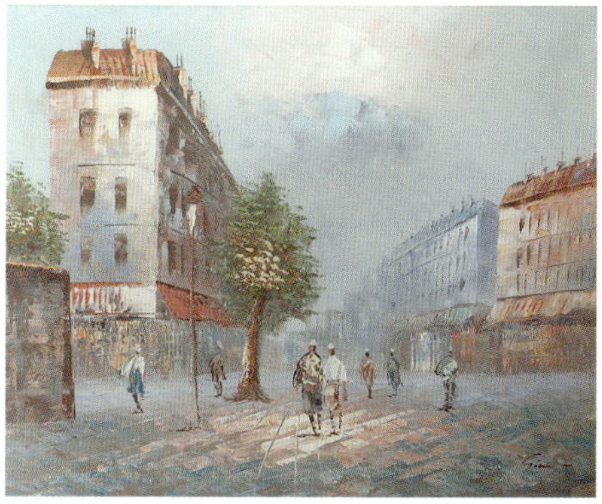

Gina
Neustadt, Germany, Street Scene 6
oil on canvas 50 x 65
7

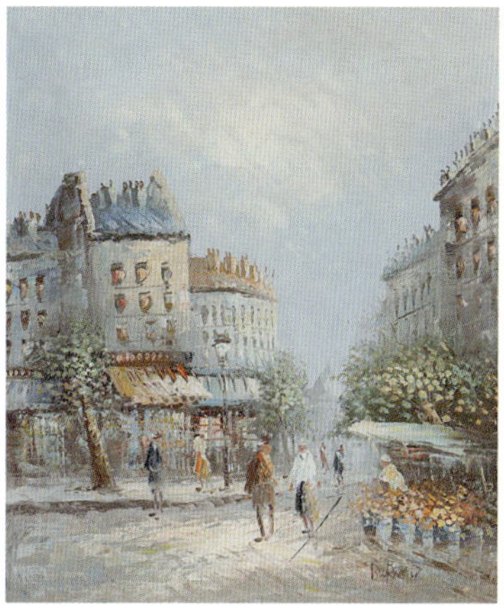

Gina
Neustadt, Germany, Street Scene 7
oil on canvas 60 x 50
8

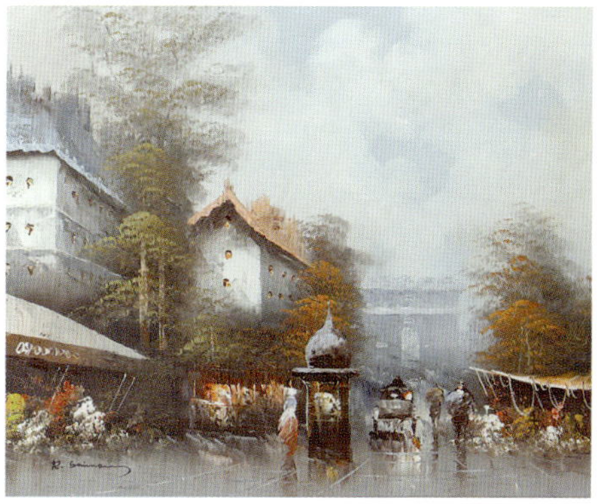

Sainsbury, R.
Neustadt, Germany, Street Scene 2
oil on canvas 50 x 65
3

The Royal Lincolnshire Regimental Museum Trust

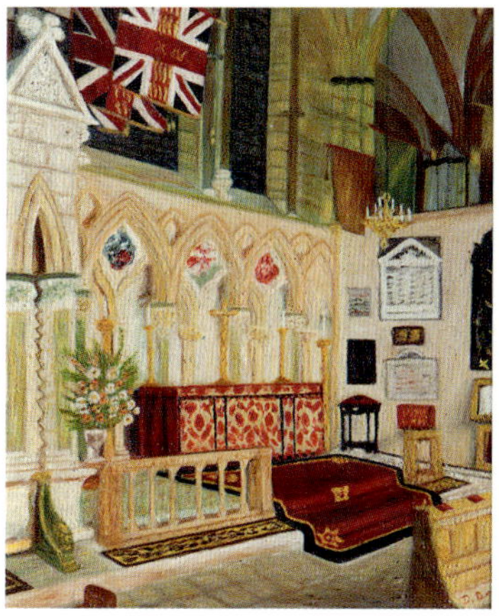

Arnold, Dorothy
The Soldiers' Chapel of St George, Lincoln Cathedral 1967
oil on board 33 x 28
1984/1772

University of Lincoln

The University of Lincoln, created in 2001, has fast established itself as a leading university in the field of Art and Design. We pride ourselves on our reputation and continue to focus on innovation and creativity in an environment where the student focus is paramount.

The history of Art and Design in Lincoln dates back many years, to when the city opened the Lincoln School of Art and Design in 1868 as a means of creating skilled draftsmen for the newly developing engineering industry. The University has built upon this foundation with the continuance of the Lincoln School of Art and Design within the Faculty of Art, Architecture and Design. We have a reputation for excellence in the School, offering courses in Illustration, Fine Art, Product and Graphic Design and our collection of art work is representative of the high standards and creativity that exist within all areas of the School.

The pieces in this catalogue are a relatively small representation of the overall collection which predominantly holds works from the student body and staff members acquired over the last nine years. Our policy is to develop the collection by purchasing significant works from students and commissions from practising staff members.

Dr Rachel Faulding, Senior Researcher & Lecturer

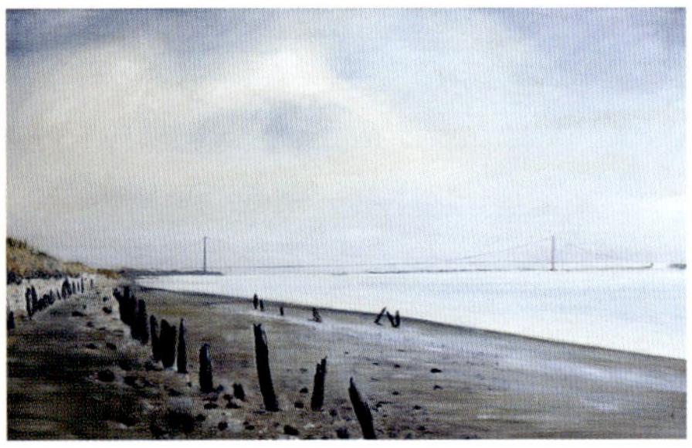

Bettles, John James b.1924
The Bridge
oil on canvas 66.5 x 92
PCF21

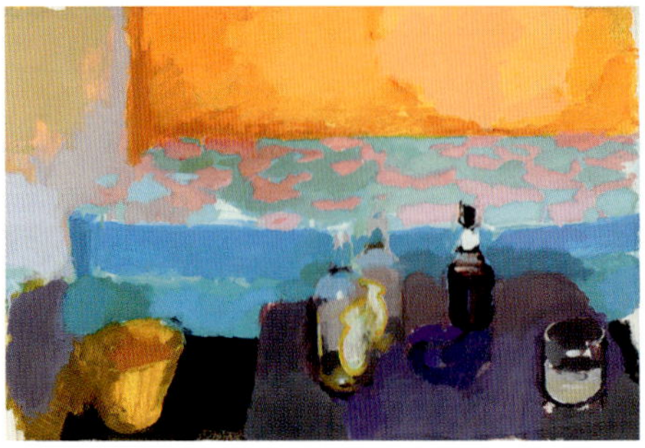

Edwards, Paul b.1954
*Beer Table**
oil on paper 56 x 78
AC09/00200

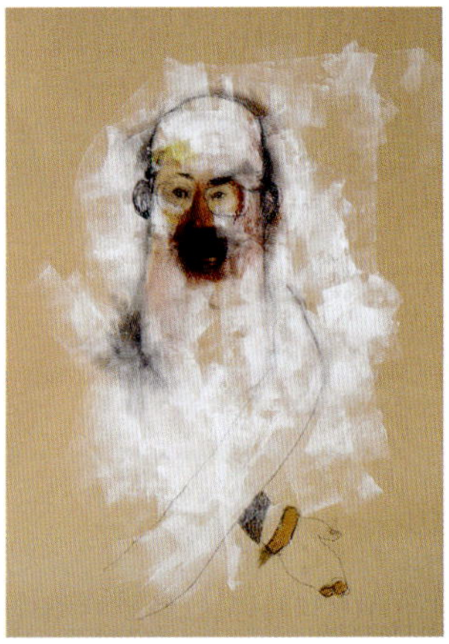

Essafiry, Savida
*Portrait of a Gentleman with Spectacles** 2006
oil on paper 92.5 x 65.5
PCF30

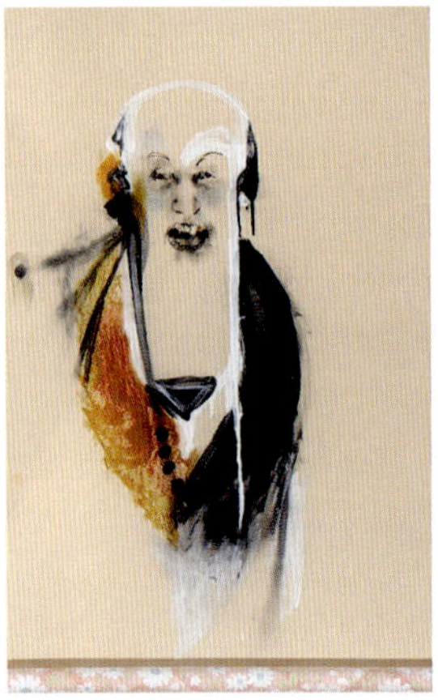

Essafiry, Savida
*Portrait of a Japanese Gentleman** 2006
oil on wallpaper 83 x 52
PCF29

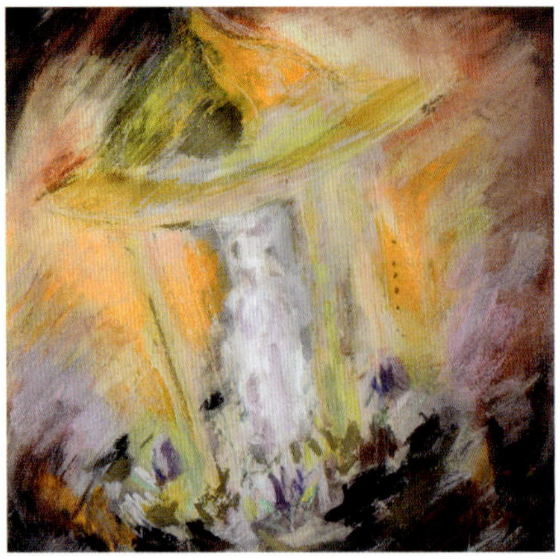

Hammad, Medina b.1963
Fountain Lamp 1992
oil on paper 26.5 x 26.5
PCF8

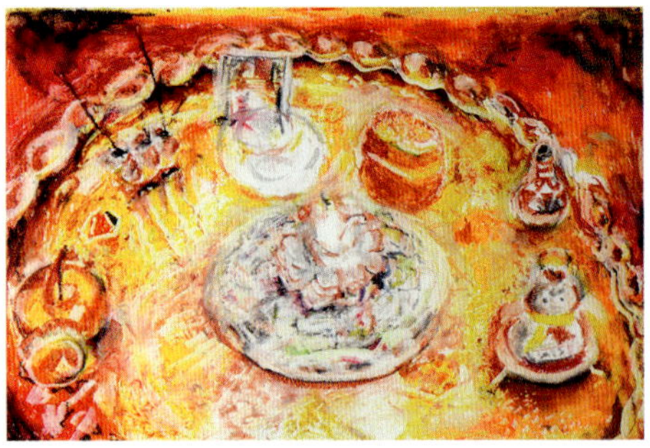

Hammad, Medina b.1963
Dad's Song Table 1993
oil on paper 20 x 30
PCF16

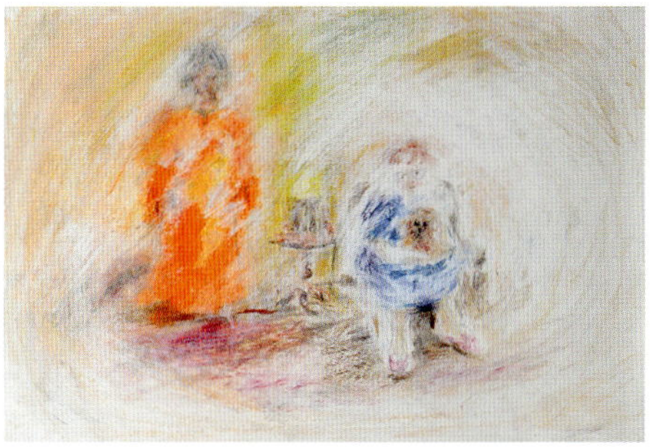

Hammad, Medina b.1963
Estrangement (study)
oil on paper 20 x 30
PCF23

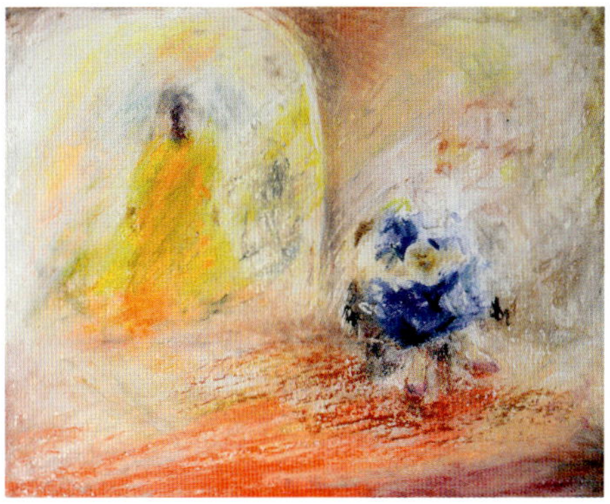

Hammad, Medina b.1963
Estrangement 1993
oil on paper 18 x 25
PCF22

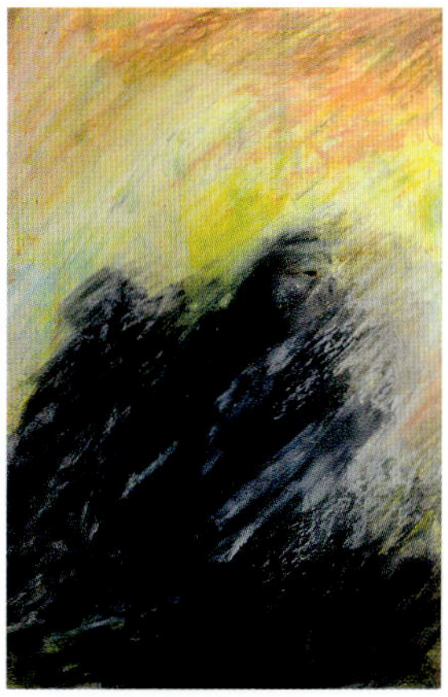

Hammad, Medina b.1963
Yellow Corridor (study) 1994
oil on paper 30 x 20
AC09/00210

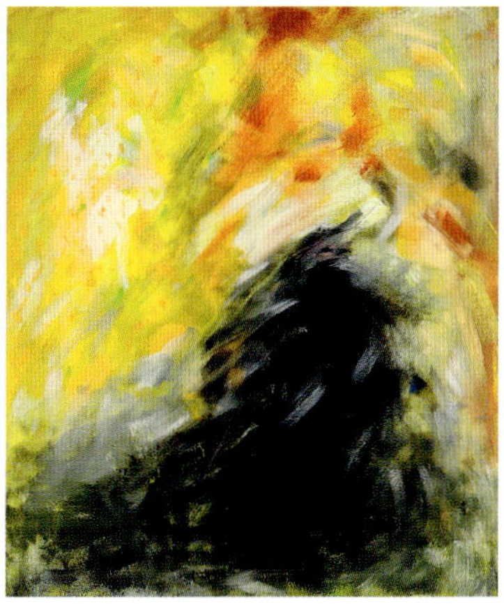

Hammad, Medina b.1963
Yellow Corridor (part of a triptych)
oil on canvas 61 x 51
AC09/00211

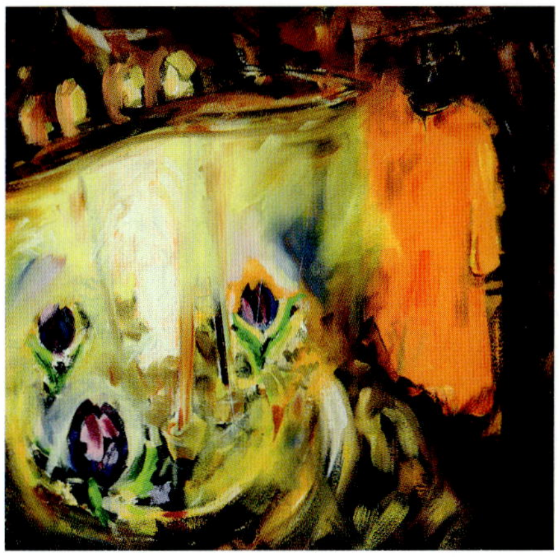

Hammad, Medina b.1963
Fountain Lamp and Rose
oil on canvas 70.5 x 70
AC09/00208

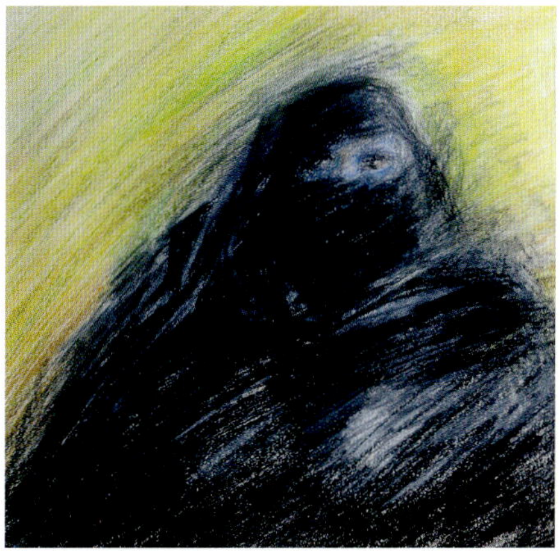

Hammad, Medina b.1963
Gulf Woman against Yellow Wall Prayer
oil on paper 15.5 x 16
PCF15

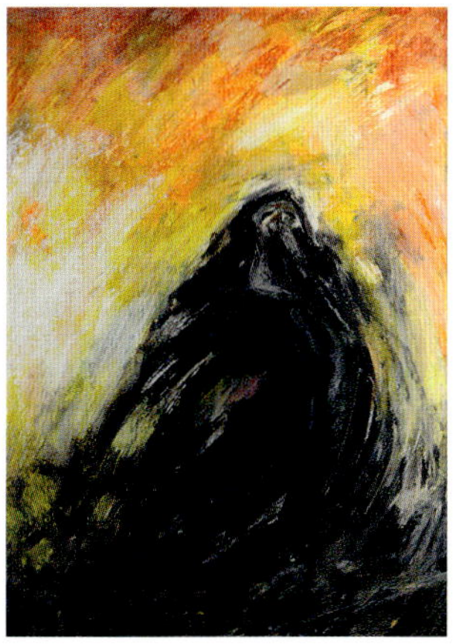

Hammad, Medina b.1963
Departure (study)
oil on paper 56 x 40
PCF14

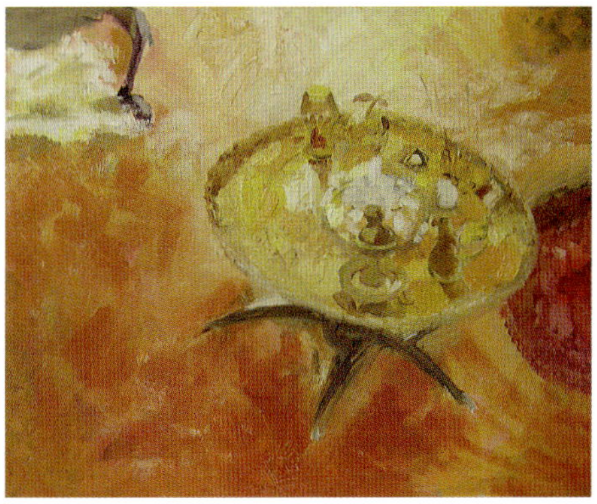

Hammad, Medina b.1963
*Yellow Table**
oil on canvas 120 x 140 (E)
PCF32

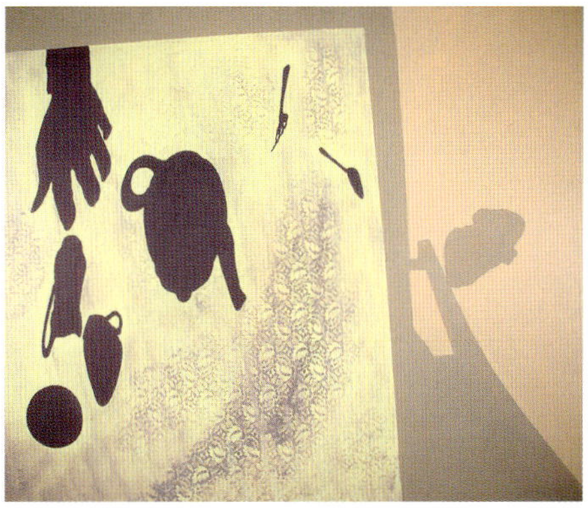

Lamb, Lynne b.1953
Untitled
acrylic on board 122.5 x 153
AC09/00237

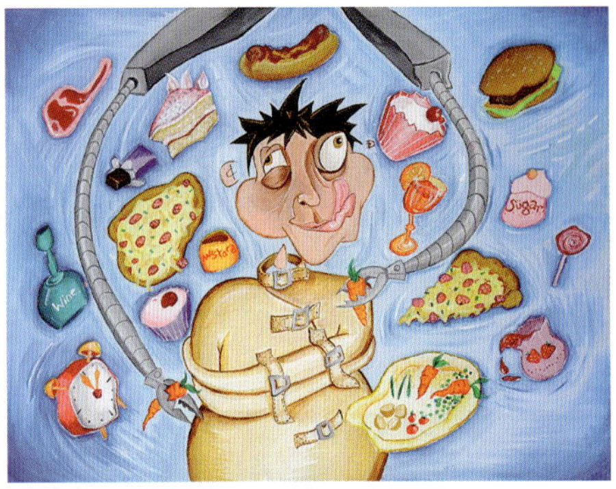

Mistry, Vanisha
*Temptation**
acrylic on canvas 40.5 x 51
AC09/00266

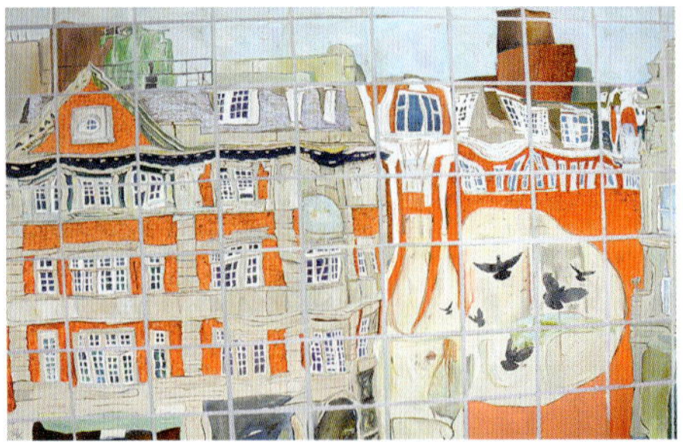

Neil, J.
*From a Window**
acrylic on canvas 90 x 135
AC09/00285

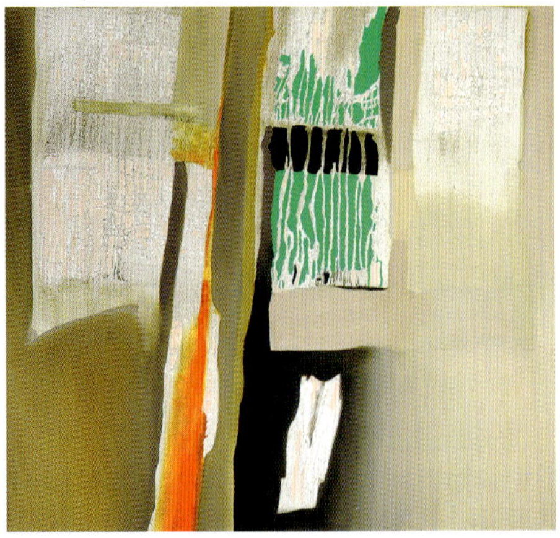

Newman, Mike b.1934
Phase
oil on canvas 91 x 91
AC09/00263

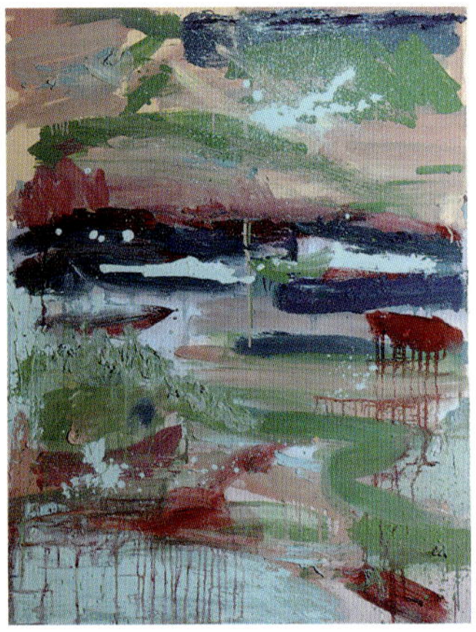

Richardson, Alexandra
West Common 1990
oil on canvas 117 x 87
AC09/00250

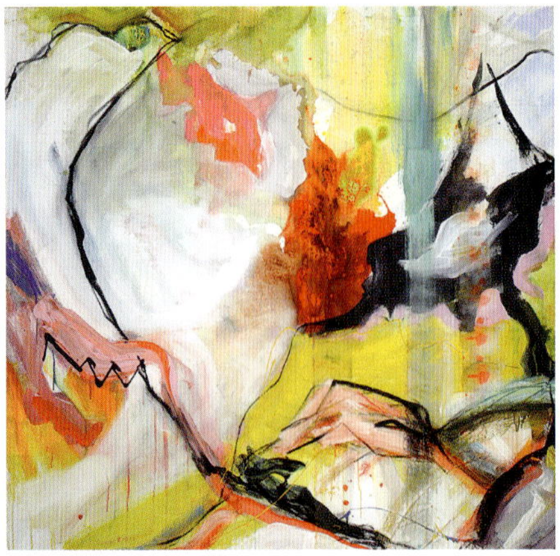

Stoneham, Leslie b.1947
Grass over Barbed Wire No.1
acrylic on canvas 152.5 x 152.5
AC09/00292

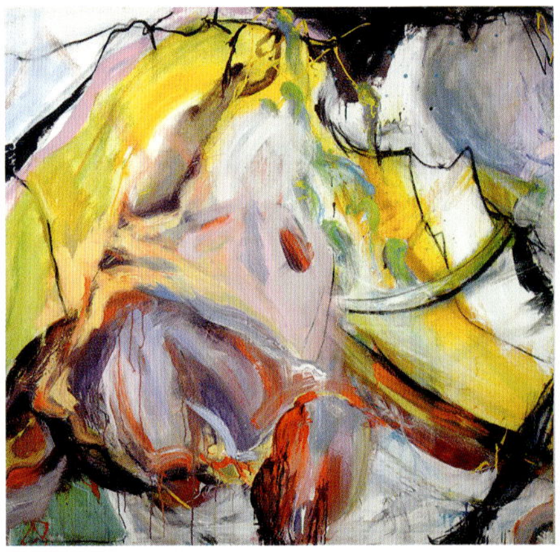

Stoneham, Leslie b.1947
Grass over Barbed Wire No.2
oil on canvas 152 x 152
PCF3

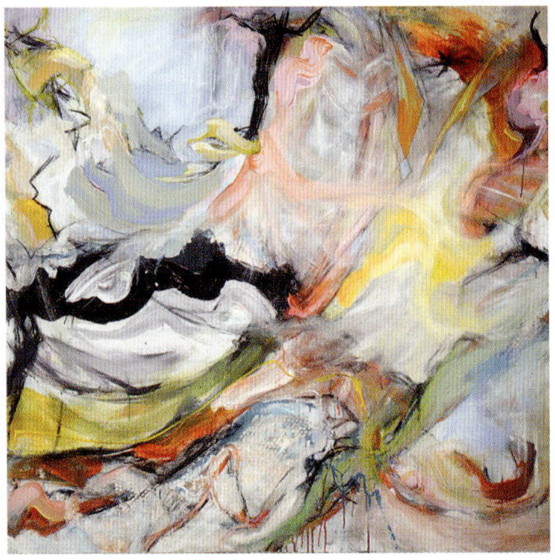

Stoneham, Leslie b.1947
Grass over Barbed Wire No.3
oil on canvas 153 x 153
PCF12

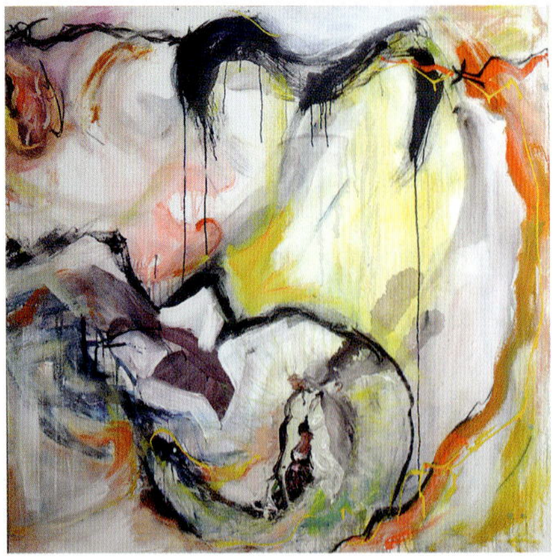

Stoneham, Leslie b.1947
Grass over Barbed Wire No.4
acrylic on canvas 152.5 x 152.5
AC09/00291

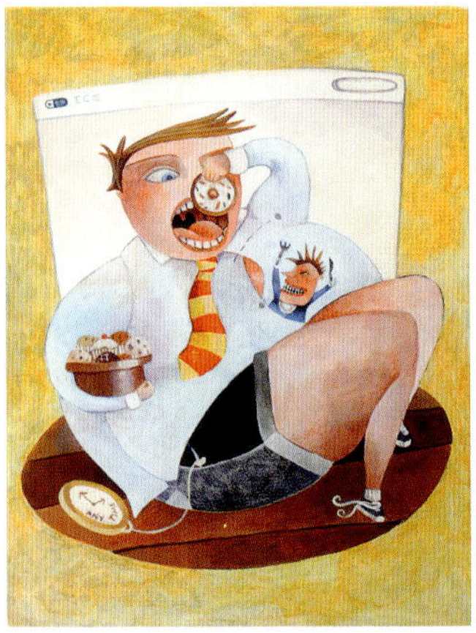

unknown artist
*Any Time**
acrylic on paper 38 x 27
PCF6

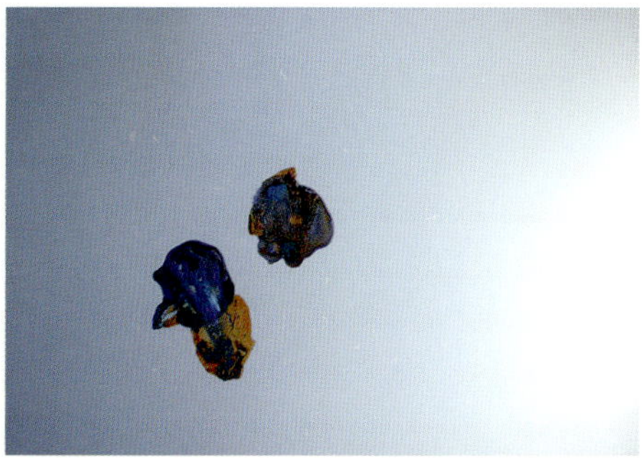

unknown artist
*Blue Jelly Fish**
oil & glass on board 122 x 183
PCF9

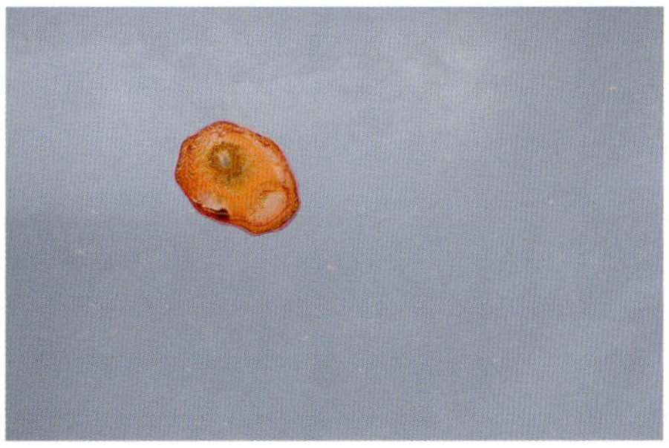

unknown artist
*Red Jelly Fish**
oil & glass on board 122 x 182.5
PCF1

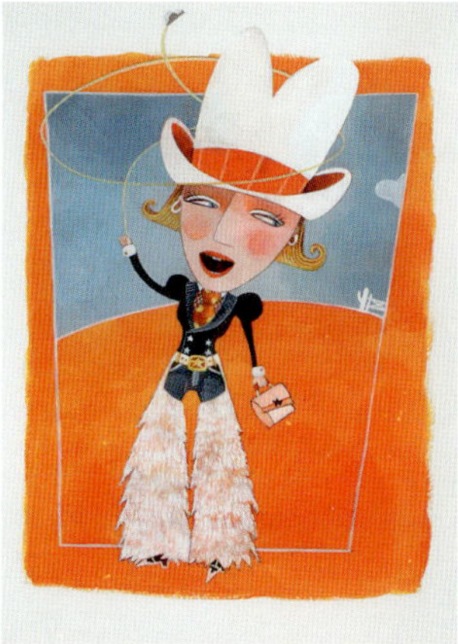

unknown artist
*Cow Girl**
acrylic on paper 38 x 27
PCF7

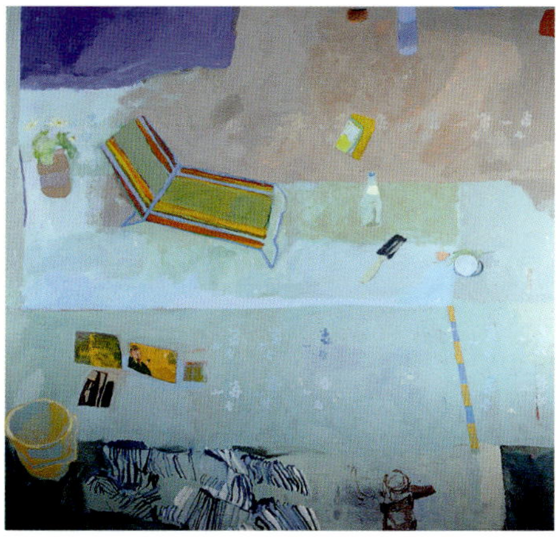

unknown artist
*Deckchair in Blue**
oil on canvas 182.5 x 183
PCF2

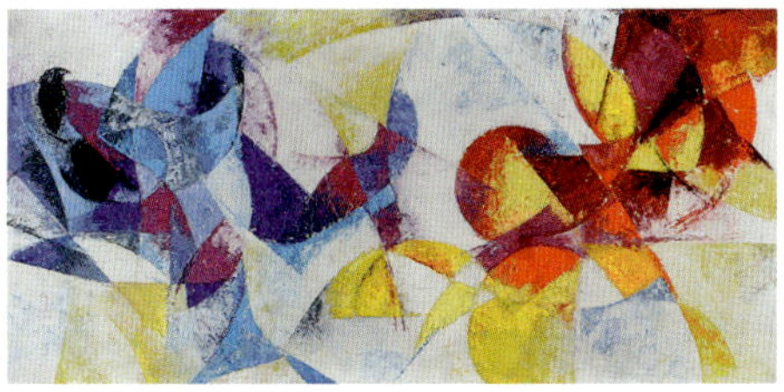

unknown artist
*Geometric**
acrylic on board 60.5 x 122
PCF28

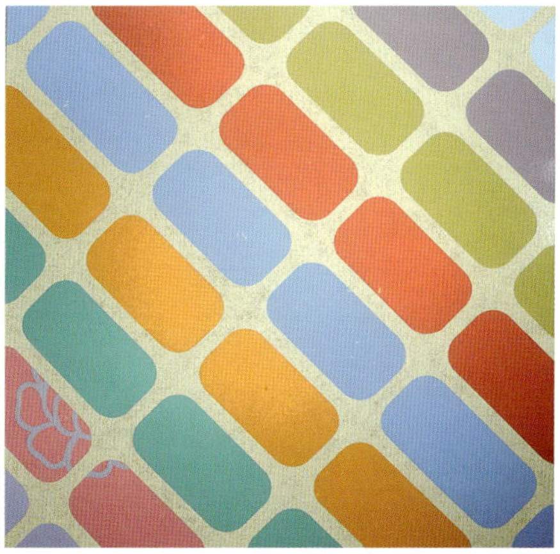

unknown artist
*Lozenge Lattice**
oil, gloss paint & glitter on canvas 180 x 180
PCF4

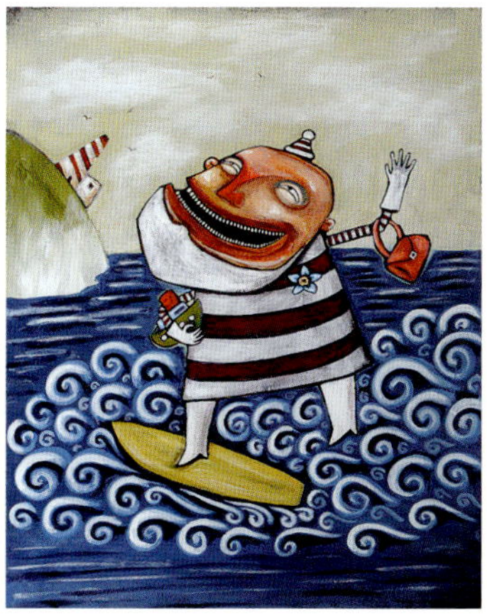

unknown artist
*Surf**
oil on canvas 49.5 x 39
PCF5

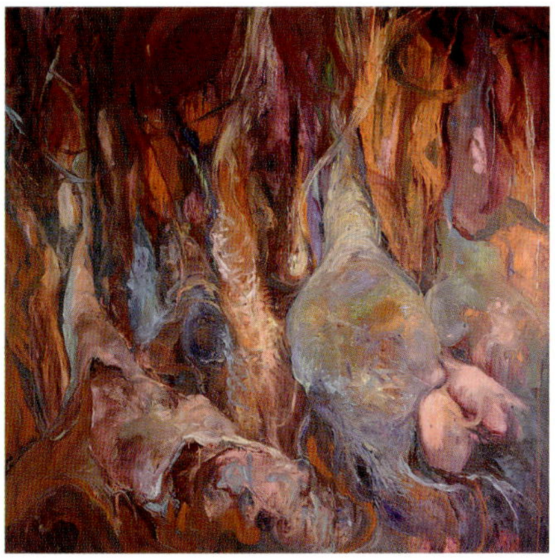

Warburton, Kay B. b.1955
*Organic Root Tuber**
oil on canvas 152 x 152
AC09/00233

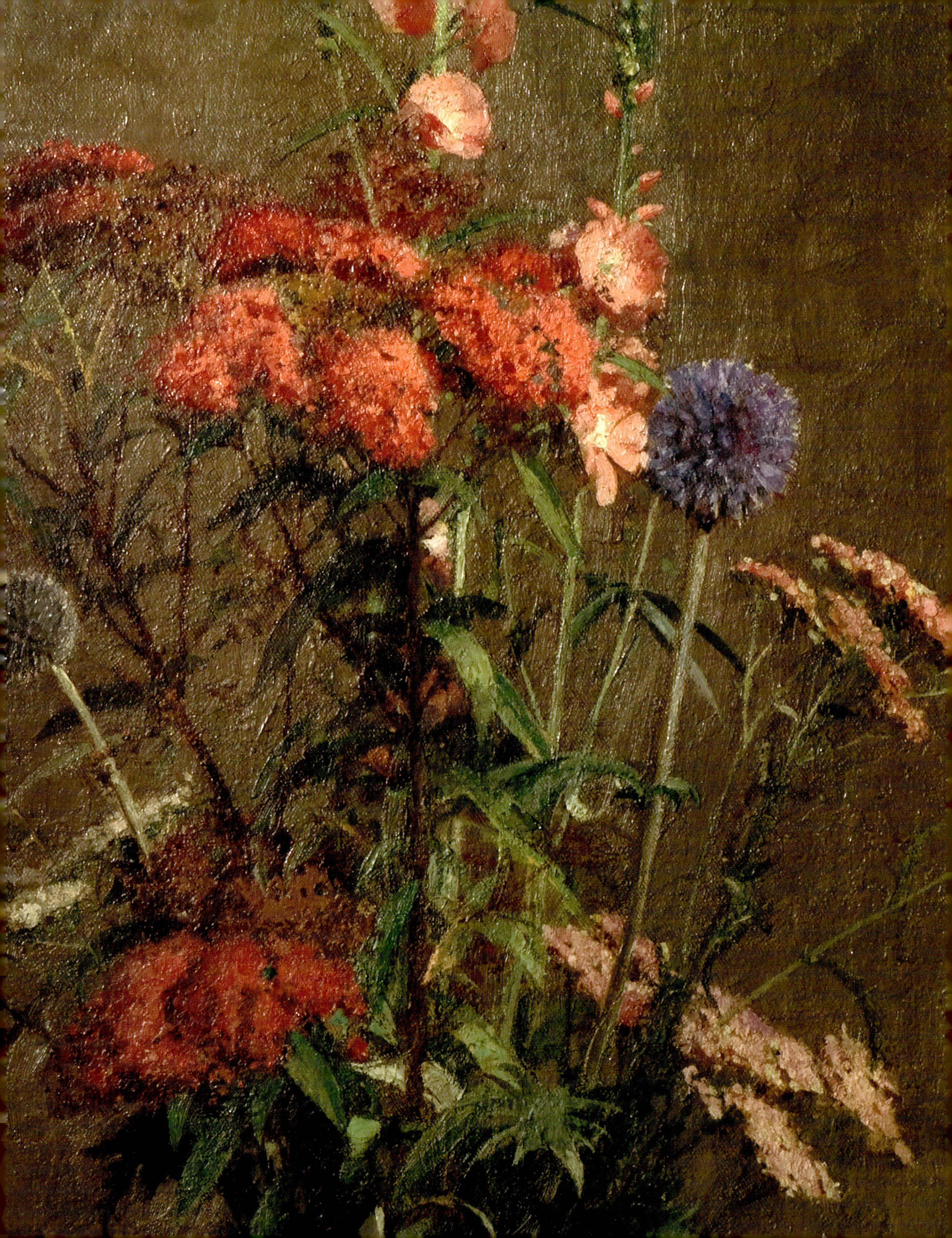

Louth Museum

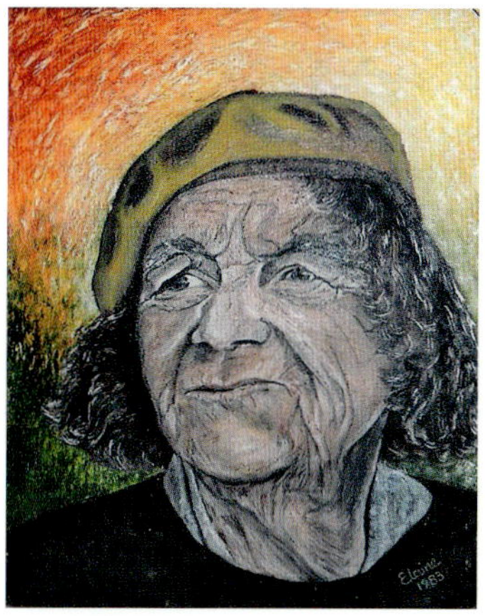

Drewery, Elaine b.1939
Miss Kent 1983
oil on canvas 50.8 x 40.7
W204

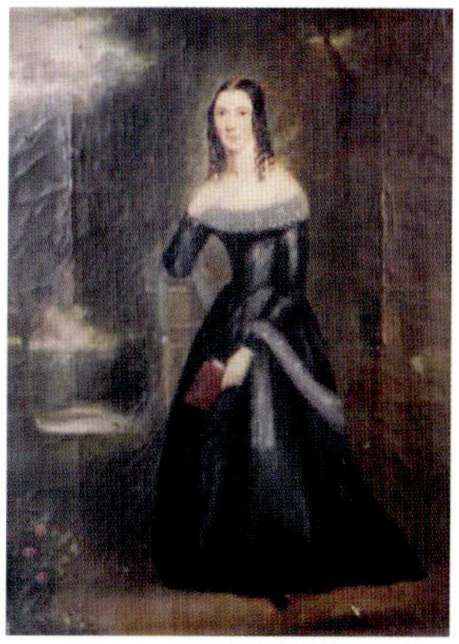

Hubbard, Bennett 1806–1870
Portrait of an Unknown Female 1843
oil on canvas 55.9 x 43.2
W25

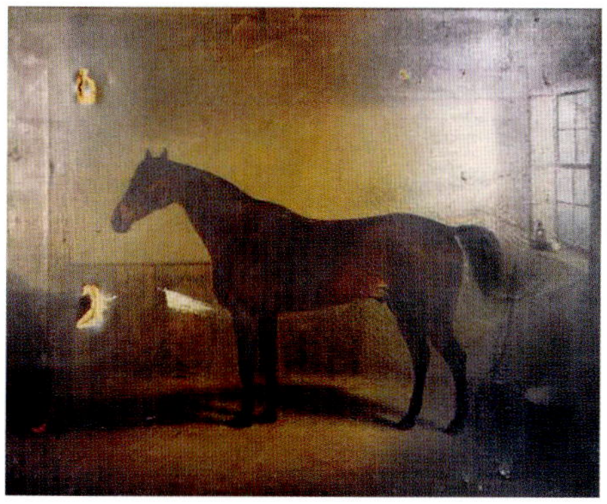

Hubbard, Bennett 1806–1870
Chestnut Horse (before restoration) 1845
oil on canvas 85.1 x 96.5
W30

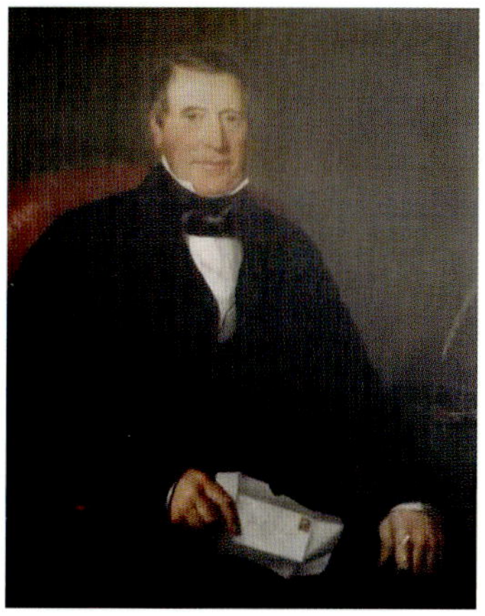

Hubbard, Bennett 1806–1870
Nathaniel Hammond Batterham 1846
oil on canvas 92 x 71.5 (E)
W17

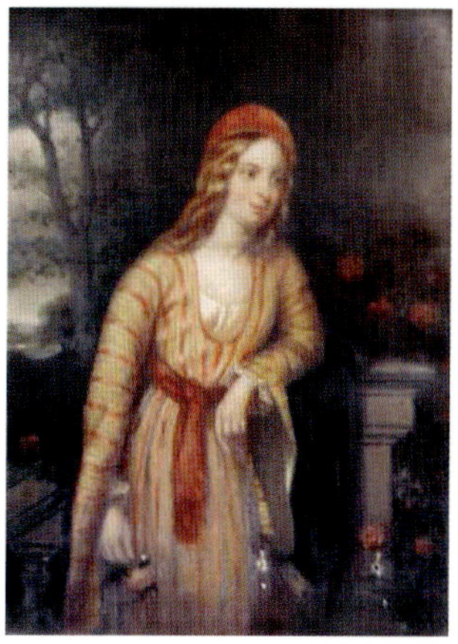

Hubbard, Bennett 1806–1870
Portrait of an Unknown Female 1856
oil on canvas 58.4 x 47
W28

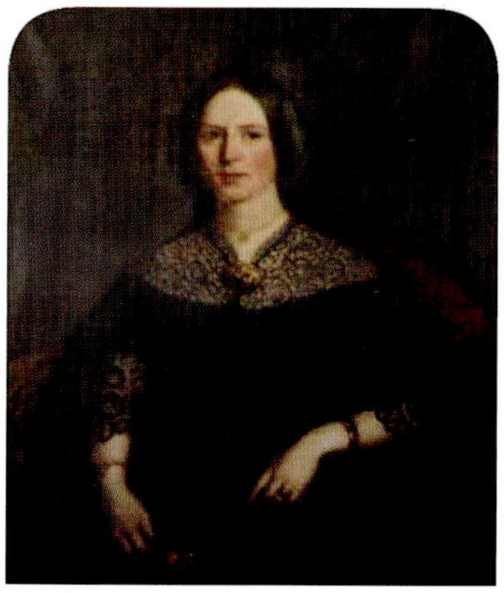

Hubbard, Bennett 1806–1870
Portrait of an Unknown Lady 1862
oil on canvas 116.8 x 96.5
W16

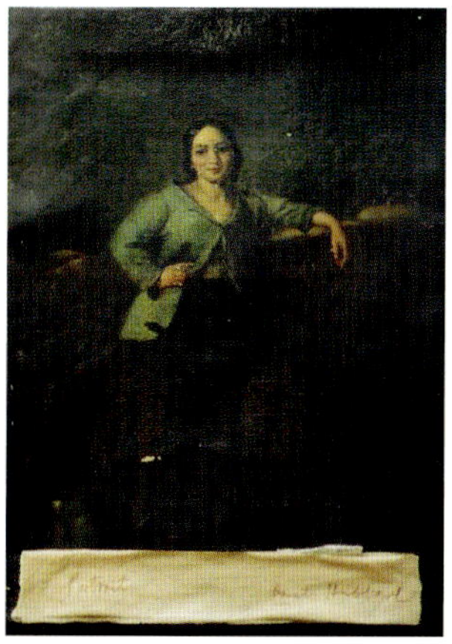

Hubbard, Bennett 1806–1870
A Welsh Milk Girl 1866
oil on canvas 48.3 x 35.6
W121

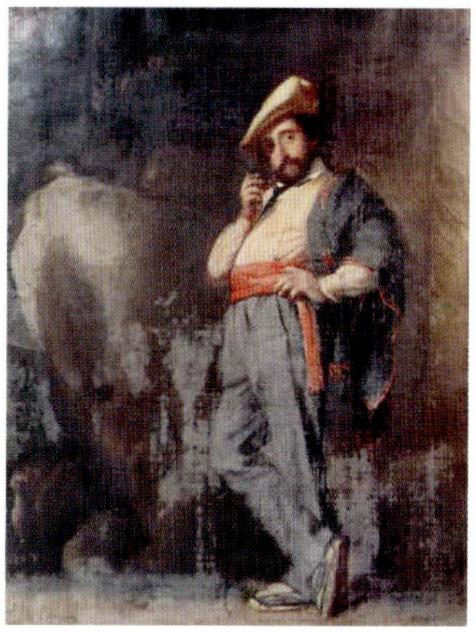

Hubbard, Bennett 1806–1870
Spanish Peasant of the Basque Provinces 1868
oil on canvas 63.5 x 52.1
W26

Facing page: Logsdail, William, 1859–1944, *Garden Flowers* (detail), c.1935, The Collection: Art & Archaeology in Lincolnshire (Usher Gallery) (p. 313)

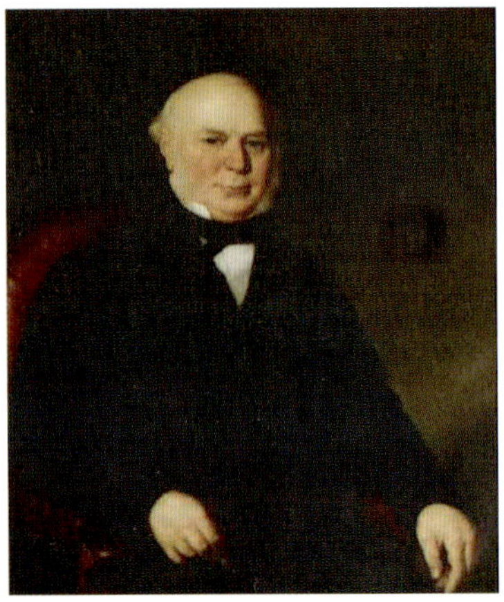

Hubbard, Bennett 1806–1870
Portrait of an Unknown Man (thought to be Charles Goodwin Smith) 1869
oil on canvas 114.9 x 94
W19

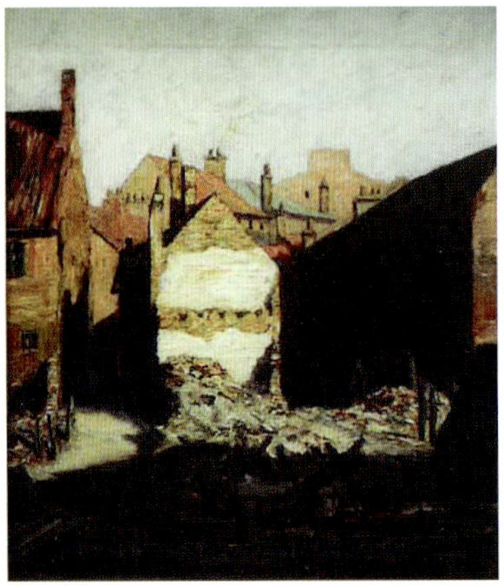

Morton, Charles Reginald (attributed to) active 1917–1936
Ruined House (Louth Flood Damage, 29 May 1920) 1920
oil on canvas 43.2 x 38.1
W122

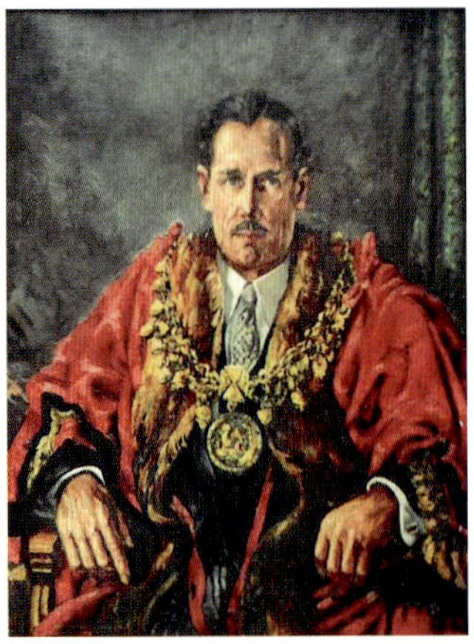

Rodgerson, W. A. active 1940s–1960s
Portrait of an Unidentified Mayor of Louth 1954
oil on canvas 88.9 x 71.1
W80

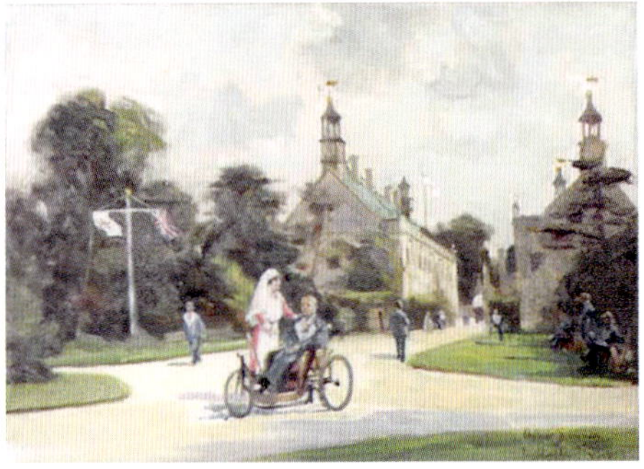

Spooner, Arthur 1873–1961
Scene of the Gatehouse at Welbeck Abbey, Nottinghamshire 1918
oil on canvas 44.5 x 52.1
W36

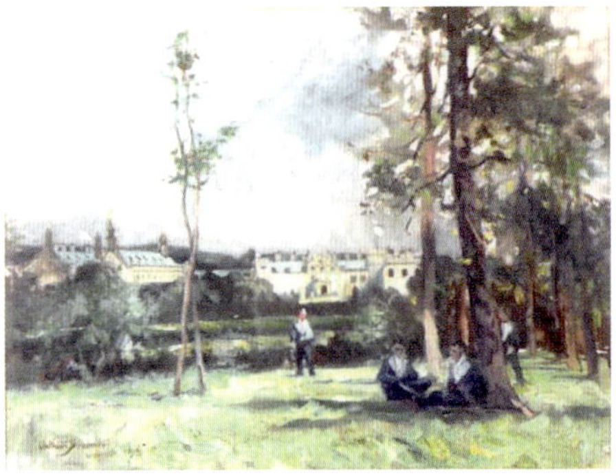

Spooner, Arthur 1873–1961
Welbeck Abbey and Park, Nottinghamshire 1918
oil on canvas 47.6 x 55.2
W37

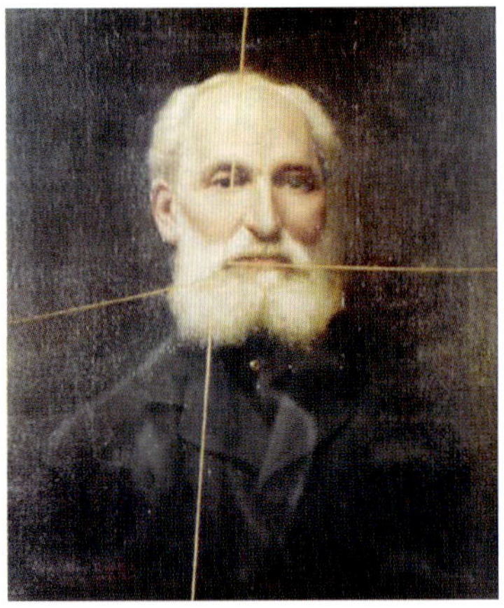

Spooner, Arthur 1873–1961
John William Goulding of Louth (1844–1922)
oil on canvas 81.3 x 71.1
W33

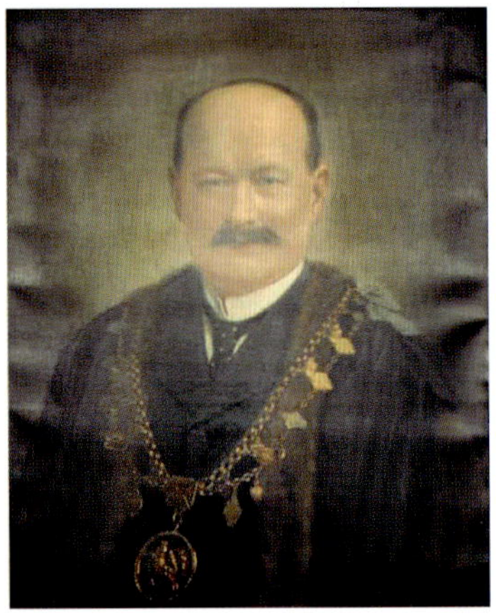

unknown artist
Alderman George Blaze, Mayor of Louth (1911)
oil on canvas 62.2 x 53.3
W81

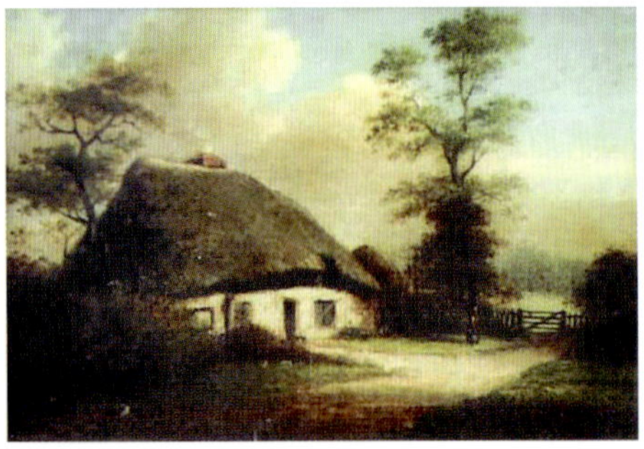

unknown artist
Thatched House and a Gate
oil on canvas 31.8 x 43.2
W120

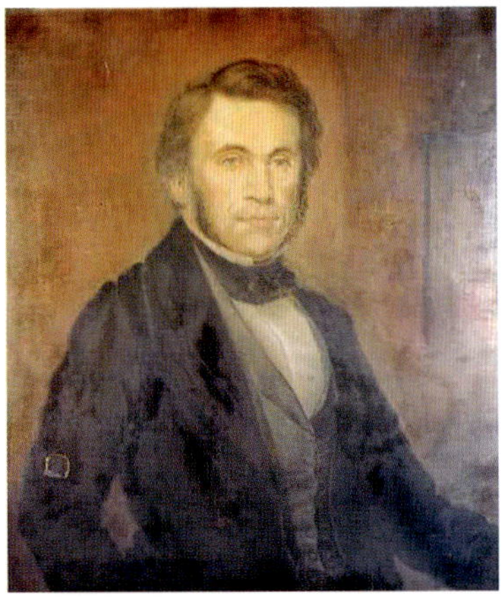

Wallis, Thomas Wilkinson 1822–1903
Self Portrait 1845
oil on canvas 99.1 x 86.4
W31

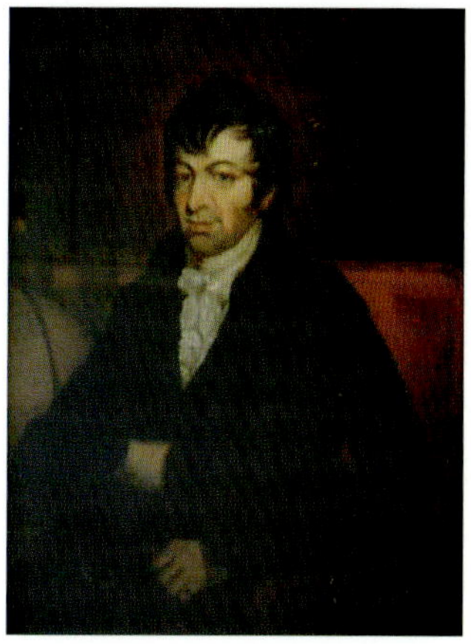

Wallis, Thomas Wilkinson 1822–1903
Thomas Espin (1767–1822), FSA (after Richard Jones) 1895
oil on canvas 111.8 x 91.4
W18

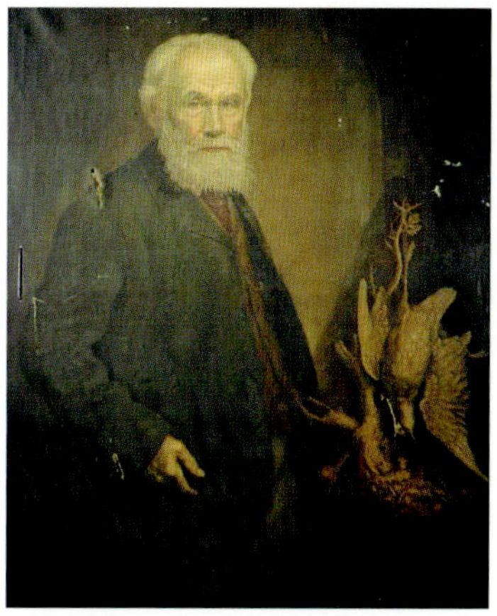

Wallis, Thomas Wilkinson 1822–1903
Self Portrait (before restoration) 1897
oil on canvas 110.5 x 85.1
W15

Owston Ferry Parish Council

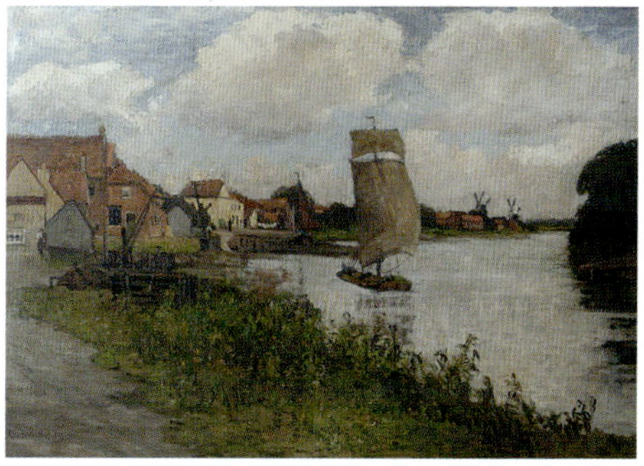

Smith, Gabell active c.1900–1930
On the Trent, Owston Ferry, Lincolnshire c.1900
oil on canvas 66 x 92
1

North Lincolnshire Museums Service

North Lincolnshire Museums Service holds a great variety of artwork, from seventeenth-century oil paintings, to work by local artists.

Some of our most fabulous oil paintings were originally collected to furnish Normanby Hall in the 1960s, and the collection has grown from this point. It was during this time that the then curator's attention was brought to a small painting on an oak panel, which was attributed to the school of Titian. With a feeling that the painting was in fact the school of Rubens, the curator purchased it reputedly for £5. After much research and collaboration with a Rubens expert, it was finally confirmed that the painting was in fact by Rubens himself. Not only that, but it is in fact the missing *Emperor Otho* from Rubens' Twelve Caesars series, three of which are still missing. We are very proud to have a painting by an Old Master in our collection.

When the Museums Service was a member of the Contemporary Art Society, a student's painting was donated each year for the collection. One student's large triptych has since become more of a treasure as the painter has evolved into a senior Royal Academician – this painting is *Lovemaking in Lissenden Gardens* by Anthony Green.

North Lincolnshire Museums Service has always supported local art by providing exhibition space. Our Collection houses a range of paintings acquired from artists who have won competitions held by the local art group.

Some of these paintings are being viewed by the public for the first time in decades through this catalogue. Our art collection on display can be viewed at three sites; in a country house setting at Normanby Hall, and in the more conventional gallery spaces at North Lincolnshire Museum. In addition a small number of paintings related to Barton-upon-Humber can be viewed at Baysgarth House Museum.

Madeleine Grout, Collections Assistant (Decorative Arts)

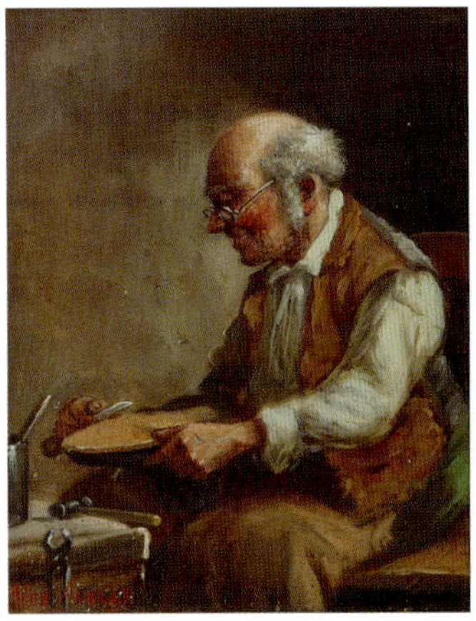

Austen, Alexander b.1859
The Cobbler
oil on canvas 25 x 19.5
1975. 166. 2 (P)

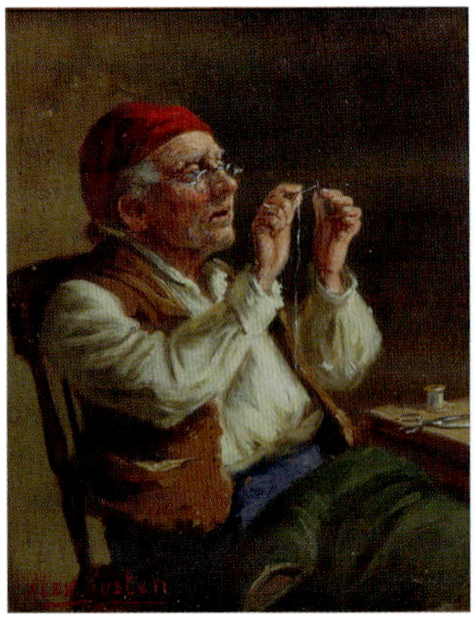

Austen, Alexander b.1859
The Tailor
oil on canvas 25 x 19.5
1975. 166. 1 (P)

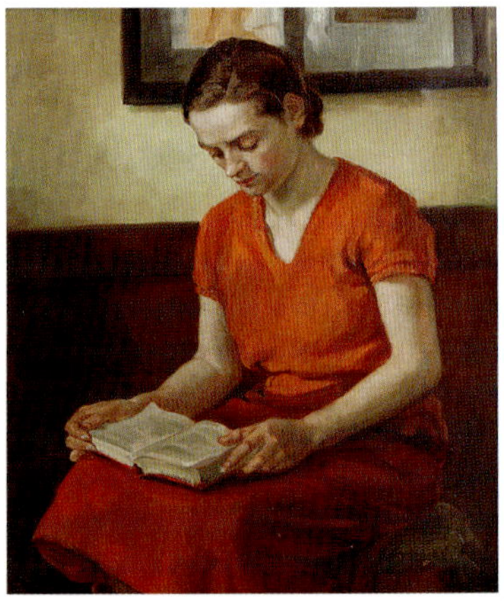

Barlow, G. B.
Portrait of a Young Woman Reading c.1938
oil on canvas 66 x 56
1967. 069. 3

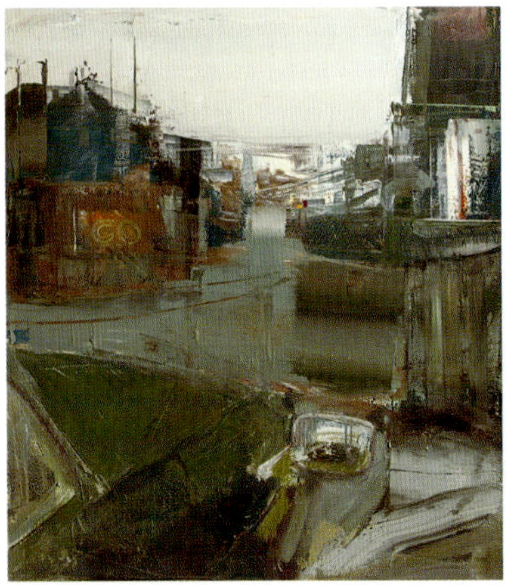

Barrie, Mardi 1930–2004
East Side c.1970
oil on canvas 76 x 63
1975. 126

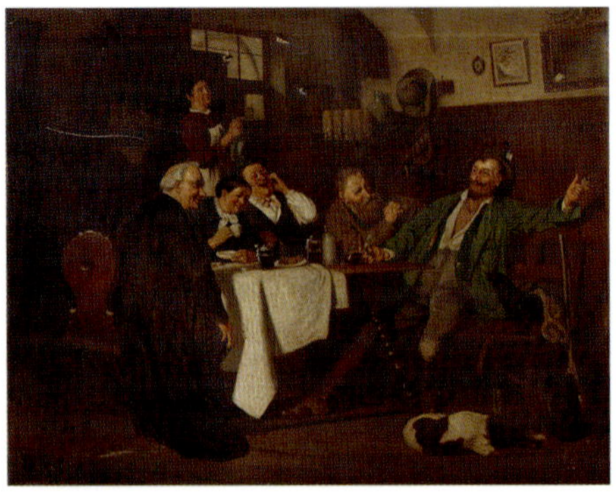

Bary, E.
Interior Scene c.1850
oil on canvas 55 x 68
1964. 104

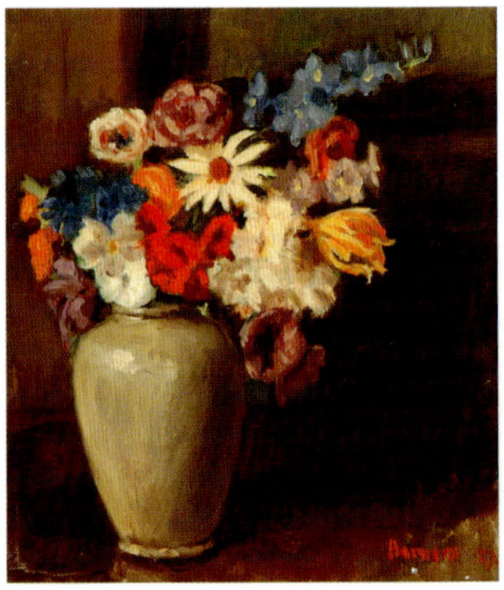

Berners, Gerald Hugh 1883–1950
Flowers in a Pottery Vase 1927
oil on canvas 36 x 30
1965. 094. 1

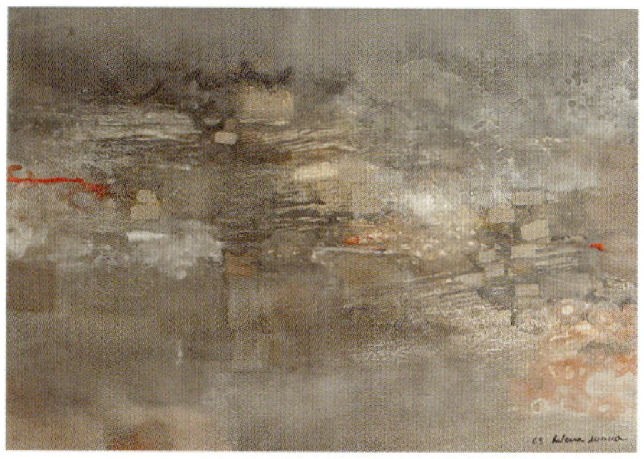

Bilbao de Barros, H. M.
Landscape 1963
oil on card 50 x 70
1972. 042

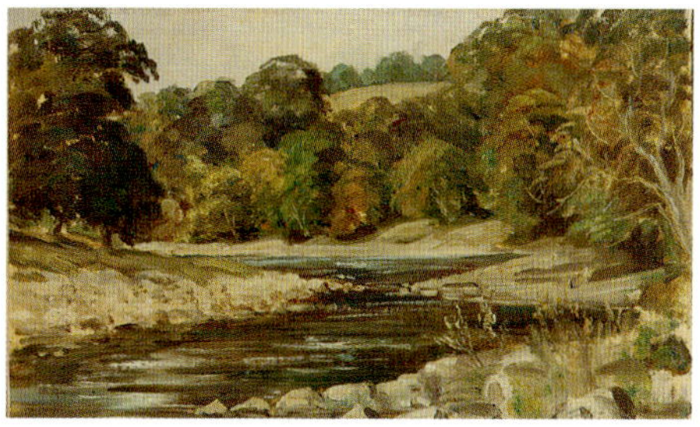

Birch, Samuel John Lamorna 1869–1955
River Landscape
oil on canvas 25 x 40
1970. 165

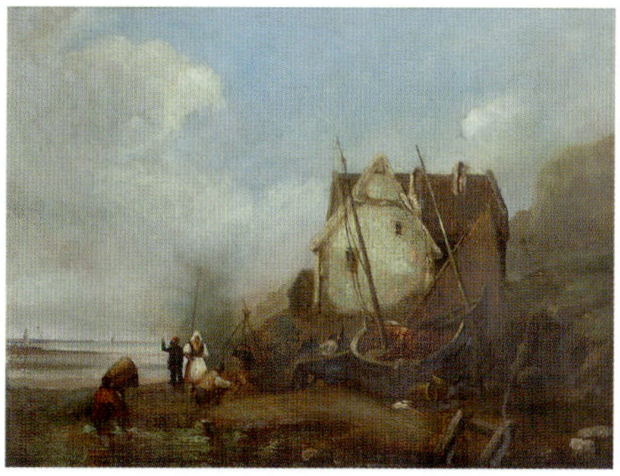

Bonington, Richard Parkes 1802–1828
On the Brittany Coast, France c.1825
oil on board 44.5 x 60
1964. 037. 2

Bower, Edward d.1667
Portrait of a Gentleman Cleric
oil on canvas 125 x 110
1967. 026. 2

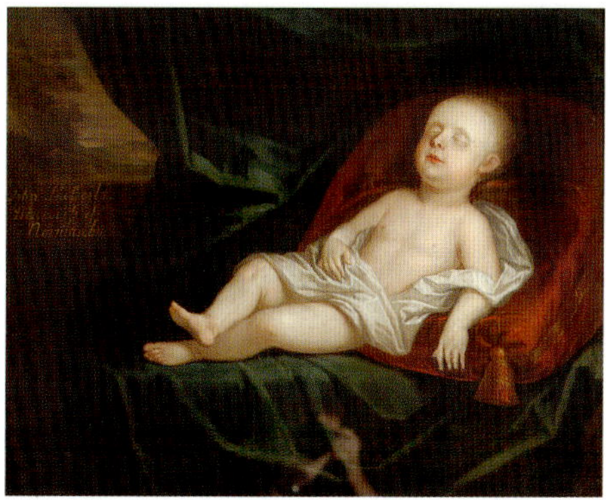

British (English) School
John Sheffield (1647–1721), 1st Duke of Buckingham and Normanby, KG, PC 1710
oil on canvas 55 x 67
1973. 215

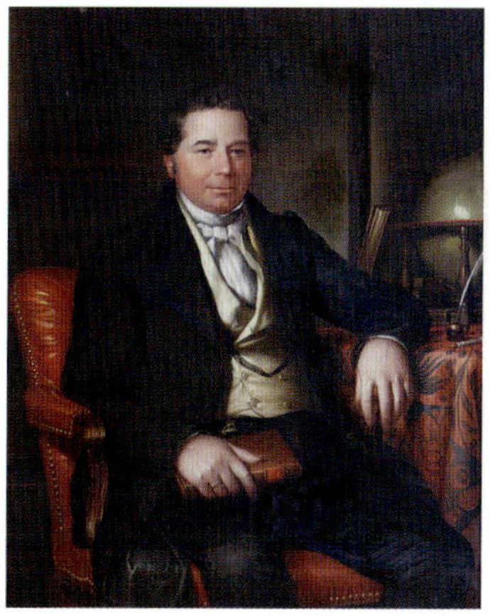

British (English) School
Matthew Pearson of Selby c.1830
oil on canvas 110 x 90
28

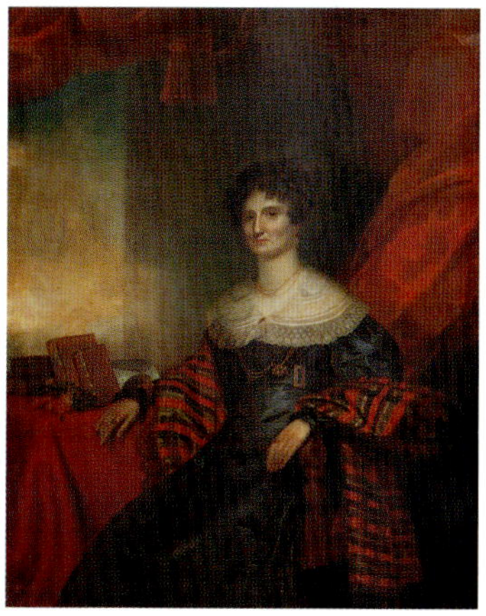

British School
Mrs Bennett of Edinburgh c.1830
oil on canvas 128.5 x 102
1968. 207. 3

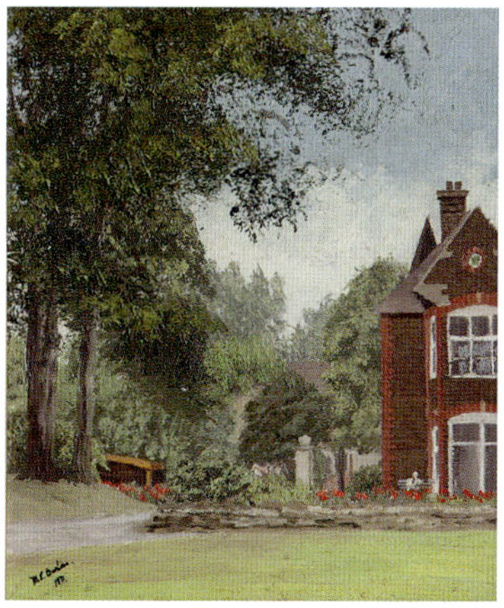

Burton, Marjorie E. active 1971–1980
Museum Garden, Scunthorpe, Lincolnshire
1971
oil on board 29.5 x 24.5
1974. 075

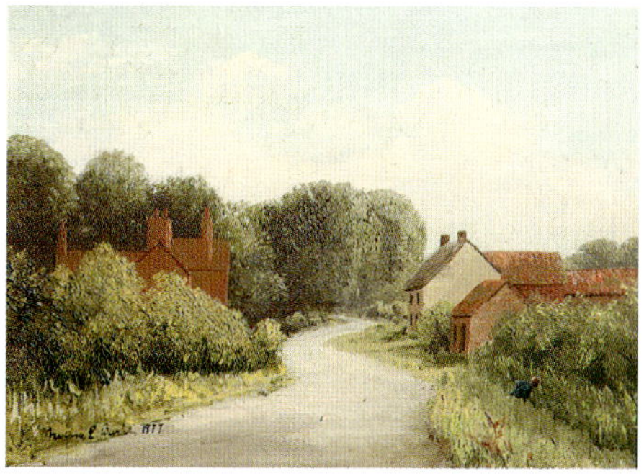

Burton, Marjorie E. active 1971–1980
Castlethorpe, Lincolnshire 1977
oil on canvas 21 x 29
1978. 162

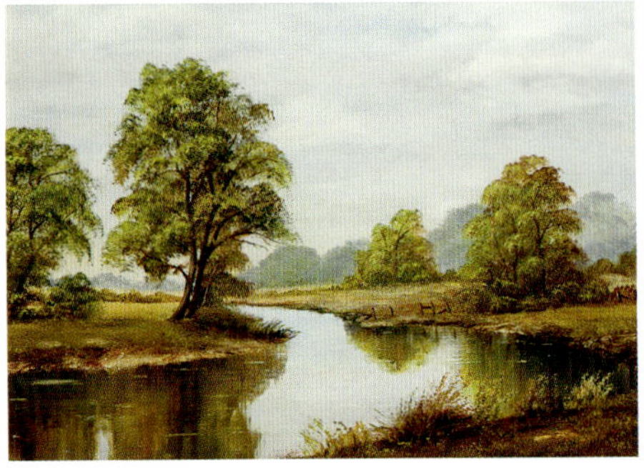

Button, Eva active 1977–1978
Winding River 1977
oil on board 29 x 39
1978. 160

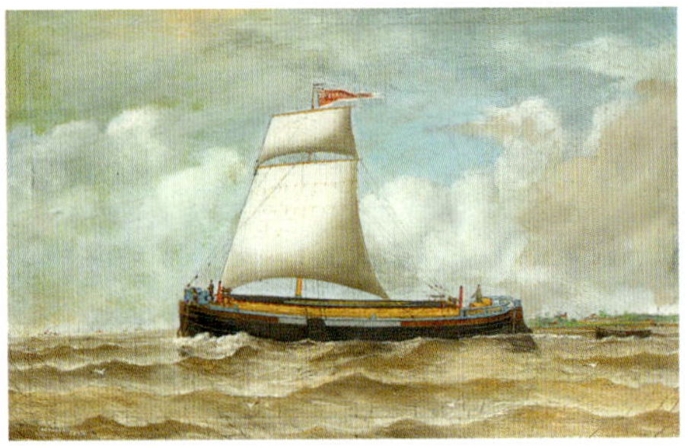

Chappell, Reuben 1870–1940
'Ceres' of Saxilby
oil on canvas 49.5 x 76.5
1964. 089

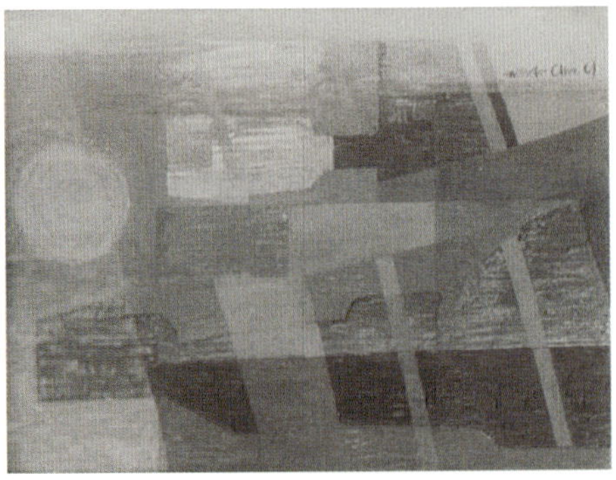

Clive, Nicholas
Illuminated Bottles 1961
oil on board 92.5 x 122.5
1973. 217. 1

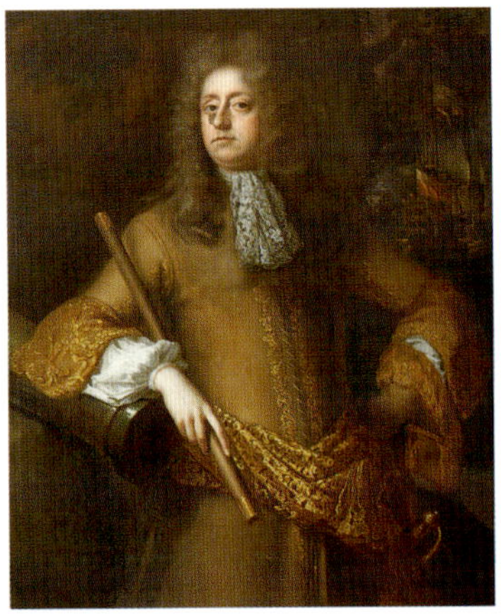

Closterman, John 1660–1711
Arthur Herbert (c.1648–1716), 1st Earl of Torrington c.1700
oil on canvas 123 x 101
1969. 195

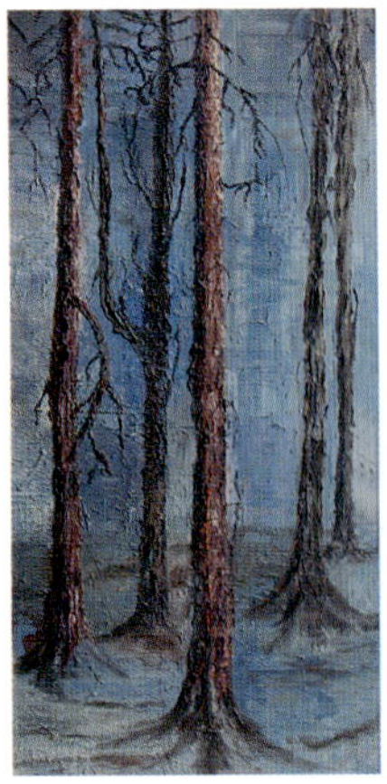

Cole, R. A.
Five Tall Trees c.1961
oil on board 122.5 x 57
1961. 124

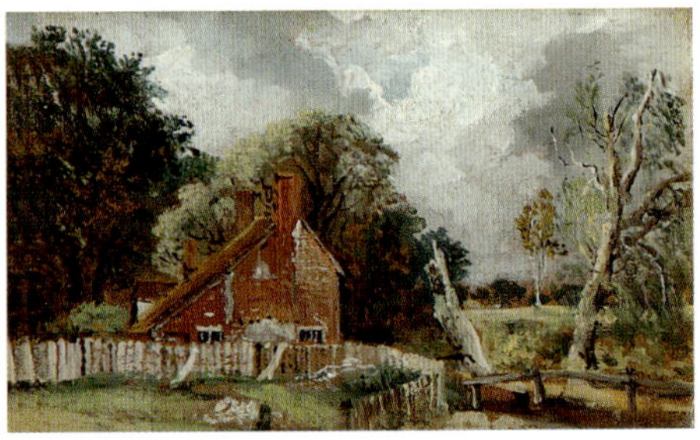

Constable, John (attributed to) 1776–1837
Cottage c.1810
oil on canvas 11.5 x 18
1969. 061

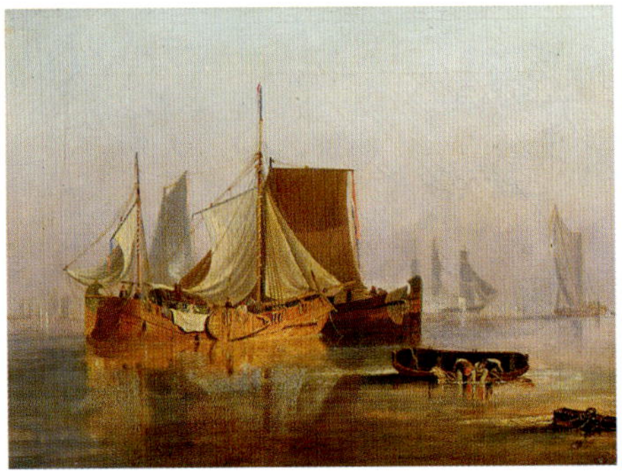

Cooke, Edward William 1811–1880
Dutch Boats in the Calm c.1850
oil on board 37 x 49
1963. 031. 3

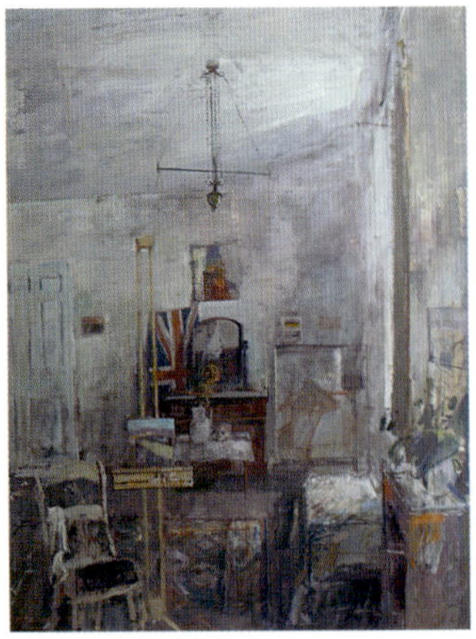

Cuming, Frederick b.1930
Studio Interior c.1950
oil on board 152.5 x 111
1970. 110

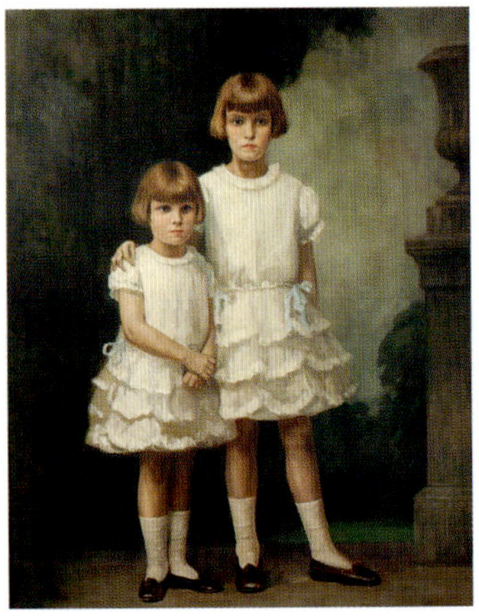

Dixon, Harry 1861–1942
Diana Mary (d.1995), and June Ramsden 1929
oil on canvas 152.5 x 121.5
2002. 030

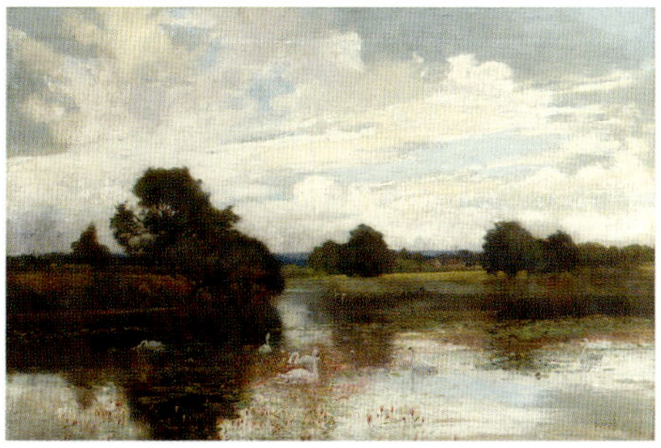

East, Alfred 1844–1913
Warnham Lake, Sussex c.1890
oil on canvas 59 x 89
1960. 090

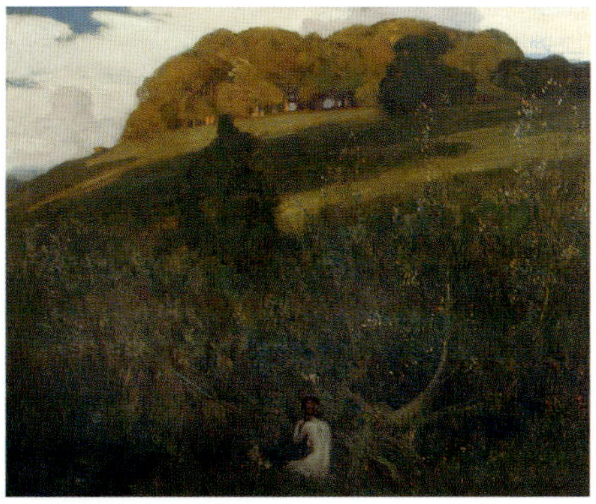

East, Alfred 1844–1913
A Mystic Pool c.1909
oil on canvas 116 x 146
1967. 069. 2

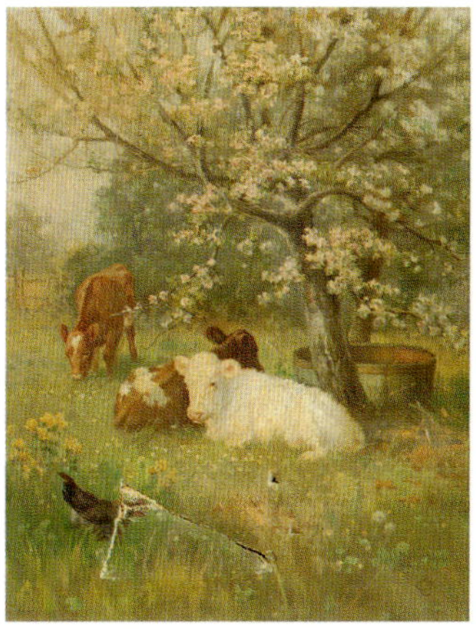

Elwell, Frederick William 1870–1958
Farm Scene c.1900
oil on canvas 40 x 30
1967. 216. 1

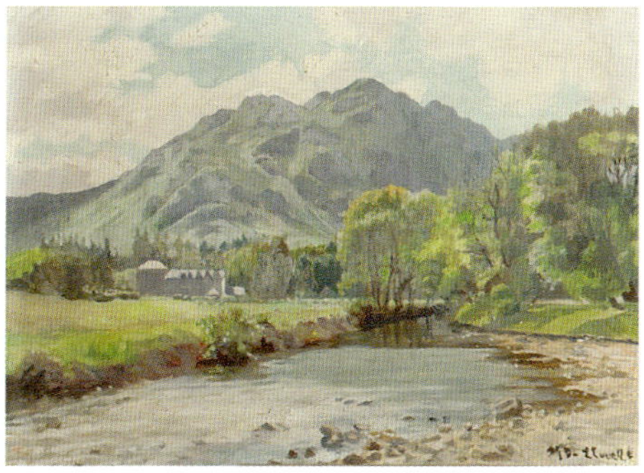

Elwell, Mary Dawson 1874–1952
In the Trossachs, Highlands c.1900
oil on board 24.5 x 34
1967. 216. 2

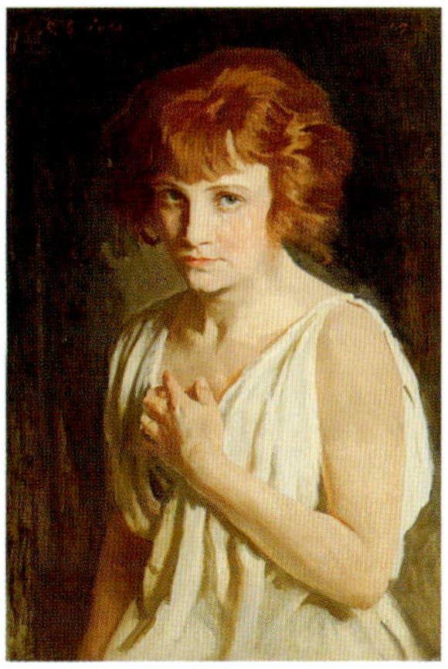

Eves, Archie
Fay Compton (1894–1978) 1922
oil on canvas 75 x 49.5
1969. 187. 2

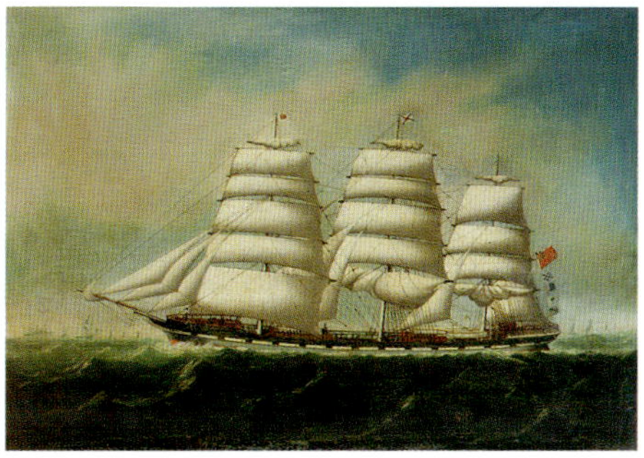

Fong, Lai active c.1870–c.1905
'Allan Shaw' 1887
oil on canvas 62 x 88
1966. 185

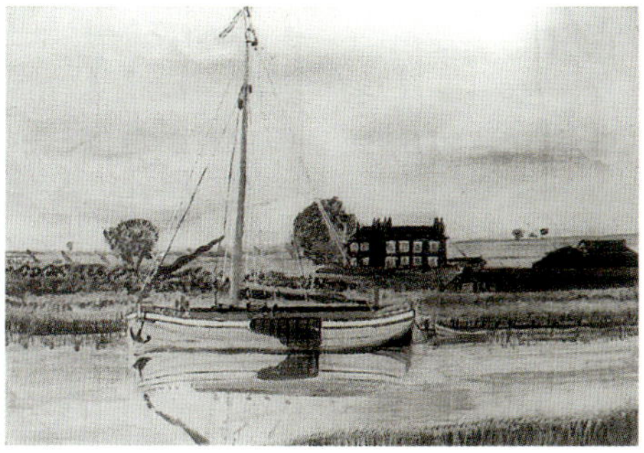

Franks, John active c.1950–1975
Sloop 'Nero' on the Trent at Burton upon Stather c.1950
oil on paper 25.3 x 35
1971. 050. 2

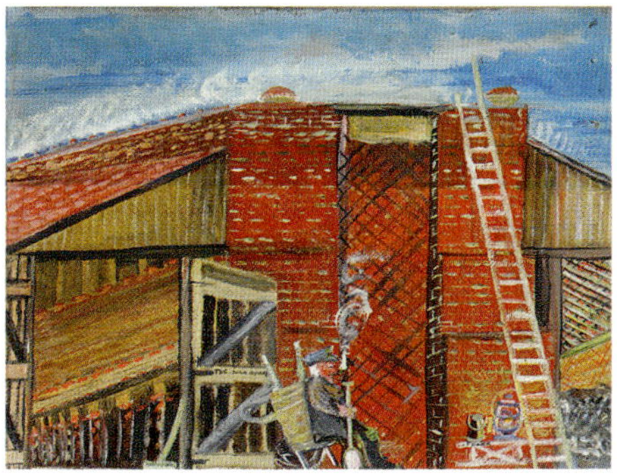

Franks, John active c.1950–1975
Brickyards
oil on board 32 x 41
1975. 079. 2

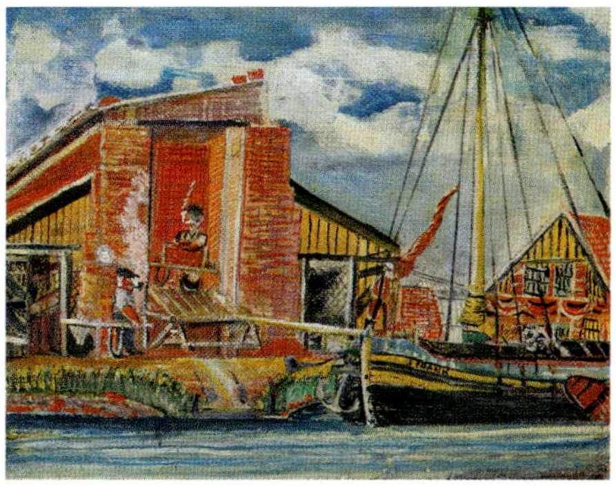

Franks, John active c.1950–1975
Brickyards
oil on board 32 x 41
1975. 079. 3

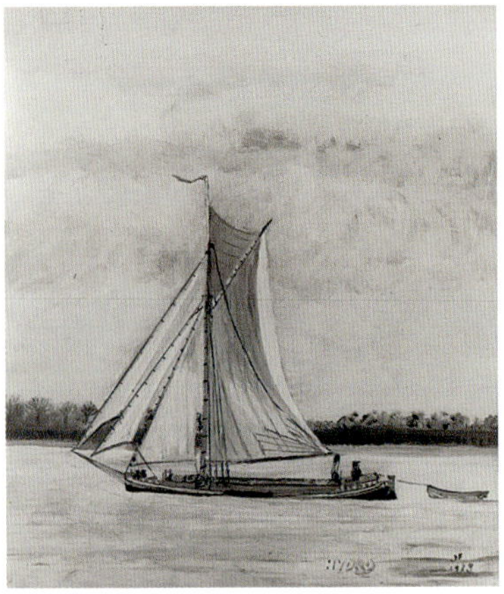

Franks, John active c.1950–1975
Sloop 'Hydro' of Goole
oil on hardboard 32 x 26 (E)
1973. 020

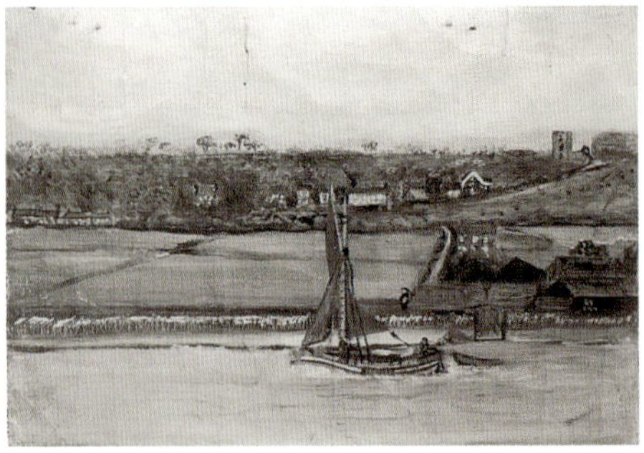

Franks, John active c.1950–1975
Sloop 'Nero' on the River Ancholme at Ferriby Sluice, Lincolnshire
oil on paper 25.3 x 35
1971. 050. 1

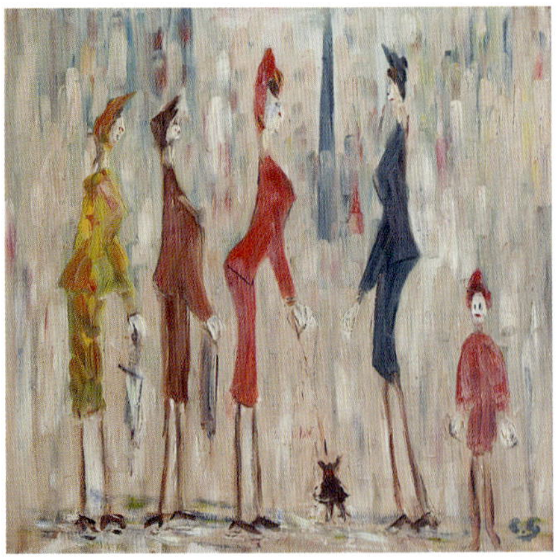

Garton, C.
The Dog c.1966
oil on board 56 x 55
1966. 083

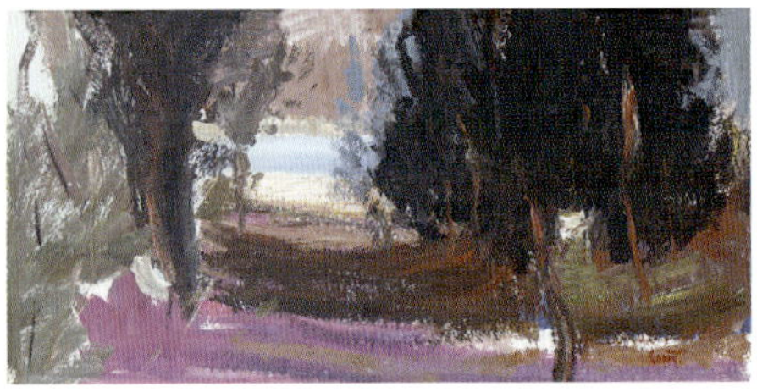

Gaunt
Woodland Vista
oil on board 40 x 76
PCF1

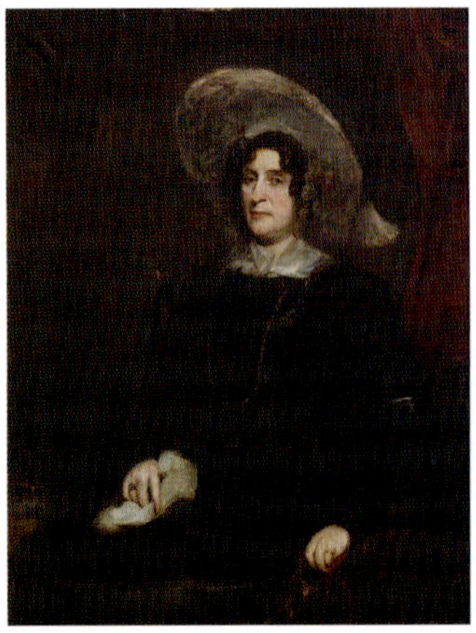

Gordon, John Watson 1788–1864
Anne Sherriff (1866–1781) (later Mrs Charles Young) 1830–1835
oil on canvas 127 x 100
1968. 207. 4

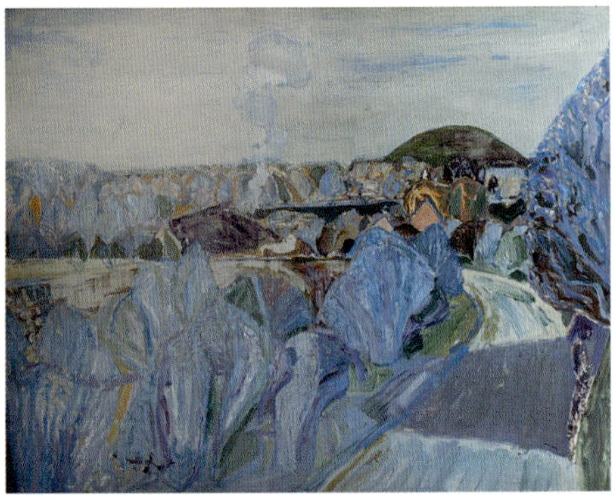

Grant, Keith b.1930
Blue Cloud c.1968
oil on board 75 x 97.5
1968. 164. 1A

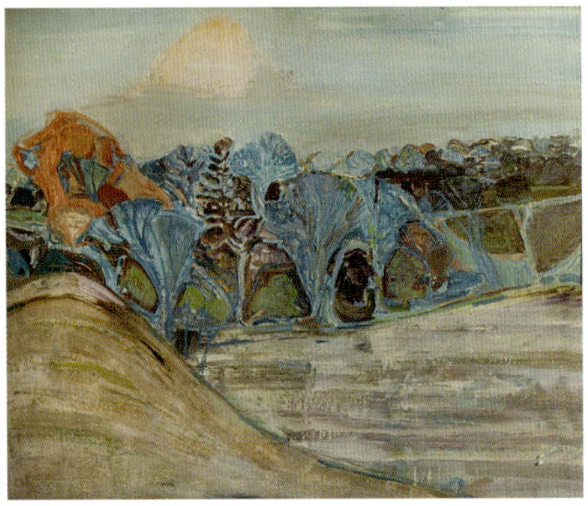

Grant, Keith b.1930
White Cloud c.1968
oil on board 74 x 90
1968. 164. 1B

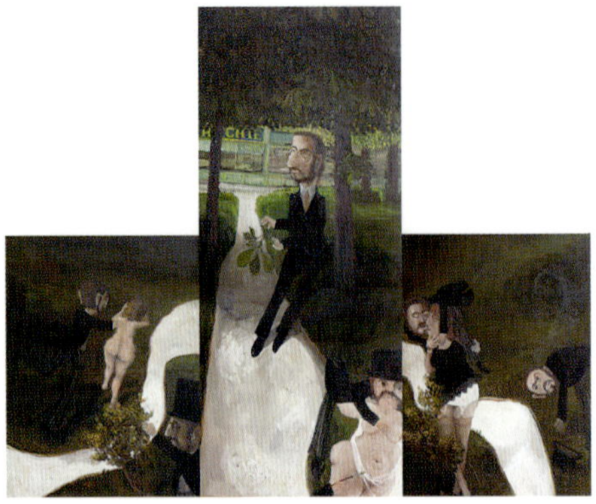

Green, Anthony b.1939
Lovemaking in Lissenden Gardens 1964
oil on board 122 x 91; 214 x 92; 122 x 91
1970. 139

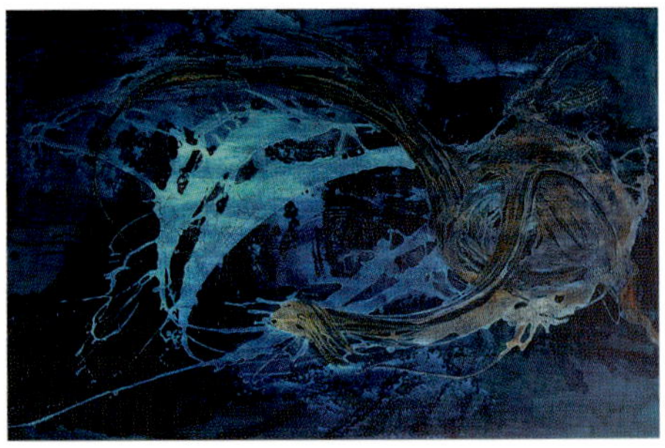

Haddock, Edwin Aldridge 1921–1996
Plesiosaurus 1978
oil on board 118 x 178
34

Facing page: Lawrence, Thomas, 1769–1830, *Mrs Alice Wood* (detail), 1830, North Lincolnshire Museums Service (p. 364)

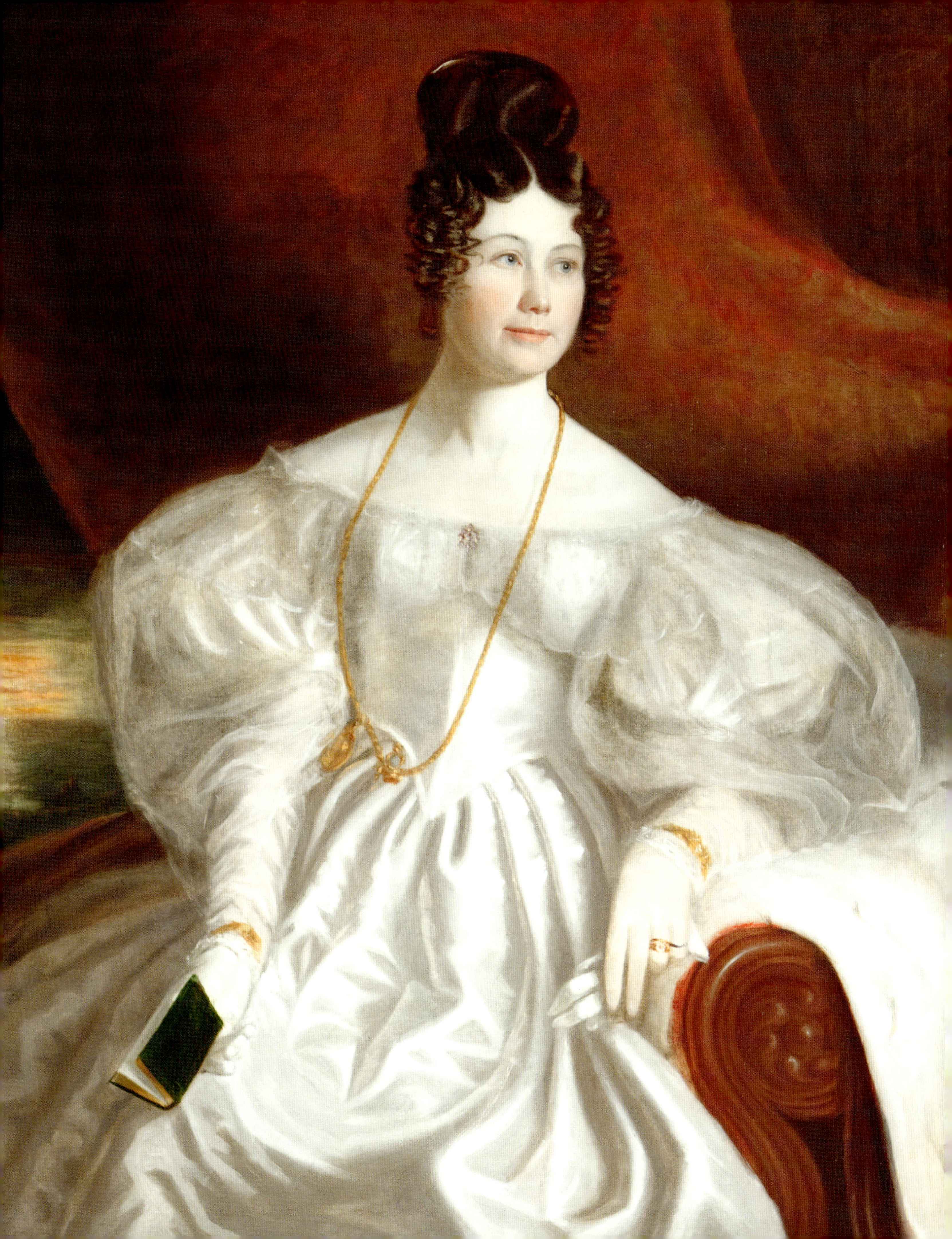

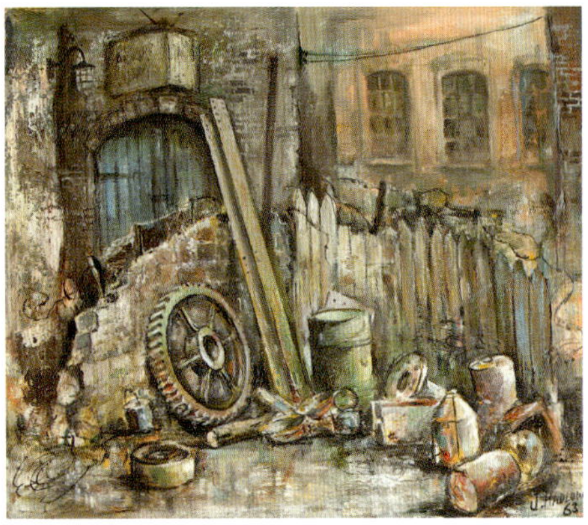

Hadlow, J.
Scrap 1963
oil on board 50 x 60
1970. 109

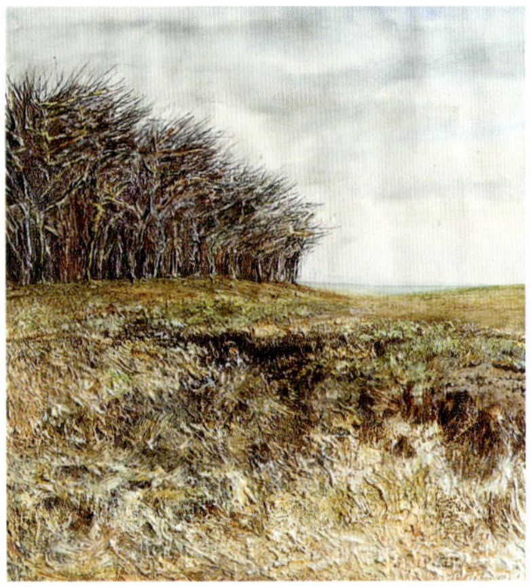

Henry, Sue
Wolds, Lincolnshire, Early March c.1981
acrylic on paper 26 x 23.5
1991. 440

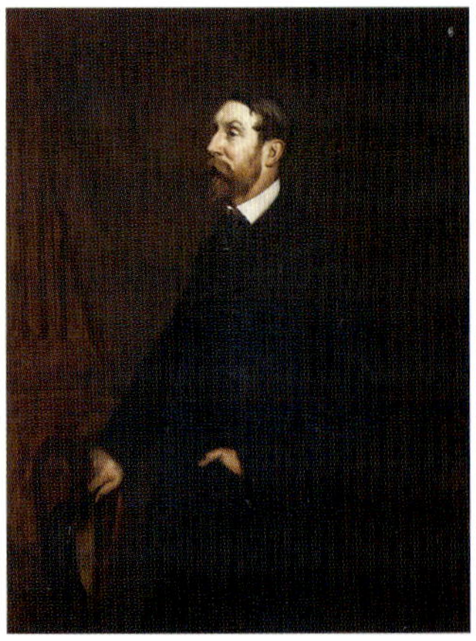

Herkomer, Herman 1863–1935
William Henry Forester Denison (1834–1900), 1st Earl of Londesborough 1900
oil on canvas 143 x 111
1973. 214. 1

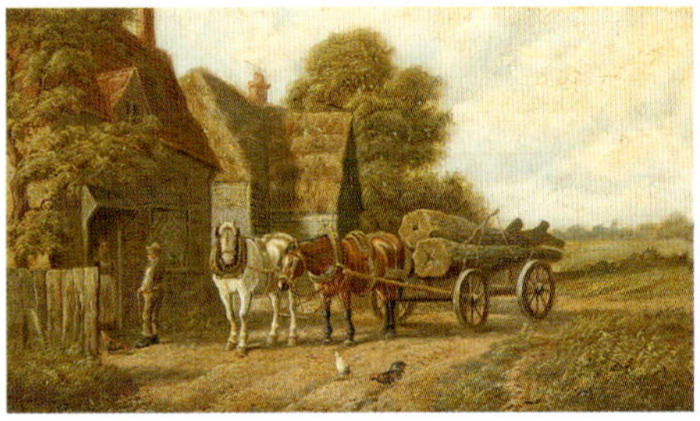

Herring, John Frederick I 1795–1865
Timber Drug c.1840
oil on canvas 30.5 x 51
1970. 111

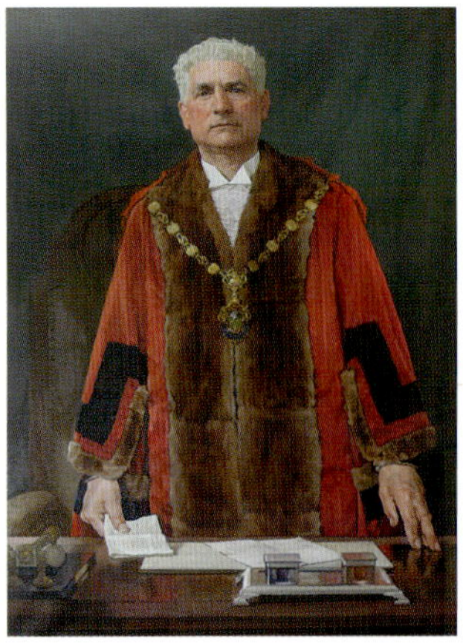

Hersch, Eugen 1887–1967
Portrait of an Unidentified Mayor of Scunthorpe 1945
oil on board 145.5 x 94
1975. 173. 1

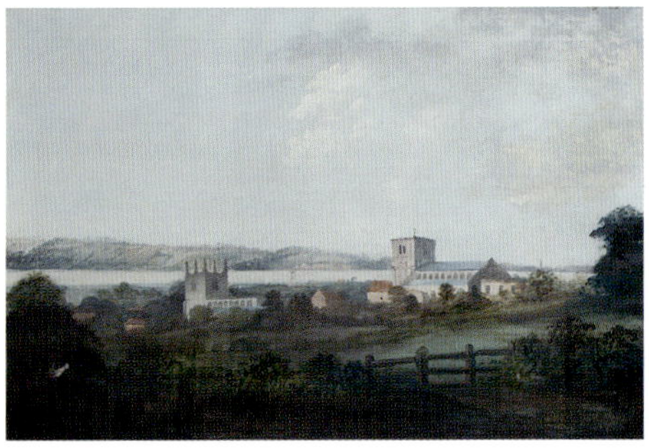

Hesledon, Edmund
View of the Churches of St Peter and St Mary, Barton-on-Humber, Lincolnshire 1812
oil on canvas 72 x 90
BABDM. 2. 1

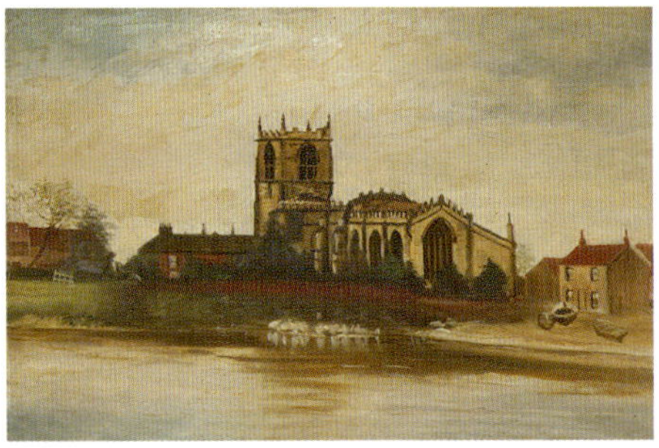

Hest, G.
St Oswald's Church, Althorpe, Lincolnshire
oil on board 29.5 x 45.5
1965. 197

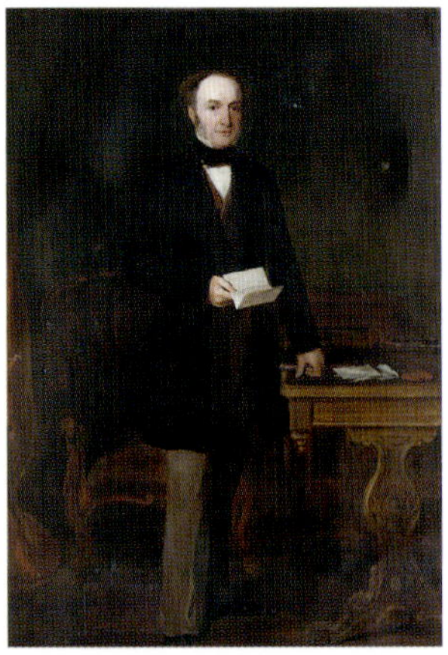

Horsley, John Callcott 1817–1903
William Henry Dawes 1871
oil on canvas 116 x 76.5
1958. 125

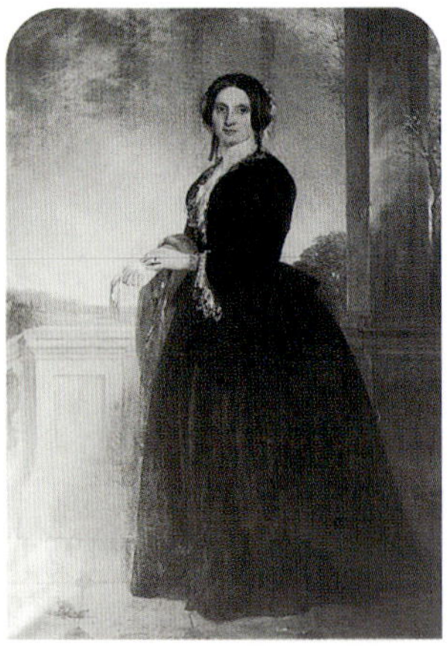

Horsley, John Callcott 1817–1903
Mrs William Henry Dawes 1871
oil on canvas 113 x 72
1958. 126

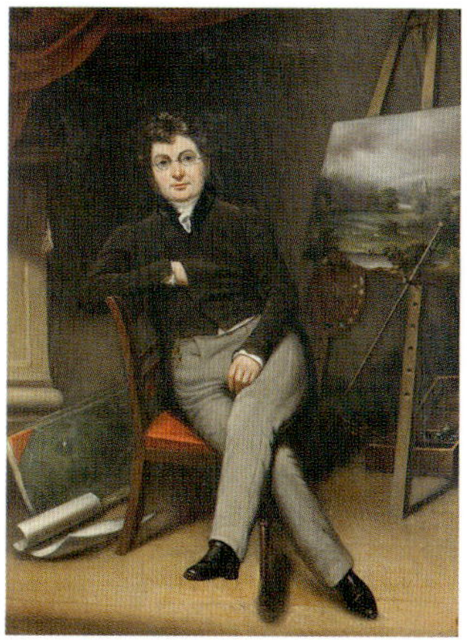

Hunter, John
Batty Tootal, Artist 1827
oil on canvas 74 x 54
1991. 002. 2

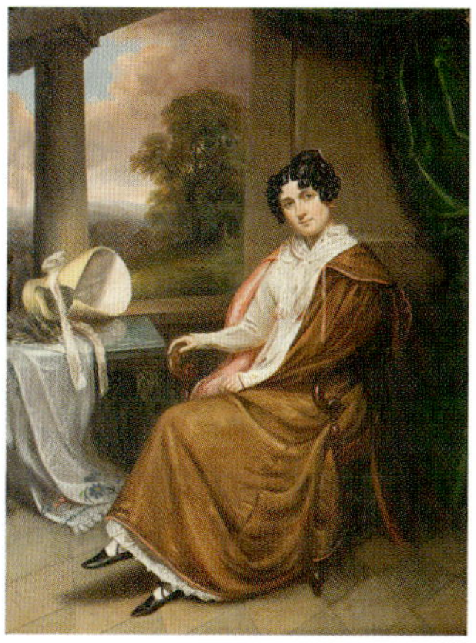

Hunter, John
Mrs Batty Tootal 1827
oil on canvas 75 x 54
1991. 002. 1

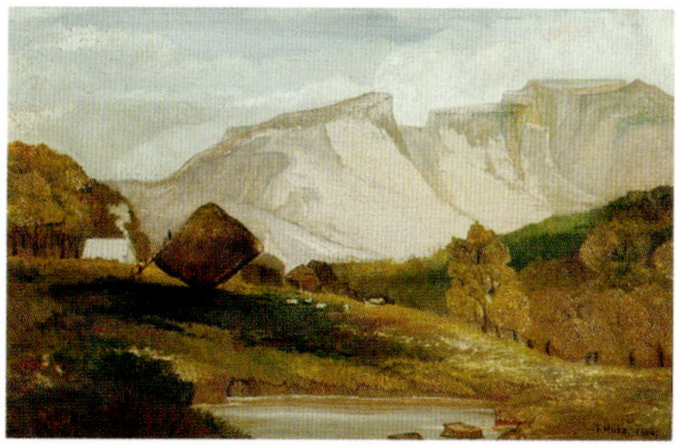

Hurd, F.
Bowder Stone, Keswick, Cumberland 1906
oil on canvas 29.5 x 44.5
1965. 065. 5

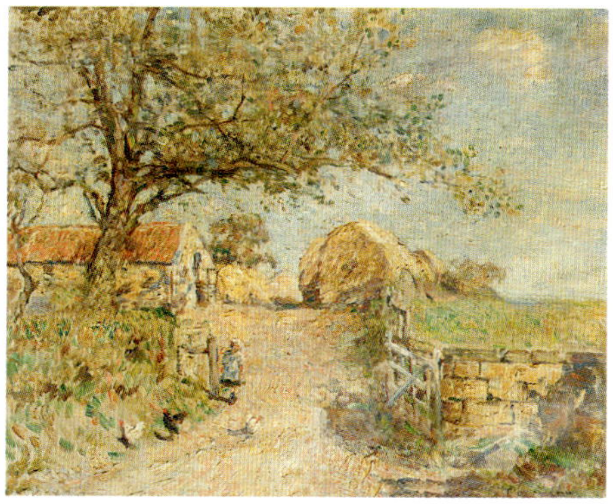

Jackson, Frederick William 1859–1918
The Road to the Farm c.1910
oil on canvas 48.5 x 59
1970. 060. 2

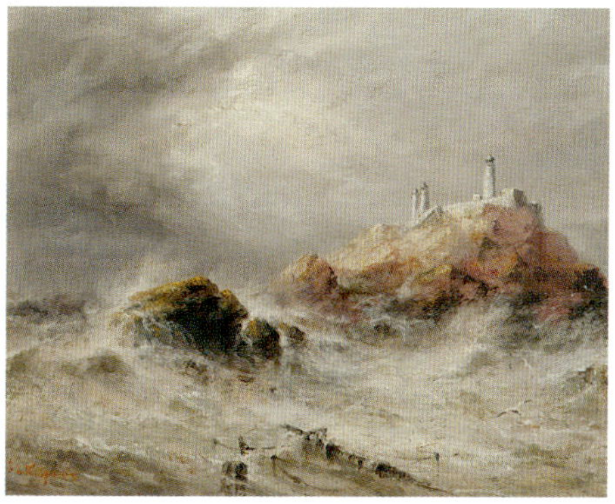

Kilpack, Sarah Louisa 1839–1909
The Casquettes near Alderney, Channel Islands
oil on panel 23.5 x 29
1970. 060. 1

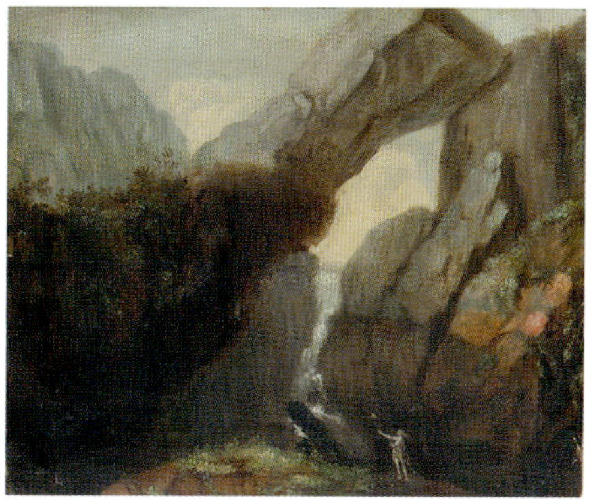

Knapton, George (after) 1698–1778
Falls of Terni (Rock of Ages) c.1800
oil on canvas 43 x 52
1963. 031. 2

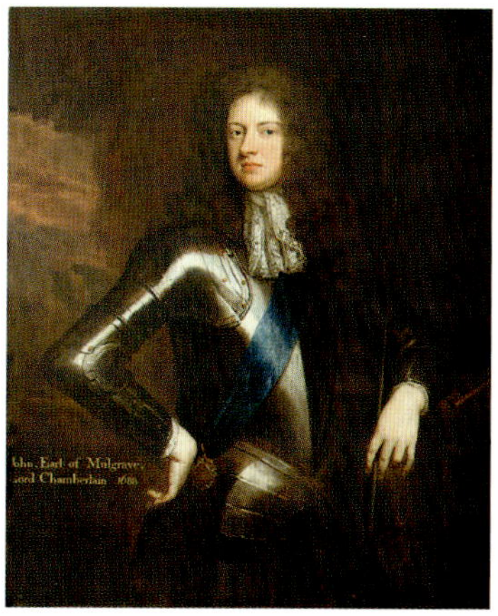

Kneller, Godfrey 1646–1723
John Sheffield (1647–1721), 1st Duke of Buckingham and Normanby, KG, PC 1688
oil on canvas 125 x 100
L. 0190

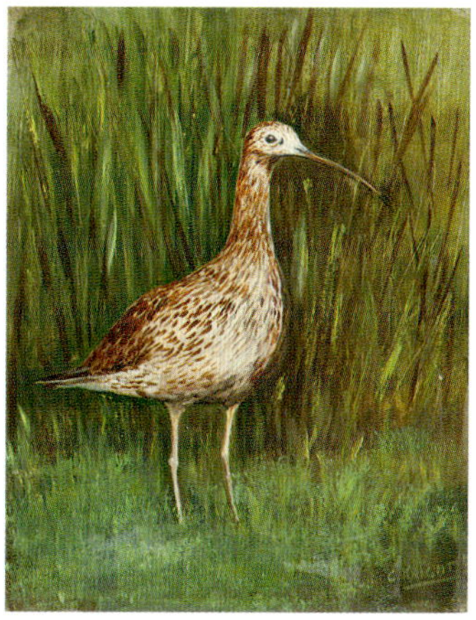

Knight, George
Curlew
oil on board 40 x 29.5
43 (P)

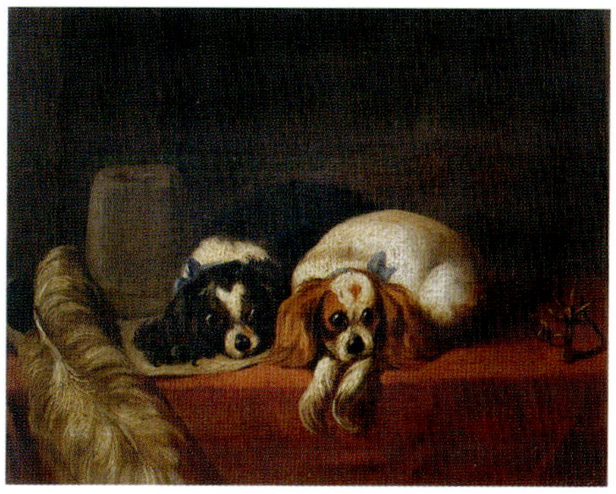

Landseer, Edwin Henry (copy of) 1802–1873
King Charles Spaniels (The Cavalier's Pets) c.1845
oil on canvas 29 x 39.5
1965. 052

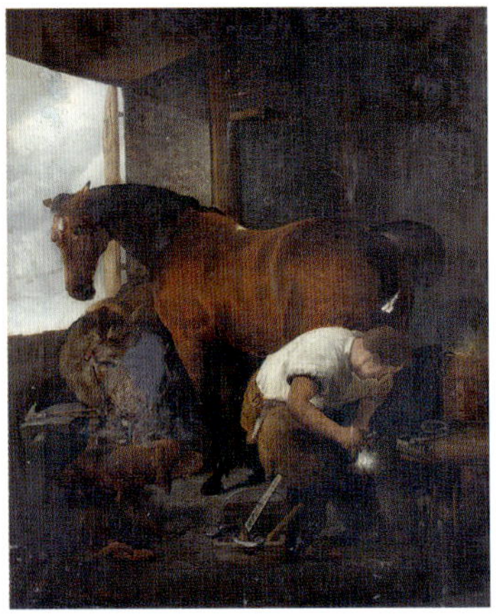

Landseer, Edwin Henry (copy of)
1802–1873
Shoeing
oil on canvas 91.5 x 71
1975. 042

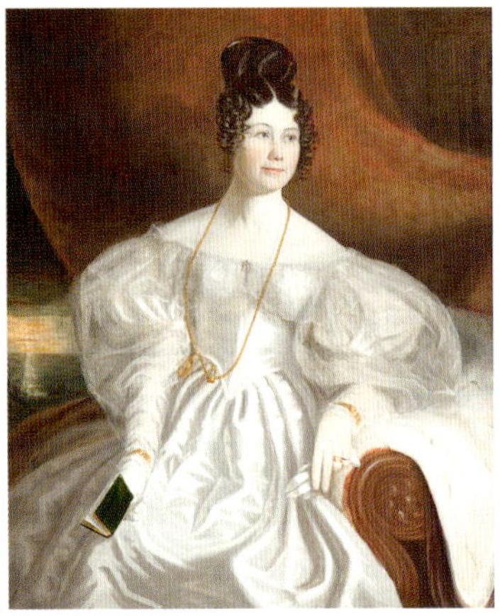

Lawrence, Thomas 1769–1830
Mrs Alice Wood 1830
oil on canvas 125 x 100
1968. 013

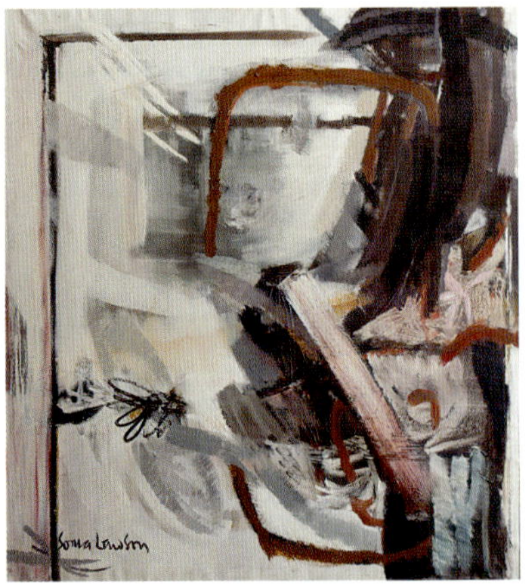

Lawson, Sonia b.1934
Journey through March Weather c.1960
oil on canvas 122 x 112
1970. 138

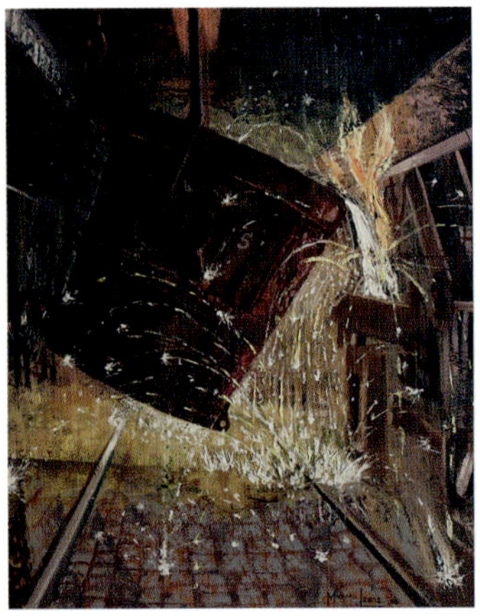

Lewis, Michael
Steel Tipping from a Ladle c.1956
oil on board 87.5 x 68.5
44

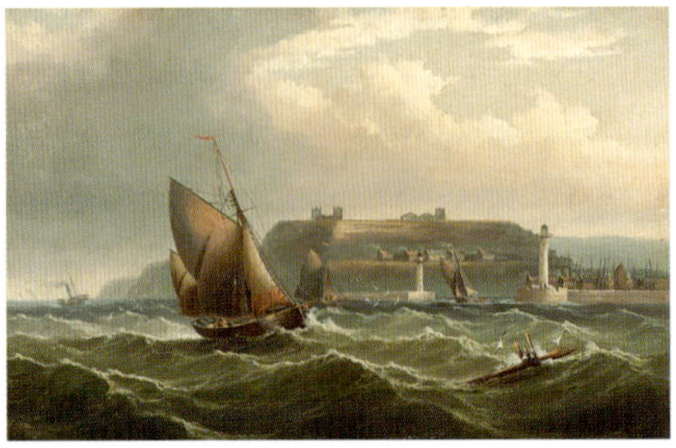

Moore, Henry 1831–1895
Storm at Whitby, North Yorkshire 1870
oil on canvas 49 x 74
ART1953. 004

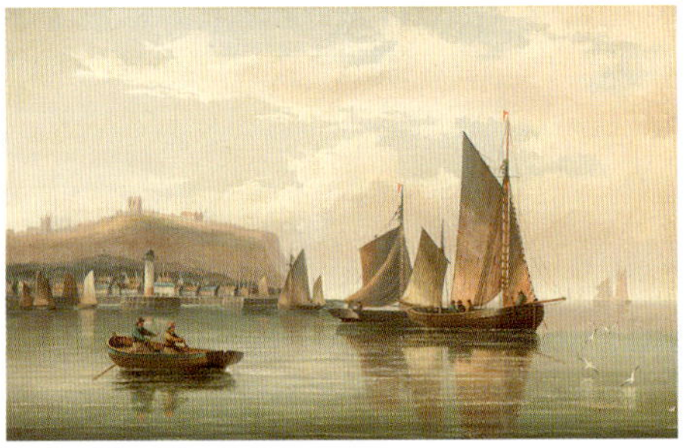

Moore, Henry 1831–1895
Calm at Scarborough, North Yorkshire c.1870
oil on canvas 49 x 74
ART1953. 005

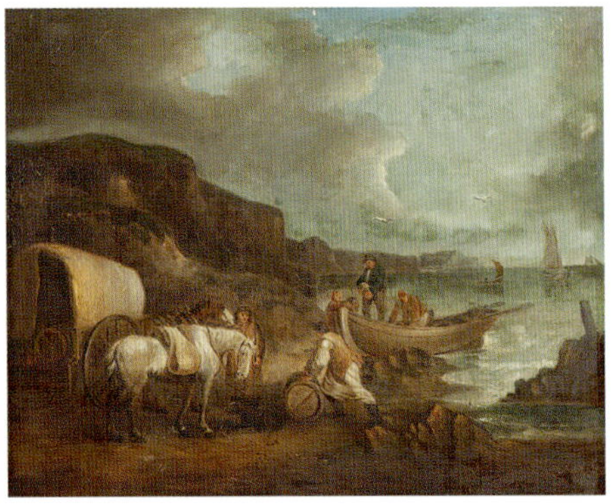

Morland, George (after) 1763–1804
Smugglers, Coastal Scene
oil on board 54 x 64
1975. 166. 5 (P)

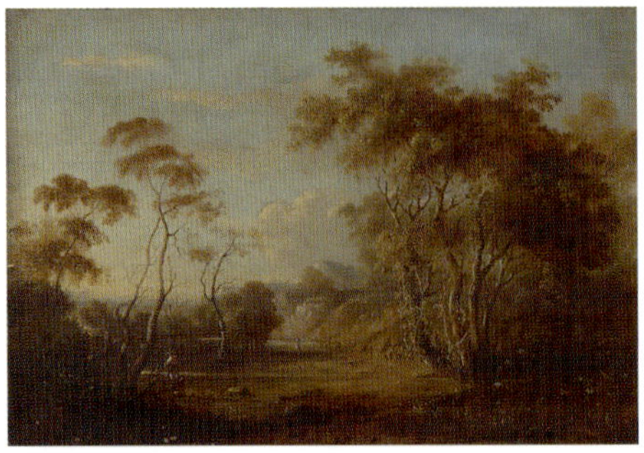

Morris, J. D. active c.1830–1905
Epping Forrest, Essex c.1830
oil on canvas 24.5 x 34.5
ART1953. 002

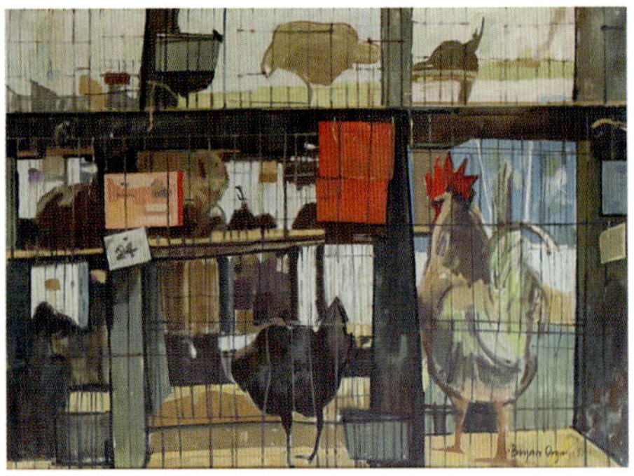

Organ, Bryan b.1935
Cage Birds at a Show 1958
oil on canvas 103 x 140
1960. 114

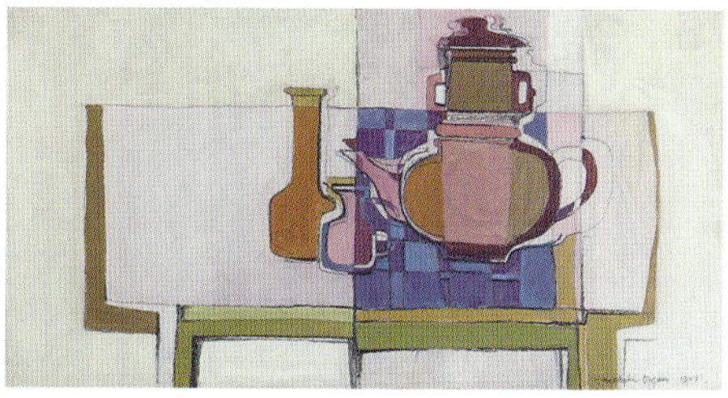

Organ, Elizabeth 1934–2009
Coffee Pot 1967
oil on canvas 33 x 61
1970. 137

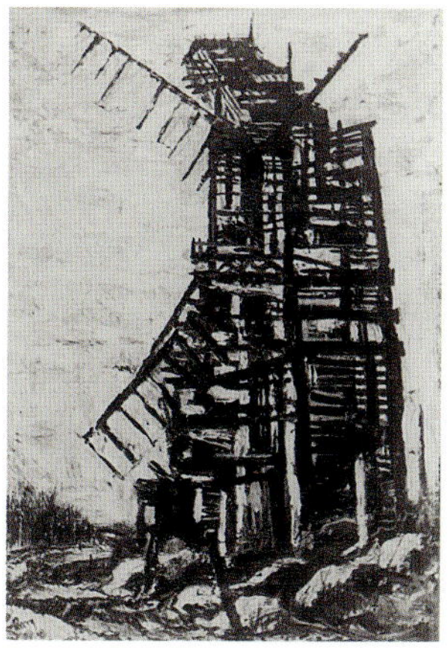

Perry, Roy 1935–1993
Wrawby Post Mill, Lincolnshire c.1960
oil on canvas 76.5 x 52.5
1963. 017

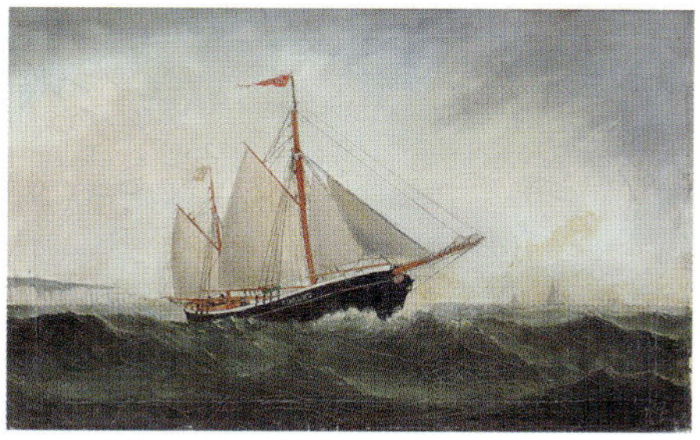

Preston, William F. active 1885–1889
'Starling' 1889
oil on canvas 43 x 68.5
1960. 111

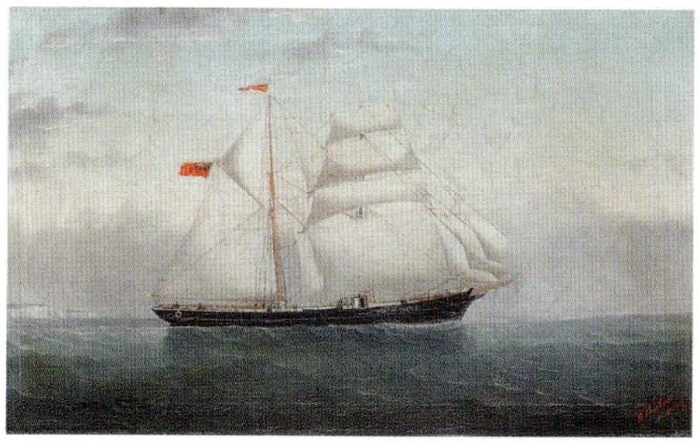

Preston, William F. active 1885–1889
'Morton Castle'
oil on canvas 42.5 x 69.5
1973. 189. 3

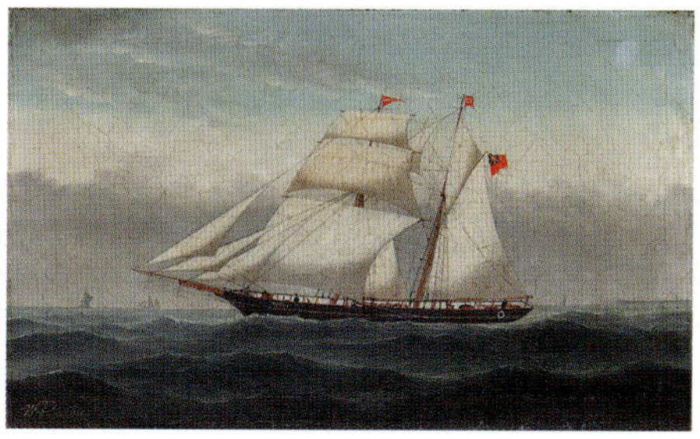

Preston, William F. active 1885–1889
'Topsy'
oil on canvas 43 x 68.5
1973. 189. 2

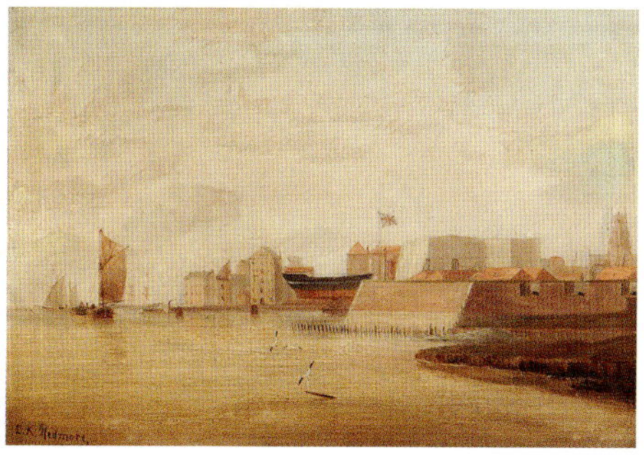

Redmore, Edward King 1860–1941
View of Hull, Hull Garrison Fortifications
oil on canvas 34 x 49
1965. 050

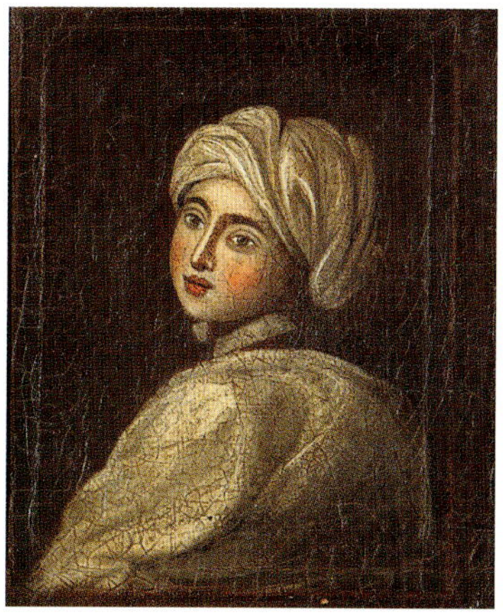

Reni, Guido (copy after) 1575–1642
Beatrice Cenci 18th C
oil on canvas 21.5 x 16.5
ART1953. 006

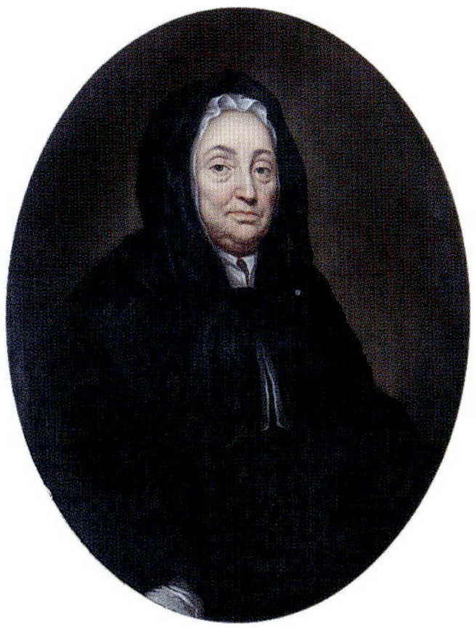

Reynolds, Joshua (school of) 1723–1792
Portrait of an Unknown Lady c.1760
oil on canvas 80 x 65
BABDM. L. 79. 1

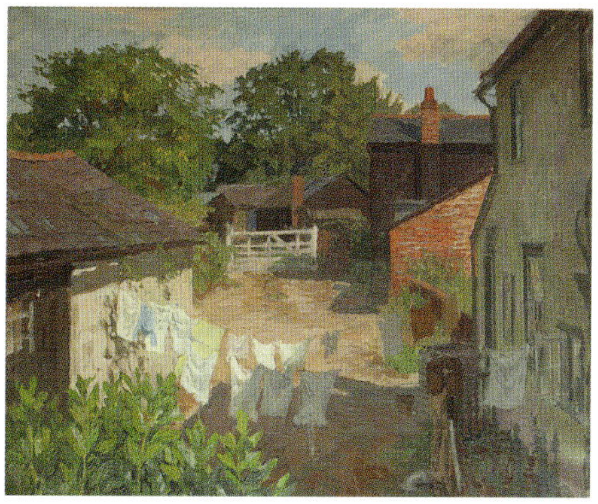

Rhoades, Geoffrey 1898–1980
The White Gate
oil on canvas 57 x 67
1969. 187. 4

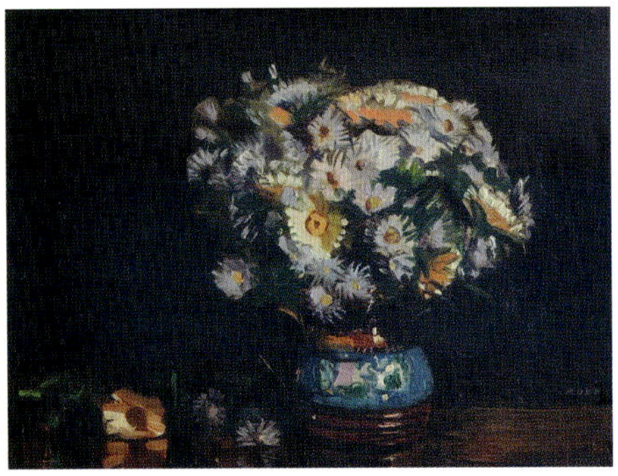

Robb, William George 1872–1940
Michaelmas Daisies and Marigolds 1926
oil on canvas 29 x 36.5
46

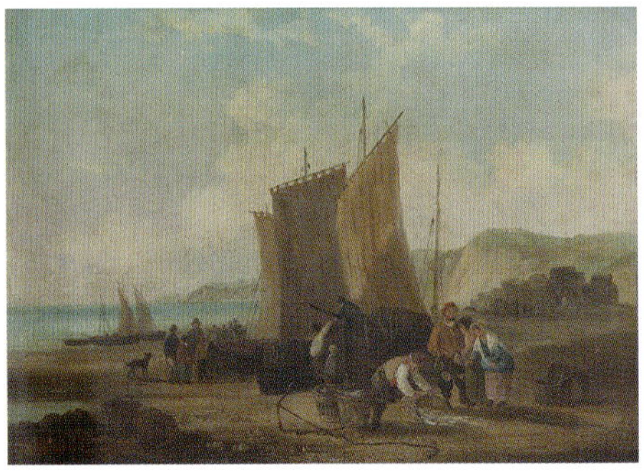

Rogers, Philip Hutchins c.1786–1853
Coastal Scene c.1830
oil on canvas 30 x 40
1970. 056

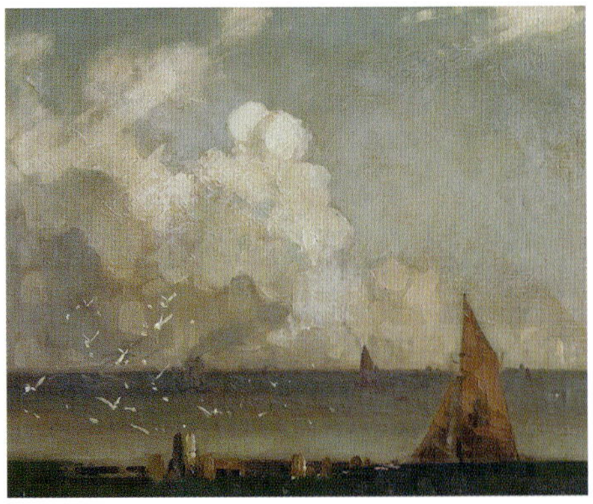

Rollett, Herbert 1872–1932
Seascape
oil on canvas 40.6 x 50.8
1971. 040. 1

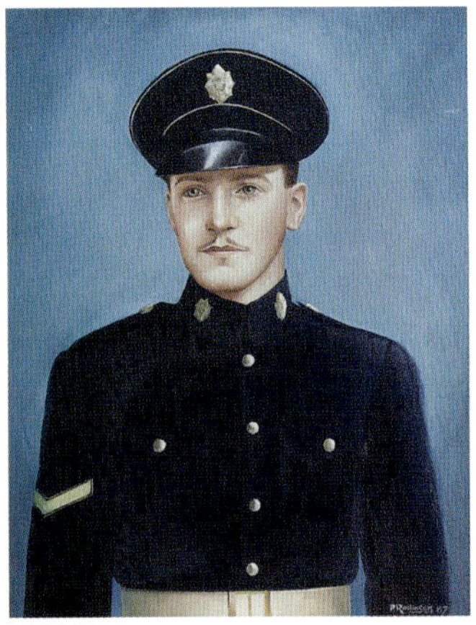

Rollinson, P.
Joseph Herbert Tomlin, MM 1987
oil on canvas 46 x 36
2002. 055. 3

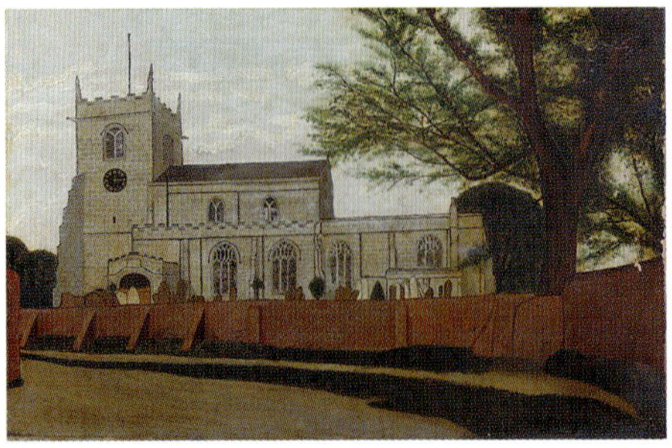

Ross, William Arthur active 1906–1937
Belton Church, Grantham, Lincolnshire 1907
oil on canvas 40.5 x 61
1960. 027. 2

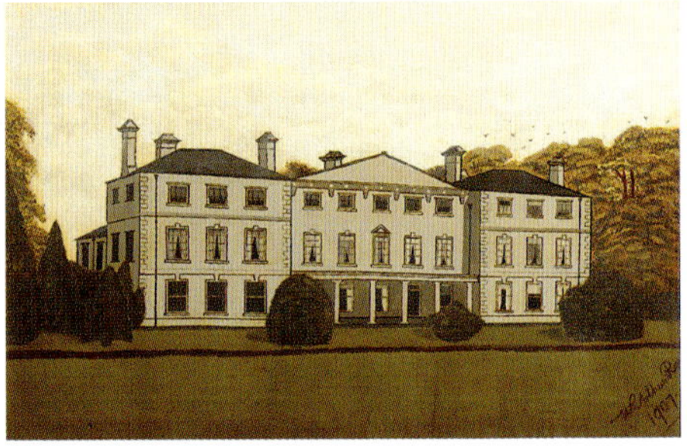

Ross, William Arthur active 1906–1937
Temple Belwood House, Lincolnshire 1907
oil on canvas 41 x 60.5
1960. 027. 1

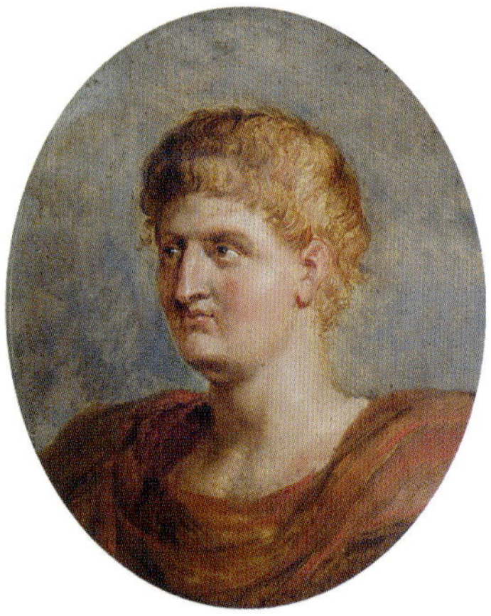

Rubens, Peter Paul 1577–1640
Emperor Otho (from the 'Twelve Caesars' series) c.1625
oil on wood 31 x 25
1967. 114. 3

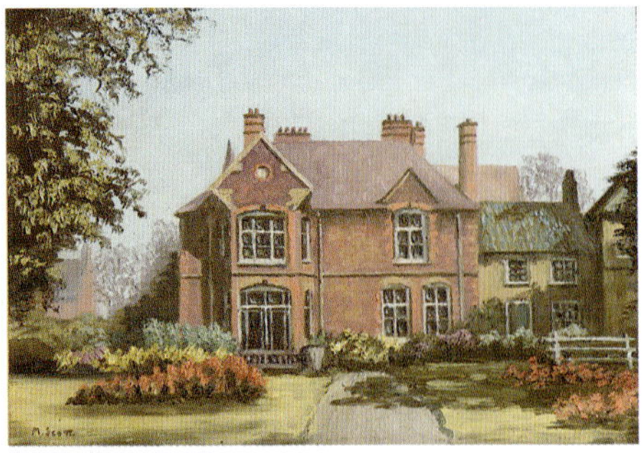

Scott, M.
Scunthorpe Museum, Lincolnshire c.1978
oil on board 24.5 x 34.5
1978. 161

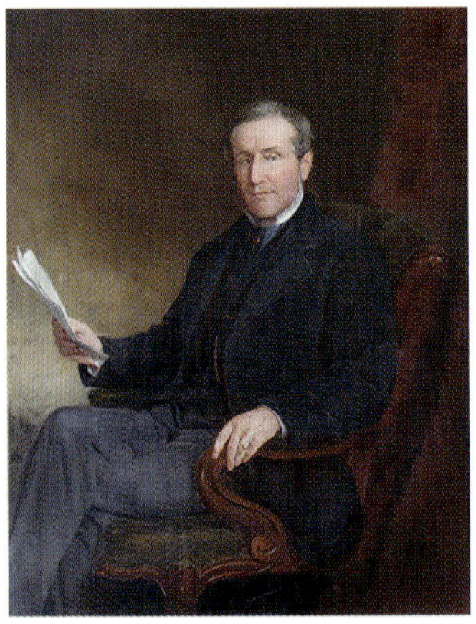

Smith, Richard 1818–1890
George Dawes (1817–1888) c.1863
oil on canvas 130 x 100
1943. 148

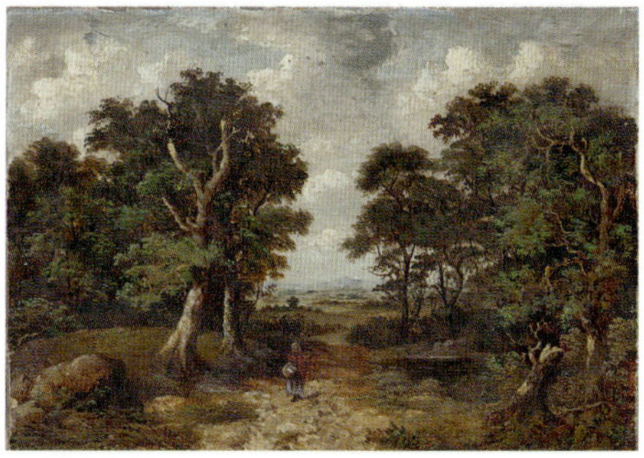

Spinks, Thomas 1847–1927
The Path through the Woods
oil on canvas 28 x 39
1965. 191. 5B

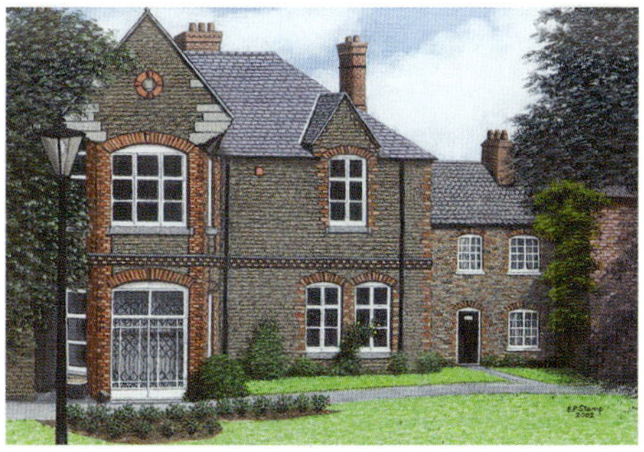

Stamp, Elaine P.
Scunthorpe Museum, Lincolnshire 2002
acrylic on board 25 x 35
2002. 040

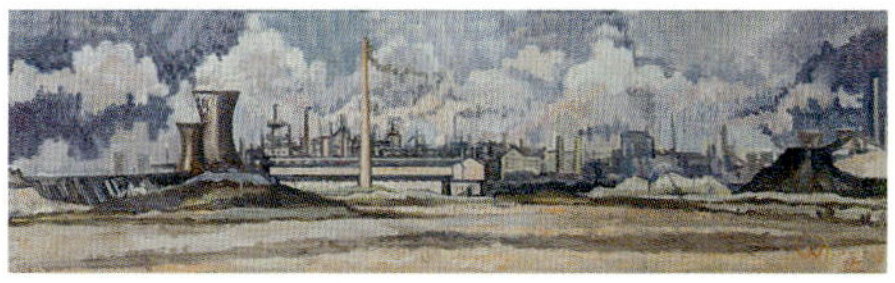

Staves, W. D. active 1964–1965
Industrial Skyline 1964
oil on board 35.5 x 117
1965. 218

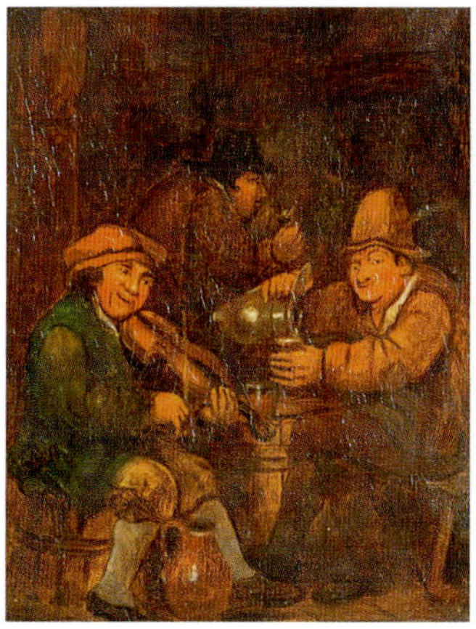

Steen, Jan (attributed to) 1626–1679
Dutch Interior
oil on oak panel 21.5 x 16.5
ART1953. 001

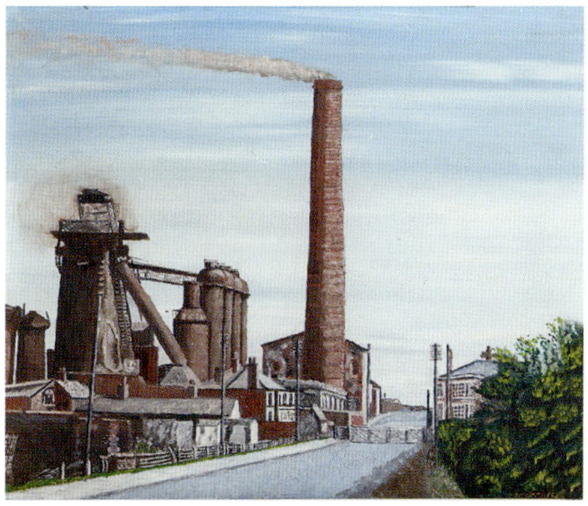

Taylor, J. M.
As I Remember (View of Old Station Road, Scunthorpe, Lincolnshire) 1965
oil on board 42 x 50
1965. 156

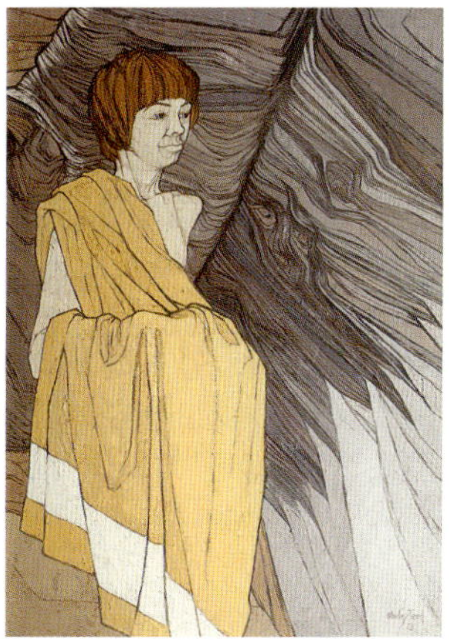

Teed, Shirley Brenda b.1933
Rockface with a Boy in a Yellow Towel 1973
oil on canvas 127 x 89
50

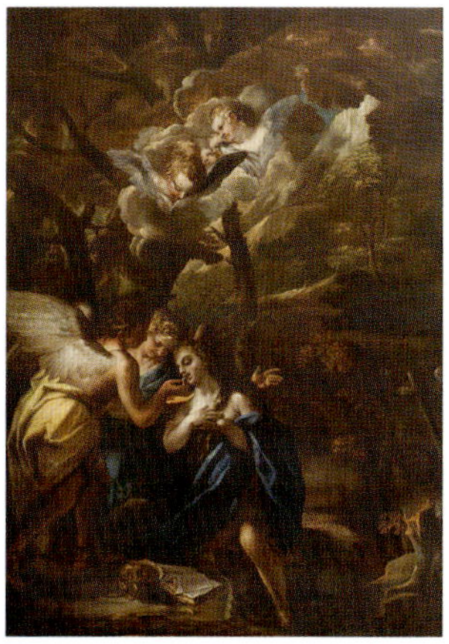

Trevisani, Francesco (attributed to) 1656–1746
Saint Mary Magdalene of Egypt c.1720
oil on canvas 285 x 190
1962. 139. 2

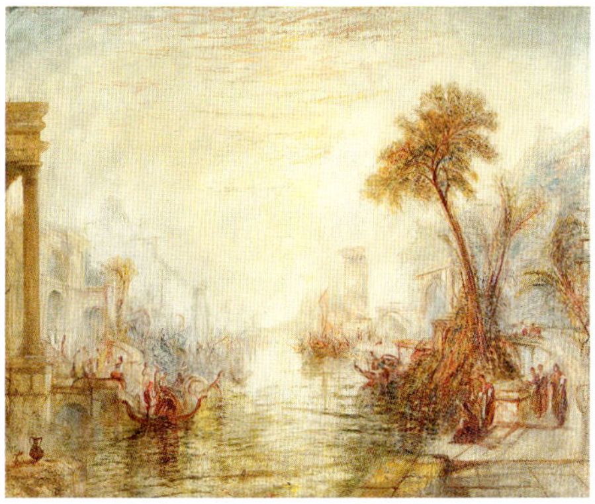

Turner, Joseph Mallord William (after) 1775–1851
Ancient Italy 1820–1845
oil on canvas 98 x 120
1964. 037. 1

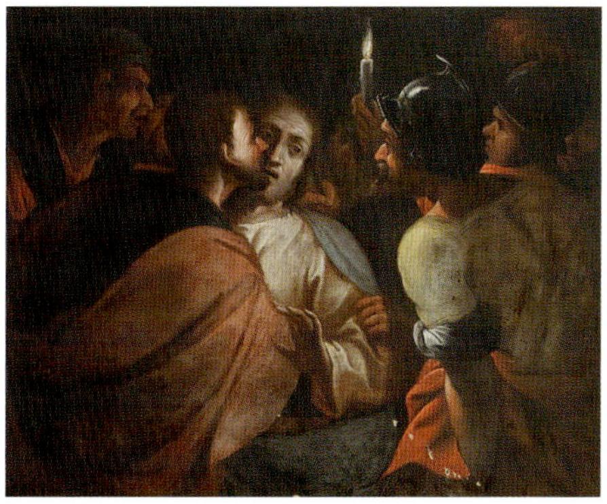

unknown artist
The Betrayal of Christ c.1640
oil on canvas 91.5 x 109
1962. 139. 1

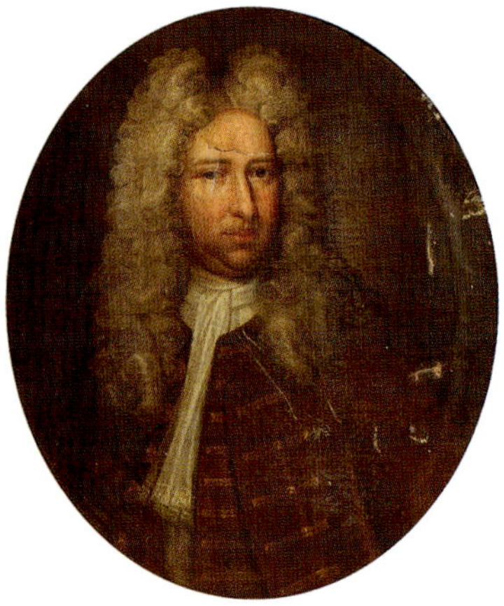

unknown artist
Portrait of an Unknown Officer 1690–1720
oil on canvas 72 x 60.5
1963. 085. 3b

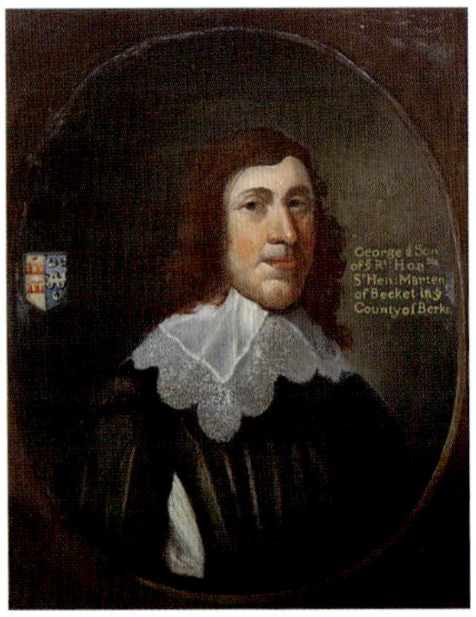

unknown artist 17th C
George Marten of Becket, Berkshire
oil on canvas 76 x 64
1974. 013. 3

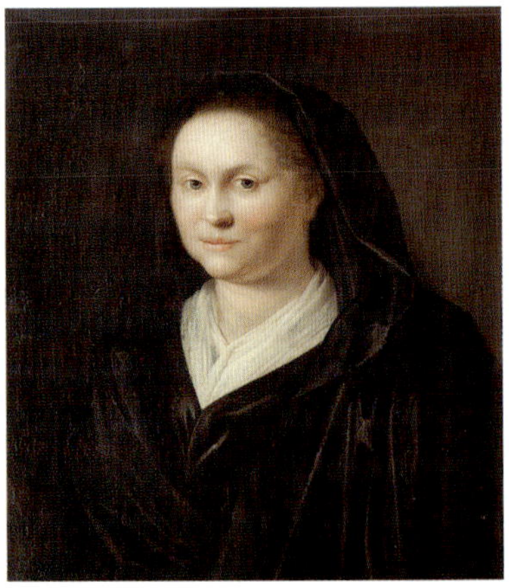

unknown artist 17th C
Portrait of a Lady in Black
oil on canvas 66 x 56
1969. 187. 3

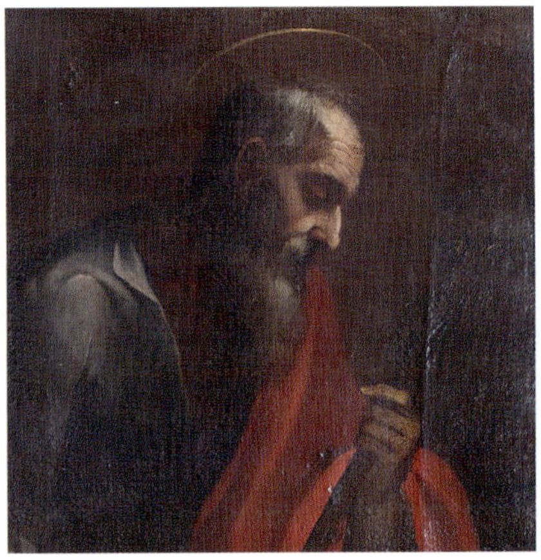

unknown artist 17th C
Saint Jerome Contemplating the Crucifix
oil on canvas 58 x 62
1962. 073

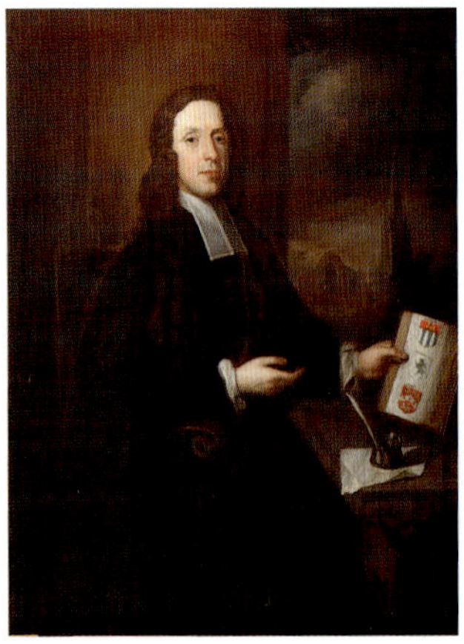

unknown artist
Reverend Thomas Lodington c.1710
oil on canvas 120 x 96
1970. 136

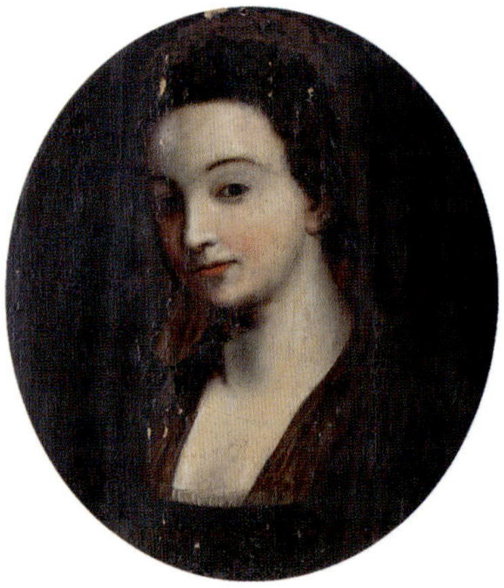

unknown artist 18th C
Bust of a Lady
oil on wood 56.5 x 47
1954. 104

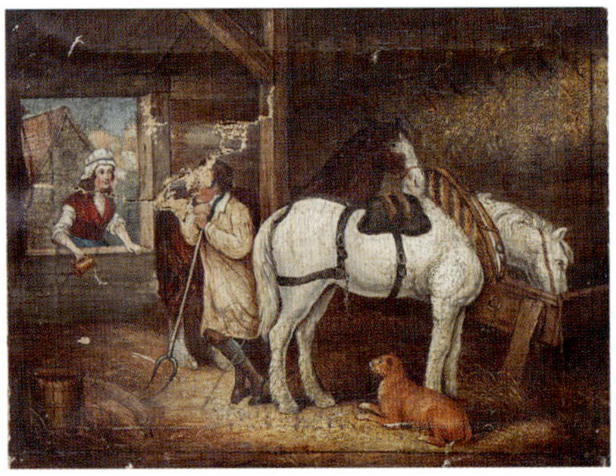

unknown artist
Conversation in a Barn c.1810
oil on canvas 37.5 x 47.5
1966. 029. 2

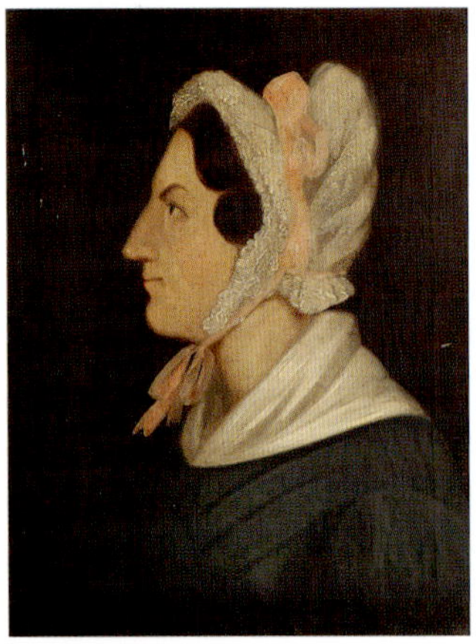

unknown artist
Mary Stead c.1840
oil on canvas 53.5 x 41
1962. 112. 1

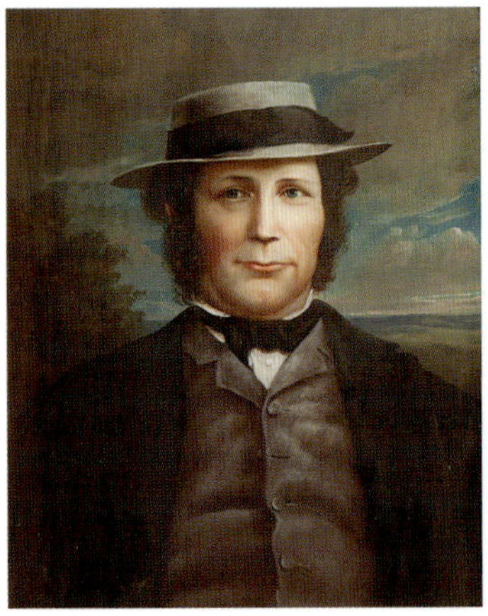

unknown artist
Mr G. F. Brunyee of Eastoft c.1860
oil on canvas 50 x 40
1964. 064

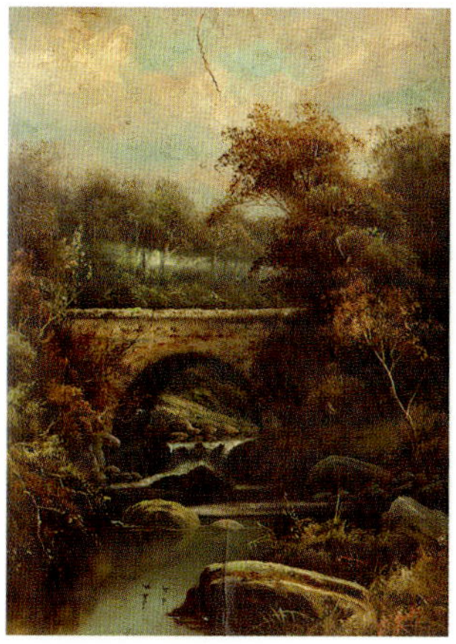

unknown artist
Landscape with a Bridge 1870
oil on board 56 x 40
1962. 141. 1

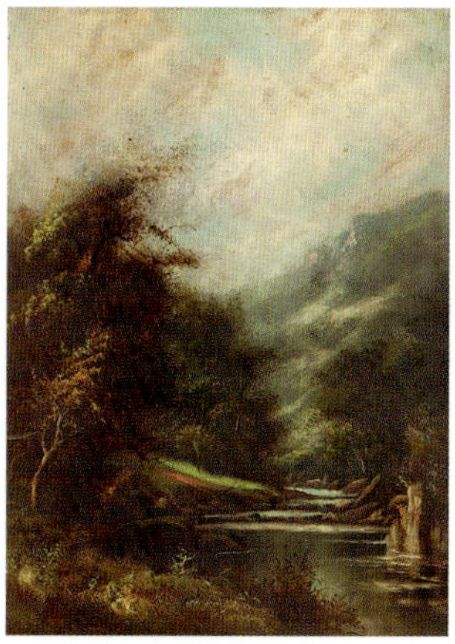

unknown artist
Landscape with a Stream 1870
oil on board 56.5 x 40.5
1962. 141. 2

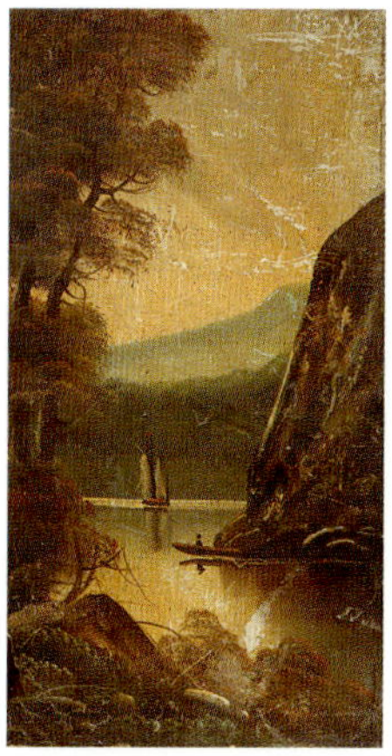

unknown artist
Lake Scene c.1880
oil on card 41 x 21
1965. 092A

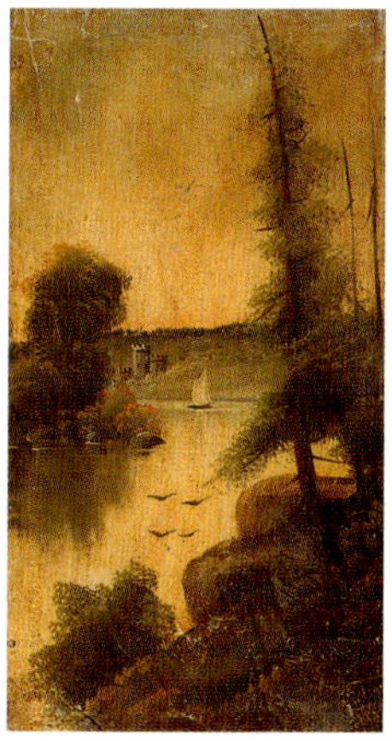

unknown artist
Lake Scene c.1880
oil on card 41 x 21.5
1965. 092B

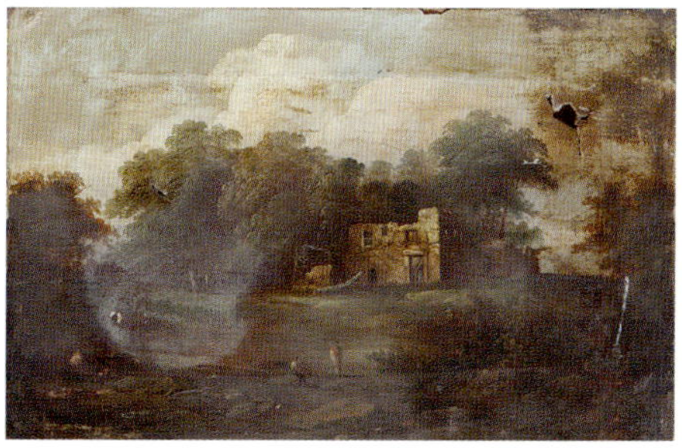

unknown artist
Rustic Scene with a Cottage c.1880
oil on canvas 30 x 46
1965. 094. 2

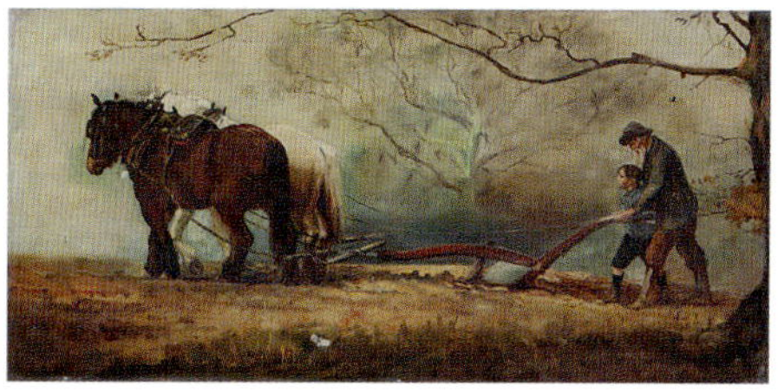

unknown artist
The Ploughing Lesson c.1890
oil on canvas 31 x 61
1965. 087. 2

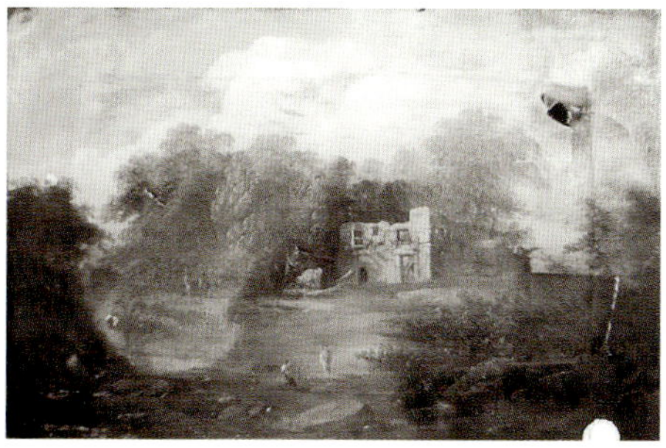

unknown artist 19th C
Rustic Scene: Derelict Stone Cottage in Woodland
oil on canvas 30.5 x 45 (E)
69b

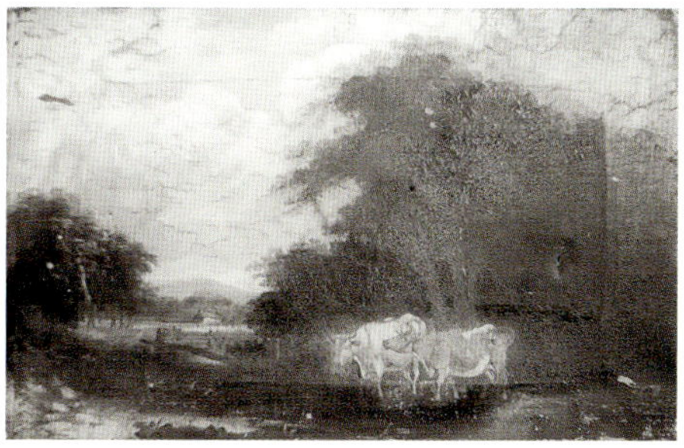

unknown artist 19th C
Rustic Scene: Two Cows by a Stream
oil on canvas 30.5 x 45 (E)
69a

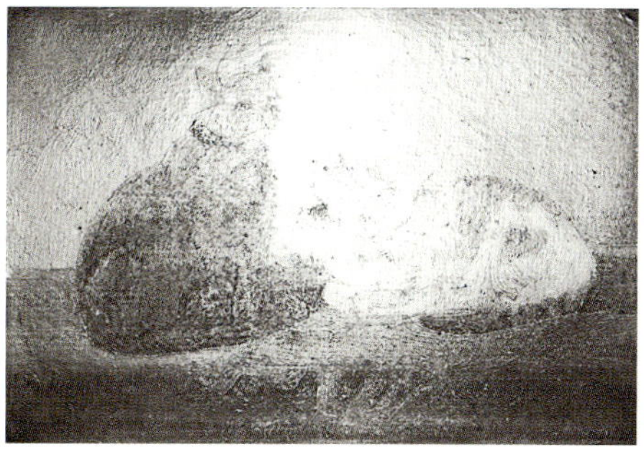

unknown artist 19th C
Two Cats
oil on canvas (?) 31 x 40
1962. 112. 2

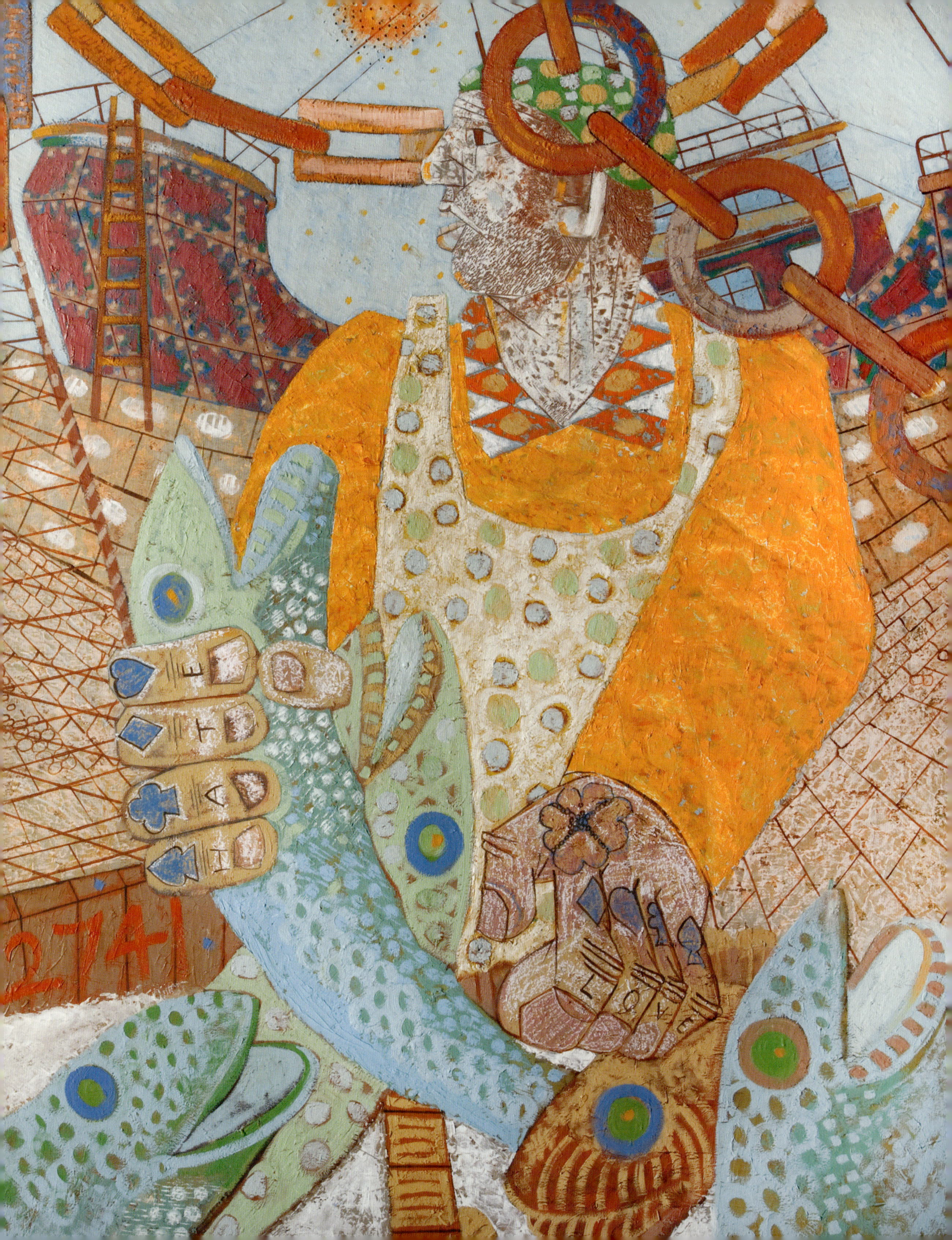
2741

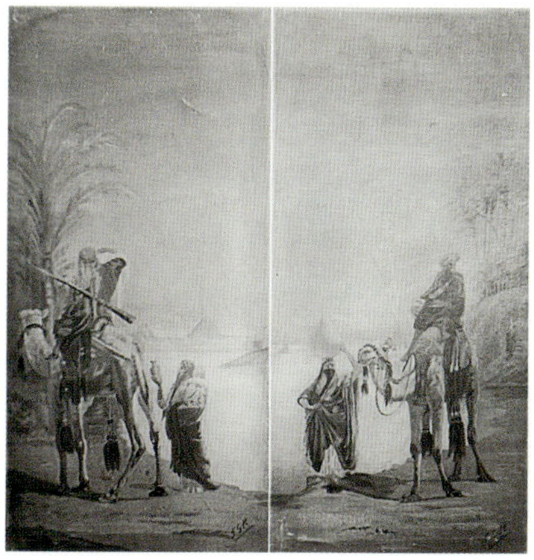

unknown artist 19th C
Two Landscapes with a Camel and Palm Trees (diptych)
oil on canvas 72.5 x 35; 72.5 x 35
64

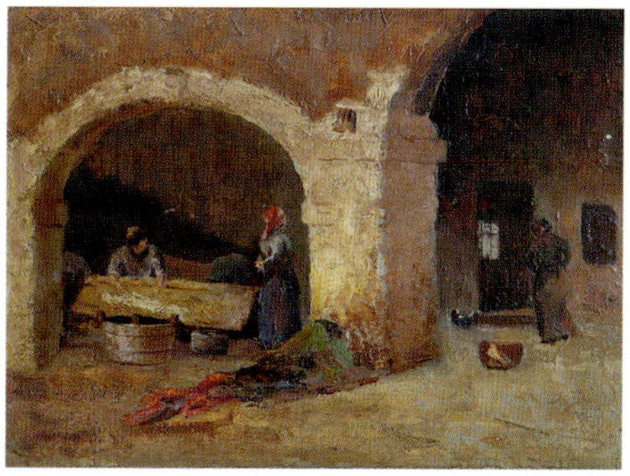

unknown artist
Washing Scene c.1900
oil on board 30 x 40.5
1970. 022

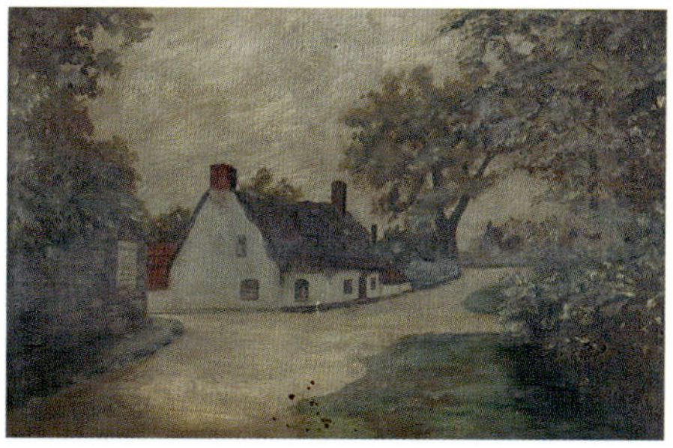

unknown artist
Frodingham Cottage, Lincolnshire 1912
oil on canvas 31 x 46
1961. 034. 4

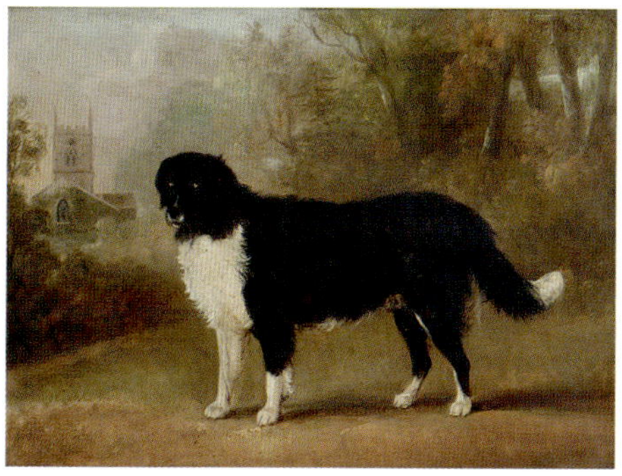

unknown artist
A Dog in Butler's Pantry, Lea Park, Lincolnshire (?)
oil on board 25 x 36
PCF2

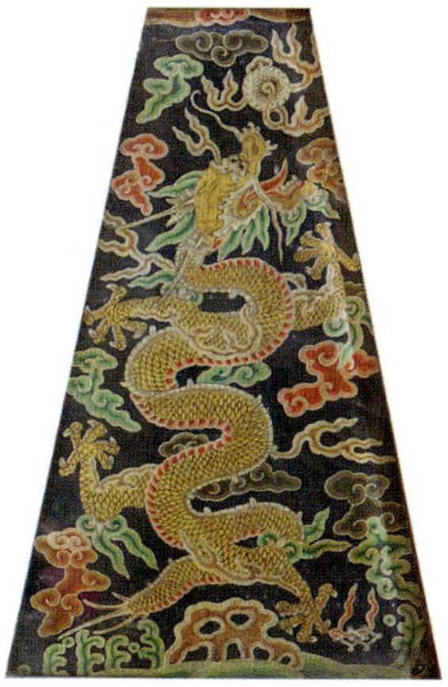

unknown artist
Chinese Dragon
oil on canvas 73 x 47
1965. 051. 1

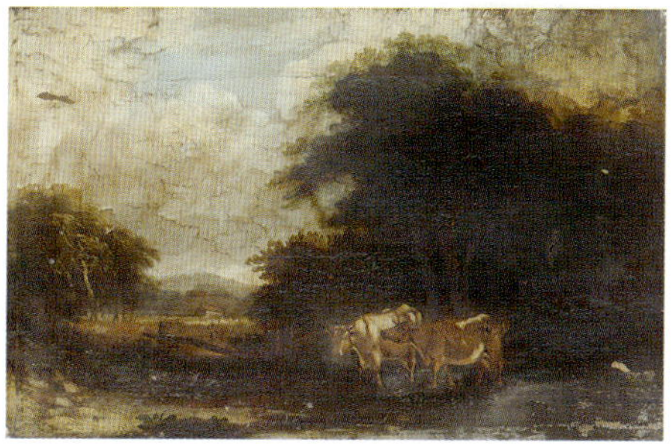

unknown artist
Cows Drinking from a River
oil on canvas 30.5 x 46
1975. 166. 6 (P)

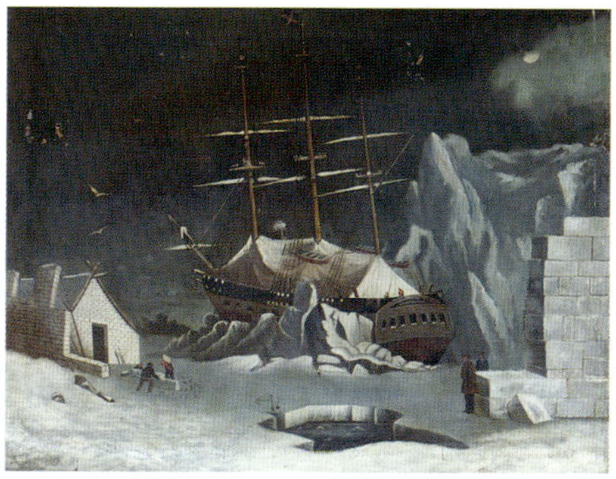

unknown artist
The Ice Ship
oil on canvas 71 x 92
1970. 096

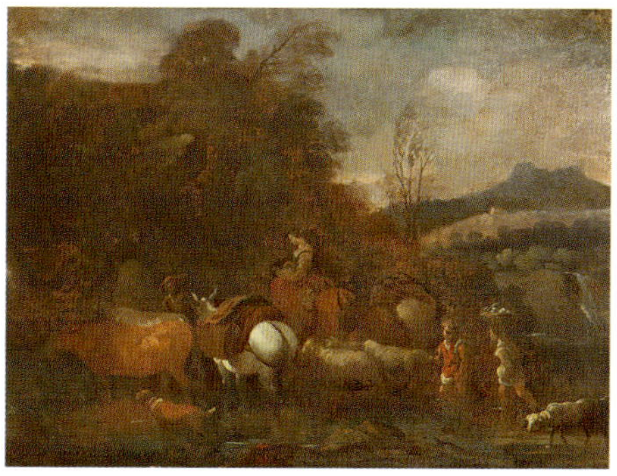

Van Bergen, Dirck 1645–1690
Pastoral Scene
oil on canvas 63.5 x 86
55

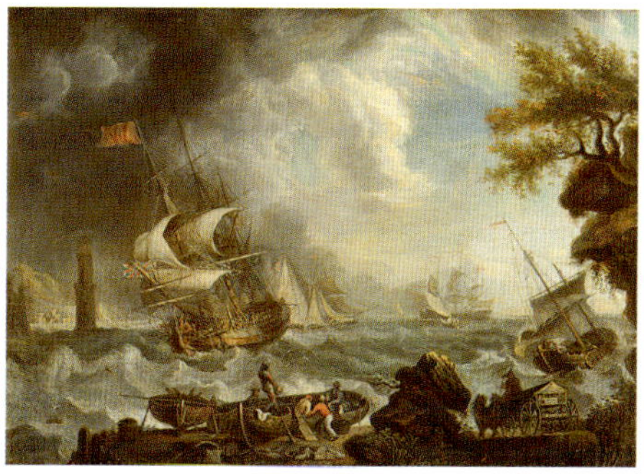

Vernet, Claude-Joseph 1714–1789
Seascape
oil on canvas 35.5 x 49.5
1963. 031. 4a

Facing page: Hopkinson, John, b.1941, *Souvenirs* (detail), 1980, North East Lincolnshire Museum Service (p. 242)

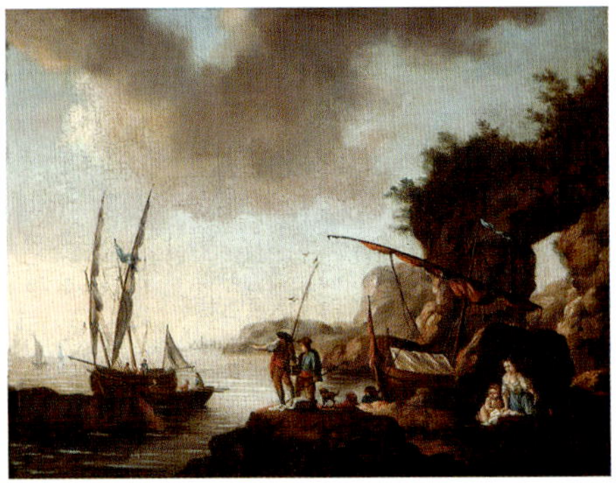

Vernet, Claude-Joseph (after) 1714–1789
Seaport in the Mediterranean 19th C
oil on canvas 39 x 47
1970. 121. 2

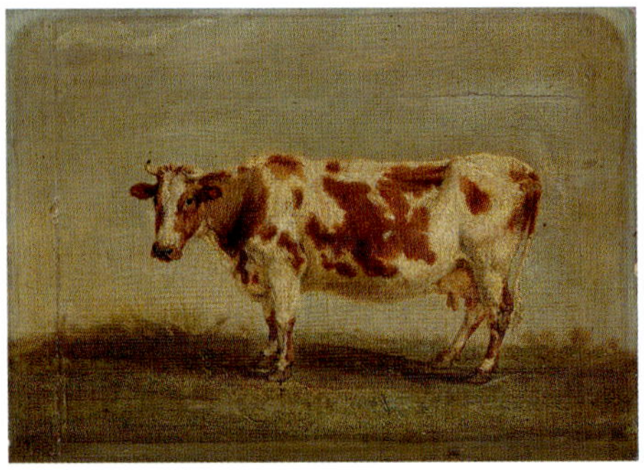

Ward, James 1769–1859
Roan Shorthorn Cow
oil on board 33 x 45
1967. 044

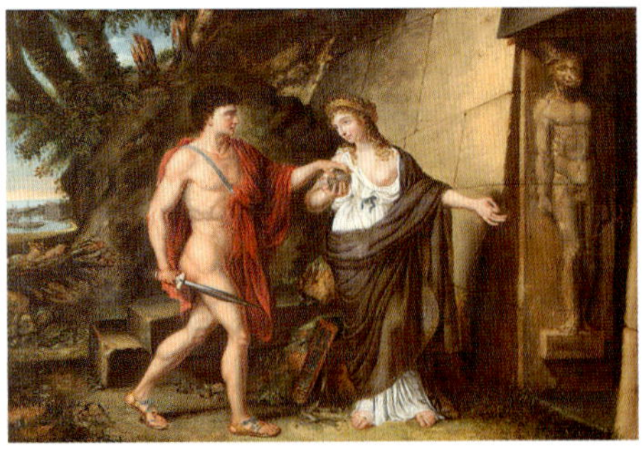

Westall, Richard 1765–1836
Theseus and Ariadne at the Entrance of the Labyrinth c.1810
oil on canvas 67 x 98
1965. 045. 1

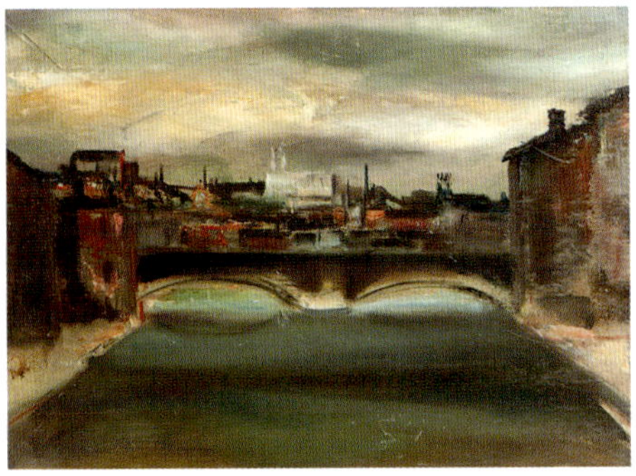

Whitehead, Tom 1886–1978
View from the Bridge c.1920
oil on card 44 x 56
1961. 123

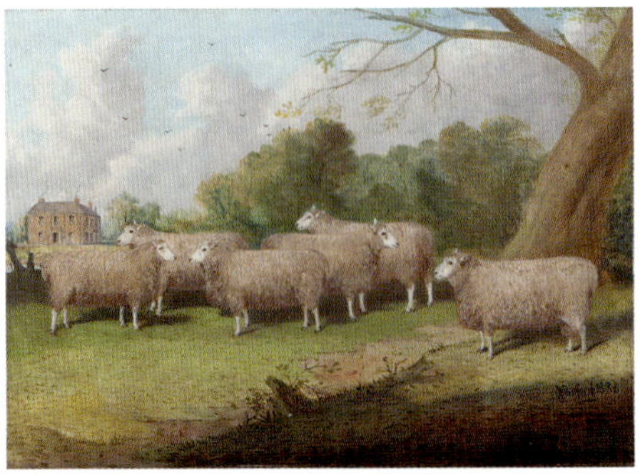

Whitford, Richard c.1821–1890
Six Lincolnshire Longwool Sheep 1888
oil on canvas 51 x 69
1972. 031. 2

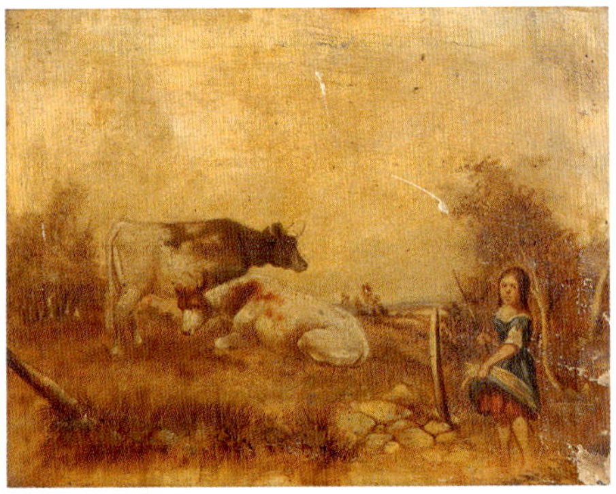

Wilkinson
Pastoral c.1858
oil on canvas 31 x 38
1961. 034. 3

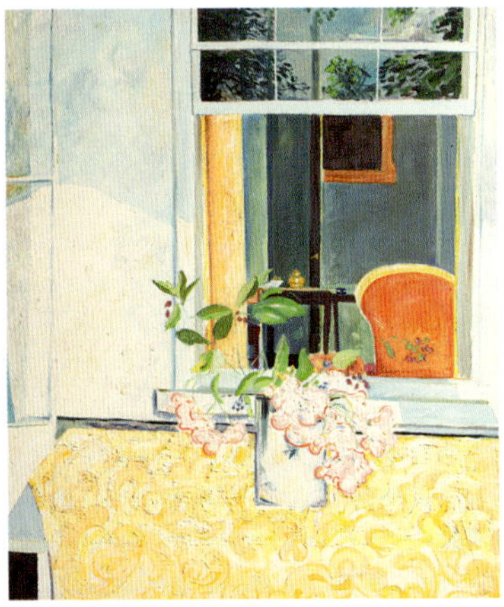

Willson, Graeme b.1951
Still Life
oil on canvas 91 x 76
1974. 034

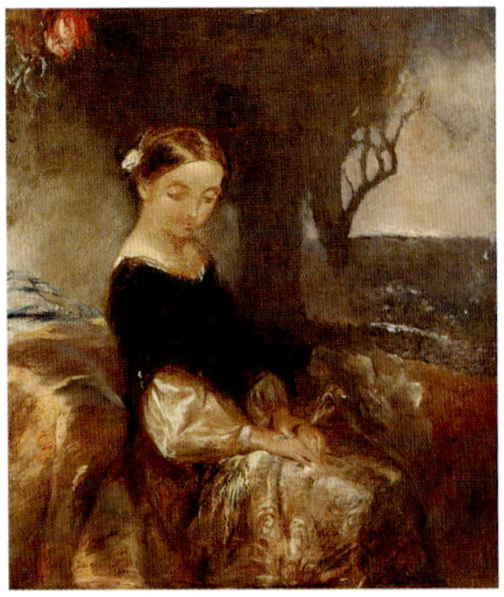

Woolmer, Alfred Joseph 1805–1892
Portrait of a Young Girl 1830–1840
oil on canvas 35 x 30
1970. 121. 1

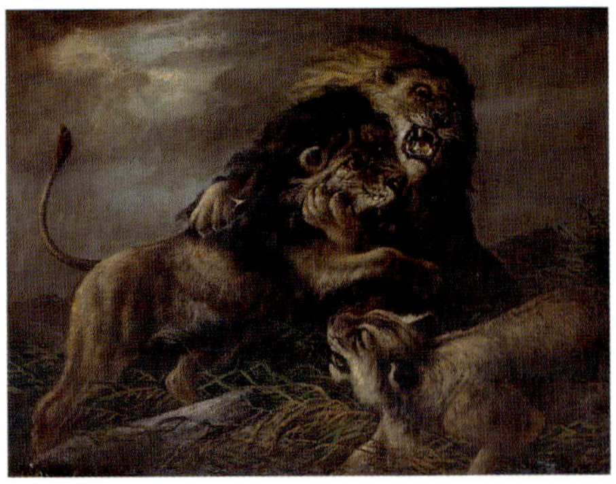

Worthington, A. 1822–1915
Fighting Lions c.1880
oil on canvas 66 x 97
1965. 065. 3

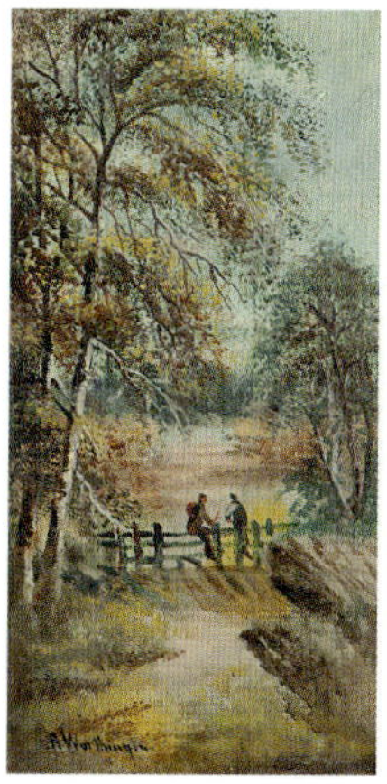

Worthington, A. 1822–1915
Rustic Scene with a Stile c.1880
oil on canvas 51 x 26
1965. 065. 4

Magdalen College Museum

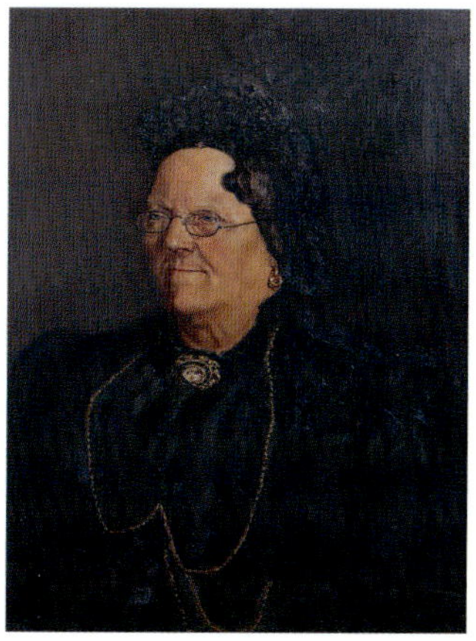

Turner, Ernest 1886–1976
Mary Paulett (d.1923)
oil on canvas 59 x 41
1

Ayscoughfee Hall Museum and Gardens

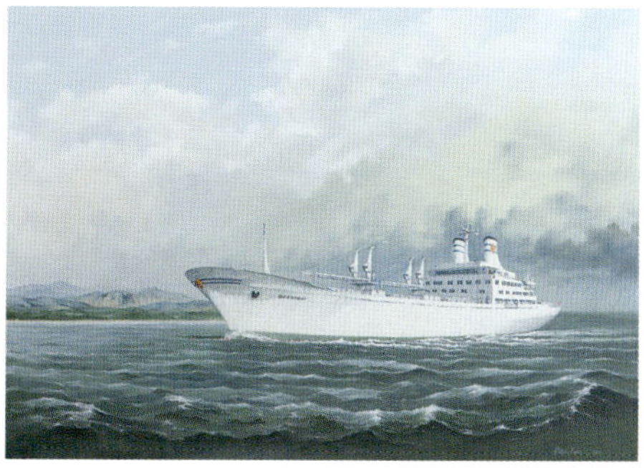

Eaton, Wilcox
MV 'Geest Bay' 1980
oil on canvas 142.8 x 150
SPAAH 2008.1

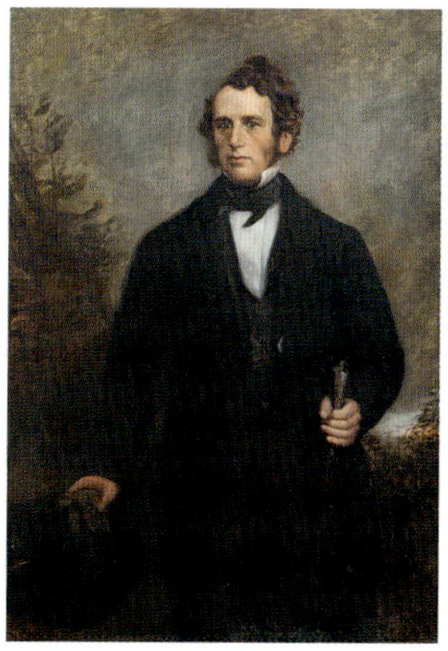

unknown artist mid-19th C
Maurice Johnson VI (1815–1864)
oil on canvas 140 x 96
SPAAH 2008.8

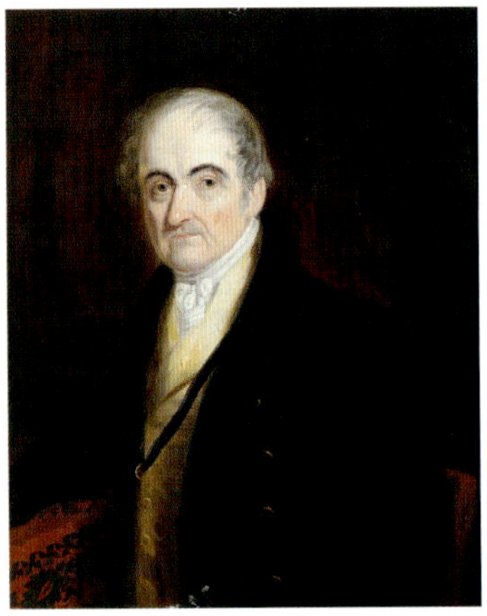

unknown artist mid-19th C
Thomas Pear II (1770–1858)
oil on canvas 69.4 x 54.9
SPAAH 2006.4

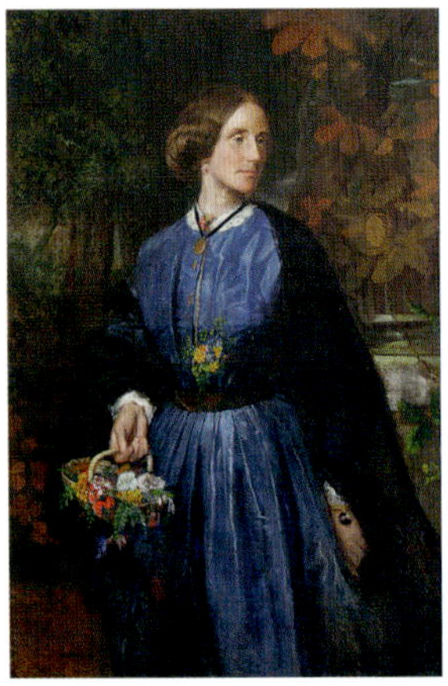

unknown artist late 19th C–20th C
Isabella Johnson (d.1905)
oil on canvas 140 x 95
SPAAH 2008.7

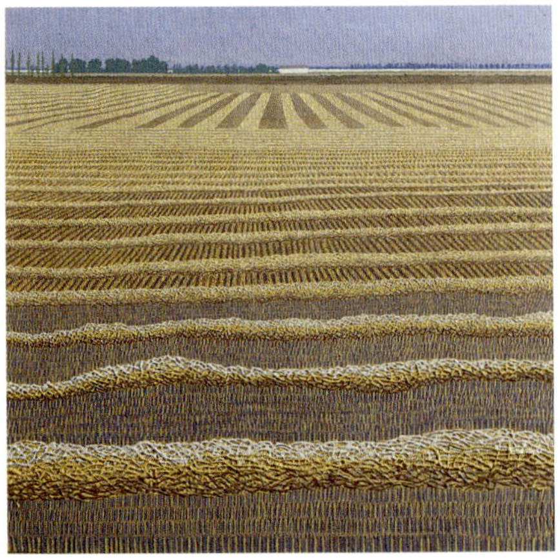

Webber, Helen active 1966–2008
Cutter Patterns 1991
acrylic on flax 100 x 100 (E)
AHM 1998.11

Stamford and Rutland Hospital

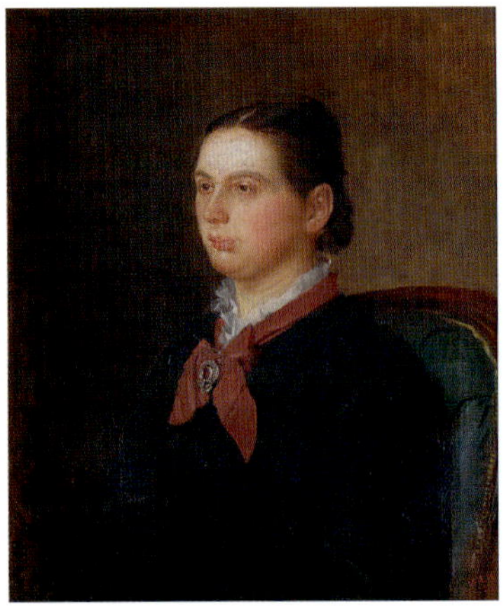

W. E. M.
Miss Michelson
oil on canvas 60 x 50
2

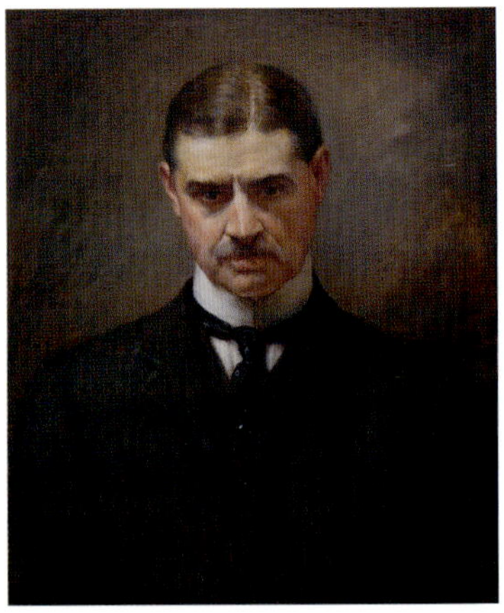

unknown artist
Dr T. P. Greenwood (1855–1927), Surgeon of Stamford and Rutland Hospital
oil on canvas 60 x 50
6

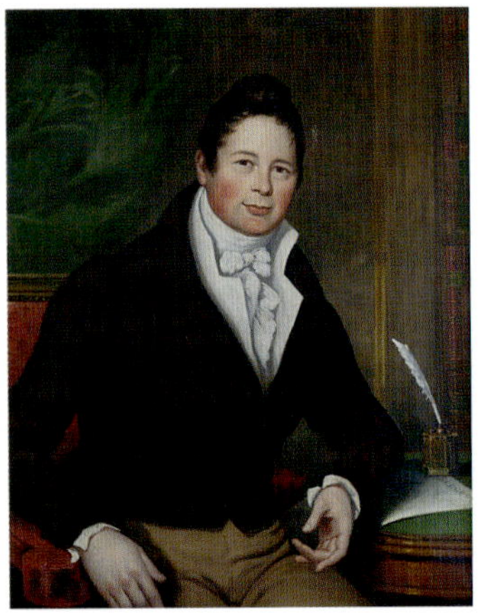

unknown artist
Henry Fryer (1762–1823), Surgeon, Founder and Benefactor of Stamford and Rutland Hospital
oil on canvas 90 x 70
5

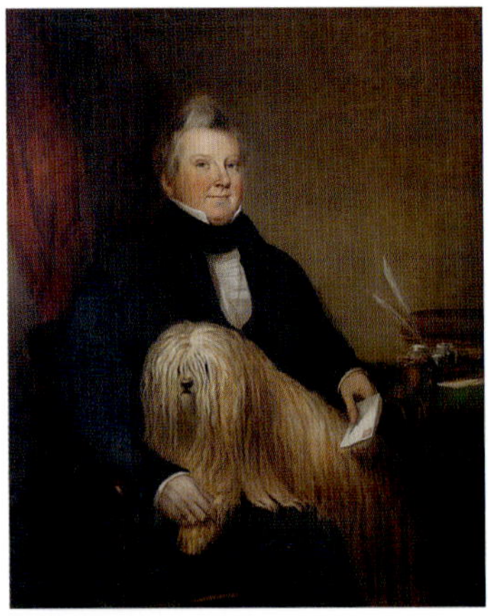

unknown artist
Portrait of an Unknown Man and a Dog
oil on canvas 125 x 100
3

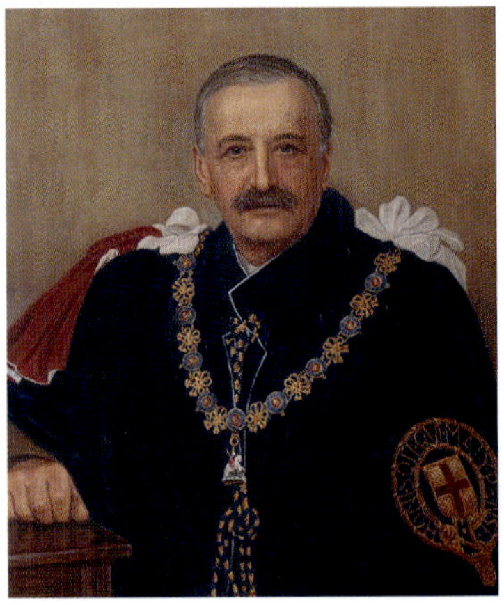

unknown artist
William Cecil (1876–1956), 5th Marquess of Exeter
oil on canvas 60 x 50
4

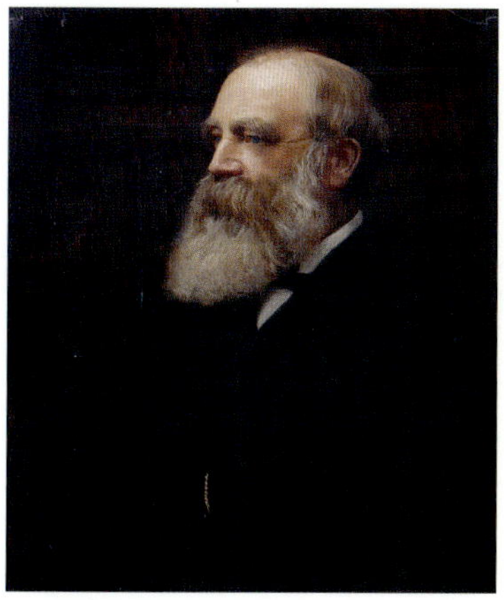

unknown artist
William Newman, MD
oil on canvas 74 x 62
1

Stamford Museum

Founded in its present form in 1980, Stamford Museum inherited the core of its collections from an earlier museum which had previously occupied the top floor of the local library. Like many early museums, the collections of this original museum consisted of an eclectic mix of items, not all of which related to Stamford. This accounts for the diverse subject matter of some of the paintings currently to be found in our Collection. However, in common with the other museums of Lincolnshire County Council Heritage Service, Stamford Museum now confines its general collecting to items of local significance, and collects paintings by local artists, or which show local topography.

These paintings often provide a valuable record of a changed landscape, for example, the painting of the site of the old Cascelloids plastics factory on West Street by a B. Baker. Painted in 1942, this area of the town is today occupied by a large modern supermarket and is unrecognisable as the area depicted in the painting. The topographical paintings of the town also include the painting of *All Saints' Church, Red Lion Square, Stamford, Lincolnshire* by an unknown artist. This hung in Mr Johnson's chemist shop in Red Lion Square for over 50 years, and so the painting serves to commemorate not only the landscape of the square as it was in the 1860s, but also Mr Johnson's business.

Other artworks in the Stamford Collection are more tenuously connected with local buildings, for example, the still life paintings of fruit by George H. Jauncey which hung in the 'Crown and Anchor' pub during the early-twentieth century and were rescued from this building when it closed down.

The landscape paintings in Stamford's Collection also reflect the geographical position of the town, which is on the border of four counties. In consequence, views of the Fenland landscape around Peterborough, and also a painting of *The Wothorpe Fields, Lincolnshire* by Cyril J. Mayes have found their way into the Collection. *The Wothorpe Fields* was exhibited in the Welland Valley Arts Society annual exhibition in 1981 and we are lucky that there are such active arts societies locally supported by the Stamford Arts Centre.

Stamford Museum's Collection also features portraits of well-known people with local connections, most notably the two images of *Daniel Lambert (1770–*

1809), one of which is on loan from Stamford Town Council. The other was acquired last year with assistance from the Museums, Libraries and Archives/ Victoria and Albert Museum Purchase Grant Fund and the Art Fund. Daniel was, at the time of his death, the largest man in England, weighing over 52 stone. He came to Stamford to attend the races in 1809 and sadly died whilst staying overnight. He is buried here in St Martin's graveyard, and has evermore been associated with the town. Less famous local people also feature, for example *William Virtue Ellis,* landlord of the 'Lord Nelson' pub during the nineteenth century.

Stamford Museum is thankful for the generosity of those who have donated works of art to the Museum, and also grateful to the Museums, Libraries and Archives/Victoria and Albert Museum Purchase Grant Fund and the Art Fund; without their assistance we could have not purchased many of our most significant paintings.

Deborah Bircham, Collections Officer

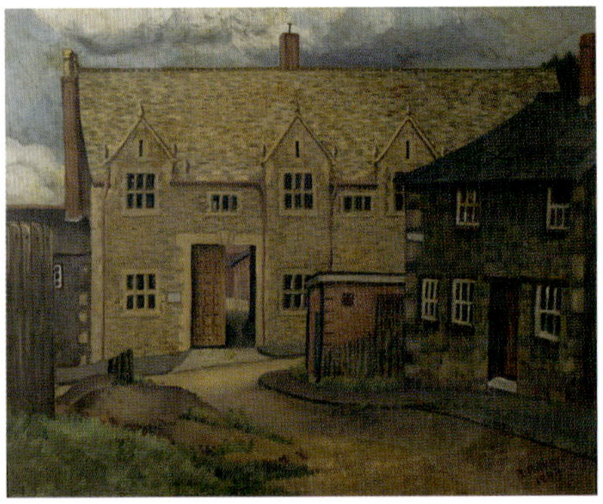

Baker, B.
West Street (Cascelloids Factory, now demolished*)* 1942
oil on canvas 64 x 76
LCNST:4784

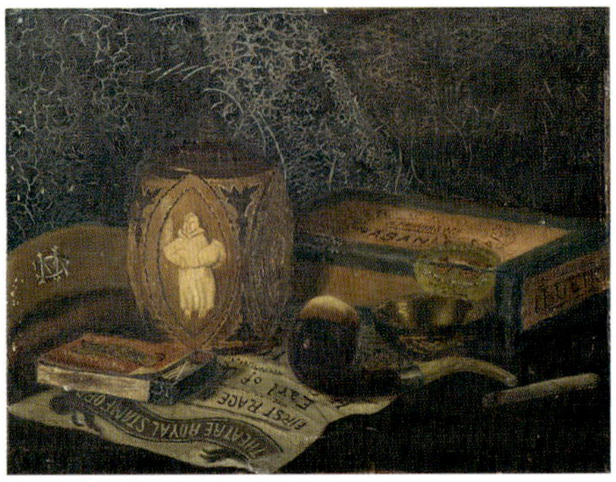

Carver (attributed to)
Still Life
oil on canvas 28 x 35.5
LCNST:1883

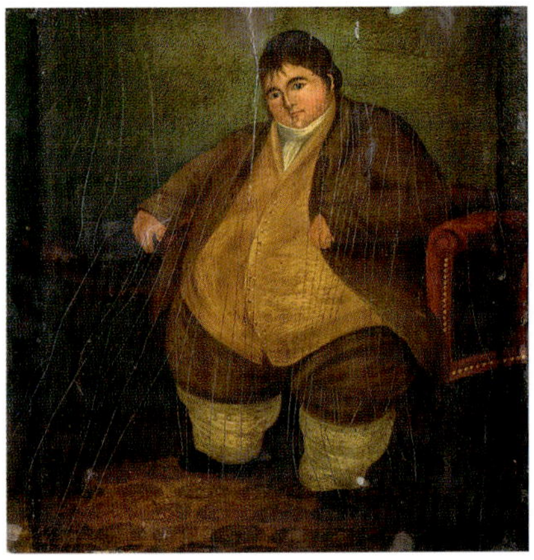

Harston, I. (attributed to)
Daniel Lambert (1770–1809) 1808
oil on wood 48 x 44 (E)
LCNST:5600

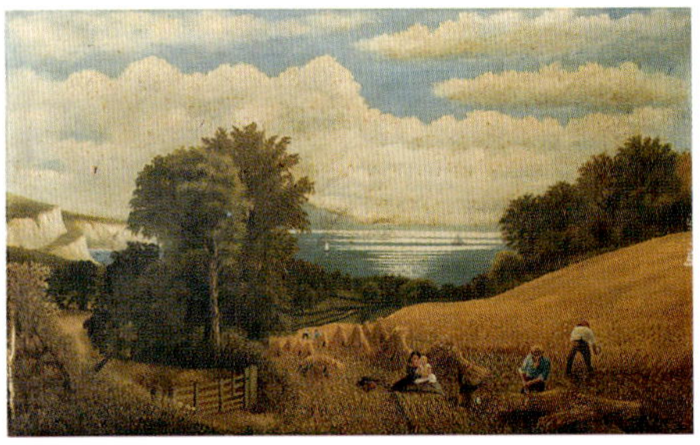

Jackson, C.
Harvesting Scene
oil on canvas 51 x 81.5
LCNST:1213

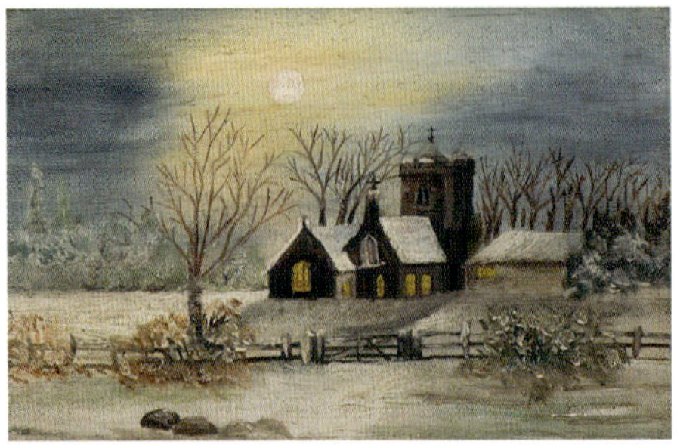

Jauncey, George H. active 1903–1907
Church and Countryside in the Snow 1903
oil on canvas 18.7 x 29.4
LCNST:161

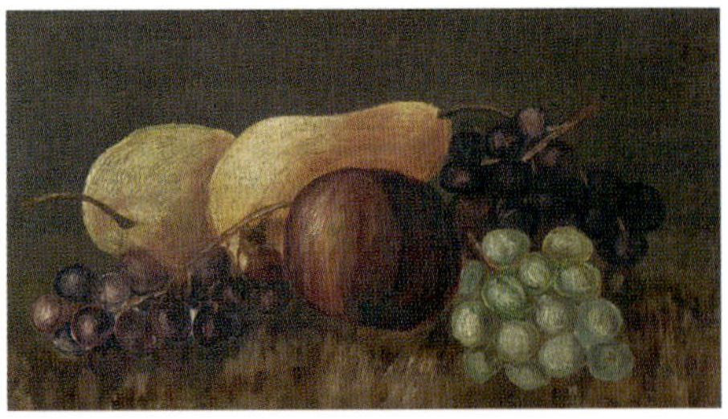

Jauncey, George H. active 1903–1907
Still Life with an Apple, Pears and Grapes 1907
oil on canvas 19.6 x 35
LCNST:160.2

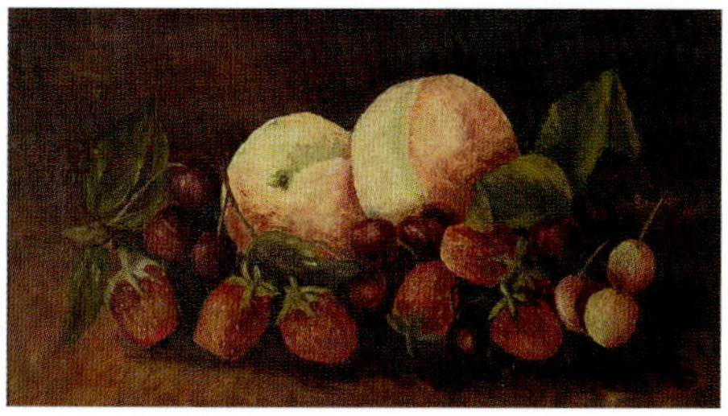

Jauncey, George H. active 1903–1907
Still Life with Peaches, Cherries and Strawberries 1907
oil on canvas 19.6 x 35
LCNST:160.1

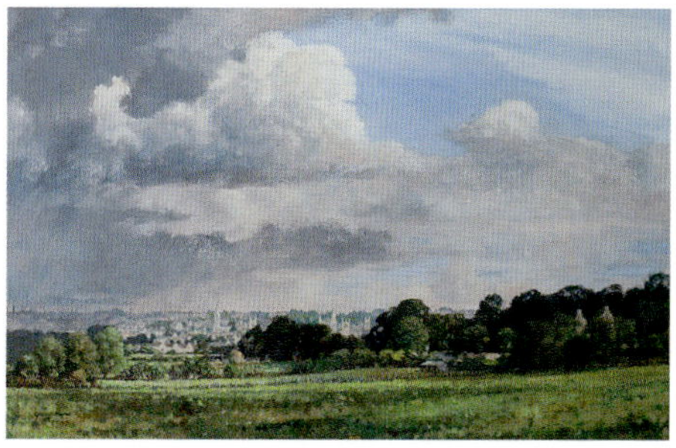

Mayes, Cyril J.
The Wothorpe Fields, Lincolnshire 1981
acrylic on canvas 49 x 74
LCNST:2872

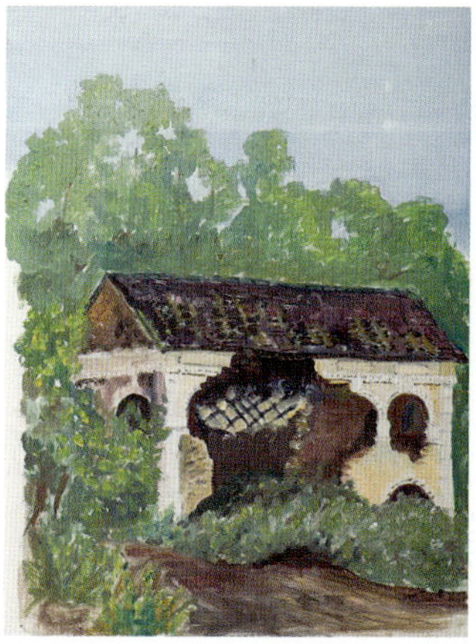

Miles, Ellis 1919–2006
The Old Grandstand, Racecourse Road, Stamford, Lincolnshire 1974
oil on paper 40 x 30
LCNST:5462.144

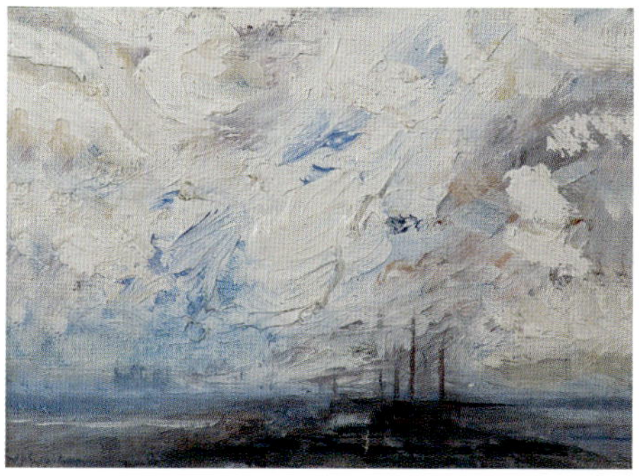

Robotham, Ruth b.1930
Cloudy Day, Peterborough, Cambridgeshire 1983
acrylic on paper 12.1 x 16
LCNST:3114.1

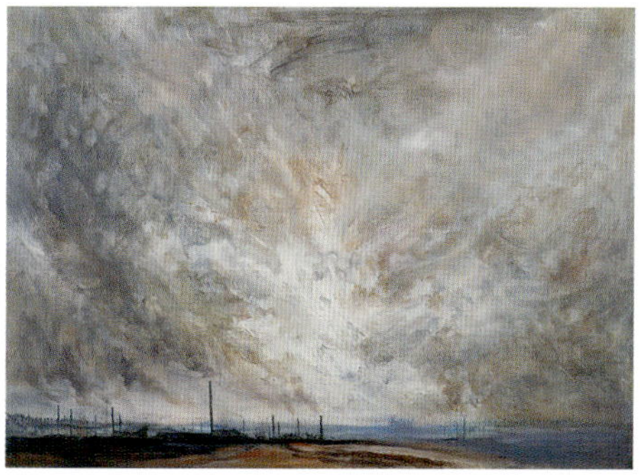

Robotham, Ruth b.1930
Fenland Landscape 1983
acrylic on paper 43.9 x 59.2
LCNST:3114.2

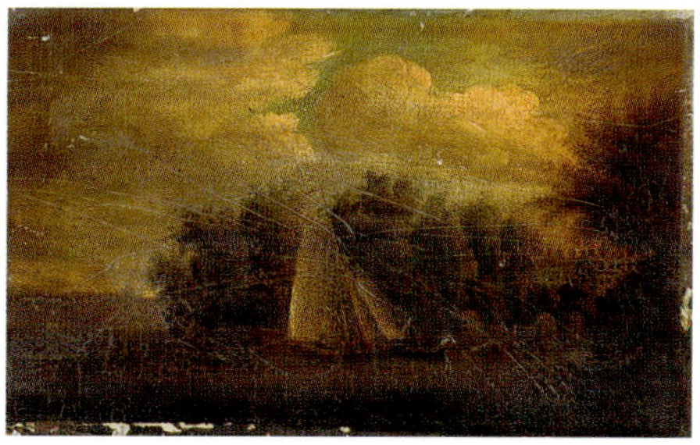

unknown artist
Sailing Scene c.1800
oil on wood 21.5 x 34.5
LCNST:1882

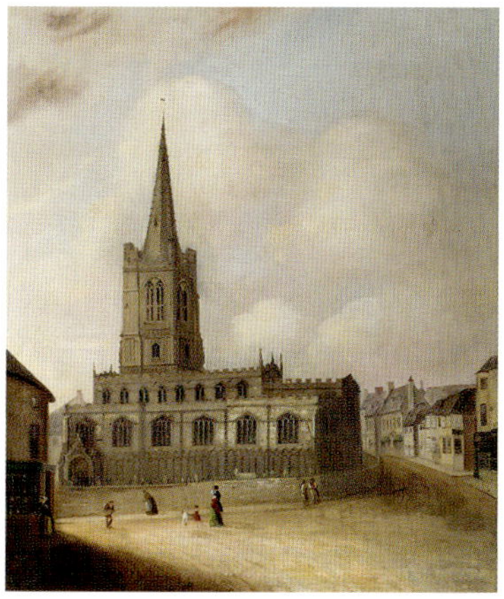

unknown artist
All Saints' Church, Red Lion Square, Stamford, Lincolnshire 1860s
oil on canvas 76 x 63.5
LCNST:3346

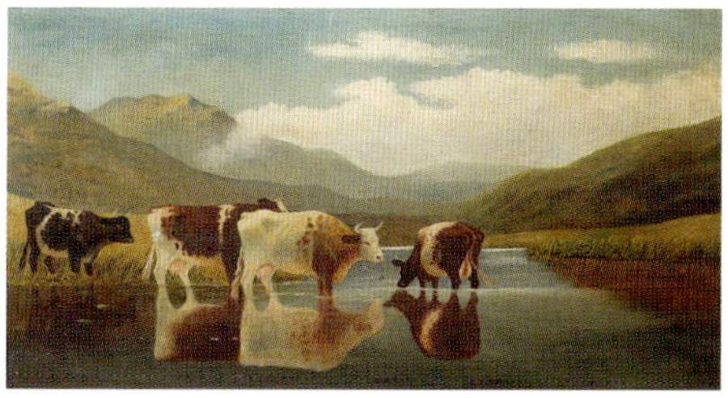

unknown artist mid-19th C–late 19th C
Mountain Landscape with Cattle
oil on canvas 29.5 x 54.5
LCNST:1886.1

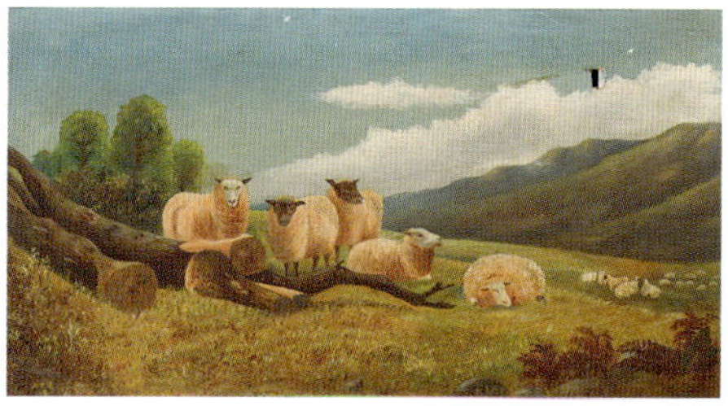

unknown artist mid-19th C–late 19th C
Mountain Landscape with Sheep
oil on canvas 29.5 x 54.5
LCNST:1886.2

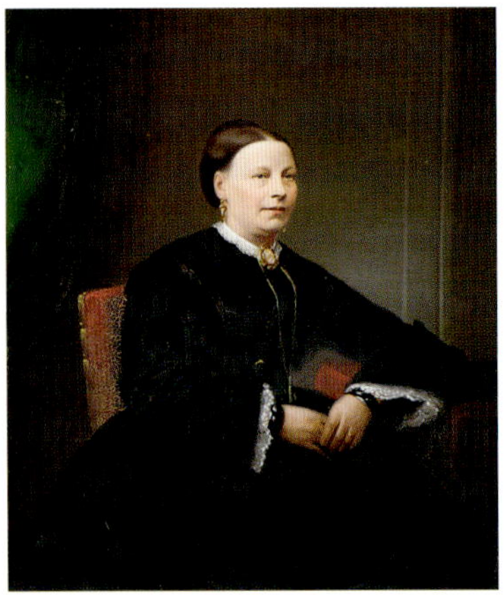

unknown artist late 19th C
Florence Ellis
oil on board 27.5 x 22.5
LCNST:1885.2

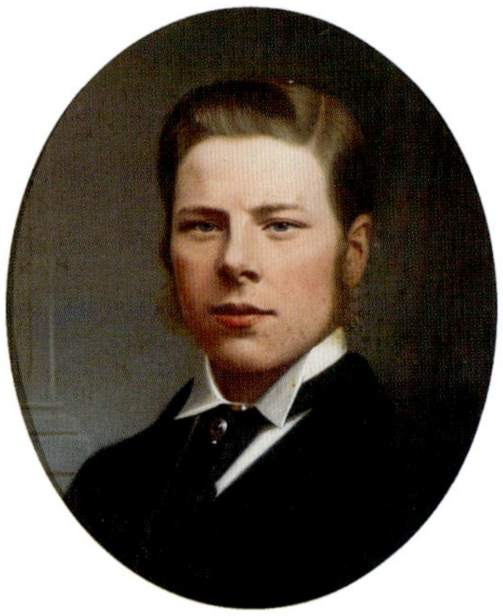

unknown artist late 19th C
George William Ellis
oil on board 24.5 x 20
LCNST:1885.3

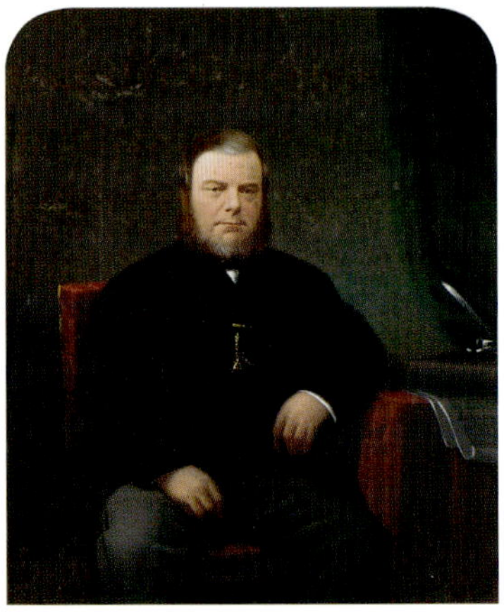

unknown artist late 19th C
William Virtue Ellis, Landlord of the 'Lord Nelson' Pub During the Nineteenth Century
oil on board 27.5 x 22.5
LCNST:1885.1

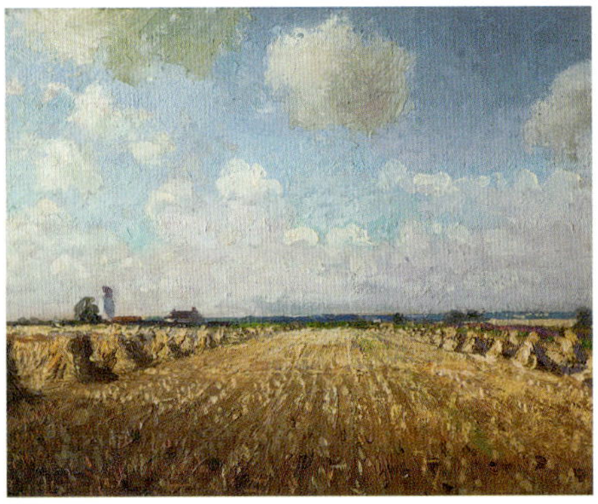

unknown artist
Fenland Scene with a Cornfield and a Windmill 1959
oil on canvas 23 x 27.5
LCNST:4

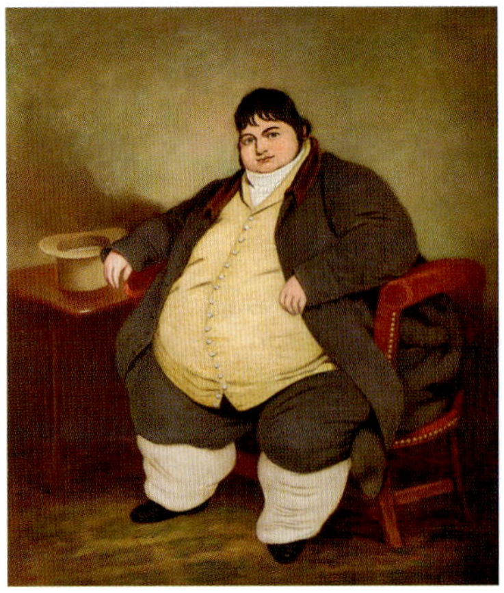

unknown artist
Daniel Lambert (1770–1809) (copy of an earlier painting)
oil on canvas 74.7 x 62.7
LCNST:2697L

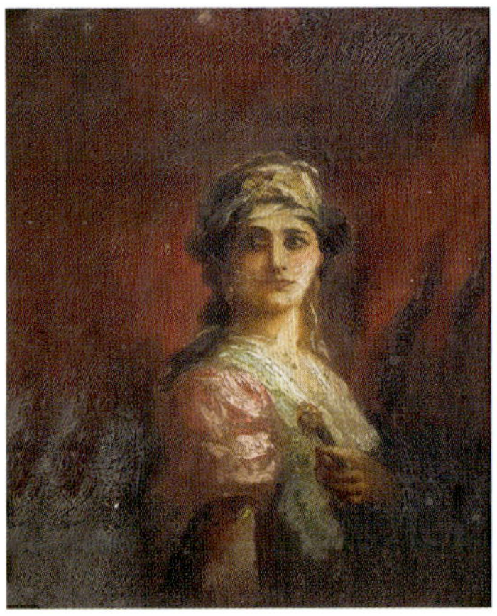

unknown artist
Portrait of an Unknown Lady in Continental Dress
oil on panel 10 x 8
LCNST:753

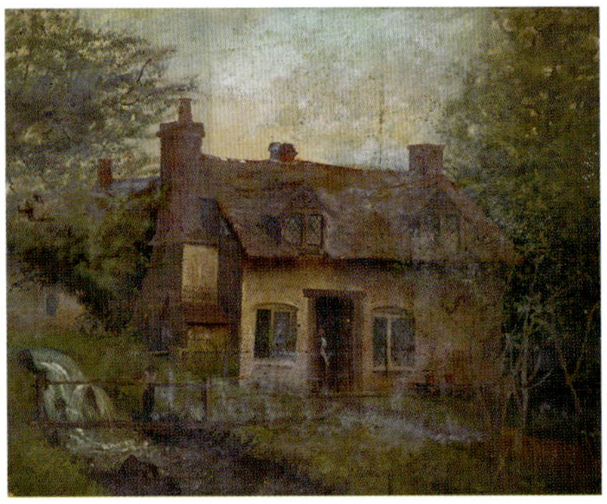

unknown artist
View of a Cottage by a Stream
oil on card 30 x 36
LCNST:1965

Facing page: Feiler, Paul, b.1918, *Italian Village Square with a Lake* (detail), 1954, Leicestershire County Council Artworks Collection (p. 116)

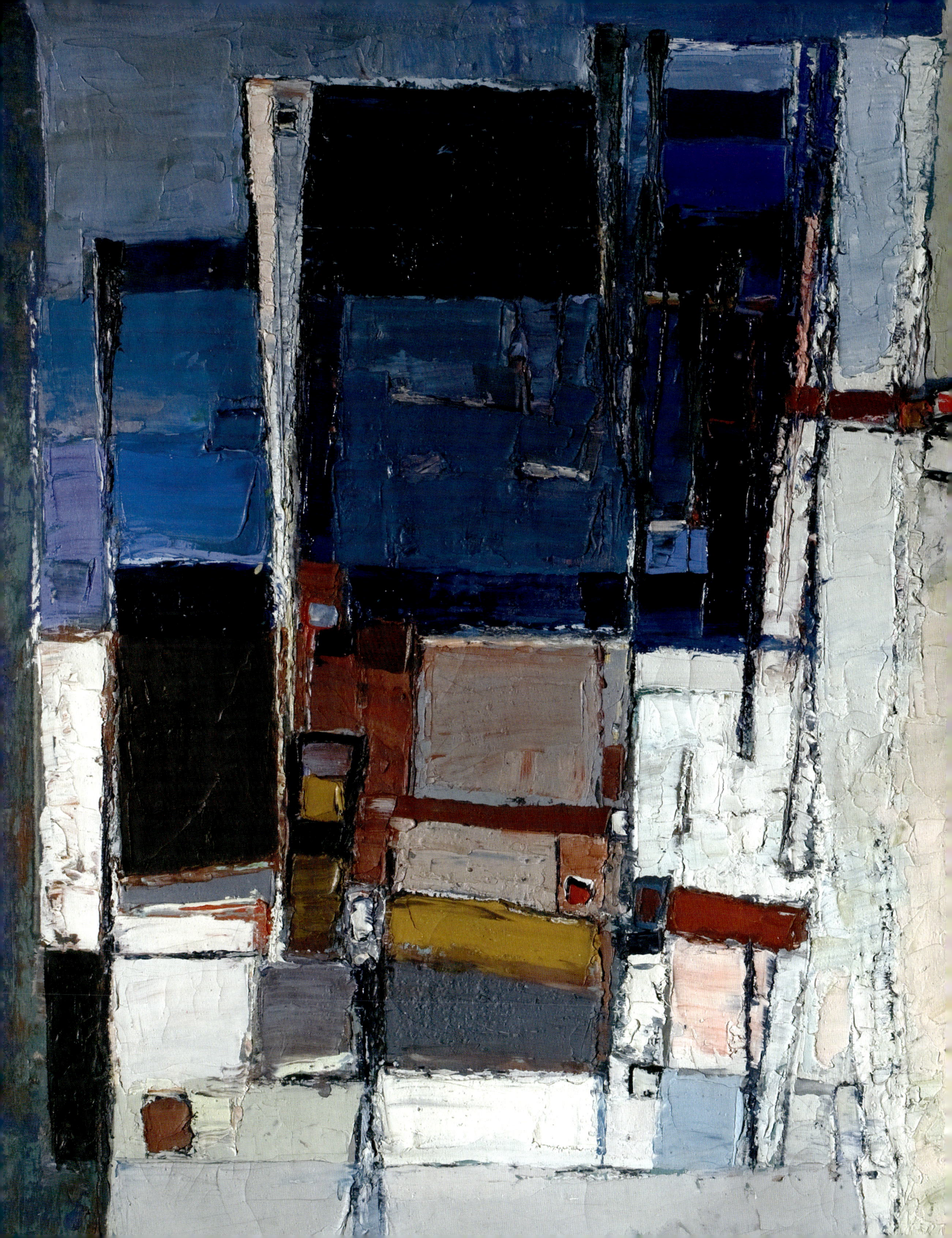

The Hospital of William Browne

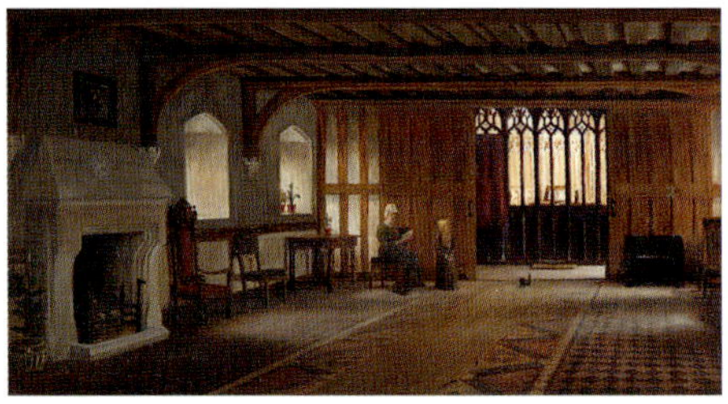

unknown artist
The Common Room at Browne's Hospital
c.1870
oil on canvas 24 x 32
1

Catmose College

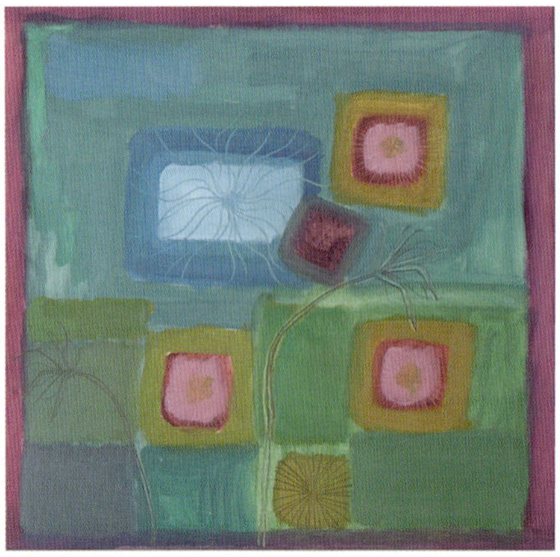

Boyfield, Caroline b.1962
Seed Heads 2005
oil on board 41 x 41
2

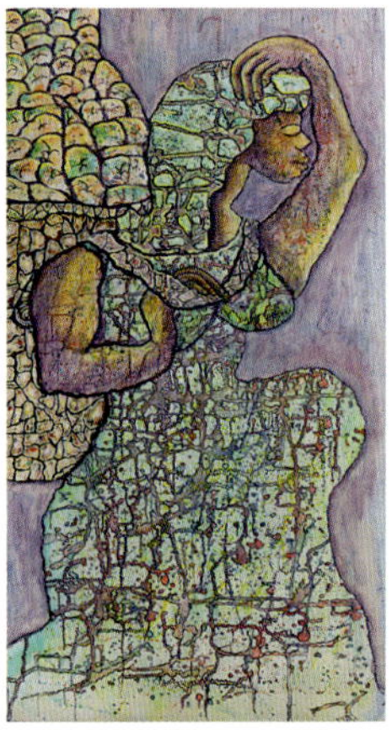

Njeiu Njeri, Patricia
Harvest Time 2004
acrylic on canvas 131 x 66
3

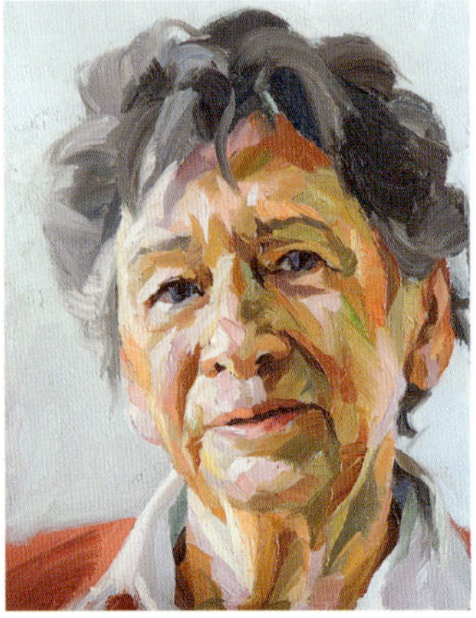

Wright, Paul b.1973
Joy Gregg II 2007
oil on wood 24.5 x 18
1

Rutland County Council

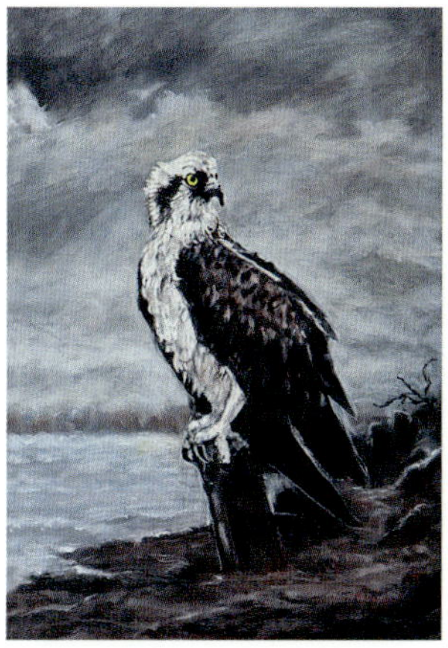

Snowdon
Osprey 2005
oil on board 49 x 34.5
1

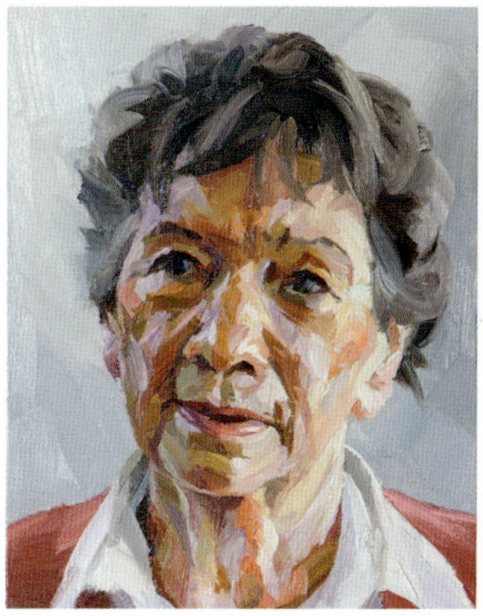

Wright, Paul b.1973
Joy Gregg I
oil on wood 40 x 30
4

Rutland County Museum

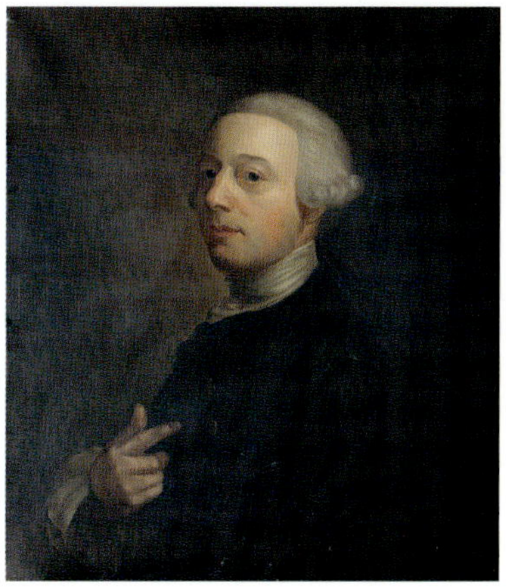

Eagleton, Aileen 1902–1984
Edward Eagletony 1933
oil on canvas 76 x 63.5
1992.39

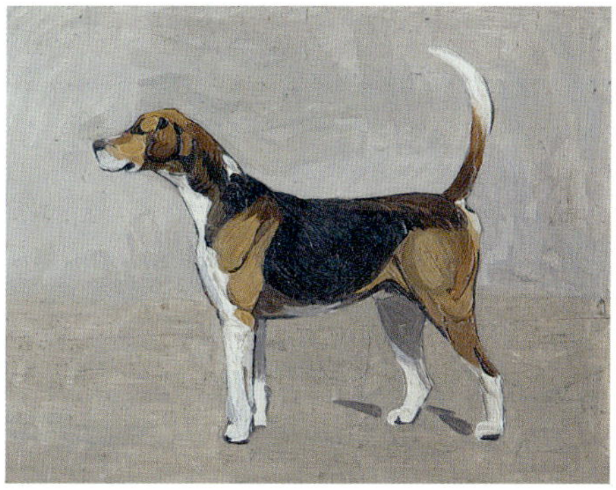

Wilson, Violet d.c.1970
Cottesmore Guider Hound
oil on wood 20 x 25.5
1999.42

Uppingham Town Hall

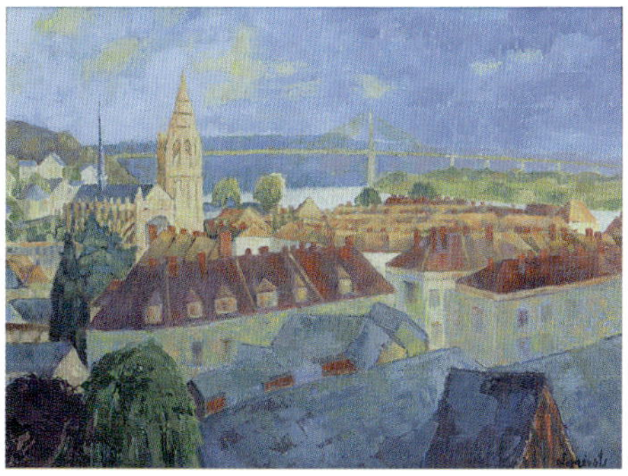

unknown artist
Caudebec-en-Caux, France 1983
oil on canvas 46.5 x 61.5
1

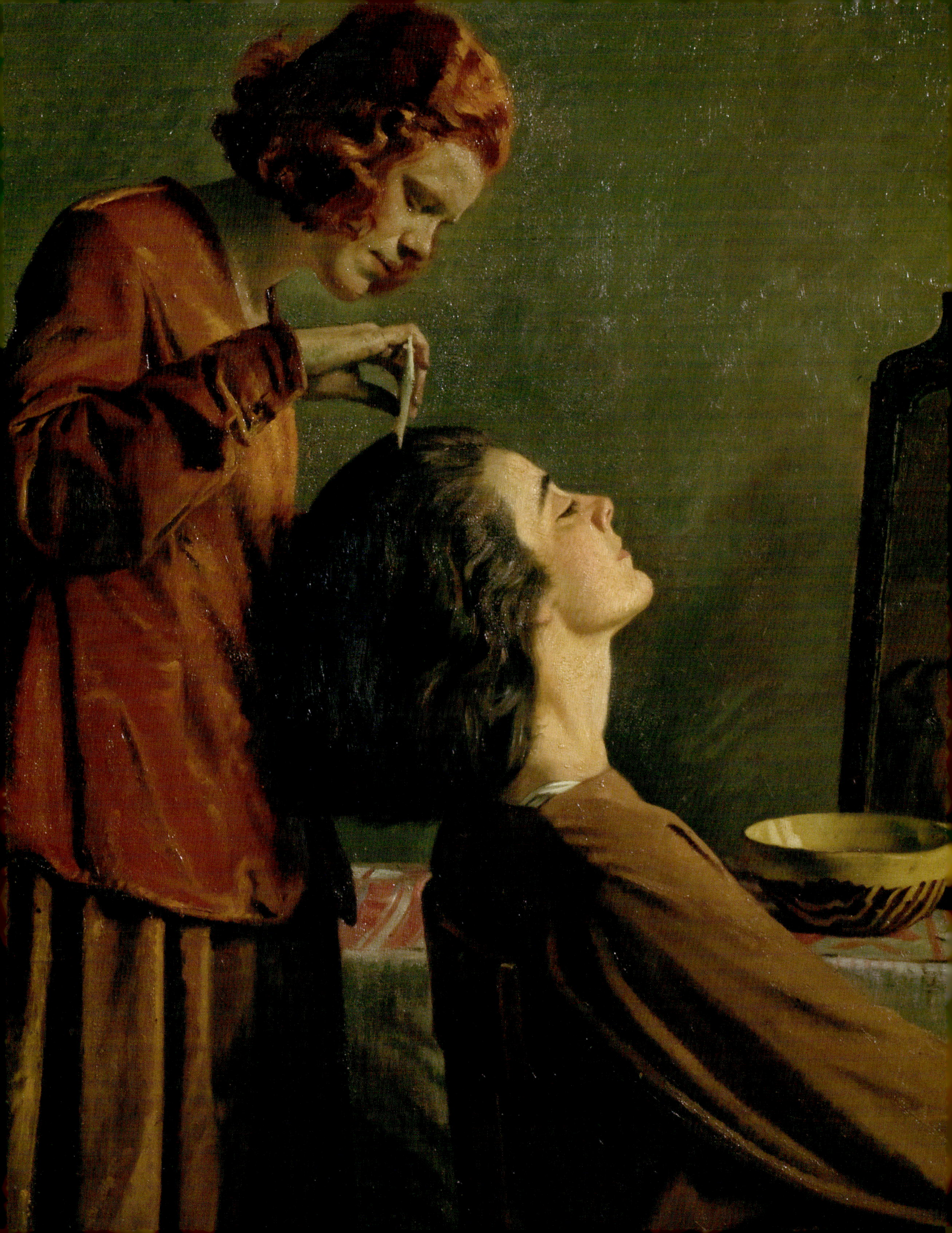

Paintings Without Reproductions

This section lists all the paintings that have not been included in the main pages of the catalogue. They were excluded as it was not possible to photograph them for this project. Additional information relating to acquisition credit lines or loan details is also included. For this reason the information below is not repeated in the Further Information section.

Leicestershire

Hinckley and Bosworth Borough Council

Bass, W. M. *The Easter Ceremony*, 62.5 x 74, oil on canvas, PCF4, untraced find, collection refused permission to reproduce images

Bass, W. M. *The Mouse Hunt*, 63 x 75, oil on canvas, PCF2, untraced find, collection refused permission to reproduce images

Ben *Grey Church*, 1985 (?), 30 x 23, oil on board, PCF8, untraced find, collection refused permission to reproduce images

Billinghame, Wilfred Ernest c.1882–1965, *River and Trees*, 39 x 49, oil on canvas, PCF1, untraced find, collection refused permission to reproduce images

British (English) School *Shepherd Boy and His Dog at a Pond*, 50 x 75, oil on canvas, PCF3, untraced find, collection refused permission to reproduce images

Dorr, Harry 1872–1950, *A Middleburg Mill*, 30 x 40, oil on canvas, PCF6, untraced find, collection refused permission to reproduce images

Haddon, Trevor 1864–1941, *A Street in Spain*, 86 x 110, oil on canvas (?), PCF5, untraced find, collection refused permission to reproduce images

Hayes, M. J. (attributed to) *Children by a Stream*, 45 x 60, oil on canvas, PCF14, untraced find, collection refused permission to reproduce images

Landseer, Edwin Henry (copy of) 1802–1873, *A Distinguished Member of the Humane Society*, 71 x 91, oil on canvas, PCF12, untraced find, collection refused permission to reproduce images

Linnell, James Thomas 1826–1905, *Driving Home the Flock*, 79 x 127, oil on canvas, PCF11, untraced find, collection refused permission to reproduce images

Moore, J. E. *Eddlesborough Church, Buckinghamshire*, 33.5 x 43.5, oil on canvas, PCF7, untraced find, collection refused permission to reproduce images

Ross, Robert Thorburn 1816–1876, *O Wha's at the Window*, 90 x 74.5, oil on canvas, PCF9, untraced find, collection refused permission to reproduce images

unknown artist *Garden Scene with Ladies and a Gentleman Seated*, 45 x 75, oil on canvas, PCF13, untraced find, collection refused permission to reproduce images

unknown artist *Italian Landscape with an Angel, a Mother and a Child*, 100 x 125.5, oil on canvas, PCF10, untraced find, collection refused permission to reproduce images

Leicester Arts and Museums Service

Allen, Hugh *Hoby, Leicestershire*, oil, L.F216.1954.6.0, purchased from A. de la Poer Rowbotham, 1954, not available at the time of photography

Bosher, Donald 1912–1977, *Leicester from Enderby Lane*, 38 x 53.5, oil, L.F25.1989.0.0, gift from Mrs E. E. Bosher, 1989, not available at the time of photography

Bright, Henry 1814–1873, *Welsh Ravine*, 143.5 x 109.2, oil on canvas, L.F13.1882.0.0, gift from William Whetstone, 1882, not available at the time of photography

British School *Guildhall Lane, Leicester*, 1840–1850, 38.7 x 48.9, oil, L.F1.1958.0.0, not available at the time of photography

British School *Ellen Winks, née Goadby, of Ashby-de-la-Zouch (1798–1864)*, 75 x 61, oil on canvas, L.F31.1959.0.0, gift from Mr Louis F. Winks, 1959, not available at the time of photography

British School *Joseph Foulkes Winks*, 75 x 61, oil on canvas, L.F32.1959.0.0, gift from Mr Louis F. Winks, 1959, not available at the time of photography

British School *Old West Bridge*, oil, L.F69.1932.0.0, gift from Miss A. D. West, 1932, not available at the time of photography

British School *St Mary's Church, Leicester*, oil, L.F70.1932.0.0, gift from Miss A. D. West, not available at the time of photography

Cope, Charles West 1811–1890, *Sheep Shearing*, 30.5 x 15.9, oil, L.F16.1969.0.0, bequeathed by Mr Colin Dare Bernard Ellis, 1969, not available at the time of photography

Davies, Edward 1841–1920, *The Road to Kyle Rae, Isle of Skye*, 20.3 x 30.5, oil on cardboard, L.F21.1910.0.0, purchased from the artist, 1910, not available at the time of photography

Dawson, Henry 1811–1878, *Landscape with Children*, 21.6 x 31.8, oil, L.F20.1947.0.0, purchased from the sale of the effects of J. Moore, 1947, not available at the time of photography

Glenton, F. Ivor b.c.1936, *A Lock near Aylestone, Leicestershire*, 14.6 x 29.2, oil on canvas, L.F361.1956.0.0, purchased from the artist, 1956, not available at the time of photography

Hill, H. *Old Belgrave*, 1901, 43.8 x 29.2, oil, L.F1110.1951.0.0, gift from W. A. Jones, 1951, not available at the time of photography

Lithiby, Beatrice Ethel 1889–1966, *The Oldest Industry*, oil on board, L.F3.1996.3.0, transferred from Hinckley Library, 1996, not available at the time of photography

Marshall, Benjamin 1767–1835, *'Lord Rous Shrapnel' with Boyce the Trainer and Ridden by W. Arnull*, oil on canvas, L.F36.1987.0.0, not available at the time of photography

Nunney, Reginald 1895–1922, *Factories on the Canal, Leicester*, 37 x 32, oil on canvas & millboard, L.F4.1939.0.0, gift from Mrs Florie Gregory, 1939, not available at the time of photography

O'Connor, James Arthur 1791–1841, *On the Dargle, County Wicklow, Ireland*, 17.3 x 22.5, oil on millboard, L.F7.1889.0.0, purchased from the Palser Gallery, 1889, not available at the time of photography

Pettinger, John Frederick 1877–1939, *Evening, Wells, Somerset*, 37.5 x 47.6, oil on canvas, L.F2.1927.0.0, purchased from the artist, 1927, not available at the time of photography

Pettinger, John Frederick 1877–1939, *Harbour, St Ives, Cornwall*, 40 x 47, oil on canvas, L.F40.1944.1.0, purchased from Mrs J. F. Pettinger, 1944, not available at the time of photography

Pettinger, John Frederick 1877–1939, *The Sluice Hole, Wells, Somerset*, 50.8 x 76.2, oil on canvas, L.F40.1944.3.0, purchased from Mrs J. F. Pettinger, 1944, not available at the time of photography

Pettinger, John Frederick 1877–1939, *Two Figures on the Quay*, 28.5 x 30.6, oil on cardboard, L.F40.1944.4.0, purchased from Mrs J. F. Pettinger, 1944, not available at the time of photography

Reeve-Fowkes, Amy 1886–1968, *Old Aylestone Bridge, Leicestershire*, 1906, 25.3 x 33, tempera on board, L.F119.1981.0.0, gift from Mrs Margaret J. Cook, 1982, not available at the time of photography

Roberts, Albert Thomas 1868–1923, *Courtyard, Hotel Petit Andely, France*, 27.3 x 33.3, oil on canvas, L.F19.1923.0.0, gift from Mrs A. T. Roberts in memory of the artist, 1923, not available at the time of photography

Roberts, Albert Thomas 1868–1923, *Le quai, Caudebec-on-Caux, France*, 23 x 32, oil on board, L.F17.1923.0.0, gift from Mrs A. T. Roberts in memory of the artist, 1923, not available at the time of photography

Staynes, George *Hoby, near Leicester*, 24.1 x 31.7, oil on canvas, L.F216.1954.8.0, purchased from A. de la Poer Rowbotham, 1954, not available at the time of photography

Thorpe, George O. *Cottage at Barwell, Leicestershire, in Snow*, 50.8 x 68.6, oil on canvas, L.F35.1952.0.0, gift from Miss L. F. Thorpe, 1952, not available at the time of photography

unknown artist 18th C, *George (1653–1708), Prince of Denmark*, 128 x 104, oil on canvas, L.F6.1894.2.0, bequeathed by Mr William Kelly, 1894, not available at the time of photography

unknown artist 18th C, *Landscape with a Figure and Boats*, 25.2 x 30.7, oil, L.F20.1935.13.1, bequeathed by Mr John William Cutler Bickley, 1935, not available at the time of photography

unknown artist 18th C, *Queen Anne of Denmark (1574–1619)*, 127.5 x 104, oil on canvas, L.F6.1894.1.0, bequeathed by Mr William Kelly, 1894, not available at the time of photography

unknown artist 19th C, *Portrait of a Man*, 30 x 25, oil, L.F20.1935.12.0, bequeathed by Mr John William Cutler Bickley, 1935, not available at the time of photography

unknown artist *Portrait of a Young Lady*, 94 x 81.3, oil on canvas, L.F432.1953.0.0, gift from Mrs E. F. Neep, not available at the time of photography

unknown artist *The Guildhall*, 38.7 x 49.5, oil, L.F62.1952.0.0, not available at the time of photography

unknown artist *Thomas Rose, Last Town Crier*, oil, L.F37.1939.0.0, acquired, 1939, not available at the time of photography

Ward, George *Old Granby Toll House*, 24.5 x 39.4, oil on panel, L.F631.1951.0.0, bequeathed by Mrs Anna Clowes, 1905, not available at the time of photography

Warren, William White (attributed to) 1832–1915, *St Mary de Castro from the River Soar, Leicester*, 1892, 35 x 53, oil on board, L.F87.1991.0.0, not available at the time of photography

Facing page: Rothenstein, William, 1872–1945, *The Toilet* (detail), 1924, Leicester Arts and Museums Service (p. 78)

West, Benjamin (attributed to) 1738–1820, *The Holy Family*, 24.8, oil on paper & card, L. F26.1936.0.0, purchased from Mr A. Renals, 1936, not available at the time of photography

Leicestershire County Council Artworks Collection

Southall, Derek b.1930, *Trails*, oil on canvas, 811, not available at the time of photography

Leicestershire County Council Museums Service

Hollams, Florence Mabel 1877–1963, *Margot*, 29 x 39, oil on wood, L.H278.1957.1.0, gift from Dr Henry Field, 1957, not available at the time of photography

Charnwood Borough Council Art Collection

Morris, Will active 2002, *That's When the Lights Went Out*, APPW24, purchased from the artist, 2002, not available at the time of photography

Platts, Christian active 2000, *Time Flies*, mixed media, APPW16, purchased from the artist, 2000, not available at the time of photography

Raper, Danny active 2005, *Eeee Heee in Blue*, household paint on aluminium, APPW28, purchased from the artist, 2005, not available at the time of photography

Lincolnshire

Loughborough University

Oliver, Peter 1927–2006, *Mending Nets*, 1960, 39.5 x 106, oil on canvas, PCF45, purchased from Leicestershire County, 1960, not available at the time of photography

Boston Borough Council

Sharp, H. *St Botolph's Church, Boston, Lincolnshire*, 22.5 x 14.5, oil on canvas, 1957.21, untraced find, not available at the time of photography

White, Charles Ernest 1891–c.1970, *Landscape Scene*, 24 x 32.5, oil on canvas & board, 1971.32, bequeathed, 1971, not available at the time of photography

Willoughby, W. *Two Horses*, 62.5 x 24, oil on canvas, 1948.6, purchased, not available at the time of photography

Gainsborough Old Hall

Bartholomew, F. W. active 1878, *Stormy Seascape*, 43.7 x 74.2, oil on canvas, GANOH1378, untraced find, not available at the time of photography

Bell, J. S. *Bridge over a River**, 75 x 45, oil on canvas, GANOH1390, untraced find, not available at the time of photography

Brotherton, L. A. active 1902, *Landscape with Buildings, a Woman and Cows*, 51.2 x 61, oil on canvas, GANOH1384, untraced find, not available at the time of photography

Callcott, Augustus Wall 1779–1844, *Scene across a Bay with Figures*, 64 x 77, oil on canvas, GANOH1373, untraced find, not available at the time of photography

Crane, I. active 19th C, *The River Trent at Gainsborough, Lincolnshire, with a view of the Wharfs*, 40.5 x 50.8, oil on canvas, GANOH4220, untraced find, not available at the time of photography

Crome, John 1768–1821, *Landscape with Trees*, 34.5 x 46.5, oil on canvas, GANOH4299, untraced find, not available at the time of photography

N. S. H. D. *Landscape with a Mountain**, 10.9 x 14.7, oil on board, GANOH1394, untraced find, not available at the time of photography

De Wys, K. *Portrait of a Man with a Bow Tie*, 46 x 56.5, oil on canvas, GANOH1369, untraced find, not available at the time of photography

Duckmanton, Nellie active 1903–1907, *View of a Beach with a Cliff, and a Man Carrying a Red Flag*, 40.5 x 61, oil on canvas, GANOH1385, gift, not available at the time of photography

Duckmanton, Nellie (attributed to) active 1903–1907, *Still Life with a Fan, Wine Glass and Cape Gooseberries*, 1907, 40.5 x 61, oil on canvas, GANOH1368, gift, not available at the time of photography

Goldenshorr, F. *Landscape**, 14.6 x 20.5, oil on hardboard, GANOH1393, untraced find, not available at the time of photography

G. E. H. active c.1850–1899, *A Seated Man Smoking a Clay Pipe*, 40.3 x 30, oil on millboard, GANOH4594, untraced find, not available at the time of photography

Hannam, S. L. active c.1850–1899, *A White Dog and a Black Cat*, 26.8 x 36.5, oil on canvas, GANOH1346, untraced find, not available at the time of photography

F. K. active 1882, *A Young Boy Seated in a Red Armchair, Dressed Up in His Father's Slippers and Spectacles, Taking Snuff from a Snuff Box*, 20.5 x 15.4, oil on canvas, GANOH1349, untraced find, not available at the time of photography

F. K. active 1882, *A Young Girl Seated on a Wooden Chair, Dressed up in Her Mother's Spectacles and White Bonnet, Holding Knitting Needles*, 20.4 x 15.3, oil on canvas, GANOH1348, untraced find, not available at the time of photography

Linley, A. *Landscape with a Thatched Cottage and a Figure**, 29.5 x 39, oil on canvas, GANOH1377, gift, not available at the time of photography

Linley, A. *Sailing Ship, YH787**, 59.6 x 29, oil on canvas, GANOH1362, gift, not available at the time of photography

Mark, Anthony *Woman in a Landscape**, 18 x 51, oil on canvas, GANOH1392, untraced find, not available at the time of photography

Mars, A. *Landscape with a Cottage and the Sea**, 18 x 28.5, oil on canvas, GANOH1383, untraced find, not available at the time of photography

McCausland, Kathleen 1859–1930, *Unknown Gentleman with Spectacles*, 59.5 x 50, oil on canvas, GANOH1359, untraced find, not available at the time of photography

Meadows, William George c.1825–1907, *Bridge with Gondolas**, 49 x 74.5, oil on canvas, GANOH1381, gift, not available at the time of photography

Meadows, William George c.1825–1907, *Canal with Moored Gondolas**, 49.3 x 75, oil on canvas, GANOH1391, gift, not available at the time of photography

Miller, William active 19th C, *Stream with a Small Waterfall, Trees and Hills, with Sheep Grazing*, 63.5 x 89, oil on canvas, GANOH1387, untraced find, not available at the time of photography

Millner, William Edward 1849–1895, *Returning from Ploughing*, 1891, 30.5 x 51, oil on card, GANOH4596, untraced find, not available at the time of photography

Rose, Arthur active 1902, *Cob Horse*, 43.5 x 59, oil on canvas, GANOH2358, untraced find, not available at the time of photography

Taylor, T. active c.1850–1899, *Lea Green and Pump at Gainsborough, Lincolnshire*, 29.2 x 43.5, oil on canvas, GANOH5001, gift, not available at the time of photography

unknown artist *Landscape with a River Bank and Figures*, c.1750–1799, 24.5 x 45, oil on canvas, GANOH2354, untraced find, not available at the time of photography

unknown artist *A Middle-Aged Lady, Seated*, c.1800–1850, 89.7 x 68.8, oil on canvas, GANOH1352, untraced find, not available at the time of photography

unknown artist *Mary Patrington, née Hardy, Wife of Thomas Patrington*, c.1800–1850, 75.5 x 63, oil on canvas, GANOH1360, untraced find, not available at the time of photography

unknown artist *Thomas Patrick (?)*, c.1820–1850, 75 x 62, oil on canvas, GANOH1355, untraced find, not available at the time of photography

unknown artist *A Seated Man, Holding a Snuff Box*, c.1828, 90.5 x 70.5, oil on canvas, GANOH5019, untraced find, not available at the time of photography

unknown artist *An Old Gentleman with a Clarinet*, c.1850–1899, 42 x 29, oil on canvas, GANOH1363, untraced find, not available at the time of photography

unknown artist *William Hargrave Caldicott (d.1877)*, c.1855, 74.5 x 62.5, oil on canvas, GANOH2275, untraced find, not available at the time of photography

unknown artist 19th C, *A Middle-Aged Gentleman*, 90 x 69.5, oil on canvas, GANOH1353, untraced find, not available at the time of photography

unknown artist 19th C, *Fishing Scene, Walkerith Ferry, Lincolnshire*, 34.2 x 76, oil on canvas, GANOH4219, gift, not available at the time of photography

unknown artist *A Lady Wearing an Apron**, 37.9 x 28.9, oil on board, GANOH1367, untraced find, not available at the time of photography

unknown artist *Boot on a Book**, 27.5 x 38, oil on panel, GANOH4599, untraced find, not available at the time of photography

unknown artist *Cobbled Street**, 22.6 x 17.8, oil on panel, GANOH3836, untraced find, not available at the time of photography

unknown artist *Fruit with a Red Admiral Butterfly**, 29.5 x 36.5, oil on canvas, GANOH4293, untraced find, not available at the time of photography

unknown artist *Lady with Flowers**, 55 x 45, oil on canvas, GANOH2351, untraced find, not available at the time of photography

unknown artist *Landscape**, 36.5 x 49.5, oil on hardboard, GANOH1376, untraced find, not available at the time of photography

unknown artist *Landscape with Mountains**, 49.5 x 36.5, oil on hardboard, GANOH1379, untraced find, not available at the time of photography

unknown artist *Madonna and Child**, 33.1 x 26.6, oil on canvas, GANOH1372, untraced find, not available at the time of photography

unknown artist *Moses with the Ten Commandments**, 28.5 x 24.2, oil on millboard, GANOH1347, untraced find, not available at the time of photography

unknown artist *North Wing, Tower and East Wing of Gainsborough Old Hall, Lincolnshire**, 27.6 x 37.5, oil on canvas, GANOH4221, untraced find, not available at the time of photography

unknown artist *Rough Sea with a Sailing Ship**, 21.3 x 28.8, oil on millboard, GANOH2353, untraced find, not available at the time of photography

unknown artist *Rowing Boat with a Sail and Three Fishermen**, 21.5 x 28.5, oil on millboard, GANOH1345, untraced find, not available at the time of photography

unknown artist *Seascape with a Steam Ship**, 68.5 x 93, oil on canvas, GANOH5004, untraced find, not available at the time of photography

unknown artist *Still Life with Pink Geraniums*, 75 x 25, oil on canvas, GANOH5021, untraced find, not available at the time of photography

unknown artist *Still Life with White Lilies*, 75 x 24.3, oil on canvas, GANOH5020, untraced find, not available at the time of photography

unknown artist *Tumbling Stream**, 34.2 x 59.5, oil on canvas, GANOH1389, untraced find, not available at the time of photography

unknown artist *Unknown Gentleman, Seated**, 90.5 x 72.5, oil on canvas, GANOH1350, untraced find, not available at the time of photography

unknown artist *View of a Church**, 62.5 x 40.2, oil on hardboard, GANOH2352, gift, 1974, not available at the time of photography

unknown artist *Young Lady Seated*, 74 x 61.5, oil on canvas, GANOH2276, untraced find, not available at the time of photography

unknown artist *Young Lady Seated Underneath a Tree**, 49.5 x 38, oil on canvas, GANOH1371, untraced find, not available at the time of photography

Wall, B. active 19th C, *Seascape**, 29.4 x 60, oil on canvas, GANOH1380, untraced find, not available at the time of photography

Wilson, G. *Below Corton, Looking Towards Gunton and Lowestoft, Suffolk*, 20.3 x 25.4, oil on board, GANOH3658, untraced find, not available at the time of photography

North East Lincolnshire Museum Service

Bourne, J. active 1890s–1914, *SS 'Cerelia'*, oil on board, A.251, not available at the time of photography

Bunting, William Richard active 1886–1944, *The Brewster*, 1886, canvas, A.189, not available at the time of photography

Griffiths, Frederick *Two Fishermen*, oil on board, A.233, not available at the time of photography

Skelton, George 1855–1932, *Corporation Bridge*, 1927, oil, A.219, purchased, not available at the time of photography

unknown artist *Ships*, oil on board, A.186, not available at the time of photography

unknown artist *Steam Trawler, GY 487*, oil on canvas, A.263, not available at the time of photography

unknown artist *Steam Trawler, GY 1220*, oil on canvas, A.262, not available at the time of photography

unknown artist *The Quail, GY 215*, oil on board, A.266, not available at the time of photography

The Franklin Trust

Lee, Ken *The Bay of Naples, Italy*, 152 x 122, oil on canvas, 118, gift from Lincolnshire and Humberside Arts, 1991, not available at the time of photography

University of Lincoln

Pallas, G. *Untitled*, oil, AC09/00222, unknown acquisition method, not available at the time of photography

Louth Museum

Beale, Mary (attributed to) 1633–1699, *Portrait of an Unknown Youth*, 63.5 x 52.1, oil on canvas, W27, unknown acquisition method, not available at the time of photography

Dutch School *Interior Scene with Musicians*, 45 x 35, oil on oak panel, W268, found in Thorpe Hall, Louth, c.1850; purchased from Thorpe Hall, 1992, not available at the time of photography

Fitzroy, Harry (attributed to) *Hetty Sorrel's Toilette*, 50.8 x 38.1, oil on canvas, W211, purchased at auction, 2006, not available at the time of photography

Hubbard, Bennett 1806–1870, *Miss Cresswell's Paternal Grandfather*, 1843, 34.3 x 31.8, oil on canvas, W24, acquired from Louth Mechanics' Institute, 1957, not available at the time of photography

Hubbard, Bennett 1806–1870, *Ann Cresswell (1819–1840)* (painted from an engraving by Henry Thomas Ryall), 1846, 69.9 x 88.9, oil on canvas, W77, acquired from Louth Mechanics' Institute, 1957, not available at the time of photography

Hubbard, Bennett 1806–1870, *St James's Church, Louth, Lincolnshire, from Westgate Fields*, 1846, 33 x 43.2, oil on canvas, W61, acquired from Louth Mechanics' Institute, 1957, not available at the time of photography

Hubbard, Bennett 1806–1870, *Mr Tom Lawrence of Louth, Lincolnshire*, 1849, 81.3 x 68.6, oil on canvas, W32, acquired from Louth Mechanics' Institute, 1957, not available at the time of photography

Hubbard, Bennett 1806–1870, *John Campbell (1782–1852)*, 1851, 82 x 64, oil on canvas, W79, acquired from Louth Mechanics' Institute, 1957, not available at the time of photography

Hubbard, Bennett 1806–1870, *Mrs Creswell's Maternal Grandfather, Mr Beastle (or Beastall?)*, 1855, 33.7 x 30.5, oil on canvas, W23, acquired from Louth Mechanics' Institute, 1957, not available at the time of photography

Hubbard, Bennett 1806–1870, *Samuel Cresswell (1816–1909)*, 1857, 69.9 x 88.9, oil on canvas, W78, acquired from Louth Mechanics' Institute, 1957, not available at the time of photography

Hubbard, Bennett 1806–1870, *Little Cawthorpe, near Louth, Lincolnshire*, 1864, 47 x 58.4, oil on canvas, W42, gift from Mrs White, not available at the time of photography

Hubbard, Bennett 1806–1870, *Portrait of an Unknown Male*, 1867, 81.9 x 69.2, oil on canvas, W29, acquired from Louth Mechanics' Institute, 1957, not available at the time of photography

Hubbard, Bennett (attributed to) 1806–1870, *Scene Depicting a Canal Lock, Its Gates, Houses and a Bridge*, c.1850–1860, 52.1 x 76.8, oil on canvas, W189, acquired from Louth Mechanics' Institute, 1957, not available at the time of photography

Morton, Charles Reginald active 1917–1936, *Hubbard's Hills Watermill, Louth, Lincolnshire*, 1917, 68.6 x 54.6, oil on canvas, W213.2, donated by Miss Cherry Lill, 2007, not available at the time of photography

Morton, Charles Reginald active 1917–1936, *James Street, Louth, Lincolnshire, from the West*, 1917, 43.9 x 52.1, oil on canvas, W213.5, donated by Miss Cherry Hill, 2007, not available at the time of photography

Morton, Charles Reginald active 1917–1936, *Gable End of a Tower at the Edge of a Lake*, 1918, 74.3 x 48.9, oil on canvas, W123.3, donated by Miss Cherry Lill, 2007, not available at the time of photography

Morton, Charles Reginald active 1917–1936, *Sun, Roofs and St James's Church, Louth, Lincolnshire*, 1927, 83.3 x 73.7, oil on canvas, W75, gift, 1937, not available at the time of photography

Morton, Charles Reginald active 1917–1936, *St James's Church, Louth, from Gospelgate, Lincolnshire*, 1936, 129.6 x 89.9, oil on board, W213.1, donated by Miss Cherry Lill, 2007, not available at the time of photography

Morton, Charles Reginald active 1917–1936, *Half-Timbered Jettied Building in a Street Scene*, 56.5 x 36.2, oil on canvas, W213.4, donated by Miss Cherry Lill, 2007, not available at the time of photography

Sharpley, Stella active 1890s–1920s, *Two-Mast Sailing Ships Stranded on Mablethorpe Beach, Lincolnshire*, 1894, 15.2 x 22.9, oil on canvas, W118, gift from the artist, not available at the time of photography

Smith, Peter G. *Scene of a Modern Chapel, Louth, Lincolnshire*, 33 x 42.5, oil, W124, gift from the artist's widow, not available at the time of photography

Smith, Peter G. (attributed to) *A Chapel and a House, Louth, Lincolnshire*, 35.6 x 45.7, oil on canvas, W125, gift from the artist's widow, not available at the time of photography

Smith, Peter G. (attributed to) *Landscape of a Chapel, Louth, Lincolnshire*, 30.5 x 43.2, oil, W123, gift from the artist's widow, not available at the time of photography

Spooner, Arthur 1873–1961, *Scene of Crocquet Players at Welbeck Abbey, Nottinghamshire*, 1918, 44.5 x 52.1, oil on canvas, W35, acquired from Louth Mechanics' Institute, 1957, not available at the time of photography

Spooner, Arthur 1873–1961, *Richard William Goulding of Louth (1868–1929), FSA*, 1922, 65.5 x 52.5, oil on canvas, W34, acquired from Louth Mechanics' Institute, 1957, not available at the time of photography

unknown artist *The Last Voyage of the Sloop 'Annieforlander'*, 1914, 45 x 65, oil on canvas, W165, gift from Mr A. Brooks, not available at the time of photography

unknown artist *North Facade of the Methodist Chapel, Eastgate, Louth, Lincolnshire*, 43.2 x 53.3, oil on canvas, W83, gift from Councillor P. Smith, not available at the time of photography

unknown artist *Primitive Methodist Chapel, New Market, Louth, Lincolnshire*, 38.1 x 43.2, oil on canvas, W84, acquired from Louth Mechanics' Institute, 1957, not available at the time of photography

Wallis, Thomas Wilkinson 1822–1903, *Self Portrait*, 1897, 59 x 49, oil on canvas, W76, acquired from Louth Mechanics' Institute, 1957, not available at the time of photography

Zuccaro, Federico (copy of) c.1541–1609, *Sir John Bolle (1560–1606)*, 1812, 232.4 x 223.5, oil on canvas, W201, gift from Mrs E. Hunter, 2002, not available at the time of photography

North Lincolnshire Museums Service

W. B. *Wild Roses*, 1909, 19.5 x 15, oil, 12, not available at the time of photography

Callow, John 1822–1878, *Shipping in the River*, 1865, 98 x 148, oil on canvas, 1955. 219. 1, gift from Mr W. H. Millett, 1955, not available at the time of photography

Cocking *Winterton Weir Pond, Lincolnshire*, oil, BABDM. 570. 1, gift from Mrs B. Burkill, 1993, not available at the time of photography

Holtby *Baysgarth House, Barton-upon-Humber, Lincolnshire*, c.1998, oil, 1999. 060, gift from the artist, 1999, not available at the time of photography

Jewitt, George 1894–1949, *Untitled*, 1925, 17 x 21.5, oil, BABDM. 125, gift from M. Straw, 1983, not available at the time of photography

Melby, Wilhelm 1824–1882, *Paddle Steamer off a Rocky Coast*, 1858, 101 x 150, oil, 1973. 214. 2, acquired, 1965, not available at the time of photography

Steen, Jan (after) 1626–1679, *Dutch Peasants*, 1837–1901, 21 x 16.5, oil on panel, ART1953. 010, gift from Mrs C. Burkill, 1953, not available at the time of photography

M. E. T. *Two Daffodils and a Rose Bush*, 1899, 67.5 x 26.5, oil on board, 49, not available at the time of photography

Torr, Anne *Sheep Dog*, 1882, oil on board, 1972. 031. 1, purchased from Thornborrow and Co., 1972, not available at the time of photography

unknown artist *Matthew Pearson of Selby (1794–1870)*, c.1830, 113.4 x 89, oil, 65, gift from Selby Museum, not available at the time of photography

unknown artist 19th C, *Portrait of a Seated Man Holding Papers and Spectacles*, 110 x 90, oil on canvas, 67, not available at the time of photography

unknown artist *Burning Ship*, oil, 1961. 034. 2, gift from Mr Cross, 1961, not available at the time of photography

Wright, Richard (copy of) 1735–1773, *Fishing in the Straits*, 41.3 x 55.5, oil on canvas, 1963. 031. 4b, gift from Mr R. Hawke, 1963, not available at the time of photography

Further Information

The paintings listed in this section have additional information relating to one or more of the five categories outlined below. This extra information is only provided where it is applicable and where it exists. Paintings listed in this section follow the same order as in the illustrated pages of the catalogue.

I The full name of the artist if this was too long to display in the illustrated pages of the catalogue. Such cases are marked in the catalogue with a (...).

II The full title of the painting if this was too long to display in the illustrated pages of the catalogue. Such cases are marked in the catalogue with a (...).

III Acquisition information or acquisition credit lines as well as information about loans, copied from the records of the owner collection.

IV Artist copyright credit lines where the copyright owner has been traced. Exhaustive efforts have been made to locate the copyright owners of all the images included within this catalogue and to meet their requirements. Any omissions or mistakes brought to our attention will be duly attended to and corrected in future publications.

V The credit line of the lender of the transparency if the transparency has been borrowed. Bridgeman images are available subject to any relevant copyright approvals from the Bridgeman Art Library at www.bridgemanart.com

Ashby-de-la-Zouch Museum

British (English) School *View of Ashby-de-la-Zouch Castle, Leicestershire, with Passers-By*, purchased at Christie's, 1997

Castle Donington Museum

Charlton, Margaret c.1905–c.1980, *Little Lane in Derbyshire*, gift from Mrs Lillah Hooley, 2000
Hurt, Henry d.c.1980, *St Edward's Church, Castle Donington, Leicestershire*
Jones, Dorothy d.c.1990, *Castle Donington Wakes, Leicestershire*, gift from Mrs Lillah Hooley, 2000
Redgate, Arthur Walker 1860–1906, *Chain Bridge, King's Mills, Leicestershire*, gift from Mrs Lillah Hooley, 2000
Redgate, Arthur Walker 1860–1906, *Cottage in Fields*, gift from Mrs Lillah Hooley, 2000
Trotter, Diana b.1923, *Shardlow Water Meadows, Derbyshire*, gift from the artist, 2010, © Castle Donington Museum

Hinckley and District Museum

Billinghame, Wilfred Ernest c.1882–1965, *Open Country*, gift from a private donor, 1997

John Cleveland College

Bass, Stanley *Dr Cheshire, First British Orthopaedic Surgeon*
Bate, William *Boxers*, acquired, c.1988
Bate, William *Gymnast*, acquired, c.1988
Cartwright, Reg b.1938, *The Schoolgirl*, © the artist/Bridgeman Art Library
Jarvis, Timothy *Age of Aspirations*
Littlehales, Thomas Paul b.1945, *Endangered Species*, © the artist
Organ, Bryan b.1935, *Frank Oldham, Former Headmaster of John Cleveland College*, commissioned, 1963, © Bryan Organ & the Redfern Gallery, London
Whitrow, Kirsty b.1960, *The Beast Is Asleep*, © the artist
Wilson, Frank Avray 1914–2009, *Paris* (3 panels), © the artist's estate

Kegworth Museum

Hudson, George Frederick 1895–1966, *Sir John Kirk's Birthplace*, on long-term loan from Mrs G. Youngs
Stanway, S. *Sir Winston Churchill (1874–1965)*, donated, 2005
Toon, Tommy d.1962, *Mill Lane, Kegworth, Leicestershire*, gift, 2007

Kibworth C. of E. Primary School

Cartwright, Reg b.1938, *View of Gumley Lake, Leicestershire*, commissioned, © the artist/ Bridgeman Art Library

Leicester Arts and Museums Service

Adams, Charles James 1859–1931, *The Ferry*, gift from Mr G. F. Adnitt in memory of his late wife, 1973
Adams, Norman 1927–2005, *Brants Ghyll, North Yorkshire, through Foliage*, gift from the Friends of the Museums Fund, 1958, © the artist's estate
Adams, Norman 1927–2005, *Rainbow Painting 4, Easter Series*, gift from the Contemporary Art Society, 1973, © the artist's estate
Adcock, John Wilton 1863–1930, *Cattle at a Stream*
Adcock, John Wilton 1863–1930, *On the Cornish Coast*
Adcock, John Wilton 1863–1930, *Stream with Harvesters*
Akkerman, Philip b.1957, *Self Portrait No.92*, gift from the Contemporary Art Society, 2000, © the artist
Akkerman, Philip b.1957, *Self Portrait No.42*, gift from the Contemporary Art Society, 2000, © the artist
Akkerman, Philip b.1957, *Self Portrait No.31*, gift from the Contemporary Art Society, 2000, © the artist
Akkerman, Philip b.1957, *Self Portrait No.38*, gift from the Contemporary Art Society, 2000, © the artist
Alberti, Cherubino (follower of) 1553–1615, *Judith with the Head of Holofernes*, gift from Mrs Clifford in memory of her husband, Alderman R. S. Clifford; transferred from Loughborough County Libraries, 1980
Anderson, Sophie 1823–1912, *A Neapolitan Boy*, bequeathed by Mr Henry Snow, 1894
Armfield, George 1810–1893, *The Breakfast Party*, bequeathed by Miss Emily Frances Dalton, 1900
Artaud, William 1763–1823, *Portrait of a Lady*, bequeathed by Miss Emily Frances Dalton, 1900
Auerbach, Frank Helmuth b.1931, *Bruton Street Building Site, London*, purchased from Mrs Monika Kinley with the assistance of the Museums and Galleries Commission/Victoria and Albert Museum Purchase Grant Fund, 1976, © the artist
Bacon, Francis 1909–1992, *Lying Figure No.1*, purchased from Marlborough Fine Art Ltd with the assistance of the Museums and Galleries Commission/ Victoria and Albert Museum Purchase Grant Fund, 1960, © estate of Francis Bacon. All rights reserved, DACS 2012
Baker, Thomas 1809–1869, *Felling Timber*, gift from Mr George Stannage, 1881
Balmer, Barbara b.1929, *Domenica*, purchased from the artist, 1996, © the artist
Banner, Delmar Harmond 1896–1983, *Scafell from Birker Moor, Eskdale, Cumberland*, gift from Mrs Delmar Banner, 1948, © the artist's estate
Barnard, Thomas Henslow 1898–1992, *Still Life*, transferred from Hinckley Library, 1996
Bassano, Jacopo the elder (follower of) c.1510–1592, *Two Peasants with Animals*, purchased from Thomas Agnew and Sons Ltd, 1939
Bayes, Walter 1869–1956, *The Bather*, gift from the Contemporary Art Society, 1929, © the artist's estate
Baynes, Keith 1887–1977, *Still Life, Flowers*, purchased from Messrs Reid and Lefevre, 1944
Beaton, Angus b.1948, *Sid Barrett's Garden*, gift from Allen Freer, 2006, © the artist
Beaumont, George Howland 1753–1827, *Derwentwater, Cumberland*, purchased from Warner, Sheppard and Wade, 1953
Beaumont, George Howland 1753–1827, *Peel Castle in a Storm, Isle of Man*, purchased from Sir Francis Beaumont with the assistance of the Museums and Galleries Commission/Victoria and Albert Museum Purchase Grant Fund, 1989
Beaumont, George Howland 1753–1827, *View near Keswick, Cumberland*, purchased from Mr R. Beaumont, 1971
Beaumont, George Howland 1753–1827, *A Ruined Abbey*, purchased from Warner, Sheppard and Wade, 1953
Beaumont, George Howland 1753–1827, *Keswick Lake, Cumberland*, purchased from

Warner, Sheppard and Wade, 1953
Beaumont, George Howland 1753–1827, *Landscape with a Bridge*, purchased from Warner, Sheppard and Wade, 1953
Beaumont, George Howland 1753–1827, *Derwentwater, Cumberland*, purchased from Warner, Sheppard and Wade, 1953
Beaumont, George Howland 1753–1827, *Derwentwater, Cumberland*, on long-term loan from a private collection, since 1982
Beaumont, George Howland 1753–1827, *Coleorton, Leicestershire*, purchased from Mr B. Halliday, 1916
Beaumont, George Howland 1753–1827, *Wooded Landscape*, purchased from Mr F. T. Turner, 1946
Beaumont, George Howland 1753–1827, *Banks of the Greta, Keswick, Cumberland*, purchased from Warner, Sheppard and Wade, 1953
Beaumont, George Howland 1753–1827, *Broughton Castle, Lancashire*, purchased from Warner, Sheppard and Wade, 1953
Beaumont, George Howland 1753–1827, *Grange Bridge in Borrowdale, Cumberland*, purchased from Warner, Sheppard and Wade, 1953
Beaumont, George Howland 1753–1827, *River Scene with Figures*, purchased from Warner, Sheppard and Wade, 1953
Beaumont, George Howland 1753–1827, *Keswick Lake, Cumberland* (recto), on long-term loan from the National Coal Board
Beaumont, George Howland 1753–1827, *Landscape with a Waterfall* (verso), on long-term loan from the National Coal Board
Beaumont, George Howland 1753–1827, *Swiss Landscape*, purchased from Warner, Sheppard and Wade, 1953
Beaumont, George Howland 1753–1827, *Swiss Landscape*, purchased from Warner, Sheppard and Wade, 1953
Beaumont, George Howland 1753–1827, *View near Coleorton, Leicestershire*, purchased from Warner, Sheppard and Wade, 1953
Beaumont, George Howland 1753–1827, *St Lorice, Ariccia, Albano, Italy*, purchased from Warner, Sheppard and Wade, 1953
Beaumont, George Howland 1753–1827, *Landscape with Figures*, purchased from Warner, Sheppard and Wade, 1953
Beaumont, George Howland 1753–1827, *Near Coleorton, Leicestershire*, on long-term loan from a private collection, since 1982
Beaumont, George Howland 1753–1827, *A View in Italy*, on long-term loan from the National Coal Board
Beaumont, George Howland 1753–1827, *An Autumn Wood*, on long-term loan from a private collection, since 1982
Beaumont, George Howland 1753–1827, *Applethwaite, Cumberland*, on long-term loan from the National Coal Board
Beaumont, George Howland 1753–1827, *Hills with Trees in the Foreground* (recto), on long-term loan from the National Coal Board
Beaumont, George Howland 1753–1827, *Landscape* (verso), on long-term loan from the National Coal Board
Beaumont, George Howland 1753–1827, *Landscape*, on long-term loan from the National Coal Board
Beaumont, George Howland 1753–1827, *Landscape*, gift from Mr A. C. Sewter, 1962
Beaumont, George Howland 1753–1827, *Landscape*, purchased at Sotheby's, 1953
Beaumont, George Howland 1753–1827, *Landscape with a Bridge*, on long-term loan from the National Coal Board
Beaumont, George Howland 1753–1827, *Mountain Road*, on long-term loan from the National Coal Board
Beaumont, George Howland 1753–1827, *Mountain Scenery*, on long-term loan from the National Coal Board
Beaumont, George Howland 1753–1827, *Mountain, Trees and a Lake*, on long-term loan from the National Coal Board
Beaumont, George Howland 1753–1827, *Mountainous Landscape with a Lake*, on long-term loan from the National Coal Board
Beaumont, George Howland 1753–1827, *Mountainous Landscape with a Waterfall and Figures*, on long-term loan from the National Coal Board
Beaumont, George Howland 1753–1827, *View near Applethwaite, Cumberland*, on long-term loan from the National Coal Board
Beaumont, George Howland 1753–1827, *Weymouth Bay, Dorset*
Beccafumi, Domenico 1484–1551, *The Holy Family with Saint John the Baptist*, purchased from P. and D. Colnaghi and Co. Ltd with the assistance of the Museums and Galleries Commission/Victoria and Albert Museum Purchase Grant Fund and the Friends of the Museum Fund, 1965
Beechey, William 1753–1839, *William Salte (c.1746–1817)*, bequeathed by Miss E. F. Lockwood, 1924
Bell, Trevor b.1930, *Strange Blue*, purchased from the Waddington Galleries, 1960, © the artist
Bell, Vanessa 1879–1961, *The Spanish Lady*, gift from the Contemporary Art Society, 1924, © 1961 estate of Vanessa Bell courtesy Henrietta Garnett
Bell, Vanessa 1879–1961, *Clive Bell (1881–1964), and Family*, gift from the Contemporary Art Society, 1927, © 1961 estate of Vanessa Bell courtesy Henrietta Garnett
Bellany, John b.1942, *Lune de miel (Towards the Lighthouse)* (triptych, left wing), purchased from Mrs Monika Kinley with the assistance of the Museums and Galleries Commission/Victoria and Albert Museum Purchase Grant Fund, 1982, © the artist/Bridgeman Art Library
Bellany, John b.1942, *Lune de miel (Towards the Lighthouse)* (triptych, centre panel), purchased from Mrs Monika Kinley with the assistance of the Museums and Galleries Commission/Victoria and Albert Museum Purchase Grant Fund, 1982, © the artist/Bridgeman Art Library
Bellany, John b.1942, *Lune de miel (Towards the Lighthouse)* (triptych, right wing), purchased from Mrs Monika Kinley with the assistance of the Museums and Galleries Commission/Victoria and Albert Museum Purchase Grant Fund, 1982, © the artist/Bridgeman Art Library
Bembo, Bonifazio (attributed to) c.1420–1482, *A Martyr*, purchased at Sotheby's, 1950
Bembo, Bonifazio (attributed to) c.1420–1482, *Saint Lawrence*, purchased at Sotheby's, 1950
Benson, Edward 1808–1863, *George Bristow (1803–1896)*, gift from Miss Elizabeth Cann, 1943
Bevan, Robert Polhill 1865–1925, *Polish Landscape*, gift from Miss Edith Bevan, 1937
Bevan, Robert Polhill 1865–1925, *From the Artist's Window*, purchased from Messrs Reid and Lefevre, 1944, photo credit: Bridgeman Art Library
Bizley, Roy 1930–1999, *Terrace*, acquired, 1999, © the artist's estate
Bizley, Roy 1930–1999, *Terrace*, acquired, 1999, © the artist's estate
Bizley, Roy 1930–1999, *Terrace*, acquired, 1999, © the artist's estate
Bizley, Roy 1930–1999, *Terrace*, acquired, 1999, © the artist's estate
Bizley, Roy 1930–1999, *Iceland I*, purchased from Mrs Pat Bizley by the friends of the artist and presented to Leicester Arts and Museums Service with the assistance of the City of Leicester Museums Trust, 1999, © the artist's estate
Blaas, Eugen von 1843–1931, *A Venetian Courtship*, purchased from Arthur Tooth & Sons Ltd, 1907
Blinks, Thomas 1860–1912, *Pointers in a Landscape*, bequeathed by Ernest Edward Cook through the National Art Collections Fund, 1955
Blinks, Thomas 1860–1912, *Two Setters in a Landscape*, bequeathed by Ernest Edward Cook through the National Art Collections Fund, 1955
Bloch, Martin 1883–1954, *Fehrbelliner Platz, Berlin*, purchased from Campbell and Franks Ltd with the assistance of the Museums and Galleries Commission/Victoria and Albert Museum Purchase Grant Fund, 1978, © Martin Bloch Trust
Bloch, Martin 1883–1954, *Laburnum and May Trees*, acquired, 1955, © Martin Bloch Trust
Bloomfield, Rib b.1948, *Landscape 19*, purchased from Susan Loppert with the assistance of the Calouste Gulbenkian Foundation, 1976, © the artist
Blow, Sandra 1925–2006, *Composition*, purchased from the artist with the assistance of the Calouste Gulbenkian Foundation, 1963, © the artist's estate
Bomberg, David 1890–1957, *Grief*, purchased from Mrs Margaret Fisher, 1982, © estate of David Bomberg. All rights reserved, DACS 2012
Bomberg, David 1890–1957, *Flowers in Sunlight*, gift from Mrs D. Davies-Rees, 1987, © estate of David Bomberg. All rights reserved, DACS 2012
Bomberg, David 1890–1957, *Landscape*, purchased from Mrs Lillian Bomberg, 1961, © estate of David Bomberg. All rights reserved, DACS 2012
Bombled, Louis Charles 1862–1927, *A Squall from the North-East*, purchased from Mr George Stannage, 1881
Bone, Stephen 1904–1958, *Liberty Men, Weymouth, Dorset*, transferred from Hinckley Library, 1996, © estate of Stephen Bone. All rights reserved, DACS 2012
Bonington, Richard Parkes 1802–1828, *The Old Jetty, Boulogne, France*, purchased from Mrs L. D. Pearson, 1936
Bosch, Hieronymus (follower of) c.1450–1516, *The Temptation of Saint Anthony*, purchased from Tomas Harris Ltd, 1936
Boudin, Eugène Louis 1824–1898, *Le Havre, France, l'avant-port*, bequeathed by Mrs Gladys E. M. Calthrop through the National Art Collections Fund, 1980
Boyd, Arthur 1920–1999, *Bridegroom Drinking from a Creek*, purchased from the Zwemmer Gallery with the assistance of the Friends of the Museum Fund, 1963
Boyd, Fionnuala b.1944 & **Evans, Leslie** b.1945, *Old Picture*, purchased from Susan Loppert with the assistance of the Calouste-Gulbenkian Foundation, 1977, © the artists
Boyd, Fionnuala b.1944 & **Evans, Leslie** b.1945, *Christopher Wright (b.1945)*, gift from the sitter, 1988, © the artists
Brandard, Robert 1805–1862, *Landscape*, purchased from the Palser Gallery, 1882
Brenner, Adam 1800–1891, *Christ Calling His First Disciples*, gift from Mrs Jarratt, 1964
Bristow, Edmund 1787–1876, *Still Life, Spaniel and Dead Game*, purchased at Christie's, 1889
British (English) School late 19th C, *Catherine Elizabeth Biggs, née Holland*, bequeathed by Mrs Lola Biggs
British School *Sir George Hastings (1540–1604), Later 4th Earl of Huntingdon, and His Son Francis*, purchased from Messrs Leggatt with the assistance of the Museums and Galleries Commission/Victoria and Albert Museum Purchase Grant Fund and the Friends of the Museum Fund, 1938
British School *Sir William Herrick (1557–1653)*, transferred to Leicester Museum from Leicester Corporation, City Estates, 1926
British School *Sir Robert Herrick (1540–1618)*, transferred to Leicester Museum from Leicester Corporation, City Estates, 1926
British School *Reverend Thomas Hayne (1582–1645), MA*, transferred to Leicester Museum from Leicester Corporation, City Estates, 1926
British School *Thomas Staveley (1626–1684)*, purchased from Reverend W. C. Hall, 1946
British School 17th C, *Mary Staveley (d.1699)*, purchased from Reverend W. C. Hall
British School *George III (1738–1820)*, transferred from the Leicester Corporation, 1926
British School 18th C, *John Darker (1722–1784)*, gift from Edward L. Lovedon; transferred from Leicester Corporation, 1926
British School 18th C, *Landscape, a Castle and a Man Fishing*, bequeathed by Mr John William Cutler Bickley, 1935
British School 18th C, *Portrait of a Lady*, gift from Mr C. Hedley Haddon, 1946
British School 18th C, *Rear Admiral Sir Cloudesley Shovell (1650–1707)*, gift from Mr C. Hedley Haddon, 1943
British School late 17th C, *John Valentine (1730–1792)*, purchased from Jane Howells, 2000
British School *John Biggs (1801–1871), MP, and His Nephew Arthur Biggs*, bequeathed by Mrs Lola Biggs, 2005
British School *Quartermaster J. Kirk, Leicestershire Yeomanry*, purchased at Sotheby's, 1987
British School *Thomas Burbidge (1784–1855)*, gift from R. B. Burbidge, 1957, photo credit: Leicester Arts and Museums Service
British School *Mr Creswell and His Daughter Charlotte (1854–1918)*, gift from Mr N. P. Greatorex, 1967
British School *Seascape*, gift from Mr R. E. Parker, 1977
British School *Seascape*, gift from

Mr R. E. Parker, 1977
British School *The East Side of West Bridge, Leicester*, gift from Mr Colin Dare Bernard Ellis, 1951
British School 19th C, *Alderman James Richards (1765–1845)*, gift from Mr C. R. Shakespear, 1949
British School 19th C, *Flower Piece*, gift from Mr C. Hedley Haddon, 1943
British School 19th C, *John Ellis (1789–1862)*, gift from Miss Edith Ellis, 1951
British School late 19th C, *Mrs Holland*, bequeathed by Mrs Lola Biggs, 2005
British School 20th C, *Alderman John Parsons*, transferred from the Town Hall, 1957
British School *A Boy with a Parrot*, gift from Mr C. Hedley Haddon, 1943
British School *Alderman Edward Wood (1839–1917)*, unknown acquisition method; found in store, 2009
British School *Bishop Dodridge*, purchased from Langdon and Co., 1920
British School *Bridge Street, View of 'The Mitre and Keys Inn', Leicester*, gift from Mr A. Looms, 1957
British School *Cock with a Hatched Chick*, purchased from Mr E. W. Keymer, 1961
British School *Two Cocks Fighting*, purchased from Mr E. W. Keymer, 1961
British School *Daniel Lambert (1770–1809)*, purchased from King's Lynn Museum, 1957
British School *Daniel Lambert (1770–1809)*, gift from Miss Evelyn Thirlby, 1956
British School *Dr George Shaw (1801–1888), MD*, gift from Miss Irene Browning, 1966
British School *Horse-Drawn Fire Engine*, gift from Leicester City Fire Brigade, 1967
British School *Joseph Goddard (1813–1877)*, gift from Mr M. Herald Goddard, 1969
British School *Lady Rachel Russell*, bequeathed by Mr William Kelly, 1894
British School *Landscape with Cattle*, unknown acquisition method; found in store, 2009
British School *The Midland Counties Railway Board*, gift from S. H. Bowers, 1973
British School *Miss Harriman*, gift from Mr A. Warner, 1977
British School *Mr Harriman*, gift from Mr A. Warner, 1977
British School *'Old Blue Boar' Inn, Leicester*, gift from Miss A. M. Allen, 1920
British School *Old West Bridge, Leicester*, gift from Mr H. S. Leete, 1957
British School *Portrait of a Gentleman at a Desk*, transferred from the Leicestershire County Council Department of Property, 1987
British School *Portrait of a Lady* (possibly Queen Caroline or Queen Elizabeth), gift from Mr C. Hedley Haddon, 1943
British School *Portrait of an Unknown Gentleman*, bequeathed by Miss Emily Frances Dalton, 1900
British School *Portrait of an Unknown Lady*
British School *Portrait of an Unknown Man*
British School *Portrait of an Unknown Man*
British School *Queen Victoria (1819–1901)*, gift from Market Bosworth Magistrates, 1990
British School *Reverend John Taylor (1711–1772)*, gift from Mr Edward R. Marshall, 1964
British School *Reverend Robert Hall (1764–1831)*, purchased from E. A. Lane and Sons, 1958
British School *Romantic Landscape*
British School *Romantic Landscape, Ruins in the Moonlight*, gift from Mr W. Mace, 1947
British School *St Mary de Castro, Leicester*, gift from Mr F. Benson, before 1914
British School *Sir Charles William Packe (1792–1867), MP*, transferred from the Leicestershire County Council Department of Property, 1987
British School *Sir Thomas White (1492–1566)*, presented to the Town of Leicester by Sir William Herrick, 1616; transferred to Leicester Museums from Leicester Corporation, City Estates, 1926
British School *Sir William Herrick (1557–1653)*, bequeathed by Miss I. M. Macaulay, 1937; on loan from Leicestershire Museums
British School *Sir William Russell*, bequeathed by Mr William Kelly, 1894
British School *Sir William Walker*, gift from Mrs M. M. Woodcock, 1949
British School *Stag Shooting in Mountainous Country*, bequeathed by Mr John William Cutler Bickley, 1935
British School *View of Leicester*
British School *William Biggs (1804–1881), 19th Lord Mayor of Leicester*, purchased from Olive Biggs, 1995
British School *William Gardiner (1770–1853)*, gift from Leicester Literary and Philosophical Society, before 1882
British School *William Stenson of Whitwick (1771–1861)*, gift from Mr J. Stenson Turner, 1960
British School *Winter Scene*, transferred from Hinckley Library, 1996
Brown, W. *Captain James Jones (1777–1866), RM*, gift from Miss B. Dunn, 1945
Brown, W. *The Wife of Captain James Jones*, gift from Miss B. Dunn, 1945
Brown, W. *John Mansfield (1739–1798)*, gift from Mr W. Beasley, 1918
Buckley, Stephen b.1944, *Two Step*, gift from the Contemporary Art Society, 2007, © the artist
Buckley, Stephen b.1944, *Dosover*, gift from the Contemporary Art Society, 2007, © the artist
Bulmer, Lionel 1919–1992, *The Shelving Beach*, purchased from the Royal Academy, 1956, © the studio estate of Lionel Bulmer and Margaret Green is represented by David Messum Fine Art Ltd
Burgess, John Bagnold 1830–1897, *Catechising*, purchased at Christie's, photo credit: Leicester Arts and Museums Service
Burne-Jones, Edward 1833–1898, *Christ and the Twelve Apostles*, purchased at Sotheby's, 1946
Burroughs, Albert Leicester 1865–after 1915, *Interior with Three Men round a Fire*
Burton, Ida *Aylestone Mill, Leicestershire*, gift from Miss F. G. Hubbard, 1955
Carracci, Annibale 1560–1609, *Youthful Bacchus*, purchased from P. and D. Colnaghi and Co. Ltd with the assistance of the Museums and Galleries Commission/ Victoria and Albert Museum Purchase Grant Fund, 1967
Carter, Christopher *Henry Hastings (c.1535–1595), 3rd Earl of Huntingdon*, commissioned by Leicester Corporation, 1623; transferred to Leicester Museum from Leicester Corporation, City Estates, 1926
Cartwright, Reg b.1938, *The Hedge Layer*, gift from the artist, 1981, © the artist/Bridgeman Art Library
Cattermole, George 1800–1868, *The Monastery Door*, purchased from Mr Grindley, 1882
Clarke, Harry Harvey 1869–1948, *The Silver Beeches of Pentre Du, Conwy*, purchased from the artist, 1925
Clays, Paul Jean 1819–1900, *A Calm on the Kel near Dordrecht, The Netherlands*, purchased at Christie's, 1891
Clough, Prunella 1919–1999, *Industrial Interior 1*, purchased from Mrs Monika Kinley, 1975, © estate of Prunella Clough 2012. All Rights Reserved DACS
Clough, Prunella 1919–1999, *Slag Heap*, purchased at Christie's, 1982, © estate of Prunella Clough 2012. All Rights Reserved DACS
Clough, Prunella 1919–1999, *Commemorate*, purchased from Mrs Monika Kinley with the assistance of the Museums and Galleries Commission/Victoria and Albert Museum Purchase Grant Fund, 1977, © estate of Prunella Clough 2012. All Rights Reserved DACS
Clutton-Brock, Evelyn Alice b.1876, *Flower Study*, transferred from Hinckley Library, 1996, © the artist's estate
Cluysenaar, André 1872–1939, *Britannia with Belgian Refugees*, gift from Belgian refugees in Leicester, 1917
Cole, George 1810–1883, *Milking Time on the Swale, Yorkshire*, bequeathed by Mr Stephen Bennett, 1902
Cole, George 1810–1883, *Fittleworth Old Mill, River Rother, Sussex*, bequeathed by Mr Henry Snow, 1894
Cole, George Vicat 1833–1893, *Harvesting in the Thames Valley*, gift from Lady Selma Lennard in memory of Sir Thomas J. Lennard, 1939
Conder, Charles 1868–1909, *Mrs Conder in Pink*, purchased from Roland, Browse and Delbanco, with the assistance of the Friends of the Museum Fund, 1956
Constable, John 1776–1837, *Portrait of a Gentleman* (unfinished), purchased from Mr J. W. Simpson, 1935
Constable, John (after) 1776–1837, *Noon, West End Fields, Hampstead, London* (sketch), purchased in memory of Alderman Charles Squire from Arthur Tooth & Sons Ltd with the assistance of the Friends of the Museum Fund, 1948
Cook, Jenny b.1942, *Cattle Market Clock Tower, Leicester*, purchased from the artist, 1982, © the artist
Cook, Jenny b.1942, *'Harris', Granby Corner, Leicester*, purchased from the artist, 1982, © the artist
Cook, Jenny b.1942, *'Kirby & West' Building, Western Boulevard, Leicester*, purchased from the artist, 1982, © the artist
Cook, Jenny b.1942, *'Roy Vickers' Flower Shop, YMCA Corner, Granby Street, Leicester*, purchased from the artist, 1982, © the artist
Cook, Jenny b.1942, *Turkey Café, Granby Street, Leicester*, purchased from the artist, 1982, © the artist
Cooke, Edward William 1811–1880, **Francis, Charles** & **unknown artist** *The Old Mill, Kirby Bellars, Leicestershire*, purchased from A. de la Poer Rowbotham, 1954
Cooper, Thomas Sidney 1803–1902, *Cattle in a Landscape*, purchased at Christie's, 1887
Cooper, Thomas Sidney 1803–1902, *Landscape with Cattle*, purchased from Mr Thomas McLean with the assistance of a bequest from Miss Emily Frances Dalton, 1900
Cope, Charles West 1811–1890, *The Village Schoolmaster*, purchased at Christie's, 1888
Corinth, Lovis 1858–1925, *Carl Ludwig Elias, Aged 7 1/4*, purchased from Mrs B. Levy with the assistance of the Museums and Galleries Commission/Victoria and Albert Museum Purchase Grant Fund, 1968
Cotes, Francis 1726–1770, *Miss Elizabeth Adney (d.1783)*, purchased from Mr Thomas McLean, 1908
Cox, David the elder 1783–1859, *Pont-y-Pair, Conwy*, purchased at Christie's, 1892
Cramphorn, Frank Leslie 1908–2000, *The Theatre Royal, Leicester*, gift from Mrs Diana Smith, 2000, © The Theatre Royal, Leicester
Cranach, Lucas the elder (follower of) 1472–1553, *Martin Luther (1483–1546)*, bequeathed by Miss E. K. Adderley, 1941
Cranach, Lucas the elder (follower of) 1472–1553, *Philip Melanchthon (1497–1560)*, bequeathed by Miss E. K. Adderley, 1941
Daintrey, Adrian Maurice 1902–1988, *The Windmill*, gift from the Contemporary Art Society, 1931, © the artist's estate
Daniell, William (attributed to) 1769–1837, *Egg Boats off Macao, China*, purchased from Thomas Agnew and Sons Ltd, 1955
Davies, Edward 1841–1920, *A Welsh Cottage*, purchased from the artist, 1910
Davies, Edward 1841–1920, *Landscape, near Peel, Isle of Man*, gift from Mrs W. E. Tyler (or Taylor?)
Davies, Edward 1841–1920, *Llugwy, Betws-y-Coed, Conwy*, purchased from the artist, 1910
Davies, Edward 1841–1920, *The Duck Pond*, purchased from the artist
Davies, Edward 1841–1920, *The Old Mill, Aylestone, Leicestershire*, purchased from the artist, 1900
Dawson, Henry 1811–1878, *On the Ribble*, purchased from Mr George Stannage, 1881
Dawson, Henry 1811–1878, *Pilgrims in Sight of the Celestial City*, bequeathed by Mr John Stafford, 1911
Dawson, Henry 1811–1878, *Landscape Sketch*, gift from Mr John E. Hodges, 1881
Dawson, Henry 1811–1878, *St Paul's, London*, gift from Mr G. H. Hodges, 1893
de Bylant, Alfred active 1853–1879, *Italian Landscape*
De Heer, Margarethe c.1603–c.1665, *Two Frisian Beggars Fighting*, purchased from Major H. S. Sutherland, 1937
de Maistre, Leroy Leveson Laurent Joseph 1894–1968, *The Crucifixion*, gift from the Contemporary Art Society, 1952, © the artist's estate
Degas, Edgar 1834–1917, *La rentrée du troupeau*, purchased from Peter Koppel with the assistance of the Museums and Galleries Commission/Victoria and Albert Museum Purchase Grant Fund, 1969, photo credit: Bridgeman Art Library
Delaney, Barbara b.1941, *Mikado's Gambit*, purchased from the artist with the assistance of City of Leicester Museums Trust, 2001, ©

the artist
Deloos, H. active 19th C, *The Pedlar*
Dent, Ann Langford b.1924, *Trafalgar Square, London*, transferred from Hinckley Library, 1996, © the artist
Devis, Arthur 1712–1787, *Edward Gordon, His Sister Mrs Miles, and Her Husband in Their Garden at Bromley*, gift from Mrs Joan L. Cross, 1955
Di Stefano, Arturo b.1955, *Edgar Degas (1834–1917)*, gift from the Contemporary Art Society, 1992, © the artist
Di Stefano, Arturo b.1955, *The New Walk Museum and Art Gallery, Leicester*, purchased from the artist, 1999, © the artist
Diaz de la Peña, Narcisse Virgile (after) 1808–1876, *A Wooded Landscape*, purchased from Mr Dickinson, 1938
Dicksee, Frank 1853–1928, *The Foolish Virgins, 'Too late, ye cannot enter now'*, purchased from Messrs Leggatt, 1902
Dicksee, Thomas Francis 1819–1895, *At the Opera*, bequeathed by Mrs Mary Hodges, 1941
Dodd, Phyllis 1899–1995, *Girl in National Costume, in an Interior*, gift from Leicestershire County Libraries Service, 1979, © P. and R. Bliss
Doig, Peter b.1959, *Concrete Cabin*, gift from the Contemporary Art Society, 1996, © Peter Doig
Donne, Walter J. 1867–1930, *God's Acre*, gift from the artist, 1929
Dowling, Robert Hawke 1827–1886, *Edward Shipley Ellis (1817–1879)*, transferred from Leicester Corporation, City Estates, 1949
Drummond, Malcolm 1880–1945, *Chelsea Public Library*, purchased from Mrs Monika Kinley, 1978, © the artist's estate
Drummond, Malcolm 1880–1945, *Seated Nude*, purchased from Mrs M. Drummond, via Mrs Monika Kinley with the assistance of the Museums and Galleries Commission/Victoria and Albert Museum Purchase Grant Fund, 1980, © the artist's estate
Duffield, William 1816–1863, *Still Life with Dead Rabbits*, gift from Alderman John Bennett, 1881
Dugdale, Thomas Cantrell 1880–1952, *Motherhood*, purchased from the artist, 1923, © Joanna Dunham
Dunlop, Ronald Ossory 1894–1973, *Les deux bateaux*, transferred from Hinckley Library, 1996
Dunlop, Ronald Ossory 1894–1973, *The Thames near Rotherhithe, London*, purchased from the Redfern Gallery, 1936
Dutch School 17th C, *William III (1650–1702), on Horseback*, bequeathed by Mr John William Cutler Bickley, 1935
Dutch School *Portrait of a Boy in the Reign of Charles II*, gift from Mr C. Hedley Haddon, 1943
Dyce, William 1806–1864, *The Meeting of Jacob and Rachel*, purchased from Thomas Agnew and Sons Ltd, 1937
East, Alfred 1844–1913, *Autumn in the Valley of the Seine*, purchased from the artist, 1910
Eastham, Frank *Harold Trevor Hawsley Peck*, gift from Mr Richard C. Timms, 1991
Eddis, Eden Upton 1812–1901, *Sir George Beaumont (1828–1882), 9th Bt*, gift from Mrs Felicity Owen, 1973
Egg, Augustus Leopold 1816–1863, *Launce's Substitute for Proteus' Dog* (from 'The Two Gentlemen of Verona' by William Shakespeare), purchased at Christie's, 1891
Egg, Augustus Leopold 1816–1863, *'The Taming of the Shrew'* (from the play by William Shakespeare), purchased from the sale of the effects of J. Moore, 1947
Ellis, Edwin 1841–1895, *The Captain's Birthday*, purchased from the Hartshorn sale, Nottingham, 1905
Ellis, Norman 1913–1971, *Old Hall Farm, Groby, Leicestershire*, gift from Mrs Norman E. Ellis, 1971
Ellis, Norman 1913–1971, *Old Manor Farm, Groby, Leicestershire*, gift from Mrs Norman E. Ellis, 1971
Ellis, Norman 1913–1971, *Leicester City Centre*, gift from Mrs Norman E. Ellis, 1971
Ellis, Norman 1913–1971, *A Leicester Vista*, purchased from the artist, 1956
Ellis, Norman 1913–1971, *Old Hall Farm, Groby, Leicestershire*, gift from Mrs Norman E. Ellis, 1971
Ellis, Norman 1913–1971, *Old Hall Farm, Groby, Leicestershire*, gift from Mrs Norman E. Ellis, 1971
Ellis, Norman 1913–1971, *Wharf Street Vista, Leicester*, gift from Mrs Norman E. Ellis, 1971
Ellis, Norman 1913–1971, *Boston Stump, Leicestershire*, gift from Mrs Norman E. Ellis, 1971
Ellis, Norman 1913–1971, *Burnham Overy Mill across the Cornfield, Norfolk*, gift from Mrs Norman E. Ellis, 1971
Ellis, Norman 1913–1971, *The Last Days of Leicester Palace*, gift from Mrs Norman E. Ellis
Engelbach, Florence 1872–1951, *Tulips and Irises*, gift from the Contemporary Art Society, 1933
Etty, William 1787–1849, *The Bowman*, purchased from Lord Derwent, 1947
Etty, William 1787–1849, *Sabrina and Her Nymphs*, purchased from Mrs L. D. Pearson, 1936
Faed, Thomas 1826–1900, *The Orphans*, purchased from Mrs Elizabeth Hassell, 1944
Faed, Thomas 1826–1900, *Pot Luck*, purchased from Thomas Agnew and Sons Ltd, 1890
Fairweather, Ian 1891–1974, *Procession in Bali*, purchased from the Redfern Gallery, 1936, © estate of Ian Fairweather. All rights reserved, DACS 2012
Farman, Agnes Ethel 1863–1947, *Castle View, Gateway, Chantry House and St Mary de Castro Church, Leicester*, purchased from Miss Isabella M. Charters, 1951
Farquhar, Keith b.1969, *'Woman I can hardly express'*, gift from the Contemporary Art Society, 2005
Farthing, Stephen b.1950, *Monument to a Propagator*, purchased from the Paton Gallery, 1985, © the artist
Feigl, Bedrich 1884–1965, *Knighton, Church Lane, Leicester*, transferred from the Schools' Loans Service
Feininger, Lyonel 1871–1956, *Hinter der Stadtkirche*, purchased from Mrs T. Hess, 1944, © DACS 2012
Ferneley, John E. 1782–1860, *Two Children with a Hurdy-Gurdy*, gift from Arthur Ackermann and Sons Ltd, 1968
Filmer, D. active c.1972, *'For what we are about to receive'*, purchased from the artist, 1972
Filmer, D. active c.1972, *The Dolly Boys Tuning Up*, purchased from the artist, 1972
Flemish School *Adoration of the Magi*, gift from Mrs M. C. Beardsworth, 2009
Flemish School *A Pastoral Scene*, purchased from the sale of the effects of Henrietta S. Butler, 1935
Flemish School *Saint Jerome*, transferred to Leicester Museum from Leicester Corporation, City Estates, 1926
Forbes-Robertson, Eric 1865–1935, *Breton Children, Pont Aven, France*, purchased from the Leicester Galleries with the assistance of the Museums and Galleries Commission/Victoria and Albert Museum Purchase Grant Fund, 1968
Foster, Herbert Wilson 1846–1929, *Breton Girl*, gift from Reverend L. Wilson Foster, 1968
Fowler, Robert 1853–1926, *Light and Laughter in the Kent Hopfields*, gift from Lord Aberconway, 1932
Frankl, Gerhardt 1901–1965, *Still Life: Lemons and a Clay Pipe*, gift from the Contemporary Art Society, 2005
Freer, Allen b.1926, *Ilam Tor, Derbyshire*, gift from the artist in memory of his parents Arthur Clement and Elsie May Freer through the National Art Collections Fund, 2004, © the artist
Freestone, William Henry 1876–1953, *Canal Bridge at Aylestone, Leicestershire*, gift from Owen Cox, 1958, © the artist's estate
Frith, William Powell 1819–1909, *The Railway Station*, purchased at Christie's, 1892
Frith, William Powell 1819–1909, *The Miniature*, purchased from Miss Kirby, 1953
Frost, Terry 1915–2003, *Red and Blue*, purchased from Mrs Monika Kinley with the assistance of the Museums and Galleries Commission/Victoria and Albert Museum Purchase Grant Fund, 1977, © estate of Terry Frost. All rights reserved, DACS 2012
Fry, Roger Eliot 1866–1934, *Samothrace, Greece*, gift from Mr Sydney Ansell Gimson, 1934
Fulleylove, John 1845–1908, *The Old Wyggeston Hospital, Leicester*, gift from Mr Joseph Wallis Goddard, 1926
Fulleylove, John 1845–1908, *High Cross Street and 'The Nag's Head', Leicester*, bequeathed by Mrs Helen Florence Evans, 1936
Fulleylove, John 1845–1908, *The Old Town Hall, Leicester*, bequeathed by Mrs Helen Florence Evans, 1936
Fulleylove, John 1845–1908, *Old West Bridge Street, Leicester*, purchased from Mr Arthur Renals, 1937
Fulleylove, John 1845–1908, *Hampton Court*, purchased from the artist
Fulleylove, John 1845–1908, *South Porch, St Nicholas, King's Lynn, Norfolk*, gift from Councillor Sydney Ansell Gimson, 1914
Gainsborough, Thomas (after) 1727–1788, *View of Drinkstone Park, Stowmarket, Suffolk*, bequeathed by Ernest Edward Cook through the National Art Collections Fund, 1955
Gardner, Daniel 1750–1805, *Wilson Gale-Braddyll (1756–1818), MP*, bequeathed by Miss Emily Frances Dalton, 1900
Garland, Henry 1834–1913, *A Cool Retreat*, gift from Mr Stephen Bennet, 1881
Gerstl, Arnold 1888–1956, *The Violinists*, purchased from Uwe Arnold Gerstl with the assistance of the Museums and Galleries Commission/Victoria and Albert Museum Purchase Grant Fund, 1989, © the artist's estate
Gertler, Mark 1891–1939, *The Fruit Sorters*, gift from the Contemporary Art Society, 1924
Gill, Edmund Marriner 1820–1894, *The Yellowstone Falls, Wyoming, USA*, bequeathed by Mr Thomas J. Gunn, 1917
Gilman, Harold 1876–1919, *Meditation*, purchased from Thomas Agnew and Sons Ltd, 1978
Gilpin, Sawrey (attributed to) 1733–1807 & **Barret, George the elder (attributed to)** 1728/1732–1784, *Landscape with Mares, Foals and Deer*, purchased from Arthur Ackermann and Sons Ltd, 1970
Ginner, Charles 1878–1952, *Cottages, Brook Green, Isle of Wight*, purchased at Christie's, 1956
Ginner, Charles 1878–1952, *Garden in Spring*, purchased from Messrs Reid and Lefevre, 1944
Ginsborg, Michael b.1943, *The Harp*, purchased from Mrs Monika Kinley with the assistance of the Museums and Galleries Commission/Victoria and Albert Museum Purchase Grant Fund, 1980, © the artist
Goodall, Frederick 1822–1904, *An Irish Eviction*, purchased at Christie's, 1890
Gore, Spencer 1878–1914, *Harold Gilman's House at Letchworth, Hertfordshire*, purchased from the Anthony d'Offay Gallery, 1974, photo credit: Bridgeman Art Library
Gorman, Michael b.1938, *Mr Treadwell Meets the Critics*, gift from the Contemporary Art Society, 1975, © the artist
Gosse, Laura Sylvia 1881–1968, *A Nun with Children*, purchased from the Leger Galleries, 1952, © the artist's estate/Bridgeman Art Library
Gotlib, Henryk 1890–1966, *Four Girls at Forte dei Marmi, Italy*, purchased from Mrs J. Gotlib with the assistance of the Museums and Galleries Commission/Victoria and Albert Museum Purchase Grant Fund, 1980, © the artist's estate
Gould, Julian 1891–1917, *Self Portrait*, bequeathed by Miss R. B. Gould, 1967
Graham, Peter 1836–1921, *The Highland Pastures*, purchased from Arthur Tooth & Sons Ltd, 1897
Graham, Peter 1836–1921, *The Inchcape Rock*, purchased from the artist, 1909
Grant, Duncan 1885–1978, *Vanessa Bell (1879–1961)*, purchased from Roland, Browse and Delbanco, 1955, © estate of Duncan Grant. All rights reserved, DACS 2012
Grant, Duncan 1885–1978, *Lewes Landscape, East Sussex*, purchased from the Leger Galleries, 1945, © estate of Duncan Grant. All rights reserved, DACS 2012
Grant, Duncan 1885–1978, *The Pink Vase*, purchased from Messrs Reid and Lefevre, 1937, © estate of Duncan Grant. All rights reserved, DACS 2012
Grant, Francis 1803–1878, *Mary Isabella Grant (d.1854)*, purchased from Thomas Agnew and Sons Ltd, 1954
Gray, Eileen 1878–1976, *Collage*, purchased from Mrs Monika Kinley, 1976
Greaves, Derrick b.1927, *Studies for Hiroshige II*, purchased from Mrs Monika Kinley with the assistance of the Calouste Gulbenkian Foundation, 1975, © the artist
Greaves, Walter 1846–1930, *The River in Winter, Sunset*, purchased from Roland, Browse and Delbanco, 1947
Greaves, Walter 1846–1930,

Nocturne in Blue and Gold, purchased from M. De Beer, 1944
Green, Charles 1840–1898, *The Girl I Left behind Me*, purchased from the artist, 1882
Green, Kenneth 1905–1986, *Borghese Gardens, Rome*, purchased from the artist, 1945, © the artist's estate
Grevatte, Jenny b.1951, *Castle in Cephalonia, Greece*, gift from the artist, 1992, © the artist
Grigg, Ronald Edwin 1917–1957, *A Barn Door*, purchased from the artist, 1943
Groves, T. *Hunter and Groom**
Harding, James Duffield 1798–1863, *A Shady Nook*, purchased from Mr Newcombe, 1890
Hardy, Frederick Daniel 1827–1911, *Interior of a Sussex Farmhouse*, purchased at Christie's, 1890
Harvey, George 1806–1876, *Catechising in a Scottish School*, purchased from Arthur Tooth & Sons Ltd, 1886
Hashem, Satta b.1959, *Freedom No.1*, purchased from the artist with the assistance of the City of Leicester Trust, 2010, © the artist
Hayes, Edwin 1819–1904, *Trawling off Gorleston Harbour, Norfolk*, purchased from the artist, 1881
Hayman, Francis (attributed to) 1708–1776, *Portrait of a Lady* (possibly the actress Margaret 'Peg' Woffington, 1720?–1760), purchased at Sotheby's, 1937
Heath, Adrian 1920–1992, *Painting Blue and White*, purchased from the Hanover Gallery, 1961, © the estate of Adrian Heath
Henton, George W. Moore 1861–1924, *Old Town Hall Library, Guildhall, Leicester*, purchased from Mrs M. Fosbrooke, 1934
Henton, George W. Moore 1861–1924, *Courtyard, Guildhall, Leicester*, purchased from Mrs M. Harpin, 1989
Henton, George W. Moore 1861–1924, *St Mary-in-the-Elms, Woodhouse, Leicestershire*, purchased from Mrs M. Fosbrooke, 1934
Henton, George W. Moore 1861–1924, *The New Walk, Leicester*, purchased from Abbott and Holder, 1960
Henton, George W. Moore 1861–1924, *November Sunshine, Lowesby Church, Leicestershire*, purchased from Mrs M. Fosbrooke, 1934
Henton, George W. Moore 1861–1924, *St Denys' Church, Evington, Leicestershire*, purchased from Mrs M. Fosbrooke, 1934
Herberte, Edward Benjamin active 1857–1893, *A Horse Race in Victoria Park, Leicester*, purchased from Mrs B. Walker, 1953
Herman, Josef 1911–2000, *Evenfall, Ystradgynlais, Powys*, purchased from Roland, Browse and Delbanco, 1950, © estate of Josef Herman. All rights reserved, DACS 2012
Herring, John Frederick I 1795–1865, *The Halt*, bequeathed by Mr Stephen Bennett, 1902
Herrmann, Curt 1854–1929, *Sunflowers*, anonymous gift, 1986
Higgins, Charles S. 1893–1980, *La lutte angelique*, gift from the Contemporary Art Society, 1952
Higgins, Charles S. 1893–1980, *Bedouin and Horses*, gift from Mrs Anne Kessler, 1983
Highmore, Joseph 1692–1780, *James Wigley of Scraptoft Hall (c.1700–1765)*, gift from Edward Hartopp Wigley; transferred from Leicester Corporation, 1926
Hill, Adrian Keith Graham 1895–1977, *The Estuary*, transferred from Hinckley Library, 1996
Hilton, Roger 1911–1975, *Spiral*, gift from the Contemporary Art Society, 1962, © estate of Roger Hilton. All rights reserved, DACS 2012
Hilton, Roger 1911–1975, *Untitled*, purchased from Mrs Monika Kinley, 1975, © estate of Roger Hilton. All rights reserved, DACS 2012
Hitchens, Ivon 1893–1979, *Flower Piece*, purchased from Messrs Brown and Phillips, 1942, © Ivon Hitchens' estate/Jonathan Clark & Co.
Hogarth, William 1697–1764, *The Wollaston Family*, on long-term loan from a private lender, since 1943
Hogarth, William (after) 1697–1764, *A Modern Midnight Conversation*, bequeathed by Mrs Anna Clowes, 1905
Holland, James 1799–1870, *English Landscape*, purchased at Christie's, 1887
Holst, Laurits Bernhard 1848–1934, *The Derelict, Morning after a Storm*
Hook, James Clarke 1819–1907, *Carting for Farmer, Pengelly, Cornwall*, purchased from Mr Thomas McLean, 1900
Hooper, John b.1939, *Untitled (To Bernstein's 'Big Bluff')*, gift from the Contemporary Art Society, 2005, © the artist
Horemans, Jan Josef the elder 1682–1752 & **Horemans, Jan Josef the younger** 1714–1790, *A Music Party*, bequeathed by Mr John William Cutler Bickley, 1935
Hosali, Nina 1898–1987, *Movement 3, Dance at Sunrise*, gift from Free Painters and Sculptors, 1988
Hosking, Hugh Richard 1904–1991, *The Finding of Moses*, purchased from the artist, 1933, © Hosking Houses Trust, founded by the artist's daughter
Hublin, Émile Auguste 1830–1891, *The Orphan*, purchased at Christie's, 1891
Hudson, Thomas 1701–1779, *Mrs Matthew Michell and Her Children, Matthew and Anne*, purchased from Thomas Agnew and Sons Ltd, 1938
Hulme, Frederick William 1816–1884, *Scene in Sussex*, bequeathed by Mr Stephen Bennett, 1902
Hunt, Edward Aubrey 1855–1922, *Greenwich Reach, London, Evening*, purchased from A. Pickering and Son, 1914
Hunt, Edward Aubrey 1855–1922, *Venice*, purchased from the Hartshorn sale, Nottingham, 1905
Hunt, Walter 1861–1941, *Kittens and a Dog*, on long-term loan from the Leicester Royal Infirmary Nurses' League
Hunter, Colin 1841–1904, *Three Fishers*, purchased at Christie's, 1891
Hunting, Leonard b.1926, *Landscape, Martigues, France*, purchased from the artist, 1958
Ibbetson, Julius Caesar 1759–1817, *Masham Castle, North Yorkshire*, purchased from the Palser Gallery, 1882
Italian School 19th C, *Andrea del Sarto (1486–1530)*, presented by the executrix of the estate of Miss Henrietta S. Butler, in her memory, 1935
Jack, Richard 1866–1952, *Colin McAlpin (1870–1942)*, gift from Mrs F. McAlpin, 1968, © the artist's estate
Jackson, John 1778–1831, *George Dance (1741–1825)*, purchased at Sotheby's, 1948
Jacquemon, Pierre 1936–2002, *Triptych*, purchased from the Temple Gallery with the assistance of the Friends of the Museum Fund, 1963
Jessel, Jeremy George b.1939, *Winter of '47*, purchased from the artist with the assistance of the Calouste Gulbenkian Foundation, 1975, © the artist
Jessop, D. E. *South End of the Library in the Guildhall, Leicester*
John, Augustus Edwin 1878–1961, *Admiral Lord Fisher of Kilverstone (1841–1920), GCB, OM, GCVO, First Sea Lord (1905–1910)*, purchased from the Chenil Gallery, 1920, © the artist's estate/ Bridgeman Art Library
Johnson, Frank 1917–1998, *Paul Oxford*, purchased from Mr James E. G. Johnson with the assistance of the City of Leicester Museums Trust Fund, 2007, © estate of the late Frank Johnson (James Edward George Johnson)
Johnson, P. M. b.1916, *Old Belgrave, Leicester*, unknown acquisition method
Keene, Ezra Elmer 1853–1929, *Old Evington Village, Leicester, c.1900*
Kiddier, William 1859–1934, *The Cottage*, gift from Mr F. S. Merriman, 1933
Kiddier, William 1859–1934, *The Inn*, gift from the artist, 1934
Kikoine, Michel 1892–1968, *Still Life with Fish*, purchased from the Crane Kalman Gallery Ltd with the assistance of the Museums and Galleries Commission/Victoria and Albert Museum Purchase Grant Fund, 1963
King, Henry John Yeend 1855–1924, *Landscape with a Windmill*, transferred from the Leicestershire County Council Department of Property, 1987
Knight, John Prescott 1803–1881, *The Merry Pedlar*, purchased at Christie's, 1891
Knight, Laura 1877–1970, *The Three Clowns*, purchased from the artist, 1934, © reproduced with permission of the estate of Dame Laura Knight, DBE, RA, 2012. All rights reserved
Knight, William 1872–1958, *Autumn Afternoon*, unknown acquisition method; found in store, 2009
Knight, William 1872–1958, *Autumn Evening*, purchased from the artist, 1925, © Leicester Arts and Museums Service
Knight, William 1872–1958, *Russet and Gold*, purchased from the artist, 1925, © Leicester Arts and Museums Service
Koelz, Johannes Mattheus 1895–1971, *Portrait of the Artist's Son, Siegfried, Aged 12*, gift from Mrs Ava M. Farrington, 1998, © estate of Johannes Koelz. All rights reserved, DACS 2012
Koelz, Johannes Mattheus 1895–1971, *Self Portrait*, gift from Mrs Ava M. Farrington, 1998, © estate of Johannes Koelz. All rights reserved, DACS 2012
Koelz, Johannes Mattheus 1895–1971, *Boy's Praying Hands*, gift from Mrs Ava M. Farrington, 1998, © estate of Johannes Koelz. All rights reserved, DACS 2012
Koelz, Johannes Mattheus 1895–1971, *Dead Soldier*, gift from Mrs Ava M. Farrington, 1998, © estate of Johannes Koelz. All rights reserved, DACS 2012
Koelz, Johannes Mattheus 1895–1971, *Girl in National Costume*, gift from Mrs Ava M. Farrington, 1998, © estate of Johannes Koelz. All rights reserved, DACS 2012
Koelz, Johannes Mattheus 1895–1971, *Heads of Two Old People*, gift from Mrs Ava M. Farrington, 1998, © estate of Johannes Koelz. All rights reserved, DACS 2012
Koppel, Heinz 1919–1980, *The Engine Shed, Dowlais* (recto), purchased from the Gillian Jason Gallery with the assistance of the Museums and Galleries Commission/Victoria and Albert Museum Purchase Grant Fund, 1989, © the artist's estate
Koppel, Heinz 1919–1980, *Classroom* (verso), purchased from the Gillian Jason Gallery, with the assistance of the Museums and Galleries Commission/Victoria and Albert Museum Purchase Grant Fund, 1989, © the artist's estate
Kossoff, Leon b.1926, *Outside Kilburn Underground, Summer 1976*, purchased from Fischer Fine Art with the assistance of the Museums and Galleries Commission/Victoria and Albert Museum Purchase Grant Fund, 1978, © the artist
La Tour, Georges de 1593–1652, *The Choirboy*, purchased from an anonymous vendor with the assistance of the Museums and Galleries Commission/Victoria and Albert Museum Purchase Grant Fund and the Friends of the Museum Fund, 1983
Lamb, Henry 1883–1960, *A French Farm*, on long-term loan from Dr J. S. Steward, since 1980, © estate of Henry Lamb
Lamb, Lynton Harold 1907–1977, *The Victorian Chair*, purchased from Mrs Lynton Lamb via Allen Freer with the assistance of the Museums and Galleries Commission/Victoria and Albert Museum Purchase Grant Fund, 1981, © the artist's estate
Langlois, Mark William 1848–1924, *The Tinker*, bequeathed by George Henry Brown, 1990
Langlois, Mark William 1848–1924, *Unwilling to School*, bequeathed by George Henry Brown, 1990
Large, George b.1936, *Typist*, gift from the artist, 2005, © the artist
Laserstein, Lotte 1898–1993, *Self Portrait with a Cat*, purchased from the artist through Thomas Agnew and Sons Ltd, 1988
Laserstein, Lotte 1898–1993, *The Yellow Parasol*, purchased from the artist through Thomas Agnew and Sons Ltd
Lawrence, Thomas 1769–1830, *William Brabazon (1744–1806), 1st Baron Ponsonby*, purchased from Thomas Agnew and Sons Ltd with the assistance of the National Art Collections Fund and the Museums and Galleries Commission/Victoria and Albert Museum Purchase Grant Fund, 1973
Le Bas, Edward 1904–1966, *Still Life with a Wine Bottle and a Glass*, purchased from Messrs Reid and Lefevre, 1944
Leader, Benjamin Williams 1831–1923, *A Surrey Meadow*, bequeathed by Mrs Helen Florence Evans, 1936
Lee, Frederick Richard 1798–1879 & **Cooper, Thomas Sidney** 1803–1902, *Cattle in a Landscape*, gift from Mrs Elizabeth Hassell, 1943
Legueult, Raymond Jean 1898–1971, *Le bocage*, gift from the Contemporary Art Society, 1956, © ADAGP, Paris and DACS, London 2012
Leighton, Frederic 1830–1896, *Head of an Arab*, bequeathed by

Mrs Mary Hodges, 1941
Leighton, Frederic 1830–1896, *Perseus, on Pegasus, Hastening to the Rescue of Andromeda*, purchased from Messrs Leggatt, 1902
Lely, Peter 1618–1680, *Sir Thomas Lee (1635–1691), 1st Bt*, purchased from Thomas Agnew and Sons Ltd, 1938
Lessore, Thérèse 1884–1945, *Circus at Bath*, gift from the Sickert Trust, 1947, © Henry & John Lessore
Lever, Ward active 1920–1959, *Tarn*, transferred from Hinckley Library, 1996
Lewis, Kathleen Edith 1907–2003, *Bottles*, gift from Mrs Penelope Harris, 2007, © the artist's estate
Lewis, Kathleen Edith 1907–2003, *Chinese Lady*, gift from Mrs Penelope Harris, 2007, © the artist's estate
Lhote, André 1885–1962, *Bust of a Young Woman*, purchased from Victor Waddington with the assistance of Mr Herald Goddard, 1971, © ADAGP, Paris and DACS, London 2012
Liebermann, Max 1847–1935, *Die Enkelin des Künstlers mit ihrem Kindermädchen*, purchased from Mrs Margaret Fisher with the assistance of the Museums and Galleries Commission/Victoria and Albert Museum Purchase Grant Fund and an anonymous donation, 1974
Lin, Richard b.1933, *Painting, Relief with Aluminium Square*, purchased from the Gimpel Fils Gallery, 1963, © the artist
Linde, Adriaen van der (attributed to) c.1560–1609, *Portrait of a Child with a Rattle*, gift from Sir William Burrell, 1944
Linton, James Dromgole 1840–1916, *Valentine*, purchased from Mr Thomas McLean, 1882
Lorenzo Monaco c.1370–1425, *Saint John the Baptist Entering the Wilderness*, purchased from P. and D. Colnaghi and Co. Ltd with the assistance of the National Art Collections Fund and Museums and Galleries Commission/ Victoria and Albert Museum Purchase Grant Fund, 1959
Loutherbourg, Philip James de 1740–1812, *A River Scene with a Ferry*, purchased from Mr Kempson, 1882
Loutherbourg, Philip James de 1740–1812, *The Battle between Richard Coeur de Lion and Saladin in Palestine*, purchased from Thomas Agnew and Sons Ltd with the assistance of the Museums and Galleries Commission/Victoria and Albert Museum Purchase Grant Fund, 1977
Loveroff, Frederick Nicholas 1894–1960, *Snow on the Hillside*, purchased from the artist, 1925
Lowry, Laurence Stephen 1887–1976, *Industrial Landscape, River Scene*, purchased from the artist, 1952, © the estate of L. S. Lowry. All rights reserved, DACS 2012
Lucas, Seymour 1849–1923, *A Whip for Van Tromp, the Admiralty*, purchased at Christie's, 1892
Ludlow, Mary Sophia 1869–1951, *Belgrave Hall, Leicestershire*, gift from Miss Edith M. Ellis, 1937
Luti, Benedetto 1666–1724, *The Agony in the Garden*, purchased from P. and D. Colnaghi and Co. Ltd with the assistance of the Museums and Galleries Commission/Victoria and Albert Museum Purchase Grant Fund, 1961
Lyle, M. W. *Flowers and Cushions*, transferred from Hinckley Library, 1996
MacKinnon, Sine 1901–1996, *A White Horse Drinking from a Stream*, gift from Mr Roger Peach
Maclise, Daniel 1806–1870, *The Rat Catcher*, gift from Lady Selma Lennard, in memory of Thomas J. Lennard, 1939
Maes, Nicolaes 1634–1693, *Portrait of an Unknown Gentleman*, bequeathed by Miss E. K. Adderley, 1941
Marc, Franz 1880–1916, *Rote Frau*, purchased from Mr S. Pauson, 1944
Marinot, Maurice 1882–1960, *Femme à la tête levée*, gift from Mlle Florence Marinot, 1974
Marinot, Maurice 1882–1960, *Paysage aux grands arbres*, gift from Mlle Florence Marinot, 1974
Marinot, Maurice 1882–1960, *Intérieur d'église*, gift from Mlle Florence Marinot, 1974
Marinot, Maurice 1882–1960, *Nature mort aux pommes*, gift from Mlle Florence Marinot, 1974
Marlow, William 1740–1813, *View of the Bay of Naples with Vesuvius in the Distance*, purchased from Thomas Agnew and Sons Ltd, with the assistance of the Museums and Galleries Commission/Victoria and Albert Museum Purchase Grant Fund, 1981
Marlow, William (attributed to) 1740–1813, *Classical Landscape*, bequeathed by Mrs Mary Hodges, 1941
Marshall, Benjamin 1767–1835, *Daniel Lambert (1770–1809)*, gift from Mr S. J. Pegg, 1919
Maufra, Maxime 1861–1918, *Bords du Loire*, acquired via the Fulford bequest through the National Art Collections Fund, 1946
McAlpine William (attributed to) active 1840–1880, *Off Sheerness, Kent*, bequeathed by Miss Emily Frances Dalton, 1900
McEvoy, Ambrose 1878–1927, *The Seasons*, purchased from the Redfern Gallery, 1946
McEvoy, Ambrose 1878–1927, *The Artist's Wife in an Interior*, purchased from Mrs A. Bazell, 1970
Meckseper, Friedrich b.1936, *Magia horographica*, purchased from the Lords Gallery, 1963, © DACS 2012
Meerhout, Jan (attributed to) 1633–1677, *View of Gorinchem* (or Gorkum?), *The Netherlands*, purchased from Mr Arthur Renals, 1937
Mees, Jérôme active 1915, *A Flemish Lace Embroiderer*, purchased from the artist, 1915
Meidner, Ludwig 1884–1966, *Apocalyptic Vision*, purchased from Mr Siegfried Oppenheimer with the assistance of the Museums and Galleries Commission/Victoria and Albert Museum Purchase Grant Fund, 1968
Melville, John 1902–1986, *Self Portrait*, gift from Mr John Hampson, 1946
Metzmacher, Emile Pierre 1815–1890, *Courtship*, gift from Dr W. S. Russell, 1964
Mexican School *Indios otomíes que ban a la feria*, gift from Dr Joseph William Noble, 1852
Mexican School *Indios bárbaros*, gift from Dr Joseph William Noble, 1852
Mexican School *De español y negra se produce un mulato*, gift from Dr Joseph William Noble, 1852
Mexican School *De negro y india se produce un lobo*, gift from Dr Joseph William Noble, 1852
Mexican School *De indio y lobo se produce un grifio que es tente en el aire*, gift from Dr Joseph William Noble, 1852
Michie, David Alan Redpath b.1928, *The Swimming Pool*, bequeathed by Mrs Diana Maud Stirling King through the National Art Collections Fund, 2003, © the artist/Bridgeman Art Library
Miller, William P. active 1843, *Elizabeth Thompson*, gift from Mr A. H. Renold, 1955
Miller, William P. active 1843, *James Thompson (1817–1877)*, gift from Mr A. H. Renold, 1955
Mintchine, Abraham 1898–1931, *Personnage assis et bouquet de fleurs*, purchased from Gimpel Fils Ltd, 1963
Mobbs, William (attributed to) *John Kelley, Leicester Chimney Sweep*, gift from Mrs Haymes, 1965
Mobbs, William (attributed to) *Sarah Kelley*, gift from Mrs Haymes, 1965
Monticelli, Adolphe Joseph Thomas 1824–1886, *Réunion dans un parc*, purchased from Arthur Tooth & Sons Ltd with the assistance of the Friends of the Museum Fund, 1963
Morland, George 1763–1804, *Bargaining for Sheep*, bequeathed by Ernest Edward Cook through the National Art Collections Fund, 1955
Morland, George 1763–1804, *Calm off the Coast of the Isle of Wight*, purchased at Christie's, 1890
Morland, George 1763–1804, *Portrait of a Girl*, purchased from Mr B. E. Walls, 1944
Morley, Harry 1881–1943, *Doctor Alfred Wilson Emms (1850–1920)*, gift from D. H. Woodfield, 1957, © the artist's estate
Morley, Harry 1881–1943, *A Framework Knitter*, gift from Mr Arthur Morley, 1952, © the artist's estate
Morley, Harry 1881–1943, *Jessie Elizabeth Morley, the Artist's Sister*, gift from Mrs J. E. Alexander, 1959, © the artist's estate
Morley, Harry 1881–1943, *Lighting the Lamp of Peace*, gift from Mr Thomas A. Morley, 1938, © the artist's estate
Morley, Harry 1881–1943, *A Wayside Madonna*, purchased from the artist, 1929, © the artist's estate
Morley, Harry 1881–1943, *Arthur Richard Johnson (1854–1918), Co-Founder of Hawley and Johnson*, gift from Hawley and Johnson Ltd, 1980, © the artist's estate
Moynihan, Rodrigo 1910–1990, *Still Life with a Jug*, gift from the Contemporary Art Society, 1941, © the artist's estate
Moynihan, Ursula 1912–1995, *Blue Cineraria*, purchased from Mrs Ursula E. Brown, 1943
Muller, William James 1812–1845, *The Slave Market, Cairo*, purchased from William Permain, 1907
Muller, William James 1812–1845, *A Wooded Landscape*, purchased at Christie's, 1890
Munger, Gilbert Davis 1837–1903, *On the Seine*, gift from Mr F. J. Nettlefold, 1948
Munter, Gabriele 1877–1962, *Anna Roslund (1891–1941)*, purchased at Sotheby's with the assistance of the National Art Collections Fund, the Museums and Galleries Commission/ Victoria and Albert Museum Purchase Grant Fund and the Friends of the Museum Fund, 1991, © DACS 2012
Musin, Auguste Henri 1852–1920, *Rotterdam Harbour, The Netherlands*, gift from Mr H. H. Gimson, 1946
Nash, John Northcote 1893–1977, *Wakes Colne Mill, Colchester, Essex*, purchased by the Friends of the Museum Fund from the artist through the Art Exhibitions Bureau, © the artist's estate/ Bridgeman Art Library
Nash, Paul 1889–1946, *Nostalgic Landscape*, purchased from Roland, Browse and Delbanco, 1947, © Tate, London 2012
Naviasky, Philip 1894–1982, *Head of a Woman*, gift from the Contemporary Art Society, 1931, © the artist's estate
Neer, Aert van der 1603–1677, *Winter Landscape at Sunset*, gift from HM Government, 1979
Nesbit, Ian *Griswold Knitting Machine*, gift from S. Lakin, 1978
Nesbit, Ian *Partridge Wilson Milk Float*, purchased from Partridge Wilson and Co. Ltd, 1986
Nessler, Walter H. 1912–2001, *Southern Landscape*, purchased from the Redfern Gallery, 1956
Neuschul, Ernst 1895–1968, *Messias*, purchased at Christie's, Amsterdam with the assistance of the Art Fund, the Victoria and Albert Museum Purchase Grant Fund and the City of Leicester Museums Trust Fund, 2006, © the artist's estate
Neuschul, Ernst 1895–1968, *Negermutter*, purchased from Campbell and Franks Ltd with the assistance of the Museums and Galleries Commission/Victoria and Albert Museum Purchase Grant Fund, 1978, © the artist's estate
Nevinson, Christopher 1889–1946, *One Summer's Day*, gift from Mrs K. Nevinson, 1947, © the artist's estate/Bridgeman Art Library
Nevinson, Christopher 1889–1946, *Oxford, on the Cherwell*, anonymous gift in memory of Reverend Timothy Jones of St Margaret's by Knighton, 1924, © the artist's estate/Bridgeman Art Library
Newton, George *The Old Workhouse (Poor House), the Green, Belgrave, Leicestershire*, gift from Mr A. Walter West, 1968
Nicholas, Hilda Rix 1884–1961, *His Land*, purchased from the artist, 1928
Nicholson, Ben 1894–1982, *1948 (still life)*, purchased at Sotheby's, 1962, © Angela Verren Taunt 2012. All rights reserved, DACS
Nicholson, Winifred 1893–1981, *Crystals*, purchased from Mrs Monika Kinley with the assistance of the Museums and Galleries Commission/Victoria and Albert Museum Purchase Grant Fund, 1977, © trustees of Winifred Nicholson
Nicol, Erskine 1825–1904, *Kept In*, bequeathed by Mr George Hodges, 1924
Nicol, Erskine 1825–1904, *Signing the New Lease*, purchased from Mr Thomas McLean, 1900
Niemann, Edmund John 1813–1876, *Filey Brigg, North Yorkshire*, bequeathed by Sir Edward Wood, 1918
Niemann, Edmund John 1813–1876, *Richmond, North Yorkshire, from the Swale*, bequeathed by Sir Edward Wood, 1918
Nolan, Sidney 1917–1992, *Mrs Fraser with Convict*, purchased from Mrs Monica Kinley with the assistance of the Museums and Galleries Commission/Victoria and Albert Museum Purchase Grant Fund, 1980, © the artist's estate/Bridgeman Art Library
Nolan, Sidney 1917–1992, *Kelly*, purchased with the assistance of

the Museums and Galleries Commission/Victoria and Albert Museum Purchase Grant Fund, 1980, © the artist's estate/ Bridgeman Art Library
Nolan, Sidney 1917–1992, *The Explorer Burke on a Camel*, purchased from Marlborough Fine Art Ltd with the assistance of the Calouste Gulbenkian Foundation, 1967, © the artist's estate/ Bridgeman Art Library
Núñez de Villavicencio, Pedro 1644–1700, *Two Boys Feeding a Beggar*, presented by Mrs Beatrice Seal and H. D. Seal in memory of Harry Seal, 1949
Núñez de Villavicencio, Pedro 1644–1700, *Two Boys Playing Pitch-and-Toss*, purchased from the executors of the estate Sir Lindsay Everard, 1950
Nunney, Reginald 1895–1922, *Self Portrait*, gift from Mrs Florie Gregory, 1939
Oakes, John Wright 1820–1887, *Picking up Wreckage on a Rocky Shore*, purchased at Christie's, 1888
O'Connor, Patrick 1909–1997, *Jack Butler Yeats (1871–1957)*, on long-term loan from Mrs M. Farrell, since 1971
Ommeganck, Balthazar Paul 1755–1826, *Landscape with Figures*, bequeathed by Mr John William Cutler Bickley, 1935
Opie, John 1761–1807, *Boy with a Hoop*, purchased from Thomas Agnew and Sons Ltd, 1953
Opie, John 1761–1807, *Head of a Girl*, gift from Mr C. Hedley Haddon, 1943
Organ, Bryan b.1935, *Sir Richard Attenborough (b.1923)*, purchased from the artist, © Bryan Organ & the Redfern Gallery, London
Organ, Bryan b.1935, *St Pancras Station, London*, gift from Mr Herald Goddard, 1969, © Bryan Organ & the Redfern Gallery, London
Organ, Elizabeth 1934–2009, *Coffee Pot*, transferred from the Schools' Loans Service
Organ, Elizabeth 1934–2009, *Blue Flowers*, transferred from the Schools' Loans Service, 1977
Orpen, William 1878–1931, *Lady on a Couch*, purchased from Mrs M. E. Rhoades, 1945
Orrock, James 1829–1913, *Kneeton Ford, Nottingham, on the Trent*, gift from the artist, 1884
Orrock, James 1829–1913, *On the Nith, Scotland*, gift from Mr Edward V. Stibbe, 1945
Pace del Campidoglio, Michele (attributed to) 1610–probably 1670, *Still Life with Fruit*, purchased from the Lisson Gallery, 1964
Parker *Emily Comber Fortey (1866–1946), Councillor*
Parker *Francis Paul Armitage, Esq., Director of Education, Leicester County Borough (1910–1940)*
Parker, Alan b.1965, *Muktaben Bhogaita and Daughter Alka*, gift from the artist, 2004
Parker, Alan b.1965, *Debbie Loves Jesus*, purchased from the artist with the assistance of the Museums, Libraries and Archives Council/Victoria and Albert Museum Purchase Grant Fund and the Art Fund, 2004
Pechstein, Hermann Max 1881–1955, *Nidden Coastline with Fishing Boats*, purchased from the Leger Galleries, 1952, © Pechstein Hamburg/Toekendorf/DACS 2012
Peng, Shi b.1954, *A Mountain Boy*, gift from the artist, 1990
Percy, Sidney Richard 1821–1886, *Highland Landscape*
Pettinger, John Frederick 1877–1939, *Wee Annie*, gift from Mr J. Wardley, 1943
Pettinger, John Frederick 1877–1939, *Percival James Atkins (1871–1955)*, gift from Mr Clive N. Atkins, 1998
Pettinger, John Frederick 1877–1939, *From the Artist's Window, Leicester Art School*, purchased from Mrs J. F. Pettinger, 1944
Pettinger, John Frederick 1877–1939, *Pont Neuf, Paris*, purchased from the artist, 1925
Pettinger, John Frederick 1877–1939, *The Jester*, gift from Mrs J. F. Pettinger, 1946
Phillip, John 1817–1867, *The Balcony*, purchased at Christie's, 1891
Phillips, Thomas 1770–1845, *George Anthony Legh-Keck (1774–1860)*, purchased from Spink and Son Ltd, 1957
Pidding, Henry James 1797–1864, *The Enthusiast*, purchased from Mrs F. Newcombe, 1889
Piper, John 1903–1992, *Derelict Cottage, Deane, Hampshire*, gift from the Contemporary Art Society, 1941, © the artist's estate
Pissarro, Camille 1831–1903, *La route, effet de neige*, purchased from Thomas Agnew and Sons Ltd with the assistance of the Museums and Galleries Commission/ Victoria and Albert Museum Purchase Grant Fund and the Friends of the Museum Fund, 1980
Pittoni, Giovanni Battista the younger 1687–1767, *The Assumption of the Virgin*, purchased from P. and D. Colnaghi and Co. Ltd with the assistance of the Museums and Galleries Commission/Victoria and Albert Museum Purchase Grant Fund, 1964
Poole, Paul Falconer 1807–1879, *Arlète, a Peasant Girl of Falaise in Normandy, First Discovered by Duke Robert le Diable*, purchased at Christie's, 1891
Poole, Paul Falconer 1807–1879, *An Italian Family*, purchased at Christie's, 1891
Poussin, Nicolas (attributed to) 1594–1665, *The Holy Family with the Infant Saint John*, gift from Mr C. Hedley Haddon, 1943
Procter, Ernest 1886–1935, *The Day's End*, purchased from the artist, 1928
Proctor, J. F. *Winter in South Wales*, unknown acquisition method
Pryde, James 1866–1941, *The Monument*, purchased from the Beaux Arts Gallery, 1941
Pullée, Edward 1907–2002, *Receding Floodwater*, purchased from the artist, 1961, © the artist's estate
Pyne, James Baker 1800–1870, *Whitby, North Yorkshire*, purchased at Christie's, 1892
Ramsay, Allan 1713–1784, *The Honourable William Finch*, purchased from Thomas Agnew and Sons Ltd, 1982
Read, Ada *Carting Fish at Mount's Bay, Cornwall* (copy after Edmund Morison Wimperis)
Régnier, Nicolas (attributed to) c.1590–1667, *The Death of Sophonisba*, purchased from A. Wiggins and Sons, 1949
Rego, Paula Figueiroa b.1935, *Three Guchi Faces, Guchi Face with Cutlery*, purchased from Mrs Monika Kinley, with the assistance of the Museums and Galleries Commission/Victoria and Albert Museum Purchase Grant Fund, 1984, © the artist
Rego, Paula Figueiroa b.1935, *Three Guchi Faces, Guchi Face with Banana*, purchased from Mrs Monika Kinley, with the assistance of the Museums and Galleries Commission/Victoria and Albert Museum Purchase Grant Fund, 1984, © the artist
Rego, Paula Figueiroa b.1935, *Three Guchi Faces, Guchi Face with Bride*, purchased from Mrs Monika Kinley, with the assistance of the Museums and Galleries Commission/Victoria and Albert Museum Purchase Grant Fund, 1984, © the artist
Reid, John Robertson 1851–1926, *Little Cornish Fishermen, Polperro*, purchased from the artist, 1906
Renals, Richard Beswick 1833–1900, *Landscape with Cattle and Sheep by a Stream*, bequeathed by Miss S. F. Clarke, 1988
Renison, G. *Summer Landscape with Hills*, transferred from Hinckley Library, 1996
Ribeiro, Lancelot 1933–2010, *Purple Still Life*, purchased from the artist, © the artist's estate
Ribeiro, Lancelot 1933–2010, *Still Life with a Pitcher*, purchased from the artist, 1987, © the artist's estate
Ribeiro, Lancelot 1933–2010, *Accented Landscape, Series 1*, purchased from the artist, 1987, © the artist's estate
Ribeiro, Lancelot 1933–2010, *Accented Landscape, Series 2*, purchased from the artist, 1987, © the artist's estate
Ribeiro, Lancelot 1933–2010, *Curvilinear Directions II*, purchased from the artist, 1987, © the artist's estate
Richards, Albert 1919–1945, *Escape from the Circus*, purchased from Allen Freer with the assistance of the Museums and Galleries Commission/Victoria and Albert Museum Purchase Grant Fund, 1979
Richards, Ceri Geraldus 1903–1971, *Return of the Patient* (version 1), purchased from Mrs Frances Richards and Mrs Monika Kinley with the assistance of the Museum and Galleries Commission/Victoria and Albert Museum Purchase Grant Fund, 1978, © estate of Ceri Richards. All rights reserved, DACS 2012
Richardson, Jonathan the elder (after) 1664/1665–1745, *Baron Carter, Lord Chief Justice Carter*, bequeathed by Miss Emily Frances Dalton, 1900
Robb, Brian 1913–1979, *Weesen, Switzerland*, purchased from the London Group Exhibition, 1954, © the artist's estate
Roberts, Albert Thomas 1868–1923, *Cider Press, Normandy, France*, gift from Mrs A. T. Roberts in memory of the artist, 1923
Roberts, David 1796–1864, *Jerusalem from the Mount of Olives*, purchased at Christie's, 1890
Roberts, David 1796–1864, *View of Tiberias on the Sea of Galilee*, gift from Mr Colin Ellis, 1966
Roberts, William Patrick 1895–1980, *At the Hippodrome*, gift from the Contemporary Art Society, 1935, © estate of John David Roberts. By courtesy of The William Roberts Society
Rothenstein, William 1872–1945, *The Toilet*, purchased from the artist through the Goupil Gallery, 1931, © the artist's estate/ Bridgeman Art Library
Rowe, Cliff 1904–1989, *The Fried Fish Shop*, purchased from the artist, 1936, © the artist's estate
Russell, George William (attributed to) 1867–1935, *Three Figures in a Landscape with Birds*
Russian School 17th C, *Ikon with Saint Theodore and Saint Aloysius*, gift from Mr William Stringer, 1856
Ruysdael, Salomon van c.1602–1670, *River Scene with a Distant View of Vianen, The Netherlands*, bequeathed by Ernest Edward Cook through the National Art Collections Fund, 1955
Ryan, Adrian 1920–1998, *Pheasants*, gift from Mr Roger Evans, 1953, © estate of Adrian Ryan
Sargent, John Singer 1856–1925, *Field Marshal Viscount Allenby (1861–1936), GCB, GCMG* (sketch), purchased from Knoedler and Co., 1925
School of Fontainebleau *The Rape of Lucrece* (from the poem by William Shakespeare), bequeathed by Mr John William Cutler Bickley, 1935
Scott, A. *Thomas Crick (d.1879)*, on permanent loan from the Trustees of Crick's Charity
Scott, William 1797–1862, *John Flower (1793–1861)*, bequeathed by Mrs Anges Middleton, 2001
Seguier, John 1785–1856, *Newarke Gateway, Leicester*, purchased from Martyn Gregory with the assistance of the Museums and Galleries Commission/Victoria and Albert Museum Purchase Grant Fund, 1974
Setch, Dianne b.1945, *Soldiers 2*, gift from the Collection of the Arts Council of Wales, 2005, © the artist
Setch, Dianne b.1945, *Soldiers 4*, gift from the Collection of the Arts Council of Wales, 2005, © the artist
Sharma, Ram Krishan *Bagor House, Gangor Festival, India*, purchased from the City Gallery with the assistance of the City of Leicester Museums Trust, 2001
Sharma, Ram Krishan *City Palace, Sawar, India*, purchased from the City Gallery with the assistance of the City of Leicester Museums Trust, 2001
Sharma, Ram Krishan *Jag Mandir, India*, purchased from City Gallery with the assistance of the City of Leicester Museums Trust, 2001
Sharma, Ram Krishan *Small Hunting Scene*, purchased from the City Gallery with the assistance of the City of Leicester Museums Trust, 2001
Shayer, William 1788–1879, *The Timber Wagon*, purchased from Mr Palser, 1883
Shayer, William (style of) 1788–1879, *At the Farm*, purchased from Messrs Withers, 1946
Sheikh, Nilima b.1945, *Champa, before Her Marriage, and with Her Mother*, purchased from the artist, 1986
Sheikh, Nilima b.1945, *Champa, on the Swing, a Traditional Motif of Love and Girlhood, on the Eve of Her Marriage*, purchased from the artist, 1986
Sheikh, Nilima b.1945, *Marriage and Departure to the In-Laws' Village*, purchased from the artist, 1986
Sheikh, Nilima b.1945, *Arrival and Welcome 'aati' at the In-Laws and the Kitchen, the Bride's Place*, purchased from the artist, 1986
Sheikh, Nilima b.1945, *The Womenfolk of the House Inspect Champa, the New Bride*, purchased from the artist, 1986
Sheikh, Nilima b.1945, *Conflict between the Daughter-in-Law and Mother-in-Law, while the Husband Enjoys a Rest*, purchased from the artist, 1986
Sheikh, Nilima b.1945, *Tensions in the Household and Persecution of the New Bride*, purchased from the artist, 1986
Sheikh, Nilima b.1945, *The*

Husband, Sister-in-Law and Mother-in-Law Plot to Kill Champa, while She Dozes Battered and Exhausted from the Chores Given to Her, in the Kitchen, purchased from the artist, 1986
Sheikh, Nilima b.1945, *Conspiracy to Murder while Champa Works in the Kitchen*, purchased from the artist, 1986
Sheikh, Nilima b.1945, *Fire and Smoke from the Kitchen*, purchased from the artist, 1986
Sheikh, Nilima b.1945, *Champa's Funeral Pyre*, purchased from the artist, 1986
Sheikh, Nilima b.1945, *Ritualised Mourning, Marshia*, purchased from the artist, 1986
Sickert, Walter Richard 1860–1942, *The Yellow Sleeve*, purchased from Thomas Agnew and Sons Ltd with the assistance of the Friends of the Museum Fund, © estate of Walter R. Sickert. All rights reserved, DACS 2012
Sickert, Walter Richard 1860–1942, *The Bart and the Bums* (after John Gilbert), purchased from the Leicester Galleries, 1931, © estate of Walter R. Sickert. All rights reserved, DACS 2012
Sickert, Walter Richard 1860–1942, *Dover, Kent*, purchased from Messrs Brown and Phillips, © estate of Walter R. Sickert. All rights reserved, DACS 2012
Singh, Sarup active 1968–2001, *Martin Luther King Junior (1929–1968)*, gift from the artist, 2001
Sisley, Alfred 1839–1899, *Le Loing, gelée blanche*, purchased from Mrs F. Leverton-Harris, 1935
Slater, Joseph Edward 1902–1994, *Charles Street, Leicester*, purchased from the artist, 1947
Slaughter, Stephen 1697–1765, *James Thomson (1700–1748), Poet*, purchased at Christie's, 1937
Small, William 1843–1931, *The Good Samaritan*, purchased from Messrs Leggatt, 1900
Smith, J. H. *Leicester from the River*
Smith, Jack 1928–2011, *64 Activities in Blue*, purchased from Mrs Monika Kinley with the assistance of the Calouste Gulbenkian Foundation, 1975, © the artist's estate/courtesy Flowers Gallery, London
Smith, Matthew Arnold Bracy 1879–1959, *Reclining Nude*, purchased from Arthur Tooth & Sons Ltd, 1948, © by permission of the copyright holder
Smith, Matthew Arnold Bracy 1879–1959, *Landscape, South of France*, gift from the Contemporary Art Society, 1954, © by permission of the copyright holder
Solomon, Abraham 1824–1862, *The Flight from Lucknow*, purchased at Christie's, 1891
Spanish School early 18th C, *The Virgin*, gift from Mr C. Arnold, 1954
Spear, Ruskin 1911–1990, *The Tea Shop*, gift from the Contemporary Art Society, 1947, © the artist's estate/Bridgeman Art Library
Spencer, J. L. *Portrait of a Scottish Huntsman*
Spencer, Stanley 1891–1959, *Adoration of Old Men*, purchased at Sotheby's with the assistance of the Museums and Galleries Commission/Victoria and Albert Museum Purchase Grant Fund, 1964, © the estate of Stanley Spencer 2012. All rights reserved DACS
Spencer, Stanley 1891–1959, *Distant View of Maidenhead, Berkshire*, gift from Tom Lawson and Ruth Oliver in memory of their parents Norma and Josef Oplatek, with the assistance of the National Art Collections Fund, the Museums and Galleries Commission/Victoria and Albert Museum Purchase Grant Fund and the City of Leicester Museum Trust, © the estate of Stanley Spencer 2012. All rights reserved DACS
Spencer, Stanley 1891–1959, *J. L. Behrend*, gift from Tom Lawson and Ruth Oliver in memory of their parents Norma and Josef Oplatek, with the assistance of the National Art Collections Fund, the Museums and Galleries Commission/Victoria and Albert Museum Purchase Grant Fund and the City of Leicester Museum Trust, © the estate of Stanley Spencer 2012. All rights reserved DACS
Stanfield, Clarkson 1793–1867, *Macbeth and the Witches*, purchased at Christie's, 1890
Steer, Henry Reynolds 1858–1928, *Christmas Eve, Highcross Market, Leicester, Sixteenth Century*, purchased at Sotheby's, 1997
Steer, Henry Reynolds 1858–1928, *De Montfort Hall Gardens, Leicester*, gift from H. A. Orton, 1975
Steer, Henry Reynolds 1858–1928, *Charles I Leaving the Cavendish Mansion, Leicester, on His Way to Relieve Oxford, May 1645*, bequeathed by Mrs Alfred Corah, 1927
Steer, Henry Reynolds 1858–1928, *The Old Woodgate, Leicester*, bequeathed by Mrs Alfred Corah, 1927
Steer, Philip Wilson 1860–1942, *Evening, near Bridgnorth, Shropshire*, on long-term loan from Dr J. S. Steward, since 1975, © Tate, London 2012
Stevenson, William Grant 1849–1919, *Church Road, Belgrave, Leicestershire*, purchased from Warner, Sheppard and Wade, 1982
Sutherland, Graham Vivian 1903–1980, *Narrow Road between Hedges*, purchased from Messrs Reid and Lefevre, 1946, © estate of Graham Sutherland
Sutherland, Graham Vivian 1903–1980, *The Laughing Woman* (study), gift from Mrs Anne Kessler, 1958, © estate of Graham Sutherland
Sutton, Philip b.1928, *Landscape*, purchased from Roland, Browse and Delbanco with the assistance of the Friends of the Museum Fund, 1956, © Philip Sutton. All rights reserved, DACS 2012
Sweerts, Michael 1618–1664, *Portrait of a Girl*, gift from HM Government, 1975
Syer, John 1815–1885, *Landscape*, purchased from Mr Cox, 1893
Tempest, Herbert Victor 1913–2003, *View of Leicester Museum*, purchased from the artist, 1941
Thomas, Susan *Chris Ofili (b.1968)*, gift from the Multicultural Education Service, Leicester City Council, 2008
Thornton, Albert James 1873–1947, *View of the New Granby Toll House, London Road, Leicester*, purchased from Warner, Sheppard and Wade, 1953
Thorpe, George O. *View from Narborough, Leicestershire, Looking towards Lubbesthorpe*, gift from Miss L. F. Thorpe, 1952
Thorpe, George O. *Old Cottage, Knighton, Leicester*, gift from Miss L. F. Thorpe, 1952
Thorpe, George O. *The Old Mill, Aylestone, Leicestershire*, gift from Miss L. F. Thorpe, 1952
Tibble, Geoffrey Arthur 1909–1952, *Reclining Woman*, purchased from the Storan Gallery, 1938
Tindle, David b.1932, *Back Room*, gift from the Linbury Trust, via the Contemporary Art Society, 1988, © the artist
Topham, Frank William Warwick 1838–1924, *A Roman Triumph*, purchased from the artist, 1888
Towne, Francis 1739/1740–1816, *The Valley of the Teign, Devonshire*, purchased from Thomas Agnew and Sons Ltd, 1953
Townsend, William 1909–1973, *Trees at Rolvenden, Kent*, purchased from the Leicester Galleries, 1957, © the artist's estate
Trevelyan, Julian 1910–1988, *Tuscan Landscape*, purchased from the artist, 1955, © the artist's estate
Tunnard, John 1900–1971, *Metamorphosis*, purchased from the Redfern Gallery, 1942
Turkiewicz, Zygmunt 1913–1973, *The Sun*, gift from Mrs Herald Goddard, 1969
Turner, Joseph Mallord William 1775–1851, *Cilgerran Castle*, purchased from Mr R. B. Beckett, 1955
Uff, Emmeline Sarah 1872–1942, *Trinity Hospital, Leicester*, gift from Mrs M. B. Martin, 1963
unknown artist late 15th C, *Head of the Virgin*, gift from Mr Roger Peach, 1955
unknown artist *Mary Herrick*, bequeathed by Miss I. M. Macaulay, 1937; on loan from Leicestershire County Council, until May 2012
unknown artist 16th C, *Portrait of a Man* (said to be James Butler, 2nd Earl of Ormonde), bequeathed by Miss E. K. Adderley, 1941
unknown artist *Portrait of a Herrick Boy*, bequeathed by Miss I. M. Macaulay, 1937; on loan from Leicestershire County Council, until May 2012
unknown artist *Interior, Tavern Scene*, bequeathed by Mr John William Cutler Bickley, 1935
unknown artist 17th C, *Mary Bond (1514–1611)*, bequeathed by Miss I. M. Macaulay, 1937; on loan from Leicestershire County Council until May 2012
unknown artist early 18th C, *Portrait of a Lady*, gift from Mrs W. Hawes, 1955
unknown artist 18th C, *Portrait of the Artist*, bequeathed by Mr John William Cutler Bickley, 1935
unknown artist 19th C, *Reverend Robert Hall (1764–1831)*, on long-term loan from the Trustees of Belvoir St Chapel
unknown artist *Landscape*, gift from Miss J. MacDonald, 1993
unknown artist *Portrait of an Unknown Man*
unknown artist *Country Ford*, transferred from Hinckley Library, 1996
unknown artist *Head of an Old Woman*, bequeathed by Mr John William Cutler Bickley, 1935
unknown artist, *Portrait of a Gentleman in Robes* (possibly Sir John Vaughan, 1769–1839), gift from Mr C. Hedley Haddon, 1943
unknown artist *Portrait of a Man* (copy of an earlier painting)
unknown artist *Portrait of a Young Man in Military Costume*, gift from Mr C. Hedley Haddon, 1943
unknown artist *The Return of the Princeton Heroes*, gift from Mr P. D. Griffen, 1988
Uwins, Thomas 1782–1857, *A Neapolitan Saint Manufactory*, purchased at Phillip's, 1892
Vandergucht, Benjamin 1753–1794, *Scene from 'The Register Office' by Joseph Reed*, purchased from Thomas Agnew and Sons Ltd, 1954
Varley, John II 1850–1933, *Mosque of Mohammed Bey, Cairo*, gift from the artist, 1882
Vaughan, John Keith 1912–1977, *Vertical Tree Forms*, gift from the Contemporary Art Society, 1960, © the estate of Keith Vaughan. All rights reserved, DACS 2012
Velde, Willem van de II 1633–1707, *Seascape, Ships and Boats in a Calm off a Rocky Shore*, bequeathed by Mr John William Cutler Bickley, 1935
Venables, Adolphus Robert (attributed to) c.1805–1892, *Peter Alfred Taylor (1819–1891), MP for Leicester (1868)*, gift from Miss Alice Whitehead, 1924
Verelst, Johannes d.1734, *Portrait of a Lady*, gift from Mrs W. Hawes, 1955
Vernet, Antoine-François 1730–1779, *A River Landscape*, bequeathed by Mr John William Cutler Bickley, 1935
Vernet, Antoine-François 1730–1779, *A River Landscape*, bequeathed by Mr John William Cutler Bickley, 1935
Vernet, Antoine-François 1730–1779, *A River Landscape*, bequeathed by Mr John William Cutler Bickley, 1935
Vickers, Alfred 1786–1868, *The Undercliff, Isle of Wight*, bequeathed by Miss Emily Frances Dalton, 1900
Vickers, Alfred 1786–1868, *Morning, Pen Pole Point, Bristol Channel*, purchased at Christie's, 1888
Vickers, Alfred 1786–1868, *Okehampton, Devon*, bequeathed by Miss Emily Frances Dalton, 1900
Vickers, Alfred 1786–1868, *Plumstead Common, London*, bequeathed by Miss Emily Frances Dalton, 1900
Vlaminck, Maurice de 1876–1958, *La route Napoléon*, purchased from the Redfern Gallery, 1943, © ADAGP, Paris and DACS, London 2012
Von Hofmann, Ludwig 1861–1945, *Zusammenbruch*, purchased from the Piccadilly Gallery, London with the assistance of the Museums and Galleries Commission/Victoria and Albert Museum Purchase Grant Fund, 1971
Wadsworth, Edward Alexander 1889–1949, *Rue Fontaine de Caylus, Marseilles, France*, purchased from Rosenberg and Helft Ltd, 1937, © estate of Edward Wadsworth 2012. All rights reserved, DACS
Wake, John Cheltenham c.1837–1882, *Landing the Catch*
Walker, Ethel 1861–1951, *In the Land of Ecstasy*, gift from Mr I. Montague Harris and Mr W. Harris, 1955, © the artist's estate/ Bridgeman Art Library
Walker, Ethel 1861–1951, *The Arrival*, gift from Mr I. Montague Harris and Mr W. Harris, 1955, © the artist's estate/Bridgeman Art Library
Walker, Ethel 1861–1951, *September Morning*, purchased from Reid and Lefevre Ltd, 1944, © the artist's estate/Bridgeman Art Library
Wallis, Alfred 1855–1942, *Two Black Boats Sailing up Dark Grey Waves*, purchased from Mrs Monika Kinley, 1976
Ward, Bryan 1921–1987, *Small Building in Buxton, Derbyshire*, purchased from the Leicester Society of Artists, 1988
Ward, George *New Granby Toll House, London Road, Leicester*, bequeathed by Mrs Anna Clowes, 1905
Ward, Henrietta Mary Ada 1832–1924, *Palissy the Potter*, purchased from Messrs Foster, 1887

Watson, Sydney Robert 1892–1971, *Portloe, Cornwall*, purchased from the artist, 1933
Watts, George Frederick 1817–1904, *Mrs Anne Gertrude Toller*, gift from Miss Lucy Jarvis, 1931
Watts, George Frederick 1817–1904, *Orlando Pursuing the Fata Morgana*, gift from the artist, 1888
Watts, George Frederick 1817–1904, *Woman and Child*, purchased from Abbott and Holder, 1961
Webb, James 1825–1895, *Dinant, Belgium*
Webb, James 1825–1895, *Men Must Work and Women Must Weep*, gift from the artist, 1884
Webb, James 1825–1895, *Namur, Belgium*, bequeathed by William Stanyon, 1907
Webb, James 1825–1895, *The Vale of Ross*, gift from Alderman George Viccars, 1881
Weissbon, G. *Portrait of a Woman with Books*, transferred from Hinckley Library, 1996
Whishaw, Anthony b.1930, *Still Life on a Round Table*, gift from Roland, Browse and Delbanco via the Friends of the Museum Fund, 1959, © the artist, www.anthonywhishaw.com
Whood, Isaac 1688/1689–1752, *Portrait of a Lady in White Satin*, gift from Mr C. Hedley Haddon, 1943
Whood, Isaac 1688/1689–1752, *Two Boys with Greyhounds*, gift from Mr C. Hedley Haddon, 1943
Wilde, Samuel de 1748–1832, *Mr Bannister Junior and Mr Parsons as Scout and Sheepface in 'The Village Lawyer'*, purchased from Mr Marshall C. Spink, 1941
Wilkie, David 1785–1841, *Washington Irving in the Archives of Seville*, purchased from Mr Thomas McLean, 1890
Willcock, George Burrell 1811–1852, *Holy Street Mill, Chagford, Devon*, gift from Mr F. J. Nettlefold, 1948
Williams, Alfred Walter 1823–1905, *Reigate Heath, Surrey*, gift from Mr Benjamin Russell, 1881
Williams, Aubrey 1926–1990, *Chac-Mool*, purchased from the Commonwealth Institute, 1985, © Aubrey Williams. All rights reserved, DACS 2012
Williams, Aubrey 1926–1990, *Maya Confrontation*, purchased from the Commonwealth Institute with the assistance of the Museums and Galleries Commission/Victoria and Albert Museum Purchase Grant Fund, 1985, © Aubrey Williams. All rights reserved, DACS 2012
Willis, Henry Brittan 1810–1884, *Cattle Watering at a Stream*, purchased at Christie's, 1891
Wilson, Frank Avray 1914–2009, *Configuration, Black and Blue*, purchased from the Redfern Gallery via the Friends of the Museum Fund, 1958, © the artist's estate
Wilson, Muriel Gertrude 1893–1977, *Chrysanthemums*, gift from the Contemporary Art Society, 1931
Wilson, Richard 1712/1713–1782, *Head of a Capuchin*, purchased from the Leger Galleries, 1955
Wilson, Richard 1712/1713–1782, *Landscape with Bathers*, purchased from Mr Marshall C. Spink, 1937
Wimperis, Edmund Morison 1835–1900, *Carting Fish, Mount's Bay, Cornwall*, purchased from the artist, 1882
Winks, Frederick c.1805–1880, *Joseph Winks (1767–1835), the Artist's Father*, gift from Mr Louis F. Winks, 1959
Wissing, Willem (school of) 1656–1687, *Portrait of a Lady*, gift from Mrs E. A. Hames, 1947
Wissing, Willem (school of) 1656–1687, *Portrait of a Lady*, gift from Mrs E. A. Hames, 1947
Wood, Christopher 1901–1930, *Dancing Sailors, Brittany, France*, purchased from Mr W. K. Elmhirst via the Reynold's Gallery, 1979
Woods, Henry 1846–1921, *The Water Wheels at Savassa, Italy*, purchased from Mr Thomas McLean with money from a bequest by the late Miss Emily Frances Dalton of Leicester, 1900
Woolmer, Alfred Joseph 1805–1892, *Lalla Rookh* (from the poem by Thomas Moore), gift from Mrs Elizabeth Hassell, 1943
Woolmer, Alfred Joseph 1805–1892, *The Bathers*, bequeathed by Mr John Ward, 1903
Wright, Joseph of Derby 1734–1797, *Mrs Catherine Swindell*, purchased from Thomas Agnew and Sons Ltd, 1938
Wright, Joseph of Derby 1734–1797, *High Tor, Matlock, Derbyshire*, purchased from Roland, Browse and Delbanco, 1946

Leicester City Council (Adult Skills and Learning)

Hashem, Satta b.1959, *Sight and Insight 1*, commissioned, 2002, © the artist
Hashem, Satta b.1959, *Sight and Insight 2*, commissioned, 2003, © the artist

Leicester Town Hall

British School 19th C, *Alderman John Biggs (1801–1871), Mayor of Leicester (1840, 1847 & 1855)*, transferred from Leicester Corporation, 1949; transferred from Leicester Arts and Museums Service, 2010
British School 19th C, *Thomas Paget (1778–1862), Mayor of Leicester (1836–1837)*, transferred from Leicester Arts and Museums Service, 2010
Bunney, Peter b.1932, *Council Chambers*, © Leicester City Council
Cobb, J. *HMS 'Renown' Polaris Submarine's Maiden Voyage*
Cope, Arthur Stockdale 1857–1940, *Sir Israel Hart (1935–1911), Mayor of Leicester (1884–1888 & 1893–1894)*, transferred from Leicester Corporation
Davies, Edward 1841–1920, *A Stream from the Hills, Brecon, Powys*, bequeathed by Mrs Helen Florence Evans, 1936; on long-term loan from Leicester Arts and Museums Service
Dawson, Henry 1811–1878, *The Mouth of the Dart, Devon*, purchased at Christie's; on long-term loan from Leicester Arts and Museums Service
Dawson, Henry Thomas 1841/1842–after 1896, *The River Tamar*, bequeathed by Mr Henry Snow, 1894; on long-term loan from Leicester Arts and Museums Service
Ellis, Norman 1913–1971, *Haymarket, Leicester*, gift from Mrs Norman E. Ellis, 1971; on long-term loan from Leicester Arts and Museums Service
Foster, Zena b.1931, *View of Old John, Bradgate Park, Leicestershire*, gift from the artist, © the artist
Fulleylove, John 1845–1908, *Interior of the Mosque of Omar, Jerusalem*, gift from Miss Joan E. Fulleylove on behalf of the artist's children, 1923; on long term-loan from Leicester Arts and Museums Service
Gotzenburg *The Mayor and Town Council of Leicester in the Mayor's Rooms*, commissioned, 1850s (?); on long-term loan from Leicester Arts and Museums Service
Hacker, Arthur 1858–1919, *Sir Herbert Marshall (1851–1918), Mayor of Leicester (1896–1897)*, transferred from Leicester Corporation
Hare, St George 1857–1933, *Alderman Thomas Windley (1835–1932), Mayor of Leicester (1899)*, transferred from Leicester Corporation
Kuhn, Willy *Cour du Corbeau, Strasbourg, France*
Le Bas, Edward 1904–1966, *Still Life with Flowers*, purchased from Roland, Browse and Delbanco, 1947; on long-term loan from Leicester Arts and Museums Service
Lurçat, Jean 1892–1966, *The Olive Tree*, gift from Mrs Anne Kessler; on long-term loan from Leicester Arts and Museums Service, © ADAGP, Paris and DACS, London 2012
Muncaster, Claude 1903–1974, *Landing Stage, Venice*, transferred from Hinckley Library, 1996; on long-term loan from Leicester Arts and Museums Service, © the artist's estate
Napier, John James 1831–1877, *The Right Honourable Sir John Mellor (1808–1887), Bt, Judge*, transferred from Leicester Corporation
Ouless, Walter William 1848–1933, *Alderman Edward Wood (1839–1917), JP, Mayor of Leicester (1888, 1895, 1901 & 1906)*, transferred from Leicester Corporation
Pettie, John 1839–1893, *Sir Thomas Wright (1838–1905)*, presented to Leicester Corporation by the citizens of Leicester; transferred from Leicester Corporation
Pettinger, John Frederick 1877–1939, *Low Tide*, purchased from the artist, 1930; on long-term loan from Leicester Arts and Museums Service
Pratt, Jonathan 1835–1911, *Alderman William Grimsley (1832–1878), Mayor of Leicester (1878)*, transferred from Leicester Corporation
Rowe, Cliff 1904–1989, *Machine Minder*, gift from the artist to Leicester Arts and Museums Service, 1986; on long-term loan from Leicester Arts and Museums Service, © the artist's estate
Sarson, George 1880–1969, *Changing Moods, near Stoneleigh Abbey, Kenilworth, Warwickshire*, purchased from the artist at the Leicester Society of Artists exhibition, 1967
Singh, Sarup active 1968–2001, *Elizabeth II (b.1926)*
unknown artist 19th C, *Sir William Wilkins Vincent (1843–1916), Mayor of Leicester (1902 & 1910)*, transferred from Leicester Corporation
unknown artist *Plans for Civic Centre 1 (Albion Hill Project)*
unknown artist *Plans for Civic Centre 2 (Albion Hill Project)*
Watt, George Fiddes 1873–1960, *Alderman Sir Jonathan North (1855–1939), JP*, transferred from Leicester Corporation, © the artist's estate
Wirgman, Theodore Blake 1848–1925, *Alderman William Kempson (1805–1893), JP, Mayor of Leicester (1873 & 1890)*, transferred from Leicester Corporation

Leicestershire County Council Artworks Collection

Aberlard, Gesner b.1922, *Birds and Flowers*, purchased from the Portal Gallery, 1969
Adnams, Marion Elizabeth 1898–1995, *Coloured Ending*, © the artist's estate
Akers, John Michael 1936–2009, *Willowherb*, purchased, 1970, © the artist's estate
Almquist, John *Exiles*, purchased from the Temple Gallery, 1961
Ayrton, Michael 1921–1975, *The Sweep and Others*, purchased from the Redfern Gallery, 1951, © the artist's estate
Ayrton, Michael 1921–1975, *Constant Lambert (1905–1951)*, purchased from the Redfern Gallery, 1955, © the artist's estate
Banks, Lesley b.1962, *From Bearsden to Partick*, purchased from the artist, 1990, © the artist
Barat, Pierre b.1935, *Village in the Camargue, France*, acquired, 1971
Barker, Kit 1916–1988, *Tranquil Forms*, purchased from the Bear Lane Gallery, 1962, © the artist's estate
Barra Barra, Sambo b.c.1946, *Waterbirds Feeding in Yellow*
Bassingthwaighte, Lewin 1928–1983, *Girl with a Headband*, © estate of Lewin Bassingthwaighte, 2012. All rights reserved, DACS
Bassingthwaighte, Paul b.1963, *Red Earth, Forest*, purchased, 1993, © the artist
Baxter, G. *Diver*
Beers, Robin b.1943, *Pepper and Salt*, purchased from the Angela Flowers Gallery, 1978
Bellany, John b.1942, *My Son, Tristan*, © the artist/Bridgeman Art Library
Bellany, John b.1942, *Portrait of My Grandmother*, purchased from the Redfern Gallery, 1968, © the artist/Bridgeman Art Library
Berrisford, Peter 1932–2003, *Church and Gondolas*
Billington, Bob b.1948, *Pentimento*, © the artist
Billington, Bob b.1948, *Seriatim (36 elements)*, © the artist
Blackett, Vivien b.1955, *Mountains and Molecules II*, © the artist
Blow, Sandra 1925–2006, *Small Painting*, purchased from the artist, 1969, © the artist's estate
Bodimeade, Nick b.1957, *Triptych*, acquired from the Contemporary Art Society, 1986, © the artist
Boothby, Daphne b.1931, *Sea Inlet*, acquired from the artist, 1971, © the artist
Bowen, Denis A. 1921–2006, *Atomic Image*, purchased from the Redfern Gallery, 1958, © the estate of Denis A. Bowen
Boyd, Fionnuala b.1944 & **Evans, Leslie** b.1945, *Rhinoceros*, purchased from the Angela Flowers Gallery, 1972, © the artists
Boyd, Fionnuala b.1944 & **Evans, Leslie** b.1945, *Vacuum Raft*, purchased from the Angela Flowers Gallery, 1976, © the artists
Boyd, Fionnuala b.1944 & **Evans, Leslie** b.1945, *Air Corridor*, purchased from the Angela Flowers Gallery, 1978, © the artists
Bradford, Jill active 1990–1991, *Doorway*, purchased from the artist, 1991
Bramble, Richard b.1968, *Manta*

Rays, purchased from the artist, 1991, © the artist
Bratby, John Randall 1928–1992, *Jean with a Bicycle*, purchased from Beaux Arts, 1960, © the artist's estate/Bridgeman Art Library
Bratby, John Randall 1928–1992, *Self Portrait with Sandals*, purchased from Beaux Arts, 1958, © the artist's estate/Bridgeman Art Library
Brereton, Ann *Introversion*, gift from the artist, 1974
Buhler, Robert A. 1916–1989, *Cornfield, Rogate, Hampshire*, purchased from the Piccadilly Gallery, 1959, © the artist's estate/Bridgeman Art Library
Buhler, Robert A. 1916–1989, *Suffolk Lane*, purchased from the Piccadilly Gallery, © the artist's estate/Bridgeman Art Library
Burr, James b.1926, *Night Flowers*, purchased, 1966
Bush, Jack 1909–1977, *Tan Band*, purchased from the Waddington Galleries, 1969, © DACS 2012
Butler, Elizabeth *6/77*
Caloutsis, Valerios b.1927, *Stress*, purchased from the Redfern Gallery, 1962
Campion, Oliver 1928–2000, *The Kitchen*, purchased from the artist, 1968, © the artist's estate
Carr, Thomas James 1909–1999, *Girl with a Lace Collar*, purchased from the Redfern Gallery, 1954, © the artist's estate
Carradice, Michael *Irontide*, acquired, 1971
Cartwright, Reg b.1938, *Landscape between Two Buildings*, acquired from the artist, 1979, © the artist/Bridgeman Art Library
Chandra, Avinash 1931–1991, *Crab Tree*, purchased from the Hamilton Galleries, 1967, © by kind permission of Osborne Samuel Ltd
Chandra, Avinash 1931–1991, *Early Figures*, purchased from the Hamilton Galleries, 1967, © by kind permission of Osborne Samuel Ltd
Chandra, Avinash 1931–1991, *Figures in the Sand*, purchased from the Hamilton Galleries, 1967, © by kind permission of Osborne Samuel Ltd
Chery, Jacques-Richard b.1928, *Picking Fruit*, purchased from the Portal Gallery, 1969
Christoforou, John b.1921, *Landscape with a Church*, purchased from Gallery One, 1949, © ADAGP, Paris and DACS, London 2012
Cohen, Harold b.1928, *Woman in the Window*, purchased from the Marlborough Galleries, 1956, © the artist
Cohen, Harold b.1928, *Gentleman in Academic Dress*, purchased from the Marlborough Galleries, 1959, © the artist
Cohen, Harold b.1928, *Water Garden*, gift, 1964, © the artist
Cohen, Harold b.1928, *Fiesta*, donated, © the artist
Cohen, Harold b.1928, *Plan for a City*, gift, 1963, © the artist
Collins, Niamh b.1956, *Red Kangaroo*, purchased from the artist, 1986, © the artist
Collinson, Hugh 1909–2009, *The Green Bowl, Derbyshire Limestone*, © the artist's estate
Colquhoun, Robert 1914–1962, *The Peasant Woman*, purchased from the Piccadilly Gallery, 1957, © the artist's estate/Bridgeman Art Library
Colquhoun, Robert 1914–1962, *The Goatherd*, purchased from the Redfern Gallery, 1958, © the artist's estate/Bridgeman Art Library
Colquhoun, Robert 1914–1962, *Seated Figure*, unknown acquisition method, © the artist's estate/Bridgeman Art Library
Colquhoun, Robert 1914–1962, *Woman Ironing*, purchased from the Whitechapel Art Gallery, 1958, © the artist's estate/Bridgeman Art Library
Cook, Frank b.1940, *Fécamp Market, France*, acquired, 1990, © the artist
Cook, Jenny b.1942, *Mtahleb, Malta II*, purchased from the artist, 2003, © the artist
Cook, Jenny b.1942, *Return to Beaumont*, purchased from the artist, 2003, © the artist
Cook, Jenny b.1942, *Spirit of Malta*, purchased from the artist, 2003, © the artist
Cook, Jenny b.1942, *Citadel Valetta, Malta*, purchased from the artist, 2004, © the artist
Cook, Jenny b.1942, *Chevron Fish*, purchased from Beaumanor Hall, 1997, © the artist
Cook, Roger b.1940, *Slightly Imperfect*, purchased from the artist, 1994, © the artist
Copnall, John 1928–2007, *Elephant*, purchased from the Piccadilly Gallery, 1957, © the artist's estate
Copnall, John 1928–2007, *Tiger*, purchased from the Piccadilly Gallery, © the artist's estate
Craxton, John 1922–2009, *Fish Hawker, Athens*, purchased from the Redfern Gallery, 1958, © John Craxton 2012. All rights reserved, DACS
Crook, P. J. b.1945, *Staff Meeting*, purchased from the artist, 1990, © the artist/Bridgeman Art Library
Crook, P. J. b.1945, *Expresso*, purchased from the artist, 1999, © the artist/Bridgeman Art Library
Crook, P. J. b.1945, *Comic Strip*, purchased from the artist, 2001, © the artist/Bridgeman Art Library
Crook, P. J. b.1945, *Armchair Supporters*, purchased from the artist, 2004, © the artist/Bridgeman Art Library
Crook, P. J. b.1945, *The Ark*, purchased from the artist, 2004, © the artist/Bridgeman Art Library
Crook, P. J. b.1945, *The Beautiful Game*, purchased from the artist, 2004, © the artist/Bridgeman Art Library
Crook, P. J. b.1945, *The Whale*, purchased from the artist, 1999, © the artist/Bridgeman Art Library
Culbert, Bill b.1935, *Descent from Château Lacoste II*, purchased from the Piccadilly Gallery, 1964, © the artist
Cyster, Poppy b.1983, *Tormaukin I*, purchased from the De Montfort University Degree Show, 2007, © the artist
Cyster, Poppy b.1983, *Tormaukin II*, purchased from the De Montfort University Degree Show, 2007, © the artist
Daborn, Erica b.1951, *Hat Bargains*, purchased from the artist, 1978
D'Aguilar, Michael b.1924, *Folk Dancers, Spain*, purchased from the Redfern Gallery, 1956
D'Aguilar, Michael b.1924, *Boy Trumpeter*, purchased from the Temple Gallery, 1960
Davies, Hugh b.1946, *Youth*, purchased from the artist, 1986, © the artist
De Souza, Pascoal b.1928, *Child Study*, purchased from the Redfern Gallery, 1961
Deacon, Peter b.1945, *Aberration I*, acquired, 1976, © the artist
Denison, David b.1939, *Bald Blindman*, purchased from the artist, 1977
Dillon, Gerard 1916–1971, *Still Life with Mackerel*
Dixon, Bob *Walk This Way*, unknown acquisition method
Donaldson, Antony b.1939, *Medal for Jim Clark*, purchased from the Rowan Gallery, 1970, © Antony Donaldson
Dorman, Arabella b.1975, *A Quick Turnaround, the Queen's Royal Lancers, Maysaan*, © the artist
Dorman, Arabella b.1975, *Another Beautiful Day in Shaibah*, © the artist
Dorman, Arabella b.1975, *Leaving Camp*, © the artist
Drawbridge, John 1930–2005, *Crustacea*, acquired, 1963, © the artist's estate
Drawbridge, John 1930–2005, *Portrait of a Man*, purchased from the Redfern Gallery, 1962, © the artist's estate
Dubsky, Mario 1939–1985, *Flying High*, acquired, 1968, © the artist's estate
Duffy, Terry b.1948, *Out of the Green*, purchased from the artist, 1991, © the artist
Dukes, Robert b.1965, *Portrait of a Girl*, © the artist
Dunn, Stephen *Black Corner*
Feiler, Paul b.1918, *Italian Village Square with a Lake*, purchased from the Redfern Gallery, 1956, © the artist/Bridgeman Art Library
Feiler, Paul b.1918, *Lamorna Grey and Black*, acquired, 1957, © the artist/Bridgeman Art Library
Feiler, Paul b.1918, *Porth Ledden Grey*, purchased from the Redfern Gallery, 1959, © the artist/Bridgeman Art Library
Fletcher, David 1948–2008, *Temple Cat*, purchased from the artist, 1973, © the artist's estate
Foord, Susan b.1945, *Untitled*, unknown acquisition method, © the artist
Francois, Roger b.c.1928, *Birds*, purchased from the Portal Gallery, 1969
Frost, Terry 1915–2003, *Blues*, purchased from the Waddington Galleries, 1966, © estate of Terry Frost. All rights reserved, DACS 2012
Fussell, Michael 1927–1974, *Low Tide, Aldeburgh, Suffolk*, purchased from the Piccadilly Gallery, 1959
Garanjoud, Claude 1926–2005, *Flowers II*, purchased from the Piccadilly Gallery, 1960, © the artist's estate
Garanjoud, Claude 1926–2005, *Valansole, Provence, France*, © the artist's estate
Garanjoud, Claude 1926–2005, *Composition with Sails*, purchased from the Piccadilly Gallery, 1960, © the artist's estate
George, Andrew Scott b.1952, *Cairngorms, Highlands*, purchased from the artist, 2005, © the artist
George, Andrew Scott b.1952, *Dream Topping*, purchased from the artist, 2005, © the artist
George, Andrew Scott b.1952, *Rothiemurchus, Inverness*, purchased from the artist, 2005, © the artist
George, Andrew Scott b.1952, *Above the Swyre, Dorset*, purchased from the artist, 2005, © the artist
George, Andrew Scott b.1952, *Bullock's Hill*, purchased from the artist, 2005, © the artist
George, Andrew Scott b.1952, *Abernethy, Perthshire*, purchased from the artist, 2005, © the artist
George, Andrew Scott b.1952, *Downland*, purchased from the artist, 2005, © the artist
George, Andrew Scott b.1952, *Dunes*, purchased from the artist, 2005, © the artist
Ghosh, Amal b.1933, *Secrets*, purchased from the artist, 1990, © the artist
Gibbs, Evelyn 1905–1991, *Erosion*, purchased from the Redfern Gallery, 1970, © the artist's estate
Gore, Frederick John Pym 1913–2009, *Provence in Silver*, purchased from the Redfern Gallery, 1953, © estate of Frederick Gore. All rights reserved, DACS 2012
Gore, Frederick John Pym 1913–2009, *Swirly Olive Trees, Les Baux, France*, purchased from the Redfern Gallery, © estate of Frederick Gore. All rights reserved, DACS 2012
Gore, Frederick John Pym 1913–2009, *Cornfield, Meopham, Kent*, purchased from the Redfern Gallery, 1956, © estate of Frederick Gore. All rights reserved, DACS 2012
Gore, Frederick John Pym 1913–2009, *Flower Farm, near Arles, France*, purchased from the Redfern Gallery, 1959, © estate of Frederick Gore. All rights reserved, DACS 2012
Gore, Frederick John Pym 1913–2009, *Near Les Baux, Provence, France*, purchased from the Redfern Gallery, 1959, © estate of Frederick Gore. All rights reserved, DACS 2012
Graham, Rigby b.1931, *Turbulent Landscape, Dorset*, purchased from the artist, © the artist
Graham, Rigby b.1931, *Cornish Landscape with Lime Workings*, purchased from the artist, 1969, © the artist
Graham, Rigby b.1931, *Mine Workings, East Cornwall*, purchased from the artist, 1969, © the artist
Grant, Keith b.1930, *Swamp on the Road to Sinnamary, French Guiana*, purchased from the artist, 1984, © the artist
Grant, Keith b.1930, *Spring, the North Tyne, Chollerford, Northumberland*, © the artist
Greaves, Derrick b.1927, *Goat*, purchased from the Midland Group of Artists, 1956, © the artist
Greaves, Derrick b.1927, *Italian Peasants*, purchased from the Piccadilly Gallery, 1959, © the artist
Greaves, Derrick b.1927, *Bloomfield*, purchased from the Zwemmer Gallery, 1963, © the artist
Greaves, Derrick b.1927, *Iris*, purchased from Brian Robertson, 1966, © the artist
Grebby, Anne b.1944, *Duladna Moonshine*, purchased from the artist, 1983
Green, Alan 1932–2003, *Key*, © the artist's estate
Green, Alan 1932–2003, *Painting with Grey, Yellow and Ochre*, purchased from East Midlands Arts, © the artist's estate
Green, Anthony b.1939, *Punch and Judy*, purchased from the Juda Rowan Gallery, 1964, © Anthony Green RA
Greep, Jenny *Gleaming Things*
Gurney, Julia b.1955, *Hot Water Bottle Still Life No.2*, purchased from the artist, 1982, © the artist
Hambling, Maggi b.1945, *Mac Laughing*, purchased from Moira Kelly, 1982, © the artist/Bridgeman Art Library
Hanley, Liam b.1933, *The Chimney*, unknown acquisition method, © the artist/Bridgeman Art Library
Hardie, Gwen b.1962, *Hand Two*, acquired from the Contemporary Art Society, 1986, © the artist
Harrison, Claude 1922–2009, *Fête Canaveral*, acquired, 1967, © the artist's estate
Hart, John 1921–1996, *Imps of*

Fancy on the Moors, purchased from the artist, 1973
Heath, Adrian 1920–1992, *Taza*, purchased from the Redfern Gallery, 1966, © the estate of Adrian Heath
Henderson, Sonia *Untitled (Green Window)*, purchased from the artist, 2004
Henderson, Sonia *Untitled (Kiwi)*, purchased from the artist, 2004
Henderson, Sonia *Untitled (Pink Window)*, purchased from the artist, 2004
Heron, Patrick 1920–1999, *Two Women in a Café*, purchased from the Redfern Gallery, 1954, © Susanna Heron. All rights reserved, DACS 2012
Hill, Elizabeth *Sombrero*, purchased from the artist, 1989
Hillier, Tristram Paul 1905–1983, *The Breakwater at Dieppe, France*, acquired, 1953, © the artist's estate/ Bridgeman Art Library
Hippisley, Julian 1938–1972, *Old Mill Pond, Leeds, Kent*, acquired, 1971
Hitchcock, Raymond 1922–1992, *Falling Soldier*, purchased from the Bear Lane Gallery
Hitchens, Ivon 1893–1979, *Woodpecker Tree*, purchased from Leicester Galleries, © Ivon Hitchens' estate/Jonathan Clark & Co.
Hitchens, John b.1940, *Torn Hill Landscape*, unknown acquisition method, © the artist
Hitchens, John b.1940, *June Hay*, unknown acquisition method, © the artist
Hosking, Knighton Stephen b.1944, *Earth, Sky and Water*, © the artist
Hosking, Knighton Stephen b.1944, *Sun Maker*, © the artist
Hosking, Knighton Stephen b.1944, *Pool of Water* (study), acquired, 1979, © the artist
Houthuesen, Albert Anthony 1903–1979, *Barrier*, purchased from the Mercury Gallery, 1969, © reproduced by permission of the trustees of the Albert Houthuesen Trust
Howard, Ian b.1952, *Staged*, acquired from the Contemporary Art Society, 1989
Hoyland, John 1934–2011, *31.3.69*, purchased from the Waddington Galleries, 1969, © John Hoyland. All rights reserved, DACS 2012
Hughes, Jack *Nina with Flowers*, purchased from the Piccadilly Gallery, 1959
Hughes, Jack *Small Girl in a Chair*, purchased from the Piccadilly Gallery, 1959
Hughes, Jack *The Bridesmaid*, purchased from the Piccadilly Gallery, 1958
Hughes, Jack *Small Boy with a Feather*
Hughes, Jack *Boy Sleeping under the Moon*
Hughes, Patrick b.1939, *Pile of Discarded Rainbows*, gift from the Contemporary Art Society, 1976, © the artist/courtesy of Flowers Gallery, London
Hughes, Patrick b.1939, *Darkness Falls*, purchased from the Angela Flowers Gallery, 1985, © the artist/ courtesy of Flowers Gallery, London
Huson, Eric b.1930, *A Ploughed Field*, unknown acquisition method, © the artist
Huxley, Paul b.1938, *Ceriff*, © Paul Huxley
Jacquemon, Pierre 1936–2002, *Composition in Crimson*, purchased from the Temple Gallery, 1962
James, Louis 1920–1996, *Evening Panorama, Spain*, purchased from the Redfern Gallery, © DACS 2012
James, Louis 1920–1996, *The Port I*, © DACS 2012
Jaray, Tess b.1937, *Dark Green with Four*, purchased from East Midlands Arts, 1971, © the artist
Jariwala, Caroline b.1965, *Mendi Hands*, purchased from the artist, 1991, © the artist
Jefferson, Anna b.1965, *Harbour*, purchased from the artist, 1991, © the artist
Jennings, Ceri active 1989–1991, *Mother and Baby*, purchased from the artist, 1991
Jirwulurr, Amy Johnson b.1953, *River Life in Pink*, purchased the Rebecca Hossack Art Gallery, 2004, © Rebecca Hossack Art Gallery
Jirwulurr, Amy Johnson b.1953, *River Life in Red*, purchased the Rebecca Hossack Art Gallery, 2004, © Rebecca Hossack Art Gallery
John, Augustus Edwin 1878–1961, *B. O. Schonegevel*, purchased from the Redfern Gallery, 1963, © the artist's estate/Bridgeman Art Library
Jones, Tim b.1950, *Piano with Light*, purchased from the artist, 1982, © the artist
Jones, Tim b.1950, *Construct II*, © the artist
Kalkhof, Peter b.1933, *Space and Colour I*, unknown acquisition method, © the artist
Kalkhof, Peter b.1933, *Hot Centre*, unknown acquisition method, © the artist
Keane, John b.1954, *Individual in Relation to the Masses*, © the artist/ courtesy Flowers Gallery, London
Keirle, Gordon *Guardian of Sleep*, unknown acquisition method
Kennelly, Peter b.1965, *On the Beach*, purchased from the artist, 1989, © the artist
Kenny, Michael 1941–1999, *Signs and Symbols IV*, purchased from the Juda Rowan Gallery, 1983, © the artist's estate
Khayatt, Dora c.1912–1986, *Downhill to the Severn*, purchased from the Redfern Gallery, 1951
Khayatt, Dora c.1912–1986, *The Little Port*, purchased from the Redfern Gallery, 1953
Kibart, James b.1912, *Leicestershire Landscape*, acquired, 1970
Kinley, Peter 1926–1988, *Monkey* (study), acquired, 1984, © the artist's estate
Klein, Anita b.1960, *Bedtime Story*, purchased from the artist, 1992, © Anita Klein. All rights reserved, DACS 2012
Kneale, Bryan b.1930, *Head of a Man*, purchased from the Redfern Gallery, 1957, © the artist
Kneale, Bryan b.1930, *Watching Head*, purchased from the Redfern Gallery, 1962, © the artist
Kneale, Bryan b.1930, *Blind Man*, acquired, 1954, © the artist
Kneale, Bryan b.1930, *Peel Child*, acquired, 1954, © the artist
Lancaster, Mark b.1938, *Bloomingdale*, acquired, 1965, © the artist
Lancaster, Mark b.1938, *King Study II*, purchased from the Rowan Gallery, 1970, © the artist
Lavarenne, Pierre b.1928, *Head of a Girl*, purchased from the Piccadilly Gallery, 1959
Lavarenne, Pierre b.1928, *Arbres bleus*, purchased from the Piccadilly Gallery, 1960
Le Bas, Philip Hubert b.1925, *Beach Scene*, © the artist
Lersy, Roger b.1920, *Concours hippique*, purchased from the Redfern Gallery, 1959
Leverett, David b.1938, *Greenfields*, purchased from the Redfern Gallery, 1972, © the artist
Leverett, David b.1938, *Split Shift*, acquired, 1974, © the artist
Liddell, Peter b.1954, *Galloway*, acquired, 1973
Lurlinski, David *Hanoko*, gift from East Midlands Arts
Luther, Peter b.1926, *Don Quixote Number 2*, purchased from the John Wibley Gallery, 1964
Luther, Peter b.1926, *French Farm Hand*, acquired, 1965
Luther, Peter b.1926, *The Cockerel*, acquired, 1970
Lyons, Peter active 1970–1972, *Spacemaker II*, acquired, 1974
MacBeth, Lorna Barbara b.1948, *Apocalypse*, unknown acquisition method, © the artist
MacBryde, Robert 1913–1966, *Man with a Melon*, purchased from the Redfern Gallery, 1952
MacBryde, Robert 1913–1966, *Melon on a Table*, purchased from the Redfern Gallery, 1953
Manchester, George 1922–1996, *Nuns on the Beach* (recto), purchased from the Redfern Gallery
Manchester, George 1922–1996, *City View** (verso), purchased from the Redfern Gallery
Manchester, George 1922–1996, *Black Boats*, purchased from the Redfern Gallery
Martin, Patrick b.1958, *Woman's Head*, purchased from the artist, 1992
Marzé, Émile b.1930, *Boats by the Mediterranean*, purchased from the Piccadilly Gallery, 1959
Marzé, Émile b.1930, *La mer*, purchased from the Piccadilly Gallery, 1959
Mason, Robert b.1946, *From Oumach*, purchased from the artist, 1978, © the artist
Mehta, Tyeb 1925–2009, *The Fall*
Messenger, Tony 1936–2001, *Composition*, gift from the Contemporary Art Society, 1980
Middleditch, Edward 1923–1987, *Butterfly and Sunflower*, purchased from Beaux Arts, 1958, © the estate of Edward Middleditch, courtesy James Hyman Gallery, London
Middleditch, Edward 1923–1987, *Pigeons in Trafalgar Square*, © the estate of Edward Middleditch, courtesy James Hyman Gallery, London
Miller, Elaine *Staircase*, donated
Miller, Peter active 1970–1989, *Hokey Pokey Man*
Mistry, Dhruva b.1957, *Maya Medallion*
Moddy, Coleen *Morning Exercises*
Murison, Neil b.1930, *South Coast Blue*, © the artist
Nash, John Northcote 1893–1977, *The Dingle Winter*, purchased from the Redfern Gallery, 1949, © the artist's estate/Bridgeman Art Library
Nash, John Northcote 1893–1977, *Autumn Berkshire*, acquired, 1951, © the artist's estate/Bridgeman Art Library
Nash, John Northcote 1893–1977, *The Garden*, purchased from the Redfern Gallery, 1951, © the artist's estate/Bridgeman Art Library
Nash, Thomas Saunders 1891–1968, *Choristers*
Nathan, Janet b.1938, *Ionian Sound*, © the artist
Nathan, Janet b.1938, *Off-Shore Sound*, purchased from the artist, 1987, © the artist
Newsome, Victor b.1935, *Medicine Chest*, purchased from the Contemporary Art Society, 1979, © the artist
Nolan, Sidney 1917–1992, *Blackboy Flower*, purchased from the Redfern Gallery, 1954, © the artist's estate/Bridgeman Art Library
Nolan, Sidney 1917–1992, *Australian Foliage*, purchased from the Redfern Gallery, 1955, © the artist's estate/Bridgeman Art Library
Nolan, Sidney 1917–1992, *Australian Landscape*, © the artist's estate/Bridgeman Art Library
Nolan, Sidney 1917–1992, *Australian Honeyeater*, purchased from the Redfern Gallery, 1979, © the artist's estate/Bridgeman Art Library
Norton, Margaret *West Gate, Winchester, Hampshire*, acquired, 1968
O'Brien, Kevin b.1956, *Circus Animals' Desertion*, gift from the Contemporary Art Society, © the artist
Oliver, Ken b.1948, *Martyrdom*, purchased from Moira Kelly, 1982
Oliver, Ken b.1948, *Small Saint George*, purchased from Moira Kelly, 1982
Oliver, Peter 1927–2006, *Winter Pier*, © the artist's estate
Organ, Bryan b.1935, *Number 3 Composition*, purchased from the Redfern Gallery, © Bryan Organ & the Redfern Gallery, London
Organ, Bryan b.1935, *Pendulum Number 3*, purchased from the Redfern Gallery, 1965, © Bryan Organ & the Redfern Gallery, London
Organ, Bryan b.1935, *Tippett at De Montfort Hall*, © Bryan Organ & the Redfern Gallery, London
Organ, Bryan b.1935, *Eric Pinkett (1911–1979)*, © Bryan Organ & the Redfern Gallery, London
Ormond, Tom b.1974, *Garden Folly (Goose)*, purchased from Beaumanor Hall, © the artist
Owen, Sally *Figure in a Frame No.1*, purchased from the artist, 1991
Oxtoby, David Jowett Greaves b.1938, *Ecclusiastics*, purchased from the Redfern Gallery, 1964, © the artist
Parkinson, Gerald b.1926, *Brittany Landscape III*, acquired, 1970
Parmar, Daxa b.1972, *Cityscape*, gift from the artist, 2008, © the artist
Partridge, David 1919–2006, *Mesozoic No.1*, purchased from the artist, 1973
Partridge, Susan *Disappear*
Pascal, Léopold 1900–1957, *Brittany Beach Scene, France*, purchased from the Piccadilly Gallery, 1956
Pass, David *Swan Alighting*, unknown acquisition method
Paterson, Guy *Breakers*, acquired, 1990
Peacock, Brian 1935–2004, *Hotel Balcony*, purchased from the Piccadilly Gallery, 1969, © the artist's estate
Pearson, John *Untitled*, gift from the Contemporary Art Society, 1987
Phillips, Peter b.1939, *Black Panther*, purchased from the artist, 1965, © Peter and Zoe Phillips
Piper, John 1903–1992, *Norwich Market, Norfolk*, purchased from the Leicester Galleries, 1952, © the artist's estate
Potworowski, Peter 1898–1962, *Ch,teau de Jumilhac-le-Grand, France*, © the artist's estate
Price, Rebecca b.1966, *Sunshine*, unknown acquisition method, © the artist
Procktor, Patrick 1936–2003, *Anemones: The Last Day*, purchased from the Redfern Gallery, 1959, © the artist's estate
Procktor, Patrick 1936–2003, *Red Army Ensemble*, purchased from the Redfern Gallery, 1963, © the artist's estate
Procktor, Patrick 1936–2003, *Two Chinese Generals*, purchased from the Redfern Gallery, 1968, © the

artist's estate

Reason, Cyril b.1931, *Cavalry*, purchased from Beaux Arts, 1960

Reiman, Maarja *Summertime*, acquired, 1971

Reynette James, Phyllis May 1911–1973, *New Walk at Night, Leicester*, unknown acquisition method

Reynette James, Phyllis May 1911–1973, *Potato Pickers near Melton, Leicestershire*, unknown acquisition method

Reynolds, Alan b.1926, *Moth Barn Interior*, purchased from the Redfern Gallery (?), 1955, © the artist

Reynolds, Alan b.1926, *Autumn Movement*, purchased from the Redfern Gallery, 1954, © the artist

Reynolds, Alan b.1926, *Forms Grey and Green*, purchased from the Redfern Gallery, 1961, © the artist

Reynolds, Alan b.1926, *Dialogue*, acquired, 1974, © the artist

Richards, Ceri Geraldus 1903–1971, *Girl at a Piano*, purchased from the Marlborough Galleries, 1955, © estate of Ceri Richards. All rights reserved, DACS 2012

Richards, Ceri Geraldus 1903–1971, *The Beekeeper*, purchased from the Redfern Gallery, 1959, © estate of Ceri Richards. All rights reserved, DACS 2012

Robb, Tom b.1933, *Summer Clouds*

Roberts, William Patrick 1895–1980, *The Dentist*, purchased from the Piccadilly Gallery, 1956, © estate of John David Roberts. By courtesy of The William Roberts Society

Romyn, Dick 1915–2007, *No.1 (Figures on a Beach)*, purchased from the Piccadilly Gallery, 1971, © the artist's estate

Roobottom, Joan b.1919, *Woodland Landscape*, acquired, 1971, © the artist

Roth, Frank b.1936, *Spirit for Annie*, purchased from Annely Juda, 1968

Rowell, Kenneth Leslie 1920–1999, *Man and Spectres*, purchased from the Bear Lane Gallery, 1963, © the artist's estate

Rowntree, Kenneth 1915–1997, *Spanish Girl*, purchased from the Redfern Gallery, 1963, © the artist's estate

Saxton, Colin b.1927, *Dark Horizon*, unknown acquisition method, © the artist

Schwab, Linda b.1960, *Painting Myself*, © the artist

Scott, William George 1913–1989, *Flowers on a Blue Cloth*, purchased from the Redfern Gallery, 1955, © estate of William Scott, 2012

Scott, William George 1913–1989, *Girl at a Blue Table*, purchased from the Gimpel Fils Gallery, 1953, © estate of William Scott, 2012

Scott, William George 1913–1989, *Still Life, Fish*, purchased from the Gimpel Fils Gallery, 1952, © estate of William Scott, 2012

Scott, William George 1913–1989, *Red Herrings*, purchased from the Gimpel Fils Gallery, 1956, © estate of William Scott, 2012

Scully, Sean b.1945, *20.7.74, No.2*, purchased from the Rowan Gallery, 1974

Scully, Sean b.1945, *Jan 4/74*, purchased from the Rowan Gallery, 1974

Sedgley, Peter b.1930, *Target Dive*, purchased from McRoberts & Tunnard Ltd, 1966, © the artist

Sen, Paritosh b.1918, *Rain over Benares, India*, purchased from Gallery One, 1962

Setch, Terry b.1936, *Racing in the Bay*, purchased from the Contemporary Art Society, 1989, © the artist

Shaw, Jack *Feeling through a Bach Brandenburg Concerto*

Simcock, Jack b.1929, *The Farm, Mow Cop, Staffordshire*, purchased from the Piccadilly Gallery, 1961, © the artist

Simcock, Jack b.1929, *The Haystack*, purchased from the Piccadilly Gallery, 1961, © the artist

Slater, Richard b.1927, *Garden Trellis, Evening*, acquired, 1971

Smith, Jack 1928–2011, *Shirt in Sunlight*, purchased from the Whitechapel Art Gallery, 1959, © the artist's estate/courtesy Flowers Gallery, London

Smith, Jack 1928–2011, *Bottles III*, purchased from the Whitechapel Art Gallery, 1959, © the artist's estate/courtesy Flowers Gallery, London

Smith, Paul *The Old Testament*, purchased from the Loughborough University Degree Show, 2007

Soo Pieng, Cheong 1917–1983, *Paysage chinois*, purchased from the Redfern Gallery, 1963

Southall, Derek b.1930, *Small Painting*, purchased from the artist, 1969

Southall, Derek b.1930, *Pale Fire No.2*

Southall, Derek b.1930, *Blue Orchid*

Southall, Derek b.1930, *Implode*, purchased from the artist, 1970

Southall, Derek b.1930, *Song I*, purchased from the artist, 1970

Southall, Derek b.1930, *Song II*

Southall, Derek b.1930, *Song III*, acquired, 1972

Souza, Francis Newton 1924–2002, *The Emperor*, purchased from Gallery One, 1958, © estate of F. N. Souza. All rights reserved, DACS 2012

Stahl, Andrew b.1954, *Head and Window*, © the artist

Stahl, Andrew b.1954, *Boat*, purchased from the artist, 1991, © the artist

Stahl, Andrew b.1954, *Figure and Rocket*, purchased from the artist, 1991, © the artist

Steele, Elaine active 1983–1984, *Miss Victoria*, purchased from the artist, 1984

Sujo, Glenn b.1952, *Gentle Portrait of the Artist and His Sister*, © courtesy of the artist, photo credit: the artist

Sumpter, Peter b.1933, *Tree Form, Rolleston, Leicestershire*, unknown acquisition method, © the artist

Sumpter, Peter b.1933, *Yellow Field on Greys, Praa Sands, Cornwall*, © the artist

Sutton, Philip b.1928, *Iken Wood, Suffolk*, © Philip Sutton. All rights reserved, DACS 2012

Symonds, Ken b.1927, *Godolphin Landscape*, purchased from the artist, © the artist

Taylor, Anita b.1961, *Revealed, Concealed*

Tindle, David b.1932, *Hastings Harbour, East Sussex*, purchased from the Piccadilly Gallery, 1957, © the artist

Tindle, David b.1932, *Shell Site, South Bank, London*, acquired, 1959, © the artist

Tippett, Bruce b.1933, *Untitled*, © the artist

Tirr, Willy 1915–1991, *Yellow and Black*, purchased from East Midlands Arts Association, © the artist's estate

Townsend, William 1909–1973, *Cornfield, August*, © the artist's estate

Trengrove, Barry *Himmelfarb and Miss Hare*, purchased from the Redfern Gallery, 1963

Trevelyan, Julian 1910–1988, *Taormina, Sicily*, acquired from the Gimpel Fils Gallery, 1950, © the artist's estate

Trevelyan, Julian 1910–1988, *White Oxen*, © the artist's estate

Tunnard, John 1900–1971, *Trio*, purchased from Alex Reid-LeFevre Ltd, 1951

Twist, Anthony *Breton Peasant Women*

Twist, Anthony *Cyprus Village*

Tyzack, Michael 1933–2007, *Saratoga*, © the artist's estate

Tyzack, Michael 1933–2007, *Pavan*, purchased from East Midlands Arts Association, © the artist's estate

Uhlman, Fred 1901–1985, *New York*, purchased from the artist, 1956, © the artist's estate/Bridgeman Art Library

Uhlman, Fred 1901–1985, *Lead Mine*, acquired, 1965, © the artist's estate/Bridgeman Art Library

unknown artist *Girl Holding a Cat*

Vaughan, John Keith 1912–1977, *Woodmen in a Clearing*, acquired, 1953, © the estate of Keith Vaughan. All rights reserved, DACS 2012

Vaughan, Michael b.1938, *Food Objects*, gift from the Tate Gallery, 1968, © the artist

Vielfaure, Jean-Pierre b.1930, *Vision d'apocalypse*, purchased from the Lincoln Gallery, 1962

Volley, Nicholas 1950–2006, *Hare*, purchased from the Jan Birkstead Gallery, 1985

Walker, Ethel 1861–1951, *Mother and Baby*, purchased from the Redfern Gallery, 1951, © the artist's estate/Bridgeman Art Library

Waplington, Paul Anthony b.1938, *Kelvin Flats, Sheffield*, © the artist

Ward, Irene *The Eel Pond*, acquired, 1971

Watkiss, Reg b.1933, *North Coast*, © the artist

Watson, John 1923–1992, *The Cockle Woman of Llansaint*, purchased from the artist, © the artist's estate

Watts, Percy active c.1962–1969, *Untitled Red Abstract with Crucifixes*

Wills, Dennis Frederick b.1928, *City Allotments*, © the artist

Wilson, Frank Avray 1914–2009, *Alleluia*, © the artist's estate

Wilson, Frank Avray 1914–2009, *Abstract Composition*, gift from the Redfern Gallery, 1957, © the artist's estate

Wilson, Frank Avray 1914–2009, *Blue Effigy*, purchased from the Redfern Gallery, 1959, © the artist's estate

Wilson, Frank Avray 1914–2009, *Participate*, purchased from the Redfern Gallery, © the artist's estate

Wood, Christopher 1901–1930, *Studio Window, Rue des Saints-Pères, Paris*, purchased from the Redfern Gallery, 1951

Wood, Christopher 1901–1930, *Constant Lambert (1905–1951), as a Young Man*, purchased from the Redfern Gallery, 1957

Wood, Christopher 1901–1930, *Flowers in a Glass*, purchased from the Redfern Gallery, 1941

Wood, Christopher 1901–1930, *Mother and Sleeping Child*, purchased from the Redfern Gallery

Wood, Christopher 1901–1930, *Woman in Black*, purchased from the Redfern Gallery, 1950

Wood, Christopher 1901–1930, *Woman with a Dog*, purchased from the Redfern Gallery

Wood, Christopher P. b.1961, *Undersea World No.5*, purchased the Rebecca Hossack Art Gallery, 2004, © DACS

Worthington, Maurice *Cliff Wall*

Yhap, Laetitia b.1941, *Mackerel and Cod and Oxo and Leon Coming up the Beach*, purchased from the artist, 1986, © the artist

Younie, Esther *Ten Paces Left*

Żulawski, Marek 1908–1985, *The Gardener*, © the artist's estate

Leicestershire County Council Beaumanor Collection

Bartram, David *Trees and Snow*, purchased, 1986

Bramall, Janella *Untitled 2*, purchased, 1987

Breen, Bernadette *Still Life on a Table*, purchased, 1989

Brill, Vicky *The Aroma of Coffee*

Cook, Jenny b.1942, *Chinese Creatures*, purchased, 1985, © the artist

Cook, Jenny b.1942, *Circus Toys*, purchased, 1984, © the artist

Cottam, Haydn b.1959, *Between the Devil and the Deep Blue Sea*, purchased, 1986, © the artist

Cottam, Haydn b.1959, *The Venus de Mile End*, acquired, 1998, © the artist

Cottam, Haydn b.1959, *View through the Eye of the Great Northern Shore*, purchased, 1985, © the artist

Croft, Tamsen *Reflections on Derwentwater*, acquired with the assistance of the Contemporary Art Society, 1990

Crowley, Graham b.1950, *Sanctuary*, purchased, 1982, © courtesy of Beaux Arts

Doubleday, Peter *Is It Only Virgins That Can Catch a Unicorn?*, purchased, 1988

Four Unknown Artists *Six Scenes of Beaumanor, Leicestershire*

Haselden, Ron b.1944, *Water Trap*, purchased, 1982, © the artist

Hatton, Rosamunde *Record*, purchased, 1982

Haywood, Rosie *Where Sheep May Safely Graze II*, purchased, 1989

Jarvis, Timothy *The Wavering Balance of My Feeling*, purchased, 1987

Lawley, Madonna *Graves in Sun and Wind*, purchased, 1988

Littlehales, Thomas Paul b.1945, *Untitled*, purchased, 1985, © the artist

Martin, Ross active 1985–1990, *Still Life: 3/11/86*, purchased with the assistance of East Midland Arts, 1987

Martin, Ross active 1985–1990, *Still Life: 26/11/85*, purchased with the assistance of East Midland Arts, 1987

Murdoch, Sadie b.1965, *Amoureuse (Marie Bashkirtseff)*, acquired, 1989, © the artist

Norton, Paul b.1946, *Horse*, purchased, 1984

Potter, Clare *Untitled 1*, purchased, 1985

Sujo, Glenn b.1952, *Gentle Portrait of the Artist and His Sister: Anxious Moments*, purchased with the assistance of the Arts Council, 1982; work currently out on loan, © courtesy of the artist

Sujo, Glenn b.1952, *Triptych I: Harlequin, une parade* (left panel)*; Crispin, Diary of an Insurgent* (centre panel)*; Ce qui joue le rôle d'un fou* (right panel), purchased, 1982; work currently out on loan, © courtesy of the artist

Sujo, Glenn b.1952, *Where Play Ends (Come Out and Play)*, purchased, 1982; work currently out on loan, © courtesy of the artist

Tiffany, Francis *Mother and Child*,

purchased, 1982
Unsworth, Peter *Landscape, Rape Field**
Vaughan, Alan b.1959, *Trombone Player with Bananas and Fish*, purchased, 1990, © the artist
Vaughan, Kraig *Untitled Abstract*, presented to Leicester County Council, 1994
Volley, Jo b.1953, *Daffodils*, purchased, 1982, © the artist
Walker, John b.1939, *Tense Study 1*, purchased, 1968, © the artist
Whitehouse, Mark *Vase of Flowers*, purchased, 1985

Leicestershire County Council Civic Collection

Birley, Oswald Hornby Joseph 1880–1952, *Lieutenant Colonel Sir Robert Martin, CMG, TD, JP, DL, Chairman of Leicestershire County Council (1924–1960)*, © the artist's estate
Collier, John 1850–1934, *Colonel Sir Henry St John Halford (1828–1897), Bt, CB, VD, Chairman of Leicestershire County Council (1889–1893)*, gift from the sitter to the county, 1896
Eves, Reginald Grenville 1876–1941, *Sir Thomas Cope (1840–1924), Bt, DL, Chairman of Leicestershire County Council (1908–1922)*, gift from the sitter to the county, 1919
Ferneley, John E. 1782–1860, *Melton Mowbray Horse Fair*, gift to the county from Major Guy Paget, 1933
Hepple, Norman 1908–1994, *Victor Robert Pochin, CBE, JP, DL, Chairman of Leicestershire County Council (1960–1961)*, © the artist's estate/Bridgeman Art Library
Hepple, Norman 1908–1994, *Colonel Philip Henry Lloyd, CBE, TD, JP, DL, Chairman of Leicestershire County Council (1961–1974)*, © the artist's estate/ Bridgeman Art Library
unknown artist *Mr Hussey Packe, DL, Chairman of Leicestershire County Council (1893–1908)*
unknown artist *The Right Honourable Arthur Grey Hazlerigg (1878–1949), 1st Baron Hazlerigg of Noseley, Lord Lieutenant of Leicestershire (1925–1949)* (copy of R. Swan)
Wright, Lawrence 1906–c.1985, *The County Rooms Leicester, Exterior View*, purchased, 1968
Wright, Lawrence 1906–c.1985, *The County Rooms Leicester, Interior of the Council Chamber*, purchased, 1968

Leicestershire County Council Museums Service

Artaud, William 1763–1823, *Portrait of a Lady of the Herrick Family*, bequeathed by Miss I. M. Macaulay, 1937
Artaud, William 1763–1823, *Portrait of a Gentleman of the Herrick Family*, bequeathed by Miss I. M. Macaulay, 1937
Beach, Thomas 1738–1806, *Dr Richard Pulteney (1730–1801), FRS, FLS*, purchased, 1911
Beach, Thomas 1738–1806, *Portrait of a Girl of the Burnaby Family*, gift from Dr Henry Field, 2009
Becker, Nicolas active 1922–1932, *Algernon Burnaby (1868–1938)*, gift from Dr Henry Field, 1957
Boultbee, John 1753–1812, *Robert Bakewell Mounted on a Bay Cob*, purchased with the assistance of the Museums, Libraries and Archives Council/Victoria and Albert Museum Purchase Grant Fund, 1967
Bown, Sydney *A Hunter*, purchased, 1957
Bradley, Cuthbert 1861–1943, *'Fallible' and 'Ranter'*, acquired, before 1994
Bradley, Cuthbert 1861–1943, *Quorn Hounds, 'Cruiser' and 'Woeful'*, gift from Dr Henry Field, 1957
Bradley, Cuthbert 1861–1943, *Quorn Hounds, 'Batsman', 'Baffler', 'Weaver' and 'Batchelor'*, gift from Dr Henry Field, 1957
Bradley, Cuthbert 1861–1943, *Quorn Hound 'Wonderful'*, gift from Dr Henry Field, 1957
Cave, F. *East Farndon, Leicestershire*, acquired from the Market Harborough Historial Society Collection, 1983
Cawthorne, Neil b.1936, *Summer Days*, purchased, 2003, © the artist
Coales, Kathleen Wallis 1893–1982, *Still Life*, purchased, 1998
Cooke, Arthur Claude 1867–1951, *Ragdale Hall, Leicestershire*, donated by the artist's family, 1984
Cope, Arthur Stockdale 1857–1940, *Equestrian Portrait of Captain Burns Hartopp with Hounds*, transferred from the Department of Property, 1987
Cowley, David M. *View of the Deacon Workshop, Barton in the Beans, Leicestershire*, donated, 2010
Davies, Edward 1841–1920, *Raven Hill, Charnwood Forest, Leicestershire*, purchased with the assistance of the Samuel Mather Bequest, 1902
Davis, William Henry 1786–1865, *Black Bull*, gift from Miss F. G. Mann, 1956
Ferneley, Claude Lorraine 1822–1891, *A Hunter*, bequeathed by Mr John William Cutler Bickley, 1935
Ferneley, Claude Lorraine 1822–1891, *A Hunter*, bequeathed by Mr John William Cutler Bickley, 1935
Ferneley, Claude Lorraine 1822–1891, *A Hunter*, bequeathed by Mr John William Cutler Bickley, 1935
Ferneley, Claude Lorraine 1822–1891, *A Hunter*, bequeathed by Mr John William Cutler Bickley, 1935
Ferneley, Claude Lorraine 1822–1891, *A Shooting Party in a Wood*, bequeathed by Mr John William Cutler Bickley, 1935
Ferneley, Claude Lorraine 1822–1891, *Two Huntsmen in a Landscape*, bequeathed by Mr John William Cutler Bickley, 1935
Ferneley, John II 1814–1862, *Playmate*, purchased with the assistance of the Friends of the Museum Fund, 1982
Ferneley, John E. 1782–1860, *Dr Thomas Ford (1742–1821)*, on loan from Melton Mowbray Town Estates, until 2015
Ferneley, John E. 1782–1860, *Portrait of the Artist and His Family in His Studio*, purchased with the assistance of the Museums, Libraries and Archives Council/ Victoria and Albert Museum Purchase Grant Fund, 1981
Ferneley, John E. 1782–1860, *John, Henry and Francis Grant at Melton*, purchased with the assistance of the Museums, Libraries and Archives Council/Victoria and Albert Museum Purchase Grant Fund, 1967
Ferneley, John E. 1782–1860, *Mr Pare's Coachman with a Newfoundland Dog*, purchased with the assistance of the Museums and Galleries Commission/ Victoria and Albert Museum Purchase Grant Fund, the National Heritage Memorial Fund, the Friends of the Museum Fund and the Museums Association in memory of Edgar Tyler, 1982
Ferneley, John E. 1782–1860, *Sir John Palmer on His Favourite Mare with His Shepherd, John Green, and His Prize Leicester Longwool Sheep*, purchased with the assistance of the Museums and Galleries Commission/Victoria and Albert Museum Purchase Grant Fund, the National Heritage Memorial Fund, the Friends of the Museum Fund and the Museums Association in memory of Edgar Tyler, 1982
Ferneley, John E. 1782–1860, *The Quorn at Quenby* (sketch), purchased, 1936
Ferneley, John E. 1782–1860, *Mr Green's Bay Mare*, purchased, 1948
Ferneley, John E. 1782–1860, *The Ferneley Family Pew in Melton Mowbray Parish Church, Leicestershire*, purchased with the assistance of the Museums, Libraries and Archives Council/ Victoria and Albert Museum Purchase Grant Fund, 1972
Ferneley, John E. 1782–1860, *Hunter in a Landscape*, bequeathed by Mr John William Cutler Bickley, 1935
Ferneley, John E. 1782–1860, *The Opening of the Leicester and Swannington Railway (The Arrival of the First Train at Bagworth, 17 July 1832)*, purchased, 1978
Ferneley, John E. 1782–1860, *Mountsorrel, Leicestershire, the Market Place*, purchased, 1949
Ferneley, John E. 1782–1860, *Carthorses with Grooms at a Fair*, bequeathed by Mr John William Cutler Bickley, 1935
Ferrow, Anton Mark active 1974–1989, *Tubes Factory, Desford, Leicestershire*, donated, 2008
Fisher, Tim b.1958, *The Melton Mowbray Hunt Meet*, purchased, 2003, © the artist
Fulleylove, John 1845–1908, *Ragdale Hall, Leicestershire*, purchased, 2008
Hancock, Lulu *Dawn, Mountsorrel Quarry, Leicestershire*
Hancock, Lulu *Dusk, Mountsorrel Quarry, Leicestershire*, acquired, 2000
Hancock, Lulu *Dusk, Mountsorrel Quarry, Leicestershire*
Handmann, Emmanuel Jakob (attributed to) 1718–1781, *Ambassador John Burnaby (1701–1774), Minister to the Swiss at Turin (1743–1749)* (after Pompeo Batoni), gift from Dr Henry Field, 1957
Hudson, Thomas 1701–1779, *Lord Edward Noel (1715–1774), 9th Baron, 1st Viscount Wentworth*, purchased, 1944
Hudson, Thomas 1701–1779, *Judith Lamb (1726–1797), Lady Wentworth*, purchased, 1944
Janssens van Ceulen, Cornelis 1593–1661, *George Villiers (1592–1628), 1st Duke of Buckingham*, purchased, 1938
Jervas, Charles c.1675–1739, *John Manners (1676–1721), 2nd Duke of Rutland*, purchased, 1935
Jill, E. W. *Two Greyhounds and a Hare*, acquired from the Market Harborough Historical Society Collection, 1983
Kirkby, Thomas 1775–c.1848, *Charlotte Jane Cope*, purchased, 1968
Kirkby, Thomas 1775–c.1848, *Thomas Cope*, purchased, 1968
Latham, William *Melton Mowbray, Leicestershire, from the Canal*
Madin, M. *The Square*, purchased, 2009
Marriott, Samuel 1932–1997, *The Meet of the Fernie Hunt*, purchased, 2008
Marshall, Benjamin 1767–1835, *Dr John Bowles (1765–1834)*, purchased with the assistance of the Museums, Libraries and Archives Council/Victoria and Albert Museum Purchase Grant Fund, 1972
Millar, James 1735–1805, *Reverend John Fisher (1755–1837)*, donated, 1981
Nedham, William active 1815–1849, *The Poacher*, donated, 1963
Nedham, William active 1815–1849, *Horse and Rider*, purchased, 1950
Nedham, William active 1815–1849, *A Hunter and Dog in the Grounds of Quenby Hall, Leicestershire*, donated, 1958
Organ, Bryan b.1935, *The Brickyard, Glenfield, Leicestershire*, purchased, 1959, © Bryan Organ & the Redfern Gallery, London
Paul, John Dean 1775–1852, *Greyhound in a Landscape*, bequeathed by Mr John William Cutler Bickley, 1935
Paul, John Dean 1775–1852, *Greyhound in a Landscape*, bequeathed by Mr John William Cutler Bickley, 1935
Reynette James, Phyllis May 1911–1973, *A Leicestershire Landscape*, bequeathed, 1973
Reynolds, Joshua 1723–1792, *Charles Boothby Skrymshire (1740–1800)*, purchased, 1949
Scott, William Wallace 1820–1905, *Mrs William Scott*, bequeathed, 1988
Scott, William Wallace 1820–1905, *William Scott of Barsby, Leicestershire (1797–1862)*, bequeathed, 1988
Sharp, Miles Balmford 1897–1973, *Barn at Sheepy Magna, Leicestershire*, gift from the artist, 1968
Shayer, William Joseph 1811–1892, *Coursing*, purchased, 1890
Smith, Charles Lorraine 1751–1835, *The Billesdon Coplow Run, Leicestershire*, donated, 1958
Stirling-Brown, Albert Edward D. G. active 1896–1929, *'Tiger', Grey Mare*, donated, 1994
Sumpter, Peter b.1933, *Aviation*, purchased, 1994, © the artist
Towne, Francis 1739/1740–1816, *Mrs Martha Nichols (1756–1788)*, purchased with the assistance of the Museums, Libraries and Archives Council/Victoria and Albert Museum Purchase Grant Fund, 1982
Treen, James *Mountsorrel Cottage, Leicestershire*, purchased, 1943
unknown artist *Sir William Herrick (1562–1653)*, purchased, 1959
unknown artist *Mary, Lady Herrick*, purchased, 1959
unknown artist *Humphrey de Burnaby*, donated, 1957
unknown artist *Portrait of a Lady of the Herrick Family*, bequeathed by Miss I. M. Macaulay, 1937
unknown artist *David Papillon (1581–1659)*, bequeathed by David Pelham Papillon, 1981
unknown artist *Portrait of a Gentleman of the Herrick Family*, bequeathed by Miss I. M. Macaulay, 1937
unknown artist *Portrait of a Girl of the Herrick Family*, bequeathed by Miss I. M. Macaulay, 1937
unknown artist *Portrait of a Young Lady of the Herrick Family*, bequeathed by Miss I. M. Macaulay, 1937
unknown artist *Captain Burnaby*,

donated, 1957
unknown artist *Reverend Andrew Burnaby (1734–1812)*, donated, 1957
unknown artist *Dimminsdale Quarries on the Ferrers Estate, Staunton Harold, Leicestershire*, purchased with the assistance of the Science Museum
unknown artist *John Heycock of Ouston (1758–1823)*, purchased, 1972
unknown artist *John Hippisley Heycock (b.1793)*, purchased
unknown artist *The Village Feast, Coleorton Hall, Leicestershire*, purchased, 1953
unknown artist *Jane Anne Oakley, née Fisher (b.1828)*, donated
unknown artist *Mr Oakley Junior (b.1852)*, donated, 1981
unknown artist *Thomas William Oakley*, donated, 1981
unknown artist 19th C, *Coleorton Church, Leicestershire*, purchased, 1953
unknown artist *Levi Lovett, Secretary of the Leicestershire Miners' Association (1887–1919)*, donated in memory of George and Reenie Clay and family, 2009
unknown artist *Coleorton Hall, Leicestershire*, purchased, 1997
unknown artist *H. W. Penistone, Esq., of Oakham*, purchased, 1946
unknown artist *Henry Woodcock (b.1775), LLB*, purchased, 1957
unknown artist *Interior, the Marriage Breakfast*, bequeathed by Mr John William Cutler Bickley, 1935
unknown artist *John Skevington (1801–1850)*, donated, 1955
unknown artist *John Wycliffe (1330–1384), Rector of Lutterworth*, donated, 1898
unknown artist *Lady in a Red Corset*, purchased, 1968
unknown artist *Portrait of a Child*, purchased from T. W. Deacon, 1951
unknown artist *Portrait of a Gentleman of the Herrick Family*, bequeathed by Miss I. M. Macaulay, 1937
unknown artist *Portrait of a Young Lady of the Herrick Family*, bequeathed by Miss I. M. Macaulay, 1937
unknown artist *Tobias Herrick, Rector (1605–1627)*, bequeathed by Miss I. M. Macaulay, 1937
unknown artist *View of Donington Hall and Grounds, Leicestershire*, purchased, 1981
unknown artist *View of Hinckley, Leicestershire*, purchased, 1981
unknown artist *View of Melton Mowbray, Leicestershire*, purchased, 1981
unknown artist *'Windmill Inn'*, acquired, before 2009
Verelst, Johannes (attributed to) d.1734, *Honest George Ashby (1656–1728), the Planter*, bequeathed by Mr John William Cutler Bickley, 1935
Waplington, Paul Anthony b.1938, *Snibston Mine, Leicestershire*, acquired, 2001, © the artist
Ward, James 1768–1859, *Leicestershire Longhorn Bull*, purchased with the assistance of the Museums, Libraries and Archives Council/Victoria and Albert Museum Purchase Grant Fund, 1981
Whood, Isaac 1688/1689–1752, *David Papillon (1691–1762), MP*, bequeathed by David Pelham Papillon, 1981
Wynn, Kenneth James 1922–2009, *The Glenfield Farmer*, purchased with the assistance of the Museums, Libraries and Archives Council/Victoria and Albert Museum Purchase Grant Fund, 1984, © the estate of Kenneth Wynn

Leicestershire County Cricket Club

Ferrow, Anton Mark active 1974–1989, *David Gower (b.1957)*, gift from the artist, 1989
Gregory, Roy *F. M. Turner*, gift from the artist, 1972
Preater, L. V. T. active 1970–1972, *George Geary (1893–1981)*, commissioned by William Bentley, 1970
Preater, L. V. T. active 1970–1972, *William Ewart Astill (1888–1948)*, commissioned by William Bentley, 1970
Preater, L. V. T. active 1970–1972, *Raymond Illingworth (b.1932)*, commissioned by R. Gardner, 1971
Preater, L. V. T. active 1970–1972, *Maurice Tompkin (1919–1956)*, gift from the artist, 1972
Sumpter, Peter b.1933, *Lewis Cage, Aged 13, 1763* (after Francis Cotes), commissioned by L. Eardley-Wilmot, © the artist

Leicestershire Libraries

Gowham, Roger *The Birstall Cedar Tree*, gift from the Birstall and Wanlip History Society, 2008
Mason, A. *The Mill, Anstey, Leicestershire*, gift
Morgan, G. *Loughborough Library, Leicestershire*, gift, 2009

The Leicestershire Fire and Rescue Service Collection

Lowe, Pamela Ann *The Old Lutterworth Fire Station, Leicestershire*, gift from the artist, 2005
Weston, David b.1935, *Men of Fire*, © David Weston

The Royal Leicestershire Regiment Museum Trust

Cuneo, Terence Tenison 1907–1996, *Lieutenant John Cridlan Barrett, VC, 1/5th Battalion, Leicestershire Regiment during the Attack on Machine Guns in Forgan's Trench, 24 September 1918*, commissioned by the Leicestershire Regiment, 1958; transferred to the Museum, 1964, © reproduced with kind permission of the Cuneo estate
Cuneo, Terence Tenison 1907–1996, *2nd Battalion The Leicestershire Regiment, as Chindits, during Operations against the Japanese at Indaw Lake, Burma, 1944*, commissioned by the Leicestershire Regiment, 1959; transferred to the Museum, 1964, © reproduced with kind permission of the Cuneo estate
Cuneo, Terence Tenison 1907–1996, *German Paratroops Landing on Top of the 2nd Battalion, The Leicestershire Regiment in Crete, 20 May 1941*, commissioned by the Leicestershire Regiment, 1959; transferred to the Museum, 1964, © reproduced with kind permission of the Cuneo estate
Cuneo, Terence Tenison 1907–1996, *Lance Sergeant Philip Smith Winning the Leicestershire Regiment's First Victoria Cross for Bringing In Wounded Comrades at the Great Redan, Sevastopol, 18 June 1855*, commissioned by the Leicestershire Regiment, 1962; transferred to the Museum, 1964, © reproduced with kind permission of the Cuneo estate
unknown artist *General Sir Frederick Augustus Wetherall (1754–1842), GCH*

William Carey Museum

Scott, F. J. *Interior of the Central Baptist Church, Leicester (1920–1983)*, on loan from the Central Baptist Church, since 1983

University of Leicester

Alizon, Henri active 1885–1886, *Winter Scene*, purchased, 2000
Davie, Alan b.1920, *Untitled Abstract*, purchased, 2007, © the artist
Goodwin, Leslie Albert b.1929, *Blaemauon, South Wales*, donated, 2008, © the artist
Goodwin, Leslie Albert b.1929, *Tapestry Study*, donated, 2008, © the artist
Gowing, Lawrence 1918–1991, *Lord Adrian*, commissioned, © estate of Sir Lawrence Gowing
Hersey, Edward b.1948, *Wooden Water Butt*, unknown acquisition method
Ismay, D. B. *Study with Leaves*, unknown acquisition method
Kynoch, Kathryn b.1942, *Sir Fraser Noble (1918–2003), MBE*, commissioned, © the artist
Lancaster, John b.1930, *Tundra Excavation I*, on loan from the artist, since 2005, © the artist
Morrocco, Alberto 1917–1998, *Sir Charles Wilson (1909–2002)*, commissioned, © the artist's estate
Organ, Bryan b.1935, *Sir Alan Hodgkin (1914–1998)*, commissioned, 1983, © Bryan Organ & the Redfern Gallery, London
Organ, Bryan b.1935, *Sir Maurice Shock*, commissioned, 1983, © Bryan Organ & the Redfern Gallery, London
Organ, Bryan b.1935, *Lord Potter*, commissioned, 1984, © Bryan Organ & the Redfern Gallery, London
Organ, Bryan b.1935, *Dr Ken Edwards*, commissioned, 1995, © Bryan Organ & the Redfern Gallery, London
Organ, Bryan b.1935, *Michael Atiyah (b.1929)*, commissioned, 2000, © Bryan Organ & the Redfern Gallery, London
Perry, A. F. *F. L. Attenborough*, commissioned
Swann, Edwin b.1873, *Dr Astley V. Clarke (1870–1945)*, commissioned, 1924
Tindle, David b.1932, *The Reader*, unknown acquisition details, © the artist
van der Putten, Daniel *Winter Hill at Sulgrave, Northamptonshire*, purchased, 2007, © the artist
Watt, George Fiddes 1873–1960, *Sir Jonathan North (1855–1939)*, unknown acquisition method, © the artist's estate
Wright, Peter *Ambio Hill, Leicestershire*, purchased

Charnwood Borough Council Art Collection

Bird, Lynsey active 1999, *Interaction*, purchased from the artist, 1999
Cumming, Gemma b.1983, *Loughborough, Leicestershire*, purchased from the artist, 2006, © the artist
Fraser, Rhiannon b.1986, *David*, purchased from the artist, 2008, © the artist
Fraser, Rhiannon b.1986, *Ethel*, purchased from the artist, 2008, © the artist
Fraser, Rhiannon b.1986, *Graham*, purchased from the artist, 2008, © the artist
Fraser, Rhiannon b.1986, *Jaida*, purchased from the artist, 2008, © the artist
Fraser, Rhiannon b.1986, *Rose*, purchased from the artist, 2008, © the artist
Hantman, Anne *Durham Coastal Town*
Mitchell, Sue active 1994, *Loughborough Fair, Leicestershire*, purchased from the artist, 1994
Ratcliff, Charlotte *Blue Circle Study*, purchased from the artist, 2009
Rutter, Neil *Self 1*, purchased from the artist, 2007
Tomlinson, Rachel *Jewish Temple*, purchased from the artist, 1998
unknown artist *Queen Victoria (1819–1901)*

Loughborough University

Aldridge, Sue active 1994–1997, *Pink Flower*, purchased from Loughborough College of Art and Design, 1997
Allen, Lara Z. *Guitarist*, purchased by Viv Green on behalf of the Music Centre
Allen, Lara Z. *Orchestra*, purchased by Viv Green on behalf of the Music Centre
Allen, Lara Z. *Violinist*, purchased by Viv Green on behalf of the Music Centre
Atkinson, Eric b.1928, *Grand Canal, Venice*, © the artist
Berrisford, Peter 1932–2003, *Torcello, Italy*
Birley, Oswald Hornby Joseph 1880–1952, *Herbert Schofield (1882–1963), Principal of Loughborough College (1915–1950)*, commissioned, © the artist's estate
Birley, Oswald Hornby Joseph 1880–1952, *Herbert Schofield (1882–1963), Principal of Loughborough College (1915–1950)*, commissioned, © the artist's estate
Boswell, Sophie *Untitled 1*, purchased, 2009
Bowyer, William b.1926, *Professor E. J. Richards (1914–1995), Vice-Chancellor of Loughborough University (1967–1975)*, commissioned, © William Bowyer. All rights reserved, DACS 2012
Bowyer, William b.1926, *Professor J. G. Phillips (1933–1987), Vice-Chancellor of Loughborough University (1986–1987)*, © William Bowyer. All rights reserved, DACS 2012
Bratby, John Randall 1928–1992, *Baby Asleep in the Garden*, purchased from Leicestershire County Council, 1961, © the artist's estate/Bridgeman Art Library
Brookes, Lionel b.1915, *Sir William Brockington (1871–1959), Director of Education for Leicestershire (1903–1946)*
Brookes, Lionel b.1915, *Professor J. F. Peck (1897–1971), Emeritus Professor of Engineering at Loughborough College of Technology*
Brookes, Lionel b.1915, *Dr Herbert Leslie Haslegrave (1902–1999), Principal at Loughborough College of Technology (1953–1966), First Vice-Chancellor at Loughborough University of Technology (1966–1967)*
Caloutsis, Valerios b.1927, *London*
Challinor, T. *Industrial Scene*
Charon, Guy b.1927, *The Canal Saint-Martin*, © ADAGP, Paris and DACS, London 2012

Chatburn, Margaret active 1994–1997, *Heavy Rain*, purchased, 1997
Clarke, Matthew b.1970, *Roaches 15*, © the artist
Clarke, Matthew b.1970, *Roaches 18*, © the artist
Clarke, Matthew b.1970, *Roaches 19*, © the artist
Clarke, Matthew b.1970, *Roaches 20*, © the artist
Coantury, R. (attributed to) *Untitled*
Cohen, Harold b.1928, *Happy Day*, purchased from the artist, 1967, © the artist
Cole, Dan *Monkey*
Copplestone, Trewin b.1921, *Dartmoor Village, Devon*, © the artist
Cuming, Frederick b.1930, *Rochester Snowscape, Kent*, purchased, 1964, © the artist/ Bridgeman Art Library
Davies, L. *Ships at Sea*
Deakins, George 1911–1981, *Sail Cluster*, purchased
Divine, Jack A. F. 1912–1960, *Haystack and Barn*
Elford, Victor 1911–2003, *April Sunshine*, © the artist's estate
Fraser, Rhiannon b.1986, *Rehearsal*, © the artist
Gaff, David b.1959, *Bowstring Bridge, Leicester*, donated, © the artist
Gaff, David b.1959, *Braunstone High Street, Leicester*, donated, © the artist
Gallagher, Rachel b.1953, *The Applause Grew Louder*, © the artist
Gray, W. *Life Painting*
Halliday, Edward Irvine 1902–1984, *Sir Harry Pilkington (1905–1983), Chancellor of Loughborough University of Technology (1966–1980)*, commissioned, 1979, © the artist's estate
Hammonds, A. L. *Loco Sheds at Saltley, Birmingham*
Hartshorne, Ian b.1968, *Cardinal Humerment*, © the artist
Hartshorne, Ian b.1968, *Keeping Mum*, © the artist
Hellawell, Edward *Tree Form*, purchased, 1975
Hitchens, John b.1940, *September Hills*, © the artist
Hitchens, John b.1940, *West Wind*, purchased from Leicestershire County Council, 1960, © the artist
Holt, Stephen *Life Painting*
Howell, Matt *Mission Statement*, commissioned by the Students' Union
Huggins, Anna Michela active 1994–1997, *To See a Sea*, purchased from Loughborough College of Art and Design, 1997
Hunting, Leonard b.1926, *The Harbour at Dieppe, France*, purchased for the College Halls in Loughborough town, 1961
McConkey, Sarah b.1973, *Can We Go Home Yet?*
McGraw, Rachel *Untitled*
McIntyre, Ian *Blackbrook, Derbyshire*
Mendoza, June b.1945, *Sir Denis Rooke (1924–2008), Chancellor of Loughborough University (1986–2003)*, © the artist
Mendoza, June b.1945, *Sir David Wallace (b.1945), Vice-Chancellor of Loughborough University (1994–2006)*, © the artist
Middleditch, Edward 1923–1987, *Sunflowers*, purchased, 1961, © the estate of Edward Middleditch, courtesy James Hyman Gallery, London
Nuttall, Matthew *Greed*
Organ, Bryan b.1935, *Race Meeting*, © Bryan Organ & the Redfern Gallery, London
Organ, Bryan b.1935, *Sir David E. N. Davies (b.1935), Vice-Chancellor of Loughborough University (1988–1993)*, © Bryan Organ & the Redfern Gallery, London
Palmer, Margaret b.1922, *Claudia Parsons (1900–1998), First Woman to Circumnavigate the World by Car*, on loan from the Women's Engineering Society, © the artist
Parker, Elizabeth *Still Life*
Pullu *Twilight*
Radcliffe, Charlotte *Scrapyard*, purchased, 2009
Ratcliffe, Andrew b.1948, *Sir Clifford Butler (1922–1999), Vice-Chancellor of Loughborough University (1975–1985)*, © the artist
Salih, Zaid *Crianlarich, Stirling*
Salih, Zaid *Thorpe Acre, Leicestershire*
Saxton, Colin b.1927, *Fiery Landscape*, © the artist
Saxton, Colin b.1927, *Fallen Giant*, © the artist
Stevenson, Lesley *Male Figure*
Stevenson, Lesley *Bride and Groom*
Stevenson, Lesley *Man Carrying a Lady*
Stevenson, Lesley *Military Award*
Stubley, Trevor 1932–2010, *Sir Arnold Hall (1915–2000), Chancellor of Loughborough University (1980–1989)*, © the artist's estate
Suff, Gregory b.1949, *The Iron Gate*, © the artist
Timlin, William Mitcheson 1893–1943, *Bush Landscape with Figures*, presented to Loughborough College of Technology by Sir Edward Herbert
Tindle, David b.1932, *Seascape*, © the artist
Trautmann, M. B. *James White, Lecturer in Civil Engineering (1924–1955)*
Turnbull, Julie *Where the Grass Is Greener*, purchased from Loughborough College of Art and Design, 1996
Turnbull, Julie *Still Breathing*, purchased from Loughborough College of Art and Design, 1996
unknown artist *Geometry*
unknown artist *A. T. Eggington (1888–1982), Headmaster of Loughborough College School (1919–1952)*
unknown artist *Baroque Lady*
unknown artist *Life Painting*
unknown artist *Lights on the Water*
unknown artist *Red Abstract*
unknown artist *Still Life (Flowers)*
unknown artist *Still Life (Flowers)*
unknown artist *Stripe Painting*
unknown artist *The Haunted House*
unknown artist *Voodoo*
Vielfaure, Jean-Pierre b.1930, *Accusé Einstein levez-vous!*, purchased from the Lincoln Gallery, 1963
Whittall, Sam *Landscape: Horizontal Line, Blue and Green Tones*, purchased, 2009
Wilson, Frank Avray 1914–2009, *Deep End*, purchased, 1961, © the artist's estate
Wishart, John Michael 1928–1996, *Waterfall*, purchased from Leicestershire County Council, 1960, © the artist's estate

Loughborough War Memorial Museum

Bradley, Jack *Nijmegen Bridge, The Netherlands*
Byrne, E. H. *Soldiers at Rest*

RNIB College Loughborough

Cook, S. *Sun Garden*, gift from Loughborough University
Hadley, Ross *Constellation of Eyes*, gift from Loughborough University
Hall, Louise M. *Ariel*, gift from Loughborough University
Huxley *Figures* (sketch), gift from Loughborough University
Lakey, Andrew b.1959, *Angel of Hope*, gift from Loughborough University, © the artist
March, Tony *Abstract*, gift from Loughborough University
Scott, Margaret *Ettrick*, gift from Loughborough University
unknown artist *Dragon and Figure*, gift from Loughborough University
unknown artist *Abstract Geometry*, gift from Loughborough University
unknown artist *Batman*, gift from Loughborough University
unknown artist *Four Squares*, gift from Loughborough University
unknown artist *The Purple Lady*, gift from Loughborough University

Allington Parish Council

Hayman, Godfrey *Sir George Welby (1851–1936)*, gift in memory of Harold Burton, 1999

Boston Borough Council

Baines, Henry 1823–1894, *St Botolph's from the Witham, Boston, Lincolnshire*, untraced find
Baker, Thomas 1809–1869, *Wooded Landscape with a Village*, untraced find
Beucherie, Paul *Scène champêtre Mayennaise, France*, gift from Laval Museum of Art, to celebrate town-twinning of Boston and Laval, 1969
Brough, M. *September Evening*, gift, 1964
Brownlow, George Washington 1835–1876, *John Wesley Preaching from His Father's Tomb at Epworth*, untraced find
Bullock, George Henry d.1999, *Bruce James Veal (1917–1990), Mayor of Boston (1968–1969)*, gift, 2009
Cheales, Edith May 1872–1964 *Freiston Shore, Boston, Lincolnshire*, gift, 1966
Dorr, Ray *Boston Dock, Lincolnshire*, purchased, 1995
Enderby, Samuel George 1860–1921, *Cupid Guarding Psyche*, gift, 1926
Enderby, Samuel George 1860–1921, *Entangled*, bequeathed
Etty, William 1787–1849, *Hero Waiting for Leander*, untraced find
Etty, William 1787–1849, *Study of a Female Nude*, untraced find
Etty, William 1787–1849, *Youth at the Prow and Pleasure at the Helm*, untraced find
Grimble, John d.1997, *Lade Bank Pumping Station, Hobhole Drain, East Fen*, untraced find
Grimble, John d.1997, *River Haven, Boston, Lincolnshire*, gift, 1966
Houghton, Arthur Boyd 1836–1875, *Street Gymnasts*, untraced find
Ibbetson, Julius Caesar 1759–1817, *Cows*, untraced find
Kennedy *Portrait Study of a Bearded Gentleman from Two Angles*, untraced find
Morland, George 1763–1804, *Landscape with an Approaching Storm*, untraced find
Morland, George 1763–1804, *Wooded Landscape with a Toll Gate*, untraced find
Pawley, A. *Flower Study*, untraced find
Phillips, Thomas 1770–1845, *Sir Joseph Banks (1743–1820), 1st Bt, GCB, PRS*, untraced find
Rose, William S. 1810–1873, *Wooded Landscape*, untraced find
Smith, H. *Fishing Boat 'Alsatian' BN73*, gift, 1987
Smith, H. *Steam Trawler*, purchased, 1957
Stothard, Thomas 1755–1834, *A Scene from William Shakespeare's 'A Comedy of Errors'*, untraced find
Stothard, Thomas 1755–1834, *A Scene from William Shakespeare's 'A Winter's Tale'*, untraced find
Thistlewaite, Clara Olive *William Bedford*
Townsend, Ernest 1885–1944, *Mayor John Beaulah (1841–1926), Mayor of Boston (1921–1922)*, untraced find
unknown artist *Ann Twell, Wife of Charles Twell*, gift, 1954
unknown artist *Charles Twell, Mayor of Boston (1729–1730)*, gift, 1954
unknown artist *Samuel Thornton*, gift, 1954
unknown artist *John Caistor, Mayor of Boston (1838–1839)*, donated
unknown artist *Boston Stump from the Market Place, Lincolnshire*, gift, 1977
unknown artist *William Caistor, Mayor of Boston (1865–1866)*, gift, 1987
unknown artist *Alderman Joseph Cooke, Mayor of Boston (1902–1904)*, untraced find
unknown artist *Boston Market Place and St Botolph's, Lincolnshire*, untraced find
unknown artist *Dog and Ducks*, gift, 1996
unknown artist *Poodle*, untraced find
unknown artist *Portrait of an Unknown Man*, untraced find
unknown artist *Sailing Ship 'Eagle'*, gift, 1961
unknown artist *Skirbeck Church, Lincolnshire*, gift, 2009
unknown artist *Steam Trawler BN178*, untraced find
unknown artist *Windmill*, gift, 2009
White, Charles Ernest 1890–1971, *Landscape Scene*, bequeathed, 1971
White, Charles Ernest 1890–1971, *Landscape Scene*, bequeathed, 1971
White, Charles Ernest 1890–1971, *Landscape Scene*, bequeathed, 1971
White, Charles Ernest 1890–1971, *Landscape Scene*, bequeathed, 1971
White, Charles Ernest 1890–1971, *Landscape Scene*, bequeathed, 1971
White, Charles Ernest 1890–1971, *Landscape Scene*, bequeathed, 1971
White, Charles Ernest 1890–1971, *Landscape Scene*, bequeathed, 1971
White, Charles Ernest 1890–1971, *Landscape Scene*, bequeathed, 1971
White, Charles Ernest 1890–1971, *Landscape Scene*, bequeathed, 1971
White, Charles Ernest 1890–1971, *Landscape Scene*, bequeathed, 1971
Wilson, Richard 1712/1713–1782, *River Landscape*, untraced find

Fydell House

Kiddey *Canon A. M. Cook (d.1964), Vicar of St Botolph's, Boston, Lincolnshire (1932–1946)*, donated by the Boston Preservation Trust
Pine, Robert Edge c.1720/1730–1788, *Richard Fydell, Junior (1747–1793)*, purchased from the Boston Preservation Trust, after 1935
unknown artist *Elizabeth Fydell (1767–1797), Niece of Richard Fydell*, purchased from the Boston Preservation Trust, after 1935
unknown artist *Sir John Leverett (1616–1679), Governor of Massachusetts (1673–1679)*, purchased from the Boston Preservation Trust, after 1935

Bourne Heritage Centre

Gardner, Robert Arthur 1850–1926, *Rose Garden*, gift, 1980

Epworth Old Rectory

Douglas, Richard Gilmore b.c.1937, *Epworth Rectory Fire, 1909* (after Henry Perlee Parker), gift from the children of Everatt and Gertrude Morwood Oates, 1991, photo credit: Donald Ryan
Douglas, Richard Gilmore b.c.1937, *John Wesley (1703–1791), Mounting His Horse*, photo credit: Donald Ryan
Douglas, Richard Gilmore b.c.1937, *Charles Wesley (1707–1788), Epworth* (after John Russell), photo credit: Donald Ryan
Douglas, Richard Gilmore b.c.1937, *John Wesley (1703–1791)* (after George Romney), photo credit: Donald Ryan
Douglas, Richard Gilmore b.c.1937, *Samuel Wesley, Senior (1662–1735)*, photo credit: Donald Ryan
Douglas, Richard Gilmore b.c.1937, *John Wesley (1703–1791), Riding a Horse Whilst Reading a Book*, photo credit: Donald Ryan
Douglas, Richard Gilmore b.c.1937, *John Wesley at Wroot, Lincolnshire*, photo credit: Donald Ryan
Douglas, Richard Gilmore b.c.1937, *Susanna Wesley with Five Children*, photo credit: Donald Ryan
Douglas, Richard Gilmore b.c.1937, *John Wesley (1703–1791), Holding a Quill Pen*, photo credit: Donald Ryan
Douglas, Richard Gilmore b.c.1937, *Charles Wesley (1707–1788), Epworth* (after John Russell), photo credit: Donald Ryan
Douglas, Richard Gilmore b.c.1937, *Samuel Wesley, Senior (1662–1735), Susanna Wesley and Samuel Wesley, Junior*, photo credit: Donald Ryan
Douglas, Richard Gilmore b.c.1937, *Susanna Wesley, Sewing*, photo credit: Donald Ryan
Douglas, Richard Gilmore b.c.1937, *Susanna Wesley with Samuel Wesley, Junior and a Cat*, photo credit: Donald Ryan
Grose, Margaret active early 20th C, *John Wesley (1703–1791)* (after Nathaniel Hone), donated, photo credit: Donald Ryan
Harley, J. *Reverend John Wesley (1703–1791)* (after John Michael Williams), photo credit: Donald Ryan
Hudson, Thomas (after) 1701–1779, *Reverend Charles Wesley (1707–1788)*, donated, 2009, photo credit: Donald Ryan
Jackson, John (after) 1778–1831, *Reverend John Wesley (1703–1791)*, photo credit: Donald Ryan
Keal, David Ernest b.1930, *John Wesley (1703–1791)* (superimposed on a purple cross, surrounded by four views of Epworth, Lincolnshire), © the artist, photo credit: Donald Ryan
Keal, David Ernest b.1930, *The Epworth Rectory on Fire and the Rescue of John Wesley, Aged 6* (after Henry Perlee Parker), © the artist, photo credit: Donald Ryan
Keal, David Ernest b.1930, *Samuel Wesley Senior (1662–1735)*, © the artist, photo credit: Donald Ryan
Keal, David Ernest b.1930, *Sarah Wesley, née Gwynne (1726–1822)*, © the artist, photo credit: Donald Ryan
Keal, David Ernest b.1930, *Charles Wesley Junior (1757–1834)*, © the artist, photo credit: Donald Ryan
Keal, David Ernest b.1930, *Samuel Wesley (1766–1837), Son of Charles*, © the artist, photo credit: Donald Ryan
Keal, David Ernest b.1930, *Sarah Wesley Junior (1759–1823)*, © the artist, photo credit: Donald Ryan
unknown artist mid-18th C, *Mrs Susanna Wesley*, photo credit: Donald Ryan

Gainsborough Old Hall

Devis, Arthur (attributed to) 1712–1787, *Sir Neville Hickman (1725–1781), Bt*, on loan from a private collection
Dyck, Anthony van (after) 1599–1641, *Thomas Wentworth (1593–1641), Earl of Strafford*, on loan from a private collection
Gordon, R. *Gainsborough Old Hall, Lincolnshire*, gift from the artist
Jackson, Gilbert active 1615–1658, *Willoughby Hickman (1659–1720), Bt*, on loan from a private collection
Lutyens, Charles Augustus Henry 1829–1915, *Elizabeth (1829–1885), Daughter of Sir Thomas Beckett, Bt, Wife of Sir Henry Hickman Bacon, Bt*, on loan from a private collection
Millner, William Edward 1849–1895, *Brown Horse*, gift
Millner, William Edward 1849–1895, *Thonock Lodge Gates, Lincolnshire*, gift
Millner, William Edward 1849–1895, *Two Women (Greek Girls)*, gift, 1964
Millner, William Edward 1849–1895, *'Will he come?'*, untraced find
Millner, William Edward 1849–1895, *A Woman with a Soldier*, untraced find
Millner, William Edward 1849–1895, *Loading Mangold Wurzels into a Tumbril*, untraced find
Millner, William Edward 1849–1895, *Preparing for Market, a Man and a Boy Loading Rhubarb*, untraced find
Millner, William Edward 1849–1895, *Group of Horses and a Foal*, gift
Millner, William Edward 1849–1895, *Two Horses Grazing, with a Parish Church Tower in the Distance*, gift
Millner, William Edward 1849–1895, *An Old Woman Knitting and a Girl Holding a Pot Plant*, untraced find
Millner, William Edward 1849–1895, *Homeward Bound*, gift
Millner, William Edward 1849–1895, *Horses and Figures in a Turnip Field*, untraced find
Millner, William Edward 1849–1895, *Men, Horses and a Hay Cart*, purchased, 1986
Millner, William Edward 1849–1895, *Reclining Lion*, purchased, 1986
Millner, William Edward 1849–1895, *'Spot' and His Friend*, gift
Millner, William Edward 1849–1895, *Three Brown Horses Standing Outside a Stable*, gift
Millner, William Edward 1849–1895, *Two Dogs*, gift
Millner, William Edward 1849–1895, *Two Horses by a Wood*, gift
Millner, William Edward 1849–1895, *White Horse*, gift
Millner, William Edward (attributed to) 1849–1895, *A Lady with a Guitar*, untraced find
Squint Master active c.1660–c.1685, *Sir William Hickman (1629–1682), Bt*, on loan from a private collection
Squint Master active c.1660–c.1685, *Elizabeth Hickman (1635–1691), Lady Hickman, Daughter of John Nevill, Esq.*, on loan from a private collection
unknown artist *Henry VIII (1491–1547)*, on loan from a private collection
unknown artist *Francis Bacon (1561–1626), Baron Verulam, Viscount St Albans*, on loan from a private collection
unknown artist *Rose Hickman (1526–1596), Daughter of Sir William Lock, Wife of Anthony Hickman*, on loan from a private collection
unknown artist *Sir William Hickman (d.1625), Kt*, on loan from a private collection
unknown artist 16th C, *Sir Nicholas Bacon (1510–1597), Lord Keeper*, on loan from a private collection
unknown artist 16th C, *Sir Nicholas Bacon (1510–1597), Lord Keeper*, on loan from a private collection
unknown artist *Walter Hickman*, on loan from a private collection
unknown artist *Antony Hickman*, on loan from a private collection
unknown artist *Lady Anne Wentworth*, on loan from a private collection
unknown artist *Portrait of a Bearded Gentleman*, on loan from a private collection
unknown artist *Sir Nathaniel Bacon (1585–1627), KB*, on loan from a private collection
unknown artist *Elizabeth Willoughby, Lady Hickman, Daughter of William, Lord Willoughby of Parham*, on loan from a private collection
unknown artist *George Villiers (1592–1628), Duke of Buckingham*, on loan from a private collection
unknown artist *Thomas Windsor Hickman (c.1627–1687), 1st Earl of Plymouth*, on loan from a private collection
unknown artist *Frances Elizabeth, Lady Hickman, Daughter of Christopher Tower, Esq.*, on loan from a private collection
unknown artist *Frances Hickman, Daughter of Edward Hall, Wife of Sir Neville Hickman, Bt*, on loan from a private collection
unknown artist 18th C, *Ann Hickman, Lady Hickman, Daughter of Sir Stephen Anderson, Bt*, on loan from a private collection
unknown artist *Sir Henry Hickman Bacon (1820–1872), Bt*, on loan from a private collection
unknown artist *Sir Henry Hickman Bacon (1820–1872), Bt*, on loan from a private collection
unknown artist *Elizabeth Beckett (1829–1885), Daughter of Sir Thomas Beckett, Wife of Sir Hickman Bacon, Bt*, on loan from a private collection
unknown artist *Cloaked Man with a Staff and Keys**, untraced find
unknown artist *Lady with a Sword**, untraced find
unknown artist *Fryar Bacon*, on loan from a private collection
unknown artist *Henry VIII (1491–1547)*, on loan from a private collection
unknown artist *Portrait of a Young Lady*, untraced find
Walton, Henry 1746–1813, *Sir Edmund Bacon (1749–1820), 8th Bt*, on loan from a private collection
Zuccaro, Federico (attributed to) c.1541–1609, *Sir Nicholas Bacon (d.1624)*, on loan from a private collection

West Lindsey District Council

Bell, A. *Trent Bridge*, untraced find
Schublaus, A. M. (attributed to) *Dingle Halbinsel, Süd-Irland*, gift
unknown artist *Sweyn's Last Journey to England, 1013*, untraced find

Grantham Museum

Clef, M. *Christ*
Connett, Isa *Self Portrait*, gift from Mrs Connett
Cross, Joe *View of Watergate with Sharpley's Building, Grantham, Lincolnshire*
Cross, Joe *Still Life*, gift from Mrs B. Teague, 1993
Dawson, Henry 1811–1878, *Self Portrait*, gift from Ethert Brand, 1927
Edwards, Alice M. active c.1930–1938, *Miss Norah Hall as Mrs Milsom in 'Call It a Day' by Dodie Smith*, gift from Mr B. Edwards, 1993
Edwards, Alice M. active c.1930–1938, *Mr Forsgate-Weekly (b.1872), Mayor of Grantham (1920–1937)*, gift from W. Shaw, 2003
Edwards, Alice M. active c.1930–1938, *Captain Spriggs, Ruston and Hornsby Fire Brigade*, gift from F. Cox, 1968
Kneller, Godfrey 1646–1723, *Sir Isaac Newton (1642–1727)*, acquired with the assistance of the Museums and Galleries Commission/Victoria and Albert Museum Purchase Grant Fund, the National Art Collections Fund, the Art Fund, South Kesteven District Council, BMARC Ltd and Suter Plc, 1987
Massey, George Edward 1919–2007, *Lancaster Crew's View of a Dam, 1943* (painted from a still of the film 'The Dam Busters'), gift from the artist, 1997, © the artist's estate
Pether, William 1731–1819, *View of a Castle*
Rhodes *My Father's Old Hovel*, gift from the Misses Hardwick, 1933
Shelbourne, Terry b.1930, *Baroness Margaret Thatcher (b.1925)*, purchased from the artist, 1996, © the artist
unknown artist *William Richard Middlemore of Grantham and Somerby Hall (1731–1772)*, gift from Mrs Rosemary Smith, 1983
unknown artist *Mid Lent Fair, Grantham Market Place, Lincolnshire*, purchased from the Crane Galleries, Folk Art and Americana, London, with the assistance of the Victoria and Albert Museum Purchase Grant Fund, Lincolnshire County Council and South Kesteven District Council, 1989
unknown artist *Mrs Mary Middlemore*, gift from Mrs Rosemary Smith, 1983
unknown artist *William Richard Middlemore of Nottingham (1767–1815)*, gift from Mrs Rosemary Smith, 1983
unknown artist *Mrs Susanna Middlemore of Orston Hall (c.1770–1849), Wife of William Richard Middlemore of Nottingham*, gift from Mrs Rosemary Smith, 1983
unknown artist *Robert Frederick Middlemore (1816–1890), Colonel of 91st Regiment*, gift from Mrs Rosemary Smith, 1983
unknown artist *Henry Preston, Founder of Grantham Museum*, commissioned by a group of local

people; presented to the sitter at the opening of the Museum, 1926
unknown artist *Algernon Gray Tollemache (1805–1892)*, gift from the Lincolnshire Archives, 1997
unknown artist *'Beehive' Public House and Landlady Elizabeth Wood*
unknown artist *Landscape with River and Trees*
unknown artist *Mr Palmer of Manthorpe Mill*
unknown artist *Mrs William Hornsby*, gift from Mr J. Martin, 1979
unknown artist *Richard Hornsby Senior (1790–1864)*
unknown artist *Ponies and Carts on Grantham Wharf, Lincolnshire*
unknown artist *Portrait of an Unknown Lady*
unknown artist *Portrait of an Unknown Man* (possibly William Knott Dunn)
unknown artist *Portrait of Two Unknown Ladies*
unknown artist *St Wulfram's Church, Grantham, Lincolnshire*, gift from Mr F. Hind, 1940
unknown artist *Toll House*, gift from Mrs Back
unknown artist *View of Grantham from Sedgwick Meadows, Lincolnshire*

Grimsby Institute of Further & Higher Education

Green, Roberta *Love Birds*, gift, c.2005
Green, Tracy *Black*, gift, 2008
Hadlington, Chris *Man in a Suit*, gift, c.2003
Holnb, Louiza *Berlin in Pink*, gift, c.2006
Holnb, Louiza *Berlin with Cars*, gift, c.2006
Jerome, Lindsey *Untitled*, gift
King, John *Man with a Book*, gift
King, John *Humber Factories*, gift
Mather, Louise *Blue*, gift
Maughton, Jane *Underwater*, gift, c.2006
McCoy, Debbie *Mixed Media*, gift, c.1989
McCoy, Debbie *Orange Squares**, gift, 1991
Mumby, John *Abstract**, gift, 1991
Osborne, Robert *We are Just Free Spirits in the Presence of Fate*, gift
Owen, David active 1981–1982, *Self Portrait*, gift
Owen, Mark b.1963, *Wooded Scene*, gift
Penketh, Andrew b.1966, *Art Studio*, gift, © the artist
Reeves, Aimie b.1971, *Yellow Field*, gift
Roberts, Darren *Yellow Rape Field*, gift, 2008
unknown artist *Backyard Scene*, gift, before 1965
unknown artist *Black Pants*, gift
unknown artist *City Parkland*, gift, c.1970
unknown artist *Lips*, gift
unknown artist *Street Scene at Night*, gift
unknown artist *Stripes and Beads*, gift
unknown artist *Welcome*, gift
Vernau, Madeleine *Fraser*, gift
Vernau, Rosie *Abstract*, gift
Volley, Nicholas 1950–2006, *Brown Cockerel*, gift
Volley, Nicholas 1950–2006, *Green Girl*, gift
Walters, Claire *Horse Skeleton*, gift

Grimsby Town Hall

Bugion, S. *Councillor James Keay, Mayor of Grimsby (1941–1942)*
Fildes, Denis 1889–1974, *Dame Madge Kendal (1848–1935), CBE*
Hailstone, Bernard 1910–1987, *Councillor C. H. Wilkinson, MBE, JP*, © the artist's estate
Jennison, George *Edward VII (1841–1910)*
Jennison, George *Robert William Roberts, Mayor of Grimsby (1909)*
Jennison, George *Alderman C. W. Hewson, JP, Mayor of Grimsby (1944–1945)*
Jennison, George *Alderman J. H. Tate, JP, Mayor of Grimsby (1913–1914)*
Kennington, Thomas Benjamin 1856–1916, *Edward John Bannister, Mayor of Grimsby (1868–1869)*
Kennington, Thomas Benjamin 1856–1916, *Frank Barrett, Mayor of Grimsby (1908 & 1924)*
Kennington, Thomas Benjamin 1856–1916, *Henry James Veal, Mayor of Grimsby (1877–1878)*
Kennington, Thomas Benjamin 1856–1916, *Jack Sutcliffe, Mayor of Grimsby (1896–1897)*
Kennington, Thomas Benjamin 1856–1916, *Sir George Doughty, MP (1895), Mayor of Grimsby (1892–1893)*
Turner, James (attributed to) *J. Carl Ross, Esq., High Steward of the Borough of Great Grimsby*
unknown artist *Henry Smethurst Senior, Mayor of Grimsby (1885–1886)*
Wade, George A. active 1950–1960, *Margaret Larmour, Mayor of Grimsby (1949)*

North East Lincolnshire Museum Service

Adam, Edouard Marie 1847–1929, *Schooner off the Coast*
Anderson, W. I. L. *The Mouth of the Humber from Grimsby Docks, Lincolnshire*, bequeathed by Wilfred Vere Doughty, 1941
Anong (attributed to) *Dock Tower, Grimsby Dock, Lincolnshire*
Appleyard, Frederick 1874–1963, *Yachts*, © the artist's estate
Barclay (Captain) *Three-Masted Sailing Ship 'Gladova' of Sunderland*
Bauckham, R. *Waterside Scene*, gift from Mr Rees
Boulen, J. *The 'Fawn', GY 1008*, gift from Mr F. E. Rice
British (English) School *Lady Anne Meres*
British (English) School *Man-of-War with Shipping off Gibraltar*, bequeathed by Wilfred Vere Doughty, 1941
British (English) School *Malta*, bequeathed by Wilfred Vere Doughty, 1941
British (English) School *The 'Yorkshireman' at Sea with a Storm Threatening*, bequeathed by Wilfred Vere Doughty, 1941
British (English) School *Ships off the Coast*, bequeathed by Wilfred Vere Doughty, 1941
British (English) School *The 'Fury', Moored in the Medway*
British (English) School *The 'Tigress'*, bequeathed by Wilfred Vere Doughty, 1941
British (English) School *Three English Sailing Ships*
British (English) School *Three-Masted Frigate*
British (English) School *The 'Falls of Dee'*, bequeathed by Wilfred Vere Doughty, 1941
British (English) School *The Thames at Greenwich, London*, bequeathed by Wilfred Vere Doughty, 1941
British (English) School *The 'Campanil'*
British (English) School *Hunting Scene*, gift from Alderman Frank Barrett, JP, 1935
British (English) School 19th C, *Lady with a Fan*
British (English) School late 19th C, *Portrait of an Unknown Gentleman*, gift
British (English) School *A Man with a Flintlock Pistol*
British (English) School *A Woman on a Balcony at Night*, bequeathed by Wilfred Vere Doughty, 1941
British (English) School *Grimsby Docks and Tower, Lincolnshire*, gift from Miss A. E. Bell
British (English) School *Man-of-War and Other Shipping*
British (English) School *The 'Horwood'*, bequeathed by Wilfred Vere Doughty, 1941
Brooking, Charles (attributed to) 1723–1759, *Man-of-war off the Coast*, bequeathed by Wilfred Vere Doughty, 1941
Bunting, William Richard 1866–c.1944, *Two-Masted Ship at Sea*
Bunting, William Richard 1866–c.1944, *Help at Last*, bequeathed by Wilfred Vere Doughty, 1941
Bunting, William Richard 1866–c.1944, *Each Fishing Boat Seemed Scarce Afloat*
Bunting, William Richard 1866–c.1944, *Still Life, Roses*
Bunting, William Richard 1866–c.1944, *Jack Bell, Shipbuilder*, gift from Miss A. E. Bell
Bunting, William Richard 1866–c.1944, *Mrs Jack Bell*, gift from Miss A. E. Bell
Bunting, William Richard 1866–c.1944, *The Last Phase of Grimsby's Old Harbour Entrance, Lincolnshire*
Bunting, William Richard 1866–c.1944, *The Old Boundary Mark, Oxford Street and Albert Street, Grimsby, Lincolnshire*
Bunting, William Richard 1866–c.1944, *Riverside Pastime and Pleasure*
Bunting, William Richard 1866–c.1944, *Ships at Sea*, bequeathed by Wilfred Vere Doughty, 1941
Bunting, William Richard 1866–c.1944, *Ships at Sea*, bequeathed by Wilfred Vere Doughty, 1941
Bunting, William Richard 1866–c.1944, *The Stowboat, No.2 Fish Dock, Grimsby, Lincolnshire*, gift from the artist, 1937
Burton, Thomas *Old Clee Church, Lincolnshire*, gift from Mr George E. Capes
Burwood, George Vemply 1844–1917, *The 'Leslie'*, gift
Burwood, George Vemply 1844–1917, *Grimsby Docks, Lincolnshire*, bequeathed by Wilfred Vere Doughty, 1941
Burwood, George Vemply 1844–1917, *The 'Tubal Cain'*
Butler, Joseph *The Departure of Princess Victoria*, bequeathed by Wilfred Vere Doughty, 1941
Calvert, Frederick c.1785–c.1845, *The Wreck of the 'Royal George'*
Campling, Herbert John 1879–1939, *Three Boats Tied up for the Night*, gift from Mr N. Handy
Carmichael, John Wilson 1800–1868, *The Construction of the Royal Dock, Grimsby, Lincolnshire*, bequeathed by Wilfred Vere Doughty, 1941
Carmichael, John Wilson 1800–1868, *Margate Harbour, Kent*, bequeathed by Wilfred Vere Doughty, 1941
Carmichael, John Wilson 1800–1868, *The 'Peruvian'*, bequeathed by Wilfred Vere Doughty, 1941
Carmichael, John Wilson 1800–1868, *Three-Masted Ship near a Lighthouse*, bequeathed by Wilfred Vere Doughty, 1941
Chapman, E. *Near Sandilands, Lincolnshire*
Chinese School *A Three-Masted British Man-of-War*, bequeathed by Wilfred Vere Doughty, 1941
Codd, Tony active 2009, *Life Painting, Woman Seated*, gift from the artist, 2009
Codd, Tony active 2009, *Life Painting, Woman Standing*, gift from the artist, 2009
Codd, Tony active 2009, *Portrait of a Woman Reading*, gift from the artist, 2009
Codd, Tony active 2009, *Portrait of a Woman Seated*, gift from the artist, 2009
Collins, Charles II 1851–1921, *Gypsy Encampment with Horses and Cattle*
Condy, Nicholas (attributed to) 1793–1857, *Two Ships near a Lighthouse*
Cook, A. R. *People's Park, Grimsby, Lincolnshire*
Cooke, A. *The Apprentice's First Voyage*
Cooke, Edward William 1811–1880, *A Dutch Galliot Entering Aberdeen Harbour in a Storm*
Daniell, William 1769–1837, *Landing on the Beach at Madras, India*
Davis, G. W. *The 'Lord Jellicoe', GY 709*, gift from Mr McKenzie
De Baeker, Mary *Zeebruge, Belgium*
De Pommayrac, Pierre Paul 1807–1880, *Henri Josse (1828–1893), MP for Great Grimsby*
De Simone, Tommaso 1805–1888, *British Man-of-War 'Hong Kong' in the Bay of Naples, Italy*, bequeathed by Wilfred Vere Doughty, 1941
Delewar, V. *River Scene*
Delewar, V. *River Scene*
Easton, J. *Trawler GY174 with Zeppelin L19*
Elwell, Frederick William 1870–1958, *John Travers Cornwell (1900–1916), VC*
Emmerson, Henry Hetherington 1831–1895, *Fishing Vessels off the Coast*, bequeathed by Wilfred Vere Doughty, 1941
Emmerson, Henry Hetherington (attributed to) 1831–1895, *Two Fishing Smacks*, bequeathed by Wilfred Vere Doughty, 1941
Engers *Sir George Doughty, MP (1895), Mayor of Grimsby (1892–1893)*
England, Reg *Riverhead, Grimsby, Lincolnshire*
Erdy, John William (attributed to) b.1760, *Two Ships in a Harbour*
Everett, John 1876–1949, *The 'Viveria'*
Friston, Frederick Edwin c.1844–1901, *The 'Harry Sinclair'*, commissioned by the ship's owner, Robert Sinclair
Green, Peter H. *Swallow Crossroads, Grimsby, Lincolnshire*
Greensmith, W. *Portrait of an Unknown Gentleman*
Hakava, Aale 1909–1995, *Ogakeghtio Toppila*, gift
Hancocks, Peter *Grimsby Fish Docks, Lincolnshire*
Headgren *The 'Alchemist' off Dover, Kent*
Herring, John Frederick I (school of) 1795–1865, *Farmyard Scene*
Hopkinson, John b.1941, *The Family*, © the artist
Hopkinson, John b.1941, *The Return of the Prodigal Son*, © the artist
Hopkinson, John b.1941, *Shipyard*, © the artist
Hopkinson, John b.1941, *Resentment*, © the artist
Hopkinson, John b.1941, *Souvenirs*, © the artist
Hopkinson, John b.1941,

Conversation, © the artist
Hopkinson, John b.1941, *Do Fish Scream?*, © the artist
Hopkinson, John b.1941, *Artists in the Pub*, donated by Mr Robert Briggs, 2009, © the artist
Hopkinson, John b.1941, *Fish Workers' Canteen*, donated by Mr Robert Briggs, 2009, © the artist
Hopkinson, John b.1941, *School Playground*, donated by Mr Robert Briggs, 2009, © the artist
Hornbrook, Thomas Lyde 1780–1850, *Dockyard Fire, 1840*
Hote, Kenneth *Fleeting*
Huggins, William John 1781–1845, *SS 'James Wyatt' Towing the Royal Yacht, 'Royal George' on the Visit of George IV to Edinburgh, August 1824*, bequeathed by Wilfred Vere Doughty, 1941
Huggins, William John 1781–1845, *The 'Leguan'*
Huggins, William John 1781–1845, *Three-Masted Frigate*
Huggins, William John (attributed to) 1781–1845, *The 'Newark'*, bequeathed by Wilfred Vere Doughty, 1941
Hyam, B. active 1912–1914, *SS 'Titanic'*
Hyam, B. active 1912–1914, *The 'Acquitania'*
Ingham, Linda b.1964, *Three Generations (Thomas Brian Ingham, Richard Coulbeck, Richard Harris)*, gift from the artist, 2009, © the artist
Jacobsen, Antonio 1850–1921, *SS 'Buffalo'*, bequeathed by Wilfred Vere Doughty, 1941
Jacobsen, Antonio 1850–1921, *The 'Hindoo'*, bequeathed by Wilfred Vere Doughty, 1941
James, Frederick Charles 1873–1926, *Lighthouse*
James, Frederick Charles 1873–1926, *Royal Dock Tower, Grimsby, Lincolnshire*
James, Frederick Charles 1873–1926, *Lighthouse*
James, Frederick Charles 1873–1926,*Royal Dock Tower, Grimsby, Lincolnshire*
James, Frederick Charles 1873–1926, *The 'Manx Hero', GY 585*
Jansen, A. J. active c.1906–c.1932, *The 'Ashton'*, gift from Mr Buckley, 1971
Jansen, A. J. active c.1906–c.1932, *The 'City of Bradford'*, bequeathed by Wilfred Vere Doughty, 1941
Jansen, A. J. active c.1906–c.1932, *The 'Immingham'*
Jansen, A. J. active c.1906–c.1932, *The 'Staveley'*
Jillot, James (attributed to) 1800–1880, *Landscape with a Church*
Kaufman, Adolf 1848–1916, *Unloading a Boat at a Quayside, Paris*
Kaufman, Adolf 1848–1916, *Harbour Scene*
Kennington, Thomas Benjamin 1856–1916, *Portrait of a Lady with a White Cap*
Kennington, Thomas Benjamin 1856–1916, *Portrait of an Unknown Man with a Beard*
Kennington, Thomas Benjamin 1856–1916, *Portrait of an Unknown Lady*
Kennington, Thomas Benjamin 1856–1916, *George Skelton (1855–1932)*
Kennington, Thomas Benjamin 1856–1916, *John Wintringham, Mayor of Grimsby (1864–1865)*
Kennington, Thomas Benjamin 1856–1916, *Mrs Wintringham*
Kennington, Thomas Benjamin 1856–1916, *Portrait of an Unknown Man*
Kennington, Thomas Benjamin 1856–1916, *Portrait of an Unknown Man*
Kennington, Thomas Benjamin (attributed to) 1856–1916, *Charles Bartholomew Moody, Mayor of Grimsby (1855–1856)*
Knell, William Adolphus 1802–1875, *A Man-of-War and Other Shipping in Harbour*, bequeathed by Wilfred Vere Doughty, 1941
Knell, William Adolphus 1802–1875, *The Old Hulk*
Lely, Peter (attributed to) 1618–1680, *George Monck (b.1608), 1st Duke of Abermarle*, bequeathed by Wilfred Vere Doughty, 1941
Lolie, M. *William Grange (1861–1913), Town Clerk of Grimsby*
Lonsdale, F. G. *A Ship Sinking*
Lonsdale, F. G. *Convoy off a Lighthouse*
Lothian, Lewis *River Scene with Fishermen*
Loveridge, Alan John *HMS 'Nerissa'*, gift from Mr V. Lease, 1980
Loveridge, Alan John *The 'Real Madrid', GY 674*, gift from the artist, 1993
Ludlam, Alf b.1941, *Cod War*, © the artist
Luny, Thomas 1759–1837, *Portsmouth Harbour, Hampshire*
Lynn, John active 1826–1845, *Shipping off the Coast*, bequeathed by Wilfred Vere Doughty, 1941
A. J. M. *The 'Ross Renown', GY 666*
Major, O. *Foreshore*
Marsden, Walter Major 1851–after 1900, *Dr Thomas Bell Keetley, Mayor of Grimsby (1883–1884)*
Marsden, Walter Major 1851–after 1900, *Portrait of an Unknown Gentleman*
Marston, Frank William b.1931, *Checking the Nets*, gift from Frank Manston, 1995, © the artist
McColvin, John A. 1864–1920, *Girl Leaning on a Fence*
McColvin, John A. 1864–1920, *Gypsy Fruit Seller*
Milnie *The 'Vivaria', GY 648*, gift
Mitchell, Alfred 1854–1914, *Two-Masted Brig*
Moore, H. (attributed to) *Street Scene*, gift from Mrs Howard Humberstone, 1983
Moore, Jack *HMS 'St Barbe'*, gift
Moorhall, R. *Ship Taking Pilots in the Channel*
Moras, S. (attributed to) *A Girl in a Wood with a Letter*
Munga, G. *Still Life, Flowers*
Munga, G. *Still Life, Flowers*
Murray, G. *The 'Iranian'*
Murray, G. *The 'Ross Jackal', GY 637*, gift from Mr B. Moore
Murray, G. *The 'Ross Zebra', GY 653*
Ovenden, F. W. active 1834–1843, *Recovering Wreckage*
Payne, Roland W. *The Old Pier, Grimsby, Lincolnshire, 1975*
Pocock, Nicholas (attributed to) 1740–1821, *HMS 'Endymion' Rescuing a French School Two-Decker off the Coast of Spain, 1805*, gift from the Earl of Yarborough, High Steward of Grimsby, 1871
Prescott, David *HMS 'Arnold Bennett'*
Race, George 1872–1957, *The 'Clyde', GY317*, bequeathed by Wilfred Vere Doughty, 1941
Race, George 1872–1957, *The 'Saxon', GY722, Outward Bound*
Race, George 1872–1957, *The 'Champion'*, bequeathed by Wilfred Vere Doughty, 1941
Race, George 1872–1957, *The 'Diamond', GY603*, gift from Mr A. G. Ramsden, 1965
Race, George 1872–1957, *The 'Dominican', GY406*, gift
Race, George 1872–1957, *The 'Egyptian', GY492*, gift from Mr A. Kirman
Race, George 1872–1957, *The 'Albatross', GY 279, Outward Bound*, purchased from Mr Freeman
Race, George 1872–1957, *The 'Albatross', GY 279, Homeward Bound*, purchased from Mr Freeman
Race, George 1872–1957, *The 'Bermuda', GY56*
Race, George 1872–1957, *SS 'Passing', GY 877*, gift from Mr K. R. Mingay
Race, George 1872–1957, *SS 'Sweeper', GY 853*
Race, George 1872–1957, *Fishing Smack, GY732*
Race, George 1872–1957, *The 'Somerville', GY301, Homeward Bound*, gift A. G. Ramsden, 1965
Race, George (attributed to) 1872–1957, *The 'Marylebone'*, gift from Mr J. Elliot, 1983
Ramsey, G. active 1856–1889, *The 'Dahlia', GY223*
Redmore, Edward King 1860–1941, *Fishing Vessels off the Coast*
Reynolds, Roy Peter b.1929, *Across the Bows*, © the artist
Rollett, Herbert 1872–1932, *Lincolnshire Scene*, gift from Mrs Taylor
Rollett, Herbert 1872–1932, *Arden Wood, Healing, Lincolnshire*, purchased from Miss Wilson
Rollett, Herbert 1872–1932, *Landscape with a Large Cloud*
Rollett, Herbert 1872–1932, *Victoria Mill and Alexandra Dock, Grimsby, Lincolnshire*
Rollett, Herbert 1872–1932, *Woodland Scene*
C. V. S. *Herbert Rollett (1872–1932)*
S. S. *The 'Sons of the Thames'*
Schade, Frederick *SS 'Uxbridge', Grimsby*, gift from Mrs Gaiter
Schade, Frederick *The 'Abronia', Grimsby*, gift from Mr Ceraiter
Schäfer, Heinrich c.1815–1905, *Utrecht, The Netherlands*
Scott, F. *Two-Masted Ship off the Coast in Three Positions*, bequeathed by Wilfred Vere Doughty, 1941
Skelton, George 1855–1932, *Tudor Portrait of an Unknown Gentleman*
Skelton, George 1855–1932, *Elizabethan Portrait of an Unknown Gentleman*
Skelton, George 1855–1932, *Building of the Second Corporation Road Bridge, Lincolnshire*, purchased
Skelton, George 1855–1932, *The Back of Bennett's Mill, Old Bone Mill and Gasworks, Grimsby, Lincolnshire*
Skelton, George 1855–1932, *The Moll All Alone*, gift from W. E. R. Hallgarth
Skelton, George 1855–1932, *Beelsby Mill, Grimsby, Lincolnshire*
Skelton, George 1855–1932, *Nun's Farm, Sunset*
Smith, H. *The 'Hungarian', BN89*
Somerscales, Thomas Jacques 1842–1927, *The Rescue of the 'Anna Mathilda' by the Trawler 'Clyde', GY 317*, purchased
Sonley, L. *High Street, Bridlington, East Riding of Yorkshire*
Speechley, J. H. *The Lying in State of George VI*, gift from Mr P. F. Speechley
Spencer, William Barnett c.1810–c.1880, *Three-Masted Sailing Ship off the Coast*
Tarttelin, David *South Quay, No.3 Fish Dock, Grimsby, Lincolnshire*
Tarttelin, David *The Riverhead in Winter*
Tindall, J. T. *The 'Emma Sharp'*
Townsend, Ernest 1885–1944, *Councillor W. R. Womersley, Mayor of Grimsby (1922–1923)*, presented by Members of the Grimsby and Cleethorpes Chamber of Trade
Truman, P. J. *Major Lushby*, gift from Mr F. M. Capiter, 1954
Tscharner, Theodore *Evening Scene with a Hay Cart*, gift from Alderman Frank Barrett, JP, 1935
Tscharner, Theodore *Evening Scene with a Plough*, gift from Alderman Frank Barrett, JP, 1935
Tudgay, Frederick J. 1841–1921, *Three-Masted Ship by Night*, bequeathed by Wilfred Vere Doughty, 1941
Tudgay, Frederick J. 1841–1921, *Launching of the 'Royal George'*, bequeathed by Wilfred Vere Doughty, 1941
Tudgay, Frederick J. 1841–1921, *Shipping at a Harbour Entrance*
unknown artist *Ships off Madras, India*
unknown artist *John Skelton, JP*
unknown artist *Victoria Street*
unknown artist *Royal Dock, Grimsby, Lincolnshire*, bequeathed by Mrs W. H. Hitzen, 1936
unknown artist *Portrait of a Man with a Moustache*
unknown artist *'Northern Pride', Arctic Trawler, Built in Germany for 'Northern Trawlers', Grimsby*, gift from Mr M. H. Thomas
unknown artist *Bremerhaven Docks, Germany*
unknown artist *First Train Leaving Grimsby, Lincolnshire, 1848*
unknown artist *GER Steamship 'Lincoln'*
unknown artist *John James Earle (Smack Owner)*, gift from Miss L. E. Earle
unknown artist *Landscape*
unknown artist *Portrait of a Child with a White Face*
unknown artist *Portrait of a Young Boy Dressed in Tartan*
unknown artist *Portrait of an Unknown Lady*
unknown artist *Portrait of an Unknown Mayor*
unknown artist *Ship in Distress off the Coast*
unknown artist *Ship in Dry Dock*
unknown artist *Sir George Doughty, MP (1895), Mayor of Grimsby (1892–1893)*, bequeathed by Wilfred Vere Doughty, 1941
unknown artist *Sluice Mill, South Ferriby, Lincolnshire*, gift from Mr Andrew
unknown artist *Still Life, Interior*
unknown artist *Sunrise, Old Outfall, Grimsby, Lincolnshire*, gift from Miss A. E. Bell
unknown artist *Thatched Cottage*
unknown artist *The 'Achilles', GY182*
unknown artist *The 'Argo'*
unknown artist *'The Commodore', Charles Anderson-Pelham (1781–1846), 1st Earl of Yarborough*, gift from Ian Sime
unknown artist *The 'Elk'*
unknown artist *The Wheelright's Shed*
unknown artist *Theatrical Scene*
unknown artist *Waltham Hall, Melton Mowbray (?)*
H. W. *Grimsby Docks from the West Pier, Lincolnshire*, gift
Wade, Albert Edward active 1911–1948, *Last of Pie Jetty, Grimsby Fish Dock, Lincolnshire*
Wade, Albert Edward active 1911–1948, *Still Life, Autumn*
Wade, Albert Edward active 1911–1948, *Jesse Flower*, gift from Mrs F. K. Wade, 1971
Wade, Albert Edward active 1911–1948, *Slipway, Grimsby Docks, Lincolnshire*, gift from Mrs F. K. Wade, 1971
Wade, Albert Edward active 1911–1948, *Councillor Max Bloom, JP, Mayor of Grimsby (1943–1944)*

Wade, Albert Edward active 1911–1948, *Ship Building, Grimsby Docks, Lincolnshire*, gift from Mrs F. K. Wade, 1971
Wade, Albert Edward active 1911–1948, *Still Life, Flowers*
Wade, Albert Edward active 1911–1948, *Captain H. Turnbull, MBE, Former Harbour Master of Grimsby*, gift from Mrs F. K. Wade, 1971
Wade, Albert Edward active 1911–1948, *Kenneth Gilmour Younger, MP*, gift from the artist
Webster, George 1797–1864, *Ships off Holyhead at the Beginning of a Storm*, gift from the Earl of Yarborough, High Steward of Grimsby
Whitcombe, Thomas c.1752–1824, *Ships at Sea*, bequeathed by Wilfred Vere Doughty, 1941
Whitcombe, Thomas (attributed to) c.1752–1824, *The Battle of the Nile, 1–2 August 1798*, bequeathed by Wilfred Vere Doughty, 1941
William, A. G. *Men-of-War at the Beginning of a Storm*, bequeathed by Wilfred Vere Doughty, 1941
Wilson, G. (attributed to) *The 'Ronsay', H387*, gift from Miss S. Coates, 1962
Wilson, John Glen 1774–1855, *Small Ships and Boats off the Coast*
Witham, Isaac Joseph 1832–1901, *The 'Oweenee'*, bequeathed by Wilfred Vere Doughty, 1941
Wozencroft, A. *The 'Ross Tiger', GY 398*, gift from Mr Dennis Avery
Yorke, William Horde 1847–1921, *The 'Lord Templeshore'*, bequeathed by Wilfred Vere Doughty, 1941

The Franklin Trust

Ashton, Stuart *Self Portrait*, purchased from an exhibition at Grimsby Art College, 1982
Atkinson, Albert *My Road through the Woods*, gift from the artist, 1980
Avison, Michelle b.1965, *Nude*, purchased from an exhibition at Grimsby Art College, 1984, © the artist
Barker, Geoffrey *Barges*, purchased from Lincolnshire and Humberside Arts, 1991
Binns, Andrew b.1964, *Lincoln Cathedral*, acquired, 2001
Boucher, John *Drawing*, gift from Lincolnshire and Humberside Arts, 1991
Bowey, Olwyn b.1936, *Landscape*, purchased from an exhibition at the Royal Academy, 1983, © the artist
Carr, Colin b.1929, *Blue Seiner*, purchased, 1991
Clatter, Malcolm b.1953, *Full Fathom Five*, gift from W. G. Baines, 1991
Clilverd, Jason *Rooftops*, purchased from the annual exhibition at Grimsby Art College, 1982
Collins, Lesley *Self Portrait*, purchased from an exhibition at Grimsby Art College, 1984
Constance, Diana 1934–2011, *Abstract Landscape*, gift from Duncan Smith, 1985, © the artist's estate
Crowe, Victoria b.1945, *Flowers on the Fridge*, gift from Lincolnshire and Humberside Arts, 1991, © Victoria Crowe
Davies, Hugh b.1946, *The Neapolitan Girl*, gift from Duncan Smith, 1995, © the artist
Davis, Katherine *Still Life, Flowers*
Dean, Margaret b.1939, *Church Interior*
Ellerby, Nick b.1958, *Pillbox, Horseshoe Point, Lincolnshire*, purchased, 2009, © the artist
Elliott, Mike *Hello*, purchased from Lincolnshire and Humberside Arts, 1991
Fegan, David 1955–2006, *Seascape*, gift from Mrs N. Fitzwilliams, 2002
Felcey, Trevor b.1945, *Nude*, gift from students and staff at Grimsby Art College in memory of Councillor Matt Lamour, 1981, © the artist
Foster, John *Sierpinski Curve Variation*, gift from Lincolnshire and Humberside Arts, 1991
Gables, Gina *Reclining Male*, purchased from an exhibition at Grimsby Art College, 1984
Gillett, Stephen *Man Reading a Newspaper*, purchased, 1984
Haddock, Edwin Aldridge 1921–1996, *Pink Pride (Pink Perfection)*, purchased, 1990, © the artist's estate
Haigh, Paul active 1983–1990, *Boy Fishing*, gift from Clixby Fitzwilliams, 2009
Haigh, Paul active 1983–1990, *Cyclamen with Apples*, gift from the artist, 1990
Haigh, Paul active 1983–1990, *Ipswich Docks, Suffolk*, purchased, 1986
Haswell, Malcolm *Model*, purchased, 1981
Hennes, Jolyon b.1950, *Greek Girl*, purchased from an exhibition at the Royal Academy, 1980
Hill, Carol *Grant Thorold Park, Grimsby, Lincolnshire*, purchased from an exhibition at Grimsby Art College, 1984
Holmes, Mark *Children*, purchased from an exhibition at Grimsby Art College, 1989
Holzer, Henry 1907–2007, *Sun over Willows*
Hopkinson, John b.1941, *Mr Beau Williams, Outsider*, purchased, 1979, © the artist
Hopkinson, John b.1941, *Trawler (Still Life)*, gift from the artist, 1987, © the artist
Hoult, Ken 1928–1990, *Hurdis Sandpits, Nettleton, Lincolnshire*, purchased from Lincolnshire and Humberside Arts, 1991
Humphreys, George *Studio Interior*, purchased at the Royal Academy, 1982
Ingham, Linda b.1964, *Shell* (study), purchased, 2009, © the artist
Ingham, Linda b.1964, *Shell*, gift from the artist, 2009, © the artist
Jensen, Andreas *The Pair Fishers*, gift from Clixby Fitzwilliams
Jessup, Ann *Triple Echo*, gift from Duncan Smith
Ludlam, Alf b.1941, *Portrait of a Young Lady*, gift from the artist, 1980, © the artist
Lundy, Fiona b.1963, *Still Life with a Kettle*, purchased, 1981, © the artist
Moffat, Mark J. *Still Life*, purchased from an exhibition at Grimsby Art College, 1985
Owen, David active 1981–1982, *Rape Field at Caistor, Lincolnshire*, purchased from an exhibition at Grimsby Art College, 1982
Owen, Mark b.1963, *Still Life*, purchased from an exhibition at Grimsby Art College, 1982
Palmer, Albert Harold 1911–1985, *Park Bench*, gift from the artist's widow, 1991
Penketh, Andrew b.1966, *Still Life*, purchased, 1985, © the artist
Rae, Annette *Still Life*, purchased, 1984
Rawson, Philip 1924–1995, *Landscape*, purchased, 1981
Reeves, Aimie b.1971, *Diptych*
Rider, Gordon *Figure*, purchased from an exhibition at the Royal Academy, 1984
Robinson, Mark active 1982, *Still Life*, purchased from an exhibition at Grimsby Art College, 1982
Rollett, Herbert 1872–1932, *The Freshney, Lincolnshire*, gift from Mrs B. Chapman, 2000
Rosoman, Leonard Henry 1913–2012, *'Blitz' (London Docks)*, gift from Rhoda Cowen, 1998, © the artist
Ross-Kelsey, Gillian *Children at Play*, purchased, 1984
Smith, David *Lily Pool at Healing, Lincolnshire*, gift from Mrs B. Chapman, 2002
Smith, Margaret *Seated Nude*, purchased, 1986
Swift, Nigel *Trees*, purchased from an exhibition at Grimsby Art College, 1981
Upton, Steve b.1947, *Molly*, purchased, 2009, © the artist
Volley, Nicholas 1950–2006, *Flowers*, gift from the artist, 1980
Volley, Nicholas 1950–2006, *Self Portrait*, gift from the artist, 1980
Waldron, E. W. *Hillside Community No.2*, purchased from Lincolnshire and Humberside Arts, 1991
Warmoth, Pip Todd b.1962, *Church Lane*, purchased from an exhibition at Grimsby Art College, 1982, © the artist
Webb, Sarah b.1964, *The Point, Cleethorpes, Lincolnshire*, purchased with an Awards for All Grant, 2009, © the artist
White, Harry *Central Market*, gift from P. H. Green, 1958
Worrall, Ernest J. 1898–1972, *Snow Scene, Healing, Lincolnshire*, gift from Clixby Fitzwilliams, 1982
Yeung, Hai Shuet b.1936, *Bridge*, gift from the artist, 1990, © the artist

Immingham Museum

Bunting, William Richard 1866–c.1944, *Habrough Mill, Lincolnshire*, donated

Bishop Grosseteste University College Lincoln

Adams, Bernard 1884–1965, *River Scene**, gift

Doddington Hall

Reynolds, Joshua 1723–1792, *The Earl and Countess of Mexborough with Their Son, Lord Pollington (1719–1778)*, commissioned as a gift to Lady Mexborough's brother, and sold to the government in lieu of tax, 1973

Museum of Lincolnshire Life

Alston, Rowland Wright 1895–1958, *Teapot Hall, Lincolnshire*, gift, 2006
Burgess, Arthur James Wetherall 1879–1957, *SS 'Mercian'*, gift from the Officers of the Lincolnshire Yeomanry, 1974, © the artist's estate
Clark, William Albert active 1908–1936, *'Strowan Butterfly'*, donated by the Dunning Family, 1972
Clark, William Albert active 1908–1936, *Lincoln Red Cow*, purchased, 1982
Clark, William Albert active 1908–1936, *The Heaviest Beast of the Smithfield Show*, purchased, 1982
Cook, Evelyn active 1897–1918, *Pastoral Scene*, gift, 1989
Davis, William Henry 1786–1865, *Prize Sheep*, gift, 1971
Day, William Cave 1862–1924, *Threshing Drum 1*
Day, William Cave 1862–1924, *Threshing Drum 2*
Garnt, F. M. *Derelict*
Hailstone, Bernard 1910–1987, *Charles W. Heathcote, Chairman of Robey & Co. Ltd of Lincoln (1969–1972)*, gift, 1997, © the artist's estate
Hutchinson, Sybil *Henry Dudding and His Shepherd, Richard Aves*, commissioned, 1906 (?); purchased by the Friends of Lincoln Museums and Art Gallery, 1984
Kennington, Thomas Benjamin 1856–1916, *Henry Dudding*
Lee, G. *Windmill by the Sea*, gift, 1981
Morris, E. M. C. d.1970, *Bicker Windmill, Lincolnshire*, bequeathed by the artist, 1970
Morris, E. M. C. d.1970, *Girl in the Sky over the Sea*, bequeathed by the artist, 1970
Morris, E. M. C. d.1970, *Heathen Shrine*, bequeathed by the artist, 1970
Morris, E. M. C. d.1970, *House at Skegness, Lincolnshire*, bequeathed by the artist, 1970
Morris, E. M. C. d.1970, *Landscape with Trees*, bequeathed by the artist, 1970
Morris, E. M. C. d.1970, *Sand Dunes at Gibraltar Point, Lincolnshire*, bequeathed by the artist, 1970
Morris, E. M. C. d.1970, *The Mysterious Being (A Donington Cat)*, bequeathed by the artist, 1970
Morris, E. M. C. d.1970, *The Parallel Universe*, bequeathed by the artist, 1970
Morris, E. M. C. d.1970, *The Rifle Range at Skegness, Lincolnshire*, bequeathed by the artist, 1970
Morris, E. M. C. d.1970, *The Wrekin, Shropshire*, bequeathed by the artist, 1970
Morris, E. M. C. d.1970, *Trees on a River Bank*, bequeathed by the artist, 1970
Pears (Mrs) *Thatched Cottage, Driby Top, Lincolnshire*, acquired, 1977
J. R. *Thatched Cottage by a Pool*, acquired, 1974; on loan to Church Farm Museum, until 2011
Robinson, Ken *Curly-Coated Pig*, donated by the Meat Research Institute, Agricultural Research Council, 1979
unknown artist *William Hornsby, Manager of Hornsby's Bank, Gainsborough, Lincolnshire*, gift, 1970
unknown artist *'Riby Swell', First and Champion at Wharfedale and Otley, First and Reserve Champion at Nottinghamshire, First at Newarke*
unknown artist *Ley Maleable Works, Lincoln*, gift, 1976
unknown artist *Bardney Mill, Lincolnshire*, gift, 1984
unknown artist *Church*, gift, 1976
unknown artist *Dunston, Lincolnshire*, gift, 1973
unknown artist *Harvesting*, unknown acquisition method
unknown artist *Mary Ann Dudding*
unknown artist *Maud Foster Mill, Boston, Lincolnshire*, gift, 1974
unknown artist *Mountains*, gift, 1976
unknown artist *Mr Wardall in Hunting Clothes*, gift, 1978
unknown artist *Newport Arch, Lincoln*, gift, 1968
unknown artist *Portrait of an Unknown Man*
Wells, F. V. *Paper Mill at Washdyke Bridge, Evedon, Lincolnshire*

The Collection: Art & Archaeology in Lincolnshire (Usher Gallery)

Airy, Anna 1882–1964, *Children Blackberrying*, gift from the artist, 1945
Airy, Anna 1882–1964, *Roses Triumphant*, purchased from the artist, 1930
Aitchison, Craigie Ronald John 1926–2009, *The Tree*, gift from the Contemporary Art Society, 2000, © the artist's estate/Bridgeman Art Library
Aldridge, John Arthur Malcolm 1905–1983, *Still Life*, purchased, 1968
Alston, Rowland Wright 1895–1958, *Peregrine Falcon*, bequeathed by Mrs R. Alston, 1960
Alston, Rowland Wright 1895–1958, *Trained Hawk on the Fist*, bequeathed by Mrs R. Alston, 1960
Andrew *Alderman Edward James Willson*, gift from Reverend E. H. Willson, 1948
Andrews, John active 1824–1870, *Charles Delaet Waldo Sibthorp (1815–1861)*, gift from the Honourable Mrs Dudley Pelham, 1964
Andrews, John active 1824–1870, *Reverend Humphrey Waldo Sibthorp (1786–1865)*, bequeathed by the Sibthorp family
Appleyard, Frederick 1874–1963, *Cleethorpes Foreshore, Lincolnshire*, gift from Sir Hickman B. Bacon, Bt, JP, 1935, © the artist's estate
Appleyard, Frederick 1874–1963, *Farm Buildings*, gift from Sir Hickman B. Bacon, Bt, JP, 1935, © the artist's estate
J. D. B. *Lincoln Cathedral and the Exchequer Gate*, gift by Mrs B. M. Ford, 1958
Baker, Joseph d.1770, *A View of Lincoln Cathedral from the West*, purchased from Sir Geoffrey Harmsworth, 1976
Baker, Joseph (attributed to) d.1770, *Lincoln from Brayford*, purchased from Shelton, 1934
Balmer, Barbara b.1929, *Deserted Cemetery*, purchased from the artist, © the artist
Barabino, Nicolò 1832–1891, *The Death of Pope Boniface VIII*, gift from E. W. Kirk, 1920
Bartl, Antonin Karel 1912–1998, *Reclining Nude*, gift from Angela Brewer, 1997
Bartl, Antonin Karel 1912–1998, *John Piper (1903–1992)*, purchased from the artist, 1977
Bartl, Antonin Karel 1912–1998, *Portrait of an Architect*, purchased, 1960
Beale, Mary 1633–1699, *Judith Sibthorp*, gift from the Honourable Mrs Dudley Pelham, 1964
Bell, Stuart Henry 1823–1896, *The Expedition Entering Baffin Bay in Search of John Franklin*, bequeathed by Sir James William Francis Hill, 1980
Bell, Vanessa 1879–1961, *Zinnias*, gift from the Contemporary Art Society, 1954, © 1961 estate of Vanessa Bell courtesy Henrietta Garnett
Blakesley, Alicia 1861–1939, *Thatched Cottage and a Poppy Field*
Blakesley, Alicia 1861–1939, *Common with Gorse and a Distant Church*, gift from Mrs Blakesley, 1948
Blane, Frances Aviva b.1954, *Self Portrait*, purchased from the artist, 1996, © the artist
Boden, George Alfred 1888–1956, *Church, Brant Broughton, Lincolnshire*, bequeathed by Mrs G. M. Pease, 1957
Boden, George Alfred 1888–1956, *Breton Oxcart*, gift from Miss Spencer, 1967
Boden, George Alfred 1888–1956, *Staple Inn, Holborn, London*, bequeathed by the artist
Boden, Leonard 1911–1999, *Sir Francis Hill (1899–1980)*, gift from the Heslam Trust, 1984, © the artist's estate
Bonjean, Antonia active 19th C, *Sheep on a Hillside*, gift from Joan Webster, 1957
Boyd, Fionnuala b.1944 & **Evans, Leslie** b.1945 *Looking Out*, gift from the Contemporary Art Society, 1979, © the artists
Bramley, Frank 1857–1915, *Neapolitan Fisher Boy*, gift from Richard Whitton Richard, 1938
Bramley, Frank 1857–1915, *Weaving Nets*, bequeathed by Trotter Alexander to Lincoln Library, 1922; transferred
Bramley, Frank 1857–1915, *Self Portrait*, purchased via Thomas Agnew and Sons Ltd at Sotheby's, 1996
Bramley, Frank 1857–1915, *Alexander S. Leslie Melville of Lincoln (d.1881)*, gift from Miss Melville, 1943
Brannan, Peter 1926–1994, *Street Scene*, purchased from the artist, 1953, © the artist's estate
Brannan, Peter 1926–1994, *Winter Street Scene*, unknown acquisition method, © the artist's estate
Brannan, Peter 1926–1994, *On the Beach*, purchased, 1960, © the artist's estate
Brannan, Peter 1926–1994, *Corn Exchange, Lincoln*, purchased from the Trafford Gallery, 1974, © the artist's estate
Brannan, Peter 1926–1994, *Rag Day, Lincoln*, purchased from the Trafford Gallery, 1974, © the artist's estate
Brannan, Peter 1926–1994, *Flowers in a Jug*, bequeathed by the artist © the artist's estate
Brannan, Peter 1926–1994, *At Frank's, Bradford, West Yorkshire*, bequeathed by the artist © the artist's estate
Brannan, Peter 1926–1994, *Cleethorpes, Beach Scene, Lincolnshire*, bequeathed by the artist © the artist's estate
Bratby, John Randall 1928–1992, *Taffy Roberts*, purchased, 1968, © the artist's estate/Bridgeman Art Library
Brigham, Isobel b.1963, *Tennis Court Self Portrait*, purchased from the artist, 1996, © the artist
Briscoe, Arthur John Trevor 1873–1943, *In Ballast*, purchased from the artist, 1937
British (English) School *Charles Caldecote, Esq., of Holton Beckering*, gift from the Honourable Mrs Dudley Pelham, 1975
Brown, Agnes Augusta 1847–1932, *Moonlight on the Yorkshire Coast*, gift from Sir Hickman B. Bacon, Bt, JP, 1933
Brown, Agnes Augusta 1847–1932, *North Sea Sunrise*, gift from Sir Hickman B. Bacon, Bt, JP, 1936
Brown, Agnes Augusta 1847–1932, *Shades of Evening*, gift from Sir Hickman B. Bacon, Bt, JP, 1935
Brown, John 1887–1966, *A Break in the Clouds*, gift from Sir Hickman B. Bacon, Bt, JP, 1933
Brown, John 1887–1966, *November Sky*, gift from Sir Hickman B. Bacon, Bt, JP, 1936
Browne, Clive Richard 1901–1991, *St Mary's Church, Stow, Lincolnshire*, bequeathed by Sir James William Francis Hill, 1980
Browne, Clive Richard 1901–1991, *Before Sunrise*, gift from Sir Hickman B. Bacon, Bt, JP, 1938
Browne, Clive Richard 1901–1991, *Early Morning*, gift from Sir Hickman B. Bacon, Bt, JP, 1936
Browne, Clive Richard 1901–1991, *Housel Bay, Cornwall*, gift from Sir Hickman B. Bacon, Bt, JP, 1939
Browne, Clive Richard 1901–1991, *Low Tide on the Humber*, gift from Sir Hickman B. Bacon, Bt, JP, 1933
Browne, Clive Richard 1901–1991, *The Haunt of the Seagull*, gift from Sir Hickman B. Bacon, Bt, JP, 1939
Browne, Clive Richard 1901–1991, *The Humber in a Sullen Mood*, gift from Sir Hickman B. Bacon, Bt, JP, 1933
Bruce, Allan b.1943, *Interior V*, purchased from the artist, 1983
Buffam, H. M. *Whitefriars House, Akrill's Passage, Lincoln*, bequeathed by Mrs P. E. M. Birchby, 1976
Bullock, Stephen 1889–1971, *Farmstead, Donington On Bain, Lincolnshire*, gift from J. J. Collinson, 1964
Callcott, Augustus Wall 1779–1844, *Sea Pier*, gift from Algernon Curtois, 1933
Carline, George F. 1855–1920, *The Ploughing Match*, gift from Sidney and Richard Carline, 1913
Carline, Sydney William 1888–1929, *Village by Lake Orta, Italy*, gift from Mrs G. F. Carline and Mr S. W. Carline, 1931
Carmichael, John Wilson 1800–1868, *The Brayford Pool and Lincoln Cathedral*, gift from the Heslam Trust, 1969
Carter, Tony b.1943, *Flag for Pericles*, gift from the Contemporary Art Society, 1980, © the artist
Carter, William 1863–1939, *Reverend Canon Frederic Pretyman (1820–1905)*, gift from the Trustees of the George Woofindin Convalescent Home, Mablethorpe, 1982
Chuhan, J. b.1955, *Self Portrait II*, purchased from the artist, 1996, © J. Chuhan
Clausen, George 1852–1944, *A. G. Webster (1852–1916)*, gift from Joan Webster, 1956, © Clausen estate
Clausen, George 1852–1944, *The Mowers*, purchased from the Fine Art Society, 1949, © Clausen estate
Clausen, George 1852–1944, *John Thomas Tweed (1823–1910), Town Clerk of Lincoln (1855–1905)*, transferred from the Guildhall, Lincoln, 1952, © Clausen estate
Clausen, George 1852–1944, *Orchard Scene*, gift from Joan Webster, 1957, © Clausen estate
Clayton, G. *George Clayton Tennyson (1778–1831), Father of Alfred Tennyson*, gift from the Tennyson family, 1961
Clements, Helen d.1934, *Chapel Doorway, Lincoln Cathedral*, bequeathed by the artist, 1934
Clements, Helen d.1934, *Corner of Judgement Porch, Lincoln Cathedral*, bequeathed by the artist, 1934
Clements, Helen d.1934, *Morning Chapel, Lincoln Cathedral*, bequeathed by the artist, 1934
Clements, Helen d.1934, *Staircase, Lincoln Cathedral*, bequeathed by the artist, 1934
Clements, Helen d.1934, *The Tomb of Sir Bartholomew Burghersh, Lincoln Cathedral*, bequeathed by the artist, 1934
Clouse, M. 1820–1880, *A View of Lincoln Cathedral from Drury Lane*, purchased at Christie's, 1995
Collier, John 1850–1934, *The Prodigal Daughter* (sketch), purchased from Abbott and Holder, 1987
Collier, John 1850–1934, *The Prodigal Daughter*, gift from the Honourable Mrs Collier, 1935
Cook, A. active 20th C, *Watermill, Hatcliffe, Lincolnshire*, gift from Sir Hickman B. Bacon, Bt, JP, 1935
Cooke, Jean 1927–2008, *Not Waving, Just Painting*, purchased from the artist, 1996, © the artist's estate
Corbet, Matthew Ridley 1850–1902, *Autumn Rains, the Marshes of Florence, Italy*, gift from Lieutenant Colonel E. F. Ridley Corbet, 1927
Curtois, Mary Henrietta Dering 1854–1929, *Young Girl Sitting in a Deck Chair*, purchased from Abbott and Holder, 1986
Curtois, Mary Henrietta Dering 1854–1929, *Ruston Ward, Lincoln County Hospital*, gift from the artist, 1928
Curtois, Mary Henrietta Dering 1854–1929, *Willow Trees, Winter*, gift from the Misses Harrison, 1964
Dahl, Michael I (style of) 1656/1659–1743, *Elizabeth Browne, Daughter of Humphry Browne*, gift from the Honourable Mrs Dudley Pelham, 1964
Dahl, Michael I (style of) 1656/1659–1743, *Mary Sibthorp, Wife of John Sibthorp*, gift from the Honourable Mrs Dudley Pelham, 1964
Dawson, Henry 1811–1878, *Lincoln Cathedral from Brayford*, gift from Mary Pennell, 1945
De Coene, Jean Henri 1798–1866, *Landscape*, gift from Miss Frankish, 1943
De Coene, Jean Henri 1798–1866, *River Scene with Men in a Boat*, gift from Miss Frankish, 1943
de Maistre, Leroy Leveson Laurent Joseph 1894–1968, *Flowers*, bequeathed by Mrs Dora M. Bond, 1985, © the artist's estate
De Wint, Peter 1784–1849, *Lincolnshire Cornfield near Horncastle*, purchased from the P. M. Turner Collection, 1947
De Wint, Peter 1784–1849, *A View of Lincoln from the South at Little Bargate*, purchased at Christie's, 1995
De Wint, Peter 1784–1849, *A Drover at the Edge of a Wood, Lincoln in the Distance*, purchased at Christie's, 1995
De Wint, Peter 1784–1849, *The Burning of the Houses of Parliament*, gift from Miss E. Scrivenor, 1951
De Wint, Peter 1784–1849, *Carnations*, gift from Miss E. Scrivenor, 1951
De Wint, Peter 1784–1849, *Cattle in a Landscape*, purchased from the Fine Art Society, 1945
De Wint, Peter 1784–1849, *Cornfield with a Windmill*, purchased from Thomas Agnew and Sons Ltd, 1946
De Wint, Peter 1784–1849, *Horses and Figures at a Ford*, purchased with the assistance of the National Art Collections Fund, 1975
De Wint, Peter 1784–1849, *Landscape with a Castle*, gift from Geoffrey Harmsworth, 1937
De Wint, Peter 1784–1849, *Landscape with a Rainbow*, gift from Miss G. Muriel Bostock, 1937
De Wint, Peter 1784–1849, *Lincoln Cathedral from the North East*, purchased with the assistance of the Friends of Lincoln Museums and Art Gallery, 2000
De Wint, Peter 1784–1849, *Lincoln from the River at Sunset*, purchased from Andrew Wyld, 1985
De Wint, Peter 1784–1849, *Lincoln from the South*, purchased at Christie's, 1941
De Wint, Peter 1784–1849, *Mrs Peter De Wint (1791–1866)*, gift from Miss G. Muriel Bostock, 1935
De Wint, Peter 1784–1849,

Newport Arch, Lincoln, purchased from H. K. Henderson, 1935
De Wint, Peter 1784–1849, *Portrait of the Artist's Mother*, purchased from Miss E. Scrivenor, 1948
Delvaux, Edouard 1806–1862, *Trees by the Side of a Watermill*, gift from Miss Frankish, 1943
Does, Jacob van der the elder 1623–1673, *Mother and Child with Cattle in a Landscape*, gift from Edwin Hitchon, 1946
Domenichino (attributed to) 1581–1641, *Saint John in a Mountain Landscape*, gift from Edwin Hitchon, 1946
Donaldson, Andrew Benjamin 1840–1919, *The Beginning of the Pilgrimage of Grace Lincoln, 1537*, gift from the family of the artist, 1919
Downton, John 1906–1991, *Child with Roses*, gift from the John Downton Trust, 1998, © The Collection: Art & Archaeology
Downton, John 1906–1991, *Young Woman in a Landscape*, gift from the John Downton Trust, 1998, © The Collection: Art & Archaeology
Downton, John 1906–1991, *The Arrival*, gift from the John Downton Trust, 1998, © The Collection: Art & Archaeology
Drake, Nathan c.1728–1778, *Newport Arch, Lincoln*, gift from Mrs W. S. Richardson, 1926
Dudding, Mary 1914–1994, *A Lincoln Model*, gift from the artist, 1992
Dunlop, Ronald Ossory 1894–1973, *The Girl of Montparnasse*, bequeathed by Mrs Dora M. Bond, 1985
Dunlop, Ronald Ossory 1894–1973, *Girl's Head*, bequeathed by Mrs Dora M. Bond, 1985
Dunlop, Ronald Ossory 1894–1973, *Gravesend, Kent*, bequeathed by Mrs Dora M. Bond, 1985
Dunlop, Ronald Ossory 1894–1973, *Head of a Girl*, bequeathed by Mrs Dora M. Bond, 1985
Dunlop, Ronald Ossory 1894–1973, *Martigues, France*, bequeathed by Mrs Dora M. Bond, 1985
Dunlop, Ronald Ossory 1894–1973, *Near Cannes, France*, bequeathed by Mrs Dora M. Bond, 1985
Dunlop, Ronald Ossory 1894–1973, *Portrait of an Unknown Woman*, bequeathed by Mrs Dora M. Bond, 1985
Dunlop, Ronald Ossory 1894–1973, *Portrait of an Unknown Woman*, bequeathed by Mrs Dora M. Bond, 1985
Dunlop, Ronald Ossory 1894–1973, *Still Life*, bequeathed by Mrs Dora M. Bond, 1985
Dunlop, Ronald Ossory 1894–1973, *Teddington, Middlesex*, bequeathed by Mrs Dora M. Bond, 1985
Dunlop, Ronald Ossory 1894–1973, *Walberswick, Suffolk*, bequeathed by Mrs Dora M. Bond, 1985
Elwell, Frederick William 1870–1958, *Bric-à-brac*, gift from the artist, 1946
Enderby, Samuel George 1860–1921, *Portrait Study*, gift from Mrs Brame, the artist's daughter, 1935
Fairweather, Ian 1891–1974, *Outside Hangchow, China*, bequeathed by Mrs Dora M. Bond, 1985, © estate of Ian Fairweather. All rights reserved, DACS 2012
Falens, Carel van 1683–1733, *Soldier on Horseback*, bequeathed by Sir James William Francis Hill, 1980
Ferneley, John E. 1782–1860, *The Burton Hunt*, gift from the Heslam Trust and the Sandars Charitable Trust, 1974
Ferneley, John E. 1782–1860, *Lincoln High Street, Two Years after the Coming of the Railways*, purchased from the Kingston-upon-Hull Corporation, 1954
Ferrari, Gaudenzio c.1470–1546, *Saint Catherine of Alexandria*, gift from the Wickham Family, 1936
Ferrari, Gaudenzio c.1470–1546, *Saint Mary Magdalene*, gift from the Wickham Family, 1936
Fisk, Roy 1916–2008, *Roman Bailgate, Lincoln*, gift from Mr Arthur Melton, 1979, © the artist's estate
Flanagan, Terence Philip 1929–2011, *Sand Dunes*, gift from the Contemporary Art Society, 1972, © the artist's estate
Fleming, Ian 1906–1994, *Danger Point, Arbroath, Scotland*, gift from Peter Brannan, 1988, © the artist's estate
Fowler, Robert 1853–1926, *The Widow's Mite*, gift from Robert Fowler, the artist's son, 1931
Frost, Terry 1915–2003, *Autumn Rings Andeuze, September 1971*, gift from the Contemporary Art Society, 1986, © estate of Terry Frost. All rights reserved, DACS 2012
Garland, Austin 1887–1966, *Portrait of an Unknown Man*, purchased, 1947
Garland, Valentine Thomas 1840–1914, *An Anxious Mother*, bequeathed by James Ward Usher, 1921
Gernez, Paul-Elie 1888–1948, *Dahlias et marguerites*, bequeathed by Mrs Dora M. Bond, 1985, © ADAGP, Paris and DACS, London 2012
Girardot, Ernest Gustave 1840–1904, *Alfred Tennyson (1809–1892)*, gift from the Tennyson family, 1961
Grant, Duncan 1885–1978, *The Wool Staple in Medieval Lincoln*, purchased, 2000, © estate of Duncan Grant. All rights reserved, DACS 2012
Grant, Duncan 1885–1978, *Woman in a Shawl*, gift from the Heslam Trust, 1990, © estate of Duncan Grant. All rights reserved, DACS 2012
Grant, Duncan 1885–1978, *Sheep Shearer* (study for 'The Russell Chantry, Lincoln Cathedral'), purchased from Richard Stone, 2002, © estate of Duncan Grant. All rights reserved, DACS 2012
Green, Margaret 1925–2003, *Festival Gardens*, bequeathed by Mrs Dora M. Bond, 1985, © the studio estate of Lionel Bulmer and Margaret Green is represented by David Messum Fine Art Ltd
Gribble, Kenneth 1925–1995, *Steep Hill, Lincoln*, purchased, 1964
Gribble, Kenneth 1925–1995, *The Spinney*, purchased, 1964
Grigoriev, Alexei b.1949, *Bound by Love*, purchased from the artist, 1997
Grimble, John d.1997, *Boston Skyline, Lincolnshire*, purchased from the artist, 1970
Hall, Frederick 1860–1948, *The Judgement Porch, Lincoln Cathedral*, unknown acquisition method, © the artist's estate/ Bridgeman Art Library
Hall, Henry active late 19th C, *Distant View of Lincoln Cathedral from the South*, bequeathed by Sir James William Francis Hill, 1980
Hammad, Medina b.1963, *Father's Robe, Fountain Lamp and Satin Cushion*, unknown acquisition method
Hammad, Medina b.1963, *Fred and Trevor*, commissioned, 1995
Hammad, Medina b.1963, *Midsummer Ball*, commissioned, 1995
Hammad, Medina b.1963, *From Sea to Sky*, commissioned, 1995
Hardy, Frederick Daniel 1827–1911, *An Interesting Story*, bequeathed by James Ward Usher, 1921
Hartnell, Kathleen 1886–c.1965, *Still Life*, bequeathed by Mrs Dora M. Bond, 1985
Hassall, John 1868–1948, *Short Seaplane*, unknown acquisition method, © the artist's estate
Hassall, John 1868–1948, *A Tank in Action*, gift from Allen Gwynes Pumps Ltd, 1968, © the artist's estate
Haughton, Benjamin 1865–1924, *Winter Morning on the Otter*, gift from Mrs J. Haughton, 1937
Havell, Edmund the younger 1819–1894, *Henry A. M. Waldo Sibthorp*, gift from the Honourable Mrs Dudley Pelham, 1961
Havell, Edmund the younger 1819–1894, *Maria, Widow of Charles Delaet Waldo Sibthorp*, gift from the Honourable Mrs Dudley Pelham, 1961
Held, Julie b.1958, *The Swimmer (Cosham Painting)*, purchased from the artist, 1996, © the artist
Herkomer, Hubert von 1849–1914, *Captain Philip Blundell Bicknell (1818–1905)*, purchased from Mrs H. Bicknell, 1985
Herring, John Frederick I 1795–1865, *Midday Rest*, gift from J. Cyril Collingham, 1938
Hilton, Joseph or **Hilton, William II** 1786–1839 or **De Wint, Peter** 1784–1849, *John Keats (1795–1821)* (copy of Joseph Severn), gift from Miss E. Scrivenor, 1951
Hilton, William I 1752–1822, *Self Portrait*, gift from Miss G. Muriel Bostock, 1941
Hilton, William I 1752–1822, *Still Life with Parrot*, gift from Miss H. H. Tatlock to the City and County Museum, Lincoln, 1921; transferred to the Usher Gallery
Hilton, William II 1786–1839, *Harriet Hilton (1791–1866) and Child (Helen Hilton, 1811–1873)* (sketch), gift from the Usher Gallery Trust, 1994
Hilton, William II 1786–1839, *Harriet Hilton (1791–1866) and Child (Helen Hilton, 1811–1873)*, purchased at Christie's, 1941
Hilton, William II 1786–1839, *The Miracle of Saint Mark* (after Jacopo Tintoretto), gift from Miss H. H. Tatlock to the City and County Museum, Lincoln, 1921; transferred to the Usher Gallery
Hilton, William II 1786–1839, *Cupid Armed*, purchased from W. H. Acford, 1952
Hilton, William II 1786–1839, *Harriet Hilton (1791–1866)*, purchased from Geoffery Harmsworth
Hilton, William II 1786–1839, *Justina Hilton, née Kent*, gift from Sir O. B. Giles, 1963
Hilton, William II 1786–1839, *Justina Hilton, née Kent*, gift from Sir O. B. Giles, 1963
Hilton, William II 1786–1839, *Portrait of an Unknown Man*, gift from Sir O. B. Giles, 1963
Hilton, William II 1786–1839, *Portrait of the Artist's Father*, gift from Miss E. Scrivenor, 1947
Hilton, William II 1786–1839, *Portrait of the Artist's Mother*, gift from Miss E. Scrivenor, 1947
Hilton, William II 1786–1839, *Reverend la Tour*, bequeathed by Mrs Mason
Hilton, William II 1786–1839, *Saint Peter, Martyr* (after Titian), gift from Miss Tatlock, 1918
Hilton, William II 1786–1839, *Self Portrait*, gift from Miss H. H. Tatlock to City and County Museum, Lincoln, 1921; transferred to Usher Gallery
Hilton, William II 1786–1839, *Self Portrait*, gift from Sir O. B. Giles, 1963
Hilton, William II 1786–1839, *Study of a Classical Subject*, purchased from A. S. Maltby, 1939
Hilton, William II 1786–1839, *The Birth of Triton*, gift from Geoffrey Harmsworth, 1937
Hilton, William II 1786–1839, *The Crucifixion*, gift from Miss Tatlock, 1918
Hilton, William II 1786–1839, *The Elopement*, purchased from G. Birrell, 1954
Hilton, William II 1786–1839, *The Holy Family* (after Jacopo Palma il vecchio), gift from Miss Tatlock, 1918
Hilton, William II 1786–1839, *Una and the Satyrs*, gift from the Lincoln School of Art Governors, 1930
Hitchens, Ivon 1893–1979, *Autumn Painting*, bequeathed by Mrs Dora M. Bond, 1985, © Ivon Hitchens' estate/Jonathan Clark & Co.
Hitchens, Ivon 1893–1979, *Boat on a Lake No.2*, bequeathed by Mrs Dora M. Bond, 1985, © Ivon Hitchens' estate/Jonathan Clark & Co.
Hitchens, Ivon 1893–1979, *Poppies in a Green Bowl*, bequeathed by Mrs Dora M. Bond, 1985, © Ivon Hitchens' estate/Jonathan Clark & Co.
Hitchens, Ivon 1893–1979, *Study for a Painting*, bequeathed by Mrs Dora M. Bond, 1985, © Ivon Hitchens' estate/Jonathan Clark & Co.
Hodge, Francis Edwin 1883–1949, *Preparation for the Ballet*, gift from Mrs H. B. Fish, 1950
Hoevenaar, Cornelis William 1802–1873, *Interior Scene with Two Ladies*, gift from Miss Frankish, 1943
Holder, Edward Henry 1847–1922, *Victoria Falls on the Zambezi, Zimbabwe*, gift from Mr R. C. Hayward, 1974
Holl, Frank 1845–1888, *Joseph Ruston (1835–1897)*, gift from Ruston Gas Turbines Ltd, Lincoln, 1990
Holzer, Henry 1907–2007, *Summer Evening after Rain*, purchased from the artist, 1971
Houston, Ian b.1934, *Lincoln Cathedral from the Water Meadows*, bequeathed by Sir James William Francis Hill, 1980, © the artist
Hubbard, Bennett 1806–1870, *The Habertoft Heifer*, gift from the Lincolnshire County Branch of the National Farmers' Union, 1994
Hughes, Arthur 1832–1915, *Rest*, transferred from the City and County Museum, Lincoln, 1935
Hulbert, Thelma 1913–1995, *Leaves and Gauze Screen*, gift from the Contemporary Art Society, 1968
Hutton, R. W. *A Lincoln Red Prize Shorthorn Bullock, Aged 4 Years and 10 Months*, purchased at Sotheby's, 1988
Hyman, Timothy b.1946, *The Dean and Chapter Meeting in the Martha and Mary Room*, purchased from the artist, 1984, © the artist
Ilett, R. A. *Morning Tide*, gift from Sir Hickman B. Bacon, Bt, JP, 1938
Jackson, F. A. active c.1900, *Lincoln High Street*, bequeathed by H. Jackson, 1959

Jackson, F. A. active c.1900, *Lincoln High Street*, bequeathed by H. Jackson, 1960
Jamieson, Robert Kirkland 1881–1950, *Essex Farm*, purchased from the artist, 1948
Jelley, James Valentine 1856–1950, *The Doctor's Car*, gift from the artist, 1939
Jervas, Charles c.1675–1739, *Queen Caroline (1768–1821)*, transferred from the Guildhall, Lincoln, 1952
Jones, Lucy b.1955, *Self Portrait*, purchased from the Angela Flowers Gallery, 1996, © the artist/courtesy Flowers Gallery, London
Kelly, J. E. T. *Kingston Manor, Angmering-on-Sea, Sussex*, gift from Mrs E. F. Gordon, 1977
Kennedy, Alex G. *Major John Hermaine Smith, City Sheriff*, unknown acquisition method
Kerr, Antony b.1924, *Ferry at Tilbury, Essex*, purchased from the artist, 1963, © the artist
Kidder, Norah b.1888, *Humber Foreshore*, gift from Sir Hickman B. Bacon, Bt, JP, 1939
Kneller, Godfrey 1646–1723, *Mary II (1662–1694)*, transferred from the Guildhall, Lincoln, 1952
Kneller, Godfrey 1646–1723, *Queen Anne (1665–1714)*, transferred from the Guildhall, Lincoln
Kneller, Godfrey (after) 1646–1723, *William III (1650–1702)*, transferred from the Guildhall, Lincoln, 1952
Koekkoek, Johannes Herman Barend 1840–1912, *Snow Scene*, anonymous gift, 1975
Laing, Patricia b.1928, *Cornish Fishing Boat*, purchased from Mrs Tennyson d'Eyncourt, 1960
Lamb, Lynton Harold 1907–1977, *Nude*, gift from the Contemporary Art Society, 1954, © the artist's estate
Lander, John Saint-Hélier 1869–1944, *Captain T. D. Trollope-Bellew*, bequeathed by Mrs D. N. Trollope-Bellew, 1976
Lane, Samuel 1780–1859, *John Willis*, gift from Miss Ella Rosa Curtois, 1935
Lawrence, Thomas 1769–1830, *George Tennyson (1749/1750–1835), Grandfather of Alfred Tennyson*, gift from the Tennyson family, 1961
Lehmann, Rudolph 1819–1905, *Maria Albina*, gift from the Honourable Mrs Dudley Pelham, 1964
Lehmann, Rudolph 1819–1905, *Montagu Richard Waldo Sibthorp*, gift from the Honourable Mrs Dudley Pelham, 1964
Lessore, Thérèse 1884–1945, *Hop-Pickers*, gift from the Sickert Trust, 1947, © Henry & John Lessore
Lewis, Simon b.1965, *'Step inside luv'*, gift from the Contemporary Art Society, 1996
Lewis, Simon b.1965, *Where's Walter?*, gift from the Contemporary Art Society, 1996
Logsdail, Marian b.1862, *Minster Yard, Lincoln*, bequeathed by Charles Gunnel, 1930
Logsdail, William 1859–1944, *Lincoln Cathedral*, bequeathed by Thomas Henry Denman, 1950, © the artist's estate/Bridgeman Art Library
Logsdail, William 1859–1944, *James Marr Snow (1808–1885), MRCS, LSA*, gift from Mr E. Mason, 1977, © the artist's estate/Bridgeman Art Library
Logsdail, William 1859–1944, *Alms Houses, Antwerp, Belgium*, bequeathed by H. Newsum, 1956, © the artist's estate/Bridgeman Art Library
Logsdail, William 1859–1944, *Church Interior*, gift from R. D. Tweed, 1942, © the artist's estate/Bridgeman Art Library
Logsdail, William 1859–1944, *Mestre, near Venice*, gift from E. E. Tweed, 1934, © the artist's estate/Bridgeman Art Library
Logsdail, William 1859–1944, *Venice*, gift from E. E. Tweed, 1934, © the artist's estate/Bridgeman Art Library
Logsdail, William 1859–1944, *A Corner of Old Venice*, gift from Trotter Alexander to Lincoln public library, 1923; transferred to the Usher Gallery, © the artist's estate/Bridgeman Art Library
Logsdail, William 1859–1944, *By the Lion of St Mark, Venice*, gift from C. T. Parker Alderman, 1926, © the artist's estate/Bridgeman Art Library
Logsdail, William 1859–1944, *Church of Santa Maria della Salute, Venice*, gift from E. E. Tweed, 1934, © the artist's estate/Bridgeman Art Library
Logsdail, William 1859–1944, *Alfred Shuttleworth (1843–1925), JP for Lincoln*, gift from Mrs Sophia Harris, 1936, © the artist's estate/Bridgeman Art Library
Logsdail, William 1859–1944, *Lincoln Cathedral, Exchequer Gate and Castle Square*, gift from C. T. Parker Alderman, 1926, © the artist's estate/Bridgeman Art Library
Logsdail, William 1859–1944, *An Early Victorian*, gift from Mrs Logsdail, 1950, © the artist's estate/Bridgeman Art Library
Logsdail, William 1859–1944, *Katherine A. Ourovssoff*, gift from the sitter, 1965, © the artist's estate/Bridgeman Art Library
Logsdail, William 1859–1944, *Patricia Theophila Anley (1908–1923)*, bequeathed by Mrs Anley, 1968, © the artist's estate/Bridgeman Art Library
Logsdail, William 1859–1944, *John D. Binns*, bequeathed by Dr Muriel Emily Binns, 1972, © the artist's estate/Bridgeman Art Library
Logsdail, William 1859–1944, *Guy Bedford*, gift from Mrs M. H. Bedford, 1978, © the artist's estate/Bridgeman Art Library
Logsdail, William 1859–1944, *Flowers in a Persian Bottle*, gift from Goldwynne R. Jones, 2002, © the artist's estate/Bridgeman Art Library
Logsdail, William 1859–1944, *Goldwynne*, gift from Goldwynne R. Jones, 2002, © the artist's estate/Bridgeman Art Library
Logsdail, William 1859–1944, *Daffodils*, gift from Goldwynne R. Jones, 2002, © the artist's estate/Bridgeman Art Library
Logsdail, William 1859–1944, *Garden Flowers*, gift from Goldwynne R. Jones, 2002, © the artist's estate/Bridgeman Art Library
Logsdail, William 1859–1944, *The Four Seasons*, gift from Goldwynne R. Jones, 2002, © the artist's estate/Bridgeman Art Library
Logsdail, William 1859–1944, *A Quiet Lane*, bequeathed by Miss F. Paulger, 1968, © the artist's estate/Bridgeman Art Library
Logsdail, William 1859–1944, *Byzantine Church at Torcello*, gift from Captain H. F. C. Crookshank, 1937, © the artist's estate/Bridgeman Art Library
Logsdail, William 1859–1944, *George Logsdail (1827–1905)*, purchased at Mallams, 1983, © the artist's estate/Bridgeman Art Library
Logsdail, William 1859–1944, *Self Portrait*, purchased at Mallams, 1983, © the artist's estate/Bridgeman Art Library
Logsdail, William 1859–1944, *Venice*, bequeathed by John D. Ruddock, 1954, © the artist's estate/Bridgeman Art Library
Lowry, Laurence Stephen 1887–1976, *View of a Town*, purchased from the artist, 1942, © courtesy of the estate of L. S. Lowry
Lowry, Laurence Stephen 1887–1976, *Britain at Play*, gift from the Contemporary Art Society, 1943, © courtesy of the estate of L. S. Lowry
Lowry, Laurence Stephen 1887–1976, *Lincoln*, on loan from the Usher Gallery Trust, since 1996, © courtesy of the estate of L. S. Lowry
Mabbutt, Mary b.1951, *Blue Kitchen*, purchased from the artist, 1996, © the artist
Manton, George Henry Grenville 1855–1932, *In the Year of Our Lord*, gift from Mrs Manton, 1934
Manton, George Henry Grenville 1855–1932, *Colonel Edward Snow-Mason*, bequeathed by Mrs Mason
Manton, George Henry Grenville 1855–1932, *Miss Dorothy Brook*, gift from W. H. B. Brook's Family, 1935
Manton, George Henry Grenville 1855–1932, *Dr E. Mansell Sympson*, unknown acquisition method
Marshall, Benjamin 1767–1835, *Daniel Lambert (1770–1809)*, purchased at Sotheby's, 1979
McCall, Charles James 1907–1989, *Maquillage*, gift from the Contemporary Art Society, 1952, © the artist's estate/Bridgeman Art Library
Miereveld, Michiel Jansz. van 1567–1641, *Maria van Wassenaer Hanecops (c.1542–after 1612)*, gift from Mrs V. Stapylton-Smith through the Art Fund, 2006
Milano, Francesco Figini active 1502–1548, *Madonna and Child Enthroned*, gift from the Lincoln School of Art Governors, 1932
Montford, Rosemary b.1951, *Daffodils on a Green Cloth*, purchased from the artist, 1988
Morton, Charles Reginald active 1917–1936, *Ely Cathedral, Cambridgeshire*, gift from Mrs H. M. Morton, 1938
Muirhead, David 1867–1930, *Lincoln, 1913*, purchased from the Dean of York, 1952
Munnings, Alfred James 1878–1959, *Colonel Lord Barnby on 'Crusader' with the Blankney Hounds*, purchased from the Lady Barnby Foundation, 1991, © Sir Alfred Munnings Art Museum
Nessler, Walter 1912–2001, *Sèvres, France*, gift from the Contemporary Art Society, 1956
Niemann, Edmund John 1813–1876, *Distant View of Lincoln*, bequeathed by Sir James William Francis Hill, 1980
Niemann, Edmund John 1813–1876, *Lincoln from Brayford*, gift from the Heslam Trust, 1965
Niemann, Edmund John 1813–1876, *Lincoln from the Holmes*, gift from James William Francis Hill Alderman, 1953
Niemann, Edmund John 1813–1876, *The Glory Hole, Lincoln*, purchased from Roland, Browse and Delbanco, 1948
Noble, Robert 1857–1917, *On the Dean, East Linton, Scotland*, purchased with the assistance of the National Art Collections Fund, 1927
Norwich, Anne b.1929, *Reading*, gift from the Contemporary Art Society, 1980, © the artist
Nyberg, Henning 1903–1964, *Plaice*, gift from the Contemporary Art Society, 1952
Olsson, Albert Julius 1864–1942, *Seascape Evening*, gift from Edwin Hitchon, 1946
Onofri, Crescenzio (attributed to) c.1632–c.1712, *Classical Landscape*, gift from J. Hermanie Smith, 1950
Onofri, Crescenzio (attributed to) c.1632–c.1712, *Classical Landscape*, gift from J. Hermanie Smith, 1950
Park, J. R. S. active 20th C, *Breezy Sea*, gift from Sir Hickman B. Bacon, Bt, JP, 1936
Park, J. R. S. active 20th C, *Seascape*, gift from Sir Hickman B. Bacon, Bt, JP, 1938
Parker, Alan b.1965, *Study for Cathedral Painting I*, gift from the Usher Gallery Trust, 2008
Parker, Alan b.1965, *Study for Cathedral Painting II*
Parker, Alan b.1965, *Study for Cathedral Painting III*
Parker, Alan b.1965, *Study for Cathedral Painting IV*
Parker, Alan b.1965, *Study for Cathedral Painting V*
Parker, Alan b.1965, *Study for Cathedral Painting VI, Stuart Bonfield, Supervisor*
Parker, Alan b.1965, *Study for Cathedral Painting VII*
Parker, Alan b.1965, *Study for Cathedral Painting VIII, Paul Ellis, Master Carver*
Parker, Alan b.1965, *Study for Cathedral Painting IX*
Pearce, Stephen 1819–1904, *Lord Kesteven on a Horse, with Hounds*, bequeathed by Mrs D. N. Trollope-Bellew, 1976
Pears, Charles 1873–1958, *Moonlight Barque*, purchased from the artist, 1937, © the artist's estate
Philips, Charles 1708–1747, *Thomas Becke (1690–1757)*, transferred from the Guildhall, Lincoln, 1952
Pickering, Roy b.1954, *Landscape, Derbyshire I*, purchased from the artist, 1984, © the artist
Piper, John 1903–1992, *Octagonal Church, Hartwell, Buckinghamshire*, gift from the Contemporary Art Society, 1946, © the artist's estate
Piper, John 1903–1992, *Saint-Riquier, Somme, France*, gift from the Heslam Trust, 1972, © the artist's estate
Poingdestre, Charles 1825–1905, *Italian Harvest Scene*, gift from Edwin Hitchon, 1946
Potter, Mary 1900–1981, *Sea Defences*, bequeathed by Mrs Dora M. Bond, 1985, © estate of Mary Potter. All rights reserved, DACS 2012
Potter, Mary 1900–1981, *Spring Landscape*, bequeathed by Mrs Dora M. Bond, 1985, © estate of Mary Potter. All rights reserved, DACS 2012
Potter, Mary 1900–1981, *Still Life*, bequeathed by Mrs Dora M. Bond, 1985, © estate of Mary Potter. All rights reserved, DACS 2012
Poulsen, Georg 1911–1997, *Seine*, purchased, 1964
Poulsen, Georg 1911–1997, *Shorescape*, purchased, 1964
Price, Alan 1926–2002, *The Bird Market*, purchased, 1953
Ranken, William Bruce Ellis 1881–1941, *Portrait of a Lady in Green*, gift from Mrs Ernest Thesiger, 1946
Rapp, Ginette 1928–1998, *Canal in Volendam, The Netherlands*, bequeathed by Mrs Dora M. Bond, 1985
Rayner, W. J. active early 20th C, *The White Bull*, gift from Mrs Rayner, 1951

Redmore, Edward King c.1860–1941, *Seascape*, bequeathed by A. Fotherby, 1945
Redmore, Edward King c.1860–1941, *Seascape*, bequeathed by A. Fotherby, 1945
Redpath, Anne 1895–1965, *Sweethearts*, bequeathed by Mrs Dora M. Bond, 1985, © the artist's estate/Bridgeman Art Library
Reynolds, Joshua 1723–1792, *Isabella Thorold of Syston (d.1803)*, purchased at Sotheby's with the assistance of the Art Fund, the Friends of Lincoln Museums and Art Gallery, the Usher Gallery Trust and the Heslam Trust, 2008
Reynolds, Joshua 1723–1792, *Thomas Middleton Trollope of Casewick (1721–1779)*, purchased at Sotheby's with the assistance of the Art Fund, the Friends of Lincoln Museums and Art Gallery, the Usher Gallery Trust and the Heslam Trust, 2008
Rhys-James, Shani b.1953, *Lead White*, purchased from the artist, 1996, © the artist
Richard, Frederick active c.1800–1850s, *Mrs Richard Mason*, bequeathed by Mrs Mason
Robinson, William H. *'The Flea'*, bequeathed by Snow-Mason family
Rollett, Herbert 1872–1932, *Summer Fallows*, gift from Mrs A. Mackay, 1984
Rollett, Herbert 1872–1932, *Blue Sky*, gift from Mrs M. A. Mackay, 1996
Rollett, Herbert 1872–1932, *June Morning*, gift from the Lincolnshire Artists' Society, 1932
Rollett, Herbert 1872–1932, *Landscape* (recto), gift from Mrs A. Mackay, 1984
Rollett, Herbert 1872–1932, *Landscape* (verso), gift from Mrs A. Mackay, 1984
Rollett, Herbert 1872–1932, *Landscape* (recto), gift from Mrs A. Mackay, 1984
Rollett, Herbert 1872–1932, *Landscape* (verso), gift from Mrs A. Mackay, 1984
Rollett, Herbert 1872–1932, *Louth, Lincolnshire*, gift from Mrs A. Mackay, 1984
Rollett, Herbert 1872–1932, *Louth, Lincolnshire*, gift from Mrs M. A. Mackay, 1996
Rollett, Herbert 1872–1932, *Sheep*, gift from Mrs M. A. Mackay, 1996
Roussel, Théodore Casimir 1847–1926, *Approaching Storm, Dover, Kent*, gift from Miss Herriot, 1947
Rowntree, Kenneth 1915–1997, *View of Lincoln Cathedral*, unknown acquisition method, © the artist's estate
Russell, J. active late 19th C, *Elizabeth Russell, née Tennyson*, gift from the Tennyson family, 1961
Russell, John Bucknell 1819–1893, *Salmon*, gift from Mrs Purvis, 1939
Salmon, James Marchbank 1916–1994, *Boats and Nets, South Coast*, purchased from Mrs R. Tennyson d'Eyncourt, 1960
Salmon, James Marchbank 1916–1994, *The White Yacht*, purchased from the artist, 1951
Schoor, Lodewijk van 1666–1726 or **Schoor, Nicholas van** active c.1690, *Landscape with a Tree*, gift from Edwin Hitchon, 1946
Shackleton, William 1872–1933, *Winter Sunrise, Malham, Yorkshire*, transferred from Lincoln Public Library, 1959
Shannon, Charles Haslewood 1863–1937, *Salt Water*, purchased from Preston Kerrison, 1953
Shannon, Charles Haslewood 1863–1937, *The Infant Bacchus*, purchased from Preston Kerrison, 1953
Shannon, Charles Haslewood 1863–1937, *Miriam*, purchased from Simon Reynolds, 1990
Shannon, Charles Haslewood 1863–1937, *The Toilet*, purchased from the artist, 1937
Shannon, Charles Haslewood 1863–1937, *The Capture*, purchased from the artist, 1937
Shannon, Charles Haslewood 1863–1937, *Study*, unknown acquisition method
Shannon, Charles Haslewood 1863–1937, *The Sower and the Reaper*, gift from Miss C. E. Shannon, 1950
Shannon, Charles Haslewood 1863–1937, *The Wood Nymph*, purchased at Sotheby's, 1977
Shayer, William 1788–1879, *Landscape with a Ruined Castle*, gift from Edwin Hitchon, 1946
Sherlock, William P. 1780–1825, *Landscape with a Castle and a River*, gift from Edwin Hitchon, 1946
Sickert, Walter Richard 1860–1942, *Nude Figure Reclining*, gift from the Contemporary Art Society, 1936, © estate of Walter R. Sickert. All rights reserved, DACS 2012
Smith, David T. b.1920, *Bombing Up*, gift from the Imperial War Museum, 1947
Smith, Edward Blount (attributed to) active 1877–1898, *Nettleton Church, Lincolnshire*, gift from Sir Hickman B. Bacon, Bt, JP, 1938
Smith, John Raphael 1752–1812, *Self Portrait*, purchased from Martin Gregory, 1978
Solomon, Solomon Joseph 1860–1927, *An Allegory of the Dead Christ* (study), gift from Sir Hickman B. Bacon, Bt, JP, 1930
Spear, Ruskin 1911–1990, *Interior with Nude*, gift from the Contemporary Art Society, 1949, © the artist's estate/Bridgeman Art Library
Spender, John Humphrey 1910–2005, *Still Life in White*, bequeathed by Mrs Dora M. Bond, 1985, © the Humphrey Spender Archive
Stanfield, Clarkson 1793–1867, *River Scene with Shipping*, gift from Edwin Hitchon, 1946
Steggles, Walter James 1908–1997, *Boston, Lincolnshire*, gift from the Contemporary Art Society, 1933
Storey, Thomas George 1865–1935, *Blossom*, purchased from J. P. D. Wheeldon, 1966
Storey, Thomas George 1865–1935, *Lincoln from the South*, purchased from J. P. D. Wheeldon, 1966
Storey, Thomas George 1865–1935, *Lincoln from the South West*, purchased from J. P. D. Wheeldon, 1966
Storey, Thomas George 1865–1935, *The Sanctuary*, purchased from the Lincoln Cathedral Fabric Fund, 1978
Stubbs, George 1724–1806, *A Clumber Spaniel*, gift from HM Government, 1996
Sully, Thomas 1783–1872, *Old Stables of the 'Dolpinn' Inn, Lincoln*, gift from James William Francis Hill Alderman, 1934
Taylor, Edward Richard 1838–1912, *Lincoln Cathedral from the Witham*, gift from Mrs G. Rawlinson and Mr A. F. Smith, 1965
Taylor, George active 1911–1931, *Double Asters*, bequeathed by Mrs Flora Shuttleworth Taylor, 1971
Taylor, George active 1911–1931, *Wallflowers*, bequeathed by Mrs Flora Shuttleworth Taylor, 1971
Taylor, George active 1911–1931, *Wallflowers*, bequeathed by Mrs Flora Shuttleworth Taylor, 1971
Taylor, George active 1911–1931, *Wedgwood and Wallflowers*, bequeathed by Mrs Flora Shuttleworth Taylor, 1971
Thorburn, Archibald 1860–1935, *Grouse*
Townshend, Arthur Louis b.1848, *Horses Returning from Exercise, Newmarket Heath, Suffolk*, gift from Mrs Elizabeth Hill
Toynbee, Edith *The Ruins of the Bishop's Palace, Lincoln*, bequeathed by Helen Clements, 1934
Tuke, Samuel 1797–1857, *Mr Kendal*, gift from Mrs G. R. Parker
Tuke, Samuel 1797–1857, *Miss Emma Tuke*, gift from Mrs Jessie Kirkby
Tyson, Kathleen 1898–c.1982, *Westwell, Kent (?)*, gift from Mrs D. Jacklin, 1966
Underwood, Leon 1890–1975, *Still Life*, gift from the Contemporary Art Society, 1933, © the estate of Leon Underwood, courtesy of the Redfern Gallery
unknown artist *Sir Peter Eure (1549–1612)*, gift from Viscount P. C. Rothermere, 1927
unknown artist *Sir Philibert Vernatti (c.1590–1646)*, gift from Jonkheer Frederick G. L. O. Van Kretschmar, 1979
unknown artist 17th C, *Turkish Battle Piece*, gift from Alan Wark, 1946
unknown artist *Reverend John Cunnington*, purchased from P. Mallalieu, 1962
unknown artist *William Mawer*, gift from Miss Margaret Emily Habgood, 1984
unknown artist 18th C, *Colonel Coningsby Sibthorp (1706–1779), LLD*, donated by the Sibthorp family
unknown artist 18th C, *Mr Gibbon Hawker (1703–1778)*, bequeathed by W. Sibthorp
unknown artist *Charles Hayward, Town Clerk*, transferred from the Guildhall, Lincoln, 1952
unknown artist *Louisa Amcotts Cracroft (1590–1643), Wife of Gervais Tottenham Waldo Sibthorp*, gift from the Honourable Mrs Dudley Pelham, 1961
unknown artist *Gervaise Tottenham Waldo Sibthorp (1815–1861)*, gift from the Honourable Mrs Dudley Pelham, 1964
unknown artist *Mary Georgiana, Wife of Coningsby Charles Sibthorp*, unknown acquisition method
unknown artist *Coningsby Charles Sibthorp*
unknown artist *Madame Frieda Rholl*, bequeathed by Peter Brannan, 1995
unknown artist early 19th C, *Interior Scene with a Man Smoking a Pipe*, bequeathed by Mrs Kathleen Zealand, 1980
unknown artist mid-19th C, *Gervaise Tottenham Waldo Sibthorp (1815–1861)*, bequeathed by the Sibthorp family
unknown artist 19th C, *Portrait of an Unknown Man*, unknown acquisition method
unknown artist 19th C, *Tree Study*, gift from Edwin Hitchon, 1946
unknown artist mid-20th C, *Farm Buildings and a Wagon*, unknown acquisition method
unknown artist *Alfred Shuttleworth (1843–1925), JP for Lincoln*, unknown acquisition method
unknown artist *Anne de Ronay (d.1757), Wife of Gervaise Tottenham Waldo Sibthorp*, gift from the Honourable Mrs Dudley Pelham, 1972
unknown artist *Archbishop Thomas Tenison (1636–1715), Archbishop of Canterbury*, gift from the Tennyson family, 1961
unknown artist *Charles C. Waldo Sibthorp (1817–1896)*
unknown artist *Charles Delaet, Esq. of Potterells (d.1792)*
unknown artist *Charles Tennyson Turner (1808–1879)*, gift from the Tennyson family, 1961
unknown artist *Classical Scene*, gift from Edwin Hitchon, 1946
unknown artist *Dr William Dodd (1729–1777)*, gift from Kings Lynn Museum Committee, 1958
unknown artist *Eleanor and Lionel, Grandchildren of Alfred Tennyson*, gift from the Tennyson family, 1961
unknown artist *Elizabeth Tennyson, née Fytche (1781–1865), Mother of Alfred Tennyson*, gift from the Tennyson family, 1961
unknown artist *Emma Maria Russell (d.1870), Viscountess Boyne*, gift from the Tennyson family, 1961
unknown artist *Frederick Louis (1707–1751), Prince of Wales*, transferred from the Guildhall, Lincoln, 1952
unknown artist *George II (1683–1760)*, transferred from the Guildhall, Lincoln, 1952
unknown artist *George II (1683–1760)*, transferred from the Guildhall, Lincoln, 1952
unknown artist *Caroline (1768–1821), Wife of George II*, transferred from the Guildhall, Lincoln, 1952
unknown artist *Jane Usher*, bequeathed by James Ward Usher, 1921
unknown artist *John Thomas Tweed (1823–1910), Town Clerk of Lincoln (1855–1905)*, gift from R. D. Tweed, 1942
unknown artist *Landscape in Wales*, gift from Edwin Hitchon, 1946
unknown artist *Landscape with a Building, Cows and Sheep*, gift from Miss Frankish, 1943
unknown artist *Mary Elizabeth, Daughter of Humphrey Sibthorp*, unknown acquisition method
unknown artist *Mary Tennyson, née Turner (d.1825), Grandmother of Alfred Tennyson*, gift from the Tennyson family, 1961
unknown artist *Nathaniel Clayton (1811–1890)*, gift from Alfred Shuttleworth, 1916
unknown artist *Portrait of a Man*
unknown artist *Portrait of a Man*
unknown artist *Portrait of an Unknown Boy*, bequeathed by the Sibthorp family
unknown artist *Portrait of an Unknown Man*, unknown acquisition method
unknown artist *Portrait of an Unknown Man with a Book*, bequeathed by the Sibthorp family
unknown artist *Portrait of an Unknown Woman*, unknown acquisition method
unknown artist *Robert Bertie (1582–1642), Earl of Lindsey*, purchased from W. J. Hill, 1950
unknown artist *Sir Richard Worsley (1751–1805)*, unknown acquisition method
unknown artist *William Rudgard, Mayor of Lincoln (1839)*, transferred from the Guildhall, Lincoln, 1952
unknown artist *Woman at a Spinning Wheel*, gift from Joan Webster, 1957
Verboeckhoven, Charles Louis 1802–1889, *Seascape*, gift from Miss Frankish, 1943
Verboeckhoven, Eugène Joseph 1799–1881, *A Horse Feeding in a*

Stable, gift from Miss Frankish, 1943
Verdonck, Cornelis active c.1715, *Mountainous Landscape with a River and a Castle*, gift from Mrs G. Roberts, 1952
Verhoesen, Albertus 1806–1881, *Farmyard Scene*, gift from Miss Frankish, 1943
Violante, Italo b.1916, *I Sassi, Matera, Italy*, gift from the artist, 1979
Voordecker, Henri 1779–1861, *Cocks Fighting*, gift from Frederick Higgs, 1934
Walker, Barbara b.1964, *Self Portrait*, acquired as part of artist's residency at the Usher Gallery, 2000, © the artist
Warrener, William Tom 1861–1934, *Portrait of an Unknown Man*, gift from Mr S. Scorer
Warrener, William Tom 1861–1934, *Oephea*, purchased from Miss Hilary Healey, 1981
Warrener, William Tom 1861–1934, *Landscape with Trees*, purchased from Mrs Edna Hoult, 1993
Warrener, William Tom 1861–1934, *Landscape with Trees*, purchased from Mrs Edna Hoult, 1993
Warrener, William Tom 1861–1934, *Leonline*, purchased from Mrs Edna Hoult, 1993
Warrener, William Tom 1861–1934, *Quadrille I*, purchased from Mrs Edna Hoult, 1993
Warrener, William Tom 1861–1934, *Quadrille II*, purchased from Mrs Edna Hoult, 1993
Warrener, William Tom 1861–1934, *Reflections*, purchased from Mrs Edna Hoult, 1993
Warrener, William Tom 1861–1934, *Undergrowth*, purchased from Mrs Edna Hoult, 1993
Warrener, William Tom 1861–1934, *Vineyard*, purchased from Mrs Edna Hoult, 1993
Warrener, William Tom 1861–1934, *December Day at Grez-sur-Loing, France*, purchased from Mrs Edna Hoult, 1993
Warrener, William Tom 1861–1934, *Garden Pathway*, purchased from Mr D. Bannister
Warrener, William Tom 1861–1934, *Grez-sur-Loing, France*, purchased from Joseph Ritter-Tscherv, 1972
Warrener, William Tom 1861–1934, *Le lavoir*, gift from Maud Warrener, 1958
Warrener, William Tom 1861–1934, *Mary Ann Carlton*, gift from Mrs A. Leggett, 1973
Warrener, William Tom 1861–1934, *Un aveu*, gift from the Friends of Lincoln Museums and Art Gallery, 1974
Watts, George Frederick 1817–1904, *Emily Tennyson (1813–1896), Wife of Alfred Tennyson*, gift from the Tennyson family, 1961
Watts, George Frederick 1817–1904, *Hallam and Lionel Tennyson*, gift from the Tennyson family, 1961
Webster, Alfred George 1852–1916, *Lectern, Lincoln Cathedral*, bequeathed by Miss Florence Harrison, 1952
Webster, Alfred George 1852–1916, *Spring*, bequeathed by Miss Florence Harrison, 1952
Webster, Alfred George 1852–1916, *Summer*, bequeathed by Miss Florence Harrison, 1952
Webster, Alfred George 1852–1916, *Autumn*, bequeathed by Miss Florence Harrison, 1952
Webster, Alfred George 1852–1916, *Winter*, bequeathed by Miss Florence Harrison, 1952
Webster, Alfred George 1852–1916, *Narcissus*, bequeathed by Miss Florence Harrison, 1952
Webster, Alfred George 1852–1916, *Frederick Andrew (1840–1916)*, gift from Andrew and Co., 1985
Webster, Alfred George 1852–1916, *Canterbury Pilgrims*, bequeathed by Mrs G. J. Newsum, 1946
Webster, Alfred George 1852–1916, *Castle Hill, Lincoln*, bequeathed by Miss Florence Harrison, 1952
Webster, Alfred George 1852–1916, *Dean's Eye, Lincoln Cathedral from the Clerestory*, bequeathed by Miss Florence Harrison, 1952
Webster, Alfred George 1852–1916, *Gainsborough Old Hall, Lincolnshire*, bequeathed by Miss Florence Harrison, 1952
Webster, Alfred George 1852–1916, *Mablethorpe Shore, Lincolnshire*, bequeathed by Miss Florence Harrison, 1952
Webster, Alfred George 1852–1916, *Mr Bland's Orchard, Heighington, Lincoln*, bequeathed by Mrs P. E. M. Birchby, 1976
Webster, Alfred George 1852–1916, *Newark Castle, Nottinghamshire*, bequeathed by Miss Florence Harrison, 1952
Webster, Alfred George 1852–1916, *Somerton Castle, Lincolnshire*, bequeathed by Miss Florence Harrison, 1952
Webster, Alfred George 1852–1916, *Whitefriars, Lincoln*, bequeathed by Miss Florence Harrison, 1952
Weiss, José 1859–1919, *Landscape*, bequeathed by A. Fotherby, 1945
West, Benjamin 1738–1820, *Sir Joseph Banks (1743–1820), 1st Bt, GCB, PRS*, purchased from Alan Bond, 1989
West, John active 1839–1844, *'Celerity'*, transferred from the City and County Museum, Lincoln, 1975
West, John active 1839–1844, *Samuel Tuke (1784–1857)*, transferred from the City and County Museum, Lincoln, 1975
White, Alfred Ernest 1873–1953, *Akrill's Passage, Lincoln*, bequeathed by Mrs H. M. Gostling, 1955
White, Harry active 20th C, *Boulby Cliffs, Yorkshire*, gift from Sir Hickman B. Bacon, Bt, JP, 1938
White, Harry active 20th C, *Concert in the Club Room*, gift from Sir Hickman B. Bacon, Bt, JP, 1939
White, Harry active 20th C, *Evening Effect over Grimsby, Lincolnshire* (sketch) (recto), gift from Sir Hickman B. Bacon, Bt, JP, 1934
White, Harry active 20th C, *Unfinished Sketch* (verso), gift from Sir Hickman B. Bacon, Bt, JP, 1934
White, Harry active 20th C, *Portrait*, gift from Sir Hickman B. Bacon, Bt, JP, 1935
White, Harry active 20th C, *Seashore at Whitby, North Yorkshire*, gift from Sir Hickman B. Bacon, Bt, JP, 1939
White, Harry active 20th C, *Sporting Pink*, gift from Sir Hickman B. Bacon, Bt, JP, 1935
White, Harry active 20th C, *The Billposter*, gift from Sir Hickman B. Bacon, Bt, JP, 1933
White, Harry active 20th C, *The Charlatan*, gift from Sir Hickman B. Bacon, Bt, JP, 1936
White, Harry active 20th C, *The Fourpenny Entrance*, gift from Sir Hickman B. Bacon, Bt, JP, 1934
White, Harry active 20th C, *Woodland Study*
Wilmot, J. H. *Brixham Trawlers*, gift from Sir Hickman B. Bacon, Bt, JP, 1937
Wilson, Geoffrey b.1920, *The Green Umbrella*, gift from the artist, 1969
Wilson, Richard 1712/1713–1782, *View in the Wye Valley, Wales*, gift from Mrs Reynolds Scorer, 1945
Wilson, Susan b.1951, *On the Gothic Line*, gift from the Contemporary Art Society, 1992, © the artist
Wilson, Susan b.1951, *Self Portrait with Hands*, purchased from the artist, 1996, © the artist
Wolfsfeld, Erich 1884–1956, *Caravan Resting*, gift from Mrs Wolfsfeld, 1959, © Dr Max Block
Wolfsfeld, Erich 1884–1956, *Plucking Chickens*, gift from Mrs Wolfsfeld, 1959, © Dr Max Block
Wolfsfeld, Erich 1884–1956, *Young Arab with a Donkey*, gift from Mrs Wolfsfeld, 1959, © Dr Max Block
Worrall, Ernest J. 1898–1972, *Limekilns*, gift from Sir Hickman B. Bacon, Bt, JP, 1935
Worrall, Ernest J. 1898–1972, *Snow at Healing, Lincolnshire*, purchased from the artist, 1954
Wortley, Archibald J. Stuart 1849–1905, *The Poacher's Daughter*, gift from R. D. Tweed, 1952
Wortley, Archibald J. Stuart 1849–1905, *The Sleep of an Acorn*, gift from E. E. Tweed, 1915
Wright, Nora active 20th C, *Sheep*, gift from Sir Hickman B. Bacon, Bt, JP, 1942
Wynter, Bryan 1915–1975, *Sandspoor III*, purchased from the Contemporary Art Society, 1963, © Bryan Wynter. All rights reserved, DACS 2012
Yglesias, Vincent Philip 1845–1911, *The Golden Common*, gift from Mrs Yglesias, 1929
Ysenbrandt, Adriaen (attributed to) c.1500–before 1551, *Crucifixion*, gift from Joan Webster, 1956
Zinkeisen, Anna Katrina 1901–1976, *Mediaeval Lincoln*, gift from the London and North Eastern Railway Company, 1937, © the artist's estate

The Guildhall, Lincoln

Bentley, Joseph Herbert 1866–1934, *Queen Victoria (1819–1901)*
Boden, George Alfred 1888–1956, *Richard II Presenting the Sword to the Mayor of Lincoln, 1386*
Brian *'Sir Nigel Gresley' Steam Train*
Pearson, Stewart *Sword Bearer*, on loan from Mr J. J. Cooke
Philips, Charles 1708–1747, *William Gylby*
Stotthard, C. J. *Vulcan over Lincoln*
Stratt, J. G. *Richard Mason (1827–1855)*
unknown artist *George III (1738–1820)*
unknown artist *John Rudyard, Mayor of Lincoln (1836)*

The Lawn

Burnett *Bridge in Neustadt, Germany*, gift to Lincoln from its twin town, Neustadt
Burnett *Neustadt, Germany, Street Scene 1*, gift to Lincoln from its twin town, Neustadt
Gina *Neustadt, Germany, Street Scene 3*, gift to Lincoln from its twin town, Neustadt
Gina *Neustadt, Germany, Street Scene 4*, gift to Lincoln from its twin town, Neustadt
Gina *Neustadt, Germany, Street Scene 5*, gift to Lincoln from its twin town, Neustadt
Gina *Neustadt, Germany, Street Scene 6*, gift to Lincoln from its twin town, Neustadt
Gina *Neustadt, Germany, Street Scene 7*, gift to Lincoln from its twin town, Neustadt
Sainsbury, R. *Neustadt, Germany, Street Scene 2*, gift to Lincoln from its twin town, Neustadt

The Royal Lincolnshire Regimental Museum Trust

Arnold, Dorothy *The Soldiers' Chapel of St George, Lincoln Cathedral*, gift from the artist

University of Lincoln

Bettles, John James b.1924, *The Bridge*, purchased, 2003, © the artist
Edwards, Paul b.1954, *Beer Table**, untraced find, © the artist
Essafiry, Savida *Portrait of a Gentleman with Spectacles**, unknown acquisition method
Essafiry, Savida *Portrait of a Japanese Gentleman**, unknown acquisition method
Hammad, Medina b.1963, *Fountain Lamp*, unknown acquisition method
Hammad, Medina b.1963, *Dad's Song Table*, unknown acquisition method
Hammad, Medina b.1963, *Estrangement* (study), unknown acquisition method
Hammad, Medina b.1963, *Estrangement*, unknown acquisition method
Hammad, Medina b.1963, *Yellow Corridor* (study), unknown acquisition method
Hammad, Medina b.1963, *Yellow Corridor* (part of a triptych), unknown acquisition method
Hammad, Medina b.1963, *Fountain Lamp and Rose*, unknown acquisition method
Hammad, Medina b.1963, *Gulf Woman against Yellow Wall Prayer*, unknown acquisition method
Hammad, Medina b.1963, *Departure* (study), unknown acquisition method
Hammad, Medina b.1963, *Yellow Table**, unknown acquisition method
Lamb, Lynne b.1953, *Untitled*, unknown acquisition method, © the artist
Mistry, Vanisha *Temptation**, unknown acquisition method
Neil, J. *From a Window**, unknown acquisition method
Newman, Mike b.1934, *Phase*, purchased, 2003, © the artist
Richardson, Alexandra *West Common*, unknown acquisition method
Stoneham, Leslie b.1947, *Grass over Barbed Wire No.1*, unknown acquisition method, © the artist
Stoneham, Leslie b.1947, *Grass over Barbed Wire No.2*, unknown acquisition method, © the artist
Stoneham, Leslie b.1947, *Grass over Barbed Wire No.3*, unknown acquisition method, © the artist
Stoneham, Leslie b.1947, *Grass over Barbed Wire No.4*, unknown acquisition method, © the artist
unknown artist *Any Time**, unknown acquisition method
unknown artist *Blue Jelly Fish**, unknown acquisition method
unknown artist *Red Jelly Fish**, unknown acquisition method
unknown artist *Cow Girl**, unknown acquisition method

unknown artist *Deckchair in Blue**, unknown acquisition method
unknown artist *Geometric**, unknown acquisition method
unknown artist *Lozenge Lattice**, unknown acquisition method
unknown artist *Surf**, unknown acquisition method
Warburton, Kay B. b.1955, *Organic Root Tuber**, unknown acquisition method, © the artist

Louth Museum

Drewery, Elaine b.1939, *Miss Kent*, gift from Mr C. Ladbrook, © Louth Museum
Hubbard, Bennett 1806–1870, *Portrait of an Unknown Female*, acquired from Louth Mechanics' Institute, 1957
Hubbard, Bennett 1806–1870, *Chestnut Horse* (before restoration), acquired from Louth Mechanics' Institute, 1957; restored by Dian Hall Conservation, 2009
Hubbard, Bennett 1806–1870, *Nathaniel Hammond Batterham*, acquired from Louth Mechanics' Institute, 1957
Hubbard, Bennett 1806–1870, *Portrait of an Unknown Female*, acquired from Louth Mechanics' Institute, 1957
Hubbard, Bennett 1806–1870, *Portrait of an Unknown Lady*, acquired from Louth Mechanics' Institute, 1957
Hubbard, Bennett 1806–1870, *A Welsh Milk Girl*, acquired from Louth Mechanics' Institute, 1957
Hubbard, Bennett 1806–1870, *Spanish Peasant of the Basque Provinces*, acquired from Louth Mechanics' Institute, 1957
Hubbard, Bennett 1806–1870, *Portrait of an Unknown Man* (thought to be Charles Goodwin Smith), acquired from Louth Mechanics' Institute, 1957
Morton, Charles Reginald (attributed to) active 1917–1936, *Ruined House (Louth Flood Damage, 29 May 1920)*, acquired from Louth Mechanics' Institute, 1957
Rodgerson, W. A. active 1940s–1960s, *Portrait of an Unidentified Mayor of Louth*, acquired from Louth Mechanics' Institute, 1957
Spooner, Arthur 1873–1961, *Scene of the Gatehouse at Welbeck Abbey, Nottinghamshire*, acquired from Louth Mechanics' Institute, 1957 © the artist's estate/Bridgeman Art Library
Spooner, Arthur 1873–1961, *Welbeck Abbey and Park, Nottinghamshire*, acquired from Louth Mechanics' Institute, 1957 © the artist's estate/Bridgeman Art Library
Spooner, Arthur 1873–1961, *John William Goulding of Louth (1844–1922)*, acquired from Louth Mechanics' Institute, 1957 © the artist's estate/Bridgeman Art Library
unknown artist *Alderman George Blaze, Mayor of Louth (1911)*, acquired from Louth Mechanics' Institute, 1957
unknown artist *Thatched House and a Gate*, acquired from Louth Mechanics' Institute, 1957
Wallis, Thomas Wilkinson 1822–1903, *Self Portrait*, acquired from Louth Mechanics' Institute, 1957
Wallis, Thomas Wilkinson 1822–1903, *Thomas Espin (1767–1822), FSA* (after Richard Jones), acquired from Louth Mechanics' Institute, 1957
Wallis, Thomas Wilkinson 1822–1903, *Self Portrait* (before restoration), acquired from Louth Mechanics' Institute, 1957; restored by Dian Hall Conservation, 2005

Owston Ferry Parish Council

Smith, Gabell active c.1900–1930, *On the Trent, Owston Ferry, Lincolnshire*, gift from Fred and Tom Claphan, 1930

North Lincolnshire Museums Service

Austen, Alexander b.1859, *The Cobbler*, on loan from T. M. Lister, since 1975
Austen, Alexander b.1859, *The Tailor*, on loan from T. M. Lister, since 1975
Barlow, G. B. *Portrait of a Young Woman Reading*, purchased from Henry Spencers & Sons Ltd, 1967
Barrie, Mardi 1931–2004, *East Side*, purchased from the artist, 1975
Bary, E. *Interior Scene*, gift from Mr C. O. Pidd, 1964
Berners, Gerald Hugh 1883–1950, *Flowers in a Pottery Vase*, purchased from Henry Spencers & Sons Ltd,1965
Bilbao de Barros, H. M. *Landscape*, gift from the Contemporary Art Society, 1972
Birch, Samuel John Lamorna 1869–1955, *River Landscape*, purchased from Henry Spencers & Sons Ltd, 1970, © the artist's estate
Bonington, Richard Parkes 1802–1828, *On the Brittany Coast, France*, purchased from Henry Spencers & Sons Ltd, 1964
Bower, Edward d.1667, *Portrait of a Gentleman Cleric*, purchased from Henry Spencers & Sons Ltd, 1967
British (English) School *John Sheffield (1647–1721), 1st Duke of Buckingham and Normanby, KG, PC*, gift from the Sheffield Family, before 1969
British (English) School *Matthew Pearson of Selby*
British School *Mrs Bennett of Edinburgh*, purchased from Henry Spencers & Sons Ltd, 1968
Burton, Marjorie E. active 1971–1980, *Museum Garden, Scunthorpe, Lincolnshire*, gift from the artist, 1974
Burton, Marjorie E. active 1971–1980, *Castlethorpe, Lincolnshire*, purchased from the artist, 1978
Button, Eva active 1977–1978, *Winding River*, purchased from the artist, 1978
Chappell, Reuben 1870–1940, *'Ceres' of Saxilby*, gift from Mr L. A. Spicer, 1964, © the artist's estate
Clive, Nicholas *Illuminated Bottles*, gift from N. Giles, 1961
Closterman, John 1660–1711, *Arthur Herbert (c.1648–1716), 1st Earl of Torrington*, gift from J. V. Sheffield, 1969
Cole, R. A. *Five Tall Trees*, purchased from the artist, 1961
Constable, John (attributed to) 1776–1837, *Cottage*, purchased from Henry Spencers & Sons Ltd, 1969
Cooke, Edward William 1811–1880, *Dutch Boats in the Calm*, gift from Mr R. Hawke, 1963
Cuming, Frederick b.1930, *Studio Interior*, © the artist/Bridgeman Art Library
Dixon, Harry 1861–1942, *Diana Mary (d.1995), and June Ramsden*, bequeathed by Diana Myburgh, 1995
East, Alfred 1844–1913, *Warnham Lake, Sussex*, gift from Mr and Mrs T. J. Lewis, 1960
East, Alfred 1844–1913, *A Mystic Pool*, purchased from Henry Spencers & Sons Ltd, 1967
Elwell, Frederick William 1870–1958, *Farm Scene*, gift from Mrs A. Duffin, 1967
Elwell, Mary Dawson 1874–1952, *In the Trossachs, Highlands*, gift from Mrs A. Duffin, 1967
Eves, Archie *Fay Compton (1894–1978)*, purchased from Henry Spencer & Sons, 1969
Fong, Lai active c.1870–c.1905, *'Allan Shaw'*, gift from Mr A. Brelsford, 1966
Franks, John active c.1950–1975, *Sloop 'Nero' on the Trent at Burton upon Stather*, gift from Mr A. Horne, 1971, photo credit: North Lincolnshire Museums Service
Franks, John active c.1950–1975, *Brickyards*, gift from the artist, 1975
Franks, John active c.1950–1975, *Brickyards*, gift from the artist, 1975
Franks, John active c.1950–1975, *Sloop 'Hydro' of Goole*, gift from the artist, 1973, photo credit: North Lincolnshire Museums Service
Franks, John active c.1950–1975, *Sloop 'Nero' on the River Ancholme at Ferriby Sluice, Lincolnshire*, gift from Mr A. Horne, 1971, photo credit: North Lincolnshire Museums Service
Garton, C. *The Dog*, purchased from the artist, 1966
Gaunt *Woodland Vista*
Gordon, John Watson 1788–1864, *Anne Sherriff (1866–1781)* (later Mrs Charles Young), purchased from Henry Spencers & Sons Ltd, 1968
Grant, Keith b.1930, *Blue Cloud*, gift from Mr J. A. McIver, 1968, © the artist
Grant, Keith b.1930, *White Cloud*, gift from Mr J. A. McIver, 1968, © the artist
Green, Anthony b.1939, *Lovemaking in Lissenden Gardens*, gift from the Contemporary Art Society, 1970, © Anthony Green RA
Haddock, Edwin Aldridge 1921–1996, *Plesiosaurus*, purchased, 1978, © the artist's estate
Hadlow, J. *Scrap*, purchased from the artist (?), c.1963
Henry, Sue *Wolds, Lincolnshire, Early March*, purchased from the artist, 1981
Herkomer, Herman 1863–1935, *William Henry Forester Denison (1834–1900), 1st Earl of Londesborough*, acquired, 1965
Herring, John Frederick I 1795–1865, *Timber Drug*, gift from Mr Pacey, 1967
Hersch, Eugen 1887–1967, *Portrait of an Unidentified Mayor of Scunthorpe*, gift from Scunthorpe Council, 1976
Hesledon, Edmund *View of the Churches of Saint Peter and St Mary, Barton-on-Humber, Lincolnshire*, gift from Brigg Rural District Council, 1974
Hest, G. *St Oswald's Church, Althorpe, Lincolnshire*, gift from Mrs H. Clark, 1965
Horsley, John Callcott 1817–1903, *William Henry Dawes*, gift from John Lysaghts Ltd, 1958, photo credit: North Lincolnshire Museums Service
Horsley, John Callcott 1817–1903, *Mrs William Henry Dawes*, gift from John Lysaghts Ltd, 1958
Hunter, John *Batty Tootal, Artist*, purchased from Reverend Denzil Wright, 1979
Hunter, John *Mrs Batty Tootal*, purchased from Reverend Denzil Wright, 1979
Hurd, F. *Bowder Stone, Keswick, Cumberland*, gift from Mr R. P. Jacklin, 1965
Jackson, Frederick William 1859–1918, *The Road to the Farm*, purchased from Henry Spencers & Sons Ltd, 1970
Kilpack, Sarah Louisa c.1840–1909, *The Casquettes near Alderney, Channel Islands*, purchased from Henry Spencers & Sons Ltd, 1970
Knapton, George (after) 1698–1778, *Falls of Terni (Rock of Ages)*, gift from Mr R. Hawke, 1963
Kneller, Godfrey 1646–1723, *John Sheffield (1647–1721), 1st Duke of Buckingham and Normanby, KG, PC*, on loan from the National Maritime Museum, since 2005
Knight, George *Curlew*, on loan from a private collection
Landseer, Edwin Henry (copy of) 1802–1873, *King Charles Spaniels (The Cavalier's Pets)*, gift from Mr J. Sparks, 1965
Landseer, Edwin Henry (copy of) 1802–1873, *Shoeing*, gift from Mr C. Haines, 1975
Lawrence, Thomas 1769–1830, *Mrs Alice Wood*, purchased from Henry Spencers & Sons Ltd, 1968
Lawson, Sonia b.1934, *Journey through March Weather*, gift from the Contemporary Art Society, 1970, © the artist
Lewis, Michael *Steel Tipping from a Ladle*
Moore, Henry 1831–1895, *Storm at Whitby, North Yorkshire*, gift from Mr W. H. Millett, 1953
Moore, Henry 1831–1895, *Calm at Scarborough, North Yorkshire*, gift from Mr W. H. Millett, 1953
Morland, George (after) 1763–1804, *Smugglers, Coastal Scene*, on loan from T. M. Lister, since 1975
Morris, J. D. active c.1830–1905, *Epping Forrest, Essex*, gift from Mr W. H. Millett, 1953
Organ, Bryan b.1935, *Cage Birds at a Show*, purchased, 1960, © Bryan Organ & the Redfern Gallery, London
Organ, Elizabeth 1934–2009, *Coffee Pot*, gift from the artist, 1970
Perry, Roy 1935–1993, *Wrawby Post Mill, Lincolnshire*, purchased from the artist, 1963
Preston, William F. active 1885–1889, *'Starling'*, gift from Mr John Franks, 1960
Preston, William F. active 1885–1889, *'Morton Castle'*, gift from Mr John Franks, 1973
Preston, William F. active 1885–1889, *'Topsy'*, gift from Mr John Franks, 1973
Redmore, Edward King 1860–1941, *View of Hull, Hull Garrison Fortifications*, purchased from W. N. Lewendon and Sons, 1965
Reni, Guido (copy after) 1575–1642, *Beatrice Cenci*, gift from Mr W. H. Millett, 1953
Reynolds, Joshua (school of) 1723–1792, *Portrait of an Unknown Lady*, on loan from Scunthorpe Borough Museum and Art Gallery, 1988
Rhoades, Geoffrey 1898–1980, *The White Gate*, purchased from Henry Spencers & Sons Ltd, 1969
Robb, William George 1872–1940, *Michaelmas Daisies and Marigolds*
Rogers, Philip Hutchins c.1786–1853, *Coastal Scene*
Rollett, Herbert 1872–1932, *Seascape*, purchased from Mr Parker, 1971
Rollinson, P. *Joseph Herbert*

Tomlin, MM, donated by Mrs Tomlin, 2002
Ross, William Arthur active 1906–1937, *Belton Church, Grantham, Lincolnshire*, gift from Mr M. Ellerton, 1960
Ross, William Arthur active 1906–1937, *Temple Belwood House, Lincolnshire*, gift from Mr M. Ellerton, 1960
Rubens, Peter Paul 1577–1640, *Emperor Otho* (from the 'Twelve Caesars' series), purchased from Henry Spencers & Sons Ltd, 1967
Scott, M. *Scunthorpe Museum, Lincolnshire*, purchased from the artist, 1978
Smith, Richard 1818–1890, *George Dawes (1817–1888)*, gift from Lysaghts Works, 1943
Spinks, Thomas 1847–1927, *The Path through the Woods*, gift from Mr A. W. Cansfield, 1965
Stamp, Elaine P. *Scunthorpe Museum, Lincolnshire*
Staves, W. D. active 1964–1965, *Industrial Skyline*, purchased from the artist, 1965
Steen, Jan (attributed to) 1626–1679, *Dutch Interior*, gift from Mr W. H. Millett, 1953
Taylor, J. M. *As I Remember (View of Old Station Road, Scunthorpe, Lincolnshire)*, gift from Mr F. H. Taylor, 1965
Teed, Shirley Brenda b.1933, *Rockface with a Boy in a Yellow Towel*, purchased from the artist, 1978, © the artist
Trevisani, Francesco (attributed to) 1656–1746, *Saint Mary Magdalene of Egypt*, on loan from Lindsey County Council, since 1962
Turner, Joseph Mallord William (after) 1775–1851, *Ancient Italy*, purchased from Messrs H. Spencers, 1964
unknown artist *The Betrayal of Christ*, on loan from Lindsey County Council, since 1962
unknown artist *Portrait of an Unknown Officer*, purchased from Messrs H. Spencers, 1963
unknown artist 17th C, *George Marten of Becket, Berkshire*, purchased from Reverend Denzil Wright, 1979
unknown artist 17th C, *Portrait of a Lady in Black*, purchased from Henry Spencers & Sons Ltd, 1969
unknown artist 17th C, *Saint Jerome Contemplating the Crucifix*, purchased from B. L. Wells, 1962
unknown artist *Reverend Thomas Lodington*, purchased from Reverend Denzil Wright, 1978/1979
unknown artist 18th C, *Bust of a Lady*, gift from Mrs E. Stone, 1954
unknown artist *Conversation in a Barn*, gift from Mr T. M. Lister, 1966
unknown artist *Mary Stead*, gift from Mrs A. S. Alletson, 1962
unknown artist *Mr G. F. Brunyee of Eastoft*, gift from Mr F. Jackson, 1964
unknown artist *Landscape with a Bridge*, gift from Mrs J. Piercy, 1962
unknown artist *Landscape with a Stream*, gift from Mrs J. Piercy, 1962
unknown artist *Lake Scene*, gift from Mrs Graham, 2001
unknown artist *Lake Scene*, gift from Mrs Graham, 2001
unknown artist *Rustic Scene with a Cottage*, purchased from Henry Spencers Ltd,1965
unknown artist *The Ploughing Lesson*, gift from Mrs Drinkall, 1965
unknown artist 19th C, *Rustic Scene: Derelict Stone Cottage in Woodland*, photo credit: North Lincolnshire Museums Service
unknown artist 19th C, *Rustic Scene: Two Cows by a Stream*, photo credit: North Lincolnshire Museums Service
unknown artist 19th C, *Two Cats*, gift from Mrs A. S. Alletson, 1962, photo credit: North Lincolnshire Museums Service
unknown artist 19th C, *Two Landscapes with a Camel and Palm Trees* (diptych), photo credit: North Lincolnshire Museums Service
unknown artist *Washing Scene*, purchased from Henry Spencers & Sons Ltd, 1970
unknown artist *Frodingham Cottage, Lincolnshire*, gift from Mr Cross, 1961
unknown artist *A Dog in Butler's Pantry, Lea Park, Lincolnshire (?)*
unknown artist *Chinese Dragon*, purchased from W. N. Lewendon and Sons, 1965
unknown artist *Cows Drinking from a River*, on loan from T. M. Lister, since 1975
unknown artist *The Ice Ship*
Van Bergen, Dirck 1645–1690, *Pastoral Scene*
Vernet, Claude-Joseph 1714–1789, *Seascape*, gift from Mr R. Hawke, 1963
Vernet, Claude-Joseph (after) 1714–1789, *Seaport in the Mediterranean*, purchased from Henry Spencers & Sons Ltd, 1970
Ward, James 1768–1859, *Roan Shorthorn Cow*, gift from Mrs Hanson, 1967
Westall, Richard 1766–1836, *Theseus and Ariadne at the Entrance of the Labyrinth*, purchased from Messrs H. Spencers, 1965
Whitehead, Tom 1886–1978, *View from the Bridge*, purchased, 1961
Whitford, Richard c.1821–1890, *Six Lincolnshire Longwool Sheep*, purchased from Thornborrow and Co., 1972
Wilkinson *Pastoral*, gift from Mr Cross, 1961
Willson, Graeme b.1951, *Still Life*, purchased from the artist, 1974, © the artist
Woolmer, Alfred Joseph 1805–1892, *Portrait of a Young Girl*, purchased from Henry Spencers & Sons Ltd, 1970
Worthington, A. 1822–1915, *Fighting Lions*, gift from Mr R. P. Jacklin, 1965
Worthington, A. 1822–1915, *Rustic Scene with a Stile*, gift from Mr R. P. Jacklin, 1965

Magdalen College Museum

Turner, Ernest 1886–1976, *Mary Paulett (d.1923)*, donated, 2004

Ayscoughfee Hall Museum and Gardens

Eaton, Wilcox *MV 'Geest Bay'*, gift from the World Wide Fruit Company of Spalding, 2008
unknown artist mid-19th C, *Maurice Johnson VI (1815–1864)*
unknown artist mid-19th C, *Thomas Pear II (1770–1858)*, gift from a private donor, 2003
unknown artist late 19th C–20th C, *Isabella Johnson (d.1905)*
Webber, Helen active 1966–2008, *Cutter Patterns*, purchased from the artist, 1991

Stamford and Rutland Hospital

W. E. M. *Miss Michelson*
unknown artist *Dr T. P. Greenwood (1855–1927), Surgeon of the Stamford and Rutland Hospital*, purchased via public subscription, 1926
unknown artist *Henry Fryer (1762–1823), Surgeon, Founder and Benefactor of the Stamford and Rutland Hospital*
unknown artist *Portrait of an Unknown Man and a Dog*
unknown artist *William Cecil (1876–1956), 5th Marquess of Exeter*
unknown artist *William Newman, MD*, gift from Mrs Newman

Stamford Museum

Baker, B. *West Street* (Cascelloids Factory, now demolished), acquired, 2003
Carver (attributed to) *Still Life*
Harston, I. (attributed to) *Daniel Lambert (1770–1809)*, purchased with the assistance of the Museums, Libraries and Archives Council/Victoria and Albert Museum Purchase Grant Fund and the Art Fund, 2009
Jackson, C. *Harvesting Scene*, gift from M. Goddard-Jackson, 1969
Jauncey, George H. active 1903–1907, *Church and Countryside in the Snow*, recovered from the 'Crown and Anchor' Inn during its demolition, 1960
Jauncey, George H. active 1903–1907, *Still Life with an Apple, Pears and Grapes*, recovered from the 'Crown and Anchor' Inn during its demolition, 1960
Jauncey, George H. active 1903–1907, *Still Life with Peaches, Cherries and Strawberries*, recovered from the 'Crown and Anchor' Inn during its demolition, 1960
Mayes, Cyril J. *The Wothorpe Fields, Lincolnshire*, gift from the artist, 1981
Miles, Ellis 1919–2006, *The Old Grandstand, Racecourse Road, Stamford, Lincolnshire*, gift from John Smith, 2006
Robotham, Ruth b.1930, *Cloudy Day, Peterborough, Cambridgeshire*, gift from the artist, 1983, © the artist
Robotham, Ruth b.1930, *Fenland Landscape*, gift from the artist, 1983, © the artist
unknown artist *Sailing Scene*
unknown artist *All Saints' Church, Red Lion Square, Stamford, Lincolnshire*, purchased from Mr Johnson, 1988
unknown artist mid–late 19th C, *Mountain Landscape with Cattle*
unknown artist mid–late 19th C, *Mountain Landscape with Sheep*
unknown artist late 19th C, *Florence Ellis*, gift from Mr W. Ellis
unknown artist late 19th C, *George William Ellis*
unknown artist late 19th C, *William Virtue Ellis, Landlord of the 'Lord Nelson' Pub during the Nineteenth Century*, gift from Mr W. Ellis
unknown artist *Fenland Scene with a Cornfield and a Windmill*, gift from Mrs O. Armstrong, c.1959
unknown artist *Daniel Lambert (1770–1809)* (copy of an earlier painting), on loan from Stamford Town Council, since 1974
unknown artist *Portrait of an Unknown Lady in Continental Dress*, gift from Mrs Liddle, 1964
unknown artist *View of a Cottage by a Stream*

The Hospital of William Browne

unknown artist *The Common Room at Browne's Hospital*, gift (?)

Catmose College

Boyfield, Caroline b.1962, *Seed Heads*, purchased, 2005, © the artist
Njeiu Njeri, Patricia *Harvest Time*, purchased, 2006
Wright, Paul b.1973, *Joy Gregg II*, donated by the artist, 2007, © the artist

Rutland County Council

Snowdon *Osprey*
Wright, Paul b.1973, *Joy Gregg I*, © the artist

Rutland County Museum

Eagleton, Aileen 1902–1984, *Edward Eagletony*, bequeathed by Mrs M. U. Ivimey, 1992, © Rutland County Council
Wilson, Violet d.c.1970, *Cottesmore Guider Hound*, gift from Mrs Jean Booth, 1999

Uppingham Town Hall

unknown artist *Caudebec-en-Caux, France*

Collection Addresses

Leicestershire

Ashby-de-la-Zouch

Ashby-de-la-Zouch Museum
North Street, Ashby-de-la-Zouch LE65 1HU
Telephone 01530 560090

Castle Donington

Castle Donington Museum
The Stone House, 4 Apiary Gate
Castle Donington, Leicestershire DE74 2JA
Telephone 01332 812711

Hinckley

Hinckley and Bosworth Borough Council
Council Offices, Argents Mead, Hinckley LE10 1BZ
Telephone 01455 238141

Hinckley and District Museum
Framework Knitters' Cottages, Lower Bond Street
Hinckley LE10 1QU
Telephone 01455 251218

John Cleveland College
Butt Lane, Hinckley LE10 1LE
Telephone 01455 632183

Kegworth

Kegworth Museum
52 High Street, Kegworth, Derbyshire DE74 2DA
Telephone 01509 670137

Kibworth

Kibworth C. of E. Primary School
Hillcrest Avenue, Kibworth, Leicestershire LE8 0NH
Telephone 0116 279 2485

Leicester

Leicester Arts and Museums Service:

Leicester Arts and Museums Service
New Walk Museum and Art Gallery
53 New Walk, Leicester LE1 7EA
Telephone 0116 225 4900

New Walk Museum & Art Gallery
53 New Walk, Leicester LE1 7EA
Telephone 0116 225 4900

Newarke Houses Museum & Gardens
The Newarke, Leicester LE2 7BY
Telephone 0116 225 4980

The Guildhall, Leicester
Guildhall Lane, Leicester LE1 5FQ
Telephone 0116 253 2569

Leicester City Council (Adult Skills and Learning)
Satta Hashem Hall, Leicester Adult Education College,
Welford Place, Leicester, Leicestershire LE1 6ZG
Telephone 0116 252 6505

Leicester Town Hall
Town Hall Square, Leicester LE1 9BG
Telephone 0116 252 7000

Leicestershire County Council Artworks Collection
c/o County Hall, Glenfield, Leicester LE3 8RA
Telephone 0116 305 5536

Leicestershire County Council Beaumanor Collection
Leicestershire County Council Communities & Well
Being Department, County Hall, Leicester Road
Glenfield, Leicester LE3 8RA
Telephone 0116 232 3232

Leicestershire Outdoor and Residential Learning
Service
Beaumanor Hall, Woodhouse LE12 8TX
Telephone 0116 232 3232

Leicestershire County Council Civic Collection
County Hall, Leicester Road, Glenfield, Leicester LE3
8RA
Telephone 0116 232 3232

Leicestershire County Council Museums Service:

Leicestershire County Council Museums Service
County Hall, Leicester Road, Glenfield, Leicester LE3
8RA
Telephone 0116 232 3232

Charnwood Museum
Queens Hall, Granby Street
Loughborough LE11 3DU
Telephone 01509 233754

Collections Resources Centre
County Hall, Leicester Road, Glenfield
Leicester LE3 8RA
Telephone 01509 815514

Harborough Museum
Council Offices, Adam and Eve Street
Market Harborough LE16 7AG
Telephone 01858 821085

Melton Carnegie Museum
Thorpe End, Melton Mowbray LE13 1RB
Telephone 01530 278444

Snibston Discovery Museum
Ashby Road, Coalville LE67 3LN
Telephone 01530 278 444

Leicestershire County Cricket Club
County Ground, Grace Road, Leicester LE2 8AD
Telephone 0116 245 2400

Leicestershire Libraries:

Anstey Library
Paper Mill Close, Anstey, Leicester LE7 7AU
Telephone 0116 305 3536

Birstall Library
Wanlip Lane, Birstall, Leicester LE4 4JU
Telephone 0116 305 8756

Loughborough Library
Granby Street, Loughborough LE11 3DZ
Telephone 0116 305 2420

The Leicestershire Fire and Rescue Service Collection
Headquarters, Anstey Frith, Leicester Road, Glenfield
Leicester LE3 8HD
Telephone 0116 287 2241

The Royal Leicestershire Regiment Museum
Territorial Army Centre, Ulverscroft Road
Leicester LE4 6BY
Telephone 0116 225 4900

New Walk Museum and Art Gallery
53 New Walk, Leicester LE1 7EA
Telephone 0116 225 4900

Newarke Houses Museum
The Newarke, Leicester LE2 7BY
Telephone 0116 2254980

William Carey Museum
Central Baptist Church, Charles Street, Leicester LE1 1LA
Telephone 0116 2873864

University of Leicester
University Road, Leicester LE1 7RH
Telephone 0116 252 2522

Loughborough

Charnwood Borough Council Art Collection
Council Offices, Southfields Road
Loughborough LE11 2TN
Telephone 01509 268903

Loughborough University
Epinal Way, Loughborough LE11 3TU
Telephone 01509 263171

Loughborough War Memorial Museum
Queen's Park, Granby Street
Loughborough LE11 3DU
Telephone 01509 263370

RNIB College Loughborough
Radmoor Road, Loughborough LE11 3BS
Telephone 01509 611077

Lincolnshire

Allington

Allington Parish Council
Allington Village Hall, Side Street, Allington NG32 2DZ
Telephone 01400 281517

Boston

Boston Borough Council:

Boston Guildhall
South Street, Boston PE21 6HT
Telephone 01205 365954

The Haven Gallery
2 South Square, Boston PE21 6JU
Telephone 01205 356656

Fydell House
South Square, Boston PE21 6HU
Telephone 01205 351520

Bourne

Bourne Heritage Centre
Baldocks Mill, 21 South Street, Bourne PE10 9LY
Telephone 01778 422775

Epworth

Epworth Old Rectory
1 Rectory Street, Epworth DN9 1HX
Telephone 01427 872268

Gainsborough

Gainsborough Old Hall
Parnell Street, Gainsborough DN21 2NB
Telephone 01427 612669

West Lindsey District Council
Guildhall, Marshall's Yard, Gainsborough DN21 2NA
Telephone 01427 676676

Grantham

Grantham Museum
St Peter's Hill, Grantham NG31 6PY
Telephone 01476 568783

Grimsby

Grimsby Institute of Further & Higher Education
East Coast School of Art and Design, Grimsby Institute
Westward Ho, Grimsby DN34 5AW
Telephone 01472 311231

Grimsby Town Hall
Town Hall Square, Grimsby DN31 1HX
Telephone 01472 313131

North East Lincolnshire Museum Service
Fishing Heritage Centre, Alexandra Dock
Grimsby DN31 1UZ
Telephone 01472 313131

The Franklin Trust
Franklin College, Chelmsford Avenue
Grimsby DN34 5BY
Telephone 01472 875000

Immingham

Immingham Museum
Margaret Street, Immingham DN40 1LE
Telephone 01469 577066

Lincoln

Bishop Grosseteste University College Lincoln
Lincoln LN1 3DY
Telephone 01522 527347

Doddington Hall
Doddington, Lincoln LN6 4RU
Telephone 01522 694308

Museum of Lincolnshire Life
Burton Road, Lincoln LN1 3LY
Telephone 01522 528448

The Collection: Art & Archaeology in Lincolnshire (Usher Gallery):

> The Collection: Art & Archaeology in Lincolnshire
> Danes Terrace, Lincoln LN2 1LP
> Telephone 01522 550990
>
> Usher Gallery
> Lindun Hill, Lincoln LN2 1NN
> Telephone 01522 550990

The Guildhall, Lincoln
Saltergate, Lincoln LN2 1DH
Telephone 01522 541727

The Lawn
Union Road, Lincoln LN1 3BL
Telephone 01522 568080

The Royal Lincolnshire Regimental Museum Trust
Burton Road, Lincoln LN1 3LY
Telephone 01522 552899

University of Lincoln
Chad Varah House, Wordsworth Street, Lincoln LN1 3BP
Telephone 01522 882000

Louth

Louth Museum
4 Broadbank, Louth LN11 0EQ
Telephone 01507 601211

Owston Ferry

Owston Ferry Parish Council
Owston Ferry Coronation Hall, High Street
Owston Ferry DN9 1RL
Telephone 01427 728444

Scunthorpe

North Lincolnshire Museums Service
Normanby Hall Museum and Country Park
Normanby, Scunthorpe DN15 9HU
Telephone 01724 720588

Baysgarth House Museum
Baysgarth Park, Barton upon Humber
Scunthorpe DN18 6AN
Telephone 01724 843533

Normanby Hall Museum and Country Park
Normanby, Scunthorpe DN15 9HU
Telephone 01724 720588

North Lincolnshire Museum
Oswald Road, Scunthorpe DN15 7BD
Telephone 01724 843533

Skegness

Magdalen College Museum
St John Street, Wainfleet, Skegness PE24 4DL
Telephone 01754 820859 or 01754 881548

Spalding

Ayscoughfee Hall Museum and Gardens
Churchgate, Spalding PE11 2RA
Telephone 01775 764555

Stamford

Stamford and Rutland Hospital
Ryhall Road, Stamford PE9 1UA
Telephone 01780 764151

Stamford Museum
Broad Street, Stamford PE9 1PJ
Telephone 01780 766317

The Hospital of William Browne
Broad Street, Stamford PE9 1PF
Telephone 01780 763153

Rutland

Oakham

Catmose College
Huntsman Drive, Oakham LE15 6RP
Telephone 01572 722286

Rutland County Council
Catmose House, Catmose Street, Oakham LE15 6HP
Telephone 01572 722577

Rutland County Museum
Catmose Street, Oakham LE15 6HW
Telephone 01572 758440

Uppingham

Uppingham Town Hall
High Street East, Uppingham LE15 9PY
Telephone 01572 822681

Index of Artists

In this catalogue, artists' names and the spelling of their names follow the preferred presentation of the name in the Getty Union List of Artist Names (ULAN) as of February 2004, if the artist is listed in ULAN.

The page numbers next to each artist's name below direct readers to paintings that are by the artist; are attributed to the artist; or, in a few cases, are more loosely related to the artist being, for example, 'after', 'the circle of' or copies of a painting by the artist. The precise relationship between the artist and the painting is listed in the catalogue.

Acknowledgements

The Public Catalogue Foundation would like to thank the individual artists and copyright holders for their permission to reproduce for free the paintings in this catalogue. Exhaustive efforts have been made to locate the copyright owners of all the images included within this catalogue and to meet their requirements. Copyright credit lines for copyright owners who have been traced are listed in the Further Information section.

The Public Catalogue Foundation would like to express its great appreciation to the following organisations for their kind assistance in the preparation of this catalogue:

Bridgeman Art Library
Flowers East
Marlborough Fine Art
National Association of Decorative & Fine Arts Societies (NADFAS)
National Gallery, London
National Portrait Gallery, London
Royal Academy of Arts, London
Tate

The participating collections included in this catalogue would like to express their thanks to the following organisations and individuals who have so generously enabled them to acquire paintings featured in this catalogue:

Mrs Dora Bond
Calouste Gulbenkian Fund
City of Lincoln Council
City of Leicester Museums Trust
Contemporary Art Society
Richard Gilmore Douglas
The Honourable Mrs Dudley-Pelham
Esmée Fairbairn Charitable Trust
Heritage Lottery Fund
Sir Francis Hill
Mr Edwin Hitchon
David Keel 'De Keal'
MLA/V&A Purchase Grant Fund
National Art Collections Fund (The Art Fund)
National Heritage Memorial Fund
The children of Everatt and Gertrude Morwood Oates
The Friends of Leicester and Leicestershire Museums
The Friends of Lincoln Libraries, Museums and Art Gallery
The Heslam Trust
The Methodist Archives and History Committee
The Methodist Publishing House
The Pilgrim Trust
The Trustees of The Royal Leicestershire Regiment Museum
The Usher Gallery Trust

The Public Catalogue Foundation

The Public Catalogue Foundation is a registered charity. It was launched in 2003 to create a photographic record of the entire national collection of oil, tempera and acrylic paintings in public ownership in the United Kingdom.

Whilst our public galleries and civic buildings hold arguably the greatest collection of oil paintings in the world, over 80 per cent of these are not on view. Few collections have a complete photographic record of their paintings let alone a comprehensive illustrated catalogue. What is publicly owned is not publicly accessible.

The Foundation is publishing a series of fully illustrated, county-by-county catalogues that will cover, eventually, the entire national UK collection. To date, it has published over 30 volumes, presenting over 72,000 paintings.

In partnership with the BBC, the Foundation will make its database of the entire UK collection of 200,000 oil paintings available online through a new website called *Your Paintings*. The website was launched in the summer of 2011.

Your Paintings (*www.bbc.co.uk/arts/yourpaintings*) offers a variety of ways of searching for paintings as well as further information about the paintings and artists, including links to the participating collections' websites. For those interested in paintings and the subjects they portray *Your Paintings* is an unparalleled learning resource.

Collections benefit substantially from the work of the Foundation, not least from the digital images that are given to them for free following photography, and from the increased recognition that the project brings. These substantial benefits come at no financial cost to the collections.

The Foundation is funded by a combination of support from individuals, charitable trusts, companies and the public sector although the latter provides less than 20 per cent of the Foundation's financial support.

Supporters

Master Patrons

The Public Catalogue Foundation is greatly indebted to the following Master Patrons who have helped it in the past or are currently working with it to raise funds for the publication of their county catalogues. All of them have given freely of their time and have made an enormous contribution to the work of the Foundation.

Peter Andreae *(Hampshire)*
Sir Henry Aubrey-Fletcher, Bt, Lord Lieutenant of Buckinghamshire *(Buckinghamshire)*
Sir Nicholas Bacon, DL, High Sheriff of Norfolk *(Norfolk)*
Sir John Bather, Lord Lieutenant of Derbyshire *(Derbyshire)*
The Hon. Mrs Bayliss, JP, Lord Lieutenant of Berkshire *(Berkshire)*
Ian Bonas *(County Durham)*
Peter Bretherton *(West Yorkshire: Leeds)*
Michael Brinton, Lord Lieutenant of Worcestershire *(Worcestershire)*
Sir Hugo Brunner, KCVO, JP *(Oxfordshire)*
Mr John Bush, OBE, Lord-Lieutenant of Wiltshire *(Wiltshire)*
Lady Butler *(Warwickshire)*
Richard Compton *(North Yorkshire)*
George Courtauld, DL, Vice Lord Lieutenant of Essex *(Essex)*

The Countess of Darnley, Lord Lieutenant of Herefordshire *(Herefordshire)*
The Marquess of Downshire *(North Yorkshire)*
Martin Dunne, Lord Lieutenant of Warwickshire *(Warwickshire)*
Sir Henry Elwes, KCVO, Lord-Lieutenant of Gloucestershire *(Gloucestershire)*
Jenny Farr, MBE, DL *(Nottinghamshire)*
John Fenwick *(Tyne & Wear Museums)*
Mark Fisher, MP *(Staffordshire)*
Patricia Grayburn, MBE, DL *(Surrey)*
The Earl of Halifax, KStJ, JP, DL *(East Riding of Yorkshire)*
Lord Roy Hattersley, PC *(South Yorkshire: Sheffield)*
Algy Heber-Percy, Lord Lieutenant of Shropshire *(Shropshire)*
The Lady Mary Holborow, Lord Lieutenant of Cornwall *(Cornwall)*
Sarah Holman *(Warwickshire)*
Tommy Jowitt *(West Yorkshire)*
Alderman Sir David Lewis, The Rt Hon. The Lord Mayor of London, 2007–2008 *(The City of London)*
Sir Michael Lickiss *(Cornwall)*
Magnus Linklater *(Scotland)*
Lord Marlesford, DL *(Suffolk)*
Dr Bridget McConnell *(Glasgow)*
Lady Sarah Nicholson *(County Durham)*
Malcolm V. L. Pearce, MP *(Somerset)*
Sir John Riddell, Lord Lieutenant of Northumberland *(Northumberland)*
Venetia Ross Skinner *(Dorset)*
The Most Hon. The Marquess of Salisbury, PC, DL *(Hertfordshire)*
Julia Somerville *(Government Art Collection)*
Tim Stevenson, OBE, Lord Lieutenant of Oxfordshire *(Oxfordshire)*
Phyllida Stewart-Roberts, OBE *(East Sussex)*
Lady Juliet Townsend, Lord Lieutenant of Northamptonshire *(Northamptonshire)*
Leslie Weller, DL *(West Sussex)*
Sir Samuel C. Whitbread, KCVO, Lord Lieutenant of Bedfordshire *(Bedfordshire)*

Financial support

The Public Catalogue Foundation is particularly grateful to the following organisations and individuals who have given it generous financial support since the project started in 2003.

National Sponsor

Christie's

Benefactors (£10,000–£50,000)

The 29th May 1961 Charitable Trust
Arts Council England
The Barbour Trust
Binks Trust
City of Bradford Metropolitan District Council
Deborah Loeb Brice Foundation
The Bulldog Trust
A. & S. Burton 1960 Charitable Trust
Christie's
City of London Corporation
The John S. Cohen Foundation
Covent Garden London
Creative Scotland
Department for Culture, Media and Sport
Sir Harry Djanogly, CBE
Mr Lloyd Dorfman
Dunard Fund
The Elmley Foundation
Fenwick Ltd
Fidelity UK Foundation
Marc Fitch Fund
The Foyle Foundation
J. Paul Getty Jr Trust
Hampshire County Council
The Charles Hayward Foundation
Peter Harrison Foundation
Mr Robert Hiscox
Hiscox plc
David Hockney, CH, RA
ICAP plc

The Jordan Charitable Foundation
Kent County Council
The Linbury Trust
The Manifold Trust
Paul Mellon Centre for Studies in British Art
The Mercers' Company
Robert Warren Miller
Mr & Mrs A. Mittal
The Monument Trust
Miles Morland
Allan and Carol Murray
National Gallery Trust
Stavros Niarchos Foundation
Norfolk County Council
Northern Rock Foundation
Nottingham City Council
Malcolm V. L. Pearce, MP
P. F. Charitable Trust
The Pilgrim Trust
Provident Financial
RAB Capital plc
The Radcliffe Trust
Renaissance East Midlands
Renaissance West Midlands
Renaissance Yorkshire
Saga Group Ltd
Scottish Government
The Bernard Sunley Charitable Foundation
Townsend Family Trust
University College, London
University of Leeds
The Walker Trust
The Wolfson Foundation
Sir Siegmund Warburg's Voluntary Settlement
Garfield Weston Foundation
Mr & Mrs A. H. Wilkinson
The Wixamtree Trust

Series Patrons (Minimum donation of £2,500)

James & Lindsay Adam
Sir John Bather
Harry Bott
Janey Buchan
Mrs Rhona Callander
Dr Peter Cannon-Brookes
The John S. Cohen Foundation
Bushey Museum in memory of Lavender Watson
Mr Lloyd Dorfman
Lord Douro
Jenny Farr, MBE, DL
Mrs Greta Fenston
The FIRS Trust
Glasgow Museums
Patricia Grayburn, MBE, DL
G. Laurence Harbottle
R. K. Harrison Insurance Services Limited
Paul & Fiona Hart
Paul & Kathrine Haworth
Lord & Lady Heseltine
Patrik Holden & Lin Hinds
Neil Honebon
Michael Jacobson
Grace Jenkins
Dr David Johnson, DL
The Keatley Trust
John Kendall, Esq.
Michael A. Lambert, CBE
David & Amanda Leathers
Miles Morland
Allan & Carol Murray
North East Regional Museums Hub
The University of Northampton
Nottingham Civic Society
Richard & Amika Oldfield
The Roper Family Charitable Trust
Adam Sedgwick
Sir Harry & Lady Soloman
Stuart M. Southall
Simon Still
Chloe Teacher
University of Surrey
David & Cissy Walker
Tony Wilkinson
Mr & Mrs Jo Windsor
Mr & Mrs Charles Wyvill

Catalogue Patrons (£1,000–£10,000)

The 29th May 1961 Charitable Trust
ACE Study Tours
Adams & Remers
Marcus & Kate Agius
The AIM Foundation
D. C. R. Allen
John Alston, CBE
Amberley Castle
The Astor Foundation
The Aylesford Family Charitable Trust
Chairman of Cornwall County Council, Mrs Doris Anson, OBE, JP
Archant Ltd

G. F. Armitage Family Charitable Trust
Mr Ian Askew
Aurelius Charitable Trust
The Bacon Charitable Trust
Lawrence Banks, CBE, DL
Barlow Robbins LLP
Mr James & Lady Emma Barnard
Basingstoke and Deane Borough Council
Bath & North East Somerset District Council Heritage Services
Robert Baxter, DL
Birmingham Common Good Trust
Sir Christopher Bland
Johnnie Boden
The Charlotte Bonham-Carter Charitable Trust
H. R. Pratt Boorman Family Foundation
A. J. H. du Boulay Charitable Trust
The Bowerman Charitable Trust
Viscountess Boyd Charitable Trust
Lord & Lady Bradbury
Bramdean Asset Management LLP
Peter Bretherton
Brewin Dolphin
J. & M. Britton Charitable Trust
Mrs T. Brotherton-Ratcliffe
Janey Buchan
Mr & Mrs Patrick Burgess
Mr & Mrs Mark Burrell
Arnold J. Burton Charitable Trust
Bushey Museum in Memory of Lavender Watson
Mrs Anne Cadbury, OBE, JP, DL
Roger Cadbury
C. J. R. & Mrs C. L. Calderwood
Sir Ralph Carr-Ellison
Mr & Mrs J. Chambers
Chichester District Council
His Honour Richard Cole, DL & Mrs Sheila Cole
The Timothy Colman Charitable Trust
Mr & Mrs Derek Coombs
The Helen Jean Cope Trust
Mr & Mrs Ian Copesteak
Cornwall County Council
Mr S. J. D. Corsan
Graeme Cottam & Gloriana Marks de Chabris
Coutts Charitable Trust
David Crane Trust
Elaine Craven, Earl Street Employment Consultants Ltd
Harriett Cullen
Culture North East
Rt Hon. Viscount Daventry
N. Davie-Thornhill
Brigadier Mike Dauncey, DSO, DL
De La Rue Charitable Trust
Mr Robert Dean
Deborah Gage (Works of Art) Ltd
Derek Johns Ltd, London
Derby City Council
Derby High School Trust Ltd
Derbyshire Building Society
Derbyshire Community Foundation (The Ashby Fund)
J. N. Derbyshire Trust
The Duke of Devonshire's Charitable Trust
S. Dewhirst Charitable Trust
Sir Harry Djanogly, CBE
Dorset County Council
Lord Douro
Professor Patrick & Dr Grace Dowling
Dunn Family Charitable Trust
East Sussex County Council
Eastbourne Borough Council
EEMLAC, through the Association for Suffolk Museums
Lord & Lady Egremont
Sir John & Lady Elliott
Andrew & Lucy Ellis
Peter & Judy Ellwood
Essex County Council
John & Felicity Fairbairn
Fairfield Charitable Trust
Jenny Farr, MBE, DL
John Feeney Charitable Trust
The Trustees of the Finnis Scott Foundation
The Fishmongers' Company
David & Ann FitzWilliam-Lay
Elizabeth & Val Fleming
The Follett Trust
Richard & Elizabeth Fothergill

Christopher & Catherine Foyle
Freemasons of Derbyshire
The Friends of Historic Essex
The Friends of the Laing Art Gallery
The Friends of the Royal Pavilion, Art Gallery & Museums, Brighton
The Friends of Southampton's Museums, Archives and Galleries
The Friends of Sunderland Museums
The Friends of York Art Gallery (E. J. Swift Bequest)
Philip Gibbs
The Hon. H. M. T. Gibson's Charity Trust
Lewis & Jacqueline Golden
The Goldsmiths' Company
Gorringes
Charles Gregson
The Grocers' Company
The Gulland Family
David Gurney
Philip Gwyn
Sir Ernest Hall
The Earl of Halifax, KStJ, JP, DL
The W. A. Handley Charity Trust
The Hartnett Charitable Trust
Hazlitt, Gooden & Fox Ltd
Heartwood Wealth Management Ltd
The Trustees of the King Henry VIII Endowed Trust, Warwick
The Rt Hon. the Lord Heseltine, CH, PC & Lady Heseltine
The Lady Hind Trust
Hobart Charitable Trust
Edward and Anna Hocknell
David Hockney CH, RA
Patrick Holden & Lin Hinds
Mrs Michael Hollingbery
The Holman Family
Mr & Mrs A. Holman-West
The Honourable Company of Gloucestershire
The Hope Scott Trust
David & Prue Hopkinson
Major & Mrs Bill Hutchinson
His Honour Gabriel Hutton
Isle of Wight Council
The J. and S. B. Charitable Trust
Alan & Penny Jerome
James & Lucilla Joll Charitable Trust
Mr & Mrs Peter Jones
Tommy Jowitt
The Keatley Trust
Kent Messenger Group
Garrett Kirk, Jr
Mr John Kirkland, OBE & Mrs Sheila Kirkland
Robert Kirkland
Kirklees Council
The David Laing Foundation
Landau Foundation
Lord Lea of Crondall, OBE
The Leche Trust
Leeds Art Collections Fund
Leeds City Council
Leeds Philosophical and Literary Society
The Hon. David Legh, DL
Lord Leverhulme's Charitable Trust
Mr & Mrs John Lewis
Mark & Sophie Lewisohn
Tom Lugg & the Lane Family
The Orr Mackintosh Foundation
The MacRobert Trust
Maidstone Borough Council
John Manser
Mr & Mrs Derek Mapp
Walter & Barbara Marais
The Marlay Group
Marshall Charitable Trust
Stephen & Carolyn Martin
Tom & Anne Martin
The Medlock Charitable Trust
The Piet Mendels Foundation
MLA East of England
MLA North East of England
Museums Galleries Scotland
Mr Paul Myners
Rupert Nabarro
Nancie Massey Charitable Trust
Newcastle City Council
Bryan Norman
Lord & Lady Northampton
The University of Northampton
NP Aerospace Ltd
Oakmoor Trust
Jasper & Virginia Olivier
The Orr Mackintosh Foundation
Mr Christopher Oughtred
The Owen Family Trust

Sir Idris Pearce
Roger Neville Russ Peers
The Pennycress Trust
Perkins Family
The Lord & Lady Phillimore
Mrs Margaret Pollett
Simon & Ursula Pomeroy
The Portland Family
Portsmouth City Council
George Pragnell Ltd
The Prince Philip Trust Fund for the Royal Borough of Windsor and Maidenhead
Provident Financial plc
Mr John Rank
Rathbone Investment Management Ltd
The Hans and Märit Rausing Charitable Trust
Roger & Jane Reed
Renaissance North East
Renaissance South East
Renaissance South West
Michael Renshall, CBE, MA, FCA
Sir John Riddell
Sir Miles & Lady Rivett-Carnac
Rockley Charitable Trust
Rolls-Royce plc
The Roper Family Charitable Trust
Rothschild Foundation
Royal Cornwall Museum
Graham & Ann Rudd
Sir Nigel Rudd
Russell New
The J. S. & E. C. Rymer Charitable Trust
The Earl St Aldwyn
The Sammermar Trust
Scarfe Charitable Trust
Andrew & Belinda Scott
The Trustees of the Finnis Scott Foundation
Shaftesbury PLC
Mr W. Sharpe
The Shears Foundation
Robert Shields, DL
Smith & Williamson
South West of England Regional Development Agency
Caroline M. Southall
Stuart M. Southall
Southampton City Council
The Jessie Spencer Trust
Hugh & Catherine Stevenson
Mrs Andrew Stewart-Roberts, OBE
Mr Michael Stone
Mr Peter Stormonth Darling
The Stratford-upon-Avon Town Trust
Strutt and Parker
Suffolk County Council, through the Association for Suffolk Museums
Surrey County Council
The John Swire 1989 Charitable Trust
The Tanner Trust
Tennants Auctioneers
Tesco Charity Trust
The Thistle Trust
Prof. Caroline Tisdall
Trusthouse Charitable Foundation
Gladwyn Turbutt
TWM Business Partners
Tyne & Wear Museums
University College Falmouth
University of Derby
University of Essex
David & Grizelda Vermont
Wakefield Metropolitan District Council
Robert & Felicity Waley-Cohen
The Peggy Walker Charitable Trust
The Walland Trust Fund
John Wates Charitable Trust
Leslie Weller, DL
The Welton Foundation
West Sussex County Council
Mr & Mrs David Wigglesworth
Wilkin & Sons Ltd
Mr & Mrs Jo Windsor
Peter Wolton Charitable Trust
Michael J. Woodhall, FRICS
Sir Philip Wroughton
Mrs Angela Yeoman

First published in 2012 by The Public Catalogue Foundation, Printed Catalogue Division, 8 Frederick's Place, London, EC2R 8AB

The responsibility for the accuracy of the information presented in this catalogue lies solely with the holding collections. Suggestions that might improve the accuracy of the information contained in this catalogue should be sent to the relevant collection and emailed to info@thepcf.org.uk.

ISBN 978-1-904931-79-9

Designed by Sally Jeffery

Printed in Hong Kong by Paramount Printing Company Limited